CROSSWORD
PUZZLE
DICTIONARY

CROSSWORD PUZZLE DICTIONARY

4th Edition

ANDREW SWANFELDT

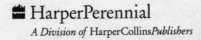
HarperPerennial

A Division of HarperCollins*Publishers*

A hardcover edition of this book was published by Thomas Y. Crowell, Publishers.

CROSSWORD PUZZLE DICTIONARY (*Fourth Edition*). Copyright 1940, 1944, 1967, 1977 by Harper & Row, Publishers, Inc. Copyright renewed 1968, 1972 by P. K. Starr, S. J. Prevatte, and J. J. Ford, Trustee. All rights reserved. Printed in the United States of America. No part of this book may be used or reproduced in any manner whatsoever without written permission except in the case of brief quotations embodied in critical articles and reviews. For information address Harper & Row, Publishers, Inc., 10 East 53rd Street, New York, N.Y. 10022.

First PERENNIAL LIBRARY edition published 1985. This larger-format edition published 1986.

Library of Congress Cataloging in Publication Data

Swanfeldt, Andrew.
  Crossword puzzle dictionary.

  Reprint. Originally published: 4th ed. New York : Crowell, c1977.
  1. Crossword puzzles—Glossaries, vocabularies, etc.
I. Title.
GV1507.C7S85 1986   793.73′2′0321   84-48628
ISBN 0-06-272034-1 (pbk.)

92 93 94 95 MPC 10 9 8

Publisher's Preface

Since its first appearance in 1940, the *Crossword Puzzle Dictionary*, compiled by Andrew Swanfeldt, has acquired such a widespread and loyal following among crossword fans that three successive improved and expanded editions have been needed to keep abreast of the demand.

The most notable improvement was the breakthrough device first incorporated in the 3rd edition: the Instant Finder System. On the surface it is a simple device—the answer words are listed according to the number of letters—but it was not, in fact, practical to produce a large book with this feature until the development of computer technology made it possible to count the letters by mechanical means.

Regrettably, Andrew Swanfeldt did not see the fruit of his years of research; he died soon after submitting the revised text for the 3rd edition. The publisher's staff, ably headed by Anne Vaughan, prepared his manuscript for processing by the computer.

This new edition is still very much a reflection of Mr. Swanfeldt's work: the publisher has kept practically all of his 3rd edition text (as well as the Instant Finder System). But the number of clues and answer words has been considerably increased. The result, we trust, is the most efficient and comprehensive puzzle dictionary of all.

The publisher is indebted, for all of the new material in the 4th edition, to lexicographer Sheila Brantley.

Abbreviations Used in This Book

abbr.	abbreviation	It.	Italian
Ar.	Arabic	L.	Latin
c.	capital	pert. to	pertaining to
comb. form	combining form	P.I.	Philippine Islands
D.	Dutch	pl.	plural
F.	French	Russ.	Russian
G.	German	Sc.	Scottish
Gr.	Greek	Sp.	Spanish
Ind.	Indian	W.	Welsh
Ir.	Irish	Yid.	Yiddish

A

A, a: an, ay; per 4 each
  Greek: 5 alpha
  Hebrew: 5 aleph
aa: 4 lava
aal, al: 8 mulberry
  dye: 8 morindin
aalii: 4 tree, wood
aardvark: 8 anteater, edentate
Aaron: *associate:* Hur
  brother: 5 Moses
  burial place: Hor
  father: 5 Amram
  sister: 6 Miriam
  son: 5 Abihu, Nadab 7 Eleazar, Ithamar
Aaronic: 9 Levitical
Aaron's rod: 7 mullein
ab-: off 4 away, from
aba: 4 robe 5 cloth 6 fabric 7 garment
abaca: 4 hemp 5 fiber, lupis 6 linaga
aback: 4 back 6 behind 8 backward, unawares
abaculus: 4 tile 7 tessera
abacus: 4 slab 5 stone 10 calculator
abaddon: 4 hell 5 hades
Abadite, Ibidite: 6 Muslim
abaft: aft 4 back, baft 5 abaff 6 astern, behind 8 rearward
abalienate: 8 alienate
abalone: ear 5 awabi, ormer, shell 6 asseir, sea-ear 7 mollusk
abandon: ego 4 cast, drop, flee, junk, quit 5 allay, ditch, expel, leave, remit, scrap, waive, yield 6 abjure, banish, desert, divest, disuse, maroon, recant, reject, relent, resign, vacate 7 discard, forsake 8 abdicate, forswear, rashness, renounce 9 surrender 10 enthusiasm, exuberance, relinquish
abandoned: bad 4 left, lost 7 corrupt, forlorn 8 derelict, flagrant, forsaken 9 desolated, destitute, dissolute, shameless, unbridled 10 dissipated, profligate 12 unrestrained
abandonment instrument: 6 waiver
abase: 5 lower, shame 6 bemean, debase, defame, deject, demean, depose, humble,

lessen, reduce 7 degrade, depress, mortify 8 disgrace, dishonor 9 denigrate, humiliate 10 depreciate
abash: awe, cow 4 dash 5 shame 6 humble 7 mortify 8 bewilder, browbeat, confound 9 discomfit, embarrass, humiliate 10 disconcert, intimidate
abashed: 7 ashamed 8 sheepish
abate: ebb, end 4 fall, omit, slow, void, wane 5 allay, annul, let up, lower, quash, relax, remit, slake 6 deduct, lessen, reduce, relent 7 abolish, assuage, nullify, slacken, subside 8 decrease, diminish, mitigate, moderate 9 alleviate
abatement: 6 rebate 8 decrease 9 allowance, deduction, reduction 10 diminution, relaxation, subsidence
abatis: 8 obstacle 9 barricade 13 fortification
abba: 5 title 6 father
abbe: 4 monk 6 cleric, curate, priest 12 ecclesiastic
abbess: 4 amma 9 prelatess
abbey: 6 priory 7 convent, nunnery 8 cloister 9 monastery, sanctuary
  pert. to: 8 abbatial
abbot: 5 coarb, abbas
  assistant: 5 prior
abbreviate: cut 4 clip, dock 5 prune 6 digest 7 abridge, curtail, shorten 8 contract, condense, truncate 9 epitomize
abdicate: 4 cede, quit 5 demit, expel, leave, remit 6 depose, disown, forego, resign, retire, vacate 7 abandon 8 disclaim, renounce 9 surrender 10 disinherit, relinquish
abdomen: 5 belly, pleon, tharm 6 paunch
  fluid in: 7 ascites
abduct: 4 lure, take 5 steal 6 kidnap 7 capture
abecedarian: 4 tyro 6 novice 7 learner 8 beginner, neophyte 9 fledgling 10 tenderfoot 12 alphabetical
abecederium: 4 book 6 primer
abed: 4 sick 7 resting, retired 8 sleeping

Abel: *brother:* 4 Cain, Seth
parent: Eve 4 Adam
Abelard's beloved: 7 Heloise
abele: 6 poplar
aberrant: 4 wild 7 deviant 8 abnormal, straying 9 wandering
aberration: 4 slip 5 error, fault, lapse, mania 8 delirium, delusion, insanity 9 deviation 12 eccentricity 13 hallucination
abet: aid, egg 4 back, help 5 boost, coach 6 assist, foment, incite, second, succor, uphold 7 connive, espouse, forward, further, support, sustain 8 advocate, befriend 9 encourage, instigate, subsidize 11 countenance
abettor: 6 fautor 8 advocate, promoter 9 accessory, auxiliary 10 accomplice 11 confederate, conspirator
abeyance: 9 cessation 10 expectancy, suspension 11 suppression
abhor: 4 hate, shun 6 detest, loathe 7 despise, dislike 8 execrate 9 abominate
abhorrence: 5 odium 6 hatred 7 disgust 8 aversion 9 antipathy 10 repugnance 11 detestation
Abi: *father:* 9 Zechariah
husband: 4 Ahaz
mother: 8 Hezekiah
abide: be 4 bear, bide, last, live, stay 5 await, delay, dwell, exist, pause, tarry 6 endure, linger, remain, reside, submit 7 sojourn, sustain 8 continue, tolerate 9 acquiesce, withstand
Abiel's son: Ner
abies: 4 firs 5 trees 10 evergreens
abigail: 4 maid
Abigail: *husband:* 5 David, Nabal
son: 5 Amasa
Abihail's husband: 8 Rehoboam
ability: can 5 force, power, skill 6 energy, talent 7 caliber, faculty, potency 8 aptitude, capacity, strength 9 dexterity, ingenuity 10 capability, competence, efficiency 11 proficiency
Abimelech's friend: 8 Ahuzzath
Abital: *husband:* 5 David
son: 10 Shephatiah
abject: low 4 base, mean, poor, sunk, vile 5 helot 6 paltry, sordid, supine 7 forlorn, ignoble, servile, slavish 8 beggarly, cringing, degraded, downcast, listless, wretched 9 groveling, miserable 10 despicable 12 contemptible
abjure: 4 deny 5 spurn 6 eschew, recall, recant, reject, resign, revoke 7 abandon, disavow, retract 8 abnegate, disclaim, forswear, renounce 9 repudiate
ablation: 7 aciurgy, surgery

ablaze: 4 alow 5 afire, alowe 7 burning, glowing, radiant 8 gleaming, inflamed
able: apt, can, fit 5 adept, smart 6 clever, facile, strong 7 capable 8 dextrous, skillful, suitable, talented, vigorous 9 competent, dexterous, effective, efficient, qualified, versatile 10 proficient
ablution: 4 bath 6 lotion 7 baptism, washing 9 cleansing
vessel: 5 basin 9 washbasin
abnegate: 4 deny 6 abjure, forego, refuse, reject 7 disavow 8 disclaim, forswear, renounce 10 relinquish
Abner: *cousin:* 4 Saul
father: Ner
abnormal: 5 queer, utter 7 erratic, unusual 8 aberrant 9 anomalous, eccentric, irregular, unnatural 10 exorbitant 11 exceptional 13 extraordinary
aboard: on 4 onto 6 across 7 athwart
abode: cot, dar, hut 4 bode, cell, flat, home 5 bower, house, manor, suite 6 estate 7 cottage, habitat, lodging, mansion 8 domicile, dwelling, tenement 9 apartment, residence 10 habitation
animal: zoo 9 menagerie
of Dead: Dar 4 Aaru, Hell 5 Aralu, Hades, Orcus, Sheol 6 Heaven 9 Purgatory
of gods: 4 Meru 6 Asgard 7 Asgarth, Olympus 8 Asgardhr
abolish: end 4 kill 5 abate, annul, erase, quash 6 cancel, recall, repeal, revoke, vacate 7 destroy, nullify, rescind 8 abrogate 9 eradicate 10 invalidate, neutralize 11 countermand, discontinue, exterminate
aboma: boa, bom 5 snake 7 serpent
abominable: 4 vile 6 odious 9 atrocious, execrable, loathsome 10 unpleasant 12 disagreeable
abominable snowman: 4 yeti 7 monster
habitat: 9 Himalayas
abominate: 4 hate 5 abhor 6 detest, loathe 8 execrate
abomination: 4 evil 5 crime, curse 6 horror, plague 7 disgust 8 aversion 9 antipathy 10 abhorrence, odiousness, repugnance 11 detestation
aboriginal: 5 first, natal 7 primary 8 original 9 beginning, primitive 10 indigenous
aborigine: 6 Indian, native, savage 10 autochthon
abortion: 7 failure 8 feticide, misbirth 9 foeticide 11 miscarriage, monstrosity 13 misconception
abortive: 4 idle, vain 6 futile 9 fruitless 12 unsuccessful
abound: 4 flow, teem 5 fleet, swarm 8 overflow 9 exuberate

abounding: 4 rife 5 flush 7 replete, teeming 8 abundant 9 luxuriant, plenteous, plentiful

prefix: 4 poly

about: in, re 4 in re, near, some 5 anent, astir, circa 6 active, almost, around 8 circiter 10 concerning, throughout 11 surrounding 13 approximately

prefix: amb

above: on, up; oer 4 atop, over, past, upon 6 beyond, higher 8 overhead, superior 9 exceeding, foregoing 12 transcendent

comb. form: 5 hyper, super, supra

abracadabra: 5 spell 11 incantation

abrade: rub 4 bark, file, fret, gall, rasp, sand, wear 5 chafe, erase, grate, grind 6 scrape 8 irritate 9 excoriate

abrader: 4 file, rasp 5 emery 6 grater, sander 7 grinder, scraper 9 sandpaper 10 grindstone

Abraham: *birthplace:* Ur

bosom: 6 heaven 8 paradise

brother: 5 Nahor

concubine: 5 Hagar

father: 5 Terah

grandfather: 5 Nahor

grandson: 4 Esau

nephew: Lot

shrine: 5 Caaba, Kaaba

son: 5 Isaac, Medan, Shuah 6 Midian, Zimran 7 Ishmael

wife: 4 Sara 5 Hagar, Sarah, Sarai 7 Keturah

abramis: 4 carp, fish 5 bream

abrasion: 4 gall, scar 9 attrition

abrasive: 4 sand 5 emery 6 pumice, quartz 7 erodent 8 corundum 9 sandpaper 11 rottenstone

abraxas: gem 5 charm, stone 6 amulet

abreast: 4 even 6 beside 8 parallel 9 alongside

of the times: 6 modern 7 popular

abret: 5 bread, wafer

abridge: cut 4 dock 5 brief, limit, rasee, razee 6 reduce, shrink 7 curtail, deprive, shorten 8 abstract, compress, condense, contract, diminish, retrench 10 abbreviate

abridgement: 6 digest, precis, sketch 7 epitome, summary 8 synopsis 9 lessening 10 compendium, diminution

abrii: 4 shed 5 cover 6 cavity, dugout 7 shelter

abrini: 8 licorice

abroad: off 4 asea, away 5 astir, forth 6 afield, astray, widely 7 distant

abrogate: 5 annul, quash, remit 6 cancel, repeal, revoke 7 abolish, nullify, rescind 8 overrule

abrogation: 9 abolition, cassation 11 dissolution

abrupt: 4 bold, curt, fast, rude 5 bluff, blunt, brief, hasty, quick, rough, sharp, sheer, short, steep, terse 6 craggy, rugged, sudden 7 angular, brusque, violent 8 headlong, vertical 9 impetuous 10 unexpected 11 precipitate, precipitous 12 disconnected 13 perpendicular, unceremonious

Abruzzi city: 4 Atri

Absalom: *captain:* 5 Amasa

father: 5 David

sister: 5 Tamar

slayer: 4 Joab

abscess: 4 boil, moro, sore 5 ulcer 6 fester, lesion 9 gathering

abscond: fly, run 4 bolt, flee, hide, quit 5 elope, scram 6 decamp, depart, desert, eloine, escape, levant 8 withdraw

absence: 4 lack, void, want 5 blank, leave 6 vacuum 7 vacancy 8 furlough 10 deficiency, withdrawal 13 nonappearance, nonattendance

absent: off, out 4 away, AWOL, gone 7 lacking, missing 8 absorbed 10 abstracted

absent-minded: 6 musing 8 distrait, dreaming 9 engrossed 10 abstracted 11 inattentive, preoccupied

absent without leave: 4 AWOL

absolute: 4 dead, fine, free, mear, meer, mere, plat, pure, rank, real, true 5 plumb, sheer, stark, total, utter, whole 6 entire, simple 7 certain, perfect, plenary 8 complete, explicit, implicit, positive 9 arbitrary, downright 10 autocratic, disengaged, peremptory 11 categorical, terminative, unalienable 13 authoritative, unconditional

monarch: 6 despot

absolutely: yea, yes 4 amen 6 wholly 8 evendown 10 thoroughly 13 unequivocally

absolution: 6 pardon 8 shriving 9 acquittal, cleansing, remission 11 exculpation, forgiveness

payment: 7 sin rent

absolve: 4 free 5 clear, remit 6 acquit, excuse, exempt, finish, pardon, shrive, unbind 7 cleanse, forgive, release 8 dispense, liberate, overlook 9 discharge, exculpate, exonerate, vindicate

absorb: eat, sop 4 soak, take 5 amuse, drink, merge, unite 6 devour, engage, engulf, imbibe, occupy 7 combine, consume, engross, immerse, occlude, swallow 10 assimilate 11 incorporate

absorbed: 4 deep, lost, rapt, sunk 6 absent, buried, intent 7 plunged, riveted 8 immersed 9 engrossed 11 preoccupied

absorbent: 5 fomes

absquatulate: sit 5 elope, scram 6 decamp

abstain: 4 deny, fast 5 avoid, cease, spurn, waive 6 desist, eschew, forego, refuse, reject 7 forbear, refrain 8 restrain, teetotal, withhold

abstemious: 5 sober 7 ascetic 8 moderate 9 abstinent, temperate

absterge: 4 wipe 5 bathe, clean, purge, rinse

abstract: 4 cull, deed, draw, part, take 5 brief, ideal, steal 6 deduct, divert, precis, remove 7 abridge, excerpt, purloin, summary 8 abstruse, argument, separate, synopsis, withdraw 9 difficult, epitomize, recondite, summarize 10 compendium 11 abridgement, theoretical

being: ens 4 esse 5 entia (pl.)

abstruse: 4 dark, deep 6 hidden, mystic, remote, subtle, 7 obscure 8 abstract, acroatic, esoteric, profound 9 concealed, recondite 10 acroamatic, mysterious 16 incomprehensible

absurd: 4 wild 5 droll, false, inane, inept, silly 6 stupid 7 asinine, foolish 8 fabulous 9 fantastic, ludicrous, senseless 10 irrational, ridiculous 11 incongruous, nonsensical 12 inconsistent, inharmonious, preposterous, unreasonable

abundance: 4 flow, mort 5 depth, store 6 foison, plenty, riches, wealth 8 fullness, opulence 9 affluence, amplitude, plenitude 10 exuberance

suffix: ose

abundant: 4 free, lush, much, rife 5 ample, flush 6 galore, hearty 7 copious, fertile, fulsome, profuse, replete, teeming 8 fruitful, generous, numerous 9 abounding, bountiful, plenteous, plentiful 10 sufficient 11 overflowing

abuse: mar, tax 4 flay, harm, hurt, maul, rail, ruin, slam 5 crime, curse, fault, scold, spoil 6 berate, defile, ill-use, injure, insult, malign, misuse, punish, ravish, revile, vilify, yatter 7 affront, bedevil, deceive, falsify, misbede, miscall, obloquy, outrage, pervert, slander, traduce, upbraid, violate 8 dishonor, maltreat, misapply, mistreat, reproach 9 blaspheme, contumely, desecrate, disparage, invective, objurgate 10 adulterate, opprobrium, scurrility 12 vituperation

abusive: 4 foul 7 corrupt 8 cheating, insolent, libelous 9 offensive, perverted 10 calumnious, fraudulent, scurrilous 11 blasphemous 12 catachrestic, vituperative

abut: 4 join, rest 5 touch 6 adjoin, border 7 project

abutment: 4 pier 6 alette 8 buttress

abysmal: 4 deep 6 dreary 8 profound, unending, wretched 10 bottomless

abyss: pit 4 deep, gulf, hell, void 5 abysm, chaos, chasm, depth, gorge 6 bottom, vorago 7 gehenna 8 downfall, interval

Abyssinia: See **Ethiopia**

acacia: gum 4 tree 5 babul, boree, garad, myall, siris 6 arabic, coobah, locust 9 boobyalla 11 kameeldoorn

academic: 5 rigid 6 formal 7 classic, erudite, learned 9 scholarly 10 collegiate, scholastic 11 quodlibetic, theoretical 12 conventional

academy: 4 USMA, USNA 6 lyceum, manege, school 7 college, society 8 seminary 9 Annapolis, institute, West Point 10 university

Acadian: 5 Cajun

acaleph: 9 jellyfish

acantha: fin 5 spine, thorn 7 prickle

acanthopterygian: 4 bass, fish 5 perch

acarus: 4 mite, tick 6 insect

acaudal: 6 bobbed 7 anurous 8 ecaudate, tailless

accede: let 5 agree, allow, grant, yield 6 accord, assent, comply, concur 7 concede, conform, consent 9 acquiesce 11 acknowledge

accelerate: rev, run 4 race, urge 5 drive, hurry, speed 6 hasten 7 advance, forward, further, quicken 8 dispatch, expedite, increase 9 stimulate 11 precipitate

accelerator: 8 throttle

accent: 4 beat, burr, mark, tone 5 ictus, pitch, pulse, sound, throb 6 brogue, rhythm, stress 8 emphasis 9 emphasize, pronounce, underline 10 accentuate, inflection, intonation

accented: 7 marcato

syllable: 5 arsis

accentuate: 6 accent 9 emphasize, intensify

accept: 4 fang, take 5 admit, adopt, agree, allow, honor, marry 6 assent 7 approve, believe, embrace, espouse, receive 9 acquiesce 10 understand 11 acknowledge

acceptable: 7 welcome 8 pleasant 9 palatable 11 comfortable 12 satisfactory

accepted: 7 popular 8 admitted, approved, credited, orthodox, standard 9 canonical, prevalent 12 acknowledged, conventional, countenanced

access: way 4 adit, door, gate, path, road 5 entry, going, route 6 accost, avenue, entree, portal, street 7 advance 8 approach, entrance, paroxysm 9 admission 10 admittance, passageway 13 accessibility

accessible: 4 near, open 5 handy 6 at hand, patent 7 affable 8 familiar, pervious, sociable 9 available, reachable 10 attainable, convenient, obtainable, procurable 12 approachable

accession: 5 enter 8 addition, increase 9 agreement, inaugural, induction 11 acquisition, enlargement 13 reinforcement

accessorius: 5 nerve

accessory: 4 aide, ally, tool 5 extra, scarf 6 helper 7 abettor, adjunct 8 additive 9 adjective, appendage, assistant, auxiliary 10 accidental, accomplice, attachment, incidental, subsidiary 11 appurtenant, concomitant, confederate, contingency, subservient 12 accompanying, appurtenance, circumstance, contributary 13 accompaniment, supplementary

accident: hap 4 case, luck 5 event 6 chance, hazard, injury, mishap 7 fortune 8 calamity, casualty, disaster, fortuity, incident 9 mischance 10 misfortune 11 catastrophe, contingency, contretemps 12 misadventure

accidental: 6 casual, chance, random 9 dependent, extrinsic, haphazard, secondary 10 collateral, extraneous, incidental, undesigned, unexpected, unforeseen, unintended 11 conditional, subordinate 12 adscititious, adventitious, nonessential, unexpectedly 13 unintentional 14 unpremeditated

acclaim: cry 4 clap, hail, laud, root 5 cheer, claim, eclat, extol, shout 6 praise, salute 7 applaud, approve, commend, endorse, ovation, plaudit, welcome 8 applause 10 compliment 11 acclamation, approbation

acclimate: 5 inure 6 harden, season 8 accustom 9 habituate 10 naturalize 11 acclimatize

acclivity: 4 bank, brow, hill, rise 5 grade, pitch, slope, slant 6 ascent, height 7 incline 9 ascendant, ascendent 11 inclination

accolade: 4 Emmy, kiss, rite, sign 5 award, honor, medal, Oscar, token 6 salute, symbol 7 embrace 8 ceremony 9 laudation 10 salutation

accommodate: aid, bow, fit 4 give, help, hold, lend, suit 5 adapt, board, defer, favor, house, lodge, serve, yield 6 adjust, comply, favour, oblige, settle 7 conform 8 attemper, suitable 9 reconcile

accompaniment: 7 descant 9 accessory, obbligato

accompany: see 4 fare, join, lead 5 pilot 6 assist, attend, concur, convey, convoy, escort, follow, squire 7 coexist, conduct, consort 9 associate, companion

accomplice: pal 4 aide, ally, chum 5 buddy, crony 6 helper 7 abettor, partner 9 accessory, assistant, associate, colleague 10 cooperator 11 confederate 12 participator

accomplish: do; end, win 4 fill, work 5 enact, equip, forth 6 afford, attain, effect, finish, fulfil, manage 7 achieve, chevise, compass, execute, fulfill, furnish, operate, perfect, perform, realize, succeed 8 complete, contrive, dispatch, engineer 9 implement, negotiate 10 consummate, effectuate

accomplished: apt 4 able, done 5 adept, ended 6 expert 8 talented 10 proficient

accomplishment: art 4 deed, feat 5 craft, skill 8 learning 10 attainment 11 achievement, performance

accord: 4 give, jibe 5 agree, allow, atone, award, grant, tally, unity 6 accede, adjust, assent, bestow, beteem, comply, concur, settle, unison 7 comport, compose, concede, concert, concord, consent, consort, rapport, respond 9 harmonize, reconcile 10 compliance, conformity, correspond, permission 11 composition, concurrence

accordant: 4 even 7 attuned 8 agreeing, coherent, suitable 9 congruous, consonant 10 compatible, concentual, consistent, harmonious 11 concentuous, conformable 13 correspondent

accordingly: so 4 then, thus 5 hence 9 therefore, wherefore 12 consequently 15 correspondingly

accost: 4 hail, meet 5 board, greet, speak 6 halloo, salute, waylay 7 address, solicit 8 approach, confront, greeting 9 encounter

account: tab, 4 bill, deem, item, rate, sake, tale 5 chalk, count, judge, score, story, value, worth 6 credit, detail, esteem, profit, reckon, record, relate, report, repute 7 compute, explain, narrate, recital 8 consider, estimate, 9 advantage, biography, chronicle, discourse, inventory, narrative, reckoning, rehearsal, statement 10 commentary, importance, recitation 11 calculation, computation, description, enumeration, explanation

accountable: 6 liable 10 answerable, explicable 11 responsible 12 attributable

accountant: CPA 5 clerk 7 auditor 8 reckoner 10 bookkeeper, calculator

accoutre, accouter: arm, rig 4 gird 5 array, dress, equip 6 attire, clothe, outfit 7 furnish, provide

accoutrements, accouterments: 9 equipment, trappings

accredit: 5 allot, vouch 6 credit, depute 7 appoint, approve, ascribe, believe, certify, confirm, endorse, license 8 sanction 9 attribute, authorize 10 commission

accretion: 4 gain 6 growth 7 deposit, exudate 8 addition, abhesion, increase 9 coherence 11 enlargement

accrue: add 4 earn, gain, grow 5 arise, ensue, inure, issue 6 mature, result, spring 7 acquire, collect, redound 8 cumulate, increase

accumulate: 4 grow, heap, pile, save 5 amass, hoard, store, total 6 accrue, garner, gather, muster 7 collect 8 increase 9 aggregate

accumulation: 4 fund, heap, mass, pile 5 stack, store 6 budget 7 cumulus 8 dividend, interest 10 acervation, congestion, cumulation

accurate: 4 just, leal, nice, true 5 close, exact, right 6 strict 7 careful, correct, precise 8 faithful 9 veridical 10 particular

accursed: fey 6 cursed, damned, doomed 9 execrable, execrated 10 detestable 13 anathematized

accuse: tax 4 call, file, show, slur, wray 5 argue, blame 6 attack, charge, defame, indict 7 appeach, arraign, attaint, censure, impeach 8 chastise, denounce, reproach 9 challenge 10 calumniate 11 incriminate, recriminate

accuser: 7 charger, delator 8 libelant 9 plaintiff 10 prosecutor 11 complainant

accustom: use 4 haft, wont 5 adapt, enure, drill, inure, train 6 addict, season 7 consort, toughen 9 acclimate, habituate 10 naturalize 11 familiarize

ace: jot, one, pip 4 a-one, atom, card, hero, mark, tops, unit 5 adept, basto, flyer, point 6 expert 7 aviator 8 particle, quantity 10 topnotcher

acerb: 4 acid, sour, tart 5 acrid, harsh, sharp, surly 6 bitter, severe 10 astringent 11 acrimonious

acerbate: 8 embitter, irritate 10 exasperate

acetaldehyde: 5 ethyl 7 ethanal

acetic: 4 sour 5 sharp

acetic acid: 7 vinegar

salt: 7 acetate

acetylene: gas 5 tolan 6 ethine, tolane

ache: 4 hurt, long, pain, pang, pine 5 smart, throb, throe 6 desire, stitch, twinge 7 anguish 8 soreness

achieve: do; end, get, win 4 earn, gain 5 reach 6 afford, attain, effect, finish, obtain 7 compass, fulfill, produce, realize, succeed, triumph 8 complete, conclude, contrive 9 terminate 10 accomplish, consummate

achievement: act 4 deed, feat 6 action, career, result 7 exploit 9 execution, fosterage 11 performance 14 accomplishment

Achilles: *advisor:* 6 Nestor

charioteer: 9 Automedon

father: 6 Peleus

friend: 9 Patroclus

horse: 7 Xanthus

lover and captive: 7 Briseis

mother: 6 Thetis

slayer: 5 Paris

soldier: 8 Myrmidon

teacher: 6 Chiron 7 Centaur

victim: 6 Hector

vulnerable part: 4 heel

achiote: 4 tree 7 annatto, arnatta, arnatto

achira: 5 canna 8 acheiria, handless

acid: dry 4 keen, sour, tart 5 acrid, amino, eager, harsh, sharp, ulmic 6 biting, bitter, oleate 7 acetose, acetous, vinegar 9 corrosive 11 acrimonious

comb. form: oxy 4 acer

nitric: 10 aquafortis

pert. to: 7 oleatic

radical: 4 acyl 6 acetyl 7 malonyl, benzoyl

acidity: 4 acor 8 acerbity, verjuice

measure: 10 acidimeter

acknowledge: nod, own 4 aver, avow, sign 5 admit, allow, grant, thank, yield 6 accede, accept, answer, assent, avouch, reward 7 concede, confess, declare, observe, profess 8 disclose 9 recognize

acme: cap, top 4 apex, peak 5 crest 6 apogee, climax, crisis, height, heyday, summit, zenith 8 pinnacle 11 culmination

acolyte: boy 6 helper, novice 7 learner 9 satellite

acomia: 8 baldness

aconic acid: 4 salt 7 aconate

aconite: 4 bikh 6 remedy 9 monkshood

acorn: nut 4 mast 5 ovest

dried: 6 camata

edible: 7 ballote, bellote

acorn-shaped: 8 balanoid

acouchi: 5 elemi, resin 7 protium

acquaint: 4 know, tell 5 teach, verse 6 advise, inform, notify, school 7 apprise, apprize, possess 11 familiarize

acquaintance: 4 kith 6 friend 8 affinity, intimate 9 companion, knowledge 10 fellowship

acquainted: 7 versant 10 conversant

acquiesce: bow 5 abide, agree, chime, yield 6 accede, accept, assent, comply, concur, submit 7 concede, conform, consent

acquire: add, buy, get, win 4 earn, gain, grab, reap 5 adopt, amass, learn, reach, steal 6 attain, effect, obtain, secure, snatch 7 collect, conquer, procure, receive 8 contract 9 cultivate

acquit: 4 free 5 clear 6 behave, excuse, pardon, parole 7 absolve, amnesty, comport, conduct, release, requite 8 liberate, overlook 9 discharge, exculpate, exonerate, quitclaim, vindicate

acre: 4 land 5 field 6 arpent 7 measure 8 farmhold
  one hundred: 7 hectare
  quarter: rod 4 rood
acreage: 5 ranch 6 estate 8 farmland
acrid: 4 acid, keen 5 harsh, rough, sharp, surly 6 biting, bitter 7 caustic, pungent, reeking 8 unsavory, virulent 9 acidulous, corrosive 10 irritating
acrimonious: mad 4 acid, keen 5 acrid, angry, gruff, harsh, irate, sharp, surly 6 bitter 7 caustic 8 stinging 9 rancorous
acroamatic: 4 oral 6 arcane, secret 8 abstruse, esoteric, profound
acrobat: 4 zany 7 gymnast, tumbler 8 balancer 10 ropedancer 13 contortionist, schoenobatist
  garment: 7 leotard
acrogen: 4 fern, moss
acropolis: 4 fort, hill 7 citadel
across: 4 over, span 6 aboard 7 athwart 8 opposite 9 crosswise 10 transverse
  prefix: dia 5 trans
acrostic: 4 agla, game, poem 6 phrase, puzzle 9 crosswise 11 composition
act: do, go; ape, law 4 actu, bill, deed, feat, play, skit, turn, work 5 actus, drama, edict, emote, exert, feign, karma, model, scene, stunt 6 behave, bestir, decree 7 comport, execute, exploit, perform, portray, pretend, statute 8 function, pretense, simulate 9 ordinance, portrayal, represent 10 observance 11 impersonate, instruction, performance
  by turns: 6 altern 9 alternate
  suffix: ure
act for: 9 represent
act like: ape 7 imitate
act up: 5 emote 9 misbehave
action: 4 case, deed, fray, push, step, work 5 doing, edict, fight 6 affair, battle 7 conduct, process 8 behavior, conflict, function 9 animation, behaviour 10 deportment, enterprise 11 performance, transaction
  field of: 4 bowl 5 arena, stage 7 stadium
  legal: res 4 suit 5 actus 8 replevin 9 gravamina
  pert. to: 9 practical
  put out of: KO 7 disable
  to recover property: 6 trover 8 replevin
  word: 4 verb
active: 4 busy, pert, spry 5 about, agile, alert, astir, brisk, quick, ready, smart 6 hearty, lively, moving, nimble, prompt 7 kinetic 8 animated, athletic, diligent, spirited, vigorous 9 assiduous, effective, energetic, sprightly, unpassive 10 productive 11 industrious, progressive

activity: ado, gog, vir 4 life, stir 5 rally 6 action, bustle 8 business, exercise, function, movement
actor: ham 4 doer, hero, lead, mime, star 5 agent, extra, heavy, mimic 6 artist, mummer, player, stager 7 artiste, guisard, histrio, protean, stormer, trouper 8 aisteoir (Ir.), comedian, juvenile, stroller, thespian 9 performer, portrayer, tragedian 10 personator 11 barnstormer, entertainer, pantomimist, protagonist
  cue: 4 hint, word 6 prompt
  group of: 4 cast 6 troupe 7 company 8 troupers
  lines: 4 role, side
  part: 4 role
  supporting: bit 5 super 6 walk-on 7 ripieno
actress: 4 diva, star 7 ingenue 8 thespian 9 soubrette 10 comedienne 11 entertainer
actual: 4 real, true 5 posit 6 bodily 7 factual, genuine 8 concrete, existing, material, positive, tangible 9 effective, veritable 11 substantial
actuality: 4 fact 5 being 6 verity 7 reality 9 existence, substance
actuate: egg, run 4 draw, move, urge 5 enact, impel, rouse, start 6 arouse, compel, incite, induce 7 agitate, animate, enliven, inspire, pointed, sharpen 8 motivate, persuade 9 instigate
acumen: wit 7 insight 8 keenness, sagacity 9 acuteness, mentality, sharpness 10 perception, shrewdness 11 discernment 12 perspicacity 14 discrimination
acute: 4 fine, high, keen 5 quick, sharp, smart, snell 6 astute, shrewd, shrill, subtle, urgent 7 intense, pointed 8 critical, incisive, poignant 9 ingenious, sensitive 10 discerning, perceiving 11 intelligent, penetrating 13 perspicacious 14 discriminating
ad-lib: 9 improvise
ad patres: 4 dead 8 deceased
adage: saw 4 dict 5 axiom, maxim, motto 6 homily, saying, truism 7 bromide, precept, proverb 8 aphorism, apothegm
Adah: *husband:* 4 Esau 6 Lamech
  son: 5 Jabal, Jubal
Adam: *grandson:* 4 Enos 5 Enoch
  rib: Eve
  son: 4 Abel, Cain, Seth
  teacher: 6 Raisel
  wife, first: 6 Lilith
Adam-and-Eve: 9 puttyroot
Adam Bede author: 5 Eliot
adamant: 4 firm, hard 5 stony 8 obdurate 9 loadstone, lodestone 10 inflexible, unyielding

adamantine: 4 firm 5 stone 9 immovable 10 unyielding
pert. to: 5 boric

Adam's ale: 5 water

Adam's apple: 6 larynx

Adam's flannel: 7 mullien

Adam's needle: 5 yucca

adapt: apt, fit 4 suit 5 agree, apply, inure 6 adjust, change, comply, temper 7 arrange, conform, convert, prepare, qualify 8 attemper, equalize, regulate 9 acclimate, calculate, harmonize 10 assimilate 11 accommodate

adaptable: 7 pliable 8 flexuous 9 tractable 10 adjustable, changeable 11 conformable 12 reconcilable

add: say, sum, tot 4 gain, give, join, plus, tote 5 affix, annex, total, unite 6 accrue, append, attach, figure, reckon 7 accrete, augment, combine, compile, compute, enlarge, subjoin 8 increase 9 aggregate 10 supplement

adda: 5 scink, skink 6 lizard

added: and, eke 4 plus

adder: 5 krait, snake, viper 7 machine, serpent 13 mathematician

addict: fan 4 buff, user 5 fiend, hound, slave 6 devote 7 deliver, devotee, hophead, pothead 8 accustom, acidhead 9 habituate, mainliner 10 enthusiast

addiction: 5 habit 9 surrender 10 attachment 11 disposition, enslavement, habituation

addition: and, ell 4 also, else, plus 5 rider 6 prefix 7 addenda (pl.), adjunct, advance, codicil, joining 8 addendum, additory, increase 9 accession, accretion, amendment, appendage, extension 10 ascription 11 enlargement 12 augmentation
prefix: 5 super

additional: new 4 else, more 5 extra, fresh, other 7 besides, further 9 auxiliary

addle: 4 earn, home, idle, mire 5 amaze, filth, ripen, spoil 6 muddle, thrive 7 agitate, confuse 8 befuddle, bewilder, confound 9 fruitless

addled: 4 asea 5 empty, upset 6 putrid 7 spoiled, unsound 9 befuddled 10 bewildered

address: aim, sue, woo 4 call, hail, home, pray, tact, talk, turn 5 abode, apply, court, greet, poise, skill 6 accost, adjust, aplomb, appeal, devote, direct, eulogy, manner, salute, speech 7 consign, entrust, lecture, oration 8 approach, delivery, dispatch, facility, harangue, petition 9 dexterity, discourse, residence, statement 10 allocution, buttonhole, deportment, management, peroration 11 application

adduce: 4 cite, give, name 5 allay, argue, infer, offer, quote 6 allege, assign 7 advance, mention, present

ade: 8 beverage

adeps: fat 4 lard

adept: ace, apt 4 A-one, able 5 handy, sharp 6 adroit, artist, expert, versed 7 capable, dabster 8 skillful 9 alchemist, dexterous, masterful 10 consummate, conversant, proficient

adequate: due, fit 4 full, meet 5 ample, equal 6 enough, proper 7 condign 8 suitable 9 competent, effective 10 answerable, sufficient 12 commensurate, satisfactory 13 proportionate

Adhem: 4 Abou

adhere: 4 cleg, glue, hold 5 affix, cling, stick, unite 6 attach, cleave, cohere 7 accrete, persist 9 persevere

adherence: 8 devotion, fidelity 9 constancy 10 allegiance, attachment 11 concurrence 12 perseverance

adherent: ist, ite 4 aide, ally 6 factor, votary 8 believer, disciple, follower, partisan, servitor, upholder 9 supporter
suffix: ist, ite

adhesive: gum, wax 4 bond, glue, tape 5 epoxy, paste 6 cement, gluten, mastic, sticky, viscum 7 stickum 8 birdlime, mucilage 9 tenacious

adhibit: use 5 admit, affix, apply 6 attach 10 administer

adieu: 5 adios 6 good-by 7 good-bye 8 farewell 11 valediction

adipose: fat 4 hard, suet 5 fatty, obese, pursy, squat 6 tallow

adit: 5 entry, stulm 6 access 7 passage 8 approach, entrance 9 admission 10 passageway

adjacent: 4 near, next, nigh 5 close, handy 6 beside, hard by 7 against, meeting 8 abutting, touching 9 adjoining, bordering 10 contiguous, juxtaposed 11 neighboring 12 conterminous

adjective: 7 epithet 8 modifier 9 accessory, dependent
demonstrative: 4 that, this 5 these, those
limiting: the
suffix: ed, ic, il; ent, ial, ian, ile, ine, ish, ive, ous 4 ical, ular
verbal: 9 gerundive

adjoin: add 4 abut, butt, join 5 touch, verge 6 append, attach, border 7 contact 8 neighbor 9 juxtapose

adjourn: end 4 move, rise, stay 5 close, defer, delay 6 recess 7 suspend 8 dissolve, postpone, prorogue 11 discontinue 13 procrastinate

adjudge: try 4 deem, find, give, hold, rate 5 allot, award, grant, judge, order 6 assign,

decide, decree, ordain, regard **7** condemn **8**
sentence **9** determine, forejudge **10** adjudicate

adjudicate: act, try **4** hear, pass, rule **5**
judge **6** decide, esteem, reckon, regard,
settle **8** consider, sentence **9** determine

adjunct: aid **4** help, word **5** annex **6** device,
phrase **7** pertain, teacher **8** addition, appanage **9** accessory, appendage, associate,
auxiliary, colleague **10** complement **11**
contingency **12** appurtenance

adjure: ask, beg, bid **4** bind, pray **5** crave,
plead, swear **6** appeal, charge **7** beseech,
command, conjure, contest, entreat, request, unswear

adjust: fit, fix, set **4** form, free, gear, line,
pare, rate, size, suit, trim, true **5** adapt,
admit, align, frame **6** accord, attune, settle, temper, wangle **7** address, arrange,
balance, conform, compose, dispose, justify, prepare, rectify **8** compound, regulate
9 harmonize **10** concinnate, coordinate,
straighten **11** accommodate, systematize

adjutage: **4** pipe, tube **5** spout **6** nozzle **7**
opening

adjutant: **4** aide, ally **6** helper **7** officer **9**
assistant, auxiliary
bird: **5** crane, stork **6** argala **7** marabou

adjuvant: **4** aide **6** helper **7** helpful **9** assistant, auxiliary

admeasure: **4** mete **7** measure **9** ascertain,
apportion, determine

Admetus' wife: **8** Alcestis

administer: run **4** deal, dose, give, rule **5**
apply, treat **6** direct, govern, manage, settle, supply **7** adhibit, conduct, control, execute, furnish, husband **8** dispense **10** distribute **11** superintend

administration: **4** rule, sway **6** policy **7** regimen **10** regulation

administrator: **7** manager, trustee **8** director, executor **9** dispenser, executive, executrix

admirable: **4** high **7** amiable, capital, elegant, ripping **9** estimable, excellent, marvelous, wonderful

Admiralty island: **5** Manus

admire: **4** like, love **5** adore, extol, honor,
prize, value **6** esteem, marvel, regard, revere, wonder **7** approve, delight, idolize,
respect **8** venerate

admirer: fan **4** beau **5** beaux (pl.), lover,
swain **7** devotee **10** dilettante

admission: fee **4** adit **6** access, charge, entree, ticket **7** consent, ingress **8** entrance
10 admittance, agregation, concession,
confession, disclosure **15** acknowledgement
receipts: **4** gate

admit: ken, own **4** avow, take **5** agree, allow,
enter, grant **6** accept, accede, adjust, assent, avouch, enroll, induct, permit, suffer
7 adhibit, concede, confess, include, profess, receive **8** initiate **9** recognize **11** acknowledge, matriculate

admixture: **5** alloy, blend, shade, tinge **6** flavor **7** mixture, soupcon **8** compound, infusion **11** composition

admonish: **4** warn **5** chide, scold **6** advise,
enjoin, exhort, notify, rebuke, remind **7**
caution, counsel, monitor, reprove **9** reprehend, sermonize

admonisher: **7** monitor

adnoun: **9** adjective

ado: **4** fuss, stir, to-do, work **6** bother, bustle,
effort, flurry, hubbub, pother, ruckus **7**
trouble, turmoil **9** commotion **10** excitement, hullabaloo

adobe: mud **4** clay **5** brick, house **6** mudcap

adolescence: **5** teens, youth **6** nonage **7** puberty **8** minority

adolescent: lad **4** girl, lass **5** young, youth **6**
nubile, subdeb **7** hebetic **8** immature, teenager **9** pubescent

Adonis: *beloved:* **9** Aphrodite
slayer of: **4** boar

adopt: **4** take **6** accept, assume, borrow,
choose, follow, foster **7** acquire, embrace,
espouse, receive, welcome **8** advocate,
maintain **9** affiliate **10** naturalize **11** appropriate

adorable: **6** lovely **7** angelic, lovable, winsome **8** charming, kissable **9** appealing **10**
cuddlesome, delightful

adoration: **6** homage **8** devotion

adore: **4** dote, laud, love **5** honor **6** admire,
esteem, praise, revere **7** glorify, idolize,
worship **8** venerate

adorn: dub **4** deck, gaud, gild, pink, trim **5**
array, begem, dight, drape, dress, grace,
primp, prink **6** attire, bedeck, blazon,
clothe, emboss, enrich, suborn, tassel **7** apparel, bedight, bedizen, commend, dignify,
furnish, garnish, glorify, implume **8** beautify, decorate, emblazon, ornament **9** bespangle, caparison, embellish

Adriana's servant: **4** Luce

Adriatic: *city:* **6** Venice
island: Bua, Eso **7** Lagosta, Lastovo
peninsula: **6** Istria
port: **4** Pola **5** Fiume **6** Rimini **7** Trieste
resort: **4** Lido
river into: Po **4** Reno **5** Adige, Bosna, Drini,
Kerka, Piave
wind: **4** bora **10** tramontana, tramontane
(pl.)

adrift: 4 asea, lost 5 awaft, loose 6 afloat 8 derelict, floating, unmoored 10 unanchored

adroit: apt 4 deft, neat 5 adept, handy, ready, sharp, smart 6 artful, clever, expert, habile 7 cunning 8 dextrous, masterly, skillful 9 dexterous, ingenious, masterful 10 proficient 11 quick-witted, resourceful

adroitness: 4 ease, tact 5 knack 7 address 8 facility 9 dexterity, ingenuity

adulate: 4 fawn, laud 5 gloss, gloze 6 praise 7 flatter 10 compliment, overpraise

adulator: fan 5 toady 6 yes-man 9 flatterer, sycophant 10 bootlicker

adult: man 4 ripe 5 grown, imago, woman 6 mature, nubile 7 grown-up 8 seasoned 9 developed 12 marriageable

adulterate: cut, mix 5 alloy, alter, taint 6 debase, defile, dilute, doctor, weaken 7 corrupt, falsify 8 denature 11 contaminate

adulterated: cut 6 impure 8 spurious 11 counterfeit

adumbrate: 5 shade, vague 7 obscure 8 intimate 10 foreshadow, overshadow

aduncuous: 4 bent 6 hooked

adust: 5 burnt, fiery 6 gloomy, sallow 7 parched 8 scorched, sunburnt

advance: aid, pay 4 gain, help, laud, lend, lift, loan, move, near, nose, pass, push, rise 5 avant, boost, exalt, extol, favor, offer, raise, serve 6 adduce, allege, amount, assign, better, favour, hasten, stride, thrive 7 benefit, elevate, forward, further, improve, proceed, process, promote, propose, succeed 8 addition, heighten, progress 9 encourage, promotion 10 accelerate, aggrandize, appreciate

guard: van 8 vanguard

military: 8 anabasis, anabases (pl.)

slowly: 4 inch, worm 5 creep

advanced: far 5 ahead 11 enlightened, progressive

equally: 7 abreast

most: 8 foremost, headmost

advantage: use 4 boot, edge, gain, odds 5 avail, favor, start, stead 6 behalf, behoof, profit 7 account, benefit, exploit, further, utility 8 handicap, interest, leverage, overplus 9 emolument, privilege 11 opportunity, superiority

advantageous: 6 useful 9 expedient, favorable, strategic 10 auspicious, beneficial, commodious, favourable, profitable, propitious 11 encouraging

advent: 6 coming 7 arrival 8 approach 11 incarnation

adventitious: 6 casual 7 foreign 8 acquired, episodic 9 extrinsic 10 accidental, fortuitous, incidental 12 adscititious, nonessential

adventure: 4 gest, lark, risk 5 event, geste, peril, quest, 6 chance, danger, hazard, 7 fortune, venture 8 escapade, jeopardy 9 mischance 10 enterprise, experience 11 undertaking

story: 4 gest, yarn 5 geste

adventurer: 7 gambler 9 almogavar 10 filibuster 11 condottiere, condottieri (pl.), enterpriser 12 entrepreneur

adventuress: 7 demirep 12 demimondaine

adventurous: 4 rash 6 daring, errant 8 reckless 9 audacious, foolhardy, hazardous 10 courageous

adverb: *ending:* ly; ily

old: 4 erst

adversaria: 5 notes 10 miscellany 12 commentaries

adversary: foe 5 enemy, rival, Satan 6 foeman 8 opponent 10 antagonist, competitor

adverse: foe, ill 4 evil 5 loath 6 averse 7 awkward, counter, diverse, froward, opposed 8 contrary, opposing, opposite 9 diametric, reluctant, repugnant 10 afflictive, calamitous 11 conflicting, disinclined, unfavorable 12 antagonistic, inauspicious, unfavourable, unpropitious

adversity: woe 5 decay 6 misery, sorrow 7 illness, trouble 8 calamity, distress 9 suffering 10 affliction, misfortune 11 contrariety

advert: 4 heed 5 recur, refer 6 allude, attend, return, revert 7 observe 8 consider

advertise: 4 plug, warn 5 blurb, bruit, noise 6 blazon, inform, notify, parade 7 declare, exploit, observe, publish 8 announce, proclaim, skywrite 9 broadcast, publicize, spotlight 10 promulgate

advertisement: ad 4 bill, sign 5 blurb 6 dodger, notice, poster, teaser 7 affiche, placard 8 handbill 10 commercial

book jacket: 5 blurb

outdoor: 5 flyer 6 poster 7 marquee 9 billboard

advertiser: 6 barker 7 plugger, spieler 8 huckster

advice: 4 lore, news 6 notice 7 caution, counsel, opinion, tidings 8 monition 10 admonition, suggestion 11 instruction 12 consultation, deliberation 14 recommendation

seek: 6 huddle 7 consult

advisable: 6 proper 7 prudent 9 befitting, desirable, expedient

advise: 4 read, rede, warn 5 aread, areed, coach, guide 6 confer, exhort, inform, reveal **7** apprise, apprize, counsel **8** acquaint, admonish **9** encourage, recommend

adviser, advisor: 4 aide, tout **5** coach, tutor **6** doctor, lawyer, nestor **7** monitor, teacher **8** attorney, preacher **9** counselor, physician **10** admonisher, counsellor, instructor

advisory: 6 urging **7** prudent **9** expedient, hortative, hortatory
　body: **5** board **7** cabinet, council

advocate: pro **4** abet **5** adopt, favor, plead **6** assert, backer, defend, lawyer **7** abettor, apostle, endorse, espouse, scholar, support **8** attorney, champion, partisan **9** apologist, barrister, counselor, paraclete, proponent, recommend **11** intercessor
　of new laws: **9** neonomian

adytum: 6 shrine **7** sanctum **9** sanctuary

adz, adze: ax; axe **7** hatchet

Aeacus: *father:* **4** Zeus
　son: **6** Peleus **7** Telamon

Aeetes' daughter: 5 Medea

Aegean Sea: *ancient peoples:* **5** Psara, Psyra **6** Samian **7** Leleges, Samiote
　gulf: **5** Saros
　island: Ios **4** Nios, Rodi, Scio **5** Chios, Melos, Naxia, Naxos, Paros, Patmo, Psara, Samos, Tenos, Thera **6** Ikaria, Ipsara, Kariot, Lemnos, Patmos, Rhodes, Skyros **7** Amorgos, Nikaria **8** Cyclades, Mytilene, Mytilini, Santorin, Sporades **10** Dodecanese, Samothrace, Samothrake **11** Castelrosso **12** Castellorizo
　port: **4** Enos
　river into: **6** Struma, Vardar **7** Marista
　rock: Aex

Aegeon's wife: 7 Aemilia

aeger: ill **4** sick **6** excuse

Aegir's wife: Ran

aegis, egis: 6 shield **7** auspice, defence, defense **9** patronage **10** protection **11** sponsorship

Aegisthus' father: 8 Thyestes

Aegyptus: *brother:* **6** Danaus
　father: **5** Belus
　son: **7** Lynceus

Aello: 5 Harpy

Aeneas: *beloved:* **4** Dido
　companion: **7** Achates
　father: **8** Anchises
　grandfather: **5** Capys
　great-grandson: **4** Brut
　mother: **9** Aphrodite
　rival: **6** Turnus
　son: Iulus **8** Ascanius
　wife: **6** Creusa **7** Lavinia

Aeneid: *author:* **6** Vergil, Virgil
　first word: **4** arma
　hero: **6** Aeneas

　second word: **8** virumque
　third word: **4** cano

Aengus' mother: 5 Boann

Aeolian lyricist: 6 Sappho

Aeolus' daughter: 6 Canace **8** Halcyone

aeon, eon: age, era **5** cycle, Kalpa **6** period

aeonian, eonian: 7 eternal, lasting **8** infinite **11** everlasting

aerate: 6 aerify, charge **7** inflate **9** oxygenate, ventilate

aerial: 4 aery, airy **5** aeric, lofty **6** unreal **7** antenna **8** antennae (pl.), ethereal **9** imaginary **13** unsubstantial

aerialist: 10 trapeze man **11** entertainer
　garment: **7** leotard

aerie: 4 nest **5** brood **9** penthouse

aeriform: 6 unreal **7** gaseous

aerify: 6 aerate, infuse **8** vaporize

aerobatics: 4 loop, roll **5** stunt

aerobe: 8 organism **9** bacterium

aerodrome: 7 airport **8** airfield

aerolite: 9 meteorite **10** brontolite

aeronaut: 5 pilot **8** operator, traveler

aeronautics: 7 science **8** aviation
　pert. to: **4** aero

aerose: 6 brassy

aerostat: 7 airship, balloon **8** aircraft

aerugo: 4 rust **6** patina **9** verdigris

aery: 6 aerial **8** ethereal **9** visionary **11** incorporeal

aes: 4 coin **6** bronze

Aesculapian: 6 doctor **7** medical **9** medicinal, physician

Aesculapius' teacher: 6 Chiron

Aeson's son: 5 Jason

Aesop work: 6 Fables
　character: ox; ant, ass, dog, fox **4** frog, hare, lion **5** eagle, mouse **8** tortoise **11** grasshopper

aesthetic, esthetic: 8 artistic, tasteful **9** beautiful

Aeta: Ita **8** Filipino **10** Philippino

Aether's father: 6 Erebus

Aetolian prince: 6 Tydeus

aevia: 8 alleluia

afar: off **4** away, saho **6** remote **7** distant

affable: 4 open **5** civil, frank, suave **6** benign, facile, urbane **7** amiable, likable **8** charming, familiar, friendly, gracious, pleasant, sociable **9** courteous **10** accessible **11** complaisant

affair: 4 case, duel **5** event, fight, levee, party, thing **6** action, battle, matter **7** concern **8** business, endeavor, intrigue, occasion **9** endeavour, rickmatic **10** engagement, proceeding **11** transaction **12** circumstance

affect: hit **4** melt, move, stir **5** allot, alter, fancy, feign, haunt, impel, mince, touch **6** aspire, assign, assume, change, desire, soften, strike, thrill **7** attinge, concern, emotion, feeling, impress, operate, passion, pretend, profess **8** allocate, disposed, frequent, interest, simulate **9** cultivate, distemper, influence **11** counterfeit, disposition, hypothecate, inclination

each other: **8** interact

affectation: air **4** pose, sham **5** mince **7** display, foppery, grimace, pietism **8** fondness, pretense **9** arrogance, hypocrisy, mannerism

affected: **4** airy **5** ailed, apish, moved **6** formal, seized **7** minikin, smitten, stilted, touched **8** attacked, disposed, mannered **9** cherished, unnatural **10** artificial **11** pretentious

affection: **4** love **5** amour, heart **6** cherte, esteem, malady, regard **7** ailment, charity, emotion, feeling, symptom **8** fondness, tendency **10** attachment, friendship, propensity, tenderness **11** disposition, inclination

parental: **6** storge

affectionate: **4** fond, warm **6** ardent, doting, loving, tender **7** amorous, devoted, earnest, zealous **8** attached, parental, sisterly **9** brotherly

affeer: **6** affirm, assess

afferent: **4** bear **6** esodic **7** sensory **9** ascending **11** centripetal

affiance: **5** faith, trust **6** assure, engage, ensure, fiance, pledge, plight **7** betroth, promise **8** contract, reliance **9** assurance, betrothal **10** confidence

affiant: **8** deponent **9** affidavit

affidavit: **4** oath **7** affiant **9** statement **10** deposition **11** declaration

affiliate: **4** ally, unit **5** adopt, merge, unite **6** attach, branch, relate **7** ascribe, chapter, connect **9** associate **10** fraternize, subsidiary **11** incorporate

affinity: **6** family, liking **7** kinship, rapport **8** alliance, relation **10** attraction, conformity, connection **11** propinquity, resemblance **12** acquaintance, friendliness, relationship **13** companionship, consanguinity

affirm: **4** affy, aver, avow **5** posit, state, swear, vouch **6** allege, assert, attest, avouch, depose, ratify, verify **7** confirm, declare, profess, testify **8** maintain **9** predicate, pronounce **10** asseverate

affirmation: vow, yes **4** amen, oath, word **9** affidavit, assertion, statement **10** deposition **11** declaration, proposition **12** asseveration, ratification

by negative understatement: **7** litotes

affirmative: ay; aye, nod, yah, yea, yep, yes **4** amen, yeah **8** dogmatic, positive **10** cataphatic **11** affirmatory, declarative, predicative **12** conformative

affix: add, fix, pin **4** clip, join, nail, seal, **5** annex, stamp, unite **6** anchor, append, attach, fasten, settle, staple **7** adhibit, connect, entitle, impress, subjoin

afflatus: **4** fury **5** furor **6** frenzy, vision **7** impulse **9** breathing **11** inspiration

afflict: ail, rue, try, vex **4** hurt, pain, rack **5** array, beset, gripe, grill, harry, wound **6** burden, grieve, harass, humble, infect, pester, remord **7** chasten, oppress, torment, trouble **8** distress **9** overthrow, persecute

afflicted: sad **5** sorry **6** ailing, woeful **7** grieved, smitten **8** impaired, troubled **9** depressed, lacerated

affliction: woe **4** evil, loss, pain, sore **5** cross, grief **6** duress, misery, pathos, plague, sorrow **7** ailment, disease, illness, scourge, trouble **8** calamity, distress, hardship, severity, sickness **9** adversity, grievance, martyrdom **10** misfortune **12** wretchedness

afflue: **4** flow

affluence: **4** ease **6** afflux, influx, plenty, riches, wealth **7** fortune **8** opulence **9** abundance, concourse, plenitude, profusion, substance **10** prosperity **11** sufficiency

affluent: fat **4** rich **5** flush, river **6** stream **7** copious, flowing, opulent, wealthy **8** abundant **9** plenteous, tributary

afflux: **4** flow

afford: **4** bear, give, lend **5** grant, incur, spare, stand, yield **6** confer, manage, supply **7** achieve, forward, furnish, further, produce, provide **8** minister **10** accomplish

affray: **4** feud, fray, riot **5** alarm, brawl, broil, fight, melee, scare **6** attack, battle, fright, strife, terror, tumult **7** assault, contest, quarrel, scuffle, startle **8** frighten **9** encounter **11** disturbance

affright: cow **4** fear **5** alarm, daunt, dread, scare **6** agrise, appall, dismay **7** confuse, startle, terrify **8** frighten **10** intimidate

affront: cut **4** defy, slap **5** abuse, beard, peeve **6** harass, injure, insult, nettle, offend, slight **7** outrage, provoke **8** confront, disgrace, illtreat, irritate **9** encounter, indignity, sobriquet **10** soubriquet

affusion: **7** pouring **8** infusion

affy: **4** join, rely **5** trust **6** affirm **7** betroth, confide, espouse **8** affiance

afghan: rug **7** blanket **8** coverlet

Afghan: dog **5** hound Pashto **8** language

Afghan carpet: **5** Herat

Afghan fox: 6 corsac
Afghanistan: *carpet:* **7** Bukhara
city: **5** Cabul (c.), Herat, Kabul (c.) **6** Ghuzni **8** Kandahar
coin: pul **6** abbasi, anania **7** afghani
language: **6** Pashto, Pushto
mountain: **8** Sulaiman **9** Himalayas, Hindu Kush
native: **7** Sistani
pony: **4** yabu **5** yaboo
prince: **4** amir, emir **5** ameer, emeer
river: **5** Cabul, Indus **7** Hari Rud, Helmund **9** Archandab
tribe: **4** Safi, Ulus
aficionado: fan **7** amateur, devotee **8** follower
afield: 6 abroad, astray
afire: 4 alow **5** alowe, eager **6** ablaze, ardent **7** burning, flaming
afloat: 4 asea **5** awaft, awash **6** adrift, buoyed, natant **7** flooded, unfixed **8** floating
afoot: 5 about, astir **6** abroad **7** walking **9** unmounted
aforesaid: 5 ditto, named, prior **8** previous **9** foregoing **10** antecedent
aforethought: 8 prepense **10** deliberate **11** forethought **12** premeditated
aforetime: ere **8** formerly
afraid: rad (Sc.) **5** timid **6** aghast, craven, scared **7** afeared, alarmed, anxious, fearful, gastful **8** cowardly, ghastful, timorous **9** shrinking, terrified **10** affrighted, frightened **12** fainthearted **13** pusillanimous
afreet: 4 jinn **5** afrit, demon, giant, jinni **6** afrite
afresh: 4 anew, anon, over **5** again, newly **6** denovo, encore **8** repeated
Africa: *animal:* ayu **4** arui **5** civet, genet, okapi, potto, ratel, zebra, zoril **6** aoudad, aye-aye, quagga, serval **7** nandine **8** aardvark, pangolin, suricate
antelope: gnu, kob **4** bisa, guib, koba, kudu, oryx, tolo, topi, tora, zenu **5** addax, beisa, bongo, eland, nagor, oribi, peele **6** duiker, grimme, impala, koodoo, rhebok **7** blaubok, blesbok, boshbok, defassa, gemsbok, grysbok, reitbok, sassaby, stembok **8** blesbuck, bontebok, bosehbok, steenbok, steinbok **9** steenbock **10** duikerbuck, hartebeest
Arab tribe: **9** Battakhin
ash: **4** atar
ass: **6** quagga
aunt: **5** tanta
baboon: **5** drill **8** mandrill
bass: iyo
bat: **10** hammerhead
bean: **7** calabar

beer: **5** pombe
bird: **4** lory, taha **6** weaver **7** touraco, xurakoo **8** umbretti **9** hammerkop
blaubok: **5** etaac **8** antelope
boat: **4** dhow
boss: **4** baas
bread: **5** kisra
buffalo: **5** niare
burrowing animal: **6** gerbil **8** aardvark, suricate
bushman: **4** Qung
bustard: **4** kori **5** paauw
caffeine tree: **4** cola, kola
camp: **4** boma **5** lager **6** laager
canoe: **7** almadia, almadie
cape: ras **4** juby, vert, yubi
carnivore: **4** lion **5** hyena, ratel **7** cheetah, leopard
cataract: **8** Victoria
catfish: **4** shal **5** schal **6** docmac
cattle: **5** niata
cattle pen: **5** kraal **6** zareba **7** zareeba
charm: **4** juju **5** saffi, safie **6** grigri, saphie **8** greegree
chief: **4** kaid **8** caboceer
city: **4** Oran **5** Accra, Cairo, Dakar, Lagos, Rabat, Tunis **6** Bangui, Ibadan **7** Algiers, Tripoli, Yaoundi **8** Cape Town, Freetown, Khartoum, Monrovia, Pretoria **9** Timbuctoo **10** Addis Ababa, Alexandria, Casablanca **11** Brazzaville, Dar es Salaam **12** Johannesburg, Leopoldville **14** Elisabethville
civet: **7** nandine
cloak: **5** jelab **6** jellab
coin: **4** akey, pesa **5** rupie, toque
colonist: **4** Boer
colony: see *country* below
coney: das **6** dassie
conference: **6** indaba
corn: **6** mealie
corn lily: **4** ixia
country: **4** Chad, Mali, Togo **5** Egypt, Gabon, Ghana, Kenya, Libya, Natal, Niger, Sudan, Zaire **6** Angola, Gambia, Guinea, Malawi, Uganda **7** Algeria, Burundi, Dahomey, Lesotho, Liberia, Morocco, Nigeria, Senegal, Somalia, Tunisia **8** Cameroon, Ethiopia, Malagasy, Tanzania **9** Swaziland **10** Mozambique **11** Sierra Leone
dance: **4** juba
deity: **6** nyambe, nzambi
desert: **5** Igidi **6** Libyan, Sahara **8** Kalahari
desert region: erg
dialect: Twi **4** Akan, Geez, Saho, Taal **5** Bantu, Fanti **7** Swahili
dish: **8** couscous
district: **4** Rand, Tibu **5** Nubia **6** Ruanda

dog: 7 basenji
dried meat: 7 biltong
drink: 8 skokiaan
dunes: erg
eagle: 8 berghaan
enclosure: 5 bomar, kraal
farmyard: 4 werf
fetish: see *charm* above
finch: 7 senegal
fly: 5 kivus 6 tsetse
food: 6 paw-paw 7 cassava
fox: 4 asse 5 caama 6 fennec
fruit: 5 terfa 6 terfez
gangster: 7 tsotsis
garden: 6 shamba
garment: 4 haik, tobe 6 kaross
gazelle: 4 admi, cora, dama, kudu, mohr,
  nohr, oryx 5 ariel, mhorr 7 buffalo, diba-
  tag 9 springbok
giraffelike animal: 5 okapi
gold region: 4 Rand
gorge: 5 kloof
grass: 4 alfa 5 fundi 7 esparto
grassland: 5 veldt
greenhorn: 5 ikona
groundnut: 5 gobbe
guard: 5 askar
gulf: 5 Gabes, Sidra 6 Guinea
gully: 5 donga 6 nullah
gun: 4 roer
harp: 4 nanga
headland: kop, ras
headman: 8 caboceer
helmet: 4 topi 5 topee
hemp: ife
hill: kop
hornbill: 4 tock
horse: 4 barb
horse disease: 5 surra
Hottentot: 4 Nama
house: 5 tembe
hunt: 6 safari
hut: 5 kraal, tembe
instrument: 5 nanga, rebab, zanze 6 balafo
iris: 4 ixia
Islamic sect: 9 Almohades
island: 6 Azores, Djerba 7 Bourbon, Como-
  ros, Madeira, Reunion, Socotra 8 Canar-
  ies, St. Helena 9 Ascension, Cape Verde,
  Mauritius 10 Fernando Po, Madagascar,
  Seychelles 12 Prince Edward
jackal: 5 diebs
king: 5 negus 8 Selassie
lake: 4 Asal, Chad, Lifu, Tana 5 Abayo,
  chott, Moero, Mweru, Ngami, Nyasa,
  Rirwa, Shott, Tchad, Tsana, Tumba 6 Albert, Dembel, Dilolo, Nyanza, Nyassa,

Rudolf, Shirwa 7 Leopold, Malumba 8 Victoria 9 Bangweulu, Stephanie 10 Tanganyika 12 Albert Edward
language: 5 Bantu, Hausa 6 Hamite 7 Swahili
legislature: 4 raad
lemur: 5 potto 6 maholi 8 kinkajou 10 angwantibo
lily: 4 aloe, ixia
livestock: fe
lynx: 7 caracal
mahogany: 9 cailcedra
measure: ton 4 doti, muid, rood, rope 5
  curba, darah, mkono 6 morgen 7 schepel 8
  Cape foot
monkey: 4 mona, mono, waag 5 patas 6
  grivet, guenon 7 guereza 8 talapoin
mortar: 5 swish
mountain: 4 Pare 5 Atlas, Kenia, Natal 7
  Cathkin, Kabylic 8 Cameroon 10 Draken-
  berg 11 Kilimanjaro
Muslim: 6 Berber
narcotic: 5 dagga
native(see also *people*below): Jur, Vai, Vei
  4 Bari, Egbo 5 Bantu, Felup, Sotik 6
  Fellup 7 Dahoman 8 Gabunese
nurse: aja 4 ayah
nut: 4 cola, kola
oak: 7 turtosa
old name: 5 Libya
ostrich: 4 rhea
palm: 4 doom, doum 6 raffia, raphia
palmyra: 6 ronier
pass: Nek
peasant: 4 kopi
people: Ga; Abo, Edo, Ewe, Ijo, Jur, Kru,
  Vai, Vei, Yao 4 Akim, Akka, Akra, Arab,
  Asha, Bari, Boni, Doma, Efik, Egbe, Ekoi,
  Golo, Habe, Hutu, Ibok, Kali, Leda, Lozi,
  Luri, Madi, Majo, Moor, Nama, Nuba,
  Riff, Sara, Suto, Tshi, Viti, Yako, Zulu 5
  Afifi, Bantu, Batwa, Dinka, Hausa, Inkra,
  Kafir, Mandi, Masai, Mende, Pygmy,
  Sanye, Temne, Tutsi, Wa-yao 6 Berber,
  Damara, Djerma, Dorobo, Fulani, Hamite, Kikuyu, Somali, Sousou, Tuareg,
  Ubangi, Wabena 7 Ashanti, Bambute,
  Bapindi, Batonga, Dahoman, Kindiga,
  Malinke, Nilotic, Sandawe, Songhai, Vol-
  taic
pigeon: 7 namaqua
pine: 6 ronier
plant: 4 ocra 5 argel, calla 6 arghel
plateau: 5 karoo
poison: 7 calabar
polecat: 5 zoril 6 musang
port: 5 Dakar 8 Freetown 10 Casablanca
Portuguese colony, former: 6 Angola
pygmy: 4 Akka 5 Afifi

reedbuck: 5 bohor, nagor 7 reitbok
region: 5 Nubia 6 Sahara
religious sect: 6 Coptic 7 Abelite
residence: 4 tato 5 kraal
rhinoceros: 6 umhofo
ridge: 4 rand
river: Job, Nun, Omo 4 Athi, Geba, Liba, Nile, Tana 5 Beira, Binue, Chobe, Congo, Kongo, Niger, Shari, Volta 6 Chinde, Gambia, Joliba, Rovuma, Sabaki, Ubangi 7 Atabara, Calabar, Limpopo, Semliki, Senegal, Zambesi 9 Crocodile
river bed: 5 donga
rosewood: 7 mulompi
scrub: 4 bito
seaport: Ibo 4 Oran 5 Dakar, Lagos, Tunis
secret society: Mau 6 Mau-Mau
servant: 4 volk
shallow lake: 5 chott, shott
sheep: 4 zenu
snake: boa 5 elaps, mamba 12 schaapsteker
soldier: 5 spahi 6 askari
sorcery: obe, obi 5 obeah
sorghum: 4 imfe 6 imphee
soup powder: 4 lalo
spear: 7 assagai, assegai
spiritual power: 4 ngai
squirrel: 5 xerus
stockade: 4 boma 6 zareba 7 zareeba
stork: 6 simbil 7 marabou
tableland: 5 karoo
tick: 6 tampan
title: 4 baas, sidi 5 bwana
tree: 4 akee, baku, bito, cola, etua, kola, moli, odum, olax, shea 5 abura, artar, bumbo, njave, odoom, sassy, siris, tenio 6 baobab, dukuma 7 assagai, assegai 8 gamdeboo 9 sassywood
tribe: See *people* above
valley: 4 daal, wadi, wady
village: 4 stad 5 kraal, stadt
wading bird: 4 ibis 8 ombrette
war dance: 7 calinda
wheat: 6 imphee
wild hog: 4 boar 7 warthog 9 boschvark
wild sheep: 4 arui 6 aoudad
wildcat: 6 serval
wind: 9 harmattan
witchcraft bean: 7 calabar
wolf: 4 aard
wood: 4 teak 5 ebony
worker: 4 volk
worm: loa
Afrikaans: 4 Boer, Taal
aft: 4 back, rear 5 abaft, after 6 astern, behind 9 posterior
opposite of: 4 fore

after: eft 4 anon, next, past 5 infra, later, since, apres (F.) 6 behind, beyond, follow, hinder 9 afterward, following, hereafter 10 subsequent, succeeding
awhile: 4 anon 5 later
prefix: 4 meta, post
after-dinner: 12 postprandial
afterbreast: 10 metathorax
aftermath: 4 loss 5 issue, rowen 6 eddish, effect, profit, result, sequel, upshot 7 stubble 11 consequence
aftermost: 4 last 8 hindmost
afternoon nap: 6 siesta
afternoon performance: 7 matinee
afterpiece: 5 epode, exode 8 postlude
aftersong: 5 epode
afterthought: 6 regret 7 remorse 15 reconsideration
in letter: PS10 postscript
afterward: 4 then 5 later 9 afterhend 10 thereafter 12 subsequently
afterwrist: 10 metacarpus
aga: 4 lord 5 chief 9 commander
wife: 5 begum
agacella: 8 antelope
Agag's slayer: 6 Samuel
again: bis, eft 4 anew, anon, back, more, over 6 afresh, denovo, encore, iterum (L.) 7 further 8 moreover
prefix: re
against: vs (abbr.); con, non 4 anti 5 anent 6 anenst, versus 7 opposed 8 adversus
prefix: ob 4 anti, para 6 contra
against the law: 7 illegal 8 unlawful
agal: 4 cord, rope
agalloch: 5 garoo 8 calambac 9 aloeswood, calambour, eaglewood
agallochum: 5 aloes
agama: 6 iguana, lizard
Agamemnon: *avenger:* 7 Orestes
brother: 8 Menelaus
daughter: 7 Electra 9 Iphigenia
father: 6 Atreus
rival: 9 Aegisthus
son: 7 Orestes
wife: 12 Clytemnestra
agape: 4 love, open 5 feast 6 gaping 7 yawning 10 bewildered
agar, agar-agar: 4 moss 6 gelose
agaric: 6 fungus
agasp: 5 eager 7 gasping 9 astounded
agate: taw 4 ruby 6 achate, marble, pebble, quartz 9 burnisher, drawplate 10 chalcedony
agave: 4 aloe 5 amole, datil 6 maguey, mescal, pulque 9 amaryllis
fiber: 4 pita 5 istle, sisal
Agaz: 6 Indian
age: eld, eon, era 4 aeon, olam, time 5 cycle, epoch, ripen, years 6 mature, mellow, pe-

riod, siecle, wither **7** century **8** duration,
eternity, lifetime, majority, maturity **9** se-
nectude **10** generation

geological: See **geology** *age*

modern: **6** atomic

pert. to: **4** eval **6** senile **9** geriatric

same: **6** coeval

aged: old **5** anile, hoary, olden, passe **6** feeble, infirm, mature, senile, ogyian **7** ancient, elderly **9** nestorian, senescent, venerable **10** antiquated

agee: 4 awry **5** agley, askew

ageless: 7 eternal **8** timeless

agency: 4 dint, hand **5** force, lever, means,
moyen, proxy **6** bureau, medium, office **9**
influence, operation **10** management **14**
intermediation **15** instrumentality

news: AP; UPI **4** Tass **5** Domei **7** Reuter's

suffix: eer, fic, ier **4** ator, ific

agendum: 5 slate **6** record, ritual **7** liturgy,
program **10** memorandum

Agenor: *daughter:* **6** Europa

father: **7** Antenor

son: **6** Cadmus

agent: spy **4** doer, gene, g-man, T-man **5** actor, buyer, cause, envoy, means, organ,
proxy **6** broker, commis, dealer, deputy,
factor, peskar, seller **7** bailiff, channel,
coucher, facient, proctor **8** aumildar, emissary, executor, operator, promoter, salesman **9** canvasser, consignee, go-between,
protector **10** commissary, instrument **11**
facilitator **12** intermediary **14** representative

appoint: **6** depute **8** deputize

insurance: **11** underwriter

narcotics: **4** nark

native: **8** aumildar

servile: **6** minion

suffix: see **agency** *suffix*

symbol: Agt

agger: 4 road, tide **5** mound **7** rampart **9**
earthwork **10** prominence

agglomerate: 4 heap, lump, mass, pile,
wind **6** gather **7** cluster, collect **10** collection **12** conglomerate

agglutination: 8 adhesion

aggrandize: 4 lift **5** boost, exalt, raise **7** advance, augment, dignify, elevate, enlarge,
magnify, promote **8** increase

aggravate: irk, nag, vex **4** load, twit **5** anger,
annoy, taunt, tease **6** burden, pester,
worsen **7** enhance, enlarge, magnify, provoke **8** aggrieve, heighten, increase, irritate **9** intensify **10** exacerbate, exaggerate,
exasperate

aggregate: add, all, sum **4** bulk, mass **5**
bunch, gross, total, unite, whole **6** amount,

volume **7** collect **9** accretion, composite **10**
accumulate, collection **11** combination,
composition

aggregation: 4 herd **5** flock, group **7** cluster
9 congeries **10** assemblage, collection **11**
association

aggression: war **4** raid **6** attack, injury **7**
assault, offense **8** invasion **9** intrusion **11**
provocation **12** encroachment

aggressive: 7 pushing **9** assertive **12** enterprising

aggressor: 9 assailant

aggrieve: try **4** harm, hurt, pain **5** harry,
wrong **6** injure **7** afflict, oppress, trouble **8**
distress **9** aggravate, persecute

aggrieved: 4 sore

aggroup: See **group**

aggry, aggri: 4 bead **5** charm

agha: See **aga**

aghast: 6 afraid **7** shocked **8** appalled **9** horrified, petrified, terrified

agile: 4 deft, fast, lish, spry, wiry **5** alert,
brisk, lithe, quick, withy **6** active, lissom,
lively, nimble, supple **7** lissome, salient,
springy **8** dextrous **9** dexterous

agio: 5 batta **7** premium **8** discount, exchange **9** allowance, brokerage, deduction
10 percentage

agist: tax **4** feed, rate **5** graze **7** pasture

agitate: fan, irk, jar, vex, wey **4** fret, move,
plot, rile, rock, seek, stir, teem **5** alarm,
churn, drive, harry, rouse, shake **6** arouse,
debate, devise, excite, foment, harass, incite, jumble, manage, rattle, ruffle, seethe
7 actuate, canvass, commove, concuss, discuss, disturb, perturb, revolve, trouble **8**
activate, contrive, convulse, disquiet, distract, transact **10** administer, discompose

agitation: gog **4** fear, gust, heat **5** hurry,
storm **6** bustle, energy, flight, flurry, jabble, quiver, tumult **7** emotion, ferment,
flutter, rampage, tempest, turmoil **8** paroxysm, upheaval **9** carfuffle, commotion,
confusion, estuation **10** combustion, ebullition, excitement, turbulence **11** trepidation **13** effervescence

prone to: **9** emotional

Aglaia: 5 Grace

aglet, aiglet: tab, tag **4** lace, stud **5** plate **7**
pendant, spangle **8** hawthorn, staylace

agley: 4 awry **5** aside, askew, wrong

agnate: 4 akin **6** allied **7** cognate, kindred

agnomen: 4 name **5** alias **7** epithet, surname **8** cognomen, nickname

agnomination: 7 echoing **10** repetition **12**
alliteration

agnostic: 7 doubter, skeptic **8** nescient **10**
unbeliever **11** freethinker

agnus dei: 4 bell, lamb **6** prayer

ago: by **4** erst, past, syne, yore **5** agone, since

agog: 4 avid, keen **5** astir, eager **6** lively **7** excited **8** vigilant **9** expectant, impatient

agon: 6 debate **7** contest **8** argument, struggle

agonize: 4 bear, rack **6** strain, writhe **10** excruciate

agony: 4 pain, pang **5** dolor, grief, panic, throe, trial **6** aching **7** anguish, anxiety, emotion, torment, torture, travail **8** distress, paroxysm **9** suffering **11** tribulation

agora: 8 assembly

agouti, agouty: 4 paca **5** color **6** animal, rodent

agra: 4 pain **7** seizure

Agra tomb: 8 Taj Mahal

agrafe, agraffe: 4 hook **5** clamp, clasp **6** eyelet

agrarian: 5 rural **8** pastoral **10** campestral **12** agricultural

agree: fit, gee, pan, yes **4** gibe, jibe, side, suit **5** admit, allow, atone, grant, hitch, match, tally, yield, unite **6** accede, accord, assent, comply, concur, condog, cotton, engage, settle, square, submit **7** arrange, comport, concede, conform, consent, promise **8** coincide, contract, covenant, quadrate **9** acquiesce, congruous, co-operate, harmonize, reconcile, stipulate **10** astipulate, correspond, homologate

agreeable: 4 easy, good, joli, lief, nice **5** amene, jolie, ready, suave, sweet **6** comely, dulcet, savory **7** adapted, amabile, amiable, couthie, greable, welcome, willing **8** amenable, charming, grateful, pleasant, pleasing, sociable, suitable **9** accordant, appealing, compliant, consonant, desirable **10** acceptable, compatible, convenient, harmonious **11** acquiescent, conformable **13** companionable

render: **7** dulcify

agreeableness of letters: 6 eutony

agreeing: 11 consentient

agreement: nod **4** bond, deal, mise, pact **5** lease, terms **6** action, assent, cartel, treaty, unison **7** bargain, closure, compact, concert, consent, entente, harmony, oneness, paction, rapport **8** contract, sympathy **9** accedence, accession, character, collusion, communion, concordat, condition, congruity, consensus, convenant, indenture, statement, unanimity **10** accordance, compliance, compromise, conformity, consonance, conspiracy, convention, obligation **11** arrangement, concordance, concurrence, resemblance, stipulation **12** capitulation **13** understanding

in opinion: **9** consensus

written: **6** cartel **8** contract

agremens, agrements: 6 graces **9** amenities, ornaments **14** embellishments

agrestic: 5 rural **6** rustic **7** bucolic **10** unpolished

agricultural: 8 geoponic

agriculture: 7 farming, tillage **8** agronomy **9** husbandry **10** agrotechny

area: **11** breadbasket

building: **4** barn, silo

chemical: **10** fertilizer

college student: **5** aggie

comb. form: **4** agro

establishment: **4** farm **5** grove, ranch **7** orchard

god: **4** Nabu, Nebo, Thor **6** Faunus, Tammuz **8** Amaethon

goddess: Ops **5** Ceres **7** Demeter

machine: **4** disk, plow **5** baler, drill, mower **6** binder, harrow, header, reaper, seeder, tedder **7** combine, tractor **8** thrasher, thresher **9** separator **10** cultivator **11** caterpillar

overseer: **8** agronome **10** agronomist

pert. to: **7** georgic

science: **11** arviculture

worker: **4** okie, peon **5** Arkie **6** cocker, farmer **7** migrant, peasant **8** farmhand

agriculturist: 6 farmer, grower **7** planter, rancher **10** agricolist, husbandman, orchardist

agrimony: 4 hemp **6** bidens **7** borwort

Agrippina's son: 4 Nero

agrise: 5 abhor, dread **6** loathe **7** shudder, terrify, tremble **8** affright

aground: 6 ashore **7** beached **8** stranded

agrypnia: 8 insomnia **13** sleeplessness

agua: 4 toad **5** water

aguacate: 7 avocado

aguamas: 7 pinguin

ague: 5 chill, fever **7** malaria

ague tree: 9 sassafras

agueweed: 7 boneset, comfrey, gentian **10** eupatorium

aguja: gar **6** marlin **9** spearfish

Ahab: *daughter* **7** Athalia **8** Athaliah

father: **4** Omri

wife: **7** Jezebel

Ahasuerus: *minister:* **5** Haman

wife: **6** Vashti

Ahaz: *son:* **8** Hezekiah

wife: Abi

Ahaziah's sister: 9 Jehosheba **11** Jehosobeath

ahead: on **4** fore **5** afore **6** before, onward **7** forward, leading **8** adelante, advanced, anterior **9** preceding

prefix: pre

Ahinoam: *husband:* **4** Saul **5** David

son: **5** Amnon

Aholibamah's husband: 4 Esau
Ahriman's angel: div 4 deev, deva
ahu: 4 heap 5 mound 7 gazelle
ahuehuete: 5 cedar 6 sabino 7 cypress
ai: 5 sloth 8 edentate
aid: key 4 abet, back, beet, help, pony 5 allay, boost, coach, favor, grant, serve, treat
   6 assist, favour, relief, remedy, rescue, second, succor, uphold 7 advance, forward,
   further, relieve, subsidy, support 8 befriend 9 alleviate, auxiliary 10 assistance,
   facilitate 11 collaborate, countenance
Aida: *composer:* 5 Verdi
   father: 8 Amonasro
   lover: 7 Radames
   rival: 7 Amneris
aide: 6 deputy, second 7 officer, orderly 8
   adjutant 9 assistant 11 subordinate 12 underofficer
aigrette: 5 egret, heron, plume, spray 8
   feathers
ail: 4 fail, pain, pine 6 affect, bother, falter,
   suffer 7 afflict, decline, trouble 8 complain, distress 13 indisposition
Ailie: 5 Helen
ailment (see also **disease**): ail 6 malady 7
   disease, illness 8 disorder, sickness, weakness 9 affection, complaint, infirmity 13
   indisposition
aim: end, lay, try 4 bent, butt, goal, head,
   plan 5 essay, guess, level, point, sight,
   train 6 aspire, design, direct, esteem, intend, intent, object, scheme, strive 7 address, purpose 8 consider, endeavor, estimate 9 calculate, endeavour, intention,
   objective 10 aspiration, conjecture, estimation
aimless: 4 idle 5 blind 6 chance, random 8
   drifting 9 desultory 10 undirected 11 purposeless
aimlessness: 8 flanerie
aine: 5 elder 6 senior
air: sky 4 aria, aura, lilt, mien, neon, pose,
   song, tell, tune, vent 5 beach (Sc.), ether,
   ozone, voice 6 aerate, aether, allure, aspect, broach, cachet, helium, manner,
   melody, ostent, regard, vanity, welkin 7
   bearing, display, exhibit, krypton 8 attitude, behavior, carriage, sandbank (Sc.) 9
   behaviour, semblance, ventilate 10 appearance, atmosphere, deportment 11 affectation, haughtiness 12 stratosphere
   comb. form: aer, atm 4 aeri, aero, atmo
   containing: 9 pneumatic
   current: 4 wind 5 draft 6 breeze 7 draught
   downward motion (pert. to): 9 katabatic
   element: 5 argon, xenon 6 oxygen 8 nitrogen
   in the: 5 aloft

   measuring device: 9 aerometer, airometer
   musical: see **melody**
   overcast: 4 haze
   upper: 5 ether 6 aether
air fleet arrangement: 7 echelon 8 squadron
air navigation officer: 8 avigator
air plant: 8 epiphyte
air pressure: 5 baric
air propeller: fan
air spirit: 5 Ariel, sylph
aircraft (see also **airplane**): 4 kite 5 blimp,
   plane 6 copter, glider 7 balloon, chopper 8
   aerostat, airplane, autogyro, zeppelin 9 dirigible, orthopter 10 helicopter
   carrier: 7 flattop
   fleet formation: 7 echelon
   manufacturer: 4 Vega 5 Astra 6 Bendix,
     Boeing, Curtis, Hughes, United, Vultee,
     Wright 7 Convair, Douglas, Grumman 8
     Lockheed, American, Northrop, Republic
   motorless: 6 glider
   part: fin 4 keel, tail, wing 5 cabin 6 cabane
     7 aileron, cockpit, nacelle 8 fusilage 9 em-
     pennage
   pilotless: 5 drone
   route: 6 skyway
   route marker: 5 pylon
   shelter: 6 hangar
   unit: 5 squad 10 escadrille
   vapor: 8 contrail
airing: 4 walk 6 pasear 8 exposure
airn: 4 iron
airplane (see also **aircraft**): jet, MIG, SST 4
   gyro, zero 5 avion (F.), liner 6 bomber, copter, glider, 7 biplane, clipper, fighter 9
   monoplane
   inventor: 6 Wright
   maneuver: 4 buzz, dive, loop, roll 8 nosedive
     9 chandelle
   operator: 5 flier, flyer, pilot 7 aviator 8
     aeronaut
airport: 5 drome 8 airdrome, airfield 9 aerodrome
airs: 6 vanity 10 mannerisms, pretension 11
   affectation, haughtiness, preciseness
airship: See **aircraft, airplane**
airt: See **direct**
airtight: 6 sealed 8 hermetic 12 impenetrable
airy: gay 4 cool, rare, thin 5 empty, huffy,
   light, merry 6 aerial, breezy, jaunty, jocund, lively 7 airlike, haughty 8 affected,
   animated, debonair, delicate, ethereal,
   flippant, graceful, trifling, volatile 9
   sprightly, visionary, vivacious 11 atmo-
   spheric 13 insubstantial, unsubstantial
aiseweed: 8 goutweed

PATh

aisle: way 4 lane, walk 5 alley 7 passage 8 corridor 10 ambulatory, passageway

ait: oat eyot, holm, isle 5 islet

aitchbone: 9 natchbone

aith: 4 oath

aitu: god 5 demon 6 spirit

aizle: 5 ember, spark

ajaja: 4 bird 9 spoonbill

ajar: 4 open 10 discordant

Ajax's father: 7 Telamon

ajonjoli: 6 sesame

ajuga: 4 herb 7 bugloss 9 bugleweed

akia: 6 poison

akimbo: 6 angled

akin: sib 4 like, near, nigh 5 alike, close 6 agnate, allied 7 cognate, connate, germane, related, similar 10 correlated 11 appropriate 14 consanguineous

aku: 10 victorfish

akule: 4 fish 7 goggler

al, aal: 8 mulberry

dye: 8 morindin

ala: 4 axil, drum, wing 6 axilla, recess 8 winglike

Alabama: *city:* 5 Selma 6 Mobile 8 Anniston 10 Birmingham (c.)

county: Lee 4 Bibb, Clay, Dale, Hale, Pike 5 Coosa, Lamar 6 Etowah 7 Chilton

river: 5 Coosa

state flower: 9 goldenrod

alabarch: 10 magistrate

alabaster: 6 gypsum

alack: 4 alas 9 alackaday

alacrity: 5 haste, speed 8 celerity, rapidity 9 briskness, eagerness, readiness 11 promptitude, willingness 13 sprightliness

Aladdin's spirit: 4 jinn (pl.) 5 genie, genii (pl.)

a la diable: 7 deviled 8 seasoned

alameda: 4 mall, walk 9 promenade

Alamo: 4 fort, tree 6 battle, poplar, shrine 7 mission

hero: 5 Bowie 8 Crockett

a la mode: 4 mood 7 stylish 11 fashionable

alan: dog 9 wolfhound

alant: 10 sneezeweed

alantin: 6 inulin

alar: 6 pteric, winged 8 axillary, winglike 10 wing-shaped

alarm: din, SOS 4 bell, fear, gast 5 alert, broil, clock, larum, noise, panic, rouse, scare, siren, upset 6 affray, alarum, appall, arouse, attack, buzzer, dismay, excite, fright, outcry, signal, terror, tocsin 7 disturb, gloppen, startle, terrify, warning 8 frighten, surprise 9 commotion, diversion 11 disturbance, trepidation 13 consternation

alarmist: 9 pessimist, terrorist 11 scaremonger

alarum: See **alarm**

alas: ay; ach, heu, och, woe 5 alack, oimee 6 ochone 8 welladay, wellaway 12 interjection

Alaska: *animal:* 4 bear 6 Kadiak, Kodiak

auk: 5 arrie, murre

bear: 6 Kadiak, Kodiak

bird: auk 5 arrie, murre

blizzard: 5 purga

boat: 5 kayak, umiak 6 oomiac 7 angeyok, bidarka 8 bidarkee

city: 4 Nome 5 Sitka 6 Juneau (c.), Kodiak, Seward, Valdez 7 Cordova, Douglas, Klawock, Skagway 8 Latouche, Wrangell 9 Anchorage, Fairbanks, Ketchikan 10 Metlakatla, Petersburg

cotton grass: 10 eriophorum

fish: 4 atka 5 wacha 6 salmon 7 inconnu

garment: 5 parka

glacier: 4 Muir

highway: 5 Alcan

island: 4 Adak, Atka, Attu, Unga 5 Riska 6 Tanaka 8 Pribilof 9 Andreanof

island group: Fox, Rat 4 Near 8 Aleutian

liquor: 9 hoochinoo

mountain: Ada 4 Muir 5 Logan 8 McKinley 9 Blackburn 10 Saint Elias 11 Fairweather

native: auk 5 Aleut, Sitka 6 Ahtena, Eskimo 7 Tlingit 8 Aleutian

purchaser: 6 Seward

river: 4 Atna 5 Yukon 6 Copper, Innoko, Noatak, Tanana 7 Koyukuk, Susitna 9 Kuskokwim, Matanuska, Porcupine 10 Whitehorse

tree: 5 sitka 6 spruce

alate: ant 5 aphid 6 insect, winged

alb, albe: 7 camisia 8 vestment

albacore: 4 tuna 5 tunny 6 germon

Albania: *city:* 5 Berat 6 Avlona, Durres, Tirana (c), Tirane (c.), Valona 7 Chimara, Coritza, Durazzo, Elbasan, Koritza, Prevesa, Scutari 8 Tepeleni

coin: lek 5 franc 6 qintar

dialect: Geg 4 Cham, Gheg, Tosc, Tosk 7 Ghegish, Toskish

former king: Zog

lake: 7 Ochrida, Scutria

river: 4 Arta, Drin

soldier: 7 palikar

albatross: 4 bird 5 nelly 6 fabric 9 mallemuck

albeit: but, tho 5 altho 6 though 8 although 15 notwithstanding

albertin: 4 coin

Albion: 6 Anglia 7 England

albula: 4 fish 5 chiro

album: 4 book 6 record 8 register 9 scrap-book 10 collection

albumen seed: 9 endosperm

albuminoid: 7 elastin, keratin, protein 8 collagen

alburnum: 7 sapwood

alcalde, alcade: 5 judge 10 magistrate 11 burgomaster

alcazar: 6 castle, palace 8 fortress

Alcestis: *father:* 6 Pelias
  husband: 7 Admetus
  rescuer: 8 Heracles, Hercules

alchemist: 5 adept 8 hermetic

alchemy: art 5 magic 11 thaumaturgy
  god: 6 Hermes
  iron: 4 Mars

alchitran: oil 5 pitch 7 bitumen

Alcidice: *husband:* 9 Salmoneus
  daughter: 4 Tyro

alcidine bird: auk 6 puffin 9 guillemot

Alcinous: *daughter:* 8 Nausicaa
  wife: 5 Arete

Alcmaeon: *father:* 10 Amphiaraus
  wife: 10 Callirrhoe

Alcmene's husband: 10 Amphitryon

alcohol (see also **alcoholic drink**)**:** 5 ethyl, vinyl 6 liquor, methyl 7 ethanol 8 methanol
  crystalline: 6 guaiol, talite 7 talitol
  desire for: 10 dipsomania
  liquid: 8 farnesol
  radical: 4 amyl
  solid: 6 sterin, sterol 11 cholesterol
  standard: 5 proof
  suffix: ol

alcoholic: 9 spiritous 11 dipsomaniac 12 intoxicating

alcoholic drink: ale, gin, rum 4 beer, grog, wine 5 julep, lager, negus, vodka 6 brandy, liquor, whisky 7 liqueur, whiskey 8 cocktail, highball

Alcoran: 5 Koran

Alcott heroine: Jo; Amy, Meg 4 Beth

alcove: bay 4 nook 5 bower, niche, oriel 6 recess 7 cubicle, dinette, tablina (L. pl.) 8 alhacena (Sp.), tablinum 11 compartment

alder: arn (Sc.) 4 tree 5 shrub
  genus: 5 almus

alderman: 6 bailie, senior 7 headman 10 magistrate

ale: mum 4 beer, bock, brew, flip 5 clink, lager, nappy, stout 6 alegar, liquor, porter, stingo, swanky 8 beverage, hugmatee
  mixed with sweetener: 7 bragget

ale mug: 4 toby 5 stein

Alea: 5 light 6 Athena

alee: 5 ahead 7 leeward
  opposite of: 5 stoss 8 aweather

alegar: ale

alehouse: pub 6 tavern 7 barroom 9 host-house

alembic: 5 still 6 retort, vessel 7 changer, furnace 9 distiller

Alençon product: 4 lace

alert: 4 gleg, warn, wary 5 agile, alarm, alive, awake, brisk, eager, ready, sharp, siren 6 active, alarum, bright, lively, nimble, prompt, tocsin 7 wakeful 8 vigilant, watchful 9 observant, wide-awake 11 circumspect

alette: 4 wing 8 abutment, door jamb

Aleut: 4 Atka 8 Unalaska

Aleutian Island: 4 Adak, Attu 5 Kiska, Umnak 6 Akutan, Amukta, Kodiak, Seguam 7 Kagamil 8 Amchitka, Unalaska

alewife: 4 fish 6 allice 7 herring, pompano, walleye 9 gaspereau (F.)

Alexander: *birthplace:* 5 Pella
  horse: 10 Bucephalus
  kingdom: 9 Macedonia
  mistress: 8 Campaspe
  victory: 5 Issus 6 Arbela

Alexandria: *bishop:* 10 Athanasius
  magistrate: 8 alabarch
  patriarch: 4 papa
  theologian: 5 Arius

alfa: 7 esparto

alfalfa: hay 6 fodder, lucern 7 lucerne

alforja: bag 5 pouch 6 wallet 9 saddlebag

alga: 4 nori 6 desmid, diatom, nostoc 7 seaweed 8 rockweed
  genus: 5 dasya 6 alaria, padina 10 gloeocapsa
  study: 8 algology

algarroba: 4 tree 5 carob 6 calden

algate, algates: yet 6 always, wholly 10 completely, everywhere 15 notwithstanding

Algeria: 7 Algerie, Numidia
  cavalryman: 5 spahi 6 spahee
  city: 4 Bona, Oran 5 Blida, Media 7 Algiers (c.), Tlemcen 11 Constantine
  department: 4 Oran 7 Algiers 11 Constantine
  grass: 7 esparto
  measure: pik 5 rebis, tarri 6 termin 9 pik halebi
  monastery: 5 ribat
  mountain: 5 Atlas
  people: 5 Arabs 7 Berbers, Kabyles
  river: 6 Shelif
  ruler: bey, dey
  seaport: 4 Bona, Bone, Oran, Orel
  ship: 5 xebec
  tirailleur: 5 Turco
  weight: 4 rotl

algesia: 4 ache, pain 7 algesis

algid: 4 cold, cool 6 chilly, clammy

Algiers', native quarters: 6 Casbah, Kasbah

algodon: 6 cotton

algodoncillo: 7 majagua

Algonquin (see also **Indian**): Sac
spirit: 7 Manitou

Alhambra site: 7 Granada

Ali: *descendant:* 7 fatimid 8 fatimite
wife: 6 Fatima

Ali Baba: *brother:* 6 Cassim
word: 6 sesame

alias: 4 else, name 5 other, title 7 assumed, epithet, pen name 9 pseudonym, sobriquet

alibi: 4 plea 6 excuse 7 apology, pretext

Alice in Wonderland: *author:* 7 Carroll
character: cat 5 Queen 6 rabbit, Walrus 9 Mad Matter 11 Cheshire cat, White Rabbit

alien: ger 5 fremd, metic 6 exotic, remote 7 foreign, invader, strange 8 stranger, transfer 9 foreigner, immigrant, outlander, peregrine 10 irrelevant, tramontane 11 incongruous 12 inconsistent 13 unsympathetic

alienate: 4 part, wean 5 avert 6 convey, devest 8 amortize, disunite, estrange, separate, transfer, withdraw 10 abalienate

alienist: 12 psychiatrist

aliform: 8 winglike 10 wing-shaped

alight: 4 land, rest, stop 5 lodge, perch, roost 6 arrive, settle 7 descend, lighted 8 dismount 9 disembark

align, aline: 4 tram, true 5 array, range 6 adjust 7 arrange, marshal 10 straighten

alike: 4 akin, like, same 5 equal, twins 7 equally, similar, uniform 9 congruent, duplicate, identical
comb. form: iso

aliment: pap 4 food 5 broma, manna 6 viands 7 alimony, pabulum, rations 9 allowance, nutriment, substance 10 sustenance 11 nourishment

alimentation: 7 support 9 nutrition 10 sustenance 11 maintenance, nourishment

alimony: 7 aliment 9 allowance 11 maintenance

aline: See **align**

alive: 4 busy, keen, spry, vive (F.) 5 agile, alert, astir, brisk, quick, vital 6 extant, living 7 animate, vibrant 8 animated, existent, sensible, swarming 9 breathing, sensitive, sprightly, unexpired 14 unextinguished

alkali: lye, reh 4 kali, soda, usar
volatile: 7 ammonia

alkaline: *remedy:* 7 antacid
salt: 5 borax

alkaloid: 6 aricin, codein, conine, eserin 7 arabine, aricine, caffein, cocaine, codeine 8 atropine, caffeine, morphine 10 strychnine 13 physostigmine

all: sum 5 gross, quite, total, totum (L.), whole 6 entire, solely, wholly 7 plenary 8 entirely, everyone, totality 9 aggregate, everybody 10 altogether, completely, everything, thoroughly 11 exclusively
comb. form: pan 4 omni

all-fired: 7 extreme 9 excessive 10 inordinate

all in: 5 tired, weary

all-knowing: 10 omniscient

all right: OK; yes 4 okay 6 agreed 9 hunky-dory

all there: 4 sane

allanite: 6 cerite 7 mineral

allay: aid 4 calm, cite, cool, ease, help, hush 5 abate, allay, charm, check, quell, quiet, slake, still 6 adduce, pacify, quench, reduce, soften, soothe, stanch, subdue, temper 7 appease, assuage, comfort, compose, lighten, mollify, relieve, repress, staunch 8 mitigate, palliate 9 alleviate

allee: See **alley**

allege: 4 aver, avow, cite 5 offer, plead, quote, state, swear 6 adduce, affirm, assert, assign, charge, depose 7 advance, ascribe, declare, lighten, present, profess, propose 8 allegate, maintain 9 attribute 10 asseverate

alleged force: od 4 odyl

allegiance: tie 4 duty 5 honor 6 fealty, homage 7 loyalty, tribute 8 devotion, fidelity 9 constancy, obedience 10 obligation
violation of: 7 treason 9 treachery

allegory: 4 myth, tale 5 fable, story 7 parable 8 apologue, metaphor

alleviate: aid 4 ease, help 5 abate, allay 6 allege, lenify, lessen, pacify, soften, solace, soothe 7 assuage, compose, console, correct, lighten, relieve 8 diminish, mitigate, moderate, palliate 9 extenuate 11 tranquilize

alley: way 4 lane, mall, path, walk 5 allee, byway, chare, tewer 6 vennel 7 passage 10 passageway 12 thoroughfare
back: 4 slum

alliance: 4 pact 5 union 6 accord, fusion, league, treaty 7 compact, entente, society 8 affinity, agnation, covenant 9 coalition 10 federation, fellowship 11 association, combination confederacy, partnership 13 confederation

allice: 4 shad

allied: 4 akin 6 agnate, joined, linked, united 7 cognate, germane, kindred, related, similar 9 analogous

alligator: 5 niger 6 caiman, cayman, jacare, yacare 7 lagarto 9 crocodile

alligator pear: 7 avocado 8 aguacate

alliteration: 10 repetition 12 agnomination

allium: 4 leek 5 onion 6 garlic

allmouth: 6 angler

allocate: 4 deal, dole, mete, rate 5 allot, award, share 6 affect, assign 9 apportion 10 distribute

allonge: 4 pass 5 lunge, rider 6 thrust

allophanamide: 6 biuret 8 compound

allot: fix 4 cast, deal, dole, mete 5 award, grant, share 6 assign, bestow, depute, design, ordain, ration 7 appoint, destine, prorate, specify, tribute 8 allocate 9 apportion, attribute, authorize, prescribe 10 distribute

allow: let 4 bear, lend 5 admit, defer, grant, stand, thole, yield 6 accept, accord, assign, bestow, beteem, endure, permit, suffer 7 approve, concede, confess, suppose 8 consider, sanction, tolerate 9 authorize 11 acknowledge

allowance: fee 4 agio, edge, gift, hire, odds, size 5 leave, share 6 bounty, margin, salary 7 aliment, alimony, pension, portion, stipend 8 appenage, approval, discount, quantity, sanction, 9 admitting, allotment, conceding, deduction, reduction, tolerance 10 permission 11 appointment, approbation 13 authorization

short: 6 ration 9 scrimping

traveling: 7 mileage

weight: 4 tare, tret 7 scalage

allowing for that: if

alloy: mix 5 mokum 6 garble 7 mixture 9 admixture 10 adulterate, amalgamate

black copper: 6 niello

carbon and iron: 5 steel

Chinese: 7 paktong 8 packtong

copper and aluminum: 9 duralumin

copper, iron and zinc: 4 aich 7 paktong, rheotan 8 packtong

copper and tin: 6 bronze, oreide, oroide, pewter

copper and zinc: 5 brass 6 oreide, oroide 8 arsedine

costume jewelry: 6 oreide, oroide

fusible: 6 solder

gold and silver: 4 asem

gold-like: 6 oreide, oroide 8 doralium

heat resistant: 6 cermet 7 ceramal

lead and tin: 5 calin, terne 6 pewter

mercurial: 7 amalgam

nickel and silver: 8 alfenide

nickel and steel: 7 elinvar

nonferrous: 4 tula

pewter: 5 bidri

silver with copper or tin: 6 billon

sulphuric: 6 niello

tin: 5 terne 6 pewter

All's Well That Ends Well character: 5 Diana, Lafeu 7 Bertram

allspice tree: 7 pimento

allude: 4 hint 5 imply, point, refer 6 advert, relate 7 connote, mention, suggest 8 indicate, intimate 9 attribute, insinuate

allure (see also **lure**): air, woo 4 bait, draw, lead, lure, move, sway 5 angle, bribe, charm, court, decoy, snare, tempt 6 entice, entrap, induce, seduce 7 attract, beguile, ensnare 8 blandish, inveigle, persuade 9 captivate, fascinate, influence

allurement: 4 cord 6 glamor 7 gudgeon 9 incentive 10 enticement, temptation 11 fascination

allusion: 4 hint, twit 7 inkling, mention 8 innuendo, instance 9 quotation, reference 10 intimation

alluvial: *clay:* 5 adobe

deposit: mud 4 sand, silt, wash 5 delta, drift, geest 6 gravel, placer

fan: 5 delta

alluvion: 4 flow, wash 5 flood 10 inundation 11 overflowing

ally: pal 4 aide, join 5 union, unite 6 backer, friend, helper 7 connect, partner 8 adherent 9 affiliate, assistant, associate, auxiliary, colleague, supporter 10 accomplice 11 confederate

almanac: 4 ordo 8 calendar 9 ephemeris

almandine: 6 spinel, garnet 9 almandite

almighty: 5 great 7 extreme 8 powerful, puissant 10 omnipotent 12 irresistible

Almighty: God 7 Creator

almond: nut 5 badam 6 kanari

paste: 8 marzipan

pert. to: 10 amygdaline

syrup: 6 orgeat

almost: 4 nigh 5 anear, close 6 amaist, feckly (Sc.), nearly 13 approximately

prefix: pen 4 pene

alms: 4 dole, gift 6 aumous (Sc.), bounty, relief 7 charity, handout 8 donation, gratuity, offering, pittance 11 benefaction 12 philanthropy

box: 4 arca 7 poor box

dispenser: 7 almoner, almsman 11 eleemosynar

almshouse: 9 poorhouse, workhouse

almsman: 6 beggar, pauper

almuce: 4 hood 6 tippet 9 headdress

alodium, allodium: 6 estate 8 property

aloe: 4 pita 5 agave 6 maguey

compound: 5 aloin

extract: 5 orcin 7 orcinol

powder: 5 picra

aloes: 5 tonic 8 agalloch 10 agallochum

aloft: up 4 high 5 above 6 upward 7 skyward
8 overhead

aloha: 4 love 8 farewell, greeting, kindness
9 affection 10 salutation

alone: one 4 bare, lorn, only, sole, solo 5
aloof, apart, solus 6 single, unique 8 desolate, detached, isolated, separate, solitary
9 exclusive, matchless, unmatched 11 exclusively 12 incomparable, unparalleled
13 companionless, unaccompanied
comb. form: 4 soli

along: on; via 4 away, with 5 ahead 6 beside,
onward 7 forward 8 parallel, together 10
lengthwise

alongside: at, by 5 close 6 aboard 7 abreast
8 parallel
prefix: 4 para

Alonso's son: 9 Ferdinand

aloof: shy 4 cold, cool 5 aback, alone, apart,
proud 6 abeigh, frosty, remote, silent 7 distant, removed 8 detached, reserved, secluded, windward 11 indifferent

alopecia: 8 baldness 11 phalacrosis

alopecoid: 7 foxlike, vulpine

alouatte: 6 monkey

aloud: 4 oral 5 vocal 7 audible

alp: 4 peak 5 demon, mount, witch 8 mountain 9 bullfinch, nightmare

alpaca: 4 paco 5 llama

alpenstock: 5 staff 9 bergstock

alpha: 5 chief, debut, first
and omega: all 5 whole 6 entire

alphabet: 4 ABC's, order 6 primer, sarada
10 abcedarium
character: 4 ogam, ogum, rune 5 ogham 6
letter
pert. to: 11 abecedarian
Runic: 7 Futharc, Futhork

alphabetize: 7 arrange

Alpine: hat 5 stick 9 alpestral
dance: 5 gavot
dress: 6 dirndl
dwelling: 6 chalet
goat: 4 ibex 8 steinbok
herdsman: 4 senn
pass: col
plant: 9 edelweiss
primrose: 8 auricula
wind: 4 bora 5 foehn

Alps: *Austrian:* 5 Tirol, Tyrol
division of: 7 Bernese 8 Maritime 9 Lepon-
tine
Italian: 9 Dolomites
mountain: 5 Blanc 7 Bernina 8 Jungfrau 10
Matterhorn
pass: 5 Cenis 7 Brenner, Simplon
tunnel: 5 Cenis 7 Arlberg, Gothard, Simplon 11 Loetschberg
Yugoslav: 6 Julian 7 Dinaric

already: een, now 6 before

Alsatian clover: 4 herb 6 alsike

also: and, eke, too, yet 4 erst, more, plus 5
ditto 7 besides, further 8 likewise, moreover 9 similarly

also-ran: 5 loser 9 candidate

altar: ara 5 table 6 autere, shrine 7 chancel,
chantry 9 sanctuary
area: 4 apse
boy: 7 acolyte
carpet: 6 pedale
cloth: 6 coster 7 frontal
curtain: 6 coster, riddel
enclosure: 4 bema
hanging: 6 dorsal, dossal, dossel
ledge: 7 retable
platform: 8 predella
portable: 10 superaltar
screen: 7 reredos
top: 5 mensa
vessel: pyx 7 piscina

alter: 4 geld, move, turn, vary, veer 5 adapt,
amend, break, emend, reset, shift 6 adjust,
change, modify, mutate, revise, temper 7
convert 9 transform 11 interpolate

alter ego: 5 agent 6 friend 8 henchman

altercation: 4 spat, tiff 5 brawl, broil, fight
6 bicker, jangle, strife 7 contest, dispute,
quarrel, wrangle 10 contention 11 controversy

alternate: 4 else, sway, vary 5 other, recur,
shift 6 change, rotate, seesaw 8 intermit 9
oscillate 10 substitute 11 interchange, reciprocate

alternative: or 6 choice, either, option 8
election 10 preference
word introducing: 7 whether

althaea: 6 mallow

Althaea's husband: 6 Oeneus

althorn: sax 4 alto 7 saxhorn

although: een 4 even 5 while 6 albeit,
though 7 despite 15 notwithstanding

altitude: 4 apex, peak 6 height 7 stature 9
elevation, loftiness
measuring device: 8 orometer 9 altimeter

altitude sickness: 7 soroche

alto: 4 part 6 singer 7 althorn, saxhorn 8
vocalist

altogether: all 5 quite 6 wholly 7 totally,
utterly 10 completely, thoroughly 12 collectively

altruism: 10 generosity 11 benevolence 12
philanthropy 13 unselfishness

alture: 6 height

aludel: pot

alula: 4 lobe, wing

alum: 7 styptic 10 astringent
rock: 7 alunite

alumina: 5 argil

aluminum: *calcium silicate:* 7 epidote
discoverers: 4 Davy 6 Wohler
hydrousphosphate: 9 wavellite
oxide: 7 alumina
sulphate: 4 alum
alumnus: 4 grad 5 pupil 8 graduate
alure: 7 gallery, passage 10 ambulatory
alveary: 4 hive 7 beehive 9 alvearium
alveolar plasma: 11 trophoplasm
alveolate: 6 pitted 9 faveolate 11 honeycombed
always: ay; aye, een, e'er 4 ever 6 semper
(L.), 7 algates, forever 8 evermore 9 eternally, uniformly 10 constantly, habitu-
ally, invariably 11 continually, perpetually, unceasingly 13 everlastingly
alyssum: 6 alison
am: See **be**
ama: cup 5 amula, cruet, diver 6 vessel 7
chalice 9 candlenut
amabile: 6 gentle, tender 9 agreeable
amability: 11 lovableness
Amadis' beloved: 6 Oriana
amadou: 4 punk 6 tinder 9 touchwood
amah: 5 nurse 7 servant
amain: 7 greatly 8 forcibly 9 violently 10
vigorously 11 exceedingly
Amalekite king: 4 Agag
amalgamate: mix 4 fuse, join 5 alloy, blend,
merge, unite 6 mingle 7 combine 8 coalesce, compound 11 consolidate
Amalthea: 4 goat
horn: 10 cornucopia
nursling: 4 Zeus
amanita: 6 agaric
amanuensis: 6 penman, scribe, typist 8 recorder 9 scrivener, secretary 11 transcriber 12 stenographer
amara: 6 beetle
amaryllis: 4 girl, lily 5 agave 10 sweetheart
11 shepherdess
Amasa's father: 6 Jether
amass: 4 heap, mass, pile, save 5 gross,
hoard, stack, store 6 gather 7 collect, compile 8 assemble 10 accumulate
amate: 4 tree 5 daunt, match 6 subdue 10
dishearten
amateur: ham 4 tiro, tyro 6 novice, votary 7
admirer, dabbler, devotee, fancier 8 beginner 10 dilettante, aficionado 15 nonprofessional
amative: 4 fond 6 ardent, loving 7 amatory,
amorous 10 passionate
amaze: awe 4 stun 5 alarm 6 astony 7 astound, confuse, perplex, stagger, stupefy 8
astonish, bewilder, confound, dumfound,
surprise 9 dumbfound, overwhelm
amazement: 5 ferly 6 frenzy, wonder 7 madness 13 consternation

Amazon: 5 river, woman 7 warrior
cetacean: 4 inia
discoverer: 8 Orellana
estuary: 4 Para
headstream: 7 Maranon
mat: 4 yapa
queen: 9 Hippolyta 12 Penthesileia
rain forest: 5 selva 6 silvas
tributary: Ica 4 Napo
ambage: 4 path 7 circuit, quibble 9 ambiguity 14 circumlocution
ambari: da 4 hemp 5 fiber 7 cordage
ambassador: 5 agent, envoy 6 deputy, legate, nuncio 8 diplomat, minister 9 messenger 10 ambassiate 12 intermediary 14 representative 15 plenipotentiary
pert. to: 8 legatine
amber: 4 gris 5 resin 6 yellow 8 amberoid,
electrum 9 ambergris
amber-colored: 8 resinous
ambiance, ambience: 6 milieu 11 environment 12 surroundings
ambiguity: 6 ambage 7 paradox 9 duplexity, obscurity 10 hesitation 12 doubtfulness
ambiguous: 4 dark 5 vague 6 double 7 cryptic, dubious 8 doubtful 9 bifarious, equivocal, uncertain, unsettled 10 indefinite, indistinct, mistakable 11 problematic 12 inexplicable, questionable 13 indeterminate
ambit: 5 limit, scope, space 6 bounds, extent,
sphere 7 circuit, compass 8 boundary, precinct 13 circumference
ambition: 4 goal, hope, wish 5 glory 6 desire
7 purpose 9 intention 10 aspiration
ambitious: 4 avid, bold, keen 5 eager, showy
7 emulous 8 aspiring
amble: 4 gait 7 meander, saunter
ambo: 4 desk 6 pulpit
Amboina button: 4 yaws
Amboina pine: 8 galagala
ambos: 5 incus
ambrosia: 5 honey 6 nectar
ambrosial: 6 divine 8 fragrant 9 delicious
ambry: 4 safe 5 chest, niche 6 closet, pantry,
recess 7 almonry, armoire 8 armarium,
cupboard 10 repository
ambulate: gad 4 hike, move, walk
ambush: 4 lurk, trap 5 await, blind, snare
6 waylay 7 forelay 9 ambuscade, ambus-
cado
ameer: See **emir**
ameliorate: 4 ease, help, mend 5 amend 6
better, reform 7 improve, promote 9 meliorate
amen: yea 5 truly 6 assent, verily, so-be-it 8
approval, sanction 9 assuredly, certainly
11 termination 12 ratification
Amen-Ra's wife: Mut

amenable: 4 open 6 liable, pliant 7 subject 9 tractable 10 answerable, responsive 11 accountable, responsible

amend: end 4 beet, mend 5 alter, emend 6 better, change, reform, remedy, repair, repeal, revise 7 convert, correct, improve, recover, rectify, redress, restore 8 chastise

amends: 6 reward 7 apology, redress 9 atonement, expiation 10 recompense, reparation 12 compensation, satisfaction

amenities: 8 agremens, niceties 9 agrements, etiquette 11 formalities

amenity: joy 6 comity 7 feature, suavity 8 civility, courtesy, mildness 9 geniality 10 gentleness 12 complaisance, pleasantness 13 agreeableness

ament: 4 cjat 5 idiot, moron 6 catkin 7 cachrys, cattail, gosling 8 imbecile, nucament

amerce: 4 fine 5 mulct 6 affeer, punish, sconce 7 condemn, forfeit 8 penalize

America (see also **North America, South America,** and specific countries, e.g., **Brazil, Canada, United States**): 8 New World 9 continent 10 hemisphere

animal: 4 puma 5 bison, tapir, vison 6 argali, marten, martin, ocelot, wapiti 7 musquaw, opossum 9 assapanic, chickaree

apple: 7 Roxbury

ash: 5 rowan, rowen

balsam: 4 tolu

bear: 7 musquaw

bird: 4 rhea, sora 5 colin, urubu 6 condor 7 shrupsh, tanager 8 squealer

butterfly: 7 viceroy

buzzard: 5 buteo 7 vulture

deer: 6 wapiti

discoverer of: 5 Cabot 7 Ericson 8 Columbus

elk: 6 wapiti

elm: 5 ulmus

finch: 5 junco

fir: 5 abies

lion: 4 puma 6 cougar

monkey: 4 titi

moth: io

plains: 6 pampas 7 prairie

rodent: 4 paca 6 gopher 8 capybara

shrub: 4 majo 5 guava, majoe, wahoo 10 frangipane, frangipani

tiger: 6 jaguar

toad: 4 agua, bufo, rana

tree: fir, lin, oak 4 pine 5 maple, savin 6 tupelo, walnut 7 hickory, redwood, sequoia 8 oneberry, zapetero

tropical tree: 5 acapu, balsa, dalli, guama, guara 6 babeen, grigri, grugru, mammee, pawpaw, sapota 7 wacapou 8 amarillo, sweetsop 10 manchineel

American: 4 Yank 6 Gringo, Yankee, Yanqui

American Indian: See **Indian** *American*

Amerind: 6 Eskimo, Indian, native 8 American

clan symbol: 5 totem

memorial post: xat

amethyst: gem 7 onegite

Amfortas' father: 7 Titurel

ami: 5 lover 6 friend

amiable: 4 kind, warm 5 sweet 6 loving, mellow, tender 7 affable, lovable, winsome 8 charming, engaging, friendly, pleasing 9 admirable, agreeable, courteous 11 kindhearted

amicable: 8 friendly 9 peaceable 10 harmonious, neighborly

amice: 4 cape, cowl, hood 5 ephod 6 almuce, tippet, vakass 8 vestment

amid: in 5 among 6 amidst, during 7 amongst, between 10 surrounded

amino acid: 7 protein

amino compound: 7 diamide, diamine 8 triamine

amir: See **emir**

amiss: ill 4 awry, bias 5 agley, askew, wrong 6 astray, faulty 7 mistake 8 improper 9 erroneous, incorrect 10 inaccurate

amit: 4 lose

amity: 5 peace 6 accord 7 concord, harmony 10 friendship 12 friendliness

amm 6 abbess, mother

ammonia: 9 hartshorn 11 refrigerant

derivative: 4 amid, amin 5 amide, amine 6 anilid 7 anilide, diamine

ammoniac plant: 5 oshac

ammunition: 4 ammo, ammu, arms, shot 5 bombs 6 powder, shells 7 bullets 8 grenades, materiel, ordnance, shrapnel 9 munitions

case: 9 bandolier

depot: 7 arsenal

holder: gun 4 tray

wagon: 7 caisson

amnesia: 5 fugue, lapse 8 blackout 13 forgetfulness

amnesty: 6 pardon 11 overlooking

amnion: sac 6 serosa 8 membrane

amoeba, ameba: olm 7 proteus

amok, amuck: mad 5 crazy 6 crazed 7 violent 8 frenzied

amole: 4 salt, soap 5 agave, plant

Amon's son: 6 Josiah

among: in; mid 4 amid, with 5 amang, midst 6 amidst 7 between

prefix: epi

amor: 4 Eros, love 5 cupid 7 amoroso

amora: 5 rabbi

amoral: 7 neutral 8 nonmoral 9 objective

Amorc member: 11 Rosicrucian

amorous: 4 fond 6 ardent, erotic, loving, tender 7 amatory, fervent 10 passionate 12 affectionate

amorphous: 5 vague 8 formless, resinous 9 irregular, shapeless 14 uncrystallized

amort: 8 dejected, lifeless 9 inanimate 10 spiritless 11 discouraged

amortize: 7 destroy 8 alienate 9 liquidate 10 extinguish

amotion: 7 ousting, removal 11 deprivation

amount: gob, lot, sum 4 dose, feck, ream, rise, unit 5 chunk, price, reach, stack, store, total, whole 6 degree, dosage, extent, number 7 advance, scruple, signify, slather 8 increase, quantity 9 aggregate
fixed: 4 rate
indefinite: any 4 some
made: lot 5 batch
relative: 5 ratio 6 degree
small: bit, tot 4 dash, dite, flow, lick, wisp 5 pinch, shred, taste, trace 6 morsel, trifle 7 dribble, driblet, modicum 8 fragment, spoonful 10 pennyworth
smallest: jot 4 iota, whit 5 grain, least 7 minimum

amour propre: 5 pride 6 egoism, vanity 7 conceit 8 self-love

ampere unit: 4 volt, watt

ampersand: and 4 also, plus 9 character

amphibian: eft, olm 4 frog, hyla, newt, rana, toad 5 anura 7 caudate, proteus 8 tree toad 10 salamander
extinct: 5 eryop
family: 7 Ranidae
order of: 5 anura 7 aglossa
young: 7 tadpole 8 polliwog

amphibole: 7 edenite, oralite, uralite 9 tremolite 10 hornblende

Amphion: *father:* 4 Zeus 5 Iasus
mother: 7 Antiope
twin brother: 6 Zethus
wife: 5 Niobe

amphitheater: 4 bowl, oval 5 arena, cavea 6 circus 7 stadium 10 auditorium

Amphitrite: *father:* 6 Nereus
husband: 8 Poseidon
mother: 5 Doris

Amphitryon's wife: 7 Alcmena, Alcmene

amphora: jar, urn 4 cadi (pl.), vase 5 cadus 6 pelike

ample: 4 full, good, much, rich, wide 5 broad, great, large, roomy 6 enough, plenty 7 copious, liberal, opulent 8 abundant, adequate, generous, handsome, spacious 9 bounteous, bountiful, capacious, extensive, plenteous, plentiful, unstinted 10 munificent, sufficient

amplification factor: mu

amplify: mu; pad 5 farse, swell, widen 6 dilate, expand, extend, stress 7 augment, enlarge 8 ampliate, increase, lengthen, multiply 10 exaggerate

amputate: cut, lop 5 prune, sever 7 curtail 12 exarticulate

ampyx: 4 band 5 plate 6 diadem, fillet 9 headdress

amuck: See **amok**

amula: ama 6 vessel

amulet: gem 4 mojo 5 charm, saffi, safie, token 6 fetish, grigri, saphie, scroll 7 periapt 8 greegree, ornament, talisman 10 protection

Amulius' brother: 7 Numitor

amuse: 6 absorb, delude, divert, engage, please, tickle 7 beguile, disport, gratify 8 bewilder, distract 9 entertain 10 exhilarate

amusement: fad, fun 4 game, jest, play 5 mirth, sport 7 pastime 8 pleasure 9 avocation, diversion, merriment 10 recreation, relaxation 13 divertisement, entertainment
place (see also **entertainment:** *place*): 4 park 5 movie 6 casino, cinema, circus, midway 7 theater

amusing: 5 droll, funny 7 comical, risible 8 humorous, pleasant 9 laughable, ludicrous, quizzical 10 ridiculous

Amy's sisters: Jo; Meg 4 Beth

Amycus: *enemy:* 5 Lycus 8 Dascylus
father: 8 Poseidon
friend: 8 Hercules
mother: 5 Melie

amygdala: 6 almond, tonsil

amyl: 6 pentyl, starch 7 alcohol

an: one 7 article

ana: 6 events 7 sayings 9 anecdotes, anthology 10 collection 11 memorabilia

anabasis: 7 advance 10 expedition

anabatic: 9 ascending

anaconda: boa 5 snake

Anacreon's birthplace: 4 Teos

anadem: 5 crown 6 diadem, fillet, wreath 7 chaplet, coronet, garland

anagogic: 6 occult 8 abstruse

anagram: 4 game 5 rebus 6 puzzle 9 logogriph 13 transposition

analabos: 5 cloak

analgesic: 5 opium 6 codein 7 anodyne, aspirin, codeine

analogous: 4 akin, like 5 alike 6 allied 7 cognate, related, similar 8 parallel 10 comparable, equivalent 11 correlative 13 correspondent

analogy: 10 congruence, proportion, similarity, similitude 11 resemblance

analysis: 4 test 5 study 8 solution, synopses 9 reduction, titration 10 exposition 13 investigation

analyze: 5 assay, parse, study, weigh 6 reduce 7 dissect, examine, resolve 8 diagnose, separate 9 decompose, determine

Anam: See **Annam**

Ananas: 5 anana 9 pineapple

Ananias: 4 liar
wife: 8 Sapphira

anarchist: 5 rebel 8 nihilist 10 antisocial

anarchy: 4 riot 5 chaos 6 revolt 7 license, misrule 8 disorder 9 confusion 11 lawlessness

anathema: ban 4 oath 5 curse 7 censure 9 blasphemy 11 imprecation, malediction 12 denunciation

Anatolia: 7 Armenia
goddess: Ma 6 Cybele
rug: 5 Tuzla

anatomize: 7 analyze, dissect

anatomy: 4 body 8 analysis, skeleton 9 structure
animal: 7 zootomy
microscopic: 9 histology
quick: 11 vivisection

Anaximander's principle: 7 apeiron

ancestor: 4 Adam, sire 5 elder 6 author, beldam, parent 7 beldame 8 forebear, relative 9 grandsire, precursor 10 forefather, forerunner, progenitor 11 predecessor
having common: 14 consanguineous
law: 6 stipes, stirps
remote: 6 atavus
worship: 10 ancientism

ancestral: 4 aval 6 avital, lineal 10 hereditary 11 patrimonial

ancestry: 4 race 6 family 7 descent, lineage 8 pedigree 9 paternity 11 antecedents
relating to: 6 atavic 9 atavistic

Anchises' son: 6 Aeneas

anchor: fix 4 bind, hook, moor, rest, stop 5 affix, berth, bower, kedge, rivet 6 attach, drogue, fasten, hermit, secure 7 chaplet, connect, grapnel, killick, support 9 anchorite
bill: pee 4 peak
hoist: 7 capstan
lift: cat
part: arm 4 palm 5 fluke, shank, stock
position: 5 atrip
ring: 4 tore 6 toroid
shaped: 8 ankyroid
tackle: cat
timber: 7 grouser

anchor bed: 9 billboard

anchorage: 4 dock, rade(Sc.) 6 harbor, refuge 7 moorage 8 berthage, location 9 roadstead

anchored: 4 stay

anchorite: 4 monk 6 hermit 7 ascetic, eremite, recluse, stylite 8 anchoret 9 pillarist

anchorman: key 5 emcee 6 editor 7 feature 8 mainstay 11 commentator

anchovy: 6 spratt 7 herring
sauce: 4 alec

ancient: eld, old 4 aged, auld(Sc.) 5 early, elder, hoary, olden 6 bygone, ensign 7 antique, archaic, archean, classic, oxygian 8 historic, obsolete, primeval, pristine 9 grandeval, primitive, venerable 10 antiquated 11 patriarchal
comb. form: 5 arche, paleo

Ancient of Days: God

ancilla: 6 helper 7 adjunct, servant 8 handmaid 9 accessory

ancillary: 9 auxiliary 10 subsidiary 11 subordinate

ancon: 5 elbow 6 corbel 7 console 9 olecranon

and: et(F., L.); ant, too 4 also, plus 7 besides, further 8 moreover 9 ampersand 10 connective 11 furthermore

and so forth: etc 4 more 6 others 8 etcetera

Andean: 5 grand, lofty 8 Peruvian

Andes: *animal:* 5 llama
bird: 6 condor
camel: 5 llama
deer: 4 pudu 6 vanada
grass: 4 ichu
tableland: 4 puna 6 paramo
tribe: 4 anti 5 campa

andiron: dog 7 cobiron, firedog, hessian

andradite: 6 aplome, garnet

android: 5 robot 9 automaton

Andromache's husband: 6 Hector

Andromeda: 5 heath, plant
father: 7 Cepheus
husband: 7 Perseus
mother: 10 Cassiopeia

ane: one 4 once

anecdote: 4 joke, tale, yarn 5 story 6 sketch 9 narrative
collection: ana

anele: 5 bless 6 anoint, shrive

anemia: 5 surra 6 surrah

anemic: low 4 pale, weak 6 watery 8 lifeless 9 bloodless 10 exsanguine

anemone: 9 buttercup 10 windflower

anent: on, re 5 about 6 anenst, beside, toward 7 against 8 opposite 9 regarding 10 concerning

aneroid: 9 barometer

anesthetic: gas 5 ether 6 acoine, obtuse, opiate 7 cocaine, dulling, menthol 8 sedative 9 novacaine 10 chloroform

anew: 4 over 5 again, newly 6 afresh, denovo, iterum(L.), 8 recently

anfractuous: 6 spiral 7 bending, sinuous, winding 8 tortuous

angel: 4 deva 5 daeva, seraf(Sp.), yaksa 6 backer, cherub, seraph, spirit, yaksha 7 sponsor **8** cherubim, guardian, seraphim **9** harbinger, messenger

apostate prince: **5** Eblis **7** Lucifer

biblical: **7** Gabriel, Raphael

bottomless pit: **7** Abaddon **8** Apollyon

of death: **6** Azrael **7** Sammael

Paradise Lost: **5** Uriel **6** Belial **7** Ariocha

worship: **5** dulia

angelfish: 9 chirivita, isabelita, isabelite

angelic: 7 saintly **8** cherubic, heavenly, seraphic **9** celestial **10** beneficent

angelica: 4 herb **7** jellica

angelico: 5 nondo

angelus: 4 bell **6** prayer **8** devotion

painter: **6** Millet

anger (see also **angry**): ire, irk **4** bile, fell, fury, gall, rage, rile, roil, teem **5** annoy, pique, wrath **6** choler, dander, enrage, excite, grieve, nettle, offend, rancor, spleen, temper **7** burning, dudgeon, emotion, incense, inflame, passion, provoke **8** acrimony, distress, irritate, vexation **9** displease **10** affliction, antagonism, antagonize, resentment **11** displeasure, indignation

express: **5** snort

Angevin: 11 Plantagenet

angle: ell, tee **4** cant, coin, fish, fork, knee, peak **5** arris, bevel, bight, coign, elbow, phase, point, slant **6** allure, aspect, canton, corner, scheme **7** bastion, perigon **8** decalage, fishhook, intrigue

acute: **6** akimbo

equal (pert. to): **8** isogonal, isogonic

external: **4** cant

forty-five degree: **6** octant

geological: **4** hade

having no: **6** agonic

mathematical: **6** octant, radian **9** incidence

measuring device: **10** semicircle

of branch and leaf: **4** axil

of keel and bowsprit: **6** steeve

of ore vein: **4** hade

without: **6** agonic

angler: 5 thief **7** rodster **8** allmouth, piscator **9** fisherman, sportsman

angleworm: ess

Anglian kingdom: 5 Deira

Anglo Saxon: *armor:* **7** hauberk

army: **4** fyrd

assembly: **4** moot, mote **6** mancus

coin: ora **5** sceat

council: **9** heptarchy

court: **4** leet **5** gemot **6** gemote

deity: Ing **4** Frey, Wyrd **5** Freyr

epic: **7** Beowulf

freeman: **5** thane, thegn

king: Ine **5** Edgar **6** Harold

king's council: **5** witan

letter: edh, eth, wyn **4** wynn **5** thorn

money: ora

nobleman: **4** earl **5** thane, thegn

poet: **4** scop

sheriff: **5** reeve **6** gerefa

slave: **4** esne

tax: **4** geld

village: ham

writer: **4** Bede

Angola: *coin:* **6** macuta, macute **7** angolar

river: **6** Coanza, Kunene, Kwanza

town: **6** Luanda(c.) **8** Benguela **10** Mossamedes

angora: cat **4** goat, hair, wool, yarn **6** rabbit

angry (see also **anger**): mad **4** grim, sore, wraw **5** cross, grame, huffy, irate, vexed, wroth **6** crouse, fuming, ireful **7** fretful, furious, iracund, painful **8** choleric, inflamed, rigorous, vehement **9** indignant, irascible, resentful **11** exasperated

anguilla: eel

anguish: woe **4** ache, pain, pang, rack **5** agony, dolor, grief, throe **6** misery, regret **7** remorse, torment, torture **8** distress

angular: 4 bone, bony, slim, thin **5** gaunt, sharp **6** abrupt **7** pointed, scrawny **8** angulose, angulous, cornered, rawboned

ani: 6 cuckoo **9** blackbird

anil: dye **6** indigo

anile: old **5** silly **6** doting, feeble, infirm, senile, simple **7** flighty, foolish **9** doddering **11** old-womanish

animadversion: 5 blame **6** remark **7** censure, comment, reproof, warning **8** monition, reproach **9** aspersion, criticism **10** perception, punishment **11** observation **12** chastisement, condemnation

animal (see also **amphibian, bird, carnivore, fish, insect, invertebrate, mammal, reptile, vertebrate**): **5** beast, biped, brute, fauna, gross, lusty **6** carnal, fleshy, mammal, rodent **7** sensual **8** creature, organism, physical **9** carnivore, marsupial, quadruped

arboreal: ai **4** unau **5** lemur, sloth **6** marten **7** dasyure, opossum, raccoon, tarsier

Biblical: **4** reem **8** behemoth

body: **4** soma

burrowing: **4** mole **6** badger, gopher, rabbit, wombat **8** squirrel **9** armadillo

class: **5** genus **6** genera(pl.)

coat: fur **4** hair, hide, pelt, skin, wool **6** pelage

collection: zoo **4** herd **5** drove **9** menagerie

crawling: **4** worm **5** snake

cross-bred: **4** mule **5** hinny **6** hybrid

doctor: vet **12** veterinarian

domestic: cat, cow, hog, pet, pig **4** mare, mule **5** horse, stock **6** cattle *draft:* ox **4** mule, oxen(pl.) **5** horse **8** elephant

enclosure: pen, sty **4** cage, coop, cote, yard **5** hutch, kraal, stall **6** corral **7** pasture

equine: ass **5** horse, zebra

extinct: **8** dinosaur, mastodon

fat: **4** lard, suet **5** cetin **6** tallow **7** lanolin

feathered: **4** bird, fowl

feline: cat **4** pard **5** tiger **6** jaguar **7** cheetah

female: cow, dam, doe, ewe, gyp, hen, roe, sow **4** hind, mare, slut **5** bitch, filly, jenny, nanny, vixen **6** heifer **7** tigress

footless: **4** apod **5** apoda

group: gam, pod **4** herd, pack **5** drove, flock, pride **6** gaggle

hibernating: **4** bear

hunted: **4** game, prey

life: **4** bios **5** fauna

life (god of): **6** Faunus

lover: **8** zoophile **10** zoophilist

male: mas, tom **4** bull, jack, stag **5** steed, steer **8** stallion

many-footed: **6** insect **7** decapod, hexapod **8** multiped **9** centipede

marine: orc **4** brit, fish, inia, seal **5** coral, otter, polyp, salpa, whale **6** dugong, walrus **7** dolphin, manatee, rotifer **9** jellyfish **10** ctenophore, ctenophran

microscopic: **5** ameba, monad **6** acarid, amoeba **8** rhizopod **9** protozoan **10** animalcule

monkey-like: **5** lemur, loris

mythical: **4** faun **5** snark **6** acephal, bagwyn, bunyip, dragon, garuda **7** alborak, centaur, griffen, unicorn **8** dingmaul, minotaur **9** rosmarine

nocturnal: bat, owl **4** coon **5** lemur, ratel, tapir **6** possum, racoon **7** opossum

one-celled: **5** ameba, monad **6** amoeba **8** protozoa **9** protozoan

ovine: **5** sheep

pack: ass **4** mule **5** burro, camel, horse, llama **6** donkey

parasitic: **8** entozoon

pert. to: **7** leonine **8** zoologic

porcine: hog, pig **4** boar

pouched: **6** possum **7** opossum **8** kangaroo **9** marsupial

rabbit-like: **4** pika **6** marmot

ruminant: cow **4** deer, goat **5** camel, sheep **8** antelope

science: **7** zoology

scrawny: **5** scrag

symbol: **5** totem

ten-footed: **7** decapod

timid: **4** deer, hare **5** sheep

track: **5** spoor

undersized: **4** runt

ursine: **4** bear

vulpine: fox

water: **4** fish, seal **5** coral, otter, whale **6** beaver, walrus

winged: bat **4** bird

young: cub, kid, pup **4** babe, calf, colt, fawn, foal, lamb **5** bruin, chick, filly, puppy, whelp **6** kitten, lionet **8** chipling

animal and plant life: 5 biota

Animal Farm author: 6 Orwell

animalcule: fly **5** ameba **6** amoeba **7** rotifer **8** rotifera(pl.)

animate: pep **4** fire, move, perk, stir, urge **5** alive, brisk, cheer, drive, flush, imbue, impel liven, rouse **6** arouse, bright, ensoul, excite, incite, induce, living, prompt, vivify **7** actuate, comfort, enliven, inspire, quicken **8** activate, energize, inspirit, vitalize **9** encourage, stimulate **10** exhilarate, invigorate

animated: gay **4** glad **5** brisk, vivid, vital **6** active, ardent, blithe, lively **7** buoyant, jocular, sthenic **8** spirited, vigorous **9** sprightly, vivacious **12** enthusiastic

anime: 5 copal, elemi, resin, rosin **7** animato **9** oleoresin

animism: 8 naturism

animosity: 4 hate, **6** animus, enmity, hatred, malice, rancor **7** dislike **9** hostility **10** antagonism, opposition, resentment **11** acharnement, malevolence

animus: 4 mind, will **6** effort, spirit, temper **8** attitude **9** intention **10** antagonism **11** disposition, inclination

anion: ion **8** particle

opposed to: **6** cation

anise: 4 anet, dill **5** cumen **6** fennel

anisette: 7 cordial, liqueur

anisic acid salt: 7 anisate

anito: 6 spirit

Anius' daughter: 5 Elais

ankle: 4 coot, cuit, hock, tali(pl.), **5** talus, tarsi(pl.) **6** tarsus

comb. form: tar **5** tarso

ornament: **6** anklet

pert. to: **6** tarsal

anklebone: 5 talus **8** astragal **10** astragalus, hucklebone

anklet: 4 sock **6** fetter

anlage: 4 base **6** embryo, source **8** blastema, rudiment **10** primordium

ann: 7 stipend

anna: 4 coin **7** hoatzin **8** hoactzin

annal: 6 record **7** archive, history **8** register **9** chronicle **11** publication

annalist: 6 writer **8** recorder **9** historian **12** chronologist

Annam: *boat:* **6** gayyou **8** gaydiang

city: Hue(c.) **4** Haoi

division: **7** Tonquin **11** Cochin China

measure: ly; con, dam, gon, mao, ngu, quo, sao, tat, vai 4 chai, phan, that 5 shita, thouc 6 tac tao, troung

money: 4 quan

river: 6 Songka

tribe: Moi

weight: li; can, fan, hao, nen, yen 4 binh, dong

Annapolis student: 4 pleb 5 plebe 10 midshipman

annates: 6 bounty 8 benefice

annatto, annotto, arnatto: dye 4 tree 5 urucu 6 salmon 7 achiote

derivative: 7 orellin

anneal: 4 bake, fuse, heat 5 smelt 6 temper 7 inflame, toughen

annectent: 7 linking 10 connecting

annelid: 4 worm

fresh water: 4 naid

marine: 4 lurg 9 autolytus

annex: add, ell 4 join 5 affix, seize, unite 6 adject, append, attach, fasten 7 acquire, fixture, subjoin 8 addition 11 appropriate 12 appurtenance

Annie Oakley: 4 pass 6 ticket

annihilate: end 4 kill, raze, slay 5 annul, erase, wreck 6 devour, quench, reduce 7 abolish, destroy, expunge 8 decimate 9 eradicate, extirpate 10 extinguish, obliterate 11 exterminate

anniversary: 4 fete 5 feast 6 annual 7 jubilee 8 birthday, festival 11 celebration

hundreth: 10 centennial

one hundred fiftieth: 16 sesquicentennial

tenth: 9 decennial

third: 9 triennial

thousandth: 10 millennial 11 millenniary

twentieth: 12 vigentennial

wedding: see **wedding:** *anniversary*

annotate: 4 edit, note 5 gloss 6 remark 7 comment, explain 9 elucidate 10 illustrate

annotation: 7 scholia(pl.) 8 scholium

announce: bid, cry 4 bode, call, deem, tell 5 bruit 6 assert, blazon, herald, inform, report, reveal, steven 7 declare, divulge, publish 8 foretell, intimate, proclaim 9 advertise, broadcast, enunciate, pronounce 10 annunciate, promulgate

announcement: 4 hat 5 banns, blurb, edict 6 decree, dictum, notice 8 bulletin 9 manifesto 11 declaration 12 notification, proclamation

announcer: 4 page 5 crier, emcee 6 nuncio 7 gongman, spieler 8 nunciate 9 messenger

of coming events: 4 seer 6 herald 7 prophet 9 harbinger

annoy: dun, get, hox, ire, irk, nag, try, vex 4 bait, bore, fret, gall, grig, hale, harm, nark, pain, rile roil 5 chafe, chase, devil,

harry, peeve, pique, spite, tease, upset, weary, worry 6 badger, bother, caddle, harass, heckle, hector, injure, molest, needle, nettle, offend, pester, rattle 7 disturb, trouble 8 distress, irritate 9 aggravate, displease, embarrass, incommode, persecute 10 exasperate 13 inconvenience

annoyance: 4 pest 5 thorn 6 insect 8 nuisance 11 disturbance 13 inconvenience

annual: 4 book 5 plant 6 flower, yearly 7 etesian 8 periodic, yearbook 11 anniversary, publication

annuity: 5 censo 6 income 7 pension, tontine

annul: 4 cass, undo, void 5 blank, elide, erase, quash, remit 6 cancel, negate, recall, repeal, revoke 7 abolish, cassate, nullify, rescind 8 abrogate, derogate, overrule 9 disaffirm 10 annihilate, extinguish, invalidate, neutralize, obliterate 11 countermand

annular: 6 banded, cyclic, ringed 8 cingular, circular

annulet: 4 ring 5 ridge 6 fillet 7 molding

annunciate: 8 announce

anoa: ox 8 sapiutan

anode: 9 electrode

deposit: 5 anion

anodic: 9 ascending

anodyne: 4 balm 6 opiate, remedy 7 soother 8 narcotic, sedative 10 painkiller, palliative

anoesia: 5 anoia 6 idiocy

anoint: oil, rub 4 balm, beat, cere, nard 5 anele, anoil, cream, crown, prune, slave, smear 6 chrism, grease, spread, thrash 7 moisten 8 chastise 10 consecrate

anole: 6 lizard

anomalous: odd 7 strange, unusual 8 aberrant, abnormal, atypical, peculiar 9 eccentric, irregular 10 dissimilar 11 exceptional

anomy: 7 miracle

anon: 4 once, soon 5 again, later 6 afresh, bedeen, bedene, thence 7 shortly 9 afterward, forthwith, presently 11 immediately, straightway

anonymous: 7 unknown 8 nameless, unavowed, unsigned 9 incognito

another: new 5 alias 6 second 7 further 9 different 10 additional

ansa: 4 loop 6 handle

anserine: 4 dull 6 stolid, stupid 9 gooselike

answer: do 4 echo, plea, suit 5 atone, avail, react, reply, serve 6 result, retort, return, result, ripost 7 defense, fulfill, respond, satisfy 8 pleading, rebuttal, repartee, response, solution 9 rejoinder 11 acknowledge 16 counterstatement

answerable: 5 equal 6 liable 7 fitting 8 adequate, amenable 10 equivalent 11 accountable, responsible 12 commensurate 13 proportionate

ant: 4 anai, anay, mire 5 emmet 6 eciton, insect 7 pismire, termite 8 formicid, micraner 9 myramicid 10 formicidae(pl.), hymenopter, myrmicidae(pl.), 11 hymenoptera(pl.), 12 hymenopteron
comb. form: 6 myrmec 7 myrmeco
leaf-cutting: 4 atta
male: 9 ergataner 15 ergatandromorph
nest: 9 formicary
nonworker: 5 drone
queen: 4 gyne
stinging: 5 kelep
white: 4 anai, anay 7 termite
worker (comb. form): 6 ergate, ergato

ant bear: 8 aardvark 12 myrmecophaga
ant cow: 5 aphid
ant lion: 5 aphid 9 myrmeleon
ant shrike: 6 batara
anta: 4 pier 5 tapir 8 pedestal, pilaster
Antaeus: enemy: 8 Hercules
father: 8 Poseidon
mother: 4 Gaea

antagonism: 6 enmity 9 animosity, antipathy, hostility 10 opposition 11 contrariety
antagonist: foe 5 enemy, rival 7 battler, warrior 8 copemate, opponent, wrangler 9 adversary, combatant 10 competitor
antagonistic: 7 counter, hostile 8 contrary, inimical 9 dissonant
Antarctica: bird: 4 skua 7 penguin
explorer: 4 Byrd, Cook, Ross 5 Scott 7 Wilkins
mountain: 5 Siple 9 Admiralty
sea: 4 Ross
seal: 4 Ross 9 sterrinck

ante: pay 5 stake 6 before
anteater: 5 tapir 6 animal 7 echidna, tamandu 8 aardvark, aardwolf, edentate, tamandua
scaly: 5 manis 8 pangolin

antecedent: 4 fore 5 cause, prior 6 former, reason 7 premise 8 anterior, previous 9 foregoing, foretaste, precedent, preceding
antechamber: See **anteroom**
antedate: 7 precede, predate 10 anticipate
antediluvian: 10 antiquated
antelope (see also specific countries, e.g., Africa: antelope):gnu, sus 4 poku 5 eland, peron, takin, yakin 6 dik-dik, impala, mammal 7 bloubok, gazelle, gemsbok, leather, stembok 8 ruminant, steenbok 9 pronghorn 10 hartebeest
brown: 5 nagor
female: doe
forest: 5 bongo
four-horned: 6 chouka 7 chikara 10 chousingha

gazelle-like: 5 beira 7 gerenuk
genus: 4 oryx
goat-like: 5 goral, serow 7 chamois
golden: 6 impala
harnessed: 4 guib
large:gnu 4 aste, kudu, oryx 5 addax, beisa, bongo, eland 6 impala, koodoo, nilgai, nilgau 7 bubalis, defassa, gemsbok, sassaby 10 hartebeest
male: 4 buck
mountain: 7 chamois
mythical: 4 yale
pied: 8 bontebok
pronghorn: 6 cabree, cabrie, cabret, cabrit
reddish: 7 grysbok
royal: 5 ipete 9 kleeneboc
sheep-like: 5 saiga
short-maned: gnu 6 nilgau
small:6 duiker, grimme 7 grysbok 9 duikerbok
tawny: 5 oribi
tiger-like: 8 agacella
young: kid

antelope-like: 5 bovid 6 bovine
Antelope State: 8 Nebraska
antenna: 4 horn, palp 6 aerial, feeler, lead-in
insect: 5 clava
radar: 7 scanner

Antenor: father: 8 Aesyetes
son: 6 Agenor 11 Archelochus
wife: 6 Theano

anterior: 5 front, prior 6 atloid, before 7 ventral 8 atlantal, previous 9 foregoing, preceding 10 antecedent
anteroom: 4 hall 5 foyer, lobby 8 entrance 9 vestibule 11 antechamber
anthelion: 4 halo 6 nimbus 7 antisun, aureole 10 countersun
anthem: 4 hymn, song 5 motet, psalm 9 antiphony, offertory 10 responsory
anther: tip 6 pollen, stamen
anthesis: 5 bloom 7 blossom 13 efflorescence
anthill: 4 bank 5 mound 9 formicary
anthology: ana 4 book 6 corpus 7 garland 9 potpourri 10 collection 11 compilation
Anthony Adverse author: 5 Allen
anthozoan: 5 coryl, polyp 7 anemone
anthropoid: ape, lar 5 orang 6 gibbon, simian 7 gorilla, primate, siamang 9 orangutan 10 chimpanzee, troglodyte
anthropophagite: 8 cannibal
anti: 6 contra 7 against, opposed
anti-aircraft: fire: 4 flak
gun: 5 archy 6 pom-pom

antic: 4 dido, fool, wild 5 caper, clown, comic, droll, prank, stunt 6 gambol 7 buffoon, caprice, gambado 9 grotesque, ludicrous 11 merry-andrew, monkeyshine

anticipate: 4 balk, hope 5 augur, await 6 divine, expect, thwart 7 devance, forerun, foresee, obviate, portend, prepare, prevene, prevent 8 antedate 9 apprehend, forestall, foretaste

anticipation: 5 odium 6 augury 9 intuition, prolepsis 11 forethought 12 presentiment 13 preoccupation

anticipator: 4 seer 6 omener 7 prophet, seeress 8 foreseer

antidote: 4 cure, soda 6 bezoar, emetic, remedy 10 preventive 11 restorative

Antigone: *mother:* 7 Jocasta
sister: 6 Ismene

Antilles: *god:* 4 Zeme
native: 5 Ineri
pearl: 4 Cuba

antimacassar: 4 tidy 5 doily

antimony: Sb 4 kohl 7 stibium
pert. to: 7 stibial

Antioch proselyte: 7 Nicolas

antipasto: 6 relish 9 appetizer, foretaste 12 hors d'oeuvres

antipathy: 6 enmity, nausea, rancor 7 disgust, dislike 8 aversion, distaste, loathing 9 disrelish, hostility 10 abhorrence, antagonism, reluctance, repugnance 11 contrariety, detestation 14 disinclination 15 incompatibility

antiquated: old 4 aged 5 passe 6 fossil, voided 7 ancient, archaic 8 obsolete, outdated, outmoded 9 primitive 12 antediluvian 13 superannuated

antique: 5 relic, virtu 9 venerable 12 old-fashioned

antiquity: eld 4 hpar, yore 5 relic 8 ancience, anciency, monument 9 anciently

antiseptic: 5 amido, amine, eupad, eusol, salol 6 iodine, phenol 7 alcohol, aseptic, loretin, sterile 8 creosote, metaphen 9 germicide 12 disinfectant
powder: 6 formin

antisocial: 7 hostile 11 anarchistic 12 misanthropic

antisociability: 14 anthropophobia

antispasmodic: 9 asadulcis

antithalian: 7 killjoy

antithesis: 8 contrast 9 antipodes 10 opposition

antitoxin: 4 sera(pl.) 5 serum

antler: 4 horn
bay: 9 bezantler
branch: bay, bey 4 beam, brow, snag, tine, tyne 5 crown, royal 7 speller 8 tresting
knob: 6 croche

main stem: 4 beam
unbranched: dag 4 horn 5 dague, spike 7 pricket 9 greenhorn

Antony and Cleopatra character: 4 Eros, Iras 5 Menas, Philo 6 Gallus, Taurus 7 Agrippa

antrum: 5 sinus 6 cavern, cavity

anuran: 4 toad 10 salientian

anurous: 8 tailless

Anu's consort: 4 Anat

anvil: 5 block 6 stithy 7 bickern 8 beakiron
bone: 4 amos 5 incus 7 incudes(pl.)
point: 4 horn, beak
tinsmith's: 5 teest

anxiety: 4 care, fear 5 alarm, anger, doubt, dread, panic, worry 7 caution, chagrin, concern, scruple, trouble 8 disquiet, suspense 9 misgiving 10 foreboding, perplexity, solicitude, uneasiness 12 apprehension

anxious: 4 agog 5 eager 6 uneasy 7 carking, unquiet 8 desirous, restless, watchful 9 disturbed, expectant, impatient

any: an; ary, oni 4 part, some 8 quantity 11 appreciable

anybody: one 7 someone

anything: 5 aught

anyway: 6 anyhow 12 nevertheless

Anzac: 7 soldier 10 Australian 12 New Zealander

aorist: 4 past 5 tense

aoristic: 10 indefinite 12 undetermined 13 indeterminate

aorta: 5 trunk 6 artery

aoudad: 4 arui 5 sheep

apa: 7 wallaba

apace: 4 fast 5 quick 7 quickly, rapidly 8 speedily

Apache: 4 Yuma 6 Indian 10 Chiricahua
beverage: 6 tiswin
chief: 7 Cochese 8 Geronimo
jacket: 6 bietle

Apache State: 7 Arizona

apar: 9 armadillo

apart: by 4 away, lone 5 alone, aloof, aside, riven, solus, split 6 atwain, lonely 7 asunder, enisled, removed, severed 8 divorced, secluded, separate 10 abstracted 11 dissociated
prefix: se; dia, dis

apartment: 4 digs, flat 5 abode, rooms, suite 7 chamber 8 building, dwelling, tenement 11 compartment
upper: 5 solar 6 sollar

apathetic: 4 calm, cold, cool, dead, dull 5 inert, stoic 6 torpid, supine 7 passive, unmoved 8 listless, sluggish 9 impassive, incurious, unfeeling 10 insensible, phlegmatic **11** indifferent, unemotional **12** uninterested **13** dispassionate, sensationless

apathy: 6 acedia, phlegm, torpor **7** languor **8** doldrums **9** lassitude, unconcern **12** indifference

apatite: 7 ijolite

ape (see also **anthropoid**): **4** boor, copy, dupe, fool, maha, mime, mock **5** clown, magot, mimic **6** baboon, gelada, langur, monkey, parrot, simian **7** buffoon, copycat, emulate, imitate, portray, primate **8** imitator, simulate **10** anthropoid, quadrumane **11** impersonate
dog-headed: **4** aani **11** cynocephali(pl.) **12** cynocephalus
largest: **7** gorilla
like animal: **5** lemur

apeak: 8 vertical

apeman: 6 alalus **15** pithecanthropus

aper: 4 boar, mime, snob **5** clown **6** mocker **7** buffoon, copycat

apercu: 6 digest, glance, sketch **7** insight, outline **10** conspectus

aperitif: 5 drink **9** appetizer

apert: 4 bold, open **7** evident **9** outspoken **15** straightforward

aperture: gap, vue **4** hole, leak, pore, rima, slit, slot, vent **5** chasm, cleft, crack, mouth, stoma **6** window **7** fissure, opening, orifice, ostiole **8** loophole, spiracle **11** perforation

apex: tip, top **4** acme, cone, cusp, noon, peak **5** crest, point, spire **6** apogee, climax, crisis, summit, tittle, vertex, zenith **7** cacumen **8** fastigia(pl.), pinnacle **9** fastigium **11** culmination
covering: epi
elbow: **5** ancon
ornament for: **6** finial
pert. to: **6** apical **9** cacuminal
rounded: **6** retuse

Aphareus: *brother:* **7** Lynceus
son: **4** Idas

aphid: 5 aphis, louse

aphorism: saw **5** adage, axiom, dicta(pl.), gnome, maxim, motto, sutra, sutta **6** dictum, saying **7** epigram, precept, proverb **8** apothegm **10** apophthegm

aphoristic: 6 gnomic **8** gnomical **10** proverbial

Aphrodite: 5 Venus **6** Urania **9** priestess
consort: **4** Ares
mother: **5** Dione
priestess: **4** Hero
son: **4** Eros **5** Eneas **6** Aeneas
temple site: **6** Paphos

apiary: 4 hive, skep **8** beehouse

apiece: per **4** each **8** seriatim **14** distributively

apina: 7 apoidea

apis: bee **8** honeybee

Apis' manifestation: 7 Serapis

apish: 5 silly **7** foppish **8** affected

apishamore: bed **7** blanket

aplomb: 4 tact **5** nerve, poise **6** surety **8** coolness **9** assurance, stability **10** confidence, resolution

apocopate: 5 elide **7** shorten

apocryphal: 4 sham **5** false **6** unreal **8** doubtful, fabulous, mythical, spurious **9** imitative **10** fictitious, unorthodox **11** counterfeit, uncanonical, unauthentic

Apocryphal book: 5 Tobit **6** Baruch, Esdras, Judith **9** Maccabees

apodal: 8 footless

apode: eel **5** moray

apogee: 4 acme, apex, peak **6** climax, zenith **11** culmination

apograph: 4 copy **6** ectype **7** replica **9** imitation **10** transcript

apoidea: bee **4** apis **5** apina **6** apidae

Apollo: 6 Delius **7** Phoebus
abode of: **7** Helicon
beloved of: **6** Cyrene, Daphne **8** Calliope
birthplace: **5** Delos
father: **4** Zeus **7** Jupiter
festival: **5** Delia **6** Carnea
instrument: **4** lute, lyre
mother: **4** Leto **6** Latona
oracle site: **6** Delphi
priest: **7** Calchas
sacred vale: **5** Tempe
sister: **5** Diana **7** Artemis
son: Ion
traveler: **6** Abaris
twin: **5** Diana

Apollyon: 5 Satan, devil **7** Abaddon **9** archfiend, Beelzebub, destroyer

apologetic: 5 sorry **9** defensive **10** remorseful

apologue: 4 myth **5** fable, story **7** parable **8** allegory
pert. to: **7** fabular

apology: 4 plea **5** alibi **6** amends, excuse, regret **11** explanation, vindication **13** justification **14** acknowledgment **15** acknowledgement

apoplexy: 4 esca **5** plant **6** stroke **12** black measles

apostate: rat **7** heretic, pervert, seceder **8** deserter, disloyal, recreant, renegade, turncoat **9** faithless **10** recidivist

apostle: 4 John, Jude, Paul **5** James, Judas, Peter, Silas, Simon **6** Andrew, Philip, Thomas **7** Matthew, teacher **8** Barnabas, disciple, follower, preacher **9** messenger **10** apprentice **11** Bartholomew
of Indies: **6** Xavier
pert. to: **7** petrine

to Franks: 4 Remi
to Gauls: 5 Denis
to Goths: 7 Ulfilas

apothecary: 8 druggist, gallipot 10 pharmacist, posologist

weight: 4 dram 5 grain, pound 7 scruple

apothegm, apophthegm: saw 4 dict 5 adage, axiom, dicta(pl.), gnome, maxim, sutra 6 dictum, saying, suttah 7 proverb 8 aphorism

apotheosize: 5 deify, exalt 7 elevate, glorify 10 consecrate

Appalachian range: 6 Ramapo

appall, appal: 4 stun 5 daunt, shock 6 dismay, reduce, revolt, weaken 7 astound, depress, disgust, dismiss, horrify, terrify 8 affright, astonish, enfeeble, frighten, overcome 10 discourage, dishearten

appalling: 5 awful 7 awesome 8 terrible, terrific 9 frightful, unearthly

appanage, apanage: 5 grant 7 adjunct 9 allowance, privilege, territory 10 dependency, perquisite 11 prerogative 12 appurtenance

apparatus (see also **device, instrument**): 4 gear, tool 6 dingus, gadget, graith, outfit 7 machine, utensil 8 equipage 9 appliance, equipment, machinery, mechanism, trappings 10 furnishing 11 contrivance 12 appurtenance

apparel (see also **dress, vestment**): 4 deck, fare, garb, gear, robe, wear 5 adorn, array, equip, tunic 6 attire, clothe, graith, outfit 7 costume, furnish, garment, prepare, raiment, vesture 8 clothing, wardrobe 9 embellish, equipment 11 habiliments

apparent: 4 open 5 clear, overt, plain 6 patent 7 certain, evident, glaring, obvious, seeming, visible 8 distinct, manifest, palpable, probable 9 appearant 10 ostensible 11 discernible, perceptible, unconcealed 12 unmistakable

apparition: 4 hant 5 dream, ghost, haunt, shade, spook 6 aspect, eidola(pl.), idolum, spirit, sprite, wraith 7 display, eidolon, fantasy, phantom, specter, spectre 8 phantasm, revenant 9 hobgoblin, semblance 10 appearance, phenomenon 13 demonstration

appay: 5 repay 6 please, reward 7 content, satisfy

appeach: 6 accuse 7 asperse, impeach

appeal: ask, beg 4 call, case, plea, seek, suit 5 apply, refer 6 accuse, adjure, avouch, invoke, prayer, summon 7 address, conjure, entreat, implôre, request, solicit 8 approach, petition 9 challenge, importune 10 appelation, supplicate

appealing: 4 cute, nice 6 catchy, clever 8 pleasant 9 agreeable 10 attractive

appear: 4 come, dawn, look, loom, seem 5 arise, enter, issue, occur 6 arrive, beseem, emerge 7 compear(Sc.), develop

appearance: air, hue 4 form, idea, look, mien, show, view 5 blush, front, guise, sight 6 aspect, manner, ostent 7 arrival, display 8 illusion, presence, pretense 9 semblance 10 disclosure, likelihood, phenomenon 11 countenance, probability 13 manifestation

first: 4 dawn 5 debut 8 premiere

appease: lay 4 calm, ease, hush 5 allay, alone, mease(Sc.), quiet, slake 6 defray, pacify, please, soften, soothe 7 assuage, content, gratify, mollify, placate, satisfy 8 mitigate 10 conciliate, propitiate 11 tranquilize

appellation: nom (F.), 4 name, term 5 style, title 6 appeal 7 calling, epithet, surname 8 cognomen, nickname 9 sobriquet 11 description, designation 12 denomination, nomenclature

appellee: 9 defendant 10 respondent

appenage: See **appanage**

append: add, pin, tag 4 clip, hang, join 5 affix, annex 6 adjoin, attach, fasten 7 augment, subjoin 8 appendix

appendage: arm, awn, tab, tag 4 aril, barb, caud, flap, lobe, tail 5 ceras, rider 6 adnexa(pl.), bracht, palpus, suffix 7 adjunct, eodicil 8 addition, pendicle 9 accessory, belonging 10 dependency 12 appurtenance

appendix: 5 organ 6 append 7 addenda(pl.), 8 addendum 10 supplement

operation: 12 appendectomy

appertain: 5 refer 6 belong, relate 7 pertain

appetite: yen 4 lust, urge, zest 5 gusto, taste 6 desire, hunger, liking, orexis, relish 7 craving, longing, passion, wanting 8 cupidity, tendency 9 appetency 10 preference, propensity

abnormal: 4 pica 7 bulimia

excessive: 5 greed 8 gluttony, gulosity 10 polyphagia

pert. to: 7 oretic

voracious: 7 edacity 8 rapacity

appetizer: 5 sauce 6 canape, relish, savory 8 aperitif 9 antipasto 11 hors d'oeuvre

applaud: 4 clap, laud, root 5 cheer, extol 6 praise 7 acclaim, approve, commend, endorse 10 compliment

applauders: 6 claque

applause: 4 clap, hand 5 bravo, cheer, eclat, huzza, salvo 6 hurrah 7 acclaim, ovation 8 clapping, plaudits 11 approbation

device: 8 claptrap

applause-seeking: 9 captation

apple: 4 crab, pome 6 Esopus, pippin, russet 7 Baldwin, Fameuse, winesap, wealthy 8 Ben Davis, Cortland, Greening, Jonathan, McIntosh 9 Delicious, Oldenberg 10 Rome Beauty 11 Gravenstein, Northern Spy, Spitzenburg 12 Yellow Newton, York Imperial 17 Yellow Transparent
acid: 5 malic
blight: 5 aphid 8 eriosoma
cider-making: 8 coccagee
crushed: 6 pomace
dried: 6 beefin, biffin
family: 8 Malaceae
genus: 5 malus
immature: 6 codlin 7 codling
juice: 5 cider 9 applejack
juice (pert. to): 5 malic
old variety: 6 rennet
pastry: 7 strudel
pulp: 6 pomace
ribbed: 7 costard
seed: pip 7 putamen
seller: 6 coster 12 costermonger
shriveled: 9 crumpling
tree: 4 sorb 5 malus, papaw 6 pawpaw
wild: 4 crab 6 doucin
apple butter: 6 spread 9 condiment
apple grunt: pie 8 dumpling
apple of one's eye: 7 darling 8 favorite
apple-polish: 7 flatter
apple-shaped: 8 pomiform
applelike fruit: 4 pome
applesauce: 4 bunk, pulp 5 hokum 6 relish 7 baloney, dessert 8 nonsense
appliance (see also **tool**): 4 gear 6 device, gadget 7 utensil 9 implement 10 instrument 11 application, contrivance 12 appurtenance
applicable: apt, fit 4 meet 6 proper, useful 7 fitting, pliable 8 apposite, relative, relevant, suitable 9 compliant, pertinent 11 appropriate
applicant: 8 prospect 9 candidate, declarant
application: use 4 form 5 blank, topic 6 appeal, effort 7 address, request 8 petition, practice, sedulity 9 diligence 10 compliance 11 requisition
applique: 6 attach, design 8 ornament 10 decoration
apply: ask, put, rub, use 4 give, toil, work 5 adapt, grind, labor, liken, smear 6 appeal, appose, bestow, betake, comply, devote, direct, employ 7 adhibit, compare, conform, overlay, pertain, request, solicit, utilize 8 dedicate, petition 9 persevere 10 administer
appoggiatura: 8 ornament 9 grace note
appoint: arm, fix, set 4 call, deck, name 5 allot, array, award, crest, dight, elect, enact, equip, place 6 assign, assize, attach, decree, detail, devise, direct, ordain, outfit, settle, steven 7 arraign, confirm, destine, dispose, furnish, resolve 8 delegate, indicate, ordinate, nominate 9 designate, determine, establish, prescribe 10 constitute
as agent: 6 depute 8 delegate, deputize
appointment: 4 date 5 berth, order, tryst 6 billet, office, steven 7 command, station 8 position 9 allowance, equipment, interview, ordaining, ordinance 10 assignment, engagement, nomination, perquisite, rendezvous 11 assignation, designation 12 capitulation 13 establishment
apport: 4 port 5 rents 7 bearing, produce, tribute 13 contributions
apportion: lot 4 deal, dole, mete 5 allot, award, grant, paral, share 6 assess, assign, divide 7 arrange 8 allocate 10 distribute
apportionment: 4 deal 8 dividend, division 9 allowance 12 distribution
appose: add, put 5 apply, place
apposite: apt, pat 6 timely 7 germane 8 relative, relevant suitable 9 pertinent 11 appropriate
appraise (see also **apprise**): 4 gage, rate 5 assay, judge, price, value 6 assess, esteem, evalue, ponder 7 adjudge, analyze, commend 8 estimate, evaluate 10 adjudicate, appreciate
appreciable: any 11 perceptible
appreciate: 4 feel, love 5 judge, prize, raise, value 6 admire, esteem 7 advance, apprize, approve, cherish, realize 8 increase, treasure
appreciation: 5 gusto 9 gratitude 11 recognition 12 gratefulness
apprehend: cop, nab, see 4 fear, know, note, take, view 5 catch, dread, grasp, gripe, intue, seize 6 arrest, detain, intuit 7 believe, capture, imagine, realize 8 conceive, discover, overtake, perceive 9 recognize 10 anticipate, appreciate, comprehend, understand
apprehensible: 6 noetic 7 sensate 12 intelligible
apprehension: 4 fear, fray 5 doubt, dread, worry 6 arrest, dismay 7 anxiety, concern 8 distrust, mistrust, suspense 9 awareness, misgiving, suspicion 10 cognizance, conception diffidence, foreboding, perception, solicitude, uneasiness 11 premonition 12 anticipation, intellection, presentiment 13 signification
apprehensive: apt 5 jumpy 6 morbid 7 nervous 9 cognizant, conscious 10 discerning
apprentice: 4 tyro 6 helper, jockey, novice 7 learner, trainee 8 beginner, servitor 9 draftsman

apres: 5 after 10 afterwards

apprise, apprize (see also **appraise**): 4 warn 5 learn, teach 6 advise, inform, notify, reveal 8 acquaint, disclose 9 ascertain 10 appreciate, certiorate

apprised: 5 aware 7 knowing

approach: try 4 adit, come, near, nere, road 5 board, coast, essay, stalk, verge 6 access, accost, advent, appeal, broach, impend 7 advance, seagate 9 introduce 11 approximate 13 appropinquate

approbation: 4 test 5 favor, proof, trial 6 assent, favour, praise, regard, repute 7 plaudit 8 applause, approval, sanction 9 allowance 10 admiration 11 attestation 12 commendation, confirmation

appropinquate: 8 approach

appropriate: add, apt, due, fit 4 akin, grab, meet, suit, take 5 annex, happy, right, steal, usurp 6 assign, assume, borrow, pilfer, pirate, proper, timely, worthy 7 apropos, cabbage, condign, convert, fitting, germane, grabble, impound, preempt, purloin, related 8 accroach, becoming, deserved, idoneous, relevant, suitable 9 attribute, pertinent 10 applicable, assimilate, confiscate, convenient, felicitous, plagiarize 11 conformable,

approval: 4 amen 5 eclat 6 assent 7 approof, support 8 sanction 10 imprimatur 11 approbation

approve: ok; try 4 like, okay, pass, test, vote 5 allow, favor, value 6 accept, admire, concur, ratify 7 applaud, certify, commend, confirm, consent, endorse, exhibit, indorse 8 accredit, manifest, sanction 9 authorize, establish 10 appreciate, experience 11 countenance 12 adscititious, authenticate

approximate: 4 near 5 about, circa, close 8 approach, estimate 10 resembling 11 approaching

approximately: 4 nigh 5 about 6 almost, around, nearly 7 roughly

appurtenance: 4 gear 5 annex 7 adjunct 8 appanage, appenage 9 accessory, apparatus, appliance, belonging

apricot: ume 4 ansu, tree 5 color, fruit 8 Blenheim
confection: 5 mebos 6 meebos
cordial: 7 perisco 8 periscot
vine: 6 maypop

apron: bib 4 base, boot, brat, tier 5 cover 6 barvel, bishop, napron, runway, shield, tarmac, touser 7 gremial 8 lambskin, pinafore 9 barmcloth 10 coverslut, protection
leather: 4 dick 6 barvel 7 barvell 8 barmskin

apropos: apt, fit, pat 4 meet 6 timely 8 relevant, suitable 9 opportune, pertinent 11 appropriate

apse: 5 niche 6 recess 10 projection

apt: fit, pat 4 able, deft, keen 5 adept, alert, happy, prone, quick, ready 6 clever, docile, liable, likely, suited 7 apropos, capable, fitting, willing 8 apposite, dextrous, disposed, idoneous, inclined, prepared, skillful, suitable 9 competent, consonant, dexterous, pertinent, qualified 10 proficient 11 appropriate

apteral: 8 apterous, wingless

apteryx: 4 bird, kiwi

aptitude: art 4 bent, gift, turn 5 craft, flair, knack 6 genius, talent 7 ability, faculty, fitness, leaning 8 capacity, instinct, tendency 10 propensity 11 disposition 12 suitableness

aqua: 5 water

aquamarine: gem 4 blue 5 beryl, color

aquarium: 4 bowl, pool, pond, tank 5 globe

aquatic plant: 4 lily 5 coral, lotus 6 enalid, sugamo 7 elatine, seaweed 10 hydrophyte

aqueduct: 4 duct 5 canal 7 channel, conduit, passage 9 conductor
of Sylvius: 4 iter

aquifer: bed 6 bearer 7 stratum

aquila: 5 eagle

aquiline: 6 curved, hooked 7 curving 9 prominent

Aquinas work: 5 Summa

aquosity: 7 wetness 8 moisture 10 wateriness

ara: 5 macaw

Arab: 4 Oman, sleb, waif 5 gamin, horse, nomad, Saudi, tatar 6 Semite, urchin 7 Arabian, bedouin, Saracen 8 wanderer, Yemenite 9 Himyarite

araba: cab 5 coach, wagon 6 monkey 7 vehicle

Arabia: *abode:* dar 4 tent
alphabet: See **Arabic:** *alphabet*
ancient: 4 Saha 5 Sheba
antelope: 5 addax
author: 6 lokman
banquet: 5 diffa
bazaar: suq
bird: 7 phoenix
caliph: Ali 6 sharif, sherif 7 shareef, shereef
caravan: 6 cafila
chief: 4 amir, emir 5 ameer, emeer
city: 4 Aden, Bida, Hail, Riad, Sana 5 Mecca, Mocha 6 Medina 7 Oneizah
cloak: aba
coffee: 5 mocha
coin: 4 lari 5 carat, dinar, kabik, riyal
cosmetic: 4 kohl

country: 4 Asir, Iran, Iraq, Oman 5 Egypt, Syria, Yemen 6 Arabia, Jordan 7 Lebanon

demon: 4 jinn 5 afrit, genie, jinni 6 afreet, jinnee

desert: Nyd 5 Ankaf, Dehna, Nefud 6 Syrian

dish: 8 couscous

division: 4 Oman, Suez 5 Mecca, Sinai 6 El Hasa, El Nejd, Mahara 7 El Yemen, Medinah 8 El Hedjáz, El Tehama 9 Hadramaut

drink: 4 bosa, boza 5 bozah 6 lebban

drum: 9 tara-booka

fabric: aba 4 haik

father: abu 4 abba, abou

flour source: 4 samh

garment: aba 4 haik 6 cabaan 7 burnous 8 burnoose

gazelle: 4 cora 5 ariel

goddess: 5 Allat

grammar: 7 ajrumya

gulf: 4 Aden, Oman

horse: 6 anezeh 8 kadischi, palomino

infantryman: 5 askar

jasmine: 4 bela 10 sampaquita

judge: 4 cadi

kingdom: 4 Nejd

land: 6 feddan

measure: den, saa 4 ferk, foot, kist 5 achir, barid, cabda, cafiz, covid, cuddy, makuk, mille, qasab, teman, woibe, zudda 6 artaba, assbaa, covido, feddan, gariba, ghalva 7 caphite, farsakh, farsang, kiladja, marhale, nusfiah

mountain: 4 Nebo 5 Horeb, Sinai

noble: 4 amir, emir 5 ameer, emeer

nomad: 7 Saracen

palm: 4 doom, doum

peasant: 6 fellah

peninsula: 5 Sinai

philosopher: 6 Farabi 8 Averroes

plant: kat 5 retem

prince(see also *ruler*below): 6 sherif 7 shereef

raiders: 8 fedayeen

river bed: 4 wadi, wady

romance: 5 antar 6 antara

ruler: 4 amir, emir 5 ameer, emeer

scripture: 5 Koran 7 Alkoran

shrine: 5 Kaaba

shrub: kat 5 alhaj, retem

tambourine: 4 taar 5 daira

tea shrub: kat

tent encampment: 5 douar

tribe: Aus 4 Asir, Irad, Tema 5 Kedar 7 Diendel, Shukria 9 Hagarenes

vessel: 4 dhow 6 boutre, sambuk

weight: 4 rotl 5 cheki, kella, nasch, nevat, ocque, oukia, ratel, toman, vakia 6 bokard, dirhem, miskal, tomand 8 farsalah

wind: 6 simoom, simoon

Arabian Nights: *bird:* roc 4 aqib

character: Ali 4 Sidi 5 Amina 7 Zobeide

dervish: 4 Agib

merchant: 7 Sindbad

poet: Kab 5 Antar

prince: 7 Alasnam

sailor: 6 Sinbad 7 Sindbad

sorceress: 5 Amine

youth: 7 Aladdin

Arabic: *alphabet:* ba, ta, ha, ra, za, fa, ya; tha, jim, kha, dal, zay, sin, sad, dad, ayn, qaf, kaf, lam, mim, nun, waw 4 alif, dhal, shin 5 ghayn

script: 5 neski

arabic acid salt: 7 arabate

arable: 7 fertile 8 plowable, tillable

land: 5 laine

araca: 4 tree 6 timber 10 terminalia

aracanga: 5 macaw

aracari: 6 toucan

araceous: 5 aroid

plant: 4 arum, lily, taro

arachnid: 4 crab, mite, tick 6 acarus, spider 8 scorpion 9 tarantula

arachnoid: 4 thin 5 hairy 8 araneous, delicate 10 cobweblike

Aram: 5 Syria

children: Uz; Hul 4 Mash 6 Gether

city: 5 arpad 6 arphad

deity: 6 Rimmon

nomads: 7 Akhlame

Aramaic: 6 Syriac 9 Samaritan

araneous: 4 thin 8 delicate 9 arachnoid 10 cobweblike

araphorostic: 7 unsewed 8 seamless

araponga: 8 bellbird

Arawakan: *Indian:* 4 Uran 5 Araua, Bares, Guana, Moxos, Piros 6 Campas 7 Atorais, Banivas, Jucunas, Lucayos, Tacanan, Ticunan 8 Lorenzan

language: 5 Taino

arbiter: 5 judge 6 critic, oddman, umpire 7 adviser, daysman, oddsman, overman, referee 10 arbitrator

arbitrary: 6 severe, thetic 7 willful 8 absolute, despotic, masterly 9 imperious 10 autocratic, capricious, highhanded, peremptory, tryannical 11 determinate 13 irresponsible

arbitrate: 6 decide 7 mediate 9 determine, intercede

arbitrator: ref 5 judge 6 umpire 7 arbiter, munsiff, referee 8 mediator 11 conciliator

arbor, arbour: bar 4 axle, beam 5 abode, bower, shaft 6 garden 7 mandrel, orchard, pergola, retreat, spindle, trellis 8 platform 11 latticework

arbustum: 5 copse 7 orchard 10 plantation

arc: bow 4 arch, bend, halo 5 curve, orbit, spark 6 radian 7 rainbow 9 spotlight
chord of: 4 sine
horizon: 7 azimuth
arc lamp rod: 6 carbon
arca: box 5 chest, paten 9 reliquary
arcade: 6 avenue, loggia, street 7 gallery, portico 8 arcature 9 collonade 10 passageway
Arcadia: 4 Eden 6 Arcady 8 paradise
huntress: 8 Atalanta
princess: 4 Auge
town: 4 Alea
woodland spirit: Pan
arcadian: 5 ideal, rural 6 rustic, simple 7 bucolic 8 pastoral, shepherd
arcane: 6 hidden, secret 10 mysterious
arcanum: 6 elixir, remedy, secret 7 mystery
Arcas: *father:* 4 Zeus
mother: 8 Callisto
son: 4 Azan 8 Apheidas
arch: arc, bow, coy, sly 4 bend, span 5 arcus, chief, curve, great, prime, saucy, vault 6 arcade, clever, fornix, impish 7 archway, cunning, eminent, roguish, support, waggish 9 principal 11 mischievous
inner curve of: 8 intrados
kind of: 4 flat 5 round, Tudor 6 lancet 7 rampant, trefoil 9 horseshoe, primitive, segmental 10 shouldered 11 equilateral 12 basket-handle, four-centered 13 three-cornered
memorial: 6 pailoo, pailou, pailow
molding: 9 accoclade
part: 8 keystone, springer, voussoir
pointed: 4 ogee 5 ogive
arch-enemy: 5 devil, Satan
archaic: old 7 ancient 8 historic, obsolete 9 venerable 10 antiquated 12 old-fashioned
archangel: 5 Satan, Uriel 7 Gabriel, Michael, Raphael
archbishop: 7 prelate, primate
archbishopric: see
archer: 4 Clim, Clym, Tell 5 cupid 6 bowman 9 Robin Hood 10 archerfish 11 Sagittarius
archery: *deity:* 6 Apollo 7 Artemis
locker: 6 ascham
lover: 11 toxophilite
target center: 5 clout
archetype: 4 idea 5 model 6 figure, sample 7 example, paragon, pattern 8 exemplar, original 9 prototype 10 manuscript
architect: 5 maker 6 artist, author 7 artisan, builder, creator, planner 8 designer 9 contriver, draftsman
architectural: 8 tectonic
architecture: *convexity:* 7 entasis
order: 5 Doric, Ionic 10 Corinthian

ornament: ove 5 gutta 6 dentil, rosace 7 rosette
style: 5 Doric, Greek, Ionic, Tudor 6 French, Gothic, Lancet, Modern, Norman 7 Baroque, Cape Cod, English, Italian, Moorish, Spanish 8 Academic, Colonial, Egyptian, Etruscan, Georgian 9 Byzantine, Palladian 10 Corinthian, Romanesque 11 Renaissance
archive: 5 annal 6 museum, record 7 library 8 document, register 9 chronicle
archon: 5 ruler 8 director, official 10 magistrate
arctic: icy 4 cold, cool, shoe 5 gelid, polar 6 boreal, chilly, frigid, galosh 8 northern, overshoe
Arctic: *base:* 4 Etah
bird: auk
canoe: 5 kayak, umiak 6 oomiak
current: 8 Labrador
dog: 7 samoyed 8 samoyede
explorer: Rae 4 Byrd, Eric, Kane, Ross 5 Davis, Peary 6 Baffin, Bering, Button, Greely, Hudson, Nansen 7 McClure, Wilkins, Wrangel 8 Amundsen 9 Frobisher, Stefanson 10 Willoughby
falcon: 9 gyrfalcon
gull (genus): 4 xema
headland: 5 Odden
inhabitant: 4 Lapp 5 Aleut 6 Eskimo 7 Alaskan 9 Laplander
jacket: 6 anorak
musk ox: 6 ovibos
native: 4 Lapp 5 Aleut 6 Eskimo 7 Alaskan 9 Laplander
plain: 6 tundra
plant: 5 ledum
sea: 7 Barents
sea animal: 6 narwal 8 narwhale
Arctic Sea gulf: Ob
Arcturus: 4 star
arcuate: 4 bent 5 bowed 6 arched, curved, hooked
ardent: hot 4 avid, fond, keen, warm 5 eager, fiery, rethe(Sc.) 6 ablaze, fervid, fierce 7 amorous, earnest, feeling, fervent, flaming, forward, intense, shining, zealous 8 desirous, vehement 9 impetuous, perfervid 11 inflammable 12 enthusiastic
ardor, ardour: 4 dash, elan, glow, heat, love, zest 5 gusto, verve 6 desire, fervor, mettle, spirit 7 ardency, passion 8 devotion, vivacity 9 animation, calenture, constancy 10 enthusiasm
arduous: 4 hard 5 lofty, steep 6 trying 7 onerous 8 exacting, tiresome, toilsome 9 difficult, laborious, strenuous 10 exhausting
are: 5 exist

area: 4 belt, size, zone 5 court, field, range, realm, scene, scope, space, tract 6 areola, extent, locale, region, sector, sphere, volume 7 areaway, circuit, compass, environ, expanse, purlieu, surface 8 district, province 9 bailiwick, extension, territory 12 neighborhood
  measure: 6 parish
  pert. to: 7 spatial
aread, areed: 4 read, tell, warn 5 guess 6 advise, decree, direct, divine 7 adjudge, counsel, declare, explain 9 interpret
areca: 4 palm 5 betel
arena: 4 area, oval, ring, rink 5 court, field, scene, scope, space, stage 6 circus, region, sphere, stadia(pl.), 7 cockpit, stadium, theater 8 province 10 hippodrome 12 amphitheater
  sports: see **field** *athletic*
arenaceous: 5 sandy 6 gritty 8 sabulous
areola: pit 4 area, ring, spot 5 space 9 periphery 10 interstice
areometer: 10 hydrometer
Ares: 4 Mars
  father: 4 Zeus
  mother: 4 Enyo, Hera
  sister: 4 Eris
  son: 6 Cycnus
arete: 4 crag 5 crest, ridge, valor 6 virtue 8 fishbone 9 manliness 10 excellence
argala: 7 marabou 8 adjutant
argali: 5 sheep 6 aoudad
argent: 4 coin 5 money, white 6 silver 7 shining, silvery 9 whiteness
Argentina: *armadillo:* 6 peludo
  barge: 7 chalana
  city: 4 Acha, Azul, Goya, Puan 5 Bahia, Jujuy, Lanus, Salta 6 Blanca, Burras, Parana 7 Cordoba, La Plata, La Rioja, Mendoza, Rosario, Santa Fe, Tucuman 11 Buenos Aires (c.)
  coin: 4 peso 7 centavo 9 argentino
  cowboy: 6 gaucho
  dance: 5 tango 6 cuando
  estuary: 5 Plata
  garment: 7 chiripa
  Indian: 4 Lule
  Indian village: 8 tolderia
  measure: 4 sino, vara 5 legua 6 cuadra, fanega 7 manzana
  mesquite: 6 calden 9 algarroba
  mountain: 9 Aconcagua
  plain: 5 pampa
  port: 7 Rosario
  province: 5 Chaco, Jujuy, Pampa, Rioja, Salta 6 Estero 7 Cordova, Formosa, Mendoza, San Juan, San Luis, Santa Fe, Tucuman 8 Santiago 9 Catamarca, Entre Rios, Patagonia 10 Corrientes

  ranch: 8 estancia
  river: 5 Negro, Plata 6 Parana, Salado 7 Vermejo 8 Colorado, Paraguay, Picomayo 9 Rio Grande
  tree: 4 coco, tala 5 ambay, timbo
  weight: 4 last 5 grano 7 quintal 8 tonelada
argil: 4 clay 7 alumina
argillaceous: 5 slaty 6 clayey, cledgy, doughy, spongy
argol, argal: 6 tartar
Argonaut: 5 Jason 8 wanderer 10 adventurer
Argos: *king:* 4 Abas 6 Danaus 7 Lynceus 8 Acrisius, Adrastus
  princess: 5 Danae
argosy: 4 boat, ship 5 craft, fleet 6 vessel 7 galleon
argot: 4 cant 5 flash, lingo, slang 6 jargon, patois 7 dialect
argue: 4 moot, spar 5 cavil, orate, plead, prove, treat 6 accuse, adduce, caffle, debate, reason 7 arraign, contend, contest, discuss, wrangle 8 indicate, maintain, persuade 9 argy-bargy, discourse 11 expostulate, ratiocinate, remonstrate
argument: row 4 agon, case, fuss, plea, spar, text 5 clash, proof, set to, theme 6 combat, debate, hassle 7 dispute, polemic, rhubarb, summary 8 abstract, evidence 9 argy-bargy, discourse 10 indication 11 altercation, argey-bargey, controversy, disputation
  conclusive: 6 corker 7 crusher 8 clincher 9 knockdown 11 sockdolager, sockdologer
  fallacious: 7 sophism
  negative side: con
  positive side: pro
  specious: rot 8 claptrap, nonsense 9 sophistry 10 paralogism
  starting point: 7 premise
argumentative: 7 eristic 8 forensic 10 rhetorical 11 presumptive 12 disputatious 13 controversial
Argus-eyed: 8 vigilant
argute: 5 acute, sharp 6 shrewd, shrill, subtle 9 sagacious
argy-bargy, argey-bargey: 5 argue 6 haggle 7 dispute, wrangle
arhat: 4 monk 5 lohan, saint
aria: air 4 solo, song, tune 6 melody 7 arietta, ariette, sortita
arid: dry 4 bald, bare, dull, lean 6 barren, desert, jejune, meager 7 parched, sterile 8 withered 9 unfertile, waterless 10 desiccated, siccaneous 12 moistureless 13 uninteresting
ariel: 7 gazelle
Aries: ram
  mother: 4 Enyo

aril: pod 7 arillus, coating 8 covering 9 appendage 10 integument
  false: 8 arillode
ariose: 7 melodic 8 songlike 9 melodious
aris: See **arris**
arise: 4 flow, lift, rear, rise, soar, stem 5 awake, begin, exist, issue, mount, raise, stand, surge, tower, waken 6 accrue, amount, appear, ascend, attain, derive, emerge, happen, spring 7 develop, emanate, proceed 8 develope 9 originate
arista: awn 5 beard 9 appendage
aristocracy: 4 rule 5 class, elite 8 nobility 10 government, patriciate
aristocrat: 4 lord 5 noble 7 grandee, parvenu 9 patrician
aristocratic: 4 tony 7 high-hat
Aristophanes work: 5 Birds, Frogs
Aristotle: 5 Greek 11 philosopher
  birthplace: 6 Thrace 7 Stagira
  category: 4 time 5 place 6 action 7 quality 8 position, quantity, relation 9 passivity, substance 10 possession
  disciple: 11 Peripatetic
  father: 10 Nicomachus
  school: 6 Lyceum
  teacher: 5 Plato
arithmetic: 4 sums 8 textbook 11 mathematics
  rule: 10 allegation
Arius' follower: 5 Arian
Arizona: *city:* 4 Yuma 5 Tempe 6 Tucson 7 Nogales, Phoenix
  county: 4 Gila, Pima 5 Pinal 6 Apache, Mohave, Navajo 7 Cochise, Yavapai
  desert: 7 Painted
  flower: 7 saguaro
  Indian: 4 Hopi, Pima, Yuma 6 Navaho, Navajo
  river: 4 Gila
  town: see *city* above
Arizona gourd: 11 calabazilla
ark: bin, box 4 boat, ship 5 barge, chest, hutch 6 basket, coffer, refuge, wangan 7 retreat, shelter, wanigan 8 flatboat
  builder: Noe 4 Noah
  resting place: 6 Ararat
Arkansas: *city:* 10 Booneville, Little Rock
  county: Lee 4 Clay, Drew, Pike, Poke, Polk, Yell 5 Scott
  mountains: 5 Ozark
arkose: 9 sandstone
arm: fin 4 limb, wing 5 bough, equip, fiord, firth, force, inlet, might, power, rifle 6 branch, energy, member, outfit, sleeve, tappet, weapon 7 flipper, forearm, fortify, furnish, prepare, protect, provide, support 8 soupbone, strength 9 appendage 10 instrument, projection 12 ramification

bone: 4 ulna 5 radii(pl.), ulnae(pl.) 6 humeri(pl.), radius 7 humerus
  comb. form: 6 brachi 7 brachio
  hollow at bend: 8 chelidon
  joint: 4 ares 5 elbow, wrist
  muscle: 6 biceps 7 triceps
  part: 4 ares 5 elbow, wrist
  pert. to: 8 brachial
armada: 4 army, navy 5 fleet 8 flotilla, squadron, warships
armadillo: 4 peva 5 poyou 6 mulita 7 tatouay 8 pangolin 10 pichiciago
  giant: 4 tatu 5 tatu 6 peludo
  small: 4 peba 11 quirquincho
  three banded: 4 apar 5 apara 6 mataco
armamentarium: 5 store 6 armory 7 arsenal 8 armament, magazine 9 equipment 10 collection
armariolum: 5 ambry 8 armarium
armarium: 5 ambry 10 armariolum
armband: 7 maniple 8 brassard
Armenia: 5 Minni 8 Anatolia
  angel or devil worshiper: 6 Yezidi
  cap: 6 calpac
  city: 6 Erivan(c.) 7 Erzurum, Yerevan
  cumin: 7 caraway
  lake: Van 8 Urumiyah
  mountain: 6 Ararat, Taurus
  people: 5 Gomer
  river: Kur 4 Aras 5 Cyrus, Halys 6 Araxes, Tigris 9 Euphrates 10 Kizil-Trmak
  town: see *city* above
armet: 6 helmet
armful: 6 yaffle
armhole: 4 mail, scye 7 armscye
armistice: 4 lull 5 peace, truce 9 cessation 10 suspension
armoire (see also **ambry**): 8 cupboard, wardrobe 12 clothespress
armor: 4 arms, egis, mail, tace 5 amure, plate, tasse 6 armour, brinie, brunie, byrnie, cuisse, graith, shield, tasset, tuille 7 cuirass, defense 8 materiel, ordnance 10 protection
  arm: 8 brassard, brassart 9 gardebras
  bearer: 6 squire 7 armiger, custrel
  body: 4 tace 6 byrnie, corium, lorica 7 cuirass
  cap: 10 cerveliere
  elbow guard: 9 cubitiere
  face: 6 beaver 7 ventail 8 aventail
  foot: 7 chausse
  horse: 5 barde 7 peitrel, peytrel, poitrel 8 poitrail, testiere
  knee: 11 genouillere
  leg: 4 boot, jamb 5 cuish, jambe 6 cuisse, greave, tuille 7 jambeau 11 braconniere
  neck: 6 gorget 8 aventail, gorgelet
  part: 6 lorica(L.)

shoulder: 7 ailette 9 epauliere
skirt: 4 tace 5 tasse 6 taslet, tasset
thigh: 5 cuish
throat: 6 gorget
armored: 6 mailed 8 equipped, ironclad, mailclad 9 panoplied 11 encuirassed
armpit: ala 5 oxter 6 axilla 7 axillae(pl.)
pert. to: 7 axillar
arms depository: 7 arsenal
army: 4 here, host 5 array, crowd, force, horde 6 cohort, legion, number, throng, troops 7 militia 8 soldiers, warriors 9 battalion, multitude
base: 5 depot
camp: 6 campoo(Ind.)
car: 4 jeep
chaplain: 5 padre
commission: 6 brevet
engineer: 6 sapper 7 pioneer
enlisted man in ranks: 7 mustang
follower: 6 sutler
mascot: 4 mule
meal: 4 chow
officer: tab 4 aide 5 major 7 captain, general 8 sergeant 9 centurion 10 lieutenant
pert. to: 7 martial 8 military
post: 4 base, camp, fort
postal abbreviation: APO
school: OCS, OTS 7 academy
storehouse: 6 armory 7 arsenal
unit: 5 corps, squad, troop 7 brigade, company, platoon 8 division, regiment 10 detachment
vehicle: 4 jeep, tank 9 half-track
wing: ala(L.)
army ant: 6 driver 9 legionary
arnotto: See **annatto**
aroba: See **araba**
aroid: 4 taro 5 apium, tania 6 tanier 8 araceous
aroint: 6 begone
aroma: 4 odor 5 nidor, savor, scent, smell, spice 6 flavor 7 bouquet, perfume 9 fragrance, redolence
aromatic: 5 balmy, spicy, sweet 7 odorous, piquant, pungent 8 fragrant, redolent
gum: 5 myrrh
herb: 4 mint, nard 5 anise, clary, nondo 8 lavender
seed: 5 anise, cumin 6 nutmeg 7 aniseed
spice: 4 mace 5 clove
tree: 6 balsam 8 huisache 9 sassafras
weed: 5 tansy
around: 4 near 5 about, circa 10 encircling, enveloping
prefix: 4 peri
arouse: 4 call, fire, move, spur, stir, wake, whet 5 alarm, awake, evoke, pique, raise, rally, rouse, roust, waken 6 awaken, excite, foment, incite, kindle, revive, summon, thrill 7 actuate, agitate, animate, enliven, incense, inflame 8 inspirit 9 stimulate

arpeggio: 5 sweep 7 roulade 8 division, flourish
arpent: 4 acre
arraign: try 4 cite 5 argue 6 accuse, charge, impute, indict, indite, summon 7 appoint, impeach 8 denounce 9 challenge, prosecute
arraignment: 6 charge 10 accusation
arrange: fix, set 4 edit, file, form, plan, size, sort, tier 5 adapt, aline, align, array, drape, ettle, frame, grade, range, score, space 6 adjust, design, devise, fettle, settle 7 bespeak, catalog, compone, compose, dispose, gradate, marshal, permute, prepare, seriate 8 classify, conclude, organize, regulate, tabulate 9 catalogue, collocate, construct, determine 10 distribute 11 alphabetize
mutually: 5 agree 7 concert
arranged alternately: 4 paly
arrangement: 4 deal 5 index, order, setup 6 scheme, system, treaty 8 contract 9 direction 10 allocation 11 composition, disposition, permutation 12 dispensation
arrant: bad 5 thief 6 outlaw, robber 7 vagrant 8 rascally 9 confirmed, downright, itinerant, notorious, shameless 11 unmitigated 13 thoroughgoing
arras: 7 drapery 8 tapestry
array: don, fig 4 army, busk, deck, doll, garb, host, pomp, robe 5 adorn, align, aline, dress, habit, order 6 attire, attrap, bedeck, clothe, finery, invest, plight, series 7 address, affaite, afflict, apparel, arrange, company, envelop, furnish, marshal 8 accouter, accoutre 10 assemblage 11 preparation
arrear: 4 debt 6 behind, unpaid 7 arriere 8 backward
arrect: 5 alert, erect 6 direct, raised 9 attentive
arrest: cop, fix, nab 4 balk, curb, grab, halt, hold, jail, keep, pull, sist, stay, stop 5 arret, catch, check, delay, pinch, seize, stunt 6 attach, collar, decree, detain, engage, hinder, pledge, retard, thwart 7 capture, custody, suspend 8 imprison, obstruct, restrain 9 apprehend, intercept, interrupt 11 concentrate
arresting: 8 pleasing, striking 10 impressive
arret: 5 edict 6 arrest, decree 8 decision, judgment
arride: 5 laugh, smile 6 please 7 delight, gratify
arrie: 5 murre

arris, aris: 4 pien 5 angle, piend

arrival: 5 comer 6 advent

arrive: 4 come, flow, gain, land 5 occur, reach 6 appear, attain, happen 7 compass

arrogance: 5 pride 6 hubris, hybris 7 conceit, disdain, egotism, hauteur 9 insolence 10 effrontery 11 affectation

arrogant: 4 bold 5 lofty, proud 6 lordly, uppish 7 forward, haughty 8 affected, assuming, cavalier, fastuous, impudent 9 audacious, conceited, insulting, presuming 10 hoity-toity 11 dictatorial, domineering, impertinent, overbearing, overweening 12 contemptuous, contumelious, presumptuous, supercilious

arrogate: 4 grab, take 5 claim, seize, usurp 6 assume

arrondissement: 4 ward 8 division

arrow: pin, rod 4 bolt, dart, reed 5 shaft 6 sprite, weapon 7 missile, pointer 9 indicator

case: 6 quiver

comb. form: 4 belo

feathered: 4 vire

maker: 6 bowyer 8 fletcher

part: 4 barb, butt, head, nock 5 shaft, stele 7 feather

pert. to: 8 sagittal

point: neb 4 barb

poison: 4 haya, inee, upas 5 urali 6 antiar, curare, sumpit, wagogo 7 woorali

rotating: 4 vire

arrow-shaped: 6 beloid 8 sagittal 9 sagittate

arrowroot: pia 4 musa 5 araru, canna, tacca, tikor 6 ararao

family: 11 marantaceae

Arrowsmith author: 5 Lewis

arrowstone: 9 belemnite

arrowweed: 7 pluchea

arrowwood: 8 viburnum 10 burrobrush

arroyo: 5 brook, creek, gulch, gully, hondo, zanja 6 ravine, stream 7 channel 11 watercourse

ars artium: 5 logic

arsenal: 6 armory, supply 8 dockyard, magazine 10 storehouse 13 armamentarium

arsenate: *copper:* 7 erinite

hydrous zinc: 7 adamite

red manganese: 9 sarkinite

arsenic: 6 poison 8 chemical

antimony: 10 allemonite

comb. form: 6 arseno

compound: 8 arsenide

sulfide: 7 realgar

trisulfide: 8 orpiment

arsenic acid salt: 8 arsenate

arsenillo: 9 atacamite

arsenopyrite: 7 danaite

arsis: 4 beat 5 ictus 6 accent, rhythm

opposed to: 6 thesis, theses (pl.)

arson: 4 fire 5 crime 7 burning 12 incendiarism

arsonist: 10 pyromaniac

art: ars(L.) 4 wile 5 craft, knack, magic, skill, trade 7 calling, cunning, faculty, finesse, science 8 artifice, business, learning, 9 dexterity, duplicity, ingenuity 10 profession 11 contrivance, cultivation

black: 5 magic 7 alchemy 8 wizardry 9 diablerie 10 demonology, necromancy 11 conjuration

fancier of: 6 votary 7 esthete, devotee 8 aesthete 10 dilettante 11 connoisseur

gallery: 5 salon 6 museum

manual: 5 craft, sloid, slojd, sloyd

school: 4 Dada 5 Dutch 6 ashcan, French, Paduan 7 Flemish, Italian, Lombard, Umbrian 8 American, eclectic, Milanese Scottish 9 Bolognese 10 Raphaelite

style: pop 4 Dada 5 genre 6 cubism 7 baroque, fauvism 10 surrealism 11 objectivism, primitivism 13 impressionism 14 abstractionism

Artemis: 4 Upis 5 Delia, Diana 6 Phoebe

brother: 6 Apollo

father: 4 Zeus

mother: 4 Leto

priestess: 9 Iphigenia

artel: 5 union 11 association, cooperative

artery: way 4 path, road 5 route 6 course, street, vessel 7 anonyma, conduit, highway 9 maxillary

main: 5 aorta 6 aortae(pl.)

neck: 8 caratoid

pulsation: 5 ictus

artful: apt, sly 4 foxy, wily 5 agile, suave 6 adroit, clever, facile, shrewd, smooth, tricky 7 crooked, cunning, politic, vulpine 8 stealthy 9 deceitful, deceptive, designing, dexterous, imitative, practical

artfulness: 8 subtlety 9 diplomacy, duplicity, stratagem 10 refinement

arthritis: 4 gout

arthron: 5 joint 12 articulation

arthropoda: 4 crab 6 phylum, spider

Arthur: See King Arthur

artichoke: bur 6 Canada, Cynara 7 Chorogi 9 Jerusalem

leafstalk: 5 chard

article: an, ye; one, the 4 item, term 5 essay, paper, piece, plank, point, story, theme, thing 6 clause, detail, object, report 7 feature 8 causerie, doctrine 9 condition, paragraph, statement 10 particular 11 composition, stipulation

French: la, le, un; les, une

German: das, der, die, ein

Spanish: el, un; las, los, una

articulate: 4 join 5 clear, speak, unite, utter, vocal 6 fluent, verbal 7 express, jointed 8 distinct 9 enunciate, pronounce 10 formulated 13 particularize

articulation: 5 joint, voice 6 arthra(pl.), suture 7 arthron 9 arthrosis, utterance 10 connection

artifice: art 4 gaud, hoax, plan, plot, ruse, wile 5 blind, cheat, dodge, feint, fraud, guile, skill, trick 6 cautel, deceit, device, 7 cunning, evasion, finesse, sleight 8 intrigue, maneuver, pretense, strategy, trickery 9 deception, expedient, imposture, ingenuity, invention, strategem 10 artfulness, subterfuge 11 contrivance, machination 13 ingeniousness

artificer: See **artisan**

artificial: 4 sham 5 faked, false 6 ersatz, forced, forged, unreal 7 assumed, bastard, feigned 8 affected, falsetto, spurious 9 insincere, synthetic, unnatural 10 factitious, fictitious, theatrical 11 adulterated, counterfeit 12 supposititious

artillery: 4 arms, guns 6 cannon 8 ordnance
emplacement: 7 battery
fire: 5 salvo 6 rafale 7 barrage
wagon: 6 camion 7 caisson

artilleryman: 6 gunner, lascar 8 topechee 9 cannoneer 10 bombardier

artiodactyl: ox; pig 4 deer, goat 5 camel, sheep 6 artiad 7 giraffe 8 antelope 12 hippopotamus

artisan: 5 smith 6 artist 7 artifex, workman 8 opificer, mechanic 9 artificer, craftsman, operative 14 handicraftsman

artist: dab 5 actor, adept 6 dancer, etcher, expert, fictor, master, singer, wizard 7 artisan, artiste, operant, painter, schemer 8 magician, musician, sculptor, sketcher 9 craftsman, performer 12 professional, practitioner
equipment: 5 brush, easel 7 palette
medium: oil 7 tempera 10 watercolor
primitive: 5 Moses
signature word: 5 fecit
workshop: 6 studio 7 atelier

artistic: 6 daedal, expert 8 esthetic 9 aesthetic

artless: 4 naif, open 5 frank, naive, plain 6 candid, rustic, simple 7 natural 8 innocent 9 guileless, ingenuous, untutored 10 unaffected 11 undesigning 15 unsophisticated

arts: *goddess:* 4 Muse 6 Athena
liberal: 5 logic 6 trivia(pl.) 7 grammar, trivium 8 rhetoric

arui: 5 sheep 6 aoudad

arum: 4 arad, taro 5 aroid, plant 10 cuckoopint

family: 7 araceae
water: 5 calla

arundinaceous: 5 reedy

Aryan: 4 Mede, Slav 9 Caucasian
deity: 6 Ormazd, Ormuzd
god of fire: 4 Agni
language: 8 Sanskrit
of India: 5 Hindu

as: for, qua 4 like, that, thus, when 5 equal, since, while 7 because, equally, similar 9 therefore
above: 5 ditto, ut sup 7 ut supra
far as: to
if: 5 quasi
she is: 4 dyce
stated: so 4 thus
usual: 6 solito
well as: and
written: sic, sta 4 stet

As You Like It character: 5 Celia 6 Jaques 8 Rosalind

Asa: 6 healer 9 physician
father: 4 Abia
son: 11 Jehoshaphat

asafetida: 4 hing 5 laser 6 ferula

ascend: up 4 rise, soar 5 climb, mount, scale, tower 7 clamber 8 escalate, progress

ascendancy: 4 sway 5 power 7 control, mastery, success 8 dominion, prestige 9 authority, influence, supremacy 10 domination 11 sovereignty 13 preponderance

ascent: sty 4 hill, ramp, rise, rist 5 glory, grade, mount, scend, slope, steps 6 stairs 7 incline, upswing 8 eminence, gradient 9 acclivity, ascension 11 advancement

ascertain: get 4 find 5 count, learn, prove 6 assure, attain 7 apprise, apprize, measure, unearth 8 discover 9 determine

ascetic: nun 4 monk, yogi 5 fakir, friar, stoic, Yogin 6 Essene, strict 7 austere, bhikshu, devotee, eremite, recluse, stylite 8 anchoret 9 anchorite 10 abstemious

ascot: tie 5 scarf 6 cravat 7 necktie 9 racetrack

ascribe: lay 4 aret 5 blame, count, guess, infer, refer 6 accuse, allege, arette, assign, attach, charge, credit, impute, reckon 8 accredit, dedicate, inscribe 9 affiliate, attribute

ascription: 8 addition 11 declaration
of praise: 6 gloria
popular: 6 repute

ascus: bag, sac

asea: 4 lost 6 addled, adrift 7 puzzled, sailing 8 confused 9 befuddled, uncertain 10 bewildered

aseptic: 5 clean 6 barren 7 sterile

Asgard: *bridge to:* 7 Bifrost
watchman: 8 Heimdall

ash: ase(Sc.), ron 4 coke, sorb, tree 5 artar,
ember, rowan 6 cinder, corpse 7 clinker,
residue 8 fraxinus
  receptacle: bin, box, urn
  reduce to: 7 cremate
  tobacco: 6 dottel, dottle
ash holder: urn
ashamed: 7 abashed, hangdog 10 humili-
ated
Ashanti pepper: 5 cubeb
ashen: wan 4 gray, grey, pale 5 waxen 6
pallid 7 ghastly 8 blanched 9 cinereous 11
cineritious
Asher: *daughter:* 5 Serah 6 Beriah
  father: 5 Jacob
  son: 4 Usui 6 Jimnah
ashkoko: 4 cony 5 daman, hyrax
ashore: 7 aground, beached, 8 stranded
ashweed: 8 goutweed
Asia (see also **Asia Minor, Southeast Asia**):
4 East 6 Orient
  ancient region: 4 Aria 5 Akkad, Sumer 6
  Canaan 7 Babylon
  animal: 5 bison 8 pangolin 10 chevrotain
  antelope: 5 goral, serow 6 dzeren, dzerin,
  dzeron
  ass: 6 onager, koulan
  bean: soy 4 gram, soya 5 mungo
  bird: 4 mina, myna 5 mynah, pitta 7
  minivet 8 dotterel 9 brambling
  blizzard: 5 buran
  carnivore: 5 panda
  cattle: 4 zobo
  central: 6 Tatary
  Christian: 5 Uniat
  city: 4 Amoy, Sian 5 Dacca 6 Bagdad, Bombay, Singan 7 Comilla 9 Singapore
  comb. form: 4 Indo
  conjurer: 6 shaman
  country: 4 Elam, Irak, Iran, Iraq, Laos,
  Siam 5 Accad, Akkad, Annam, Araby, Assam, Burma, China, India, Japan, Korea,
  Nepal, Syria, Tibet 6 Arabia, Malaya,
  Persia, Russia, Sikkim, Turkey 7 Armenia, Chaldea, Siberia, Vietnam 8
  Cambodia, Pakistan, Thailand
  crowfoot: 9 buttercup
  deer: roe 4 axis
  desert: 4 Gobi
  disease: 4 yaws 7 cholera, malaria 9 tracho-
  man
  district: 7 Fartary
  dog (wild): 5 dhole
  drink: 5 airan
  eskimo: 4 Yuit 6 Innuit
  esplanade: 6 maidan
  falcon: 6 laggar 8 lanneret
  fiber: 4 hemp 5 ramie
  fox: 6 corsac

gangster: 6 dacoit
gazelle: ahu 4 cora
goat: 4 tahr
goddess: 4 Anta
grass: 4 coix, munj
greeting: 6 salaam
herb: 4 hemp
holiday: Tet
horse: 6 tarpan
island: 4 Java 5 Japan, Luzon, Malay 6 Borneo, Ceylon 7 Celebes, Formosa, Sumatra,
Wrangel 8 Mindanao, Sakhalin 11 Philippines
isthmus: Kra
jay: 7 sirgang
lake: Tai 4 Tami 6 Baikal 8 Balkhash
language: 5 Malay, Pamir, Tamil
lemur: 5 loris 6 macaco
lynx: 7 caracal
mammal: 5 panda 10 chevrotain
market: 6 bazaar
measure: mou 4 tael
medicine man: 6 shaman
millet: 4 dari
mink: 8 kolinsky
mongoose: 4 urva
monkey: 6 rhesus
mountain: 5 Altai, Sayan 6 Zagros 7 Everest 9 Himalayas, Hindu-Kush 14 Kan-
chininjinga
mystic: 5 fakir
nomad: 4 Arab 5 Tatar 6 Mongol 7 Kipchak
oasis: 4 merv
oil plant: 4 odal
owl: 4 utum
ox: yak
partridge: 6 seesee
peninsula: 5 Corea, Korea, Malay 6 Arabia
9 Kamchatka
people: Meo, Tai 4 Huns, Miao, Shan, Yuit
5 Kurds, Medes, Seres, Tatar, Todas 6 Tartar 10 Mongolians
pert to: 8 Chaldean
pheasant: 8 tragopan
plain: 4 chol
plant: tea 4 atis, odal, soya 5 akebi, betel
plant (fiber source): 5 ramie
region: 7 Siberia, Tartary
religion: 5 Islam 8 Buddhism, Hinduism
river: Ob; Ili, Obi 4 Amur, Lena, Onon,
Yalu 5 Amoor, Eelee, Indus, Putra 6
Branma, Ganges, Mekong, Tigris 7
Hwang-Ho, Yang-Tse, Yeinsei 8 Chao
Phya, Irawaddy 9 Euphrates
rodent: 4 pika 6 gerbil, marmot 7 gerbile
sandstorm: 6 simoon, tebbad
seaport: 5 Macao 6 Bombay 9 Singapore
shrub: tea
sea: 4 Aral, Azof 7 Caspian

sheep: sha **5** argal, urial **6** argali, bharal, nahoor, oorial

shrub: tea **4** tche, thea

snake: **6** bongar, daboia, jessur

squirrel: **8** jelerang **10** polatouche

storm: **5** buran **6** tebbad **7** monsoon, typhoon

tableland: **5** Tibet

tree: **4** asak, asok, dita, rata **5** asoka, siris **6** banyan, medlar, wampee

warehouse: **6** godown

weapon: **5** adaga

weight: **4** tael **5** catty

wolf: **6** chanco

Asia Minor (see also **Asia**): **8** Anatolia

animal: **5** daman

city: **4** Myra, Myus, Teos, Troy **5** Haran, Perga, Ushak **6** Aintab, Sardis, Tarsus **7** Ephesus, Miletus

coast: **5** Ionia

island: **5** Samos

mountain: Ida

mountain range: **4** Alai

region: **4** Aria **5** Caria, Eolis, Ionia, Troad, Troas **6** Pontus

river: **5** Halys **8** Monderez

sea: **6** Aegean

seaport: **5** Issus

aside: off **4** away, gone, near, past **5** agley, aloof, apart **6** aslant, astray, beside, beyond, byhand **7** lateral, private, whisper **8** reserved, secretly, separate, sidewise **9** alongside **10** indirectly

asinego: ass **4** fool

asinine: 4 dull **5** crass, dense, inept, silly **6** absurd, obtuse, simple, stupid **7** doltish, fatuous, foolish, idiotic **9** gooselike, senseless

ask: beg, sue **4** pray, quiz **5** claim, crave, exact, frayn, plead, query, speer(Sc.), **6** adjure, demand, expect, frayne, invite **7** beseech, bespeak, consult, entreat, implore, inquire, request, require, solicit **8** petition, question **9** obsecrate **11** interrogate

askance: 4 awry **5** askew **6** askant, askile **7** crooked **8** sideways **9** obliquely, suspicion **13** distrustfully

askew: cam **4** agee, alop, awry **5** agley, amiss, atilt **6** askant, aslant, atwist **7** asquint, crooked, oblique **9** distorted **10** catawampus

asleep: 4 dead, idle **6** latent, numbed **7** dormant, napping **10** motionless, slumbering **11** unconscious

asomatous: 10 immaterial **11** incorporeal

asp: 5 adder, aspen, snake, viper **7** serpent **8** ophidian

representative headdress: **6** uraeus

asparagus: 5 sprue

aspect: air **4** face, look, mien, side, view **5** angle, facet, guise, phase, sight, stage **6** glance, manner, visage **7** bearing, feature, outlook **8** carriage, prospect **9** semblance **10** appearance **11** countenance **13** consideration

aspen: aps, asp **4** tree **6** poplar **7** quaking **9** quivering, trembling, tremulous

asper: 4 coin **5** harsh, rough, stern **6** bitter

asperse: 4 spot, slur **5** abuse, decry, libel, spray **6** defame, defile, malign, revile, shower **7** appeach, blacken, detract, lampoon, slander, tarnish, traduce **8** besmirch, forspeak, sprinkle **9** bespatter, discredit, disparage **10** besprinkle, vituperate

aspersion: 7 baptism, calumny **8** innuendo

asperity: ire **5** rigor **8** acerbity, acrimony, hardship, severity, sourness, tartness **9** briskness, harshness, roughness **10** bitterness, difficulty, unevenness **11** crabbedness **16** disagreeableness

aspersorium: 4 font **5** basin, stoup **11** aspergillum

asphalt: 4 brea **7** bitumen **9** chapapote **10** wurtzilite **11** courtzilite

asphyxia: 5 apnea **6** apnoea **8** acrotism **11** suffocation

aspic: asp **5** jelly **7** gelatin **8** gelatine, lavender

aspirant: 9 candidate

aspiration: 4 goal **5** ideal **8** ambition

aspire: aim **4** hope, long, rise, seek, soar, wish **5** ettle, mount, tower, yearn **6** desire, ascend, attain

ass: 4 dolt, duff, fool, moke **5** burro, chump, cuddy, dunce, jenny, kiang, kulan, neddy **6** donkey, koulan, onager, quagga **7** asinego **8** imbecile **9** blockhead, simpleton **10** rattlepate

comb. form: ono

in lion's skin: **8** imposter

male: **4** jack

assai: 4 very **6** enough

assail: woo **4** pelt **5** assay, beset, stone, whack, whang **6** accuse, attack, bullet, hurtle, impugn, invade, malign, molest, rattle, scathe **7** assault, belabor, bombard **9** encounter **11** assassinate

assailant: 9 aggressor

Assam: *city:* **4** Ledo **10** Shillangle (c.)

dialect: Ao; Aka **5** Lhota

rubber: **7** rambong

silkworm: eri **4** eria

tribesman: Ao; Aka **4** Ahom, Garo, Naga

assart: 4 grub **8** clearing

assassin: 4 thag, thug **5** bravo **6** cuttle, killer, slayer **7** ruffian **8** murderer **9** cutthroat

Abel's: 4 Cain

Kennedy's: 6 Oswald, Sirhan

Lincoln's: 5 Booth

assation: 6 baking 8 roasting

assault: 4 beat, raid, slug 5 assay, brunt, onset, pound, smite, storm 6 affray, assail, attack, buffet, breach, charge, invade 7 attempt, bombard, violate 8 outburst 9 incursion, onslaught 10 aggression

assay: try 4 test 5 prove, trial 6 attack, effort 7 analyze, attempt, examine, tasting 8 analysis, appraise, endeavor, hardship 9 determine 10 affliction, experiment

assaying: 8 docimasy

cup: 5 cupel

assemblage: 4 army body, camp, crew, herd, host, mass, pack 5 bunch, crowd, drove, flock, levee, posse, salon, swarm 6 convoy, galaxy, hookup, throng 7 cluster 9 community 11 aggregation 13 constellation

assemble: fit 4 call, mass, meet 5 amass, piece, rally, unite 6 couple, gather, huddle, muster, summon 7 collect, convene, convoke, recruit 9 aggregate 10 congregate, foregather

assembly: hui 4 baud, bevy, diet, feis, moot, raad 5 forum, group, junta, party, press, setup, synod, troop 6 assize, gemote, powwow, senate 7 comitia, company, council, husting, meeting, session, society 8 audience, conclave, congress, tribunal 10 consistory, convention, parliament 11 convocation, legislature

ecclesiastical: 6 coetus 8 sederunt

full: 5 plena

people's: 7 folcmot, folkmot 8 folkmote, folkmout 9 folcgemot

place: 5 agora

room: 4 hall 10 auditorium

assembly line: 5 plant 7 factory, process

assent: aye, bow, nod, yea, yes 4 amen 5 admit, agree, yield 6 accede, accept, accord, chorus, comply, concur, submit 7 approve, concede, conform, consent 8 adhesion, sanction 9 acquiesce, subscribe 10 compliance, condescend 11 acknowledge

assert: say 4 aver, avow, cite 5 claim, plead, posit, state, swear, utter, vaunt, voice 6 affirm, allege, assure, avouch, defend, depone, depose, uphold 7 advance, betoken, contend, declare, protest, support 8 advocate, champion, maintain 9 attribute, predicate, vindicate 10 asseverate

positively: 5 swear

assertive: 8 dogmatic, positive 9 defensive, pragmatic 10 aggressive 11 affirmatory

assess: tax 4 cess, levy, mise, rate, scot, toll 5 cense, price, value 6 assize, charge, impose 7 measure 8 appraise, estimate 9 apportion

assessment: fee, tax 4 duty, levy, scot, toll 5 price, ratal, tithe, worth 6 extent, impost, surtax, tariff 7 scutage 9 valuation

assessor: 5 judge, rater 8 adsessor 11 adjudicator

assets: 5 goods, means, money 6 credit, wealth 7 capital, effects 8 accounts, property, resource 9 valuables

asseverate: say, vow 4 aver, avow 5 state 6 affirm, allege, assert, assure 7 asseover, declare, protest

asseveration: 4 oath

assiduous: 4 busy 6 active 7 devoted 8 diligent, frequent, sedulous, studious 9 attentive, laborious, unwearied 10 persistent 11 industrious, painstaking, persevering, unremitting 13 indefatigable 14 unintermittent

assign: fix, set 4 cede, deal, dole, give, mete, rate, seal, show, sign 5 allot, allow, award, endow, refer 6 adduce, affect, allege, charge, convey, delate, depute, detail, reckon, select, settle 7 adjudge, advance, appoint, ascribe, consign, dispose, specify, tribute 8 allocate, delegate, transfer 9 apportion, attribute, designate, determine 10 commission, distribute 11 appropriate

assignation: 4 date 5 tryst 7 meeting 11 appointment

assignment: 4 duty, task 5 stent, stint 6 lesson 11 assignation

assimilate: mix 4 fuse 5 adapt, alter, blend, learn, merge 6 absorb, digest, imbibe 7 compare, concoct 8 resemble 9 transform 10 metabolize, understand 11 appropriate, incorporate

assist: aid 4 abet, back, help, join 5 avail, boost, coach, favor, nurse, serve, speed 6 attend, escort, prompt, second, squire, succor 7 benefit, relieve, support, sustain 8 befriend 9 accompany 10 facilitate

assistance: aid 4 alms, gift, help 5 heeze 6 relief, remedy 8 easement 9 patronage 11 furtherance

assistant: 4 aide, ally, hand, maid, mate, zany 5 clerk, groom, usher, valet 6 aidant, deputy, second 7 abettor, partner 8 adjutant, adjuvant, servitor 9 associate, auxiliary, secretary 10 accomplice 11 confederate, subordinate

to pastor: 6 curate

assistants: 4 crew 5 staff 7 retinue 9 entourage

assize: fix 4 oyer, rate 5 court, edict, trial 6 assess, decree 7 hearing, measure, session, sitting, statute 8 assembly, standard, tri-

bunal 9 enactment, ordinance 10 regulation
associate: mix, pal 4 aide, ally, band, chum,
join, link, mate, moop, moup, peer, yoke,
wife 5 blend, buddy, crony 6 cohort, fellow,
friend, helper, hobnob, mingle, relate,
spouse 7 adjunct, comrade, connect, consort, husband, partner 8 copemate, federate, intimate 9 accompany, affiliate, assistant, attendant, coadjutor, colleague,
companion, conrector, socialize 10 accomplice, fraternize 11 concomitant
in crime: 10 accomplice
association: 4 body, bond, club, gild 5 artel,
guild, hansa, hanse, union 6 cartel,
league, pledge 7 company, consort, society
8 alliance, converse, intimacy, sodality 9
syndicate 10 assemblage, fellowship, sisterhood 11 aggregation, brotherhood,
combination, confederacy, conjunction,
partnership 12 conversation 13 confederation
literary: 6 lyceum 9 athenaeum
merchants': 5 hanse
secret: 5 cabal, lodge
workers': 5 guild, union
association football: 6 soccer
assoil: rid 5 atone, clear, solve 6 acquit, pardon, refute 7 absolve, deliver, expiate, forgive, release, resolve 9 discharge
assonance: pun 5 rhyme 8 paragram 11 resemblance
assort: 4 file, rank, sort, type 5 group, order
8 classify
assortment: lot, set 4 olio 5 batch, group,
suite 7 mixture 10 collection, miscellany
assuage: 4 calm, ease 5 abate, allay, delay,
slake 6 lessen, modify, pacify, quench, reduce, soften, solace, soothe, temper 7 appease, comfort, mollify, relieve, satisfy 8
diminish, mitigate, moderate 9 alleviate
11 tranquilize
assuasive: 4 mild 7 lenient 8 lenitive, soothing 9 emollient
assume: don 4 dare, fang, mask, sham, take
5 adopt, cloak, elect, feign, indue, infer,
raise, usurp 6 accept, affect, betake, clothe
7 believe, premise, pretend, receive, suppose, surmise 8 accroach, arrogate, simulate 9 undertake 11 appropriate, counterfeit
assumed: 5 alias 9 fictional, uncertain 10
artificial, fictitious, precarious 12 hypothetical, suppositious
assumed name: 5 alias 9 pseudonym
assuming: 5 lofty 8 arrogant, superior 10
assumptive 11 pretentious 12 presumptuous
different form: 7 protean

assurance: 4 seal 5 brass, faith, nerve, trust
6 aplomb, belief, credit, safety 7 courage,
promise 8 audacity, boldness, coolness, firmance, security 9 certainty, certitude, impudence 10 confidence, effrontery 12 cock-
sureness
assure: 4 aver 5 hight 6 assert, avouch, ensure, insure, pledge, secure 7 betroth, confirm, declare, hearten, promise, protest 8
affiance, convince, embolden, reassure 9
ascertain, encourage, guarantee, vouchsafe 10 asseverate, certiorate, underwrite
assuredly: 4 amen 6 surely, verily 10 in-
trepidly, truthfully 11 indubitably, un-
doubtedly
Assyria: 5 Ashur, Assur 6 Asshur
capital: 5 Calah 7 Nineveh
city: 4 Hara, Opis 5 Al Sur, Calah 6 Arbela,
Asshur, Kalakh 7 Antioch(c.), Nineveh(c.)
9 Dur Sargon
god: El, Zu; Ira, Sin 4 Adad, Anet, Asur,
Nebo 5 Ashir, Ashur, Hadad, Ninip 6 Asshur, Nergal, Shamas
goddess: 4 Nana, Nine 5 Istar 6 Allatu, Ishtar 9 Sarpanitu
king: Pul 5 Belus 6 Sargon 8 Asnapper, Os-
nappar 9 Asenappar
measure: 4 cane, foot 5 makuk, gasab 6 artaba, gariba, ghalva 7 mansion
queen: 9 Semiramis
river: Zab 6 Adhiam
astart: 8 suddenly
asteism: 5 irony 8 derision, raillery, ridicule
aster: *family:* 10 carduaceae, compositae
herb: 5 alant 6 arnica 7 boneset 10 elecampane
asterisk: 4 mark, star
Asterius: 8 argonaut, minotaur
father: 10 Hyperasius
mother: 8 Pasiphae
wife: 6 Europa
astern: aft 4 baft, hind, rear 5 abaft, apoop
6 behind 7 occiput 8 backward
asteroid: 4 Eros, Hebe, Iris, Juno 5 Ceres,
Flora, Irene, Metis, Vesta 6 Astrea, Egeria, Europa, Hygeia, Pallas, planet,
Psyche, Thetis 7 Eunomia, Fortuna,
Lutetia 8 Massalia, starfish, starlike, Victoria 9 Melpomene, planetoid 10 Parthenope, star-shaped
first: 5 Ceres
nearest earth: 4 Eros
asthmatic: 5 pursy 6 wheezy 7 panting,
puffing
astipulate: 5 agree 6 assent 11 exstipulate
astir: up 4 agog 5 about, afoot, alert, going
6 active, moving, roused 7 abroach, excited 8 stirring, vigilant
Astolat's Lily Maid: 6 Elaine

astonish: awe 4 daze, stam 5 amaze 7 astound, impress, startle 8 bewilder, confound, surprise 11 flabbergast

astonished: 5 agape

astonishing: 8 fabulous

astonishment: 5 ferly 6 dismay, wonder 10 admiration 13 consternation

astound: 4 stun 5 amaze, appal, shock 6 appall 7 stagger, stupefy, terrify 8 astonish, confound 9 overwhelm

astragal: 5 talus 7 molding 9 anklebone

astrakhan: 5 apple, cloth 7 caracul, karakul

astral: 6 remote, starry 7 stellar 8 sidereal, starlike 9 visionary

astray: 4 awry, lost 5 agley, amiss, aside, wrong 6 abroad, afield, errant, erring, faulty 7 sinning 8 mistaken, straying 9 wandering

astride: 4 atop 7 acheval 8 spanning 9 astraddle 10 bestriding, straddling

astringent: 4 acid, alum, sour, tart 5 acerb, harsh, stern 6 severe, tannin 7 austere, binding, styptic 11 acrimonious, compressive, contracting 12 constrictive
extract: 7 catechu
gum: 4 kino

astrologer: 4 Josh 6 Merlin 9 stargazer 10 astronomer 11 Nostradamus

astronaut: 9 cosmonaut
American: 5 Glenn, Scott, White, Young 6 Aldrin, Anders, Borman, Cernan, Conrad, Lovell 7 Collins, Grissom, Schirra, Shepard 8 McDivitt, Mitchell, Stafford 9 Armstrong 10 Cunningham
Soviet: 7 Gagarin, Komarov

astronomer: 10 Hipparchus

astronomical: far 4 huge 5 great 6 uranic 7 distant, immense 8 colossal, infinite
instrument: aba 9 telescope 10 equatorial
measurement: 5 apsis 7 azimuth
Muse: 4 Clio 6 Urania

astute: sly 4 foxy, keen, wily 5 acute, canny, quick, sharp, smart 6 clever, crafty, shrewd 7 cunning, skilled 9 astucious, sagacious 10 discerning 14 discriminating

asunder: 5 apart, split 6 atwain, sunder 7 divided 8 divorced 9 separated
prefix: dis

asylum: ark 4 home, jail 5 altar, cover, grith, haven 6 bedlam, harbor, refuge 7 alsatia, hospice, retreat, shelter 9 sanctuary 11 institution

asymmetrical: 4 skew

asymmetry: 13 disproportion

at: al, au, by, to; als 5 atten, there 6 hereat
all: any, ava, eer 4 ever 5 aught 6 anyway, soever
hand: by 4 near, nigh 7 present

home: in; tea 4 here 5 levee, party 9 reception

last: 7 finally 10 ultimately

odds: out

once: now, PDQ 4 anon 5 amain 6 presto 9 instanter 11 immediately

that: 4 then 7 thereat, whereat 9 thereupon, whereupon

this: 6 hereon 8 hereupon

Ata, Aeta: Ita 7 Negrito

atabal, attabal: 4 drum 5 tabor 10 kettledrum

atacamite: 9 arsenillo

Atahaulpa: 4 Inca 6 Indian

ataman: 5 chief, judge 6 hetman 7 Cossack, headman

atap: 4 nipa, palm

atavism: 9 reversion

atavus: 8 ancestor 11 grandfather

atelier: 6 studio 7 bottega 8 botteghe(pl.), workshop

ates: 8 sweetsop

Athamas: *daughter:* 5 Helle
son: 7 Phrixos, Phrixus 8 Learchus
wife: Ino

athanor: 4 oven 7 furnace

Athapascan Indian: 4 Dene, Hupa 5 Hoopa

atheist: 7 doubter 8 agnostic 11 nonbeliever

Athena, Athene: 4 Alea, Auge, Nike 5 Alera, Areia 6 Ergane, Hippia, Hygeia, Itonia, Pallas, Polias 7 Minerva 8 Apaturia, Athenaia 9 Parthenos, Poliuchos, Promachos 10 Chalinitis 11 Chalcioecus, Tritogeneia
pert. to: 9 Palladian
temple: 9 Parthenon

Athens (see also **Attica, Greece**):
alien resident: 5 metic
assembly: 4 pnyx 5 boule
assembly platform: 4 bema
astronomer: 5 Meton
clan: obe
coin: 5 oboli 6 obolus 7 chalcus, chalkos
family: 11 Alcmaeonids 12 Alcmaeonidae
festival: 8 Apaturia, Athenaea 11 Scirophoria
founder: 7 Cecrops
general: 6 Nicias 7 Phocion 8 Zenophon
hill: 9 Acropolis 10 Lycabettus
historian: 8 Xenophon
king: 6 Codrus 7 Cecrops, Pandion
lawgiver: 5 Draco, Solon
magistrate: 5 draco 6 archon, dicast
marketplace: 5 agora
mountain: 6 Parnes
orator: 9 Isocrates
pert. to: 5 Attic
philosopher: 5 Plato 8 Socrates 9 Aristotle
platform: 4 bema 6 bemata(pl.)

rival: 6 Sparta
ruler: 6 archon
sculptor: 7 Phidias
seaport: 7 Piraeus
statesman: 8 Pericles 9 Aristides
temple: 4 Nike
Athens of: *America:* 6 Boston
Ireland: 7 Belfast
Switzerland: 6 Zurich
the North: 9 Edinburgh
the West: 7 Cordoba
athlete: pro 4 star 5 boxer 7 amateur, acrobat, gymnast, tumbler 8 wrestler 9 aerialist
athletic: 5 agile, burly, lusty, vital 6 brawny, robust, sinewy, strong 8 muscular, powerful, vigorous 9 acrobatic, energetic, strapping
contest: 4 agon, game, meet, race 8 Olympics
field: 4 oval, ring, rink 5 arena, court, green 6 course 7 diamond, stadium 8 gridiron
prize: cup 5 medal 6 ribbon
athletics: 5 games, sport 8 exercise
athwart: 6 aboard, across, aslant 7 oblique 8 sidewise, traverse 10 perversely
atlantal: 6 atloid 8 anterior, cephalic
Atlantic: *island:* 4 Cuba 6 Azores, Canary 7 Iceland 9 Greenland
seaport: 5 Colon 6 Boston 7 New York, Norfolk 8 Savannah 9 Baltimore 12 Philadelphia
Atlantides: 8 Pleiades 10 Hesperides
atlas: 4 bone, book, list, maps, tome 5 titan 8 mainstay
Atlas: *daughter:* 4 Maia 6 Merope 7 Alcyone, Calypso, Electra, Kelaine, Taygete 8 Asterope, Pleiades
mother: 7 Clymeme
atloid: 8 atlantal
atmosphere: air 4 aura, mood, tone 5 ether 6 frowst, miasma, nimbus, welkin 7 feeling, qualify 10 background 11 environment
disturbance: 5 storm 6 static
gas: 5 argon 6 oxygen 8 nitrogen
phenomenon: 6 aurora, meteor
prefix: 4 atmo 5 atmos
pressure: 10 barometric
atole: 4 meal 5 gruel 8 porridge
atoll: 4 reef 6 Bikini, island, Tarawa
atom: ace, bit, jot 4 haet, iota, mite, mote, whit 5 atomy, monad, shade, speck, tinge 7 atomize 8 molecule, particle, quantity 9 corpuscle, scintilla
adsorbed: 6 adatom
component: 6 proton 7 neutron
electrically charged: ion
nucleus: 6 proton

atomic: 4 tiny 6 minute 7 nuclear 9 molecular 13 infinitesimal
particle: 4 beta, pion 5 alpha, meson 6 photon 7 neutron
physicist: 4 Bohr, Rabi 5 Fermi, Pauli 7 Compton, Meitner
pile: 7 reactor
submarine: 5 Sargo, Skate 6 Triton 8 Nautilus
theory originator: 6 Dalton
atomize: 5 grate, spray 6 reduce 8 nebulize 9 devastate, pulverize
atomy: 4 atom, mite, mote 5 pygmy 8 skeleton
atone: 5 agree, amend 6 accord, redeem, repent 7 appease, expiate, restore 9 harmonize, reconcile 10 conciliate, propitiate
atonement: 7 penance 10 reparation 12 satisfaction
atonic: 7 unheard 9 voiceless 10 unaccented
atrabilious: 4 glum 6 gloomy, morose, sullen 10 melancholy
atramentous: 4 inky 5 black
Atreus: *brother:* 8 Thyestes
father: 6 Pelops
half brother: 10 Chrysippus
mother: 10 Hippodamia
slayer: 9 Aegisthus
son: 8 Menelaus 9 Agamemnon 11 Pleisthenes
wife: 6 Aerope
atrio: 6 atrium, valley 10 depression
atrip: 6 aweigh
atrium: 4 hall 5 atrio, court 6 cavity 7 auricle, chamber, passage 8 entrance
atrocha: 5 larva
atrociou bad 4 dark, rank, vile 5 awful, black, cruel, gross 6 brutal, odious, savage, wicked 7 heinous, ungodly, violent 8 grievous, horrible, terrible 9 execrable, frightful, nefarious 10 abominable, villainous
atrophy: 4 rust 5 stunt, tabes 6 shrink, starve, wither 8 stultify 10 emaciation
Atropos: 4 Fate
attach: add, fix, tag, tie 4 bind, glue, join, link, take, vest, weld 5 affix, annex, hitch, paste, seize, unite 6 accuse, addict, adhere, adjoin, append, arrest, cement, fasten, indict 7 adhibit, appoint, ascribe, connect, subjoin 9 affiliate, associate, garnishee
attache: 4 aide 8 diplomat
attached (see also **attach**): 4 fond 6 doting
at base: 7 sessile
to the land: 7 predial 8 praedial
attachment: 4 love 8 devotion, fondness 9 accessory, addiction, adherence, affection 10 engagement, friendship 11 inclination
attack: fit 4 bout, fray, pang, raid, rush, wade 5 alarm, assay, begin, beset, blitz, drive, fight, foray, ictus, onset, sally,

spasm, storm **6** accuse, action, affray, assail, battle, charge, invade, onrush, pounce, sortie, strike, stroke, thrust **7** assault, beseige, censure, descent, offense, potshot, seizure **8** paroxysm **9** diversion, encounter, onslaught **10** aggression

false: **5** feint

suicidal: **8** kamikaze

attacker: 9 aggressor **10** iconoclast

attain: get, hit, win **4** earn, gain, rise **5** reach, touch **6** accede, amount, arrive, aspire, effect, obtain, secure, strike **7** achieve, acquire, compass, procure, succeed **8** overtake **9** ascertain **10** accomplish, comprehend

attainment: 4 feat **5** skill **6** wisdom **14** accomplishment

attar: oil **4** atar **7** essence, perfume

attempt: try **4** dare, fist, mint, mird, osse, seek, shot, stab, wage **5** assay, begin, essay, frame, onset, start **7** attack, effort **7** venture **8** endeavor, exertion **9** undertake **10** enterprise, experiment

attend: go, ho; see **4** hear, heed, mind, tend, wait **5** await, guard, nurse, serve, treat, visit, watch **6** assist, convey, follow, harken, listen, shadow **7** consort **8** champion, minister **9** accompany

attendance: 4 gate **6** number, regard **8** presence **9** attention **11** application, expectation

attendant: 4 maid, page, zany **5** gilly, guide, usher, valet **6** escort, famuli(pl.), friend, minion, porter, squire, varlet, waiter **7** chobdar, courier, famulus, footboy, orderly, pageboy **8** chasseur, follower, henchboy, henchman **9** assistant, associate, attentive, companion **10** consequent, subsequent **11** chamberlain, concomitant **12** accompanying

attendants: 5 train, suite **7** cortege, retinue **9** entourage

attention: ear **4** care, heed, hist, note **5** study **6** notice, regard **7** achtung(G.), respect **9** diligence, obedience, vigilance **10** observance **11** observation **13** concentration, consideration

attentive: 4 wary **5** alert, awake, civil **6** intent, polite **7** careful, gallant, listful, mindful **8** studious, watchful **9** advertent, assiduous, courteous, listening **11** circumspect

attenuate: sap **4** thin **5** water **6** dilute, lessen, rarefy, reduce, weaken **7** slender **8** decrease, diminish, enfeeble, tapering **9** subtilize

attest: 4 seal **5** prove, swear, vouch **6** adjure, affirm, invoke **7** certify, confess, confirm, testify, witness **8** evidence, manifest **9** subscribe **12** authenticate

attic: 4 loft **6** garret **8** cockloft

Attic: 5 Greek **8** Athenian

Attic salt: wit

Attica (see also **Athens, Greece**): *alien:* **5** metic

festival: **5** Haloa **8** Diipolia **9** Diipoleia

legendary king: **6** Ogyges, Ogygos

township: **4** deme

valley: **6** Icaria

Attila: Hun **5** Etzel

attire: See **dress**

attitude: air, set **4** bias, mien, mood, pose **5** angle, phase, slant, stand **6** action, aspect, manner **7** bearing, feeling, posture **8** behavior, position **11** disposition

attorney: 4 doer **5** agent, proxy **6** deputy, factor, lawyer, legist, muktar **7** proctor **8** advocate **9** barrister, counselor, solicitor **10** counsellor

attract: 4 bait, draw, lure, pull **5** catch, charm, court, fetch, tempt **6** allure, engage, entice, invite, seduce **8** interest **9** captivate, fascinate, influence, magnetize

attracting: 9 allicient, attrahent

attraction: 4 card **6** magnet **7** gravity **8** affinity, penchant, witchery

attractive: 4 chic, cute, fair **5** bonny **6** lovely, pretty, taking **7** winning, winsome **8** alluring, charming, fetching, graceful **9** beautiful

attribute: fix, owe **4** mark, sign, type **5** asign, badge, blame, place, power, refer **6** allege, allude, assert, bestow, charge, impute, symbol **7** ascribe, pertain, quality **8** accredit, property **10** reputation **11** peculiarity **14** characteristic

attribution: 6 theory **8** etiology

attrition: 4 wear **5** grief **6** regret, sorrow **7** anguish **8** abrasion, friction **10** contrition

attune: key **4** tune **5** adapt, agree **6** accord, adjust, temper **7** prepare **9** harmonize

atua: 5 being, demon **6** spirit

atwain: 7 asunder

Au: 4 gold

au fait: 6 expert, proper **8** skillful **10** proficient

auberge: inn **7** albergo

auction: 4 cant, roup, sale, sell, vend **5** trade **6** barter, bridge **8** disposal

hammer: **5** gavel

platform: **5** block

price: bid **5** upset

audacious: 4 bold **5** brash, hardy, saucy **6** audace, brazen, cheeky, daring **7** forward **8** arrogant, fearless, impudent, insolent, intrepid, spirited **9** barefaced, bodacious, imprudent, shameless **10** courageous **11** adventurous, impertinent, venturesome **12** presumptuous

audacity: 5 nerve **7** courage **8** boldness, temerity **9** assurance, hardihood, impudence, insolence, sauciness **10** effrontery **12** impertinence

audible: 5 aloud, heard

audience: ear **4** fans **5** audit, court, house **6** public **7** gallery, hearing **8** assembly, auditory, tribunal **9** audiencia, interview, reception

audio-visual aid: 4 film, tape **5** slide

audit: 4 scan **5** check, probe **6** reckon, verify **7** account, examine, inquire, inspect **8** estimate

audition: 4 test **5** trial **6** tryout

auditor: CPA **6** censor, hearer **7** apposer, audient **8** disciple, listener **10** accountant, catechumen **11** comptroller

auditorium: 4 hall, room **5** cavea, odeum **7** theater **8** auditory

auditory: 4 oral, otic **5** aural **8** acoustic

auger: bit **4** bore, tool **5** grill **6** gimlet, wimble

aught: 5 owned **6** cipher, naught, worthy **7** nothing, valiant **8** anything, property **9** possessed

Augie March creator: 6 Bellow

augite: 8 pyroxene

augment: add, eke **4** grow **5** exalt, swell **6** append, dilate, expand, extend **7** amplify enhance, enlarge, improve, magnify **8** heighten, increase, multiply **9** increment **10** aggrandize

augur: 4 bode, omen, seer **6** auspex, divine **7** betoken, foresee, portend, predict, presage, prophet, promise, signify **8** forebode, foreshow, foretell, forewarn, indicate, prophesy **9** auspicate, **10** anticipate, conjecture, soothsayer **13** prognosticate

augury: 4 rite, sign **5** token **6** hansel, ritual **7** handsel **8** ceremony **10** foreboding, forerunner

august: 5 awful, grand, noble **6** solemn **7** exalted, stately **8** imposing, majestic **9** dignified, venerable **11** magisterial

Augustus' death place: 4 Nola

auk: 4 loom **5** arrie, lemot, noddy **6** puffin, rotche **7** dovekey, dovekie, **9** guillemot
family: **7** alcidae
genus: **4** alca, alle
razorbill: **4** falk **5** murre

aula: 4 hall, room **5** court **6** emblic

aumildar: 5 agent **6** factor **7** manager **9** collector

auncel: 7 balance

aunt: tia(Sp.) **4** bawd **5** tante(F.) **6** gossip **8** relative

aura: air **4** halo, odor **5** aroma, savor **6** breeze **7** buzzard, feeling **9** emanation **10** atmosphere, exhalation

aural: 4 otic **7** audible **9** auricular
appendage: ear

aureate: 6 golden, ornate, rococo, yellow **8** aurelian

aureole: 4 halo **5** crown, glory, light **6** corona, nimbus **8** gloriole

auricle: ear **5** pinna **6** atrium, earlet **7** trumpet
part: **7** earlobe

auricular: 4 otic **7** hearsay **12** confidential

aurochs: tur **4** urus **5** bison **6** wisent

Aurora: Eos **4** dawn **7** morning

auroral: 4 eoan, rosy **7** eastern, radiant

aurum: 4 gold

auscultate: 6 listen

auspex: 5 augur

auspicate: 5 augur **7** portend, predict **8** initiate **10** inaugurate

auspice: 4 care, egis, omen, sign **5** aegis **6** augury **7** portent **8** guidance **9** patronage **10** indication, protection **11** observation, sponsorship

auspicious: 4 fair, good **6** dexter **9** favorable, fortunate, opportune **10** favourable, propitious, prosperous **12** advantageous

Aussie: 9 Australia **10** Australian

austere: 4 cold, hard, sour **5** budge, grave, gruff, harsh, rigid, rough, sharp, stern, stiff **6** bitter, formal, severe, simple, somber, strict **7** ascetic, earnest, serious **8** rigorous **9** unadorned, unsmiling **10** astringent, forbidding, relentless **13** unembellished

Australia: *animal:* **4** tait **5** coala, koala, panda **6** bunyip, cuscus, wombat **7** dasqure, wallady **8** duckbill, kangaroo, platypus **9** bandicoot, phalanger
apple: **6** colane
badger: **6** wombat
bag: **5** dilli
bear: **5** coala, koala
beefwood: **5** belar
beverage: **4** kava
bird: emu **4** emeu, lory **5** arara, crake, grebe, stint **6** gannet, leipoa **7** bittern, boobook, bustard, figbird **8** berigora, dabchick, dotterel, lorikeet, lyrebird, morepork, whimbrel **9** bower-bird, cassowary, coachwhip, friarbird, stipiture, **10** paradalote, pratincole, sanderling
boomerang: **5** kiley, kilie
brushwood: **6** millee
bush: ake
bustard: **7** bebilya
cake: **6** damper **7** brownie
call: **5** cooee, cooey

cape: 4 Howe
cat: 7 dasyure
catfish: 6 tandan
cattle stealer: 6 duffer
cedar: 4 toon
channel: 5 cowal 9 anabranch, billabong
city: see town below
clover fern: 6 nardoo
cockatoo: 5 galah
coin: 4 dump
colonist: 8 sterling
countryman: 8 Billijim
crayfish: 5 yabby 6 yabbie
cycad: 5 banga
dog: 5 dingo 6 Kelpie
duckbill: 8 platypus
eucalyptus: 6 bimbil, mallee 7 carbeen
fern: 5 nardu 6 nardoo
fish: 4 dart, mado, mako 5 yabby 6 tandan, yabbie
flightless bird: emu 4 emeu
fruit: 5 nonda
gum tree: 4 kari 6 tewart, tooart, touart
herb: 8 piripiri
horse: 7 brumbee 8 yarraman
hut: 6 miamia
insect: 4 laap, lerp
island: 5 Timor 8 Tasmania
kangaroo: 4 joey 5 tungo 7 bettong
kiwi: roa
lake: 4 Eyre 5 Carey, Cowan, Frome, Moore, Woods 6 Austin, Barlee, Bulloo, Harris, Mackay 7 Amadeus, Blanche, Eyerard, Torrens 8 Carnegie, Gairdner 9 Macdonald 14 Disappointment
language: 6 yabber
lizard: 6 goanna
lorikeet: 6 parrot, warrin
mahogany: 6 jarrah 7 gunning
marsupial: 4 tait 5 koala 6 wombat 8 kangaroo
measure: 4 saum
mile: 4 naut
moth: 6 bogong
mountain: Ise 5 Bruce 6 Cradle, Garnet, Magnet, Morgan 7 Bongong 8 Cuthbert, Mulligan 9 Kosciusko, Murchison
mountain range: 7 Darling 8 Flinders
native: 4 Mara 5 binge 6 digger 7 Billjim 8 Warragal, Warrigal
no: 4 baal, bail, bale
ostrich: 4 emeu
owl: 7 boobook 8 morepoke, morepork
palm: 8 bangalow
parakeet: 6 budgie 7 corella 10 budgerigar
parrot: 4 lory 7 corella, lorilet 8 lorikeet 9 cockateel, cockatiel
pepper: 4 arva, kava, yava 6 ava-ava
petrel: 4 titi

phalanger: 5 ariel
plant: 5 lakea 6 correa 7 calomba, waratah 8 warratau
pine: 5 kauri, kaury
pond: 9 billabong
rat: 8 hapalote 9 hapalotis
ratite: 4 emeu
rifleman: 5 yager
river: Hay 4 Avon, Daly, Swan, Yule 5 Comet, Namoi, Paroo, Roper, Yarra 6 Barcoo, Barwon, Bulloo, Culgoa, Dawson, De Grey, Hunter, Isaacs, Murray, Nepean, Norman 7 Darling, Fitzroy, Georges, Gilbert, Lachlan, Staaten 8 Brisbane, Burdekin, Clarence, Drysdale, Flinders, Gascoyne, Georgina, Goulburn, Mitchell, Thompson, Victoria, Werribee, Wooramel 9 Ashburton, Fortescue, Macquarie, Murchison, Saltwater 10 Diamantina, Leichhardt 11 Murrumidgee
rustler: 6 duffer
shark: 4 mako
shield: 8 heelaman, heilaman, hielaman, yeelaman
snake: 6 elapid
soldier: 5 Anzac 6 digger, swaddy 7 Billjim
sorcerer: 5 boyla 6 boolya
spear: 7 womerah, wommala, woomera 8 wommerah, woomerah 9 woomerang
state: 8 Tasmania, Victoria 10 Queensland 13 New South Wales 14 South Australia 16 Western Australia 17 Northern Territory
territory: 5 Papua
thicket: 6 mallee
throwing stick: 5 kiley, kylie 7 womerah, wommala 8 hornerah, wommerah, woomerah 9 boomerang, woomerang
town: Ayr 4 Yass 5 Dubbo, Perth, Wagga 6 Albury, Casino, Darwin, Hobart, Mackay, Sydney 7 Geelong, Ipswich, Kogarah, Mildura, Warwick, Waverly 8 Adelaide, Brighton, Brisbane, Canberra (c.), Hamilton, Maylands, Richmond, Toowomba 9 Bankstown, Caulfield, Melbourne, Newcastle 10 Hurtsville, Townsville, Wollongong 11 Rockhampton
toy: 8 weet-weet
tree: 4 toon 5 belah, belar, boree, gidya, penda 6 gidgea, gidgee, gidyea, marara 7 alipata 8 beefwood, curajong, flindosa, flindosy, ironbark 9 koorajong 10 bunya-bunya
tulip: 7 waratah 8 warratau
valley: 5 Grose 8 Jamieson, Kangaroo, Megalong 11 Burragorang
war club: 5 waddy
weapon: 5 hulla, waddy 6 hullah 7 liangle 8 leeangle 10 hullanulla

wilderness: **7** outback
wombat: **5** koala
wood: emu
workman: **7** Bill jim
Austria: *city:* **4** Graz, Linz, Wien(c.) **5** Gratz **6** Vienna(c.) **7** Noricum **8** Salzburg
coin: **5** ducat, krone **6** florin, heller, zehner **8** groschen **9** schilling
composer: **4** Berg **7** Strauss **8** Bruckner
crownland: **8** Dalmatia
dance: **6** dreher
former ruling family: **8** Habsburg, Hapsburg
legislature: **10** Herrenhaus
measure: **4** fass, fuss, joch, mass, muth, yoke **5** halbe, linie, meile, metze, pfiff, punkt **6** achtel, becher, seidel **7** klafter, viertel **8** dreiling **10** muthmassel **12** futtermassel
measure of weight: **4** marc, saum, unze **5** denat, karch, pfund, stein **7** centner, pfennig **8** vierling **9** quentchen
money: **5** ducat
native: **7** Styrian **8** Tyrolese
nobility: **6** Ritter
province: **4** Gorz **5** Tirol, Tyrol **6** Istria, Styria, Triest **7** Bohemia, Galicia, Moravia, Selesia **8** Bukowina, Carniola, Dalmatia, Gradisca, Salzburg **9** Carinthia **10** Vorarlberg
psychiatrist: **5** Adler, Freud
river: Inn, Mur **4** Elbe, Enns, Isar, Raab **6** Danube, Moldau
writer: **5** Kafka
austringer: **8** falconer
Austronesian language: **4** Niue **7** Tagalog
autarch: **6** despot **8** autocrat
authentic: **4** pure, real, sure, true **5** exact, right, valid **6** actual, proper **7** correct, genuine, sincere **8** bonafide, credible, official, original, reliable **9** veritable **10** authorized **11** trustworthy **13** authoritative
authenticate: **4** seal **5** prove **6** attest, verify **7** approve, confirm
author: **4** doer **5** maker, ruler **6** factor, parent, source, writer **7** creator, founder **8** ancestor, begetter, compiler, composer, inventor, producer **10** bookwright, instigator, originator
authoritative: **8** official, oracular, positive **9** canonical, effectual, imperious, masterful **10** conclusive, convincing, legitimate, peremptory **11** dictatorial, excathedral, magisterial
authority: **4** sway **5** adept, board, power, riche, right, title **6** artist, author, expert, regent, regime, weight **7** command, dynasty, scepter, sceptre, warrant **8** dominion, prestige, sanction **9** influence **10** ascendancy, ascendency, commission, competence **12** jurisdiction **13** authorization, justification
judicial: **4** banc
preponderant: **8** hegemony
symbol: **7** scepter
woman's: **7** distaff
authorize: let **4** vest **5** allow **6** clothe, permit, ratify **7** approve, empower, endorse, entitle, indorse, justify, license, warrant **8** accredit, delegate, legalize, sanction **10** commission, legitimize
authorless: **9** anonymous
auto: See **automobile**
auto court: inn **5** motel
auto race: **4** drag **5** derby
autobiography: **4** vita **6** memoir
autochthonous: **6** native **7** edaphic, endemic **10** aboriginal, indigenous
autocrat: **4** czar, tsar, tzar **5** mogul **6** Caesar, despot **7** autarch, monarch **8** dictator **9** sovereign
autocratic: **8** absolute **9** arbitrary **10** tyrannical
autograph: **4** name, sign **9** signature
automatic: **7** machine **10** automatous, mechanical, self-acting **11** instinctive, spontaneous
automaton: **5** golem, robot **7** android, machine
automobile: **4** heap, jeep **5** coupe, crate, racer, sedan **6** jalopy **7** flivver, machine, phaeton **8** roadster **11** convertible
army: **4** jeep
British: AC, MG **5** Alvis, Riley, Rover **6** Allard, Anglia, Austin, Consul, Humber, Jaguar, Jowett, Morgan, Morris, Rapier, Singer, Zephyr **7** Bentley, Daimler, Hillman, Sunbeam, Triumph **8** Berkeley, Vauxhall **10** Rolls-Royce **11** Austin-Healy, Hillman-Minx, Morris-Minor **12** Metropolitan **13** Sunbeam-Talbot
Czech: **5** Skoda
early: EMF, Reo **4** Alco, Benz, Cord, Knox, Moon, Olds, Sear, Star **5** Brush, Regal, Stutz **6** Auburn, Dupont, Duryea, Graham, Haynes, Kissel, Lozier, Marmon, Mercer, Saxson, Thomas, Winton **7** Autocar, Bugatti, La Salle, Maxwell, Oakland, Premier, Rambler, Simplex, Stevens, Tourist **8** Apperson, Chalmers, Chandler, Franklin, Mercedes, National, Overland, Peerless **9** Hupmobile **10** Cunningham, Duesenberg, Jackrabbit, Locomobile **11** Graham-Paige, Pierce-Arrow **12** Crane-Simplex, Owen-Magnetic, Pope-Hartford, White-Streamer **13** Baker-Electric, Ofeldt-Steamer, Stevens-Duryea, Wills-St.

Claire 14 Stanley-Steamer 16 Columbia-Electric 22 International Auto Buggy

Europe: BMW 4 Benz 5 Aston, Metro, Prinz, Skoda 6 Martin, Denzel, Isetta, Zodiac 7 Bugatti, Prefect 9 Facel-Vega

French: DB 5 Simca 7 Citroen, Panhard, Peugeot, Renault 8 Dauphine

German: DKW 4 Opel 6 Taunus 7 Goliath, Porsche, Weidner 8 Borgward, Rometsch, Wartburg 10 Golomobile, Lloyd-Wagon, Volkswagen 12 Mercedes-Benz

Italian: 4 Fiat 6 Lancia 7 Ferrari 8 Maserati 9 Alfa-Romeo

Japanese: 5 Honda 6 Datsun, Toyota 13 Pringe-Skylark

part: 4 hood 5 motor, trunk 6 engine 7 chassis, magneto, tonneau 8 ignition

Russian: Zim 6 Pobeda 9 Moskvitch

Swedish: 4 Saab 5 Volvo

supercharged: 6 hot rod

United States: 4 Ford, Jeep, Nash, Nova, Vega 5 Buick, Capri, Comet, Dodge, Edsel, Pinto 6 Cougar, De Soto, Duster, Hudson, Impala, LeMans, Torino, Willys 7 Caprice, Lincoln, Mercury, Montego, Mustang, Packard, Pontiac, Rambler, Ventura 8 Cadillac, Chrysler, Corvette, Imperial, Maverick, Plymouth 9 Chevrolet 10 Oldsmobile, Studebaker 11 Continental, Thunderbird

autonomous: 4 free 11 independent

autopsy: 8 necropsy 10 dissection 11 examination

autumn: 4 fall 6 season 8 maturity 11 harvest-time

auxiliary: aid, sub 4 aide, ally 6 branch, helper 7 abetter, abettor, adjunct, partner 8 adjutant 9 accessory, adminicle, ancillary, assistant, coadjutor, secondary, tributary 10 additional, foederatus, subsidiary, supporting 11 confederate, cooperating, subordinate, subservient

ava: 4 kava

avail: do; aid, dow, use 4 boot, help 5 serve, stead, value 6 moment, profit 7 benefit, bestead, succeed, suffice, utilize 9 advantage 10 assistance

available: fit 4 free, open 5 handy, ready 6 patent, usable 7 present 9 effectual, practical 10 accessible, attainable, convenient, obtainable 11 efficacious

aval: 8 acceptor, indorser 9 ancestral

avalanche: 5 slide 9 landslide

avale: 4 doff, flow, sink 5 abase, lower, yield 6 submit 7 descend 8 dismount

Avalon, Avilion: 4 isle 6 island

tomb: 6 Arthur

avania: tax 6 impost

avanious: 12 extortionate

avantgarde: 8 vanguard

avarice: 7 avidity 8 cupidity, rapacity

spirit of: 6 Mammon

avaricious: 5 close 6 greedy, hungry, stingy 7 gripple, miserly 8 covetous, grasping 9 niggardly, penurious 12 parsimonious

avast: 4 hold, stay, stop 5 cease

avatar: 8 epiphany 10 embodiment 11 incarnation

avaunt: 5 boast, vaunt 6 begone, depart 7 advance, forward 9 dismissal

ave: 4 bead, hail 6 prayer 8 farewell, greeting 10 salutation, veneration

avellane: nut 5 hazel 7 filbert

avelonge: 4 oval 6 oblong 8 slanting

avenaceous: 4 oaty 5 oaten

avenge: 5 repay, wrack 6 awreak, punish 7 requite, revenge 8 chastise 9 retaliate, vindicate

avenger: 7 nemesis 10 vindicator

avens: 4 geum, herb

avenue: rue(F.), way 4 gate, mall, pike, road 5 allee, alley, drive, entry 6 access, arcade, artery, street 7 opening 9 boulevard 10 passageway 12 thoroughfare

aveolate: 6 favose

aver: say 5 claim, prove, state, swear 6 affirm, allege, assert, assure, avouch, depose, verify 7 declare, justify, protest 9 predicate 10 asseverate 11 acknowledge

average: par, sum 4 duty, fair, mean, norm, rule, so-so 5 ratio, usual, value 6 charge, medial, median, medium, middle, normal, tariff 8 estimate, mediocre, moderate, ordinary, quantity, standard 10 proportion 13 approximation

averse: 4 loth 5 balky, loath 7 adverse, against, opposed 8 inimical, opposite 9 disliking, reluctant, unwilling 11 disinclined, unfavorable

aversion: 4 hate 5 odium 6 enmity, hatred, horror 7 disdain, disgust, dislike 8 distaste 9 antipathy 10 repugnance 11 abomination 12 estrangement 14 disinclination

avert: 4 bend, fend, move, shun, ward 5 avoid, deter, dodge, evade, parry, sheer, twist 6 defray, divert, retard, shield 7 deflect, expiate, prevent 8 alienate, estrange, forefend 9 forestall

aviary: 4 cage 5 house 6 volery 8 ornithon 9 birdhouse, enclosure

keeper: 8 aviarist

aviation: 6 flying 10 airplaning 11 aeronautics

maneuver: 8 Immelman

aviator: ace 5 flier, flyer, pilot 6 airman, flying, Icarus 8 operator

signal: out 4 over 5 roger

aviatrix: 13 Amelia Earhart

avid: 4 agog, keen, warm 5 eager 6 ardent, greedy, hungry, jejune 7 anxious, athirst, craving, longing 8 desirous, grasping 9 devouring

avidity: 7 avarice 8 cupidity 10 greediness

avifauna: 5 birds, ornis

avile: 5 abase 6 debase, vilify 10 depreciate

avital: 6 avitic 9 ancestral

avocado: 4 coyo, pear, tree 6 chinin 8 aguacate, alligato

avocation: 4 work 5 hobby, trade 7 calling 9 amusement, diversion 10 recreation

avocet: 4 bird 5 stilt 6 godwit, plover

avoid: 4 balk, quit, shun 5 annul, avert, dodge, elude, evade, feign, hedge, parry, shirk, slack, spair(Sc.), 6 blench, escape, eschew, refute, remove, vacate 7 abstain, evitate, forbear, forsake, refrain 8 sidestep

avoidance: 6 outlet 10 dismissing, withdrawal

avoirdupois weight: ton 4 dram 5 ounce, pound 7 long ton 13 hundredweight 17 long hundredweight

avolate: fly 6 escape 9 evaporate

avow: own 4 bind 5 admit, state 6 affirm, avouch, depone, depose, devote 7 confess, declare, justify, profess 8 maintain 11 acknowledge

avowal: 4 oath, word 14 representation

awa: 4 kava 8 milkfish

awabi: 8 abalone

await: 4 bide, heed, pend, wait 5 abide, tarry, watch 6 attend, expect, impend, waylay

awake: daw 4 stir, wake 5 alert, alive, aware, rouse 6 active, arouse, awaken, excite 7 careful, heedful 8 open-eyed, vigilant 9 attentive, conscious

awakening: 7 revival 14 expergefacient, expergefaction

award: 4 give, meed, mete 5 allot, grant, medal, prize 6 accord, addeem, assign, bestow, bounty, confer, decide 7 adjudge, appoint, consign, custody, keeping 8 accolade, sentence 9 apportion, determine, judgement 10 adjudicate
  academic: 7 diploma 11 scholarship
  cinema: 5 Oscar
  television: 4 Emmy

aware: hep 4 reck, sure, wary 5 alert, alive 6 beware 7 knowing, mindful 8 apprised, apprized, informed, sensible, vigilant, watchful 9 cognizant, conscious 11 intelligent

away: awa(Sc.), fro, off, out, via 4 gone 5 along, apart, aside, forth, hence 6 abroad, absent, begone, onward, thence 7 distant, froward 8 fromward 9 fromwards, herehence
  prefex: aph, apo

awe: cow 5 amaze, daunt, scare 6 fright, regard, terror, wonder 7 buffalo, respect 8 astonish, bewilder, overcome 9 fascinate, overpower 10 intimidate

aweband: 4 band, rope 5 check 9 restraint

aweigh: 5 atrip

awesome: 4 eery 5 awful, eerie, weird 6 solemn 7 dreaded, ghostly 9 appalling, unearthly

awful: 4 dire, ugly 6 august, horrid 7 awesome, fearful 8 dreadful, shocking, terrible 9 appalling, frightful 10 tremendous

awk: odd 6 clumsy 7 adverse 8 perverse

awkward: 4 gaum 5 gawky, inapt, inept 6 clumsy, gauche, rustic, uneasy 7 adverse, boorish, froward, loutish, stilted, uncouth, unhandy 8 bungling, clownish, lubberly, perverse, ungainly, untoward, unwieldy 9 graceless, inelegant, lumbering, maladroit, ponderous 10 backhanded, blundering, ungraceful, unskillful 11 heavyhanded 12 inconvenient

awl: 4 brog 5 brode, elsen, elson(Sc.) 6 elshin, gimlet

awn: ear 4 barb 5 beard 7 aristae, bristle 9 appendage

awning: 5 velum 6 canopy, tienda 8 velarium 9 shameeana, shamianah(Ind.)
  fastening: 6 earing

awreak: 6 avenge 7 condemn

awry: 4 agee, bias 5 agley(Sc.), amiss, askew, gleed, gleyd, wrong 6 cammed 7 askance, asquint, crooked, oblique 8 perverse 9 distorted 10 crisscross

ax: adz 4 adze 5 hache 6 twibil 7 besague, boucher, cleaver, hatchet, twibill 8 tomahawk
  blade: bit
  butt: 4 poll
  handle: 5 helve

axeman: 8 woodsman 9 lumberman 10 woodcutter 11 woodchopper

axial: 7 central

axilla: ala 6 armpit 8 shoulder

axiom: saw 5 adage, dicta(pl.), maxim, motto 6 byword, dictum, saying, truism 7 precept, proverb 8 aphorism, apothegm, sentence 9 principle 11 proposition

axis: 4 axle, deer 5 stalk 6 chitra 7 spindle

axle: bar, cod, pin 4 axis 5 arbor, shaft 6 axtree 7 mandrel, spindle

axletree pin: 8 linchpin

axoloti: 4 newt 10 salamander

axweed: 8 goutweed

ay: 9 champagne

ayah: 4 maid 5 nurse 9 nursemaid

aye, ay: pro, yea, yes 4 ever 6 always, assent 7 forever 11 affirmative, continually

aye-aye: 5 lemur

Azerbaijan city: 4 Baku(c.) 11 Elizavetpol 12 Yelisavetpol

Azores: *district:* 5 Horta
 island: 4 Pico 5 Fayal 6 Flores
 port: 5 Horta
 volcano: 4 Pico

Aztec: *ball game:* 8 tlachtli
 god: 4 Xipe 9 Xipetotic 11 Xiuhtecutli
 language: 7 Nahuatl
 myth: 4 Nana, Nata
 stone: 9 temelactl 12 chalchihuitl
 temple: 6 teopan 8 teocalli

azure: 4 bice, blue 8 cerulean 9 cloudless, unclouded

azygous: odd 6 single

B

baa: 5 bleat
baahling: 4 lamb
Baal: god 4 idol 5 deity
  consort: 6 Baltis
baba: 4 baby, cake, male 5 child
babacoote: 5 lemur
babassu: oil 4 palm, soap
babblative: 9 garrulous, talkative 10 loquacious
babble: 4 chat, gash 5 haver, prate 6 cackle, gabble, glaver, gossip, murmur, palter, tumult 7 blabber, blather, bluster, brabble, chatter, chipper, clatter, prattle, smatter, twaddle 8 glaister 11 stultiloquy
babel: din 5 clang, tower 6 jargon, medley, racket, tumult 7 discord 9 charivari, confusion
babiche: 5 thong 6 lacing, thongs
babillard: 4 bird 11 whitethroat
baboon: ape 4 papa 5 drill 6 chaema 7 babuina 8 mandrill
babul: gum, lac 4 tree, wood 6 acacia, mimosa
  pod: 5 garad
babushka: 5 scarf 8 kerchief 11 grandmother
baby: 4 baba, babe, doll 5 bairn(Sc.), child, humor, spoil 6 coddle, fondle, infant, moppet, pamper, puppet, weanie(Sc.) 7 bambino(It.), papoose 9 youngster
  carriage: 4 pram 6 gocart 8 stroller 12 perambulator
  cry: mew 6 squall
  food: pap 4 milk 6 pablum
  outfit: 7 layette
  shoe: 6 bootee
babyish: 6 simple 7 puerile 8 childish
Babylonia: *abode of the dead:* 5 Aralu
  Adam: 5 Adapa
  army officer: 11 samagarnebo
  city: 5 Akkad 6 Calneh, Cunaxa, Cuthah
  cycle of moon: sar 5 saros
  division: 4 Elam 5 Sumer, Sumir
  era: 5 sumer 10 Nabonassar
  foe: 7 Elamite

  god: Ea, Zu; Anu, Aya, Bel, Hea, Hes, Ira, Ler, Sin, Utu 4 Adad, Anat, Apsu, Baal, Gula, Irra, Nebo, Utug 5 Alala, Alalu, Dagan, Enlil, Etana, Ninib, Nusku, Siris, Urash 6 Ishtar, Nergal, Oannes, Tammuz 7 Ninurta, Shamash 8 Merodach 10 Adramelech 11 Adrammelech
  goddess: Ai; Aya 4 Erua, Nana, Nina 5 Belit, Istar 6 Belili, Beltis, Ishtar 7 Mylitta
  hero of myth: 5 Adapa, Etana 9 Gilgamesh
  king: 14 Nebuchadnezzar, Nebuchadrezzar
  language: 5 Accad, Akkad
  mountain: 6 Ararat
  people: 7 Elamite
  priest: En
  priestess: 5 Entum
  region: 5 Aralu, Sumer, Sumir
  river: 6 Tigris 9 Euphrates
  ruler: 8 Exilarch
  sea: 4 Nina
  sun god's attendant: 6 Bunene
  tower: 7 zikurat 8 ziggurat
  waters: 4 Apsu
  weight: 4 mina 5 maneh
Babylonian: 5 Accad 8 Sumerian
bacalao: 5 murre 7 codfish, grouper 9 guillemot
bacca: 5 berry
baccalaureate degree: B.A. 8 bachelor
baccarat: 4 game
  player: 6 punter
  term: 5 banco
  variety of: 11 chemin-de-fer
baccate: 5 pulpy 7 berried
bacchanal: 7 devotee, reveler 8 carouser
Bacchanal's cry: 4 evoe 5 evohe
bacchante: 6 maenad 9 priestess
bachelor: 4 seal 6 garcon 8 benedict, celibate 11 holluschick 13 holluschickie(pl.)
bachelor button: 8 milkwort 10 bluebottle
bacillus: 4 germ 5 virus 7 microbe
back: aid, fro, tub, vat 4 abet, beck, hind, nape, nata, rear, tail 5 again, angel, chine, dorsa(pl.), notum, splat, spine, stern 6 assist, dorsum, second, trough, uphold, verify 7 cistern, endorse, finance, sponsor,

support, sustain 8 backward 9 encourage, posterior, reinforce 10 strengthen

at the: aft 5 abaff, abaft, arear 6 astern 7 postern

comb. form: 5 notus

lower part of: 4 loin

pain: 8 notalgia

pert. to: 6 dorsal, lumbar, tergal

prefix: re 5 retro

toward: aft 5 abaft 6 astern, dorsad 7 postern

back off: ebb 6 recede, retire 7 retreat, reverse 10 retrograde

back out: 4 funk 5 welsh 8 crawfish, withdraw

back scratcher: 7 strigil

Back Street author: 5 Hurst

back talk: lip 4 sass 9 insolence

backbite: 5 abuse 6 defame, vilify 7 asperse, slander

backbone: 4 grit, guts 5 chine, nerve, pluck, spina, spine 6 mettle, spinae, spirit 7 stamina 8 vertebra

backer: 5 angel

backgammon: 6 fayles 10 tricktrack

term: 4 blot 6 gammon

background: 4 rear 6 offing 7 setting 8 distance, training 9 education

backing: aid 6 lining, refuse 7 support 9 financing 10 embankment 11 endorsement

backlog: 7 reserve, surplus 12 accumulation

backslide: 4 fall 5 lapse 6 desert, revert 7 relapse 11 deteriorate

backward: fro, lax 4 back, dull, loth 5 arear, inapt, loath, unapt 6 astern, averse, bygone, stupid 7 bashful, laggard, lagging, reverse 8 dilatory, perverse, rearward 9 recessive, reluctant, unwilling 10 behindhand, hesitating, regressive, retrograde 11 unfavorable 13 retrogressive, retrospective, unprogressive

backwater: ebb 5 bayou 7 retract, retreat

backwoodsman: 4 hick 9 hillbilly

backwort: 7 comfrey

bacon: pig 4 pork 5 prize 6 rustic

fat: 5 speck

side: 6 gammon

slice: 6 rasher, collop

Bacon work: 12 Novum Organum

bacteria, bacterium: 4 germ 6 aerobe 7 aerobia, microbe 10 aerobacter

chain: 6 torula 7 torulae(pl.)

culture: 4 agar 6 agar-agar

dissolver: 5 lysin

free from harmful: 7 asepsis, aseptic

rod-shaped: 7 bacilli(pl.) 8 bacillus

vaccine: 8 bacterin

bacteriologist: *culture:* 4 agar

wire: 4 oese

bactrian: 5 camel

bad: big, ill, sad 4 evil, full, lewd, poor, qued, sick, vile 5 gammy, nasty, sorry, worst, wrong 6 arrant, faulty, nought, rotten, severe, sinful, wicked 7 baleful, baneful, corrupt, harmful, hurtful, immoral, inutile, naughty, noughty, spoiled, tainted, unlucky, unmoral, unsound, vicious 8 annoying, criminal, depraved, flagrant, inferior, unsuited 9 abandoned, atrocious, blemished, dangerous, defective, incorrect, injurious, offensive, perverted, worthless 10 aggravated, distressed, inadequate, iniquitous, pernicious, unsuitable 11 deleterious, displeasing, inopportune, unfavorable 12 disagreeable, inauspicious

comb. form: dys, mal 4 caco, kako

prefix: mal, mis

bad blood: 4 hate 5 anger 6 enmity 10 bitterness, resentment

bad debt: 7 default

bad habit: 4 vice

bad luck: 7 ambsace, ill wind 9 adversity 10 misfortune

badderlocks: 6 murlin 7 henware, seaweed 9 honeyware

badge: pin 4 mark, sign 5 token 6 emblem, ensign, symbol 8 insignia 10 cognizance

policeman: 4 star 6 busser, shield

badger: nag 4 bait, mele, pate 5 annoy, brock, brush, chevy, chivy, phani, rated, tease, worry 6 bauson, bother, chivvy, haggle, harass, hawker, heckle, pester, teledu, wombat 7 torment 8 carcajou, huckster, irritate 9 bandicoot, mistonusk 10 badgerweed 12 pasqueflower

cape: 4 cony 5 coney, daman, hyrax

Badger State: 9 Wisconsin

badgerweed: 12 pasqueflower

badigeon: 5 paste 6 cement 11 composition

badinage: 4 fool 5 joker 6 banter 8 raillery, trifling 9 badinerie

badly: ill 4 illy, sick 6 poorly, unwell 8 faultily, wickedly 9 viciously 11 imperfectly 12 disagreeable, unskillfully 13 unfortunately

baff: 4 bang, beat, blow, thud 6 strike, stroke 9 worthless

baffle: get 4 balk, foil, pose 5 cheat, check, elude, evade, fling, stump 6 blench, boggle, defeat, delude, infamy, outwit, resist, thwart 7 confuse, deceive, quibble 8 bewilder, confound, disgrace, juggling 9 confusion, discomfit, frustrate 10 circumvent, disappoint, disconcert

baft: 5 abaft 6 astern

bag: cod, net, pod, pot, sac 4 grip, poke, sack, trap, womb 5 belly, bouge, bulse, catch,

pouch, purse, scrip, seize, snare, steal **6** budget, cavity, entrap, pocket, sachet, valise, wallet **7** alforja, balloon, capture, gamebag, handbag, reticle, satchel **8** entrails, knapsack, reticule, suitcase **9** cartridge, container, gladstone, haversack **10** collection, pocketbook **11** portmanteau
botanic: sac **4** asci **5** ascus, spore
canvas: **7** musette
fishing net: **4** bunt, fyke
hop: **7** sarpler
muslin: **6** tillot
traveling: **9** telescope
bagatelle: 4 game **5** verse **6** trifle
baggage: 4 arms, gear, minx **5** huzzy, nasty, tents, trash, wench **6** harlot, refuse, trashy, trunks **7** clothes, effects, rubbish, valises **8** carriage, rubbishy, utensils **9** munitions, viaticals, worthless **10** prostitute **11** impedimenta
baggy: 5 loose **6** flabby, puffed
Baghdad: *capital:* **4** Irak
merchant: **6** Sinbad **7** Sindbad
bagman: 5 tramp **7** swagman **8** henchman **9** collector
bagnio: 4 bath **5** bagne **6** prison **7** brothel **8** hothouse
bagpipe: 5 drone **7** musette **8** zampogna **10** doodlesack, sordellina
mouthpiece: **4** muse
pipe: **6** drones **7** chanter
play: **5** skirl
player: **5** piper **7** doodler
sound: **5** skirl
tune: **4** port
bah: foh, pah, rot **5** faugh, pshaw **8** nonsense
Bahama Islands: 5 Abaco **6** Andros, Bimini **9** Eleuthera
capital: **6** Nassau
bahia: bay
baikie: 5 stake, stick
bail: dip **4** bond, hoop, lade, lave, ring, rynd, yoke **5** ladle, scoop, throw, vouch **6** bucket, handle, secure, surety **7** custody, deliver, release **8** bailsman, bulwarks, security **9** guarantee
bailiff: 4 hind **5** agent, reeve, staff **6** bailie, bailli, beadle, deputy, factor, grieve, office, porter, staves(pl.), varlet **7** sheriff, steward **8** huissier, overseer, tipstaff **9** constable **10** magistrate **12** understeward
farm: **4** hind
bailiwick: 4 area **6** domain, office **8** province **9** bailiffry, bailliage **12** jurisdiction
bain: 4 near **5** lithe, ready, short **6** direct, limber, supple **7** forward, willing
bairn: 5 child
bait: bad **4** bite, chum, feed, halt, lure **5** decoy, tempt, worry **6** allure, attack, badger, entice, harass, repast **7** fulcrum, gudgeon,

provoke, torment **9** persecute **10** allurement, enticement, exasperate, inducement, temptation **11** refreshment
artificial: **6** hackle
bird enticing: **5** shrap **6** shrape
salmon fishing: **5** baker
baize: 6 fabric **7** drapery
bake: dry **4** cook, fire **5** batch, broil, grill, parch, roast **6** anneal, harden **7** biscuit **8** clambake
baker: 4 oven **6** baxter **7** furnace, roaster, utensil
sheet: pan
shovel: **4** pale, peel
tool: **4** pale, peel
baker's dozen: 8 thirteen
baker's itch: 4 rash **9** psoriasis
bakie: 6 trough, vessel
baking chamber: 4 kiln, oast, oven
baking dish: 7 cocotte, ramekin
baking ingredient: 4 soda **5** flour, yeast
baking soda: 9 saleratus
Bakongo goddess: 6 Nyambe, Nzambi
Balaam's beast: ass **6** donkey
balance: 4 even, rest **5** peise, poise, scale, weigh, weihe **6** adjust, equate, offset, sanity **7** residue **8** equality, equalize, serenity **9** composure, equipoise, remainder, stability **10** neutralize, steadiness **11** equilibrium **12** counterpoise
lose: **4** trip **7** stagger
weighing: **6** auncel
balancer: 7 acrobat, athlete, gymnast
balate: 7 trepang
balcony: 5 oriel, porch **6** piazza, sollar **7** balagan, gallery, mirador, pergola, terrace **8** brattice, verandah
church singer: **8** cantoria
projecting: **6** gazabo, gazebo
bald: 4 bare, base **5** crude, naked, plain **6** callow, paltry, pilled, simple **7** epilose, literal **8** glabrous, hairless **9** unadorned, uncovered **11** undisguised, unvarnished
Balder: *father:* **4** Odin
mother: **5** Frigg
murder weapon: **9** mistletoe
slayer: **4** Hoth, Loke **5** Hothr
son: **7** Forsete, Forseti
wife: **5** Nanna
balderdash: rot **5** trash **6** drivel, jargon **8** nonsense **9** balductum, rigmarole **10** flumdiddle
baldicoot: 4 coot, monk
baldmoney: 7 gentian **8** spicknel
baldness: 6 acomia **7** calvity **8** alopecia **10** calavities **11** phalacrosis
baldric, baldrick: 4 belt **6** girdle, zodiac **7** balteus, support **8** baltheus, necklace
bale: no; not, woe **4** evil, fire, harm, pyre **5** crate, death **6** ballot, bundle, sorrow **7**

package 8 compress, disaster 9 influence, suffering

of wool: 7 sarpler

Balearic Island: 5 Iviza 7 Cabrera, Majorca, Minorca 10 Formentera

language: 7 Catalan

measure: 5 palmo 6 misura, quarta, quarte 7 quartin 8 barcella, quartera

port: 5 Palma

weight: 5 artal, artel, cargo, corta, libra, mayor, ratel, rotel 8 quartano

baleen: 5 whale 9 whalebone

baleful: bad 4 evil 6 deadly, malign 7 noxious, ruinous 8 sinister, wretched 10 calamitous, pernicious 11 destructive

baleise: 4 flog

Bali (see also **Indonesia**):

dance: 5 ardja, baris, kriss 6 barong, ketjak, monkey 7 djanger 9 sanghyang 14 barong-landoeng

musical instrument: 7 gamelan 8 gamelang

religion: 8 Hinduism

rice field: 6 sawaii

balk: hue, jib, shy 4 beam, bilk, foil, heap, lick, loft, miss, omit, shun, skip, slip, stop 5 avoid, block, check, hunch, mound, rebel, reest(Sc.), ridge, waver 6 baffle, defeat, falter, hinder, impede, outwit, rafter, refuse, thwart 7 blunder, isthmus, mistake 8 omitting, overlook, skipping 9 discomfort, frustrate 10 disappoint 14 disappointment

Balkan: 4 Serb, Slav 7 Serbian 8 Albanian, Rumanian, Yugoslav

bandit: 6 haiduk, heydue 7 heyduck, heyduke

coin: 6 novcic

country: 6 Serbia, Servia 7 Albania, Rumania 10 Yugoslavia

instrument: 5 gusla, gusle

balky: 6 mulish 8 stubborn 9 obstinate

ball: bal(F.), bob, orb, toy 4 bead, pill 5 dance, globe, glome 6 bullet, muddle, pellet, pompon, rundle, sphere 7 confuse, mandrel, ridotto 8 spheroid 11 glomeration

lofted: fly, lob

low: 5 liner

minced meat: 5 pinda 7 rissole

wooden: 4 knur

ball and chain: 4 wife 6 burden

ball club: 4 nine, team 6 eleven

ball game: cat 5 rugby 6 pelota, soccer 7 cricket 8 baseball

ball of fire: 4 whiz 6 genius

ball up: 7 confuse, perplex

ballad: lai(F.) 4 lilt, poem, song 5 derry 6 ballet, sonnet 7 ballant, canzone

ballast: 4 load, trim 5 poise, stone 6 burden, gravel, weight 7 balance 9 saburrate

ballerina: 4 pony 6 dancer 8 danseuse

ballet: 5 dance, drama 6 ballad, masque 9 pantomime 12 choreography

leap: 4 jete

movement: 4 jete 5 brise 8 glissade

posture: 9 arabesque

skirt: 4 tutu

ballistic missile: 4 ICBM, IRBM

balloon: bag 5 blimp 6 expand, gasbag 7 airship, distend, inflate 8 aerostat 9 dirigible

basket: car 7 gondola, nacelle

ballot: 4 bale, poll, vote 5 elect, voice 6 billet, choice, ticket

cast: 4 vote

balm: oil 4 bito, daub, case 5 salve 6 balsam, embalm, lotion, relief, soothe, solace 7 annoint, anodyne, besmear, comfort, cure-all, heal-all, perfume, soother, unguent 8 mitigate, ointment 11 assuagement

horse: 10 citronella

of Gilead: 6 balsam

balmy: 4 mild, soft 5 bland, daffy, moony, spicy, sunny, sweet 6 gentle, insane 7 healing, lenient 8 aromatic, dressing, fragrant, soothing 9 assuaging 10 refreshing 11 odoriferous

balneary: 9 bathhouse

balneation: 4 bath

balneum: 4 bath 8 bathroom

baloney: 4 bunk 5 hooey 6 humbug 8 nonsense

balsa: 4 raft, tree, wood 5 float

balsam: 4 balm, riga, tree, tolu 6 storay 7 copaiba 8 bdellium, ointment

apple: 4 vine 7 creeper 8 amargosa, amargoso, ampalaya

Balt: Yod 4 Esth, Lett 8 Estonian 10 Lithuanian

balteus: 4 band, belt 7 baldric

Baltic: *barge:* 5 praam

city: 4 Riga 6 Danzig

gulf: 4 Riga

island: 4 Dago, Faro, Osel 5 Alsen, Oesel, Oland

language: 6 Lettic

seaport: 4 Kiel, Riga 5 Memel, Reval 6 Talinn

Baltic Sea: *canal:* 4 Kiel

river: 4 Oder, Odra 5 Dvina, Peene, Wilsa

Baluchistan: *native:* 4 Mari 5 Marri 6 Marree

province: Lus 5 Kalat 6 Khelat

balustrade: 6 barrer 7 parapet, railing 8 balconet, baluster, banister 10 balconette

Balzac character: 4 Nana 6 Goriot

bam: 4 hoax, sham 5 cheat, trick 7 wheedle

Bambi: 4 deer 7 animal
bambino: 4 baby 5 child 6 infant
bamboo: 4 cane, reed, tree
 sacred: 6 nandin
 sprouts: 5 achar
 sugar: 9 tabasheer
 woven: 6 sawali
bamboozle: 4 dupe 5 cheat, cozen, grill 6 cajole, humbug 7 buffalo, defraud, deceive, mystify, perplex 11 hornswoggle
ban: bar, woe 4 tabu, veto 5 banal, block, curse, edict, order, taboo 6 banish, enjoin, forbid, hinder, invoke, notice, outlaw 7 condemn, exclude 8 anathema, denounce, execrate, prohibit 9 interdict, proscribe 10 inhibition 11 forbiddance, imprecation, malediction 12 anathematize, denunciation, interdiction, proclamation 15 excommunication
Bana: *conqueror:* 7 Krishna
 daughter: 4 Usha
banal: 4 flat 5 corny, inane, silly, stale, trite, vapid 6 jejune 7 trivial 9 hackneyed 11 commonplace 13 platitudinous
 phrase: 6 cliche
banana: 4 musa 6 ensete 7 platano(Sp.) 8 plantain
 bunch: 4 hand, stem
 family: 4 musa 6 pesang 8 musaceae
 leaf: 5 frond
 wild: fei
banana fish: 6 albula 8 ladyfish
banana oil: 8 soft soap
Bananaland: 10 Queensland
band: bar, tie 4 belt, bond, came, cord, crew, fess, gang, girt, hoop, ring, zona, zone 5 ampyx, bandy, corse, label, strap, strip, tribe, unite, zonae(pl.) 6 armlet, binder, bundle, cohort, collar, collet, copula, fascia, fetter, fillet, girdle, hyphen, norsel, pledge, string, stripe, swathe, tether 7 aweband, bandeau, binding, circlet, company, fasciae(pl.), garland, orphrey, promise, shackle 8 banderol, biliment, bracelet, cincture, cingulum, faisceau, ligament, ligature, tressour, tressure 9 associate, banderole, bandoleer, guarantee, orchestra 10 obligation
 armed: 5 posse
 armor: 6 tonlet
 brain: 6 ligula 7 ligulae
 decorative: 7 cornice
 garment fastening: 5 patte
 narrow: 4 tape 5 stria 6 striae(pl.)
 small: 8 bandelet 10 bandelette
bandage: 4 bind, tape 5 blind, clout, dress, sling, spica, truss 6 fettle, fillet, ligate, swathe 8 cincture, ligature 9 blindfold
 fastener: 7 ligator

 nose: 9 accipiter
 surgical: 5 spica 6 fascia, spicae(pl.) 7 fasciae
bandeau: 4 band 5 strip 6 fillet
bandicoot: rat 6 badger
bandikai: 4 okra
bandit: 4 caco 5 bravo, thief 6 banish, outlaw, robber 7 bandido, brigand, ladrone 8 marauder, picaroon 10 highwayman
bandleader: 6 master 7 choragi, maestro 8 choragus 9 conductor
bandmaster: 5 Sousa
bandy: 4 band, cart, swap 5 trade 6 league, strive 7 chaffer, contend, discuss 8 carriage, exchange 11 reciprocate
bane: woe 4 evil, harm, kill, pest, ruin 5 curse, death, venom 6 injury, murder, poison, slayer 7 nemesis, scourge 8 mischief, murderer, nuisance
baneful: bad, ill 4 evil, vile 7 harmful, hurtful, noxious, ruinous 8 venomous 9 sinistral 10 pernicious
bang: rap 4 baff, beat, blow, dash, dock, drub, slam 5 blaff, clash, drive, excel, force, impel, pound, sound, thump, whack, whang 6 bounce, cudgel, energy, strike, thrash, thunge, thwack 7 sardine, surpass 8 forelock
 into: hit 5 crash 7 collide
bang-up: 5 crack 6 tiptop 9 first-rate
bangle: 4 flap, roam 5 droop, waste 7 circlet, fritter, trinket 8 bracelet, ornament
Bani's son: Uel 4 Amzi 5 Amram
banish: ban 5 eject, exile, expel, fleme 6 bandit, deport, dispel, forsay, outlaw 7 abandon, condemn, dismiss, exclude 8 displace, relegate 9 ostracize, proscribe, transport 10 expatriate, repatriate
banished: 8 fugitive
banister: 7 railing 8 baluster 10 balustrade
bank: bar, bay, cop, rim, row 4 bink, brae, brew, caja, dike, dune, dyke, edge, hill, mass, pile, ramp, rive, sand, seat, tier, weir 5 banco, bench, bluff, brink, fence, levee, marge, mound, ridge, stack, share, shelf, shoal, shore, slope, stage, trust 6 causey, degree, depend, margin, reckon, rivage, strand 7 anthill, deposit, pottery, shallow 8 barranca, barranco, platform 9 acclivity, 10 depository, elevation, embankment
 clerk: 6 teller
 examiner: 10 accountant
 requirement: 5 funds, money 6 assets 7 surplus 8 deposits
 river: 4 ripa
bankroll: wad 5 bills 8 currency
bankrupt: sap 4 bung 5 broke, drain, smash, strip 6 busted, devour, ruined,

quisby 7 failure 8 beggarly, depleted 9 destitute, insolvent 12 impoverished

banner: 4 fane, flag, jack 5 color 6 ensign, fannon, pennon 7 leading, pennant, salient 8 banderol, foremost, gonfalon, standard, vexillum 9 banderole, exemplary, oriflamme 10 surpassing

banns: 4 bans 6 notice 12 proclamation

banquet: 4 fete, meal 5 feast 6 dinner, junket, regale, repast 8 carousal, festival
room: 8 cenacula(pl.) 9 cenaculum

banquette: way 4 seat 5 shelf 7 footway 8 platform, sidewalk 10 embankment

banshee: fay 5 fairy, sidhe 6 goblin

bant: 4 diet, fast 6 reduce

bantam: 4 cock 5 saucy 7 chicken 9 combative 10 diminutive
breed: 8 Sebright

banteng: ox 5 tsine

banter: kid, rag 4 fool, jest, joke, josh, mock, quiz, rail 5 borak, chaff, rally, roast, trick 6 delude, deride, haggle, satire 7 badiner, stashie 8 badinage, chaffing, raillery, ridicule 10 persiflage, pleasantry

bantering: 9 quizzical

bantling: 5 child 6 infant

Bantu: *dialect:* 6 Chwana 8 Sechuana
language: Ila 4 Suto 5 Ronga 6 Thonga 7 Nyanaja 8 Nyamwezi 10 Wanymawezi
people: 4 Baya, Bihe, Bule, Fang, Gogo, Gola, Guha, Hehe, Jaga, Luba, Maka, Nama, Vira, Yaka, Zulu 5 Duala, Kafir 6 Banyai, Damara, Kaffir, Waguha, Yakala 7 Swahili, Wachaga 8 Bechuana

banxring: 4 tana 6 tupaia

banyan: bur 4 burr 6 banian

banzai: cry 6 attack

baobab: 4 tree 7 tebeldi

baptism: 9 aspersion, cleansing, immersion 11 christening
robe: 7 Chrisom
vessel: 4 font 6 fontal, spring 7 piscina
water: 5 laver

baptize: dip 4 full, name 5 heave 6 purify 7 cleanse 8 christen, sprinkle

bar: ban, dam, fid, gad, law, rod 4 axle, band, bank, beam, bolt, cake, gate, hide, joke, lock, oust, pole, rail, reef, save, shut, stop 5 arbor, bench, bilco, block, close, court, deter, estop, fence, hedge, lever, perch, shade, shaft, strap, strip 6 billet, brooch, except, fasten, grille, hinder, meagre, saloon, stripe 7 barrage, barrier, confine, counter, exclude, prevent 8 conclude, handicap, obstacle, obstruct, preclude, prohibit, restrain, restrict, surround, tribunal 9 barricade, fastening, gatehouse,

hindrance, interpose, ostracize 10 crosspiece, difficulty, impediment, inhibition, portcullis 11 obstruction
acrobat: 7 trapeze
bullion: 5 ingot
legally: 5 estop
millstone: 4 rynd
resisting pressure: 5 strut
supporting: fid, rod 9 stanchion
tamping: 7 stemmer
window: 5 jemmy, jimmy 7 forcing

barb: awn, bur, jag, mow 4 burr, clip, file, flue, hair, herl, hook, jagg 5 beard, horse, point, ridge 6 pigeon 7 bristle 8 kingfish 9 appendage 10 projection
anchor: 4 flue
feather: 4 harl, herl 5 ramus 7 pinnula, pinnule 8 pinnulae

Barbados: *capital:* 10 Bridgetown
liquor: rum
native: Bim

barbarian: Hun 4 boor, Goth, rude, wild 5 alien, brute 6 savage, vandal 7 ruffian 9 foreigner, untutored 10 Philistine, unlettered 11 uncivilized
North African: 6 Berber

barbarism: 4 cant 8 savagism, solecism 10 savageness

barbarity: 6 ferity 7 cruelty 8 ferocity, rudeness, savagery 9 brutality 10 inhumanity

barbarous: 4 fell, rude, wild 5 cruel 6 brutal 7 foreign, Hunnish, inhuman, slavish, uncivil 8 ignorant 9 ferocious, primitive 10 illiterate, outlandish, tramontane, unpolished 11 uncivilized 12 uncultivated

Barbary: ape 5 magot 6 simian
sheep: 6 aoudad
states: 5 Tunis 7 Algiers, Morocco, Tripoli

barbecue: 4 bake 5 broil, grill
rod: 4 spit 6 skewer

barbed: 4 bent 6 hooked 8 uncinate

barber: 6 Figaro, poller, shaver, tonsor 7 scraper, tonsure 11 chirotonsor

barber's itch: 8 ringworm

bard: 4 poet, scop 5 druid, runer, scald 6 singer 8 minstrel, musician
India: 4 bhat

Bard of Avon: 11 Shakespeare

bardy: 4 bold 7 defiant 9 audacious

bare: 4 bald, mere, nude 5 alone, crude, empty, naked, plain, stark, strip 6 barren, callow, denude, divert, divest, expose, histie, meager, meagre, paltry, pilled, reveal, simple 7 divulge, exposed, unarmed, uncover 8 desolate, disclose, stripped 9 unadorned, uncovered, worthless 10 threadbare 11 defenseless, unconcealed, unfurnished 13 unaccompanied

bare skin: 4 buff

barefaced: 7 glaring 8 impudent 9 audacious, shameless 11 undisguised

barefooted: 6 unshod 9 discalced

barely: 4 only 5 faint 6 hardly, merely, poorly 8 scantily, scarcely, slightly 13 unqualifiedly 14 insufficiently

barfly: 5 drunk, stiff 8 carouser

bargain: 4 deal, huck, mise, pact, pick, sale, sell 5 cheap, fight 6 barter, dicker, haggle, higglo, palter 7 chaffer, compact, contend, contest, traffic 8 contract, covenant, purchase, struggle 9 agreement, negotiate, situation, stipulate 10 engagement 11 transaction

bargain-basement: 5 cheap 6 tawdry

bargain for: 6 expect

barge: ark, box, boy, tow, tub 4 bark, boat, pram, raft, scow 5 foist, lunge, lurch, praam, scold, shrew, vixen 6 barque, berate, praham, rebuke, thrust, tender, vessel 7 gabbard, gabbart, gondola, lighter, omnibus 9 houseboat, interfere

charge: 10 lighterage

coal: 4 keel

bargeman: pug 6 bargee 7 huffler

barium sulphate: 6 barite

bark: bag, bay, rub, wap, yap, yip 4 boat, coat, howl, husk, peel, pelt, pill, rind, ross, ship, skin, yawp 5 balat, barca, barge, cough, shell, shout, strip 6 abrade, cortex, girdle, vessel 7 solicit, tanbark 8 cortices, covering

aromatic: 6 sintoc 7 canella 9 sassafras

at: 5 scold 6 rebuke

cloth: 4 tapa 5 tappa 8 mulberry

covered with: 9 corticate 10 corticated

medicinal: 4 coto 5 casca, madar, nudar, niepa 7 quinine 8 cinchona 9 sassafras

outer: 8 periderm

pert. to: 8 cortical

remove: 4 ross 5 scale

resembling: 8 cortical

rough: 4 ross

tanning: 5 alder

up the wrong tree: err 5 stray

barkeeper: 6 barman 7 tapster

barker: dog 6 jumper, pistol, tanner 7 spieler 9 solicitor

barking: 4 spud 7 latrant 9 latration

barking deer: 7 muntjac, muntjak

barley: 5 grain

ground: 6 tsamba

pert. to: 11 hordeaceous

steep: 4 malt

variety: big 4 bere, bigg

barman: 7 tapster 9 barkeeper, barrister 11 metalworker

barmy: 5 foamy, silly 6 frothy, yeasty 7 flighty, foolish, idiotic

barn: 4 byre 5 stall 6 stable 10 storehouse

storage area: bag, mow 4 loft 7 hayloft

barn dance official: 6 caller

barnacle: *genus:* 5 Lepas

plate: 5 terga(pl.), 6 tergum

barnstorm: 4 tour

barometric line: 6 isobar

baron: 4 peer 5 noble 7 freeman

baronet: sir 8 commoner

barony: han 4 rank 6 domain 7 dignity

baroque: 6 ornate, rococo 9 grotesque, irregular 11 extravagant

barrack: 4 camp 6 casern 7 cuartel(Sp.), 8 quarters

barraclade: 7 blanket

barracuda: 4 fish, spet 5 barry, pelon 6 becuna, picuda, sennet 10 guaguanche 12 guanchepelon

barrage: bar 6 attack, volley 7 barrier 9 cannonade 10 barricuade, obtruction

barranca, barranco: 4 bank 5 bluff 6 ravine

barras: 5 linen 7 galipot 8 gallipot

barrator: 5 bully, rowdy 7 fighter

barred: 6 ribbed 7 striped

barrel: fat, keg, tun, vat 4 butt, cade, cask, drum, knag 6 runlet, tierce, vessel 7 cistern, rundlet 8 cylinder, hogshead 9 container, kilderkin

herring: 4 cade

maker: 6 cooper

part: 4 side, hoop 5 stave

raising device: 9 parbuckle

stopper: 4 bung

support: 4 hoop 6 gantry 7 gauntry

barren: dry 4 arid, bare, dull, gast, geld 5 blunt, drape, empty, gaunt, stark, stern 6 desert, effete, fallow, histie, hungry, jejune, meager, stupid 7 sterile 8 impotent, treeless 9 exhausted, fruitless, infertile, penurious 10 unfruitful 12 unproductive, unprofitable

barren oak: 9 blackjack

barren privet: 7 alatern 9 houseleek

barrette: bar 8 ornament

barricade: bar 4 stop 5 block, close, fence 6 abatis, prison 7 barrage, defense, fortify 9 roadblock 11 obstruction 13 fortification

Barrie character: 5 Peter, Wendy

barrier: bar, dam 4 door, gate, line, wall, weir 5 bound, chain, fence, hedge, limit 6 hurdle, screen 7 barrage, parapet, railing 8 boundary, fortress, frontier, stockade 9 palisades, restraint 10 difficulty, partcullis, tournament 11 obstruction

movable: 4 bars, door 5 blind, shade 6 window 7 certain 8 shutters

barring: 4 save 6 except 7 without

barrio: 4 slum 6 ghetto 7 village

barrister: 6 barman, lawyer 7 counsel 8 advocate, attorney

barroom: pub 4 cafe 6 saloon 7 cantina(Sp.), doggery 8 dramshop, exchange

barrow: hod, hog 4 bank, dune, hill, mote 5 grave, gurry, mound 6 tumuli 7 hillock, trolley, tumulus 8 mountain

bartender: 7 tapster

barter: 4 chap, chop, cope, coup, hawk, sell, swap, vend 5 corse, trade, troke, truck 6 dicker 7 bargain, cambium, permute, traffic 8 commerce, exchange 9 excambion 11 reciprocate

Bartered Bride composer: 7 Smetana

bartizan: 6 turret 7 lookout

bas: low

bas-relief: 9 plaquette

basal: 5 basic 7 basilar 11 fundamental

basalt: 6 marble, navite 7 pottery

base: bed, low 4 clam, evil, foot, foul, lewd, mean, poor, root, stem, step, vile 5 basis, cheap, dirty, muddy, petty, snide 6 abject, bottom, common, ground, menial, paltry, podium, shabby, sordid, vulgar 7 bastard, caitiff, comical, debased, hangdog, hilding, housing, ignoble, servile, slavish, support 8 coistrel, coistril, degraded, infamous, inferior, pedestal, scullion, shameful, stepping, unworthy, wretched 9 absorbent, degrading, establish, worthless 10 despicable, foundation, villainous 11 ignominious 12 contemptible, dishonorable, disreputable 13 dishonourable

architectural: 5 socle 6 plinth

attached by: 7 sessile

military: HDQ 4 camp 5 depot 12 headquarters

structural: 6 plinth

base hit: 6 bingle, single

base on balls: 4 pass, walk

baseball: *field:* 7 diamond

founder: 9 Doubleday

hit: 4 bunt

official: ump 5 coach 6 umpire 7 manager

team: 4 nine

term: bag, bat, box, fan, fly, hit, lob, low, out, peg, RBI, run, tap, top 4 ball, bean, beat, bunt, burn, deck, foul, high, hill, hole, home, hook, miss, pill, pole, sack, save, turn, walk, wild 5 alley, apple, bench, booth, clout, coach, count, curve, drive, error, field, first, force, frame, glove, homer, lined, mound, pitch, plate, popup, punch, score, slide, swing, third 6 assist, batter, bungle, bottom, charge, clutch, double, dugout, groove, hitter, inside, lifted, lumber, middle, popout, putout, rubber, runner, screen, second, series, single, sinker, stance, strike, string, target, triple, wind-up 7 arbited, arbiter, battery,

blooper, bullpen, circuit, cleanup, diamond, fielder, floater, infield, manager, nothing, outside, pitcher, side-arm, squeeze, stretch, thumbed 8 delivery, grounded, grounder, knuckler, outfield, pinch-hit, powdered, soupbone, spitball 9 full-count, hot corner, sacrifice, smothered, strike-out, two-bagger 10 scratch-hit 11 three-bagger

baseless: 4 idle 9 unfounded 10 gratuitous, groundless

basement: 4 base 6 cellar

bash: bat, lam 4 beat, blow, dent, mash, swat, wham, whop 5 abash, smash 6 bruise, strike

Bashan king: Og

Bashemath's husband: 4 Esau

bashful: coy, shy 4 helo 5 blate, heloe, timid 6 modest 7 daunted 8 backward, blushing, dismayed, retiring, sheepish, verecund 9 diffident, shrinking

Bashkir capital: Ufa

basic: 5 basal, vital 7 central 9 elemental 11 fundamental 13 indispensable

basil: 4 herb 5 plant, royal 6 fetter

basilica: 6 canopy, church, shrine, temple 7 Lateran

part of: 4 apse

basin: pan 4 bowl, dish, dock, ewer, font, tank 5 laver, stoup 6 chafer, marina, valley, vessel 7 cuvette, piscina 8 lavatory, receptor, washbowl 9 reservoir 10 aspersoria, depression 11 aspersorium

geological: 4 tala

basis: 4 base, fund, root, sill 5 axiom 6 bottom, ground 7 footing, premise, support 10 foundation, groundwork

bask: sun 4 beek, warm 5 acrid, bathe, enjoy, revel 6 bitter 7 rejoice 9 luxuriate

basket: ark, fan, ped 4 kipe, trug 5 cassy(Sc.), cesta, chest, crate, scull 6 cassie, coffin, dorsel, dorser, dosser, gabion, hamper, hoppet, panier 7 canasta, hanaper, pannier, scuttle 9 container 10 receptacle

coal mine: 4 corf

eel: 4 buck

fig: 4 caba 5 frail 6 tapnet

fire: 5 grate 7 cresset

fish: pot 4 caul, cawl, corf, hask, skip, weel 5 creel, crate, maund 6 courge, gabion, hamper 7 pannier

fruit: 6 pottle, funnet

material: 5 otate

twig: 6 wattle

water-tight: 7 wattape

wicker: cob 4 cobb, coop 5 willy 6 hamper 7 hanaper 8 bassinet

willow: 5 osier 7 prickle

work: 4 caba 5 cabas, slath 6 slarth

basket-ball team: 4 five 7 cagemen
Basque: 5 waist 6 scoter 7 Iberian
  cap: 5 beret
  dance: 7 auresca 8 aurrescu, zortzico
  game: 6 pelota
  language: 6 Uskara 7 Eskuara, Euskara,
    Euskera
  people: 7 Euscara, Euscaro
  petticoat: 8 basquine
  province: 5 Alava 6 Biscay
bass: low 4 deep, fish 5 voice 6 singer 7 achi-
    gan, jewfish
bassinet: 6 basket, cradle
basswood: lin 4 bast 5 tilia 6 linden
bast: 4 bark, flax, hemp, jute 5 fiber, ramie
    6 phloem 8 piassava
basta: 4 stop 6 enough
bastard: 4 base 5 false 6 cannon, galley, hy-
    brid, impure 7 byspell, lowbred, mongrel 8
    bantling, spurious 10 artificial 11 adulter-
    ated 12 illegitimate
baste: sew 4 beat, cane, cook, drub, lard,
    tack 6 cudgel, punish, stitch, thrash
bastion: *defensive:* 4 fort 13 fortification
  shoulder: 6 epaule
bat: hit, wad 4 bate, beat, club, gait, lump,
    mass, swat, wink 5 brick, piece, spree,
    stick 6 aliped, backie(Sc.), baston, beetle,
    cudgel, racket, strike, stroke 7 flutter, noc-
    tule, vampire 8 bludgeon, serotine 9 rere-
    mouse 10 battledore, chiroptera, packsad-
    dle 11 rattlemouse 12 chauvesouris, flit-
    termouse
  around: 4 roam 6 ponder 7 debate
  European: 9 barbastel 11 barbastelle
  species: 9 pipistrel 11 pipistrelle
Bataan: *bay:* 5 Subic
  city: 7 Balanga
Batavia: 7 Jakarta 8 Djarkarta
batch: lot 4 mass, mess, sort 5 group 6 bak-
    ing 7 mixture 8 quantity 10 collection
bateau: 4 boat
batfish: 6 diablo
bath: dip 4 bate, pert 5 therm 6 plunge,
    shower 7 balneum 8 ablution 10 natato-
    rium
  comb. form: 6 balneo
  pert. to: 7 balneal
  public: 7 piscine
  sponge: 5 luffa 6 loofah
  treatment by: 13 balneotherapy .
Bath river: 4 Avon
bathe: bay, tub 4 bask, lave, stew, wash 5
    embay 6 enwrap 7 immerse, pervade, suf-
    fuse 8 permeate
bathhouse: 6 cabana 8 balneary
bathing suit: 6 bikini, trunks 7 maillot
bathos: 8 comedown 10 anticlimax

bathroom: W.C.(abbr.) 6 hammam 8 suda-
    tory 10 sudatorium 11 water closet
Bathsheba: *husband:* 5 Uriah
  son: 7 Solomon
baton: rod 4 bend 5 staff, stick 6 baston,
    cudgel 7 bourdon, scepter, sceptre 9 trun-
    cheon
batrachian: 4 frog, toad
batsman: 6 batter, hitter 7 striker
batten: 6 enrich, fatten, thrive 9 fertilize
batter: ram 4 beat, dent, maim 5 clour,
    dinge, frush, paste, pound 6 bruise, ham-
    mer, hatter, hitter, pummel 7 batsman,
    bombard, cripple, destroy, shatter, striker
    8 demolish
battery: *floating:* 4 cell 5 praam 7 parapet 9
    artillery 11 bombardment
  plate: 4 grid
battle: war 4 duel, fray, meet, tilt 5 brush,
    fight, joust 6 action, affray, combat 7 con-
    tend, contest, hosting, warfare 8 conflict,
    skirmish, struggle 9 encounter 10 engage-
    ment, tournament 11 competition
  area: 5 arena, front 6 sector 7 terrain
  cry: 6 slogan 9 catchword
  formation: 5 herse 6 deploy
  line: 5 front
  order: 7 regalia 8 battalia
  royal: 5 melee 9 scrimmage
  site: 6 Shiloh 7 Bull Run 8 Manassas 10
    Armageddon, Gettysburg
  trophy: 5 medal, scalp 6 ribbon
Battle Hymn of the Republic author: 4
    Howe
battleship: 7 carrier 11 dreadnaught 16
    superdreadnaught
battologize: 6 repeat 7 iterate
batty: 5 crazy, silly 7 batlike, foolish
bauble: bow, toy 4 bead, gaud 6 button, gew-
    gaw, trifle 7 trinket 8 gimcrack 9 play-
    thing 10 knickknack
bauxite derivative: 8 aluminum
Bavaria: *beer:* 10 Wurzburger
  city: Hof 6 Munich(c.), 8 Augsburg, Nurn-
    berg, Ratisbon, Wurzburg 10 Regensburg
  community: 6 Passau
  division: 7 Neuburg 8 Schwaben 9 Franco-
    nia 10 Palatinate, Regensburg 13 Aschaf-
    fenburg
  lake: 4 Wurm 5 Ammer, Chiem 8 Starbber
  measure: 4 fass, fuss, rute 5 linie, metze,
    ruthe 6 massel, morgen 7 juchert, tag-
    werk 10 dreissiger
  mountain: 6 Vosges 8 Watzmann 9 Zug-
    spitze
  river: Inn, Nab 4 Eger, Isar, Iser, Lech 5
    Iller, Regen, Saale 7 Altmuhl, Wornitz
  university site: 8 Erlangen
  weight: 4 gran 9 quentchen

bawd: 4 aunt, hare 5 dirty 6 defile 7 commode 8 procurer 9 procuress 10 fruitwoman

bawdry: 5 mirth 6 filthy, finery, gaiety, gayety 9 obscenity

bawdy: 4 foul, lewd 5 dirty 7 obscene 8 unchaste

bawl: cry 4 howl 5 golly, shout 6 bellow, boohoo, outcry 8 glaister 10 vociferate

out: 5 scold 9 reprimand

bawling: 10 vociferous

bay: dam, ria, voe 4 bank, bark, cove, gulf, hole, hope, howl, loch(Sc.), roan, tree, yaup, yawp 5 bahia(Sp.), berry, bight, color, creek, fiord, fjord, fleet, haven, horse, oriel, sinus 6 laurel, recess, window 7 enclose, estuary, silanga, ululate 11 compartment, indentation

bird: 5 snipe 6 curlew, godwit, plover

camphor: 6 laurin

Bay State: 13 Massachusetts

bayard: 5 horse

bayardly: 5 blind 6 stupid

Baylor University site: 4 Waco

bayonet: 4 stab 5 knife 6 pierce, weapon

bayou: 5 brook, creek, inlet, river 6 outlet, stream 7 rivulet 9 backwater

Bayou State: 11 Mississippi

bazaar, bazar: 4 fair, fete, sale 5 agora, burse 6 market 7 canteen 8 emporium 9 bezesteen 10 exposition

bazoo: 4 talk 5 kazoo, mouth

be: are 4 live 5 abide, exist, occur 6 remain 7 breathe, subsist 8 continue

beach: 4 bank, moor, ripa, sand 5 coast, plage(F.), playa(Sp.), shore 6 ground, shilla, strand 7 hardway, seaside, shingle

beachcomber: 7 vagrant 8 vagabond

beachhead: van 7 landing 8 foothold

beacon: 4 mark, sign 5 baken, fanal, guide, phare 6 ensign, pharos, signal 7 cresset, seamark, warning 8 signpost 10 lighthouse, watchtower

light: 7 cresset, lantern

Beaconsfield: 8 Disraeli

bead: 4 drop, foam 5 sewan, sight 6 bauble, bubble, prayer, wampum 7 globule, molding, sparkle, trinket

string: 6 rosary 7 chaplet 8 necklace

beadel: 5 crier, macer, usher 6 bedell, bumble, herald 7 bailiff, officer 8 servitor, summoner 9 apparitor, messenger 10 mace-bearer

beadsman, bedesman: 6 beggar, hermit 10 petitioner

beady: 5 round, small 8 globular 10 glistening

beak: neb, nib 4 bill, nose, prow 5 lorum, snout 6 master, speron 7 molding, rostrum 8 mandible 10 magistrate 11 stipendiary

ship's: bow, ram 4 prow

without: 9 erostrate

beaker: cup 4 tass 5 bocal, bouse, glass 6 bareca, bareka, vessel

beam: bar, ray 4 balk, emit, glow, I-bar, sile(Sc), stud, T-bar 5 arbor, caber, flash, gleam, gleed, joist, light, shine, smile 6 binder, girder, rafter, timber, walker 7 bumpkin, chevron, radiate, support, trimmer 10 architrave

beaming: gay 4 rosy 6 bright, lucent 7 radiant, shining

beamy: 5 broad 6 joyous, lucent 7 massive, radiant 8 mirthful

bean: urd 4 chap, gram, head, Lima, pole 5 brain, skull 6 caster, collar, fellow, kidney, lentil, nipple, noggin, strike, thrash, trifle 7 calabar, frijole(Sp.) 11 castigation

Asian: 4 gram 5 mungo

climbing: 4 lima, pole

cluster: 4 guar

eye: 4 hila 5 hilum

kind: goa, soy, wax 4 lima, navy 6 castor, kidney, string 7 calabar

lima: 4 haba 5 sieva

locust: 5 carob

lubricant: ben

Mexican: 6 frejol, frijol 7 frijole

poisonous 4 loco 7 calabar

bean shooter: 8 catapult 9 slingshot

Bean Town: 6 Boston

bear: cub, lug 4 gest, tote, ursa 5 abide, allow, beget, breed, bring, brook, brown, bruin, carry, drive, geste, koala, Polar, press, stand, yield 6 afford, behave, endure, kadiak, kodiak, pierce, render, suffer, thrust, uphold 7 comport, conduct, forbear, grizzly, produce, support, sustain, undergo 8 forebear, tolerate 9 carnivore, transport 13 constellation

Alaskan: 6 kadiak, kodiak

genus 5 ursus

bear bane: 9 wolfsbane

bear bush: 8 inkberry

bear cat: 4 paud 9 binturong

bear down: 5 exert, press 6 stress 8 approach

bear-shaped: 8 ursiform

Bear State: 8 Arkansas

bear upon: 6 affect 7 concern

beard: ane, awn 4 avel, barb, defy 6 arista, goatee 7 affront, aristae, Vandyke 8 whiskers

grain: awn

bearded: 5 hairy 6 barbed 7 barbate, hirsute 9 whiskered 11 barbigerous

grain: rye **5** awned, wheat **8** aristate

bearer: 5 macer **6** beadle, porter **7** carrier **8** escudero, portator **9** supporter **10** pallbearer **11** gonfalonier

bearing: aim, air **4** gest, mien, orle, port **5** birth, front, geste, habit, poise, trend **6** allure, apport, aspect, course, gerent, manner, orient, thrust **7** address, conduct, meaning, posture, purport, support **8** amenance, attitude, behavior, carriage, demeanor, pressure, relation, tendency, yielding **9** behaviour, demeanour, direction, gestation, influence, personage, producing **10** cognizance, deportment **11** comportment, countenance **12** significance.

fine: **6** belair

heraldic: **4** ente, orle **5** pheon

plate: gib

beast: 4 bete(F.) **5** brute **6** animal **7** monster **8** blighter **9** quadriped

mythical: **4** ogre, Rahu **5** Apepi, giant, harpy, hydra, Rahab **6** dragon, ellops, Empusa, garuda, Geryon, gorgon, Kraken, scylla, sphinx, triton **7** centaur, chimera, echidna, figfaun, griffin, griffon **8** chimaera, minotaur **9** bucentaur **10** jabberwock **11** chichevache

pertaining to: **7** leonine

royal **4** lion

beast fly: 6 gadfly

beast of burden: ox; ass, yak **5** burro, camel, horse, llama **6** donkey, onager

beastly: 5 gross **6** brutal **7** bestial, brutish, inhuman, swinish **9** offensive **10** abominable, disgusting

beat: KO; bat, cob, dad, fan, fib, tap, taw, tew **4** baff, bang, bash, bate, belt, best, blow, bolt, bray, cane, chap, club, daud, ding, dint, drub, dump, dunt, fell, flap, flax, flog, frat, haze, lash, lump, maul, mill, pant, pelt, poss, prat, rout, scat, slam, tack, tick, tund, whip, whop **5** baste, berry, churn, clink, douse, feeze, fight, filch, flail, knock, pound, pulse, round, scatt, scoop, skelp, strap, threp, throb, thump, trump, whang, worst **6** accent, batter, beetle, bensel, buffet, cotton, cudgel, defeat, dowsel, feague, fettle, hammer, hamper, larrup, outrun, pummel, raddle, rhythm, squash, strike, stroke, swinge, switch, thrash, threap, threip, threpe, thresh **7** assault, battuta, belabor, blister, cadence, canvass, conquer, contuse, exhaust, fatigue, pulsate, reeshie, shellac, surpass, trounce, vibrate **8** belabour, fatigued, lambaste, overcome, shellack, slaister, vanquish **9** exhausted, pulsation, throbbing **10** assignment

back: **7** repulse

into plate: **8** malleate

beat it: 4 scat **5** scram **7** vamoose

beater: rab **4** maul, seal **5** caner, lacer **6** dasher, mallet **8** thresher **9** scrutcher

beatify: 6 hallow **7** enchant, glorify **8** sanctify

beatitude: joy **5** bliss **7** benison **9** happiness **11** blessedness

beau: 5 beaux(pl.), blade, dandy, flame, lover, spark, swell **6** garcon, escort, fellow, steady, suitor **7** admirer, bravery, courter, coxcomb, cupidon, gallant **8** follower

Beau Brummell: fop **5** dandy **7** coxcomb

beau geste: 5 favor

beau ideal: 5 model **8** paradigm

beau monde: 7 fashion, society

beaut: 4 lulu

beautician: 10 beautifier, cosmetiste(F.) **11** cosmetician

beautifier: 8 cosmetic

beautiful: 4 fair, fine, glad, mear, meer, mere **5** belle, bonny **6** blithe, bonnie, comely, decore, freely, lovely, poetic, pretty **7** elegant **8** charming, delicate, fairsome, gorgeous, graceful, handsome **9** exquisite

comb. form: bel **4** calo **5** calli

beautify: 4 gild **5** adorn, grace, hight, preen, primp, prune **6** bedeck **7** adonize, garnish **8** decorate, fairhead **9** embellish

beauty: 5 belle, charm, grace **6** looker, polish **10** comeliness, goodliness, loveliness **11** pulchritude

goddess: Sri **5** Freya, Venus **6** Freyja **7** Lakshmi **9** Aphrodite

lover: **7** esthete **8** aesthete

beaver: hat **4** coin **6** castor, rodent

cloth: **6** kersey

eater: **9** wolverine

skin: **4** plew

Beaver State: 6 Oregon

because: as, so; for **4** that **5** since **8** inasmuch

because of that: 7 thereby **9** therefore

bechance: 6 befall, chance

beche-de-mer: 4 grub, worm **6** pidgin **7** trepang **8** language

beck: vat **5** becon, brook

becken: 7 cymbals

beckon: bow, nod **4** wave **6** curtsy, summon **7** bidding, command, curtsey, gesture **10** salutation

becloud: 4 hide **5** bedim **6** darken **7** mystify, obscure **8** befuddle, overcast

become: get, wax **4** grow, pass, suit **5** adorn, befit, grace **6** accord, befall, beseem, betide, change **7** behoove, flatter

becoming: 4 good 5 right 6 comely, gainly 7 decorum, farrand, farrant 8 decorous, handsome, suitable 10 convenient 11 appropriate

becscie: 9 merganser

becuna: 9 barracuda

bed: cot, pad 4 base, bunk, doss, lair, plot 5 berth, couch, layer 6 bottom, couche(F.), litter, matrix, pallet, strata 7 channel, lodging, stratum 8 matrices, plancher 9 basegrave, stretcher 10 apishamore, foundation
　feather: tye
　small: cot 4 crib 6 cradle, pallet 7 hammock, truckle, trundle 8 bassinet
　straw: 9 shakedown

bed stay: 4 slat

bedbug: 5 cimex 6 chinch 7 cimice(pl.) 8 conenose

bedding: 6 quilts, sheets 8 blankets 10 bedclothes

bedeck: gem 4 lard 5 adorn, array, dight, grace 8 ornament 9 embellish

bedevil: 5 abuse, annoy, worry 6 muddle, pester 7 bewitch, confuse, torment

bedim: fog 4 mist 5 cloud 6 darken 7 becloud, obscure

bedizen: 4 daub 5 adorn, array, dizen 6 bedaub 9 overdress

bedlam: 4 riot 5 noise, rudas(Sc.) 6 asylum, madman, tumult, uproar 7 lunatic, madness 8 madhouse 9 confusion

Bedouin: 4 Arab, Moor 5 nomad
　head cord: 4 agal
　official: 4 cadi 5 sheik
　tribe: 4 Harb

bedridden: ill 6 ailing

bedrock: 5 nadir 6 bottom

bedroll: 6 bindle

bedroom: 4 flat 5 berth, cabin 11 compartment

bee: dor, fly 4 apis, ring 5 party 6 dingar, insect, notion, torque 7 stinger 9 gathering 11 hymenoptera 12 hymenopteron
　colony of: 5 swarm, yeast
　comb. form: api
　family: 5 apina 6 apidae
　female: 5 queen
　genus: 4 apis
　girl named for: 7 Melissa
　house: gum 4 butt, hive, scap, skep 6 apiary 7 alveary, bee-butt 9 alvearium
　house covering: 6 hackle
　male: 5 drone
　nose: 4 lora(pl.) 5 lorum
　pert. to: 8 apiarian
　pollen brush: 5 scopa 6 scopae(pl.), 9 sarothrum

beebread: 8 ambrosia

beech: 4 buck, tree 6 myrtle
　genus: 5 fagus

beechnut: 4 mast

beef: 4 meat 5 gripe 8 complain
　cut: 4 loin, rump, side 5 baron, chine, chuck, flank, roast, round, shank, steak 6 cutlet, saddle 7 brisket, knuckle, quarter, sirloin 8 short-rib, shoulder 9 aitchbone, rattleran 11 porterhouse
　dried: 5 bucan, jerky, vifda, vivda 6 buccan 7 charqui
　pickled: 5 bully
　salted: 4 junk
　spiced: 8 pastroma, pastromi

beefy: 5 hefty, heavy 6 brawny, fleshy, stolid

Beehive State: 4 Utah

beekeeper: 8 apiarist, skeppist 12 apiculturist

been: be; see

beep: 4 tone, toot 6 signal

beer: ale, mum 4 bock, brew, grog, scud(Sc.) 5 kvass, lager, stout 6 liquor, porter, stingo, swanky 8 beverage
　barley: 5 chang
　cask: 4 butt
　ingredient: 4 hops, malt
　king: 9 Gambrinus
　maize: 5 chica 6 chicha
　mug: see *vessel,* below
　shop: pub 6 saloon
　unfermented: 4 wort
　vessel: mug 4 Toby 5 stein 6 flagon, seidel, tanker 8 schooner 9 blackjack

beer and skittles: fun 4 play

beery: 7 maudlin, muddled

beeswax substitute: 7 ceresin

beet: 5 chard, sugar 6 mangel 8 beetrave 9 vegetable
　genus: 4 beta

Beethoven: *birthplace:* 4 Bonn
　opera: 7 Fidelio
　symphony: 5 fifth, first, ninth, sixth, third 6 eighth, Eroica, fourth, second 7 seventh 8 Pastoral

beetle: bat, bug, jut, ram 4 beat, goga, gogo, maul, stag 5 amara, drive, gogga, hispa, meloe 6 chafer, golach, goloch, jutout, mallet, pestle, scarab, weevil 7 prinoid, project 8 lowering, overhang 9 prioninae(pl.) 10 battledore, projecting
　bark: 5 borer
　bright: 7 ladybug
　family: 10 elateridae 11 clavicornes, clavicornia
　fire: 6 cucuyo
　genus: 5 fidia
　grain: 7 cadelle
　grapevine: 6 thrips

ground: 5 amara
horny substance of: 6 chitin
mustard: 9 blackjack
rhinoceros: 4 uang
sacred: 6 scarab
wing cover: 5 shard
wood: 6 sawyer
beetle-browed: 6 morose 8 scowling
beetle-head: 6 plover 9 blockhead
befall: hap 4 come 5 occur 6 astart, become, betide, happen 7 pertain 8 bechance
befile: 4 soil 6 defile
befit: dow 4 suit 5 beset 6 become, behove, beseem, betide 7 behoove
beflum: 7 deceive
befog: 5 cloud 6 obsane 7 confuse, mystify
before: ere 4 said 5 ahead, afore, avant, coram(L.), first, forby, front, prior 6 forbye, former, rather, sooner 7 already, earlier, forward 8 anterior, hitherto 10 beforehand, heretofore, previously
prefix: pre, pro 4 ante, prae
before long: 4 anon, soon 9 presently
before now: ere 4 gone, over 6 erenow
befoul: 4 soil 5 dirty 6 bemire, defile 7 pollute 8 entangle 11 contaminate
befriend: aid 4 abet, help 5 favor 6 assist, favour, foster, succor 7 benefit, support, sustain 11 countenance
befuddle: 5 addle, besot 6 muddle 7 becloud, confuse, fluster, mystify, stupefy
beg: ask, bid, sue, woo 4 coax, pray, sorn(Sc.) 5 cadge, crave, mooch, plead 6 adjure 7 beseech, entreat, implore, request, solicit 8 petition 9 importune, panhandle 10 supplicate
beget: ean 4 bear, sire 5 breed, yield 6 author, create, father 7 acquire, engraff 8 engender, generate 9 germinate, procreate
begetter: 4 sire 6 author, father, mother, parent
beggar: 4 ruin 5 asker, randy, rogue 6 alsman, bacach, bidder, canter, devour, mumper, pariah, pauper, wretch 8 palliard, stroller 9 maunderer, mendicant, schnorrer, suppliant 10 impoverish, panhandler, petitioner, starveling 12 hallan-shaker
saint: 5 Giles
speech: 4 cant
beggarly: 4 mean, poor 5 cheap, petty, sorry 6 abject, paltry 8 bankrupt, indigent 10 despicable 12 contemptible
Beggar's Opera author: Gay 6 Brecht
begin: 4 fang, lead, open, rise 5 arise, enter, start 6 attack, spring 8 commence, inchoate, initiate 9 institute, introduce, originate 10 inaugurate

begin again: 4 anew, over 5 renew 6 resume 7 restart
beginner: 4 boot, tiro, tyro 5 rooky 6 novice, rookie 7 amateur, entrant, noviate, recruit, trainee, student 8 freshman, neophyte 9 candidate, debutante, postulate, 10 apprentice
beginning: egg 4 dawn, edge, germ, rise, root, seed 5 alpha, birth, debut, start 6 source 7 genesis, geneses(pl.), initial, nascent 8 entrance, exordium, inchoate, rudiment 9 embryonic, inception, incipient 10 conception, foundation, incunabula(pl.), initiation 11 incunabulum 12 commencement
begone: off, out 4 away, scat, shoo 5 scoot, scram 6 aroint, avaunt, depart 7 vamoose
begrudging: 6 loathe, grudge 7 envious, grumble 9 reluctant
beguile: fox 4 coax, foil, gull, lure 5 amuse, charm, cheat, cozen, elude, evade, trick 6 brique, delude, divert, entrap 7 deceive, ensnare, flatter, mislead 9 entertain
behalf: 4 part, sake, side 5 stead 6 affair, matter, profit 7 benefit, defence, support 8 interest 9 advantage
behave: act 4 bear, work 5 carry, react, treat 6 acquit, demean, deport, handle 7 comport, conduct, gesture, manager 8 function, regulate, restrain
behavior, behaviour: air 4 port, mien 5 guise 6 action, manner 7 bearing, comport, decorum 8 amenance, breeding, carriage 9 demeanour 10 deportment, governance
behead: 9 decollate 10 decapitate, guillotine
behemoth: 4 huge 5 beast, giant, hippo 7 monster
behest: bid, law 4 hest, rule 5 order 6 demand 7 command, mandate 10 injunction
behind: aft 4 past, rear, ward, rump 5 abaff, abaft, after, ahind(Sc.), arear, later, passe, tardy 6 arrear, astern 8 backward, dilatory 9 posterior 10 afterwards
behold: lo; eye, see, spy 4 ecce, espy, gaze, hold, keep, look, scan, stop, view, wait 5 sight, voila, watch 6 descry, regard, retain 7 discern, observe, witness 8 consider, maintain, perceive
beholden: 7 obliged 8 indebted
behoof: use 6 profit 7 benefit 8 interest 9 advantage
behoove: dow, fit 4 need, suit 5 befit, ought 6 belong, proper 7 require 8 suitable 9 incumbent
beige: tan 4 ecru 5 color, grege(F.) 10 unbleached
being: ens 4 self 5 entia, entre(F.), gnome, human, troll 6 animal, entity, extant, living, mortal, person 7 essence, present, re-

ality 8 creature, ontology, standing 9 actuality, existence 11 subsistence 12 constitution
abstract: ens 5 entia
actual: 4 esse
in front: 6 anteal
physiological: 4 bion
science of: 8 ontology
suffix: ure
beken: 7 commend, deliver, entrust, intrust
beknow: 7 confess 9 recognize 11 acknowledge
Bela's son: Ard, Iri 4 Uzzi 5 Ezbon
Bel's wife: 5 Belit 6 Beltis
belabor, belabour: ply 4 beat, drub, lash,
work 6 assail, cudgel, hammer, hamper,
thrash, thwack
belair: 7 bearing 10 deportment
Belait: 6 Europe
belamour: 5 lover 6 flower 8 ladylove
belated: 5 lated, tardy 7 delayed, overdue
belay: 5 beset 6 invest, waylay 7 besiege 8
encircle
belaying pin: 5 kevel 7 bollard
belch: 4 boke, bolk, galp, rasp 5 eruct 8 eruc-
tate 10 eructation
beldam, beldame: hag 4 fury 5 crone, jixen
6 alecto, erinys, virago 7 Jezebel 8 ancestor 9 Tisiphone 11 grandmother
beleaguer: 5 belay, beset 6 invest 7 assault,
besiege 8 blockade, surround 9 encompass
belfry: 4 shed 5 tower 7 clocher 9 campanile
Belgian: 7 Fleming, Walloon
Belgian Congo: See **Zaire**
Belgium: *anthem:* 11 Brabanconne
city: Ans, Huy, Spa 4 Gand, Mons 5 Alost,
Ciney, Eupen, Ghent, Jumet, Liege, Namur, Ypres 6 Bruges, Deurne, Lierre,
Merxem, Ostend, Turnai 7 Antwerp, Ber-
chem, Herstal, Hoboken, Ixelles, Louvain,
Mechlin, Roulers, Seraing 8 Brussels(c.),
Courtrai, Muscron, Turnhout, Verviers 9
Charleroi, Molenbeek 10 Anderlecht, Bor-
gerhout, Schaerbeek
coin: 5 belga, franc 7 centime
commune: Ans, Ath, Ely, Hal, Mol, Spa 4
Aath, Boom, Geel, Genk, Lier, Niel, Roux,
Zele 5 Aalst, Alost, Evere, Genck, Jette,
Namur, Ronse, Uccle, Ukkel
endive: 7 witloof
Gaul tribe: 4 Remi 6 Nervii
horse: 9 Brabancon
marble: 5 rance
measure: vat 4 aune, last, pied 5 carat 6
perche 8 boisseau
province: Spa 5 Liege, Namur 7 Antwerp,
Brabant, Hainaut, Limburg 8 Flanders 9
Luxemburg

river: Lys 4 Dyle, Leie, Maas, Yser 5 Meuse,
Rupel, Senne 6 Dender, Ourthe, Sambre 7
Schelde, Scheldt
seaport: 6 Ostend
tribe: 9 Bellovaci
violinist: 5 Ysaye
weight: 4 last 5 carat, livre, pound 6 charge
7 chariot 8 esterlin
Belgrade native: 4 Serb
Belial: 5 devil, Satan
belie: 6 belong, defame 7 besiege, falsify,
pertain, slander, traduce 8 disguise,
strumpet, surround 9 encompass 10 calumniate, contradict 11 counterfeit 12
misrepresent
belief: fay, ism 4 mind, sect, view 5 credo,
creed, dogma, faith, tenet, troth, trust 6
credit 7 opinion 8 credence, doctrine, reliance 9 assurance 10 confidence, conviction, persuasion
liable to: 7 credent 9 credulous
believe: wis 4 deem, trow, ween 5 judge,
think, trust 6 accept, credit 7 suppose 8
accredit, consider, credence
believer: ist 8 adherent
in all religions: 7 omnist
in God: 5 deist 6 theist
in predestination: 13 particularist
Belili's brother: 6 Tammuz
belittle: 5 decry, dwarf, sneer 6 slight 7 detract 8 minimize 9 denigrate, discredit,
disparage 10 depreciate
bell: 4 call, fair, gong, ring, roar 5 chime,
cloak, codon, flare, knell, swell 6 bellow,
bubble(Sc.), crotal, curfew, tocsin 7 blossom, campana, campane, corolla 9 beautiful 13 tintinnabulum
alarm: 6 tocsin
axle bearing: cod
clapper: 6 tongue
kind of: cow 4 door, gong, hand 5 ship's 6
church, jingle, school 8 electric
part: 7 baldric 8 baldrick
pert. to: 10 campanular 11 campanulate
ringer: 6 toller 12 carillonneur
room: 6 belfry
sound: 4 ding, dong, toll 5 knell 6 tinkle
tower: 6 belfry 9 campanile
bell, book, and candle: 15 excommunication
bell bottoms: 8 trousers
bell ear: 6 cannon
Bell for Adano author: 6 Hersey
bell-mouthed: 5 evase(F.)
bell-shaped: 11 campanulate
belladonna: 5 dwale, plant 6 remedy 7
manicon 8 narcotic 9 dwayberry 10 nightshade
extract: 7 atropin 8 atropine

bellbird: 6 shrike 8 arapunga
bellboy: 4 page 6 porter, redcap
Bellerophon: *father:* 7 Glaucus
  spring: 7 Pelrene
belles-lettres: 10 literature
bellicose: mad 5 irate 7 hostile, warlike 8
  militant 10 pugnacious 11 belligerent
belligerent: 7 hostile, warlike 8 choleric,
  fighting, jingoist 9 bellicose, combative,
  irascible, litigious, wrangling 10 pugnacious 11 contentious, quarrelsome 12 disputatious
Bellini: *opera:* 5 Norma
  sleepwalker: 5 Amina
bellow: cry, low, moo, yap 4 bawl, beal, bell,
  roar, rout, yaup, yawp 5 belve, blart,
  croon, roust(Sc.), shout 6 buller, clamor 7
  bluster, clamour, ululate 10 vociferate
bellware: 4 kelp
bellweed: 8 knapweed
bellwether: 5 sheep 6 leader
belly: bag, cod, gie(Sc.), gut, pod 4 bouk, ky-
  te(Sc.) 5 bingy, bulge, pleon 6 hunger
  paunch 7 abdomen, stomach 8 appetite
bellying: 7 bunting
belong: 4 bear 5 apply, belie 6 inhere, relate
  7 pertain 9 appertain
belongings: 4 gear 5 goods, traps 6 assets,
  estate 7 effects 8 chattels, property 9
  household 10 appendages 11 possessions
  13 appurtenances
beloved: 4 dear, idol 5 cheri(F.) 6 adored,
  cherie(F.) 7 darling 8 precious 9 inamorata, valentine
below: 4 alow, down 5 ablow, infra, sot-
  to(It.), under 7 beneath 8 downward, inferior 10 downstairs, underneath
belt: 4 area, band, beat, blow, cest, gird,
  mark, ring, sash, zone 5 girth, strap, strip,
  tract, whack, zonar 6 bodice, cestus, cingle, fettle, girdle, invest, region, strait,
  stripe, zonnar, zonule 7 circuit, passage 8
  cincture, encircle, surround 9 bandoleer,
  encompass 10 cummerbund, kummer-
  bund
  conveyor: 5 apron
  ecclesiastical: 7 balteus 8 baltheus
  non-Mohammedan: 5 zonar
  sword: 7 baldric 8 boldrick
belted: 6 zonate 7 girdled 9 cinctured
bema: 4 pace, step 7 chancel
bemoan: 4 wail 6 grieve, lament, sorrow 7
  deplore
bemuse: 5 addle 7 confuse 8 distract
bench: bar, pew 4 banc, seat 5 board, judge,
  ledge, stool 6 settee 7 discard
  church: pew, pue 6 sedile(L.)
bench hook: 5 clamp
bend: bow, nid, ply, sag 4 arch, flex, kink,
  turn 5 angle, baton, bulge, crimp, crook,

curve, stoop, twist 6 buckle, cotice, cotise,
  crouch, direct, divert, fasten, inflex, submit 7 bendlet, incline, refract 9 genuflect
  backward: 6 retort
  in timber: sny
bender: leg 5 drunk, spree 7 whopper 8 guz-
  zling, sixpence
bending: 5 lithe 6 pliant, supple 7 anfract,
  flexion 8 flection
beneath: 5 aneth(Sc.), below, lower, under 6
  aneath 10 underneath 11 underground
benedict: 4 mild 6 benign, kindly 7 blessed
  8 bachelor, gracious, salutary 9 benignant, favorable, wholesome 10 propitious
Benedictine: 4 monk 7 Cluniac, liqueur
  title: dom
benediction: 4 amen 6 prayer 7 benison 8
  blessing 10 invocation
benefaction: 4 alms, boon, gift 7 benefit,
  present 8 benefice, donation, gratuity 11
  beneficence
benefactor: 5 agent, angel, donor 6 friend,
  helper, patron, savior 8 promoter 14 philanthropist
benefice: feu 4 fief 5 favor 6 curacy, favour,
  living 7 benefit, rectory 8 kindness, vicarage 10 beneficium 11 benefaction
  first fruit: 5 annat 6 annate
beneficence: 4 boon, gift 5 grace 6 bounty 7
  charity 8 goodness, kindness 11 benefaction
beneficial: 4 good 6 useful 7 helpful 8 salutary 9 available, benignant, desirable, enjoyable, healthful, lucrative, wholesome
  10 beneficent, profitable, salubrious 11
  serviceable 12 advantageous, remunerative
beneficiary: 4 heir, user 5 donee 6 vassal 7
  legatee 9 feudatory
benefit: aid, use 4 boon, boot, gain, gift,
  help, prow, sake 5 avail, boost 6 assist,
  behalf, behoof, better, profit, usance 7 advance, bespeak, concert, deserve, improve,
  service, utility 8 benefice, befriend, interest 9 advantage, emolument 11 benefaction, performance
benevolent: 4 good, kind 6 benign, loving 7
  amiable, liberal 8 generous 9 benignant 10
  altruistic, charitable, munificent 13 philanthropic
Bengal: *boat:* 5 batel 6 baulea 7 bauleah
  capital: 5 Dacca
  caste member: 6 baidya
  city: see *town* below
  cotton: 5 adati, adaty
  district: 5 Dacca, Nadia
  gentlemen: 5 baboo
  grass: 6 millet
  hemp: 4 sunn

measure: 5 cotta 6 cottah 8 chattack
native: Ebo, Kol 4 Eboe 6 Banian
quince: bel 4 bael, bhel
root: 10 cassumunar
singer: 4 baul
town: 5 Dacca(c.) 6 Madras 7 Barisal, Rangoon 8 Calcutta 9 Tittacarh
tree: 4 bola

benign: 4 boon, good, kind, mild 5 bland 6 genial, gentle 7 affable 8 benedict, gracious, salutary 9 benignant, favorable, wholesome 10 benevolent, favourable, propitious, salubrious

benison: 8 blessing 9 beatitude 10 invocation 11 benediction

Benjamin: *descendant:* 4 Aher
grandson: Iri
son: Ehi 4 Gera, Rosh

benne: 6 sesame

bent: aim, bow, set 4 bias, gift, turn 5 bound, bowed, crank, crump, flair, knack, prone, taste, trend 6 akimbo, biased, braced, courbe, course, curved, energy, genius, hooked, swayed, talent 7 crooked, curvant, flexion, flexure, impetus, leaning, leveled, pronate, purpose, stooped, tension 8 aptitude, declined, flection, penchant, tendency 9 curvature, direction, prejudice 10 determined, proclivity, propensity 11 disposition, inclination 13 prepossession 14 predisposition

benthonic plant: 6 enalid

benthos: 5 fauna, flora

benumb: nip 4 daze, dunt, numb, stun 5 daver 6 cumber, deaden 7 fretish, fretize, stupefy

benzine derivative: 6 phenol

Beowulf: 4 epic, poem

bequeath: 4 give, will 5 endow, leave, offer 6 bestow, commit, demise, devise, legate, quethe 7 bequest, commend 8 transmit 9 testament

bequest: 4 gift, will 6 legacy 8 bequeath, heritage, pittance 9 endowment

berate: jaw, nag 4 lash, rail 5 abuse, chide, scold, score 6 revile 7 censure, reprove, upbraid 8 chastise 10 vituperate

Berber: 4 Moor 6 Hamite, Kabyle 7 Haratin
chief: 4 caid, qaid
dialect: 6 Tuareg
tribe: 4 Daza, Riff, Tibu 6 Tuareg

Berea: 6 Aleppo

bereave: rob 5 strip 6 divest, sadden 7 deprive, despoil 10 dispossess

bereft: orb 4 lorn, lost, poor 7 forlorn 9 destitute 12 dispossessed

beret: cap, hat, tam 7 biretta, chapeau 8 berretta, chapeaux(pl.), headgear

berg: ice 4 floe 6 barrow 8 eminence, mountain

bergamot: 4 bose, mint, pear 5 snuff 6 orange 7 Bergama, essence, perfume

bergstock: 10 alpenstock

beriberi: 5 kakke

Berkshire: *race course:* 5 Ascot
village: 5 Ascot

Berlin park: 10 Tiergarten

berm, berme: 4 bank, edge, path 5 ledge, shelf 7 terrace

Bermuda: *arrowroot:* 5 aruru 6 ararao
barracuda: 4 spet
berry: 9 soapberry
capital: 8 Hamilton
catfish: 6 coelho
ceremony: 6 gombay
grass: 4 doob

berry: bay, dew, haw 4 beat, cran, rasp 5 acini, bacca, black, fruit, mound, salal, savin 6 acinus, baccae, burrow, sabine, thresh 7 currant, hillock
comb. form: 5 bacci
disease: 8 bluestem
medicinal: 5 cubeb
oil: 5 olive

berry-like: 7 baccate

berserk: mad 5 bravo 6 pirate 7 enraged, warrior 8 frenzied, maniacal

berth: bed, job 4 bunk, dock, slip 5 place 6 billet, office 7 lodging, mooring 8 position 9 anchorage, situation 11 appointment

bertha: 4 cape 6 cannon, collar

beryl: gem 5 jewel 7 emerald 10 aquamarine
green: 11 davidsonite
yellow: 8 heliodor

beryx: 8 alfonsin

beseech: ask, beg, sue 4 pray 5 crave, plead 6 adjure, appeal, obtest 7 entreat, implore, solicit 9 impetrate, obsecrate 10 supplicate

beseeching: 9 precative

beset: ply 4 sail, stud 5 allot, belay, harry, siege, spend 6 assail, attack, harass, infest 7 arrange, besiege, perplex 8 blockade, encumber, obstruct, surround 9 beleaguer

beshrew: 5 curse 8 execrate

beside: by 4 hear 5 along, aside 7 abreast 8 adjacent
comb. form: 4 para 5 juxta

besides: by; and, but, too, yet 4 also, else, over, then 6 beside, beyond, except 8 moreover 10 additional 11 furthermore

besiege: 4 gird, girt 5 belay, belie, beset, siege, storm 6 attack, pester, plague 7 solicit 8 surround 9 beleaguer

besmear: ray 4 balm, daub, soil 5 apply,
cover, muddy, smear, sully, taint 6 bedaub
7 beslime, smother 8 besmirch

besmirch: 4 soil 5 smear, sully 6 smirch 7
asperse, blacken 8 discolor

besom: map 4 drab(Sc.), 5 broom, sweep 6
sloven(Sc.), 7 heather

besot: 4 dull 6 muddle, stupid 7 stupefy 8
befuddle 9 infatuate

bespangle: dot 4 stud, star 5 adorn 8 sprinkle

bespatter: 4 blot, dash, soil, spot 5 muddy,
plash, stain, sully 6 sparge 7 asperse, scatter 8 reproach, sprinkle

bespeak: 4 cite, hint, show 5 argue, imply,
order, speak 6 accost, attest, engage, steven 7 address, arrange, benefit, betoken,
discuss, exclaim, reserve 8 foretell, indicate 9 stipulate

best: ace 4 a-one, beat, most, tops, wale 5
elite, excel, worst 6 choice, defeat, finest,
flower, outwit, utmost 7 conquer, largest,
optimum 8 greatest, outmatch, outstrip,
vanquish 9 excellent, overmatch 11 superlative

comb. form: 5 arist 6 aristo

bestial: low 4 vile, wild 5 brute, feral 6 brutal, filthy 7 beastly, brutish, inhuman,
sensual 8 depraved 10 irrational

bestir: 5 rouse

bestow: add, put, use 4 deal, dote, give 5
allot, allow, apply, award, beset, grant,
lodge, place 6 accord, beteem, confer, demise, devote, divide, donate, employ, entail, extend, impart, render 7 collate, dispose, instate, present, quarter, tribute 8
bequeath 11 communicate

bestraddle: 8 bestride

bestride: 6 stride 8 straddle 10 bestraddle

bet: lay 4 ante, gage, play, plot, risk, wage 5
hedge, stake, wager 6 gamble, pledge

broker: 6 bookie 9 bookmaker

fail to pay: 5 welch, welsh

faro: 7 sleeper

roulette: bas 4 noir 5 carre 6 milieu 7 dernier, encarre, enplein

betake: go; hie 4 move 5 apply, catch, grant
6 assume, commit, repair, remove, resort
7 commend, journey

bete: 5 beast, silly 6 stupid 7 foolish

bete noir: 4 hate 5 dread 6 terror 7 bugaboo,
bugbear

betel: 4 ikmo, itmo, siri

leaf: pan 4 buyo

betel palm: 5 areca

extract: 7 catechu

masticatory: pan 4 buyo

seed: 8 betel nut

Betelgeuse: 4 star

bethel: 6 chapel

Bethesda: 4 pool 6 chapel

bethink: 5 think 6 devise, recall 7 reflect 8
consider, remember 9 recollect 10 deliberate

Bethlehemite: 4 Boaz

Beth's sister: Jo; Amy, Meg

Bethuel's son: 5 Laban

betide: hap 5 befit, occur, trite 6 become,
befall, chance, happen 7 betoken, presage

betimes: 4 anon, rath, soon 5 early, rathe 8
speedily 9 forthwith 10 seasonably 12 occasionally

betise: 5 folly 9 silliness, stupidity

betoken: 4 mark, note, show 5 augur 6 assert, betide, denote, evince, import 7 bespeak, express, forbode, oblique, portend,
presage, signify 8 forebode, foreshow, indicate 9 symbolize 10 foreshadow 13 prognosticate

betray: 4 blab, blow, boil, gull, sell, sile,
sing, tell, undo, wray 5 peach, spill 6 accuse, delude, descry, reveal, seduce,
snitch, squeal 7 beguile, deceive, falsify,
mislead 8 disclose, discover

betrayer: rat 5 Judas, skunk 7 seducer, traitor 8 derelict

betroth: 4 affy 6 assure, engage, ensure,
pledge, plight 7 espouse, promise 8 affiance, contract, handfast

better: aid, top 4 mend 5 amend, emend,
excel, safer, wiser 6 bigger, exceed, reform
7 advance, choicer, correct, greater, improve, promote, rectify, relieve, support,
surpass 8 increase, superior 9 meliorate
10 ameliorate, preferable

better half: 4 wife

betting: *adviser:* 4 tout

figures: 4 odds

odds: 5 price

betty: 7 dessert

between: 4 amid 5 amell, among, entre(F.)
7 average, betwixt 12 intermediate

law: 5 mesne

prefix: dia 4 meta 5 inter

between the lines: 6 latent, secret

bevel: 4 blow(Sc.), cant, edge, push(Sc.) 5 angle, bezel, miter, mitre, slant, slope 6
aslant 7 chamfer, incline, oblique

corners: 5 splay

end of timber: 5 snape

out: 4 ream

beverage: ade, ale, nog, pop, tea 4 beer,
grog, mead, milk, soda, wine 5 cider, cocoa,
draft, drink, lager, leban, negus, morat,
punch, treat, water 6 coffee, eggnog, liquid, liquor, nectar, posset 7 potable 8 cocktail, potation 9 metheglin 10 melicratum

alcoholic: see **alcoholic drink**

container: vat 6 kettle 7 charger 9 separator

extract: 4 kola

malted wheat: 6 zythem, zythum

mixed: 5 negus, punch, smash 6 bishop

mulberry and honey: 5 morat

Oriental: rak 4 sake 5 rakee 6 arrack

pepper: 4 kava

Polynesian: 4 kava

South American: 4 mate

bevy: 4 herd, pack 5 covey, drove, flock, group, swarm 6 flight, school 7 company 8 assembly 9 gathering, multitude 10 collection

bewail: cry, rue 4 keen, moan, sigh, wail, weep 5 mourn 6 bemoan, grieve, lament, plaint, sorrow 7 deplore 8 complain

beware: 4 cave, heed, shun 5 avoid, spend 6 eschew 7 warning

bewilder: fog 4 daze, foil, gaum 5 abash, addle, amaze, amuse, deave 6 baffle, bemist, bother, dazzle, muddle, puzzle 7 buffalo, confuse, mystify, perplex, stagger, stupefy 8 astonish, confound, distract, entangle, surprise 9 embarrass, obfuscate 10 spifflicate 11 spifflicate

bewildered: 4 asea, lost, mang 5 agape, dazed 8 confused, helpless 9 perplexed

bewilderment: awe, fog 4 daze 9 amazement, confusion 10 perplexity 11 distraction 13 embarrassment

bewitch: hex 5 charm, fasci, spell 6 enamor, entice, glamor, grigri, hoodoo, thrill 7 bedevil, delight, enchant, glamour 8 ensorcel, forspeak, greegree 9 captivate, ensorcell, fascinate

bewith: 9 makeshift 10 substitute

bewray: 4 show, tell 6 accuse, betray, expose, malign, reveal 7 divulge 8 disclose

bey: 6 beylic, beylik 8 governor

Beyle's penname: 8 Stendhal

beyond: by 4 free, over 5 above, aside, forby, ultra 6 forbye, yonder 7 besides, further 8 superior 9 hereafter

prefix: sur 4 meta 5 ultra

the sea: 11 ultramarine

the threshold: 12 ultraliminal

bezel, basil: rim 4 edge, ouch, seal 5 bevil, bezil, crown, facet 6 chaton, flange 8 template

bezezteen: 5 bazar 6 bazaar

bezzle: 5 drink, revel, waste 7 consume, plunder 10 gluttonize

bhagavat: 7 blessed

bhakta: 7 devotee 9 bhagavata, worshiper

bhalu: 4 bear

bhandar: 5 store 7 library 10 storehouse

bhandari: 7 steward 9 treasurer

bhang, bang: 7 hashish 8 narcotic 10 intoxicant

product of: 6 majoon

bhangi: 6 mehtar 7 sweeper

bharal: tur 5 sheep 6 nahoor

bhat: 4 bard 8 minstrel

bhikku: 4 monk 5 friar 6 priest 9 mendicant

bhikshu: 5 friar 7 ascetic 9 mendicant

bhoosa: 5 chaff, husks, straw

b'hoy: 5 rowdy 8 gangster

bhut: 5 ghost 6 goblin

Bhutan: *disease:* dha

pine: 4 kail

religion: 9 shamanism

robe: 6 bakkhu

bias: 4 awry, bent, sway 5 amiss, color, slant, slope 7 bigotry, incline, oblique 8 clinamen, diagonal, tendency 9 clinamina(pl.), prejudice, procedure 10 favoritism, partiality, prepossess, propensity 11 declination, disposition, favouritism, inclination 12 predetermine, predilection 13 prepossession

biased: 11 tendentious

bib: sip 4 brat, fish 5 apron, drink 6 tipple, tucker 7 bavette(F.), 9 neckpiece 10 protection

bibelot: 5 curio 7 trinket 8 ornament

Bible: *angel:* 5 Micah 7 Raphael

animal: 4 reem 5 daman 6 hydrax 8 behemoth

apocrypha: 5 Tobit 6 Baruch, Esdras, Jeremy, Judith, Syriac, Wisdom 7 Vulgate 8 Manasses 9 Maccabees 10 Septuagint 14 Ecclesiasticus

ascetic order: 6 Essene

battle scene: 10 Armageddon

book: Job 4 Acts, Amos, Ezra, Joel, John, Jude, Luke, Mark, Ruth 5 Hosea, James, Jonah, Kings, Micah, Peter, Titus 6 Daniel, Esther, Exodus, Haggai, Isaiah, Joshua, Psalms, Romans, Samuel 7 Ezekiel, Genesis, Hebrews, Matthew, Numbers, Obadiah, Timothy 8 Habakkuk, Jeremiah, Nehemiah, Philemon, Proverbs 9 Apocrypha, Ephesians, Galatians, Leviticus, Zechariah 10 Chronicles, Colossians, Revelation 11 Corinthians, Deuteronomy, Philippians 12 Ecclesiastes, Lamentations 13 Song of Solomon, Thessalonians

character: see *name* below

city: Ain, Dan 4 Arad, Aven, Cana, Elim, Elon, Gath, Gaza, Geba, Maon, Rome, Tyre, Zoar 5 Akkad, Arvad, Ashur, Assur, Joppa, Sidon, Sodom 6 Bethel, Biblos, Gadara, Jerico, Tarsus 7 Babylon, Nineveh 8 Gomorrah, Nazareth 9 Jerusalem

clan: 6 Shelah

country: Nod, Pul **4** Aram, Bela, Edam, Elam, Gath, Hali, Moab, Seba, Seir **5** Ammon **6** Canaan **7** Galilee, Samaria

garden: **4** Eden

giant: **4** Anak, Emim **7** Goliath

giant killer: **5** David

hunter: **6** Nimrod

judge: **4** Agog, Elon

king: Og; Asa, Gog, Iva **4** Agag, Ahab, Ahaz, Amon, Bera, Jehu, Omri, Reba, Saul **5** David, Herod, Hiram, Joram, Nadab, Rezin, Tidal, Zimri **6** Birsha, Hezion, Japhia, Jotham, Uzziah **7** Jehoram, Solomon

kingdom: **4** Elam, Moab **5** Judea, Judah **6** Israel **8** Chaldeae

land of plenty: **6** Goshen

liar: **7** Ananias

money: **4** beka **5** bekah **6** shekel

mountain: Hor **4** Ebal, Nebo, Peor, Sina, Sion, Zion **5** Heres, Horeb, Sinai, Tabor **6** Ararat, Gilead, Moriah, Olivet, Pisgah

name: Ai, Ar, Ir; Ahi, Asa, Eri, Eve, Evi, Hor, Iri, Koa, Lot, Ner, Ono, Reu, Toi, Uel, Uri **4** Abel, Acan, Acub, Adam, Ader, Adna, Ador, Agee, Aher, Aman, Anak, Anam, Aner, Aram, Arem, Arie, Asan, Asom, Ater, Aven, Azal, Cain, Cana, Dura, Edar, Edec, Edes, Eker, Enan, Enos, Eran, Esau, Etam, Gera, Irad, Iram, Isac, Mary, Neri, Obal, Omar, Oreb, Oren, Paul, Reba, Sami, Sara, Seth, Suba, Ucal, Vale **5** Ahlab, Alian, Amasa, Aroer, Bedan, Besai, Caleb, Elias, Ephai, Esrom, Hadad, Hanes Isaac, Mered, Nehum, Oseas, Peleg, Rahad, Tarah, Vania **6** Naaman, Pilate, Ramath **7** Abadias, Abigail, Antioch, Elmodam, Idithum, Sidrach, Tabitha

navigator: **4** Noah

ornament: **4** urim **7** thummin

patriarch: Reu **4** Seth, Shem **5** Jacob, Nahor, Peleg **6** Israel, Lamech

people: **4** Moab, Phut, Seba **5** Ammon **6** Hamite, Hivite, Kenite **7** Amorite, Dodanim, Moabite

plain: **5** Mamre **7** Jericho

plotter: **5** Haman

pool: **6** Siloam

priest: Eli **5** Aaron **6** Levite

pronoun: ye; thy **4** thee, thou **5** thine

prophet: **4** Amos, Ezra **5** Elias, Hosea, Jonah, Micah, Nahum **6** Elijah, Isaiah **7** Ezekial **8** Jeremiah

psalmist: **5** David

queen: Abi **5** Sheba **6** Esther, Vashti **7** Jezebel

region: **4** Enon **5** Ophir, Perea **6** Bashan

reproach: **4** raca

river: Zab **4** Nile **5** Abana. Arnon **6** Kishon, Jordan

ruler: see *king* above

scholar: **7** Biblist **9** Biblicist

sea: Red **4** Dead **7** Galilee **8** Tiberias **10** Gennesaret

shepherd: **4** Abel **5** David

spice: **5** myrrh **6** stacte **12** frankincense

spy: **5** Caleb

stone: **4** ezel **6** ligure

tower: **4** Edar **5** Babel

town: see *city* above

tribe: see *people* above

valley: **4** Baca, Elah **6** Shaveh, Siddim

version: Av, RV **4** Geez **5** Douay, Itala **6** Syriac **7** Vulgate **8** Bohairic **9** Apocrypha, King James **10** New English **15** Revised Standard

weed: **4** tare

witch's home: **5** Endor

Bible society: **7** Gideons

Biblical: **10** scriptural

bicker: war **4** bowl, spar, tiff **5** argue, brawl, cavil, fight **6** assail, attack, battle **7** contend, dispute, quarrel, wrangle **8** pettifog, skirmish, squabble **10** contention

bicycle: **4** bike **5** wheel

for two: **6** tandem

rider: **7** cyclist

bid: beg **4** call, hist, pray **5** clepe, offer, order **6** adjure, charge, direct, enjoin, invite, reveal, tender **7** command, declare, entreat, proffer **8** announce, proclaim, proposal

biddable: **6** docile **8** obedient

biddy: hen **7** chicken

bide: **4** face, stay, wait **5** abide, await, dwell, tarry **6** endure, remain, suffer **7** sojourn **8** continue, tolerate **9** encounter, withstand

bield: den **4** cozy **5** dwell **7** comfort, courage, hearten, protect, shelter **8** boldness, embolden **9** sheltered **10** confidence, habitation

bien, bein: **4** fine, good, snug **6** genial **8** pleasant, thriving **10** prosperous **11** comfortable

bier: **4** pyre **5** frame, grave **6** coffin, hearse, litter **7** support **10** catafalque, handbarrow

bifarious: **7** twofold **9** ambiguous

biff: **4** blow

bifid: **6** forked

bifocal: **4** lens

bifold: **6** double **7** twofold

bifurcation: wye **4** fork **5** split **6** branch **8** division

big: **4** bold, huge, vast **5** bulky, chief, grand, great, gross, large **6** mighty **7** bumping, eminent, leading, massive, pompous, violent **8** boastful, bouncing, enormous, generous, gigantic, imposing, pregnant **9** notorious **10** tremendous **11** magnanimous, outstanding, pretentious, threatening

Big Bend State: 9 Tennessee

big shot: VIP

big toe: 6 hallux

bigener: 4 mule **6** hybrid

bighorn: 5 sheep **6** argali, aoudad **8** cimarron

bight: bay **4** bend, coil, gulf, loop **5** angle, curve, inlet, noose **6** corner, hollow

bignou, biniou: 7 bagpipe

bigot: 6 cafard, zealot **7** fanatic ʮ nypocrite

bigoted: 6 biased, narrow **9** hidebound, illiberal, sectarian **10** intolerant, prejudiced **12** narrow-minded

bijou: 5 jewel **7** trinket

bilbie: 6 refuge **7** shelter

bile: 4 boil, gall, hump **5** venom **6** choler, growth

bilge: 4 scum **5** bouge, bulge

bilingual: diglot

bilk: do; gyp **4** balk, hoax **5** cheat, cozen, trick **6** delude, fleece **7** deceive, defraud, swindle **9** frustrate **10** disappoint

bill: act, dun, law, neb, nib, tab **4** beak, note, peck **5** libel, score **6** caress, charge, indict, pickax, poster, strike **7** invoice, lampoon, mattock, placard, statute **8** billhook, document, headland, petition **9** memoranda(pl.), statement **10** broadsword, memorandum, promontory **13** advertisement
anchor: pee
five dollar: fin, vee
one dollar: **4** buck **8** frogskin
ten dollar: **7** sawbuck

bill of fare: 4 card, menu **5** carte

billabong: 8 waterway

billet: bar, gad, log **4** loop, note, pass, post **5** berth, enrol, house, lodge, order, stick, strap **6** ballot, enroll, harbor, letter, notice, ticket **7** bearing, epistle, harbour, missive, pollack **8** coalfish, document, firewood, ornament, position, quarters **11** appointment, requisition

billfish: gar **8** sailfish **9** spearfish

billiard: *cue:* **4** mace
shot: **5** carom, masse **7** bricole
rod: cue

billiards: 4 game, pool

billingsgate: 5 abuse **7** obloquy **8** ribaldry **12** vituperation

billionaire: 6 nabob

billow: sea **4** wave **5** bulge, float, surge, swell **6** ripple, roller **7** breaker **8** undulate

billowing: 5 tidal **7** surging

billy: caw **4** chap, club, goat, mate **6** cudgel, fellow **7** brother, comrade **8** billikin, bludgeon **9** blackjack

billycock: 5 derby **6** bowler

bin: ark, box, cub **4** bing, cart, crib, vina **5** frame, hutch, pungi, stall, store, wagon **6** basket, bunker, hamper, manger, trough, within **9** container **10** receptacle
coal: **6** bunker
fish: **5** canch, kench

binate: 4 dual **6** double, paired **7** coupled, twofold

bind: jam, tie **4** gird, hold, tape **5** stick **7** confine
comb. form: **5** desmo
to secrecy: **4** tile, tyle
tightly: **4** frap
up in: **6** absorb

binder: 4 band, beam, bond, cord, rope **5** baler, cover, frame, lever **6** fillet, folder, girder, header **9** bondstone

binding: 4 band, cord, rope, tape **5** valid **6** edging, ribbon **7** galloon, mousing, webbing **9** stringent **10** astringent, obligatory **11** restraining, restrictive
limp: **4** yapp

bindle stiff: 4 hobo **5** tramp

binge: bow, hit **4** blow, soak **5** beano, party, spree **6** cringe **8** carousal **9** obeisance

bingo: 4 game, keno **5** lotto **6** brandy

biography: 4 life, vita(It.) **6** memoir **7** account, history, memoire(F.), recount
saint's: **11** hagiography

biological class: 5 genus **6** genera(pl.) **7** species

biological factor: id **4** gene **5** idant

biology: 7 ecology **8** genetics

biose: 11 disaccharid **12** disaccharide

biotic community: 5 biome

biotite: 4 mica **7** anomite

biplane: 4 spad **8** airplane

birch: 4 cane, flog, tree, whip **5** canoe **6** betula **7** hickory

bird: ani, daw, nun, pie, tit **4** avis(L.), crow, kite, lark, ruff, tern, wren **5** brant, egret, finch, hobby, pewee, pewit, raven, robin, snipe, terek, vireo **6** bulbul, dunlin, falcon, hoopoe, linnet, marten, mocker, oriole, phoebe, plover, shrike, thrush **7** bluejay, bustard, buzzard, catbird, flicker, halcyon, irrisor, jackdaw, kinglet, ortolan, peacock, redwing, skylark, sparrow, swallow, tanager, warbler, waxwing **8** airplane, bluebird, boatbill, bobolink, bobwhite, chicadee, grosbeak, kingbird, pheasant, redstart, starling, thrasher **9** blackbird, blackcock, brambling, bullfinch, goldfinch, partridge, phalarope, sandpiper **10** bufflehead, meadowlark, tropicbird, woodpecker **11** butcherbird, hummingbird **12** yellowhammer

bird

adjutant: 5 stork 6 argala 7 hurgila, marabou

African: 4 taha 8 umbrette

American: 4 sora 5 robin, vireo 6 darter, fulmar, turkey 7 grackle, tanager 8 cardinal 10 bufflehead

Antarctic: 4 skua 7 penguin

aquatic: 4 duck, gull, loon, swan, tern 5 goose, grebe, small, terne 7 penguin 8 dabshick, flamingo

aquiline: 5 eagle

Arabian Nights: roc

Arctic: auk 6 fulmar

Asiatic: 4 mine, myna 5 pitta 7 hilltit 8 dotterel 9 brambling, feng-huang, fenghwang

Attic: 11 nightingale

Australian: emu, roa 4 emeu, lory 5 arara 6 leipoa 7 boobook, bustard 8 lorikeet, lyrebird, platypus 9 cassowary, coachwhip, friarbird, pardalote

black: ani, ano, daw, pie 4 crow 5 merle, raven 6 oriole 7 jackdaw 8 starling

brillant plumage: 4 tody 5 jalep 6 oriole, trogon 7 jacamar, tanager 8 pheasant

Central American: daw 4 crow, rave, rook 5 raven 6 magpie 7 corvine, jacamar 8 puffbird

crane-like: 5 wader 6 chunga

crow-family: daw, jay, pie 4 craw 5 raven 7 jackdaw

crying: 6 ramage 7 limpkin

diving: auk

dressing of feathers: 5 preen

emu-like: 11 cassowaries

European: ani, daw, emu, mew, qua 4 cirl, darr, emeu, gled, kite, mall, moro, osel, rook, stag, whim, yite 5 amsel, boonk, glede, mavis, merle, ousel, ouzel, sacer, saker, serin, tarin, terek, terin, whaup 6 avocet, avoset, cushat, gaylag, godwit, linnet, loriot, marten, merlin, missel, redcap, whewer, windle, winnel, wranny 7 bittern, bustard, haybird, kestrel, motacil, ortolan, sakeret, starnel, whiskey, winnard, witwall 8 bargoose, chepster, dotterel, garganey, redstart, wheybird, whimbrel, wrannock, yoldring 9 brambling, gallinule, goldfinch, goosander, peregrine, swinepipe, wheybeard 10 chiffchaff, lammegeyer, turtledove, whitterick 11 capercailie, lammergeier 12 capercailzie

extinct: moa, roc 4 dodo, jibi, kiwi, mamo, rukh 7 offbird

finch-like: 7 chewink, tanager

fish-catching: 6 osprey 9 cormorant

flightless: emu, moa 4 emeu, kiwi 7 apteryx, ostrich, penguin, ratitae 9 solitaire

fly-catching: 8 redstart 9 solitaire

flying backwards: 7 swallow, humming

food: hen 5 capon 6 pullet, turkey 7 chicken, rooster

frigate: ioa, iwa 6 tropic

gallinaceous: 6 peahen 7 peacock, peafowl

game: 5 quail, snipe 6 grouse 8 pheasant

genus: 4 alca, crax, otis 7 certhia 9 apatornis

gull-like: 4 tern 6 jaeger

Hawaiian: io, oo; ava, ioa, iwa 4 iiwi, mamo, moho

heron family: 4 benu, ibis 7 bittern

honey eater: 4 moho

humming: ava 5 carib 7 colibri

insectiverous: owl 5 vireo

jay: gae 6 magpie

large: emu 4 emeu, guan 5 eagle 6 curlew, willet 7 bustard, megapod, ostrich, pelican, seriema 8 curassow, shoebill

lark-like: 5 pipit

long-billed: 5 snipe 7 pelican

long-legged: io 4 sora 5 heron, snipe, stilt, wader 6 avocet, avoset, curlew 7 seriema

long-necked: 4 swan 5 agami, crane, goose, geese(pl.), stork 7 ostrich

male: cob, tom 4 cock 5 drake 6 gander 7 peacock, rooster 11 chanticleer

marsh: 4 sora 5 snipe, stilt

meadow: 8 bobolink

Mexican: 6 jacana, towhee 7 jacamar

mythological: roc 5 hansa 6 simurg 7 phoenix, simurgh

New Zealand: kea, moa 4 kaka, kiwi, kulu, ruru, titi, weka 6 kakapo 7 apterix, apteryx 8 morepork, notornis 10 blightbird

nonpasserine: 4 tody 6 hoopoe, motmot 8 hornbill 10 kingfisher

Northern: auk 6 gannet, puffin

of Athena: owl

of Juno: 7 peacock

of paradise: 8 manucode

of prey: owl 4 hawk, kite 5 eagle, elant 6 eaglet, elanet, owelet 7 goshawk, vulture 9 accipeter

of Zeus: 5 eagle

oldest known: 13 archaeopteryx

oscine: 4 chat 6 dronge, oriole 7 tanager

ostrich-like: emu, moa 4 emeu, rhea 10 cassowarie

parrot-like: 11 budgereegah, budggerygah

parson: poe, tue, tui

parts of body: neb, nib 4 bill, cere, knee, lora, mala 5 lores 6 pecten, pileum, pinion, rostra, syrinx 7 ambiens 8 pectines(pl.)

passerine: 5 finch 7 sparrow, starnel 9 chatterer, coachwhip

pert. to: 5 avian, avine 8 ornithic 9 volucrine

pink: 8 flamingo
plover-like: 5 drome 7 lapwing
Poe's: 5 raven
predatory: owl 4 kite 5 yager 6 falcon, shrike 9 cormorant
protuberance at base of bill: 4 cere
rare: 8 rara avis
ratite: emu, moa 4 emeu 7 ostrich 9 cassowary
red-tailed: 4 koae
sacred: 4 ibis
sea: auk, ern 4 erne, gony, gull, smew, tern 5 eider, solan 6 gannet, petrel, puffin 7 pelican 9 albatross 10 shearwater
shore: ree 4 rail, sora 5 snipe, stilt, wader 6 avocet, avoset, curlew, plover, willet
Sindbad's: roc 4 rock, rukh
singing: 4 lark, wren 5 finch, mavis, robin, shama, veery, vireo 6 canary, linnet, mocker, oriole, oscine, thrush 7 mocking, robinet 8 bobolink, redstart 12 whippoorwill
small: tit 4 tody, wren 5 dicky, pipit, vireo 6 dickey, linnet, siskin, todies(pl.), tomtit 7 creeper, humming, sparrow, titlark, wheater 8 starling 9 didappers
South American: 4 guan, mina, myna 5 chaja, mynah 6 barbet, becard 7 cariama, oilbird 8 bellbird, boatbill, caracara, guacharo, hoactzin, puffbird
swallow-like: 4 cran 5 swift
swimming: 4 loon 5 grebe
talking: 4 crow, mina, mino, myna 5 mynah 6 parrot
tall: 6 avocet, avoset
tropical: ani 4 koae, tody 6 barbet, trogon
unfledged: gor 4 eyas 6 gorlin 8 bubbling, nestling
wading: 4 hern, ibis, rail, sora 5 crane, heron, snipe, stilt, stork 6 avocet, jacana 8 flamingo 9 sandpiper
web-footed: 4 duck, swan 5 drake, goose 6 avocet, avoset, gander
West Indies: 4 tody
white-tailed: ern 4 erne 5 egret
woodcock: 5 pewee
young: eya 4 gull 5 piper 7 flapper, nestler 8 birdikin, nestling 9 fledgling
bird cage: 6 aviary, pinjra, volary, volery 7 paddock
bird clapper: 9 scarecrow
bird crest: 4 tuft
bird eye: 12 cuckoo flower
bird nest: 4 aery, eyry 5 aerie, eyrie
bird of passage: 8 wanderer 9 transient
bird route: 6 flyway
birdman: 6 airman 7 aviator 13 ornithologist
birds: 4 aves

collective: 4 fowl
domesticated: 7 poultry
bird's-eye view: 6 apercu
birdwoman: 8 aviatrix 9 aviatress, aviatrice
biretta, berretta: cap 5 beret 8 skullcap
biri: 9 cigarette
birl: 4 spin, toss, whir 5 whirr 6 rattle, rotate 7 revolve
birma: 6 calaba
birn: 5 brand 6 burden
birr: bur 4 blow, burr, push, rush, wind 5 force, storm, vigor 6 energy, thrust, onrush 7 impetus
birse: 6 temper 7 bristle 8 bristles 10 irritation
birsle: 5 broil, toast 6 scorch 9 scorching
birsy: 7 bristly 9 irritable
birth: 4 bear 6 burden, origin 7 descent, genesis, lineage 8 delivery, geniture, nascency, nativity 9 beginning, naissance, parentage 10 extraction
after: 9 postnatal
before: 8 prenatal
by: nee
goddess: 5 Parca
help with: 8 accouche
new: 10 renascence 11 Renaissance
nobleness: 6 eugeny
pert. to: 5 natal 13 primogenitive
birth flower: *April:* 5 daisy
August: 9 gladiolus
December: 9 poinsetta
February: 8 primrose
January: 9 carnation
July: 8 sweet pea
June: 4 rose
March: 6 violet
May: 15 lily of the valley
November: 13 chrysanthemum
October: 6 dahlia
September: 5 aster
birth stone: *April:* 7 diamond 8 sapphire
August: 9 carnelian
December: 4 ruby
February: 8 amethyst
January: 7 garnet
July: 9 turquoise
June: 5 agate
March: 6 jasper 10 bloodstone
May: 7 emerald
November: 5 topaz
October: 5 beryl
September: 10 chrysolite
birthday: 11 anniversary, celebration
ode: 12 genethliacon
pert. to: 10 genethliac 12 genethliacal
birthmark: 4 mole 5 naeve, nevus 6 naveus 7 blemish, spiloma

pert. to: **7** naevoid
birthplace: 10 incunabula(pl.) **11** incunabulum
birthrate: 8 natality
birthright: 8 heritage
bis: 5 again, twice **6** encore, repeat **7** replica **9** duplicate
Biscay: *island:* Re; Yeu
  language: **6** Basque
biscuit: bun **4** bake(Sc.), roll, rush, snap **5** scone, wafer **6** cookie **7** cracker, pentile, pretzel **8** harutack **9** porcelain **11** earthenware
bisect: 4 fork **5** cross, halve, split **6** cleave, divide **8** separate
bishop: 4 pope **5** angel **6** archer, bustle, priest **7** pontiff, prelate, primate **8** director, overseer **9** clergyman, inspector **13** administrator **14** superintendent
  apron: **7** gremial
  assistant: **6** verger **9** coadjutor
  buskin: **6** caliga **7** caligae(pl.)
  cap: **4** hura **5** miter, mitre **7** biretta **8** berretta, mitrella
  first year revenue: **5** annat **6** annate
  jurisdiction: see **7** diocese
  private room: **9** accubitus
  robe: **6** chimar, chimer **7** chimere
  staff: **7** crosier
  stave: **6** baculi(pl.) **7** baculus
  throne: **4** apse
  title: **4** abba, anba **7** prelate, primate
  vestment: alb **4** cope **6** chimer, rochet **7** gremial, tunicle **8** dalmatic **10** omophórion
bishopric: see **7** diocese **10** episcopacy, episcopate
bishop's weed: 4 ammi **6** ammeos **8** goutweed
bismar: 9 steelyard
bismer: 5 scorn, shame **8** reproach
bison: 6 bovine **7** aurochs, boñasus, buffalo
bisque: 4 soup **5** point **8** ceramics
bisson: 5 blind **8** blinding, purblind
bistro: bar **6** tavern **10** restaurant
bisulcate: 6 cloven
bit: ace, jot, ort, wee **4** atom, bite, curb, doit, food, iota, item, mite, mote, part, snap, tool, whit **5** blade, check, crumb, drill, pezzo, piece, scrap, shred, speck **6** bridle, cannon, eating, morsel, smidge, splice, tittle, trifle **7** morceau(F.), portion, scatche, smidgen, smidgin, smigeon, snaffle **8** fraction, fragment, quantity, smitchin, victuals **9** restraint
  horse's curb: **6** pelham
  Irish: **7** traneen
bit by bit: 9 gradually
bit part: 6 walk-on

bite: bit, cut, eat, nip **4** bait, cham, chew, food, gash, gnap, gnaw, hold, knap, meal, snap **5** chack, chamm, champ, cheat, pinch, seize, smart, snack, sting, trick **6** crunch, morsel, nibble, pierce **7** cheater, corrode, impress, partake, sharper, slander **8** lacerate, puncture, victuals **9** denticate
bite one's tongue: 6 regret
biting: 4 acid, hoar, keen **5** acrid, sharp, snell **6** bitter, rodent, severe **7** caustic, cutting, mordant, nipping, pungent **8** incisive, poignant, scathing, stinging **9** corrosive, sarcastic, trenchant, vitriolic
biting dragon: 8 tarragon
biting of nails: 12 phaneromania
bito: 4 balm, tree **7** hajilij
  oil **6** zachun
bitt: 4 post **5** block
bitter: 4 acid, bask, gall, keen, sore, sour, tart **5** acerb, acrid, amara, bleak, harsh, irate, sharp **6** biting, picric, severe **7** austere, caustic, crabbed, cutting, galling, painful, pungent, satiric **8** poignant, stinging, virulent **9** malicious **11** acrimonious, distressful
bitter apple: 9 colocynth
bitter bush: 9 snakeroot
bitter gentian: 9 baldmoney
bitter grass: 9 colicroot
bitter oak: 6 cerris
bitter spar: 8 dolomite
bitter vetch: ers **5** vicia
bitter wintergreen: 10 pipsissewa
bittern: 4 bump **5** boonk, heron **6** kakkak
bitterness: rue **4** acor, bile, fell, gall **5** atter **6** enmity, malice, rancor **7** amarity **8** acerbity, acrimony, severity **9** amaritude, hostility, poignancy, virulence **11** malevolence
bitters: 4 amer(F.) **5** tonic **6** liquor
  pert. to: **9** amaroidal
bittersweet: 10 confection, nightshade
bitterweed: 7 ragweed **9** horseweed **10** sneezeweed
bitterwort: 7 felwort **9** dandelion
bitumen: tar **5** pitch **7** asphalt **8** alkitran **9** alchitran, elaterite
bivalve: 4 clam, spat **6** cockle, diatom, mussel, oyster **7** mollusk, Pandora, scallop **10** brachiopod
  genus: **5** pinna **6** anomia **7** toheroa **12** gastrochaena
bivocal: 9 diphthong
bivouac: 4 camp **5** etape, watch **6** encamp **10** encampment
biwa: 6 loquat

bizarre: odd 5 antic, dedal, outre, queer 6 quaint 7 curious 8 fanciful 9 eccentric, fantastic, grotesque 10 ridiculous 11 extravagant

Bizet opera: 6 Carmen

blab: 4 chat 5 blart, blate, clack 6 babble, betray, gossip, reveal, tattle 7 blabber, chatter 8 telltale

black: jet 4 calo, dark, ebon, foul, inky 5 dusky, murky, Negro, noire(F.), raven, sable, sooty 6 atrous, dismal, gloomy, pitchy, sullen 7 melanic, Negrito, swarthy, unclean 8 mournful 9 atrocious 10 blackamoor, calamitous, forbidding
and white: 11 chiaroscuro
comb. form: 4 atra, atro, mela 5 melan 6 melano

black and blue: 5 livid
spot: 6 bruise, shiner 10 ecchymosis

black art: 5 magic 7 alchemy 8 wizardy 10 necromancy 11 conjuration

black cod: 6 beshow

black death: 6 plague

black diamond: oil 4 coal 8 hematite

black earth: 4 mold 9 chernozem

black elder: 9 hackberry

black eye: 5 shame 6 bruise, shiner 7 scandal

black-eyed Susan: 6 ketmia 10 coneflower

black grunt: 10 tripletail

black hole: 4 cell 7 dungeon 8 solitary

black plague: 7 bubonic

Black Sea: *city:* 5 Batum 6 Odessa
old name: 6 Euxine
peninsula: 6 Crimea
pert. to: 6 Pontic
river to: Bug, Don 4 Prut 6 Danube 7 Dnieper 8 Dniester

black sheep: 7 deviate 9 reprobate

black widow: 6 spider 7 pokomoo

blackamoor: 5 bleck, Negro 7 negress

blackball: 4 pill 6 ballot 7 exclude, heeball 9 ostracize

blackberry: 6 agawam 8 dewberry

blackbird: ani, daw, pie 4 crow, merl 5 amsel, colly, merle, ousel, ouzel, raven 6 colley 7 jackdaw

blackboard: 5 slate

blackcap: 4 gull 7 warbler 8 chicadee, titmouse 9 raspberry

blackdamp: 9 chokedamp

blacken: ink, tar 4 char, soot 5 bleck, cloud, japan, sully 6 darken, defame, malign, vilify 7 asperse, slander, traduce 8 besmirch 10 calumniate

blackface: 5 actor, comic, sheep 8 boldface, minstrel

blackfin: 4 fish 5 cisco, sesis

blackfish: 5 whale 6 tautog 10 nigrescent

school: 5 grind

blackguard: 4 shag 5 gamin, guard, snuff 7 vagrant 8 criminal, hanger-on, vagabond 9 scoundrel

blackhead: 6 comedo

blackjack: oak 4 club, duck, flag, game, jack 5 billy 6 beetle, jerkin, vessel, weapon

blackleg: 4 scab, snob 7 disease, gambler 8 apostate, swindler 13 strikebreaker

blacklist: ban 4 veto

blackmail: 5 bribe 6 coerce, extort 7 payment, tribute

blackmailer: 5 ghoul 7 leecher

blackmailing: 8 chantage 9 extortion

Blackmore heroine: 10 Lorna Doone

blackout: 6 darken 8 darkness, scrounge 11 suppression

blacksmith: gow 5 shoer, smith 6 plover, smithy, stithy 7 farrier, striker 10 horseshoer
shop: 5 anvil, stith 6 smithy, stithy 8 smithery

blacksnake: 4 whip 5 racer, quirt

blackhorn: haw 4 sloe

Blackwater State: 8 Nebraska

blackwort: 8 comfrey

bladder: sac 7 blister, inflate, vesicle
comb. form: 4 asco

blade: bit, fop, oar 4 blow, bone, edge, leaf, shiv 5 blood, dandy, fluke, grain, knife, spark, spear, spire, sword 6 cutter, lamina, scythe, sickle 7 gallant, laminae(pl.), scapula 9 propeller

blae: blo 4 blue, gray 5 bleak, livid 7 sunless 10 unbleached

blague: lie 4 hoax 6 humbug 8 claptrap, raillery

blah: 4 bunk 8 nonsense

blain: 4 sore 5 bulla 7 blister, inflame, pustule 8 swelling

blake: wan 4 pale 6 yellow 9 colorless

Blake's symbol: 4 Zoas

blamable: 6 faulty 8 culpable 11 blameworthy 13 reprehensible

blame: 4 call, hurt, onus, twit 5 chide, fault, guilt, odium, shend 6 accuse, charge, dirdum, rebuke, revile, scance 7 ascribe, censure, condemn, obloquy, reproof, reprove, upbraid 8 reproach 9 challenge, criticism, inculpate 10 accusation 11 culpability, reprobation 12 reprehension 13 animadversion
deserving: 8 culpable

blameless: 7 perfect 8 innocent, spotless 9 faultless, righteous 14 irreproachable

blanch: 4 fade, pale 5 chalk, scald, white 6 argent, bleach, blench, whiten 8 etiolate 9 whitewash

bland: 4 kind, mild, oily, open, soft 5 suave 6 benign, genial, gentle, smooth, urbane 7 affable, amiable, lenient 8 gracious 9 benignant, courteous

blandish: 4 coax 5 charm 6 allure, blanch, cajole 7 flatter, wheedle 10 compliment

blank: 4 bare, flan, form, shot, void 5 annul, blind, break, clean, empty, range, space 6 vacant 7 nonplus, unmixed, vacuous 8 unfilled 9 colorless, downright, fruitless, frustrate

blanket: 4 brot, wrap 5 cotta, cover, layer, manta, quilt, sheet, throw 6 afghan, poncho, serape 8 coverlet 10 barraclade

cowboy: 5 sugan 6 soogan, sougan, sugann

goat's hair: 6 cumbly

horse: 5 manta

Indian: 6 stroud

blare: 4 peal 5 blast, noise 6 blazon 7 fanfare, tantara, trumpet 11 flamboyance

blarney: 5 stone 6 butter 7 flatter, wheedle 8 flattery

blase: 5 bored, sated, weary 8 satiated 9 surfeited 11 indifference

blaspheme: 5 abuse, curse 6 revile 7 defame, profane 10 calumniate

blasphemy: 7 calumny, cursing, impiety 8 anathema, swearing 9 profanity, sacrilege 10 execration 11 imprecation, irreverence, malediction 12 vilification

blast: bub, nip, wap 4 bang, blow, gale, gust, ruin, wind 5 split, stunt 6 attack, blight, wither 7 bluster, explode, shatter, shrivel 8 dynamite, outburst, proclaim 9 discharge, explosion 10 detonation

blast furnace: *lower part:* 4 bosh

nozzle: 6 tuyere

blat: 5 bleat, blurt

blatant: 4 glib, loud 5 gross, noisy, silly, vocal 6 coarse, vulgar 8 brawling 9 bellowing, clamorous, inelegant, obtrusive 10 vociferous

blate: 4 blab, dull, pale, slow 5 blunt, prate, timid 7 bashful, ghastly 8 sheepish 9 diffident 10 spiritless

blather: 4 stir 5 bleat 6 babble 7 blither, prattle 8 nonsense 9 commotion

blaubok: 5 etaac 8 antelope

blaw: 4 blow, brag 5 boast

blaze: 4 burn, fire, glow, mark, shot 5 flame, flare, flash, glare, gleam, glory, shine, torch 6 bleeze 7 bonfire, pioneer 8 splendor 9 firebrand 10 effulgence 11 coruscation 13 conflagration

blazer: 6 jacket

blazon: 4 deck, show 5 adorn, blare, boast 6 depict, shield 7 declare, display, exhibit, publish 8 emblazon, inscribe 9 delineate, embellish 11 description, publication 14 representation

bleach: sun 5 chalk 6 blanch, blench, chlore, purify, whiten 7 decolor, lighten 8 etiolate

bleachers: 5 seats, stand 10 grandstand

bleaching vat: 4 keir, kier

bleak: dim, raw 4 blae, blay, cold, gray, pale 5 sprat 6 bitter, bleach, dismal, dreary, frigid, pallid 7 cutting 8 desolate 9 cheerless 10 depressing

fish: 4 blay, bley 5 sprat

blear: dim 4 blur, dull 6 darken 7 deceive, mislead 8 hoodwink, protrude

bleared: 4 inky 5 dusky 6 rheumy

bleat: baa 4 blat, blea 5 blart 7 blather, bluster, whicker

bleb: 4 blob 5 bulla 6 bubble 7 blister, pustule, vesicle 8 swelling

bleed: 4 flow, leak, shed 6 escape, extort 7 agonize

bleeding heart: 8 dicentra

blemish: mar 4 blot, blur, dent, flaw, gall, lack, mark, rift, scar, slur, spot, vice, want 5 blame, breck, crack, fault, mulct, speck, sully, tache, taint 6 blotch, breach, defame, defect, impair, injure, macula, macule, smirch, stigma 7 default, failing, fissure, maculae(pl.) 9 birthmark, deformity, discredit, disfigure 10 defacement, deficiency 12 imperfection 13 disfigurement

wood: 4 mote

wound: 4 scar 8 cicatrix 9 cicatrice

blench: 4 foil, shun, wile 5 avoid, elude, evade, quail, shake, shirk, trick 6 baffle, blanch, bleach, flinch, recoil, shrink 7 deceive 9 stratagem 10 disconcert

blend: mix 4 blot, fuse, join, meng 5 blind, cream, merge, shade, spoil, stain, tinge, unite 6 commix, dazzle, mingle 7 combine, confuse, corrupt, deceive, mixture, pollute 8 coalesce, tincture 9 admixture, associate, commingle, harmonize 10 amalgamate 11 incorporate

blended: 5 fondu, mixed 6 merged 7 mingled 9 confluent

blesbok: 5 nunni 8 antelope, blesbuck

bless: 4 keep, sain, wave 5 adore, anele, bensh(Yid.), extol, favor, guard, thank, wound 6 favour, hallow, praise, thrash 7 approve, beatify, glorify, protect 8 macarize, preserve, sanctify 10 consecrate, felicitate

blessed: 4 holy 5 happy 6 divine, joyful, sacred 8 benedict, bhagavat, blissful, hallowed 9 beatified, benedight 11 consecrated

blessing: 4 boon, gift 5 bliss, grace 6 praise 7 benison, worship 8 felicity 9 beatitude 10 benedicite, beneficent 11 benediction

blether: See blather

blight: nip 4 ruin, rust, smut 5 blast, frost 6 mildew, wither 7 destroy 9 frustrate

blimp: 7 airship, balloon, colonel

blind: bet, pot 4 ante, dark, dull, hood 5 blank, blend, dunch, shade, stake, wager 6 ambush, bisson, dazzle, screen, secret 7 aimless, bandage, benight, eclipse, execate, eyeless, obscure, pretext, shutter 8 abortive, artifice, bayardly, blinding, hoodwink, ignorant, involved, jalousie, outshine, purblind 9 benighted, concealed, deceitful, defective, insensate, intricate, senseless, sightless 10 incomplete, misleading, subterfuge
as a hawk: 4 seel
part of: 4 slat
printing for: 7 braille

blind alley: 7 dead end, impasse 8 cul-de-sac

blind god: 4 Hoth 5 Hoder, Hothr

blind me: 5 blimy

blind pig: 4 dive 6 saloon

blind spot: 6 hang-up 7 bigotry

blind staggers: gid 7 vertigo

blind worm: 5 orvet

blinder: 4 flap 5 bluff 7 blinker 8 hoodwink 9 blindfold 11 obstruction

blindfold: 4 dark 5 blink, bluff 7 bandage, blinder, obscure 8 heedless, hoodwink, reckless 9 concealed

blindness: 6 bisson, cecity 7 ablepsy, anopsia 8 ablepsia 9 ignorance
color: 13 achromatopsia 14 monochromatism
day: 11 hemeralopia
partial: 7 meropia 10 cecutiency
snow: 10 chiona-blepsia

blink: 4 shun, wink 5 blush, cheat, flash, gleam, shine, trick 6 glance, ignore, obtuse 7 blinter, condone, glimmer, glimpse, neglect, nictate, sparkle, twinkle 9 blindfold

blinker: eye 5 bluff, light 6 signal 7 blinder, goggles 8 coquette, hoodwink, mackerel

blinking: 5 utter 8 blooming, complete

blintze: 7 pancake

bliss: joy 4 Eden, kaif, seil(Sc.) 5 glory 7 delight, ecstacy, gladden, rapture 8 felicity, gladness, paradise, pleasure 9 happiness 11 contentment
place of: 4 Eden 6 Utopia 7 Elysium 8 Paradise

blissful: 4 holy 6 blithe 7 blessed, Elysian, Utopian 9 beatified, glorified

blister: 4 beat, bleb, blob, lash 5 blain, bulge 6 bubble, scorch 7 vesicle 8 vesicate 10 vesicatory

blithe: gay 4 glad 5 bonny, happy, jolly, merry 6 bonnie, jovial, joyous, lively 7 gaysome, jocular, winsome 8 cheerful, gladsome 9 sprightly

blitzkrieg: 4 raid 5 blitz 6 attack 11 bombardment

blizzard: 4 blow, gale, wind 5 purga 6 retort 9 snowstorm, squelcher

Blizzard State: 11 South Dakota

bloat: 5 puffy, swell 6 expand, tumefy 7 distend, ferment, inflate 8 drunkard

bloated: 5 bloat, cured 6 sodden, turgid 7 pompous

blob: lip, wen 4 bleb, blot, boil, daub, drop, lump, mark, mass 6 bubble, pimple, splash 7 blemish, blister, blossom, globule, postule, splotch 8 globular

bloc: 4 ring 5 cabal, party, union 6 clique 7 faction 11 combination

block: ame, bar, cob, dam, hob, nog, row, vol 4 bloc, cake, clog, cube, foil, head, mass, stop 5 check, chump, deter, nudge, parry, shape, spike, stump 6 hamper, hinder, impede, oppose, outwit, square, street, stymie, taplet, thwart 7 buckler, inhibit, outline, prevent 8 blockade, obstacle, obstruct, stoppage 9 barricade, blockhead, frustrate, hindrance 11 obstruction
architectural: 6 dentil, mutule
electrically insulated: 6 taplet
football: 4 clip
for shaping metal objects: ame
ice: 4 cube 5 serac
mechanical: 6 pulley
metal type: 4 quad, quod
nautical: 7 deadeye
perforated: nut
small: 7 tessera

blockade: dam 5 beset, block, siege 6 whisky 7 embargo 8 obstruct 9 beleaguer 11 obstruction, restriction

blockhead: ass, oaf 4 bust, coof, dolt, fool, mome 5 block, chump, cuddy, idiot, ninny 6 noodle 7 dizzard, half-wit, tomfool 8 beefhead, clodpate, gamphrel, hardhead 9 blockpate, grouthead, hoddy-peak, numbskull, screwball, simpleton 10 beetlehead, dunderhead, hoddy-doddy

blockhouse: 4 fort

bloke: man 4 chap, toff 6 fellow 9 personage

blonde: 4 fair 5 light 6 flaxen, golden, yellow

blood: kin, sap 4 gore, life, mood, race 5 blade, fluid, serum, stock 6 indred 7 gallant, kinship, kinsman, lineage, youstir(Sc.) 8 relation 9 lifeblood 14 consanguineous
comb. form: 4 hema, hemo 5 haemo
deficiency: 6 anemia 7 anaemia

disease: 8 leucemia, leukemia 9 leucaemia, leukaemia

fluid part: 5 serum 6 plasma 7 opsonin

mixed: See **hybrid**

of the gods: 4 icor 5 ichor

particle in: 7 embolus

poisoning: 6 pyemia 7 pyaemia, toxemia 10 septicemia

stagnation: 4 clot 5 cruor, grume 6 stasis, stases

strain: 4 race 5 stock 6 family

testing instrument: 13 hemabarometer 14 haemabarometer

blood and thunder: 6 uproar 8 violence 9 melodrama

blood brother: 6 friend 8 intimate

blood feud: 8 vendetta

blood fine: cro(Sc.) 4 eric 7 galanas, wergild 9 bloodwite

blood horse: 12 thoroughbred

blood money: cro 7 breaghe

blood pudding: 7 sausage

blood relationship: 7 kinsman 8 relative 13 consanguinity

blood vessel: 4 vein 5 hemad 6 artery 9 capillary

comb. form: vas

rupture: 6 rhexis

bloodbath: 8 massacre

bloodcurdling: 8 horrible 10 terrifying

blooded: 9 pedigreed 12 thoroughbred

bloodhound: 4 lyam, lyme

bloodless: 4 dead 6 anemic 7 anaemic, inhuman 8 lifeless 9 unfeeling 10 exsanguine

bloodroot: 7 puccoon 10 tetterwort

bloodshed: 5 death 7 carnage 8 violence 9 slaughter

bloodshot: red 8 inflamed

bloodstone: 10 chalcedony

bloodsucker: 5 leech 7 sponger 11 extortioner

bloodthirsty: 6 bloody, carnal 9 ferocious, murderous 10 sanguinary

bloody: 4 gory 5 cruel 6 cruent 8 bleeding, hematose, infamous 9 cruentous, ferocious, haematose, merciless, murderous 10 sanguinary 12 bloodstained, bloodthirsty, contemptible

bloodybones: 7 specter 9 hobgoblin

bloom (see also **flower**): dew 4 blow 7 blossom, blowing 8 floreate, flourish 13 efflorescence

bloomer: 5 error 6 blower 7 blunder, failure

bloomery: 5 forge 6 hearth 7 furnace

blooming: 4 rosy 5 green 6 abloom, florid

blooper: 5 error, radio 7 blunder, blowing, roseate 8 blinking 10 prospering.

blossom (see also **flower**): bud 4 blob 5 bloom 7 prosper 8 flourish 13 efflorescence

small: 8 floweret

blot: mar 4 blob, blue, daub, soil, spot 5 blend, erase, smear, speck, stain, sully 6 blotch, cancel, damage, efface, impair, macula, shadow, smirch, smudge, smutch, stigma 7 blemish, eclipse, expunge, maculae(pl.), obscure, tarnish 8 disgrace, reproach 9 bespatter 10 obliterate, stigmatize 12 obliteration 13 disfigurement

blotch: dab 4 blot, gout, spot 5 patch, smear, stain 6 macula, mottle, smirch, stigma 7 blemish, maculae(pl.), pustule, splotch 8 eruption, maculate

blouse: 5 shirt, smock, tunic 7 casaque 10 shirtwaist

bushman's: 5 bluey

blow: bob, cob, cop, dub, jab, pat, rap, tap, wap 4 ande, baff, bang, bash, beat, belt, biff, birr, blad, blaw, brag, buff, bump, chap, conk, crig, cuff, daud, dint, dird, drub, dunt, dush, fleg, gale, gowf, huff, jolt, knap, lash, mint, oner, pant, plug, puff, scud, slam, slap, slug, sock 5 binge, blade, blast, blizz, bloom, boast, brunt, burst, clink, clour, clout, clump, crump, curse, douse, dowse, filip, flack, flick, gowff, ictus, impel, knock, peise, shock, skite, slipe, sound, spend, storm, swipe, thump, whack, whang 6 bensel, bensil, betray, bounce, buffet, depart, dirdum, expand, fillip, flower, frolic, larrup, wallop 7 assault, attaint, bensail, bensall, bensell, blossom, blowout, bluster, boaster, destroy, inflate, publish, shatter, whample 8 boasting, calamity, confound, disaster, disclose 9 bastinado

in: 5 enter 6 arrive

mock: 5 feint

over: end 4 pass 7 subside

to: 5 treat

up: 5 scene 7 explode, inflate 8 dynamite, outburst

blower: fan 5 whale 6 puffer 7 bloomer 8 braggart 9 swellfish 11 sacheverell

blowfish: 6 puffer

blowfly: 10 bluebottle

blowgun: 10 peashooter

blowhard: 8 braggart

blowhole: 7 nostril 8 spiracle

blown: 5 stale, tired 6 opened 7 blossom, swollen, tainted 8 betrayed, flyblown, inflated 9 distended, exhausted, worthless

blowout: 4 blow, feed, meal 6 valley 10 depression

blowze: 5 trull, wench, woman 6 hoyden 8 slattern

blowzed: red 5 ruddy 7 flushed

blowzy: 5 dowdy 6 frowzy 10 disheveled, slatternly

blub: 4 bulb 5 swell 6 puffed 7 blubber, swollen

blubber: cry, fat 4 blub, foam, wail, weep 5 swell, thick, whine 6 bubble, flitch, medusa, nettle, seethe 7 blobber, bluster, swollen, whimper 9 disfigure

remove: 6 flense

whale: 5 fenks, speck 6 muktuk

blubbery: fat 5 obese 7 swollen 9 quivering 10 gelatinous 11 protuberant

bludgeon: bat, hit 4 club, mace 5 billy, stick 6 coerce, weapon

blue: low, sad, sky 4 aqua, bice, glum 5 azure, livid, perse, small 6 cobalt, gloomy, indigo, severe 7 celeste, gentian, learned, lobelia 8 cerulean, cynanine, dejected, literary 9 turquoise 10 despondent, melancholy

asbestos: 11 crocidolite

gray: 5 merle, pearl, slate 7 cesious 8 caesious

green: 4 bice, teal 5 beryl 8 calamine

red: 5 smalt 6 mallow 8 gridelin, mazarine 9 gris-de-lin

sheep: 6 bharal

blue blood: 5 noble 10 aristocrat 12 bluestocking

blue boneset: 10 mistflower

blue catalpa: 9 paulownia

blue-chip: 9 exemplary 11 prestigious

blue dandelion: 7 chicory

blue dye herb: 4 woad

Blue Eagle agency: NRA

blue earth: 10 kimberlite

Blue Grotto site: 5 Capri, Italy•

blue gum: 4 tree 10 eucalyptus

Blue Hen State: 8 Delaware

blue huckleberry: 11 tangleberry

blue jaundice: 8 cyanosis

blue jeans: 5 levis 6 denims

blue Joe: 8 bluegill

blue John: 4 milk

Blue Law State: 11 Connecticut

blue-pencil: 4 edit 6 delete, redact

blue peter: 4 coot, flag 9 gallinule

blue-ribbon: top 4 best 7 supreme

Bluebeard's wife: 6 Fatima

bluebonnet: cap 4 Scot 7 bluecap 8 Scotsman 10 cornflower

bluebottle: 5 bluet 7 barbeau, blowfly 8 hyacinth

bluecap: 4 Scot 10 bluebonnet

bluefish: 4 bass, tuna 5 saury 8 weakfish

bluegill: 7 sunfish

bluegrass: poa 9 agropyron 10 andropogon

Bluegrass State: 8 Kentucky

bluejacket: gob, tar 6 sailor

bluejoint: 6 redtop

bluenose: 4 snob 8 moralist 11 Nova Scotian

bluepoint: 6 oyster

blueprint: map 4 plan, plot 5 draft, trace 6 sketch 7 diagram 9 cyanotype

bluer: 4 anil

bluerocket: 9 monkshood

blues: 4 song 5 dumps 6 cafard 7 megrims 10 melancholy, mulligrubs 11 despondency

bluestocking: 5 woman 12 intellectual

bluet: 5 plant 10 bluebottle 11 farkleberry

bluethroat: 7 warbler

bluey: 6 bundle 7 blanket

bluff: 4 bank, brag, curt, fool, rude 5 blunt, burly, cliff, frank, gruff, short, surly 6 abrupt, crusty 7 blinder, blinker, brusque, deceive, uncivil 8 barranca, barranco, churlish, hoodwink, impolite 9 blindfold, outspoken, precipice 13 unceremonious

Bluff King Hal: 5 Henry

blunder: err, mix 4 balk, bull, flub, gaff, roil, slip, stir 5 boner, botch, break, error, fault, lapse, misdo 6 boggle, bumble, bungle, gazabo, gazebo, mingle, muddle 7 bloomer, confuse, derange, failure, fauxpas, mistake, stumble 8 solecism 9 confusion, mismanage 11 disturbance

blunderbuss: gun 9 espingole

blunge: mix 5 blend 10 amalgamate

blunk: 6 bungle 9 mismanage

blunt: 4 bald, curt, damp, dull, flat 5 bluff, brusk, inert, plain, plump, stunt 6 clumsy, deaden, obtund, obtuse, stupid 7 brusque 8 hebetate 9 depressed, downright 10 point-blank 11 insensitive 13 unceremonious

mentally: 8 hebitate

blur: dim, hum 4 blob, blot, mist, soil, spot 5 blear, cloud, smear, stain, sully 6 mackle, macule, smudge, stigma 7 blemish, obscure 9 disfigure

blurb: ad 4 puff, rove 5 brief 6 notice 12 announcement, commendation 13 advertisement

blush: 4 glow, look 5 blink, color, flush, gleam, tinge 6 glance, mantle, redden 8 likeness 10 appearance, rubescence

blushing: red 4 rosy 5 ruddy 7 roseate 8 flushing 9 rosaceous 10 erubescent 11 embarrassed

bluster: 4 blow, huff, rage, rant 5 blast, bleat, boast, bully, noise, storm, swank 6 babble, bellow, bounce, hector, huffle, tumult 7 blubber, bravado, gauster, roister, swagger 8 boasting, bullying, threaten 9 confusion, gasconade 10 swaggering, turbulence 11 fanfaronade, rodomontade

bo, boh: 5 chief 6 leader 7 captain

boa: 5 aboma, scarf, snake 8 anaconda 9 neckpiece

boa contrictor: 5 snake 6 giboia

Boadicea's people: 5 Iceni

boar: hog, sus 4 aper 5 swine 6 barrow, hogget 8 sanglier 9 hoggaster
head: 4 hure
wound: 4 gore 5 ganch

board: 4 deal, diet, eats, fare, keep, lath, slat 5 enter, found, house, lodge, meals, panel, plank, stage 6 accost, planch, shield 7 cabinet, council, duoviri, enplane, entrain, planche 8 approach, tribunal 9 authority, shipboard 10 commission, management, provisions 11 switchboard 13 entertainment

boast: gab 4 blaw, blow, brag, crow, pomp, rave 5 brave, extol, exult, glory, prate, roose, scold, skite, vapor, vaunt 6 bounce, clamor, extoll, flaunt, menace(Sc.), outcry, splore 7 bluster, clamour, display, glorify, swagger 8 flourish, threaten 9 gasconade 11 rodomontade

boaster: 5 skite 6 crower, gascon, pedant 7 bouncer, bravado, cracker, ruffler 8 blowhard, braggart, cacofogo, fanfaron, glorioso, jingoist, rodomont 9 cacafuego 11 braggadocio

boastful: big 6 parado 8 fanfaron 9 gasconade, kompology 11 rodomontade, thrasonical

boat (see also **canoe, ship, vessel**): ark, cat, cot, gig, tub 4 bark, brig, carv, dory, junk, raft, scow, ship, skag, tack, trow, yawl 5 aviso, barca, barge, bully, canoe, coble, craft, dingy, ferry, ketch, liner, shell, skiff, skift, smack, xebec, zebec 6 baidak, bateau, carvel, chebec, cruise, cutter, dinghy, dugout, garvey, packet, vessel, zebeck 7 bateaus, chebeck, coracle, gondola, lighter, nacelle, pinnace, scooter, steamer 8 pessoner, schooner 9 submarine, transport 10 watercraft
coal cargo: 7 collier
comb form: 5 scapo
deck: 4 poop 5 orlop
engine-driven: 6 sampan
fishing: 8 bracozzo
flat-bottomed: bac 4 dory, punt, scow 5 barge 6 bateau
freight: 7 lighter
front: bow 4 prow
garbage: 6 hopper
harbor: tug 5 barge 7 bumboat
joint: 4 jerl
merchant: 6 argosy, holcad
ornamental: 9 navicella
part: bow 4 beam, deck, hold, keel, prow 5 bilge, cabin, stern 6 bridge, gunnel, kelson, saloon, thwart 7 capstan, gunwale,

keelson, painter, scupper 12 companionway
pin: 5 thole
post: poy 4 biff 7 bollard, capstan 9 sternpost
power: tug
propellant: oar, row 4 pole 5 motor, scull
racing: gig 5 scull
ride: row 4 sail 6 cruise
round: 4 gufa 5 goofa 6 goofah
sailing: 4 pram, proa 5 praam, prahu
undersea: sub 9 submarine 11 submersible

boatman: 6 barger, Charon 7 hobbler, hoveler, huffler 8 hoveller 9 gondolier 10 barcajuolo

boatswain: 5 bosun 6 serang
whistle: 4 pipe

Boaz: *son:* 4 Obed
wife: 4 Ruth

bob: bow, cut, dab, job, rap, tap 4 ball, blow, buff, calf, clip, coin, cork, duck, grub, jeer, jerk, jest, knob, mock, worm 5 bunch, cheat, dance, filch, float, flout, shake, taunt, trick 6 bingle, buffet, curtsy, delude, pommel, strike, weight 7 bobsled, bobtail, cluster, curtesy, haircut, pendant, refrain 8 shilling 9 bobsleigh

bobac: 6 marmot

bobber: 4 cork, duck 5 float 6 bobfly 7 dropper 8 deadhead

bobbery: 6 hubbub, tumult 8 squabble 11 disturbance

bobbie, bobby: cop 4 bull 6 peeler 7 officer 9 policeman

bobbin: pin 4 cord, pirn, reel 5 braid, quill, spool 7 ratchet, spindle 8 cylinder 10 cuckoopint
frame: 5 ereel
pin: 7 spindle

bobble: dib 6 fumble

bobcat: 4 lynx

bobolink: 4 bird, reed 7 bunting, ortolan 10 butterbird

bobsled: bob 6 ripper

bobtail: bob, cur 4 dock 6 rabble, strunt(Sc.) 7 curtail 8 sheepdog 9 deficient 11 abbreviated

bobwhite: 4 bird 5 colin, quail

bocardo: 6 dokhma, prison 7 bokardo

Boccaccio work: 9 Decameron

bodacious: 8 reckless

bode: 4 omen, stop 5 augur, offer 6 herald 7 message, portend, presage 8 forebode, forecast, foreshow, foretell, indicate 9 messenger 10 inaugurate 13 foreshadowing, prognosticate

bodice: 4 jupe 5 choli, gilet, waist 6 basque, corset

bodiless: 9 trunkless 11 incorporeal

bodily: 5 solid 6 actual, carnal 7 fleshly, somatic 8 corporal, entirely, material, physical 9 corporeal 10 completely 11 corporeally, substantial
bodily motion: 5 shrug 7 gesture
boding: 7 ominous 10 foreboding, prediction, prognostic
bodkin: awl, pin 6 dagger, needle 7 hairpin, poniard 8 stiletto 9 eyeleteer
body: 4 bole, bouk, bulk, form, mass, nave, rupa, soma, stem 5 flesh, stiff, torso, trunk 6 corpse, corpus, extent, licham, person 7 cadaver, carcass, company 8 extensum, majority 9 curcurbit, substance 10 assemblage, foundation 11 association, corporation
  anterior part of: 7 prosoma
  armor: 4 tace 6 corium
  away from center: 6 distal
  cavity: 5 sinus 6 coelom 7 coelome
  comb. form: 4 soma 6 somato
  fluid: 5 blood, lymph, serum 6 plasma, saliva
  heavenly: sun 4 luna, moon, star 5 comet 6 meteor, planet 8 asteroid, luminary
  joint: hip 4 knee 5 elbow, wrist 8 shoulder
  motion: 7 gesture
  of men: 5 posse 10 authorized
  of persons: 5 corps, posse
  of water: bay, sea 4 gulf, lake, pond, pool 5 ocean 6 lagoon, sealet 9 reservoir
  path: 5 orbit
  pert. to: 5 somal 8 physical, systemic
  wagon: box
  wall: 6 paries, septum
body politic: 4 weal 9 community
bodyguard: 5 thane 6 escort 7 retinue, trabant 9 lifeguard
Boeotia: *capital:* 6 Thebes
  region: 5 Ionia
Boer: *dialect:* 4 Taal
  general: 5 Botha
bog: bug, car, fen, gog, hag 4 bold, carr, cess, mire, moor, moss, ooze, sink, slew, slue, syrt 5 marsh, saucy, swamp 6 morass, muskeg, slough 7 forward 8 quagmire 9 conceited
bog down: 4 mire 5 stall 6 bemire
bogey: bug, cow, hag 5 bogie, bogle, devil, gnome 6 boggle, booger, goblin 7 boggard, boggart, bugaboo, bugbear, gnomide, specter, spectre 9 hobgoblin, scarecrow 10 bullbeggar
boggle: jib, shy 4 balk, foil, stop 5 alarm, botch, demur, scare, start 6 baffle, bungle, goblin, shrink 7 bauchle, blunder, perplex, scruple 8 frighten, hesitate 9 dissemble, embarrass 10 difficulty

boggy: wet 4 miry, soft 5 gouty, fenny, haggy, mossy 6 quaggy, swampy 7 boggish, queachy
bogle: 5 alarm, scare 6 goblin
bogus: 4 fake, sham 5 false, phony 8 spurious 10 fictitious 11 counterfeit
bogy: See **bogey.**
Bohemian: 4 arty 5 gipsy, gypsy 6 Picard
  dance: 6 redowa
boil: sty 4 bile, blob, buck, coct, cook, rage, sore, stew, stye, teem 5 botch, brede, steam 6 betray, bubble, buller, burble, decoct, seethe, simmer 7 anthrax, estuate, inflame 8 aestuate, ebullate 10 ebbulliate, effervesce
  almost: 5 scald
  down: 6 decoct
boiler: 4 reef 6 copper, kettle, retort 7 alembic, caldron, furnace 8 cauldron
  plate: 4 sput
  tube scaler: 6 sooter
boisterous: 4 gurl, loud, rude 5 burly, gurly, noisy, rough, windy 6 coarse, stormy, strong, unruly 7 furious, massive, roaring, violent 8 cumbrous, strident, vehement 9 clamorous, excessive, excitable 10 blustering, tumultuous, unyielding
bold: big, bog, yep 4 derf, pert, rash, rude, yepe 5 bardy, bield, brash, brave, brent, frack, freak, freck, gally, hardy, large, manly, nervy, peart, saucy, steep, stout 6 abrupt, audace, brassy, brazen, crouse, daring, fierce, heroic, strong 7 assured, dashing, defiant, forward, grivois, haughty, massive, valiant 8 arrogant, familiar, fearless, grivoise, immodest, impudent, intrepid, malapert, powerful, resolute 9 audacious, bodacious, confident, dauntless, imprudent, undaunted 10 courageous, forritsome 11 venturesome 12 enterprising, overassuming, presumptuous, stout-hearted 13 overconfident
boldness: 4 brow 5 bield, nerve, vigor 6 daring 7 bravery, courage 8 audacity, temerity 9 assurance, hardiesse, hardihood, hardiness 10 brazenness, confidence, effrontery 11 intrepidity, presumption 13 dauntlessness
bole: 4 clay, dose, stem 5 bolus, crypt, trunk 7 opening
bolero: 5 dance, waist 6 jacket
Bolero composer: 5 Ravel
bolide: 6 meteor 7 missile
Bolivia: *animal:* 6 vicuna
  city: 5 La Paz(c.), Oruro, Sucre(c.) 6 Potosi 10 Chuquisaca, Cochabamba
  coin: 5 tomin 7 bolivar, centavo 9 boliviano

district: 5 La Paz, Oruro 6 Elbeni, Potosi, Tarija 7 Colinas, El Chaco 9 Santa Cruz 10 Chuquisaca, Cochabamba

dried mutton: 7 chalone

Indian: Uro, Uru 4 Iten, Moxo, Uran 6 Arawak, Aymara, Charca, Chicha, Tacana 7 Aymaran, Puquina, Sirione 10 Chiriguano

lake: 8 Aullugas, Titacaca 11 Desaguadero

measure: 6 league 7 celemin

mountain: 5 Andes, Cusco, Cuzco 6 Sajama, Sorata 8 Illimani

plateau: 9 Altiplano

river: 4 Beni 5 Orton 6 Mamore 7 Guapore 8 Paraguay 9 Pilcomayo, San Miguel 10 Cordillera 11 Madre de Dios

weight: 5 libra, macro

boll: pod 4 bulb, grow, knob 5 onion 6 bubble 7 capsule, measure 8 pericarp 12 protuberance

boll weevil: 6 picudo

bollard: 4 bitt, post

bolo: 5 knife 7 machete, sundang 8 pacifist 9 defeatist

Bolshevist: 7 Russian 9 socialist

leader: 5 Lenin

bolster: aid, pad 6 pillow 7 cushion, support 8 compress, maintain

bolt: bar, pen, pin, rod, run 4 beat, dart, flee, gulp, lock, pawl, sift 5 arrow, bilbo, close, elope, flash, gorge, latch, rivet, shaft 6 assort, decamp, desert, fasten, flight, garble, pintle, purify, refine, secure, strong, toggle, winnow 7 missile, shackle, thunder 8 fastener, separate, stampede 9 lightning

bolus: cud 4 bole, clop, lump, mass, pill, rock

bomb: dud, egg 5 blare, shell 6 ashcan 7 bombard, grenade, marmite 9 pineapple 10 projectile 11 blockbuster

guide: fin

hole: 6 crater

bombard: 4 bomb 5 crump, shell 6 batter, bottle, strafe, vessel

bombardier: 6 gunner 12 artilleryman

bombardment: 5 blitz, siege 6 attack, rafale, strafe 9 cannonade

bombardon: 4 oboe, tuba 7 bassoon

bombast: gas, pad 4 rage, rant, rave 5 stuff 6 padded 7 bluster, stuffed, tympany 8 boasting 9 turgidity 11 rodomontade 12 altiloquence 14 grandiloquence

bombastic: 5 tumid, vocal 6 fluent, heroic, turgid 7 bombast, flowery, fustian, orotund, pompous, ranting, stilted 8 inflated 9 expansive, flatulent, grandiose, plethoric 10 lexiphanic 12 magniloquent

Bombay: *arrowroot:* 5 tikor

division: 4 Sind

fabric: 5 rumal

hemp: 4 sunn 6 ambary

mountain: Abu

native: 5 Parsi 6 Parsee

state: 4 Edar

town: 5 Miraj, Poona, Surat

vessel: 7 patamar

bombinate: hum 4 boom

bombproof chamber: 8 casemate

bombyx: eri 4 eria, moth 8 silkworm

bon ami: 5 lover 6 friend 10 sweetheart

bon mot: pun 4 jest, quip 9 witticism

bonafide: 7 genuine 9 authentic

bonanza: 4 mint 6 eureka 7 jackpot

Bonanza State: 7 Montana

bonasus: ox 5 bison 7 aurochs

bonbon: 5 candy, cream 6 dainty 7 caramel 8 confetto, confetti 9 sugarplum

bond: tie, vow 4 bail, band, duty, glue, knot, link, note, yoke 5 bound, chain, nexus 6 binder, cement, connex, engage, escrow, fetter, league, pledge 7 husband, manacle, shackle 8 adhesive, contract, covenant, guaranty, ligament, ligature, mortgage, security 9 agreement, composure, guarantee 10 constraint, husbandman, obligation 11 association, householder

chemical: 5 diene 7 valence

bondage: 4 yoke 7 helotry, serfdom, slavery 9 captivity, restraint, servitude, thralldom

bondsman: 4 carl, esne, peon, serf 5 churl, Helot, slave 6 stooge, surety, thrall, vassal 7 chattel, peasant, servant, villein

bondstone: 6 binder

bone: os; rib 4 ossa(pl.) 5 blade 6 fillet, radius 7 humerus

anvil: 5 incus 7 incudes(pl.)

arm: 4 ulna 6 radius 7 humerus

breast: 6 sterna(pl.) 7 sternum

cartilage: 6 ossein

cavity: 5 antra(pl.), sinus 6 antrum

cell: 10 osteoblast

change into: 6 ossify

comb. form: os 5 osteo

dorsal: 4 ilia(pl.) 5 ilium

elbow: 4 ulna

formation: 7 ostosis 10 parostosis

girdle: 12 sphenethmoid

manipulator: 9 osteopath

pert. to: 6 osteal 7 osseous

prefix: 4 oste

scraper: 6 xyster

bonefish: 8 ladyfish

bonelet: 7 ossicle

boner: 5 error 7 blunder, mistake

bones: 4 dice, ossa 8 skeletoa

boneset: 7 comfrey 8 hempweek 12 thoroughwort

boneyard: 5 store 6 supply 9 scrap heap

bonefire: 5 blaze

bongo: 4 drum 8 antelope

boniata: yam

boniface: 8 landlord 9 innkeeper

bonito: aku, atu 4 fish, nice 5 cobia 6 bonita, pretty, robalo 8 skipjack

Bonjour Tristesse author: 5 Sagan

bonne: 5 nurse 9 nursemaid 11 maidservant

bonnet: cap, hat 4 hood 5 cover, decoy, toque 6 capote, slouch 7 chapeau, coronet 8 headgear 9 headdress 10 accomplice, chinquapin

brim: 4 poke

string: 5 bride

bonnet monkey: 4 zati 5 munga

bonny, bonnie: gay 4 fine 5 merry, plump 6 blithe, pretty, strong 7 healthy 8 budgeree, handsome 9 beautiful 11 goodlooking

bonnyclabber: 4 curd, milk, skyr

bonton: 5 elite

bonus: tip 4 gift, meed 5 award, bribe, bunce, pilon, prize, spiff 6 reward 7 cumshaw, premium, subsidy 8 dividend, lagnappe 9 allowance, lagniappe 12 compensation

bony: 4 hard, lank, leaw, thin 5 stiff, tough 6 osteal, skinny 7 osseous 8 skeletal

boo: 4 hoot, jeer 5 decry

boob: ass 4 fool 5 dunce, goony, neddy 6 nitwit

boobook: owl 6 cuckoo

booby: 5 dunce, idiot, loser, prize 6 sleigh, stupid 8 goosecap 9 simpleton

booby hatch: 4 jail 6 asylum

boodle: 4 swag 5 crowd, graft 6 noodle 7 plunder 8 caboodle

boohoo: sob 4 hoot, weep 5 shout 8 sailfish

boojum: 5 snark

book: mo; log, mss. 4 opus, text, tome 5 Bible, canto, diary, divan, enter, folio, liber, libri(pl.) 6 manual, record, volume 7 blotter, catalog, writing 8 brochure, document, libretto, register 9 catalogue, potboiler

accounts: day 5 bilan, liber 6 ledger 7 journal

alphabet: 9 abecedary

Apocrypha: 5 Tobit

back: 5 spine

best selling: 5 Bible

binding material: 5 cloth, paper 6 canvas 7 buckram, leather

blank: 5 album, diary 6 tablet

church music: 6 hymnal

collector: 12 bibliomaniac

cover ornamentation: 7 tooling

covering: 6 jacket 7 binding

design: 6 format, lay-out

destroyer: 11 biblioclast

devotional: 5 Bible 6 gospel, missal 7 diurnal, psalter

division: 7 chapter

elementary reading: 6 primer

fiction: 5 novel

group: 7 trilogy

Islam: 5 kitab, Koran

jacket notice: 5 blurb

large: 4 tome 5 folio

lover: 11 bibliophile

make-up: 6 format

manuscript: 5 codex, draft 7 codices(pl.)

map: 5 atlas

mass: 6 missal

navigator's: log 7 logbook 9 portolano

obscene: 11 pornography

of hours: 4 Hora 5 Horae(pl.)

of masses: 6 missal

of nobility: 7 peerage

of psalms: 7 psalter

page: 5 folio

palm: 4 tara 7 taliera

part: 4 leaf, page 5 cover 7 binding, chapter, section 9 signature

pert. to: 13 bibliographic

school: 6 primer, reader 7 grammar, speller 9 geography 10 arithmetic

size: 6 octavo, quarto 8 twelvemo 9 duodecimo

title page: 6 rubric

translation: 4 pony

words of opera: 8 libretto

yearbook: 7 almanac

Zoroastrian: 6 Avesta

book dealer: 10 bibliopole 11 bonguiniste

bookbinder: 12 bibliopegist

bookcase: 5 forel 6 forrel

bookkeeper: 7 auditor 10 accountant

bookkeeping term: 4 post 5 debit, entry 6 credit 9 statement

booklet: 8 brochure 10 literature

bookman: 6 bookie, dealer 7 scholar 9 publisher 11 litterateur

bookplate: 8 exlibris

bookworm: 6 reader 7 scholar 11 bibliophile

boom: jib 4 bump, crib, pole, roar, spar 5 croon 7 bumpkin, resound, support 8 bowsprit, flourish 9 bombilate, bombinate 10 prosperity

boomerang: 5 kiley, kalie 6 recoil 7 rebound 8 backfire, ricochet

boon: gay 4 bene, gift, good, kind 5 favor, grant, merry, order 6 benign, bounty, favour, goodly, jovial, prayer 7 benefit, command, present 8 blessing, intimate, petition 9 congenial, convivial, favorable 10 concession, prosperous 11 benefaction

boon companion: pal 4 chum 5 buddy

boondocks: 6 sticks 9 backwoods 10 wilderness

boondoggle: 6 trifle 9 goldbrick

boor: cad, oaf 4 Boer, carl, lout, pill 5 chuff, churl, clown, slave 6 carlot, clunch, hoblob, lubber, lummox, rustic 7 cauboge, grobian, peasant, villain 8 bosthoon 9 barbarian, roughneck 10 clodhopper, countryman, husbandman, tramontane

boorish: 4 rude 5 gawky, rough, surly 6 clumsy, rustic, sullen, vulgar 7 awkward, crabbed, hoblike, loutish, roister, uncouth 8 churlish, cloddish, clownish, lubberly, ungainly 9 bourgeois 10 uncultured, unmannerly

boost: aid 4 abet, back, help, lift, plug, push 5 coach, exalt, hoist, raise 6 assist, rear up 7 advance, commend, elevate, endorse, indorse, promote 8 increase 9 encourage 10 assistance 12 commendation

booster: 4 shot 9 injection 10 enthusiast

boot: pac, use 4 cure, gain, help, kick, shoe, sock 5 avail, booty, eject, jemmy, kamik, spoil 6 bootee, buskin, casing, crakow, enrich, fumble, galosh, sheath 7 benefit, galoshe 8 chassure(F.), covering 9 advantage, discharge, dismissal

half: pac 4 pack 6 buskin, cocker 7 blucher, bottine 8 cothurni(pl.) 9 cothurnus

heavy: pac 5 stogy 6 Brogan 8 Balmoral

high-water: 5 wader

loose-topped: 10 wellington

riding: 5 jemmy 7 gambado

small: 7 bottine 8 bottekin

Boot: 5 Italy

booted: 4 shod 7 ocreate

booth: 4 loge, shed, shop, sook 5 bothy, cabin, crame, house, stall, stand 6 tienda 7 balagan

bootleg: 7 illegal, illicit 11 clandestine 12 illegitimate 13 surreptitious

bootless: 7 useless 9 incurable 10 remediless, unavailing 12 unprofitable

bootlick: 4 fawn 5 toady 7 flatter

booty: 4 boot, gain, loot, pelf, prey, swag 5 cheat, graft, prize 6 spoils 7 despoil, pillage, plunder 10 chevisance

booze: 4 bout 5 budge, drink, spree 6 fuddle, liquor

boozer: pub 5 toper 6 bouser

boquet: See **bouquet**

bora: 4 wind

borax: 6 tincal

Bordeaux wine (see also **wine**): 5 Bourg, cosne, medoc 6 claret 7 Margauz

border: hem, rim 4 abut, brim, dado, eave, edge, line, nark, orle, rand, rund(Sc.), roon, side, trim 5 bound, braid, brink, coast, costa, flank, forel, frame, limit, march, marge, plait, skirt, strip, touch, verge 6 adjoin, costae, edging, forrel, fringe, impale, margin, purfle, stripe 7 bordure, confine, selvage 8 boundary, frontier, neighbor, tressour, tressure 9 extremity, periphery 10 sidepieces

fluted: 5 frill

ornamental: 4 dado

wall: 4 dado, ogee 7 cornice

Border State (Civil War): 8 Arkansas, Delaware, Kentucky, Maryland, Missouri, Virginia 9 Tennessee 13 North Carolina

bordering: 6 edging 8 abutting, adjacent

bore: bit, irk, tap 4 drag, hole, pall, poke, push, ream, size, tide, tire, tool 5 annoy, augur, chink, drill, eagre, gauge, prick, punch, tewel, trick, weary 6 befool, gimlet, pierce, thrust, tunnel 7 caliber, calibre, carried, crevice, opening 8 aiguille, diameter 9 annoyance, penetrate, perforate, terebrate 11 perforation 12 buttonholder

Boreas: 4 wind 7 norther

son: 5 Butes 6 Calais

borecole: 4 kail, kale

bored: 7 ennuyee(F.)

boredom: 5 ennui 6 tedium

borer: 6 insect 7 hagfish, termite 8 shipworm

boric acid salt: 6 borate

boring: dry 4 flat 6 broach, tiring 7 tedious 8 piercing, tiresome 9 wearisome 11 displeasing, penetrating 13 uninteresting

boring tool: bit 5 auger, drill 6 gimlet, wimble

born: nee(F.) 6 innate 7 nascsent, natural 9 delivered

dead: 9 stillborn

prematurely: 8 abortive

well: 4 free 5 noble 7 eugenic

borne (see also **bear**): 4 rode 6 narrow 7 carried, endured

by the wind: 6 eolian

Borneo (see also **Indonesia**): *ape:* 5 orang 9 orangutan

city: 5 Bruni

island near: 4 Java

measure: 5 ganta 7 gantang

mountain: 8 Kini-Balu

native: 4 Dyak, Iban 5 Dayak

pepper plant: ara

pirates: 5 bajau

river: 5 Bruni, Kajan

sea: 4 Sulu

seaport: 4 Miri 5 Balik, Papan

snake: 5 boiga

timbertree: 7 billian

tribe: 4 Dyak, Iban 6 Dusuns

weight: 4 para 6 chapah

boron: 5 borax, boric 7 ulexite

borough: 4 burg, town 5 brush, burgh 6 burgus, castle 7 citadel, village 8 fortress, township

borracho: 5 drunk 8 drunkard

borrow: 4 copy, loan, take 5 adopt, steal 6 pledge, surety 7 chevise, hostage, tithing 11 frankpledge

bosc: 4 pear

boscage: 4 wood 5 grove 7 thicket

bosh: end, rot 4 joke, show, talk, tosh 5 trash 6 bushwa, figure, flaunt, humbug, trivia 8 nonsense 9 poppycock

bosky: 5 bushy, tipsy, woody 7 fuddled 11 intoxicated

Bosnian native: 4 Slav 5 Croat

bosom: 4 barm(Sc.) 5 close, sinus 6 breast, cavity, desire, recess 7 beloved, embrace, inclose 8 intimate 9 cherished 11 inclination, indentation 12 confidential

boss: bur, pad 4 baas, buhr, burr, knob, stud 5 bully, chief, empty, knosp, order, owner 6 brooch, button, direct, emboss, hollow, manage, master, shield 7 capataz, cushion, foreman, hassock, headman, manager, phalera 8 director, domineer, overseer 9 supervise 10 politician, supervisor 12 protuberance 14 superintendent
logging camp: 4 bully
political: 7 cacique
shield: 4 umbo

bossy: cow 4 calf 11 dictatorial, domineering

Boston: 4 game 5 waltz 8 Beantown
district: Hub 7 Back Bay
leader: 7 Brahmin

bot: 5 larva

botanist: Ray 5 Brown 6 Mendel

botany: *angle:* 4 axil
cell: 5 spore
depression: 5 fovea 7 variole

botch: mar, mux 4 boil, mend, mess, sore 5 bitch, bodge, spoil 6 boggle, bumble, bungle, cobble, jumble, repair 8 swelling 10 hodge podge

botcher: 6 grilse, salmon 7 bungler, butcher, clouter, cobbler

botfly larva: bot

both: bo; two 7 equally
handed: 12 ambidextrous
prefix: bi 4 ambi

bother: ado, ail, nag, vex 4 fuss 5 annoy, deave, tease, worry 6 badger, bustle, dither, flurry, gravel, harass, meddle, moider, molest, pester, pother, puzzle, tamper 7 confuse, disturb, perplex, trouble 8 bewilder, irritate, nuisance

bothy: cot, hut 5 booth, lodge 6 bothie 8 barracks

bottle: jug 4 vial 5 cruet, cruse, flask, glass, gourd, house, phial 6 bundle, carafe, carboy, fiasco, flagon, magnum, vessel 7 canteen, costrel 8 building, decanter, demijohn, jeroboam, preserve 9 aryballos, aryballus, container
sealer: 6 capper
size: 4 pint, pipe 5 fifth, quart 6 magnum 8 jeroboam
small: 4 vial 5 ampul, cruet, phial 6 doruck, flacon 7 ampoule, costrel 8 decanter 11 vinaigrette

bottleneck: 7 barrier 8 blockade

bottom: bed 4 base, dale, fund, holm, lees, root 5 abyss, basis, dregs, floor, nadir 6 ground 7 bedrock, grounds, lowland, support, surface 8 buttocks, sediment 10 foundation, groundwork

boudoir: 4 room 5 cabin 7 bedroom, cabinet

bouffant, bouffante: 4 full 6 puffed 7 bulging

bough: arm, leg 4 limb, twig 5 shoot, spray, sprig 6 branch, ramage 7 gallows 8 offshoot, shoulder

bouillabaisse: 4 stew 7 chowder

bouillon: 4 soup 5 broth 8 consomme

boulder: 4 rock 5 stone
monument: 8 megalith
transported by ice: 7 erratic

boulevard: 6 avenue, street 7 highway 12 thoroughfare

boulevardier: 4 roue 5 dandy, idler

bounce: 4 bang, blow, brag, bump, fire, jump, leap, sack 5 boast, bound, bully, carom, chuck, eject, knock, scold, thump, verve 6 spirit, spring, strike 7 address, bluster, dismiss, rebound, swagger 8 proclaim, ricochet 9 discharge, explosion, expulsion 10 resilience

bouncing: big 5 buxom, lusty, stout 7 healthy 9 excessive

bound: dap, end, hop 4 bent, bind, bond, brow, butt, dart, girt, jump, leap, mere, ramp, scud, skip, stem 5 ambit, bourn, going, limit, ready, stend, sting, tiled, vault, verge 6 border, bounce, bourne, curvet, define, domain, finish, hurdle, oblige, prance, spring 7 barrier, certain, chained, closure, confine, costive, delimit, dressed, rebound, saltate, secured, trussed 8 boundary, confined, destined, enclosed, frontier, handfast, landmark, precinct, prepared, shackled 9 compelled, inhibited, obligated 10 borderland 11 constrained, termination 12 circumscribe 13 circumference
back: 5 carom 6 resile
by a vow: 6 votary

boundary: ahu, end, rim 4 dole, dool, edge, line, mear, meer, mere, meta, mete, term, wall 5 ambit, bourn, fence, hedge, limit, march, metae, mound, verge 6 border,

bourne, define 7 barrier, bounder, termini(pl.) 8 frontier, precinct, terminus 9 demarcate, perimeter 11 termination 13 circumference
comb. form: ori

bounder: cab, cad, cub 4 snob, rake, roue 7 dogcart

boundless: 4 vast 6 untold 7 endless, eternal 8 infinite 9 limitless, unlimited 10 immoderate, unconfined, unmeasured 11 illimitable, measureless 12 immeasurable, interminable

bountiful: 4 good, lush, rich 5 ample 6 freely, lavish 7 liberal, profuse 8 abundant, generous 9 bounteous, plenteous, plentiful 10 munificent

bounty: 4 boon, gift, meed 5 award, bonus, grant, valor, worth 6 reward, virtue 7 largess, premium, present, prowess, subsidy 8 goodness, gratuity, kindness 9 allowance 10 generosity, liberality, recompense 11 beneficence, munificence

Bounty captain: 5 Bligh

bouquet, boquet: 4 aura, odor 5 aroma, cigar, posey, spray 7 corsage, nosegay 9 fragrance 10 compliment 11 boutonniere

bourgeois: 6 common, stupid 7 boorish, burgher 8 mediocre 9 hidebound 12 capitalistic, conservative

bourn, bourne: 4 goal 5 bound, brook, limit, realm 6 bourne, domain, stream 7 rivulet 8 boundary 11 destination

bouse: cup 4 haul, lift, pull, tope 5 booze, drink 6 beaker 7 carouse

bout: go; job 4 turn 5 booze, essay, fight, match, round, set-to, trial 6 attack, fracas 7 attempt, carouse, circuit, contest, debauch, outside, without 8 conflict 10 knobkerrie

boutique: 4 shop

boutonniere: 6 boquet 7 bouquet 10 buttonhole

bovine: ox; bos, cow 4 bull, calf, dull, neat, slow, zebu 5 bison, taurine 8 longhorn, sluggish
hybrid: 4 mule 6 catalo
genus: bos

bow: arc, nod, tie 4 arch, beck, bend, bent, duck, fold, knot, prow, stem, turn, wend 5 binge, conge, crush, curve, defer, kneel, noued, stoop, yield 6 archer, assent, bauble, buckle, curtsy, fiddle, ribbon, salaam, submit, swerve, weapon 7 depress, incline, inflict, rainbow 8 crescent, greeting 9 obeisance, prostrate
facing sea: 4 atry
of ship: 4 beak, prow, stem
oriental: 5 salam 6 salaam
toward: 5 afore

wood for: yew

bow-shaped: 6 arcate

bowdlerize: 6 censor 9 expurgate

bowed: 4 bent 5 kneed 6 arcate, curved 7 bulging

bowels: gut 5 belly, colon 8 entrails 10 compassion 11 disembowels, eviscerates

bower: 4 jack, nook 5 abode, arbor, joker, knave 6 anchor 7 berceau, chamber, cottage, embower, enclose, pergola, retreat, shelter

bowfin: 4 amia 6 lawyer 7 grindle, mudfish

bowie: tub 4 bowl, cask, pail 5 knife

Bowie State: 8 Arkansas

bowl: cap, cup, pan 4 coup 5 arena, basin, bowie, depas, phial, rogan 6 beaker, crater, syphus, tureen, vessel 7 stadium, whiskin

bowler: hat 5 derby 6 kegler 8 trundler

bowling: 7 tenpins
division: 5 frame
pin: 7 ninepin, skittle
place: 5 alley
score: 5 spare 6 strike

bowman: 5 cupid 6 archer

box: bin, lug, pix, pyx 4 arca, cage, caja, case, cist, crib, cuff, cyst, loge, pack, scob, seat, slap, slug, spar, stow, till, tray 5 barge, boist, buist, buxus, caddy, chest, clout, crate, fight, hutch, punch, shrub, stall, trunk 6 arcana(pl.), buffet, bunker, carton, casket, coffin, hopper, shrine, strike 7 arcanum, cabinet, caisson, casquet, cassone, confine, enclose, fostell, hanaper, package, trummel 9 container, fisticuff 10 receptacle
alms: 4 arca
ammunition: 7 caisson 9 bandoleer, bandolier
document: 7 hanaper
tea: 8 canister

box office: 4 gate 6 income 8 receipts

box sleigh: 4 pung

boxcar: 7 carrier

boxer: dog, hat, pug 5 champ 6 bantam 7 bruiser, fighter, sparrer 8 pugilist 11 heavyweight
hand covering: 5 cesti, glove 6 cestus

boxing contest: 4 bout 5 match
blow: jab 5 feint, punch
knockout: KO; TKO
pert. to: 6 fistic 10 pugilistic

boxwood: 4 tree 5 seron

boy: bub, lad, tad 4 chap, nino(Sp.), page, puer(L.) 5 buddy, chabo, child, gamin, knave, rogue, valet, youth 6 garcon, nipper, rascal, shaver, urchin 7 gossoon, servant 8 henchboy 9 stripling, youngster

boy friend: 4 beau 5 beaux(pl.) 6 steady 10 sweetheart

boycott: 4 shun 5 avoid, debar 9 blackball 10 ostracized

brabble: 5 argue 7 quarrel

brace: leg, tie, two 4 bind, case, frap, gird, mark, pair, prop, stay 5 nerve, strut 6 clench, couple, crutch, fasten, fathom, splint 7 embrace, refresh, stiffen, support 8 buttress, encircle 9 reinforce, stimulate, suspender 10 strengthen 11 mantelpiece

bracelet: 4 band, ring 5 chain 6 armlet, bangle, grivna 7 armilla, circlet, manacle, poignet 8 handcuff 10 calombigas

bracer: 5 drink, tonic 6 breeze 9 stimulant

brachyuran: 4 crab 10 crustacean

bracing: 5 crisp, quick, tonic 10 salubrious 11 stimulating 12 invigorating 13 strengthening

brack: 4 crag 5 brine, crack

bracken: 4 fern 5 plaid

bracket: 5 brace, class, level, shelf, strut 6 corbel, couple, sconce 7 console, fixture, spotted 8 category, speckled 9 merganser

brackish: 5 foist, salty 6 bracky, saline 7 saltish 8 nauseous 11 distasteful

bract: 5 glume, palea, palet 6 spadix, spathe

brad: pin 4 nail 5 rivet, sprig

brae: 4 bank, brow, hill 5 cleve, slope 6 cleeve, valley 8 hillside

brag: 4 blaw, blow, crow, defy, huff, yelp 5 bluff, boast, flird, preen, strut, vaunt 6 bounce, splore 7 display, gauster, roister, swagger 8 braggart, flourish, pretense, threaten 9 gasconade 11 rodomontade

braggadocio: 7 boaster 8 braggart, rodomont 9 swaggerer 10 pretension

braggart: 4 brag 5 boast 6 blower, crower, gascon, potgun 7 boaster, cracker, ruffler 8 bangster, blowhard, fanfaron, rodomont 9 renommist 10 burgullian 11 braggadocio, rodomontade

Bragi's wife: 4 Idun 6 Ithunn

Brahma: 5 Hindu 7 creator
first woman created by: 6 Ahalya

Brahman: 4 zebu 5 Aryan, Hindu 6 priest, pundit 9 Bostonian
land grant: 5 sasan
precept: 5 sutra, sutta
title: aya

braid: cue 4 band, jerk, lace, plat, trim 5 brede, fancy, freak, jiffy, lacet, onset, plait, pleat, queue, start, tress, trick, twine, vomit, weave 6 bobbin, border, moment, plight, ribbon, sennet, snatch, string 7 caprice, entwine, upbraid 8 brandish, ornament, reproach, soutache, trimming 9 deceitful, interlace 10 interweave
gold and silver: 5 orris

hemp: 5 tagal
knotted: 5 lacet

brain: mad 4 bean, harn(Sc.), mind, utac, wits 5 skull 6 psyche 7 furious 8 cerebrum(L.), conceive 9 intellect
box: pan 5 skull 7 cranium
comb. form: 7 cerebro
layer: 4 obex 6 cortex
membrane: 4 tela 8 meninges
operate on: 6 trepan
orifice: 4 lura
part: 4 aula 8 cerebrum 10 encephalon 11 pericranium
passage: 4 iter
pert. to: 8 cerebral 10 cerebellar, encephalic
tumor: 6 glioma
white matter: pia 4 alba, dura

brain trust: 5 panel 7 council 8 advisers

brainchild: 4 opus, work

brainless: 5 silly 6 stupid 7 foolish, witless 11 thoughtless

brainstorm: 9 confusion

brake: 4 cage, curb, drag, fern, rack, slow, trap 5 block, check, copse, delay, deter, snare, vomit 6 bridle, harrow, hinder, retard 7 dilemma, thicket 9 brushwood

brakeman: 6 brakie 8 trainman

bramble: 5 brier, thorn 6 bumble 10 cloudberry

brambly: 5 spiny 6 thorny 7 prickly

bran: 5 treat 6 cereal, chisel

branch: arm, bow 4 brog, bush, chat, fork, limb, part, rame, rami, snag, spur, stem 5 bough, creek, ramus, shoot, spray, sprig, vimen, withe 6 divide, member, outlet, raddle, ramage, ramify, stolon, stream 7 diverge, tendril 8 district, offshoot 10 department 11 bifurcation 12 ramification
angle of: 4 axil
of nerves: 4 rami(pl.) 5 ramus
pert. to: 5 ramal 6 remeal

branch herring: 7 alewife

branch-like: 4 ramal 6 ramose, ramous

branched: 5 forky 6 forked, ramate, ramose 7 cladine, cladose

branchia: 4 gill

brand: 4 birn, blot, burn, flaw, kind, mark, sear, smit, sort 5 buist, stain, stamp, sword, taint, torch 6 stigma 8 flambeau 9 cauterize, character, trademark 10 stigmatize
on stolen cattle: 4 duff
sheep: 4 smit

brandish: 4 dart, wave 5 bless, braid, shake, swing, wield 6 flaunt, hurtle 7 flutter, glitter, swagger, vibrate 8 flourish 9 coruscate, irradiate

brandling: 4 parr. 9 earthworm

brandy: 4 marc 5 bingo 6 cognac 11 aguardiente(Sp.)
and soda: peg
cocktail: 7 sidecar, stinger 9 alexander
mastic: 4 raki 5 rakee
plum: 9 slivovitz

brank: 5 caper, mumps, strut 6 bridle, prance 7 pillory

brannigan: 5 brawl

brant: 4 rout 5 erect, goose, proud, quink, sheer, steep 7 steeply 8 straight

brash: 4 bold, rash 5 hasty, saucy, storm 6 attack 7 brittle, forward 8 impudent, tactless 9 irascible

brass: 4 cash 5 alloy, money, nerve 6 brazen 7 officer 9 impudence, insolence

brass hat (army slang): 7 general, officer

brass tacks: 5 facts 10 essentials

brassard, brassart: 5 badge 6 bracer 7 armband

brassbound: set 5 rigid 10 inflexible

brassica: 4 cole, rape 6 turnip

brassy: 4 bold 6 aerose, brazen 8 impudent

brat: bib, imp 4 film, scum 5 apron, bairn, bilsh, child, cloak 6 infant, mantle, urchin 7 garment 8 clothing 9 offspring

bravado: 4 pomp 5 brave, pride, storm 6 bravor, hector 7 bluster, bombast, bravade, bravery, swagger 9 gasconade

brave: 4 bold, braw(Sc.), dare, defy, face, fine, game, good, prow 5 adorn, boast, bravo, bully, felon, hardy, manly, Roman, stout, vaunt 6 breast, daring, heroic, manful, plucky 7 bravado, gallant, soldier, swagger, valiant, venture, warrior 8 cavalier, defiance, embolden, fearless, intrepid, stalwart, superior, valorous, virtuous 9 challenge, dauntless, excellent, undaunted 10 courageous 11 venturesome 12 stouthearted

Brave New World author: 6 Huxley

bravery: 4 grit 5 valor 6 spirit, valour 7 bravado, bravura, courage, heroism 8 boldness 9 fortitude, gallantry, gentleman, hardihood

bravo: ole(Sp.), rah 4 thug 5 brave, bully 6 bandit, Indian 7 bravado, villain 8 applause, assassin 9 cutthroat, desperado

brawl: din, row 4 clem, fray, riot 5 broil, fight, melee, revel, scold 6 affray, bicker, fracas, habble, revile, rumpus, shindy, strife, tumult, uproar 7 brabble, discord, dispute, quarrel, scuffle, wrangle 8 complain, squabble 10 contention 11 altercation, disturbance

brawling: 5 noisy 7 blatant 9 clamorous 10 clamourous, vociferous 11 quarrelsome

brawn: 4 boar 5 flesh 6 fatten, muscle 8 strength 10 headcheese

brawny: 5 beefy 6 fleshy, robust, sinewy, strong, sturdy 7 callous 8 muscular, powerful, stalwart

bray: cry, mix, rub 4 beat, rout, tool 5 grind, noise, pound 6 bruise, heehaw, outcry, pestle, thrash, whinny

brazen: 4 bold, pert 5 brass, harsh, sassy 6 brassy 7 callous, forward 8 immodest, impudent, insolent, metallic 9 shameless

Brazil: *ant:* 9 tucandera
bird: ara, iva 4 soco 5 agami, macaw 6 arvara, darter, tiriba 7 maracan, seriema
city: Rio 4 Lapa, Para 5 Bahia, Belem, Ceara, Natal 6 Manaos, Santos 8 Brasilia(c.), Campinas, Sao Paulo 10 Pernambuco 11 Porto Alegre 12 Rio de Janeiro
coffee plantation: 7 fazenda
coin: 4 reis 5 conto, dobra 7 milreis 8 cruzeiro
dance: 5 samba 6 maxixe
discoverer: 6 Cabral
drink: 5 assai
duck: 7 muscovy
estuary: 4 Para
fiber: 4 imbe
fish: 8 arapaima
forest: 5 matta
Indian: 4 Anta 5 Acroa, Arara, Arana, Bravo, Carib, Guana, Hauri 6 Arawak, Caraja 7 Tariana 8 Amiranha, Araquaju, Botocudo
mammal: 5 tapir
measure: pe 4 moio, pipa, sack, vara 5 braca, fanga, legoa, milha, palmo, passo, tonel 6 canada, covado, cuarta, league, quarto, tarefa 7 alquier, garrafa 8 alqueire 9 pollegada, quartilho
monkey: sai 6 miriki 9 belzebuth
mountain: 5 Organ 8 Maririme 10 Serra do Mar 14 Serra dos Orgaos
palm: 4 jara 5 assai, inaja, tucum 6 babaca, jupati 7 babassu 9 barriguda
paste: 7 guarana
plant: 4 imbe, para, yage, yaje 5 caroa 7 ayapana, seringa 9 jaborandi
promontory: 4 frio
river: Apa 4 Para, Paru 5 Jurua, Negro, Purus, Xingu 6 Amazon, Parana 7 Madeira, Orinoco, Tapajos 8 Paraguay 9 Tocantins 12 San Francisco
rubber: ule 4 hule, Para 6 caucho
seaport: Rio 4 Para 5 Bahia, Belem, Natal 6 Santos 7 Pelotas
state: 4 Para 5 Bahia, Ceara, Goyas 6 Parana, Piauhy 7 Alagoas, Sergipe 8 Amazonas, Maranhao, Parahiba, Sao Paulo 10 Mato Grosso, Pernambuco 11 Minas

Geraes 13 Espirito Santo 14 Rio Grande do Sul, Santa Catharina 16 Rio Grande do Norte

tree: apa, ule 4 anda, assu, uhle 5 araca, tingi 6 biriba, brauna, satine 7 araroba, becuiba, gomavel, paraiba, seringa, wallaba 8 bakupari 10 barbatimao, dal guarabu

weight: bag 4 onca 5 libra 6 arroba, oitava 7 arratel, quilate, quintal 8 tonelada

wood: 6 embuia 8 kingwood

breach: gap 4 chap, flaw, gool, rent, rift 5 brack, breck, chasm, cleft, crack, pause, split, wound 6 bruise, harbor, hernia, hiatus, inroad, schism 7 assault, blemish, dispute, fissure, opening, quarrel, rupture 8 breaking, fraction, fracture, interval, trespass 9 violation 10 disruption, infraction 12 infringement, interruption 14 nonfulfillment 16 misunderstanding

of etiquette: 5 gaffe 8 solecism

breach pin: 4 tige

bread: bun 4 diet, fare, food, loaf, pone, roll, rush 5 batch 7 aliment, bannock(Sc.) 10 livelihood, sustenance

boiled: 4 cush 6 panada

browned: 5 toast 6 sippet 7 crouton

communion: 4 azym 5 azyme

crust: 4 rind

leavened: 5 kisra 6 cocket

Passover: 5 matzo 6 matzoh, matzos(pl.), matzot(pl.) 7 matzoth(pl.)

pert. to: 6 panary

unleavened: 4 azym 5 azyme 6 matzos 7 bannock, matzoth 8 afikomen

bread spread: 4 oleo 6 butter 9 margarine 13 oleomargarine

breadth: 4 span 5 brede, scope, width 6 extent 8 diameter, distance, latitude 9 amplitude, dimension

breadwinner: 6 earner, worker

break: gap 4 boon, bust, dash, hint, knap, pick, plow, rend, rent, rift, rive, ruin, rush, slip, snap, stop, tear 5 alter, blank, burst, cleft, crack, craze, frush, lapse, pluck, sever, smash, wound 6 bruise, change, cleave, defeat, hiatus, impair, lacuna, pierce 7 blunder, caesura, crackle, crevice, crumble, destroy, disable, dispart, disrupt, exhaust, fissure, lacunae(pl.), opening, respite, rupture, shatter 8 caesurae, fraction, fracture, interval, separate 9 interrupt, penetrate 10 invalidate 12 interruption 14 discontinuance

down: 7 debacle, failure 8 collapse 9 cataclasm 10 catabolism

in: 4 slip 5 stave 7 blunder 8 initiate 9 interrupt

of day: 4 dawn, morn 5 sunup 7 morning

out: 4 rash 5 erupt 6 escape

up: 5 split 7 disband, disrupt 8 disperse, dissolve, separate

breakable: 7 brittle, bruckle, friable 8 delicate

breakbone fever: 6 dengue

breaker: 4 surf, wave 6 billow, comber, roller

breakwater: cob, dam 4 cobb, dike, mole, pier, pile, quay 5 jetty 6 refuge 11 obstruction

bream: tai 4 fish, scup 5 broom 7 sunfish

sea: 4 shad 6 sargus

breast: 4 crop 5 bosom, brave, chest 6 thorax 9 encounter

ornament: 8 pectoral

breastbone: 6 sterna(pl.) 7 sternum, xiphoid 9 gladiolus

pert. to: 7 sternal

breastplate: *armor:* 4 urim 6 gorget, lorica, shield 7 poitrel, thummin 8 poitrail

ecclesiastical: 4 urim

breastwork: 4 fort 5 redan 7 brattle, parapet, rampart 10 forecastle

breath: 4 ande, gasp, huff, life, pant, pech, puff, sigh, wind 5 pause, scent, smell, vapor, whiff 6 breeze, pneuma 7 halitus, instant, respite 10 exhalation

breathe: 4 ande, live, pant, pech, puff, sigh 5 exist, speak, utter 6 aspire, exhale, inhale, wheeze 7 afflate, emanate, respire, suspire

hard: 4 gasp, pant

breather: 4 rest 5 break, pause, truce 6 recess, repose 9 armistice

breathing: 5 alive 7 gasping 9 spiration 11 respiration

difficult: 7 dyspnea 8 dyspnoea

harsh: 4 rale

orfice: 4 nose, pore 5 mouth, nares 7 nostril 8 spiracle

smooth: 4 lene

sound: 4 rale 5 snore, snort 7 stridor

breathless: 4 dead 5 stale, tense 6 stuffy 10 motionless

bred well: 6 polite 7 genteel 9 pedigreed

breech: 4 bore, butt, doup 5 block 7 droddum 8 buttocks, derriere 9 posterior

breeches: 5 chaps, jeans, levis 8 jodhpurs, knickers, trousers 10 pantaloons

breeching: 4 rope 7 harness

breed: ilk 4 bear, kind, race, rear, sort 5 beget, brood, caste, cause, class, hatch, raise, stock, train 6 create, strain 7 educate, nourish, produce, progeny, species, variety 8 engender, instruct, multiply 9 offspring, orginate, propagate 10 generation

breeding: 6 origin 7 descent 8 behavior, training 9 education, gestation 10 deportment, extraction **11** development, instruction

science: **8** eugenics

breeze: air **4** aura, blow, flaw, gale, gust, pirr, stir, wind **5** blast, rumor **6** breath, report, zephyr **7** freshen, quarrel, whisper **11** disturbance

land: **6** terral

breezy: **4** airy **5** brisk, fresh, windy **6** airish **9** vivacious

bressumer: **4** beam **6** girder, lintel **7** support

breve: **4** bird, mark, note, writ **5** brief, minium, order **6** letter **7** compose, precept **8** syllable

brevet: **6** confer **9** promotion **10** commission

breviary: **4** ordo **6** digest, portas **7** coucher, epitome, summary **8** abstract **10** compendium **11** abridgement

brevity: **9** briefness, shortness, terseness **11** conciseness **12** succinctness

brew: ale, mix **4** beer, boil, make, plot, pour **5** hatch **6** devise, dilute, foment, gather, liquor, seethe **7** concoct, incline, prepare **8** beverage, contrive

brewer: *grain:* rye **4** corn, malt **6** barley

vat: tun

yeast: **4** barm **6** leaven

briar: saw **4** pipe

bribe: fee, oil, rob, sop, tip **4** bait, gift, hire, meed **5** bonus, cuddy, graft, offer, steal, sugar, tempt **6** extort, grease, payola, suborn **7** corrupt **8** gratuity **10** allurement

bric-a-brac: **5** curio **7** bibelot **11** knick-knacks

brick: **4** pave, tile **5** block, quarl, stone **6** fellow, quarle

handler: **6** hacker

oven: **4** kiln

sun-baked: bat **5** adobe

tray: hod

vitrified: **7** clinker

wood: nog **4** dook **6** scutch

bridal: **7** nuptial

bride: bar, tie **4** loop, rein, rose **6** bridle, kallah

bridesmaid: **9** attendant

bridewell: **4** gaol, jail **6** prison **9** workhouse

bridge: way **4** game, link, pons, pont, span **5** cross **6** ponton **7** auction, bascule, connect, pontoon, trestle, viaduct **8** contract, traverse **9** alcantara, gangplank

combination: **6** tenace

forerunner: **5** whist

lever: **7** bascule

of musical instrument: **5** magas **10** ponticello

part: **4** arch, deck, pier **5** cable, pylon **7** caisson **8** spandrel

player: **4** east, west **5** north, south

pontoon plank: **5** chess

score: leg

support: **4** pier **5** truss

term: bid, bye, leg, set **4** book, game, pass, ruff, slam, suit, void **5** raise, trick, trump **6** renege, revoke **7** finesse **9** part-score

bridle: bit **4** curb, rein, rule **5** brake, brank, bride, check, guard, guide, strut **6** direct, govern, halter, master, simper, subdue **7** blinder, control, repress, snaffle, swagger **8** restrain, suppress **9** restraint

noseband: **6** musrol **8** cavesson

brief: few **4** curt, list, rife, writ **5** blurb, breve, charm, pithy, quick, short, terse **6** abrupt, common, letter **7** abridge, compact, compose, concise, invoice, laconic, mandate, outline, precept, summary **8** breviate, condense, fleeting, succinct, syllabus **9** catalogue, condensed, ephemeral, memoranda(pl.), prevalent **10** compendium, memorandum, transitory **11** compendious

briefness: **7** brevity

brier, briar: **4** barb, pipe **5** thorn **6** similax

briery: **5** sharp, spiny

brig: **4** boat, jail **6** prison, vessel **10** guardhouse

brigand: **5** thief **6** bandit, pirate, robber **7** cateran, ladrone, soldier **8** picaroon **10** highwayman

bright: apt, gay **4** fine, glad, rosy **5** acute, aglow, alert, anime, beamy, clear, fresh, gemmy, light, lucid, nitid, quick, riant, sharp, smart, sunny, vivid, witty **6** cheery, clever, florid, garish, limpid, lively, lucent, orient **7** forward, fulgent, radiant, ringing, shining **8** animated, cheerful, flashing, gleaming, luminous, lustrous, splendid, splendor **9** brilliant, cloudless, effulgent, refulgent, sparkling **10** brightness, epiphanous, glistening, glittering **11** illustrious, intelligent, resplendent, transparent

brighten: **4** gild **5** cheer, clear, light, liven, shine **6** cantle, engild, polish **7** animate, burnish, enliven, furbish, lighten **8** illumine **9** irradiate

brightness: **5** eclat, flame, gleam, gloss, nitor, sheen **6** acumen, bright, fulgor, luster **7** clarity, fulgour, sparkle **8** splendor **9** clearness **10** brilliance, effulgence

brilliance: **4** fame **5** eclat, flame, glory **8** keenness, radiance, splendor **10** brightness, effulgence

brilliant: gay **4** good, keen, sage, wise **5** breme **6** bright, clever, signal **7** eminent, flaming, radiant, shining **8** dazzling, glorious, luminous **9** effective, prismatic, refulgent, sparkling **10** glittering **11** prismatical, resplendent **13** distinguished

brim: lip, rim, rut, sea **4** edge **5** bluff, brink, marge, ocean, verge, water **6** border, margin **8** copulate, strumpet **9** periphery

brimming: 4 full

brimstone: 6 virago **7** sulphur **8** spitfire

brindled: 5 tawny **7** flecked **8** streaked

brine: sea **4** main, salt **5** ocean, tears **6** pickle **8** marinade

preserve in: **4** corn, cure, salt

brine shrimp: 7 artemia

bring: 4 bear, take **5** carry, fetch **6** convey, deduce **7** conduce, procure, produce **9** transport

about: **5** cause **6** create **7** achieve **10** accomplish

back: **6** effect, recall, return, revive **7** produce, restore **8** occasion, retrieve, transact **9** instigate **10** consummate

forth: ean(Sc.) **4** bear **5** educe, hatch, incur **6** adduce, beteem **7** produce

forward: **7** present **9** introduce

in: **5** usher **6** import, report, return **9** introduce

near to: **6** appose

off: **7** achieve, succeed **8** complete

on: **6** induce

out: **7** display, publish

to: **11** resuscitate

to earth: **4** land

to light: **6** elicit, reveal **7** unearth **8** disclose, discover

to naught: **4** dash **6** negate **7** confute **9** frustrate

together: **4** join **5** unite **7** compile

up: **4** rear **5** nurse, raise, train **7** educate **11** regurgitate

up to date: **4** post **5** brief **6** inform

brink: end, eve, lip, rim, sea **4** bank, brim, edge, foss **5** marge, shore, verge **6** border, margin

briny: 5 brack, salty **6** saline

brioche: 4 roll **6** stitch **7** cushion, pudding, savarin

Briseis' lover: 8 Achilles

brisk: gay **4** busy, fast, keen, pert, racy, spry, yern **5** agile, alert, alive, budge, crisp, fresh, frisk, peart, perky, quick, sharp, smart, yerne **6** active, breezy, cocket, crouse, lively, nimble, snappy **7** allegro **8** animated, friskful, spirited **9** energetic, sprightly, vivacious **11** stimulating **12** effervescing

bristle: awn **4** barb, hair, seta, tela **5** birse, brush, parch, preen, setae, strut, toast **6** chaeta, palpus, ruffle, setula **7** chaetae, setulae, stubble

comb. form: **4** seti

surgical: **4** seta **5** seton

bristled: 7 horrent **8** echinate

bristlelike: 5 setal **8** setiform

bristling: 5 rough **6** hispid, horrid, setose, thorny **7** horrent, scrubby

brit, britt: 5 sprat **7** herring **10** crustacean

Britain: See **England**

British Columbia: *Indian:* **5** Haida **7** Shuswap

river: **6** Nicola

Britomartis: 7 Artemis **8** Dictynna

mother: **5** Carme

Briton: 4 Celt, Scot

Brittany: *ancient name:* **8** Armorica

canvas: **8** vandelas

king: Ban

native: **6** Breton

poetry: **6** soniou

saint: **4** Anne

brittle: 4 frow, weak **5** brash, candy, crisp, crump, eager, frail, frowy, frush, short **6** crispy, crumpy, feeble, fickle, frough, infirm, slight **7** brickle, bruckle, fragile, friable, froughy **8** delicate, snappish **9** breakable, crumbling, frangible, irritable **10** perishable

broach: air, awl, cut, pin, rod, tap **4** open, ouch, shed, spit, spur, stab, veer, vent **5** begin, dress, drift, prick, rimer, spool, voice **6** boring, brooch, launch, pierce, reamer **7** enlarge, publish, spindle, violate **8** approach, broacher, deflower, incision **9** introduce **11** perforation

broad: 4 deep, free, vast, wide **5** ample, beamy, large, plain, roomy, thick, woman **6** coarse **7** evident, general, grivois, liberal, obvious, platoid **8** grivoise, spacious, tolerant **9** capacious, expansive, extensive, outspoken **12** unrestrained **13** comprehensive

comb. form: **4** lati

broad-footed: 8 platypod

broad-minded: 7 lenient, liberal **8** Catholic, tolerant

broadbill: 4 bird, gaya, raya **5** scaup **8** shoveler **9** swordfish

broadcast: sow **4** seed, send **5** radio, strew **6** spread **7** publish, scatter **8** announce, televise, transmit **9** advertise

broadcloth: 6 cotton, fabric, woolen **7** suiting **8** material

broaden: 5 brede, widen **6** dilate, expand, extend, spread **7** ennoble **9** expatiate **10** generalize

broadside: 4 bill **5** salvo **8** circular

broadsword: 4 bill, kris **6** glaive, spatha **7** cutlass, Ferrara **8** claymore, scimitar

brobdingnagian: big 4 huge 5 giant 8 colossal, gigantic

brocade: 5 cloth 6 broche, kincab 8 baudekin 9 baldachin

brocard: 4 gibe, rule 5 maxim 6 speech 7 sarcasm 9 principle

brochure: 4 book 5 tract 8 pamphlet, treatise

brocket: 4 deer, pita, stag 5 brock 7 spitter

brogan: 4 shoe 5 stogy 6 brogue

brogue: 4 hose, shoe 5 fraud, trick 6 accent, brogan 7 dialect 8 trousers

broil: row 4 burn, char, feud, fray, heat 5 alarm, brawl, grill, melee, scrap 6 affray, birsle, braise, splore, tumult 7 brulyie(Sc.), contest, discord, dispute, embroil, garboil, quarrel 8 conflict, grillade 10 contention, dissension 11 altercation, disturbance

broiler: 4 bird 5 grill 7 chicken

broke: 8 bankrupt 9 insolvent, penniless

broken: 4 rent, torn 5 burst, gappy, rompu(F.), rough, tamed 6 hackly, ruined, shaken 7 crushed, fracted, reduced, subdued 8 outlawed, ruptured, weakened 9 cashiered, dispersed, fractured, shattered 10 incoherent, incomplete 11 fragmentary 12 disconnected, intermittent

broker: 5 agent 6 corser, dealer, factor, jobber 7 brogger, changer, courser, peddler, realtor, scalper 8 broacher, huckster, merchant 10 pawnbroker

brokerage: fee 4 agio 10 commission

brolly: 8 umbrella

bromide: 5 trite 8 compound, sedative 9 platitude

bronco: 5 horse 6 cayuse 7 broncho, mustang 9 estrapade(Sp.)

bronco buster: 6 cowboy, ginete

Bronte: 4 Anne 5 Emily 9 Charlotte
hero: 9 Rochester 10 Heathcliff
heroine: 8 Jane Eyre
pen name: 4 Bell

Bronx cheer: boo 9 raspberry

bronze: aes(L.), tan 4 bust 5 alloy, brown 6 statue
film: 6 patina
gilded: 6 ormolu
nickel: 11 cupronickel
pert. to: 7 aeneous

brooch: bar, pin 4 boss, ouch 5 cameo, clasp 6 fibula, plaque, shield 8 ornament 9 brochette

brood: fry, nye, set, sit 4 mope, nest, nide, race, weep 5 aerie, breed, covey, flock, group, hatch, issue, sedge, worry, young 6 cletch, clutch, family, litter, ponder 7 progeny, species 8 cogitate, incubate, meditate 9 multitude, offspring 11 contemplate

brook: run 4 bear, beck, burn, ghyl, gill, rill, rush, sike 5 abide, bayou, bourn, creek, stand 6 arroyo(Sp.), bourne, canada, endure, gutter, rindle, rivose, runlet, stream, suffer 7 comport 8 quebrada, tolerate 11 watercourse

brooklet: 4 beck, rill 6 rillet, runnel 7 rillock, rivulet 9 arroyuelo(Sp.)

broom: mop 4 fray, swab 5 besom, bream, brush, spart, sweep, whisk 8 splinter

broom plant: 5 hirse, spart 7 cyticus, genista, heather 8 deerweed

broomcorn millet: 5 hirse

broth: 4 bree, broo, soup 5 stock 6 brewis, jussal, jussel 7 pottage 8 consomme, jusshell

brothel: 4 crib, stew 6 bagnio, bordel 8 bordello

brother: bub, fra, kin, pal, sib 4 mate, monk, peer 5 billy, buddy, cadet, frere(F.), friar 6 fellow, fraile, frater(L.) 7 comrade, sibling
pert. to: 9 fraternal

brotherhood: 4 gild 5 guild, lodge 6 friary 8 bratstro, sodality 10 fellowship, fraternity 11 association 13 brotherliness, companionship, confraternity

brotherly: 4 kind 6 tender 9 fraternal 12 affectionate

brougham: 8 carriage

brought up: 4 cade

brow: top 4 brae, bree, edge, mien, snab(Sc.) 5 bound, brink, crest, front, ridge, slope 8 boldness, forehead 9 acclivity, gangplank 10 effrontery 11 countenance

browbeat: 5 abash, bully 6 hector 7 depress 10 disconcert, intimidate

brown: dun, tan 4 coin, cook, dark, sear 5 dusky, penny, sedge, sepia, tawny, tenne, toast, umber 6 gloomy, russet, sennet, tanned 9 half-penny
cocoa: 6 sahara
dark: 6 bister, bistre
light: tan 4 ecru, fawn 5 beige, khaki, tenne
purple: 4 puce
red: bay 4 cuba, roan 5 henna, sepia 6 auburn, russet, sorrel 8 chestnut
rich: 5 sepia

brown Bess: 6 musket

brown Betty: 7 pudding 10 coneflower

brown study: 10 absorption 11 abstraction

browned: 7 rissole

brownie: elk, nis 4 cake 5 cooky, nisse, urisk 6 goblin, uruisg(Sc.) 9 sandpiper

browse: 4 brut, crop, feed 5 graze 6 forage, nibble 7 pasture

bruin: 4 bear

bruise: 4 bash, bray, dent, dunt, hurt, maim, maul 5 break, crush, curry, delve, dinge, pound **6** batter, breach, hatter, injury, mangle, shiner **7** contuse, dammish, disable **9** pulverize, triturate

bruised: 4 hurt **5** livid **6** humble **7** froisse

bruiser: 5 boxer **8** pugilist

bruit: din **4** fame, rale, tell **5** noise, rumor, sound **6** blazon, clamor, report **7** declare, hearsay

brume: fog **4** haze, mist, smog **5** vapor

brumous: 5 foggy, misty **6** hiemal, sleety **7** wintery

brunette: 4 dark **5** brown, brune, gipsy, gypsy **7** swarthy

brunt: jar **4** blow, jolt **5** clash, force, onset, shock **6** attack, effort, impact **7** assault **8** outburst

brush: 4 comb, fray, skim **5** broom, clean, copse, fight, graze, sweep **6** badger, battle, brosse(F.), stroke **7** thicket **8** skirmish **9** brushwood, encounter **11** undergrowth

brushwood: 4 rone **5** brake, brush, copse, frith, scrog, scrub **6** rammel **7** coppice, thicket

brushy: 5 hairy **6** shaggy **7** hirsute

brusque: 4 curt, rude **5** bluff, blunt, brusk, gruff, hasty, rough, short **6** abrupt **7** violent **8** cavalier, impolite **12** discourteous

brut: dry **6** browse

brutal: 5 cruel, feral, gross **6** carnal, coarse, savage **7** bestial, beastly, brutish, caddish, inhuman **8** ruthless **9** atrocious, barbarous, ferocious, insensate

brute: 5 beast, yahoo **6** animal, savage **7** ruffian **9** scoundrel

bryophyte: 4 moss **5** plant **9** liverwort

Brython: 5 Welsh **6** Celtic **7** Cornish

god: Dea, Ler **4** Bran **5** Dylan, Lludd **8** Amaethon

goddess: Don **8** Rhiannon **9** Arianrhod

bubal: 4 topi **8** antelope

bubble: air, bub **4** bead, bell(Sc.), bleb, blob, boil, boll, dupe, foam, glob, seed, suds **5** caper, cheat, empty **6** burble, delude, seethe, trifle **7** blister, blubber, deceive, globule **8** delusive **10** effervesce **11** speculation

bubbling: gay **8** effusive **9** sparkling

buccal: 4 oral

buccaneer: 6 pirate, rifler, robber, viking **7** corsair, mariner, spoiler **8** Picaroon **10** freebooter

standard: **5** roger

Bucephalus: 5 steed **7** charger

buck: fob, ram **4** boil, butt, deer, dude, male, prig, rear, soak, stag, toff, wash **5** dandy, steep **6** basket, dollar, oppose, resist **7** sawbuck **8** antelope, prickett, sawhorse **9** buckwheat

first year: **4** fawn

fourth year: **4** sore

buckaroo: 6 cowboy **8** horseman

buckboard: 8 carriage

bucket: tub **4** bail, bowk, cage, pail **5** cheat, scoop, skeel **6** bailer, drench, hoppet, situla(L.), vessel **7** swindle **8** cannikin

handle: **4** bail

molten glass: **7** cuvette

Buckeye State: 4 Ohio

buckle: bow **4** bend, curl, kink, tach, warp **5** clasp, marry, twist **6** fibula(L.) **7** contend, fermail, fibulae(L.pl.), grapple **8** fastener, struggle **10** distortion

part: **5** chape **6** tongue

buckler: 4 crab **5** block **6** shield **7** rotella, roundel, shutter

buckram: 6 fabric **7** precise **10** cuckoopint, stiffening

buckthorn: 5 rhamn **7** alatern, cascara **8** lotebush **9** alaternus, chaparral

buckwheat: 4 buck **8** sarrazin

buckwheat tree: 4 titi **6** teetee

bucolic: 4 idyl **5** local, naive, rural **6** farmer, rustic, simple **7** cowherd, eclogue **8** agrestic, herdsman, pastoral

bud: eye, gem, imp, pip **4** bulb, cion, germ, girl, grow, knop **5** child, graft, scion, shoot, youth **6** button, flower, germin, sprout **7** blossom, brother, gemmule **8** bourgeon **9** germinate

arrangement: **11** aestivation

social: deb **8** debutant **9** debutante

Buddha: Fo; Foh **7** Gautama **10** Shakyamuni

cause of infinite existence: **6** nidana

center: **5** Lassa, Lhasa

church: **4** Tera

column: lat

disciple: **6** Ananda

dryad: **6** Yaksha, Yakshi

enlightenment: **5** bodhi

evil spirit: **4** Mara

fate: **5** karma

fertility spirit: **6** Yaksha, Yakshi

festival: bon

final beatitude: **4** raga **7** nirvana

for justice: **5** dharna, dhurna

gateway: **5** toran, torii **6** torana

god: **4** deva

greater: **8** Mahayana

hatred: **4** dosa

hell: **6** Naraka

Japanese image: **8** Daibutsu

language: **4** Pali

lesser: **8** Hinayana

life cycle: **6** anicca

mendicant: **6** bhikku **7** bhikshu

monastery: **4** Tera **6** Vihara

monk: bo 4 lama 5 arhat, yahan 7 poongee 8 poonghee, poonghie, talapoin

monument: 5 stupa

mother: 4 Maya

novice: 5 goyim

paradise: 4 Jodo

passion: 4 raga

prayer: 4 mani

priest: 4 lama 7 mahatma

relic mound: 5 stupa

retribution: 5 karma

rock temple: 4 rath 5 ratha

sacred city: 5 Lassa, Lhasa

scripture: 5 sutra

sect: Zen 7 Jodo-shu

shrine: 4 tope 5 stupa 6 dagoba 7 chorten

son: 6 Rahula

stupa site: 9 Amaravati

throne: 5 asana

title: 7 Mahatma

tree: 5 pipal 6 botree

will to live: 5 Tanha

buddy: bo; boy, pal 4 mate 7 brother, comrade 8 tentmate 9 companion

budge: fur 4 move, stir 5 booze, brisk, stiff, thief 6 jocund, liquor, solemn 7 austere, pompous 8 movement 11 nervousness

budget: bag 4 boot, pack, plan, roll 5 batch, bunch, stock, store 6 bottle, bundle, parcel, socket, wallet 7 program 12 accumulation

buds: 8 burgeons, dehisces

pickled: 6 capers

buff: ox; bob, fan, tan 4 blow, coat, curt, firm 5 shine 6 buffet, polish, sturdy 7 leather, stammer, stutter 8 nonsense, seladang 10 enthusiast

buffalo: ox 5 anoa, buff, stag 5 bison, bugle 6 buffle, hamper 7 cariboo, caribou, gazelle, overawe, timarau, zamouse 8 bewilder 9 bamboozle

large: 4 arna, arni 5 arnee

meat: 7 biltong

wild: 4 arna, arni 5 arnee 8 seladang

buffalo gourd: 11 calabazilla

buffalo tree: 10 rabbitwood

buffer: dog, pad 6 bumper, fender, pistol 7 cushion

buffet: bar, bob, box 4 beat, blow, buff, cuff, slap, toss 5 filip, smite, stool 6 abacus, batter, fillip, strike, strive, thrash 7 contend, counter, hassock 8 credence, credenza, cupboard 9 footstool, sideboard 10 affliction

bufflehead: 4 duck, fool 5 clown 6 buffle 9 merrywing

buffleheaded: 4 dull 6 stupid

buffoon: dor, wag, wit 4 aper, fool, jape, mime, mome 5 actor, antic, buffo, clown, comic, drole, droll, mimer 6 harlot, jester, mummer, stooge 7 playboy 8 balatron, gracioso, humorist, merryman, ridicule 9 harlequin 10 harlequina, hobby-horse 11 merry-andrew, Punchinello

bug: bog, dor 4 flaw, germ, idea, mite 5 bogey, bulge, roach 6 beetle, chinch, elater, insect, scheme 7 bellied, bugbear, forward, pompous 8 hemipter, hobbyist 9 conceited, hobgoblin, prominent 10 enthusiast, flashlight 11 hunchbacked

June: dor

lightning: 7 firefly

needle: 7 ranatra

bugaboo: 4 bogy, fear, goga, gogo, ogre 5 alarm, bogey, bogie, gogga 6 bodach, goblin 7 bugbear, specter, spectre 8 worricow(Sc.) 9 hobgoblin, scarecrow, worriecow(Sc.) 10 mumbo-jumbo

bugbane: 4 herb 9 hellebore 10 rattleroot

bugbear: See **bugaboo**

bugger: 4 chap 6 fellow, person, rascal 7 heretic 8 sodomite 11 Albigensian

buggy (see also **carriage**): 4 cart, shay, trap 5 nutty 7 caboose, foolish, vehicle 8 demented, infested, stanhope 9 gladstone

bughouse: 5 crazy, nutty 6 asylum, insane

bugle: ox 4 bead, horn 5 black 7 buffalo, bullock, clarion, trumpet

blare: 7 tantara

call: 4 taps 6 alerte(F.), sennet, tattoo 7 retreat 8 reveille

note: mot

yellow: iva

bugleweed: 4 mint 6 indigo

build: big 4 bigg, form, make, rear 5 edify, erect, found, frame, raise, set up, shape 6 create, graith 7 fashion 8 assemble 9 construct, establish, fabricate

nest: 6 nidify

up: 7 enhance 8 increase 9 publicity 10 strengthen

builder: 5 maker 7 erector 8 tectonic 9 carpenter 11 constructor

labyrinth: 8 Daedalus

of wooden horse: 5 Epeus 6 Epeius

building: 4 casa(Sp.), pile 5 aedes, hotel, house 6 biggin, bottle, fabric 7 edifice, factory 8 dwelling 9 apartment, structure 10 storehouse 11 edification

addition to: ell 4 apse, wing 5 annex 6 lean-to

dilapidated: 7 rookery 8 firetrap, tenement

exhibition: 6 museum

farm: 4 barn, crib, shed, silo

gateway: 5 pylon

material: 4 iron, wood 5 brick, glass, steel 6 cement

medieval: 6 castle

part: ell 4 apse

projection: ell 4 apse, wing 5 annex 6 dormer, lean-to 7 cornice

public: 5 edile 6 aedile, casino, church, museum, temple 7 capitol, library, theater 10 auditorium

rib: 9 tierceron

round: 7 rotunda

sacred: 4 fane 6 church, mosque, temple 7 edicule 8 pantheon 9 cathedral

stately: 6 castle, palace 7 edifice, mansion

buirdly: 5 husky 6 strong 8 athletic

bulb: bud 4 blub, corm, knob, lamp, root 5 globe, swell, tuber 6 bulbus 9 expansion 12 protuberance

edible: yam 4 sego 5 onion 6 garlic. potato

bulbous: 5 round 7 swollen

bulbul: 4 bird, kala

Bulgar: 4 Slav 5 Tatar 6 Slavic 9 Bulgarian

Bulgaria: *assembly:* 8 Sobranje, Sobranye

capital: 5 Sofia

coin: lev, lew 8 stotinka

commune: 6 Sliven, Slivno 7 Sistova

liquor: 8 slivovic 9 slivovitz, slivowitz

measure: oka, oke 5 krine, lekha

river: 5 Mesta 6 Danube, Marica, Struma 7 Marista

ruler: 4 czar, tsar 5 Boris

town: 4 Ruse 5 Byclu, Sofia(c.), Stara, Varna 6 Bleven, Burgas, Plevna, Shumen, Shumla, Sliven, Slivno, Widdin, Zagora 7 Plovdiv, Sistova, Tirnova 8 Rustchuk 9 Silistria

weight: oka, oke 5 tovar

bulge: bag, bug, jut 4 bump, cask, hump, knob, lump 5 belly, bilge, bloat, bouge, flask, pouch, swell 6 billow, cockle, extend, pucker, wallet 7 blister 8 protrude 9 convexity, gibbosity 10 projection 11 indentation 12 protuberance

bulged: 5 bombe

bulging: 4 full 5 bombe, bowed, pudgy 6 convex 7 gibbous 8 bouffant

bulk: 4 body, heap, hold, hulk, hull, mass, pile, size 5 cargo, gross, might, power, stall, swell 6 expand, extent, figure, volume 7 bigness 8 majority, quantity 9 aggregate, dimension, largeness, magnitude 11 massiveness

bulkhead: 5 check 9 partition, structure

bulky: big 5 burly, gross, large, stout 6 clumsy, stody 7 hulking, massive, weighty 8 unwieldy 9 corpulent, policeman, ponderous

bull: cop 4 apis, jest, male, seal, slip, toro(Sp.), zebu 5 bobby, boner, drink, edict, error 6 bovine, letter, peeler, taurus(L.) 8 cajolery, document, flattery 9 detective, policeman, quadruped 10 zapaterito(Sp.)

angry: 5 gorer

castrated: 4 stot 5 steer 7 bullock

half man: 8 minotaur

hornless: 5 doddy 6 doddie

pert. to: 7 taurine

young: 4 stot(Sc.) 5 stirk 7 bullock

bull-like: 7 taurine

Bull Run: *battle:* 8 Manassas

hero: Lee

bull session: 4 talk 7 rapping 10 discussion

bulla: 4 bleb, case, seal 5 blain 7 vesicle

bullate: 8 puckered

bulldoze: cow, dig, ram 5 bully, force, scoop 6 coerce, pistol 8 browbeat, restrain

bulldozer: 5 bully 6 grader 7 machine

bullet: 4 ball, lead, shot, slug 6 pellet, sinker, tracer 7 missile

diameter: 7 caliber

fake: 6 pellet

bulletin: 4 memo 6 notice, poster, report 7 program 9 statement 11 publication 12 announcement

bullfight cheer: ole

bullfighter: 6 torero 7 matador, picador 8 capeador, matadore, toreador

foot: 6 torero

mounted: 8 toreador

bullfinch: alp, olp 4 monk, nope, olph, pope 5 hedge

bullheaded: 6 stupid 8 stubborn 9 obstinate 10 headstrong

bullion: bar 5 ingot, metal 6 billot

bullock: 4 stot 5 bugle, steer, stirk 6 bovine 9 quadruped

bull's eye: 6 target

bully: 4 boat, boss, fine, good, huff, mate 5 brave, bravo, great 6 bounce, harass, hector, jovial, tyrant 7 bluster, bouncer, bullock, darling, dashing, gallant, gauster, huffcap, roister, ruffian 8 bangster, barrater, barrator, browbeat, bulldoze, domineer, frampler 9 blusterer, bulldozer, companion, excellent, scrimmage 10 burgullian, intimidate, sweetheart

bulrush: 4 reed, rush, tule 5 sedge 6 bumble 7 cattail, papyrus, scirpus

bulwark: 4 bail, fort, wall 5 fence, mound 7 bastion, defence, defense, parapet, protect, rampart 10 breakwater 12 propugnacula(L.pl.) 13 propugnaculum(L.)

bum: beg, din 4 hobo 5 drink, drone, idler, mooch, tramp 6 frolic, guzzle, sponge 7 guzzler 8 vagabond

bumble: bee 4 veil 5 botch, drone, idler 6 beadle, bungle, jumble, muffle 7 bittern, blunder, bramble, bulrush, bungler

bumblebee: dor 6 bumbee, bumble, insect

bump: cry, hit 4 blow, boom, jolt, lump, whop 5 bulge, clout, knock, thump 6 bounce, nodule, strike 7 bittern, collide 8 swelling 10 projection 12 protuberance

bumper: 4 bowl, fine, good 5 facer, glass 6 buffer, fender, goblet 8 carangid

bumpkin: yap 4 beam, boom, clod, gawk, hick, lout, rube, swab 5 churl, clown, robin, yahoo, yokel 6 lummox 7 cauboge, hawbuck 9 chawbacon

bumptious: 8 insolent 9 obtrusive

bumpy: 5 rough 6 uneven

bun: jag, wig 4 boat, bunt, roll, stem, tail 5 stalk 6 rabbit 7 biscuit, chervil, stubble 8 squirrel 11 drunkenness

bunch: bob, set 4 bale, club, herd, hump, kick, pack, tuft, wisp 5 clump, fagot, flock, knoll, pahil(Ir.), thump 6 budget, bundle, finial, hobble, 8 quantity, swelling 9 aggregate 10 collection

of grapes: bob

pert. to: 5 comal

buncombe: rot 4 bunk 6 drivel 9 poppycock

bund: 4 band, quay 5 praya 6 league 7 society 10 embankment, federation 11 confederacy

bundle: lot, wad, wap 4 bale, band, bolt, garb, hank, pack, roll, swag 5 bunch, fadge, group, sheaf 6 bindle, fardel, fascis(L.), gather, number, packet, parcel 7 package 10 collection

maker: 5 baler

bundle of: arrows: 5 sheaf

firewood: 5 bavin

grain: 5 sheaf

sticks: 5 fagot 6 faggot

straw: 4 bolt

bung: 4 cork, dead, maul, plug, stop 5 plumb, purse, spile 6 parcel 7 smashed, squared, stopper, stopple, tampeon, tampion, tampoon 8 bankrupt, bunghole, 9 falsehood 10 pickpocket

bungalow: 5 house 7 cottage

bungle: err 4 goof, mess, muff 5 blunk, botch, spoil 6 boggle, bumble, foozle, fumble 7 bauchle, blunder 9 mismanage

bungling: 6 clumsy 7 awkward 9 maladroit, unskilled 10 blundering

bunk: bed, car 4 case 5 abide, berth, bunko, frame, hokum, hooey, leave, lodge, sleep, truck 6 bunkum, timber 7 baloney, boloney, chicory, hemlock, twaddle 8 buncombe, nonsense 9 crossbeam, skedaddle 10 humbuggery

bunker: bin, box 5 chest 6 hazard 8 obstacle, sandhole 11 compartment 12 entanglement

bunko: 5 bunco, cheat 6 scheme 7 swindle

bunt: bun 4 butt, push, sift, smut, tail 5 shove, 6 kernel, strike

bunting: 4 bird, flag, pape 5 dumpy, finch, plump 6 cotton, stocky, towhee, untidy 7 cowbird, etamine, garment, ortolan, rounded 8 bellying, bobolink, slovenly

bunyip: 4 sham 6 humbug, poster 8 impostor

buoy: dan 5 baken, elate, float, raise 6 marker 7 sustain 8 deadhead, levitate

mooring: 7 dolphin

trawling marker: dan

buoyant: gay 5 happy, light 6 blithe, floaty, lively 7 elastic, hopeful, lilting, springy 8 animated, cheerful, sanguine, spirited, volatile 9 resilient, vivacious 12 lighthearted

bur: See burr.

burble: 4 boil 6 bubble, gurgle, jabber, muddle, pimple 7 confuse, prattle, trouble 8 disorder

burbot: cod 4 fish, ling, lota 7 eelpout

burd: 4 lady 5 woman 6 maiden

burden: tax, vex 4 birn(Sc.), care, cark, clag, clog, duty, load, onus, seam 5 birth, cargo 6 charge, cumber, fardel, hamper, impose, lading, weight 7 ballast, fraught, freight, oppress, refrain, trouble 8 capacity, carriage, encumber, handicap, quantity 9 aggravate, grievance 10 imposition 11 encumbrance 14 responsibility

of complaint: 8 gravamen

with care: 4 cark

burden bearer: 4 Amos 5 Atlas

burdensome: 5 heavy 7 irksome, onerous, weighty 8 cumbrous, grievous, grinding 10 chargeable, cumbersome, oppressive 11 importunate, troublesome

burdock: 5 clite, lappa, plant 7 cadillo, clotbur, harebur, hurr-bur 9 cocklebur

bureau: 4 desk 5 chest 6 agency, office 7 dresser 10 chiffonier, department, escritoire

burg, burgh: 4 city, town 6 burgus 7 borough 9 community

burgeon: bud 4 grow 5 shoot 6 sprout

burgess: 7 citizen, freeman 8 commoner 10 magistrate

burglar: 4 yegg 5 thief 6 gopher, robber 7 yeggman 8 peterman 10 burglarize

burglary: 5 theft 7 larceny, robbery 8 stealage

burgomaster: 4 gull 5 mayor 7 alcalde 10 magistrate

burgoo, burgout: 4 soup, stew 5 gruel 7 pudding 8 porridge

burial: 9 interment 10 deposition

case: box 6 casket, coffin

ceremony: 7 funeral

litter: 4 bier

mound: low 5 grave 6 barrow 7 tumulus

pile: 4 pyre

place: 4 tomb 5 grave 7 pyramid 8 catacomb, cemetery, golgotha 9 graveyard, mausoleum 10 necropolis

preparation for: 4 cere 11 pollincture

buried (see also **bury**): 6 hidden 8 absorbed, imbedded

burin: 4 tool 6 graver

burke: 4 kill, slay 6 murder 7 smother

burl: 4 knot, lump 6 pimple 7 pustule 11 excrescence

in mahogany: roe

burlap: 5 gunny 6 fabric 7 bagging 8 wrapping

fiber: 4 hemp, jute

burler: 6 spiler 9 inspector

burlesque: ape, odd 4 copy, jest, mime 5 droll, farce, revue 6 comedy, overdo, parody 7 jocular, mockery, overact 8 ridicule, travesty 9 imitation, laughable, ludicrous 10 caricature

serenade: 9 charivari

burly: fat 5 bluff, bulky, heavy, husky, large, lusty, noble, obese, stout, thick, tramp 7 stately 8 imposing 9 corpulent, excellent, policeman 10 boisterous

Burma: *canopy:* 7 tazaung

chief: bo; boh, wun 4 woon

city: Ava 4 Pegu 5 Akyah, Prome 6 Lashio 7 Rangoon(c.) 8 Mandalay

dagger: dah 4 dout

deer: 6 thamin 7 thameng

demon: nat

district: 7 Toungoo

division: 4 Pegu 6 arakam

garment: 6 tamein

gate: 5 toran

gibbon: lar

girl: 4 mima

head hunter: 4 Naga

hill: 4 chin 6 kachin

hill dweller: Lai

knife: dah, dow

language: Wa; Lai 4 Chin, Pegu 6 Kachin

measure: dha, lan, tha 4 byee, dain, seit, taim, teng 6 palgat

musical instrument: 4 turr

native: Vu, Wa; Lai, Mon 4 Shaw 5 Karen 6 Kachin, Pequan

river: 6 Salwin, Sutang 7 Salween 8 Chindwin, Irrawadi 9 Irrawaddy

robber: 6 dacoit

sash: 7 tubbeck

skirts: 5 engis

spirit: nat

town: 4 Paan 5 Akyab, Manle 7 Bassein 8 Moulmein

traveler's shed: 5 zayat

tree: 4 acle 7 yamanai

tribe: Ao; Tai 4 Chin, Kuki, Shan, Thai, Tsin 6 Kachin, Karens 8 Kakhyens

tribesman: Lai

weight: mat, moo, vis 4 kait, ruay, viss 5 candy, tical, ticul

burn: 4 brew, char, fire, plot, raze, rill, sear, sere 5 adust, blaze, broil, brook, cense, flame, parch, scald, singe, waste, water 6 scorch, stream 7 combure, combust, consume, cremate, flicker, oxidize, rivulet, smolder 8 squander 9 cauterize 10 incinerate

midnight oil: 6 stay up 9 lucubrate

surface: 5 singe 6 scorch

burn up the road: 5 speed

burned: 5 baked 6 seared 7 charred 8 ustulate

burner: 6 Bunsen, censer 8 thurible

burning: hot 4 fire 5 afire, angry, blaze, calid, eager, fiery, flame, gledy 6 ablaze, ardent, fervid, torrid 7 caustic, cautery, fervent, flaming, glaring, glowing, mordant, shining 8 ardurous, exciting, inustion 9 consuming, cremating, inflaming 10 combustion, phlogistic 13 conflagration

bush: 5 wahoo

malicious: 5 arson

mountain: 7 volcano

taste: 5 acrid

burnish: rub 5 glaze, gloss 6 polish 7 furbish

burnisher: 4 tool 5 agate 6 buffer 7 frottom 8 polisher

burnoose, burnous: 5 cloak 7 garment 8 albornoz

burnsides: 5 beard 8 whiskers

burnt work: 10 pyrography

burr: nut, pad, rib 4 barb, birr, boss, buzz, halo, knob, ring, whir 5 briar, whirr 6 banyan, circle, corona, tunnel, washer 7 sticker 8 parasite 9 whetstone 10 sweetbread

burro: ass 6 donkey 9 quadruped

burrow: den, dig 4 heap, hole, mine, mole, root, tube 5 berry, couch, mound 6 furrow, tunnel 7 passage, shelter 8 excavate

bursa: sac 4 hall, sack 5 pouch 6 cavity 9 residence

bursar: 6 purser, terrar 7 boucher, cashier, student 9 treasurer

bursary: 8 treasury 11 scholarship

burse: 4 case, shop 5 bazar, purse 6 bazaar, bourse, pocket 8 exchange, treasury 11 scholarship

burst: pop 4 blow, bust, loss, rend, scat 5 blast, break, erupt, flash, reave, salvo, scatt, split **6** broken, damage, injury, sprout **7** explode, rupture, shatter **8** outbreak, sundered **9** interrupt

forth: **5** erupt, sally **9** blasted

inward: **7** implode

burster: **4** gale **7** cracker **9** explosive

bursting: **8** erupting **10** dehiscence

comb. form: **6** rrhage **7** rrhagia

bury: **4** hide, mool, veil **5** cloak, cover, earth, grave, inter, inurn **6** entomb, hearse, inhume, shroud **7** bedelve, conceal, engross, immerse, repress, secrete **8** submerge **9** overwhelm

bus: **6** jitney **7** vehicle **9** charabanc

busby: cap, wig **7** bearskin **9** headdress

bush: tod **4** buss, butt **5** bosch, clump, grove, shrub **6** branch, tavern **7** boscage, cluster, thicket **11** advertising

bushed: **4** worn **5** spent **9** exhausted

bushel: foo(Sc.), gob, lot **4** full

quarter of: **4** peck

forty: wey

bushing: **5** drill **6** collet, lining **7** padding

machine: **6** sleeve

bushman: san(pl.) **4** gung, saan(pl.) **5** bushy **6** Abatoa, Abatua, Abatwa, rustic **8** woodsman

blanket: **5** bluey

bushmaster: **5** snake, viper

bushwa: **4** bosh, bull **5** hooey, trash **7** baloney **8** bodewash

bushwacker: **5** papaw **6** pawpaw, scythe **8** guerilla

bushy: **5** bosky **6** dumose, dumous **7** bushman, queachy

hair: **4** shag

heap: tod

business: ado, art, job **4** care, firm, fuss, game, line, task, work **5** cause, trade **6** affair, custom, matter, metier, office **7** calling, concern, trading, traffic **8** activity, commerce, industry, vocation **9** diligence, following, patronage, rickmatic **10** employment, enterprise, occupation, solicitude **11** disturbance, importunity, intercourse, transaction **13** attentiveness, establishment

custom: **9** patronage

memorandum: **4** note **7** agendum

place of: **4** mart, shop **5** store **6** market, office, shoppe **8** emporium

businessman: **9** executive

powerful: **6** tycoon

busk: hie **4** seek, stir, tack **5** array, dress **6** corset, hasten **7** prepare, stiffen

buskin: **4** boot, shoe **7** bottine, tragedy **8** cothurni(L. pl.), half-boot, stocking **9** brodequin, cothurnus(L.)

buss: **4** boat, bush, calf, deck, kiss **5** dress, smack **6** vessel **9** transport

bussock: **6** donkey

bussu: **4** palm **7** troolie

bust: **4** fail, ruin, tame **5** bosom, break, burst, chest, flunk, spree **6** bronze, demote, reduce, statue **7** degrade, dismiss, failure **8** bankrupt **9** blockhead

sculptured part: **5** gaine **6** pillar

bust-up: **5** party, spree **7** failure **8** collapse, outbreak **11** dissolution

bustard: **4** bird, kori **5** paauw **7** bebilya, houbara **8** gompaaum

genus: **4** otis **6** otidae

bustee: **4** slum **6** hamlet **7** village

buster: **4** crab, wind **5** blade, child, spree **6** fellow

bustle: ado **4** fray, fuss, stir, todo, whir **5** frisk, haste, whirr **6** bishop, energy, fissle, fistle, flurry, fustle, huddle, hustle, pother, racket, tumult, unrest, uproar **7** clatter, contend, scuffle **8** activity, struggle, tournure **9** agitation, commotion, stirabout

woman's: **6** bishop

busy: **4** fell **5** brisk **6** active, eident, intent, lively, occupy **7** engaged, humming, operose, trouble **8** diligent, employed, occupied, sedulous, tireless, untiring **9** assiduous, attentive, detective, laborious, officious, unwearied **11** industrious, painstaking, persevering, unremitting **13** indefatigable

busybody: **4** busy **5** snoop **7** marplot, meddler, snooper **8** factotum, quidnunc

but: lo, ma(It.); sed(L.), yet **4** mere, only, save **5** still **6** except, unless **7** besides, howbeit, however **12** nevertheless

butcher: **4** kill, slay **5** spoil **6** bungle, murder, vendor **7** botcher, britten **8** pigstick **9** slaughter **10** pigsticker **11** executioner, slaughterer

hook: **7** gambrel

rabbi: **8** shochtim

tool: saw **5** knife, steel **7** cleaver

butcher-bird: **6** shrike

butchery: **6** murder **7** carnage **8** massacre, shambles **9** martyrdom, slaughter **12** manslaughter **14** slaughterhouse

butler: **6** yeoman **7** servant, spencer, steward **10** manservant

butt: jut, mot, pit, ram, run, tup **4** buck, bunt, burt, bush, cart, cask, fool, goad, goal, goat, jolt, poll, push, stub, tope **5** bound, hinge, joint, mound, stump **6** breech, target, thrust **7** beehive, buttock, parapet, project **8** flatfish, flounder

cigar or cigarette: **5** snipe

one third: **5** terce **6** tierce

butte: 4 hill 7 picacho 8 mountain

butter: 4 shea 6 beurre(F.), cajole, spread 7 blarney, flatter
artificial: 4 oleo, suin 8 margarin 9 butterine, margarine 12 oleomargarin 13 oleomargarine
comb. form: 6 butyro
lump: pat
pert. to: 7 butyric
semifluid: ghi 4 ghee
shea: 5 galam 6 bambui, bambuk 7 bambara
tree: 4 shea 5 fulwa 8 phulwara
tub: 6 firkin

butter-and-eggs: 6 clover 7 ransted 8 ramstead, ranstead, toadflax

butterbur: 5 eldin, plant

buttercup: 6 flower 7 anemone 8 reindeer 10 butter-rose
fruit: 6 achene

butterfish: 6 blenny, gunnel

butterfly: io 4 kiho 5 satyr 6 idalia, morpho, ursula 7 admiral, buckeye, monarch, skipper, vanessa, viceroy 8 arthemis, cecropia, grayling 9 aphrodite, underwing 10 fritillary, lepidopter
expert: 13 lepidopterist
fish: 6 blenny
genus: 8 melitaea 10 heliconius
larva: 11 caterpillar
lily: 4 sego 8 mariposa
peacock: io

buttermilk: 8 sourdook(Sc.)

butterwort: 9 steepweed

buttery: 6 larder, pantry, spence 9 apartment, storeroom, wheedling 10 flattering

button: bud 4 boss, chin, hook, knob, knop 5 badge, catch, pearl 6 bauble, buckle 8 fastener
ornamental: 4 stud
part: 5 shank
three jewel: 6 troche

buttonhole: 4 loop, slit 6 detain, eyelet 11 boutonniere

buttress: 4 pier, pile, prop, stay 5 brace 7 support 8 abutment 11 counterfort

butty: 4 chum 6 worker 7 partner, workman 9 companion, middleman

buxom: 4 mild 5 jolly, plump, prone, sonsy 6 blithe, florid, humble, pliant, sonsie 8 bouncing, flexible, obedient, obliging, yielding 9 compliant, courteous, tractable 10 submissive 11 complaisant

buy: 4 chap, coff(Sc.), coup, gain, shop 5 bribe, trade 6 market, ransom, redeem, secure 7 acquire 8 purchase
cheaply: 4 snup
to sell at a profit: 7 regrate

buyer: 4 chap 5 agent 6 emptor, patron 7 chapman, shopper 8 customer, prospect 9 purchaser
stolen property: 5 fence

buying and selling: 11 nundination

buzz: hum 4 burr, call, hiss, huss, huzz, ring, whir 5 fancy, fling, phone, rumor 6 notion 7 whisper 9 bombilate, telephone

buzzard: 4 aura, fool, hawk, pern 5 buteo 6 beetle, curlew, stupid 7 vulture 9 senseless
bald: 6 osprey
honey: 4 pern

buzzer: bee 4 bell 5 alarm, badge 6 signal 7 whizzer 10 pickpocket, talebearer

by: at; ago, per 4 abut, anon, near, past 5 apart, aside, close 6 beside, toward 7 besides, through 9 alongside 10 concerning
means of: per 4 from, with 7 through
mouth: 4 oral

by-pass: 4 shun 5 evade, shunt 6 detour 7 circuit

bygone: 4 past, yore 5 olden 6 former 7 ancient, elapsed 8 backward, departed

byname: 6 byword 7 surname 8 cognomen, nickname 9 sobriquet

bypath: 4 lane 5 byway

byre: 4 barn 6 stable

Byron character: 4 Inez, Lara 6 Haidee 7 Don Juan

byssin: 4 flax 5 linen

byssoid: 7 cottony 9 fiberlike 10 byssaceous

bystander: 7 witness 9 spectator

byway: 4 lane, path 5 alley

byword: 5 axiom, motto 6 byname, phrase, saying 7 proverb 8 nickname 9 catchword

Byzantine: *capital:* 6 Nicaea 14 Constantinople
coin: 6 bezant
empress: 5 Irene
mosaic: 4 icon
scepter: 6 ferula

C

C: 7 hundred

Caaba: 6 shrine

caama: fox 4 asse 10 hartebeest

cab: 4 hack, taxi 6 hansom

cab driver: 5 cabby 6 cabbie, cocher(F.) 7 cochero(Sp.)

cabal: 4 plot, ring 5 junta, party 6 brigue, clique, scheme, secret 7 chatter, consult, council, dispute, faction, talking 8 intrigue 9 occultism, tradition 10 conspiracy 11 combination
pert. to: 9 factional

cabalistic: 6 mystic 10 mysterious

caballero: 6 knight 8 cavalier, horseman 9 gentleman

caballo: 5 horse

cabana: 9 bathhouse

cabaret: 4 cafe 5 table 6 tavern 9 nightclub 10 restaurant

cabbage: cab 4 chou, crib, kale, wort 5 filch, steal 6 pilfer, tailor 7 bowkail, purloin 8 borecole, colewort 11 appropriate, translation
daisy: 11 globeflower
family: 12 brassicaceae
salad: 4 slaw 8 coleslaw
seed: 5 colza
soup: 4 kale(Sc.)
tree: 7 angelin
variety: 4 cale, kale 5 colza, savoy 8 colewort, kohlrabi

cabbagehead: 5 dunce 9 screwball

cabbageworm: 6 looper 7 cutworm

cabby: 6 cabbie, cabman 9 cabdriver

caber: 4 beam, pole, spar 6 rafter

cabin: cot, den, hut 4 cave, cell, shed 5 booth, coach, hovel, lodge, shack 6 litter, saloon, shanty 7 bedroom, boudoir, cottage 9 stateroom

cabin boy: 7 grummet

cabin car: 7 caboose

cabinet: box 4 buhl, case 5 habut, board, chest 6 bureau, closet 7 almirah, boudoir, console, council, etagere, whatnot 8 cellaret, cupboard, ministry 10 chiffonier

cable: 4 boom, link, rope, wire 6 ganger 8 telegram
lifter: 7 wildcat
post: 4 bitt

cable car: 6 telfer 7 telpher

cabling: 7 molding 9 rudenture

cabochon: gem 5 stone 8 ornament

caboodle: kit, lot 10 collection

caboose: cab, car 5 buggy 6 galley

cabotin: 5 actor 9 charlatan

cabrilla: 4 bass 7 grouper

cacao: 4 bean 5 broma, cocoa 6 arriba 9 chocolate
shell extract: 6 martol

cache: 4 bury, hide 5 store 6 screen 7 conceal 8 treasure 10 storehouse

cachet: 4 seal 5 stamp, wafer

cachexia: 7 illness, wasting 9 morbidity 12 malnutrition

cacholong: 4 opal

cackle: 4 cank 5 clack, laugh 6 babble, gabble, giggle, gossip, keckle, titter 7 chackle, chatter, snicker, twaddle 8 laughter

cacoethes: 4 itch 6 desire

cacography: 11 misspelling

cacophonous: 5 harsh 7 raucous 8 jangling, strident 9 dissonant 10 discordant 11 unmelodious

cactus: 4 bleo 5 dildo, nopal, plant 6 cereus, chaute, chende, cholla 7 airampo, saguaro 8 chichope
drug: 6 peyote
fruit: 6 cochal
plantation: 7 nopalry

cad: cur 4 boor, chum, heel 5 churl 6 rascal, rotter 7 bounder, dastard 9 scoundrel

cadaver: 4 body 5 stiff 6 corpse 7 carcass 8 skeleton

cadaverous: 4 pale 5 gaunt 7 ghastly, haggard

caddis fly: 4 bait 5 cadew 6 cadbit 7 cadbait, cadbote

caddle: 4 fuss, mess 5 annoy, tease, worry 6 gossip 7 confuse, trouble 8 disarray 9 confusion 13 embarrassment

caddow: 5 quilt 7 jackdaw 8 coverlet

caddy: box, boy, can 5 chest

cade: keg, pet 4 cask, lamb 6 barrel, coddle 7 indulge, juniper

cadence: 4 beat, lilt, pace, tone 5 meter, metre, sound, swing, throb 6 rhythm, 8 clausula 10 modulation

cadent: 7 falling 10 descending, rhythmical

cadet: son 5 plebe, youth 6 embryo, junior 10 midshipman

cadew: 4 worm

cadge: beg, tie 4 bind, hawk 5 carry, mooch 6 peddle, sponge 8 scrounge

cadger: 6 dealer, hawker 7 carrier, packman, sponger 8 huckster

cadgy: 6 wanton 7 lustful 8 cheerful, mirthful

Cadmus: *daughter:* Ino 5 Agave 6 Semele 7 Autonoe

father: 6 Agenor

sister: 6 Europa

wife: 8 Harmonia

cadre: 4 core 5 frame, group 6 scheme 9 framework

caduceus: 4 wand 5 staff 6 symbol 7 insigne, scepter, sceptre

caducity: 5 lapse 8 senility 10 feebleness 14 perishableness

caecum: See **cecum**

Caen stone: 9 freestone, limestone

Caesar (see also **Augustus**): 6 tyrant 7 emperor

assassin: 6 Brutus 7 Cassius

capital: 4 Roma

colleague: 7 Bibulus

country conquered by: 4 Gaul

fatal day: 4 Ides

place of victory: 6 Actium

river crossed by: 7 Rubicon

sister: 4 Atia

site of famous message: 4 Zela

wife: 8 Cornelia 9 Calpurnia

caesura: 4 rest, stop 5 break, pause 8 interval 12 interruption

cafard: 5 bigot, blues 6 apathy, humbug 9 hypocrite 10 depression

cafe: 7 barroom, cabaret 8 teahouse 10 restaurant 11 coffeehouse

caffeine: 5 thein 6 theine 8 alkaloid 9 stimulant

cage: box, car, pen 4 coop 5 brake 6 aviary, basket, bucket, chapel, prison 7 chantry, confine 8 imprison, scaffold, strainer 9 enclosure, inclosure

cage hawk: mew 5 meute

caged: 4 pent

cagey, cagy: sly 4 wary

cahoots: 6 league 9 collusion 11 partnership

caiman: 6 cayman, jacare 9 alligator

Cain: 8 murderer 10 fratricide

brother: Pur 4 Abel, Seth

descendant: 6 Lamech

father: 4 Adam

land: Nod

mother: Eve

nephew: 4 Enos

son: 5 Enoch

cairn: 4 pike 5 mound 8 stoneman

cairngorm: 6 quartz

caisson: box 4 pont 5 chest, wagon 6 ponton 7 chamber, pontoon

disease: 5 bends

caitiff: 4 base, mean, vile 6 coward, wicked 7 captive 8 cowardly, prisoner, wretched 10 despicable

cajole: cog 4 coax, flam, palp 5 carny, cheat, curry, decoy, jolly, tease 6 carney, delude, entice, fraise, humbug, whilly 7 beguile, flatter, wheedle 8 blandish 9 bamboozle 10 honey-fogle

cajolery: 5 fraik 6 butter 8 flattery

cake: bar, bun, wig 4 bake, flae, fool, lump, mass, tart 5 batty, block, crust, scone, torte, wafer, wedge 6 barkle, cimbal, eclair, harden, nacket, pastry 7 bannock, oatcake, pancake 8 solidify 9 coagulate, simpleton 11 griddlecake

almond: 7 macaron 8 macaroon

boiled in honey: 8 teiglech

corn: 4 pone 7 fritter

custard: 6 eclair 9 creampuff

dough: 6 batter

filled: 4 flan

fried: 7 cruller 8 doughnut

griddle: 7 bannock(Sc.), crumpet, hotcake, pancake

plum: 4 baba

rich: 5 torte 8 madeline 9 madeleine

sacrificial: 6 hallah

seed: wig 4 wiff

small: bun 4 tart 5 batty 6 jumble 7 cupcake

tea: 5 scone

thin: 5 scone, wager 8 tortilla(Sp.)

unleavened: 5 matzo 6 damper 8 tortilla

cakewalk: 4 walk 5 dance, march, strut 6 prance

calaba: 4 tree 5 birma

calabash: 5 gourd 6 curuba

calaboose: jug 4 brig, gaol, jail 6 prison 8 bastille

caladium: 4 taro

calamanco: 5 manco 6 fabric 7 garment

calamitous: sad 4 dire, evil 5 black, fatal 6 bitter, dismal, tragic, woeful 7 adverse, baleful, direful, hapless, ruinous, unhappy, unlucky 8 grievous, tragical,

wretched 9 miserable 10 afflictive, deplorable, disastrous 11 distressful, unfortunate

calamity: 4 blow, evil, ruin 5 storm, wrack 6 misery, sorrow 8 accident, disaster, distress, fatality 9 adversity, mischance 10 affliction, misfortune 11 catastrophe, unhappiness 12 misadventure, wretchedness

calamus: pen 4 cane, reed 9 sweetflag

calangay: 8 cockatoo

calash: 6 calesa

calcar: 4 oven, spur 7 furnace

calcareous: See calcite

calced: 4 shod

calcite: *animal:* 8 skeleton
deposit: 4 spar, tufa 5 tatar 10 stalactite, stalagmite
soil with: 4 marl

calcium: *carbonate:* 4 tufa
oxide: 9 quicklime
sulphate: 5 hepar 6 gypsum

calculate: aim 4 plan, rate, tell 5 count, frame, think 6 design, expect, figure, number, reckon 7 average, compute, prepare 8 consider, estimate, forecast 9 determine, enumerate

calculation: 4 care 5 share 7 account, caution 8 forecast, prudence 9 logistics, reckoning 10 adjustment, discretion 11 computation

calculator: 5 table 6 abacus 7 soroban 10 accountant

Calcutta: *hemp* 4 jute
river: 5 Hugli 7 Hooghly
weight: 4 pank, raik 5 hubba, pally

calderite: 6 garnet

caldron, cauldron: pot, red, vat 4 afet 6 boiler, kettle, vessel 8 go-ashore

Caleb's son: Hur, Iru

Caledonia: 8 Scotland

Caledonian: 4 Pict, Scot 8 Scotsman

calefy: 4 heat, warm

calendar: 5 diary 7 almanac, calends, journal, kalends 8 register, schedule 9 repertory, ephemeris
church: 4 ordo
former: 6 Julian
French revolution: 6 Nivose 7 Floreal, Ventose 8 Brumaire, Fervidor, Gernubak, Messidor, Pluviose, Prairial 9 Fructidor, Thermidor 11 Vendemiaire

calenture: 4 fire, glow 5 ardor, fever 7 passion 9 sunstroke

calf: bob, boy, leg 4 buss, dolt 5 bobby, bossy, dogie, moggy, youth 6 bovine, muscle 7 bulchin, fatling 9 quadruped
flesh: 4 veal, veau(F.)
jelly: 7 fisnoga
motherless: 4 dogy 5 dogie 8 maverick

muscle: 9 plantaris
pert. to: 5 sural

Caliban: 5 beast, slave
adversary of: 8 Prospero
deity of: 7 Setebos
witch mother: 7 Sycorax

caliber: 4 bore, rank 6 degree, talent 7 ability, breadth, compass, quality 8 capacity, diameter

calibrate: 7 measure 11 standardize

calico: 4 girl 5 pinto, sallo, woman 6 salloo 7 spotted 8 goldfish 9 womankind 12 multicolored
horse: 5 pinto
mix colors for: 4 teer
pigment: 7 canarin 8 canarine
printing: 4 teer 5 fondu, lapis

calid: hot 4 warm 7 burning

Calif: 6 Caliph

California: *bay:* 8 Monterey
bulrush: 4 tule
capital: 10 Sacramento
condor: 8 gymnogyp
county: 4 Inyo, Kern, Lake, Napa, Yolo, Yuba 5 Butte, Costa, Glenn, Kings, Marin, Modoc 6 Alpine, Amador, Colusa, Contra, Fresno, Lassen, Madera, Merced, Nevada, Orange, Plumas, Obispo, Shasta, Sierra, Solano, Sonoma, Sutter, Tehama, Tulare 7 Alameda, San Luis, Trinity, Ventura 8 Del Norte, Eldorado, Humboldt, Imperial, Mariposa, Monterey, San Diego, Siskiyou, Toulumne 9 Calaveras, Mendocino, Riverside, San Benito, Santa Cruz, San Joquin 10 Los Angeles, Sacramento, Santa Clara, Stanislaus 12 San Francisco, Santa Barbara 13 San Bernardino
dam: 6 Shasta
desert: 6 Mohave, Mojave
fan palm: 7 erythea
fish: 5 reina, sprat
fort: Ord
Indian: 4 Hupa, Pomo, Seri, Yuma 5 Hoopa, Yurok 10 Weitspekan
island: 4 Goat, Mare 7 Anacapa 8 Alcatraz, Catalina, Coronado, Nicholas, Treasure 9 Farollone, San Miguel, Santa Cruz, Santa Rosa 11 San Clemente 12 Santa Barbara
lake: 5 Tahoe
laurel: 7 cajeput, cajuput
motto: 6 Eureka
oak: 5 roble 6 encina
observatory: 4 Lick 7 Palomar 8 Mt. Wilson
pass: 6 Donner, Sonora
peak: 6 Lassen, Shasta
plant: 7 tarweed

river: Eel, Mad, Pit 4 Kern 5 Kings, Smith 6 Merced, Salmon 7 Feather, Klamath, Russian, Salinas, Trinity 10 Sacramento, San Jacinto, Stanislaus

rockfish: 4 rena 5 reina, viuva 6 rasher 8 bocaccio

sea: 6 Salton

shrub: 5 salal 7 chamise, chamiso, tarbush 9 chaparral, manzanita

town: 4 Asti, Napa 5 Tracy 6 Arcata, Eureka, Fresno, Salina 7 Alameda, Arcadia

tree: 6 torrey 7 redwood, sequoia 12 Wellingtonia

valley: 4 Napa

wine area: 4 Napa

caliginous: dim 4 dark 5 misty 7 obscure

Caligula's horse: 9 Incitatus

caliph, calif: Abu, Ali 4 Bekr, Imam, Omar 6 Othman 9 caliphate

descendant: 5 Alide 7 Fatamid 8 Fatamite

fourth: Ali

calix: cup 7 chalice

calk: nap 4 copy, stop 5 close 7 occlude, silence

calking: 5 oakum

call: bid, cry, dub 4 cite, hail, name, page, stop, term, yell 5 claim, clepe, clock, elect, phone, rouse, shout, style, utter, visit, waken, yodel, yodle 6 accuse, appeal, arouse, demand, invite, invoke, muster, quethe, summon 7 address, appoint, collect, command, convene, convoke, entitle, impeach 8 announce, assemble, nominate, proclaim, vocation 9 challenge, reprimand, telephone, terminate 10 denominate

back: 6 revoke 8 retrieve

distress: S.O.S.

down: 5 scold 6 berate, invoke, rebuke 7 censure, reprove 8 denounce, execrate 9 reprimand

for: 4 page 5 exact 6 demand 7 request, require

forth: 5 evoke 6 arouse, elicit, invoke, signal, summon 7 evocate

off: end 6 cancel

out: 5 ascry, evoke 6 muster

to: 4 hail 5 ascry 6 accost, halloo 7 address

to attention: hop 6 remind

to mind: 4 cite 6 recall 8 remember

together: 6 muster, summon 7 convoke

call girl: 10 prostitute

Call of the Wild author: 6 London

callan, callant: boy, lad 4 chap 6 fellow 8 customer

calligrapher: 6 penman, writer 7 copyist 9 engrosser

calling: art, job 4 rank 5 trade 6 career, metier, naming, outcry 7 pursuit, station, summons 8 business, function, position, shouting, vocation 9 condition, summoning, utterance 10 employment, invitation, occupation, profession 11 appellation, convocation, undertaking 13 circumstances

Calliope's son: 7 Orpheus

Callisto's son: 5 Arcas

callous: 4 hard 5 horny, tough 6 brawny, obtuse, torpid 8 obdurate 9 indurated, unfeeling 11 hardhearted, indifferent 14 pachydermatous

callow: 4 bald, bare 5 crude, green 6 marshy 7 meadown 8 immature, unformed, youthful 9 unfledged 13 inexperienced 15 unsophisticated

calm: lee 4 cool, dill, easy, fair, hush, lull, mees(Sc.), mild, rest 5 abate, allay, charm, mease, peace, quell, quiet, sober, still, stoic 6 docile, gentle, irenic, pacify, placid, sedate, serene, smooth, soothe, steady 7 appease, assuage, halcyon, mollify, pacific, patient, placate, restful, unmoved 8 composed, decorous, peaceful, restrain, tranquil 9 collected, impassive, temperate, unexcited, unruffled 10 halcyonian, phlegmatic, unconfused 11 complacence, tranquilize, undisturbed 13 dispassionate, imperturbable 15 undemonstrative

calmness: 5 poise 6 repose 8 ataraxia, serenity 9 composure, placidity, quietness, sang-froid, stillness 10 equanimity 11 self-control, tranquility 12 peacefulness 13 impassiveness

calorie, calory: 5 therm 6 therme

calotte: 4 coif 6 summit

calumet: 4 pipe

calumniate: 4 slur 5 belie, libel 6 accuse, attack, defame, malign, revile, vilify 7 asperse, blacken, slander, traduce 9 blaspheme

calyx: 4 leaf 5 sepal

helmet-shaped: 5 galea

of flower: 8 perianth

cam: cog 4 awry, lobe 5 askew, catch, wiper 6 tappet 7 crooked, trippet 8 perverse

camail: 4 hood 5 guard 6 tippet

camalig: hut 5 cabin 10 storehouse

camara: 5 house 7 chamber

camarilla: 4 cell, ring 5 cabal, junta 6 clique 7 chamber, company 11 combination

camas, cammas: 5 plain 7 lobelia, prairie

Cambodia: *ancient capital:* 6 Angkor

capital: 8 Pnompenh

lake: 8 Tonle Sap

native: 5 Khmer

official name: 13 Khmer Republic

river: 6 Mekong

temple: 9 Angkor Wat

Cambria: 7 Camboja 8 Cambodge

Cambria: See **Wales**

cambric: 5 linen 7 batiste
Cambridge: *boat races:* 4 Lent
  college official: 6 bedell
  council: 5 caput
  honor examination: 6 tripos
  student: 5 sizar, spoon 6 optime
camel: 4 cont 6 mehari 7 tylopod 8 bactrian,
  ruminant 9 dromedary 10 camelopard
  driver: 6 sarwan 8 cameleer
  female: 4 naga
  fermented milk: 5 kumys 6 koumis, kumiss
  7 koumiss, koumyss
  keeper: 4 obil
  two-humped: 8 Bactrian
camellia: 8 japonica
Camelot: *lord:* 6 Arthur
  magician: 6 Merlin
camel's hair: aba 5 cloth 6 camlet 8 came-
line
  garment: aba
cameo: gem 7 camaieu(F.), carving, relievo,
  rilievo, phalera 8 anaglyph 9 sculpture
  cutting tool: 5 spade
  stone: 4 onyx 8 sardonyx
camera: 7 chamber 10 department, instrument
  part: 4 lens 6 finder 7 bellows, shutter
  platform: 5 dolly
cameraman: 8 camerist, operator 12 photographer 13 projectionist
Cameroon: *inhabitant:* 4 Sara
  river: 5 Shari
camion: bus 4 dray 5 truck, wagon 7 motor-
bus
camlet: 6 Angora, fabric, mohair 9 camel-
teen, camletine
Camorra: 5 Mafia
camouflage: 4 fake, hide 6 muffle, screen 7
  conceal 8 disguise 9 deception
camp: 4 pest, tent 5 etape(F.), horde, siege,
  tabor 7 bivouac, shelter 8 quarters 10 settlement
  follower: 5 bidar(Ind.) 6 gudget(Sc.)
  pert. to: 7 castral
  provision seller: 6 sutler
campaign: 5 drive, plain 7 canvass, crusade,
  solicit 9 champaign, operation
campanero: 8 arapunga, bellbird
campanile: 5 tower 6 belfry 7 clocher, steeple
camphol: 7 borneol
camphor: 7 menthol, asarone
campus: 4 quad 5 field 7 grounds
Camus work: 5 Rebel
can: cup, jug, may, tin 4 able, fire, jail 5
  caddy, could, eshin, skill 6 vessel 7 ability,
  capable, dismiss 8 conserve, preserve 9
  competent, container, discharge, knowledge 10 cleverness, receptacle

Canada: *airport:* 6 Gander
  boat: 6 bateau 7 bateaux(pl.), batteau 8 bat-
teaux(pl.)
  city: 5 Banff, Levis, Sorel 6 Ottawa(c.), Regina 7 Calgary, Toronto 8 Edmonton,
Montreal, Victoria, Winnipeg 9 Carstairs,
Saskatoon, Vancouver
  court decree: 5 arret
  fur company employee: 8 voyageur
  gannet: 6 margot
  goose: 5 brant 6 honker
  lake: 4 Cree, Gras, Seul 6 Louise, Teslin
  land measure: 6 arpent, roture
  lynx: 5 pishu
  measure: ton 5 minot, perch, point 6 arpent
7 chainon
  mountain: 4 Gold 5 Logan 7 Cascade, Rockies, St. Elias 9 Notre Dame 10 Laurentian,
Shickshock
  peninsula: 5 Gaspe
  physician: 5 Osler
  policeman: 6 mounty 7 mountie
  poplar: 5 liard
  porcupine: 5 urson 7 cawquaw
  province: 6 Quebec 7 Alberta, Ontario 8
Manitoba 10 Nova Scotia 12 New Brunswick, Newfoundland, Saskatchewan 15
British Columbia 18 Prince Edward Island
  river: 4 Back, Leaf 5 Peace, Trent 6 Albany,
Fraser, Nelson, Ottawa, Skeena 8 Gati-
neau, Saguenay, Stickeen 9 Athabasca,
Churchill, Great Bear, Great Fish, Mac-
kenzie, Richelieu, St. Maurice 10 Copper-
mine, Great Slave, Peace Slave, St. Lawrence 12 Saskatchewan
  territory: 5 Yukon 9 Northwest
Canadian: 6 Canuck
canadine: 8 alkaloid
canaille: mob 5 flour 6 rabble 7 rifraff
canal: cut 4 cano, duct, tube 5 ditch, drain,
  fossa(L.), graff, zanje 6 fossae(L.pl.),
  groove, strait, trench 7 acequia(Sp.), channel, conduit, raceway, towpath 8 aqueduct
  10 waterspout 11 watercourse
  dredging machine: 7 couloir
  famous: Soo 4 Erie, Kiel, Suez 6 Morris,
Panama 7 Welland
  footpath: 7 towpath
Canal Zone: *city:* 6 Balboa
  lake: 5 Gatun
canape: 6 relish 9 appetizer 11 hors d'oeuvre
canard: 4 hoax 9 grapewine 11 fabrication
canary: 4 bird 5 dance 6 singer 8 informer,
  squealer
  forerunner of: 5 serin
canary broom: 7 genista
Canary Islands: 4 Roca 5 Ferro, Lobos,
  Palma, Clara 6 Gomero 7 Inferno 8 Graci-

osa, Rocca Sta., Tenerife 9 Lanzarote, Teneriffe 10 Allegranza 11 Grand Hierro 13
Fuerteventura
city: 6 Laguna 9 Santa Cruz(c.)
commune: 4 Icod
measure: 8 fanegada
mountain: 6 La Cruz 8 El Cumbre, Tenerife
9 Teneriffe 11 Gran Canaria
canary yellow: 6 meline
canasta: 4 game 5 cards, crate 6 basket,
hamper
play: 4 meld
cancel: 4 blot, dele, omit 5 annul, erase,
quash, remit 6 delete, efface, recall, remove, revoke 7 abolish, destroy, expunge,
nullify, rescind, retract, scratch 8 abrogate 10 obliterate 11 countermand
cancion: 4 song 5 lyric
candent: hot 7 fervent, glowing
candescent: 7 glowing 8 dazzling 11 lumi-
nescent 15 autoluminescent
Candia: 5 Crete
candid: 4 fair, just, open, pure 5 blunt,
clear, frank, naive 6 honest 7 artless, sincere 8 splendid 9 guileless, honorable, impartial, ingenuous, outspoken 10 immaculate 11 illustrious 15 straightforward
candidate: 7 nominee 8 aspirant, prospect 9
applicant
list: 4 leet 5 slate 6 roster
religious: 9 postulant
winning: 7 electee
Candiot, Candiote: 6 Cretan
candle: dip, wax 5 light, taper 6 cierge(F.) 9
chandelle
holder: 6 lampad, sconce, sconse 9 girandole 10 candelabra 11 candlestick
kind of: 8 bayberry
place of keeping: 9 chandlery
wax: 5 taper 6 bougie
candlelight: 4 dusk 8 twilight 9 nightfall
candlelighter: 5 spill 7 acolyte
candlenut tree: ama 5 kukui 6 bankul
candlestick: 6 lampad, sconce 8 flambeau,
standard 9 flambeaux(pl.)
bracket: 6 sconce, sconse
branched: 5 jesse 8 dicerion, dikerion 9 girandole, tricerion, trikerion 10 chandelier
11 candelabrum
candlewood: 4 tree 5 shrub 9 coachwhip
candor, candour: 6 purity 8 fairness, kindness 9 frankness, innocence, unreserve,
whiteness 10 brightness, brilliance, kind-
liness 12 impartiality 13 outspokenness
candy: 5 fudge, gundy, lolly, sweet, taffy 6
bonbon, comfit, nougate 7 brittle, caramel, congeal, fondate, flatter, sweeten 8
lollipop 9 granulate, sweetmeat 10 confection 11 crystallize

base: 7 fondant
mixture: 6 fourre
nut: 7 praline
pulled sugar: 5 taffy 6 penide
sugar: 7 fondant 8 alphenic
candytuft: 5 plant 6 flower, iberis
cane: rod 4 beat, dart, flog, pipe, reed, stem,
tube, whip 5 birch, lance, staff, stick 6
bamboo, punish, rattan 7 calamus, hickory, malacca, scourge 9 crabstick
dense growth: 9 canebrake
knife: 7 machete
part: 7 ferrule
sugar: 7 sucrose
Canfield: 8 Klondike 9 solitaire
cangle: 7 dispute, quarrel, wrangle
canine (see also **dog**): cur, dog, fox, pup 4
fisc, wolf 5 canis(L.) 7 doglike
tooth: 7 laniary
caning: 6 rattan
canister: box 9 container
canker: 4 rust 6 infect 7 consume, corrode,
corrupt, tarnish 9 verdigris
cannabis: 4 hemp
drug: 5 bhang 7 hashish 9 marijuana
Cannery Row author: 9 Steinbeck
cannibal: 6 savage 15 anthropophagite
cannikin: can, cup 4 pail 6 bucket
cannon: bit, gun 5 crack, thief 6 mortar 7
bastard 8 howitzer, ordnance 9 artillery
10 pickpocket
breech-end knob: 8 cascabel
early: 5 aspic, saker 7 robinet
fire: 7 barrage
firing stick: 8 linstock
fodder: 8 infantry
handle: 4 anse
muzzle plug: 7 tampion
part: 4 bore 5 chase 6 breech, muzzle 7
chamber, rimbase 8 cascabel, trunnion
shot: 5 grape
support: 8 trunnion
cannonade: 7 barrage
cannoneer: 12 artilleryman
cannot: 6 unable
cannular: 6 hollow 7 tubular
canny: sly 4 cozy, snug, wary, wily, wise 5
lucky, pawky, quiet 6 clever, frugal, gentle, shrewd 7 careful, cunning, knowing,
prudent, quietly, thrifty 8 cautious, skillful, watchful 9 carefully, dexterous, fortunate, sagacious 10 cautiously 11 comfortable, sharpwitted
canoe: 4 boat, kiak, pahi, proa, waka 5
birch, kayak, prahu, skiff, umiak, waapa 6
ballam, dugout, oomiak, pitpan 7 almadia,
bidarka, coracle, currane, pirogue
bark: 7 cascara

dugout: **5** banca **6** baroto, corial **7** pirogue, piroque **12** pambanmanche

large: pah **5** bungo

sailing: **4** proa **5** prahu

skin-covered: **4** kiak **5** bidar, kayak **7** baidara

war: **4** proa

canon: law **4** code, hymn, laud, list, rule, song **5** axiom, gorge, gulch, model, table, tenet **6** decree **7** precept, statute **8** decision, standard **9** catalogue, clergyman, criterion **10** regulation **12** constitution

enigmatical: **4** nodi(pl.) **5** nodus

resident: **8** stagiary

canonical: **8** accepted, orthodox **13** authoritative

hour: **4** laud, none, sext **5** matin, prime **6** tierce **7** vespers **8** compline

canonicals: alb **4** cope, cowl, robe **5** stole

canopy: sky **4** ceil, cope, dais, hood **5** shade, vault **6** awning, celure, finial, tester **7** marquee, shelter **8** covering **9** baldachin, baldaquin, pavillion **11** baldacchino

altar: **7** ciboria(pl.) **8** baldakin, ciborium **9** baldachin, baldaquin **10** baldachino **11** baldacchino

bed: **6** tester **7** sparver

canorous: **5** clear **7** musical **8** sonorous **9** melodious **10** euphonious

cant: tip **4** coax, heel, lean, list, nook, sing, tilt, turn **5** argot, bevel, chant, hield, lingo, lusty, merry, niche, pitch, share, slang, slant, slope, whine **6** careen, corner, herald, intone, jargon, lively, patois, snivel **7** auction, incline, portion, singing, wheedle **8** cheerful, pretense, vigorous **9** barbarism, hyprocrisy, vulgarism **10** intonation **13** colloquialism **17** sanctimoniousness

cantabank: **6** singer **7** chanter

cantaloupe, cantaloup: **9** muskmelon

cantankerous: **6** ornery **8** perverse **9** irritable, malicious **10** brabagious **11** contentious **12** crossgrained

cantata: **4** mote, poem **8** serenata **11** composition

cantatrice: **6** singer **9** chanteuse

canteen: K.T., P.X., bar **5** bazar, flask **6** bazaar **7** cantina

canter: jog, run **4** gait, lope, pace, rack **5** rogue **6** beggar, whiner **8** vagabond

Canterbury: *archbishop:* Odo **4** Lang **6** Anselm, Becket **7** Crammer

gallop: **5** aubin

canticle: ode **4** hymn, laud, song **5** canto **6** anthem, cantic, hirmos **7** bravura

church: **6** Te Deum, venite **10** magnificat

cantilena: **6** legato, melody **8** graceful

cantillate: hum **5** chant **6** intone, recite

cantina: bag **5** pouch, store **6** pocket, pommel, saloon **7** canteen

canting: **5** atrip, pious **12** hypocritical

cantle: **4** join, nook, part **5** cheer, piece, raise, slice **6** corner **7** portion, segment **8** brighten, fragment **11** cornerpiece

canto: air, fit **4** book, pace, song **5** verse **6** melody, passus

canton: **4** part **5** angle **6** corner **7** portion, quarter, section **8** district, division

cantor: **6** leader, singer **7** chanter, soloist **9** precentor

cantoria: **7** balcony, gallery

cantrip: **5** charm, spell, trick

cantus: **4** song **5** chant

canty: **6** lively **8** cheerful **9** sprightly

Canuck: **8** Canadian

canvas: **4** duck, sail, tarp, tent, tewk **5** scrim **6** burlap **7** picture, poldavy **8** painting

waterproof: **9** tarpaulin

canvasback: **4** duck **6** cheval

canvass: **4** beat, hawk, poll, sift **5** randy, study **6** debate, peddle, search **7** agitate, discuss, examine, solicit, trounce **8** campaign, consider **11** electioneer, investigate

canvasser: **5** agent **6** poller, rodman **7** counter **8** salesman

canyon: **5** cajon, chasm, gorge, gulch **6** arroyo, ravine

mouth: **4** abra

small: **6** canada

canzonet: air **4** song **5** canto **6** ballad **7** canzona, canzone **8** madrigal

caoba: **5** quira **8** mahogany, muskwood

caoutchouc: **6** rubber

source: ule **6** caucho

cap: fez, hat, lid, taj, tam, tip, top **4** acme, coif, cork, dome, eton, hood, hure, mate, topi **5** beret, chief, cover, crown, excel, match, outdo, seize, topee **6** arrest, beanie, bonnet, climax, cornet, helmet, puzzle, summit, turban **7** commode, ferrule, overlie, overtop, perplex, surpass **8** headgear, surprise, tarboosh **9** detonator, headpiece **11** mortarboard

child's: **5** mutch, toque **6** biggin, bonnet

close-fitting: **4** coif **5** toque **6** cloche **7** calotte

covering: **8** havelock

ecclesiastical: **5** beret **6** barret **7** biretta, galerum, galerus **8** barretta

hunter's: **7** montero

ignition: **4** fuse, fuze

military: **4** kepi **5** busby, shako

muslin: **5** mutch

part: **4** bill, peak **5** visor

Roman: **6** pileus

Scotch: tam **8** balmoral **9** glengarry **11** tamoshanter

sheepskin: **6** calpac **7** calpack

skull: 5 beame 6 callot, pileus 7 calotte, yamilke 8 yarmulka
steel: 10 cerveliere
cap-a-pie: 7 utterly 10 throughout
capa: 5 cloak 6 mantle
capability: 6 stroil 7 ability 8 capacity 9
potential 10 competence, efficiency
capable: apt, can, fit 4 able 5 adept 6 expert
7 skilled 9 competent, effective, efficient,
qualified 10 proficient 12 accomplished
of being cut: 7 sectile 8 scissile
of being defended: 7 tenable
of being heard: 7 audible
of being molded: 7 plastic
of being touched: 8 tangible
of endurance: 4 wiry 5 tough
of extension: 7 tensile
of flying: 6 volant
of suffering: 8 passible 9 sensitive
render: 6 enable
capacious: 4 full, wide 5 ample, broad,
large, roomy 6 goodly 8 captious, spacious
9 extensive 10 commodious 12 considerable
capacitate: 7 qualify
capacity: 4 bent, gift, size, turn 5 knack,
power, skill, space 6 burden, extent,
spread, talent, volume 7 ability, caliber,
calibre, content, faculty, fitness 8 aptitude, strength 9 continent, endowment,
intellect 10 capability, competence
Capaneus: *father:* 9 Hipponous
mother: 8 Astynome
son: 9 Sthenelus
wife: 6 Evadne
caparison: 4 deck, trap 8 covering 9 adornment 10 decoration
capatas: 4 boss 7 capataz(Sp.), foreman 8
overseer
capcase: bag 4 case 5 chest 10 receptacle
cape: ras 4 cope, gape, head, look, neck,
ness, writ 5 amice, cappa, cloak, fanon,
fichu, orale, point, sagum, stare, stole,
talma 6 bertha, chapel, mantle, sontag,
tabard, tippet 7 leather, manteel 8 headland, lambskin, mantilla 9 inverness, peninsula, sheepskin 10 projection, promontory
crocheted: 6 sontag
lace: 5 fichu 6 bertha 8 collaret
Cape anteater: 8 aardvark
Cape armadillo: 8 pangolin
Cape Colony plateau: 5 karoo 6 karroo
Cape Dutch: 9 Afrikaans
Cape elk: 5 eland
Cape gooseberry: 4 poha 12 ground cherry
Cape jasmine: 8 gardenia
Cape lancewood: 7 assagai
cape merchant: 10 supercargo

Cape polecat: 5 zoril 8 muishond
Cape Province: *people:* 4 Xosa 5 Pondo
Cape Ruby: 6 garnet, pyrope
Cape Verde: *capital:* 5 Praia
island: Sal 4 Fago
native: 5 Brava, Serer
Capek: *play:* RUR
creature: 5 robot
capel: 4 rock, wall 5 horse 6 quartz
caper: hop 4 dido, jump, leap, romp, skip,
skit 5 antic, brank, dance, flisk, frisk,
prank, sauce, shrub 6 cavort, frisco, frolic,
gambol, gamond, prance, spring, tittup,
vagary 7 corsair, courant, friscal, gambado 8 capricci(pl.), capriole, marigold 9
capriccio, condiment, privateer
family: 13 capparidaceae
capercaillie: 4 cock 6 grouse
courtship: lak
capernoited: 7 crabbed, peevish 9 irritable
11 intoxicated 12 muddleheaded
capernoitie: 4 head 6 noddle
capeskin: 7 leather 9 sheepskin
capful: 4 puff 8 quantity
capias: 4 writ 7 process
capillary: 6 minute 7 slender 8 filiform,
hairlike
capillus: 4 hair
capilotade: 4 stew 5 sauce 6 ragout
capital: 4 cash, city, good, main, rare, seat 5
basic, chief, fatal, great, major, money,
stock, vital 6 deadly, letter, mortal, primal, wealth 7 central, chattel, leading,
radical, serious, weighty 9 copacetic, excellent, paramount, principal, prominent
10 pre-eminent 11 scrumptious
ancient: 4 Roma
impairment of: 7 deficit 9 depletion
provide: 4 back 5 angel 7 finance
capital punishment: 7 hanging 8 shooting
12 death penalty 13 electrocution
capitalist: 8 investor 9 plutocrat
capitano: 5 chief 7 captain, headman, soldier
capitate: 8 headlike
Capitol Hill group: 5 House 6 Senate
capitulate: 4 fall 5 agree, title, yield 8 headline 9 enumerate, surrender
caporal: 7 foreman, tobacco 8 overseer
capote: 4 hood 5 cloak 6 bonnet, mantle,
topper 8 overcoat
capric acid salt: 6 rutate
caprice: fad 4 kink, mood, whim 5 antic,
braid, fancy, freak, humor, quirk 6 maggot, notion, temper, vagary, whimsy 7 boutade, conceit, crochet, impulse, whimsey 9
capriccio 12 inconsistent
capricious: 5 dizzy, doddy, fluky, moody 6
fickle 7 comical, erratic, flighty, wayward
8 fanciful, freakish, humorous, unsteady,

volatile 9 arbitrary, crotchety, fantastic, humorsome, whimsical 10 changeable, inconstant

Capricorn: 4 Goat 6 beetle 13 Constellation
star within: 5 Deneb

capriole: 4 leap 5 caper 6 spring 9 headdress

capripede: 4 goat 5 satyr

caprylate: 4 acid, salt 5 ester 7 octoate

capsize: 4 coup, keel 5 upset 8 overturn

capstan: 4 drum 5 hoist, lever 8 cylinder, windlass
catch: 4 pawl

capsule: pod 4 boll, case, pill 5 shell, theco, wafer 6 ampule, sheath 7 ampoule 8 pericarp 9 cartridge, detonator 10 repository

captain: bo; boh 4 head 5 chief 6 leader, master 7 capitan, foreman, headman, manager, skipper 8 capitano, governor 9 centurion, commander, principal 14 superintendent
boat: gig

caption: 5 title 6 leader, legend 7 heading 8 headline, subtitle

captious: 5 testy 6 crafty, severe 7 carping, cynical, fretful, peevish 8 alluring, caviling, contrary, critical 9 capacious, insidious, irascible 10 capricious, censorious 12 faultfinding 13 hypercritical

captivate: win 4 take 5 catch, charm 6 allure, enamor, please, ravish, subdue 7 attract, bewitch, capture, enamour, enchant 8 enthrall, overtake 9 enrapture, fascinate, infatuate

captive: 5 slave 6 enamor 7 caitiff 8 prisoner

captivity: 4 bond 6 duress 7 bondage, serfdom, slavery 9 servitude, thralldom 10 subjection 11 confinement 12 imprisonment

captor: 5 taker 6 victor 7 catcher

capture: bag, cop, get, nab, net, win 4 fang, grab, hook, land, prey, take, trap, tree 5 catch, prize, raven, seize 6 arrest, collar, obtain 9 apprehend, captivate 10 circumvent 12 apprehension

capuche: 4 cowl, hood

Capuchin: 5 friar 6 monkey, pigeon

caput: top 4 head 7 chapter, council, section 8 division 9 paragraph

capybara: 6 rodent

car (see also **automobile**): box, bus 4 auto, jeep, rath 5 coach, hutch, ratha, sedan, train, wrong 6 basket 7 awkward, chariot, trailer, trolley, vehicle 8 roadster, sinister 10 automobile, left-handed 11 convertible
aerial cable: 6 telfer 7 telpher
armored: 4 tank
railroad: box, oil 4 club, flat, mail, tank 5 chair, coach, diner 6 buffet, hopper, parlor

7 baggage, caboose, express, freight, gondola, pullman, sleeper, tourist 9 furniture, passenger 12 refrigerator

car barn: 5 depot

carabao: 7 buffalo

caracara: 4 hawk

caract: See **character**

carafe: 6 bottle

caramel: 5 candy, sweet 6 bonbon 9 flavoring 10 confection

carapace: 5 crust, shell 6 lorica

carara: 9 coronopus

caravan: van 4 trek, trip 5 fleet 6 cafila, convoy, safari, travel 7 journey, vehicle
slave: 6 coffle

caravansary: inn 4 chan, khan 5 hotel, serai 6 hostel, imaret 8 choultry, hostelry 9 resthouse

carbine: gun 5 rifle 6 musket, weapon 7 escopet 9 escopette

carbohydrate: 5 sugar 6 starch 8 dextrose 9 cellulose

carbon: 4 coal, coke, copy, soot 6 crayon 7 replica 8 graphite
deposit: 4 soot
point: 6 crayon

carbonate: 4 burn, char, fizz 6 aerate 7 enliven 9 carbonize

carborundum: 5 emery 8 abrasive

carboy: jug 6 bottle

carbuncle: 4 boil 5 jewel 6 garnet 7 abscess

carcajou: 4 lynx 6 badger, cougar 9 wolverine

carcanet: 5 chain 6 collar 8 headband, necklace

carcass: 4 body 6 corpse 7 carrion

carcel: 4 jail 6 prison

carcoon: 5 clerk 7 manager

card: map, pam, wag 4 comb, menu, plan 5 chart, fiche, joker, tease 6 cartel, ticket 7 program 8 schedule 9 character, eccentric 10 attraction, pasteboard
spot: pip
wool: tum 4 comb, rove, toom

card game: lu; gin, hoc, loo, pam 4 bank, faro, hock, keno, ruff, skat, slam, snap, solo, spin, vint 5 beast, chico, cinch, comet, crimp, decoy, gilet, gleek, monte, omber, ombre, pedro, pique, pitch, poker, rummy, stuss, trump, two-up, waist, whist 6 basset, boston, bridge, casino, commit, ecarte, euchre, fantan, flinch, hearts, masset, piquet, rounce, sledge, smudge 7 baccara, bezique, cayenne, Chicago, canasta, coon-can, sevenup 8 baccarat, commerce, conquian, contract, cribbage, handicap, Napoleon, patience, pinochle, tresillo, vederuff 9 Newmarket, panguinui, solitaire 10 blackstone 11 everlasting, speculation *bid:* 4 slam 6 misere

holding: 6 tenace

old: hoc, loo, pam 4 brag, ruff 5 comet, gilet, omber, ombre, trump 7 primero, reversi 8 penneech, penneeck

player who cuts: 4 pone

playing card: ace, pam, ten 4 jack, king, trey 5 basto(Sp.), deuce, joker, knave, queen, taroc, tarot

term: bid, bye, cat, pic 4 book, card, deal, hand, meld, pair, pass, suit 5 flush, raise, trump 6 renege, tenace, tricon 8 sequence, straight 9 doubleton, singleton 10 Yarborough

widow: 4 skat

wild: 5 joker

cardigan: 6 fabric, jacket, wampus 7 sweater

cardinal: 4 bird, main 5 basic, chief, cloak, color, vital 6 cleric 7 radical 9 principal 10 underlying

assembly at Rome: 7 college

notification of elevation: 9 biglietto

office: hat 6 datary 7 dataria

title: 8 eminence

cards (see also **card game**): 4 deck, pack, suit

care: 4 cark, cure, duty, fret, heed, mind, reck, soin(F.), tend, wish, yeme 5 grief, guard, nurse, pains, worry 6 burden, desire, grieve, lament, regard, sorrow 7 anxiety, auspice, caution, cherish, concern, keeping, scruple, thought, tuition 8 business 9 attention, diligence, direction, oversight 10 management, solicitude 11 calculation, heedfulness 12 watchfulness 14 responsibility

for: 4 like, mind, tend 5 guard, nurse, treat 6 foster, relish

requiring: 7 fragile 8 ticklish

under another's: 4 ward 6 charge 7 protege 10 apprentice

careen: .ip 4 cant, heel, keel, list, tilt, veer 5 lurch, slope 7 incline

career: run, way 4 life, road 5 trade 6 charge, course, gallop 7 calling, pursuit, running 8 business, vocation 10 occupation, profession, racecourse 11 achievement

carefree: 4 easy 5 frank, happy 10 insouciant 12 lighthearted

careful: 4 wary 5 canny, chary, exact 6 eident, frugal 7 anxious, guarded, heedful, prudent, thrifty 8 accurate, cautious, diligent, discreet, dreadful, gingerly, mournful, troubled, vigilant, watchful 9 advertent, attentive, exquisite, observant, provident 10 economical, meticulous, respect-ful, respective, scrupulous, solicitous, thoughtful 11 circumspect, considerate, painstaking, punctilious

carefully: 7 charily 8 gingerly

careless: lax 4 cool, easy, lash, rash 5 slack 6 casual, overly, remiss, supine, untidy, unwary 7 languid 8 heedless, listless, reckless, slattern, slipshod, slovenly 9 forgetful, haphazard, negligent, unheeding, unmindful 10 neglectful, nonchalant, regardless 11 inadvertent, inattentive, indifferent, perfunctory, spontaneous, thoughtless, unconcerned

caress: coy, hug, pat, pet 4 bill, dant(Sc.), kiss, neck 6 coddle, cosset, fondle, pamper, stroke 7 cherish, embrace 10 endearment

caretaker: 6 keeper 7 janitor 9 custodian 11 housekeeper

Carew's love: 5 Celia

careworn: 5 lined

carfuffle: 6 flurry, ruffle 8 disorder 9 agitation 10 disarrange

cargador: 6 porter 7 carrier 9 stevedore

cargo: 4 bulk, load 6 burden, lading 7 freight 8 property, shipment 10 freightage

discarded: 6 jetsam

loader: 9 stevedore

space in ship: 4 hold

stabilizer: 7 ballast

take on: 4 lade, load

wrecked ship: 7 flotsam

Caribbean: *bird:* 4 tody

gulf: 6 Darien

island: 4 Cuba 6 Nassau

caribe: 4 fish 6 pirana, piraya 7 piranha

caribou: 4 deer 8 reindeer

carica: 4 tree 6 papaya, pawpaw

caricature: ape 4 copy, mock, skit 5 farce, libel, mimic, squib 6 overdo, parody, satire 7 cartoon 8 travesty 9 burlesque 12 exaggeration

caries: 5 decay 10 ulceration 11 saprodontia

carillon: 5 bells 6 chimes 12 glockenspiel

cark: vex 4 care, heed, load 5 cavil, pains, worry 6 burden, charge, harass 7 anxiety, perplex, trouble 8 distress

carl: lad 4 boor, hemp 5 churl, snarl 6 carlot, fellow, rustic 7 bondman, villein 10 husbandman, pinchpenny

carling: 6 rafter 7 support

Carmelite: 4 monk 5 friar

barefoot: 8 Teresian

carmen: 4 poem, song 11 incantation

Carmen composer: 5 Bizet

carmine: red 7 crimson, scarlet 8 coloring

carnage: 6 murder, pogrom 8 butchery, massacre 9 bloodshed, slaughter

carnal: 4 crow, lewd 6 animal, bodily, sexual, worldly 7 brutish, earthly, fleshly, secular, sensual 8 material, temporal 9

' corporeal 11 unspiritual 12 bloodthirsty, unregenerate

carnation: 4 pink 5 flake 6 flower 7 picotee 9 grenadine(F.)

carnelian: 4 sard 10 chalcedony

carnival: 4 fete 7 revelry 8 festival 11 merrymaking

wild man: 4 geek

carnivore: cat, dog, fox 4 bear, coon, lion, lynx, mink, puma, seal, wolf 5 civet, coati, genet, hyena, otter, panda, pekah, ratel, sable, stoat, tiger 6 cougar, ermine, feline, ferret, jackal, jaguar, marten, ocelot, possum, serval, weasel 7 dasyure, genette, glutton, leopard, opposum, polecat, raccoon, tigress 8 mongoose 9 ichneuman

carnose: 6 fleshy

carob: 4 tree 6 locust 9 algarroba

carol: lay 4 noel, sing, song 5 ditty, yodel, yodle 6 alcove, warble 8 madrigal

Caroline island: Yap 4 Palu, Truk 5 Pelew 6 Ponape

carom: 4 shot 6 bounce, glance, strike 7 rebound 8 ricochet

carousal: 4 lark, orgy, riot, romp, toot 5 binge, feast, randy, revel, spree 6 frolic, shindy, splore 7 banquet, carouse, wassail 8 festival, jamboree 9 bacchanal

carouse: 4 bout 5 birle(Sc.), bouse, drink, revel, quaff, spree, toast 7 wassail 8 carousal

carp: nag 4 fish, sing, snag, talk, yerk 5 cavil, prate, scold, speak 6 censor, nibble, recite 7 censure, chatter, quibble 8 complain, goldfish 9 criticize, discourse

carpel: 9 carpophyl 10 carpophyll

carpenter: ant 6 framer, joiner, wright 8 tectonic 9 artificer 10 woodworker 12 cabinetmaker

machine: 5 lathe 6 planer, shaper

ship: 5 chips

tool: adz, awl, saw 4 adze 5 level, plane 6 gimlet, hammer, square 7 hatchet

carpet: mat, rug 4 kali 5 scold, tapet, tapis 6 fabric 8 covering 9 reprimand

design: 9 medallion

variety: 4 Agra 6 velvet, Wilton 7 ingrain 8 Brussels, moquette, Venetian 9 Axminster, broadloom

carping: 8 captious, caviling, critical 10 censorious 12 faultfinding 13 hypercritical

carplike fish: 4 dace, rudd

carpus: 5 wrist

carr, car: bog, fen 4 pool 5 grove

carrack, carack: 4 boat 7 galleon

carrageen: 4 alga, moss 7 seaweed

carriage: air, gig 4 gait, garb, hack, load, mien, shay 5 bandy, brake, break, buggy, coach, front, midge, poise, wagon 6 burden, convoy, landau, manner, surrey 7 baggage, bearing, conduct, gesture, hackney, phaeton, vecture, vehicle 8 behavior, demeanor, dormeuse, equipage, portance 9 behaviour, execution 10 conveyance, deportment, management 14 administration

baby: 4 pram 6 gocart 8 stroller 12 perambulator

closed: cab 4 hack, taxi 6 calash 7 caleche 8 brougham, clarence

covered: 6 Berlin, landau 7 ricksha 8 carryall, dearborn, stanhope

four-wheeled: 5 coupe 6 surrey, whisky 7 phaeton, whiskey 8 barouche, clarence, rockaway, victoria 9 chariotee, gladstone

French: 6 fiacre

one-horse: fly, gig 4 ekka (Ind.), shay, trap 5 sulky 6 dennet 7 cariole, dogcart 8 carriole

open: 7 dogcart, dos-a-dos 8 sociable

portable: 5 sedan

three-horse: 6 troika

two-seated: 6 tandem

two-wheeled: gig 4 shay, trap 5 essed, sulky, tonga 6 chaise, cisium, esseda, hansom 7 carreta, chariot, tilbury 8 carretta 9 caretella, carromata 11 jinrickshaw

carriage trade: 7 society

carried: 5 borne, giddy, toted 6 carted, lugged, wafted 8 drifting, ravished 10 abstracted 11 transported

carrier (see also **conveyance**): hod 4 ship 5 hamal, macer, plane 6 bearer, cadger, hamaul, hammal, khamal, porter 7 drayman, flattop, hammaul, postman, remover 8 cargador, portator, railroad, teamster 9 messenger

carrion: 4 vile 6 corpse, refuse, rotten 7 carcass, corrupt 9 loathsome

Carroll character: 5 Alice 6 hatter, rabbit 7 duchess

carrot: 4 root 5 plant 6 daucus 10 enticement

deadly: 5 drias

family: 8 ammaicea

genus: 5 carum

top: 7 red-head

wild: 8 hilltrot 10 laceflower

carrottop: 7 redhead

carrousel: 4 ride 12 merry-go-round

carry: hug, jag, lug 4 bear, cart, gest, hold, lead, take, tote, tump 5 bring, cadge, geste, guide, poise 6 behave, convey, convoy, delate, derive, extend 7 conduct, contain, produce, support, sustain, undergo 8 continue, transfer, transmit 9 prosecute, transport 11 comportment

away: 4 kill, take 5 eloin, reave, steal 6 eloign, kidnap, remove 9 transport *on:* 4 rant, rave, wage 6 manage 7 conduct, perform, proceed 8 continue, maintain, transact 9 misbehave, prosecute

out: 6 effect 7 execute, perform, sustain 8 complete

over: 4 tide 5 table 6 extend, shelve 8 contango, postpone, transfer

the day: win 7 prevail

carryall: bag, bus 4 case 8 carriage

carrying: 6 gerent 9 gestation

cart: 4 butt, char, dray, haul, tote, wain 5 araba, bandy, bogie, carry, sulky, tonga, wagon 6 charet, convey 7 chariot, hackery, trolley, trundle, tumbler, tumbrel, tumbril, vehicle 8 charette

farmer: 7 morfrey 8 morphrey

freight: 8 carreton

horse: 8 cartaver(Sc.)

license: 6 caroon 7 caroome, carroon

racing: 5 sulky

rope: 5 wanty(Sc.)

strong: 4 dray

two-wheeled: bin, gig 4 shay 5 dandy, sulky, tonga 6 reckla 7 tumbril 8 carretta(Sp.)

cartage: 7 drayage, haulage

carte: map 4 card, list, menu 5 chart 7 charter, diagram

cartel: 4 card, defy, pact, pool, ship 5 paper, trust 6 corner, letter, treaty 8 contract 9 agreement, challenge 10 convention

carter: 7 drayman, trucker 8 horseman, teamster

Carthage: *citadel:* 5 Bursa, Byrsa

emblem: 4 palm

foe: 4 Cato

founder: 4 Dido

general: 5 Hanno 8 Hannibal

god: 6 Moloch

goddess: 5 Tanit 6 Tanith

language: 5 Punic

magistrate: 7 suffete

pert. to: 5 Punic

queen: 4 Dido

subject: 6 Libyan

victor at Zama: 6 Scipio

Carthusian: 4 monk 7 eremite

monastery: 5 Pavia 7 Certosa

noted: 4 Hugh

superior: 5 prior

cartilage: 6 tissue 7 gristle

ossified: 4 bone

cartload: 6 fother

cartograph: map 4 plat 5 chart

carton: box 4 case 9 container 10 receptacle

cartoon: 10 caricature

cartoonist: 4 Arno, Capp, Ding, Nast 6 Disney

cartridge: bag 4 case 5 shell 7 capsule

holder: 4 clip

carucate: 4 hide, land 5 field

caruncle: 4 comb, gill 6 growth, wattle

carving: *in stone:* 5 cameo 8 intaglio 10 engrailing

pert. to: 7 glyphic, glyptic

relief: 5 cameo

carya: 5 pecan 6 pignut 9 bitternut

caryatid: 6 figure 9 priestess

male: cap 7 telamon

casa: 5 house 8 building, dwelling

casaba: 5 melon 9 muskmelon

Casanova: 4 rake, roue 5 lover

cascade: lin(Sc.) 4 fall, linn(Sc.) 5 force(Sc.) 8 cataract 9 waterfall

casco: 5 barge 7 lighter

case: bag, box, hap, pod 4 bunk, burr, deed, file, pack, pair, suit 5 brace, bulla, burse, casus, cover, crate, event, folio, state, theca, trial 6 action, affair, binder, carton, chance, coffin, couple, matter, quiver, sheath, survey 7 cabinet, capcase, capsule, enclose, envelop, example, holster, inclose, lawsuit, satchel 8 accident, argument, cupboard, envelope, instance, situated 9 cartridge, condition, container, happening 10 occurrence, receptacle, sabretache 11 contingency

book holder: 5 forel 6 forrel

cigar: 7 humidor

cosmetic: 7 compact

document: 7 hanaper

explosive: 5 shell 6 petard 11 firecracker

grammatical: 6 dative 8 ablative, genitive, vocative 9 objective 10 accusative, nominative

small: tye 4 etui 5 bulla, etwee 6 trouse

toiletries: 4 etui 5 etwee

case history: 5 story 6 record

casement: 6 window 8 covering

cash: 4 coin, cush, dump, dust, jack, jake 5 blunt, brass, clink, darby, dough, funds, money 6 specie 7 capital, hemlock 8 currency 10 spondulics

keeper: 6 bursar, teller 7 cashier 9 treasurer

cashbox: 4 till 6 coffer

cashew: nut 4 tree 7 maranon

casing: 4 boot, shoe, tire 5 gaine 6 coffin, collet, lining, sheath 8 covering 9 framework

cask: keg, tub, tun, vat 4 butt, cade, cowl, knag, pipe 5 bowie, bulge, foist 6 bareca, bareka, barrel, cardel, casque, firkin, tierce 7 barrico, fostell 8 cassette, hogshead, puncheon 9 kilderkin

bulge: 5 bilge

oil: 4 rier

orifice: 8 bunghole

rim: 5 chimb, chime

stave: lag
wine: fat, tun 4 butt, fust, pipe 6 tierce
casket: box, pix, tye 4 case, cask, cist, till,
tomb 5 chest 6 Accera, chasse, coffer, coffin 7 casquet, fostell 8 cassette 9 reliquary
Caspian Sea: 5 Tates
ancient region: 7 Parthia
harbor: 4 Baku
river to: 4 Kura, Ural 5 Terek, Volga
casque: hat 4 cask 5 armor 6 helmet 9 headdress
Cassandra: 7 prophet, seeress
father: 5 Priam
cassation: 8 quashing 9 annulling, cancel-
ing 10 abrogation
cassava: 4 aipi, juca 5 aipim 6 casiri, manioc
7 tapioca
cassena: 6 yaupon
cassette: 6 casket, holder, sagger
cassia: 4 drug, herb, tree 5 senna, shrub
bark: 8 cinnamon
cassie: 6 basket 8 huisache
Cassiopeia: *daughter:* 9 Andromeda
husband: 7 Cepheus
cassock: 4 gown 5 gippo 6 priest 7 pelisse,
soutane 9 clergyman
cassone: box 5 chest
cassowary: emu 4 bird 5 murup 6 moorup
cast: 4 hurl, mold, molt, shed, spew, tint,
toss 5 eject, fling, found, heave, mould,
pitch, shade, sling, throw, tinge 7 cashier,
deposit, discard
aside: see *away* below
away: 4 jilt, junk, shed 5 scrap, wreck 6
maroon, reject 7 abandon, discard, dismiss 8 squander 9 shipwreck
down: 5 abase 6 abattu, deject, sadden 7
abattue, depress, destroy 8 demolish,
dispirit 10 discourage
lots: 5 cavel
off: 4 free 5 untie 6 disown, unmoor 7 discard 9 eliminate
out: 5 eject, expel 6 banish
up: add 5 total, vomit 6 reckon 7 compute,
measure 8 reproach
castaway: 4 waif 5 tramp 6 reject 7 outcast
8 derelict, stranded 9 shipwreck
caste: 4 rank 5 breed, class, grade, order 6
degree, status
group: 5 varna
merchant: 6 banian, banyan
priestly: 4 magi(pl.) 5 magus
caster: 4 vial 5 cruse, cruet, phial, wheel 6
castor, hurler, roller 7 pitcher, trundle
castigate: 5 emend, scare 6 berate, punish,
revise, strafe, subdue 7 censure, chasten,
correct, reprove 8 chastise, lambaste 9
criticize

castigatory: 5 penal 8 punitive 10 corrective
Castile: *hero:* Cid
province: 5 Avila, Soria
river: 4 Ebro, Esla 5 Douro, Duero
Castilian: 7 Spanish
casting: *mold:* die 6 matrix 7 matrice
rough: pig
castle: 4 fort, rock, rook 5 abode, morro 7
bastile, chateau, citadel 8 bastille, castillo,
fastness, fortress 10 stronghold 13 fortification
in the air: 5 dream 6 vision 7 fantasy 8
daydream 9 imagining
part: 4 bawn, moat 6 donjon 10 drawbridge,
portcullis
tower: 4 keep
wall: 6 bailey
warden: 6 disdar, dizdar 9 castellan
castor: hat 4 bean, star 6 beaver 7 leather
Castor: *and Pollux:* 5 twins 6 Gemini 8 Dioscuri
brother: 6 Pollux
father: 4 Zeus 9 Tyndareus
horse: 8 Cyllaros
mother: 4 Leda
slayer: 4 Idas
castor-bean poison: 5 ricin
castrate: gib 4 geld, spay, swig 5 alter, capon, prune 6 eunuch, neuter 7 evirate 8
caponize, mutilate 10 emasculate
casual: 5 stray 6 chance, random 7 cursory,
natural, offhand 8 informal 9 haphazard,
uncertain 10 accidental, contingent, fortuitous, incidental, nonchalant, occasional
11 indifferent 14 unconventional, unpremeditated
casualty: 4 loss 5 death 6 chance, hazard,
injury, mishap 8 accident, disaster 9 mischance 10 misfortune 11 contingency 12
misadventure
casus: 4 case 5 event 8 occasion
cat: 4 flog, lion, lynx, pard, puma, puss 5
civet, felid, gatol(Sp.), moggy, ounce,
pussy, tiger 6 cougar, feline, jaguar, malkin, mawkin, ocelot, tibert 7 cheetah, leopard, panther, tigress, wildcat 8 bau-
drons(Sc.) 9 carnivore, grimalkin 11 caterpillar 12 catamountain
breed: 4 Manx 5 alley, tabby 6 Angora 7
Maltese, Persian, Siamese
civetlike: 5 genet
comb. form: 5 aelur 6 aeluro
cry: mew 4 hiss, meow, miau, purr 5 miaou,
miaow, miaul
disease: 9 distemper
Eugene Field's: 6 calico
female: 9 grimalkin
genus: 5 felis 7 felidae(pl.)

cat-o-nine-tails: 4 lash, whip 7 cattail

cataclysm: 5 flood 6 deluge 7 debacle 8 disaster, overflow, upheaval 11 catastrophe

catacomb: 4 tomb 5 crypt, vault 8 cemetery

catafalque: 4 bier 6 coffin

cataian: 5 thief 7 sharper 9 scoundrel

catalepsy: 6 trance 7 seizure

catalog, catalogue: 4 book, list, roll, rota 5 brief, canon, index 6 record, roster 7 arrange 8 classify, register, schedule 9 enumerate, inventory, repertory 11 systematize

Catalonia: *dance:* 7 sardana
  marble: 8 brocatel 10 brocatelle

catamaran: 4 raft, trow 5 balsa, float 6 vessel 8 auntsary

catamount: 4 lynx, puma 6 cougar

cataplasm: 8 poultice

catapult: 5 throw 6 launch, onager 7 bricole 8 ballista, crossbow 9 slingshot

cataract: lin 4 linn 5 falls, flood 6 deluge 7 cascade, Niagara 8 Victoria 9 waterfall

cataria: 6 catnip

catarrh: 4 cold 5 rheum

catastrophe (see also **cataclysm**): 8 accident, calamity, disaster 10 denouement, misfortune

catbird: 7 mimidae

catcall: boo 4 hoot 6 deride

catch: bag, cop, get, nab, net 4 draw, hasp, haul, hawk, hold, hook, land, pawl, snap, stop, trap, tree 5 grasp, hitch, ketch, knack, seize, snare, trick 6 button, clutch, corner, detect, detent, engage, enmesh, entrap, snatch 7 attract, capture, ensnare, grapnel 8 entangle, overtake, surprise 9 intercept
  sight of: 4 espy 6 descry
  up with: 8 overtake

catchall: bag 6 basket 10 receptacle

catchfly: 5 plant 6 silene 7 campion

catching: 6 catchy 8 alluring 10 contagious, entrapping, infectious 11 captivating

catchwork: cue, tag 5 motto 6 byword, phrase, slogan

catchy: 9 appealing

cate: 4 food 6 viands 8 dainties 10 delicacies, provisions

catechism: 5 guide 6 manual 8 carritch 10 carritches(Sc.)

catechumen: 5 pupil 7 audient, auditor, convert 8 beginner, neophyte

categorical: 8 absolute, explicit 11 dictatorial, unequivocal, unqualified

category: 4 rank 5 class, genus, genre(pl.), order 6 family 7 species 8 division 12 denomination 14 classification

catena: 4 link 5 chain 6 series

catenate: 4 link 11 concatenate

cater: 4 feed 5 humor, serve, treat 6 pander, purvey, supply 7 provide

caterpillar: cat 4 muga 5 aweto, eruca, larva 6 canker, erucae(pl.), risper, woubit 7 tractor

caterwaul: cry 4 wail 5 miaul

catface: 4 scar

catfish: mud 4 cusk, elod, pout, raad, shal 5 bagre, raash 6 docmac, hassar, raasch, tandau 7 candiru 8 bullhead 9 sheatfish
  genus: 13 saccobranchus

catgut: 4 cord, ropp 5 tharm 6 string, violin

cathartic: 8 lapactic, laxative 9 cleansing, purgative

cathedral: dom 6 church
  passage: 5 slype

cathode: 9 electrode

catholic: 5 broad, papal 7 general, liberal 8 tolerant 9 universal 10 ecumenical

Catholic: See **Roman Catholic**

catkin: 5 ament, spike

catlike: 6 feline 8 stealthy 9 noiseless

catmint: nep, nip 4 herb

catnap: 4 doze

catnip: nep 6 catnep 7 cataria, catwort

Catoism: 9 austerity, harshness

Catreus: *daughter:* 6 Aerope 7 Clymene 9 Apemosyne
  father: 5 Minos
  mother: 8 Pasiphae

cat's-cradle: 7 ribwort

cat's-paw: 4 dupe, gull, tool 5 cully

cattail: 4 flag, musk, rush 5 ament, cloud, raupo, reree 6 catkin 7 bulrush, matreed
  family: 9 typhaceae

cattle: 4 cows, dhan(Ind.), kine, neat, oxen 5 beefs, bulls, stock 6 beasts, beeves, steers 7 bovines
  assemblage: 4 herd 5 drove
  brand: 4 duff 5 buist
  breed: 4 Nata, Zobo 5 Angus, Devon, Dutch, Niata(dwarf) 6 Durham, Belted, Jersey, Sussex 7 Brahman, Brangus, Kerries 8 Ayrshire, Bradford, Charbray, Guernsey, Hereford, Holstein, Longhorn 9 Red Polled, Shorthorn, Teeswater 10 Beefmaster, Brown Swiss 11 Charollaise, Dutch Belted 14 French Canadian, Santa Gertrudis
  call: 4 sook
  dealer: 6 drover, herder
  dehorned: 5 muley 6 mulley
  genus: bos
  goddess: 6 Bubona
  group: 4 herd 5 drove 7 creaght(Ir.)
  plague: 10 rinderpest
  shelter: 4 byre 5 barth
  tick: 8 carapato
  yard: 6 cancha

cattleman: 6 cowboy 7 byreman 8 stockman

catwalk: 7 footway, walkway

catwort: 6 catnip

Caucasia: *goat:* tur

ibex: zac

language: Laz, Udi 4 Andi, Avar, Laze, Lazi, Udic 5 Udish 7 Semitic 9 Itranican

race: 5 Aryan, Osset 6 Ossete

rug: 4 baku, kuba 5 chila 7 derbend

tribe: 4 Imer, Kurd, Laze, Lazi, Svan 5 Pshav 7 Kubachi

caucho: ule 4 tree 6 rubber

caucus: 7 council, meeting, primary 8 election

caudal: 4 rear 9 posterior

appendage: 4 tail

caudata: 4 newt 5 snake 10 salamander

cauk: 5 chalk 9 limestone

caul: web 4 cawl, trug, veil 7 network, omentum 8 membrane, tressour, tressure

cauldrife: 4 cold 6 chilly 8 chilling 9 cheerless

cauldron: See caldron

cauliflower: 7 cabbage 8 broccoli 9 disfigure

caulk, calk: 6 chinse 7 chintze

cauma: 4 heat 5 fever 6 warmth

cause: aim, gar(Sc.), key 4 case, chat, move, root, spur, suit 5 agent, basis, breed 6 create, effect, gossip, ground, induce, malady, motive, object, origin, reason, source, spring 7 concern, disease, lawsuit, produce, provoke 8 business, engender, movement, occasion 9 originate, wherefore 10 mainspring

causerie: 4 chat, plea, talk 6 debate 10 discussion 12 conversation

causes, science of: 8 etiology

causeuse: 4 sofa 9 tete-a-tete

causeway: way 4 dike, road 7 chausse(F.), highway

causey: dam, way 4 bank, pave, road 5 mound 6 street 7 highway 8 sidewalk

caustic: lye 4 tart 5 acrid, sharp 6 biting, bitter, severe 7 burning, cutting, erodent, mordant, pungent, satiric 8 alkaline, scathing, snappish, stinging 9 corrosive, sarcastic, satirical, vitriolic 10 malevolent 11 acrimonious

agent: 7 cautery, erodent

cauterize: 4 burn, char, fire, sear 5 brand, inust, singe 9 sterilize

caution: 4 care, heed, warn 6 advice, cautel, caveat, exhort 7 anxiety, counsel, precept, proviso 8 admonish, forecast, monition, prudence, wariness 9 diligence, vigilance 10 admonition, precaution, providence 11 calculation, forethought, reservation 12 watchfulness

cautious: 4 wary 5 alert, canny, chary, siker 6 fabian, sicker 7 careful, guarded, prudent 8 discreet, vigilant 10 scrupulous 11 circumspect

cavalcade: 4 raid, ride 5 march 6 parade, safari 7 journey, pageant 10 procession

cavalier: gay 4 curt, easy, fine 5 brave, frank, rider 6 escort, knight 7 brusque, gallant, haughty, offhand, soldier 8 Royalist 9 caballero, chevalier 10 disdainful 12 high-spirited, supercilious

Cavalleria Rusticana character: 4 Lola 5 Alfio 7 Turiddu

cavalry: 6 horses, troops 8 horsemen 10 knighthood

horse: 6 lancer

weapon: 5 lance, saber

cavalryman: 5 spahi 6 hussar, lancer, spahee 7 courier, dragoon, soldier, trooper 8 gendarme, horseman

cave: den, tip 4 cove, hole, lair, rear, sink, toss, weem 5 antre, cavea, crypt, speos, store, upset 6 beware, cavern, cavity, cellar, forgou, grotto, hollow, larder, luster, pantry, plunge 7 reserve, spelunk 8 collapse, overturn 9 storeroom

dweller: 10 troglodyte

researcher: 9 spelunker 12 speleologist

science of researching: 10 speleology

cave in: 5 stove, yield 6 submit 8 collapse

cavea: den 4 cage, cave 10 auditorium

caveat: 6 beware 7 caution, warning

cavern: 4 cave, grot, hole, lair, weem 5 antra(pl.), croft 6 antrum, cavity, grotto, hollow 7 spelunk

cavetto: 7 molding

caviar, caviare: ova, roe 4 eggs, ikra 5 ikary 6 relish 8 delicacy

source: 7 sterlet 8 sturgeon

cavie: 4 cage, coop 7 hencoop

cavil: 4 cark, carp, haft 6 haggle 7 quibble 9 criticise, criticize, exception, objection

caviling: 8 captious, picayune

cavity: bag, pit, sac 4 abri, cave, dalk, dent, hole, mine, vein, void 5 antra(pl.), atria(pl.), fossa, geode, lumen, mouth, sinus 6 antrum, atrium, camera, cavern, fossae(pl.), grotto, hollow, vacuum 7 cistern, vesicle 8 cul-de-sac 10 depression, excavation

anatomical: 5 antra(pl.), fossa 6 antrum, fossae(pl.)

brain: 6 coelia

gun: 4 bore

heart: 7 auricle 9 ventricle

lode: vug 4 voog, vugg, vugh

pert. to: 5 sinal 6 atrial, geodic

sac-like: 5 bursa 6 bursae(pl.)

skull: 4 aula 5 fossa, sinus

stone: 5 geode

cavort: 4 play 5 bound, caper 6 curvet, gambol, prance

cavy: 4 paca, pony 6 agouti, aperea, cayuse, rodent 8 capybara 9 guinea pig

caw: cry 4 call, cawl 5 croak, quark, quawk

cawl: 4 trug 6 basket

caxi: 4 fish 7 snapper

cay: See **key**

cayenne: 5 whist 6 canary, pepper 8 capsicum

cayuse: 4 cavy, pony 6 bronco 7 broncho

cease: end 4 halt, liss, quit, rest, stop 5 avast, douse, dowse, lisse, pause, peter 6 desist, devall, finish 7 abstain, refrain 8 intermit 9 terminate 11 discontinue

cease-fire: 5 truce 9 armistice

ceaseless: 4 ever 7 endless 8 unending 9 continual, incessant, unceasing

ceasing: 9 cessation

cecidium: 4 gall

cecity: 9 blindness

Cecrops' daughter: 5 Herse 8 Aglauros

cecum: pit 4 pore 6 cavity

cedar: 4 toon, tree 5 savin 6 deodar, sabina, sabine, savine 7 waxwing
camphor: 6 cedrol
green: 5 cedre(F.), color
moss: 8 hornwort

cede: 4 cess, give 5 award, grant, leave, waive, yield 6 assign, resign, submit 8 renounce, transfer 9 surrender 10 relinquish

cedrat: 6 citron

cedula: 8 document, schedule 11 certificate

ceil: 4 line 7 overlay 8 wainscot

ceilidh: 4 call 5 visit 12 conversation 13 entertainment

ceiling: 6 lining, screen, soffit 7 curtain, testudo 8 covering, paneling 10 testudines(pl.) 11 wainscoting
covering: 9 calcimine, kalsomine
division: 5 trave
mine: 5 astel
wooden: 8 plancher

Celebes: *bovine:* ox 4 anoa
island: 4 Muna
people: 6 toraja 7 toradja

celebrate: 4 keep, sing 5 extol, honor, revel 6 extoll, praise 7 glorify, observe 8 emblazon, eulogize, proclaim 9 solemnize 11 commemorate

celebrated: 4 kept 5 famed, noted 6 famous 7 eminent, feasted, renomme 8 glorious, observed, renowned 9 distingue, prominent 10 solemnized 11 conspicuous, illustrious 13 distinguished

celebration: 4 fete, rite 6 renown 9 celebrity, festivity

celebrious: 6 famous 7 festive 8 renowned, thronged 10 frequented

celebrity: VIP 4 fame, lion, name, star 5 eclat 6 renown, repute 11 celebration

celerity: 5 haste, hurry, speed 8 dispatch, rapidity, velocity 9 prestezza, quickness, swiftness

celery: *family:* 9 ammiaceae
wild: 8 smallage

celeste: 4 stop 5 pedal 7 sky-blue

celestial: 4 holy 6 divine, uranic 7 angelic, Chinese, ethered 8 empyreal, ethereal, heavenly
being: 5 angel 6 cherub, seraph 8 seraphim(pl.)
body: sun 4 star 5 comet 6 meteor, nebula, planet
elevation of mind: 7 anagoge
matter: 6 nebula

celibacy: 8 chastity

celibate: 6 chaste, single 8 bachelor, spinster 9 unmarried

cell: egg 4 cage, germ, jail 5 cabin, crypt, group, vault 6 cytode, prison 7 cellule, chamber, cubicle, dungeon 9 hermitage 10 ergastulum 11 compartment
bull: 5 toril 7 toriles(pl.)
coloring: 10 endochrome
colorless: 10 achroacyte, lymphocyte
connecting: 10 heterocyst
division: 7 spireme
generative: 6 gamete
group: 6 ceptor 7 cascade 8 blastema
layer: 8 blastula 10 blastoderm
lens-shaped: 8 lenticel
migratory: 9 leucocyte
pert. to: 6 cytoid
star-shaped: 10 astroblast
structural unit: 7 energid, nucleus 10 protoplast
study of: 8 cytology
substance: 5 linin

cell-like: 6 cytoid

cella: 4 naos

cellar: 4 cave 8 basement 9 storeroom

cellaret: 4 case 7 cabinet 8 tantalus 9 sideboard

cellular: 6 favose 7 areolar 8 faviform 9 alveolate

cellulose: *acetate:* 7 acetose
elastic: 5 rayon

celsitude: 6 height 8 altitude 10 exaltation

Celt: 4 Gael, Gaul, Manx 5 Irish, Welsh 6 Breton, Briton, Eolith 7 Cornish

Celtic: 4 Erse 7 Scotch
abbot: 5 coarb
chariot: 5 essed
chieftain: 6 tanist
divinity: 7 Taranis

foot soldier: 4 kern

giant: 5 Fomor

god: Ler 4 Leir, Llyr

harp: 5 telyn 11 clairschach

hero: 5 Fionn

language: 4 Erse, Manx 5 Irish, Welsh 6 Celtic, Cymric, Gaelic 9 Brythonic

peasant: 4 kern

priest: 5 Druid

sword: sax 4 seax

cembalo: 8 dulcimer 11 harpsichord

cement: fix 4 glue, join, knit, lime, lute 5 imbed, paste, putty, stick, unite 6 cohere, fasten, gulgul(Ind.), mortar, solder 7 asphalt 8 adhesive, hadigeon(F.), solidify 11 agglutinate

hydraulic: 4 paar

infusible substance: 4 lute

plastic: 8 albolite, albolith

quick-drying: 6 mastic

substance: 6 celite

window glass: 5 putty

cemetery: 6 litten 7 charnel 8 catacomb, Golgotha 9 graveyard 10 necropolis 11 polyandrium

cenchrus: 5 grass 6 millet

cenobite: nun 4 monk 5 friar 6 essene 7 recluse 8 monastic 9 anchorite

cenoby: 5 abbey 6 priory 7 convent

cense: 4 rank 6 assess, rating 7 perfume 8 estimate, position

censer: 8 thurible

censor: 6 critic 8 restrict, suppress 9 detractor

censorious: 6 severe 7 carping 8 blameful, captious, critical 9 satirical

censurable: 8 blamable, culpable 13 reprehensible

censure: 4 carp, flay 5 blame, chide, decry, judge, slate 6 accuse, berate, charge, rebuff, rebuke, remord, targue(Scot.), tirade 7 chasten, condemn, impeach, inveigh, reprove 8 disallow, reproach 9 challenge, criticize, reprimand 10 animadvert, exprobrate, vituperate 11 disapproval 12 reprehension 13 animadversion 15 discommendation

census: 4 list, poll 5 count 11 enumeration

cent: 4 coin 5 penny 6 copper

centaur: *bull's head:* 9 bucentaur

father: 5 Ixion

killed by Hercules: 6 Nessus

Centennial State: 8 Colorado

center, centre: cor, hub, mid 4 axis, core, foci(pl.), nave, seat 5 focus, heart, midst, pivot, spine 6 middle 7 lineman, nucleus 8 centrate 12 headquarters

away from: 6 distal

toward: 4 orad 5 entad 10 centerward

centerpiece: 7 epergne

centigrade: 5 scale 11 thermometer

centipede: 4 veri 6 earwig, golach, goloch 8 chilopod, myriapod 9 geophilus

central: mid 5 axial, basic, chief, focal, prime 6 median, middle 7 capital, centric, leading, pivotal, primary 8 dominant 11 equidistant

Central Africa: See Africa

Central America: *agave:* 5 sisal

ant: 5 kelep

bird: 7 jacamar 8 puffbird

canoe: 6 pitpan

country: 6 Panama 8 Honduras, Salvador 9 Costa Rica, Guatemala, Nicaragua

fishing boat: 6 cayuco

gopher: 7 quachil

Indian: 4 Maya 5 Carib

measure: 7 cantaro, manzana

monkey: 4 mono

mullet: 4 bobo

rodent: 4 paca

snake: 10 bushmaster

stockade: 4 boma

tragon: 4 bird 6 quezal 7 quetzal

tree: ebo, ule 4 eboe 5 amate 9 sapodilla

village: 4 boma

weight: 5 libra

Central Asia: See Asia

central cylinder: 5 stele

centric: 5 focal 6 middle, tarete 7 central 9 clustered 11 cylindrical 12 concentrated

centrifugal: 9 radiating

centripetal: 8 afferent

century: age 6 siecle(F.)

ten: 7 chiliad 10 millennium

century plant: 4 aloe 5 agave 6 maguey

fiber: 4 pita, pito

ceorl: 5 churl, thane 7 freeman, villein

cepa: 5 onion

cephalagia: 8 headache

cephalic: 8 atlantal, cerebral

cephalopod: 5 squid 6 cuttle 7 inkfish, octopus

secretion: ink

Cepheus: *daughter:* 9 Andromeda

wife: 10 Cassiopeia

ceral: 4 waxy 7 waxlike

ceramics: 5 tiles 7 pottery 9 stoneware

oven: 4 kiln

sieve: 4 laun

cerate: wax 4 lard 5 salve 8 ointment

ceratoid: 5 horny

ceratose: 5 horny

Cerberus: dog 7 monster 8 guardian 9 custodian

cere: wax 4 sere, wrap 6 anoint, embalm

cereal: rye 4 bean, bran, corn, mush, oats, rice 5 grain, maize, spelt, wheat 6 barley, farina, hominy 7 oatmeal, soybean 8 por-

ridge **9** buckwheat
coating: **4** bran
grass: oat, rye **4** ragi, rice **5** grain, wheat **6** barley, raggee
seed: **6** kernel
spike: ear
cereal grass genus: 6 secale
cerebral: 6 mental
cerebration: 7 thought
cerebrospinal axis: 4 cord **5** brain, spine
cerement: 6 shroud **9** cerecloth
ceremonial fuss: 10 panjandrum
ceremonious: 5 grand, lofty, stiff **6** formal, proper, solemn **7** precise, stately, studied **10** respectful **11** punctilious **12** conventional
ceremonious leave-taking: 5 conge
ceremony: 4 fete, pomp, rite, show, sign **5** state **6** augury, parade, powwow, review, ritual **7** display, pageant, portent, prodigy **8** accolade, function, marriage, occasion **9** formality, solemnity **10** ceremonial, observance **11** celebration
cerer: 10 undertaker
Ceres: 7 Demeter
mother: Ops
cerise: red **6** cherry
cerite: 7 mineral **8** allanite
cernuous: 7 nodding **8** drooping **9** pendulous
cero: 4 fish **6** sierra **7** cavallo, pintado
certain: 4 firm, real, sure, true **5** bound, clear, exact, fixed, plain, siker(Sc.) **6** actual, sicker, stated **7** assured, precise, settled **8** absolute, apparent, constant, official, positive, reliable, resolved, unerring **9** confident, steadfast, undoubted **10** dependable, inevitable, infallible, undeniable **11** determinate, indubitable, trustworthy **12** indisputable **13** incontestable **14** unquestionable **16** incontrovertible
certainly: 4 amen, ywis **5** iwiss, truly **6** certes, indeed, verily **7** hardily **8** forsooth
certie, certy: 5 faith, troth
certificate: 4 bond **5** check, libel, scrip **6** attest, ticket, verify **7** diploma, voucher **9** statement, testimony **10** credential **11** attestation, declaration, testimonial **13** certification
cargo: **8** navicert
debt: IOU **9** debenture
land: **6** amparo(Sp.)
medical, for ill student: **8** aegrotat
money owed: **9** debenture
certify: 4 avow, vise **5** swear **6** affirm, assure, depose, evince, verify **7** endorse, license, testify **9** determine, guarantee
under oath: **6** attest
certiorari: 4 writ **6** review

certiorate: 6 assure **7** apprise, certify
cerulean: 4 blue **5** azure **6** coelin **7** skyblue
cervine: elk **4** deer, stag **5** moose **6** cervid **8** cervidae(pl.), reindeer
cervix: 4 neck
cespitose: 6 matted, tufted **7** tangled
cess: bog, tax **4** cede, duty, levy, luck, rate, tyrf **5** slope, yield **6** impost **7** measure **9** surrender **10** assessment, estimation
cessation: end **4** halt, liss, lull, rest, stay, stop **5** letup, lisse, pause, truce **6** recess **7** ceasing, respite **8** interval, stoppage, surcease **9** armistice, remission **12** intermission, interruption **14** discontinuance
of being: **8** desition
cession: 8 yielding **9** surrender **10** compliance, concession
cesspool: 4 sump **7** cistern
cest: 4 belt **6** cestus, girdle
cesta: 6 basket
cetacean: orc **4** cete, orca **5** whale **6** beluga **7** dolphin, grampus **8** porpoise
blind: **4** susu
genus: **4** inia
cete: 5 whale **7** cetacea
Ceylon: *aborigine:* **4** Toda **5** Vedda **6** Veddah
bay: **4** Palk
boat: **4** done, doni **5** balsa, dhoni, doney **11** warkamoowee
city: **7** Colombo(c.)
coin: **4** cent
Dravidian: **5** Tamil
garment: **6** sarong
gooseberry: **10** ketembilla
governor: **6** disawa
hemp: **6** sina-wa
hill dweller: **4** Toda
language: **4** Pali **5** Tamil
measure: **4** para **5** parah
monkey: **4** maha **5** toque **6** langur, rilawa, rillow **10** wanderoock
moss: **4** agar, alga **5** jaffa **7** gulaman
native: **5** Vedda **6** Veddah
oak: **5** kusam
palm: **7** talipat, talipot
rat: **9** bandicoot
resthouse: **6** abalam
rice: **4** padi **5** paddy
rose: **8** cleander
seaport: **5** Galle
sedan: **6** tomjon, tonjon
skirt: **6** reddha
snake: **7** adjiger
soldier: **4** peon
tea: **5** pekoe
tree: **4** doon, tala **7** talipot
chabouk, chabuk: 4 whip
chabutra: 4 dais **7** terrace **8** platform

chack: 4 bite, snap 5 clack, snack 8 wheatear

chackle: 6 cackle, rattle 7 chatter

chacma: 6 baboon

chacra: 4 farm 5 milpa, ranch

chaeta: 4 seta 5 spine 7 bristle

chafe: irk, rub, vex 4 fret, frig, frot, fume, gall, heat, josh, rage, warm, wear 5 anger, annoy, grind, scold 6 abrade, banter, excite, fridge, harass, injury, nettle 7 incense, inflame 8 friction, irritate, raillery

chaff: guy, hay, pug 4 bran, caff(Sc.), guff, josh, quiz 5 borak, chyak, dross, glume, hulls, husks, straw, tease, trash 6 banter, bhoosa, chyack, refuse 7 tailing 8 raillery, ridicule

chaffer: 5 bandy, sieve, wares 6 buying, dicker, haggle, higgle, market 7 bargain, chatter, selling, traffic 8 exchange 9 negotiate 10 bargaining 11 merchandise

chaffinch: 7 robinet

chaffy: 5 scaly 7 acerose, acerous, paleate, trivial 9 bantering, worthless 10 paleaceous

Chaillot resident: 8 madwoman

chain: guy, row, set, tew, tie, tye 4 bind, bond, file, gyve, join, link 5 cable, leash, suite, train 6 catena, chigon, collar, fasten, fetter, hobble, secure, series, string, tether 7 bobstay, catenae(pl.), connect, embrace, enslave, manacle, network, shackle 8 bracelet, restrain 9 constrain 10 chatelaine 13 concatenation

collar: 4 tore 6 torque

key: 10 chatelaine

mountain: 5 range, Rocky 7 Sierras

of quotations: 6 catena

of rocks: 4 reef

pert. to: 8 catenary

set with precious stones: 7 sautoir

chain cable: 4 boom

chain grab: 7 wildcat

chain-like: 8 catenate

chains: 7 bondage, serfdom

lady in: 9 Andromeda

chair: 4 seat 5 sedan, stool 6 office, pulpit, rocker

back: 5 splat

bath: 11 vinaigrette

bishop's official: 8 cathedra

cover: 4 tidy 12 antimacassar

decoration: 8 claw foot

easy: 6 morris, rocker

folding: 9 faldstool

litterlike: 4 kago

occupy: 7 preside

portable: 5 sedan

chairman: 4 head 5 emcee 8 director 9 moderator 10 supervisor

chaise: gig 4 shay 7 curicle 8 carriage

chaitya: 6 shrine 8 monument

chalcedony: 4 onyx, opal, sard 5 agate 6 jasper, quartz 7 opaline 9 carnelian 11 chrysoprase

orange: 4 sard

Chalcodon: *father:* 4 Abas

son: 9 Elephenor

Chaldea: *astronomical cycle:* 5 saros

city: Ur

measure: 4 cane, foot 5 makuk, qasab 6 artaba, gariba, ghalva 7 mansion

chalet: hut 5 cabin, house 7 cottage 8 lavatory

chalice: ama, cup 4 bowl 5 calix, grail 6 goblet 7 calices(pl.)

cover: 4 pall 8 animetta

chalk: 4 cauk, pale, scar, talc, tick 5 creta, score 6 blanch, bleach, crayon, credit, rubble, whiten 7 account 9 limestone, reckoning

chalky silicate: 4 talc

challenge: 4 call, dare, defy, gage 5 blame, brave, claim, query, stump 6 accuse, appeal, cartel, charge, dacker, daiker, demand, forbid, impugn, invite 7 arraign, censure, impeach, provoke, reprove, summons 8 question, reproach 9 exception, objection 10 controvert 11 impeachment

judge: 6 recuse

to a duel: 6 cartel

challenger: 7 duelist 8 pugilist

chamber: oda 4 cell, flat, hall, kiva, room 5 atria(pl.), bower, solar, soler 6 atrium, camara, camera, hollow, sollar 7 bedroom, caisson, cubicle, lochlus 9 apartment, camarilla, vestibule 11 compartment

annealing: 4 leer

bombproof: 8 casemate

council: 10 consistory

drying: 4 kiln, oven

judge's: 6 camera

pert. to: 7 cameral

private: 5 adyta(pl.) 6 adytum 7 sanctum 8 conclave

underwater construction: 7 caisson

chamberlain: 6 factor 7 officer, servant, steward 9 attendant, chamberer, treasurer 10 camerlengo 14 superintendent

papal: 10 camerlengo, camerlingo

chambray: 5 cloth 6 fabric 7 gingham

chameleon: 5 anole, anoli 6 lizard

chameleonic: 6 fickle 10 changeable, inconstant

chamfer: 5 bevel, flute 6 furrow, groove 7 channel 11 countersink

chamois: 4 gems, skin 5 cloth, gemse 6 chammy, shammy, shamoy 7 leather 8 antelope *male:* 7 gemsbok

champ: 4 bite, chaw, firm, hard, mash 5 field, gnash 7 trample 11 battlefield

champagne: ay 4 wine

center: 6 Troyes

champerty: 7 contest, rivalry 10 conspiracy

champion: ace, aid 4 abet, back, defy, hero 6 assert, attend, defend, squire, victor 7 espouse, fighter, protect 8 advocate, defender 9 challenge, combatant, firstrate 10 unexcelled

championship: 5 title 7 defense 8 advocacy 9 supremacy 10 leadership

champleve: 6 enamel, inlaid

chance: die, hap, lot 4 case, dint, fate, luck, odds, risk, tide 5 ettle, stake 6 betide, casual, gamble, happen, hazard, mishap, random 7 aimless, fortune, stumble, venture 8 accident, casualty, fortuity 9 adventure, haphazard, happening, mischance 10 contingent 11 contingency, opportunity, probability

by: 5 haply

even: 6 tossup

favorable: 4 odds

chancel: *part:* 4 bema 5 altar

screen: 4 jube

seat: 6 sedile 7 sedilia(pl.)

chancery petitioner: 7 relator

chandelier: 6 pharos 7 fixture 11 candelabrum

chandelle: lob 4 turn, zoom 5 climb 6 candle 7 support

chandler: 6 dealer 10 chandelier 11 candlestick

chang: 4 beer 5 noise 6 uproar

change: mew 4 move, turn, vary, veer 5 adapt, alter, amend, break, coins, shift 6 modify, mutate, remove, revamp, revise, switch 7 commute, convert, deviate 8 revision, transfer 9 diversity, permutate, rearrange, transform, transmute, transpose, variation 10 alteration, correction, difference, transition 11 vicissitude 13 metamorphosis 15 diversification

appearance: 6 obvert

back: 6 return, revert

character of: 8 denature

color: dye 5 blush 6 redden

course: 4 tack, turn, veer 5 sheer

into: 6 become

music: 4 muta

subject to: 7 mutable 8 amenable, variable

changeable: 5 eemis, giddy, immis 6 fickle, fitful, mobile 7 bruckle, erratic, mutable, protean, variant 8 amenable, catching, unstable, volatile 9 alterable, irregular, mercurial, uncertain, unsettled 10 capricious, inconstant, irresolute 11 chameleonic

in form: 9 metabolic

changeling: oaf 4 dolt, fool 5 child, dunce, idiot 7 waverer 8 imbecile, renegade, turncoat 9 simpleton 10 substitute

changing: *color:* 11 allochroous

pattern and color: 13 kaleidoscopic

channel: gat, ree, rut 4 cano, cava, dike, duct, dyke, gool, gote, gout, pipe, vein, wadi, wady 5 canal, chase, ditch, drain, drill, flume, flute, glyph, media(pl.), regal, rigol, river, sinus, stria 6 arroyo, artery, furrow, groove, gutter, medium, rabbet, rivose, sluice, strait, stream, striae(pl.), trough 7 conduct, conduit, passage, rivulet, silanga, tideway 8 aqueduct, guideway

artificial: gat 4 leat 5 canal, drain, flume 6 sluice 7 drainer

brain: 4 iter

formed by cutting: 5 scarf

longitudinal: 6 rabbet

marker: 4 buoy

narrow: 6 furrow, strait

near port: 5 deeps

river: bed 6 alveni(pl.) 7 alvenus

ship: gat

vertical: 5 glyph

vital: 6 artery

water: gat 4 gote, gurt, leat, pipe, race 5 canal, drain, flume 6 sluice 7 conduit 8 aqueduct, millrace, tailrace

channel bone: 8 clavicle 10 collarbone

Channel Island: 4 Sark 8 Guernsey

measure: 4 cade 5 cabot

seaweed: 5 vraic

channelbill: 8 rainfowl

channeled: 7 voluted 8 furrowed 9 chamfered

channels: 5 media 6 striae

chanson: 4 song 5 lyric 6 ballad 7 refrain

chant: 4 cant, sing, song 5 carol, psalm 6 anthem, cantus, intone, warble 7 introit, worship 10 cantillate

chantage: 9 extortion 12 blackmailing

chanter: 6 cantor, singer 7 bagpipe 8 songster 9 chorister

chanteuse: 6 singer 10 cantatrice

chantey, chanty: 4 song

chanticleer: 4 cock 7 rooster

Chantilly: 4 lace

chantry: 5 altar 6 chapel, shrine

chanty, chantey: 4 song

chaos: pie 4 gulf, mess, void 5 abyss, babel, chasm 6 jumble 7 anarchy, mixture 8 disorder, shambles 9 confusion

primordial: 4 Apsu

utter: 6 tophet 7 topheth

Chaos: *Babylonian:* 4 Apsu
daughter: Nox, Nyx
Maori: 4 kore
primeval fluid of: Nu
son: 6 Erebus
chaotic: 5 snafu 7 muddled 8 confused, formless
chap: boy, buy, man, rap 4 bean, beat, blow, chip, chop, cove, duck, kibe, mash 5 billy, bloke, bully, buyer, chink, cleft, crack, knock, lover, split, trade, youth 6 barter, breach, bugger, callan, choose, fellow, shaver, strike, stroke 7 callant, chapman, chappie, fissure, husband, roughen 8 blighter, customer, division
odd: 6 galoot
old: 6 geezer
young: 6 gaffer
chaparral: 9 buckthorn
chapel: 4 cage, cape, cope, cowl, hood 5 cloak 6 bethel, church, shrine 7 chantry, service 8 bethesda 9 reliquary, sanctuary
private: 7 oratory
sailor's 6 bethel
chaperon: 4 hood 6 attend, duenna(Sp.), escort, matron 7 protect 8 guardian, trapping 10 escutcheon 11 gouvernante(F.)
chaplain: 5 padre 9 clergyman
chaplet: 4 bead, orle 5 crown 6 anadem, anchor, circle, fillet, rosary, trophy, wreath 7 coronal, coronet, garland 8 moulding, necklace, ornament
chapman: 4 chap 5 buyer 6 dealer, hawker, trader 7 peddler 8 customer, merchant
chaps: 4 boys, jaws, lads 5 flews 8 breeches, overalls
chapter: 4 body, cell, post 5 caput, lodge 6 branch 7 correct, meeting, section 8 assembly 9 reprimand 10 contingent
member: 9 capitular
char: 4 burn, cart, sear 5 broil, chark, chore, singe, trout 6 scorch 7 blacken, chariot 8 sandbank 9 carbonize
charabanc: bus 5 coach 7 vehicle
charact: 6 emblem
character: 4 bent, card, kind, mark, mold, note, part, rune, sign, sort, tone 5 brand, fiber, stamp, tenor, token, trait, write 6 caract, emblem, figure, letter, mettle, nature, repute, stripe, symbol 7 edition, essence, engrave, impress, quality 8 inscribe 9 agreement, ampersand 10 reputation 11 disposition
assumed: 4 role
bad: 5 drole(F.)
chief: 4 hero, lead, star 7 heroine
group: 5 ethos
of a people: 5 ethos
vein: 6 streak

word-representing: 8 logogram 9 logograph
characteristic: 4 cast, mark, mien 5 trait 6 nature 7 feature, impress, quality, typical 8 property, symbolic 9 attribute, lineament 11 distinctive, pathognomic, peculiarity
individual: 9 idiopathy
characterize: 4 mark 6 define, depict 7 engrave, entitle, imprint, portray 8 describe, indicate, inscribe 9 delineate, designate, represent 11 distinguish
charade: 6 enigma, puzzle, riddle 7 picture, tableau
charco: 4 pool 6 puddle, spring
charcoal: 5 carbo, chark 6 carbon, fusain, pencil 7 blacken, drawing
animal: 9 boneblack
reduce to: 4 char
chard: 4 beet 7 thistle 9 artichoke
chare, char: job 4 lane, task, turn 5 alley, chore 6 finish, street 7 perform
charge: fee 4 bill, cark, cost, duty, fill, lien, load, onus, rate, rush, toll, ward 5 debit, onset, order, price, refer 6 accuse, adjure, allege, assess, attack, burden, career, credit, defame, demand, enjoin, impute, indict, tariff, weight 7 arraign, ascribe, assault, average, censure, command, concern, custody, expense, impeach, keeping, mandate, mission 8 chastise, overload 9 challenge, oversight 10 commission, impetition, impregnate, injunction, management 11 arraignment, encumbrance, incriminate, instruction 14 responsibility
customary: 4 dues
grazing: 5 agist
with gas: 6 aerate
chargeable: 6 costly, liable 7 weighty 9 expensive, important, momentous 10 burdensome 11 responsible, troublesome
charged: 5 tense 9 emotional 10 purposeful
with electricity: 4 live
chargeman: 7 blaster, foreman 10 batteryman
charger: 4 dish 5 horse, mount, plate, steed 6 vessel 7 accuser, courser, platter
charges: *boat carrying:* 7 boatage
legal: 4 dues, fees 5 costs 9 retainers
repairs to barrister's quarters: 9 detriment
charily: 8 frugally, gingerly 9 carefully 10 cautiously
chariness: 7 caution 9 frugality, integrity 11 heedfulness, sparingness
chariot: car 4 cart, char, wain 5 buggy, essed, wagon 6 charet, esseda, essede 7 vehicle 8 carriage, charette
for carrying image of god: 4 rath 5 ratha
Greek: 8 quadriga
Roman: 5 essed 6 esseda, essede

two-horse: 4 biga
chariotee: 8 carriage
charioteer: 5 pilot 6 auriga, driver 7 wagoner 9 charioter
charisma: 5 charm, power 6 impact
charitable: 4 kind 6 benign, humane 7 lenient, liberal 8 generous 9 favorable, forgiving, indulgent 10 beneficent, benevolent 12 eleemosynary 13 compassionate, philanthropic
charity: 4 alms, dole, gift, love, pity, ruth 5 mercy 6 bounty 7 handout, largess 8 lenience 9 affection 10 almsgiving, generosity, liberality, tenderness 12 philanthropy
dispenser: 7 almoner
charivari: 5 babel 8 serenade, shivaree 10 callithump 11 celebration
chark: cup 4 burn, char, coal, coke 5 glass 6 cinder, noggin 8 charcoal
charlatan: 5 cheat, faker, fraud, quack 7 cabotin, empiric 8 imposter, magician 9 pretender 10 medicaster, mountebank
Charlemagne: *brother:* 8 Carloman
conquest: 5 Avars
court hero: 6 Roland
father: 5 Pepin
knight: 4 Gano 7 Ganelon, Paladin
nephew: 7 Orlando
peer: 6 Oliver 7 Paladin
pert. to: 8 Caroline
sword: 7 Joyeuse
Charles' Wain: 4 Bear, Ursa 6 Dipper
Charlie Chan creator: 7 Biggers
charlock: 4 weed 5 kraut 7 mustard
charlotte: 7 custard, dessert
Charlotte Corday's victim: 5 Marat
charm: obi 4 calm, juju, jynx, mojo, play, song 5 allay, freet, freit, grace, obeah, magic, saffi, safie, spell, weird 6 allure, amulet, beauty, caract, enamor, entice, fetich, fetish, glamor, grigri, melody, please, scarab, saphie, soothe, subdue, summon 7 assuage, attract, beguile, bewitch, cantrip, conjure, control, delight, enamour, enchant, enthral, flatter, glamour, periapt, singing, sorcery 8 breloque, enthrall, entrance, greegree, practice, talisman 9 agreeable, captivate, fascinate, seduction 10 attraction, demonifuge 11 incantation
protective: 6 amulet
charmer: 5 siren 8 exorcist, magician, sorcerer 9 sorceress 11 spellbinder
charming: 7 amiable, eyesome, winning, winsome 8 adorable, delicate 9 agreeable, beautiful, glamorous 10 attractive, glamourous
charnel: 7 ghastly 8 cemetery 10 sepulchral
house: 7 ossuary 8 mortuary
Charon: 7 boatman 8 ferryman

payment to: 4 obol 6 obolus
river: 4 Styx
Charpentier opera: 6 Louise
charpoy: bed, cot
charqui: 4 beef, meat 5 jerky
chart: map 4 card, plat, plan, plot 5 carte, graph 6 record, scheme 7 diagram, explore, outline, project 8 document, platform 10 cartograph
chartaceous: 6 papery
charter: let 4 deed, hire, rent 5 carte, chart, grant, lease 6 charta, permit 9 privilege 10 commission, conveyance
chary: shy 4 dear, wary 5 chere, scant 6 frugal, prized, skimpy 7 careful, sparing 8 cautious, hesitant, precious, reserved, vigilant 9 diffident, reluctant, treasured 10 economical, fastidious, scrupulous 11 circumspect
Charybdis rock: 6 Scylla
chase: 4 hunt, shag, sick 5 annoy, catch, chevy, chivy, harry, score 6 chivvy, emboss, follow, frieze, furrow, gallop, groove, harass, hollow, indent, pursue, quarry, scorse, trench 7 channel, engrave, pursuit 8 ornament
away: 4 rout 5 drive
goddess: 4 Dian 5 Diana
chaser: ram 5 drink 8 airplane, engraver
chasm: gap, pit 4 gulf, rift 5 abyss, blank, canon, chaos, cleft, gorge 6 breach, canyon, hiatus 7 fissure 8 aperture, crevasse, interval
glacial: 7 crevass 8 crevasse
chasse: 4 step 5 glide 6 liquor, shrine 7 dismiss 9 reliquary
chasseur: 6 hunter 7 footman 8 huntsman 9 attendant
chassis: 5 frame
chaste: 4 pure 5 clean 6 decent, honest, modest, proper, severe, vestal 7 refined 8 celibate, innocent, virtuous 9 continent, undefiled 10 immaculate
chasten: 4 rate 5 abase, smite, smote, sober 6 humble, punish, refine, subdue, temper 7 afflict, censure, correct 8 chastise, moderate, restrain 9 castigate, reprimand 10 discipline
chastise: 4 beat, flog, lash, slap, trim, whip 5 amend, blame, scold, spank, strap, taunt 6 accuse, anoint, berate, charge, punish, purify, rebuke, refine, swinge, temper, thrash 7 chasten, correct, reprove, scourge, suspect 9 castigate
chastity: 6 purity, virtue 7 modesty 8 goodness
chasuble: 6 deacon 8 vestment
chat: mag 4 bird, chin, cone, coze, gist, talk, tove, twig 5 ament, cause, dally, point, prate, speak, spike 6 babble, branch, cat-

kin, confab, gabble, gibber, gossip, jabber, potato, samara 7 chatter, prattle 8 causerie, converse, spikelet, strobile 9 dalliance 11 confabulate 12 conversation

chateau: 5 house 6 castle 7 mansion 8 fortress

Chateaubriand work: 5 Atala

chatelaine: pin 4 etui, hook 5 chain, clasp, etwee, purse 6 brooch 8 mistress

chaton: 5 basil, bezel, bezil 7 setting

chatta: 8 umbrella

chattels: 4 gear 5 goods, money, wares 6 slaves 7 capital 8 bondsmen, property 9 livestock, principal
distraint: 4 naam
tenant's: 6 farleu, farley
to recover: 7 detinue

chatter: gab, jaw, mag, yap 4 blab, carp, chat, hack, rick, talk, tear, yirr 5 cabal, clack, garre, haver, prate, shake 6 babble, gabble, gibber, gossip, jabber, palter, rattle, shiver, tattle, yammer, yatter 7 blabber, brabble, chackle, chaffer, chipper, chitter, clitter, nashgob, prabble, prattle, shatter 8 verbiage 11 goosecackle
conjurer's: 10 hanky-panky

chatterbox: jay, mag 4 piet 5 clack 6 gossip, magpie 10 chatterbag, chattermag 13 chatterbasket

chattering: 8 babbling 9 prattling, talkative 10 loquacious

Chaucer: *inn:* 6 Tabard
Knight's Tale character: 7 Palamon
pilgrim: 5 reeve
title: Dan

chauffeur: 5 drive 6 driver 8 operator

chaussee: 4 road 6 street 7 highway 8 causeway

chaussure: 4 boot, shoe 7 slipper 8 footgear

chauve-souris: bat

chauvinism: 8 jingoism 10 patriotism

chavel: 4 gnaw 6 mumble, nibble

chaw: jaw, vex 4 chew, envy, mull 5 champ, grind 6 ponder 7 portion 8 ruminate 9 chawbacon, masticate

chawbacon: 4 chaw 5 yokel 6 rustic 7 bumpkin

chawn: gap 4 gape 5 cleft 6 cleave

cheap: low 4 base, poor, vile 5 close, gaudy, kitch, price, tight, tinny, value 6 abject, common, plenty, shoddy, sordid, stingy, tawdry, trashy 7 bargain, dealing 8 inferior, purchase 9 innkeeper 10 despicable 11 depreciated, inexpensive 12 contemptible

cheap jack: 6 hawker, pedlar, pedler 7 peddler 8 huckster 9 Cheap-John

cheat: do; bam, bob, cog, con, fob, gip, gum, gyp, nip 4 bilk, bite, clip, dupe, fake, flam, geck, gull, hoax, jilt, jouk, liar, mump,

rook, sell, sham, sile, skin 5 blink, booty, bunco, bunko, cozen, cully, dodge, faker, fling, foist, fraud, gleek, gouge, guile, knave, mulct, rogue, scamp, spoil, trick, welsh 6 baffle, blanch, bubble, bucket, chiaus, chisel, chouse, daddle, delude, deride, doodle, duffer, fiddle, fleece, grease, humbug, illude, jockey, outwit, raddle, renege, shaver 7 abusion, beguile, deceive, defraud, escheat, faitour, finesse, foister, gudgeon, juggler, mislead, plunder, quibble, sharper, skelder, swindle 8 artifice, delusion, dry-shave, hoodwink, imposter 9 bamboozle, fainaigue, hypocrite, imposture, scoundrel, stratagem, victimize 10 mountebank 15 prestidigitator

cheater: 4 bite, gull 5 knave 6 bilker, topper 7 sharper 9 trickster

check: bit, dam, nab, nip, tab 4 balk, curb, damp, rein, snub, stay, stem, stop, stub, test, twit, were 5 abort, allay, block, brake, catch, chide, chink, choke, crack, daunt, delay, deter, draft, limit, quell, repel, stall, still, stunt, tally, taunt, token 6 arrest, attack, baffle, bridle, defeat, detain, detent, gravel, hinder, impede, oppose, outwit, quench, rabbet, rebate, rebuff, rebuke, scotch, stifle, ticket, verify 7 backset, command, control, inhibit, monitor, refrain, repress, reproof, reprove, repulse, setback 8 bulkhead, encumber, obstruct, restrain, withhold 9 constrain, frustrate, interrupt, overpower, reprimand, restraint, supervise 10 difficulty 11 certificate, counterfoil, examination

check growth of: 5 stunt 7 shorten

check in: 6 arrive 8 register

check out: die 5 leave 6 depart 7 confirm 11 investigate

check over: 7 examine, inspect

checker: 5 freak, freck 6 damper

checkerboard: 7 dambrod 8 damboard
marked like: 10 tessellate

checkered: 4 pied, vair 5 diced, plaid 6 motley 10 changeable, variegated 11 diversified

checkers: 4 game 6 damrod, drafts 8 draughts
move: 4 dyke, fife, huff 5 cross 7 bristol
opening: 6 souter
term: 4 king 5 block, crown

checkerwork: 7 tessera 8 tesserae(pl.)
inlay: 6 mosaic

checkmate: 4 gain, lick, stop, undo 6 baffle, corner, defeat, outwit, stymie, thwart 9 frustrate

checkrein: 4 curb 7 saccade

cheddar: 6 cheese

cheechako, chee-chaco: 10 tenderfoot

cheek: 4 chap, gall, gena, jole, jowl, leer, sass 5 bucca, chyak, genae(pl.), nerve, sauce 6 chyack, haffet, haffit 8 audacity, temerity 9 impudence

bone: 5 malar 6 zygoma

comb. form: 5 bucco

distended: 7 buccate

muscle: 10 buccinator

pert. to: 5 genal, malar 6 buccal

cheep: pip, yap, yip 4 hint(Sc.), peep, pule 5 chirp, creak(Sc.), tweet 6 squeak, tattle

cheer: ole(Sp.), rah 4 fare, food, root, viva, yell 5 bravo, elate, feast, heart, huzza, mirth, shout, whoop 6 cantle, gaiety, hurrah, huzzah, solace, viands 7 acclaim, animate, applaud, cherish, comfort, console, enliven, gladden, hearten, jollity, refresh, rejoice 8 applause, brighten, inspirit, pheasant, vivacity 9 animation, encourage, merriment 10 exhilarate, invigorate 11 acclamation, hospitality 13 entertainment, hospitability

burst: 5 salvo

cheerful: gay 4 cant, glad, gleg(Sc.), rosy 5 cadgy, canty, chirk, douce, happy, jolly, merry, peart, ready, sunny 6 blithe, bright, cheery, chirpy, crouse, genial, hearty, hilary, jocund, lively 7 buoyant, chipper 8 cheering, gladsome, homelike, sanguine 9 contented, lightsome, sprightly 10 enlivening 11 comfortable 12 lighthearted

cheerless: sad 4 cold, drab, glum, gray 5 bleak, drear 6 dismal, dreary, gloomy 7 forlorn, joyless 8 dejected 10 dispirited, melancholy 11 comfortless 12 disconsolate

cheese: 4 Brie, Edam, Jack 5 cream, Gouda, mysost, Swiss, Ziega 6 Barrie, Dunlop, Glarus, Zieger 7 Cheddar, cottage, Gruyere, Stilton 8 American, Parmesan 9 Camembert, Gammelost, Limburger, Roquefort 10 Gorgonzola, Neufchatel 11 Liederkranz

brown: 6 mysost

curdy: 4 trip

dish: 4 cake 6 fondue, omelet 7 rarebit, souffle

green: 7 sapsago

large: 7 kebbock, kebbuck

milk whey: 5 ziega 6 zieger

Normandy: 7 angelot

pert. to: 6 caseic 7 caseous

poached: 10 gnocchetti

white: 11 Neufchatel

cheese maggot: 7 skipper

cheesecake: 7 dessert 10 photograph

cheeseparing: 6 penury 9 parsimony 10 stinginess

cheesy: 4 fine 5 cheap, smart 6 shabby, sleazy 7 caseous 9 excellent, worthless

cheetah: cat 5 youse, youze 7 guepard 8 gueparde

chef: 4 cook 9 cuisinier 10 cuisiniere

chela: 4 claw 5 slave 6 pincer 7 servant 8 disciple

chelicera: 8 mandible 9 appendage

chelonian: 6 turtle 8 tortoise

chemical: 4 acid, salt 7 alkalai 10 alchemical 13 iatrochemical

agent: 8 catalyst

compound: 4 imin 5 amide, azine, ceria, ester, imine, purin 6 boride 7 inosite, leucine, metamer

element: see **element:** *chemical*

measure: 4 dram, gram 5 liter, titer

salt: sal

suffix: ac, ol; ane, ein, ene, ile, ine, ion, ite, ole, ose 4 idin, olic 5 ylene

chemise: 5 shift, shirt, smock 6 camisa 8 lingerie

chemisette: 4 sham 6 guimpe

chemist: 7 analyst 8 druggist 9 alchemist 10 apothecary

vessel: 4 vial 5 ampul, cupel, phial 6 aludel, ampule, beaker, retort 7 ampoule

workroom: lab 10 laboratory

chequeen: 6 basket, sequin, zequin 8 zecchino

cheri, cherie: 4 dear 7 beloved, darling 9 cherished 10 sweetheart

cherish: aid, hug, pet 4 dote, hope, like, love, save 5 adore, cheer, cling, enjoy, nurse, prize, value 6 caress, esteem, faddle, fondle, foster, harbor, nestle, pamper, pettle, revere 7 comfort, embosom, embrace, indulge, nourish, nurture, protect, support, sustain 8 enshrine, inspirit, preserve, treasure 9 cultivate, encourage, entertain

cheroot: 5 cigar

cherry: 4 bing, duke, gean 5 morel 7 capulin, chapman, lambert, morello, oxheart 8 amarelle, napoleon 9 bigarreau

acid: 7 cerasin

color: red 6 cerise

extract: 8 cerasein

sour: 8 amarelle

sweet: 4 bing 7 lambert, oxheart

wild: 4 gean 7 marasca, mazzard

cherry finch: 8 hawfinch

cherry holly: 5 islay

cherry laurel: 7 cerasus

cherry orange: 7 kumquat

cherub: 5 angel 6 seraph, spirit 8 seraphim(pl.)

chervil: bun 4 herb

Cheshire district: 4 Hale 5 Hoole 6 Marple

chess: *draw game:* 9 stalemate

finish: 4 draw, mate 7 endgame 9 checkmate, stalemate
Japanese: 5 shogi
move: 5 debut 6 castle, fidate, gambit 10 fianchetto
opening: 5 debut 6 gambit 10 fianchetto
pert. to: 8 scacchic
piece: man 4 king, pawn, rook 5 horse, queen 6 bishop, castle, knight
chest: ark, box, kit 4 arca, bust, cist, cyst, fund, safe 5 ambry, bahut, front, hoard, hutch, trunk 6 basket, breast, bunker(Sc.), casket, coffer, coffin, hamper, locker, shrine, stripe, thorax 7 caisson, capcase, cassone(It.), commode, deposit, enclose 8 cupboard, treasury 9 container, strongbox 10 contention, receptacle, repository 11 controversy, gardeviance
alms: 6 almoin 7 almoign
animal: 7 brisket
bone: 5 costa
human: 6 breast, thorax
meal: 6 girnal, girnel
pert. to: 8 thoracic
sacred: ark 4 arca, cist
sound: 4 rale 7 rhonchi(pl.) 8 rhonchus
stone: 4 cist, kist
supply: 6 wangan, wangun 7 wanigan 8 wannigan
chesterfield: 4 coat, sofa 5 divan 8 overcoat 9 davenport
chestnut: 4 joke, ling, rata, tree 5 brown, horse 6 marron(F.), sativa 7 crenata, dentata
and gray: 4 roan
dwarf: 9 chincapin 10 chinquapin
genus of: 8 castanea
water: 4 ling 5 trapa
chevalier: 5 noble 6 knight 7 gallant 8 cavalier, horseman 10 greenshank
cheverel, cheveril: 6 pliant 7 elastic, kidskin 8 flexible
chevet: 4 apse 11 termination
chevin: 4 chub
chevisance: 5 booty, issue, spoil 6 remedy, supply 8 chivalry, resource 9 expedient, substance 10 enterprise, provisions 11 achievement, transaction
chevron: 4 beam, mark 5 glove 6 rafter, stripe 7 molding 10 gravystain
chevrotain: 4 napu 7 deerlet, kanchil, tragule
chevy: See **chivy**
chew: cud 4 bite, cham, chaw, gnaw, quid 5 chamm, grind, munch, rumen 6 mumble 8 meditate, ruminate 9 denticate, manducate, masticate
inability to: 8 amasesis
the rag: 6 gossip 7 chatter

chewing gum base: 6 chicle
chewink: 4 bird 5 finch, joree 6 towhee
chiastolite: 5 macle
chiaus: 5 cheat 8 sergeant, swindler 9 messenger
Chibcha: 4 zipa 5 zaque 6 Indian, zacqua
chic: 4 pert, posh, trig, trim 5 natty, nifty, smart 6 dapper, modish 7 elegant, stylish
chicadee: 8 titmouse
Chicago district: 4 Loop
chicanery: 4 ruse, wile 5 feint, trick 8 artifice, intrigue, trickery 9 deception, duplicity, sophistry, stratagem
chick: 4 girl, tick 5 child, natty 6 screen, sequin, sprout 7 chicken
chick-pea: 4 gram, herb 5 chich, cicer 8 garbanzo, garvance, garvanzo 9 garavance
chickadee: 8 titmouse
chickaree: 8 squirrel'
chicken: hen 4 cock, fowl 5 biddy, capon, chick, child, chuck, fryer, layer, manoc, poult 6 chicky, pullet 7 broiler, rooster 8 cockerel 11 chickabiddy
breed: 7 Leghorn 9 Wyandotte 11 Rhode Island
raising device: 7 brooder
young: 5 chick, fryer, poult 6 pullet 7 broiler
chicken out: 4 quit 6 renege
chicken snake: 4 boba
chickenhearted: 5 timid 8 cowardly
chickweed genus: 6 alsine
chicle: gum 5 latex
chicory: 4 bunk, root 5 plant 6 endive 7 succory, witloof
family: 12 cichoriaceae
chide: 4 rail, rate 5 blame, check, flite, flyte, scold 6 berate, rebuff, rebuke, threap, threep, threpe 7 censure, reprove, upbraid, wrangle 8 admonish, reproach 9 objurgate, reprehend, reprimand
chief: bo; aga, big, boh, cap, cob, dux, mir 4 agha, arch, boss, duce, duke, head, high, khan, main, rais, raja, reis, tyee 5 alder, elder, first, great, major, prime, rajah, ruler, thane, titan, vital 6 adalid, cabeza, leader, master, rector, sachem, staple 7 capital, captain, central, eminent, foreman, overman, palmary, prelate, premier, supreme 8 dominant, especial, foremost, intimate, sagamore 9 chieftain, commander, paramount, principal, prominent 11 predominant
chiffonier: 6 bureau 7 cabinet, commode
chigger: 4 mite 6 chigoe, insect, jigger, red-bug
chignon: 4 knot 5 chain, twist 6 collar
chigoe: 4 flea 7 chigger
chilblain: 4 kibe, mule(F.) 5 blain 6 pernio

child (see also **children**): ben (Heb.), boy, bud, imp, kid, son, tad, tot 4 baba, babe, baby, bata, brat, chit, girl, page, tike, tyke 5 bairn(Sc.), chick, chiel(Sc.), gamin, issue 6 cherub, enfant, filius(L.), infant, moppet, urchin 7 bambino(It.), progeny 8 bantling, chiseler(Ir.), daughter 9 firstling, offspring, youngster 10 descendant 11 chickabiddy

advancement: 9 precocity

chubby: 8 rolypoly 10 butterball

comb. form: ped 4 paed, pedo 5 paedo

dainty: elf 5 fairy

homeless: 4 waif

illegitimate: 6 by-blow 7 bastard

killer: 11 infanticide

parentless: 6 orphan

patron saint: 8 Nicholas

pert. to: 6 filial

puckish: imp

roguish: 6 urchin

spoiled: 4 brat 5 mardy 7 cockney

street: 5 gamin

tiny: tot 4 babe, baby 6 infant, peewee

unmannerly: 7 smatche(Sc.)

childbirth: 5 labor 7 lying-in, travail 11 confinement, parturition

goddess: 4 Apet, Auge, Upis 5 Damia 6 Lucina 7 Auxesia

childish: 4 weak 5 naive, petty, silly 6 puling, simple, weanly(Sc.), young 7 asinine, babyish, foolish, kiddish, puerile, unmanly 8 bairnish, brattish, immature, juvenile 9 credulous, childlike, infantile, kittenish

childish talk: 7 prattle

childish walk: 6 toddle

childlike: 4 meek 6 docile, filial 7 babyish, dutiful 8 childish, innocent, trusting 9 confiding, frivolous 10 submissive

children: 7 progeny 9 offspring

dislike of: 9 misopedia 10 misopaedia

medical science: 10 pediatrics 11 paediatrics

room: 7 nursery

study: 8 pedology 9 paedology

tender of: 4 amah 6 sitter 9 nursemaid

Chile: *arborvitae:* 6 alerce, alerse

city: 6 Arauco, Cobija, Serena 7 Caldera, Copiapo 8 Coquimbo, Santiago(c.), Valdivia 10 Concepcion, Valparaiso

coastal wind: 5 sures

coin: 4 peso 5 libra 6 condor, escudo

desert: 7 Atacama

Indian: Ona

island: 5 Hoste

measure: 4 vara 5 legua, linea 6 cuadra, fanega

money: 6 condor

mountain: 5 Maipu, Pular

mountain range: 5 Andes

national police: 11 carabineros

province: 5 Arica, Aysen Maule, Nuble, Talca 6 Bio-Bio, Cautin, Chiloe, Curico 7 Atacama 8 Coquimbo, Santiago, Tarapaca, Valdivia 9 Aconcagua, Colchagua 10 Concepcion, Valparaiso 11 Antofagasta

river: Loa 5 Itata, Maipu, Maule 6 Bio-Bio, Chuapa, Lontue 7 Illapel 8 Valdivia

rodent: 10 chinchilla

seaport: 4 Lota, Tome 5 Arica 8 Coquimba

shrub: 5 lithi 6 pepino

tree: 4 brea, pelu, ulmo 5 coleu, rauli, roble 6 alerce, alerse, coigue, muermo

volcano: 6 Antuco, Lascar, Llaima 7 Calbuco

weight: 5 grano, libra 7 quintal

workman: 4 roto

chill: ice, raw 4 ague, cold, cool, dazy(Sc.) 5 algor, gelid, rigor, shake 6 frappe, freeze, frigid, frosty, shiver 7 depress, frisson, malaria 8 coldness 11 refrigerate

chilling: 4 eery 5 eerie

chills and fever: 4 ague 7 malaria

chilly: raw 4 cold, cool, lash 5 algid, bleak, hunch 6 arctic, frosty 9 cauldrife

chilver: 4 lamb

chimaera: 7 ratfish

chime: din, rim 4 bell, edge, peal, ring, suit, ting 5 agree, prate 6 accord, cymbal, jingle, melody 7 concord, harmony 8 singsong

chimera: 5 fancy 6 mirage 8 illusion ◆

chimerical: 4 vain, wild 7 utopian 8 delusive, fanciful, romantic 9 fantastic, imaginary, unfounded, visionary

chimes: 5 bells 8 carillon

chimney: lum 4 flue, pipe, tube, vent 5 gully, stack, tewel 6 funnel 7 fissure, opening, orifice 10 smokestack

cover: 4 cowl 7 turncap

deposit: 4 soot

piece: 5 parel 6 mantel

post: 5 speer

chimney corner: 8 fireside 9 inglenook

chimpanzee: ape 5 pigmy 10 anthropoid, troglodyte

chin: jaw 4 chat 5 menta(pl.) 6 mentum

comb. form: 5 genio

double: 4 fold 7 buccula

china: 4 ware 6 dishes 7 ceramic, pottery 8 Cinchona, crockery 9 porcelain 11 earthenware

fine: 5 Spode 6 Sevres 7 Limoges 8 Wedgwood

China: *aborigine:* Yao 4 Mans, Miao 6 Mantzu, Yao-min 7 Miaotse, Miaotze

alloy: 7 paktong 8 packtong
ancient name: 4 Tsao 5 Seres 6 Cathay
antelope: 6 dzeren
arch: 6 pailoo, pailou, pailow
artichoke: 7 chorogi
bamboo: 7 whangee
banker: 6 shroff
bat: ia
bean: soy 6 cowpea
black tea: 6 oolong
boat: 4 bark, junk 6 sampan
brigand: 9 hunghutze, hunghutzu
Buddha: Fo; Foh
Buddhist paradise: 7 Chingtu
cabbage: 7 pakchoi
calculator: 7 suan pan, swan pan
canton: Fu 5 Hsein
city: Su; Nom, Ude 4 Amoy, Tsin, Wuhu 5 Jehol, Macao, Macau, Pekin 6 Canton, Fachan, Fuchau, Hankau, Hankow, Huchau, Kalgan, Nankin, Ningpo, Suchau, Swatow, Tsinan, Yunnan 7 Chengte, Chengtu, Chingtu, Fatshan, Foochow, Hanyang, Kaifeng, Lanchau, Nanking, Paoting, Taiyuen, Tunkuan, Wenchau, Wuchang, Yenping 8 Changsha, Chaochau, Fancheng, Hangchau, Hangchow, Kiaochau, Nanchang, Shanghai, Shaohing, Siangtan, Tengchau, Tientsin, Tungchau, Tunghwan, Yanphing 9 Changchau, Chinkiang, Chungking, Lienkiang 10 Chingkiang, Kingtechen
city (walled): 6 Peking
civet: 5 rasse
clay: 6 kaolin
cloth: sha 4 moxa, pulo, silk 6 nankin 7 nankeen
cloth-stiffening gelatin: 7 haitsai
coin: le, pu; fan, neu, sen 4 cash, cent, mace, tael, tiao, yuan 5 liang, tsien 6 dollar, ticket 9 candareen 10 Kupingtael 11 Haikwantael
comb. form: 4 Sino 5 Sinic
cooking style: 5 Honan 6 Fukien, Peking 8 Szechuan 9 Cantonese
cosmic order: tao
customs collector: 5 hoppo
decigram: li
deer: 8 elaphure
department: Fu 5 Hsien
dialect: Wu 4 Amoy 5 Hakka 6 Canton, Ningpo, Swaton 7 Foochow, Wenchow
dish: 4 rice 7 fooyung 8 fooyoung
division: 4 chow, Miao 5 Hsien 6 canton
dog: 4 chow, peke
dragon: 6 chilin
drink: 6 samshu
duck eggs: 5 pidan
dulcimer: 7 yang-kin

dynasty: Fo; Han, Sui, Wei, Yin 4 Chin, Chou, Hsia, Ming, Sung, Tang, Tsin, Yuan 5 Shang
exchange medium: 5 sycee
factory: 4 hong
festival: 9 Ching Ming
feudal state: Wei
figurine: 5 magot
fir: 5 nikko
fish: 7 trepang
flute: che 4 tche
fruit: 6 lichee, litchi
ginger: 9 galingale
god: 4 Ghos, Joss, Shen 5 Kuant
gong: 6 tamtam
gooseberry: 9 carambola
grass: bon 5 ramie
grass linen: 8 barandos
gruel: 6 congee, conjee
herb: tea 7 ginseng
herb genus: 7 nandina
houseboat: 5 tanka
idol: 4 joss 6 pagoda
indigo: 6 isatis
isinglass: 4 agar 8 agar-agar
island: 4 Amoy 5 Macao 6 Hainan 7 Formosa
jute: 7 chingma
laborer: 6 coolie
lake: 6 Po-yang 8 Tung-ting
language: Wu 4 Shan 8 Mandarin 9 Cantonese
lemon: 6 citron
magistrate: 8 mandarin
magnolia: 5 yulan
mandarin's residence: 6 oyamen
measure: ho, hu, ko, li, mu, pu, ta, to, tu, yu; cho, fen, tou, yan, yin 4 chih, fang, kish, quei, shih, teke, tsan, tsun 5 chang, ching, sheng, shing 6 kung ho, kung li, kung mu, tching, tchung 7 kung fen 8 kung chih, kung shih 9 kung ching, kung sheng
measure of distance: li
measure of weight: 4 chin 5 catty
mile: li
money (see also *coin* above): mo, pu 4 mace, tael, tiao 5 sycee, tsien
mongol: hu
mountain: Omi 4 Omei, Sung 5 Tsins 6 Inshan, Pu-ling 7 Alashan, Kuen-lun, Kuliang 8 Ta-yu-ling 9 Funiu-shan, Tsing-Ling
musical instrument: kin 5 cheng, sheng 7 samisen
Nationalist Party: 11 Kuomintang
noodles: 4 mein
nurse: ama 4 amah
official: 4 kuan, kwan 5 amban
oil: 4 tung

old name: 6 Cathay
orange: 7 kumquat 8 mandarin
ounce: 4 tael
ox: 4 zebu
pagoda: ta; taa 4 taag
parasol tree: 6 aogiri
peony: 6 moutan
pert. to: 4 Sino
philosopher: 4 Moti 5 Motzu 6 Laotse, Laotzu 9 Confucius
plant: tea, udo 4 rice, tche 5 ramie 7 ginseng
poet: 4 Li Po 7 Li Tai-Po
pony: 7 griffin
porcelain: 7 Celadon, Nankeen
porcelain glaze: 7 eelskin
porgy: tai
positive principle: 4 yang
pottery: 4 Kuan, Ming, Ting 5 Chien 7 boccaro, Tzuchou
pound: 5 catty
prefecture: fu
province: 4 Amur (Heilungkiang) 5 Chili, Honan, Hunan, Hupeh, Kansu 6 Fokien, Fukien, Shansi, Shensi, Yunnan 7 Kiangsi, Kiangsu, Kwangsi, Nganhui 8 Che-Kiang, Kweichau, Shantung, Szechuan, Szechwan 9 Kwangtung, Manchuria
provincial chief: 6 taoyin
puzzle: 7 tangram
race: 4 Lolo 5 Sinic, Soyot 6 Mongol
religion: 6 Taoism 12 Confucianism
river: Si; Han, Ili, Kan, Min, Pei, Wei 4 Hwai, Tung, Yuan, Yuen 5 Hwang, Peiho, Pieho, Tarim 7 Hoangho, Sikiang 12 Yangtsekiang ⊢YANGTZE
roller: 7 sirgang
salutation: bow 6 kowtow
sauce: soy
sea port: 4 Amoy, Wuhu 5 Aigun, Shasi 6 Antung, Canton, Chefoo, Dairen, Harbin, Ichang, Ningpo, Pakhoi, Swaton, Szemao, Wuchow, Yochow 7 Foochow, Hangkow, Hunchun, Lungkow, Mengtsz, Nanking, Nanning, Samshui, Santuao, Soochow, Wenchow 8 Changsha, Hangchow, Kiukiang, Kongmoon, Lungchow, Shanghai, Tengyueh, Tientsin, Tsingtao, Wanhsien 9 Chinkiang, Chungking, Kiungchow, Newchwang 10 Chiankiang 12 Chingwangtao 14 Lungchingstsun
secret society: hui 4 tong
sedge: 4 mati
shrub: tea 5 ramie
silk: sha 5 pekin, tasar 6 pongee, tussah 7 taysaam, tsatlee 8 shantung
silkworm: 4 sina 6 tussah, tusser 10 ailanthus
silver: 5 sycee

skiff: 6 sampan
sky: 4 tien
sleeping platform: 4 kang
society: 4 Hoey, Huey, Hung, Tong 5 Triad
squash: 6 cushaw
state(anc.): 4 Tsao 6 Cathay
stocks: 6 cangue
street: 6 hutung
student: 9 sinologue
sugar cane: 5 sorgo
taa: 6 pagoda
Tartar tribe: 4 Toda
tax: 5 likin
tea: cha 4 Tsia 5 bohea, congo, congu, Emesa, hyson
Temple: taa 6 pagoda
toy: 7 tangram
treaty port: 4 Amoy
tree: 5 nikko 6 kinkan, litchi 7 gingkgo, hagbush, kumquat 9 bandoline, soapberry
tribe: Hu 4 Shan, Toba
vegetable: udo
vine: 5 kudzu 7 yangtao
walking stick: 7 whangee
warehouse: 4 hong
wax: 4 cere, pela
weight: li; fen, hao, kin, ssu, tan, yin 4 chee, chin, mace, shih, tael 5 catty, chien, liang, picul, tsien 6 kung li 7 haikwan, kung fen, kung ssu, kung tun 8 king chin 9 candareen 10 kuping tael 11 haikwan tael
wind instrument: 5 cheng, sheng
wormwood: 4 moxa
China Sea: *gulf:* 4 Siam
island: 6 Hainan 7 Formosa
Chinaberry: 9 soapberry
chinch: 6 bedbug
chine: 4 back, grow 5 chink, crack, crest, ridge, spine 6 cleave, ravine, sprout 7 crevice, fissure 8 backbone
Chinese (see also **China**): 5 Cerai, Seres, Seric, Sinic 6 Mongol, Sinico 7 Asiatic, Cataian, Sangley 9 Celestial
pert. to: 5 Seric 6 Serian 7 Sinitic 8 Senesian
chink: gap 4 bore, cash, coin, kink, rent, rift, rime 5 boore, check, chine, cleft, crack, grike, money 6 cranny, sprain 7 chinkle, crevice, fissure 8 aperture 9 chaffinch 10 interstice
chinky: 5 rifty 6 rimose
Chinook: 4 wind 6 indian 8 Flathead
chief: 4 Tyee
god: 8 tamanoas
people: 7 tilikum 8 tillicum
powwow: 4 wawa
salmon: 7 quinnat
woman: 10 klootchman
Chinook State: 10 Washington

chinquapin: oak 6 bonnet 8 chestnut, wankapin 9 rattlenut

chinse: 4 calk, seam 5 close

chintz: 5 cloth 7 pintado

Chios: 4 Scio(It.) 5 Khios(Gr.) 6 island 10 Sakis-Adasi

chip: bit, cut, hew, nig 4 chap, clip, knap, nick, pare 5 crack, flake, piece, scrap, spale, spalt, waste 6 chisel 7 counter 8 fragment, splinter
of stone: 5 spall 6 gallet

chipmunk: 6 chippy, hackee, rodent 8 squirrel

chipper: gay 4 spry 5 chirp, perky 6 babble, cockey, lively 7 chatter, chirrup, twitter 8 cheerful

chirk: 5 chirp 6 lively 7 chirrup 8 cheerful

chirm: din, hum 5 chirp, croon, noise 6 clamor

chiro: 4 fish

chirognomy: 9 palmistry 10 chiromancy

chirography: 6 script 7 writing 10 engrossing 11 handwriting

chiromancy: 9 palmistry 10 chirognomy

chiroptera: bat

chirp: pip 4 peek, peep, pipe 5 cheep, chelp, chirk, chirl, chirm, chirt, tweet 7 chipper, chirrup, chitter, rejoice, twitter, wheetle

chirrup: 5 chirk, chirp, tweet 7 chipper

chirurgeon: 7 surgeon

chisel: cut, gad 4 chip, form, pare, tool 5 burin, carve, cheat, gouge, hardy 6 chesil, gravel, haggle 7 bargain, engrave, quarrel, shingle
ancient stone: 4 celt
engraving: 7 scooper, scorper
mine: gad 6 peeker
sculpture: 7 gradine 9 ebauchoir
stonemason's: 5 drove
toothed: 6 jagger

chiseled: 6 cisele(F.)

chiseler: 5 cheat, crook 6 gouger 9 bargainer

chiselled: 8 clearcut

chiselly: 6 gritty 8 gravelly 10 unpleasant 12 disagreeable

chit: dab, IOU 4 bill, girl, mind, note, rice 5 child, draft, shoot 6 infant, letter, sprout 7 voucher 9 offspring 10 memorandum

chitarra: 6 guitar

chitchat: 4 talk 6 banter, gossip 12 conversation

chiton: 4 gown, robe 5 tunic 7 mollusk

chitter: 5 chirp 6 shiver 7 chatter, twitter

chivalrous: 5 brave, civil, noble 6 gentle, polite 7 gallant, genteel, valiant, warlike 8 knightly 9 courteous, honorable

chive: cut 4 stab 5 clout, clove, knive, onion 6 bulbet

chivy, chivvy: run, vex 4 hunt, race 5 chase, tease 6 badger, flight, harass, pursue 7 pursuit, scamper, torment 8 maneuver 9 confusion

chlamys: 5 cloak 6 mantle 7 garment

chloral: 8 sedative

chloride: 4 salt 5 ester 7 calomel 8 compound

chlorine remover: 9 antichlor

chloroform: 4 kill 10 anesthetic
discoverer: 6 Liebig 7 Guthrie 9 Soubeiran
ingredient: 7 acetone
liquid used: 7 acetone

chobdar: 5 usher 9 attendant

chock: 5 block, chuck, cleat, wedge

chocolate: 5 candy, cocoa 8 beverage
family: 13 sterculiaceae
machine: 6 conche
powder: 5 cocoa 6 pinola
seed: 5 cacao
stick for mixing: 7 molinet
tree: 4 cola 5 cacao

choice: 4 a-one, best, fine, pick, rare, wale, weal, will 5 cream, elite, prime, voice 6 chosen, dainty, flower, option, picked, select 8 delicate, election, eximious, uncommon, volition 9 excellent, exquisite, recherche 10 preferable, preference 11 alternative

choicy: 6 choosy 10 fastidious

choir: 5 quire 6 chorus
leader: 6 cantor 9 precentor
member: 4 alto, bass 5 basso 7 songman, soprano 9 chorister
vestment: 4 gown 5 cotta 8 surplice

choke: dam, gag 4 clog, plug, quar 5 check, close, grane 6 hinder, impede, stifle 7 querken, repress, silence, smother 8 obstruct, stoppage, strangle, suppress, throttle 9 constrict, neckcloth, suffocate 10 extinguish

choke coil: 7 reactor

chokedamp: 9 blackdamp

choler: ire 4 bile, fury, rage 5 anger, wrath 6 spleen, temper 9 distemper 10 resentment 11 biliousness 12 irascibility

choleric: mad 5 angry, cross, fiery, huffy, testy 6 fumish, touchy 7 bilious, enraged, iracund, peevish, peppery, waspish 8 wrathful 9 impatient, irascible 10 passionate 11 belligerent, quarrelsome
render: 6 enrage

choose: opt 4 chap, cull, pick, vote, wale, weal 5 adopt, chuse, elect 6 prefer, select 7 embrace, espouse

choosy, choosey: 7 finical 9 selective 10 fastidious

chop: cut, hew, jaw, lop 4 chap, dice, gash, hack, hash, jowl, rive, slit 5 carve, cleft, crack, knock, mince, slash, stamp, trade,

truck, whang 6 barter, change, cleave, incise 8 exchange 9 cotolette
down: 4 fell, raze 5 level
eye of: 8 noisette
off: lop 4 drib 5 prune 8 amputate
chop-chop: 7 quickly 8 promptly
chophouse: 10 restaurant
Chopin's country: 6 France, Poland
chopping block: 7 hacklog
chopping tool: ax; axe 7 cleaver, hatchet
choppy: 5 rough
choragus: 6 leader 10 bandleader
chord: 4 cord, tone 5 nerve, triad 6 string, tendon 7 harmony 8 filament 9 harmonize
arc: 4 sine
harplike: 8 arpeggio
musical: 5 major, minor
ninth: 4 none
seventh: 6 tetrad
succession: 7 cadence
Chorda filum: 7 sealace
chore: job 4 char, duty, task 5 chare, stint 6 errand 9 housework
chorister: 6 singer 7 chanter 8 choirboy
chorten: 5 stupa 6 shrine 8 monument 9 reliquary
chortle: 5 laugh, snort 7 chuckle
chorus: 4 song 5 choir 6 accord, assent, unison 7 refrain, singers 8 response
girl: 6 dancer, singer 7 chorine
leader: 7 choragi(pl.) 8 choragus 9 conductor
chose: 5 thing
chosen: 5 elect, elite 7 elected 8 selected
Chosen: 5 Corea, Korea
chosen people: 10 Israelites
chough: 4 bird, crow
chouse: 4 dupe, gull, sham 5 chase, cheat, trick 6 harass 7 defraud 8 swindler 10 imposition
chow: dog 4 eats, food, grub, meal 6 fodder
chowchow: dog 4 bird, olio 7 mixture 8 mishmash 10 hodgepodge, miscellany
chowk: 5 bazar 6 bazaar, market
Christ: 4 Lord 7 Messiah, Saviour
christen: 4 name 7 baptize 10 denominate
Christian: 7 Gentile 8 Nazarene
early: 8 Galilean
Eastern: 6 Uniate
Egyptian: 4 Copt
persecuted: 6 martyr
unity: 7 irenics
Christian Science founder: 4 Eddy
Christiania: 4 Oslo
Christianity: *heretical sect:* 7 Docetae
love feast: 5 agape
martyr: 7 Stephen
symbol: 5 cross, orant 7 lehthus

theologian: 4 Kuhn 7 Aquinas, Niebuhr, Tillich 8 Bultmann 9 Augustine, deChardin 10 Bonhoeffer 11 Kierkegaard
writer: 6 Origen
Christ's thorn: 4 nabk, nubk 5 shrub 6 jujube
Christmas: 4 noel, yule 7 holiday 8 festival, nativity, yuletide
carol: 4 noel 5 nowel
crib: 6 creche
decoration: 5 holly 6 tinsel 9 mistletoe
midnight mass supper: 9 reveillon
Christmas Carol: *author:* 7 Dickens
character: Tim 7 Scrooge
Christmas rose: 9 hellebore
chromium: 7 element, mineral
group element: 7 uranium 8 tungsten 10 molybdenum
symbol: Cr
chromo: 7 picture 10 lithograph
chromolithograph: 7 picture
chronic: 5 fixed 6 severe 7 intense 8 constant 9 confirmed, continual, lingering, prolonged 10 continuous, inveterate 12 disagreeable
chronicle: 5 annal, diary 6 record 7 account, archive, history, recital 8 register 9 narrative
chronicler: 6 writer 8 compiler, recorder 9 historian 11 memorialist
chronology: 6 record 11 arrangement 14 classification
according to: 5 datal
error in: 9 prolepsis 11 anachronism
chronometer: 5 clock 9 metronome, timepiece 10 timekeeper
chronometry: era 4 date 5 epoch
chrysalis: 4 pupa 5 pupae(pl.)
chrysolite: 7 olivine, peridot
chrysoprase: 10 chalcedony
chthonian: 8 infernal
chub: 4 dace, dolt, fool, lout 5 chopa 6 chevin, shiner 8 fallfish, mackerel 9 hornyhead, squawfish
chubby: 5 chuff, fubsy, plump 6 choaty, rotund 8 rolypoly
chuck: hen, log, pig 4 beef, food, fowl, grub, hurl, jerk, lump, toss 5 chock, cluck, pitch, throw 6 bounce, collet 7 chicken, discard 9 dismissal
chuckle: 5 cluck, exult, laugh 6 giggle, titter 7 chortle
chuff: fat 4 boor 5 brick, churl, cross, miser, proud, sound, sulky, surly 6 chubby, elated, rustic 7 swollen 9 conceited 11 ill-tempered
chug: 4 puff

chum: cad, pal 4 bait, mate, pard 5 buddy, butty, crony 6 cobber, copain, friend 8 roommate 9 associate, companion

chump: ass 4 dolt, head 5 block 8 endpiece 9 blockhead, schlemiel, schlemihl

chunk: dab, gob, pat, wad 4 junk, slug 5 claut, piece, throw, whang

chunky: 4 game 5 lumpy, plump, squat, stout, thick

church: 4 tera(Jap.) 7 edifice 9 sanctuary, structure

altar end: 4 apse

altar offering: 8 altarage

attendant: 8 altarboy, choirboy

balcony: 8 cantoria

bench: pew, pue 4 seat

bishopric: see 7 diocese 10 episcopacy, episcopate

body of: 4 nave

calendar: 4 ordo

chapel: 7 oratory

congregation: 7 synaxis

council: 5 synod 6 Nicene

court: 4 Rota

deputy: 5 vicar 6 curate

dignitary: 4 dean, pope 5 abbot, canon 6 bishop 7 prelate, primate

dissenter: 7 sectary

district: 6 parish 7 diocese

dominion of: 11 sacerdotium

doorkeeper: 7 ostiary

early Christian: 8 basilica

endowed: 8 benefice

entrance chapel: 7 galilee

episcopacy: 7 prelacy

field: 5 glebe

government: 9 hierarchy

home: 5 manse 7 deanery 8 convento 9 parsonage

law: 5 canon

member: 11 communicant

morning service: 5 matin

officer: 5 elder, vicar 6 beadle, deacon, lector, sexton, warden 7 prelate, sacrist 8 reverend 9 clergyman, moderator, presbyter, sacristan 11 headborough

part of: 4 apse, bema, nave 5 altar, solea 7 chancel, narthex 8 cantoria, transept 10 clearstory, clerestory

prayer: 5 kyrie 12 kyrie eleison

property: 5 glebe

reader: 6 lector

recess: 4 apse

revenue: 5 tithe 8 benefice

Roman: 7 lateran 8 basilica

room: 6 vestry 7 galilee 8 sacristy

seat: pew, pue 5 bench 6 sedile 7 sedilia(pl.)

service: 4 mass, rite 5 matin 7 vespers, nocturn 8 evensong

stand: 4 ambo

stipend: 7 prebend

vault: 5 crypt

vessel: ama, pyx 4 font 5 amula 7 columba, piscina 9 colymbion 10 monstrance

vestry room: 8 sacristy

wall: 6 cashel

warden's aide: 7 hoggler

wing: 5 aisle

church council (previous to): 10 antenicene

churchgoer: 11 communicant

Churchill: *forte:* 5 prose

Order: 6 Garter

trademark: 5 cigar

churchly: 9 religious, spiritual

churchyard: 6 litten 8 cemetery 9 graveyard

churl: cad, man 4 boor, carl, gnof, hind, lout, serf 5 carle, ceorl, chuff, gnoff, knave, miser 6 bodach, carlot, lubber, rustic, vassal, yeoman 7 bondman, freeman, haskard, husband, niggard, peasant, villain, villein 10 countryman, curmudgeon

churlish: 4 mean 5 bluff, gruff, rough, surly 6 crabby, rustic, sordid, sulkly, sullen, vulgar 7 boorish, crabbed, uncivil, violent 9 illiberal 10 ungracious, unyielding 12 cross-grained

churn: 4 beat, kirn(Sc.), stir 5 drill, shake 7 agitate

part: 6 dasher

chute: 4 rush, tube 5 flume, hurry, rapid, shoot, slide 6 hopper, trough 7 decline, descent 8 downfall, stampede

cibarious: 6 edible

cibol: 5 onion 7 shallot

ciborium: pix, pyx 6 canopy, coffer, vessel

cicada: 6 cagale, cigala, locust

noise: 5 chirr

cicala: 6 locust 11 grasshopper

cicatrix: 4 mark, scab, scar, seam

cicatrization: 8 scarring

cicely: 5 myrrh

Cicero's target: 8 Catiline

cicerone: 5 guide, pilot 6 mentor, orator 7 courier 9 conductor

cichlid food dish: 5 bolti 7 sunfish

cid: Ruy 4 epic, hero, poem 5 Bivar, chief, title 9 commander

sword of: 6 colada, tizona

cider: 5 perry 6 perkin, swanky 8 beverage

pulp: 6 pomace

cienega: 5 marsh, swamp

cigar: 4 toby 5 claro, smoke 6 boquet, Corona, maduro, stogie 7 bouquet, cheroot, culebra 8 perfecto 9 Belvedere

crude: 7 cheroot, culebra

long thin: 8 panatela, panetela 9 panatella, panetella

cigarette: fag 4 biri, pill 5 cubeb, smoke 6 gasper, reefer 9 cigarillo

cigarfish: 4 scad 8 quiaquia

cilium: 4 hair, lash 7 eyelash 8 barbicel

cima: See **cyma**

cimarron: 5 slave 6 maroon 7 bighorn

cimbia: 4 band 6 fillet

cimex: 6 bedbug, insect

cimmerian: 4 inky 5 black 6 gloomy

cinch: 4 belt, gird, grip, pipe, snap 5 girth 6 fasten 8 sinecure 9 certainty

cinchona: 4 bark, tree
extract: 7 quinine

cinct: 4 girt 9 encircled

cincture: 4 band, belt, gird, halo, list, ring 5 girth 6 cestus, collar, fillet, girdle 7 baldric, compass 8 encircle 9 enclosure 11 environment, surrounding

cinder: ash 4 gray, slag 5 chark, dross, ember 6 scoria 7 clinker, lapilla, residue

cinders: 5 gleed, track

cinema (see also **motion picture**): 4 film, show 5 flick, movie 6 screen

cinerarium: urn 8 mortuary

cinerator: 6 ashery 9 crematory 11 incinerator

cinerous: 5 ashen

cingle: 4 belt 5 girth 6 gírdle

cingular: 7 annular 8 circular

cingulum: 4 band 5 ridge 6 girdle

cinnabar: ore 7 mineral 9 vermilion
derivative: 11 quicksilver

cinnamic acid derivative: 7 sinapic

cinnamon: 4 tree 5 canel, spice 6 canela, canell, canelo, cassia 7 canella, canelle 8 barbasco

cinnamon apple: 8 sweetsop

cinnamon oak: 8 bluejack

cinnamon stone: 6 garnet 8 essonite

cinquefoil: 6 clover 7 frasier

cion: bud 5 graft, scion, shoot, uvula 10 descendant

Cipango: 5 Japan 6 Nippon

cipher: key, nil 4 code, null, zero 5 aught, ought 6 device, decode, figure, letter, naught, nought, number, symbol 9 nonentity 10 cryptogram

cipo: 4 vine 5 liana

cippus: 6 pillar 8 landmark 10 gravestone

circa: 5 about 6 around 13 approximation

Circassian: *dialect:* 6 Adighe 8 Cherkess 9 Abkhasian, Kabardian
king: 9 Sacripant

Circe: 5 siren 7 tempter 9 sorceress 11 enchantress
brother: 6 Aeetes
father: 6 Helios

island: 5 Aeaea
niece: 6 Medea
son: 5 Comus 9 Telegonus

circle: lap, set 4 disk, gyre, halo, hoop, loop, maru(Jap.), orbe, ring, rink, turn 5 class, crown, cycle, frame, group, monde, realm, rhomb, rigol, round, swirl, twirl 6 bezant, cirque, clique, collet, cordon, corona, diadem, girdle, rotate, rundle, spiral, system 7 chukkar, chukker, circlet, circuit, company, compass, coronet, coterie, enclose, revolve, ringlet 8 encircle, surround 9 circulate, encompass 13 circumference
around sun or moon: 6 corona
geographic: 6 tropic
great: 7 equator
heraldry: 7 annulet
longest chord: 8 diameter
luminous: 4 aura, halo 6 corona, nimbus
part of: arc 5 chord 6 degree, radius, secant, sector 7 segment

circlet: 4 band, hoop, ring 6 bangle, cirque 7 circuit 8 bracelet, headband
of light: 7 aureola, aureole

circuit: lap 4 area, bout, iter, loop, tour, zone 5 ambit, cycle, orbit, round, route 6 ambage, circle, detour 7 compass, itinera(pl.) 8 district 10 revolution 13 circumference
auxiliary: 5 relay
court: 4 eyre

circuitous: 4 mazy 6 curved 7 crooked, devious, oblique, sinuous, twisted, vagrant, winding 8 circular, flexuous, indirect, rambling, tortuous 9 ambagious, ambiguous, deceitful, underhand, wandering 10 roundabout, serpentine 12 disingenuous, labyrinthine

circular: 4 bill 5 libel, orbed, round 6 ringed 7 annular, cycloid, discoid, perfect 8 cingular, complete, encyclic, globular, pamphlet 9 orbicular 10 circuitous, roundabout 11 publication
indicator: 4 dial
motion: 4 eddy, gyre
plate: 4 disc, disk

circulate: air, mix 4 move, turn 6 rotate, spread 7 diffuse, publish 9 propagate 10 promulgate 11 disseminate
publicly: 6 report 9 broadcast

circumference: arc 5 ambet, girth 6 border, bounds, limits 7 circuit 8 boundary, surround 9 dimension, perimeter, periphery

circumlocution: 6 ambage 7 winding 8 verbiage 10 periphrase, redundancy, roundabout

circumscribe: 5 bound, fence, limit 6 define 7 confine, enclose, environ 8 encircle, restrain, restrict, surround 9 encompass

circumspect: 4 wary, wise 5 alert, chary 7 careful, guarded, prudent 8 cautious, discreet, watchful 9 attentive 10 deliberate

circumstance: fix 4 fact, item 5 event, phase, state 6 affair, detail, factor, pickle 7 element, episode 8 incident, position 9 condition, situation 10 occurrence, particular 11 environment, opportunity 12 surroundings

circumstantial: 5 exact 6 minute 7 precise 8 detailed 9 pertinent 10 incidental, particular 11 inferential 12 nonessential

circumstantiate: 7 support 8 evidence

circumvent: 4 balk, dupe, foil 5 cheat, check, cozen, evade, trick, 6 baffle, delude, entrap, outwit, thwart 7 capture, deceive, defraud, ensnare, prevent 8 surround 9 encompass, frustrate, overreach, underfong

circus: 4 ring 5 arena 6 circle, cirque 9 spectacle 10 hippodrome 12 amphitheater 13 entertainment

arena wall: 5 spina

column: 4 meta

employee: 5 clown, tamer

gear: 4 tent 5 rings 7 trapeze

rider: 8 desultor

cirque: 5 basin 6 circle, circus, corrie, recess 7 circlet, erosion

cirrus: 5 cloud 7 tendril 8 filament

cisco: 8 blackfin, whitefin

cist: box 4 tomb 5 chest 6 casket 7 chamber 9 cistavaen

cistern: sac, tub, vat 4 tank, well 6 cavity 7 cuvette 8 cisterna 9 reservoir, impluvium

cit: 8 townsman 9 tradesman 10 shopkeeper

citadel: arx 4 fort, hall 5 alamo, tower 6 castle 7 borough 8 fastness, fortress 10 stronghold 13 fortification

of Carthage: 5 Bursa, Byrsa

of Moscow: 7 Kremlin

citation: 6 notice 7 mention, summons 8 monition 9 quotation, reference 10 allegation 11 enumeration

cite: 4 call, tell 5 allay, quote, refer 6 accite, accuse, adduce, allege, arouse, avouch, excite, notify, repeat, summon 7 arraign, bespeak, excerpt, extract, mention 8 indicate

citizen: cit 5 voter 6 native 7 burgess, burgher, citoyen(F.), denizen, elector, freeman, oppidan 8 civilian, commoner, occupant, resident 9 citoyenne(F.) 10 inhabitant

suffix: ese, ian, ist, ite

citizenship: *admission to:* 14 naturalization 15 enfranchisement

pert. to: 5 civic

citrine: 5 color 7 rhubarb

citron: 4 lime 5 lemon 6 cedrat, yellow

citrullus: 7 pumpkin 10 watermelon

citrus: *belt:* 7 Florida 10 California

disease: 8 buckskin

drink: ade 5 juice

fruit: 4 lime 5 lemon 6 citron, orange 7 kumquat, tangelo 8 mandarin, shaddock 9 tangerine 10 grapefruit

city: 4 burg, dorp, town, urbs(L.) 5 ville 6 ciudad, staple 9 community 10 metropolis 12 municipality

celestial: 4 Zion

district: 4 slum 6 barrio, ghetto, uptown 8 business, downtown, red-light 11 residential

eternal: 4 Roma, Rome

hanging gardens: 7 Babylon

holy: 5 Mecca 6 Medina 9 Jerusalem

leaning tower: 4 Pisa

official: 5 mayor 7 manager, marshal 8 alderman 10 councilman

oldest inhabited: 8 Damascus

pert. to: 5 civic, urban 7 oppidan 9 municipal 12 metropolitan

problem: 4 riot, slum, smog 5 crime 6 ghetto 7 poverty, traffic

section: 4 ward 5 block, plaza 6 square

wicked: 5 Sodom 8 Gomorrah

City: *of Bells:* 9 Strasburg 10 Strasbourg

of Bridges: 6 Bruges

of Brotherly Love: 12 Philadelphia

of Churches: 8 Brooklyn

of David: 9 Jerusalem

of God: 6 church, heaven 8 Paradise

of God author: 9 Augustine

of Hundred Towers: 5 Pavia

of Kings: 4 Lima

of Lilies: 8 Florence

of Masts: 6 London

of Rams: 6 Canton

of Refuge: 6 Medina

of Saints: 8 Montreal

of Seven Hills: 4 Rome

of Violet Crown: 6 Athens

of Victory: 5 Cairo

Cius: 6 Gemlik

civet: cat, cit 5 rasse, zibet 6 bondar, musang, zibeth 7 fossane, nandine

civet-like animal: 5 genet

civic: lay 5 civil, suave, urban 6 polite, urbane 7 secular

civil: 4 hend 5 hende, suave 6 polite, urbane 7 affable, courtly, elegant, politic, refined 8 discreet, gracious, obliging, polished, wellbred 9 civilized, courteous 10 cultivated, respectful 11 complaisant 13 condescending

civil rights (extinction of): 9 attainder

Civil War: *admiral:* 8 Farragut

battle: 6 Shiloh 8 Antietam
commander: Lee 4 Pope 5 Ewell, Grant, Meade, Sykes 7 Forrest, Jackson
civil wrong: 4 tort
civilian: cit 5 civvy 7 citizen, teacher 12 noncombatant, practitioner
dress: 5 mufti
civility: 6 comity 7 amenity 8 courtesy 9 propriety 10 affability, compliance, politeness 11 complacence 12 complaisance
civilization: 6 kultur(G.) 7 culture 10 refinement 11 cultivation
civilize: 4 tame 5 teach, train 6 polish, refine 7 educate 8 humanize, urbanize 9 cultivate 11 domesticate
clabber: mud 4 mire 6 curdle, lopper 12 bonnyclabber
clack: 4 blab 5 chack, cluck, crack 6 cackle, gossip, rattle, tongue 7 chatter, clacket, clatter, prattle 10 chatterbox
clad: 5 drest, robed 6 beseen, decked 7 adorned, arrayed, attired, clothed, covered, dressed 8 sheathed
cladose: 6 ramose 8 branched
clag: mud 4 clog, clot, daub, mire 5 fault, stick 6 adhere, burden
claggum: 5 taffy 7 treacle 8 molasses 9 sweetmeat
claim: ask 4 aver, call, case, lien, mine, name 5 exact, right, shout, title 6 assert, demand, elicit 7 acclaim, derecho, pretend, profess, require 8 maintain, pretence, pretense, proclaim 9 challenge, homestead, postulate, vindicate 11 encumbrance
claimant: 7 usurper 9 pretender, arrogator
clairvoyance: 7 insight 8 sagacity 10 divination 11 discernment, penetration
clairvoyant: 4 seer 6 omener 7 prophet, seeress
clam: 4 base, clog, daub, glam, hush, mean 5 clamp, crash, glaum, grasp, grope, smear, stick 6 adhere, clutch, sticky 7 bivalve, clangor, mollusk, steamer 8 adhesive
genus of: mya
kinds of: 4 mega 5 blunt, chama, razor, solen 6 gweduc, quahog 7 geoduck, quahaug
clamant: 4 loud 6 crying, urgent 9 clamorous
clambake: 4 bake 5 movie, rally 6 defeat 7 failure 9 gathering 11 performance
clamber: 5 climb, scale 6 claver 7 rammack 8 scramble, struggle
clamjamfry: mob 5 crowd 6 rabble 7 rubbish
clammy: 4 damp, dank, soft, wack 5 moist, sammy 6 sticky, waughy

clamor: cry, din 4 bere, bunk, roar, rout, wail 5 blare, boast, bruit, noise, shout 6 bellow, hubbub, outcry, racket, tumult, uproar 7 stashie 10 hullabaloo, vociferate
clamorous: 4 loud 5 noisy 7 blatant, clamant, yelling 8 brawling, decrying 9 clamatory, turbulent 10 boisterous 11 openmouthed
clamp: lug, nip, pin 4 bolt, glam, grip, nail, vise 5 block, clasp, glaum 6 fasten 8 fastener, holdfast 10 clothespin
clan: set, sib 4 cult, race, sect, sept, unit 5 class, group, horde, party, tribe 6 clique, family 7 society 8 division 10 collection, fraternity
emblem: xat 5 totem
head of: 5 chief, elder, thane
pert. to: 6 tribal
clancular: 6 secret 11 clandestine
clandestine: bye, sly 4 foxy 5 privy 6 covert, hidden, secret 7 bootleg, furtive, illicit 8 phratria, stealthy 9 clancular, concealed 10 fraudulent 12 hugger-mugger 13 surreptitious
clang: din 4 ding, peal, ring 5 clank, clash, noise 6 jangle, timbre
clangor: din 4 clam, roar 5 clang 6 hubbub, uproar
clank: 4 ring 5 sound 6 rackle
clannish: 5 close 6 secret, tribal, united
clansman: 10 Highlander
clap: 4 bang, flap, peal, slap 5 cheer, clink, crack 6 poster, strike, stroke 7 applaud, chatter, plaudit 9 explosion 11 thunderpeal
clapper: 6 rattle, tongue 7 knacker, knocker
support: 7 baldric 8 baldrick
claptrap: 5 trash 6 blague, device 7 fustian 8 nonsense, trickery 10 pretension 11 insincerity
clarify: 5 clean, clear 6 purify, refine, render, settle 7 cleanse, explain, glorify 8 depurate, eliquate, simplify 10 illuminate 11 transfigure
clarinet: 4 reed, wind 10 instrument
mouthpiece: 4 birn
snake charmer's: 4 been
clarion: 5 clear 7 trumpet
clarity: 5 glory 8 splendor 9 clearness 10 brightness, brilliance 11 pellucidity
claro: 4 mild 5 cigar
clart: 4 clot, daub 5 smear, trash 6 sloven
clarty: 4 foul 5 dirty, gooey, muddy 6 sticky
clash: jar 4 bang, bolt, dash, news, slam 5 brawl, brunt, crash, fight, occur, prate, shock 6 affray, differ, gossip, hurtle, impact, strife, strike, tattle 7 collide, discord, scandal 8 argument, conflict 9 collision, interfere

clasp: hug, pin 4 fold, grab, grip, hasp, hold, hook, hoop, ouch, tach 5 cling, grasp, morse, preen, seize, tache 6 agrafe, brooch, buckle, clench, clutch, enfold, enwrap, fasten, fibula, gimmer, gimmor, infold 7 agraffe, amplect, embrace, entwine, fermail, tendril 8 barrette, fastener, surround 9 constrain, safety-pin 10 chatelaine

class: ilk 4 clan, kind, race, rank, sect, sort, type 5 breed, caste, genus, genre, grade, group, order, tribe 6 circle, family, gender, rating 7 seminar, species, variety 8 category, division 9 abteilung 11 description 12 denomination

animal: 5 genus 6 genera

biological: 5 genus 6 genera(pl.)

member: 4 coed 6 junior, senior 8 freshman 9 sophomore

pert. to: 7 generic

classic: 4 book 5 Attic, model 7 ancient 8 standard 9 venerable 11 composition, masterpiece

classical: 4 pure 5 Attic, Greek, Latin, Roman 6 chaste 8 academic, masterly 9 firstrate

classification: 4 file, rank, rate, sort 5 genre, genra(pl.), genus, grade, order, taxis 6 genera(pl.), rating, system 8 analysis, category, division, taxonomy 12 distribution

classify: 4 list, rank, rate, size, sort, type 5 grade, group, label, range 6 assort, codify, divide, ticket 7 arrange, catalog, dispose, marshal 8 register 9 catalogue, segregate 10 categorize, distribute

classy: 4 tony 5 nifty, slick, smart 7 stylish

clat: 4 clod, clot, mess 5 dirty, prate 6 bedaub, gossip 7 chatter

clatter: din, jar 5 clack, noise, rumor 6 babble, gabble, gossip, rackle, rattle, tattle 7 blatter, chatter, clutter, prattle, reeshie 9 commotion 11 disturbance

Claudia's husband: 6 Pilate

claudicant: 4 lame 7 limping

Claudius' wife: 9 Messalina

clause: 4 part 5 close, plank, rider 6 phrase 7 article, passage, proviso 8 sentence 9 condition, provision 10 conclusion 11 stipulation

claut: 4 hand, lump, rake, tear 5 chunk 6 clutch, scrape 7 handful, scratch

clavecin: 11 harpsichord

clavel: 6 lintel, mantel

claver: 5 prate 6 clover, gossip 7 chatter, clamber

clavichord: 6 spinet

clavicle: 4 bone 10 collarbone

clavis: key 8 glossary

clavus: 4 band, corn 5 strip 6 bunion 7 callous

claw: dig 4 clee, fawn, hand, hook, nail, pull, sere, tear, unce 5 chela, cloof, clufe, court, grasp, griff, seize, talon, uncus 6 clutch, nipper, scrape, ungula 7 crubeen, flatter, scratch, wheedle 8 lacerate

clawk: 4 claw 6 snatch 7 scratch

clay: cob, pug 4 bole, galt, loam, lute, marl, mire 5 argil, brick, cloam, earth, gault, loess, ochre, rabat, tasco 6 cledge, clunch, kaolin 8 lifeless 9 inanimate

bed: 5 gault

box: 6 saggar, sagger

building: 5 adobe, tapia

casting: 4 slip

comb. form: pel 7 argillo 10 argillaceo

constituent: 7 alumina

covered with: 6 lutose

deposit: 4 marl

fragment: bat

friable: 4 bole

layer: 4 lias 5 sloam

lump: 4 clag, clod

made of: 7 fictile

mineral: 7 nacrite

mold: dod

musical instrument: 7 ocarina

pert. to: 5 bolar

piece: 4 tile

pottery: 6 kaolin 7 kaoline

tropical: 8 laterite

claybrained: 4 dull 6 stupid

clayey: 5 bolar, heavy, malmy, marly 6 cledgy, lutose 9 argillous 12 argillaceous

clead: 6 attire, clothe

cleam: 4 daub 5 smear, stick 6 adhere 7 plaster

clean: fay, fey, hoe, mop 4 dust, fair, pure, smug, swab, trim, wash, wipe 5 bream, clear, curry, empty, feigh, grave, scour, scrub, smart 6 chaste, clever, kosher, purify 7 apinoid, cleanse, clearly, furbish, perfect 8 absterge, brightly, dextrous, entirely, renovate, spotless, unsoiled 9 destitute, dexterous, guiltless, speckless, undefiled 10 immaculate 11 butterworth, untarnished 13 unadulterated

Hebrew: 6 kosher

cleaner: 4 soap 5 borax, purer 6 ramrod 8 cleanser 9 detergent 10 dentifrice

fish: 6 scaler

cleaning agent: 4 soap 5 borax 9 detergent

cleaning implement: mop 4 swab 5 broom 6 ramrod 7 sweeper

cleanly: 4 pure 6 adroit, artful, chaste 7 correct, elegant 8 innocent, skillful 9 dexterous

cleanse: 4 farm, heal, soap, wash 5 brush, clean, dight, purge, rinse, scour, scrub 6 purify, refine **7** baptize, clarify, deterge, sweeten **8** renovate

cleanser: lye **10** clarifiant

cleansing: 4 bath **7** abluent, clysmic, washing **8** ablution, lavation **9** acquittal, cathartic, detergent **10** emundation **12** purification

cleansing agent: 4 soap **5** borax

cleansing process: 4 bath **7** washing

clear: net, rid **4** free, gain, open, over, pure, quit **5** atrip, breme, brent, clean, lucid, plain, prune, sharp, vivid **6** acquit, assoil, bright, candid, clever, exempt, fluted, limpid, lucent, patent, purify, settle, smooth **7** absolve, clarion, clarify, crystal, deliver, evident, glaring, graphic, lighten, obvious, release **8** apparent, brighten, definite, distinct, explicit, manifest, pellucid, revelant **9** cloudless, discharge, disengage, elucidate, enigmatic, exculpate, exonerate, extricate, vindicate **10** unconfused **11** disentangle, perspicuous, transparent **12** intelligible

as crystal: **7** evident, obvious

away: fay, fey **5** feigh **6** dispel **8** evacuate **9** eliminate, expurgate

out: **6** decamp, desert

up: **5** solve **6** settle

clear-cut: 5 lucid, sharp **7** concise **8** definite, distinct, incisive **9** chiselled **10** unconfused

clear-sighted: 10 discerning **13** perspicacious

clearing: *in woods:* **5** glade, tract **8** slashing

of land: **4** sart **6** assart

cleat: 4 bitt **5** block, chock, kevel, wedge **6** batten **7** bollard, coxcomb, support **9** butterbur

cleavage: 7 fission, fissure **8** division **9** partition **10** separation

cleave: cut, rip **4** chop, hold, join, link, part, rely, rend, rift, rive, slit, tear **5** break, carve, chawn, chine, clave, cleft, cling, clove, crack, sever, shear, split, stick **6** adhere, bisect, cohere, divide, pierce, sunder **7** dispart, fissure **8** separate

cleaver: ax; axe **4** froe, frow

cleche: 4 urde **5** urdee **11** cross-shaped

cleek: 4 club, hook, link **5** crook, pluck, seize **6** clutch, snatch **8** fishhook

clef: key **9** character

bass: eff

treble: gee

cleft: gap **4** chap, chop, fent, flaw, reft, rift, rima, rive **5** break, chasm, chawn, chink, clove, crack, crena, riven, split **6** breach, cleave, cloven, cranny, crotch, divide, recess **7** crevice, divided, fissure, opening **8** aperture, fracture

cleft-lip: 7 harelip

cleg: 4 gleg **6** gadfly **8** horsefly

Cleite: *father:* **6** Merops

husband: **7** Cyzicus

clem: 4 riot **5** brawl, fight **6** clutch, starve, thirst

clemency: 4 pity **5** mercy **6** lenity **7** quarter **8** kindness, leniency, mildness **10** compassion, indulgence

clement: 4 mild, soft, warm **6** gentle **7** lenient **8** merciful **9** forgiving **13** compassionate

clench: 4 fist, grip, grit, hold **5** brace, clasp, clint, close, grasp **6** clinch, clutch **9** interlock **10** strengthen

cleome: 5 caper

Cleopatra: *attendant:* **4** Iras **8** Charmian

killer: asp

lover: **6** Antony, Caesar **10** Mark Antony

river: **4** Nile

sister: **7** Arsinoe

Cleopatra's Needle: 7 obelisk

clepe: bid, cry **4** call, name **5** shout **6** appeal, invite, invoke, summon **7** address, mention

clepsydra: 5 clock

clergy: 4 cloth **9** clergyman

body of: **6** pulpit **7** college

clergyman: 4 abba, abbe, dean, Papa **5** canon, clerk, padre, pilot, prior, rabbi, vicar **6** bishop, cleric, curate, deacon, divine, domine, parson, pastor, priest, rector **7** cassock, prelate **8** cardinal, chaplain, minister, preacher, reverend **9** blackcoat, dignitary, presbyter **12** ecclesiastic

office: **4** cure **6** curacy **8** ministry **9** pastorate, priorship, rectorate

residence: **5** manse **6** priory **8** vicarage **9** parsonage

clergywoman: nun **8** rectress **9** priestess **10** religieuse

cleric: See **clergyman**

clerical clothing: alb **5** rabat, stole, amice, cloth, fanon, orale **6** collar **7** biretta

clerk: nun **4** monk **5** agent, write **6** cleric, commis, hermit, layman, priest, scribe, teller, yeoman **7** carcoon, compose, gomasta, scholar **8** employee, greffier(F.), recorder, salesman **9** assistant, clergyman, registrar **10** accountant **11** salesperson **12** ecclesiastic

court: **11** protonotary **12** prothonotary

passenger ship: **6** purser

clerkly: 7 learned, scribal **9** scholarly

cletch: 5 brood **6** clique, clutch, family **8** hatching

cleuch: 5 cleft **6** clough, ravine **7** descent

cleve, cleeve: 4 brae **5** cliff **8** hillside

clever: apt, sly **4** able, cute, deft, fine, gnib, hend, keen **5** agile, alert, clean, clear, handy, hende, lithe, quick, slick, smart, witty **6** active, adroit, artful, astute, bright, expert, habile, heppen, neatly, nimble, pretty, shrewd **7** amiable, cunning, parlous **8** dextrous, handsome, obliging, skillful, talented **9** dexterous, ingenious **10** well-shaped **11** clean-limbed, dexterously, intelligent

cleverness: can **4** tact **5** skill **6** esprit **9** dexterity, ingenuity **10** adroitness, astuteness

clevis: 4 hake **5** copse **6** muzzle **7** fitting **10** connection

clew, clue: 4 ball, hint **5** globe, glome, skein **6** hurdle, thread

cliche: 6 truism **7** bromide **8** banality

click: 4 pawl, tick **5** agree, catch **6** detent **7** ratchet

click beetle: 6 elater

client: 5 ceile **6** patron **7** patient **8** customer, henchman, retainer **9** dependent

clientele: 9 following

cliff: hoe **4** crag, hill, rock, scar **5** bluff, cleve, heuch, heugh, scarp, shore, slope **6** cleeve, height **7** clogwyn **8** hillside, palisade **9** precipice

cliff-hanger: 8 suspense **9** melodrama

climate: 4 mood **6** region, temper **8** attitude **9** condition

climax: cap, top **4** acme, apex, near, peak, shut **5** mount, scale, tight **6** apogee, ascend, finish, opogee, summit, zenith **9** gradation **11** culmination

climb: gad **4** ramp, rise, shin **5** creep, grimp, mount, scale, speed(Sc.), twine **6** ascend, ascent, shinny **7** clamber

climb down: 7 descend **8** dismount

climb on: 5 mount, scale

climber: 6 rigger, scaler **11** mountaineer **12** alpenstocker

climbing device: 6 ladder

climbing plant: ivy **4** vine **5** liana, liane **7** creeper

clime: See **climate**

clinamen: 4 bias, turn **5** twist

clinch: fix, get, hug **4** bind, grip, nail, seal **5** clamp, cling, clink, clint, grasp, rivet, seize **6** clench, clutch, fasten, secure, snatch **7** confirm, embrace, grapple, scuffle **8** complete, conclude, holdfast **9** establish

cling: hug **4** bank, hang, hold, rely **5** clasp, stick, trust **6** adhere, cleave, clinch, cohere, depend, fasten, shrink, wither **7** cherish, embrace, shrivel **8** contract **9** persevere

clingfish: 6 testar

clink: ale, jug, put, rap **4** beat, blow, brig, cash, clap, coin, jail, move, ring, slap **5** latch, money, rhyme, seize **6** clinch, jingle, lockup, moment, prison, strike, tinkle **7** instant **9** assonance **10** guardhouse

clinker: 4 slag **5** waste

clinquant: 5 clink, showy **6** tinsel **8** tinseled **10** glittering

Clio's sister: 5 Erato

clip: bob, cut, dod, hug, lip, lop, mow, nip **4** barb, chip, coll, crop, dock, dodd, hold, pace, pare, poll, snip, trim **5** clasp, force, prune, shear **6** clutch, fasten, hinder, holder **7** curtain, curtail, embrace, scissor, shorten **8** diminish, encircle **9** encompass **10** abbreviate

clipper: 4 boat, ship **6** vessel **7** shearer, workman

clique: cot, mob, set **4** bloc, clan, club, gang, ring **5** cabal, group, junto, write **6** circle, cletch **7** coterie, faction **8** conclave, sodality **9** camarilla **11** combination

clit: 5 caked, close, heavy **6** doughy, sticky

clitter: 5 noise **6** rattle **7** chatter **10** stridulate

cloaca maxima: 5 drain, sewer

cloak: aba **4** brat, capa, cape, hide, mant, mask, pall, rail, robe, veil, wrap **5** capot, cover, guise, manta, manto, sagum **6** assume, bautta, capote, caster, chapel, dolman, mantle, mantua, pharos, screen, serape, shield, shroud, tabard, visite **7** bavaroy, chlamys, conceal, garment, manteau, manteel, pelisse, pretext, shelter, zimarra **8** albornoz, burnoose, disguise, intrigue, mantilla, palliate **9** dissemble **10** roquelaure **11** portmanteau

African: **5** jelab **6** jellab

Arabian: **7** feridgi, ferigee, feri jee **8** feridjee

baptismal: **7** chrisom

bishop's: **10** mantelleta

ecclesiastical: **4** cope

Greek: **6** abolla **7** chlamys

hooded: **6** camail

Indian: **5** choga

Jewish: **6** kittel **9** gaberdine

large-sleeved: **10** witzchoura

loose: **5** palla

monk's: **8** analabos

Punjabi: **5** choga

Roman: **5** sagum **7** alicula, paenula

Roman military: **10** paludament **11** paludamenta(pl.) **12** paludamentum

sleeveless: aba **6** dolman **7** paenula

Spanish: **4** capa **5** manta **6** mantle

worn over armor: **6** tabard

cloam: 4 daub **8** crockery **11** earthenware

clobber: 4 beat **5** patch, pound, smear **6** cobble, defeat, strike

cloche: hat, jar **4** bell **5** cover

clocher: 6 belfry **9** bell tower, campanile

clock: nef **4** bell, call, dial, gong, time **5** cluck, hatch, hurry, meter, watch **6** beetle, Big Ben, crouch **8** horologe, incubate, ornament, recorder **9** clepsydra, hourglass, indicator, taximeter, timepiece 11 chronometer, speedometer

ancient water: 9 clepsydra

astronomical: 8 sidereal

maker: 9 horologer 10 horologist

part of: 4 dial 5 bundy 6 detent, foliot 8 pendulum, recorder

regulating body: 8 pendulum 10 escapement

ship-shaped: nef

weight: 5 peise

clocker: 5 timer 8 railbird 11 embroiderer

clockmaker: 9 horologer

clockwise: 6 deasil, dessil 7 deiseal 8 positive

clod: sod 4 clat, clot, dolt, dull, lout, lump, turf 5 clout, clown, divot, earth, glebe, gross, knoll, yokel 6 ground, stupid 7 bumpkin 9 coagulate 10 clodhopper

cloddish: 5 gross 6 stupid 7 boorish

clodhopper: 4 boor, clod, shoe 6 rustic 7 plowman

clodpate: 4 clot, dolt, fool 7 ramhead 8 clodpole, clodpoll, imbecile 9 blockhead

clog: gum, jam, log 4 clag, clam, cloy, curb, load, lump, shoe, skid, stop 5 block, check, choke, dance, sabot 6 adhere, burden, chopin, fetter, galosh, hamper, hobble, impede, pattern, remora, sandal, secque, weight 7 galoshe, perplex, shackle, trammel 8 coalesce, encumber, obstruct, overshoe, restrain 9 embarrass, hindrance, restraint 10 difficulty 11 encumbrance

with mud: 4 daub 6 daggle

cloggy: 5 heavy, lumpy 6 sticky

clogwyn: 5 cliff 9 precipice

cloister: 4 hall, stoa 5 abbey, aisle, stoae(pl.) 6 arcade, friary, immure, piazza, priory 7 closter, convent, nunnery 9 cloistral, enclosure, hermitage, monastery, sanctuary 11 ambulatoria(pl.) 12 ambulatorium

pert. to: 9 claustral, cloistral

Cloister and the Hearth author: 5 Reade

cloistered: 7 recluse 11 sequestered

cloistress: nun 10 religieuse(Fr.)

cloof, clufe: 4 claw, hoof 6 cleave

clop: 4 limp 5 sound 6 hobble

close: by; cap, end, hot 4 clit, firm, hard, hide, near, nigh, quit, seal, shut, slam, snug, stop 5 anear, block, cease, cheap, dense, finis, garth, gross, muggy, thick, tight 6 clause, clench, effect, expiry, finale, finish, narrow, nearby, period, stingy, strait 7 adjourn, compact, context, extreme, miserly, occlude, similar 8 accurate, adjacent, complete, conclude, familiar, imminent, intimate 9 barricade, extremity, niggardly, terminate 10 avaricious, conclusion 11 termination 12 parsimonious

a hawk's eyes: 4 seel

comb. form: 4 sten 5 steno

firmly: bar 4 lock, seal 5 tight 6 batten, cement

closefisted: 4 near 6 stingy 7 miserly 8 handfast 9 niggardly

closely: 4 just 6 almost, barely, narrow, nearly 9 compactly

closeness: 7 secrecy 8 fidelity, intimacy 9 parsimony, proximity 10 stinginess, strictness 11 conciseness, literalness 14 oppressiveness

closest: 4 next 7 nearest 9 proximate

closet: 4 ewry, room, safe 5 ambry, cuddy 6 armary, locker, pantry, secret 7 cabinet, conceal, private 8 conclave, cupboard, gardevin, wardrobe 9 gardevine 12 confidential

closing device: 4 lock 6 zipper

closure: end, gag 5 bound, limit 7 cloture 8 clausure 9 agreement, enclosure 10 conclusion 11 confinement, containment 12 entrenchment

clot: dot, gel 4 clag, clat, clod, gout, jell, lump, mass 5 clart, grume 6 balter, cotter 7 clodder, embolus, thicken 8 clodplate, coagulum, concrete, solidify 9 blockhead, coagulate 12 crassamentum

cloth (see also **fabric,** and names of individual fabrics: **cotton, linen, silk,** etc.): rag 5 bluet, toile(F.), tweed, twill 6 canvas, clergy, drapet, fabric, livery, napkin 7 acetate, drapery, garment, raiment, textile, worsted 8 dwelling, material, sheeting 10 cassinette

baptismal: 7 chrisom

bark: 4 tapa 9 tapa cloth

blemish: yaw 4 snag, tear 5 amper

camel's hair: aba 6 camlet

coarse: 4 duck 5 crash, gunny 6 burlap, linsey

crinkled: 5 crape, crepe 10 seersucker

dealer: 6 draper, mercer

decorative: see *ornamental* below

dryer: 6 tenter

dye method: tie 5 batik

figured: see *patterned* below

fine-textured: 4 mull, pima, silk 7 percale

finisher: 7 beetler

flaw in: 4 rase

flaxen: 5 linen

glazed: 5 tammy

goat's hair: 5 tibet 6 camlet, mohair

heavy: 9 petersham

hemp: 4 jute 5 gunny 6 baline, burlap, canamo

homespun: 4 kelt
instrument: 8 ringhead
knitted: 6 jersey, tricot
light: 6 tissue 7 challis, etamine
lining: 5 serge 8 sarcenet, sarsenet
measure: ell 4 nail
mesh: net 5 super, tulle 11 cheesecloth
metallic: 4 acca, tash
mourning: 5 crape, crepe
muslin: 5 adati
narrow: 4 tape 5 braid 6 edging, ribbon
old kind: 4 acca, tuke 5 tewke 6 samite
ornamental: 4 gimp, lace 6 lampas, riband
   8 tapestry
poplin: 7 tabinet 8 tabbinet
print: 6 calico 7 percale
printer: 7 candroy
raised design: 7 brocade
remnant: 4 fent
ridge in: 4 wale
roll: 4 bolt
rug: mat 7 matting
satin: see **fabric:** *satin*
shop: 7 mercery
silk: see **fabric:** *silk*
soft: 5 panne, plush, surah 6 fleece 9 montagnac
stiff: 7 taffeta 9 crinoline
stretcher: 6 tenter
synthetic: 5 nylon, rayon 6 dacron 7 acetate
toweling: 5 terry
twilled: rep 4 jean 5 denim, serge
used as a dressing: 5 stupe
velvet: 5 panne
weatherproof: 4 tarp 6 canvas
woolen: 6 kersey
clothe: don, dub, rig, tog 4 deck, garb, gird,
   gown, robe, vest 5 adorn, array, clead,
   cleed, dress, endow, endue, frock 6 attire,
   enrobe, invest, swathe 7 address, apparel,
   vesture 8 accouter, accoutre 9 authorize,
   represent
clothes (see also **dress**): 4 duds, garb, gear,
   suit, tack, wear 5 habit 6 attire 7 apparel,
   baggage, costume, raiment, regalia, toggery, vesture 8 clothing, frippery, garments 9 vestments 10 bedclothes 11 habiliments
basket: 6 hamper
civilian: 5 mufti
dealer: 6 ragman 7 fripper 9 fripperer
informal: 5 smock 6 halter, shorts, slacks,
   trunks
pert. to: 8 vestiary 10 habilatory
presser: 7 sadiron
clothesmoth: 5 tinea
clothespress: 5 chest 7 armoire 8 wardrobe
clothing: (see also **garment**): 4 wear 6 attire
   7 apparel

coarse: 4 brat 5 burel
protective: 5 armor
woman's: 6 fardel
cloud: fog, nue(F.) 4 blur, dust, haze, hide,
   mist 5 bedim, befog, gloom, nubia, stain,
   sully, swarm, taint, vapor 6 cirrus, damage, darken, deepen, defame, nebula, nimbus, screen, shadow, stigma 7 blacken,
   confuse, cumulus, eclipse, obscure, tarnish 8 overcast 9 obfuscate 10 overspread
   11 thunderhead
comb. form: 5 nepho
kinds of: nue 4 rack, scud 6 cirrus, nebule,
   nimbus 7 cumulus, stratus, tornado 9
   mare's tail
morning: 4 velo
pert. to: 7 nebular 12 nephological
study of: 9 nephology
wind-driven: 4 rack, scud
cloud-built: 4 airy 9 imaginary 13 unsubstantial
cloud-like: 7 nebular
cloudburst: 6 deluge 9 rainstorm
cloudless: 5 azure, clear 6 bright
cloudy: dim 4 dark, dull, hazy 5 filmy,
   foggy, misty, murky, shady 6 gloomy, lowery, opaque 7 blurred, clouded, nebular,
   obscure 8 confused, nubilous, overcast, vaporous 9 cloudlike 10 indistinct, lackluster
clough: 5 cleft 6 cleuch, cleugh, ravine, valley
clour: 4 blow, bump, dint 5 thump 6 batter
clout: bat, box, hit 4 beat, blow, bump, clod,
   club, cuff, join, mend, nail, slap, slug, swat
   5 patch, smite 6 strike, target, thrash,
   washer 7 bandage 8 bosthoon 12 handkerchief
clouter: 7 botcher, cobbler
clove: gap 4 tree 5 cleft, spice 6 cleave, ravine
cloven: 5 cleft, split 9 bisulcate
cloven-footed: 8 fissiped
clover: red 5 lotus, medic, nardu 6 alsike,
   luxury, nardoo 7 alfalfa, comfort, lucerne,
   melilot, trefoil 10 prosperity
cloverleaf: fan 7 freeway 8 crossway
clown: hob, oaf 4 aper, boor, fool, goff, joey,
   lout, mime, mome, zany 5 churl, comic,
   mimer, punch, zanni(It.) 6 august, bodach,
   hobbil, jester, lubber, rustic, stooge 7 buffoon, bumpkin, peasant, playboy 8 merryman 9 harlequin, joculator 10 bufflehead,
   countryman, harlequina 11 merry-andrew, punchinello 13 pickle-herring
clown's allheal: 8 woudword 9 clownheal

clownish: raw 4 rude, zany 5 gawky, rough 6 clumsy, coarse, rustic 7 awkward, boorish, hoblike, ill-bred, loutish, uncivil 8 ungainly 9 untutored

cloy: 4 clog, glut, nail, pall, sate 5 gorge, prick 6 pierce 7 satiate, satisfy, surfeit

club: bat, hit, set 4 beat, cane, join, mace, maul, polt, team 5 billy, bunch, clout, kebby, lodge, order, staff, stick, unite, yokel 6 clique, cudgel, kebbie, menage, weapon 8 bludgeon, sorority, spontoon 9 blackjack, truncheon 10 fraternity, knobkerrie, shillelagh 11 association

famous: 5 Lambs 6 Friars 7 Garrick

kinds of: bat 4 arum, mere 5 billy, plant 6 nullah, tawkee, tawkin, taiaha 7 pantoon 8 spantoon, spontoon 9 blackjack, espantoon, truncheon 10 knobkerrie, pogamoggan 12 nullahnullah

social: 4 card 6 bridge, cercle 10 fraternity

woman's: 7 Sorosis 8 sorority

club moss: 8 buckhorn

club-shaped: 7 clavate

clubfoot: 7 talipes 9 deformity

clubfooted: 7 taliped

clubs: 4 suit 5 cards, basto

clubstart: 5 stoat

clubweed: 8 knapweed

cluck: hen 4 call, fuss 5 chuck, clack, click, clock, sound

clue: key, tip 4 ball, clew, hint, idea 5 guide, twine 6 thread 8 innuendo 10 indication, intimation, suggestion 11 fingerprint

clump: tod 4 blow, bush, heap, lump, mass, mott, tope, tuft 5 bunch, group, grove, patch, tread 6 clunch, dollop 7 cluster, thicket

clumsy: awk 4 numb, rude 5 blunt, bulky, gawky, hulky, inapt, inept, stiff 6 gauche 7 awkward, boorish, ill-made, unhandy 8 benumbed, bungling, clownish, footless, tactless, ungainly, unwieldy 9 lumbering, maladroit, misshapen 10 cumbersome 11 heavy-handed 13 inappropriate

clunch: 4 clay, lump 5 clump, lumpy 9 limestone

clung: 5 stiff 8 shrunken, starving 9 collapsed, shriveled, toughened

Cluny product: 4 lace

cluster: bog 4 bush, cyme, knot, lump, tuft 5 bunch, clump, group 7 bourock, cluther 8 fascicle 9 glomerule 10 collection 11 agglomerate, aggregation

fern spore: 4 sori(pl.) 5 sorus

fiber: nep

flower: 4 cime, cyme 5 ament, umbel 6 raceme 7 panicle 8 anthemia

flower-like: 7 rosette

growing in: 8 acervate

of seven stars: 8 Pleiades

clustered: 6 tufted 8 racemose 9 aciniform, aggregate, glomerate 10 coacervate

clutch: nab 4 clam, claw, clem, clip, fist, glam, grab, grip, nest 5 brood, catch, clasp, claut, cleek, glaum, grasp, gripe, hatch, lever, power, seize, talon 6 cleach, clench, cletch, clinch, retain, snatch 7 control 8 coupling

clutter: 4 mess 6 bustle 7 clatter 8 disorder 9 confusion 10 disarrange

Clymene's son: 5 Atlas

clyster: 5 enema 9 injection

Clytemnestra: *daughter:* 7 Electra

half-sister: 5 Helen

husband: 9 Agamemnon

mother: 4 Leda

paramour: 9 Aegisthus

son: 7 Orestes

cnemis: 4 shin 5 tibia 7 legging

coach: bus, car 4 hack, help 5 araba, cabin, prime, teach, train, tutor 6 advise, direct, fiacre(F.), saloon 7 adviser, prepare, tallyho 8 carriage, dormeuse 10 instructor, stagecoach

railway: 7 Pullman, sleeper

coach dog: 9 Dalmatian

coachman: fly 4 fish, jehu, whip 5 pilot 6 coachy, driver 7 coachee, coacher 8 yemschik

assistant: 10 postillion

Russian: 7 yamshik 8 yemschik 9 yamstchik

coadjuster: 6 bishop 7 partner 8 coworker 9 assistant, associate

coagulant: 6 rennet 7 styptic 8 gelatine

coagulate: gel, set 4 cake, clod, clot, curd, jell 5 quail 6 cotter, curdle, posset 7 clabber, congeal, thicken 8 solidify

coagulation: 4 gout 7 clotter

coal: 4 bass, fuel 5 chark, ember, gleed, stoke 6 carbon, cinder

agent: 6 fitter

bed: 4 seam

block: jud

carrying box: hod 7 scuttle

comb. form: 7 anthrac 8 anthraco

constituent: 4 goaf 6 carbon, ethene, phenol, pyrene 7 benzene 8 creosote 11 naphthalene

distillate: tar

dust: 4 coom, culm, smut, soot, swad 5 coomb

immature form of: 7 lignite

kind of: jud 4 dant, hard, soft 6 cannel 7 lignite 9 tasmanite 10 anthracite, bituminous

lump: cob

mine explosive: 9 Bobbinite

miner: 7 collier
miner's disease: 11 anthrocosis
mining implement: 7 breaker
oil: 8 kerosene
refuse: 4 coke, dust, slag 6 cinder 7 backing, clinker
size: cob, ett, nut, pea 4 lump 5 slack, stove 6 broken 8 chestnut 9 buckwheat
wagon: 4 corb, carf, tram
worker: 7 collier, geordie 8 chaffman
coal car part: 6 hopper
coalbin: 6 bunker
coalesce: mix 4 fuse, join 5 blend, merge, unite 6 embody 7 combine 10 amalgamate
coalescence: 5 union 6 fusion, league 11 combination
coalfish: sey 4 parr 5 cuddy 6 beshow, billet, cudden, podler, sarthe 7 baddock, glashan, pollack
coalition: 5 trust, union 6 fusion, league, merger 8 alliance 11 combination, confederacy, conjunction 13 confederation
coarse: low, raw 4 dank, hard, hask, lewd, loud, rank, rude, vile 5 bawdy, broad, crass, crude, dirty, gross, harsh, heavy, loose, randy, routh, thick 6 brutal, callow, common, earthy, impure, ribald, rustic, vulgar 7 blatant, fulsome, goatish, obscene, raucous, sensual 8 clownish, homespun, immodest, indecent, unchaste 9 inelegant, offensive, unrefined 10 boisterous, indelicate, unpolished
coast: 4 bank, land, ripa 5 beach, blide, shore, slide 6 adjoin, border, rivage, strand 7 seaside 8 approach, seaboard, seashore
area: 7 seaside 8 seacoast 9 coastline, shoreline
dweller: 7 orarian
pert. to: 7 coastal, orarian 8 littoral, riparian
projection: 4 cape, ness 8 headland 9 peninsula
Coast Guard: *boat:* 6 cutter
service-woman: 4 Spar
coaster: mat 4 sled 5 trout 8 toboggan 9 container
coat (see also **cloak**): 4 bark, daub, husk, rind, zinc 5 cloth, cover, crust, glaze, habit, layer, paint, plate, shell, terve 6 enamel, jacket, mantle, parget, pelage, veneer 7 garment, incrust, overlay, plaster, vesture 8 membrane, tegument 9 petticoat 10 integument
animal: fur 4 hair, hide, wool 6 pelage
fastener: 4 frog 6 button
Irish: 9 coatamore
kind of: pea 4 cape, jupe, mail, robe, sack, toga 5 armor, simar, tails 6 coatie, duster, jerkin, kirtle, mantle, reefer, rocket, top-

per 7 cassock, cutaway, haubeck, paletot, pelisse, surcoat, curcote, surtout 8 benjamin, mackinaw, overcoat 9 gaberdine, newmarket, redingote 12 chesterfield
neck: 6 george
part: 4 cuff 5 lapel, skirt 6 collar, george, pocket, sleeve
seaman's: 5 grego
soldier's: 5 tunic
coat of arms: 5 crest
pert. to: 8 heraldic
coati: 5 nasua 6 animal, narica
coating: 4 aril, film 6 patina, veneer 8 mucilage
coax: beg, coy, pet 4 cant, dupe, fawn, lure, urge 5 tease 6 cajole, cuitle, entice 7 beguile, cuittle, flatter, implore, wheedle 8 blandish, collogue, inveigle, persuade 9 influence 10 manipulate
coaxial: 12 conterminous
cob: ear, mew 4 beat, blow, gull, loaf, lump, mole, mule, pier, pony, swan, toss 5 block, break, chief, excel, horse, outdo, piece, stump, throw, thump 6 basket, cobnut, leader, muffin, peapod, spider, strike 7 beating, seagull, surpass, threash 8 dumpling 10 breakwater
cobber: pal 4 chum, mate 6 friend 9 companion
tool: awl
cobble: 4 darn, make, mend, pave 5 botch, patch, stone 6 bungle, repair 7 clobber 11 cobblestone
cobbler: pie 4 snob 5 sheep, soler, sutor 6 souter 7 botcher, catfish, crispin, dessert, pompano, saddler 8 chuckler, scorpion 9 killifish, shoemaker
pitch: 4 code
cobbra: 4 head 5 skull
cobby: 5 stout 6 hearty, lively, stocky 10 headstrong
cobia: 4 fish 6 bonito
cobra: asp, nag 4 naga, naja 5 snake, viper 6 uraeus
genus: 4 naja
tree: 5 mamba
cobweb: net 4 trap 5 snare, wevet 8 gossamer 9 intricacy
cocaine: 4 snow 8 alkaloid, narcotic 10 anesthetic
source: 4 coca
Cochin-China: See **Vietnam**
cochleate: 6 spiral
cock: tap 4 bank, fowl, heap, kora, pile, rick 5 fugie, fight, gallo, shock, stack, strut, valve, yowle 6 faucet, leader 7 chicken, contend, gorcock, rooster, swagger 8 gamecock, malemass 10 cockalorum 11 chanticleer

gun: nab

cock-a-hoop: 4 awry 6 elated, lively 8 boastful, cockeyed

cock-and-bull story: lie 6 canard

cockade: 4 knot 5 badge 7 rosette

Cockade State: 8 Maryland

Cockaigne: 6 utopia 8 paradise

cockatoo: ara 5 arara, cocky, galah, macaw 6 abacay, cockie, parrot 8 calangay, ganggang

genus: 7 cacatua, kakatoe

cockatrice: 7 serpent 8 basilisk

cockboat: cog 7 rowboat

cockchafer: 6 beetle

cocker: dog, pet 4 shoe 6 coddle, fondle, pamper, quiver, reaper 7 fighter, indulge, legging, nurture, spaniel

cockerel: 4 cock 6 bantam

cocket: 4 join, pert, seal 5 bread, brisk, merry, saucy 6 lively 7 mortise 8 document

cockeyed: 4 alop, awry 5 askew

cockfight: 4 game, spar 5 match 7 contest

cockfighting: 13 alectryomachy

cockhorse: 5 lofty, proud 7 astride, upstart 8 exultant

cockle: 4 boat, gall, gith, kiln, oast 5 bulge, shell, stove 6 darnel, pucker, ripple, wabble 7 mollusk, wrinkle 9 whimsical

cocklebur: 5 plant 7 burdock

cockpit: pit 4 ring, rink, well 5 arena, cabin, field 7 gallera

cocksure: 4 sure 5 cocky 8 confident

cocktail: 5 Bronx, drink 7 apertif, martini, sidecar 8 daiquiri 9 appetizer, Manhattan

cocky: 4 pert 6 crouse, farmer, jaunty 8 arrogant 9 conceited

cocoa, coco: 4 head, palm, tary 5 broma 6 yuntia 9 chocolate

cocoanut: 7 coquito

dried meat: 5 copra

fiber: 4 coir, kyar

cocoon: pod 4 clew, clue 5 shell 11 incubabulum

cod: bag, cor, pod 4 axle, bank, cusk, fish, fool, hoax, husk, rock 5 belly, pouch, scrod, torsk 6 burbot, codger, cultus, fellow, pillow 7 bacaloa, cushion

family: 7 gadidae

genus: 5 gadus

young: 5 scrod, sprag 7 codling

cod-like: bib 4 hake, ling 5 gadus

coda: 4 part 5 rondo 6 finale 10 conclusion

coddle: pet 4 baby, cade, cook 5 humor, nurse, spoil 6 caress, cocker, cotton, fondle, pamper 7 parboil

code: law 4 flag 5 canon, codex 6 cipher, digest, secret, signal 7 precept

inventor: 5 Morse

message: 6 cipher 10 cryptogram

coded message: 10 cryptogram

codex: 4 code 5 annal 9 formulary 10 manuscript

codfish: See **cod**

codger: cod 5 churl, crank, miser 6 fellow 7 niggard

codicil: 5 rider 6 sequel 8 appendix

codify: 5 index 6 digest 8 classify 11 systematize

coehorn: 6 mortar

Coelebs: 8 bachelor

coelenterate: 5 polyp 8 cnidaria

coerce: cow 4 curb, make 5 bully, check, drive, force 6 compel 7 concuss, enforce, repress 8 bludgeon, bulldoze, restrain, restrict 9 blackmail, constrain, terrorize 10 intimidate

coercion: 5 force 6 duress

Coeus' daughter: 4 Leto

coeval: 12 contemporary

coffee: *after dinner:* 9 demitasse

alkaloid: 7 caffein

bean: nib

beverage: Rio 4 Java, Kona 5 Milds, Mocha 6 Bogota, Brazil, Santos 7 Sumatra 8 Medellin 9 Maracaibo

maker: urn 5 silex

refuse: 6 triage

coffee house: inn 4 cafe

coffeeberry: 6 jojoba 7 cascara, soybean 8 peaberry 9 buckthorn, chaparral

coffeepot: 6 biggin 9 cafetiere

coffer: ark, box, dam 5 chest, hutch, trunk 6 casket, forcer, trench 7 caisson 8 ciborium, standard

coffin: 4 bier, case, cist, mold 6 basket, casing, casket 11 sarcophagus

cloth: 4 pall 5 cloak

support: 4 bier

cog: cam, lie 4 gear, jest 5 catch, cheat, cozen, tenon, tooth, trick, wedge, wheel 6 cajole 7 deceive, produce, quibble, wheedle 8 cockboat 9 fabricate, falsehood

cogent: 5 valid 6 potent, strong 7 telling 8 forcible, powerful 9 trenchant 10 conclusive, convincing, legitimate, persuasive

cogitate: 4 mull, muse, plan 5 think 6 ponder 7 connate, reflect 8 consider, meditate

cognate: kin 4 akin 5 alike 6 allied 7 kindred, related, similar 8 bandhava, relative

cognizance: ken 4 heed, mark 5 badge, crest 6 emblem, notice 7 bearing, cockade 9 knowledge 11 observation, recognition 12 apprehension

cognizant: 4 onto, ware 5 awake, aware 8 sensible 9 conscious 10 conversant 11 intelligent 12 apprehensive

cognize: 4 know 8 perceive 9 recognize

cognomen (see also **name**): 4 name 6 by-name 7 agnomen, surname 8 nickname, patronym 11 appellation

cohabit: 4 live 5 dwell 6 occupy 8 accustom 9 accompany

coheir: 8 parcener 10 coparcener

cohere: fit 4 glue, suit 5 agree, cling, stick, unite 6 adhere, cement, cleave 7 connect 8 coincide 9 glutinate

coherence: 5 union 8 cohesion 9 congruity 10 accordance, connection, continuity 11 consistency

cohort: 4 band 7 company

coif, coiffe: cap 4 hood 6 beggin, burlet, hairdo 7 arrange 8 skullcap 9 headdress

coiffure: 6 hairdo 9 headdress

coign: 5 wedge 6 corner 8 position 10 projection

coil: ado, wip 4 ansa, clew, curl, fuss, hank, loop, roll, wind 5 helix, querl, tense, twine, twist 6 rundle, spiral, tumult, windup 7 haycock, ringlet, trouble 8 encircle 9 confusion, encounter 10 difficulty 11 convolution
electric: 6 teaser

coilet: 7 sinuous, tortile

coin: die, ori 4 cash, dime, make, mint 5 angle, brown, chink, clink, metal, money, quoin, shape, . stamp, token, wedge 6 change, corner, create, invent, specie, strike 7 convert 8 currency 9 fabricate, neologize, originate 11 cornerstone
ancient: 4 obol 6 obolus
box: pyx 4 till 5 meter 8 register
collector: 11 numismatist
copper: 4 cent 5 penny, bodle, brown
counterfeit: 9 brummagem
difference: 5 value 11 seigniorage
edge corrugation: 7 reeding
front: 4 head 7 obverse
imperfectly minted: 8 brockage
kind of: lap, ora 4 dime, doit, mite, rial, rosa 5 cuyne, daric, disme, ducat, eagle, groat 6 bawbee, beaver, besant, bezant, cunzie 7 bezzant, carolus, crocard, louleau 8 bezantee, crockard 10 castellano
pert. to: 10 numismatic 12 numismatical
reverse side: 4 tail 5 verso
roll: 7 rouleau
science: 11 numismatics
silver: 4 batz, dime, dump, pina, tara 5 bezzo 6 tester, teston
stamper: 4 mill
weight: 6 shekel

coin new words: 9 neologize

coinage: 7 fiction, mintage
collector: 11 numismatist

coincide: gee 4 jibe 5 agree, tally 6 concur 9 harmonize 10 correspond

coincidence: 9 concourse 11 concurrence 12 concomitance, simultaneity

coincident: 4 even 8 together 9 consonant 10 concurrent 11 concomitant 12 contemporary 15 contemporaneous

coiner of new words: 9 neologian, neologist

coistrel: 4 base 6 menial, varlet 7 servile, soldier

coition: 7 meeting 10 attraction 11 conjunction

cojuror: 12 compurgator

coke: ask 4 coal, core, dope 5 chark 7 cocaine

cokes: 4 gull 9 simpleton

col: 4 pass 10 depression

colander: 5 sieve 7 utensil 8 strainer

colate: 6 filter, strain

Colchean: See **Colchis**

Colchis: *king:* 6 Aeetes
princess: 5 Medea

cold: flu 4 dead, dull 5 algid, bleak, frore, gelid, rheum, virus 6 arctic, chilly, frigid, frosty, wintry 7 catarrh, chilled, distant, glacial 8 reserved, rhigosis, unheated 9 apathetic, cheerless 10 insensible, spiritless 11 hyperborean, indifferent, unemotional 12 unresponsive 13 dispassionate, marble-hearted 15 undemonstrative
comb. form: 4 cryo 5 frigo
pert. to: icy 5 gelid 6 frigid, frozen 10 frigorific
remedy: 13 antihistamine

cold and damp: raw 4 dank 5 bleak

cold-blooded: 7 callous 9 unfeeling 14 poikilothermal

cold feet: 4 fear 5 doubt 9 cowardice 12 apprehension

cold mist: 4 drow

cold-shoulder: 4 snub 6 ignore, rebuff

cold steel: 5 sword 6 dagger 7 bayonet

cold sweat: 4 fear 5 shock 11 trepidation

colder: 4 husk 6 refuse 7 rubbish

coleoptbera insect: 6 beetle, insect, weevil

Coleridge's sacred river: 4 Alph

colewort: 4 cole, kale 7 cabbage

colic: 10 mulligrubs

coliseum: 4 hall 7 stadium, theater 8 building 12 amphitheater

coll: hug 4 clip, poll 5 prune 7 embrace

collaborate: aid 9 cooperate

collagen: 7 protein 10 albuminoid

collapse: 4 cave, fall, fold 5 crash, slump, wreck 6 bust-up 7 crumple, debacle, deflate, failure, flummox, smashup 8 contract, downfall 9 breakdown, telescope 11 prostration

collar: nab 4 band, eton, gill, grab, ring, ruff 5 chain, fichu, ruche, seize 6 bertha, gor-

get, tackle, torque **7** capture, chignon, circlet, shackle **8** cincture, neckband, necklace **9** neckpiece
horse: **6** hounce
jeweled: **8** carcanet
kind of: **4** ruff **5** fanon, orale, phano, ruche, rabat **6** cangue, carcan, rabato, rebato, **7** bargham, panuelo, **8** carcanet **10** chevesaile
collar cell: **10** choanocyte
collarbone: **8** clavicle
collared monad: **16** choanoflagellate
collate: **6** bestow, confer, verify **7** compare, emamine
collateral: **4** side **8** indirect, parallel, security **9** ancillary **10** subsidiary **11** accidential, concomitant, subordinate
collation: tea **4** meal **5** lunch **6** repast, sermon **7** address, reading **8** dejeuner, parallel, treatise **10** collection, comparison, conference **12** consultation, contribution
collator: **6** critic **7** machine
colleague: **4** aide, ally **5** unite **6** deputy **7** adjunct, consort, partner **8** confrere, conspire **9** assistant, associate
collect: tax **4** call, heap, levy, pile, pool, save **5** amass, glean, group, hoard, raise **6** accoil, accrue, confer, garner, gather, muster, prayer, sheave **7** compile, engross, impound **8** assemble, contract **9** aggregate **10** accumulate, congregate **11** agglomerate
collected: **4** calm, cool **5** sober **6** serene **8** composed **9** aggregate, clustered **10** coacervate **11** agglomerate **13** dispassionate
collection: ana **4** bevy, clan, olio **5** batch, group, store, suite **6** bundle, conger, sorite **8** assembly, caboodle **9** aggregate, anthology, collation, repertory **10** assemblage, assortment, cancionero
literary: ana **7** library **8** analects
miscellaneous: **4** olio **6** fardel
poems: **5** divan, sylva **9** anthology **10** cancionero
proper names: **11** onomasticon
wild animals: zoo **9** menagerie
collector: *bird egg:* **8** oologist
book: **11** bibliophile
coin: **11** numismatist
item: **5** curio **11** collectible
stamp: **11** philatelist
collectorship: **5** staff **6** office **9** residence **12** jurisdiction
colleen: **4** girl, lass, miss **5** belle **6** damsel, lassie, maiden
college (see also **university**): **5** lycee **6** school **7** academy **8** seminary **10** assemblage, university **11** institution **12** organization
accounts: **6** battel

building: gym, lab
campus: **4** quad **10** quadrangle
course: **5** major, minor **7** seminar
court: **4** quad
degree: A.B., B.A., B.S., C.E., D.D., M.A., M.D., M.S.; B.L.S., B.Sc., LL.B., LL.D., M.Sc., S.C.B., Ph.D. **5** Litt.D.
girl: **4** coed
graduate: **6** alumna, doctor, master **7** alumnus **8** bachelor
kind of: **9** electoral
living quarters: **4** dorm, hall
official: **4** dean **5** prexy **6** beadle, bursar, regent **7** proctor **9** president, registrar
pert. to: **8** academic **10** collegiate
professor: don **6** docent, doctor
session: lab **5** class **7** lecture, seminar **8** tutorial
student group: **4** frat **8** sorority **10** fraternity
term: **8** semester
treasurer: **6** bursar
tree: elm
U.S. oldest: **7** Harvard
U.S. woman's oldest: **9** Mt. Holyoke
collet: **4** band, ring **5** chuck **6** casing, circle, collar, flange, socket **7** bushing, ferrule **8** neckband
collide: hit, ram **4** bump, dash, hurt **5** clash, crash, wreck **6** hurtle, strike
collier: fly **4** boat **5** miner **6** plover, vessel **7** geordie
boy: **6** hodder
lung disease: **11** anthracosis
colliery: **4** mine
collieshangie: row **5** brawl **6** uproar **7** quarrel **8** squabble **11** disturbance
colliquate: **4** melt **7** liquefy
collision: **5** clash, crash, shock **7** smashup **8** clashing **9** encounter **10** opposition, percussion **12** interference
collocate: set **5** place **7** arrange
collogue: **4** coax, talk **5** gloze **6** confer **7** collude, flatter, wheedle **8** conspire, intrigue **12** conversation
colloquial: **8** familiar, informal **9** unstudied **14** conversational
colloquy: **4** chat, talk **6** parley **8** dialogue **9** discourse **10** conference **12** conversation
colluctation: **8** struggle **10** contention
collude: **4** plot **6** scheme **7** connive **8** collogue, conspire
collusion: **6** deceit **7** cahoots, secrecy **9** agreement **10** connivance
law: **5** covin
collusive: **8** covinous **10** fraudulent
colly: **4** dust, smut, soot **5** black, grime, sooty **9** blackbird
coloboma: **6** defect **7** fissure

Cologne: *German spelling:* 4 Koln
  king: 6 Caspar, Jaspar
Colombia: *city:* 4 Cali 5 Neiva, Pasto, Tunja 6 Bogota(C.), Cucuta, Ibaque, Quibdo 7 Leticia, Popayan 8 Medellin 9 Cartagena, Manizales, San Andres 10 Santa Maria 11 Bucaramanga 12 Barranquilla 13 Villavicencio
  coin: 4 peso, real 6 condor, peseta 7 centavo
  gulf: 6 Darien
  Indian: 5 Boros 6 Betoya, Chitas, Tahami, Yahuna 7 Tunebos 8 Guacicos, Morcotes, Pedrazas, Quimbaya, Sinsigas
  mahogany: 7 albarco
  measure: 4 vara 7 celemin
  plant: 5 yocco
  province: 5 Cauca, Choco, Huila, Valle 6 Boyaca, Caldas, Narina, Tolima, Vaupes 7 Bolivar 9 Antioquia, Atlantico, Magdalena, Santander 12 Cundinamarca
  river: 4 Sinu, Tomo 6 Atrato, Atroto, Pattia, Yapura 7 Putumay 8 Guaviara 9 Magdalena
  seaport: 6 Lorica 9 Cartagena 10 Santa Marta 12 Barranquilla
  volcano: 5 Huila, Pasto 6 Purace
  weight: bag 4 saco 5 carga, libra 7 quilate, quintal
colon: 4 coin 6 farmer 7 planter 8 colonist 10 husbandman
colonial teak: 8 flindosa
colonist: 5 colon 7 pioneer, settler 8 emigrant
colonize: 5 found 6 gather, settle 7 migrate 9 establish
colonizer: ant 6 oecist 7 settler
colonnade: row 4 stoa 7 pergola, portico, terrace 9 peristyle
colony: 5 swarm 9 community 10 dependency, settlement
colophon: 6 device, emblem
colophonite: 6 garnet 9 andradite
colophony: 5 resin, rosin
color (see also next entry): dye, hue 4 blee, cast, flag, tint, tone 5 badge, blush, paint, shade, stain, tenne, tinge 6 banner, ensign, redden 7 distort, pennant, pigment 8 standard, tincture 10 complexion
  achromatic: 4 gray 5 black, white
  change: 8 iridesce, opalesce
  dull: dun 4 drab 5 terne
  full of: 9 chromatic
  graduation: 5 shade
  healthy: tan
  light: 4 tint
  line of: 6 streak
  malachite: 4 bice
  mat white: 9 alabaster
  mulberry: 7 morello

  neutral: 4 ecru, gray 5 beige, black, white
  painter: 6 Titian
  pale: 6 pastel
  primary: red 4 blue 5 black, green, white 6 yellow
  quality: 4 tone
  secondary: 5 green 6 orange, purple
  shade of difference: 6 nuance
  unhealthy: 6 sallow
  uniform in: 4 flot
  value: see *quality* above
  varying: 10 iridescent, opalescent
color: For colors see their names: **red, green, purple,** etc.; for shades see main color. EXAMPLES: "reddish brown": see **brown;** "grayish green": see **green.**
color bar: 11 segregation 14 discrimination
color blindness: 9 Daltonism 13 achromatopsia 14 monochromatism
color organ: 8 clavilux
color photography inventor: 4 Ives
Colorado: *army camp:* 6 Carson
  city: 5 Aspen, Delta, Lamar 6 Denver, Meeker, Pueblo 7 Alamosa, Boulder, Greeley, Manassa 8 Trinidad 10 Walsenburg
  county: Ada 4 Baca, Bent, Mesa, Park, Weld, Yuma 5 Adams, Grand, Kiowa, Logan, Otero, Ouray 6 Custer, Denver, Elbert, Moffat 7 Conejos, Crowley, Dolores, Douglas, Jackson, Lincoln, Prowers 8 Arapahoe 9 Archuleta, Montezuma
  fort: 5 Logan
  Indian: Ute 8 Arapahoe
  mountain: Oso 5 Eolus 7 Massive
  mountain pass: 6 Alpine 7 Fremont 8 Marshall 9 Argentine, Tennessee 10 Cottonwood
  mountain range: Elk 4 Book, Park, Roan 5 Raton 7 Sawatch
  park: 5 Estes 9 Mesa Verde
  peak: Oso 4 Yale 5 Baldy, Ethel, Evans, Grays, James, Pikes 6 Castle, Elbert, Long's, Maroon 7 Audubon, Harvard, Rosalie, Torreys 8 Arapahoe, Snowmass 9 Princeton
  resort: 5 Aspen 7 Manitou
  river: 4 Bear 5 Grand, Green, White, Yampa 7 Dolores, Laramie 8 Arkansas, Colorado, Gunnison
  river tributary: 4 Gila
  state flower: 9 Columbine
  valley: 5 Estes
colorant: dye 4 anil 7 pigment
coloratura: 6 singer 7 soprano 8 vocalist
colored: 6 biased 9 distorted, prismatic 14 misrepresented
  partly: 4 pied 6 motley 7 piebald 10 variegated
colorful: gay 5 vivid 9 brilliant

colorimeter: 10 tintometer

coloring: *cell:* 10 endochrome
matter: dye 5 morin 7 pigment 8 clorofil 10 endochrome 11 chlorophyll

colorless: wan 4 drab, dull, pale 5 ashen, blake, blank, plain 6 pallid 7 hueless, neutral 8 blanched 9 impartial 10 achromatic 11 transparent 13 uninteresting

colors, set of: 7 palette

colossal (see also **huge**): big 4 huge, vast 5 great, large 7 immense 8 enormous, gigantic 9 monstrous

colosseum: See **coliseum**

colossus: 5 giant, titan 6 statue 7 monster, prodigy

colporteur: 6 hawker 7 peddler 11 distributor

colt: gun 4 foal 5 filly 6 pistol 9 quadruped, youngster

coluber: 5 snake 7 serpent

colubrine: 6 crafty 7 cunning 9 snakelike

Columbia River rapids: 6 Dalles

Columbia University symbol: 4 lion

columbine: 4 bird, dodo 5 plant 6 flower 8 dovelike

Columbus: *birthplace:* 5 Genoa
burial place: 7 Seville
companion: 5 Ojeda
embarkation port: 5 Palos
patron: 8 Isabella 9 Ferdinand
ship: 4 Nina 5 Pinta 10 Santa Maria
son: 5 Diego

column: lat, row 4 file, line, post 5 shaft, stela, stele 6 pillar 7 support 8 cylinder, pilaster 9 formation
arrange in: 8 tabulate
base: 9 stylobate
part: 4 anta, fust 5 galbe, socle, scape, shank 6 plinth 7 entasis, capital 8 pilaster
pert. to: 8 columnar
shaped like human figure: 7 telamon 8 atlantes, caryatid
small: 5 stele
support: 5 socle
type of: 5 Doric, Ionic 10 Corinthian

columnar: 6 terete 7 stelene 8 vertical

columnist: 6 writer

columns: *series of:* 9 colonnade
set in: 7 tabular
without: 7 astylar

coma: 4 tuft 5 bunch, carus, sleep 6 stupor, torpor, trance 7 cluster 8 lethargy 13 insensibility

comate: 5 hairy 6 comose 9 companion

comatose: out 6 drowsy 9 lethargic 10 insensible

comb: 4 card, lash, rake 5 brush, clean, crest, curry, tease 6 smooth 11 disentangle
comb. form: 4 cten 5 cteno

flax: 6 hackle, heckle 7 hatchel
horse: 5 curry

comb jelly: 10 ctenophore

comb-like: 8 pectinal 9 pectinate

comb rat: 5 gundi

combat: war 4 bout, cope, duel, fray, meet, rush, tilt 5 clash, fight, joust, repel, set-to 6 action, battle, oppose, resist, strife 7 contend, contest, counter, scuffle 8 argument, conflict, struggle 9 encounter, withstand 10 antagonize, contention
challenge to single: 6 cartel
code: 6 duello
place: 5 arena

combatant: 6 dueler 7 battler, fighter 8 champion 10 contestant

combative: 6 bantam 8 militant 9 agonistic 10 pugnacious 11 agonistical, belligerent

comber: 4 wave 7 breaker 11 beachcomber

combinate: 6 joined 8 combined 9 betrothed

combination: key 4 bloc, gang, pact, pool, ring 5 cabal, junto, party, trust, union 6 cartel, clique, corner, merger 7 combine, consort, coterie, faction 8 alliance, ensemble 9 aggregate, camarilla, coalition, composite, composure, synthesis 10 concoction, conspiracy 11 association, coalescence, composition, confederacy, conjunction, corporation 12 undergarment 13 incorporation

combine: add, mix, wed 4 bloc, join, pool 5 blend, marry, merge, total, unite 6 absorb, concur, merger, mingle, splice 7 conjoin, conjure, machine 8 coalesce, compound, concrete, condense, contract, federate 9 construct, cooperate 10 amalgamate 11 combination, consolidate

combining form (see also **prefix, suffix**): For all definitions beginning with this phrase, look under main word or phrase. EXAMPLES: "combining form for cat": see **cat:** *comb. form;* "combining form for foot": see **foot:** *comb. form.*

comble: 4 acme, heap, load 6 summit

comboy: 6 sarong

combust: 4 burn 5 burnt 8 consumed 10 incinerate

combustible: 4 fuel, peat 5 fiery 9 irascible 10 accendible 11 inflammable
material: gas, oil 4 coal, coke, peat 6 tinder

combustion: 4 fire, heat 5 therm 6 tumult 7 burning 9 agitation, confusion, consuming, cremation, oxidation 12 inflammation 13 conflagration
residue: ash, gas 7 clinker

come: 4 grow 5 arise, issue, occur, reach 6 accrue, appear, arrive, befall, emerge, happen, spring 7 advance, develop, emanate 8 approach, practice 9 eventuate

a cropper: 4 fail, fall
across: 4 find, meet 9 encounter 10 contribute
after: 5 ensue 6 follow 7 succeed
again: 6 return
along: 4 fare 7 improve 8 progress
apart: 5 break
at: 6 attack
before: 7 precede, prevene 8 antecede
between: 8 alienate 9 interpose
by: get 4 gain 6 obtain 7 acquire, inherit
down with: 5 catch 8 contract
forth: 6 appear, emerge
from: 5 ensue 6 result
in: 5 crash, enter 6 arrive 7 intrude
into view: 4 loom 6 appear, emerge
of age: 6 mature
out: 6 appear, emerge, emerse, extend 8 protrude
to a head: 6 climax 9 suppurate
to nothing: end 4 stop 5 cease
to terms: 4 join 5 agree 6 assent, settle 7 approve, consent 8 coincide 9 acquiesce
together: 4 bump, join, meet 5 clash 7 collide, convene 8 assemble, converge
under: 7 subvene
up: 5 arise, occur 6 appear
comeback: 5 rally 6 answer, retort, return 7 rebound 8 recovery, repartee
comedian: wag, wit 4 card 5 actor, antic, clown, comic 6 jester 7 buffoon
comedown: 4 land 6 alight, bathos 7 descend
comedy: 5 drama, farce, revue 8 comoedia(L.), travesty 9 burlesque, slapstick
character: 9 Pantaloon
muse: 6 Thalia
pert. to: 7 thalian
symbol: 4 sock
Comedy of Errors servant: 4 Luce
comeling: 8 newcomer 9 immigrant, sojourner
comely: 4 fair, hend, pert 5 bonny, hende 6 decent, goodly, liking, lovely, pretty, proper 7 farrant 8 becoming, decorous, graceful, handsome, pleasing, suitable 9 agreeable, beautiful 10 gratifying, personable
comer: one 6 person 7 arrival
comestible: 4 food 5 manna, viand 6 edible 7 eatable, victual 8 esculent
comet: 6 meteor
discoverer: 5 Biela, Encke, Swift 6 Donati, Halley, Olbers 8 Kohoutek
part: 4 coma
tail: 8 streamer
comeuppance: 6 rebuke 7 deserts 12 chastisement

comfit: 5 candy 7 confect, praline 8 conserve, preserve 9 sweetmeat 10 confection
comfort: aid 4 ease, rest 5 bield(Sc.), cheer 6 endure, relief, repose, solace, soothe, succor 7 animate, assuage, cherish, confirm, console, enliven, gladden, refresh, relieve, support, sustain 8 inspirit, nepenthe, pleasure, reassure 9 encourage, well-being 10 strengthen 11 consolation
comfortable: 4 bein, bien, cosh, cozy, easy, like, snug, trig 5 comfy, scarf 7 relaxed 8 cheerful, euphoric, wristlet 9 contented 10 acceptable, commodious, complacent, gratifying 11 consolatory, encouraging
comforter: 4 puff 5 cover, quilt, scarf 6 tippet 7 cheerer 8 pacifier
comfortless: 7 forlorn 8 desolate 9 cheerless 12 inconsolable
comfrey: 5 daisy 9 blackwort
comic: 5 droll, funny 8 comedian, farcical 9 burlesque
comical: low 4 base 5 droll, funny, queer, witty 7 amusing, jocular, risible, strange, trivial 8 humorous, ticklish 9 diverting, laughable, ludicrous, quizzical, whimsical 10 capricious
coming: due 4 next 6 advent, future 7 arrival, forward 8 deserved 9 impending 11 approaching
coming out: 5 debut 8 issuance
command: bid 4 beck, bode, boon, call, fiat, hest, rule, sway 5 beken, check, edict, exact, force, hight, order, power, ukase 6 adjure, behest, charge, compel, degree, demand, direct, enjoin, govern, impose, master, ordain 7 appoint, behight, bidding, control, dictate, mandate, officer, precept, require 8 domineer, restrain 9 authority, direction, influence, ordinance, prescribe 10 commission 11 appointment
supreme: 9 hegemony
to a horse: gee, haw, hup 4 whoa
commander: cid, cio 4 head 5 chief 6 leader, master, rammer 7 captain, drungar, emperor, general, officer 10 commandant 11 commendador(Sp.) 13 generalissimo
of a thousand men: 9 chiliarch
commanding: 8 dominant, imposing 9 imperious, masterful 10 imperative 13 authoritative
commandment: law 4 rule 5 order 7 precept
commmando: 6 raider, ranger
comme il faut: 6 proper 7 fitting
commemoration: 5 award, medal 6 plaque 7 service 8 memorial 11 celebration 13 solemnization

commence: 4 fall, open 5 arise, begin, found, start 6 incept, spring 8 initiate 9 institute, originate

commencer: 4 tyro 8 beginner

commencing: 7 initial, nascent 9 incipient

commend: pat 4 give, laud 5 adorn, boost, extol, grace, offer 6 bestow, betake, commit, praise, resign 7 applaud, approve, bespeak, deliver, entrust, intrust 8 bequeath 9 predicate, recommend 10 compliment, ingratiate
highly: 5 extol 8 eulogize 10 panegyrize
to favor: 10 ingratiate

commendable: 4 good 6 worthy 8 laudable 9 exemplary, honorable

commensurate: 4 even 5 equal 6 enough 8 adequate 10 answerable, convenient 11 appropriate 12 proportional 13 corresponding, proportionate

comment: 4 note, talk, word 5 aside, gloss, gloze 6 notate, postil, remark 7 descant, discuss, explain, expound 9 criticise, criticism, criticize, discourse 10 animadvert, annotation, commentary 13 animadversion

commentaries: 10 adversaria

commentary: 5 gloss 6 memoir 7 account, comment 8 glossary, treatise

commentator: 6 critic, glozer 9 annotator, expositor, glossator, scholiast 10 glossarist 13 glossographer

commerce: 5 trade 6 barter 7 traffic 8 business, exchange 10 connection 11 interchange
vehicle: 5 truck

commercial: 9 mercature 10 mercantile 13 advertisement

commingle: mix 4 fuse, join 5 blend, merge, unite 6 mingle 7 combine, embroil 10 amalgamate

comminute: 4 mill 5 crush, grind 9 pulverize, triturate

commiseration: 4 pity 7 empathy 8 sympathy 10 compassion, condolence

commission: 4 send, task 5 board, trust 6 brevit, charge, demand, depute, errand, office, ordain, permit 7 command, consign, empower, mandate, mission, warrant 8 delegate, encharge 9 allowance, authority, authorize, brokerage, establish 10 constitute 11 instruction 12 compensation, dispensation, perpetration 13 authorization

commissioner: 5 envoy 7 officer 8 delegate

commissure: 4 seam 5 joint, miter, mitre 8 juncture 10 miter joint

commit: do 4 give 5 allot, refer 6 assign, betake, remand 7 command, confide, consign, deposit, entrust, intrust 8 bequeath, delegate, imprison, relegate 9 recommend 10 perpetrate

committee: 4 body 5 board, group, junta 7 council 9 executors, guardians

Commius' kingdom: 9 Atrebates

commixture: 7 mixture 8 compound

commode: cap 5 chest 8 cupboard 10 chiffonier

commodious: fit 5 ample, roomy 6 proper, useful 8 spacious, suitable 9 capacious 10 beneficial, convenient 11 comfortable, serviceable 12 advantageous

commodity: 4 ware 5 goods 6 staple 7 article

common: low 4 base 5 banal, brief, cheap, joint, stale, trite, usual 6 coarse, mutual, ornery, vulgar 7 average, current, general, generic, natural, plebian, popular, regular, trivial, unnoble 8 familiar, frequent, habitual, mediocre, ordinary, pandemic, trifling 9 bourgeois, customary, defective, hackneyed, prevalent, universal, unrefined 10 second-rate 11 commonplace

common effort: 8 teamwork

common fund: pot 4 pool 5 purse

common law: 6 custom 9 tradition

common man: 4 pleb 8 plebeian

common sense: 5 sense 8 judgment

common stock: 8 security

commoner: 5 ceorl, plebe 7 burgess, citizen, student 8 roturier 12 participator

commonly: *accepted:* 7 popular, vulgate
thought: 7 reputed 8 putative

commonplace: 4 dull, fade, worn 5 banal, daily, plain, prose, stale, trite, usual 6 common, garden, truism 7 humdrum, prosaic, tedious, trivial 8 ordinary 9 hackneyed 11 unimportant
remark: 5 style 6 cliche, truism 9 platitude

commonwealth: 5 state 6 public 9 community 10 commonweal, res publica

Commonwealth country: 6 Canada 8 Rhodesia 9 Australia 10 New Zealand

commotion: ado, din 4 bree, fray, fuss, heat, riot, stir, to-do, whir 5 alarm, flare, hurry 6 bustle, cathro(Sc.), fracas, flurry, garray, mutiny, pother, tumult, unrest, welter 7 clatter, tempest, turmoil 8 disorder, upheaval, uprising 9 agitation, confusion 10 concussion, convulsion, ebullition, excitement, turbulence 11 disturbance 12 perturbation

commune: 4 area, talk 5 argue, realm, share, treat 6 advise, confer, debate, import, parley, reveal 7 consult, discuss, divulge 8 converse, district, township 11 communicate, intercourse, participate 12 conversation

embrace, deflate, flatten, repress, squeeze 8 astringe, condense, contract, restrain 9 constrain, epitomize 11 consolidate
medical: 5 stupe 7 bandage, pledget

compressor: 4 pump 6 device 7 machine

comprise, comprize: 4 hold 5 cover, imply, seize 6 attach, confer, embody 7 compose, contain, embrace, enclose, include, involve 8 conceive, perceive 10 comprehend

comprised: 4 rapt 8 included 9 engrossed 14 comprehensible

compromise: 8 compound, endanger 9 surrender 10 concession
opposition to: 13 intransigence

compt: 4 neat 6 spruce 8 polished

comptroller: 7 auditor, officer 10 controller

compulsion: 4 need, urge 5 force 6 duress, stress 7 impulse 8 coaction, coercion 10 constraint

compulsory: coercive, forcible 10 imperative, obligatory

compulsory service: 6 angary 7 angaria, slavery

compunction: 5 qualm 6 regret, sorrow 7 remorse, scruple 9 misgiving 10 conscience, contrition, repentance

compute: add, sum 4 cast, rate 5 count, tally 6 assess, figure, number, reckon 7 account 8 estimate 9 calculate, enumerate

computer: 6 univac 7 machine
algebraic language: 5 algol
correct: 5 debug
information: 4 data 5 input 6 output
inventor: 7 Babbage
plan for action: 7 program
program symbol: 5 block
symbol system: 4 code
worker: 9 programer 10 programmer

comrade: pal 4 ally, chum, mate, peer 5 billy, buddy, crony 6 copain(F.), digger, fellow, frater, friend, hearty 7 brother 8 copemate 9 associate, companion

comte: 5 count

comtesse: 8 countess

con: rap 4 anti, know, lead, look, pore, read, scan 5 cheat, guide, knock, learn, steer, study 6 direct, peruse, regard, versus 7 against, deceive, examine, inspect, opposed, swindle 10 understand

conation: 4 will 7 conatus 8 tendency, volition 11 inclination

conative state: 5 nisus

concatenate: 4 join, link 5 chain, unite 7 connect 8 catenate

concave: 4 void 6 arched, dished, hollow 7 vaulted 8 incurved 9 depressed

concavity: dip, pit 4 bowl, dent, hole 6 crater, hollow

conceal: 4 bury, hide, mask, sile, veil 5 cache, cloak, couch, cover, feign 6 closet,

emboss, pocket, screen, shroud 7 secrete 8 bescreen, disguise, ensconce, withhold 9 dissemble 10 camouflage
goods: 5 cache, eloin 6 eloign

concealed: 4 dern(Sc.) 5 blind 6 covert, hidden, latent, occult, perdue, secret, veiled 7 covered, larvate 8 abstruse 9 blindfold, disguised, insidious, recondite, withdrawn 11 clandestine

concealing: 10 obvelation

concede: own 4 cede 5 admit, agree, allow, grant, waive, yette, yield 6 accord, assent 7 confess 9 surrender 10 condescend 11 acknowledge

conceit: ego 4 idea 5 fancy, pride 6 notion, vagary, vanity 7 caprice, egotism, tympany 9 arrogance, conundrum 10 conception

conceited: bug 4 fess, väin 5 chuff, cocky, flory, huggy, proud 6 clever 8 arrogant, dogmatic, priggish, snobbish 9 pragmatic, whimsical 11 coxcombical, egotistical, opinionated

conceive: 4 form, make, plan, ween 5 begin, brain, dream, fancy, frame, think 6 devise, ideate, ponder 7 imagine, realize, suppose, suspect 8 comprise, comprize, contrive 9 apprehend, formulate 10 comprehend, understand

concent: 9 harmonize 10 accordance 11 consistency

concentrate: aim, fix 4 mass, pile 5 coact, exalt, focus, unify 6 arrest, attend, center, gather 7 compact, essence, thicken 8 approach, assemble, condense, contract 9 intensify 10 centralize 11 consolidate 12 conglomerate

concentration: 7 extract 10 absorption 11 application

concentration camp: 6 prison, stalag

concept: 4 idea 5 fancy, image 7 opinion, thought 11 disposition

conception: ens 4 idea 5 fancy, fetus, image 6 belief, design, embryo 7 conceit, purpose 8 notation 9 beginning 10 cogitation, impression 12 apprehension 13 comprehension

concern: 4 bear, care, firm, reck, sake 5 apply, cause, event, grief, touch, worry 6 affair, affect, behold, charge, employ, matter, regard 7 anxiety, article, company, disturb, involve, pertain, respect, trouble 8 business, interest 9 implicate, rickmatic 10 solicitude 11 corporation, distinguish 12 apprehension

concerned: 6 intent 7 anxious, worried 8 bothered

concerning: by, of, on, re; for 4 in-re 5 about, anent 6 anenst 9 regarding

communicable: 4 open 5 frank 8 catching, sociable 9 knowledge, talkative 10 diffusible, infectious 13 communicative

communicant: 6 member 8 adherent 9 informant

communicate (see also **commune**): 4 tell 6 bestow, convey, impart, inform, reveal, signal 7 declare, dictate, divulge 8 converse

communication: 4 note 5 favor 6 favour, letter 7 message 8 telegram 9 communion 10 communique, connection
means: 4 drum, flag, note, post 5 phone, radio, smoke 6 letter, movies, speech, tom-tom 9 telegraph, telephone 10 television

communion: 4 cult, host, mass, sect, talk 5 creed, faith, share, unity 6 church, homily 7 concord 8 antiphon, converse, viaticum 9 agreement, eucharist, sacrament 10 confession, fellowship 11 intercourse 12 conversation, denomination 13 communication, participation
case: 5 burse
cloth: 8 corporal 9 corporale
consecrated food: 5 hagia
cup: ama
plate: 5 paten
table: 5 altar
vessel: pyx

communique: 6 report 7 message 12 announcement 13 communication

communism: 8 Leninism 10 Bolshevism

communist: Red 6 Soviet

community: mir 4 body, burg, city 5 firca, state, thorp 6 cenoby, colony, hamlet, nation, polity, public 7 society, village 8 district, likeness, province, township 9 frequency 10 commonness 12 commonwealth, neighborhood
pert. to: 8 societal

commute: 5 alter 6 change, travel 7 convert 8 exchange 10 substitute 11 interchange

Comoro island: 6 Moheli

comose: 5 hairy 6 comous, tufted

compact: 4 bond, case, firm, hard, knit, pact, plot, snug, trim 5 brief, close, dense, gross, pithy, solid, terse, thick 6 vanity 7 bargain, concise, concord, serried 8 alliance, condense, contract, covenant, solidify, succinct 9 agreement, concordat 10 compaction, compressed, conspiracy, federation 11 compendious, concentrate, confederacy, consolidate, sententious 13 understanding

compadre: pal 5 buddy 6 friend 9 companion

companion: pal 4 chum, fere, mate, peer, twin, wife 5 buddy, bully, butty, crony, cully, matey 6 attend, comate, escort, fellow, friend, spouse 7 compeer, comrade,

consort, husband, partner 8 compadre, helpmate 9 accompany, associate, attendant 11 concomitant 12 acquaintance
constant: 6 shadow
equal: 4 peer 7 compeer
faithful: dog 7 Achates

companionable: 6 social 7 cordial 8 gracious, sociable 9 agreeable

company: mob, set 4 band, bevy, body, core, crew, fare, fere, firm, gang, gest, ging, host, rout, team 5 coven, covey, crowd, flock, geste, group, guest, horde, party, squad, troop 6 actors, circle, clique, cohort, covine, curney(Sc.), throng, troupe 7 battery, college, consort, society, visitor 8 assembly 9 camarilla, cavalcade, concourse, gathering 10 fellowship 11 association, partnership 13 companionship

comparable: 4 like 7 similar 9 analogous

comparative: as 4 than 5 equal, rival 7 compeer 8 relative
suffix: er, or; ior

compare: vie 4 even 5 apply, liken, match, scale 6 confer, relate 7 collate, examine, senible 8 contrast, estimate 10 assimilate

comparison: 6 simile 7 analogy, parable 8 likeness, likening, metaphor 9 collation 10 conference, similitude 11 examination

compartment: bay, bin 4 cell, part 5 abode, stall 6 alcove, bunker, region 7 cellule, chamber, section 8 division 9 apartment 10 pigeonhole
granary: 8 grintern

compass: 4 area, gain, room, size 5 admit, field, gamut, range, reach, scope 6 arrive, attain, bounds, circle, degree, device, effect, extent, sphere 7 achieve, caliber, circuit, confine, divider, enclose, environ, horizon, pelorus 8 boundary, cincture, circuity, surround 10 accomplish
beam: 7 trammel
card: 4 rose
housing: 8 binnacle
ink leg: pen
kind of: sun 4 gyro 5 solar
part: pen 4 airt, vane 5 rhumb 6 gimbal, needle 7 gimbals, trammel 8 trammels
pocket: 6 diacle
point: E., N., S., W.; N.E., N.W., S.E., S.W.; E.N.E., E.S.E., N.N.E., N.N.W., S.S.E., S.S.W., W.N.W., W.S.W. 4 airt 5 airth, rhumb 7 azimuth
sight: 4 vane
suspender: 6 gimbal

compassion: rue 4 pity, ruth 5 heart, grace, mercy, sorry 6 lenity 7 remorse 8 clemency, synipathy 10 condolence 12 misericordia 13 commiseration

compatible: 8 suitable 9 accordant, agreeable, congenial, congruous, consonant 10 consistent, harmonious 16 noncontradictory

compatriot: 10 countryman

compeer: 4 mate, peer, rank 5 equal, match 7 comrade 9 colleague, companion 11 comparative

compel: gar(Sc.) 4 make, move, urge 5 cause, drive, exact, force, impel, press 6 coerce, enjoin, extort, incite, oblige 7 actuate, command, dragoon, enforce, require 9 constrain, influence, instigate, overpower 11 necessitate, subjudicate

compelled: has 4 must 5 bound

compelling: 6 cogent 7 telling 8 forceful 9 demanding 10 conclusive, convincing, persuasive

compendious: 5 brief, short 6 direct 7 compact, concise 8 succinct 9 condensed 11 expeditious 13 comprehensive

compendium: 4 list 5 brief 6 apercu, digest, precis, sketch 7 catalog, compend, epitome, medulla, outline, summary 8 abstract, breviary, syllabus, synopsis 10 abridgment 11 compilation, composition, contraction 12 abbreviation

compensate: pay 4 jibe 5 agree, atone, repay, tally 6 recoup, reward, square 7 correct, redress, requite, restore, satisfy 8 compense 9 indemnify 10 recompense, remunerate 11 countervail 12 counterpoise 14 counterbalance

compensation: fee, pay, utu 4 hire 5 bonus, wages 6 amends, angild, gersum, offset, reward, salary 7 damages, payment, redress, stipend 8 pittance, requital 9 emolument, indemnity 10 recompense 11 restitution 12 counterpoise, remuneration, satisfaction 15 indemnification

compete: pit, vie 4 cope, tend 5 match, rival 6 strive 7 contend, contest, emulate

competent: apt, can, fit 4 able, good, meet, sane 5 adept, capax, smart 6 worthy 7 capable, endowed, skilled 8 adequate, suitable 9 effective, efficient, qualified 10 proficient, sufficient

competition: 4 game, heat 5 match, trial 7 contest, rivalry 8 conflict 9 emulation 10 contention, free-for-all, opposition

competitor: foe 5 enemy, rival 6 player 7 entrant 8 opponent 9 adversary, candidate, combatant 10 antagonist, contestant

Compiegne's river: 4 Oise 5 Aisne

compilation: ana 4 book, code 5 cento 6 digest 9 accretion 10 collection, compendium, confection

compile: add 4 edit 5 amass 6 gather, select 7 arrange, collect, compose, prepare 11 anthologize

compiler: 6 author, editor

complacent: 4 calm, smug 7 fatuous 9 satisfied 11 comfortable 13 self-satisfied

complain: ail, yip 4 beef, carp, fret, fuss, kick, moan, rule, wail, yelp, yirn 5 brawl, croak, croon, gripe, whine 6 bewail, charge, cotter, grieve, grizze, grouse, murmur, repine, yammer 7 deplore, grumble, protest 8 bellyache 11 expostulate

complainant: 5 asker 7 accuser, querent, relator 9 plaintiff

complaining: 9 plaintive, querulous

complaint: 6 lament, malady, plaint 7 ailment, disease, illness, protest 8 disorder, gravamen, jeremiad 9 exception, grievance 10 accusation 11 lamentation

complaisant: 4 able, easy, kind 5 buxom, civil, suave 6 polite, smooth, urbane 7 affable, amiable, lenient 8 gracious, obliging, pleasing 9 compliant, courteous, favorable 10 favourable 12 ingratiating

complect: 5 plait 7 embrace 9 interwine 10 interweave

complement: 4 crew, gang 5 force 6 amount 7 adjunct, obverse 10 completion, supplement 11 counterpart

complete: do; all, end 4 dead, deep, fill, full 5 close, every, plumb, quite, ripen, total, utter, whole 6 effect, entire, finish, intact, mature 7 achieve, execute, fulfill, germane, perfect, plenary, realize 8 absolute, blinking, circular, conclude, implicit, thorough 9 implement, surfeited, terminate 10 accomplish, consummate, effectuate 11 unqualified 12 wholehearted

completely: all 5 quite

completeness: 5 depth 9 entelechy

completion: end 6 finish 9 plenitude

complex: 4 hard, mazy 5 mixed 6 knotty 7 network, tangled, twisted 8 involved, manifold, syndrome 9 composite, difficult, entangled, intricate, perplexed 10 interlaced 11 complicated

of communities: 5 biome

complexion: hue 4 blee, look, rudd, tint 5 color, humor, state, tenor, tinge 6 aspect, temper 10 appearance

compliance: 7 harmony 8 civility 9 obedience 10 concession, submission 11 application 12 complaisance

compliant: 4 easy, oily 6 pliant, supple 7 ductile, dutiful, willing 9 indulgent 10 applicable, manageable, obsequious, sequacious 11 complaisant

complicate: 6 intort, puzzle, tangle 7 involve, perplex 8 bewilder

complicated: 4 hard 6 knotty, prolix 7 complex, gordian, snarled, tangled 8 involved 9 difficult, elaborate, embroiled, intricate, plexiform 10 disordered

complication: 4 node, plot 5 nodus, snarl 9 complexus, confusion, intricacy 10 difficulty, perplexity

compliment: 4 gift, laud 5 extol 6 boquet, eulogy, praise 7 adulate, applaud, encomium, flummery, gratuity 9 adulation, panegyric 12 blandishment, commendation, congratulate

compline: 4 hour 7 prayers, service

comply: 4 cede, obey 5 abide, adapt, agree, apply, yield 6 accede, accord, assent, enfold, submit 7 conform, embrace, observe 9 acquiesce 11 accommodate

component: 4 item, part, unit 6 factor, member 7 element 8 integral 10 compounder, ingredient 11 constituent

comport: act 4 bear, jibe, suit 5 agree, brook, carry, tally 6 accord, acquit, behave, demean, endure, square 7 conduct 9 behaviour, harmonize 10 correspond, deportment 11 comportance

comportable: 8 suitable 9 endurable, tolerable 10 consistent

comportment: 7 conduct, dealing 8 behavior, demeanor 9 behaviour, demeanour 10 deportment

compose: pen, set 4 calm, dite, form, lull, make 5 allay, brief, clerk, dight, order, write 6 accord, adjust, create, design, indite, settle, soothe 7 arrange, compone, concoct, conform, dispose, fashion, produce 8 compound, comprise, comprize, regulate 9 alleviate, construct, formulate 10 constitute 11 tranquilize

compose type: set

composed: 4 calm, cool 5 quiet, sober, wrote 6 demure, placid, sedate, serene 7 written 8 compound, decorous, tranquil 9 collected, composite, unruffled 13 dispassionate

composer: 4 poet 5 odist 6 author, writer 7 elegist 8 monodist, musician 10 compositor, typesetter

composition (see also **musical composition**): ana 4 mass, opus, work 5 cento, ditty, drama, piece, poesy, theme 6 accord, lesson, make-up, thesis 7 article, compost, mixture, picture, writing 8 acrostic, compound, fantasia 9 admixture, aggregate, composure, congruity, formation, invention, structure, synthesis 10 adjustment, compendium, composture, confection, manuscript 11 arrangement, combination, compositure, conjunction 12 constitution, composture, construction

art of: 8 rhetoric

for two: 6 duetto 7 duetino

literary: ms(abbr.) 5 cento, drama, novel, theme 6 satire, thesis 7 tr[...] treatise

metrical: 4 poem, rime 5 poesy, rh[...]

mournful: 5 dirge

compositor: 4 type 6 setter 7 ca[...] printer

compost: 6 mingle 7 compote, mix[...] compound 10 composture, fertili[...] composition

composure: 4 bond, mien 5 quiet, u[...] repose 7 balance, posture 8 calmn[...] renity 10 composture, equanimity, [...] ness 11 combination, composition[...] quility

compote, compot: 4 bowl 5 fruit 7 [...]

compound: 4 fill, join 5 alloy, blend[...] unite 6 adjust, jumble, medley, s[...] amalgam, combine, complex, con[...] compose, compost 8 ceromide 9 [...] ture, aggregate, composite, enclos[...] amalgamate, commixture, compr[...] concoction, confection, cons[...] hodge-podge, settlement

alkaline: 4 soda

amorphous: 7 phenose

chemical: 4 amid, amin, azin, imid, [...] amide, amine, azine, azola, borid[...] ester, imide, imine, osone 6 borids[...] site, metamer, leucine 8 chloride

containing double bonds: 5 diene 6 [...]

containing two hydroxyl groups: 4 d[...]

crystalline: 5 aloin, oscin 6 amarin, [...] phenol 7 tropine

hypnotic: 7 trional

organic: 4 amin 5 amine, ester, k[...] ketole, ketone

compound interest: 9 anatocism

comprehend: get, see 4 know 5 gras[...] ply, savvy, seize, sense 6 attain, diges[...] body, fathom, follow, uptake 7 co[...] discern, embrace, enclose, imagin[...] clude, involve, realize 8 comprise[...] prize, conceive, conclude, perceive[...] prehend 10 understand

comprehensible: 8 exoteric, inclu[...] comprised 11 conceivable 12 intelli[...]

comprehension: 5 grasp 6 noesis 7 gra[...] knowing, summary 9 inclusion, int[...] 10 conception 11 connotation

comprehensive: big 4 full, wide 5 [...] grand, large 7 concise, generic 8 en[...] spacious 9 expansive, extensive, [...] oramic 11 compendious

compress: nip, tie 4 bale, bind, firm, [...] cling, cramp, crowd, crush, press 6 g[...] shrink 7 abridge, bolster, compact, c[...]

concert: 4 plan 5 unite 6 accord, devise 7 arrange, benefit, concent, concord, consort, consult, harmony, recital 9 agreement 11 performance 13 entertainment

concert hall: 5 odeon, odeum

concertina: 9 bandonion

concession: 4 boon 5 favor, grant, lease 6 assent, favour, gambit 7 cession 9 admission, privilege 10 compliance, compromise 12 acquiescence 13 condescension 15 acknowledgement

conch: 5 shell 6 cockle, mussel

conchie, conchy: 8 objector

Conchobor's wife: 4 Medb

concierge: 6 porter, warden 7 janitor 9 attendant 10 doorkeeper

conciliate: get 4 calm, ease 5 atone 6 adjust, pacify 7 acquire, appease, concile, mollify, placate, satisfy 9 reconcile 10 propitiate

conciliatory: 4 mild 6 gentle, giving, irenic 7 lenient, pacific, winning 8 irenical, lenitive 9 forgiving 10 mollifying 12 propitiating

concilium: 7 council

concinnity: 7 harmony 8 elegance

concise: 4 curt, neat 5 brief, crisp, pithy, short, terse 7 compact, laconic, pointed, precise, serried 8 mutilate, pregnant, succinct 9 condensed 10 compedious, contracted 11 sententious 12 epigrammatic 13 comprehensive

concision: 6 schism 7 faction 8 division 10 mutilation

conclave: 6 closet 7 chamber, meeting 8 assembly

conclude: bar, end 4 rest 5 close, estop, infer, judge, limit 6 clinch, deduce, figure, finish, gather, reason, settle 7 achieve, arrange, confine, embrace, enclose, resolve, suppose 8 complete, dispatch, graduate, restrain 9 determine, speculate, terminate 10 comprehend

conclusion: end 4 amen, coda, last 5 finis 6 finale, finish, period, result, upshot 7 finding, outcome 8 epilogue, judgment 9 diagnosis, inference 10 conjecture, settlement 11 probability, termination

conclusive: 4 last 5 final, valid 6 cogent 7 certain, extreme, telling 8 decisive, definite, ultimate 10 convincing, peremptory 11 irrefutable 12 unanswerable 13 determinative

concoct: mix 4 brew, cook, plan, plot, vamp 5 frame, hatch 6 decoct, devise, digest, invent, refine, scheme 7 compose, perfect, prepare 8 compound, intrigue 9 fabricate 10 assimilate

concomitant: 9 accessory, associate, attendant, attending, companion, conjoined, cooperant 10 coincident, concurrent 11 synchronous 12 accompanying 13 accompaniment

concord: 4 part 5 agree, amity, peace, union, unity 6 treaty, unison 7 compact, concent, concert, harmony, oneness 8 covenant 9 agreement, communion, congruity 10 accordance, consonance

concordant: 8 unisonal 9 agreeable, congruous, consonant 10 harmonious 13 correspondent

concourse: 5 crowd, place, point 6 throng 7 company 8 assembly 9 affluence, frequency, gathering 10 assemblage, confluence 11 coincidence, concurrence, conjunction, cooperation

concredit: 6 commit 7 entrust, intrust

concrete: 4 clot, firm, hard, real 5 beton, solid, unite 6 actual 7 combine, congeal, special 8 coalesce. compound, tangible 9 concresce 10 particular

construction: 6 tremie 7 caisson

concretion: 4 clot, mess 5 pearl 6 nodule 8 calculus

concubine: 5 woman 7 adalisk 8 mistress 9 odalisque

concur: 4 jibe, join 5 agree, chime, unite 6 accede, accord, assent 7 approve, combine, consent 8 coincide, converge 9 acquiesce, cooperate 10 correspond

concurrence: 5 union 6 assent, bestow 7 consent, consort, meeting 8 adhesion 9 adherence, agreement, concourse 10 conspiracy 11 coincidence, conjunction

concurrent: 6 coeval, united 7 meeting 10 associated, coincident 11 concomitant, synchronous 12 accompanying

concuss: jar 4 jolt 5 clash, force, shake, shock 6 coerce 7 agitate

condalia: 9 chaparral

condemn: ban 4 damn, doom, file, fine 5 blame, decry, judge 6 amerce, attain, awreak, banish, detest 7 adjudge, censure, convict 8 denounce, reproach, sentence 10 confiscate, disapprove

condemnation: 4 doom 5 blame 7 censure, decrial 11 reprobation 13 animadversion 14 disapprobation

condense: cut 5 brief, unite 6 decoct, digest, harden, lessen, narrow, reduce, shrink 7 abridge, combine, compact, deflate, distill, shorten, thicken 8 compress, diminish, solidify 9 constrict, epitomize, evaporate, intensify 11 concentrate, consolidate

condensed: 4 curt 5 brief 7 compact, concise 8 absorbed 11 compendious

condenser: 4 cric 6 aludel

condescend: 5 deign, favor, grant, stoop 6 assent, oblige, submit 7 concede, descend 9 patronize, vouchsafe

condescension: 7 disdain 8 courtesy 10 affability, concession 12 complaisance

condign: due, fit 4 fair, just 6 severe, worthy 8 adequate, deserved, suitable 11 appropriate

condiment: rea 4 herb, kari, mace, sage, salt 5 caper, curry, sauce, spice, thyme 6 catsup, cloves, pepper, relish 7 chutney, cuminos, ketchup, mustard, paprika, vinegar 8 allspice, turmeric 9 appetizer, seasoning

container: 5 cruet

stand: 6 caster

condisciple: 7 student 12 schoolfellow

condite: 7 pickled 8 seasoned 9 preserved

condition: if 4 case, mode, rank, rote, term 5 angle, birth, cause, class, estre, facet, place, stage, state 6 estate, fettle, gentry, morale, plight, status 7 article, calling, premise, proviso, station 8 covenant, occasion, position 9 agreement, exception, provision, requisite, situation 10 limitation 11 predicament, stipulation 13 circumstances

comb. form: ate 4 ance, ancy, ence, ency 6 blasty

critical: 9 emergency

favorable: 4 odds

suffix: ile

conditional: 9 qualified 10 accidental

conditioned: 6 finite 7 limited

condolence: 4 pity, ruth 7 empathy 8 sympathy 10 compassion 13 commiseration

condone: 5 blink, remit 6 acquit, excuse, forget, ignore, pardon 7 absolve, forgive 8 overlook

condor: 4 coin 6 tiffin 7 vulture 8 gymnogyp

conduce: aid 4 help, hire, lead, tend 5 bring, guide 6 confer, effect, engage 7 advance, conduct, further, redound 10 contribute

conduct: act, run 4 bear, deed, gest, lead, mien, rule, wage 5 carry, geste, guard, guide, usher 6 action, attend, behave, convey, convoy, demean, deport, direct, escort, govern, manage, squire 7 bearing, channel, comport, conduce, conduit, control, execute, officer, operate 8 behavior, carriage, chaplain, demeanor, guidance, regulate, transact 9 accompany, behaviour, demeanour, supervise 10 administer, deportment, governance, government, proceeding 11 comportment, countenance, superintend

scandalous: 9 esclandre(F.)

conductor: cad 4 gude 5 guard 6 convoy, copper, escort, leader 7 cathode, maestro 8 aqueduct, cicerone, conveyor, director, employee 10 bandleader, propagator 11 impressario

stick: 5 baton

conduit: 4 duct, main, pipe, tube, wire 5 cable, canal, sewer 6 trough 7 channel, conduct, culvert, passage 8 aqueduct

cone: 4 chat 5 crack, solid, spire 6 bobbin, object 7 cluster, fissure, strobil 8 strobile 9 container

section: 8 parabola

cone-shaped: 5 conic 6 pineal 7 conical

conenose: 6 bedbug

conepate: 5 skunk

coney: See cony

confab: 4 chat, talk 6 powwow 7 prattle 10 conference 11 confabulate 12 conversation

confect: mix 4 form, make 6 pickle 7 prepare 8 preserve 9 construct

confection: 5 candy, dulce, sweet 6 bonbon, comfit, cimbal, dainty, nougat 7 caramel, confect, fondant, mixture, praline, sherbet, succade 8 compound, delicacy, preserve, sherbert 9 confiture, marmalade, sweetmeat 10 concoction 11 bittersweet, compilation, composition, preparation

Confederacy: banknote: 8 blueback

general: Lee 5 Bragg, Price 6 Morgan 7 Jackson 10 Beauregard

guerilla: 11 bushwhacker

president: 5 Davis

soldier: reb

vice-president: 8 Stephens

victory: 7 Bull Run 11 Chickamauga 16 Chancellorsville

confederate: aid, pal, reb 4 ally 5 rebel, stall, unite 6 league 7 abetter, abettor, conjure, fedarie, federal, partner 8 conspire, federate 9 accessory, assistant, associate, auxiliary 10 accomplice

confederation: 4 body 5 union 6 league 7 compact, society 8 alliance, covenant 9 coalition 10 conspiracy, federation 11 association, confederacy

confer: dub 4 give, meet, talk 5 award, endow, grant, treat 6 advise, bestow, donate, impart, invest, parley 7 commune, compare, conduce, consult, counsel, discuss, instate, present 8 comprise, converge 10 contribute, deliberate

conference: 4 talk 5 synod, trust 6 confab, huddle, parley, pow-wow 7 council, meeting, palaver 8 colloque, colloquy, congress 9 collation, comparing, discourse, interview 10 comparison, discussion 11 association 12 consultation, conversation

technique: 13 brainstorming

confess: own 4 avow, sing 5 admit, grant 6 attest, avouch, beknow, reveal, shrive 7 concede, divulge 8 disclose, discover, manifest 11 acknowledge

confession: 5 credo, creed 6 avowal, shrift, shrive 9 admission, communion, statement 10 profession

confetti: 4 tape 5 candy 7 bonbons 9 sweetmeat 10 confection

container: 8 cascaron

confidant: 8 intimate

confide: 4 affy, rely, tell 5 trust 6 commit, depend 7 believe, consign, entrust, intrust

confidence: 4 hope 5 bield, faith, trust 6 aplomb, belief, credit, mettle, morale, secret, spirit 7 courage 8 affiance, boldness, credence, reliance, sureness 9 assurance, certitude, hardihood, hardiness 10 effrontery 11 presumption 12 impertinence

game: 5 bunco, bunko 7 swindle

lack: 10 diffidence

confident: 4 bold, smug, sure 5 hardy, siker 6 crouse, secure, sicker 7 assured, certain, hopeful, reliant 8 constant, fearless, impudent, sanguine, trustful 9 dependent, undaunted 10 dogmatical 11 trustworthy 12 presumptuous

confidential: 5 bosom, privy 6 covert, secret 7 private, subrosa 8 esoteric, intimate 9 auricular 11 trustworthy

law: 9 fiduciary

configuration: 4 form 5 shape 6 figure 7 contour, outline 10 topography

confine: bar, box, dam, hem, new, pen, pin, sty, tie 4 bind, cage, coop, hasp, jail, keep, lock, seal 5 bound, cramp, delay, impen, limit, pinch, stint 6 border, compas, corral, fetter, forbar, hamper, hurdle, immure, impale, intern, pinion, pocket, tether 7 astrict, impound 8 boundary, conclude, imprison, restrain, straiten 9 carcerate, constrain, restraint 11 incarcerate 12 circumscribe

confined: ill 4 pent 5 bound, caged 6 sealed 7 cramped, cribbed, limited 8 impended, interned 9 impounded 10 cloistered 13 incommunicado

to select group: 8 estoeric

confinement: mew 8 clausure, firmance 9 captivity, restraint 10 childbirth, constraint, internment 11 contraction 12 accouchement, imprisonment

place of: mew, pen 4 brig, cage, coop, goal, jail, stir 5 limbo 6 asylum, corral, prison 7 dungeon 9 calaboose 12 penitentiary

confirm: fix, set 4 firm, seal 5 prove 6 affirm, assent, assure, attest, avouch, clinch, ratify, settle, verify 7 approve, comfort, endorse, fortify, sustain 8 accredit, convince, sanction, validate 9 approbate, establish 10 comprobate, strengthen 11 corroborate, countersign 12 adminiculate, authenticate, substantiate

confirmed: set 5 fixed 6 arrant, stable 7 chronic 8 habitual, ratified 9 fortified, initiated 10 encouraged, inveterate 11 established

confiscate: 4 grab 5 seize, usurp 7 condemn 9 sequester 11 appropriate

conflagration: 4 fire 5 blaze, fever 7 burning 10 combustion 12 inflammation

conflict: war 4 bout, duel, fray, rift 5 broil, brush, clash, fight, grips, mix-up 6 action, battle, combat, mutiny, oppose, strife 7 contend, contest, discord, warfare 8 disagree, militate, struggle 9 collision, encounter, rebellion 10 contention 11 competition

final: 10 Armageddon

conflicting: 7 adverse 10 contending 12 incompatible, inharmonious

confluence: 5 crowd 7 conflux, meeting 8 junction 9 concourse 12 assimilation

conform: go; fit 4 lean, obey, suit 5 adapt, agree, apply, yield 6 accede, adjust, assent, comply, settle, submit 7 compose 9 acquiesce, harmonize, reconcile 10 correspond 11 accommodate

conformist: 6 pedant 7 babbitt 9 precisian 10 philistine 11 reactionary

conformity: 7 harmony 8 affinity, likeness, symmetry 9 agreement, congruity, obedience 10 accordance, compliance, similarity, submission 11 affirmative 12 acquiescence, complaisance

to law: 6 dharma 8 legality

confound: mix 4 blow, dash, maze, rout, stam, stun 5 abash, addle, amaze, spend, spoil, waste 6 baffle, dismay, muddle, rattle 7 astound, confuse, confute, corrupt, destroy, flummox, perplex, stupefy 8 astonish, bewilder, distract, surprise 9 discomfit, dumbfound, embarrass, frustrate, overthrow 10 disconcert 11 intermingle

confraternity: 4 body 5 union 7 society 11 brotherhood

confrere: 6 fellow 7 comrade 9 colleague

confront: 4 defy, face, meet 5 beard, brave 6 oppose, resist 7 affront, compare 8 envisage, threaten 9 challenge, encounter

confuse: mix 4 dash, daze, maze, muss, rout 5 abash, addle, amaze, befog, blend, cloud, snarl 6 baffle, bemuse, bother, burble, caddle, flurry, fuddle, jumble, muddle, puzzle, rattle 7 bedevil, blunder, derange, fluster, mystify, nonplus, perplex, stupefy 8 befuddle, bewilder, confound, distract 9 barbulyie, discomfit, dumbfound, obfuscate 10 demoralize, disarrange, discompose, disconcert

confused: 4 asea, lost 5 foggy, muddy, vague 6 doiled, doited 7 chaotic, obscure 8 deranged 9 chagrined 10 bewildered, hurly-burly, topsy-turvy, tumultuous **13** helter-skelter

confusion: din **4** coil, dust, fuss, harl, mess, moil, riot **5** babel, chaos, chevy, chivy, deray, mix-up, snafu, snarl, strow **6** babble, bedlam, caddle, chivvy, habble, hubbub, huddle, jabble, jumble, muddle, pother, rabble, rumpus, tophet, tumult, uproar, welter **7** farrage, blunder, bluster, clutter, farrage, flutter, garboil, topheth, turmoil, widdrim **8** disarray, disorder **9** agitation, commotion **10** hullabaloo, hurly-burly **11** disturbance, trepidation **12** hugger-mugger, perturbation **13** embarrassment

confute: **4** deny **5** rebut **6** expose, refute **7** silence **8** confound, convince, disprove, infringe, overcome **9** overwhelm

conge: bow **6** curtsy **7** license, molding **8** farewell, passport **9** clearance, dismissal **10** permission **11** leavetaking

congeal: gel, ice, set **4** geal, jell **5** candy **6** cotter, curdle, freeze, harden **7** stiffen, thicken **8** concrete, solidify **9** coagulate **11** crystallize

congealing agent: **6** pectin **8** gelatine

congee: **5** gruel **9** departure

congener: **4** kind, race **5** class, genus

congenial: **4** boon **5** natal **6** native **7** connate, kindred **10** compatible **11** sympathetic

conger: eel **8** cucumber

congeries: **4** mass **5** group **10** collection

congestion: jam **4** heap **8** crowding, stoppage **9** gathering **12** accumulation

conglaciate: **6** freeze **7** congeal

conglobation: **4** ball

conglomerate: **4** heap, mass, pile, rock **5** stack **9** clustered **10** assemblage **11** agglomerate **12** concentrated

Congo (see also **Zaire**): *tribe:* **4** Susa **6** Wabuma **7** Bangala

tributary: **4** Uele **6** Ubangi **7** Aruwima

congou: tea

congratulate: **4** laud **5** greet **6** salute **8** macarize **10** compliment, felicitate

congregate: **4** herd, mass, meet, teem **5** group, swarm, troop **6** gather, muster **7** collect, convene **8** assemble

congregation: **4** body, fold, host, mass **5** flock, swarm **6** church, parish **7** meeting, synaxes **8** assembly, brethren **9** gathering **10** collection **11** convocation

congress: **4** dail, diet **5** synod **7** council, meeting **8** assembly, conclave **10** conference, convention, parliament **11** convocation, legislature

Congress: *building:* **7** Capitol

member: **7** senator

upper house: **6** Senate

congressman: **14** representative

congruity: **6** accord **7** concord, fitness, harmony **8** symmetry **9** agreement, coherence **10** conformity, consonance **11** composition, consistency, correctness, suitability **13** compatability **14** correspondence

conical: **8** tapering

conifer: fir, yew **4** pine, tree **5** cedar, larch **6** spruce **7** pinacle, pinales

conium: **7** hemlock

conjecture: aim **4** plot, shot, view **5** augur, ettle, fancy, guess, opine **6** belief, divine, theory **7** imagine, opinion, presume, suppose, surmise, suspect **9** inference, speculate, suspicion **10** conclusion, estimation **11** contrivance, supposition

conjoined: **6** joined, linked **8** conjunct, touching **11** concomitant

conjoint: **8** combined **9** conjoined **10** associated **11** correlative **12** simultaneous

conjugal: **9** connubial **11** matrimonial

conjugate: **5** yoked **6** joined, united **7** coupled

conjunction: as, et, if, or; and, but, nor, tie **4** than **5** joint, since, union **7** coition, consort **9** coalition, concourse **10** connection **11** association, combination, composition, concurrence

conjuration: art **5** charm, magic, spell **6** voodoo **10** necromancy **11** incantation, legerdemain

conjure: **4** pray **5** charm, halse **6** adjure, invent, invoke **7** beseech, combine, entreat, imagine **8** conspire, contrive, exorcise, exorcize **10** supplicate **11** confederate

conjuror: **4** mage, sear **6** pellar, shaman, wizard **7** juggler, warlock **8** magician, sorcerer **9** coswearer, enchanter **15** prestidigatator

conk: **4** fail, head, nose **5** faint, knock, stall

Conlaech: *father:* **10** Cuchulainn

mother: **5** Aoife

connach: **5** spoil, waste

Connacht king: **6** Ailill

connate: **4** akin, born **5** fused **6** allied, inborn, innate **7** cognate **9** congenial **10** congenital

connect: tie **4** ally, bind, glue, join, knit, link **5** affix, chain, marry, unite **6** attach, bridge, cement, cohere, connex, couple, fasten, relate **7** combine **8** continue **9** affiliate, associate, correlate, interlock **11** communicate

Connecticut: *city:* **4** Avon **6** Bethel, Darien **7** Meriden **8** Hartford(c.)

river: **10** Housatonic

connection: tie **4** bond, link **5** nexus, union **6** family **7** contact, kinship **8** affinity, alliance, commerce, intimacy, junction, rela-

communicable: 4 open 5 frank 8 catching, sociable 9 knowledge, talkative 10 diffusible, infectious 13 communicative

communicant: 6 member 8 adherent 9 informant

communicate (see also **commune**)**:** 4 tell 6 bestow, convey, impart, inform, reveal, signal 7 declare, dictate, divulge 8 converse

communication: 4 note 5 favor 6 favour, letter 7 message 8 telegram 9 communion 10 communique, connection

means: 4 drum, flag, note, post 5 phone, radio, smoke 6 letter, movies, speech, tom-tom 9 telegraph, telephone 10 television

communion: 4 cult, host, mass, sect, talk 5 creed, faith, share, unity 6 church, homily 7 concord 8 antiphon, converse, viaticum 9 agreement, eucharist, sacrament 10 confession, fellowship 11 intercourse 12 conversation, denomination 13 communication, participation

case: 5 burse

cloth: 8 corporal 9 corporale

consecrated food: 5 hagia

cup: ama

plate: 5 paten

table: 5 altar

vessel: pyx

communique: 6 report 7 message 12 announcement 13 communication

communism: 8 Leninism 10 Bolshevism

communist: Red 6 Soviet

community: mir 4 body, burg, city 5 firca, state, thorp 6 cenoby, colony, hamlet, nation, polity, public 7 society, village 8 district, likeness, province, township 9 frequency 10 commonness 12 commonwealth, neighborhood

pert. to: 8 societal

commute: 5 alter 6 change, travel 7 convert 8 exchange 10 substitute 11 interchange

Comoro island: 6 Moheli

comose: 5 hairy 6 comous, tufted

compact: 4 bond, case, firm, hard, knit, pact, plot, snug, trim 5 brief, close, dense, gross, pithy, solid, terse, thick 6 vanity 7 bargain, concise, concord, serried 8 alliance, condense, contract, covenant, solidify, succinct 9 agreement, concordat 10 compaction, compressed, conspiracy, federation 11 compendious, concentrate, confederacy, consolidate, sententious 13 understanding

compadre: pal 5 buddy 6 friend 9 companion

companion: pal 4 chum, fere, mate, peer, twin, wife 5 buddy, bully, butty, crony, cully, matey 6 attend, comate, escort, fellow, friend, spouse 7 compeer, comrade, consort, husband, partner 8 compadre, helpmate 9 accompany, associate, attendant 11 concomitant 12 acquaintance

constant: 6 shadow

equal: 4 peer 7 compeer

faithful: dog 7 Achates

companionable: 6 social 7 cordial 8 gracious, sociable 9 agreeable

company: mob, set 4 band, bevy, body, core, crew, fare, fere, firm, gang, gest, ging, host, rout, team 5 coven, covey, crowd, flock, geste, group, guest, horde, party, squad, troop 6 actors, circle, clique, cohort, covine, curney(Sc.), throng, troupe 7 battery, college, consort, society, visitor 8 assembly 9 camarilla, cavalcade, concourse, gathering 10 fellowship 11 association, partnership 13 companionship

comparable: 4 like 7 similar 9 analogous

comparative: as 4 than 5 equal, rival 7 compeer 8 relative

suffix: er, or; ior

compare: vie 4 even 5 apply, liken, match, scale 6 confer, relate 7 collate, examine, senible 8 contrast, estimate 10 assimilate

comparison: 6 simile 7 analogy, parable 8 likeness, likening, metaphor 9 collation 10 conference, similitude 11 examination

compartment: bay, bin 4 cell, part 5 abode, stall 6 alcove, bunker, region 7 cellule, chamber, section 8 division 9 apartment 10 pigeonhole

granary: 8 grintern

compass: 4 area, gain, room, size 5 admit, field, gamut, range, reach, scope 6 arrive, attain, bounds, circle, degree, device, effect, extent, sphere 7 achieve, caliber, circuit, confine, divider, enclose, environ, horizon, pelorus 8 boundary, cincture, circuity, surround 10 accomplish

beam: 7 trammel

card: 4 rose

housing: 8 binnacle

ink leg: pen

kind of: sun 4 gyro 5 solar

part: pen 4 airt, vane 5 rhumb 6 gimbal, needle 7 gimbals, trammel 8 trammels

pocket: 6 diacle

point: E., N., S., W.; N.E., N.W., S.E., S.W.; E.N.E., E.S.E., N.N.E., N.N.W., S.S.E., S.S.W., W.N.W., W.S.W. 4 airt 5 airth, rhumb 7 azimuth

sight: 4 vane

suspender: 6 gimbal

compassion: rue 4 pity, ruth 5 heart, grace, mercy, sorry 6 lenity 7 remorse 8 clemency, sympathy 10 condolence 12 misericordia 13 commiseration

compatible: 8 suitable 9 accordant, agreeable, congenial, congruous, consonant 10 consistent, harmonious 16 noncontradictory

compatriot: 10 countryman

compeer: 4 mate, peer, rank 5 equal, match 7 comrade 9 colleague, companion 11 comparative

compel: gar(Sc.) 4 make, move, urge 5 cause, drive, exact, force, impel, press 6 coerce, enjoin, extort, incite, oblige 7 actuate, command, dragoon, enforce, require 9 constrain, influence, instigate, overpower 11 necessitate, subjudicate

compelled: has 4 must 5 bound

compelling: 6 cogent 7 telling 8 forceful 9 demanding 10 conclusive, convincing, persuasive

compendious: 5 brief, short 6 direct 7 compact, concise 8 succinct 9 condensed 11 expeditious 13 comprehensive

compendium: 4 list 5 brief 6 apercu, digest, precis, sketch 7 catalog, compend, epitome, medulla, outline, summary 8 abstract, breviary, syllabus, synopsis 10 abridgment 11 compilation, composition, contraction 12 abbreviation

compensate: pay 4 jibe 5 agree, atone, repay, tally 6 recoup, reward, square 7 correct, redress, requite, restore, satisfy 8 compense 9 indemnify 10 recompense, remunerate 11 countervail 12 counterpoise 14 counterbalance

compensation: fee, pay, utu 4 hire 5 bonus, wages 6 amends, angild, gersum, offset, reward, salary 7 damages, payment, redress, stipend 8 pittance, requital 9 emolument, indemnity 10 recompense 11 restitution 12 counterpoise, remuneration, satisfaction 15 indemnification

compete: pit, vie 4 cope, tend 5 match, rival 6 strive 7 contend, contest, emulate

competent: apt, can, fit 4 able, good, meet, sane 5 adept, capax, smart 6 worthy 7 capable, endowed, skilled 8 adequate, suitable 9 effective, efficient, qualified 10 proficient, sufficient

competition: 4 game, heat 5 match, trial 7 contest, rivalry 8 conflict 9 emulation 10 contention, free-for-all, opposition

competitor: foe 5 enemy, rival 6 player 7 entrant 8 opponent 9 adversary, candidate, combatant 10 antagonist, contestant

Compiegne's river: 4 Oise 5 Aisne

compilation: ana 4 book, code 5 cento 6 digest 9 accretion 10 collection, compendium, confection

compile: add 4 edit 5 amass 6 gather, select 7 arrange, collect, compose, prepare 11 anthologize

compiler: 6 author, editor

complacent: 4 calm, smug 7 fatuous 9 satisfied 11 comfortable 13 self-satisfied

complain: ail, yip 4 beef, carp, fret, fuss, kick, moan, rule, wail, yelp, yirn 5 brawl, croak, croon, gripe, whine 6 bewail, charge, cotter, grieve, grizze, grouse, murmur, repine, yammer 7 deplore, grumble, protest 9 bellyache 11 expostulate

complainant: 5 asker 7 accuser, querent, relator 9 plaintiff

complaining: 9 plaintive, querulous

complaint: 6 lament, malady, plaint 7 ailment, disease, illness, protest 8 disorder, gravamen, jeremiad 9 exception, grievance 10 accusation 11 lamentation

complaisant: 4 able, easy, kind 5 buxom, civil, suave 6 polite, smooth, urbane 7 affable, amiable, lenient 8 gracious, obliging, pleasing 9 compliant, courteous, favorable 10 favourable 12 ingratiating

complect: 5 plait 7 embrace 9 interwine 10 interweave

complement: 4 crew, gang 5 force 6 amount 7 adjunct, obverse 10 completion, supplement 11 counterpart

complete: do; all, end 4 dead, deep, fill, full 5 close, every, plumb, quite, ripen, total, utter, whole 6 effect, entire, finish, intact, mature 7 achieve, execute, fulfill, germane, perfect, plenary, realize 8 absolute, blinking, circular, conclude, implicit, thorough 9 implement, surfeited, terminate 10 accomplish, consummate, effectuate 11 unqualified 12 wholehearted

completely: all 5 quite

completeness: 5 depth 9 entelechy

completion: end 6 finish 9 plenitude

complex: 4 hard, mazy 5 mixed 6 knotty 7 network, tangled, twisted 8 involved, manifold, syndrome 9 composite, difficult, entangled, intricate, perplexed 10 interlaced 11 complicated

of communities: 5 biome

complexion: hue 4 blee, look, rudd, tint 5 color, humor, state, tenor, tinge 6 aspect, temper 10 appearance

compliance: 7 harmony 8 civility 9 obedience 10 concession, submission 11 application 12 complaisance

compliant: 4 easy, oily 6 pliant, supple 7 ductile, dutiful, willing 9 indulgent 10 applicable, manageable, obsequious, sequacious 11 complaisant

complicate: 6 intort, puzzle, tangle 7 involve, perplex 8 bewilder

complicated: 4 hard 6 knotty, prolix 7 complex, gordian, snarled, tangled 8 involved 9 difficult, elaborate, embroiled, intricate, plexiform 10 disordered

complication: 4 node, plot 5 nodus, snarl 9 complexus, confusion, intricacy 10 difficulty, perplexity

compliment: 4 gift, laud 5 extol 6 boquet, eulogy, praise 7 adulate, applaud, bouquet, commend, flatter, tribute 8 encomium, flummery, gratuity 9 adulation, panegyric 12 blandishment, commendation, congratulate

compline: 4 hour 7 prayers, service

comply: 4 cede, obey 5 abide, adapt, agree, apply, yield 6 accede, accord, assent, enfold, submit 7 conform, embrace, observe 9 acquiesce 11 accommodate

component: 4 item, part, unit 6 factor, member 7 element 8 integral 10 compounder, ingredient 11 constituent

comport: act 4 bear, jibe, suit 5 agree, brook, carry, tally 6 accord, acquit, behave, demean, endure, square 7 conduct 9 behaviour, harmonize 10 correspond, deportment 11 comportance

comportable: 8 suitable 9 endurable, tolerable 10 consistent

comportment: 7 conduct, dealing 8 behavior, demeanor 9 behaviour, demeanour 10 deportment

compose: pen, set 4 calm, dite, form, lull, make 5 allay, brief, clerk, dight, order, write 6 accord, adjust, create, design, indite, settle, soothe 7 arrange, compone, concoct, conform, dispose, fashion, produce 8 compound, comprise, comprize, regulate 9 alleviate, construct, formulate 10 constitute 11 tranquilize

compose type: set

composed: 4 calm, cool 5 quiet, sober, wrote 6 demure, placid, sedate, serene 7 written 8 compound, decorous, tranquil 9 collected, composite, unruffled 13 dispassionate

composer: 4 poet 5 odist 6 author, writer 7 elegist 8 monodist, musician 10 compositor, typesetter

composition (see also musical composition): ana 4 mass, opus, work 5 cento, ditty, drama, piece, poesy, theme 6 accord, lesson, make-up, thesis 7 article, compost, mixture, picture, writing 8 acrostic, compound, fantasia 9 admixture, aggregate, composure, congruity, formation, invention, structure, synthesis 10 adjustment, compendium, composture, confection, manuscript 11 arrangement, combination, composture, conjunction 12 constitution, construction

art of: 8 rhetoric

for two: 6 duetto 7 duetino

literary: ms(abbr.) 5 cento, drama, essay, novel, theme 6 satire, thesis 7 tragedy 8 treatise

metrical: 4 poem, rime 5 poesy, rhyme

mournful: 5 dirge

compositor: 4 type 6 setter 7 caseman, printer

compost: 6 mingle 7 compote, mixture 8 compound 10 composture, fertilizer 11 composition

composure: 4 bond, mien 5 quiet, union 6 repose 7 balance, posture 8 calmness, serenity 10 compompsture, equanimity, sedateness 11 combination, composition, tranquility

compote, compot: 4 bowl 5 fruit 7 dessert

compound: 4 fill, join 5 alloy, blend, ester, unite 6 adjust, jumble, medley, settle 7 amalgam, combine, complex, compone, compose, compost 8 ceromide 9 admixture, aggregate, composite, enclosure 10 amalgamate, commixture, compromise, concoction, confection, constitute, hodge-podge, settlement

alkaline: 4 soda

amorphous: 7 phenose

chemical: 4 amid, amin, azin, imid, imin 5 amide, amine, azine, azola, borid, ceria, ester, imide, imine, osone 6 borids 7 inosite, metamer, leucine 8 chloride

containing double bonds: 5 diene 6 triene

containing two hydroxyl groups: 4 diol

crystalline: 5 aloin, oscin 6 amarin, anisil, phenol 7 tropine

hypnotic: 7 trional

organic: 4 amin 5 amine, ester, ketol 6 ketole, ketone

compound interest: 9 anatocism

comprehend: get, see 4 know 5 grasp, imply, savvy, seize, sense 6 attain, digest, embody, fathom, follow, uptake 7 contain, discern, embrace, enclose, imagine, include, involve, realize 8 comprise, comprize, conceive, conclude, perceive 9 apprehend 10 understand

comprehensible: 8 exoteric, included 9 comprised 11 conceivable 12 intelligible

comprehension: 5 grasp 6 noesis 7 epitome, knowing, summary 9 inclusion, intension 10 conception 11 connotation

comprehensive: big 4 full, wide 5 broad, grand, large 7 concise, generic 8 encyclic, spacious 9 expansive, extensive, panoramic 11 compendious

compress: nip, tie 4 bale, bind, firm, wrap 5 cling, cramp, crowd, crush, press 6 gather, shrink 7 abridge, bolster, compact, curtail, embrace, deflate, flatten, repress, squeeze 8 astringe, condense, contract, restrain 9 constrain, epitomize 11 consolidate

medical: 5 stupe 7 bandage, pledget

compressor: 4 pump 6 device 7 machine

comprise, comprize: 4 hold 5 cover, imply, seize 6 attach, confer, embody 7 compose, contain, embrace, enclose, include, involve 8 conceive, perceive 10 comprehend

comprised: 4 rapt 8 included 9 engrossed 14 comprehensible

compromise: 8 compound, endanger 9 surrender 10 concession

opposition to: 13 intransigence

compt: 4 neat 6 spruce 8 polished

comptroller: 7 auditor, officer 10 controller

compulsion: 4 need, urge 5 force 6 duress, stress 7 impulse 8 coaction, coercion 10 constraint

compulsory: coercive, forcible 10 imperative, obligatory

compulsory service: 6 angary 7 angaria, slavery

compunction: 5 qualm 6 regret, sorrow 7 remorse, scruple 9 misgiving 10 conscience, contrition, repentance

compute: add, sum 4 cast, rate 5 count, tally 6 assess, figure, number, reckon 7 account 8 estimate 9 calculate, enumerate

computer: 6 univac 7 machine

algebraic language: 5 algol

correct: 5 debug

information: 4 data 5 input 6 output

inventor: 7 Babbage

plan for action: 7 program

program symbol: 5 block

symbol system: 4 code

worker: 9 programer 10 programmer

comrade: pal 4 ally, chum, mate, peer 5 billy, buddy, crony 6 copain(F.), digger, fellow, frater, friend, hearty 7 brother 8 copemate 9 associate, companion

comte: 5 count

comtesse: 8 countess

con: rap 4 anti, know, lead, look, pore, read, scan 5 cheat, guide, knock, learn, steer, study 6 direct, peruse, regard, versus 7 against, deceive, examine, inspect, opposed, swindle 10 understand

conation: 4 will 7 conatus 8 tendency, volition 11 inclination

conative state: 5 nisus

concatenate: 4 join, link 5 chain, unite 7 connect 8 catenate

concave: 4 void 6 arched, dished, hollow 7 vaulted 8 incurved 9 depressed

concavity: dip, pit 4 bowl, dent, hole 6 crater, hollow

conceal: 4 bury, hide, mask, sile, veil 5 cache, cloak, couch, cover, feign 6 closet, emboss, pocket, screen, shroud 7 secrete 8 bescreen, disguise, ensconce, withhold 9 dissemble 10 camouflage

goods: 5 cache, eloin 6 eloign

concealed: 4 dern(Sc.) 5 blind 6 covert, hidden, latent, occult, perdue, secret, veiled 7 covered, larvate 8 abstruse 9 blindfold, disguised, insidious, recondite, withdrawn 11 clandestine

concealing: 10 obvelation

concede: own 4 cede 5 admit, agree, allow, grant, waive, yette, yield 6 accord, assent 7 confess 9 surrender 10 condescend 11 acknowledge

conceit: ego 4 idea 5 fancy, pride 6 notion, vagary, vanity 7 caprice, egotism, tympany 9 arrogance, conundrum 10 conception

conceited: bug 4 fess, vain 5 chuff, cocky, flory, huggy, proud 6 clever 8 arrogant, dogmatic, priggish, snobbish 9 pragmatic, whimsical 11 coxcombical, egotistical, opinionated

conceive: 4 form, make, plan, ween 5 begin, brain, dream, fancy, frame, think 6 devise, ideate, ponder 7 imagine, realize, suppose, suspect 8 comprise, comprize, contrive 9 apprehend, formulate 10 comprehend, understand

concent: 9 harmonize 10 accordance 11 consistency

concentrate: aim, fix 4 mass, pile 5 coact, exalt, focus, unify 6 arrest, attend, center, gather 7 compact, essence, thicken 8 approach, assemble, condense, contract 9 intensify 10 centralize 11 consolidate 12 conglomerate

concentration: 7 extract 10 absorption 11 application

concentration camp: 6 prison, stalag

concept: 4 idea 5 fancy, image 7 opinion, thought 11 disposition

conception: ens 4 idea 5 fancy, fetus, image 6 belief, design, embryo 7 conceit, purpose 8 notation 9 beginning 10 cogitation, impression 12 apprehension 13 comprehension

concern: 4 bear, care, firm, reck, sake 5 apply, cause, event, grief, touch, worry 6 affair, affect, behold, charge, employ, matter, regard 7 anxiety, article, company, disturb, involve, pertain, respect, trouble 8 business, interest 9 implicate, rickmatic 10 solicitude 11 corporation, distinguish 12 apprehension

concerned: 6 intent 7 anxious, worried 8 bothered

concerning: by, of, on, re; for 4 in-re 5 about, anent 6 anenst 9 regarding

concert: 4 plan 5 unite 6 accord, devise 7 arrange, benefit, concent, concord, consort, consult, harmony, recital 9 agreement 11 performance 13 entertainment

concert hall: 5 odeon, odeum

concertina: 9 bandonion

concession: 4 boon 5 favor, grant, lease 6 assent, favour, gambit 7 cession 9 admission, privilege 10 compliance, compromise 12 acquiescence 13 condescension 15 acknowledgement

conch: 5 shell 6 cockle, mussel

conchie, conchy: 8 objector

Conchobor's wife: 4 Medb

concierge: 6 porter, warden 7 janitor 9 attendant 10 doorkeeper

conciliate: get 4 calm, ease 5 atone 6 adjust, pacify 7 acquire, appease, concile, mollify, placate, satisfy 9 reconcile 10 propitiate

conciliatory: 4 mild 6 gentle, giving, irenic 7 lenient, pacific, winning 8 irenical, lenitive 9 forgiving 10 mollifying 12 propitiating

concilium: 7 council

concinnity: 7 harmony 8 elegance

concise: 4 curt, neat 5 brief, crisp, pithy, short, terse 7 compact, laconic, pointed, precise, serried 8 mutilate, pregnant, succinct 9 condensed 10 compedious, contracted 11 sententious 12 epigrammatic 13 comprehensive

concision: 6 schism 7 faction 8 division 10 mutilation

conclave: 6 closet 7 chamber, meeting 8 assembly

conclude: bar, end 4 rest 5 close, estop, infer, judge, limit 6 clinch, deduce, figure, finish, gather, reason, settle 7 achieve, arrange, confine, embrace, enclose, resolve, suppose 8 complete, dispatch, graduate, restrain 9 determine, speculate, terminate 10 comprehend

conclusion: end 4 amen, coda, last 5 finis 6 finale, finish, period, result, upshot 7 finding, outcome 8 epilogue, judgment 9 diagnosis, inference 10 conjecture, settlement 11 probability, termination

conclusive: 4 last 5 final, valid 6 cogent 7 certain, extreme, telling 8 decisive, definite, ultimate 10 convincing, peremptory 11 irrefutable 12 unanswerable 13 determinative

concoct: mix 4 brew, cook, plan, plot, vamp 5 frame, hatch 6 decoct, devise, digest, invent, refine, scheme 7 compose, perfect, prepare 8 compound, intrigue 9 fabricate 10 assimilate

concomitant: 9 accessory, associate, attendant, attending, companion, conjoined, cooperant 10 coincident, concurrent 11 syn-

chronous 12 accompanying 13 accompaniment

concord: 4 part 5 agree, amity, peace, union, unity 6 treaty, unison 7 compact, concent, concert, harmony, oneness 8 covenant 9 agreement, communion, congruity 10 accordance, consonance

concordant: 8 unisonal 9 agreeable, congruous, consonant 10 harmonious 13 correspondent

concourse: 5 crowd, place, point 6 throng 7 company 8 assembly 9 affluence, frequency, gathering 10 assemblage, confluence 11 coincidence, concurrence, conjunction, cooperation

concredit: 6 commit 7 entrust, intrust

concrete: 4 clot, firm, hard, real 5 beton, solid, unite 6 actual 7 combine, congeal, special 8 coalesce. compound, tangible 9 concresce 10 particular

construction: 6 tremie 7 caisson

concretion: 4 clot, mess 5 pearl 6 nodule 8 calculus

concubine: 5 woman 7 adalisk 8 mistress 9 odalisque

concur: 4 jibe, join 5 agree, chime, unite 6 accede, accord, assent 7 approve, combine, consent 8 coincide, converge 9 acquiesce, cooperate 10 correspond

concurrence: 5 union 6 assent, bestow 7 consent, consort, meeting 8 adhesion 9 adherence, agreement, concourse 10 conspiracy 11 coincidence, conjunction

concurrent: 6 coeval, united 7 meeting 10 associated, coincident 11 concomitant, synchronous 12 accompanying

concuss: jar 4 jolt 5 clash, force, shake, shock 6 coerce 7 agitate

condalia: 9 chaparral

condemn: ban 4 damn, doom, file, fine 5 blame, decry, judge 6 amerce, attain, awreak, banish, detest 7 adjudge, censure, convict 8 denounce, reproach, sentence 10 confiscate, disapprove

condemnation: 4 doom 5 blame 7 censure, decrial 11 reprobation 13 animadversion 14 disapprobation

condense: cut 5 brief, unite 6 decoct, digest, harden, lessen, narrow, reduce, shrink 7 abridge, combine, compact, deflate, distill, shorten, thicken 8 compress, diminish, solidify 9 constrict, epitomize, evaporate, intensify 11 concentrate, consolidate

condensed: 4 curt 5 brief 7 compact, concise 8 absorbed 11 compendious

condenser: 4 cric 6 aludel

condescend: 5 deign, favor, grant, stoop 6 assent, oblige, submit 7 concede, descend 9 patronize, vouchsafe

condescension: 7 disdain 8 courtesy 10 affability, concession 12 complaisance

condign: due, fit 4 fair, just 6 severe, worthy 8 adequate, deserved, suitable 11 appropriate

condiment: rea 4 herb, kari, mace, sage, salt 5 caper, curry, sauce, spice, thyme 6 catsup, cloves, pepper, relish 7 chutney, cuminos, ketchup, mustard, paprika, vinegar 8 allspice, turmeric 9 appetizer, seasoning
container: 5 cruet
stand: 6 caster

condisciple: 7 student 12 schoolfellow

condite: 7 pickled 8 seasoned 9 preserved

condition: if 4 case, mode, rank, rote, term 5 angle, birth, cause, class, estre, facet, place, stage, state 6 estate, fettle, gentry, morale, plight, status 7 article, calling, premise, proviso, station 8 covenant, occasion, position 9 agreement, exception, provision, requisite, situation 10 limitation 11 predicament, stipulation 13 circumstances
comb. form: ate 4 ance, ancy, ence, ency 6 blasty
critical: 9 emergency
favorable: 4 odds
suffix: ile

conditional: 9 qualified 10 accidental

conditioned: 6 finite 7 limited

condolence: 4 pity, ruth 7 empathy 8 sympathy 10 compassion 13 commiseration

condone: 5 blink, remit 6 acquit, excuse, forget, ignore, pardon 7 absolve, forgive 8 overlook

condor: 4 coin 6 tiffin 7 vulture 8 gymnogyp

conduce: aid 4 help, hire, lead, tend 5 bring, guide 6 confer, effect, engage 7 advance, conduct, further, redound 10 contribute

conduct: act, run 4 bear, deed, gest, lead, mien, rule, wage 5 carry, geste, guard, guide, usher 6 action, attend, behave, convey, convoy, demean, deport, direct, escort, govern, manage, squire 7 bearing, channel, comport, conduce, conduit, control, execute, officer, operate 8 behavior, carriage, chaplain, demeanor, guidance, regulate, transact 9 accompany, behaviour, demeanour, supervise 10 administer, deportment, governance, government, proceeding 11 comportment, countenance, superintend
scandalous: 9 esclandre(F.)

conductor: 4 cad 4 gude 5 guard 6 convoy, copper, escort, leader 7 cathode, maestro 8 aqueduct, cicerone, conveyor, director, employee 10 bandleader, propagator 11 impressario

stick: 5 baton

conduit: 4 duct, main, pipe, tube, wire 5 cable, canal, sewer 6 trough 7 channel, conduct, culvert, passage 8 aqueduct

cone: 4 chat 5 crack, solid, spire 6 bobbin, object 7 cluster, fissure, strobil 8 strobile 9 container
section: 8 parabola

cone-shaped: 5 conic 6 pineal 7 conical

conenose: 6 bedbug

conepate: 5 skunk

coney: See **cony**

confab: 4 chat, talk 6 powwow 7 prattle 10 conference 11 confabulate 12 conversation

confect: mix 4 form, make 6 pickle 7 prepare 8 preserve 9 construct

confection: 5 candy, dulce, sweet 6 bonbon, comfit, cimbal, dainty, nougat 7 caramel, confect, fondant, mixture, praline, sherbet, succade 8 compound, delicacy, preserve, sherbert 9 confiture, marmalade, sweetmeat 10 concoction 11 bittersweet, compilation, composition, preparation

Confederacy: *banknote:* 8 blueback
general: Lee 5 Bragg, Price 6 Morgan 7 Jackson 10 Beauregard
guerilla: 11 bushwhacker
president: 5 Davis
soldier: reb
vice-president: 8 Stephens
victory: 7 Bull Run 11 Chickamauga 16 Chancellorsville

confederate: aid, pal, reb 4 ally 5 rebel, stall, unite 6 league 7 abetter, abettor, conjure, fedarie, federal, partner 8 conspire, federate 9 accessory, assistant, associate, auxiliary 10 accomplice

confederation: 4 body 5 union 6 league 7 compact, society 8 alliance, covenant 9 coalition 10 conspiracy, federation 11 association, confederacy

confer: dub 4 give, meet, talk 5 award, endow, grant, treat 6 advise, bestow, donate, impart, invest, parley 7 commune, compare, conduce, consult, counsel, discuss, instate, present 8 comprise, converge 10 contribute, deliberate

conference: 4 talk 5 synod, trust 6 confab, huddle, parley, pow-wow 7 council, meeting, palaver 8 colloque, colloquy, congress 9 collation, comparing, discourse, interview 10 comparison, discussion 11 association 12 consultation, conversation
technique: 13 brainstorming

confess: own 4 avow, sing 5 admit, grant 6 attest, avouch, beknow, reveal, shrive 7 concede, divulge 8 disclose, discover, manifest 11 acknowledge

confession: 5 credo, creed 6 avowal, shrift, shrive 9 admission, communion, statement 10 profession

confetti: 4 tape 5 candy 7 bonbons 9 sweetmeat 10 confection
container: 8 cascaron

confidant: 8 intimate

confide: 4 affy, rely, tell 5 trust 6 commit, depend 7 believe, consign, entrust, intrust

confidence: 4 hope 5 bield, faith, trust 6 aplomb, belief, credit, mettle, morale, secret, spirit 7 courage 8 affiance, boldness, credence, reliance, sureness 9 assurance, certitude, hardihood, hardiness 10 effrontery 11 presumption 12 impertinence
game: 5 bunco, bunko 7 swindle
lack: 10 diffidence

confident: 4 bold, smug, sure 5 hardy, siker 6 crouse, secure, sicker 7 assured, certain, hopeful, reliant 8 constant, fearless, impudent, sanguine, trustful 9 dependent, undaunted 10 dogmatical 11 trustworthy 12 presumptuous

confidential: 5 bosom, privy 6 covert, secret 7 private, subrosa 8 esoteric, intimate 9 auricular 11 trustworthy
law: 9 fiduciary

configuration: 4 form 5 shape 6 figure 7 contour, outline 10 topography

confine: bar, box, dam, hem, new, pen, pin, sty, tie 4 bind, cage, coop, hasp, jail, keep, lock, seal 5 bound, cramp, delay, impen, limit, pinch, stint 6 border, compas, corral, fetter, forbar, hamper, hurdle, immure, impale, intern, pinion, pocket, tether 7 astrict, impound 8 boundary, conclude, imprison, restrain, straiten 9 carcerate, constrain, restraint 11 incarcerate 12 circumscribe

confined: ill 4 pent 5 bound, caged 6 sealed 7 cramped, cribbed, limited 8 impended, interned 9 impounded 10 cloistered 13 incommunicado
to select group: 8 estoeric

confinement: mew 8 clausure, firmance 9 captivity, restraint 10 childbirth, constraint, internment 11 contraction 12 accouchement, imprisonment
place of: mew, pen 4 brig, cage, coop, goal, jail, stir 5 limbo 6 asylum, corral, prison 7 dungeon 9 calaboose 12 penitentiary

confirm: fix, set 4 firm, seal 5 prove 6 affirm, assent, assure, attest, avouch, clinch, ratify, settle, verify 7 approve, comfort, endorse, fortify, sustain 8 accredit, convince, sanction, validate 9 approbate, establish 10 comprobate, strengthen 11 corroborate, countersign 12 adminiculate, authenticate, substantiate

confirmed: set 5 fixed 6 arrant, stable 7 chronic 8 habitual, ratified 9 fortified, initiated 10 encouraged, inveterate 11 established

confiscate: 4 grab 5 seize, usurp 7 condemn 9 sequester 11 appropriate

conflagration: 4 fire 5 blaze, fever 7 burning 10 combustion 12 inflammation

conflict: war 4 bout, duel, fray, rift 5 broil, brush, clash, fight, grips, mix-up 6 action, battle, combat, mutiny, oppose, strife 7 contend, contest, discord, warfare 8 disagree, militate, struggle 9 collision, encounter, rebellion 10 contention 11 competition
final: 10 Armageddon

conflicting: 7 adverse 10 contending 12 incompatible, inharmonious

confluence: 5 crowd 7 conflux, meeting 8 junction 9 concourse 12 assimilation

conform: go; fit 4 lean, obey, suit 5 adapt, agree, apply, yield 6 accede, adjust, assent, comply, settle, submit 7 compose 9 acquiesce, harmonize, reconcile 10 correspond 11 accommodate

conformist: 6 pedant 7 babbitt 9 precisian 10 philistine 11 reactionary

conformity: 7 harmony 8 affinity, likeness, symmetry 9 agreement, congruity, obedience 10 accordance, compliance, similarity, submission 11 affirmative 12 acquiescence, complaisance
to law: 6 dharma 8 legality

confound: mix 4 blow, dash, maze, rout, stam, stun 5 abash, addle, amaze, spend, spoil, waste 6 baffle, dismay, muddle, rattle 7 astound, confuse, confute, corrupt, destroy, flummox, perplex, stupefy 8 astonish, bewilder, distract, surprise 9 discomfit, dumbfound, embarrass, frustrate, overthrow 10 disconcert 11 intermingle

confraternity: 4 body 5 union 7 society 11 brotherhood

confrere: 6 fellow 7 comrade 9 colleague

confront: 4 defy, face, meet 5 beard, brave 6 oppose, resist 7 affront, compare 8 envisage, threaten 9 challenge, encounter

confuse: mix 4 dash, daze, maze, muss, rout 5 abash, addle, amaze, befog, blend, cloud, snarl 6 baffle, bemuse, bother, burble, caddle, flurry, fuddle, jumble, muddle, puzzle, rattle 7 bedevil, blunder, derange, fluster, mystify, nonplus, perplex, stupefy 8 befuddle, bewilder, confound, distract 9 barbulyie, discomfit, dumbfound, obfuscate 10 demoralize, disarrange, discompose, disconcert

confused: 4 asea, lost 5 foggy, muddy, vague 6 doiled, doited 7 chaotic, obscure 8 deranged 9 chagrined 10 bewildered, hurly-burly, topsy-turvy, tumultuous 13 helter-skelter

confusion: din 4 coil, dust, fuss, harl, mess, moil, riot 5 babel, chaos, chevy, chivy, deray, mix-up, snafu, snarl, strow 6 babble, bedlam, caddle, chivvy, habble, hubbub, huddle, jabble, jumble, muddle, pother, rabble, rumpus, tophet, tumult, uproar, welter 7 farrage, blunder, bluster, clutter, farrage, flutter, garboil, topheth, turmoil, widdrim 8 disarray, disorder 9 agitation, commotion 10 hullabaloo, hurly-burly 11 disturbance, trepidation 12 hugger-mugger, perturbation 13 embarrassment

confute: 4 deny 5 rebut 6 expose, refute 7 silence 8 confound, convince, disprove, infringe, overcome 9 overwhelm

conge: bow 6 curtsy 7 license, molding 8 farewell, passport 9 clearance, dismissal 10 permission 11 leavetaking

congeal: gel, ice, set 4 geal, jell 5 candy 6 cotter, curdle, freeze, harden 7 stiffen, thicken 8 concrete, solidify 9 coagulate 11 crystallize

congealing agent: 6 pectin 8 gelatine

congee: 5 gruel 9 departure

congener: 4 kind, race 5 class, genus

congenial: 4 boon 5 natal 6 native 7 connate, kindred 10 compatible 11 sympathetic

conger: eel 8 cucumber

congeries: 4 mass 5 group 10 collection

congestion: jam 4 heap 8 crowding, stoppage 9 gathering 12 accumulation

conglaciate: 6 freeze 7 congeal

conglobation: 4 ball

conglomerate: 4 heap, mass, pile, rock 5 stack 9 clustered 10 assemblage 11 agglomerate 12 concentrated

Congo (see also Zaire): tribe: 4 Susa 6 Wabuma 7 Bangala
tributary: 4 Uele 6 Ubangi 7 Aruwima
congou: tea

congratulate: 4 laud 5 greet 6 salute 8 macarize 10 compliment, felicitate

congregate: 4 herd, mass, meet, teem 5 group, swarm, troop 6 gather, muster 7 collect, convene 8 assemble

congregation: 4 body, fold, host, mass 5 flock, swarm 6 church, parish 7 meeting, synaxes 8 assembly, brethren 9 gathering 10 collection 11 convocation

congress: 4 dail, diet 5 synod 7 council, meeting 8 assembly, conclave 10 conference, convention, parliament 11 convocation, legislature

Congress: building: 7 Capitol
member: 7 senator

upper house: 6 Senate

congressman: 14 representative

congruity: 6 accord 7 concord, fitness, harmony 8 symmetry 9 agreement, coherence 10 conformity, consonance 11 composition, consistency, correctness, suitability 13 compatability 14 correspondence

conical: 8 tapering

conifer: fir, yew 4 pine, tree 5 cedar, larch 6 spruce 7 pinacle, pinales

conium: 7 hemlock

conjecture: aim 4 plot, shot, view 5 augur, ettle, fancy, guess, opine 6 belief, divine, theory 7 imagine, opinion, presume, suppose, surmise, suspect 9 inference, speculate, suspicion 10 conclusion, estimation 11 contrivance, supposition

conjoined: 6 joined, linked 8 conjunct, touching 11 concomitant

conjoint: 8 combined 9 conjoined 10 associated 11 correlative 12 simultaneous

conjugal: 9 connubial 11 matrimonial

conjugate: 5 yoked 6 joined, united 7 coupled

conjunction: as, et, if, or; and, but, nor, tie 4 than 5 joint, since, union 7 coition, consort 9 coalition, concourse 10 connection 11 association, combination, composition, concurrence

conjuration: art 5 charm, magic, spell 6 voodoo 10 necromancy 11 incantation, legerdemain

conjure: 4 pray 5 charm, halse 6 adjure, invent, invoke 7 beseech, combine, entreat, imagine 8 conspire, contrive, exorcise, exorcize 10 supplicate 11 confederate

conjuror: 4 mage, sear 6 pellar, shaman, wizard 7 juggler, warlock 8 magician, sorcerer 9 coswearer, enchanter 15 prestidigatator

conk: 4 fail, head, nose 5 faint, knock, stall

Conlaech: father: 10 Cuchulainn
mother: 5 Aoife

connach: 5 spoil, waste

Connacht king: 6 Ailill

connate: 4 akin, born 5 fused 6 allied, inborn, innate 7 cognate 9 congenial 10 congenital

connect: tie 4 ally, bind, glue, join, knit, link 5 affix, chain, marry, unite 6 attach, bridge, cement, cohere, connex, couple, fasten, relate 7 combine 8 continue 9 affiliate, associate, correlate, interlock 11 communicate

Connecticut: city: 4 Avon 6 Bethel, Darien 7 Meriden 8 Hartford(c.)
river: 10 Housatonic

connection: tie 4 bond, link 5 nexus, union 6 family 7 contact, kinship 8 affinity, alliance, commerce, intimacy, junction, relative, syndetic **9** coherence, reference, relevance **10** continuity **11** association, conjunction, intercourse **12** articulation, relationship **13** communication

connective: 8 syndetic **11** conjunction

connective tissue: 6 fascia

conniption fit: 7 tantrum

connive: 4 abet, plot, wink **5** blink, cabal **6** assent, foment, incite **7** collude **8** intrigue, overlook

connoisseur: 5 judge **6** critic, expert **7** epicure, gourmet **8** gourmand **9** collector **11** cognoscente

connotation: 6 intent **7** meaning **10** denotation **13** comprehension, signification

connote: 5 imply **8** indicate

connubial: 7 marital **8** conjugal, domestic **11** matrimonial

conquer: get, win **4** beat, best, down, gain, lick, rout, tame **5** crush, daunt **6** defeat, evince, humble, master, reduce, subdue, victor **7** acquire, prevail, subject, triumph **8** overcome, surmount, vanquish **9** checkmate, discomfit, overpower, overthrow, overwhelm, subjugate

conqueror: 4 hero **6** victor, winner **12** conquistador

conquest: 7 mastery, triumph, victory **8** invasion

conquistador: 6 Cortez

consanguineous: 4 akin **7** kindred, related

consanguinity: 5 blood, nasab **7** kinship **8** affinity **12** relationship

conscience: 5 grace, inwit, qualm. sense **6** erinys, psyche, virtue **7** monitor, probity, scruple, thought **9** casuistry, punctilio **11** compunction

conscientious: 4 fair, just **5** exact, rigid **6** honest, strict **7** dutiful, upright **8** faithful **9** honorable **10** scrupulous **11** punctilious

conscious: 4 keen **5** alive, awake, aware **7** feeling, knowing **8** rational, sensible, sentient **9** attentive, cognizant, concerned **10** perceptive **12** apprehensive

consciousness: 9 awareness

loss of: **4** coma **5** faint **8** apoplexy

consciousness-altering: 11 psychedelic

conscript: 5 draft, enrol **6** enlist, muster **7** recruit

consecrate: vow **4** fain, seal **5** bless, deify, devot **6** anoint, hallow, ordain **8** sanctify, dedicate **10** inaugurate **11** apotheosize

consecrated: 5 blest **6** oblate, sacred, votive **8** hallowed

cloth: **11** antimension

oil: **6** chrism

thing: **6** sacrum

consent: 5 agree, allow, grant, yield **6** accede, accord, assent, beteem, comply, permit **7** approve **9** recognize **10** permission **11** concurrence **12** acquiescence

consequence: end **4** bore **5** event, fruit, issue, worth **6** effect, import, moment, repute, result, sequel, weight **7** concern, outcome **8** aftering, interest, occasion **9** aftermath, emanation, inference **10** importance **11** consecution **13** consideration

consequently: so **4** ergo, then, thus **5** hence, later **8** pursuant **9** therefore **11** accordingly **12** subsequently **13** consecutively

conservative: 4 safe, Tory **5** staid **6** stable **7** diehard **8** moderate **9** bourgeois **11** reactionary **12** preservative

conservatory: 6 school **7** academy **10** glasshouse, greenhouse

conserve: can, jam **4** save **5** guard, jelly **6** defend, secure, shield, uphold **7** husband, protect, sustain **8** maintain, preserve **9** sweetmeat

consider: see **4** deem, heed, mull, muse, rate **5** ettle, judge, study, think, weigh **6** behold, debate, expend, impute, ponder, reason, reckon, regard **7** account, believe, canvass, examine, inspect, reflect, suppose **8** cogitate, estimate, meditate, ruminate **9** calculate, entertain, speculate **10** adjudicate, deliberate **11** contemplate

considerable: 5 geyan(Sc.), large, smart, smert **7** notable, several **9** capacious, important **10** cognizable, noteworthy, remarkable **11** perceptible, significant

considerate: 4 kind, mild **6** gentle **7** careful, heedful, prudent, serious **8** delicate **9** observant, regardful **10** deliberate, reflective, respectful, thoughtful

consideration: 4 sake **5** price, topic **6** aspect, esteem, motive, notice, reason, regard **7** respect, thought **9** attention, deference, incentive, influence **10** importance, inducement, recompense, reputation **11** consequence

considering: if 5 since

consign: 4 doom, give, mail, send, ship **5** allot, award, dight, remit, shift, yield **6** assign, commit, devote, remand, resign **7** address, confide, deliver, deposit, entrust, intrust **8** delegate, relegate, transfer **9** recommend **10** commission

consignee: 5 agent **8** receiver

consist: lie **4** hold **5** exist, stand **6** inhere, reside **7** contain, embrace **8** comprise **9** harmonize

consistency: 4 body **5** union **6** degree **7** concord, harmony **8** firmness, solidity, symmetry **9** adherence, coherence, congruity

10 consonance, uniformity 11 composition, persistency 14 correspondence, substantiality

consistent: 4 firm 7 durable, logical, uniform 8 coherent, enduring, suitable 9 accordant, congruous, consonant 10 changeless, compatible, persisting

consociate: 9 associate 11 confederate

consolation: sop 4 fine 6 relief, solace 7 comfort 10 booby prize

console: 4 calm 5 allay, ancon, cheer, organ, table 6 solace, soothe 7 bracket, cabinet, comfort, relieve, support, sustain 9 alleviate, encourage

consolidate: mix 4 knit, mass, pool, weld 5 blend, merge, unify, unite 6 harden, mingle 7 combine, compact 8 coalesce, compress, condense, organize, solidify 10 amalgamate, strengthen 11 concentrate

consomme: 4 soup

consonance: 6 accord 7 harmony 9 resonance

consonant: 5 linis 6 dental, fortis, letter, sonant 7 palatal, spirant, unified 8 harmonic, suitable 9 accordant, agreeable, congruous 10 coincident, compatible, concordant, consistent, harmonious
hard: 6 fortis
hissing: 8 sibilant
pert. to: 7 palatal 9 fricative
smooth: 4 lene 5 lenis
voiceless: 4 lene, surd 6 atonic 7 spirate

consort: cot 4 aide, ally, join, mate, wife 5 group, unite 6 accord, attend, escort, mingle, spouse 7 company, concert, husband, partner 8 accustom, assembly 9 accompany, associate, colleague, companion, forgather 10 foregather 11 association, combination, concurrence, conjunction

consortium: 5 group 8 alliance

conspectus: 4 list 6 survey 7 outline 8 synopsis 11 abridgement

conspicuous: 5 clear, famed, plain 6 extant, famous, marked, patent, signal 7 eminent, glaring, notable, obvious, pointed, salient, visible 8 apparent, manifest, striking 9 egregious, prominent 10 celebrated, noticeable 11 discernable, distinctive, illustrious, outstanding, perspicuous 13 distinguished

conspiracy: 4 coup, plan, plot, ring 5 cabal, junto 6 scheme 7 compace 8 intrigue 9 agreement, champerty 11 combination, concurrence, confederacy, machination

conspire: 4 abet, plot 5 unite 6 league, scheme 7 collude, complot, conjure 8 contrive 9 cooperate 11 confederate

constable: cop 4 bull 6 beadle, harman, keeper, warden 7 bailiff, officer 8 tipstaff 9 policeman

constancy: 4 zeal 5 ardor 6 fealty 7 loyalty 8 devotion, fidelity 9 adherence, diligence, eagerness, integrity, stability 10 allegiance, attachment 11 earnestness 12 perseverance
symbol of: 6 garnet

constant: set 4 even, firm, leal, true 5 fixed, loyal, solid, still, tried 6 stable, steady 7 certain, chronic, durable, forever, lasting, regular, staunch, uniform 8 enduring, faithful, positive, resolute 9 confident, continual, immovable, incessant, permanent, perpetual, steadfast, unvarying 10 invariable, persistent, unwavering

Constantine: *birthplace:* 4 Nish
mother: 6 Helena
wife: 6 Fausta

Constantinople: See Istanbul

constate: 6 assert 9 establish

constellation (see also **star**): 5 group 6 dipper 7 cluster, pattern 10 assemblage 13 configuration
altar: Ara
archer: 11 Sagittarius
Argo division: 4 Vela
arrow: 7 Sagitta
balance: 5 Libra
bear: 4 Ursa
bird of paradise: 5 Apus
bull: 6 Taurus
Champion: 7 Perseus
charioteer: 6 Auriga
Charles' Wain: 6 Dipper
clock: 10 Horologium
compass: 5 Pyxis 8 Circinus
crab: 6 Cancer
crane: 4 Grus
cross: 4 Cruz
crow: 6 Corvus
crown: 6 Corona
dipper: 4 Ursa
dog: 5 Canis
dolphin: 9 Delphinus
dove: 7 Columba
dragon: 5 Draco
eagle: 6 Aquila
fish: 6 Pisces
goat: 9 Capricorn
herdsman: 6 Bootes
hunter: 5 Orion
lady, chained: 9 Andromeda
lady in the chair: 10 Cassiopeia
lion: Leo
lyre: 4 Lyra
maiden: 5 Virgo
northern: Leo 4 Coma, Lynx, Lyra, Ursa 5 Aries, Canes, Draco 6 Aquila, Auriga.

Bootes, Cancer, Cygnus, Gemini, Taurus 7 Cepheus, Lacerta, Pegasus, Sagitta 8 Hercules 9 Andromeda, Delphinus, Vulpecula 10 Cassiopeia

peacock: 4 Pavo

rabbit: 5 Lepus

ram: 5 Aries

sails: 4 Vela

southern: Ara 4 Apus, Argo, Crux, Grus, Pavo, Vela 5 Canis, Cetus, Hydra, Indus, Lepus, Libra, Mensa, Musca, Norma, Virgo 6 Antlia, Carina, Corvus, Crater, Dorado, Fornax, Pictor, Pisces, Puppis, Tucana, Volans 7 Columba, Phoenix, Sextans 8 Aquarius, Circinus, Sculptor, Scorpius 9 Centaurus, Chameleon, Monoceros, Reticulum 10 Horologium 11 Capricornus, Sagittarius 12 Microscopium

stern: 6 Puppis

swan: 6 Cygnus

twins: 6 Gemini

water bearer: 8 Aquarius

whale: 5 Cetus

winged horse: 7 Pegasus

wolf: 5 Lupus

consternation: 4 fear 5 alarm, panic 7 dismay, fright, horror, terror 9 amazement, trepidity 11 trepidation 12 befuddlement

constituent: 4 item, part 5 piece, voter 6 detail, factor, matter, member 7 elector, element 9 component 10 ingredient

constitute: fix, set 4 form, make 5 enact, forge, found, shape 6 depute, graith, ordain 7 appoint, compose, station 8 compound, comprise 9 determine, establish 10 commission

constitution: law 4 code 5 being, canon, humor, state 6 custom, health, nature, temper 7 charter 8 physique 9 enactment, ordinance, structure 11 composition, disposition 12 organization

Constitution: 9 Ironsides

Constitution State: 11 Connecticut

constitutional: 4 walk 6 innate 8 exercise 9 essential, organical 10 congenital

constrain: 4 bend, bind, curb, fain, urge 5 chain, check, clasp, cramp, deter, drive, force, impel, limit, press 6 coerce, compel, oblige, ravish, secure 7 astrict, confine, enforce, oppress, repress, violate 8 compress, distress, restrain 9 constrict 10 constringe 11 necessitate

constraint: 4 bond 5 force 6 duress, stress 7 reserve 8 coercion, distress, pressure 9 captivity, restraint, stiffness 10 compulsion, obligation 11 compression, confinement

constrict: tie 4 bind, curb, grip 5 choke, cramp, limit 6 hamper, shrink, strait 7 astrict, deflate, squeeze, tighten 8

astringe, compress, condense, contract, restrict 9 constrain 10 constipate, constringe

breath: 8 strangle

constrictor: boa 5 snake 6 python 8 anaconda 9 sphincter

constringe: See **constrict**

construct: 4 form, make, rear 5 build, dight, erect, frame, model 6 devise 7 arrange, combine, compose, confect, fashion 8 construe, engineer 9 fabricate, originate

construction: 7 synesis 8 building

constructive: 7 helpful 8 creative, implicit, inferred

construe: 5 infer, parse 6 render 7 analyze, dissect, explain, expound, resolve 9 construct, interpret, translate

consuetude: use 4 wont 5 habit, usage 6 custom 8 practice

consuetudinary: 6 manual, ritual

consul's recognition: 9 exequatur

consult: ask 5 cabal, refer 6 advise, confer, decree, devise 7 concert, counsel, discuss, meeting 8 consider, contrive, decision 9 agreement, determine 10 deliberate

consultant: 6 expert 7 adviser

consultation: 6 advice 7 council, counsel 9 collation, interview 10 conference, discussion 12 deliberation

consume: eat, use 4 burn, fret, rust, wear 5 drink, raven, spend, waste 6 absorb, absume, bezzle, canker, devour, engage, expend, perish 7 corrode, destroy, dwindle, engross, exhaust, swallow 8 squander 9 dissipate 10 incinerate, monopolize

consumer: 4 usee, user

consummate: end 4 fine, full, ripe 5 ideal, sheer 6 arrant, effect, finish 7 achieve, consume, crowned, perfect, perform 8 absolute, complete 9 culminate, exquisite 10 accomplish

consumption: use 5 decay, waste 7 expense 8 phthisis 11 destruction, expenditure 12 tuberculosis

contact: 4 abut, join, meet 5 touch, union 6 arrive, impact, syzyzy 7 meeting 8 junction, tangency, touching 10 connection, contiguity 11 contingency 13 juxtaposition

contagion: pox 5 taint, virus 6 miasma, poison 9 infection 13 contamination

preventative: 4 shot 8 antidote 10 alexiteric 11 prophylaxis

contagious: 7 noxious 8 catching 9 pestilent, spreading 10 infectuous

contain: 4 have, hold, keep 5 carry, check, cover, house 6 embody, retain 7 embrace, enclose, include, subsume, sustain 8 comprise, restrain 10 comprehend

container: bag, bin, box, can, cup, jug, keg, pan, pod, pot, tin, tub, urn, vat 4 cage, case, cask, crib, ewer, sack, silo, tank, vase 5 crate, cruet, gourd, pouch 6 barrel, basket, bottle, carboy, carton, hamper, hatbox, holder, shaker 7 bandbox, capsule, hanaper 8 canister, decanter, demijohn, hogshead, puncheon 10 receptacle

containing: For all phrases beginning with this word, see under the main word or phrase. EXAMPLES: "containing gold": see **gold** *containing;* "containing air": see **air** *containing.*

contaminate: 4 foul, harm, slur, soil 5 stain, sully, taint 6 befoul, debase, defile, infect, injure, poison 7 corrupt, debauch, pollute, tarnish, vitiate 8 dishonor 9 desecrate 10 adulterate

conte: 4 tale 9 narrative, novelette

contemn: 4 hate 5 flout, scorn, spurn 6 reject, slight 7 despise, disdain 8 contempt

contemplate: 4 muse, plan, scan, view 5 deign, study, think, weigh 6 ponder, regard, survey 7 propose, reflect 8 consider, meditate 9 speculate

contemplation: 5 study 6 musing, prayer, regard, theory 7 request 8 petition 9 intention 10 meditation 13 consideration

contemporaneous: 6 coeval, living, modern 7 current 8 existing, up-to-date 10 coincident 12 contemporary, simultaneous

contemporary: 6 coeval 7 current
comb. form: neo

contempt: 5 scorn, shame, sneer 6 slight 7 contemn, disdain, mockery 8 derision, disgrace 9 contumacy, contumely 10 disrespect 11 indignation
exclamation of: bah, foh 4 pooh

contemptible: low 4 base, mean, vile 5 cheap, petty, sorry 6 abject, paltry, scurvy, shabby, sordid, yellow 7 pitiful, scorned 8 beggarly, infamous, inferior, sneaking, unworthy, wretched 9 groveling, worthless 10 despicable 11 ignominious 12 dishonorable 13 insignificant

contemptuous: 7 haughty 8 arrogant, flouting, insolent, scornful 9 hubristic, insulting 10 despicable, disdainful 12 contemptible, supercilious

contend: vie, war 4 cope, race, wage 5 argue, bandy, brawl, claim, fight 6 assert, battle, bicker, buffet, bustle, combat, debate, oppose, reason, strive 7 bargain, compete, contest, dispute, quarrel 8 conflict, contrive, maintain, militate, squabble, struggle

contender: 7 entrant 10 contestant 11 protagonist

content: 4 calm, ease, gist, paid 5 happy 6 amount, please 7 appease, gratify, replete,

satiate, satisfy, suffice, willing 8 capacity 9 satisfied 12 satisfaction

contented: 4 cozy 5 sated 8 cheerful 9 satisfied

contention: war 4 bait, bate, feud, riot, tiff 5 broil 6 combat, debate, strife 7 contest, discord, dispute, opinion, quarrel, rivalry, wrangle 8 argument, conflict, squabble, struggle, variance 9 rebellion 10 dissension, litigation 11 altercation, competition, controversy 12 disagreement

contentious: 7 peevish 8 perverse 9 litigious, wrangling 10 pugnacious 11 belligerent, quarrelsome 12 cantankerous, disputatious

contentment: 4 ease 5 bliss 8 pleasure 9 happiness 11 complacence 12 satisfaction 13 gratification

conterminous: 4 next 8 adjacent, proximal 9 adjoining

contest: bee, sue, try, vie 4 agon, bout, cope, duel, feud, fray, game, pitt, race, spar, tiff, tilt 5 broil, clash, fight, setto, trial 6 action, adjure, affray, battle, combat, debate, defend, oppose, resist, strife, strive 7 bargain, brabble, compete, contend, dispute, protest, tourney, warfare 8 argument, conflict, skirmish, struggle 9 champerty, encounter 10 controvert, tournament 11 altercation
kind of: 6 tryout 7 lawsuit 10 litigation

contestant: 4 vier 5 rival 6 player 7 agonist, entrant 8 finalist, prospect 9 combatant, candidate, contender, defendant, plaintiff 10 competitor 12 participator

contiguous: 4 next, nigh 6 nearby 8 abutting, adjacent, touching 9 adjoining, immediate, proximate 10 contacting 11 neighboring

continence: 6 virtue 8 chastity

continent: 4 Asia, land, mass 5 sober 6 Africa, chaste, Europe 7 content 8 capacity, mainland, moderate 9 Greenland, temperate 10 Antarctica, receptacle, restrained 12 South America
hypothetical: 8 Cascadia
lost: 8 Atlantis

contingency: 4 case 5 event 6 chance 7 adjunct, contact 8 fortuity, incident, prospect 9 accessory 11 possibility, uncertainty

contingent: 6 casual, chance 8 doubtful, touching 9 dependent 10 accidental, fortuitous 11 provisional
on discretion: 9 arbitrary

continual: 7 endless, lasting, regular, undying, uniform 8 constant, enduring, unbroken 9 ceaseless, connected, incessant, perennial, permanent, unceasing 10 continuous, invariable 11 everlasting, unremitting **12** imperishable **13** unintermitted, uninterrupted

continually: aye **4** ever **6** always, hourly, steady **7** endless, eternal, forever **9** perpetual **10** constantly **11** incessantly, unceasingly

continuance: 4 stay **5** delay **6** sequel **8** duration **9** endurance, procedure **10** continuity **11** adjournment **12** postponement, perseverance

continue: be **4** bide, dure, last, live, stay **5** abide, carry, exist, unite **6** beleve, endure, extend, remain, resume **7** beleave, connect, persist, proceed, prolong, sustain **8** protract **9** persevere

continued: 5 still **6** serial **7** chronic **8** constant **9** continual, extending **10** continuous, protracted

continuity: 6 script **8** cohesion, scenario **9** coherence **10** connection

contort: wry **4** bend, coil, turn, warp **5** gnarl, screw, twist, wrest **6** deform, writhe **7** distort, pervert **8** obvolute **9** convolute

contortionist: 7 acrobat

contour: 4 form, line **5** curve, graph, shape **6** figure **7** outline, profile **9** lineament **10** appearance, silhouette **13** configuration

outline: **13** configuration

contra: 6 offset **7** against, counter, opposed **11** contrasting **12** contrariwise

contraband: 5 goods **7** illegal, illicit **8** smuggled, unlawful

contract: get **4** bond, knit, pact **5** catch, cramp, incur, lease, limit **6** cartel, engage, lessen, narrow, pledge, pucker, reduce, shrink, treaty **7** abridge, bargain, compact, crumple, curtail, promise, shorten, shrivel, wrinkle **8** condense, covenant, restrict **9** agreement, betrothal, constrict, indenture **10** abbreviate, constringe, convention, obligation **11** arrangement, concentrate, stipulation

addition to: **5** rider **7** codicil

furnishing slaves: **8** assiento

part: **6** clause **7** proviso

unlawful: **10** chevisance

contraction: tic **5** cramp, spasm **6** intake, twitch **7** elision, epitome **9** gathering, reduction, shrinkage, stricture **10** abridgment, compendium, limitation **11** conciseness, confinement **12** abbreviation

common: een, eer, oer, oft, tis **5** arent, shant

heart: **8** systolic

contractor: 7 builder, remover **8** supplier

contradict: 4 deny **5** belie, rebut **6** forbid, impugn, negate, oppose, recant, refute **7** counter, gainsay **8** disprove **9** disaffirm **10** contravene, controvert

contradiction: 6 denial **7** paradox **8** antilogy

contradictory: 6 oppose **9** dissonant **12** incompatible, inconsistent

contraption: rig **4** tool **6** device, gadget **7** machine **11** contrivance

contrary: 5 snivy **6** averse, contra, ornery, snivey **7** adverse, counter, hostile, opposed, reverse, wayward **8** captious, contrair, inimical, opposite, perverse, petulant **9** refactory, repugnant, unpopular, vexatious **10** discordant, discrepant **11** prejudicial, unfavorable **12** antagrepant, cantankerous

to fact: **5** false

to law: **7** illegal **16** unconstitutional

to reason: **6** absurd

contrast: 6 strife **7** compare, contend **8** opposite **9** diversity **10** difference

contravene: 4 defy, deny **6** hinder, oppose, thwart **7** dispute, violate **8** infringe, obstruct **9** disregard **10** contradict

contravention: sin **4** vice **5** crime **6** breach **7** offense **9** violation **13** contradiction, transgression

contretemps: 4 slip **5** boner, hitch **6** mishap, scrape **8** accident **9** mischance **10** occurrence

music: **11** syncopation

contribute: aid **4** ante, give, help, tend **5** cause, grout **6** assist, bestow, concur, confer, donate, supply, tender **7** conduce, further **9** cooperate, subscribe

contribution: sum, tax **4** alms, boon, gift **5** essay, share **6** impost **7** article, largess, payment, present, renewal, writing **8** donation, offering **9** collation **10** imposition

contrite: 4 worn **5** sorry **6** humble, rueful **8** penitent **9** repentant, sorrowful

contrition: 7 penance, remorse

contrivance: art, gin **4** gear, plan, tool **5** shift **6** deceit, design, device, gadget, scheme **7** fiction, machine, project **8** adaption, artifice, resource **9** apparatus, appliance, doohickey, invention **10** conjecture, instrument **11** contraption

contrive: 4 brew, make, plan, plot **5** frame, fudge, hatch, weave **6** afford, design, devise, divine, invent, manage, scheme, wangle **7** achieve, agitate, concoct, consult, contend, fashion, procure, project **8** conspire, engineer, intrigue **9** fabricate, machinate **10** accomplish

contrived: pat **10** artificial

contriver: 8 Daedalus **9** architect **10** originator

control: law, run **4** curb, hold, rein, rule, sway **5** charm, check, grasp, gripe, guide, power, skill, steer **6** bridle, direct, empire, govern, handle, manage, regime, subdue **7**

command, conduct, mastery, preside 8 attemper, dominate, dominion, hegemony, regulate, restrain 9 influence, ordinance, prescribe 10 ascendancy, manipulate, moderation, possession, regulation 11 predominate, superintend

controversial: 7 eristic 9 debatable, polemical 12 disputatious 13 argumentative

controversy: 4 spat, suit 5 chest 6 debate, strife 7 dispute, quarrel, wrangle 8 argument 10 contention, difference, difficulty, discussion, litigation 11 altercation 12 disagreement

controvert: 4 deny, face, moot 5 argue 6 debate, oppose, oppugn, refute 7 contest, dispute, gainsay 9 challenge 10 contradict

contumacious: 6 unruly 7 riotous 8 insolent, mutinous, perverse, stubborn 9 obstinate, seditious 10 disdainful, headstrong, rebellious, refractory, unyielding 11 disobedient, intractable 13 insubordinate

contumelious: 8 arrogant

contumely: 5 abuse, scorn 6 contek, insult 7 conteck, disdain 8 contempt, rudeness 9 arrogance 10 opprobrium 11 humiliation

contuse: 4 beat 5 pound 6 bruise, injure 7 squeeze

contusion: 4 blow, bump 6 bruise

conundrum: pun 4 whim 6 enigma, puzzle, riddle 7 conceit 8 crotchet

convalesce: 4 mend 7 recover 10 recuperate

convene: sit 4 call, meet 5 unite 6 gather, muster, summon 7 convoke 8 assemble, converge 10 congregate, foregather

convenience: 7 benefit, comfort 8 plumbing 9 appliance

convenient: fit 5 handy, ready 6 proper, useful 7 adapted, helpful 8 becoming, suitable 9 agreeable, available, congruous, favorable, opportune 10 accessible, commodious 11 appropriate 12 commensurate

convent: 5 abbey 6 priory 7 convent, meeting 8 cloister 9 community, monastery, sanctuary

head: 5 abbot 6 abbess 8 hegumene 10 hegumeness

member: nun 4 monk 8 cenobite

pert. to: 6 friary

reception room: 8 arlatory

room: 9 parlatory

superior: see *head* above

convention: 4 diet, feis, mise, rule 5 synod, usage 6 cartel, caucus, custom, treaty 7 decorum, meeting 8 assembly, congress, contract, covenant, practice 9 agreement, gathering, tradition 10 conference 11 convocation

conventional: 4 more 5 nomic, right, trite, usual 6 decent, formal, modish, proper 7 correct, regular 8 academic, accepted 9 customary, hidebound 10 ceremonial, stipulated 11 contractual

conventionalize: 7 conform, stylize

converge: 4 join, meet 5 focus 6 concur 8 approach

conversant: 5 adept 6 busied, expert, versed 7 skilled 8 familiar, occupied 9 concerned, practiced 10 acquainted, proficient

conversation: 4 chat, talk 6 confab, parley 7 conduct, palaver 8 behavior, chitchat, colloquy, dialogue, parlance 9 discourse 10 conference 11 association, interchange, intercourse 13 communication, interlocution

of three: 7 trialog 9 trialogue

private: 7 ceilidh(Sc.) 8 collogue 9 tete-a-tete

converse: 4 chat, chin, live, move, talk 5 dwell, speak 6 confer, homily, parley 7 commune, obverse, reverse 8 colloque, exchange, opposite 9 discourse 11 association, confabulate

convert: 4 turn 5 alter, amend, apply, renew 6 change, decode, direct, novice 7 restore, reverse 8 converse, neophyte, persuade 9 acetalize, proselyte, transform, translate, transmute, transpose 10 regenerate

convertible: 4 auto 7 soft-top 10 automobile, changeable, equivalent, reciprocal, synonymous 15 interchangeable

convex: 5 bowed 6 arched, camber, curved 7 bulging, gibbous, rounded 9 cymbiform 11 protuberant

molding: 5 ovolo, torus

convey: 4 bear, cart, cede, deed, lead, mean, pass, send, take, tote, will 5 bring, carry, grant, guide, hurry, steal 6 assign, convoy, delate, demise, devise, eloign, impart, import, remove 7 auction, conduct, deliver, dispone, dispose 8 alienate, bequeath, transfer, transmit 9 accompany, transport 11 communicate

conveyance: bus, car, sak 4 auto, cart, deed, sled, taxi, tram 5 grant, stage, theft, train, wagon 6 demise 7 charter, conduct, rattler, trailer, trolley, vecture, vehicle, waftage 8 carriage, carrying, stealing, transfer 9 transport 10 automobile 11 transmittal

public: el; bus, cab, car 4 taxi, tram 5 train 6 subway 7 omnibus, ricksha, steamer 8 airplane, elevated, railroad, rickshaw 10 jinricksha, jinrikisha

convict: 4 find 5 argue, felon, lifer, prove 6 attain, termer, trusty 7 attaint, captive, condemn, culprit 8 criminal, jailbird, prisoner, sentence 10 malefactor

collar: 6 carcan

conviction: 5 creed, dogma, faith, tenet 6 belief, credit 7 opinion 8 sentence

convinced: 4 sold, sure 6 assure, subdue 7 certain 8 overcome, positive 9 persuaded

convincing: 5 sound, valid 6 cogent, potent 7 telling 8 forcible 10 conclusive, persuasive

convivial: gay 4 boon 6 festal, genial, jovial, social 7 festive, jocular 8 reveling

convocation: 4 diet 5 synod 7 calling, council, meeting 8 assembly, congress 9 gathering 10 convention 12 congregation

convoke: bid 4 call, cite, meet 6 gather, muster, summon 7 convene 8 assemble

convolute: 4 coil, roll, wind 5 twist 6 tangle, writhe 7 contort 8 obvolute

convolution: 4 coil, curl, fold 5 gyrus, whorl 9 sinuosity

of brain: 5 gyrus

convolve: 5 twist 6 enwrap, enfold, infold, writhe

convolvulus: 4 vine

convoy: 4 lead 5 carry, guard, guide, pilot, watch 6 attend, convey, escort, manage 7 conduct 9 accompany, conductor, safeguard

convulse: 4 rock, stir 5 shake 6 excite 7 agitate, disturb

convulsion: fit 5 shrug, spasm, throe 6 attack, tumult, uproar 8 laughter, paroxysm 9 agitation, commotion 11 disturbance

cony: das 4 hare, pika 5 daman, dassy, ganam, hutia, hyrox, lapen 6 burbot, dassie, gazabo, gazebo, rabbit 7 ashkoko

catcher: 5 cheat 7 sharper 8 swindler

coo: 4 curr(Sc.), woot 6 murmer

coof: 4 dolt, lout 9 blockhead

cook: fix, fry 4 bake, boil, chef, make, sear, stew 5 broil, grill, poach, roast, shirr, steam 6 braise, decoct, sautee, seethe, simmer 7 prepare, process, servant 8 cusinero, magirist 9 cuisinier

in simmering liquid: 4 poach

one's goose: 5 spoil 6 defeat

partially: 7 parboil

cooked: 4 done

cookery: 7 cuisine, science 8 magirics

cookie, cooky: 4 cake, snap 6 hermit 7 brownie, oatcake 8 seedcake 10 confection, gingersnap

cooking: *art:* 7 cuisine 8 magirics

device: 4 etna 5 range, stove 7 brazier, griddle 10 rotisserie

odor: 5 nidor

pert. to: 8 culinary

room: 5 cuddy 6 galley 7 kitchen

vessel: pan, pot 4 etna, olla 6 caster, chafer, spider, tureen 7 broiler, griddle, roaster, skillet, steamer 8 colander, fleshpot 9 autoclave

cool: air, fan, ice 4 calm, cold 5 algid, allay, chill, fresh, gelid, nervy, sober, staid,

whole 6 chilly, placid, quench, sedate, serene 7 unmoved 8 careless, cautious, composed, mitigate, moderate, tranquil 9 apathetic, collected, officious, temperate, unruffled 10 deliberate, nonchalant, unfriendly 11 indifferent, refrigerate, unconcerned 12 unresponsive 13 dispassionate, imperturbable 15 undemonstrative

one's heels: 4 wait

cooled: 6 frappe

cooler: 4 icer, jail, olla 5 drink 6 icebox, lockup, prison 11 refrigerant 12 refrigerator

coolie: 7 changar

cooling device: fan 7 freezer 12 refrigerator 14 air-conditioner

coolness: 5 nerve 6 aplomb 8 serenity 9 assurance

coom, coomb: 4 smut, soot 5 frame, grime 6 grease, refuse

coony: sly 4 cute, foxy 6 clever, crafty

coop: cot, cub, mew, pen, pot 4 cage, cote, jail 5 cramp, hutch 6 basket, corral 7 confine 9 enclosure 11 cooperative

cooperate: 4 tend 5 agree, coact, unite 6 concur 7 combine, conduce, connive 8 coadjute, conspire 10 contribute 11 collaborate

cooperation: 8 teamwork

cooperator: 9 auxiliary, colleague 10 accomplice

coordinate: 5 adapt, equal 6 adjust 7 arrange, syntony 8 classify 9 harmonize 10 concurrent

coordination: 4 bond 7 harmony, liaison 12 relationship

inability: 6 abasia

lack: 8 asynergy

coorie: 5 cower, stoop 6 crouch

cooser: 8 stallion

coot: 4 duck, fowl, rail 5 smyth 6 beltie, person, scoter 7 henbill 13 phalacrocorax

cooter: 4 idle 6 loiter, turtle 8 tortoise

cottie: nit 4 bowl, game 5 louse 6 vessel 8 grayback

cop: bag, nab, rob 4 bank, blow, bull, head, heap, lift, pile, trap, tube 5 catch, crest, filch, mount, quill, shock, snare, steal, stock, swipe 6 peeler, spider, strike 7 capture 9 patrolman, policeman

cop-out: 7 retreat 9 defection

copacetic: 4 fine 5 dandy, prime 6 snappy 7 capital 12 satisfactory

copaiba: 4 tree 6 balsam 9 oleoresin

copain: pal 4 chum 7 comrade

copal: 5 anime, resin

cope: vie, war 4 cape, duty, face 5 cappa, cloak, cover, dress, equal, fight, match, notch, rival, vault, wield 6 barter, canopy, chapel, combat, mantel, muzzle, oppose, strike, strive **7** contend, contest **8** complete, exchange, struggle, vestment **9** encounter

copemate: 7 comrade, partner **9** associate **10** antagonist

Copenhagen: *park:* **6** Tivoli
shopping district: **7** Stroget

copestone: 5 crown **6** coping

copier: 4 stat **5** Xerox

copious: 4 full, good, lush, rich **5** ample, large **6** fluent, lavish **7** diffuse, flowing, fulsome, profuse, replete, teeming, uberous **8** abundant, affluent, numerous **9** exuberant, plenteous, plentiful, redundant **11** overflowing

copper: cu; cop **4** bull, cent **5** bobby, metal, penny **6** cuprum, peeler **9** butterfly, policeman
alloy: **5** brass **6** oroide **7** rheotan
arsenic sulfide: **8** enargite
coin: **4** cent **5** brown, penny
comb. form: **5** cupro **6** chalco
engraving: **9** mezzotint
sulphate: **7** vitriol

copper nickel: 9 niccolite

Copperfield's wife: 4 Dora **5** Agnes

copperhead: 5 snake, viper

coppice: 4 wood **5** copse, firth, grove **6** forest, growth **7** thicket **9** brushwood, underwood

Copreus: *father:* **6** Pelops
son: **10** Periphetes
victim: **7** Iphitus

copse: cut, hag **4** hasp, trim **6** clevis **7** coppice, shackle

Copt: 8 Egyptian **9** Christian **11** monophysite
dialect: **8** Bohairic
title: **4** anba

copula: 4 band, link **5** union **7** coupler

copy: ape **4** echo, edit, mime **5** dummy, image, mimic **6** ectype, effigy, follow, record **7** emulate, estreat, imitate, redraft, replica, reprint, tracing **8** apograph, likeness **9** abundance, antigraph, duplicate, imitation, reproduce **10** transcribe, transcript **11** counterpart **12** reproduction
kind of: **6** carbon, ectype **7** estreat, extract, pattern, replica **9** duplicate, facsimile
true: **7** estreat

copying: 7 mimicry **8** mimetism

copyist: 6 scribe **7** copycat **10** plagiarist
pert. to: **8** clerical

copyread: 4 edit

copyright: 6 patent
infringe: **6** pirate **10** plagiarize

coque: bow **4** loop **8** trimming

coquette: toy **5** dally, flirt **6** trifle **9** philander **11** hummingbird

coquettish: coy

coquila: 4 palm **6** cohune **7** attalea

cora: 7 gazelle

coral: red **4** pink **5** polyp **6** palule **8** skeleton, zoophyte **9** madrepore, millepore **10** stalactite
division: **7** aporosa
formation: **5** palus
island: key **4** reef **5** atoll

corbel: 5 ancon **6** timber **10** projection

corbie: 4 crow **5** raven

cord: rib **4** band, bind, bond, cord, welt **5** nerve, twine **6** bobbin, sennet, string, tendon **7** amentum, measure **10** aiquilette, cordeliere
drapery: **7** torsade
goat's hair: **4** agal
parachute: **7** ripcord

cordage: da **4** rope, coir, eruc, feru, hemp, imbe, jute **5** fiber **6** sennit **7** rigging

Corday's victim: 5 Marat

corded: 4 tied **6** repped, ribbed, welted **7** stacked, twilled

Cordelia: *father:* **4** Lear
sister: **5** Regan **7** Goneril

cordelle: tow **4** cord, rope **7** towline, towrope

cordial (see also **liqueur**)**: 4** real, warm **5** shrub **6** ardent, elixir, genial, hearty **7** liqueur, sincere, zealous **8** anisette, friendly, gracious, vigorous **9** courteous, unfeigned **10** hospitable
apricot: **8** periscot
flavoring: **7** aniseed

cordiality: 5 ardor **6** regard, warmth **10** friendship, heartiness

cordon: 4 cord **5** braid, group, guard **6** ribbon
bleu: **10** decoration
sanitary: **10** quarantine

core: cob, hub, nut **4** coke, gist, nave, pith **5** focus, heart, nowse, spool **6** center, centre, kernel, matrix, middle, nodule **7** company, corncob, essence, nucleus **9** substance

corf: tub **4** cage, corb, skip **5** creel **6** basket, dosser

corge: 5 score **6** twenty

corinne: 7 gazelle

Corinth's king: 7 Polybus

corium: 5 layer **6** dermis

cork: oak **4** plug **5** float, shive **6** bobber **7** soberin, stopper, stopple
pert. to: **7** suberic
tissue: **5** suber
wax: **5** cerin

corking: 4 fine **8** pleasing **9** excellent

corkscrew: 6 defect, spiral

corkwood: 5 balsa **6** blolly

cormorant: 4 bird, shag 5 norie, scart 6 gormaw, scarth 7 glutton 8 ravenous 13 phalacrocorax

young: 7 shaglet

corn: 4 salt, samp 5 grain, maize, mealy 6 clavis, heloma, kernel 7 callous 8 preserve 9 granulate

bread: 4 pone

dealer: 10 cornmonger

ear: cob 5 mealy 6 mealie, nubbin

food: 6 hominy

ground: 4 meal 5 grist

hulled: 4 samp 6 hominy

Indian: zea

knife: 7 machete

spike: cob, ear

corn bread: 4 pone 8 tortilla

Corncracker State: 8 Kentucky

corndodger: 4 pone 5 bread 8 dumpling

corned: 6 salted

cornel: 4 tree 6 cherry 7 dogwood

corner: in; get, wro 4 bend, cant, coin, nook, pool, trap, tree 5 angle, bight, catch, coign, elbow, herne, ingle, niche, quoin, trust 6 cantle, canton, coigne, cranny, recess 8 monopoly

cornerpiece: 6 cantle

cornerstone: 4 coin 5 basis, coign 6 coigne 7 support 9 curbstone 10 foundation

cornet: 4 horn 8 woodwind 10 instrument

cornflower: 7 barbeau 10 bluebottle

cornhouse: 7 granary 8 corncrib

Cornhusker State: 8 Nebraska

cornice: 4 band, drip, eave 5 crown 6 geison 7 molding 8 astragal

basket: 4 caul

diamond: 6 quartz

support: 5 ancon

wolframite: cal

cornmeal: 4 masa, samp 5 atole 7 hoecake 10 johnnycake

cornucopia: 4 horn

Cornwall: *castle:* 8 Tintagel

mine: bal 5 wheal

ore: 5 whits

Cornwallis' surrender site: 8 Yorktown

corny: 5 banal, stale, trite 11 sentimental

corolla: 4 bell 8 perianth

part: 5 galea, petal

corollary: 5 dogma 6 result, truism 7 adjunct, theorem 9 deduction, inference 11 consequence, proposition

geometric: 6 porism

corona: 5 cigar, crown, glory 6 fillet, rosary, wreath 7 aureole, circlet, garland, scyphus

coronation: 9 inaugural

stone: 5 Scone

coroner: 6 elisor 7 officer 8 examiner

coronet: 4 band, burr 5 crown, tiara 6 anadem, circle, diadem, timbre, wreath 7 chaplet

coronopus: 4 herb 6 carara

corporal: NCO 4 fano 5 fanon, fanum, phano 6 bodily

corporal punishment: 5 death 7 penalty 8 spanking, whipping

corporate: 6 united 8 combined 9 aggregate

corporation: 4 body, firm 5 trust 10 fellowship, foundation 11 association, combination

corporeal: 4 real 5 hylic, somal 6 actual, bodily, carnal 7 somatic 8 material, physical, tangible 11 substantial

corpse: DOA 4 body 5 mummy, relic, stiff 7 cadaver, carcass, carrion

fat of: 9 adipocere

pert. to: 7 deathly 10 cadaverous

corpulent: fat 5 bulky, burly, husky, obese, plump, stout 6 fleshy, portly, rotund 7 adipose, bellied, weighty 8 rolypoly

corpus: 4 body 8 writings 10 literature

corpuscle: 4 cell 9 leucocyte

lack of red: 6 anemia

redblood: 7 hematid 8 haematid 11 polkilocyte, schistocyte

corral: pen, sty 4 coop 5 atajo, pound 7 confine, enclose 8 stockage, surround 9 enclosure, inclosure

correct: O.K.; due, fit, fix 4 edit, lean, nice, okay, smug, true 5 amend, check, emend, exact, right 6 adjust, better, change, inform, proper, punish, rebuke, reform, remedy, repair, revamp, revise, strict 7 chasten, improve, perfect, precise, rectify, redress, reprove 8 accurate, chastise, definite, emendate, regulate, rigorous, truthful 9 castigate, faultless 10 immaculate, particular, scrupulous 11 punctilious 12 conventional

comb. form: 5 ortho

correctable: 10 corrigible

correlated: 4 akin 7 related

correlative: or; nor 4 then 5 equal, still 6 either, mutual 7 neither 8 analogue, conjoint 9 analogous 10 reciprocal 13 correspondent

correspond: fit, gee 4 jibe, suit 5 agree, match, tally, write 6 accord, concur, square 7 conport, respond 8 coincide, parallel, quadrate 9 analogous, harmonize 11 communicate

correspondence: 4 mail 7 analogy, letters, traffic 8 homology 9 assonance, congruity 10 similarity

costly: 4 dear, fine, high, rich 6 lavish 8 gorgeous, precious, prodigal, splendid 9 dearthful, expensive, priceless, sumptuous 11 extravagant

costmary: 4 herb 5 plant, tansy 7 alecost

costrel: keg 4 head 5 flask 6 bottle

costume (see also dress, vestment): rig 4 garb, robe, sari, suit 5 dress, getup, habit 6 attire 7 apparel, clothes, raiment, uniform 8 clothing, ensemble 10 habiliment

costus root: 4 herb 6 pachak, pochok

cot: bed, hut, mat, pen 4 boat, coop, cote, fold 5 abode, cabin, couch, cover, house, stall 6 pallet, sheath, tangle 7 charpai, charpoy, cottage, shelter 8 bedstead, dwelling 9 sheepfold, stretcher 11 fingerstall

cote: cot, hut 4 coop, fold, shed, wine 5 house, quote 7 cottage, shelter 8 hillside, outstrip, vineyard 9 inclosure, sheepfold

Cote d'Azur: 7 Riviera

coterie: set 4 ring 5 junto, monde 6 circle, clique, galaxy 7 platoon, society 9 camarilla

cothamore: 8 overcoat 9 greatcoat

cothurnus: 4 boot 6 buskin

cotta: 6 mantle 7 blanket 8 surplice, vestment

cottage: cot, hut 4 bari, cosh 5 bower, cabin, house, lodge, shack 6 bohawn, cabana, chalet 7 shelter 9 hosthouse 10 guesthouse
partition: 5 speer 6 hallan

cottage cheese: 9 smearcase

cotter, cottar: 4 mat, pin, vex 4 clot 6 fasten, potter, pucker, shrink, toggle, wither 7 congeal, cottier, peasant, shrivel, villein 8 cottager, cotterel, entangle 9 coagulate

cotton: 4 beat, flog 5 agree, bayal, derry 6 coddle, dhurry, fabric, nankin 7 algodon, dhurrie, garment, succeed 8 perceive 9 harmonize 10 fraternize, understand
and linen: 7 fustian
cleaner: 5 willy 6 willow
cloth: 4 baft, jean, lawn, leno, susi 5 bafta, bluet, denim, doria, khaki, lisle, manta, surat, terry, vichy, wigan 6 baline, calico, cangan, hum-hum 7 cambric, cotonia, galatea, jaconet, nankeen, percale, silesia
cloth blemish: nit
Egyptian: sak 4 Pima 5 sakel
extraction: 5 bolly
fabric: 4 leno
fiber: 4 lint 6 stapel
flowered: 6 chintz
gauze: 4 leno
handkerchief: 7 malabar
knot in: nep 4 slub
lawn: 7 batiste
light: 7 etamine
long-staple: 4 maco

measure: lea 4 hank
printed: 6 calico
refuse: 8 grabbots
seed pod: 4 boll 5 bolly
seed remover: gin
sheeting: 5 manta 6 muslin 7 percale 8 drilling
striped: 5 bezan 7 express
strong: 4 duck 5 scrim 6 canvas
thread: 5 lisle
twilled: 4 jean 7 silesia
waste: 4 noil 6 linter

cotton gin inventor: 10 Eli Whitney

Cotton State: 7 Alabama

cottonseed kernel: 4 meat

cottontail: 4 hare 7 leveret

cottonwood: 4 tree 5 alamo 6 poplar

couch: bed, cot, lie 4 hide, lair, lurk, sofa 5 divan, inlay, lodge, press, skulk, slink, sneak, squat, stoop, utter 6 burrow, litter, pallet, settee 7 conceal, express, overlay, recline 8 disguise 9 accubitus(L.), davenport, embroider

couch grass: 5 quack, quick 6 quitch, scutch

couchant: 4 abed 5 prone 6 supine 7 lurking 9 crouching, squatting

cougar: cat 4 puma 7 panther 9 catamount

cough: 4 bark, hack 5 hoast 6 tussis 9 pertussis
pert. to: 7 tussive

cough drop: 6 pastil, troche 7 lozenge 8 pastille

cough up: 4 ante 5 yield 10 contribute

coulee: 4 lava 5 gorge, gulch 6 ravine

council: 4 body, dael, diet, rede 5 board, boule, cabal, divan, junta, junto, synod 6 senate 7 cabinet, consult, meeting 8 assembly, conclave, congress, hustling, ministry 10 conference, consistory, federation 11 convocation 12 consultation
church: 5 synod
pert. to: 7 cameral
political: 5 cabal, junta
table cover: 5 tapis

councilman: 11 concionator

counsel: 4 lore, rede, rule, warn 5 chide 6 advice, advise, confer 7 caution 8 admonish, advocate, prudence 9 barrister, counselor, recommend 10 counsellor 11 exhortation, instruction 12 consultation, deliberation

counselor, counsellor: 4 sage 6 lawyer, mentor, nestor 7 adviser, advisor, counsel, proctor 8 attorney 9 barrister

counselor-at-law: 9 barrister

count: add, tot 4 bank, cast, earl, foot, graf, name, rely, tell, tote 5 comte(F.), judge, score, tally 6 census, depend, esteem, figure, impute, number, reckon **7** account, ascribe, compute **8** numerate, sanction **9** ascertain, calculate, enumerate

Count of Monte Cristo: 6 Dantes

count on: 4 lean, rely **6** expect

countenance: aid, mug **4** abet, brow, face, mien, puss, show, vult **5** favor, front **6** aspect, favour, visage **7** approve, bearing, conduct, endorse, feature, proffer, support **8** befriend, demeanor, sanction **9** demeanour, encourage, semblance **10** appearance **11** physiognomy

counter: bar **4** chip, dump, eddy, pawn **5** shelf, stand, table **6** combat, marker, oppose **7** adverse, contend, current **8** contrary, opposite **10** contradict

counter-irritant: 4 moxa **5** seton, stupe **6** arnica, iodine, pepper **7** mustard **8** liniment

counteract: 5 check **6** oppose, resist, thwart **7** balance, destroy, nullify **8** antidote **9** frustrate **10** compensate, neutralize **11** countermand **12** counterpoise

counterattack: 6 answer, charge

countercurrent: 4 eddy **5** swirl **9** whirlpool

counterfeit: tin **4** base, copy, coin, duff, fake, mock, sham **5** belie, bogus, dummy, false, feign, forge, fudge, phony, queer **6** affect, assume, forged, pseudo, tinsel **7** falsify, feigned, imitate **8** deformed, simulate, spurious **9** brummagem, disguised, dissemble **10** adulterate, artificial, fictitious, fraudulent

counterfoil 4 stub **5** check

countermand 4 stop **5** annul **6** cancel, forbid, recall, revoke **7** abolish, rescind, reverse **8** abrogate, prohibit **9** frustrate **10** counteract

counterpart: 4 copy, like, mate, twin **5** image, match **6** double **7** obverse **8** parallel **9** duplicate, facsimile **10** complement, equivalent, similitude

counterpoint: 4 foil **7** descant **8** contrast **11** arrangement **13** juxtaposition

counterpoise: 6 offset **7** balance **8** equalize **10** compensate, counteract **13** counterweight **14** counterbalance

countersign: 4 mark, seal, sign **6** signal **7** confirm, endorse **8** consigne, password, sanction **9** signature, watchword **11** corroborate

countersink: 4 ream **5** bevel **7** chamfer

countertenor: 4 alto **8** falsetto

counting frame: 6 abacus

countless: 8 infinite **10** numberless **12** incalculable

country: 4 home, land, pais(Sp.) **5** addle, realm, state, tract, weald **6** ground, nation, people, region, sticks **8** district **9** champaign, territory **12** commonwealth

ancient: **4** Aram, Elam, Elis **5** Sheba

man: **4** jake, rube **5** swain, yokel **6** farmer, rustic **7** bumpkin, hayseed, plowman **10** compatriot, inhabitant

mythical: Oz

open: **4** moot, wold **5** heath, weald

pert. to: **5** rural **6** rustic **7** predial **8** agrestic, pastoral, praedial

place: **4** farm, peat **5** ranch, villa

reside in: **9** rusticate

road: **4** lane, path **5** byway

county: 4 seat **5** shire **6** domain, parish **7** borough **8** district

coup: buy **4** blow, plan, play **5** scoop, upset **6** attack, barter, strike, stroke **7** capsize, traffic **8** overturn **9** stratagem

coup-cart: 8 dumpcart

coup de grace: end **7** quietus **9** deathblow

coup d'etat: 9 stratagem **10** revolution

couple: duo, tie, two **4** bond, case, dyad, join, link, mate, pair, span, team, twin, yoke **5** brace, leash, marry, twain, unite **7** bracket, connect, coupler **8** assemble

coupled: 5 yoked **6** joined, wedded **7** gemalad **8** geminate **9** conjugate

coupler: 4 link, ring **7** drawbar, shackle, tirasse

couplet: 4 pair, poem **5** brace **7** distich

coupon: 4 form, slip, stub **5** check, stamp **7** portion

courage: 4 grit, guts, prow, sand, soul **5** heart, nerve, pluck, spunk, valor **6** daring, mettle, spirit **7** bravery, heroism, prowess **8** audacity, boldness, firmness, tenacity **9** assurance, fortitude, gallantry, hardihood **10** resolution

symbol of: **10** bloodstone

courageous: 4 bold, game **5** brave, hardy, manly, stout **6** daring, heroic, manful, plucky **7** gallant, spartan, staunch, valiant **8** fearless, intrepid, valorous **9** undaunted **11** adventurous **12** enterprising

courant, courante: 4 romp **5** caper, dance, music **6** letter **7** current, gazette, running **9** messenger, newspaper

courier: 4 post **5** guide, scout **7** estafet, orderly, postboy, soilage **8** cicerone, dragoman, estafeet, horseman **9** attendant, messenger **10** cavalryman

courlan: 4 bird **7** limpkin

course: lap, run, way **4** bent, flow, game, heat, line, mode, path, race, rill, rink, road, rote, went **5** cycle, drift, orbit, route, tenor, track, trail, trend **6** artery, career, cursus, gallop, manner, method, series, stream, street, system **7** beeline, conduct, highway, passage, pathway, process, routine, running, subject, traject 8 curricle, progress, sequence, tendency 9 direction 10 curriculum, proceeding, racecourse, succession 11 watercourse

alter: 4 veer 6 detour

easy: 4 pipe, snap 5 cinch 8 sinecure

habitual: rut, way 4 rote 7 regimen, routine

of action: 6 career 8 demarche 9 procedure

of study: 7 seminar 8 syllabus 10 curriculum

roundabout: 6 detour 11 indirection

courser: 5 horse, racer, steed 7 charger

court: bar, bid, see, sue, woo 4 area, body, quad, rota, seek, yard 5 arena, curea, curry, favor, forum, judge, patio, space, spark, tempt, train 6 allure, atrium, gemote, homage, invite, palace 7 address, attract, retinue, solicit 8 hustling, serenade, tribunal 9 attention, enclosure 10 quadrangle

action: 4 case, suit 5 trial

attendant: 5 staff 6 elisor, staves

bring into: sue 4 sist 6 arrest

call to: 4 oyes, oyez 7 summons 8 subpoena 11 arraignment

circuit: 4 eyre, iter

crier: 6 beadle

cry: 4 oyes, oyez

ecclesiastical: 10 consistory

exemption: 6 essoin

hearing: 4 oyer, suit 5 trial 6 action

inner: 5 patio

Mikado's: 5 dairi

minutes: 4 acta

of equity: 8 chancery

official: 5 clerk, crier, macer(Sc.) 7 bailiff

old: 4 leet 5 gemot 6 gemote 8 woodmote

order: 4 nisi, rule, writ 6 decree

panel: 4 jury

participant: 4 jury 5 crier, judge 6 elisor 7 pleader 8 advocate, talesman 9 defendant, plaintiff

pert. to: 5 aulic 10 fornaneous

session: set 4 oyer 6 assize 7 sitting 8 sederunt 11 downsitting

writ: 6 capias 7 summons 8 subpoena

court game: 6 tennis 9 badminton

court-martial: 8 drumhead

courteous: 4 fair 5 buxom, civil, suave 6 polite, urbane 7 affable, cordial, gallant, genteel, gentile, refined 8 debonair, gracious 9 attentive 10 complaisant, respectful 11 considerate, gentlemanly

courtesan: 10 prostitute

courtier: 4 bean 5 beaux(pl.), wooer 7 courter 8 courtman 9 attendant, courtling, flatterer

courtly: 4 hend 5 aulic, civil, hende 6 polite 7 elegant, refined, stately 8 polished 9 dignified

courtship: 4 suit 7 romance

courtyard: 4 area 5 patio 7 cortile 9 curtilage 10 quadrangle

cousin: coz, kin 4 akin 6 allied 8 relative

couthie: 4 smug 6 kindly, smooth 8 friendly, pleasant 9 agreeable 11 comfortable

couturier, couturiere: 8 designer 10 dressmaker

cove: bay, den 4 cave, chap, gill, hole, nook, pass 5 basin, bight, creek, inlet 6 fellow, hollow, recess, valley 7 molding

covenant: 4 bind, bond, mise, pact 5 agree 6 accord, cartel, engage, pledge, treaty 7 bargain, compact, concord, promise 8 alliance, contract, document 9 agreement, concordat, condition, stipulate, testament, undertake 10 convention 11 confederacy, stipulation

cover: cap, lid 4 coat, hide, mask, pave, roof, span, veil 5 drape, hatch 6 mantle, screen, shield 7 obscure, overlay, shelter

a bet: 4 fade

a fire: 4 bank

a hatch: 6 batten

ground: 5 speed 7 advance

the eyes: 9 blindfold

up: 4 hide 7 conceal

up for: 6 shield 7 protect

with mud: 6 belute

with straw: 6 thatch

with strips of bacon: 4 lard

covered: 4 clad, shod 5 mossy 6 covert, hidden 7 encased 8 screened 9 cleithral, concealed, panoplied, sheltered

covering: fur, hap 4 aril, bark, boot, case, hood, hull, husk, mask, pall, roof, tarp, tile 5 apron, armor, crust, quilt, shell, testa 6 awning, canopy, drapet, facing, heling, helmet, jacket, pelage, screen, sheath, shroud 7 capsule, ceiling, healing, overlay, pericap, wrapper 8 casement, clothing, coverlet, umbrella 9 coverture, operculum 10 integument 11 smokescreen

defensive: 5 armor 6 helmut 10 camouflage 11 smokescreen

seed: 4 aril

thin: 4 film 6 veneer

coverlet: 5 quilt, rezai, throw 6 afghan, caddow, spread 7 blanket 8 coverlid 9 comforter 11 counterpane

coverslut: 5 apron 7 garment

covert: den, lie, sly 4 lair 5 niche, privy 6 asylum, harbor, hidden, latent, masked, refuge, secret 7 covered, defense, harbour, private, shelter, subrosa, thicket **9** concealed, disguised, insidious, shrubbery **10** underbrush **12** confidential

covet: 4 ache, envy, pant, want, wish **5** crave, yearn **6** desire, grudge, hanker

covetous: 4 avid, gair, gare **5** eager **6** frugal, greedy, stingy **7** miserly **8** desirous, grasping **9** mercenary **10** avaricious **12** parsimonious

covey: 4 bevy **5** brood, flock, hatch **7** company

covin, covine: 4 band, crew **5** fraud **7** company **8** assembly, trickery

cow: awe **4** beef, bogy, cowl, cush, faze, kine, vaca **5** abash, alarm, bossy, brock, bully, daunt, dompt, moggy, scare **6** bovine, goblin, heifer, subdue, vacha **7** bugbear, depress, overtop, squelch, terrify **8** browbeat, dispirit, frighten, threaten **9** quadruped **10** intimidate

barn: **4** byre **7** vaccary
barren: **5** drape
cud: **5** rumen
dung: **4** upla
group: **4** herd, kine **6** cattle
hornless: not **4** moil **5** doddy, muley **6** doddie, mulley **7** pollard
hybrid: **7** cattabu, cattalo
pasture: **7** vachery
sound: low, moo
young: **4** calf **5** stirk **6** heifer

cow-headed deity: 4 Isis

cow pilot: 4 fish **9** chirivita **10** damselfish

cowardly: shy **4** argh **5** timid **6** afraid, cowish, craven, yellow **7** caitiff, chicken **11** lily-livered **12** fainthearted **13** pusillanimous

cowbird: 7 bunting **9** blackbird

cowboy: 5 rider, roper, waddi **6** gaucho, herder **7** llanero, puncher, vaquero **8** buckaroo, buckayro, wrangler **10** cowpuncher **12** broncobuster
breeches: **5** chaps, levis **8** jodhpurs
contest: **5** rodeo

cowcatcher: 5 guard, pilot

cowed: 8 downcast **11** crestfallen

cower: 4 fawn **5** quail, stoop, toady, wince **6** coorie, cringe, crouch, hurkle, shrink

cowfish: 4 toro **7** manatee, sirenia

cowherd: 7 bucolic **8** herdsman, neatherd

cowl: cap, lid, tub **4** hood, monk **6** bonnet, vessel **7** capuche

cowle: 5 grant **7** amnesty **10** engagement **11** safe-conduct

cowled: 6 hooded **9** cucullate

cowpea: 5 sitao

cowpuncher: 6 cowboy **7** puncher

cowslip: 8 auricula, marigold, primrose

coxa: hip

coxcomb: fop, nob **4** buck, dude, fool, toff **5** cleat, dandy, hinge **7** princox **8** popinjay

coy: pal, shy **4** arch, coax, nice **5** aloof, chary, decoy, quiet, still **6** allure, caress, demure, modest, proper **7** bashful, distant **8** reserved **9** diffident **10** coquettish, disdainful, hesitating

Coyote State: 11 South Dakota

coypu: 6 nutria, rodent

coze: 4 chat, talk **6** gossip **8** converse

cozen, cosen: cog, con **4** bilk, gull **5** cheat, trick **6** chisel **7** beguile, deceive, defraud, swindle **8** hoodwink **9** bamboozle

cozy: 4 easy, safe, snug **5** bield **6** chatty, secure, toasty **8** covering, familiar, homelike, sociable **9** contented, gemutlich, talkative **11** comfortable

cozy retreat: den **4** lair, nest, nook **5** ingle

crab: gin **5** anger, maian, racer, winch **6** buster, cancer, grouse, heemit, peeler **7** buckler, fiddler, grumble **8** arachnid, irritate, windlass **9** horseshoe **10** crosspatch, crustacean, curmudgeon
abdomen: **5** apron
claw: **5** chela **6** nipper
fiddler: uca
genus: uca **6** birgus **7** squilla
suborder: **9** brachyura

crab apple: 5 malus, scrog

crabbed: 4 ugly **5** cabby, cross, testy **6** bitter, crusty, morose, rugged, sullen, trying **7** boorish, cramped, cornish, crooked, gnarled, knotted, obscure, peevish **8** churlish, contrary, petulant, vinegary **9** difficult, fractious, intricate, irregular **10** perplexing **11** intractable

crabgrass: 9 digitaria

crabstick: 4 cane **5** crank, stick **6** cudgel

crabwood: 8 andiroba

crack: gag, pop **4** a-one, bang, blow, chap, chip, chop, clap, cone, flaw, jest, jibe, joke, kibe, leak, quip, rend, rift, rime, snap, yerk **5** brack, break, check, chine, chink, clack, cleft, craze, split **6** cleave, cranny **7** blemish, crackle, crevice, crevise, fissure **8** fracture

crack down on: 6 attack **10** discipline

crack up: 5 amuse, crash, extol, smash **8** collapse **9** break down

crackbrain: 8 crackpot **9** screwball

crackbrained: 5 crazy, nutty **7** erratic **12** unreasonable

cracker: 4 bake, liar **5** wafer **7** biscuit, boaster, breaker, burster, redneck, snapper **8** braggart **11** firecracker

Cracker State: 7 Georgia

crackle: 4 snap **5** break, crack **7** brustle, crinkle, sparkle, sputter **9** crackling, crepitate

crackpot: 7 erratic, lunatic 9 screwball

cracksman: 4 yegg 7 burglar, peteman

cradle: bed, cot 4 rest, rock 5 cader, frame 6 creche 7 berceau, shelter 8 cunabula 9 framework 11 incunabulum
song: 7 lullaby 8 berceuse
wicker: 8 bassinet

craft (see also **boat**): art 4 boat 5 fraud, guile, skill, trade 6 deceit, metier, talent, vessel 7 ability 8 aptitude, artifice, vocation 9 dexterity 10 employment, occupation 12 skillfulness

craftsman: 4 hand 5 navvy 6 artist, writer 7 artisan, workman 8 mechanic 9 artificer
aid: cad

crafty: sly 4 arch, foxy, wily 5 adept 6 adroit, astute, callid, shrewd, subtle, tricky 7 cunning, vulpine 8 captious, fetching 9 cautelous, deceitful, ingenious 10 fallacious, fraudulent 13 Machiavellian 15 Mephistophelean

crag: tor 4 craw, neck, rock, scar, spur 5 arete, brack, cliff 6 throat 9 precipice

craggy: 5 rough 6 abrupt, knotty, rugged

crake: 4 bird, crow, rail, rook 5 raven 8 railbird

cram: wad 4 bone, fill, glut, pack, stow, urge 5 crowd, crush, drive, force, gorge, grind, learn, press, study, stuff, teach

crame: 4 tent 5 booth, stall

cramp: 4 coop, kink, pain 5 crick, crowd, pinch, stunt 6 hamper, hinder, knotty 7 confine 8 compress, contract, restrain, restrict 9 constrict, difficult 11 contraction
one's style: 5 queer 9 frustrate

cranberry: 7 pembina 8 bilberry, foxberry 9 mossberry, sourberry
habitat: bog

crane: job 4 bird, grus 5 davit, heron, jenny, raise, wader 6 sarsus 7 derrick 9 cormorant
arm: gib, jib
charges: 7 cranage
genus: 4 grus
Malayan: 5 sarus
neck: 4 gaze 5 stare
pert. to: 6 gruine
ship: 5 davit
small: 10 demoiselle
traveling: 5 jenny, titan

crane fly: 6 tipula

cranial nerve: 4 vagi(pl.) 5 vagus
root: 5 radix 7 radices(pl.)

craniometrical point: 5 inion 7 pterion, stenion

cranium: pan 4 head 5 skull 8 brainpan
nerve root: 5 radix
part: 7 calotte 8 calvaria
pert. to: 7 cranial

crank: wit 4 bent, sick, weak, whim, wind 5 brace, loose, rogue, shaky, winch 6 ailing, boldly, grouch, handle, infirm 7 awkward, bracket, fanatic, lustily 9 distorted, eccentric, sprightly 10 monomaniac, vigorously

crankle: 4 bend, turn 5 twist 6 zigzag

cranky: 4 ugly 5 crazy, cross, lusty, shaky, testy 6 ailing, infirm, sickly 7 crooked, grouchy 8 tortuous 9 crotchety, difficult, irritable

cranny: 4 hole, nook 5 chink, cleft, crack 6 corner 7 crevice, fissure

cranreuch: 4 rime 9 hoarfrost

crants: 6 wreath 7 garland

crap: 5 dregs, money 7 gallows, greaves, rubbish 8 nonsense, sediment

crape: 4 band, curl, friz 5 crepe, crimp, drape, gauze 6 shroud 8 mourning

crapehanger: 7 killjoy 10 spoilsport

crapulence: 7 surfeit 8 gluttony 11 overfeeding 12 intemperance, intoxication

crash: 4 fail, fall 5 blast, burst, cloth, crush, shock, smash, sound 6 fiasco 7 failure, shatter 8 collapse, splinter 9 collision

crass: raw 4 dull, rude 5 crude, dense, gross, rough, thick 6 coarse, obtuse, stupid 9 unrefined

cratch: 4 crib, rack 6 manger 7 grating

crate: box, car 4 case, crib 5 plane, seron 6 basket, cradle, encase, hamper, hurdle 7 canasta, vehicle 9 container 10 receptacle
bar 4 slat

crater: cup, pit 4 cone, hole 5 fovea 6 hollow 7 caldera
edge: lip

cravat: tie 4 teck 5 ascot, scarf, stock 7 bandage, necktie, overlay 8 crumpler 9 neckcloth 10 fourinhand 11 neckerchief

crave: ask, beg 4 long, need, pray, seek 5 covet, yearn 6 desire, hanker, hunger, thirst 7 beseech, entreat, implore, request, require, solicit 10 supplicate

craven: 6 afraid, coward, scared 7 dastard 8 cowardly, defeated, overcome, poltroon, recreant, sneaking 10 vanquished 12 fainthearted

craw: maw 4 crop 7 stomach 9 ingluvies

crawl: lag 4 drag, fawn, inch, ramp, swim 5 creep, kraal 6 cringe, grovel, scride 7 slither

crayfish: 5 yabby 6 yabbie 7 crawdad, lobster 8 cambarus, crawfish 9 ecrevisse 10 crustacean

crayon: 4 plan 5 chalk 6 pastel, pencil, sketch 7 drawing

craze: fad 4 flaw, mode, rage 5 break, crack, crush, furor, mania, vogue 6 defect, impair, madden, weaken, whimsy 7 derange, destroy, fashion, shatter, whimsey 8 distract 9 bedlamize, infirmity 11 infatuation

crazed: mad, ree 4 amok, loco, wild, wood, zany 5 balmy, batty, daffy, dotty, manic, nutty, potty, wacky 6 coocoo, dottle, insane, looney 7 lunatic 8 deleerit, delieret, demented, deranged 10 crackbrain, distraught

creak: gig 4 rasp, yirr 5 cheep(Sc.), croak, grind, groan 6 squeak

cream: 4 beat, best 5 creme, elite, froth, sauce 6 bonbon 8 emulsion, ointment

cream of tartar: 5 argol

cream puff: 6 pastry 8 weakling

creamery: 5 dairy

creamy: 4 rich 5 reamy 6 smooth 8 luscious

crease: 4 fold, lirk, ruck, ruga, seam 5 crimp, pleat 7 crumple, wrinkle

create: 4 coin, form, make, plan 5 build, cause, forge, shape, write 6 design, invent 7 compose, fashion, imagine, produce 8 generate 9 establish, originate

creation: 5 world 6 cosmos, effect 7 fashion, product 8 creature, universe 10 production 11 masterpiece

creative: 9 demiurgic, inventive 10 productive 12 constructive

creativity: 6 genius

creator: 5 maker 6 author 8 designer 9 architect

creature (see also **animal**): man 4 tool 5 beast, being, slave, thing 6 animal, minion, person, wretch 8 hellicat(Sc.) 9 dependent 10 animalcule, individual

fabled: elf 5 gnome 6 dragon, merman 7 centaur, mermaid

ogre: 5 pixie 6 wyvern

creche: 4 crib 6 manger 7 nursery

credence: 5 faith, trust 6 belief, buffet, credit 8 credenza 10 acceptance, confidence 11 reliability 15 trustworthiness

credential: 7 voucher 8 credence 11 certificate, testimonial

credenza: 5 niche, shelf, table 6 buffet 8 credence, cupboard 9 sideboard

credible: 6 likely 7 credent 8 probable 9 authentic, plausible, reputable 11 trustworthy

credit: 4 loan 5 asset, chalk, faith, honor, merit, tenet, trust 6 belief, charge, esteem, impute, renown, repute, weight 7 ascribe, believe 8 accredit, credence 10 estimation

credulous: 4 fond 8 credible, gullible

creed: ism 4 cult, sect 5 credo, dogma, faith, tenet 6 belief 7 trowing 8 doctrine 10 confession

Christian: 6 Nicene 8 Apostle's

creek: bay, ria, rio 4 burn(Sc.), cove, kill, pill, rill, slue 5 bayou, bight, bogue, brook, crick, fleet, inlet, zanja 6 arroyo, estero,

Indian, slough, stream 7 estuary, rivulet 11 watercourse

creel: 4 caul, cawl, rack, trap 6 basket

creem: hug 4 mash 5 crush 6 shiver 7 shudder, squeeze

creep: 4 fawn, inch, ramp 5 crawl, prowl, skulk, slink, steal 6 cringe, grovel, scride 7 cramble

creeper: ivy 4 shoe, vine, worm 5 snake 6 ipecac, romper, tecoma

creeping: 4 slow 7 reptant, servile 9 reptilian 11 reptatorial

creese: 4 kris, stab 5 sword 6 dagger, weapon

cremate: 4 burn 9 incremate 10 incinerate

Cremona: 5 Amati 6 violin

crena: 5 cleft, notch 7 scallop 11 indentation

crenic acid salt: 7 crenate

creole: 6 patois 7 mestizo

Creole State: 9 Louisiana

crepe: 6 fabric 7 frizzed, pancake 8 crinkled, wrinkled

crepitate: 4 snap 6 rattle 7 crackle

crepuscule: 8 twilight

crescent: 4 horn, lune, moon, rool 5 curve, lunar 6 lunule 7 lunette, menisci(pl.) 8 meniscus 10 semicircle

point: 4 cusp

crescent-shaped: 6 bicorn, lunate 7 lunular 9 semilunar

crescive: 7 growing 10 increasing

cresset: 5 torch 6 basket, beacon, signal 7 furnace 8 flambeau

crest: cop, tip, top 4 acme, apex, comb, edge, knap, peak, seal, tuft 5 chine, crown, plume, ridge 6 copple, crista, finial, height, helmet, summit 7 bearing 8 pinnacle, whitecap 10 cognizance

rugged: 6 arete

crested: 6 muffed 7 crisate, crowned 8 pileated 9 coronated

crestfallen: 5 cowed 8 dejected 10 dispirited

creta: 5 chalk

cretaceous: 6 chalky

Crete: 6 Candia

cape: 4 krio 5 krios

city: Hag 5 Canea(c.), Khora 6 Kisamo, Malemi, Mallia, Meleme, Retimo 7 Kasteli 8 Nikolacs, Sphakion 9 Heraclion, Tympakion 11 Palaiokhora

earth spirit: 6 Curete

flier: 6 Icarus

goddess: 8 Dictynna

king: 5 Minos 9 Idomeneus

language: 6 Minoan

man of brass: 5 Talos

monster: 8 minotaur

mountain: *Ida* 9 Psiloriti

princess: 7 Ariadne

seaport: 5 Canea 6 Candia, Khania
Cretheus: *son:* 8 Amythaon
  wife: 7 Biadice
cretin: 5 idiot
cretism: 5 lying 9 falsehood
cretose: 6 chalky
Creusa: *father:* 5 Priam
  husband: 6 Aeneas
  mother: 6 Hecuba
  son: 8 Ascanius
crevasse: 5 chasm, split 8 cleavage
crevice: 4 bore, leak, nook, seam, vein 5
  break, chine, chink, cleft, crack, grike 6
  cranny 7 fissure, opening 8 crevasse, peephole 10 interstice
crew: men, mob, set 4 band, gang, herd,
  oars, team 5 hands, party, squad, staff 6
  seamen, throng 7 company, faculty, mem-
  bers, retinue 8 equipage, mariners 10 assemblage, complement
crewel: 6 caddice 7 caddice 10 crewelwork,
  embroidery
crib: bed, bin, box, cab, cot, cub, hut, key 4
  boom, dive, pony, rack, raft 5 boose, boosy,
  cheat, crate, frame, hovel, stall, steal 6
  bunker, cratch, creche, manger, pilfer 7
  purloin 8 cribbage 9 enclosure 10 plagiarize, storehouse
cribbage score: nob, peg
crick: 5 creek, hitch, spasm, twist
cricket: 4 game, grig 6 insect
  genus: 7 gryllus
  run: bye
  side: ons
  sound: 5 chirp 12 stridulation
  team: 6 eleven
  term: off, ons, rot 4 over 5 smick 6 yorker
crier: 6 beadle, herald, wailer 7 muezzin
crime: act, sin 4 evil 5 abuse, arson, blame,
  wrong 6 felony, murder, piacle 7 misdeed,
  offense 8 iniquity 9 violation 10 wickedness 11 abomination, malefaction 13
  transgression
  ecclesiastical: 6 simony
  goddess of: Ate
  organized: 10 underworld
  scene of: 5 venue
Crimea: 4 Krym
  city: 5 Kerch, Yalta 10 Sevastopol
  people: 5 Tauri
  river: 4 Alma
  sea: 4 Azof, Azov
criminal: bad 4 yegg 5 crook, felon 6 guilty,
  inmate, nocent, slayer, wicked 7 convict,
  culprit, illegal 8 culpable, gangster 9 desperado, wrongdoer 10 blackguard, deplorable, flagitious, malefactor, malfeasant 11
  blameworthy, disgraceful 13 reprehensible

habitual: 8 repeater 10 recidivist
refuge: 7 Alsatia 11 Whitefriars
crimonology branch: 8 penology
crimp: 4 bend, curl, fold, friz, pote, wave,
  weak 5 cramp, flute, frizz, pinch, plait 6
  goffer, ruffle 7 crinkle, friable, gauffer,
  wrinkle 8 obstacle 9 corrugate 12 inconsistent
crimson: dye, lac, red 4 pink 6 bloody, maroon, modena 7 carmine, scarlet
crine: 4 hair, mane 6 shrink 7 shrivel
cringe: bow 4 bend, fawn, jouk 5 binge,
  cower, crawl, quail, sneak, stoop, wince,
  yield 6 crouch, grovel, shrink, submit 7
  crinkle, distort, truckle
cringing: 6 abject 7 hangdog
cringle: orb 4 disk 6 eyelet, terret 7 grommet
crinite: 5 hairy 6 fossil
crinitory: 5 hairy 7 crinose
crinkle: 4 bend, curl, kink, turn, wind 6
  pucker, ripple, rumple, rustle 7 crackle,
  wrinkle 9 corrugate 11 convolution
cripple: mar 4 halt, harm, hurt, lame,
  maim, wing 6 bacach, hobble, impair, injure, scotch, spavin, weaken 7 crapple,
  crumpet, disable, lamiter(Sc.) 8 handicap,
  mutilate, paralyze 9 hamstring 12 incapacitate
crisis: 4 acme, crux, pass, turn 5 panic, peril,
  pinch, trial 6 strait 8 decision, juncture 9
  criterion, emergency 11 conjunction
  having no: 9 acritical
crisp: new 4 cold 5 brisk, clear, curly, fresh,
  nippy, pithy, sharp, short, stiff, terse 6 biting, bright, lively 7 bracing, brittle, concise, cutting, friable 9 crackling
crispin: 4 coat 9 shoemaker
crisscross: 4 awry 7 network 8 confused 9
  intersect
cristate: 6 ridged, tufted 7 crested
criterion: law 4 norm, rule, test, type 5 axiom, canon, gauge, nodel, proof 6 metric 7
  measure 8 standard 9 yardstick 10 indication, touchstone
critic: 5 booer, judge, momus 6 carper, censor, expert, slater 8 collator, reviewer 9
  detractor, literator 11 connoisseur, critic-
  aster, faultfinder
critical: 4 edge 5 acute, exact 6 urgent 7
  carping, exigent 8 captious, decisive, exacting 10 censorious, fastidious 12 faultfinding 14 discriminating
critical mark: 6 obelus 7 obelisk
criticism: 5 blame 6 review 7 comment 8
  critique, diatribe, judgment 9 stricture 13
  animadversion
criticize: hit, pan, rap, rip 4 carp, flay, slam,
  slur, yelp 5 blame, blast, cavil, judge,
  knock, roast 6 rebuke, review 7 censure,

comment, examine **8** critique **9** castigate **10** animadvert

Crius: *father:* **6** Uranus
  mother: Ge **4** Gaea, Gaia
  sister: **7** Eurybia

cro: 7 payment **12** satisfaction

croak: caw, die **4** gasp, kill **5** creak, quark, speak **7** forbode, grumble **8** complain

Croatia: *capital:* **5** Agram **6** Zagreb
  city: **5** Fiume, Rieka
  mountain: **6** Kapela
  people: **4** Serb, Slav, Sorb, Wend **5** Sclav **6** Hrvati **7** Hervati, Slovene **8** Croatian, European

crochet: 4 hook, knit **5** braid, plait, weave **8** crotchet

crock: jar, pig, pot **4** smut, soil, soot **5** stool **6** critch, smudge **8** potsherd

crockery: 5 china, cloam **6** dishes, plates **11** earthenware

crocodile: goa **5** gator **6** cayman, gavial, jacare, mugger **7** reptile **9** alligator
  genus: **11** goniopholis

crocus: 7 saffron

Croesus: 4 king **9** moneybags, plutocrat
  country: **5** Lydia

croft: 4 farm **5** crypt, field, garth, vault **6** bleach, cavern

cromlech: 6 circle, dolmen **7** gorsedd **9** cyclolith

Cromwell: 4 Noll **6** Oliver
  son-in-law: **6** Ireton
  victory site: **6** Naseby

crone: hag **4** cive **5** witch **6** beldam **7** beldame **9** cailleach, cailliach

Cronus: *daughter:* **4** Hera **6** Hestia **7** Demeter
  father: **6** Uranus
  mother: **4** Gaea
  wife: **4** Rhea

crony: pal **4** chum **9** associate, companion

crook: 4 bend, turn, warp **5** cheat, cleek, crump, curve, pedum, staff, thief, trick **7** crosier, crozier **8** artifice, swindler **10** camshachle(Sc.)

crooked: cam **4** agee, awry, bent **5** agley(Sc.), askew, false, gleed **6** akimbo, artful, aslant, crabby, crafty, curved, tricky, zigzag **7** askance, asquint, corrupt, crabbed, oblique, turning, twisted, winding **8** tortuous **9** dishonest, distorted, irregular **10** circuitous, fraudulent, misleading **12** dishonorable
  comb. form: **5** ankyl **6** ankylo

croon: hum, low **4** boom, lull, sing, wail **5** chirm, whine **6** lament, murmur **8** complain

crop: cut, maw, top **4** clip, craw, knap, reap, trim, whip **5** fruit, quirt, shear **6** gather, gebbie, silage **7** curtail, harvest, tillage **8** gleaning, ingulies
  goddess of: **6** Annona
  second growth: **5** rowen
  year's: **6** annona

cropper: 8 collapse, disaster

croquet: 5 roque

croquette: 5 cecil

crosier, crozier: 5 crook, cross, staff

cross: go; mix **4** ford, rood, span **5** angry, testy, trial **6** bisect, crabby, cranky, crouch, emblem, gibbet, grumpy, outwit, signum, sullen, symbol, thwart, touchy **7** athwart, crabbed, fretful, froward, oblique, peevish, pettish, potence **8** crotched, crucifix, petulant, snappish, suastica, swastika, traverse, vexillum **9** frustrate, intersect, irritable, plaintive **10** affliction, ill-humored, transverse **12** disagreeable
  barred: **11** trabeculate
  fiery: **8** crantara **9** crostarie
  Greek: **6** fylfot
  stroke: **5** serif **6** ceriph
  swords: **4** duel **5** fight **6** combat
  tau: **4** crux **5** ankih
  type: **5** Greek, Latin, Papal **6** Celtic **7** Maltese **8** Egyptian
  wires: **7** confuse

cross-examine: 5 grill **8** question

cross-grained: 7 gnarled **8** churlish, perverse **9** irascible **12** cantankerous

cross out: 4 dele **5** blank, erase **6** cancel, delete **9** eliminate

cross-rib: 4 arch **6** lierne

cross section: 4 part **14** representation

crossbar: 4 axle, rung **5** round **10** horizontal

crossbeam: bar **5** trave **6** girder

crossbow: 6 weapon **8** arbalest

crossbreed: 5 husky **6** hybrid **9** hybridize

crosshatch: 7 engrave

crossing: 7 passage **8** opposing

crosspatch: 4 bear, crab **6** grouch

crosspiece: bar **4** spar, yoke **5** grill **8** crossarm **10** doubletree

crossroads: 9 carrefour **12** intersection
  goddess: **6** Hecate, Hekate, Trivia

crossruff: 6 seesaw **9** alternate

crosswise: 6 across **7** athwart **8** acrostic, diagonal

crotch: 4 fork, pole, post **5** cleft, notch, stake **9** stanchion

crotchet: fad **4** hook, whim **5** fancy **6** vagary **9** conundrum **11** peculiarity **12** eccentricity

crotchety: 6 cranky **10** capricious

crouch: 4 bend, fawn, ruck **5** cower, squat, stoop **6** cringe **7** scrooch

crouching: 8 couchant

crouse: 4 bold 5 brisk, cocky 6 lively 8 cheerful 9 confident

crouton: bit 5 toast 7 garnish

crow: aga, caw, cry, daw 4 bird, brag, rook 5 boast, exult, raven, vaunt 6 carnal, corvas 7 grapnel, jackdow, swagger 9 blackbird

cry: caw

pert. to: 7 corvine

crow-like: 7 corvine

crowbar: pry 5 jemmy, jimmy, lever 7 gablock 8 gavelock

crowd: jam, mob, set 4 bike, cram, herd, host, pack, push, rock, rout, stow, swad 5 bunch, cramp, crush, drove, flock, group, horde, posse, press, serry, shoal, swarm, three, wedge 6 boodle, clique, hubble, huddle, jostle, rabble, throng 7 bourock(Sc.), company, squeeze 9 multitude 10 assemblage, clamjamfry(Sc.), confluence

penetrate: 5 elbow 6 needle

crowded: 5 close, dense, thick 6 filled 7 bunched, compact, serried, stipate, stuffed, teeming 9 congested

crowder: 6 loader 7 fiddler 8 thatcher

crown: cap, top 4 coin, pate, peak, poll 5 adorn, basil, bezel, bezil, crest, miter, mitre, tiara 6 anadem, circle, climax, corona(L.), diadem, fillet, invest, laurel, potong, reward, summit, trophy, wreath 7 aureole, chaplet, coronet, garland, install 8 coronate, enthrone, pinnacle, surmount 9 headdress, sovereign

pert. to: 8 coronal

crown prince: 4 heir 8 atheling

cru: 8 vineyard

crucial: 5 acute 6 severe, trying 7 pivotal, telling 8 critical, decisive

cruciation: 7 torture

crucible: pot 4 dish, etna, test 6 cruset, retort 7 furnace

crucifix: pax 4 rood 5 cross

crucify: vex 4 hang, kill 5 harry 7 mortify, torment, torture 8 cruciate 9 persecute

crud: 4 curd 6 refuse 7 thicken

crude: raw 4 bald, bare, rude 5 crass, green, harsh, rough 6 callow, coarse, savage, unripe, vulgar 7 uncouth 8 immature, impolite 9 primitive, unglossed, unrefined, untrained 10 incomplete, unpolished 11 undeveloped 13 inexperienced

cruel: 4 fell, hard 5 harsh 6 bloody, brutal, fierce, savage, severe, unjust, unkind 7 bestial, brutish, inhuman, neronic 8 barbaric, diabolic, fiendish, inhumane, pitiless, ruthless, sadistic, tyrannic 9 atrocious, draconian, ferocious, heartless,

merciless, rapacious, unfeeling 10 diabolical, sanguinary, vindictive 11 hardhearted

lover of: 6 sadist

cruet: ama, jar, jug 4 vial 5 cruse 6 bottle, caster, guttus, vessel 7 ampulla, burette 9 container

cruise: 4 boat, sail, trip 9 excursion

cruiser: 4 ship 6 vessel 7 warship

cruising: 4 asea

cruller: 7 olycook, olykock 8 doughnut 9 friedcake

crumb: bit, ort 5 piece 6 little, morsel 7 remnant 8 fragment

crumb covered: 7 breaded

crumble: rot 5 break, crush, decay, slake, spoil 6 molder, perish 7 moulder 9 decompose, pulverize 12 disintegrate

crumbly: 7 friable

crumpet: 4 cake 6 muffin 7 pikelet

crumple: 4 fold, muss 5 crush 6 crease, furrow, raffle, rumple 7 crunkle, wrinkle 8 collapse, contract 9 corrugate

crunch: 4 bite, chew 5 chomp, crump, crush, gnash, grind, munch, press 6 cranch 7 craunch, scrunch

cruor: 4 gore 5 blood

crural joint: 4 knee

crus: 5 shank

crusade: war 5 jehad, jihad 8 campaign 10 expedition

crusader: 7 pilgrim, Templar 8 reformer

enemy: 7 Saladin, Saracen

port: 4 Acre

crush: bow, jam 4 cram, dash, mash, mill, mull 5 brake, break, crash, craze, crowd, force, grind, press, quash, quell, smash, tread, unman 6 bruise, burden, crunch, squash, subdue, thwack 7 conquer, crumple, depress, destroy, oppress, overrun, repress, scrunch, scrunge, shatter, squeeze, squelch 8 compress, overcome, suppress 9 overpower, overwhelm, pulverize

crust: 4 cake, hull, rind 5 shell 6 eschar, harden 7 coating 8 pellicle

crustacean: 4 crab, flea, scud 5 louse, prawn 6 endite, isopod, shrimp 7 lobster, squilla 8 barnacle

appendage: 5 exite

claw: 5 chela

feeler: 7 antenna

genus: 5 eryon, hippa 6 tripos

group: 7 caridea

larva: 5 alima

limb: 6 podite

small: 6 isopod 7 copepod 8 barnacle

ten-footed: 4 crab

crusty: 4 curt 5 bluff, blunt, testy 6 morose 7 crabbed, peevish, pettish 8 snappish 11 ill-tempered

crux: nub 4 ankh, gist, pith 5 cross, point 6 puzzle, riddle 7 problem 10 difficulty

cry (see also **exclamation**): ho; boo, caw, cri(F.), fad, hue, ole, sob, yip 4 bawl, bump, call, evoe, hawk, hoot, howl, keen, mewl, pule, rage, scry, wail, weep, yell, yelp 5 clepe, crede, greet, groan, rumor, shout, sound, utter, vogue whewl, whine 6 bellow, boohoo, clamor, demand, lament, outcry, quethe, scream, shriek, slogan, snivel, squeal, squall, wimick, yammer 7 clamour, exclaim, fashion, screech 8 proclaim 11 acclamation, lamentation

court: 4 oyes, oyez

derisive: bah, boo 4 hiss, hoot 6 phooey 7 catcall

for: 4 need 6 demand, desire

gang's signal: 4 whyo

havoc: 8 mobilize

of approval: ole, rah 5 bravo

of pain: 4 ouch

of relief: 4 phew, whew

of sorrow: ay; woe 4 alas 5 alack

of triumph: aha 6 hurrah

out: 5 blame, crake, deery 7 censure, protest 8 complain, denounce

political: 6 slogan 10 shibboleth

Cry the Beloved Country author: 5 Paton

crying: 6 urgent 7 clamant, heinous 8 pressing, recreant 9 notorious 11 exclamatory

crying bird: 7 limpkin

crying hare: 4 pika

crying out: 10 childbirth 11 confinement

crypt: pit 5 croft, vault 6 cavern, grotto, recess 7 chamber 8 follicle 10 depression

cryptic: 4 dark 5 vague 6 hidden, occult, secret 7 obscure 9 enigmatic, recondite 10 mysterious 12 hieroglyphic

cryptogram: 4 code 6 cipher 11 cryptograph

crystal: ice 4 dial, hard 5 clear, glass, lucid 6 limpid, pebble 7 acicula, diamond 8 pellucid 11 crystalline, transparent

gazer: 4 seer 7 seeress

ice: 6 frazil

twin: 5 macle

crystalline: 4 pure 7 crystal 8 pellucid 11 transparent

acid: 7 alanine

compound: 5 alban 6 anisil, oscine 7 aconite, amarine 8 atropine

mineral: 4 mica, spar 6 quartz 7 apatite 8 boracite, elaterin

phenol: 5 orcin 6 orcine

pine tar: 6 retene

salt: 5 borax 8 analgene, racemate

structure: 6 sparry 8 siderite

substance: 4 urea 6 dulcin 9 scopoline

crystallize: 5 candy, sugar 7 congeal 8 solidify 9 granulate

ctenophora: 4 nuda 5 beroe 6 cestus

cub: fry, pen 4 bear, coop, shed 5 stall, whelp 6 lionet, novice 7 codling 8 reporter 9 youngster

Cuba: *asphalt:* 9 chapapote

beverage: 4 pina

bird: 6 trogon 8 tocororo

carriage: 7 volante

castle: 5 Morro

cigar: 6 Havana

city: 6 Guines, Havana(c.) 7 Palmira 8 Camaguay, Matanzas, Santiago 9 Cienfuego 10 Santa Clara 14 Puerto Principe

coin: 4 peso 7 centavo 8 cuarenta

dance: 5 conga, rumba 6 danzon, rhumba

dictator: 6 Castro 7 Batista

dollar: 6 gourde

fish: 6 diablo 7 viajaca

hutia: 6 pilori

measure: 4 vara 5 bocoy, tarea 6 cordel, fanega 10 caballeria

mountain: 6 Copper 11 Pinar del Rio 12 Guaniguanico 13 Pico Turquinos

province: 6 Havana 7 Oriente 8 Camaguey, Matanzas 10 Santa Clara 11 Pinar del Rio

rodent: 5 hutia 6 pilori

root: 7 malanga

rum: 7 Bacardi

secret police: 5 porra

snake: 4 juba

storm: 6 bayamo

tobacco: 4 capa 6 vuelta

tree: 4 cuya 5 culla

ward: 6 barrio

weapon: 7 machete

weight: 5 libra 6 tercio

cubage: 6 volume 7 content

cubbyhole: 4 nook

cube: cut, die 4 dice 5 block, solid 10 hexahedron

cube spar: 9 anhydrite

cubic: 5 solid 9 isometric

decimeter: 5 liter, litre

meter: 5 stere

shape: 6 cuboid

cubicle: bay 4 cell, noak, room 5 booth, niche 6 alcove

cubitus: 4 ulna 7 forearm

Cuchullin's wife: 4 Emer 5 Eimer

cuckoo: ani 4 bird, fool, gowk, koel 5 clock, crazy, silly 7 boobook 8 rainfowl

kind: 6 coucal, kobird 7 kowbird, wryneck 8 coccyzus

cuckoopint: 4 arum 5 aaron, plant 9 wake-robin

cormorant: 4 bird, shag 5 norie, scart 6 gormaw, scarth 7 glutton 8 ravenous 13 phalacrocorax
young: 7 shaglet
corn: 4 salt, samp 5 grain, maize, mealy 6 clavis, heloma, kernel 7 callous 8 preserve 9 granulate
bread: 4 pone
dealer: 10 cornmonger
ear: cob 5 mealy 6 mealie, nubbin
food: 6 hominy
ground: 4 meal 5 grist
hulled: 4 samp 6 hominy
Indian: zea
knife: 7 machete
spike: cob, ear
corn bread: 4 pone 8 tortilla
Corncracker State: 8 Kentucky
corndodger: 4 pone 5 bread 8 dumpling
corned: 6 salted
cornel: 4 tree 6 cherry 7 dogwood
corner: in; get, wro 4 bend, cant, coin, nook, pool, trap, tree 5 angle, bight, catch, coign, elbow, herne, ingle, niche, quoin, trust 6 cantle, canton, coigne, cranny, recess 8 monopoly
cornerpiece: 6 cantle
cornerstone: 4 coin 5 basis, coign 6 coigne 7 support 9 curbstone 10 foundation
cornet: 4 horn 8 woodwind 10 instrument
cornflower: 7 barbeau 10 bluebottle
cornhouse: 7 granary 8 corncrib
Cornhusker State: 8 Nebraska
cornice: 4 band, drip, eave 5 crown 6 geison 7 molding 8 astragal
basket: 4 caul
diamond: 6 quartz
support: 5 ancon
wolframite: cal
cornmeal: 4 masa, samp 5 atole 7 hoecake 10 johnnycake
cornucopia: 4 horn
Cornwall: *castle:* 8 Tintagel
mine: bal 5 wheal
ore: 5 whits
Cornwallis' surrender site: 8 Yorktown
corny: 5 banal, stale, trite 11 sentimental
corolla: 4 bell 8 perianth
part: 5 galea, petal
corollary: 5 dogma 6 result, truism 7 adjunct, theorem 9 deduction, inference 11 consequence, proposition
geometric: 6 porism
corona: 5 cigar, crown, glory 6 fillet, rosary, wreath 7 aureole, circlet, garland, scyphus
coronation: 9 inaugural
stone: 5 Scone
coroner: 6 elisor 7 officer 8 examiner

coronet: 4 band, burr 5 crown, tiara 6 anadem, circle, diadem, timbre, wreath 7 chaplet
coronopus: 4 herb 6 carara
corporal: NCO 4 fano 5 fanon, fanum, phano 6 bodily
corporal punishment: 5 death 7 penalty 8 spanking, whipping
corporate: 6 united 8 combined 9 aggregate
corporation: 4 body, firm 5 trust 10 fellowship, foundation 11 association, combination
corporeal: 4 real 5 hylic, somal 6 actual, bodily, carnal 7 somatic 8 material, physical, tangible 11 substantial
corpse: DOA 4 body 5 mummy, relic, stiff 7 cadaver, carcass, carrion
fat of: 9 adipocere
pert. to: 7 deathly 10 cadaverous
corpulent: fat 5 bulky, burly, husky, obese, plump, stout 6 fleshy, portly, rotund 7 adipose, bellied, weighty 8 rolypoly
corpus: 4 body 8 writings 10 literature
corpuscle: 4 cell 9 leucocyte
lack of red: 6 anemia
redblood: 7 hematid 8 haematid 11 polkilocyte, schistocyte
corral: pen, sty 4 coop 5 atajo, pound 7 confine, enclose 8 stockage, surround 9 enclosure, inclosure
correct: O.K.; due, fit, fix 4 edit, lean, nice, okay, smug, true 5 amend, check, emend, exact, right 6 adjust, better, change, inform, proper, punish, rebuke, reform, remedy, repair, revamp, revise, strict 7 chasten, improve, perfect, precise, rectify, redress, reprove 8 accurate, chastise, definite, emendate, regulate, rigorous, truthful 9 castigate, faultless 10 immaculate, particular, scrupulous 11 punctilious 12 conventional
comb. form: 5 ortho
correctable: 10 corrigible
correlated: 4 akin 7 related
correlative: or; nor 4 then 5 equal, still 6 either, mutual 7 neither 8 analogue, conjoint 9 analogous 10 reciprocal 13 correspondent
correspond: fit, gee 4 jibe, suit 5 agree, match, tally, write 6 accord, concur, square 7 conport, respond 8 coincide, parallel, quadrate 9 analogous, harmonize 11 communicate
correspondence: 4 mail 7 analogy, letters, traffic 8 homology 9 assonance, congruity 10 similarity

correspondent: 8 quadrate, suitable 9 accordant, analogous, congruous 10 accomplice, concordant, equivalent 11 conformable, contributor, correlative

corresponding: *in sound:* 5 rimic 6 rhymic *part:* 7 isomere

corrida: 9 bullfight

corridor: 4 hall 5 aisle, oriel 6 arcade 7 couloir, gallery 8 coulisse 10 passageway

corrie: 6 cirque, hollow

corrigible: 8 amenable 10 corrective, punishable 11 correctable

corroborant: 5 tonic 10 supporting 12 invigorating 13 strengthening

corroborate: 5 prove 7 confirm, support, sustain 9 establish 11 countersign 12 substantiate

corrode: eat 4 bite, burn, etch, gnaw, rust 5 decay, erode, waste 6 be-gnaw, canker, impair 7 consume

corrosive: 4 acid 6 ardent, biting 7 caustic, erosive, fretful, mordant 9 sarcastic 11 destructive 14 disintegrating

corrugate: 5 crimp 6 furrow, rumple 7 crinkle, crumple, wrinkle

corrugation: 4 fold 6 crease, pucker 7 wrinkle

corrupt: bad, low, rot 4 evil, vile 5 blend, bribe, spoil, stain, sully, taint, venal 6 augean, canker, debase, impure, poison, putrid, ravish, rotten 7 abusive, attaint, carrion, crooked, defiled, degrade, deprave, envenom, falsify, immoral, pervert, pollute, putrefy, violate, vitiate 8 confound, empoison 9 abandoned, dishonest 10 adulterate, demoralize, flagitious, profligate 11 contaminate, purchasable

corsage: 5 waist 6 bodice, boquet 7 bouquet, flowers

corsair: bug 6 pirate, robber 8 picaroon, rockfish 9 privateer 10 buccanneer *body:* 5 armor, cover

corset: 4 belt, busk 6 girdle 7 support *covering:* 8 camisole *strip:* 4 bone, busk

Corsica: *seaport:* 6 Bastia *town:* 7 Ajaccio

corslet: 6 bodice 8 corselet 11 breastplate

cortege: 5 suite, train 6 parade 7 retinue 10 procession

cortex: 4 bark, peel, rind 8 peridium

corundum: 4 ruby, sand 5 emeru, emery 7 alumina 8 abrasive, sapphire

coruscate: 5 blaze, flash, gleam, shine 7 glisten, glitter, radiate, sparkle 8 brandish 11 scintillate

corviform: 7 corvine 8 crowlike

corvine bird: daw 4 crow, rook 5 raven

coryza: 4 cold

symptom: 6 sneeze

cos: 7 lettuce, romaine

cosa nostra: 5 Mafia 9 syndicate

cosh: 4 neat, snug, tidy 5 happy, quiet, still 6 attack, lively, strike, weapon 7 assault 8 familiar, friendly 11 comfortable

cosher: pet 4 chat 5 feast, visit 6 pamper, sponge

cosmetic: 5 cream, henna, liner, paint, rouge 6 enamel, pomade, powder 7 mascara 8 lipstick *medicated:* 6 lotion *paste:* 4 pack *white lead:* 6 ceruse

cosmic: 4 vast 7 orderly 8 catholic, infinite 9 universal 10 harmonious *opposed to:* 7 chaotic

cosmonaut: See **astronaut**

cosmopolitan: 5 urban 8 ecumenic 10 ecumenical 13 sophisticated

cosmos: 5 earth, globe, order, realm, world 6 flower 7 harmony 8 universe *opposed to:* 5 Chaos

Cossack: 4 Turk 5 tatar 6 ataman, hetman, tartar 7 Russian 10 cavalryman *captain:* 6 Sotnik *chief:* 6 ataman, hetman *district:* 6 voisko *mount:* 5 steed 7 charger *regiment:* 4 polk, pulk *squadron:* 6 sotnia, sotnya *village:* 8 stanitza *whip:* 5 knout

cosset: pet 4 lamb 6 caress, coddle, cuddle, fondle, pamper

cossette: 4 chip 5 slice, strip 9 schnitzel

cossid: 9 messenger

cost: 4 loss, pain 5 price, value 6 charge, outlay 7 expense 8 estimate 9 detriment, sacrifice, suffering 11 deprivation, expenditure 14 characteristic

costa: rib 4 side, vein 5 ridge 6 border, midrib

Costa Rica: *city:* 7 Heredia, San Jose(c.) 8 Alajuela *coin:* 5 colon 7 centimo *measure:* 6 fanega, tercia 7 cajuela, manzana 10 caballeria *mountain:* 6 Blanco 8 Chirripo *people:* 6 Guaymi 7 Guaymie *port:* 10 Porto Limon 11 Punta Arenas *volcano:* 5 Barba *weight:* bag 4 caja

costate: 6 ribbed

costermonger: 6 coster, hawker, nipper 7 peddler

cucullate: 6 cowled, hooded 7 covered 10 hood-shaped

cucumber: 4 cuke, pepo 6 conger, pepino(Sp.) 7 gherkin 9 elaterium

cucurbit: 5 flask, gourd 6 vessel 7 alembic, matrass

cud: chew, quid 5 bolus, rumen 6 cudgel

cuddle: hug, pet 6 caress, cosset, fondle, nestle 7 embrace, snuggle

cuddy: ass 4 lout 5 bribe, cabin 6 donkey, galley, pantry 9 blockhead

cudgel: bat 4 beat, cane, club, drub, rack 5 baste, drive, kebby, kevel, staff, stave, stick 6 alpeen, ballow, baston, kebbie, thrash, weapon 7 belabor, bourdon 8 bludgeon, shillala 9 bastinado, crabstick, fustigate, truncheon 10 shillelagh

cue: nod, tip 4 hint, mast, tail, wink 5 braid, cluff, plait, queue, twist 6 prompt, signal 7 pigrail 9 catchword 10 intimation

cuff: box 4 bank, blow, gowf, slam, slap, slug, swat 5 clout, fight, gowff, miser, smite 6 buffet, codger, mitten, strike 7 scuffle 8 gauntlet, handcuff

cuirass: 4 mail 5 armor, loric, plate 6 lorica

cuisine: 4 food, menu 5 table 7 cookery

cuittle: 4 coax 6 tickle 7 wheedle

cul-de-sac: 6 pocket, strait 7 deadend, impasse 10 difficulty

culicid: 8 mosquito

cull: opt 4 dupe, gull, pick, sift, sort 5 elect, glean, pluck 6 assort, choose, gather, remove, select 8 separate

cully: 4 dupe, gull, mate 5 cheat, trick 7 deceive 9 companion

culm: 5 slack 6 refuse 7 deposit

culmen: top 4 acme 5 ridge

culmination: end 4 acme, apex, noon 5 crown 6 apogee, climax, summit, vertex, zenith 10 completion 12 consummation

culpa: 5 fault, guilt 10 negligence 12 carelessness

culpable: 6 faulty, guilty, laches 7 immoral 8 criminal 10 censurable 11 blameworthy 13 reprehensible

culprit: 5 felon 7 convict 8 criminal, offender 10 malefactor

cult: 4 clan, sect 5 creed 6 church, ritual, school 7 worship 12 denomination

cultivate: ear, hoe 4 disk, farm, grow, plow, rear, tend, till 5 nurse, raise, study, train 6 affect, foster, harrow, plough 7 acquire, cherish, educate, husband, improve, nourish, prepare 8 civilize 9 encourage

cultivated: 5 civil 6 polite 7 refined 8 cultured 12 domesticated

land: 4 farm 5 arada, tilth

cultivation: 7 culture, tillage 9 culturing, husbandry 10 refinement 12 civilization

art: 9 geoponics

cultivator: 6 farmer, harrow, tiller 7 grubber, husband 10 husbandman

culture: art 4 agar 5 taste 6 polish 7 tillage 9 knowledge 10 discipline, refinement 12 civilization

medium: 4 agar

culver: 4 dove 6 pigeon

culvert: 5 drain 6 bridge 7 conduit

cumbersome: 5 heavy 6 clumsy 7 onerous, weighty 8 cumbrous, unwieldy 10 burdensome

combrous: 8 clogging, unwieldy 9 difficult, vexatious 10 burdensome, cumbersome

cumin: 5 anise, cumic

cummer, kimmer: 4 girl, lass 5 witch, woman 6 friend 7 midwife 9 companion, godmother

cummerbund: 4 band, belt, sash

cumshaw: tip 5 bonus 6 thanks 7 present 8 gratuity

cumulate: 4 heap 6 gather 7 combine 10 accumulate

cunabula: 6 cradle

cuneal: 7 cuneate 11 wedge-shaped

cuneiform: 4 bone 6 wedged 7 writing 8 sphenoid

cunner: 5 canoe 6 nipper, wrasse

cunning: sly, wit 4 arch, cute, foxy, keen, wily 5 downy, guile, sharp, smart 6 adroit, artful, astute, callid, clever, crafty, deadal, deceit, shrewd, subtle, tricky, wisdom 7 curious, finesse, politic, vulpine 8 dextrous, skillful, stealthy 9 chicanery, colubrine, designing, dexterity, ingenious, knowledge, sagacious 10 fraudulent, witchcraft 13 Machiavellian

cup: ama, dop, mug, tyg 4 tass 5 bouse, calix, cruse, glass, grail, phial, stein, tazza 6 beaker, crater, goblet, noggin, potion, vessel 7 chalice, stirrup

assay: 4 test 5 cupel 6 beaker

diamond cutting: dop

eared: 6 quaich, quaigh

earthenware: mug

fungus: 6 aecium

handle: ear, lug

holder: 4 zarf

horn-shaped: 6 holmos

large: 5 grail, jorum

looped handles: 5 kylix 9 cantharus, kantharos

loving: tyg 5 award, prize

of tea: 5 forte, thing 6 metier

pastry: 7 dariole

resembling: 9 oalicular

small: 4 shot 5 chark, cruse 6 noggin 8 cannikin 9 demitasse

two-handled: tig, tyg 5 depas

cup-shaped: 10 cyathiform

cupbearer of the gods: 4 Hebe 8 Ganymede

cupboard: kas 4 case, safe 5 ambry, cuddy 6 buffet, closet, larder, pantry 7 armoire, cabinet, dresser 8 credenza 9 sideboard

cupel: 4 burn, test 6 refine

Cupid: Dan 4 Amor, Eros, love 7 Amorino
beloved of: 6 Psyche
mother: 5 Venus

cupidity: 4 lust 5 greed 6 desire 7 avarice, avidity, longing 8 appetite 12 covetousness
demon of: 6 Mammon

cupidon: 5 cupid

cupola: 4 dome, kiln 5 vault 6 turret 7 furnace, lantern, lookout

cur: dog, yap 4 fice, mutt, tike, tyke 5 feist 6 canine, messan, messin 7 bobtail, mongrel 9 goldeneye

curacao: 7 liqueur

Curacao island: 5 Aruba

curare: 5 urare, urari 6 oorali, poison

curassow: 4 bird, crax, mitu

curate: cur 4 abbe 5 agent 7 dominie 8 minister 9 assistant, clergyman

curative: 7 healing 8 remedial, salutary, sanative 9 medicinal 11 restorative

curator: 6 keeper 7 manager, steward 8 guardian, overseer 9 custodian 14 superintendent

curb: bit 4 foil, rein 5 brake, check, curve, guard, limit 6 arrest, bridle, govern, hamper, thwart 7 control, inhibit, repress, shackle 8 moderate, restrain, restrict, withhold 9 constrain, hindrance 10 hamshackle

curculio: 6 weevil

curd: 6 curdle 7 caseine, clabber, congeal 8 fleeting 9 coagulate

curdle: 4 earn(Sc.), leep, quar, sour, yern 5 quail, quarl, spoil 6 posset, quarle 7 clabber, congeal, thicken 8 condense 9 coagulate
agent causing: 6 rennet

cure: dry 4 boot, care, heal, heed, help, jerk, salt, save 5 reest, smoke 6 charge, curate, priest, remedy, season 7 restore, therapy 8 antidote, preserve
by salting: 4 corn
in sun: 6 rizzar

cure-all: 4 balm 5 avens 6 elixir, remedy 7 panacea 10 catholicon

curfew: 4 bell 6 signal

curio: 5 relic, virtu 7 bibelot 8 keepsake, souvenir 9 bric-a-brac, curiosity

curious: odd 4 nosy, rare 5 queer 6 prying, quaint 7 cunning, strange, unusual 8 freakish, meddling, peculiar, singular 9 intrusive, wondering 11 inquisitive

curl: 4 bend, coil, kink, lock, roll, wave, wind 5 acker, crisp, tress, twist 6 buckle, frowse, ripple, spiral, writhe 7 crimple, flexure, ringlet, tendril 11 convolution 12 heartbreaker

curled: 7 savoyed

curlew: 4 bird, fute 5 kioea, snipe, whaup 6 marlin 7 bustard

curlicue: ess 5 caper, curve 6 paraph 8 flourish

curling mark: tee

curly: 4 wavy 5 crisp 7 rippled 8 crinkled

curmudgeon: 4 crab 5 churl, miser 6 grouch 7 niggard

curn: 4 corn 5 grain

currant: 5 berry 6 raisin, rizzar
genus: 5 ribes

currency: 4 cash, coin 5 bills, money, scrip 6 specie 10 greenbacks

current: now, way 4 eddy, flow, flux, ford, rife, tide 5 drift, going, rapid, tenor, trend, usual 6 coeval, common, course, living, motion, moving, recent, stream 7 counter, flowing, general, present, running, thermal, torrent 8 frequent 9 prevalent 10 prevailing 11 electricity 15 contemporaneous
generator: 12 electromotor
measuring device: 7 ammeter
pert. to: 7 voltaic

currish: 4 base 7 cynical, ignoble 8 snarling 12 mean-spirited

curry: 4 comb, drub 5 clean, dress, groom 6 bruise, cajole, powder 7 prepare 9 condiment, seasoning
favor: 4 fawn 6 cajole, smooge

curse: ban 4 bane, blow, damn, oath 5 spell, swear 6 malign 7 beshrew, malison 8 anathema 9 blaspheme, imprecate, maranatha 10 execration, vituperate 11 deprecation, malediction 12 anathematize 13 excommunicate

cursed: bad 6 odious 8 blighted, virulent 9 execrable

cursory: 4 fast 5 brief, hasty, quick, short 6 fitful, speedy 7 passing, shallow 8 careless, rambling 9 desultory, irregular, transient 10 discursive, evanescent 11 superficial

curt: 4 buff, rude, tart 5 bluff, blunt, brief, brusk, short, terse 6 abrupt 7 brusque, concise 8 cavalier, succinct 9 condensed

curtail: cut, lop 4 clip, crop, dock, pare, stop 5 abate, short, slash, stunt 6 lessen, reduce, teaser 7 abridge, bobtail, shorten 8 diminish, minorate, retrench 9 decurtate, epitomize 10 abbreviate

curtain: end 4 boom, drop, mask, veil, wall 5 blind, drape, shade 6 purdah, screen, shroud 7 ceiling, conceal, drapery 8 portiere

half: 4 bise, cafe 5 brise
raiser: 9 forepiece
curtilage: 4 area, yard 5 court
curtsy, curtsey: bob, bow 4 beck 5 conge 9 obeisance
curvature (see also **curve**): are 4 bool, curl 8 kyphosis, lordosis 9 arcuation, scoliosis
center locus: 7 evolute
convex: 6 camber
surface: 5 plane
curve: arc, bow, ess 4 arch, bend, curb, ogee, turn, veer 5 ambit, bight, crook, crump, swirl, twist 6 bought, spiral 7 circuit, concave, contour, curvity, ellipse, flexure, inflect, sinuate 8 parabola, sinusaid 9 convexity, curvature
cusp: 7 spinode
double point of: 6 acnode
kind: 9 parabolic 10 memniscate
mathematical plane: 5 polar
parallel to an ellipse: 6 toroid
curved: 5 round, wound 6 convex, hamate, turned 7 arcuate, arrondi, crooked, curvant 8 anchoral, aquiline, arciform
inward: 5 adunc 6 hooked 8 aduncous
curvet: hop 4 leap, lope, skip, turn 5 bound, caper, frisk, prank 6 cavort, frolic, gambol, prance 8 corvetta(F.) 9 courbette
cuscuta: 5 plant 6 dodder 8 parasite
Cush: *father:* Ham
son: 4 Seba 6 Nimrod
cushat: 4 bird, dove 6 pigeon
cushion: bag, cod, mat, pad 4 boss, seat 5 gaddi, squab 6 buffer, insole, jockey, pillow, sachet 7 bolster, hassock 9 upholster
stuffing: 4 baru, down 5 kapok 8 feathers
cusk: 4 fish, tusk 5 torsk 6 burbot
cusp: 4 apex, horn, peak 5 angle, point, tooth 6 corner 8 paracone 10 projection
custard: 4 flan 5 flawn 6 doucet, dowcet, dowset 8 flummery 9 charlotte
custard apple: 5 anona 6 annona, paw-paw 8 sweetsop
custodian: 5 guard 6 bailee, keeper, warden 7 curator, janitor 8 guardian 9 caretaker, protector
custody: 4 care 5 trust 6 charge 7 control, durance, keeping, tuition 11 safekeeping 12 guardianship
custom: fad, law, mos(L.), tax, use 4 duty, form, garb, mode, more, rite, rote, rule, toll, wont 5 habit, haunt, usage, vogue 6 dastur, impost 7 costume, fashion, tribute 8 business, practice 9 costumbre, patronage 10 consuetude, convention, observance 12 constitution
of peoples: 5 mores
with force of law: mos
customary: 5 nomic, usual 6 common 7 general 8 familiar, habitual, orthodox 10 accustomed 11 traditional 12 conventional 14 consuetudinary
customer: 4 chap 5 buyer 6 client, patron 7 callant, patient, shopper 8 prospect 9 purchaser
group: 9 clientele
customhouse: 6 aduana(Sp.), dogana(It.) 9 chophouse
customs: tax 4 cess, duty, levy, rate, toll 5 mores 6 tariff 7 trewage
officer: 8 douanier
cut: bob, hew, lop, mow, nip, rit 4 bite, chip, chop, clip, crop, dock, fell, gash, hack, knap, mode, nick, pare, raze, slit, snee, snip, snub, trim 5 carve, flick, knife, lance, mince, notch, prune, razee, scarp, sever, shear, shorn, slash, slice, slish, snick, split 6 ablate, bisect, broach, chisel, cleave, divide, excise, haggle, ignore, incise, lessen, mangle, reduce, scotch, slight, swinge 7 affront, curtail, whittle 8 lacerate, retrench 9 engraving, intersect
a melon: 5 allot 8 dispense
a rug: 5 dance
across: 5 slice 8 transect 9 intersect, transcend
along: go 5 speed
capable of being: 7 sectile
down: 4 pare 5 clear, slash 9 economize
in: mix 9 interpose, interrupt, introduce
in half: 5 halve 6 bisect, secant 8 dimidate
in small pieces: 4 dice, hash 5 mince 6 sliver
off: lop, nig 4 clip, crop, drib, poll 5 elide, roach, shave 7 deprive, divorce, exscind 8 amputate, truncate 9 apocopate, intercept 10 disinherit
out: 6 exsect 7 exscind 9 eliminate
roughly: jag 4 hack, snag 7 butcher
short: bob 4 clip, crop, dock, poll 5 abort, check, clipt 6 arrest 7 curtail
slanting: 4 bias 5 bevel, miter, mitre
with die: 4 dink
with shears: 4 snip 5 shirl
wool: dod 4 dodd 5 shear
cut and dried: 5 trite
cutaneous: 6 dermal
cutaway: 4 coat
cute: coy 4 keen 5 coony, dinky, sharp 6 clever, pretty, shrewd 7 cunning 10 attractive
cuticle: 4 hide, skin 8 membrane, pellicle 9 epidermis 10 integument
blister: 4 bleb 5 bulla
ingredient: 5 cutin
cutis: 4 skin 5 derma 6 corium
cutlass: 5 sword 6 dusack, tesack 7 machete
cutout: 9 decoupage
cutpurse: 5 thief 10 pickpocket

cutter: 4 beef, boat, sled 5 bravo, sloop, smack 6 cotter, editor, sleigh, slicer 7 clipper, incisor, ruffian 9 cutthroat, foretooth

cutthroat: 5 bravo 7 ruffian

cutting: hag, raw 4 curt, keen, kerf, slip, tart, twig 5 acute, bleak, crisp, scion, scrap, scrow, sharp 6 biting, bitter, secant, severe 7 caustic, mordant, painful, satiric 8 chilling, incisive, piercing, poignant, wounding 9 sarcastic, trenchant 10 blustering 11 abridgement, curtailment 12 adulteration
  edge: 5 blade
  implement: ax; axe, bit, hob, saw 4 adze 5 knife, lathe, mower, plane, razor 6 chisel, reaper, scythe, shears 8 scissors
  of last letter: 7 apocope

cuttle: 4 thug 5 bully, knife 7 ruffian 8 assassin 9 swaggerer

cuttlefish: 5 sepia, squid 7 octopus, scuttle
  ink: 5 sepia

cuvette: pot, tub 4 tank 5 basin 6 bucket, trench 7 cistern

cyanogen compound: 7 cyanide

Cybele: 4 Rhea
  sweetheart: 5 Attis

Cyclades Island: Ios, Zea 4 Keos, Milo, Nios, Sira, Syra 5 Delos, Melos, Naxia, Naxos, Paros, Syros, Tenos, Tinos 6 Andros 7 Amorgos

cycle: age, eon, era 4 aeon, bike 5 epoch, pedal, round, saros, wheel 6 circle, course, period 7 bicycle, circuit, vehicle 8 tricycle 10 revolution

cyclone: 4 gale, gust, wind 5 blast, storm 6 baguio 7 tornado, twister, typhoon 9 hurricane, windstorm

cyclopean: 4 huge, vast 6 strong 7 massive 8 colossal, gigantic 9 herculean

Cyclopes: 5 Arges 7 Brontes 8 Steropes

Cyclops: 5 giant 7 monster
  feature: 6 one eye

cyclostome: 7 lamprey

Cycnus' father: 4 Ares

cygnet: pen 4 fowl, swan

cygnus: 4 swan

cylinder: 4 beam, drum, pipe, prim, tube 6 barrel, bobbin, gabian, piston, platen, roller 7 sleever

cylindrical: 5 round 6 terete 7 centric, tubular 8 teretial

cyma: 4 gola, gula, ogee 7 molding

cymar: 4 robe 5 shift, simar

cymbal: tal, zel 8 doughnut

cymbals: 6 becken, piatti

Cymbeline's daughter: 6 Imogen

Cymric: 5 Welsh
  god of dead: 5 Pwyll
  god of sky: 7 Gwydion
  god of sun: 4 Lleu, Llew
  god of underworld: 4 Gwyn

cynic: 5 Timon 7 doubter 9 pessimist 11 misanthrope

cynical: 6 sullen 7 currish, doglike 8 captious, snarling

cynosure: 8 lodestar, polestar

cypress: 9 belvedere

cyprinoid: See **fish**

Cyprus: *city:* 6 Paphos 7 Limasol, Nicosia(c.) 9 Famagusta
  coin: 4 para 7 piaster
  measure: oka, oke, pik 4 cass 5 donum, kouza 6 gomari, kartos 7 medimno
  mountain: 7 Troodos
  weight: oka, oke 5 moosa 6 kantar

cyrenaic: 7 hedonic

Cyrus: *daughter:* 6 Atossa
  treasurer: 10 Mithredath

cyst: bag, sac, wen 5 pouch 6 ranula 7 vesicle

Cyzicus: *mother:* 6 Aenete
  slayer: 5 Jason
  wife: 6 Cleite

czar, csar: 4 Ivan, tsar, tzar 5 Peter 8 Nicholas
  daughter: 8 czarevna, tsarevna
  son: 10 czarevitch, tsarevitch
  wife: 7 czarina, tsarina

Czechoslovakia: *capital:* 5 Praha 6 Prague
  city: As 4 Asch, Brno, Eger, Hron 5 Opava, Praha, Tuzla 6 Aussig, Pilsen, Prague 7 Budweis, Teplitz 9 Pressburg 10 Bratislava 11 Reichenberg
  coin: 5 ducat, haler 6 heller, koruna
  county: Ung
  dance: 5 polka 6 redowa 7 furiant
  leader: 5 Benes
  measure: lan, sah 4 mira 5 latro, liket, stopa 6 merice
  mountain: 5 Tatra
  munitions plant: 5 Skoda
  province: 7 Bohemia, Moravia
  reformer: 4 Huss
  river: Vag, Vah 4 Eger, Elbe, Gran, Hron, Isar, Iser, Labe, Oder, Ohre, Waag 5 Nitra 6 Moldau

czigany: 5 gypsy

D

dab: dap, hit, pat 4 blow, chit, lump, peck, spot 5 clout, dight, smear 6 blotch, expert, strike 7 dabster, portion, splotch 8 flatfish, flounder

dabble: dib 4 mess 5 dally 6 dibble, meddle, paddle, potter, splash, tamper, trifle 7 moisten, spatter 8 sprinkle

dabbler: 7 amateur, dabster 10 dilettante

dabby: wet 4 damp 5 moist 8 adhesive

dabchick: 5 grebe

dabster: See **dab**

dace: 4 chub

dacoit: 6 robber 8 criminal 9 plunderer

dactyl: toe 6 finger 7 piddock

dactylogram: 11 fingerprint

dactylopodite: 6 pollex

dactyloscopy: 14 classification, identification

dad: 4 beat, blow, hunk, lump, papa 5 knock, thump 6 father, strike

daddle: 4 fist, hand 6 dawdle

daddy longlegs: 5 stilt 7 spinner, tipulid 8 arachnid

dado: 6 groove 7 solidum

daedal: 4 rich 6 varied 7 bizarre 8 artistic, skillful 9 ingenious, intricate 10 variegated

Daedalus: *son:* 6 Icarus
victim: 5 Talos

daemon (see also **demon**): 8 eudaemon

daffing: fun 7 fooling

daffodil: 5 dilly

daffy: See **daft**

daft: gay 4 luny, wild 5 balmy, crazy, giddy, potty, silly 6 insane 7 foolish, idiotic 8 imbecile

dag: jag 4 stab 5 slash 6 daggle, pierce 7 daglock

Dag's horse: 8 Hrimfaxi 9 Skinfaksi

Dagda's kin: 5 Boann 6 Aengus, Brigit

dagger: 4 dirk, itac(Pl), kris, snee, spud, stab 5 crise, katar(Ind.), skean(Ir.) 6 anlace, bodkin, coutel, creese, diesis, kreese, panade, stylet, weapon 7 baslard, corteau, dudgeon, lalarao, poniard 8 puncheon, stiletto 10 misericord 11 misericorde
Burmese: dah, dow
handle: 4 hilt
Malay: 4 kris
Scotch: 4 dirk
stroke: 4 stab 8 stoccado

Dahomey people: Fon 4 Fong

daily: 4 aday 7 diurnal 9 hodiernal, newspaper, quotidian

daintily: 8 gingerly

dainty: 4 cate, nice, rare 5 acate, denty 6 bonbon, choice, costly, friand, mignon, minion, picked, scarce 7 elegant, finical, finicky, minikin 8 delicacy, delicate, migniard 9 exquisite, finicking, squeamish 10 confection, fastidious

dairy: 7 vaccary 8 creamery
food: 6 yogurt 7 yoghurt, yohourt 8 yoghourt
tool: 9 separator

dairymaid: dey 8 deywoman, milkmaid

dairyman: 7 milkman

dais: 4 seat 5 bench, podia(pl.), stage, table 6 canopy, podium, settle 7 estrade, terrace 8 chabutra, platform

daisy: 5 gowan, oxeye 6 shasta 10 moonflower

dak: 4 post

Dakota Indian: 5 Sioux 6 Mandan 7 Arikara 8 Arikaree

Daksha's father: 6 Brahma

Dalai Lama: 5 ruler 13 reincarnation

dale: 4 dell, dene, glen, vale 5 spout 6 bottom, dingle, trough, valley

dalles: 6 rapids

dalliance: toy 4 chat, play, talk 6 gossip, trifle, tousel, tousle

dally: toy 4 chat, fool, idle, jake, jauk, play, wait 5 delay, flirt, sport, tarry 6 dabble, dawdle, linger, loiter, trifle

Dalmatia: *channel:* 7 Narenta
seaport: 7 Spalato

dam: bar, bay 4 stay, stem, stop, weir 5 block, check, choke, garth, mound 6 anicut, causey, mother, parent **7** annicut, barrier **8** blockade, obstacle, obstruct, restrain

dama: 7 gazelle

damage: mar **4** blot, cost, harm, hurt, loss, ruin, teen **5** burst, cloud, spoil, wound **6** charge, deface, defect, impair, injure, injury, scathe **7** expense, scratch **8** accident, disserve, mischief, sabotage **9** detriment, disprofit, vandalism **10** impairment **11** deleterious, impeachment **12** disadvantage

pert. to: **5** noxal

damages: 5 award **7** payment

daman: 5 hyrax

Damascus: *people:* **6** Syrian

river: **5** Abana **6** Abanah, Barada **7** Pharpar

damask: 5 linen

dame: 4 lady **5** woman **6** matron

correlative: **4** sire

dammar: 5 resin, rosin

damn: 5 curse

damnable: 6 odious **8** infernal **9** execrable **10** detestable

damnation: 9 perdition

damned: 5 bally **6** bloody **8** accursed

damnum: 4 harm, loss **9** detriment

damourite: 4 mica **9** muscovite

damp: deg, fog, wet **4** dank, dewy, dull, mist, roky **5** dabby, humid, moist, muggy, musty, rafty, rainy, soggy **6** clammy, dampen, deaden, muffle, quench, stupor **7** bedewed, depress, moisten **8** dejected, dispirit, humidity, moisture **9** depressed, stupefied **10** discourage

damper: 5 bread **7** checker **8** register

damsel: 4 girl **6** maiden **8** donzella, princess **10** demoiselle

Dan: *prince:* **7** Ahiezer

town: **4** Elon

Danae's kin: 4 Zeus **7** Perseus **8** Acrisius

danaite: 12 arsenopyrite

dance: bal(F.), bob, hop **4** ball, frug, haka, hoof, prom, shag **5** caper, flisk, frike, frisk, rumba, tango, tread, stomp, twist, waltz **6** balter, Boston, hormos, masque, minuet, monkey **7** foxtrot, saltate **8** cotillon, fandango **9** allemande(G.), cotillion, farandole **10** roundabout, tripudiate

ancient: see *old* below

art of: **8** orchesis **12** choreography

ballroom: **5** polka, waltz **7** czardas, foxtrot, mazurka, twostep

basket-carrying: **11** calathiscus

ceremonial: **6** areito

chorus: **5** strut **6** cancan, cordax

college: hop **4** prom

country: hay, hey **7** argeers, auresca **8** aurrescu, haymaker **10** villanella

designer: **12** choreographer **13** choreographer

drama: **6** ballet

English: **6** althea, morris

exhibition: tap **6** ballet

fast: see *lively* below

formal: **4** prom **5** pavan, paven, pavin **7** mazurka **9** farandole

gypsy: **7** farruca **10** zingaresca

Hawaiian: **4** hula

Hebrew: **4** hora

involuntary: **8** tricotee

Italian: **5** volta **8** courante **9** rigoletto **10** tarantella

Latin American: **5** conga, rumba, samba, tango **6** maxixe, rhumba **7** carioca, criolla

lively: jig **4** reel, trot **5** fling, galop, gavot, polka, rumba **6** bolero, branle, canary,, rhumba **7** coranto **8** galliard, rigadoon **9** allemande, schottish, shakedown, tambourin **10** corybantic **11** schottische

masked: **7** ridotto

modern: toe **4** dump, frug, pony, shag **5** twist **6** chacha, monkey **7** twostep **10** Charleston **12** mashed potato

movement: pas **4** jete, step **5** brise, coule, coupe **6** chasse, coupee **7** chassed, fouette, gambado **8** glissade **9** entrechat, pirouette

Muse: **11** Terpsichore

music: **10** gymnopedie

nineteenth-century: **7** tempete

old: **5** galop, gavot, loure, pavan, paven, pavin, rondo, volta **6** bource, branle, canary, carole, cebell, corant, minuet, morris, pavane **7** boutade, chaccon, chacona, coranto, courant, furlana, gavotte, lavolta **8** chaconne, faradole, gilliard **9** allemande, farandola, horedance, sarabande **10** tarantella, tarantelle

pert. to: **6** gestic **13** terpsichorean

Peruvian: **5** cueca

round: **5** carol, waltz **6** carole **10** Charleston

rustic: See *country* above

shoes: **4** taps **5** pumps **8** slippers, toeshoes

slow: **5** waltz **6** adagio, minuet, valeta

square: **7** argeers, lancers **8** lanciers **9** quadrille

step: See *movement* above

sword: **8** matachin **11** Flamborough

voluptuous: **5** belly **8** habanera

dance of death: 7 macaber, macabre

dancer: 6 artist, hoofer, happer **7** danseur **11** terpsichore **13** terpsichorean

Biblical: **6** Salome

female: **7** artiste, chorine **8** bayadere, coryphee, danseuse, devadasi **9** ballerina **15** terpsichorienne

garment: 7 leotard
instrument: 8 castanet
rope: nat
sword: 8 matachin
dancing: 7 saltant 11 choregraphy 12 choreography
dancing girl: See **dancer** *female*
dandelion: 7 chicory 10 bitterwort
stalk: 5 scape
dander: 5 anger, scurf 6 stroll, temper, wander 7 passion, saunter 8 dandruff
dandified 6 spruce 8 adonized
dandiprat: 5 dwarf, pygmy 6 urchin
dandle: 6 diddle, fondle, pamper
dandruff: 5 scurf
dandy: fop 4 beau, buck, dand, dude, fine, jake, prig, toff, yawl 5 dildo, swell 7 capstan, coxcomb, foppish, jessamy 8 sailboat 9 exquisite 11 scrumptious
female: 10 dandisette, dandizette
Dane: See **Denmark**
danger: 4 fear, risk 5 doubt, peril 6 hazard 7 pitfall, venture 8 distress, jeopardy 9 adventure
signal: 4 bell 5 alarm, siren 6 tocsin
dangerous: bad, rum 5 nasty 6 fickle 7 parlous 8 insecure 9 desperate 10 precarious
dangle: lop 4 hang, loll 5 droop, swing 7 shoggle, suspend
Danish: See **Denmark**
dank: wet 4 damp 5 humid, moist 6 clammy, coarse, dampen 7 drizzle, wetness 8 moisture
danseuse: 6 dancer 9 ballerina
danta: 5 tapir
Dante: *beloved:* 8 Beatrice
circle of hell: 5 Caina
illustrator: 4 Dore
patron: 5 Scala
verse form: 7 sestina
Danube: 5 Ister
fish: 4 huch 5 hucho
people: 6 Dacian
town: Ulm
tributary: 4 Drau, Raab, Raba 5 Drava, Drave, Siret
Danzig: *coin:* 6 gulden 7 pfennig
liqueur: 7 ratafia
dap: dab, dib, dip 4 skip 6 bounce, dibble 7 rebound
Daphne: 8 Mezereon
father: 5 Ladon
mother: 6 Creusa
Daphnis' lover: 5 Chloe
dapper: 4 neat, trim 5 natty 6 spruce 7 finical, foppish
dappled: 6 dotted 7 flecked, mottled, spotted 8 freckled 10 variegated
darbies: 8 manacles 9 handcuffs

Dardanelles: 10 Hellespont
dare: 4 dast, defy, face, osse, risk 5 brave 6 assume 7 attempt, venture 9 challenge, undertake
dare not: 5 dasn't 6 daurna
daredevil: 6 madcap 12 swashbuckler
daring: 4 bold, rash 5 brave, hardy, manly, nerve 6 heroic 7 courage 8 boldness, devilish, fearless 9 audacious 10 courageous, jeopardous 11 adventurous, venturesome
dariole: cup 5 shell
Darius: *father:* 9 Ahasuerus
prince: 6 Daniel
dark: dim, mum, sad, wan 4 dern, ebon, mirk, murk 6 black, blind, brown, cloud, dingy, dusky, faint, mirky, murky, shady, sooty, swart, unlit, vague 6 closed, cloudy, dimpsy, dismal, gloomy, opaque, swarth, wicked 7 melanic, obscure, rayless, stygian, swarthy 8 abstruse, darkling, gloomful, ignorant, lowering, sinister 9 ambiguous, atrocious, blindfold, Cimmerian, infuscate, recondite, secretive, tenebrous, uncertain, unlighted, unrefined 10 caliginous, indistinct, mysterious
dark-complexioned: 7 swarthy
dark horse: 9 candidate 10 contestant
darken: dim 4 dull 5 bedim, cloud, gloam, shade, sully, umber 6 deepen, shadow 7 becloud, benight, blacken, eclipse, obscure, opacate, perplex, tarnish 8 overcast 9 obfuscate, overcloud 10 overshadow
darkness: 4 dark, dern, dusk, murk 5 gloom, night, shade 6 shadow 7 dimness, privacy, secrecy 8 gloaming, iniquity, twilight 9 blackness 10 wickedness
realm: Po 6 Erebus
darling: jo; joe(Sc.), pet 4 dear, duck 5 aroon(Ir.), aruin, bully, cheri, deary, lieve, sweet 6 cherie, dautie(Sc.), dawtie(Sc.), minion, moppet 7 acushla(Ir.), pigsney, querida 8 favorite 9 favourite
darn: 4 mend 5 patch 6 repair
darnel: 4 tare, weed 5 grass 6 cockle
darner: 6 needle
dart: 4 bolt, flit, jouk, leap, plan 5 arrow, bound, fling, flirt, lance, skite, spear, speed, start 6 dartle, elance, method, scheme, spring 7 javelin, missile 9 flechette
throwing machine: 10 anisocycle
dart-like: 8 dartling, spicular
D'Artagnan: *companion:* 5 Athos 6 Aramis 7 Porthos
creator: 5 Dumas
Dartmouth College Location: 7 Hanover 12 New Hampshire
Darwin: *boat:* 6 Beagle
theory: 9 evolution

Darwinian: 12 evolutionist
das: 6 dassie
Das Kapital author: 4 Marx
dash: pep 6 bang, ding, elan, gift, hurl, line, pelt, race, ruin, rush, show, slam 5 abash, ardor, break, clash, crash, crush, fling, knock, smash, speed, spice, style, swash, throw 6 energy, hurtle, hyphen, shiver, spirit, splash, sprint, stroke, thrust 7 bravura, collide, depress, display, shatter, spatter, splotch 8 confound, gratuity, splinter 9 animation, bespatter, frustrate, overthrow
dasheen: 4 taro
dasher: 6 beater 7 plunger
dashing: 4 bold 5 bully, showy 6 swanky, veloce 7 stylish, swagger 8 spirited 11 fashionable
dastard: cad, sot 5 sneak 6 coward, craven 7 dullard 8 poltroon
dastardly: 4 foul
data: 5 facts 8 material 11 information
datary: 7 dataria
date: age, day, era 5 epoch, fruit 6 reckon 10 engagement, rendezvous 11 anniversary, appointment
erroneous: 11 anachronism
on coin: 7 exergue
dated: 5 passe 8 outmoded 12 old-fashioned 13 unfashionable
dateless: 8 timeless 10 immemorial
dating: 6 timing
datum: 4 fact, item 11 information
daub: 4 balm, blob, blot, clag, clam, clat, coat, gaum, soil 5 clart, cleam, cover, paint, slake, smear 6 bedaub, grease 7 besmear, plaster, splotch 8 slaister
daughter: 4 bint 5 fille, filly 6 alumna 7 cadette
pert. to: 6 filial
Daughter of Moon: 7 Nokomis
daunt: awe, cow, daw 4 daze, faze, stun, tame 5 abash, amate, break, check, deter, dompt 6 dismay, subdue 7 conquer, control, overawe, repress, stupefy, terrify 8 dispirit, overcome 10 disconcert, discourage, dishearten, intimidate
dauntless: 4 bold, good 5 brave 7 aweless 8 fearless, intrepid 9 undaunted 10 courageous
davenport: 4 desk, sofa 5 couch, divan 12 chesterfield
daver: 4 fade, stun 5 droop 6 benumb, wither 7 stupefy
David: *chief ruler:* Ira
companion: 6 Hushai
daughter: 5 Tamar
employer: 5 Nabal
favorite son: 7 Absalom

friend: 5 Ittai
kin: 5 Jesse, Tamar 6 Michal 7 Abigail, Absalom, Solomon
man of: Ira 4 Igal 7 Shammah
musician: 5 Asaph
prophet: 6 Nathan
scribe: 7 Shavsha
traitor to: 10 Ahithophel
valley of Goliath's death: 4 Elah
David Copperfield character: 4 Dora, Heep, Rosa 5 Agnes, James, Uriah 6 Dartle 8 Micawber 9 Wickfield 10 Steerforth
daviely: 10 listlessly 12 spiritlessly
Davy: 4 lamp
daw: 4 dawn, drab 5 color, daunt 6 magpie 7 jackdaw 8 slattern, sluggard 9 blackbird, simpleton
dawdle: lag 4 idle, poke 5 dally 6 daddle, daidle, diddle, linger, loiter, pickle, piddle, putter, trifle 7 finnick, quiddle
dawn: 4 morn 5 sunup 6 aurora 7 morning, sunrise 8 daybreak 9 beginning
comb. form: eo
goddess: Eos 5 Ushas 6 Aurora
pert. to: 4 eoan 7 auroral
symbol: dew
toward the: 8 eastward
dawny: 4 puny 5 small
day: yom(Heb.) 4 date, time 5 epoch 6 period 8 lifetime
before: eve 9 yesterday
early: see **daybreak**
father of: 6 Erebus
god of: 5 Horus
hot: 8 scorcher
joyful: 8 festival
judgment: 8 doomsday
pert. to: 6 ferial
day blindness: 11 hemeralopia
daybreak: 4 dawn, morn 5 sunup
daydream: 4 muse 6 vision 7 reverie
days: *fateful:* 4 Ides
fifty: 13 quinquagesima
fourteen: 9 fortnight
daysman: 6 umpire 7 arbiter 8 mediator
daze: fog 4 stun 5 daunt 6 astony, bemuse, benumb, dazzle, muddle, trance 7 confuse, stupefy 8 bewilder, dumfound
dazed: 4 asea 6 doiled, rotten 7 spoiled 8 astonied, withered 10 doitrified
dazzle: 4 daze 5 blind, glaik, shine 6 fulgor 7 eclipse 8 bewilder, outshine, surprise
dazzling: 5 flare, flash 6 garish 7 fulgent, glaring, radiant 8 gorgeous 9 brilliant 10 candescent, foudroyant 11 pyrotechnic
deacon: 5 adept 6 cleric, doctor, layman, master 10 adulterate
prayers: 6 ectene
stole: 7 orarion

dead: 4 bung, cold, dull, flat, gone, mort(F.), numb, tame 5 amort, inert, napoo, quiet, slain 6 asleep, lapsed, napooh, refuse 7 defunct, exactly, expired, extinct, insipid, sterile, tedious 8 absolute, complete, deceased, departed, inactive, lifeless, obsolete 9 apathetic, bloodless, inanimate, nerveless, unsalable 10 breathless, lusterless, monotonous, motionless, spiritless, unexciting 11 indifferent, ineffectual, inoperative 12 extinguished, unproductive, unprofitable
city of: 10 necropolis
house of: 4 tomb 5 grave 6 morgue 7 ossuary 8 mortuary 9 crematory, ossuarium
mass for: 5 black
region of: Po 5 Hades 6 Erebus
dead duck: 5 goner
Dead Sea: *city:* 5 Sodom
mountain: 6 Pisgah
pass: 8 Akrabbin
plateau: 4 Seir
river to: 5 Arnon 6 Jordan
territory: 4 Moab
Dead Souls author: 5 Gogol
deadbeat: bum 7 sponger 8 parasite
deaden: 4 damp, dull, kill, mute, numb, stun 5 blunt 6 benumb, dampen, muffle, obtund, opiate, retard, weaken 7 petrify, repress 8 amortize, enfeeble 10 devitalize
deadfall: 4 trap
deadhead: 6 bobber
deadhouse: 6 morgue 8 mortuary
deadline: 5 limit 8 boundary
deadlock: tie 4 draw 7 impasse 8 stoppage 9 stalemate 10 standstill
deadly: 4 dire, fell, mort 5 fatal 6 lethal, mortal 7 capital, deathly, fateful, ruinous 8 venomous, virulent 9 pestilent 10 implacable, pernicious 11 destructive, internecine
deadpan: 6 vacant 9 impassive
deaf: 5 dunch 9 unheeding
deaf and dumb person: 9 surdomute
deafness: 6 asonia 8 anacusia, anacusis, cophosis
cause: 4 stun 5 deave(Sc.)
deal: 4 dole, part, sale 5 allot, board, plank, sever, share, trade, wield 6 bestow, divide, handle, parcel 7 bargain, deliver, inflict, portion, scatter, wrestle 8 dispense, separate 9 apportion, negotiate 10 administer, distribute 11 transaction
in: 4 sell 5 trade 6 purvey
with: 4 cope 6 handle
dealbate: 5 white 8 whitened
dealer: 5 agent 6 badger, broker, cadger, jobber, monger, seller, trader 7 chapman

8 merchant, operator 9 middleman, tradesman 10 negotiator, trafficker 11 distributer, distributor
secondhand goods: 6 broker 10 pawnbroker
dealing: 7 trading, traffic 8 exchange 11 intercourse
shrewd: 6 deceit 9 chicanery
dean (see also **dene**): 5 doyen 6 senior, verger 8 official
dear: jo; gra, joe, pet 4 agra, cara(It.), cher(F.), fond, high, lief, near 5 chary, chere(F.), honey, loved 6 costly, dearly, scarce, severe, worthy 7 beloved, darling, lovable, pigsney, querida 8 esteemed, glorious, precious, valuable 9 cherished, expensive, heartfelt, honorable, important 10 sweetheart 12 affectionate
dearly: 6 deeply, keenly, richly 8 heartily 9 earnestly
dearness: 6 dearth
dearth: 4 lack, want 6 famine 7 paucity, poverty 8 dearness, scarcity 10 costliness, deficiency
death: end 4 bale, bane, doom, mors, mort(F.), obit 5 decay 6 demise, expiry, murder 7 decease, quietus 8 biolysis, rawbones 9 bloodshed, departure, forthfare 10 expiration, extinction, pestilence
after: 10 posthumous
angel of: 6 Azrael
aware of portending: fey
bringing: 6 funest
eternal: 9 perdition
goddess: Hel 4 Dana, Danu
march: 5 dirge 7 cortege, funeral
meditation: 11 thanatopsis
mercy: 10 euthanasia
notice: 4 obit 5 orbit 8 obituary
personification: 4 Mors 5 Ankou 6 Charos, Charus
put to: gas 4 hang, kill, slay 5 choke 6 murder, noyade, starve, stifle 7 garrote 8 strangle 9 suffocate 11 assassinate, electrocute
rate: 9 mortality
rattle: 4 rale
register: 9 necrology
song: 5 dirge, elegy 8 threnody
symbol of: 5 orant
type of: 5 lynch 6 halter, noyode 10 lapidation
death-defying: 4 bold, rash 6 heroic 9 audacious, imprudent
deathless: 7 eternal, undying 8 immortal 12 imperishable
deathlessness: 9 athanasia 11 immortality
deathlike: 7 deathly, ghastly, macaber, macabre 8 ghastful, moribund

deathly: 5 fatal 6 deadly, mortal 8 mortally
9 deathlike 11 destructive

deave: din 4 stun 6 bother, deafen 7 stupefy
8 bewilder

debacle: 4 rout 7 failure 8 collapse, stampede 9 breakdown, cataclysm

debar: 4 deny, tabu 5 estop, taboo 6 forbid,
hinder, refuse 7 boycott, deprive, exclude,
prevent, seclude, suspend 8 preclude, prohibit 9 foreclose, interdict 10 disqualify

debark: 4 land 9 disembark

debarrass: 7 relieve 12 disembarrass

debase: 5 abase, alloy, avile, lower, stoop 6
defile, demean, impair, reduce, revile, vilify 7 corrupt, degrade, deprave, traduce,
vitiate 10 adulterate, degenerate, depreciate 11 deteriorate

debased: 4 base, vile 7 corrupt

debatable: 4 moot

debate: 4 agon, moot 5 argue, fight 6 reason,
strife 7 agitate, canvass, contend, contest,
discuss, dispute, examine, palaver, quarrel, wrangle 8 argument, consider, militate, question 9 dialectic, quodlibet 10 contention, controvert, deliberate 11 controversy 12 dissertation 13 argumentation
pert. to: 8 forensic
place of: 5 forum
stoppage of: 7 cloture

debater: 16 controversialist

debating: 11 contentious
association: 6 lyceum

debauch: 4 bout 5 spree, taint 6 defile, guzzle, seduce, splore, vilify 7 corrupt, deprave, mislead, pollute, violate 8 squander, strumpet 10 depreciate, hellbender 11
contaminate

debauched: 4 lewd 8 rakehell 9 dissolute

debauchee: rip 4 rake, roue 6 lecher 8 rakehell 9 libertine

debilitated: 4 weak 5 seedy 6 feeble, infirm,
sapped 9 enervated

debility: 5 atony 7 languor 8 weakness 9
infirmity, lassitude 10 feebleness

debit: 4 loss 6 charge

deblaterate: gab 7 chatter

debonair: 4 airy 6 jaunty, polite 8 graceful,
gracious

Deborah's husband: 8 Lapidoth

debouche: 4 exit 6 emerge, outlet 7 passage
9 emergence

debris: 5 trash, waste 6 refuse, rubble 7 rubbish 8 detritus

debt: sin 5 debit, fault 7 arrears 8 trespass
9 arrearage, liability 10 obligation
acknowledgement: IOU 4 bill, note

debtor: 6 dyvour
note: IOU
proceed against: 6 excuss

debut: 7 opening 8 entrance 9 beginning 12
introduction

debutant, debutante: bud, deb 5 debby

decad: ten

decade: 9 decennium

decadent: 6 effete 7 decayed 9 declining 10
retrograde 12 deteriorated 13 retrogressive

decamp: 4 bolt 5 elope, scoot, vamos 6 depart, levant, mizzle, vamose 7 abscond, vamoose 8 clear out

decant: 4 emit, pour 6 unload 8 transfer

decanter: 6 carafe

decapitate: 6 behead 10 guillotine

decapod: 4 crab 5 prawn, squid 7 lobster 10
crustacean

decay: ebb, rot 4 conk, dote, doze, fade, fail,
ruin 5 death, spoil, waste 6 caries, mildew,
wither 7 decline, failure 8 decrease 9 adversity, decadence, decompose 11 destruction, deteriorate, dissolution 12 dilapidation, disintegrate, putrefaction 13 decomposition, deterioration 14 disintegration
comb. form: 5 sapro
dental: 6 caries
in fruit: 4 blet

decaying: 4 doty

decease: die 5 death 6 demise 9 departure
11 dissolution

deceased: 4 dead 7 defunct 8 departed

deceit: See deception

deceitful: 5 false, gaudy 6 fickle, hollow 7
sirenic 8 tortuous 9 faithless, insidious, insincere 10 circuitous, fallacious 11 disaffected 13 machiavellian

deceivable: 8 gullible

deceive: cog, con, lie 4 bilk, dupe, flam, fool,
gaff, gull, hoax, jilt 5 abuse, blear, blend,
blind, bluff, catch, cheat, cozen, cully,
dodge, gleek, hocus, trick 6 baffle, beflum,
befool, betray, bubble, delude, divert,
humbug, illude 7 beguile, defraud, mislead 8 flimflam, hoodwink 9 bamboozle,
frustrate 11 doublecross 12 misrepresent

deceiver: 6 trepan 7 juggler, sharper, warlock 8 magician

decelerate: 4 slow

decency: 7 decorum 9 propriety

decennium: 6 decade

decent: 4 fair 6 chaste, comely, honest, modest, proper, seemly 7 fitting, gradely,
shapely 8 decorous 11 appropriate, respectable

deception: dor 4 dole, gaff, ruse, sham, wile
5 cheat, covin, craft, fraud, guile, magic,
trick 6 cautel, deceit, humbug 7 blaflum,
cunning, evasion, fallacy, fiction, knavery, pretext, slyness 8 artifice, fal-
sedad(Sp.), intrigue, prestige, subtlety,
trickery, trumpery, wiliness 9 chicanery,
collusion, duplicity, falsehood, hypocrisy,
imposture, mendacity, sophistry, treach-

ery **10** artfulness, camouflage, dishonesty, imposition, infidelity **11** contrivance, counterfeit, dissembling **13** deceitfulness, dissimulation

deceptive: 5 false **8** delusive, illusory **10** fallacious

decided: 4 firm, flat **6** formed **8** clear-cut, decisive **14** unquestionably

decima: 5 tenth, tithe

decimal base: ten

decimate: 7 destroy

decipher: 4 read **6** decode, detect, reveal **8** discover, indicate **9** translate

decision: end **4** doom, fiat, grit **5** arret, canon, pluck **6** crisis, decree, ruling **7** consult, verdict **8** finality, judgment, sentence **9** precedent **10** conclusion, resolution **12** adjudication **13** determination

maker: **5** judge **6** umpire **7** referee **9** executive

sudden: **4** whim **7** impulse

decisive: 5 final **6** crisic **7** crucial **8** critical **10** conclusive, peremptory

deck: tog **4** buss, dink, heap, pink, trig **5** adorn, array, cover, dizen, dress, equip, floor, prink, store **6** blazon, clothe, fettle **7** apparel, bedight, bedizen, feather **8** beautify, decorate, platform **9** embellish **10** overspread

kind: gun **4** boat, main, poop, spar **5** berth, orlop, upper **6** bridge **7** shelter **8** platform, splinter **9** hurricane, promenade **10** forecastle, protective

lowest: **5** orlop

part: **7** scupper

deck out: 5 adorn, array **6** attire

decked: 4 clad **6** beseen

deckle-edged: 5 erose

declaim: 4 gale, rant, rave **5** orate, speak, spout **6** recite **7** elocute, inveigh **8** denounce, harangue, perorate **9** discourse

declaration: 4 word **5** fuero, libel **6** oracle, placet **7** promise **9** affidavit, assertion, statement **10** allegation, deposition, exposition, intimation **11** affirmation, certificate, description, enunciation **12** announcement, asseveration, proclamation **13** advertisement, pronouncement **14** interpretation **15** acknowledgement

declare: 4 bid, say, vow **4** aver, avow, deny, make, read, show, trow **5** aread, areed, posit, state **6** affirm, allege, assert, assure, avouch, blazon, depone, herald, indict, notify, relate **7** behight, express, profess, protest, signify, testify **8** announce, denounce, describe, indicate, maintain, manifest, proclaim **9** advertise, enunciate, nuncu-

pate, pronounce **10** annunciate, asseverate, promulgate **11** acknowledge, communicate

in cards: **4** meld

declination: 4 bias **5** decay, slope **6** regret **7** decline, descent, refusal **8** swerving **10** declension **11** declinature, inclination **13** deterioration

decline: dip, ebb, set **4** bend, fade, fail, fall, flag, sink, turn, wane **5** chute, droop, heald, hield, lower, repel, slope, slump, stoop, stray **6** debase, refuse, reject, renege, weaken **7** descend, descent, deviate, disavow, dwindle, failure, forbear **8** decrease, forebear, languish, withdraw **9** decadence, declivity, recadence, repudiate **10** declension, retrograde **11** declination, degradation **13** deterioration

declining: 5 awane **8** decadent **13** deteriorating

declivity: 4 hang **5** cliff, scarp, slope **6** calade **7** decline, descent, hanging **9** acclivity, precipice

declivous: 5 prone **7** sloping

decoct: 4 boil, cook **5** smelt **6** excite, kindle, refine **7** extract **8** condense, diminish

decoction: 4 dish, sapa **5** drink **6** cremor **7** extract **8** infusion

decode: 8 decipher

decompose: rot **5** decay, spoil **7** putrefy

decorate: 4 bind, cite, deck, pink, trim **5** adorn, dress, inlay, panel **6** decore, emboss, parget **7** festoon, garnish, miniate **8** ornament, titivate **9** embellish

decorated: 6 ornate **7** damasse, wrought **9** sigillate

decoration: 4 bahl **5** medal **6** frieze, plaque, tinsel **7** epergne, garnish, regalis **8** flourish, ornament **9** furniture, sgraffito **10** chambranle, decorament, decorement, sgraffiato

metalware: **4** tole

military: DSC, DSM, DSO **5** medal **6** ribbon

pert. to: **8** medallic

decorative: 5 fancy **9** beautiful **10** ornamental

decore: 5 adorn **8** beautify, decorate

decorous: 4 calm, good, prim **5** grave, quiet, sober, staid **6** decent, demure, modest, polite, proper, sedate, seemly, serene, steady **7** fitting, orderly, regular, settled **8** becoming, composed, mannerly **9** befitting, dignified, unruffled **11** appropriate

decorticate: 4 flay, hull, husk, pare, peel, pill, skin **5** strip **6** denude **9** excoriate

decorum: 9 propriety **10** convention

decoy: 4 bait, lure, tole **5** drill, plant, shill, tempt **6** allure, entice, entrap, pigeon **8** inveigle **9** shillaber

decrease: ebb 4 drop, fall, loss, sink, wane 5 abate, decay, taper, waste 6 impair, lessen, shrink 7 decline, dwindle, slacken, subside 8 diminish, moderate, retrench 9 decession, decrement 10 diminution

decree: act, law 4 fiat, rede, rule, will 5 aread, areed, arret, canon, edict, enact, irade, order, tenet, ukase 6 arrest, assize, decern, dictum, firman, indict, ordain 7 adjudge, appoint, command, decreet, mandate, statute 8 decision, decretum, rescript, sentence 9 determine, enactment, ordinance, preordain 10 adjudicate, plebiscite 12 adjudication, announcement

authoritative: 5 arret, canon

imperial: 4 fiat

papal: 4 bull

decrement: 4 loss 5 waste 8 decrease 10 diminution

decrepit: 4 lame, weak, 6 feeble, infirm, senile 7 failing, invalid 9 bedridden

decrown: 6 depose 8 unthrone

decry: boo 4 slur 5 lower 6 lessen 7 asperse, censure, condemn, debauch, degrade, detract 8 belittle, derogate 9 discredit, disparage, underrate 10 depreciate, undervalue

decuman: 4 huge 5 large

decuple: 7 tenfold

decussate: 9 intersect

dedal: See **daedal**

dedicate: vow 6 devote, direct, hallow, oblate 7 ascribe 8 inscribe 9 nuncupate 10 consecrate

deduce: 4 draw, lead 5 bring, drive, infer, trace 6 derive, elicit, evolve, gather 7 extract 8 conclude

deduct: 4 bate, dock, take 5 abate, allow 6 defalk, remove 7 curtail 8 abstract, discount, separate, subtract

deduction: 4 agio 6 rebate 7 reprise 8 illation 9 corollary, induction

deed: act 4 case, fact, feat, fiat, gest 5 actum, actus, chart, doing, title 6 action, convey, escrow, pottah, remise 7 charter, exploit 8 transfer 10 instrument 11 achievement, performance 14 accomplishment

benevolent: 4 boon 5 favor 8 benefice

evil: sin 11 malefaction

deeds: 4 acta 9 res gestae

deem: say 4 hope, reck, tell 5 judge, opine, think 6 esteem, expect, ordain, reckon, regard 7 account, adjudge, believe, surmise 8 announce, consider, judgment, proclaim 10 adjudicate

deep: low, sea 4 howe, rapt 5 abyss, grave, great, gruff, heavy, ocean 6 hollow, intent 7 abysmal, intense, serious, unmixed 8 absorbed, abstruse, complete, powerful, profound, thorough 9 entangled, insidious, recondite 11 far-reaching

deepen: 5 cloud 6 darken 7 enhance, thicken 9 intensify 10 strengthen

deer: red, roe 6 animal, cervid, fallow, mammal 7 barking

antler: dag

Asian: 4 axis, maha, napu, shou, sika 5 maral 6 chitra, hangul, sambar 10 barasingha

barking: 7 muntjac, muntjak

cry: 4 bell

fallow: 4 dama

family: 8 cervidae

female: doe 4 hind

genus of: 8 cervilla

large: elk 5 moose 6 wapiti 7 caribou

male: 4 buck, hart, spay, stag 7 roebuck

meat: 5 jerky 7 charqui, venison

North American: elk 5 moose 6 wapiti

path: run 4 slot 5 trail

pert. to: 6 damine 7 cervine

small: roe 7 roebuck

South American: 4 pudu 6 guemal, guemul, vanada 7 brocket

young: 4 fawn, spay 7 spitter

deerlet: 4 napu 10 chevrotain

deface: mar 4 foul, ruin, scar 5 erase, shame, spoil 6 damage, defame, defoil, deform, defoul, efface, injure, injury 7 destroy, detract, distort, slander 8 disgrace, dishonor, mutilate, outshine 9 blemished, discredit, disfigure, disvisage, vandalize 10 disfeature

defame: 4 foul 5 abase, belie, cloud, libel, smear 6 accuse, charge, deface, infamy, injure, malign, vilify 7 asperse, blacken, blemish, debauch, detract, publish, scandal, slander, traduce 8 dishonor 9 blaspheme, denigrate 10 calumniate, defamation

default: 4 fail, flaw 5 error, fault 6 offend 7 blemish, failure, mistake, neglect, offense 8 omission 12 imperfection 13 nonappearance

defeasance: 6 defeat 7 undoing 9 overthrow

defeat: win 4 balk, beat, best, drub, foil, loss, rout, ruin, undo 5 break, check, facer, floor, skunk, worst, wrack 6 baffle, cumber, derout, master, thwack, weaken 7 conquer, deprive, destroy, preempt, reverse, shellac 8 overcome, vanquish, Waterloo 9 discomfit, disfigure, frustrate, overpower, overthrow, overwhelm 10 defeasance, defeatment, disappoint 12 discomfiture

at chess: 4 mate 9 checkmate

defeated: 4 lost 5 kaput 6 craven

defeatist: 4 Bolo 8 fatalist 9 handupper, pessimist 10 handsupper

defect: 4 flaw, lack, vice, want 5 craze, fault, minus 6 damage, desert, injury 7 blemish, debauch, detract, publish, scandal, slander, traduce 8 dishonor 12 imperfection
in cloth: 4 scob
in timber: 4 knot
without: 5 sound 7 perfect

defective: bad, ill 4 poor 6 faulty 7 halting 8 vitiated 9 deficient, imperfect 10 inaccurate, incomplete

defend (see also **defense**): 4 fend, hold, save, wear 5 guard, watch 6 assert, forbid, screen, secure, shield, uphold 7 contest, espouse, justify, prevent, protect, shelter 8 advocate, champion, conserve, maintain, preserve, prohibit 9 exculpate, patronage, vindicate

defendant: 8 appellee
answer: 4 plea 14 nolo contendere

defender: 11 propugnator

defense, defence (see also **fortification**): 4 egis, fort 5 aegis, alibi, fence, grith 6 answer, behalf, covert, sconce 7 contest, shelter 8 apologia, boundary, security 9 coverture, safeguard 10 protection 11 maintenance
in law: 6 answer
means of: 6 abatis
movement: 4 spar
outwork: 8 barbican
position: 7 rampart 10 bridgehead
unit: AAF 4 army, NATO, navy 5 SEATO 7 marines

defenseless: 4 bare 5 naked 7 unarmed 8 helpless 9 unguarded

defensible: 7 tenable 9 excusable

defensive: 9 shielding 10 apologetic

defer: boy 4 wait 5 delay, honor, yield 6 esteem, humble, retard, revere, submit 8 consider, postpone, prorogue, protract 13 procrastinate

deference: 6 homage, regard 9 obeisance

defiance: 6 defial

defiant: 4 bold 5 brave 6 daring 8 insolent 11 challenging

deficiency: 4 lack, want 5 fault, minus 6 dearth, defect 7 absence, blemish, deficit, failing, failure 8 scarcity, shortage 9 indigence 10 inadequacy 11 destitution, shortcoming 12 imperfection 13 insufficiency

deficient: 6 meager, meagre 7 bobtail

defile: gut 4 file, gate, gowl, hals, pass, soil 5 abuse, beray, dirty, gorge, reveal, sully, taint 6 debase, infect, ravish 7 corrupt, deprave, distain, passage, pollute, tarnish, violate 8 dishonor, maculate 9 desecrate 10 adulterate 11 contaminate

defiled: 6 impure 7 unclean 8 maculate

definable: 6 finite

define: end, fix, set 4 mere, term 5 bound, limit 6 decide 7 clarify, delimit, explain, expound 8 describe, discover 9 demarcate, determine, interpret, prescribe 11 distinguish 12 characterize, circumscribe

definite: 4 sure 5 clear, final, fixed, sharp 7 certain, limited, precise 8 distinct, explicit, limiting 10 conclusive 11 determinate, determining, unequivocal 12 determinable, unmistakable

definitive: 5 final

deflect: 4 bend, warp 5 parry 6 divert, swerve 7 deviate, inflect, reflect, refract

deflower: 6 ravage, ravish 7 despoil, violate

Defoe character: 4 Moll, Xury 6 Crusoe, Friday

deform: mar 6 deface 7 blemish, contort, distort 8 disguise, dishonor, misshape 9 disfigure 10 disarrange

deformed: 7 crooked, hideous 8 formless 9 amorphous, loathsome, monstrous, shapeless, unshapely 11 counterfeit

deformity: 4 flaw 6 defect 7 blemish 13 disfigurement
of foot: 5 varus 7 talipes

defraud: rob 4 bilk, fake, gull, rook, trim 5 cheat, cozen, gouge, mulct, trick 6 chouse 7 deceive, swindle 8 dry-shave

defray: pay 5 avert 6 expend, prepay 7 appease, requite, satisfy 8 disburse 9 discharge, reimburse

deft: 4 neat, trim 5 agile, handy, quick 6 adroit, expert, heppen, nimble, spruce 7 deliver 8 dextrous, skillful 9 dexterous

defunct: 4 dead 7 extinct 8 deceased, departed, finished

defy: 4 dare, face 5 beard, brave, stump, tempt 6 forbid, reject 7 affront, despise, disdain, outface 8 champion, defiance, renounce 9 challenge, repudiate 10 contravene

deg: 6 dampen 8 sprinkle

degenerate: rot 6 debase 7 degrade, deprave 11 deteriorate

degradation: 7 descent 8 ignominy

degrade: 4 bust 5 abase, decry, lower, shame, strip 6 debase, demean, demote, depose, humble, reduce, vilify 7 corrupt, decline, depress 8 disgrace, dishonor 9 disparage, humiliate 10 degenerate, depreciate 11 deteriorate

degraded: 4 base 5 seamy 6 abject, fallen 7 debased, grieced 10 degenerate, diminished

degrading: 4 base 6 menial 8 shameful

degree: 4 bank, heat, rank, rate, rung, step, term, tier 5 class, grade, grece, honor, order, pitch, point, stage, stair 6 extent, me-

dium, soever **7** measure, station **8** quantity, standing **9** gradation **10** attainment
academic: A.B., B.A., B.S., C.E., D.D., M.A., M.D., M.S., B.L.S., B.Sc., L.L.B., L.L.D., M.Sc., Ph.D. **4** D.Lit. **5** Litt.D.
conferral: **10** laureation
equal: as
highest: sum **6** summit, utmost **7** extreme **8** cum laude
kind of: nth **5** third
seeker: **9** candidate
slight: ace, nth **4** hair, inch **5** shade **8** slightly **9** gradation

degust, degustate: 5 savor, taste **6** relish
dehisce: 4 gape
dehort: 4 urge **8** dissuade
dehydrate: dry **9** desiccate, evaporate
deific: 6 divine **7** godlike
deification: 10 apotheosis
deiform: 6 divine **7** godlike
deify: 10 consecrate **11** apotheosize
deign: 5 stoop **10** condescend
deigning: 11 patronizing
deity (see also **god** and next entry)**:** god **4** deva, idol, muse **6** genius **7** creator, demigod, godling, godhead, godship **8** Almighty, divinity, governor
half-fish: Ea **6** Oannes
half-goat: **4** faun
hawk-eyed: Ra **5** Horus **6** Sokari **7** Sokaris
jackal-headed: **6** Anubis
tutelary: **5** genie, lares, numen **7** Hershef, penates
deity: For definitions using this word, see *god* and *goddess* under appropriate country or function. EXAMPLES: "Roman deity" see **Rome** *god;* "war deity" see **war** *god.*
deject: 5 abase, lower **6** humble, lessen **7** flatten **8** dispirit **9** overthrow **10** discomfort, discourage, dishearten
dejected: low, sad **4** damp, glum, sunk **5** amort **6** abased, gloomy, pining **7** alamort, humbled, unhappy **8** repining, wretched **9** cheerless, depressed, prostrate, woebegone **10** despondent, spiritless **11** crestfallen, downhearted **12** disconsolate, disheartened, fainthearted
dejection: 6 dismay **10** melancholy
dejeuner: 5 lunch **9** breakfast, collation
dekko: 4 look, peep
delapse: 5 lapse **7** descend
delate: 5 carry **6** accuse, assign, convey, inform, report, submit, tender **7** publish **8** denounce
Delaware: *county:* **4** Kent **6** Sussex
Indian: **6** Lenape
seaport: **5** Lewes
town: **5** Dover, Lewes **7** Chester **10** Wilmington

delay: lag **4** bode, mora, stay, stop, wait **5** abide, abode, allay, check, dally, defer, demur, deter, dwell, frist, stall, tarry **6** arrest, belate, detain, dilate, dilute, dretch, hinder, impede, linger, loiter, quench, remora, retard, taigle, temper, weaken **7** adjourn, assuage, barrace, confine, prolong, respite **8** demurral, hesitate, macerate, mitigate, moration, obstruct, postpone, stoppage **9** detention, hindrance, lingering **10** cunctation, moratorium, suspension **13** procrastinate **15** procrastination
delayed: 4 late **5** tardy **7** belated, overdue
delaying: 8 dilatory
dele: 4 omit **5** erase **6** cancel, delete, efface, remove **7** expunge **9** eradicate, extirpate **10** obliterate
delectable: 5 tasty **8** pleasing **9** delicious, desirable, diverting, enjoyable **10** delightful **11** pleasurable
delegate: 4 name, send **6** assign, commit, depute, deputy, legate, nuncio **7** appoint, consign, empower, entrust **8** emissary, transfer **9** authorize, surrogate **10** commission **12** commissioner **14** representative
delegation: 7 mission **9** committee **10** deputation
delete: 4 dele, omit **5** erase, purge **6** cancel, remove **7** destroy, expunge **9** eliminate, eradicate **10** obliterate
deleterious: bad **7** harmful, hurtful, noxious **8** damaging **9** injurious, malignant **10** pernicious **11** destructive, detrimental, prejudicial
delf, delft: pit, sod **4** mine, pond **5** ditch, drain, grave **6** quarry
Delhi district: 5 Simla
Delian god: 6 Apollo
delibate: sip **5** taste **6** dabble
deliberate: 4 cool, pore **5** think **6** advise, confer, debate, ponder **7** bethink, consult, reflect, resolve, studies **8** consider, measured, meditate **9** determine, leisurely, speculate, voluntary **10** purposeful **11** circumspect, intentional **12** premeditated **13** dispassionate
deliberation: 7 counsel **10** reflection
without: **4** rash **8** headlong
Delibes ballet: 5 Naila
delible: 10 eradicable
delicacy: roe **4** cate, ease, nori, tact **5** acate, taste **6** caviar, dainty, delice, luxury, nicety **7** caviare, finesse **8** niceness, pleasure, subtlety **9** exactness, precision **10** daintiness, effeminity, femininity, refinement **13** gratification
lacking: **5** gross

delicate: 4 airy, fine, lacy, nice 5 frail, light, silky 6 dainty, minion, petite, puling, queasy, slight, tender 7 elegant, finical, fragile, minikin, refined, subtile, tenuous 8 araneose, araneous, charming, ethereal, graceful, luscious, migniard, pleasant 9 agreeable, beautiful, delicious, exquisite, palatable, sensitive 10 delightful, fastidious 11 comfortable, considerate

delicatessen: 11 charcuterie

delicious: 8 delicate 9 ambrosial, exquisite, luxurious, nectareal, nectarean 10 delectable, delightful, nectareous, voluptuous

delict: 7 offense 13 transgression

delight: joy 4 glee, love 5 bliss, charm, feast, mirth, revel 6 admire, divert, liking, please, ravish, regale 7 ecstasy, enchant, gladden, gratify, rapture, rejoice 8 entrance, gladness, pleasure, savoring 9 delectate, enjoyment, enrapture, happiness 11 delectation
in: 6 relish

delightful: 4 nice 6 savory 7 elysian 8 adorable, delicate, glorious 9 delicious 10 delectable 11 pleasureful

Delilah's paramour: 6 Samson 7 Sampson

delimit: See **define**

delineate: map 4 draw, limn, line 5 trace 6 blazon, depict, design, sketch, survey 7 outline, picture, portray 8 describe 9 represent 12 characterize

delineation: 10 expression

delinquency: 5 fault 7 failure, misdeed, offense 8 omission 9 violation 10 misconduct 11 malfeasance, misdemeanor, misfeasance

deliquesce: 4 give, melt 7 liquify 8 dissolve

delirious: mad 4 frey, gyte 5 manic 6 insane, raving 7 frantic, lunatic 8 brainish, deleerit, delieret, deranged, frenetic, frenzied 9 phrenetic 11 lightheaded

delirium: 4 fury, maze 8 idleness 10 aberration 13 hallucination

delirium tremens: 7 horrors 9 oenomania

delitescent: 6 latent

deliver: rid 4 bail, deal, free 5 serve, speak, utter 6 assoil, commit, convey, redeem, render, rescue, resign, succor, unbind 7 beteach, consign, declaim, dictate, present, release, relieve 8 dispatch, exorcise, exorcize, liberate 9 enunciate, pronounce, surrender 10 emancipate

deliverer: 7 drayman 9 preserver

deliverly: 6 deftly, nimbly 8 actively

delivery: 6 rescue 7 address 8 shipment 9 rendition 11 deliverance, parturition 12 accouchement

dell: den 4 dale, dean, dene, drab, glen, vale 5 trull, wench 6 dingle, ravine, valley

Delphi: 6 oracle, shrine
modern name: 6 Kastri
priestess: 5 Pythia

delphinium: 8 larkspur

delta: 8 alluvium, triangle

delude: bob 4 bilk, dupe, fool 5 cheat, elude, evade, trick 6 befool, bubble, illude 7 beguile, deceive, mislead 8 hoodwink 9 mislippen 10 circumvent

deluge: sea 4 flow 5 flood, swamp 8 inundate, overflow, submerge 9 cataclysm, overpower, overwhelm, rainstorm 10 overspread

delusion: 5 trick 6 mirage, vision 7 chimera, fallacy, fantasm 8 illusion, phantasm 9 deception 13 appersonation, hallucination
Buddhist: 4 moha
of grandeur: 11 megalomania
partner of: 5 snare

delusory: 8 delusive

delve: den, dig, dip, pit 4 cave, dint, mine 5 ditch, plumb 6 bruise, exhume, fathom, indent 7 impress 8 excavate, inscribe

demagogic: 8 factious

demagogue, demagog: 6 leader, orator, rouser 7 speaker

demand: ask, cry 4 call, need 5 claim, exact, order, query 6 charge, elicit, expect, summon 7 command, inquire, mandate, request, require 8 question 9 challenge 10 commission 11 requisition

demandable: due

demarcate: 6 demark 7 delimit 8 separate 12 discriminate

demean: 5 abase, lower 6 debase 7 degrade 8 demeanon, maltreat

demeanor: 4 mien, port 5 habit 6 action, havior 7 bearing, conduct 8 behavior, carriage, portance 9 treatment 10 deportment, management 11 comportment, countenance

demented: mad 4 luny 5 buggy, crazy, nutty 6 insane 7 fatuous

demerit: 4 mark 5 fault 6 desert

demesne: 5 manor, place, realm 6 domain, estate, region 8 district

Demeter: 5 Ceres
daughter: 4 Cora, Kore 8 Despoina 10 Persephone, Proserpina, Proserpine 11 Persephassa
headdress: 5 polos
mother: 4 Rhea
shrine: 9 anaktoron

demigod: 4 hero 7 godling
pert. to: 7 satyric
sylvan: 5 satyr

demirep: 11 adventuress

demise: 4 will 5 death 6 convey 7 decease 8 bequeath

demiss: 6 humble
demit: 5 lower 6 humble, resign 8 abdicate 10 relinquish 11 resignation
demiurgic: 8 creative
demoded: 5 passe
demoiselle: 5 crane 7 kaikara
demolish: 4 rase, raze, ruin 5 level, waste, wreck 6 batter 7 destroy, ruinate 9 devastate, overthrow
demon: hag, imp, nat 4 aitu, atua, ogre 5 devil, fiend, genie, lamia, Satan, witch 6 Abigor, afreet 7 villain, warlock 9 cacodemon 10 cacodaemon
assembly of: 6 sabbat
female: 6 empusa 8 succubus
Hebrew: 8 Asmodeus
Iroquois: 5 otkon
possessed by: 9 energumen
prince of: 9 Beelzebub
worship of: 11 demonolatry
Zoroastrian: 5 daeva
demoniac: 7 demonic, lunatic 8 devilish, diabolic, fiendish, infernal 10 diabolical
demonstrate: 4 show 5 prove 7 display, portray 8 manifest
demonstration: 4 show, sign 5 proof 9 manifesto, portrayal 10 apparition 12 illustration 13 manifestation
demonstrative: 4 that, this 5 these, those 8 effusive 9 ostensive 12 ostentatious
demoralize: 6 weaken 7 confuse, corrupt, deprave, pervert 9 undermine 10 discourage, dishearten 11 disorganize
demos: 4 deme 6 people 8 citizens, populace
Demosthenes: *follower:* 5 Bryan 6 orator
oration: 9 philippic
demote: 4 bust 6 reduce 7 degrade
demotic: 7 popular
demulcent: 8 soothing 9 softening 10 mollifying
demur: 4 stay 5 delay, doubt, pause 6 boggle, linger, object 7 scruple, suspend 8 hesitate, suspense 9 objection 12 irresolution
demure: coy, mim, shy 4 prim 5 grave, staid, suant 6 modest, sedate 8 composed, decorous
demurral: See **demur**
den: mew 4 cave, cove, dell, dive, glen, hole, lair, nest, room 5 bield, cabin, couch, haunt, study 6 burrow, cavern, covert, grotto, hollow, ravine 7 retreat 8 hideaway, snuggery, workroom
denary: 7 tenfold
dendroid 11 arborescent
dendrophilous: 8 arboreal
dene, dean: 4 dell, vale 5 mound 6 valley
denial (see also **deny**)**:** nó; nay
denizen: 6 native 7 citizen 8 resident 9 indweller 10 inhabitant

Denmark: *city:* 6 Odense 7 Aalborg, Aarhuus, Horsens, Randers 8 Elsinore 9 Helsingor 10 Copenhagen(c.) 13 Frederiksberg
anatomist: 5 Steno
animal: 7 aurochs
artist: 5 Bloch
astronomer: 5 Brahe
author: 5 Bajer 8 Andersen
borough: 4 borg
chief: 4 jarl, yarl
coin: ore 5 krone
comb. form: 4 Dano
composer: 4 Gade
county: Amt 4 Soro 7 Aalborg 8 Aabenraa
downs: 7 Klitten
embroidery: 6 hedebo
flag: 9 Dannebrog
inlet: Ise 5 fjord
island: Oe; Als 4 Aero 5 Faroe, Samso 7 Seeland
king: 4 Cnut, Knut 6 Canute 9 Christian
knighthood order: 9 Dannebrog
measure: ell, fod, mil, pot 4 alen, favn, rode 5 album, kande, linje, paegl, tomme 6 achtel, paegel, paegle, skeppe 7 landmil, oltonde, skieppe, viertel 8 fjerding 9 korntonde, ottingkar
musical instrument: 4 lure
parliament: 7 Rigsdag
peninsula: 7 Jutland
physicist: 4 Bohr
possession: 5 Faroe 6 St. John 7 Iceland 8 St. Thomas 9 Greenland, Santa Cruz
prince: 5 Ogier
river: Asa 4 Holm, Stor 5 Guden 7 Lonborg
seaport: 6 Aarhus
settlers: 6 Ostmen
tribunal: 7 Rigsret
weight: es; lod, ort, vog 4 eser(pl.), last, mark, pund, unze 5 carat, kvint, pound, quint, tonde 6 toende 7 centner, lispund, quintin 8 lispound, skippund 9 ship pound, skibslast 10 bismerpund
dennet: gig 8 carriage
denominate: 4 call, name 5 title 6 denote 8 christen, indicate, nominate 9 designate
denomination: 4 cult, sect 5 class, title 7 society 8 category 9 communion 11 appellation
religious: 7 Baptist 8 Lutheran 9 Methodist, Unitarian 12 Episcopalian, Presbyterian 14 Congregational
denotation: 4 sign 5 token
denote: 4 give, mark, mean, name, show 6 import 7 betoken, connote, express 8 indicate 9 designate, recommend, represent 10 denominate

denouement: end 5 issue 7 outcome 8 solution 11 catastrophe

denounce: ban 6 accuse, delate, descry, menace, scathe 7 arraign, condemn, declare, upbraid 8 proclaim, threaten 9 fulminate 10 stigmatize

de novo: 4 anew 5 again, newly 6 afresh

dense: 4 firm 5 close, foggy, gross, heavy, murky, silly, solid, thick 6 obtuse, stupid 7 compact, crowded, serried 11 thickheaded 12 impenetrable

density: 4 mass 11 compactness

dent: 4 bash, dint, nick 5 dinge, notch, tooth 6 batter, hallow, indent 7 blemish, depress 10 depression, impression 11 indentation

dental: See **dentistry, tooth**

dentate: 6 jagged 7 serrate, toothed

dentation: 5 serra 10 projection

denticulate: 7 serrate

denticulation: jag 5 tooth 8 denticle

dentil: 5 block

dentine, dentin: 5 ivory 6 enamel

dentistry: *appliance:* dam 4 burr

  branch: 9 exodontia 11 orthodontia 12 orthodontics

  plastic: 6 cement

  tool: 6 scaler 7 forceps

denture: 5 teeth, plate

denude: 4 bare 5 scalp, strip 6 devest, divest 8 denudate 11 decorticate

denunciation (see also **denounce**): 6 threat 8 diatribe 9 philippic 11 malediction 12 proclamation

deny: nay 5 debar, repel 6 abjure, disown, forbid, impugn, negate, refuse, refute, reject, renege 7 confute, deprive, disavow, dispute, forsake, gainsay, protest 8 abnegate, disclaim, forswear, renounce, withhold 9 disaffirm 10 contradict, contravene, controvert

deodand: 7 forfeit

deodar: 5 cedar

depart: go; die, mog 4 blow, pass, quit, vary 5 found, leave, mosey, sever 6 begone, decamp, demise, desist, divide, perish, recede, retire, sunder 7 abscond, deviate, forsake, get away, retreat, vamoose 8 farewell, separate, withdraw

departed: 4 dead 6 bygone 7 defunct 8 deceased, decedent

department: 4 part 5 realm 6 branch, bureau, sphere 7 portion 8 division, province 11 subdivision

departure: 4 exit 5 death, exode 6 congee, egress 7 decease 9 decession 11 abandonment, forthfaring, leavetaking

depend: 4 bank, hang, lean, rely, rest, turn 5 count, hinge, trust 7 confide

dependable: 5 siker, solid 6 sicker 7 certain 8 reliable 11 trustworthy

dependency: 5 taluk 6 colony 7 apanage 8 appanage

dependent: 6 client, minion, sponge, vassal 7 sponger, subject 8 clinging, follower 9 adjective, corollary 10 accidental, contingent, sequacious 11 subordinate

depict: 4 draw, limn 5 paint 6 blazon 7 picture, portray 8 describe 9 delineate, represent 12 characterize

depilate: 4 husk 5 shave

depilatory: 5 rusma

depilous: 8 hairless

deplete: 5 drain, empty 6 reduce, unload 7 exhaust 8 diminish 10 impoverish

deplorable: sad 8 wretched 10 calamitous

deplore: rue 4 moan, sigh, wail 5 mourn 6 bemoan, bewail, grieve, lament, regret 8 complain

deploy: 6 unfold 7 display

deplume: 5 pluck, strip

depone: 5 swear 6 depose 7 testify

deponent: 7 affiant 10 incomplete

depopulate: 6 ravage 9 devastate, dispeople

deport: 5 exile 6 banish, behave, demean 7 bearing, conduct 9 transport 10 deportment

deportment: air 4 gest, mien 5 geste, havit 6 action, deport, manner 7 address, bearing, comfort, conduct 8 behavior, breeding, carriage, demeanor 9 behaviour, demeanour

depose: 4 aver 5 abase 6 affirm, assert, depone, divest, remove 7 degrade, deposit, testify 8 dethrone, displace 10 dispossess 11 disenthrone

deposit: lay, set 4 bank, cast, dump, fund, hock, pawn 5 chest, lodge, place, store 6 entomb, pledge, repose, settle 7 consign, deposit, entrust 10 deposition, depository

  alluvial: 5 delta, geest

  black: 4 soot

  earthy: as; ore 4 asar(pl.), gobi, lode, marl, sand, silt 5 delta, eskar, esker, geest, loess, manto, trona 6 placer, sludge 7 alluvia, moraine 8 alluvium

  geyser: 6 sinter

  gold-containing: 6 placer

  gravel: 5 apron

  ore: vug

  roric: dew

  teeth: 6 tartar

  wine cask: 6 tartar

deposition: 6 burial 7 deposit, opinion 8 sediment 9 affidavit, statement, testimony 10 allegation 11 declaration 12 displacement 13 precipitation

depository: 4 bank, safe 5 attic, vault 7 ossuary 10 repository

depot: 4 base, gare(F.) 6 aurang(Ind.), aurung 7 station 8 magazine, terminal, terminus 9 warehouse 10 storehouse

deprave: 5 taint 6 debase, defile, malign, revile 7 corrupt, pervert, vitiate 10 degenerate, depreciate

depraved: bad 4 evil, ugly, vile 6 rotten, wicked 7 bestial, immoral, vicious 9 abandoned, graceless 10 profligate 11 demoralized 12 incorrigible

depravity: 4 vice 8 villainy

deprecate: 4 pray 6 invoke 7 beseech 10 depreciate, disapprove, supplicate

deprecation: 8 petition 14 disapprobation

depreciate: 4 fall 5 abase, avile, decry, slump 6 debase, lessen, reduce, shrink 7 cheapen, debauch, degrade, deprave, depress, detract 8 belittle, derogate, disprize, disvalue, minimize 9 disparage, dispraise, extenuate 10 undervalue

depreciation: 4 agio 8 discount 9 misprison

depredate: rob 4 prey, raze 5 spoil 6 thieve 7 despoil, destroy, pillage, plunder

deprehend: 5 seize 6 detect 7 capture 8 discover 9 apprehend

depress: bow, cow 4 dash, dent, fall, sink 5 abase, appal, chill, crush, lower, slump 6 appall, dampen, dismay, humble, indent, lessen, sadden, weaken 7 degrade, flatten, oppress, repress 8 browbeat, diminish, dispirit, enfeeble 9 disparage, subjugate 10 depreciate, discourage, dishearten

depressed: 4 sick 6 gloomy, hipped, hollow, lonely, oblate, somber, triste 8 dejected, downcast 9 afflicted, debruised 10 spiritless 11 downhearted, melancholic

depressing: 5 bleak 6 dreary

depression: col, dip, gat, pit 4 delk, doke, fall, foss, howe 5 atrio, basin, cowal, crypt, dinge, fossa, fosse, nadir 6 cafard, cavity, crater, dismay, gulley, ravine, valley 7 alveola, blowout 8 doldrums 9 dejection 11 despondency 13 disparagement

between mountains: col

pert. to: 6 bathic

deprivation: 4 cost, loss, want 7 amotion 9 privation, restraint 10 diminution 11 destitution

deprive: bar, rob 4 bate, deny 5 debar, spoil, strip 6 amerce, defeat, depose, devest, dismay, divest, hinder, remove 7 abridge, bereave, cashier, despoil, exhaust 8 denature, desolate, evacuate 9 dismantle, forestall 10 dispossess

deprived: 4 reft

depth: 5 abyss, midst 8 deepness, strength 9 abundance, intensity 10 profundity 12 abstruseness, completeness, profoundness

depth charge: 4 mine 10 projectile

depths: 5 heart

depurant: 8 purifier 11 purificator

deputation: 7 mission 10 delegation

depute: 4 send 5 allot 6 assign, devote 7 appoint 8 delegate 10 commission, constitute

deputy: 4 aide 5 agent, envoy, proxy, vicar 6 commis, legate 7 bailiff 8 delegate 9 assistant, surrogate, vigilante 10 substitute

deracinate: 9 eradicate, extirpate

derange: 5 upset 7 disturb, perturb 8 displace, unsettle 9 interrupt 10 disarrange, discompose

deranged: 5 crazy 6 crazed 7 frantic 10 distraught, unbalanced

derangement: 5 mania 6 lunacy 7 madness, rummage 8 delirium, disorder, insanity 9 confusion 11 distraction, disturbance 12 irregularity 15 disorganization

deray: 8 disorder 9 confusion 11 disturbance

derby: hat 4 race, town 5 shire 6 bowler

derelict: 7 failure 8 betrayer, castaway 9 abandoned 10 delinquent, neglectful, unfaithful

derf: 4 bold 6 daring

deride: 4 geck, gibe, hoot, jape, jeer, mock, twit 5 fleer, rally, scoff, scorn, taunt 6 illude 8 ridicule

derision: 8 contempt

derive: get 4 draw, stem 5 carry, infer, trace 6 deduce, evolve, gather, obtain 7 extract, proceed, receive 9 originate

derm: 4 skin 7 cuticle

derma: 5 layer 6 corium, dermis

dermal filament: 4 hair

dern: 4 dark, darn, dire, evil, hide 5 drear 6 crafty, hidden, secret, somber, sombre 7 conceal 9 concealed, underhand

dernier: 4 last 5 final

dernier cri: 7 fashion, novelty

derogate: 5 annul, decry 6 lessen, repeal 7 detract, slander 8 restrict, withdraw 9 disparage 10 depreciate

derrick: jib, rig 4 lift, spar 5 crane, davit, hoist 6 tackle 7 gallows, hanging, hangman

part: jib, leg 4 boom

derring-do: 4 gest 8 audacity

derringer: 6 pistol, weapon

derry: 7 dislike 8 aversion

dervish: 5 fakir 6 fakeer

cap: taj

descant: 4 sing, song 6 melody, remark, warble 7 comment 9 discourse 11 observation 12 counterpoint, dissertation 13 accompaniment

descend: 4 fall, sink 5 avale, lower, stoop 6 alight, derive 7 decline, delapse 9 originate 10 condescend

descendant: son 4 cion, heir, seed 5 child, scion 9 offspring

descendants: 7 progeny 9 posterity 10 generation

descended from same mother: 5 enate 6 enatic

descent: 4 drop, fall 5 birth, chute, issue, scarp, slope, stock 6 escarp, strain 7 assault, decline, extract, lineage 8 ancestry, breeding, downfall, pedigree 9 avalanche, declivity, onslaught 10 declension, extraction, generation 11 declination, degradation, inclination

describe: 4 tell 6 define, depict, relate, report 7 declare, explain, express, narrate, outline, picture, portray, recount 8 inscribe 9 delineate, designate, discourse, enumerate, represent 10 transcribe 12 characterize

descry: see, spy 4 espy 5 sight 6 behold, betray, detect, reveal 7 discern, display 8 denounce, disclose, discover, perceive 9 determine 11 distinguish

Desdemona: *husband:* 7 Othello

traducer: 4 Iago

desecrate: 5 abuse 6 defile 7 pollute, profane, violate 8 unhallow 11 contaminate

desert: due, erg, rat 4 areg, arid, bolt, fail, flee, sand 5 waive, waste 6 barren, defect, lonely, renege, reward 7 abandon, abscond, demerit, forsake, hornada 8 desolate, renounce 9 backslide, wasteland 10 excellence, punishment, relinquish, wilderness

beast: 5 camel

driver: 8 cameleer 9 camelteer

dweller: 4 Arab 5 nomad

group: 7 caravan

hallucination: 6 mirage

pert. to: 6 eremic

rat: 10 prospector

region: erg

science: 9 eremology

ship: 5 camel

shrub: 5 retem 6 alhagi, raetam

train: 7 caravan

valley: 6 bolson

watering spot: 5 oasis

wind: 6 simoom, simoon 7 sirocco

desert candle: 5 plant 8 ocotillo

desert-like: dry 4 arid, sere

deserted: 6 lonely 7 forlorn 8 desolate, forsaken 9 abandoned 11 uninhabited

deserter: rat 6 bolter 8 apostate, fugitive, recreant, renegade

desertion: 14 tergiversation

deserve: 4 earn 5 merit, repay 7 benefit

deserved: 6 worthy 7 condign 11 appropriate

desiccate: dry 4 arid, sere 5 drain 9 dehydrate

desideratum: 4 need 6 desire

design: aim, end, map 4 draw, goal, idea, mean, plan, plot 5 allot, decor, drift, ettle, model, motif, shape 6 device, intend, intent, invent, layout, object, sketch 7 destine, diagram, fashion, outline, pattern, project, propose, purpose 8 contrive 9 calculate, delineate, intention 10 conception 11 contemplate, contrivance

of scattered objects: 4 seme

perforated: 7 stencil

skin: 6 tattoo

designate: set 4 mark, mean, name, show 5 label, style, title 6 assign, denote, intend, settle 7 appoint, entitle, specify 8 describe, identify, indicate 9 appellate, nuncupate 10 denominate 11 distinguish 12 characterize

designed: 8 prepense 11 intentional

designer: 7 planner, plotter, schemer 8 engineer 9 architect, intriguer

designing: 6 artful 7 cunning 8 planning, plotting, scheming 10 foreseeing, fraudulent, intriguing

desinential: 8 terminal

desipience: 5 folly 8 trifling

desipient: 5 silly 7 foolish

desirable: 7 amiable, welcome 8 desirous, eligible, pleasing, salutary 9 advisable, agreeable 10 beneficial

desire: yen 4 care, hope, itch, lust, need, urge, want, will, wish 5 ardor, bosom, covet, crave, mania, yearn 6 affect, aspire, hanker, hunger, prefer, thirst, yammer 7 craving, fantasy, inkling, longing, passion 8 appetite, cupidity 9 appetency, cacoethes 10 benedicite, desiderium

want of: 11 inappetence

desirous: 4 fain, fond 5 eager, frack, freck 6 ardent 7 willing, wishing 8 covetous, spirited 10 delectable, solicitous

desist: ho 4 ease, halt, quit, stop 5 cease 6 depart 7 forbear 11 discontinue

desk: pew 4 ambo 5 board, table 6 pulpit 7 lectern 8 prie-dieu 9 davenport, monocleid, secretary 10 escritoire, monocleide

desman: 4 mole 7 muskrat

Desmanthus: 5 Acuan

desmid: 4 alga 5 algae(pl.)

desolate: sad 4 bare, lorn, ruin, sack, sole 5 alone, bleak, drear, gaunt 6 desert, dreary, gloomy, gousty, lonely, ravage 7 destroy, forlorn, goustie, lacking 8 deprived, deserted, forsaken, solitary **9** abandoned, destitute, dissolute, woebegone **11** comfortless, uninhabited **12** disconsolate

desolation: woe **4** ruin **5** gloom, grief, havoc **6** ravage **7** sadness **10** gloominess, loneliness, melancholy **11** deprivation, destitution, destruction, devastation **12** solitariness

area of: **5** waste **6** desert

Desmodium: 7 trefoil

despair: 5 gloom **11** desperation, despondency **12** hopelessness

despect: 8 contempt

desperado: 6 bandit **7** ruffian **8** criminal **10** lawbreaker

desperate: mad **4** rash **7** extreme, frantic **8** headlong, hopeless, perilous, reckless **9** dangerous **10** despairing, despondent, infuriated, outrageous **11** precipitate **13** irretrievable

despicable: 4 base, vile **5** cheap, dirty **6** abject, paltry, shabby, sordid **7** caitiff, pitiful **8** unworthy, wretched **9** beggardly, miserable **11** ignominious **12** contemptible, contemptuous

despise: 4 defy, hate **5** scorn, scout, spurn **6** detest, loathe, slight **7** contemn, despite, disdain **8** disprize, misprize, vilipend **9** disregard

despite: vex **7** despise **15** notwithstanding

despiteful: 5 cruel **8** insolent **9** insulting, malicious **12** contemptuous, contumelious

despiteous: 5 cruel **8** pitiless **9** malicious, merciless **12** contemptuous

despoil: rob **4** poll, raid, ruin **5** booty, harry, reave, rifle, spoil, strip **6** divest, fleece, ravage, ravish, remove **7** bereave, deprive, disrobe, pillage, plunder **8** deflower, disarray, unclothe **9** depredate

Despoina: 4 Kore **10** Persephone

despondency: 6 misery **7** despair **10** depression, melancholy **11** desperation

despondent: sad **4** blue **8** dejected, downcast, hopeless **9** desperate, heartless **10** despairing **12** heavy-hearted

despot: 4 czar, tsar, tzar **6** satrap, tyrant **7** autarch, monarch **8** autocrat **10** autocratix

despotic: 6 lordly **8** absolute, dominant **9** arbitrary **10** tyrannical

despumate: 4 scum, skim **5** froth

dessert: ice, pie **4** cake **5** fruit, glace(Fr.) **6** eclair, mousse, pastry, sweets **7** banquet, pudding, sherbet, strudel **8** ice cream, Napoleon, sillabub **9** poundcake, sweetmeat **10** blanc-mange

destination: end **4** goal **5** bourn **6** bourne

destine: 4 doom, fate **5** allot **6** depute, design, devote, intend, ordain **7** appoint **9** designate, destinate **10** foreordain, predestine **12** predetermine

destiny: lot **4** dole, doom, fate **5** karma, stars **6** kismet **7** fortune **8** foredoom

goddess: **4** Fate, Norn **5** Moira **6** Ciotho, Laches **7** Atripos

oriental: **6** kismet

destitute: 4 poor **5** clean, needy **6** bereft, devoid, wasted **7** forlorn, lacking, wanting **8** bankrupt, beggared, defeated, deprived, desolate, forsaken, helpless, indigent **9** abandoned, defaulted, driftless **10** devastated, frustrated **12** disappointed, impoverished

destroy: eat, end, gut **4** blow, full, rase, raze, ruin, rush, slay, undo **5** break, craze, elide, erase, erode, fordo, havoc, quell, shend, smash, smite, spoil, stroy, wrack, wreck **6** blight, cancel, cumber, deface, defeat, delete, efface, famish, foredo, ravage **7** abolish, consume, expunge, forfare, nullify, overrun, perempt, ruinate, unbuild, whittle **8** amortize, confound, decimate, demolish, desolate, dissolve, infringe, mutilate, overturn, sabotage **9** depredate, devastate, discreate, dismantle, eradicate, extirpate, liquidate, overthrow **10** annihilate, counteract, disappoint, discomfort, extinguish, neutralize **11** assassinate, exterminate

destroyed: 5 kaput

destroyer: hun **6** vandal **7** warship **8** saboteur

Destroyer: 4 Siva

Destroying Angel: *fungus:* **7** amanita

Mormon: **6** Danite

destruction: end **4** bane, doom, loss, ruin **5** decay, havoc, waste **7** Abaddon(Heb.) **8** downfall, excision, shambles **9** holocaust, perdition **10** extinction, subversion

god: **4** Siva

goddess: Ara

of species: **8** genocide

destructive: 4 fell **5** fatal **6** deadly, mortal **7** baleful, deathly, fateful, harmful, hurtful, noisome, noxious, ruinous **8** wasteful **9** poisonous, truculent **10** catawampus, pernicious **11** catawampous, deleterious, internecine

desuetude: 6 disuse **12** obsolescence **14** discontinuance

desultory: 4 idle **5** hasty, loose **6** roving **7** aimless, cursory **8** rambling, unsteady, wavering **9** irregular, unsettled **10** discursive, inconstant **12** disconnected

detach: 5 sever **7** disjoin, isolate **8** disunite, separate, unfasten, withdraw **9** disengage detached: 4 free 5 alone, aloof 8 unbiased 11 unconcerned, unconnected

detail: 4 item 6 assign, nicety, relate 7 account, appoint, article, itemize, minutia, narrate, specify 8 rehearse, salience 9 enumerate, narrative 10 particular 11 stipulation 12 circumstance 14 accountability 15 circumstantiate

detailed: 6 prolix 8 tiresome 9 wearisome 10 protracted

detain: 4 hold, keep, stay, stop 5 check, delay 6 arrest, hinder, retard 8 imprison, restrain, withhold
in time of war: 6 intern

detainment: 6 arrest 9 detention

detect: see, spy 4 espy, nose, spot 5 catch 6 descry, divine, expose, reveal 7 develop, discern, uncover 8 decipher, discover, overtake 9 deprehend

detection device: 5 radar

detective: tec 4 bull, dick 6 sleuth, tracer 7 gumshoe, scenter, spotter 8 flatfoot, operator, Sam Spade, The Saint 9 James Bond, Nero Wolfe 10 Martin Kane, Miss Marple, Nick Carter, Perry Mason, Peter Salem, Philo Vance 11 Charlie Chan, Ellery Queen, Green Hornet 12 investigator, Simon Templar 13 Hercule Poirot, Michael Shayne 14 Sherlock Holmes
story writer: 10 Ian Fleming 11 Ellery Queen 14 Agatha Christie 16 Arthur Conan Doyle 19 Earle Stanley Gardner

detector: 7 reagent
defect: 14 troubleshooter
storm: 7 sferics

detent: dog 4 pall, pawl 5 catch, click 7 ratchet

detention: 5 delay 7 capture 9 hindrance, restraint 10 arrestment, detainment

deter: bar 5 block, check, delay 6 hinder, retard 7 prevent 8 dissuade, restrain 9 constrain 10 discourage, dishearten, intimidate

deterge: 5 purge 7 cleanse

detergent: 4 soap 7 purging, smectic, solvent 8 cleanser 9 cleansing

deteriorate: 4 fail, wear 5 decay 6 debase, impair 7 decline, pervert 9 backslide 10 degenerate

determinable: 5 fixed 8 definite 9 judicable 10 mensurable, terminable

determinate: 7 certain 8 definite, resolute, resolved, specific 9 arbitrary 10 invariable 11 established

determinative: 5 final 7 shaping 8 limiting 9 directing 10 conclusive 13 authoritative

determine: end, fix, get 4 test 5 assay, award 6 assess, assign, decide, decree, define, descry, settle 7 adjudge, analyse, analyze, appoint, arrange, dispose, resolve 8 conclude 9 admeasure, arbitrate, ascertain, calculate, terminate 10 adjudicate, constitute, deliberate, predestine

determined: set 4 bent, firm 6 dogged, intent, mulish, sturdy 7 decided, settled 8 foregone, perverse, resolute, resolved, stubborn 9 obstinate, pigheaded 10 persistent, unyielding 12 determinable

deterrent: 9 hindrance 14 discouragement

detersion: 7 washing 8 ablution

detest: 4 damn, hate 5 abhor, curse 6 loathe 7 condemn, despise, dislike 8 denounce, execrate 9 abominate

detestable: 4 foul 6 horrid, odious 8 infamous 9 nefarious 12 antipathetic

dethrone: 6 depose, divest

detonate: 4 fire 5 blast 7 explode 9 fulminate

detonator: cap 7 torpedo 9 explosive

detour: 6 bypass 7 circuit 9 deviation

detract: 5 decry 6 defame, divert, villify 7 asperse, traduce 8 belittle, derogate, distract, minimize, protract, subtract, withdraw 9 disparage 10 depreciate

detraction: 7 calumny, scandal, slander

detriment: 4 cost, hurt, loss 5 damna(pl.), wound 6 damage, damnum, injury 8 mischief 9 disprofit 10 impediment 12 disadvantage

detrimental: 7 harmful, hurtful 9 injurious 10 pernicious 11 deleterious

detritus: 4 tuff 5 chaff, waste 6 debris 7 garbage, rubbish

deva: 5 angel, deity

Devaki's son: 7 Krishna

deval: 4 stop 5 cease, pause 9 cessation

devance: 8 outstrip 9 forestall 10 anticipate

devastate: 5 exile, havoc, waste 6 ravage 7 destroy, pillage, plunder, scourge 8 demolish 10 depopulate

devel: 4 blow 6 strike

develop, develope: 4 form, grow 5 arise, ripen 6 appear, detect, evolve, expand, flower, mature, reveal, unfold, unfurl 7 educate, enlarge, expound, uncover 8 disclose, discover, engender, generate, manifest 9 elaborate, germinate

development: 6 growth 7 stature 8 breeding, increase 9 evolution, expansion, formation, unfolding 11 elaboration
arrested: 7 aplasia
full: 8 maturity, ripeness
going back: 13 retrogression

devest: 5 strip 6 denude, divest 7 abandon, deprive, undress 8 alienate

Devi: *beneficent:* 5 Guari
consort: 4 Siva
fierce: 4 Kali
light: Uma

malignant: **5** Durga

riding a tiger: **6** Chandi

deviate: err, yaw **4** lean, miss, vary, veer **5** drift, lapse, sheer, stray **6** change, depart, detour, recede, squint, swerve, wander **7** decline, deflect, digress, diverge

from the norm: **6** mutate

from the vertical: **4** hade

deviation: 7 anomaly **11** declination

device: gin, mot **4** tool **5** drift, meter, motto, shift **6** design, emblem, gadget, scheme **7** compass, fiction, impresa, imprese, project, vehicle **8** artifice, fastener, gimcrack **9** apparatus, appliance, doohickey, expedient, invention, regulator, stratagem **10** concoction, instrument **11** contraption, contrivance

curve measuring: **9** rotameter

holding: **4** vise **5** clamp

devil: imp **4** bogy, Deil(Sc.), haze, mahu **5** annoy, bogey, bogie, demon, fiend, Satan, tease **6** Amamon, diablo(Sp.), diable(F.), pester **7** Amaimon, Apollyn, clootie, diaboli(pl.), dickens, gremlin, torment, warlock **8** diabolus, Mephisto **9** archfiend, Beelzebub, cacodemon, deevilick, diablotin **10** cacodaemon

Dante's: **8** Cagnazzo

pert. to: **7** satanic **10** diabolical

printer's: **10** apprentice

ruler: **10** diabolarch

tree: **4** dita

worship: **8** satanism

devil's bones: 4 dice

devil-may-care: 8 reckless

deviled: 9 a la diable

devilfish: ray **5** manta

devilish: 6 daring, rakish, wicked **7** demonic, extreme, hellish, inhuman, satanic **8** demoniac, diabolic, fiendish, infernal **9** excessive **10** diabolical **15** Mephistophelian

devilkin: imp

devious: 6 errant, roving, shifty, tricky **7** vagrant, winding **8** indirect, rambling, tortuous **9** eccentric, irregular **10** circuitous, farfetched, roundabout

devise: 4 plan, plot, will **5** array, frame, fudge, weave **6** convey, decoct, divide, divine, invent, scheme **7** appoint, arrange, bethink, concoct, consult, prepare **8** bequeath, contrive **9** construct, fabricate **10** distribute **11** distinguish

devitalize: 6 deaden **10** eviscerate

devoid: 4 free, void **5** empty **6** barren, vacant **7** wanting **9** destitute

devoir: 4 duty, task **6** effort

devolve: 4 pass **8** overturn, transfer, transmit

Devonshire: *boat:* **9** mumblebee

river: **4** Exe

devote: vow **4** ally, avow, doom, give **5** apply **6** addict, attach, bestow, depute, resign **7** address, consign, destine **8** dedicate, venerate **10** consecrate **11** appropriate

devoted: 4 true **5** liege, loyal, pious **6** devout, doomed, fervid **7** adoring, arduous, zealous **8** attached, constant, faithful **9** assiduous, religious **10** obsequious, venerating **11** whole-souled **12** affectionate, wholehearted

devotee: fan, nun **4** monk **6** votary, zealot **7** admirer, amateur, fanatic **8** follower, partisan **10** enthusiast

devotion: 4 aves(pl.) **6** bhakti, novena **7** loyalty, worship **8** fidelity

excessive: **13** ecclesiolatry

object of: **4** idol **5** totem **6** fetich, fetish

period of: **4** Lent **6** novena

devour: eat **4** fret **5** raven, waste **6** engulf **7** consume, engorge **10** annihilate

devout: 4 good, holy, warm **5** godly, pious **6** hearty, solemn **7** cordial, devoted, godlike, saintly, sincere **8** reverent **9** religious, righteous, spiritual **13** sanctimonious

devow: 7 disavow **8** disclaim, renounce

dew: 4 rime **5** bloom **7** moisten, refresh **8** moisture

dewlap: 4 jowl **7** wattles

dewy: 4 damp **5** moist, roral, roric **6** gentle, roscid **9** sparkling **10** refreshing

dexter: 5 right **6** honest **9** fortunate **10** auspicious **15** straightforward

dexterity: art **5** craft, knack, skill **6** stroil **7** ability, address, agility, aptness, cunning, finesse, sleight **8** aptitude, deftness, facility **9** adeptness, diplomacy, quickness, readiness **10** adroitness, cleverness, expertness, nimbleness

dextral: 10 auspicious **11** right-handed

dey: 5 pasha, ruler **7** servant **9** dairymaid

dhan: 6 cattle, wealth **8** property

diabetes remedy: 7 insulin, orinase

diablerie: 7 devilry, sorcery **8** demology, mischief

diabolical, diabolic: 5 cruel **6** wicked **7** demonic, hellish, inhuman, satanic, violent **8** demoniac, devilish, fiendish, infernal **9** demonical, fiendlike

diacope: cut **5** wound **8** incision

diacritic: 4 mark **5** tilde **6** umlaut **11** distinctive

diadem: 5 crown, tiara **6** anadem, circle, emblem, fillet **7** coronet **8** headband **11** sovereignty

diagnose: 7 analyze **8** identify

diagonal: 4 bias

diagram: map 4 plan, tree 5 carte, chart, epure(F.), graph 6 design, schema 9 blueprint

dial: 7 crystal 8 horologe 9 horoscope, indicator, telephone, timepiece

dialect: 5 argot, idiom, lingo 6 brogue, debate, patois, patter, speech 8 language 10 vernacular 11 phraseology

dialogue, dialog: 6 epilog, patter 8 epilogue 12 conversation
having nature of: 13 interlocutory 14 conversational

diameter: pi 4 bore 5 width
half: 5 radii(pl.) 6 radius

diamond: gem, ice 4 bort, rock 5 bortz, field, jager, jewel 7 lozenge 8 corundum 9 briolette
coarse: 4 bort
crystal: 7 glassie
cutter: 12 brilliandeer
famous: See stone: *famous*
fragments: 4 bort
glazier's: 6 emeril
holding device: dop 4 dopp
imitation: 5 paste 9 schlenter
necklace: 7 riviere(F.)
surface: 5 facet

diamond-hard: 7 adamant

Diamond State: 8 Delaware

Diana: 7 Artemis
father: 7 Jupiter
mother: 6 Latona
twin: 6 Apollo

diana monkey: 7 roloway

diaper: 6 hippen, hippin, napkin

diaphanous 5 sheer 11 transparent

diaphragm: 4 riff 7 midriff
pert. to: 7 phrenic

diary: log 6 record 7 journal 8 register 9 ephemeris

diaskeuast: 6 editor 7 reviser, revisor

diastase: 4 malt 6 enzyme

diatribe: 6 screed 8 harangue 9 criticism, invective, philippic 10 discussion 12 denunciation

Diaz de Bivar's title: Cid

dib: bob, dap, dip 5 rupee 6 dibble

dibble: dap, dib 6 dabble, trifle

dibs: 5 syrup

dice: 4 cube 5 bones 6 reject 7 checker
cheater: 6 topper
throw of six: 4 sice
trick: cog

dicer: 5 derby 7 gambler

dick: lad 4 dike, whip 5 agent, apron, ditch 6 fellow 8 flatfoot 9 detective

Dickens: *character:* Tim 4 Dora, Nell 5 Fagin 6 Cuttle 7 Dorritt, Podsnap 9 Bill Sikes, Uriah Heep

pen name: Boz

dicker: 4 swap 5 daker 6 barter, haggle 7 bargain, chaffer 8 exchange 9 agreement, negotiate

dickey, dicky: 4 weak 5 shaky 6 donkey, rumble 7 haddock 9 petticoat

dict: saw 5 adage, maxim 6 saying 8 apothegm 10 apophthegm

dictate: say 4 dite, tell 5 dicta(pl.), utter 6 dictum, enjoin, impose 7 command, deliver, require, suggest 9 prescribe 11 communicate

dictatorial: 6 lordly 7 pompous 8 arrogant, dogmatic, positive 9 imperious, masterful, pragmatic 10 autocratic, peremptory 11 categorical, domineering, magisterial, opinionated, overbearing 13 authoritative

diction: 5 style 6 phrase 8 language, parlance, verbiage 10 vocabulary 11 enunciation, phraseology

dictionary: 7 lexicon 8 wordbook 10 vocabulary 11 onomasticon
compiler: 13 lexicographer
geographical: gazetteer
poet's: 6 gradus

dictum: 5 adage, axiom, edict 6 decree, saying 7 dictate, opinion 8 apothegm 9 principle, statement

Dictynna: 11 Britomartis

did: See do

didactic: dry 7 preachy 10 moralistic

didacticism: 6 homily 8 pedantry

diddle: 4 hoax 6 befool, dandle, dawdle, jiggle, toddle 7 swindle

dido: 5 antic, caper, trick

Dido: *father:* 5 Belus
founder of: 8 Carthage
husband: 7 Acerbas
sister: 4 Anna
wooer: 6 Aeneas

die: dod 4 coin, fade, mold, seal, wane 5 croak, stamp 6 chance, depart, expire, finish, perish, vanish, wither 7 decease, succumb 8 languish, puncheon 9 plaything
loaded: 6 fulham, fullam
symbol: ace

die-hard: 4 Tory

diet: 4 fare, fast, food 5 board 6 reduce, viands 7 regimen 8 congress 10 convention 11 convocation, legislature
convalescent: 5 broth
rule of: 7 dietary

difference: 5 clash 6 change 7 discord, dispute 8 division 10 alteration, dissension, unlikeness 11 controversy, discrepancy 12 disagreement

different: 4 many 5 other 6 divers, sundry, unlike 7 diverse, several, unalike, unusual, variant, various **8** distinct, manifold, separate **9** disparate, divergent **10** dissimilar, variegated **11** diversified

differentiate: 8 contrast **11** distinguish **12** discriminate

difficult: 4 hard **5** cramp, crank, spiny **6** crabby, cranky, strait, uneasy, uneath **7** arduous, crabbed, diffuse, labored, obscure, painful, practic **8** abstract, puzzling, stubborn **9** difficile, intricate, laborious **11** complicated, troublesome

prefix: dys

difficulty: ado, bar, rub **4** clog, coil, node, nodi(pl.), snag **5** cheek, nodus **6** boggle, habble, hobble, plight, scrape, strait **7** barrier, pitfall, problem **8** asperity, obstacle, severity, struggle **9** hindrance **10** impediment **11** controversy, obstruction **12** complication, disagreement

lack of: **4** ease

pert. to: **5** spiny **7** crucial

diffidence: 5 doubt **7** modesty, reserve, shyness **8** distrust, humility, timidity **9** suspicion **10** hesitation **11** bashfulness **12** apprehension

diffuse: 4 full, shed **5** strew **6** derive, dilate, divide, expand, extend, prolix, spread **7** copious, perplex, pervade, publish, radiate, scatter, verbose **8** confused, disperse **9** circulate, difficult, dissipate, expatiate, garrulous, irradiate, propagate **10** widespread **11** disseminate

diffusion: 6 osmose **7** osmosis

diffusive: 7 osmotic

dig: hoe **4** claw, grub, howk, mine, moot, pion, poke, root **5** delve, dwell, graft, lodge, spade, start **6** burrow, exhume, plunge, thrust **7** unearth **8** excavate

dig out: 5 scoop, shove, spade **8** excavate

digest: 4 code **5** ripen **6** codify, mature **7** concoct, epitome, pandect, summary **8** condense **10** abridgment, assimilate, compendium, comprehend **11** abridgement

digestion: 7 eupepsy **8** eupepsia **9** dyspepsia

agent: **6** pepsin, rennin **7** maltase

ailment: **5** colic **6** gripes **7** pyrosis **9** dyspepsia **12** constipation

having good: **8** eupeptic

digger: pal **4** plow **5** miner **6** bildar, drudge **7** comrade, plodder **10** Australian **12** New Zealander

digging, fitted for: 7 fodient

dight: dab, rub **4** deck, wipe **5** adorn, dress, equip, order, raise, treat **6** manage, repair, winnow **7** appoint, consign, perform, prepare **9** construct

digit: toe **4** unit **5** thumb **6** figure, finger, number **7** dewclaw

podal: toe

shield for: cot **5** stall **7** thimble

diglot: 9 bilingual

dignified: 5 grand, lofty, manly, noble, staid **6** august, sedate, solemn **7** courtly, exalted, togated **8** ennobled, majestic **11** magisterial

dignify: 5 adorn, exalt, grace, honor **7** elevate, ennoble, promote

dignitary: don **4** raja **5** rajah **6** priest **7** prelate **9** clergyman

dignity: 4 rank **5** honor, pride, state **6** barony, repose **7** bearing, decorum, fitness, gravity, majesty, station **8** nobility **9** nobleness **10** excellence

digraph: 8 ligature

digress: 4 veer **6** swerve, wander **7** deviate, diverge **8** divagate **10** transgress

digression: 7 episode **8** excursus **9** excursion

dike, dyke: 4 bank, dick, pond, pool **5** digue, ditch, levee **7** channel **8** causeway **10** embankment **11** watercourse

dilapidation: 4 ruin **5** decay **9** disrepair **10** raggedness **14** disintegration

dilatation: 7 ectasia, ectasis **8** dilation

dilate: 5 delay, plump, swell, widen **6** expand, extend, spread **7** amplify, broaden, diffuse, distend, enlarge, inflate, prolong, stretch **8** disperse, increase, lengthen, protract **9** expatiate

dilatory: 4 slow **5** slack, tardy **6** fabian, remiss **8** backward, delaying, inactive, sluggish **10** behindhand **15** procrastinating, procrastinative

dilemma: fix **4** node **5** brake **8** quandary **11** predicament **12** complication

dilettante, dilettant: 5 lover **7** admirer, amateur, dabbler, dabster, esthete **8** aesthete

diligence: 4 heed **6** effort **7** caution **8** industry **9** constancy **11** application, earnestness, heedfulness

diligent: 4 busy, hard **6** active, eident, steady **7** careful, earnest, heedful, operose **8** cautious, constant, sedulous **9** assiduous, attentive, laborious **11** industrious, painstaking

dill: 4 calm **5** anise **6** pickle, soothe

seed: **4** anet

dillydally: lag, toy **4** loaf **5** stall **6** loiter, trifle **9** vacillate

dilute: dil(abbr.) **4** thin **5** delay, water **6** rarefy, reduce, weaken **8** diminish **9** attenuate, distemper

dim: wan **4** blur, dark, dull, fade, gray, hazy, mist, pale, veil **5** bleak, blear, dusky, faint, foggy, misty **6** bemist, cloudy, darken, dimpsy, gloomy, obtuse, shadow **7** darkish, eclipse, obscure, shadowy, tarnish **8** overcast **9** obfuscate **10** indistinct, mysterious **11** crepuscular

dime: 4 coin 5 disme

dimension: 4 bulk, size 5 scope 6 extent, height, length 7 breadth 9 magnitude, thickness 10 importance, proportion 11 measurement 13 circumference

diminish: ebb 4 bate, ease, fade, fret, melt, pare, sink, wane, wear 5 abate, lower, peter, taper 6 decoct, dilute, lessen, rebate, reduce, vanish, wither 7 abridge, assuage, curtail, deplete, depress, dwindle, qualify, relieve 8 adminish, condense, decrease, diminute, minorate, moderate, retrench 9 alleviate, epitomize, extenuate

diminution: 8 decrease 9 abasement, abatement, decrement 11 abridgement, attenuation, curtailment, degradation, deprivation, extenuation

diminutive: wee 4 tiny 5 banty, dwarf, petty, runty, small 6 bantam, little, petite 9 minuscule 11 disparaging
  suffix: el, et, ie; cle, ole, ule 4 cula, ette 5 culus

dimmet: 4 dusk 8 twilight

dimness: 5 gloom 8 darkness 9 obscurity

dimple: 4 doke 6 ripple 8 fossette

din: bum 4 riot 5 alarm, bruit, clang, noise 6 clamor, hubbub, racket, rattle, steven, tumult, uproar 7 clamour, clangor, clatter, discord, turmoil 9 commotion, confusion 10 hullabaloo

dindle: 4 ring 6 quiver, thrill, tingle, tinkle, tremor 7 vibrate 9 vibration

dine: eat, sup 5 feast 6 regale

diner: 7 epicure

dinette: 6 alcove 10 kitchen set

ding: 4 beat, dash, push, ring 5 clang, drive, excel, fling, knock, pound, thump 6 stroke, thrash, thrust

dinge: 4 dent, dint 6 batter, bruise 10 depression

dinghy, dingy: 4 boat 5 skiff 7 rowboat, shallop

dingle: 4 dale, dell, glen, vale 6 valley

dingus: 6 gadget 9 doohickey, doohickus, doohinkey, doohinkus

dingy: dun 4 dark 5 dirty, dusky, grimy, ourie, smoky 6 dinghy 8 smirched

dining: *room:* 7 cenacle, dinette 9 refectory
  science: 10 aristology

dink: 4 deck, neat, trim 7 elegant

dinkey: 10 locomotive

dinkum: 4 fair 5 truly 6 honest, square 7 genuine 8 honestly, reliable

dinky: 4 cute, neat, poor 13 insignificant

dinner: 4 meal 5 feast 6 repast 7 banquet 9 beanfeast
  course: 4 nuts, soup 5 fruit, salad 6 entree 7 dessert
  pert. to: 8 cenatory

dinornis: moa

dinosaur: 11 morosaurian, stegosauria, stegosaurus, triceratops, tyrannosaur 12 brontosaurus 13 tyrannosaurus
  genus of: 10 diplodocus 11 apatosaurus

dint: 4 beat, blow, dent, nick 5 clour, delve, dinge, force, notch, onset, power, press, shock 6 attack, chance, effort, strike, stroke 7 imprint 8 efficacy, striking 10 impression 11 indentation

diocese: see 8 district 12 jurisdiction
  division: 6 parish 8 parishen(Sc.)

Dione: *consort:* 4 Zeus
  daughter: 9 Aphrodite

Dionysus: *attendant:* 6 Maenad
  festival: 7 Agrania 8 Agrionia
  mother: 6 Semele
  pert. to: 7 Bromian

diopside: 7 alalite 8 pyroxene

diorite: 7 diabase

Dioscuri: 5 twins 6 Anaces, Castor, Gemini, Pollux
  father: 4 Zeus 9 Tyndareus
  mother: 4 Leda
  sister: 5 Helen 12 Clytemnestra

diose: 14 glycolaldehyde

dip: sop 4 bail, drop, dunk, lade, sink, soak 5 delve, ladle, lower, slope 6 candle, hollow, plunge 7 decline, immerge, immerse, incline, moisten 8 submerge 10 depression, pickpocket
  in water: 5 douse, rinse, souse

diploma: 6 degree 7 charter 11 certificate

diplomacy: 4 tact 9 dexterity 10 artfulness

diplomat: 4 dean 6 consul 7 attache 8 minister 10 ambassador
  corps head: 4 dean 5 doyen

dipody: 6 syzygy

dipper: 5 ladle, scoop 10 pickpocket

dippy: mad 7 foolish 9 screwball

dipsomania: 9 potomania 10 alcoholism

dipteran: fly 4 gnat 8 mosquito
  lobe of wing: 5 alula

dipthong, diphthong: 4 ae, oe 7 bivocal

dird: 4 blow 5 thump 9 buffeting

dirdum: 4 blow 5 blame 6 rebuke, tumult, uproar 8 scolding 10 punishment

dire: 4 dern, evil 5 awful, fatal 6 deadly, dismal, funest, tragic, woeful 7 doleful, drastic, fearful 8 dreadful, horrible, terrible, ultimate 10 calamitous, oppressive, portentous 12 overpowering

direct: aim, bid, con 4 airt, bain, bend, boss, edit, even, flat, head, helm, lead, open, rein, sway, turn 5 apply, blank, coach, frank, guide, order, point, refer, steer, teach, train, utter, write 6 ensign, govern, handle, honest, impart, lineal, manage 7 address, appoint, command, conduct, control, convert, execute, express, officer, preside 8 dedicate, instruct, marshall, regulate, straight 9 categoric, downright, immediate 10 administer, forthright, point-blank 11 categorical, compendious, superintend, superscribe 15 straightforward

direction: way 4 airt, bent, care, duct, east, road, rule, west 5 north, order, route, south, trend 6 course 7 address, bearing, command, control, mandate, precept 8 guidance, tendency 9 ordinance 10 injunction, management, regulation 11 appointment, arrangement, inclination, information, instruction 13 determination 14 superscription 15 superintendence

Biblical: 5 selah

court: 5 order

line of: 5 range

musical: see **musical direction**

pole to pole: 5 axial

printer's: 4 stet

without: 7 astatic

direction finder: 7 compass

directly: 4 soon 8 promptly 9 instantly, presently 11 immediately, straightway

director: 4 boss, head 5 coach, guide, pilot 6 archon, bishop, leader, rector 7 manager, prefect, trainer 8 governor, producer 9 conductor, intendant 13 administrator 14 superintendent

directors, board of: 10 management

directory: 9 phonebook 10 collection, directoire(F.)

dirge: 4 keen, song 5 elegy 6 hearse, lament 7 epicede 8 epicedia(pl.), threnody 9 epicedium

part: fin 7 nacelle

dirk: 4 snee 5 skean, sword 6 dagger, weapon

dirl: 4 ring 6 pierce, thrill, tingle 7 vibrate

dirndle: 5 dress, skirt

dirt: fen, mud 4 dust, gore, muck, nast, soil 5 earth, filth, grime, trash 6 gravel, ground, refuse 7 mullock 8 muckment 9 excrement

dirty: low 4 base, clat, foul, soil 5 bawdy, cabby, dingy, foggy, grimy, gusty, horry, muddy, nasty, sully 6 bemire, clarty, defile, filthy, greasy, grubby, impure, mussed, smutty, soiled, sordid, stormy 7 begrime, brookie, bruckle, clouded, muddied, squalid, sullied, tarnish, unclean 10 despicable

dirty dig: 5 taunt

dirty look: 5 frown

Dis: 5 Pluto

disable: 4 lame, maim 5 break, gruel, wreck 6 bruise, dismay, weaken 7 cripple 9 hamstring 10 disqualify 12 incapacitate

disaccharide: 5 biose 7 lactose, maltose, sucrose 10 saccharose

disadvantage: 4 hurt, risk 6 damage, injury 7 penalty 8 handicap 9 detriment

disadvantageous: 7 hurtful 10 derogatory 11 detrimental, prejudicial, unfavorable

disaffected: 5 false 6 untrue 8 disloyal, forsworn, perjured, recreant 9 estranged, faithless, insidious 10 perfidious, traitorous 11 treacherous

disaffection: 6 deceit 7 disease, disgust, dislike 8 disorder 9 distemper, hostility 10 disloyalty, alienation, discontent 13 indisposition 14 disinclination

disaffirm: 4 deny 5 annul 7 reverse 9 repudiate 10 contradict

disagree: 4 vary 6 differ 7 dissent, quarrel 8 conflict

disagreeable: bad 4 sour, vile 5 cross, harsh, nasty 7 chronic, hateful 8 terrible 9 invidious, irritable, offensive, repugnant 10 abominable, forbidding, unpleasant 11 displeasing, distasteful 13 uncomfortable

disagreement: 5 clash, fight 7 discord, dispute, dissent, wrangle 8 variance 9 diversity 10 contention, difference, difficulty, dissension, dissidence, divergence, unlikeness 11 contrariety, controversy, discrepancy, displeasure, incongruity 16 misunderstanding

disallow: 6 forbid, reject 7 censure 8 disclaim, disprove, prohibit 10 disapprove

disappear: fly 4 fade, flee 6 vanish 7 evanish 8 evanesce

disappoint: 4 balk, bilk, fail, fall, mock, undo 6 baffle, defeat, delude, outwit, thwart 7 deceive, destroy, nullify 9 frustrate, mislippen

disappointment: rue 7 letdown 11 frustration

disapprobation: 5 odium 11 deprecation, disapproval 12 condemnation

disapproval: 4 booh, hiss, veto 7 catcall, censure 9 disliking 14 disapprobation

disapprove: 6 reject, resent 7 condemn, protest 8 disallow, disprove 9 deprecate

disarm: 6 subdue

disarrange: 4 muss 6 deform, ruffle 7 clutter, confuse, derange, disturb, rummage 8 dishevel, disorder, unsettle 9 dislocate 10 discompose, disconcert 11 disorganize

disarray: 4 mess 5 strip 6 caddle 7 despoil 8 dishevel, disorder 9 confusion 10 dishabille

disassociate: 8 separate 10 dissociate

disaster: woe 4 bale, blow, evil, ruin 6 mishap, stroke 7 reverse 8 accident, calamity, casualty, fatality 9 cataclysm, extremity, mischance 10 misfortune 11 catastrophe 12 misadventure

disavow: 4 deny 5 devow 6 abjure, disown, recant, refuse 7 decline, retract 8 abnegate, disclaim, renounce 9 repudiate

disband: 7 breakup, dismiss, release, scatter 8 dissolve 9 discharge 12 disintegrate

disbelieve: 5 doubt 6 reject 7 suspect 9 discredit

disbeliever: 7 atheist, heretic

disburden: rid 4 ease 7 relieve 9 exonerate 11 disencumber

disburse: 5 spend 6 defray, expend, outlay 10 distribute

disc: 4 dial 5 medal, paten, plate, quoit 6 record 7 platter

discalced: 6 unshod 10 barefooted

discard: 4 cast, jilt, junk, omit, oust, shed 5 chuck, ditch, scrap, shuck, sluff 6 disuse, divest, excuss, reject 7 abandon, cashier, dismiss, forsake 9 eliminate, repudiate

pile: 4 heap 5 trash 8 boneyard

discern: ken, see, spy 4 espy, read 5 sight 6 behold, descry, detect, notice 8 discover, perceive 10 understand 11 distinguish

discernible: 7 evident, visible 8 apparent, manifest 11 conspicuous, perceptible 15 distinguishable

discernment: eye 4 tact 5 flair, taste 6 acumen 7 insight 8 sagacity 9 sharpness 10 divination, perception, shrewdness 11 penetration 12 clairvoyance, perspicacity 14 discrimination

discharge: can 4 boot, cass, dump, emit, fire, free, pour, sack 5 eject, empty, expel, exude, shoot, speed 6 acquit, assoil, bounce, defray, effect, exempt, unlade, unload 7 absolve, cashier, disband, dismiss, exhaust, release, relieve 8 disgorge, displace, evacuate, mittimus 9 acquittal, dismissal, exculpate, exonerate, exudation, liquidate 10 discompose, liberation 11 acquittance, exoneration, performance, transaction

dishonorable: 7 bobtail, cashier

discharged from active service: 8 emeritus

disciple: ite 4 John, Mark 5 Judas, Peter, teach, train 6 hearer, punish 7 apostle, auditor, Matthew, scholar, student 8 adherent, follower 10 discipline

disciplinarian: 4 czar, tsar 6 tyrant 7 trainer 8 martinet

discipline: 4 whip 5 inure, teach, train 6 ferule, govern, punish 7 chasten, culture, educate, scourge 8 doctrine, instruct, learning, regulate, restrain, teaching, training, tutoring 9 education 10 punishment 11 instruction 12 chastisement

disclaim: 4 deny 5 devow 6 abjure, disown, refuse 7 disavow 8 abdicate, abnegate, disallow, renounce 9 repudiate

disclose: ope 4 bare, blow, open, tell 5 utter 6 betray, bewray, descry, expose, impart, reveal, shrive, unseal, unveil 7 confess, develop, display, divulge, exhibit, unclose, uncover 8 discover, indicate, manifest

disclosure: 6 expose 10 revelation

discolor: 4 fade, spot 5 stain, tinge 6 smirch, streak 7 distain, tarnish 8 besmirch

discoloration: 4 spot 5 stain

discolored: old 5 dirty, moldy 7 stained 8 ustulate 9 tarnished

discomfit: 4 rout 5 abash, upset 6 baffle, defeat 7 confuse, conquer, disturb, scatter 8 confound 9 embarrass, frustrate, overthrow 10 disconcert

discomfort: 4 pain 6 dismay, grieve, sorrow, unease 7 disturb 8 distress 9 annoyance, embarrass 10 discourage, uneasiness 11 displeasure 13 inconvenience 14 discouragement

discommendation: 5 blame 7 censure 8 reproach 9 dispraise

discommode: 7 trouble 9 incommode 13 inconvenience

discompose: 4 fret 5 upset 6 flurry, ruffle 7 agitate, confuse, derange, disturb, fluster, perturb 8 disorder, displace, disquiet, unsettle 9 discharge 10 disarrange, disconcert

disconcert: 4 faze 5 abash, daunt, feeze, upset, worry 6 baffle, blench, rattle 7 confuse, disturb, nonplus, perturb, squelch 8 browbeat, disorder 9 discomfit, embarrass, frustrate 10 disarrange, discompose 14 discountenance

disconnect: 4 undo 5 sever 6 divide 7 disjoin 8 dissolve, disunite, separate, uncouple

disconnected: 6 abrupt, broken 7 cursory 8 rambling 9 desultory, scattered 10 abstracted, disjointed, incoherent

disconsolate: sad 6 gloomy, woeful 7 forlorn 8 dejected, desolate, hopeless 9 cheerless, miserable, sorrowful 10 dispirited, melancholy 12 inconsolable

discontent: 8 disquiet 9 displease 10 dissatisfy, malcontent, uneasiness 11 displeasure 12 disaffection 15 dissatisfaction

discontinue: end 4 drop, quit, stop 5 break, cease, letup 6 desist, disuse, sunder 7 disrupt 8 intermit

discord: din, jar 5 broil 6 strife 7 faction 8 conflict, variance 9 cacophony, diversity 10 contention, difference, dissension, dissonance 12 disagreement
goddess of: Ate 4 Eris

discordant: 4 ajar 5 harsh 6 hoarse 7 jarring 8 contrary, jangling 10 discrepant 11 incongruous, quarrelsome 12 antagonistic, inconsistent, inharmonious 14 irreconcilable
musically: 8 scordato
serenade: 9 charivari

Discordia: 4 Eris

discotheque: 5 agogo 7 cabaret

discount: 4 agio 5 batta 6 rebate, reduce 9 allowance, deduction, disregard, reduction 12 depreciation

discourage: 4 carp 5 daunt, deter 6 dampen, deject, dismay 7 depress 8 dispirit, dissuade 10 discomfort, dishearten

discourse: 4 carp, talk, tell 5 orate, paper, speak, tract 6 eulogy, homily, parley, preach, sermon 7 account, address, comment, declaim, discuss, dissert, lecture, narrate, oration, prelect 8 argument, colloquy, converse, parlance, treatise 9 expatiate, narration, narrative, panegyric, sermonize, soliloquy 10 conference 11 description 12 conversation, dissertation
art of: 8 rhetoric
long: 6 screed, tirade 7 descant 9 philippic

discourteous: 4 rude 6 scurvy 7 uncivil 8 impolite, ungentle 10 unmannerly 11 ill-mannered, uncivilized 13 disrespectful

discover: see, spy 4 espy, find 5 learn 6 define, descry, detect, expose, invent, locate, reveal 7 confess, discern, display, divulge, exhibit, explore, uncover, unearth 8 decipher, disclose, manifest 9 apprehend, ascertain, deprehend 11 reconnoiter

discoverer: spy 5 scout 8 explorer, inventor 10 originator

discovery: 5 trove 6 espial 10 disclosure, revelation
gold: 6 strike

discreate: 7 destroy 10 annihilate

discredit: 5 decry, doubt, refel 6 deface 7 asperse, blemish, impeach, scandal, suspect 8 belittle, disgrace, dishonor, distrust 9 disparage, disrepute 10 disbelieve

discreet: 4 wary 5 civil 6 polite, silent 7 careful, guarded, politic, prudent 8 cautious, reserved, reticent 11 circumspect

discrepant: 8 contrary 9 different 10 discordant 11 disagreeing 12 inconsistent

discrepate: 6 differ 11 distinguish 12 discriminate

discrete: 8 distinct, separate

discretion: 4 tact 6 wisdom 8 courtesy 9 restraint 13 secretiveness

discriminate: 6 secern 8 perceive 9 demarcate 10 discrepate 11 distinguish 13 differentiate

discriminating: 4 nice 5 acute 6 astute 7 choosey 8 critical 10 discerning 11 distinctive

discrimination: 5 taste 6 acumen 11 discernment, distinction, penetration

discursive: 6 roving 7 cursory 8 rambling 9 desultory 10 digressive

discus: 4 disk 5 quoit
thrower: 10 Discobolus

discuss: air 4 moot 5 argue, bandy, treat 6 confer, debate, excuss, parley 7 agitate, bespeak, canvas, consult, dispute, dissert, examine, narrate 9 discourse, exagitate, ventilate 11 expostulate

discussion: 5 forum 6 hassel 8 causerie, diatribe, entreaty 12 dissertation
group: 5 class, panel 7 seminar
medium of: 5 forum
open to: 4 moot

disdain: tut 5 pride, scorn, spurn 7 contemn, despise 8 contempt 9 arrogance 11 haughtiness, indignation

disease: 4 harm 5 pinta 6 malady, morbus 7 ailment, illness, malaria, trouble, yellows 8 beriberi, distress, sickness 9 complaint, distemper, infirmity 10 discomfort, pestilence, uneasiness 12 disaffection
agent of: 4 germ 9 bacterium, contagium
animal: coe, pip, rye 4 rout 5 braxy, coath, colic, farcy, hoose, hooze, mange, nenta 6 amoeba, garget, hammer 7 dartars, spavins, takosis 8 asthenia, glanders, sacbrood 9 distemper, tularemia 11 myxomatosis, psittacosis
blood: 8 leucemia, leukemia 9 leucaemia
brain: 8 paranoia 13 schizophrenia
comb. form: nos 4 noso
contagious: pox 5 mumps 7 measles
crippling: 9 arthritis, sclerosis 10 rheumatism 13 poliomyelitis
declining stage: 9 catabasis
deficiency: 6 scurvy 8 pellagra
diver's: 5 bends 7 caisson
eye: 8 glaucoma, trachoma 9 pterygium 14 conjunctivitis
fatal: 5 lyssa 10 malignancy
favorable termination of: 5 lysis
fowl: pip 4 roup 7 perosis
fungus: 5 ergot, tinea
hair: 5 plica 7 xerasia 8 psilosis
heart: 8 aneurism, aneurysm
liver: 9 cirrhosis, hepatitis
local: 7 endemic

lung: 8 phthisis 9 emphysema, pneumonia 11 consumption 12 tuberculosis

nervous: see **mental disorder**

pert. to: 6 clinic, loimic 7 endemic

plant: fen 4 bunt, rust, scab, smut 5 ergot, speck 6 calico, coleur, mildew 7 erinose, viruela, walloon 8 brindled, melanose

prediction about: 9 prognosis

recognition of: 9 diagnosis

science of children's: 10 pediatrics 11 paediatrics

science of origin: 8 etiology

skin: 4 acne, pian, rash 5 favus, hives, psora, tinea 6 courap, dartre, eczema, herpes, lichen, tetter 7 scabies, serpigo 8 impetigo, ringworm 9 frambesia, psoriasis, xeroderma 10 framboesia 11 scleroderma

spreader: fly 6 vector 7 carrier

suffix: 4 itis

tropical: 5 sprue 7 malaria

wasting: 8 phthisic

disembark: 4 land 6 alight, debark

disembodiment: 4 soul 6 spirit

disembowel: gut 4 hulk 6 paunch 8 gralloch 10 eviscerate

disembroil: 8 untangle 9 extricate

disencumber: rid 4 free 9 disburden, disengage

disengage: 4 free 5 clear, untie 6 detach, evolve, loosen 7 release, unravel 8 liberate 9 extricate 11 disencumber, disentangle 12 disembarrass

disentangle: 4 comb, free 5 clear, loose, ravel 6 evolve, sleave 7 unravel 8 untangle 9 disengage, extricate 12 disembarrass

disenthrone: 6 depose

disfavor, disfavour: 5 odium 7 umbrage 9 disesteem 11 displeasure

disfigure: mar 4 blur, scar 6 deface, defeat, deform, injure, mangle 7 blemish 8 mutilate 10 disfashion

disgorge: 4 spew, vent 5 eject, empty, vomit 9 discharge 10 relinquish

disgrace: 4 blot, slur, soil, spot 5 abase, crime, odium, shame, stain 6 infamy 7 affront, attaint, degrade, scandal, slander 8 contempt, dishonor, ignominy, reproach 9 discredit, disesteem, disfigure, humiliate 10 attainture, defamation, opprobrium 11 displeasure, humiliation 13 disparagement

disgruntled: 4 sore 7 peevish

disguise: 4 hide, mask, mumm, veil 5 belie, cloak, couch, feign, gloze, guise 6 covert, deform, masque 7 conceal, obscure, pretend 8 palliate 9 coverture, dissemble, incognito 10 camouflage, intoxicate, masquerade 11 dissimulate

disgust: 5 repel, shock 6 degout(F.), horror, nausea, offend, revolt, sicken 8 aversion, distaste, loathing, nauseate 9 antipathy 10 abhorrence, repugnance 11 abomination 12 disaffection

disgusting: 4 foul, vile 5 nasty 6 filthy 7 beastly, fulsome, hateful, noisome, obscene 8 shocking

dish (see also **food**): cap 4 caup 5 basin, comal, nappy, paten, plate 6 bassie, critch, panada, patera, recipe, saucer, tureen 7 charger, cresset, epergne, patella, plateau, platter, ramekin, scuttle 9 casserole, clackdish

gravy: 4 boat

main: 6 entree

dishabille: 8 disarray, disorder, negligee

Dishan's son: Uz 4 Aran

dishearten: 5 amate, daunt 6 deject 7 depress, flatten, unnerve 8 dispirit 10 demoralize, discourage

disheartened: 6 gloomy 8 downcast

dishevel: 4 muss 6 ruffle, tousel, tousle, tumble 8 disarray, disorder 10 disarrange

dishonest: 4 foul, lewd 5 cronk, false 7 corrupt, crooked, knavish 8 indecent, shameful, unchaste 9 deceitful, repulsive 10 fraudulent, perfidious 12 dishonorable 13 untrustworthy

dishonor, dishonour: 5 abase, abuse, shame, stain 6 defame, defile, infamy 7 degrade, obloquy, violate 8 disgrace, ignominy, reproach 9 discredit, disparage, disrepute 10 defamation, disworship, opprobrium 11 contaminate, impeachment, irreverence 13 disparagement

dishonorable, dishonourable: 4 base, foul, mean 5 nasty 6 yellow 7 ignoble 11 disesteemed

dishwasher: 7 machine 8 domestic

disillusion: 10 disenchant

disinclination: 7 dislike 8 aversion, distaste 9 antipathy 10 reluctance, repugnance 12 disaffection

disinclined: 6 averse 9 reluctant, unwilling 10 indisposed

disinfect: 7 cleanse 9 sterilize

disinfectant: 5 iodin 6 iodine, phenòl 9 germicide 10 antiseptic

disingenuous: 5 false 10 circuitous

disinherit: 7 deprive 10 exheredate

disintegrate: 4 melt 5 decay, erode 7 crumble, disband 8 dissolve, separate 9 decompose

disinter: 6 exhume, unbury

disinterested: 4 fair 9 apathetic, impartial 11 unconcerned

disjasked, disjaskit: 5 jaded 7 decayed

disjoin: 4 part, undo 5 sever 6 detach, sunder 8 dissolve, disunite, separate 10 disconnect, dissociate

disjune: 9 breakfast

disk: 4 dial 5 cakra, medal, paten, plate, sabot, wheel 6 bezant, chakra, harrow, record, washer 7 medalet, phalera 9 cultivate, faceplate, medallion, millstone
hockey: 4 puck
metal: 4 flan, gong 6 ghurry, sequin 8 zecchino
pert. to: 6 discal 7 discoid
solar: 4 Aten

dislike: 4 loth, mind 5 loath 6 detest 8 aversion, distaste 9 antipathy, disesteem, disrelish 11 detestation, displacency, displeasure 12 disaffection 14 disinclination
comb. form: mis 4 miso
object of: 8 anathema
of children: 9 misopedia 10 misopaedia

dislocate: 5 splay 8 disjoint, displace 10 disarrange

dislodge: 5 expel 6 remove

disloyal: 5 false 6 untrue 9 faithless 10 inconstant, perfidious, unfaithful 11 disaffected, treacherous

dismal: sad, wan 4 dark, dire, dull, glum, gray 5 black, bleak, drear, sorry 6 dreary, gloomy, triste 7 doleful, ghastly, joyless, ominous, unhappy 8 dolorous, funereal, lonesome 9 cheerless, sorrowful 10 acherontic, calamitous, lugubrious, melancholy 11 unfortunate

dismantle: 4 rase, raze 5 strip 6 divest 7 deprive, destroy, uncloak 8 dismount

dismay: 4 fear, ruin 5 alarm, appal, daunt, dread 6 appall, fright, subdue, terror 7 depress, deprive, horrify, terrify 8 affright, confound 9 dejection 10 depression, discomfort, discourage 11 trepidation 12 apprehension 13 consternation 14 discouragement

dismember: 4 maim, part, rend 5 sever 6 mangle 7 dissect 8 disjoint, mutilate

dismiss: can 4 boot, bust, drop, oust 5 chuck, eject 6 banish, bounce, reject, remove 7 cashier, disband, discard 8 relegate 9 discharge, overthrow

dismissal: 5 conge 6 avaunt 8 mittimus

dismount: 5 avale 6 alight 9 dismantle

disobedient: 7 forward, froward, naughty, ungodly, wayward 8 mutinous 10 rebellious, refractory 11 intractable 12 contumacious 13 insubordinate

disoblige: 6 offend 7 affront

disorder: pie 4 mess, muss, riot 5 chaos, deray, snafu, touse 6 burble, jumble, litter, malady, mucker, muddle, ruffle, tousle, tumu't 7 ailment, clutter, confuse, derange, disturb, embroil, flutter, illness, misdeed, perturb, trouble 8 disarray, dishevel 9 commotion, complaint, confusion, distemper 10 disarrange, discompose, disconcert, misconduct 11 derangement, disorganize, disturbance, misdemeanor 12 disaffection, discomposure, irregularity 13 indisposition 14 disarrangement 15 disorganization
visual: 10 strabismus

disordered: 6 frouzy, frowsy, frowzy 10 topsy-turvy 11 lightheaded

disorderly: 5 randy 6 unruly 8 slipshod, slovenly 12 hugger-mugger, ungovernable, unmanageable

disorganize: 5 upset 7 confuse, derange, disband, disrupt 8 disorder, dissolve 10 disarrange

disour: 6 jester 11 storyteller

disown: 4 deny 6 reject 7 disavow, retract 8 abdicate, disclaim, renounce 9 reprobate, repudiate

disparage, desparage: 4 slur 5 abuse, decry, lower 6 slight 7 degrade, depress, detract, impeach 8 belittle, derogate, dishonor, disprize, minimize 9 discredit, dispraise, extenuate 10 depreciate

disparate: 7 unequal 8 separate 9 different 10 dissimilar 16 disproportionate

dispart: 4 open, rend, rive 5 break, sever, split 6 cleave, divide 8 separate

dispassionate: 4 calm, cool, fair 5 stoic 6 sedate, serene 8 composed, moderate 9 collected, impartial, temperate, unruffled 10 deliberate, unimpaired 12 unprejudiced

dispatch: rid 4 free, kill, mail, note, post, send 5 haste, hurry, speed 6 hasten 7 deliver, depeche(F.), dispose 8 celerity, conclude, expedite 9 quickness 10 accelerate, accomplish, promptness

dispatch boat: 5 aviso 6 packet

dispatcher: 8 trainman 9 motor boss

dispel: 6 banish 7 scatter 8 disperse 9 dissipate

dispend: 5 spend 6 expend 8 dispense, squander

dispendious: 6 costly 9 expensive 11 extravagant

dispensation: 4 plan 6 scheme 7 economy, license 9 allotment 12 distribution

dispense: 4 deal, dole 6 effuse, excuse, exempt, forego, manage 7 absolve, arrange, dispend 9 exemption 10 administer, distribute 12 dispensation

dispenser: 7 manager, steward 10 pharmacist 13 administrator
information: 4 tout 7 tipster 11 stoolpigeon

dispeople: 10 depopulate

disperse: sow 4 fray, part, rout 5 strew 6 dilate, dispel, sparse, spread, vanish 7 diffuse, scatter 8 separate, squander 9 dissipate 10 dispergate, distribute 11 disseminate

dispirit: cow 4 damp 5 daunt 6 deject 7 depress, flatten 10 discourage, dishearten, intimidate

dispirited: 6 abattu 7 abattue 8 downcast 9 cheerless, woebegone 11 crestfallen 12 disconsolate

dispiteous: 5 cruel 8 pitiless, spiteful

displace: 6 banish, depose, mislay, remove 7 derange 8 dislodge, misplace, supplant 9 discharge, dislocate, superseded 10 discompose

display: air 4 brag, pomp, show, wear 5 boast, emote, scene, sight, sport, stage 6 blazon, deploy, descry, expose, extend, flaunt, ostent, parade, reveal, uncase 7 approve, etalage, exhibit, flutter, pageant, uncover 8 ceremony, disclose, discover, emblazon, exercise, flourish, indicate, manifest, splendor 9 spectacle 10 exhibition 11 affectation, demonstrate 13 demonstration, manifestation

displease: vex 4 miff 5 anger, annoy, pique 6 offend 7 provoke 8 irritate 10 discontent, dissatisfy

displeasing: bad, dry 7 irksome 9 offensive 10 unpleasant 11 distasteful 12 disagreeable

displeasure: ire 5 anger, mumps, pique 6 injury 7 dislike, offense, trouble, umbrage 8 disfavor, disgrace, distaste 10 discomfort, discontent, resentment, uneasiness 11 indignation

show: cry 4 pout 5 frown

dispone: 8 transfer 10 distribute

disport: 4 play 5 amuse, frisk 6 divert, frolic, gambol

disposal: 8 bestowal 11 arrangement, disposition

dispose: set 4 bend, give, mind 5 array, order, place 6 adjust, attire, bestow, settle 7 appoint, arrange, prepare 8 dispatch, regulate 9 determine 10 distribute

disposed: apt 5 fixed, prone, ready 7 tending 8 arranged, inclined

disposition: 4 bent, bias, mood, turn 5 tache 6 affect, animus, health, nature, temper 7 concept 8 aptitude, attitude, disposal, positure 9 affection, character, diathesis 10 adjustment, management, proclivity, propension, propensity 11 arrangement, inclination, temperament 12 constitution, distribution, organization 14 relinquishment

dispossess: 4 oust 5 eject, evict, expel, strip 6 depose, divest 7 bereave, deprive 8 disseize

dispraise: 5 blame 7 censure 9 disparage 10 depreciate, detraction 13 disparagement 15 discommendation

disprize: 10 undervalue 13 underestimate

disproof: 10 refutation 11 confutation

disproportion: 9 disparity 10 inequality

disproportionate: 14 incommensurate

disprove: 5 rebut, refel 6 negate, refute 7 confute, explode 8 disallow, redargue 10 disapprove

disputable: 5 vague 6 unsure 7 dubious, fallible 8 doubtful, insecure 9 uncertain 10 indefinite, precarious

disputant: 6 arguer 7 debater

disputation: 7 polemic 8 argument 9 dialectic 10 discussion 11 controversy 12 conversation

disputatious: 7 eristic 13 argumentative

dispute: 4 deny, feud, fuss, moot, riot, spat 5 argue, brawl, broil, cabal, hurry 6 barney, bicker, cangle, dacker, daiker, debate, differ, fratch, haggle 7 brabble, contend, contest, discuss, dissert, faction, gainsay, quarrel, wrangle 8 argument, question, squabble 9 argy-bargy, encounter 10 contravene, controvert, litigation 11 altercation, controversy 12 disagreement

disqualify: 5 debar 6 outlaw 7 disable 9 indispose 12 incapacitate

disquiet: vex 4 fear, fret, pain 6 excite, unease, unrest 7 agitate, anxiety, disturb, inquiet, trouble, turmoil 9 incommode 10 discompose, discontent, uneasiness 12 inconvenience, restlessness

disquieted: 6 uneasy

disquisition: 5 essay 10 discussion

disregard: 4 omit 5 waive 6 forget, ignore, slight 7 despise, neglect 8 discount, disvalue, overlook 9 pretermit 10 contravene 11 inattention

disrelish: 7 dislike 8 distaste 9 antipathy

disreputable: low 4 base, hard 5 seamy, shady 7 raffish 8 shameful 13 discreditable

disrepute: 7 disfame 8 dishonor, reproach 9 discredit, disesteem

disrespect: 8 rudeness 9 disesteem, insolence 10 incivility 11 discourtesy

disrespectful: 7 uncivil 8 impolite, impudent 10 irreverent 11 impertinent

disrobe: 5 strip 6 divest 7 despoil, undress

disrupt: 4 rend, tear 5 break 7 disrump 11 discontinue, disorganize

dissatisfaction: 8 distaste 9 annoyance 10 discontent 11 displeasure

dissect: 7 analyze 9 anatomize, dismember

disseize: 10 dispossess

dissemble: 4 hide, mask 5 cloak, feign 6 boggle 7 conceal 8 disguise, simulate 11 counterfeit, dissimulate

dissembler: 9 hypocrite

disseminate: sow 5 strew 6 effuse, spread 7 diffuse, publish, scatter 8 disperse 9 circulate, propagate 10 distribute

dissent: 4 vary 6 differ 7 contend, protest 8 disagree 9 exception 10 dissidence 12 disagreement, nonagreement 13 nonconformity 14 nonconcurrence

signal of: nay

dissenter: 7 heretic 8 recusant 9 meetinger, protestor 10 Protestant 13 nonconformist

pert. to: 7 pantile

dissentious: 8 factious 11 contentious

dissepiment: 9 partition

dissert: 7 discuss, dispute 9 discourse

dissertation: 5 essay, theme, tract 6 debate, thesis, theses(pl.) 7 descant, lecture 8 treatise 9 discourse 10 discussion

Dissertation on a Roast Pig (author): 11 Charles Lamb

disservice: 4 harm 6 damage, injury 8 mischief

dissever: 4 part 6 sunder 8 disunite

dissidence: 7 dissent 12 disagreement 13 nonconformity

dissimilar: 6 unlike 7 difform, diverse 9 anomalous, different, disparate 13 heterogeneous

dissimulate: 5 feign 7 deceive, pretend 8 disguise 9 dissemble

dissipate: 4 fray 5 spend, waste 6 dispel, expend 7 diffuse, scatter, shatter 8 disperse, dissolve, embezzle, evanesce, squander 9 evaporate

dissocial: 7 selfish 8 unsocial 10 unfriendly

dissociate: 5 sever 7 disjoin 8 disunite, separate

dissolute: lax 4 lewd, wild 5 loose, slack 6 rakish, wanton 7 immoral, lawless 8 desolate, rakehell, reckless, uncurbed 9 abandoned, debauched, libertine, unbridled 10 licentious, negligence 12 unrestrained

dissolution: 4 ruin 5 decay 6 bust-up 7 breakup, decease, divorce 10 abrogation 14 disintegration

comb. form: lys

dissolve: end 4 fade, fuse, melt, thaw 5 fleet, solve 6 relent, unbind 7 adjourn, destroy, disband, disjoin, divorce, liquefy 8 discandy, disunite, separate 9 decompose, dissipate 10 deliquesce, disconnect 11 disorganize 12 disintegrate

dissolved: 6 solute

dissolving: 7 diluent

dissonant: 5 harsh 7 grating, jarring 8 jangling 10 discordant 11 cacophonous, incongruous, unmelodious 12 inconsistent, inharmonious, unharmonious 13 contradictory

dissuade: 5 deter 6 dehort, divert 10 discourage, disincline

distaff: 4 axis 5 woman 6 female

distain: 5 stain 6 defile 7 tarnish 8 discolor

distal: 6 remote 7 distant

angle: 4 axil

opposite of: 8 proximal

distance: 4 step 5 depth, range, space 7 farness, mileage, reserve, yardage 8 interval, outstrip 10 background, remoteness

measuring device: 6 stadia 8 odograph, odometer, viameter 9 pedometer, telemeter

on earth's surface: 8 latitude 9 longitude

distant: coy, far, off 4 afar, away, cold, yond 5 aloof 6 remote, yonder 7 faraway, foreign, removed 8 reserved 9 separated 10 discrepant

prefix: tel 4 tele

distaste: 6 degout 7 disgust, dislike 8 aversion 9 disrelish 11 displeasure 14 disinclination

distasteful: 7 hateful 8 brackish, nauseous, unsavory 9 loathsome, offensive, repugnant, repulsive 10 unpleasant 11 unpalatable 12 disagreeable

distemper: 4 soak 5 steep 6 choler, dilute, malady 7 ailment, disease, illness 8 disorder, sickness, unsettle 12 disaffection 13 indisposition

distend: 4 fill, grow 5 bloat, plump, swell, widen 6 dilate, expand, extend, spread 7 balloon, enlarge, inflate, stretch

distended: 4 wide 5 blown 8 patulous

distich: 7 couplet

distill, distil: 4 emit 6 infuse 7 trickle

distillation: 9 ascension

device: 6 retort 7 alembic

product: dew 6 liquor 7 spirits

tube: 7 matrass

distinct: 5 breme, clear, plain, vivid 7 diverse, legible, obvious, several, special 8 apparent, separate 9 different 10 articulate, individual 11 well-defined 13 distinguished

distinction: 4 note, rank 5 glory, honor 6 laurel, luster, lustre, renown 9 variation 10 prominence, reputation, separation 14 discrimination 15 differentiation

distinctive: 8 peculiar, talented 9 prominent 11 conspicuous 14 characteristic, discriminating

air: 6 cachet

distingue: 7 eminent 8 affected 10 celebrated

distinguish: 6 decern, define, descry, secern 8 perceive, separate 9 designate, punctuate 10 discrepate 12 characterize, discriminate 13 differentiate

distinguished: 5 noted 6 famous, marked 7 eminent, notable, special 8 distinct, laureate, renowned 9 brilliant, prominent 10 celebrated 11 conspicuous, illustrious 13 extraordinary

distort: 5 screw, twist 6 cringe, deface, deform 7 contort, pervert 10 camshachle, disfeature

distorted: wry 4 awry 5 askew, crank 7 crooked, gnarled 9 misshapen 10 anamorphic 11 anamorphous

distract: mad 5 amuse, craze 6 bemuse, divert, harass, insane, madden, moider, puzzle, twitch 7 agitate, confuse, disturb, embroil, perplex 8 bewilder, confound 9 tosticate 10 distraught

distraught: mad 6 crazed 7 frantic 8 deranged, distract 9 perplexed

distress: ail 4 hurt, need, pain, teen 5 agony, anger, annoy, dolor, grief, gripe, worry, wound 6 danger, dolour, grieve, harass, harrow, misery, sorrow 7 afflict, anguish, anxiety, disease, misease, oppress, perplex, torture, trouble 8 aggrieve, calamity, straiten 9 adversity, constrain, martyrdom, necessity 10 affliction, constraint, discomfort 11 tribulation
   call: S.O.S. 6 mayday

distressing: sad 4 hard, sore 7 carking, fearful, painful 9 sorrowful 11 troublesome

distribute: 4 deal, dole, mete, sort 5 allot, issue, share 6 assign, assort, divide, expend, impart, parcel 7 arrange, dispose, prorate 8 allocate, classify, dispense, disperse, separate 9 apportion, partition 10 administer 11 disseminate

distributee: 4 heir

distributively: 4 each 6 apiece 9 severally 10 separately 12 individually, respectively

distributor: 6 dealer 10 colporteur

district: 4 area, slum, ward 5 harsh, tract, vicus(L.) 6 canton, member, parish, region 7 circuit, country, demesne, diocese, quarter 8 distrito, precinct, province, rigorous 9 community, territory 12 neighborhood 13 neighbourhood
   theater: 6 rialto

District of Columbia: See **Washington, D.C.**

distrust: 4 fear 5 doubt 7 suspect 8 mistrust 9 suspicion 12 apprehension

distrustfully: 7 askance

disturb: vex 4 rile, roil 5 alarm, annoy, feeze, rouse, upset 6 harass, molest, ruffle, uncalm 7 agitate, commote, commove, derange, garboil, inquiet, perturb, trouble 8 convulse, disorder, disquiet, distract 9 discomfit, interfere, interrupt 10 disarrange, discomfort, discompose, disconcert

disturbance: 4 bree, dust, riot, rout 5 alarm, brawl, broil, deray, hurry, storm, strow, sturt, touse 6 affray, bother, breeze, cathro, fracas, hubbub, pother, rumpus, tumult, uproar 7 blunder, brulyie, brulzie, clatter, emotion, ferment, trouble, turmoil 8 business, disorder 9 agitation, annoyance, commotion, confusion, violation 10 convulsion, excitement 11 derangement, distraction, trepidation 12 discomposure, interruption, perturbation 13 collie-shangie(Sc.), inconvenience
   emotional: 8 neurosis
   ocean: 7 tsunami

disunite: rip 4 part 5 sever, untie 6 detach, divide, sunder 7 disband, disjoin, dissent, divorce, unravel 8 alienate, dissever, dissolve, estrange, separate 10 disconnect, dissociate

disuse: 6 misuse 7 abandon, discard 8 misapply 9 desuetude, disrepair 11 disaccustom, discontinue

disvalue: 9 disesteem, disregard 10 depreciate, undervalue

disyllabic foot: 7 trochee

disyoke: 6 unteam

dit, ditt: 4 poem, said, song 5 adage, ditty 6 saying 7 reputed 8 obstruct, surnamed 9 appointed 10 expression

ditch: rut, sap 4 delf, dick, dike, dyke, foss, gool, gout, ha-ha, holl, moat, rine, sike 5 canal, delft, delve, fence, fossa(L.), fosse, graff, graft, grave, rhine, zanja 6 fossae(pl.), gutter, trench, zanjon 7 abandon, channel, grindle, gripple, zanjona
   side: 5 scarp

dite: 4 mite, song 5 ditty 6 indict, indite 7 compose, dictate, diction 11 composition

dither: 5 shake 6 bother, shiver 7 trouble 9 trembling

dithyrambic: 4 wild 10 boisterous

ditto: 4 same 6 repeat 8 likewise 9 duplicate

ditty: dit, lay 4 dite, poem, sing, song 5 theme, verse 6 saying 7 dictate 9 utterance 11 composition

diuretic: 8 evacuant

diurnal: 5 daily 9 ephemeral

divagate: 6 wander 7 digress

divan: 4 book, hall, room, sofa 5 couch, court 6 canape(F.), leewan, lounge, saloon, senate, settee 7 council 9 davenport 12 chesterfield

divaricate: 6 forked

dive: den 4 crib, duck, leap 5 haunt, swoop 6 header, plunge, resort 7 explore 8 submerge, tailspin 9 penetrate
   kind of: 4 swan 6 gainer 8 jacknife

dive into: try 5 begin, start

diver: 4 loon 7 pearler, plunger 9 submarine 10 pickpocket

disease: 5 bends

gear: 4 tank 7 flipper

diverge: 6 branch, differ, divide, ramify, spread 7 deviate, digress 8 disagree

divers: 4 evil, many 5 cruel 6 sundry 7 several, various 8 perverse 9 different

diverse: 4 evil 6 motley, sundry, unlike, varied 7 adverse, several, various 8 distinct, perverse, separate, varietal 9 different, multiform 10 dissimilar 13 heterogeneous

comb. form: 4 vari

diversify: 4 vary 5 freck 7 variate 9 variegate 13 differentiate

with colors: 6 begary 7 begarie 9 bespatter

diversion: jeu 4 game, play 5 alarm, feint, hobby, sport 6 attack 7 pastime 9 amusement, avocation, merriment 10 deflection, recreation, relaxation 11 delectation, distraction 13 divertisement, entertainment

diversity: 6 change 7 discord, variety 10 difference, inequality 11 variegation 12 disagreement

divert: 5 amuse, relax 7 beguile, deflect, delight, detract, reflect 8 dissuade, distract, estrange, recreate 9 entertain

diverting: 5 droll 8 pleasant 9 laughable

divest: 4 bare, doff, reft 5 spoil, strip 6 delawn, denude, depose, devest 7 bereave, deprive, despoil, disrobe, uncover 8 denature, dethrone, unclothe 9 dismantle 10 disfurnish, dispossess

of sham: 6 debunk

divide: cut, lot 4 deal, fork, mere, part, rift, zone 5 cleft, divvy, sever, share, slice, space, split 6 bisect, branch, cleave, coteau, depart, devise, differ, parcel, ramify, sleave, sunder 7 aliquot, britten, diffuse, dispart, diverge, fissure, partake, prorate 8 classify, crossect, disunite, graduate, separate 9 apportion, dismember, intersect, multisect, partition, watershed 10 distribute

into feet: 4 scan

into parts: 4 paly 6 bisect, gobbet 7 quarter, trisect 9 bifurcate, septinate

divided: 4 ente, reft 7 fissate, partite 8 aerolate, areolate, camerate 10 incomplete

comb. form: 6 schist

dividend: 5 bonus

divider: 7 compass

dividing wall: 5 septa(pl.) 6 septum 9 partition

divination: 4 omen 6 augury 9 sortilege 11 discernment, rhabdomancy, sideromancy 12 clairvoyance 13 machairomancy

by dreams: 11 oneiromancy

by figures: 8 geomancy

by monstrosities: 11 teratoscopy

by rods: 7 dousing, dowsing

divine: 4 holy 5 aread, areed, guess, pious 6 detect, devise, halsen, priest, sacred 7 blessed, foresee, godlike, portend, predict, presage 8 ariolate, contrive, forebode, foreknow, foretell, heavenly, immortal, minister, perceive 9 ambrosial, celestial, clergyman, religious 10 anticipate, conjecture, superhuman, theologian 12 supernatural

artificer: 8 tvashtar, tvashtri

being: 4 deva

communication: 6 oracle

favor: 5 grace

gift: 5 grace

messenger: 7 apostle

render: 5 deify

spirit: 5 numen

word: 5 logos

work: 7 theurgy

Divine Comedy author: 5 Dante

divinely inspired: 7 entheal 8 entheate

diviner: 4 seer 5 augur, sibyl 7 augurer, prophet 8 haruspex 10 soothsayer 11 clairvoyant 14 prognosticator

diving: 8 plunging 10 acrobatics, submerging

bird: auk 4 loon 5 grebe

hazard: 5 bends

divinity: See god; goddess

divisible: 9 dividable, separable

division: 4 chap, clan, dole, neat, part, rift 5 group, realm, share 6 canton, schism, sector 7 roulade, section 8 arpeggio, category, cleavage 9 Abteilung, allotment, concision, departure, partition 10 department 11 bifurcation, compartment, disjunction 13 apportionment, disconnection, dismemberment

between torrid and temperate zones: 6 tropic

house: 5 estre

into hundred: 12 centuriation

plant: 15 archichlamydeae

play: act 5 scene

poem: 5 canto

political: 4 city, ward 5 state 6 county, parish 7 borough 8 district

property: 9 gavelkind

religious: 6 schism

shield: 4 ente, paly

social: 5 caste, class, tribe 6 clique

time: day, eon 4 aeon, week, year 5 month 6 decade, minute, moment, second 7 weekend 9 fortnight

word: 8 syllable

divisional: 10 fractional, separative

divorce: 5 sever 6 sunder 7 asunder 8 dissolve, disunion, disunite, separate 10 separation 11 dissolution
Jewish law: get 4 gett
mill: 4 Reno
divot: 4 clod
divulge: 4 bare, show, tell 5 voice 6 bewray, impart, reveal, spread, unfold 7 publish, uncover 8 disclose, discover, evulgate, proclaim 9 eliminate 11 communicate
divvy: 5 share 6 divide 7 portion
Dixie Land: 5 South
dizen: 7 bedizen 9 overdress
dizzard: 4 fool 6 jester 9 blockhead
dizziness: 6 megrim 7 vertigo 9 giddiness
pert. to: 5 dinic 7 dinical
with headache: 10 scotodinia
dizzy: 4 dunt 5 crazy, giddy 6 fickle, stupid 7 foolish 8 swimming, unsteady 10 capricious 11 lightheaded, vertiginous
djebel: 4 hill
Dnieper tributary: Bug 4 Psel, Sula 5 Desna, Psiol
do: act 4 bilk, dost, make, suit 5 avail, cheat, guise, serve, trick 6 answer, render 7 achieve, execute, perform, produce, satisfy, suffice 8 transact 10 accomplish, administer
musical: ut
poetic: 5 didst
do away with: rid 4 kill 7 abolish, destroy 9 liquidate 11 discontinue
do in: 4 kill 6 defeat 7 destroy
do out of: 5 cheat 7 deceive
do-re-mi: 4 song 5 money
do up: 4 wrap
do well: 7 prosper
dobbin: 4 mare
docent: 7 teacher 8 lecturer
docile: 4 calm, meek, tame 6 gentle 7 ductile, dutiful 8 biddable 9 tractable 10 manageable
dock: cut 4 bang, clip, moor, pier, quay 5 basin, wharf 6 marina, strunt 7 bobtail, curtail, shorten 8 canaigre 9 perforate
post: 4 pile 7 bollard
ship's: 4 slip 5 basin, berth
worker: 9 stevedore
yard: 7 arsenal
doctor: 4 dose 5 sugar, treat 6 deacon, healer, intern 7 teacher 9 internist, physician 11 aesculapian
aide: 5 nurse
animal: vet 10 veterinary 12 veterinarian
oath of: 11 hippocratic
specialist: 6 aurist, goofer, intern 7 interne, oculist, surgeon 9 hippiater, otologist 10 podiatrist 11 chiropodist, neurologist, optometrist, orthopedist 12 chiropractor, gynecologist, obstetrician, orthodontist, or-

thopaedist, psychiatrist, proctologist 13 cranioscopist, gynaecologist 15 ophthalmologist
doctrine: ism 4 doxy, lear, rule 5 credo, creed, dogma, maxim, tenet 6 belief, gospel, theory 7 article, opinion, precept 8 position 9 principle 10 discipline
pert. to: 10 dogmatical 12 teleological
secret: 7 esotery
single principle: 6 henism, monism
specific: 6 cabala, heresy, malism, Mishna 7 egotism, Mishnah 8 fatalism, hedonism 10 agathology, pragmatism 13 monarchianism
spreader: 12 propagandist
document: 4 bill, book, deed, writ 5 chart, lease, paper, teach 6 billet, patent, school 7 archive, missive, precept, writing 8 contract, covenant, instruct, mortgage 9 indenture 10 manuscript 11 instruction
addition: 5 rider 7 codicil 9 amendment
file: 7 dossier
original record: 8 protocol
provisional: 5 scrip
receptacle: 7 hanaper
signed by all parties: 8 syngraph
true copy: 7 estreat
dod, dodd: lop 4 clip, poll
Dodecanese Island: Coo, Cos 4 Caso, Lero, Simi, Syme 5 Leros, Lipso, Lisso, Patmo, Tilos 6 Calchi, Calino, Lipsos, Nisiro, Patmos 7 Nisyrós, Piscopi 9 Karpathos, Scarpanto, Stampalia 10 Astropalia
dodder: 5 shake 6 totter 7 tremble
doddering: old 5 inane 6 infirm, senile 7 foolish
dodge: 4 duck, jink, jouk, ruse 5 avoid, cheat, elude, evade, shift, trick 6 escape 7 deceive, evasion 8 artifice, gilenyie 9 expedient 10 equivocate
dodger: 7 haggler 8 handbill 10 corndodger 13 advertisement
corn: 4 pone
doe: roe, teg 4 faun, hind 6 female
doer: 5 actor, agent, maker 6 author, factor, feasor 7 facient, manager 8 attorney, executor 9 performer
suffix: er, or; ast, eer, ier, ist 4 ator, euse, ster
does: 4 doth
doff: off 4 daff, vail 5 avale, douse, dowse, strip 6 divest, remove 7 undress
dog: cur, mut, pug, pup, yap 4 mutt, pawl, tike, tyke 5 canis(L.), pooch, puppy, whelp 6 bowwow, buffer, canine, detent, yapper 7 mongrel, yapster 9 carnivore
African: 7 basenji
Australian: 5 dingo
breed: pug 4 Dane 5 boxer, hound, Husky, pelon, sauki, spitz 6 Afghan, basset, bea-

gle, borzoi, Briard, collie, Eskimo, gun dog, poodle, setter, Sussex 7 Basenji, bulldog, griffon, harrier, Maltese, mastiff, Mexican, owtchar, pincher, pointer, Scottie, sleughi, spaniel, starter, terrier, whippet 8 Airedale, Alsatian, Aleutant, chow chow, coach dog, Doberman, elkhound, Flanders, foxhound, labrador, landseer, Malemute, Malinois, papillon, Pekinese, Pyrenees, Samoyede, Sealyham, shepherd, springer 9 boarhound, Brabancon, Chihuahua, dachshund, Dalmation, deerhound, Great Dane, greyhound, kerry blue, police dog, retriever, St. Bernard, schnauzer, shorthair, wolfhound, wolf spitz, Yorkshire 10 Bedlington, bloodhound, Boston bull, fox terrier, Manchester, otter hound, Pomeranian, Rottweiler, schipperke, toy terrier, weimaraner, wire-haired 11 bull terrier, Groenendael, ruby spaniel, Skye terrier 12 cairn terrier, field spaniel, gazelle hound, Gordon setter, gossett hound, Newfoundland, water spaniel, Welsh terrier 13 Boston terrier, Chesapeake Bay, cocker spaniel, Great Pyrenees, Prince Charles, yankee terrier 14 Chinese crested, clumber spaniel, highland collie, Tibetan spaniel 15 Brussels griffon, highland terrier, Riesenschnauzer 17 Bouvier de Flandres

close-haired: pug 5 boxer

Eskimo: 5 husky 7 samoyed 8 Malemute, samoyede

famous: 4 Asta, Fala, King, Tige, Toby 5 Devil 6 Feller, Lassie 8 Checkers 9 Rin-tin-tin 11 Strongheart

F.D.R.'s: 4 Fala

fox-like: 6 colpeo

genus: 5 canis

German origin: 5 boxer 8 Doberman 9 Drahthaar 10 Weimaraner

hauling: 5 husky 7 samoyed 8 Malemute, samoyede 9 Dalmatian

house: 6 kennel

howling of: 9 ululation

hunting: 4 alan, rach 5 aland, alant, hound, rache, ratch, toler 6 basset, borzoi, beagle, saluki, setter, talbot 7 courser, harrier, pointer 8 Elkhound 9 retriever, wolfhound 10 bloodhound

iron: 7 firedog

large: 4 alan, Dane 5 boxer, bawty 6 briard, bawtie, collie, police 7 mastiff 12 Newfoundland

long-haired: 4 alco, chow 7 spaniel

multi-headed: 8 cerberus

Orphan Annie's: 5 Sandy

pack: 8 canaglia, canaille

reward: 6 hallow

small: Pom, pug, pup 4 alco, fist, purp 5 ascob, feist 6 messan, messin 7 spaniel 8 Pekinese 9 chihuahua, Pekingese 10 Pomeranian

underworld: 8 Cerberus

upper lip: 5 flews

Welsh: 8 Sealyham

wild: 5 adjag, dhole, dingo 6 jackal 7 agouara 8 cimarron

dog days: 8 canicule

dog-like: 13 cynocephalous

dog rose: 5 bucky 6 canker 9 eglantine

fruit: hip

dog salmon: 4 keta

dog star: 4 sept, sopt 6 sirius

dogboat: pig

dogcart: 6 tumtum 7 bounder 8 gadabout

dogfish: hoe 4 huss, tope 9 roussette

dogged: 6 sullen 7 doggish, doglike 9 malicious, obstinate, tenacious 10 determined 12 pertinacious

doggerel: 6 trivia 9 burlesque

doggery: 7 barroom 8 grogshop

doggish: 5 sulky 7 currish, cynical, stylish 8 snapping

dogie: 5 stray

dogma: 5 creed, tenet 6 dictum 8 doctrine, document

pert. to: 9 levitical

dogmatic: 9 assertive, confident, pragmatic 10 intolerant, peremptory 11 affirmative, dictatorial, magisterial, opinionated, pragmatical

saying: 6 dictum 8 levitism

dogmatism: 10 positivism, pragmatism 11 intolerance 13 pontificality

Dogpatch depicter: 4 Capp

dogs: 4 feet

dogwood: 5 osier, sumac 6 cornel, cornus

flowering: 7 boxwood

genus: 6 cornus

doily: mat 6 napkin

doing: act 4 deed, stir 5 event 6 action 8 function

doings: ado 6 hustle 8 activity

doldrum: 5 dumps, ennui 6 tedium 7 dullard 8 confused, dullness 10 depression 12 listlessness

dole: lot 4 alms, deal, gift, goal, mete, part 5 allot, fraud, grief, guile, mourn, share 6 deceit, grieve, relief, sorrow 7 charity, dealing, destiny, handout, payment, portion 8 boundary, dispense, division, gratuity, landmark, pittance 9 allotment, apportion 10 distribute, misfortune 12 distribution

doleful: sad 5 drear, heavy 6 dismal, dreary, funest, rueful 7 flebile 8 dolesome, dolorous, mournful 9 sorrowful 10 lugubrious, melancholy

dolent: 9 sorrowful

dolente: 9 plaintive

dolesome: 6 dismal, gloomy 7 doleful 9 sorrowful

doll: toy 4 babe, baby 5 array, puppe(G.) 6 maumet, moppet, muneca(Sp.), poupee(F.), puppet 8 mistress 9 golliwogg 10 sweetheart

doll up: 5 adorn, dress

dollar: 4 bean, buck 5 berry, eagle 8 frogskin, simoleon

Doll's House heroine: 4 Nora

dolly: car 4 cart, doll, drab, tray 5 truck 7 carrier 8 mistress, slattern 10 sweetheart

dolor, dolour: 5 calor, grief 6 sorrow 7 anguish, sadness 8 distress, mourning 11 lamentation

dolorous: sad 6 dismal 7 doleful 8 grievous 9 sorrowful

dolphin, delphin: 4 fish, inia 6 dorado 8 porpoise 9 goosebeak 10 bottlenose
river: 5 bouto

dolt: ass, oaf 4 asse, calf, chub, clod, coof, dult, fool, moke 5 chump, dummy, dunce, idiot 6 befool, cudden, doodle 7 bluntie(Sc.), dawcock, dullard, half-wit 8 bosthoon, clodpate, imbecile, mooncalf, numskull 9 blockhead, ignoramus, simpleton 10 dunderhead

doltish: 4 dull 6 stupid 7 foolish, sottish 8 blockish, doltlike 11 thickheaded

domain: 5 bound, bourn, realm, scope, state, world 6 barony, bourne, empery, empire, estate 7 demesne 8 dominion, province 9 bailiwick 12 commonwealth

Dombey and Son: 6 Cuttle

dome: cap 4 cima 6 cupola 7 calotte, edifice

domed: 7 vaulted

domestic: 4 hind, maid 5 domal 6 hameil, hamelt, hamilt, homely, homish, housal, inland, inmate, native 7 servant 8 homebred, homemade, intimate 9 enchorial, home-grown
establishment: 6 menage

domesticate: 4 tame 6 entame 7 amenage, reclaim 8 civilize 10 naturalize 11 domiciliate

domicile: 4 home 5 abode, house 6 menage 8 dwelling 9 residence 10 habitation
identification: 9 doorplate

dominant: 5 bossy, chief 6 ruling 7 central, regnant, supreme 8 superior 9 ascendant, imperious, paramount, prevalent, princi-pal 10 commanding, pre-eminent, prevailing 11 outweighing, predominant 12 preponderant 13 overbalancing

dominate: 4 rule 5 reign 6 govern 7 control 8 domineer 11 predominate

domination: 7 control 8 dominion 9 supremacy 10 ascendancy, ascendency 11 sovereignty 12 predominance 14 possessiveness

domine: 4 Lord, rule 6 master 9 clergyman 11 predominate

domineer: 4 boss, lord, rule 5 bully, feast, revel, tower 7 command, swagger 8 dominate, overlord 11 predominate

domineering: 6 lordly 7 haughty 8 arrogant, masterly 9 imperious, masterful 10 tyrannical 11 dictatorial, magisterial, overbearing

Dominican: 9 predicant

dominie: 6 pastor 9 pedagogue 12 schoolmaster

dominion: 4 rule, sway 5 realm, reign 6 domain, empire 7 control, dynasty, poustie, regency 9 authority, hierarchy, ownership, supremacy 10 ascendancy, ascendency, domination 11 sovereignty 12 jurisdiction
church: 11 sacerdotium
joint: 11 condominium

domino: die 4 mask

dominoes: 4 game 5 bones 7 ivories

dompt: cow 5 daunt 6 subdue

domus: 4 home 5 house

don: 4 wear 5 array, dress 6 assume, clothe, invest 8 nobleman 9 gentleman, professor 10 instructor

Don Juan's mother: 4 Inez

Don Quixote: *companion:* 11 Sancho Panza
steed: 9 Rosinante, Rozinante

Donar: 4 Thor

donate: gie(Sc.) 4 give 6 bestow 7 present 10 contribute

donatio: 4 gift 8 donation

donation: 4 gift 5 grant 7 donatio, present 10 foundation 11 benefaction 12 contribution

done: 4 over 5 baked, ended 6 cooked 7 through 8 finished 9 completed, exhausted 12 accomplished

donee: 7 heritor 8 receiver 9 recipient 11 beneficiary

donkey: ass 4 moke 5 burro, cuddy, dicky, neddy 6 dickey, onager 7 bussock, fussock 9 quadruped
comb. form: ono
cry: 4 bray 6 heehaw

donkey engine: 6 yarder

donna: 4 lady, wife 5 madam, woman 8 mistress

donor: 4 give 5 giver 10 benefactor 11 contributor 14 philanthropist

donsie: 6 ailing 7 sickish 9 squeamish

doodle: 4 dolt, draw 5 cheat 7 cartoon, trifler

doodlesack: 7 bagpipe

doodling: 9 scrolling

doohickey: 6 device, gadget 11 contrivance

doolee: 6 litter

doom: law, lot 4 damn, fate, ruin 5 death 6 decree, devote, steven 7 condemn, destine, destiny, fortune, statute 8 decision, sentence 9 destinate, enactment, judgement, ordinance 10 adjudicate, predestine 11 destruction, discernment 12 condemnation 13 righteousness

doomed: fey 5 fatal 8 accursed 9 sentenced

door: 4 gate 5 hatch 6 portal 7 barrier, doorway, opening, passage, postern 11 entranceway
back: 7 postern
cross piece: 6 lintel
fastener: bar 4 bolt, hasp, lock 5 catch 8 fastener
frame: 4 jamb
holder: 5 hinge
holy: 11 amphithyron
part: 4 jamb, knob, risp 5 panel 6 alette, lintel
storm: 6 dingle
trap: 4 drop
way: 4 exit 8 entrance

doorkeeper: 5 tiler, usher 6 durwan, porter, warden 7 durwaun, janitor, ostiary 8 huissier, janitrix 9 concierge(F.), janitress, ostiarius

doorknocker: 6 hammer, rapper

doorlatch: 8 haggaday

doormat: rug 8 weakling

doorpost: 4 durn, jamb 6 alette

doorway: 4 door, exit 6 portal 7 opening 11 entranceway

dope: hop 4 drug 5 opium, paste 6 heroin, opiate 7 predict, stupefy 8 narcotic 9 marijuana 13 nitroglycerin

doped: 10 narcotized, prophesied

dopester: 4 tout 6 touter 7 tipster

doppelganger: 6 double, spirit, wraith 10 apparition 11 counterpart

dor, dorr: bee 4 joke, mock 5 joker, scoff, trick 6 beetle 7 buffoon, deceive, mockery 9 deception 11 drumbledore

dorbel: 6 pedant

dorcas: 7 gazelle

dorian: 6 simple

Dorian festival: 6 Carnea 7 Carneia

doric: 6 rustic

Doric: *frieze bottom:* 6 taenia
frieze slab: 6 metope

Doris' king: 8 Aegimius

dormancy: 6 torpor 8 abeyance 10 quiescence

dormant: 5 fixed 6 asleep, latent, torpid 7 resting, sleeper 8 dormient, inactive, sleeping 9 quiescent, unaroused 10 stationary

dormer: 6 window 7 lucarne

dormeuse: 4 seat 5 coach 8 carriage, nightcap

dormient: 7 dormant 8 sleeping

dormitory: 4 dorm 5 house 8 quarters
monastery: 6 dorter 7 dortour

dormouse: 4 loir 5 lerot
pert. to: 7 myoxine

dornick: 5 linen

dorp: 4 city, town 5 thorp 6 hamlet, thorpe 7 village 8 township

dorsal: 5 notal 6 dorsel, dorser, dosser, tergal 7 hanging 9 posterior
opposed to: 7 ventral
pert. to: 5 notal 6 tergal

dorsum: 4 back

dorty: 5 saucy, sulky 7 haughty

dose: 4 bole 5 draft, treat 6 doctor, drench, potion 7 draught 8 quantity

doss: 4 tuft

dosseret: 6 abacus

dossil: 4 tent 6 spigot 7 pledget

dot: 4 clot, lump, mote, peck 5 dowry, point, speck 6 period 7 speckle, stipple 8 particle, sprinkle 9 bespangle 10 besprinkle, distribute
over the letter i: 6 tittle

dotage: 4 dote 5 folly 6 drivel 8 senility 10 feebleness, imbecility

dotard: 5 silly 6 senile 8 imbecile

dote: rot 4 dove, doze, love 5 adore, decay, endow 6 bestow, dotage, dotard, drivel, stupor 8 imbecile

doting: 4 fond

dotish,, doatish: 4 weak 7 foolish 8 imbecile

dotted: 7 spotted 8 speckled, stippled 9 scattered 11 distributed, diversified

dotterel: 4 dupe, gull, wind 6 plover 7 morinel

dottle: 4 fool, plug 5 silly 6 dotard

dotty: 5 crazy 6 feeble, spotty

doty: 10 discolored

Douay Bible: 4 Aree

double: ply 4 dual, fold, twin 5 duple, fetch 6 bifold, binary, binate, duplex 7 twofold 8 geminate 9 ambiguous, duplicate 11 counterpart
prefix: di

double dagger: 6 diesis

double dealing: 6 deceit

double-edged: 9 ancipital

double-hue: 7 bicolor

doublecross: 5 cheat 6 betray 7 deceive, swindle 9 treachery

doublecrosser: rat

doubled: 5 gemel

doublet: 9 pourpoint

doubling: 4 loop

doubloon: 4 coin, onza

doubly: 5 twice

doubt: 4 fear 5 demur, dread, query, waver 7 dubiate, scruple, suspect 8 distrust, dubitate, hesitate, mistrust, question 9 discredit, misgiving, suspicion 10 diffidence, disbelieve, indecision 11 uncertainty 12 apprehension

doubter: 5 cynic 7 skeptic 10 unbeliever

doubtful: 7 dubious, fearful, perhaps 8 dreadful, perilous, wavering 9 ambiguous, dangerous, diffident, equivocal, uncertain, undecided 10 apocryphal, hesitating, irresolute, suspicious 11 distrustful, vacillating 12 apprehensive, questionable, undetermined 13 problematical

doubtfulness: 9 ambiguity

douce: 4 neat, tidy 5 sober, sweet 6 genial, modest, sedate 7 prudent 8 cheerful, pleasant 10 hospitable

douceur: 5 bonus 9 pourboire

dough: 4 cash, duff 5 money, paste 6 noodle, sponge 7 brioche

doughnut: 6 cymbal, sinker 7 cruller, olycook, olykoek, simball 9 freidcake

doughty: 4 fell 7 valiant 8 intrepid

dour: 4 glum, grim, hard, sour 5 rough, stern 6 gloomy, morose, severe, strong, sullen 7 ominous 9 obstinate 10 inflexible

douse, dowse: 4 beat, blow, doff, duck, quit, stow 5 cease, rinse, souse 6 drench, plunge, strike, stroke 7 immerse 8 downpour 9 drenching 10 extinguish

douzepers: 4 Ivon, Oton 5 Ivory, Gerin, Ogier, peers 6 Anseis, Gerier, nobles, Oliver, Roland, Samson, Turpin 7 knights 8 Engelier, paladins 9 Berengier 17 Gerard de Rousillon

dove: 4 doze 5 color 6 culver, cushat, pigeon 7 namaqua, slumber

home: 4 cote

pert. to: 9 columbine

sound: 4 curr

young: 8 doveling

dovecot, dovecote: 9 columbary 11 columbarium

dovekey, dovekie: auk 4 alle 5 rotch, rotge 6 rotche 8 dovelike 9 guillemot

dovelike: 4 pure 6 dovish, gentle 7 lovable 9 columbine

dover: 4 doze, stun 6 drowse

dovetail: 5 tenon

dovish: 8 dovelike, harmless, innocent

dow: 4 dull, fade 5 avail, befit, endow 6 thrive 7 behoove, prosper

dowd: 5 frump

dowdy: 4 poky 5 frump, pokey 6 blowzy, shabby, untidy 8 slovenly 10 slatternly

dowel: peg, pin 4 coak 6 pintle

dower: dos 5 dowry, endow 7 portion 9 endowment

dowitcher: 5 snipe

down: 4 dowl, fell, flix, flue, fuzz, hill, lint 5 below, dowle, floor, fluff 6 bedown 7 hillock, plumage 9 overthrow

comb. form: bas(F.) 4 cata(Gr.)

poetic: 5 adown

prefix: de

down at the heel: 5 seamy, seedy

down in the mouth: 4 glum 7 unhappy 9 depressed 11 discouraged

down under: 8 Tasmania 9 antipodes, Australia 10 New Zealand

down wind: 7 leeward

down with: 4 a bas

downcast: sad 6 abject, gloomy 8 hopeless 9 depressed 10 despondent, dispirited, melancholy 11 discouraged 12 disheartened

downfall: pit 4 fate, ruin, trap 5 abyss 7 descent, undoing 8 collapse 9 precipice, ruination 11 destruction, ecroulement 12 degringolade

heavy: 7 torrent

downhearted: 8 dejected 9 depressed 10 melancholy

downpour: 4 pour, rain 5 douse, dowse, spill 7 torrent

downright: 4 flat, pure, rank 5 blank, blunt, plain, plumb, sheer, stark 6 arrant, direct 8 absolute, even-down, positive, thorough 10 completely, forthright, thoroughly 11 straightway 13 perpendicular, unceremonious 15 perpendicularly

downstairs: 5 below

downward: 5 below, lower 11 netherwards

poetic: 5 adown

slope: 9 declivity

downy: 4 soft 5 mossy, nappy, pilar, quiet 6 fluffy, placid 7 cunning, knowing 8 soothing

dowry: dos, dot 4 gift 5 dower 6 talent 7 portion 9 endowment

pert. to: 5 dotal

doxology: 13 glorification

doxy: ism 5 wench 6 harlot 7 opinion 8 doctrine

doyen: 4 dean

doze: nap, nod, rot 4 dote, dove 5 decay, dover, sleep, sloom 6 catnap, drowse, muddle, snooze 7 perplex, slumber, snoozle, stupefy

drab: box, daw 4 dell, drug, dull 5 besom, dolly, graze, wench, whore 6 malkin, poison **7** prosaic **9** colorless **10** monotonous, prostitute **13** uninteresting

drachma: 4 coin, dram
one-sixth: **4** obol

draconian: 5 cruel **6** severe

Dracula: 5 demon, devil **7** vampire
home: **4** Bran **6** Risnov **9** Hunedoara

draff: 4 lees **5** dregs, drink **6** refuse **7** hogwash

draft: nip, sip **4** dose, dram, gust, levy, plan, swig, toot **5** drink, epure, swipe **6** drench, godown, minute, potion, redact, scroll, sketch, waucht, waught **7** drawing, outline, pattern, project **8** beverage, potation, protocol **9** conscript

draftsman, draughtsman: 6 drawer **7** tippler **9** architect

drag: lug, tow, tug **4** draw, hale, harl, haul, pull, snig, tear, tump **5** brake, drawl, rally, tease, trail, trawl **6** linger, school, taigle **7** grapnel
out: **6** elicit, extend **8** protract
through mud: **7** bemire

dragnet: 5 trawl **7** trainel

dragoman: 5 agent, guide **11** interpreter

dragon: 7 monster **8** basilisk
Biblical: **5** Rahab
biting: **8** tarragon
Chinese: **5** lung
Norse: **6** Fafner, Fafnir
Vedic: Ahi

dragonfly order: 8 odonata

dragoon: 10 cavalry-man, carabineer, carabinier

drain: dry, gaw, sap **4** delf, gout, grip, gurt, lade, milk, sike, sink **5** bunny, canal, delft, dreen, empty, fleet, gully, rhine(dial.), sewer, silver **6** filter, furrow, guzzle, siphon, syphon, trench, zanjon **7** acequia, alberca, channel, deplete, exhaust, grindle, gripple, zanjona **8** thurrock **9** undermine **11** watercourse
arched: **7** culvert
blood: **12** exsanguinate
forces: **5** spend

drainage: 4 adit
area: **5** basin

drainpipe: 6 leader

dram: nip **4** mite, slug **5** draft, drink **6** drachm **7** snifter **8** potation, quantity **11** indifferent

drama: 4 mime, play **5** opera **6** comedy **7** atellan, history, theater, tragedy **8** operetta, pastoral **9** pantomime **11** composition
court: **5** trial
division: act **5** scene
for single actor: **8** monodram
main act: **8** epitasis

part: **4** role
short: **4** skit **7** saynete
spectacular: **12** extravaganza
third most important actor: **11** tritagonist

dramatic: 4 wild **5** vivid **6** scenic **10** theatrical **12** melodramatic
expression system: **8** delsarte
representation: **13** impersonation

dramatist: 5 actor **10** playwright

drank: See **drink**

drape: 4 hang **5** adorn, cover, weave **7** curtain, hanging, valance

drapeau: 4 flag **8** standard

draper: 6 tailor

drapery: 5 baize, cloth **7** curtain, valance **8** mourning

drapet: 5 cloth **8** covering

drastic: 4 dire **5** harsh **7** extreme, radical **8** rigorous

drasty: 4 vile **9** worthless

draught: See **draft**

Dravidian (see also **India**): **4** Gond, Kota, Toda, Tulu **5** Arava, Gondi, Khond, Malto, Oraon, Tamil **6** Andhra, Brahui, Kodagu, Kurukh, Telegu, Telugu **8** Kanarese **9** Malayalam
demon: **4** bhut
tribe: **6** Badaga **7** Colleri, Collery **9** Colleries

draw: lug, tie, tow, tug **4** drag, duct, hale, haul, lade, limn, lure, pull **5** catch, educe, train **6** allure, deduce, depict, derive, design, elicit, entice, induce, inhale, select, sketch **7** attract, detract, extract, inspire, portray **8** inveigle **9** delineate, reproduce, statement
again: **5** remap **6** replat
away from: **6** shrink
back: **4** fawn **5** wince **6** cringe, rebate, recede, recoil, resile, retire, shrink **7** retract, retreat **9** deduction, hindrance
close: **4** near **5** steal **8** approach
finely: **4** etch
forth: tug **4** pull **5** educe **6** derive, elicit
near: hie **4** near **5** coast **8** approach
off: sap **5** drain **6** siphon, syphon **7** extract **8** abstract, withdraw
out: **4** lade, pump **5** educe **6** elicit, exhale **7** extract, tweezer **8** protract **9** exantlate **11** interrogate **12** cross examine
tight: **4** frap, furl, lace **5** brace, cinch **7** stretch
together: **4** coul, frap **8** assemble

draw game: 9 stalemate

drawer: 4 till

drawers: 5 pants **7** panties **9** shintiyan
chest of: **7** commode

drawing: 5 draft, envol, epure **7** hauling, pulling **8** traction **9** attrahent **10** attracting, extracting **11** delineation, centripetal

absent-minded: 8 doodling
exaggerated: 7 cartoon 10 caricature
instrument: 9 eidograph 10 pantograph
drawing room: 5 salon 6 parlor, saloon
drawl: 5 drant, drunt 6 draunt, loiter
drawlatch: lag 6 dawdle 11 latchstring 12 eavesdropper
drawn: 7 haggard
drawstring: 5 latch
dray: 4 cart 5 wagon 6 camion 7 go-devil
drayage: 7 cartage, haulage
drayman: 6 carter 7 carrier, remover, wagoner
dread: awe 4 fear, fray 5 awful, doubt 6 adread, agrise, dismay, eschew, horror, terror 7 anxiety, dismiss 8 affright, dreddour, terrible 9 reverence 12 apprehension
object of: 4 bogy 5 bogey, bogie 7 bugaboo, bugbear
dread of: See **fear**
dreaded: 7 awesome
dreadful: 4 dire 5 awful 6 grisly, horrid 7 careful, direful, fearful, ghastly, grimful, hideous 8 doubtful, ghastful, horrible, shocking, terrible, terrific 9 frightful 10 formidable
dreadnaught, dreadnought: 4 tank 7 warship 8 fearless 10 battleship
dream: 4 muse, reve(F.) 5 fancy 6 sweven, vision 7 fantasy, imagine, reverie, romance 8 phantasm 9 nightmare 10 apparition
god of: 8 Morpheus
interpretation: 13 oneirocritics 15 oneirocriticism
pert. to: 7 oneiric, somnial 9 oneirotic
dreamed: 7 fancied 8 visioned
dreamer: 4 poet 7 fantast 8 idealist 9 visionary 10 ideologist
dreaminess: 7 languor
dreamy: kef 4 soft 5 vague 6 poetic 7 faraway, languid, pensive 8 fanciful, soothing 9 visionary 11 imaginative
drear: 4 dern 5 gloom 6 dismal, gloomy 7 doleful, sadness 9 sorrowful 10 melancholy
dreary: sad 4 dire, dree, dull, flat 5 bleak, cruel, ourie 6 dismal, elenge, gloomy, gousty, lonely 7 doleful, goustie, howling, wilsome 8 grievous 9 cheerless, sorrowful 10 depressing, monotonous 11 distressful
dredge: mop 4 sift 5 scoop 6 deepen 8 excavate, springle 9 sweetmeat
dredger: 6 duster 9 sprinkler
dree: 4 dull, slow 5 grief 6 dismal, dreary, endure, suffer 7 tedious 9 suffering 10 persistent
dregs: 4 crap, faex, lees 5 draff, dross, feces, grout, magma 6 bottom, dunder, faeces,

refuse 7 grounds, grummel, residue 8 grummels, remnants, sediment, settling 9 excrement, feculence 10 subsidence 12 crassamentum
drench: 4 dose, hose, sind, sink, soak 5 douse, dowse, draft, drink, drouk, drown, souse, steep 6 bucket, douche, imbrue, potion 7 immerse 8 permeate, saturate, submerge
drenched: wet 4 asop 6 soaked
dress (see also **garment, gown, robe, vestment**): don, dub, fig, ray, rig, tog 4 be-go, busk, buss, deck, garb, gear, gown, hone, knap, mill, rail, robe, suit, tire, trim, wear 5 adorn, array, curry, dight, equip, frock, guise, habit, magma, preen, primp, prink, prune 6 attire, broach, clothe, enrobe, fangle, fettle, graith, invest, outfit, revest, toilet 7 affaite, apparel, bandage, clothes, costume, garment, garnish, raiment, toggery, vesture 8 cleading, clothing, decorate, ornament, vestment 9 embellish, equipment, vestiture 10 garmenture, habiliment, habilitate, investment 12 accouterment, accoutrement
clerical: 5 cloth
cloth: 4 burl
court: 4 robe
feathers: 5 preen
flax: ted 5 dizen
gaudily: 5 primp, prink 6 dizene 7 bedizen
in full armor: 7 panoply
informal: 6 shorts, slacks 8 negligee 9 bluejeans
kind of: alb 4 huke 5 crape, crepe, ephod, get-up, mufti, tails, tenue, tunic, weeds 6 dirndl, finery, gaiter, kirtle, livery, tuxedo 7 regalia 8 lava-lava, negligee, peignoir 9 canonical, decollete, polonaise
leather: tan, taw, tew 5 curry
mean: 4 rags
odd: rig 5 getup
ornament: 4 frog, lace 5 jabot, ruche 6 sequin, zequin 7 ruching 8 chequeen, zecchino 10 embroidery
riding: 5 habit 8 breeches, jodhpurs
stone: nig 5 nidge, spall 7 scabble
surgically: 5 dight
trimming: 4 gimp, lace 5 braid
dress up: tog 5 preen, primp, prink
dressed: 4 clad 5 bound 7 habited
well: 4 braw 5 smart 7 dallack, stylish 9 spruced-up
dresser: 5 rober 6 bureau 7 modiste 8 cupboard 9 appreteur 10 escritoire
leather: 7 currier 8 levanter
scrupulous: 4 dude 7 preener 11 Beau Brummel
dressing: 7 beating 8 scolding 11 castigation

kind of: 4 lint 5 salve 7 pledget 8 ointment, remolade

dressing room: 7 camarin

dressing stone: 9 scotching

dressmaker: 5 sewer 6 seamer 7 modiste 8 stitcher 9 couturier 10 couturiere, seamstress

model: 7 manikin 8 mannikin 9 mannequin

dretch: 5 delay 6 dawdle 7 trouble

drew (see also **draw**): 8 eelgrass

dribble: 4 drip, drop

driblet: 5 piece

dried: See **dry**

dried out: 5 stale 6 effete

drift: sag 4 dene, dune, ford, herd, plot, tide, till 5 drove, fleet, float, flock, tenor, trend 6 broach, course, design, device, scheme, tunnel 7 impetus, impulse, pasture, purport 8 tendency 9 deviation 10 propulsion

along: 4 tide 5 float

sidewise: 4 crab 8 crescent

driftage: 7 flatsam 8 wreckage

drill: gad, sow, tap 4 bore, spud 5 auger, borer, churn, decoy, train, tutor, twirl, whirl 6 allure, entice, furrow, pierce, school, seeder, stoper 7 channel 8 exercise, instruct, practice 9 perforate

drilled: 9 practiced

drilling: 5 denim

drink (see also **beverage**): bib, bum, lap, peg, rum, sip, tea 4 dram, grog, horn, lush, mead, shot, slug, soak, swig, tiff, toot, tope 5 bever, booze, bouse, draft, julep, morat, punch, quaff, skink, sniff, snort, souse, toast, toddy, vodka 6 absorb, bezzle, bracer, chaser, coffee, drench, godown, guzzle, hooker, imbibe, potion, ptisan, swinge, tipple 7 diluent, draught, snifter, swallow 8 beverage, cocktail, highball, potation, refresco 9 decoction 10 intoxicant

alcoholic: ade, ale, gin, hum, rye 4 beer, beno, bosa, boza, chia, flip, mead, nipa, nogg, soma, swig 5 airah, bombo, bozah, bubud, bumbo, julep, lager, negus, posca, sling, vodka, zombi 6 brandy, casiri, caudle, fuddle, mescal, posset, rickey, zombie, 7 cobbler, guarapo, sidecar 8 aperitif, rumbarge, sangaree, tequilla 9 cointreau, ship belly 10 tangle-foot 13 whistle-belley

carbonated: fiz, pop 4 fizz, soda 9 gingerade, gingerale

Christmas: nog 7 wassail

farinaceous: 6 ptisan

frozen: 6 frappe

fruit: ade 5 assai, bland, julep, morat 6 rickey 7 ratafee, ratafia

honey: 4 mead 5 morat

hot: tod 5 cocoa, copus, negus, toddy 6 caudle

magic: 8 nepenthe

mixer of: 6 barman 9 barkeeper, bartender

molasses and vinegar: 6 swanky

money for: 8 bonamano 9 pourboire

much: 4 swig, tope 5 bouse, quaff, swill 6 waucht, waught 7 carouse

of gods: 6 nectar

Oriental: 4 sake

portion: 4 shot 5 ounce 6 dollop, jigger

Russian: 5 vodka

sassafras: 6 saloop

small: hum, nip, peg, tot 4 bull, dram, pony, shot 5 sniff, snort, tabor 6 chaser 7 diluent snifter

sweet: 6 nectar

Tatar: 6 kumiss

drinkable: 7 potable

drinker: sot 5 toper 6 bender 7 imbiber, intaker, quaffer 8 drunkard 9 inebriate

drinking: 5 bever 6 guzzle 8 carousal 10 poculation

bout: 4 orgy 5 binge, spree 6 fuddle, shindy, splore 7 gaedown, wassail 8 carousal, potation 11 downsitting

horn: 6 rhyton

salutation: 5 skoal 6 prosit

vessel: cup, mug 4 bowl, tass 5 glass, gourd, hanap, jorum, stein, stoop, stoup 6 beaker, cappie, dipper, goblet, noggin, patera, rumkin 7 bombard, canikin, hanaper, tankard 8 cannikin, schooner

drip: sie, sye 4 drop, leak, sile 5 eaves 7 dribble, dripple, trickle

frozen: 6 icicle

drive: cot 4 bang, bear, butt, cram, ding, goad, hunt, ride, send, spur, urge 5 chase, co-act, crowd, feeze, force, hurry, impel, infer, press, repel, roust, shove, sweep 6 attack, beetle, bensel, compel, cudgel, deduce, derive, hasten, plunge, propel 7 overtax 9 constrain

away: 5 chase, repel 6 banish, dispel 7 repulse

down: 4 tamp

frantic: 7 bedevil

out: 4 rout 5 exile, expel 9 eradicate

public: 9 esplanade

drive-in: 7 open-air 10 restaurant

drivel: 4 dote 5 drool 6 dotage, drudge, footle, menial, slaver 7 twaddle 8 nonsense

driveler: 4 fool 5 doter

driver: 4 jenu 5 drabi 6 cabman, caller, drover, jarvey, mallet 7 catcher, spanker, speeder 8 coachman, engineer, galloway, overseer, teamster 9 chauffeur, izvozchik, propeller 10 charioteer, taskmaster

of golden chariot: 6 Helios

drizzle: deg, mug 4 dank, haze, ling, rain, smur 5 misle, smurr 6 mizzle 8 sprinkle

drole: 7 buffoon

droll: odd 5 comic, drole, funny, merry, queer 6 jester, jocose 7 amusing, buffoon, comical, jocular, strange, waggish 8 farcical, humorous 9 burlesque, diverting, laughable, ludicrous, whimsical 10 ridiculous

drollery: wit 4 jest 5 farce, humor 10 buffoonery

drome: 6 ployer 7 airport

dromedary: 5 camel, delul 7 camelus, dromond

dromond: 7 warship

drone: bee, bum, hum 4 drum, slug 5 drant, idler, snail 6 bumble, draunt, lubber 7 bagpipe, humming, shirker, sleeper, speaker 8 loiterer, sluggard 9 bombilate

dronish: 4 slow 8 indolent, sluggish

drool: 6 drivel, slaver 7 slobber

droop: fag, lob, lop, sag 4 bend, drop, flag, hang, loll, pine, sink, wilt 5 daver, heald, hield 6 bangle, dangle, nutate, slouch 7 decline, flitter 8 languish

drooping: lop 4 limp 6 flaggy, nutant 7 nodding

of eyelid: 6 ptosis

on one side: 4 alop

drop: dap, sie, sye 4 bead, bede, blob, drib, drip, fall, gout, omit, shed, sile, sink, stop 5 droop, lower, minim, plump, plunk, slump 6 drappy, plunge 7 abandon, curtain, descent, dismiss, drappie, dribble, forsake, globule, guttula, guttule, plummet, release 8 decrease, quantity 10 relinquish 11 discontinue

lachrymal: 4 tear

syllable: 5 elide 7 elision

drop in: 5 enter 6 arrive 8 surprise

drop off: nap 4 doze 5 sleep 8 decrease

droplet: 7 globule

dropped: 6 fallen

dropper: 7 pipette

dropsical: 5 puffy 6 edemic 8 hydropic

dropsy: 5 edema

dross: 4 lees, scum, slag 5 chaff, dregs, sprue, waste 6 garble, refuse, scoria, scruff, sinter 7 cinders, leaving 9 recrement

iron: 6 sinter

drossel: 4 slut 5 hussy 6 drazel, drazil 9 dratchell

drought, drouth: 4 soka 6 thirst 7 aridity, dryness

drought plant: 9 xerophyte

drouk: 4 soak 6 drench 9 overwhelm

drove (see also **drive**)**:** mob 4 sent 5 atajo, crowd, drift, flock 6 manada 7 disturb, trouble 8 driftway 10 assemblage

drover: 6 dealer, driver 8 herdsman

drovy, druvy: 5 muddy 6 filthy, turbid

drown: 6 drench 8 inundate

drowse: nod 4 doze 5 dover, sleep 6 snooze 7 slumber

drowsiness: 8 dullness 9 oscitance, oscitancy 10 sleepiness 12 sluggishness

drowsy: 4 dull, logy 5 noddy 6 sleepy, stupid, supine 7 lulling 8 comatose, oscitant, sluggish 9 somnolent, soporific 11 heavy-headed

drub: tap 4 bang, beat, blow, drum 5 array, curry, stamp, thump 6 cudgel, thrash 7 belabor, shellac 8 belabour, shellack

drubbing: 9 thrashing

drubly: 5 muddy 6 turbid 8 troubled

drudge: fag 4 grub, moil, plod, toil 5 grind, scrub, slave 6 digger, drivel, endure, slavey, suffer 7 hackney, plodder, slavery

literary: 4 hack 5 devil

drudgery: 4 moil, toil, work 5 labor, swink 7 faggery

piece of: fag

drug: 4 aloe, alum, dope, drab, dull, hemp, numb 5 hocus, japop, locus, opium, salol, senna, tonga, truck 6 heroin, ipecac, locust(pl.), opiate, peyote, peyotl 7 atebrin, stupefy, zedoary 8 medicine, nepenthe 9 asedulcis, marijuana 11 barbiturate, ipecacuanha 14 sulphapyridine

and ship: 8 shanghai

container: 7 capsule 8 gallipot

convulsion causing: 7 tetanic

crocus species: 7 saffron

for neuralgia: 5 tonga

Hippocratic: 5 mecon

of forgetfulness: 8 nepenthe

sleeping: 8 narcotic, sedative 12 somnifacient

drugged: 4 high 5 hyped 6 zonked 7 freaked 8 turned on 9 spaced out

drugget: mat, rug

druggist: 8 gallipot 10 apothecary, pharmacist 13 pharmaceutist

bible: USP

drugstore: 8 pharmacy

Druid: 6 priest

lodge: 4 cove

priestess of opera: 5 Norma

stone: 6 sarsen

symbol: 9 mistletoe

drum: 4 drub 5 drone, tabor 6 barrel, tambor, tympan 7 tambour, timbrel 8 cylinder, tympanum 9 reiterate

call to arms: 6 rappel

flourish: 7 roulade

kettle: 5 naker 6 atabal, nagara, timbal 7 attabal, timbale, timpano, timpani(pl.), tympani(pl.) 8 tympanum 9 tamburone

kind of: 4 base, gong, toph 5 gumbe, gumby, snare, tabor, tombe 6 kettle, tabour, tam-tam, timbre, tom-tom 7 capstan, taboret, timbrel 8 bamboula, darbukka, derbukka, tabouret 9 darabukka, tambouret, tambourin

roll: 4 dian 5 diana

string: 5 snare

tighten cords: 4 frap

drumbeat: dub 8 berloque, breloque

at hour for sleep: 6 tattoo

drummer: 7 roadman 8 salesman

drumstick: 6 tampon

drunk: See **drunken**

drunkard: sot 4 soak 5 bloat, dipso, souce, souse, sowce, toper 7 fuddler, potshot, tippler, tosspot 8 borachio 9 alcoholic, inebriate 11 dipsomaniac

drunken: ree 4 gone 5 bousy, drown 6 blotto, fluffy 7 pickled, sottish 8 drenched, saturate, squiffed 9 drunkelew 10 inebriated 11 intoxicated

drunkenness: bun 7 potshot 9 inebriacy, inebriety 12 intoxication

bout of: 4 bust

drupelet: 5 acini(pl.) 6 acinus

dry: sec, ted 4 adry, arid, bake, brut, dull, geld, hask, sere, wipe 5 drain, hasky, parch, prosy, vapid, wizen 6 barren, boring, gizzen, jejune 7 brustle, insipid, sapless, sub-arid, sterile, thirsty, xerotic 8 tiresome 9 dehydrate, desiccate, drinkless, exsiccate, exsuccous, fruitless, pointless, sarcastic, waterless 10 desicated, evaporated, siccaneous, teetotaler 11 displeasing 12 moistureless, unprofitable 13 uninteresting

comb. form: ser, xer 4 xero

grass: hay

leather: sam

out: 5 steam, toast 6 rizzar 7 siccate

up: 4 sere 5 parch 6 shrink 9 dehydrate, desiccate, evaporate, exsiccate 10 dehumidify

dry goods: 4 wear 6 linens, napery

dry run: try 8 maneuver 9 rehearsal

dry shave: 5 cheat 7 defraud

dry spell: 7 drought

dryad: 5 nymph 6 yaksha, yakshi

dryness: 6 drouth 7 drought, siccity

abnormal: 7 xerosis 9 xerostoma 10 xerostomia

dryth: 6 thirst 7 drought, dryness

duad: 4 pair

dual: 4 twin 6 binary, double 7 twofold

dub: rub 4 blow, call, name, pool 5 adorn, array, dress, style, thump 6 clothe, puddle, smooth, strike 7 entitle 8 beginner, drumbeat, ornament 9 schlemiel, schlemihl

dubious: 8 doubtful, doubting 9 ambiguous, equivocal, uncertain, unsettled 10 disputable, precarious 12 questionable, undetermined

ducal: 5 noble

duck: bob, bow, mig, pet 4 chap, dive, jouk 5 dilly, dodge, douse, dowse, mommy, shirk, souse 6 fellow, person, plunge 7 darling, gadwall 9 sheldrake

black: 9 blackjack

bluebill: 5 scaup

brood: 4 team

dead: 5 goner

diving: 4 smew

eider: 4 colk, wamp

for cooking: 7 caneton

fresh-water: 4 teal

fresh-water genus: aix

genus: 4 anas 7 nettion

goldeneye: 7 gowdnie

group: 4 sord, team 5 skein

heraldic: 6 cannet 8 cannette

hooked-bill: 9 merganser

kind of: 4 smee, smew, teal 5 eider, scaup 6 scoter 7 mallard, pintail, scooter 9 merganser 10 bufflehead, butterball

longtailed: 6 hareld

male: 5 drake

Muscovy: 4 pato

old squaw: 4 quandy

Old World: 7 pochard 9 sheldrake

pert. to: 7 anatine

pintail: 4 smee, smew 8 piketail 11 querquedule

rare: 5 merse

ring-necked: 5 bunty

river: 4 smee, teal 7 pintail 8 piketail, shoveler 9 greenwing

ruddy: 6 bobber 9 blackjack

scaup: 9 blackjack

sea: 4 coot 5 eider, scaup 6 scoter 7 scooter 9 harlequin

tree: 7 yaguaza

wild: 4 teal 5 scaup 7 gadwall, mallard

wooden: 5 decoy

yellow-billed: 7 geelbec 8 geelbeck

young: 8 duckling

duck-on-the-rock player: 6 tenter

duck out: 4 flee 7 escape

duckbill: 8 platypus 10 mallangong

duckweed: 5 lemna

duct: vas 4 main, pipe, tube, vasa(pl.) 5 canal 7 conduit, ductule, leading, passage, trachea 8 aqueduct, guidance 9 direction

ductile: 4 soft 6 docile, facile, pliant 7 plastic, pliable, tensile 8 flexible, tractile 9 compliant, malleable, tractable 10 manageable, sequacious

ductless gland: 6 pineal, thymus

dud: 7 failure
dude: fop 5 dandy 6 dudine 7 coxcomb
stage door: 7 Johnnie
dudeen: 4 pipe
dudgeon: ire 5 anger, pique 6 dagger 10 resentment
duds: 7 clothes 8 clothing, garments
due: owe 4 just, meed, owed, toll 5 endow, endue, fated, owing 6 desert, extent, lawful, mature, proper, unpaid 7 exactly, fitting 8 adequate, directly, rightful, suitable 10 demandable, inevitable, sufficient 11 appropriate 12 attributable
duel: 4 tilt 5 fence, fight 6 affair, combat 7 contest 8 conflict
duelist: 7 fighter
aide: 6 second
duena: 8 landlady, mistress
duenna: 8 chaperon
dues: 5 tolls 6 droits 7 payment
duet: duo, two 7 twosome
upper part: 5 primo
duff: 5 alter, brand 7 pudding
duffer: 4 sham 5 cheat 6 hawker 7 peddler
dugong: 6 seacow
dugout: 4 abri, boat, cave 5 canoe, donga, dunga 6 cayuca, cayuco 7 pirogue, shelter 10 excavation
duke: duc(F.) 4 peer 5 chief 6 leader
dukedom: 4 duchy 8 ducatus
dulcet: 5 sweet 8 soothing 9 agreeable, melodious 10 harmonious
dulcimer: 6 citole, santir 7 cembalo, yang-kin 9 pantaleon
dull: dim, dow, dry, lax, mat, sad 4 clod, cold, dead, drab, dree, drug, dumb, flat, gray, grey, logy, mope, poky, slow, tame 5 besot, blate, blear, blind, blunt, crass, dingy, dunch, fishy, foggy, gross, heavy, inert, matte, moron, noose, plump, pokey, prose, prosy, shade, unapt, vapid 6 barren, bovine, cloudy, dampen, darken, deaden, dismal, dreary, drowsy, glassy, hebete, leaden, muffle, obtund, obtuse, sleepy, somber, stodgy, stolid, stupid, torpid, triste 7 blunted, doltish, humdrum, irksome, lumpish, mumpish, prosaic, sottish, stupefy, tedious, vacuous 8 backward, blockish, boeotian, hebetate, lifeless, listless, overcast, sluggish, stagnant, tiresome 9 apathetic, colorless, heavisome, inanimate, lethargic, pointless, saturnine, tarnished, tasteless, unfeeling 10 insensible, lusterless, melancholy, monotonous, slow-witted 11 claybrained, displeasing, heavy-headed, thickheaded 12 buffle-headed 13 unimaginative
become: 4 pall 8 hebetate
finish: mat 5 matte

noise: 4 klop
dullard: 4 dolt 5 dunce, idiot, moron 6 stupid 7 dastard, doldrum, pothead
dullness: 7 dimness, doldrum, duncery, fatuity, languor 8 hebetude, slowness, vapidity 9 bluntness, oscitancy, platitude, stupidity 10 drowsiness
of hearing: 9 baryecoia
duly: 5 fitly 8 properly 9 regularly 13 appropriately
Dumas: *character:* 5 Athos 6 Aramis 7 Porthos
heroine: 7 Camille
dumb: 4 dull, mute 6 silent, stupid 9 senseless 10 speechless 11 meaningless 12 inarticulate, inexpressive
dumbbell: 9 screwball
dumfound, dumbfound: 4 daze, stun 5 amaze 7 confuse 8 confound, surprise 9 embarrass
dummy: 4 copy, dolt, mute, sham 6 silent 9 imitation 10 fictitious, figurehead 11 counterfeit
dump: sum 4 beat, cash, coin, fall, hole, jail, muse, nail 5 empty, house 6 grieve, plunge, unload 7 counter, deposit, reverie, sadness, storage 9 halfpenny 10 melancholy 11 despondency
dumping ground: 4 toom
dumpling: cob 7 gnoccho, gnocchi(pl.) 8 quenelle 10 appleberry
dumps: 8 doldrums
dumpy: 5 pudgy, squat
dun: tan 4 fort, urge 5 annoy, brown, crave, dingy, mound, sepia 6 pester, plague 7 swarthy 9 importune
dunce: ass 4 dolt, dult, gony 5 booby, idiot, ninny 6 hobbil, pedant 7 dullard, half-wit, sophist 8 numskull 9 ignoramus, simpleton 10 dunderhead
dunderhead: oaf 4 dolt 5 dunce 9 blockhead, numbskull
dune: bar 5 mound, towan 6 barkan 7 barchan, barkhan
dung: 4 gore, muck 5 filth, fumet 6 billet, manure, ordure 9 billeting, excrement, poppycock
dungeon: 4 cell, hell, hole 5 vault 6 donjon, prison 8 revolver 9 oubliette 10 ergastulum
dunghill: 5 mixen 7 mixhill 10 muckmidden
dunk: dip, sop 4 soak 5 steep 7 immerse, moisten
dunker: 7 tumbler
dunlin: 4 stib 9 sandpiper
dunt: 4 beat, blow 5 dizzy, knock, thump 6 benumb, bruise, strike, stupid 7 stupefy 10 heartthrob

duo **226**

duo: 4 duet, pair 6 couple

dupe: ape, fob, mug 4 coax, cull, fool, geck, gull, tool 5 cheat, cully, heald, mouth, trick 6 bubble, choose, delude, deride, plover, sucker, victim 7 catspaw, deceive, gudgeon, mislead, pidgeon, swindle 8 dotterel

dupery: 4 ramp

duple: 7 twofold

duplex: 6 double 7 twofold 8 dwelling

duplexity: 9 ambiguity

duplicate: bis 4 copy 5 alike, ditto, spare 6 double, repeat 7 estreat, mislead, replica, twofold 8 likeness 9 facsimile, reproduce 10 transcript 11 counterpart

duplicity: art 6 deceit 8 trickery 9 deception, falsehood 13 dissimulation

durable: 4 firm 6 stable, staple 7 lasting 8 constant, enduring 9 permanent 10 consistent, continuing, persistent 11 everlasting

durance: 6 duress 12 imprisonment

Durante byword: 8 Calabash

duration: age 4 span, term, time 5 space 6 period 7 durance 8 lifetime 9 extension 11 continuance

note: 4 time 5 clock

of ministerial charge: 9 pastorate

without beginning or end: 8 eternity

D'Urberville lass: 4 Tess

dure: 4 hard, last 5 rough 6 endure, severe, strong 7 sustain 8 continue

duress: 7 cruelty, durance 8 coercion, hardness, pressure 9 captivity, harshness 10 affliction, compulsion, constraint 12 imprisonment

durgah, dargah: 4 tomb 5 court 6 mosque, shrine

during: 4 time 5 while 6 whilst 7 pending 10 throughout

durra: 7 sorghum

durst: 8 ventured

dusk: eve 5 gloom 6 dimmet, dimpsy 7 dimness 8 darkness, gloaming, twilight 11 crepusculum

dusky: dim, sad, wan 4 dark 5 adusk, brown, dingy, tawny 6 gloomy, somber, sombre, swarth 7 swarthy 8 blackish 10 melancholy

dust: row 4 dirt, pilm, smut 5 clean, flour, pouce, stive 6 pollen, powder 7 eburine, remains, turmoil 9 commotion, confusion 10 kryokonite 11 disturbance

measuring device: 9 koniscope

reduce to: 4 mull

speck: 4 mote

dust-like: 7 powdery

dusty: 5 adusk 6 poucey 9 pulverant

Dutch: See **Netherlands**

Dutch East Indies: See **East Indies, Indonesia**

Dutch Guiana: See **Surinam**

Dutch South Africa: See **South Africa**

Dutch uncle: oom

Dutchware blue: 5 delft

duteous: 7 dutiful 8 obedient 10 respectful 11 subservient

dutiful: 6 docile 7 duteous 8 obedient, reverent 9 childlike, compliant 10 submissive 11 reverential 13 conscientious

duty: job, tax 4 care, onus, role, task, toll 5 chore, stint 6 burden, charge, devoir, excise, exitus, heriot, impose, impost, rivage, tariff 7 average, bailage, service, station, tribute 8 function, malikana 10 allegiance, obligation

Hindu: 6 dharma

on commodities: 6 excise

shirking: 7 truancy

spell of: 5 shift, trick, watch

dux: 5 chief 6 leader

dwarf: elf 4 grig, grub, runt 5 crile, crowl, elves(pl.), Galar, gnome, midge, pigmy, pygmy, scrub, stunt, troll 6 ablach, droich, durgan, durgen, midget 7 blastie, manikin, overtop, Pacolet 8 belittle, Cercopes, homuncio, homuncle, huckmuck, nander 9 dandiprat, homuncule 10 diminutive, homunculus, overshadow

king: 8 Alberich

race: 8 Nibelung 9 Nibelungs 10 Nibelungen

dwarfish: 5 pigmy, pygmy 6 grubby, nanoid 7 pigment, runtish, stunted

dwarfishness: 6 nanism

dwell: big, cot, dig 4 bide, bigg, haft, harp, live, stay 5 abide, bield, brood, delay, lodge, pause, tarry 6 linger, remain, reside 7 cohabit, inhabit 8 converse 9 expatiate 12 intermission, interruption

dweller: 6 tenant 8 habitant, occupant, resident 10 inhabitant

around city: 11 suburbanite

cave: 10 troglodyte

city: 8 urbanite

desert: 4 Arab 5 nomad 9 sourdough

earth: 9 tellurian

fellow: 6 inmate

formicary: ant

jungle: 5 beast 6 monkey

monastery: 8 cenobite

prairie: 9 plainsman

seacoast: 7 coaster 11 beachcomber

temporary: 6 lodger 7 boarder 9 transient

underground: 4 mold 5 gnome

dwelling: dar, hut 4 casa(It.), flat, haft, home, nest, slum, tent 5 abode, cabin, hotel, house, hovel, motel 6 duplex, shanty, teepee 7 cottage, lodging, mansion, trailer, triplex 8 building, bungalow, domicile, tenement 9 apartment, habitance, residence 10 habitation

dwindle: 4 melt, pine, wane 5 peter, taper, waste 6 shrink 7 consume, decline 8 decrease, diminish, fordwine

Dyak: *blowgun:* 8 sumpitan
 knife: 6 parang

Dyak Sea: 4 iban

dye: aal 4 anil, tint 5 color, eosin, fucus, imbue, stain, tinge 6 litmus, madder 7 aniline, toluene 8 colorant
 blue: wad 4 anil, wade, woad
 blue-red: 6 orchal, orchil
 brown: 5 sumac 6 sumach
 coal-tar: 6 magena
 hair: 5 henna 6 rastik
 indigo: al; aal 4 anil
 morindin: al; aal
 mulberry: al
 purple: 8 murexide
 quercitron bark: 6 flavin
 red: 5 aurin, eosin 7 annatto, magenta 8 rhodamin 9 rhodamine 10 orseilline
 red-brown: 5 henna
 red-orange: 5 chica 7 fuchsin 8 morindin
 source: 5 murex

 violet: 6 archil
 yellow: 4 weld, wold 5 arusa, woald, would
 yellow-red: 6 anatta, anatto 7 annatto, annotto

dyeing apparatus: vat 4 ager
 scrape: 6 harass

dyestuff: See dye

dying: 8 moribund

dynamic: 6 potent 8 forceful 9 energetic

dynamite: 5 blast 9 explosive
 kind of: 6 dualin 7 dualine 9 fulgurite 10 kieselguhr
 inventor: 5 Nobel

dynamo: 9 generator
 in distributing system: 7 booster
 inventor: 7 Faraday
 part: 5 rotor 7 brushes 8 armature 10 commutator

dynast: 5 ruler 6 prince 8 governor

dynasty: 4 race 5 realm, ruler 6 prince 7 monarch 8 dominion, governor, lordship 10 succession 11 sovereignty
 Chinese: Fo; Han, Yin 4 Isin, Ming
 French: 5 Capet

dysentery: 7 toxemia 8 diarrhea, epidemic
 remedy: 14 sulfaguanidine

dysphoria: 7 anxiety

E

ea: **5** river **6** stream
Ea's daughter: **4** Nina
each: ea; all, ilk, uch **4** ilka, uche **5** every **8** everyone
eager: hot **4** acid, avid, gair, keen, sour, warm, wave **5** afire, agasp, itchy, ready, sharp **6** ardent, greedy, hetter, intent **7** anxious, athirst, brittle, burning, excited, fervent, forward, provoke **8** desirous, irritate, spirited, vigorous, yearning **9** desireful, impatient, impetuous, strenuous **12** enthusiastic, forereaching
eagerness: gog **4** elan, zeal **5** ardor **6** fervor **7** ardency, avidity **8** alacrity, cupidity, fainness, fervency **9** alertness, constancy, readiness **10** enthusiasm, impatience **13** impetuousness
eagle: ern **4** erne, gier, tern **6** aquila, bergut, eaglet, formal, formel **8** allerion, bataleur, berghaan **9** ossifrage
Biblical: **4** gier
comb. form: **4** aeto
constellation: **6** Aquila
genus of: **10** haliaeetus
nest: **4** aery, eyry **5** aerie, eyrie
sea: ern **4** erne
eaglestone: **7** aetites
eagre: **4** bore, wave
ear: lug(Sc.) **4** hear, heed, obey, plow, till **5** auris(L.), spike **6** listen **7** auricle, hearing **8** audience **9** attention, cultivate
absence of: **6** anotia
bone: **5** ambos, incus **6** stapes **7** malleus, stirrup
canal: **5** scala
cavity: **6** meatus **7** cochlea
cleaning device: **8** aurilave
comb. form: oto **4** auri
covering: **4** muff **6** earcap, earlap **7** earmuff
doctor: **6** aurist **9** otologist
inflammation of: **6** otitis
middle: **4** drum **8** tympanum
near: **7** parotic
part of: **4** burr, lobe **5** helix, pinna **6** tragus
pert. to: **4** otic **5** aural **7** entotic **9** auricular

science of: **7** otology
ear shell: **7** abalone
ear stone: **7** otolite, otolith
earache: **6** otalgy **7** otalgia
earbob: **7** earring
eardrop: **7** earring, pendant
eardrum: **8** membrane, tympanum
eared seal: **5** otary
earl: **4** eorl, lord, peer **5** noble **8** nobleman
pert. to: **7** comital
earldom: **5** derby
earlet: **7** auricle
earlier: ere **4** erst, fore **5** elder **6** before, former, sooner **8** previous
early: air, ere, old **4** rath **5** forme, rathe **6** timely **7** ancient, betimes **9** matutinal, premature **10** forehanded
earmark: bit **14** identification
earn: get, win **4** fang, gain **5** addle, ettle, merit **6** obtain **7** achieve, acquire, chevise, deserve
earner: **6** winner, worker **11** breadwinner
earnest: **4** hard **5** grave, sober, staid **6** ardent, hearty, intent, sedate, solemn **7** engaged, forward, serious, sincere, zealous **8** diligent, emphatic **9** heartfelt **10** expressive, thoughtful **12** affectionate, wholehearted
earnest money: **5** arles **7** deposit, forfeit **8** security
earring: **4** grip **8** ornament **9** girandole
earshot: **7** hearing
earsplitting: **4** loud **5** shrill
earth: erd(Sc.), orb **4** bury, clay, dirt, grit, land, loam, marl, mool, muck, rock, soil, sory **5** glebe, globe, groot, inter, loess, regur, terra(L.), trass, umber, world **6** coarse, ground **7** tierras, topsoil **8** magnesia **10** terra firma
comb. form: geo
compound: **7** tierras
crust constituent: **6** silica
deposit: **4** marl, silt **5** loess **8** alluvium
dweller: **9** tellurian
god: Geg, Keb, Seb **5** Dagan

goddess: 4 Gaea 5 Ceres, Terra 6 Semele 7 Demeter
layer of: 5 sloam
lump of: 4 clod
metallic: ore
opposite side of: 9 Antipodes
pert. to: 4 geal 5 terra 8 telluric 9 planetary 11 terrigenous
pigment: 5 ochre, umber
prepare for seeding: 4 plow 5 spade 6 harrow 9 cultivate
ridge of: 4 kame 6 rideau
satellite of: 4 moon
science: 7 geodesy, geology 9 geography
surface gravel: 6 eratum 8 erratice
earth bob: 4 grub 6 maggot
earth hog: 8 aardvark
earth lodge: 5 hogan
earthborn: 11 terrigenous 13 autochthonous
earthbred: low 6 vulgar
earthdrake: 6 dragon
earthenware: 4 delf 5 china, cloam, crock, delft 7 biscuit, faience, pottery 8 crockery 9 porcelain, stoneware 10 terra-cotta
maker: 6 potter
peddler: 6 mugger
piece of: 5 shard
earthfall: 9 landslide
earthkin: 7 terella
earthling: 5 human 6 mortal
earthly: 6 carnal 7 mundane, secular, terrene, worldly 8 temporal 11 terrestrial
earthnut: 5 arnot, chufa 6 peanut 7 truffle
earthquake: 5 quake, seism 7 temblor
measuring device: 10 seisometer
pert. to: 7 seismic
point directly above: 9 epicenter
science: 10 seismology
earthstar: 6 fungus 7 geaster
earthwork: 5 agger 7 rampart 10 breastwork 13 fortification
earthworm: ess 7 annelid, ipomoea
earthy: low 5 gross 6 carnal, coarse, fleshy 7 sensual 11 terrestrial
earwax: 7 cerumen
earwig: 6 golach, goloch
ease: 4 calm, rest 5 allay, knack, peace, quiet, relax 6 loosen, pacify, reduce, relief, repose, smooth, soften, soothe 7 appease, assuage, comfort, faculty, freedom, leisure, liberty, lighten, relieve, slacken 8 diminish, facility, mitigate, moderate, palliate, pleasure, security, unburden 9 alleviate, disburden, enjoyment 10 ameliorate, facilitate, relaxation, solicitude 11 contentment, naturalness, tranquility 12 satisfaction
at: 6 degage, otiose 7 relaxed

ease off: 4 slow 5 slack
easel: 5 frame 7 support
easily: 6 gently, glibly 7 readily 8 smoothly
east: 4 Asia 6 Levant, Orient 9 direction
pert. to: 4 eoan 8 oriental
East Africa: See **Africa**
East Asia: *people:* 5 Seres
weight: 4 tras
East India: *agent:* 8 gomashta, gomastah
animal: 7 tarsier
aroid: 4 apii
arrowroot: 5 tikor
bark: 4 lodh 5 niepa
bead tree: nim 4 neem 6 neemba
bird: 4 baya
boatswain: 6 serang
broadbill: 4 raya
bush: 4 sola
cattle: 4 dhan, gaur
cavalry troop: 7 ressala
cheroot: 6 lunkah
civet: 6 musang
dancing girl: 4 dasi
disease: 5 lanas
drink: 4 nipa
dye: aal
dye tree: 4 dhak, toon
fish: 5 dorab 7 gourami
food: 4 sago
freight boat: 5 oolak
fruit: 6 durian, durion 8 belleric, cardamom 9 myrobalan
gateway: 5 toran 6 torana
granary: 4 gola
grass: 4 kasa, ragi, usar 5 glaga, ragee, raggi, raggy 6 glagah, raggie
gulf: 4 Boni
harbor master: 9 shabandar, shabunder
hawk: 5 bacha
hemp: 7 pangane
herb: pia, rea, til 4 chay, sola 6 sesame 7 roselle 8 eggplant
hog: 8 babirusa 9 babirussa 10 babiroussa
island: 4 Bali, Muna, Nias 5 Misal, Timor 6 Borneo 7 Celebes, Sumatra
juniper berry: 5 abhol
liquor: 6 arrack
maid: 4 ayah
mammal: 7 tarsier
mangrove: 7 ceriops
market: 5 pasar
measure: kit, kos 4 bouw, depa, rood, rope 5 depoh, kilan, parah, takar 6 bamboo, coyang 7 gantang, tjenkal, toenbak
millet: 4 dura 5 durra 6 dhurra
money: 4 bonk, duit
money changer: 6 shroff
monkey: 8 entellus
musical instrument: 4 bina, vina

muskmelon: 6 wungee
muslin: ban
nose flute: 6 upanga
nut: ben
palm: tal 4 nipa 7 jaggery, palmyra, tokopat
plant: da; rea 4 amil, jute, sola, sunn 5
benne 6 ambari, ambary, madder, sesame
7 ambaree
poison: 4 bikh
police chief: 7 darogah
post: dak 4 dawk
race: 4 swat
robber: 6 dacoit
rubber tree: saj
sailing vessel: 4 doni 5 dhoni
sardine: 4 lile
shrub: ak 4 odal, sola 5 mudar
snake: 7 bokadam
songbird: 5 shama
squirrel: 6 taguan
starch: 4 sago 5 tikor
sugar cane: 5 glaga 6 glagah 7 talthib
sword: 4 pata
tree: ach, bel, ber, bih, dar, eng, hur, mee,
nim, saj, sal 4 alof, dhak, moli, neem, odal,
poon, toon 5 dadap, fulwa, mahua, neeba,
niepa, oodal, rohan, roman, salai, sapan,
simal, siman, siris, sissu, tikur, uadal 6
banyan, chalta, chogak, deodar, illupi, sissoo, tikoor 7 champac, dhamnoo, gumihan, hollong, margosa 8 phulwbra 11
chaulmaugra, hursinghair
vehicle: 5 tonga
vessel: 7 patamar 8 gallivat
vine: 4 odal, soma
viper: 6 kupper
warrior: 5 singh
weight: 4 hoen, wang
wood: eng
wood apple: bel
xylophone: 5 saron
East Indies: See **East India**
Easter: 5 Pasch 6 Eostre, Pascha
first Sunday after: 9 Quasimodo
pert. to: 7 paschal
Sunday before: 4 Palm
eastern: 6 ortive 7 auroral
Eastern Church: *bishop:* 4 abba
choir platform: 5 solea
convent head: 8 hegumene
festival day: 8 apodosis
monk: 7 caloyer
prayer: 6 ectene, ektene
Eastland: 8 estriche
easy: 4 calm, cozy, eath, eith, glib, mild 5
cushy, light, suave 6 facile, gentle, secure,
simple 7 lenient, natural 8 carefree, careless, cavalier, familiar, graceful, homelike, moderate, tranquil, unforced 9 com-

pliant, indulgent, tractable, unhurried 10
manageable, unaffected 11 comfortable,
complaisant, susceptible, unconcerned 13
unconstrained
easy job: 4 pipe, snap 5 cinch 8 sinecure
easy mark: 5 chump 6 sucker
easygoing: 6 placid 7 relaxed
eat: sup 4 bite, dine, fare, feed, fret, gnaw,
grub, rust 5 erode, feast, munch, taste,
waste 6 absorb, begnaw, devour, ingest,
ravage 7 consume, corrode, destroy, swallow 9 manducate
between meals: 5 bever
by regimen: 4 diet
fastidiously: 7 epicure 8 gourmand
grass: 5 graze 6 forage
greedily: 4 cram, wolf 5 gorge, raven 6 gobble, goffle 8 gourmand 10 gormandize
pert. to: 7 dietary 8 dietetic, edacious
sparingly: 4 diet
sumptuously: 6 regale
eatable: 6 edible 8 esculent 10 comestible
eatage: 9 pasturage
eating: 6 dining 7 caustic, erosive 8 corrosive
eating-place: inn 4 cafe 5 diner, grill, hotel
6 tavern 7 automat, tearoom 8 grubbery 9
cafeteria, chophouse
eave: 7 cornice
eavesdrop: 6 harken 7 hearken
eavesdropper: 9 drawlatch
ebb: 4 fail, sink, wane 5 abate, decay 6 recede, reflux, retire 7 decline, subside 8 decrease, diminish 9 backwater
ebb and flow: 5 estus 6 aestus
ebbing: 5 awane 8 refluent 9 refluxing
Eber's son: 6 Joktan
ebon: 4 dark 5 black, sable
ebony: 5 black
eboulement: 9 landslide
ebriate: 9 inebriate 11 intoxicated
ebrious: 5 tipsy
ebullate, ebulliate: 4 boil
ebullience: 8 overflow
ebullient: 7 boiling 12 effervescent
ebullition: 7 ferment 8 outburst 9 agitation,
commotion 10 excitement 12 fermenta-
tion 13 effervescence
ecaudate: 8 tailless
ecce: lo 6 behold
eccentric: odd 4 card 5 crank, queer 6
cranky 7 bizarre, devious, erratic, strange
8 abnormal, peculiar, singular 9 anomalous, erratical, irregular, quizzical, screwball, whimsical 15 idiosyncratical
eccentricity: 5 ferly 6 oddity 8 crotchet 9
queerness 10 aberration 11 peculiarity,
strangeness 12 idiosyncrasy

ecclesiastic: 4 abbe 5 abbot, clerk 6 priest 7
    prelate 9 clergyman
belt: 7 balteus 8 baltheus
council: 5 synod
court: 4 rota
garment: alb 4 cope 5 amice, fanon, orale,
    stole, cappa, rabat 6 callot 7 cassock, bi-
    retta, calotte 8 berretta
head: 6 rector
land: 5 glebe
living: 8 benefice
ruler: 8 hierarch
service: 5 matin
unit: 6 parish
ecclesiastics: 11 gens d'eglise
ecdysiast: 11 stripteaser
eche: 4 grow 7 enlarge 8 increase
echelon: 8 maneuver 11 arrangement
echidna: 8 anteater
    food: 4 ants
    three-toed: 6 nodiak
echinate: 5 spiny 7 bristly, prickly
echinoderm, armed: 8 starfish
echo: eco 4 ring 6 repeat, second 7 imitate,
    iterate, resound, respond, revoice 8 re-
    sponse 9 imitation 10 repetition 11 rever-
    berate 13 reverberation
eciton: ant
eclat: 4 fame, pomp 5 glory 6 praise, renown,
    repute 7 acclaim, scandal 8 applause, fa-
    cility, splendor 9 notoriety 10 brilliance,
    brilliancy 11 ostentation
eclectic: 7 liberal
eclipse: dim 4 bind, blot, hide 5 blind, cloud,
    shade, sully 6 darken, dazzle, exceed 7 ob-
    scure, travail 8 outrival 10 extinguish,
    overshadow 11 obscuration, occultation
    demon of: 4 Rahu
    shadow: 8 penumbra 9 penumbrae
eclogue: 4 idyl, poem 5 idyll 7 bucolic
ecology, oecology: 9 bionomics
economical: 5 chary 6 frugal, saving 7 care-
    ful, prudent, thrifty 9 provident
economics: element: 9 commodity
    theoretical: 9 plutology
economize: 4 save 5 skimp, stint 6 scrimp 7
    husband, utilize 8 retrench 9 housewife
economy: 6 saving, thrift 9 frugality, hus-
    bandry 10 compendium, providence
    bad: 11 cacoeconomy
    practice: 7 scraped 8 scrimped
ecostate: 7 ribless
ecru: 5 beige, linen 10 unbleached
ecstasy: joy 5 bliss, swoon 6 trance 7 de-
    light, emotion, madness, rapture 9 enrap-
    ture, happiness, transport
ecstatic: 4 rapt 8 glorious 9 entranced, rap-
    turous, rhapsodic 10 enraptured
ectad: 5 outer 7 outward 8 exterior

opposite of: 5 entad
ectal: 5 outer 8 exterior
ectype: 9 imitation
ecu: 4 coin 6 shield
Ecuador: animal: 6 vicuna
    capital: 5 Quito
    city: 4 Loja, Suyo 5 Banos, Guano, Luisa,
        Mocha, Piura, Quito, Zunga 6 Ambato,
        Cuenca, Ibarra, Patate, Pujili, Tulcan 7
        Azogues, Cayambe, Guamote, Machala,
        Pelileo, Pillaro, Salcedo, Salinas, Squisil 8
        Babahoyo, Cevallos, Cujibies, Guaranda,
        Pansaleo, Riobamba 9 Guayaquil, Lata-
        gunga 10 Esmeraldas 11 Puertoviejo
    coin: 5 sucre 6 condor 7 centavo
    Indian: 4 Cara 5 Palta 6 Canelo, Jibaro,
        Jivaro
    island: 9 Galapagos
    measure: 5 libra 6 cuadra, fanega
    mountain:7 Cayambe 8 Antisana, Cotopaxi
        9 Cotacachi, Pichincha 10 Chimborazo
    province: 4 Loja 5 Azuay, Canar, El Oro 6
        Carchi, Guayas, Manabi 7 Bolivar, Los
        Rios 8 Cotapaxi, Imbabura 9 Pichincha 10
        Chimborazo, Esmeraldas, Tungurahua
    river: 4 Napo 5 Tigre 6 Ambato 7 Pastaza
        9 Guayaquil 10 Esmeraldas
    town: See Ecuador: city
    tree: 5 balsa
    volcano: 8 Antisana
ecumenic: 12 cosmopolitan
ecumenical: 7 liberal 8 catholic, tolerant 9
    worldwide 12 cosmopolitan
ecumenical council: 4 Lyon 5 Lyons, Trent
    7 Vatican
eczema: 6 herpes, tetter 9 malanders 10 der-
    matitis
edacity: 8 appetite, voracity 12 ravenous-
    ness
edaphic: 5 local 13 autochthonous
Edda: 4 saga
Eddaic god: 4 Odin
eddish: 6 arrish 7 eegrass 9 aftermath
eddo: 4 taro
eddy: 4 gulf, purl, weel 5 acker, gurge, shift,
    swirl, whirl 6 vortex 7 backset 9 whirlpool
    14 countercurrent
eddying: 4 wale
edema: 5 tumor 6 dropsy 8 swelling 9 puffi-
    ness 12 intumescence
Eden: 6 heaven, utopia 7 arcadia, elysium 8
    paradise
Edenic: 7 elysian, elysium 8 blissful 10 par-
    adisaic
Edenite: 9 amphibole
edental: 9 toothless
edentate: ai 5 sloth 7 ant bear 8 aardvark,
    anteater, pangolin, tamandua 9 arma-
    dillo, toothless

Edessa's king: 5 Abgar

edge: hem, jag, lip, rim 4 bank, berm, brim, brow, rand, side, trim, whet 5 arris, berme, bevel, blade, brink, crest, frill, knife, marge, ruler, sidle, splay, verge 6 border, flange, impale, margin 7 margent, sharpen, selvage 8 boundary, keenness, selvedge 9 advantage, beginning, sharpness 10 escarpment

run along: 5 skirt

sharp: 5 beard

uneven: 4 wane, wany 5 waney

edged: 5 sharp, erose 7 crenate

edger: 7 whetter 9 sharpener

edging: hem 4 lace 5 frill, picot 6 border, fringe 7 binding 8 rickrack 10 embroidery

loop: 5 picot

edgrew, edgrow: 5 rowen 9 aftermath

edgy: 5 sharp 7 angular 8 critical, snappish 9 irritable

edible: 7 eatable 8 esculent 9 cibarious, vegetable 10 comestible

arum: 4 taro

fungus: 5 morel

gallingale: 5 chufa

mollusk: asi

parts of fruit: 4 pulp

rush: 5 chufa

seaweed: 4 agar 5 dulse, laver 6 delisk 8 agaragar

seed: pea 4 bean

tuber root: oca, uva, yam 4 beet, eddo, taro 6 turnip 7 parsnip 8 rutabaga

edict: act, ban, law 4 bull, fiat 5 arret, bando, bulla, irade, order, ukase 6 decree, dictum, notice 7 command, embargo, program, statute 9 ordinance, programma 12 announcement, proclamation

papal: 4 bull

edification: 7 edifice 8 building 11 instruction 13 enlightenment

edifice: 4 dome 6 church 8 building 9 structure 11 edification

kind: 6 palace, church, temple 7 capitol 10 tabernacle

edifier: 7 teacher

edify: 4 grow 5 build, teach 7 improve, prosper 8 instruct, organize 9 construct, establish

edile: 10 magistrate

Edina: 9 Edinburgh

Edinburgh: 5 Edina

part of: 5 Leith

edit: 5 emend 6 direct, redact, review, revise 7 arrange, compile, correct, prepare, publish, rewrite 8 copyread 9 supervise

edition: 4 kind 5 issue, print, stamp 6 source 7 version 9 character 10 extraction

kind of: 5 extra 7 revisal, reprint

editor: 8 redactor 9 emendator, publisher, redacteur 10 diaskeuast, journalist

room: 7 sanctum

Edom: 7 Idumaea

chieftain: 4 Iram

district: 5 Teman

king: 5 Hadad

mountain: Hor

Edomite's ancestor: 4 Esau

educate: 4 rear 5 breed, teach, train 6 expand, inform, school 7 develop, nurture 8 develope, instruct 9 cultivate, enlighten 10 discipline, strengthen 12 indoctrinate

educated: 4 bred 6 taught 7 trained 8 lettered, literate

education: 7 nurture 8 breeding, learning, training 9 erudition 10 background, discipline 11 scholarship

institution: 6 school 7 college 8 seminary 10 university

organization: PTA 6 lyceum

educator: 7 teacher

educe: 5 evoke 6 elicit, evolve 7 extract 9 eliminate

edulcorate: 7 sweeten

eegrass: 6 eddish 7 stubble

eel: ele 4 grig, ling, opah, snig 5 elver, moray, siren 6 conger, carapo, moreia, murene 7 eel pout, lamprey, muraena, sniggle, wriggle 8 Anguilla 9 snipefish

cut and cooked: 10 spitchcock

fish for: 7 sniggle

marine: 6 conger

migration: 7 eelfare

sand: 6 launce

trap: 6 eelpot

young: 5 elver

eel-shaped: 12 anguilliform

eelboat: 6 schuit

eeler: 9 fisherman

eelgrass: 9 grassweed

eellike: 10 anguilloid

eelpot: 4 trap

eelpout: 4 pout 6 burbot, guffer, yowler 10 muttonfish

eelworm: 4 nema

eely: 7 elusive, evasive, wriggly 8 slippery 9 wriggling

eemis, immis: 8 insecure 10 changeable

e'en: 4 even 7 evening

eerie, eery: 5 scary, timid, weird 6 dismal, gloomy, spooky 7 awesome, ghostly, macabre, strange, uncanny 8 eldritch, ghoulish 9 unearthly, unnatural, unworldly 10 frightened 11 phantomlike

efface: 4 blot, dele, rase, raze 5 erase 6 cancel, deface 7 destroy, dislimn, expunge 10 obliterate

effacement: 7 erasure

effect: 4 does, feck, prey 5 cause, close, eclat, enact, ettle 6 intent, result, sequel 7 achieve, acquire, compass, conduce, emotion, execute, fulfill, operate, outcome, perform, produce, purport, realize 8 complete 9 execution, influence 10 accomplish, consummate, expression, impression 11 consequence, fulfillment, performance 13 manifestation 14 accomplishment
of past experience: 5 mneme
of wind on a shot: 7 windage

effective: 4 able, real 5 siker 6 active, actual, causal, potent, sicker 7 capable, telling 8 adequate, forceful, powerful, striking, vigorous 9 brilliant, competent, effectual, efficient 10 perficient 11 efficacious, influential

effectiveness: 10 efficiency

effects: 5 goods 7 baggage 8 movables 10 belongings

effectual: 8 adequate, powerful 9 available, effective, efficient 10 perficient, sufficient 13 authoritative

effectuate: 6 fulfil 7 fulfill 8 complete 10 accomplish

effeminancy: 10 muliebrity

effeminate: 5 milky 6 female, tender, weakly 7 citizen, epicene, womanly 8 feminate, feminine, oversoft 9 emolliate 10 voluptuous 12 overdelicate 13 overemotional

effervesce: 4 huff 6 bubble

effervescence: 10 ebullition

effervescing: 5 brisk 9 ebullient

effete: 4 sere 5 spent 6 barren 8 decadent, moribund 9 exhausted

efficacious: 5 valid 6 mighty, potent 8 forcible, powerful, vigorous, virtuous 9 available, effective, officious, prevalent 10 legitimate 11 efficiently

efficaciousness: 10 efficiency

efficacy: 4 dint, feck 5 force, grace, might, power 6 virtue 7 potency 10 efficiency

efficiency: 5 power, skill 6 agency 7 ability 8 efficacy 10 capability, competence, competency 11 proficiency 13 effectiveness 15 efficaciousness

efficient: 4 able 6 potent 7 capable, feckful 8 powerful 9 competent, effective, effectual

efficiently: 13 efficaciously

effigy: 5 image 8 likeness 9 jackstraw

efflorescence: 5 bloom 7 blossom 8 anthesis

effluence: 5 issue 6 efflux 7 emanate 9 emanation

effluvium: 4 aura 9 emanation 10 exhalation

efflux: 7 outflow 8 effusion 9 effluence, emanation

effluxion: 7 outflow 9 effluence, emanation

effodient: 9 burrowing, fossorial

effort: try 4 dint, fist, toil 5 assay, brunt, drive, essay, labor, nisus, pains, power, trial 6 devoir, fizzle, fuffle, strain 7 attempt, trouble 8 endeavor, exertion, struggle 9 diligence 11 application
single: 4 solo 5 trice
violent: 4 adit 5 burst 8 struggle

effrontery: 4 brow, gall 5 front 8 audacity, boldness, temerity 9 hardihood, impudence, sauciness 10 confidence, incivility

effulgence: 5 blaze, glory 7 radiant 8 radiance, splendor 10 brightness, brilliance

effulgent: 6 bright 7 fulgent, radiant

effuse: 4 gush, shed 5 fling 7 emanate 8 dispense 11 disseminate

effussion: 6 efflux, foison

effusive: 5 gushy 7 gushing 8 bubbling 9 exuberant, rhapsodic 13 demonstrative

eft, evet: 4 newt 6 lizard, triton 10 salamander

eftsoon: 4 anon 5 again 9 afterward

egad: 4 ecod

egality: 8 equality 10 equanimity

egall: 5 equal

egeran: 11 vesuvianite

egeria: 7 adviser

egest: 4 void 7 excrete

egg: ova(pl.) 4 abet, goad, ovum, prod, seed, spur, urge 5 ovule, spore 6 incite 7 actuate, cokeney 9 instigate
case: 5 shell 6 ovisac 7 outheca
collector: 8 oologist
combining form: oo; ovi
fertilized: 4 zoon 7 oosperm
fish: roe 5 berry 6 caviar
insect: nit
measuring device: 7 oometer
nest: 6 clutch
part of: 4 yolk 5 shell, white 7 albumen, latebra
Philippine duck: 5 balut
prefix: oo
small: 5 ovule
tested: 7 candled
unfertilized: 8 oosphere
white of: 5 glair 7 albumen

egg case: 4 ovum 6 ovisac

egg on: 4 abet, goad, urge 6 incite

egg-shaped: 4 ooid, oval 5 ovate, ovoid 6 ooidal 7 obovoid, ovaloid, oviform

egg to anger: 7 provoke

egg yolk: 7 liaison 8 lecithin

egger: 4 moth

eggnog: nog 8 beverage

eggplant: 7 brinjal 8 brinjaul 9 berengena

eggs: roe 5 spawn 6 graine 7 ahuatle
feeding on: 9 ovivorous

poached in cream: 7 shirred
eggshell: 8 cascaron
Egil's brother: 6 Volund
egis: 5 aigis, armor 6 shield 7 defence, defense 10 protection
Eglah: *husband:* 5 David
    son: 7 Ithream
eglantine: 8 eglatere, woodbine 10 sweetbrier 11 honeysuckle
Eglon's king: 5 Debir
ego: 4 self 7 conceit 11 personality, selfishness
egoism: 5 pride 6 oneism, vanity
egoist: 8 believer
egotism: 5 pride 6 vanity 7 conceit
egotistic: 7 selfish 9 conceited
egotistical: 7 selfish 9 conceited
egregious: 4 fine 5 gross 7 eminent 8 flagrant, shocking 9 excellent, prominent 10 remarkable 13 distinguished
egress: 4 exit 5 issue 6 outlet 7 outgate, passage, regress 9 departure
egret: 5 heron, plume 6 gaulin 8 gaulding
egrimony: 6 sorrow
Egypt: UAR 18 United Arab Republic
    air god: Shu
    animal: fox 4 adda, lynx 5 genet, hyena 6 jackal, jerboa 7 gazelle 9 ichneumon
    antelope: 5 bubal
    army chieftain: 6 sirdar
    beer: 6 zythum
    beetle: 6 scarab
    bird: 6 sicsac
    boat: 5 baris 8 dahabeah
    body: Ka 4 Sahu
    bottle: 6 doruck
    bull: 4 apis
    burial jar: 7 Canopus
    calendar: 4 Ahet, Apap, Tybi 5 Choik, Payni, Shemu, Thoth 6 Hathor, Mechir, Mesore, Paophi 7 Pachons 9 Phamenoth, Pharmuthi
    cap: fez
    capital: 5 Cairo 10 Alexandria
    cat-headed goddess: 4 Bast 5 Pakht
    Christian: 4 Copt
    city: No 4 Sais 5 Cairo, Gizeh, Luxor, Tanis 6 Abydos, Armant, Thebes 10 Alexandria
    civilization: 6 Tasian
    clover: 7 berseem
    cobra: 4 haje
    coin: 5 girsh, pound 7 piaster 8 millieme
    concubine: 5 Hagar
    cosmetic: 4 kohl
    cotton: Sak 4 Pima
    crocodile-headed god: 4 Sobk 5 Sebek
    cross: 4 ankh
    crown: 4 atef
    dam: 4 sadd, sudd 5 Aswan

    dancers: 7 ghawazi 8 ghawazee
    deity: Hor, Mut, Nut 4 Anta, Apet, Bast, Isis, Maat, Sati 5 Anaka 6 Hathor, Seshat, Tefnut 7 Nepthys 8 Nechebit
    descendant: 4 copt 6 fellah
    desert: 5 Scete, Skete
    dog: 6 saluki
    drink: 4 bosa, boza 5 bozah
    drug: 8 nepenthe
    elysium: 4 Aalu
    emblem: 4 aten 5 lotus
    gateway: 5 Pylon
    god: Set 4 Ptah, Seth 5 Thoth 6 Anubis 7 Serapis
    goddess: Mut, Nut 4 Bast, Isis 5 Pakht 6 Sekhet 8 Nekhebet
    governor: 5 Pasha
    guard: 6 ghafir 7 ghaffir
    gunde: 8 dragoman
    hawk-headed god: 5 Horus
    herb: 5 anise
    instrument: 7 arghool, arghoul, sistrum
    isthmus: 4 Suez
    judge of the dead: 6 Osiris
    king: So; Tut 4 Fuad, Mena 5 Menes 6 Ramses 7 Pharaoh, Ptolemy, Rameses 9 Amenhotep 11 Tutankhamen
    laborer: 5 aperu
    lake: 8 Menzaleh 13 Birket-el-Kurun
    language: 6 Arabic, Coptic
    lighthouse: 6 pharos
    lily: 6 calla, lotos, lotus
    lion-headed goddess: 4 Bast 5 Pakht 6 Sekhet
    lizard: 4 adda 5 scink, skink
    love goddess; 6 Hathor
    lute: 5 nabla
    maternity goddess: 4 Apet
    measure: apt, dra, hen, rob 4 dira, draa, kada, khet, ocha, roub, theb 5 abdat, ardab, ardeb, cubit, farde, keleh, kilah, sahme 6 artaba, aurure, baladi, kantar, kedlah, robhah, scheme 7 choryos, daribah, malouah, roubouh, toumnah 8 kassabah, kharouba 10 dira baladi, dira mimari, kerat kamel, nief keddah 11 feddan nasri
    monarch: 7 Pharaoh
    monument: 7 obelisk
    mountain: 5 Sinai
    native: 4 Copt 5 Nilot
    negro: 6 Nubian
    oasis: 4 Siwa 6 Dakhel 7 Farafra, Khargeh 8 Bahriyeh 12 Wah-el-Khargeh
    official: 5 mudir
    paper: 6 papyri 7 papyrus
    peasant: 6 fellah
    peninsula: 5 Sinai
    Pharaoh's headdress: 7 pschent

plant: 5 cumin 6 cummin, lentil
province: 4 Giza
queen: 9 Cleopatra, Nofretete
relic: 5 mummy
river: 4 Bahr, Nile
rulers: 9 Ptolemeis
sacred bird: 4 ibis
sacred bull: 4 apis
sacred flower: 5 lotos, lotus
sanctuary: 5 secos, sekos
seal: 6 scarab
serpent: 5 apepi
shrub: kat
solar disk: 4 Aten
soul: Ba
stone: 7 rosetta
sun god: Ra; Tem, Tum 4 Atmu, Atum
symbol: uta 4 ankh 6 scarab
talisman: 5 angle
temple: 4 Idfu 5 Luxor 6 Abydos, Karnak,
 Osiris 7 Dendera
title: 4 atef 5 pasha 7 Pharaoh
tomb: 7 mastaba, pyramid
underworld: 4 Aaru, Duat 6 Amenti
vase: 7 canopic
viper: 8 cerastes
vulture-headed goddess: Mut 8 Nekhebet
waterway: 4 Nile
weight: ket, oka, oke 4 dera, heml, khar,
 okia, rotl 5 artal, artel, deben, kerat,
 okieh, ratel, uckia 6 hamlah, kantar 7
 drachma, quintal
wind: 6 kamsin 7 chamsin, kamseen, khamsin 8 khamseen
Egyptian: 4 Arab, Copt 7 African, Ptolemy
Ehud's son: 6 Naaman
eident: 4 busy 7 careful 8 diligent
eider duck: 4 colk
eidetic: 5 vivid
eidolon: 4 icon 5 ghost, image 7 phantom 10
 apparition
eight: eta(G.) 6 ogdoad
 combining form: 4 octo
 group of: 5 octad, octet 6 octave 7 octette
 set of: 5 octad 6 ogdoad
eight-sided: 9 octagonal
eighth: *circle:* 6 octant
 day after nones: 4 ides
 order: 5 octic
eighty: pi(G.) 9 fourscore
Eire: 4 Erin
 capital: 6 Tralee
 legislature: 4 Dail
Eireannach: 8 Irishman
ejaculate: 5 blurt, eject 7 exclaim
ejaculation: 7 begorra 8 uttering 11 exclamation
eject: 4 boot, cast, emit, oust, spat, spew,
 spit, void 5 avoid, erupt, evict, expel,
 spout, spurt, vomit 6 banish, bounce 7 dismiss, exclude, extrude, obtrude 8 disgorge
 9 discharge, ejaculate 10 disembogue, dispossess
ejection: 6 ouster 8 eviction 9 expulsion
eke: 4 also 7 augment, enlarge, husband,
 stretch 8 appendix, increase, lengthen,
 likewise 10 postscript, supplement
eking: 7 piecing 8 addition 12 augmentation
el: 4 bend
El Salvador: *coin:* 4 peso 5 colon 7 centavo
 measure: 4 vara 6 fanega, tercia 7 botella,
 cajuela, manzana
 weight: 4 caja
elaborate: 5 great 6 ornate, refine 7 develop, enlarge, labored, perfect 9 embellish, perfected 11 complicated, extravagant, painstaking
elaborated: 7 wrought 9 superfine
elaboration: 10 production 11 development
Elam: *capital:* 4 Susa
 king: 12 Chedorlaomer
elan: 4 dash 5 ardor, gusto, verve 6 spirit,
 warmth 7 potency 9 eagerness 10 enthusiasm
elanet: 4 kite
elapse: go 4 pass, slip 6 expire
elasmobranch fish: ray
elastic: 6 garter, spongy 7 buoyant, springy
 8 cheverel, cheveril, flexible, stretchy 9
 expansive, resilient 10 propulsive
 fluid: gas
 material from whales: 6 baleen
elasticity science: 9 elaterics
elastin: 10 albuminoid
elate: 4 buoy 5 cheer, exalt, exult, flush,
 lofty, raise 6 excite, please, thrill 7 elevate, gladden, inflate, success 8 elevated,
 heighten, inspirit 9 stimulate 10 exhilarate
elated: 5 chuff, happy, vogie 6 jovial 7 excited, exulted, jocular 8 exultant, inflated,
 jubilant 9 cock-a-hoop
elater: 6 beetle 8 skipjack
elaterite: 7 bitumen
Elatha's son: 4 Bres
elation: joy 4 glee 10 exaltation
Elatus' daughter: 6 Caenis 7 Caeneus
Elbe tributary: 4 Eger, Iser
elbow: 4 bend 5 ancon, joint, nudge, shove
 6 jostle
 bend: 4 tope 5 drink
 bone: 4 ulna 5 ulnae
 pert. to: 5 ulnar 8 anconeal
elbowroom: 6 leeway
elcaja: 6 mafura
elchee, elchi: 5 envoy 10 ambassador
eld: 9 antiquity

elder: ain, iva 4 aine 5 prior 6 senior 7 ancient 8 ancestor, danewort 9 elderwort, presbyter 10 forefather

elderly: 4 aged, gray 6 senile

eldest: 5 eigne 6 oldest

eldritch: 4 eery 5 eerie, weird 7 uncanny 9 frightful

Eleanor's husband: 7 Henry II

eleatic: 11 xenophanean

elect: 4 call, pick 6 assume, choose, chosen. decide, prefer, select 9 legislate

election: 6 choice 9 balloting 10 plebiscite 11 alternative
majority of votes: 9 plurality

electioneer: 5 stump

elective: 8 optional 9 voluntary

elector: 5 voter 6 elisor 7 chooser 11 constituent

Electra: *brother:* 7 Orestes
father: 9 Agamemnon
husband: 7 Thaumas
mother: 12 Klytemnestra
son: 8 Dardanus

electric: 4 elod 6 static 8 magnetic
appliance: 4 iron, oven 5 dryer, mixer, stove 6 heater, washer 7 blender, broiler, toaster
carrier: 9 conductor
circuit regulator: 7 booster
coil: 5 tesla
conductor: 6 ohmage
current: AC., DC.
current meter: 7 ammeter 9 voltmeter
current moderator: 5 coder 9 rheometer 10 attenuator
device: 6 dynamo 8 divertor, rheostat 9 amplifier, capacitor, condenser
generator: 6 dynamo
instrument: 6 dynamo 8 rheostat, rheotome 9 condenser, generator
light: arc 4 neon 12 incandescent
measuring unit: es; amp, ohm, rel 4 volt, watt 5 barad, farad, henry, joule 6 ampere, proton 7 coulomb 8 kilowatt
motion: 14 electrodynamic
motor part: 10 commutator
od: 4 elod
particle: ion
pole: 5 anode 7 cathode
power: 7 wattage
resistance: 6 ohmage
safety device: 4 fuse
strength: 8 amperage
transmission: 5 radio
wave meter: 9 ondometer

electrify: 7 startle

electrocute: 7 execute

electrode: 5 anode 7 cathode, kathode
controlling electron tube: 4 grid

negative: 7 cathode, kathode

electronic tube: 6 triode, vacuum 8 klystron

electrum: 5 amber

Electryon: *brother:* 6 Mestor
daughter: 7 Alcmene
father: 7 Perseus
mother: 9 Andromeda
wife: 5 Anaxo

eleemosynary: 4 free 7 almoner 9 dependent 10 charitable, gratuitous

elegance: 4 chic 5 grace, taste 6 finery, luxury, polish 8 courtesy, grandeur, splendor 9 propriety, recherche 10 concinnity, refinement 12 gracefulness

elegant: 4 chic, dink, fine, posh 5 civil 6 dainty, dressy, facete, minion, superb, urbane 7 cleanly, courtly, featish, featous, genteel, minikin, refined 8 delicate, graceful, handsome, polished, tasteful 9 admirable, beautiful, excellent, exquisite 10 concinnous, fastidious

elegantly: 8 gingerly

elegiac: 8 mournful 9 plaintive

elegiacal: 8 mournful

elegist: 4 Gray, poet 6 Milton 10 Propertius

elegit: 4 writ

elegy: 4 poem, song 5 dirge 6 lament 7 epicede 9 epicedium 11 lamentation

element: 5 metal, stuff 7 essence 8 rudiment 9 component 10 ingredient 11 constituent, environment
chemical: tin(Sn) 4 gold(Au), Iron(Fe), lead(Pb), neon(Ne), zinc(Zn) 5 argon(A), boron(B), radon(Rn), xenon(Xe) 6 barium(Ba), carbon(C), cerium(Ce), cesium(Cs), cobalt(Co), copper(Cu), erbium(Er), helium(He), indium(In), iodine(I), nickel(Ni), osmium(Os), oxygen(O), radium(Ra), silver(Ag), sodium(Na) 7 arsenic(As), bismuth(Bi), bromine(Br), cadmium(Cd), calcium(Ca), gallium(Ga), hafnium(Hf), holmium(Ho), iridium(Ir), krypton(Kr), lithium(Li), mercury(Hg), niobium(Cb), rhenium(Re), rhodium(Rh), silicon(Si), sulphur(S.), terbium(Tb), thorium(Th), thulium(Tm), uranium(U), yttrium(Y) 8 actinium(Ac), aluminum(Al), antimony(Sb), astatine(At), chlorine(Cl), chromium(Cr), Europium(Eu), fluorine(F), hydrogen(H), illinium(Il), lutecium(Lu), masurium(Ma), nitrogen(N), platinum(Pt), polonium(Po), rubidium(Rb), samarium(Sm), scandium(Sc), selenium(Se), tantalum(Ta), thallium(Tl), titanium(Ti), tungsten(W), vanadium(V) 9 beryllium(Be), columbium(Cb), germanium(Ge), lanthanum(La), magnesium(Mg), manganese(Mn), neodymium(Nd), palladium(Pd), potassium(K), ruthenium(Ru),

strontium(Sr), tellurium(Te), virginium(Vi), ytterbium(Yb), zirconium(Zr) 10 dysprosium(Dy), gadolinium(Gd), molybdenum(Mo) 11 phosphorous(P), 12 praseodymium(Pr) 13 protoactinium(Pa)

combining power: 7 valence

decomposed: 5 anion

different weight: 7 isotope

even valence: 6 artiad

family: 7 halogen

minute: 5 monad

nonmetallic: 5 boron 6 bromin, iodine 7 bromine, silicon

nonvolatile: 6 barium

of air: 5 argon 6 oxygen 8 nitrogen

poisonous: 7 arsenic

rare earth: 6 erbium

elemental: 4 pure 5 basic 6 primal, simple 7 primary 10 elementary 11 fundamental, rudimentary

elemental spirit: 5 genie

elementary: 6 simple 7 initial 8 inchoate 9 elemental 10 rudimental, uncombined 11 fundamental, rudimentary

organism: 5 monad

reader: 6 primer

elemi: 5 anime, resin 9 oleoresin

pert. to: 7 elemine

elenge: 6 dreary, remote 7 tedious 9 miserable

elephant: cow 4 bull, calf 5 rogue, hathi 6 tusker, muckna 7 marmoth 8 oliphant, mastodon 9 pachyderm

call: 4 barr 7 trumpet

cry: 4 barr

dentin: 5 ivory

driver: 6 mahout

ear: 4 taro

enclosure: 5 kraal

extinct: 8 mastodon

goad: 5 ankus

group: 4 herd

keeper: 6 mahout

male: 4 bull

pert. to: 11 pachydermic

saddle: 6 howdah

seat: 6 howdah

trappings for: 5 jhool

trunk: 9 proboscis

tusk: 5 ivory 9 scrivello

young: 4 calf

elephant boy: 4 Sabu

elephantine: 4 huge 8 enormous, ungainly 9 ponderous

goddess: 4 Sati

elevate: 4 hain, lift, rear, rise 5 elate, erect, exalt, extol, heave, hoist, raise, setup,

tower 6 uplift 7 advance, dignify, enhance, ennoble, glorify, promote 8 heighten, inspirit 10 exhilarate

elevated: el 4 high 5 great, lofty, noble, risen, steep 6 elated, raised, rising 7 exalted 8 majestic

elevation: 4 bank, hill, rise, toot 5 horst, mound, ridge 6 height, uplift 8 altitude, eminence, highness, swelling 10 exaltation

of mind: 7 anagoge

elevator: bin 4 cage, lift, silo 5 hoist 9 ascenseur

elf: fay, hob, imp, oaf, pug 4 fane, peri, pixy 5 dwarf, elfin, fairy, gnome, ouphe, pigmy, pixie 6 elfkin, goblin, sprite 7 brownie, incubus, succubi 8 succubus 10 changeling, leprechaun

elf dock: 10 elecampane

elfin: elf 5 child 6 urchin

elfish: 5 elfin 6 elvish, impish 7 elflike, tricksy 11 mischievous

elfland: 9 fairyland

elfwort: 10 elecampane

Elgin marbles: 10 sculptures

Eli: 4 Yale

son: 6 Hophni 8 Phinehas

Eliam's daughter: 9 Bathsheba

Elian: 8 Eretrian

elicit: 4 draw, milk, pump 5 claim, educe, evoke, exact, wrest, wring 6 deduce, demand, entice, extort, induce 7 extract 9 elicitate

elide: 4 omit, skip 5 annul 6 ignore 7 destroy, nullify 8 demolish, suppress 9 apocopate

eligible: fit 6 worthy 8 suitable 9 desirable, qualified

Elijah: 5 Elias 7 prophet 8 Tishbite

eliminate: 5 educe, expel 6 delete, except, ignore, remove 7 divulge, exclude, excrete, release, silence 8 separate

elimination: 9 excursion

Eliot: *hero:* 6 Marner

heroine: 6 Romola

eliquate: 4 melt 5 smelt 6 strain 7 clarify, liquate, liquefy

elision mark: 10 apostrophe

elisor: 7 elector

Elisha: *father:* 7 Shaphat

home: 11 Abelmeholah

servant: 6 Gehazi

Elissa: See **Dido**

elite: 4 best 6 choice, flower, select 9 oligarchy 10 uppercrust 11 aristocracy 12 quintessence

gathering: 6 galaxy

elixir: 6 spirit 7 arcanum, cordial, cureall, panacea 12 quintessence *of life:* 6 amrita 7 amreeta

Elizabeth I: 4 Bess 6 Oriana

   mother: 6 Boleyn

elk: 4 alce, deer 5 aland, eland, moose 6 sambar, wapiti 7 sambhur

   genus of: 5 alces

ell: 6 alnage 8 addition

ellipse: 4 oval

ellipsoidal: 4 oval

elliptical: 4 oval 5 ovate

elm: *family of:* 8 ulmaceae

   fruit of: 6 samara

   rock: 5 wahoo

Elmo's fire: See **Saint Elmo's fire**

elocute: 7 declaim

elocution: 7 oratory 9 eloquence

elocutionist: 6 reader 7 reciter

elodian: 8 tortoise

eloge: 6 eulogy 7 oration 8 encomium 9 panegyric

elogium: 7 oration 11 inscription

eloign: 6 convey, remove 7 conceal

eloine: 7 abscond

elongate: 6 remove 7 stretch 8 lengthen, protract

elongated: 4 lank, long 6 linear, oblong 7 prolate, slender 9 stretched

elope: 6 decamp 7 abscond, getaway

eloquence: 6 facund 7 fluency, oratory 9 elocution, facundity, loftiness

   teacher of: 6 rhetor

eloquent: 6 facund, fervid, fluent 7 renable 10 expressive, meaningful, oratorical, persuasive 11 impassioned, significant

else: or; ens 4 ense 5 other 7 besides, instead 9 otherwise 10 additional

elsewhere: 5 alibi

elt: 5 knead

elucidate: 5 clear, lucid 7 explain 8 simplify 9 interpret 10 illustrate

elude: 4 flee, foil, mock 5 avoid, dodge, evade 6 baffle, befool, delude, escape, illude 7 beguile, deceive 9 frustrate

elusive: 4 eely 6 subtle, tricky 7 elusory, evasive, subtile 8 baffling 9 lubricous 10 impalpable

elusory: 7 elusive, evasive

elver: eel

elves: See **elf**

elvish: 11 mischievous

Elysian: 8 beatific, blissful 10 delightful

Elysium: 4 Eden 8 Paradise

elytrin: 6 chitin

elytrum of beetle: 5 shard

emaciated: 4 lean 5 gaunt 6 peaked, skinny, wasted

emaciation: 5 niton, tabes 7 atrophy 8 marasmus 11 attenuation

emanant: 9 radiating

emanate: 4 flow 5 arise, issue 6 effuse 7 breathe, outcome, proceed, radiate 9 effluence, originate

emanation: 4 aura 5 aurae(pl.), niton 6 efflux 7 outcome 9 ectoplasm, effluence 10 exhalation 11 consequence

emanative: 7 issuant

emancipate: 4 free 7 manumit, release 8 liberate, unfetter 11 affranchise, enfranchise

emancipation: 7 freedom, release 10 liberation 11 deliverance, manumission 15 enfranchisement

emancipator: 5 freer, Moses 7 Lincoln 9 deliverer

emasculate: 4 geld 6 soften 8 castrate, enervate

embale: 4 pack

embalm: 4 balm, cere 5 mummy 6 balsam

embalmer: 5 cerer 10 undertaker

embankment: 4 bank, bund, dike, fill, quay 5 digue, levee, mound, revet 6 staith 7 backing 9 banquette

embar: 4 stop 6 hinder

embargo: 5 edict, order 8 blockade, stoppage 10 impediment, inhibition 11 prohibition, requisition

embark: 4 sail, ship 6 engage, enlist, invest

embarrass: 4 clog 5 abash, annoy, shame, upset 6 boggle, gravel, hamper, hinder, hobble, impede 7 confuse, flummox, nonplus 8 bewilder, confound, dumfound, encumber, entangle, handicap, obstruct, straiten 9 discomfit 10 complicate, disconcert

embarrassment: fix 5 shame 6 caddle, hobble 9 abashment, confusion 10 discomfort, impediment, perplexity 11 encumbrance, involvement 12 bewilderment, discomfiture, discomposure, entanglement 13 inconvenience

embassy: 7 ambassy 9 ambassade, embassage 10 ambassiate

embattle: 6 crenel 7 fortify

embattled: 7 crenele 8 crenelee, crenelle

embattlement: 7 parapet

embay: 5 bathe 7 shelter, suffuse 8 encircle, surround

embed: set 6 engage

embellish: 4 deck, gild, trim 5 adorn, dress, grace 6 bedeck, blazon, emboss, enrich, flower 7 apparel, bedrape, emblaze, garnish, varnish 8 beautify, decorate, flourish, ornament 9 elaborate, embroider

embellished: 6 florid, gested, ornate

embellishment: 7 agremen 8 agrement, mounting, ornament 9 fioritura, furniture, garniture 13 ornamentation

ember: ash 4 coal 5 aizle 6 cinder

embezzle: 5 steal 8 peculate, squander 9 dissipate

embezzlement: 5 theft

embitter: 4 sour 7 acidify, envenom 8 acerbate 9 acidulate 10 exacerbate, exasperate

emblaze: 5 adorn, honor 6 kindle 9 embellish

emblazon: 4 laud 5 adorn, extol 6 blazon 7 display, exhibit, glorify 8 celebrate

emblem: bar 4 aten, mace, orle, sign, star, type 5 badge, image, tiara, token 6 device, diadem, figure, sabcat, symbol 7 impresa, imprese, scepter, sceptre 8 allegory, colophon, insignia 9 character, laticlave, prototype 10 cognizance
of authority: 4 mace
of clan: 5 totem
of U.S.: 5 eagle

emblematic: 5 typal 7 typical 8 symbolic 10 figurative

emblic: 4 aula 5 aulae(pl.)

embodiment: map 6 avatar 11 incarnation 15 personification
of Ptah: 4 Apis

embody: 5 unite 7 contain 8 coalesce, organize 9 incarnate, personify 10 comprehend 11 incorporate

embolden: 5 bield, brave, nerve 6 assure 7 hearten 9 encourage, enhearten

embolism: 8 stoppage 9 occlusion 11 obstruction 13 intercalation

embolus: 4 clot

embosom, imbosom: 6 foster 7 cherish, enclose, shelter 8 surround

emboss: 4 boss, hide, knob 5 adorn, chase 6 indent 7 conceal, enclose, exhaust, inflate 8 ornament 9 embellish, embroider, insheathe

embossing: 8 celature

embowed: 5 bowed

embower: 5 bower

embrace: hug 4 clip, coll, fold, love, neck, side 5 adopt, bosom, brace, chain, clasp, cling, enarm, grasp, halch, halse, inarm 6 abrazo, accept, caress, clinch, comply, cuddle, enfold, huddle, inclip, infold, plight 7 amplect, cherish, contain, enclose, espouse, include, involve 8 accolade, complect, compress, comprise, comprize, conclude, encircle 9 encompass 10 comprehend 11 amplexation

embrangle: 7 confuse 8 entangle

embrocation: 6 arnica 8 liniment

embroider: tat 4 lace 5 couch, panel 6 emboss, frieze, stitch 8 ornament 9 embellish 10 exaggerate

embroidered: 5 brode 6 brodee 7 browden

embroidery: 4 lace 5 brede 6 bonnaz, edging, hedebo 7 orphrey 8 arrasene

figure: 6 etoile
frame: 7 taboret
hole: 6 eyelet
machine-made: 6 bonnaz
thread: 5 floss

embroil: 5 broil 6 jumble 7 perplex, trouble 8 disorder, distract, entangle 9 commingle, implicate 10 complicate

embrown: tan

embryo: 5 cadet, fetus, ovule 6 foetus 9 peritroch 10 conception
young: 8 blastema

embusque: 7 shirker, slacker

eme: 5 uncle 6 friend, gossip 8 relative

emeer, emir: 5 pasha, ruler

emend: 4 edit, mend 5 alter, amend 6 better, reform, repeal, revise 7 correct, improve, rectify, redress

emendate: 7 correct, rectify

emendator: 6 editor

emerald: 5 beryl, color, green 7 smaragd

Emerald Isle: 4 Erin 7 Ireland

emerge: dip 4 loom, rise 5 issue 6 appear, plunge 10 disembogue

emergence: 4 need 8 debouche, exigence 9 occurrence, outgrowth

emergency: 5 pinch 6 crisis, crises(pl.), strait 8 exigency, juncture 9 necessity

emergent: 6 rising

Emerson: *friend:* 7 Thoreau
philosophy: 17 transcendentalism

emery: 8 abrasive, corundum 11 carborundum

emetic: 8 evacuant

emetic holly: 6 yaupon

emeute: 6 tumult 8 outbreak

emigrant: 6 emigre 7 exodist, settler 8 colonist, stranger

emigrate: 4 move

emigre: 7 refugee

eminence: 4 berg, mote, note, rise, scar, toot 6 ascent, height, renown, rideau 9 elevation, loftiness 10 projection, prominence 12 protuberance 13 transcendency

eminent: big 4 arch, high 5 chief, great, lofty, noble, noted 6 famous, marked, signal 8 glorious, renowned, singular, towering 9 egregious 10 celebrated, noteworthy 11 conspicuous, illustrious, outstanding 13 distinguished

emir, emeer: 5 noble, ruler, title 6 leader, prince 8 governor 9 chieftain, commander
province: 7 emirate

emissary: spy 5 agent, scout 8 delegate

emission: 9 radiation

emissive: 8 exhalant

emit: 4 beam, cast, give, pour, send, shed, vent 5 avoid, eject, exert, exude, fling, issue, utter **6** decant, evolve, exhale, expire **7** distill, exhaust, radiate **8** transmit **9** discharge, irradiate

heat: **4** glow

light: **4** glow **9** luminesce

offensive odors: **4** reek

emmer: 5 spelt, wheat

emmet: 4 ant **7** pismire **8** formicid

emolliate: 6 soften **10** effeminate

emollient: 7 lenient **8** lenitive

emolument: 4 fees **5** wages **6** income, profit, salary **7** benefit, stipend **9** advantage **12** compensation

Emory University site: 7 Atlanta

emote: act **7** overact

emotion: ire **4** love **5** agony, anger, grief, heart **6** affect, effect, raptus, snivel **7** ecstasy, feeling, passion **8** gramercy, movement **9** affection, agitation, sentiment **11** disturbance **14** susceptibility

without: **9** apathetic

emotionable: 11 sensational

emotional: 7 emotive **9** rhapsodic **10** hysterical, passionate

emotionalism: 8 hysteria

emotionless: 5 staid **6** torpid **9** apathetic, unfeeling

empathy: 4 pity, ruth **8** affinity, sympathy **13** understanding

emperor: 4 czar, king, tsar **5** Akbar, ruler **6** sultan **7** Baginda, monarch **9** commander, imperator, sovereign

Holy Roman: **4** Otho, Otto

empery: 6 empire **8** dominion **11** sovereignty

emphasis: 6 accent, stress **8** salience

emphasize: 6 accent, betone, stress **9** punctuate **10** accentuate

emphatic: 7 earnest, marcato **8** enfatico, forcible, positive **9** energetic

empire: 4 rule, sway **5** power, realm, reign, state **6** domain, empery **7** control, kingdom **8** dominion **11** sovereignty

Empire State: 7 New York

empiric: 5 quack **8** impostor **9** charlatan **10** mountebank

emplacement: 7 battery **8** platform

employ: fee, use **4** busy, hire, wage **5** beset **6** bestow, engage, infold, occupy, supply **7** concern, enclose, involve, service, utilize **8** exercise

employed: 4 busy **6** unidle **7** engaged

employee: 5 clerk **11** salesperson

bank: **5** guard **6** teller **7** cashier **8** watchman **10** bookkeeper

minor: cog **6** helper **9** assistant

slaughterhouse: **5** sider

employees: men **4** help **5** hands

employer: 4 boss, user **6** gaffer **7** manager **12** entrepreneur

employment: use **4** task, toil, work **5** craft, trade, usage **7** calling, purpose **8** business, vocation **10** engagement, occupation, profession

empoison: 5 taint **6** poison **7** corrupt, deprave, envenom

emporium: 4 mart, shop **5** bazar, store **6** bazaar, market, staple

empower: 6 enable **7** entitle **8** delegate, deputize **9** authorize **10** commission

empresa: 5 motto **6** device **7** tsarina

empress: 5 queen, ruler

Byzantine: **5** Irene

Russian: **7** czarina, tsarina

empress tree: 9 paulownia

empresse: 6 ardent **9** impetuous

emprise, emprize: 9 undertake **10** enterprise

empt: 5 empty

emptiness: 4 void **7** inanity, vacancy, vacuity **9** inanition

emptio: 6 buying **8** purchase

empty: rid **4** bare, boss, dump, empt, farm, free, howe, idle, leer, pour, toom, void **5** addle, avoid, blank, drain, equal, expel, inane **6** barren, bubble, devoid, hollow, jejune, unload, vacant, vacate **7** deplete, exhaust, untaken, vacuate, vacuous **8** disgorge, evacuate, evanesce, negation, unfilled **9** discharge, moonshine **10** unburdened, unoccupied **11** rodomontade

comb. form: ken **4** keno

empty space: 4 void **5** blank **6** vacuum

emptying: 8 evacuant **9** avoidance

Empusa: 7 specter **9** hobgoblin

empyreal: 7 sublime **9** celestial

empyrean: 5 ether **7** heavens **9** firmament

emu: 4 rhea **6** ratite

emulate: ape, vie **4** copy **5** equal, excel, rival **7** compete, imitate

emulation: 6 strife **7** contest **10** contention **11** competition

emulator: 5 rival

emulsive: 9 softening

emyd: 6 turtle

enable: 7 empower, entitle, qualify

enact: 4 pass **6** decree, effect, ordain **7** actuate, appoint, perform, portray **9** legislate, personate, represent **10** constitute

enactment: law **4** doom **6** assize, decree **7** statute **12** constitution **14** representation

enactor: 6 player **10** legislator

enamel: 5 glaze, gloss, paint **6** aumail **7** dentine, schmelz **8** cosmetic, schmelze

enamelled: 10 variegated

enamelware: 7 Limoges

enamor, enamour: 4 love 5 charm 7 captive 9 captivate, fascinate

enamorata, inamorata: 5 lover 10 sweetheart

enamored, enamoured: 4 fond 5 epris 6 eprise 7 amorous, charmed, smitten 10 fascinated, infatuated

Enan's son: 5 Ahira

enarm: 4 lard 7 embrace, enhance

enarme: 5 strap

enate: 7 related

encamp: 4 tent 5 lodge, pitch 7 bivouac

encampment: 5 siege 7 bivouac, castrum(L.)

encase: 7 inclose

encave: 6 entomb

enchain: 6 fetter

enchant: 5 charm 6 delude, glamor 7 bewitch, delight, glamour 8 ensorcel 9 captivate, enrapture, ensorcell, fascinate, spellbind

enchanted: 4 rapt

enchanting: 10 bewitching

enchantment: hex 5 charm, magic, spell 7 chantry, gramary, sorcery 8 gramarye, witchery 9 chantment 10 necromancy, witchcraft 11 fascination, incantation

enchantress: 5 Circe, fairy, Medea 9 sorceress

encharge: 7 entrust 10 commission

enchase: 7 engrave

enchiridion: 6 manual 8 handbook

enchorial: 6 native 8 domestic

encina: oak

encipher: 4 code

encircle: orb 4 belt, clip, coil, gird, girt, hoop, pale, ring, rink, zone 5 belay, brace, embay, embow, girth, inorb 6 circle, emball, engirt, enlace, girdle, impale 7 betrend, embrace, enclose, environ, wreathe 8 cincture, ensphere, surround 9 encompass 12 circumscribe 13 circumference

encircled: 4 girt 6 ringed 10 surrounded

encircling: 6 around 8 encyclic

encircling band: 4 zone

encloak: 6 mantle

enclose: bay, box, hem, mew, orb, pin, rim 4 case, gird, pale, wall, yard 5 bound, bower, bught, chest, fence, hedge, house 6 bought, circle, corral, emboss, empark, employ, encase, encyst, enfold, enlock, impark, incase, picket, pocket 7 contain, embosom, embrace, envelop, harness, imbosom 8 comprise, comprize, conclude, encircle, imprison, palisade, surround 9 encompass 10 comprehend 12 circumscribe

enclosure: hag, haw, mew, pen, ree, sty 4 bawn, cage, coop, fold, sept, wall, yard 5 atajo, court, fence, kraal, pleck, pound, reeve 6 aviary, corral, cowpen, garden, hurdle, kennel, paling, prison 7 closure,

paddock, puddock 8 cincture, clausure, cloister, sepiment

animal: pen, sty, par 4 yard, cage, cote, weir, yair, yare 5 booly, crawl, kench, gotra, kraal, atajo 6 booley, corral, runway, cancha, keddah 8 poundage 9 sheepcote

kind of: 4 bawn, boma, cage 5 bomar, carol, crawl 6 cruive 7 nacelle, paddock, stadium 8 delubrum, stockade 9 cofferdam

encomiast: 8 eulogist 10 panegyrist

encomium: 5 eloge 6 eulogy, praise 7 plaudit, tribute 9 panegyric 10 compliment

encompass: 4 be-go, belt, clip, gird, ring, wall 5 belie, beset 6 begird, circle, engird 7 embrace, enclose, environ, include 8 encircle, engirdle, surround 9 beleaguer, circulate 10 circumvent 12 circumscribe

encompassed: 5 bayed 6 begirt 10 surrounded

encompassing: 13 circumambient

encore: bis 5 again 6 recall, repeat 10 repitition

anti: boo 4 hiss 7 catcall

encorel: 5 again

encounter: 4 bide, coil, face, meet, rink 5 brush, fight, force, incur, onset 6 accost, affray, assail, attack, battle, breast, combat, oppose 7 address, affront, contest, counter, dispute, hosting 8 conflict, confront, skirmish 9 collision, interview 10 engagement, foregather, occurrence, tournament

courageously: 5 beard, brave 7 weather

encountered: 4 moot

encourage: 4 abet, back 5 boost, cheer, impel, nerve 6 advise, assure, exhort, foment, foster, incite, induce, second, uphold 7 advance, animate, cherish, comfort, confirm, console, enliven, forward, hearten, inspire, promote 8 embolden, inspirit, reassure 9 instigate, stimulate 10 strengthen 11 comfortable, countenance

encouragement: 5 flush 6 hurrah 7 fomento 9 incentive, patronage 11 fomentation

encouraging: 8 favoring 11 comfortable, inspiriting 12 advantageous

Encratite: 6 Tatian 9 Tatianist

encraty: 10 abstinence

encroach: 5 poach 6 invade, trench 7 impinge, intrude 8 entrench, infringe, intrench, trespass

encroachment: 6 inroad 10 aggression, infraction

encuirassed: 7 armored 8 loricate

encumber: 4 clog, load 5 beset, check 6 burden, hamper, hinder, impede, moider, retard, saddle, weight **7** involve, oppress **8** entangle, handicap, obstruct, overcome, overload **9** embarrass **10** overburden

encumbered: 5 heavy

encumbrance: 4 clog, lien, load **5** claim **6** burden, charge **7** trouble **8** mortgage **9** cumbrance **10** impediment, perplexity **11** impedimenta(pl.) **13** embarrassment

encyclic: 8 circular **10** encircling **13** comprehensive

encyclopedia: 4 tome

encyclopedic learning: *person of:* **7** scholar **10** polyhistor

end: aim, tip **4** fate, goal, heel, stop, tail **5** amend, cease, close, death, ensue, finis, issue, limit, napoo, omega, raise, scrap, stash **6** define, design, expire, finale, finish, napooh, object, period, upshot, windup **7** abolish, achieve, closure, destroy, lineman, outgive, purpose, remnant **8** boundary, complete, conclude, dissolve, finality, surcease, terminal, terminus **9** cessation, determine, extremity, intention, objective, terminate **10** completion, conclusion, denouement, expiration **11** consequence, destruction, discontinue, termination **12** consummation **14** accomplishment

comb. form: **4** telo

loose: tag

musical: **4** coda, fine

remove: tip **4** clip

tending to: **5** telic

upper: tip **4** apex, head

End of World: 15 Gotterdammerung

end result: 7 product

endamage: 4 harm **6** injure

endanger: 6 hazard **7** imperil **10** compromise, jeopardize

endearing: 7 lovable **9** caressing

endearment: 6 caress

term of: hon **4** dear **5** aroon, honey **7** acushla, sweetie **10** mavourneen

endeavor, endeavour: aim, try **4** best, mint, seek **5** assay, essay, ettle, exert, study, tempt, trial **6** affair, effort, strife, strive **7** afforce, attempt **8** exertion, struggle **9** undertake

ended: 4 done, over, past **8** finished

endemic: 5 local

ending: 6 finale **11** termination

adjective: ic

adverbial: ly

having same: **11** coterminous **12** conterminous

participial: ed

superlative: est

endive: 7 chicory **8** escarole

endless: 7 eternal, forever, undying **8** immortal, infinite, unending **9** boundless,

ceaseless, continual, incessant, perpetual, unceasing **10** continuous **11** everlasting, measureless **12** interminable **13** uninterrupted

endlessly: 7 forever

endlong: 5 along **10** lengthwise **14** longitudinally

endmost: 8 farthest, remotest

endoderm: 8 entomere

endorse, indorse: 4 back, sign **5** boost **6** second **7** approve, certify, support **8** advocate, sanction **9** authorize, guarantee **11** countenance

endorsement: 4 fiat, visa **5** rider **7** backing **8** approval, sanction **9** signature

endow: dow, due **4** dote, vest **5** dower, endue, equip, found, indue **6** clothe, dotate, enrich, invest **7** furnish, instate **8** bequeath

with bodily form: **11** materialize

with power: **8** energize

endowment: 4 gift **5** dower, dowry **6** talent **7** apanage, chantry **8** appanage, dotation **9** mentality **10** foundation

endpiece: 5 chump

endue: due **5** endow, teach **6** clothe, invest **8** instruct

endurable: 7 livable **8** bearable **9** tolerable **10** sufferable **11** supportable

endurance: 5 pluck **7** durance, stamina **8** gameness, hardship, patience, strength **9** fortitude, suffering **10** sufferance **11** continuance, persistance, resignation **12** perseverance

endure: vie, **4** bear, bide, dree, dure, last, tide, wear **5** abear, abide, allow, brook, stand, thole **6** abrook, drudge, harden, remain, suffer **7** comfort, forbear, persist, sustain, toughen, undergo **8** continue, forebear, tolerate **9** exantlate, withstand **10** strengthen

endured: 5 borne

enduring: 4 fast **6** biding **7** durable, eternal, lasting, patient **8** immortal, remanent **9** continual, perennial, permanent **11** everlasting **12** imperishable

endwise: 7 erectly

Endymion: *mother:* **6** Calyce

son: **7** Aetolus

loved by: **6** Selene

enemy: fae, foe **4** Axis, feid **5** devil, fiend, Satan **6** foeman **7** hostile **8** opponent **9** adversary, ill-wisher **10** antagonist, backfriend

energetic: 4 fast, hard, live **5** brisk, dashy **6** active, hearty, hustle **7** arduous **8** emphatic, forceful, forcible, vigorous **9** dynamical, strenuous **10** expressive **12** enterprising

energize: 7 animate

energumen: 7 fanatic 8 demoniac 10 enthusiast

energy: go; pep, vim, zip 4 bang, bent, birr, life 5 force, nerve, power, steam, vigor 6 intake, output, spirit 7 potency 8 activity, strength 9 animation
lack: 5 atony 6 anergy 7 aneuria
measuring device: 9 ergometer
pert. to: 7 actinic
potential: 4 edar 5 ergal
unit: erg 4 dyne 5 ergon, joule 7 atomerg, quantum 8 dinamode 9 megajoule 10 horsepower

enervate: sap 6 weaken 7 unnerve 8 enfeeble 9 enslumber 10 debilitate

enfeeble: 4 numb 5 shake 6 appall, deaden, impair, soften, weaken 7 depress 8 enervate 9 attenuate, undermine 10 debilitate

enfeebled: fey 4 numb 9 dissolute

enfilade: 4 rake

enfold: lap 4 wrap 5 clasp, cover, enrol 6 comply, enlace, enroll, enwrap, swathe 7 embrace, enclose, envelop

enforce: 5 exact 6 coerce, compel 7 execute, implant 9 constrain, prosecute

enfranchise: 4 free 7 deliver, manumit, release 8 liberate 10 emancipate

engage: 4 book, gage, hire, join, mesh, rent, sign 5 agree, catch, enter, lease, trade 6 absorb, arrest, embark, employ, enlist, induce, oblige, occupy, pledge 7 bespeak, betroth, conduce, consume, engross, involve, promise 8 contract, covenant, entangle, interest, persuade 9 interlock, undertake

engaged: 4 busy 5 hired 6 bonded, meshed 7 assured, earnest, entered, pledged, versant 8 embedded, employed, involved, occupied, promised 9 affianced, betrothed

engagement: 4 aval, date 5 cowle 6 affair, battle, escrow 7 bargain 9 betrothal, encounter 10 attachment, employment 11 appointment, involvement

engager: 6 surety

engaging: 5 sapid 6 taking 10 attractive 11 interesting

engastrimyth: 13 ventriloquist

engender: 5 beget, breed, cause 6 excite, gender 7 develop, produce 8 generate, occasion 9 procreate, propagate

engild: 8 brighten

engine: gas 5 motor, steam 7 turbine 8 gasoline 10 locomotive
covering: 4 cowl
kind of: gin, ram 4 goat 5 dinky, mogul 6 diesel, helper, mallet, pusher 7 turbine 8 dollbeer 10 locomotive
military: ram 4 tank 6 onager 7 robinet 8 ballista, helepole 9 espringal 11 ribaudequin

part: cam 4 gear 6 boiler, piston, stator 8 cylinder 9 crankcase 10 carburetor 12 differential, transmission
speed up: rev

engineer: 4 plan 6 driver, manage 7 planner, plotter 8 contrive, designer, inventor, maneuver 9 construct 10 accomplish 11 constructor, superintend
degree: C.E., E.E., M.E.

enginous: 6 crafty 9 ingenious

engirdle: 4 gird 9 encompass

engirt: 6 engird 7 envelop 8 encircle

England: 6 Albion 7 Britain 9 Britannia 12 Great Britain
aborigine: 4 Pict
actor: 4 Tree 5 Donat, Evans 6 Arliss 7 Burbage, Olivier 8 Guinness
actress: 4 Gwyn 5 Leigh, Terry
admiral: 6 Nelson, Rodney, Vernon
admirer of: 10 anglophile
air force: R.A.F.
Antarctic explorer: 5 Scott
apartment: 4 flat
apple: 6 beefin, biffin, coling, rennet 7 beaufin, costard 8 coccagee 9 guarenden, guarender
apron: 8 barmskin
archbishop: 4 Lang, Laud 6 Becket 7 Cranmer
architect: 4 Wren
art gallery: 4 Tate
bailiff: 5 reeve
bed: 4 doss
biologist: 6 Huxley
boat: 7 coracle
castle site: 7 Arundel, Windsor
cathedral city: Ely
cattle: 5 Devon
cattle tender: 7 byreman
Channel Island: 4 Sark
charity school scholar: 8 blue coat
cheese: 7 stilton, truckle
chinaware: 5 Spode 8 Wedgwood
church caretaker: 6 verger
church officer: 6 beadle
circuit court: 4 eyre
city: Ely 4 Bath, Hull, York 5 Derby, Erith, Leeds, Truro, Wigan 6 Bolton, Bootle, Exeter, Hanley, Jarrow, Leyton, London, Oldham, Rippon 7 Bristol, Burnley, Croydon, Grimsby, Halifax, Hornsey, Ipswich, Newport, Norwich, Preston, Reading, Salford, Seaford, Walsall, West Ham 8 Bradford, Brighton, Coventry, Dewsbury, Hastings, Plymouth, Rochdale, Wallasey, Wallsend 9 Birkenhead, Blackburn, Devonport, Gateshead, Leicester, Liverpool, Rotherham, Sheffield, Smethwick, Stockport, Tottenham, Willesden 10 Aston Manor, Birmingham, Manchester, Nottingham,

Portsmouth, Sunderland, Warrington 11 Bournemouth, Northampton, Saint Helens, Southampton, Walthamstow 12 Huddersfield, Southshields, West Bromwich 13 Middlesbrough, South-end-on-sea, Wolverhampton 14 Stoke-upon-Trent, West Hartlepool 15 Barrow-in Furness 17 Newcastle-upon-Tyne

class: 4 form

clergyman: 4 Inge 5 Donne, Oates 6 Becket, Newman 7 Latimer

cloth: 5 tweed

coin: ora 4 rial, ryal 5 ackey, angel, crown, groat, pence, pound 6 bawbee, florin, guinea, seskin, teston 7 angelet, carolus 8 farthing, shilling, sixpence, twopence 9 dandiprat, fourpence, halfcrown, halfpenny, sovereign 10 threepence

composer: 4 Arne 5 Elgar, Neale 6 Delius, Handel 7 Britten, Stainer 8 Williams

conservative: 4 Tory

conspirator: 6 Fawkes

conveyance: 4 tram 6 waggon

county: 4 Kent 5 Derby, Devon, Essex, Hants, Shire 6 Dorset, Surrey, Sussex

court: 4 eyre, leet 5 gemot 6 gemote 8 hustling 9 Old Bailey

crown tax: 4 geld

dance: 6 morris

dandy: 4 toff

diarist: 5 Pepys 6 Evelyn

dramatist: 4 Shaw 5 Peele, Reade, Wilde 6 Coward, Dryden, Pinero 7 Marlowe 8 Beaumont, Fletcher 11 Shakespeare

early conqueror: 5 Horsa 7 Hengist

economist: 6 Keynes 7 Gresham, Ricardo

elevator: 4 lift

emblem: 4 Lion

entertainment: 4 busk 7 ridotto

essayist: 4 Elia, Lamb, Lang 5 Bacon 6 Steele 7 Addison

estate: 4 este

explorer: 4 Cook, Ross 5 Cabot, Drake, Scott 6 Hudson

field: 5 croft

fish: 5 sewen 8 dragonet

flood: 5 spate

flower: 4 rose

food dealer: 12 costermonger

forest: 5 Arden

freeman: 5 ceorl

game: 5 darts, rugby 6 soccer 7 cricket

gold: 4 rial, ryal

gun carrier: 4 bren

historian: 5 Acton, Grote 7 Toynbee 8 Macaulay

hog: 5 Essex

humorist: 4 Lear

inspector: 9 exciseman

invader: 4 Dane 5 Engle, Roman, Saxon 6 Norman

island: Man 4 Holy 5 Farne, Lundy 6 Scilly, Thanet, Walney 7 Ireland, Sheppey 8 Anglesey, Holyhead, Shetland 11 Isle of Wight

jacket: 4 Eton

king: Hal, Lud 4 Bran, Brut, Cnut, Cole, Knut, Lear 5 Brunt, Henry, James, Sweyn 6 Alfred, Arthur, Bladud, Cnaute, Edward, Egbert, George 7 Artegal, Elidure, Richard, Stephen, William 8 Gorboduc

laborer: 5 navvy

lake: 7 Derwent 8 Coniston 9 Ullswater 10 Windermere

land: 5 laine

law: 4 soke 6 esnecy 7 danelaw 9 common law

lawyer: 7 bencher 9 barrister, solicitor

liberal: 4 Whig

lunch: 6 tiffin

machine gun: 4 Bren, Sten

magistrate: 4 beak

man: 6 Briton 9 Britisher, Sassenach

measure: ell, pin, rod, ton, tun, vat 4 acre, bind, boll, comb, cran, foot, gill, goad, hand, hide, inch, last, line, mile, once, palm, peek, pint, pipe, pole, pool, rood, sack, span, trug, wist, yard, yoke 5 bodge, carat, chain, coomb, cubit, digit, float, floor, fluid, hutch, mimim, perch, point, prime, quart, skein, stack, truss 6 barrel, bovate, bushel, cranne, fathom, firkin, gallon, hobbet, jugrum, league, manent, oxgang, pottle, runlet, strike, sulung, thread, tieree 7 furlong, hobbitt, quarter, quarten, rundlet, spindle, tertian, virgate 8 carucate, chaldron, hogshead, landyard, puncheon, quadrant, standard 9 kilderskin, shaftment, shaftmont 10 barleycorn, barn gallon, winchester 13 tablespoonful

minister: 4 Peel, Pitt 7 Walpole 8 Disraeli

molasses: 7 treacle

monk: 4 Beda, Bede 5 Baeda

mountain: 7 Pennine 8 Cumbrian, Scawfell

news agency: 7 Reuters

noble family: 6 Talbot

nobleman (see also *title* below): 4 peer 6 milord

novelist: 5 Arlen, Hardy, Reade, Waugh, Wells 6 Austen, Bronte, Huxley, Sterne 7 Dickens 8 Fielding, Trollope

officer's civilian dress: 5 mufti

old kingdom: 6 Sussex

old letter: wen 5 thorn

order: 6 Garter

painter: 4 Opie 6 Turner 7 Hogarth, Millais, Poynter

pamphleteer: 5 Defoe, Swift

Parliament proceedings: 7 Hansard
party member: 4 Tory, Whig 7 Liberal 8 Laborite 9 Labourite 12 Conservative
patron saint: 5 George
peasant: 5 churl
pert. to: 8 Anglican 10 Anglo-Saxon
philosopher: 4 Hume 5 Bacon, Locke 6 Hobbes 7 Russell, Spencer 9 Whitehead
pirate: 4 Kidd 5 Drake 6 Morgan 7 Hawkins
poet: 4 Gray, Pope 5 Auden, Blake, Byron, Carew, Donne, Eliot, Keats 6 Brooke, Landor 7 Barrett, Caedmon, Shelley 8 Browning 9 Masefield 11 Shakespeare
policeman: 5 bobby 6 copper, peeler
pottery: 5 Spode
prairie: 4 moor 5 heath
printer: 6 Caxton
prison: 4 gaol
public school: 4 Eton 5 Rugby 6 Harrow 9 Sandhurst
queen: 4 Anne, Mary 8 Victoria 9 Elizabeth
racing town: 5 Ascot 10 Epsom Downs
rebel: 5 Essex, Tyler 8 Cromwell 10 Washington
resort: 4 Bath 8 Brighton
rifle: 7 Enfield
river: Dee, Esk, Exe, Nen, Ure, Wye 4 Aire, Avon, Eden, Nene, Ouse, Tees, Tyne, Wash, Wear 5 Alton, Dudin, Trent 6 Humber, Mersey, Ribble, Severn, Thames 7 Caulder 8 Walbrook
royal house: 4 York 5 Tudor 6 Stuart 7 Hanover, Windsor 9 Lancaster 11 Plantagenet
royal household officer: 7 equerry
royal residence: 7 Windsor
scientist: 6 Darwin, Huxley
seaman: 5 limey 6 rating
seaport: 4 Deal 5 Dover, Poole 8 Wallasey 9 Liverpool 11 Southampton
serf: 6 thrall
settler: 4 Jute, Pict 5 Angle, Saxon 6 Norman
sheep: 8 costwold 11 Wensleydale
shoemaker: 4 snob
sixpence: 5 sprat
slave: 4 esne
socialist: 6 Fabian
soldier: 5 tommy 7 redcoat 8 fusileer, fusilier 10 carabineer, carabinier
spy: 5 Andre
stable: 4 mews
statesman: 4 Eden, Grey, Peel, Pitt 5 Bevin, Simon 6 Attlee 7 Asquith, Baldwin 8 Disraeli 9 Churchill, Gladstone, MacDonald, Macmillan 10 Walsingham 11 Chamberlain, Lloyd George
stone monument: 8 cromlech
streetcar: 4 tram
tavern: pub

taxpayer: 9 ratepayer
tea muffin: 7 crumpet
thicket: 7 spinney
thrush: 5 mavis
title: 4 dame, duke, earl, king, lady, lord, peer 5 baron, noble, queen 6 knight, prince 7 baronet, duchess, marquis 8 baroness, countess, marquess, princess, viscount 11 marchioness, viscountess
tourist: 7 tripper
tribe: 5 Iceni
truck: 5 lorry
tutor: don
university: 6 London, Oxford 9 Cambridge
uplands: 5 downs
valley: 4 Eden, Tees, Tyne 5 coomb 6 coquet
weight: 5 stone
engorge: 4 glut 5 gorge 6 devour
engraft: 9 inoculate
engrave: cut 4 etch 5 carve, chase, grave, print, sculp 6 chisel, incise 7 enchase, impress, imprint, stipple 8 inscribe, ornament 9 character, sculpture
by dots: 7 stipple
engraver: 6 chaser, etcher, graver 7 artisan 13 siderographer
tool of: 5 burin
engraving: *wax:* 8 intaglio 9 cerograph, xylograph 11 glyptograph
instrument: 6 stylet
pert. to: 7 glyphic, glyptic
engross: 4 bury 5 amass 6 absorb, engage, enroll, enwrap, occupy 7 collect, consume, immerse 9 fascinate, overwhelm, preoccupy
engrossed: 4 rapt 6 intent
engrosser: 12 calligrapher
engrossing: 11 chirography
engulf: 5 swamp, whelm 6 absorb, devour 7 swallow 8 submerge 9 overwhelm
enhance: 4 lift 5 enarm, exalt, raise 6 deepen 7 augment, elevate, enlarge, greaten, improve, sharpen 8 heighten, increase 9 aggravate, intensify 10 exaggerate
enhearten: 8 embolden
enigma: 5 griph, rebus 6 riddle, sphinx 7 griphus, mystery, problem 9 conundrum
enigmatic: 6 mystic 7 cryptic, obscure 8 mystical, puzzling 9 equivocal 12 inexplicable
enisle: 7 isolate
enisled: 5 alone, apart 8 solitary
enjoin: bid 5 order 6 decree, forbid 7 command, dictate, require 8 admonish, prohibit

enjoyment: use 4 bask, ease, zest 5 gusto 6 liking, relish 7 delight 8 felicity, pleasure 9 happiness 11 delectation 12 satisfaction 13 gratification

enkerchief: 5 drape

enkindle: 7 incense, inflame 9 enlighten

enlace: tie 5 twine, twist, weave 6 enfold 7 entwine 8 encircle, entangle 10 interweave

enlarge: add, eke(Sc.) 4 grow, huff, ream 5 swell, widen 6 broach, dilate, expand, extend, fraise, spread 7 amplify, augment, distend, enhance, greaten, magnify, stretch 8 flourish, increase 9 elaborate, expatiate, intumesce 10 aggrandize, exaggerate

enlarged: 8 varicose

enlargement: 9 accession, accretion 10 ampliation 13 magnification

enlarging gradually: 5 evase

enlighten: 5 edify, teach 6 inform 7 educate 8 enkindle, instruct 9 irradiate 10 illuminate

enlightened person: 10 illuminato

enlightenment: 5 bodhi 6 wisdom

enlist: 4 join 5 enter 6 embark, engage, enroll, induct 7 impress 8 register 9 volunteer

enlisted man: GI

enlistment: 5 hitch 7 listing

enliven: 4 warm 5 cheer, rouse 6 revive 7 animate, comfort, inspire, refresh 8 brighten, inspirit 9 encourage, stimulate 10 exhilarate, invigorate

enclose: 6 genial 9 sprightly

enlock: 7 enclose

enmesh: 4 trap 5 catch 7 ensnare 8 entangle

enmity: war 4 feud 5 spite 6 hatred, malice, rancor 8 aversion 9 animosity, antipathy, hostility 10 antagonism, repugnance, resentment 11 malevolence

ennead: 4 nine 8 ninefold

ennoble: 5 exalt, honor, raise 6 uplift 7 dignify, elevate, glorify

ennui: 4 bore 6 tedium 7 boredom, doldrum

Enoch: *father:* 4 Cain 5 Jared
son: 4 Irad 10 Methuselah

enorm: 8 abnormal, enormous 9 monstrous 10 outrageous 13 extraordinary

enormous: big, gob 4 huge, ream, vast 5 enorm, great, large 6 heroic, mighty 7 immense 8 abnormal, colossal, gigantic 9 excessive, monstrous 10 gargantuan, prodigious, stupendous 11 elephantine

Enos: *father:* 4 Seth
grandfather: 4 Adam
grandmother: Eve
uncle: 4 Abel, Cain

enough: 4 enow 5 ample, basta 6 plenty 7 suffice 8 adequate 10 sufficient 12 satisfactory

enounce: 5 state, utter 8 proclaim 9 enunciate, pronounce

enow: 9 presently

enrage: 5 anger 6 grieve, madden 7 incense, inflame 9 infuriate 10 exasperate

enraged: 5 irate 7 berserk 8 choleric, maddened

enrapture: 6 ravish 7 ecstasy, enchant 8 enravish, entrance 9 captivate, fascinate

enraptured: 4 rapt 11 imparadised

enravished: 4 rapt 10 enraptured

enrich: 4 boot, lard 5 adorn, endow 6 batten, fatten 7 furnish 8 ornament 9 embellish, fertilize

enrobe: 6 attire, clothe

enroll, enrol: 4 join, list 5 enter, write 6 billet, enfold, enlist, induct, record 7 ascribe, impanel 8 initiate, inscribe, register 11 matriculate 13 immatriculate

enroot: 7 implant

ens: 5 being 6 entity 9 existence

ensaint: 8 canonize

ensconce: 4 hide 5 cover 6 settle 7 conceal, shelter 9 establish

ensemble: 5 decor, whole 7 costume 11 combination

ensiform: 6 ensate 7 xiphoid

ensign: 4 flag, sign 5 badge 6 banner, signal, symbol 7 officer 8 gonfalon, standard 9 oriflamme
of Othello: 4 Iago
of sovereignty: 7 regalia
papal: 8 gonfalon

ensilage: 4 feed 6 fodder, silage

enslave: 5 chain 7 slavish 8 enthrall

ensnare: net, web 4 mesh, trap 5 benet, catch, noose, snarl 6 allure, attrap, enmesh, entoil, entrap, tangle, trepan 7 beguile, springe 8 overtake 10 circumvent, intertwine

ensorcell, ensorcel: 5 charm 7 bewitch, enchant 9 fascinate

ensoul, insoul: 7 animate

ensuing: 4 next 9 following, resulting 10 subsequent, succeeding

ensure: 6 assure, insure, secure 7 betroth, espouse, warrant 8 affiance 9 guarantee

entablature: 10 trabeation

entad: 6 inward
opposite of: 5 ectad

entail: 6 impose 7 involve, require 11 necessitate

ental: 5 inner
opposite of: 5 ectal

entame: 11 domesticate

entangle: mat, web 4 foul, harl, knit, knot, mesh, mire 5 catch, ravel, snafu, snare, snarl, twist **6** befoul, cotter, engage, enlace, enmesh, entrap, hankle, inmesh, puzzle **7** confuse, embroil, ensnarl, involve, perplex **8** bewilder, encumber **9** embarrass, embrangle, imbroglio **10** intertwine, interweave

entangled: 4 deep **5** cotty **7** complex **10** interwoven

entanglement: 4 knot **6** bunker **8** obstacle **13** embarrassment

entellus: 6 monkey

entente: 6 treaty **8** alliance **9** agreement **13** understanding

enter: 4 join, post **5** admit, begin, share **6** accede, appear, engage, enlist, enroll, entrer(F.), hamper, incept, pierce, record **7** intrude **8** initiate, inscribe, register **9** introduce, penetrate **11** matriculate
militarily: **6** invade

enter into: 10 participate

enter upon: 5 begin **6** embark

enteric: 10 intestinal

enterprise: 5 essay **6** action, spirit **7** attempt, emprise, project, venture **8** business, gumption **9** adventure **10** initiative, management **11** undertaking

enterpriser: 12 entrepreneur

enterprising: 4 bold **9** energetic **10** aggressive, courageous **11** progressive

entertain: 4 fete, hold **5** amuse, treat **6** divert, regale **7** beguile, cherish **8** consider, interest

entertainer: 4 host **5** actor **6** amuser, dancer, singer **7** actress, hostess, regaler, speaker **8** comedian, magician, minstrel **9** soubrette(F.) **10** comedienne

entertainment: 4 fare, fete, glee, play **5** board, cheer, feast, opera, revue, sport **6** kermis, shivvo **7** banquet, ceilidh(Ir.), concert, festine, festino, kermess, pastime, ridotto **8** function, musicale **9** amusement, diversion, festivity, reception, wayzgoose **10** recreation
of strangers: **9** xenodochy
place: **4** gaff, park **5** movie **6** casino, cinema, circus, midway **7** cabaret, theater, theatre

enthrall, enthral: 5 charm **7** enslave **9** captivate

enthrone: 5 crown, exalt **6** throne

enthusiasm: 4 elan, fire, zeal, zest **5** ardor, flame, furor, mania, verve **6** fervor, spirit **7** ardency **9** animation, eagerness **10** ebullience, fanaticism

enthusiast: bug, fan, nut **5** bigot **6** rooter, zealot **7** devotee, fanatic **8** follower **9** energumen

enthusiastic: 4 keen, warm **5** rabid **6** ardent **10** forthgoing

enthymeme: 8 argument **9** syllogism

entice: win 4 bait, coax, draw, lure, tole, wile **5** charm, decoy tempt **6** allure, cajole, incite, induce, invite, seduce **7** attract, bewitch **8** inveigle, persuade

entire: all 4 full, mear, mere **5** clean, every, quite, sound, stark, total, utter, whole **7** perfect, plenary **8** absolute, allwhole, complete, unbroken **9** exclusive, integrate, undivided **10** unimpaired **11** unqualified **12** undiminished

entitle: dub 4 call, name, term **5** affix **6** enable **7** empower, qualify **8** nominate **9** authorize, designate **10** denominate, habilitate **12** characterize

entity: ens 4 unit **5** being, thing **7** essence, integer **9** existence

entoil: 5 snare **7** ensnare

entomb: 4 bury **5** inter, inurn **6** encave, hearse, inhume

entourage: 5 train **7** retinue **9** associate, attendant

entracte: 8 interval **9** interlude **12** intermission

entrail: bag, gut 5 bowel **6** giblet, mugget **7** viscera **8** gigerium

entrain: 5 board

entrance: 4 adit, boca(Sp.), door, gate, hall **5** charm, debut, entry, foyer, mouth, stulm, toran **6** access, atrium(L.), entree, portal, ravish, torana, zaguam **7** delight, gateway, hallway, ingoing, ingress, initial, postern **9** admission, beginning, enrapture, fascinate, incursion, induction, overpower, threshold, vestibule **10** admittance **12** introduction

entranced: 4 rapt **8** ecstatic

entrant: 7 intrant, starter **8** beginner **11** participant

entrap: bag, net 5 catch, decoy, snare **6** allure, ambush, taigle(Sc.), tangle, trepan **7** beguile, ensnare **8** entangle, inveigle

entre(F.): 7 between

entreat: ask, beg, bid, sue 4 pray, seek **5** crave, plead **6** appeal, invoke **7** beseech, conjure, implore, prevail, request, solicit **8** persuade, petition **9** impetrate, importune **10** supplicate

entreaty: 4 plea, suit **8** petition **9** treatment **11** importunity, negotiation

entree: 5 entry **6** access **8** entrance **9** admission **10** permission

entrench, intrench: 6 invade **8** encroach, trespass

entrenchment: 7 closure

entrepot: 5 depot **9** warehouse **10** storehouse

entrepreneur: 7 manager **8** employer **10** impresario **11** enterpriser

entresol: 9 mezzanine

entrust, intrust: 4 give 6 commit 7 address, commend, confide, consign, deposit 8 delegate, encharge 9 concredit, recommend

entry: 4 adit, hall, item 5 debit 6 credit, entree, postea, record, ringer 7 ingress, passage 8 entrance, notandum, register 9 vestibule 10 adjustment, enlistment, enrollment

entwine: 4 lace 5 braid, twine, twist, weave 6 enlace 7 wreathe 9 interlace 10 intertwine

enucleate: 7 explain

enumerate: 4 tell 5 count 6 detail, number, recite, reckon, relate 7 compute, itemize, recount 8 estimate 9 calculate 13 particularize

enumeration: 4 list 6 census 7 account, catalog 9 catalogue

enunciate: 5 utter 7 declare, enounce 8 announce, proclaim 9 pronounce 10 articulate

enure: See **inure**

envelop, envelope: 4 case, coma, husk 5 cover, round 6 bemist, enfold, engirt, enwrap, infold, invest, muffle, sheath, shroud, swathe 7 enclose, environ, wrapper 8 ensphere, surround 9 chevelure 10 integument
of fruit: bur 4 burr

envenom: 7 corrupt, vitiate 8 embitter, empoison

envious: 7 jealous 8 enviable 9 invidious

environ: hem 4 gird 5 limit 6 girdle, suburb 7 envelop, inclose, involve, jealous, purlieu 8 district, encircle, surround 9 encompass, territory 12 circumscribe

environment: 6 medium, milieu 7 element, habitat, setting 8 ambiance, precinct
comb. form: eco
science of: 7 ecology

envisage: 4 face 8 confront 9 visualize

envision: 5 dream

envoy: 5 agent, envoi(F.) 6 deputy, legate 8 ablegate 9 messenger, missioner 10 ambassador 12 commissioner 14 representative 15 plenipotentiary

envy: 5 covet 6 grudge 8 begrudge, jealousy

enwrap: 4 roll 5 clasp 6 enfold, infold, kirtle 7 engross, envelop 8 convolve, envelope

enzyme: ase 6 cytatase, lipase, olease, papain, pepsin, rennin, urease 7 adenase, amylase, casease, diatase, erepsin, ferment, guanase, inulase, maltase, pectase, pepsine, tannase 8 catalase, cytolist, eraptase, esterase, protease 9 biogenase, deamidase, deaminase, invertase, trehalase 10 amygdalase 11 gaultherase 14 acetaldehydase
leather-making: 7 tannase
opposite of: 5 azyme

eoan: 7 auroral

eolith: 4 celt

eon: age 8 eternity

eonic: 4 eral

epee: 5 blade, sword

epergne: 11 centerpiece

ephah: 7 measure
one-tenth: 4 omer
ten: 5 homer

ephelis: 7 freckle

ephemeral: 5 brief, vague 7 passant, passing 9 temporary, transient 10 evanescent, short-lived, transitory 11 impermanent

ephemeris: 5 diary 7 almanac, journal 8 calendar, magazine 10 periodical 11 publication

Ephialtes' slayer: 6 Apollo 8 Hercules

Ephraim's descendant: 7 Resheph

epi: 5 spire 6 finial 8 pinnacle

epic: 4 Edda, epos, saga 5 grand, Iliad, noble 6 epopee, heroic 7 Beowulf 8 epyllion, Ramayana 9 narrative 11 Mahabharata

epicarp: 4 husk, rind

epicede, epicedium: ode 4 song 5 dirge, elegy

epicene: 7 sexless 10 effeminate

epichoric: 5 local

Epictetus: 4 Stoic 10 philosopher
birthplace: 10 Hierapolis
expelled from: 4 Rome
home: 6 Epirus

epicure: 6 friand 7 glutton, gourmet 8 gourmand 10 gastronome 11 connoisseur

epicurean: 7 Apician 8 hedonist 9 luxurious

epidemic: flu 6 plague 8 pandemic 9 influenza 10 pestilence

epiderm appendage: 4 horn

epidermis: 7 cuticle

epigram: 4 poem 6 englyn 11 inscription

epigrammatic: 7 concise, piquant, pointed

epigraph: 7 imprint 11 inscription 14 superscription

epilogue, epilog: 8 appendix 10 conclusion

Epimetheus: *daughter:* 7 Pyrrha
wife: 7 Pandora

epinard: 7 spinach

Epiphany: 9 uphellyaa(Sc.)

Epirus: *native:* 5 Greek 6 Epirot 7 Epirote
town: 6 Dodona

episcopacy: 9 bishopric

Episcopal parish head: 6 rector

Episcopalian: 9 prelatist

episcopate: 9 bishopric

episode: 5 event, scene, story 8 incident 9 happening

episperm: 5 testa

epistaxis: 9 nosebleed

epistle: 6 letter 7 missive, writing

epitaph: 8 hicjacet 11 inscription

epithet: 4 name, term 5 title 6 phrase 7 agnomen 9 sobriquet 10 soubriquet 11 appellation

epitome: 6 digest, precis 8 abstract, synopsis 9 comprisal, statement 10 compendium 11 abridgement, contraction 13 comprehension

epitomize: 6 resume 7 curtail 8 compress, condense, diminish 9 summarize 10 abbreviate

epityphlitis: 12 appendicitis

epoch: age, era 4 date, time 5 event 6 period

epochal: 4 eral

epode: 7 refrain 9 aftersong

epopee: 4 epic, epos

epoptic: 6 mystic

epure: 5 draft 7 diagram, drawing, pattern

equability: 10 equanimity

equable: 4 even, just 5 equal, suant 6 smooth, steady 7 uniform 8 tranquil 9 equitable

equal: par, tie 4 cope, egal(F.), even, fere, isos(Gr.), just, like, meet, peer, same 5 alike, level, match, rival 6 equate 7 abreast, compeer, emulate, equable, identic, uniform 8 adequate, equalize, tranquil 9 equitable, identical, unruffled 10 answerable, equivalent, tantamount 11 comparative, countervail 12 commensurate, counterpoise 13 unfluctuating
combining form: iso 4 equi, pari

equal-angled figure: 6 isogon

equalire: 4 even

equality: 6 equity, parity 7 balance, egality 8 evenness, fairness 12 impartiality
legal: 7 isonomy

equally: as 4 both 5 alike 6 evenly, justly

equanimity: 5 poise 7 egality 8 calmness, evenness, serenity 9 composure 10 equability 11 tranquility

equate: 7 balance 8 equalize

equatorial: 8 tropical

equestrian: 5 rider 7 vaquero(Sp.) 8 horseman

equidistant: 7 central, halfway

equilibrium: 5 poise 7 balance 9 equipoise
being in: 7 astatic
science: 8 astatics

equine: 4 colt, foal, mare 5 filly, horse, zebra

equine water sprite: 5 kelpy 6 kelpie

equip: arm, rig 4 deck, gear, gird, heel, reek 5 array, dress, enarm, endow 6 attire, fit out, outfit, suborn 7 apparel, appoint, bedight, furnish, prepare, qualify 8 accouter, accoutre 10 accomplish, habilitate

equipage: 4 crew 5 suite, train 6 supply 7 retinue, turnout 8 carriage 9 apparatus, furniture 10 habiliment

equipment: 4 gear 6 attire, tackle 7 fitment, harness, panoply 8 armament, material,

mounting 11 appointment 13 paraphernalia

equipoise: 5 poise 7 balance 11 equilibrium

equiponderate: 14 counterbalance

equitable: 4 even, fair, just 5 equal, right 6 honest 7 equable, upright 9 impartial, righteous 10 reasonable

equitation: 12 horsemanship

equity: law 7 honesty, justice 8 equality, fairness 9 rectitude 11 uprightness 13 righteousness

equivalent: 9 identical 10 synonymous, tantamount

equivocal: 7 dubious, obscure 8 doubtful, puzzling 9 ambiguous, enigmatic, uncertain 10 indefinite, mysterious, perplexing, suspicious 12 questionable, undetermined 13 indeterminate, problematical

equivocate: lie 5 dodge, evade, shift 6 escape, palter, trifle, weasel 7 quibble, shuffle 11 prevaricate

equivogue: mot, pun 4 quip 9 witticism 10 paronomasia 12 adnomination

era: A.D., B.C.; age 4 aeon, date, time 5 epoch, stage 6 period

eradicate: 4 dele, weed 5 erase 6 delete, remove, uproot 7 abolish, destroy, outroot 9 extirpate 10 annihilate, deracinate 11 exterminate

eral: 7 epochal

erase: 4 blot, dele, rase, raze 5 annul 6 cancel, deface, delete, efface, excise, remove 7 destroy, expunge, scratch 9 eradicate 10 obliterate

erd: 4 land 5 earth 6 region

ere: 4 soon 5 early, prior 6 before 8 erewhile, formerly 9 aforetime 10 previously

Erebus: *parent:* 5 Chaos
sister: Nox
son: 6 Charon

erect: big 4 bigg, rear, step 5 build, exalt, setup, stand 6 arrect, uplift 7 address, elevate, upright 8 straight, vertical 9 construct, establish, institute 10 upstanding 13 perpendicular

erelong: 4 anon, soon

eremite: 6 hermit 7 ascetic, recluse 8 anchoret 9 anchorite
hut: 4 cell

erewhile: ere 10 heretofore

Erewhon: 6 utopia

ergastulum: 4 cell 7 dungeon

ergo: so 5 hence 9 therefore

erica: heath 7 heather

Erin: 4 Eire 7 Ireland 8 Hibernia 9 Innisfail

Erinys: 4 Fury 6 Alecto 7 Megaera 9 Tisiphone

Eriphyle: *brother:* 8 Adrastus
daughter: 8 Eurydice

father: 6 Talaus
son: 7 Alcmeon
Eris: *brother:* 4 Ares
 daughter: Ate
 missile: 5 apple
eristic: 12 disputatious 13 controversial
Eritrea: See **Ethiopia**
ermine: fur 5 stoat, white 6 weasel 7 ermelin, miniver
erode: eat 4 gnaw, wear 7 corrode, destroy 9 undermine 12 disintegrate
Eros: 4 Amor 5 Cupid
 beloved: 6 Psyche
 brother: 7 Anteros
 father: 6 Hermes 7 Mercury
 mother: 5 Venus 9 Aphrodite
erose: 6 uneven 9 irregular
erotic: 6 loving 7 amatory, amorous
err: sin 4 miss, slip 5 lapse, misgo, stray 6 bungle, wander 7 blunder, deviate, misplay, mistake 8 misjudge 10 transgress 12 miscalculate, misinterpret
errand: 5 chore 7 journey, mission
errand boy: 4 page 7 courier 9 messenger
errant: 5 stray 6 astray, erring 9 deviating, itinerant, wandering 10 journeying 11 adventurous
erratic: 5 queer, wacky 6 whacky 7 strange, vagrant 8 vagabond 9 eccentric, irregular, wandering 10 capricious, changeable
erratum: 5 error 7 mistake
errhine: 7 sneezer
erring: 6 astray, errant
erroneous: 5 amiss, false, wrong 6 untrue 7 erratic 8 mistaken, straying, wrongful 9 incorrect, wandering
error: sin 4 bull, flub, muff, slip 5 bevue, boner, fault, fluff, lapse 6 fumble, miscue 7 bloomer, blunder, default, erratum, fallacy, falsity, misplay, misstep, mistake, offense, rhubarb 8 solecism 9 violation 10 inaccuracy 12 irregularity, malformation
 measuring device: 11 aberrometer
ers: 5 vetch
ersatz: 10 artificial, substitute 11 replacement
Erse: 5 Irish 6 Celtic, Gaelic 8 Scottish
erst: 8 formerly
erstwhile: 6 former 8 formerly 10 heretofore
eruca: 11 caterpillar
erudition: 4 lore 7 letters 8 learning 9 education, knowledge 11 instruction, scholarship
erupt: 5 burst, eject
eruption: 4 rush 5 rupia, storm 6 blotch 8 outbreak, outburst 9 commotion
Eryx: *father:* 5 Butes
 mother: 5 Venus 9 Aphrodite

Esau: 4 Edom
 brother: 5 Jacob
 country: 4 Edom
 descendant: 7 Edomite
 father: 5 Isaac
 father-in-law: 4 Elon
 grandson: 6 Amalek
 mother: 7 Rebekah
 son: 5 Korha, Reuel 7 Eliphaz
 wife: 4 Adah 10 Aholibamah
escapade: 5 prank, sally 7 runaway 9 adventure, excursion
escape: lam 4 flee, gate, jink(Sc.), miss, slip 5 avoid, dodge, elope, elude, evade, issue, spill 6 eschew, outlet 7 getaway, leakage, mistake, outflow 9 evaporate
 means: 8 loophole
escargot: 5 snail
escarole: 6 endive
escarp: 5 scarp, slope
eschalot: 5 onion
eschar: 4 scab 5 crust
escheat: 4 fall 5 lapse 6 revert 7 forfeit
eschew: 4 shun 5 avoid 6 escape 7 abstain
escolar: 8 mackerel
escort: see 4 beau, lead, show 5 guard, usher 6 attend, convoy, squire 7 conduct, consort, gallant 8 cavalier, chaperon 9 accompany, attendant, bodyguard, safeguard
escritoire: 4 desk 6 bureau 9 secretary
escrow: 4 bond, deed
esculent: 6 edible 7 eatable 10 comestible
escutcheon: 6 shield
 band: 4 fess 5 fesse
 cord: 10 cordeliere
Esdras' angel: 5 Uriel
eserine: 13 physostigmine
eshin: tub 4 pail
esker, eskar: as 4 kame
Eskimo: *Aleutian Islands:* 4 Atka 5 Aleut, Husky
 Asiatic: 4 Yuit 6 Innuit
 bird: 4 fute
 boot: 5 kamik
 canoe: 5 cayak, kayak, umiak 6 oomiac, oomiak 7 oomiack
 coat: 5 parka 6 parkee, temiak
 Diomede Islands: 11 Yikirgaulit
 dog: 5 husky 8 Malamute, Malemute
 dwelling: 4 iglu 5 igloo, topek, tupek, tupik 9 barrabora
 goddess: 5 Sedna
 Greenland: Ita
 knife: ulu
 medicine man: 7 angakok, angakut, angekok, angekut 8 angekkok
 mountain: 7 nunatak
 settlement: 4 Etah
 Siberian: 4 Yuit

sledge: 7 komatik
esne: 4 serf 7 bondman 8 hireling
esodic: 8 afferent
esophagus: 6 gullet
esoteric: 5 inner 6 mystic, secret 7 private 8 abstruse 9 recondite 10 acroamatic, mysterious 12 confidential
esoteric doctrine: 6 cabala
esoteric knowledge: 6 gnosis
ESP: 9 intuition 12 clairvoyance
espadon: 9 swordfish
espalier: 7 lattice, railing, trellis
Espanol: 7 Spanish
espantoon: 4 club 8 spontoon
esparto: 4 alfa
especial: 5 chief 8 peculiar, uncommon 10 particular
esperance: 4 hope 11 expectation
espial: spy 5 scout 6 notice 9 discovery 11 observation
espiegle: 7 roguish 10 frolicsome
espionage: 4 espy 6 spying
  agent: spy
esplanade: 4 walk 5 drive 6 maidan, marina 9 promenade
esplee: 6 profit 7 product
espousal: 8 ceremony
espouse: wed 4 affy, mate 5 adopt, marry 6 defend, spouse 7 betroth, embrace, husband, support 8 advocate, maintain
esprit: wit 6 spirit 10 cleverness 12 intelligence
esprit de corps: 8 devotion
espy: see 4 spot 5 sight, watch 6 behold, descry, detect, locate, notice 7 discern, observe 8 discover 9 espionage
esquire: 7 armiger
ess: 4 worm 5 curve, sigma 7 sigmoid 8 curlicue, curlycue
essay: try 4 seek 5 chria(L.), paper, theme, tract, trail 6 effort, satire, thesis 7 article, attempt, venture, writing 8 endeavor, exertion, treatise 10 enterprise, experiment 12 disquisition, dissertation
essayist: 4 Elia, Lamb 5 Paine 6 Holmes, Steele 7 Addison, Emerson
esse: 5 being 9 existence
essence: ens 4 atar, core, crux, gist, odor, otto, pith, soul 5 attar, basic, being, heart, ottar, ousia(G.) 6 nature 7 element, extract, medulla, perfume 9 existence, principle, substance 10 extraction
Essene: 7 ascetic
essential: 5 per se, vital 7 needful 8 inherent, material 9 intrinsic, necessary 11 fundamental 13 indispensable 14 constitutional
essonite: 6 garnet
establish: fix, set 4 base, rear, rest, seat 5 build, edify, erect, found, plant, prove,

setup, state 6 avouch, clinch, create, ground, locate, ordain, ratify, settle, verify 7 appoint, approve, confirm, enstate, install, instate, preempt 8 colonize, constate, ensconce, identify, radicate, regulate, validate 9 determine, institute, originate 10 accomplish, constitute 11 corroborate
established: 4 fast, firm, sure 7 certain
establishment: 4 mill 5 plant 6 ecesis, menage 7 dounset(Sc.), factory 8 business, hacienda
estafette: 7 courier 9 messenger
estancia(Sp.)**:** 4 farm 5 ranch
estate: 4 alod, fief, home, pomp, rank 5 acres, allod, finca, habit, manor, state, taluk 6 domain, ground 7 alodium, demesne, dignity, dislay, fortune 8 allodium, freehold, hacienda, position, property, standing 9 condition, situation 11 latifundium
  fourth: 5 press 9 newspaper
  manager: 7 steward 8 executor, guardian 9 committee 13 administrator
  owner: 9 hacendero
  purchaser: 9 acquereur(F.)
  rent deduction: 7 reprise
  third: 9 tiers etat(F.)
  to hold: 7 tenancy
esteem: 4 deem 5 adore, count, favor, honor, pride, prize, value, worth 6 credit, favour, regard, repute 7 account, opinion, respect 8 appraise, venerate 9 deference, reckoning, reverence 10 admiration, appreciate, estimation 13 consideration
ester: 6 oleate 7 acetate, tropate 8 compound, stearate
estero: 5 inlet 7 channel, estuary
Esther: 8 Hadassah
  festival: 5 Purim
  foster father: 8 Mordecai
  husband: 6 Xerxes 9 Ahasuerus
esthesiometer: 10 tactometer
esthetic: See **aesthetic**
estimable: 4 good 5 solid 6 worthy 9 admirable, honorable 11 respectable
estimate: set 4 rank, rate 5 cense, guage, guess, judge, prize, value 6 assess, budget, esteem, reckon 7 average 8 appraise, consider 9 calculate 11 computation
  low: 14 undervaluation
  smallest: 7 minimum
  too high: 8 overrate
estimation: air 4 fame 5 honor 6 regard, repute 7 opinion 9 judgement 10 conjecture
estivate: 6 summer
estoc: 5 sword
estocada: 6 thrust
Estonia: *city:* 5 Reval 7 Tallinn

coin: 4 sent 5 kroon 7 estmark
island: 4 Dago 5 Oesel, Saare
measure: tun 4 elle, liin, pang, sund, toll,
   toop 5 faden, verst 6 sagene, versta, verste
   7 kulimet, verchoc, verchok, 8 tonnland 9
   lofstelle
weight: 4 lood, nael, puud
estop: bar 4 fill, plug, stop 5 debar 6 hinder,
   impede 7 prevent 8 preclude, prohibit
estrade: 4 dais 8 platform
estrange: part, wean 6 divert 8 alienate, disunite
estray: 4 waif 5 dogie 6 wander
estreat: 4 copy, fine 5 exact 6 record 7 extract 9 duplicate
estrepe: 5 spoil
estuary: ria 5 firth, frith, inlet 6 estero
estuate: 4 boil 5 heave, surge 7 agitate
esurient: 6 greedy, hungry 9 voracious
et al: 6 others 9 elsewhere
etaac: 7 blaubok 8 antelope
etagere: 7 whatnot
etalon: 14 interferometer
etat: 5 state
etch: 7 engrave 8 inscribe
Eteocles: *father:* 7 Oedipus
   kingdom: 6 Thebes
   mother: 7 Jocasta
   son: 8 Laodamas
eternal: 6 eterne 7 ageless, endless, lasting,
   unaging 8 enduring, immortal, timeless 9
   boundless, continual, deathless, immutable, perpetual, unceasing 10 perdurable
   11 everlasting 12 imperishable, unchangeable 13 uninterrupted
Eternal City: 4 Rome
eternal home: 6 heaven 8 paradise
eternal sleep: 5 death
eternal verity: 5 truth
eternally: ake, eer 4 ever 6 always 7 forever
eterne: 7 eternal
eternity: age, eon 4 aeon, olam
etesian: 6 annual 8 periodic
ethenol: 7 alcohol
etheostomoid: 4 fish 6 darter
ether: air, sky 5 ester 7 solvent 8 empyrean
   10 anesthetic, atmosphere
ethereal, etherial: 4 aery, airy 6 aerial 7
   airlike, etheric, fragile, slender 8 delicate,
   heavenly 9 celestial 10 spiritlike
ethical: 5 moral
ethics: *system of:* 8 hedonics
   teacher of: 8 moralist
   without: 6 amoral
Ethiopia: 4 Kafa 5 Kaffa 9 Abyssinia
   ancient capital: 5 Meroe
   animal: 4 kudu, lion, oryx 5 zebra 6 baboon,
   gelada, impala, jackal, monkey 7 gazelle,
   giraffe, redbuck 12 hippopotamus

area: 6 Amhara 7 Eritrea
battleground: 5 Adowa
bishop: 5 abuna
Catholic: 4 Cush, Geez 5 Uniat 6 Uniate
cattle: 5 sanga
cereal: 4 teff
city: 4 Axum, Gore 5 Adowa, Assab, Harar
   6 Antalo, Asmara, Gondar, Harrar,
   Napata 7 Ankober, Gambela, Magdala 10
   Addis Ababa(c.)
coin: 4 besa, harf 5 amole, girsh 6 kharaf,
   talari 7 ashrafi, piaster, tallero
district: 4 Shoa 5 Harer, Tigre 6 Amhara
dollar: 6 Levant, talari 12 Maria Theresa
emperor: 5 Negus 6 Memnon 7 Menelik 8
   Selassie
fly: 4 zimb
garment: 6 chamma
governor: ras
Hamite: 4 Afar
lake: 4 Tana 5 Tanna, Tsana, Tzana 6 Dembel 8 Stefanie
language: Ago 4 Afar, Geez, Saho 5 Galla,
   Tigre 6 Harari 7 Amharic
lyre: 6 kissar
measure: tat 4 cubi, kuba 5 derah, messe 6
   cabaho, sinjer, sinzer, tanica 7 entelam,
   farsakh, farsang, ghebeta
mountain: 9 Ras Dashan
people: 4 Kala 5 Bejas, Negro 6 Ethiop,
   Hamite, Harari 7 Somalis 10 Abyssinian
prince: ras
princess: 4 Aida 9 Andromeda
province: 4 Jima 5 Arusi, Gojam, Tigre,
   Wallo 6 Harage, Sidamo, Walaga 8
   Bagemder, Gamagofa, Ilubabor
pygmy: 4 Doko
queen: 7 Candace
river: Omo 4 Baro, Gibe, Juba 5 Abbai, Al-
   bai, Giubo, Rahad, Webbe 7 Tacazze
tableland: 4 amba
title: ras 5 abuna, negus
torah: 5 tetel
tree: 4 koso 5 cusso
tribe: 4 Afar 5 Agows, Galas 6 Amhara,
   Tigres 7 Donakus, Somalis
violin: 7 masinko
weight: pek, 4 kasm, natr, oket, rotl 5
   alada, artal, mocha, neter, ratel, wakea 6
   wogiet 8 farasula 9 mutagalla
wolf: 7 kaberu
etiolate: 4 pale 6 bleach
etiquette: 4 form 6 manner 7 chanoyu, decorum 9 propriety
   breach of: 8 solecism
etna: 4 lamp
Etruria: *city:* 4 Veii
   god: 5 Tinia
   goddess: Uni 6 Menfra

king: 4 Lars 7 Porsena
pert. to: 8 Etruscan
pottery: 8 bucchero
Etruscan (see also **Etruria**)**:** 8 Etrurian, Tursenoi, Tyrrheni
ettle: aim 4 plan 6 aspire, design, intend, intent, nettle 8 endeavor
etui, etwee: 4 case 8 reticule 10 needlecase
etymology: 6 origin
etymon: 4 root 5 radix 7 radical
eucalyptus: *gum:* 4 kino
  insect secretion: 4 laap, larp, lerp 5 laarp
Eucharist: *box:* pix, pyx
  bread plate: 5 paten
  cloth: 4 fano 5 fanon
  cup: 5 calix 7 chalice
  wafer vessel: 8 ciborium
  wine vessel: ama 5 amula
Euchite: 8 satanist
Euclid: 11 philosopher
  place of origin: 6 Megara
  proposition: 11 asses' bridge 12 pons asinorum
eugenic: 8 wellborn
eulogistic: 9 laudatory 11 encomiastic, panegyrical 12 commendatory
eulogize: 4 laud 5 extol 7 glorify 9 celebrate
eulogy: 5 eloge 6 hesped(Heb.), praise 7 address, oration 8 encomium 9 panegyric 11 composition
eunuch: 7 gelding 8 castrate
  pert. to: 8 spadonic
euphonium: 4 tuba
euphony: 5 meter 6 melody 7 harmony
euphorbia: 5 plant 6 spurge
euphoria: 4 ease 7 comfort 9 well-being
Euphrates tributary: 5 Habor 6 Tigris
euplexoptera: 6 earwig
Eurasia: *range:* 4 Ural 5 Urals
  region: 6 Tatary
eureka red: 4 puce
Euripides: *hero:* Ion
  heroine: 5 Helen, Medea
euripus: 4 flow 5 canal 6 strait 7 channel
Europa: *father:* 6 Agenor
  husband: 8 Asterius
Europe: 9 continent
  antelope: 7 chamois
  ape: 6 baboon
  ash: 4 sorb
  badger: 5 brock
  barracuda: 4 spet
  bass: 6 brasse
  bat: 8 serotine
  bellflower: 7 rampion
  bird: See **bird:** *Europe*
  bison: 7 aurochs
  boar: sus(L.) 4 aper(L.)
  boxing: 6 savate

broadcloth: 6 suclat
buckthorn: 7 alatern 9 alaternus
canal: 4 kiel
cavalryman: 4 Ulan 5 Uhlan 6 Hussar
cherry: 4 gean
city: Osb 4 Riga, Rome 5 Paris, Posen, Soest, Vichy 6 Berlin, Lisbon, Pilsen 9 Stockholm
clover: 6 alsike
coal basin: 4 Saar
coin: 5 ducat, taler 7 pistole
country: 5 Italy, Spain 6 France, Greece, Latvia, Norway, Poland 7 Austria, Belgium, Denmark, Finland, Germany, Holland, Hungary, Rumania 8 Bulgaria 9 Luxemburg 11 Switzerland
deer: roe 6 fallow
elder: 8 danewort
fish: id; gar, ide 4 blay, boce, dace, lote, rudd, tope 5 alose, barse, roach, ruffe, sprat, tench 6 barbel, besugo, braise, meagre, morgay, plaice, turbot 7 eperlan, homelyn, lavaret, osseter, picarel, topknot 8 John Dory, scirenga 9 John Doree
grape: 6 muscat
gulf: 4 Riga
herb: 4 dill, meum, woad 6 borage, lovage, yarrow 7 henbane 8 spicknel, tarragon
hundredweight: 7 zentner
industrial region: 4 Ruhr, Saar
invaders: 4 Huns 5 Alani, Alans, Arabs, Turks 7 Mongols
island: 4 Erin 5 Aland
juniper: 4 cade
kingdom: 5 Arles, Italy 6 Aragon, Norway, Sweden 7 Belgium, England, Holland, Navarre 11 Netherlands
lake: 5 Enare, Inari 6 Geneva
language: 5 Ugric
larkspur: 10 stavesacre
lavender: 5 aspic
lime: 4 teil
measure: aam 5 liter, metre
mint: iva 6 hyssop 9 horehound
mountain: Alp
mountain ash: 4 sorb 5 rowan, rowen
mountainous region: 4 Alps 5 Tyrol
mouse: 4 loir, vole 5 lerot
nationality: 4 Dane, Finn, Goth, Lapp, Lett, Pole, Serb, Slav 5 Croat, Swede, Welsh
oak: 4 holm 7 durmast
ox: 4 urus
peninsula: 7 Iberian
plain: 6 steppe
plant: 4 ulex 7 azarole, eelware 8 lavender 9 elderwort, escobilla 10 sneezewort
polecat: 7 fitchet, fitchew
rabbit: 4 cony 5 coney

republic: 4 Eire 5 Hesse 7 Andorra, Andorre

resort: Ems, Spa 5 Baden 7 Riviera

river: Po; Bug 4 Drau, Eder, Eger, Elbe, Oder, Oise, Ruhr, Saar, Ural 5 Meuse, Mosel, Rhine, Rhone 6 Danube 7 Narenta

rodent: erd 7 hamster

rustic: 7 peasant

sea: 4 Aral, Azov 5 North 6 Baltic

sedge: 5 chufa

squirrel: 5 sisel 10 polatouche

strait: 8 Bosporus

valley: 4 Ruhr

weasel: 5 stote 8 whitrack

wheat: 5 emmer 6 whizen 7 einkorn

worm: sao

Eurydice's husband: 7 Orpheus

Eurytus' daughter: 4 Iole

Euterpe: 4 Muse

lover: 7 Strymon

son: 6 Rhesus

evacuant: 6 emetic 8 diuretic, emptying 9 cathartic, purgative

evacuate: 4 void 5 empty, expel 6 vacate 7 deprive, excrete, exhaust, nullify, vacuate 9 discharge

evade: 4 bilk, foil, jouk, shun 5 avert, avoid, dodge, elude, shirk 6 baffle, blench, escape, illude 7 beguile

evaluate: 6 ponder 8 appraise

evanesce: 4 fade 5 empty 6 vanish 9 disappear, dissipate

evanescent: 7 cursory, evasive 8 fleeting, fugitive 9 ephemeral, fugacious, transient, vanishing 11 impermanent 13 infinitesimal

evangel: 6 gospel

Evangeline's home: 6 Acadia

evangelist: 4 John, Luke, Mark 6 Graham, Sunday, writer 7 apostle, Edwards, Matthew 8 disciple 9 McPherson, patriarch 10 revivalist

evaporate: dry 8 condense, vaporize 9 dehydrate

evasion: 4 jink 5 dodge, shift 6 escape 9 avoidance 10 subterfuge 12 equivocation

evasive: sly 4 eely 5 dodgy 6 shifty 7 elusive, elusory 9 deceitful 12 tergiversate

eve: 4 dusk 6 sunset 7 sundown 9 threshold

Eve: rib 6 female

even: een, tie 4 fair, just 5 aline, equal, exact, flush, grade, level, match, plain, rival, suant 6 direct, placid, smooth, square, steady 7 abreast, balance, equable, flatten, regular, uniform 8 moderate, parallel 9 equitable, impartial 10 coincident 15 straightforward

even if: tho 8 although

even-tempered: 4 calm, mild 5 plane, still 9 impartial

evener: 7 leveler 9 equalizer 10 doubletree

evening: eve 4 ereb(Heb.), sera(It.), soir(F.) 5 abend(G.) 6 sunset 8 eventide, twilight

party: 6 soiree

pert. to: 6 vesper 11 crepuscular

prayer: 6 vesper 7 vespers

song: 6 serena

star: 5 Venus 6 Hesper, Vesper 8 Hesperus

evenness: 8 equality 10 equanimity, uniformity

event: hap 4 case, fact, fate, feat, tilt 5 casus(L.), doing, epoch 6 factum(L.), result 7 episode, miracle, tragedy 8 incident, occasion 9 adventure, happening, milestone 10 occurrence, phenomenon 11 catastrophe, consequence, termination 12 circumstance

first: 6 opener 8 premiere

happy: hit 5 birth 7 godsend 8 marriage

eventful: 7 notable 9 important, momentous

eventide: 6 vesper 7 evening

eventual: 4 last 5 final 8 ultimate

eventuate: 6 result

ever: ay; aye, eer 6 always 7 forever 10 constantly 11 continually, perpetually

Everglade State: 7 Florida

Everglades: 5 marsh, swamp

evergreen: fir, ivy 4 ilex 5 heath, holly, savin 6 laurel, savine 7 jasmine 9 mistletoe 12 rhododendron

genus of: 4 olax 9 cupressus 11 pittosporum

tree: fir, yew 4 pine 5 carob, cedar 6 balsam, calaba, larche

everlasting: 6 eterne 7 aeonial, aeonian, durable, endless, eternal, forever, lasting, tedious 8 enduring, immortal, infinite, timeless 9 continual, incessant, perpetual, unceasing, wearisome 10 everduring, perdurable 12 imperishable 13 unintermitted, uninterrupted

everlasting flower: 6 orpine

everlastingly: 6 always 7 forever

evermore: 6 always

evert: 7 subvert 9 overthrow

every: all, ilk(Sc.) 4 each, ilka(Sc.) 6 entire 8 complete

everybody: all 8 everyone

everyday: 7 prosaic 8 ordinary

everything: all

evict: 4 oust 5 eject, expel 10 dispossess

evidence: 4 show 5 proof, scrip, token, trace 6 attest, reveal 7 exhibit, support 8 argument, manifest, muniment 9 testimony 10 indication 15 circumstantiate

piece of: 7 probate

evident: 5 apert, broad, clear, plain 6 patent 7 glaring, obvious, visible 8 apparent, manifest, palpable 10 noticeable 11 discernible, indubitable, transparent 12 demonstrable

evil: bad, ill, sin 4 bale, base, harm, poor, vice, vile 5 crime, malum(L.), wrong 6 menace, wicked 7 adverse, corrupt, disease, hurtful, immoral, misdeed, noxious, satanic, unsound 8 calamity, depraved, disaster, improper, iniquity, mischief, sinister 9 injurious, malicious, malignant, malignity, offensive, worthless 10 malevolent, misfortune, pernicious 11 malefaction, unwholesome 12 unpropitious 14 unsatisfactory
combining form: mal
incarnation of: 5 Satan

evil spirit: imp 5 demon, devil 6 daemon
Hebrew: 8 Asmodeus
Iroquois: 5 otkon
Zoroastrian: 5 daeva

evildoer: 5 cheat, crook, felon 6 sinner 7 culprit, villain 8 criminal 9 miscreant 10 malefactor

evince: 4 show 5 prove 6 subdue 7 conquer, display, exhibit 8 indicate, manifest

evirate: 8 castrate 10 emasculate

eviscerate: gut 10 devitalize, disembowel, exenterate

evoke: 5 educe 6 arouse, elicit, summon 7 evocate

evolute: 6 evolve, unfold

evolution: 7 biogeny 8 maneuver 11 development

evolutionist: 9 Darwinian

evolve: 4 emit 5 educe 6 derive, unfold, unroll 7 develop, evolute 9 disengage 11 disentangle

evulgate: 7 divulge, publish

ewe: teg 5 crone, sheep 6 theave
old: 5 crone

ewer: jug 5 basin, udder 7 pitcher 9 container

ewest: 4 next 7 nearest

ex: 6 former

exacerbate: irk 5 tease 6 enrage, excite, worsen 7 provoke 8 embitter, increase, irritate 9 aggravate, infuriate 10 exasperate

exact: ask 4 even, fine, levy, true 5 wreak, wrest 6 compel, demand, elicit, extort, formal, minute, square, strict 7 careful, certain, command, correct, enforce, estreat, extract, literal, precise, regular, require 8 accurate, critical, explicit, rigorous, specific 9 religious 10 methodical, meticulous, scrupulous 11 punctilious 13 hypercritical 14 circumstantial
satisfaction: 6 avenge 7 revenge

exacting: 6 severe 7 arduous, exigent 8 pressing

exactly: due 4 dead 5 spang, truly 6 evenly, nicely 9 precisely

exactness: 8 delicacy, identity, severity

exaggerate: 6 extend, overdo 7 amplify, enhance, enlarge, magnify, romance, stretch 8 increase 9 aggravate, embroider, overstate

exaggerated: 5 outre 11 exceptional, extravagant

exaggeration: 9 hyperbole 10 caricature

exagitate: 6 harass 7 agitate, censure, discuss

exalt: 5 arear, elate, erect, extol, heeze, honor, raise, set up, tower 6 ascend, refine 7 advance, augment, dignify, elevate, enhance, ennoble, glorify, greaten, inspire, magnify, promote 8 enthrone, heighten 9 intensify 10 aggrandize

exaltation: 7 elation, rapture 9 celsitude, elevation 10 apotheosis

exalted: 4 high 5 grand, noble 7 haughty, sublime 11 illustrious, magnanimous

examen: 7 inquiry 11 examination 13 investigation

examination: 4 exam, oral, quiz, test 5 assay, audit, check, trial 6 examen, review, survey, tripos 7 autopsy, inquest, inquiry 8 necropsy, research, scrutiny 10 comparison, inspection 11 exploration, inquisition 13 consideration, investigation 14 reconnaissance
taker: 6 testee

examine: spy, try 4 feel, scan, sift, view 5 assay, probe, quest 6 candle, ponder 7 analyze, canvass, palpate, rummage 8 overhaul 10 introspect, scrutinize 11 expostulate, interrogate, reconnoiter, reconnoitre
critically: 4 sift 6 censor
judicially: try
secretly: spy 9 eavesdrop

examiner: 6 censor, conner 7 analyst, auditor, coroner 9 inspector 10 inquisitor

example: 4 case, norm, tipe(Sp.), type 5 model 6 praxis, sample 7 pattern 8 exemplar, exemplum(L.), foregoer, instance, paradigm, specimen 9 precedent 11 description 12 illustration 15 exemplification

exanimate: 8 lifeless 9 inanimate 10 spiritless

exasperate: ire, irk 4 bait, gall, heat 5 annoy 6 enrage, excite, nettle 7 inflame, provoke, roughen 8 irritate 9 aggravate

exasperated: 5 wroth 9 indignant

excavate: dig 4 mine, mole, pion 5 delve, scoop 6 burrow, dredge

excavation: cut, pit 4 hole, mine 5 grave, stope 6 cavity, groove, trench
for ore: 4 mine 5 stope

into bank: **7** remblai
surface: **8** opencast
excavator: 6 bildar(Ind.), cleoid, digger **7** pioneer
exceed: top **4** best, pass **5** excel, outdo, outgo **6** better, outrun, outvie, overdo **7** eclipse, overtax, surpass **8** outrange, outstrip, overcome, overstep **9** overshoot, transcend **11** predominate
exceedingly: 4 tres(F.), very **5** amain **7** parlous **9** extremely
excel: cap, cob **4** best **5** outdo, outgo, shine **6** better, exceed **7** emulate, outpeer, surpass **8** outclass, outrival, outstrip **9** transcend
excellence: 5 arete(Gr.), merit **6** virtue **7** dignity **8** goodness **10** perfection
excellent: 4 best, braw(Sc.), fine, good **5** brave, bully, great, prime, super, wally(Sc.) **6** choice, famous, gentle, proper, select, spiffy, worthy **7** capital, corking, elegant, quality **8** eximious, generous, superior, valuable **9** admirable, first-rate **10** inimitable, preeminent **12** transcendent
excelse: 5 lofty **7** eminent
except: but **4** bate, omit, only **6** exempt, unless **7** besides, exclude **9** eliminate
exception: 5 demur **7** dissent, offense **9** complaint, condition, objection
exceptional: 4 rare **7** unusual **8** abnormal, uncommon **9** anomalous **10** remarkable **11** outstanding **13** extraordinary
excerpt: 4 cite **5** quote, scrap **7** extract
excess 4 over, plus, riot **5** flood **7** nimiety, overage, profuse, surplus **8** overmuch, overplus, plethora **10** exuberance, redundancy **11** excrescence, superfluity **12** intemperance **13** overabundance **14** superabundance
of solar year: **5** epact
excessive: too **4** over **5** enorm(Sc.), undue **6** de trop(F.) **7** extreme, nimious **8** allfired, enormous, horrible, overmuch **9** exuberant **10** boisterous, exorbitant, immoderate, inordinate **11** extravagant, intemperate **12** extortionate, unreasonable
excessively: 11 parlous
exchange: set **4** cash, chop, cope, mart, sell, swap, swop **5** bandy, bolsa, corse, store, trade, truck **6** barter, bourse, dicker, excamb(Sc.), market, resale, rialto, scorse, shoppe **7** barroom, chaffer, commute, dealing, traffic **9** excambion(Sc.), transpose **10** substitute **11** interchange, reciprocate **12** headquarters
business: **5** bolsa
medium: **7** coinage
rate: **4** agio **5** batta
exchequer: 4 fisc(Sc.) **5** purse **7** finance **8** treasury

excise: tax **4** duty, toll **6** impost, resect **7** exscind **8** alcabala(Sp.) **9** extirpate **10** overcharge
officer: **8** revenuer
excision: cut **7** erasure **9** expulsion **11** destruction, extirpation **15** excommunication
excitability: 12 irritability
excitable: 9 spasmodic
excite: 4 fire, spur, stir, urge **5** alarm, amove, anger, chafe, elate, impel, pique, rouse **6** arouse, awaken, decoct, foment, incite, kindle **7** agitate, animate, inflame, provoke **8** disquiet **9** electrify, galvanize, instigate, stimulate, titillate **10** exasperate, intoxicate
excited: hot **4** agog **5** eager, ranty **6** heated **7** fevered, wakened **8** flurried, startled
excitement: ado **4** stir **5** fever, furor, larry **6** warmth **7** widdrim(Sc.) **9** commotion **10** irritation **11** disturbance
exciting: 6 hectic **8** stirring, terrific
exclaim: 6 clamor, outcry **9** ejaculate
exclamation: ah, ai, ay, bo, ha, hi, ho, la, lo, oh, ow, so; aha, aie, bah, boo, fie, foh, hep, hey, hic, huh, och, oho, pah, poh, suz, tut, ugh, wow, yah **4** adad, ahem, alas, arra(Ir.), drat, egad, evoe, garn, hech, heck, hein(F.), hist, hoch(G.), hola, phew, pish, psha, pugh, rats, rivo, tush, wugg **5** alack, arrah(Ir.), bravo, faugh, feigh, heigh, holla, humph, ohone(Ir.), pshaw **6** clamor, hurrah, indeed, ochone(Ir.) **7** hosanna **9** alackaday, expletive **12** interjection
of contempt: foh, pah
of disgust: ugh **4** rats
of exhilaration: **4** evoe
of pain: ow **4** ouch
of sorrow: **4** alas **9** alackaday
of surprise: oh; aha, gee, oho, wow
of reproach: fie
exclude: bar **5** debar, eject, expel **6** banish, except, exempt, reject **7** foreign **9** blackball, eliminate, forestall, ostracize **13** excommunicate
exclusive: all **4** only, rare, sole **5** alone, whole **6** select **8** cliquish, entirely
excommunicate: 8 unchurch
excommunication: ban **8** excision
excoriate: 4 flay, gall **5** score, strip **6** abrade **11** decorticate
excrement: lee **4** dirt, dreg, dung, fece **5** faece **6** ordure, refuse
excrescence: 4 burl, lump, wart **6** excess, pimple **9** outgrowth, tubercule **11** superfluity
excrete: 5 egest **8** defecate **9** eliminate
excruciate: 4 rack **5** grind **7** agonize, torture
exculpate: 4 free **5** clear, remit **6** acquit, excuse, pardon **7** absolve, forgive, justify,

release 8 palliate 9 discharge, exonerate, vindicate

excursion: row 4 ride, sail, tour, trip 5 jaunt, sally, tramp 6 cruise, junket, outing, ramble, voyage 7 journey 8 campaign, escapade 10 digression, expedition

excusable: 6 venial 9 allowable 10 defensible, pardonable 11 justifiable

excuse: 4 plea 5 alibi, remit 6 acquit, essoin, pardon 7 absolve, apology, condone, essoign, essoine, forgive, pretext 8 dispense, occasion, overlook 9 exculpate, exonerate, extenuate, vindicate

for nonappearance: 6 essoin

for sickness: 5 aeger

excuss: 7 discard, discuss

execrable: bad 8 accursed, damnable, wretched 9 nefarious 10 abominable, detestable, horrifying

execrate: ban 5 abhor, curse 9 imprecate, objurgate 12 anathematize

execute: do; act 4 hang, kill, obey, play, slay 5 lynch 6 direct, effect, finish, manage 7 conduct, enforce, perform 8 complete 10 accomplish, administer 11 electrocute

execution: 7 garrote, technic 8 garrotte 9 technique 10 fulfilment 11 achievement, fulfillment

executioner: 7 butcher, hangman, headman, lockman 9 deathsman, Jack Ketch

executive: 4 dean 5 mayor 7 cashier, manager, premier 8 governor, official 9 president 13 administrator

executor: 4 doer 5 agent 8 enforcer 9 performer 13 administrator

exegesis: 10 exposition 11 explanation 14 interpretation

exegete: 6 critic 11 interpreter

exemplar: 5 model 7 example, pattern 9 archetype

exemplary: 8 laudable 11 commendable 12 praiseworthy

exemplification: 7 example 12 illustration

exemplify: 10 illustrate

exemplum: 7 example 12 illustration

exempt: 4 exon, free 6 fidate 7 exclude, release 8 excepted 9 discharge 11 exceptional

exemption: 7 freedom 8 immunity 12 dispensation

exenterate: 10 disembowel, eviscerate

exequy: 4 rite 7 obsequy 8 ceremony 10 procession

exercise: ply, ure, use 5 drill, etude, exert, longe 6 employ, lesson, parade, praxis, school 7 aufgabe, display, problem 8 activity, practice 9 athletics 10 exhibition, gymnastics, recitation 14 constitutional

system of: 8 aerobics

exercise book: 8 notebook

exerciser: 5 groom

exert: 4 emit 5 spend 6 reveal, strain 8 endeavor, exercise

exertion: 5 essay, labor, trial 6 action, effort, strife 7 attempt 8 endeavor

exfoliate: 5 scale 10 desquamate

exfoliation: 7 scaling

exhalation: 5 steam 9 effluvium, emanation 10 expiration 11 evaporation

exhale: 4 cast, emit 6 expire 7 breathe, respire 9 transpire

exhaust: sap 4 emit, fail, jade 5 break, drain, empty, peter, waste, weary 6 abrade, overdo 7 deplete, deprive, fatigue 8 evacuate 9 discharge 10 impoverish

exhausted: 4 done, worn 5 blown, spent, tired 6 barren, beaten, effete 7 emptied, fordone 8 consumed, foredone, forspent 10 forwearied

exhausting: 7 arduous

exhaustion: 7 fatigue 9 depletion, inanition, lassitude 11 exinanition, prostration

exheredate: 10 disinherit

exhibit: air 4 fair, shew, show 5 stage 6 blazon, evince, expose, ostend, parade, reveal 7 approve, display, perform, produce 8 disclose, discover, emblazon, evidence, manifest 9 represent 11 demonstrate

exhibition: 4 fair, show 5 sight 6 salary 7 display, pageant, pension, present 8 exercise 9 allowance, cosmorama, spectacle 10 exposition, sustenance 11 maintenance 13 manifestation 14 representation

exhibitioner: 8 servitor

exhilarate: 5 cheer, elate 7 animate, enliven, gladden 10 invigorate

exhilarated: rad 9 ebullient

exhilaration: 6 gaiety 7 jollity 8 gladness, hilarity 9 merriment 10 joyousness

exhort: 4 urge, warn 6 advise, dehort, incite, preach 7 caution 8 admonish 9 encourage

exhortation: 6 advice 7 counsel 9 hortation

exhume: dig 5 delve 7 unearth 8 disinter, exhumate

exigency: 4 need, want 7 urgency 8 juncture

exigent: 5 vital 8 critical, exacting, pressing 13 indispensable

exiguity: 7 paucity

exiguous: 4 fine, tiny 5 scant, small, spare 6 meager, sparse 7 slender 10 diminutive

exile: 4 poor, ruin, thin 5 expel 6 deport, outlaw, scanty 7 outcast, refugee, slender 8 fugitive 9 devastate, foreigner, ostracize 10 banishment, expatriate 12 proscription

exility: 7 tenuity 8 fineness, subtlety, thinness 9 smallness 10 meagerness 11 slenderness

eximious: 6 choice, select 9 excellent

exinanition: 9 abasement 10 exhaustion 11 humiliation

exist: am, be, is; are 4 live
at same time: 15 contemporaneous
in name only: 7 nominal, titular
passively: 7 subsist 8 vegetate

existed: was 4 been, were, wert

existence: ens 4 esse, life, sein 5 being 6 entity, inesse 7 essence, reality 9 actuality
beginning of: 5 birth, origin 9 nascency
having no: 4 dead, null, void 7 defunct
pert. to: 5 ontal, ontic

existent: 4 real 5 alive, being 6 extant 8 existing

Existentialist leader: 6 Sartre

existing: 5 alive, being 6 extant

exit: 4 door, gate 5 going, leave 6 egress, exitus, outlet 7 outgate, passage 8 debouche 9 departure

exitus: 4 exit 5 issue 6 exodus, outlet 7 outcome

exlex: 6 outlaw

exode: 9 departure 10 afterpiece

exodus: 5 exody 6 exitus 9 migration

exonerate: 4 free 5 clear 6 acquit, excuse, exoner, unload 7 absolve, relieve 9 disburden, discharge, exculpate, vindicate

exorbitant: 5 undue 8 abnormal 9 deviating, excessive, wandering 10 immoderate, outrageous 11 extravagant 12 extortionate, unreasonable

exorcism: 5 charm, spell 9 expulsion 11 incantation

exordium: 7 preface 9 beginning 12 introduction

exoteric: 4 open 6 public 8 external, outsider

exotic: 5 alien 7 foreign, strange 9 glamorous, peregrine 10 extraneous, outlandish

expand: ope, wax 4 blow, bulk, flue, grow, open 5 splay, swell, widen 6 dilate, extend, spread, unfold, unfurl 7 amplify, balloon, broaden, develop, diffuse, display, distend, educate, enlarge, explain, inflate, stretch 8 dispread, increase, lengthen 9 disspread, expatiate, explicate, intumesce

expanded: 8 patulous

expanse: 4 area, room 5 reach, tract 6 extent, spread 7 stretch 8 separate
vast: 5 ocean 6 desert, empire

expansion: ala 6 growth 8 increase 9 extension 10 dilatation, distention 11 development, enlargement

expansive: 4 free 5 broad 6 genial 7 elastic, liberal 8 spacious 9 bombastic, diffusive, grandiose

expatiate: 5 dwell 6 dilate, expand, spread 7 broaden, descant, diffuse, enlarge

expatriation: 5 exile 10 banishment

expect: 4 deem, hope, stay, trow, wait, ween 5 await 6 attend, demand 7 require, suppose 8 calculate 10 anticipate

expectation: 9 esperance

expectorate: 4 spit

expedient: 4 wise 5 dodge, knack 6 device 7 politic, stopgap 9 advisable, makeshift 10 profitable 12 advantageous

expedite: hie 4 easy, free 5 hurry, speed 6 hasten 7 quicken 8 dispatch 9 expediate 10 accelerate, facilitate

expedition: 4 fare, trek 5 drave(Sc.), haste, hurry 6 safari, voyage 7 crusade, journey 8 progress 9 excursion

expeditious: 4 fast 5 hasty, quick, rapid, ready 6 prompt, speedy

expel: 4 oust 5 eject, evict, exile 6 banish, deport 7 exclude 8 dislodge, for judge 9 discharge, eliminate, forejudge 10 dispossess, expatriate

expend: 5 spend, waste 6 occupy, ponder 7 dispend, overuse 9 dissipate 10 distribute

expenditure: 4 cost 5 outgo 6 outlay 10 lavishment 11 consumption 12 disbursement

expense: 4 cost, loss 5 batta, price 6 charge, gersum, outlay 8 overhead 11 consumption, expenditure 12 disbursement

expensive: 4 dear, high 6 costly, lavish 7 liberal 11 dispendious, extravagant

experience: see 4 feel, have, live, test 5 assay, skill, taste, trial 6 ordeal, suffer 7 calvary, feeling, undergo 9 adventure, knowledge

experienced: had, met 6 expert 7 veteran 9 practiced, underwent

experiment: try 4 test 5 assay, essay, trial 7 attempt

experimental: 9 empirical, tentative

expert: ace, dab 4 deft, good 5 adept 6 adroit, artist, au fait, clever, habile 7 artiste(F.), capable, skilled 9 authority 10 proficient 11 experienced 12 professional

expertness: 8 facility 9 dexterity, expertise

expiate: 5 atone, avert 6 assoil 10 propitiate

expiatory: 8 piacular

expiration: end 5 death 10 exhalation, extinction 11 termination

expire: die, end 4 emit 5 expel, lapse 6 elapse, exhale, perish

expiry: 5 close, death 10 extinction 11 termination

explain: 4 rede 5 aread, areed, gloze, solve 6 define, expand, unfold 7 expound 8 describe, exegesis, manifest 9 elucidate, enucleate, explicate, interpret 10 understand

explanation: key 7 account, apology 10 exposition 11 description 13 clarification

expletive: gee 4 bosh, egad, gosh, oath 5 begad

explicate: 6 expand, unfold 7 account, explain 9 interpret

explicit: 4 open 5 clear, exact, fixed, plain 7 express, precise 8 absolute, definite, implicit, positive, specific 9 categoric, outspoken 11 categorical, unambiguous, unequivocal 13 unconditional 14 discriminating

explode: 4 fire 5 blast, burst 8 backfire, detonate 9 fulminate

exploding meteor: 6 bolide

exploding star: 4 nova

exploit: act 4 deed, feat, gest, milk 5 geste, stunt 7 perform, success 9 advantage 11 achievement, performance

exploits: 9 res gestae(L.)

exploration: 5 probe 6 search 11 examinaion 13 investigation

explore: map 4 dive, feel 5 chart, range 8 discover

explorer: 4 Cook, Eric 5 Bruce, Cabot, Davis, diver, Drake 6 Baffin, Carter, Cortes, De Soto, Hearne, Hudson 7 pioneer, Pizarro, Raleigh 8 Amundsen, Columbus, Magellan, Vespucci 9 Frobisher 10 Chancellor, discoverer

explosion: pop 5 blast 6 blow-up, report 8 outburst 10 detonation

explosive: TNT 4 mine 6 amatol, powder, tonite 7 ammonal, lyddite, melnite 8 cheddite, dynamite, eruptive 9 fulminate, guncotton 10 detonative 13 nitroglycerin 15 trinitrotoluene

coal mine: 9 Bobbinite

device: cap 6 petard 9 initiator

high: TNT 7 cordite

igniter: 4 fuse

picric acid: 7 lyddite

place of manufacture: 4 Lydd

projectile: 5 shell 7 grenade 9 cartridge

sound: 4 bang, boom, chug 5 pluff, vroom

exponent: 9 explainer, expounder 11 interpreter 14 representative

expose: 4 bare, open, risk 5 strip 6 betray, detect, reveal, unmask 7 display, exhibit, expound, pillory, publish, uncover, unearth 8 disclose, discover, muckrake, ridicule, satirize, unclothe 10 exposition, jeopardize

exposed: 6 unsafe 11 unprotected

exposition: 4 fair 5 tract 6 expose 8 analysis, exegesis, exposure, treatise 10 exhibition, expounding 11 declaration, explanation 14 interpretation

expostulate: 5 argue 7 discuss, examine, protest 8 complain 11 remonstrate

expound: 5 gloze, treat 6 define, expose 7 develop, explain, exposit, express 8 construe 9 interpret

express: 4 vent 5 emote, opine, speak, state, utter, voice 6 denote, direct, phrase 7 declare, dictate, expound, testify 8 definite, describe, explicit, manifest 9 expatiate 10 articulate, particular, peremptory

appreciation: 5 thank

approval: 6 praise 7 applaud

pity: 6 bemoan

regret: 9 apologize

expression: 4 form, pose, show, sign, term, word 5 idiom, token, voice 6 byword, oracle, phrase, symbol 8 laconism 9 euphemism, statement, utterance 10 holophrase 11 delineation, holophrasis 13 manifestation 14 representation

facial: 4 grin, 5 laugh, scowl, smile 7 grimace

hackneyed: 6 cliche

mathematical: 8 equation

metaphorical: 6 figure

of approval: 4 clap 5 smile 7 ovation 8 applause

of assent: 6 placet

of contempt: bah, fie 4 geck, hiss 5 pshaw, sneer

of gratitude: 12 thanksgiving

of incredulity: 6 indeed

of opinion: 4 vote

of sorrow: ay 4 alas 11 lamentation

of weariness: 4 sigh

expressionless: 5 stony 6 vacant 8 toneless

expressive: 6 poetic 8 eloquent, emphatic 10 indicative 11 significant

expressly: 6 namely

expressway: 4 road 7 freeway, highway

exprobrate: 7 censure, upbraid 8 reproach

expugn: 5 storm 6 attack 8 vanquish

expulsion: 5 exile 6 bounce 8 ejection 10 banishment

expunge: 4 blot, dele 5 erase 6 cancel, delete, efface, excise 7 destroy, scratch 10 annihilate, obliterate

expurgate: 4 gelt 5 purge

exquisite: fop 4 dude, nice 5 dandy, exact 6 choice, dainty 7 careful, elegant, refined 8 affected, delicate 9 beautiful, delicious, excellent, matchless, perfected, recherche 10 consummate, farfetched, fastidious 12 accomplished 14 discriminating

exsanguine: 6 anemic 9 bloodless

exscind: 6 excise 9 extirpate

exsert: 8 protrude

exsiccate: dry

exsuccous: dry 7 sapless

extant: 5 alive, being 6 living 7 visible 8 existing, manifest 10 protruding 11 protuberant

extempore: 7 affloof(Sc.), offhand 9 forthwith 11 immediately 14 extemporaneous, unpremeditated

extend: eke, lie, run 4 grow, rise, span 5 bulge, cover, reach, renew, seize, widen 6 amount, deepen, deploy, dilate, expand, spread, strain 7 amplify, broaden, diffuse, display, distend, enlarge, overlap, overrun, proffer, prolong, radiate, stretch 8 continue, increase, lengthen, protract, protrude 10 exaggerate, generalize

extended: 4 long, open 12 outstretched

extending widely: far

extension: 4 area 5 scope 8 addendum, addition, duration, increase 9 expansion 11 enlargement 12 augmentation 13 amplification

building: ell 4 wing 6 lean-to

of time: 4 stay 7 respite 8 reprieve

trench: sap

extensive: 4 vast, wide 5 ample, broad, large 7 immense 8 expanded 9 capacious 10 widespread 11 far-reaching 13 comprehensive

extent: due, tax 4 area, body, bulk, levy, writ 5 ambit, limit, range, reach, scope, space 6 amount, attack, degree, spread 7 acreage, assault, breadth, compass, expanse, seizure 8 increase, latitude, quantity 9 dimension, extension, magnitude, territory, valuation 10 assessment

extenuate: 4 thin 5 gloze 6 excuse, lessen, weaken 8 diminish, palliate 9 alleviate, attenuate, disparage, underrate 10 depreciate 13 underestimate

extenuation: 10 dimunition

exterior: 5 ectad, ectal, outer, shell 6 extern 7 outside, outward, surface 8 external

exterminate: 5 expel 6 uproot 7 abolish, destroy 9 eradicate, extirpate 10 annihilate

extern: 7 outward 8 exterior, external 9 extrinsic

external: out 5 outer 6 extern 7 outside, outward 8 exterior 9 extrinsic 10 peripheral 11 superficial

comb. form: 4 ecto

extinct: 4 dead 7 defunct 8 quenched 12 extinguished

extinction: 5 death 6 expiry 9 abolition 10 expiration 11 destruction 12 annihilation, obliteration

extinguish: 4 dout 5 annul, choke, douse, dowse, quell 6 quench, stanch, stifle 7 destroy, eclipse, obscure, staunch 8 suppress 9 suffocate 10 annihilate

extinguished: 4 dead 7 extinct

extirpate: 4 dele 5 erase, expel 6 excise, uproot 7 destroy, exscind 8 supplant 9 eradicate 10 annihilate, deracinate 11 exterminate

extirpation: 8 excision 11 destruction, eradication 12 annihilation

extol, extoll: 4 laud 5 bless, exalt 6 praise 7 applaud, commend, elevate, enhance, glorify 8 emblazon, eulogize 9 celebrate

extort: 5 exact, force, wrest, wring 6 compel, elicit, wrench 7 extract 9 blackmail

extortion: 7 bribery 8 chantage, exaction, rapacity 10 oppression, overcharge

extortionate: 4 hard 9 excessive 10 exorbitant, oppressive

extortioner: 6 poller, shaver 11 blackmailer

extra: odd 4 more, orra(Sc.), over plus 5 added, spare 7 special, surplus 8 superior 9 accessory, lagniappe 10 additional

extract: dig, pry 4 cite, draw, pull 5 educe, exact, quote, steep, wring 6 decoct, deduce, derive, elicit, evulse, extort, remove, render 7 descent, essence, estreat, excerpt, exhaust, summary 8 withdraw 9 decoction, quotation 11 preparation

information: 4 pump

extraction: 5 birth, stock 6 origin 7 descent, essence, extract 8 breeding, tincture 9 parentage

extraneous: 5 outer 6 exotic 7 foreign 9 extrinsic 10 accidental

extraordinary: odd 4 rare, unco(Sc.) 5 byous(Sc.), enorm 6 signal 7 notable, special, strange, unusual 8 abnormal, singular, uncommon 9 irregular, monstrous, wonderful 10 additional, phenomenal, remarkable, surprising, tremendous 11 exceptional 13 distinguished

extravagance: ela

extravagant: 4 wild 5 outre 6 costly, heroic, lavish 7 baroque, bizarre, fanatic, nimious, profuse, vagrant 8 prodigal, reckless, romantic, wanderer, wasteful 9 excessive, expensive, fantastic, luxurious 10 exorbitant, thriftless 11 dispendious 12 unreasonable, unrestrained

extreme: 4 last, rank, sore 5 close, final, great, limit, ultra, undue, utter 6 heroic, severe, utmost 7 drastic, forward, howling, intense, outward, radical, violent 8 devilish, farthest, greatest, terrible, terrific 9 desperate, excessive, outermost, stringent, uttermost 10 conclusive, immoderate

comb. form: 4 acro, arch

extremely: so 4 very 6 mighty 10 mortacious 11 exceedingly

extremist: 7 radical

extremity: end, tip **4** need, tail **5** close, limit, verge **6** border **8** disaster, terminal **9** bitter end

extricate: **4** free **5** clear, loose **6** rescue **8** liberate, untangle **9** disengage **10** disembroil **11** disentangle

extrinsic: **5** every **7** foreign, outward **8** external **10** accidental, extraneous, incidental **11** unessential **12** adventitious, nonessential

extrude: **4** spew **5** eject, expel **7** project **8** protrude

exuberance: **6** plenty **8** overflow **9** abundance, profusion **11** excrescence **14** superabundance

exuberant: **6** lavish **7** copious, fertile, rampart **8** effusive **9** abounding, excessive, luxuriant, plentiful

exudation: gum, lac, sap, tar **5** pitch, resin, rosin **9** discharge, secretion

exude: **4** emit, ooze **5** sweat **7** secrete **8** perspire **9** discharge, percolate

exult: **4** crow, leap **5** boast, gloat, glory **6** spring **7** rejoice

exultant: **6** elated

exultation: joy **7** rapture **10** jubilation

exulted: **6** prided **7** vaunted

exuviate: **4** molt **5** moult

eyas: **4** bird **8** nestling

eye: ee(Sc.); orb **4** disc, gaze, glim, lamp, loop, mien, ogle, scan, view **5** glare, watch **6** behold, goggle, oculus(L.), peeper, regard, vision **7** blinker, observe, witness **10** scrutinize **11** discernment

　black: **5** mouse **6** shiner

　cavity: **5** orbit

　colored portion: **4** iris

　comb. form: **4** opia

　cosmetic: **4** kohl, kuhl

　covering: **6** eyelid **9** blindfold

　defect: **4** cast **6** anopia, myopia **11** astigmatism

　disease: **6** iritis **8** glaucoma, trachoma **14** conjunctivitis

　doctor: **15** ophthalmologist

　hollow: **5** orbit **6** socket

　instrument for examining: **8** otoscope **14** ophthalmoscope

　opening in: **5** pupil

　part: **4** disc, iris, uvea **5** pupil **6** areola, cornea, retina

　pert. to: **5** irian, optic **7** areolar, corneal, retinal **9** ocellated

　protector: **5** patch, visor **7** blinker

　pupil dilater: **8** atropine **10** belladonna

　science: **13** ophthalmology

　simple: **6** ocelli(pl.) **7** ocellus

eye-like: **9** ocellated

eyebrow: **4** bree(Sc.) **6** eebree(Sc.) **11** supercilium

eyedropper: **7** pipette

eyeglasses: **5** specs **6** lenses **7** lorgnon, nippers **8** monocles, pince-nez **9** lorgnette

eyelash: **4** lash **5** cilia(pl.) **6** cilium

　dye: **7** mascara

　loss: **9** madarosis

eyeless: **5** blind **9** sightless

eyelet: **6** agrafe, gromet, oillet **7** agraffe **8** peephole **10** buttonhole **11** perforation

eyeleteer: **6** bodkin **8** stiletto

eyelid: *drooping of:* **6** ptosis

　pert. to: **9** blepharal

eyer: **8** beholder **9** spectator

eyeshot: **5** range, reach

eyesight: **4** view **5** sight **11** observation

eyesome: **11** good-looking

eyesore: **6** defect **7** blemish

eyetooth: **6** cuspid

eyewash: **6** excuse **8** flattery

eyot: ait **5** islet

eyra: **7** wildcat

eyrie: See **aerie**

Ezekiel: *father:* **4** Buzi

　four beasts: **5** Aniel **6** Azriel, Haniel **7** Kafziel

F

fabes: 10 gooseberry
fabian: 8 cautious
fabiform: 10 bean-shaped
fable: 4 myth, tale 5 feign, story 6 legend 7 fiction, parable, untruth 8 allegory, apologue 9 falsehood, narrative 10 fabulosity
animal of: 6 dragon 7 centaur, unicorn
being of: 4 ogre 5 dwarf, giant, troll
bird of: roc 7 phoenix
collection: 8 bestiary
serpent of: 8 basilisk
fabric: rep, web 4 felt, repp 5 baize, beige, build, crepe, frame, lisle, rayon, serge, terry, tulle 6 creton, etoile 7 texture 8 cretonne, material 9 construct, cottonade
calico: 5 sallo 6 sallco
coarse: mat 5 crash 6 burlap
corded: rep 4 repp 5 pique
cotton: 4 susi 5 pique, wigan 6 burrah 7 buckram, galatea, hickory 8 bourette
cotton knit: 10 balbriggan
cotton of light quality: 4 leno 7 jaconet, organza 9 silka line
cotton mixture: 6 mashru 7 delaine, satinet, zanella 9 bombasine, grusaille
cotton print: 6 calico 7 percale 8 cretonne
cotton twilled: 5 denim, sallo 6 salico 7 fustian, silesia
cotton with silk embroidery: 8 agabanee
curtain material: 4 leno 5 scrim 6 moreen, velvet 7 silesia
dealer: 6 draper, mercer
finisher: 6 beetle
flag material: 7 buntine, bunting
heavy: 5 denim 6 canvas
linen: 4 crea(Sp.), ecru 5 carde, crash 6 barras 7 buckram, drabbet, sinelon
linen and cotton: 9 huckaback
linen of light quality: 4 lawn 5 scrim
lustrous: 6 poplin, sateen
medieval: 4 acca 6 samite
metallic: 4 lame
old: 9 ciclatoun
plaid: 6 tartan
printed: 5 batik 6 calico 7 challis

satin: 5 pekin 6 etoile
satin imitation: 6 sateen
sheer: 4 lawn 5 gauze, voile
silk: 4 alma, gimp, gros, ikat 5 caffa, carde, crepe, ninon, rumal, satin, surah 6 blatta, camaka, patola, samite 7 alamode, chiffon, taffeta, Xmantua, 8 barathea, bourette, sarcenet, sarsenet 9 charmeuse, levantine, matelasse 10 bombay-cine
silk (thin): 4 moff 5 tulle 6 pongee 7 hernani 8 eolienne
silk and cotton: 6 crepon, gloria 9 bombasine, bombazine
silk and linen: 8 brocatel 10 brocatelle
silk and wool: 6 crepon, gloria 7 challie, challis 8 eolienne
silk imitation: 5 rayon 7 satinet
silk mixture: kin 4 acca 5 balda 6 mashru 7 grogram 9 baldachin, baldaquin, farandine
silk-ribbed: rep 4 repp 6 faille 7 epingle 8 marocain
silk yarn: 7 schappe
straw: mat 7 matting
striped: aba
suiting: 6 dacron 7 acrilan
surface: nap
synthetic: 5 nylon, orlon, rayon 7 plastic
textile: rep 5 moire 7 etamine
texture: 4 woof
thin: 5 gauze 8 gossamer, tarlatan 9 grenadine
towel: 4 huck 5 terry
Turkish: 6 agaric 7 chekmak 8 cottonee 10 terry cloth
twilled: 4 alma 5 sallo, serge, surah 6 coburg, sallco 8 corduroy, shalloon, whipcord 9 bombasine, bombazine, gabardine, levantine, messaline, tricotine 10 kerseymere
unbleached: 5 beige
upholstery: rep 4 repp 6 frieze 7 tabaret
velvet-like: 5 panne 6 velure 8 duvetine 9 velveteen
waste material: 5 mungo

watered silk: 5 moire
waterproof: 8 burberry
white: 8 coteline
wide: 6 cotele
wool: 5 baize, beige, casha, serge, tweed 6 burnet, frisca, moreen 7 bolivia, debeige, delaine, droguet, frisado, frizado, hernani, worsted 8 cataloon, harateen, rattinet, zibeline 9 catalowne, gabardine, grenadine, harrateen, montagnac, zibelline
wool (coarse): 6 djersa, duffel, kersey, witney 7 bocking
wool dress: 5 beige 7 delaine 8 wildbore 9 grenadine
wool mixture: 7 delaine, zanella 9 grisaille
wool-ribbed: rep 4 repp 8 marocain
worsted: 7 etamine
woven: 4 lame 5 tweed, twill 6 tissue, tricot 7 blanket, damasse, textile
fabricate: 4 coin, form, make, mint 5 build, frame 6 devise, invent 7 concoct, fashion, produce 8 contrive 9 construct 11 manufacture
fabrication: lie 7 fiction, forgery, untruth 8 pretense 9 falsehood
fabricator: 4 liar 6 forger 12 manufacturer
fabricature: 9 structure 12 construction
fabula: 5 story
fabulist: 4 liar 5 Aesop, Grimm 6 fabler 8 Andersen 10 parabolist
fabulous: 7 feigned 8 mythical, romantic 9 legendary 10 apocryphal, fictitious 11 astonishing
facade: 4 face 5 front
face: map, mug, pan 4 dare, defy, dial, leer, line, meet, moue 5 cover, front, stand 6 facade, oppose, veneer, visage 7 feature, grimace, surface 8 confront, envisage 9 encounter, semblance 11 countenance, physiognomy
artery: 9 maxillary
bone: 5 malar 6 zygoma 7 maxilia 8 manduble
covering: 4 mask, veil
defect: 7 harelip
false: 4 mask
guard: 6 beaver
ornament: 4 veil 5 jewel, patch 9 cosmetics
paint: 4 fard 6 parget
part: eye, jaw, lid, lip 4 brow, chin, nose 5 cheek
with masonry: 5 revet
face eastward: 9 orientate
face-to-face: 7 affront, vis-a-vis
face value: par
facer: 6 bumper 7 tankard
facet: 5 bezel, culet, phase
facete: 5 witty 9 facetious

facetious: 5 witty 6 facete, jocose 7 jocular 8 humorous, polished 9 laughable
facia: 5 plate 6 tablet
facient: 4 doer 5 agent
facile: 4 able, easy 5 quick, ready 6 expert, fluent, gentle 7 affable, lenient
facilitate: aid 4 ease, help 5 speed 6 assist 8 expedite
facility: art 4 ease 5 eclat, knack, skill 7 address, freedom 9 dexterity, readiness 10 adroitness, expertness, pliability
facing: 5 front, panel 6 veneer 7 surface 8 covering, opposite
inward: 8 introrse
outward: 8 extrorse
facsimile: 4 copy 5 model 7 replica 9 duplicate, imitation 10 similitude 11 counterpart
fact: 4 data(pl.), deed, fait(F.) 5 datum, event, truth 6 factum(L.) 7 keynote, lowdown, reality 9 actuality 12 circumstance
support: 15 circumstantiate
faction: 4 bloc, sect, side 5 cabal, junto, party 6 brigue, clique 7 dispute, quarrel 8 intrigue 9 concision 11 combination
factious: 9 seditious 11 dissentious
factitious: 4 sham 9 unnatural 10 artificial
factor: gen 4 doer, gene 5 agent, maker 6 author, detail 7 bailiff, factrix, steward 8 adherent, aumildar, gomashta, gomastah 11 chamberlain, constituent
factory: 4 mill, shop 5 plant 6 aurang, aurung 8 building, fabrique(F.), officina(Sp.), workshop 11 manufactory 13 establishment
book: 7 bindery
factotum: 5 agent 7 servant 8 handyman
factual: 4 real, true 6 actual 7 literal
factum: 4 fact 5 event 8 memorial
faculty: wit 4 ease, gift 6 talent 7 ability 8 aptitude, capacity
fad: 4 rage, whim 5 craze, fancy, hobby 7 crochet, fashion 9 amusement
faddle: 6 trifle 8 nonsense
fade: die, dim, dow, wan 4 flat, pale, vade, wilt 5 daver, decay, passe, peter 6 perish, vanish, wither 7 decline, insipid, lighten 8 diminish, discolor, dissolve, evanesce, languish 11 commonplace
camera device: 4 iris 9 diaphragm
faded: dim 4 dull 5 faint, passe
fadge: fit 4 suit 6 bundle 7 succeed
faerie: See **fairy**
Faerie Queen: *author:* 7 Spenser
character: Una 4 Alma 5 Guyon 6 Amoret 7 Artegal 8 Calidore, Gloriana 11 Britomartis
Faeroes: *district manager:* 4 foud
island: 6 Ostero

whirlwind: oe
Fafnir: *brother:* 5 Regin
slayer: 6 Sigurd 7 Sigurth 9 Siegfried
fag: 4 flag, tire, toil 5 droop, weary 6 drudge, menial 7 exhaust, fatigue, frazzle 9 cigarette
fagot, faggot: 5 fadge 6 bundle
faik: 6 lessen
fail: ebb 4 flag, fold, lose, sink, wane 5 flunk, peter 6 desert, falter 7 exhaust, flicker, founder 8 languish
failing: 5 fault 6 foible 7 blemish, frailty, weakness 9 infirmity 10 deficiency 11 delinquency, diminishing 12 imperfection
failure: dud 4 bust, flop, lack, loss, miss 5 bilge, decay, fault, lapse, lemon 6 fiasco, fizzle 7 bloomer, debacle, decline, default, neglect 8 abortion, collapse, omission 10 bankruptcy, deficiency 11 delinquency, miscarriage, shortcoming 13 deterioration 14 disappointment
fain: 4 fond, glad 5 eager 7 pleased, willing 8 desirous, inclined 11 constrained
fainaigue: 5 shirk 6 revoke, renege
faineant: 4 idle, lazy 5 idler 8 inactive, sluggard
fainness: 8 gladness 9 eagerness 11 willingness
faint: dim 4 dark, pale, pall, soft, weak 5 swoon, timid, waugh 6 evanid, feeble, sickly 7 feigned, languid, obscure, syncope 8 cowardly, delicate, languish, listless, sluggish, timorous 9 simulated 10 indistinct
fainthearted: 5 timid 6 afraid, craven 8 cowardly, timorous
faintness: 7 tenuity 8 weakness 9 dejection 10 feebleness 12 timorousness 16 faintheartedness
fair: 4 calm, even, just, mart 5 bazar, blond, clear, feria(L.), right 6 bazaar, blonde, decent, honest, kermis 7 exhibit, kermess 8 distinct, middling, unbiased 9 beautiful, equitable, impartial 10 auspicious, exhibition, reasonable 12 unprejudiced 13 disinterested, dispassionate
fair game: 4 butt, dupe 6 victim
fair-haired: 5 blond 6 blonde
fair-mindedness: 6 equity 7 justice
fairest: 6 flower
fairly: 4 well 7 plainly 8 properly, suitably 9 favorably, tolerably 10 handsomely 12 legitimately
fairness: 6 equity 7 honesty 8 equality 12 impartiality
fairy: elf, fay, hob, imp 4 peri, perl, pixy, puck, shee, vila 5 pixie, sidhe 6 faerie, spirit, yaksha, yakshi 7 banshee, sylphid 8 folletto 10 leprechaun 11 enchantress

abode: 4 shee 5 sidhe
air: 5 sylph
chief: 4 Puck
king: 6 Oberon
queen: Mab, Una 7 Titania
shoemaker: 10 leprechaun
spirit of death: 7 banshee
tricky: 4 Puck
fairy-like: 5 elfin
fairyland: 7 elfland
fait: 4 deed, fact
faith: 5 certy(Sc.), creed, troth, trust 6 belief, certie(Sc.), credit 8 affiance, reliance 9 bona fides 10 confidence
article: 5 tenet 8 credenda 9 credendum
faithful: 4 fast, feal, firm, leal, true 5 liege, loyal, pious, tried 6 honest, steady, trusty 7 devoted, sincere 8 accurate, constant 9 steadfast, veracious 13 conscientious
faithfulness: 8 fidelity
faithless: 5 false, punic 6 fickle, hollow, unjust, untrue 7 atheist 8 apostate, delusive, disloyal, shifting, unstable 9 deceptive, mercurial 10 inconstant, perfidious 11 disaffected, incredulous, treacherous 12 unsatisfying
faithlessness: 7 falsity, perfidy, untruth 8 betrayal 10 infidelity
faitour: 5 cheat 8 imposter
fake: 4 hoax, sham 5 bogus, cheat, false, feign, fudge, phony 7 falsify, furbish, pretend, swindle 8 simulate, spurious 9 imitation 10 fictitious, fraudulent 11 counterfeit, manufacture
comb. form: 5 pseud 6 pseudo
faker: 5 quack 6 humbug 7 peddler 9 charlatan, pretender
fakir: 4 monk, yogi 7 ascetic, dervish 9 mendicant
falbala: 7 flounce 8 furbelow, trimming
falcon: 4 hawk 5 hobby, saker 6 lanner, luggar, lugger, merlin, musket, tercel 7 kestrel 9 peregrine
bait: 4 lure
blind: 4 seel
genus: 5 falco
male: 6 tercel 7 tiercel
nestling: 4 eyas
strap for: 4 jess
falconer: 6 hawker 8 ostreger 10 austringer
summons: wo
fall: sag 4 drip, drop, flop, plop, ruin, ruse, sile, sink, slip 5 abate, cloit(Sc.), crash, hance, lapse, plump, rapid, shoot, slump 6 autumn, happen, perish, recede, season, topple, tumble 7 cascade, decline, degrade, depress, descend, devolve, dribble, escheat, plummet, retreat, stumble, subside 8 cataract, collapse, commence, decrease 9

backslide, prostrate, surrender 10 capitulate, depreciate, disappoint 11 precipitate
back: 6 recede 7 relapse, retreat
in: 4 cave 5 agree, lapse 6 concur 9 terminate
short: shy 4 fail, lack, miss
fall guy: 5 patsy 9 scapegoat
fallacious: sly 6 untrue 8 delusive, guileful, illusory 9 deceitful, deceptive, insidious 10 fraudulent, misleading 11 treacherous
fallacy: 5 error 6 idolum
fallal: 4 ruff 6 finery, gewgaw
fallfish: 4 chub
fallible: 7 errable
falling: 6 cadent 8 prolapse, windfall 10 subsidence
fallout: 9 radiation
fallow: 4 pale 6 barren 9 yellow-red, yellowish 12 uncultivated
fallow deer: 6 damine
false: 4 fake, sham 5 bogus, fause(Sc.), paste, phony, wrong 6 fickle, hollow, pseudo, untrue 7 bastard, crooked, feigned 8 disloyal, illusive, recreant, spurious 9 deceitful, deceptive, dishonest, erroneous, faithless, incorrect, insincere, irregular, pretended 10 apocryphal, artificial, calumnious, fictitious, groundless, mendacious, misleading, perfidious, traitorous, untruthful 11 counterfeit, disaffected, treacherous, unveracious 12 hypocritical
comb. form: 6 pseudo
falsehood: cog, fib, lie 4 flam, tale 5 fable 7 falsity, fiction, perfidy, romance, untruth 8 roorback 9 deception, duplicity, imposture, mendacity, treachery 10 pseudology 11 fabrication
falsify: lie 4 fake 5 belie, feint, forge 6 betray, doctor 7 violate 9 dissemble 10 adulterate 11 counterfeit
falsity: lie 5 error 7 untruth 9 falsehood, falseness, mendacity 13 deceitfulness, faithlessness 17 untrustworthiness
show: 5 belie 8 disprove
Falstaff: *follower:* Nym
ancient: 6 Pistol
prince: Hal
falter: 4 fail 5 pause, waver 6 boggle, flinch, totter 7 fribble, stumble, tremble 8 hesitate
faltering: 4 hink
Fama: 5 rumor
fame: 5 bruit, glory, honor, kudos, rumor 6 renown, report, repute 7 hearsay 9 celebrity 10 reputation
famed: 5 known, noted 7 eminent, renomee(F.) 11 illustrious, outstanding 13 distinguished
familiar: 4 bold, cozy, easy, free, tosh 5 usual 6 common, homely, versed 7 affable

8 frequent, habitual, intimate, sociable 9 customary, household, presuming, well-known 10 accustomed, conversant 12 acquaintance 13 unconstrained
familiarize: 4 haft 8 accustom 9 habituate 10 naturalize
family: lik, kin 4 clan 5 class, flesh, group, house 6 cletch 7 kindred, lineage, progeny 8 category 9 household 10 generation
head: 7 goodman, husband 9 patriarch 11 householder 13 pater familias(L.)
pert. to: 7 nepotic 12 genealogical
famine: 6 dearth, hunger 8 scarcity 10 starvation 11 destitution
famish: 4 kill 6 starve 7 destroy
famous: 5 grand, noted 6 namely 7 eminent, namable, notable 8 renowned 9 excellent, notorious 10 celebrated, celebrious 11 conspicuous, outstanding 13 distinguished
famulus: 7 servant 9 attendant
fan: 4 beat, cool 5 punka 6 basket, blower, colmar, punkah, rooter, shovel, spread, winnow 7 admirer, devotee 8 follower 9 flabellum, propeller 10 enthusiast
alluvial: 5 delta
form of: 7 plicate
fan-shaped: 10 flabellate
fanal: 5 light 6 beacon
fanatic: mad 5 bigot, crazy, rabid, ultra 6 zealot 7 devotee 8 frenetic 9 energumen, phrenetic 10 enthusiast, monomaniac 11 extravagant
fancied: 6 unreal 7 dreamed 9 imaginary 10 fictitious
fanciful: odd 5 ideal, queer 6 dreamy, quaint, unreal 7 bizarre, strange 8 romantic 9 conceited, fantasque, fantastic, grotesque, visionary, whimsical 10 capricious, chimerical, notionable 11 imaginative, unrealistic
fancy: fad 4 idea, love, maze, ween, whim 5 dream, freak, guess, humor 6 humour, ideate, liking, megrim, notion, ornate, vagary, vision, whimsy 7 caprice, chimera, conceit, crochet, fantasy, romance, suspect 8 chimaera, conceive, illusion, phantasm, phantasy 9 capriccio, fantaisie 10 conception, conjecture, decorative, impression, ornamental 11 imagination, inclination
fandango: 4 ball, tune 5 dance
fane: 4 flag 6 banner, church, temple 7 pennant 9 cathedral, sanctuary 11 weathercock
fanfare: 7 tantara 8 fanfaron, flourish 9 fanfarade 11 fanfaronade
fanfaron: 7 boaster, fanfare 8 braggart 9 swaggerer

fanfaronade: 7 bluster, fanfare 8 boasting 10 swaggering 11 ostentation

fanfoot: 5 gecko 6 lizard

fang: 4 earn, take, tusk, vang 5 begin, seize, snare, tooth 6 assume, obtain 7 capture, procure 9 undertake

fange: mud 4 dirt, mire

fangle: 4 mode 5 dress 6 geegaw 7 fashion

fanion: 4 flag 6 guidon

fanlight: 7 transom

fanon: 4 cape 5 orale 7 maniple

fantasque: 4 whim 5 fancy 7 fantasy 8 fanciful 9 fantastic

fantast: 7 dreamer 9 visionary

fantastic: odd 5 queer 6 absurd, unreal 7 bizarre 8 fanciful, freakish, romantic, singular 9 fantasque, grotesque, whimsical 10 capricious, chimerical 11 extravagant, imaginative 12 unbelievable

fantasy: 4 idea 5 dream, fancy 6 desire, vision 7 caprice, chimera, phantom, romance 8 chimaera, phantasm 9 fantasque 10 apparition 11 imagination, inclination 13 hallucination

fantoccini: 5 shows 7 puppets

fantod: pet 4 fuss 6 fidget

fantom: See **phantom**

far: 4 long 6 remote 7 distant
across: 4 wide
comb. form: tel 4 tele
down: 4 deep

far-reaching: 4 deep, vast 7 intense 8 profound

faraway: 6 dreamy, remote 7 distant 10 abstracted

farce: 4 mime 5 stuff 6 comedy 7 mockery 8 drollery 9 forcemeat

farceur: wag 5 joker

farcical: 5 comic, droll 7 Atellan 9 ludicrous 10 ridiculous

fardel: lot 4 furl, pack 6 bundle, burden 10 collection

fare: eat 4 diet, food, path, rate, wend 5 cheer, going, price, track, viand 6 happen, travel 7 journey, passage, proceed, prosper 8 progress 9 equipment, passenger, provision, sagaciate 10 expedition 11 nourishment 13 entertainment

farer: 8 traveler

farewell: ave(L.) 4 vale(L.) 5 adieu, adios, aloha, conge, final 7 goodbye, leaving, parting 9 bon voyage, departure 11 valedictory

farfetched: 6 forced 7 devious 8 strained 9 recherche 10 roundabout

farina: 4 meal 5 flour 6 starch

farinaceous food: oat, rye 4 meal 5 flour, grain, salep, spelt, wheat 6 barley, cereal 7 pudding 10 cornstarch

farm: 4 till 5 croft, empty, haras, ranch, range 6 barton, chacra, grange, rancho 7 cleanse, hennery, potrero 8 estancia, hatchery, hacienda 9 cultivate, farmstead
building: 4 barn, crib, shed, silo 7 farmery
grazing: 5 ranch
laborer: 4 hand, hind
machine: See **agriculture** *machine;* **machine** *farm*
steward: 7 granger
tenant: 6 cotter 7 cottier, cropper, metayer 12 sharecropper

farm out: let 4 hire

farmer: 4 tate 6 grower, tiller, yeoman 7 granger, hayseed, planter, plowman, rancher 8 producer 9 hacendero(Sp.), ploughman 10 cultivator, husbandman 13 agriculturist
Egyptian: 6 fellah 8 fellahin(pl.)
migratory: 4 Okie
South African: 4 Boer

farmhouse: 6 grange 7 caserio(Sp.), onstead(Sc.)

farming: 9 husbandry

farmland: 7 acreage

farmyard: 6 barton

farnesol: 7 alcohol

faro: 5 monte
bet: 7 sleeper
card: 4 soda
card combination: 5 split 6 cathop
player: 6 punter

Faroes: See **Faeroes**

farouche: shy 4 wild

farrago: 6 medley 7 mixture

farrier: 5 shoer, smith 10 blacksmith, horseshoer 12 veterinarian

farrow: pig, row 4 rake 6 litter

farseeing: 10 telescopic

farsighted: 6 shrewd 9 hyperopia, provident, sagacious 11 foresighted 13 hypermetropia

farther: 6 longer 7 remoter

farthest: 7 endmost, extreme, farmost, longest, outmost 8 remotest 11 farthermost

farthing: 4 coin 8 quadrans

fascia: 4 band, sash 6 fillet 7 molding

fascicle: 6 bundle 7 cluster

fascinate: 5 charm 6 allure, enamor 7 attract, bewitch, enchant, engross, philter, philtre 8 entrance, interest, intrigue 9 captivate, enrapture, spellbind

fascinating: 9 glamorous 10 attractive, glamourous

fascination: 5 charm, spell 11 enchantment

fashion: fad, ton(F.) 4 form, make, mode, mold, rage 5 craze, forge, frame, guise, model, mould, shape, style, vogue 6 create,

custom, design, fangle, invent, manner,
method 7 compose, portray 8 contrive 9
construct, fabricate

fashionable: 5 dashy, smart 6 modish 7 a la
mode, dashing, stylish

fashioned: 6 carved 7 wrought

fast: 4 firm, Lent 5 agile, apace, brisk, fixed,
fleet, hasty, quick, rapid, stuck, swift 6
lively, secure, speedy, stable, starve 7
abiding, settled 8 enduring, faithful 9 immovable, indelible, steadfast, unfadable,
velocious 10 abstinence, stationary, unyielding 11 expeditious

day of: 5 Ember

period of: 4 Lent

fasten: bar, fix, pen, pin, tag, tie 4 bend,
bind, bolt, clip, gird, girt, glue, knit, lace,
lash, link, lock, moor, nail, rope, seal, snib,
soud, weld, wire 5 affix, annex, belay,
brace, chain, clamp, clasp, cling, latch,
paste, rivet, seize, strap, truss 6 anchor,
attach, batten, cement, clinch, picket, secure, solder, staple, tether 7 connect, padlock 8 transfix

comb. form: 4 desm 5 desmo

fastener: bar, gib, nut, pin 4 agal, bolt, frog,
hasp, lock, nail, snap 5 catch, clamp, clasp,
latch, rivet, screw, strap, thong 6 buckle,
button, hatpin, staple, zipper 7 latchet,
padlock 8 staylace

fastidious: 4 fine, nice 5 chary, fussy, natty
6 choicy, choosy, dainty 7 choosey, elegant, finical, finicky, haughty, refined 8
critical, delicate, gingerly, overnice, scornful 9 exquisite, finicking, squeamish 10
meticulous, particular 14 overparticular

fastigate: 7 conical, pointed

fastness: 4 fort 6 castle 7 citadel 8 fortress
10 stronghold

fastuous: 7 haughty 8 arrogant 12 ostentatious

fat: oil, tub 4 lard, lipa, rich, suet 5 adeps,
brosy, cetin, chuff, ester, fleck, gross, lipid,
lipin, obese, plump, podgy, pudgy, pursy,
squab, stout, thick 6 fleshy, grease, lipide,
portly, pubble, stocky, tallow 7 adipose,
blubber, fertile, fulsome, lanolin, opulent,
pinguid, stearin 8 extended, fruitful, lanoline, stearine, unctuous 9 corpulent 10
profitable 11 flourishing

comb. form: pio 4 lipo, sebi 5 adipo, steat 6
steato

hard: 4 suet

liquid: 5 elain, olein 6 elaine, oleine

of geese: 6 axunge

pert. to: 6 adipic

render: try 4 lard

wool: 7 lanolin 8 lanoline

fat person: 4 lump 5 blimp, squab, tubby 8
roly-poly 12 humpty-dumpty

fata morgana: 6 mirage

fatal: fey 4 dire 6 deadly, doomed, funest,
lethal, mortal 7 capital, fateful, ominous,
ruinous 8 destined 9 condemned, prophetic 10 calamitous, disastrous, pernicious, portentous 11 destructive

fatality: 5 wreck 8 calamity, disaster

fatbird: 8 guacharo

fate: end, lot 4 doom, ruin 5 event, karma 6
chance, kismet 7 destiny, fortune, outcome 8 downfall 14 predestination

goddess: Ker 4 Nona, Norn 5 Morta, Tyche
8 Adrastea 9 Adrasteia

fated: 6 doomed 7 decreed 8 destined 10 inevitable

fateful: 5 fatal 6 deadly 7 ominous 9 momentous, prophetic 10 inevitable, portentous
11 destructive, predestined

Fates: *Greek:* 5 Moera, Moira 6 Clotho, Mo-
erae 7 Atropos 8 Lachesis

Roman: 4 Nona 5 Decum, Morta, Parca 6
Parcae

father: bu(Ar.), pa; abu(Ar.), ama, dad, pop
4 abba, abou(Ar.), baba(Ar.), bapu, papa,
pere(F.), sire 5 adopt, babbo, beget, daddy,
friar, padre(Sp.), vader(Dan.) 6
old man, parent, priest 7 tatinek(Czech.) 8
beaupere(F.), generate 9 confessor, paternity, procreate 11 acknowledge

of English learning: 4 Bede

of geometry: 6 Euclid

of gods and men: 4 Zeus

of human race: 4 Adam

of plenty: 8 Abiathar

pert. to: 6 agnate 8 paternal

Father of Waters: 11 Mississippi

fatherhood: 9 paternity

fatherly: 8 parental, paternal

fathom: 5 brace, delve, solve 7 measure 9
penetrate

fathomless: 16 incomprehensible

fatidic: 9 prophetic

fatigue: fag 4 jade, tire 5 spend, weary 6
overdo, taigle(Sc.) 7 exhaust 8 fatigate

fatigued: 4 beat 8 tuckered 9 forjaskit,
forjesket

fatiloquent: 9 fatidical, prophetic

Fatima: *husband:* Ali 9 Bluebeard

descendant: 7 Fatimid 8 Fatimite

sister: 4 Anne

stepbrother: Ali

fatness: 10 pinguitude

fatten: 4 lard 6 batten, enrich, thrive

fatty: 5 suety 6 greasy 7 adipose, pinguid 8
unctuous

fatty tumor: 6 lipoma

fatuous: 5 inane, silly **6** stupid, unreal **7** foolish, idiotic, witless **8** demented, illusory, imbecile **9** frivolous, insensate

faucal: 10 pharyngeal

faucet: tap **4** cock **5** valve **6** spigot **7** hydrant

faugh: bah

fault: sin **4** debt, flaw, flub, lack, slip, vice **5** abuse, blame, culpa(L.), error, guilt, lapse, tache(Sc.) **6** defect, foible, vitium(L.) **7** blemish, blunder, default, demerit, failure, frailty, mistake, neglect, offense **10** peccadillo **11** culpability, delinquency, misdemeanor **12** imperfection **13** transgression

in mining: **4** hade

faultfinder: 5 momus **6** carper, critic **7** caption, knocker, nagster

faultless: 4 pure **5** right **7** correct, perfect, precise **8** flawless **9** blameless **10** impeccable **13** unimpeachable **14** irreproachable

faulty: bad, ill **5** amiss, unfit, wrong **9** incorrect **10** inaccurate

faun: 5 satyr

of Praxiteles: **6** marble

fauna and flora: 5 biota

Faunus: *grandfather:* **6** Saturn

son: **4** Acis

Faust: *author:* **6** Goethe

composer: **6** Gounod

fautor: 6 patron **7** abetter, abettor, favorer **8** partisan **9** protector

faux pas: 4 bull, slip **5** boner, error, gaffe, lapse **6** booboo, bungle **7** blooper, misstep, mistake

faveolate: 6 favose **9** alveolate **11** honeycombed

favonian: 4 mild

favor, favour: aid, for, pro **4** boon, face, gree, help **5** bless, grace, leave, spare **6** esteem, letter, uphold **7** advance, feature, forward, support **8** advocacy, befriend, goodwill, kindness, resemble **9** patronage, privilege, subscribe **10** assistance, concession, indulgence, permission **11** accommodate, approbation, countenance **13** communication

pay: woo **5** court

favorable: 4 good, kind, rosy **5** clear **6** benign **7** benefic, optimal, popular **8** friendly, gracious, pleasing **9** approving, opportune **10** auspicious, charitable, convenient, propitious **12** advantageous

favored: 6 gifted **9** fortunate, preferred

favorer: 6 fautor **9** supporter

favorite: pet **6** minion **7** darling, popular

favoritism: 4 bias **8** nepotism **9** prejudice

favose: 8 aveolate **9** faveolate, honeycomb

fawn: 4 buck, deer, jouk **5** color, cower, crawl, kotow, toady, whelp **6** cringe, grovel, kowtow, shrink **7** adulate, flatter,

hangdog, servile, toadeat, truckle **9** parasitic, sycophant **10** ingratiate

skin: **6** nebris

fay: elf, fit **4** join **5** fairy, unite **6** sprite

faze: 5 daunt, worry **10** disconcert

F.D.R.: See **Roosevelt, F.D.**

fe: 4 iron

feal: 5 loyal **7** conceal **8** faithful

fealty: 6 homage **7** loyalty **8** fidelity **9** constancy, obeisance **10** allegiance

fear: awe **5** alarm, doubt, dread, panic **6** danger, dismay, fright, horror, phobia, terror **7** anxiety, suspect **8** affright, disquiet, distrust, venerate **9** agitation, reverence, revulsion **10** solicitude **12** apprehension **13** consternation

of animals: **9** zoophobia

of being alone: **10** monophobia

of burial alive: **11** taphephobia

of cats: **12** aelurophobia, ailurophobia

of crowds: **11** ochlophobia

of darkness: **11** nyctophobia

of dirt: **10** mysophobia

of drafts: **10** aerophobia

of enclosed places: **14** claustrophobia

of fire: **10** pyrophobia

of great heights: **10** acrophobia

of open spaces: **11** agoraphobia

of pain: **10** algophobia

of poisons: **10** toxiphobia

of strangers: **10** xenophobia

of thunder: **12** brontophobia **13** tonitrophobia

of water: **11** hydrophobia

fearful: 4 dire **5** awful, pavid, timid **6** afraid **7** ghastly, nervous, panicky, worried **8** cautious, doubtful, dreadful, grewsome, gruesome, horrible, horrific, shocking, terrible, timorous **9** appalling, frightful, trembling **10** formidable, horrendous, meticulous **11** distressing **12** apprehensive

comb. form: **4** dino

fearless: 4 bold **5** brave **6** daring, heroic **7** impavid **8** intrepid **9** audacious, confident, dauntless, undaunted **10** courageous

fearsome: 5 timid **8** timorous **9** frightful

feasible: 6 likely **8** possible, probable, suitable **9** practical **10** reasonable

feast: eat, foy(Sc.), sup **4** dine, fete, luau, meal **5** festa, treat **6** regale, repast **7** banquet, delight, festino, gratify **8** festival, potlatch **10** burrakhana

comb. form: mas

Christian: **5** agape **9** eucharist

funeral: **5** arval, arvel, dirgy(Sc.), **6** arthel, averil, dirgie(Sc.)

January 6: **8** Epiphany

of lanterns: Bon

of lights: 7 Hanukka 8 Chanukah, Hanuk-
kah
of lots: 5 Purim
of nativity: 9 Christmas
of tabernacles: 7 Succoth
of weeks: 8 Shabuoth
passover: 5 seder
feasting: 9 epulation
companion: 7 convive
feat: act 4 deed, gest 5 geste, stunt, trick 7
exploit, miracle 11 achievement, performance 14 accomplishment
feather: 4 deck, down, vane 5 adorn, penna,
pinna(L.), pluma(L.), plume, quill, 6
clothe, fledge, fletch, hackle, pinion
barb: 4 harl, herl 7 pinnula
comb. form: 5 ptile
down: 4 dowl 5 dowle 7 plumule
mature: 10 teleoptile
quill: 5 remex 7 calamus
shaft: 5 scape
shank: 4 boot
shoulder: 4 cape
feather alum: 8 alunogen 12 halotrichite
feather-brained: 7 foolish 9 frivolous
feather-headed: 5 giddy 7 foolish
feather key: 6 spline
feather star: 8 comatula 9 comatulae(pl.),
comatulid
feathered: 7 pennate, pinnate
feathers: *provide with:* 6 fletch
shed: 4 molt 5 moult
feathery: 6 fluffy
featly: 6 neatly, nimbly 8 graceful, properly
feature: 4 face 5 favor, motif, token, trait 6
aspect, favour 7 amenity, outline 8 salience 9 lineament 11 countenance 14
characteristic
natural: 9 geography
feaze: 4 fray 7 roughen, unravel, untwist
febris: 5 fever
feces, faeces: 4 dreg 5 drast, drest 6 ordure,
refuse 8 sediment 9 excrement, feculence
feck: 5 value 6 amount 8 quantity
fecket: 9 waistcoat
feckful: 6 strong 8 powerful 9 efficient
feckless: 4 weak 9 shiftless, worthless
feckly: 6 almost, mostly
feculence: 5 dregs, feces 6 faeces 8 foulness
9 muddiness
fecund: 7 fertile 8 fruitful, prolific
fecundate: 9 fertilize, pollinate 10 impregnate
fed up: 5 bored 7 wearied 8 satiated 9 surfeited
fedarie: 10 accomplice 11 confederate
federacy: 8 alliance 11 confederacy
federation: 5 union 6 league, nation 8 alliance 11 association, confederacy

fedity: 8 impurity, vileness
fedora: hat
fee: 4 dues, feal, feul(Sc.), fier, hire, rate,
wage 5 price 6 charge, dastur, employ, reward, salary 7 payment, stipend, storage,
tribute 8 gratuity, malikana, retainer 9
allowance, bienvenne, emolument, pourboire 10 assessment, honorarium, perquisite, recompense 12 compensation
feeble: 4 flue, lame, mean, poor, puny, weak
5 faint 6 dotage, flabby, flimsy, foible, infirm, scanty, sickly, wankle, weanly 7
fragile, invalid, languid, queechy 8 decrepit, impotent, inferior, thewless(Sc.),
yielding 9 miserable 10 inadequate, indistinct 11 debilitated
feeble-minded: 5 anile, dotty 7 moronic 10
irresolute 11 vacillating
feed: eat, hay 4 bait, bran, fill, glut, grub,
meal, oats, sate 5 agist, gorge, grass, graze,
nurse 6 fodder, foster, repast, suckle, supply 7 blowout, furnish, gratify, herbage,
indulge, nourish, nurture, satiate, satisfy,
surfeit, sustain 9 replenish
to excess: 4 glut 6 agrote, pamper 7 surfeit
8 overfill 9 crapulate
feeder: 9 tributary
fire: 6 stoker
feel: 5 grope, sense, touch 6 handle 7 examine, explore, sensate 8 perceive 10 appreciate, experience
feeler: 4 palp 6 palpus 7 antenna, smeller 8
proposal, tentacle
feeling: 4 pity, tact, view 5 humor, touch 6
morale 7 emotion, opinion, passion 8 attitude, sentient 9 affection, sensation, sentiment 10 atmosphere, experience, perception 11 sensibility 13 consciousness 14 susceptibility
capable of: 8 sentient
evocative of: 7 emotive
lack of: 8 numbness 9 apathetic, insensate
10 anesthesia 11 anaesthesia 13 insensibility
feet (see also **foot**): 4 dogs
feeze: 4 rush 5 drive 6 impact 7 disturb
fegary: 4 whim 5 prank 6 finery, gewgaw
feign: act 4 fake, seem, sham 5 avoid, fable,
shape, shirk 6 affect, assume, invent 7 conceal, fashion, imagine, pretend, romance 8
disguise, simulate 9 dissemble, personate
11 counterfeit, dissimulate, make-believe
ignorance: 7 connive
sickness: 8 malinger
feigned: 5 false 6 pseudo 7 fictive 9 insincere
10 artificial, fictitious
feil: 4 neat 11 comfortable
feint: 4 ruse 5 shift, trick 7 falsify, feigned 8
pretense 9 diversion

in fencing: 5 appel
feirie: 6 active, nimble
feis: 8 assembly 10 convention
feist: dog, pup
feldspar: 6 albite, gneiss 7 odinite, syenite 9 anorthite 11 labradorite
  yield: 6 kaolin
felicitate: 12 congratulate
felicitous: 5 happy
felicity: joy 9 happiness, well-being
felid: cat
felidae: cat
feline: cat, sly, tom 4 lion, lynx, pard, puma 5 civet, tiger 6 jaguar 7 cheetah, leonine, leopard, wildcat 8 stealthy 9 grimalkin 11 treacherous
  breathing: 4 purr
felis: *domestica:* cat
  leo: 4 lion
  pardus: 7 leopard
fell: cut, fen, hew 4 down, hide, hill, moor, pelt, ruin, skin, very 5 cruel, eager, field, great, sharp 6 deadly, fierce, fleece, intent, mighty, savage, shrewd 7 brutish, crashed, doughty, hideous, inhuman, tumbled 8 mountain, spirited, vigorous 9 barbarous, ferocious, marshland, momentous, prostrate 11 destructive
fellah: 7 peasant
fellow (see also **man; person**): bo; cod, guy, lad, man 4 bean, beau, bozo, carl, chal, chap, cove, dick, duck, hind, mate, peer 5 billy, bloke, chiel, match 6 bugger, callan, chield, codger, hombre(Sp.), person, sirrah 7 callant, chappie, comrade, cullies, partner, scroyle 8 neighbor 9 associate, companion 10 sweetheart 12 contemporary
  awkward: oaf 4 club, gawk, lout, slam 5 booby, clown 6 galoot 7 bumpkin 9 dromedary 11 hobble-de-hoy
  beggardly: 8 bezonian
  brutish: 5 yahoo
  conceited: 7 dalteen
  craven: 6 coward
  dissolute: 4 rake, roue 9 debaucher
  dull: 4 drip, fogy 5 fogey 8 codshead
  fat: 7 glutton
  fine: 5 brick, bully 7 bawcock 8 bonhomme(F.)
  foolish: sop 4 goff
  funny: wag, wit 4 card 5 clown
  honest: 6 trusty 9 truepenny
  idle: 6 footer, stochah
  ignorant: 6 gobbin
  lazy: bum 9 drawlatch
  little: bub 5 caddy 6 birkie, caddie, shaver 9 dandiprat

  mean: cad 4 boor, carl, pleb 5 bucko, bully, catso, cavil, churl, yahoo 6 fouter, foutre 7 cullion 8 blighter, coistrel, coistril, smatchet(Sc.)
  old: 6 geezer, gleyde
  old-fashioned: 4 fogy
  queer old: 6 geezer 10 curmudgeon
  ragged: 10 ragamuffin 14 tatterdemalion
  reckless: 4 buck 5 blade 9 daredevil, hell-raker
  rowdy: 6 roarer 8 larrikin
  shrewd: 6 gazabo, gazebo
  silly: 8 dotterel
  stupid: ass 4 clod, daff, dolt, gump, hash, simp 5 booby, dunce, moron 6 bayard, foozle 8 codshead 9 blockhead, heavyhead 10 bufflehead 11 blunderbuss, blunderhead
  tricky: 5 knave, scamp 6 rascal
  vain: fop
  worthless: bum, cur 5 rogue, scamp 6 budzat 7 bobtail, brothel, budzart, vaurien(F.) 9 schlemiel(Yid.), schlemihl(Yid.), scoundrel
fellowship: 5 guild, union 7 company 8 alliance 9 communion 10 membership 11 association, brotherhood, camaraderie, comradeship, corporation, familiarity, intercourse, partnership 12 acquaintance, friendliness 13 companionship
felly: rim 6 keenly 7 cruelly 8 bitterly, fiercely, savagely, terribly 11 barbarously 13 destructively
felo-de-se: 7 suicide
felon: 4 wild 5 cruel 6 fetlow, fierce, wicked 7 convict, culprit, villain, whitlow 8 criminal 9 murderous 10 malefactor
felony: 5 arson, crime 7 offense
felt: hat 6 fabric, sensed
felwort: 7 gentian
female: 4 girl, gyne 5 woman 6 weakly 7 feminal, womanly 8 feminine, ladylike, womanish 9 womanlike 10 effeminate
  animal: cow, doe, ewe, hen 4 mare, slut 5 bitch, filly, jenny 6 sheder 7 lioness, tigress
  assistant: 8 adjutrix 9 adjutrice
  camel: 4 naga
  comb. form: gyn 4 gyne, gyno
  figure: 5 orant 8 caryatid
  fish: 4 raun
  fox: 5 vixen
  monster: 6 gorgon
  principle: 5 Sakti
  red deer: 4 hind
  saint: ste
  sandpiper: 5 reeve
  sheep: ewe
  slave: 7 odalisk 9 odalisque
  spirit: 7 banshee

warrior: 6 Amazon

feminine: 4 soft, weak 5 woman 6 female, tender 8 womanish 10 effeminate

femininity: 10 effeminacy, muliebrity 11 womanliness 12 womanishness

fere: 4 mate, peer 5 equal 9 companion

femme fatale: 5 siren 7 Lorelei

femoral: 6 crural

femur: 9 thighbone

fen: bog 4 carr, fowl, moor 5 marsh, snipe, swamp 6 morass 8 quagmire

fence: bar 4 bank, duel, ha-ha, pale, rail, wall 5 guard, hedge 6 paling, picket, raddle, rasper 7 barrier, bulwark, defense 8 palisade, palisado 9 enclosure 12 circumscribe

fish: net 4 weir

interwoven: 6 raddle

picket: 4 pale 6 paling

sunken: 4 ha-ha

fencer: 7 duelist, parrier 9 gladiator, swordsman

cry of: 6 touche 7 en garde

fencing: *attack:* 7 reprise

breastplate: 8 plastron

cry: 4 sasa

hit: 5 punto

maneuver: 5 appel

movement: 4 volt

position: 5 carte, prime, sixte, terce 6 octave, quarte, quinte, tierce 7 seconde, septime

position of hands: 9 pronation 10 supination

redoubling of attack: 7 reprise

sword: 4 epee, foil 6 rapier

term: 4 bind 5 lunge 6 thrust, touche

thrust: 7 riposte

weapon: 4 epee, foil 5 saber, sabre, sword 6 rapier

fend: 4 ward 5 parry 6 defend, forbid, resist 7 support

fender: 5 guard 6 buffer, bumper, shield 11 splashboard

fenestra: 6 window 7 foramen, opening 8 aperture, fontanel

fennel: 4 hemp

fent: 4 slit 7 opening

fer-de-lance: 5 snake

feracious: 8 fruitful

feral: 4 wild 6 deadly, savage 7 bestial, untamed 8 funeral, unbroken 11 uncivilized 14 undomesticated

Ferdinand's wife: 8 Isabella

feretory: 6 chapel, shrine

feria: 4 fair 6 fiesta 7 holiday

ferine: 4 rude, wild 6 savage 7 untamed 9 barbarous, ferocious 11 uncivilized

ferly: 6 marvel, wonder 9 amazement 12 astonishment

fermail: 5 clasp 6 buckle

ferment: 4 barm, heat, turn, work, zyme 5 fever, yeast 6 enzyme, foment, tumult, uproar 7 agitate 8 disorder 10 ebullition, exacerbate, excitement, turbulence

fermenting mixture: bub

fern: 4 tara, weki 5 frond

climbing: 4 nito

edible: roi 4 tara

genus: 7 onoclea, osmunda 8 psilotum

kind of: 4 nito 5 brake 6 pteris 7 bracken 8 polypody 10 maidenhair

leaf: 5 frond

royal: 6 osmund

scale: 7 ramenta(pl.) 8 ramentum

fern-like: 7 pteroid 13 pteridophytic

ferocious: 4 fell, grim, wild 5 cruel, feral 6 bloody, brutal, fierce, raging, savage 7 inhuman, ominous, violent 8 pitiless, ravenous, ruthless 9 barbarous, malignant, merciless, murderous, rapacious, truculent 10 implacable, malevolent, relentless, sanguinary 11 remorseless 12 bloodthirsty

ferret: hob 4 tape 6 weasel 7 polecat

male: hob

ferric oxide: 5 rouge 6 powder

ferrotype: 7 tintype

ferrule: cap 4 ring, virl(Sc.) 6 collet, pulley, verrel 7 bushing, verrell

ferry: 4 pont, scow 7 traject

ferryman: 6 Charon

fertile: fat 4 rank, rich 5 gleby 6 fecund, hearty 7 teeming 8 abundant, fruitful, generous, prolific 9 exuberant, feracious, inventive, luxuriant, plenteous, plentiful 10 productive, profitable

render: 6 enrich

fertility god: 4 Frey 5 Freyr

fertilize: 6 batten, enrich 8 fructify 9 fecundate 10 impregnate, inseminate

fertilizer: 4 marl 5 guano, humus 6 alinit, manure, pollen, potash 7 compote, nitrate 8 nitrogen 11 phosphorous 14 superphosphate

ferule: rod 5 ruler 6 fennel, ferula 10 discipline, punishment

fervency: See **fervor**

fervent: hot 4 keen, warm 5 eager, fiery 6 ardent, bitter, fervid, fierce, raging, savage 7 boiling, burning, glowing, intense 8 vehement 9 religious 10 passionate 11 impassioned

fervid: hot 6 ardent, tropic 7 boiling, burning, fervent, zealous 8 vehement 9 impetuous 11 impassioned

fervor: 4 fire, heat, rage, zeal 5 ardor 7 passion 8 candency 9 eagerness, vehemence 10 enthusiasm 11 earnestness

fess: bar 4 band, pert 5 smart 6 lively 9 conceited

festa: 5 feast 7 holiday 8 festival

festal: gay 4 gala 5 gaudy 7 festive

fester: rot 4 scar 6 rankle 7 pustule, putrefy 9 cicatrice, cicatrize

festival: mas 4 fair, fete, gala, Holi 5 feast, feria, festa, gaudy, Haloa, Hooli, revel 6 fiesta, Hohlee 7 banquet, holiday 8 carnival, carousal 9 festivity

church: 4 Lent 6 Easter 9 Christmas

comb. form: mas

epiphany: 7 uphelya

festive: gay 4 gala 6 festal, genial, joyous 7 holiday, jocular 8 mirthful, sportive 9 convivial 10 celebrious 11 merry making

festivity: 4 gala 5 mirth, randy, revel 6 gaiety, splore 7 jollity 8 festival, function 9 festivity 10 joyfulness 11 celebration, merrymaking 12 conviviality 13 entertainment, glorification

god: 5 Comus 7 Bacchus 8 Dionysus

festoon: 6 wreath 7 garland 8 decorate

fetch: fet 4 gasp, tack, take 5 bring, sweep, trick 6 double, wraith 7 achieve, attract 8 artifice, interest 9 strategem

fetching: 6 crafty 8 alluring, pleasing, scheming 10 attractive 11 fascinating

fete: 4 fair, gala 5 bazar, feast 6 bazaar, fiesta, regale 7 banquet, holiday 8 ceremony, festival 9 entertain 11 celebration 13 entertainment

fetid: 4 foul, olid, rank 5 fusty, musty 6 putrid, rancid, rotten, virose 8 mephitic, stinking 9 offensive 10 malodorous

fetish, fetich: obi 4 idol, obia 5 charm, huaca, obeah, obiah, totem 6 grigri, voodoo 7 sorcery 8 greegree, talisman 10 mumbo-jumbo

fetter: 4 band, bond, find, gyve, iron 5 basil, chain 6 anklet, garter, hamper, hobble, hopple, impede 7 confine, enchain, manacle, shackle, trammel 8 restrain 9 restraint

fettle: 4 beat, deck, fuss, mull, tidy 5 dress, groom 6 repair, strike 7 arrange, bandage, harness 9 condition

fetus, foetus: 5 birth, child, young 6 embryo 10 conception

human: 10 homunculus

limbless: 5 ameli(pl.) 6 amelus

feud: 4 fray 5 broil 6 affray, enmity, strife 7 contest, dispute, quarrel 8 vendetta 9 hostility 10 contention

blood: 8 vendetta

feudal: *estate:* 4 feod, fief

jurisdiction: soc 4 soke

lord: 7 vavasor 8 suzerain, vavasour

penalty: 7 sursise

pert. to: 5 banal

tenant: 6 vassal 7 homager

tenure: 6 socage

feudatory: 4 fief 11 beneficiary

fever: 4 ague, fire 6 febris 7 ferment 9 calenture 10 excitement 11 temperature 13 conflagration

kind of: 4 ague 5 octan 6 dengue, sextan, sodoku 7 feveret, helodes, malaria, quartan 10 calentural 11 brucellosis

without: 8 apyretic

feverish: 5 fiery 6 hectic 7 excited, febrile, frantic 8 restless 9 overeager 11 impassioned

few: 4 less, some 5 scant 7 limited 8 exiguous

comb. form: 4 olig 5 oligo, pauci

fewness: 7 paucity

fey: 4 dead 5 fatal 7 unlucky 8 accursed 9 delirious, enfeebled, visionary

fez: cap 8 tarboosh

fiacre: 4 hack 5 coach

fiance: 5 trust 7 promise 8 affiance 10 confidence

fiasco: 5 crash, flask 6 bottle 7 failure

fiat: 5 edict, order 6 decree 7 command 8 decision, sanction 9 ordinance 12 announcement, proclamation

fib: lie, yed 4 beat, flaw, whid 6 pummel 9 falsehood 11 tarradiddle

fibber: 4 liar 12 prevaricator

fiber, fibre: 5 grain 6 strand, thread

band: 6 fillet

bark: 5 olona, terap

hat: 5 datil

kind of: nap, nep, tal, tow 4 adad, aloe, bast, buri, coir, eruc, feru, flax, hemp, ixle, jute, kyar, lint, marl, noil, pita, silk, sola 5 abaca, civil, erizo, floss, istle, istli, ixtle, kapok, linen, mudar, nylon, oakum, orlon, ramee, ramie, rayon, sisal 6 amiray, cotton, dacron, manila, raffia, staple 7 acetate, acrilan, castuli, haurizo, sabutan 8 filament, fibrilla, keratose 9 gamelotte 10 anodendron, escobadura

knot: nep

palm: 4 eruc 6 raffia 7 coquita, coquito

synthetic: 5 nylon, orlon, rayon 6 dacron 7 acetate, acrilan

yarn: 6 strand

fibril: 4 hair 8 filament

fibrin: 6 gluten

fibrose: 6 sinewy 7 stringy

fibula: 5 clasp 6 brooch, buckle 9 safety-pin

fickle: 4 gery 5 dizzy, false, giddy 6 mobile, puzzle, shifty, volage, wankle 7 casalty, caselty, cazelty, flatter, mutable 8 cassalty, casselty, gossamer, unstable, unsteady, variable, volatile, wavering 9 changeful, dangerous, deceitful, faithless, unsettled 10 capricious, changeable, inconstant, irresolute, highheaded 11 treacherous, vacillating

fico: fig 4 snap 6 trifle

fictile: 6 molded 7 plastic

fiction: 4 tale 5 fable, false, novel 6 deceit, device, fabula, legend 7 coinage, fantasy, figment, forgery, romance 9 falsehood, invention 10 concoction, pretending 11 contrivance, dissembling, fabrication 14 counterfeiting

fictional: 7 assumed 11 make-believe

fictitious: 5 bogus, dummy, false, phony 7 assumed, feigned 8 fabulous, mythical, spurious 9 imaginary, imitative, pretended 10 apocryphal, artificial 11 counterfeit

fictive: 9 imaginary

fiddle: bow 4 viol 5 cheat, gique 6 potter, trifle, violin 7 swindle

fiddler: 4 crab 7 crowder, scraper 8 sixpence 9 violinist

fiddler crab: uca

fiddlesticks: 5 pshaw

fidelity: 5 troth, truth 6 fealty 7 honesty 8 adhesion, devotion, veracity 9 adherence, closeness, constancy 10 allegiance 12 faithfulness
symbol of: 5 topaz 7 diamond

fidget: 4 fike, fuss, roil 5 hotch, worry 6 brevit, fissle, fistle, fridge, fusser 7 nervous 8 restless 9 impatient 10 uneasiness 12 restlessness

fidgety: 5 fussy 6 uneasy 7 restive 8 restless 9 impatient

fiducial: 4 firm 7 trusted 8 trustful 9 confident 11 trustworthy

fiduciary: 7 trustee

fief: fee, han 4 feud 8 benefice 9 feudatory

field: lea, lot 4 acre, ager(L.), area, fell, list, mead, rand, wong 5 campo, champ, croft, glebe, paddy, range, rowen, sawah 6 arrish, campus, champe, furrow, ground, machar, meadow, sphere 7 compass, garston, paddock, terrain 8 clearing 9 grassland 11 battlefield
athletic: 4 oval, ring, rink 5 arena, court, green 6 course, stadia(pl.) 7 diamond, stadium 8 gridiron
common share: 4 dale
edge: 4 rand
extensive: 7 savanna 8 savannah
god: 4 Faun
goddess: 5 Fauna
pert. to: 8 agrarian, agrestic 10 campestral
Roman: 4 ager
stubble: 5 rowen

field mouse: 4 vole

field of blood: 4 ager 8 aceldama, akeldama 9 sanguinis

fieldwork: 5 lunet, redan 7 lunette 13 fortification

fiend: foe 5 demon, devil, enemy, Satan, trull 6 wizard

fiendish: 5 cruel 6 wicked 7 demonic 8 demoniac, devilish, diabolic 10 diabolical

fierce: 4 bold, fell, grim 5 breme, cruel, felon, rethe 6 ardent, gothic, hetter, raging, savage 7 brutish, fervent, furious, grimful, scaddle, violent 9 felonious, ferocious, impetuous, truculent 10 catawampus, forbidding, passionate 11 catawampous 13 catawamptious

fiercely: 4 fell 5 felly

fiery: hot, red 5 adust 6 ardent, flashy, ignite 7 burning, fervent, flaming, furious, glowing, parched, peppery, violent 8 choleric, feverish, frampoid, inflamed, spirited, vehement 9 hotheaded, impetuous, irascible, irritable 10 mettlesome, passionate, phlogistic 11 combustible, inflammable

fiesta: 4 fete 5 feria, party 7 holiday 8 festival 9 festivity

fife: 4 pipe 5 flute

fifty: nu(Gr.)

fig: rig 4 fico 5 array, breba, dress, eleme, elemi, pipal 6 trifle 7 furbish
basket: 5 cabas
crate: 5 seron
genus: 5 ficus
sacred: 5 pipal
Smyrna: 5 eleme, elemi

fig-shaped: 8 ficiform

Figaro: 6 barber

fight: box, war 4 beat, bout, clem, cock, cope, cuff, duel, flog, fray, mell, tilt, wage 5 brawl, clash, hurry, melee, scrap 6 affair, affray, barney, battle, bicker, combat, debate, impugn, oppose, resist, rippit, strife, strike, strive 7 bargain, contend, contest, ruction 8 conflict, militate, struggle 9 encounter, pugnacity 10 free-for-all 11 altercation 12 disagreement 13 combativeness
against the gods: 9 theomachy

fighter: pug 4 vamp 5 boxer 6 cocker 7 battler, duelist, soldier, warrior, 8 andabata, barrater, barrator, champion, pugilist, guerilla, scrapper 9 combatant, guerrilla

fighting: 7 warlike 8 militant 10 pugnacious 11 belligerent
street: 4 riot 5 brawl

fighting fish: 5 betta

figlike: 8 caricous

figment: 7 fiction 9 invention 11 fabrication

figuration: 4 form 5 shape 7 outline

figurative: 6 florid 7 flowery, typical 9 allegoric 10 rhetorical 12 emblematical
use of words: 5 trope

figure: hue, vol 4 bosh, form, idea, star 5 digit, image, magot, shape 6 emblem, number, symbol, tattoo 7 chiffer, chiffre, compute, contour, numeral, outline 8 likeness 9 archetype, calculate 13 configuration
geometrical: 4 cone, cube, lune 5 prism, rhomb, solid 6 circle, gnomon, oblong, sector, square 7 ellipse, lozenge, pelcoid, rhombus 8 crescent, pelecoid, pentacle, triangle 9 ellipsoid, rectangle 16 parallelepipedon
human form: 4 nude 5 dummy, glyph, orant 7 telamon 8 Atlantes, caryatid
many-sided: 4 cube 6 isogon 7 decagon, hexagon, nonagon, octagon, polygon 8 pentagon, tetragon 10 hexahedron, octahedron 11 icosahedron 12 dodecahedron 13 quadrilateral
of speech: 5 trope 6 aporia, simile 7 imagery 8 metaphor, metonymy
praying: 5 orant
symbolic: 6 emblem

figure out: 4 dope 5 solve
figured: 7 adorned, faconne(Fr.) 8 computed
figurine: 7 tanagra 9 statuette
motion picture: 5 Oscar
Fiji Island: *capital:* 4 Suva
chestnut: 4 rata
group: lau
drug: 5 tonga
filament: 4 dowl, hair, harl 5 fiber, fibre 6 mantle, strand, thread
lamp: 12 incandescent
filbert: nut 5 hazel
filch: bob, nim, rob 4 beat, fake, prig 5 fetch, steal 6 pilfer, strike 7 purloin
file: row 4 line, list, rank, rasp, rate, risp, roll, tool 5 grail, index, track 6 accuse, carlet, befoul, defile, rascal 7 arrange, condemn, graille, quannet 10 procession
combmaker's: 6 carlet
document: 7 dossier
flat: 7 quannet
filet: net 4 lace
filial: 9 childlike
filibeg: 4 kilt 5 skirt
filibuster: 5 orate 11 obstruction
filigree: 8 fanciful 13 unsubstantial
filing: 5 lemel 6 rasion 8 limation
Filipino: See **Philippines**
filippic: See **philippic**
fill: pad 4 cram, feed, glut, hold, pang, sate 5 estop, gorge 6 charge, fulfil, occupy 7 distend, enlarge, execute, fraught, fulfill, inflate, perfect, perform, pervade, plenish, satiate, satisfy, suffuse 8 complete, compound, permeate 9 replenish 10 accomplish, embankment 11 sufficiency
cracks: 4 calk, shim 5 caulk
with zeal: 7 enthuse
fille: 4 girl 8 daughter
filled: SRO 5 sated, solid 6 loaded 7 implete, replete 9 saturated 11 preoccupied
fillet: 4 band, bone, orle, orlo, sole, tape 5 ampyx, crown, label, miter, snood, stria, tiara, vitta 6 anadem, binder, cimbia, diadem, fascia, norsel, quadra, ribbon, striae(pl.), taenia, turban 7 bandage, bandeau, fasciae(pl.), molding, taeniae(pl.), tresson 8 bandelet, cincture, tressour, tressure 9 sphendone 10 bandelette
architectural: 6 cimbia, lintel, listel, regula, taenia
filling: *dental:* 5 inlay
fabric: 4 weft, woof
fillip, filip: 4 blow, flip, snap, urge 5 flash, flirt, flisk 6 buffet, moment 7 project 8 stimulus 9 stimulate
filly: 4 colt, foal, girl, mare 9 youngster
film (see also **motion picture**): 4 brat, haze, mist, scum, skin, veil 5 flake, layer 6 mother, patina 8 beeswing, negative, pellicle 10 photograph
filmy: 4 hazy 5 gauzy, misty, wispy 6 cloudy 7 clouded 8 gossamer 13 unsubstantial
filter: 4 sift, sile 5 drain, sieve 6 colate, purify, refine, strain 8 strainer 9 percolate
sugar: 4 clay
filth: 4 dirt, dung, gore, nast, slut 5 addle, gleet 6 defile, ordure, vermin 7 squalor 8 muckment 9 obscenity, scoundrel 10 acartharsy 11 acartharsia
filthiness: 5 mucor 7 squalor 8 cenosity
filthy: low 4 foul, miry, vile 5 dirty, drovy, gross, nasty 6 bawdry, impure, sordid 7 bestial, hoggish, obscene, squalid, unclean 8 sluttish 9 polluting 10 disgusting, licentious 11 disgraceful
fimbriate: hem 5 hairy 6 fringe
fin: arm 4 hand, keel 5 pinna 7 acantha, flipper, ventral
fin-footed: 8 pinniped
finagle, fenagle: 5 cheat, trick 6 revoke 7 deceive
final: 4 last 6 latter 7 dernier, extreme, outmost 8 decisive, definite, eventual, farewell, ultimate 9 uttermost 10 concluding, conclusive, definitive 11 terminating 13 determinating
final outcome: 5 issue 6 upshot
finale: end 4 coda 5 close, finis, fugue, shank 6 ending 7 closing 9 uttermost 10 conclusion 11 termination
finalist: 10 contestant

finality: end 11 termination 12 decisiveness 14 conclusiveness

finance: tax 4 back 5 goods 7 revenue 8 taxation, treasure 10 underwrite

finances: 5 funds, purse 6 assets 9 exchequer

financial: 6 fiscal 7 solvent 8 monetary 9 pecuniary

financing: 7 backing

finch: 4 fink, moro, pape 5 serin, terin 6 burion, citril, linnet, siskin 7 chewink, redpoll, senegal, tanager 8 amadavat 9 snowflake

find: get 5 catch 6 locate 8 discover
by keen search: 5 probe 6 ferret

find fault: nag 4 carp, crab, fret 5 cavil, scold 8 complain 9 belly-ache, criticise, criticize

find guilty: 7 convict

find out: 5 learn 6 detect 8 discover 9 ascertain

fine: cro, rum, tax 4 bein, bien, braw, eric, good, jake, levy, nice, pure 5 bonny, brave, bully, dandy, frail, mulct, noble, sharp, sheer, wally 6 amerce, bonnie, bright, clever, crafty, finish, gersum, ornate, proper, slight, spiffy, tender 7 cunning, elegant, estreat, forfeit, fragile, penalty, perfect, refined, tenuous 8 absolute, bloodwit, delicate, handsome, penalize, pleasant, skillful, splendid, superior 9 beautiful, bloodwite, excellent, ingenious, sensitive 10 consummate, fastidious, pulverized, punishment, surpassing
for killing: cro 7 wergild
for misdemeanor: 5 mulct
record of: 7 estreat

fineness: 5 trick 6 finery, purity 7 exility 8 delicacy 9 clearness

finery: 4 gaud, waly 5 wally 6 bauble, bawdry, beauty, fegary 7 gaudary 8 elegance, fineness, ornament 9 fallalery 10 hufty-tufty, lavishness

finespun: 4 hair, thin

finesse: art 5 cheat, skill 6 purity, serene 7 cunning 8 artifice, delicacy, subtlety, thinness 9 clearness, dexterity, stratagem 10 artfulness, refinement

Fingal's cave: *island:* 6 Staffa
kingdom: 6 Morven

fingent: 7 molding 10 fashioning

finger: toy 5 digit, index, pinky 6 handle, meddle, pilfer, pinkie 7 annular, minimus, purloin
comb. form: 6 digiti
guard for: cot 5 stall 7 thimble
inflammation of: 5 felon 7 whitlow
pert. to: 7 digital
resembling: 8 digitate

snap with: 5 filip 6 fillip

finger board: 4 fret

fingerlike: 6 dactyl

fingerling: 4 parr 8 troutlet

fingernail moon: 6 lunule

fingerprint: 11 dactylogram
mark: 4 arch, loop 5 whorl 9 composite
science: 12 dactyloscopy

finial: epi, tee, top 4 knot 5 bunch, crest, final 8 ornament, pinnacle

finical: 4 nice 5 fussy 6 choosy, dainty, dapper, jaunty, prissy, spruce 7 choosey, finicky, foppish, mincing 8 delicate 9 squeamish 10 fastidious, meticulous 11 overprecise 14 overscrupulous

finikin, finnikin: 6 pigeon

finis: end 4 goal 5 close 10 conclusion

finish: die, end 4 char, mill 5 bound, cease, chare, cheve, close enden(G.), glaze, limit 6 fulfil, windup 7 achieve, execute, fulfill, perfect, surface 8 complete, conclude, terminal 9 erudition, terminate 10 accomplish, completion, conclusion, consummate, perfection
dull: mat 5 matte
glossy: 6 enamel

finished: did, oer, pau 4 done, fine, gone, over, ripe 5 ended, kaput 6 closed, ornate 7 refined, stopped 8 climaxed, lustered, polished 9 completed, concluded, perfected, performed 10 terminated 11 consummated 12 professional

finisher: 4 eyer 5 ender 7 beetler 8 enameler

finishing line: 4 tape

finite: 7 limited 9 definable 10 restricted, terminable 11 conditioned

fink: 8 informer, squealer 13 strikebreaker

Finland: 5 Suomi
bathhouse: 5 sauna
city: Aba, Abo 11 Helsingfors
coin: 5 penni 6 markka
composer: 8 Sibelius
dialect: 5 Karel
division: 5 Ijore 9 Villipuri
forest god: 5 Tapio
fortress: 11 Suomenlinna
god: 6 Jumala
harp: 7 kantele
island: 5 Aland 6 Aaland
isthmus: 7 Karelia
lake: 5 Enare
language: 4 Avar, Lapp 5 Ugric 6 Magyar, Ostyak, Tarast 7 Samoyed 8 Estonian
measure: 5 kannu, tunna, verst 6 fathom, sjomil 7 tunland 8 ottinger, skalpund, tunnland
parliament: 9 Eduskunta
pert. to: 6 Suomic 7 Suomish
town: 5 Enare

tribe: 4 Veps, Wote 5 Vepse 6 Ugrian

Finlandia composer: 8 Sibelius

Finnegan's Wake author: 5 Joyce

fiord, fjord: ise 5 inlet

fippenny bit: fip

fir: 9 evergreen
   genus: 5 abies

Firbolg queen: 6 Tailte 7 Talitiu

fire: can, feu(F.) 4 bale, burn, heat, zeal 5 ardor, arson, fever, gleed, light, shoot, stoke 6 arouse, excite, fervor, ignite, incite, kindle, spirit 7 animate, burning, dismiss, explode, fervour, glimmer, inflame, inspire 8 detonate, illumine, irritate, vivacity 9 calenture, cauterize, discharge, holocaust 10 combustion, enthusiasm, illuminate 12 inflammation 13 conflagration
   artillery: 7 barrage
   comb. form: 4 igni, pyro
   containing: 7 igneous
   fighter: 4 vamp
   god: 4 Agni 6 Vulcan 10 Hephaestus
   military: 4 flak 5 salvo 6 rafale 7 barrage
   particle: arc 5 spark
   pert. to: 7 igneous
   sacrificial: 4 agni
   set: 6 accend, ignite, kindle 7 inflame 8 enkindle, irritate
   worshipper: 5 Parsi 6 Parsee 9 pyrolater 10 ignicolist

fire basket: 5 grate 7 cresset

fire extinguisher: 6 pyrene 9 pyroleter

fire feeder: 6 fueler, stoker

firearm: gun 5 piece, rifle 6 musket, pistol 7 demihag 8 revolver

fireback: 7 reredos 8 pheasant

fireboat: 8 palander

firebrand: 5 blaze 6 bleery

firebug: 10 incendiary, pyromaniac

firecracker: 5 squib 6 petard 7 cracker, snapper 9 skyrocket

firedamp: gas 7 methane

firedog: 7 andiron

fireman: 4 vamp 6 stoker, tizeur 9 fireeater

fireplace: 5 focus, fogon, forge, foyer, ingle 6 heath 8 cheminee
   part: hob 6 mantel 9 ingleside 11 hearthstone

firer: 6 stoker 10 incendiary

fireside: 9 ingleside 11 hearthstone

firestone: 5 flint

firewood: 4 lena 5 fagot 6 billet, billot

fireworks: 4 gerb 5 gerbe 7 fizgigs, rockets 9 sparklers 10 girandoles 11 tourbillion 12 pyrotechnics
   resembling: 11 pyrotechnic

firing: 4 fuel

firm: hui 4 buff, fast, hard, sure, trig 5 champ, dense, firma, fixed, hardy, house, loyal, rigid, solid, sound, stith, stout, tight 6 hearty, secure, settle, sinewy, stable, stanch, steady, stolid, strong 7 adamant, certain, compact, company, confirm, context, decided, durable, staunch, unmoved 8 constant, faithful, fiducial, obdurate, resolute, unshaken 9 backboned, establish, immovable, immutable, standfast, steadfast 10 consistent, determined, unslipping, unwavering, unyielding 11 established, partnership, substantial, substantive, well-founded

firmament: sky 7 heavens 8 empyrean

firmance: 9 assurance, stability 11 confinement

firmly fixed: 6 rooted, stable

firmness: 4 iron 7 courage 8 solidity, strength, tenacity 9 constancy, stability 10 immobility, steadiness 11 consistency 13 determination 15 indissolubility

firn: ice 4 neve, snow

first: 4 erst, head, high, main 5 alpha, chief, forme, nieve, prime 6 primal, primus 7 highest, initial, leading, primary 8 earliest, foremost, original 9 primitive, principal 10 aboriginal, primordial
   comb. form: 5 proto
   appearance: 5 debut 8 premiere

first-born: 5 eigne 11 protogenist

first class: 5 prime 9 excellent, topdrawer 10 first-cabin

first-rate: 4 A-one, good, jake 5 prime 6 tiptop 7 skookum 8 clipping, topnotch 9 admirable, excellent

firth: 4 kyle 5 frith, inlet 7 coppice, estuary

Firth of Clyde Island: 4 Bute

fisc: 9 exchequer

fiscal: 8 monetary 9 financial

fiscus: 8 treasury

fish: net 4 cast, quab 5 angle, drail, seine, troll 7 poisson(F.)
   Alaska: 6 iconnu
   ascending river from sea: 7 anadrom
   Atlantic Coast: 4 opah, pogy 6 bunker, salema 7 alewife, bugfish, bughead, fatback, oldwife 8 bonyfish, menhaden 9 greentail 10 mossbunker
   Australian: 4 mado 6 groper 7 grouper
   bait: 5 killy 9 killifish
   barbed tail: 8 stingray 9 stingaree
   California: 4 rena 5 reina 6 rasher 9 garibaldi
   carangold: 4 scad 5 jurel
   carp: id; ide, orf
   catfish: 6 hassar 9 sheatfish
   caviar-yielding: 7 sterlet 8 sturgeon
   cod: bib 4 cusk, hake, ling 5 torsk 6 gadoid 7 bacalao, beardie
   colorful: 4 opah

cyprinoid: id; ide 4 dace
devil: ray 5 manta
eel-like: 4 link, opah 6 conger, cuchia 7 eel-pout, lamprey
electric: 4 raad 7 torpedo
elongated: eel, gar 6 saurel
European: id; ide, rud 4 boce, dace, rudd, spet 5 alose, bleak, bream 6 angler, barbel, braice, meagre, plaice 7 gudgeon, lavaret, picarel
female: 4 raun 7 henfish
flat: dab, ray 4 butt, dace, sole 5 bream, fluke, skate 6 plaice, turbot 7 halibut, sanddab, sunfish, torpedo 8 flounder
Florida: 5 crunt 6 atinga, salema 7 burfish, tomtate 8 burrfish
food: cod, eel, gar, iki, sey 4 bass, boga, carp, haik, hake, scup, shad, sole, stew, tile, tuna 5 bolti, cisco, hilsa, jurel, siera, skate, smelt, trout 6 baleen, groupa, hilsah, mullet, pompon, salema, salmon, tautog, wahoon, weever, wrasse 7 alewife, escolar, garlopa, halibut, herring, pompano, pompoon, sardine, snapper 8 mackerel 9 barracuda 10 barracouta
fresh water: id; gar, ide, orf 4 bass, carp, chub, dace, orfe, pike, rudd 5 bream, loach, roach, tench 6 darter, redeye, sucker 7 crappie, mooneye
game: 4 bass, cero, tuna 5 trout 6 grilse, marlin, salmon, tarpon 8 grayling 9 swordfish
grunt: 5 ronco
Hawaiian: aku 4 ulua 5 akule, lania
herring: 4 shad, brit 5 sprat, sprot 7 alewife 8 pilchard
Japanese: tai, ayu
kind of: id; cat, cod, dab, eel, gar, ide, orf 4 bass, carp, chub, dace, dorn, hake, hiku, jocu, lant, lija, ling, mado, masu, meat, mero, mola, opah, orfe, pega, peto, pike, pogy, pout, rena, roud, rudd, ruff, scad, scup, shad, sier, skil, sole, spot, spet, tope, ulua 5 bream, lance, midge, otter, perch, pogie, porgy, prane, roach, ruffe, scrod, seine, skate, smelt, trout, umbra, wahoo 6 barbel, caribe, launce, mullet, porgie, sauger, saurel, shiner, tomcod, turbot, wrasse 7 alewife, grunion, haddock, machete, pegador, pintado, piranha, poisson 8 gourhead, hardhead, pilchard, sturgeon 9 teleostei 10 candlefish
large: 4 cusk, opah 5 chiro, sargo, shark 6 bichir, tarpon 7 escolar, gourami, sennett 8 arapaima, sturgeon 10 blanquillo, maskalonge, maskinonge 11 muskellunge
little: see *small* below.
long: eel, gar 7 lamprey

mackerel-like: 4 cero 5 tunny 6 coelho 7 escolar, pintado
Mediterranean: 5 porgy, sargo 6 chivey 9 menominee
nest-building: 5 acara 11 stickleback
New England: 4 hake
New Zealand: ihi 5 hikus
newly-hatched: fry
Nile: 4 erse 5 saide
olive green: 7 lutfisk 8 ludefisk
one-horned: 9 monoceros
parasitic: 6 remora
pert. to: 7 piscine 8 ichthyic 9 piscatory
pike: gar 4 lude
pilot: 6 romero
ray-like: 5 skate
river: 8 arapaima 10 barramunda
rock: 4 rena 5 reina 8 buccacio
scaleless: 9 alepidote
serpentine: eel
shark-eating: som 4 pega 7 catfish
shell: 7 abalone
small: id; fry, ide, ihi 4 brit, dace, goby, spet 5 saury, sprat 6 blenny, cunner, limpet, minnow, riggle, sennet, shiner 7 sardine 8 halfbeak, seahorse, spearing
small bait: 5 killy 9 killifish
South American: 4 gogy, mapo 5 acara 6 acoupa, aimara, almara, caribe
sparoid: tai 5 porgy, sargo
spear-snouted: gar
star: 7 asteria
sucking: 6 remora
teleost: eel 6 iniomi
toad: 4 sapo 6 slimer
toothed: 7 piranha
total haul: 4 mess 5 catch
tree-climbing: 6 anabas
tropical: 8 coachman
tunny: 4 tuna
voracious: 4 pike 5 shark 6 caribe 9 barracuda
West Indies: 4 Boga, cero, sier 5 chopa 6 Blanco 7 guapena 12 walleyed pike
young: fry 4 parr 6 alevin
fish basket: pot 4 caul 5 creel, slath
fish gig: 5 spear
fish handler: 4 icer
fish hawk: 6 osprey
fish hide: 7 eelskin
fish limb: fin
fish net: 4 bunt 5 seine, trawl 6 sagene
fish net line: 5 meter
fish net mender: 8 beatster
fish peddler: 6 ripier, ripper 7 rippier
fish pole: pew
fish preserve: 6 warren
fish relish: 7 botargo
fish roe: 6 caviar 7 caviare

fish sauce: 4 alec 5 garum

fish spear: gig 7 trident

fish trap: 4 coop, fyke, weel, weir 5 willy 6 eelpot

fisher: 5 eeler, pecan 6 seiner, wejack 7 trawler, troller

fisherman: 5 eeler 6 angler, seiner 7 prawner, trawler 8 peterman, piscator 9 harpooner 11 Izaak Walton

fishery: 7 piscary 9 piscation

fishes: 5 raiae

fishhook: gig 5 angle, Kirby 6 Sproat 7 Kendall 8 Aberdeen, barbless, Carlisle, limerick

feathered: fly 5 sedge 6 hackle

fishing duck: 9 merganser

fishing gear: lam, rod, tew 4 cork, flew, flue, gaff, gimp, hook, line, reel, trot 5 cadar, cader, float, sedge, seine, snell, shood 8 trotline

fishing ground: 4 haaf

fishing vessel: 5 smack 6 seiner 7 trawler

fishlike: 8 ichthyic

fishline: 5 snell 7 boulter

fishmonger: 8 pessoner

fishpond: 7 piscina

fishwife: 9 buttwoman

fishy: 4 dull 6 vacant 10 improbable, lusterless, suspicious, unreliable 11 extravagant

fissate: 7 divided 8 fissured

fissile rock: 5 shale

fission: 8 breaking, cleavage, cleaving 9 splitting 12 reproduction

fissle: 4 fuss, hiss 6 bustle, fidget, rustle 7 whistle 9 fidgeting

fissure: gap 4 chap, cone, flaw, gool, leak, lode, rent, rift, rima, rime, seam, vein, vent 5 chasm, chine, chink, cleft, crack 6 cleave, cranny, divide, lesion 7 blemish, crevice, opening 8 aperture, cleavage, coloboma, crevasse, quebrada

fissured: 6 rimate 7 fissate, rimosed

fist: job 4 nave, neif 5 grasp, nieve 6 clench, clutch, daddle, effort, strike 7 attempt 8 puffball, tightwad 11 handwriting

fistic: 10 pugilistic

fisticuff: box

fistula: 4 pipe, reed, tube 5 sinus 6 cavity

fit: apt, fay, gee, pan, rig 4 able, ague, good, hard, meet, ripe, suit, well, whim 5 adapt, adept, besit, chink, fancy, ictus, ready, right, spasm 6 adjust, attack, become, behove, besort, habile, heppen, proper, seemly, stroke, strong, suited 7 adapted, behoove, capable, condign, conform, correct, healthy, prepare, qualify, tantrum 8 adequate, becoming, eligible, glooming, idoneous(L.), outbreak, paroxysm, passable, suitable, syncopes 9 befitting, competent, congruous, covenable, opportune,

pertinent, qualified 10 applicable, commodious, correspond, convenient 11 accommodate, appropriate

out: 6 outfit 7 habille, prepare 9 equipment

together: fay 4 mesh, nest 5 panel 8 dovetail

fitful: 4 gery 7 cursory, flighty 8 restless, unstable, variable 9 impulsive, irregular, spasmodic, uncertain 10 capricious, convulsive 12 intermittent

fitly: pat 4 duly 6 gladly, meetly 7 happily 8 properly, suitably

fitness: 7 aptness, decency, decorum, dignity 8 aptitude, capacity, justness 9 rectitude 10 competence 11 suitability

fitout: 6 outfit 9 equipment

fitted: apt 4 able 6 suited 7 adapted 8 adjusted 9 qualified 10 convenient

for digging: 7 fodient, laniary

fitting: apt, due, pat 4 meet 5 happy 6 become, proper, seemly 8 decorous, graceful, suitable 9 befitting 10 adjustment, answerable, habiliment 11 appropriate

five: 4 cinq(F.), funf(G.) 6 cinque(It.) 7 epsilon(Gr), quinque(L.)

comb. form: 4 pent 5 penta

group of: 6 pentad

five-dollar bill: "V"; fin, vee

five-finger: 4 fish 5 oxlip, plant 10 cinquefoil

Five Nations: 7 Cayugas, Mohawks, Oneidas, Senecas 9 Onondagas

founder: 8 Hiawatha

five-year period: 6 pentad 7 lustrum

fivefold: 9 quintuple

fix: peg, pin, set 4 glue, mend, moor, nail, seal 5 affix, allot, found, imbed, limit, tryst 6 adjust, anchor, arrest, assign, assize, attach, cement, clinch, define, fasten, ficche, freeze, repair, revamp, settle, temper 7 appoint, arrange, confirm, delimit, dilemma, impress, imprint, prepare, station 8 renovate, transfix 9 determine, establish, stabilize 10 constitute 11 predicament 13 embarrassment

firmly: set 4 moor 5 brace, grave, imbed, stamp 6 anchor, cement, enroot 7 engraff

fixed: pat, set 4 fast, firm 5 siker, staid 6 frozen, intent, mended, sicker, stable 7 certain, dormant, settled, statary 8 arranged, attached, constant, definite, explicit, fastened, immobile, moveless, resolute, stubborn 9 immovable, indelible, inerratic, permanent 10 stationary 12 determinable, refrigerated

amount: 4 rate 6 ration 7 stipend 10 remittance

star: 4 Vega

fixer: 8 handyman

fixture: 5 annex 7 bracket, shelves 8 counters, shelving 10 furnishing

fizgig: 9 fireworks, whirligig

fizzle: 4 fuss 6 barney 7 failure, flivver, hissing 9 agitation

flabby: lax 4 fozy, lash, limp, weak 5 frush 6 feeble 7 flaccid

flabellate: 9 fan-shaped

flabent: 10 flickering

flaccid: 4 limp 6 flabby, flaggy 8 yielding

flack: 4 blow, flap 5 throb 6 stroke 7 flutter

flacker: 5 throb 7 flutter, tremble

flag: fag, sag, sod 4 fail, fane, pine, turf, waif, wilt 5 droop, woman 6 banner, colors, ensign, flower, pennon, signal 7 ancient, cattail, decline, drapeau, pennant 8 banderol, brattach, languish, standard, streamer, vexillum 9 banderole, flagstone, fourpence

kind of: 5 Roger 6 burgee, colors, danger, ensign, fanion, guidon, muleta 7 calamus, curtain, pennant 8 banderol, brattach, masthead, standard, streamer, vexillum 9 banderole, blackjack 10 Jolly Roger

flagellants: 4 albi

flagellate: 4 flog, whip 5 throw 6 thrash 7 flutter, scourge

flagellum: 4 whip 5 shoot 6 runner 7 scourge

flageolet: 4 pipe 6 zufolo 7 basaree, zuffolo
Hindu: 7 basaree

flagging: 4 weak 7 languid 10 spiritless

flaggy: 4 weak 7 flaccid, languid 8 drooping

flagitious: 6 wicked 7 corrupt, heinous 8 criminal, flagrant, grievous 10 scandalous, villainous

flagon: 5 stoup 6 bottle, vessel 7 flacket

flagrant: bad 4 rank 5 gross 6 odious, wanton, wicked 7 glaring, hateful, heinous, scarlet, violent 8 shameful 9 abandoned, atrocious, egregious, monstrous, nefarious, notorious 10 flagitious, outrageous, profligate, villainous

flagstone layer: 5 paver

flail: 4 beat, flog, whip 6 thrash, thresh
part: 7 swingle

flair: ray 4 bent, odor 5 skate, smell, taste 6 talent 7 leaning 8 aptitude 11 discernment

flake: 4 chip, film, flaw, rack, snow 5 fleck, flock, scale, strip 6 hurdle, lamina, paling 7 flaught 8 fragment

flaky: 5 scaly 7 laminar 8 laminose

flam: 4 whim 5 cheat, false, freak, trick 6 cajole, humbug, untrue 7 deceive, pretext, rubbish 8 drumbeat, illusory, nonsense, pretense 9 deception, deceptive, falsehood

flambeau: 5 torch 6 kettle 11 candlestick

flamboyant: 6 florid, ornate 7 flaming 9 flamelike 11 resplendent

flame: 4 fire, glow 5 ardor, blaze, flare, flash, glare, gleed, light 7 burning 9 affection 10 brightness, brilliance, sweetheart
fire without: 4 punk
movement: 4 dart, lick

flaming: 5 afire, fiery, vivid 6 ardent 7 blazing, burning, flaring 9 brilliant, consuming, flamelike 10 flamboyant, passionate 12 illuminating

Flanders capital: 5 Ghent

flanerie: 6 stroll 7 loafing 8 idleness 9 aimlessly, strolling 10 pillowcase

flaneur: 6 loafer 7 trifler

flank: 4 leer, side 5 thigh 6 border

flannel: 4 lana 6 stamin

flap: rob, tab, tag, wap 4 clap, flip, loma, slam, waff 5 alarm, flack, flaff, flipe, lapel, skirt 6 bangle, faffle, lappet, strike, tongue 7 aileron, blinder, flounce, flutter, swindle 9 appendage, operculum 10 epiglottis
furnished with: 5 lobed

flapper: 7 snicket 9 backfisch 10 backfische

flare: 4 bell, flue 5 blaze, flame, flash, fleck, fusee, light, torch 6 signal, spread 7 flicker 8 outburst 10 illuminate 11 ostentation

flaring: 4 bell, flue 5 evase(F.), gaudy 7 flaming, glaring 8 dazzling

flash: 4 pool 5 blash, blaze, burst, flare, flame, fluff, glaik, gleam, glent, glint, marsh, spark 6 bottle, fillip, glance 7 fouldre, glimmer, glimpse, glisten, glitter, instant, shimmer, sparkle 11 coruscation, fulguration, scintillate

flashing: 6 bright, flashy 7 forward 8 meteoric, snapping 9 fulgurant, fulgurous

flashy: gay 4 flat, gaud, loud 5 fiery, gaudy, showy 6 frothy, slangy, sporty 7 insipid, tinhorn 8 dazzling, flashing, vehement 9 impetuous 10 spiritless

flask: 4 olpe 5 betty, bulge, girba 6 bottle, fiasco, flacon, guttus 7 ampulla, canteen, matrass 8 cucurbit 9 aryballos

flask-shaped: 10 lageniform

flat: 4 dead, dull, fade, plat 5 abode, aflat, banal, blunt, level, molle, plane, prone, vapid 6 boring, dreary, flashy 7 decided, insipid, platoid, prosaic, uniform 8 directly, dwelling, lifeless, unbroken 9 apartment, downright, prostrate, tasteless 10 homaloidal, horizontal, monotonous, unanimated 12 unmistakable 13 uninteresting
comb. form: 5 plani

flat-nosed: 6 simous

flatboat: ark 4 scow 5 barge

flatfish: dab, ray 4 butt, dace, sole 5 bream, fluke 6 acedia, plaice, turbot 7 sanddab, sunfish, torpedo 8 flounder

flatiron: 7 sadiron

flatten: 4 even 5 level 6 deject, smooth 7 depress 8 compress, dispirit 9 prostrate 10 complanate, discourage, dishearten

flattened: 6 oblate 7 planate

flatter: 4 bull, claw, coax, fage, fume, palp 5 charm, float, gloze, honey, smalm 6 become, cajole, fickle, fleech, fraise, glaver, smooge, soothe 7 adulate, beguile, blarney, flether, flutter, wheedle 8 blandish, bootlick, collogue 10 compliment, ingratiate

flatterer: 6 cogger, glozer 7 soother 8 courtier 9 sycophant 10 assentator, greasehorn

flattering: 7 buttery, candied 11 assentatory

flattery: 4 bull, bunk 5 fraik, gloze, salve, taffy 6 butter, fleech 7 blarney, fawning, flether, palaver 8 cajolery 9 adulation 10 compliment 14 obsequiousness

flatulent: 5 gassy, windy 6 turgid 7 pompous, ventose 8 inflated 9 bombastic

flatworm: 9 trematode 13 plathelminth

flaunt: 4 bosh, wave 5 boast, vaunt 6 parade, trapes 7 display, flutter, traipse 8 brandish

flavicant: 6 yellow

flavor, flavour: 4 gamy, odor, rasa, salt, tang, zest 5 aroma, devil, sapid, sapor, sauce, savor, scent, taste, tinge 6 asarum, relish, season 7 perfume 8 hautgout, piquancy 9 fragrance

flavorable: 5 sapid, sipid 6 savory 9 palatable

flavoring material: 4 mint, sage 6 orgeat 7 cumarin 8 coumarin, cumarone 9 coumarone

flavorless, flavourless: 5 stale, rapid 9 tasteless

flaw: fib, gap, lie, mar 4 gall, hole, rase, rift, spot, wind 5 brack, cleft, crack, craze, fault, flake 6 breach, defect 7 blemish, default, fissure, nullify, violate, whitlow 8 fracture, fragment, gendarme 10 intoxicate 12 imperfection

flawless: 5 sound 7 perfect 9 faultless

flax: pob, tow 4 card, harl, lint 5 hards, hurds, linen, linin, pouce 6 bobbin
filament: 4 harl
holder: 7 distaff
prepare: ret
refuse: pob
remove seed: 6 ribble
tool: 7 hatchel, swingle

flaxen-haired: 4 bawn

flaxseed: 7 linseed

flay: 4 skin 5 strip 6 fleece 7 censure, pillage, reprove 9 excoriate 11 decorticate

flea: 6 chigoe 10 sandhopper
genus: 5 pulex

flebile: 7 doleful, tearful

fleck: fat 4 flea, flit, spot, tuft 5 flake, flare 6 dapple, streak, stripe 7 flutter, speckle 8 particle 9 variegate

fledgling, fledgeling: 5 squab

flee: fly, lam, run 4 bolt, fleg, loup, shun 5 elude, speed 6 escape, vanish 7 abandon, abscond, forsake 8 liberate 9 disappear, skedaddle

fleece: abb, jib, teg 4 bilk, fell, flay, gaff, wool 5 cheat, fleck, pluck, shear 6 toison 7 despoil

fleecy: 5 wooly 6 linten, woolly

fleeing: 7 fugient 8 fugitive

fleer: 4 gibe, grin, jeer, leer, mock 5 flout, laugh, scoff, sneer, taunt 7 grimace 8 derision

fleet: bay 4 fast, flit, navy, sail, skim, swim 5 creek, drain, drift, evand, float, flote, hasty, inlet, quick, rapid, swift 6 abound, argosy, armada, hasten, nimble, speedy 7 estuary 8 flotilla 10 evanescent, transitory

fleeting: 5 brief 6 caduke, volage 7 flighty, passing 8 caducous, fugitive 9 ephemeral, fugacious, transient 10 evanescent, transitory 11 impermanent

fleetings: 5 curds 9 skimmings

fleg: fly 4 flee, kick 5 fling, scare 6 fright

Flemish: *geographer:* 8 Mercator
painter: 5 Bouts 6 Mabuse, Massys, Rubens 7 Gossart, Memling, Patinir, van Eyck 8 Breughel, Brueghel, Gossaert, van Cleve 12 van der Weyden

flesh: kin 4 body, meat, race 5 stock 6 family, muscle 7 kindred, mankind 8 humanity 9 mortality 10 sensuality
appendage: 5 palpi(pl.) 6 palpus
formation: 8 sarcosis
kind of: 5 brawn 6 chevron, chiver 7 carrion
pert. to: 7 sarcoid
resembling: 7 sarcoid

fleshbrush: 7 strigil

flesh-eating: 11 carnivorous

fleshy: fat 5 beefy, human, obese, plump, pulpy, stout 6 animal, bodily, brawny, carnal 9 corpulent
fruit: 4 pear, pome 5 berry, drupe, melon 6 tomato

fleur-de-lis: lis, lys 4 iris, liss, luce, lucy

fleuret: 4 epee 5 sword 6 flower

flex: 4 bend

flexible: 4 limp, lush, soft 5 buxom, lithe, withy 6 limber, pliant, supple 7 ductile, elastic, flexile, lissome, pliable, willowy 8 cheverel, cheveril, yielding 9 tractable 10 manageable

shoot: 4 bine

tube: 4 hose

flexile: 6 pliant 7 plastic, pliable 8 flexible 9 tractable, versatile

flexuous: 6 zigzag 7 relaxed 8 softened, wavering 9 adaptable 10 circuitous, flickering

flexure: 4 bend, bent, curl, fold 5 curve 6 bought

flichter: 6 quiver 7 flicker, flutter, vibrate

flick (see also **motion picture**): cut, hit 4 blow, flip, flit, snap, toss, whip 5 flisk, throw 6 flitch, propel 7 flutter

flicker: 4 fail, flit 5 flare, flunk, waver 6 fitter, shiver, yucker 7 blinter, flimmer, flitter, flutter, tremble 8 flichter 9 flaughter, palpitate 10 woodpecker

flickering: 7 flabent, lambent 8 flexuous, unsteady

flier: ace 5 pilot 6 airman 7 aviator 8 operator

female: 8 aviatrix 9 aviatress, aviatrice

flight: hop 4 bolt, rout 5 chevy, chivy, flock, scrap, volee 6 chivvy, exodus, hegira, hejira 7 flaught, migrate, mission, scamper 8 stampede, swarming 9 agitation, migration 12 perturbation

of fancy: 5 sally

of steps: 6 perron

of wild fowl: 5 skein

pert. to: 5 volar

put to: 4 rout

flightiness: 9 lightness

flightless bird: emu, moa 4 dodo, kiwi, weka 7 ostrich, penguin

flighty: 5 barmy, giddy, swift 6 fitful, nimshi, volage, whisky 7 foolish, giggish 8 fleeting, freakish 9 transient 10 capricious 11 harum-scarum 13 shuttlewitted

flim-flam: fob 5 freak, trick 6 humbug, tricky, trifle 7 swindle 8 nonsense, trifling 9 deception, deceptive 11 nonsensical

flimmer: 7 flicker, glimmer

flimsy: 4 limp, vain, weak 5 frail, gaudy 6 feeble, paltry, sleazy, slight 7 shallow, tenuous 10 gossamered 11 superficial 13 insubstantial, unsubstantial

flinch: 4 funk, game 5 feign, start, wince 6 blench, falter, flense, recoil, shrink

fling: 4 buzz, cast, dart, dash, ding, emit, fleg, gibe, hurl, kick, toss 5 cheat, dance, flirt, pitch, sling, sneer, throw, whang 6 baffle, effuse, hurtle, plunge, rebuff, spirit 7 flounce, repulse, sarcasm, scatter, swindle 9 overthrow

flint: 5 chert, miser, silex 6 quartz 9 firestone, skinflint

flintlock: 6 musket

flinty: 4 hard 5 cruel 8 obdurate

flip: tap 4 flap, snap, toss, trip 5 flick, flirt, slirt 6 fillip, limber, nimble, pliant, propel 7 journey 10 somersault

flipe: 4 flap, fold, peel

flippant: 4 airy, glib 6 fluent, limber, nimble 9 talkative

flipper: arm, fin, paw 4 hand

flirt: tap, toy 4 dart, fike, flip, gibe, jeer, jest, joke, mash, mock, play, toss 5 dally, flick, fling, throw 6 coquet, fillip, masher, spring, trifle 7 trifler 9 philander

flirtatious: coy 4 arch 10 coquettish

flit: 4 dart, flow, scud 5 fleck, fleet, flick, float, flurr, hover, quick, scoot, swift 6 nimble 7 flicker, flutter, migrate

flite, flyte: 4 gibe, jeer 5 chide, scold 6 strife 7 contend, dispute, quarrel, wrangle

flitter: rag 5 droop, hover, piece, waver 6 tatter 7 flicker, flutter, shuffle 8 fragment

flittermouse: bat

float: fly, sea 4 buoy, cork, flow, flux, hove, pont, raft, ride, sail, scow, soar, swim, waft, wave 5 balsa, drift, fleet, flood, hover, ladle 6 billow, bobber, bungey, ponton 7 flatter, flotter, pontoon 8 overflow 9 catamaran, podoscaph

aloft: 4 soar

floating: 4 free 5 awash, loose 6 adrift, afloat, flying, natant 7 movable 8 drifting, fluitant, shifting, variable 9 wandering

flocculent: 6 woolly

flock: mob 4 bevy, fold, herd, pack 5 brood, bunch, charm, covey, crowd, drift, drove, flake, fleck, group, sedge, shoal, swarm 6 flight, hirsel 7 company 9 multitude 10 assemblage 11 aggregation

kind of: nid, nye, pod 4 nide, sord 5 covey, sedge, tribe

pert. to: 6 gregal

flocks (god of): Pan

floe: 4 raft

flog: cat, tan 4 beat, cane, hide, lash, toco, toko, wale, whip 5 birch, excel, fight, flail, linge, quilt, skeeg 6 cotton, larrup, strike, switch, thrash 7 baleise, belabor, scourge, sjambok, surpass, trounce 8 slaister 10 flagellate

flood: sea 4 bore, flow, flux 5 eagre, float, spate 6 deluge, excess 7 debacle, freshet, torrent 8 alluvion, inundate, overflow 9 cataclysm 14 superabundance

flooded: 6 afloat 10 surrounded

floodgate: 5 hatch 6 sluice

floodlight: 5 klieg

floor covering: mat, rug 4 tile 5 tapis(Fr.) 6 carpet, planks 8 linoleum, oilcloth

floor plank: 5 chess

flop: 4 whop

flora: 6 plants 9 florilege 11 florilegium

flora and fauna: 5 biota

floreate: 5 bloom

Florence: *coin:* 6 florin 7 ruspone
devotees: 4 neri
family: 6 Medici
gallery: 6 Uffizi
iris: 5 ireos, orris

Florentine (see also **Florence**): 4 gold 6 finish

floret bract: 5 palea, palet

florid: 5 buxom, fresh, ruddy 6 ornate 7 flowery 8 blooming, rubicund, vigorous 10 figurative, flamboyant, rhetorical 11 embellished, full-blooded

Florida: *beach:* 4 Vero
city: 5 Miami, Ocala, Tampa 7 Orlando, Palatka, Pompano 8 Sarasota 9 Pensacola 11 Tallahassee(c.)
county: Bay, Lee 4 Clay, Dade, Gulf, Lake, Leon, Levy, Polk 5 Pasco
fish: 6 tarpon, tetard
fishing boat: 7 smackee
islands: 6 Bahama
palm: 5 royal
plain: 7 savanna 8 savannah
region: 10 Everglades

floss: 5 fluff, skein, waste 6 sleave, stream

flotage: 8 buoyancy

flotilla: 5 fleet

Flotow opera: 6 Martha

flotsam: 8 driftage

flounce: 4 flap, slam 5 fling, frill 6 ruffle 7 falbala, falbelo 8 flounder, furbelow, struggle

flounder: dab 4 butt, keel, roll, toss 5 bream, fluke, megin 6 grovel, muddle, plaice, turbot, wallow 7 flounce, plounce, stumble, sunfish, topknot, vaagmar, vaagmer 8 flatfish, struggle, vaagmaer

flour: *bleach:* 5 agene
diabetic: 9 aleuronat
maker: 6 miller
sifter: 6 bolter
sprinkle with: 6 dredge
testing device: 11 farinometer
wheat: 4 atta

flourish: 4 boom, brag, grow, riot, rise, show, wave 5 adorn, bloom, boast, cheve, gloss, quirk, vaunt 6 parade, paraph, thrive 7 blossom, display, enlarge, fanfare, prosper, roulade 8 arpeggio, brandish, curlicue, curlycue, increase, ornament 9 embellish 10 decoration 11 ostentation

flourishing fat 4 frim 5 green, palmy 7 florent 8 thriving 10 prosperous, successful

floury: 4 meal

flout: bob 4 gibe, jeer, mock 5 fleer, flite, flyte, frump, scoff, scorn, scout, sneer, taunt 6 deride, insult 7 jeering, mockery 8 betongue

flow: ebb, jet, run 4 bore, flit, flux, fuse, gush, hale, lava, lave, melt, pour, roll, shed, sile, teem, well 5 avale, drain, eagre, exude, fleam, float, flood, glide, issue, river, spill, spurt 6 abound, afflux, deluge, recede, stream 7 current, emanate, flutter, meander, spurtle 8 alluvion, inundate 9 streaming 10 menstruate, outpouring 12 menstruation

flower (see also **plant**): bud 4 best, blow, flag, iris, ixia, pink, posy, rose 5 aster, bloom, elite, lilac, pansy, tulip 6 azalia, crocus, dahlia, orchid, posies(pl.), unfold 7 blethia, blossom, develop, fairest, gentian 8 camellia, choicest, daffodil, freshest, gardenia, geranium, hyacinth, ornament 9 carnation, embellish, gladiolus 13 chrysanthemum
appendage: 5 bract
artificial: 7 rosette 8 gloxinia
band: 6 wreath
bell-shaped: 4 lily 5 tulip
blooming once a year: 6 annual
blue: 6 lupine 8 harebell
bud: 5 ament, caper 6 spadix
cluster: 4 cime, cyme 5 ament, bract, umbel 6 corymb, raceme 7 panicle 9 glomerule
of death: 8 asphodel
desert: 6 cactus
extract: 4 atar, otto 5 attar, ottar
fall: 5 aster 6 cosmos
of forgetfulness: 5 lotus
garden: 4 iris, ixia, lily, pink, rose 5 aster, canna, daisy, lilac, pansy, peony, phlox, tulip 6 asalia, olivia, orchid, violet 7 freesia, petunia, verbena 8 bletilla, camellia, daffodil, gloxinia, hyacinth, primrose 9 buttercup, carnation, gladiolus, narcissus 10 heliotrope, ranunculus 11 honeysuckle
goddess: 5 Flora
imaginary: 7 amarant 8 amaranth
large: 5 canna, peony
late-blooming: 5 aster
mass: 8 anthemia
meadow: 5 bluet
modest: 6 violet
obsolete: 5 pense
part: 5 calyx, sepal 6 anther, pistil, stamen 7 nectary, petiole 8 peduncle, perianth, pericarp
passion: 6 maypop
pink: 4 rose 7 rhodora

prickly: 4 burr
purple: 5 lilac, pense
receptacle: 4 vase 5 torus
spring: 4 iris 5 lilac, peony, tulip 7 arbutus
  8 hepatica
stand: 7 epergne
stylized: lis
unfading: 7 amarant 8 amaranth
unknown kind: 8 belamour
white: 5 gowan
wild: 4 sage 5 bluet, daisy 6 lupine 7 anemone, arbutus 8 bluebell, hepatica 9 buttercup, innocence
wind: 7 anemone
yellow: 5 daisy, gowan, pense 7 jonquil 8
  daffodil, marigold 9 buttercup
flower holder: pot 4 frog, vase 5 lapel
Flower State: 7 Florida
flowering: 7 flowery 8 anthesis, blooming
  11 florescence
flowering plant: rue 4 arum 5 avens, calla,
  canna, comos, orpin, phlox, yucca, zamia 6
  alalea, bareta, oxalis, spirea, teasel 7 bar-
  reta, gentian, lobelia, pavonia, petunia,
  rhodora, spiraea, tamarix, torenia, waratah 8 acanthus, ageratum, damewort, geranium, gerardia, valerian 9 candytuft,
  coreopsis, gloxinias, goldenrod, hollyhock,
  monkshood 10 pulsatilla, snapdragon
flowerless plant: 4 fern, moss 6 lichen 7
  acrogen
flowerlike: 7 anthoid
flowerpot: 10 jardiniere
flowery: 6 florid 7 florent 9 flowering 10
  figurative, flosculous
flowing: 4 flux 5 fluid, fluor, tidal 6 afflux,
  fluent 7 copious, current, cursive, ema-
  nent, fluxing 9 affluxion, emanation 10
  transitive
together: 9 confluent
flu: 6 grippe
flub: 4 muff 5 error
fluctuate: 4 sway, vary, veer 5 waver 7 vibrate 8 undulate, unsteady 9 oscillate,
  vacillate 10 irresolute 12 undetermined
fluctuating: 8 unstable, unsteady
flue: net 4 barb, down, open, pipe, thin 5
  flare, fluff, fluke 6 expand, feeble, funnel,
  sickly, tunnel 7 chimney, flaring, passage,
  shallow
fluency: 9 eloquence, profusion 10 smooth-
  ness
fluent: 4 glib 5 fluid, ready 6 facile, liquid,
  smooth, stream 7 copious, flowing, fluidic,
  renable, verbose, voluble 8 eloquent, flippant 9 talkative 13 talkativeness
fluff: nap 4 down, flue, lint, puff 5 flash,
  floss, whiff

fluffy: 4 soft 5 downy, drunk, fluey, fuzzy 6
  linten 8 feathery, unsteady 12 undependable
fluid: ink 5 rasa 5 water 6 fluent, liquid,
  watery 7 flowing, fluible, fluxile, gaseous
  8 floating, fluxible
  kind of: gas, ink, oil, sap, tar 4 bile, icor,
  milk 5 blood, ether, grume, ichor, latex,
  nerol, plasm, serum 6 naptha 7 acetone,
  coaloil, tearlet 8 gasoline, kerosene
  measure: rhe
  pert. to: 7 humoral
  without: 7 aneroid
fluidity unit: rhe
fluke: 4 fish, flue 5 blade 8 flounder
fluky: 8 unsteady 9 uncertain 10 capricious
flume: 4 leat 5 chute, gorge, water 6 ravine,
  sluice, stream 7 channel
flunk: 4 bust, fail 7 flicker
flunky, flunkey: 4 snob 5 toady 6 cookee 7
  footman, servant, steward
flurry: ado 4 gust, stir 5 haste, skirl 6
  bother, bustle, scurry, squall 7 confuse,
  flusker, fluster, flutter, footser 9 agitation, carfuffle 10 discompose
flush: 4 even, glow, pool, rose 5 blush, elate,
  rouge, vigor 6 aflush, excite, lavish, mantle, morass, redden, thrill 7 animate 8
  abundant, affluent, prodigal, rosiness 9
  abounding, encourage 10 prosperous
flushed: red 4 ruby 5 aglow 6 florid 7 scarlet
  8 vigorous 10 prosperous
flushing: 8 blushing 9 rubescent
fluster: 5 shake 6 flurry, fuddle, muddle,
  pother, rattle 7 confuse, flusker, footser 8
  befuddle, flustrum 10 discompose
flute: nay 4 fife 5 crimp 6 flauto, goffer,
  zufolo 7 chamfer, channel, gauffer, magadis, piccolo, zuffolo 8 flautino
  ancient: 5 tibia
  Hindu: bin 5 pungi
  player: 5 piper 6 aulete 7 flutist, tootler 8
  auletris, flautist
  stop: 7 ventage
  wood for: 5 kokra
fluting: 5 strix 7 gadroon, godroon, strigil 10
  gadroonage, godroonage
flux: 4 flow, fuse, melt 5 float, flood, resin,
  rosin, smear, smelt 6 fusion, stream 7 euripus, flowing, outflow
fluxible: 5 fluid 7 pliable 8 changing 10 inconstant
fly: bee, hop 4 flee, fleg, flit, leap, melt, scud,
  soar, solo, whir, whiz, wing 5 agile, alert,
  float, midge, pilot, quick, sharp, whirr 6
  aviate, insect, nimble, spring, vanish 7
  avigate, avolate, knowing 8 coachman 9
  disappear
  African: 4 zimb 5 zebub 6 tsetse

enemy: 6 spider

fishing: bee 4 lure 5 nymph, sedge 6 Cahill 7 Babcock, grannom, huzzard 8 coachman, Ferguson, hare's ear 9 alexandra 10 Barrington

genus: 5 dacus

kind of: bee, bot, fag, mau, plu 4 gnat, kivu, zimb 5 alder, cadew, horse, midge, whame 6 breeze, gadfly, seroot, tsetse 7 butcher, collier, tachina 8 housefly 9 shoemaker 10 bluebottle 11 caterpillar, trichoptera

small: 4 gnat 5 midge

two winged: 8 dipteron

flyaway: 5 giddy 7 flighty 8 restless 12 unrestrained

flybane: 12 cinnamonroot

flyblow: 5 larva

flycatcher: 5 pewee 6 phoebe, yetapa 7 fielder, grignet, grinder

flyer: ace 5 pilot 7 Pegasus 8 aeronaut, operator

flying: 5 awing 6 flight, volant, waving 8 aviation, floating 9 fugacious

pert. to: 7 aviatic

flying adder: 9 dragonfly

flying boat: 8 seaplane 9 amphibian

flying body: 6 meteor

flying device: 4 kite 6 glider

Flying Dutchman heroine: 5 Senta

flying expert: ace

flying fish: 5 saury 7 gurnard

flying machine: 5 plane 8 aerostat 9 gyroplane 10 helicopter

flying mammal: bat

flying ship: 5 blimp 7 aeronat, biplane 8 airplane 9 amphibian, dirigible, monoplane 10 helicopter

Fo: 6 Buddha

foal: 4 colt 5 filly

foam: fob, sud 4 fume, head, scud, scum 5 frost, froth, spume, yeast 6 bubble, freath, lather 7 blubber

foaming: 6 yeasty 7 spumous

foamy: 5 barmy, spumy 6 frothy

fob: 4 buck, foam 5 cheat, froth, trick 6 impose, pocket 8 flimflam, imposter, ornament, swindler

focal: 7 central, centric, nuclear, nucleus 13 concentrative

focus: 4 foci(pl.) 5 point, train 6 center, hearth 8 converge 9 fireplace 11 concentrate

fodder: hay 4 feed, food, vert 5 mange 6 forage, silage 9 provender

kind of: ers, oat, rye 4 corn, rape 5 batad, maize, vetch, wheat 6 barley, clover, millet 7 alfalfa 8 deerweed 11 bitter vetch

storing place: 4 silo 5 bakie 6 haymow, silage 8 ensilage

trough for: 6 manger

fodgel: fat 5 plump, squat, stout

foe: 5 enemy, fiend, rival 7 adverse, hostile, opposer, saracen 8 opponent 9 adversary, ill-wisher 10 antagonist

foederatus: 4 ally

foeman: 5 enemy 9 adversary

fog: dag, rag 4 damp, daze, haar, haze, mist, moke, moss, murk, prig, roke, smog 5 bedim, brume, cloud, grass, vapor 6 nebula, salmon, stupor 7 obscure, pogonip 8 bewilder, moisture 10 aftergrass 12 bewilderment

foggy: dim 4 dull, hazy, moky, roky 5 dense, dirty, misky, misty, murky, rooky 6 cloudy, marshy 7 brumous, muddled, obscure 8 confused, nubilous 9 beclouded

foghorn: 5 siren

fogy: 6 foozle

foible: 4 weak 5 fault, ferly 6 feeble 7 frailty 8 weakness 9 infirmity 12 imperfection

foil: 4 balk, soil, tain 5 blade, blunt, elude, evade, stain, stump, sword, track, trail 6 baffle, blench, boggle, defeat, defile, outwit, stigma, stooge, thwart 7 beguile, failure, pollute, repulse, trample 8 disgrace 9 frustrate, overthrow 11 frustration

foist: 4 cask 5 barge, cheat, fudge, fusty 6 galley, suborn 7 swindle 8 brackish 9 rascality 11 interpolate

fold: bow, lap, pen, ply, wap 4 bend, cote, fail, flap, furl, loop, plie, ruga, tuck 5 clasp, crimp, drape, flipe, flock, layer, plait, pleat, plica, prank, sinus, yield 6 bought, crease, double, hurdle, infold, plight, pucker, rimple 7 crumple, enbrace, flexure, placate, plicate 8 surround 9 enclosure, overthrow, plicature

kind of: 4 loop 5 bight, lapel, plica, quire 6 bought, dewlap, octavo 7 plicate 9 replicate

of skin: 5 plica

folded: 4 shut 6 closed 7 plicate

folder: 5 cover, folio 6 binder 7 leaflet 8 pamphlet

folderol, falderal: 8 nonsense

foliage: 6 leaves 7 leafage

foliated: 5 lobed 7 spathic

folio: fo 4 case, leaf, page

folk: 6 daoine, people 7 friends 9 intimates, relatives

folklore: 4 myth 6 custom, history, legend 9 tradition 12 superstition

genie of: 7 sandman

folks: 6 people

folkway: mos 5 mores(pl.) 6 custom 7 pattern

folle: mad 8 reckless 11 extravagant

folletto: imp 5 fairy 6 goblin, spirit

follicle: 5 crypt

follow: 4 copy, hunt, next, seek, shag, tail 5 adopt, after, chase, ensue, snake, spoor, trace, track, trail 6 attend, pursue, result, shadow 7 imitate, observe, replace, succeed 8 practice, supplant 9 accompany, alternate, supervene 10 comprehend, understand

follow behind: dog, lag, tag 4 heel, hunt, nose, tail 5 hound, trace 6 shadow, trail 7 draggle 9 supervene

follower: fan, ist, ite, son 4 aper, beau, zany 5 gilly 6 bildar, ensuer, gillie, gudget, sequel, sulter, votary 7 devotee, grifter, pursuer, retinue, spaniel 8 adherent, disciple, henchman, partisan, retainer, servitor 9 attendant, caudatory, cuadrilla, dependent, satellite, successor 10 aficionado, sweetheart 11 cuadrillero
suffix: ite

following: 4 next, sect 5 after, suant, train 6 sequel 7 ensuing, sequent 8 business, trailing, vocation 9 clientele 10 posthumous, profession, sequential, subsequent, succeeding, successive
exact words: 7 literal
laws of arithmetical algebra: 6 scalor

folly: sin 6 betise, dotage, lunacy 7 daffery, daffing, foolery, foppery, madness, mistake 8 fondness, idleness, lewdness, morology, nonsense, rashness 9 silliness 10 imprudence, wantonness 11 foolishness 12 indiscretion

foment: 4 abet, brew, spur 5 rouse, stupe 6 arouse, excite, incite 7 agitate, ferment 9 encourage, instigate

fond: tid 4 dear, dote, fain, fool, fund, weak 5 silly, stock, store 6 ardent, befool, caress, dearly, doting, fondle, loving, simple, tender 7 amatory, amorous, beguile, browden, foolish, insipid 8 desirous, enamored, sanguine, trifling, uxorious 9 credulous, enamoured, indulgent, savorless 10 curcuddoch, infatuated, passionate 12 affectionate
of dainties: 6 friand 9 friandise
of drink: 8 bibulous
of hunting: 7 venatic

fonda: inn 5 hotel 6 fonduk 7 fondouk, funduck

fondle: pet 4 baby, coax, fond, neck, waly 5 daunt, wally 6 caress, cocker, coddle, cosset, dandle, pamper, stroke 7 cherish 8 blandish, canoodle

fondling: pet 4 fool 5 ninny 9 caressing, dalliance, simpleton

fondly: 4 fond 6 dearly 7 foolish 8 tenderly 9 foolishly 14 affectionately

fondness: gra 4 love 5 folly, taste 8 dearness, weakness 9 affection 10 attachment, tenderness 11 affectation, foolishness 12 predilection 15 Philotherianism

fondu: 6 cheese 7 blended

fons: 6 source 8 fountain

font: 4 pila 5 basin 6 source, spring 7 piscina 8 delubrum, fountain 10 aspersoria(pl.) 11 aspersorium

fontal: 8 original 9 baptismal

food: bit, pap 4 bite, cate, chow, diet, eats, fare, farm, gear, grub, meat, peck, prog 5 bread, broma, cheer, foray, scaff, tripe 6 fodder, foster, morsel, viands, wraith 7 aliment, edibles, handout, pabulum 8 flummery, grubbery, victuals 9 nutriment, provender 10 provisions, sustenance 11 nourishment
animal: 4 feed 5 grain, grass 6 fodder, forage 9 provender
choice: 4 cake 6 pastry
comb. form: 4 sito 5 troph 6 tropho
container: jar 4 bowl, dish, olla 5 crock, plate 6 saucer
craving for: 4 pica 7 bulimia
devotee: 7 epicure, gourmet
dislike of: 6 asitia 9 sitomania 10 cibophobia
dressing: 5 sauce
element: 6 gluten 7 protein, vitamin
farinaceous: 4 sago
garnish: 5 sauce
heavenly: 5 manna
invalid: pap 5 broth
kind of: pap, poi, sop 4 ants, chum, crum, mess, mush, sago 5 acate, balut, bread, broma, cates, gruel, jelly, manna, puree, salep, scaff, souse, tripe 6 cagmag, cereal, farina, forage, hominy, vivres 7 abalone, boscage, pemican, tapioca 8 ambrosia, aperient, beebread, pemmican 9 aperitive, rechauffe 10 rechauffe
list: 4 diet, menu 5 carte
of gods: 6 amrita 7 amreeta 8 ambrosia
pert. to: 8 cibarial 9 cibarious
protein: 4 fish, meat 6 cheese
provision of: 4 mess 6 ration 8 catering
seller: 6 grocer 7 viander
semidigested: 5 chyme
soft: pap
storage pit: 4 cist
southern: 4 okra, pone 5 gumbo 6 hominy 7 hoecake 11 chitterling
special dish: 4 hogo, olla, stew 5 bredi, pilaf, pilau, pilaw, pizza 6 haslet, hominy, majoon, omelet, panada, pilaff, ragout, salmis, scouse, sundae, zimmis 7 chowder, custard, rarebit, ravioli, souffle 8 cabeliau, hautgout, omelette, sillabub, sukiyaki 9 cabilliau, colcannon, galantine, succotash 10 salmagundi, shish-kebab

starchy: 8 macaroni 9 spaghetti 10 vermicelli

unclean: 4 tref

food and drink: 4 diet, fare 5 bouge, found 6 bouche 10 provisions

fool: ape, ass, cod, fop, fox, mug, nup, toy 4 butt, cake, chub, dolt, dupe, fond, gowk, gype, jape, jest, joke, mome, nizy, simp, toot, zany 5 bluff, clown, dally, goose, idiot, knave, moron, ninny, nizey, noddy, sammy, silly, snipe, spoof, trick 6 buffle, cudden, cuckoo, delude, dotard, dottle, jester, nidget, nimshi, nincom, nupson, tamper 7 asinego, buffoon, coxcomb, deceive, dizzard, foolish, fribble, gomeral, gomeril, haveral, haverel, mislead, omadawn, playboy, witling 8 badinage, driveler, fondling, hoodwink, omadhaun 9 blockhead, capocchia, driveller, fopdoodle, hoddy-peak, hoddy-poll, simpleton 10 bufflehead, hoddy-doddy, nincompoop

fool's gold: 6 pyrite

fool's paradise: 7 chimera 8 illusion

fool's stitch: 6 tricot

foolable: 8 gullible

foolhardy: 4 rash 11 adventurous 12 presumptuous

fooling: 6 banter 7 daffery, daffing 12 harlequinade

foolish: mad 4 bete, daft, fond, fool, rash, zany 5 barmy, batty, boggy, buggy, dizzy, gawky, goofy, goosy, inane, inept, noddy, silly 6 absurd, dotish, fondly, gotham, harish, mopish, simple, stupid, unwise 7 asinine, doatish, doltish, fangled, fatuous, flighty, foppish, gullish, idiotic, witless 8 fopperly, headless, heedless 9 brainless, childlike, desipient, doddering, imprudent, insensate, ludicrous, senseless 10 half-witted, hulver-head, indiscreet, irrational 12 preposterous 13 feather-headed 14 feather-brained

foolishness: 5 folly 6 barney, levity, rubble 8 fondness 9 absurdity 10 insipience

foot: paw, pes 4 base, hoof 6 gammon

animal: pad, paw 4 hoof 7 fetlock, pastern

armor: 7 chausse

comb. form: 4 pedi, pode

deformity: 5 varus

metric: 4 iamb 5 arsis, paeon 6 dactyl, iambic, iambus 7 anapest, spondee, triseme 8 bacchius, epitrite, molossus, trochee

pain: 8 talalgia

part: toe 4 arch 6 instep, tarsus, thenar 10 metatarsus

pert. to: 5 pedal, podal

poetic: See *metric* above

worked by: 5 pedal 7 treadle

foot bone: 6 cuboid, tarsus 8 scaphoid 10 astragulus, metatarsus

foot doctor: 10 podiatrist 11 chiropodist

foot lever: 5 pedal 7 treadle

foot-like part: pes

foot-loose: 4 free 10 ambulatory 11 untrammeled

foot soldier: 8 infantry

football: 5 rugby 6 rugger, soccer 7 pigskin

coach: 5 Jones, Morre, Stagg, Wilce 6 Bezdek, Dorais, Harlow, Rockne, Romney 7 Crisler, Heisman, Higgins 8 Morrison 9 Cavanaugh

kick: 4 punt 6 spiral

play: 4 buck, pass, punt 7 spinner

score: 4 down, goal 6 safety 9 touchback, touchdown

term: 6 onside 7 offside

footband: 6 canvas

footboy: 4 page 9 attendant

footed: 6 pedate

multiple: 7 bipedal, octopod 8 multiped

large: 7 megapod

footer: 4 fall, idle, jump 6 plunge, potter, trifle, walker

footfall: 5 tread

footgear: See **footwear**

foothold: 7 toehold

footing: par 5 basis, track 7 toehold 9 footprint

footle: 5 silly 6 drivel, potter, trifle 7 trivial, twaddle

footless: 4 apod 5 apoda, apode, inapt 6 apodal, clumsy, stupid 13 unsubstantial

footman: 6 flunky, lackey, varlet, walker 7 flunkey, footpad, servant 8 chasseur 10 pedestrian

footnote: 9 reference 11 explanation

footpad: pad 4 whyo 6 padder, robber 7 footman 10 highwayman

footpath: 4 lane 5 senda, trail 8 trottoir

footprint: 5 trace, track, tread

fossil: 9 ichnolite

rabbit: 5 prick

footrest: 4 rail 7 hassock 9 footstool

footrope: 5 horse 8 boltrope

footstalk: 7 pedicel, petiole 8 peduncle

footstep: 7 vestige

footstool: 4 mora 6 buffet 7 cricket, hassock, ottoman 8 footrest

footway: 4 path 9 banquette

footwear: pac 4 boot, clog, pack, shoe, sock 5 kamik, sabot 6 arctic, bootee, brogan, brogue, buskin, galosh, kamika(pl.), patten, rubber, sandal 7 galoshe, slipper 8 moccasin, overshoe, stocking

footy: 4 mean, poor 6 paltry

fooyoung, fooyung: 6 omelet 8 omelette

fop: 4 buck, dude, dupe, fool 5 dandy 7 coxcomb, jessamy 8 gimcrack, popinjay 9 exquisite

foppery: 9 absurdity

foppish: 5 apish, dandy, silly 6 dapper, spruce, stupid 7 fangled, finical, foolish 8 dandyish

foppishness: 13 dandification

for: 7 because 8 favoring 9 favouring 10 concerning
prefix: pro

for all voices: 5 tutti

for cash: 9 alcontado (Sp.)

for each: per

for example: e.g.

for fear that: 4 lest

for nothing: 6 gratis, lanyap 8 gratuity 9 lagniappe

for shame: fie

for temporary use: 4 jury

for that reason: 4 ergo(L.) 9 therefore

for which reason: 6 whence

forage: ers, oat, rye 4 corn, mast, raid, rape 5 grass, maize, raven, spoil, wheat 6 barley, browse, clover, fodder, millet, ravage, russud 7 alfalfa 8 deerweed 9 pasturage 10 provisions 11 bitter vetch

foramen: 4 pore

forane: 6 remote 7 foreign

foray: 4 rade, raid 5 melee 6 ravage, sortie 7 chappow, hership, pillage 9 incursion

forbear, forebear: 4 bear, help, shun, sire 5 avoid, forgo, spare 6 desist, endure, forego, parent 7 abstain, decline, refrain 8 ancestor 10 ancestress, forefather, foreparent

forbearance: 5 mercy 6 lenity 8 mildness, patience 9 tolerance 10 abstinence, self-denial 13 self-restraint

forbearing: 7 patient 8 tolerant 9 desisting

forbid: ban 4 defy, deny, fend, tabu, veto 5 debar, taboo 6 defend, enjoin, impede, refuse 7 forfend, forwarn, gainsay, inhibit 8 disallow, forefend, forspeak, preclude, prohibit 9 challenge, interdict, proscribe 10 contradict 11 countermand

forbiddance: ban 4 veto 12 interdiction, proscription

forbidden: 4 tabu 5 taboo 6 banned, denied 8 verboten 10 prohibited
Jewish law: 4 tref

Forbidden City: 5 Lhasa

forbidding: 4 grim 5 black, gaunt, stern 6 fierce, odious, strict 9 offensive, repellent 10 unpleasant 11 displeasing, prohibiting 12 disagreeable, interdicting

forbode: See **forebode**

force: gar, gut, vim, vis 4 bang, birr, clip, cram, dint, feck, make 5 co-act, drive, exert, farce, impel, might, peise, poach, power, press, repel, shear, stuff, wrest 6 coerce, compel, cudgel, energy, extort, oblige, ravish, stithy 7 ability, afforce, cascade, impetus, impulse, require, violate 8 coaction, coercion, efficacy, momentum, pressure, strength, validity, violence, virility 9 constrain, influence, puissance, restraint, waterfall 10 compulsion, constraint, constringe 11 necessitate
air upon: 4 blow
down: 4 tamp 5 stuff
into smaller space: 8 compress
kinds of: od 4 army, birr, dyne, elod, soul, task 5 agent, cadre, dynam, enemy, fohat, nerve, posse, steam, tonal 6 nature 7 voltage 8 bionergy, battalia, sanction 13 reinforcement
onward: 4 urge 6 propel
out: 5 evict 6 banish, unseat
producing rotation: 6 torque
to do without: 7 deprive
with full: 5 amain

forced: 7 labored 8 spurious 9 reluctant 10 artificial, compulsory, farfetched 11 constrained, involuntary, spontaneous 12 artificially
contribution: tax 4 duty, levy, toll 6 demand, excise, impost 7 tribute 8 exaction 10 assessment
feeding: 6 gavage

forceful: 6 mighty, strong, virile 7 dynamic, violent 8 eloquent, enfatico, forcible, vigorous 9 effective, energetic

forcemeat: 5 farce

forceps: 7 pincers 8 dentagra

forces: 4 army 6 troops

forcible: 5 stout, valid 6 cogent, mighty, potent 7 violent, weighty 8 emphatic, forceful, powerful, puissant, vigorous 9 energetic, impetuous, necessary 10 compulsory, convincing, impressive, obligatory 11 efficacious, influential

forcibly: 5 amain 6 hardly 9 violently 10 vigorously

ford: 4 wade, wath 5 drift 6 stream 7 current 8 crossing 9 wathstead

Fordham's team: 4 Rams

fore: van, way 5 afore, ahead, front, prior, track 6 former 7 earlier, further, journey 8 advanced, formerly 10 antecedent, previously

forearm: arm
bone: 4 ulna
pert. to: 7 cubital

forebear: See **forbear**

forebode, forbode: 4 bode, omen 5 augur, croak 6 divine 7 betoken, portend, predict, presage 8 foretell 13 prognosticate 15 prognostication

foreboding, forboding: 4 omen 5 black 6 augury, boding, gloomy 7 anxiety 8 bodement, sinister 10 prediction 11 pessimistic, presagement 12 apprehension, presentiment

forecast: 4 bode 6 scheme 7 caution, foresee, fortune, predict 8 foredeem, foretell, prophesy 9 calculate, foregleam, forepoint, forescent, foretoken, prognosis 10 foreordain, prediction, prognostic 11 calculation, foredestiny 12 predetermine 15 prognostication

forecaster: 4 seer 6 oracle 8 dopester 11 nostradamus 13 meteorologist

foreclose: 5 debar 6 hinder 7 prevent 8 preclude

foredoom: 7 destiny 10 predestine

forefather: 4 sire 5 elder 6 parent 7 forbear 8 ancestor 9 grandsire 10 forerunner, progenitor

forefinger: 5 index

forefoot: paw, pud

forefront: van 5 front

foregather: 4 meet 7 consort, convene 8 assemble 9 encounter 10 fraternize

forego, forgo: 5 waive 7 abstain, neglect, precede, refrain 8 dispense, renounce

foregoer: 7 example 8 ancestor 10 forerunner 11 predecessor

foregoing: 4 past 5 above 8 anterior, previous 10 antecedent

foregone: 4 past 8 previous
conclusion: 9 certainty

forehanded: 5 early 6 timely 7 prudent, thrifty

forehead: 4 brow 5 frons, front 7 frontes 8 sinciput
pert. to: 7 metopic
prominence: 8 glabella
strap: 4 tump

foreign: 5 alien, fremd 6 exiled, exotic, forane, remote 7 distant, ecdemic, exclude, strange 8 barbaric, peregrin 9 barbarous, extrinsic, peregrine 10 extraneous, outlandish, tramontane 12 adventitious, exallotriote, exterraneous
comb. form: 4 xeno
geology: 7 epigene

foreign quarter: 6 barrio, ghetto 7 enclave

foreign service: *official:* 6 consul 7 attache 8 diplomat 10 ambassador
residence: 9 consulate

foreign to: 6 dehors

foreigner: 5 alien, haole 6 gringo, pakeha 7 greener, pardesi 8 outsider, stranger 9 barbarian, estranger, outlander 10 tramontane 12 ultramontane

forejudge: 7 adjudge

foreknow: 6 divine 7 foresee 9 prescient 11 preconceive

foreknowledge: 10 prescience

forel: 4 case 6 border, sheath 7 selvage 8 slipcase

foreland: 8 headland 10 promontory

forelay: 6 ambush, hinder, waylay 8 obstruct

forelock: 4 bang 6 cotter 8 linchpin

foreman: 4 boss 5 chief 6 gaffer, ganger, leader 7 capataz, captain, headman, manager, steward 8 overseer 9 chargeman 10 supervisor

foremost: 4 head, high, main 5 chief, first, forme, front, grand 6 banner 7 leading, supreme 9 principal
part: van 5 front

forensic: 8 forensal 10 rhetorical 13 argumentative

foreordain: 7 destine, foresay, predoom 8 forecast 9 preordain 10 predestine 12 predestinate, predetermine

forepart: 5 front 9 stomacher
of horse's hoof: toe

forerun: 6 herald, outrun 7 precede, prelude 8 announce 9 forestall, introduce, precourse, prefigure 10 anticipate, foreshadow

forerunner: 4 omen, sign 5 usher 6 augury, herald 8 ancestor, foregoer, fourrier 9 harbinger, messenger, precedent, precursor 10 forefather, foreganger, progenitor, prognostic 11 predecessor

foresaid: 9 aforesaid

foresee: 4 read 6 divine 8 forecast, foreknow 10 anticipate

foreseeing: 9 designing

foreshadow: 7 forerun 9 adumbrate, prefigure

foreshank: 4 shin

foreshow: 4 bode 5 abode, augur 7 betoken 8 foretell, prophesy 9 auspicate, foretoken 13 prognosticate

foresight: 6 vision 8 prudence 9 prevision 10 prescience, prevoyance, providence 11 forethought 12 anticipation 14 farsightedness

foresighted: 9 prescient, provident 10 farsighted

forest: 4 gapo, wood 5 Arden, glade, gubat, sylva(L.), taiga, waste 6 jungle, timber 7 boscage 8 caatinga, woodland 10 wilderness
deity: 4 faun 5 satyr 7 Aegipan
glade: 5 camas 6 camass, cammas 7 quamash
god: Pan 5 Tapio
love of: 9 hemophily
open place: 5 glade
pertaining to: 6 sylvan 7 nemoral 9 forestral
road: 4 ride 5 trail

subarctic: 5 taiga
treeless: 4 wold
warden: 6 ranger
Forest City: 8 Portland, Savannah 9 Cleveland
forest fire locator: 7 alidade
forester: 7 montero, treeman, woodman 8 woodsman
forestland for tillage: 7 thwaite
foretaste: 4 gust 6 teaser 8 prospect 12 anticipation
foretell: 4 bode, erst, read, spae 5 augur, insee, weird 6 divine 7 bespeak, foresay, portend, predict, presage 8 forebode, forecast, foreshow, prophesy, soothsay 9 predicate, prefigure, prophetic 10 vaticinate 13 prognosticate
foretelling: 9 fatidical, prophetic
forethought: 7 caution 8 prepense, prudence 9 foresight, provident 12 aforethought, anticipation 13 premeditation
foretoken: 4 omen 7 promise 8 forecast, foreshow, foresign 9 auspicate 10 presignify 13 prognosticate
foretold: 10 annunciate
foretooth: 5 biter 6 cutter 7 incisor
forever: ay; ake, aye 4 ever 5 etern 6 always, eterne 7 endless 8 eternity 9 endlessly, eternally, perpetual 10 constantly, invariably 11 ceaselessly, continually, everlasting, incessantly, perpetually, unceasingly 12 interminably, unchangeably 13 everlastingly
forewarn: 5 augur
forewarning: 7 portent 11 premonition
foreword: 5 proem 7 preface 8 preamble 12 introduction
forfeit: 4 fine, lose 5 crime, dedit, forgo 6 forego 7 escheat, misdeed, penalty 8 forfault
law 7 abandum
forfeiture: 4 fine 5 mulct 7 penalty 9 decheance 10 amercement
forfend, forefend: 5 avert 6 forbid, secure 7 prevent, protect 8 preserve, prohibit
forfex: 6 shears
forge: 4 mint 5 feign 6 smithy, swinge 7 falsify, fashion 8 bloomery 9 fabricate 11 counterfeit, fabrication, manufacture
nozzle: tew 5 tewel
on: 5 drive
tongs: tew
waste: 5 dross, sprue
wrought iron: 8 bloomery
forged: 10 artificial 11 counterfeit
forger: 5 smith 9 falsifier 10 coachsmith, fabricator
forgery: 4 sham 7 fiction 8 bloomery 11 counterfeit, fabrication 13 falsification

forget: 4 omit 7 neglect 8 overlook 9 disregard 11 disremember
one's lines: 5 fluff
forgetful: 8 careless, heedless 9 oblivious 10 neglectful 11 inattentive
forgetfulness: 7 amnesia, amnesty 8 oblivion
fruit of: 5 lotus
river of: 5 Lethe
forging: 11 fabrication
forgivable: 6 venial
forgive: 5 remit, spare 6 excuse, pardon 7 absolve, condone 8 overlook 9 exculpate
forgiven: 7 excused
forgiveness: 6 pardon 9 remission 10 absolution 11 condonation
forgiving: 6 humane 7 clement 8 merciful, placable 9 remissive 10 charitable
forgo, forego: 4 quit 5 leave 7 abstain, forbear, forfeit, forsake, neglect, refrain 8 agnegate, forebear, overlook, renounce 10 relinquish
forgoing: 5 above
forjudge, forejudge: 4 oust 5 expel 7 adjudge, condemn
fork: 4 tine 5 prong 6 bisect, branch, crotch, divide 7 fourche 10 divaricate, fourchette
kinds of: 4 croc, evil 5 graip, pikle, glack 7 biprong 9 tormentor
forked: 5 bifid 6 furcal 7 divided, furcate 8 branched 9 furciform 10 bifurcated 11 forficulate
forleave: 7 abandon
forlorn: 4 lorn, lost, reft 5 stray 6 abject, bereft, ruined 7 forfare 8 deserted, desolate, forsaken, helpless, hopeless, pitiable, wretched 9 abandoned, cheerless, desperate, destitute, miserable 10 friendless 11 comfortless 12 disconsolate
form: ame 4 blee, body, make, mode, mold, plan, rite, thew 5 bench, build, frame, guise, image, model, shape 6 adjust, create, figure, invent, manner, ritual, schema, sponge 7 arrange, compose, confect, contour, develop, fashion, outline, pattern, portray, produce, profile 8 ceremony, conceive, likeness, organize, schemata(pl.) 9 construct, etiquette, fabricate, formation, structure 10 appearance, constitute, expression, figuration, observance, similitude 12 conformation 13 configuration, questionnaire
carved: 8 statuary
display: 4 rack 7 manikin 9 mannequin
geometrical: see **figure:** *geometrical*
into arc: 5 embow
into ball: 8 conglobe
into chain: 8 catenate
into fabric: 4 knit

into network: 10 reticulate
literary: ode 5 novel, poesy 6 satire, sonnet 7 romance
liturgical: 6 litany 7 service
lyrical: 6 rondel 7 sestina, sestine(pl.)
of government: 6 polity
of greeting: bow 5 hello, salam 6 salaam, salute 7 curtsey
pert. to: 5 modal
formal: set 4 prim 5 exact, stiff 6 solemn 7 orderly, precise, regular, solward, starchy, stilted 8 academic, affected, formular, starched 9 essential, officious 10 ceremonial, methodical 11 ceremonious, punctilious, superficial 12 conventional
formality: 8 ceremony 15 conventionality
format: 4 size 5 shape, style 7 pattern
formation: 4 form, rank 9 structure 10 procession 11 composition, development 12 construction
bone: 7 ostosis 10 parostosis
cell: 6 tissue
flesh: 8 sarcosis
geological: lia 4 ione 5 atoll, ledge 6 schist 7 tapeats, terrain, terrane
military: 4 line 5 herse 7 echelon
sand: 4 dene, dune
formative: 7 plastic
forme: 5 bench, early, first 6 former 8 foremost
formed: 5 built 7 decided, matured, settled, wrought 10 constitute
at foot of mountain: 8 piedmont
by law: 9 corporate
crudely: 9 roughhewn
from above: 8 catogene
ingeniously: 5 dedal 6 daedal
of clustered grains (bot.): 7 grumose
on earth's surface: 7 epigene
former: ex; die, old 4 erst, fore, late, once, past 5 forme, gauge, guide, maker, prior 6 whilom 7 ancient, creator, earlier, further, pattern, quondam, templet 8 previous, sometime 9 aforetime, erstwhile 10 antecedent
prefix: ex
formerly: ere, nee 4 erst, fore, once, then 5 grave 7 onetime, quondam 8 sometime 9 aforetime, anciently, erstwhile 10 heretofore
formicary: ant 7 anthill, dweller
formicid: ant
formidable: 7 fearful 8 alarming, dreadful, menacing, terrible 11 redoubtable, threatening
formless: 5 arupa 7 anidian, chaotic 8 deformed 9 amorphous, shapeless 13 indeterminate
comb. form: 6 amorph 7 amorpho

Formosa city: 6 Taipei, Taiwan 7 Dai-Hoku
formula: law 4 rule 6 method, recipe, theory 7 receipt
formular: 5 model 6 formal, proper 7 regular 9 formulary
formulated: 6 stated 10 articulate
forsake: 4 deny, drop, flee, quit, shun 5 avoid, forgo, leave, waive 6 beleve, defect, depart, desert, forego, refuse, reject 7 abandon, beleave, discard 8 renounce, withdraw 9 surrender 10 relinquish
forsaken: 4 lorn 7 forlorn 8 deserted, desolate 9 abandoned, destitute
forset: bar 5 beset 6 invest, waylay 8 surround
forspeak: 4 help 5 avert, curse 6 forbid, hinder 7 asperse, bewitch, devance, exclude, forerun, obviate, prevent 8 renounce 9 intercept 10 anticipate
forswear: 4 deny 6 abjure, reject 7 abandon, perjure 8 abnegate, renounce
forsworn: 8 perjured 11 disaffected
fort: pa; dun, lis, pah 4 liss, shee 5 gotta, redan, sidhe 6 castle, strong 7 bastile, bastion, bulwark, citadel, fortify 8 bastille, castillo, fastness, fortress 10 blockhouse, protection, stronghold
sloping bank of: 6 glacis
forte: bag 5 skill, thing 6 metier 7 calling 8 strength 9 specialty
forth: out 4 away 6 abroad, manage, onward 7 forward 8 outdoors 10 accomplish
forthink: 6 regret, repent 10 reconsider
forthright: 7 frankly 9 downright 11 straightway 13 straightforth 15 straightforward
forthwith: now 6 bedene, believe, direct 7 betimes 8 directly 9 extempore, presently, therewith 11 immediately
fortification (see also **defense**): 4 boma, moat, wall 5 redan, tower 6 abatis, castle, glacis, shield 7 bastion, bulwark, citadel, parapet, rampart, ravelin, redoubt 8 fortress 9 barricade 10 stronghold 12 machiolation
kind of: 4 fort 5 redan 6 abatis, sconce 7 lunette, ravelin, redoubt, parados 8 ceinture, demilune, estacade 9 fortalice, bastionet
part: 5 redan 7 bastion, ravelin 8 barbette
fortify: arm, man 4 fort 5 spike 6 abatis, picket 7 bastile, confirm 8 bastille, embattle, fortress, palisade 9 barricade 10 invigorate, strengthen, stronghold
fortitude: 6 mettle 7 bravery, courage, heroism, stamina 8 strength 9 endurance 10 resolution 12 resoluteness 14 impregnability
fortress: 4 fort, keep 5 rocca 6 castle 7 alcazar, barrier, bastile, borough, castlet, cas-

trum, chateau, citadel, fortify **8** alcalzar,
alcazava, bastille, chateaux(pl.), fastness
10 stronghold **13** fortification, propug-
naculum
outwork of: **6** tenail **8** tenaille
fortuitous: **6** casual, chance, random **9** hazardous **10** accidental, contingent, incidental **12** adventitious
fortuity: **4** luck **6** chance **9** accidence
fortunate: edi, hap, sri **4** good, shri **5** faust,
happy, lucky, shree **6** dexter **7** favored **8**
gracious **10** auspicious, prosperous, successful
fortune: hap, lot **4** bahi, doom, fate, hail,
luck **5** weird **6** chance, estate, mishap,
riches, wealth **7** destiny, success **8** accident, hacienda **9** adventure **10** prosperity
13 circumstances
goddess: **5** Tyche
fortune teller: **4** seer **5** gypsy, sibyl, sybil **7**
diviner, palmist
forty: **13** quadragesimal
forty days: **4** Lent
forty winks: nap **6** snooze
forty-five degree angle: **6** octant
forty-five inches: ell
forty-third asteroid: **4** Eros
43,560 square feet: **4** acre
forum: **5** court **8** tribunal
forward: on, to; aid, bog, bug **4** abet, bain,
bold, free, help, pert, send, ship, step **5**
ahead, along, brash, eager, favor, forth,
frack, freck, front, hasty, ready, relay, remit, saucy, serve, spack, ultra **6** afford, ardent, avaunt, before, bright, coming, favour, forthy, hasten, onward, prompt **7** advance, earnest, extreme, further, promote, radical **8** adelante, arrogant,
immodest, impudent, perverse, petulant,
transmit **9** audacious, encourage, forth-
ward, obtrusive, overready **10** accelerate,
forritsome, precocious **11** disobedient, progressive
fosette: **5** ulcer **6** dimple, hollow
fossa: pit **4** foss, moat **5** canal, ditch, fosse,
fovea, graff, grave **6** cavity, trench **10** depression
fosse (see also **fossa**): pit **4** hole, moat
fossil: **6** dolite **7** antique, lituite **8** calamite,
conodont
egg: **7** ovulite
footprint: **7** ichnite
mollusk: **6** dolite
resin: **5** amber **8** retinite
science: **12** paleontology
shell: **6** dolite
toothlike: **8** conodont
worm track: **7** nereite
fossorial: **9** effodient

fostell: box **4** cask **6** casket
foster: **4** feed, food, help, rear **5** nurse **6** harbor **7** cherish, embosom, gratify, imbosom,
indulge, nourish, nursing, nurture, promote, sustain **8** befriend, forester, nursling **9** cultivate, encourage, fosterage, offspring **11** nourishment
foster child: **5** nurry **7** stepson **12** step-
daughter
fosterage: **11** achievement
foudroyant: **8** dazzling, stunning **10** thundering
fougue: **5** ardor **11** impetuosity
foul: **4** base, hory, roil, vile **5** bawdy, black,
dirty, grimy, horry, muddy, nasty, sully,
weedy **6** clarty, defame, dirten, filthy, impure, malign, odious, putrid, rotten,
soiled, unfair **7** abusive, defaced, fulsome,
hateful, illegal, noisome, obscene, profane, smeared, squalid, unclean, vicious **8**
entangle, indecent, stinking, wretched **9**
dastardly, dishonest, loathsome, nasti-
ness, obnoxious, offensive **10** detestable,
disgusting, scurrilous **11** contaminate, unfavorable **12** dishonorable, inauspicious
foulard: tie **11** neckerchief **12** handkerchief
foulmouthed: **7** abusive, obscene, profane
10 scurrilous **11** opprobrious
foulness: **9** feculence
found: fix, try **4** base, cast, rest **5** board,
build, endow, erect **6** attach, depart **8**
equipped, practice, provided, supplied **9**
establish, institute, originate, supported
10 foundation
foundation: bed **4** base, body, fund, gist, sill
5 basis, bases(pl.), found, stock **6** bottom,
legacy, reseau, riprap **7** bedding, bedrock,
chantry, roadbed **8** donation, pedestal **9**
beginning, endowment **11** corporation **12**
substructure
founder: **4** fail **6** author, caster, dismay, dynast **7** stumble **8** miscarry **9** supporter, undermine **10** maintainer **11** dumbfounder,
establisher
metal: **5** yeter **6** yetter
founding: **8** settling
foundling: oaf **4** waif **6** infant, orphan **8**
nursling
fount: **4** fons **6** source **8** fountain **9** reservoir
fountain: **4** fond, head, syke, well **5** fount **6**
phiale, pirene, source, spring **7** bubbler **8**
aganippe **9** reservoir **12** fountainhead
god of: **4** Fons
nymph: **5** naiad
Fountain of Youth site: **6** Bimini
fountainhead: **6** origin, source
four: IV
comb. form: **5** tetra

group of: 6 tetrad 7 guartet 8 quadriad 9 quartette

four-footed: 9 quadruped

Four Horsemen: war 5 death 6 famine 8 conquest

four hundred: 5 creme, elect, elite 6 select

four-in-hand: 7 necktie

four inches: 4 hand 7 measure

four-sided: 13 quadrilateral

fourchette: 4 fork 8 wishbone

fourflusher: 9 pretender

fourgon: car, van 5 wagon 7 tumbril

fourpence: 5 groat

fourrier: 9 harbinger 10 forerunner 13 quartermaster

fourscore: 6 eighty

foursome: 6 tetrad 7 quartet

fourth: 5 quart 6 fardel 7 quarter 8 quadrant

fourth estate: 5 press 10 newspapers

foveated: 6 pitted

fowl: hen 4 bird, cock 5 chick, chuck, manoc 7 chicken, rooster 8 volaille

kinds of: 4 keel, coot 5 malay, banty, snipe, poult, brant 6 Houdan, bantam, Sussex, rumkin 7 minorca, galeeny

fox: tod 4 fool 5 trick 6 canine, outwit 7 beguile, stupefy, vulpine 10 intoxicate, perplexity

foot: pad

hunter's cry: 4 soho 5 yoick

kinds of: cub 4 asse, stag 5 vixen, zorro 6 fennec, corsac 7 Reynard, karagan

scent of: 4 drag

fox trot: 5 dance

foxglove: 7 popdock

leaf: 9 digitalis

foxlike: 9 alopecoid

foxtail: 5 brush, grass

foxy: sly 4 wily 5 coony 6 shrewd 7 cunning, vulpine 10 fraudulent

foy: 4 gift 5 faith, feast

foyer: 5 lobby 6 hearth 8 anteroom, entrance 9 fireplace, greenroom

fra: 4 monk 5 friar 6 priest 7 brother

Fra Diavolo composer: 5 Auber

frab: nag 5 scold, worry 7 contend 8 struggle

fracas: 4 bout 5 brawl, melee, set-to 6 rumpus, uproar 7 quarrel 8 fraction 9 commotion 11 disturbance

fraction: bit 4 part 5 break, piece, scrap 6 breach, fracas, little 7 ruction, rupture 8 breaking, fracture, fragment

fractional: 7 partial

fractious: 4 ugly 5 cross 6 unruly 7 crabbed, peevish, waspish 8 perverse, snappish 9 irritable

fracture: 4 flaw, rend 5 break, cleft, crack 6 breach 7 rupture 8 fraction

fragile: 4 fine, frow, weak 5 frail, frowy, light 6 feeble, frough, infirm, slight 7 brickle, brittle, froughy, slender 8 delicate, ethereal 9 frangible

fragility: 8 delicacy 12 delicateness

fragment: bit, ort 4 blad, chip, flaw, grot, part, snip, wisp 5 broke, crumb, flake, groat, piece, relic, scrap, shard, sherd, shred, spall 6 gobbet, morsel, parcel, screed, sheard, sippet, sliver 7 cantlet, flinder, flitter, fritter, oddment, portion, remnant 8 fraction 10 smithereen

biographical: 8 anecdote

diamond: 4 bort

ice afloat: 5 brash

fragmentary: 5 hashy 6 broken

fragments: 5 frush 7 gubbins

literary: ana 7 analect

Fragonard painting: 7 Bathers

fragrance: 4 odor 5 aroma, scent, smell 6 flavor 7 flavour, incense, perfume 9 perfumery, redolence

fragrant: 5 balmy, olent, spicy 7 odorant, odorous, perfumy, scented 8 aromatic, redolent 9 ambrosial 11 odoriferous

fragrant ointment: 4 balm, nard

fragrant wood: 5 aloes, cedar

fraicheur: 5 chill 8 coolness 9 freshness

frail: 4 fine, puny, weak 5 crazy 6 basket, flimsy, infirm, sickly 7 brittle, bruckle, fragile 8 delicate 12 destructible 13 insubstantial

frailty: 5 fault 6 foible 7 failing 9 frailness, infirmity 10 peccadillo 12 imperfection

fraise: 4 fray, fuss, ream, ruff 6 cajole, defend, praise 7 defense, enlarge, flatter, pancake 8 cajolery 10 strawberry 11 disturbance

fraist: ask, try 4 seek 7 attempt 10 experience

fram: 5 spear

frambesia: 7 disease, sibbens, sivvens

frame (see also **framework**): go; bin 4 bunk, form, mold, plan, plot, sill 5 build, cadre, easel, panel, serve, shape, trave 6 abacus, adjust, binder, border, devise, fabric, invent, manage, profit, redact, resort, tenter 7 arrange, attempt, chassis, fashion, furnish, outline, portray, prepare, proceed, prosper 8 contrive, regulate 9 calculate, construct, fabricate, structure

kinds of: ame, mat 4 bier, calm, caum, gill, sash, sess, sime, sley 5 airer, cadar, cader, dekle, easel, grate, herse, knape, trave, scray 6 abacus, deckel, deckle, tenter 7 drosser, hayrack, taboret

frame of mind: 4 bent, mood 5 humor

frame-up: 4 plot 10 conspiracy

framework: 4 rack, sill 5 cadge, cadre, racke 6 replum, stroma 7 chassis, nacelle, trestle 8 skeleton

frampoid: 5 cross, fiery 7 peevish 8 spirited 9 vexatious 11 quarrelsome

franc: *piece of twenty:* 5 louis
twentieth part of: 7 centime

France: 4 Gaul 6 Gallia
airplane: 5 avion
among: 5 entre
ancient name: 4 Gaul 6 Gallia
and: et
annuity: 5 rente
appellation: nom
architect: 7 Lenotre 9 Corbusier
article: la, le, un; les, une
author: 4 Gide, Hugo, Loti, Sand, Zola 5 Benda, Camus, Dumas, Renan 6 Balzac, Proust, Racine, Sartre 8 Stendhal, Voltaire
axe: 5 hache
baby: 4 bebe 6 enfant
bachelor: 6 garcon
bacteriologist: 7 Pasteur
ball: bal
ballad: lai 7 virelai
bay: 6 Biscay
beach: 5 plage
beast: 4 bete
bed: lit 5 couche
beef: 5 boeuf
billiards: 7 bouchon
bitters: 4 amer
blessed: 4 beni 5 sacre
boat: 8 chaloupe
bond: 5 rente
boxing: 6 savate
boy: 6 garcon
brandy: 8 armagnac
brewery: 9 brasserie
brush: 6 brosse
butcher shop: 11 charcuterie
cafe: 9 estaminet
cape: 5 talma
capital: 5 Paris
card game: 6 ecarte 7 baccara 8 baccarat
cardinal: 7 Mazarin 9 Richelieu
care: 4 soin
cathedral city: 5 Reims, Rouen 6 Nantes, Rheims
champagne: Ay
chanteuse: 4 Piaf
chaperon: 11 gouvernante
cheese: 4 Brie 9 Roquefort
chemist: 5 Curie 7 Pasteur
chestnut: 6 marone, maroon
citizen: 7 citoyen
city: Ay; Aix, Pau 4 Caen, Metz, Nice, Riom, Sens, Vimy 5 Aries, Arles, Arras, Brest, Dijon, Harve, Lille, Lisle, Lyons, Nance, Nancy, Nerac, Nesle, Nimes, Paris, Reims, Rouen, Sedan Seine, Tours, Tulle, Vichy 6 Amiens, Angers, Calais, Lemans, Nantes, Pantin, Perret, Rennes, Rheims, Senlis, Sevres, Tarare, Toulon 7 Bareges, Ferrand, Limoges, Orleans, Roubaix, Valence 8 Bordeaux, Clermont, Mulhouse, Rochelle, Toulouse 9 Levallois, Marseille, Tourcoing 10 Saint-Denis, Strasbourg, Strassburg 11 Montpellier 12 Saint-Etienne
cleric: 4 abbe
cloth: ras 5 toile 8 blancard
cloud: nue
coffee house: 9 estaminet
coin: ecu, sol, sou 4 gros 5 agnel, blanc, blank, franc, obole, livre 6 denier, dizain, teston 7 centime, dizaine, testoon 8 cavalier, Louis d'or, Napoleon
commune: Pau 4 Auby, Bron, Dole, Laon, Loos, Orly, Reze, Vimy 5 Ancre, Rodez, Vichy 6 Pessac, Sanvic, Stains, Tarare
composer: 4 Lalo 5 Bizet, Ravel, Thome 6 Gounod, Halevy 7 Debussy
comrade: ami
concrete: 5 beton
conjunction: et
cordial: 8 anisette
cotton: 7 jasmine
couturier: 4 Dior
cowardly: 5 lache
cowboy: 6 baille 7 gardian
creamcake: 7 dariole
critic: 5 Taine
crown: ecu
curate: 4 abbe
custom: 9 Gallicism
daffodil: 10 polyanthus
daisy: 10 marguerite
dance: bal 5 gavot 6 branle, canary, cancan 7 bourree, boutade
dash: 4 élan
daughter: 5 fille
dead: 4 mort
dean: 5 doyen
dear: 4 cher
delicatessen: 11 charcuterie
department: Ain, Lot, Var 4 Aube, Aude, Cher, Eure, Gard, Gers, Jura, Nord, Oise, Orne, Tarn 5 Aisne, Corse, Doubs, Drome, Indre, Isere, Loire, Marne, Meuse, Rhone, Seine, Somme, Yonne 6 Allier, Ariege, Cantal, Creuse, Landes, Loiret, Lozere, Manche, Nievre, Sarthe, Savoie, Vendee, Vienne, Vosges 7 Ardeche, Aveyron, Correze, Dordgne, Gironde, Herault, Mayenne, Meurthe, Moselle 8 Ardennes, Calvados, Charente, Morbihan, Vaucluse 9 Finistere

designer: **4** Dior, Gres **5** Patou **6** Chanel **8** Givenchy **9** Courreges, St. Laurent **10** Balenciaga
devil: **6** diable
diplomat: **5** Segur, Senet **7** Ronsard
directory: **10** directoire
division: **6** canton **7** commune **10** department **14** arrondissement
division, ancient: **5** Arles **6** Arelas **7** Arelate **9** Aquitaine
doorkeeper: **9** concierge
dramatist: **5** Piron **6** Halevy, Racine, Sardou **7** Moliere
dressmaker: **9** couturier **10** couturiere
duke: duc
dungeon: **6** cachot
dynasty: **5** Capet **6** Valois
ecclesiastic: **4** abbe
egg: **4** oeuf
empress: **7** Eugenie
essayist: **4** Gide
evening: **4** soir
exclamation: **4** hein
F.B.I.: **15** Surete Nationale
farmhouse: mas
father: **4** pere
finally: **5** enfin
friar: **5** frere
friend: ami
gala: **4** fete
game: jeu **4** jeux(pl.)
god: **4** dieu
good: bon
goodbye: **5** adieu
green: **4** vert
hairdresser: **7** friseur
hat: **5** beret **7** chapeau **8** chapeaux
health: **5** sante
heaven: **4** ciel
here: ici
high: **5** haute
horse stable: **6** ecurie
husband: **4** mari
income: **5** rente
inn: **5** hotel **7** auberge
island: ile **4** Elba
judgment: **5** arret
king: roi **5** Louis, Capet
knife: **7** couteau
lace: **10** colberteen colbertine **12** Valenciennes
lake: **6** Annecy **7** Bourget
language: **7** Catalan **9** Provencal
laugh: ris **4** rire
laundry: **13** blanchisserie
leather: **4** cuir
lenten season: **6** Careme
liqueur: **5** creme **8** anisette **9** Cointreau
lord: **8** seigneur

lover: **5** amant
lyric: **6** rondel **7** descort, rondeau
magistrate: **7** echevin
maidservant: **5** bonne **7** lisette
marshal: Ney **4** Foch, Saxe **5** Murat **6** Petain
mask: **5** loups
mathematician: **5** Borel
me: moi
measure: pot **4** aune, line, mile, mine, muid, pied, sack, velt **5** arpen, carat, lieue, ligne, minot, perch, pinte, point, pouce, toise, velte **6** arpent, hemine, league, perche, quarte, setier **7** chopine, heminee, poisson, septier **8** boisseau, quartaut, roquille **9** decillion, quarteron **12** tonneau de mer
milk: **4** lait
money: See **coin** above
mountain: **4** Alps, Jura **6** Vosges **8** Auvergne, Cevennes, Cote d'Or, Pyrenees **9** Mont Blanc, Puy de Dome, Vignemale **10** Puy de Sancy
museum: **5** Musee
nail: **4** clou
name: nom
national anthem: **12** Marseillaise
national flower: **4** lily
no: non
noon: **4** midi
nose: nez
nothing: **4** rien
novelist: **4** Gide, Hugo, Loti, Zola **5** Camus, Dumas, Ohnet, Sagan, Verne **6** Halevy, Proust **7** Merimee **8** Flaubert
nursemaid: **5** bonne
of: de
officer: **7** prefect
old money: **6** besant
one: une
opera: **5** Faust, Manon **6** Carmen, Mignon
painter: **4** Dore **5** Corot, Degas, Manet, Monet **6** Cormon, Legros, Renoir, Vernet **7** Chardin, Deveria, Lorrain, Poussin, Watteau **8** Steinlen **9** Deschamps
palace: **6** elysee
pancake: **5** crepe
parish priest: **4** cure
Parliament chamber: **5** senat
party: bal
pastry shop: **10** patisserie
patron saint: **5** Denis, Denys **6** Martin
peer: duc **8** seigneur
philosopher: **4** Caro **5** Camus **6** Pascal, Sartre **8** Rousseau **9** Descartes
physicist: **5** Arago, Binet **6** Ampere
pocket: **5** poche
poem: dit, lai **7** rondeau
poet: **4** Labe **6** Racine **7** Rimbaud, Rostand **9** Deschamps, Desportes

police: 6 Surete 8 gendarme
porcelain: 7 Limoges
port: 4 Caen
preposition: de
president's residence: 6 elysee
pretty: 4 joli 5 jolie
priest: 4 abbe, cure, pere
pronoun: tu; moi 4 elle 6 tienne
psychologist: 5 Binet
pupil: 5 eleve
queen: 5 reine
rabbit: 5 lapin
race course: 7 Auteuil
railroad: 10 tortillard
railroad station: 4 gare
read: 4 lire
rear: 7 arrière
region: 6 Alsace
Republic calendar: 6 Nivose 7 Floreal, Ventose 8 Brumaire, Fervidor, Frimaire, Germinal, Messidor, Pluviose, Prairial 9 Fructidor, Thermidor 11 Vendemiaire
resort: Pau 4 Nice 5 Vichy 6 Cannes, Menton 7 Riviera
rest: 5 repos
restaurant: 6 bistro
Revolutionary hero: 6 Danton
Revolutionary leader: 5 Marat
Revolutionary radical: 7 Jacobin
river: Ain, Lot, Lys 4 Aire, Aude, Cher, Eure, Gard, Gers, Loir, Oise, Orne, Saar, Tarn, Yser 5 Adour, Aisne, Drome, Indre, Isere, Loire, Maine, Marne, Meuse, Rance, Rhone, Saone, Sarre, Seine, Seyre, Somme, Veste, Yonne 6 Allier, Ariege, Escaut, Loiret, Nievre, Sambre, Scarpe, Vienne 7 Ardeche, Durance, Garonne, Gironde, Moselle, Scheldt 8 Charente, Dordogne, Nantaise
roast: 4 roti 5 rotir
room: 5 salle
royal family: 5 Capet 6 Valois
saint: 5 Denis, Denys 6 Martin
savant: 7 Diderot
school: 5 ecole, lycee 8 Barbison, Barbizon
scientist: 5 Curie 7 Pasteur
sculptor: 5 Barye, Rodin 9 Bartholdi
sea: mer
seaport: 4 Caen 5 Brest, Havre 6 Calais, Toulon 8 Bordeaux 9 Dunkerque
shelter: 4 abri
shield: ecu 5 targe
shoe: 9 chaussure
shopgirl: 9 midinette
sister: 5 soeur
slang: 5 argot
soldier: 5 assis, poilu 6 Zouave 8 chasseur
son: 4 fils

song: 5 caira 6 aubade 7 Madelon, virelai, virelay
soul: ame
south: sud 4 Midi
spirit: ame 4 elan 6 esprit
stable: 6 ecurie
star: 6 etoile
state: 4 etat
stock exchange: 6 bourse
store: 8 boutique
story: 5 conte
street: rue
summer: ete
symbol: 4 lily 10 Fleur-de-lis
the: la, le; les(pl.)
theater: 5 odeon
then: 5 alors
ticket window: 7 guichet
title: duc 5 comte
tobacco: 5 tabac
town: 4 Agen, Aire, Caen, Sens, Sete 5 Douai, Ernee, Laval, Nerac, Ornes 6 Longwy, Sarlat, Tarbes, Troyes, Verdun 7 Castres 8 Le Perche, Rochelle
true: 4 vrai
Verdun battle: 4 Vaux
verse: 4 vers
verse form: lai 4 alba 6 rondel 7 ballade, virelay
very: 4 tres
vessel: 7 navette
vinegar: 8 vinaigre
vineyard: cru
waiter: 7 garcon
wall: mur
water: eau 4 eaux(pl.)
weight: 4 gros, marc, once 5 carat, livre, pound, tonne, uckia 7 tonneau 8 esterlin 9 esterling
who: qui
wicket: 7 guichet
wine: vin 4 Bois 8 sauterne 10 Roussillon
wine district: 5 Medoc 8 Burgundy 9 Champagne
wine shop: 6 bistro
woman: 5 femme
world: 5 monde
you: tu 4 vous
Franciscan: 8 Minorite, Capuchin 9 Cordelier
nun: 5 Clare
franchise: soc 5 grant 6 patent 7 license 8 freelage, suffrage 9 privilege
old English: soc 4 soke
francolin: 4 bird 5 titar 9 partridge
frangible: 7 brittle, fragile 9 breakable
frank: 4 free, open, rank 5 bluff, lusty, naive, plain 6 candid, direct, honest 7 artless, genuine, liberal, profuse, sincere 8 carefree, cavalier, generous, vigorous 9 ingen-

uous, luxuriant, outspoken 10 licentious, unreserved 15 straightforward, unsophisticated

frankincense: 8 olibanum

Frankish hero: 6 Roland

Franklin's nickname: 11 Poor Richard

frankly: 6 freely, openly 7 plainly 8 candidly 9 artlessly, liberally, sincerely, willingly 10 forthright 11 ingenuously 12 unreservedly 13 undisguisedly

frankness: 6 candor 7 freedom 8 openness 9 telltruth, unreserve

frankpledge: 6 borrow

Franks: 7 Salians

  hero: 6 Roland

  king: 5 Pepin 6 Clovis

  law of: 5 Salic

  peasant: 4 liti(pl.) 5 litus

  vassal: 4 leud

frantic: mad 5 rabid 6 insane 7 furious, lunatic, violent 8 deranged, feverish, frenetic, frenzied 9 delirious, desperate, phrenetic 10 distracted, distraught

frap: 4 beat 5 brace 6 strike 7 tighten 10 strengthen

frappe: ice 4 iced 5 chill 6 cooled, freeze, frozen 9 milkshake

frat: 11 brotherhood

fratch: 7 dispute, quarrel, wrangle

frater: 7 brother, comrade

fraternal: 9 brotherly

fraternity: 4 club 8 sorority 10 sisterhood 11 brotherhood

fraternize: 6 cotton 9 affiliate, associate, forgather 10 foregather

fraud: 4 dole, fake, gaff, gaud, gull, jape, ruse, sham, wile 5 cheat, craft, faker, guile, hocus, quack, trick 6 brogue, deceit, humbug 7 defraud, knavery, roguery, swindle 8 artifice, impostor, subtlety, trickery, trumpery 9 collusion, deception, imposture, stratagem 10 imposition 11 fraudulency 13 circumvention

fraudulent: 4 fake, wily 5 snide 6 crafty, quacky 7 abusive, crooked, cunning 8 cheating, covinous, guileful, spurious 9 deceitful, deceiving, deceptive, designing, dishonest, horsefair, insidious, underhand 10 fallacious, misleading 11 clandestine, counterfeit, treacherous

fraught: 4 fill, lade, load 5 cargo, equip, laden 6 burden, supply 7 freight 9 freighted, transport

fraxinus: ash 4 tree

fray: 4 feud, fret, riot 5 alarm, broil, broom, dread, feaze, fight, melee, panic, ravel 6 affray, assail, attack, battle, bustle, combat, fraise, fridge, fright, inroad, terror, tumult 7 contest, frazzle, ruction, terrify 8 disperse, frighten 9 commotion, dissipate 12 apprehension

frayed: 4 worn 7 raveled 10 threadbare

freak: 4 bold, flam, lune, mood, whim 5 braid, fancy, fleck, humor, prank, sport 6 frolic, greedy, humour, megrim, streak, vagary, whimsy 7 caprice, checker, crochet, monster, whimsey 8 capricci(pl.), flimflam 9 capriccio, variegate 11 monstrosity 12 whimsicality

freakish: odd 6 screwy 7 curious, flighty 9 fantastic, whimsical 10 capricious

fream: 4 roar

freath: 4 foam 5 froth 6 lather

freck, frack: 4 bold, hale 5 eager, lusty, ready, stout 6 dapple, strong 7 checker, forward 8 desirous 9 diversify

freckle: 4 spot 7 ephelis, frecken, lentigo

  remover: 6 adarce

Frederick I's nickname: 10 Barbarossa

Frederick the Great: 6 Alaric

free: lax, rid 4 liss, open, quit, void 5 broad, clear, enode, frank, lisse, loose, ready, siker, slake, spare, untie 6 acquit, adjust, beyond, degage, devoid, exempt, gratis, immune, lavish, loosen, remove, rescue, sicker, unbind 7 absolve, deliver, forward, grivois, inexact, leisure, liberal, manumit, outside, release, relieve, unbound, willing 8 abundant, detached, dispatch, distinct, expedite, familiar, floating, generous, grivoise, indigent, innocent, liberate, overfree, separate, unfasten, unhamper 9 discharge, disengage, exculpate, exonerate, expansive, extricate, foot-loose, guiltless, ingenuous, outspoken, separated, unbridled, unchecked, unimpeded, unleashed 10 autonomous, emancipate, gratuitous, immoderate, licentious, openhanded, unattached, uncombined, unconfined, unfettered, unimpaired, unreserved 11 disencumber, disentangle, independent, magnanimous, spontaneous, untrammeled 12 uncontrolled, unencumbered, unrestrained, unrestricted 13 communicative, unconstrained

  from bacteria: 7 aseptic, sterile

  from blame: 5 clear 6 acquit 7 absolve, relieve 9 exonerate

  from bondage: 7 manumit 10 emancipate 11 affranchise

  from dirt: 7 apinoid

  from discount: net

  from moisture: dry 9 dehydrate

  from restraint: 5 untie

  from suspicion: 5 clear, purge 6 acquit 7 absolve 9 exculpate, exonerate

free-for-all: 4 race 5 fight, melee 6 barney 11 competition

free of charge: 8 buckshee

free time: 4 rest 6 recess 7 leisure

freebooter: 5 rider 6 pirate 7 cateran, corsair 8 pillager 9 buccaneer, plunderer 10 filibuster

freed: 8 absolute 13 disencumbered

freedom: 4 ease 7 abandon, content, leisure, liberty, license, release 8 facility, freelage, immunity, latitude, openness 9 exemption, frankness, readiness 10 generosity, liberality, liberation 11 manumission, willingness 12 emancipation, independence 13 outspokenness 14 unreservedness
from activity: 4 rest 6 recess 7 respite
from fraud: 7 honesty 9 bonafides
from pain: 6 aponia
from strife: 5 peace
of access: 6 entree

freehold: 4 alod 5 allod 6 estate, tenure 7 alodium 8 allodium

freeholder: 6 yeoman

freeing: 8 acquital 11 manumission

freely: 4 lief 5 noble, nobly 6 gratis 7 frankly, largely, readily 8 heartily 9 beautiful, bounteous, bountiful, copiously, excellent, liberally, voluntary, willingly 10 abundantly, generously 11 beautifully, bounteously, bountifully, excellently, plenteously, plentifully, voluntarily 12 munificently 13 spontaneously 14 unobstructedly 15 unconditionally

freeman: 4 aire 5 ceorl, churl, thane, thegn 6 yeoman 7 burgess, burgher, citizen

Freestone State: 11 Connecticut

freethinker: 7 infidel, skeptic 8 agnostic 10 espritfort, unbeliever

freeze: ice 4 rime 5 chill 6 frappe, harden 7 chilled, congeal, impound 11 conglaciate, refrigerate

freezer: 4 icer

freezing: 4 cold 6 frigid, frosty

freight: 4 load 5 cargo, laden 6 lading 7 fraught 9 transport 10 freightage

freightage: 5 cargo 6 lading 7 freight

freighted: 5 laden 7 fraught

fremd: 5 alien 7 foreign, strange

French: See France

French-Belgian river: Lys 4 Yser

Frenchman: 4 Gaul 6 Picard 8 Parisian

frenetic, phrenetic: mad 4 wild 5 crazy, fresh 6 insane, madman 7 fanatic, frantic, madness, violent, zealous 9 delirious 10 distracted, ornamental, passionate 12 absent-minded

frenzied: 4 amok, mang 5 amoke, amuck, rabid 6 ramage 7 berserk, frantic, furious 8 frenetic, furibund, maddened 9 delirious

frenzy: mad 4 amok, fury, rage 5 amoke, amuck, furor, mania 7 frantic, madness, oestrus 8 delirium, insanity, maniacal 9 amazement 11 distraction

frequency: 5 crowd 6 throng 7 crebity 9 community, concourse 11 familiarity
unit: 7 fresnel

frequent: 5 haunt, howff, often, usual 6 affect, common, effect, hourly, sundry 7 current, enhaunt, prevail 8 familiar, habitual 9 assiduous, crebrouse, habituate 10 persistent

frequented places: 5 dives 6 haunts 7 resorts

frequenter: 7 habitue

frequently: oft 5 often 6 hourly 8 ofttimes 10 repeatedly

fresco: 5 mural, shade 8 coolness

frese: 4 bend, furl 5 slack 6 unbend 7 untwine

fresh: new 4 cool, good, pure, racy 5 brisk, green, ruddy, saucy, sound, sweet, vivid 6 breezy, bright, caller, florid, lively, recent, strong, unused 7 unfaded, untired, untried 9 obtrusive, unspoiled 10 additional, meddlesome, refreshing, unimpaired 12 invigorating, presumptuous
and lively: 4 racy

freshen: 5 renew 6 breeze, revive 7 refresh, sweeten

freshet: 5 spate 9 streamlet 10 inundation

freshly: 5 again

freshman: 5 bejan, frosh, plebe 6 bejant, novice

freshness: 4 verd 8 verdancy 9 fraicheur
lose: dry 4 fade, wilt 6 wither

fret: nag, rub, vex 4 care, fray, gall, gnaw, pout, rage, stew 5 chafe, grate, pique, tease, worry 6 abrade, devour, harass, murmur, nettle, plague, rankle, ripple, ruffle, strait 7 agitate, consume, disturb, grizzle, roughen 8 diminish, disquiet, irritate, vexation

fretful: 5 angry, cross 6 repine, sullen 7 carking, frecket, gnawing, peevish, pettish 8 captious, corroded, fretsome, petulant, restless 9 corrosive, impatient, irascible, irritable, plaintive, querulous 10 ill-humored, ill-natured

Freudian term: id; ego

Frey: *sister:* 5 Freya 6 Freyja
wife: 4 Gerd

Freya's husband: 4 Oder

friable: 5 crimp, crisp, crump, loamy, mealy
clay: 4 bole

friar: fra 4 fish, monk 5 frere 6 Bhikku; fraile, frater 7 Bhikshu, brother 8 monastic 9 Carmelite 10 Franciscan 11 Augustinian

black: 9 Dominican

mendicant: 7 Servite

friary: 8 cloister 9 monastery 11 brotherhood

fribble: 4 fool 6 falter, totter, trifle 7 stammer 8 trifling 9 frivolity, frivolous

fricassee: 6 potpie 10 blanquette 11 blanc-manger

friction: rub 5 chafe 9 attrition 10 dissension

air: 7 windage

fridge: rub 4 fray 5 chafe 6 fidget 8 irritate

fried: 4 frit 7 sauteed

fried cake: 7 cruller 8 doughnut

friend: ami(F.), amy, eme, pal 4 ally, amie(F.), chum, kith 5 amigo(Sp.), amiga(Sp.), crony 6 bonami(F.), cummer, gimmer, kimmer 7 comrade, gremial, kinsman 8 cockmate, compadre, paramour, relative 9 associate, attendant, bonne amie(F.), broadbrim, companion, confidant 10 confidante 12 acquaintance

Friend: 6 Quaker

church founder: 9 George Fox

friendless: 7 forlorn

friendliness: 5 amity 8 affinity, amicable, goodwill 10 fellowship 13 companionship

friendly: sib 4 cosh, good, kind 5 chief, howdy 6 blithe, genial, homely, howdie 7 affable, amiable, amicous, cordial 8 amicable, homelike, intimate, sociable 9 favorable 10 favourable, hospitable 11 warmhearted

Friendly island: 5 Tonga

friendship: 5 amity 6 amitie 8 relation 9 affection 10 attachment

Friendship author: 6 Cicero

frier: 6 pullet

frieze: 4 kelt(Sc.) 5 adorn, chase 8 trimming 9 embroider 10 decoration

band: 6 taenia

frigate (see also **boat, ship**): 5 zabra(Sp.)

frigate bird: iwa

Frigg's son: 5 Baldr 6 Balder

fright: awe, cow 4 fear, fray, funk, gast 5 alarm, gliff, panic, scare, shock 6 affray, dismay, horror, schrik, terror 7 startle 13 consternation

frighten: awe, cow 4 fray, funk, hare, haze, shoo 5 afear, alarm, appal, gliff, hazen, scare 6 affray, appall, ascare, boggle 7 frecken, startle, terrify 8 affright 10 intimidate

frightened: 4 awed, eery, gast 5 eerie, timid 6 afraid 8 skittish

frightful: 4 grim 5 awful, ferly 6 horrid, ugsome 7 affreux, fearful, gashful, ghastly, hideous 8 alarming, dreadful, fearsome,

horrible, horrific, shocking, terrible, terrific 10 horrendous, tremendous

frightfulness: 13 atrociousness 15 schrecklichkeit(Ger.)

frigid: icy 4 cold 5 acold, bleak 6 arctic, frosty 8 freezing

frill: 4 purl 5 jabot, ruche 6 ruffle 7 flounce 8 furbelow 9 balayeuse 11 chitterling

fringe: 4 loma 6 border, edging, margin 8 ciliella, trimming

fringed: 9 laciniate 10 frimbriate

frisk: 4 leap, skip, whid 5 brisk, caper, dance, flisk 6 curvet, frisco, frolic, gambol, lively, search 7 disport, friscal 8 caracole 10 frolicsome

frisky: gay 4 pert 6 lively 7 playful 8 frisking, sportive 10 frolicsome

frisson: 5 chill 6 quiver, shiver, thrill 7 shudder

frith: 4 help 5 firth, hedge 6 hurdle, wattle 7 coppice, estuary, freedom 8 liberate, security 9 brushwood, copsewood, underwood 10 protection

fritter: 5 shred, spend, waste 6 bangle 7 pancake, scatter 8 fragment

frivol: 6 trifle 9 frivolous

frivolity: 6 levity 7 fribble, inanity 8 nonsense 9 lightness

frivolous: gay 5 giddy, inane, petty 6 frivol, futile 7 fatuous, fribble, shallow, trivial 8 gossamer 9 childlike, worthless 11 lightheaded 14 featherbrained

frizzed: 5 crepe 6 crispy

fro: 4 away, back, from 5 hence, since 8 backward

frock (see also **dress**): jam 4 gown, slip, wrap 5 tunic 6 cleric, jersey, mantle 7 workman 9 gaberdine

frog: 5 frosh, frosk, jakie 6 peeper 7 paddock, quilkin 8 ferreiro 9 amphibian

order of: see *zoological order* below.

pert. to 6 ranine

rearing place: 7 ranaria(pl.) 8 ranarium

zoological order: 5 anura 6 anoura 9 salientia

frogman: 5 diver 7 swimmer

gear: 5 scuba

frohlich: gay 5 happy 6 joyous

froise: 7 pancake

frolic: bum, gay 4 blow, game, gell, jink, lark, orgy, play, ramp, romp 5 caper, freak, frisk, merry, prank, randy, sport, spree 6 curvet, gambol, plisky, prance, rollix, shindy, splore 7 disport, gammock, pliskie, scamper, stashie, wassail 8 carousal 9 gilravage 10 masquerade

frolicsome: gay 4 roid 5 gilpy 6 frisky, gilpey 7 jocular, waggish 8 espiegle, friskful, gamesome, sportive

from: fro
  beginning to end: 4 over 7 through
  head to foot: 7 capapie
  here: 5 hence
  that time: 6 thence
  the egg: 5 ab ovo
  the time that: 5 since
  this time: 5 hence
front: bow, van 4 brow, face, fore, head,
  prow 5 afore 6 before, facade, facing, oppose, sector 7 forward, further, obverse 8
  forehead, foremost, forepart 9 forefront 10
  appearance, effrontery 11 countenance
  toward the: 8 anterior
frontal: 6 sindon 7 metopic
frontier: 4 face 5 bound, march 6 border,
  oppose 7 barrier, defense 8 boundary
frontiersman: 4 Cody 5´Boone 6 Carson 7
  settler
fronton: 7 jai-alai
frore: 4 cold 6 frosty, frozen
frost: ice, nip 4 foam, hoar, rime 7 failure
frosted: 4 iced 5 glace 6 frozen
frostfish: 5 smelt 6 tomcod 9 whitefish
frosting: ice, mat 5 icing
frosty: icy 4 cold, rimy 5 chill, frore, gelid,
  glary 6 frigid, froren 8 chilling, freezing
froth: fob 4 barm, foam, scum, suds 5 spume
  6 freath, lather
frow: 4 frau, froe, wife 5 vrouw, woman
froward: 4 away 5 cross 7 adverse, awkward, peevish, wayward 8 contrary, perverse, petulant, untoward 9 obstinate 10
  refractory, unyielding 11 disobedient, unfavorable 12 ungovernable
frown: 4 lour 5 gloom, glout, lower, scowl 6
  glower, glunch 7 frounce
frowst, froust: 4 loll 5 stale 6 lounge, stuffy
  10 atmosphere
frowsy, frowzy: 5 musty 6 blowzy 7 raffish,
  unkempt 8 slovenly 10 disordered
frozen: 4 hard 5 fixed, frore, gelid, glary 6
  chilly, frappe, froren 7 chilled, frosted 8
  hardened, immobile 9 congealed 10 unyielding 11 coldhearted 12 refrigerated 13
  unsympathetic
fructify: 9 fertilize 10 impregnate
frugal: 4 mild 5 chary, roman, spare 6 saving 7 careful, sparing, thrifty 9 economize,
  provident 10 economical, unwasteful 12
  parsimonious
frugality: 6 thrift 7 economy 9 chariness
fruit: fig 4 date, lime, pear, plum, pome 5
  apple, berry, drupe, grape, lemon, melon,
  olive, peach 6 cherry, orange, result 7
  apricot, azarole, product 8 dewberry 9
  blueberry, nectarine, offspring, pineapple,
  tangerine 10 production
  aggregate: 7 etaerio

  apple-like: 4 pome 6 quince
  astringent: 4 sloe
  baccate: 5 berry
  beverage: ade 4 wine
  blackthorn: 4 sloe
  buttercup: 5 akene 6 achene 7 achenia(pl.)
    8 achenium
  citrus: 4 lime 5 grape, lemon 6 orange 7
    tangelo 9 tangerine
  collective: 7 syncarp 10 syncarpium
  cooked in syrup: 7 compote
  decay: 4 blet
  desert region: 5 terfa 6 terfez
  dish: 7 compote
  dried: 5 prune 6 orejon
  dry: 5 regma 6 achene, samara
  early maturing: 8 rareripe
  elm tree: 6 samara
  fleshy: 4 pear, plum, pome 5 berry, drupe,
    melon 6 tomato
  fleshy part: 9 sarcocarp
  goddess of: 6 Pomona
  gourd family: 4 pepo
  horseradish tree: ben
  husk: 5 lemma
  hybird: 7 tangelo
  imperfect: 6 nubbin
  juicy: 4 lime, pear, plum 5 grape, lemon,
    peach 6 orange 7 apricot 9 pineapple 10
    grapefruit
  layer: 7 epicarp
  lime & lemon: 6 citron
  many-seeded: 11 pomegranate
  maple: 6 samara
  mild acid: 5 guava
  multiple: 4 cone
  of rose: 11 cynorrhodon
  of strawberry: 7 etaerio
  oily: 5 olive
  one-seeded: 5 akene 6 achene, samara 7
    achenis(pl.) 8 achenium
  palm tree: 4 date
  peach-like: 7 apricot 9 nectarine
  pear-shaped: fig 7 avocado
  plum-like: 4 sloe
  pome: 4 pear 5 apple 7 azarole
  preserving: 6 medlar
  pulp: pap
  pulpy: uva 4 pome 5 drupe, grape, berry
  red: 4 plum 5 apple 6 cherry 9 raspberry 10
    strawberry
  refuse: 4 marc
  rind: 7 epicarp
  rose-bush: hip
  science of: 8 pomology
  seed: pip, pit
  spore: 6 aecium
  stalk: 8 peduncle

stone: 4 paip, plum 5 drupe, peach, prune 6 cherry 7 apricot 9 nectarine

strawberry-family: 7 etaerio

tropical: fig 4 date 5 guava, gourd, mango 6 banana, papaya, pawpaw 9 sapodilla

vine: 5 grape

winged: 6 samara

withered: 6 nubbin

yellowish: 5 papaw 6 quince

fruit basket: 6 pottel, pottle

fruit bats: 8 pteropid 10 pteropidae

fruit dealer: 9 frontsman, fruiterer 11 greengrocer

fruit of Jove: 9 persimmon

fruit of paradise: 6 pomelo 10 grapefruit

fruit stone: pit 4 paip 6 pyrene 7 putamen

fruitful: fat 6 fecund 7 fertile 8 abundant, prolific 9 feracious, plenteous, plentiful, procreant 10 productive

fruitgrower: 8 fruitist 10 orchardist 11 pal-mologist 14 horticulturist

fruition: 8 pleasure 9 enjoyment 11 realiza-tion

fruitless: dry 4 geld, vain 5 addle, blank 6 barren 7 sterile, useless 8 abortive 10 prof-itless 11 ineffectual 12 unprofitable, un-successful

frump: vex 4 mock, snub, sulk 5 dowdy, flout 6 gossip 7 provoke 8 irritate

frush: din, rub 4 rush 5 break, carve, crush, onset 6 batter, debris, flabby, polish 7 brit-tle, scratch 9 fragments

frustrate: 4 balk, bilk, dash, foil, null, vain, void 5 baulk, blank, block, check, cross, crush, elude 6 baffle, blight, defeat, de-lude, outwit, scotch, thwart 7 deceive, nul-lify, prevent, useless 8 confound, infringe, nugatory 9 checkmate, discomfit 10 cir-cumvent, counteract, disappoint, discon-cert, neutralize 11 countermand, ineffec-tual 12 unprofitable

frustration: 4 foil 6 fiasco 12 discomfiture 15 disillusionment

fry: 4 sile 5 brook, roast, saute, young 9 off-spring

frying pan: 6 spider 7 griddle, skillet

fubsy: 5 fubby, plump, short 6 chubby, stuffy

fuddle: 5 booze, tiple 6 muddle 7 fluster

fuddled: fap, ree 5 bosky, tipsy 7 muddled

fudge: 4 fake 5 candy, foist, hunch 6 devise, humbug 8 contrive, nonsense 9 interlope, makeshift 10 substitute 11 counterfeit

fuel: gas, oil 4 coal, coke, peat, wood 5 argal, argol, argul, stoke 6 acetol, elding, firing, petrol 7 pabulum 8 charcoal, gasoline, ker-osene 9 petroleum 11 combustible

fuff: 4 puff 5 whiff 8 splutter

fuffy: 5 huffy, light, puffy

fugacious: 6 flying 8 fleeting, volatile 10 evanescent

fuggy: 6 smelly, stuffy

fugient: 7 fleeing 8 retiring

fugitive: 5 exile, fleme 6 emigré, exiled, outlaw 7 fleeing, refugee, roaming, run-away 8 banished, deserter, fleeting, runa-gate, unstable, vagabond, volatile 9 fuga-cious, strolling, transient, uncertain 10 ev-anescent

fugue: 4 fuga 9 ricercare

exponent: 4 Bach 6 Handel

Fukien river: Min

fulcrum: 4 bait, prop 5 thole 7 support

fulfill: 4 fill, full, meet 6 effect, finish, oc-cupy 7 achieve, execute, perform, satisfy 8 complete 9 implement 10 accomplish, ef-fectuate

fulfillment, fulfilment: 6 effect 9 execution 10 completion 11 performance, realization 14 accomplishment

fulgent: 6 bright 7 shining 8 dazzling 9 efful-gent

full: bad 4 good 5 ample, round, sated, solid, total 6 entire, fulfil, honest 7 baptize, copi-ous, destroy, diffuse, fulfill, fulsome, oro-tund, perform, plenary, replete, teeming, trample 8 adequate, bouffant, brimming, complete, resonant 9 bouffante, capacious, plentiful 10 consecrate, exhaustive 13 comprehensive

suffix: ose 5 itous, ulent

full-blooded: 6 florid 8 rubicund 12 thor-oughbred

full force: 5 brunt

full-grown: 6 mature 9 developed

full of: *cracks:* 6 rimose

glands: 7 adenose

hollows: 8 lacunose

minute openings: 6 porous

sand: 7 arenose

sap or juice: 7 succous 9 succulent

thorns: 6 briary

twists: 5 kinky 7 winding

wrinkles: 6 rugose

fuller: 7 creaser

fuller's grass: 8 soapwort

fullness, fulness: 5 fulth 6 plenty 7 satiety 8 pleonasm 9 abundance, amplitude, plumpness, repletion 10 fleshiness, perfec-tion 12 completeness

fully: 5 amply 6 wholly 7 clearly, largely, utterly 8 entirely, maturely 9 perfectly 10 abundantly, completely, distinctly 11 plenteously, plentifully

fulmar: 4 bird 5 nelly 7 malduck

fulminate: 7 explode, inveigh 8 detonate

fulsome: fat 4 foul, full 5 gross, plump, suave 6 coarse, wanton 7 copious, lustful, overfed 8 abundant, nauseous 9 offensive, overgrown, repulsive, satiating, sickening 10 disgusting, indelicate, nauseating

fumble: paw 4 boot 5 abase, error 6 bobble, bungle, faffle, haffle, huddle, mumble

fume: 4 foam, odor, rage, rant, reek 5 ewder, fumet, smoke, storm, vapor 6 exhale 7 flatter, fumette 8 fumigate, outburst 10 exhalation

fumid: 5 smoky 8 vaporous

fun: gag, gig 4 game, gell, hoax, jest, joke, play 5 mirth, sport 6 gaiety, gayety 9 amusement, horseplay, merriment 10 pleasantry

function: act, run, use 4 duty, role, work 5 doing 6 action, office 7 calling, operate, service 8 activity, ceremony, occasion 9 festivity, gathering, operating, operation 10 occupation, profession, providence 11 performance 13 entertainment

social: tea 4 ball 5 party 6 soiree 9 reception

trigonometrical: 4 sine 6 cosine, secant 7 tangent

fund: 4 fond, pool 5 basis, stock, store 6 bottom, ground, supply 7 deposit, reserve 10 foundation, groundwork 12 accumulation

fundamental: 5 basal, basic, vital 7 basilar, organic, primary, radical 8 original, rudiment 9 elemental, essential, important, principle 10 elementary

funds: 4 caja, cash 5 money 9 resources

funebre: sad 7 funeral 8 funereal

funeral: 6 burial, dismal, exequy 7 cortege, funebre 8 exequial, funereal 9 forthfare, obsequies 10 sepulchral

bell: 5 knell

oration: 5 eloge 6 eulogy 8 encomium 9 panegyric

pile: 4 pyre

song: 5 dirge, elegy, elogy, nenia 6 elegie 7 elogium, epicede 8 threnody 9 epicedium

structure: 10 catafalque

funereal: 5 feral 6 dismal, solemn 7 funebre, funeral 8 mournful 9 funebrial, funebrous 10 funebrious

funest: sad 4 dire 5 fatal 7 doleful

fungus: 4 bunt, cepe, mold, rust, smut 5 ergot, fungo, morel, moril, uredo, yeast 6 agaric, fungal, mildew, oidium, telium 7 agarics, amanita, blewits, fungoid, fungous, geaster, truffle 8 amanitin, mushroom, puffball 9 stinkhorn, toadstool 10 fungaceous

edible: 4 cepe 5 morel 7 truffle 8 mushroom

parasitic: 5 ergot

fungus-like: 6 agaric

funk: 4 kick, odor, rage 5 shirk, spark 6 coward, flinch, fright, recoil, shrink 8 frighten 9 cowardice, touchwood

funnel: 6 hopper

funny: odd 5 comic, droll, queer 7 comical, jocular, risible, strange 8 humorous 9 laughable, ludicrous

funnyman: wit 8 comedian

fur: 4 flix, pell, pelt 5 budge, stole 6 furrow, pelage

coat: 6 pelage

collection of: 5 pelts 6 peltry

kind of: fox 4 mink, paen, scut, seal, vair, woom 5 budge, civit, coney, fitch, lapin, otter, sable 6 ermine, galyac, galyak, marten, martin, moutin, nutria 7 calabar, caalaber, caracul, karakul, miniver, platina, sealine 8 karakule, ragondin 9 silver fox

piece: 5 stole

refuse: 4 kemp

fur-bearing animal: fox 4 mink, seal 5 genet, otter, sable 6 marten, martin

furbelow: 5 frill 6 ruffle 7 falbala, falbelo, flounce 8 trimming

furbish: fig, rub 4 fake, vamp 5 clean, scour 6 polish 7 burnish 8 renovate

Furies: 5 Dirae 7 Erinyes

individual: 6 Alecto, Erinys 7 Erinnys, Erinyes, Megaera 9 Tisiphone

furious: mad 5 angry, brain, irate, rabid 6 fierce, furied, insane, stormy 7 frantic, mankind, rushing, violent 8 frenzied, vehement, wrathful 9 impetuous, turbulent 10 boisterous, tumultuous, uproarious

furl: 4 fold, roll, wrap 5 frese 6 fardel, furdel, furdle

furlana: 5 dance, music

furlong: 5 stade 7 stadium 10 quarentene

furlough: 5 leave 6 permit 8 passport

furnace: 4 bosh, dome, kiln, oven 5 stove, tisar 6 calcar, cupola, heater 7 athanor, howells, rotator, smelter 8 bloomery, bruckner 9 scorifier 11 incinerator

part: 4 bosh, flue 5 grate

furner: 5 baker

furnish: arm 4 feed, give, lend 5 array, endow, equip, frame, indue 6 afford, graith, insure, render, supply 7 apparel, appoint, garnish, provide 8 minister, palisade 10 accomplish, administer

crew: man

with battlements: 9 crenelate

with meals: 5 board, cater

furnished: 5 boden, garni 8 equipped, provided, supplied 9 garnished

furnishing: 7 fitment 8 fixtures, muniment, ornament 9 adornment, apparatus, furniture 10 enrichment, habiliment

furniture: 6 graith, outfit 7 fitment, tallboy 8 equipage 9 equipment 10 decoration, encoignure, furnishing 13 embellishment *style:* 6 Empire 8 Colonial, Sheraton 11 Chippendale, Hepplewhite, Renaissance

furor: 4 fury, rage 5 craze, mania 6 frenzy 7 madness

furrow: fur, rut 4 grip, plow, rout 5 chase, drain, drill, field, rigol, score, stria 6 groove, sulcus, trench 7 channel, crumple, windrow, wrinkle

furrowed: 6 rivose 7 sulcate, porcate 8 porcated 10 corrugated

furry: 5 hairy

furse: 4 whin 5 gorse

further: aid, and, yet 4 abet, also, fore, help, more 5 again, front, serve 6 afford, beyond, former 7 advance, earlier, forward, promote, remoter 8 moreover 9 advantage 10 accelerate, additional

furtherance: 6 assist 8 facility, progress 9 promotion 10 assistance 11 advancement

furthermore: and 7 besides 8 moreover

furthersome: 4 rash 7 helpful 11 venturesome 12 advantageous

furtive: sly 6 secret, sneaky 7 hangdog 8 mystical, sneaking, stealthy 10 creepmouse 11 clandestine

fury: ire 4 rage 5 anger, breth, furor, rigor, vixen, wrath 6 beldam, choler, frenzy 7 beldame, madness, oestrus 8 delirium, violence 9 furiosity, vehemence 10 fierceness, turbulence 11 indignation

fuse: 4 flux, frit, melt, weld 5 blend, smelt, unite 6 anneal, mingle, solder 7 liquefy 8 dissolve 10 amalgamate 11 incorporate

fusee: 5 flare, torch 6 signal

fusion: 4 flux 6 fusure, merger 8 alliance, blending 9 coalition 11 coalescence

fuss: ado, row, tew, vex 4 busk, fike, rout, spat, stir, todo 5 bearm, touse, whaup, worry 6 bother, bustle, caddle, fantad, fantod, fettle, fidget, fissle, fistle, fizzle, fraise, fuffle, fustle, pother, potter, tumult 7 dispute, friggle, fussock, quarrel, sputter, trouble 8 business 9 confusion 10 disconcert

fussy: 6 bustle, fidfad, spruce 7 fidgety, finical 8 overnice 10 fastidious, meticulous 14 overparticular

fustanella: 8 petticoat

fustian: 4 rant 5 tumid 7 bombast, pompous 8 claptrap, inflated 9 bombastic, worthless

fustigate: 4 beat, whip 6 strike

futile: 4 idle, vain 6 otiose 7 useless 8 hopeless, trifling 9 frivolous, worthless 11 ineffectual

futility: 11 uselessness 13 frivolousness

future: 5 later 6 coming 9 hereafter

fuzz: nap 4 down, lint 5 fluff 8 puffball

fyke: net

fylfot: 5 cross 6 emblem 8 swastika

G

Gaal's father: 4 Ebed

gab: lie, yap 4 talk 5 boast, mouth, prate, scoff 6 gossip 7 chatter, deceive, prattle

Gabael's son: 5 Aduel

gabardine: 5 cloth 6 fabric

gabbard, gabbart: 4 scow 5 barge 6 vessel 7 lighter

gabble: rai(Sc.), yap 4 cank, chat, talk 6 babble, cackle, gossip, habble, jabber, yabble 7 chatter, clatter, twaddle

gabbro: 4 rock 6 norite

gabelle: tax 4 duty 6 excise, impost

gaberdine: 4 coat, gown 5 frock, smock 6 mantle 7 garment 8 pinafore

gabi: 4 taro

gabirit: 4 mold 5 gauge, model

gable: 4 wall 6 dormer, pinion

gablock: See **gavelock**

Gabriel's instrument: 4 horn 7 trumpet

gaby: 4 fool 5 dunce 9 simpleton

gad: bar, rod 4 band, goad, roam, rope, rove, whip 5 climb, ingot, prowl, spear, spike, staff, stick, stray 6 billet, chisel, ramble, switch, wander 7 traipse 9 gallivant

Gad: *chieftain:* Ahi

  descendant: Zia

  father: 5 Jacob

  mother: 6 Zilpah

  son: Eri 5 Ezbon

  tribe of: 6 Erites

gadfly: 4 pest 6 botfly 7 annoyer, oestrid, tabanid 8 busybody 9 breezefly

gadget: 4 tool 5 gibbe(Sc.) 6 device, doodad, jigger 9 doohickey 11 contrivance

Gadhelic: 4 Erse 6 Celtic, Gaelic

gadus: cod 4 fish

gadwall: 4 duck

gadzooks: 4 egad

Gaea: Ge 6 Tellus

  consort: 6 Uranus

  offspring: 5 Titan 6 Pontus, Titans, Uranus

  parent: 5 Chaos

Gaelic (see also **Irish**): 4 Erse 8 Highland

  clan: 4 Sept

  hero: 6 Ossian

  John: Ian

  land distribution: 7 rundale

  poem: 4 Duan

  spirit: 5 kelpy 6 kelpie 7 banshee

  warrior: 5 Dagda 6 Fenian

gaff: 4 hoax, hook, pick, spar, spur, talk 5 fraud, laugh, spear, trick 6 clamor, deceit, fleece, gamble, outcry 7 prating 8 raillery

gag: 4 gegg, hoax, joke 5 choke, heave, retch 6 muffle, muzzle 7 prevent, silence 8 obstruct, throttle 9 imposture 13 interpolation

gage (see also **gauge**): bet 4 pawn, risk 5 stake, wager 6 pledge 8 appraise, defiance, security 9 challenge

gain: buy, get, net, win 4 boot, earn, good, pelf, reap 5 clear, lucre, reach 6 attain, effect, income, obtain, profit, secure 7 achieve, acquire, advance, benefit, conquer, prevail, procure, realize 8 increase 9 accretion, advantage, increment 12 appreciation

  ill-gotten: 4 pelf 5 graft, lucre 6 payola 9 extortion

gainly: 7 shapely 8 becoming, gainsome, graceful, suitable

gainsay: 4 deny 6 forbid, impugn, oppose, refute, resist 7 dispute 10 contradict, controvert

Gainsborough painting: 7 Blue Boy

gair: 4 keen 5 eager, piece 6 greedy, stingy 8 covetous 12 parsimonious

gait: bat, run, way 4 lope, pace, rack, step, trip, trot, volt, walk 5 amble, strut, tread 6 allure, canter, gallop 7 journey, shamble 8 distance

gaiter: 4 boot, spat 6 gaskin, puttee 7 cutikin(Sc.), legging 8 bootikin, gamashes 11 galligaskin

gala: gay 4 fete 5 merry 6 festal, fiesta 8 festival

galago: 5 lemur 6 monkey

Galahad: *father:* 8 Lancelot

  mother: 6 Elaine

  quest: 5 grail

Galapagos Islands resident: 8 tortoise
Galatea: *lover:* 4 Acis
  suitor: 10 Polyphemus
galaxy: 6 nebula
gale: 4 blow, gust, wind 5 blast, storm 6
  breeze, easter 7 declaim, tempest 8 outburst 9 hurricane, windstorm 11 northeaster, northwester, southeaster, southwester
galea: 6 helmet
Galen: 9 physician
Galician river: San 4 Styr
galilee: 5 porch 7 portico
Galilee: *ruler:* 5 Herod
  town: 4 Cana, Nain 8 Nazareth, Tiberias 9
  Capernaum
Galileo's birthplace: 4 Pisa
galimatias: 6 jargon 8 nonsense 9 gibberish
galipot, gallipot: sap 5 rosin 6 barras
gall: vex 4 bile, fell, flaw, fret 5 annoy, chafe,
  cheek, spite 6 abrade, harass, injure, poison, rancor 7 blemish 8 acerbity, cecidium,
  irritate, temerity 9 excoriate, impudence
  10 bitterness, effrontery, exasperate
Gallagher's partner: 5 Shean
gallant: gay 4 beau, prow 5 blade, brave,
  bully, lover, noble, showy, swain 6 escort,
  heroic, polite, suitor 7 amatory, amorist,
  amorous, conduct, stately, younker 8 cavalier, cicisbeo(It.), galliard, handsome, polished, splendid 9 attentive, chamberere,
  chevalier, courteous 10 chivalrous, courageous 11 fashionable 12 high-spirited
gallantry: 7 bravery, courage 11 intrepidity
galled: mad, raw 4 sore 6 peeved 9 sensitive
galleon: 4 ship 6 carack, vessel 7 carrack
  cargo: oro 4 gold
gallery: 5 alure, boyau(F.), porch, salon 6
  arcade, dedans(F.), loggia, piazza 7 balcony, terrace, veranda 8 audience, brattice, cantoria, catacomb, corridor 9 promenade 10 ambulatory
galley: 4 aesc, tray 5 cuddy, foist 6 bireme,
  carvel, galiot, hearth 7 birling, birlinn,
  caravel, galliot, hexeris, kitchen, trireme,
  unireme 8 cookroom, crumster, galleass,
  hepteris, ramberge 9 caravelle 10 tria-
  conter 13 tesseraconter
gallfly: 11 hymenoptera(pl.) 12 hymenopteron
galliard: 5 hardy 6 lively 7 gallant, valiant
Gallic: 6 French
gallimaufry: 4 hash 6 jumble, medley, ragout 7 mixture 10 hodgepodge
gallinae: 6 grouse, quails 7 rasores, turkeys
  8 peafowls 9 curassows, pheasants
gallinule: hen 4 coot, fowl, rail
gallivant: gad 4 flit, roam 6 travel
galloon: 4 lace 8 trimming

gallop: run 4 gait, pelt 5 chase, speed 6 canter, career, course, hasten, pursue
galloping dominoes: 4 dice
gallows: 4 crap 5 bough 6 gibbet 7 potence
  pert. to: 10 patibulary
galluses: 10 suspenders
gally: 5 worry 7 terrify 8 frighten
galoot: 6 fellow, marine, person 7 soldier 9
  screwball
galore: 7 profuse 8 abundant 9 plentiful
galosh: 4 boot, clog, shoe 6 arctic, patten 8
  overshoe
galvanize: 4 coat 6 excite 7 startle 9 stimulate
Galway islands: 4 Aran
galyak: fur, yak 6 cattle, hybrid
gam: leg 5 mouth, tooth, visit
gamb, gambe: leg 5 shank
gambado: 4 boot 5 antic, caper 6 spring 7
  legging
gambit: 4 move 7 comment, opening 8 maneuver 9 launching
gamble: bet 4 dice, gaff, game, risk, spec 5
  stake, wager 6 chance, hazard, plunge 9
  speculate 11 uncertainty
gambler: 5 dicer, shill 6 carrow(Ir.), player
  7 playman, plunger, sharper 8 blackleg,
  gamester 10 speculator
  accomplice: 5 shill
gambling (see also **game:** *gambling*): *pert.
  to:* 8 aleatory
  place: 4 Reno 6 casino
  stake: pot 4 pool
gambol: hop 4 play 5 caper, frisk, prank 6
  cavort, frolic
game: fun, jeu(F.) 4 lame, lark, plan, play,
  prey 5 brave, dodge, prank, sport, trick 6
  course, frolic, gamble, gritty, plucky,
  quarry, racket, spunky 7 contest, foolery,
  pastime, project 8 enduring, resolute 9
  amusement, diversion 10 courageous
  ball: cat, tut 4 golf, polo, pool 5 fives, rugby
  6 hockey, pelota, soccer, squash, tennis,
  tipcat 7 cricket, croquet 8 baseball, football, handball 9 billiards
  board: 4 keno 5 bingo, chess, halma, lotto,
  salta 6 squail 7 pachisi 8 checkers, cribbage, parchesi, parchisi, scrabble 9 croki-
  nole, parcheesi 10 backgammon
  card: gin, hoc, loo, lus, nap, pam 4 bank,
  brag, faro, hock, jass, ruff, skat, slam,
  snap, solo, spin, vint 5 beast, chico, cinch,
  comet, crimp, decoy, gilet, gleek, monte,
  omber, ombre, pedro, pique, pitch, poker,
  rummy, stuss, trump, two-up, waist, whist
  6 basset, birkie, boston, bridge, commit,
  ecarte, flinch, hearts, loadum, masset, piquet, rounce, sledge, smudge 7 bezique, canasta, cassino, cayenne, Chicago, cooncan,
  hundred, oldmaid, primero, reversi, sev-

en-up **8** baccarat(F.), commerce, conquian, contract, cribbage, handicap, napoleon, patience, penneeck, tresillo, videruff **9** cinq-cents, grabouche, montebank, new market, solitaire, tredrille **10** heartsette **11** everlasting, speculation

carnival: **5** darts **6** hoopla

confidence: **5** bunco, bunko

court: **5** roque **6** pelota, squash, tennis **7** jai alai **8** handball **10** volleyball

dice: **4** ludo **5** craps **7** pachisi **8** dominoes, trey-trip

gambling: **4** beno, faro, keno, pico **5** beano, bingo, boule, craps, keeno, lotto, monte(Sp.), pique, pitch, poker, rondo, stuss **6** brelan(F.), fan-tan(Ch.), piquet, policy **7** baccara, barbudi, primero, rondeau(F.) **8** baccarat, crackloo, roulette **9** black-jack, crackaloo, ꞇ montebank, twenty-one, vingt-et-un(F.) **10** panguingui(Phil. Is.)

goal: run **4** home **5** first, score, spare, tally **6** basket, strike **9** touchdown

kind of: **4** mora(It.) **6** merels, morris, quoits **7** diabolo, loggats, loggets, marbles **9** philopena **10** jackstraws, spillikins

official: **5** judge, timer **6** umpire **7** referee, starter **8** linesman **10** timekeeper

outdoor: **4** polo **6** tennis **7** cricket, croquet **9** badminton

parlor: **4** dibs **5** jacks **7** matador **8** charades **13** tiddledywinks

pin: **7** bowling, kegling, tenpins **8** ninepins, skittles

racket: **5** bandy **6** squash, tennis **8** lacrosse **9** badminton

small: **4** bird, fowl

stewed in wine: **5** salmi **6** ragout

war: **10** kriegspiel

word: **6** crambo **7** anagram **8** acrostic, scrabble

gamekeeper: 8 warrener

gamester: 5 dicer **6** player **7** gambler, playman

gamete: 6 zygote **8** oosphere

gamin: tad **6** urchin **7** hoodlum

domain: **6** street

gaming cube: die

gammon: leg **4** bosh, dupe, foot, gull **5** bacon, cozen, feign, thigh **6** delude, humbug **7** beguile, deceive, mislead, pretend **10** backgammon

gammy: bad **4** lame, sore

gamp: 8 umbrella

gamut: 5 orbit, range, reach, scale **6** extent, series **7** compass

gamy: 5 spicy **7** lustful **8** spirited **10** malodorous **12** disreputable

ganch: 4 kill **6** impale **7** execute

gander: 5 goose **6** stroll, wander **9** simpleton

Gandhi: *name:* Bu; Aba, Abu **4** Abba, Abou, Bapu **7** Mahatma

publication: **7** Harijan

gandul: 6 loafer

ganef: 5 thief **6** rascal

gang: go; mob, set **4** band, crew, ging, pack, road, team, walk **5** group, horde, shift **6** clique, course, outfit, travel **7** company **9** pasturage **10** passageway **11** combination

member of: **4** b'hoy **5** rowdy, tough

Ganges River: *city:* **7** Benares

dolphin: **4** susu

goddess: **9** Gangadevi

vessel: **6** puteli **7** putelee

gangling: 5 lanky **7** awkward **9** spindling

ganglion: 5 tumor

gangplank: 4 brow **6** bridge **8** platform **9** gangboard

gangrene: rot **7** mortify **8** necrosis **9** sphacelus

gangster: 4 b'hoy, thug, whyo, yegg **5** rough, thief **6** bandit **7** mobster, ruffian **8** criminal, hireling

female companion: **4** moll

gangway: 7 couloir **8** corridor **10** passageway

gannet: 4 bird, fowl **5** goose, solan

family: **4** sula

ganoid fish: gar **6** bowfin **8** sturgeon

gaol: 4 brig, jail **6** prison

gaoler: 5 guard **6** warden

gap: col **4** flaw, pass, rent **5** break, breck, chasm, chawn, cleft, clove, meuse, notch, space **6** breach, hiatus, lacuna, ravine **7** fissure, lacunae(pl.), opening **8** aperture, interval, quebrada **10** interstice **12** interruption **13** discontinuity

gape: ope **4** cape, gasp, gaum, gaup, gawp, gaze, pant, rent, yaup, yawn, yawp **5** chawn, shout, stare **6** rictus, vacuum **7** dehisce **8** oscitate

gapeseed: 6 starer

gaping: 4 open **7** cracked, ringent

of plant capsule: **10** dehiscence

garage: 6 hangar, siding **8** building

garb (see also **dress**)**: 5** array, dress, habit, style **6** attire, bundle, clothe, custom, method **7** apparel, clothes, costume, fashion, raiment **8** carriage, clothing, vesiture, vestment **10** appearance, habiliment

kinds of: **4** toga **8** mourning **9** sackcloth

garbage: 5 offal, trash **6** bundle, faggot, refuse, scraps

garble: 4 bolt, cull, geld, sift, sort **5** alloy **6** jumble, mangle, refine, refuse, select **7** distort, pervert, rubbish **8** disguise, mutilate

garboil: 9 confusion **10** turbulence

garcon: boy, lad **6** waiter **8** bachelor

garden: 4 Eden, hall, park, yard 5 arbor, patch, tract 6 arbour 8 outfield 9 cultivate, enclosure 11 commonplace

implement: hoe 4 rake 5 mower 6 scythe, sickle, trowel, weeder

kind of: 4 herb 5 oasis, truck 6 cactus, flower, formal 7 kitchen 8 chinampa, kailyard(Sc.), kaleyard(Sc.) 9 botanical, terrarium, vegetable 10 zoological

protector: 7 Priapus

Garden City: 7 Chicago

garden plant: See **plant** *garden*

gardener: 9 topiarist 14 horticulturist

garfish: 8 hornbeak, hornfish

Gargantua'a son: 10 Pantagruel

gargantuan: 4 huge, vast 5 giant 7 titanic 8 enormous, gigantic 9 monstrous

gargle: 9 mouthwash 11 collutorium

garish: 4 loud 5 cheap, gaudy, showy 6 bright, tawdry 8 dazzling 9 offensive

garland: bay, lei 4 band 5 crown, glory 6 anadem, corona, crants, diadem, laurel, rosary, wreath 7 chaplet, coronal, festoon 9 anthology

garlic: 4 moly, ramp 5 chive, clove 6 ramson

garment (see also **undergarment**)**:** 4 brat, cape, coat, gear, gown, jupe, rail, robe, sari, vest 5 cloak, dress, habit 6 attire, kimono 7 apparel, leotard, raiment 8 vestment 10 investment

ancient: 4 toga 5 palla, stola 6 chiton 7 chlamys 8 himation

ecclesiastical: see **vestment**

infant's: 6 woolly 7 bunting

Malay: 6 cabaya, kabaya, sarong

medieval: 5 simar 6 kirtle, rochet, tabard 8 chausses

men's: cap, hat, tie 4 belt, coat 5 pants, shirt, short, socks 6 jacket, slacks 7 drawers 8 trousers 10 suspenders 11 windbreaker

mourning: 5 weeds

outer: 4 coat, wrap 5 cloak, dress, pants, parka, shawl, skirt, stole 6 jacket, slacks 7 sweater 9 coverslut, polonaise

protective: 4 brat 5 apron, armor, chaps, smock 7 cuculla 8 overalls, pinafore 9 coveralls, gaberdine

rain: 6 poncho 7 oilskin, slicker

sleeveless: aba 4 cape, vest 6 mantle 7 sweater 8 slip-over

upper: 4 coat, vest 5 jupon, shirt, tunic, waist 6 blouse, jersey, peplos, peplus 7 sweater 8 guernsey, slip-over

garn: 4 yarn 7 worsted 11 exclamation

garner: 4 reap 5 store 6 gather 7 collect, granary 10 accumulate

garnet: 5 jewel, stone 7 garnate 8 essonite

black: 8 melanite

deep-red: 9 almandine, almandite

green: 7 olivine

garnish: 4 trim 5 adorn, dress, equip 7 furnish 8 decorate, meringue, ornament 9 embellish

garret: 4 head 5 attic, solar, soler 6 gallet, soller, turret 7 mansard 8 cockloft 10 watchtower

garrot: 4 duck, fowl 9 goldeneye

garrote, garrotte: 4 kill 7 execute 8 strangle, throttle

garrulous: 5 talky, wordy 7 diffuse, voluble 8 fanfaron 9 talkative 10 long-winded, loquacious

garter: 4 garten 7 elastic 9 supporter

garth: dam 4 hoop, yard 5 close, girth 9 enclosure

garvey: 4 boat, scow

gas: 4 fuel, fume, reek, talk 5 radon, vapor 6 gossip, petrol 7 bombast 8 hydrogen 10 anesthetic, asphyxiate, illuminant

air: 4 neon 5 argon, ozone, xenon 6 oxygen 7 ammonia, krypton, sulfate 8 nitrogen

balloon: 6 helium

blue: 5 ozone

charcoal: 5 oxane

charge with: 6 aerate

colorless: 5 keten, ozone 6 arsine, ethane 7 ammonia

comb. form: aer 4 aero

inert: 5 argon, xenon 6 helium 8 nitrogen

inflammable: 6 butane, ethane 7 methane

marsh: 7 methane

mustard: 7 yperite

nitrogen and carbon: 8 cyanogen

oxygen: 5 ozone

poisonous: 6 arsine 7 mustard, stibine

gasbag: 7 balloon

gascon: 7 boaster 8 braggart 10 swaggering 12 swashbuckler

gasconade: 4 brag, crow 5 boast, vaunt 7 bluster, bravado 8 boasting

gaseous: 4 thin 5 fluid, light 7 tenuous 8 aeriform, gasiform, volatile 13 unsubstantial

gash: cut 4 bite, chop, slit, talk, trim, wise 5 sharp, slash, witty 6 babble, gossip, tattle 7 knowing 8 incision 9 talkative 11 well-dressed

gasket: 4 lute, ring, seal

gasoline: gas 6 petrol

gasp: 4 gape, pant 5 croak, fetch

gassy: 5 windy 8 inflated 9 flatulent

gast: 5 alarm, scare 8 frighten

gasthaus: inn 6 tavern

gastronome: 7 epicure 11 connoisseur

gastropod: 4 slug 5 harpa, oliva, snail 6 nerita, nerite, volute 7 mollusk 8 pteropod

ear-shaped: 7 abalone

marine: 5 cowry, murex 6 cowrie, limpet, tethys 7 aplysia

gat: gun 7 channel, passage 8 revolver

gata: 5 shark

gate: bar, dar, way 4 door, exit, hole, pass 5 hatch, valve 6 defile, escape, method, portal, wicket, zaguan 7 barrier, opening, postern 8 entrance 9 threshold, turnstile
flood: 6 sluice

gate money: fee 5 price 9 admission

Gates of Hercules: 9 Gibraltar

gatehouse: bar 5 lodge

gatekeeper: 6 porter, warden 8 guardian, watchman

gatepost: 4 durn

gateway: dar 5 pylon, toran, torii(Jap.) 6 portal, torana 8 entrance

gather: 4 bale, brew, cull, furl, herd, mass, meet, pick, rake, reap 5 amass, bunch, flock, glean, group, infer, pleat, pluck, raise, shirr 6 bundle, deduce, derive, garner, muster, scrape, summon 7 collect, compile, convene, convoke, harvest, recruit 8 assemble, colonize, compress, conclude, contract, increase 10 accumulate, congregate 11 agglomerate, concentrate 12 conglomerate

gatherer: 5 miser 7 gleaner 9 collector

gathering: bee, tea 4 bevy, fest, stag 5 crowd, party, troop 6 galaxy, plisse, shivoo, smoker 7 abscess, company, meeting, mooting 8 assembly, function, swelling 9 concourse 10 assemblage, collection, congestion, convention 11 contraction 12 accumulation, congregation

gauche: 4 skew 5 gawky 6 clumsy 7 awkward, twisted 8 tactless 10 left-handed

gaucho: 6 cowboy 8 herdsman
knife: 4 bolo
lariat: 5 bolas
weapon: 7 machete

gaud: 4 joke 5 adorn, fraud, paint, sport, trick 6 bauble, finery, flashy, gewgaw 7 trinket 8 artifice, ornament

gaudy: gay 4 loud 5 cheap, feast, showy 6 festal, flashy, flimsy, garish, tawdry, tinsel, tricky 7 brankie(Sc.), flaring, glaring, trinket 8 festival 9 brummagem, deceitful, flaunting, luxurious 11 pretentious 12 meretricious, ostentatious 13 entertainment

gaufre: 5 wafer 6 waffle

gauge, gage: 4 carp 5 judge 6 former 7 measure, scantle 8 estimate, udometer 9 indicator, manometer, manoscope 10 anemometer

Gaul: 6 France, Gallia(L.)
chariot: 5 esses 6 esseda, essede
city: 6 Alesia

god of thunder and rain: 7 Taranis
god of vegetation: 4 Esus
magistrate: 9 vergobret
people: 4 Remi
priest: 5 druid
river goddess: 8 Belisama
seer: 5 vates

gaulding: 4 bird 5 egret, heron

gaum: paw 4 daub, gape, heed, hold, mess 5 smear, stuff 8 perceive 9 attention 10 perception 13 understanding

gaunt: 4 bony, grim, lank, lean, slim, thin 5 spare 6 barren, hollow, meager, meagre 7 haggard, slender 8 desolate, rawboned 9 emaciated 10 attenuated, cadaverous, forbidding

gauntlet: 4 test 5 glove 6 ordeal

gauster: 4 brag 5 bully 6 gossip 7 bluster, swagger

Gautama: 6 Buddha 10 Siddhartha
wife: 6 Ahalya

gauze: 4 film, leno 5 crape, crepe, lisse 6 fabric, tissue 7 bandage

gavel: 4 mace, maul, rent 5 usury 6 hammer, mallet

gavelock: 4 gaff 5 lever, spear 7 crowbar, javelin

gavial: 9 crocodile

gaw: god 4 gape 5 drain 6 trench

Gawain: *brother:* 7 Gaheris
father: Lot
son: 5 Lovel 8 Florence, Gyngalyn

gawk: 4 gowk, left, lout 5 stare 6 gawney, lubber 7 bumpkin, rammack 9 simpleton 10 left-handed

gawky: 6 clumsy, gauche 7 awkward, foolish 8 clownish

gawn: tub 4 pail

gawney: 4 gawk 9 simpleton

gawp, gaup: 4 gape 5 stare 7 swallow 9 simpleton

gay: 4 airy, boon, daft, glad, gleg 5 bawdy, bonny, brisk, happy, jolly, loose, merry, riant, showy 6 blithe, bonnie, bright, flashy, frisky, garish, jocund, jovial, joyful, lively, wanton 7 festive, gleeful, jocular 8 cavalier, cheerful, colorful, mirthful, sportive 9 brillante, brilliant, convivial, sprightly, vivacious 10 frolicsome, licentious 12 lighthearted

gazabo: guy 6 fellow, person

gaze: eye, pry 4 gape, gouk, gowk, leer, look, moon, ogle, peer, pore, scan, toot 5 glare, gloat, sight, stare 6 behold, glower, regard

gazebo: 8 pavilion 11 summerhouse

gazelle: ahu, goa 4 admi, cora, dama, kudu, mohr, oryx 5 ariel, mhorr 7 buffalo, chikara, corinne 8 antelope 9 springbok

gazelle hound: 6 saluki

gazette: 7 courant, journal 9 newspaper
gazetteer: 5 atlas 6 writer 10 dictionary
Ge: See Gaea
geal: ice 5 jelly 7 congeal
gean: 6 cherry
gear: cam, cog, rig 4 food, tack 5 dress, equip, goods, stuff, tools 6 affair, aludel, doings, graith, liquor, matter, pinion, tackle, things, wealth 7 apparel, concern, harness, rigging, rubbish, trapeze 8 business, clothing, cogwheel, garments, material, ornament, property 9 equipment, mechanism, trappings, vestments 10 appliances, belongings, implements 12 appurtenance 13 accoutrements
geason: 4 rare 5 scant 6 scarce 12 unproductive
geaster: 9 earthstar
Geb: *daughter:* 4 Isis 8 Nephthys
father: Shu
son: Set 6 Osiris
wife: Nut
gecko: 6 lizard 7 tarente
gel: set 6 harden 7 congeal, thicken 8 solidify 9 coagulate
gelatin, gelatine: 6 collin 7 sericin 8 agar-agar
geld: dry 4 spay 5 alter, prune 6 barren, garble 8 castrate, mutilate 9 expurgate, fruitless 10 emasculate
gelid: icy 4 cold, iced 6 frozen
gell: fun 5 spree 6 frolic 8 carousal
gelt: 4 gold 5 money
gem: bud 4 keas, naif, onyx, opal, ruby, sard 5 agate, beryl, cameo, jewel, paste, pearl, stone, topaz 6 amulet, bedeck, garnet, muffin, scarab, spinel 7 diamond, emerald, paragon 8 intaglio, sapphire, tigereye 9 carnelian, germinate 10 aquamarine 11 masterpiece
blue: 8 sapphire 9 turquoise 10 aquamarine
face: 5 facet
green: 7 emerald, peridot 10 chrysolite
imperfect: 5 loupe
iridescent: 4 opal 5 pearl 7 cat's-eye 8 tigereye 9 moonstone
measure of weight: 5 carat
of fidelity: 5 topaz
of immortality: 7 emerald
of law: 4 ruby
of love: 8 amethyst
of peace: 7 diamond
of purity: 5 pearl
of truth: 8 sapphire
paste: 6 strass
purple: 8 amethyst
rectangular: 6 baguet 8 baguette
red: 4 ruby, sard 5 avena 6 garnet, pyrope 9 carnelian

relief-carved: 5 cameo
setting for: 4 ouch, pave 6 chaton
support: 7 setting
surface: 5 bezel, bezil, facet
Gem State: 5 Idaho
gemel: 4 twin 5 pairs, twins 6 hinged, paired 7 coupled, doubled
geminate: 6 binate, double 7 coupled
Gemini: 5 twins 6 Castor, Pollux
gemmule: bud 5 ovule
gemot, gemotte: 5 court 7 meeting 8 assembly
gemsbok: 4 oryx 8 antelope
gemutlich: 4 cozy 6 genial, kindly 8 cheerful 9 agreeable 11 comfortable, good-natured
gendarme: 7 soldier 9 policeman 10 cavalryman
gender: sex 4 kind, male, sort 5 class, genus 6 female, neuter 8 copulate, engender, generate
gene: 6 factor 10 determiner, uneasiness 13 embarrassment
genealogy: 4 tree 7 account, history, lineage, progeny 8 pedigree 9 offspring 10 generation
general: 5 broad, gross 6 common, leader 7 average, officer 8 catholic 9 commander, customary, prevalent, universal 10 prevailing, widespread
Civil War: Lee 5 Grant, Meade 7 Sherman
generalize: 5 widen 6 extend, spread 7 broaden
generate: 4 make 5 beget, breed, steam 6 create, gender 7 develop, produce 8 develope, engender 9 originate, procreate, propagate
generation: age, era 4 kind, race 5 breed, stock 6 family 7 descent, progeny 8 geniture 9 genealogy, offspring, posterity 11 abiogenesis, descendants, procreation
spontaneous: 11 abiogenesis
generative: 8 prolific 10 productive
generic: 12 encompassing 13 comprehensive
generosity: 7 largess 8 largesse
generous: big 4 free, good, kind, rich 5 ample, frank, noble 6 honest 7 fertile, liberal 8 abundant, gracious, handsome, highborn, spirited 9 bountiful, excellent, honorable, plenteous, unselfish, unstinted 10 benevolent, charitable, courageous, munificent, openhanded 11 magnanimous, stimulating, warmhearted
genesis: 5 birth 6 origin 9 beginning 11 origination
genet: 5 berbe, horse
genial: 4 bein, bien, warm 5 douce 6 benign, forthy, inborn, jovial, kindly, native 7

cordial, festive 8 cheerful, friendly, pleasant 9 benignant, expansive, gemutlich 10 enlivening, generative

genie: See **jinni**

genitor: 6 parent 7 creator 10 procreator

geniture: 5 birth 8 nativity 9 offspring 10 generation

genius: 5 genio 6 talent, wizard 8 aptitude 9 intellect 10 brilliance

Genoa: *coin:* 4 jane 8 genovino
   family: 5 Doria
   magistrate: 4 doge

genos: 4 clan, gens 6 family

genouillere: 7 kneelet 9 kneepiece

genre: 4 kind, sort, type 5 class, style 7 species 8 category 11 description 14 classification

gens: 4 clan 5 nomen 6 people

gent: 4 fine 5 noble 6 pretty 7 elegant 8 graceful

genteel: 4 nice 6 polite 7 stylish 8 graceful, lady-like, well-bred 11 fashionable

gentian: 6 flower 7 felwort 9 baldmoney

Gentile: 7 heathen 9 Christian

gentility: 8 breeding 10 refinement

gentle: moy 4 calm, deft, dewy, easy, fair, kind, meek, mild, soft, tame 5 bland, light, milky, quiet, sweet, tamed 6 benign, docile, facile, placid, polite, tender 7 amabile, bonaire, clement, gradual, lenient 8 amenable, dovelike, lenitive, maidenly, mansuete, moderate, peaceful, soothing, tranquil, well-born 9 courteous, excellent, honorable, tractable 10 chivalrous 11 considerate 12 compassionate
   in music: 7 amabile

gentlemen: don, rye, sir 5 sahib, senor 6 bayard, mister 7 younker 8 cavalier 9 caballero

Gentlemen Prefer Blondes author: 4 Loos

gentlewoman: 4 lady

gentry: 4 rank 5 birth 6 people 8 gentrice 9 condition 10 gentlefolk

genty: 5 noble 7 genteel 8 graceful 9 courteous

genu: 4 bend 7 flexure

genuflect: 5 kneel

genuine: 4 leal, pure, real, true, vrai(F.) 5 frank, plain, pucka, pukka 6 actual, dinkum, honest 7 germane, gradely, sincere 8 bonafide 9 authentic, heartfelt, intrinsic, simon-pure, true-penny, unalloyed, unfeigned, veridical, veritable 10 legitimate 13 unadulterated 15 unsophisticated

genus: 4 kind, sort 5 class, order 6 gender 8 category 14 classification
   pert. to: 7 generic

geode: 5 druse 6 nodule

geology: 12 earth science

age: 7 Permian 8 Cambrian, cenezoic, Devonian, Jurassic, mesozoic, Silurian, Triassic 9 paleozoic 10 Cretaceous, cryptozoic, Ordovician 13 Mississippian, Pennsylvanian
division: age, era 4 lias, lyas 5 epoch, trias
period: 6 eocene 7 miocene 8 pliocene, tertiary 9 oligocene 10 quaternary 11 pleistocene
remains: 7 fossils
science: 12 paleontology 13 palaeontology

geometry: *angle:* 9 incidence
curve: 6 spiral 7 ellipse, evolute 8 parabola, sinusoid
father: 6 Euclid
figure: 4 cone, lune 5 prism, rhomb 6 circle, gnomon, oblong 7 ellipse, rhombus 8 triangle
proposition: 7 theorem
ratio: pi
solid: 4 cube 5 prism 7 pyramid
surface: 5 nappe, torus

geoponic: 5 rural 11 agriculture 12 agricultural

Georgia (Caucasus): *city:* 6 Iberia, Kutais, Tiflis
island: 7 Sapelo
people: 4 Svan 5 Svane
queen: 6 Tamara 7 Thamara

Georgia (U.S.): *city:* 5 Macon 6 Dalton 7 Atlanta, Cordele
college: 5 Emory
county: Lee 4 Bibb, Clay, Cobb, Cook, Dade, Hall, Hart, Long, Pike, Polk, Tift, Ware 5 Bacon, Burke, Butts, Crisp, Early, Rabun, Troup

Geraint's wife: 4 Enid

germ: bud, bug 4 seed 5 spore, virus 6 embryo, germen, sprout 7 germule, microbe 8 rudiment 9 bacteriam, beginning 13 microorganism

germ cell: egg 4 ovum

German: 4 Goth 5 Boche, Saxon 6 Teuton

German measles: 7 rubello

germane: 4 akin, true 6 allied 7 genuine, related 8 relevant 9 pertinent 11 appropriate

Germany: *ancient:* 6 Almain 7 Almaine
ancient tribesman: 4 Jute 6 Teuton 9 Ostrogoth
angry: 4 bose
animal: 4 tier
article: das, der, des, die
artist: 5 Durer
association: 6 verein 12 gesellschaft
bacteriologist: 4 Koch
beautiful: 5 schon
blue: 4 blau
bread: 4 brot

bright: 4 hell
but: 4 aber
cake: 5 torte 9 lebkuchen 11 pfeffernuss
canal: 4 Kiel
capital: 6 Berlin
castle: 7 schloss
cheese: 4 kase
chicken: 4 huhn
child: 4 kind
Christmas: 11 Weihnachten
city: Aue, Ede, Ems, Ulm 4 Bonn, Gera,
Jena, Kiel, Koln, Linz, Oder 5 Emden, Essen, Furth, Gotha, Hagen, Halle, Herne,
Mainz, Pirna, Trier 6 Aachen, Altona,
Barmen, Berlin, Bochum, Bremen, Cassel,
Dessau, Erfurt, Kassel, Linden, Lubeck,
Munich, Plauen 7 Breslau, Cologne, Cre-
feld, Dresden, Gorlitz, Hamburg, Hanover, Harburg, Krefeld, Leipzig, Mayence,
Munchen, Munster, Potsdam, Rostock,
Spandau, Stettin, Zwickau 8 Augsburg,
Chemnitz, Dortmund, Duisburg, Frei-
burg, Liegnitz, Nurnberg, Steglitz, Wur-
selen, Wurzburg 9 Bielefeld, Brunswick,
Darmstadt, Elberfeld, Flensburg, Karls-
ruhe, Magdeburg, Nuremberg, Offenbach,
Osnabruck, Pforzheim, Remscheid, Stuttgart, Wiesbaden 10 Braunsberg, Dusseldorf, Heidelberg, Konigsberg, Oberhau-
sen, Schoneberg, Tuttlingen 11 Lichten-
berg, Saarbrucken 12 Ludwigshafen 13
Gelsenkirchen 14 Charlottenburg, Mann-
heim-on-Ruhr 15 Frankfort-on-Main,
Frankfort-on-Oder
clever: 4 klug
clock: uhr
coal region: 4 Ruhr, Saar 5 Sarre
code: 5 Salic
coin: 4 mark 6 kronen, thaler 7 pfennig 8
groschen
cold: 4 kalt
day: tag
dead: tot
dear: 4 lieb
deep: 4 tief
dog: 4 hund
door: tur
early: 4 fruh
earth: 4 erde
evening: 5 abend
eye: 4 auge
field: 4 feld
forest: 4 wald
forest-keeper: 9 waldgrave
gnome: 6 kobold
good: gut
hair: 4 haar
hall: 4 aula, saal 5 diele
happy: 4 froh

head: 4 kopf
heart: 4 herz
highway: 8 autobahn
home: 4 heim
industrial area: 4 Ruhr
iron region: 4 Saar 5 Sarre
knight: 6 ritter
lake: 9 Constance
lancer: 4 ulan
language: 7 Deutsch
leaf: 5 blatt
letter: 5 brief
measure: aam, imi 4 last, sack, stab 5 carat,
eimer, kanne, kette, maass 6 strich 7
klafter 8 scheffel, schoppen, stubchen 9
masskanne
mister: 4 herr
moon: 4 mond
mountain: 4 Alps, Berg, Harz
never: nie
nine: 4 neun
no: 4 nein
nobleman: 4 graf 5 adlig 6 junker, ritter 7
younker
overture: 8 vorspiel
parliament: 9 Bundestag, Reichstag
philosopher: 4 Kant 5 Hegel
port: 5 Emden 6 Bremen 7 Hamburg,
Stettin
resort: 4 Ems 5 Baden
river: Ems, Inn, Ulm 4 Alle, Eder, Eger,
Elbe, Eser, Isar, Main, Oder, Ruhr, Saar 5
Aller, Hunte, Rhine, Saale, Spree, Werra,
Weser 9 Constance
school: 10 realschule, volkschule 14 ober-
realschule
shoe: 5 schuh
singing festival: 10 sangerfest 11 saenger-
fest
society: 4 bund 6 verein 10 turnverein 12
gesellschaft
son: 4 sohn
song: 4 lied
spa: see *resort* above
star: 5 stern
stone: 5 stein
teacher: 6 docent, dozent
tooth: 4 zahn
tower: 4 turm
two: 4 zwei
village: 4 dorf
vowel change: 6 umlaut
weight: lot
white: 5 weiss
wine: 4 hock, wein 5 Rhine 7 Moselle
woman: 4 frau, frow 8 fraulein
world: 4 welt
year: 4 jahr
young: 4 jung

germicide: 5 iodin **6** iodine **10** antiseptic **11** bactericide **12** disinfectant

germinate: bud, gem **5** geget, sprit **6** braird, evolve, sprout **7** develop **10** effloresce

geryon 7 monster

gesso: 5 paste **7** plaster

gest, geste: 4 deed, feat, jest, tale **5** route, stage **7** bearing, company, conduct, gesture, lampoon, romance **9** adventure **10** deportment

gestation: 7 bearing **8** breeding, carrying **9** pregnancy

gesticulate: 4 bend **6** motion **7** gesture

gesture: act, fig, nod **4** beck, bere, gest **5** geste, sneer **6** behave, motion, salute **7** posture **8** carriage **11** gesticulate **13** gesticulation

get: pen, win **4** earn, find, gain, take, trap **5** annoy, beget, catch, fetch, learn, reach, seize **6** appear, attain, baffle, become, corner, derive, induce, obtain, puzzle, secure, suffer **7** achieve, acquire, capture, conquer, possess, prepare, procure, realize, receive, recover **8** contract, irritate, overcome, persuade, retrieve, vanquish **9** ascertain, determine **10** comprehend, conciliate, understand

get along: 4 fare **5** hurry **7** advance, prosper, succeed **8** progress

get away: lam **4** flee, scat, shoo **6** escape

get back: 6 redeem **7** recover

get on: 4 fare **5** board **6** embark

get out: 5 scram **6** elicit, escape, reveal **8** evacuate

get-together: bee **4** stag **6** social **7** meeting

get up: 5 arise, array, dress, style **6** invent **7** arrange, costume, prepare **9** construct

get well: 4 heal **10** recuperate

getaway: lam **4** scat **5** elope, leave, start **6** depart, escape

gewgaw: toy **4** gaud **6** bauble, fangle, fegary, trifle **7** trinket **8** gimcrack **10** knickknack

gey: 4 very **5** quite **6** pretty, rather **9** tolerable **12** considerable

ghastful, gastful: 6 afraid **7** alarmed, ghostly **8** dreadful **9** frightful **10** frightened

ghastly: wan **4** grim, pale **5** ghast, lurid **6** dismal, gashly, gousty, grisly, pallid **7** charnel, deathly, fearful, gashful, goustie, hideous, macaber, macabre **8** dreadful, grewsome, gruesome, horrible, shocking, terrible **9** deathlike, frightful, horrified, terrified **10** cadaverous

ghat: 4 pass **5** range **7** landing **8** mountain

gherkin: 6 pickle **8** cucumber

ghost: hag **4** bhut, hant **5** bugan, duppy, shade, spook, umbra **6** daemon, spirit, sprite **7** eidolon, haunter, lemures(pl.), phantom, specter, spectre **8** guytrash, phantasm, revenant **10** apparition, glimmering **11** poltergeist

ghostly: 4 eery **5** eerie, scary, weird **6** spooky **7** gastful **8** ghastful, spectral **9** spiritual

ghoul: 4 ogre **5** fiend **7** vampire

ghoulish: 4 eery **5** eerie

giant: 4 Bara, eten, huge, ogre, rahu, Ymir **5** Argus, Cacus, jumbo, titan, troll **6** afreet, nozzle, ogress **7** Antaeus, Cyclops, monster, warlock **8** behemoth, Bellerus, colossus **9** monstrous **10** gargantuan, prodigious, tremendous

gibber: 5 stone **6** pebble **7** boulder, chatter

gibberish: 6 jabber, jargon **9** rigmarole **10** galimatias

gibbet: 4 stob, tree **6** cudgel **7** gallows, potence

gibbon: ape, lar **6** monkey, wou-wou **7** hoolock, siamang **10** anthropoid

gibbous: 6 convex, humped **7** hunched, rounded **11** hunchbacked, protuberant

gibe, jibe: 4 gird, jape, jeer, mock, quib, quip, twit **5** agree, fleer, fling, flirt, flout, gleek, scoff, sneer, taunt **6** deride, heckle **7** prepare, sarcasm **8** ridicule

giddy: 4 daff, daft **5** dizzy **6** fickle, giglot, volage **7** carried, flighty, glaiket, glaikit **8** halucket, heedless **9** frivolous, hellicate **11** hairbrained **13** featherheaded

gift: sop **4** bent, boon, dash, dole **5** bonus, bribe, dower, dowry, favor, grant, knack, pilon, power, token **6** bounty, donary, gersum, hansel, legacy, talent **7** aptness, benefit, faculty, handsel, largess, present, subsidy **8** aptitude, bestowal, blessing, donation, gratuity, largesse, offering, pittance, potlatch **9** endowment, gratitude, lagniappe, readiness **10** compliment **11** benefaction, beneficence, serendipity **12** contribution

gifted: 8 talented **9** ingenious

gig: fun, top **4** boat, fool, goad, joke, spur, whim **5** rouse, spear, sport **6** kibble **7** provoke **8** carriage, hilarity

gigantic: big **4** huge, vast **5** giant, large **7** immense, mammoth, titanic **8** colossal, enormous **9** cyclopean, gigantean, monstrous **10** gargantuan, prodigious

giggle: 5 tehee **6** teehee, titter **7** snicker, snigger

gila: 5 trout **6** lizard **10** woodpecker

Gilbert island: 5 Makin **6** Tarawa

gild: 4 adorn, tinge **7** overlay **8** brighten, inaurate **9** embellish

Gilda's father: 9 Rigoletto

gilded: 5 aural **6** aurate **7** aureate **8** inaurate **11** embellished

gilet: 4 vest 6 bodice 9 waistcoat

gill, ghyl: ivy 4 cove, girl, lass 5 brook 6 collar, ravine, stream, tipple, valley, wattle 10 sweetheart

four: 4 pint

gilt: hog, sow 4 gold 5 money 6 gilded, golden

gimcrack: fop, toy 6 bauble, flimsy, gewgaw, trifle 7 trinket, trivial 8 ornament, trumpery 9 frivolous 10 knickknack 13 unsubstantial

gimmer: ewe 5 clasp, hinge

gimp: jag, vim 4 trim 5 notch, orris 6 indent, spirit 7 cripple 8 trimming

gin: net 4 crab, grin, rack, sloe, trap 5 snare, trick 6 device, diddle, liquor, scheme 7 springe 8 artifice, beverage, schnapps 10 intoxicant 11 contrivance

ging: 4 crew, gang 5 troop 7 company, retinue

ginger: pep, vim 5 spice, vigor 6 mettle, revive, spirit 8 piquancy, spirited

genus: 8 zingiber

wild: 6 asarum

ginger cookie: 4 snap

ginger root: 4 race

gingerbread: 4 cake 5 money 6 wealth 8 trimming 13 pfefferkuchen(Ger.)

gingerbread tree: 4 doom

gingerly: 6 warily 7 charily 8 daintily 9 carefully, elegantly, finically, guardedly, mincingly 10 cautiously 12 fastidiously

gingham: 8 chambray

ginseng: 4 herb 5 panax 6 aralia

gipsy: See **gypsy**

giraffe: 5 piano 6 animal, spinet 10 camelopard

girasol, girasole: 4 opal 5 thorn 9 artichoke

gird: 4 belt, bind, gibe, girt, hasp, hoop, jerk, mock, yerk 5 brace, equip, scoff, sneer 6 clothe, fasten, girdle, secure 7 besiege, enclose, prepare, provide 8 engirdle, surround 9 encompass

girder: 4 beam 6 binder

girdle: obi 4 band, bark, belt, bind, cest, gird, ring, sash, zona, zone 5 girth, sarpe 6 bodice, cestus, circle, circum, corset, moocha, zonule 7 baldric, balteus, environ, equator, griddle 8 batheus, cincture, cingulum, encircle

girl: gal, sis 4 bint, chit, coed, gill, jill, lass, maid, minx 5 child, fille, filly, gilpy, quean, skirt, sylph, wench 6 amoret, calico, damsel, female, hoyden, kimmer, tomboy 7 camilla, colleen, flapper, ingenue 9 backfisch, debutante 10 jeune fille, sweetheart 11 maidservant

name: see **name** *female*

girlish: 5 sissy 7 artless 8 immature

girt: 4 gird 6 belted, fasten 7 besiege 8 prepared 9 encircled 13 circumference

girth: 4 band, belt, gird, hoop 5 cinch, cinct, garth, strap, width 6 girdle 7 girding, measure 8 cincture, encircle 13 circumference

gist: 4 core, crux, pith 5 heart, point 7 essence 10 foundation

gitano, gitana: 5 gipsy, gypsy

give: gie(Sc.) 4 cede, dole, emit, hand, mete 5 apply, endow, grant, serve, yield 6 accord, afford, bestow, commit, confer, denote, devote, donate, impart, render, supply 7 consign, dispose, furnish, intrust, present, proffer, propose 8 bequeath 9 surrender, vouchsafe 10 administer, contribute, deliquesce

give a hand: aid 4 abet, help

give away: 5 grant, yield 6 bestow, betray 7 present, succumb 8 disclose, telltale 9 sacrifice

give back: 4 echo 6 recede, remise, retire, return 7 replace, restore, retreat

give forth: 4 emit 8 eradiate

give in: 5 yield 6 relent 7 succumb 9 surrender

give off: 4 emit, quit 5 cease, exude, issue 7 publish

give out: 4 deal, emit, mete 5 exude, issue, peter, print 7 publish, release 9 circulate

give rise: 6 gender 7 produce 8 engender, occasion 9 originate

give up: 4 cede, emit, quit 5 demit, forgo, spare, waive, yield 6 betray, devote, forego, resign, reveal, vacate 7 abandon, deliver, despair, present 8 abdicate, renounce 9 sacrifice, surrender 10 relinquish

given: 5 fixed 6 stated 7 donated, granted 8 addicted, disposed, inclined 9 specified

givey: 4 soft

gizz: wig

gizzen: dry 5 leaky 7 parched 10 shrivelled

glabrous: 4 bald 6 smooth 8 levigate

glace: ice 6 glazed 8 polished

glacial: icy 4 cold 5 gelid 6 arctic, frigid, frosty, frozen 9 congealed

glacier: 6 icecap 7 iceberg

chasm: 6 crevas

deposit: as 4 asar(pl.) 5 eskar, esker 6 placer 7 moraine

direction: 5 stoss

fissure: 8 crevasse

fragment: 5 serac

hill: 4 paha 7 drumlin

ridge: as, os 4 kame, osar(pl.) 5 eskar, esker

snow: 4 neve

snow field: 4 firn, neve

glacis: 5 slope 6 buffer 7 incline

glack: 6 ravine, valley

glad: gay **4** fain **5** eager, happy, merry, sunny **6** blithe, bright, joyous **7** pleased, shining, willing **8** animated, cheerful, gladsome **9** beautiful, delighted, gratified, satisfied **11** exhilarated **12** lighthearted

gladden: **5** cheer, elate **6** please **7** gratify, rejoice

gladdy: **12** yellowhammer

glade: **4** vale **5** marsh **8** clearing
comb. form: **4** nemo

gladiator: **5** boxer **6** fencer **7** fighter
competition: **5** ludus
trainer: **7** lanista

gladness: joy **5** bliss, mirth **6** blithe **8** fainness, pleasure **9** happiness **12** cheerfulness, exhilaration

glaiket, glaikit: **5** giddy **6** stupid **7** foolish **11** lightheaded, thoughtless

glamor, glamour: **5** charm, magic, spell **7** bewitch, enchant, mystery, romance **9** fascinate

glamorous, glamourous: **6** exotic **8** alluring, charming, romantic **11** fascinating

glance: **4** gleg, leer, ogle, peek, peep, scan, scry, skew **5** blink, blush, flash, glent, gliff, glime, glint, glisk, prink **6** aspect, scance **7** glimpse

gland: **5** liver, lymph **6** carnel, thymus **7** adrenal, parotid, thyroid **8** exocrine **9** endocrine **11** paranephros
comb. form: **4** aden **5** adeno
edible: **5** liver **6** thymus
enlargement: **7** adenoma
secretion: **5** sebum **7** hormone
swelling: **4** bubo

glandular: **7** adenoid, adenose

glare: **4** gaze **5** blaze, flame, glaze, stare **7** glitter **8** radiance **9** showiness

glaring: **4** rank **5** clear, gaudy, glary, gross, plain, vivid **6** aglare **7** burning, evident, flaring, obvious, staring, visible **8** apparent, flagrant, manifest **9** barefaced **11** conspicuous

glary: **6** frosty, frozen **7** glaring, shining **8** slippery

glass: **4** frit, lens, pane **6** beaker, bottle, cloche, cullet, goblet, mirror **7** tumbler **9** barometer, telescope
alcohol: mug **4** pony **5** stein **6** rummer, seidel **8** schooner
colored: **5** smalt **7** opaline **10** aventurine
container: jar **6** bottle **7** matrass
design: **4** etch
molten: **5** metal **7** parison
partly fused: **4** frit
pert. to: **6** vitric
remove bubbles: **5** plane

glassmaking: *device:* **7** ironman
frame: **7** drosser

material: **4** frit **5** fritt
oven: **4** lehr

glassworker: **6** teaser

glasswort: **4** kali **5** plant **8** kelpwort

glassy: **4** hard **5** sharp **6** shrill **8** strident **9** apathetic **10** forbidding, lackluster, unwavering, unyielding

Glaucus: *father:* **8** Sisyphus
son: **11** Bellerophon

glaver: **7** flatter, wheedle

glaze: **4** coat, slip **5** cover, glare, sleet, stare **6** enamel, finish, polish, veneer, window **7** burnish, glidder, incrust, overlay, vitrify **8** couverte

glazier: **11** glassworker

gleam: ray **4** beam, glow **5** blink, blush, flash, glaik, glent, glint, glisk, sheen, shine **7** glimmer, glitter, shimmer, sparkle **8** radiance, splendor **9** coruscate **10** brightness **11** coruscation, scintillate

gleaming: **6** ablaze, bright

glean: **4** cull, reap **6** gather **7** collect

gleaning: **4** crop

glebe: sod **4** clod, land, soil **5** earth, field

glebe house: **5** manse **9** parsonage

glee: joy **4** song **5** mirth, sport **6** gaiety **7** delight, elation **8** hilarity **9** merriment **10** minstrelsy **12** cheerfulness **13** entertainment

gleeful: gay **5** merry **6** joyous **7** jocular **8** gleesome

gleek: **4** gibe, jest, joke

gleeman: **8** minstrel, musician

gleg: gay **4** keen **5** alert, quick, sharp **6** bright, lively, nimble **8** cheerful

glen: den **4** dale, dell, vale **5** griff, heuch, heugh, kloof **6** dingle, valley **10** depression

glent: **4** slip **5** flash, gleam, glint, shine **6** glance **7** sparkle

glib: pat **4** easy, oily **5** slick **6** casual, fluent, smooth **7** offhand, shallow, voluble **8** flippant, unforced **9** impromptu, talkative, unstudied **10** nonchalant, unthinking **11** superficial

glibbery: **6** smooth **8** slippery **10** changeable, unreliable

glide: **4** flow, sail, sile, skim, slip, soar **5** coast, creep, merge, slide, steal **6** glance **7** slither **8** glissade

gliding over: **6** labile **7** eliding

gliff: **4** look **5** scare, shock **6** fright, glance, moment **7** glimpse, instant **8** frighten

glim: bit, eye **5** light, watch **12** illumination

glimmer: **4** fire, glow **5** blink, flash, gleam **7** flimmer, glimpse, glitter, shimmer, sparkle

glimmering: **5** ghost

glimpse: 4 idea 5 blink, flash, glint, glisk, tinge, trace 6 glance, luster 7 glimmer, inkling

glint: 4 peep 5 flash, gleam, glent, shine 6 glance, luster 7 glimpse, sparkle 10 brightness

glisten: 5 flash, glisk, gliss, shine 7 glitter, sparkle 9 coruscate

glister: 5 shine 6 luster 7 sparkle

glitter: 5 flash, glare, gleam, glore, sheen, shine 6 scance 7 glimmer, glisten, glister, spangle, sparkle, twinkle 8 radiance 9 coruscate 10 brilliancy 11 coruscation, scintillate

glittering: 5 gaudy, gemmy 6 bright, fulgid 9 brilliant, clinquant, sparkling, twinkling

gloaming: eve 4 dusk 8 twilight

gloat: 4 gaze 5 exult

globe: orb 4 ball, clew 5 earth, monde, world 6 sphere 7 globule

half: 10 hemisphere

pert. to: 7 spheric

globular: 5 beady, round 6 beaded, globed 7 globose, spheric 9 globulous, orbicular, spherical 10 orbiculate

globule: 4 bead, blob, drop 6 bubble 7 droplet 8 particle, spherule

glockenspiel: 4 lyra 8 carillon 9 xylophone

glom, glaum: 4 take 5 steal, swipe, watch 10 understand

gloom: 4 dusk, murk 5 cloud, drear, frown 7 despair, dimness, sadness 8 darkness 9 dejection, heaviness, obscurity 10 cloudiness, depression, desolation, melancholy

gloomy: dim, sad, wan 4 blue, dark, dour, eery, glum 5 adusk, adust, black, brown, drear, dusky, heavy, moody, murky, stern 6 cloudy, dismal, dreary, morose, somber, sullen 7 clouded, obscure, stygian 8 darkling, darksome, detected, desolate, dolesome, downcast, overcast 9 cheerless, darkening, depressed, saturnine, tenebrous 10 depressing, despondent, foreboding, lusterless, melancholy, sepulchral, tenebrific 11 pessimistic 12 disconsolate, disheartened

glorify: 4 hery, laud 5 adore, adorn, bless, boast, exalt, extol, glory, honor, vaunt 6 praise 7 clarify, elevate, ennoble, magnify 8 emblazon, eulogize 9 celebrate 11 apotheosize

gloriole: 4 halo 7 aureole

glorious: 4 dear, mear, meer, mere 5 grand, noble 6 bright 7 eminent, haughty, radiant 8 boastful, ecstatic, gorgeous, renowned, splendid 9 hilarious, wonderful 10 celebrated, delightful 11 illustrious, intoxicated, magnificent, resplendent 12 praiseworthy, vainglorious

glory: 4 fame, halo 5 blaze, bliss, boast, eclat, exult, honor, kudos, pride 6 beauty, corona, heaven, praise, renown 7 aureole, clarity, garland, glorify 8 ambition, splendor 10 admiration, brilliancy, effulgence, reputation 11 distinction 12 magnificence, resplendence

gloss: 4 glow 5 dodge, gloze, sheen, shine 6 blanch, enamel, excuse, luster polish, remark, veneer 7 burnish 8 annotate, flourish, palliate, pretense 9 semblance, sleekness 10 brightness, commentary 14 interpretation

glossal: 7 lingual

glossary: 6 clavis, claves(pl.)

glossy: 5 nitid, silky, sleek 6 bright, sheeny, smooth 7 shining 8 lustrous, polished, specious 9 plausible

glove: mit 4 cuff, mitt 6 mitten, sheath 7 chevron, dannock, gantlet 8 gauntlet

fabric: 4 silk, wool 5 nylon 6 cotton

leather: kid 4 napa 5 mocha, suede 7 pigskin

shape: 5 trank

glow: 4 beam, halo 5 ardor, blush, flame, flush, gleam, gloss, shine 6 warmth 7 glimmer 13 incandescence

glower: 4 gaze 5 frown, glore, scowl, stare

glowing: hot, red 5 aglow, fiery, vivid 6 ardent 7 burning, candent, fervent, radiant, shining 10 candescent

gloze: 4 fawn, glow, peer, pore 5 gleam, gloss, shine 6 speech 7 comment, deceive, explain, expound, flatter, wheedle 8 brighten, collogue, disguise, flattery, palliate, pretense 9 adulation, interpret

Gluck opera: 5 Orfeo 7 Alceste

glucose: 5 sugar 6 starch 7 sucrose 8 dextrose

glue: fix 5 mount, paste, stick 6 adhere, attach, cement, fasten, gluten, sizing 7 sericin 8 adhesive, mucilage

glum: 4 dour, grum 5 moody, surly 6 dismal, gloomy, glummy, glumpy, morose, sullen 8 dejected, frowning, overcast 10 melancholy 11 threatening

glume: 4 leaf 5 bract

glut: 4 cloy, fill, gulp, sate 5 draft, gorge 6 englut, excess, pamper 7 engorge, satiate, surfeit, swallow 8 overfeed, overload, plethora, saturate

gluten: gum 4 glue 7 fibrin 8 adhesive

glutinous: 4 ropy, sizy 5 gluey, gummy 6 sticky 7 viscous

glutton: hog, pig 4 gulo 5 gulch 6 lecher, rascal, wretch 7 epicure 8 gourmand 9 scoundrel 11 gormandizer

gluttonous: 6 greedy 7 hoggish 9 voracious

gnar, gnarr: 5 growl, snarl

gnarl: 4 gnaw, knor, knot, nurl 5 growl, knurl, snarl, twist 6 nibble, tangle 7 contort, distort

gnarled: 6 knarry, knotty, rugged 7 crabbed, knarred, twisted 12 crossgrained

gnash: 5 champ, grind

gnat: fly 4 pest 5 midge 6 insect

gnaw: eat 4 bite, chew, fret 5 erode, gnarl, waste 6 be-gnaw, chavel, nibble 7 corrode

gnede: 6 scanty 7 sparing

gnib: 5 ready, sharp 6 clever

gnome: elf, saw 5 adage, bogey, dwarf, elves(pl.), maxim, motto, pigmy, troll 6 goblin, kobold, sprite 8 aphorism, apothegm 10 apophthegm

gnomon: 4 nose 5 canon, style, tenet 9 indicator

gnostic: 4 wise 6 clever, shrewd 7 knowing 12 intellectual

gnu: 5 takin 6 mammal 8 antelope

go: be; act, bet, bid, die, gae, mog, run 4 fall, fare, gang, lead, mosy, move, pass, read, ride, turn, walk, wane, wend, work 5 break, elope, leave, occur, set-to, steal, visit 6 amount, attain, become, belong, betake, depart, elapse, follow, happen, intend, resort, result, retire, travel 7 conduce, operate, proceed, succeed 8 diminish, traverse, withdraw 9 circulate, harmonize, undertake

aboard: 6 embark 7 entrain

ahead: 7 proceed 8 continue, progress

around: 6 detour 10 circumvent

ashore: 4 land 6 debark 9 disembark

astray: err 8 aberrate, miscarry

away: 4 exit, scat, shoo 5 imshi, leave, scram 6 begone, depart, retire 7 amscray

back: ebb 6 recede, return, revert 7 regress, retreat 10 retrogress

back on: 6 betray, recede 7 abandon, retrace

before: 4 lead 7 precede 8 antecede

between: 7 mediate 9 interpose

down: sag 4 fall, sink 5 lower 7 decline, descend, founder 8 decrease 11 deteriorate

forward: 4 fare 7 advance 8 progress

into: 5 audit, delve, enter, probe 7 examine

mad: 4 rage, rave, roar 5 erupt

on: 5 enter 7 proceed 8 continue

over: 5 renew 7 retrace 9 backtrack

swiftly: run 5 scoot, speed

to and fro: 5 waver 6 totter, wig-wag 7 stagger 9 fluctuate, vacillate 11 shuttlecock

to glory: die 6 perish

to pot: die 4 fail 7 decline

up: 4 rise 5 arise, raise 6 ascend

go-between: 4 bhat 5 agent 7 arbiter 8 mediator 10 mouthpiece 11 internuncio 12 intermediary

go-cart: 4 pram 5 wagon 12 perambulator

goa: 6 mugger 7 gazelle

goad: egg, gad, rod 4 brod, dice, edge, move, prod, spur, urge, yerk 5 ankus, decoy, impel, pique, prick, sting, thorn 6 incite 7 inflame, stimuli(pl.) 8 irritate, stimulus 9 incentive, instigate, stimulate 10 incitement

goal: aim, end 4 base, butt, dole, hail, mark, mete 5 bourn, finis, score, tally 6 object 7 purpose 8 ambition 9 intention, objective 10 aspiration 11 destination 12 consummation

goat: kid, ram, tur 4 ibex, tahr 5 beden, billy, goral 6 alpaca, chamal, pasang, victim 7 markhor 8 aegagrus, ruminant 9 bouquetin, stambecco, steinbock

constellation: 9 Capricorn

disease: 7 takosis

flesh: 6 chevon

genus: 5 capra

god of: Pan

male: 4 buck 5 billy

pert. to: 6 capric 7 caprine, hircine

wild: 4 ibex

goatee: 5 beard

goatherd: 5 Damon

goatish: 4 lewd 6 coarse 7 caprine, hircine, lustful 9 salacious 10 lascivious

goatskin: 9 chevrette

gob: 4 hunk, lump, mass 5 chunk 6 sailor, seaman 7 mariner 8 quantity

gobbet: gob 4 lump, mass 5 piece 6 morsel 7 portion 8 fragment, mouthful

gobble: 4 gulp 6 gorble

Gobi Desert site: 4 Asia

goblet: cup 5 glass, hanap 6 vessel 7 chalice 8 standard

goblin: bog, cow, elf, hag, nis 4 bhut, pook 5 bogey, bogle, bucca, gnome, nisse, ouphe, pooka 6 boggle, booger, churel, kobold, sprite 7 brownie, bugaboo, bugbear 8 barguest, bogey-man, folletto, folletti(pl.)

god (see also **deity** and next entry): As, Ea, Ra, Ve; Ada, Ani, Asa, Bel, Bes, Geb, Keb, Ler, Min, Pan, Ran, Seb, Tiu, Tyr, Ull, Van 4 aitu, Amen, Amon, Aten, Aton, Baal, deus(L.), deva, dieu(F.), Frey, Hler, idol, Kama, Loke, Loki, Nora, Odin, Orra, Ptah, Rama, Surt, Thor, Vali, Yama, Zeus 5 Aeger, Aegir, Asura, Baldr, Brage, Brama, Donar, Freyr, Hades, image, Othin, Pluto, Shiva, Surtr, Woden 6 Apollo, Brahma, Cronus, Elohim, Ganesa, Hermes, Hoenir, Kronus, Marduk,

Njorth, Osiris, Saturn, Vulcan, Yahweh **7**
Bacchus, creator, Forsete, godhead, Heimdal, Jehovah, Jupiter, Krishna, Mercury,
Serapis, Vitharr **8** Almighty, Dionysus **9**
Heindallr, Hlorrithi **10** Hephaestus **11**
Ramachandra
false: **4** Baal **6** Mammon
love for: **5** piety **6** amadis, bhakti
god: For gods of specific localities, religions,
or functions, see under the specific locality, religion, or function. EXAMPLES: "god
of Thebes": see **Thebes** *god of;* "hindu
god": see **Hinduism** *deity;* "god of war" :
see **war** *god.*
God be with you: 5 adieu, adios **7** good-bye
God blind me: 5 blimy
god-fearing: 5 pious **6** devout **9** religious
god-horse: 6 mantis
god-like: 5 pious **6** deific, devout, divine **8**
immortal **9** religious
god of: For all definitions beginning with
this phrase, see next important word. EXAMPLE: "god of flocks": see **flocks** *god of.*
goddess (see also **god**): Bau, Dis, Eir, Eos,
Hel, Mut, Nut, Uma **4** Anta, Bast, Devi,
Gaia, Hela, Hera, Isis, Juno, Kali, Nina,
Norn, Saga, Urth, Wyrd **5** Belit, Ceres, Diana, Durga, Freya, Frigg, Gauri, Nanna,
Venus **6** Athena, Aurora, Chandi, Freyja,
Frigga, Hecate, Hestia, Shakti, Tiamat **7**
Artemis, Asynjur, Demeter, Mylitta, Parvati **9** Aphrodite, Haimavati **10** Persephone, Proserpina
godfather: 7 sponsor
godforsaken: 8 desolate, wretched **9** neglected.
godless: 6 wicked **7** impious, profane, ungodly **9** atheistic
godliness: 5 piety **13** righteousness
godling: 5 deity **6** godkin, godlet
woodland: **7** Selenus
godly: 5 pious **6** devout **8** gracious **9** religious, righteous
godmother: 6 cummer, kimmer **7** sponsor
gods' abode: 6 heaven **7** Olympus
God's body: 7 bodikin
Goethe drama: 5 Faust **6** Egmont
goety: 5 magic **10** necromancy
goffer, gauffer: 5 crimp, flute, plait
gog: bog **4** stir **8** activity, quagmire **9** agitation, eagerness
goggle: bug, eye **4** roll **5** stare **6** squint
goggler: 4 scad **5** akule
goggles: 8 blinkers
going: run, way **4** exit, fare, gait, gate, path,
road **5** bound **6** access **8** behavior **9** departure **10** passageway
goiter: 6 struma **7** strumae(pl.)
gola: 4 cyma **7** granary **9** storeroom

Golan Heights town: 8 Kuneitra
gold: oro(Sp.) **4** gelt, gilt **5** aurum, metal **6**
riches, wealth **7** bullion **9** clinquant
bar: **5** ingot
black: oil
comb. form: **4** auro
deposit: **6** placer
fool's: **6** pyrite
heraldry: or
imitation: **6** ormolu, oroide
measure of weight: **5** carat
pert. to: **4** dore **6** aurous
symbol: Au
thin sheet of: **4** foil **6** latten
uncoined: **7** bullion
gold braid: 5 orris
gold-brick: 7 swindle
Gold Bug author: Poe
gold-plate: 4 gild, gilt
golden: 4 gilt, rich **5** auric, blest, blond,
goldy **6** aureal, blonde, goldie, mellow, yellow **7** aureate, aureous, halcyon, shining **8**
aurelian, precious **9** aureoline, Pactolian,
yellowish **10** auriferous
golden age: 9 siecle d'or(F.)
golden apple giver: 5 Paris
golden bough: 9 mistletoe
golden chain: 8 laburnum
Golden Fleece: *keeper of:* **6** Aeetes
land of: **7** Colchis
seeker: **5** Jason **8** Argonaut
ship used: **4** Argo
golden oriole: 5 pirol **6** loriot
goldeneye: cur **9** merrywing
goldenrod: 8 solidago
goldfinch: 8 graypate, greypate **12** yellowhammer
goldfish: 4 carp **6** calico **9** garibaldi, shubunkin
goldsmith: 7 artisan **9** artificer
crucible: **6** cruset
golem: 5 robot **9** automaton, blockhead
golf: *assistant:* **5** caddy **6** caddie
club: **4** iron, wood **5** baffy, cleek, mashy,
spoon **6** brassy, driver, jigger, mashie, putter **7** brassie, midiron, niblick
course: cup **4** link **5** green, links
cry: **4** fore
cup: **5** Ryder **6** Walker
hazard: **4** trap **5** stymy **6** bunker, stymie
mound: tee
score: par **4** bogy **5** bogey, bogie, eagle **6**
birdie, Nassau
stroke: **4** hook, loft, putt **5** drive, slice
target: cup **4** flag **5** green
term: lie, par, tee **4** baff, fore, hook **5** bogey,
bogie, divot, dormy, eagle, green, slice,
stimy **6** birdie, dormie, stymie, stroke **7**
gallery

tournament: 4 open
goliath: 5 giant
Goliath: *home:* 4 Gath
  place of death: 4 Elah
  slayer: 5 David
gollar, goller: 4 roar 5 growl, shout 6 gurgle
golly: 4 oath, yell
Gomer: *father:* 7 Japheth
  husband: 5 Hosea
gondola: car 4 boat 5 barge, coach
gone: 4 left, lost 6 ruined 8 absorbed, advanced, finished, involved
gone by: ago, o'er 4 over, past 5 agone 6 bygone, passed
Goneril: *father:* 4 Lear
  sister: 5 Regan 8 Cordelia
gonfalon: 4 flag 6 banner, ensign
goober: 6 peanut
good: bon(F.), fit 4 able, bein, bien(F.), boon, braw, fine, full, gain, kind, nice, prow 5 ample, brave, bueno, bully, moral, nifty, pious, sound, valid 6 benign, devout, expert, profit, proper 7 copious, gradely, helpful, liberal, trained, upright 8 becoming, budgeree, decorous, friendly, gracious, interest, orthodox, pleasant, pleasing, salutary, skillful, suitable, virtuous 9 agreeable, bountiful, competent, dauntless, enjoyable, estimable, excellent, favorable, fortunate, indulgent, reputable, righteous, well-being 10 auspicious, beneficial, benevolent, courageous, gratifying, profitable, sufficient 11 pleasurable, respectable, responsible, well-behaved 12 considerable, satisfactory, stouthearted, well-disposed
good-bye, good-by: 4 tata 5 addio, adieu(F.), adios(Sp.), ciaou(It.) 6 so-long 7 cheerio 8 farewell
Good Earth author: 4 Buck
good-for-nothing: 4 orra 7 useless 8 spalpeen(Ir.) 9 worthless 10 ne'er-do-well, 11 rapscallion
good health: 5 skoal 6 prosit 7 slainte
good-looking: 4 fair 5 bonny 6 comely, pretty 7 eyesome, winsome 9 beautiful 10 personable
good luck: 7 fortune
  image: 6 alraun
good-natured: 9 gemutlich
good spirit: 8 eudaemon
goodliness: 5 grace 6 beauty 8 goodness, kindness 10 comeliness, excellence
goodly: 4 kind 5 large 6 comely, portly 8 gracious, handsome 9 capacious, excellent 12 considerable
goodness: 6 bounty, purity, virtue 8 chastity, kindness 10 excellence, generosity, goodliness 11 beneficence, benevolence

goods: 4 fent, gear 5 stock, wares, wrack 7 chattel, finance 8 property 11 merchandise, possessions
cast overboard: 5 lagan, ligan 6 jetsam, lagend
in animal hides: 6 ceroon, seroon
in law: 4 bona
lost in shipwreck: 7 flotsam
smuggled: 10 contraband
stolen: 4 loot, pelf 5 booty, spoil 6 spoils
goodwill: 4 love 5 favor 9 readiness 10 heartiness 11 benevolence 12 friendliness
goody: 5 candy 9 sweetmeat
goof: 5 spoil 7 blunder
goofy: 5 silly 7 foolish 8 gullible
gool: 5 ditch 6 breach, sluice 7 channel, fissure
goon: sap 4 boob, dope, thug 6 bomber 7 slugger
goosander: 9 merganser
goose: 4 hiss 5 hansa, ninny, solan 6 cagmag, gander, goslet 7 gosling, widgeon 9 screwball, simpleton
cry: 4 honk, yang 5 cronk
flock: 4 raft 6 gaggle
genus: 4 chen 5 anser, brant
mackerel: 9 phalarope
male: 6 gander
pert. to: 8 anserine 9 grossular
resembling: 8 anserine
snow: 4 chen 5 brant, wavey 9 whitehead
tailor's: 8 flatiron
young: 7 gosling
gooseberry: 4 fabe 6 groser 7 currant 8 feaberry, goosegog 9 honey-blob
gooseflesh: 4 cold 7 pimples
goosefoot: 5 blite, plant, shrub
gooseherd: 7 gozzard
gopher: 4 tuza 6 rodent 8 squirrel
Gopher State: 9 Minnesota
Gorboduc's son: 6 Porrex
Gordian: 9 intricate 11 complicated
gore: mud 4 burt, dirt 5 blood, cruor, filth, slime 6 gusset, insert, pierce 9 penetrate
gorge: 4 fill, gaum, glut, pass, sate 5 cajon, canon, chasm, flume, gulch, gully, kloof, strid 6 canyon, coulee, defile, englut, nullah, ravine, valley 7 couloir, overeat, pitcher, satiate 8 quebrada 10 gluttonize
gorgeous: 4 vain 5 grand, showy 6 costly 8 dazzling, glorious, splendid 9 beautiful, luxurious 11 magnificent, resplendent
Gorgon: 6 Medusa, Stheno 7 Euryale
watcher for: 4 Enyo 5 Deino 6 Graeae(pl.) 8 Pephredo
gorilla: ape 10 anthropoid
gorse: 4 whin 5 furze 7 juniper
gory: 6 bloody 9 murderous 10 sanguinary 12 bloodstained

goshawk: gos 6 tercel
keeper: 8 ostreger 10 austringer
gospel: 7 evangel, tidings 8 doctrine, teaching 9 veritable
harmony of the four: 11 diatessaron
gossamer: web 5 filmy 6 cobweb 8 raincoat
gossip: cat, gab, gup 4 aunt, chat, clat, gash 5 cause, clack, clash, clepe, clype, crony, rumor 6 babble, caddle, callet, claver, gabble, glaver, norate, tattle 7 chatter, chin-wag, clatter, comment, gauster, nashgob, scandal, sponsor, tattler 8 informer, quidnunc 9 chatterer 10 newsmonger, talebearer, tattletale 11 scuttlebutt
gossoon: boy, lad 5 youth
got: see **get**
gotch: jug 7 pitcher
gote: 6 sluice, stream 7 channel
Goth: 8 Visigoth 9 barbarian, Ostrogoth
hero: 5 Wudga
last: 8 Roderick
Gothamite: 9 New Yorker
Gothic: 4 rude 5 rough 6 fierce 8 barbaric, Teutonic
gouge: 4 tool 5 cheat, fraud 6 cavity, chisel, groove 7 defraud 9 extortion 10 overcharge
Gounod opera: 5 Faust
gourd: 4 hole, pepo 5 melon, pepos 6 bottle, vessel 7 anguria 8 calabash, cucurbit 9 colocynth 11 chilacayote
rattle: 6 maraca
sponge: 5 loofa, luffa
gourmand: 7 epicure, glutton, gourmet 11 connoisseur
gourmandise, gormandize: 6 guttle
gourmet: 7 epicure 8 gourmand 11 connoisseur
gousty: 6 dreary 7 ghastly 8 desolate 13 preternatural
gout: 4 clot, drop 5 ditch, drain, taste 6 blotch, sluice, splash 7 channel, podagra 9 arthritis 11 coagulation, discernment
goutweed: 8 aiseweed
govern: run 4 curb, rein, rule, sway 5 guide, regle, steer 6 bridle, direct, manage, police 7 command, conduct, control, preside, refrain 8 dominate, regulate, restrain 9 influence, supervise 10 administer, discipline
governance: 7 control 10 government, management
governante, gouvernante: 8 chaperon 9 governess 11 housekeeper
governess: 6 abbess 8 mistress 11 gouvernante
governing: 6 regent 7 leading 11 gubernative

government: 4 rule 5 power 6 empire, habits 7 conduct, regency, regimen 8 demeanor, monarchy, republic 9 autocracy, democracy, hierarchy, oligarchy 10 governance, management 11 aristocracy, gubernation
agent: 5 envoy 6 consul 8 diplomat, minister 10 ambassador
art of: 8 politics 13 statesmanship
by a few: 9 oligarchy
by church: 9 hierarchy 10 hierocracy
by people: 9 democracy
by rich: 10 plutocracy
by three: 8 triarchy 11 triumvirate
by women: 8 gynarchy 11 gynecocracy
derived from: 9 political
head: 4 czar, king, tzar 5 queen 7 emperor, empress, premier 8 dictator 9 president 10 presidente
official: 6 syndic 10 bureaucrat
opposition to: 10 antarchism
representative: 6 consul 10 ambassador
science: 8 politics
system: 6 regime
without: 6 acracy 7 anarchy
governor: bey 4 lord 5 deity, nabob, pilot, ruler 6 author, dynast, grieve, rector, regent 7 captain, control, dynasty, manager, viceroy 8 director 9 president, regulator 10 gubernator, magistrate
castle: 6 alcaid 7 alcaide 9 castellan
gowk: 4 fool, gawk 6 cuckoo 9 simpleton
gowl: 4 howl, yell 5 whine 6 throat
gown (see also **dress, garment**): 4 robe, toga 5 frock, habit, manto, toosh 6 clothe, invest, mantua 7 garment
dressing: 4 robe 6 kimono 8 peignoir
loose: 6 banian, camise, chimer 7 cassock, chemise, chimere
Moslem: 4 jama 5 jamah
Goya painting: 4 Maja
goyle: 5 gully 6 hollow, ravine, valley
gozzard: 9 gooseherd
gra: 5 lover 6 liking 8 fondness 10 sweetheart
grab: nab, rap 4 boat 5 catch, clasp, grasp, seize 6 arrest, beclap, clutch, collar, snatch 7 capture, grapnel, grapple 11 appropriate
grabble: 4 grab 5 grope, seize 6 snatch, sprawl 7 grapple 11 appropriate
grace: 4 este 5 adorn, charm, favor, leave, mercy 6 beauty, become, bedeck, favour, polish, prayer, virtue 7 commend, dignify, gratify 8 beautify, easiness, efficacy, elegance, kindness 9 embellish, privilege 10 comeliness, goodliness, permission, refinement, seemliness 12 dispensation 14 attractiveness

Grace: 6 Aglaia, Charis, Thalia **10** Euphrosyne
mother of: **5** Aegle
graceful: 4 airy, easy, gent **5** genty **6** comely, gainly, mignon, seemly **7** elegant, fitting, genteel, tactful **8** charming, debonair, delicate **9** beautiful **11** appropriate
graceless: 4 ugly **5** cruel **7** awkward **8** depraved **9** abandoned, inelegant, merciless **10** ungracious **11** unfortunate
gracenote: 12 appoggiatura
graces: 8 agremens **9** agrements
gracile: 4 thin **6** slight **7** slender **8** graceful
gracious: 4 good, hend, kind, mild **5** civil, godly, happy, lucky, suave **6** benign, goodly, kindly **7** affable **8** benedict, debonair, generous, handsome, merciful, pleasing **9** benignant, courteous, favorable, fortunate **10** beneficent, forthcoming, regenerate **11** complaisant
grackle: 4 myna
gradation: 4 rank, step **5** scale, stage **6** climax, degree, series **8** position **10** exaltation, succession
grade: peg **4** mark, rank, rate, size, sort **5** class, level, order, stage **6** ascent, assort, degree, rating, select **7** incline, inspect **8** classify, gradient, graduate **14** classification
grader: 9 bulldozer
gradient: 4 ramp **5** grade, slope
gradine, gradin: 5 shelf **7** retable
gradual: 4 easy, slow **6** gentle **9** leisurely
graduate: 5 grade **6** alumna **7** alumnus
Graeae, Graiae: 4 Enyo **5** Deino **8** Pephredo
father: **7** Phorcus, Phorcys
sister: **6** Gorgon, Medusa **7** Gorgons
graff: 5 canal, ditch, fosse **6** trench
graft: dig **4** cion, toil, work **5** ditch, gravy, labor, scion, trade **6** boodle, inarch, trench **7** engraff **10** occupation
grafted: 6 united **8** attached
heraldry: **4** ente
grail: ama, cup **4** bowl **7** chalice, platter **8** sangraal, sangreal
knight of: **4** Bors **7** Galahad **8** Percival
grain: jot, rye **4** corn, curn, grit, meal, oats, rice, seed, wale **5** fiber, glebe, maize, scrap, spark, trace, wheat **6** barley, cereal, kernel, russud(Russ.) **7** granule, texture **8** particle **9** granulate
beard: awn
brewing: **4** malt
bundle: **5** sheaf
chaff: **4** bran, grit
coating: **4** bran
comb. form: **4** sito
disease: **4** smut **5** ergot
dried: **5** straw **6** groats, rissom, rizzom

ear of: **5** spike **6** ressum
foodstuff: **6** cereal
fungus: **5** ergot
funnel: **6** hopper
goddess of: **5** Ceres **7** Demeter
ground: **4** meal **5** flour, grist
line: **5** swath
measure: **6** thrave
mixture: **6** fodder **7** farrage **9** bullimong
outer membrane: **6** extine
parched: **7** graddan
price: **4** fiar(Sc.)
receptacle: bin **8** elevator
refuse: pug **5** chaff
scoop: **5** shaul
spike: ear
stack: **4** rick
tool: **5** flail
warehouse: **8** elevator
graip: 5 gripe
graith: 4 gear **5** adorn, build, dress, stuff **6** wealth **7** apparel, compose, furnish, prepare **8** material **9** apparatus, furniture **11** possessions **12** acoutrements **13** accouterments
gram: *one-tenth:* **8** decigram
molecule: mol **4** mole
gramary: 5 magic **7** grammar **8** learning **10** necromancy **11** enchantment
gramercy: 6 thanks **7** emotion
grammar: 6 syntax **9** accidence **11** linguistics
case: nom **6** dative **8** ablative, genitive, vocative **9** objective **10** accusative, nominative
describe: **5** parse
direct address: **8** vocative
example: **8** paradigm
term: **6** phrase, simile **8** metaphor
grampus: orc **4** orca **5** whale **7** cetacea, dolphin **8** cetacean, scorpion
granada: 11 pomegranate
granary: bin **4** gola **6** garnel, garner, girnal, girnel, grange **8** cornloft **9** cornhouse **10** repository, storehouse
grand: 4 epic, main **5** chief, great, lofty, noble, showy **6** august, epical, famous, superb, swanky **7** exalted, immense, stately, sublime **8** foremost, glorious, gorgeous, majestic, splendid **9** dignified, grandiose, principal, sumptuous **10** impressive, preeminent **11** ceremonious, illustrious, magnificent **13** comprehensive
Grand Canyon state: 7 Arizona
Grand Duke of Hell: 6 Abogor
grand slam: 4 vole **5** homer **7** home run
grandchild: oe, oy; oye
great: **5** ieroe

grandee: 6 bashaw 7 magnate 8 nobleman 10 clarissimo(It.)

grandeur: 4 pomp 5 state 6 parade 7 majesty 8 elegance, splendor, vastness 9 greatness, immensity, loftiness, nobleness, sublimity 10 augustness 12 magnificence

grandeval: 7 ancient

grandfather: 6 atavus 8 grandfer, gudesire(Sc.)

pert. to: 4 aval

grandiloquent: 6 heroic, turgid 7 pompous 9 bombastic 13 grandiloquous

grandiose: 4 epic 5 grand 6 turgid 7 pompous 8 imposing 9 bombastic, expansive, flaunting 10 impressive

grandmother: 6 beldam, granny, gudame(Sc.) 7 beldame, grandam, grannie 8 babushka(Russ.), grandame 9 eldmother

Devil's: 4 Baba

grange: 4 farm 7 granary 9 farmhouse

granger: 6 farmer

granite: 6 aplite 7 haplite, syenite 8 alaskite

granitic: 4 hard 7 austere 10 inflexible

grant: aid 4 boon, cede, gift, give, lend, loan, mise 5 admit, allot, allow, bonus, chart, cowle, spare, yette, yield 6 accede, accord, afford, assent, bestow, betake, beteem, bounty, confer, octroi, patent, permit, remise 7 adjudge, concede, consent, promise, subsidy, tribute 8 bestowal, donation, transfer 9 franchise, undertake 10 concession, permission, relinquish 11 acknowledge

granting: if 6 ceding, remise 7 lending 9 allowance, conceding

granular: 5 sandy 6 coarse, grainy 9 granulose

granulate: 5 grain 7 coarsen 11 crystallize

granule: 4 pill 5 grain 6 nodule, pellet 8 particle

grape: uva 5 Tokay 6 Agawam, Lalang, Malaga, Malage, Muscat 7 Catawba, Concord, Hamburg, Mission, Niagara 8 Delaware, Riesling, Thompson 8 muscadine 11 Scuppernong

acid: 7 racemic

cluster: 10 racemation

comb. form: 5 botry 6 botryo

conserve: 5 jelly, uvate

cultivation: 11 viniculture, viticulture

dried: 6 raisin

drink: 4 dibs, sapa, wine

fermentation: 6 cuvage(Fr.)

gatherer: 8 vintager

genus of: 5 vitis

juice: 4 dibs, must, sapa, stum

pert. to: 4 uval 10 botryoidal

refuse: 4 marc

residue: 4 marc, rape 6 pomace

seed: 6 acinus

spirit: 4 marc

sugar: 8 dextrose, fructose

grapefruit: 6 pomelo 8 shaddock

Grapes of Wrath: *author:* 9 Steinbeck

family: 4 Joad

grapevine: 4 caro 5 rumor 6 canard, report

pest: 10 phylloxera

graph: 5 chart 7 contour 8 quantity

graphic: 5 vivid 11 picturesque

graphite: 6 carbon

grapnel: 4 drag, grab 5 catch, seize 6 anchor 7 grapple

grapple: 4 grab, hold 5 grasp, gripe 6 buckle, clinch, tackle 7 contend, grabble, grapnel, gripple, seizing, seizure, wrestle 8 struggle

grasp: nap, see 4 clam, fist, glam, grab, grip, hand, hent, hold, holt, take 5 catch, clasp, glaum, gripe, seize, snare 6 clench, clinch, clutch, grappe, snatch 7 control, embrace, grapple, gripple, seizure 8 handfast 9 apprehend 10 comprehend, understand 13 comprehension

grasping: 4 avid, hard 6 greedy, grippy 7 miserly 8 covetous 10 avaricious 12 apprehension, parsimonious

adapted for: 10 prehensile, prehensive

grass (see also **cereal**): 4 lawn, reed, turf 6 darnel 7 hassock, herbage, pasture 9 colieroot, vetiveria 10 greensward

blade of: 7 traneen

dried: hay 6 fodder

fiber: 4 flax 5 istle, ramee, ramie 6 bhabar

fodder: 4 dura, gama 6 millet

forage: 7 setaria

genus of: 5 stipa 6 clover, lygeum 7 setaria

kinds of: eel, fog, hay, poa 4 alfa, bent, cane, diss, leaf, reed 5 avena, grama, sedge, spart, spike, stipa 6 enalid, marram, quitch, redtop, sesame, sorrel 7 esparto, traneen 8 calfkill 9 bouteloua

tuft: 7 tussock

grasschat: 8 whinchat

grasshopper: 4 grig 6 locust

grassland: lea 4 lawn, rakh(Ind.), vale 5 field, range, veldt 6 meadow 7 pasture, prairie

grassplot: 4 lawn 6 meadow

grassweed: 8 eelgrass

grate: jar 4 fret, grid, grit, rasp 5 grill, grind 6 abrade, basket, offend, prison, scrape 7 grating 8 imprison, irritate

grateful: 8 thankful 9 agreeable 12 appreciative

gratification: 4 gust 6 reward 8 delicacy, gratuity, pleasure 9 enjoyment 10 recompense 11 contentment 12 satisfaction

gratified: 4 glad 5 proud 7 pleased 9 delighted

gratify: 4 feed, sate 5 adorn, amuse, feast, grace, humor, wreak 6 arride, foster, pamper, please 7 appease, content, delight, flatter, gladden, indulge, requite, satisfy, welcome 9 gratulate 10 remunerate

grating: 4 grid, heck, rasp 5 grate, gride, grill, harsh, raspy, rough 6 cratch, grille, hoarse 8 gridiron, grinding, strident 9 dissonant 11 latticework

gratis: 4 free 10 gratuitous

gratitude: 4 gift 5 favor 6 thanks 7 tribute 8 gratuity 12 thankfulness

gratuitous: 4 free 6 gratis, wanton 8 baseless, needless 10 groundless 11 superfluous, unwarranted

gratuity: fee, tip 4 dash, dole, gift, vail 5 bonus, bribe, pilon, spiff 6 bounty 7 cumshaw, pension, present 8 bakshish, bonamano, buckshee, lagnappe 9 baksheesh, buona-mano, gratitude, lagniappe, pourboire 10 compliment 11 benefaction 13 gratification

grave: dig, pit 4 bier, bury, deep, foss, slow, tomb 5 carve, ditch, fossa, fosse, heavy, inter, sober, staid, suant 6 burial, grieve, hearse, sedate, solemn, somber, sombre, trench 7 austere, earnest, engrave, serious, steward 8 decorous, overseer, sermonic 9 important, momentous, ponderous, sepulcher 11 influential 13 authoritative

cloth: 8 cerement

comb. form: 5 serio

robber: 4 goul 5 ghoul

gravecloth: 6 sudary 8 cerement 9 cerecloth

gravedigger: 6 burier, fossor 7 fossore(pl.)

gravel: 4 dirt, grit, sand, stop 5 check 6 bother, chisel, eratum, sammel 7 perplex 8 alluvium, erratice 9 embarrass

graven: 6 etched 8 engraved 10 sculptured

graver: 5 burin 8 engraver, sculptor

gravestone: 5 blank, stela, stele 6 cippus, marker 8 monument 9 tombstone 11 sarcophagus

graveyard: 8 cemetery 10 churchyard

gravid: 8 pregnant

graviers: 4 dice

graving tool: 5 burin

gravity: 7 dignity 8 enormity, sobriety 9 heaviness, influence, solemnity 10 importance 11 earnestness, seriousness, weightiness 12 significance 13 momentousness 17 authoritativeness

law discoverer: 6 Newton

gravy: jus(F.) 4 lear 5 graft, juice, sauce

gravy boat: 9 sauceboat

gray: dim 4 ashy, dull, gris, hoar 5 ashen, bleak, hoary, lyard, lyart, slate 6 dismal, leaden, mature 7 elderly, grisard, grizzly, hueless, neutral 9 cheerless 10 achromatic

bluish: 7 cesious

comb. form: 5 polio

dark: 5 taupe 6 Oxford 8 charcoal

light: 4 ashy 5 pearl

Quaker: 5 acier

Gray's churchyard opus: 5 Elegy

gray matter: 4 obex 5 brain

gray whale: 7 ripsack

grayish: 7 grizzle 8 grizzled

graylag: 5 goose

grayling: 4 fish 9 butterfly

graze: 4 drab, feed, rase, skim 5 agist, brush, shave 6 browse, ripple, scrape 7 pasture

grazing ground: 4 colp 5 range 6 collop, meadow 7 pasture

grease: fat, oil 4 daub, lard, mort, seak, soil 5 bleck, bribe, cheat, cozen, smear 6 creesh(Sc.) 7 lanolin 9 lubricate, overreach

greaser: 6 stoker

greasewood: 5 chico, orach, yolky 6 orache

greasy: fat 4 oily, rich 5 dirty, fatty, gross, porky, thick 7 smeared 8 indecent, unctuous 10 indelicate 11 threatening

great: big 4 deep, fell, huge, much, rial, unco, vast 5 ample, chief, grand, large, yeder 6 grande(F.), heroic, mickle 7 capital, eminent, extreme, howling, immense, intense, titanic, violent 8 almighty, elevated, enormous, favorite, horrible 9 elaborate, excellent, important, prolonged 10 delightful, omnipotent 11 magnificent

comb. form: 4 mega 5 macro, megal

prefix: 4 arch

great albacore: 5 tunny 7 bluefin

great-aunt: 9 grandaunt

Great Barrier island: 4 Otea

great blue heron: 5 crane

Great Britain: See **England**

great deal: 4 gobs, lots

Great Divide: 7 Rockies

Great Expectations hero: Pip

Great Lake: 4 Erie 5 Huron 7 Ontario 8 Michigan, Superior

great many: lac 4 lakh

Great Sea: 5 Black 13 Mediterranean

Great White Brother: 7 Mahatma

greatcoat: 5 grego, jemmy, jimmy 8 overcoat 9 cothamore

greaten: 5 exalt 7 enhance, enlarge, magnify 8 increase

greater: 6 better 8 majority, mightier

greatest: 4 arch, best, most 6 utmost 7 extreme, noblest, supreme

greatly: 4 fell, much 5 amain, nobly

greatness: 8 grandeur 9 magnitude 11 magnanimity

greave: 5 armor, grove 7 thicket
greaves: 9 crackling
grebe: 4 fowl 8 dabchick
Grecia: 6 Greece
Grecian: 5 Greek 9 Hellenist
gree: 5 favor, prize 7 mastery 8 gladness, pleasure 11 superiority 12 satisfaction
Greece (see also **Athens, Sparta**): 6 Hellas
abode of gods: 7 Olympus
administrator: 10 amphodarch
alphabet: mu, nu, xi, pi; eta, rho, tau, phi, chi, psi 4 beta, zeta, iota 5 alpha, gamma, delta, theta, kappa, sigma, omega 6 lambda 7 epsilon, omicron, upsilon
altar: 7 eschara
ancient district: 4 Elis 5 Doris 6 Achaea, Achaia, Attica, Epirus, Hellas, Sparta 7 Epeiros, Macedon 12 Peloponnesus
Argolis valley: 5 Nemea
army corps: 6 evzone
assembly: 4 Pnyx 5 agora
avenging spirit: 6 Erinys
basin: 6 louter
beauty: 4 Lais
bondman: 6 penest
cape: 5 Malea 7 Matapan
castanet: 8 crotalum
Catholic: 5 Uniat 6 Uniate
chamber: 12 bouleuterion
chariot: 4 biga
church: 8 Orthodox
citadel: 9 Acropolis
city: 4 Elis 5 Barca, Chios, Drama, Eolis, Pella, Samos, Zante 6 Athens(c.), Edessa, Janina, Kozane, Larisa, Lesbos, Locris, Phocis, Phokis, Serrai, Serres, Sparta, Yanina 7 Corinth, Epeiros, Laconia, Larissa, Megaris, Rhodope 8 Ioannina, Komotine, Lassithi, Lessenia, Lessinia, Salonica, Salonika, Thessaly, Trikkala 9 Korinthos, Lasethion, Lasithion, Phthiotis, Rethymnon, Zakynthos 10 Negroponte 15 Alexandroupolis
clan: 4 obes 5 genos
cloak: 6 abolla 7 chlamys
coin: 4 mine, obol 5 hecte, nomas 6 lepton, phenix, stater 7 diobolo, drachma
colony: 4 Elea 5 Ionia
column: 5 Doric, Ionic 10 Corinthian
contest: 4 agon
counselor: 6 Nestor
courtesan: 5 Thais 7 Aspasia
cup: 5 depas
dialect: 5 Doric, Elean, Eolic, Ionic 6 Aeolic
dirge: 5 linos
district: 4 Arta, deme 5 Canea, Chios, Corfu, Drama, Evros, Khios, Pella, Samos, Zante 6 Achaea, Attica, Epirus, Euboea, Khania, Kozane, Lesbos, Phocis, Serrai, Yanina 7 Achaiam, Aetolia, Arcadia, Ar-

golis, Boeotia, Corinth, Florina, Kavalla, Laconia, Larissa, Rhodope 8 Cyclades, Ioannina, Messenia, Rethymne, Salonica, Thessaly, Trikkala 9 Acarnania, Korinthos, Lasithion, Macedonia, Phthiotis, Zakynthos 10 Cephalonia, Chalcidice, Khalkidike 11 Kephallenia
doom: ker
dramatist: 9 Aeschylus, Euripides, Sophocles 12 Aristophanes
enchantress: 5 Circe, Medea
epic: 5 Iliad 7 Odyssey
essence: 5 ousia
fabulist: 5 Aesop
Fate: 6 Clotho 7 Atropos 8 Lachesis
festival: 5 delia, haloa 8 Apaturia
flask: 4 olpe
fleet commander: 7 navarch
flute: 7 hemiope
folk dance: 7 romaika
foot-race course: 6 stadia(pl.) 7 diaulos, stadium
foot soldier: 7 hoplite
Fury: 6 Alecto, Erinys 7 Erinyes, Megaera 9 Tisiphone
galley: 6 bireme 7 trireme, unireme
garment: 5 tunic 6 abolla, chiton, peplos, peplus 7 chlamys
giant: 4 Otus 5 Mimas 7 Aloadae 9 Enceladus, Ephialtes
gift: 6 xenium
god: Dis, Pan 4 Ares, Eros, Zeus 5 Hades, Momus, Pluto, satyr 6 Apollo, Cronus, Hermes, Kronos, Nereus, Triton 7 Bacchus 8 Dionysus, Poseidon
god of love: 4 Eros
god of sea: 6 Triton 8 Poseidon
god of war: 4 Ares
god of wind: 6 Aeolus
goddess: Ge, Io; Ara, Ate, Eos, Not, Nyx, Ops 4 Alea, Dice, Dike, Enyo, Gaea, Gaia, Hebe, Hera, Leto, Nike 5 Horae, Irene, Metis, Moera, Niobe, Vesta 6 Athena, Eirene, Hecate, Hestia, Selena, Selene, Semele 7 Ariadne, Artemis, Astarte, Demeter, Eunomia, Nemesis 9 Aphrodite
Gorgon: 4 Enyo 5 Deino 6 Graeae, Graiae, Medusa, Stheno 7 Euryale 8 Pephredo
governor: 6 eparch
gymnasium: 4 xyst 9 palaestra
hero: 4 Aias, Ajax, Idas 5 Jason 7 Cecrops, Theseus 8 Heracles
historian: 7 Ctesias 8 Polybius, Xenophon 10 Thucydides
hobgoblin: 6 Empusa
hunter: 5 Orion
huntress: 7 Artemis 8 Atalanta
instrument: 5 aulos 8 barbiton
invader: 6 Dorian

island: Ios, Kos, Nio **4** Keos, Milo, Paxi, Syra **5** Chios, Corfu, Crete, Delos, Khios, Krete, Melos, Milos, Naxos, Paros, Psara, Samos, Syros, Thera, Tinos, Zante **6** Andros, Candia, Cerigo, Ikaria, Ionian, Ithaka, Lemnos, Lesbos, Leukas, Patmus, Rhodes, Sifnos **7** Amorgos, Cythera, Kimolos, Kythera, Kythnos, Myconos, Mykonis, Serifus **8** Cyclades, Mytelene, Santorin **9** Antiparos, Santorini **10** Cephalonia, Samothrace **11** Anticythera

jar: **7** amphora

judge: **6** dikast **7** heliast

jug: **5** ascos

king: **5** Minos **6** Nestor

lake: **6** Copais

lawgiver: **5** Minos, Solon

legislative council: **5** boule

letter: see *alphabet* above

letter(primitive): san **5** koppa, sampi **7** digamma

lover: **7** Rhoecus

lyre player: **5** Arion

man of brass: **5** Talos

marker: **5** stela, stele

market place: **5** agora

marriage: **5** gamos

mathematician: **6** Euclid **10** Archimedes

measure: pik **4** bema, piki, pous **5** baril, cados, chous, cubit, diote, doron, pekhe, pygon, xylon **6** acaena, bachel, bacile, barile, cotula, dichas, hemina, koilon, lichas, milion, orgyia, palame, pechys, schene, xestes **7** amphora, choemix, cyathos, diaulos, hekteus, metreta, stadion, stadium, stremma **8** condylos, daktylos, dekapode, dolichos, medimnys, palaiste, plethron, spithame, stathmos **9** hemiekton, oxybaphon

monster: **5** Hydra

mountain: Ida **4** Oeta, Ossa **5** Athos, Parus, Visti **6** Othrys, Pelion, Pindus **7** Helicon, Olympus **8** Hymettus, Taygetus **9** Cambunian, Cithaeron, Parnassus, Psiloriti **10** Lycabettus, Pentelucus

musical interval: **6** ditone, meseme

musical note: **4** mese, nete

musical system: **5** neume

mustard: **6** sinapi

nome: see *district* above

numeral: mu, nu, xi, pi; eta, san **4** beta, zeta, iota **5** alpha, gamma, delta, theta, kappa, koppa, sampi **6** lambda **7** epsilon, digamma, omicron

nymph: **5** Oread **8** Arethusa

old testament: **10** Septuagint

overseer: **5** ephor

paradise: **7** Elysium

patriarch: **5** Arius

patriot: **6** klepht

peninsula: **4** Alte **5** Morea

people: **5** demos **6** Argive, Cretan, Ionian **7** Hellene, Spartan **8** Athenian

pert. to: **6** Ionian **8** Hellenic **9** classical **11** Panhellenic

philosopher: **4** Zeno **5** Galen, Plato **6** Thales **8** Diogenes **9** Aristotle **10** Pythagoras

physician: **5** Galen

pilaster: **4** anta

pillar: **5** stele

pitcher: **4** olla, olpe **8** oenochoe

platform: **4** bema **6** logeum

poem: **5** Iliad **7** Odyssey

poet: Ion **5** Arion, Homer **6** Pindar **9** Simonides, Sophocles

poetess: **5** Sapho **6** Sappho **7** Corinna

port: **4** Syra **5** Corfu **6** Patras **7** Piraeus

portico: **4** stoa, xyst

precinct: **7** temenos

priest: **4** papa

priestess: **4** Auge, Hero, Iole **8** Caryatid

promontory: **6** Actium

province: **4** nome **5** nomos **7** eparchy

resistance group: Eam **4** Elas

river: **4** Arta **5** Lerna **6** Peneus, Ruphia **7** Alpheus, Eurotas **8** Achelous, Arachtus **11** Aspropitamo **12** Basilipotamo

rose: **7** glaieul

sacred place: **6** abaton

sage: **5** Solon **6** Thales **8** Socrates

sanctuary: **5** hiera

sculptor: **5** Myron **7** Phidias

seaport: **4** Enos, Volo **5** Pylos **8** Salonica, Salonika **9** Gallipoli

senate: **5** boule

serpent: **4** seps

settler: **5** metic

shield: **5** pelta

ship: **4** saic **5** diota

shrine: **5** secos, sekos

skeptic: **5** Timon

slave: **5** helot **6** penest

slave woman: **5** Baubo, Iambe

soldier: **7** palikar

song: ode **5** melos, paeon

soothsayer: **7** Calchas

sorceress: **5** Circe, Medea, Siren

speech: **6** rhesis

statesman: **8** Pericles **9** Aristides **12** Themistocles

statue: **6** xoanon

storm wind: **6** lelaps **7** laelaps

subdivision: **5** phyle

temple: **4** naos **5** cella **7** Theseus

territory: see *district* above

theater: **5** odeon, odeum

time: **7** chronos

town: 4 Elea 5 Nemea 6 Actium 7 Eleusis 9 Pharsalus

township: 4 deme

tribal division: 7 phratry

underworld: Dis 5 Hades

valley: 5 Nemea

vase: 5 dinos

verse: 6 Alcaic

village: obe

weight: mna, oka, oke 4 mina 5 litra, maneh, minah, obole, pound 6 diobol, dramme, kantar, obolos, obolus, stater, talent 7 chalcon, chalque, drachma 8 diobolon, talanton 12 tetradrachma

wine pitcher: 4 olpe

word: 5 logos

greed: 7 avarice, avidity 8 cupidity, gulosity, voracity 11 miserliness

greedy: 4 avid 5 eager, gutty 6 stingy 7 miserly 8 covetous, esurient, grasping, ravenous 9 devouring, rapacious, voracious 10 avaricious, gluttonous, insatiable

Greek: See Greece

green: new, raw 4 bice, live, verd, vert(Fr.) 5 cedre, crude, fresh, mossy, virid, young 6 callow, recent, unripe 7 untried, verdant 8 blooming, gullible, ignorant, immature, inexpert 9 malachite, undecayed, unskilled, untrained 11 flourishing 13 inexperienced 15 unsophisticated

blue: 4 cyan, saxe 7 sistine

gray: 5 olive

pale: 7 celadon

←*shade:* 4 nile 5 apple, kelly 6 bottle 7 emerald

woodbine: 7 peridot

yellow: 7 opaline

Green Mansions author: 6 Hudson

Green Mountain Boys' leader: 10 Ethan Allen

Green Mountain state: 7 Vermont

green peak: 10 woodpecker

greenback: 8 frogskin

greenery: 7 verdure

greengage: 4 plum

greenhorn: yap 4 jake, tyro 5 ikona 6 novice 9 cheechaco, cheechako 10 tenderfoot

Greenland: *base:* 4 Etah

discoverer: 4 Eric

Eskimo: Ita

geological division: 4 kome

town: 4 Etah 8 Godthaab 11 Julianehaab 12 Angmagssalik

greenlet: 5 vireo

greenroom: 5 foyer

greens: 5 salad

greenstone: 4 jade 7 pounamu 8 nephrite 9 malachite

greensward: 4 turf 5 grass

greet: cry 4 hail 5 halse 6 accost, salute 7 address, receive, welcome

greeting: ave, bow 4 hail 5 aloha, hello, salut(Fr.) 6 accost, salute 7 address, slainte, welcome 8 saluting 9 reception 10 salutation 12 commendation

gregarious: 6 gregal, social 8 sociable 11 amadelphous

grego: 5 cloak 6 jacket 9 greatcoat

gremlin: imp 5 devil

grenade: 4 bomb 5 shell 11 pomegranate

grenadier: 4 fish 7 rattail, soldier

grenier: 5 attic

gres: 8 ceramics 9 stoneware

Gretna Green visitor: 6 eloper

grey: See gray

Greya's husband: 4 Oder

greyhound: 4 grew 9 grewhound

grid: 5 grate 6 buccan 7 grating 8 gridiron

griddle: 5 grill 8 gridiron

griddle-cake: 7 crumpet, pancake 8 chapatty

gridiron: 5 field, grill 7 brander, grating, griddle

grief: woe 4 care, dole, dool, dree, harm, hurt, pain, ruth, teen 5 agony, dolor, tears, trial, wrong 6 dolour, mishap, regret, sorrow 7 anguish, chagrin, emotion, failure, offense, sadness, trouble 8 disaster, distress, hardship 9 grievance, suffering 10 affliction, desolation, heartgrief 11 lamentation

Grieg's dancer: 6 Anitra

grievance: 5 anger, grief 6 burden 8 gravamen, hardship 9 complaint, injustice 10 affliction, oppression 11 displeasure

grieve: rue 4 care, dole, pain, pine, sigh, 5 anger, grave, mourn, wound 6 bewail, enrage, lament, sadden, sorrow 7 afflict, bailiff, condole, manager, sheriff, steward, trouble 8 complain, distress, governor, overseer 10 discomfort

grieved: 4 sore 5 vexed 9 afflicted

grievous: sad 4 sore 5 heavy, sorry 6 bitter, dready, severe 7 heinous, intense 8 dolorous 9 atrocious 10 burdensome, calamitous, deplorable, flagitious, oppressive 11 gravaminous

griff: 4 glen 6 ravine

griffon: 4 lion 5 eagle 7 monster

grifter's henchman: 5 shill

grig: eel 5 annoy, dwarf 7 cricket, heather 8 irritate 9 tantalize 11 grasshopper

grigri: 5 charm 6 amulet, fetish 8 talisman

grike: 5 chink 6 ravine 7 crevice

grill, grille: vex 4 reja(Sp.) 5 broil, grate, harsh 6 offend 7 grating, griddle, torment 8 distress, gridiron, grillade, irritate 12 cross-examine grilse: 5 trout 6 salmon 7 botcher

grim: 4 dour, sour 5 angry, cruel, gaunt, harsh, stern 6 fierce, grisly, horrid, raging, savage, sullen 7 furious, ghastly, hideous, ominous 8 horrible, pitiless, ruthless, sinister 9 ferocious, frightful, merciless, repellent 10 forbidding, inexorable, relentless, unyielding

grimace: mop, mow, mug 4 face, mock, moue, mowe, mump, sham 5 fleer, smirk, sneer 8 pretense 11 affectation

grimalkin: cat 6 feline, she-cat

grime: 4 dirt, smut, soil, soot 5 colly, sully 7 begrime

grimly: 4 grim 5 stern 7 hideous

grimp: 5 climb

grimy: 4 foul 5 dingy, dirty 6 grubby, soiled 7 swarthy 8 begrimed

grin: gin 4 girn 5 fleer, smile

grind: vex 4 bray, chaw, chew, grit, joke, mill, mull, whet 5 chafe, crush, gnash, grate, study 6 abrade, crunch, drudge, harass, pestle, polish, powder, satire 7 oppress, sharpen 8 satirize 9 blackfish, comminute, pulverize, triturate 12 steeplechase

grim: 4 dour, sour 5 angry, cruel, gaunt, harsh, stern 6 fierce, grisly, horrid, raging, savage, sullen 7 furious, ghastly, hideous, ominous 8 horrible, pitiless, ruthless, sinister 9 ferocious, frightful, merciless, repellent 10 forbidding, inexorable, relentless, unyielding

grinder: 5 molar, tooth, tutor 9 announcer 10 flycatcher, goatsucker

grinding: 7 grating 10 burdensome 12 excruciating

grindle: 5 ditch, drain 6 bowfin

gringo: 8 American 9 foreigner 10 Englishman

grip: bag 4 holt, vice 5 cinch, clamp, clasp, cleat, ditch, drain, grasp, gripe, seize, spasm 6 clench, clinch, clutch, furrow, gutter, handle, trench, valise 7 earring, grapple, handbag, handful 8 gripsack, handfast, handgrip 9 constrict 12 sceneshifter

gripe: 4 grip 5 grasp, pinch 6 clench, clutch, grouse, handle, harass, snatch, timber 7 afflict, control, grapple, handful, mastery, vulture 8 complain, distress 9 apprehend 10 affliction, oppression

griph, griphus: 6 enigma, puzzle, riddle

grippe, grip: flu 9 influenza

gripper: 6 nipper

gripping device: dog 4 hand, vise 5 tongs 6 pliers

gripple: 5 grasp 7 grapple 9 tenacious 10 avaricious

gripsack: 4 grip 7 handbag

griskin: 4 chop, loin 5 steak

grisly: 4 grim 7 ghastly, hideous 8 dreadful, grewsome, gruesome, horrible, terrible

grison: 5 huron 6 weasel

grist: lot 8 quantity 9 provision

gristle: 9 cartilage

grit: 4 sand, soil 5 earth, grain, grate, grind, nerve, pluck 6 clench, gravel 7 bravery, courage 8 decision 12 perseverance

grith: 5 mercy, peace 6 asylum, refuge 7 defense, quarter 8 security 9 sanctuary 11 self-conduct

gritty: 4 game 5 sandy 6 plucky 7 arenose, arenous 8 resolute, sabulous 10 persistent

grivet: 6 monkey

grivois: 4 bold, free 5 broad 8 indecent

grizzle: 4 fret 7 grayish, whimper 8 complain

grizzly: 4 bear

Grizzly Bear State: 10 California

groan: 4 moan 5 creak, grank, grunt

grocer: 7 epicier(F.) 11 storekeeper

grog: rum 5 drink, rumbo 6 liquor 8 beverage

groggery: 7 shebeen(Ir.)

groggy: 5 shaky, tipsy 8 unsteady, wavering 9 tottering

groom: 4 mafu, syce, tidy 5 curry, dress, mafoo, strap 6 fettle 7 hostler, marshal, prepare, servant, shopboy 8 coistrel 9 assistant 10 bridegroom, manservant, palfrenier 11 horsekeeper

grooming: 8 toilette

groove: rut 4 dado, rake, slot 5 canal, chase, flute, glyph, regal, rigol, scarf, shaft, stria, sulci(pl.) 6 furrow, gutter, hollow, rabbet, raglet, scrobe, striae(pl.), sulcus 7 channel, striate 10 excavation

groovy: 6 modern 9 excellent 10 marvellous

grope: 4 clam, feel, glam, test 5 glaum, probe, sound 6 handle 7 examine, grabble, gropple

grosbeak: 7 warbler 8 hawfinch

groser: 10 gooseberry

gross: big, fat, low, sum 4 bulk, clod, dull, mass, rank, rude 5 amass, broad, brute, bulky, burly, close, crass, dense, heavy, plain, rough, thick, total, whole 6 animal, brutal, coarse, earthy, entire, filthy, greasy, impure, vulgar 7 beastly, brutish, compact, fulsome, general, glaring, massive, obscene, obvious, sensual, swinish, witless 8 cloddish, flagrant, indecent 9 egregious, unlearned, unrefined 10 indefinite, indelicate, scurrilous

grot: 6 cavern, grotto

grotesque: 5 antic 7 baroque, bizarre 8 fanciful 9 fantastic, whimsical 11 incongruous 12 preposterous

grotto: den 4 cave, grot, hole 5 crypt, speos, vault 6 cavern, recess

grouch: 4 sulk 6 grouse 7 grumble

ground: 4 base, dirt, fund, land, root, soil 5 earth, field, train 6 bottom, estate, reason 7 country, premise, terrain 8 initiate 9 establish, territory 10 foundation, fundamenta(pl.) 11 fundamentum

kinds of: bog, lot 4 moor, acre, farm, plat, park 5 arada, glebe, tilth, range, marsh, swale, patch 6 meadow, calade, reseau, maidan 7 pasture, cripple, curragh

raised: 5 ridge 7 hillock, hummock

ground pine: iva

ground squirrel: 6 gopher 8 chipmunk

groundhog: 6 marmot 9 woodchuck

Groundhog Day: 9 Candlemas

groundless: 4 idle 5 false 8 baseless 9 unfounded 10 gratuitous 11 unwarranted

groundnut: 5 chufa, gobbe 6 goober, peanut

grounds: 4 lees 5 basis, dregs, grout 6 bottom 8 sediment

college: 6 campus

military: 4 camp, fort 8 presidio 11 reservation

groundwork: 4 base, fund 5 basis, bases(pl.) 6 bottom, fundus

group: fry, mob, set 4 bevy, gang, herd, mass, ring, sect, team 5 batch, brood, cabal, class, clump, drove, firca, flock, genus, horde, party, squad, suite, tribe 6 bundle, clique, family, galaxy, gather, nation 7 arrange, cluster, collect, company, consort 8 assemble, assembly, classify, division 10 assemblage, assortment, collection, congregate 11 aggregation

animal: 4 herd 5 drove

pert. to: 7 generic

suffix: ery

group together: 4 band, file, meet 7 cluster 8 assemble

grouper: 4 fish, hind, mero 5 guasa

grouse: 5 ganga, gripe 6 gorhen, grouch, repine 7 attagen, cheeper, gorcock, grumble 8 complain, squealer 9 gelinette, ptarmigan 10 whitebelly 12 capercaillie

grout: 4 less, root 5 dregs, larry 7 grounds 8 porridge

grouty: 5 cross, sulky 6 sullen

grove: 4 bush, hewt, tope, wood 5 copse, hurst, lucus(L.) 6 aboret, bosket, greave, pinery 7 alameda, boscage, boskage, bosquet, coppice, thicket

pert. to: 7 nemoral

grovel: 4 fawn, roll 5 crawl, creep 6 cringe, tumble, wallow 7 grabble 8 flounder

groveling: 6 abject 7 hangdog 12 contemptible

grow: age, bud, get, wax 4 come, eche, rise 5 edify, raise, swell 6 accrue, batten, become, expand, extend, thrive 7 augment, develop, distend, enlarge, improve, nourish 8 develope, flourish, increase 9 cultivate 10 accumulate

grow old: age 5 ripen 7 senesce

grower: 6 farmer, raiser 7 rancher 10 orchardist 13 agriculturist 15 arboriculturist

growing: 6 rising 8 crescive

growl: 4 gnar, gurl, gurr, wirr, yirr 5 gnarl, snarl 6 gollar, goller, mutter, rumble 7 grumble, maunder 9 complaint

grown: 5 adult, risen 6 mature 7 matured 8 expanded

grownup: man 5 adult 7 matured

growth: wen 4 rise 5 swell 7 stature 8 increase, swelling 9 accretion, expansion, heterosis 11 development, enlargement 12 augmentation

in clusters: 8 racemose

on another: 8 parasite

on surface: 9 epigenous

organic: 9 accretion

promoting: 8 nutrient 9 nutriment

retarding: 9 paratonic

grub: bob, dig, eat 4 chow, feed, food, moot, plod, root 5 dwarf, larva, stump 6 drudge, larvae(pl.), maggot, search 7 plodder 8 victuals

grubby: 5 dirty, grimy, small 8 dwarfish, slovenly

grudge: 4 envy 5 covet, pique, spite 6 grutch 8 begrudge 10 resentment

grue: ice 4 snow 6 shiver 7 shudder 8 particle

gruel: 5 atole 6 burgoo, crowdy 8 porridge, wangrace

gruesome, grewsome: 4 ugly 6 grisly, horrid, sordid 7 fearful, ghastly, hideous, macabre 8 horrible

gruff: 4 deep, sour 5 bluff, harsh, rough, surly 6 hoarse, morose, severe, sullen 7 austere, brusque, quarrel

grumble: 4 crab, hone, kick 5 croak, growl, munge, snarl 6 grouch, grouse, mumble, murmur, mutter, repine, rumble, yammer 7 channer, gnatter, gruntle, maunder 8 begrudge, complain

grumpy: 5 cross, moody, surly 7 grumphy

grunt: 4 fish 5 groan, snork, snort 6 grumph 7 gruntle

grutch: 6 grudge, murmur 8 complain

guacharo: 7 fatbird, oilbird

guaiol: 7 alcohol

Guam: *breadfruit tree:* 6 nangca, nangka

capital: 5 Agana
idol: 5 anito
native: 8 Chamorro
port: 4 Apra
guan: 4 bird, fowl 10 chachalaca
genus: 6 pipile 7 ortalis
guanaco: 5 llama
guar: 4 bean
guarantee: 4 bail, band, bond, seal 6 assure, avouch, ensure, insure, surety 7 certify, endorse, hostage, warrant 8 guaranty, security, warranty 9 assurance, vouchsafe
guarantor: 5 angel 6 backer, patron 7 sponsor 11 underwriter
guaranty: 4 bond, pawn, seal 6 pledge 7 warrant 8 security, warranty 9 guarantee
guarapucu: 4 fish, peto 5 wahoo
guard: 4 care, curb, herd, hold, keep, rail, tend, ward 5 bless, fence, hedge, watch 6 bantay, bridle, convey, custos, defend, dragon, escort, fender, gaoler, jailer, jailor, keeper, patrol, police, sentry, shield, warden 7 keeping, lineman, protect 8 conserve, preserve, restrain, security, sentinel, watchman 9 attention, custodian, protector, safeguard 10 cowcatcher, protection
foil: 6 button
line of: 6 cordon
on: 4 wary 5 alert, ready 8 vigilant, watchful 9 observant
guarded: 4 wary 6 manned 7 careful 8 cautious, defended, discreet, watchful 9 protected 11 circumspect
guardhouse: 4 brig 5 clink 6 prison 8 hoosegow
guardian: 4 herd 6 keeper, parent, pastor, patron, warden 7 curator, trustee, tutelar 8 defender, guardant 9 custodian, protector
church relics: 10 mystagogue
heavenly: 5 angel
legal: 7 trustee
pert. to: 7 tutelar 8 tutelary
subject of: 4 ward
watchful: 5 Argus 8 Cerberus
guardianship: 7 custody, keeping, tuition 8 custodia, tutelage 9 custodiae(pl.) 10 guardiancy
guasa: 7 grouper
Guatemala: *ant:* 5 kelep
city: 6 Salama 9 Guatemala 11 Ciudad Viega, Totonicapan 13 Quezaltenango
coin: 4 peso 7 centavo, quetzal
fruit: 4 anay
Indian: 4 Itxa, Ixil, Maya 5 Xinca
lake: 5 Dulce, Peten 7 Atitlan 10 Amatitland

measure: 4 vara 6 cuarta, fanega 7 cajuela, manzana 10 caballeria
port: 7 San Jose 10 Champerico, Livingston
river: 6 Chixoy, Pasion 8 San Pedro
volcano: 4 Agua 5 Fuego 7 Atitlan
Guaycuruan Indian: 4 Toba
gubbins: 6 refuse, scraps 9 fragments
gudame: 11 grandmother
gudesire: 11 grandfather
gudgeon: pin 4 bait, dupe, fish 5 cheat, pivot 7 journal 10 allurement
Gudrun: *brother:* 6 Gunnar
husband: 4 Atli
guenon: 4 mona 6 grivet, monkey
guerdon: 6 reward 8 requital 10 recompense
guess: aim 4 shot 5 areed, fancy, infer 6 divine 7 opinion, presume, surmise, suspect 8 estimate 9 speculate 10 conjecture
guest: 4 host 6 caller, inmate, lodger, patron, roomer 7 visitor 8 visitant
guesthouse: inn 5 hotel 11 caravansary
guff: 4 puff, talk 5 chaff, whiff 6 humbug
guffaw: 5 laugh 6 heehaw 8 laughter 10 horselaugh
Guiana: *cassava drink:* 7 paiwari
coin: bit
fowl: 4 keet
hut: 5 benab
river turtle: 8 matamata
tree: 4 dali, mora 5 dalli 6 camara
guidance: 4 duct, helm 7 auspice, conduct, guidage 8 steerage 9 direction 10 leadership, management 15 superintendence
guide: guy 4 airt, buoy, clue, lead, pole, rein, rule, show 5 airth, carry, longe, order, pilot, reign, steer, teach, treat, tutor, usher 6 bridle, convey, convoy, direct, former, govern, leader, manage 7 conduce, conduct, control, marshal, mercury 8 cicerone, director, instruct, polestar, regulate, textbook 9 catechism, conductor, guidebook, guidepost, itinerary, prescribe, regulator 11 superintend
guidebook: 8 baedeker, handbook 9 itinerary
guideway: 4 sley, slot 5 track 7 channel 8 slideway
guiding: 5 polar 7 leading
Guido: *fifth note:* sol
first note: ut
fourth note: fa
high note: la
highest note: E la
second note: re
third note: mi
guild, gild: hui 6 gremio 7 society 10 fellowship 11 association, brotherhood
merchant: 5 hansa, hanse 6 cartel

guile: 4 dole, wile 5 cheat, craft, fraud 6 deceit, humbug 7 cunning 9 duplicity, treachery

guileful: 9 deceitful, insidious 10 fallacious, fraudulent 13 Machiavellian

guileless: 5 naive 6 candid, honest 7 artless 8 innocent 9 ingenuous

guillemot: auk 4 loom, quet 5 murre 7 dovekey, dovekie

guillotine: 6 behead 10 decapitate
wagon for: 7 tumbrel, tumbril

guilt: sin 5 culpa, fault 6 piacle 7 offense 8 iniquity 10 wickedness 11 criminality, culpability

guiltless: 4 free 8 innocent 9 righteous

guilty: 6 nocent, wicked 7 correal 8 culpable

Guinea: *measure:* 7 jacktan
seaport: 4 Bata
tree: 4 akee, dali, mora 5 dalli
weight: 4 akey, piso, uzan 5 benda, seron 6 quinto 8 aguirage

guinea fowl: 4 keet 7 galeeny, pintado

guinea pig: 4 cavy

Guinevere's husband: 6 Arthur

guise: hue 4 form, garb, mask, mien 5 cloak, cover, dress, habit, shape 6 aspect, attire, deceit, manner 7 arrange, fashion 8 behavior, disguise, likeness, practice 9 semblance 10 appearance, masquerade

guitar: uke 5 sitar, tiple 6 sancho 7 samisen, ukulele 8 chitarra 10 calascione
guitarlike instrument: 4 lute, rota 7 bandore, pandora, samisen
half step in pitch: 5 dital
key: 5 dital
of India: 4 vina 5 sitar
play: 5 strum
small: uke 7 ukelele

guitguit: 6 pitpit

gula: 4 cyma, ogee 6 gullet, throat 7 molding

gulch: 4 gulp 5 canon, gorge, gully 6 arroyo, canyon, coulee, ravine 7 glutton

gulf: 4 eddy 5 abyss, chaos, chasm 6 vorago 9 barathrum, whirlpool 10 separation

Gulf of Mexico islet: cay

Gulf States: 5 Texas 7 Alabama, Florida 9 Louisiana 11 Mississippi

gull: 4 mew 4 dupe, fool, geck, sell, tern 5 cheat, cokes, cully, fraud, larid, trick 6 chouse, nilgai, teaser, victim, whilly 7 cheater, deceive, defraud, gosling, mislead 8 dotterel, impostor 9 kittiwake 10 mountebank
kinds of: cob 4 skua 5 allan, annet, pewit 6 larine, teaser, waggel 11 burgomaster
pert. to: 6 larine, laroid

gullet: maw 6 throat, weason 7 weasand 9 esophagus

gullible: 5 goofy, green, naive 9 credulous

Gulliver: *author:* 5 Swift
flying island: 6 Laputa
human beast: 5 Yahoo
island kingdom: 8 Lilliput

gully: gut 4 sike 5 drain, gorge, goyal, goyle, gulch, knife, sword, zanja 6 arroyo, gutter, nullah, ravine, valley 7 couloir 11 watercourse

gulp: 4 glut, swig 5 gulch, quilt, swipe 6 glutch, gobble 7 swallow

gulp down: 4 bolt 6 englut

gum: 4 clog, hive, kino 5 cheat, nyssa, stick, trick 6 chicle, gluten, hashab, humbug, impede, tissue, tupelo 7 bilsted, gingiva 8 mucilage 10 eucalyptus 11 masticatory
derivative: 8 bassorin 10 tragacanth, traganthin 12 tragacanthin
kinds of: 5 tuart 6 acacia, acacin, balata, touart 7 acacine, dextrin
resin: 5 elemi, gugal, myrrh 6 salban 9 sagapenum 12 frankincense

gum tree: 5 xylan

gumbo: 4 ocra, okra, soup 7 melange

gumma: 5 tumor

gummy: 6 mastic 7 viscous 8 adhesive

gumption: 10 enterprise, initiative, shrewdness

gums: ula 7 alveoli
comb. form: ulo
pain in: 7 ulalgia
pert. to: 6 uletic 8 gingival

gun: gat, rod 5 rifle, tommy 6 cannon, heater, pistol, weapon 7 carbine, shotgun 8 revolver 9 matchlock 11 blunderbuss
barrel cleaner: 6 ramrod
kinds of: 4 bore, bren, roer 5 baril 6 ack-ack, archie, barker 7 aerogun, bazooka 8 amusette
mount: 6 turret
part: 4 lock 5 stock 6 barrel, hammer, muzzle, rammer, safety 7 trigger
platform: 11 emplacement

gunfire: 4 rake 5 salvo 6 strafe 7 barrage 8 enfilade

gunlock: *catch:* 4 sear
hammer: 7 doghead
pawl: 4 sear

gunner: 7 shooter 9 cannoneer 10 bombardier 12 artilleryman

gunny: tat 4 jute 6 burlap

gunpowder: 5 nitro

gunroom: 8 quarters

gunshot: pop

Gunther's uncle: 5 Hagen

gunwale: 8 portoise

gurge: 4 eddy 5 surge, swirl

gurgle: 6 gargle, gollar, goller, guggle

Gurkha's sword: 5 kukri

gurl: 4 howl 5 growl, snarl

gurnard: 6 elleck, rochet 8 dragonet
guru: 5 guide 7 teacher
gush: 4 flow, pour, teem 5 issue, smarm, spate, spout, spurt 6 effuse, stream 10 outpouring
gushing: 5 agush 7 teeming 8 effusive, unctuous
gusset: 4 gore 8 piecette
gussie: pig 5 swine
gust: bub 4 flan, gale, puff, scud, waft, wind 5 blast, draft, gusto, storm, taste, whiff 6 flurry, liking, relish, squall 8 outburst 9 enjoyment, foretaste 11 inclination 13 gratification
gusto: 4 elan, gust, zest 5 taste 6 liking, relish 12 appreciation
gusty: 5 windy 6 savory, stormy 7 gustful, squally 8 agitated 11 tempestuous
gut: 5 belly, force, gully 6 bowels, defile, strait 7 courage, destroy, passage, plunder, stamina, stomach 8 entrails, gluttony 9 intestine 10 disembowel, eviscerate
gutta: 8 ornament
gutta-percha: 5 latex 6 balata
gutter: 4 grip, sink 5 brook, ditch, gully, siver(Sc.) 6 groove, guzzle, trench, trough, vennel 7 channel, scupper 11 watercourse
guttural: 5 burry, harsh, velar 7 rasping, throaty
guy: kid, rod 4 josh, rope, stay, twit 5 chain, guide, spoof, tease 6 decamp, fellow, gazabo, gazebo, person 8 ridicule
guy rope: 4 stay, vang
guzzle: 4 tope 5 drain, drink 6 gutter, throat
guzzler: bum 6 bender
gwyniad: 7 schelly

gymnast: 6 turner 7 acrobat, athlete, tumbler 8 balancer 10 gymnasiast
gymnastic: *stunt:* kip 9 handstand, headstand 10 handspring, headspring
  swing: 7 trapeze
gyp: 5 cheat, steal 7 sharper, swindle 8 swindler 10 overcharge
gypsum: 6 parget 8 selenite 9 alabaster
  resembling: 11 alabastrine
gypsy, gipsy: 4 calo 5 caird, nomad 6 Gitana, Gitano, roamer 7 czigany, tzigany, zincala, zincalo, zingana, zingano, zingara, zingaro 8 Bohemian, brunette, wanderer, zigeuner
  boy: 4 chal
  camp: tan
  dance: 10 zingaresca
  devil: 4 beng
  dialect: 6 Romany 7 Rommany
  fortune: 4 bahi
  gentleman: rye
  girl: chi 4 chai
  horse: gri, gry
  husband: rom
  nongypsy: 4 gajo
  paper: lil
  Syrian: 5 Aptal
  thief: 4 chor
  village: gav
  wife: 4 romi
gyrate: 4 gyre, spin, turn 5 twirl, whirl 6 rotate 7 revolve
gyrator: top
gyre: 4 ring 6 gyrate, vortex 7 circuit 10 revolution
gyrfalcon: 6 jerkin
gyve: 4 iron 5 chain 6 fetter 7 shackle

H

H: 5 aitch 8 aspirate
sound of: 8 aspirate
H-shaped: 5 zygal
haar: fog
habeas corpus: 4 writ
haberdashery: hat 5 shirt 6 gloves 7 necktie 8 menswear
habile: fit 4 able 6 adroit, clever, expert 8 skillful, suitable
habiliment (see also **dress, gown**): 4 garb 5 habit 6 attire 7 apparel, clothes, costume, raiment 8 billiment, clothing, equipage, fittings, ornament, vestment 9 equipment, faculties 11 furnishings
habilitate: 5 dress, equip 6 clothe 7 entitle, qualify
habit (see also **dress**): rut, use 4 coat, garb, gown, suit, vice, wont 5 array, guise, haunt, thews, usage 6 attire, clothe, custom, estate, groove 7 bearing, clothes, costume, garment 8 demeanor, habitude, practice, tendency 9 cacoethes 10 consuetude, deportment, habiliment
habitant: 7 dweller
habitat: 4 home 5 abode, range 6 patria 7 station 8 locality 11 environment
combining form: eco 4 oeco, oiko
habitation: 4 home, tent 5 abode, house, hovel, igloo 6 harbor, warren 7 harbour, lodging 8 domicile, dwelling, tenement 9 chaumiere(F.), residence
habited: 6 garbed, gowned 7 arrayed, clothed, dressed 9 inhabited 10 accustomed
habitual: 5 usual 6 common, hectic 7 regular 8 familiar, frequent, ordinary 9 customary 10 accustomed, inveterate
habituate: use 5 enure, inure 6 addict, season 8 accustom, frequent 9 acclimate, 11 acclimatize, familiarize
habitude: 5 habit 11 familiarity
habitue: 10 frequenter
hacendero: 6 farmer
Hachaliah's son: 8 Nemehiah
hachure: 4 line, mark 5 shade

hacienda: 4 farm 5 ranch 6 estate 7 finance 10 plantation 13 establishment
proprietor: 9 hacendado
hack: cab, cut, hag, hew 4 chop, taxi 5 coach, cough 6 drudge, fiacre, hacker, hackle, haggle, mangle 7 butcher, chatter, hackney, stammer, stutter 8 carriage, mutilate 9 mercenary
hack writer: 7 penster
hackberry: 8 oneberry 10 sugarberry
hackee: 8 chipmunk
hackle: 4 bait, comb, hack 6 heckle 11 stickleback
hackly: 5 rough 6 broken, jagged
hackney: nag 4 hack, pony 5 horse, noddy 6 drudge 8 carriage, hireling
hackneyed: old 4 worn 5 banal, stale, trite 6 common 7 forworn 8 foreworn 10 habituated, threadbare 11 commonplace, stereotyped
had: See **have**
Hades: dis, pit 4 hell 5 Orcus, Sheol 8 Tartarus 11 netherworld
god: 5 Pluto
inhabitant of: 7 hellion
lake to: 7 Avernus
mother: 4 Rhea
pert. to: 7 sheolic 8 infernal
river: 4 Styx 5 Lethe 7 Acheron
wife: 10 Persephone
hadj, hajj: 10 pilgrimage
haet: bit 4 atom, whit
haff: 6 lagoon
haffet, haffit: 5 cheek 6 temple
haft: 5 dwell 6 handle, settle 8 accustom, dwelling 11 familiarize
hag: bog, cut 4 bogy, hack, wood 5 copse, crone, demon, ghost, marsh, notch, rudas(Sc.), witch 6 beldam, goblin, harass, spirit 7 beldame, fatigue, haggard, pasture, terrify 8 harridan, quagmire 9 cailleach, cailliach, enclosure, hobgoblin
Hagar's son: 7 Ishmael
hagdon: 7 seabird 10 shearwater
hagfish: 5 borer

haggard: 4 bony, lank, lean, pale, thin, wild 5 drawn, gaunt, spare 6 hagged, wanton 7 anxious, haglike, untamed 8 harrowed, unchaste 9 suffering, untrained 10 cadaverous 11 intractable

Haggard novel: She

haggle: cut, hew 4 hack, prig 5 cavil 6 badger, banter, chisel, dicker, higgle, huckle, palter, scotch 7 bargain, chaffer, dispute, stickle, wrangle

haggler: 6 dodger 8 huckster

haggy: 5 boggy 6 uneven

hagioscope: 6 squint 7 opening

hagride: 4 ride 6 harass 7 torment

hail: ave 4 ahoy, call, goal 5 greet, sleet, sound, whole 6 accost, health, salute 7 address, fortune, graupel 8 greeting 10 salutation 13 precipitation

hain: 4 save 5 raise, spare 7 elevate

hair: fax, fur 4 barb, coma, mane, shag 5 crine, tress 6 crinet, nicety, trifle 7 bristle 8 capillus, filament, finespun 9 chevelure
  accessory: 8 barrette
  Angora goat: 6 mohair
  braid: cue, pig 5 queue 7 pigtail
  coarse: 4 kemp, seta, shag 7 bristle
  comb. form: pil 4 pilo
  curl: 7 ringlet
  disease: 8 dandruff, psilosis
  dye: 5 henna
  excessive: 7 pilosis
  false: rat, wig 6 peruke 7 periwig
  fringe: 8 frisette, frizette
  having: 6 pilose 7 barbate, hirsute, villous 8 crinated
  horse: 4 mane 5 seton 7 fetlock
  intestinal: 6 villus
  knot: bun 7 chignon
  lock: 4 curl, feak, tate 5 flock, tress 6 berger 7 cowlick, elflock 8 lovelock 9 harigalds
  loss: 8 alopecia, baldness
  ornament: bow 4 comb 5 tiara 6 ribbon 7 coronet 8 barrette
  pert. to: 6 crinal
  plant: 6 villus
  remover: 8 epilator 9 depilator, epilatory 10 depilatory
  roll: 4 puff 5 twist 7 chignon 9 pompadour
  short: 6 setula, setule
  soft: 4 down 6 villus
  unruly: mop 6 tousle 7 cowlick
  white: 4 snow

hairbrained: 5 giddy 8 heedless, volatile

hairbreadth: ace 6 margin

haircloth: aba 6 cilice

haircut: 7 tonsure

hairdo: bob 4 glib(Ir.) 5 braid 6 bubble, marcel 7 beehive, pageboy, pigtail, shingle 8 bouffant, ponytail 9 horsetail

hairdresser: 7 friseur 8 coiffeur 9 coiffeuse

hairless: 4 bald 8 depilous

hairnet: 5 snood

hairpin: 4 bend 6 bodkin 8 bobbypin

hairy: 5 pilar 6 comate, comous, pilary, piline, pilose, shaggy 7 crinose, hirsute

Haiti: *bandit:* 4 caco
  city: 12 Port-au-Prince
  coin: 6 gourde
  island: 4 Mona 6 Gonave
  liberator: 9 Toussaint
  magic: obi
  ruler: 8 Duvalier
  spirit: 4 baka, bako
  sweet potato: 7 batatas

hake: 4 idle 5 tramp 6 loiter, trudge

Halakoth collection: 6 mishna 7 mishnah

halberd: 4 bill 6 glaive, weapon 8 battle-ax

halcyon: 4 bird, calm 5 happy, quiet 6 golden 8 peaceful, tranquil 9 unruffled 10 kingfisher

Halcyone: *father:* 6 Aeolus
  husband: 4 Ceyx

hale: lug, tug, vex 4 draw, haul, heal, pull 5 annoy, frack, freck, sound 6 harass, hearty, robust, strong, summon, wholly 7 healthy 8 contract, vigorous

Halevy opera: 5 Juive

half: 4 demi, hemi, part, semi, term 6 moiety 7 partial, partner, portion 8 semester 11 imperfectly

half-ape: 5 lemur 7 tarsier

half breed: 5 metif, metis 6 mestee, metive, mustee 7 metisse, mestizo, mestiza, mulatto, mulatta 8 octoroon, quadroon

half brother: 7 half-sib 11 half-sibling

half circumference: 10 semicircle

half diameter: 6 radius

half-man: 4 faun 6 garuda 7 centaur 8 minotaur

half mask: 4 loup 6 domino

half-month: 9 fortnight

half-moon: 9 semilunar
  figure: 4 lune

half-turn: 8 caracole

half-wit: 4 dolt 5 dunce 6 nimshi 9 blockhead

half-witted: 5 dotty, silly 7 foolish 9 senseless

halfbeak: ihi 5 balao

halfpenny: mag 4 dump 5 brown 6 bawbee

halfway: mid 7 midship, partial 9 equivocal, partially 11 equidistant

halibut steak: 6 flitch

Halicarnassian: 9 Dionysius, Herodotus

halicore: 6 dugong

halidom, halidome: 8 holiness, sanctity 9 sanctuary

Halifax citizen: 10 Haligonian

halite: sal 4 salt

halitus: fog 4 aura 5 vapor 6 breath 10 exhalation

hall: 4 aula, room, saal(G.) 5 entry, foyer, lobby, manor, odeon, odeum, salle 6 atrium, durbar, saloon 7 chamber, gallery, hallway, passage 8 anteroom, corridor 9 vestibule 10 auditorium, misericord, passageway 11 misericorde

  music: 4 gaff 5 odeon, odeum

  reception: 5 salon 6 parlor

  student residence: 4 dorm 5 bursa 9 dormitory

hallanshaker: 5 scamp 6 beggar 8 vagabond

halloo: 5 shout 6 accost

hallow: 5 bless 8 dedicate 10 consecrate

hallowed: 4 holy

hallowed place: 4 fane 5 altar 6 bethel, chapel, church, shrine, temple 9 cathedral, synagogue

hallucination: d.t.'s 6 mirage 7 fantasy 8 delirium, delusion

halma: 4 game, jump

halo: arc 4 glow, nimb 5 glory 6 areola, areole, brough(Sc.), circle, corona, nimbus 7 aureola, aureole 8 cincture, gloriole

halogen: 6 iodine 7 bromine 8 chlorine 8 cyanogen, fluorine

halse, hals: col, hug 4 neck 5 greet 6 defile, salute, throat 7 conjure, embrace, entreat

halt: hop 4 bait, lame, limp, stem, stop 5 cease, hilch, hitch, pause, stand 6 arrest, desist, docked 7 limping 8 lameness, stoppage 9 cessation, mutilated, terminate

halter: 4 rope 5 leash, noose, strap, widdy 6 bridle, hamper 8 cavesson, restrain 9 hackamore

halting: 4 lame 7 limping 8 spavined 9 defective 10 hesitating 11 vacillating

halting place: 4 camp

halucket: 4 wild 5 crazy, giddy 10 halfwitted

ham: pig 4 port 7 amateur

Ham: *brother:* 4 Shem

  father: 4 Noah

  son: 4 Cush 6 Canaan

  son's land: 8 Ethiopia

hamadryad: 5 nymph 6 baboon

hamate: 6 curved, hooked 7 hamular 8 hamiform

hameil: 5 homey 8 domestic

Hamilcar: 5 Barca

  conquest: 5 Spain

  home: 8 Carthage

  son: 8 Hannibal

Hamite: *father:* 4 Abel

  language: 4 Afar, Agao, Beja 5 Belin, Galla 6 Berber, Kabyle, Shilha, Somali, Zenaga 8 Cushitic, Numidian, Tamashek 9 Ethiopian, Gaetulian 11 Mauretanian

  people: 4 Beja, Bogo 5 Fulah 6 Berber, Gallas, Somali

hamlet: 4 dorp 5 aldea(Sp.), casal, hamel, moray, vicus(L.) 6 bustee, casale(It.), thorpe 7 clachan(Sc.), village 10 settlement

Hamlet: *beloved:* 7 Ophelia

  castle: 8 Elsinore

  character: 7 Laertes, Ophelia 8 Gertrude, Polonius

  country: 7 Denmark

  friend: 7 Horatio

hammer: bit, tup 4 beat, claw, jack, maul, mell, reel, tack, tamp 5 gavel 6 batter, beetle, mallet, martel, pummel, sledge, strike, swinge 7 belabor 8 malleate 11 door-knocker

  blacksmith's: 6 fuller, oliver

  bricklayer's: 6 scutch

  face: 4 trip

  firearm: 4 cock 7 doghead

  half-round: 6 fuller

  head: 4 peen, poll

  medical: 6 plexor 7 plessor

  stone: 5 kevel, spall

hammerhead: 5 shark

hammock: 7 machila

hamper: bin, ped 4 beat, clog, curb, load, slow 5 block, cramp, crate, rusky(Sc.), seron(Sp.) 6 basket, burden, fetter, halter, hinder, hopple, impede, panier 7 buffalo, confine, hanaper, manacle, pannier, perplex, shackle, trammel 8 encumber, entangle, obstruct, restrain, restrict 9 container, embarrass

hamstring: hox 4 hock, lame 5 hough 7 cripple, disable

hamulus: 4 hook

Hananiah: *father:* 4 Azur

  son: 8 Zedekiah

hanaper: 6 basket, hamper 10 receptacle

hance: 4 arch, fall 5 raise 6 lintel

hand: fin, paw, pud 4 claw, give, mano, mitt, neif, pass 5 claut (Sc.), grasp, nieve, power, share 6 clunch, daddle, famble, pledge, worker 7 ability, flipper, forepaw, laborer, proffer, workman 8 applause, bestowal, transmit 9 betrothal, craftsman, indicator, operative, signature 11 handwriting

  back: 10 opisthenar

  clenched: 4 fist

  comb. form: 4 manu 5 chiro

  covering: 4 mitt, muff 5 glove 6 cestus(L.) 7 gantlet 8 gauntlet

  deformity: 11 talipomanus

hollow: 6 gowpen, gowpin
palm: 6 thenar
part: 4 palm 5 thumb 7 fingers
pert. to: 6 manual
without: 7 amanous
hand-me-down: 5 cheap 9 ready-made 10 secondhand
hand mjll: 5 quern 7 grinder
hand out: 10 administer, distribute
hand over: 4 ante, cede 5 yield
hand-picked: 5 elite 8 selected
handbag: bag 4 etui, grip 5 cabas, etwee, purse 6 valise 7 satchel 8 gripsack, pochette, reticule
handball: *game:* 6 pelota 7 jai alai
point: ace
handbarrow: 4 bier
handbill: 5 libel 6 dodger 13 advertisement
handbook: 6 manual 9 guidebook 11 enchiridion
handbreath: 4 span 6 spread
handcar: 6 gocart 7 go-devil
handcloth: 5 towel 6 napkin 12 handkerchief
handcuff: 4 cuff, iron 5 darby 6 nipper 7 manacle 8 bracelet, handbolt, handlock
Handel: *composition:* 5 Largo
opera: 4 Nero 6 Xerxes
oratorio: 7 Messiah
handfast: 4 bind, grip 5 bound, grasp 7 betroth, manacle 11 closefisted
handful: 4 grip, wisp 5 claut, gripe 6 gowpen, gowpin, yaffle 7 maniple 8 quantity
handicap: bar, law 4 lame, lisp 6 burden, hinder, impede 7 stammer, stutter 8 encumber 9 advantage, embarrass 12 disadvantage
handicapper: 5 rater
handicraft goddess: 7 Minerva
handicraftsman: 7 artisan, workman 9 craftsman
handiwork: tat 7 sampler 10 embroidery
handjar: 5 knife 6 dagger 7 khanjar
handkerchief: 5 clout, fogle 6 madras 7 bandana, belcher, sneezer 9 barcelona, handcloth, muckender, neckcloth 11 neckerchief
handle: ear, fan, lug, nob, paw, ply, use 4 ansa, bail, bool, deal, feel, gaum, grip, haft, hank, hilt, knob 5 gripe, grope, helve, lever, shaft, swipe, touch, treat, wield 6 behave, direct, finger, manage 7 control 8 handgrip 10 manipulate
ancient: 4 ansa
bucket: 4 bail, bale
cup: ear
equipped with: 6 ansate
pail: 4 bail
printing press: 6 rounce

pump: 5 brake
scythe: 5 snath, snead, thole 6 snathe
sword: 4 haft, hilt
whip: 4 crop
handled: 5 dealt 6 ansate
handling: use 7 control 9 treatment 10 management
handlock: 8 handcuff
handout: aid 4 alms, dole, food, gift, meal, mete 5 snack 7 charity
handreading: 9 palmistry
hands: men 4 crew 8 pointers
hands off: 4 tabu 5 taboo
hand's spread: 4 span
handsel, hansel: 4 gift, luck, omen 5 money, token 6 augury
handsome: 4 braw(Sc.), fair, fine, pert 5 ample, belle, bonny, handy, ready 6 bonnie, clever, comely, goodly, heppen, limber 7 elegant, gallant, liberal 8 becoming, budgeree, generous, gracious, suitable 9 beautiful, dexterous 10 convenient, manageable 11 appropriate 12 considerable
handspring: 9 cartwheel
handstone: 4 mano
handwriting: 4 fist, hand 5 ronde 6 script 10 griffonage, manuscript 11 chirography
on the wall: 4 mene 6 tekel 8 upharsin
study of: 10 graphology
handy: 4 deft, near 5 adept, ready 6 adroit, clever, heppen 8 adjacent, dextrous, handsome, skillful 9 available, dexterous, versatile 10 accessible, convenient
Handy Andy's catch 5 Oonah
handyman: 5 fixer 8 repairer
hang: lop, sag 4 kilt, loll, pend, rest 5 drape, droop, hinge, knack, slope, swing 6 append, dangle, depend, gibbet, talter 7 crucify, execute, stretch, suspend 9 declivity 11 inclination
around: 4 loaf 6 loiter
back: 6 falter 8 hesitate
down: 6 dangle 7 suspend
onto: 5 cling
hang fire: 4 pend 8 hesitate
hangar: 4 shed 6 garage, stable 7 shelter 9 penthouse
hangdog: 4 base 6 shifty 7 ashamed, fawning, furtive 8 cringing, sneaking 9 groveling
hanger-on: bur 5 toady 6 hangby, heeler 7 adjunct, dangler, slinger 8 bottomer, loiterer, onsetter, parasite 9 appendage, dependent, sycophant 10 blackguard
hanging: 5 arras, drape 6 celure, tippet 7 pendent, pensile, valance 8 inclined 9 declivity, execution, suspended 11 inclination
Hanging Gardens site: 7 Babylon

hangman: 6 hangie 9 Jack Ketch 11 executioner

hangnail: 6 agnail 10 backfriend

hangout: 5 joint 10 rendezvous

hangover: 8 residuum 11 aftereffect

hank: 4 coil, loop 5 skein 6 bundle, handle 7 control 9 influence

hanker: 4 long 5 crave, yearn 6 desire

hankle: 5 twist 6 fasten 8 entangle

Hannay: *creator:* 6 Buchan
special number: 10 thirty-nine

Hannibal: *father:* 8 Hamilcar
place of victory: 6 Cannae

Hanse merchant: 7 hansard

hansom: cab

hap: lot 4 case, luck, wrap 5 check, seize 6 befall, chance, clothe, snatch 7 fortune, venture 8 covering 9 happening 10 occurrence, prosperity

haphazard: 6 casual, chance, random 8 careless 10 accidental

hapless: 4 poor 7 unlucky 11 unfortunate

happen: 4 come, fall, fare 5 evene, occur 6 arrive, befall, betide, chance, mayhap 7 perhaps, stumble 9 eventuate, transpire

happen again: 5 recur

happening: hap 4 case, fact 5 event 6 chance, faring 7 episode 8 incident, occasion 10 occurrence

happily: 5 fitly, haply 6 gladly 7 luckily 10 gracefully 11 contentedly, fortunately, opportunely 12 felicitously, peradventure, prosperously, successfully 13 appropriately

happiness: joy 4 sele(Sc.), weal 5 bliss, mirth 6 felice 7 delight, ecstasy, felicia, rapture 8 felicity, gladness, hilarity 9 beatitude, enjoyment, eudaemony, transport, well-being 10 exaltation, prosperity 11 blessedness
god: 5 Ebisu
incapacity for: 9 anhedonia

happy: apt, gay 4 cosh, glad, gleg 5 blest, lucky, merry, ready, seely, sonsy, sunny 6 elated, sonsie 7 blessed, content, fitting, halcyon, radiant 8 carefree, frohlich, gracious, mirthful 9 contented, fortunate 10 felicitous, propitious, prosperous

happy-go-lucky: 9 easygoing

happy hunting ground: 6 heaven 8 paradise

Haran: *brother:* 7 Abraham
daughter: 6 Milcah
father: 5 Terah
son: Lot

harangue: nag 4 rave 5 orate, spiel 6 screed, sermon, speech, tirade 7 address, declaim, oration 8 diatribe, perorate 10 concionate

harass: fag, hag, nag, try, vex 4 bait, fret, gall, hake, hale, haze, jade, rack, raid, tire 5 annoy, beset, bully, chafe, chase, grind, gripe, harry, herry(Sc.), hurry, pique, tease, weary, worry 6 badger, bother, bucket, cumber, hatter, heckle, impede, molest, obsess, pester, plague, pother, scrape 7 afflict, affront, agitate, disturb, exhaust, fatigue, hagride, oppress, perplex, provoke, scourge, torment, trouble 8 distract, distress, irritate 9 exagitate, persecute, tantalize

harbinger: 4 camp, host 5 usher 6 herald 7 presage, shelter 8 fourrier, harbinge, harborer 9 messenger, precursor 10 forerunner
spring: 5 robin 6 crocus

harbor, harbour: inn 4 hold, port 5 haven 6 billet, breach, bunder, covert, foster, refuge 7 fairway, lodging, quarter, retreat, seaport, shelter 9 harborage
entrance: 4 boca
harbor master: 7 havener

harborage, harbourage: 6 harbor 7 shelter

hard: fit 4 acid, cold, dear, dere, dure, firm, iron, mean, oaky, sour 5 champ, close, cruel, hardy, harsh, horny, rigid, rocky, rough, solid, stern, stiff, stony 6 coarse, frozen, knotty, marble, robust, severe, steely, strict, strong 7 adamant, arduous, austere, callous, compact, earnest, intense, onerous, scleral 8 diligent, granitic, grasping, hardened, obdurate, renitent, rigorous, scleroid, toilsome 9 difficult, energetic, fatiguing, inclement, intricate, laborious, petrified, repelling, reprobate, resistant, strenuous, stringent, unfeeling, wearisome 10 inflexible, oppressive, perplexing, persistent, relentless, ungraceful, unyielding 11 complicated, distressing, impregnable, persevering, unremitting 12 disreputable, extortionate, impenetrable, incorrigible, unalleviated 13 unsympathetic
comb. form: dys

hard coal: 10 anthracite

hard corn: rye 5 wheat

hard drawn: 4 taut 5 tense

hard-shell: 9 confirmed, extremist

hard times: 9 recession 10 depression

harden: gel, set 4 bake, cake, salt, sear 5 beath, enure, inure, steel 6 endure, freeze, ossify, temper 7 congeal, petrify, stiffen, thicken, toughen 8 concrete, condense, indurate, solidify 11 acclimatize

hardened: 4 hard 5 caked 6 frozen, gelled, inured 7 callous, steeled 8 obdurate 9 abandoned, reprobate 10 impenitent, impervious inveterate, solidified 12 impenetrable

hardhead: 4 fish 5 whale 7 ribwort 8 knap-weed, mackerel, menhaden 9 blockhead 10 niggerhead

hardheaded: 4 keen 6 shrewd 7 willful 8 stubborn 9 sagacious 10 longheaded 11 sharp-witted

hardhearted: 4 mean 5 cruel, stern 7 callous 8 obdurate, pitiless 9 unfeeling 13 marblehearted, unsympathetic

hardihood: 5 pluck, vigor 7 bravery, courage 8 audacity, boldness, temerity 9 hardiness, impudence, stoutness 10 confidence, effrontery, imprudence, resolution, robustness 11 intrepidity 13 audaciousness

hardly: 6 barely 7 faintly, hardily, harshly, roughly 8 forcibly, scarcely, severely, unfairly 11 unfavorably

hardness: 6 durity 8 severity, solidity 9 substance
measuring device: 9 durometer

hardpan: pan 7 bedrock 8 ortstein

hardship: 5 assay, rigor, trial 6 injury 7 penalty 8 asperity, hardness 9 endurance, grievance, injustice, privation 10 affliction

hardtack: 7 biscuit, galette(F.), pantile

hardwood: ash, oak 4 pelu, teak 5 maple 6 walnut 7 hickory 8 mahogany
genus: 7 quercus

hardy: 4 bold, firm, hard, rash, wiry 5 brave, lusty, manly, stout, tough 6 chisel, daring, robust, rugged, strong, sturdy 7 compact, spart n 8 galliard, intrepid, resolute, stubborn, vigorous 9 audacious, confident 10 courageous

Hardy heroine: 4 Tess

hare: dol 4 bawd(Sc.), pika 5 harry, lepus, tease, worry 6 malkin, rabbit 7 leporid, leveret 8 frighten, leporide
comb. form: lag 4 lago
female: doe
genus of: 5 lepus
male: 4 buck
pert. to: 8 leporine
tail: 4 scut
track: 4 file, slot
young: 7 leveret

harem: oda 4 odah 5 serai 6 serail, zenana 8 seraglio
male attendant: 6 eunuch
room: oda
slave: 9 odalisque

haricot: 4 stew 6 ragout

harish: 7 foolish

hark: 4 hear, heed hist 6 harken, listen 7 hearken, whisper

harl: 4 barb, drag, knot 5 leash, snarl 6 scrape, tangle 7 confuse, plaster, scraper 8 entangle 9 confusion

harlequin: 5 clown 7 buffoon 9 fantastic 11 masquerader

harlot: low, pug 4 base, doxy, lewd, slut 5 churl, knave, quean, rogue, whore 6 menial, rascal, wanton 7 buffoon, juggler 8 strumpet, vagabond 10 fricatrice, prostitute

harm: hob, ill 4 bale, bane, evil, hurt, pain, teen 5 abuse, annoy, grief, shend, wound, wrong 6 damage, damnum, injure, injury, scathe, sorrow 7 disease, impeach 8 disserve, endamage, nuisance 10 disservice, misfortune, wickedness 11 impeachment

harmful: bad 4 evil 5 nasty 6 nocent 7 baneful, hurtful, malefic, noisome, noxious 8 damaging, sinister 9 injurious 10 pernicious 11 contrarious, deleterious, detrimental, mischievous

harmless: 4 safe 6 dovish 9 innocuous 11 inoffensive

Harmonia: *father:* 4 Ares
husband: 6 Cadmus
mother: 9 Aphrodite

harmonious: 6 cosmic, dulcet 7 cordial, musical, spheral, tuneful 8 amicable, peaceful 9 accordant, agreeable, congruous, consonant, harmonial, melodious, peaceable 10 compatible, concentive, concordant 11 harmoniacal, symmetrical 12 proportional

harmonize: go; gee, key 4 jibe, tone, tune 5 adapt, agree, blend, chime, hitch, rhyme 6 accord, adjust, attune, cotton 7 concent, concord, consist, consort 9 reconcile 10 correspond, sympathize

harmony: 4 tune 5 amity, music, peace 6 cosmos, melody 7 concert, concord, rapport 9 agreement 10 accordance, atmosphere, conformity, congruence, consonance 11 cooperation
bring into: 6 attune
lack: 7 discord

harness: 4 gear 5 heald 6 fettle, tackle 7 enclose, hitch-up 9 equipment, trappings
maker: 7 knacker, lorimer
part: bit, tug 4 hame, rein 5 blind, trace 6 billet, bridle, collar, saddle, terret 7 crouper 9 breeching, circingle, martingal, ridgeband, surcingle 10 breastband, crownpiece, martingale

harp: 4 arpa, koto, lyre 5 nanga 6 trigon 8 bedlamer 11 clairschach

harper: 4 coin 8 minstrel, musician

harpoon: 5 spear 7 javelin

harpsichord: 6 spinet 8 clavecin, virginal 12 clavicembalo

harpy: 5 Aello 7 Celaeno, Ocypete, Podarge 11 extortioner

harquebus: 6 hagbut 7 hackbut

harquebusier: 7 soldier 10 arcabucero

harridan: hag 5 crone, horse, vixen, woman 8 strumpet

harrier: dog 4 hawk

harrow: vex 4 disk, drag 5 brake, harry, wound 6 spader 7 oppress, torment 8 distress, lacerate 9 cultivate 10 cultivator

harrowed: 7 haggard

harry: rob, vex 4 sack 5 annoy, hound, hurry, spoil, steal, worry 6 harass, harrow, hector, plague, ravage 7 agitate, despoil, pillage, plunder, torment 9 persecute

harsh: raw 4 grim, hard, hask 5 acerb, acrid, asper, brute, crude, cruel, grill, gruff, raspy, rough, sharp, stern, stiff 6 bitter, brazen, coarse, severe, strict, sullen, unkind 7 austere, braying, drastic, grating, rasping, raucous 8 acerbate, catonian, clashing, croaking, district, guttural, jangling, rigorous, strident, ungentle 9 dissonant, inclement, insensate, repellent, squawking, truculent, unfeeling 10 astringent, discordant, oppressive, relentless 11 acrimonious, disagreeing 12 disagreeable

harshness: 5 rigor 6 duress 7 crudity, raucity 8 acerbity, acrimony, asperity, severity

hart: roe 4 deer, hert, stag 5 spade

hartebeest: 4 asse, tora 5 caama, kaama 6 lecama 8 antelope

hartshorn: 7 ammonia

harum-scarum: 4 rash, wild 7 flighty 8 reckless 11 thoughtless 13 irresponsible

Harun-Al-Rashid's wife: 7 Zobeide

haruspex: 7 diviner 10 soothsayer 14 prognosticator

Harvard book prize: 5 detur

harvest: 4 bind, crop, reap 6 foison, gather 8 ingather
  festival: 6 Opalia
  god: 5 Ceres 6 Cronus
  goddess: Ops 5 Carpo

harvest home: 4 kern, kirn(Sc.)

harvester: 8 spalpeen

has: See **have**

hash: 4 chop 5 mince 6 jumble 7 mixture 11 gallimaufry, olla podrida

hashish: 4 hemp 5 bhang 8 cannabis

hashmark: 6 stripe

hask: dry 4 cold 5 harsh 6 coarse

hasp: 4 gird 5 catch, clasp 7 confine 8 fastener

hassle: 4 talk 6 hustle 7 quarrel, wrestle 8 argument, squabble 9 commotion 10 discussion

hassock: 4 boss, pess 5 grass, sedge 6 buffet 7 cushion, tussock 8 footrest 9 footstool

haste: hie 4 rush 5 hurry, speed 6 bustle, flurry 7 urgency 8 dispatch, rapidity 9 quickness, swiftness 10 expedition, nimbleness 11 festination, impetuosity 12 precipitance 13 precipitation

hasten: hie, run 4 pell, race, rush, trot 5 crowd, drive, fleet, hurry, speed 6 expede, gallop, scurry 7 advance, scamper 8 dispatch, expedite 9 festinate 10 accelerate 11 precipitate

hastily: 6 nimbly 8 speedily 11 impatiently 13 precipitately

hasty: 4 fast, rash 5 brash, fleet, quick, swift 6 abrupt, daring, nimshi, speedy, sudden 7 cursory, forward, hurried 8 headlong, pell-mell, succinct 9 hotheaded, hurrisome, impatient, impetuous 10 indiscreet 11 expeditious, precipitate, precipitous

hasty pudding: 4 mush 6 supawn 9 stir-about

hat: cap, dip, fez, lid, nab, tam 4 baku, felt, topi 5 beany, benjy, benny, beret, boxer, cordy, derby, dicer, kelly, terai, topee, toque 6 Alpine, beaver, boater, bonnet, bowler, castor, claque, cloche, fedora, panama, shovel, turban 7 biretta, caubeen, chapeau, Homburg, petasus, salacot, shallow 8 capeline, copatain, headgear, sombrero 9 Dunstable, stovepipe, wide-awake 10 belltopper 11 mortarboard
  covering: 8 havelock
  crown: 4 poll
  ecclesiastic: 7 biretta
  fiber: 4 felt, sola 5 straw
  fur used in: 4 mink 5 coney 6 beaver, ermine 8 coonskin
  ladies: 5 caddy, cooie 6 Breton, caddie, slouch 7 leghorn 8 duckbill 9 harlequin 12 Gainsborough
  medieval: 6 abacot 7 bycoket
  military: 5 shako
  oilskin: 5 squam 9 sou'wester
  opera: 5 crush, gibus 6 claque, topper
  palm-leaf: 7 salacot
  pert. to: 9 castorial
  pith: 4 topi 5 topee
  Quaker: 9 broadbrim
  silk: lum(Sc.) 4 tile 5 opera 6 topper 7 catskin 8 gossamer
  soft: 6 fedora
  stovepipe: 8 caroline
  straw: 6 boater
  three-cornered: 7 tricorn
  ventilated: 5 terai

hatch: 4 brew, door, gate, vent 5 breed, cleck, clock, cover 6 clutch, wicket 7 concoct 8 contrive, hatchway 9 floodgate
  covering: 4 tarp

hatchel: 5 tease, worry 7 torment

hatchet: ax; adz, axe 4 adze, mogo 8 tomahawk

hatchet man: 4 tool 6 stooge 8 henchman

hatching: 6 cletch 8 breeding

hatchway: 7 scuttle

hate: 4 teen 5 abhor 6 detest, loathe, rancor, revile 7 contemn, despise 8 aversion 9 abominate, malignity 11 detestation

hateful: 4 foul 5 black 6 odious 7 heinous 8 flagrant 9 abhorrent, invidious, loathsome, malignant, obnoxious, offensive, revolting 10 abominable, detestable, disgusting, malevolent 11 distasteful 12 disagreeable

hatful: 4 lots, many, much 8 quantity

hatred: 5 odium 6 enmity, rancor 8 aversion 9 animosity, hostility, malignity 10 abhorrence, repugnance 11 abomination, detestation, malevolence

of argument: 8 misology

of children: 9 misopedia 10 misopaedia

of mankind: 11 misanthropy

of marriage: 8 misogamy

of strangers: 10 xenophobia

hatter: 5 worry 6 batter, bruise, harass 7 exhaust 8 milliner

haught: 4 high 5 noble 7 exalted, haughty

haughtiness: 4 airs 5 pride 6 morgue 7 hauteur 9 arrogance, insolence

haughty: 4 airy, bold, high 5 dorty, lofty, noble, proud 6 haught, snooty 7 exalted, fatuous, hontish, paughty, stately 8 arrogant, cavalier, glorious, scornful 9 imperious, masterful 10 disdainful, fastidious 11 domineering, magisterial, overbearing 12 contemptuous, presumptuous, supercilious

haul: lug, tow, tug 4 cart, drag, draw, hurl, pull, tote 5 bouse, catch, heave, trice 8 cordelle 9 transport

haulage: 6 towage 7 cartage, drayage

hauler: 7 tractor

haulm: 4 culm, stem 5 stems 6 stalks

haunch: hip 4 huck 5 hance 12 hindquarters

haunt: den 4 dive, hawf, lair, nest 5 ghost, habit, hawff, skill 6 custom, infest, obsess, resort, spirit 7 terrify 8 frequent, practice 9 companion 10 fellowship

haunted: 6 filled, spooky 8 infested

haunty: 6 unruly 8 restless

hautboy, hautbois: 4 oboe 10 strawberry

hauteur: 5 pride 9 arrogance 11 haughtiness

Havana suburb: 5 Regia

have: hae(Sc.), own 4 hold 5 enjoy 6 retain 7 contain, possess 10 experience

on: 4 wear

to do with: 4 deal

haven: bay, lee 4 hope, port 5 hotel, inlet 6 asylum, harbor, recess, refuge 7 shelter 9 sanctuary

haver: oat 6 babble, holder 7 chatter, maunder, twaddle 8 nonsense 9 possessor

haversack: bag

havior, haviour: 8 behavior, demeanor

havoc: hob 4 ruin 5 waste 7 destroy 9 devastate 10 desolation 11 destruction, devastation

haw: gee 4 sloe, yard 5 fence, hedge 8 hawthorn 9 enclosure

Hawaii: *ballad:* 4 mele

basket: ie

beverage: 4 kava 8 kava-kava

bird: io, oo; ioa, iwa 4 iiwi, koae, mamo, omao, ooaa 6 palila 8 drepanis

breechcloth: 4 malo

bush: See *shrub* below

canoe: 5 waapa

channel: 4 Auau

chant: 4 mele

city: 4 Hilo 7 Wailuku 8 Honolulu(c.)

cloak: 4 mamo 6 ahuula

cloth: 4 kapa, tapa 5 tappa

cookout: 4 luau

cord: aea

crater: 7 Kilauea

dance: 4 hula

discoverer: 4 Cook

district: 4 Puna, Kona

farewell, hello: 5 aloha

feast: 4 luau 7 ahaaina

fern: 4 heii 5 ekaha, uluhi 6 iwaiwa 7 amaumau

fiber: 4 pulu

fish: ahi 4 ulua 5 akule

fish poison: 4 hola 6 auhuhu

flower: 5 ilima

food: poi 4 kalo, taro

game: hei

garland: lei

garment: 6 holoku, muumuu 7 holomuu

god: 4 Kane 5 Wakea

goddess: 4 Pele

goose: 4 nene

grass: 6 emoloa

greeting: 5 aloha

harbor: 5 Pearl

hawk: io

herb: ape, pia 4 hola 5 awiwi 6 auhuhu

instrument: uke 7 ukalele, ukelele, ukulele

island: 4 Maui, Oahu 5 Kauai, Lanai 6 Hawaii, Niihau 7 Molokai 9 Kahoolawe

lava: aa 8 pahoehoe

loincloth: 4 malo, maro

lomilomi: rub 7 massage, shampoo

love: 5 aloha

massage: 8 lomilomi

morning glory: 5 koali
mountain: Kea 5 Mauna 7 Waianae 8 Mauna Loa
musical instrument: uke 7 ukulele
native: 6 Kanaka
octopus: hee
pantheon: 4 Kane
parrot fish: 5 lauia
partnership: hui
pepper: ava
pine: ie
pit for baking: imu
plant: pia 4 hala, taro 5 olona 8 pandanus
poem: 4 mele
porch: 5 lanai
precipice: 4 pali
priest: 6 Kahuna
raven: 5 alala
root: 4 taro
root paste: poi
seaweed: 4 limu
shaman: 6 Kahuna
shrub: 4 akia 5 akala, olona 6 aupaka
song: 4 mele
staple: poi 4 taro
starch plant: pia
starch root: pia 4 taro
swordfish: au
temple: 5 heiau
thrush: 4 amao 6 olomao
tree: koa 4 aulu, ohia 5 aalii, alani 7 amau-mau, walahee 8 mokihana
valley: 5 Manoa
vine: 5 kaiwi 9 awikiwiki
volcano: 7 Kilauea 8 Mauna Kea, Mauna Loa
white man: 5 haole
wind: 4 kona
windstorm: 4 kona
woman: 5 haole
wreath: lei
yam: hoi
hawfinch: 8 grosbeak
hawk: io; cry, gos 4 eyas, kite, nyas, sell, vend 5 astur, cadge, catch, reach, retch 6 elanet, falcon, formal, formel, higgle, musket, osprey, peddle, rifler, tarcel, tarsel, tercel 7 buzzard, canvass, colport, harrier, kestrel, puttock, sparrow, vulture 8 brancher, caracara 9 accipiter 11 mortarboard
cage: mew
male: 6 tercel 7 tiercel
leash: 4 jess, lune
nest: 5 aerie
nestling: 4 eyas
pinion feather: 6 sarcel
hawk-headed deity: Ra
hawkbit: 9 dandelion

hawker: 6 badger, cadger, coster, duffer 7 chapman, mercury, packman, peddler 8 falconer, huckster 9 colporter 10 colporteur 12 costermonger
Hawkeye State: 4 Iowa
hawklike: 11 accipitrine
hawser: 4 line, rope
block: 4 bitt
post: 4 bitt 7 bollard
hawthorn: haw, may 5 aglet 6 aiglet 8 cockspur, maybloom, quickset
hay: bed, net 4 park 5 chaff, fence, grass, hedge 9 provender
bundle: mow 4 bale, rick, wisp 5 gavel, stack, truss 7 hayrick
kind of: 6 clover 7 alfalfa, timothy
line: 5 swath 7 windrow
second cutting: 5 rowen
spreader: 6 tedder
storage: mow 4 loft
haycock: 4 coil
hayfork: 4 evil 5 pikel
hayloft: mow 9 hay-tallat
hayseed: 5 yokel 6 farmer, rustic 10 countryman
hazard: die, lay, lot 4 risk 5 peril, stake 6 chance, danger, gamble 7 imperil, venture 8 accident, casualty, endanger, jeopardy 9 adventure 10 jeopardize
hazardous: 5 risky 6 chance, chancy, queasy, unsafe 8 insecure, perilous 9 dangerous, uncertain 10 fortuitous, jeopardous, precarious 11 adventurous
haze: fog 4 beat, film, mist 5 cloud, devil, scold, vapor 6 harass, vapour 7 drizzle 8 frighten
hazel: 8 noisette 11 avellaneous
hazelnut: nit 6 cobnut
Hazor king: 5 Jabin
hazy: dim 5 filmy, foggy, misty, smoky, thick, vague 7 nebular, obscure, unclear 8 nebulous 9 uncertain 10 indistinct
head: aim, cop, mir, nab, nob 4 bean, cape, coco, conk, crop, lead, pate, poll, tete(F.), turn 5 caput(L.), chief, chump, first, front, start, tibby 6 cabeza, cobbra, direct, garret, leader, manage, noggin, noodle, sconce, source, spring 7 captain, coconut, costrel, cranium, crumpet, leading, prelate 8 director, foremost, fountain, headland, initiate 9 intercept, president, principal 10 caper-nutie, headmaster, promontory 11 caper-noitie
army camp: 10 commandant
back part: 7 occiput
bald: 9 pilgarlic
boar: 4 hure
bone: 8 parietal

covering: cap, hat, tam **4** caul, hair, hood **5** beret, snood, toque

crown: **6** cantle

muscle: **11** occipitalis

ornament: hat, wig **4** hair, veil **5** tiara **7** coronet

part: **4** pate **5** scalp **6** earlap, temple **7** cranium

pert. to: **8** cephalic

shaven: **7** tonsure

shrunken: **7** tsantsa

side of: **4** lore **5** lorum **6** temple

top: **4** pate **5** scalp **7** coxcomb

head cook: 4 chef

head covering (see also **cap, hat**): cap, fez, hat, tam, wig **4** barb, coif, hair, hood **5** beret, scalp, snood **6** bonnet, coiffe, peruke, toupee **7** biretta, chapeau, periwig **8** berretta, maharmah, sombrero **9** rigolette **10** fascinator

head-shaped: 8 capitate

head to foot: 7 cap-a-pie

headache: 6 megrim **8** headwork, migraine **10** cephalalgia

headband: 5 miter, mitre, vitta **6** diadem, fillet, infula **7** circlet, coronet **8** frontlet **9** sphendone

headdress: 4 caul, coif, pouf **5** ampyx, crown, cupee, miter, mitre, tiara, toque **6** almuce, bonnet, coiffe, faille, hennin, mobcap, pinner, turban **7** bandore, bycoket, coronet, topknot **8** biliment, binnogue, capriole, coiffure, stephane, tressure **9** rigolette

medieval: **6** abacot

military: **5** busby, shako **6** casque

sacerdotal: **5** miter **7** biretta

sacred: **6** uraeus

headgear: See **headdress**

headily: 6 rashly **9** violently

heading: 5 title, topic **7** caption **8** headline

topical: **5** trope

headland: ras **4** bill, cape, head, nase, naze, ness, peak **5** Morro, ridge, strip **8** foreland **10** promontory

headless: 4 rash **6** stupid **8** beheaded **10** acephalous

headline: 7 caption, feature, heading

headliner: 4 star **11** personality

headlong: 4 rash **5** hasty, steep **6** abrupt, sudden **8** reckless **9** desperate, headfirst, impetuous, impulsive **11** precipitate, precipitous

headman: 4 boss **5** chief **6** ataman, cabeza, hetman **7** capitan, captain, foreman **8** alderman, caboceer, capitano **11** executioner

headmaster: 4 head **9** principal **11** gymnasiarch

headpiece: See **headdress**

headquarters: 5 yamen **6** center **8** exchange, precinct

headstrong: 4 rash **5** cobby **6** unruly **7** hotspur, violent **8** stubborn **9** obstinate **10** bullheaded, forthright, hotspurred **11** intractable **12** contumacious, ungovernable

heady: 4 rash **7** huffcap, violent, willful **9** impetuous **11** precipitate **12** intoxicating

heal: 4 cure, hale, knit, mend, sain **5** amend **6** remedy, repair **7** restore **10** recuperate

heal-all: 4 balm **7** allheal, figwort, panacea

healer: asa **4** balm **6** doctor **9** naprapath **12** practitioner

healing: 5 balmy **8** covering, curative, sanative

agent: **6** balsam

goddess: Eir

pert. to: **7** medical **9** medicinal

science: **8** medicine **9** iatrology, latrology

health: 4 hale, hail **5** sante(F.), toast **7** slainte **8** eucrasia **11** disposition

goddess: **7** Minerva

poor: **4** sick **5** dawny

resort: spa

healthy: fit **4** hale, sane, well **5** bonny, hoddy **6** bonnie, hearty, robust **8** salutary, vigorous **9** wholesome **10** healthsome, salubrious

combining form: **4** sani

heap: ahu, cob, cop, mow **4** balk, bing, bulk, deck, dess(Sc.), hill, lump, mass, pile, pyre, raft, rick, ruck **5** amass, cairn, clump, crowd, spire, stack **6** burrow, hipple, jumble, plenty, throng **7** bourock, cumulus, hurrock **9** congeries, multitude **10** accumulate, collection, congestion, cumulation

hear: ear, see **4** feel, hark, heed, obey **6** attend, harken, listen **7** hearken **8** perceive **10** adjudicate

hear ye: 4 oyes, oyez

hearer: 7 audient, auditor **8** disciple, listener

hearing: ear **5** sound, trial **6** assize, report **7** earshot, lecture **8** audience, audition, scolding **9** attention, audiencia, interview, knowledge **10** attendance

court: **4** oyer

judicial: **5** trial **7** retrial

pert. to: **8** acoustic

hearken, harken: 4 hark, hear, heed, wait **6** attend, listen **7** inquire, whisper **9** eavesdrop

hearsay: 4 fame **5** rumor **6** report

hearse: 4 bier, bury, tomb **5** dirge, grave **6** coffin **8** monument, threnody

heart: ab; cor 4 core, gist, hati, love 5 cheer
6 center, centre, depths, middle, ticker 7
courage, emotion, essence, feeling 9 affection
cavity: 6 atrium
chamber: 7 auricle 9 ventricle
contraction: 7 systole
covering: 11 pericardium
expansion: 8 diastole
record: 17 electrocardiogram
stimulant: 8 thialdin 9 digitalis, thialdine
10 adrenaline, epinephrin 11 epinephrine
heart-shaped: 7 cordate
heartache: 4 pang 5 grief 6 sorrow
heartbeat: 5 pulse, throb 7 systole 9 pulsation
heartbreak: 5 grief 6 sorrow 7 tragedy
heartbroken: 12 inconsolable 13 broken-
hearted, grief-stricken
heartburn: 4 envy 6 enmity 7 pyrosis 8 jealousy 10 cardialgia, discontent, heartscald,
heartscaud
hearten: 5 cheer 6 spirit 7 refresh 8 embolden, inspirit, reassure 9 encourage
heartfelt: 4 dear, deep, real, true 7 earnest,
genuine, sincere
hearth: 5 cupel, focus, fogon, foyer 8 bloomery, fireside
god: 6 Hestia
line: 6 fettle
heartily: 6 dearly, freely, warmly 8 actively,
strongly 9 cordially, earnestly, profusely,
sincerely, zealously, zestfully 10 abundantly, completely, vigorously 14 whole-
heartedly
heartiness: 4 soul 8 goodwill, strength 9
soundness 10 cordiality
heartless: 5 cruel 8 hopeless, listless 9 merciless, unfeeling 10 despairing, despondent, spiritless 13 unsympathetic
heartsease, heartease: 5 pansy, peace 12
tranquillity
heartthrob: 4 dunt, love
heartwood: 4 dura 7 duramen
hearty: 4 firm, hale, real, rich, warm, well
5 cobby, heavy, sound 6 active, cheery, devout, robust, sailor, stanch 7 comrade,
cordial, earnest, fertile, healthy, sincere,
staunch 8 abundant, cheerful, heartful,
vigorous 9 energetic, unfeigned, wholesome 10 nourishing 11 substantial, warmhearted
heat: ire 4 fire, mull, rage, warm 5 ardor,
cauma, chafe, fever, roast, tepor 6 anneal,
choler, degree, warmth 7 ferment, inflame, passion 8 fervency 9 agitation, animation, chauffage, commotion, vehemence 10 excitement 11 temperature 12
exasperation 14 passionateness

comb. form: 5 therm 6 calori, thermo
measure: 5 therm 6 calory, therme 7 calorie
10 centigrade, fahrenheit 11 calorimeter,
pyronometer
pert. to: 7 thermic
quantity: 6 degree 11 temperature
unit of: 5 therm 7 calorie
white: 13 incandescence
heated: 7 excited 8 vehement 10 phlogistic
heater: 4 etna, oven 5 stove 6 boiler 7 chof-
fer(Sc.), furnace 8 radiator
heath: 4 ling, moor 5 erica, plain
scrub: 9 chaparral
tree: 5 briar, brier
heathen: 5 pagan 6 ethnic, paynim 11 irreligious
deity: 4 idol
non-Jewish: 6 ethnic
non-Muslim: 7 infidel
heather: 4 grig, ling 5 erica
family: 9 ericaceae
heatless: 8 athermic
heautarit: 7 mercury 11 quicksilver
heave: gag 4 cast, haul, heft, hurl, lift, pant,
pull, push, quap, toss 5 hoist, pitch, raise,
scend, throw 7 elevate, estuate 8 struggle
heaven: sky 5 dyaus, ether, glory 6 Him-
mel(G.), welkin, zodiac 7 Elysium, Nirvana, Valhall, Vahalla 8 devaloka, empyrean, paradise 9 firmament
combining form: 5 urano
pert. to: 6 uranic 9 celestial
queen: 7 Astarte
heavenly: 6 divine 7 angelic, olympic, sublime, uranian 8 ethereal, supernal 9 angelical, celestial, celestine
heavenly being: 5 angel 6 seraph
heavenly belt: way 6 galaxy, nebula, zodiac
heavenly body: sun 4 luna, moon, star 5
comet 6 planet 8 luminary
heavenly city: 4 Sion, Zion
heavenly twins: 6 Castor, Gemini, Pollux
heaviness: 5 gloom 6 weight 7 gravity, sadness 9 thickness 10 oppression 12 sluggishness
heavy: 4 clit, deep, dull, logy, loud 5 actor,
beefy, burly, dense, grave, gross, hefty,
hoggy, massy, thick 6 clayey, cloggy,
coarse, gloomy, hearty, leaden, stodgy,
strong, stupid 7 doleful, intense, massive,
onerous, serious, villain, violent, weighty
8 burdened, grievous, inactive, lifeless,
lowering, overcast, pregnant, profound,
sluggish 9 heavisome, laborious, lethargic,
ponderous, saturnine 10 afflictive, burdensome, cumbersome, encumbered, oppressive 13 consequential
heavy-headed: 4 dull 6 drowsy, stupid

heavy-hearted: sad 10 despondent, melancholy

hebdomad: 4 week 5 seven

hebetate: 4 dull 5 blunt

Hebrew (see also **Israel, Judaism**): Jew 6 Semite 7 Semitic 8 Hebraean 9 Israelite
acrostic: 4 agla
alphabet: He, Pe; Mem, Nun, Sin, Taf, Tav, Tet, Vav, Yod, Yud 4 Alef, Ayin, Beth, Caph, Kaph, Koph, Ooph, Resh, Shin 5 Aleph, Cheth, Gimel, Lamed, Sadhe, Tsade, Zayin 6 Daleth, Samekh
ancestor: 4 Eber
clean: 6 kosher
dance: 4 hora
day: yom
gentile: goi, goy 5 goyim(pl.)
God: El 5 Eloah 6 Adonai, Elohim 7 Jehovah
greeting: 6 shalom
high priest: Eli 5 Aaron
infinity: 6 adalam
Jehovah: 5 Jahve, Yahve, Yahwe 6 Jahvah, Jahveh, Yahveh, Yahweh 7 Jahaveh
juniper: 4 ezel
lawbreaking: 6 averah
lesson: 9 Haphtarah
man: rab 5 bahur, hakam
measure: cab, hin, kab, kor 4 epha, ezba, omer, reed, seah 5 cubit, ephah, homer
month: Ab 4 Adar, Elul 5 Iyyar, Nisan, Tebet 6 Kislew, Shebat, Tammuz, Tishri, Veadar 7 Heshwan
name for God: 6 Adonai, Elohim, Yahweh 7 Jehovah
parchment: 6 mezuza 7 mezuzah
school: 5 heder, schul
scriptures: 4 Tora 5 Torah
son: ben
teacher: 5 rabbi
thief: 5 ganef, ganof, gonof 6 gonoph
title: rab 4 abba
weight: 4 beka, reba

Hebrides island: 4 Skye, Uist

hecatomb: 9 sacrifice, slaughter

heckle: nag 4 gibe 5 tease 6 badger, hackle, harass, hector, needle

hectic: 8 exciting, feverish, habitual, restless 11 consumptive 13 constitutional

hector: nag 5 bully, harry, worry 6 harass, heckle, plague 7 bluster, torment 8 braggart, browbeat, irritate 9 roisterer, swaggerer 10 intimidate

Hector: *companion:* 8 Diomedes
father: 5 Priam
mother: 6 Hecuba
rescuer: 6 Agenor
slayer: 8 Achilles
wife: 10 Andromache

Hecuba: *daughter:* 9 Cassandra
husband: 5 Priam
son: 5 Paris 6 Hector 7 Helenus 9 Deiphobus

hedenbergite: 8 pyroxene

hedge: bar, haw, hem 4 boma 5 beard, fence, frith, guard, skulk 6 hinder, hurdle, privet 7 barrier, enclose, protect 8 boundary, obstruct, quickset, separate, sepiment, straddle, surround 14 counterbalance

hedgehog: 6 urchin 7 echinus 8 herisson, hurcheon 9 porcupine

hedonic: 8 cyrenaic

heed: ear 4 care, cark, cure, gaum, hark, hear, mind, note, obey, reck 5 await, watch 6 attend, beware, harken, listen, notice, regard, remark 7 caution, hearken, observe, respect 8 consider 9 attention, diligence 10 cognizance, solicitude 11 observation

heedful: 4 wary 5 chary 6 attent 7 careful, mindful 8 diligent, watchful 9 advertent, attendant, attentive, observant 10 respectful 11 considerate

heedless: 4 rash 5 giddy 6 remiss, unwary 7 languid, witless 8 careless, reckless 9 blindfold, forgetful, negligent 10 incautious, indiscreet, insouciant, regardless, unthinking 11 hairbrained, inadvertent, inattentive, indifferent, lightheaded, thoughtless, unobservant

heehaw: 4 bray 6 guffaw 10 horselaugh

heel: cad, end, tip 4 calx, cant, knob, tilt 5 talon 6 careen 7 incline 12 protuberance
bone: 9 calcaneus

heeze: 4 help 5 exalt, hoist, raise 6 assist

heft: 5 heave, raise 6 strain, weight 8 exertion 9 influence 13 ponderousness

hefty: 5 heavy, rough 6 rugged 7 massive, weighty 8 vehement, vigorous

hegemonic: 6 ruling 7 leading 11 controlling, predominant

hegemony: 9 authority, influence 10 leadership

hegira, hejira: 6 exodus, flight 9 migration

heifer: 4 quey 5 stirk 10 colpindach(Sc.)

height: 4 acme, apex, mote 5 crest 6 summit 7 stature 8 altitude, eminence 9 celsitude, dimension, elevation, procerity, steepness 11 magnanimity

heighten: 4 lift 5 elate, exalt, raise 7 advance, augment, elevate, enhance 8 increase 9 aggravate, intensify

heinous: 6 crying, malign, odious, wicked 7 hateful 8 flagrant, grievous 9 atrocious, malicious, nefarious 10 flagitious, outrageous

heir: son 5 heres, scion 7 heritor, legatee 9 firstborn, inheritor, successor 11 beneficiary

heiress: 5 begum 8 heretrix, heritrix

Hejaz city: 5 Mecca

Hel: *dog:* 4 Garm
father: 4 Loki
mother: 9 Angurboda
realm: 7 Niflhel 8 Niflheim

held: See hold

Helen of Troy: *abductor:* 5 Paris
brother-in-law: 9 Agamemnon
daughter: 8 Hermione
half-sister: 12 Clytemnestra 13 Clytaemnestra
husband: 8 Menelaus
mother: 4 Leda

heliacal: 5 solar

helical: 6 spiral

helicon: 4 tuba

Helios: *daughter:* 5 Circe 8 Heliadae, Heliades
father: 8 Hyperion
son: 8 Phaethon

heliotrope: 6 Clytie

helix: 4 coil 6 spiral

hell: 5 limbo 6 prison 7 dungeon, inferno 9 barathrum

hell-bent: 8 reckless 10 determined

hellebore: 7 bugbane

Hellen: *father:* 9 Deucalion
son: 5 Dorus 6 Aeolus, Xuthus

Hellene: See Greece

Hellenistic school: 9 Pergamene

Hellespont: 11 Dardanelles
swimmer: 7 Leander

hellgrammite: 6 dobson 8 sialidae

hellier: 5 tiler 6 slater 8 thatcher

hellish: 6 wicked 7 stygian 8 devilish, diabolic, infernal 9 malignant 10 detestable, diabolical

hello: 8 greeting 10 salutation

helm: 5 helve, steer, wheel 6 direct, tiller 8 guidance
position: 4 alee 5 aport

helmet: cap 4 sola, topi 5 armet, galea, topee 6 casque, heaume, morion, salade, sallet 7 basinet 8 schapska 9 casquetel, headpiece
part: 4 bell 5 crest 7 ventail 8 aventail

helmet-shaped: 7 galeate

helmsman: 5 pilot 9 steersman

Heloise's lover: 7 Abelard

helot: 4 serf 5 slave 6 vassal 7 bondman

help: aid, bot, S.O.S. 4 abet, boot, bote, cure, lift, mend, rede, tide 5 avail, boost, favor, frith, heeze, serve, speed, stead 6 assist, favour, relief, remedy, repair, succor 7 advance, benefit, forbear, forward, further, improve, promote, relieve, support, sustain 8 befriend, facility 9 adminicle, allevi-

ate, forestall 10 assistance, contribute, facilitate, strengthen

helper: aid 4 ally 5 aider 7 abetter, abettor, striker 8 adjutant, adjutrix, helpmate 9 adjutrice, assistant, samaritan 10 apprentice, benefactor

helpful: 4 good 6 aidant, useful 8 adjuvant, helpsome, salutary 9 auxiliary 10 beneficial, profitable 11 furthersome

helpless: 4 numb, weak 6 unable 7 forlorn 8 unaiding 9 destitute, powerless 10 bewildered, unsupplied 11 defenseless, incompetent, unprotected 12 irremediable

helpmate: 4 wife 6 helper 8 helpmeet 9 companion

helpmeet: See **helpmate**

helve: 4 haft 5 lever 6 handle

Helvetian: 5 Swiss 6 Suisse

hem: 4 edge, seam 5 hedge 6 border, edging, margin, stitch 7 confine, enclose, environ, inclose 8 surround 9 fimbriate

hem in: 5 beset, limit 6 impale 7 enclose, inclose 8 surround

hematite: 7 iron ore

hemeralopia: 6 defect 9 blindness

hemi: 4 half

hemlock: 4 bunk, herb, tree 5 tsuga 6 conium
poison: 6 conium

hemmel: 4 shed 5 hovel 7 shelter 11 outbuilding

hemp: ife, pua, tow 4 bang, carl, flax, harl, jute, rine, sunn 5 abaca, bhang, istle, ramie, sisal, sizal 6 ambary, banana, cabuja, cabuya, fennel, manila 7 hashish

hen: pea 4 fowl, rail, wife 5 biddy, chuck, woman 6 gorhen, nester, pullet, towdie 7 chicken 9 gallinule

hen coop: 4 cavy(Sc.) 5 cavie
feature: 4 nest

henbane: 10 nightshade

hence: so; fro 4 away, ergo(L.), thus 5 since 7 hereout, thither 9 therefore 11 accordingly

henceforth: 6 thence 12 henceforward

henchboy: boy 4 page 9 attendant

henchman: 4 page 6 gillie, squire 7 mobster 8 follower 9 attendant, supporter

Hengist: *brother:* 5 Horsa
daughter: 6 Rowena

Henley's poem: 8 Invictus

henna: dye 6 alcana 7 alcanna

Henry II: *adversary:* 6 Becket
drama about: 15 The Lion in Winter
surname: 5 Anjou 11 Plantagenet
wife: 7 Eleanor

Henry VII's surname: 5 Tudor

Henry VIII: Hal
first wife: 9 Catherine

second wife: 4 Anne

third wife: 4 Jane

fourth wife: 4 Anne

fifth wife: 9 Catherine

sixth wife: 9 Catherine

hent: get 5 catch, grasp, reach, seize 6 intent, obtain 11 opportunity

hepar: 5 liver

Hephaestus' wife: 6 Charis 8 Charites

heppen: fit 4 deft, neat 5 handy 6 clever 8 handsome 11 comfortable

heptad: seven 11 septivalent

Hera: 4 Juno

husband: 4 Zeus

mother: 4 Rhea

rival: Io

son: 4 Ares

herald: 4 bode 5 crier, usher 6 beadle, Hermes 7 declare, forerun 8 announce, blazoner, foretell, proclaim 9 harbinger, introduce, messenger, precursor 10 forerunner

heraldry: *band:* 4 fess 5 fesse

bastardy mark: 4 bend 5 baton 7 bendlet 8 sinister

bearing: 4 orle

bell: 7 compane 10 campanella

blood-red: 6 murrey

chaplet: 4 Orle

charge: vol 7 boterol, saltier, saltire 8 boteroll, tressor, tressure

circle: 6 bezant

cross: 4 paty 5 patee, patte 6 ermine, moline, pattee 7 erminee, patonce, saltier, saltire

device: 4 ente, orle 5 crest 6 altier

fleur-de-lis: lis, lys

gold: or

grafted: 4 ente

green: 4 vert

keylike: 4 urde

knot: 4 Lacy, Wake 5 Bowen, Dacre 7 Heneage 8 Stafford 9 Bourchier 10 Harrington

leg: 4 gamb, jamb 5 gambe, jambe

line: 4 unde

scattered: 4 seme

shield: 10 escutcheon

tincture: or 5 tenne 6 argent

triangle: 5 giron

winged: 4 aile

wreath: 4 orle 5 torse

herb: iva 4 anet, balm, dill, leek, mint, moly, sage, wort 5 anise, basil, chive, plant, sedge, thyme 6 annual, borage, catnip, clover, lovage, sesame, yarrow 7 caraway, oregano, parsley 8 marjoram, tarragon

aromatic: 4 anet, dill, hemp, mint, nard, sage 5 anise, basil, clary, nondo, tansy,

thyme 6 catnip, fennel, hyssop 7 chervil, mustard 8 wormseed 9 basilmint, spearmint

bitter: rue 4 aloe, woad 7 aletris, boneset 8 centaury 10 turtlehead

bog: 5 calla 9 steepweed, steepwort

climbing: 4 faba 5 vicia

coarse: 5 tansy 6 eringo, eryngo 7 leafcup 8 pokeweed

flowering: 7 anemone, dittane 8 stapelia 9 celandine

genus: iva 4 ruta 5 canna, cicer, cruca, galax, gavra, inula, lemna, loasa, rheum 6 aralia, asarum, cassia, dondia, isatis, mentha, nerine 7 anemone, cirsium, hedeoma, torenia 8 psoralea 9 grindelia

medicinal: rue 4 aloe 5 senna, sumac, tansy 6 arnica, lovage, tutsan 7 aconite, boneset

mythical: 4 moly

narcotic: 4 hemp

perennial: pia 4 balm, irid 5 sedum 6 fennel, madder, yarrow 7 bugbane, lopweed 8 sainfoin, soapwort 9 digitalis

poisonous: 4 loco 6 conium 7 hemlock, henbane 9 hellebore

salad: 6 endive 7 chicory 10 watercress

shoot: udo

sweet-scented: 8 woodruff

trinity: 8 hepatica

woody: rue

herbage: 5 grass 7 foliage, pasture

herbbane: 9 broomrape

herculean: 4 huge 10 superhuman

Hercules: *capitve:* 4 Iole

companion: 5 Hylas

friend: 6 Iolaus

lion's home: 5 Nemea

mother: 7 Alcmene

stone: 9 loadstone

sweetheart: 4 Iole

victim: 5 Hydra

wife: 4 Hebe 8 Deianira

herd: mob 4 crew, ruck 5 bunch, crowd, drift, drove, flock, group, guard 6 hirsel, pastor, rabble 7 creaght, shelter 8 guardian 9 associate 10 assemblage, congregate 11 aggregation

herdsman: 5 booly 6 booley, cowboy, drover, gaucho, herder 7 bucolic, vaquero 8 garthman, ranchero(Sp.), wrangler

god: 5 Pales

here: ici(F.), 4 army, host 5 ready 6 hither 7 present

hereafter: 5 after, later 6 beyond, future

hereditary: 6 innate, lineal 8 heirship 9 ancestral, descended 11 inheritable, patrimonial

heredity: 4 line 10 inheritance

factor: 4 gene

heresy: 7 dissent 10 radicalism 11 unorthodoxy 13 nonconformism

heretic: 7 Patarin 8 Patarine 9 dissenter, miscreant, sectarian 10 schismatic, unbeliever 13 nonconformist

heretofore: 4 erst 6 before 8 erewhile, formerly, hitherto, previous 9 erstwhile

heritage: 9 heritance, patrimony 10 birthright 11 inheritance

heritor: 4 heir 5 donee 9 inheritor

heritrix, heretrix: 7 heiress

herl: fly 4 barb

hermaphrodite: 9 androgyne 10 androgynus

Hermes: 7 Mercury
  birthplace: 7 Cyllene
  cap: 7 petasos, petasus
  father: 4 Zeus
  mother: 4 Maia
  son: 7 Evander 9 Autolycus
  winged cap: 7 petasos, petasus
  winged shoes: 7 talaria

hermetic: 8 airtight 9 alchemist

Hermione: *father:* 8 Menelaus
  husband: 7 Orestes 11 Neoptolemus
  mother: 5 Helen

hermit: 4 monk 5 clerk 6 anchor 7 ascetic, eremite, incluse, inclusa, recluse, stylite 8 anchoret, beadsman, bedesman, inclusus, marabout 9 anchorite
  hut: 4 cell

hermit crab: 8 pagurian

hermitage: 7 ashrama 8 cloister 9 monastery, reclusery

hermitical: 8 eremitic

hernia: 6 breach 7 rupture

hero: ace 4 idol 5 darer 7 demigod 8 champion 9 conqueror 10 topnotcher 11 protagonist
  deified: 7 demigod
  legendary: 6 Amadis, Roland 7 Paladin

Hero's lover: 7 Leander

Herodias: *daughter:* 6 Salome
  husband: 5 Herod

heroic: 4 bold, epic, huge 5 brave, great, large, noble 6 daring, epical 7 extreme, gallant, spartan, valiant 8 enormous, fearless, intrepid, powerful 9 bombastic 10 courageous 11 extravagant, illustrious, magnanimous, outstanding, venturesome 13 grandiloquent

heroin: 4 drug 8 narcotic

heroine: 11 demigoddess

heroism: 5 valor 6 valour 7 bravery, courage 9 fortitude 13 unselfishness

heron: 4 hern, rail, soco 5 crane, egret, herne, quawk, wader 7 bittern, hernser, quabird 8 aigrette, gaulding, heronsew 9 cormorant, herneshaw, heronsewe, heronshaw
  genus: 5 ardea

herpes 6 eczema 8 shingles

herring: 4 raun 7 alewife, anchovy 8 scud-dawn
  barrel: 4 cade, cran
  catch: 4 tack
  family: 8 pilchard
  female: 4 raun
  fry: 4 sile
  genus: 6 clupea
  head: cob
  lake: 5 cisco
  young: 4 brit 5 sprat, sprot

Hersey setting: 5 Adano

hership: 4 loot, raid 5 foray

Hertha: 4 Erda 7 Nerthus

hery: 6 praise 7 glorify, worship

hesitancy: 10 hesitation, indecision, reluctance

hesitant: 4 loth 5 chary, loath 8 timorous 9 reluctant

hesitate: 4 wait 5 delay, demur, doubt, pause, stall, waver 6 boggle, falter, loiter, scotch 7 stammer

hesitating: coy 4 hink 7 halting 8 backward, doubtful 9 ambiguous 10 indecisive 11 vacillating

hesped: 6 eulogy 7 oration

Hesperides: 5 Aegle 6 Hestia 7 Hespera 8 Arethusa, Erytheia, Erytheis

Hesperus: *father:* 8 Astraeus
  mother: Eos

hessonite: 6 garnet

hest: bid 6 behest, pledge 7 command, precept, promise 10 injunction

Hestia: *father:* 6 Cronus
  mother: 4 Rhea

hetaera, hetaira: 8 mistress, paramour 9 companion

heterogeneous: 5 mixed 6 motley, unlike 7 diverse 10 dissimilar 13 miscellaneous 14 indiscriminate

Heteroousian: 5 Arian

hetman: 6 ataman 7 headman

heu: 4 alas

heugh, heuch: 4 bank, crag, glen 5 cliff, shaft 6 hollow

hew: cut 4 chip, chop, fell, hack 5 carve, wound 6 haggle, strike, stroke

hex: 4 jinx 7 bewitch

hexad: 6 sextet

hexadecene: 6 cetene

hexastich: 6 sestet, stanza 7 strophe

hexoctahedron: 10 adamantoid

heyday: joy, May 4 acme 8 wildness 14 frolicsomeness

Hezekiah: *kingdom:* 5 Judah
  mother: Abi
Hg: 7 mercury
hi: 8 greeting 10 salutation
hiatus: gap 5 break, chasm 6 breach, lacuna
  7 opening 8 interval 12 interruption
Hiawatha: *grandmother:* 7 Nokomis
  mother: 7 Wenonah
Hibernia: 4 Erin 7 Ireland
hiccup, hiccough: 4 burp 5 spasm 9 singultus
hick: 4 jake, rube 6 hiccup, rustic 7 bumpkin
hickory: 5 pecan 9 bitternut, shellbark
hidage: tax
hidalgo: 8 nobleman
hidden: 4 lost 5 inner, overt, perdu 6 arcane,
  buried, cached, closed, innate, latent,
  masked, occult, secret, veiled 7 arcanum,
  covered, cryptic, obscure, recluse 8
  screened, secluded, secreted 9 concealed,
  invisible, recondite 10 mysterious 11 clandestine, delitescent 12 subterranean
hide: bar, kip, lie 4 bury, coat, dern, fell, hill,
  hood, lurk, pelt, skin, stow, veil 5 cache,
  cloak, cloud, couch, cover, derne(Sc.),
  skulk 6 huddle, screen, shroud 7 abscond,
  conceal, eclipse, leather, secrete, shelter 8
  carucate, disguise, ensconce, hoodwink,
  palliate, suppress, withhold 9 dissemble
  10 camouflage
  cleaning instrument: 6 slater
  measured in: 8 hidation
  remove hair from: 4 moon
  undressed: kip 4 pelt
  worker: 6 tanner
hideaway: den 4 cave, lair 7 retreat
hidebound: 6 narrow 7 bigoted, miserly 9
  barkbound, bourgeois, illiberal, niggardly
  10 restrained 12 conventional
hideous: 4 fell, grim, ugly 5 awful 6 grisly,
  horrid, odious, ogrish 7 ghastly, ogreish 8
  deformed, dreadful, grewsome, gruesome,
  horrible, shocking, terrible 9 dismaying,
  frightful, revolting 10 detestable, discordant, terrifying
hideout: mew 4 lair 5 cache
hides: 4 furs 5 skins 6 peltry
hiding: 7 secrecy 8 flogging 9 coverture
hie: 5 haste, hurry, speed 6 betake, hasten,
  scurry, strive 8 expedite
hield: 4 heel, lean, tilt 5 droop, slope, yield
  7 decline, incline
hiemal: 6 wintry
hierarchical: 9 episcopal
hieroglyphic: 7 cryptic 9 illegible
hieroglyphics key: 7 Rosetta
higgle: 6 haggle 7 bargain, chaffer
high: alt 4 dear, haut(F.), main, much, tall
  5 acute, chief, first, lofty, sharp, steep 6

costly, shrill 7 eminent, exalted, haughty,
  violent 8 elevated, foremost, piercing, towering 9 admirable, expensive, important,
  principal, turbulent 10 tumultuous 11
  mountainous
  combining form: 4 alti
high-and-mighty: 8 arrogant 9 imperious
  11 overbearing
high-brow: 7 egghead 14 intelligentsia
high-class: 6 classy 10 first-class
high-flying: 7 icarian 11 pretentious
high-handed: 6 lordly 8 arrogant, despotic
  9 arbitrary 11 dictatorial, domineering,
  overbearing
high-hat: 4 snub 8 snobbish 12 aristocratic
high-pitched: 6 shrill 8 inclined
high-pressure: 8 forceful, pressing 9 insistent 10 aggressive
high-priced: 4 dear 6 costly 9 expensive
high priest: Eli
high sea: 4 main
high-sounding: 7 fustian, pompous 8 imposing 9 bombastic 10 altisonant
high-spirited: 5 fiery 6 lively 7 gallant 8
  cavalier 10 mettlesome
high-strung: 5 tense 7 nervous 9 excitable
high-toned: 7 stylish 8 elevated 9 dignified
  11 fashionable
highborn: 5 noble 8 generous 12 aristocratic
highbred: 7 genteel, refined
higher: 8 superior
highest: 6 upmost 8 bunemost, overmost
highest point: 4 acme 6 zenith
Highland war cry: 6 slogan
Highlander (see also **Scotland**)**:** 4 Celt,
  Gael, Kelt, Scot 6 Tartan 8 clansman 9
  Gluneamie
  dance: 4 reel 5 fling
  language: 4 Erse
  pouch: 6 sporan 7 sporran
  weapon: 8 claymore, skeandhu
highroad: 7 highway
highway: way 4 bahn(G.), iter(L.), path,
  pike, road 5 Alcan 6 Appian, artery, causey, course, rumpad, street 7 Lincoln 8 autobahn, causeway, chaussee(F.), highroad,
  turnpike 9 boulevard 12 thoroughfare
highwayman: pad 5 rider, thief 6 bandit,
  padder, robber 7 brigand, footpad, ladrone
  8 hightoby 9 bandolero
Highwayman: *author:* 5 Noyes
hike: 4 jerk, toss, walk 5 march, raise,
  throw, tramp
hilarious: mad 5 funny, merry, noisy 6 jovial 7 jocular 8 mirthful 9 ludicrous

hilarity: gig, joy 4 glee 5 mirth 6 gaiety 7 jollity 9 happiness, joviality, merriment 10 joyousness 12 cheerfulness, exhilaration

hilch: 4 halt, limp

hill: ben, hoe, kop, pap, tor 4 bank, brae, bult, dagh, dune, fell, heap, hide, knap, knob, loma, mesa 5 bargh, butte, cerro(Sp.), cliff, cover, hurst, morro, mound, mount 6 ascent, barrow, copple, djebel 7 colline, picacho 9 acclivity, elevation, monadnock

glacial: 4 kame, paha 7 drumlin

Jerusalem: 6 Olivet

range: 5 ridge

sand: 4 dene, dune

top of: tor 4 peak 6 summit

hillock: 4 tump 5 croft, hurst, knoll, kopje, mound, toman(Sc.)

over grave: 7 tumulus

hillside: 4 brae, cote 5 cleve, cliff, falda(Sp.), slade, slope 6 cleeve

hilly: 5 steep

hilt: 6 handle 8 handgrip

hilum: 5 porta 7 nucleus

Himalaya: *animal, bear-like:* 5 panda

antelope: 5 goral, serow

bear: 5 bhalu

bearcat: 5 panda

cedar: 6 deodar

cypress: 6 bhutan

dweller: 8 Nepalese

goat: 4 kras, tahr, tair, thar

oxen: yak

peak: Api 7 Everest

pheasant: 5 monal

sheep: 6 bharal, nahoor

swamp: 5 Terai

tableland: 5 Tibet

Himavat's daughter: 4 Devi

himene, himine: 4 hymn, song

himself: 4 ipse(L.)

Himyarite: 4 Arab 7 Axumite, Sabaean

Hinayana Buddhism: 5 shojo 6 lesser

hind: doe, lad, roe 4 back, chap, stag 6 fellow, rustic, worker 7 bailiff, peasant, servant, steward 8 cabrilla, domestic 9 posterior 11 hindquarter

hinddeck: 4 poop

hinder: bar, let 4 slow 5 after, block, cheat, check, choke, cramp, debar, delay, deter, embar, estop, hedge 6 arrest, detain, hamper, harass, impede, impend, injure, retard, scotch 7 deprive, forelay, impeach, inhibit, prevent 8 encumber, handicap, obstruct, preclude, prohibit 9 embarrass, foreclose, forestall, interrupt, posterior

hindmost: 4 last, rear 9 aftermost

hindrance: bar, rub 4 clog, curb, snag, stop 5 block, check, delay, hitch 6 arrest 7 barrier 8 obstacle 9 detention, deterrent, restraint 10 difficulty, impediment 11 impeachment, obstruction 12 interruption

Hindu (see also **India**): 4 Babu, Koli, Sikh 5 Tamil 6 Gentoo, Hindoo 8 Kolarian

abode of gods: 4 Meru

adherent: Sik 4 Jain, Seik, Sikh 5 Jaina, Seikh

age of world: 4 yuga

alphabet: 6 Sarada

ancestral race: 5 Aryan

apartment: 5 mahal

Aryan race: 4 Swat

ascetic: 4 jogi, sadh, yati, yogi 5 sadhu

atheist: 7 nastika

book: 4 Veda 6 Tantra 11 Yajna-valkya

calendar: Pus 4 Jeth, Asin, Kaur, Magh 5 Asarh, Sawan, Katik, Aghan, Chait 6 Bhadon, Kartik, Phagun 7 Baisakh, Sarawan, Phalgun

call to prayer: 4 azan

caste: Dom, Mal, Meo 4 Dasi, Gola, Koli, Kori, Mali, Pasi, Teli 5 Goala, Palli, Sudra 6 Babhan, Soodra 7 Brahman

caste member: Jat 4 Jain 6 Banian, Banyan, Rajput, Vaisya 7 Rajpoot 9 Kshatriya, Vakkaliga

charm: 6 mantra

chief: mir 6 sirdar

coin: ana, pai, pie 4 anna, pice 5 paisa, rupee

congregation: 5 samaj, somaj

convert to Islam: 6 shaikh

cremation: 4 sati 6 suttee

dancer: 8 devadasi

deity: Dev 4 Deva, Dewa, Maya, Rama, Yama 6 Ganesa, Varuna, Vishnu 7 Ganesha, Krishna 9 Jagannath 10 Jagannatha, Juggernaut 11 Ramachandra

demon: 4 Bali, Bhut, Ketu, Rahu 5 Asura 6 Daitya

devotee: 4 yati

disciple: 4 sikh

divine being: dev 4 deva

doctrine: 5 Karma 6 dharma

drink: 4 soma

duty: 6 dharma

ejaculation: om, um

essence: 4 rasa, rata 5 atman 6 amrita

family: 5 gotra

female energy: 5 Sakti 6 Shakti

festival: 4 Holi, mela 6 Dewali, Hoolee 7 Dashara

flute: bin 5 pungi

garment: 4 sari 5 saree

gentleman: 4 babu 5 baboo, sahib

god (see also *deity* above): 4 Agni, Deva, Kama, Siva, Vayu, Yama 5 Asura, Shiva, Simia 6 Brahma, Ganesa, Skanda, Varuna 7 Ganesha

goddess: Sri, Uma, Vac 4 Devi, Kali, Shri, Vach 5 Durga, Gauri, Sakti, Shree, Ushas 6 Chandi, Shakti 7 Parvati 9 Haimavati

guitar: 5 sitar

headdress: 5 rumal

heaven: 5 dyaus

hermitage: 7 ashrama

hero: 4 Nala, Rama

holy book: 4 Veda 6 Sastra

holy sage: 5 rishi

hymn: 6 mantra

idol worship: 5 arati

incarnation: 6 avatar

Indra: 5 Sakka, Sakra

king: 4 Nala 5 Sesha 6 Shesha

lady: 4 devi, rani 5 ranee

language: 4 Pali, Urdu 5 Hindi, Tamil 8 Sanskrit 10 Hindustani

lawgiver: 4 Manu

leader: 5 Nehru 6 Gandhi, sirdar

life principle: 4 jiva 5 atman, prana

literature: 4 Veda 5 sruti 6 shruti

loincloth: 5 dhoti

magic: 4 jadu, maya 5 jadoo

magician: 5 fakir 6 fakeer

mantra: om, um

master: 5 sahib

mendicant: 4 naga 7 bairagi, vairagi 8 sannyasi

mental discipline: 4 yoga

monastery: 4 math

monkey god: 7 Hanuman

month: see *calendar* above

mother goddess: 6 matris

mystic: 4 yogi

noble: 5 rajah 8 maharaja

non-violence: 6 ahimsa

offering: 4 bali, lepa 5 pinda

paradise: 7 Nirvana

patriarch: 5 pitri

philosophy: 4 yoga 5 tamas

poem: 8 Ramayana 11 Mahabharata 12 Bhagavad-Gita

poet: 6 Tagore

policeman: 5 sepoy

prayer rug: 4 asan 5 asana

priest: 5 hotar

prince: 4 raja, rana 5 rajah 8 maharaja 9 maharajah

princess: 4 rani 5 ranee

pundit: 5 swami

queen: 4 rani 5 ranee 8 maharani 9 maharanee

religion: 5 Prana 7 Jainism, Sivaism 8 Shivaism

rice: 4 boro

rite: 5 achar

ruler: 5 rajah

scripture: Li; rig 4 Veda 5 Sruti 6 Purana, Sastra, Smriti, Tantra 7 Shastra

sect: 4 Sikh, siva 6 Aghori

social division: 5 caste

soldier: 4 Sikh 5 sepoy

soul: 4 atma 5 atman

spirit: 4 Jiva, Mara 5 Asura, Atman, Prana 7 Muktama

supreme being: 6 Vishnu

teacher: pir 4 guru

temple: 4 deul 6 vimana

title: aya, sri 4 mian, raja, shri, sidi 5 rajah, sahib, shree, swami 7 bahadur

tower: 5 stupa

triad god: 4 Siva

tunic: 4 jama 5 jamah

unknown god: Ka

unorthodox: 4 Jain 5 Jaina

Upanishad: 4 Isha, Veda 7 Vedanta

worship: 4 puja 5 pooja

Hindustan: Ind

language: 4 Urdu 5 Hindi

tribesman: 4 toda

hinge: har 4 butt, hang, turn 5 gemel, joint, pivot, stand 6 depend, gimmer, gimmor, hingle, lamina, pintle

Hinnom Valley: 7 Gehenna

hint: cue, tip 4 clew, clue, time, turn 5 cheep(Sc.), imply, trace 6 allude, moment 7 inkling, mention, suggest 8 allusion, innuendo, intimate, occasion 9 catchword, insinuate 10 indication, intimation, suggestion 11 insinuation

hip: hop 4 coxa, huck, limp, miss, skip 6 haunch, huckle

pert. to: 7 sciatic

hip boots: 6 waders

hipbone: 5 ileum, ilium

hippie: mod 5 rebel 6 copout

Hippocrates: *birthplace:* kos

drug: 5 mecon, opium

hippodrome: 5 arena 6 circus 7 contest

hippopotamus: 6 seacow 9 pachyderm

hire: buy, fee, let, use 4 rent, sign, wage 5 bribe, lease, price, wages 6 employ, engage, retain, reward, salary 7 charter, conduce, stipend 9 allowance 12 compensation

hireling: 4 esne, serf 5 slave 8 gangster 9 mercenary

hirple: 4 limp 6 hobble

hirsel: 4 herd, land 5 flock

hirsute: 5 hairy, rough 6 coarse, shaggy

hispid: 7 bristly 8 strigose, strigous

hiss: 4 hish, sizz, whiz 5 whizz 6 fissle, fistle 8 goose cry 10 assibilate

hissing: 6 fizzle 8 sibilant 9 sibilance

hist: 4 hark, hush

historian: 8 annalist 10 chronicler

history: 4 tale 5 drama, story 6 annals, memoir, record 7 account 8 relation 9 biography, chronicle, genealogy, narrative
muse: 4 Clio

histrion: 5 actor

histrionics: 6 acting 11 theatricals

hit: bat, lam, lob, ram, rap, tap 4 bump, bunt, cast, club, slog, slug, sock, swat, wham 5 clout, flick, knock, smack, smite, smote, throw, touch 6 attain, batted, bingle, strike 7 collide, success 8 bludgeon 10 production, succession

hit-or-miss: 6 casual, chance, habnab 8 careless 9 haphazard

hitch: hop, tie, tug 4 halt, hook, join, knot, limp, pull 5 agree, catch, crick, hotch, marry, unite 6 attach, enlist, hobble 8 obstacle, stoppage 9 harmonize, hindrance 10 enlistment, impediment 11 contretemps, obstruction

hitchhiker: 8 stowaway

hither: 4 here

hitherto: ago, yet 6 before

Hitler: *aerie:* 13 Berchtesgaden
chosen race: 5 Aryan
follower: 4 Nazi

hitter: 6 batter 7 batsman, slugger

Hittite: *ancestor:* 4 Heth
capital: 6 Pteria
storm god: 6 Teshub, Teshup

hive: 5 store, swarm 6 apiary 9 multitude

hives: 5 uredo 7 allergy 9 urticaria

ho: 4 long, stop 5 yearn 6 attend, desist

hoar: 4 cold, gray, rime 5 hoary, musty, stale 6 biting 7 ancient 9 antiquity, venerable 13 venerableness

hoard: 4 save 5 amass, chest, hutch, stock, store 6 supply 7 husband 8 quantity, treasure, treasury 10 accumulate, collection

hoarder: 5 miser 6 storer 9 treasurer

hoarfrost: rag 4 rime 9 cranreuch(Sc.)

hoarse: 5 gruff, harsh, rocky, rough 7 grating, raucous 10 discordant

hoarseness: 4 frog 5 croup

hoary: old 4 aged, gray, hoar 5 moldy, mossy, musty 7 ancient, hoarish, whitish 9 canescent, venerable

hoax: bam, cod, fun, hex, kid 4 bilk, fake, gaff, gegg, gunk, joke, ruse, sell, sham 5 bluff, cheat, spoof, trick 6 canard, diddle, humbug, string 7 deceive 8 artifice 9 bamboozle, string 11 hornswoggle

hob: elf, peg, pin, tap 4 game, mark, nail, nave 5 clown, fairy, ledge 6 ferret, rustic, sprite 7 mandrel 8 mischief 10 countryman, projection

hobbil: 4 dolt 5 clown, dunce, idiot

hobble: 4 clog, clop 5 bunch, cramp, hitch 6 fetter, hopple 7 cramble, perplex, shackle, spancel 9 embarrass 10 difficulty, perplexity 13 embarrassment

hobbledehoy: lad 5 youth

hobbler: 5 pilot 7 boatman, hoveler, laborer 8 retainer 12 longshoreman

hobbly: 5 rough 6 uneven

hobby: fad 5 horse 6 falcon 7 pastime 9 avocation, diversion

hobgoblin: bug, elf, hag, imp 4 bogy, Puck 5 bogey, bogie, bugan, poker, spook 6 boodie(Sc.), sprite 7 bugaboo 8 boggle-bo, worricow(Sc.) 9 coltpixie 10 apparition

hobo: bo; boe, bum 5 tramp 7 vagrant 8 vagabond

hock: ham, hox 4 pawn 5 ankle, hough, thigh 6 mallow, pledge 9 hamstring 10 houghsinew

hocket: 6 hiccup 8 obstacle 12 interruption

hockey: 5 bandy 6 shinny
disk: 4 puck
goal: 4 cage

hocus: 4 drug 5 cheat, fraud 7 deceive 8 cheating, deceiver, trickery 10 adulterate

hocus-pocus: 5 cheat, trick 6 humbug 7 juggler 8 flimflam, quackery 9 trickster 12 charlatanism

hod: 4 soil 6 barrow 7 scuttle

hoddy-doddy: 4 fool 5 snail 7 cuckold 9 blockhead

hodgepodge: ana 4 mess, olio, stew 5 cento 6 medley 7 mixture 10 hotchpotch, miscellany 11 gallimaufry, ollapodrida 12 mingle-mangle

hoe: dig 4 brod, hill, till 5 clean, cliff, padle, worry 6 sarcle, scrape 7 dogfish, trouble 8 griffaun 9 cultivate 10 promontory

hog (see also **pig**): sow 4 bene, boar, dime, galt, gilt 5 shoat, shote, swine 6 barrow 7 hogling 8 shilling 9 boschvark 10 backfatter
breed: 5 Essex 9 Hampshire
food: 4 mash 5 slops, swill 6 acorns
genus: sus
young: pig 5 shoat

hog peanut: 8 earthpea

hog plum: 4 amra

hog side: 6 flitch

hog thigh: ham

hogfish: 8 scorpene

hoggish: 5 hoggy 7 selfish, swinish 10 gluttonous

hognut: 5 ouabe 6 pignut 8 earthnut

hogo: 5 taint 6 flavor, stench

hogshead: 4 cask 6 barrel, hogget, vessel

hogtie: 4 clog 6 fetter, hamper

hogwash: 5 draff 7 pigwash

hoi polloi: mob 6 masses, rabble 8 populace

hoick: 4 lift, yank

hoist: cat, gin 4 jack, lift 5 boost, crane, davit, heave, heeze, horse, lewis, raise, setup, winch 7 derrick, elevate 8 elevator

hoist sail: 4 swig

hoistman: 8 bandsman 9 engineman

hoity-toity: 5 giddy, proud 6 snooty 7 flighty, haughty 8 arrogant 11 harum-scarum, patronizing, thoughtless 13 irresponsible

hokum: 4 bunk 11 foolishness

hold: own 4 bind, bite, bulk, clip, fill, have, hook, keep, rely, seat, stow, tend 5 avast, carry, catch, grasp, guard, rivet 6 adhere, arrest, behold, cleave, clench, defend, detain, harbor, occupy, retain 7 adjudge, contain, control 8 interest, maintain, thurrock 9 entertain 10 possession, stronghold

hold a brief for: 6 defend 8 advocate

hold back: dam 4 stem, stop 5 deter 6 detain, retard 7 inhibit, repress 8 restrain

hold fast: hug 5 cling, stick 6 cohere

hold forth: 5 offer 7 exhibit 8 continue, maintain, propound

hold in custody: 4 jail 6 detain, intern

hold off: 5 avert 7 refrain

hold on: 4 stop, wait 7 forbear 8 continue

hold out: 4 last 6 endure 7 exclude, protend 8 continue

hold up: rob 4 halt, lift, rein 5 boost, check, raise 7 display, exhibit, robbery, support, sustain

hold water: 5 sound 10 consistent

holder: 5 haver 6 tenant 9 container 10 receptacle

holdfast: 5 clamp, miser 6 clinch 7 support 9 tenacious 10 persistent

holding: 5 asset 6 estate, tenure 8 property

adapted for: 10 prehensile

hole: bay, den, pit 4 bore, cave, cove, deep, dump, flaw, gate, gulf, leak, mine, nook, peck, rent, vent 5 abyss, chasm, shaft 6 burrow, cavern, cavity, cranny, crater, eyelet, grotto, hollow, pierce, prison, recess 7 dungeon, mortise, opening, orifice, ostiole 8 aperture, bunghole, peephole 10 excavation 11 perforation, predicament

instrument for making: awl 4 bore 5 drill 8 stiletto

wall: 4 muse 5 meuse, niche

Holi, Hoolee: 8 festival

holia: 4 fish 6 salmon

holiday: 4 fete 5 feria, festa, merry 6 fiesta, jovial, outing 7 festive, playday 8 festival, vacation 9 convivial, Mardi Gras

holiness: 5 piety 7 halidom 8 halidome, sanctity 9 sanctuary 11 saintliness 13 righteousness

Holland: See **Netherlands**

holler: 4 yell 6 shriek 7 protest

hollow: den, dip 4 boss, cave, cove, deep, dent, doke, glen, hole, holl, howe, huck, lean, thin, vain, void 5 bight, chase, cuppy, empty, false, gaunt, goyal, goyle, heugh, scoop, sinus, stria 6 cavern, cavity, cirque, groove, hungry, socket, sunken, vacant 7 concave, muffled, unsound 8 alveolus, fossette, specious 9 cavernous, deceitful, depressed, faithless, worthless 10 depression, sepulchral 11 treacherous 12 unsatisfying

comb. form: 5 coelo

hollow-eyed: 7 haggard

hollowed: 7 glenoid

hollowed out: 6 cavate

hollowness: 6 vanity 7 vacuity

holly: 4 assi, holm, ilex 5 yapon, yupon 6 hulver, yaupon, youpon

pert. to: 6 ilicic

holm: ait 5 holly, islet 7 bottoms, lowland

holm oak: 4 ilex 5 holly

Holmes' word: 10 elementary

holobaptist: 12 immersionist

holocaust: 9 sacrifice 11 destruction

holster: 4 case 7 housing 8 scabbard

holt: den 4 grip, hill, hold, lair, wood 5 copse, grasp 7 retreat

holy: 5 pious, sacre(F.), saint, santo 6 devout, divine, hallow, sacred 7 blessed, perfect, sainted, saintly 8 blissful, hallowed 9 inviolate, sanctuary, spiritual 10 sacrosanct 13 sanctimonious

combining form: 5 hagio

Holy City: 4 Kiev, Rome, Zion 5 Mecca, Lhasa, Medina, Moscow 7 Benares 9 Allahabad, Jerusalem

Holy Grail: 8 Sangraal, Sangreal

castle: 9 Monsalvat

knight: 7 Galahad

Holy Joe: 9 clergyman

Holy Land: 9 Palestine

pilgrim: 6 palmer

holy oil: 6 chrism

Holy One: God 6 Christ 7 Jehovah 12 Supreme Being

Holy Roman emperor: 4 Otho, Otto

Holy Rood: 5 cross 8 crucifix

holy statue: 4 icon, ikon 5 ikono

holy water: *font:* 5 paten

receptacle: 5 stoup

sprinkler: 11 aspergillum

homage: 5 honor 6 eulogy, fealty, regard 7 loyalty, manrent, ovation, respect 9 adoration, deference, obeisance, reverence 10 allegiance

homager: 6 vassal

homaloidal: 4 even, flat

homard: 7 lobster

hombre: guy, man 6 fellow

Homburg: hat 4 felt

home: den 4 nest 5 abode, being, domus, house 6 asylum, estate, maison(F.), 7 habitat, hospice, village 8 domicile, dwelling 9 homestead, residence 10 habitation 11 hearthstone

at: 4 chez(F.)

wheeled: 7 trailer

home base: den 5 plate

homeborn: 6 native 10 indigenous

homefelt: 6 inward 7 private

homelike: 4 cozy 5 homey 6 homely, homish 8 cheerful, friendly, homesome 11 comfortable

homeliness: 9 plainness 10 simplicity 11 domesticity 17 unpretentiousness

homely: 4 rude, ugly 5 plain 6 hameil, hamelt, hamilt, kindly, simple 7 plainly 8 domestic, familiar, friendly, homelike, intimate 9 unsightly 10 intimately 12 unpretending 15 unpretentious

homemade: 5 plain 6 simple 8 domestic

Homer: *birthplace:* 5 Chios

character: 4 Ajax 6 Nestor 8 Achilles, Odysseus

poem: 5 Iliad 7 Odyssey

Homeric: 4 epic 6 epical

homesickness: 9 nostalgia

homespun: 4 kelt(Sc.), rude 5 plain 6 coarse

homestead: 4 toft, tref(W.) 7 onstead

homicide: 6 murder

homilist: 8 preacher

homily: 5 adage 6 sermon 8 assembly 9 communion, discourse 11 exhortation

hominy: 4 bran, corn, samp 5 grits

homo: man

Homo Americanus: 6 Indian

Homo sapiens: man

homogeneity: 8 equality, identity, sameness

homogeneous: 4 like 5 equal, solid 7 similar 10 comparable

homologous: 9 identical

homonym: 7 synonym 8 namesake

homunculus: 5 dwarf 7 manikin

Honduras: *city:* 4 Yoro 6 Cedros, Iriona 7 Gracias 9 Juticalpa 11 Tegucigalpa(c.)

coin: 4 peso 7 centavo, lempira

Indian: 4 Ulua, Ulva 5 Lenca

measure: 4 vara 5 milla 6 mecate, tercia 7 cajuela, manzana 10 caballeria

mountain: 5 Ceiba, Colon

port: 8 Truxillo 10 San Lorenzo

river: 4 Ulua 5 Aguan, Negro 6 Patuca, Sulaco 9 Choluteca 10 Chemelicon

weight: 4 caja

hone: 4 long, pine 5 delay, dress, strop 6 lament 7 grumble, sharpen 8 oilstone 9 whetstone

honest: 4 fair, full, just, open 5 frank, roman 6 candid, chaste, decent, dexter, dinkum, proper, rustic, square 7 genuine, sincere, upright 8 bonafide, faithful, rightful, reliable, straight, suitable, truthful, virtuous 9 equitable, guileless, honorable, ingenuous, veracious 10 creditable 11 trustworthy 13 conscientious, incorruptible, unadulterated 15 straightforward

honestly: 5 truly 6 dinkum, justly 8 directly 9 telltruth

honesty: 5 honor 6 equity 7 decency, justice, probity 8 fairness, fidelity, veracity 9 constancy, integrity 10 generosity, liberality 11 uprightness 12 suitableness, truthfulness 13 honorableness 15 trustworthiness 19 straightforwardness

honesty plant: 8 moonwort

honey: mel 4 dear, niel(F.) 5 sweet 6 nectar 7 flatter 8 precious

combining form: 5 melli

fermented drink: 4 mead

source: bee 6 nectar

honey badger: 5 ratel

honey bear: 8 kinkajou

honey buzzard: 4 hawk, pern

honey eater: iao 6 manuao

honeybee: 7 deseret 8 angelito

disease: 8 sacbrood

honeyberry: 4 tree 5 genep, genip

honeycomb cell: 7 alveola 8 alveolus

honeycombed: 6 favose, pitted 8 alveolar

honeydew: 5 melon 6 mildew, orange

honeyed: 5 sweet 6 sugary 7 candied 11 mellifluous

honeysuckle: 6 azalea, widbin

Hong Kong: *bay:* 4 Mirs

city: 8 Victoria

coin: 4 cent 6 dollar 13 British dollar 14 Hong Kong dollar

honor: 4 fame, fete, prow 5 adore, exalt, glory, grace, izzat 6 credit, decore, esteem, homage, laurel, praise, regard, repute, revere 7 dignify, dignity, emblaze, ennoble, glorify, honesty, respect, worship 9 celebrate, deference, reverence 10 estimation, reputation

pledge: 6 parole

honorable: 4 dear 5 moral, noble, white 6 gentle, honest 7 upright 8 generous, honorary **9** dearworth, estimable, reputable **10** creditable **11** commendable, illustrious, magnanimous, meritorious, respectable

honorarium: fee, tip **6** reward, salary **7** douceur, payment **8** gratuity

Honshu: *bay:* Ise
port: **4** Kobe

hood: cap **4** coif, cowl, hide **5** amice, blind **6** biggin, bonnet, burlet, camail, canopy, chapel, tippet **7** calotte, capuche, surtout **8** capsheaf, caputium, chaperon, covering
academic: **8** liripipe, liripoop
monk's: **4** atis, cowl **5** atees
saddle: **8** tapadera, tapadero
vehicle: **6** bonnet, capote

hooded: **9** cucullate **10** capistrate

hoodlum: yap **5** rowdy **6** goonda **8** hooligan

hoodoo: **4** jinx **5** Jonah **6** voodoo **7** bewitch, unlucky

hoodwink: **4** fool, hide, wile **5** blear, blind, bluff, cheat, cosen, cover, cozen **6** befool, delude **7** blinder, blinker, deceive, mislead **9** blindfold

hooey: **4** bunk **6** bunkum **7** baloney, boloney **8** buncombe, nonsense

hoof: **4** clee, foot, walk **5** cloof, cloot, cluif, dance, tramp **6** ungula

hoofer: **6** dancer, walker

hook: **4** barb, gaff, hake, hock, hold, huck **5** catch, cleek, hamus, hitch, larin, seize, steal **6** agrafe, anchor, larree, pilfer, tenter **7** agraffe, capture, grunter, hamulus, hitcher **8** crotchet **10** chatelaine

hook money: **5** larin **6** larree

hooka, hookah: **4** pipe **7** nargile **8** narghile **9** narghileh

hooked: **6** hamate **7** hamular, uncinal **8** ankyroid, aquiline, uncinate

hookey player: **6** truant

hooligan: **6** loafer **7** ruffian

hooly: **4** slow, soft, wary

hoop: **4** bail, band, ring, tire **5** clasp, garth, girth, shout **6** circle, frette **7** circlet, trundle **8** encircle, surround

hoopskirt: **9** crinoline

hoosegow: jug **4** jail **6** lockup, prison **10** guardhouse

hoosh: **4** lift, urge **5** boost, hoist

Hoosier State: **7** Indiana

hoot: boo **4** jeer, whoo **5** shout, whoop **6** boohoo **7** ululate

Hoover Dam lake: **4** Mead

hop: fly, hip **4** dope, halt, jump, leap, limp, skip **5** bound, dance, hitch **6** flight, gambol, spring

hop back: vat

hop kiln: **4** oast

hop-o'-my-thumb: **5** dwarf **6** midget

hop stem: **4** bine

hopbush: **6** akeake

hope: **4** deem, spes(L.), want, wish **5** haven, trust **6** aspire, desire, expect, morale **7** cherish, confide **8** prospect, reliance **9** esperance **10** aspiration **11** expectation **12** anticipation
goddess of: **4** Spes
lack of: **7** despair
symbol of: **4** opal

hopeful: **8** sanguine **9** confident, expectant **10** optimistic

hopeless: **4** gone, vain **6** futile **7** forlorn, useless **8** downcast **9** desperate, heartless, incurable **10** despairing, despondent, desponding, remediless **11** ineffectual **12** disconsolate, irremediable **13** irrecoverable, irretrievable

hophead: **6** addict

Hophni: *brother:* **8** Phinehas
father: Eli

Hopi Indian: **4** Moki **5** Moqui
god: **7** Kachina, Katcina **8** Katchina

hoplite: **7** soldier

hopper: box **5** chute **6** dancer, leaper **10** receptacle

hoppet: **4** yard **6** basket, bucket

hopple: **6** fetter, hamper, hobble **8** entangle

hopscotch: **7** pallall
stone: **5** potsy **6** peever

hopvine: **4** bine

Horae: **4** Dike **6** Eirene **7** Euromia

horde: **4** army, camp, clan, pack **5** crowd, group, swarm **6** legion, throng **9** multitude

horehound: **6** henbit

Horite chief: **4** Seir

horizon: rim **4** edge, goal **8** prospect

horizontal: **4** flat **5** level

hormigo: **5** quira **7** ant tree

horn: **4** scur, tuba **5** brass, bugle, cornu, drone, siren **6** antler, cornet, rhyton **7** antenna, trumpet **8** oliphant **9** alpenhorn **10** cornucopia
blast: **4** mort, toot **7** fanfare, tantara **9** tantarara
combining form: **4** kera
crescent moon: **4** cusp
deer: **4** tine **5** prong **6** antler
drinking: **6** rhyton
Hebrew: **6** shofar **7** shophar
player: **6** bugler **9** cornetist, trumpeter
without: **5** doddy **6** doddie, polled **7** acerous

hornbill: **4** bird, tock **6** homrai
genus of: **7** buceros

hornet: **4** wasp

hornpipe: **4** tune **5** dance **8** matelote

hornswoggle: **4** hoax **9** bamboozle

horny: **4** hard **8** ceratoid **9** calloused **10** semiopaque

hornyhead: **4** chub

horologe: 4 dial 5 clock, watch 9 timepiece
horoscope: 4 dial 7 diagram
horrendous: 7 fearful 8 horrible 9 frightful
horrible: 4 dire, grim 5 great 6 grisly, horrid 7 fearful, ghastly, hideous, horrent 8 dreadful, gruesome, horrific, shocking, terrible 9 atrocius, excessive, frightful, horrified, nefarious 10 horrendous, tremendous
horrid: 4 grim, ugly 5 awful, rough 6 rugged 7 hideous 8 dreadful, grewsome, gruesome, horrible, shocking 9 bristling, frightful, obnoxious, offensive, revolting 10 detestable, terrifying 13 objectionable
horrific: 7 fearful 8 horrible 9 frightful 10 horrifying
horrified: 6 aghast 7 ghastly
horrify: 5 shock 6 appall, dismay
horrifying: 8 horrific 9 execrable
horror: 4 fear 5 dread 6 terror 8 aversion 10 abhorrence 11 abomination, detestation 13 consternation
hors d'ouevre: 6 canape, relish 7 zakusha 8 apertif 9 antipasto, appetizer
Horsa's brother: 7 Hengist
horse: gee, nag, pad 4 barb, mare, plug, prad 5 brock, caple, capul, draft, filly, hobby, hoist, mount, pacer, raise, shier, steed, waler 6 cheval, equine, geegee, ladino, pelter, rouncy 7 caballo(Sp.), cavallo(Sp.), cavalry, charger, clipper, courser, hackney, mustang, saddler, sheltie, sleeper, stepper, trestle 8 bathorse, cartaver(Sc.), footrope, jackstay 10 breastband
Achilles': 7 Xanthus
ankle: 4 hock
breastplate: 7 peytrel, poitrel
breed: 4 Arab, Barb 5 Shire 6 hunter, Morgan 7 Belgian, harness, Suffolk, trotter 8 Galloway, Normandy, Shetland 9 Percheron 10 Clydesdale
brown: bay 6 sorrel 8 chestnut
buyer: 5 coper 6 trader 7 knacker
calico: 5 pinto
color: bay 4 pied, roan 5 pinto 6 calico, sorrel 8 chestnut, palomino, schimmel
combining form: 5 hippo
command: gee, haw, hup 4 whoa 6 giddap
covering: 9 caparison
cry: nie 5 neigh 6 whinny
dappled: 4 roan 5 pinto 7 piebald
dark: 4 zain
dealer: 7 chanter, scorser
disease: 5 surra 6 heaves, lampas 7 lampers, quittor, spavins 9 distemper
docked-tail: 6 curtal 8 cocktail
draft: 4 aver 5 aiver, hairy
driver: 6 jockey 7 sumpter 8 coachman
farm: 6 dobbin

feeding box: 6 manger
female: 4 mare, yaud 5 filly
foot: 4 frog, hoof 7 coronet, fetlock, pastern
forehead: 8 chanfrin
gait: run 4 lope, pace, rack, trot, vott, walk 6 canter, gallop
genus: 5 equus
goddess of: 5 Epona
golden: 8 palomino
gray: 8 schimmel
guide: 4 rein 5 longe
harness: 5 pacer 7 trotter
hired: 4 hack 7 hackney
horned: 7 unicorn 9 monoceros
leg: 6 instep 7 fetlock
lover: 10 hippophile
male: 4 stud 6 entire 7 gelding 8 stallion
measure: 4 hand
menage: 6 school 7 academy
pace: 4 lope, trot 5 amble 6 canter
pack: 5 bidet 7 sumpter
pair: 4 span, team
pert. to: 6 hippic
piebald: 5 pinto
prehistoric: 8 Eohippus
racing: 4 turf
rearing: 6 pesade
relay: 6 remuda
round-up: 5 rodeo
saddle: cob 5 mount 7 palfrey
small: cob, nag, tit 4 pony 5 bidet, genet 6 cayuse, jennet(Sp.) 8 galloway, Shetland
sorrel: 4 roan 8 chestnut
spirited: 4 Arab 5 steed 6 rearer 7 courser
stable of: 6 string
talking: 5 Arion
track slope: 6 calade
trainer: 5 valet
trapping: 6 tackle 7 harness 9 caparison
trotting: 6 Morgan
turn: 7 passade
war: 5 steed 7 charger, courser 8 destrier
white-streaked face: 4 shim 5 blaze, reach
wild: 6 bronco, brumby, tarpan 7 mustang 8 warragal, warrigal
winged: 7 Pegasus
working: 4 aver 5 aiver 6 dobbin
worn-out: nag 4 hack, jade, moke, plug 5 crock, skate 6 garran, garron, gleyde 7 knacker 8 harridan 9 rosinante
horse-and-buggy: rig 12 old-fashioned
horse collar: 7 bargham(Sc.)
horse mackerel: 4 fish, scad 5 atule, tunny 6 bonita, saurel
horse opera: 7 western
horse tackle: 7 harness
horseback: *on:* 7 a cheval(F.)
horsefly: 4 cleg 5 clegg 6 botfly, gadfly
horsehair: 4 mane 9 haircloth

horsehide: 8 cordovan
horsekeeper: 5 groom 7 hostler
horselaugh: 5 snort 6 guffaw, heehaw
horseman: 5 rider 6 carter, cowboy centaur, courier, vaquero 8 buckaroo, chevalier 10 cavalryman, equestrian 12 broncobuster, equestrienne
horseman goad: 4 spur
horsemanship: 6 manege 10 equitation
  rearing: 6 pesade
  sidewalk: 4 volt
  turn: 8 caracole
horsemen: 7 cavalry 11 equestrians
horseradish tree: ben 5 behen
horseshoe: *point:* 6 sponge
  spur: 4 calk
  rim: web
horseshoer: 7 farrier 10 blacksmith
horsewhip: 4 flog 5 quirt 7 chabouk
horticulturist: 8 gardener
Horus: Ra, Re
  brother: 6 Anubis
  father: 6 Osiris
  mother: 4 Isis
hory, horry: 4 foul 5 dirty 6 impure
hose: 4 sock, tube, vamp 5 water 6 drench 8 stocking
Hosea's wife: 5 Gomer
hospice: inn 5 house 6 asylum, imaret 9 hospitium
hospitable: 5 douce 6 cheery 7 cordial 8 friendly 9 receptive 10 hospitious
hospital: 6 creche, refuge, spital 9 infirmary 10 sanatorium 11 xenodochium 12 ambulatorium
  attendant: 5 nurse 7 orderly
  mobile: 9 ambulance
  user: 7 patient
hospitality: 7 welcome 10 cordiality
  to strangers: 9 xenodochy
host: inn 4 army, here 5 crowd, guest, swarm 6 housel, legion, myriad, throng 7 company, lodging 8 landlord 9 harbinger, multitude, sacrifice 10 assemblage 11 entertainer
  receptacle for: pyx 5 paten 8 ciborium
hostage: inn 5 hotel 6 pledge 8 security 9 guarantee
hostel: inn 5 hotel, lodge 7 lodging 12 lodginghouse 13 entertainment
hostelry: inn 5 hotel 6 hostel, hostry, tavern 11 caravansary 12 lodginghouse
hostile: foe 5 black, enemy, fremd 7 adverse, opposed, warlike 8 contrary, inimical 9 resisting 10 malevolent, unfriendly 11 belligerent 12 antagonistic 13 unsympathetic
hostility: 4 feid, feud 6 animus, enmity, hatred, rancor 7 ill-will, warfare 9 animos-

ity, antipathy 10 antagonism, bitterness, opposition, resistance 12 disaffection 14 unfriendliness, vindictiveness
hosting: 6 battle 9 encounter, gathering, incursion
hostler: 5 groom 6 ostler 9 innkeeper, stableman
hot: 5 acrid, calid, eager, fiery, spicy 6 ardent, biting, fervid, recent, strong, sultry, torrid, urgent 7 burning, excited, fervent, flaming, glowing, intense, lustful, peppery, pungent, thermal 8 sizzling, vehement 9 impatient, impetuous 10 passionate
hot cakes: 7 kneepad, pancake 11 griddle cake
hot-tempered: 7 iracund 8 choleric 9 irascible
hot-water bottle: pad, pig
hotbed: 4 nest
hotchpotch: 4 stew 6 jumble 8 hotchpot 9 tripotage(F.) 10 hodgepodge
hotel: inn 5 fonda, haven, house 6 hostel, imaret, tavern 7 gasthof, hostage 8 building, dwelling, gasthaus 11 caravansary 12 caravanserai, lodginghouse
  auto: 5 motel
  keeper: 4 host 7 padrone 8 boniface, hotelier
hothead: 5 raver 7 inciter 11 reactionary
hotheaded: 5 fiery, hasty 8 reckless 9 impetuous
hothouse: 6 bagnio 10 greenhouse
hotspur: 4 rash 6 madcap 7 violent 8 reckless 9 impetuous 10 headstrong
Hottentot: *dialect:* 4 Gona, Kora, Nama
  garment: 6 kaross
  instrument: 4 gora 5 gorah, goura
  tribe: 4 Gona, Kora, Nama 6 Damara, Griqua 7 Sandawe, Sandawi
  war club: 10 knobkerrie
hound: dog 4 hunt 5 harry 6 addict, talbot 7 harrier 9 persecute
  tail: 5 stern
hounds: 4 pack 8 avantlay
hour: *canonical:* 4 none, sext
  class: 6 period
  lights out: 4 taps 6 curfew
hourly: 5 brief, horal 6 horary, recent 7 quickly 8 frequent 9 continual 10 frequently 11 continually
hourglass: 5 clock 7 shapely
house: cot, hut 4 casa(It.), cote, dorm, dump, firm, flat, flet, haus(G.), home, nest 5 abode, bahay, booth, cabin, cover, dacha, domus(L.), hovel, lodge, manor, shack, villa 6 biggin, billet, bottle, camara, casino, duplex, family, grange, maison(F.), palace, shanty 7 cabildo, chateau, cottage, enclose, mansion, quarter, shelter, thea-

ter **8** ancestry, audience, building, domicile, dwelling, tenement **9** dormitory, playhouse, residence **10** habitation

cluster: **4** dorp **6** hamlet **7** village

combining form: eco

commercial: **4** firm **5** store **8** emporium

eating: inn **4** cafe **6** tavern **9** chophouse **10** restaurant

English royal: **5** Tudor **6** Stuart **7** Windsor

guest: inn **5** hotel **11** caravansary

Newfoundland: **4** tilt

Oriental: **5** serai

pert. to: **5** domal

public: inn **5** hotel **6** hostel, tavern **7** hospice **8** hostelry

religious: **4** kirk **6** chapel, church, priory, temple **9** cathedral, synagogue **10** tabernacle

Russian: **4** isba **5** dacha

summer: **6** gazebo **9** belvedere

Upper: **6** Senate

house organ: 8 magazine **10** periodical

house servant: 4 maid **8** domestic

houseboat: 5 barge **6** wangan, wangun **7** wanigan **8** dahabeah, wannigan

housefly: 4 pest **5** musca **6** insect

household: 5 meiny **6** common, family, housal, menage **8** familiar **9** belonging

gods: **5** Lares **7** Penates

regulation: **6** thrift **7** economy **9** husbandry

housekeeper: 6 matron **7** janitor **8** janitrix **9** caretaker, janitress

housel: 9 Eucharist

houseleek: 8 sengreen

housemaid: 6 duster **7** servant

houseplant: ivy **5** aphis, calla **6** coleus **7** begonia, violets **10** asphidistra

housewarming: 6 infare

housewife: 8 hausfrau(G.) **9** economize

housework: 5 chore **8** drudgery

housing: box, pad **4** cowl **5** cover, niche **6** garage **7** shelter **8** covering **10** protection

Houston college: 4 Rice

hove: See **heave**

hovel: hut, sty **4** crib, hulk, hull, shed **5** cabin, hutch, lodge **6** cruive, hemmel, shanty **7** shelter **10** tabernacle

hoveler: 7 boatman, hobbler

hover: 4 flit **5** float, pause **7** flitter, flutter

howdy, howdie: 7 midwife **10** salutation

howe: 4 deep **5** empty, lowly **6** hollow, humble, hungry **10** depression

however: but, tho, yet **5** still **6** though **8** although **10** howsomever **12** nevertheless **15** notwithstanding

howf, howff: 4 loaf **5** haunt, lodge **6** resort, tavern **7** shelter, sojourn **8** frequent

howitzer: 6 cannon

howl: bay, cry, wow(Sc.) **4** bawl, gowl, gurl, hurl, wail, wawl, yawl, yell, yowl, yowt **5** whewl **6** lament, steven **7** ululate

howling: 4 wild **5** great **6** baying, dreary, savage **7** extreme, ululant **10** pronounced

howling monkey: 5 araba

howsoever: 8 although

howsomever: 8 although **12** nevertheless

hox: 4 hock **5** annoy, worry **6** pester **7** trample **9** hamstring

hoyden, hoiden: 4 romp, rude **6** blowze, tomboy **7** ill-bred **10** roistering

Hreidmar's son: 5 Otter, Regin **6** Fafnir, Reginn

huaca: 4 holy, idol, tomb **6** fetish, sacred, shrine, temple

hub: 4 core, nave **6** center, centre

Hub: 6 Boston

hubble: 5 crowd **6** hubbub, uproar

hubble-show: 6 rabble **9** commotion, confusion

hubbub: ado, din **4** stir **5** noise **6** clamor, hubble, racket, rumpus, tumult, uproar **7** bobbery **8** hubbuboo **9** commotion, confusion **11** disturbance

hubby: 7 husband

hubristic: 4 vain **7** insolent **8** arrogant **12** contemptuous

huck: hip **4** husk **6** haunch, higgle **7** bargain

huckle: hip **6** haunch

huckleberry: 9 blueberry

family: **9** ericaceae

Huckleberry Finn: *author:* **9** Mark Twain **13** Samuel Clemens

character: Jim

huckster: 5 adman, cheap **6** badger, broker, cadger, cagier(Fr.), hawker **7** haggler, peddler **8** regrater, retailer **9** middleman

hud: 4 hull, husk **5** shell

huddle: hug **4** hide, raff **5** crowd, hurry **6** bustle, fumble, jumble, mingle **7** conceal, embrace, scrunch **8** assemble, disorder **9** confusion **10** conference **14** conglomeration

Hudibras author: 6 Butler

hue: 4 balk, blee, form, tint **5** color, guise, shade, shout, tinge **6** aspect, clamor, depict, figure, outcry **7** clamour **8** shouting **10** appearance, complexion

hueless: 4 gray **9** colorless

huff: dod, pet **4** blow, brag, puff **5** bully, peeve, swell **6** hector **7** bluster, enlarge **8** boasting, offended

huffcap: 5 bully, heady **6** strong **9** blusterer **10** blustering, swaggering

huffy: 4 airy **5** fuffy, puffy, windy **7** pettish **8** arrogant **9** conceited **10** swaggering

hug: lug 4 clip, coll 5 carry, clasp, cling, creem, halse, press 6 cuddle, huddle, huggle 7 cherish, embrace, squeeze

huge: big 4 stor(Sc.), vast 5 enorm, giant, great, jumbo, large 6 heroic 7 banging, bumping, immense, massive, monster 8 colossal, enormous, gigantic, titanic 9 monstrous, pyramidal 10 gargantuan, prodigious, tremendous, unmeasured 11 elephantine

hugger-mugger: sly 6 jumble, muddle, secret 7 secrecy 8 confused, secretly 9 confusion 10 disorderly 11 clandestine 13 clandestinely

hui: 4 firm 5 guild 7 society 8 assembly 11 partnership

huisache: 4 wabe, wabi 5 aromo, shrub 6 cassie 7 popinac

huitain: 6 octave, stanza

huke: 4 cape 5 cloak, dress

hulk: 4 bulk, hull, loom, ship 5 hovel 10 disembowel

hulking: 5 bulky, hulky, husky 7 loutish, massive 8 unwieldy

hull: hud, hut, pod 4 bulk, hulk, husk, shed 5 hovel, shell, strip 8 covering 11 decorticate

grain: 4 bran

hullabaloo: ado, din 5 noise 6 clamor, hubbub, racket, tumult, uproar 7 clamour 9 confusion

hulver: 5 holly

hum: 4 blur, buzz, huss, huzz, sing, whiz 5 croon, drink, drone, feign, whizz 6 murmur 9 bombinate 11 bombilation, bombination

human: 6 humane, mortal 7 hominid 9 enigmatic

comb. form: 7 anthrop 8 anthropo

human being: man 6 mortal, person 7 Adamite 8 creature

humane: 4 kind 6 kindly, tender 8 merciful 9 forgiving 11 sympathetic 13 compassionate, tenderhearted

humanitarian: 14 philanthropist

humanity: 5 flesh 6 lenity 8 kindness 9 mortality

humanize: 6 refine 8 civilize

humble: low 4 mean, meek, mild, poor 5 abase, abash, lower, lowly, plain, stoop 6 debase, deject, demean, demiss, modest, reduce, simple 7 afflict, conquer, degrade, depress, mortify 8 contrite, deferent, disgrace, reverent 9 humiliate 10 submissive

humbug: gum, kid, pah 4 bosh, flam, guff, hoax, sham 5 cheat, faker, fraud, fudge, guile, trick 6 barney, blague, bunkum, cafard, cajole, gammon 7 deceive, flummer, mislead 8 flimflam, flummery, huckmuck, pretense 9 bamboozle, deception, imposture, stratagem 10 flumdiddle 11 flumadiddle

humdinger: 4 oner 6 corker

humdrum: 4 dull 7 irksome, prosaic 10 monotonous 11 commonplace, indifferent 13 uninteresting

humect: wet 7 moisten

humerus: 4 bone

humid: wet 4 damp, dank 5 moist 6 sultry 8 humorous, vaporous

humidity: 8 dampness

humiliate: 5 abase, abash, shame 6 debase, humble 7 degrade, mortify 8 belittle, disgrace

humility: 7 modesty 8 meekness, mildness 9 lowliness 10 diffidence

humming: big 5 brool 6 strong 7 buzzing, droning 8 frothing, seething 13 extraordinary

humming bird: ava 5 carib 6 hummer 8 froufrou 9 sheartail

genus of: 6 sappho

hummock: 4 hump 5 knoll

humor, humour: pet, tid, wit 4 baby, mood, whim 5 fancy, freak, vapor 6 levity, megrim, please, temper 7 caprice, gratify, indulge 8 drollery, moisture 11 inclination, temperament

humorist: wag 5 joker

humorous, humourous: 5 comic, droll, funny, humid, moist 6 watery 7 amusive, comical, jocular, playful 8 pleasant 9 facetious, laughable, whimsical 10 capricious

hump: 4 bile, hunk, lump 5 bouge, bulge, bunch, crump, hunch, mound, ridge 6 gibber, gibbus, hummie 7 hummock 12 protuberance

humpback: 9 hunchback 10 huckleback

Humperdinck girl: 6 Gretel

Hun: 6 vandal 9 barbarian

leader: 5 Etzel 6 Attila

Hunan river: 4 Yuan, Yuen

hunch: 4 balk, bend, hump, hunk, lump, push 5 fudge, shove 6 chilly, frosty, thrust 9 intuition 12 protuberance

Hunchback of Notre Dame: 9 Quasimodo

hundred: 7 cantred, cantref

combining form: 5 centi, hecto

division into: 12 centuriation

hundred-eyed being: 5 Argus

hundred percent: 6 entire 7 genuine, perfect 9 unalloyed 13 thoroughgoing 14 unquestionable

hundred years: 7 century 9 centenary

Hundred Years' War battle: 6 Cressy

hundredfold: 8 centuple 12 centuplicate

hundredweight: cwt 6 cental 7 quintal

hung: See **hang**

Hung Wu: 4 Ming

Hungary: *army:* 6 Honved 9 Honvedseg
cavalryman: 6 Hussar
city: 5 Erlau 8 Budapest(cap.), Debrecen, Szegedin 9 Budapesth, Debreczin, Kecskemet 16 Hodmezo-Vasarhely
coin: 4 gara 5 balas, pengo 6 filler, korona
commune: Mor
composer: 5 Lehar 6 Bartok
dance: 7 czardas
dog: 4 puli 6 kuvasz
gypsy: 7 tzigane
hero: 5 Arpad
lake: 7 Balaton 9 Blaten See 13 Neusiedler See
measure: ako 4 hold, joch, yoke 5 antal, itcze, marok, metze 7 huvelyk, merfold
mountain range: 10 Carpathian
people: 6 Magyar
poet: 5 Arany
river: 4 Raab 5 Drave, Maros 6 Danube, Poprad, Theiss 7 Vistula
Slav: 5 Croat 8 Croatian
weight: 7 vamfont 8 vammazsa
wine: 5 tokay

hunger: 4 long, want 5 belly 6 desire, famine, starve 7 craving 8 appetite, voracity 9 esurience
abnormal: 7 bulimia 10 polyphagia

hungry: 4 avid, howe, poor 6 barren, hollow, jejune 7 uneaten 8 esurient, hungered 10 avaricious

hunk: dad 4 daud, hump, lump 5 hunch, piece

hunks: 5 miser

hunt: dig 4 drag, seek 5 chase, chevy, chivy, delve, drive, hound, probe, quest, stalk, track, trail 6 chivvy, ferret, follow, forage, hunter, pursue, search, shikar 11 inquisition
god of: 5 Ninip 6 Apollo

hunted: 4 game, prey

hunter: 4 hunt 5 jager, yager 6 chaser, nimrod 7 stalker 8 chasseur, huntsman 9 sportsman
assistant: 5 gilly, jager
attendant: 5 gilly(Scot.) 6 gillie
mythological: 5 Orion
Golden Fleece: 5 Jason
patron saint: 6 Hubert

hunting: *cry:* yoi 4 toho 5 chevy, chivy, hoick 6 chivvy, hoicks, yoicks
expedition: 6 safari
game: 6 shikar, venery
horn note: 4 mort
pert. to: 7 venatic

hunting dog: 5 hound 6 basset, beagle, setter 7 pointer

huntress: 5 Diana 7 Artemis 8 Atalanta

huntsman: 5 jager 6 hunter 7 catcher, venerer 8 chasseur
changed into stag: 7 Actaeon

Hur's son: Uri

hurdies: 4 hips, rump 8 buttocks

hurdle: pen 4 clew, fold, leap 5 bound, cover, crate, frith, hedge 6 raddle 7 barrier, confine 8 obstacle, surmount 9 enclosure

hurdy-gurdy: 4 lira, rota

hurkle: 5 squat 6 crouch

hurl: 4 cast, dash, haul, howl, hurl, pelt, roar, send, toss, turn 5 fling, heave, pitch, sling, smite, throw, twist, whang 6 elance 9 overthrow

hurlement: 6 tumult 9 confusion

hurly: 6 uproar 7 turmoil 9 confusion

hurly-burly: 4 hurl 5 storm 6 tumult, uproar 8 confused 9 confusion 10 tumultuous

huron: 6 grison

hurrah: joy 5 cheer, huzza, shout 7 triumph 8 applause 13 encouragement

hurricane: 4 wind 5 storm 7 cyclone, prester, tempest 8 chubasco 9 hurricano, windstorm
center of: eye

hurried: See **hurry**

hurry: ado, hie, run 4 pass, pell, race, rese, rush, scud, stir, trot, urge, whir 5 drive, fight, haste, impel, slide, speed, worry 6 convey, harass, hasten, hustle, scurry, tumult 7 agitato(It.), dispute, quarrel, quicken 8 dispatch, expedite 9 agitation, commotion 10 expedition 11 disturbance, festination, precipitate

hurst: 4 hill, wood 5 copse, grove 7 hillock 8 sandbank

hurt: 4 harm, maim, pain 5 abuse, blame, grief, sorry, wound 6 damage, grieve, impair, injure, injury, mittle, scathe, strike 7 afflict, collide, hurting 8 distress, mischief, nuisance 9 detriment 12 disadvantage

hurtful: bad 4 evil 6 nocent 7 baneful, malefic, noisome, noxious 10 pernicious 11 deleterious, destructive, detrimental, prejudicial

hurtle: 4 dash 5 clash, fling, whirl 6 assail, jostle 7 collide 8 brandish

husband: eke, man, rom 4 bond, buck, chap, keep, mate, save 5 churl, hoard, marry, store 6 manage, spouse, tiller 7 consort, espouse, partner, plowman, steward 8 conserve 9 cultivate, economize 10 cultivator, husbandman
more than one: 9 polyandry
property right: 7 curtesy

husbandman: 4 bond, boor, carl 5 colon 6 farmer, tiller 7 acre-man, husband 8 agricole 10 cultivator

husbandry: 6 thrift 7 economy 8 managery 11 cultivation
god: 6 Faunus
hush: tut 4 calm, clam, hist, lull 5 allay, quiet, still 6 soothe 7 appease, repress, silence
husk: cod, hud 4 bark, bran, coat, hulk, hull, leam, rind 5 lemma, scale, shack, shell, shuck, straw, strip 6 colder 7 envelop, epicarp 8 covering, envelope 11 decorticate
husks: 5 chaff 6 bhoosa
Husky: dog 6 Eskimo
huss: 7 dogfish
hussar: 7 soldier 10 cavalryman
headdress: 5 busby
uniform jacket: 6 dolman
hussy: 4 jade 5 besom(Sc.), gipsy, gypsy, madam, quean 7 drossel 9 housewife 11 housekeeper
hustle: 4 push 5 crowd, hurry, shove 6 bustle, jostle, thrust 7 pushing 8 activity
hustler: 6 peeler 8 go-getter
hut: cot 4 bari, cote, crib, hulk, shed 5 benab, bohio, bothy, cabin, choza, house, hovel, humpy, hutch, kraal, lodge, scale, shack, toldo, wurly 6 bohawn, canaba, chalet, gunyah, gunyeh, rancho, shanty 7 balagan, bourock, camalig, cottage, huddock, wickiup 8 barabara, chantier
fisherman's: 4 skeo
hermit's: 4 cell
military: 6 Nissen
mining: coe
shepherd's: 5 bothy
hutch: ark, bin, box, car, hut, pen 4 coop 5 chest, hoard, hotch, hovel 6 coffer, humped, shanty 7 hunched, shelter 9 inclosure
huzza: 5 cheer, shout 6 hurrah, huzzah 9 roisterer
huzzar: 6 hussar
huzzy: See **hussy**
hyacinth: 7 greggle 8 bluebell, harebell
hyalite: 4 opal
hybrid: 5 blend 7 mongrel 9 composite
bovine: 7 cattalo
dog: 4 mutt 7 mongrel
horse and ass: 4 mule 5 hinny
horse and zebra: 7 zebrula, zebrule 8 zebrinny
zebra and donkey: 7 zebrass
hydra: 5 polyp 7 serpent
hydrant: 4 plug 6 faucet
hydraulic engine: ram
hydrazoate: 4 azid 5 azide
hydrocarbon: 6 butane, carane, nonane, retene 7 benzene, olefine, pentane

gaseous: 6 ethane, ethene
liver oil: 8 pristane
tree: 7 terpene
hydrocyanic acid: 7 prussic
hydrogen: gas 5 arsin 6 arsine
hydromel: 4 mead 5 aloja 10 melicratum
hydrometer: 9 aerometer
hydromica: 4 mica 9 muscovite
hydrophobia: 5 lyssa 6 rabies
hydrophyte: See **aquatic plant**
hygienic: 8 sanitary
hymenopteron: ant, bee 4 wasp 6 sawfly 7 gallfly 9 ichneumon
hymn: ode 4 sing, song 5 psalm 6 himene, himine, hirmos, hirmus 7 introit 8 canticle 11 recessional 12 processional
following psalm: 9 sticheron
funeral: 5 dirge
praising: 4 pean 5 paean
ritual: 8 encomium
sung in unison: 6 choral 7 chorale 9 plainsong
tune: 6 choral 7 chorale
victory: 9 epinicion, epinikion
hyoscyamus: 8 narcotic
hyperbole: 12 exaggeration 13 overstatement
Hyperborean sage: 6 Abaris
hypercritical: 7 carping 8 captious 12 overcritical, supercilious
Hyperion: *daughter:* Eos 6 Selene
son: 6 Helios
hyphen: 4 band, dash
hypnotic: 6 opiate 8 narcotic 9 soporific 12 somnifacient
hypnotic condition: 4 coma 6 trance 8 lethargy
hypnotism: 5 sleep 8 hypnosis 9 mesmerism
hypnotist: 6 Mesmer 9 mesmerist
hypnotize: 5 charm 9 mesmerize
hypnum: 4 moss
hypochondria: hyp 6 megrim
hypocrisy: 4 cant 10 simulation
hypocrite: 6 Levite 7 Tartufe
hypocritical: 4 nice 5 exact, false 7 bigoted, canting, carping 8 captious, specious 9 deceptive, insincere 11 dissembling, pharisaical 13 sanctimonious
hypostatic: 5 basic 9 elemental
hypotenuse: 5 slant
hypothesis: ism 6 system, theory 9 postulate 10 assumption 11 supposition
hypothetical being: ens 6 entity
hypocrisy: 6 deceit
hyrax: 8 procavia
Hyrtacus' son: 5 Nisus
hyssop: 4 mint 11 aspergillum
hysteria: 6 nerves
hysterical: 9 emotional 12 uncontrolled

I

I, Claudius *author:* 6 Graves
I do not wish to contend: 14 nolo conten-
dere(L.)
I have found it: 6 eureka
I understand: 5 roger
Iago's wife: 6 Emelia
Iasion's father: 4 Zeus
Iberian: 4 Pict
ibex: tur, zac
ibis: 5 guara, stork 9 gourdhead
Ibsen: *character:* Ase 4 Gynt, Nora
  native country: 6 Norway
  play: 11 Rosmersholm
Icarian: 4 rash 6 daring 9 foolhardy
Icarius' daughter: 7 Erigone 8 Penelope
Icarus' father: 8 Daedalus
ICBM: 5 Atlas 6 weapon 7 missile
ice: 4 cool, geal, grue(Sc.), rime 5 chill, frost,
  glace(F.) 6 freeze 7 congeal, diamond, hauteur 10 confection 11 refrigerant, refrigerate
  crystals: 4 snow 5 frost
  floating: 4 berg, floe
  fragment: 5 brash
  glacier: 4 neve 5 serac
  mass: 4 berg, floe
  patch: 4 rone(Sc.)
  pendant: 6 icicle
  sea: 6 sludge
  sheet: 4 floe
  slushy: 4 sish
ice cream dish: 4 soda 6 frappe, sundae 7
  parfait
ice river: 7 glacier
icebox: 6 cooler 12 refrigerator
icecap: 7 calotte
Iceland: *assembly:* 7 Althing
  bishopric: 5 Holar 8 Skalholt
  capital: 9 Reikjavik, Reykjavik
  coin: 5 aurar, eyrir, krona
  epic: 4 Edda
  giant: 4 Atli
  hero: 4 Bele
  language: 5 Norse
  legislature: 7 Althing

  measure: fet 4 alin, lina 5 almud, turma 6
    almenn, almude, ferfet, pottur 7 fathmur,
    feralin, fermila, oltunna, sjomila 9 korn-
    tunna 10 ferfathmur, kornskeppa, thum-
    lungur 11 angjateigur 12 tundagslatta 13
    ferthumlungur
  mountain: 5 Jokul 10 Orafajokul
  musician or poet: 5 scald, skald
  volcano: 4 Laki 5 Hekla
  weight: 4 pund 5 pound 11 tunna smjors
ichneumon: 8 mongoose 11 hymenop-
  tera(pl.) 12 hymenopteron
ichnography: map
ichnolite: 6 fossil 9 footprint
ichthyosis: 9 sauriosis
icicle: 7 shoggle
  limestone: 10 stalactite, stalagmite
icing: 7 topping 8 frosting
icon, ikon: 5 image 6 eidola(pl.), idolon,
  symbol 7 eidolon, picture 8 portrait 12 illustration
iconolater: 9 worshiper
iconoscope: 6 finder
icterine: 9 yellowish
icterus: 8 jaundice
ictus: fit 4 blow 6 attack, stress, stroke
icy: 4 cold 5 gelid 6 arctic, frigid, frosty 8
  chilling
Idaho: *capital:* 5 Boise
  county: Ada 5 Butte, Katah, Lewis
  motto: 12 esto perpetua
  nickname: 8 Gem State
  river: 7 Kutenai, Kutenay 8 Kootenai, Koo-
    tenay
  town: 5 Boise, Nampa 7 Preston 9 Pocatello
Idas' consort: 8 Marpessa
ide: orf
idea: 4 idee(F.) 5 fancy, ideal, image 6 design, figure, notion 7 conceit, concept, fantasy, inkling, opinion, project, thought 8
  gimcrack 9 archetype 10 appearance, cogitation, conception, impression, reflection
  comb. form: 4 ideo
  impracticable: 7 chimera 8 chimaera
  prompting action: 6 motive

ideal: 5 dream, model 6 mental 7 paragon, perfect, Utopian 8 abstract, fanciful, standard 9 imaginary, visionary 10 aspiration, conceptual, consummate 12 intellectual

ideal state: 4 Eden 6 Oceana, Utopia

ideate: 5 fancy 7 imagine 8 conceive 9 prefigure 11 preconceive

identic: 4 same 5 equal

identical: one 4 same, self, very 5 alike, equal, samen(Sc.) 8 selfsame 10 equivalent, tantamount

identify: 4 mark, name 5 brand, prove 7 earmark 9 designate, establish

identity: 4 name 5 unity 7 oneness 8 sameness 9 exactness 11 homogeneity
false: 5 alias

ideologist: 7 dreamer 8 theorist 9 visionary

idiasm: 11 peculiarity 12 idiosyncrasy

idiocy: 7 anoesia, fatuity

idiograph: 9 signature, trademark

idiom: 6 phrase 11 peculiarity

idiosyncrasy: way 6 idiasm, manner 11 peculiarity 12 eccentricity

idiot: oaf 4 dolt, fool 5 booby, dunce 6 cretin, hobbil, nidget 7 dullard, omadawn 8 imbecile, omadhuan 9 blockhead, simpleton 10 changeling

idiotic: 4 daft, zany 5 barmy, inane 7 asinine, fatuous, foolish 9 senseless

idle: 4 lazy, loaf, sorn(Sc.), vain 5 dally, empty, shool 6 asleep, cooter, dawdle, futile, loiter, otiant, otiose, unused, vacant 7 aimless, loafing, sluther, useless 8 baseless, faineant, inactive, indolent, slothful, trifling 9 desultory, unfounded, worthless 10 groundless, unemployed, unoccupied 11 ineffectual

idle talk: 5 rumor 6 gossip

idleness: 5 folly 6 vanity 7 inertia 8 flanerie, inaction, laziness 9 silliness 10 inactivity 15 lightheadedness

idler: bum 4 hake 5 drone 6 bodaud, bumble, loafer, stoach 7 faitour 8 faineant, loiterer

Idmon: *father:* 6 Apollo
killer: 4 boar
mother: 6 Cyrene
ship: 4 Argo

idol: 4 god 4 Baal, hero 5 afgod, image, satyr 6 fetish 7 phantom 8 impostor 9 pretender
matinee: 4 star

idolater: 5 pagan 6 adorer 7 Baalite 9 worshiper

idolatrous: 5 pagan

idolize: 5 adore 6 admire, revere 7 worship 8 venerate

idolon: 5 image 6 eidola(pl.) 7 eidolon, phantom 10 apparition

idolum: 7 fallacy 8 phantasm

idoneous: apt, fit 8 suitable 11 appropriate

idyl, idyll: 4 poem 7 eclogue

idyllic: 7 bucolic 8 pastoral

if: si(F., It., L.) 8 granting, provided 9 supposing

i'faith: 5 truly 6 indeed

iffy: 8 doubtful

igloo: hut 4 home

igneous rock: 4 trap 6 basalt, gabbro 7 granite, periodot

ignite: hot 4 fire 5 fiery, light 6 ardent, kindle

ignition cap: 4 fuse, fuze

ignoble: low 4 base, mean, vile 6 adject, sordid 8 shameful 11 disgraceful 12 dishonorable

ignominious: 4 base 6 odious 8 infamous, shameful 9 degrading 10 despicable, mortifying 11 disgraceful, humiliating 12 contemptible, dishonorable

ignoramus: 4 dolt 5 dunce 6 nitwit

ignorance: 6 agnosy

ignorant: 4 dark 5 green, young 6 stupid 7 artless, unaware, uncouth 8 nescient, untaught 9 unlearned, unskilled, untutored 10 illiterate, unlettered 11 unconscious

ignore: cut 4 omit, snub 5 blink, elide 6 slight 7 neglect 8 overlook 9 disregard, eliminate

Igorot, Igorrote: 6 Bontok 7 Nabaloi 8 Kankanai
chief: Apo

iguana: 6 lizard 7 tuatara

Iguvine: 7 Umbrian 8 Eugubine

ihi: 4 fish 7 skipper 8 halfbeak 9 stichbird

Ihlat: 8 Sunnites

ijolite: 7 apatite, calcite 8 titanite

ikary: 6 caviar

ikbal: 7 arrival 8 prestige 10 prosperity

ikey: 5 proud

ikon: 5 image 6 symbol 7 picture 8 portrait 12 illustration

ikona: 9 greenhorn, simpleton

ikra: 6 caviar

ilex: 5 holly

Iliad: 4 epic, poem
character: 4 Ajax 5 Priam 6 Hector 8 Achilles 9 Agamemnon, Cassandra

ilium: 4 bone

Ilium, Ilion: 4 Troy

ilk: 4 each, kind, same, sort 5 breed, class, every 6 family

ill: bad 4 evil, harm, poor, sick 5 amiss, badly, wrong 6 ailing, faulty, wicked 7 adverse, ailment, baneful, noxious, trouble, unlucky 8 improper 9 adversity, defective 10 indisposed, iniquitous, misfortune 11 unfortunate
prefix: mal

ill at ease: 7 awkward

ill-boding: 4 dire 12 inauspicious

ill-bred: 6 hoiden, hoyden 7 plebian, uncivil 8 clownish, impolite, malapert 9 bourgeois 11 impertinent

ill-favored: 4 ugly 9 offensive 10 unpleasant 12 disagreeable

ill-humor: tid 5 anger 7 dudgeon

ill-humored: 5 cross 6 cranky, morose 7 fretful, peevish

ill-natured: 4 dour 5 nasty, surly 6 crabby 7 fretful

ill-smelling: 5 fetid 10 malodorous

ill-tempered: 5 cross, moody 6 crusty 7 bilious

ill-treat: 5 abuse 8 maltreat

ill will: 5 spite 6 animus, malice, mauger 9 hostility

showing: 7 hostile 8 choleric 9 bellicose, irascible, litigious, wrangling 10 pugnacious 11 belligerent, contentious, quarrelsome 12 disputatious

ill-wisher: foe 5 enemy

illation: 9 deduction 11 inferential

illegal: 4 foul 7 bootleg, illicit 8 unlawful 10 contraband

illegitimate: 7 bastard, bootleg, unusual 8 abnormal, improper, spurious, unlawful, wrongful 9 illogical

illiberal: 6 stingy 7 bigoted 8 churlish 9 hidebound 13 ungentlemanly

illicit: 7 bootleg, illegal 8 improper, unlawful 10 contraband

illimitable: 4 vast 8 infinite 9 boundless 11 measureless 12 immeasurable

Illinois: *county:* Lee 4 Cook, Ogle, Polk 6 Hardin

river: 5 Spoon

town: 4 Pana 5 Alton, Elgin 6 Aurora, Breese, Joliet, Moline 7 Decatur, Wheaton 8 Streator 10 Springfield(c.)

illiterate: 6 unread 8 ignorant, untaught 9 barbarous, unlearned, untutored 10 unlettered

illness: 5 colic 6 malady, morbus 7 ailment, cachexy, disease 8 cachexia, disorder, sickness 9 complaint, distemper 10 affliction, wickedness 13 indisposition

feign: 8 malinger

mental: See **mental disorder**

illogical: 7 invalid 12 inconsequent

illude: 4 bilk, mock 5 cheat, elude, evade 6 delude, deride 7 deceive

illume: See **illuminate**

illuminant: gas 9 petroleum

illuminate: 4 fire 5 adorn, flare, light 6 illume, kindle 7 clarify, emblaze, lighten 8 brighten, illumine 9 enlighten, irradiate 10 illustrate

illumination: *device:* 4 lamp 5 torch 7 lantern 10 flashlight

in eclipse: 8 penumbra

measure: 4 phot

illumine: See **illuminate**

illusion: 5 fancy 6 mirage 7 chimera, fallacy, mockery, phantom 8 delusion 9 deception 10 appearance

illusive: 4 flam 5 false 6 unreal 7 fatuous 8 illusory 9 deceitful, deceptive, fantasmal 10 fallacious, phantasmal 16 phantasmagorical

illusory: See **illusive**

illustrate: 5 adorn 7 picture 9 elucidate, exemplify, represent 10 illuminate

illustration: 4 icon, ikon 7 example, exempla(pl.) 8 exemplum, vignette 13 demonstration 15 exemplification

illustrator: 6 artist

illustrious: 5 famed, grand, noble, noted 6 bright, candid, heroic 7 eminent, exalted 8 glorious, renowned 9 honorable 10 celebrated 11 conspicuous 13 distinguished

ilvaite: 6 yenite

image: god 4 copy, form, icon, idol, ikon 5 eikon, image 6 effigy, eidola(pl.), emblem, figure, idolon, statue, symbol 7 eidolon, phantom, picture, portray 8 likeness 9 semblance, simulacre 10 conception, reflection, similitude, simulacrum

good luck: 6 alraun

maker: 10 iconoplast

mental: 4 idea 6 recept 7 concept 8 phantasm 10 conception

pert. to: 6 iconic 10 simulacral

rainbowlike: 7 spectra(pl.) 8 spectrum

religious: 4 icon

stone: 5 herma 6 hermae(pl.)

televised: 5 video

wooden: 4 tiki 6 xoanon

worship: 5 arati 8 idolatry

image-breaker: 10 iconoclast

image-like: 10 simulacral

image-worshiper: 8 idolator 9 conolater

imaginary: 5 ideal 6 unreal 7 fancied, feigned 8 mythical, notional 9 fantastic, visionary 10 artificial, chimerical, fictitious

imagination: 5 fancy 7 fantasy

imaginative: 6 dreamy, poetic 8 fanciful 9 fantastic

imagine: 4 ween 5 dream, fancy, feign, think 6 vision 7 picture, suppose, surmise 8 conceive, envision 9 apprehend 10 comprehend, conjecture

imago: bee

imam: 5 calif 6 caliph

last: 5 Mahdi

imaret: 7 hospice 11 caravansary, caravaserai

imbar: 5 guard 7 fortify

imbecile: 4 dolt, dote 5 anile, daffy, idiot, moron 6 cranky, dotard, dotish 7 fatuous 9 driveling 10 changeling, half-witted

imbed: fix 5 embed, inset 6 cement

imbibe: sip 4 soak 5 drink, imbue, steep 6 absorb 7 swallow 8 saturate 10 assimilate

imbosom: 7 cherish, embrace, shelter

imbricate: 5 tiled 6 scaled

imbroglio: 12 disagreement 16 misunderstanding

imbrue: wet 4 soak 5 stain, steep 6 defile, drench 7 moisten 8 saturate

imbue: dye 4 soak 5 steep, tinge 6 imbibe, infuse, leaven 7 animate, ingrain, inspire, instill, pervade 8 permeate, saturate, tincture 9 inoculate 10 impregnate

imburse: pay 10 recompense

imidogen compound: 4 imid, imin 5 imide, imine

imitant: 9 imitation 11 counterfeit

imitate: ape 4 copy, echo, mime, mock 5 mimic 6 follow, repeat 7 copycat, emulate 8 resemble, simulate 9 dissemble 11 counterfeit

imitation: 4 copy, echo, fake, sham 5 dummy, paste 6 parody 7 imitant 9 emulation, facsimile, imitative, schlenter

derisive: 7 mimicry, mockery

fantastic: 8 travesty

imitation gem: 5 glass, paste

imitation pearl: 6 olivet

imitator: 4 mima 5 mimae(pl.)

immaculate: 4 pure 5 clean 6 candid, chaste 7 correct, perfect 8 innocent, spotless, unsoiled 9 faultless, undefiled, unspotted, unstained, unsullied

immalleable: 10 unyielding

immane: 4 huge, vast 5 great 6 fierce 7 immense, inhuman 9 atrocious, monstrous

immanent: 8 inherent 9 intrinsic 10 indwelling

immaterial: 6 slight 8 trifling 9 asomatous, spiritual 10 impalpable, intangible 13 insignificant, unsubstantial

immatriculate: 6 enroll 11 matriculate

immature: 5 crude, green, young 6 callow, unripe 7 girlish, puerile, untried 8 youthful 9 premature 10 incomplete, unfinished 11 undeveloped

immaturity: 5 youth 6 nonage 7 infancy 10 callowness, unripeness

immeasurable: 7 immense 8 infinite 9 boundless, unlimited 10 indefinite 11 illimitable, measureless 12 immensurable

immediate: 4 next 6 direct 7 instant 8 imminent 9 proximate 10 contiguous, succeeding

immediately: now 4 anon 6 presto 8 directly 9 extempore, forthwith, presently

immemorial: 7 ageless, ancient 8 dateless 11 prehistoric, traditional

immense: 4 huge 5 grand, great, large 7 titanic 8 enormous, gigantic, infinite 9 extensive, monstrous 10 prodigious, unmeasured 12 immeasurable

immensurable: See **immeasurable**

immerge: See **immerse**

immerse: dip 4 bury, duck 5 bathe, douse, dowse, souse 6 absorb, drench, plunge 7 engross, ensteep, immerge

immigrant: 8 comeling

Israel: 6 halutz 7 chalutz

imminent: 9 impending

immitigable: 10 implacable

immobile: set 4 firm 5 fixed, inert 6 frozen, stable 8 moveless 9 immovable 10 motionless, stationary

immoderate: 4 free 5 undue 7 extreme 9 boundless, excessive, voracious 10 exorbitant, inordinate 11 intemperate 12 unreasonable

immodest: 4 bold 6 brazen, coarse 7 forward, obscene 8 indecent, unchaste 9 shameless 10 indecorous

immolation: 9 sacrifice

immoral: bad 4 evil 5 loose, wrong 7 corrupt, vicious 8 culpable, depraved, indecent 9 dissolute 10 licentious 11 unwholesome

immortal: 6 divine 7 endless, eternal, godlike 8 enduring 9 ceaseless, deathless 11 amaranthine, everlasting 12 imperishable 13 incorruptible

immortality: 8 athanasy 9 athanasia 13 deathlessness 15 everlastingness

Hindu: 6 amrita

immovable: pat, set 4 fast, firm 5 fixed, rigid 7 adamant 8 constant, immobile, obdurate 9 steadfast 10 adamantine, stationary

immunity: 7 freedom 9 exemption 11 unrestraint

immunize: 7 vastate 9 inoculate 10 haffkinize

immunizer: 5 serum 7 vaccine

immure: 4 wall 7 confine 8 cloister, imprison 11 incarcerate

immutable: 4 firm 7 eternal 10 invariable, unchanging 11 unalterable 13 unadulterated

Imogen's mother: 9 Cymbeline

imp: bud, elf 4 brat, cion, slip 5 child, demon, devil, graft, rogue, scamp, scion 6 sprite, urchin 7 gremlin, implant, progeny 8 devilkin, folletto, folletti(pl.) 9 hobgoblin, offspring 13 mischiefmaker 15 flibbertigibbet

impact: 4 pack, slam 5 brunt, feeze, shock, wedge, whang 6 stroke 7 impulse

impair: mar 4 blot, harm, hurt, wear 5 break, spoil, waste 6 damage, debase, injure, lessen, reduce, sicken, weaken 7 blemish, impeach, vitiate 8 decrease, enfeeble

impaired: 9 afflicted

impala: 7 rooibok 8 rooyebok

impale: 4 edge, spit 5 spear, spike 6 border, pierce 7 confine 8 encircle, surround

impalpable: 7 elusive 10 immaterial, intangible

impar: odd 7 unequal

impark: 7 enclose

impart: 4 give, lend, tell 5 share, yield 6 bestow, confer, convey, direct, impute, reveal 7 divulge, inspire, instill 8 disclose, discover 10 distribute 11 communicate

impartial: 4 even, fair, just 6 candid 8 unbiased 9 colorless, equitable 12 irrespective 13 disinterested, dispassionate

imparting motion: 7 kinetic

impassable: 5 solid 10 impervious

impasse: 8 cul-de-sac(F.) 9 stalemate

impassible: 9 impassive, unfeeling 11 unendurable

impassioned: 6 fervid 7 fervent 8 eloquent, feverish

impassive: 4 calm 5 stoic 6 serene, stolid 7 passive 9 apathetic 10 impassible 13 imperturbable

impatient: hot 5 eager, hasty, testy 7 fidgety, fretful, peevish 8 choleric, petulant, restless 9 irascible, irritable

impavid: 8 fearless

impeach: 4 call, harm 6 accuse, charge, hinder, impair, impede, indict 7 appeach, arraign, censure, prevent 9 challenge, discredit, disparage

impeachment: 4 harm 6 damage, injury 8 dishonor, reproach 9 challenge, hindrance 10 accusation, impediment 11 obstruction

impeccable: 9 faultless

impecunious: 4 poor 9 penniless

impede: gum, let 4 clog 5 block, check, choke, delay, estop 6 fetter, forbid, hamper, harass, hinder, retard, stymie 7 impeach, prevent 8 encumber, handicap, obstruct, preclude 9 embarrass
legally: bar 5 debar, estop

impediment: bar, bur, rub 4 clog, snag 5 hitch 6 defect, malady, remora 7 embargo 8 obstacle 9 detriment, hindrance 10 difficulty 11 encumbrance, impeachment, obstruction 13 embarrassment

impedimenta: 7 baggage

impel: pat 6 blow, goad, move, send, spur, urge 5 drive, feeze, force, hurry 6 compel, excite, incite, induce 7 actuate 8 motivate 9 constrain, encourage, influence, instigate, stimulate

impelling force: 7 impetus 8 momentum

impend: 4 hang, loom 6 menace 8 approach

impending: 8 imminent, menacing 9 hindering 11 threatening

impenetrable: 4 hard 5 dense 8 airtight, hardened 10 impervious 11 inscrutable 12 unfathomable

impenitent: 8 hardened, obdurate 11 unrepentant

imperative: 8 pressing, verb form 9 imperious, mandatory 10 commanding, compulsory, peremptory

imperator: 6 leader 7 emporer, general

imperceptible: 10 insensible, intangible 13 inappreciable, indiscernible 17 indistinguishable

imperfect: 4 cull, poor 5 rough 6 faulty, second 9 defective 10 inadequate, incomplete, unfinished
prefix: mal 5 atelo

imperfection: 4 flaw, vice 5 fault 6 defect, foible 7 blemish, default, failing, frailty 8 weakness 10 deficiency 11 shortcoming

imperfectly: 4 half 5 badly

imperial: 5 regal, royal 6 kingly 8 majestic
cap: 5 crown
domain: 6 empery, empire 8 emperies(pl.)
officer: 8 palatine

imperial woodpecker: 9 ivorybill

imperil: 4 risk 6 expone, hazard 8 endanger 10 jeopardize

imperious: 6 lordly 7 haughty 8 arrogant, despotic, dominant, pressing 10 commanding, imperative, tyrannical 11 dictatorial, domineering, magisterial, overbearing 13 authoritative

imperish: 6 impair, injure

imperishable: 7 eternal, undying 8 enduring, immortal 9 continual, deathless 11 everlasting 14 indestructible

impermanent: 8 fleeting 9 ephemeral, temporary, tentative, transient 10 evanescent

impersonal: 4 cold 7 general

impersonate: act, ape 4 pose 6 typify 9 exemplify, personify

impersonator: 5 actor 7 actress

impertinence: 4 sass 8 audacity 9 insolence 10 confidence, incivility 11 impropriety, irrelevance

impertinent: 4 rude 5 sassy, saucy 7 ill-bred 8 arrogant, impudent 9 audacious, officious 10 inapposite 12 inconsequent 13 disrespectful

imperturbability: 8 ataraxia
imperturbable: 4 cool 6 placid, serene 8 tranquil 9 impassive 10 phlegmatic
impervious: 5 tight 8 hardened 10 impassable 12 impenetrable
impetition: 6 charge 10 accusation
impetrate: 7 beseech, entreat, procure
impetuosity: 5 haste 6 fougue
impetuous: hot 4 ramp, rash 5 eager, fiery, hasty, heady, sharp 6 abrupt, ardent, fervid, fierce, flashy, sudden 7 furious, hotspur, violent 8 forcible, headlong, vehement 9 impulsive 10 hotspurred 11 precipitate
impetus: 4 bent, birr, fard 5 drift, faird, force 6 swinge 7 impulse 8 momentum, stimulus 9 incentive
imphee: 5 plant 7 sorghum
impi: 8 soldiers, warriors
impiety: 9 blasphemy 11 irreverence, ungodliness
impignorate: 6 pawned 7 pledged
impinge: 6 strike 8 encroach
impious: 6 unholy 7 godless, profane, ungodly 9 atheistic, nefandous, undutiful 10 irreverent 11 irreligious
impish: 6 elfish 7 warlock 11 mischievous
implacable: 6 deadly 9 ferocious 11 immitigable 12 unappeasable 14 irreconcilable
implant: sow 4 root 5 infix, inset 6 enrace, enroot, infuse 7 enforce, engraft, impress, inspire, instill 9 inculcate, inoculate, insinuate, introduce
implement (see also **tool**): 4 gear 7 enforce, fulfill, utensil 8 complete, material 9 apparatus, appliance 10 accomplish, instrument
ancient: 4 celt 6 amgarn, eolith 9 paleolith
baker's: 4 peel
barbed: 7 harpoon
cleaning: mop 4 swab 5 broom, brush 6 vacuum 7 sweeper
cutting: 5 knife, mower, razor 6 reaper, scythe, shears 8 scissors 9 jackknife 11 pocketknife
enlarging: 6 reamer 7 dilator
farm: 4 disc, disk, plow, rake 6 seeder, tiller 7 tractor
furcate: 4 fork
garden: hoe 4 rake 5 mower 6 sickle, weeder
grasping: 5 tongs 6 pliers 8 tweezers
hand printing: 6 brayer, roller
hide cleaning: 6 slater
kind of: 5 dolly 6 fraise, mortar, pestle, rabble 7 mattock, sadiron, scraper
kitchen: pot, pan 5 corer 6 kettle 7 skillet, spatula
lifting: pry 5 lever, tongs

logging: 4 tode 5 peavy, peevy 6 peavey, peevey
nap-raising: 5 tease 6 teasel, teasle, teazel, teazle
pounding: 4 maul 6 hammer, pestle
printer's: 5 biron, press
reaping: 5 mower 6 reaper, scythe, shears, sickle
shovel-like: 5 scoop, spoon 6 trowel
surgical: 7 scalpel 9 tenaculum
threshing: 5 flail
war: 6 armory, onager, petard
implete: 6 filled 7 replete
implicate: 7 concern, embroil, entwine, involve 10 interweave
implicit: 5 tacit 8 absolute, complete, explicit 12 constructive
implied: 5 tacit 6 hinted 11 inferential
implore: ask, beg 4 coax, pray 5 crave, plead 6 appeal 7 beseech, entreat, solicit 8 petition 10 supplicate
imply: 4 hint 5 infer 6 infold 7 connote, involve, premise, signify 8 comprise, intimate 9 insinuate, predicate 10 comprehend
impolite: 4 rude 5 bluff, crude, rough 7 ill-bred, uncivil 10 indecorous, ungracious, unmannerly, unpolished 12 discourteous 13 disrespectful
impolitic: 6 unwise 10 indiscreet 11 inexpedient, injudicious 12 undiplomatic
imporous: 5 close, dense, solid
import: 5 sense, value 6 convey, denote 7 betoken, meaning, signify 8 indicate 9 substance
tax: 4 duty 6 tariff
importance: 4 bore 6 moment, weight 7 account, gravity 8 prestige 9 dimension 11 consequence 13 consideration
to be of: 6 matter
important: 4 dear, high 5 grave, great 6 urgent 7 pompous, serious 8 eventful, material 9 momentous, ponderous 10 chargeable 11 considerate, fundamental, influential, significant 12 considerable 13 consequential
important person: VIP 6 bigwig 7 magnate
importunate: 6 urgent 7 teasing 8 exigeant, pressing 9 exigeante 10 burdensome 11 inopportune, troublesome
importune: beg, dun, nag, ply, woo 4 urge 5 plead 6 appeal 7 entreat, solicit 10 supplicate
importunity: 8 business, entreaty
impose: fob 4 dupe, fool, levy, sorn 6 burden, charge, delude, entail 7 blaflum, command, dictate, inflict, obtrude
impose upon: fob 4 dupe, palm
imposing: big 5 burly, proud 6 august 7 stately 9 grandiose, pyramidal 10 com-

manding, impressive, obligatory 11 outstanding

imposition: tax 4 duty, levy 5 fraud, gouge, trick 6 burden, chouse 7 penalty 8 artifice 9 deception, imposture

impossible: 13 impracticable

impost: tax 4 duty, levy, task, toll 6 annale, avania, custom, excise, surtax, tariff, weight 7 tribute 8 chaptrel

India: 5 abwab

salt: 7 gabelle

impostor: fob 4 gull, idol, sham 5 cheat, fraud, gouge, quack 6 bunyip 7 empiric, faitour 8 deceiver 9 charlatan, pretender 10 mountebank

imposture: gag 4 sham 5 cheat, fraud, trick 6 deceit, humbug 8 artifice, delusion 9 deception, falsehood 10 imposition

impotence: 7 acratia 8 weakness 10 feebleness

impotent: 6 barren, unable 7 sterile 9 powerless

impound: 5 seize, store 6 freeze 7 collect 11 appropriate

impouring: 6 influx

impoverish: 4 ruin 6 beggar, weaken 7 deplete, exhaust

impoverished: 4 poor 8 bankrupt

impracticable: 10 impossible

impractical: 9 visionary

imprecate: 4 pray 5 curse 6 invoke 8 execrate 10 supplicate

imprecation: ban 4 oath 5 curse 8 anathema 9 blasphemy 10 execration 11 deprecation, malediction

impregnability: 9 fortitude

impregnable: 4 hard 12 inexpugnable

impregnate: 4 soak 6 charge, infuse, leaven 8 fructify, permeate, saturate 9 fecundate, fertilize

impresa: 5 maxim, motto 6 device, emblem 7 proverb

impresario: 7 manager 9 conductor, projector 12 entrepreneur

impress: fix 4 bite, levy, mark, seal, tool 5 affix, brand, delve, infix, press, print, stamp 6 enlist 7 engrave, implant, impress, imprint 9 character, inculcate, influence 14 characteristic

impressed: 4 awed 8 affected

impression: 4 dent, dint, idea, mark 5 fancy, print, stamp 6 effect, signet 7 opinion 8 reaction 10 conception

printing: 6 macule

impressionable: 7 plastic 9 sensitive 10 responsive 11 susceptible

impressionist painter: 5 Manet, Monet 6 Renoir 8 Pissarro

impressive: 5 grand 6 solemn 8 forcible, imposing 9 arresting, grandiose

imprevu: 10 unforeseen

imprimatur: 7 license 8 approval, sanction

imprint: fix 4 dint, mark 5 press, stamp 7 engrave, impress 12 characterize

imprison: 4 cage, jail, seal 5 grate, limit 6 arrest, commit, detain, immure 7 confine, enclose 8 restrain 9 carcerate 11 incarcerate

imprisonment: 6 arrest, duress 7 durance 8 coercion 9 captivity, restraint 11 confinement 13 incarceration

improbable: 5 fishy 8 unlikely

impromptu: 7 offhand 9 extempore 14 extemporaneous

improper: ill 4 evil 5 amiss, undue, unfit, wrong 6 unjust 7 illegal, illicit 8 indecent, shameful, unseemly 9 incorrect 10 inaccurate, indecorous, indelicate, unbecoming 12 illegitimate

improperly: 5 amiss

impropriety: 5 shame 8 solecism 12 impertinence

improve: 4 grow, help, mend 5 amend, edify, emend, moise 6 better, enrich 7 advance, augment, benefit, correct, enhance, perfect, promote, rectify, retouch 9 cultivate, intensify, meliorate 10 ameliorate

improvident: 8 prodigal, wasteful 9 negligent 10 thriftless 11 thoughtless

improvise: 5 ad-lib 6 devise, invent 7 compose 8 contrive 11 extemporize

music: 4 vamp

imprudent: 4 rash 6 unwary, unwise 7 foolish 8 reckless 10 incautious, indiscreet 11 injudicious 12 shortsighted

impudence: lip 4 gall 5 brass, cheek, folly 8 audacity 9 arrogance, assurance, hardihood, insolence 10 confidence, effrontery 11 presumption 13 shamelessness

impudent: 4 bold, pert, rude 5 brash, sassy, saucy 6 brazen 7 forward 8 insolent 9 barefaced, officious 11 impertinent 13 disrespectful

impugn: 4 deny 5 fight 6 assail, resist 7 gainsay 9 insinuate 10 contradict

impulse: 4 urge 5 drift, force 6 impact, motive 7 impetus 8 instinct 9 incentive 11 instigation

blind: ate

characterized by: 7 sensory

divine: 8 afflatus

traveling: 10 wanderlust

impulsive: 5 quick 6 fitful 8 headlong 9 impellent, impetuous

impure: 4 foul, hory, lewd, vile 5 dirty, gross, mixed 6 coarse, filthy, unholy 7 bastard, defiled, obscene, unclean, vicious 8 indecent, inferior, unchaste 10 unhal-

lowed **11** adulterated, incongruous, unwholesome
impurity: 6 defect, fedity **8** solution **9** pollution **10** corruption
impute: 4 give **5** count **6** charge, credit, impart, reckon **7** arraign, ascribe **8** consider
9 attribute
impy: 11 mischievous
in: at **4** amid, into, nook **5** among **6** corner **7**
arrived **9** incumbent
 a bad way: **4** sick **5** upset
 a chamber: **8** incamera
 a flutter: **7** pitapat
 a frenzied manner: **5** amuck
 a row: **4** arow **6** alined, serial **7** aligned
 a standing position: **7** statant
 a vertical line: **5** apeak
 abeyance: **7** pending
 abundance: **6** galore, plenty
 accordance with: **8** pursuant
 addition: too, yet **4** also, more, plus **5** aside
 7 besides
 advance: **5** ahead **6** before
 another direction: **4** away
 any case: **4** ever
 any event: **15** notwithstanding
 as much: **5** since **7** because
 capacity of: qua
 case: **4** lest
 common: **5** alike
 company of: **4** with
 concert: **8** together
 contact: **9** attingent
 due course: **4** soon **11** opportunely
 Dutch: **9** disgraced
 equal degree: as
 every way: **5** fully **6** wholly **7** totally **8** entirely **10** completely, thoroughly
 excess: too **4** over
 existence: **6** extant
 fact: **5** truly **6** indeed **7** de facto(L.)
 favor of: pro
 few cases: **6** seldom
 good season: **5** early **6** betime
 great need: **7** straits
 manner of: ala
 name only: **7** nominal **10** supposedly
 place of: for **5** stead **7** instead
 prefix: en, il
 regard to: **5** anent
 same place: **4** ibid
 shape: fit **4** neat, trim **5** ready
 so far as it is: qua
 spite of: **4** over **6** mauger, maugre **7** despite
 stitches: **6** amused **8** laughing
 store: **8** awaiting
 that case: so **4** then
 the case of: **4** in re(L.)
 the center of: **4** amid

 the interim: **9** meanwhile
 the know: hep, hip
 the main: **9** generally
 the manner of: a la
 the mood: **5** eager **7** willing
 the raw: **4** nude **10** dishabille
 the red: **5** broke **8** bankrupt, strapped
 the same period: **15** contemporaneous
 the time of: **6** during
 this: **6** herein
 this way: **4** thus
 toto: all **5** whole **8** complete **10** completely
 truth: **6** certes, indeed, verily **8** forsooth
 what way: how **7** quomodo
 year of: **4** anno
inability: 9 impotence **10** incapacity **12** incompetence
 to articulate: **7** anaudia
 to chew: **8** amasesis
 to comprehend: **11** acatalepsia
 to name correctly: **9** paranomia
 to read: **6** alexia
 to speak: **6** anepia
 to stand erect: **7** astasia
 to swallow: **7** aphagia
 to understand speech: **7** aphasia
inaccessible: 12 unattainable **14** inap-
proachable, unapproachable
inaccuracy: 5 error **7** mistake
inaccurate: 5 loose **6** faulty, unjust **7** inexact **8** improper **9** defective, imperfect **10**
unfaithful
Inachus's daughter: Io
inaction: 8 idleness **9** inertness
 temporary: **5** pause **6** recess **7** abeyant, respite
inactive: lax **4** dead, idle, slow **5** heavy, inert, prone, slack, still **6** latent, otiose, supine **7** dormant, passive **8** dilatory, faineant, indolent, sleeping, slothful, sluggish **9**
quiescent, recumbent, sedentary **10** unemployed
inadequate: bad **4** lean **6** feeble **9** deficient,
imperfect **12** insufficient
 perilously: **7** Icarian
inadvertence: 10 negligence **12** carelessness, heedlessness **15** thoughtlessness
inadvisable: 4 rash **10** indiscreet
inalterable: 9 steadfast
inamorato: 7 amorado **8** amoretto
inane: 5 empty, silly, vapid **6** vacant **7** fatuous, foolish, idiotic, vacuous **8** trifling **9**
doddering, frivolous, pointless, senseless,
worthless **11** nonsensical **13** characterless
inanimate: 4 dead, dull, flat **5** brute, inert **6**
stolid **8** lifeless **10** insensible **11** insensitive, unconscious
inanition: 7 fasting **9** emptiness

inanity: 7 vacuity 9 emptiness, frivolity, silliness 10 flimsiness, triviality 13 senselessness

inapposite: 10 irrelevant 11 impertinent 13 inappropriate

inappreciable: 10 invaluable 13 imperceptible

inappropriate: 5 inept, undue 6 clumsy 10 unsuitable

inapt: 5 inept 6 clumsy 7 awkward 8 backward 10 amateurish, unsuitable

inarch: 5 graft

inarm: 7 embrace

inarticulate: 4 dumb, mute

inartistic: 9 tasteless

inasmuch: as; for 5 since 7 because

inattention: 7 neglect 9 disregard 10 negligence

inattentive: lax 6 absent, remiss 8 careless, heedless 9 forgetful, negligent, unheeding, unmindful 10 abstracted, neglectful 11 inadvertent, thoughtless 13 inconsiderate

inaugurate: 4 open 5 augur, begin, start 6 induct 7 install 8 initiate 9 auspicate, introduce 10 consecrate

inauspicious: bad 4 foul 7 adverse, ominous 8 sinister 12 unpropitious

inauthentic: 5 false 6 mythic, unreal 8 doubtful, spurious 9 ambiguous, uncertain 10 apocryphal, fictitious

inborn: 6 inbred, innate, native 7 connate, natural 8 inherent 10 congenital

inborn desire: 7 conatus

inbreak: 6 inroad 8 invasion 9 incursion

inbred: 6 inborn, innate 10 congenital

Inca: 9 Atahualpa
clan: 5 ayllu
empire: 4 Peru
god: 4 Inti 5 Choun, Iraya 6 Chasca 9 Uiracocha, Viracocha 10 Pachacamac
king: 9 Atabalipa, Atahualpa
priests: 6 Amauta
ruler's sister-wife: 5 Ccoya

incalculable: 6 untold 9 boundless, countless, uncertain 11 illimitable 12 immeasurable

incandescence: 4 glow, heat

incantation: 5 chant, charm, dawut, magic, spell 6 carmen(L.) 7 sorcery 9 cantation 11 conjuration, enchantment

incapable: 6 unable 11 inefficient, unqualified 12 disqualified

incapacitate: 4 lame 7 cripple, disable 10 disqualify

incarcerate: 4 jail 6 immure 7 confine 8 imprison 9 carcerate

incarnate: 6 embody 8 embodied

incarnation: 6 advent, avatar, Christ 10 embodiment

of Vishnu: 4 Rama

incase: 5 cover 7 enclose 8 surround

incasement: 11 emboitement

incautious: 4 rash 6 unwary 8 careless, heedless, reckless 9 impolitic, imprudent, unguarded 10 indiscreet

incendiarism: 5 arson

incendiary: 4 goon 5 firer 9 seditious 12 inflammatory

incense: 5 anger 6 arouse, enrage, incite 7 provoke 8 enkindle, irritate 9 instigate
burner: 6 censer 8 thurible
spice: 6 balsam, stacte
vessel: 6 censer 7 navette(F.)

incentive: 4 goad, spur 5 spark 6 motive 7 impetus, impulse 8 stimulus 9 influence 10 incitement, inducement 11 provocation 13 consideration, encouragement

incept: 8 commence 9 undertake

inception: 6 origin 9 beginning, reception 10 initiation 12 commencement

incessant: 6 steady 7 endless, eternal 8 constant 9 ceaseless, continual 11 everlasting, unremitting

incessantly: 7 forever 11 continually, unceasingly

inch: 5 uncia
one-thousandth: mil
three-quarters of: 5 digit

inch along: 4 worm

inch forward: 4 edge 7 crowhop

inches: *forty-five:* ell
four: 4 hand
nine: 4 span
39.37: 5 meter
two and one-quarter: 4 nail

inchmeal: 9 gradually

inchoate: 5 begin 8 commence, initiate 9 incipient 10 incomplete

inchpin: 10 sweetbread

incident: 5 event 7 episode 8 accident, casualty, occasion 9 happening 11 contingency

incidental: 6 casual 8 episodic 9 accessory, extrinsic 10 accidental, contingent, fortuitous, occasional 12 adventitious 14 circumstantial

incidentally: 6 byhand, obiter 7 apropos

incinerate: 4 burn 7 combust, consume, cremate

incinerator: 7 furnace 9 crematory

incipient: 6 induct 7 initial 8 inchoate 10 commencing, inaugurate

incise: cut 4 chop, etch, rase 5 carve 7 engrave
narrowly: 9 laciniate

incision: cut 4 gash, slit 5 lance 6 broach, scotch 10 laceration

incisive: 5 acute, sharp 6 biting 7 cutting 9 sarcastic 11 penetrating

incisor: 6 cutter 9 foretooth

incite: egg, hie 4 abet, fire, goad, move, prod, sick, spur, urge 5 impel, sting 6 arouse, compel, entice, excite, exhort, foment, induce 7 actuate, agitate, animate, commove, provoke 8 motivate 9 encourage, instigate, stimulate

incitement: 6 motive 8 stimulus 9 incentive

incivility: 8 rudeness 9 surliness 10 disrespect, effrontery 11 discourtesy 12 churlishness, impertinence 14 unmannerliness

inclemency: 8 asperity

inclement: raw 4 hard, rude 5 harsh, rough 6 severe, stormy 8 rigorous 10 unmerciful

inclination: 4 bent, bias, broo, hang, love, urge, will 5 bevel, fancy, heald, hield, slant, taste, tenor, trend 6 affect, animus, ascent, device 7 conatus, descent, fantasy, hanging, inkling, leaning 8 penchant, tendency 9 acclivity, affection, direction, proneness 10 attachment, proclivity 11 declination, disposition 12 predilection 13 prepossession

incline: apt, bow, dip, tip 4 bend, brew, cant, heel, lean, list, ramp, tend, tilt 5 bevel, grade, heald, hield, humor, shape, slant, slide, slope, trend 6 careen, humour 7 upgrade

inclined: apt, dip 4 fain, wont 5 alist, atilt, prone 6 biased, leaned 7 hanging 8 addicted, affected 11 predisposed

inclip: 7 embrace, enclasp, inclasp

inclose: hem, pen 4 case 5 embar 6 encase, incase 7 environ

inclosed: 8 interior

inclosure: ree(Sc.) 8 sepiment 10 impalement
  animal: pen, sty 4 cage, cote, fold 5 hutch, kraal 6 corral

include: 7 contain, embrace, involve 8 comprise, comprize 9 encompass 10 comprehend

incognito: 7 unknown 8 disguise

incoherent: 6 broken 9 illogical 11 incongruous 12 disconnected, inconsequent, inconsistent

income: 4 gain 5 rente(F.) 6 profit, return 7 produce, revenue 8 interest, proceeds, receipts 9 emolument
  pert. to: 7 tontine
  receiver: 7 rentier

incommensurate: 7 unequal 12 insufficient 16 disproportionate

incommode: vex 5 annoy 6 molest, plague 7 trouble 8 disquiet 9 disoblige 10 discommode 13 inconvenience

incomparable: 8 peerless 9 matchless, unequaled, unrivaled 10 surpassing 11 superlative 15 incommeasurable

incompatible: 9 repugnant 11 conflicting, incongruous 12 inharmonious 13 contradictory, unsympathetic 14 irreconcilable

incompetence: 9 inability, unfitness 10 disability

incompetent: 5 inept, unfit 6 unable 8 helpless 9 incapable, unskilled 10 untalented 11 inefficient, unqualified 12 insufficient

incomplete: 5 blind, crude, rough 6 broken, undone 7 divided, lacking 8 immature, inchoate 9 defective, imperfect, partially 10 unfinished

incomprehensible: 8 abstruse 9 graspless 10 fathomless, mysterious, unreadable 11 unthinkable 12 unimaginable 13 unconceivable 14 unintelligible

inconclusive: 10 indefinite 11 ineffective

incondite: 5 crude 9 unrefined 10 unpolished

incongruity: 9 inharmony 10 dissonance 11 incoherence 12 disagreement 13 inconsistency 14 unsuitableness

incongruous: 5 alien 6 absurd, impure 9 grotesque 10 discordant, unsuitable 12 disagreeable, inconsistent, inharmonious 13 inappropriate

inconsequent: 7 invalid 9 illogical 10 irrelevant 11 unimportant 12 inconsistent 13 inconsecutive

inconsiderable: 5 petty 7 trivial 8 careless, unworthy 10 negligible 13 inconsiderate

inconsiderate: 4 rash 6 unkind 8 careless 9 imprudent, negligent 10 incautious, indiscreet, neglectful 11 improvident, injudicious, thoughtless 14 inconsiderable

inconsistent: 5 crimp 6 absurd 9 dissonant 10 capricious, discordant, discrepant, incoherent, inconstant 13 contradictory 14 irreconcilable

inconsolable: 11 comfortless, heartbroken 12 disconsolate

inconstant: 6 fickle 7 bruckle 8 disloyal, fluxible, variable 9 desultory, faithless 10 capricious, changeable 12 inconsistent

incontestable: 4 sure 7 certain 10 undeniable 11 indubitable

incontrovertible: 7 certain 10 undeniable

inconvenience: 5 annoy 8 disquiet 9 annoyance, incommode 10 discomfort, discommode, uneasiness 11 awkwardness, disturbance 12 discomfiture 13 embarrassment

inconvenient: 7 awkward, unhandy 8 annoying 10 unsuitable 11 troublesome 12 unreasonable

incorporate: mix 4 fuse, join 5 blend, merge, unite 6 absorb, embody 10 assimilate

incorporation: 10 absorption 11 combination

incorporeal: 4 aery 8 bodiless 9 asomatous, spiritual, sprightly 13 unsubstantial

incorrect: bad 5 false, wrong 6 faulty 9 erroneous

incorrect naming of objects: 9 paranomia

incorrigible: 4 hard 9 abandoned

incorruptible: 4 just 6 honest 7 upright

incrassate: 7 stupefy, swollen, thicken 10 inspissate

increase: add, eke, wax 4 eche, gain, grow, rise, rist 5 boost, raise, swell 6 accrue, amount, better, dilate, expand, extend, gather, growth 7 amplify, augment, enhance, enlarge, greaten, inflate, magnify 8 addition, ampliate, flourish, heighten, multiply 9 accession, advantage, aggravate, expansion, extension, increment, intensify 10 accelerate, accumulate, aggrandize, appreciate 11 aggravation, development, enlargement 12 augmentation 13 amplification 15 intensification

comb. form: 4 auxo

in sound: 9 crescendo

possessions: 5 amass 6 enrich

salary: 5 raise

incredulous: 8 doubting 9 faithless, skeptical

incremate: 7 cremate

increment: 4 gain 6 growth, income 8 increase 12 augmentation

increscent: 6 waxing 7 growing 9 enlarging 10 increasing

incriminate: 6 accuse 7 impeach

incrust: 4 coat 5 glaze 6 barkle

incubate: 5 brood

incubator: 8 couveuse 11 eccaleobion

incubus: 4 load 5 demon 6 burden, spirit 9 hindrance, nightmare 10 impediment 11 encumbrance

inculcate: 5 infix 6 infuse, instil 7 implant, impress, instill

inculpate: 5 blame 11 incriminate

incumbent: 9 impending 11 threatening

incunabulum: 6 cocoon, cradle, origin 7 infancy 9 beginning 10 birthplace

incur: 8 contract 9 encounter

incurable: 8 hopeless 10 remediless 11 irreparable 12 irremediable 13 irretrievable

incurious: 9 apathetic 11 unconcerned, uninquiring 12 uninterested

incursion: 4 rade(Sc.), raid 5 foray 6 inroad 7 assault, descent, hosting 8 invasion 10 dragonnade

incurved: 7 concave

incus: 5 ambos, anvil

indebted: 8 beholden 9 obligated

indecency: 8 impurity 9 immodesty, indecorum, obscenity 10 indelicacy

indecent: 4 foul 5 gross, nasty 6 coarse, greasy, impure 7 grivois, immoral, obscene 8 grivoise, immodest, improper, unseemly 9 dishonest 10 scurrilous

indecipherable: 9 illegible

indecision: 5 doubt 9 hesitancy 10 hesitation 11 uncertainty, vacillation 12 irresolution

indecorous: 4 rude 6 coarse 7 uncivil 8 immodest, impolite, improper, unseemly 10 unbecoming

indeed: aru, yea 4 awat(Sc.), iwis, ywis 5 truly 6 i'faith 8 forsooth

indefatigable: 4 busy 8 tireless, untiring 9 assiduous 10 persistent, unwearying 11 persevering

indefensible: 11 inexcusable 12 unpardonable 13 insupportable

indefinite: 5 loose, vague 7 inexact, neutral 8 aoristic 9 ambiguous, equivocal, uncertain, unlimited 10 inexplicit 12 inconclusive

pronoun: any, one 4 some

indehiscent fruit: uva

indelible: 4 fast 5 fixed 9 permanent 10 inerasable 12 ineffaceable, ineradicable, inexpungible

indelicate: raw 5 broad, gross 6 coarse, greasy 7 fulsome 8 impolite, improper, unseemly 9 offensive, unrefined 10 indecorous, unbecoming

indemnification: 10 reparation 11 restitution

indemnify: pay 6 recoup 9 reimburse 10 compensate, recompense

indemnity: 7 amnesty 9 exemption 10 protection 12 compensation

indent: jag 4 dent, gimp 5 chase, delve, inlay, notch, press, stamp, tooth 6 bruise, emboss 7 depress

indentation: bay 4 dent, dint, doke, nick 5 bulge, choil, crena, notch 6 crenae(pl.), dimple, recess 8 crenelet 10 impression

indented: 6 dented, jagged, milled 7 notched, sinuous 9 crenelate, impressed 10 undulating

indenture: 5 notch 8 contract 9 agreement

independence: 7 freedom 10 competency

independent: 4 free 5 proud 9 sovereign, uncoerced 11 self-centred 12 self-centered, uncontrolled, unrestricted

independently: 5 apart 10 absolutely

indestructible: 10 inviolable 12 imperishable

indeterminate: 5 vague 8 formless 9 uncertain, unlimited

indetermined: 9 ambiguous, equivocal

index: 4 file, list 5 table 7 catalog 9 catalogue, repertory

India (see also **Hindu**): *abuse:* 4 gali 5 galee
  acrobat: nat
  agent: 4 amin 5 ameen 6 muktar 8 go-
    mashta, gomastah
  air conditioner: 5 tatty
  alphabet: 6 Sarada 10 Devanagari
  ambassador: 5 vakil 6 vakeel
  ancestor: 4 Manu 5 Pitri
  animal, ox-like: 4 zebu
  antelope: 5 sasin 6 nilgau, nilgau 7 chikara,
    nilghai
  apartment: 6 zenana
  army officer: 4 naig, naik 6 naigue, naique
    7 jemadar, jemidar
  astrologer: 5 joshi
  attorney: 6 muktar
  awning: 9 shamianah
  baby: 4 baba
  bandit: 6 dacoit
  bard: 4 bhat
  bathing place: 4 ghat 5 ghaut
  bazaar: 5 chawk, chowk
  bean: urd
  bear: 4 balu 5 baloo
  bearer: 6 sirdar
  bed: 7 charpai, charpoy
  bed cover: 9 palampore
  bedstead: 7 charpao, charpoy
  bill of exchange: 5 hundi
  bird: 5 shama 8 amadavat, amaduvad 9
    amaduvade
  blight: 4 soka
  boat: 7 almadia, almadie, masoola
  bodice: 5 choli
  body servant: 6 sirdar
  boy: 6 chokra, Mowgli
  bracelet: 6 sankha
  bread: 8 chapatty, chupatty
  breakfast: 5 hazri
  brick: 6 soorki, soorky 7 soorkee
  British founder: 5 Clive
  buck: 5 sasin
  buffalo: 4 arna 5 arnee
  bulbul: 4 kala
  butter: ghi 4 ghee
  buzzard: 4 tesa
  cabinet: 6 almura, almyra 7 almirah, al-
    myrah
  calico: 5 saloo 6 salloo
  cannabis: 5 ganja
  canoe: 5 tanee
  cape: 4 divi
  capital: 5 Delhi
  carpet: 4 agra
  carriage: 4 ekka 5 bandy, tonga 6 gharri,
    gharry
  cashmere: 5 ulwan

  caste: Jat, Mal, Meo 4 Ahir, Gola, Mali 5
    Dhoby, Sansi 6 Dacoit, Dhanuk, Dhobie,
    Lohana, Vaisya 7 Agarwal, Brahmin,
    Dhangar, Vaishya
  cavalryman: 5 sowar 6 risala 7 ressala
  cedar: 6 deodar
  chamber: 4 Kiva 8 Tahkhana
  charm: 6 mantra
  chief: mir 4 raja, rana 5 rajah 6 sirdar
  church: 5 samaj
  cigarette: 4 biri
  city: See *town* below.
  civet: 5 rasse, zibet 6 zibeth
  clarinet: 4 been
  class: 5 caste
  clerk: 4 babu 5 baboo
  cloak: 5 choga
  cloth: 7 dhurrie
  coast: 7 Malabar
  coin: lac, pie 4 anna, dawm, fels, hoon, lakh,
    pice, tara 5 abidi, crore, paisa, rupee
  college: Tol
  colonialist: 5 Clive
  combining form: 4 Indo
  cook: 8 bawarchi
  corn: zea
  coronation: 8 abhiseka
  court official: 5 nazir
  cowrie: 5 zimbi
  crane: 5 sarus
  crocodile: 6 gavial, muggar, mugger, mug-
    gur
  crop: 4 rabi
  cymbal: tal
  dagger: 5 katar
  dais: 8 chabutra
  dance: 6 nautch 7 cantico
  dancer: nat 8 bayadere
  deer: 4 axis 5 kakar 6 chital, chitra, sam-
    bar, sambur 7 cheetal, cheetul
  demon: 4 bhut 5 asura 6 daitya
  deputy: 5 nabob, nawab
  desert: 4 Thar
  devil tree: 4 dita
  dialect: 4 Urdu 5 Hindi, Tamil 7 Prakrit
  dignitary: 5 rajah
  dill: 4 soya
  disease: 5 agrom
  district: 4 Sibi 5 Nasik, Patna, Simla 6 Zil-
    lah 7 Malabar, Nellore 8 Mofussil
  dog: 5 dhole 6 pariah
  drama: 6 nataka
  Dravidian: 5 Arava, Tamil
  drink: 4 soma 6 arrack
  drinking pot: 5 lotah
  drought: 4 soka
  drug: 5 bhang
  dust storm: 7 shaitan, sheitan
  earth: 5 regur

educated man: 4 babu 6 pundit
educated woman: 7 pundita
elephant: 5 hathi
elephant driver: 6 mahout
epic: 8 Ramayana 11 Mahabharata
fabric: 6 tanjib, zenana
falcon: 6 shahin 7 shaheen
fan: 5 punka 6 punkah
father: 4 babu
festival: 4 Holi, mela
fiber: 6 ambary
fig tree: 5 pipal 6 peepul
fish: 5 dorab
flower: 5 lotus
founder of Mogul dynasty: 5 Baber
fruit: bel
garment: 4 sari 5 burqa, saree
god: 4 Deva, Yama 5 Shiva
goddess: 4 Amma 5 Amman
gossip: gup
government: 6 sircar
governor: 5 nazim
grass: 4 kusa 5 kusha, roosa 6 bhabar, darbha, doorba
griddlecake: 8 chapatty
grinding stone: 4 mano 6 metate
grove: 5 Sarna
guard: 7 daloyet
guide: 7 shikari 8 shikaree
hall: 6 durbar
handkerchief: 7 malabar
harem: 6 zenana
harvest: 4 rabi
heiress: 5 Begum
hemp: kef 4 bang, carl, kaif, keef 5 bhang, ramie 7 chirata
herb: pie 6 sesame 7 curcuma, tumeric, zeodary
hero: 4 Rama
holy: sri 4 shri 5 shree
holy man: 5 fakir, sadhu 6 saddhu
house: 5 mahal 8 bungalow
impost: 5 abwab
instrument: 5 ruana, sarod 7 sarinda
intoxicant: 4 soma
jungle: 5 shola
justice: 7 adawlut
king: 4 Nala, raja 5 rajah
knife: dah
laborer: 4 toty 7 totyman
lady: 7 sahibah
lake: 4 jhil 5 jheel 6 Chilka, Kolair
language: 4 Urdu 5 Hindi, Tamil 6 Siouan, Telugu 8 Sanskrit
law opinion: 5 futwa
leader: 5 Nehru 6 Gandhi
legal claim: hak 4 hakh
leopard, hunting: 7 cheetah
literature: 7 akhyana

loincloth: 5 dhoti
lord: 4 mian
mahogany: 4 toon 5 toona
mail: dak 4 dawk
mangrove: 5 goran
master: 5 saheb, sahib
matting: 5 tatta
meal: ata 4 atta
measure: ady, dha, gaz, gez, guz, jow, kos, lan, ser 4 byee, coss, dain, dhan, hath, jaob, koss, kunk, moot, para, rati, raik, seit, taun, teng, tola 5 bigha, cahar, covid, crosa, danda, denda, drona, garce, gireh, hasta, krosa, pally, parah, ratti, salay, yojan 6 adhaka, amunam, angula, covido, cudava, cumbha, geerah, lamany, moolum, mushti, palgat, parrah, ropani, tipree, unglee, yojana 7 adoulie, dhanush, gavyuti, khahoon, niranga, prastha, vitasti 8 okthabah
merchant: 5 banya 6 banian 8 soudagur 9 brinjaree
millet: 4 joar
money: See *coin* above
mountain: 4 Meru 5 Ghats 7 Siwalik, Vindhya 8 Suleiman 9 Himalayas, Hindukush, Nilghiris 12 Neilgherries
mulberry: al; aal, ach 6 alroot
musical instrument: 4 vina 5 ruana
muslin: 5 adati, dorea, doria 6 gurrah 9 charkhana
narcotic: 4 bang 5 bhang 7 hashish
native: 5 Hindu, Sepoy, Tamil 8 Assamese 10 Hindustani
nonviolence: 6 ahimsa
nurse: 4 amah, ayah, dhai
old money: 5 mohur
ox: 4 zebu
peasant: 4 ryot
people: 4 Bhil 5 Kotar 6 Hubshi, Badaga
pheasant: 5 monal 6 monaul, moonal
pipe: 6 hookah
poetic name: Ind
policeman: 4 peon 5 sepoy
priest: 5 mobed, mulla 6 mullah
prince: 4 bana, rana 5 rajah
princess: 4 rani 5 begum, ranee
property: 4 dhan
province: 4 Dhar, Jath, Jind 5 Assam, Berar, Bihar 6 Bengal, Gujara, Kerala, Madras, Mysore, Orissa, Punjab 7 Kashmir, Manipur 9 Rajasthan 11 Utar Pradesh 13 Andhra Pradesh, Madhya Pradesh 14 Himachi Pradesh
Punjabi caste: 5 Sansi
Punjabi people: 4 Sikh
queen: 4 rani 5 begum, ranee 8 maharani
race: 5 Hindu 9 Dravidian
rainy season: 6 varsha 7 monsoon

region: 7 Malabar
religion: 5 Islam 8 Buddhism, Hinduism
rice: 4 boro
river: Ai; Dor 4 Kosi, Kusi, Sind 5 Bhimi, Indus, Kabul, Rapti, Tapti 6 Chenab, Ganges, Kistna, Sutlej 7 Cauvery, Irawadi, Krishna 8 Godavari, Hydaspes, Nerbudda, Vindhyas 9 Irrawaddy 10 Bhagirathi 11 Brahmaputra
rubber: 10 caoutchouc
rule: raj
ruler: 4 rana 5 nawab, rajah
sacred grove: 5 Sarna
saffron: 7 tumeric, zedoary
sage: 6 pandit, pundit
seaport: 6 Bombay, Madras 8 Calcutta
servant: 4 maty 6 bearer 10 mussalchee
sheep: 5 urial 6 oorial
shirt: 6 banian
shrine: 6 dagaba, dagoba
silk: 4 muga 6 cabeca
silkworm: eri
snake: 5 krait
soldier: 4 peon 5 sepoy 6 gurkha
song: 4 raga
spinning wheel: 6 charka 7 charkha
state: see *province* above
storm: 5 tufan 7 peesash
sun worshiper: 5 parsi 6 parsee
supreme court: 6 Sudder
tapir: 8 saladang
tariff: 6 zabeta
tax: 10 chaukidari
teacher: 4 guru 5 akhun, mulla 6 akhund, mullah, pandit, pundit 7 akhoond
tenant: 4 ryot
title: sri 4 mian, raja 5 sahib, singh 6 sirdar 7 gaekwad, gaekwar, gaikwar, sahibah 8 guicowar 9 ahluwalia
tower: 5 minar
town: 4 Agra, Gaya, Puna, Rewa 5 Adoni, Akola, Arcot, Bhera, Dacca, Daman, Delhi, Girot, Kalpi, Naida, Patan, Patna, Poona, Salem, Simla, Surat 6 Ajmere, Ambala, Bareli, Baroda, Bhopal, Bombay, Dum-Dum, Howrah, Indore, Jaipur, Lahore, Madira, Madras, Madura, Meerut, Multan, Muttra, Musore, Nagpur, Rampur 7 Aligarh, Benares, Calicut, Cawnpur, Dinapir, Gwalior, Jodhpur, Karachi, Laswari, Lucknow, Rangoon, Rangpur 8 Amritsar, Bhatinda, Bhatpara, Calcutta, Cawnpore, Dinapore, Jabalpur, Kolhapur, Mandalay, Mirzapur, Peshawar, Sholapur, Srinagar 9 Ahmadabad, Allahabad, Berhampur, Berhampir, Bhagalpur, Bungalore, Cuddalore, Darjiling, Gorakhpir, Hyderabad, Kurrachee, Moradabad, Nagapatam, Srirangam 10 Darbhangah, Darjeeling, Haidarabad, Jubbulpore, Ra-

walpindi, Saharanpur 11 Barrackpore 12 Shahjahanpur, Trichioopoli
tree: bel, dar, lin, sal 4 dita, myxa, shoq, teak 5 anjan, pipal, salai 6 banyan, deodar 7 majagua
tribe: Ao; Gor 4 Bhil 6 Badaga 7 Sherani, Shirani
turban: 8 seerband
vessel: 4 doni 6 shibar
viceroy: 5 nabob, nawab
village: 5 abadi 6 mouzah
weight: moo, pai, ser, vis 4 bhar, dhan, drum, kona, myat, pala, pank, pice, raik, rati, ruay, seer, tank, tola, yava 5 adpao, bahar, candy, catty, hubba, masha, maund, pally, pouah, ratti, retti, tical, ticul, tikal 6 abucco, dhurra, karsha, ruttee 7 chittak, peiktha 8 chittack
wheat: 4 suji 5 sujee
wife's cremation: 6 suttee
wild ox: 4 gaur
wine: 5 shrab
wood: eng, sal 4 toon 5 kokra
Indian (see also **India**): red 5 indic 7 redskin 9 aborigine
acricultural: 6 Pawnee
Alaska: 5 Aleut
Aleutian: 4 Attu
Algonquin: Sac 4 Cree, Sauk 5 Miami 6 Abnaki, Micmac, Ottawa, Sokoki 7 Arapaho, Mohican, Ojibwae, Shawnee 8 Cheyenne, Delaware, Illinois 9 Blackfoot 10 Montagnais 11 Massachuset
American: Aht, Kaw, Oto, Red, Sac, Ute 4 Cree, Dene, Erie, Hopi, Ioni, Iowa, Otoe, Pima, Tana, Taos, Yuma, Zuni 5 Banak, Caddo, Coree, Creek, Huron, Kania, Kansa, Keres, Kiowa, Miami, Omaha, Osage, Piute, Sioux, Tinne 6 Abnaki, Apache, Dakota, Kansas, Lenape, Mohave, Mojave, Navaho, Navajo, Nootka, Oneida, Ottawa, Paiute, Pawnee, Redman, Sambos, Seneca, Siwash 7 Abenaki, Amerind, Arapaho, Choctaw, Keresan, Redskin 8 Apalachi, Cherokee, Chippewa, Comanche, Hitchiti, Iroquois, Kickapoo, Onondaga, Pokonchi, Sagamore, Seminole, Shoshone 9 Algonquin, Apalachee, Chickasaw, Winnebago 10 Muskhogean 12 Narragansett
Arawakan: 5 Guana
Arikara: Ree
Arizona: 4 Pima, Yuma 6 Navaho, Navajo
Athapascan: 4 Dene, Hupa 5 Hoopa, Tinne 6 Apache, Navaho, Navajo, Tinneh
blanket: 6 stroud 9 strouding
Bolivia: Uro 4 Iten, Moxo 6 Aymara 10 Chiriguano
Brazil: 5 Bravo 7 Tariana

British Columbia: 7 Gitksan
Caddoan: Ree 4 Adai, Ioni, Waco 6 Eyeish, Hainai 7 Andarko, Arikara 8 Arikaree 9 Nachitoch
Calgary: 5 Sarsi
California: 4 Pomo
Canadian: 4 Cree, Dene 5 Tinne 6 Tinneh 7 Sanetch 9 Athabasca 10 Athabascan
Cariban: 4 Yaos 5 Arara, Trios 6 Caribs, Oyanas 7 Akawais, Aparais, Chaymas, Macusis 8 Arecunas, Bakairis, Woyaways, Yauapery 9 Tamanacos 11 Cumanagotos 12 Maquiritares
ceremonial chamber: 4 kiva
chief: 6 sachem 8 sagamore
child: 7 papoose
Copehan: 6 Wintun
corn: zea 4 samp 5 maize
council: 6 powwow
craft: 5 canoe, kayak 6 dugout
Dakota: Ree
daughter of moon: 7 Nakomis, Nokomis
Delaware: 6 Lenape
female: 5 squaw 6 mahala, mahaly
festival: 8 potlatch
fighter: 5 Boone, Miles 6 Custer
flathead: 7 Chinook
Fuegian: Ona 6 Yahgan 8 Alikuluf
game: 6 canute
Great Lake: 4 Erie 5 Huron
Great Spirit: 6 manito
guardian spirit: 5 totem
hatchet: 8 tomahawk
headdress: 7 topknot
Hopi: 4 Moki 5 Moqui
hut: 5 hogan, toldo 6 wikiup 7 wickiup
Iroquois: 4 Erie 6 Oneida, Seneca 7 Wyandot 9 Hochelaga
Keresan: Sia
liquor: 9 firewater
lodge: 5 tepee
man: 4 buck 5 brave, chief 6 sannup
Manitoba: 4 Cree
meal bread: 8 corncake
memorial post: xat 5 totem
Missouri: 5 Osage
moccasin: pac
money: 6 seawan, wampum 7 seawant
Muskhogean: 5 Creek 8 Hitchiti
Nebraska: 4 Otoe 5 Omaha
Nevada: 6 Digger, Paiute
New Mexico: Sia 4 Tano, Taos 5 Keres
New York: 4 Erie 6 Oneida, Seneca 9 Tuscarora
North Carolina: 5 Coree 7 Buffalo
Northwest: 4 Cree
Oklahoma: 5 Creek, Kansa, Osage 6 Pawnee, Quapaw 7 Choctaw 8 Cherokee
Oregon: 5 Modoc

Orinoco Valley: 9 Guahiribo
Panama: 4 Cuna 6 Guaymi 7 Guaymie
Paraguay: 8 Guayaqui
Paru River: 8 Araquaju
Payaguas: 4 Agaz
peace pipe: 7 calumet
Peban: 5 Yagua
Peru: 4 Ande, Cana, Inca, Inka, Peba, Yutu 5 Boros, Campa, Carib, Panos 6 Aymara, Jibaro, Jiyaro, Kechua, Lamano 7 Quechua
pillar: lat, xat
Piman: 5 Opata
Platte River: 6 Pawnee
pony: 6 cayuse
porridge: 4 samp
potato: 4 yamp 9 breadroot
prayer stick: 4 paho
Pueblo: 4 Hopi, Moki, Piro, Tana, Taos
Quapaw: 5 Ozark
Quechuan: 4 Inca
Rio Grande: Tao
Salishan: 7 Tulalip
Seminole chief: 7 Osceola
Shoshone: Ute 4 Hopi, Otoe, Utah 5 Piute 6 Paiute 8 Comanche
Sioux: Kaw, Oto 4 Otoe 5 Omaha, Osage 6 Biloxi, Hidata, Saponi, Tutelo
snake dancer: 4 Hopi
sorcery: ob; obe, obi
South American: Ges, Ona 4 Inca 5 Aztec, Carib
spirit: 5 totem 7 Manitou
tent: 5 tepee 6 wigwam
Tierra del Fuego: Ona 4 Agni
token of victory: 5 scalp
Uchean: 5 Uchee, Yuchi
Utah: Ute 5 Piute 6 Paiute
Vancouver Island: Aht 5 Sooke 9 Ehatisaht
Venezuela: 5 Carib 6 Timote 7 Timotex 8 Guarauno
village: 6 pueblo
Virginia: 8 Powhatan 10 Algonquian
Wakashan: 6 Nootka
wampum: 4 peag 5 peage
warrior: 5 brave
Washington: Aht, Hoh 5 Lummi, Makah 6 Callam
weapon: 8 tomahawk
Western: Kaw 4 Seri
wigwam: 5 tepee
Wisconsin: Sac
woman: 5 squaw
Wyoming: 4 Crow 5 Kiowa
Xingu River: 5 Aneto
Yucatan: 4 Maya
Yukian: 4 Yuki 5 Wappo 7 Huchnom
Zuni Land: 6 Cibola
Indiana: *and Ohio River:* 6 Maumee

bird: 8 cardinal

city: 4 Peru 5 Floyd 6 Brazil, Fowler, Marion, Muncie 7 Bedford, Hammond, Laporte 8 Danville 10 Huntington 11 Bloomington 12 Indianapolis(c.), Kendallville 14 Jeffersonville

county: 8 Lagrange

flower: 6 zinnia

native: 7 Hoosier

tree: 5 tulip

indicate: say 4 bode, cite, mark, read, show 5 argue, augur, point 6 allude, denote, evince, import, reveal 7 bespeak, betoken, connote, declare, display, signify, specify 8 decipher, disclose, evidence, manifest, register 9 designate 10 denominate 12 characterize

indicated: 6 marked, signed 9 betokened

indicating: *chemical group:* azo

literal transcript: sic

succession: 7 ordinal

indication: 4 clew, clue, hint, mark, note, omen, sign 5 proof, token, trace 6 augury, signal 7 auspice, symptom 8 argument, evidence 10 denotation 11 designation 13 manifestation

indicative: 10 expressive 13 argumentative

indicator: 4 dial, hand, sign, vane 5 arrow, clock, gauge, index 6 gnomon, marker 7 indices(pl.), pointer 11 annunciator 15 telethermometer

indices: 5 files 6 tables 8 pointers

indicium: 4 mark, sign 5 token 10 appearance, indication

indict: 4 bill, dite 6 accuse, attach, charge, decree 7 arraign, impeach 8 proclaim

indictive: 8 declared 9 appointed 10 proclaimed

indictment: 10 accusation

indifference: 6 apathy 8 coldness, froideur 9 aloofness 10 negligence 11 insouciance 12 carelessness, heedlessness, lukewarmness 13 insensibility, pococurantism

indifferent: ill 4 cold, cool, dead, dram, sick, soso 5 aloof, blase, blaze, shrug, stoic 6 casual, poorly, supine 7 neutral, uneager 8 careless, listless, mediocre 9 apathetic, Laodicean 10 nonchalant, regardless 11 adiaphorous, pococurante 12 nonessential

indigence: 4 lack, need, want 6 penury 7 beggary, poverty 10 deficiency

indigene: 6 native

indigenous: 5 natal 6 inborn, innate, native 7 endemic, natural 8 homeborn, inherent 10 aboriginal 13 autochthonous

indigent: 4 free, poor, void 5 needy 7 lacking, wanting 8 beggarly 9 destitute, penniless 11 impecunious, necessitous

indigestion: 6 apepsy 7 apepsia

indign: 8 unworthy 10 undeserved 11 disgraceful, undeserving

indignant: 5 angry, irate, wroth 7 annoyed 8 incensed, wrathful 11 exasperated

indignation: ire 4 fury 5 anger, wrath 7 disdain 8 contempt 11 displeasure

indignity: cut 6 insult, slight 7 affront 13 disparagement

indigo: 4 anil, blue

artificial source: 6 isatin

bale of: 6 seroon

derivative: 5 indol 6 indole

natural source: 4 anil 7 indican

shrub: 4 anil

wild genus: 8 baptisia

indigo bunting: 4 bird 5 finch

indirect: 4 side 7 devious, oblique 8 circular 9 dishonest 10 circuitous, collateral, misleading, roundabout

expense: 8 overhead

indirectly: 5 aside

indiscernible: 13 imperceptible 17 indistinguishable

indiscreet: 4 rash 5 hasty, silly 6 unwise 7 foolish, witless 8 careless, heedless 9 impolitic, imprudent, unadvised 10 incautious 11 injudicious 12 undiscerning 13 inconsiderate

indiscretion: 5 folly 8 fredaine 10 imprudence

indiscriminate: 5 mixed 7 mingled 9 wholesale 13 heterogeneous

indispensable: 5 basic, vital 7 exigent 9 essential, requisite 10 imperative

indisposed: ill 4 sick 6 ailing 8 unsuited 11 disinclined 12 disqualified

indisposition: ail 6 malady 7 ailment, illness, malaise 8 disorder, sickness 9 distemper 10 discomfort, reluctance 12 disaffection 13 unwillingness

indisputable: 4 sure 7 certain, evident 8 positive 10 undeniable 11 indubitable 12 irrefragable 13 incontestable 14 unquestionable 16 incontrovertible

indissolubility: 8 firmness

indistinct: dim 4 dark, hazy 5 faint, misty, vague 6 cloudy 7 blurred, obscure, shadowy 9 ambiguous, unrefined 10 indefinite 17 indistinguishable

indistinctly: 6 feeble

indite: pen 4 dite 5 write 7 compose 8 inscribe

individual (see also **person**): one 4 oner, self, sole, unit 6 person, single 7 special 8 distinct, selfsame, solitary 9 identical 11 inseparable

combining form: 4 idio

of compound animal: 4 zoon

physiological: 4 bion

selfish: **6** egoist
smug: **4** prig
individuality: **5** seity **7** oneness **14** indivisibility, inseparability
rare: **5** seity
individually: **9** severally **10** personally **14** distributively
individuate: **9** undivided **11** inseparable
Indo-Aryan: Jat **6** khatri, Rajput
diety: **5** Indra
Indo-China: *dialect:* ao
former kingdom: **4** Anam **5** Annam
language: Ao, Hu, Wa; Aka, Lai, Lao, Sai, Tai, Yao **4** Bama, Mrus, Shan, Thai **7** Burmese
linguist stock: Tai
native: see *people* below
people: Mru, Tai **4** Naga
race: see *people* above
region: **4** Laos **5** Annam
river: Te
state: **4** Laos **5** Burma **7** Vietnam **8** Cambodia, Thailand
tree: eng, mee
Indo-European: **4** Lett, Serb, Slav **5** Aryan, Croat, Czech
language: **5** Indic **6** Baltic, Celtic, Italic, Slavic **7** Iranian **8** Albanian, Germanic, Hellenic
Indo-Iranian: **5** Aryan
Indo-Portuguese: *Christian half-caste:* **5** Topas, Topaz **6** Topass
measure: **5** covid **6** covido
indoctrinate: **5** imbue, teach, tutor **7** educate **8** instruct
indolence: **5** scorn, sloth **7** inertia, languor
indolent: **4** idle, lazy **5** inert **6** otiose, supine **7** dronish **8** inactive, slothful, sluggish
indomitable: **10** invincible **11** intractable **13** unconquerable
Indonesia: *base:* Lae
capital: **7** Jakarta
coin: **6** rupiah
Indian: Ata
island: **4** Bali, Java **5** Timor **6** Flores, Lombok **7** Madoera, Sumatra **8** Soembowa **9** New Guinea
lake: **4** Toba
law: **4** adat
Luzon: **6** Igorot
market: **5** pasar
measure: **4** depa **5** depoh
news agency: **5** Aneta
people: **6** Tapiro
priest caste: **8** brahmana
pyramid: **5** stupa
race: **4** Dyak **6** Battak, Bontok, Ifugao, Igorot, Manobo **7** Lampong
sea gypsy: **6** selung

shop: **4** toko
tribe: Ata **4** Atta
volcano: **4** Awoe **5** Agung, Raung
weight: **6** soekoe
wind: **5** brubu **7** broeboe
indorse: See **endorse**
Indra: **5** Sakka, Sakra
dragon: **6** Vritra
elephant: **8** Airavata
father: **8** Tvashtri
food: **4** soma
heaven capital: **9** Amaravati
indubious: **7** certain
indubitable: **4** sure **7** assured, certain, evident **8** apparent **10** infallible, undeniable **12** irrefragable **13** incontestable **16** incontrovertible
induce: get **4** draw, lure, urge **5** infer, tempt **6** elicit, suborn **7** actuate **8** persuade **9** encourage, influence
induced: led **5** moved, urged **6** caused **7** allured, engaged, enticed, incited **8** impelled **9** motivated, persuaded **10** instigated
inducement: **4** bait **5** prize **6** motive, reason **9** incentive, influence **10** enticement **13** consideration
induct: **5** enrol **6** enlist, enroll **7** install **8** initiate **9** introduce **10** inaugurate
inductance unit: **5** henry
inductile: **10** inflexible, unyielding
induction: **8** entrance **9** accession, deduction **10** initiation **12** commencement, introduction
indue: **5** endow **6** assume, clothe, invest **7** furnish
indulge: pet **4** cade, feed, waly **5** favor, humor, wally **6** cocker, favour, foster, humour, pamper, please **7** cherish, gratify
in antics: **7** skylark
in fault finding: **5** cavil
in recreation: **4** play
in revelry: **5** roist
to excess: **6** pamper
indulgence: **5** favor, spree **6** favour **8** clemency, humoring **9** tolerance **13** gratification **17** self-gratification
indulgent: **4** easy, fond, good, kind, mild **7** lenient **8** tolerant **9** compliant **10** charitable
indurate: **5** inure **6** harden **9** calloused
indurated: **4** hard **5** inure **7** callous, scleral **8** hardened, obdurate, scleroid, stubborn **9** sclerotic
Indus tribesman: Gor
industrial magnate: **6** tycoon
industrious: **4** busy **6** active **7** zealous **8** diligent, sedulous **9** assiduous **11** painstaking **13** indefatigable

industry: 5 labor, skill 8 business 9 assiduity, diligence, ingenuity 10 occupation

indweller: 7 denizen 9 sojourner 10 inhabitant

indwelling: 8 immanent, inherent 9 immanence

inearth: 4 bury 5 inter

inebriacy: 11 drunkenness 12 intemperance

inebriate: sot 5 drunk 6 excite 7 ebriate 8 drunkard 9 stupefied 10 exhilarate, intoxicate 11 intoxicated

inebriated: 5 drunk

ineffable: 11 unspeakable, unutterable 13 indescribable, inexpressible 15 unpronounceable

ineffaceable: 9 indelible 12 ineradicable

ineffectively: 6 feebly

ineffectual: 4 dead, idle, vain, weak 6 futile 7 useless 8 hopeless, nugatory 9 fruitless, frustrate 10 unavailing 11 inefficient 13 inefficacious

inefficient: 4 poor 6 unable 7 useless 11 incompetent

inelastic: 4 limp 10 inflexible, unyielding

inelegant: 6 vulgar 7 awkward, blatant 9 graceless

ineluctable: 4 sure 5 fated 6 doomed 7 certain 10 inevitable 11 inescapable

inept: 4 dull, slow 5 unfit 6 absurd, clumsy 7 awkward, foolish 8 backward, unsuited 10 unbecoming, unsuitable 11 incompetent 13 inappropriate

inequal: 5 rough 6 uneven 7 unequal

inequality: 4 odds 9 disparity, diversity 10 unevenness 13 disproportion

inequity: 9 injustice 10 unfairness

ineradicable: 7 lasting 9 indelible, permanent 12 ineffaceable

inerrable: 8 unerring 10 infallible

inerrant: 8 unerring 10 infallible

inerratic: 5 fixed 7 settled 11 established

inert: 4 dead, dull, lazy, slow 5 still 6 stupid, supine, torpid 7 passive 8 immobile, inactive, indolent, lifeless, slothful, sluggish 9 apathetic, lethargic 10 motionless, phlegmatic

inertia: 5 sloth 8 idleness 9 indolence

inesculant: 8 inedible

inessential: 9 extrinsic 11 unimportant

inestimable: 9 priceless 10 invaluable 12 incalculable

inevitable: due 5 fated 7 certain, fateful 11 ineluctable, unavoidable

inexact: 4 free 5 rough 10 inaccurate

inexorable: 4 grim 5 stony 6 strict 7 ominous 8 rigorous 9 unbending 10 inflexible, relentless, unyielding 11 unrelenting

inexorability: 5 rigor

inexpedience: 6 unwise 9 imprudent 10 indiscreet 11 inadvisable 12 unprofitable 15 disadvantageous

inexpedient: 6 unwise 9 impolitic, imprudent 10 indiscreet 11 inadvisable, injudicious 12 unprofitable 15 disadvantageous

inexpensive: 5 cheap 6 frugal

inexperienced: raw 5 crude, green, naive, young 6 callow 7 untried 8 inexpert 10 amateurish

inexpert: 5 green 9 unskilled

inexplicable: 9 ambiguous, enigmatic 12 supernatural 13 preternatural

inexpressible: 8 nameless 9 ineffable 11 unutterable

inexpressive: 4 dull, dumb 13 unintelligent

infallible: 4 sure 7 certain 8 inerrant, unerring 9 inerrable, unfailing 11 indubitable

infamous: 4 base 6 bloody, odious 8 shameful 9 nefarious 10 detestable 11 ignominious 12 contemptible

infamy: 5 stain 6 baffle, defame 8 disgrace, dishonor, reproach 10 opprobrium

infancy: 10 incunabula(pl.) 11 incunabulum

infant: 4 babe, baby 5 child, minor 7 bambino, chrisom 8 bantling 9 foundling

in law: 5 minor

Indian: 7 papoose

murder: 11 infanticide

infantile paralysis: 13 poliomyelitis

infantryman: 6 doggie 7 dogface 8 fusilier 9 musketeer

infare: 12 housewarming

infatuate: 5 besot 6 befool 9 captivate

infatuated: mad 4 fond 6 engoue 7 engouee 8 enamored 9 enamoured

infatuatedness: 7 fatuity

infatuation: ate 4 rave 5 craze, folly 6 beguin 9 engoument 10 engouement

infeasible: 13 impracticable

infect: 5 taint 6 canker, defile, poison 7 pollute 11 contaminate

infection: 6 malady, plague 7 disease, illness

freedom from: 7 asepsis

infectious: 8 catching 9 vitiating 12 demoralizing, pestilential

infelicitous: 7 unhappy 11 unfortunate

infelicity: 6 misery 10 misfortune 11 unhappiness 12 wretchedness

infer: 4 hint 5 drive, educe, guess, imply 6 adduce, deduce, derive, gather 7 surmise 8 conclude, construe

inferal: 7 stygian

inference: 9 corollary, deduction 10 assumption, conclusion, derivation 11 consequence

inferential: 7 implied 8 illative 9 deductive

inferior: bad 4 base, cull, less, poor 5 baser, below, lower, minor, petit, petty, snide, worst 6 cagmag, common, feeble, impure, lesser, nether 7 cheaper, humbler, unequal 8 mediocre 9 underling 10 inadequate 11 subordinate 12 contemptible 13 insignificant

infernal: 7 avernal, hellish, satanic, stygian 8 all-fired, damnable, devilish, diabolic 9 tartarean 10 acherontic, demoniacal, diabolical

infernal machine: 4 bomb

inferno: 4 fire, hell

infertile: 4 poor 6 barren 7 sterile

infest: vex 5 beset, haunt 6 plague 7 overrun, torment

infester: 8 nuisance

infidel: 5 deist, pagan 6 giaour, Kaffir, paynim 7 atheist, skeptic 8 agnostic 10 unbeliever 11 freethinker

infiltrate: 4 leak, seep

infinite: 6 Ananta 7 endless, immense 9 boundless, countless, limitless, unlimited 11 everlasting, illimitable, measureless 12 immeasurable, interminable

absorption into: 7 nirvana

infinitesimal: 4 tiny 5 small 6 atomic, minute 10 evanescent

infinity: 4 olam 8 eternity

infirm: old 4 lame, weak 5 anile, crank, crazy, frail 6 cranky, feeble, senile, sickly 7 brittle, casalty, caselty, cazelty, craichy, dowless, dwaible, dwaibly, fragile 8 cassalty, casselty, decrepit 9 doddering 10 irresolute 11 debilitated, vacillating

infirmary: 8 hospital

infirmity: 4 vice 7 ailment, disease, failing, frailty 8 debility, sickness, weakness 10 feebleness

infirmness: 8 weakness

infix: 5 inset 6 insert 7 engrave, implant, impress, ingrain, instill 9 inculcate

inflame: 4 boil, fire, goad, heat, stir 5 anger, blain, chafe 6 anneal, arouse, enrage, excite, kindle, madden, rankle, redden 7 inflame 8 enkindle, irritate 10 exasperate

with love: 6 enamor

with rage: 6 madden

inflamed: red 5 angry, fiery 6 ablaze

inflaming: 7 burning

inflammable: 5 fiery 6 ardent, tinder 7 bitumen, piceous 9 excitable, irascible, irritable 10 accendible 11 combustible

inflammation: 4 fire 10 combustion, phlegmasia 13 conflagration

kind of: 4 gout 5 felon 6 iritis, omitis, otitis 7 coxitis, gonitis, rickets 8 adenitis, cystitis, myositis, rachitis, sarcitis 9 arthritis, gastritis, phlebitis, rhachitis 12 encephalitis 13 poliomyelitis

suffix: 4 itis

inflate: 4 blow, fill 5 bloat, elate, swell 6 aerify, dilate, emboss, expand, tumefy 7 bombast, distend 8 increase

inflated: 4 blew 5 blown 6 elated, turgid 7 aerated, bellied, bloated, bombast, dilated, fustian, pompous, swollen 8 expanded 9 bombastic, distended, flatulent, plethoric

inflect: bow 4 bend 5 curve 7 deflect 8 modulate

inflection: 4 tone

of words: 8 paradigm

inflex: 4 bend 7 inflect

inflexibility: 8 acampsia

inflexible: 4 dour, hard 5 eager, rigid, stiff, stony 6 strict 7 adamant 8 granitic, obdurate, rigorous 9 immovable, inelastic, unbending 10 implacable, inexorable, relentless 14 uncompromising

inflict: 4 deal 5 wreak 6 impose

great pain: 7 torture

vengeance: 5 wreak

infliction: 7 scourge

inflorescence: 6 raceme

axial circle of: 5 whorl

inflow: 6 influx, infuse

influence: win 4 bale, coax, egis, hank, heft, lead, move, pull, rule, sway 5 bribe, force, impel, lobby 6 affect, aspect, compel, effect, govern, induce, infuse, leaven, miasma, motive, sphere 7 attinge, attract, bearing, command, control, gravity, impress, inspire, mastery 8 hegemony, persuade, prestige, reaction 9 authority 10 ascendancy, ascendency, attraction, inducement 13 consideration

by fixed idea: 6 obsess

by reward: 5 bribe

region of: 5 orbit 6 sphere

influence peddling: 8 intrigue, lobbying

influenced: 6 biased 8 affected

easily: 7 pliable

influential: 5 grave 6 potent 8 forcible 9 effective, important, momentous

influenza: flu 5 virus 10 coqueluche

influx: 4 tide 6 inflow 7 illapse 9 affluence, influence, inpouring

infold: lap 4 fold, wrap 5 clasp, twine 6 employ, enwrap 7 embrace, envelop 8 envelope

inform: 4 post, tell 5 train 6 advise, notify, preach 7 apprise, apprize, educate, lighten 8 acquaint, instruct 9 advertise 11 communicate

informal: 8 sociable 10 colloquial 13 unceremonious 14 unconventional

conversation: 4 chat
information: 4 data(pl.), dope, news, word 5 aviso, datum 6 notice 7 tidings 9 direction, knowledge 11 instruction
condensed: 6 digest
detailed: 7 dossier
giver: spy 4 fink 5 stool 7 stoolie 8 informer, squealer, telltale 10 tattletale 11 stoolpigeon
personal: 7 dossier
informative: 11 instructive 12 enlightening
informed: up; hep, hip 4 wise 5 aware 6 posted 7 knowing 8 apprised 11 enlightened
informer: spy 4 fink, tout 5 stool 6 canary, gossip, pigeon, teller 7 delater, delator 8 observer, squealer, telltale 9 informant 10 discoverer, talebearer
military: spy 5 agent
infortune: 4 Mars 6 Saturn 7 Mercury 10 misfortune
infra: 5 after, below, under
infraction: 6 breach 8 trespass 10 intrustion 12 encroachment, infringement 13 transgression
infrequency: 6 rarity 8 rareness, solitude 9 isolation 12 uncommonness
infrequent: 4 rare 6 scarce, seldom, sparse 8 sporadic, uncommon, unwonted 10 occasional
infrequently: 6 rarely, seldom 12 occasionally
infringe: 6 defeat, refute 7 confute, destroy, intrude 8 encroach, trespass 9 frustrate
upon: 7 violate
infringement: 6 breach 8 trespass 9 violation 10 infraction 13 transgression 14 nonfulfillment
infuriate: vex 6 enrage, madden 7 enfelon
infuscate: 6 darken 7 obscure
infuse: 5 spoil, steep 6 aerify 7 engrain, implant, instill 9 inculcate, influence, insinuate, introduce
infusion: tea 7 extract 8 affusion, tincture 9 admixture, decoction
malt: 4 wort
infusoria: 10 vorticella
ingang: 5 porch 8 entrance 10 intestines
Inge play: 6 Picnic
ingeminate: 6 repeat 8 redouble 9 reiterate
ingenious: 4 cute, fine 5 acute, dedal, sharp, smart, witty 6 adroit, clever, crafty, daedal, gifted, subtle 7 cunning 8 dedalian, enginous, skillful, talented 9 daedalian, deviceful, inventive 11 intelligent, resourceful
ingeniousness: 5 skill 8 artifice

ingenuity: art 7 address, cunning 8 artifice 10 adroitness, cleverness 11 originality 13 inventiveness
ingenuous: 4 free, naif 5 frank, naive, noble, plain 6 candid, honest, innate, simple 7 artless, sincere 8 freeborn, innocent 9 guileless 10 unaffected, unreserved 15 unsophisticated
ingenuousness: 7 naivete 9 innocence
ingest: eat 7 swallow
ingle: 4 fire 5 blaze, flame 9 fireplace
inglenook: 11 cornerstone
ingleside: 8 fireside
ingluvies: 4 craw, crop
ingoing: 8 entrance
ingot: *metal:* gad, pig
worker: 6 barman
ingrained: 6 imbued, innate, native 7 inhered 9 saturated 10 inveterate
ingratiate: 4 fawn 7 commend, flatter 9 insinuate, introduce
ingredient: 7 element 9 component 11 constituent
baking: 4 alum, soda 5 yeast
cough-syrup: 8 glycerin
facial: 5 cream, rouge 6 powder 7 lanolin 8 lanoline
incense: 6 stacte
ink: 6 tannin
varnish: lac 5 drier, resin, rosin
ingress: 4 adit 5 entry 8 entrance
ingrowing nail: 7 acronyx
inhabit: 5 dwell 6 occupy, people, settle 7 possess 9 establish
inhabitant: cit 6 inmate, native, people, tenant 7 citizen, denizen, dweller 8 habitant, resident
desert: 4 Arab 5 nomad
earliest known: 9 aborigine
foreign: 5 alien 10 alienicola
local: 6 native
moon: 8 selenite
northern: 11 septentrion
suffix: ese, ite
inhabited: 5 lived 7 dwelled, habited, peopled 9 populated
inhabiting: *caves:* 7 spelean 8 spelaean
ground: 11 terricolous
grove: 7 nemoral
island: 7 nesiote
lake: 9 lacustral
marsh: 10 limnophile
sea: 7 pelagic
inhale: 4 draw 7 attract, breathe, respire 9 embreathe
inharmonious: 6 absurd, atonal 7 jarring 9 dissonant, unmusical 10 discordant 11 conflicting 12 antagonistic
inhere: 6 belong, innate 7 ingrain

inherent: 6 inborn, innate 7 infixed 8 immanent 9 essential, immanence, intrinsic 10 indwelling, subsistent 13 indispensable

inheritable: 10 hereditary

inheritance: 6 legacy 8 heirship, heredity, heritage 9 cleronomy, heritance
by first-born: 13 primogeniture
portion: 8 legitime
restricted: 10 entailment
Scotch law: 5 annat
seizer: 6 abator

inherited: 6 native

inheritor: 4 heir 7 heiress, heritor, legatee

inheritrix 7 heiress

inhibit: 4 curb 5 check 6 forbid, hinder 8 prohibit, restrain 9 interdict

inhibition: ban, bar 7 embargo 9 restraint 11 prohibition 12 interdiction

inhuman: 4 fell 5 cruel 6 brutal, savage 7 beastly, bestial, brutish 8 devilish 9 barbarous, bloodless, ferocious 10 diabolical

inhumane: 5 cruel 6 brutal

inhumanity: 7 cruelty 9 barbarity

inhume: 4 bury 5 inter 6 entomb 7 deposit

inimical: 6 averse, frosty 7 hostile 8 contrary 9 repugnant 10 unfriendly 11 unfavorable

iniquitous: bad, ill 5 wrong 6 sinful, unjust, wicked 9 nefarious

iniquity: sin 4 evil, vice 5 crime, guilt 8 darkness 9 injustice 10 wickedness

initial: 5 first 6 letter, paraph 7 opening 8 entrance, monogram 9 beginning, incipient 10 commencing, elementary
design of: 8 monogram

initial payment: 4 ante, down 7 deposit

initiate: 4 head, open 5 admit, begin, enrol, start 6 enroll, ground, induct 7 install, instate 8 commence, inchoate 9 introduce, originate 10 inaugurate

initiation: 9 admission, beginning, induction 10 admittance, introduced 12 commencement

initiative: 5 getup 6 energy 8 aptitude, gumption, petition

injection: 4 hypo 5 enema

injudicious: 6 unwise 9 impolitic, imprudent 10 indiscreet 11 inexpedient

injunction: 4 hest, writ 5 order 6 behest, charge 7 mandate, precept, process 9 direction

injure: mar 4 harm, hurt, maim 5 abuse, spoil, sully, wound, wrong 6 impair, insult 7 affront, cripple 8 maltreat 9 disfigure
by bruising: 7 contuse
by scorching: 4 burn, char 5 singe

injured: 9 aggrieved

injury: ill, mar 4 bane, evil, harm, hurt, loss, risk, scar, tort 5 burst, chafe, wound, wrack, wrong 6 damage, deface, lesion,

mayhem, scathe, trauma 7 hurting, scratch 8 crepance, hardship, nuisance, traumata(pl.) 9 contusion, detriment, injustice 10 aggression, disservice, impairment 11 displeasure, impeachment 12 disadvantage
causing: 7 malefic 9 traumatic
pert. to: 5 noxal
sense of: 7 umbrage

injustice: 5 wrong 6 injury 8 hardship, inequity, iniquity 9 grievance 10 imposition, unfairness

ink: 7 blacken 8 millrynd
pert. to: 10 atramental

ink fish: 5 squid 6 cuttle

inkling: 4 hint, idea 5 rumor, scent 6 desire, report 7 glimpse 10 glimmering, intimation 11 inclination

inky: 5 black 9 cimmerian 11 atramentous

inlaid: 6 mosaic 9 champleve, decorated

inland: 8 domestic, interior
sea: 4 Aral 5 Black

inlay: 5 adorn, couch 6 insert 7 enchase 8 ornament 9 marquetry
work: 6 mosaic 9 certosina, certosino, champleve

inlet: oe; arm, bay, cay, geo, gio, ria 4 cove, hope, rias(pl.), slew, sloo, slue 5 admit, bayou, bight, creek, fiord, firth, fjord, fleet, haven, inlay, sound 6 estero, slough, strait 7 estuary, orifice 8 entrance
coastline: 5 bight 6 strait

inmate: 5 guest, lifer 6 termer 8 domestic, occupant, prisoner 10 inhabitant
harem: oda

inmost: 8 intimate 9 innermost

inn: pub 4 host, khan 5 fonda, hotel, house, serai, tambo, venta 6 fonduk, harbor, hostel, hostry, imaret, public, tavern 7 albergo, auberge, boliche, fondaca, fondouk, fonduck, gasthof, harbour, hospice, hostage 8 choultry, gasthaus, hostelry, wayhouse 9 hosthouse 10 harbergage, herbergage 11 caravansary 12 caravanserai

innards: 4 guts 5 numbles 8 entrails

innate: 4 born 6 inborn, inbred, inhere, native 7 connate, natural 8 inherent 9 ingrained, intrinsic 10 congenital, hereditary 11 instinctive 14 constitutional

inner: ben 5 ental 6 inside, inward 8 esoteric, interior, internal
comb. form: ent 4 ento 5 ental

innermost: 6 inmost

innet: 7 ensnare

Innisfail: 4 Eire, Erin 7 Ireland

innkeeper: 4 host 5 cheap 7 hostler 8 boniface, caupones, traiteur 10 aubergiste

innocence: 6 purity 7 naivete 11 sinlessness 13 guiltlessness *symbol of:* **7** diamond

innocent: 4 free, naif **5** bluet, naive **6** chaste, dovish, simple **7** artless, chrisom, cleanly, upright **9** blameless, childlike, guileless, guiltless, ingenuous, stainless **10** immaculate, unblamable **12** simpleminded **15** unsophisticated

Hebrew: **8** zaccheus **9** zacchaeus

innocent one: 4 babe, lamb **5** child **6** infant

innocuous: 8 harmless, innocent **9** innoxious **11** inoffensive, unoffending

innovation: 6 novity **7** novelty

innuendo: 4 clue, hint, slur **8** allusion **10** intimation **11** implication, insinuation

innumerable: 4 many **6** legion, myriad

Ino's grandfather: 6 Agenor

inoculate: 6 immune **7** engraft, implant

inodorous: 8 odorless **9** scentless

inoffensive: 8 harmless **9** innocuous

inoperative: 4 dead

inopinate: 10 unexpected

inopportune: bad **8** ill-timed, untimely **10** malapropos **11** importunate **12** unseasonable

inorb: 8 encircle

inordinate: 5 undue **8** all'fired **9** excessive **10** disorderly, immoderate **11** unregulated **12** unrestrained

inorganic: 7 mineral

inquest: 5 quest **6** search **7** inquiry **11** examination **13** investigation

official: **7** coroner

inquiet: 6 uneasy **7** disturb **8** disquiet, restless **9** disturbed

inquire: ask, esk(Sc.) **4** seek **5** frayn, price, query, spere **6** demand, frayne, harken **7** examine, hearken **8** question **11** interrogate, investigate

inquirer: 5 asker **6** seeker **7** zetetic **8** searcher

inquiring: 7 curious

inquiry: 5 query **6** examen **7** examine **8** question, research **11** examination **13** investigation

for lost goods: **6** tracer

inquisition: 4 hunt **6** search **11** examination **13** investigation

inquisitive: 4 nosy **5** nosey **6** prying **7** curious **8** meddling **10** meddlesome

inquisitiveness: 9 curiosity

inquisitor: 5 prier **6** tracer **8** examiner

inroad: 4 raid **5** foray **6** breach **8** invasion **9** incursion, irruption **12** encroachment

insane: mad **4** daft, luny **5** balmy, crazy, daffy, loony, manic **6** cranky, crazed **7** frantic, furious **8** bughouse, demented, deranged, distract, frenetic **9** delirious, phrenetic, psychotic

house for: **6** asylum, bedlam

to make: **6** dement **7** derange

insanity: 5 folie, mania **6** frenzy, lunacy **7** madness, vesania **8** delirium, dementia **9** psychosis **10** aberration, alienation **11** derangement

temporary: **7** amentia

insatiable: 6 greedy **9** voracious

insatiate: 10 insatiable **11** unsatisfied

inscribe, enscribe: 4 etch **5** delve, enter, stamp, write **6** blazon, enroll, indite, scroll **7** ascribe, engrave **8** dedicate, describe **9** character **12** characterize

inscribed: 8 lettered **9** dedicated

on stone: **10** lapidarian

with Teutonic characters: **5** runed

inscription: 6 legend **7** epigram, writing **8** epigraph **11** description **14** superscription

appropriate: **5** motto

end of book: **8** colophon

explanatory: **6** tituli(pl.) **7** titulus

on coins: **5** sigla

tomb: **7** epitaph

inscrutable: 6 secret **10** mysterious **12** impenetrable, inexplorable, unfathomable **16** incomprehensible

insculpture: 7 carving **11** inscription

insect: ant, bee, bug, fly **4** flea, gnat, goga, gogo, lice, mite, moth, tick, wasp **5** emmet, gogga, roach **6** beetle, earwig, mantis, spider, weevil **7** cricket, katydid, termite **9** bumblebee, centipede

adult: **6** imago

antenna: **4** palp **6** feeler

back surface: **5** notum

chirping: **7** cricket

destructive: **5** scale **7** termite **8** predator

dipterous: **8** mosquito

eye: **6** ocelli(pl.), stemma **7** ocellus

female: **4** gyne

genus of: **4** nepa **5** emesa **6** acarus, cicada, cicala, mantis, termes

hard covering: **6** chitin

hymenopterous: ant, bee **4** wasp **6** sawfly **7** gallfly **10** ichneumons

immature: **4** pupa **5** larva **6** larvae(pl.) **9** chrysalis

insectivorous bird: **5** pewee, vireo **8** redstart **10** flycatcher

kind of: dun, loa **5** aphid, aphis, bicho, borer **6** cicada, earwig, tremex, tsetse, vermin **7** attacus, Diptera, stinger **9** centipede, ephemeral

long-legged: **5** emesa

molting of: **7** ecdysis

order: **7** diptera **17** palaeodictyoptera

organ: **8** plantula **9** plantulae(pl.)

parasitic: **4** lice **5** louse

part of: **4** nota **5** chirr, media, palps **7** antenna **8** pronotum, tentacle

pert. to: 11 entomologic
plate: 6 scutum
resin: lac
science: 10 entomology
secretion: lac
small: 4 flea, gnat, mite 5 aphid, aphis, micro, midge 6 garfly 8 bullhead
social: ant, bee 5 emmet
stage: 4 pupa 5 imago, larva 6 instar 9 chrysalis
stinging: ant, bee 4 wasp 6 hornet 7 sciniph 12 yellowjacket
trap: web
winged: bee 4 wasp 6 hornet 12 yellowjacket
wingless: 4 flea 6 aptera(pl.)
insecticide: DDT 9 hellebore
insecure: 5 eemis, immis, loose, risky, shaky 6 infirm, unsafe, unsure 7 casalty, caselty, cazelty 8 cassalty, casselty, perilous, unstable 9 dangerous, hazardous 10 precarious
insecurity: 5 peril
insee: 8 foretell
inseminate: sow 7 implant, instill 9 fertilize 10 impregnate
insensate: 4 surd 5 blind, harsh 6 brutal, stupid 7 brutish, fatuous, foolish 9 senseless, unfeeling, untouched 10 insensible
insensibility: 4 coma, damp 6 apathy, torpor, trance 8 lethargy 9 analgesia 10 anesthesia 11 insentience 12 indifference
insensible: 4 dull 7 brutish 8 obdurate 9 inanimate, insensate, unfeeling 10 insentient 11 insensitive, meaningless, unconscious 13 imperceptible
insensitive: 5 blunt 9 inanimate, unfeeling 10 insensible, insentient 16 unimpressionable
insentient: 10 insensible 11 insensitive
insert: 5 foist, infix, inlay, inset 9 interpose 11 intercalate, interpolate
for growth: 5 graft 7 engraft
triangular: 4 gore 5 wedge
insertion: 5 inset
kind of: 5 shinn 11 parenthesis 13 interpolation 13 intercalation
of sound in word: 10 epenthesis
inset: 4 gore 5 imbed, infix, panel 6 gusset, insert 7 appoint, engraft, implant 9 insertion
insheathe: 6 emboss
inside: 5 inner 6 lining, within 8 interior 9 partition
toward: 5 entad 6 inward
inside out: 7 everted
insidious: 4 deep 6 covert 7 cunning 8 guileful 9 concealed, deceitful 10 fallacious, fraudulent 11 disaffected, treacherous

insight: ken 11 discernment 12 clairvoyance
insignia: 4 mark 5 badge 6 emblem
kind of: tie 7 caducei(pl.), regalia 8 caduceus
insignificance: 10 effacement
insignificant: 4 puny 5 dinky, petit, petty 6 paltry 7 trivial 8 inferior, trifling 9 minuscule, senseless 10 immaterial 12 contemptible
part: bit 4 iota 5 tithe 8 molehill
insincere: 5 false 7 feigned 9 deceitful, deceptive 12 hypocritical
insinuate: 4 hint 5 imply 6 allude, infuse 7 implant, instill 9 introduce, penetrate 10 ingratiate, serpentine
insinuation: 4 hint 8 innuendo
insipid: dry 4 dead, fade, flat, fond, pale, pall, tame 5 bauch, prosy, stale, tepid, vapid, waugh 6 flashy, jejune 7 prosaic 8 lifeless 9 pointless, tasteless 10 monotonous, spiritless, unanimated 13 uninteresting
insipience: 9 stupidity 11 foolishness
insist: 6 demand 9 persevere
insistence: 7 urgency 11 persistence
insnare: web 4 trap 5 benet, noose 6 enmesh, trapan, trepan
insolence: 5 nerve 6 insult 8 audacity 9 arrogance, contumacy, contumely, impudence 11 haughtiness, presumption 12 impertinence
insolent: 4 pert, rude 5 bardy 6 brazen 7 abusive, defiant 8 arrogant, impudent 9 audacious, hubristic 11 overbearing 12 contemptuous, contumelious
insolvency: 7 failure 10 bankruptcy
insolvent: 5 broke 6 busted, ruined 8 bankrupt 9 destitute 12 impoverished
insomnia: 7 ahypnia 8 agrypnia
insouciant: 4 calm 8 carefree, heedless 10 unbothered 11 indifferent, unconcerned
inspect: pry, see 5 aview, grade, visit 6 peruse 7 examine 8 consider 9 supervise 10 scrutinize
inspection: 4 oyer 6 parade, review 8 scrutiny 11 examination
inspector: 6 bishop, conner, sealer 8 examiner, overseer
inspiration: 4 muse 6 breath 8 afflatus 9 afflation 10 aspiration
poetic: 7 pierian
pretender to: 6 eolist
inspire (see also **inspirit**): 4 draw, fire, move, stir 5 exalt, imbue 6 aspire, inhale 7 actuate, animate, enliven, implant 8 motivate 9 encourage, influence, stimulate
inspired: 5 vatic

inspirit (see also **inspire**): 4 stir 5 cheer, elate, rouse 7 cherish, comfort, hearten, quicken 10 invigorate

inspissate: 7 thicken 8 condense 10 incrassate

instability: 8 fluidity 11 flexibility 12 unsteadiness 13 changeability 14 disequilibrium

install: 4 seat, vest 6 induct, invest 7 instate 8 initiate 9 establish 10 inaugurate

installation: 9 vestiture

instance: 4 case, sign, urge 5 token 7 example, present, request, symptom 8 presence 9 importune 10 succession 11 demonstrate, instigation

instancy: 7 urgency 8 pressure 9 imminence 10 insistence 17 instantaneousness

instant: 4 urge 5 clink, flash, gliff, glisk, trice 6 breath, minute, moment, second, urgent 7 solicit 8 pressing 9 handwhile, immediate 11 importunate

instantly: now 4 just 8 directly

instate: set 5 endow 6 bestow, confer, invest 7 install 8 initiate 9 establish

instead: 4 else 6 in lieu 10 equivalent, substitute

of: for

instigate: egg 4 abet, goad, move, prod, sick, spur, urge 5 impel 6 compel, excite, foment, incite, prompt, suborn 7 provoke 8 motivate 9 encourage, stimulate

instigator: 6 author 10 ringleader

instill: 5 imbue, infix 6 impart, infuse 7 implant, pervade 9 inculcate, insinuate

instinct: 5 knack 7 impulse 8 aptitude 11 instigation

instinctive: 6 innate 7 natural 8 inherent, original 9 automatic, intuitive 11 involuntary, spontaneous

institute: 5 begin, erect, found 6 asylum, ordain 7 academy 8 academie, initiate, organize 9 establish, originate 10 inaugurate

institution: 6 clinic, school 7 academy, college 8 hospital, seminary 10 university 12 constitution

instruct: 4 lead, show 5 breed, coach, drill, edify, guide, teach, train, tutor 6 direct, inform, preach 7 counsel, educate 8 document 9 enlighten 10 discipline 12 indoctrinate

instruction: act 4 lore, news, tora 5 torah 6 advice, assize, charge, lesson 7 precept, tuition 8 practice 9 erudition, knowledge 10 commission 12 propaedeutic

art of: 8 pedagogy

period: 4 term, year 7 quarter, session 8 semester 9 trimester

place of: 13 conservatoire

instructive: 8 didactic, sermonic

instructor: don 5 coach, tutor 6 docent, mentor 7 acharya, teacher, trainer 9 preceptor, professor

instrument (see also **apparatus; device; tool**): 4 deed, writ 5 agent, means 6 medium 7 utensil, writing 9 appliance, implement 11 contrivance

altitude: aba 9 altimeter 10 altazimuth

board: 5 panel

calculating: 6 abacus 9 sliderule

copying: 10 hectograph

cutting: 5 knife, razor 6 scythe, shears, sickle 8 scissors

for studying motion: 11 stroboscope

musical: See **musical instrument**

percussion: 12 Glockenspiel

sacred: 4 urim

sealed: 4 deed 5 crypt, vault 6 escrow

sharp-edged: 5 knife, razor 6 scythe, shears, sickle 7 cutlery 8 scissors

surveying: 7 transit 10 theodolite

instrumental: 5 organ 6 needed, useful 7 helpful, organic 11 ministerial

instrumentalist: 5 luter 6 harper 7 flutist, harpist, pianist 8 minstrel 9 cornetist 10 trombonist

instrumentality: 5 means 6 agency, medium

insubordinate: 5 rebel 6 unruly 7 riotous 8 mutinous, perverse 9 seditious 10 headstrong, refractory, unyielding 11 disobedient, intractable 12 contumacious

insubstantial: 4 airy, thin 5 frail 6 flimsy 10 intangible 12 apparitional

insufficient: 4 bare, poor 5 short 6 feeble, scanty, scarce 7 unequal, wanting 9 deficient 10 inadequate 14 incommensurate

insular: 8 islander, isolated 9 separated

insulate: 7 isolate 8 isolated 9 segregate 10 quarantine

material to: 4 cork 6 Kerite, rubber

insulated: 5 isled, taped

insulator: 4 tape 5 cleat

insult: cag 4 slap, slur 5 abuse, flout, frump 6 offend, revile 7 abusion, affront, offense, outrage 9 contumely, indignity, insolence

insulting: 4 rude 8 arrogant 9 offensive 10 despiteful, scurrilous 11 opprobrious 12 contumelious

insurance: 8 guaranty, warranty 9 assurance 10 protection

computer: 7 actuary 8 adjuster

payee: 11 beneficiary

system: 7 tontine

insure (see also **ensure**): 6 assure 7 furnish 10 underwrite

jointly: 8 coinsure

insurgent (see also **insubordinate**): 5 rebel 10 rebellious

insurmountable: 10 impassable, invincible 11 insuperable 13 unconquerable

insurrection: 6 mutiny, revolt, rising 9 rebellion

insusceptible: 6 immune 9 unfeeling

intact: 5 sound, whole 8 complete, unbroken 9 undefiled, undivided, uninjured, untouched 10 unimpaired

intaglio: cut, gem 9 represent

intake: net 4 gain, gate 6 profit 8 receipts 11 contraction

intangible: 5 vague 10 immaterial, impalpable 13 imperceptible, insubstantial

integer: one 5 whole 8 integral

integral: 5 whole 8 totality

integrate: mix 4 join 5 unite 6 entire

integrity: 7 honesty, probity 9 chariness, constancy

integument: 4 aril, coat 5 testa 7 cuticle, envelop 8 covering, envelope 10 investment

intellect: wit 4 mind, nous 5 brain 6 genius, reason 9 mentality 12 intelligence
limited in: 7 moronic

intellection: 6 notion 9 cognition, knowledge 12 apprehension 13 comprehension, understanding

intellectual: 5 ideal 6 brainy, mental, noetic, sophic 7 egghead 8 highbrow 9 epistemic

intelligence: 4 chit, mind, news, word 5 sense 6 esprit, notice, wisdom 8 learning 13 understanding
used alone: 6 noesis
without: 4 dull 5 inane 6 stupid

intelligence test deviser: 5 Binet, Simon

intelligencer: spy 9 informant, messenger 10 newsmonger

intelligent: 5 acute, aware, smart 6 bright, mental 7 knowing 8 rational, sensible 9 cognizant 13 understanding

intelligentsia: 13 intellectuals

intelligible: 5 clear, plain 10 conceptual 11 perspicuous 12 apprehensive 13 apprehensible, intellectible, suprasensuous 14 comprehensible

intemperate: 4 pure 6 severe 7 extreme 9 excessive, inclement, inviolate, undefiled 10 immoderate, inordinate 12 ungovernable

intend: aim 4 mean, mint, plan 5 allot, ettle 6 design 7 destine, purpose

intended: 6 fiance 7 fiancee

intense: hot 4 deep, hard, keen 5 acute, great, heavy, vivid 6 ardent, severe, strong 7 chronic, earnest, extreme, fervent, violent, zealous 8 grievous, powerful, strained, vehement 9 assiduous, excessive, strenuous 11 far-reaching

intensify: 5 exalt 6 deepen 7 enhance 8 condense, heighten, increase 9 aggravate 10 accentuate 11 concentrate

intensity: 5 depth 6 chroma, timbre

intensive: 7 intense 8 vehement 9 ascensive

intent: aim 4 deep, dole(Sc.), fell, rapt 5 eager, ettle, fixed, tense 6 design, effect 7 earnest, meaning, purpose 8 absorbed, diligent, sedulous 9 attentive, engrossed, intention, steadfast 10 determined

intention: aim, end 4 goal, hent, will 6 animus, attent, design, intent, object 7 meaning, purpose 11 designation 13 contemplation

intentional: 8 designed 9 voluntary 10 deliberate

inter: 4 bury 5 earth, grave 6 entomb, inhume

interagent: 6 medium 12 intermediary

intercalary: 8 inserted 12 intercalated, interpolated

intercalary month: 6 Veadar

intercalate: 7 insert 9 insinuate, interpose 11 interpolate

intercede: 7 mediate 9 arbitrate, interpose, intervene

intercept: 4 bury, head 5 catch 8 gaincope, retrench 9 forestall, interrupt

intercessor: 8 advocate, mediator

interchange: 4 vary 7 commute, permute 8 converse, exchange 9 alternate 10 transposal 11 reciprocate 12 conversation

interchangeable: 10 reversible 11 convertible

intercolumniation: 7 eustyle, systyle 8 diastyle 10 araeostyle

interconnection: 5 nexus

intercourse: 7 dealing 8 business, commerce, converse 9 communion 10 connection, fellowship 12 conversation 13 communication

interdict: ban 4 veto 5 debar, fence 6 forbid 7 inhibit 8 prohibit 9 proscribe

interdiction: 4 tabu 5 taboo

interest: 4 good 5 fetch 6 behalf, behoof, engage, profit 7 attract, concern 8 sympathy 9 advantage, anatocism, entertain, fascinate
exorbitant: 5 usury
in law: 5 right, title
lose: 4 tire
rate: 5 yield
without: 6 jejune 9 apathetic

interested: 4 rapt 6 caring

interfacing: 7 dineric

interfere: 5 barge, clash 6 meddle, tamper 7 collide, disturb, intrude 8 obstruct, sabotage 9 interpose, intervene

interference: 6 static

interferometer: 6 etalon

interim: 8 interval, meantime

interior: ben 5 ental, inner 6 inland, inside 8 midlands

interjection: aw, lo; boo, hic, rah 4 ahem, alas, amen, egad, ouch, well 6 aroint 7 criminy 11 exclamation

interlace: mat 5 braid, twine, weave 6 pleach, raddle 7 entwine 9 interfret, interlink 10 intertwine, interweave 11 interpolate

interlaced: 7 complex

interlock: 4 knit 5 unite 6 clench, engage 9 interlace 11 interrelate

interlocution: 12 conversation 13 communication

interlocutory: 12 intermediate

interlope: 6 insert 7 intrude, obtrude 8 trespass 11 intermeddle, interpolate

interlude: 5 truce 6 verset 8 entracte, ritornel 10 ritornelle

short: 6 verset

intermediary: 5 agent 6 medium 8 mediator 9 go-between 10 ambassador, interagent

intermediate: 5 mesne 6 median, middle 7 between 10 interposed 11 intervening

interminable: 7 endless, eternal 8 infinite, timeless, unending 9 boundless, limitless, unlimited

interminably: 7 forever

intermingle: 8 intermix 10 infiltrate

intermission: 4 rest, stop 5 dwell, pause 6 devall, recess 7 respite 8 entracte, vacation 9 cessation 10 suspension 13 interposition 14 discontinuance

intermittent: 6 broken, fitful 8 periodic 9 recurrent, spasmodic 11 alternating, interrupted 12 pretermitted

intermix: 6 mingle 10 interweave

intern: 6 doctor, inhume 7 confine, trainee

internal: 5 inner 6 inward, mental 8 enclosed 9 spiritual

combustion engine part: 5 timer

international: 9 world-wide

International: 4 song 9 Comintern

international business: 6 cartel

international organization: UN; WHO 4 NATO 5 SEATO 6 UNESCO

internecine: 6 deadly

interpellation: 7 summons 10 prevention 12 interception, intercession, interruption

interpolate: 5 alter 6 insert 9 introduce 11 intercalate

interpose: 6 thrust 7 intrude, mediate 9 intercede, interfere, intervene

interpret: 4 read, rede 5 aread, areed, gloze 6 decode, define, expose, render 7 explain, expound 8 construe 9 elucidate, explicate, translate 10 literalize, understand

interpretation: 5 gloss, sense 6 oracle 7 anagoge 8 exegesis 11 declaration

of science: 8 exegesis 12 hermeneutics

interpreter: 5 ulema 7 exegete 8 exponent 9 exegesist, hermeneut 11 oneirocritic

interpretive: 11 explanatory, hermeneutic 12 constructive

interrogate: ask 5 query 7 examine, inquire 8 question

interrogation: 4 quiz 5 probe, query 7 inquest 8 question 11 examination

interrogation mark: 7 eroteme

interrogative: how, who, why 4 what, when 5 where 8 question

interrupt: 4 stop 5 break, burst, cease, check 6 arrest, hinder, thwart 7 derange, disturb, suspend 8 obstruct 9 intercept, pretermit 11 discontinue

interruption: gap 5 dwell, pause 6 breach, hiatus 7 caesura 9 cessation 12 intermission

intersect: cut 4 meet 5 cross 6 divide, pierce 9 decussate

intersection: 6 secant 7 chiasma

interstice: 4 mesh, pore, seam 5 chink, crack, space 6 areola, areole, cranny 7 crevice 8 interval

pert. to: 7 areolar

intervolve: 4 coil, roll, wind 5 twist

intertwine: 4 knit, lace 5 twist 6 tangle 7 ensnare, ensnarl, entwine 8 entangle 9 interlace 10 intertwist

intertwist: 10 intertwine

interval: gap 4 rest, span 5 break, space 6 breach, hiatus, recess 7 caesura, respite 8 entracte 9 cessation 12 intermission

at irregular: 12 sporadically

musical: 5 fifth, ninth, sixth, tenth, third 6 fourth, octave, second 7 seventh

intervene: 7 mediate 9 intercede, interpose

intervening: 5 mesne(law) 12 intermediate

interview: see 7 consult, hearing 8 audience, question 9 encounter 10 conference 12 consultation

interweave: mat 4 plat 5 braid, plait 6 enlace, raddle, splice, wattle 8 entangle, intermix 9 interlace

intestinal: 7 enteric

intestine: gut 5 inner 6 inward 7 viscera 8 domestic, internal

comb. form: 6 entero

part: ile 5 ileum, ilium

pert. to: 7 enteric

intice: See **entice**

intimacy: 8 affinity 10 connection

intimate: sib 4 boon, hint, homy, near 5 bosom, chief, close, homey, imply 6 allude, chummy, homely, inmost, secret 7 signify, suggest 8 announce, domestic, familiar, friendly, informal, personal 9 associate, confidant 11 contubernal 12 acquaintance, confidential

intimately: 4 inly

intimation: 4 clue, hint, wind 5 scent 6 notice 7 inkling 10 suggestion 11 declaration

intimidate: awe, cow 5 abash, bully, daunt, deter, scare 6 hector 7 overawe, terrify 8 browbeat, dispirit, frighten 9 blackmail, terrorize

into: 4 unto 5 among, until 6 inside

prefix: en

that: 9 thereinto

intolerance: 9 misoneism

intolerant: 6 narrow 7 bigoted 8 dogmatic 9 illiberal, impatient 10 prejudiced

intonation: 4 sing 5 chant, sound 7 sonance

intonational: 7 tonetic

intone: 4 cant, sing 5 chant 8 modulate 10 cantillate

intort: 4 curl 5 twist

intoxicant (see also **alcoholic drink, liquor**): fox, gin, rum 4 wine 5 drink 6 excite, liquor 7 whiskey 9 inebriate, stimulate

intoxicated: 4 high, shot, tosy 5 bosky, drunk 6 boiled, soused, stewed 7 excited, screwed 8 besotted, glorious 9 crapulous 10 crapulated, inebriated, tosticated 11 capernoited

intoxicating: 5 heady

intracellular: 8 histonal

intractable: 6 unruly, wilful 7 haggard, restive 8 indocile, mutinous, obdurate, perverse, stubborn 9 obstinate 10 headstrong, refractory 11 disobedient, unteachable 12 contumacious, ungovernable 14 uncontrollable

intrada: 7 prelude 12 introduction

intranquillity: ado 12 restlessness

intransigent: 7 radical 14 irreconcilable, uncompromising

intrepid: 4 bold 5 brave, hardy, nervy 6 daring, heroic 7 assured, doughty, gallant, valiant 8 fearless, resolute, valorous 9 dauntless, dreadless, nerveless 10 courageous

intrepidity: 4 guts 5 nerve, valor 6 daring 7 bravery, courage 8 boldness

intricate: 4 hard 5 dedal 6 daedal, knotty 7 complex, Gordian, sinuous 8 involved 9 Daedalian, difficult, involuted 10 perplexing 11 complicated 12 labyrinthine

intrigue: 4 plot 5 cabal, charm 6 brigue, deceit, design, scheme 7 faction 8 artifice, collogue 9 fascinate 10 concoction, conspiracy 11 machination

intrinsic: 4 real, true 6 inborn, inbred, innate, native 7 genuine, natural 8 immanent, inherent, intimate 9 essential, necessary 11 inseparable 13 indispensable

intrinsically: 5 per se

introduce: 5 begin, enter, start, usher 6 broach, herald, infuse, insert 7 forerun, implant, precede, preface, present, sponsor 8 approach, initiate 9 insinuate 10 ingratiate

introduction: cue 5 debut, proem 7 intrada, introit, isagoge, preface, prelude 8 entrance, exordium, foreword, preamble, prologue, protasis 11 preparation

of new word: 7 neology

to treatise: 7 isagoge

introductory: 8 exordial 9 prefatory, prelusive

introductory cry: 4 hear, oyes, oyez

introit: 8 entrance 12 introduction

intromit: 5 admit 6 insert

intrude: 6 invade, meddle 7 obtrude 8 infringe, trespass 9 interfere, interlope, interpose

intruder: 8 outsider

intrusion: 10 aggression, infraction

intrusive: 7 curious

intrust: See **entrust**

intuit: 4 feel 5 sense 8 perceive 9 apprehend

intuition: 5 hunch 8 instinct

inulase: 6 enzyme

inunction: 8 ointment 9 anointing

pert. to: 7 aliptic

inundate: 4 flow 5 drown, flood 6 deluge 8 overflow, submerge 9 overwhelm 10 overspread

inundation: 8 alluvion

inure, enure: 5 steel 6 harden, season 7 toughen 9 accustom 9 habituate 10 discipline 11 acclimatize

inurn: 4 bury 6 entomb

inustion: 7 burning 13 cauterization

inutile: bad 7 useless 8 unusable 9 worthless 12 unprofitable

inutterable: See **unutterable**

invade: 4 raid 6 irrupt, offend 7 assault, intrude, overrun 8 encroach, entrench, intrench, trespass

invader: Hun 4 Pict 6 raider 8 intruder

invalid: 4 null 6 feeble, infirm, sickly 8 nugatory 11 ineffective 14 valetudinarian

invalidate: 4 undo 5 annul, break 7 abolish

invaluable: 8 precious 9 priceless 11 inestimable 13 inappreciable

invariable: 4 same 6 steady 7 uniform 8 constant 9 continual, immutable 10 unchanging 11 determinate 12 unchangeable

invariably: 6 always 7 forever

invasion (see also **invade**): 6 inroad 9 incursion 10 aggression

invective: 5 abuse, taunt 6 tirade 7 railing 8 diatribe, reproach 12 vituperation

inveigh: 9 fulminate

inveigle: 4 coax, lure 5 snare 6 allure, entice, entrap 8 persuade

invent: 4 coin, form, make, vamp 5 feign, forge, frame 6 create, design, devise, patent 7 concoct, fashion 8 contrive, discover, engineer 9 fabricate, improvise, originate 11 manufacture

invention: 7 fiction, figment

inventive: 6 adroit 7 fertile 9 ingenious

inventor: 6 author, coiner 7 creator 8 engineer 10 discoverer, originator
  airplane: 6 Fokker, Wright
  baseball: 9 Doubleday
  condensing steam engine: 4 Watt
  cotton gin: 7 Whitney
  dynamite: 5 Nobel
  electric light: 6 Edison
  electric motor: 9 Davenport
  elevator: 4 Otis
  gun: 4 Colt 9 Remington
  internal combustion engine: 6 Lenoir 7 Daimler
  logarithm: 6 Napier
  phonograph: 6 Edison
  photography: 6 Niepce, Talbot
  power loom: 10 Cartwright
  printing: 9 Gutenberg
  printing press: Hoe
  radio: 7 Marconi 8 de Forest
  safety lamp: 4 Davy
  sewing machine: 4 Howe 6 Lester
  steam locomotive: 10 Stephenson
  steamboat: 5 Fitch 6 Fulton, Rumsey
  telegraph: 5 Morse
  telephone: 4 Bell
  television: 6 Nipkow
  wireless: 7 Marconi

inventor's right: 6 patent

inventory: 4 list 7 account, catalog, listing 8 register, schedule 9 catalogue

inveracity: fib, lie 9 falseness

inverse: 8 opposite

invert: 4 turn 7 reverse

invertebrate: 4 worm 5 polyp 6 insect, sponge 7 mollusk 8 arachnid 12 coelenterate
  group: 7 radiata

invest: don 4 belt, gird, gown, robe, vest, wrap 5 array, crown, dress, endow, endue,

imbue 6 clothe, confer, embark, ordain 7 envelop, install, instate 8 accredit, enthrone, surround

investigate: pry 4 nose 5 probe, study, trace 6 search 7 examine, explore, inquire 8 research 10 scrutinize

investigator: 6 prober, tracer 9 detective
  body of: 4 jury 5 panel 9 committee

investiture: 7 clothes, vesture 8 clothing

investment: 7 garment 8 vestment
  list: 9 portfolio

investor: 10 capitalist, shareowner 11 stockholder

inveterate: 6 rooted 7 chronic 8 habitual, hardened 9 confirmed, ingrained

invidious: 6 odious 7 envious, hateful 9 malignant 12 disagreeable

invigorate: pep 5 brace, cheer, nerve, renew 6 vivify 7 animate, enliven, fortify, refresh 9 stimulate 10 exhilarate, strengthen

invigorating: 5 tonic 11 corroborant

invincible: 10 unbeatable 11 indomitable

inviolate: 4 holy 6 sacred 9 undefiled, unstained 10 inviolable, sacrosanct 13 incorruptible 14 indestructible

invisible: hid 6 unseen 10 indistinct, unapparent 13 undiscernible

Invisible Empire: 4 Klan

invitation: bid 4 call 7 bidding 8 biddance, entreaty 9 challenge
  initials: 4 RSVP

invite: ask, bid 4 call 5 court 6 allure, entice 7 attract, provoke, request, solicit

invocation: 4 plea 6 prayer, sermon 7 benison 8 entreaty 11 benediction

invoice: 4 bill 5 brief 7 account 8 manifest 9 statement

invoke: 4 call, pray 6 appeal, attest 7 conjure, entreat, provoke, solicit 9 imprecate 10 supplicate

involucre: 5 whorl 7 rosette 8 envelope

involuntary: 6 forced 9 reluctant, unwilling 11 instinctive, spontaneous

involute: 6 curled, rolled 8 involved

involve: 4 wrap 5 imply, snare 6 bemist, employ, engage, entail, tangle 7 concern, embrace, ensnare 8 comprise, comprize, encumber, entangle 9 implicate 10 complicate, comprehend

involved: 7 complex 12 labyrinthine

inward: 5 entad, inner 6 inside 8 homefelt, interior 10 internally

Io: *father:* 7 Inachus
  guard: 5 Argus
  son: 7 Epaphus

iodine: *combining form:* iod 4 iodo
  compound: 6 iodide
  salt: 6 iodate
  source: 4 kelp

substitute: 7 aristal
treat with: 6 iodate
Iolcus king: 6 Pelias
ion: *negative:* 5 anion
  positive: 6 cation, kation
Ion: *father:* 6 Apollo
  mother: 6 Creusa
Ionia: *coin:* 4 obol 5 obolo
  gulf: 4 Arta
  island: 5 Corfu, Zante 6 Cerigo, Ithaca 7 Kythera 10 Cephalonia
  monk: 5 Aidan
iota: bit, jot 4 atom, whit 6 tittle 8 particle
Iowa: *college:* Coe
  county: 5 Adair, Onawa 7 Wapello
  religious sect: 5 Amana
  town: 4 Ames 5 Anita 7 Ottumwa 9 Davenport, Oskaloosa
  tree: oak
ipecac: 4 evea
  substance: 7 emetine
Iphicles: *brother:* 8 Heracles, Hercules
  mother: 7 Alcmene
  son: 6 Iolaus
Iphis' daughter: 6 Evadne
iracund: 8 choleric 9 irascible
irade: 5 edict 6 decree
Irak: See **Iraq**
Iran: 6 Persia
  almond: 5 badam
  angel: Mah
  assembly: 6 Majlis, Mejlis
  bed: 4 sofa 5 divan
  bird: 6 bulbul
  books: 5 Koran, Yasna 6 Avesta, Gathas, Yashts 8 Vendidad, Vispered
  capital: 7 Teheran
  carpet: 4 Kali 7 Hamadan
  caste: 4 magi
  chief: Mir
  city: 4 Amol 7 Teheran(c.)
  coin: pul 4 asar, cran, kran, lari, rial 5 bisti, daric, dinar, larin, shahi, toman 6 shahee, stater 7 ashrafi, kasbeke, pahlavi
  comedy: 7 temacha
  country: 4 Elam 5 Media
  demigod: 4 Yima
  demon: 7 Apaosha, Ahriman
  diadem: taj
  dynasty: 6 Safavi, Seljuk 7 Safavid, Safawid 10 Sassanidae
  fire-worshipper: 5 Parsi 6 Parsee
  founder: 5 Cyrus
  garment: 6 chedar
  god: 6 Ormazd 7 Mithras
  governor: 4 khan 6 satrap
  grass: 6 millet
  hat: fez 6 turban
  hero: 4 Yima

javelin: 5 jerid 6 jeerid
king: 4 shah 6 Darius, Xerxes 7 Jamshid, Jamshyd 9 Giamschid 10 Artaxerxes
Koran student: 5 hafiz
lake: 5 Niriz, Urmia 6 Sahweh 8 Urumiyeh
language: 4 Zend 7 Pahlavi, Pehlevi
measure: guz, mou, zar, zer 4 cane, foot 5 gareh, jerib, kafiz, makuk, qasab 6 artaba, charac, chebel, gariba, ghalva, ouroub 7 capicha, chenica, farsakh, farsang, mansion, mishara 8 parasang, piamaneh, sabbitha, stathmos 9 collothun, colluthun
moon: 4 Mahi
mountain: 4 Kush 5 Hindu 6 Ararat, Elburz 8 Demavend 11 Parapanisus
New Year's Day: 7 Nowroze
nomad: 4 Luri
oil center: 6 Abadan
Parliament: 6 Majlis, Mejlis
peasant: tai
people: Lur, tai 4 Kurd, Mede, sart 5 Kajar, Mukri, nomad, Perse, Tajik 6 Iranic, Tadjik 7 Hadjemi, Persian
poet: 4 Omar 5 Saadi
port: 7 Bushire 11 Bandar Abbas
province: 4 Yezd
religion founder: 9 Zoroaster 11 Zarathustra
religious doctrine: 6 babism 7 babiism
revenue officer: 9 tahsildar 10 tahseeldar
river: 4 Mand, Mund 5 Karun 6 Tigris 8 Safid Rud 9 Euphrates, Kizil Uzen
ruler: 4 shah 6 atabeg, atabek, satrap, sultan
saint: 6 Safavi 7 Safavid, Safawid
screen: 6 purdah
sect: 5 Shiah, Sunni 6 Shiite, Sunnee 7 Sunnite
supreme deity: 6 Ormazd
tapestry: 7 susanee
tax collector: 9 tahsildar 10 tahseeldar
tent-maker: 4 Omar
throne room: 5 aiwan
tiara: 7 cidaris
title: mir 4 azam, shah 5 mirza
tobacco: 6 tumbak, tumbek 7 tumbaki, tumbeki
town: Fao, Kom 5 Niriz, Resht 6 Kasvin, Kerman, Meshed, Shiraz, Tabriz, Tauris 7 Hamadan, Ispahan, Tabreez 9 Balfroosh
traders: 4 sart
trumpet: 6 kerana 7 kerrana
vessel: 6 aftaba
water-pipe: 5 hooka 6 calean, hookah 8 narghile 12 hubble-bubble
water wheel: 5 noria
weight: ser 4 dram, dung, rotl, sang, seer 5 abbas, artal, artel, maund, pinar, ratel 6

batman, dirhem, gandum, karwar, miscal, miskal, nakhod 7 abbassi 8 tcheirek 9 sad-dirham

Iraq: *capital:* 6 Bagdad 7 Baghdad
 coin: 5 dinar
 district: 5 Basra
 town: 5 Amara, Basra

irascible: 5 brash, fiery, hasty, irate, techy, testy 6 snappy, touchy 7 fretful, peevish 8 captious, choleric, petulant, snappish 9 impatient, splenetic 10 passionate 11 bad-tempered, belligerent, combustible, hot-tempered 13 quick-tempered

irate: mad 5 angry, het up, wroth 6 bitter, wrathy 7 angered, enraged, furious 8 incensed, provoked, wrathful 9 indignant, irascible

ire: vex 4 fury, heat, rage 5 anger, annoy, wrath 6 choler, temper 8 asperity, vexation 9 vehemence 10 exasperate, resentment 11 displeasure 12 exasperation

Ireland: 4 Eire, Erin 5 Ierne, Irena 7 Ivernia 9 Innisfail
 ancestor: Ir; Mil 6 Miledh 8 Milesius
 assembly: 6 aenach, aonach
 basket: 7 skeough
 battle cry: abu
 bay: 6 Galway
 boat: 7 pookaun 8 pookhaun
 cabstand: 6 hazard
 cap: 6 barrad
 capital: 4 Tara 6 Dublin
 cattle: 5 Kerry
 chamber of deputies: 4 Dail
 chemist: 5 Boyle
 chieftain: 6 Tanist
 church: kil
 church steward: 7 erenach
 clan: 4 sept 5 Cinel
 club: 8 shillala 9 shillalah, shillelah 10 shillelagh
 coin: rap 4 real
 cordial: 10 usquebaugh
 county: 4 Cork, Down, Mayo 5 Cavan, Clare, Kerry, Louth, Meath 6 Antrim, Armagh, Galway, Offaly, Tyrone, Ulster 7 Donegal, Kildare, Leitrim, Wexford, Wicklow 8 Fermangh, Kilkenny, Limerick, Longford, Monaghan 9 Tipperary, Westmeath 11 Londonderry
 dagger: 5 skean
 dance: 10 rinkafadda, rinncefada
 dirge: 4 keen
 dish: 4 stew
 dramatist: see *playwright* below
 epic tales: 4 tain, tana(pl.)
 exclamation: och 4 arra 5 arrah, ohone
 fair: 6 aenach, aonach

fairy: 4 shee 5 sidhe 7 banshee, banshie 10 leprechaun
festival: 4 feis
fort: Lis 4 rath
freebooter: 8 rapparee
freeman: 4 aire
fuel: 4 peat
garment: 4 inar
goblin: 5 pooka
god's mother: Ana, Anu
god of love: 5 Dagda 6 Aengus, Oengus
god of sea: Ler
goddess: 4 Badb, Bodb, Dana
good-for-nothing: 8 spalpeen
groggery: 7 shebeen
harvester: 8 spalpeen
herring: 8 scud-dawn
holiday: 10 Whitmonday
infantryman: 4 kern
islands: 4 Aran
king: Ri; Rig 5 Ardri
king's home: 4 Tara
lamentation: 6 ochone
landholding system: 7 rundale
lawyer: 6 brehon
legislature: 4 Dail 10 Oireachtas
liquor: 6 poteen 7 potheen
lord: 6 tanist
luck: 4 cess
measure: 4 mile 6 bandle
melody: 7 planxty
moccasin: 9 pampootee, pampootie
monk: 6 culdee
monk's cell: kil 4 kill
mountain: 7 Wicklow 10 Carrantual 11 Lugnaquilla 13 Macgillicuddy
musical festival: 4 feis
musical instrument: 4 harp, lyre
name: 4 Sean 5 Moira
national emblem: 8 shamrock
negative: 5 sorra
novelist: 4 Shaw
oath: 5 bedad
old capital: 4 Tara
parliament: 4 Dail
patriot: 5 Emmet 6 Oakboy
patron saint: 7 Patrick
peasant: 4 kern 5 kerne
peat: gor
people: 4 Celt, Erse, Gael 6 Celtic 9 Hibernian
person: 4 aire, kern 5 kerne, paddy 7 shoneen 8 spalpeen 10 Eireannach
pert. to: 6 Celtic, Gaelic
pig: 5 bonav
playwright: 4 Shaw 5 Synge, Wilde, Yeats 6 O'Casey
poem: 6 amhran
poet: 5 Moore, Wilde, Yeats

priest: 5 druid
princess: 6 Iseult
proprietor: 6 tanist
Protestant: 9 Sassenach
province (see also *county* above): 6 Ulster 7 Munster 8 Leinster 9 Connaught
republicanism: 9 Fenianism
revolutionist: 6 Fenian
river: Lee 4 Bann, Deel, Erne, Suir 5 Boyne, Clare, Feale, Flesk, Foyle, Laune 6 Bandon, Barrow, Liffey, Martin 7 Munster, Shannon 10 Blackwater
robber: 8 woodkern
saint: 5 Aidan 7 Patrick
salutation: 6 a chara
seaport: 4 Cobh 6 Tralee
servant: 5 biddy
society: 4 aire
soldier: 6 bonagh 8 rapparee
soldiers' quartering: 7 bonaght 8 bonaught
song: 4 rann
spirit: see *fairy* above
steward: 7 erenach 8 herenach
stock: 4 daer
straw load: 5 barth
surgeon: 6 Colles
sweetheart: gra
symbol: 4 harp 8 shamrock
tax: 7 bonaght 8 bonaught
tenant: 4 saer
tenure: 6 sorren 7 sorehon
term of endearment: 5 aroon, aruin 7 acushla, alannah, asthore 9 avourneen 10 mavourneen
town: 4 Cork 5 Adare 6 Dublin, Lurgan 8 Limerick 9 Killarney, Tipperary 10 Abbey Feale 12 Castle Island
tribesman: see *person* above
trout: 7 gilaroo
verse: 4 rann
whiskey: 6 poteen 10 usquebaugh
white: 4 bawn
womanhood: 4 emer
writing system: 4 ogam 5 ogham
irenic: 4 calm 5 irene 7 henotic, pacific 8 irenical, peaceful 12 conciliatory
iridescence: 9 irisation
iridescent: 6 irised 7 opaline 9 prismatic 10 opalescent
iridium: *pert. to:* 6 iridic
symbol: ir
iris: lis 4 ixia 5 orris, sedge 6 orrice 7 rainbow 10 Florentine 11 ambassadeur
comb. form: 4 irid
family: 4 irid 8 tileroot
layer: 4 uvea
part: 4 uvea 6 argola 7 argolae(pl.)
pert. to: 5 irian
problem of: 6 iritis 8 aniridia

Irish (see also **Ireland** *people*): 6 Celtic, Gaelic 9 Hibernian
Irish bit: 7 traneen
Irish confetti: 6 bricks
Irish dividend: 10 assessment
Irish Free State: See **Ireland**
Irish pennant: 6 thread 8 raveling
Irish Sweepstakes: 7 lottery
irk (see also **ire**): vex 4 bore 5 anger, annoy, chafe, peeve, tease, upset, weary 6 nettle 7 trouble 8 irritate 10 exasperate
irksome: 4 dull 6 tedium 7 humdrum, painful, tedious 8 tiresome 9 fatiguing, wearisome 10 burdensome, monotonous, unpleasant 11 displeasing
irne: 4 iron
iron: fer(F.) 4 gyve, hard, irne 5 goose, metal, power, press 6 fetter, trivet, robust, strong, yetlin 7 manacle, shackle, yetling 8 firmness, gridiron, handcuff, hematite, siderite 10 unyielding
comb. form: 6 sidero
compound: 5 steel
containing: 6 ferric
dross: 6 sinter
magnet: 8 armature
lump: pig
marking: 7 brander
meteoric: 8 siderite
pert. to: 6 ferric
sulphate: 7 ilesite
symbol: Fe
Iron City: 10 Pittsburgh
iron sand: 6 iserin
ironclad: 7 armored, monitor
ironer: 6 mangle 7 presser
ironic: 7 satiric 9 sarcastic
irons: 6 chains 7 garters 8 creepers, shackles
ironwork: 8 ferament
ironworker's tool: 6 lifter
irony: 6 satire 7 asteism, sarcasm 8 ridicule 13 dissimulation
Iroquois Indian: 4 Erie 5 Huron, Litre 6 Cayuga, Mohawk, Neuter, Oneida, Seneca 7 Wyandot 8 Cherokee, Nottoway, Onondaga 9 Conestoga, Tuscarora 10 Tionontati
irradiance: 11 irradiation
irradiate: ray 4 beam, emit 6 bright 7 diffuse, radiate 8 brighten 9 enlighten 10 illuminate 11 illuminated
irrational: 4 surd 5 brute 6 absurd, stupid 7 bestial, brutish, foolish 9 senseless 10 ridiculous 12 preposterous, unreasonable 13 unintelligent
irrational number: 4 surd
irreclaimable: 4 lost 8 hopeless 9 abandoned 11 irrevocable

irreconcilable: 9 repugnant 10 discordant, implacable 12 incompatible, inconsistent, intransigent

irrecoverable: See **irreclaimable**

irredeemable: See **irreclaimable**

irrefutable: 10 conclusive

irregular: 4 wild 5 erose, false 6 ataxic, fitful, rugged, spotty, uneven, unlike 7 atactic, crabbed, crooked, cursory, devious, erratic, snatchy, unequal, wayward 8 abnormal, atypical, sporadic, unlawful, unstable, unsteady, variable 9 anomalous, desultory, eccentric, unsettled 10 changeable, disorderly, immoderate 11 intemperate 12 uncontrolled, unsystematic 13 extraordinary

irregularity: 5 error 7 anomaly 8 disorder 11 derangement 12 perturbation

irrelevant: 9 unrelated 10 inapposite 11 inessential, unessential 12 inconsequent

irreligious: 5 pagan 6 wicked 7 godless, heathen, impious, profane

irremediable: 8 helpless, hopeless 9 desperate, incurable 11 irreparable 13 irretrievable

irreproachable: 8 spotless 9 blameless, faultless

irresistible: 8 almighty 10 resistless 11 ineluctable 12 spellbinding

irresolute: 6 fickle, infirm, unsure 8 doubtful, unstable, wavering 9 uncertain, undecided 10 changeable, inconstant 11 fluctuating 12 undetermined

irresponsible: 8 carefree 10 fly-by-night 11 harum-scarum 12 undependable 13 unaccountable

irretrievable: See **irremediable**

irreverence: 7 impiety 8 dishonor 9 blasphemy, impudence, profanity

irrevocable: 4 firm 5 final 6 stable 9 immutable 11 unalterable

irrigate: wet 5 water 6 sluice 7 moisten

irritable: 4 edgy 5 birsy, cross, fiery, techy, testy 6 cranky, ornery, tetchy, touchy 7 fretful, iracund, peevish, pettish 8 snappish 9 excitable, fractious, impatient, querulent 11 capernoited 12 disagreeable

irritate: get, irk, nag, rub, vex 4 crab, fret, gall, goad, grig, rasp, rile, roil 5 anger, annoy, chafe, cross, frump, grate, peeve, pique, spite, sting, tease 6 abrade, badger, bother, enrage, excite, fridge, harass, hector, madden, needle, nettle, ruffle 7 affront, incense, provoke 8 acerbate 9 aggravate, displease, stimulate 10 exacerbate, exasperate

irritating: 5 acrid 8 rankling

irritation: 4 itch, sore 5 birse 6 temper

is: 6 exists 10 represents 11 personifies

is not: nis, nys

Isaac's kin: 4 Esau 5 Jacob 7 Abraham

isagoge: 12 introduction

Iseult: *beloved:* 7 Tristan
husband: 4 Mark

Ishmael: 5 rover 6 pariah 7 outcast
kin: 5 Hagar 7 Abraham 8 Nebaioth

Ishtar's lover: 6 Tammuz

isinglass: 4 mica

Isis: *kin:* 5 Horus 6 Osiris
mother: Nut
shrine: 5 Iseum 6 Iseium
son: 4 Sept

Islam: *adherent:* 6 Moslem, Muslim
festival: Eed
founder: 7 Mahomet
holy city: 5 Mecca 6 Medina
judge: 4 cadi
law: 5 sheri 6 sharia, sheria 8 sheriyat
paradise: 5 jenna
place of pilgrimage: 5 Caaba, Kaaba 6 Kaabeh
priest: 4 imam
scriptures: 5 Koran
tambourine: 5 daira

island: ait, cay, ile(F.), key 4 calf, eyot, holm, ilot, inch(Sc.), isle, Qais 5 atoll, holme, islet, islot 8 insulate
group: 5 Faroe, Samoa 8 Antilles, Caroline, Marshall 11 archipelago
mythical: 4 Meru 6 Avalon, Bimini 8 Atlantis
pert. to: 7 insular
snake-free: 4 Erin

Island of Saints: 7 Ireland

isle: See **island**

Isle of Man: *city:* 4 Peel 6 Ramsey 7 Douglas 10 Castletown
division of: 5 Treen
judge: 8 deemster, dempster
legislature: 7 tynwald
measure: 6 kishen, kishon
mountain: 8 Snaefell
part: 4 Ayre
pert. to: 4 Manx
watering place: 4 Ryde

islet: See **island**

ism: 5 ology, tenet 6 belief 8 doctrine 10 hypothesis
follower of: ist, ite

isolate: 4 isle 6 detach, enisle, island 7 seclude 8 insulate, separate 9 segregate, sequester 10 quarantine

isolated: 4 sole 5 alone 6 lonely 7 insular 8 singular, solitary

Isolde's lover: 7 Tristan

Israel (see also **Hebrew, Judaism**):
anthem: 7 Hatikva 9 Hattikvah
child: 5 sabra

city: 5 Jaffa, Joppa 9 Jerusalem(c.)
dance: 4 hora
desert: 5 Negeb
dust storm: 8 khamseen
government body: 7 Knesset 9 Sanhedrin
judge: 4 Elon 6 Samson 7 Sampson, Shamgar 8 Jephthah
king: 4 Ahab, Jehu, Omri, Saul 5 David, Pekah 7 Jehoram, Solomon 8 Jehoahaz, Jeroboam, Pekahiah
labor federation: 9 Histadrut
labor party: 5 Mapai
land of plenty: 6 Goshen
lawgiver: 5 Moses
measure: cab, cor, hin, kab, kor, log 4 bath, epha, ezba, omer, reed, seah 5 cubit, ephah, homer, kaneh, qaneh 11 handbreadth
plain: 6 Sharon
priest: Eli
seaport: 4 Acre 5 Aqaba, Elath, Haifa 7 Tel Aviv
settlement: 6 moshav 7 kibbutz
tribe: Dan 4 Aser, Levi 5 Asher 6 Reuben
issuance: 5 issue 6 sortie 7 issuing 9 emanation 12 distribution
issue: end, son 4 come, emit, fate, flow, gush, pour, send 5 arise, child, sally, spout, topic, utter 6 accrue, egress, emerge, escape, exitus, expede(Sc.), source, upshot 7 descent, edition, emanate, fortune, outcome, problem, proceed, progeny 9 effluence, offspring 10 denouement, distribute
issuing: 9 affluence, affluxion
ist: 7 devotee 8 adherent, believer, disciple, follower
Istanbul: 9 Byzantium 14 Constantinople
part: 4 Pera 5 Fanar
patriarch: 9 Nestorius
isthmus: 4 neck 6 strait 9 peninsula
istle fiber: 4 pita, pito
it may be: 5 haply
Ita: Ata 4 Aeta 7 Negrito
italicize: 9 emphasize, underline 10 underscore
Italy: *actress:* 4 Duse
article: et, il
artist: 7 Cellini
astronomer: 6 Secchi 7 Galileo
author: 5 Dante
card game: 5 tarot
carriage: 7 vettura
cathedral: 5 duomo
cereal: 5 arzun
cheese: 6 Romano 8 Parmesan
chest: 7 cassone
city: Bra, Ora 4 Alba, Asti, Bari, Este, Lodi, Nola, Pisa, Pola, Roma, Rome 5 Aosta, Fiume, Genoa, Lucca, Massa, Milan, Ostia, Padua, Parma, Pavia, Siena, Trent,
Turin, Udine 6 Ancona, Foggia, Mantua, Modena, Naples, Spezia, Venice, Verona 7 Bologna, Catania, Ferrara, Leghorn, Livorno, Marsala, Messina, Palermo, Perugia, Pompeii, Ravenna, Taranto, Trieste 8 Brindisi, Cagliari, Florence, Sorrento 11 Alessandria
coin: 4 lira, sudo, tari 5 grano, paoli, soldo 6 ducato, sequin, teston, zequin 8 chequeen, zecchino 9 centisimo
commune: Bra 4 Atri, Como, Dego, Este, Nola 5 Asola, Eboli 6 Rivoli
composer: 5 Verdi 7 Puccini 8 Mascagni 9 Scarlatti
condiment: 6 tamara
country: 7 Etruria
dance: 5 volta 8 courante 9 rigoletto 10 tarantella
deity: 4 faun
department: 4 Roma 5 Marca 6 Apulia, Emilia, Umbria 7 Liguria, Sicilia, Tuscana, Venetia 8 Calabria, Compania, Piemonte, Sardinia 9 Lombardia 10 Basilicata 13 Aruzzi e Molise
dictator: 9 Mussolini
engraver: 8 Raimondi
entertainment: 6 ridoto
estate: 11 latifundium
family: 4 Asti, Este 5 Amati, Cenci 6 Medici
festival: 5 festa
food: 5 pizza 7 ravioli 10 zabaglione
gentleman: ser 6 signor
god: 5 Liber, Picus 6 Consus
goddess: Ops 4 Juno 5 Diana, Salus, Venus 6 Pomona 7 Feronia, Minerva
grape: 6 verdea
guessing game: 4 mora
gulf: 7 Salerno
hamlet: 5 casal 6 casale
hero: 7 Orlando
holiday: 5 festa
house: 4 casa 6 casino
immigrant: 6 guinea
infant cupids: 7 amorini
inlay work: 6 tarsia
inn: 7 locanda
innkeeper: 7 padrone
instrument: 10 colascione
island: Cos 4 Elba 5 Capri, Leros 6 Ischia, Lipari, Sicily 8 Sardinia
king: 4 Rene 5 Murat 6 Alonso
lady: 5 donna 7 signora
lake: 4 Como 5 Garda 6 Albano, Lugano 7 Bolsena 8 Maggiore 9 Trasimene
land: 7 maremma
landlord: 7 padrone
leader: 4 duce
limestone: 7 scaglia
lover: 7 amoroso

macaroni: 5 pasta
magistrate: 7 podesta
marble: 7 carrara
master: 7 padrone
mayor: 6 syndic
measure: pie 4 orna 5 canna, carat, palma, piede, punto, salma, staio, stero 6 barile, miglio, moggio, rubbio, tavola, tomolo 7 boccale, braccio, secchio 8 giornata, polonick, quadrato
medieval faction: 4 Neri
millet: 4 buda, moha 5 mohar, tenai
monk 5 padre 6 abbate
mountain: 4 Alps 5 Amaro, Somma 8 Vesuvius 9 Apennines, Appennino
musician: 5 Guido
native: 5 Italo 6 Tirano 7 Sienese 9 Calabrian
naval base: 7 Taranto
needlework: 8 trapunto
noblewoman: 8 marchesa
omelet: 8 frittata
opera: 4 Aida 5 Norma, Tosca 9 Pagliacci
opera house: 5 Scala
organization: 7 Balilla
painter: 4 Reni, Tisi 5 Colle, Lippi, Lotto 6 Crespi, Guardi, Sacchi, Titian 7 Amigoni, di Credi, di Paolo, Raphael, Robusti, Strozzi, Tiepolo 8 Bronzino, Cagliari, Mainardi, Sassetta 9 Correggio, del Piombo, Giorgione, Veneziano 10 Botticelli, Caracciolo, Tintoretto
painting: 9 tenebrosi
part: toe
patriot: 9 Garibaldi
peasant: 9 contadini, contadino
people: 5 Latin, Oscan, Roman 6 Sabine, Tuscan 8 Venetian
philosopher: 7 Rosmini
physicist: see *scientist* below
pie: 5 pizza
plays: 7 Vangeli
poet: 4 Redi 5 Dante, Tasso
poetic name: 7 Ausonia
police officer: 6 sbirri, sbirro
policeman: 11 carabiniere, carabinieri
porridge: 7 polenta
port: 6 Rimini
possession: 6 Dhalak 7 Eritrea, Tripoli 10 Somaliland
pottery: 8 majolica
prelate: 4 Rici
priest: fra
prince: 4 Asti, Este
printer: 6 Bodoni
procession: 5 corso 7 trionfi, trionfo
province: 4 Bari, Este, Pola, Roma, Zara 5 Aosta, Cuneo, Parma, Udine 6 Istria, Verona 7 Salerno

region: 5 Carso
resort: 4 Lido
river: Po 4 Adda, Arno, Liri 5 Adige, Melfa, Oglio, Piave, Tiber 6 Panora, Rapido, Tevere, Ticino 7 Rubicon, Secchia, Trebbia 8 Volturno 10 Garigliano
rock: 7 scaglia
saint: 4 Neri
sausage: 6 salami
scientist: 5 Fermi, Volta 7 Galileo, Galvani
sculptor: 5 Leoni 6 Canova 7 Bernini 8 Canonica 9 Egenesean
sea: 8 Adriatic
seaport: Aci 4 Bari, Mola, Pola, Zara 5 Genoa, Ostia, Trani 7 Otranto, Trieste
secret society: 5 Mafia 7 Camorra 9 Carbonari
section: 7 maremma
shore: 4 riva
soldier: 10 carabineer, carabinier 11 bersagliere, carabinieri
song: 10 villanella, villanelle
soprano: 5 Patti
soup: 8 minestra 10 minestrone
spice: 6 tamara
straits: 7 Messina, Otranto
stream: 4 rivo
summer house: 6 casino
theme: 4 tema
theologian: 7 Peronne
town: Bra 4 Alba, Elea, Este, Meda, Pisa 5 Acqui, Aosta, Capua, Genoa, Milan, Parma, Teano 6 Naples, Napoli, Torino 7 Bologna, Caserta 9 Caporetto
university: 5 Padua
vessel: 9 trabacolo 10 trabascolo
violin maker: 5 Amati
violinist: 7 Corelli, Tartini
volcano: 4 Etna 5 Somma 8 Vesuvius 9 Stromboli
weight: 5 carat, libra, oncia, pound 6 denaro, libbra, ottava 11 chilogrammo
wind: 7 sirocco
wine: 4 Asti 6 Barolo, Massic 9 Vernaccia
itch: 4 reef, yeuk(Sc.) 6 desire 9 cacoethes, hankering 10 irritation
ite: 8 adherent, disciple, follower
item (see also **object**): ad, bit 5 entry, scrap, thing, topic 6 detail 7 account, article, product 8 personal 9 paragraph 10 particular 12 circumstance
   curious: ana
itemize: 9 enumerate
iterate: See **reiterate**
Ithaca king: 8 Odysseus
Ithunn's husband: 5 Brage, Bragi

itinerant: 6 errant, roving 7 migrant, nomadic 8 traveler, wanderer 9 migratory, transient, traveling, unsettled, wandering 11 peripatetic

itinerary: 4 plan, tour 5 guide, route 6 record 8 roadbook 9 guidebook

itinerate: 6 travel 9 traveling

itineration: 4 eyre, tour 7 circuit, travels

Ivan the Terrible: 4 Tsar
wife: 9 Anastasia

Ivanhoe: *author:* 5 Scott
character: 4 Tuck 5 Isaac 6 Cedric, Rowena

ivory: 6 creamy, dentin 7 dentine, ivoride, ribzuba 8 ribazuba
carving: 9 toreutics
rasping: 5 scobs

ivy: tod 4 gill, hove 6 hedera, hibbin
crowned with: 9 hederated
pert. to: 7 hederic
poison: 5 sumac 6 sumach

Ixion's descendants: 8 Centaurs

ixtle: 4 pita 5 fiber, istle

izzat: 5 honor 6 credit 8 prestige 10 reputation

J

jaal: 4 goat, ibex 5 beden
jab: hit, jag 4 poke, prod, stab 5 lunge, punch 6 thrust
Jabal's father: 6 Lamech
jabber: 4 chat 6 burble, gabble 7 chatter 9 gibberish
jabberwocky: 4 tove 6 slithy 7 brillig 8 nonsense 9 rigmarole
jabiru: 4 ibis 5 stork
jabot: 5 frill
jacare: 6 caiman
jacent: 5 prone 9 recumbent
jack: nob 4 card, lift 5 knave, money 6 wenzel 8 zapetero
  group of 4: 8 quatorze
jack-in-the-pulpit: 4 herb 5 plant 7 figwort
jack-of-all-trades: 6 tinker
jack tree: 4 jaca
jackal: 5 diebs
jackanapes: ape, fop 4 beau 5 dandy 6 monkey 7 coxcomb
jackass: 4 dolt, fool 5 dunce 6 donkey, nitwit 9 blockhead
  comb. form: ono
jackdaw: coe, daw 6 caddow 7 dawcock 9 blackbird
jacket: 4 bajo, coat, Eton 5 acton, grego, wamus 6 anorak, banian(Ind.), bietle, blazer, bolero, dolman, reefer, sliver, wammus, wampus 7 cassock, doublet, ristori, spencer 8 camisole, chaqueta, hanselin 9 habergeon, peajacket 10 carmagnole(F.), roundabout 11 nightingale
  knitted: 5 gansy 6 gansey, sontag 7 sweater 8 cardigan, penelope
  sleeveless: 4 vest 6 bolero
jackknife: 6 barlow
jackpot: all 5 award 8 windfall
jackrabbit: 4 hare
jackstay: 4 rope 5 horse, staff
jackstones: 4 dibs
Jacob: *brother:* 4 Edom, Esau
  daughter: 5 Dinah
  descendant: 6 Levite 9 Israelite
  father-in-law: 5 Laban

  new name: 6 Israel
  parent: 5 Isaac 7 Rebekah
  retreat: 5 Haran
  son: Dan, Gad 4 Aser, Levi 5 Asher, Judah 6 Bononi, Joseph, Reuben, Simeon 7 Gershon, Zebulun 8 Benjamin, Issachar, Naphtali
  vision(scene): 6 Bethel
  wife: 4 Leah 6 Rachel
jade: fag, nag 4 hack minx, plug, tire 5 hussy, weary 6 harass 7 exhaust, fatigue, hilding, pounamu 8 nephrite 10 greenstone
jaded: 4 worn 5 blase, tired, weary 6 dulled 7 wearied 9 exhausted, for jaskit, for jesket
jaeger: 4 bird, gull, skua 6 hunter 7 diamond 8 huntsman
jag: dag, jab, rag 4 barb, hair, load, mess, stab 5 carry, notch, prick, scrap, shred, slash, souse, spree, tooth 6 indent, tatter 7 bristle, pendant, portion 8 quantity 13 denticulation
jagged: 5 erose, rough, sharp 6 hackly, ragged 7 cutting
jaguar: 5 ounce
jai alai: 4 game 6 pelota
  court: 7 fronton
  racket: 5 cesta
jail: can, jug 4 brig, dump, gaol, keep, stir 5 clink, pokey 6 asylum, carcel, cooler, lockup, prison 7 hoosgow 8 bastille, hoosegaw, hoosegow, imprison 9 calaboose 11 incarcerate
jailer, jailor: 4 caid 5 guard 6 gaoler, keeper, warden 7 alcaide, turnkey
Jairite: Ira
jake: 4 fine, hick, rube 5 dandy 6 rustic 9 first-rate, greenhorn
jako: 6 parrot
jalousie: 5 blind 7 shutter
jam: 4 bind 5 crowd, crush 6 spread 7 squeeze 9 marmalade 10 congestion
Jamaica dogwood: 8 barbasco
  ginger alcohol: 4 jake
James' father: 7 Zebedee

jangle: 4 ring 6 bicker 7 prattle, quarrel, wrangle 11 altercation

jangling: 5 harsh 9 dissonant 10 discordant 11 cacophonous

janitor: 6 porter 9 caretaker 10 doorkeeper 11 housekeeper

japan: 7 lacquer, varnish

Japan: 5 Nipon 6 Niphon, Nippon

abacus: 7 soroban

abalone: 5 awabi

aborigine: 4 Aino, Ainu

alcoholic beverage: 4 sake, saki

alloy: 5 mokum

allspice: 12 chimonanthus

apricot: ume 4 ansu

art design: 5 notan

baron: 6 daimio, daimyo

battle cry: 6 banzai

bay: ise

biwa: 6 loquat

boxes: 4 inro

brake: 6 warabi

brazier: 7 hibachi

brocade: 7 nishiki

Buddha: 5 Amida, Amita

Buddhist festival: Bon

Buddhist sect: Zen 7 Jodo-shu, Shin-shu

bush clover: 4 hagi

button: 7 netsuke

calculator: 6 abacus 7 soroban

calisthenics: 4 judo

cape: 4 mino

capital: 5 Tokyo

cherry: 4 fuji

chess: 5 shogi

chevrotain: 4 napu

church: 4 tera

circle: 4 maru

city: Ome 4 Kobe, Kura, Nara, Ueda 5 Atami, Kioto, Kyoto, Nikko, Osaka, Otaru, Sasebo, Sendai 7 Fukuoka, Niigata, Okayama, Okazaki, Sapporo 8 Hako Date, Kamakura, Kanazawa, Kumamoto, Nagasaki, Wakatama, Yokahama, Yokosuka 9 Hiroshima, Kagoshima, Tokushima 11 Akamagaseki

clan: 7 Satsuma

class: eta, roi 6 heimin 7 kwazoku, samurai, shizoku

clogs: 4 geta

clover: 4 hagi

coin: bu; rin, sen, yen 4 oban 5 koban, obang, tempo 6 cobang, ichebu, ichibu, itzebu, itzibu, kobang 7 itzeboo, itziboo

combine: 8 zaibatsu

composition: 6 haikai

costume: 7 netsuke

court: 5 dairi

crepe: 8 chirimen

crest: mon 7 kikumon

dancing girl: 6 geisha

deer: 4 sika

deity: 9 Amaterasu

dextrose: ame

dish: 7 tempura 8 sukiyaki

dog: 6 tanate

door: 6 fusuma

drama: no

drink: 4 mate, sake, saki

drum: 5 tarko

dye process: 5 yuzen

earthenware: 5 banko 8 rakuware

emperor: 6 Makado 8 Hirohito

emperor's title: 5 Tenno 6 Mikado

ethics: 7 Bushido

explosive: 7 shimose

fabric: 6 birodi 7 habutai, nishiki 8 chirimen, habutaye

family concern: 8 zaibatsu

fan: ogi

felicitation: 6 banzai

festival: Bon 7 Matsuri

fish: ayu, tai, tho 4 fugu, funa

flag: 7 sunflag

flower: 9 nelumbium

flute: 4 fuye

game: go 5 goban 6 gobang

garment: 5 haori 6 kimono, mompei

gateway: 5 torii

girdle: obi

girdle receptacle: 4 inro

girl: 6 geisha, mousme 7 mousmee

god: 5 Ebisu, Hotei 6 Benten 7 Daikoku, Jurojin 8 Bishamon 10 Fukurokuju

goddess: 9 Amaterasu

governor's title: 6 shogun, taikun, tycoon

harp: 4 koto

herb: udo

island: Iki 4 Oita 5 Bonin, Hondo, Kuril, Sikok 6 Honshu, Kiushu, Kiusiu, Kurile, Kyushu, Niphon, Riu-kiu 7 Cipango, Loo-Choo, Shikoku 8 Hokkaïdo

kelp: 4 kome

lacquer: 6 urushi

lake: 4 Biwa

legislature: 4 Diet

litter: see *palanquin* below

loquat: 4 biwa

lyric: 5 haiku, hokku

magnolia: 5 yulan

measure: bu, jo; boo, cho 4 hiro 5 tsubo 11 kujira-shaku

measure of distance: ri

measure of land: se; tan

measure of weight: mo; fun, kin, kon, rin, shi 4 kati, kwan, niyo 5 carat, catty, momme, picul 6 kwamme 8 hiyak-kin 11 komma-ichida

medicine case: 4 etui, inro

metalwork: 5 zogan

Mikado: 5 dairi

monastery: 4 tera

money: mo, ro

money of account: mo; rin, yen

mountain: Usu 4 Fuji 5 Asama, Hondo, Yesso 6 Asosan, Kiusiu 7 Fujisan 8 Fuji-yama

music and dancing: 7 san-gaku 8 sarugaku

musical instrument: 4 fuye, koto 5 tarko 8 samisen, truyume

nautical mile: 5 kairi

news service: 5 Domei

nobility: 7 kwazoku

opened by: 5 Perry

ornament: 4 inro

outcast: eta 5 ronin

overcoat: 4 mino

pagoda: taa

painting style: 4 kano 7 ukiyoye

palanquin: 4 kago 5 cango 7 norimon

paper mulberry: 4 kozo

paper screen: 5 shoji

peninsula: Izu

people: 4 Aino, Ainu 6 Nippon 9 Nipponese

persimmon: 4 kaki 7 Hyakume

pine: 5 matsu

plant: udo 5 kudzu 6 sugamo

plum: 6 kelsey

porcelain: 5 Hizen, Imari 6 Hirado 9 Nabe-shima

port: 4 Kobe 5 Hiogo, Osaka, Otaru 7 Nii-gata 8 Hakodate, Nagasaki, Wakatama, Yokohama

porter: 5 akabo

potato: imo

prefecture: 5 ehime 9 Yamaguchi

province: Ise 5 Iwaki 6 Yamato 7 Satsuma

quince: 8 japonica

radish: 6 daikon

receptacle: 4 inro

religion: 6 Shinto 8 Buddhism 9 Shintoism

rice cake: ame

rice flour: ame

rice paste: ame

rice wine: 4 sake

river: 4 Yalu 8 Tonegawa

robe: 6 kimono

ruler: 6 shogun

salad plant: udo

salmon: 4 masu

samurai: 5 ronin

sash: obi

screen: 5 shoji

seaweed: 4 nori

self-defense: 4 judo 7 jujitsu, jujutsu

Shinto temple: Sha 5 Jinja 6 Jinsha 7 Ya-shiro

ship: 4 maro, maru

shoe: 4 geta, zori

shrub: 4 fuji 5 goumi 8 japonica

silk: 7 habutai 8 chirimen, habutaye

silkworm: 7 yamamai

silkworm disease: uji

sock: 4 tabi

song: uta

sovereign: 5 tenno

storm: 7 tsunami

street: 5 Ginza

suicide: 7 seppuku 8 hara-kari, hara-kiri, hari-kari, kamikaze

suntree: 7 hinokis

sword: 5 catan 6 cattan 8 wacadash

sword guard: 5 tsuba

syllabic writing: 4 kana

tea ceremony: 7 chanoyu

tea girl: 6 mousme 7 mousmee

temple: 4 tera

throne: 6 shinza

title: 4 kami 6 shogun

tortoise shell: 5 bekko

tree: 4 kozo, sugi 5 akeki, kiaki, yeddo 6 urushi 7 camphor 8 akamatsu 10 shiraka-shi

untouchable: eta

vehicle: 7 ricksha 8 rickshaw 10 jinricksha, jinrikisha

velvet: 6 birodi

verse: 5 tanka

vine: 5 kudzu

volcano: Aso 4 Fuji 5 Asama, Asame 6 Aso-san 8 Fujiyama 9 Asamayama

wall: 5 shoji

windstorm: 5 taifu

winged being: 5 tengu

wrestling: 4 judo, Sumo 7 jujitsu, jujutsu 8 jiujitsu, jiujutsu

writing: 4 kana

zitherharp: 4 koto

Japanese-American: 5 Issei, Kibei, Nesei, Nisei 6 Kibbei, Sansei

japaneer: 9 varnisher

jape: 4 fool, gibe, jeer, jest, jibe, jipe, joke, mock 5 fraud, trick 6 deride

japery: 10 buffoonery

Japeth: *father:* 4 Noah
    son: 5 Magog, Tubal 7 Meshech

japonica: 4 bush 5 shrub 8 camellia

jar: jug, ola, urn 4 jolt, olla, vase 5 banga, clash, cruse, shake, shock 6 croppa, hydria, krater, tinaja 7 agitate, amphora, clatter, concuss, discord 10 jardiniere
    fruit: 5 mason

rubber: 4 lute
top: lid
two-handled: 7 amphora
wide-mouthed: 4 ewer
jardiniere: jar, jug, urn 4 vase 5 stand 7 garnish 9 flowerpot
jargon: 4 cant 5 argot, idiom, lingo, slang 6 pidgin 9 baragouin, gibberish 10 balderdash 11 grimgribber
jarl: 4 earl 7 headman 9 chieftain
jarring: 5 rough 9 dissonant 10 discordant
jasmine: 4 bela 5 papaw 6 flower 7 jessamy
Jason: *father:* 5 Aeson
love: 6 Creusa
men: 9 Argonauts
ship: 4 Argo
teacher: 7 Cheiron
uncle: 6 Pelias
wife: 5 Medea
jasper: 6 morlop, quartz 10 bloodstone
jauk: 5 dally 6 trifle
jaundice: 4 bias, envy 7 gulsach, icterus 8 jealousy 9 prejudice
jaunt: 4 ride, trip 5 sally, tramp 6 ramble 7 journey 9 excursion
jaunty: 4 airy 5 cocky, perky, showy, smart 7 finical, stylish 8 debonair 9 debonaire, sprightly
Java: *arrow poison:* 4 upas
badger: 5 ratel 6 teledu
berry: 5 cubeb
carriage: 4 sado 5 sadoo
city: 7 Batavia, Jakarta 8 Samarang, Surabaya 9 Surakarta 10 Jokjokarta
civet: 5 rasse
community: 5 Dessa
cotton: 5 kapok
dancers: 6 bedoyo
drama: 6 topeng
Dutchman: 6 blanda
fabric: 4 ikat
fig tree: 7 gondang
grackle: beo
island: 4 Bali
lomboy: 4 plum
measure: 4 paal 5 palen
mountain: 4 Gede 5 Lawoe 6 Raoeng 7 Semeroe, Slameta 8 Soembing
musical instrument: 5 saron 6 bonang, gender 7 gambang, gamelan 8 gamelang
orchestra: 7 gamelan 8 gamelang
ox: 7 bantens
pepper: 5 cubeb
plum: 5 duhal 6 jambul, lomboy 7 jambool
port: 7 Batavia 8 Surabaya
puppet show: 6 wajang, wayang
rice field: 5 sawah
speech: 5 krama, ngoko
straw: 6 peanit

sumac: 6 fuyang
temple: 5 candi 6 chandi, tjandi
tree: 4 upas 6 antiar 7 gondang
village: 5 Dessa
weight: 4 amat, pond, tali, 5 pound
wild dog: 5 adjag
Java almond: 7 talisay
Java cotton: 5 kapok
Javan squirrel: 8 jelerang
Javanese skunk: 6 teledu
javelin: 4 dart 5 lance, spear 7 assagai, assegai, harpoon
cord: 7 amentum
jaw: maw 4 chaw, chop, talk 5 scold 6 jabber 7 chatter 8 scolding
lumpy: 13 actinomycosis
muscle: 8 masseter
part: 4 chin
pert. to: 5 malar 7 gnathic
jawab: 5 reply 6 answer 7 balance 8 building
jawbone: 7 maxilla
Jayhawker: 6 Kansan
Jayhawker State: 6 Kansas
jazz: hot 4 cool 5 funky, swing 6 modern 7 ragtime 11 barrelhouse, progressive
jealous: 6 yellow 7 envious 10 suspicious 11 mistrustful
jeer: bob, boo 4 gibe, hoot, jape, jibe, mock 5 fleer, flite, flout, scoff, scout, sneer, taunt 6 deride 8 ridicule
jeering: 6 glaiks 7 sarcasm
Jehiada's wife: 9 Jehosheba 12 Jehoshabeath
Jehoahaz's mother: 7 Hamutal
Jehoiachin's successor: 9 Salathiel
Jehoshaphat: *father:* Asa
son: 4 Jehu
Jehovah: 4 Jave 5 Jahve, Yahve, Yahwe 6 Jahvah, Jahveh, Yahveh, Yahweh 7 Jahaveh
jehu: 6 driver
Jehu's father: 11 Jehoshaphat
jejune: dry 4 arid, avid, dull, flat 5 empty, inane, prosy, trite, vapid 6 barren, hungry, meager 7 insipid, sterile 8 foodless, lifeless
jell: 9 coagulate 11 crystallize
jellify: gel 5 jelly
jelly: gel 4 geal, sapa 5 aspic, kisel 6 cullis, pectin, spread 7 fisnoga, gelatin 8 gelatine
animal: 7 gelatin 8 gelatine
meat: 5 aspic
vegetable: 6 pectin
jellyfish: 6 medusa 7 acaleph
group: 10 discophora
part: 10 exumbrella
jellylike: 10 gelatinous
jennet: ass 5 horse 6 donkey

jeofail: 7 mistake 9 oversight
jeopardize: 6 expose 7 imperil 8 endanger
jeopardous: 6 daring 11 venturesome
jeopardy: 4 risk 5 peril 6 danger, hazard,
 menace 9 adventure
jequirity: 8 licorice
Jerahmeel's son: 4 Oren 5 Achia
jeremiad: 6 lament, tirade 9 complaint
jerez: 6 sherry
Jericho: *publican:* 8 Zaccheus 9 Zacchaeus
 woman: 5 Rahab
jerk: bob, tic, tit 4 hike, lipe, shog, yank,
 yerk 5 chuck, hitch, pluck, tweak
jerkin: 4 coat 6 jacket, salmon 9 blackjack,
 waistcoat
jerky: 5 wagon 7 charqui 8 saccadic,
 staccato
jeroboam: 4 bowl 6 bottle, goblet
jersey: 6 gansey 7 sweater
Jersey tea: 11 wintergreen 12 checkerberry
Jerusalem: 4 Sion, Zion 5 Salem
 captor: 4 Omar
 garden: 10 Gethsemane
 mosque: 4 Omar
 mountain: 4 Sion, Zion 6 Moriah, Olivet
 oak: 7 ambrose
 pert to: 14 Hierosolymitan
 pool: 6 Siloam 8 Bethesda
 priest: 5 Zadoc, Zadok
 prophetess: 4 Anna, Anne
 region: 5 Perea
 spring: 5 Gihon 6 Siloam
 temple treasury: 6 Corban
 thorn: 6 retama
 town: 14 Hierosolymitan
Jerusalem artichoke: 5 tuber 7 girasol 8
 girasole 10 topinambou
Jerusalem corn: 5 durra
Jerusalem haddock: 4 opah
jess: 5 strap, thong 7 binding
jessamy: fop 5 dandy
Jesse: *father:* 4 Obed
 son: 5 David
jest: bob, cog, fun 4 bull, fool, gaud, jape,
 joke, mime, quip, skit 5 bourd, droll, flirt,
 gleek, sport 6 banter, japery, trifle 8 drollery 9 burlesque 10 jocularity
jester: 4 fool, mime 5 clown, droll 6 disour
 7 buffoon, dizzard 8 merryman 9 joculator
 11 merry-andrew
Jesuit: *founder:* 6 Loyola
 motto: 4 A.M.D.G.
 saint: 5 Regis
Jesuits' bark: 8 cinchona
jet: 4 ebon, gush 5 black, ladle, raven, spout,
 spurt 6 nozzle 8 fountain, spouting
jet-assisted takeoff: 4 JATO
Jethro's daughter: 8 Zipporah
jetty: 4 mole, pier 5 groin, wharf 6 groyne

jeu: 4 game, play 9 diversion
jeune fille: 4 girl, miss
Jew (see also **Hebrew, Judaism**): 6 Essene,
 Semite
 ascetic: 6 essene
 harp: 8 guimbard
 horn: 6 shofar
jewel: gem 4 opal, ruby, sard 5 beryl, bi-
 jou(F.), regal 6 garnet 7 diamond 8 amethyst, ornament
 box: 6 casket 7 casquet
 case: tye
 connoisseur: 10 lapidarist
 set: 6 parure
 weight: 4 tola
jeweler: 7 gemmary
 glass: 5 loupe
jewelry: 10 bijouterie
 alloy: 6 oreide, oroide
 artificial: 5 paste 6 strass 7 costume
 cutting device: dop
 false: 5 paste 6 strass 7 costume
 piece: 4 ring 6 brooch 8 bracelet, necklace
 set: 6 parure 8 lavalier, necklace 9 lavaliere
 10 lavalliere
 setting: 4 pave
Jezebel: 4 fury 6 virago
 husband: 4 Ahab
 victim: 6 Naboth
jib: gib 4 balk, boom, sail
jibe: See **gibe**
jiffy: 5 braid, flisk, hurry, trice 6 gliffy, moment, second 7 instant
jig: top 4 boat 5 dance, prank 6 fiddle 8 carriage, fishhook
jigger: cup 4 club 5 glass 6 bridge, gadget 7
 support
jiggle: jar 5 dance, shake 6 diddle, teeter
jihad, jehad: war 6 strife 7 contest, crusade
 8 campaign
jill: 4 girl 5 woman 10 sweetheart
jilt: mau 4 girl, gunk 5 cheat, woman 6 begunk, mitten, reject 7 abandon, deceive,
 discard
jimmy: bar, pry 4 neat, spot 5 dandy, jemmy
 6 spruce 7 crowbar 9 greatcoat
Jimsonweed: 6 datura
jingle: 4 ring 5 clank, clink, rhyme, verse 6
 tinkle 7 chinkle
jingoist: 10 chauvinist
jinni: 5 genie 6 afreet, Alukah, jinnee, Yaksha, Yakshi(fem.)
jinx: hex 5 jonah 6 hoodoo
jitters: 5 panic 6 dither 11 nervousness
jittery: 5 jumpy 7 fidgety, nervous
jivatma: ego 5 atman
Joan of Arc: 7 Pucelle
 counselors: 6 voices
 victory: 7 Orleans

Joan's spouse: 5 Darby

job: 4 char, duty, snap, task 5 chare, chore 8 sinecure

Job: *daughter:* 5 Kezia 6 Jemima
friend: 6 Bildad, Zophar 7 Eliphaz
home: Uz

Job's tears: 4 coix 5 adlai, adlay, grass, plant

jobber: 6 dealer 10 wholesaler

Jocasta: *daughter:* 6 Ismene 8 Antigone
husband: 7 Oedipus
son: 7 Oedipus 8 Eteocles 9 Polynices 10 Polyneices

jockey: 4 gull 5 rider, trick 6 fellow, laddie, outwit 8 maneuver 10 manipulate
kind of: 4 disk

jocose: dry 5 droll, merry

jocular: gay 4 airy 5 droll, funny, jolly, merry, silly, witty 6 blithe, elated, jocose, jocund, jovial, joyous, lively, ribald 7 comical, festive, gleeful, jesting, playful, waggish 8 animated, cheerful, gladsome, humorous, mirthful, sportive 9 burlesque, convivial, facetious, hilarious, vivacious 10 frolicsome

joculator: fod 4 mime 6 jester 7 juggler 8 conjurer, jongleur, minstrel 11 entertainer

jog: bob, mog 4 lope, poke, prod, shog, trot 5 dunch, nudge 6 canter 7 refresh 9 stimulate

joggle: 5 hotch 7 shoggle

John: Ian 4 Ivan, Juan, Sean

John Brown's Body author: 5 Benet

John of Gaunt: 9 Lancaster

John the Baptist: *father:* 7 Zachary 9 Zachariah, Zacharias
mother: 9 Elizabeth

johnnycake: 4 pone 7 hoecake

Johnson grass: 7 sorghum

join: add, fay, mix, tie, wed 4 abut, affy, ally, club, fuse, knit, knot, link, mate, meet, seam, team, weld, yoke 5 annex, atone, blend, chain, clout, enrol, enter, graft, hitch, marry, merge, miter, nally, piece, unite 6 adject, adjoin, assist, attach, cantle, cement, cocket, concur, couple, engage, enlist, enroll, mingle, solder, splice, suture 7 combine, conjoin, connect, consort, mortise 8 accouple, coalesce, compound, copulate 9 associate 10 amalgamate, articulate, consociate 11 incorporate

joined: 8 conjugal

joiner: 7 splicer 9 carpenter 10 woodworker

joining: 6 syzygy 8 abutting, addition

joint: ell, hip, tee 4 ares, butt, coxa, knee, node, seam 5 alula, ancle, ankle, cross, elbow, hinge, scarf, tenon, wrist 6 arthra(pl.), mutual, rabbet, resort 7 arthron,

calepin, hangout, knuckle, pastern 8 coupling 12 articulation
pert. to: 5 nodal 9 articular
plant stem: 6 phyton 8 phytomer
put out of: 9 dislocate
right angle: ell, tee
turned outward: 6 valgus
without: 10 acondylose, acondylous
wooden: 5 tenon

joist: 4 beam 7 sleeper 8 studding

joke: dor, egg, fun, gag, gig, pun 4 fool, gaud, gibe, hoax, jape, jest, jibe 5 flirt, prank, rally, sport, tease 6 banter, humbug 7 bromide 8 chestnut

joker: out, wag, wit 4 card 5 catch 6 gagger, jester 7 farceur 9 mistigris

Joktan: *father:* 4 Eber
son: 5 Ophir

joll: 5 lurch

jollity: fun 5 cheer, mirth, revel 6 gaiety, gayety 7 revelry 8 hilarity 9 amusement, festivity, joviality, merriment 11 merrymaking 12 cheerfulness, exhilaration 13 jollification

jolly: 5 buxom, rally 6 cajole, jovial, mellow 7 jocular 11 merrymaking

jolly boat: 4 yawl

jolt: jar 4 blow, bump, butt, shog 5 knock, shake, shock 6 jostle, jounce

Jonah: 4 jinx 7 prophet
deliverer: 5 whale

jongleur: See **joculator**

Jonson comedy: Fox 7 Epicene, Volpone 9 Alchemist

Jordan: *region:* 5 Perea 6 Basham

joree: 7 chewink

Joseph: *brother:* Dan, Gad 4 Levi 5 Asher, Judah 6 Reuben, Simeon 7 Zebulun 8 Benjamin, Issachar, Naphtali
buyer: 8 Potiphar
father: 5 Jacob
mother: 6 Rachel
son: 4 Igal 7 Ephraim

josh: guy, kid, rib 4 joke 5 chaff, spoof, tease 6 banter, string

Joshua: *associate:* 5 Caleb
burial place: 5 Gaash
father: Nun
place of importance: 7 Aijalon

Joshua tree: 5 yucca

Josiah: *father:* 4 Amon
mother: 7 Jedidah
son: 8 Jehoahaz 9 Jehoiakim

joss: 4 idol 5 image 8 divinity

jostle: jar, jog 4 jolt, push, shog 5 crowd, elbow, shove 6 hurtle, hustle

jot: ace, bit 4 atom, iota, whit 5 grain, minim, point 6 tittle 8 particle

jouk: 4 dart, duck, fawn, hide 5 cheat, dodge, evade, skulk 6 cringe

jounce: 4 jolt 5 shake 6 bounce

journal: log 5 diary, paper 6 record 7 day-book, gazette, gudgeon, logbook 8 magazine 10 periodical
  keeper: 7 diarist

journalist: 6 editor 8 reporter 9 columnist

journey: go; run 4 eyre, fare, iter(L.), ride, sail, tour, trek, trip 5 jaunt, route 6 errand, travel, voyage 7 circuit, odyssey, passage, travail 8 navigate 9 excursion 10 expedition, pilgrimage 13 peregrination
  course of: 9 itinerary
  division of: lap, leg
  pert. to: 6 viatic 11 peripatetic

journeying: 6 errant

joust: 4 tilt 6 combat 7 tourney 10 tournament
  field: 4 list
  ready to: 5 atilt

jovial: gay 4 boon 5 bully, jolly, merry 6 elated, genial, jocose, jocund, joyous 7 jocular 9 convivial, hilarious

jowl: jaw 4 chop 5 cheek 6 dewlap, wattle 7 jawbone

joy: 4 gaud, glee 5 bliss, mirth, revel 6 gaiety, gayety 7 delight, ecstasy, elation, rapture, revelry 8 felicity, gladness, hilarity, pleasure 9 beatitude, festivity, happiness, rejoicing, transport 10 exultation, joyfulness, joyousness 12 cheerfulness, exhilaration
  Muse: 4 Tara

joya: 5 jewel

joyless: 6 dismal 9 cheerless

joyous: gay 4 glad 5 merry 6 blithe, festal, festus 7 blessed, gaudful, festive, gleeful, jocular 8 cheerful, gleesome, mirthful 9 blitheful, delighted

Jubal's father: 6 Lamech

jubilant: 6 elated 8 exulting 9 rejoicing 10 triumphant

Judah (see also **Judea**):
  brother: 4 Levi 6 Joseph, Reuben, Simeon
  daughter-in-law: 5 Tamar
  descendant: 4 Anub, Boaz 5 David, Jesse 9 Jerahmeel
  father: 5 Jacob
  king: 4 Ahaz 6 Uzziah
  mother: 4 Leah
  queen: 8 Athaliah
  son: Er 4 Onan

Judaism (see also **Hebrew, Israel**):
  abode of the dead: 5 Sheol
  ascetic: 6 essene
  Bible: 4 Tora 5 Torah
  Bible text: 5 miqra
  Book of Psalms: 8 Tehillim

  bread: 5 echem, matzo 6 hallah, matzos 7 matzoth 8 afikomen
  butcher: 6 shohet 8 shochtim
  cabalistic book: 5 Zohar
  calendar: see *month* below
  ceremony: 8 habdalah
  community: 6 aljama 8 kehillah
  confession of sins: 5 Alhet 7 Ashamnu
  convert: ger
  Day of Atonement: 9 Yom Kippur
  devil: 6 Belial
  dispersion: 5 golah 8 diaspora
  doctor of law: 6 scribe
  doctrine: 6 Mishna 7 Mishnah 8 Kodashim
  drum: 4 toph
  festival: see *holiday* below
  garment: 5 shawl, talis 7 tallith
  harp: 5 nebel
  healer: Asa
  heretical doctrine: 7 Karaism
  holiday: 5 Pesah, Purim 6 Pesach, Succos, Sukkos 7 Sukkoth 8 Hanukhah, Lagbomer, Shabouth 9 Tishahbab 11 Rosh Hashana 12 Simhath Torah
  horn: 6 shofar 7 shophar
  immigrant: 4 oleh 6 halutz 7 chalutz
  instrument: 4 asor 5 nebel
  instrument player: 9 psalterer, psaltress
  judge: 7 shophet
  land: 4 Zion
  law: 4 Chok, Tora 5 Torah 6 Chukah, Talmud 7 Halacha, Halakah 8 Kashruth
  lawgiver: 5 Moses
  liturgy: 6 Maarib, Minhah 9 Shaharith
  lyre: 4 asor
  marriage broker: 8 shadchen
  marriage custom: 8 levirate
  meat inspection: 7 bedikah
  miter: 7 petalon
  month: Ab 4 Adar, Iyar, Elul 5 Tebet, Nisan, Sivan 6 Tishri, Kislev, Shebat, Beadar, Tammuz 7 Heshvan
  mourning period: 6 Shivah
  New Year: 11 Rosh Hashana
  Old Testament division 11 Hagiographa
  patriarch: 5 Isaac
  patriot family: 8 Maccabee
  pioneer: 6 halutz 7 chalutz
  poems: 6 yigdal 8 Azharoth
  prayer: 5 Alenu, Shema 7 Geullah
  prayer book: 6 mahzor, siddur
  priest: 4 Ezra 5 Aaron, Cohen 6 Levite
  priestly caste: 7 Cohanim, Levites
  prophet: 4 Amos, Ezra 5 Elias, Hosea, Jonah, Micah, Nahum 6 Daniel, Elijah, Elisha, Haggai 8 Habakkuk, Jeremiah 9 Zechariah
  prophetess: 6 Huldah
  proselyte: ger

psalm of praise: 6 hallel
redeemer: 4 goel
revelation: 5 Torah
ritual: see *ceremony* above
sabbath: 8 Saturday
sacred objects: 4 urim
sage: 4 Agur
scarf: 5 abnet 7 tallith
scroll: 11 Sepher Torah
sect member: 6 Essene, Hassid
skullcap: 6 kippah 7 yamilke 8 yarmulka
song: 8 hatikvah 9 hattikvah
spirit: 8 Asmodeus
synagogue: 5 schul
tassel: 6 zizith
teacher: 5 rabbi
temple precentor: 6 cantor
trumpet: 6 shofar 7 shophar
vestment: 5 ephod
women's organization: 8 Hadassah

Judas: 7 traitor 8 betrayer
place of suicide: 8 Aceldama, Akeldama

Judea (see also **Judah**):
ancient name: 5 Judah
governor: 6 Pilate
king: Asa 4 Ahaz, Amon 5 Herod 7 Jehoram 8 Manesseh 10 Jehoiachin 11 Jehosphaphat
place: 5 Berea

judge: try 4 deem, gage 5 count, court, gauge, opine, trier 6 critic, decide, dicast, puisne, umpire 7 account, adjudge, arbiter, believe, referee, shamgar, suppose 8 consider, deemster, dempster, estimate, sentence 9 criticise, criticize, determine 10 adjudicate, appreciate, arbitrator, chancellor
bench: 4 banc 6 bancus
chamber: 6 camera
circuit: 4 iter
entry of, after verdict: 6 postea
gavel: 4 mace
group: 5 bench
junior or subordinate: 6 puisne
kind: 6 deputy 9 assistant
of Hades: 5 Minos
of the dead: 6 Osiris
robe: 4 toga

judgment 4 deem, doom 5 arret, award, sense, taste 6 steven 7 censure, opinion, verdict 9 criticism 10 astuteness, visitation 11 sensibility
lack of: 6 acrisy
left to one's: 13 discretionary

judicable: 12 determinable
judicial assembly: 5 court
judiciary: 5 bench
document: 4 writ 8 decision
judicious: 4 wise 9 sagacious 10 discerning

Judith: *husband:* Manasses
victim: 10 Holofernes

juego: 4 game, play

jug jar 4 ewer, jail, olla, toby 5 ascos, askos, ascus, buire, cruse, gotch 6 gomlah, lockup, prison, tinaja, urceus 7 pitcher 8 cruisken 9 container, cruiskeen 10 bellarmine, jardiniere 13 schnabelkanne
shaped like a man: 4 Toby

Juggernaut 6 Vishnu

juggle: 7 conjure, shuffle 10 manipulate

juggler: 5 cheat 6 harlot 8 conjurer, conjuror, deceiver, jongleur 14 legerdemainist

jugglery: 8 trickery 9 deception 10 escamotage(F.), hanky-panky 13 sleight-of-hand

Jugoslavia: See **Yugoslavia**

juice: jus(F.), oil, sap 4 broo 6 cremor 8 gasoline 10 succulence 11 electricity
apple: 5 cider
fruit: rob 4 must, stum, wine 5 cider 6 casiri 7 vinegar
plant: sap 4 milk 5 latex 6 achete

juicy: 4 frim, racy 5 spicy 6 lively 7 piquant 9 succulent

juju: 5 charm 6 amulet, fetish

jujube: ber, elb

julep: 5 drink 8 beverage

Juliet: *betrothed:* 5 Paris
father: 7 Capulet
lover: 5 Romeo

jumble: 4 hash, heap, mess, raff, stir 5 botch, shake 6 bumble, huddle, medley, muddle 7 agitate, confuse, embroil 8 disorder, riffraff 9 confusion 10 hodgepodge 12 hugger-mugger

jump: hop, lep 4 leap, loup, lowp 5 bound, caper, halma, scold, vault 6 prance, spring 7 saltate
stick for: 4 pogo, pole

jumper: 5 dress 6 blouse, jacket

jumpy: 7 jittery, nervous 12 apprehensive

junco: 5 finch 8 snowbird

junction: 4 axil, seam 5 joint, union 6 suture 7 contact, meeting 8 crossing, juncture 10 confluence, connection

juncture: 4 pass 5 union 6 choice, crisis, strait 7 quandry 8 exigency, junction 9 emergency 11 conjuncture, predicament

June bug: dor 4 dorr

June grass: poa

Jungfrau: 4 peak 8 mountain
site of: 4 Alps

jungle: 5 shola
dweller: 5 beast, snake 6 savage

junior: son 6 puisne 7 younger 8 namesake

juniper: 4 cade, ezel 5 gorse, retem, savin 6 sabine, savine

junk: 4 boat, bunk, dope, drug, lump, rush 5 chunk, scrap, waste 6 heroin, refuse 7 discard, rubbish 8 nonsense 9 narcotics

junker: 5 noble 6 German 12 conservative

junket: 4 trip 5 feast 6 picnic 9 excursion 13 entertainment

Juno: 4 Hera
consort: 7 Jupiter
special messenger: 4 Iris

junta: 7 council 8 tribunal 9 committee 10 government

junto: 5 cabal 6 clique 7 coterie, faction 11 combination

jupe: 4 coat 5 shirt, skirt, stays, tunic 6 bodice, jacket

Jupiter: 4 Jove, Zeus
angel: 7 Zadkiel
consort: 4 Juno
daughter: 4 Bura 7 Minerva
epithet: 6 Stator
lover: Io
Roman temple: 7 Capitol
satellite: Io 6 Europa 8 Ganymede, Callisto
son: 6 Castor, Pollux

Jupiter Pluvius: 4 rain

jural: 5 legal 8 juristic

Jurassic division: 4 Lias

juridical: 5 legal 7 juridic

jurisdiction: law, see, soc 4 soke 5 venue 6 county, parish 7 diocese 8 dominion 9 authority, bailiwick, patronate 10 patriarchy 13 collectorship
ecclesiastical: see 6 parish 7 deanery, diocese

jurisprudence: law

juror: 7 assizer, juryman 8 talesman
group: 4 jury 5 panel

jury: 5 panel
additions: 5 tales 8 talesmen
attempt to influence: 9 embracery
form: 7 impanel
person: 8 talesman
summons: 6 venire

just (see also **joust**): due, fit 4 even, fair, only, true 5 equal, exact, legal, valid 6 candid, honest, merely, normal, purely, simply 7 correct, equable, upright 8 accurate, unbiased 9 equitable, impartial 10 legitimate

justice: law 6 equity 7 honesty, nemesis
god: 7 Forsete, Forseti, Forsite
goddess: 4 Maat
pert. to: 9 juridical
seat: 4 banc 5 court 6 bancus 8 tribunal

justification: 6 excuse 7 apology 9 authority, rationale

justify: 4 avow 6 adjust, defend, excuse 7 support, warrant 8 maintain, sanction 9 authorize, exculpate, vindicate

jut: 4 butt 5 bulge 6 beetle 7 project 8 overhang, protrude 10 projection

jute: 4 desi 5 gunny 6 burlap 7 sacking

Jutlander: 4 Dane

jutting: 7 salient

juvenile: 5 actor, young 8 immature, youthful 11 undeveloped

Juventas: 4 Hebe

juxtaposition: 7 contact 8 nearness 9 adjacence, adjacency, proximity 10 contiguity

K

kaama: 10 hartebeest
kaddish: 6 prayer 8 doxology
kae: 7 jackdaw
kaffeeklatsch: 6 social 9 gathering 11 get-together
Kaffir, Kafir: 4 Xosa 5 Bantu, fondo, Tembu 8 Matabele
  corn: 7 sorghum
  language: 4 Xosa
  servant: 6 umfaan
  warriors: 4 Impi
  weapon: 4 keri, kiri 10 knobkerrie
Kafka character: 4 Olga
kaiser: 5 ruler 7 emperor
kaka: 6 parrot
  genus: 6 nestor
kakapo: 6 parrot
kaki: 4 bird 5 stilt 9 persimmon
kakkak: 7 bittern
kale: 4 cole 5 green 7 cabbage, collard 8 colewort
kalends: 7 calends
kali: 5 plant 6 carpet 8 saltwort
Kali's husband: 4 Siva 5 Shiva
kalinite: 4 alum
Kalmuck, Kalmuk: 5 Eleut 6 Mongol
Kamchatka: codfish: 6 wachna 9 wachna-cod
  salmon: 6 mykiss
kamias: 7 bilimbi
Kanaka: 8 Hawaiian 10 Melanesian, Polynesian 11 Micronesian
kanari: 6 almond
Kandh language: Kui
kangaroo: 'roo 5 bilbi, bilby 6 turatt 7 bettong, wallaby 8 bettonga, boongary, forester 11 macropodian
  female: doe, gin, roo
  male: 6 boomer
  young: 4 joey
kangaroo rat: 7 potoroo
Kansas: county: 4 Reno
  fort: 5 Riley
  river: 5 Osage

  town: 4 Iola 5 Dodge, Lyons, Paola, Sedan 6 Salina, Topeka(c.) 7 Abilene 8 Lawrence 11 Leavenworth
  tree: 10 cottonwood
Kant's category: 7 quality 8 modality, quantity, relation
kaput: 6 broken, ruined 8 defeated 9 destroyed
karakul: 5 sheep
Karelian lake: Seg
karma: 4 fate 7 destiny
Kartvelian: 4 Svan 5 Svane
karyotin: 9 chromatin
kasha: 4 mush 5 grain 6 cereal
Kashmir: alphabet: 6 sarada
  capital: 8 Srinagar
  deer: 6 hangul
  official: 6 pundit
  river: 6 Jhelum
katchung: 6 peanut
kava: ava, awa
  bowl: 5 tanoa
kayak: 5 canoe
kazoo: 5 gazoo
kea: 6 parrot
Keats poem: 5 Lamia
kebbie: 4 club 5 stick 6 cudgel
ked: 4 tick
kedge: 6 anchor
keek: spy 4 look, peep
keel: vat 4 ship 5 upset 6 careen, carina 7 capsize, carinae(pl.) 8 flounder, navigate
  part: 4 skag, skeg
  right angle to: 5 abeam
  without: 9 ecarinate
keel over: 4 seel 7 capsize
keel-shaped: 8 carinate
keelbill: ani
keeling: 7 codfish
keen: yap(Sc.) 4 avid, fell(Sc.), gleg(Sc.), nice, wide 5 acute, awake, eager, sharp 6 ardent, astute, bewail, biting, clever, hearty, lament, severe, shrewd 7 cunning, fer-

vent, intense, parlous, pungent 9 trenchant 10 hardheaded 12 enthusiastic 13 perspicacious

keenly: 6 dearly

keenness: 4 edge 6 acumen, genius, talent

keep: 4 fend, hold 5 board, guard, lodge, place 6 arrest, behold, detain, stable 7 confine, contain, husband 8 fortress, maintain, preserve, restrain, withhold 9 celebrate 10 livelihood
going: 7 sustain

keep back: bar, dam, hap 6 detain 7 reserve

keep in: 6 retain

keep on: 8 continue

keep out: 4 save 5 debar 7 exclude, reserve 8 withhold

keeper: 5 guard 6 alcade, alcaid, custos, pastor, warden 7 alcaide, alcayde, curator 8 custodes(pl.), guardian 9 constable, custodian 10 maintainer
of golden apple: 5 Ithun
of marches: 8 margrave
of park: 6 ranger

keeping: 4 care 5 award, guard, trust 6 charge 7 custody 10 caretaking, possession 11 maintenance 12 guardianship

keepsake: 5 token 7 memento 8 giftbook, souvenir

keest: sap 6 marrow 9 substance

keeve: tub, vat 5 basin

kef: 7 languor, tobacco 8 euphoria 10 dreaminess 12 tranquillity

keg: cag 4 cade, cask 6 barrel 7 barrico
open: 6 unhead

kegler: 6 bowler

kelly: hat 5 color,.derby, green

kelp: 5 varec 6 varech 7 seaweed 8 bellware(Sc.)

ken: 4 know(Sc.), view 5 admit, sight 7 discern, insight 9 knowledge, recognize 10 cognizance, understand 13 understanding

kench: bin

Kenilworth author: 5 Scott

kennel: 5 drain, sewer 6 cannel, gutter, stable 9 enclosure

Kent: *freedman:* 4 laet
sheep: 6 romney
tribal law: 4 laes

kentledge: 5 metal 7 ballast

Kentucky: *college:* 5 Berea
county: 4 Owen 6 Harlan
town: 5 Benge, Berea 7 Paducah 10 Louisville

Kentucky bluegrass: Poa

Kentucky coffee tree: 6 bonduc, chicot

Kenya: *lake:* 6 Rudolf
native: 5 Masai
reserve: 5 Masai

kerchief: 5 curch(Sc.) 7 panuelo 8 headrail 12 handkerchief

kerchoo: 6 sneeze
answer to: 10 gesundheit 11 God Bless you

Keresan Indian: Sia

kerf: cut 4 slit 5 notch 6 groove 7 cutting

kermis, kermess: 4 fair 8 carnival 11 celebration

kernel: nut 4 bunt, core, meat, pith, seed 5 acini(pl.), grain 6 acinus, nuclei(pl.) 7 nucleus

kestrel: 6 falcon, fanner 7 stannel 9 windhover

ketch: 4 boat, saic 8 sailboat

ketone: 7 acetone, camphor, shogaol 8 acridone, civetone, deguelin 9 heptanone 14 cyclopentanone
oily: 5 irone 6 carone

kettle: pot, vat 4 cazo(Sp.) 5 lebes 6 hollow 7 caldron 8 cauldron, flambeau 9 teakettle 10 kettledrum
nose: 5 spout

kettledrum: 5 naker, tabor 6 atabal, nagara(Ind.), timbal 7 attabal, timbale, timpano, timpani(pl.), tympani(pl.)

kevel: bar, bit, peg 4 bolt 5 cleat, staff 6 cudgel 7 bollard

key: cay, fin 4 clef, isle, quay, reef 5 dital, islet, pitch 6 claves(pl.), clavis, island, opener, spline, tapper 7 digital 8 clavecin, solution, tonality 11 explanation
notch: 4 ward
part: bit
pert. to: 5 tonal, tonic
skeleton: 4 gilt 5 screw 7 twirler

key chain: 10 chatelaine

keyboard: 6 manual 7 clavier 8 pedalier 10 claviature

keyed up: 4 agog 5 eager 7 excited 10 stimulated

keynote: do 5 theme, tonic, topic 7 feature

keynoter: 4 boss 6 orator

keystone: 8 voussoir

Keystone State: 12 Pennsylvania

khedive's estate: 5 daira

Khmer Republic: See Cambodia

Khnemu's consort: 6 Anukit

Khyber Pass tribe: 6 Afridi

kiang: ass

kibble: 5 grind 6 bucket

kibblings: 4 bait

kibe: 4 chap, sore 5 crack

kibitzer: 7 adviser, meddler 9 spectator

kick: toe 4 boot, fleg, funk(Sc.), punt, yerk 5 bunch, fling 6 fitter(Sc.), object, recoil 7 grumble 8 complain 10 calcitrate, enthusiasm

kickshaw: toy 6 bauble

kid: guy 4 hoax, joke 5 child, suede, tease 6 banter 7 fatling, leather 8 cheverel, cheveril 9 youngster

kidcote: 6 prison

kidnap: 6 abduct

kidney: 4 neer
comb. form: 4 reni
pert. to: 5 renal

kidney-shaped: 8 reniform

kidney stone: 4 jade 8 calculus, nephrite 10 nephrolith

Kilauea goddess: 4 Pele

kilderkin: 4 cask 6 barrel 7 measure

Kilimanjaro peak: 4 Kibo

kill: 4 fake, hang, slay 5 croak, fordo, stone 6 deaden, diddle, famish, foredo, murder 7 achieve, execute, poniard 8 deathify, dispatch, lapidate 9 slaughter 11 assassinate
by stoning: 8 lapidate
by strangling: 7 garotte, garrote

killed: 4 slew 5 slain 9 immolated

killer: 6 gunman 7 soldier, torpedo 8 genocide, homicide, murderer 10 triggerman 11 infanticide
of relative: 8 filicide 9 matricide, parricide, patricide 10 fratricide, sororicide

killer whale: orc 4 orca 7 grampus

killing: 6 murder 7 slaying 8 homicide 9 euthanasy, martyrdom, slaughter 10 euthanasia
of brother or sister: 10 fratricide
of father: 9 patricide
of king: 8 regicide
of mother: 9 matricide
of self: 7 suicide
of small child: 11 infanticide

Kilmer poem: 5 Trees

kiln: 4 oast, oven 5 clamp, stove, tiler 6 cockle 7 furnace

kiloliter: 5 stere

kilt: 4 hang 5 pleat 6 fasten 7 filibag
pouch for: 7 sporran

kilter: 5 order 9 condition

kimmer: 4 girl 5 witch 6 cummer, friend

kimono sash: obi

kin: (see also **kinship**): 4 clan, race, sept 5 flesh, tribe 6 family 7 kindred, kinfolk, related 8 affinity, cousinry, kinsfolk, relation, relative 12 relationship

kind: ilk, kin 4 boon, gest, good, kith, mild, soft, sort, type 5 breed, class, genre, genus, geste, order 6 benign, blithe, gender, genera(pl.), genial, gentle, goodly, humane, kindly, tender 7 amiable, clement, couthie, species, variety 8 amicable, benedict, friendly, generous, gracious, merciful 9 benignant, brotherly, favorable, indulgent, squeamish 10 benevolent, charitable, favourable, generation 11 considerate, description, kindhearted, sympathetic 13 compassionate
comb. form: 4 geno
same: 10 homogeneal

kindle: 4 beet, fire, move 5 beete, brood, light, young 6 alight, arouse, decoct, excite, ignite, illume, incite, litter 7 animate, emblaze, inflame, inspire, provoke

kindling: 5 fagot 6 faggot, sticks, tinder 7 akindle

kindness: 5 aloha 6 bounty 8 benefice 9 benignity 11 beneficence

kindred: kin, sib 5 blood, flesh 6 allied, family 7 cognate, kinsmen 8 affinity, kinsfolk 9 congenial 12 relationship

kine: 4 cows 6 cattle

kinetic: 6 active

king: dam, rex(L.), rey(Sp.), roi(F.) 4 czar, tzar 5 ruler 7 cacique, regulus 9 sovereign
chamber: 9 camarilla
child: 6 prince 8 princess
domestic officer: 8 palatine
family: 7 dynasty
legendary: Lud 4 Bran 5 Hogni, Lludd, Midas, Sesha 6 Oberon, Shesha 11 Prester John
murderer: 8 regicide
personnel: 5 thane 6 avener 7 avenuer, dapifer, viceroy
pert. to: 5 regal 6 regnal
symbol: 7 scepter, sceptre
title: Sir 4 Sire 7 Majesty 8 Highness

King Arthur: *abode:* 6 Avalon
birthplace: 8 Tintagel
character: 6 Elaine, Merlin
court site: 7 Camelot 8 Caerleon
crowner: 6 Dubric
death place: 6 Camlan
father: 5 Uther
fool: 7 Dagonet
forest: 7 Calydon
foster brother: Kay
hound: 6 Cavall
jester: 7 Dagonet
knight: Kay 6 Gareth, Gawain, Modred 7 Galahad 8 Lancelot, Tristram 9 Percivale
lady: 4 Enid
lance: Ron
magician: 6 Merlin
mother: 7 Igraine
nephew: 6 Gareth 7 Mordred
parent: 5 Uther 7 Igraine
queen: 8 Guinever 9 Guinevere
shield: 7 Pridwin
sister: 7 Morgain 11 Morgan le Fay
sword: 9 Excalibur

King Canute's consort: 4 Emma

king clover: 7 melilot

king crab: 7 limulus
King Henry IV character: Hal 5 Blunt, Henry, Percy, Poins 6 Scroop
King Lear: See Lear
king of beasts: 4 lion
king's evil: 8 scrofula
king's yellow: 8 orpiment
kingdom: 5 realm, world 6 empire, region
kingfish: 4 barb, haku, opah 6 bagara
kingfisher: 7 halcyon
kingly: 5 regal, royal 6 regnal 7 basilic, leonine 8 imperial, majestic
kink: 4 bend, curl, loop 5 bunch, chink, cramp, quirk, snarl, twist 6 buckle, tangle 7 caprice 11 peculiarity
kinkajou: 5 potto 6 mammal
kinship (see also kin): 5 blood, nasab 8 agnation, nearness 10 connection 11 propinquity 13 consanguinity
  father's side: 5 agnat 6 agnate 8 agnation
  mother's side: 5 enate 7 enation
kinsman (see also kin, kindred): 4 ally 6 friend 8 bandhava 9 rishtadar
kiosk: 8 pavilion 9 newsstand
kipe: 6 basket
Kipling: poem: 6 L'Envoi
  tale: Kim
kirtle: 4 coat, gown 5 cover, dress, skirt, tunic 6 enwrap 7 garment 9 petticoat
Kish: father: Ner
  son: 4 Saul
kismet: 4 fate 7 destiny
kiss: 4 bass, buss 5 smack 6 caress 8 osculate
kiss-me-quick: 6 bonnet
kiss of peace: pax
Kiss sculptor: 5 Rodin
kist: box 4 cist 5 chest 6 locker
kit: bag, box, cat, lot, set 6 kitten, outfit 7 catling 8 caboodle 10 collection
kitchen: ben(Sc.) 4 chil(Ind.) 5 calan(P.I.) 6 chilla(Ind.) 7 cuisine 8 scullery
  pert. to: 8 culinary
  ship's: galley
  tool or utensil: 5 corer, ricer 6 beater, grater, opener, sifter 7 spatula 8 colander, strainer
kitchen garden: 7 olitory
kith: 6 friend 10 associates 12 acquaintance
kittenish: coy 6 frisky 7 playful 8 childish
kittiwake: 4 gull 5 annet
kitty; 4 bowl, pool 6 stakes
kiwi: roa 7 Apteryx
kleptomaniac: 5 thief 7 filcher 8 pilferer
Klondike: See Alaska
kloof: 4 glen 5 gorge 6 ravine, valley
knabe: boy
knack: art 4 ease, gift, hang 5 catch, skill, trick 8 facility 9 dexterity 10 adroitness

knap: cut, rap, top 4 bite, blow, chip, crop, hill, snap 5 break, crest, knoll 6 nibble, strike, summit 7 hilltop
knapsack: bag 6 wallet
knapweed: 5 bluet 7 harweed 8 bellweed, clubweed, hardhead, harshwee 10 harebottle
knarred: 6 knarry, knotty 7 gnarled
knave: boy, nob, pam 4 fool, jack 5 cheat, churl, losel, rogue, scamp 6 harlot, rascal, varlet 7 villain 9 miscreant, scoundrel, trickster
knavery: 5 fraud 8 mischief 10 dishonesty 12 sportiveness
knead: elt(Sc.), mix 5 malax 7 massage 8 malaxate 9 masticate 10 manipulate 11 incorporate
knee: bow 5 joint 10 supplicate
  armor: 11 genouillere
  bend: 5 kneel
  bone: 7 patella
knee breeches: 8 knickers 12 smallclothes
kneecap: 7 patella
kneel: 4 genu 9 genuflect
kneeling desk: 8 prie-dieu
kneepan: 6 rotula 7 patella
knell: 4 bell, omen, ring, toll 6 stroke, summon 7 warning 8 proclaim
knickknack: toy 6 bauble, bawble, gadget, gewgaw, trifle 7 novelty, trinket 8 gimcrack, kickshaw
knife: cut 4 bolo, cane, corn, shiv, snee, stab 5 bowie, bread, chive, corer, gully, kurki, sword 6 barong, campit, colter, coutel, cuttle, dagger, trevet, worker 7 carving, machete, spattle, spatula, whittle, yatagan 8 belduque, serpette
  case: 6 sheath
  maker: 6 cutler
  one-bladed: 6 barlow
  plaster and paint: 7 spatula
  sharpener: 4 hone 5 steel, stone
  surgical: 6 catlin 7 catling, scalpel
knight: sir 5 eques 6 equite, Ritter 8 banneret, cavalier 9 caballero, caveliere, chevalier
  attendant: 6 squire
  banner: 8 gonfanon
  cloak: 6 tabard
  famous: 7 Caradoc, Cradock, Galahad 9 Lohengrin
  fight: 5 joust
  horse: 7 charger, palfrey
  rank above: 7 baronet
  servant: 4 page 6 varlet
  title: sir
  wife: 4 lady
  wreath: 4 orle
knight-errant: 7 paladin

knight of the road: 4 hobo 5 tramp
knighthood: 8 chivalry
  confer: dub
knightly: 5 brave 9 courteous 10 chivalrous
knit: 4 bind, heal, join, mend, purl 5 plait, unite, woven 6 cement, fasten 7 conjoin, connect, crochet, wrinkle 8 contract, entangle 10 intertwine 11 compaginate, consolidate
knitted blanket: 6 afghan
knitter: 6 legger
knitting: 5 craft 9 handiwork
  rod: 6 needle
  term: 4 purl 7 castoff
knob: bob, bur, nub 4 boss, buhr, burr, club, heel, knot, lump, node, tore, umbo 5 bulge 6 button, croche, emboss, handle, pommel 12 protuberance
  pointed: 6 finial
knobby: 5 gouty, hilly 6 knotty
knobkerrie: 4 club 5 stick
knobstick: 4 cane, club 5 stick 8 blackleg
knock: con, dad, hit, rap, tap, wap 4 beat, blow, bolt, bump, chap, chop, dash, daud, ding, dunt, hill(Sc.), jolt, knap, polt, poss, rout, slay 5 pound, thump 6 bounce 7 hillock(Sc.) 9 criticize 12 faultfinding
knock down: 4 fell 5 floor 9 prostrate
knock-kneed: 6 valgus
knock off: rob 4 kill, stop 6 deduct 8 overcome 11 discontinue
knock out: 4 daze, stun 6 defeat 7 exhaust 8 paralyze
knockabout: 5 actor, sloop, yacht
knockout: K.O. 4 kayo 5 facer
knoll: 4 knap, knob, lump 5 mound 7 hillock
knop: 5 knosp 6 button 8 ornament
knot: bow, nep, tie 4 bond, burl, burr, harl, knag, knar, knob, knur, loop, lump, node, snag 5 gnarl, hitch, knurl, nodus, snarl 6 finial, granny, nodule, puzzle, tangle 7 chignon, cockade, laniard, lanyard, rosette 8 entangle 12 entanglement, protuberance
  running: 4 slip 5 noose
  pert. to: 5 nodal
knotted: 5 noded 6 knotty 7 crabbed, nodated 9 intricate
knotted lace: 7 tatting
knotty: 4 hard 5 gouty 6 craggy 7 complex 9 difficult, intricate 10 perplexing
know: can, con, ken(Sc.), wis, wot 4 wist 7 realize 8 perceive 9 recognize 10 comprehend, experience, understand
know-it-all: 6 smarty 8 wiseacre
know-nothing: 8 agnostic 9 ignoramus 11 scissorbill
knowing: 4 able, gash, wise 5 cagey, downy, leery, smart, witty 6 scient, shrewd 7 gnostic, sapient, stylish 8 informed 9 cognitive, conscious, gnostical, wide-awake 10 expe-

rience, perceptive 11 intelligent 13 comprehension
knowledge: ken 4 lore 6 wisdom 7 cunning, hearing, science 8 learning, sapience 9 cognition, erudition 10 cognizance, experience 11 information, instruction 12 acquaintance 13 enlightenment, understanding
  instrument: 7 organon
  lack of: 9 ignorance, nescience
  object of: 7 cognita(pl.), scibile 8 cognitum
  pert. to: 7 gnostic
  seeker: 10 philonoist
  slight: 7 inkling, smatter 8 sciolism 10 smattering
  summary: 13 encyclopaedia
  systematized: 7 science
  universal: 9 pantology
known: 5 couth, famed 6 famous 7 notable 8 familiar, renowned 9 notorious
knucklebone: 4 tali(pl.) 5 dolos, talus 7 dolosse(pl.)
kobird: 6 cuckoo
kobold: nis 5 gnome 6 goblin 7 Hodeken(G.) 10 nissespire
koel: 4 bird 6 cuckoo
kohl: 8 antimony
kohlrabi: 6 turnip
kokoon: gnu
kokopu: 4 fish, para
kola: nut 6 jackal
kopecks (100): 5 ruble
kopje: 4 hill 5 mound 7 hillock
Koran: 7 Alcoran
  compiler's son: Ali
  division: 4 Sura
  interpreter: 5 ulema 7 alfaqui 8 alfaquin
  pert. to: 9 alcoranic
  register: 5 sijil 6 sijill
Korea: 6 Chosen
  money: won 4 hwan
  peninsula: 6 Ongjin
  river: Kum 4 Hans, Look, Yalu 5 Imjin 7 Naktong
  soldier: ROK
  town: 5 Fusan, Heijo(c.), Kanko, Keijo(c.), Kimpo, Moppo, Rigen, Seoul(c.) 6 Andong, Antung, Gunzan, Inchon, Jushin, Kaeson, Keishu, Pochon, Rashin, Reigui, Wonzan 7 Capyong, Kenjiho, Moonsan, Samchok, Seishin 8 Chunchon, Pingyang 9 Chinnampo, Chuminjun, Shingishu
  weight: kon
kosher: fit 4 pure 5 clean 6 proper 8 Kashruth 9 undefiled
  meat maker: 6 porger
  opposite of: 4 tref
kra: ape 7 macaque
kraal: 5 crawl 9 enclosure

krimmer: fur 4 skin 8 lambskin
Krishna: 6 Vishnu 10 Juggernaut
  grandson: 9 Aniruddha
  mother: 6 Devaki
  paradise: 6 Goloka
kudo: 4 fame 5 glory 6 praise, renown 8 prestige 9 extolling
kudu: 8 antelope
kulak: 6 farmer 7 peasant
kumiss: 5 drink

Kurd: 7 Persian
  ancestors: 9 Gordyaean
Kurile island: 6 Iturup
Kurland Peninsula inhabitant: 4 Lett
kurrajong: 4 tree 5 shrub 6 calool
kurtosis: arc 9 curvature
Kwantung seaport: 6 Dairen
kyphosis: 8 humpback 9 curvature, hunchback
Kyushu: See **Japan**

L

L: 5 fifty
La Boheme: *composer:* 7 Puccini
  heroine: 4 Mimi
laagte: 6 bottom, valley
Laban's daughter: 4 Leah 6 Rachel
label: tab, tag 4 band 5 brand 6 docket, lappet, tassel 8 classify 9 designate 10 definition
labellum: lip 5 petal
labile: 8 unstable
labium: lip
labor: 4 moil, task, toil, work 5 sweat, yakka 6 effort, labour, stress, strive 7 travail 8 business, drudgery, exertion, industry, struggle 11 lucubration
labor organization: AFL, CIO, UMW 5 union, ILGWU
laboratory equipment: 5 pipet 6 beaker, retort
labored: 5 heavy 6 forced 8 strained 9 difficult, elaborate
laborer: man 4 hand, hind, peon, prol 5 cooly, plebe 6 coolie, toiler, worker 7 bracero, dvornik, hobbler, wetback, workman 10 bluecollar
laborious: 4 hard 5 heavy 7 arduous, operose, tedious 8 diligent 9 assiduous, difficult 11 displeasing, painstaking
Labrador retriever: 12 Newfoundland
Labrador tea: 5 ledum 8 gowiddie 9 evergreen
labyrinth: 4 maze 7 circuit
labyrinthine: 8 involved, puzzling, tortuous 9 intricate 11 complicated
lac: 4 milk 5 resin 6 veneer
lace: gin, net, tat 4 band, beat, cord, lash, line 5 braid, noose, plait, snare, twine, unite 6 fasten, ribbon, string 7 ensnare, entwine, laniard, lanyard 8 biliment, openwork 9 embroider, interlace 10 embroidery, intertwine, shoestring
  barred: 6 grille
  edge: 5 picot
  frilled: 5 jabot, ruche
  front: 5 jabot

  gold and silver: 5 orris
  kind: 5 lisle, orris, tulle 7 alencon, allover, guipure, macrame, potlace 9 Alostlace 10 colberteen, colbertine 12 Valenciennes
  knotted: 7 tatting
  loop in: 5 picot
  make: tat
  opening: 6 eyelet
lacerate: cut, rip 4 bite, rend, rive, tear 6 harrow, mangle
laceration: rip 4 tear 5 wound
lacework: See lace
lachrymose: sad 5 teary, weepy
laciniate: 7 fringed
lacis: 4 lace 7 network
lack: 4 need, void, want 5 fault, minus 6 dearth 7 absence, failure, paucity, poverty 8 scarcity 9 indigence 10 deficiency 11 destitution
lackadaisical: 4 blah 7 languid 8 listless 10 spiritless 11 sentimental
lackaday: 4 alas
lackey: 5 toady, valet 7 footman, servant
lacking: shy 5 short 6 absent, barren 7 wanting 8 desolate 9 deficient, destitute
lackluster: 4 dull 6 cloudy 8 dullness
Laconia: *capital:* 6 Sparta
  people: Obe
laconic: 5 brief, pithy, short, terse 7 concise, pointed, summary 8 succinct
lacquer: 7 shellac, varnish
lactate: 4 salt 5 actol, ester
lacteal: 5 milky
lacuna: gap 5 break
lacy: 7 weblike 8 delicate
lad: boy, tad 4 carl, dick, hind 5 caddy, youth 6 caddie, shaver 9 stripling 10 adolescent
  on call: 4 page 7 bellboy 9 messenger
  serving: 7 gossoon 8 coistrel, coistril
ladder: run, sty 4 stee 7 scalade
  on fortification: 8 escalade
  step: 7 ratline
ladderlike: 6 scalar

lade: dip 4 bail, draw, lave, load, ship 5 drain, scoop 6 burden, charge, weight 7 fraught, freight

laden: 4 lade 7 fraught 9 freighted, oppressed

ladies' man: 4 beau

lading: 4 load 5 cargo 6 burden 7 freight 10 freightage

ladle: dip 4 bail 5 scoop, serve, spoon 6 dipper

ladrone: 5 rouge, thief 6 bandit, robber 7 brigand 10 highwayman

Ladrone island: 4 Guam 6 Saipan 8 Marianas

lady (see also **woman**): 4 burd, dame, dona(Sp.), rani(Ind.) 5 begum(Ind.), donna(It.), madam, ranee(Ind.) 6 domina(L.), female, senora(Sp.) 7 signora(It.) 11 gentlewoman

noble: 5 queen 7 duchess 8 countess, princess

young: 7 damozel 10 demoiselle, jeune fille(F.)

lady-killer: 4 wolf 5 sheik 7 Don Juan 8 Casanova

Lady of the Lake: 5 Ellen

lady's maid: 5 woman 9 tirewoman

lady's thumb: 9 peachwort, persicary

ladybird: bug 6 beetle

genus: 9 epilachna

ladyfish: oio 6 wrasse

ladylike: 6 female, polite 7 genteel 8 feminine

ladylove: 5 amour, lover 8 mistress 10 sweetheart

Laertes: *father:* 8 Acrisius

son: 7 Ulysses

wife: 8 Anticlea

laet: 8 freedman

lag: 4 flag, rift, tire 5 delay, stave, tarry, trail, weary 6 dawdle, linger, loiter 9 drawlatch 10 dillydally 11 retardation

lager: ale 4 beer 5 drink 8 beverage

laggard: 4 slow 6 remiss 8 backward, loiterer, sluggish 9 straggler

lagging: 5 tardy 8 backward

lagniappe: tip 4 gift 5 bonus, pilon 7 present 8 gratuity

lagomorph: 4 hare, pika 5 coney 6 rabbit

lagoon: 4 cove, haff, pond, pool 5 liman 6 laguna(Sp.)

Lagoon Islands: 6 Ellice

laic: 6 layman 7 secular 15 nonprofessional

laid-down: 5 posed 6 thetic 8 academic 10 prescribed 11 traditional

lair: den, lie 4 holt, rest 5 haunt 6 cavern 7 hideout, retreat 8 quagmire

Lais: 7 Burmese

laissez-faire: 8 inactive, tolerant 9 donothing, unconcern 11 philosophic 12 indifference, mercantilism 15 individualistic, noninterference

laity: 6 laymen

Laius' son: 7 Oedipus

lake: red, sea 4 loch, mear, mere, pond, pool, shat, shot, tarn 5 chott, color, lough, shott 7 pigment

deposit: 5 trona

highest: 8 Titicaca

Indian: 4 Erie

marshy: 5 liman

Lake Chad: *people:* 4 Maba

river: 5 Shari

Lake State: 8 Michigan

lakelet: 4 pond

lakhs (100): 5 crore

lam: hit 4 bash, beat 6 thrash

Lamaism: *dignitary:* 8 hutukhtu

priest: 6 Getsul

stupa: 7 Chorten

lamasery: 9 monastery

lamb: ean 4 yean 5 agnus(L.) 6 agneau(F.), cosset 7 chilver, fatling, hogling

hand-raised: hob

leg of: 5 gigot

pet: 4 cade 6 cosset

Lamb of God: 8 Agnus Dei

Lamb's penname: 4 Elia

lambskin: 4 case 5 suede 6 bagdad 7 baghdad

lambent: 7 glowing, radiant 8 wavering 9 brilliant 10 flickering

lame: 4 game, halt 5 gammy 6 feeble 7 cripple, halting 8 crippled, decrepit, disabled, handicap 9 defective, hamstring 12 incapacitate

Lamech: *son:* 5 Jabal, Jubal 9 Tubalcain

wife: 4 Adah 6 Zillah

lament: cry, rue 4 care, howl, keen, moan, pine, sigh, wail, weep 5 croon, dolor, dirge, elegy, greet, grief, mourn 6 bemoan, bewail, beweep dolour, grieve, lament, ochone, outcry, plaint, regret, repent, repine, yammer 7 condole, deplore, elegize 8 jeremiad 9 complaint

lamentable: sad 8 wretched 11 distressing

lamia: 5 witch 7 vampire 9 sorceress

lamina: 5 blade, flake, hinge, layer

laminated: 5 flaky 6 scaled 7 fissile, spathic, tabular 8 foliated, lamellar

lamp: 4 davy, etna 5 light, torch 7 lantern 8 lanthorn 9 veilleuse

safety: 4 davy

lampblack: 4 soot

lamplighter: 5 match, spill, torch

lampoon: 5 squib 6 satire 8 ridicule, satirize 10 pasquinade

lamprey: eel 6 ramper

migration: 7 eelfare

lanai: 5 porch 7 veranda
lanate: 5 wooly 6 woolly
Lancashire section: 6 Eccles
lance: cut 4 dart, hurl 5 joust, spear 6 faucre, lancet, launch, pierce, weapon 7 javelin
head: 5 morne
Lancelot's lover: 6 Elaine
lancer: 4 ulan 5 uhlan 7 soldier, spearer 10 cavalryman
lancet: 5 fleam
lancinate: 4 stab 5 gouge 6 pierce 8 lacerate
land: erd 4 ager(L.), soil 5 catch, earth, glebe, realm, shore, terra(L.) 6 alight, arrive, debark, ground 7 acreage, capture, country, terrene 9 disembark, territory
alluvial: 5 delta
ancestral: 5 ethel
arid: see **desert**
barren: see **wasteland**
body: 9 continent
church: 5 glebe 8 abadengo
cultivated: 4 farm 5 arada, arado, ranch, tilth 7 orchard, tillage
dealer: 7 realtor
depressed: 6 graben
elevated: alp 4 hill, mesa 5 mound, ridge 7 plateau 8 mountain
grazing: 5 field, plain, range 6 meadow 7 pasture
heritable: 4 alod, fief, odal 5 allod 7 alodium 8 allodium
hilly: 4 down
householder's: 6 barton, casate 7 demesne
in foreign territory: 7 enclave
living on: 11 terrestrial
low: 4 vale 5 carse(Sc.) 6 polder, valley 9 intervale
measure: ar; are, rod 4 acre, mile, rood 5 meter, perch 6 decare
mythical: 4 Eden 6 Utopia 7 Erewhon, Lemuria 9 Shangri-La
narrow: 4 neck 6 strake 7 isthmus 9 peninsula
open: 4 moor, vega, wold 5 heath, slash, weald
owned: see *heritable* above
pasture: ham 5 grass 6 meadow
pert. to: 11 continental
piece: lot 4 acre, farm 5 laine, ranch, range, solum (law) spong 6 estate
plowed: 5 arada, arado, field 6 arable, fallow, furrow 7 thwaite
point of: 4 cape, ness, spit
profit: 4 crop, rent 7 esplees
public: 4 parc, park
reclaimed: 6 polder 7 novalia(Sc.)
river drained: 5 basin
sandy: 4 dene

tilled: see *plowed* above
treeless: 5 llano 6 steppe 7 prairie, savanna 8 savannah
triangular: 4 gore
uncultivated: 5 heath, waste 6 desert, forest
uplifted: 5 horst
waste: see **wasteland**
waterlocked: ile(F.) 4 isle 6 island
watery: bog 4 flow, moor 5 marsh, swamp 6 morass 7 maremma(It.)
Land of Cakes: 8 Scotland
Land of the Midnight Sun: 6 Norway
Land of Nod: 5 sleep
Land of Plenty: 6 Goshen
Land of Promise: 7 Canaan 9 Palestine
Land of Rising Sun: 5 Japan
land's end guardian: 8 Bellerus
landed: See **estate; land**
landholder: 5 laird 6 coscet, yeoman
landholding: 6 tenure
landing: 8 arrivage
kind: 5 crash 10 three-point
place: 4 dock, pier 5 wharf 7 airport 8 airplace, arrivage
landlady: 5 duena 7 hostess 8 mistress 9 concierge
landlord: 4 host 5 laird(Sc.) 6 lessor
landmark: 4 copa, dole, dool, mere 5 bound, cairn, senal(Sp.) 9 milestone
landscape: 4 plan 5 plant, scene 7 scenery, paysage, picture 8 decorate
landslide: 9 avalanche 10 eboulement
landsman: 6 lubber, sailor
lane: way 4 char, path, race 5 aisle, alley, byway, chare, tewer 6 boreen, bypath, gullet, street, throat, vennel 7 pathway 8 footpath 10 passageway
Langobard king: 6 Alboin
language: 4 chib 5 argot, idiom, lingo, slang 6 jargon, speech, tongue 7 dialect, diction
ancient: 4 Pali 5 Aryan, Greek, Latin 6 Hebrew 7 Chinese 8 Sanskrit
artificial: 9 Esperanto
change: 8 misquote 9 interpret, translate 10 paraphrase
classical: 5 Greek, Latin
common: 6 French, German 7 Chinese, English, Italian, Russian, Spanish
Cretan: 6 Minoan
dead: 5 Latin
figurative: 7 imagery
international: od, ro; ido 7 volapuk 9 esperanto
nonmetrical: 5 prose
pert. to: 8 semantic
pompous: 4 bull, wind 7 bombast, oratory 8 rhetoric
principles: 7 grammar

Romance: 5 Latin 6 French 7 Catalan, Italian, Spanish 8 Rumanian 10 Portuguese
sacred: 4 Pali
secret: 5 argot
Semitic: 6 Arabic, Hebrew
spoken: 7 diction 13 pronunciation
unintelligible: 9 gibberish

languid: 4 dull, slow, weak 6 dreamy, tender 8 indolent, listless, lovesick, sluggish 9 lethargic 11 indifferent

languish: die 4 fade, fail, flag, long, pine, wilt 5 droop, dwine, faint, swoon 6 linger, repine 7 decline

languor: kef 4 kaif, keef, kief 5 ennui 7 boredom 8 debility 9 lassitude 10 stagnation

langur: 6 monkey 8 wanderoo

lanky: 4 lean, slim, tall, thin 5 gaunt, rangy, spare 6 gangly, meager, meagre, skinny 7 haggard, slender 8 gangling, ungainly 9 elongated 12 loose-jointed

lanose: 5 wooly 6 woolly

lantern: 4 lamp 5 bowet 8 absconce

lanyard, laniard: 4 cord, knot, rope

Laodamia's father: 7 Acastus

Laodicean: 8 lukewarm 9 apathetic 10 uninvolved 11 indifferent

Laomedon's son: 8 Tithonus

lap: sip 4 fold, lick, wash 5 drink, slurp 6 circle, cuddle, enfold, infold 7 circuit

lap robe: rug 5 throw 6 afghan 7 blanket

lapactic: 8 laxative 9 cathartic

lapel: 5 rever 6 revers

lapidary: 7 jeweler 8 engraver 9 gem cutter
instrument: dop 4 dial

lapidate: 4 pelt 5 stone

lapin: 6 rabbit

Lapland: *animal:* 8 reindeer
city or town: 4 Kola 6 Kiruna
sled: 4 pulk 5 pulka

lappet: 4 lobe 5 label 6 fabric

lapse: err 5 break, error, fault 6 expire 7 delapse, escheat, failure, relapse 8 caducity, slipping 9 backslide

lapsed: 4 dead, null, void

laputan: 6 absurd, dreamy 7 utopian 9 visionary 10 unfeasible 11 impractical

lapwing: 5 pewit 6 plover

lar: 6 gibbon

larboard: 4 left, port

larceny: 5 theft 7 looting, robbery 8 burglary, stealage

lard: fat, oil 4 mort 5 adeps(L.), baste, enarm, inarm 6 enrich, fatten, grease

larder: 4 cave 6 pantry, spence, spense 8 cupboard

large: big 4 bold, free, huge, main, vast, waly 5 ample, broad, bulky, burly, enorm, giant, great, hulky, massy, wally 6 goodly, heroic 7 copious, immense, liberal, massive, titanic, weighty 8 colossal, enormous,

gigantic 9 capacious, extensive, plentiful 12 considerable 13 comprehensive
comb. form: 5 macro

largess, largesse: 4 gift 6 bounty 7 charity, present 10 generosity, liberality 11 beneficence

lariat: 4 rope 5 lasso, noose, reata(Sp.), riata(Sp.)
loop: 5 honda, hondo 6 hondoo, hondou

larix: 5 larch 7 larches

lark: 6 frolic 7 carouse 8 carousal

larkspur: 10 delphinium

larrigan: 8 moccasin

larrup: 4 beat, blow, flog, whip

larry: hoe 5 grout, noise 6 mortar 9 confusion 10 excitement

larva: bot, fly, loa 4 bott, grub 5 eruca 6 botfly, woubit 7 atrocha, oestrid 8 cercaria, horsefly 11 caterpillar
aquatic: 12 hellgrammite
beetle: 4 grub

larvate: 6 masked 7 covered 9 concealed

lascar: 6 sailor 12 artilleryman

lascivious: 6 wanton 7 blissom 9 lecherous, salacious, seductive 10 libidinous, licentious

lash: 4 beat, bind, blow, flog, lace, whip, yerk 5 slash 6 berate, fasten, strike, stroke, swinge 7 belabor, eyelash, scourge

lasket: 8 latching

lass: gal 4 gill, girl, maid, miss 5 trull, woman 6 cummer, kimmer, lassie, maiden 7 colleen 10 sweetheart 11 maidservant

lassitude: 5 ennui 7 languor 8 debility, lethargy 10 exhaustion

lasso: 4 rope 5 noose, reata(Sp.), riata(Sp.) 6 lariat

last: 4 dure, tail 5 abide, final, omega 6 endure, latest, utmost 7 dernier, extreme, tail-end 8 continue, eventual, hindmost, rearmost, ultimate 9 aftermost 10 concluding
but one: 6 penult
long: 7 outwear 9 perendure

Last of the Mohicans: 5 Uncas

Last Supper: *representation:* 4 cena
room: 7 cenacle

lasting (see also **last**): 6 stable 7 chronic, lasting, eternal 8 constant 9 perennial, permanent, steadfast 11 everlasting
briefly: 9 ephemeral, temporary

latch: 5 catch, sneck 6 fasten 8 fastener

latchet: tab 5 thong

late: new 4 sere 5 tardy 6 former, recent 7 belated, overdue 8 neoteric, serotine 10 behindhand
comb. form: neo

latent: 6 hidden 7 dormant 9 concealed, potential, quiescent, suspended 11 undeveloped

later: 4 anon, soon 5 after, newer 6 behind, future, puisne 7 elderly, neozoic 9 hereafter, posterior, presently 10 subsequent 12 subsequently

lateral: 4 side 8 indirect, sideward

latest: 4 last 6 newest

latex: 5 juice 6 rubber 9 secretion

lath: 4 slat 5 spale, stave
  attachment: 7 setover
  operator: 6 turner
  part: 7 mandrel

lather: 4 foam, soap, suds 5 froth 6 freath

Latin (see also **Rome**): 5 Roman 7 Italian, Romanic
  barracks: 6 canaba
  bath: 7 balneum
  booth: 7 taberna
  bowl: 6 patina
  boxing glove: 6 cestus, ceston
  boy: 4 puer
  bronze: aes
  building: 5 aedes
  cape: 5 sagum 6 byrrus
  cistern: 9 impluvium
  connective: et
  contract: 5 nexum
  couch: 9 accubitum
  deity: 4 deus
  dish: 4 lanx 6 lances, pateral, patina
  food: 5 cibus
  foot: pes
  for example: 4 vide
  force: vis
  friend: 6 amicus
  garland: 6 corona
  ghosts: 7 lemures
  grammar: 5 donat, donet
  grammatical case: 6 dative 8 ablative, genitive, vocative 10 accusative, nominative
  hope: 4 spes
  hour: 4 hora
  javelin: 4 pile 5 aclys, pilum
  life: 4 vita
  ornament: 5 bulla
  post: 4 meta
  pronoun: tu; ego, hic 4 ille, ipse, iste
  ram: 5 aries
  rite: 4 orgy 5 sacra
  roof opening: 10 compluvium
  seat: 5 sella
  shelter: 7 taberna
  towel: 5 mappa
  trumpet: 4 tuba 6 buccin 7 buccina

Latinus' daughter: 7 Lavinia

latite: 4 lava

latitude: 5 scope, width 6 extent 7 breadth, freedom 8 distance
  complement: 10 colatitude
  measure: 6 degree 8 parallel
  zero degrees: 7 equator

latrant: 7 barking 8 snarling 11 complaining

latrine: 5 privy 6 toilet

latter: 4 last 5 final 6 latest

Latter Day Saints: 7 Mormons

latterly: 4 anew 6 lately 8 recently

lattice: 6 pinjra(Ind.) 7 trellis 8 espalier

latticework: 5 arbor, grate 6 arbour 7 grating

Latvia: *city:* 4 Riga(c.) 5 Libau 6 Dvinsk, Libava 8 Dunaburg 10 Daugavpils
  coin: lat 6 rublis 7 kapeika 8 santimas
  measure: 4 stof 5 kanne, stoff, verst 6 kulmet, sagene, versta, verste 7 verchoc, verchok 8 krouchka, kroushka, pourvete 9 deciatine, lofstelle 10 tonnstelle
  parliament: 6 Saeima
  people: 5 Letts
  river: Aa
  university site: 4 Riga
  weight: 9 liespfund

laud: 4 lute 5 extol 6 extoll, praise 7 adulate, applaud, cittern, commend, glorify, magnify 8 emblazon, eulogize 9 panegyric 10 compliment

laudable: 9 allowable, exemplary 12 praiseworthy

laugh: 4 gaff, haha 5 fleer, snort 6 cackle, giggle, guffaw, hawhaw, nicker, titter 7 chortle, grizzle, snicker 9 cachinate
  disposed to: 7 risible
  incipient: 4 grin 5 smile
  pert. to: 8 gelastic

laughable: odd 5 comic, droll, funny, merry, queer, witty 7 amusing, comical, risible, strange, waggish 8 gelastic, humorous, sportive 9 burlesque, diverting, facetious, grotesque, ludicrous 10 ridiculous

laughing: 5 riant

laughing bird: 4 gull, loon 5 pewit 10 woodpecker

laughing owl: 5 wekau

laughter: 5 mirth, risus(L.)
  pert. to: 7 risible

launder: tye 4 wash

laundry: 4 wash 10 laundromat 13 blanchisserie(F.)

laureate: 13 distinguished

laurel: bay 4 fame 5 honor 6 daphne, myrtle, tarata, trophy 7 garland, taratah 9 spoonwood 11 distinction

lava: aa, oo 4 slag 5 ashes 6 coulee, latite, scoria, verite 7 clinker 8 pahoehoe
  fragment of: 8 lapillus

sheet of: 6 coulee
lavabo: 5 basin 8 washbowl 9 cleansing
lavaliere, lavalier: 7 pendant
lavation: 4 bath 6 lavage 7 washing 9 cleansing
lavatory: 5 basin 8 washbowl, washroom
lave: 4 bail, lade, pour, wash 5 bathe, rinse
lavender: 6 pastel, purple, violet
laver: 5 basin 6 trough, vessel 7 cistern
Lavinia: *father:* 7 Latinus
  husband: 6 Aeneas
  mother: 5 Amata
lavish: 4 free, lash, rank, wild 5 flush, spend, waste 7 opulent, profuse 8 prodigal, reckless, splendid, squander 9 bountiful, expensive, exuberant, impetuous, luxuriant, sumptuous, unstinted 10 immoderate 11 extravagant, magnificent 12 unrestrained 13 superabundant
law: act, bar, ius(L.), jus(L.), lex(L.) 4 code, doom, rule, Tora 5 canon, edict, mesne, sutra, Torah 6 custom, decree, equity, noetic, sutrah 7 derecho, justice, precept, statute 8 handicap 9 enactment, ordinance, principle 11 commandment, legislation 12 constitution, jurisdiction 13 jurisprudence
  action: res 4 suit 5 actus 8 replevin 9 gravamina
  body of: 4 code
  breaker of: 5 felon 6 sinner 8 criminal
  claim: 4 lien
  contrary to: 7 illegal, illicit 8 unlawful 16 unconstitutional
  decree: 4 nisi 5 edict
  degree: LLD
  delay: 4 mora
  document: 4 deed, writ 6 capias, elegit
  expounder of: 6 jurist
  goddess: 4 Maat
  male succession: 5 Salic
  man of: 5 judge 6 jurist, lawyer 7 counsel, justice 8 attorney 9 barrister
  Manu: 5 sutra, sutta
  offender: 8 criminal 9 desperado, wrongdoer
  offense: 4 tort 5 crime, malum 6 delict
  oral: 5 parol 11 nuncupative
  order: 4 writ
  permitted by: see **lawful**
  pert. to: 5 legal 7 canonic 9 canonical, judiciary 11 legislative
  philosophy of: 13 jurisprudence
  prevent by: 5 estop
  warning: 6 caveat

lawful: due 5 legal, licit, valid 7 canonic, ennomic 10 legitimate
lawgiver: 5 Moses

lawless: 4 lewd 6 unruly 7 illegal 8 anarchic 9 dissolute 10 anarchical, disorderly, tumultuous
lawlessness: 4 riot 6 mutiny 7 anarchy, license 10 illegality
lawmaker: 5 solon 7 senator 10 legislator
lawn: 5 arbor, grass, sward 6 arbour 7 batiste 9 grassland, grassplot, grasswork
lawsuit: 4 case
  one engaged in: 8 litigant
  subject: res
lawyer: 6 avocat(F.) 8 attorney, commoner 9 barrister, counselor 10 counsellor
  bad: 7 shyster 11 pettifogger
lax: 4 dull, free, limp, open, pave, slow 5 loose, slack, tardy 6 remiss 7 lenient 8 backward, careless, inactive 9 dissolute, negligent 10 unconfined 11 inattentive 12 unrestrained
lay: bet, put, set 4 bury, poem, rest, song 5 carol, ditty, place, quiet, stake, still, wager 6 ballad, entomb, hazard, impose, impute, melody 7 appease, ascribe, deposit 14 unprofessional 15 nonprofessional
lay aside: 5 table 6 shelve 7 abandon, discard, neglect
lay away: See **lay by**
lay bare: 4 show 5 strip 6 denude, expose, reveal 7 uncover
lay by: 4 hive, save 5 amass, cache, hoard, store 7 deposit, husband, reposit 8 treasure 10 accumulate
lay down: set 5 posit 9 establish, surrender
lay hold of: 4 grab, grip 5 grasp, gripe, seize 9 apprehend
lay out: 4 plan 5 set up, spend 6 expend, extend, invest
lay up: See **lay by**
lay waste: 6 harass, ravage 7 destroy 8 desolate 9 depredate, devastate
layer: bed, hen, ply 4 coat, film, fold, seam, tier, zona 5 paver 6 folium, lamina, veneer 7 bedding, provine, stratum 8 laminate 10 substratum
  of coal: 4 seam
  of stones: 4 dess
  of wood: 6 veneer
  pert. to: 7 stratal
layered: 7 laminal, laminar 8 tunicate
layman: 4 laic
laymen: 4 laic 5 laity
layout: 4 plan 6 design, make-up 7 pattern
lazar: 5 leper
lazy: 4 idle, laze 5 inert 8 indolent, slothful, sluggard
lea: 6 meadow 7 pasture 9 grassland
leach: wet 7 moisten 9 lixiviate, percolate
lead: con, van, wad 4 head, lode, star, wadd 5 carry, first, guide, krems, metal, pilot, steer, usher 6 bullet, ceruse, convey, de-

duce, direct, escort, induce, manage **7** command, conduct, pioneer, precede **8** graphite, instruct, outstrip **9** influence
astray: **4** lure **6** allure, delude, entice, seduce **7** deceive, mislead, pervert **8** inveigle
color: **4** dull, gray **5** livid, olive
ore: **6** galena
paste: **6** strass
pig: **6** fother
sounding: **7** plummet
sulphide: **6** galena
leaden: **4** dull, gray **5** heavy **8** plumbean, sluggish **9** plumbeous
leader: bo; boh, cob, dux **4** cock, duce, duke, head, line, wire **5** chief, coach, pilot, sinew, snell **6** cantor, Fuhrer(G.), tendon **7** captain, demagog, foreman, Fuehrer(G.) **8** caudillo, choragus, headsman, preceder **9** chieftain, demagogue, drainpipe, principal **10** bellwether **11** condottiere, gymnasiarch
ecclesiastical: fra **4** pope **5** rabbi **6** bishop, father, priest **8** cardinal, minister, preacher **10** evangelist
leadership: **8** guidance, hegemony **9** authority
leading: big **4** duct, head, main **5** ahead, chief, first **6** banner **7** capital, central, guiding, premier, stellar **8** foremost **9** conducive, directing, governing, hegemonic, inductive, principal **11** controlling
leaf: ola, ole, pan **4** foil, olay, olla, page **5** blade, bract, folio, frond, palet, scale, sepal **6** areola, insert, spathe **7** tendril
angle with branch: **4** axil
aperture: **5** stoma
appendage: **6** ligula, stipel **7** stipule
aromatic: see **herb**
circle: **7** corolla
division: **4** lobe
edge: **9** crenation
fern: **5** frond
floating: pad
kind: **5** calxy, petal, sepal **7** corolla
part: pen **4** axil **5** costa, stoma **6** pagina **7** petiole, stomate
secretion on: **4** lerp
set: **5** calyx **7** corolla
vein: rib **5** costa
leafage: **7** foliage
leaflet: **5** pinna, tract **6** folder **7** booklet **8** pamphlet
leafstalk: **6** celery
leafy: **5** green, shady **6** foliar **7** sepaled
league: **4** bond **5** union **7** compact **8** alliance, covenant **9** coalition **10** federation **11** association, combination, confederacy **13** confederation
League of Nations city: **6** Geneva

Leah: *father:* **5** Laban
sister: **6** Rachel
son: **6** Simeon
leak: **4** drip, hole, loss, ooze, seep **5** crack **6** escape **7** channel, crevice, fissure
leaky: **6** gizzen
leal: **4** just, real, true **5** legal, loyal **6** lawful **7** correct, genuine **8** accurate, faithful
leam: **4** husk
lean: **4** bend, cant, lank, mean, poor, rely, slim, tend, thin, tilt **5** gaunt, lanky, scant, spare **6** depend, hollow, meager, meagre, skinny **7** conform, deviate, haggard, incline, recline, scrawny, slender **8** rawboned, scragged **9** deficient, emaciated **10** inadequate **12** unproductive
lean-to: hut **4** shed **5** shack
Leander's sweetheart: **4** Hera, Hero
leaning: **7** pronate **8** penchant **9** accumbent
leap: fly, hop **4** dart, dive, jump, loup, skip **5** bound, caper, exult, frisk, lunge, salto, vault **6** bounce, breach, cavort, curvet, gallop, gambol, hurdle, hurtle, spring **7** saltate **8** capriole **9** ballotade, entrechat
leap year: **10** bissextile
leaping: **7** salient, saltant **9** caprizant, saltation
lear: **4** lore **6** lesson **8** learning
Lear: *daughter:* **5** Regan **7** Goneril **8** Cordelia
dog: **4** Tray
follower: **4** Kent
learn: con, get **4** find, here, lere **6** master **7** acquire, apprise, apprize, realize **8** memorize **9** ascertain
learned: wot **4** blue, read, sage, wise **6** astute, doctus **7** clerkly, cunning, erudite **8** lettered, literary, literose **9** scholarly **10** omniscient
learner: **5** pupil **7** scholar, trainee **8** disciple, opsimath **10** apprentice
learning: art **4** lear, lore **6** wisdom **7** cunning **8** pedantry **9** education, erudition, knowledge **10** discipline, experience **11** scholarship
display of: **8** pedantry
love of: **9** philology
man of: **6** pundit, savant **7** scholar, teacher **9** philomath, professor **12** intellectual
lease: let **4** hire, rent **6** demise, engage, rental, tenure **7** charter **8** contract **10** concession
leash: **4** bind, cord, harl, jess, lune **5** strap **6** couple, tether
least: **6** fewest, little, lowest **7** minimal, minimum **8** shortest, smallest **9** slightest
leather: tan **4** napa, whip, yuft(Russ.) **5** balat, leder, strap **6** thrash
artificial: **7** keratol

drying: sam **4** samm **5** sammy
fine: kid **6** vellum
finish: **4** buff
inspector: **6** sealer
kind: elk, kid, kip **4** bock, buff, calf, doze, napa, roan, seal, vici **5** aluta, basil, mocha, suede, trank **6** castor, levant, oxhide, skiver **7** buffalo, canepin, chamois, morocco, saffian **8** cheverel, cheveril, Cordovan
napped: **5** suede
pare: **5** skive
piece of: **4** rand, welt **5** clout, strap, thong **6** latigo
prepare: tan, taw
sheepskin: **4** roan **6** skiver
tool: **6** skiver
waste: **6** tanite
worker: **6** chamar, tanner **8** chuckler
leatherback: **6** turtle
leatherneck: **6** marine
leave: go; let **4** bunk, exit, quit **5** favor, forgo, grace, scram **6** beleve, decamp, depart, desert, entail, favour, forego, forlet, permit, retire, vacate **7** abandon, beleave, forsake, getaway, liberty, license **8** bequeath, emigrate, furlough, vacation **9** allowance **10** permission, relinquish
behind: **11** outdistance
in the lurch: **6** desert, maroon, strand
leave of absence: **5** exeat **8** furlough
leave off: **4** quit, stop **5** cease, elide **6** desist **10** abbreviate
leave out: **4** omit, skip **5** elide
leave-taking: **5** adieu, conge **6** congee **7** parting **8** farewell **9** departure
leaven: **5** imbue, yeast **7** lighten **10** impregnate
leaves (see also **leaf; leave**): **7** foliage
having: see **leafy**
medicinal: **5** senna
leavings: See **lees; rubbish**
Lebanon: *castle:* **5** Saida, Sidon, Toron **8** Beaufort
city: **4** Arca, Tyre **5** Ehden, Saida **6** Beirut(c.) **7** Tripoli **8** Beyrouth **9** Broummana
dance: **6** dabkeh
fort: **6** Byblos
money: **5** livre **7** piastre
mountain: **4** Mzar **7** Sannine **8** Kadischa, Kenisseh
people: **4** Arab
river: **5** Lycos **6** Damour, Litani **8** Kasemieh
seaport: **4** Tyre **6** Beirut **8** Beyrouth
tree: **5** cedar
lech: **4** slab **8** capstone, monument
lecher: **7** glutton **8** gourmand, parasite **9** debauchee, libertine

lecherous: **4** lewd **7** boarish, goatish, lustful **9** salacious
lectern: **4** ambo, desk **10** escritoire
lecture: **5** scold **6** lesson, preach, sermon **7** address, hearing, lection, oration, prelect **9** discourse, sermonize **12** dissertation
lecturer: **6** docent, reader **9** prelector, professor
led: See **lead**
Leda: *lover:* **4** swan, Zeus
son: **6** Castor, Pollux
ledge: **4** berm, sill **5** bench, berme, shelf **7** retable
ledger: **4** tome **6** record
lee: **5** haven **7** shelter **10** protection
opposite of: **5** stoss **8** windward
leech: **8** parasite **9** blackmail **11** bloodsucker
leer: **4** face, lear, lehr, loin, look, lust, ogle, void **5** empty, flank, fleer, smirk **6** entice, unlade **7** grimace
leery, leary: **4** wary **7** knowing **10** suspicious **11** distrustful
lees: **5** draff, dregs, dross, grout **6** bottom, dunder, refuse, ullage **7** grounds **8** emptings, sediment, settling **9** excrement
leeward: **4** alee
drift: **4** crab
Leeward group island: **5** Nevis **7** Antigua, Barbuda, St. Kitts **8** Anguilla, Dominica, Windward **10** Montserrat
leeway: **4** room **5** space **9** elbowroom
left: **4** port **8** larboard
toward: **4** haw **5** aport **9** sinistrad
left-handed: car **6** gauche **8** southpaw **9** portsided
left-over: See **lees; rubbish**
leftist: red **7** radical **13** revolutionary
leftward: **5** aport
leg: gam **4** gamb, hoof, limb, prop, walk **5** bough, brace, gambe, shank **6** bender, gammon **8** cabriole
armor: **4** jamb **6** greave
bone: **4** shin **5** femur, ilium, tibia **6** fibula
in heraldry: **4** gamb
muscle: **8** peroneus **9** peronaeus
ornament: **6** anklet
part: **4** calf, crus, knee, shin **5** ankle, thigh **11** anticnemion
pert. to: **6** crural
legacy: **4** gift **6** legate **7** bequest **8** windfall **10** foundation
inheritor: **4** heir **7** legatee
legal (see also **law**): **5** licit, valid **6** lawful **7** juridic **9** juridical **10** authorized, legitimate
legal matter: res
legal right, by: **6** ex jure
legal tender: **4** cash, coin **5** money **6** dollar, specie

legalize: 9 authorize

legate: 5 envoy 6 deputy, legacy, nuncio 8 bequeath, delegate 9 messenger 10 ambassador 14 representative

legatee: 4 heir
joint: 6 coheir

legend: 4 edda, lore, myth, saga, tale 5 fable, story 6 record 7 fiction, proverb 9 tradition

legerdemain: 5 magic 6 deceit 8 trickery 9 conjuring

legging: 4 spat 5 chaps 6 cnemis, cocker, puttie 7 bottine, gambado 8 bootikin, chivarra, chivarro, gamashes 11 galligaskin, spatterdash 12 antigropelos

legible: 8 distinct, readable 14 understandable

legion: 4 army, host 9 multitude

legislate: act 5 elect, enact

legislation: act, law 7 statute

legislative: 12 nomothetical

legislative body: 4 diet, rada 5 house, junta 6 senate 7 althing 8 congress 9 Reichstag 10 parliament

legislator: 5 solon 7 enactor, senator 8 lawmaker 9 statesman

legislature: 4 Dail, diet 6 senate 8 assembly, congress

legitimate: 4 fair, just, real, true 5 legal, licit, valid 6 cogent, lawful 7 genuine 11 efficacious

'egume: pea, pod, uva 4 bean, soya 5 pulse 6 lentil, loment 9 vegetable

lei: 6 wreath 7 flowers, garland

leisure: 4 case, free, idle, time 5 otium(L.), spare 6 otiose 7 freedom 10 relaxation, unemployed, unoccupied 11 convenience, opportunity 12 unproductive

leisurely: 4 slow 7 gradual 12 deliberately

leman: 5 lover 8 mistress, paramour 10 sweetheart

lemma: 5 bract 8 membrane

lemonade: 5 drink 6 cooler 8 beverage

lemur: 4 maki, vari 5 avahi, indri, loris, potto 6 aye-aye, colugo, galago, macaco, maholi 7 half-ape, semiape, tarsier 8 kinkajou 9 babacoote 10 angwantibo

lend: 4 loan 5 grant, prest 6 afford, impart, settle 7 advance, furnish 11 accommodate

lene: 6 smooth 9 consonant 11 unaspirated

length: 4 pace, term 7 yardage 9 dimension
measure: mil 4 foot, inch, yard

lengthen: eke 6 dilate, expand, extend 7 amplify, produce, prolong, stretch 8 elongate, increase, protract

lengthwise: 5 along 7 endlong, endways 14 longitudinally

lengthy: 4 long 8 extended 10 protracted

lenient: lax 4 easy, kind, mild 6 facile, gentle, humane 7 clement 8 lenitive, merciful, mitigant, relaxing, soothing, tolerant 9 as-

suasive, emollient, softening 10 charitable, forbearing, palliative

Leningrad: 9 Petrograd

lens: 4 unar 5 toric 7 bifocal 8 meniscus 10 anastigmat

Lent: 6 Careme(F.)

Lenten: 5 plain 6 meager, meagre, somber, sombre 8 meatless 14 unostentatious

lentigo: 7 freckle

lentil: 6 legume

Leo star: 7 Regulus

leonine: 8 lionlike, powerful

leopard: cat 4 pard 5 ounce 7 cheetah, panther

lepidopter: 4 moth 9 butterfly

leprechaun: elf 5 fairy

leprosy: 5 lepra

lerot: 8 dormouse

Les Miserables author: 4 Hugo

lesion: cut 4 sore 5 ulcer, wound 6 injury 7 fissure

less: 5 fewer, minus, under 7 smaller 8 inferior

lessee: 6 leaser, renter, tenant 7 huurder(D.)

lessen: 4 bate, ease, wane 5 abase, abate, decry, lower, peter 6 impair, reduce, soften, shrink, weaken 7 amenuse, assuage, curtail, depress, relieve 8 belittle, condense, contract, decrease, derogate, diminish, minimize, mitigate, palliate, retrench, truncate 9 alleviate, attenuate, disparage, extenuate 10 depreciate 11 deteriorate

lesser: 5 minor

lesson: 4 lear, task 5 moral, study 6 rebuke 7 example, lecture, precept, reading, reproof, warning 8 exercise 10 assignment 11 composition, instruction

lessor: 8 landlord

lest: 8 anaunter

let: 4 hire, rent 5 allow, lease, leave 6 hinder, impede, permit, suffer 7 prevent 8 obstacle 9 hindrance
fall: 4 drop, slip 5 lower, spill 7 mention
forth: 4 emit
in: 5 admit, enter 6 insert

let it stand: sta 4 stet

letdown: 5 slump 8 comedown, drawback 10 anticlimax, relaxation, slackening

lethal: 5 fatal 6 deadly, mortal, poison 9 poisonous 12 death-dealing

lethargic: 4 dull 5 heavy, inert 6 drowsy, sleepy, torpid 8 comatose, sluggish 9 apathetic

lethargy: 5 sopor 6 stupor, torpor

Lethe: 8 oblivion 13 forgetfulness

Leto: 6 Latona
daughter: 7 Artemis
father: 5 Coeus

mother: 6 Phoebe
son: 6 Apollo
Lett: 4 Balt 7 Latvian
letter: 4 bull, chit, line, note 5 breve, brief, chain, favor, vowel 6 billet, cartel, charta, favour, screed, symbol 7 collins, courant, epistle, message, missile, missive 9 consonant, semivowel 13 communication, semiconsonant
Anglo-Saxon: edh, eth, wen, wyn 4 wynn
decorated: fac
sloping: 6 italic
letter carrier: 6 correo(Sp.) 7 mailman, postman 9 messenger
letter for letter: 9 literally, literatim
lettered: 7 learned, stamped 8 educated, literate 9 inscribed
lettuce: *kind of:* cos 4 head, leaf 6 butter 7 romaine, simpson
sea: 4 alga 5 laver
letup: 7 respite 9 abatement, cessation
leucite: 5 lenad 9 amphigene
levant: 5 wager 6 decamp 7 abscond
Levant: 4 East 6 Orient 13 Mediterranean
garment: 6 caftan
river: 4 wadi, wady
ship: 4 jerm, saic
valley: 4 wady
levee: 4 bank, dike, dyke, pier, quay 6 durbar 9 reception 10 embankment
level: aim, par 4 even, flat, rase, raze, true 5 equal, grade, peavy, plane, point, scalp 6 evenly, peavey, peavie, smooth 7 flatten, uniform 8 demolish 10 horizontal 12 standardized
comb. form: 5 plani
social: 5 caste, class
tool: 5 plane 6 gimbal
level-headed: 8 sensible
lever: bar, lam, pry 5 helve, jemmy, jimmy, peavy, pedal, prise, swipe 6 binder, garrot, peavey, peavie, tappet, tiller 7 crowbar, treadle 9 rockshaft
part: 7 fulcrum
leveret: 4 hare 8 mistress
Levi: *descendant:* 6 Levite 7 Gershon
father: 5 Jacob
son: 6 Kohath
leviathan: 4 ship 5 titan, whale 6 dragon
levigate: 6 polish, smooth
levin: 9 lightning
levitate: 4 rise 5 float
levity: 5 humor 6 gaiety, humour 8 buoyancy 9 frivolity, lightness, silliness 11 foolishness
levy: tax 4 cess, fine, wage 5 exact, stent 6 assess, extent, impose, impost 7 collect 10 assessment, imposition
lewd: 4 base, rude 5 bawdy 6 carnal, coarse 7 lustful, obscene, rammish, sensual 8 un-

chaste 9 debauched, dissolute, lecherous, salacious 10 lascivious, libidinous, licentious 12 pornographic
lexicographer: 6 author 8 compiler 9 onomastic
lexicon: 7 calepin 10 dictionary 11 onomasticon
Leyte capital: 8 Tacloban
liability: 4 debt, loan 5 debit 6 burden 10 obligation
liable: apt 8 amenable 10 answerable 11 accountable, responsible
liaison: 4 bond 8 intimacy, intrigue
liana: 4 cipo 5 plant
liang: 4 tael
liar: 5 cheat 6 fibber 7 Ananias, cracker 8 deceiver, fabulist 10 fabricator 11 pseudologue 12 prevaricator, pseudologist 14 misrepresenter
lias: 4 rock 9 limestone
libation: 5 drink 8 potation
libel: 4 bill 4 defame, malign, vilify 7 calumny, lampoon, request, scandal, slander 8 circular, handbill, roorback 10 calumniate, defamation 11 certificate, declaration 12 supplication
libelant: 7 accuser
liberal: 4 free, good, open 5 ample, broad, frank, noble 6 honest 7 electic, profuse 8 eclectic, generous, handsome 9 benignant, bounteous, bountiful, expansive, expensive, plenteous, plentiful 10 benevolent, charitable, ecumenical, munificent
Liberal: 4 Whig
liberate: rid 4 flee, free 5 clear, loose, remit 6 acquit, redeem, rescue 7 deliver, manumit, release 8 unfetter 9 discharge, disengage, extricate 10 emancipate
Liberia: *boatman:* Kru
city: 8 Buchanan, Marshall, Monrovia(c.) 10 Greenville
measure: 4 kuba
people: Gi; Kru, Kwa, Vai, Vei 4 Kroo, Toma 5 Bassa, Gibbi, Greba 6 Krooby, Kruman 7 Krooboy, Krooman
river: 5 Manna 8 San Pedro
libertine: 4 rake, roue 7 sceptic 9 debauchee, dissolute 11 freethinker
liberty: may 4 ease, play 5 leave, right 7 freedom, license 9 privilege 11 presumption
library: 7 bhandar 8 atheneum 9 athenaeum 11 bibliotheca
libretto: 4 book 5 words
Libya: *city:* 7 Tripoli
measure: 4 drah 5 bozze, donum, jabia, teman 6 barile 7 mattaro
measure of weight: 4 kele 5 uckia 6 gorraf 7 termino 8 kharouba

oasis: 5 sebka
seaport: 5 Derna, Derrn 6 Tobruk 7 Bengazi
  8 Benghazi
wind: 7 sirocco
Libya's child: 5 Belus 6 Agenor
lice: See **louse**
license: tax 5 exeat, leave 6 patent, permit
  7 dismiss, freedom, liberty 8 escambio,
  passport, sanction 9 approbate, authority,
  authorize, franchise 10 permission 11 im-
  primateur, unrestraint
licentious: gay, lax 4 free, lewd 5 frank,
  loose 6 unruly 7 immoral, obscene 9 dissolute 10 lascivious, profligate 12 pornographic, uncontrolled, unrestrained
lichen: 4 moss
  derivative: 6 archil, litmus
  genus: 5 usnea 7 evernia 10 pertusaria
lich-house: 8 mortuary
licit: 5 legal 6 lawful 9 permitted
lick: lap, win 4 flog 5 slake 6 thrash 7 conquer 8 overcome, vanquish
licorice: 5 abrin, anise 8 absinthe 9 jequirity
  pill: 6 cachou
  seed: 9 jequirity
lid: cap, hat, top 5 cover 7 shutter 9 operculum
lie: cog, fib, gab 4 bask, cram, flaw, hide, loll,
  rest 5 exist 6 covert, extend, grovel, remain, repose 7 cracker, crammer, deceive,
  falsify, falsity, pronate, untruth 8 position, roorback 9 deception, fabricate,
  falsehood, mendacity, prostrate 10 equivocate, inveracity, taradiddle 11 fabrication,
  prevaricate, tarradiddle 13 prevarication
  in ambush: 4 lurk 6 hugger 9 insidiate
Liebestraum composer: 5 Liszt
Liechtenstein: *capital:* 5 Vaduz
  monetary unit: 5 rappe
lief: 4 dear, fain 5 leave 6 freely, gladly 7
  beloved, happily 8 pleasing, precious 9
  willingly 10 permission
liege: 5 loyal 6 vassal 7 devoted, subject 8
  faithful, overlord 9 sovereign
lien: 5 claim 6 charge 8 mortgage 9 trust
  deed 11 encumbrance, garnishment
lieu: 5 place, stead 7 instead
lieutenant: 4 zany
lieve: See **lief**
life: vie 6 blood, hours 6 biosis, energy, spirit
  8 vitality, vivacity 9 animation, biography, existence 11 anilopyrine
  animal: 4 bios 5 biota, fauna
  comb. form: bio
  god of: 6 Faunus
  pert. to: 5 vital 6 biotic, mortal 8 biotical
  plant: 4 bios 5 biota, flora
  principle: 5 atman, prana, tenet

professional: 6 career
science: 7 anatomy, biology, zoology 12 paleontology
sea: 5 coral 8 halibios, plankton
simple form: 5 ameba 6 amebic, ameoba 7
  amoebic, amoebae(pl.)
staff of: 5 bread
without: 4 dead 5 azoic 9 inanimate
life insurance: 7 tontine
life jacket: 7 Mae West
life-like: 9 realistic
lifeless: 4 arid, dead, dull, flat 5 amort,
  heavy, inert, vapid 6 anemic, jejune, torpid 7 anaemic 8 inactive 9 bloodless, ex-
  aminate, inanimate, powerless, tasteless
  10 spiritless, unanimated
  comb. form: 4 abio
lifer: 7 convict
lifetime: age, day, eon 4 aeon 5 being 8 duration
lift: pry 4 help, jack, perk, rear 5 boost, exalt, heave, hoick, hoist, hoosh, raise, scend
  6 cleach, cleech 7 derrick, elevate, enhance 8 elevator, heighten
ligament: 4 band, bind, bond 6 artery 7 bandage
  comb. form: 5 desmo
ligan, lagan: 6 debris
ligate: 4 bind 7 bandage
ligature: tie 4 band, bond 6 taenia 7 bandage
light: dey, gay 4 airy, deft, easy, fire, glim,
  lamp, mild, moon, neon, soft 5 agile, blond,
  fanal, filmy, flaky, flame, flare, merry,
  torch 6 alight, beacon, bright, candle,
  floaty, gentle, ignite, kindle, lively, lumine, nimble, pastel, volant 7 buoyant,
  cresset, flyaway, fragile, trivial 8
  brighten, cheerful, delicate, ethereal, gossamer, graceful, illumine, luminary, luminous, trifling 10 illuminate
  circle: 4 halo 7 aureola, aureole
  cloud: 6 nimbus
  faint: 7 glimmer, shimmer 9 starlight 10
  glimmering, shimmering
  globe: 4 bulb
  god: 5 Baldr 6 Balder
  kind of: arc 4 lamp 5 klieg, torch 7 lantern
  9 headlight 10 flashlight 12 incandescent
  measure: lux, pyr, rad 5 lumen 6 Hefner
  overpower with: 6 dazzle
  portable: 4 lamp 5 flare, taper, torch 6 candle 7 lantern 10 flashlight
  reflector: 4 lens 6 mirror
  refractor: 5 prism
  science: 6 optics
  source: sun
  unit: lux, pyr 4 phot 5 lumen
  without: 4 dark 5 blind 7 aphotic

lighten: 4 ease, fade 5 allay, clear 6 alight, allege, bleach, illume, leaven 7 gladden, relieve 8 brighten 9 alleviate 10 illuminate

lightening: 10 levitation

lighter (see also **light**): 4 scow 5 barge, spill 7 fidibus, gabbard, gabbart, pontoon 8 chopboat

lightheaded: 5 dizzy, giddy 6 fickle 7 flighty, glaiket, glaikit 8 flippant, heedless, unstable, unsteady 9 delirious, frivolous 10 disordered, inconstant 11 thoughtless

lighthearted: gay 4 glad 5 merry 7 buoyant 8 carefree, cheerful, gleesome, volatile 9 vivacious

lighthouse: 5 phare 6 beacon, pharos 7 seamark, warning

lightness: 6 levity

lightning: 4 bolt 5 levin
   defier of: 4 Ajax
   pert. to: 8 fulgural
   protective device: 8 arrester

lightning bug: 7 firefly

lightning rod: 8 arrester

lightning stone: 9 fulgurite

lights: 5 lungs

lights out: 4 taps

ligneous: 5 woody

lignite: 4 coal

ligula: 4 band

ligulate: 11 strap-shaped

likable: 6 genial 7 winning 8 charming, pleasant 10 attractive

like: as 4 love, same 5 alike, enjoy, equal 6 admire, prefer, relish 7 similar 9 analogous, semblance 10 preference, synonymous 11 counterpart, homogeneous
   suffix: ar, ic; ose

like a: For definitions beginning with these words, see following important words. Examples: "like a cat" : see **catlike;** "like a house": see **house:** *pert. to.*

likelihood: 10 appearance 11 probability 14 verisimilitude

likely: apt 5 prone 6 liable 7 tending 8 credible, feasible, probable, suitable 9 promising 11 verisimilar

liken: 5 apply 7 compare 10 assimilate

likeness: 4 copy, form, twin 5 guise, image 6 effigy, figure, statue 7 analogy, parable, picture, replica 8 parallel, portrait 9 duplicate, facsimile, imitation, semblance, simulacre 10 comparison, photograph, similarity, similitude, simulacrum 11 counterfeit 12 reproduction 14 representation

likewise: and, nor, not, too 4 also 5 ditto 7 besides 8 moreover

liking: goo 4 gust, lust 5 fancy, gusto, taste 6 comely 7 delight 8 affinity, appetite, fondness, penchant, pleasing, pleasure 9 affection 10 sensuality 12 predilection

lilac: 5 mauve 7 syringa

Lilith's successor: Eve

lilliputian: 4 tiny 5 petty, small 6 midget 7 dwarfed

lilt: air 4 sing, song, tune 7 cadence

lily (see also **water lily**): ki, ti 4 aloe, ixia, sego 5 calla, niobe, tiger, water, yucca 6 titree 8 mariposa
   family: 9 liliaceae
   genus: 7 bessera

lily iron: 7 harpoon

Lily Maid of Astolat: 6 Elaine

lily of France: 10 fleur-de-lis

lily of the valley: 6 mugget, mugwet 10 convallily
   family: 15 convallariaceae

lily-of-the-valley tree: 8 sourwood 10 fetterbush, pepperbush

lily-shaped: 7 crinoid

lima: 4 bean

liman: bay 5 marsh 6 lagoon 7 estuary

limation: 6 filing 9 polishing

limb: arm, fin, leg 4 wing 5 bough 6 branch, member 7 flipper, pleopod, support
   adapted for swimming: 8 nectopod
   flexion: 9 anaclasis

limber: 4 bain, flip, limp 5 lithe 6 pliant, supple, swanky 8 flexible, flippant, handsome, yielding

limbo: 4 hell 9 purgatory

lime: 5 color, green 6 cement, citrus
   pendent: 10 stalactite
   phosphate: 7 apatite

lime tree: 4 teil 6 linden, tupelo

limen: 9 threshold

limestone: 4 calp, cauk, malm 5 chalk, ganil, poros(Gr.) 6 clunch, marble, oolite 7 hurlock 8 peastone, pisolite

limey: 6 sailor 7 soldier 10 Englishman

limit: end, fix 4 curb, mete 5 ambit, bound, bourn, check, fence, hedge, scant, stint, verge 6 border, bourne, curfew, define, extent, finish 7 astrict, barrier, closure, confine, environ, extreme 8 boundary, conclude, contract, deadline, restrain, restrict, terminal, terminus 9 condition, constrain, extremity 10 limitation 11 restriction, termination 12 circumscribe 13 determination, qualification
   combining form: ori

limited: few, ltd 5 local, scant 6 finite, narrow, scanty, strait 8 reserved 9 parochial 10 restricted 11 topopolitan

limiting: 10 relational

limitless: 4 vast 8 infinite 9 boundless, unbounded, unlimited 11 measureless

limn: 4 draw 6 depict, sketch 7 portray 8 describe 9 delineate

limp: hop, lax 4 himp, soft, thin 5 hilch, hitch, loose 6 flabby, flimsy, hirple, hobble, limber, wilted 7 flaccid 8 drooping, flexible 9 inelastic 13 unsubstantial

limpid: 4 pure 5 clear, lucid 6 bright 7 crystal 8 pellucid 11 translucent, transparent

limping: 4 halt 10 claudicant

limy: 6 sticky 7 viscous

Lincoln: *friend:* 5 Speed
  portrayer of: 6 Massey
  secretary of state: 6 Seward
  secretary of war: 7 Stanton
  son: Tad
  wife: 4 Mary

linden: lin 4 lime, teil 8 basswood
  genus of: 5 tilia

line: pad, ray, row, wad 4 axis, ceil, cord, dash, etch, face, file, mark, mere, race, rein, rope, rule, seam, wire 5 curve, front, leger, queue, route, serif, snell, steen, stich, stria, swath 6 border, ceriph, cordon, fettle, hawser, isobar, metier, nettle, streak, string, stripe, suture 7 barrier, carrier, contour, radiant, scratch 8 boundary, crossbar, isotherm, wainscot 9 delineate
  comb. form: 4 lino
  conceptual: 6 agonic, tropic 7 equator, isother 8 latitude, meridian 9 longitude
  diagonal: 4 bias
  geometrical: arc, ess 4 cant, sine 6 secant 7 tangent 8 parallel 9 asymptote
  mathematical: 6 vector
  nautical: 6 earing, hawser, ratlin 7 marline, painter, ratline
  of soldiers: 4 file, rank 6 column
  pertaining to: 5 filar 6 linear
  raised: 4 weal, welt 5 ridge
  with boards: 8 wainscot

lineage: 4 race 5 birth, blood, caste, tribe 6 family, havage, stirps 7 descent, stirpes(pl.) 8 ancestry, heredity, pedigree 9 genealogy 10 progenitor

lineal: 6 direct, racial 9 ancestral 10 hereditary

lineament: 7 feature 14 characteristic

linear: 9 elongated

lineate: 7 striped 8 streaked

lined: 5 ruled 6 notate 7 striate 8 careworn 9 lineolate

lineman: end 5 guard 6 center, tackle 7 wireman

linen: 4 brin, crea(Sp.), lawn 5 toile 6 barras, damask, dowlas, forfar 7 brabant, cambric, dornick 13 linsey-woolsey
  fabric: 7 taffeta
  household: 6 napery, sheets
  source: 4 flax

yarn: lea

liner: 4 boat, ship 6 vessel 7 steamer 9 steamship
  wrecked: 7 Titanic

lines: net 7 network, reticle

ling: 4 fish, hake 5 heath 6 burbot 7 heather 8 chestnut

linger: lag 4 drag, stay, wait 5 dally, delay, dwell, hover, tarry 6 dawdle, loiter, remain

lingerie: 9 underwear 11 underthings

lingering: 4 slow 7 chronic

lingo: 4 cant 5 argot 6 jargon, patter, tongue 7 dialect 8 language 10 vernacular

lingot: 4 mold 5 ingot

lingua: 6 glossa

lingual: 7 glossal 10 linguistic, tonguelike

linguist: 8 polyglot 9 pantoglot 10 vocabulist 11 interpreter, philologist

linguistics: 7 grammar 9 philology

lingy: 5 agile 6 active, healthy, limber, nimble 8 heathery

linhay: 4 shed 8 outhouse

liniment: 11 embrocation

lining: 5 stean, steen 7 backing, ceiling 8 wainscot 12 wainscotting

link: tie 4 join, yoke 5 cleek, nexus, torch, unite 6 braced, catena, copula, couple, course, fasten 7 conjoin, connect 8 catenate 10 connection, golf course 11 concatenate
  series: 5 chain 13 concatenation

linking: 9 annectant, annectent

linn, lin: 4 pool 6 linden, ravine 8 cataract 9 precipice, waterfall

linnet: 5 finch, twite 9 gorsebird

linseed: 8 flaxseed

lint: 5 fluff 7 charpie 8 raveling

lintel: 5 hance 6 clavel 7 transom

lion: 4 puma, star 5 simba 6 cougar, roarer 9 carnivore, celebrity
  group: 5 pride
  hair: 4 mane
  winged, with woman's head: 6 sphinx
  young: cub 6 lionet

Lion of God: Ali

lionlike: 7 leonine

lip: rim 4 brim, edge, kiss 5 brink, labia(pl.) 6 labium, margin 7 labella 8 labellum
  comb. form: 5 labio
  ornament: 6 labret
  part: 8 philtrum
  pert. to: 6 labial 11 labiodental

lipa: fat

liparoid: 5 fatty

liparous: 5 obese

lipless: 8 achilary

lipoma: 5 tumor

lipped: 7 labiate

liquefy: 4 fuse, melt 6 fusile 7 liquate 8 dissolve, eliquate 10 colliquate, deliquesce

liqueur: 5 creme, noyau 6 genepi 7 cordial, ratafee 8 anisette, beverage 9 cointreau 11 benedictine

liquid: 5 fluid 6 fluent, watery 8 beverage
colorless: 5 water 7 alcohol
container: cup, jar, jug, mug, pan, pot 4 etna, ewer, vase, vial 5 cruse, glass, phial 6 boiler, bottle, bucket, goblet, kettle 7 creamer, pitcher 8 decanter, demijohn
gasified: 5 steam, vapor
inflammable: see *volatile* below
measure: 4 pint 5 ounce 6 gallon, tierce
oily: 6 cresol, octane 7 aniline, picamar
particle form: 4 mist 5 spray
sweet: 5 sirup, syrup 7 treacle 8 molasses
volatile: gas 5 ether 6 butane 7 alcohol, ligroin 8 gasolene, gasoline, ligroine

liquidate: 6 settle 8 amortize 9 discharge

liquor (see also **liqueur**): ale, bub, dew, gin, rum, rye 4 arak, bang, beer, beno, brew, grog, nipa, raki, sake, saki, soma 5 bhang, booze, budge, lager, pisco, stout 6 arrack, brandy, porter, pottle, scotch, stingo, strunt, tipple 7 bitters, whiskey 8 beverage 9 moonshine
bad: 5 smoke 6 rotgut 10 balderdash
cabinet: 8 cellaret
crude: 5 hooch 6 rotgut 9 hoochinoo, moonshine
drugged: 5 hocus 6 mickey 10 mickey-finn
manufacturer: 6 abkari 9 distiller
measure: 4 dram 5 rouse 7 snifter
mix with: 4 lace
mixture: 5 bogus 7 bragget
residue: 4 must 5 dregs 8 heeltaps
server: 6 barman 7 barmaid, skinker, tapster 9 barkeeper, bartender
shop: bar 6 saloon, tavern 7 shebeen
vessel: ama, keg 4 bowl 5 amula, flask 6 barrel, bottle, flagon 7 bombard, psykter, stamnos 8 cruisken, decanter 9 cruiskeen

lira (one-twentieth): 5 soldo

liripipe, liripoop: 4 hood, task 5 scarf 6 lesson, tippet

lirk: 6 crease 7 wrinkle

lish: 5 agile, quick 6 active, nimble

lisk: 4 loin 5 flank, groin

lisp: 7 prattle

lissome, lissom: 5 agile, lithe 6 limber, nimble, supple 8 flexible

list: tip 4 bill, cant, cast, file, item, keel, leet, memo, ordo, roll, rota, rote, tilt 5 brief, canon, index, panel, scrip, slate 6 careen, docket, roster 7 catalog, incline 8 manifest, register, schedule, tabulate 9 catalogue, inventory, portfolio, repertory 10 repertoire 11 enumeration

listen: ear 4 hark, hear, heed, note 5 audit 6 attend, harken 7 hearken 8 overhear 9 eavesdrop 10 auscultate

listener: 6 hearer 7 audient

lister: 8 assessor 9 appraiser 10 cataloguer

listful: 9 attentive

listing: 5 atilt 7 tilting, tipping 8 register 10 enlistment, enrollment
individual: 4 item 5 entry

listless: 4 dull 5 faint, inert 6 abject, drowsy, supine 7 languid 8 careless, heedless, sluggish 9 apathetic, heartless 10 spiritless 11 indifferent 13 uninteresting

listlessness: 8 doldrums

litany: 6 ectene, ektene, prayer 8 rogation 11 orapronobis

liter: kan(D.) 7 measure

literal: 4 bald, dull 5 exact 7 factual, precise, prosaic 8 verbatim 13 unimaginative

literary: 6 versed 7 bookish, erudite, learned 8 lettered 9 scholarly

literate: 6 reader, writer 8 educated, lettered

literati: 14 intelligentsia

literator: 6 critic

literature: 7 letters
extracts: 9 anthology
form: 5 novel 6 poetry 7 fiction 9 technical 10 nonfiction, scientific 11 pornography

lithe: 4 bain, slim 6 clever, limber, lissom, pliant, supple, svelte 7 lissome, slender 8 flexible

lithograph: 6 chromo

Lithuania: *city:* 5 Kovno(c.), Memel, Vilna
coin: lit 5 litas, marka 6 centas, fennig 7 ostmark 8 auksinas, skatikas
dialect: 5 Zmudz
lowlander: 5 Zhmud 10 Samogitian
railroad junction: 5 Vilna

Lithuanian: 4 Balt, Lett 5 Zhmud 6 Litvak 7 Yatvyag

litigant: 4 suer 6 suitor 7 accuser

litigation: 4 moot, suit 7 contest, dispute, lawsuit 10 contention, discussion
one involved in: 8 barrater, barrator, litigant

litigious: 10 disputable 11 belligerent, contentious 14 controvertible

litten: 7 lighted 8 cemetery 10 churchyard

litter: bed, hay 4 bier, mess, raff 5 cabin, couch, dooly, mulch, straw, trash, young 6 doolie, refuse 7 cacolet, mullock, rubbish, rummage 8 brancard(F.), disorder 9 offspring, stretcher 10 untidiness

litterateur: 7 bookman

little: sma(Sc.), wee 4 poco(It.), puny, tiny 5 crumb, petit, small 6 petite 8 fraction 10 diminutive
comb. form: 5 steno

little finger: 7 minimus
little toe: 7 minimus
Little Women: Jo; Amy, Meg 4 Beth
author: 6 Alcott
surname: 5 March
littoral: 7 coastal
lituite: 6 fossil
liturate: 7 spotted
liturgy: 4 rite 6 ritual 7 service
livable: 8 bearable 9 endurable, tolerable
live: 4 fare, room 5 abide, alive, dwell, exist, green, vital, vivid 6 reside 7 animate, blazing, breathe, subsist 8 animated, continue, converse 9 energetic 10 experience
in: 7 inhabit
in the country: 9 rusticate
passively: 8 vegetate
permit to: 5 spare 8 reprieve
livelihood: 4 keep 5 being 6 living
liveliness: 6 spirit 8 vitality
lively: gay, vif(F.) 4 airy, cant, fast, pert, racy, vive, yare 5 agile, alert, alive, brisk, canty, chirk, cobby, desto(It.), fresh, peart, peppy 6 active, blithe, bright, cheery, chirpy, cocket, crouse, dapper, frisky, nimble, snappy 7 allegro(It.), animate, animato(It.), buoyant, chipper 8 animated, galliard, spirited 9 energetic, sprightly, vivacious
liven: 5 cheer 7 animate 8 brighten
liver: 4 foie 5 hepar 8 tomalley
disease: 9 cirrhosis, hepatitis
fluid: 4 bile
pert. to: 7 hepatic
liverwort: 4 moss 8 agrimony, hepatica 9 bryophyte
genus: 6 riccia
livery: 7 uniform 8 clothing
livestock: 6 cattle 7 chattel
livid: 4 blae, blue 5 bleak 10 discolored
living: 4 keep 5 alive, being, vivid 6 extant 7 animate 8 animated, benefice 10 livelihood, sustenance 11 subsistence
again: 6 reborn 9 redivivus
correct: 7 regimen 11 orthobiosis
off others: 8 entozoic 9 parasitic, raptorial
together: 11 contubernal
Livonian river: Aa
lixiviate: 5 leach
lixivium: lye
lizard: dab, eft 4 adda, dabb, dhab, evet, gila, ibid, newt, seps, uran 5 agama, anoli, dhabb, gecko, gekko, goana, scink, skink, varan, waran 6 ameiva, anolis, dragon, goanna, iguana, lacert, moloch, worral, worrel 7 cheecha, geitjie, monitor, saurian, tuatera 8 basilisk 9 chameleon, galliwasp 10 chuckwalla 12 scheltopusik
comb. form: 5 sauro

family: 12 xenosauridae
genus: uta 5 agama 6 ameiva
mammal similar to: 10 salamander
lizard-like: 8 iguanoid
llama: 6 alpaca
habitat: 5 Andes
llanero: 6 cowboy 8 herdsman
llano: 5 plain 7 lowland, prairie
Llyr's son: 4 Bran 7 Branwen
lo: but 4 ecce(L.), look 6 behold 7 observe
load: jag 4 clog, jagg, lade, onus, pack, tote, stow 5 cargo, weigh 6 burden, charge, hamper, lading, steeve, weight 7 fraught, freight, oppress 8 carriage, encumber 9 aggravate, exonerate 10 adulterate 11 encumbrance
small: jag 4 jagg 5 hurry
loader: 9 stevedore
loadstone: See **lodestone**
loaf: 4 idle, laze 6 dawdle, loiter, lounge 10 dilly-dally
loafer: bum 4 hood 5 idler 7 flaneur, hoodlum, lounger 8 hooligan, larrikin 11 chairwarmer
loam: 4 rab 4 silt 5 loess, regur(Ind.) 6 cledge
constituent: 4 clay, lime 5 chalk
deposit: 4 silt 5 loess
loan: 4 dhan(Ind.), lend 5 prest 6 borrow 7 advance 10 obligation, provisions 13 accommodation
loan shark: 6 usurer
loath, loth: 6 averse, odious 7 hateful 8 backward 9 reluctant, repulsive, unwilling
loathe: 4 hate 5 abhor 6 detest 7 adverse, condemn, despise, dislike 9 abominate
loathsome: 4 foul, ugly, vile 7 carrion, cloying, hateful 8 abhorent, deformed 9 offensive, repellent, repugnant 10 abominable, detestable, disgusting 11 distasteful
lob: hit 4 bowl, lots, lour, lump, step, till, toss, vein 5 droop, stair, throw 6 propel 7 pollack 9 chandelle
lobate: 8 lobelike
lobby: 4 hall, room 5 foyer 8 anteroom, coulisse 9 enclosure, vestibule
lobbyist: 8 promoter 12 propagandist
lobe: 5 alula 6 alular, earlap, lappet, lobule
lobelike: 6 lobate
loblolly: 4 mush, pine, tree 5 gruel 6 puddle 7 mudhole
lobo: 4 wolf
lobster: *claw:* 5 chela 6 nipper
female: hen
part: 4 claw 6 pincer, telson, thorax
roe: 5 coral
trap: pot 5 creel 6 bownet
lobster pot: pot 4 corf 5 creel, trunk

local: 7 bucolic, endemic, limited, topical **8** regional, specific **10** restricted

locale: 4 loci(pl.), site **5** locus(L.), place, scene **6** region **9** situation

locality: 4 loci(pl.), seat, site, spot **5** locus, place, situs **6** region **7** habitat **8** district, position **12** neighborhood

localize: 7 situate **8** pinpoint

locate (see also **place**): sat **4** espy, find, seat, show, site, spot **5** stand, trace **6** settle **7** situate, station **8** discover **9** establish

located: 7 bestead

locatio: 7 leasing, letting

location: 4 area, seat, site, spot **5** place, scene, situs **6** ubiety **7** habitat **9** situation

loch: bay **4** lake, pond, pool **5** lough

loci: See **locus**

lock: 4 bolt, curl, frib, hank, hasp **5** latch, sasse, tress **6** fasten **7** confine, cowlick **8** fastener
  part: **4** bolt **5** stump **8** cylinder

locker: 6 ascham

lockjaw: 7 tetanus, trismus **11** ankylostoma
  remedy: **11** antitetanic, antitetanus

lockman: 11 executioner

lockup: jug **4** jail **5** clink **6** cooler **7** hoosgow **8** hoosegaw, hoosegow **9** calaboose

loco: mad **4** crazy **6** insane

locomotive: 5 dolly, mogul **6** diesel, dinkey, engine, mallet **8** electric
  part: cab **5** pilot
  service car: **6** tender **7** coalcar

Locrine: *daughter:* **7** Sabrina
  father: **4** Brut

locus: 4 area, site **5** place **8** locality

locust: 5 bruke, cicad **6** cicada, cicala, cigala **11** grasshopper
  wingless: **4** weta

locust bird: 7 grackle **8** starling

locust plant: 5 senna

locust tree: 5 carob **6** acacia

locustberry: 5 drupe, nance **9** glamberry

lode: 4 path, road, vein **5** canal, drain, ledge **6** course **7** deposit, fissure **8** waterway
  cavity: vug **4** vugg, vugh

lodestone, loadstone: 6 magnet **7** adamant **8** terrella **9** magnetite

lodge: dig, lie **4** club **5** board, couch, dwell, hogan **6** alight, bestow, encamp, hostel **7** deposit **8** harbinge **11** brotherhood

lodger: 5 guest **6** roomer, tenant

lodging: bed, hut, inn **4** camp, gite(F.), host, howf, nest, room, tent **5** abode, cabin, hotel, house, hovel, howff **6** billet, tavern, teepee, wigwam **7** mansion **8** barracks, dwelling, hostelry, quarters **9** dormitory, harborage, residence **10** habitation, harbourage
  cost: **4** rent

loess: 4 loam, silt

loft: bin **4** balk **5** attic

lofty: 4 aery, epic, high, tall **5** aerie, elate, grand, noble, proud, steep **6** aerial, Andean, andine **7** Andesic, arduous, eminent, haughty, sublime **8** arrogant, assuming, elevated, eloquent, majestic **9** cockhorse, dignified, overproud **11** magisterial, mountainous

log: 4 clog, wood **5** diary **6** billet, loggat, logget, record, timber **7** journal
  kind: **4** slab **5** splat **8** puncheon
  mass: **5** drive
  revolve: **4** birl **7** logroll

log gin: 6 jammer

logarithm: *unit:* bel
  inventor: **6** Napier

loge: box **4** room **5** booth, stall

logger: 6 sniper **9** lumberman **10** lumberjack, woodcutter **11** woodchopper
  boot: pac **4** pack

loggerhead: 4 head **6** turtle **9** blockhead

loggerheads: 4 odds, outs

loggets, loggats: 4 game

loggia: 7 gallery

logging: *sled:* **4** tode **7** travois **8** travoise
  tool: **4** pevy **5** peavy, peevy **6** nigger, peavey

logic: 9 reasoning
  inductive: **7** epagoge
  specious: **7** sophism
  term: **5** ferio, lemma **7** ferison

logical: 4 sane **5** sound, valid **8** coherent, rational **10** consistent, reasonable

logion: 5 maxim, motto **6** saying **11** observation

logograph: 5 rebus **6** puzzle, riddle **7** anagram

logroll: 4 birl

logy: 4 dull **5** heavy **6** drowsy **8** sluggish

lohan: 4 monk **5** Arhat

Lohengrin: *character:* **4** Elsa **8** Parsifal
  composer: **6** Wagner

loincloth: 5 pagne

loir: 8 dormouse

Loire: *river:* **5** Liger
  town: **6** Nantes

loiter: lag **4** idle, loaf **5** dally, delay, drawl, shool, tarry **6** cooter, dawdle, linger **7** saunter **8** hesitate

loiterer: 4 slug **5** drone, idler **7** laggard **8** sluggard

Loki: *child:* Hel **4** Hela, Nare, Nari
  mother: **9** Angrbodha
  wife: **5** Sigyn

loll: 4 hang **5** droop, tarry **6** dangle, froust, frowst, lounge, sprawl **7** recline

loma: 4 hill

lombard: 6 cannon

Lombardy: *king:* **6** Alboin

lake: 4 Como
lomilomi: rub 7 massage, shampoo
lomita: 4 hill
London: *bus conductor:* 6 clippy
  coffee shop: 5 Wills
  district: 4 Soho 5 Acton 7 Adelphi, Alsatia, Mayfair
  fish market: 12 Billingsgate
  gallery: 4 Tate
  monument: Gog 5 Magog 8 Cenotaph
  porter: 6 George 8 Georgina
  promenade: 4 Mall
  roisterer: mun
  society: 7 Mayfair
  square: 9 Leicester
  stables: 4 mews
  street: 4 Bond 6 Savile 7 Wardour 9 Cheapside, Haymarket
  suburb: Kew
  theater: 7 Adelphi
  timepiece: 6 Big Ben
Londoner: 7 Cockney
lone: 4 sole 5 alone, apart 6 single 7 retired 8 solitary 9 unmarried 12 unfrequented
Lone Ranger's companion: 5 Tonto
Lone Star State: 5 Texas
loneliness: 8 solitude 9 dejection, isolation 10 depression, desolation 12 lonesomeness
lonely: 4 lorn, sole 5 alone, apart 6 dismal, dreary 7 deavely, forlorn 8 deserted, desolate, lonesome, secluded, solitary 11 sequestered 12 unfrequented
long: far 4 hone, hope, pine 5 yearn 6 aspire, hanker, hunger, prolix, thirst 7 lengthy, tedious 8 extended, tiresome 9 elongated, prolonged, wearisome 10 protracted
  and slender: 5 lathy, reedy 6 linear 9 elongated
  for: 4 miss, want, wish 5 covet, crave 6 desire
long ago: 4 yore
long dozen: 8 thirteen
long-suffering: 7 patient 8 patience 9 endurance 10 forbearing
long-winded: 6 prolix 9 garrulous
longe: 4 rein, rope 5 guide, strap, trout 8 exercise
Longfellow hero: 8 Hiawatha
longheaded: 4 wise 6 shrewd 10 hardheaded 11 foresighted
longing: yen 6 desire 7 athirst, craving, wistful 8 appetite, cupidity, yearning 9 nostalgia 10 desiderium
longitudinally: 7 endlong 10 lengthwise
longshoreman: 9 stevedore
loo: pam 8 napoleon
look: lo; con, pry, see 4 gaze, leer, ogle, peek, peep, peer, pore, scan, seem, skew 5 blush, dekko, fleer, glare, gliff, glime, gloat, gloom, glout, lower, sight, smile, snoop,

stare 6 aspect, behold, gander, glance, glower, glunch, regard, search, squint, visage 7 observe 8 demeanor 10 appearance
look after: 4 tend 6 attend
look at: eye, see 4 glom, view 6 behold, regard 7 examine, observe
look back: 6 recall, relive, review 7 rethink 8 remember 10 retrospect
look down on: 7 despise
look for: 4 seek 5 await 6 expect 10 anticipate
look forward to: 5 await 6 expect 10 anticipate
look into: 5 study 7 examine, inspect 11 investigate
look like: 8 resemble
look over: 6 ignore, survey 8 overlook 9 disregard 11 reconnoiter, reconnoitre
look toward: 4 face
looker-on: 8 audience, beholder 9 bystander, spectator
lookout: 6 conner 7 atalaya(P.I.) 8 bantayan(P.I.), cockatoo 10 watchtower
looks (see also **look**): 4 face 8 features 10 attraction
loom: auk 4 hulk, loon, tool 5 dobby, weave 6 appear, emerge, gentle, puffin, vessel 7 machine 9 guillemot, implement 10 receptacle
  part: bar, lam 4 caam, leaf, reed, sley 5 easer, lathe 6 hanger, heddle 7 harness
loon: nut, sap 4 dolt, lout 5 diver, rogue, scamp, wabby 6 cobble, rascal
loop: eye, tab 4 ansa, coil, fold, hank, kink, knot, oese 5 bight, bride, coque, honda, hondo, noose, picot, terry 6 becket, billet, circle 7 circuit, curette, folding 8 doubling 11 aiguillette
loop-shaped: 9 fundiform
loophole: out 4 muse 5 meuse, oilet 6 escape, eyelet 7 opening 8 aperture, weakness
loose: gay, lax 4 floa, free, open 5 baggy, bulgy, crank, loose, relax, slack, vague 6 coarse, dangly, random, unlash, wobbly 7 immoral, movable, relaxed, unbound, unleash 8 insecure, unstable, withdraw 9 desultory, dissolute, unbridled, unchecked 10 indefinite, licentious, unattached, unconfined, unfastened 11 untrammeled 12 uncontrolled, unrestrained 14 unconventional
loose ends: 4 dags 5 bored 7 tagrags 8 restless
loose-jointed: 5 lanky, rangy 6 clumsy, wobbly 7 rickety 10 ramshackle
loosen: pry 4 ease, free, undo 5 relax, untie 7 slacken 8 liberate, unfasten 9 disengage, extricate 11 disentangle

loot: rob, sum 4 sack, swag 5 booty, strip 6
pilfer, ravage, spoils 7 pillage, plunder
receipt of: 9 theftbote

lop: bob, cut, dod 4 clip, flop, hang, sned(Sc.),
snip, trim 5 droop, prune, slice 6 dangle 7
pendant, pendent 8 truncate

lope: jog 4 gait 6 canter 7 dogtrot

lopper: 4 clot 6 curdle 7 clabber 9 coagulate

lopsided: 4 alop 7 crooked 10 unbalanced

loquacious: 5 gabby 6 verbal 7 prating 8
cackling 9 garrulous, talkative 10 babblative, chattering

loquacity: 9 garrulity

loquat: 4 biwa

lord: aga 4 agha, earl, peer, rule, tsar 5 liege,
ruler 6 domine, master, prince 7 marquis,
vavasor 8 domineer, governor, nobleman,
seigneur, suzerain, vavasour, viscount 9
dominator
attendant: 5 thane

Lord have mercy upon us: 5 Kyrie 12 Kyrie eleison

Lord High Executioner: 4 Koko

Lord Jim author: 6 Conrad

Lord's Prayer: 11 Paternoster

lordly: 5 proud 6 uppish 8 arrogant, despotic
9 imperious, masterful 10 tyrannical 11
dictatorial, domineering, magisterial,
overbearing

lordship: 7 dynasty 10 allegiance

lore: 4 lear 6 advice, wisdom 7 counsel 8
learning 9 erudition, knowledge, tradition
11 instruction

Lorelei: 5 siren

lorgnette: 8 eyeglass 10 opera glass

lorica: 5 shell 7 cuirass 8 corselet

lorikeet: 6 parrot

loriot: 6 oriole

loris: 5 lemur

lorn: 6 bereft 7 forlorn 8 desolate, forsaken,
lonesome 9 abandoned

Lorraine: *capital:* 4 Metz
river: 4 Saar

lose: 4 amit, fail, miss 5 waste 6 defeat, mislay 7 forfeit 9 dissipate

losel: bum 6 loafer 10 ne'er-do-well

loss: 4 cost, leak, ruin, toll 5 price, waste 6
damage, damnum, defeat, injury, ullage 7
expense, failure 8 amission, decrease 9
decrement, detriment, privation 10 affliction, bankruptcy 11 bereavement, deper-
dition, deprivation, destruction

lost: 4 gone, lorn 5 perdu(F.) 6 absent, hidden, ruined 7 forlorn, mislaid, strayed 8
absorbed, confused, defeated, estrayed, ob-
scured, prodigal 9 abandoned, forfeited,
perplexed, reprobate, subverted 10 abstracted, bewildered, dissipated, over-
thrown 11 preoccupied 13 irreclaimable

Lost Horizon author: 6 Hilton

lot: hap 4 dole, doom, fate, land, luck, much,
plat, plot 5 batch, field, grist, group, share,
weird 6 amount, bundle, chance, divide,
hazard, parcel 7 destiny, fortune, portion
8 caboodle, quantity 9 allotment, apportion 13 apportionment
appointment by: 9 sortition
miscellaneous: 6 fardel, joblot

Lot: *father:* 5 Haran
grandson: 7 Moabite
nephew: 7 Abraham
place of flight: 5 Sodom
sister: 6 Milcah
son: 4 Moab

lotion: 4 balm, wash 6 loture 8 ablution,
linament

lots: 4 gobs 5 scads 6 plenty

lottery: 6 raffle 10 sweepstake

lotto: 4 keno 5 bingo, keeno

lotus, lotos: 7 nelumbo 10 chinquapin

lotus bird: 6 jacana

lotus tree: 4 sadr 9 persimmon

loud: 5 gaudy, heavy, noisy, showy, vivid 6
coarse, flashy, vulgar 7 blatant, clamant,
obvious, raucous 8 emphatic, strepent, vehement 9 clamorous, insistent, turbulent,
unrefined 10 blustering, boisterous, stentorian, tumultuous, vociferous 11 thersiti-
cal 12 obstreperous

louder: 9 crescendo

lough: sea 4 lake, loch, pool 5 water

Louisiana: *county:* 6 parish
decree: 5 arret
dialect: 6 creole
native: 5 Cajun 6 creole
parish: 4 Winn 5 Allen, Caddo, Union 6
Acadia, De Soto, Iberia, Sabine, Tensas,
Vernon 9 Iberville, Vermilion 10 Evangeline 11 Plaquemines
town: 4 Begg 6 Gretna 10 Shreveport
university: LSU 6 Tulane

lounge: 4 idle, loaf, loll, sofa 5 bange, couch,
divan, relax 6 froust, frowst, loiter

loup: 4 flee, jump, leap

louse: nit 5 aphid, aphis 6 cootie, slater

lousy: 9 pedicular 10 pediculous

lout: bow, oaf 4 bend, boor, clod, coof, dolt,
fool, gaum, gawk, hulk 5 clown, cuddy,
stoop, yahoo, yokel 6 curtsy, lubber 7
bumpkin, grobian

loutish: 4 rude 5 crude 6 clumsy, gauche(F.),
stupid 7 awkward

lovable, loveable: 4 dear 7 amative, amiable 8 adorable, dovelike 9 endearing

love: gra(Ir.), loe(Sc.), loo(Sc.) 4 dear, dote,
like 5 adore, aloha, amore(It.), amour(F.),
Cupid, fancy, liebe(G.), lover 6 enamor 7

charity, embrace, idolize **8** fondness, goodwill, idolatry **9** adoration, affection **10** attachment, sweetheart **11** inclination

comb. form: **4** phil **5** philo

god of: **4** Amor, Ares, Eros, Kama **5** Bhaga, Cupid

goddess of: **5** Athor, Freya, Venus **6** Freyja, Hathor, Ishtar **9** Aphrodite

science of: **9** erotology

token of: **6** amoret

love apple: 6 tomato

love feast: 5 agape **7** banquet **9** gathering

love knot: 6 amoret

love-potion: 5 charm **7** philter, philtre **11** aphrodisiac

love story: 7 romance

lovebird: 6 parrot

loveliness: 6 beauty **11** pulchritude

lovelock: 4 curl **5** tress **12** heartbreaker

lovely: 5 sweet **6** loving, tender **7** amiable, amorous, angelic **8** adorable, angelina, charming, graceful **9** beautiful **10** attractive

lover: ami(F.), gra(Ir.) **4** beau, chap **5** amant(F.), leman, Romeo **6** adorer, amadis, amante(F., fem.), bonami **7** admirer, amateur, amorist, amoroso, Don Juan, gallant **8** belamour, Lothario **9** bonne amie(fem.), enamorata, inamorata **10** dilettante, sweetheart **11** philanderer

meeting place: **5** tryst

patron saint: **9** Valentine

rustic: **7** Celadon

lovesick: 6 pining **7** longing **11** languishing

loving: 4 fond **6** erotic, lovely **7** adorant, amative, amatory, amorous **9** affecting **12** affectionate

comb. form: **4** phil **5** phile

loving cup: tig, tyg **5** prize

low: bas(F.), moo **4** base, bass, blue, deep, hill, mean, neap **5** dirty, gross, snide **6** bellow, coarse, common, earthy, feeble, filthy, humble, humbly, slight, sordid, vulgar **7** bestial, ignoble, plebian, shallow, slavish **8** dejected **9** depressed, earthbred **10** melancholy **11** undignified, unfavorable **12** contemptible, disreputable

lowan: 4 bird **6** leipoa, mallee

Low Country: 7 Belgium, Holland **9** Luxemburg **11** Netherlands

low-lived: 4 mean **10** despicable **12** contemptible

low-necked: 9 decollete

low tide: ebb **4** neap

lowbred: 5 crude **6** coarse, vulgar **11** ill-mannered

lower: dip **4** alow, bate, drop, sink, vail **5** abase, abate, baser, below, decry, demit, frown, glare, scowl, under **6** bemean, debase, deepen, demean, derate, glower,

humble, lessen, meaner, nether, reduce **7** beneath, degrade, depress, descend, subside **8** diminish, downward **9** disparage **10** depreciate, nethermore

lowering: 4 dark **5** heavy **6** beetle, cloudy, gloomy, lowery, sullen **8** overcast **11** threatening

lowest: 5 least, nadir **6** bottom **7** bedrock **10** nethermost

lowing (see also **low**): **7** mugient **9** bellowing

lowland: 4 flat, holm, spit **5** terai(Ind.) **6** valley **7** bottoms

Lowlander (see also **Scotland**): **4** Scot **9** Sassenach

language: **6** Lallan **7** Lalland

lowly: 4 base, mean, meek **6** humble, modest **7** ignoble **12** unpretending **13** unpretentious

lox: 6 salmon

loy: 4 tool **5** spade

loyal: 4 feal, firm, leal, true **5** liege, pious **6** stanch **7** devoted, staunch **8** constant, faithful

loyalty: 6 homage **10** allegiance

Loyalty island: Uea **4** Lifu, Uvea

Loyolite: 6 Jesuit

lozenge: 4 pill **5** candy **6** jujube, pastil, tablet, troche **7** diamond **8** pastille

lubber: 4 boor, gawk, lout **5** churl, drone **8** landsman

lubricate: oil **4** dope **6** grease **7** moisten

lubricous: 4 lewd **6** shifty, tricky, wanton **7** elusive **8** slippery, unstable **10** lascivious

luce: 4 pike

lucent: 5 clear, lucid **6** bright **7** shining **11** translucent, transparent

lucerne, lucern: 7 alfalfa

lucid: 4 sane **5** clear **6** bright, lucent **7** crystal, shining **8** luminous, pellucid **11** resplendent, translucent

lucidity: 6 sanity **7** clarity

Lucifer: 5 devil, Satan

luck: hap, lot, ure **4** cess, eure, fate **5** deuce **6** chance, hansel **7** ambsace, fortune, handsel, success **8** fortuity **9** mischance

bringer: **5** Jonah **6** clover, mascot **9** horseshoe **10** rabbit-foot

stroke of: **5** fluke

token for: **5** charm **6** amulet, mascot **7** periapt

lucky: 5 canny, happy, sonsy **6** sonsie **8** gracious **9** fortunate **10** propitious, prosperous, successful **12** providential

lucrative: 6 paying **7** gainful **10** beneficial, productive, profitable **12** remunerative

lucre: 4 gain, loot, pelf **5** booty, money **6** profit, riches, wealth

ludicrous: 5 antic, awful, comic, droll, funny 6 absurd 7 comical, foolish, risible 8 farcical 9 burlesque, laughable 10 ridiculous

luff: 4 sail

lug: box, ear 4 drag, draw, pull, tote, worm, haul 5 carry 10 projection

lugubrious: sad 6 dismal 7 doleful 8 mournful

lukewarm: 5 tepid

lull: 4 calm, hush, rock 5 allay, quiet, still 6 pacify, soothe 7 compose 8 calmness, mitigate 9 cessation 11 tranquilize

lullaby: 5 baloo, balow

lumber: 4 raff, wood 6 refuse, timber

lumbering: 7 awkward

lumberman: 6 logger, sawyer, scorer 10 lumberjack

boot: pac

hook: 5 peavy 6 peavey

sled: 4 tode 7 travois 8 travoise

luminary: sun 4 star 5 light 12 illumination, intellectual

lumine: 5 light 8 illumine

luminous: 5 clear, lucid 6 bright 7 shining 9 brilliant 11 illuminated, transparent 14 phosphorescent

lummox: 4 boor, lout 5 yahoo 7 bumpkin, bungler

lump: bat, cob, dab, dad, dot, gob, nub, wad 4 beat, blob, burl, cake, clog, clot, daud, heap, hump, hunk, knob, knot, mass 5 bulge, claut, clump, clunk, hunch, wedge 6 dollop, gobbet, nodule, nugget 12 protuberance

lumpfish: 6 paddle

lumpish: 4 dull 5 heavy, inert 6 stodgy, stupid 8 sluggish 9 shapeless

lumpy: 5 rough 6 choppy

lunacy: 5 folly, mania 7 madness 8 delirium, insanity 9 craziness 11 derangement

lunar (see also **moon**): 6 lunate 8 crescent 9 satellite

lunatic: mad 6 insane, madman 7 frantic 8 demoniac 9 bedlamite 10 moonstruck

lune: 5 leash 8 crescent

lung: *comb. form:* 5 pulmo

disease: 11 anthracosis

having: 9 pulmonate

sound: 4 rale

lunge: jab 4 foin, leap, stab 5 barge, longe, lurch, pitch 6 plunge, thrust

luny: 5 crazy 8 demented

lupine: 6 fierce 7 wolfish 8 ravenous, wolflike

lurch: rob 4 jolt, reel 5 barge, cheat, fraud, lunge, pitch, steal, trick 6 careen, career, swerve 7 stumble

lure: 4 bait, draw, trap 5 decoy, snare, tempt 6 allure, entice, seduce 7 attract, beguile, pitfall 8 inveigle 10 allurement, attraction, enticement

lurer: 4 bait 5 siren 7 trapper

lurid: wan 4 pale 5 gaudy, livid 6 dismal, gloomy 7 ghastly, hideous 8 gruesome, shocking, terrible

lurk: 4 hide 5 skulk, slink, sneak 6 ambush

luscious: 4 rich, ripe 5 sweet 6 creamy 7 cloying 8 delicate 9 delicious 10 voluptuous

lush: 4 soft 5 drunk 6 limber, mellow 9 alcoholic, luxuriant, succulent 11 intoxicated

lusory: 7 playful 8 sportive

lust: 6 desire, liking 7 passion 8 appetite, cupidity 11 inclination

luster, lustre: 4 cave, naif 5 sheen, shine, water 6 polish 7 glister 8 schiller, splendor 11 distinction, iridescence

lusterless: mat, wan 4 dead, dull 5 faded, fishy 6 gloomy 9 tarnished

lustful: hot 4 gamy, lewd 5 cadgy 7 fulsome, rammish 9 lecherous, salacious

lustrous: 5 nitid 6 glossy, orient 7 radiant 8 nitidous 9 brilliant 11 illustrious, transparent

lusty: 4 cant 5 crank, frack, frank, freck, hardy 6 cranky, gawsie, robust, strong, sturdy 8 bouncing, vigorous

lute: tar 4 clay, ring 6 cement 7 dyphone 10 instrument

luxe: 8 elegance, richness

Luxemburg: *measure:* 5 fuder

river: 7 Moselle

luxuriant: 4 lush, rank, rich 5 frank 6 lavish 7 fertile, opulent, profuse, teeming 8 prolific 9 exuberant 10 voluptuous

luxuriate: 4 bask, riot 5 revel

luxurious: 4 posh, rich 5 gaudy 6 costly 7 elegant, opulent 8 gorgeous, sensuous 9 sumptuous 11 comfortable, extravagant

luxury: 8 delicacy

lover of: 8 Sybarite

Luzon: *city:* 5 Gapan 6 Ilagan 10 Cabanatuan

dialect: 6 Itaves

mountain: Iba

people: Ata, Ita 4 Aeta, Atta 5 Tagal 6 Aripas, Arupas, Igorot, Isinay, Itaneg 7 Igorote, Italone, Tagalog

seaport: 6 Aparri, Manila

volcano: 5 Mayon

lyam: 5 leash 10 bloodhound

lycanthrope: 8 werewolf

lycee: 6 lyceum, school

Lycian city: 4 Myra 6 Sardis

Lydia: *king:* 5 Gyges 7 Croesus

river: 8 Pactolus

lye: 6 potash 7 caustic 8 lixivium

pert. to: 8 lixivial

lying: 4 flat 5 awald, awalt, prone 6 supine 8 couchant 9 dishonest, mendacity 10 pseudology

lying-in: 11 confinement 12 accouchement

lymph: sap 5 water 6 plasma, spring

lynch: 4 hang 6 murder 7 execute

Lynette's knight: 6 Gareth

lynx: cat 5 pishu 6 bobcat, lucern 7 caracal 8 carcajou

Lyra star: 4 Vega

lyrate: 9 spatulate

lyre: 4 asor, harp 6 kissar, trigon 7 cithara, kithara, testudo

lyre turtle: 11 leatherback

lyric: lai, lay, ode 4 alba, odic, poem 5 epode, gazel, melic 6 ghazel, poetic, rondel 7 cancion, canzone(It.), descort, rondeau 9 dithyramb

   Muse: 5 Erato 8 Polymnia 10 Polyhymnia

lyrical: 6 epodic 7 sestina

lyrichord: 11 harpsichord

lyssa: 6 rabies 11 hydrophobia

M

Maacah: *father:* Talmai
  husband: 5 David 8 Rehoboam
  son: Asa 6 Abijah 7 Absalom
mabolo: 4 plum 7 camagon
macabre: 4 eery, grim 5 eerie 7 ghastly 8
  grewsome, gruesome 9 deathlike
macaca: 5 lemur 6 monkey
macadam: tar 8 pavement
macaque: 4 bruh 6 monkey, rhesus
macaw: ara 4 arra, bird 5 arara 6 parrot 7
  maracan 8 aracanga, ararauna
Macbeth: *character:* 5 Angus 6 Banquo
  title: 5 Thane
  victim: 6 Duncan
maccaboy: 5 snuff
mace: dod, rod 4 club, maul, rush 5 spice,
  staff 6 mallet 7 swindle
  bearer: 6 beadle
  royal: 7 scepter, sceptre
Macedonia: *king:* 5 Abgar
  mountain: 5 Athos 7 Olympus 8 Olympiad
  people: 6 Greeks 8 Serbians 9 Albanians 10
   Bulgarians
  statesman: 9 Antipater
macer: 6 beadle, bearer 8 swindler
macerate: ret 4 soak 5 steep
machete: 4 bolo, fish 5 blade, knife 6 guitar
Machiavellian: 4 wily 6 crafty 7 cunning 8
  guileful 9 deceitful 11 treacherous
Machiavelli's book: 6 Prince
machila: 7 hammock
machin: 7 macaque
machinate: 4 plan, plot 5 cabal 6 scheme
machination: 4 plan, plot 5 cabal 6 scheme
  8 artifice, intrigue 10 conspiracy 11 contrivance
machine: car 4 auto 5 robot 6 device, engine
  9 apparatus, appliance, automatic, automaton, mechanism 10 automobile 11 contrivance, machination 12 organization
  hydraulic: 9 telemotor
  part: cam 5 rotor, wheel 6 piston, stator,
   tappet
machine gun: 4 Sten 5 Maxim 7 Gatling 9
  Hotchkiss 10 chatterbox

  place: 4 nest
macilent: 4 lean, thin 9 emaciated
mackeral: 4 scad 5 akule, atule, tunny 7
  escolar, tassard 8 hardhead
  genus: 7 scomber
  net: 7 spiller
  young: 5 spike 6 tinker 7 blinker
mackerel bird: 7 wryneck 9 kittiwake
mackle: See macula
macle: 8 chrystal 11 chiastolite
macula: 4 blot, blur, spot 5 stain 6 blotch,
  mackle, macule 7 blemish
maculate: 6 defile, impure 7 speckle 8 besmirch
mad: 4 gite, gyte, hyte(Sc.) 5 angry, crazy,
  folle, irate, rabid, vexed 6 frenzy, insane 7
  enraged, foolish, frantic, furious 8 demented, frenetic, incensed, maniacal 9
  desperate, fanatical, hilarious, phrenetic,
  psychotic 10 distracted, distraught, infatuated, infuriated 11 fantastical 12 arreptitious, unreasonable
Madagascar: *animal:* 6 aye-aye, tanrec,
  tenrec 7 tendrac
  city: 7 Mojanga 8 Tamatave 10 Tananarive,
   Tananarivo 12 Antananarivo(c.)
  civet: 7 fossane
  island group: 7 Aldabra
  lemur: 5 avahi, indri 6 aye-aye 9 babacoote
  measure: 7 gantang
  native: 4 Hova 8 Sakalava
  palm: 6 raffia
  people: 4 Hova
  tree: 11 antankarana
  tribe: 4 Bara 5 Hovas 8 Betsileo, Malagasy,
   Sakalava 13 Betsimasaraka
madam, madame: Mme., Mrs. 4 bawd, lady
  5 donna, hussy, title, wench 6 senora 8
  mistress 9 courtesan
madcap: 4 wild 7 hotspur 8 reckless
madder: al; aal 7 munjeet 8 dyestuff
  family: 9 rubiaceae
made: 10 artificial
Madeira: *capital:* 7 Funchal

wine: 4 bual 5 tinta, tinto 7 malmsey, sercial 8 verdelho

mademoiselle: 4 miss

madhouse: 5 chaos 6 asylum, bedlam 8 bughouse

madid: wet 5 moist

madman: 6 maniac 7 furioso, lunatic 8 frenetic 9 phrenetic, psychotic

madness: ire 4 fury 5 folly, furor, mania 6 bedlam, frenzy, lunacy, rabies 7 dewanee, ecstasy, widdrim 8 delirium, dementia, insanity 9 amazement, furiosity, nosomania, phrenetic 11 derangement

Madras: *district:* 7 Malabar, Nellore

hemp: 4 sunn

measure: 4 para 5 cawny, manei, parah 6 cawney, mercal, ollock, olluck, parrah, puddee

town: 5 Adoni, Arcot 7 Calicut

weight: ser 4 cash, powe, seer 5 fanam 6 pagoda, pollam 7 chinnam, varahan 8 mangelin

madrepore: 5 coral 6 fossil

Madrid promenade: 5 Prado

madrigal: ode 4 glee, poem 5 lyric 6 verses

Maecenas: 6 patron

maelstrom: 4 eddy 5 swirl 7 current, turmoil 9 whirlpool

maenad: 9 bacchante

maestro: 6 master 7 teacher 8 composer 9 conductor 10 bandleader 11 choirmaster 13 kapellmeister

di-cappella: 11 choirmaster 13 kapellmeister

maffle: 6 muddle, mumble 7 confuse, stammer 8 bewilder, squander

mag: 4 chat 6 magpie 7 chatter, magneto 8 titmouse 9 halfpenny 10 chatterbox

Magadha king: 9 Bimbisara 10 Ajatasatru

magadis: 5 flute 9 monochord

magazine: 4 pulp 5 depot 7 almacen, arsenal, chamber, journal 9 ephemeris, reservoir, warehouse 10 periodical, repository, storehouse 11 armamentary

mage: See **magician**

magenta: dye 7 fuchsia

maggot: 4 grub, mawk, whim 5 larva, mathe 6 gentle, notion 7 caprice

magi: 5 Sages 6 Gaspar 8 Melchior 9 Balthasar

gift of: 4 gold 5 myrrh 12 frankincense

magic: art 4 rune 5 fairy, obeah, spell, turgy 6 glamor, voodoo 7 glamour, gramary, sorcery 8 brujeria(Sp.), gramarye 9 deception, diablerie 10 necromancy, witchcraft 11 conjuration, enchantment, legerdemain, thaumaturgy 12 invultuation

act of: 11 conjuration

lantern: 11 epidiascope 12 stereopticon

perform: hex 6 sorcer 7 conjure

pert. to: 6 goetic

staff: 4 wand 7 rhabdos 8 caduceus

symbol: 5 charm 6 caract 8 pentacle

tree: 13 polemoniaceae

word: om, um 5 selah 6 presto, sesame, shelah 11 abracadabra

Magic Mountain: *author:* 4 Mann

character: 7 Castorp

magical: 5 goety 6 goetic, occult 8 charming 10 bewitching 11 necromantic

magician: 4 mage, magi 5 magus 6 goetic, Merlin, wabeno, wizard 7 juggler 8 conjurer, conjuror, mandrake, sorcerer 9 archimage, charlatan, enchanter 11 entertainer, necromancer, thaumaturge 13 thaumaturgist 15 prestidigitator

assistant: 6 famuli(pl.) 7 famulus

manual: 8 grimoire

motion: 4 pass

magirist: 4 cook

magisterial: 5 lofty, proud 6 august, lordly 7 haughty, stately 8 arrogant, dogmatic 9 dignified, imperious 11 dictatorial, domineering, overbearing 13 authoritative

magistrate: 4 beak, doge 5 edile, judge 6 alcade, alcaid, archon, bailie, bailli, syndic 7 alcalde, alcaide, bailiff, burgess, podesta(It.) 8 alderman, governor, mittimus, official 11 burgomaster

orders: 4 acta(pl.) 5 actum

magma: 4 rock 5 dregs 8 sediment

basalt: 10 limburgite

magnanimous: big 4 free 5 lofty, noble 6 heroic 7 exalted, liberal 8 generous 9 honorable, unselfish, unstinted 10 highminded, high-souled 13 disinterested

magnate: 4 lord 5 mogul, noble 6 bashaw, tycoon 7 grandee, richman 10 clarissimo 11 millionaire

magnesian limestone: 8 dolomite

magnesium: *silicate:* 4 talc

sulphate: 7 loweite

symbol: Mg

magnet: 7 terella 8 solenoid, terrella 9 loadstone, lodestone

end: 4 pole

pole: red

type of: bar 9 horseshoe

magnetic: 5 polar 10 electrical

unit: 5 weber

magnetize: 4 lure 7 attract 9 captivate

magnific: 4 vast 5 grand 7 pompous, sublime

magnificent: 4 rial, rich 5 grand, great, noble, regal 6 august, lavish 7 exalted, stately, sublime 8 glorious, gorgeous, palatial, splendid, striking 9 beautiful, sumptuous 10 munificent

magnificence: 4 pomp

magnify: 4 laud 5 exalt, extol 6 praise 7 enhance, enlarge, glorify, greaten 8 increase 9 aggravate, overstate 10 exaggerate

magniloquent: 6 turgid 9 bombastic 13 grandiloquent

magnitude: 4 bulk, mass, size 6 extent 7 bigness 9 dimension, greatness

magnolia: 5 yulan

magnum: 6 bottle

magnum opus: 4 work 11 achievement

magot: ape 6 figure

magpie: daw, mag, pie 4 pica, piet, piot, pyat, pyet 5 madge, ninut, scold 9 chatterer, haggister
  diver: 4 smew
  shrike: 7 tanager

magsman: 8 swindler

maguari: 5 stork

maguey: 4 aloe 5 agave, plant 7 cantala

magus: 4 magi 8 magician

Magyar: 6 Ugrian 9 Hungarian

maha: 4 deer

mahajan: 11 moneylender

mahala: 5 squaw

mahogany: 4 toon 6 acajou, totara 7 albarco, gunnung 8 bangalay 9 cailcedra

maholi: 5 lemur

Mahomet: See **Mohammed**

Mahometan: See **Muslim**

Mahound: 5 devil 8 Mohammed

mahout: 6 driver, keeper

mahu: 5 devil

mahua butter: 6 phulwa

Maia's son: 6 Hermes

maid: may 4 ayah, girl, help, lass 5 bonne, woman 6 damsel, maiden, slavey, virgin 7 Abigail, ancilla, colleen, servant 8 domestic, suivante 9 attendant, cameriera, tirewoman
  changed to heifer: Io
  changed to spider: 7 Arachne
  mythical: 5 nymph

Maid of Astolat: 6 Elaine

Maid of Orleans: 4 Joan 7 Pucelle

maiden: deb 4 girl, jill, lass 5 nymph, sylph 6 damsel 7 damosel, damozel 8 damozell 9 damosella, damoysell, debutante

maiden duck: 8 shoveler

maiden name: nee

maidenhair: 4 fern 8 adiantum
  tree: 6 ginkgo

maidenly: 6 gentle, modest, virgin

mail: bag 4 post, send, ship 6 wallet 8 dispatch
  boat: 6 packet
  coat: see **armor**

maim: 4 hurt 6 mangle 7 cripple, disable 8 mutilate 9 dismember

main: sea 4 duct, high, pipe 5 chief, first, grand, ocean, prime 7 capital, conduct, conduit, leading, purpose 8 foremost 9 principal

main gauche: 6 dagger

Main Street author: 5 Lewis

Maine: *bay:* 5 Casco 13 Passamaquoddy
  bird: 9 chickadee
  city: 4 Bath, Milo, Saco 5 Hiram, Orono 6 Bangor 7 Augusta(c.) 9 Skowhegan
  county: 5 Waldo
  lake: 5 Moose 6 Sebago
  motto: 6 dirigo
  mountain: 5 Kineo 8 Katahdin
  port: 6 Bangor 8 Portland
  river: 4 Saco 8 Kennebec
  symbol: 4 pine
  university town: 5 Orono

mainferre: 5 armor 8 gauntlet

mainland: 8 fastland 9 continent

mainsheet: 4 rope

mainstay: key 7 support

maintain: 4 avow, bear, fend, hold, keep 5 argue, claim 6 affirm, allege, assert, avouch, defend, retain, uphold 7 bolster, contend, declare, espouse, justify, support, sustain 8 conserve, preserve 9 vindicate
  again: 8 reassert

maintainable: 7 tenable

maintenance: 5 batta 6 upkeep 7 alimony, prebend 10 livelihood

maison: 5 house
  de sante: 6 asylum 8 hospital 10 sanatorium

maize: 4 corn, samp 5 grain 7 mealies
  genus: Zea

majagua: hau 4 baru, bola 5 guana 8 balibago 12 algodoncillo

majestic: 5 grand, lofty, noble, regal, royal 6 august, kingly 7 leonine, stately, sublime 8 elevated, imperial, splendid 9 dignified, sovereign 11 magnificent

major: wig 5 chief 7 capital, greater, officer 8 superior 9 principal
  music: dur

major-domo: 7 bailiff, steward 9 seneschal

Majorca city: 5 Palma

majority: age 4 body, more, most 6 quorum 7 greater

make: do; cut, gar(Sc.) 4 coin, form 5 build, force, frame, shape 6 compel, create, invent, render 7 compose, confect, fashion, prepare, produce 8 contrive, generate 9 construct, fabricate 11 manufacture
  suffix: fy; ify

make-believe: 4 sham 5 feign, magic 7 feigned, fiction, pretend 8 pretense

make do: eke 9 improvise

make fun of: rib 5 scoff 8 ridicule

make known: 6 impart, reveal 7 divulge, publish, uncover 8 disclose, discover, proclaim 9 advertise, publicize

make over: 4 redo 6 revamp 9 refashion

make up: 8 complete, cosmetic

make up for: 5 atone 10 compensate

maker: 4 doer 6 author, factor 7 creator 8 declarer, inventor 9 architect 10 originator 12 manufacturer

makeshift: 4 rude 9 temporary

maki: 5 lemur

makluk: 4 seal

mal: bad 4 evil

de mer: 11 seasickness

du pays: 12 homesickness

Malabar: *bark:* 5 ochna

canoe: 5 tonee

monkey: 8 wanderoo

palm: 7 talipot

people: 4 Nair

malacca: 4 cane 5 stick

Malacca: *measure:* 4 asta

weight: kip

malachite: 4 bice 7 azurite, mineral

maladive: ill 4 sick 6 sickly, unwell 9 unhealthy

maladroit: 6 clumsy 7 awkward, unhandy 8 bungling, inexpert

maladventure: 6 mishap 8 escapade

malady (see also **disease**): 7 ailment, illness 8 disorder, sickness 9 affection, complaint, distemper 10 affliction 13 indisposition

malagma: 7 plaster 8 poultice

malanders: 6 eczema

malapert: 4 bold 5 saucy 7 ill-bred 8 impudent 9 unskilled

malapropism: 7 mistake

malapropos: 11 inopportune

malar: 6 zygoma 8 zygomata(pl.) 9 cheekbone

malaria: 4 agie, ague 5 chill, fever, miasm 6 miasma

antidote: 7 quinine

carrier: 8 mosquito 9 anopheles

malarkey: 6 drivel 8 nonsense

malaxate: 5 knead

Malaya: *almond:* 6 kanari

ape: lar

archipelago: See *island* below

boat: 4 proa 5 praam, prahu 6 praham 7 cougnar

buffalo: 7 carabao 8 seladang

Christian: 7 Ilokano

coin: tra 4 trah 7 tampang

condiment: 6 sambal, sambei 7 semball

crane: 5 sarus

disease: 4 amok, lata 5 amuck, latah

form of address: 4 tuan

fruit: 8 rambutan

garment: 6 sarong

island: Aru, Goa, Kei, Oma 4 Bali, Buru, Gaga, Java, Sulu 5 Ambon, Arroe, Arrou, Banca, Banda, Buton, Ceram, Misol, Sangi, Sumba, Timor 6 Boefon, Boeroe, Borneo, Flores, Jilolo, Lombik, Madura, Musool, Sangir, Soemba, Talaur, Waigeu 7 Amboina, Amboyna, Celebes, Morotai, Salwati, Sumatra, Sumbawa 8 Belitong, Billiton, Djailolo, Moluccas, Soembawa, Tanimbar, Tenimber 9 Belitoeng, Halmahera, New Guinea, Singapore, Timorlaut 10 Sandalwood

isthmus: Kra

jacket: 4 baju

knife: 4 cris, kris 5 crise 6 crease, creese, kreese, parang

language: 7 Tagalog

mammal: 10 chevrotain

measure: 4 tael, wang

mountain: 6 Gunong, Gunung

musical instrument: 7 anklong

ox: 5 tsine 7 banteng

palm: 4 ejoo, sago 5 areng 6 arenga, gebang, gomuti, nibong, nibung 7 talipot

parrot: 4 lory 6 lories

people: Ata 5 Bajau, Tagal 6 Aripas Semang 7 Bisayan, Tagalog, Visayan

pepper: 4 siri 5 sirih

pewter: 4 trah

rice field: 5 sawah

state: 5 Kedah, Perak 6 Johore

title: 4 tuan

town: 7 Malacca

tree(see also *palm* above)*:* 4 upas 5 kapur, niepa, terap 6 durian, durion

ungulate: 5 tapir

malconformation: 9 imperfect 16 disproportionate

malcontent: reb 5 rebel 6 uneasy 8 agitator, Frondeur 10 discontent, rebellious 12 discontented

Maldives' capital: 4 Male

male: man, mas 4 gent 5 manly 7 mankind, manlike, mannish 9 masculine

animal: tom 4 buck, bull, hart, jack, stag, stud 8 stallion

figure: 7 telamon

gelded: 4 galt 5 steer 6 eunuch 7 gelding

malediction: ban 5 curse 7 malison, slander 8 anathema 9 blasphemy 11 imprecation 12 denunciation

malefactor: 5 felon 7 convict, culprit 8 criminal, evildoer, offender 9 wrongdoer

malefic: 7 harmful, hurtful 11 mischievous

malevolence: 4 evil, hate 5 pique, spite 6 enmity, hatred, malice, rancor 8 ferocity 9 animosity, hostility, malignity 10 bitterness

malevolent: 4 evil 7 hateful, hostile 9 rancorous 11 ill-disposed

malfeasance: 5 crime, wrong 8 trespass 11 delinquency

malheur: 10 misfortune

malice: 5 pique 6 enmity 9 animosity 13 maliciousness

malicious: 4 evil 5 catty, depit 6 bitter 7 heinous 8 sinister, spiteful 9 felonious, malignant, rancorous, resentful 10 calumnious, despiteful, despiteous, malevolent 11 ill-disposed 12 cantankerous, unpropitious

action: 5 arson 8 sabotage 9 vandalism

intention: 6 animus

malign: 4 evil, foul 5 abuse, curse, libel 6 bewray, defame, revile, vilify 7 asperse, baleful, blacken, deprave, hurtful, slander 8 virulent 10 calumniate, pernicious

malignant: 4 evil 6 wicked 7 hateful, heinous, hellish, noxious, vicious 8 spiteful, venomous, virulent 9 cancerous, felonious, ferocious, invidious, malicious, poisonous, rancorous 10 rebellious 11 deleterious

malignity: 10 malignancy

malikana: fee 4 duty 7 payment

malison: 5 curse 11 malediction

malkin: cat, mop 4 drab, hare 6 sponge 8 slattern 9 scarecrow

mall: 4 walk 5 allee, alley 6 mallet 7 meeting 9 promenade

mallard: 4 duck

genus: 4 anas

malleable: 4 soft 7 ductile, pliable

mallemuck: 6 fulmar, petrel 9 albatross

mallet: tup 4 club, mace, mall, maul, mell(Sc.) 5 gavel, madge 6 beater, beetle, driver, hammer

hatter's: 6 beater

presiding officer's: 5 gavel

wooden: 4 maul 6 beetle

maline: net

mallow: maw 4 hock, weed 5 altea 6 escoba 7 althaea, gemauve

malm: 4 marl 9 limestone

malmsey: 4 wine 5 grape 7 madeira

malnutrition: 7 cachexy, wasting 8 cachexia

malodorous: 4 rank 5 fetid 6 putrid, smelly 7 noisome 9 odiferous

malt: 8 diastase

beverage: ale 4 beer, brew 5 lager, stout 6 zythem

froth: 4 barm

ground: 5 grist

infusion: 4 wort

vinegar: 6 alegar

worm: 5 toper 7 tippler

Malta: *capital:* 7 Valetta

coin: 5 grain, grano

hamlet: 5 casal 6 casale

island: 4 Gozo 6 Comino

measure: 4 salm 5 canna, salma 7 caffiso

suburb: 7 Florian

weight: 4 rotl, salm 5 artal, artel, parto, ratel, salma 6 kantar

wind: 7 gregale 8 levanter

Malta fever: 11 brucellosis

maltose: 6 amylon

maltreat: 5 abuse, dight 6 defile, defoul, demean, huspel, huspil, misuse, mohock

malty: 5 drunk

malum: 4 evil 5 wrong 7 offense

malvaceous plant: 4 okra 6 cotton, escoba, mallow 7 althaea

malvasia: 5 grape

mameluke: 5 slave 7 servant

Mamers: 4 Ares, Mars

mammal (see also **animal**): cat 5 beast, ovine, swine 6 bovine, equine, feline, monkey, rodent 7 primate 8 edentate, ruminant, ungulant 9 carnivore, marsupial

amphibious: 5 otter

antlered: elk 4 deer 5 moose 7 caribou 8 reindeer

aquatic: 4 seal 5 otter, shark, whale 6 desman, dugong, manati, rytina, walrus 7 dolphin, manatee, sealion 8 sirenian 12 hippopotamus

aquatic order: 4 cete 7 cetacea

arboreal: ai 5 lemur, sloth 6 fisher, monkey 7 glutton, opposum, raccoon 8 banxring, kinkajou 9 orangutan

armored: 9 armadillo

badgerlike: 5 ratel 8 balisaur

bearlike: 5 panda

bovine: ox; bos, cow 4 bull, calf, zebu 5 bison, steer 7 taurine 8 longhorn

burrowing: 4 mole 6 badger, gopher, wombat 8 squirrel 9 armadillo

camel-like: 7 guanaco

caprine: 4 goat

carnivorous: 9 carnivore

cetacean: see *aquatic* above

civetlike: 5 genet

coat: fur 4 hide, skin 6 pelage

cud-chewing: 8 ruminant

deerlike: 10 chevrotain

desert: 5 camel

dolphinlike: 4 inia

domestic: cat, cow, dog 5 horse, sheep 6 cattle

edentate: **7** ant bear **8** anteater, pangolin, tamandua

equine: **4** colt, foal, mare **5** filly, horse, zebra **8** stallion

extinct: **6** rytina **8** mastodon

feline: cat **4** lion, lynx, puma **5** ounce, tiger **6** bobcat, cougar, jaguar, ocelot, serval **7** leopard, panther

fish-eating: **5** otter

fleet: **4** deer, hare **8** antelope

flying: bat

fur-bearing: **4** coon, mink **5** coypu, otter, sheep, skunk **6** badger, ermine, marten, martin, nutria, rabbit **7** genette, raccoon **8** squirrel

giraffe-like: **5** okapi

gnawing: **6** rodent

hands different from feet: **6** bimana

hedgehog-like: **6** tenrec

herbivorous: **5** daman, tapir **6** bovine, dugong, equine **7** manatee **8** ruminant **9** orangutan **10** rhinoceros **12** hippopotamus

highest order: **7** primate

horned: ox; cow **4** gaur, goat, reem **5** bison **7** buffalo, unicorn **8** antelope, reindeer, seladang **10** rhinoceros

insectivorous: bat **6** tenrec **7** tendrac

large: **5** whale **7** mammoth **8** behemoth, elephant, mastodon **10** rhinoceros **12** hippopotamus

largest: **5** whale

lemurine: **5** potto

leopard-like: **4** lion, lynx, pard, puma **5** tiger **6** cougar, jaguar, ocelot **7** polecat, wildcat

llama-like: **6** vicuna

lowest order: **9** marsupial **11** marsupialia

marine: see *aquatic* above

marsupial: **4** tait **5** koala **7** opossum **8** kangaroo

meat-eating: **9** carnivore

mole-like: **6** desman

monkey-like: **5** lemur, loris

mouselike: **5** shrew

musteline: **5** otter, ratel

nocturnal: bat **5** hyena, lemur, ratel, tapir **6** macaco, racoon **7** raccoon, tarsier **8** kinkajou, platypus

omnivorous: hog, pig **5** swine

ovine: **5** sheep

plantigrade: **6** racoon **7** raccoon

porcine: hog, pig **4** boar **5** swine **7** peccary

pouched: **9** marsupial

raccoon-like: **5** coati

retentive: **8** elephant

rhinoceros-like: **5** tapir **14** baluchitherium

ring-tailed: **4** coon **5** lemur

ruminant: ox; yak **4** deer, goat **5** bison, camel, llama, moose, okapi, sheep, steer **6** alpaca, cattle, chewer, vicuna **7** buffalo, giraffe **8** antelope

scaled: **8** pangolin

shelled: **7** armadillo

short-tailed: **7** bobtail

skunk-like: **5** zoril

slow-moving: **5** loris, sloth

smallest: **5** shrew

snake-eating: **8** mongoose

spiny: **6** tenrec **9** porcupine

thick-skinned: **8** elephant **9** pachyderm **10** rhinoceros

toothless: **8** edentate

tropical: **5** coati, rhino **7** peccary **9** coati-modi **10** coati-mundi, rhinoceros

tusked: **6** walrus **7** mammoth **8** elephant, mastodon

ursine: **4** bear **5** panda

viverrine: **8** falanaka

vulpine: fox **4** wolf

web-footed: **5** otter

wing-footed: **6** aliped

winged: bat

zebra-like: **6** quagga

mammock: 4 tear **5** break, scrap **6** mangle

mammon: 6 riches, wealth

mammoth: 5 large **8** gigantic

man (see also **fellow, person**): bo; guy, vir(L.) **4** aner(Gr.), chal, chap, homo(L.), male, mann(G.), uomo(It.), work **5** bloke, chiel, guard, homme(F.), human, valet **6** andros(Gr.), chield, hombre(Sp.), mensch(-Yid.) **7** counter, fortify, homines(L.pl.), husband, laborer, mankind, operate **8** creature **9** anthropos(Gr.)

aged: vet **4** cuff, sire **5** senex(L.), uncle **6** gaffer, stager **7** grandpa, starets(Russ.) **8** grandpop **9** grandsire, patriarch **10** Methuselah **11** grandfather **12** octogenarian

bad-tempered: **6** bodach **10** curmudgeon

bald: **9** pilgarlic **10** pillgarlic

big: cob

brass: **5** Talos

brave: **4** hero, lion

coarse: **5** churl, knave **7** ruffian

comb. form: **4** homo **5** andro **8** anthropo

conceited: **7** coxcomb

cruel: **4** ogre **7** monster, ruffian, villain

cunning: **5** rogue **7** shyster **9** trickster **10** mountebank

dissolute: **4** roue

eccentric: **6** codger

effeminate: **9** androgyne

elderly: see *aged* above

enlisted: GI **6** rating, sailor **7** private, soldier **8** sargeant

fashionable: fop **4** dude **5** dandy **10** Corinthian **11** Beau Brummel **12** boulevardier

handsome: **6** Adonis

hard-pressed: Job

hardheaded: **5** boche

henpecked: **10** hoddy-doddy **11** milquetoast

impetuous: **7** hotspur

important: VIP **4** hero, name **5** nabob **7** grandee

ladies': **4** beau **5** beaux(pl.)

learned: PhD **4** bhat **6** doctor, pundit savant **7** erudite, scholar, teacher **8** literati **9** literatus, professor **11** philologist

little: **6** mankin, shrimp, squirt **8** homuncio **10** homunculus

mechanical: **5** robot **9** automaton

medicine: **6** priest, shaman

money: **9** paymaster

mother of: Eve **6** Cybele

newspaper: **6** editor **8** reporter **9** columnist **10** journalist

objectionable: oaf **4** boor **5** bully **8** wiseacre

of all work: **4** joey, mozo **8** factotum, handyman

of letters: **6** savant **11** litterateur

of straw: **6** figure **9** nonentity

of the world: **6** layman **10** secularist **11** cosmopolite **12** sophisticate

old: see *elderly* above

old-clothes: **4** poco

outdoor: **6** camper, hunter **7** athlete **9** fisherman

personifying: **15** anthropomorphic

pert. to: **5** human **6** humane, mortal

political: **7** senator **8** diplomat **9** statesman **10** ambassador **11** assemblyman **14** representative

poor: **6** pauper **7** peasant **8** beadsman, bedesman

primitive: **6** savage **8** urmensch(Yid.)

resembling: **7** android **10** anthropoid

rich: **5** Midas, nabob **6** tycoon **7** Croesus, magnate **9** plutocrat **10** capitalist **11** billionaire, millionaire

science: **9** ethnology **12** anthropology

self-important: **10** cockalorum

shadowless: **6** ascian

single: **4** stag **7** widower **8** bachelor, celibate

unattractive: **4** clod, goon, jerk, lout, rube, slob **5** yokel **6** lummox **7** fathead **10** clodhopper

undercover: spy **5** agent **9** detective **12** investigator

unemployed: **6** batlan, batlon(Yid.)

unmarried: see *single* above

white: **6** buckra **7** cachila(P.I.) **8** paleface

wicked: **7** villain

wise: **4** sage, seer **5** solon **6** nestor **7** Solomon

worthless: bum **4** hobo **5** idler, tramp

young: boy **5** youth **6** varlet

man fungus: **9** earthstar

Man of Destiny: **17** Napoleon Bonaparte

Man of Galilee: **11** Jesus Christ

man of God: **5** rabbi, saint **6** pastor, priest **7** ascetic, prelate **8** minister **12** ecclesiastic

man-of-war: **7** frigate, soldier, warrior

deck: **5** orlop

Man O'War: **5** horse **6** winner

Man Without a Country: *author:* **4** Hale

character: **5** Nolan

manacle: **4** bond, cuff, iron **5** chain, darby **6** fetter, hamper **7** confine, shackle **8** handcuff **9** restraint

manada: **4** herd **5** drove, flock

manage: man, run **4** boss, head, lead, rule **5** dight, frame, guide, order, steer, wield **6** convoy, demean, direct, govern, handle **7** conduct, control, dispose, execute, husband, operate, oversee **8** contrive, dispense, engineer, maneuver **9** supervise **10** accomplish, administer, manipulate

frugally: **6** eke out **7** husband **9** economize

hard to: **6** ornery

manageable: **4** easy, tame, yare **6** docile, wieldy **7** ductile, pliable **8** flexible, maniable, workable **9** compliant, tractable **10** governable

management: **4** care **6** agency, charge, menage **7** address, economy, gestion **8** carriage, demeanor **9** demeanour, governail, ordinance **10** enterprise, governance **11** generalship

good: **6** eutaxy **7** eutaxie

poor: **11** cacoeconomy

manager: **4** doer **6** gerent, grieve **7** captain, curator, foreman, steward **8** aumildar **12** entrepreneur

managery: **7** cunning **8** artifice **9** frugality, husbandry **10** management **11** managership

Manasseh: *city:* **4** Aner

son: **4** Amon, Jair

manatee: **6** seacow **8** sirenian

Manchuria: *city:* **5** Hulan, Kirin **6** Harbin, Mukden **9** Niuchwang

province: **5** Jehol

river: **4** Amur, Liao, Yalu

manciple: **5** slave **7** servant, steward **8** purveyor

mandarin: **6** orange **7** Chinese **9** tangerine

residence: **5** yamen

mandate: **4** writ **5** brief, order **6** behest, charge, decree, demand, firman **7** bidding, command, precept **9** direction **10** commission, injunction, referendum

mandatory: **10** imperative, obligatory

mandible: jaw **4** beak **9** chelicera

part: **5** molar

mandrel: hob 4 axle, ball, pick 5 arbor 7 spindle

mandrill: 6 baboon

manducate: eat 4 chew 9 masticate

mane: 4 hair, juba 5 brush 6 grivna 8 encolure

manege gait: 4 lope, trot, volt

maneuver: 4 ploy 6 deploy, jockey, tactic 7 echelon 8 artifice, contrive, engineer 9 evolution, stratagem 10 manipulate

aviation: 4 loop, spin 7 echelon, flathat 9 chandelle, Immelmann

military: 6 tactic

manful: See **manly**

mang: 8 frenzied 10 bewildered

manga: 6 poncho

manganese symbol: Mn

mange: eat 4 itch, meal, scab 6 fodder, scurvy

cause of: 4 mite 6 acarid

manger: bin, box 4 crib, meal 5 stall 6 trough 7 banquet

mangle: cut, mar 4 hack, maim 6 bruise, garble, ironer, smooth 8 calender, lacerate, mutilate 9 dismember

mango: 4 tree 5 bauno, fruit

bird: 6 oriole 11 hummingbird

fish: 9 threadfin

tree: 4 tope

mangrove: 4 tree 5 goran, shrub

mangy: 4 mean 5 seedy 6 ronion, ronyon, scurvy, shabby 7 squalid 12 contemptible

manhandle: 4 maul

mani: 6 peanut

mania: 5 craze, furor 6 frenzy, furore 7 madness, passion 8 delirium 9 cacoethes 11 derangement

buying: 9 oniomania

stealing: 11 kleptomania

maniable: See **manageable**

maniac: 6 madman 7 lunatic

maniacal: mad 6 crazed, insane 8 demented, deranged 9 psychotic 10 hysterical

manic: 9 afflicted

manicure: cut 4 clip, pare, trim 6 polish

manifest: 4 open, show 5 argue, clear, index, overt 6 attest, evince, extant, graith, patent, reveal 7 approve, confess, declare, develop, display, evident, exhibit, explain, express, glaring, invoice, obvious, signify, visible 8 apparent, develope, disclose, discover, evidence, indicate, palpable 11 conspicuous, demonstrate, discernible, indubitable, perspicuous 12 indisputable, unmistakable

manifestation: 4 sign 5 phase 6 effect, ostent

manifesto: 5 edict 7 placard 8 evidence 9 statement 11 declaration 13 demonstration

manifold: 4 many 7 various 8 multiple, numerous 9 different, multifold, multiplex, replicate 12 multifarious

manikin: 4 puny 5 dwarf, model, pygmy 7 phantom 8 homuncio, homuncle 9 homuncule, homunculi(pl.), mannequin 10 diminutive, homunculus

Manila: *airfield:* 5 Clark

creek: 6 estero

hemp: 5 abaca, abaka 6 banana

hero: 5 Dewey

nut: 6 peanut

river: 5 Pasig

Manila Bay boat: 6 bilalo

manioc: 7 cassava, tapioca

manipulate: rig, use 4 work 5 treat, wield 6 handle, manage 7 control, operate

manis: 8 anteater, pangolin

mankind: man 4 Adam, male 5 flesh, world 6 humans, people 8 humanity

division: 4 race 5 tribe 6 people

hater: 11 misanthrope

manlike: 4 male 5 manly 7 android, mannish 9 masculine 10 anthropoid

manly: 4 bold, male 5 brave, hardy, noble 6 daring 7 manlike, mannish 8 resolute 9 dignified, masculine, undaunted 10 courageous

Mann character: 7 Castorp

manna: 7 Godsend 10 gazangabin

mannequin: See **manikin**

manner: air, way 4 cost, form, mien, mode, more, thew 5 guise, trick 6 aspect, course, method 7 address, bearing, fashion, quomodo 8 attitude, behavior 9 behaviour, technique 10 appearance, deportment

law: 4 modi(pl.) 5 modus

mannerism: 4 mode, pose 5 trait 7 bearing 11 affectation, peculiarity

mannerly: 4 nice 5 civil, moral 6 decent, polite, seemly 8 decorous

manners: 5 lates 8 courtesy 9 amenities, etiquette

Mannus' father: 6 Tuisto

mano: 4 hand 9 handstone

manoc: 4 fowl 7 chicken, rooster

manor: 4 hall 5 abode, house 6 estate 7 mansion

land: 6 barton 7 demesne

manred: 6 homage 9 vassalage

manse: 7 rectory

manservant: 4 help, mozo, syce 5 gilly(Sc.), groom, valet 6 Andrew, butler, garcon, gillie 8 factotum

manship: 5 honor 6 homage 7 courage, manhood 8 courtesy, humanity 9 manliness

mansion: 4 hall, home, stay 5 abode, house, manor, siege 7 chateau, lodging, sojourn 8 chateaux(pl.), dwelling 9 residence
papal: 7 Lateran
manslaughter: 6 murder 7 killing, slaying 8 butchery
mansuete: 4 kind, tame 6 gentle
manta: 4 wrap 5 cloak, cloth 7 blanket, bulwark, shelter 8 mantelet 9 devilfish
mantegar: ape
manteel: See **mantle**
mantel: 4 arch, beam 5 brace(Sc.), ledge, shelf, stone 6 clavel, lintel 10 manteltree
mantelet: 4 cape 5 cloak 6 mantle, screen, shield 7 shelter 8 galapago
mantilla: 4 cape 5 cloak
mantis crab: 7 squilla
mantle (see also **cloak**): 4 brat, capa, cape, coat, cope, hood, mant, robe 5 blush, cover, manto 6 capote, kittel 7 encloak, manteau, manteel, whittle 8 envelope, mantelet, mantilla 10 witzchoura
manto: 4 gown 5 cloak 6 mantle, mantua
mantoid: 6 mantis
mantra: om 4 hymn 5 charm, spell
mantua: 4 gown 5 cloak, manto 9 overdress
manual: 4 book 7 clavier, didache 8 grimoire, handbook 9 catechism 11 enchiridion
art: 5 craft
manuduction: 5 guide 7 leading 8 guidance 9 direction 12 introduction
manufactory: 7 factory
manufacture: 4 fake, make 5 forge 6 invent 7 confect, produce 9 fabricate
manufactured: 4 made 10 artificial
manufacturer: 8 employer 9 fabricant, operative 10 fabricator 12 entrepreneur 13 industrialist
manumission: 7 freedom, freeing, release 10 liberation 11 deliverance 12 emancipation
manure: 4 dung 5 addle 7 compost 10 composture
manuscript: MS 4 copy 5 codex 7 papyrus, writing 8 document 9 archetype, minuscule 11 composition, handwriting
back: 5 dorso
space: 6 lacuna
copier: 6 scribe
mark: 5 obeli(pl.) 6 obelus
many: 4 fele, raff 6 divers 7 diverse, several, various 8 manifold, numerous 9 different, multifold, multitude 10 multiplied
prefix: 4 poly, vari 5 multi
many-footed: 8 multiped
many-sided: 9 versatile 12 multilateral
mao: 7 peacock
Maori: *bird:* poe, tue, tui

canoe: 4 waka
charm: 7 heitiki
chief: 5 ariki
clan: ati 4 hapu
club: 4 mere, patu, rata
compensation: utu
dance: 4 haka
food: kai
fort: pa; pah
hen: 4 weka
hero: 4 Maui
house: 5 whare 8 wharekai 9 wherekura 12 wharewananga
over: umu
priest: 7 tuhunga
raft: 4 moki 6 moguey
sect: 7 Ringatu
store: 6 pataka
tatooing: 4 moko
tree: 5 mapau 6 manuka 9 tanehakas
tribe: Ati 4 Hapu
village: pa; pah 4 kaik 5 kaika 6 kainga
wages: utu
weapon: 4 mere, patu, rata
map: 4 card, plan 5 carte, chard, chart, image 6 design, sketch, survey 7 diagram, epitome, explore, outline, picture 8 roadbook 9 delineate 10 cartograph, embodiment 14 representation
book: 5 atlas
copier: 10 pantograph
maker: 7 charter 8 Mercator 12 cartographer
townsite: 4 plat
weather line: 6 isobar
maple: 4 acer
cup: 5 mazer
derived from: 6 aceric
family: 9 aceraceae
sap: 5 humbo
scale: 10 pulvinaria
seed: 6 samara
spout: 5 spile
mar: 4 amar, blot, scar 5 botch, spoil 6 damage, deface, deform impair, injure, mangle 7 blemish 8 obstruct 9 disfigure
marabou: 5 stork 6 argala 7 faleric 8 adjutant, marabout
maral: 4 deer
maranatha: 5 curse
maranon: 6 cashew
marasca: 6 cherry 10 maraschino
marasmus: 5 waste 10 emaciation 13 contabescence
maraud: 4 loot, raid, rove 7 pillage, plunder
marauder: 6 bandit, pirate 7 cateran(Sc.)
marble: 4 cold, hard 5 agate, rance, stone 6 basalt 7 cipolin 8 brocatel, dolomite 9 unfeeling 10 brocatelle

game: taw

mosaic: 7 tessera

playing: mib, pea, taw 4 doby 5 alley, dobie 6 glassy 7 shooter

slab: 5 dalle(F.)

Marble Faun: *author:* 9 Hawthorne

character: 5 Hilda

marble flower: 5 poppy

marblehead: 6 fulmar

marbler: 6 carver 8 sculptor

marc: 6 refuse 7 residue

marcato: 6 marked 7 pointed 8 accented, emphatic

march: 4 hike, trek 5 route, troop 6 border, defile, parade 8 boundary, frontier, smallage 9 cavalcade 10 procession

day's: 5 etape

horsemen: 9 cavalcade

spirited: 9 quickstep

March 15: 4 ides

March King: 5 Sousa

March sisters: Jo; Amy, Meg 4 Beth

marchland: 8 frontier 10 borderland

marcid: 4 weak 7 decayed, tabetic 8 withered 9 exhausted 10 emaciating

marcor: 5 decay 7 maramus

Mardi Gras: 8 carnival

king: Rex

mare: yad 4 jade, yade, yaud(Sc.) 5 gilot, horse, meare 6 dobbin, equine, grasni

young: 5 filly

mare's nest: 4 hoax 5 trick 8 disorder 9 confusion

mare's tail: 5 cloud 6 cirrus

margarine: 4 oleo

marge: See **margin**

margin: hem, lip, ori, rim 4 bank, brim, edge, orae(L.), rand, side 5 brink, shore, verge 6 border, fringe, leeway 7 margent

narrow: 4 hair

note: 7 apostil 8 scholium 10 annotation

set in: 6 indent

Marianas: 4 Guam 6 Saipan

marigold: 5 boots, caper, gools 6 buddle 7 cowslip, elkslip, golland

genus: 7 tagetes

marijuana: boo, hay, pot, tea 5 grass

cigarette: mu 6 greefa, griffo, moocah, mooter, muggle, reefer 7 mohasky 8 joy-smoke, loco weed, Mary Jane 9 Indian hay 10 bambalacha, Mary Warner, Mary Weaver 11 giggle-smoke

cigarette holder: 6 crutch

user: 7 pothead

marina: 4 dock 5 basin 9 esplanade, promenade

marinade: 5 brine 6 pickle 8 marinate

marinal: 6 marine, sailor, saline 7 mariner 8 nautical

marine: tar 5 jolly, naval, water 7 aquatic, marinal, mariner, oceanic, pelagic 8 halimous, maritime, nautical 9 aequoreal 11 leatherneck

crustacean: 8 barnacle

instrument: aba 5 radar 7 pelorus, sextant

plant: 4 alga 5 algae 6 enalid 7 seaweed

science: 10 oceanology 12 oceanography

skeleton: 5 coral

slogan: 6 gungho

marine animal: orc 4 salp 5 coral, polyp 9 jellyfish

marine fish: 8 menhaden

mariner: gob, tar 5 Jacky 6 galoot, sailor, seaman 7 buscarl 8 buscarle, seafarer, waterman 9 aequoreal

card: 5 chart

compass card: 4 rose

compass points: 6 rhumbs

marinheiro: 6 acajou

marionette: 6 puppet 10 bufflehead

marital: 9 connubial 11 matrimonial

maritime: See **marine**

marjoram: 4 herb, mint 6 origan

mark: dot, hob, tee 4 belt, goal, line, note, rist, scar, wale 5 badge, brand, grade, label, score, stamp, track, watch 6 accent, beacon, caract, denote, notice, target 7 betoken, blemish, earmark, impress, imprint, insigne, observe 8 identify, insignia(pl.), standard 9 character, designate 10 indication 11 distinguish 14 characteristic

bad: 7 demerit

diacritical: 5 breve, tilde 6 macron, umlaut 7 cedilla(F.)

down: 5 lower

out: 6 cancel, define 7 measure 10 obliterate

possessive: 10 apostrophe

printer's: 4 dele, fist, stet 5 caret, obeli 6 dagger, diesis, obelus 7 obelisk

pronunciation: see *diacritical* above

punctuation: 4 dash 5 colon, comma 6 period 8 dieresis 9 diaeresis, semicolon 11 parenthesis, parentheses(pl.)

question: 7 erotema, eroteme

reference: 4 star 6 dagger 8 asterisk

tiny: dot

white: 5 rache, ratch

with critical notes: 8 annotate

Mark Antony's wife: 7 Octavia

Mark Twain's name: 22 Samuel Langhorne Clemens

markaz: 8 district 11 subdivision

marked: 5 fated 7 eminent 10 emphasized 11 conspicuous, outstanding

with lines: 5 ruled 6 gyrose, linear, notate

marker: peg 5 arrow 6 scorer, signal 7 brander, counter, monitor 8 bookmark,

marksman, recorder **9** milestone **10** gravestone
air course: **5** pylon
floating: **4** buoy
market: 4 gunj(Ind.), mart, sale, sell, shop, sook **5** agora(Gr.), bazar, gunge, halle, pasar, plaza, store, tryst **6** bazaar, rialto, shoppe **7** chaffer **8** cheaping, debouche(F.), emporium
marketable: 8 vendible
markhor: 4 goat
marksman: 4 shot **6** sniper
marl: 4 clay, malm **6** manure **7** marlite **9** greensand **10** fertilizer, overspread
marli: 4 lace **5** gauze, tulle
marlin: 6 curlew, godwit **9** spearfish
marlinespike: fid **4** skua **6** Jaeger
marlock: 4 ogle **5** prank, sport, trick **6** frolic
marmalade: jam **6** sapote **8** preserve
quince: **8** co-diniac, quiddany
tree: **5** mamie
marmit: pot **6** kettle
marmoset: 4 mico **6** monkey, sagoin, wistit **7** tamarin, wistiti
marmot: 5 bobac **6** rodent **8** burrower, whistler **9** woodchuck
marmota: 8 arctomys **9** woodchuck
maroon: 6 enisle, strand **7** isolate, reddish **8** cimarron, purplish
marooner: 6 pirate **9** buccaneer
Marpessa's abductor: 4 Idas
marplot: 7 meddler, snooper **8** busybody **9** addle-plot
Marquand character: 4 Moto **5** Apley, Wayde **6** Pulham **7** Goodwin
marquee: 4 tent **6** canopy
marquetry: 5 inlay
marquis: 4 peer
marriage: 5 match **6** splice **7** wedding, wedlock **9** matrimony
absence of: **5** agamy
broker: **9** schatchen(Yid.)
comb. form: **4** gamy
forswearer: **8** celibate
fourth: **9** tetragamy
god: **5** Hymen
goddess: **4** Hera
hater of: **10** misogamist
more than one husband: **9** polyandry
more than one wife: **6** bigamy **8** polygamy
notice: **5** banns
of aged: **8** opsigamy
of gods: **8** theogamy
open to slaves: **12** contubernium
outside tribe: **7** exogamy
pert. to: **7** marital, spousal **8** hymeneal **9** connubial, endogamic
portion: dot **5** dowry
second: **6** digamy

secret: **9** elopement
to promise: **7** betroth **8** affiance
to two people: **6** bigamy
marriageable: 6 nubile
married: 5 wived **6** wedded **8** espoused **9** connubial
married person: 4 wife **6** spouse **7** husband **8** benedict
marrow: 4 best, pith **5** reest(Sc.) **6** inmost, medula **7** essence, medulla
bones: **5** knees
marry: 4 join, mate, wive, yoke **5** cleek, hitch, unite **6** buckle, couple **7** espouse, husband
Mars: 4 Ares **6** planet, war god
discoverer of satellites: **4** Hall
inner moon: **6** Phobos
pert. to: **5** Arean **7** Martian
planet belt: **5** Libya
planet spot: **5** oasis, oases(pl.)
priests of: **5** Salii **6** Deimos
region (dark): **4** mare
twin sons: **5** Remus **7** Romulus
Marseillaise author: 13 Rouget de Lisle
marsh: bog, fen, hag **4** jeel, mire, moor, slew, sloo, slue **5** flash, liman, slash, swale, swamp **6** morass, palude, slough **7** cienaga, maremma(It.) **8** quagmire **9** everglade
bird: **4** sora **5** snipe, stilt
crocodile: goa
elder: iva
fever: **7** helodes
gas: **7** methane **8** firedamp
grass: **4** tule **5** sedge, spart
hawk: **7** harrier
marigold: **5** boots
pert. to: **8** paludine
salt: **6** salina **7** corcass
shrub: **8** moorwort
marsh plant genus: 6 caltha **7** elatine
marshal: 4 lead **5** align, aline, array, groom, guide, usher **6** direct, parade **7** arrange, farrier, officer **8** official
marshland: fen **4** fell
marshmallow: 5 altea
marshwort: 9 cranberry
genus: **4** sium
marshy: wet **5** fenny **6** callow **7** helodes, paludal, paludic **8** paludine **9** paludinal
lake: **5** liman
marsupial: 4 tait **5** coala, koala **6** possum, wombat **7** dasyure, opossum **9** bandicoot
Australian: **4** tait **6** cuscus **7** dasyure **8** kangaroo **9** phalanger
bearlike: **5** coala, koala **6** wombat
genus: **10** diprotodom
mart: 4 fair **5** bazar **6** bazaar, market, rialto **8** emporium
martel: 6 hammer

marten: fur 5 sable 6 animal, fisher, martin
  beech: 4 foin
  genus: 7 mustela
  stone: 4 foin
martial: 7 warlike 8 military
Martial's writing: 7 epigram
Martian: 5 Arean
  comb. form: 4 areo
martin: 7 swallow
martinet: 6 tyrant 14 disciplinarian
Martinique: *garment:* 4 jupe
  volcano: 5 Pelee
martyr: 5 saint 8 sufferer 10 sacrificer
  first Christian: 7 Stephen
  royal: 7 Charles
martyrdom: 7 killing, passion, torment, torture 8 butchery, distress 10 affliction
  place of: 8 Golgotha
marvel: 5 ferly 6 admire, wonder 7 miracle, portent 8 astonish 9 horehound 12 astonishment
marvelous: 7 strange 8 wondrous 9 excellent 10 improbable, incredible
Maryland: *city:* 9 Baltimore
  county: 4 Kent 5 Cecil 6 Howard, Talbot
  founder: 7 Calvert
  race track: 5 Bowie
mas: 9 masculine
masa: 8 cornmeal
Masada: *builder:* 5 Herod
  defender: 6 zealot
  enemy: 4 Rome
  historian: 8 Josephus
masculine: mas 4 male 5 manly 6 strong, virile 7 manlike, mannish
mash: 4 chap, mess, ogle 5 champ, cream, crush, flirt, smash 6 muddle 7 farrago, mixture, trouble
mashal: 7 parable, proverb
masher: 4 chap 5 flirt, ricer
masjid: 6 mosque
mask: 4 hide, veil 5 cloak, cover, guise, visor 6 screen 7 conceal, curtain 8 defilade, disguise 9 dissemble
  half: 4 loup(Fr.) 6 domino(Fr.)
  top knot on: 5 onkos
masked: 6 covert 7 larvate, obscure 8 larvated
masker: 6 domino, mummer
maskery: 10 masquerade
maslin: 5 brass 7 mixture 9 potpourri
mason: 7 builder 11 stoneworker
  mixing rod: rab
Masons: *doorkeeper:* 5 tiler
  order: 8 Templars
masonry: 6 ashlar 7 blocage 9 stonework
masquerade: 5 guise 8 disguise
mass: bat, gob 4 blob, body, bulk, clot, heap, lump, size, swad 5 amass, batch, gross, group, store 6 gather, gobbet, prayer 7 phalanx, service 8 assemble 9 aggregate, magnitude 10 accumulate, assemblage, congregate 11 agglomerate, composition, compositure, concentrate, consolidate 12 congregation
  book: 6 missal
  cloudlike: 6 nebula 7 nebulae(pl.)
  comb. form: mas
  confused: cot 5 chaos 6 welter 9 imbroglio 10 hotchpotch
  directory: 4 ordo
  for dead: 7 requiem
  musical number: 5 Credo, Kyrie 6 Gloria 7 Sanctus
  of particulars: 9 aggregate
  pert. to: 5 molar
  small: dab, pat, wad 4 floc
  tangled: mop 4 shag
mass meeting: 5 rally
Massachusetts: *cape:* Ann
  city: 4 Lynn 5 Acton, Salem 6 Boston(c.), Hadley, Lowell, Malden, Quincy, Wianno, Woburn 7 Chelsea, Metheun, Waltham 8 Brockton, Plymouth 9 Braintree, Cambridge, Worcester 10 Framingham 11 Charlestown, Springfield, Summerville
  flower: 7 arbutus
  island: 9 Nantucket 15 Martha's Vineyard
  mountain: Tom
  mountain ridge: 7 Taconic
  oyster: 6 Cotuit
  port: 5 Salem 6 Boston
  school: 7 Andover
  state flower: 7 arbutus
massacre: 6 pogrom 7 carnage 8 butchery 9 slaughter
massage: rub 5 knead
massager: 7 masseur 8 masseuse
massed: 7 serried
Massenet's opera: 5 Manon, Thais
massive: big 4 bold, huge 5 beamy, bulky, gross, heavy, large, massy 7 hulking, weighty 9 cyclopean, ponderous 10 boisterous
mast: cue 4 spar 5 stick 6 forage 8 beechnut
  against: 5 aback
  crosspiece: fid
  inclination from perpendicular: 4 rake
  middle: 8 mainmast
  wood for: ash 4 poon
mastaba: 4 tomb 8 platform
master: get, man, rab 4 baas, boss, lord, mian, rule, sire 5 chief, rabbi, sahib(Ind.), tutor 6 bridle, buckra, defeat, doctor, domine, govern, humble, subdue 7 captain, conquer, maestro, padrone(It.) 8 amaister, overcome, regulate, surmount, vanquish 9 commander, overpower, preceptor, subjugate 10 proprietor

comb. form: 4 arch 5 archi
Eton: 4 beak
fencing: 7 lanista
harbor: 7 havener, havenor
hard: 6 despot, Legree
of house: 13 paterfamilias
pert. to: 6 herile
ship's: 7 captain, skipper
Master of Arts: A.M., M.A.
master of ceremonies: M.C. 5 emcee
master stroke: 4 coup
masterful: 6 lordly 7 haughty 8 arrogant, masterly 9 arbitrary, imperious 10 commanding 11 dictatorial, domineering, magisterial, overbearing 13 authoritative
mastermind: 4 plan 6 expert 8 wiseacre
masterpeice: 4 coup 7 triumph 10 masterwork 11 chef d'oeuvre
mastery: 4 gree 5 gripe 7 control, victory 8 conquest, facility 9 influence
mastic: 5 gummy 8 adhesive
masticate: 4 chaw, chew 5 crush, gnash, grind 6 crunch 9 manducate
masticatory: gum 7 chewing
mastiff: dog 5 burly 7 massive
mastodon: 5 giant 7 mammoth
mat: cot, rug 4 felt 5 doily, platt, snarl 6 carpet, cotter, petate(Sp.), tangle 7 cushion, drugget, gardnap 8 entangle 10 interweave, lusterless
mat grass: 4 nard
Mata Hari: spy 5 agent
Mataco: 4 apar 6 Indian 9 armadillo
matador: 11 bullfighter
  adversary: 4 bull, toro
  garment: 4 cape
  staff: 6 muleta
  sword: 7 estoque
matagasse: 11 butcherbird
match: go; cap, pit, tir(F.) 4 bout, cope, even, mate, pair, peer, side, spar, suit, team, wife 5 amate, equal, fusee(F.), marry, rival, tally, torch, vesta 6 fellow, spouse 7 compare, compeer, contest, husband, lucifer(Eng.) 8 equalize, lampwick, marriage 9 allumette(F.) 10 candlewick, correspond 11 counterpart, countervail, parallelize
matched: 6 paired, teamed
matchless: 5 alone 6 unlike 8 peerless 9 exquisite, unequaled 10 inimitable 12 incomparable
matchlock: gun
mate: cap, pal, wed 4 fear, fere, join, pair, peer, wife 5 billy, buddy, bully, cully, feere, marry, match 6 bunkle, cobber, couple, fellow, spouse 7 brother, compeer, comrade, consort, espouse, husband, partner 9 associate, companion 10 yokefellow
matelot: 6 sailor

mater: ma; mom 4 mama 6 mother
materia medica: 7 acology
material (see also **cloth, fabric, substance**): 4 data, gear 5 goods, stuff 6 bodily, carnal, graith, matter 7 weighty 8 physical, tangible 9 corporeal, essential 12 nonspiritual
  discard: 4 junk, slag 5 scrap, trash, waste 6 refuse 7 rubbish
  glass-like: 5 plass
  raw: ore 6 staple
materialism: 8 hylonism
materialize: 5 reify
materiel: 8 supplies 9 apparatus, equipment
maternal: 8 motherly
  relation: 7 enation
matey: 9 companion 13 companionable
matezite: 7 pinitol 10 caoutchouc
matgrass: 4 nard 8 fogfruit
math: 6 mowing 9 monastery 10 arithmetic 11 mathematics
mathe: 4 grub 6 maggot
mathematician: 5 adder 7 figurer
mathematics: *abbreviation:* Q.E.D.
  branch: 7 algebra, geodesy 8 calculus, geometry 9 logarithm 10 arithmetic 12 trigonometry
  constant (arbitrary): 9 parameter
  deduction: 8 analysis
  diagram: 5 graph
  equation: 4 surd
  exercise: 7 problem
  factor: 10 quaternion
  function: 4 sine 6 cosine
  instrument: 6 sector 7 compass 8 arbalest
  irrational number: 4 surd
  line: 6 vector
  number: 5 digit 12 multiplicand
  operation: 7 operand
  operator: 5 nabla 10 quaternion
  proposition: 7 theorem
  quantity: 6 scalar
  ratio: pi 4 sine 8 derivate
  symbol: 7 faciend, operand 12 multiplicand
  term: 4 root, sine 6 cosine
mathemeg: 7 catfish
mathes: 7 mayweed
matie: 7 herring
matin: 4 call, song 6 prayer 9 matutinal
  song: 6 aubade
matinee: 5 party 6 soiree 8 negligee 9 reception 13 entertainment
matinee idol: 4 lion, star 5 actor
matka: 4 seal
matranee: 7 servant, sweeper
matrass: 4 tube 5 flask 6 bottle 8 bolthead
matriculate: 5 adopt, enter 6 enroll 8 register 10 naturalize 13 immatriculate

matrimonial: 7 nuptial, spousal 8 conjugal, hymeneal 9 connubial

matrimony: 7 wedlock 8 marriage

matrix: bed, die, mat 4 form, mold, womb 5 plasm 6 gangue 7 pattern
plate: 6 stereo

matron: 4 dame, wife 5 widow 11 housekeeper

matte: 7 regulus

matter: pus 4 gear, malm, mass 5 solid, topic 6 affair, behalf 7 article, concern, problem, signify, trouble 8 business, material 11 constituent
law: res
particle: 4 atom
pert. to: 5 hylic
property: 4 mass 7 inertia
rarefied: fog, gas 4 mist 5 vapor 6 miasma

matter of fact: 7 literal, prosaic 9 pragmatic 11 utilitarian

matthiola: 5 stock

mattock: ax; axe 4 bill 5 tubal 6 twibil 7 twibill

mattress: 6 pallet
cover: 4 tick 7 ticking

mature: age, old 4 aged, form, gray, grow, ripe 5 adult, grown, ripen 6 accrue, autumn, decoct, digest, mellow, season 7 develop 8 complete, develope

maturing: 8 rathripe 9 ratheripe

matutinal: 5 early, matin

Mau Mau land: 5 Kenya

maud: rug 5 plaid, shawl

maudlin: 5 beery, corny, tipsy 7 tearful, weeping 10 lachrymose 11 sentimental

mauger: 5 spite 7 ill-will 9 unwilling 15 notwithstanding

Maugham: *heroine:* 5 Sadie
play: 4 Rain

maul: paw 4 beat, bung, club, mace, mall, mell, moth 5 abuse, gavel, staff 6 beater, beetle, bruise, hammer, mallet 9 manhandle

maumet: god, guy 4 doll, idol 5 image 6 puppet

maund: beg 6 basket, hamper

maunder: 5 growl, haver 6 beggar 7 grumble

Maupassant character: 4 Fifi

Maurois subject: 4 Hugo, Sand 5 Byron, Dumas 6 Proust 8 Disraeli

Mauser: arm, gun 5 rifle 6 weapon 7 firearm

mausoleum: 4 tomb 8 baradari(Ind.)

mauve: 5 lilac 6 purple, violet

mauvetaupe: 5 copra

maux: 8 slattern, slipshod 10 prostitute

mavis: 6 thrush

maw: 4 craw, crop 6 gullet, mallow 7 stomach

mawk: 6 maggot

mawkish: 5 vapid 6 sickly 8 nauseous 9 squeamish 10 disgusting 11 sentimental

maxilla: jaw 4 bone

maxim: saw 4 dict, rule, word 5 adage, axiom, gnome, logia(pl.), moral, motto 6 logion, saying 7 brocard, precept, proverb 8 aphorism, apothegm, doctrine, moralism 9 erudition, principle 10 apophthegm

maximum: 4 most, peak 5 limit 7 highest, largest 8 greatest

may: can 4 mote 5 might, shall 6 maiden 8 possible

May: *festival:* 7 Beltane
goddess: 4 Maia

May curlew: 8 whimbrel

May gowan: 5 daisy

Maya: *day:* 5 uayeb
month: 5 uinal
people: Mam 8 Pokonchi
year: 4 haab

mayapple: 8 mandrake

maybe: 7 perhaps 11 possibility, uncertainty

maybird: 6 thrush

maycock: 5 melon 6 maypop, plover

mayfish: 9 killifish

mayflower: 7 arbutus 8 hawthorn, marigold 10 stitchwort 12 cuckooflower

Mayflower's sister ship: 9 Speedwell

mayfly: dun

mayfowl: 8 whimbrel

mayhap: 6 happen 7 perhaps 12 peradventure

mayor: 5 maire(F.) 7 alcalde(Sp.) 8 official 10 magistrate 12 burgomeister(G.)

maze: 4 daze 5 amaze, fancy 7 confuse, stupefy 8 bewilder, confound, delirium, delusion 9 amazement, deception, labyrinth 12 bewilderment

mazed: 4 lost 5 dazed 10 bewildered

mazer: 4 bowl

mazy: 7 complex 9 intricate 10 circuitous, perplexing

mead: 5 drink 6 meadow 8 hydromel 9 metheglin

meadow: ing, lea 4 mead, vega, wish, wong 5 field, haugh 6 saeter 7 pasture 9 grassland, grassplot
piece of: 5 swale

meadow bell: 8 harebell

meadowlark: 6 medlar

meadowmouse: 4 vole 8 arvicole

meadowsweet: 7 spiraea

meager: bar 4 arid, bare, lank, lean, poor, slim, thin 5 gaunt, scant, spare 6 barren, jejune, lenten, meagre, narrow, pilled, scanty, scarce, sparse **7** scranny, starved, sterile, tenuous **9** emaciated **10** inadequate

meagerness: 7 exility

meal: tub **4** bite, dune, feed, menu **5** feast, flour, lunch, padar, salep, snack **6** bucket, dinner, morsel, nocake, repast, supper **7** banquet, blowout, potluck **8** sandbank **9** breakfast, collation, pulverize

army: **4** chow, mess

coarse: **5** grout **7** cribble **8** gurgeons

last course: **7** dessert

light: tea **5** lunch, snack **6** tiffin

main dish: **6** entree

wheat: **4** atta(Ind.)

meals: 5 board

mealy: 4 pale **6** floury, spotty **7** friable, starchy **8** farinose **9** personate **11** farinaceous

mealy back: 6 cicada

mean: low **4** base, clam, hard, lean, norm, poor **5** argue, footy, nasty, petty, ratty, snide, snivy, sorry **6** abject, chetif, coarse, common, denote, design, dirten, feeble, humble, intend, medial, medium, middle, narrow, paltry, pilled, snivey, sordid **7** average, caitiff, ignoble, pitiful, purport, purpose, signify **8** baseborn, beggarly, churlish, recreant, shameful **9** niggardly, penurious, truculent **11** disgraceful, hard-hearted **12** contemptible, dishonorable, intermediate, parsimonious

mean line: 9 bisectrix

meander: 4 roam, turn, wind **5** amble **6** wander **8** straggle **9** labyrinth

meaning: 5 sense **6** import, intent, spirit **7** anagoge, bearing, purport, purpose **9** intending, intention, knowledge **10** definition **11** designation **12** apprehension, significance **13** signification, understanding

without: **4** null

meanly: 6 humbly, poorly **8** beggarly, shabbily

means: 4 cost **5** agent **6** agency, method **7** quomodo **8** averages **10** instrument **11** wherewithal **12** intermediary

financial: **5** funds **7** capital **9** resources

of livelihood: **4** work **5** labor, trade **8** vocation **10** profession

support: **4** hold **6** income **7** aliment **11** maintenance

meantime: 7 interim **8** interval

meanwhile: 9 adinterim

mear: 8 boundary

measles: 7 rubeola

measly: 4 mean **6** skimpy, slight **9** worthless **12** contemptible

measure (see also **measuring instrument**): pe **4** bole, boll, cess, gage, mete, rule, span, tape, time **5** clock, gauge, girth, meter, ruler, scale **6** assize, degree, stadia **7** battuta, caliper **8** odometer, tapeline **9** admeasure, calculate, criterion, rotameter

area: ar; are, rod **4** acre **6** decare

astronomical: **7** azimuth

Biblical: cab, hin, kor, log **4** epha **5** cubit, aphah, homer

cable: **4** naut

capacity: **4** cask, gill, orna, peck, pint **5** liter, quart **6** barrel, bushel, gallon

cloth: ell **4** yard

cubic: **4** cord **5** stere **10** hectostere

cut wood: **4** cord

degree of angle: arc

distance: see *length* below

dry: **4** bale, peck **6** bushel

energy: erg **5** ergon, joule

established: **8** standard

fish: vog **4** cran(Sc.) **5** crane, crans

flexible: **4** tape **8** tapeline

heat: **5** therm **6** calory, therme **7** calorie **10** centigrade, fahrenheit

horse: **4** hand

land: ar; are, rod **4** acre, area, mile, rood **6** decare **7** hectare, kiliare

length: dra, ell, pik, rod **4** foot, inch, knot, mile, nail, pace, pole, yard **5** cubit, digit, meter, metre, perch, toise(F.) **6** league, micron, mikron **9** decimeter, kilometer **10** centimeter, hectometer, millimeter

liquid: aam, keg **4** gill, pint **5** lagen, liter, quart **6** barrel, gallon, magnum, minims, runlet, tierce **7** rundlet **8** hogshead **9** hectolite, kiloliter

loudness: **4** phon

medicinal: **4** dram **5** minim, ounce **7** scruple

nautical: **4** knot **6** fathom

paper: **4** page, ream **5** quire, sheet

printer's: em, en **4** pica **5** agate, empen

short: **6** ullage

sound: bel

space: **6** parsec

time: day **4** hour, week, year **5** month **6** decade, minute, moment, second

water depth: **5** sound

weight: ton **4** bale **5** carat, liter, ounce, pound **9** kiloliter **10** hectoliter

wheat: **4** trug

wine: tun **4** butt, pipe

wire: mil **5** stone

work: erg **5** ergon

yarn: lea **4** heer, typp **6** denier **7** spindle

Measure for Measure character: 5 Elbow, Froth, Lucio **6** Angelo, Juliet

measured: 7 careful, guarded **10** deliberate

measureless: 4 vast **7** endless, immense **8** infinite **9** boundless, limitless, unbounded, unlimited **11** illimitable **12** immeasurable

measurement: 9 dimension **11** mensuration

pert. to: 6 metric 11 dimensional

measuring instrument: 4 gage, tape 5 chain, gauge, meter, ruler 7 alidade 8 measurer, tapeline 9 container, yardstick 13 saccharimeter

acidity: 10 acidimeter

heat: 11 calorimeter

lumber: 6 scaler

surveying: 11 stratameter

thickness: 7 caliper

measuring wheel: 8 odometer 12 perambulator

meat: 4 beef, food, gist, lamb, pork, veal 5 flesh 6 chevon, mutton 7 chilver, venison 9 nutriment

ball: 7 rissole 9 croquette, fricandel 11 fricandelle

bony: 5 scrag 9 spareribs

cured: ham 5 bacon 6 flitch, salame, salami 7 biltong, bultong, sausage 8 pastrami, pastroma 9 biltongue

cut: ham, rib 4 chop, loin 5 flank, roast, steak 6 cutlet, rasher 7 icebone, sirloin 9 aitchbone

dish: 5 pasty 6 potpie, ragout 7 goulash, haricot, ravioli 8 fricando 10 fricandeau

dish with vegetables: 4 olla, stew 8 mulligan 9 lobscouse 10 lobscourse

dried: 5 jerky 7 biltong, bultong, pemican 8 pemmican 9 biltongue

frozen: 5 frigo

ground: 7 rissole, sausage 9 hamburger

jelly: 5 aspic

pie: 5 pasty 7 rissole

pin: 6 skewer

potted: 7 rillett 8 rillette

roasted: 5 brede, cabob, kabob

sauce: 4 A-one 5 caper, gravy 14 Worcestershire

slice: 6 collop

smoking place: 5 bucan

unwholesome: 6 cagmag

meated: fed 8 fattened

meatless: 6 lenten, maigre

meatman: 7 butcher

meatus: 4 burr, duct 5 canal 7 foramen, passage

meatworks: 8 abattoir 14 slaughterhouse

meaty: 5 pithy, solid 11 substantial

Mecca (see also **Muslim**): *deity:* 5 Hobal, Hubal

mosque: 5 Caaba, Kaaba 6 Kaabeh

pilgrim's dress: 5 ihram

pilgrimage: 4 hadj

mechanic: erk(F.) 7 artisan, workman 8 operator 9 artificer, craftsman, operative

mechanical: 9 automatic 10 uninspired 11 automatical, involuntary, perfunctory, stereotyped

mechanical man: 5 robot 9 automaton

mechanical part: 5 rotor 6 stator, tappet

mechanics branch: 7 statics 8 dynamics

mechanism: 4 gear, tool 9 apparatus, machinery

driving: 9 propeller

eccentric: cam

self-moving: 8 automata(pl.) 9 automaton

meconin: 7 opianyl

medal: 4 disk 5 badge 6 plaque 7 medalet 10 decoration

medallion: 4 coin 8 ornament 11 contorniate, contorniato

Medb's consort: 6 Ailill

meddle: 4 nose 5 snoop 6 dabble, finger, monkey, potter, tamper 7 intrude 9 interfere

meddler: 7 marplot 8 busybody

meddlesome: 4 busy 5 fresh 7 curious 8 meddling 9 officious 10 handersome

Mede: 5 Aryan, Mesne 6 Median

caste: 4 magi

king: Evi

Medea: *father:* 6 Aeetes

husband: 5 Jason

rival: 6 Creusa

media: See **medium**

medial: 6 middle 8 ordinary

median: 4 mean 6 medial, middle 7 average, central 12 intermediate

Median: See **Mede**

mediate: 7 referee 8 ruminate 9 arbitrate, intercede, interpose

mediator: 7 daysman 9 go-between 10 ambocepter, interagent 12 intermediary

medic: 6 clover, doctor, intern, medico 7 luterne, student, surgeon 8 resident 9 physician

false: 10 medicaster

medical: 6 iatric 11 aesculapian

medical officer: 7 coroner

medical student: 6 extern, intern 7 externe, interne 8 resident

medicinal: 6 curing 7 healing 8 salutary 9 relieving 11 aesculapian

bark: 6 cartex

berry: 5 cubeb

capsule: 6 cachet

compound: 4 pill, sera 5 hepar, iodin, serum 6 iodine 7 turpeth

nut: 4 cola

plant (see also *root* below): rue 4 aloe 5 ergot, senna, tansy 6 arnica, cohosh, ipecac 7 chirata 8 valerian

remedy: 8 antidote

root (see also *plant* above): 5 artar, jalap, orris 6 seneca, senega 8 licorice

solution: 8 tincture

tablet: 4 pill 6 troche 7 lozenge

medicine: 4 drug 5 tonic 6 physic, remedy 7 placebo 10 abirritant, alterative
amount: 4 dose 6 dosage
comb. form: 5 iatro, iatry
institution: 6 clinic 8 hospital
instrument: see **surgery instrument**
mild: 6 tisane
noncuring: 6 ptisan
patent: 7 nostrum
vessel: 4 vial 5 ampul, phial 6 ampule 7 ampoule 8 gallipot
medicine dropper: 7 pipette
medicine man: 4 piay 6 doctor, shaman 8 magician, sorcerer 9 physician
mediety: 6 moiety
medieval: *battle:* 4 Acre
coin: 9 bracteate
dagger: 6 anlace
fiddle: 4 giga
fort: 11 Carcassonne
gown: 6 cyclas
helmet: 5 armet 6 heaume
lyric: 4 alba
prayer book: 7 portass
shield: ecu
weapon: 5 lance, oncin 7 gisarme 8 crossbow
Medina (see also **Muslim**): Aus
citizen: 5 Ansar
mediocre: 4 mean, soso 6 common, medium 7 average 8 middling, ordinary, passable 11 commonplace, indifferent
meditate: 4 chew, mull, muse, pore 5 brook, study, think, watch, weigh 6 ponder, reason 7 reflect, revolve 8 cogitate, consider, ruminate 10 deliberate 11 contemplate
meditation: 4 yoga 8 higgaion 14 omphaloskepsis
meditative: 7 pensive
mediterranean: 6 inland 7 midland 10 landlocked
Mediterranean: sea
boat: nef 4 saic 5 setee, xebec, zebec 6 galiot, mistic, settee, tartan, zebeck 7 felucca, mistico, polacre
coast: 7 Riviera
country: 5 Italy 6 France, Greece 7 Algeria
Eastern: 6 Levant
falcon: 6 lanner
fish: aco 6 remora
fruit: 5 olive 7 azarole
galley: 6 galiot
grass: 4 diss
gulf: 5 Tunis
island: 4 Elba 5 Capri, Crete, Ibiza, Iviza, Malta 6 Candia, Cyprus, Ebusus, Lesbos, Lipari, Rhodes, Sicily 7 Majorca, Panaria 8 Sardinia 9 Stromboli
pert. to: 9 Levantine

port: 5 Tunis 7 Tunisia
resort: 4 Nice 6 Menton 7 Mentone
shrub: 7 azarole
storm: 7 borasca, borasco
tree: 5 carob 6 mastic 7 azarole
wind: 6 otesan, solano 7 gregale, mistral, sirocco 8 levanter 10 euroclyden
medium: 4 mean 5 media(pl.), midst, organ 6 degree, medial 7 average, channel, psychic 8 mediator 10 instrument, interagent 11 environment 12 intermediary, intermediate
communication: 4 note 5 cable, phone, radio 6 letter 9 telegraph, telephone 10 television
culture: 4 agar
news: TV 5 radio 7 journal 8 magazine 9 newspaper 10 periodical, television
medlar: 4 lark, tree 5 fruit 6 mespil
medley: 4 olio 6 jumble 7 farrago, melange, mixture 8 mingling 9 bariolage(F.), potpourri 10 hodgepodge 11 gallimaufry 12 mingle-mangle
musical: 8 fantasia
medrick: 4 gull, tern
medulla: 4 pith 6 marrow 7 essence, summary 10 compendium
Medusa: 6 Gorgon 7 blubber 9 jellyfish
offspring: 7 Pegasus 8 Chrysaor
representation: 9 Gorgoneum
sister: 6 Stheno 7 Euryale
slayer: 7 Perseus
meed: due 4 gift 5 award, bribe, merit, repay, worth 6 desert, reward 7 bribery 10 excellence, recompense
meek: 4 deft, kind, mild 5 lowly 6 docile, gentle, humble 7 pacific, patient 8 moderate, sheepish, yielding 9 childlike, spineless 10 spiritless, submissive
meerkat: 6 monkey 8 suricate
meerschaum: 7 seafoam 9 sepiolite
meet: fit, kep(Sc.), sit 4 duel, face, join, tidy 5 equal, occur, touch, tryst 6 battle, combat, confer, gather, proper 7 contact, convene, fitting, fulfill 8 assemble, assembly, confront, moderate, suitable 9 encounter, forgather, gathering, intersect 10 congregate, experience, foregather 11 appropriate
athletic: 8 gymkhana 10 tournament
meeting: 4 mall, moot 5 gemot, rally, union 6 caucus, gemote, huddle, parley 7 coition, consult, session 8 adjacent, assembly, conclave, congress, junction 10 concurrent, conference, confluence, rendezvous 11 convocation
meeting place: 4 fora(pl.) 5 forum
meetinger: 9 dissenter
meg: 6 guinea 9 halfpenny

Meg's sisters: Jo; Amy 4 Beth
megagamete: 11 macrogamete
megalithic chamber: 6 dolmen
megaphone: 8 vamphorn
megapod: 4 bird 5 maleo 6 leipoa
Megara king: 5 Nisus
megrim: 4 whim 5 blues, fancy, freak, humor, whiff 7 vertigo 8 flounder, headache 9 dizziness 12 hypochondria
Mehitabel: cat
  companion: 6 Archie 9 cockroach
  creator: 7 Marquis
Mekong River: *site:* 4 Asia 7 Vietnam
  tribe: Moi
mel: 5 honey
melancholia: 6 athymy 7 athymia
melancholy: sad 4 blue, dram, dull, dump, glum 5 dolar(L.), drear, dusky, gloom 6 dismal, somber, sombre, sorrow, yellow 7 chagrin, doleful, pensive, sadness, unhappy 8 atrabile, downcast, tristful 9 cheerless, dejection, plaintive 10 allicholly, depression, desolation 11 despondency, downhearted 12 disconsolate, heavy-hearted, hypochondria, mournfulness
Melanesia: *language:* 5 Santo
  people: 4 Fiji
melange: 4 olio 6 medley 7 mixture
melanic: 5 black
melanous: 4 dark 6 brunet 8 brunette
meld: 4 play 5 unite
mele: 4 poem, song 5 chant, lyric 6 ballad
melee: row 4 fray, riot 5 brawl, fight, foray, mix-up 6 affray, fracas, ruckus 7 ruction, scuffle 8 dogfight, skirmish
melicocca: 5 genip
melicratum: 4 mead 8 beverage, hydromel
melilotus: 6 clover
meliorate: 6 better, soften 7 improve 10 ameliorate
melisma: 7 cadenza
melissa plant: 4 mint
Melita: 5 Malta
Melkarth: 4 Baal 6 Moloch
mell: mix 4 maul 5 fight, honey 6 beetle, hammer, mallet, meddle, mingle
mellifluous: 7 honeyed, sugared
mellow: age 4 aged, rich, ripe, soft 5 ripen 6 mature, tender 7 matured 8 patinate
melodeon: 9 seraphine
melodious: 6 ariose, arioso, dulcet 7 lyrical, melodic, musical, tunable, tuneful 8 canorous 10 harmonious
melodist: 6 singer 8 composer 9 harmonist
melodramatic: 8 dramatic 9 emotional 10 theatrical 11 sensational

melody: air, lay 4 aria, lilt, note, raga(Ind.), solo, song, tune 5 charm, dirge, music, theme 6 strain 7 arietta, harmony, rosalia, sortita 9 cantilena 11 tunefulness
  characterization: 6 ariose, arioso
  counter: 7 descant
  outline: 5 melos
  pert. to: 6 plagal
  unaccompanied: 4 solo 6 monody
meloid: 6 beetle
melon: 4 musk, pepo 5 gourd, water 6 casaba, papaya 7 Persian 8 honeydew 10 cantaloupe, paddymelon
melon pear: 6 pepino
melongena: 8 eggplant
melos: 4 song 6 melody
melt: rin(Sc.), run 4 flow, flux, fuse, thaw 5 smelt, sweal 6 render, soften 7 dwindle, liquefy 8 discandy, dissolve, eliquate 10 colliquate, deliquesce 12 disintegrate
  down: 6 render 7 liquefy
  partly: 4 frit
Melville: *character:* 4 Ahab 5 whale
  novel: 4 Omoo 5 Typee
member: 4 limb, part 5 organ 6 branch, fellow 7 section 8 district 11 communicant
  new: 6 novice 7 entrant 8 neophyte 10 apprentice
  oldest: 4 dean
membership: 4 seat 10 fellowship
membrane: web 4 caul, coat, skin, tela 5 amnia(pl.), lemma, telae(pl.) 6 amnion, amnios, retina 7 cuticle, eardrum, velamen 8 striffen
  diffusion through: 7 osmosis
  fold of: 5 plica
  fringe: 4 loma
  of bird: 4 cere
  spore: 6 intine
  weblike: 4 tela
memento: 5 relic, token 6 trophy 8 keepsake, reminder, souvenir
memo: 4 chit 8 reminder
memoir: 4 note 5 eloge 6 record, report 7 history 8 memorial 9 biography, narrative 10 commentary
memorabilia: ana
memorable: 7 namable, notable, special 9 reminding 10 remarkable 11 reminiscent 13 distinguished, extraordinary
memorandum: 4 bill, note, stub 5 brief 6 agenda(pl.) 7 agendum, memento, minutes, notanda(pl.), proctol 8 notandum, notation, reminder
  book: 5 diary 6 agenda 7 tickler 8 calendar
  legal: 5 jurat
memoria: 6 chapel, church, shrine, temple 9 reliquary
memorial: ahu 5 facta(pl.), relic 6 factum, memoir, record, trophy 8 mnemonic, mon-

ument 11 remembrance 12 recollection 13 commemorative

carved: 5 totem

stone: 5 cairn 6 statue 9 mausoleum

memorist: 8 prompter

memory: 4 mind, rote 8 memorial 9 retention 11 remembrance 12 recollection, reminiscence 13 retrospection

aid: 8 mnemonic, reminder 10 anamnestic

goddess: 9 Mnemosyne

loss: 5 blank, lethe 7 amnesia, aphasia 13 forgetfulness

pattern: 6 engram

pert. to: 6 mnesic 7 mnestic 8 mnemonic

vivid: 7 eidetic

memory book: 5 diary 9 scrapbook

Memphis (see also **Egypt**):

chief: Evi

god: Ra 4 Ptah

men: 4 crew 6 people

armed body: 4 army 5 posse

party: 4 stag 6 smoker

section of Greek church: 6 andron

wise: 4 Magi 6 Gaspar 8 Melchior 9 Balthasar, Balthazar

menace: 5 boast, peril 6 impend, threat 8 denounce, jeopardy, threaten 9. fulminate

menacing: 10 formidable

menage: 4 club 7 society 8 domicile 9 household 10 management 12 housekeeping

menagerie: zoo 10 collection

menald: 8 speckled 10 variegated

menaspis: 5 shark

mend: fix, sew 4 beet, darn, heal, help, knit 5 amend, beete, botch, clout, emend, moise, patch 6 better, cobble, repair, solder 7 improve, restore 10 ameliorate, convalesce

mendacity: lie 5 lying 6 deceit 7 falsity, untruth 9 falsehood

mendelevium symbol: Md

mender: 6 tinker 7 cobbler 9 repairman

mendicant: 4 monk 5 fakir 6 beggar, begger, bhikku, fakeer, frater, gosain, gusain 7 ajivika, bhikshu

Menelaus: *brother:* 9 Agamemnon

daughter: 8 Hermione

father: 6 Atreus

steersman: 7 Canopus

wife: 5 Helen

meng: mix 5 blend 6 mingle

menhaden: 4 fish, pogy 5 pogie, porgy 8 bonyfish 10 mossbunker

young: 7 sardine

menial: fag 4 base 6 drivel, harlot, sordid, stocah, varlet 7 servant, servile, slavish 8 coistrel, coistril, servitor 9 degrading, underling

meniscus: 4 lens

mennom: 6 mennon, minnow

Mennonite: 5 Amish

meno: 4 less

Menominee whitefish: 6 chivey

Menotti character: 5 Amahl

mensk: 5 adorn, favor, grace, honor 6 credit 8 ornament 9 reverence 12 graciousness

mensuration: 11 measurement 13 determination

mental: 5 ideal 7 phrenic 11 intelligent 12 intellectual

mental aberration: fog 4 daze, haze 5 lapse 6 stupor 7 doldrum, madness 8 insanity

mental defective: 5 idiot, moron 8 imbecile 9 retardate

mental disorder: 6 ataxia 7 aphasia 8 neuritis, neurosis, paranoia 9 melomania, paranomia, psychosis 11 megalomania 12 hypochondria 13 schizophrenia

specialist: 12 psychiatrist

mental faculties: 4 mind, wits

mental image: 4 idea 5 dream, idola(pl.) 6 idolum 7 fantasy 8 phantasm 10 conception

mental state: 5 blues 6 morale 7 doldrum 8 euphoria

mentality: 4 mind 5 sense 6 acumen, reason 9 endowment, intellect 11 rationality 12 intelligence

mentiferous: 10 telepathic

mention: 4 cite, hint, mind, name 5 clepe, refer, speak, trace 6 allude, denote, notice, record 7 specify, vestige 8 allusion, citation 9 statement 10 indication

implied: 11 connotation

mentioned: 8 foresaid 9 aforesaid

mentor: 4 guru 7 monitor, teacher 9 counselor 10 counsellor, instructor

menu: 4 card, meal 5 carte 10 bill of fare

part of: 4 soup 5 salad 6 entree 7 dessert, special 9 appetizer

Mephistophelean: sly 4 evil 6 crafty

Mephistopheles: 5 devil, Satan

mephitic: 4 foul 6 deadly 7 noxious

mephitis: 4 odor 5 smell 6 stench

mercantile: 7 trading 10 commercial

mercenary: 4 hack 5 venal 6 sordid 7 Hessian 8 covetous, hireling, vendible 10 galloglass(Sc.) 11 gallowglass 13 stipendiarian

merchandise: 4 ware 5 goods, wares 7 chaffer

cheap: 5 borax 7 camelot, schlock

pert. to: 10 emporeutic

merchant: 4 Seth(Ind.) 6 dealer, seller, sutler, trader, vender, vendor 7 chapman, goladar, howadji, vintner 8 purveyor 9 tradesman 10 shopkeeper 11 storekeeper

group: 5 guild, hansa 6 cartel

wholesale: 6 packer
Merchant of Venice: 7 Antonio
  character: 5 Tubal 6 Portia 7 Jessica, Lorenzo, Nerissa, Shylock
merchant vessel: 6 argosy, holcad 8 bilander, indiaman
merciful: 6 benign 7 sparing 9 benignant, forgiving 10 charitable
merciless: 4 grim 5 cruel 6 savage 8 pitiless 9 ferocious, graceless, heartless 10 despiteous, relentless
mercurial: 6 clever, lively, shrewd 8 changing, thievish 9 faithless 10 inconstant
mercury: 5 azoth, guide, thief 6 hawker 9 messenger 11 quicksilver
  derivative: 11 quicksilver
  symbol: Hg
Mercury: 6 Hermes, planet 9 newspaper
  son: 5 Cupid
  staff: 8 caduceus
  winged cap: 7 petasos, petasus
  winged shoes: 7 talaria
mercury subchloride: 7 calomel
mercy: law 4 pity, ruth 5 grace, grith 6 lenity 7 charity 8 clemency, humanity, kindness, lenience, leniency, mildness 9 tolerance 10 compassion, indulgence, tenderness 11 forbearance, forgiveness
  show: 5 spare 6 pardon 7 forgive 8 reprieve
mercy killing: 10 euthanasia
mere: but, sea 4 bare, club, lake, mear, pool, pond, pure, sole 5 bound, limit, plain, sheer, utter 6 divide, entire, famous, scarce, simple 7 unmixed 8 absolute, boundary, glorious, landmark, trifling 9 beautiful, undiluted 11 unqualified
merely: 4 also, just, only 5 quite 6 anerly
merganser: 4 smee, smew 5 harle, robin 7 becscie, bracket, garbill 9 goosander
merge: 4 fuse, join, meld 5 blend, unify, unite 6 absorb, mingle 7 combine, conjoin 8 coalesce 9 commingle 10 amalgamate 11 consolidate, incorporate
mericarp: 8 hemicarp
meridian: 4 noon 6 midday 11 culmination
meringue 5 icing
merino: 4 wool 5 sheep 6 fabric 7 Delaine
merit: 4 earn, meed 5 worth 6 desert, reward 7 deserve 10 condignity, excellence
merited: fit 7 fitting 8 adequate, suitable
meritorious: 8 valorous 9 honorable
merkin: mop
merlin: 6 falcon
Merlin: 4 poem 8 magician 9 alchemist
Merlin's grass: 9 quillwort
mermaid: 5 nymph, siren 6 merrow
mero: 5 guasa 7 grouper
Merob's alphabet: 8 Armenian
meropia: 9 blindness

meropodite: 5 meros
meros: 5 thigh
merriment: fun 5 deray 9 amusement, diversion 11 galliardise
merrow: 7 mermaid
merry: gai(F.), gay 4 agog, airy, boon, cant, glad 5 bonny, droll, happy, jolly, sunny 6 blithe, bonnie, cocket, hilary, jocose, jocund, jovial, joyous, lively 7 gleeful, jocular 8 cheerful, chirping, gamesome, gleesome, mirthful, pleasant, sportive 9 hilarious, sprightly 10 blithesome, frolicsome 11 exhilarated 12 lighthearted
merry andrew: 4 zany 5 antic, clown, joker 6 jester 7 buffoon 8 merryman
merry-go-round: 8 carousel 9 carrousel
Merry Widow composer: 5 Lehar
Merry Wives of Windsor character: Nym 4 Ford 5 Robin 6 Fenton, Pistol
merrymaking: 5 jolly, revel 6 splore 7 festive, revelry, wassail 8 carnival 9 festivity, merriment 12 conviviality
merrythought: 8 wishbone
merrytrotter: 5 swing 6 seesaw
merrywing: 9 goldeneye 10 bufflehead
merse: dip 5 marsh 6 plunge 7 immerse
merycism: 10 rumination
mesa: 7 plateau 8 plateaux(pl.) 9 tableland
mescal: 5 cacti(pl.), drink 6 cactus, peyote, peyotl
mesel: 5 leper 7 leprosy
mesh: net 4 moke 5 snare 6 areola, engage, macula, tangle 7 areolae, ensnare, maculae(pl.), netting, network 8 entangle 10 reticulate
mesial: 6 median, middle
mesmerize: 9 hypnotize
mesne: 6 middle 11 intervening 12 intermediate
Mesopotamia: 4 Irak, Iraq
  ancient city or town: Ur 6 Nippur 7 Babylon
  captives' place: 5 Halah
  city: 5 Mosul 6 Bagdad(c.) 7 Edessan, Kerbela
  people: 5 Iraki, Iraqi 7 Aramean
  river: 6 Tigris 9 Euphrates
  wind: 6 shamal
mesosperm: 9 secundine
mesotais: 4 base 10 groundmass
mespil: 6 medlar
mesquin: 4 mean 6 shabby, sordid
mesquite: 9 algarroba
  genus: 8 prosopis
mess: jag, row 4 clat, jagg, meal, mull, muss, soil 5 batch, botch, cauch, dirty, lelee 6 bungle, dabble, jumble, litter, muddle, rumple, tousle 7 crumple, mixture, wrin-

kle **6** disarray, dishevel, disorder, scramble, slaister, squabble **9** commotion, confusion **10** hodgepodge, picklement

message: **4** bode, line, memo, news, note, wire, word **5** cable **6** brevet, letter **7** bodword, depeche, mission, missive, tidings **9** memoranda **10** communique, memorandum **13** communication

good news: **7** evangel

Messalina: **6** wanton **10** prostitute

husband: **8** Claudius

messenger: **4** bode, page, sand, toty **5** angel, envoy, miler **6** beadle, chiaus, herald, legate, nuncio **7** apostle, carrier, courant, courier, hi-carra, mercury, prophet, totyman **8** hi-carrah, minister, nunciate, portator **9** harbinger **10** ambassador, evangelist, forerunner **11** internuncio

mounted: **6** cossid(Ind.) **7** courier, estafet **9** estafette

of the gods: **6** Hermes **7** Mercury

Messiah: **6** Christ, Savior **7** prophet, Saviour

Messina Strait rock: **6** Scilla, Scylla

messy: **5** dirty **6** untidy

mestive: **8** mournful

mestizo: **5** cross, metis **7** mixture

met (see also **meet**): **7** measure, opposed **11** measurement

metad: rat

metagnomy: **10** divination

metagnostic: **10** unknowable

metal: ore, tin **4** gold, iron, lead, zinc **6** cobalt, copper, oroide, pewter, radium, silver, sodium, spirit **7** bullion, gallium, mercury **9** potassium, substance

alloy: **5** brass, steel

bar: gad **5** ingot

base: **5** dross, sprue

box: **8** canister

cake: **4** slag

clippings: **7** scissel

containing: **13** metalliferous

crude: **5** matte

decorate: **4** etch **6** emboss **9** damascene, damaskeen

decorative: **6** chrome, niello

deposit: **4** lode

disc: **5** paten **6** patten

fastener: pin **4** bolt, brad, nail **5** rivet, screw **6** cotter, solder

filings: **5** lemel

heavy: **6** osmium **7** uranium

impure mass: **7** regulus

layer: **4** seam **5** stope

leaf: **4** foil

lightest known: **7** lithium

lump: pig **4** slug **6** nugget

magnetized: **13** electromagnet

mixture: **5** alloy

nonexpanding: **5** invar

oblong piece: sow

patch: **6** solder

plate: gib

rare: **4** zinc **6** cerium, erbium **7** iridium, terbium, uranium, yttrium **8** lutecium, platinum

refuse: **4** slag **5** dross **6** scoria

scrap: **6** filing

shaper: **5** swage

sheet: **4** foil **5** lames, plate **6** lamina, latten, tagger

spike: gad

stannic: tin

strip: **6** spline

suit: **4** mail **5** armor

test: **5** assay

tin-like: **7** cadmium

unrefined: ore

vein: **4** lode

waste: **4** slag **5** dross **6** scoria **9** recrement

worker: **5** smith **6** barman **7** riveter **8** tinsmith **9** goldsmith **11** coppersmith, silversmith

metallic: **6** brazen **13** metalliferous

content: ory

metamere: **6** somite **8** somatome

metamerism: **12** segmentation

metamorphose: **6** change **9** transform, transmute **16** transubstantiate

metamorphosis: **4** pupa **6** change **8** mutation

metaphor: **5** trope **6** simile **8** allegory **10** comparison **11** tralatition

faulty or mixed use of: **11** catachresis

metaphorical: **10** figurative

metaphysical being: ens **5** entia(pl.)

metastrophe: **11** interchange

metayer: **6** farmer

mete: **4** dole, give, goal, post **5** allot, award, bound, limit, stake **7** measure **8** allocate **9** apportion **10** distribute

meteor: **5** bolis, Cetid, comet, Lyrid **6** Antlid, bolide, Lyraid **8** aerolite, fireball **9** Andromede **10** Andromedid

August: **8** Perseids

November: **6** Leonid

meteorite: **8** aerolite, aerolith, siderite **9** asiderite **10** siderolite

meteorological instrument: **6** bolide **9** barometer **11** thermometer

meteorologist: **10** forecaster

meter: **4** beat, time **5** metre, verse **6** rhythm **7** cadence, measure **8** measurer

cubic: **5** liter, litre, stere

one-hundredth: **10** centimeter

one-millionth: **6** micron

one-tenth: **9** decimeter

one-thousandth: 10 millimeter
square: 7 centare
unit: 4 mora 5 morae(pl.)
meterist: 10 verse-maker
meters: *10:* 9 decameter
100: 10 hectometer
100 square: ar; are
1,000: 9 kilometer
10,000: 10 myriameter
methane hydrocarbon: 8 paraffin 9 paraffine
metheglin: 4 mead 8 beverage
mether: cup
method: way 4 dart, form, garb, mode, rule 5 means, order, style, usage 6 course, manner, system 7 fashion, formula, process 9 procedure, technique 11 orderliness
customary: rut 5 habit 7 routine
methodical: 5 exact 6 severe 7 precise
methodize: 8 regulate
Methuselah: *father:* 5 Enoch
grandson: 4 Noah
son: 6 Lamech
methyl: *cyanide:* 7 nitrile
ethyl ketone: 8 butanone
ketol: 6 acetol
meticulous: 4 neat, nice, prim 5 fussy, timid 7 careful, fearful, finical 10 fastidious, scrupulous
metier: 4 line 5 trade 7 calling 8 business 10 occupation, profession
metis: 8 octoroon 9 halfbreed
metric: 8 criteria(pl.) 9 criterion
measure: ar; are 5 carat, liter, litre, meter, stere, tonne 6 decare, hectar, micron, miglio 7 centare, deciare, dekiare, hectare, kiliare, manzana, myriare 8 centiare, dekagram, milliare 9 decaliter, decameter, decastere, deciliter, decimeter, decistere, dekaliter, dekameter, dekistere, kiloliter, kilometer, kilostere, megameter 10 centiliter, centimeter, centistere, dekadrachm, hectoliter, hectometer, hectostere, microliter, milliliter, millimeter, millistere, myrialiter, myriameter 15 micromillimeter
metrical beat: 5 ictus
metrical foot: 4 iamb 6 iambic, iambus 7 anapest
accented syllable: 5 arsis
four syllables: 6 syzygy
three short syllables: 8 tribrach
two syllables: 7 spondee, trochee
two together: 6 dipody
metrist: 4 poet 9 metrician
metronome: 5 timer
metropolis: see 4 city, seat 6 center
metropolitan: cit 5 chief, urban 7 bishops, leading 9 principal

mettle: 4 fire 5 ardor, nerve, pluck, spunk 6 ginger, spirit 7 bravery, courage 9 fortitude
Metz's river: 7 Moselle
meuse: gap 4 hole, lurk 7 conceal, opening 8 loophole
mew: den 4 cage, cast, coop, gull, maas(Sc.), molt, shed 5 miaow, miaul 6 change 7 conceal, confine, enclose, garages, stables 8 spicknel 9 enclosure 11 concealment, confinement
mewl: cry, mew 6 squall 7 whimper
Mexico: *agave:* 5 datil 6 zapupe
alcoholic beverage: 6 mescal, pulque 7 tepache, tequila
American: 6 gringo
annuity: 5 censo
antelope: 9 pronghorn
bean: 6 frejol, frijol 7 frijole
bedbug: 8 conenose
beverage: 4 chia
bird: 6 jacana, towhee 7 jacamar, tinamou 8 zopilote
blanket: 6 serape
bread: 6 tamale
brigand: 7 ladrone
bull: 4 toro
cactus: 6 bavoso, chaute, chende, mescal 8 alicoche, chichipe 11 alfilerillo
candlewood: 8 ocotillo
cat: 6 margay
chaps(leather): 10 chaparajos, chaparejos
city: 4 Leon, Tula 5 Tepic 6 Colima, Jalapa, Juarez, Merida, Mexico(c.), Oaxaca, Puebla, Potosi 7 Durango, Orizaba, San Luis, Tampico 8 Culiacan, Mazatlan, Monterey, Saltillo, Vera Cruz, Victoria 9 Chihuahua, Luis Potos 10 Hermosillo 11 Guadalajara
cloak: 5 manta 6 serape
cockroach: 9 cucaracha
coin: 4 peso 5 adobe 6 azteca 7 centavo, piaster
conqueror: 6 Cortes, Cortez
cottonwood: 5 alamo
dish: 5 atole, tamal 6 tamale 9 enchilada
dollar: 4 peso
drug: 7 damiana
early dweller: 4 Maya 5 Aztec
fiber: 4 pita 5 istle, sisal 6 catena
fish: 6 salema 7 totuava
garment: 5 manga 6 serape 7 chiripa
gopher: 4 tuza 7 quachil
grapefruit: 7 toronja
grass: 5 otate 7 sacaton, zacaton 8 hanequen, hanequin
guardian spirit: 6 nagual
hero: 4 Diaz 6 Juarez
hog: 7 peccary

house: 5 jacal
Indian: see *people* below
ivy: 6 cobaea
laborer: 4 peon 7 bracero, wetback
lake: 7 Chapala
land owner: 8 ranchero
laurel: 7 madrona
masonry: 5 adobe
mat: 6 petate
measure: pie 4 alma, vara 5 almud, baril, jarra, labor, legua, linea, sitio 6 almude, fanega 7 pulgada 9 cuarteron, cuartillo 10 caballeria
measure of weight: bag 4 onza 5 carga, libra, marco 6 adarme, arroba, ochava, tercio 7 quintal
mixed blood: 7 mestizo
mountain: 7 Orizaba 12 Citlaltepetl, Ixtaccihuatl, Popocatepetl
musical instrument: 6 clarin, guiros 7 cabacas, maracas 11 chiapanecas
onyx: 6 tecali
orange: 7 choisya
painter: 6 Orozco, Rivera
pancake: 5 arepa
peasant: 4 peon
peninsula: 7 Yucatan
people: Mam 4 Cora, Maya, Seri, Xova 5 Aztec, Hauve, Lipan, Nahau, Opata, Otomi, Yaqui, Zoque 6 Indian, Mixtec, Otonia, Toltec 7 Haustec, Tepanec, Zacatec, Zapotec 8 Totonaco, Zacateco 9 Campesino 10 Cuitlateca, Cuitlateco
plant: 4 chia 5 agave, amole, datil, jalap, sotol 6 chaute, maguey, slavia 7 tequila 8 acapulco 9 sabadilla
plantation: 8 hacienda
porridge: 5 atole
porter: 5 tamen
ranch: 8 hacienda
resort: 8 Acapulco
river: 6 Panuco 7 Tabasco
rubber tree: ule
sandal: 8 gauracha, guarache, guaracho, huarache, huaracho
sandwich: 4 taco
sauce: 7 tabasco
scarf: 6 rebozo, tapalo
shawl: 6 serape
shrub: 6 anagua, anaqua, colima 7 choisya
state: 6 Colima, Sonora 7 Durango, Hidalgo, Sinaloa, Tabasco, Yucatan 9 Michoacan
sugar: 7 panocha
tea: 6 basote 7 apasote 9 alpasotes
thong: 5 romal

tree: ule 4 sero 5 abeto, amapa, ebano, ocote 6 chacte, colima, mezcal, sabino 7 capulin, colorin 8 chaparro, ulmaceae 9 ahuehuete, canadulce 10 anacahuita
village: 6 ejidos, tecali
volcano: 6 Colima 7 Jorullo 9 Paricutin 12 Popocatepetl
weight: 4 onza
yucca: 5 isote
mezereon: 5 shrub 6 daphne 8 camillia
mezzanine: 5 story 7 balcony 8 entresol
mias: 9 orangutan
miasma: 7 malaria
miaul: mew 4 meow, wraw 5 miaou, miaow, miaul 9 caterwaul
mib: 6 marble
mica: 4 talc 5 glist 7 biotite 8 silicate 9 damourite, hydromica, isinglass, muscovite 10 lepidolite
micaceous: 7 talcose
Micah: 7 prophet
  son: 5 Abdon
miche: 4 lurk 5 skulk, sneak 6 pilfer 7 conceal
Michelangelo work: 5 Pieta
micher: 5 cheat, thief 6 truant 8 panderer
Michigan: *city:* 4 Alma, Caro 5 Flint, Ionia 7 Detroit, Lansing(c.) 8 Muskegon 9 Marquette
  county: 4 Kent
  motto: 6 Tuebor
  river: 4 Cass 5 Huron
  state flower: 5 apple
mickle: 4 much 5 great
mico: 8 marmoset
micraner: ant
micro: 4 moth
microbe: 4 germ 8 bacillus, organism
microcosm: 5 world 7 village 8 universe 9 community
Micronesia island: 4 Guam, Wake 5 Palau 6 Bikini, Ellice, Saipan
microorganism: 4 germ 5 virus 6 aerobe 7 aerobia 8 aerobium 9 autoblast, spirillum 10 spirochete 11 spirochaete
microscopic: 5 small 6 minute 9 engyscope
microspore: 6 pollen
microsporophyll: 6 stamen
mid: See **midst**
mid-European: 4 Slav 7 Slovene
mid-wifery: 10 obstetrics
midday: 4 noon 8 noontide
  intermission: 5 lunch 7 nooning 8 noon hour
  nap: 6 siesta
middle: 4 mean 5 mesne, midst, waist 6 center, centre, centry, median, mesial 7 average, central, centric 11 intervening 12 intermediate 13 intermediator

combining form: mes **4** medi, meso

way: **6** midway **7** halfway **10** moderation

Middle Ages: See **medieval**

Middle East: 6 Levant

middleman: 5 agent, butty **6** dealer, trader **8** huckster, retailer **9** go-between **12** interlocutor, intermediary

middling: 4 fair, soso **6** fairly, medium **8** mediocre, moderate, ordinary, somewhat **10** moderately

middlings: 4 feed

midge: fly **5** fish, gnat **5** dwarf, stout **6** insect, midget, punkie **8** carriage

midget: 5 dwarf, small **9** miniature

Midianite: *king:* Hur **4** Reba

prince: Evi, Zur

midnoon: 4 noon **6** midday

midrib: 5 costa **6** costae(pl.)

midshipman: 5 cadet **6** reefer

midst: 4 amid, mean **5** among, depth **6** amidst, center, centre, medium, middle, mongst **7** between, halfway, setting **11** surrounding

midwife: 4 baba, dhai(Ind.), gamp **5** howdy **6** cummer, howdie, kimmer **7** hebamme **9** gracewife **11** accoucheuse, finger-smith

mien: air, eye **4** brow, vult **5** guise **6** aspect, manner, ostent **7** bearing, conduct **8** attitude, behavior, carriage, demeanor **9** behaviour, demeanour **10** appearance, deportment **11** countenance

miffed: 5 sulky, vexed **8** offended **10** displeased

mig: 4 duck **6** marble

migale: 5 mouse, shrew

migeloid fish: 4 bobo

might: arm **4** mote **7** ability

mighty: big **4** bulk, fell, vast, very **5** felon, great **6** potent, strong **7** violent **8** enormous, forceful, forcible, powerful, puissant, vigorous **9** extensive, extremely, gigantean **10** omnipotent **11** efficacious

migniard: 6 dainty, minion **7** mincing **8** delicate, mistress

mignon: 5 small **6** dainty, petite **8** delicate, graceful

mignonette: 6 reseda

vine: **7** Madeira, tarweed

migraine: 4 whim **8** headache **10** hemicrania

migrant: See **migratory**

migrate: 4 flee, flit, move, pass, trek **8** colonize, transfer

migration: 5 exode **6** exodus, flight

migratory: 6 roving **7** nomadic **9** peregrine, wandering

bird: **4** duck **5** goose, robin

farm worker: **4** Okie

mihrab: 4 slab **5** niche **7** chamber

Mikado: 9 sovereign

court: **5** dairi

office: **9** mikadoate

mike: 10 microphone

milady: 4 dame **5** madam **10** noblewoman **11** gentlewoman

Milan opera house: 5 Scala

milarite: 8 silicate

mild: moy **4** calm, easy, kind, meek, soft, tame **5** balmy, bland, claro **6** benign, gentle, humble **7** clement, lenient **8** benedict, favonian, gracious, lenitive, merciful, moderate, soothing, tranquil **9** assuasive, forgiving, indulgent, temperate **10** forbearing, mollifying **11** considerate

milder: 6 molder

mildew: 4 mold, rust **5** mould **6** blight, fungus **8** honeydew

genus of: **7** erysibe **8** erysiphe

mildness: 6 comity

mile: *nautical:* **4** knot, naut

one-eighth: **7** furlong

mileage: 8 distance

milepost: 5 stela, stele **6** marker, stelae

miler: 6 runner

milestone: 8 milepost

milfoil: 6 yarrow **9** ahartalav

milieu: 11 environment **12** surroundings

militant: 7 martial, soldier, warlike **8** fighting **9** combating, combative **10** aggressive

military (see also **army, troop**): **7** martial

advance: **5** drive **8** anabasis **11** penetration **12** breakthrough

adventurer: **10** filibuster

area: **6** sector

assistant: **4** aide **8** adjutant

base: **4** camp **5** depot, field **7** billets **8** barracks, quarters **10** encampment

call: **6** tattoo

chest: **5** funds

cloak: **5** sagum

command: **4** halt **6** at ease **9** attention

commander: **7** marshal

commission: **6** brevet

engine: ram **6** cannon, onager **7** robinet **8** catapult, mangonel

force: **5** guard **6** legion, troops **7** reserve

formation: **4** file, line **7** echelon

front: **5** lines **6** sector

guard: **6** patrol

hat: **4** kepi **5** shako **6** helmet

hat covering: **8** havelock

horsemen: **7** cavalry, Hussars

informer: spy

inspection: **5** drill **6** parade, review

landing point: **9** beachhead

machine: **4** jeep, tank

maneuver: **6** tactic

messenger: **7** estafet

obstruction: 6 abatis 7 abattis
officer: 5 major 7 captain, colonel, general 8 corporal, sergeant 9 brigadier, subaltern 10 lieutenant
operations: 8 campaign, strategy
order: 7 command
organization: 5 cadre
pit: 10 trou-de-loup
police: M.P. 9 gendarmes 12 constabulary
punishment: 9 strappado
quarters: 4 camp 7 billets 8 barracks
rank: 6 brevet 8 banneret
salute: 5 salvo
signal: 7 chamade
staff officer: 4 aide
storage place: 7 arsenal
supplies: 8 materiel, ordnance
survey: 11 reconnoiter
unit: van 4 rear 5 cadre, corps, squad, troop 7 company, platoon, 8 division, regiment
vehicle: 4 jeep, tank 6 camion 7 caisson
weapon: 4 croc 6 onager 7 robinet 8 ballista 9 catapault
work: 4 fort
militate: 5 fight 6 debate 7 contend 8 conflict
milk: lac 4 lait(F.) 5 drain, nurse 6 elicit, suckle
coagulator: 6 rennet
comb. form: 4 lact 5 lacti, lacto
curdled: 6 yogurt 7 clabber, yoghurt, yogourt 8 yoghourt
curdler: 4 ruen 6 rennet
deodorizer: 7 aerator
derived from: 6 lactic
fermented: 5 kefir, kumys 6 koumis, koumys, kumiss 7 koumiss, matzoon
first after delivery: 9 beestings, biestings, colostrum
food: 10 lacticinia
mouse: 6 spurge
pail: soa, soe 5 bowie
pert. to: 6 lactic 7 lactary, lacteal
preparation: 9 lactarene, lactarine
protein: 6 casein
sap: 5 latex
selling place: 5 dairy 9 lactarium
separator: 7 creamer
sour: 4 whig 6 blinky
sugar: 7 lactose
thickened part: 4 curd
watery: 8 blue John
watery part: 4 whey
with: 6 aulait(F.)
milk and honey: 10 prosperity
milk-and-water: 4 weak 7 insipid
milk glass: 7 opaline
milk leg: 9 phlebitis
milkfish: awa 6 sabolo

milkman: 7 chalker 8 dairyman
milksop: 5 sissy 7 cockney 11 mollycoddle
milkweed: *down:* 4 silk
family: 14 asclepiadaceae
fluid: 5 latex
milkwood: 9 paperbark
milkwort family: 12 polygalaceae
milky: 4 meek, mild, tame 5 timid, white 6 chalky, gentle 7 lacteal, opaline 8 timorous 10 effeminate
Milky Way: 6 galaxy
black spaces in: 9 coalsacks
mill: box 4 beat, nurl 5 crush, dress, fight, grind, knurl, shape, thief 6 finish, powder, thrash 7 factory, machine 8 snuffbox, vanquish 9 comminute, transform 12 housebreaker
beetle: 9 cockroach
bill: adz
end: 7 remnant
kind of: 5 quern 7 central 8 arrastra, arrastre, trapiche
race: 4 lade
run: 7 average 8 millrace, ordinary
sail: 4 vane
mill-wheel: *current:* 8 millrace
float: 5 ladle
millclapper: 10 chatterbox
millcourse: 8 millrace
millefleurs: 7 perfume
millenarian: 8 chiliast
millennium: 6 utopia 8 paradise
millepede: 8 myriapod
millepore: 5 coral
miller: ray 4 moth 5 boxer 7 harrier 8 pugilist 10 flycatcher
miller's thumb: 4 bird 7 warbler 8 cottidae, titmouse 9 goldcrest
millerite: 8 sulphide
millesimal: 10 thousandth
millet: 4 buda, moha 5 bajra, bajri, chena, cumbu, hirse, milly, mohar, proso, tenai 6 bajree, hureek 7 zaburro 8 cenchrus
millimeter: *one millionth:* 15 micromillimeter
one thousandth: 6 micron
milliner: 6 hatter
millions of millions: 9 trillions
millpond: dam
millrace: 4 lade(Sc.) 10 millcourse
below wheel: 8 tailrace
millrind: 6 moline
millstone: 6 burden 7 grinder 9 albatross 10 affliction
support: 4 rind, rynd
millstream: 5 fleam
Mills bomb: 7 grenade
milo: 5 grain
milpa: 6 chacra

milt: 6 spleen

mim: shy 4 prim 5 quiet 6 demure, modest

mime: ape 4 aper, copy, jest 5 actor, clown, drama, farce, mimer, mimic 6 jester 7 buffoon, imitate 9 represent

chief: 9 archi-mime

mimeograph: 7 stencil

mimer: 4 mime

mimesis: 7 mimicry

mimic (see also **mime**): 4 mima, mimo(G.), mock 6 parrot 7 copy-cat, copying, mimetic 9 burlesque 11 counterfeit

mimic thrush: 11 mockingbird

mimicry: 4 echo 5 apery, apism 7 mimesis 8 parrotry 9 imitation 10 camouflage

mimidae: 7 catbird 8 thrasher 11 mockingbird

mimmock: 6 dainty 10 fastidious

mimosa: 4 tree 6 acacia

mimsey: 4 prim 7 prudish

min: 5 ruler 6 memory, prince, remind 8 remember 11 remembrance

mina: 5 money

minar: 4 myna 5 tower

minaret: 4 lamp 5 tower 10 lighthouse

minatory: 8 menacing 11 threatening

minaway: 6 minuet

mince: cut 4 chop, hash 6 affect 7 finnick 9 subdivide 11 affectation

minced oath: gad, gee, lud 4 drat, heck

mincemeat: 5 gigot

minchery: 7 nunnery

minchiate: 5 tarot

mincing: 5 fussy 7 finical, minikin

mincingly: 8 gingerly

mind: min(Sc.) 4 care, chit, heed, obey, reck, tend, will 5 besee, brain, manas(Ind.), watch 6 animus, burrow, memory, notice, psyche, regard 7 dislike, dispose 9 intellect, mentality 11 inclination, remembrance 12 intelligence, recollection

keep in: 9 entertain

origin and development: 13 psychogenesis

pert. to: 6 mental, noetic 7 phrenic 13 psychological

split: 13 schizophrenic

state of: 4 mood, tune

Mindanao: *gulf:* 5 Davao

island: 5 Samal

language: Ata

people: Ata 5 Lutao 6 Bagobo, Illano, Lutayo

town: 4 Dapa

volcano: Apo

mindful: 5 aware 7 heedful 9 attentive, observant, regardful

mine (see also **mining**): my; bal, dig, mio(Sp.), pit, sap 4 delf, hole, meum(It.) 5 bargh, delft, delve 6 cavity, gopher, threat 7 gallery, passage 8 colliery 10 excavation

basket: 4 corf

ceiling: 5 astel

coal: rob

deposit: 4 lode, vein

entrance: 4 adit 5 stulm

excavation: 5 stope

floor: 4 sill

gold: 9 Homestead(S.D.)

guardian: 5 gnome

passage: 4 sill 5 stope

platform: 6 sollar, soller

product: ore 4 coal, iron

prop: 5 sprag

refuse: 4 dead 5 attle

reservoir: 4 sump 8 standage

rich: 4 lode 7 bonanza 8 golconda

roof support: nog

shaft: 4 sump

surface: 6 placer

sweeping device: 8 paravane

tunnel: 4 adit 5 stulm

vein: 4 lode

wagon: 4 tram

waste: gob 4 goaf 7 rubbish

worker: 5 cager, miner 6 canary 7 cageman, trapper 8 onsetter

mine run: 6 common 7 average 10 unassorted

mine-thrower: 6 minnie 11 minenwerfer

miner (see also **mining**): 6 dammer(Sc.), digger, sapper 7 collier

miner's anemia: 15 ancylostomiasis

miner's consumption: 8 phthisis

miner's worm: 8 hookworm

mineral (see also **ore, metal**): cal, tin 5 irite 6 barite, iolite 7 alumite, ataxite, uralite 9 celestite, galactite, inorganic, uraninite 10 gadolinite, retinalite

amorphous: 6 pinite

black: jet 4 coal 5 irite 6 cerine, yenite 7 knopite, niobite 8 graphite 10 minguetite

blue-green: 5 beryl

brittle: 7 euclase

brown: 6 cerine, egeran, rutile 8 lederite 9 elaterite

calcium and magnesium: 8 diopside

calcium carbonate: 7 calcite 8 calcspar

combining form: 4 lite

crystalline: 4 spar 6 yenite 7 apatite, felsite, felspar, knopite 8 boracite, elaterin, felspath

deposit: 4 lode, nest, vein 6 placer

deposit cavity: vug 4 voog, vugg, vugh

earth like: 5 glebe

fibrous: 8 asbestos, oakenite

flaky: 4 mica

gray-green: 7 edenite

gray-white: 5 trona 14 chromiumptrona

green: 7 alalite, apatite, epidote, erinite, prasine, uralian 9 demantoid

gunpowder: 5 niter

hard: 6 spinel 7 adamant 8 corundum, spinelle

lustrous: 4 spar 7 blendes 8 smaltine, smaltite

magnetic: 9 lodestone

mixture: 5 magma

native: ore

non-combustible: 8 asbestos

non-metallic: 4 spar 5 boron 6 gangue, iodine

plaster of paris: 6 gypsum

potash: 4 alum

potassium sulphate: 8 misenite

quartz-like: 4 opal

rare: 7 euclase, thorite

red: 5 balas 6 garnet, rutile

salt: 4 alum

seam: 4 vein

silicate: 4 mica

smelting: ore

soft: 4 talc 6 gypsum

spot: 5 macle

tallow: 11 hatchettine

tar: 4 brea 6 maltha

transparent: 4 mica 5 fluor

vitreous: 4 spar 7 apatite

wax-like: 9 ozocerite

white: 6 barite 8 smaltine, smaltite

yellow: 4 iron 5 topaz 6 pyrite

yellowish green: 7 epidote

mineral jelly: 8 vaseline

mineral oil: 5 colza

mineral spring: spa 4 well

mineral water: 6 selter 7 seltzer

Minerva: 6 Athena, Athene

shield: 5 aegis

ming: 6 remind 7 mention, recount 8 remember

minge: 5 midge

mingle: mix 4 amix, fuse, join, meng, mool 5 admix, blend, merge, unite 6 huddle 7 blender, combine, compost 8 coalesce, compound, intermix 9 associate, commingle 10 amalgamate 11 consolidate

mingle-mangle: 6 medley 7 mixture 10 hodgepodge

mingwort: 8 wormwood

mingy: 4 mean 6 stingy

minhag: 6 custom, manner 7 conduct

miniate: 5 paint 8 decorate, luminate 9 rubricate

miniature: 4 copy, tiny 5 small, teeny 6 little, minute 8 painting, portrait 9 lineament, miniating 10 diminutive 11 rubrication 12 illumination 14 representation

minikin: 6 dainty 7 elegant, mincing 8 affected, delicate 10 diminutive

minim: jot 4 drop, fish 6 minnow, minute 7 tiniest 8 smallest 9 miniature 10 diminutive

minimize: 6 reduce 7 detract 8 belittle 9 disparage 10 depreciate

minimum: 5 least 6 lowest

minimuscular: wee 4 tiny 5 small

mining: 4 gwag

chisel: gad

deposit: 4 lode, nest, vein 6 placer

extraction: ore, tin 4 gold, lead 6 silver 8 diamonds 11 quicksilver

instrument: 4 dial

lamp: 4 davy

nozzle: 5 giant

partition: 8 brattice

place: 6 minery, mining

shack: coe

terms: hat 4 hade 6 clinic

tool: van

waste: 5 attle

minion: 4 idol, neat 5 lover 6 dainty, pretty 7 darling, elegant 8 creature, delicate, favorite, ladylove, mistress, paramour 9 underling

minister: 4 tend 5 angel, serve 6 afford, attend, cleric, curate, divine, pander, parson, pastor, supply 7 furnish, provide, servant 8 executor, preacher, reverend 9 attendant, clergyman, upstander 10 administer, ambassador

home: 5 manse 9 parsonage

minestrone: 4 soup

minitant: 11 threatening

Minnesota: *city:* Ely 6 Duluth, Winona 7 Bemidji, Mankato 8 Owatonna 9 Rochester 11 Minneapolis

county: 4 Cass, Clay, Cook, Lake, Lyon, Pine, Polk, Pope, Rice, Rock, Todd 5 Dodge, Swift 6 Aitkin, Benton, Carver, Dakota, Isanti, Nobles, Ramsey, Roseau, Sibley, Steele, Wadena, Waseca, Wilkin 7 Kanabec, Kittson, Stearns, Stevens 8 Hennepin 10 Pennington

iron range: 6 Cuyuna, Mesabi 9 Vermilion

lake: Red 7 Bemidji 10 Minnewaska 12 Winniboshish

minnow: 5 guppy 6 baggie

minor: 4 less 5 petit, petty, youth 6 infant, lesser, slight 7 smaller 8 inferior 11 subordinate 15 inconsequential

minorate: 7 curtail 8 diminish

minority: 6 nonage 10 immaturity

Minos: *child:* 7 Ariadne, Phaedra

country: 5 Crete

father: 4 Zeus

lover: 6 Scylla

mother: 6 Europa
slayer: 7 Cocalus
wife: 8 Pasiphae
Minotaur: *father:* 4 bull
home: 9 labyrinth
mother: 8 Pasiphae
owner: 5 Minos
slayer: 7 Theseus
minster: 6 church 9 cathedral, monastery
minstrel: 4 bard, bhat(Ind.), moke, poet 6 harper, jockey, singer 7 gleeman, goliard, Pierrot 8 jongleur, musician 9 blackface, troubador 10 gleemaiden, mountebank, troubadour 11 entertainer
accompanist: 7 harpist
minstrel show: *endman:* 5 bones
middleman: 12 interlocutor
part: 4 olio
minstrelsy: 4 glee
mint: aim, iva 4 blow, coin, sage 5 basil, feint, money, thyme 6 catnip, hyssop, intend, mentha, ramona 7 attempt, dittany, potherb, purpose, venture 8 bergamot, calamint, endeavor, lavender, marjoram 9 fabricate, horehound
charge: see *levy* below
family: 9 lamiaceae
genus of: 7 melissa 10 moluccella
geranium: 8 costmary
herb family: 4 balm 5 basil 6 hyssop
levy: 8 brassage 11 seigniorage
mintage: 5 stamp 7 coinage
minuend: 6 lessen 8 diminish
minuet: 5 dance
movement: 7 scherzo
minus: 4 lack, less 6 defect, devoid 7 lacking, without 8 negative, subtract 10 deficiency
minuscule: 4 tiny 5 petty, small 6 minute 10 diminutive, manuscript 13 insignificant
minute: jot, wee 4 mite, nice, note, time, tiny 5 draft, exact, petty, small 6 atomic, little, moment, record, slight, tittle 7 instant, minutia, precise 8 detailed, trifling 9 memoranda(pl.) 10 memorandum 13 imperceptible 14 circumstantial
glass: 9 hourglass
minutely: 7 exactly 9 continual, unceasing
minutes: 4 acta 5 actum 6 record
minutiae: 7 details, trifles 11 particulars
minx: dog 4 girl, jade 5 woman
Minyae king: 7 Athamas
minyan: 6 quorum
mir: 4 head 5 chief 9 community
Mira: 4 star
constellation: 5 Cetus
mirabilia: 7 marvels, wonders 8 miracles
mirac: 6 mirach 7 abdomen
miracle: 4 feat 5 anomy 6 marvel, wonder 10 occurrence, phenomenon

scene of: 4 Cana
wheat: 7 Poulard
worker of: 8 magician 11 thaumaturge
miraculous: 9 unnatural 12 supernatural
mirador: 5 oriel 6 loggia, turret 7 balcony 10 watchtower
mirage: 5 serab 7 chimera 8 delusion, illusion 10 phenomenon, refraction
Miranda's father: 8 Prospero
mirandous: 8 wondrous
mirate: 6 wonder
mird: toy 6 meddle 7 attempt
mire: bog, mud, wet 4 glar, moil, ooze, slew, slob, sloo, slud, slue 5 addle, embog, glaur(Sc.), marsh, sluig, slush, stall, swamp 6 defile, slough, sludge 7 clabber, sludder 8 entangle
mire duck: 7 mallard
Miriam: *brother:* 5 Aaron, Moses
father: 5 Amram
mother: 8 Jochebed
mirific: 9 wonderful
mirky: See **murky**
mirror: 5 glass 7 reflect 8 speculum 9 girandole
pert. to: 9 catoptric 11 catoptrical
mirth: fun, joy 4 glee 5 cheer 6 bawdry, gaiety, levity, spleen 7 delight, jollity 8 gladness, hilarity, laughter 9 festivity, happiness, merriment 10 jocularity, joyousness 12 cheerfulness
god: 5 Comus
mirthful: 5 cadgy
miry: 5 boggy, muddy 6 claggy, clashy, filthy, lutose 7 guttery
mis: 5 amiss, wrong
misadventure: See **misfortune**
misanthrope: 5 cynic, hater, Timon
misanthropic: 7 cynical 10 antisocial
misapplication: 5 abuse 6 disuse 10 perversion
misappropriate: 5 steal
misbear: 9 misbehave
misbede: 5 abuse, wrong 6 injure
misbegotten: 7 bastard 12 illegitimate
misbehave: 7 disobey, misbear, mislead
misbeliever: 7 heretic, infidel 9 miscreant
misbirth: 8 abortion
miscalculate: err 9 overshoot
miscall: 5 abuse 6 revile 7 slander
miscarriage: 5 lapse 6 mishap 7 failure, misdeed, mistake 8 abortion 9 mischance 11 misdemeanor 13 mismanagement
miscarry: err 5 misgo 7 founder
miscellaneous: 5 mixed 6 sundry, varied 8 assorted 13 heterogeneous 14 indiscriminate
miscellany: 4 olio 10 adversaria, hodgepodge

mischance: See **misfortune**

mischief: ate, hob, ill 4 bane, evil, harm, hurt 5 prank, wrack 6 damage 7 cantrip 9 devilment, diablerie 10 disservice

god: 4 Loki

goddess: Ate 4 Eris

mischiefmaker: elf, imp, wag 5 knave, rogue

mischievous: sly 4 arch, impy 5 elfin, hempy 6 elfish, elvish, impish 7 harmful, knavish, malefic, mocking, naughty, parlous, roguish, teasing, waggish 8 prankish, sportive, venomous 9 injurious

mischievous child: imp 4 brat, limb 5 devil, scamp 6 monkey 7 hellion

miscible: 7 mixable

misconception: 8 abortion 16 misunderstanding

misconduct: 7 offense 8 disorder 9 mismanage 11 delinquency, malfeasance, misbehavior, misdemeanor

mark of: 7 demerit

miscreant: 5 knave 6 rascal, wretch 7 heretic, infidel, villain 8 criminal 9 heretical, scoundrel 10 unbeliever 11 misbeliever, unbelieving 12 unscrupulous

miscue: 4 miss, slip 5 error 7 mistake

misdeed: sin 5 crime, wrong 7 forfeit, offense 8 disorder 11 delinquency 13 transgression

misdemeanor sin 5 crime, fault 6 delict 7 misdeed 8 disorder 11 delinquency 12 misdemeanant

misdirect: 7 pervert

mise: 4 levy, pact 5 grant 6 layout, treaty 8 immunity 9 agreement, privilege

misease: 7 poverty 8 distress 10 discomfort, uneasiness

misenunciation: 9 lallation

miser: 4 cuff 5 churl, flint, hayne, hunks, Nabal 6 codger, huddle, nipper, snudge, wretch 7 hoarder, niggard 8 holdfast 9 skinflint 10 curmudgeon

miserable: bad 4 dawy 6 abject, chetif, elenge, feeble 7 forlorn, pitiful 8 pitiable 10 despicable, discomfort, inadequate 12 disconsolate 13 commiserative

miserere: 4 boss 7 bracket

misericord: 4 hall, pity 5 mercy 6 dagger 9 refectory 10 compassion

miserly: 4 mean 5 close, gnede 6 greedy, grippy, stingy 8 covetous, grasping 9 penurious, scrimping 10 avaricious 12 parsimonious

misery: woe 4 ache, pain 5 agony 6 sorrow 7 anguish, avarice, poverty, sadness, squalor 8 calamity, distress 9 adversity, privation, suffering 10 affliction, depression,

misfortune 11 despondency, unhappiness 12 covetousness, wretchedness 13 niggardliness 14 unpleasantness

misfare: 6 mishap 8 miscarry 9 misbehave 10 misfortune

misfeasance: See **malfeasance**

misfortune: woe 4 dole, evil, harm, slip 5 grief 6 misery, mishap, scathe 7 ill-luck, misfare, reverse, trouble 8 accident, calamity, casualty, disaster 9 adversity, holocaust, infortune, mischance 10 affliction, ill-fortune 11 catastrophe, contretemps, miscarriage 12 misadventure

misgiving: 5 doubt, qualm 7 anxiety 12 apprehension

misgo: err 8 miscarry

misguess: err

misguide: 5 abuse 6 injure 7 mislead 8 maltreat 9 misbehave, misdirect, misgovern, mismanage

mishap: See **misfortune**

mishmash: 4 olio 6 jumble 10 hodgepodge

Mishnah: 6 Talmud 9 scripture

pert. to: 7 tannaic 8 Mishnaic

section: 4 Moed 5 Aboth

supplement: 8 Toseftas

misinterpret: err 4 warp

misjudge: err

misky: 5 foggy, misty

mislay: 4 lose

misle: 4 mist, rain 6 mizzle 7 drizzle

mislead: 4 dupe, fool 5 blear, cheat 6 betray, delude, humbug 7 beguile, debauch, deceive 8 hoodwink, misguide 9 duplicate, mismanage

misleading: 5 false 7 crooked 10 fallacious, fraudulent

mismanage: 5 blunk 6 bungle

misplace: 4 lose 6 mislay

misplay: err 5 error 6 renege

misprision: 5 scorn 6 slight 7 despite, mistake 8 contempt, misprise, misprize 10 misconduct 11 misdemeanor 12 depreciation 14 undervaluation 16 misunderstanding

mispronunciation: 8 cacology

misrepresent: lie 5 belie 6 garble 7 deceive

miss: err, fau, hip 4 balk, chit, fail, lack, lass, lose, muff, omit, skip, slip, snab, want 5 lapse, title 6 escape, lassie, miscue 7 deviate, failure 8 fraulein(G.), mistress, overlook, senorita(Sp.), spinster 9 signorina(It.) 10 desiderate, jeune fille, prostitute 12 mademoiselle(F.)

missay: 5 abuse 6 vilify 7 slander

missel: 9 mistletoe

misshapen: 4 ugly 6 clumsy 8 deformed 9 distorted, misformed, monstrous 11 counterfeit

missile (see also **guided missile**): 4 bola, bolt, dart, shot 5 arrow, shaft, spear 6 bullet, weapon 7 missive, outcast 8 brickbat 9 boomerang 10 projectile

pert. to: 9 ballistic

missing: out 4 lost 6 absent

mission: 6 charge, errand 7 message 10 commission, delegation, deputation

missionary: 6 Marist 7 apostle

Mississippi: *county:* 5 Amite 8 Pontotoc

flower: 8 magnolia

mussel: 8 deerhorn

nickname: 5 Bayou

town: 5 Yazoo 6 Biloxi 7 Jackson, Memphis, Natchez 8 Gulfport, Tutwiler

Mississippi River: *mouth:* 4 pass

source: 6 Itasca

Mississippian: 15 Eocarboniferous

missive: 4 note 6 billet, letter 7 epistle, message, missile 8 document

love: 9 valentine

Missouri: *bird:* 8 bluebird

county: 4 Cass, Cole 5 Adair, Bates, Boone, Lewis, Scott, Taney 6 Benton, Dallas, Maries, Mercer, Pettis, Putnam, Shelby 7 Clinton, Johnson, Webster 8 Reynolds, Stoddard, Sullivan 9 Bollinger 10 Montgomery, Saint Clair

gourd: 11 calabazilla

monogram: HST

river: 5 Osage

skylark: 5 pipit

town: 5 Edina 7 Clayton, Sedalia

misspelling: 10 cacography

misspend: 4 lose 8 squander

misstep: 4 slip, trip 5 error 7 faux pas

mist: dag, dim, fog, hag, rag, ure(Sc.) 4 blur, damp, drow(Scot.), film, haze, moke, scud, smog, smur, soup 5 bedim, brume, cloud, dabby, drisk, misle, smurr, vapor 6 mizzle, serein, shadow 7 mystery 9 obscurity 13 precipitation

mistake: err 4 balk, bull, slip 5 amiss, boner, error, fault, folly 6 astray, erring, escape, miscue, renege 7 blunder, default, erratum, rhubarb 10 inaccuracy 12 inadvertence 13 misconception 15 misapprehension

mistaken: 5 wrong

mister: don, sir 4 herr(G.) 5 senor(Sp.), title 6 signor(It.) 8 monsieur(F.)

mistletoe: 7 allheal, gadbush

family: 12 loranthaceae

mistonusk: 6 badger

mistreat: 5 abuse 7 violate

mistress: 4 amie, doll, dozy 5 amiga, dolly, donna, duena, leman 7 hataera, hetaira, hostess 8 gudewife(Sc.), guidwife, ladylove 9 chamberer, concubine, courtesan, courtezan, governess 10 chatelaine, sweetheart

mistrust: 5 doubt 8 distrust 12 apprehension

misty: 4 roky 5 rouky, vague 10 indistinct 13 unilluminated 14 unintelligible

misunderstanding: 6 breach 7 quarrel 9 imbroglio 12 disagreement

misuse: 5 abuse 6 disuse 7 abusion, pervert 8 maltreat, mistreat 9 misemploy

mite: bit 4 atom, dite, dram, tick 5 acari(pl.), atomy, speck 6 acarid, acarus, minute, smidge 7 acarina, chigger, smidgen, smidgin 8 acaridan, arachnid, particle, smidgeon, smitchin

miter: 4 belt 5 frank, mitre, tiara 6 fillet, girdle, gusset, tavern 8 headband 9 headdress

flower: 8 cyclamen

Jewish part: 7 Petalon

mithridate: 8 antidote 9 electuary 12 alexipharmic

mitigate: 4 balm, bate, cool, ease, tone 5 abate, allay, delay, mease(Sc.), relax, remit, slake 6 lessen, pacify, soften, temper 7 appease, assuage, mollify, qualify, relieve, sweeten 8 diminish, lenitive, moderate, palliate 9 alleviate, meliorate

mitt: mit 5 glove 6 mitten

mitten: 4 cuff, jilt, mitt 5 glove, hands

mittimus: 4 writ 6 notice 7 quietus, warrant 9 discharge, dismissal 10 magistrate

mittle: 4 hurt 8 mutilate

mix: pug 4 amix, fuse, join, meng, stir 5 admix, alloy, blend, cross, knead, merge, unite 6 jumble, mingle, muddle, wuzzle 7 blunder, confect, confuse, shuffle 8 coalesce, compound, confound 9 associate, commingle 10 amalgamate 11 incorporate, intermingle

with water: 5 slake 6 dilute, weaken

mix-up: 5 fight, melee 6 tangle 8 conflict 9 confusion

mixable: 8 miscible

mixed: 6 impure, motley 7 piebald 11 farraginous 13 heterogeneous 14 indiscriminate

mixed blood: See **hybrid**

person of: 5 metis 6 Baluga, Ladino, mestee, mustee 7 mestizo, metisse, mulatta, mulatto

mixed metaphor: 11 catachresis

mixen: 7 mixhill 8 dunghill

mixer: 5 party, paver 9 bartender

mixhill: 5 mixen 8 dunghill

mixture: 4 hash, mash, olio 6 batch, blend 6 medley 7 amalgam, compost, farrage, far-

rago, melange **8** blendure **9** admixture,
potpourri **10** concoction, hodgepodge **11**
composition **12** mingle-mangle

mizar star: **5** alcor

mizmaze: **9** confusion **12** bewilderment

mizzle: **4** mist, rain **5** misle **6** decamp **7** confuse, drizzle, speckle **9** disappear, misinform

mizzy: bog **8** quagmire

mnemonic: **8** memorial

Mnemosyne: **6** Memory
  consort: **4** Zeus
  daughters: **5** Muses
  father: **6** Uranus

mo: **4** book **6** moment, volume

moa: **4** bird **6** ratite **8** dinornis **13** dinornithidae

moab: hat

Moab: *city:* Kir
  descendant: **7** Moabite
  famous woman: **4** Ruth
  god: **7** Chemosh
  king: **5** Eglon, Mesha
  mountain: **4** Nebo
  people: **5** Emims

moan: cry **4** sigh, wail **5** groan **6** bemoan,
bewail, grieve, lament **7** deplore, whimper
8 complain **9** complaint **11** lamentation
  as the wind: **4** sugh **5** sough

moat: **4** foss, lake, pond **5** ditch, fossa, fosse
6 trench

mob: set **4** crew, gang, herd, rout **5** cohue,
crowd, drove, flock, group, volge **6** clique,
masses, rabble **7** undress **9** multitude **10**
dishabille, prostitute
  member: **6** rioter
  rule: **7** anarchy **8** violence
  worship: **9** mobolatry

mobbish: **7** lawless **10** disorderly

mobile: mob **6** fickle, vision **7** movable **8** populace **9** wandering **10** changeable

moble: **4** wrap **6** muffle **8** movables **9** furniture

mobsman: **10** pickpocket

mobster: **8** gangster

Moby Dick: **5** whale
  author: **8** Melville
  character: Pip **6** Daggoo, Parsee **7** Ishmael
  pursuer: **4** Ahab

moccasin: pac **4** pack, shoe **5** snake, tegua **6**
loafer **7** slipper **8** larrigan **11** cottonmouth

moch: **4** moth

mocha: **6** coffee **7** leather
  stone: **5** agate

mochy: **4** damp **5** misty, moist, muggy

mock: ape, bob, dor, gab **4** gibe, gird, jape,
jeer, leer, sham **5** bourd, elude, false, fleer,
flirt, flout, frump, hoker, mimic, scoff,

sneer, taunt **6** banter, deride **7** deceive,
grimace, imitate **8** ridicule **9** imitation **10**
disappoint **11** counterfeit
  brawn: **10** headcheese
  cucumber: **5** apple
  nightingale: **7** warbler **8** blackcap
  orange: **7** seringa, syringa, syringe
  ore: **10** sphalerite
  plane: **8** sycamore

mocker: **4** bird **7** flauter **11** mockingbird
  nut: **7** hickory

mockery: **5** bourd, farce, glaik, irony **6** satire **7** hething, sarcasm **8** futility, illusion,
travesty **9** burlesque

mocking: **8** fleering

mockingbird: **8** imitator, songster
  genus: **5** mimus

mod: **4** bold, free **6** modern **7** offbeat

mode: cut, fad **4** form, thew **5** modus, order,
state, style, vogue **6** course, custom, fangle, manner, method, regime, system **7**
fashion **10** convention

model: act, sit **4** form, mold, norm, plan,
plot, pose, type **5** canon, ideal, shape **6** design, sitter **7** example, fashion, manikin,
paragon, pattern, templet **8** ensample, exemplar, formular, fugleman, mannikin,
paradigm, specimen, standard, template **9**
archetype, construct, exemplary, facsimile, flugelman, mannequin, miniature,
precedent, prototype

moderate: **4** bate, calm, ease, easy, even,
meek, mild **5** abate, lower, slake, sober **6**
ease-up, frugal, gentle, lessen, soften, temper **7** average, control **8** attemper, decrease, diminish **9** abstinent, alleviate,
temperate **10** abstemious, reasonable **12**
conservative **13** dispassionate

moderating: **9** remissive

moderation: **7** control **9** restraint **10** abstinence, diminution, governance, limitation, mitigation **11** restriction **13** temperateness

moderator: **6** umpire **7** arbiter **8** mediator

modern: new **4** late **6** latter, recent **8** neoteric
  comb. form: ne; neo

modernize: **8** renovate

modest: coy, mim(Sc.), shy **4** deft, prim **5**
douce, lowly **6** chaste, decent, demure,
humble **7** bashful **8** decorous, maidenly,
reserved, retiring, verecund, virtuous **9**
diffident **10** unassuming **13** unpretentious

modicum: bit **6** amount **7** portion, soupcon

modify: **4** edit, tone, vary **5** alter, limit **6**
change, master, temper **7** assuage, qualify
8 attemper, mitigate, moderate **9** influence

modish: **4** chic

modiste: 7 stylist 8 milliner 9 couturier 10 dressmaker

modulated: 5 toned 7 changed, intoned 8 softened, tempered 9 inflected, regulated

modulation: 9 inflexion 10 inflection

modus: way 5 means 6 manner, method

mog: jog 4 move, plod, walk 6 depart

moggan: leg 6 sleeve 8 stocking

moggy: cat, cow 4 calf 8 slattern 9 scarecrow

mogo: 7 hatchet

moguey: 4 moki, raft 5 mokhi

mogul: 4 lord 5 nabob, ruler, Tatar 6 Tartar 7 magnate 8 autocrat 9 Mongolian, personage 10 locomotive
capital: 4 Agra
emperor: 5 Akbar

moha: 6 millet

Mohammed: 7 Mahomet, Mahound 8 Muhammed
birthplace: 5 Mecca
daughter: 6 Fatima
descendant: Ali 5 Hasan 6 Hosein, Husain, She-rif 7 Ibrahim, She-reef
father: 8 Abdallah
flight from Mecca: 6 hegira, hejira
follower: 6 Wahabi 7 Wahabee, Wahabit, Wahhabi 8 Wahabite
horse: 7 Alborak
nephew: Ali
son-in-law: Ali
successor: 5 Calif 6 Caliph
title: 4 Iman
tomb: 6 Medina
uncle: 8 Abu-Talib
wife: 5 Aisha 6 Avesha, Ayesha 7 Khadija

Mohammedan: See **Muslim**

Mohammedanism: 5 Islam

moho: 4 bird, rail 9 gallinule

mohock: 6 attack 8 maltreat

mohr: 7 gazelle

moider: 4 toil 5 worry 6 bother, wander 7 perplex, smother 8 distract, encumber

moieter: 6 roller

moiety: 4 half, part 5 share 7 portion

moil: bar 4 mire, soil, spot, tire, toil 5 labor, taint, weary 6 defile, drudge 7 torment, trouble, turmoil 8 drudgery, vexation 9 confusion 10 defilement

moire: 7 watered

moise: 4 mend 6 thrive 7 improve

moist: 4 dank 5 humid, rainy 6 clammy 8 humorous

moisten: dew, dip, ret, wet 4 moil 5 bedew, leach 6 anoint, dabble, dampen, humect, humify, imbrue, sparge 8 irrigate, sprinkle 9 humectate

moisture: fog 4 bree(Sc.), drip, drop 5 humor, vapor, water 6 humour, liquid 8 aquosity, humidity

excess: 5 edema
remove: dry 4 wipe 5 wring 9 dehydrate

moisture-laden: 6 sodden

moistureless: dry 4 arid 6 burned 7 parched 8 scorched 10 desiccated

mojo: 4 Moxo 5 charm 6 amulet 7 majagua

mokaddam: 5 chief 7 headman

moke: fog, net 4 dolt, mesh, mist 5 horse 6 donkey 7 network 8 minstrel 9 performer

moki: 4 raft 9 trumpeter

moko: 9 tattooing

moko-moko: 6 lizard

mokum: 5 alloy

molar: 5 tooth 7 grinder 8 grinding

molarimeter: 11 thermometer

molasses: 5 syrup 7 claggum, treacle 8 theriaca 10 blackstrap

molave: 5 vitex

mold: die, fen 4 calm, cast, caum, core, form, mool, mull, must, soil 5 frame, humus, knead, model, mould, plasm, shape 6 coffin, matrix, mildew 7 fashion, matrice, moulage, pattern 9 ceroplast, character
opening: 6 ingate
part: 5 nowel, sprue
pert. to: 5 humic
pouring hole: 5 sprue

moldable: 7 fictile

Moldavia: *Rumania capital:* 4 Iasi
department: 4 Iasi 5 Jassy
measure: 7 faltche

molder: rot 5 decay 7 crumble

molding: ess 4 bead, beak, cima, cove, cyma, gula, ogee, reed, tore 5 angle, arris, conge, ogive, ovolo, splay, talon, thumb, torus 6 baguet, baston, fascia, fillet, listel, nebule, reglet, scotia 7 annulet, beading, cavetto, cornice, fingent, reeding, shaping 8 astragal, bageette, bezantee 9 trochilus
case: 5 chape
combination: 9 ledgement
concave: 4 gula 5 oxeye 7 cavetto
convex: 5 torus
curved: 4 ogee 6 nebule
flat: 6 fillet
ogee: 5 talon
pedestal: 7 surbase
rounded: 5 ovolo, torus 6 billet
rule for: 6 screed

moldy: 5 fusty, hoary, mucid, musty, stale 7 foughty 8 mildewed

mole: cob 4 cobb, pier, pile, quay 5 fault, jetty 6 anicut, burrow, rodent 7 annicut, barrier 8 excavate, starnose, tunneler 10 breakwater 12 imperfection
cricket: 9 churrworm
genus: 5 talpa

mole-like animal: 4 tape 6 desman

molecast: 8 molehill

molecule: *component:* 4 atom
  gram: mol 4 mole
molehead: 8 pierhead
moleskin color: 5 taupe
molest: vex 5 annoy, tease 6 assail, bother, harass, pester 7 disturb, trouble 9 incommode, interfere 10 discommode
molge: 8 triturus
moliminous: 7 massive 9 laborious, momentous
moline: 8 millrind
molition: 6 device, effort 11 contrivance
molka: 10 cloudberry
moll: gal 5 wench 8 mistress 9 companion 10 prostitute
mollescent: 9 softening
mollhern: 5 heron
mollichop: 8 delicate
mollicrush: 4 beat, chop 9 pulverize
mollify: 4 bate, calm, ease 5 allay, relax, sleek 6 pacify, relent, soften, soothe, temper 7 amolish, appease, placate, sweeten 8 mitigate 9 attempter 10 conciliate
mollifying: 4 mild 9 demulcent
mollitious: 8 sensuous 9 softening, luxurious
molluscous: 6 flabby 9 spineless
mollusk: 5 snail, whelk 6 chiton, limpet 7 abalone 10 cuttlefish
  bivalve: 4 leda, spat 5 chama 6 cockle, mussel, oyster 7 scallop
  cephalopod: 8 argonaut
  conical-shaped: 6 limpet
  eight-armed: 7 octopus
  fresh water: 7 etheria
  gastropod: 4 slug 5 snail, whelk 7 abalone 12 taenioglossa
  genus: 4 arca, leda(pl.) 5 eolis, ledum
  group: 8 pteropod
  large: 5 chama
  larval: 7 veliger
  marine: asi 4 welk 5 murex 7 abalone, scallop 8 nautilus
  one shell: 5 snail 8 univalve
  shell: 4 test 5 cowry, testa 6 cowrie, testae
  shell concretion: 5 pearl
  shell-less: 4 slug
  teeth: 6 radula
  ten-armed: 5 squid
  used for bait: 5 squid 6 limpet
  wrinkled shell: 6 cockle
  young: 4 spat
molly: 4 moll 6 basket 7 milksop 9 mallemuck 11 mollycoddle
mollycoddle: 6 coddle, pamper
moloch: 6 lizard
molt: mew 4 cast, mute, shed 5 moult 8 exuviate
molten rock: 4 lava 5 magma

molting: 7 ecdysis
Molucca island: 5 Banda, Ceram 6 Maluku 7 Amboina 9 Halmahera
moly: 4 herb 6 garlic
molybdenum symbol: Mo
momble: 6 jumble, tangle
mome: 4 fool 5 clown 6 critic 7 buffoon 9 blockhead
moment: mo; sec 4 gird, hint, tick, tide, time 5 avail, braid, clink, filip, gliff, point, trice, value 6 fillip, minute, second, weight 7 instant 9 handwhile, twinkling 10 importance 11 consequence 13 signification
  critical: 4 inch, nick 6 crisis, crises
  particular: 4 then, when
momentary: 9 ephemeral, transient 10 transitory 13 instantaneous
momentous: 4 fell 5 grave 7 fateful, serious, weighty 8 eventful 9 important, ponderous 10 chargeable 11 influential
momentum: 5 force, power 7 impetus
momist: 5 momus
mommy: 4 duck 5 mammy 6 mother
momus: 6 critic, momist 8 ridicule 11 faultfinder
mon: 5 badge
monachist: 7 monkish
monad: 4 atom, unit 5 deity, henad 8 particle, zoospore
monarch: 4 csar, czar, tsar, tzar 5 ruler 6 despot, prince 7 dynasty, emperor 8 autocrat 9 butterfly, potentate, sovereign
monarchal: 5 regal, royal 8 imperial
monarda: tea 4 mint 5 plant 8 bergamot
monastery: 5 abbey, badia 6 friary, mandra, priory 7 convent, hospice, minster, nunnery 8 cloister, lamasery 9 sanctuary
  Carthusian: 7 certosa
  haircut: 7 tonsure
  head: 5 abbot 7 hegumen
  officer: 5 prior
  room: 4 cell
  superior: 5 prior
  title: dom
monastic: 4 monk 5 friar 6 oblate 7 ascetic, monkish, recluse 8 abbatial, cenobite 9 cenobitic 10 conventual
monde: 5 globe, mound, world 6 circle 7 coterie, society
monetary: 9 financial, pecuniary
money (see also **bill, coin**): oof, tin, wad 4 bill, cash, coin, cush, dubs, dump, gelt, gilt, grig, jack, jake, kale, loot, lour, mina, moss, pelf 5 blunt, brass, bread, bunce, chink, clink, dough, funds, livre, lucre, maneh, rhino 6 argent, boodle, change, flimsy, hansel, mazuma, siller(Sc.),

spense, steven, wampum, wealth **7** chattel, handsel, lettuce, ooftish **8** currency **9** spondulix **10** spondulics
ancient: aes
blood: cro **7** breaghe
bag: **4** fels **6** follis, wealth **8** follicle
box: **4** arca, safe, till **5** chest **6** drawer **8** register
bribe: **6** boodle
broker: **7** changer
certificate: **5** scrip
changer: **5** saraf, seraf **6** shroff
chest for: **7** brazier
coinage: **4** mint
coined: **6** specie
counterfeit: **5** queer **6** boodle
cowrie: **6** shells
dealer: **6** broker
depreciation: **4** agio **9** inflation
earnest: **5** arles(Sc.), arrha **6** hansel **7** deposit, handsel **8** handgeld
gambler's: **6** barato
gate: **9** admission
gift: **4** alms **7** bequest, charity **9** endowment
given to lord: **6** farleu, farley
found: **5** trove **8** treasure
hearth: **6** fumage
held: **6** escrow
hole for: **4** slot
hook: **4** lari **5** larin **6** larree
lender: **6** banker, usurer **7** shylock **9** loanshark **10** pawnbroker
lots of: pot **4** heap, mint, pile
maker: **4** mint **7** moneyer
manual of exchange values: **7** cambist
metal: **4** coin **6** change, specie **7** coinage
overdue: **7** arrears
oversupply: **9** inflation
paid down: **4** cash **7** deposit **11** downpayment
paper: **4** bill, kale **6** flimsy **7** lettuce
premium: **4** agio
ready: **4** cash **5** asset, darby **9** alcontado(Sp.)
roll of coin: **7** rouleau
sent: **10** remittance
shell: **4** peag **5** cowry, peage, sewan, uhllo **6** cowrie, seawan
small amount: **4** mite **7** peanuts **11** chickenfeed
sorter: **6** teller **7** cashier
standard bank: **5** banco
transactions: **7** banking, finance
unit: ora, yen **4** lira, mark, mina, peso, real, tael **5** franc, krona, krone, maneh, pound, ruble, rupee **6** dollar, piatre, talent **7** drachma, guilder, milreis, piaster **8** cruzeiro
without: **4** poor **5** broke **11** impecunious
money of account: ora

money plant: 9 moneywort
moneyed: 4 rich **6** heeled **7** wealthy **8** affluent
moneyer: 6 banker, coiner, minter **13** counterfeiter
weight: **4** mite **5** blank, droit, perit
moneylender: 6 usurer **10** pawnbroker
mong: mix **5** crowd **6** barter, mingle **7** mixture, traffic **8** mingling **11** intercourse
monger: 6 dealer, trader
mongler: 9 sandpiper
Mongolia: *ass:* **8** chigetai
caravan leader: **5** bashi
city: **4** Urga **5** Kobdo **14** Ulan Bator Khoto
coin: **5** mungo **6** tugrik
conjurer: **6** shaman
conqueror: **9** Tamerland **11** Genghis Khan
desert: **4** Gobi
dynasty: **4** Yuan
fuel: **5** argal, argol, argul
measure: lan
monk: **4** lama
people: Hu; Lai, Rai **4** Garo, Lapp, Shan **5** Asian, Eleut, Tatar **6** Buriat, Tartar **7** Asiatic, Kalmuck, Khalkha **8** Annamese, Oriental **9** Mongoloid
priest: **6** shaman
province: **6** Chahar
religion: **9** Shamanism, Shintoism **12** Confucianism
river: Pei **4** Onon **5** Peiho
tent: **4** yurt
weight: lan
Mongoloid: See **Mongolia** *people*
mongoose: 4 urva **5** lemur **9** ichneumon
Kipling's jungle book: **14** Rikki-Tikki-Tavi
mongrel: cur, dog, mut **4** mutt **6** hybrid **7** bastard, piebald **9** sandpiper
whitefish: **8** tullibee
monial: nun
moniker: 4 name **5** alias **8** nickname
monish: 8 admonish
monition: 5 order **6** advice, notice **7** caution, summons, warning **8** citation **10** admonition, indication, intimation **11** instruction **13** animadversion
monitor: 4 ibid **6** lizard, mentor, nozzle **7** inciter **8** ironclad, reminder **9** catamaran **10** instigator
bug: **8** conenose
lizard: **4** uran **5** varan
monk: dom, fra **4** saki **5** clerk, friar, padre(Sp.) **7** devotee **8** anchoret, cenobite, monastic **9** anchorite, baldicoot, bullfinch, hieronach
Buddhist: bo **4** lama **5** arhat, goyim, yahan **6** bhikku **7** bhikshu, poongee **8** poonghee, poonghie, talapoin
cap: **5** kulah **6** kullah

Eastern Church: 7 caloyer, starets
haircut: 7 tonsure
hood: 4 cowl
Muslim: 7 dervish
Roman Catholic: 6 Culdee 8 Capuchin, Trappist
time in monastary: 9 monachate
monk's-head: 9 dandelion
monkey (see also **ape**): lar 4 fool, sime 5 burro 6 meddle, nisnas, simian, tamper, trifle 7 colobin 9 catarhina, catarhine 10 catarrhina, catarrhine
African: 4 waag 5 potto 6 grivet, vervet
American: 4 saki 5 acari 6 grison, miriki 7 ouakari 8 marmoset, orabassu 9 beelzebub
Asiatic: 4 douc 5 toque 6 langur 7 macaque
bearded: 8 entellus
beautiful: 7 guereza
bonnet: 4 zati
Callicebus: 5 yapok 6 yapock
capuchin: sai 7 sapajou
cebine: sai
Diana: 7 roloway
entellus: 7 hanuman 10 hoonoo-maun
genus of: 5 cebus 8 alouatta
god: 7 Hanuman
grivet: 4 tota
handsome: 4 mona
howling: 4 mono 5 araba 7 gauriba, stentor 8 alouatta
large: 5 sajou
long-tailed: sai 4 maha 5 patas 6 guenon, langur 7 hanuman 8 entellus, telapoin, wanderoo
macaque: 6 rhesus
proboscis: 4 kaha 7 noseape
purple-faced: 8 wanderoo
rhesus: 6 bandar
saki: 6 couxia, couxio
small: 4 titi 6 apelet, teetee 7 apeling 8 marmoset
spider: 6 ateles, coaita 9 belzebuth
squirrel: 6 samiri
tailless: ape
monkey bear: 5 koala
monkey bread: 6 baobab
monkey flower: 7 mimulus 8 toadflax
monkey-nut: 6 peanut
monkey pot: 5 fruit
monkey with: 6 meddle 9 interfere
monkey wrench: 7 spanner
monkeyboard: 9 footboard
monkeyshines: 6 antics, pranks, tricks 7 aperies
monkish: 7 ascetic 8 monastic
monkshood: 4 atis 5 atees 7 aconite 8 napellus
monoceros: 7 sawfish, unicorn 9 swordfish

monochord: 7 harmony, magadis 9 agreement, sonometer
monocle: 8 eyeglass
monocleid: 4 desk 7 cabinet
monocracy: 9 autocracy
monodist: 6 singer, writer 8 composer
monody: ode 4 poem, song 5 dirge 7 oration
monogram: 6 cipher, sketch 7 outline 8 initials 9 character
monolith: 6 menhir, pillar, statue 8 monument
monologue: 9 soliloquy
monomachy: 4 duel 6 combat
monomaniac: 5 crank 12 single-minded
monophone: 9 homophone
Monophysite: 4 Copt 8 Jacobite
monoplane: 5 Taube
monopole: 8 emporium, monopoly 11 combination
monopolize: 7 engross
monopoly: 5 grant, right, trust 6 cartel, corner 7 appalto, charter, control 9 privilege, syndicate
monosaccharide: ose 5 sugar
monostele: 8 prostele
monotonous: 4 dead, drab, dull, flat, same 6 dreary 7 humdrum, tedious, uniform 8 unvaried 9 wearisome 10 repetitive
monotony: 9 treadmill
monoxylon: 4 boat 5 canoe
monster (see also **beast**): 4 gowl, huge, ogre 5 bilsh, freak, giant, teras 6 geryon, sphinx 7 centaur, chimera, warlock
combining form: 5 terat 6 terato
fabled: 5 Argus, harpy 6 gorgon, sphinx 8 basilisk, Minotaur 9 bucentaur
female: 5 harpy 6 gorgon
fire-breathing: 6 dragon 7 chimera
handless: 8 acheirus
headless: 9 acephalus
human: 5 teras 6 terata
medical: 5 teras
nine-headed: 5 hydra
short-limbed: 9 nanomelus
study of: 10 teratology
two-bodied: 7 disomus
two-headed: 10 dicephalus
winged: 5 harpy
without hind limbs: api 4 apus
monster-like: 8 teratoid
monstrous: 4 huge, vast 5 enorm, large 7 hideous, immense, strange, titanic 8 colossal, deformed, enormous, flagrant, gigantic, horrible, shocking, 9 atrocious, unnatural 10 outrageous, prodigious, stupendous, tremendous 12 overpowering, overwhelming 13 extraordinary

Montana: *river:* Sun 4 Milk 5 Teton 6 Willow 7 Madison, Shields 8 Missouri 11 Yellowstone
  town: 4 Kipp 5 Butte, Havre, Libby 6 Circle, Helena, Laurel 8 Anaconda, Billings, Browning, Glendive, Lewiston, Missoula 9 Kalispell
montant: 6 rising 8 mounting
montanto 5 sword 10 broadsword
Monte Cristo: *author:* 5 Dumas
  hero: 6 Dantes
monteith: 4 bowl 12 handkerchief
Montenegro coin: 4 para 6 florin 7 perpera
montero: cap 6 ranger 8 forester, huntsman, mountain
Montezuma cypress: 9 ahuehuete
month: *comb. form:* 4 meno
  excess of calendar over lunar: 5 epact
  following: 7 proximo
  half: 9 fortnight
  preceding: 6 ultimo
  present: 7 instant
monticule: 4 hill 5 mount 7 hillock 8 monticle, mountain
montilla: 6 sherry
Montmorency: 6 sherry
Montrachet: 8 Burgundy
monture: 5 horse, mount
monument: 4 tomb 5 cairn, relic, vault 6 bilith, effigy, hearse, menhir, record, statue 7 chaitya, chhatri, funeral 8 bilithon, cenotaph, cromlech, memorial, monolity 9 antiquity, sepulcher 10 gravestone
  pillar-like: 5 stela, stele 6 stelae
moo: low 6 bellow
mooch: beg, bum 4 loaf 5 cadge, skulk, sneak, steal 6 loiter, pilfer, sponge 7 vagrant
moocha: 6 girdle
mood: tid(Sc.) 4 tune, vein, whim 5 freak, humor 6 humour, temper 7 caprice, feeling 10 atmosphere 11 disposition
  assumed: 4 pose
  recollection of past: 13 retrospection
moody: sad 4 glum 6 gloomy, grumpy, sullen 7 pensive 8 brooding 9 depressed 10 capricious 11 ill-tempered
mool: 4 bury, mold, soil 5 earth, grave 6 mingle 7 crumble
mools: 10 chilblains
moon: orb 4 Dian, Luna, lune(F.) 5 Diana, lunar 6 Phoebe 7 Cynthia, selenic 8 satelles, selenian 9 satellite
  above: 10 superlunar
  age at beginning of calendar year: 5 epact
  apogee: 5 apsis
  area on: 4 mare
  aspect: 5 phase

  astronaut: 6 Aldrin 9 Armstrong
  combining form: 5 selen
  crescent: 7 menisci 8 meniscus
  crescent point: 4 cusp, horn 6 apogee 7 perigee
  distance between apogee and perigee: 5 apsis
  festival: 8 neomenia
  first quarter: 8 crescent
  geographer: 13 selenographer
  god: Sin 6 Nannar
  goddess: 4 Luna 5 Diana, Tanit 6 Hecate, Hekate, Salena, Selene, Tanith 7 Artemis, Astarte
  inhabitant: 8 Selenite
  instrument: 11 selenoscope
  Jupiter's: Io
  mock: 10 paraselene
  new: 6 phasis
  perigee: 5 apsis
  pert. to: 5 lunar 7 selenic
  phase: 7 horning
  picture: 11 selenograph
  position: 6 octant
  spacecraft: 6 Apollo
  Uranus': 5 Ariel
  valley: 4 rill 5 cleft, rille
  vehicle: LEM
moon fern: 8 moonwort
moon lily: 10 moonflower
moon-mad: 7 lunatic
moon-shaped: 6 lunate
  half: 10 semilunate
moon valley: 5 rille
moonack: 9 woodchuck
moonbeam: ray
moonbill: 4 duck
mooncalf: 4 dolt, mole 7 monster 11 monstrosity
mooncreeper: 8 moonseed 10 moonflower
moondown: 7 moonset
mooned: 8 crescent
moonery: 7 madness
moonet: 9 satellite
moonfall: 7 moonset
moonfish: 4 opah 7 sunfish 9 spadefish
moonflower: 5 daisy, oxeye 6 achete
moonglow: 9 moonlight
moonish: 7 flighty 10 capricious
moonlighting: 4 raid 9 adventure 10 expedition 11 moonshining
moonman: 5 gipsy 6 robber
moonraking: 13 woolgathering
moonshine: 4 idle 5 empty, month, sauce 6 liquor 7 trivial, whiskey 8 nonsense 10 balsamweed
moonsick: 7 lunatic
moonstone: 10 hecatolite
Moonstone author: 7 Collins

moony: 5 round, silly 6 dreamy 8 listless

moor: bog, fen, fix 4 fell 5 heath, lande, marsh, swale, swamp 6 anchor, fasten, secure

Moor: 6 Berber, Moslem, Muslim 7 Bedouin, Othello, Saracen 8 Moroccan

moor blackbird: 5 ouzel

moor buzzard: 7 harrier

moor evil: 9 dysentery

moor game: 6 grouse 8 moorfowl

moor hawk: 7 harrier

moorage: 8 berthage 9 anchorage

moorbird: 6 grouse

moorburn: 7 quarrel 9 illtemper

moorcock: 6 grouse 9 blackcock

Moore character: 5 Lalla, Rookh

moorfowl: 6 grouse

moorhen: 4 coot 9 gallinule

Moorish: 8 Moresque

 alcazar: 8 Alhambra

 garment: 5 jupon 7 burnous 8 albornoz, burnoose

 horse: 4 barb

 judge: 4 cadi

 kettledrum: 5 tabor 6 atabal

 opiate: 4 kief

 palace: 8 Alhambra

moorland: fen 5 moose

moose: elk 4 alce 5 eland

 genus: 5 alces

mooseberry: 10 hobblebush

moot: dig 4 grub, plea, root, tell 5 argue, plead, speak 6 debate 7 discuss, meeting 8 argument, assembly, complain, disputed 9 debatable, encounter, gathering, undecided 10 discussion, litigation

mooth: wet 4 damp 5 misty

mop: 4 pout, swab, wash, wipe 5 bunch, clean 6 merkin, moppet, scovel 7 cleanse, grimace

mope: 4 pout, sulk 5 brood

mopish: 6 gloomy 7 foolish 8 confused

moppet: tot 4 baby, doll, tike 5 child 7 darling, toddler 9 youngster

mopsy: son 6 moppet 8 slattern

moquette: 6 carpet 10 upholstery

mora: 5 delay, stool 7 default 9 footstool 12 postponement

mora tree: 6 fustic

moral: 4 good, pure 5 ethic 7 dutiful, epimyth, ethical, upright 8 priggish, virtuous 9 honorable, righteous

 fable: 8 apologue

 failure: sin

 law: 9 Decalogue

 teaching: 5 maxim 7 precept 8 apologue 9 preaching 10 preachment 11 edification

morale: 4 hope, mood, zeal 6 spirit 8 morality 9 condition 10 confidence

morals: 6 ethics

 description: 10 ethography

morass: bog, fen 4 flow, quag 5 flush, marsh, swamp 8 quagmire

morass weed: 8 hornwort

moration: 5 delay

Moravian city: 4 Brno, Zlin 5 Brunn

moray: eel 6 conger, hamlet 7 muraena

morbid: 4 sick 6 grisly 8 diseased, gruesome, horrible 9 debatable unhealthy 11 unwholesome 12 apprehensive, pathological

morbilli: 7 measles

morbus: 7 disease, illness

mordant: 4 keen 5 sharp 6 biting 7 burning, caustic, pungent 8 scathing 9 corrosive, sarcastic

more: piu 4 also, mair, plus 5 again, extra 6 custom, manner 7 folkway, further, greater 10 additional, convention

 or less: 4 some

 than: 4 over 5 above

 than enough: too 9 excessive

 than one: few 4 many 6 couple, plural 7 several

 than this: yea

More opus: 6 Utopia

morel: 8 mushroom 10 nightshade

morena: 8 brunette

moreover: and 4 also, then 5 again 7 besides, further 8 likewise 11 furthermore

morepork: 4 peho, ruru 7 boobook

morgay: 7 dogfish

morglay: 5 sword

morgue: 8 mortuary 9 deadhouse, stolidity 11 haughtiness, impassivity

moribund: 5 dying 6 effete 8 decadent, decaying 10 acherontic, terminated

morindin dye: al

morinel: 8 dotterel

moringa oil: ben

morion: 6 helmet, quartz 8 cabasset

mormo: 7 bugbear 10 shemonster

Mormon: 6 Danite 8 mandrill

 brothers: 7 Danites

 emblem: bee

 founder: 5 Smith

 officer: 5 elder

 priesthood: 7 Aaronic 11 Melchizedek

 prophet: 6 Moroni

Mormon State: 4 Utah

Mormonweed: 6 flower, mallow

morning: 4 dawn, morn 5 matin 6 aurora 7 sunrise

 concert: 6 aubade

 coat: 7 cutaway

 performance: 7 matinee

 pert. to: 5 matin, wight 7 matinal 9 matutinal

 prayer: 5 matin 6 matins

reception: 5 levee
morning glory: nil 7 gaybine, ipomoea
family: 14 convolvulaceae
morning star: 4 Mars 5 Venus 6 Saturn 7 Daystar, Jupiter, Lucifer, Mercury
moro: 5 finch
Moro: *chief:* 4 Dato 5 Datto
dialect: 4 Sulu
island: 8 Mindanao
knife: 6 barong
people: 4 Sulu 5 Lanao, Yakan
priest: 4 atli 5 sarip
sailboat: 5 sapit
morocco: 7 leather
imitation: 4 roan
Morocco: *cape:* Nun
city (see also *port* below): Fez 4 Assa 5 Rabat 6 Rabbat 7 Morocco 9 Marrakech
coin: 4 okia, rial 5 okieh 8 mouzouna
district: Sus 4 Riff
emperor: 9 Miramolin 11 Miramomolin
government: 7 Maghzen, Makhzan, Machzen
hat: fez
island: 7 Madeira
Jews' quarter: 8 El Millah
measure: 4 sahh 6 fanega, tomini
military expedition: 5 harka
mountain: Rif
people: 4 Moor 6 Berber, Kabyle, Moslem, Muslim 7 Maghzen, Makhzan, Makhzen
port: 5 Ceuta, Rabat 6 Agadir, Rabbat, Tetuan 7 Mogador, Tangier 8 El Araish, Laraiche 10 Casablanca
ruler: 6 she-rif, sultan 7 she-reef
soldier: 5 askar
tree: 4 arar 5 argan 6 alerse 8 sandarac
weight: 4 rotl 5 artal, artel, gerbe, ratel 6 dirhem, kintar 7 quintal
morology: 5 folly 8 nonsense
moron: 4 dull, fool 5 ament 6 stupid 7 dullard 8 imbecile, sluggish
moronic: 4 dull 6 stupid 7 idiotic 8 sluggish
morose: 4 dour, glum, grum, sour 5 gruff, moody, sulky, surly 6 crusty, gloomy, sullen 7 crabbed, clumpse, clumpst, crooked, unhappy 8 strounge 9 splenetic 10 embittered, ill-humored
moroseness: 8 asperity
morphia: 8 morphine
morphine derivative: 6 heroin
morro: 4 hill 5 bluff, point 6 castle 8 headland
Mors: 5 death
morse: 5 clasp 6 brooch, walrus
Morse code signal: dit, dah
morsel: bit, ort 4 bite, snap 5 crumb, piece, scrap, snack 6 tidbit, titbit 7 morceau, rarebit 8 fragment

morsing: 7 priming
morsure: 4 bite 6 biting
mort: 4 dead, lard 5 death, fatal 6 deadly, grease, salmon 9 abundance
mortacious: 4 very 9 extremely
mortal: 4 dire 5 being, fatal, human 6 deadly, lethal 7 capital, deathly, fleshly 8 grievous 9 extremely 10 implacable 11 destructive
mortar: 5 compo, putty 6 cannon, cement, holmos, petard 7 perrier
carrier: hod
mixer: rab
tray: hod
mortarboard: cap 4 hawk
Morte d'Arthur author: 6 Malory
mortgage: 4 bond, deed, lien 5 trust 6 pledge, wadset(Sc.) 11 encumbrance
giver: 6 lienee
receiver: 6 lienor
mortician: 10 undertaker
mortification: 5 shame 7 chagrin 8 gangrene, necrosis, vexation 11 humiliation 13 embarrassment
mortified: 10 sphacelate
mortify: 5 abase, abash, spite 6 ashame, humble, offend 7 crucify
mortifying: 11 ignominious
mortise: 6 cocket
complement of: 5 tenon
law: 8 amortize
machine: 7 slotter
mortuary: 4 gift 6 morgue 7 funeral 9 deadhouse, lich-house, sepulcher
car: 6 hearse
morvin: 7 mallein
mosaic: 5 tiled, tiles
formed like a: 10 tesselated
mosaic gold: 6 ormolu
piece: 7 tessera
moschate: 5 musky
Moscow citadel: 7 Kremlin
Moses: 6 leader 8 lawgiver
brother: 5 Aaron
emissary: 5 Caleb
father: 5 Amram
father-in-law: 6 Jethro
law: 4 Tora 5 Torah 10 Pentateuch
mother: 8 Jochebed
mountain: 4 Nebo
sister: 6 Miriam
son: 7 Eliezer, Gershom
successor: 6 Joshua
wife: 8 Zipporah
mosey: 4 mosy 5 amble 6 depart, ramble, stroll, wander 7 shuffle
mosker: 5 decay 6 molder

Moslem (see also **Muslim**): 7 Islamic, Saracen 9 Moslemite, Mussulman 10 Mohammedan

mosque: 4 jami, mosk 5 Caaba, Kaaba 6 church, dargah, durgah, Kaabeh, Kiblah, masjid, shrine, temple
official: 4 imam 5 imaum
student: 5 softa
tower: 7 manarat, minaret 8 minarete
warden: 5 nazir

mosquito: 5 aedes 7 culicid 11 gallinipper
genus of: 5 aedes, Culex 9 Anopheles
killer: 8 culicide
larvae: 8 wigglers

mosquito bee: 5 karbi 8 angelito
mosquito boat: P.T.
mosquito fish: 8 gambusia
mosquito hawk: 9 dragonfly, nighthawk
mosquito plant: 4 mint 10 pennyroyal
Mosquito State: 6 Jersey

moss: bog, fog, rag 5 swamp, usnea 6 lichen, morass 9 bryophyte, treebeard
animalcule: 8 bryozoan
club: 7 lycoped
edible: 4 agar 8 agaragar
like: 7 hepatic

moss cheeper: 5 pipit 7 bunting
moss coral: 8 bryozoan
moss corn: 10 silverweed
moss duck: 7 mallard
moss fruit: 11 sporogonium
moss-grown: 10 antiquated 12 old-fashioned
moss hammer: 7 bittern
moss polyp: 8 bryozoan
moss-trouper: 6 raider 8 marauder
mossback: 4 fogy 5 fogey
mossberry: 9 cranberry
mossbunker: 8 menhaden
mosshead: 9 merganser
mosswort: 9 bryophyte
mossy: 4 dull 5 boggy, downy, green, hoary 6 marshy, stupid 7 covered 9 abounding, overgrown
most: 4 best 5 chief 6 utmost 7 maximum 8 majority 9 principal
mostly: 6 feckly
mot: 4 butt, mark, moat, word 5 motto, piece 6 device 7 epigram, opinion
mote: dot, may 4 atom, hill, iota 5 atomy, match, might, speck, squib, stalk, straw 6 barrow, fescue, height, trifle 7 tumulus 8 eminence, particle
motel: inn 5 hotel
motet: 4 song 6 anthem 11 composition 12 contrapuntal
moth: io 5 tinea 6 bogong, lappet, mallet, miller, tineah, tinean, tineid 7 tineina 8 chloasma, forester 11 yellowshell

family: 7 arctiid, tineina 9 arctiidae
genus of: 5 sesia
larva: 11 caterpillar
spot: 8 chloasma, fenestra
suborder: 10 heterocera

moth-eaten: 4 worn 7 decayed 8 decrepit, out-dated
moth hawk: 10 goatsucker
moth hunter: 10 goatsucker
mother: dam 4 dame, womb 5 adopt, dregs, mamma, mater(L.), nurse 6 foster, matron, native, origin, parent, patron 7 nurture 8 genetrix 10 ancestress
comb. form: 5 matri
of believers: 5 Aisha 6 Ayesha
of gods: 4 Rhea 9 Brigantia
of Gracchi: 8 Cornelia
of Graces: 5 Aegle
of man: 6 Cybele
of months: 4 moon
of presidents: 8 Virginia
of sorrows: 4 Mary 6 Virgin
of states: 8 Virginia
one delivery: 7 unipara
related on side of: 6 enatic
spiritual: 4 amma
three deliveries: 7 tripara
two deliveries: 6 bipara

Mother Carey's chicken: 6 petrel
Mother Carey's goose: 6 fulmar
Mother Carey's hen: 6 petrel
mother gate: 4 bord 7 tramway
Mother Hubbard: 4 gown 5 dress
mother-in-law: 9 eldmother
mother of coal: 8 charcoal
mother of pearl: 5 nacre
mother superior: 6 abbess
mother's mark: 9 birthmark
mothered: 5 thick 6 viscid
motherland: 4 home 10 fatherland
motherly: 8 maternal
motion (see also **bodily motion**): 4 fard, idea, move 5 faird 6 unrest 7 gesture, impulse, propose, request, suggest 8 movement, petition, proposal 10 suggestion 11 application, inclination 13 gesticulation
circular: 4 gyre 10 revolution
convulsive: 11 vellication
due to: 7 kinetic
expressive: 7 gesture
impetuous: 6 bensel, bensil 7 bensail, bensall, bensell
pert. to: 7 kinetic 9 kinematic 11 kinematical
producing: 6 motile
quality: 8 momentum
rate: R.P.M. 4 time 5 speed, tempo 11 steerageway
science: 10 ballistics, kinematics

motion picture

transmitter: cog 4 belt, gear
upward: 5 scend 8 upthrust
motion picture: 4 film, show 5 flick, movie, talky 6 cinema 7 flicker 9 photoplay
arc lamp: 5 kleig, klieg
award: 5 Oscar
cowboy & Indian: 7 Western
machine: 9 projector 11 kinetoscope 12 animatograph, theatrograph 13 cinematograph 14 cinematographe
outline: 6 script 8 scenario
pert. to: 9 cinematic
play: 5 movie 6 cinema 9 photoplay
prize: 5 Oscar
term: pan 4 shot, take 6 retake 7 reverse
motionless: 4 dead 5 inert, rigid, still 6 asleep 8 becalmed, immobile, stagnant, stagnate, stirless 9 quiescent, sedentary 10 breathless
motivate: 4 move 5 impel 6 incite, induce 7 inspire 9 influence, instigate, stimulate
motive: 4 sake, spur 5 cause 6 object, reason 7 impulse, purpose 8 pressure, stimulus 9 incentive, objective 13 consideration
ostensible: 7 pretext
motley: 4 fool 5 mixed 6 jester 7 diverse, mottled, piebald 9 checkered 10 variegated 13 heterogeneous
man of: 4 fool 6 jester 7 Pierrot
motmot: 4 bird
motor: car 4 auto, ride 6 engine 7 kinetic, machine 8 motorcar 10 automobile
electric: 6 dynamo
hand-powered: 9 baromotor
part: cam 4 coil 5 rotor 6 piston, stator 9 capacitor 10 carburetor
rotary: 7 turbine
motor-bike: 10 motorcycle
motor-boat: 8 palander
motor court: inn 5 motel
motor speed control: 8 rheocrat
motorman: 8 engineer, operator
motte: 5 grove
mottled: 4 pied, roed 5 pinto 6 motley 7 brocked, clouded, dappled, piebald, spotted 8 blotched 10 variegated 11 varicolored
motto: mot 4 word 5 adage, axiom, gnome, maxim 6 device, saying 7 empresa, precept 8 aphorism 10 shibboleth
mouche: 5 patch
mouchoir: 12 handkerchief
moue: 4 face, pout 7 grimace
mouflon, moufflon: 5 sheep
mould: See **mold**
moulding: See **molding**
moulrush: 7 pollack
moult: See **molt**
moulting: See **molting**

mound: ahu, cop, dam, dun, tee 4 balk, bank, butt, dene, dher, doon, dune, heap, hill, hump, pile, terp 5 agger, berry, cairn, dheri, globe, huaca, knoll, stack, toman(Scot.) 6 barrow, bounds, burrow, causey 7 bourock, bulwark, hornito, rampart, tumulus 8 boundary 9 elevation 10 embankment
pert. to: 7 tumular
prehistoric: 4 terp
mound bird: 8 megapode
Mound City: 7 St. Louis
mound of light: 8 kohinoor
mount: 4 glue, hill, pony, rise 5 arise, climb, horse, paste, steed 6 ascend, aspire 8 escalate, increase, mountain 10 promontory 13 fortification
by ladder: 8 escalade
horizontal bar: kip
two-legged: 5 bipod
Mount Etna city: 7 Catania
Mount Everest peak: 6 Lhotse
Mount Helicon fountain: 8 Aganippe
Mount Ida nymph: 6 Oenone
Mount of Olives: 6 Olivet
Mount Parnassus fountain: 8 Castalia
Mount Rainier: 6 Tacoma
mountain (see also **peak**): ben(Scot.), kop 4 berg, dagh, fell, mont(F.) 5 onlay 6 barrow, bundoc 8 bundocks
base of: 8 piedmont
beyond: 10 tramontane 11 transalpine
Biblical: See **Bible:** *mountain*
burning: 7 volcano
combining form: oro 4 oreo
depression: col
devil: 6 moloch
formation: 7 orogeny 9 orogenesy 10 orogenesis
gap: see *pass* below
highest: 7 Everest
lake: 4 tarn
low: 5 butte
mythical: Kaf, Qaf 4 Meru 5 candy, glass 7 Helicon 9 Parnassus
nymph: 5 dryad, oread
pass: col, gap 4 cove, duar, gate, ghat 5 ghaut, gorge, kotal 6 defile
pasture: alp 6 saeter
pert. to: 10 orological
range: 4 Alps, Ghat, Ural 5 Andes, chain, Coast, ridge, Rocky, Teton, White 6 Alatau 7 Rockies, Sierras 8 Cascades, Catskill, Pyrenees 9 Allegheny, Blue Ridge, Himalayas 10 San Jacinto 11 Appalachian, San Gorgonio
ridge: 4 aret, peak, spur 5 arete, crest 6 sierra, summit 7 sawbuck
rocky: 7 nunatak

science: 7 orology
sickness: 4 veta 7 soroche
snow: 5 jokul
study: 7 orology 9 orography
sunset reflection: 9 alpenglow
trail marker: 5 cairn
mountain andromeda: 10 fetterbush
mountain ash: 4 sorb 5 rowan, rowen
mountain badger: 6 marmot
mountain balsam: fir
mountain banana: fei
mountain barometer: 8 orometer
mountain beaver: 8 sewellel
mountain bluet: 8 centaury
mountain cat: 4 lynx 6 bobcat, cougar 10 cacomistle
mountain climber: 10 alpestrian
  equipment: 4 rope 5 piton
mountain climbing: 8 alpinism
  peg: 5 piton
mountain cock: 12 capercaillie
mountain curassow: 10 oreophasis
mountain dew: 7 bootleg, whiskey 9 moonshine
mountain duck: 9 harlequin, sheldrake
mountain finch: 9 brambling
mountain flax: 8 centaury
mountain fringe: 8 fumitory, wormwood
mountain goat: 4 ibex
mountain ivy: 6 laurel
mountain leather: 12 palygorskite
mountain lion: 6 cougar
mountain magpie: 10 woodpecker 11 butcher-bird
mountain mint: 5 basil 8 calamint
mountain oak: 8 chestnut
mountain panther: 5 ounce 6 cougar 7 leopard
mountain parrot: kea
mountain partridge: 4 dove 5 quail
mountain pheasant: 6 grouse
mountain quail: 9 partridge
mountain raspberry: 10 cloudberry
mountain rose: 6 laurel
mountain snow: 4 neve
mountain spinach: 5 orach 6 orache
Mountain State: 7 Montana
Mountain States: 4 Utah 5 Idaho 6 Nevada 7 Arizona, Montana, Wyoming 8 Colorado 9 New Mexico
mountain tea: 11 wintergreen
mountaineer: 5 Aaron 7 climber, hillman 9 hillbilly
  song: 5 yodel
mountainlike: 7 etiolin
mountainous: 4 high 5 alpen 6 alpine, rugged 8 elevated 10 alpestrine
mountaintop: 4 cone, peak 6 summit

mountebank: 4 gull 5 cheat, quack 7 empiric 8 impostor, minstrel 9 charlatan, pretender
  aid: 4 zany
mounting: 7 setting 9 equipment 13 embellishment
mounting horizontal bar method: kip
moup: 6 nibble 9 associate
mourn: rue 4 dole, erme, long, sigh, wail, weep 6 bemoan, bewail, grieve, lament, murmur, sorrow 7 deplore 8 mourning
mournful: sad 5 black 6 woeful 7 doleful, elegiac, pitiful 8 funereal 9 elegiacal, plaintive, sorrowful, threnodic, woebegone 10 lamentable, lugubrious, melancholy 11 distressing
mourning: 4 garb 5 dolor 6 dolour 7 drapery
  bride: 5 plant 8 scabious
  dress: 5 black, crape, weeds 6 sables
  group: 7 cortege
  song: 5 dirge
mouse: erd, pry 4 girl, hunt, knot 6 bruise, rodent 8 black-eye
  comb. form: mys
  field: 4 vole 7 harvest
  leaping: 6 jerboa
  male: 4 buck
  meadow: 5 voles
  milk: 6 spurge
  pert. to: 6 murine
mouse deer: 10 chevrotain
mouse-ear: 8 hawkweed 9 chickweed
mouse hare: 4 pika
mousebird: 4 coly 6 shrike
mouselike: shy 4 drab 5 mousy, quiet, timid 6 murine 8 retiring
mouser: cat 8 detective
mouseweb: 6 cobweb 8 gossamer
mousing: 6 prying 7 binding 8 prowling 9 rapacious 11 inquisitive
mousle: 6 rumple
mousse: 7 dessert, messboy
mousy: 4 drab 5 quiet, timid
moutan: 5 peony, plant 6 flower
mouth: os; gab, gan, gob, mow, mug, mun, ora 4 boca(Sp.), dupe 5 front, stoma 6 cavity, gebbie(Sc.), mumble, rictus 7 flummer, opening, stomata 8 entrance 9 impudence
  away from: 6 aborad, aboral
  combining form: ori 5 stome
  deformity: 7 harelip
  disease: 4 noma 6 canker 10 stomatitis
  muscle: 7 caninus
  of furnace: 5 bocca
  of river: 5 delta, firth
  part: lip 5 uvula 6 palate 7 pharynx
  pert. to: 4 oral 6 rictal 7 oscular, palatal 8 stomatic
  projecting: 5 spout

roof: 6 palate
tissue: gum
toward: 4 orad
with open: 5 agape
mouth organ: 9 harmonica
mouth-watering: 8 alluring 9 delicious
mouthful: lot, sup 4 bite, gulp 6 gobbet
mouthpiece: 5 bocal 6 lawyer 8 attorney
mouthwash: 9 collutory 11 collutorium
mouthy: 9 bombastic, talkative
mouton: fur, spy 4 wool 9 sheepskin
movable: 5 loose 6 fickle, mobile, motile 8 exorable, floating 10 changeable, inconstant 11 ephelcystic 12 figuratively
move (see also **go**): go; act, gee, mog 4 goad, pass, play, spur, stir 5 budge, cause, clink, impel, rouse, shift, start, sweep 6 affect, arouse, bestir, betake, excite, incite, induce, kindle, motion, prompt, quetch, remble, remove 7 actuate, advance, agitate, animate, inspire, migrate, propose, provoke, suggest 8 converse, emigrate, maneuver, motivate, transfer 9 influence, instigate, stimulate
along: mog 5 mosey, scram 7 maunder
away: shy 8 emigrate
back: ebb 6 recede 7 retreat
back and forth: wag 4 flap, rock, tack 5 dodge, weave 6 falter, teeter, wabble, wiggle, wigwag, zigzag 7 shuttle 9 oscillate
false: 4 balk 5 feint 7 misstep
first: 10 initiative
forward: 4 edge 5 drive, forge, surge 7 advance 8 progress
furtively: 5 skulk, slink, sneak
heaven and earth: try 6 strive
heavily: lug 6 lumber, trudge
in: 6 occupy 7 inhabit
in water: 4 swim, wade
inwardly: 6 enmove
noiselessly: 4 slip 5 creep, glide, skulk, slink, sneak, steal 6 tiptoe 9 pussyfoot
noisily: 6 bustle 7 clatter, rollick
obliquely: 4 edge, joll, skew, slue 5 sidle
on wheels: 4 roll 7 trundle
quickly: fly 4 dart, dash, flit, jump, leap, race, scud, scur, whir 5 bound, hurry, scoot, skirr, spank, sweep, start 6 career, gallop, hurtle, scurry, spring
restlessly: 6 kelter, twitch
rhythmically: bob, jig, jog 5 dance, march
round and round: 4 eddy 5 swirl, twirl
sinuously: 5 snake 6 writhe
slowly: lag, mog 4 edge, inch, worm 5 crawl 6 trudge 7 crowhop
smoothly: 4 slip 5 glide, skate, slide
together: 5 unite 8 converge
moveless: See **immovable**
movement: 5 tempo, trend 6 rhythm

biological: 5 taxis
capable of: 6 mobile, motile
music: 4 moto
surface 6 seiche
movie: See **motion picture**
moving: 7 current 8 ambulant, pathetic, poignant, touching 9 transient 10 ambulatory
moving about: 8 ambulant 10 ambulatory
moving part: cam, cog 5 rotor, wheel
moving picture: See **motion picture**
moving staircase: 9 escalator
mow: bin, cut, lay, mew 4 barb, clip, goaf, heap, mass, math, pile, rick 5 mouth, stack 6 scythe, sickle 7 grimace 8 haystack 9 cornfield
mowana: 6 baobab
mowed strip: 5 swath 6 swathe
Mowgli: *elephant:* 5 Hathi
friend: 5 Akela, Baloo
mowie: 9 stackyard
mowing: 7 mockery 8 derision 10 meadowland
mowland: 6 mowlot 10 meadowland
mowth: 6 mowing
moxie berry: 9 snowberry
moy: 4 mild 6 demure, gentle 8 affected
moyen: way 5 means 6 agency, course 8 property 9 influence, substance
Mozambique native: Yao
Mozart opera: 6 Figaro
mubarat: 7 divorce
mucago: 5 mucus 7 coating 8 mucilage
much: 4 fele, high, lots, many 5 great, heaps, scads 6 mickle 7 gaylies, geylies, greatly 8 abundant, uncommon 9 multitude
comb. form: 4 poly 5 multi
music: 5 molto
Much Ado About Nothing character: 4 Hero 6 Ursula 7 Antonio, Claudio, Leonato
mucid: 5 moldy, musty, slimy 6 mucous
mucilage: gum 5 paste 6 arabin, mucago 8 adhesive
mucilaginous: 5 gluey, slimy 6 sticky, viscid 8 adhesive
muck: 4 dirt, dung, mess 5 filth, money, slime, waste 6 manure, refuse, wealth
muckle: 4 fret 6 bother
mucoid: See **mucous**
mucor: 9 hoariness, moldiness 10 filthiness
mucous: 5 moist, slimy 6 mucoid 7 viscous 8 blennoid, muculent
mud fen 4 dirt, glar, gore, mire, ooze, slob, slud 5 glaur, gumbo, slime, slush, waise 6 sludge 7 clabber, sludder, sluther 12 offscourings
deposit: 4 silt
hole: pan 6 puddle, wallow 8 quagmire

living in: **10** limicolous
pert. to: **7** luteous
mud bath: 10 illutation
mud dab: 8 flounder
mud dabbler: 9 killfish
mud dauber: 4 wasp
mud devil: 10 hellbender
mud eel: 5 siren
mud lark: 5 gamin **6** magpie, urchin **8** shoveler **10** meadowlark
mud mark: 7 mudflow
mud peep: 9 sandpiper
mud puppy: 10 hellbender, salamander
mud snipe: 8 woodcock
mud sunfish: 4 bass **8** warmouth
mud volcano: 5 salse
mudar: 6 yercum
Mudcat State: 11 Mississippi
muddle: mix **4** ball, daze, doze, mess **5** addle, besot, snafu **6** bemuse, burble, fuddle, jumble, pother **7** bedevil, blunder, confuse, fluster, mystify, perplex, stupefy **8** befuddle, bemuddle, bewilder, confound, disorder, flounder **9** confusion **10** intoxicate **12** hugger-mugger
muddled: ree **4** asea **5** beery, crazy, drunk, foggy, tipsy
muddy: 4 miry, roil **5** dirty, drovy, druvy, slaky, vague **6** claggy, clarty, clashy, cloudy, drubly, lutose, sludgy, slushy, turbid **7** clouded, guttery, obscure, sensual **8** confused, feculent **9** besmeared, spattered **11** bespattered
mudfish: 6 bowfin
mudhold: 4 slew, sloo, slue **6** slough
mudworm: ipo **9** earthworm
mudwort: 7 mudweed
muezzin's call to prayer: 4 adan, azan
muff: fur, vex **4** flub **5** crest, error **6** bungle, warmer **8** irritate
muffet: 5 mufty, muggy **11** whitethroat
muffetee: 7 muffler, wrister **8** wristlet
muffin: cob, gem **5** bread, scone **7** crumpet, popover
muffle: gag **4** damp, dull, mute, wrap **6** bumble, dampen, deaden, shroud **7** silence **8** envelope **10** camouflage
muffled: 6 hollow
muffler: 4 mute **5** scarf **6** tippet **8** silencer
mufflin: 8 titmouse
mufti: 4 alim **8** assessor, civilian, clothing, official **9** expounder
mufty: See **muffet**
mug: cup **4** cram, dupe, face, fool, toby **5** mouth, mungo, pulse, sheep, stein, study **6** noggin, seidel **7** assault, canette, drizzle, goddard, grimace, tankard **8** schooner **10** photograph
muga: 11 caterpillar

mugger: goa **4** thug **6** tinker **7** peddler, puncher **9** crocodile
mugget: 6 mugwet **8** woodruff
muggins: 4 dupe, fool, game **9** simpleton
muggy (see also **muffet**)**: 4** damp, fozy **5** humid, moist, moldy
mughouse: 8 alehouse, pothouse
mugweed: 7 mugwort
mugwet: 8 woodruff
muir: 4 moor
mulatto: 5 metis
mulberry bird: 8 starling
mulberry family: 8 Moraceae
mulberry fig: 8 sycamore
mulberry tree: 4 more
mulch: 5 cover, straw **6** litter **7** compost, sawdust
mulct: 4 balk, fine, scot **5** cheat **6** amerce, defect, fleece, punish **7** blemish, deceive, defraud, forfeit, penalty **8** penalize **10** amercement, forfeiture
mule: 4 mewl, mool, mute **5** coble, hinny **6** hybrid **7** bat-mule, slipper, tractor **9** chilblain **10** locomotive
cry: **4** bray **6** heehaw
driver: See **muleteer**
group: **5** atajo, drove
leader in pack train: **8** cencerro
male: **4** jack
spinning: **7** ironman
untrained: **9** shavetail
mule killer: 6 mantis
muleteer: 4 peon **6** driver **7** arriero(Sp.), skinner **9** almocrebe
mulga: 6 shield, wattle
mulish: 5 balky **6** hybrid, sullen **7** sterile **8** perverse, stubborn **9** obstinate, pigheaded **10** determined
mull: cow **4** crag, dust, heat, mess, mold, muse **5** cloth, crush, grind, snout, spice, think **6** fettle, muslin, muzzle, ponder, powder **7** crumble, failure, rubbish, squeeze, sweeten **8** cogitate, consider, ointment, snuffbox **9** pulverize **10** promontory
mullein: 5 torch **6** agleaf **8** hagtaper **9** torchwort **10** hare's-beard
mullet: 4 bobo, liza **6** harder, puffin
mullet hawk: 6 osprey
mulligan: 4 stew
mulligatawny: 4 soup
mulligrubs: 5 blues, colic, sulks
mullock: 4 dirt **6** litter, refuse **7** rubbish
mulloway: 7 jewfish
mulmul: 6 muslin
multicolored: 4 pied **6** calico **7** dappled, spotted
multifarious: 7 diverse **8** manifold
multifold: 4 many **8** manifold, numerous
multiform: 7 diverse

multiple: 4 many 6 plural 8 numerous
multiplier: 7 facient
multiply: 5 breed 6 spread 7 amplify, augment, magnify 8 increase 9 reproduce
by eight: 11 octuplicate
by ten: 7 decuple
multitude: mob 4 army, heap, hive, host, many, mass, much, ruck 5 crowd, drove, flock, horde, shoal, swarm 6 legion, myriad, nation, throng
multitudinous: 8 manifold, numerous
mum ale 4 beer, dark 5 still 6 mother, silent 7 silence 9 voiceless 10 speechless 13 chrysanthemum
mumble 4 chew, mump 5 mouth 6 chavel, chavle, faffle, fumble, haffle, murmur, mutter, palter, patter 7 flummer, grumble
mumbo-jumbo: 4 idol 6 fetich, fetish 7 bugaboo
mummer: 4 mime 5 actor 6 guiser, player 7 buffoon 9 performer, puppeteer
mummery: 6 acting 8 puppetry 9 hypocrisy
mummy: 5 relic 6 corpse 7 cadaver, carcass
mummy apple: 6 papaya
mump: 5 cheat, sulks 6 mumble, mutter 7 grimace 10 sullenness 11 displeasure
mumper: 6 beggar 8 impostor
mumps: 5 brank
mumruffin: 8 titmouse
mun: it; him, may 4 face, must, them 5 mouth, shall
munch: eat 4 chew 5 champ 6 growse, growze
mundane: 6 cosmic 7 earthly, prosaic, secular, terrene, worldly 8 temporal 11 terrestrial
mungo: mug 8 mongoose
municipality: 4 city, town 7 cabildo
pert. to: 5 civic
munificent: 4 free 6 ample 6 lavish 7 liberal 8 generous 9 bounteous, bountiful 10 benevolent
muniment: 6 record 7 defense 8 document, evidence, writings 9 valuables 11 furnishings 13 fortification
munitions: 7 baggage, weapons 10 ammunition
munity: 9 privilege
Munro's penname: 4 Saki
muntjac, muntjak: 4 deer 6 kidang
muraena: 5 moray
mural: 4 wall 8 painting
muralist: 6 Benton, Giotto, Orozco, Rivera 7 Cimabue, da Vinci
murchy: 8 mischief
murder: 4 bane, kill, slay 5 death 7 butcher, carnage, killing, murther 8 homicide 9 slaughter 11 assassinate 12 manslaughter
brother: 10 fratricide

father: 9 patricide
fine: cro 7 wergild 9 bloodfine
infant: 11 infanticide
king: 8 regicide
mother: 9 matricide
own child: 9 prolicide
parent: 9 parricide
prophet: 8 vaticide
sister: 10 sororicide
son or daughter: 8 filicide
spouse: 10 mariticide
wife: 9 uxoricide
woman: 8 femicide
murderous: 4 gory 5 felon 6 bloody, brutal 9 ferocious 10 sanguinary 12 bloodthirsty
mure: 4 meek, soft, wall 6 gentle, demure, immure, modest
murgeon: 7 grimace, grumble
muriatic: 12 hydrochloric
nurid: rat 8 disciple
murky: dim 4 dark 5 black, dense, foggy, mirky, misty, thick 6 gloomy 7 obscure 12 impenetrable
murmur: coo, hum, pur 4 curr, fret, huzz, purl, purr, sugh 5 brool, grank, sough 6 babble, grutch, hummer, mumble, mutter, repine 7 grumble, whisper 8 complain 9 grumbling
nasal: hum
murphy: 6 potato
murrain: 6 plague 10 pestilence
murther: 6 murder
Musa: 6 banana
muscadine: 5 grape 11 scuppernong
muscle: 4 thew 5 brawn, flesh, sinew, teres 6 lacert 8 strength
affection: 5 crick 6 abasia, ataxia
column: 10 sarcostyle
contracting: 7 agonist
curve: 7 myogram
expansion: 7 dilator
lifting: 7 levator
limb-straightening: 8 extensor
round: 5 teres
segment: 8 myocomma
spasm: 5 tonus
straight: 6 rectus
stretching: 6 tensor
sugar: 7 inosite 8 inositol
trapezius: 10 cucullaris
triangular: 7 deltoid
turning: 7 evertor, rotator
two-headed: 6 biceps
muscovado: 5 sugar
Muscovite: Red 4 mica, Russ 7 Russian
mica: 4 talc
prince: 4 Ivan

muscular: **5** thewy **6** brawny, robust, sinewy, strong, torose, torous **8** athletic, vigorous

muse: **4** dump, mull **5** dream, think **6** loiter, ponder, trifle **7** reflect **8** cogitate, consider, meditate, ruminate **9** amusement **10** meditation **11** contemplate

Muse: **4** Clio **5** Erato **6** Thalia, Urania **7** Euterpe **8** Calliope, Pierides, Polymnia **9** Melpomene **10** Polyhymnia **11** Terpsichore

　birthplace: **6** Pieria
　epithet: **7** Pierian
　father: **4** Zeus
　Fountain: **8** Aganippe
　home: **5** Aonia **7** Helicon
　mother: **9** Mnemosyne
　mountain: **9** Parnassus
　of astronomy: **6** Urania
　of comedy: **6** Thalia
　of dancing: **11** Terpsichore
　of eloquence: **8** Calliope
　of epic poetry: **8** Calliope
　of history: **4** Clio
　of love poetry: **5** Erato
　of lyric poetry: **5** Erato
　of music: **7** Euterpe
　of pastoral poetry: **6** Thalia
　of sacred poetry: **8** Polymnia **10** Polyhymnia
　of tragedy: **9** Melpomene
　seat of worship: **6** Pieria

museful: **6** silent **10** meditative, thoughtful

musery: **4** play **9** amusement

musette: air **4** oboe **7** bagpipe, gavotte

museum: **10** repository
　custodian: **7** curator
　director: **7** curator

mush: cut **5** atole, crush, gruel, march, notch, sepon **6** indent, sepawn, supawn, travel **7** confuse, journey, pudding, suppawn **8** flattery, porridge, sagamite, umbrella **14** sentimentality

mushroom: **4** grow **6** agaric, spread **7** parvenu, upstart
　cap: **6** pileus
　disease: **5** flock
　edible: **5** morel **11** chanterelle
　fairy-ring: **10** champignon
　like: **7** fungous
　part of: **4** gill **5** stipe, trama **6** pileus **7** annulus **8** basidium, hymenium, sterigma **12** basidiospore
　poisoning: **8** mycetism
　poisonous: **7** amanita **9** toadstool
　stem: **5** stipe

mushy: **4** soft, weak **5** gushy, thick **8** effusive, yielding

music (see also **melody, song,** and entries under **musical**): air, art **4** tune **7** harmony

aftersong: **5** epode

beat: **5** ictus, pulse, tempo **6** rhythm

change to another key: **10** modulation **13** transposition

chord: **5** triad

flourish: **7** roulade

for eight: **5** octet

for five: **7** quintet

for four: **7** quartet

for nine: **5** nonet

for one: **4** soli, solo

for seven: **6** septet

for six: **6** sextet **7** sestole **8** sestolet

for three: **4** trio

for two: duo **4** duet

god: **6** Apollo

half tone: **8** semitone

machine for: **5** radio **7** juke-box, pianola **8** musicbox **10** gramophone, phonograph

major scale: **5** gamut

major third: **6** ditone

mania for: **9** melomania

melodic phrase: **9** leitmotif, leitmotiv

morning song: **6** aubade

Muse: **7** Euterpe

notation system: **5** neume

outdoor: **6** aubade **8** serenade

patron saint: **7** Cecilia

simple song: air, lay **4** tune

symbol: bar, key, tie **4** clef, flat, note, rest, slur **5** brace, sharp, staff

syncopated: **4** jazz

theme: **4** tema

timing device: **9** metronome

music hall: **4** gaff, odea(pl.) **5** odeum, odeon

musical: **4** show **5** lyric, revue **7** lyrical, melodic **8** harmonic, rhythmic **9** melodious **10** harmonious

musical comedy: hit **4** flop, show **5** revue **6** review **7** musical

musical composition: **4** glee, opus **5** cento, fugue, opera, rondo **6** ballad, sonata **7** ballade, boutade, cantata, chanson, prelude, scherzo, virelai **8** berceuse, concerto, nocturne, operetta, oratorio, serenata, serenade, sonatina, symphony **9** cabaletta, interlude **10** intermezzo

aria-like: **6** arioso

choral: **5** motet **7** chorale **9** plainsong

dancer's: **10** gymnopedie

dawn: **6** aubade

declamatory: **10** recitative

ending: **4** coda, fine **6** finale

exercise: **5** etude, study

feature: **5** motif, theme

interlude: **6** verset

jazz: rag 4 jive 5 bebop, blues, swing 7 ragtime 12 boogie-woogie
opera: 5 scena
poetic: ode
prelude: 6 verset
religious: 4 mass 5 motet, psalm 6 anthem 7 cantata 8 oratorio
round: 5 canon, fugue, troll
suite: 7 partita
musical direction: *above:* 5 sopra
accented: 8 sforzato 9 sforzando
again: DC, DS; bis 6 da capo 8 dal segno
all: 5 tutti
always: 6 sempre
animated: 7 animato 9 spiritoso
ardent: 7 ardente 12 appassionato
as written: sta
begin now: 7 attacca
below: 5 sotto
bold: 6 audace
bowed: 4 arco
bright: 5 anime
cold: 6 freddo
continue: va
devout: 6 divoto
dignified: 8 maestoso
disconnected: 8 staccato
dying away: 7 calando
emotional: 12 appassionato
emphatic: 7 marcato
evenly: 10 eugalmente
everyone: 5 tutti
excited: 7 agitato 9 spiritoso
fast: 4 vivo 5 tosto 6 presto, veloce, vivace 10 tostamente
faster: 7 stretto
freely: 9 ad libitum
furious: 7 furioso
gay: 7 giocoso
gentle: 5 dolce
half: 5 mezzo
heavy: 7 pesante
held: 6 tenuto
hurried: 7 agitato
in the style of: 4 alla
joyous: 7 giocoso
leap: 5 salto
less: 4 meno
little: 4 poco
little by little: 9 poco a poco
lively: 6 vivace 7 allegro, animato, giocoso
loud: 5 forte 10 fortissimo
louder: 9 crescendo
lovingly: 7 amabile, amoroso
lyric: 5 erato
majestic: 8 maestoso
marked: 7 marcato
moderate: 7 andante 8 moderato
more: piu

more rapid: 7 stretta, stretto
much: 5 molto
muted: 5 sorda
passionless: 6 freddo
plaintive: 7 dolente
playful: 7 giocoso 10 scherzando
plucked: 9 pizzicato
proceed: va
quick: 4 vite 5 tosto 6 presto 7 schnell
quick time: 9 alla breve
quickening: 11 affrettando
repeat: bis 6 ancoro 7 ripresa
sadly: 7 dolente 8 doloroso
sharp: 8 staccato 9 sforzando
silent: 5 tacet
singing: 9 cantabile
sliding: 9 glissando
slow: 5 grave, largo, lento, tardo 6 adagio 7 andante 9 larghetto
slower: rit 6 ritard 10 ritardando
slowing: 11 rallentando
smooth: 6 legato
so much: 5 tanto
soft: 5 dolce, piano 10 pianissimo
softer: 10 diminuendo 11 decrescendo
solemn: 5 grave
somewhat: 4 poco
spirited: 7 animato 9 spiritoso
stately: 7 pomposo
strong: 5 forte 10 fortissimo
sustained: 6 tenuto 9 sostenuto, sustenuto
sweet: 5 dolce
tempo irregular: 6 rubato
thrice: ter
throughout: 6 sempre
together: 8 ensemble
too much: 6 troppo
tranquil: 7 calmato
turn: 9 gruppetto
twice: bis
very: tre 4 tres 5 assai, molto 7 dimolto
with: con
musical disc: 6 cymbal, record 9 recording
musical drama: 5 opera 8 operetta, oratorio
musical event: 5 opera 6 ballet 7 concert, recital 8 musicale, oratorio
musical instrument: 4 drum, fife, gong, harp, horn, lute, lyre, oboe, reed, tuba 5 banjo, flute, organ, piano, viola 6 cornet, guitar, spinet, violin 7 bassoon, ocarina, piccolo, saxhorn, trumpet, ukelele 8 castanet, clarinet, dulcimer, mandolin, trombone 9 euphonium, flageolet, saxophone 11 violoncello
aid: 4 pick 8 diapason, plectrum 9 metronome, pitch pipe
ancient: 4 asor 5 rocta 6 rappel, sabeca 7 cithera, serpent 9 pantaleon
bass: 5 cello 11 violoncello

brass: 4 horn, tuba 5 bugle 6 tromba 7 alt-horn, helicon, saxhorn, trumpet 8 altohorn, trombone 10 French horn

China: kin

East Indies: 4 bina

Egypt: 7 sistrum

helicon: 4 tuba

Java: 7 gamelon 8 gamelang

keyboard: 5 organ, piano 6 spinet 7 celesta, clavier 8 melodeon 9 accordion 10 clavichord, concertina, pianoforte 11 harpsichord

lute-like: 7 angelot, bandore, cithern, cittern 9 bandurria 10 colascione

lyre-like: 4 asor 6 cither, zither 7 cithara, kithara

medieval: 5 rebab, rocta 7 chrotta

Mexico: 5 guiro 6 clarin 7 cabacas, maracas 11 chiapanecas

mouthpiece: 4 reed 6 fipple

oboe-like: 5 shawm 7 musette

old: 5 rebec 7 cittern, gittern

percussion: 4 drum, gong 5 bells, traps 6 maraca 7 cymbals, marimba, timpani, tympani 8 triangle 9 castanets, xylophone 10 tambourine 12 glockenspiel

piano-like: see *keyboard* above

reed: 4 oboe 7 bassoon 8 clarinet 9 saxophone 11 English horn

six-stringed: 6 guitar

stringed: oud, uke 4 asor, bass, harp, lute, lyre, viol, vina 5 banjo, cello, rebec, ruana, viola 6 citole, fiddle, guitar, rebeck, violin, zither 7 bandore, cythara, gittern, pandura, samisen, theorbo, ukelele 8 autoharp, dulcimer, mandolin 11 harpsichord, violoncello

supplementary: 7 ripieno

two-necked: 7 theorbo

viol-like: 5 rebec, ruana 6 rebeck 7 claviol 8 claviole

wind: jug, sax 4 fife, horn, oboe, reed, tuba 5 brass, bugle, flute, organ 6 cornet 7 althorn, bagpipe, bassoon, clarion, ocarina, panpipe, piccolo, saxhorn, serpent, trumpet 8 altohorn, clarinet, recorder, trombone, zampogna 9 flageolet, harmonica, saxophone 10 French horn 11 sarrusphone

xylophone-like: 7 marimba

musical interval: 5 fifth, major, minor, sixth, third 6 ditone, fourth, octave, second, unison 7 perfect, seventh, tritone 9 augmented 10 diminished

musical medley: 4 olio 5 cento

musical note (see also **musical syllable**): 5 breve, minim, neume 6 quaver 9 semibreve

musical piece: See **musical composition; song**

musical program: 5 opera 7 concert, recital 8 musicale

musical rhythm: 4 beat, time 5 ictus, meter, pulse, swing, tempo

measuring device: 9 metronome

musical scale (see also **musical syllable**): 5 gamut

musical sign: 5 segno

entrance: 5 presa

hold: 7 fermata, formata

key: 4 flat 5 sharp 7 natural

pitch level: 4 clef

silence: 4 rest

slur: 8 ligature

smooth: 4 slur

staff: bar

musical syllable: do, fa, la, mi, re, si, ti, ut; sol

ancient: ce, ut; alt, are, ela 5 elami, neume 7 alamire

musical term: *arrangement:* 7 ridotto

ballad style: 8 a ballata

between acts: 8 entracte

cadence: 4 half 6 plagal 7 perfect 9 deceptive, imperfect

chapel-style: 9 a cappella

dance-style: 7 da ballo

embellishment: 8 ornament 9 fioritura 12 appoggiatura

ending: 4 coda

florid: 7 bravura

flourish: 7 cadenza

half note: 5 minim

half tone: 8 semitone

major key: dur

melodic phrase: 5 motif 9 leitmotif, leitmotiv

melos: 4 song 6 melody

minor key: 4 moll

movement: 4 moto

note: 5 breve, neume

refrain: 5 epode 8 repetend

repeat: 5 rondo 7 reprise

run: 6 volata 9 glissando

shake: 5 trill 7 tremolo

soft pedal: VC 7 celeste

third: 6 tierce

thirty-second note: 14 demisemiquaver

three-note chord: 5 triad

time: see **musical rhythm**

tones: 5 chord

tremble: 5 trill 7 tremolo, vibrato

triplet: 6 tercet, triole

two notes: 5 duole

unaccompanied: 9 a cappella

upbeat: 5 arsis

vocal part: 5 canto

musical theme: 4 tema 5 motif 9 leitmotif, leitmotiv

musician: 4 bard 5 piper 6 singer 7 drummer, flutist, gleeman, pianist 8 bandsman, composer, flautist, minstrel, organist 9 cornetist, performer, serenader, violinist 10 trombonist 11 clarinetist, saxophonist

group: 4 band, duet, trio 5 choir, nonet 6 chorus, septet, sextet 7 nonetto, quartet 8 ensemble, septette, sextette 9 orchestra, quartette

patron saint: 7 Cecelia

musing: 7 reverie 10 meditation, meditative 13 contemplation

musk: 4 deer 7 perfume

musk beaver: 7 muskrat

musk cat: 5 civet

musk cavy: 5 hutia

musk cucumber: 11 cassabanana

musk deer: 10 chevrotain

musk hog: 7 peccary

musk lorikeet: 8 parakeet

musk mallow: 8 abelmosk

musk shrew: 6 desman

muskeg: bog 5 marsh

muskellunge: 4 pike

musket: 4 hawk 5 fusil 6 falcon 7 bundock, bundook, dragoon, firearm 8 biscayen 9 flintlock

Musketeers: *Three:* see **Three Musketeers**

muskmelon: 6 atimon, casaba 10 cantaloupe

muskrat: 5 shrew 6 desman

Muslim, Moslem (see also **Islam, Mohammed**): 4 Moro 6 Paynim 7 abadite, Islamic, Saracen 9 Mahometan, Mussulman 10 Mohammedan

ablution: 4 widu, wudu, wuzu

Alexandria sect: 6 Senusi

angel: 6 Azrael 7 isrefel, israfil 8 israfeel

annual fast: 7 Ramadan

antenuptial settlement: 4 mahr

ascetic: 4 sufi 5 fakir 6 fakeer

bazaar: 4 sook

belt: 5 zonar 6 zonnar

Berber dynasty: 6 Hafsid 7 Hafsite

Bible: 5 Coran, Koran 7 Alcoran

bier: 5 tabut

blood relationship: 5 nasab

calendar: 5 Rabia, Rajab, Safar 6 Jumada, Shaban 7 Ramadan, Shawwal 8 Zu'lhijah, Zu'lkadah 9 Mulharram

call to prayer: 4 adan, azan

cap: taj 5 kulah 6 kullah

caravansary: 6 imaret

caste: 5 mopla 6 moplah

chief: 4 rais, sidi 5 datto, sayid, sheik

city (sacred): 5 Mecca 6 Medina

coin: 5 dinar

convert: 5 ansar

council: 5 Ulema

creed: 5 Sunna

crusade: 5 jehad, jihad

decree: 5 irade

deity: 5 Allah, Eblis

demon: 5 afrit, eblis, jinni 6 jinnee

dervish: 6 Sadite, Santon

divorce: 5 ahsan, talak 7 mubarat

fast days: 7 Ramadan

festival: Eed 6 Bairam

freethinker: 7 Saracen 9 Aladinist

garment: 4 izar 6 jubbah

god: 5 Allah

guide (spiritual): pir

headdress: fez, taj 5 kulah 6 kullah, turban

hermit: 8 marabout

holy book: 5 Koran

holy city: 5 Mecca 6 Medina

holy war: 5 jehad, jihad

infidel: 5 kafir 6 kaffir

judge: 4 cadi, cazi, imam, kazi 5 hakim, imaum

lady: 5 begum

law: 5 halal 7 sheriat

lawyer: 5 mufti

leader: 4 amir, emir 5 ameer, emeer

men's quarters: 8 selamlik

messiah: 5 Mahdi

minaret crier: 7 muezzin

minister of state: 6 vizier

monastery: 5 tekke

month: see *calendar* above

mosque: 6 masjid

mystic: 4 Sufi

mysticism: 6 Sufism

name: Ali

nymph: 5 houri

officer: aga

official: 5 hajib, mufti

orthodox: 5 hanif 7 Sunnite

people: Laz 4 Lazi, Moro, Sufi, Swat 5 Hanif, Isawa, Salar, Samal, Sunni, Swati 6 Dehgan, Senusi 7 Bazigar, Senousi, Senussi 8 Senusite 9 Senussian

physician: 5 hakim 6 hakeem

pilgrim: 4 haji 5 hadji, hajji

pilgrimage: 4 hadj

pilgrim's dress: 5 ihram

prayer: 5 namaz, salat

prayer call: 4 adan, azan

priest: 4 imam 5 imaum 6 wahabi

priests (body): 5 ulema

prince: 4 amir, emir, seid 5 ameer, emeer, nawab, sayid

princess: 4 tola 5 begum

religion: 5 Islam

ruler: aga 4 amir, emir 5 ameer, emeer, hakim, nawah 6 hakeem, sultan *saber:* 7 yatagan 8 scimitar, scimiter, yataghan

sacred book: See *Bible* above

saint: Pir 5 Abdal 6 Santon 8 Marabout

salutation: 5 salam 6 salaam

sect: 5 Isawa 6 Wahabi 7 Abadite, dervish, Sunnite 8 Ahmadiya, Sifatite

shrine: 5 Kaaba 6 Kaabeh

spirit: 4 jinn(pl.) 5 genie, jinni 7 jinnyeh

spiritual adviser: pir

student: 5 softa

supreme being: 5 Allah

teacher: 4 alim, imam 8 mujtahid

title: sid 4 said, sidi 5 nawab, sayid 6 sayyid

warrior: 7 Saracen

washing: 4 widu, wudu, wuzu

women's quarters: 5 harem

muslin: ban 4 mull 5 adati, dorea, doria, shela 6 cossas, gurrah, shelah 7 beteela, organdy 8 nainsook, seerhand, sheeting 9 charkhana, womanhood 10 femininity

muss: See **mess**

mussel: 4 naid, unio 5 naiad 6 mucket, nerita 8 deerhorn

genus of: 8 modiolus

part: 6 byssus

mussitate: 6 mutter

Mussolini's son-in-law: 5 Ciano

Mussulman: See **Muslim**

must: 4 bood, mold, musk, sapa, stum 5 juice, ought, shall 6 refuse 10 obligation

mustang: 5 pinto 6 bronco 7 broncho

mustard: 5 nigra, senvy 6 senapi 7 cadlock 8 charlock

chemical: 5 allyl

family: 12 brassicaceae

genus of: 7 sinapis

pod: 7 silicle

mustard plaster: 8 sinapism

musteline animal: 6 weasel

muster: 4 call 5 erect 6 gather, roster, sample, summon 7 collect, marshal, pattern 8 assemble 10 accumulate, congregate

out: 7 disband, release 9 discharge

mustiness: 4 fust, mold

musty: 4 dull, sour 5 fusty, hoary, moldy, rafty, stale, trite 6 rancid 7 foughty, spoiled 10 antiquated

Mut: *child of:* 5 Chons

husband: 4 Amen, Amon

mutable: 6 fickle 8 variable 9 alterable 10 changeable, inconstant 11 vacillating

mutate: 4 vary 5 alter 6 change, modify

mutation: 6 change, revolt 9 posthouse 10 revolution, succession 11 vicissitude

mute: mum 4 dumb, lene, surd 6 deaden, muffle, silent 7 mourner, muffler 8 deadener, silencer 9 voiceless 10 speechless 12 inarticulate

mutilate: mar 4 hack, maim 6 deface, garble, injure, mangle, mittle(Sc.) 7 cripple, destroy 9 disfigure, dismember

mutinous: 6 unruly 9 seditious, turbulent 10 rebellious, refractory, tumultuous 11 disobedient, intractable 12 contumacious 13 insubordinate

mutiny: 6 revolt, strife 9 commotion 12 insurrection

mutt: cur, dog 7 mongrel 9 blockhead

mutter: 5 growl 6 mumble, murmur, patter 7 channer, grumble, maunder 9 mussitate

mutton: 4 meat 5 sheep 6 candle 10 prostitute

dried: 5 vifda, vivda

leg: 5 cabob, gigot 7 wabbler, wobbler

muttonbird: oii 6 petrel 10 shearwater

muttonchop: 7 whisker 8 burnside

muttonfish: 4 sama 5 pargo, porgy 7 eelpout, mojarra

muttonhead: 5 dunce 9 blockhead, screwball

mutual: 6 common 10 reciprocal, responsive

mutuality: 13 interrelation

mux: 4 mess 5 botch

muzhik: 7 peasant

muzz: 6 muddle

muzzle: gag 4 grub, nose, root 5 snout 6 clevis, muffle 7 sheathe 8 restrain 10 respirator

muzzy: 4 dull 5 fuzzy 7 blurred, muddled 8 confused 10 depressive

My Last Duchess author: 9 Browning

mycoid: 7 fungoid

mykiss: 6 salmon

myna: 7 grackle

myomorph: rat 5 mouse 6 rodent

myopic: 8 purblind 11 nearsighted 12 shortsighted

myotic: 6 eserin 7 eserine

myriad: 9 countless 11 innumerable 13 multitudinous

myriapod: 9 centipede

myrmicid: ant

myrmidon: 8 adherent, follower, henchman

myrrh: gum 4 tree 5 resin

myrtle: 8 ramarama 10 periwinkle 11 candleberry

myself: 5 masel(Sc.)

mysterious: dim 4 dark 5 runic 6 arcane, mystic, occult, secret 7 cryptic, uncanny 8 abstruse 9 equivocal, recondite, sphinxine 12 inexplicable, unfathomable

mystery: 4 rune 5 craft, trade 6 cabala, enigma, puzzle, riddle, secret 7 arcanum, esotery 8 thriller, whodunit

mystery novel award: 5 Edgar

mystic: 4 seer 5 epopt, runic 6 occult, orphic, secret 7 cryptic, epoptic, obscure 8 anagogic, esoteric, symbolic 9 enigmatic, recondite 10 cabalistic, mysterious
art: 6 cabala
initiate: 5 epopt
Moslem: 4 Sufi
secret sect: 5 cabal
word: om, um 4 evoe 7 abraxas 11 abracadabra

mystical: 4 dark 6 occult, secret 8 symbolic 9 spiritual
significance: 7 anagoge
mysticism: 6 cabala 8 cabalism
mystify: 5 befog 6 muddle, puzzle 7 becloud, confuse, perplex 8 befuddle, bewilder 9 bamboozle, obfuscate
myth: 4 saga, tale 5 fable, fancy, story 6 legend 7 parable 9 apocrypha
mythical: 9 imaginary 10 fictitious

N

nab: hat 4 grab, head 5 catch, seize 6 arrest, clutch, nibble, snatch 7 capture 9 apprehend

Nabal: *home:* 4 Maon
wife: 7 Abigail

nabob: 5 nawab 6 deputy 7 viceroy 8 governor 9 plutocrat 10 viceregent 11 billionaire

Nabokov novel: Ada 4 Pnin 6 Lolita

nacelle: 7 shelter 11 compartment

nacket: boy 4 cake 5 lunch

nacre: 9 shellfish 10 conchiolin 13 mother-of-pearl

nadir's opposite: 6 zenith

nag: tit 4 frab, fret, gnaw, jade, pony, twit 5 annoy, cobra, hobby, horse, scold, snake, tease 6 badger, berate, bother, harass, heckle, hector, padnag, pester, wanton 7 hackney 8 harangue, irritate 9 aggravate

naga, nag: 5 cobra, snake

nagor: 8 antelope, reedbuck

nahoor: sha, sna 5 sheep, urial 6 bharal, oorial

Nahor: *father:* 5 Serug
grandson: 7 Abraham
son: 5 Terah
wife: 6 Milcah

Nahuatlan: 5 Aztec

naiad: 5 nymph 6 mussel

naif: See naive

nail: cut, fix, hob 4 brad, brag, brod, claw, cloy, dump, spad, stub, stud, tack, trap 5 affix, catch, clout, grope, spike, sprig 6 clinch, detain, fasten, hammer, secure, unguis, ungula 7 capture 8 fastener, sparable, spikelet 9 finishing, intercept
drive at a slant: toe
headless: 5 sprig
ingrowing: 7 acronyx
marking on: 6 lunule
perforated: 4 spad
shoemaker's: 4 brad 8 sparable

nais: 5 naiad, nymph

naissance: 5 birth

naive: 5 frank 6 simple 7 artless 8 childish, untaught 9 childlike, guileless, ingenuous, untutored, unworldly 10 unaffected 13 inexperienced, unphilosophic 15 unsophisticated

naked: 4 bare, nude, open 6 cuerpo 7 exposed 8 manifest 9 unadorned, unclothed, uncovered 11 defenseless, unprotected

namaycush: 5 lunge, togue, trout

namby-pamby: 7 insipid 10 wishy-washy 11 sentimental

name: dub, nom(F.) 4 call, term 5 claim, clepe, count, nemme, nemne, neven, nomen, style, title 6 adduce, appeal, monica, select 7 appoint, behight, enstyle, entitle, epithet, intitle, mention, moniker 8 christen, delegate, identify, identity, monicker, monniker, nominate 9 designate 10 denominate, denotation, reputation 11 appellation, designation 12 denomination, nomenclature
added: 6 agname 7 agnomen
assumed: 5 alias 6 anonym 9 incognito, pseudonym, sobriquet 10 nom de plume, soubriquet
backwards: 6 ananym
based on location: 7 toponym
Biblical: See Bible: *name*
derivation: 7 eponymy
family: 7 eponymy, sirname, surname 8 cognomen
female: Ada, Amy, Ann, Ava, Dot, Ena, Eva, Eve, Fay, Ida, Ina, Jen, Lil, Lou, Mae, May, Meg, Nan, Pam, Pat, Rae, Una, Zoe 4 Alma, Alta, Anna, Anta, Avis, Caro, Cora, Dian, Dona, Dora, Edla, Edna, Ella, Elsa, Enid, Erma, Etta, Eula, Fifi, Gail, Inez, Irma, Kate, Katy, Lena, Lida, Lila, Lois, Lola, Lona, Lora, Lula, Meta, Mina, Nena, Nina, Nita, Nora, Olga, Prue, Rena, Reta, Rita, Sara, Suke, Suky, Susy, Tess, Vera 5 Adele, Agnes, Aimee, Alice, Alida, Aline, Alsie, Anita, Annie, Aphra, Bella, Betsy, Betty, Celia, Clare, Delia, Della, Doris, Dulce, Edith, Eilen, Elain, Elena, Elise, Ellen, Elsie, Essie, Ester, Ethel, Ettie, Flora, Freda, Genie, Greta, Helen, Hilda, Irene, Janet, Karen, Laura, Lelia, Leona,

Lucia, Lydia, Maida, Maria, Moira, Molly, Norah, Norma, Paula, Rhoda, Sally, Sarah, Sukey, Sukie, Susan, Susie, Tecla, Wilma **6** Adelai, Alicia, Annice, Arline, Connie, Dagmar, Daphne, Dorcas, Elaine, Esther, Fedora, Flavia, Frieda, Gertie, Gloria, Gratia, Hedwig, Hermia, Honora, Isabel, Janice, Jennie, Lenora, Lenore, Louisa, Louise, Muriel, Pamela, Persis, Sallie, Sandra, Sheila, Zebina **7** Abigale, Belinda, Cecilia, Celeste, Dolores, Eleanor, Emaline, Estelle, Eveline, Felicia, Heloise, Imogene, Juanita, Madelon, Mildred, Rosalia, Rosalie, Susanna, Waunita, Zulinde **8** Arabella, Drusilla, Hermiona, Hyacinth, Patricia **9** Anastasia

first: **9** praenomen

list: **11** onomasticon

masculine: Al, Ed, Si; Abe, Alf, Asa, Ben, Cal, Dan, Eli, Gil, Gus, Guy, Hal, Ian, Ike, Ira, Lem, Len, Lon, Moe, Nat, Ned, Ole, Pat, Ray, Rex, Roy, Sam, Sid, Ted, Tex, Tim, Ugo, Vic **4** Abel, Adam, Alan, Alex, Alva, Amos, Axel, Bart, Bert, Carl, Dian, Dick, Earl, Emil, Enos, Eric, Esme, Evan, Ezra, Gene, Hugh, Igor, Ivan, Joab, Joel, Knut, Leon, Levi, Luke, Lynn, Marc, Mark, Neal, Neil, Noah, Noel, Olaf, Otto, Owen, Paul, Phil, Pius, Rene, Saul, Stan, Tony, Zeke **5** Aaron, Abiel, Abner, Abram, Agard, Allan, Alvan, Angus, Anton, Basil, Biron, Bryan, Bryon, Byron, Caleb, Cecil, Cliff, Clive, Denis, Edgar, Elias, Elihu, Elmer, Emery, Eneas, Enoch, Ernie, Erwin, Ethan, Felix, Floyd, Giles, Hiram, Isaac, Jabez, Judah, Leigh, Leroy, Lloyd, Louis, Lysle, Moses, Nahum, Nigel, Orson, Peleg, Percy, Peter, Reuel, Roger, Rollo, Roman, Rufus, Silas, Titus, Urban, Uriah, Uriel, Zebee **6** Adolph, Adrian, Alaric, Albert, Alexis, Alfred, August, Austin, Caesar, Calvin, Caspar, Cedric, Daniel, Decius, Dexter, Donald, Dudley, Duncan, Dwight, Edmund, Egbert, Harvey, Hubert, Isaiah, Israel, Jairus, Jarvis, Joshua, Josiah, Jotham, Junius, Kasper, Lemuel, Lester, Lucius, Luther, Manuel, Marcus, Marion, Murray, Naaman, Nathan, Pierre, Reuben, Roland, Roscoe, Rupert, Samuel, Steven, Teague, Theron, Tobiah, Vergil, Victor, Vivian, Walter, Wilbur **7** Abraham, Anatole, Bertram, Chester, Clement, Dominic, Douglas, Eleazar, Elliott, Erasmus, Erastus, Eustace, Everard, Everett, Ezekiel, Flavius, Gabriel, Gifford, Gilbert, Godfrey, Isidore, Japheth, Lazarus, Leonard, Leopold, Lorenzo, Malachi, Maurice, Obadiah, Patrick, Phineas, Raphael, Raymond, Raymund, Rowland, Russell, Seymour, Stanley, Stephen, Ulysses, Zachary,

Zebedee, Zebedei, Zebedia **8** Adelbert, Algernon, Alphonso, Benjamin, Claudius, Clifford, Ebenezer, Emmanuel, Fernando, Frederic, Gamaliel, Geoffrey, Gustavus, Hezekiah, Ignatius, Jeremiah, Laurence, Lawrence, Napoleon, Nehemiah, Octavius, Percival, Schuyler, Silvanus, Terrence, Thaddeus, Zebadiah **9** Anatasius, Archibald, Celestine, Cornelius, Demetrius, Ferdinand, Frederick, Lafayette, Launcelot, Llewellyn, Marcellus, Nathaniel, Rodolphus, Rudolphus, Siegfried, Sigismund, Silvester, Zachariah, Zacharias **10** Maximilian, Theophilus

objectionable: **7** caconym

pet: **8** nickname **9** sobriquet

tablet: **5** facia

nameable: 6 famous **7** notable **9** memorable

named: 6 yclept **7** ycleped

nameless: 7 bastard, obscure **9** anonymous, unnamable **12** illegitimate **13** indescribable, unmentionable

namely: viz **5** noted, to wit **6** famous **8** scilicet **9** expressly, videlicit **10** especially **12** specifically

namesake: 6 junior

nandu: 4 rhea

nanism: 12 dwarfishness

nanny: 4 goat **5** nurse

nanny plum: 10 sheepberry

nanpie: 6 magpie

Naomi: 4 Mara

daughter-in-law: **4** Ruth **5** Orpah

husband: **9** Elimelech

son: **6** Mahlon **7** Chilion

naos: 5 cella **6** shrine, temple

nap: nod **4** calk, doze, fuzz, lint, pile, shag, wink **5** fluff, grasp, seize, sleep, steal **6** siesta, snooze

nape: nod **5** nucha, nuque **6** scruff **7** niddick

napery: 5 linen

Naphtali: *census taker:* **4** Enan

mother: **6** Bilhah

son: **4** Guni **5** Jezer **7** Jahziel, Shallum

naphtha: 9 petroleum

napkin: 5 cloth, doily, towel **6** diaper **8** kerchief **9** handcloth, serviette **11** neckerchief **12** handkerchief

Naples: *biscuit:* **10** ladyfinger

coin: **6** carlin **7** carline

king: **5** Murat

secret society: **7** Camorra

napless 10 threadbare

Napoleon: *battle:* Ulm **4** Acre, Jena **7** Dresden **8** Borodino, Waterloo **10** Austerlitz

birthplace: **7** Corsica

brother: **5** Louis **6** Jerome, Joseph, Lucien

brother-in-law: **5** Murat

island of exile: **4** Elba

marshal: Ney
nickname: 5 Boney
place of victory: 5 Ligny 10 Austerlitz
sister: 5 Elisa, Maria 8 Carlotta, Carolina
wife: 9 Josephine

nappy: ale 4 dish 5 downy, heady, wooly 6 liquor, strong 7 foaming

napu: 7 deerlet 10 chevrotain

narcotic (see also **marijuana**): kat 4 bang, dope, junk 5 bhang, dagga, ether, opium 6 heroin, opiate 7 anodyne, cocaine, hashish 8 hasheesh, hypnotic, morphine, takrouri 9 soporific 10 bella-donna, hyoscyamus, stramonium
dose: 5 locus
package: 4 deck 6 bindle
plant: kat 4 coca, cuca, hemp, kaat, khat 5 dutra, poppy
seller: 6 pusher 7 peddler

nard: 5 spice 6 anoint 7 rhizome 9 spikenard

nardoo: 6 clover

nargileh: 4 pipe 5 hooka 6 hookah 7 coconut

narial: 6 rhinal

nark: spy, vex 5 annoy 8 informer, irritate 10 spoilsport 11 stool pigeon

narrate: 4 tell 5 state 6 detail, recite, relate, report 7 discuss, recount 8 describe, rehearse 9 chronicle, discourse

narrative: 4 epic, myth, saga, tale 5 conte, drama, fable, story 6 legend 7 account, episode, history, parable 8 allegory, anecdote 9 narration

narrator: 9 reconteur

narrow: 4 mean 5 close, scant, sound, taper 6 biased, linear, meager, meagre, strait, strict 7 bigoted, limited 8 condense, contract 9 constrict, hidebound, illiberal, niggardly 10 prejudiced, restricted, straighten, ungenerous 11 reactionary 12 parsimonious 13 circumscribed
combining form: 4 sten 5 steno

narrowminded: 6 biased 7 bigoted

narsinga: 7 trumpet

narthex: 5 porch 7 portico 9 vestibule 10 antetemple

nasab: 7 kinship 13 consanguinity

nasal: 6 narine, rhinal, twangy

nascency: 5 birth 6 origin 7 genesis 9 beginning

naseberry: 9 sapodilla

nashgab: 6 gossip

nasi: 9 patriarch

nasicorn: 10 rhinoceros

nastika: 7 atheist

nasty: bad 4 foul, mean, ugly 5 dirty 6 filthy 7 harmful, obscene, squalid 8 indecent 9 dangerous, malicious, offensive 10 disgusting, ill-natured, nauseating, unpleasant 12 disagreeable, dishonorable 13 objectionable

nasutiform: 8 noselike

nat: 5 demon 6 spirit

natal: 6 native 7 gluteal 10 congenital

natant: 6 afloat 8 floating, swimming

natator: 7 swimmer

natatorium: 4 bath, pool

natchbone: 9 aitchbone

nation: 4 host, race 5 caste, class, state 6 people 7 country 9 community, multitude
symbol: 4 flag 5 crest

national: 7 citizen, federal 11 gentilitian

National Guard member: 10 militiaman

native: 5 natal 6 genial, inborn, innate, normal 7 citizen, endemic, natural 8 domestic, inherent, original, resident 9 aborigine, congenial, ingrained, unbranded 10 congenital, indigenous, inhabitant

nativity: 5 birth 8 geniture 9 horoscope

natrium: NA 6 sodium

nattle: 4 gnaw 6 nibble

natty: 4 chic, neat, tidy, trig, trim 5 smart 6 spruce 10 fastidious

natural: 4 born, easy 5 usual 6 common, cretin, inborn, inbred, innate, native, normal 7 regular 8 inherent, ordinary, physical 9 primitive, unassumed unfeigned 10 congenital 13 unenlightened

naturalize: 5 adopt 8 accustom 9 acclimate 11 acclimatize, domesticate, familiarize

nature: 4 kind, sort, type 7 essence 9 character 11 disposition, temperament
divinity: 5 nymph
god: Pan
goddess: 6 Cybele 7 Artemis
same: 10 homogeneal

naught: 4 evil, zero 5 aught, ought 6 cipher, nought, wicked 7 nothing, useless 9 worthless

naughty: bad 4 evil 5 wrong 6 wicked 7 obscene, wayward 8 improper 10 indelicate 11 disobedient, mischievous

nauntle: 4 fuss 5 raise, strut 6 potter

naupathia: 11 seasickness

nausea: 4 pall 7 disgust 8 loathing, sickness 10 queasiness

nauseating: 5 nasty, waugh 7 fulsome 8 brackish 9 loathsome, sickening 10 disgusting 11 distasteful

nautical (see also **navigation**): 5 naval 6 marine 7 oceanic 8 maritime
cry: 4 ahoy
flag: 6 cornet, pennon
instrument: 7 compass, sextant
mile: 4 knot
term: 4 atry 5 abaft, abeam, alist, avast

nautilus: 7 mollusk 9 argonauta

Navaho hut: 5 hogan

naval stores: tar 5 pitch 8 supplies 10 turpentine

nave: hob, hub, nef 4 apse, body, fist 5 aisle, nieve

navel: 9 umbilicus

navigate: 4 keel, sail 5 steer 6 direct, manage 7 journey, operate

navigation: 7 nautics 8 cabotage 10 seamanship

call: 4 ahoy 5 avast, belay

hazard: fog, sub 4 mine 9 submarine

instrument: aba 7 compass, pelorus, sextant

measure: ton 4 knot, seam 6 fathom 7 renning, sea mile 12 cable's length

signal: 4 bell, flag

term: 4 atry 5 abeam, atrip

navigator: 5 flyer, navvy, pilot 6 airman 7 aviator, copilot, laborer 8 aeronaut, seafarer, spaceman

navite: 6 basalt

navvy: 7 laborer 9 navigator

navy: 5 fleet

board: 9 admiralty

depot: 4 base

force: 5 fleet 6 armada 8 squadron

jail: 4 brig

officer: 4 aide, mate 5 bosun 6 ensign 7 admiral, armorer, captain 8 armourer 9 commander, commodore 10 lieutenant

vessel: PT; sub 7 carrier, cruiser, flattop, gun boat 9 destroyer, submarine, transport 10 battleship

wireless operator: 6 sparks

nawab: 5 nabob, ruler 7 viceroy

nay: no; nai, not 4 deny, nyet(Russ.) 5 flute, never 6 denial, refuse 7 refusal 8 negative 11 prohibition

naysay: 6 denial 7 refusal

nayword: 6 byword 7 proverb 9 watchword

naze: 8 headland 10 promontory

Nazi: 9 Hitlerite

police: SS 7 Gestapo

symbol: 6 fylfot 8 swastika

nazim: 7 viceroy 8 governor

neal: 6 anneal, temper

neanic: 8 immature, youthful

neap: 4 tide

near: by; gin, kin, nar(Sc.) 4 bain, dear, hend, nigh 5 anear, anent, aside, close, handy, hende 6 almost, around, beside, climax, narrow, stingy 7 advance, similar, thrifty, vicinal 8 adjacent, approach, intimate 9 niggardly, thriftily 10 contiguous, juxtaposed 11 approximate, closefisted 12 parsimonious 13 propinquitous

Near East: 6 Levant

ketch: 4 saic

nearest: 4 next 5 ewest(Sc.) 7 closest 9 proximate

nearsighted: 6 myopic 12 shortsighted

neat: gim 4 cosh(Sc.), deft, dink, feil(Sc.), nice, prim, pure, snod(Sc.), snug, tidy, tosh, trig, trim 5 clean, compt, dinky, douce, natty 6 adroit, cattle, clever, dapper 7 concise, orderly, precise, refined, unmixed 8 skillful, tasteful 9 dexterous, shipshape, undiluted 10 concinnous, meticulous

neath: 5 below 7 beneath

neatherd: 7 cowherd 8 herdsman

neb: nib, tip 4 beak, bill, nose 5 snout

Nebraska: *bird:* 10 meadowlark

city: 5 Omaha

river: 6 Platte

nebris: 8 fawnskin

nebula: sky 5 vapor 6 galaxy 10 atmosphere

nebulize: 7 atomize

nebulous: 4 hazy 5 foggy, misty, vague 6 cloudy 7 clouded, unclear 8 nebulose 10 indefinite, indistinct

necessarily: 8 perforce

necessary: 5 privy, vital 6 toilet 7 needful 8 forcible, integral 9 essential, mandatory, requisite 10 inevitable, undeniable 11 unavoidable, water-closet 13 indispensable

necessitate: 5 force, impel 6 compel, entail, oblige 7 require 9 constrain

necessity: 4 food, must, need, want 5 drink 7 ailment, poverty, urgency 8 distress 9 emergency 11 destitution

neck: pet 4 cape, crag, crop, hals, kiss 5 halse 6 caress, cervix, collum, fondle, strait 7 channel, embrace, isthmus

armor: 6 gorget

artery: 7 carotid

back of: 4 nape 5 nucha, nuque 6 scruff

comb. form: 6 cervic 7 cervico

muscle: 8 scalenus

part: 4 gula 7 withers

pert. to: 7 jugular 8 cervical

piece: bib, boa 5 amice, rabat, scarf, stole 6 collar 8 kerchief

neck and neck: tie 4 even 5 close

neckatee: 11 neckerchief

neckband: 6 collar, collet 10 collar-band

neckcloth: bib, boa 4 ruff 5 amice, choke, jabot, rabat, ruche, scarf, stole 6 choker, collar, cravat, dickey 7 bur-dash, pannelo 8 kerchief 9 barcelona 11 neckerchief

neckerchief: 4 gimp 7 belcher 8 kerchief, nectatee 12 handkerchief

necklace: 4 rope, torc 5 beads, chain, noose 6 collar, grivna, locket, torque 7 baldric, chaplet, haltern, necktie, riviere 8 baldrick, carcanet, lavalier 9 esclavage, lavaliere 10 lavalliere

necktie: bow, tie 4 band 5 ascot, scarf 6 cravat 10 four-in-hand

necktie party: 7 hanging 8 lynching

necrologue: 8 obituary

necromancy: art 5 goety, magic 7 grammary, sorcery 8 gramarye, wizardry 11 conjuration, enchantment

necropolis: 8 cemetery

necropsy: 7 autopsy

nectar: 5 honey 8 ambrosia

nectar bird: 7 sunbird

nedder: 5 adder

neddy: 6 donkey

nee: 4 born 8 formerly

need: 4 lack, want 5 crave 6 behove, demand, desire 7 behoove, poverty, require, urgency 8 distress, exigency 9 emergency, extremity, indigence, necessity, requisite 10 compulsion, dependence, obligation, retirement 11 destitution

needful: 5 vital 8 integral 9 essential 13 indispensable

needle: sew 4 acus(L.), darn 5 annoy 7 acicula, provoke, spicule 10 strengthen
  combining form: acu
  hole: eye
  type: 4 sail 5 blunt, style 6 bodkin, stylus 7 darning, obelisk 8 knitting 10 hypodermic, phonograph, upholstery

needle bug: 7 ranatra

needle gun: 5 rifle 6 Dreyse

needlefish: gar 8 pipefish

needlelike: 6 acuate 7 acerate, acerose, acerous, aciform 8 acicular, belonoid

needleman: 6 tailor

needless: 10 gratuitous 11 superfluous, unnecessary

needlewoman: 10 seamstress

needlwood: 10 needlebush

needlework: 6 sewing 7 sampler, seaming, tatting 8 knitting 9 hemstitch 10 embroidery, crocheting

needy: 4 poor 9 penniless

neep: 6 turnip

ne'er-do-well: bum 5 losel, loser 9 schlemiel, worthless 11 incompetent

nef: 4 nave 5 clock

nefandous: 9 execrable

nefarious: 6 wicked 7 heinous, impious 8 flagrant, horrible, infamous 9 atrocious 10 detestable, iniquitous, villainous

nefast: 6 wicked

negate: 4 deny 5 annul 6 refute 7 nullify

negation: not 5 empty 6 denial 7 refusal 9 annulment, blankness, nonentity 10 refutation 13 contradiction, nullification

negative: no, ne; nae(Sc.), nay, non(F.), nor, not 4 film, veto 5 minus, never 7 neutral
  prefix: il, im, in, ir, un; dis, non

neglect: 4 fail, omit, slip 5 fault, forgo, shirk 6 forego, forget, ignore, slight 7 default, failure 8 omission 9 disregard, oversight, pretermit 10 negligence 11 inattention 12 inadvertence, indifference

neglectful: lax 6 remiss 8 careless, derelict, heedless 9 dissolute

negligee: 4 robe 7 undress 8 peignoir 9 nightgown 10 dishabille

negligence: 7 laxness 9 disregard

negotiable: 12 transferable

negotiate: 4 deal 5 treat 6 dicker 7 bargain, chaffer, discuss 8 transact 10 accomplish

negotiation: 6 treaty 8 entreaty

negus: 8 beverage

neigh: 6 whinny

neighbor: 6 adjoin, border fellow

neighborhood: 4 area 5 venue 6 locale, region 7 section 8 district, vicinage, vicinity 9 community, proximity, territory 11 propinquity

neighboring: 4 nigh 6 near-by 7 vicinal 8 adjacent 10 contiguous

neither: not

nema: 7 eelworm 9 roundworm

nemesis: 4 bane 7 avenger

nemoral: 6 sylvan

neophyte: 4 tyro 5 epopt 6 novice 7 amateur, convert 8 beginner 9 proselyte 10 catechumen

neoteric: new 4 late 6 modern, recent

nep: 6 catnep, catnip 7 catmint

Nepal: *city:* 5 Palan 8 Bhatgaon, Katmandu 9 Khatmandu
  cloth: 5 khadi 6 changa
  coin: 5 mohar
  mountain: 7 Everest 11 Dhawalagiri 12 Kinchinjinga
  people: Rai 4 Aoul 5 Bokra, Hindu, Limbu, Murmi, Newar, Tharu 6 Bhotia, Gurkha, Lepcha 7 Kiranti 8 Gorkhali
  river: 4 Kusi 6 Gandak 7 Karnali
  ruler: 4 Rana
  sheep: 6 bharal, nahoor, nayaur
  tree: sal 4 toon 5 sisoo

nepenthe: 7 anodyne

nephew: 6 nepote(Sc.)

nephrite: 4 jade 6 pounam 10 greenstone

nepote: 6 nephew

nepotism: 9 patronage 10 favoritism

Neptune: sea 5 ocean 6 seagod
  consort: 7 Salacia
  emblem: 7 trident

Ner's son: 5 Abner

Nereides: *father:* 6 Nereus
  mother: 5 Doris
  steed: 8 seahorse

Nero: 6 tyrant 7 emperor, fiddler
  mother: 9 Agrippina

successor: 5 Galba
victim: 5 Lucan 6 Seneca
wife: 7 Octavia, Poppaea
Nero Wolfe creator: 5 Stout
nerve: 4 grit 5 cheek, pluck, sinew, spunk,
vigor 6 aplomb, daring, energy 7 courage
8 audacity, boldness, coolness, embolden,
strength, temerity 9 encourage 10 brazenness, invigorate, resolution
apparatus: 6 sensor
cell: 5 cyton 6 cytone
center: 8 ganglion
combining form: 4 neur 5 neuro
cranial: 5 optic, vagus
inflammation: 8 neuritis
malady: tic 8 neuritis
operation: 10 neurolysis
pathway: 4 rete 5 hilum 8 ganglion
pert. to: 5 neuro 6 neural
root: 5 radix
sensory: 8 afferent
tissue: 8 cinerea
tumor: 7 neuroma 9 neurinoma 11 neurocy-
toma 12 neuromatosis
nerve cell: 4 axon 6 neuron
extension: 4 axon 6 neurite
framework: 6 stroma
process: 4 axon 5 axone 7 neurite
nerveless: 4 dead, weak 5 brave, inert 8 un-
nerved 9 foolhardy, powerless 10 courageous
nervous: 5 jumpy, timid 6 fidget, sinewy,
touchy 7 fearful, fretful, jittery 8 neurotic,
timorous 9 excitable, sensitive 10 high-
strung 12 apprehensive
nervous disorder: See **mental disorder**
nervous system: *center:* 5 brain
description of: 11 neurography
nomenclature: 9 neuronymy
science: 9 neurology
nervy: 4 bold 6 brazen, sinewy, strong 7 jittery, nervous 8 impudent, vigorous 9 excitable
nescient: 7 infidel 8 agnostic, ignorant
ness: 4 cape 6 suffix 8 headland 10 promontory
nest: den, web 4 aery, bike, dray, drey, eyry,
home 5 abode, aerie, eyrie, haunt, nidus,
swarm 6 cuddle, hotbed 7 lodging, retreat
9 residence 10 nidificate
builder of: ant, bee 4 bird, wasp
eagle's: 4 aery 5 aerie
insect's: 5 nidus
squirrel's: 4 dray, drey
nester: 7 settler 8 squatter 11 homesteader
nestle: pet 4 nest 6 cuddle, pettle(Sc.) 7 cherish, shelter, snuggle
nestling: 4 baby, bird, eyas, nest 7 retreat 9
fledgling

nestor: 4 sage 7 adviser, advisor 9 counselor
10 counsellor
net: bag, gin, web 4 caul, flan, gain, lace,
lawn, mesh, moke, neat, pure, rete, toil,
trap, trim, weir 5 clean, clear, gauze, lacis,
seize, snare, tulle, yield 6 bright, cobweb,
entrap, maline, profit 7 dragnet, ensnare,
network, protect, rinsing, shelter 8 meshwork 9 reticulum 10 reticulate 13 unadulterated
fishing: lam 4 flew, flue, fyke 5 seine, trawl
6 sagene 7 trammel
hair: 5 snood
interstice: 4 hole, mesh
net-winged: 12 neuropteroid
nether: 5 lower, under 8 downward
Netherlands: 7 Holland
bailiff: 6 schout
cheese: 4 Edam 5 Gouda 7 cottage
city: Ede 5 Asten, Breda, Hague 6 Aalten,
Arnhem, Leiden 7 Commune, Haarlem,
Utrecht 8 Aalsmeer 9 Amsterdam, Groningen, Rotterdam 10 Gravenhage
coin: 4 cent, doit, raps 5 ryder 6 florin, gulden, stiver 7 ducaton, escalan, escalin,
guilder, stooter 8 ducatoon 9 dubbeltje 12
rijksdaalder
commune: Ede, Epe 4 Echt 5 Breda, Doorn,
Hague 6 Dongen, Leyden 9 Amsterdam,
Rotterdam 11 Doniawestal
council: 7 heemrad 8 heemraad, heemraat
fishing boat: 4 tode 6 hooker
former colony: 4 Java 6 Borneo 7 Celebes,
Sumatra 9 New Guinea
gin: 8 schnapps
inlet: 9 Zuider Zee
island: 5 Texel 7 Ameland 8 Vlieland 9
Schelling
island group: Aru 5 Arroe, Arrou
lake: 7 Haarlem
legislative assembly: 4 Raad
measure: el; aam, ahm, aum, ell, kan,
kop(pl.), mud, vat, zak 4 duim, lood, mijl,
rood, rope, voet 5 anker, carat, roede,
stoop, wisse 6 bunder, koppen, legger,
maatje, muddle, mutsje, streep 7 leaguer,
schepel 8 mimgelen, okshoofd, steekkan
10 vingerhoed
native: 5 Dutch 8 Dutchman
painter: Lis 4 Hals, Kalf, Neer 5 Helst,
Steen 6 Leyden 7 De Houch, Hobbema,
Seghers, Vermeer 8 Kroninck, Mostaert,
Ter Borch 9 Rembrandt 10 Van de Velde
11 Van Ruisdael 19 Geertgen Tot Sint
Jans
people: 5 Dutch 7 Flemish, Frisian
possessions: 4 Saba 7 Curacao, Surinam
pottery: 4 delf 5 delft 11 Dutch Guiana, St.
Eustacius

province: Epe **7** Brabant, Drenthe, Holland,
Limburg, Utrecht, Zeeland **9** Friesland,
Groningen **10** Gelderland, Overijssel
reclaimed land: **6** polder
river: Eem **4** Leck, Maas, Rijn, Waal, Ysel
5 Meuse, Rhine, Yssel **6** Ijssel, Kromme **7**
Scheldt
scholar: **7** Erasmus
sheriff: **6** schout
town hall: **9** stadhouse
uncle: eme, oom
vessel: **4** koff **5** yanky **6** schuit, schuyt
weight: ons **4** last, lood, pond **5** bahar, grein,
pound **6** korrel **7** wichtje **8** esterlin, **9** esterling
woman: **4** frau, frow
netlike: 9 reticular
netop: 5 crony **6** friend **9** companion
netting: 4 lint, mesh **7** network
nettle: vex **4** fret, line **5** annoy, cnida, ettle,
peeve, pique, sting **6** henbit, ruffle, splice
7 affront, blubber, knittle, provoke **8** irri-
tant, irritate **9** urticacea **10** exasperate
nettle cell: 10 nematocyst
family: **10** Urticaceae
genus of: **10** parietaria
network (see also **net**): **6** plexus, reseau
neume: 6 pneuma
neural: 6 dorsal
neuralgia: 9 costalgia
neuter: 6 gender **7** neither, neutral, sexless
9 impartial
neutral: 4 gray **8** middling, negative **9** colorless **10** achromatic, indefinite **11** adiaphorous, indifferent **12** noncombatant
comb. form: **6** neutro
neutralize: 5 annul **7** abolish, balance, destroy, nullify, vitiate **9** frustrate **10** counteract **11** countervail **14** counterbalance
neutralizer: 6 alkali
Nevada: *lake:* **5** Tahoe
town: Ely **4** Elko, Reno **6** Carson, Fallon,
Minden, Sparks **7** Sulphur **8** Lovelock,
Mesquite **9** Henderson **10** Winnemucca
neve: 4 firn, snow **7** glacier
never: nay, nie(G.), not **4** nary, ne'er
nevertheless: but, yet **5** still **7** how-be-it,
however **9** howsoever,, natheless **10** howsomever
nevus: 4 mole **5** tumor **7** spiloma **9** birthmark
new: neu(G.) **4** late, noval(L.) **5** fresh, green,
novel **6** modern, recent, unused **7** foreign,
strange, untried **8** neoteric, original, untested **10** additional, promethean, unfamiliar **11** fashionable, modernistic **12** unaccustomed **13** inexperienced
combining form: neo
New Caledonia: *bird:* **4** kagu

seaport: **5** Numea
New Deal agency: CCC, NRA, TVA
New England: *aristocrat:* **7** Brahmin
chair: **6** Carver
inhabitant: **6** Yankee
of the West: **9** Minnesota
settler: **7** Pilgrim, Puritan
New Guinea: *bay:* Oro
city: Lae **4** Daru **5** Soron **6** Rabaul
export: **5** copra
gulf: **4** Huon **5** Papua
hog: **4** bene
island: Aru **5** Ceram, Papua
island group: **7** Solomon
mountain: **6** Albert **8** Victoria **9** Carstensz
10 Wilhelmina
parrot: **4** lory
people: **5** Karon **6** Papuan
port: Lae **4** Daru
river: Fly **5** Sepik **7** Amberno **10** Strickland
15 Kaiserin Augusta
section: **8** Bunagona
New Hampshire: *academy:* **6** Exeter
city: **5** Dover, Keene **6** Antrim, Exeter,
Nashua **7** Hanover, Laconia
county: **4** Coos
lake: **7** Sunapee
river: **4** Saco
state flower: **5** lilac
New Hebrides island: Epi **4** Tana **5** Efate
port: **4** Vila
New Jersey: *city:* **6** Verona **7** Bayonne, Rar
itan, Trenton
river: **6** Ramapo **7** Raritan
New Mexico: *county:* **4** Mora, Taos
resort: **4** Taos
river: **4** Gila **5** Pecos
state flower: **5** yucca
New Testament (see also **Bible**): *book:* **4**
Acts, John, Jude, Luke, Mark **5** James,
Peter, Titus **6** Romans **7** Hebrews, Matthew, Timothy **8** Philemon **9** Ephesians,
Galatians **10** Colossians, Revelation **11** Corinthians, Philippians **13** Thessalonians
gospel: **4** John, Luke, Mark **7** Matthew
letter: **7** epistle
New York: *canal:* **4** Erie
city: Rye **4** Avon, Erie, Rome, Troy **5** Ilion,
Nyack, Olean, Owego, Tioga, Utica **6** Al-
bany, Cohoes, Elmira, Esopus, Geneva,
Goshen, Gotham, Ithaca, Malone, Oneida,
Oswego **7** Buffalo, Endwell **8** Saratoga **10**
Binghamton **11** Skaneateles **12** Niagara
Falls
county: **4** Erie **5** Tioga, Wayne, Yates **6** Cayuga, Monroe, Oneida, Oswego, Seneca **7**
Chemung, Genesee, Niagara, Ontario, Or-
leans, Steuben, Tompkin, Wyoming **8** Al-

legany, Onondaga, Schuyler **9** Chatauqua, Courtland **10** Livingston **11** Cattaraugus
early land owner: **7** patroon
harbor entrance: **14** Ambrose channel
Indian tribe: **6** Seneca
lake: **6** Cayuga, Croton, Oneida, Seneca **7** Saranac **8** Onondaga **11** Skaneateles
law: **6** Baumes
resort: **7** Saranac
river: **5** Tioga **6** Harlem, Hudson **7** Genesee, Niagara **8** Canisteo, Cohocton
state flower: **4** rose
university: **7** Colgate, Cornell **8** Columbia
New York City: 6 Gotham
island: **5** Ellis **6** Staten **7** Bedloes, Liberty, Welfare **9** Governors, Manhattan **10** Blackwells
prison: **5** Tombs
street: **4** Wall **6** Bowery
subway: BMT, IND, IRT
New Zealand: *anteater:* **7** echidna
bird: kea, moa, oii, poe, roa **4** kaka, kiwi, koko, kulu, ruru, titi, weka **6** kakapo **7** apteryx, wrybill **8** morepork, notornis
city: see *town* below
clay: **4** papa
dance: **4** haka
fern: **4** weki **5** pitau, wheki
fish: ihi **5** hikus
flax: **8** harakeke
flightless bird: **4** weka **7** apteryx
fort: pa; pah, pau
grass: **6** toetoe
gun: **6** tupara
heron: **6** kotuku
hut: **5** whare
island: **4** Otea **7** Stewart
kiwi: moa, roa **7** apteryx
lake: Ada **4** Gunn, Ohau, Rere **5** Hawea, Okaro, Taupo **6** Fergus, Pukaki, Rotoma, Sylvan, Teanau, Tekapo, Wanaka **7** Brunner, Diamond, Kanieri, Okareka, Rotoiti, Rotoroa, Rotorua **8** Okataina, Paradise, Rotoaira, Tarawera, Wakatipu **9** Manapouri, Rotokawau **10** Rotomahana **12** Rerewhakaitu, Waikaremoana
mahogany: **6** totara
mountain: **4** Cook **5** Ohope **6** Egmont **7** Aorangi, Pihanga, Raupehu, Ruapehu, Tauhara, Tauhera **8** Aspiring, Tarawera, Tauranga **9** Blackburn, Messenger, Ngauruhoe, Tongariro **10** Ngongotaha, Tapuaenuka
national bird: **4** kiwi
ostrich: moa
owl: **4** ruru
palm: **5** nikau
parrot: kea **4** kaka **6** kakapo
people: Ati **5** Arawa, Maori **7** Ringatu

pine: **4** rima **6** totara **9** kahikatea
port: Lae **7** Aukland, Dunedin **10** Wellington
reptile: **7** tuatara, tuatera
river: **7** Waikato **8** Wanganui **9** Taramakau, Tongariro, Whakapapa **10** Rangitikei **11** Waimakariri
settlement: pa; pah, pau
shark: **4** mako
shrub: **4** tutu
song: **6** waiata
spa: **5** Aroha **7** Rotorua, Tearoha
storehouse: **5** whata
town: **5** Levin, Otaki, Taupo **6** Foxton, Napier, Nelson, Oamaru, Picton, Timaru **7** Dunedin, Raetihi, Rotorua **8** Auckland, Gisborne, Hamilton, Hastings, Tauranga, Wanganui **9** Ashburton, Greymouth, Masterton, Whangarei **10** Dannenirke, Palmerston, Queenstown, Wellington **12** Christchurch, Invercargill
tree: ake **4** hino, kopi, mako, miro, pelu, puka, rata, rimu, tawa, toro, toru, whau **5** hinau, hinou, karui, mahoe, maire, mapau, ngaio **6** ake-ake, karaka, kowhai, manuka, puriri, tarata, titoki **7** akepiro, taratah, wahahen **8** hiropito, makomako **9** kaiwhiria **10** pohutukawa
vine: aka
volcano: **6** Egmont **7** Ruapehu **9** Ngauruhoe
wages: utu
welcome: **8** haeremai
newcomer: 7 settler **8** comeling **9** immigrant
newel: 4 post
newfangled: 5 novel **6** modern
Newfoundland: *cape:* **4** Race
log house: **4** tilt
newly: 4 anew **5** again **6** afresh, lately **8** recently
news: 4 word **6** notice **7** tidings **11** information, instruction **12** intelligence
agency: AP, UP; DNB, INS, UPI **4** Tass(-Russ.) **5** Domei **7** Reuters **13** International
gatherer: **8** reporter
media: TV **5** radio **7** journal **8** magazine **9** newspaper **10** periodical, television
statement: **8** bulletin
newsboy: 7 camelot
newsmonger: 6 gossip **7** tattler **8** reporter
newspaper: 4 News **5** daily, paper, sheet, Times **6** Herald **7** courant, Gazette, Mercury, tabloid, Tribune **9** newsprint **11** publication
article: **4** item
collectively: **5** press

employee: 6 editor 7 printer 8 pressman, reporter 9 columnist, linotyper 10 cartoonist, compositor, journalist 12 photographer 13 correspondent

file: 6 morgue

hoax: 6 canard

part of: ear 6 banner, sports 8 obituary 9 editorial

newsstand: 5 booth, kiosk, stall

newt: ask, eft 4 evet 6 lizard, triton 7 axolotl 10 salamander

next: 4 then 5 after, ewest(Sc.), neist(Sc.) 7 closest, ensuing, nearest 9 adjoining, following, immediate, proximate 10 contiguous, succeeding 12 conterminous

next to: 6 almost, beside, nearly 8 adjacent

nexus: tie 4 link 10 connection 15 interconnection

nib: pen 4 beak, bill 5 point, prong

nibble: eat, nab 4 bite, gnaw, knap 6 browse 7 chimble, gnabble, gnatter

Nicaragua: *city:* 4 Leon 6 Masaya 7 Granada, Managua 9 Choluteca 10 Chinandega

coin: 4 peso 7 centavo, cordoba

lake: 7 Managua

measure: 4 vara 5 cahiz, milla 6 suerte, tercia 7 cajuela, estadal, manzana 10 cabelleria

river: 4 Coco, Tuma 5 Wanks 7 San Juan

weight: bag 4 caja 8 tonelada

nice: 4 fine, good 5 exact 6 bonita, dainty, minute, peachy, queasy, subtle 7 elegant, finical, genteel, precise, prudish, refined 8 delicate, exacting, pleasant, pleasing 9 agreeable, appealing, exquisite, squeamish 10 appetizing, delightful, discerning, fastidious, particular, scrupulous 11 considerate, punctilious, scrumptious 13 hypercritical 14 discriminating

niche: 4 apse, nook 6 alcove, covert, recess 7 edicule, retreat 9 habitacle

nick: cut, nob 4 chip, slit 5 cheat, notch, tally, trick 6 arrest, record 7 defraud 9 indention

nickel alloy: 5 invar

nickel compound: 8 argenton

nickelodeon: 7 jukebox

nickname (see also **penname, pseudonym**): 6 agname, byword 7 misname, moniker 8 cognomen, monicker 9 sobriquet 10 soubriquet

James Boswell: 5 Bozzy

Winston Churchill: 6 Winnie

Georges Clemenceau: 5 Tiger

Benjamin Disraeli: 5 Dizzy

Thomas Edison: 17 Wizard of Menlo Park

Dwight Eisenhower: Ike

Elizabeth I: 11 Virgin Queen

Frederick I: 10 Barbarossa

Ernest Hemingway: 4 Papa

Andrew Jackson: 10 Old Hickory

Abraham Lincoln: 9 Honest Abe

Louis XIV: 7 Sun King

Joe Louis: 11 Brown Bomber

Mary I: 10 Bloody Mary

Napoleon I: 14 Little Corporal

Napoleon II: 7 L'Aiglon

Richard Nixon: 10 Tricky Dick

Henry Percy: 7 Hotspur

William Pitt: 13 Great Commoner

Richard I: 11 Lion-Hearted

Richard III: 10 Crouchback

Babe Ruth: 7 Bambino 12 Sultan of Swat

Joseph Stilwell: 10 Vinegar Joe

Charles Stratton: 8 Tom Thumb

nicknaming: 12 prosonomasia

nictate: 4 wink 5 blink, twink 7 twinkle 9 nictitate

niddick: 4 nape

nide: 5 brood

nidge: 5 shake 6 quiver

nidget: 4 fool 5 idiot

nidification: 7 nesting

nidor: 5 aroma, savor, scent

nidus: 4 nest

nieve: 4 fist, hand, neif

niff-naff: 6 trifle

nifty: 4 good 5 smart 7 stylish

Nigeria: *people:* Aro, Ebo, Edo, Ibo, Ijo, Vai 4 Beni, Eboe, Efik, Ejam, Ekoi, Nupe 5 Benin

port: 5 Lagos 7 Calabar

province: Isa 4 Nupe, Ondo 5 Warri

river: Oli

town: Aba, Ede, Isa 4 Bidi, Offa 5 Lagos 6 Ibadan, Yakoba 9 Ogbomosho

tree: 5 afara

walled city: 4 Kano

niggard: 8 scrimper 9 skinflint 10 curmudgeon

niggardly: 4 mean 5 close 6 narrow, scanty, stingy 7 miserly 8 churlish, wretched 10 avaricious 11 closefisted 12 parsimonious

niggle: 6 potter, putter, trifle

nigh: at 4 near 5 close 6 almost, nearly 8 adjacent 10 contiguous 11 neighboring

night: 4 nuit(F.) 8 darkness

comb. form: 4 nyct 5 nycti, nycto

goddess: Nox, Nyx

goddess of: Nyx 6 Hecate

pert. to: 9 nocturnal

night bird: 10 shearwater 11 nightingale

night blindness: 10 nyctalopia

night-wandering: 11 noctivagant

nightcap: 6 biggin

nightchurr: 10 goatsucker

nightclub: 7 cabaret

nightfall: een, eve 4 dusk, even 8 twilight

nightingale: 8 philomel 9 philomela

nightjar: 5 potoo 9 nighthawk 10 goatsucker

nightmare: 5 dream, fiend 7 incubus 9 cauchemar(F.), ephialtes

nightshade: 4 morel 7 henbane, morelle 10 belladonna 11 bittersweet

nigrescent: 9 blackfish

nihil: 7 nothing

nihilist: 9 anarchist

nil: 4 zero 7 nothing

Nile: *bird:* 4 ibis 7 wryneck
 boat: 5 baris 6 nuggar 8 dahabeah
 captain: 4 rais, reis
 dam: 5 Aswan
 falls: 5 Ripon
 fish: 5 saide 8 mormyrid 9 mormyroid
 houseboat: 8 dahabeah
 island: 4 Roda
 people: 4 Madi 5 Nilot
 plant: 4 sudd 5 lotus
 reptile: 9 crocodile
 river gauge: 9 nilometer
 town: 5 Cairo, Rejaf 7 Rosetta
 tributary: 6 Atbara, Kagera

nilgai: 8 antelope

nim tree: 4 neem 7 margosa

nimb: 4 halo

nimble: 4 deft, lish, spry 5 agile, alert, fleet, quick 6 active, adroit, clever, feirie, lissom, lively, prompt, volant 9 dexterous 11 quick-witted

nimbly: 6 featly 9 deliverly

nimbose: 6 cloudy, stormy

nimbus: 4 halo 5 cloud, vapor 6 gloria 7 aureole 10 atmosphere

nimiety: 6 excess 10 redundancy

nimmer 5 thief

nimrod: 5 ruler 6 hunter, tyrant

nimshi: 4 fool 7 halfwit

nincompoop: 4 dolt, fool 5 moron, ninny 9 simpleton

nine: 6 ennead 8 ninefold
 based on: 8 novenary
 comb. form: 5 ennea
 days' devotion: 6 novena
 group of: 5 nonet 6 ennead
 inches: 4 span

nine-eyes: 7 lamprey

nine-headed monster: 5 Hydra

nine-killer: 6 shrike

ninepin: 6 kayles 7 skittle 8 skittles

ninny: See **nincompoop**

ninth: 5 nonus(L.)

ninut: 6 magpie

Niobe: *brother:* 6 Pelops
 father: 8 Tantalus
 husband: 7 Amphion

sister-in-law: 5 Aedon

nip: cut, sip 4 bite, clip, dram, tang 5 check, clamp, draft, drink, frost, pinch, seize, sever, steal, sting 6 blight, catnip, snatch, tipple, twitch 7 squeeze 8 compress 10 pickpocket

nipa: 4 atap, palm 5 attap, drink 6 liquor

nipcheese: 5 miser 6 purser

nipper: boy, lad 4 claw, grab 5 biter 6 cunner, pliers, urchin 7 forceps, incisor, pincers 8 pincenez 9 handcuffs 10 eyeglasses

Nippon: See **Japan**

nippy: 5 brisk, quick, sharp 6 active, biting, nimble 7 nipping 8 vigorous

nisse: 6 goblin, kobold, sprite 7 brownie

nisus: 6 effort 7 impulse 8 endeavor, striving

Nisus' daughter: 6 Scylla

nit: egg, nut 5 speck 6 insect 8 hazelnut

niter, nitre: 5 peter, petre 6 potash 9 saltpeter
 combining form: 5 nitro

nither: 5 blast 6 debase, shiver 7 tremble 9 humiliate

nithing: 6 coward 7 dastard

nitid: 6 bright, glossy 7 glowing, radiant 8 lustrous, nitidous

nitrate: 4 salt 5 ester
 sodium: 5 niter, nitre

nitrocotton: 9 guncotton

nitroform: 15 trinitromethane

nitrogen: 9 quinoline
 combining form: az; azo
 compound: 7 ammonia

niveau 5 level

nivenite: 9 uraninite

niveous: 5 snowy 8 snowlike

nix: no 6 goblin, nobody, sprite 7 nothing

Njorth: *daughter:* 5 Freya 6 Freyja
 son: 4 Frey 5 Freyr
 wife: 6 Skathi

no: na(Sc.), ne; nae(Sc.), naw, nay, nea(Sc.), nit, nix, non(F.) 4 nein(G.), nyet(Russ.), play 5 drama 6 denial 7 refusal

no one: 5 nix 6 nobody

Noah: *dove:* 7 Columba
 father: 6 Lamech
 grandson: 4 Aram
 great-grandson: Uz; Hul
 place of debarkation: 6 Ararat
 raven: 6 Corvus
 son: Ham, Sem 4 Shem 7 Japheth
 wine cup: 6 Crater

nob: 4 head, jack

nobble: 5 bribe, cheat, steal 7 swindle 12 incapacitate

nobby: 4 chic 5 swell 7 stylish 9 excellent, first-rate 11 fashionable

noble: 4 epic, fine, free, gent, good, pure, rial 5 burly, ducal, grand, ideal, lofty, manly, proud 6 august, epical, famous, heroic 7 eminent, exalted, gallant, liberal, soulful, stately, sublime 8 elevated, generous, glorious, nobleman, precious, renowned, splendid 9 chevalier, dignified, excellent, honorable 10 idealistic, noblewoman 11 illustrious, magnanimous, magnificent

noble pine: 10 pipsissewa

nobleman: don 4 duke, earl, lord, peer 5 barin(Russ.), baron, count 6 knight, varlet 7 grandee(Sp.), hidalgo, marquis 8 marquess 10 aristocrat

pert. to: 5 ducal 6 lordly

nobleness of birth: 6 eugeny

noblewoman: 4 lady 7 duchess, peeress 8 baroness, countess, marquise 10 marquisess 11 marchioness

nobody: 4 none 9 nonentity

nocent: 6 guilty 7 harmful, hurtful, noxious 8 criminal

noctambulism: 12 somnambulism

noctuid: 4 moth, worm

noctule: bat

nocturnal: 5 night 7 nightly 11 nightwalker

nocturnal mammal: bat 5 lemur

nocturne: 7 lullaby 8 serenade

nocuous: See **noxious, poisonous**

nod: bow 4 beck, bend, doze, wink 5 droop 6 assent, beckon, drowse, nutate, salute 7 signify 8 nutation

nodding: 6 nutant 7 annuent 8 cernuous

noddy: auk 4 fool 5 ninny 6 fulmar, noodle 7 hackney 9 simpleton

node: bow 4 bump, knob, knot, lump 5 joint, nodus 6 nodule 7 dilemma, granule 8 swelling, tubercle 10 difficulty 12 complication, protuberance

nodule: 4 auge, node 5 geode 7 noblock 9 septarium

noel: 5 carol 9 Christmas

noetic: 12 intellectual

nog: ale, peg, pin 5 block 6 eggnog, noggin 8 beverage, treenail

noggin (see also **noodle**): cup, mug, nog 4 pate

noir: 5 black

noise (see also **sound**): air, din 5 bruit, rumor 6 gossip, norate, report

noiseless: 5 quiet, still, tacit 6 silent 7 catlike

noisemaker: 4 bell, horn 6 rattle

noisette: 5 hazel

noisome (see also **noxious**): 4 foul 5 fetid 7 harmful, hurtful 8 stinking 9 offensive 10 disgusting, malodorous, pernicious 11 destructive, unwholesome

noisy: 4 loud 6 clashy 7 blatant 8 brawling, clattery, strepent 9 clamorous, hilarious, turbulent 10 boisterous, tumultuous, vociferous 12 obstreperous

noll: See **noodle**

nom: 4 name 10 nominative

nom de plume: 7 pen name 9 pseudonym

noma: 5 ulcer

nomad: 4 Arab, Luri, Moor 5 Alani, gypsy, rover 6 roamer, roving 7 Bedouin, Saracen, scenite 8 wanderer

nomadic: 9 itinerant

nomadism: 10 wanderlust

nome: 4 Elis 5 nomos 8 nomarchy, province 10 department

nomen: 4 gens, name

nomenclature: 4 list, name 8 glossary, register 9 catalogue, recounter 10 dictionary, vocabulary 11 appellation, designation

nomic: 8 ordinary 9 customary 12 conventional

nominal: 6 slight, unreal 7 titular, trivial 8 platonic 11 theoretical 13 unsubstantial

nominalist: 8 Occamist 9 terminist

nominate: 4 call, leet(Sc.), name 5 slate 7 appoint, entitle, propose, specify 10 denominate

nominee: 9 candidate

nomothetical: 11 legislative

non-kosher: 4 tref

non-Mahometan: 5 Kafir

nonage: 10 immaturity 12 youthfulness

nonaspirate: 4 lene

nonbeliever: 5 pagan 7 atheist 8 agnostic

nonce: 7 present 8 occasion

noncentric: 8 acentric

nonchalant: 4 cool 6 casual 8 careless 10 insouciant 11 indifferent 13 imperturbable

noncleric: lay 4 laic

noncombatant: 8 chaplain, civilian, observer

noncompliance: 7 refusal 10 obstinance 13 recalcitrance

nonconcurrence: 7 dissent

nonconductor: 5 resin

nonconforming: 9 anomalous

nonconformist: 5 rebel 6 hippie 7 beatnik, heretic 8 bohemian 9 dissenter

nonconformity: 6 heresy 7 dissent 9 recusance, recusancy 10 dissidence 13 individualism

nondependent: 11 independent

nondescript: 13 indescribable 14 indeterminable

none: no; nae 4 nane(Sc.), neen

nonentity: 4 zero 6 cipher 7 nothing

nonessential: 9 extrinsic 10 adiaphoron 11 unnecessary 12 adventitious 14 circumstantial

nonesuch: 5 apple, model 7 paragon 8 paradigm 9 matchless, nonpareil, unequaled, unrivaled

nonexistent: 4 null 8 nonbeing

nonfestal: 6 ferial

nonfulfillment: 6 breach 12 infringement

nongrata: 9 unwelcome

nongypsy: 4 gajo

nonobjective: 8 abstract

nonobservance: 9 violation

nonpareil: 4 best 7 paragon, perfect, unequal 8 nonesuch, peerless 9 unrivaled

nonpasserine bird: 4 tody 6 hoopoe, motmot 8 hornbill 10 kingfisher

nonphysical: 7 psychic 9 psychical

nonplus: 5 blank, stump, trump 6 puzzle 7 perplex 9 embarrass

nonpositive: 8 negative 9 privative

nonproductive: 6 barren 7 sterile 10 unfruitful

nonprofessional: lay 4 laic 7 amateur

nonsense: bah, pah, rot 4 blah, bosh, buff, bunk, flam, tosh 5 blash, folly, fudge, haver, hooey, stite(Sc.) 6 bunkum, drivel, faddle, folder 7 blarney, blather, buncome, inanity, twaddle 8 blahblah, blathery, falderal, folderol, flimflam, trumpery 9 absurdity, fandangle, frivolity, moonshine, poppycock, silliness 10 balderdash, flapdoodle, flumdiddle, galimatias, triviality 11 flumadiddle, foolishness, monkeyshine 12 fiddle-dee-dee, flummadiddle, flummydiddle 16 preposterousness

nonsolid: 5 fluid 6 liquid

noodle: 4 bean, fool, head, nizy, noll, pate 5 ninny, nizey, noddy 6 boodle, noddle, noggin 9 blockhead, simpleton 10 caper-nutie 11 caper-noitie

nook: in; out, wro 4 cant, cove, glen, hole 5 angle, herne, niche 6 cantle, corner, cranny, recess 7 crevice, retreat

noon: 6 midday 8 meridian 11 culmination

noose: tie 4 bond, dull, grin, loop, trap 5 bight, grane, honda, snare, widdy 6 entrap, halter, lariat 7 ensnare, execute, laniard, lanyard, springe 8 slip-knot
armed with: 10 laquearian

nope: 9 bullfinch

nor: ner 7 neither 8 negative 10 connective

norate: 5 noise, rumor 6 gossip

nori: 4 alga 7 seaweed

noria: 5 wheel

norie: 9 cormorant

norite: 6 gabbro

norm: 4 rule, type 5 gauge, model, norma 7 average, pattern 8 standard, template

norma: 4 mold 5 gauge 6 square 7 pattern

normal: 5 usual 7 natural, regular, typical

Normandy: _beach:_ 5 Omaha
capital: 4 Caen 5 Rouen
conqueror: 5 Rollo 10 Eisenhower
department: 4 Eure, Orne 6 Manche 8 Calvados
duke: 5 Rollo
town: 7 Saint-Lo

Norn: 4 fate, Urth, Wyrd 5 Skuld 9 Verthandi

Norse (see also **Scandinavia**): 4 mink 8 Teutonic 9 Icelandic, Norwegian 12 Scandinavian
abode of gods: 6 Asgard
alphabet: 5 runic
bard: 5 scald, skald 7 sagaman
chieftain: 4 jarl
demigoddess of destiny: Urd
demon: 4 Mara, Surt 5 Surtr
epic: 4 Edda
explorer: 4 Eric
fate: 4 Norn
first man: 4 Askr
first woman: 5 Embla
giant: 4 Atli, Loke, Loki, Natt, Norn, Nott, Wate, Ymer, Ymir 5 Jotun, Mimer, Mimir, Thrym 6 Fafnir, Jotunn
god (see also _giant_ above): As, Ve; Asa, Ase, Ran, Tiu, Tyr, Ull, Zio 4 Frey, Hler, Hoth, Loke, Loki, Odin, Surt, Thor, Vali 5 Aeger, Aegir, Aesir(pl.), Baldr, Brage, Bragi, Donar, Freyr, Gymir, Othin, Surtr, Vanir(pl.), Wodan, Woden, Wotan 6 Balder, Hoenir, Njorth 7 Forsete, Forseti, Heimdal, Vitharr 9 Heimdallr, Hlorrithi
goddess: Dis, Eir, Hel 4 Frea, Hela, Nora, Saga, Urth, Wyrd 5 Freya, Frigg, Nanna 6 Freyja, Frigga 7 Asynjur
goddess of earth: 4 Erda
king: 4 Atli
mythological wolf: 6 Fenrir
night: 4 Natt, Nott
nobleman: 4 yarl
poem: 4 rune
poet: 5 scald, skald
saint: 4 Olaf 5 Olaus
sea serpent: 6 Kraken 7 Midgard
tale: 4 saga
toast: 5 skoal
viking: 5 Rollo
watchdog: 4 Garm 5 Garmr
world tree: 8 Ygdrasil

norsel: 4 band, line 6 fillet

North Africa: _antelope:_ 5 addax 7 gazelle
country: 7 Algeria, Tunisia
fruit: fig 4 date
lyre: 6 kissar
measure: 4 rotl

oasis: 4 wadi, wady
people: 4 Moor 5 Nilot 6 Hamite
port: 4 Sfax
sheep: 6 aoudad
valley: 4 wadi, wady
North America: *bird:* 6 fulmar 7 grackle 8
 cardinal, killdeer, kingrail 10 bufflehead
 discoverer: 5 Cabot
 herb: 4 sego
 Indian: see **Indian**
 marmoset: 7 tamarin
 mountain: 5 Logan 8 McKinley
 orchids: 9 arethusas
 owl: 7 wapacut
 people: 7 Mexican 8 American, Canadian
 reindeer: 7 caribou
 thrush: 5 robin
 tree: lin 4 mabi, sorb, titi 5 balsa, papaw 6
 balsam, pawpaw, redbud, tupelo 7 catalpa,
 hickory 8 basswood, oneberry, sweetsop 9
 sassafras
North Atlantic: *island:* 7 Britain, Iceland,
 Ireland 9 Manhattan
 seagull: 4 skua
North Britain: 8 Scotland 9 Caledonia
North Carolina: *cape:* 4 Fear 8 Hatteras
 college: 4 Elon
 county: 4 Ashe 5 Anson, Avery 6 Lenoir
 people: 7 Buffalo, Tarheel
 river: Tar 5 Neuse 6 Pee Dee
 town: 5 Boone 6 Durham, Lenoir, Oxford,
 Whynot 7 Edenton, Raleigh, Roxboro
North Dakota: *city:* 5 Fargo, Minot
 county: 6 Traill
North Pole discoverer: 5 Peary
North Sea: *arm:* 9 Skagerrak, Skager-Rak
 canal: 4 Kiel
 river: 5 Weser
North Star: 7 polaris 8 loadstar, lodestar,
 polestar 10 tramontane
North Vietnam: *capital:* 5 Hanoi
 city: 8 Haiphong
 gulf: 6 Tonkin
 monetary unit: 4 dong
north wind: 6 boreas
northeaster: 4 blow, gale, wind 5 storm
northern: 6 boreal 13 septentrional
Northern Bear: 6 Russia
Northmen: See **Norse**
Northumberland river: 4 Tyne
Norway: *bird:* 4 rype
 boat: 4 pram 5 praam 6 praham
 capital: 4 Oslo
 cart: 11 stolkjaerre
 chieftain: 4 jarl
 city: see *town* below
 coin: ore 5 krone
 counties: 5 amter

county: amt 5 fylke 6 fylker(pl.), Tromso 7
 Finmark
dance: 7 halling
embroidery: 9 hardanger
goblin: 5 nisse 6 kobold
governor: 6 amtman
haddock: 8 rosefish
inlet: 5 fiord, fjord
language: 5 Norse
measure: fot, mal, pot 4 alen, maal 5 kande
 6 fathom 7 skieppe 9 korntonde
mountain: 5 Sogne 6 Kjolen 7 Numedal 8
 Telemark, Ustetind 9 Blodfjell, Hartei-
 gen, Ramnanosi 10 Galdhoepig, Gli-
 tretind, Hallingdal, Vibmesnosi 11 Myr-
 dalfjell 14 Hallingskarvet, Hardanger-
 jokul, Skagastolstind
parliament: 8 Storting 9 Storthing
plateau: 5 Dovre, fjeld 9 Hardanger
river: Oi; Ena 4 Tana 6 Lougen, Glomma
ruler: 6 hersir
saint: 4 Olaf 5 Olaus
town: 5 Nes 4 Oslo(c.), Voss 5 Bjort, Hamar,
 Skein, Skjak 6 Bergen, Horten, Larvik,
 Narvik 7 Alesund, Drammen 9 Stavanger,
 Trondhjem 10 Kristiania(c.) 11 Chris-
 tiania(c.)
weight: lod 4 mark, pund 9 skaalpund 10
 bismerpund
nose: neb, nez(F.), pry, spy 4 beak, conk, lo-
 ra(pl.) 5 lorum, scent, smell, sniff, snoop,
 snout 6 detect, muffle, muzzle, nozzle,
 search, socket 7 advance, perfume 8 discover, informer, perceive 9 proboscis 11
 investigate
 cartilage: 6 septum
 inflammation: 6 coryza 8 rhinitis
 large: 6 nasute
 medicine: 7 errhine
 muscle: 7 nasalio
 openings: 5 nares
 partition: 5 vomer
 pert. to: 5 nasal 6 narial, rhinal
 snub: 6 simous
nosebleed: 9 epistaxis
nosegay: 4 odor, posy 5 scent 6 boquet 7
 bouquet, perfume
nosegay tree: 10 frangipani
nosepiece: 5 nasal 6 nozzle 8 noseband
nosey: See **nosy**
nosh: 4 chew 5 munch, snack
nosocomium: 8 hospital
nostalgia: 4 longing 10 melancholy 12
 homesickness
nostic: 12 paragerontic
Nostradamus: 4 seer 7 prophet 10 forecaster
nostril: 4 nare 5 nares(pl.), naris(pl.) 6 thrill
 pert. to: 5 naric 6 narial, narine

nostril-shaped: 8 nariform

nosy: 6 prying 7 curious 8 fragrant 10 malodorous 11 inquisitive

not (see also **non**): na(Sc.); nae(Sc.), nay, nor 4 baal, bail, bale, nott 5 shorn 6 nought, polled, shaven 7 neither 8 hornless, negation, negative 11 nothingness

any: no; nul 4 nane(Sc.), nary, none

at all: 5 never 6 noways, nowise

either: 7 neither

final: 13 interlocutory

otherwise than: 6 merely

prefix: il, im, ir, un; non

the same: 5 other 7 another 9 different

notable: V.I.P. 6 fabled, famous 7 eminent, storied 8 eventful, historic 9 memorable, notorious 10 noteworthy, remarkable 12 considerable 13 distinguished, extraordinary

notal: 6 dorsal

notandum: 4 note 5 entry 9 memoranda(pl.) 10 memorandum

notar: 6 notary

notarize: 6 attest 7 certify

notary: 5 notar(Sc.), noter 7 graffer, notable 8 notebook, observer, official 9 notorious, scrivener

chief: 11 protonotary 12 prothonotary

notation: 4 memo, note 7 marking 10 annotation 14 representation

phonetic: 5 Romic

notator: 5 noter 8 recorder 9 annotator

notch: cut, dag, gap, hag, jag 4 cope, dent, dint, gimp, hila(pl.), kerf, nick, step 5 crena, grade, hilum, score, tally 6 crenae(pl.), crotch, defile, degree, indent, record, scotch 7 crenate, serrate 8 undercut 9 indenture 11 indentation

notched: 5 erose 7 crenate, serrate 8 crenated, serrated

irregularly: 5 erose

note: I.O.U., jot, see 4 bill, chit, fame, heed, line, mark, memo, name, sign, sole, song, tone, tune 5 label, sound, token 6 billet, letter, minute, notice, record, regard, remark, renown, report 7 betoken, comment, message, missive, notanda(pl.), observe 8 annotate, breviate, dispatch, eminence, notandum, perceive 9 character 10 indication, memorandum, prominence, reputation 11 distinction, observation

accompanying: 8 overtone

bank: 6 finnip, flimsy 8 frogskin

bugle: mot

explanatory: 8 scholium 10 annotation

highest: ela

marginal: 6 postil 7 apostil 9 apostille

middle: 4 mese

musical: 4 half 5 breve, whole 6 eighth 7 punctus, quarter 9 semibreve

prisoner's: 4 kite

promissory: bon

writer: 9 annotator

note well: N.B.(L.) 8 nota bene(L.)

notebook: log 5 diary 6 street 7 journal 10 adversaria

notecase: 10 pocketbook

noted: 9 distingue, well-known 10 celebrated 11 illustrious

notes: *literary:* ana

miscellaneous: 10 adversaria

noteworthy: 7 eminent, notable 10 remarkable 11 outstanding 12 considerable

nothing: nil 4 free, luke, nill, zero 5 aught, nihil 6 naught, nought, trifle 7 useless 10 triviality 12 nonexistence, unimportance 14 insignificance

nothing but: 4 mere, only

nothous: 8 spurious 12 illegitimate

notice: ad; ban, see 4 espy, heed, idea, mark, mind, news, note, sign 5 await, quote 6 advice, billet, espial, notion, regard, remark 7 affiche, article, discern, mention, observe, warning 8 appraisal, citation, civility 9 attention 10 cognizance, intimation 11 garnishment 12 announcement, intelligence, notification 13 consideration

book: 5 blurb

death: 4 obit 8 obituary

favorable: 4 rave

honorable: 8 citation

leave of: 8 mittimus

marriage: ban 4 bans 5 banns

official: 5 edict 8 bulletin 12 proclamation

paid: ad 13 advertisement

Patent Office: 6 caveat

refuse: 6 ignore

noticeable: 7 evident, notable, salient 8 striking 9 prominent 10 noteworthy, remarkable 11 conspicuous, outstanding, significant

notification: 6 notice

notify: bid 4 cite, page, tell, warn 6 inform 7 apprise, declare, frutify, publish 8 acquaint

notion: bee 4 buzz, idea, idee, view, whim 5 fancy, image 6 belief, desire, maggot, notice, theory, vagary 7 conceit, inkling, opinion, thought 9 intention 10 conception 11 inclination

notoriety: 5 eclat 9 publicity

notorious: big 5 known 6 arrant, crying, famous, notour 7 evident 8 apparent, flagrant, infamous, manifest 11 conspicuous

notum: 4 back

notus: 9 southwind

notwithstanding: yet 4 even 6 algate, mauger, maugre 7 algates, despite, however 8 although 12 nevertheless

nougat: 5 candy 8 nut shell 10 confection

nought: bad, nil 4 zero 5 wrong 7 nothing, useless 9 worthless 10 wickedness

noun: 4 name, word 11 substantive
form: 4 case 6 gender
indeclinable: 6 aptote
kind of: 6 common, proper
suffix: ac, et, ia, ic; ent, ery, ial, ier, ing, ion, ior, ist 4 ence 5 orium
verbal: 6 gerund

nourish: 4 feed, grow 5 breed, nurse 6 foison, foster, suckle, supply 7 cherish, support, sustain, develop 9 cultivate, stimulate

nourishing: 4 alma 6 alible, hearty 8 nutrient 9 alimental, nutritive 10 alimentary

nourishment: 4 food, meat 5 manna 6 foison 7 aliment, pabulum 9 nutriment 10 sustenance 13 nutritiveness 14 nutritiousness

nous: 4 mind 6 reason 9 intellect

nova: new

Nova Scotia: 6 Acadia, Acadie
bay: 5 Fundy
cape: 5 Canso, Sable 6 Breton, George
mountain ash: 8 dogberry
people: 8 Acadians 9 bluenoses
port: 5 Truro

novel: new 4 book 5 fresh, story 6 recent 7 fiction, romance, strange, unusual 8 original, uncommon 10 newfangled
cut: 11 abridgement 12 condensation

novelette: 5 conte

novelty: fad 6 change 10 innovation

novice: dub 4 puny, tiro, tyro 5 rooky 6 rookie, tyrone 7 amateur, convert, learner 8 beginner, freshman, neophyte 9 greenhorn 10 apprentice 11 abecedarian

novitiate: 9 probation 14 apprenticeship

now: noo(Sc.) 4 here 5 today 7 present 9 forthwith 11 immediately

nowise: 5 navis

nowt: ox 4 lout, oxen 6 cattle 7 bullock 9 blockhead

noxious: ill 4 evil 6 nocent 7 baneful, harmful, hurtful, nocuous, noisome, vicious 8 virulent 9 injurious, miasmatic, poisonous 10 pernicious 11 deleterious, destructive, unwholesome 12 insalubrious

noy: 4 harm 5 annoy

nozzle: 4 nose, vent 5 snout

nuance: 5 shade

nub: 4 core, crux, gist, hang, knob, knot, knub, lump, neck, snag 12 protuberance

nubia: 4 wrap 5 cloud

nubile: 12 marriageable

nubilous: 5 foggy, misty, vague 6 cloudy 7 obscure 10 indefinite

nucament: 5 ament

nucha: 4 nape

nucleus: 4 core 5 focus, umbra 6 kernel
pert. to: 8 nucleate
starch: 4 hila(pl.) 5 hilum

nude: 4 bare 5 model, naked 6 statue 7 denuded, picture 8 painting, stripped 9 unclothed, uncovered, undressed

nudge: jog, nog 4 knub, lump, poke, push 5 block, elbow

nudibranch: 7 mollusk

nudist: 7 Adamite 12 gymnosophist

nugatory: 4 vain 7 invalid, trivial 8 trifling 9 frustrate, worthless 11 ineffectual

nugget: 4 hunk, lump, mass, slug

nuisance: 4 harm, hurt, pest 6 injury 9 annoyance 13 inconvenience

null: nil 7 nullify 11 nonexistent 13 insignificant

nullah: 5 gorge, gully 6 ravine

nullifidian: 7 skeptic

nullify: 4 flaw, null, undo, void 5 abate, annul, elide 6 cancel, negate, repeal 7 abolish, destroy 8 abrogate, evacuate 9 frustrate 10 counteract, disappoint, invalidate, neutralize

nullo: 4 game, task

numb: 6 asleep, benumb, deaden, stupid, torpid 7 stupefy 8 enfeeble, helpless 9 incapable 10 insensible

number: sum 4 curn(Sc.), data(pl.), many, mort, slew, herd, host 5 count, datum, digit, scads, score, total 6 bundle, encore, figure, myriad, reckon, hirsel 7 chiffer, chiffre, compute, decimal, several 8 numerate, quantity, fraction 9 aggregate, calculate, enumerate, multitude 10 collection, complement, percentage
cardinal: one, two 4 four 5 three
dice: 4 sise
indeterminate: 7 umpteen, zillion
irrational: 4 surd
ordinal: 5 first, third 6 second
prime: one, two 4 five 5 seven, three 6 eleven 8 thirteen
pure: 6 scalar
suffix: st, th; eth
third power: 4 cube
under ten: 5 digit
whole: 7 integer

numbles: 7 innards nombles 8 entrails

numen: 5 deity 6 spirit 8 divinity

numerable: 11 enumerative

numeral: 4 word 6 figure, letter
style: 5 Roman 6 Arabic

numerate: 6 number

numerical group: duo 4 trio 5 octet 6 sextet
7 octette, quartet, twosome 8 foursome,
sextette 9 threesome
numerous: 4 lots, many 7 copious, crowded
8 abundant, multiple, thronged 9 multifold, plentiful
Numidia: *bird:* 10 demoiselle
   city: 5 Hippo
nun: 4 bird, snew 5 clerk 6 pigeon, sister,
vestal 7 confine, devotee 8 titmouse, votaress 9 priestess 10 cloistress
   chief: 6 abbess
   Franciscan: 5 Clare
   headdress: 6 wimple
   Latin: 5 Vesta
   order: 6 Marist 8 Trappist 9 Dominican,
   Lorettine
Nun's son: 6 Joshua
nun moth: 7 tussock
nunbird: 6 monase
nunciate: 9 announcer, messenger
nuncio: 6 legate 8 delegate 9 messenger 14
representative
nuncupate: 7 declare 8 dedicate, inscribe,
proclaim 9 designate
nuncupative: 4 oral 9 unwritten
nunnery: 5 abbey 7 convent 8 cloister
   head: 6 abbess
nunni: 7 blesbok 8 antelope
nuphar: 12 nymphaeaceae
nupson: 4 fool
nuptial: 6 bridal, genial 7 marital, wedding
11 matrimonial
nur: 5 gnarl
nurse: 4 amah, ayah, baba, care, feed, rear,
tend 5 bonne(F.), mammy, nanny 6 attend,
cradle, foster, norice, suckle 7 cherish,
nourice, nourish, nurture, promote
nurse shark: 4 gata
nursery: 6 creche
nursling: 4 baby 9 foundling
nurture: 4 diet, feed, food, rear 5 nurse,
train 6 cocker, foster 7 cherish, educate 8
breeding, training 9 education, nutriment
nut: bur, guy, nit 4 burr, cola, core, head,
kola, nute, pili, task 5 acorn, betel, crank,
hazel, pecan 6 almond, Brazil, cashew, fellow, peanut, pyrene 7 filbert, hickory,
problem 8 beechnut, chestnut 9 eccentric
11 undertaking
   collective: 4 mast 5 shack
   edible part: 6 kernel
   ivory: 4 anta
   kola: 5 bichy 9 gourou-nut
   medicinal: 4 cola, kola
   palm: 5 betel, lichi 8 cocoanut
   pert. to: 5 nucal
   tropical: ben 4 cola, kola
Nut: *daughter:* 4 Isis 8 Nephythys

   son: Ra
nut-bearing: 10 nuciferous
nut-brown: 5 hazel 6 walnut 8 chestnut
nut coal: 10 anthracite
nut grass: 5 sedge
nutate: nod 5 droop
nutbreaker: 10 nutcracker
nutcake: 8 doughnut
nutcracker: 6 xenops 7 pillory 8 nuthatch 9
nutpecker 10 nutbreaker
nuthook: 6 beadle 9 constable
nutmeg: *covering:* 4 mace
   family: 13 myristicaceae
Nutmeg State: 11 Connecticut
nutpecker: 8 nuthatch
nutramin: 7 vitamin
nutria: fur 5 coypu
nutrice: 5 nurse
nutrient: 10 nourishing
nutrify: 7 nourish
nutriment: 11 nourishment
nutrition: 11 nourishment 12 alimentation
nutritious: 10 nourishing
nutritive: 10 nourishing
nutty: 4 gaga 5 buggy, queer, spicy 7 amorous, piquant 8 demented, pleasant 10 unbalanced 12 crackbrained, enthusiastic
nuzzle: 5 nurse 6 foster, nestle 7 snuggle
nye: 4 eyas, nest, nide 5 brood
nylon: 5 crepe, ninon, tulle
nymph: 5 Aegle, naiad, siren, oread, sylph 6
nereid 7 Corycia 9 hamadryad
   Arcadian: 6 Syrinx
   beloved of Narcissus: 4 Echo
   Cretan: 8 Cynosura
   hills: 5 Oread
   laurel tree: 6 Daphne
   Messina Strait: 6 Scylla
   Mount Ida: 6 Oenone
   mountain: 5 Oread
   Muslim: 5 houri
   ocean: 5 siren 6 Nereid 7 Galatea, Oceanid
   10 Callirrhoe
   pursued by Apollo: 6 Daphne, Syrinx 8 Arethusa
   queen: Mab
   sea bird: 6 Scylla
   water: 4 Nais 5 Naiad 6 Egeria, Lurlei, Undine 7 Apsaras, Hydriad, Lorelei 8 Arethusa
   wood: 5 Dryad 6 Nereid 9 Hamadryad
nymphaea: 7 Castaly 8 Castalia, Castalie
nyssa: 6 tupelo
nystagmus: tic
Nyx, Nox: *brother:* 6 Erebus
   daughter: Day 4 Eris 5 Light 10 Hesperides
   father: 5 Chaos
   husband: 5 Chaos 6 Erebus
   son: 6 Charon

O

O. Henry: 6 Porter

oaf (see also **fool**): 4 boor, dolt, lout 5 clown, idiot, yokel 9 blockhead, foundling, schlemiel, schlemihl, simpleton 10 changeling

oafish: 6 stupid

oak: 5 roble 6 barren, cerris, encina 7 ambrose, durmast, turtosa 8 chaparro 9 blackjack
bark: 4 crut
bitter: 6 cerris
black: 10 quercitron
blight: 5 louse
comb. form: 6 querci
evergreen: 4 holm
family: 8 fagaceae
fruit: 5 acorn 6 camata
fungus: 10 armillaria
gall: 8 oakapple
holm: 4 ilex 5 holly
immature fruit: 6 camata
seed: 5 acorn
tannin: 6 queric 9 quercinic
white: 5 roble
young: 8 flittern

oak beauty: 4 moth

oak fern: 8 polypody

oak web: 10 cockchafer

oaky: 4 hard

oam: 5 steam

oar: row 5 aloof, rower 6 paddle, propel 7 oarsman 9 propeller
blade: 4 palm, peel
collective: 6 oarage
fulcrum: 7 oarlock
part: 4 loom
short: 5 scull
steering: 5 swape, swipe

oarlock: 5 thole 7 rowlock

oarsman: 5 rower 6 stroke 7 sculler

oasis: ojo, spa 4 merv, wadi, wady

oast: 4 kiln, oven

oat: ait(Sc.) 5 grain 6 angora 7 egilops 8 aegilops
genus: 5 avena
head: 7 panicle

oaten: 10 avenaceous 11 farinaceous

oath: vow 4 aith 5 aithe, curse, haith 6 appeal, pledge 7 serment 8 anathema 9 affidavit, expletive, profanity, swearword 10 adjuration, obligation 11 affirmation, imprecation
mild: 4 darn, drat, ecod, egad, gosh 5 golly 7 gee-wizz
take: 5 swear

oatmeal: 8 porridge

oats: *paid as rent:* 7 avenage
unthreshed: 6 oathay

obclude: 4 hide

obduction: 7 autopsy

obdurate: 4 firm, hard 5 rough, stony 6 inured, rugged 7 adamant 8 hardened, stubborn 9 calloused, immovable, obstinate, unbending, unfeeling 10 impenitent, inflexible, insensible, persistent, unyielding 11 hardhearted, intractable, unrepenting 13 unsusceptible

obeah: 5 charm 6 fetish, voodoo

Obed: *father:* 4 Boaz
mother: 4 Ruth
son: 4 Jehu 5 Jesse 7 Azariah

obedience: 5 order 7 control 8 docility 10 compliance, conformity, submission 12 jurisdiction

obedient: 7 duteous, dutiful, heedful, mindful, obeying 8 biddable, yielding 9 attentive, observing, tractable

obedient plant: 10 dragonhead

obeisance: bow 5 binge, conge, salam 6 congee, curtsy, fealty, homage, saalam 7 curtsey 9 abaisance, deference, reference 10 submission 14 respectfulness

Oberon: 4 king, poem 5 fairy, opera
wife: 7 Titania

obese: fat 5 plump, pudgy, pursy, stout 6 fleshy, pyknic, rotund 8 blubbery, liparous 9 corpulent

obey: ear 4 hear 7 execute

obfuscate: dim 6 darken 7 confuse, mystify, obscure, perplex, stupefy 8 bewilder 9 obfuscous

obi: 4 sash 5 charm, obeah 6 fetich, fetish, girdle

obit: 5 death 6 notice 8 obituary 9 obsequies 10 necrologue

obiter: 12 incidentally

object: aim, end 4 goal, item 5 argue, cavil, demur, thing 6 design, entity, motive, oppose, target 7 dislike, protest, purpose, quarrel 9 challenge, intention, interpose 10 disapprove 11 expostulate, remonstrate

rare: 5 curio 7 antique

sacred: 4 urim

object lesson: 7 example

object to: 4 mind

objection: but 6 cheson 7 chesoun 9 exception

legal: 5 demur

objectionable: 4 vile 6 horrid 9 obnoxious, offensive 11 exceptional 12 disagreeable

objective: aim, end 4 goal 6 motive, realty, target 7 purpose 8 detached 9 intention 10 impersonal

objet d'art: 4 vase 5 curio, virtu 7 bibelot 8 figurine

objurgate: 5 abuse, chide 6 berate, rebuke 7 reprove, upbraid 8 execrate

oblate: 4 monk 8 dedicate, monastic

opposite of: 7 prolate

oblation: 6 corban 7 charity 8 devotion, offering 9 sacrifice

obligate: 6 fasten, oblige

obligation: vow 4 band, bond, debt, duty, loan, must, oath, onus 6 pledge 7 promise 8 contract 9 agreement, liability 10 allegiance, compulsion 11 obstruction 12 indebtedness 14 responsibility

obligato: 13 accompaniment

obligatory: 7 binding, bounden 8 forcible, imposing 9 mandatory

oblige: 4 pawn 6 engage, please 7 gratify, require 8 mortgage, obligate 9 constrain 11 necessitate

obliged: 8 beholden

obliging: 4 kind 5 buxom, civil 6 clever 7 amiable 9 agreeable, courteous 11 complaisant 13 accommodating

oblique: 4 awry, bias, skew 5 askew, bevel, cross, slant 6 aslant, aswash 7 askance, crooked, evasive, scalene 8 inclined, indirect, sidelong, sideways, sidewise, slanting 9 slantways, slantwise, underhand 10 circuitous 12 disingenuous

render: 5 splay

obliterate: 4 blot, dele, rase, raze 5 annul, erase 6 cancel, delete, efface, sponge 7 expunge 10 annihilate, extinguish

obliteration: 7 erasure, removal 10 extinction

oblivion: 5 Lethe 6 pardon 7 amnesty 13 forgetfulness

producer of: 8 nepenthe

oblong: 8 avelonge 9 elongated 11 rectangular

rounded: 7 ellipse

obloquy: 5 abuse, odium 6 infamy 7 calumny, censure 8 disgrace, dishonor 12 reprehension, vituperation

obnoxious: 4 foul, vile 6 horrid, odious, rancid 7 hateful 9 offensive, verminous 13 objectionable

oboe: 4 reed 5 shawn 6 surnai, surnay 7 hautboy, musette 8 szopelka

obrok: tax

obscene: 4 foul, lewd, nast 5 bawdy, gross, nasty 6 coarse, filthy, impure, vulgar 7 profane 8 immodest, indecent 9 loathsome, offensive, repulsive 10 disgusting, licentious 12 pornographic

obscuration: 7 eclipse

obscure: dim 4 blot, blur, dark, hazy, hide 5 bedim, befog, blind, faint, foggy, inner, murky, vague 6 bemist, cloudy, darken, darkle, gloomy, mystic, remote 7 becloud, conceal, confuse, cryptic, eclipse, shadowy, unknown, unnoted 8 abstruse, darkling, disguise, mystical, nameless, obstruse, oversile 9 ambiguous, blindfold, difficult, enigmatic, equivocal, recondite, undefined 10 caliginous, extinguish, indistinct, overshadow 14 uncomprehended

obsecrate: 4 pray 7 beseech, entreat 8 petition 10 supplicate

obsequious: 5 slick 7 devoted, dutiful, fawning, servile, slavish 8 obedient, toadying, toadyish 9 attentive, compliant 10 submissive 11 subservient

obsequy: 4 rite 6 exequy, ritual 7 funeral 8 ceremony

observance: act 4 form, rite, rule 6 custom, regard 8 ceremony, practice 9 attention, deference 11 observation 12 constitution

religious: 6 Novena 9 sacrament

observant: 5 alert 7 careful, mindful 8 watchful 10 perceptive 11 considerate

observation: 4 heed, note 6 remark 7 auspice, autopsy, descant

preliminary: 5 proem

observatory: 4 Lick 5 tower 7 lookout, Palomar 11 Mount Wilson

observe: lo; eye, see, spy 4 espy, heed, keep, look, nark, note, obey, tout, wait, yeme 5 study, watch 6 athold, behold, follow, notice, regard, remark 7 comment, discern, respect, witness 8 perceive, preserve 9 advertise, celebrate, solemnize 10 animadvert, scrutinize

observer: 8 audience, informer, onlooker 9 bystander, spectator 11 stool-pigeon

obsess: 5 beset, haunt 6 harass 9 preoccupy

obsession: 5 craze, mania 6 hang-up 7 passion 8 idee fixe(F.) 13 preoccupation

obsidian: 5 lapis

obsignate: 4 seal 5 stamp 6 ratify

obsolescence: 9 desuetude

obsolete: old 4 dead 5 passe 7 ancient, archaic, outworn 8 out-dated, outmoded 9 discarded 10 antiquated 12 old-fashioned

obstacle: bar, dam, let 4 snag 5 block, hitch 6 bunker, hocket, hurdle 7 barrier 9 hindrance 10 difficulty, impediment 11 obstruction 12 entanglement

insurmountable: 7 impasse

obstetrician: 10 accoucheur

obstetrics: 9 maieutics

obstetrix: 7 midwife

obstinate: set 4 dour 5 balky, sulky, tough 6 assish, dogged, mulish, sullen, unruly 7 froward, willful 8 crotched, obdurate, perverse, stubborn 9 foreright, pigheaded 10 bullheaded, determined, headstrong, inflexible, persistent, refractory, selfwilled 11 intractable, opinionated 12 contumacious, pertinacious, recalcitrant

obstreperous: 5 noisy 6 unruly 9 clamorous 10 boisterous, vociferous

obstriction: 10 obligation

obstruct: bar, dam, dit, gag, mar 4 clog, ditt, stop 5 beset, block, check, choke, delay, hedge 6 arrest, cumber, forbar, hamper, hinder, impede, oppose, retard 7 barrier, forelay, occlude 8 blockade, encumber, incumber 9 barricade, embarrass, interfere, interrupt 10 filibuster 11 fillibuster

obstruction: 4 snag 5 gorce, hitch 7 barrace, barrage, barrier, blinder 8 embolism, obstacle 10 difficulty, impediment 11 impeachment

obtain: beg, bum, eke, get, win 4 earn, fang, gain, hent, reap 5 cadge, ettle, reach 6 attain, derive, secure, sponge 7 achieve, acquire, capture, chevise, prevail, procure, receive, succeed

by threat: 6 extort

obtainable: 9 available

obtent: 6 design 7 purpose

obtest: 7 beseech 10 supplicate

obtrude: 5 eject, expel 6 impose

obtruncate: lop

obtrusive: 5 fresh, pushy 7 blatant, forward, pushing 9 intrusive 10 aggressive 12 presumptuous

obtund: 4 dull 5 blunt, quell 6 deaden

obtuse: dim 4 dull 5 blink, blunt, crass, dense 6 stupid 8 boeotian, hebetate, purblind 11 insensitive

obvelation: 7 veiling 10 concealing

obverse: 4 face 5 front 8 converse 10 complement 11 counterpart

obviate: 7 prevent 8 preclude 9 forestall

obvious: 4 open 5 broad, clear, gross, overt, plain 6 patent 7 evident, glaring, visible 8 apparent, distinct, manifest, palpable 11 conspicuous

obvolute: 9 contorted, convolute 11 overlapping

oca: 5 tuber 6 oxalis, sorrel

occasion: 4 hint, sele, time 5 casus, cause, event, nonce, slant 6 excuse 7 pretext 8 ceremony, engender, exigency, function, incident 9 condition, happening

festive: 7 holiday

occasional: odd 4 orra 5 stray 6 daimen 8 sporadic 10 infrequent

occasionally: 7 betimes 9 sometimes

occasive: 7 setting 8 westward

Occidental: 4 West 6 ponent 7 Western 9 Hesperian, Westerner

occlude: 5 close 6 absorb 8 obstruct

occult: 5 magic 6 hidden, mystic, secret, voodoo 7 alchemy, cryptic 8 esoteric, mystical 9 concealed, recondite 10 mysterious, necromancy 11 supernormal 12 supernatural 13 imperceptible

science: 9 esoterics

occultation: 7 eclipse 13 disappearance

occultism: 6 cabala

occupant: 6 inmate, tenant 7 citizen, dweller 10 inhabitant

occupation: job 4 note, toil, work 5 graft, trade 6 career, metier, tenure 7 calling, pursuit 8 business, function, industry, vocation 10 employment, profession

transient: 5 hobby 9 avocation

occupied: 4 rapt

occupy: sit, use 4 busy, fill, hold, take 6 absorb, employ, engage, expend, fulfil, tenant 7 cohabit, engross, fulfill, oversit, pervade, possess 8 interest

occur: be 4 come, meet, pass 5 clash 6 appear, arrive, befall, betide, happen

again: 5 recur 6 repeat

occurrence: hap 4 case 5 event 7 episode 8 incident 9 encounter, happening 12 circumstance

supernatural: 7 miracle

unusual: 6 oddity

ocean (see also **sea**): 4 brim, deep, main 5 brine 6 Arctic, Indian 7 Pacific 8 Atlantic 9 Antarctic

approach: 7 seagate

floating matter: 5 algae 7 flotsam

mammal: 5 whale
periodic motion: 4 tide
phenomenon: 4 tide
swell: sea
Oceania: 6 Malaya 9 Australia, Melanesia, Polynesia 10 Micronesia, New Zealand 11 archipelago
Oceanid: 5 nymph
Oceanus: *daughter:* 5 Doris 7 Oceanid 8 Eurynome
father: 6 Uranus
mother: 4 Gaea
sister: 6 Tethys
wife: 6 Tethys
ocellus: eye 6 stemma
ocelot: cat 7 leopard
ocher: rud, sil 5 tiver 6 abraum 7 almagra
black: 4 wadd
ocrea: 6 sheath
octahedrite: 7 anatase
octapody: 9 octameter
octave: 4 utas 5 eight 6 eighth
Octavia: *brother:* 8 Augustus
husband: 6 Antony
octet: 7 huitain
octopean: 7 octopus
octopus: 5 polyp, poulp 6 poulpe 7 polypus 8 octopean 10 cephalopod
arm: 8 tentacle
secretion: ink
ten arms: 7 decapod
octoroon: 5 metis 6 mestee, mustee 7 metisse
octose: 5 sugar
octroi: tax 5 grant 9 privilege 10 concession
octuple: 9 eightfold
ocuby: rum
ocular: 5 optic 6 visual
odd: awk 4 fell, left, lone, orra(Sc.), rare 5 droll, extra, funny, impar, outre(F.), queer, weird 6 quaint, uneven 7 azygous, bizarre, curious, strange, unusual 8 fanciful, freakish, peculiar, singular, unpaired 9 burlesque, eccentric, fantastic, grotesque, unmatched, whimsical 10 occasional 13 extraordinary
oddity: 5 quirk 8 crotchet, quiddity 12 eccentricity, idiosyncrasy
oddly: 6 featly
oddman: 6 umpire 7 arbiter, referee
oddment: ort 5 scrap 7 remnant 8 fragment
odds: 7 dispute, quarrel 8 variance 9 advantage 10 dissension 13 probabilities
odds and ends: 4 orts 6 refuse, scraps 7 mixture, seconds 8 remnants 9 leftovers
ode: 4 hymn, poem 5 lyric, paean, psalm 7 epicede 8 canticle 9 epicedium
birthday: 12 genethliacon
kind of: 8 pindaric

part: 5 epode
victory: 9 epinicion, epinikion
odeon: 4 hall 5 odeum 7 gallery, theater
Oder tributary: 6 Neisse
odeum: 5 odeon
odic: 5 lyric
odiferous: 11 odoriferous
Odin: 5 Wodan, Woden, Wotan
brother: Ve 4 Vili
descendant: 5 Scyld
father: Bor
hall: 7 Valhall 8 Valhalla
horse: 8 Sleipner
maiden: 8 Valkyrie
mother: 6 Bestla
ring: 8 Draupnir
son: Tyr 4 Thor, Vali 5 Baldr 6 Balder
spear: 7 Gungnir
sword: 4 Gram
wife: 4 Fria, Rind 5 Frigg, Rindr 6 Frigga
wolf: 4 Gere, Geri 5 Freki
odious: 4 foul, loth, vile 5 loath 7 hatable, hateful, heinous, hideous 8 damnable, flagrant, infamous 9 abhorrent, invidious, obnoxious, offensive, repugnant 10 abominable, detestable, disgusting, forbidding 11 ignominious, opprobrious
odium: 6 stigma 8 aversion, disfavor 9 antipathy 14 disapprobation
odograph: 9 pedometer
odontalgia: 9 toothache
odor: 4 fume, funk, nose, olid, tang 5 aroma, ewder, fetor, flair, fumet, nidor, odour, scent, smell, stink 6 breath, flavor, foetor, repute, stench 7 bouquet, essence, flavour, fumette, perfume 9 fragrance, redolence 10 estimation, reputation
odoriferous: 5 balmy, olent 7 odorous 9 odiferous
Odysseus: See **Ulysses**
Odyssey: *author:* 5 Homer
sorceress: 5 Circe
oecist: 9 colonizer
oecodomic: 13 architectural
oeconomus: 7 manager, steward
Oedipus: *brother-in-law:* 5 Creon
daughter: 6 Ismene 8 Antigone
father: 5 Laius
mother: 7 Jocasta
refuge: 7 Colonus
son: 8 Eteocles 9 Polynices 10 Polyneices
victim: 5 Laius 6 Sphinx
wife: 7 Jocasta
oeillade: 4 ogle 6 glance
Oeneus: *father:* 8 Porthaon
kingdom: 7 Calydon
mother: 6 Euryte
wife: 7 Althaea
Oenomaus daughter: 10 Hippodamia

oestrid fly larva: bot

oestrus: 4 fury 5 sting 6 desire, frenzy 7 impulse 8 stimulus

oeuvre: 4 opus, work

of (see also next entry): de(F.); van(D.) 4 from 5 about 10 concerning

of: For all definitions beginning with this word, see under following main word or phrase. EXAMPLES: "of the country": see **country** *pert. to;* "of necessity": see **necessity** *of*

off: 4 away, doff, gone 5 aside, wrong 6 absent, cuckoo, remote 7 distant, further, removed

off-scouring: 5 filth 6 refuse 7 garbage, rubbish

offal: 5 gurry, waste 6 refuse 7 carrion, garbage, leaving, rubbish 8 gralloch

offend: cag, sin, vex 4 hurt, miff 5 abuse, anger, annoy, grate, grill, pique, shock, wrong 6 aguilt, attack, grieve, insult, revolt 7 affront, default, mortify, outrage, violate 9 disoblige, displease 10 transgress

offended: 4 huff, sore 7 froisse

offender: 7 culprit

offense: 4 mala(pl.) 5 crime, error, fault, guilt, malum 6 felony, pritch 7 misdeed, umbrage 8 peccancy, trespass 9 indignity 10 aggression, peccadillo, resentment 11 delinquency, misdemeanor

civil: 11 stellionate

law: 5 delit 6 delict 8 delictum

moral: 4 evil

offensive: bad 4 foul 5 fetid 6 coarse, horrid 7 beastly, fulsome, hateful, noisome 8 invading 9 loathsome, obnoxious, repugnant 10 aggressive, disgusting, forbidding, ill-favored, scurrilous, ungracious, unpleasant 11 distasteful 12 disagreeable 13 objectionable

offer: bid 4 bode, tend 6 adduce, allege, tender 7 advance, commend, present, proffer, propine, propose, suggest 8 avertment, bequeath, overture 9 volunteer

last: 9 ultimatum

solemn: 6 pledge

offering: 4 gift 6 corban 7 present 9 sacrifice

religious: 7 deodate 8 anathema, oblation

sacrificial: 5 hiera 7 sphagia(pl.) 8 sphagion

offering block: 4 aloe

offhand: 4 curt 6 casual 7 brusque 8 cavalier, informal 9 impromptu 10 improvised 11 extemporary 14 extemporaneous, unpremeditated 15 autoschediastic 16 extemporaneously

office: 4 post, wike 5 place, wiken 6 bureau 7 camarin, station 8 function, position 9 bailiwick, situation 10 commission 11 appointment 13 collectorship

chief: 7 manager

divine: 9 akoluthia

help: 5 clerk 6 typist 9 secretary 12 stenographer

machine: 5 Xerox 9 stenotype 10 calculator, mimeograph, typewriter 11 comptometer

of third hour: 5 terce

paid without work: 8 sinecure

purchase or sale: 8 barratry

put in again: 7 re-elect 9 re-instate

seeker of: 7 nominee 9 candidate

officeholder: in 6 winner 8 official, placeman

officer: 4 aide 5 usher 6 direct, ensign, manage, tindal 7 command, conduct, general 8 adjutant

assistant: 4 aide

college: 4 dean 6 bursar 10 chancellor

future: 5 cadet

law: cop 7 bailiff, marshal, sheriff 9 constable, detective, patrolman, policeman

naval: 4 mate 5 bosun 6 ensign, yeoman 7 admiral, captain, striper 9 boatswain, commander, commodore 10 lieutenant

noncommissioned: 4 mate 5 chief 8 corporal, sergeant

presiding: 6 archon 7 speaker 8 chairman 9 moderator, president

warrant: 5 bosun 9 boatswain

officers: 5 staff

official: 6 formal 9 escribano(Sp.), executive, officious 10 authorized, bureaucrat, magistrate 11 ceremonious 13 authoritative

administrative: 5 reeve 6 gerefa 9 executive

assistant: 4 aide

city or town: 5 mayor 7 manager, marshal 8 alderman 10 councilman

civil: 5 judge, mayor 7 bailiff, marshal, sheriff 8 governor 9 constable, patrolman, policeman, president 10 magistrate

corrupt: 7 grafter

despotic: 6 satrap

excise: 8 reveneur 9 revenooer

former: aga

government: 6 syndic

judicial: 8 assessor, recorder 9 treasurer 11 comptroller

local: 6 bailie(Sc.), grieve 7 burgess

public: 6 notary

state: 8 minister 9 secretary

officiate: act 6 supply 7 perform 9 celebrate

officious: 4 busy, cool, pert 6 formal 8 arrogant, impudent, informal, official 10 impersonal, meddlesome 11 efficacious, impertinent, pragmatical 12 contemptuous 14 supererogatory 16 superserviceable

offing: 7 picture 10 background

offset: 6 contra 7 balance 10 compensate, complement 12 counterpoise

offshoot: rod 5 bough, scion 6 branch, sprout

offspring: fry, imp, kid, son 4 brat, chit, seed 5 brood, child, fruit, issue, scion 6 foster, result 7 outcome, produce, product, progeny 8 children, daughter, geniture 9 genealogy, youngster 10 descendant, generation

oficina: 5 works 6 office 7 factory 10 laboratory

oflete: 5 wafer 8 oblation, offering

often: 6 common 8 frequent, repeated 10 frequently 11 continually

ogdoad: 5 eight

ogee: See **molding**

Ogier: 4 Dane, hero 6 prince 8 Norseman

ogle: eye 4 gaze, leer 5 stare 7 examine

ogre: 5 demon, giant 6 tyrant, yaksha, yakshi 7 bugaboo, monster

ogtiern: son 4 lord 6 master

ogygian: 7 ancient 8 primeval

oh: ach(G.) 4 ouch

Ohio: *college:* 5 Hiram, State 7 Antioch 10 Wittenberg
county: 4 Erie, Ross
town: Ada 5 Akron, Berea, Cadiz, Niles, Xenia 6 Canton, Dayton, Girard, Lorain, Toledo 7 Bucyrus 8 Columbus, Sandusky 9 Cleveland 11 Chillicothe 13 Yellow Springs

oii: 10 muttonbird

oil: ben, fat, ile 4 balm, fuel 5 bribe, oleum 6 aceite, anoint, chrism, grease 7 lanolin 9 lubricate, petroleum
blasting: 14 nitroglycerine
bone: 6 olanin
butter: 4 ghee
cedar and juniper: 8 alkitran 9 alchitran
coal: 8 photogen
comb. form: 4 oleo
derived from: 5 elaic, oleic
in skin: 5 sebum
linseed: 6 carron
liquid compound: 5 olein
mineral: 7 naphtha
orange-blossom: 6 neroli
pert. to: 5 oleic
prefix: ol
salt: 7 bittern
torch: 7 lucigen
vegetable: 8 macassar
vessel: 4 drum, olpe 5 cruet, cruse 6 tanker 7 cresset
whale: 5 sperm

oil beetle: 5 meloe

oil bottle: 5 cruet

oil cask: 4 rier

oil fish: 7 escolar

oil lamp: 7 coal-oil 8 kerosene

oil plant: 6 sesame

oil rock: 5 shale 9 limestone

oil tree: 4 eboe, tung 5 mahwa

oil well: 6 gusher

oilbird: 8 guacharo

oilcan: 5 oiler

oilcloth: 8 linoleum

oiler: 6 oilcan, tanker

oillet: 6 eyelet

oilseed: til 4 teel 6 sesame 7 linseed 8 rapeseed 10 castorbean, cottonseed

oilstone: 4 hone 5 shale 9 whetstone

oily: fat 4 glib 5 bland, soapy, suave 6 greasy, oleose, supple 7 pinguid 8 slippery, unctuous 9 compliant, plausible 10 oleaginous 11 subservient

ointment: 4 balm, mull, nard 5 salve 6 balsam, cerate 7 unguent 9 spikenard
application: 11 embrocation
Biblical: 9 spikenard
dry: 9 xeromyron, xeromyrum
hair: 6 pomade 7 pomatum
oil: 6 carron, cerate 7 oleamen
veterinary: 8 remolade 9 remoulade
wax: 6 cerate

Oise tributary: 5 Aisne

Oisin's father: 4 Finn

oisivity: 8 laziness

ojo: 5 oasis

okay: ok 4 okeh 7 approve, correct

oket: 5 ounce

Okie: 7 migrant

Okinawa capital: 4 Naha

Oklahoma: *county:* 6 Garvin
mountain: 5 Ozark
people: 5 Okies 7 Sooners
river: Red
state flower: 9 mistletoe
town: Ada 4 Alva, Enid, Hugo 5 Miami, Sayre, Tulsa 6 Beaver, Edmond, El Reno, Guymon, Idabel, Kansas, Lawton, Pawnee 7 Buffalo, Cordell, Cushing, Newkirk, Shawnee 8 Anadarko, Cheyenne, Coalgate, Eldorado 9 Drumright, Stillwell, Wilburton 10 Kingfisher 11 Pauls Valley
tribe: 4 Otoe
university: 6 Norman 10 Stillwater

okra: 5 bendy, gumbo 6 bendee 8 bandikai

olam: 8 eternity, infinity, universe

old: agy, ald, eld 4 aged, auld 5 anile, hoary, stale 6 former, infirm, mature, senile, shabby 7 ancient, antique, archaic 8 medieval, obsolete 9 doddering, hackneyed, senescent, venerable 10 antiquated 11 experienced 12 antediluvian

old age: 10 senescence 11 senectitude

Old Bailey: 4 gaol, jail 6 prison

Old Bay State: 13 Massachusetts
old boy: man 6 alumni(pl.) 7 alumnus
Old Dominion State: 8 Virginia
Old Faithful: 6 geyser
old-fashioned: 5 passe 6 fogram, fogrum,
  quaint 7 ancient, antique, archaic 8 obsolete 9 primitive 10 antiquated
Old Franklin State: 9 Tennessee
Old Gooseberry: 5 devil, satan
Old Hickory: 13 Andrew Jackson
Old Line State: 8 Maryland
old maid: 8 cardgame, spinster
Old Noll: 14 Oliver Cromwell
Old Rough and Ready: 6 Taylor
Old Sod: 4 Erin 7 Ireland
Old Testament: See Bible
old-womanish: 5 anile
Old World: *ape:* 6 baboon 10 catarrhina,
  catarrhine
  carnivore: 5 genet
  dish: 5 tansy
  falcon: 5 saker
  goat: 4 ibex
  lizard: 5 agama 9 chameleon
  mouse: 6 jerboa
olden: 6 bygone
older: 5 elder 6 senior 8 ancestor 11 forefa-
  thers 12 predecessors
oldest: 4 dean 6 eldest
olea: 5 olive
oleaginous: 4 oily
oleander: 11 rhododaphne 12 rhododendron
olecranon: 5 ancon
olefin: 6 alkene
olena: 8 turmeric
olent: 11 odoriferous
oleo: 9 margarine
oleomargarine: 9 butterine, margarine
oleoresin: 5 anime, elemi, tolus 7 copaiba 10
  turpentine
oleum: oil
olfact: 5 smell
olfaction: 7 osmesis 8 smelling
olid: 5 fetid
olinda bug: 6 weevil
olio: 4 stew 6 medley 7 melange, mixture 8
  mishmash 9 potpourri 10 collection,
  hodgepodge, miscellany
oliphant: 4 horn 8 elephant
oliprance: 4 romp, show 7 jollity 11 merrymaking, ostentation
olitory: 6 garden 7 potherb
olive: 4 olea 9 appetizer
  enzyme: 6 olease
  overripe: 5 drupe
  pert. to: 9 oleaceous
  stuffed: 6 pimola
  wild: 8 oleaster
oliver: 6 hammer

olivet: 5 pearl
olivine: 10 chrysolite
olla: jar, jug, pot
ollapodrida: 4 hash, olio, olla 6 medley 10
  assortment, hodgepodge, miscellany
olm: 10 salamander
ology: ism 7 science
oloroso: 6 sherry
olp: 4 olph 9 bullfinch
olpe: 5 flask 6 vessel 7 pitcher
olycook: 7 cruller, olykoek 8 doughnut
Olympic cupbearer: 4 Hebe 8 Ganymede
Olympus: *deity:* see **Greece:** *god*
  pert. to: 7 exalted, godlike, Olympic 8 heavenly, majestic 9 celestial
Oman money: 5 ghazi
Omar Khayyam's country: 4 Iran 6 Persia
omber card: 5 basto
omega: end 4 last
omelet: 5 amlet 8 fooyung
omen: 4 bode, omen, sign 5 augur, boder,
  freet, freit, token 6 augury, handel, hansel
  7 auspice, portent, presage, warning 8
  bodement, forebode, foresign 9 foretoken
  10 foreboding, forerunner, indication, prediction 11 premonition
omentum: 4 caul
omer: 4 unit 7 measure
  ten: 4 epha 5 ephah
ominous: 4 dour, grim 5 fatal 6 dismal 7
  fateful 8 menacing, sinister 9 prophetic 10
  inexorable, portentous 11 threatening
  mark: 4 dele 5 caret 7 ellipse 10 apostrophe
  pretended: 10 paralepsis, paralipsis
  tacit: 7 silence
omission: cut 5 error 7 default, failure 9
  exclusion, oversight
  mark of: 5 caret
  of vowel: 7 elision
omit: cut 4 balk, dele, drop, miss, skip, slip
  5 abate, elide, spare 6 beleve, cancel, delete, except, forget, ignore 7 beleave, discard, neglect 8 overlook 9 disregard, pretermit
omneity: 7 allness
omnibus: bus 5 barge 10 shillibeer
omnipotent: God 4 able 5 deity, great 6 arrant, mighty 8 almighty, powerful 9 unequaled, unlimited 11 all-powerful
omnipresent: 10 ubiquitous 12 ubiquitar-
  ian
omniscient: 4 wise 7 learned 8 powerful 10
  all-knowing, allwitting 11 everpresent
omnitude: 7 allness 8 totality 12 universal-
  ity
omoplate: 7 scapula
omphalos: hub 4 boss, knob 5 navel 6 center
Omri: *daughter:* 8 Athaliah
  successor: 4 Ahab

on: 4 atop, upon 5 about, above, ahead, along, anent 6 anenst, within 7 forward 10 concerning
account of: for
all sides: 5 about 6 around
and on: 4 ever 7 forever, tedious
behalf: for
other side: 4 over 6 across
on the contrary: 6 rather
on the other hand: but 7 however 8 although 11 nonetheless 12 contrariwise, nevertheless
on time: 6 prompt
on what account: why
Ona: 7 Fuegian
onager: ass 8 catapult
Onam's son: 4 Jada 7 Shammai
once: ane(Sc.) 4 anes(Sc.), anis(Sc.), erst 5 aince(Sc.) 6 former 7 quondam 8 formerly, whenever
in a while: 9 sometimes 12 occasionally
more: 4 anew, echo 5 again 6 encore, repeat
upon a time: 8 formerly
once-over: 6 survey 8 scrutiny
oncorhynchus: 6 salmon
ondoyant: 4 wavy
one: ae(Sc.), an; ain(Sc.), ane(Sc.), ein(G.), tae(Sc.), una, une(F.), yae(Sc.) 4 same, sole, some, unal, unit 5 alone, unity 6 person, single, unique, united 7 numeral, pronoun 8 unbroken 9 singleton, undivided, unmarried 10 individual
after another: 8 serially, seriatim 11 consecutive 12 successively
by one: 6 apiece, singly 10 separately
comb. form: uni 4 mono
one-chambered: 10 unicameral
one-colored: 13 monochromatic
one-footed: 6 uniped
one-sided: 6 biased, uneven, unfair, unjust 7 bigoted, partial 10 prejudiced, unilateral
one-spot: 4 buck 6 dollar
one tenth: 5 tithe
one thousand: mil
one twenty-fourth: 5 carat
oneberry: 9 hackberry
onefold: 6 simple, single 7 sincere 9 guileless
onegite: 8 amethyst
O'Neill heroine: 4 Anna
oneism: 6 egoism, monism
oneness: 7 concord 8 identity, sameness 9 agreement 11 singularity
oner: 6 corker 9 humdinger
onerous: 4 hard 5 heavy 7 arduous, onerose 8 exacting 9 laborious 10 burdensome, cumbersome, oppressive
onetime: 8 formerly

onfall: 5 onset 6 attack
onion: 4 boll, cepa, leek 5 cibol, pearl 7 Bermuda, onionet, shallot 8 eschalot, rareripe, scallion
genus: 6 allium
onkos: 7 topnot
onlepy: 4 only, sole 8 solitary 9 unmarried
onlooker: 5 gazer 7 witness 8 audience, beholder 9 bystander, spectator 10 rubberneck
only: 4 just, lone, mere, sole 5 afald 6 anerly, barely, merely, simple, single, singly, solely 9 allenarly, excepting 11 exclusively
onomasticon: 7 lexicon 10 dictionary
onomatopoeic: 6 echoic
onrush: 4 birr 6 attack
onset: 4 dash, dint, fard, rese, rush 5 braid, brunt, faird, frush, start 6 attack, charge 7 assault, attempt, brattle 9 beginning, encounter, onslaught 12 commencement
onslaught: 5 onset 6 attack 7 assault, descent
onstead: 9 farmhouse, homestead
Ontario: *capital:* 7 Toronto
town: 4 Galt 9 Kitchener
onto: 4 atop 6 aboard
onus: 4 duty, load 6 burden, charge 10 obligation
onward: 4 away 5 ahead, along, forth 7 forward
onyx: 10 chalcedony
oodles: 4 heap 5 scads 8 lashings 9 abundance
oolong: tea
oomiack, oomiak: 4 boat
oomph: 5 vigor 6 energy
oont: 5 camel
oopak: tea
oorali: 6 currare
oorial: sha 5 urial
ooze: bog, mud 4 drip, leak, mire, seep, slob 5 exude, gleet, marsh, slime, weeze 6 sludge 8 transude 9 percolate
opah: 4 fish 5 cravo
opal: gem 5 noble, resin 7 girasol, hyalite 8 girasole 10 chalcedony
variety: 8 menilite 9 cacholong
opalescent: 7 opaline 8 irisated 10 iridescent
opaque: 4 dark, dull 6 obtuse, stupid 7 obscure 8 eyeshade 13 unilluminated 14 unintelligible
open: dup, ope 4 ajar, flue, free, undo 5 agape, apert, begin, clear, frank, lance, overt, naked, plain, start, untie 6 candid, direct, expand, expose, honest, patent, unbolt, unfold, unfurl, unlock, unseal, unstop 7 artless, dispart, obvious, sincere, unclose 8 apparent, commence, disclose,

dispread, explicit, extended, initiate, manifest, patulous, unfasten 9 disspread, originate, uncovered 10 accessible, forthright, inaugurate, unreserved 11 unconcealed 13 undissembling 15 straightforward

bursting: 10 dehiscence

fully: 4 wide 5 agape 7 yawning 9 dehiscent, full-blown

partly: mid 4 ajar

open-eyed: 5 awake 8 vigilant, watchful 9 receptive 10 discerning

opener: key 4 knob 5 latch 6 seseame 8 aperient

openhanded: 4 free 7 liberal 8 generous 9 receptive 10 munificent

opening: os; gap, ora(pl.) 4 bore, door, fent, gate, hole, pass, rift, rima, slit, slot, span, vent 5 brack, cleft, debut, mouth, start, width 6 avenue, breach, hiatus, lacuna, outlet, portal, spread 7 crevice, fissure, orifice 8 aperture, overture 11 opportunity

enlarge: 4 ream

escape: 4 muse 5 meuse

having: 10 fenestrate

in chess: 6 gambit

mouth-like: 5 stoma 7 stomata(pl.)

slitlike: 4 rima

small: 4 pore 5 chink 6 cranny, eyelet 7 foramen, pinhole 8 foramina(pl.)

openmouthed: 6 gaping, greedy 8 ravenous 9 clamorous 10 vociferous

openwork: 7 tracery

opera: 4 Aida 5 Faust 6 Boheme, Carmen, Otello 7 Fidelio 8 Falstaff, Parsifal, Traviata, Walkyrie 9 Lohengrin, Pagliacci, Rheingold, Rigoletto, Trovatore 10 Magic Flute, Tannhauser 11 Don Giovanni 16 Marriage of Figaro

comic: 5 buffa

division: 5 scena

horse: 7 Western

kind: 4 soap 5 horse 8 burletta

part: 4 aria

soap: 6 serial 9 melodrama

solo: 4 aria

song: 4 aria 7 sortita 8 cavatina 9 cabaletta

soprano: 4 Bori 5 Eames, Patti 6 Callas, Farrar

star: 4 diva

tenor: 6 Caruso

opera glass: 9 lorgnette 10 binoculars

opera house: 7 theater

operant: 9 operative

operate: go; act, man, run 4 work 6 affect, effect, manage 7 conduct 10 accomplish

by hand: 10 manipulate

operation: 4 deed 6 agency 7 process 8 creation, function 9 actuation, influence, procedure 10 production 11 maintenance, transaction

operative: 4 hand 6 artist 7 artisan 8 mechanic 9 detective

beyond itself: 9 transeunt

for past: 11 retroactive

operator: 5 agent, quack 6 dealer 7 manager, operant, surgeon 9 conductor, operative 10 mountebank

operculum: lid 4 flap 8 covering

operose: 4 busy 8 diligent 9 laborious 11 industrious

ophidian: asp, eel 5 snake 6 conger 7 reptile, serpent

ophthalmic: 6 ocular

opiate: 4 dope, drug, hemp 5 dwale, opium 6 deaden 7 anodine, anodyne 8 hypnotic, narcotic 9 paregoric

opificer: 7 workman 9 artificer

opine: 4 deem 5 judge 6 ponder 7 suppose

opinion: 4 idea, view, ween 5 dicta(pl.), guess, tenet 6 advice, belief, dictum, esteem, notion, repute 7 concept, feeling, thought 8 decision, doctrine, estimate, judgment 9 sentiment 10 conjecture, conviction, deposition, estimation, expression, evaluation, impression, persuasion 12 apprehension

erroneous: 13 misconception

expression: 4 vote

preconceived: 9 prejudice

united: 9 unanimous

unorthodox: 6 heresy

opinionated: 8 dogmatic 9 conceited, obstinate 11 dictatorial

opinions: *collected:* 9 anthology, symposium

professed: 5 credo

opium: 4 drug 10 intoxicant

alkaloid: 6 codein 7 codeine 8 morphine, narcotin 9 narcotine, papaverin 10 papaverine

camphorate tincture: 9 paregoric

concentrated form: 6 heroin

derivative: 7 meconic

Egyptian: 8 thebaine

poppy seed: maw

prepared: 6 chandu 7 chandoo

opossum: 9 marsupial

mouse: 7 marmosa, marmose 8 marmouse

water: 5 yapok 6 yapock

oppidan: 5 civic, urban 8 townsman

oppilate: 4 clog 5 block 8 obstruct

opponent: foe 5 enemy 7 opposer 9 adversary, assailant 10 antagonist

opportune: fit, pat 5 ready 6 timely 8 suitable 9 favorable, well-timed 10 auspicious, convenient, favourable, seasonable

opportunely: 7 apropos, happily

opportunity: 4 hent, sele 5 slant 6 chance 7 opening 8 occasion 9 advantage 12 circumstance

oppose: pit, vie 4 buck, cope, face, meet, stem, wear 5 argue, block, check, cross, fight, front, rebel, rebut, repel 6 breast, combat, object, oppugn, resist 7 contest, counter, gainsay 8 conflict, confront, contrast, frontier, obstruct 9 encounter, withstand 10 calcitrate, contradict, contravene, controvert

opposed: 4 anti 6 averse 7 adverse, against, hostile 8 contrary 11 contrariant

opposer: 8 opponent

opposite: 5 anent, polar 6 across, anenst, averse, facing 7 adverse, counter, inverse, reverse 8 contrary, contrast, converse 9 antipodal, repugnant 10 antipodean 12 antagonistic 13 contradictory

opposite to: 7 abreast, subtend

opposition: 5 atilt 9 animosity, collision, hostility, renitency 10 resistance 11 contrariety

oppress: 4 load, rape, thew 5 crush, grind, weigh, wrong 6 burden, defoil, defoul, extort, harass, harrow, ravish, subdue 7 afflict, depress, overlay, repress, trample 8 distress, encumber, pressure, suppress 9 constrain, overpower, overthrow, overwhelm 10 extinguish

oppressed: 5 laden 9 debruised 10 heavy-laden

oppression: 8 dullness 9 grievance, lassitude 11 obscuration

oppressive: 4 dire, hard 5 close, harsh, heavy 6 severe 7 onerous 8 rigorous 10 hardhanded 11 gravaminous, heavy-handed, overbearing 12 extortionate

oppressor: 4 csar, czar, Nero, tsar, tzar 6 tyrant

opprobrium: 5 abuse, odium, scorn 6 infamy, insult 7 calumny, offense, scandal 8 disgrace, dishonor, reproach 9 contumely 10 disrespect

oppugn: 6 oppose

oppugnacy: 9 hostility 10 antagonism

oppugnation: 6 attack 10 opposition

Ops: *associate:* 6 Consus
consort: 6 Saturn
daughter: 5 Ceres
festival: 6 opalia
son: 4 Zeus 8 Poseidon

opt: 4 cull, pick 5 elect 6 choose, decide, select

optic: eye 6 ocular, visual

optical: 6 ocular
instrument: 4 lens 6 alidad 7 alidade 9 eriometer, optometer, periscope, telescope 10 microscope, teinoscope 11 stereoscope 15 ultramicroscope
organ: eye

optimistic: 4 rosy 6 joyous 7 hopeful, roseate 8 sanguine

option: 6 choice 7 refusal 9 privilege 11 alternative

optional: 8 elective 9 voluntary 10 permissive

opulent: fat 4 rich 5 ample 6 lavish 7 profuse, wealthy 8 abundant, affluent 9 luxuriant, plentiful

opus: 4 work 11 composition
overlabored: 11 lucubration

oquassa: 5 trout

or: aut(L.), ere 6 either 11 alternative
heraldry: 4 gold 6 yellow

oracle: 4 seer 5 sibyl
pert. to: 8 pythonic

oracular: 4 otic 5 vatic 7 vatical 9 prophetic 10 mysterious 11 dictatorial 13 authoritative

orage: 5 storm 7 tempest

oral: 5 aloud, parol, vocal 6 sonant, spoken, verbal 7 uttered 9 unwritten 10 acroamatic

orange: 4 mock 5 chino, color, hedge, Navel, Osage 6 bodock 7 Seville 8 bergamot, chinotti, mandarin, Valencia 9 tangerine
genus: 6 citrus
heraldry: 5 tenne
membrane: 4 zest
mock: 7 seringa, syringa, syringe
piece: 4 lith(Sc.) 7 segment
red: 7 saffron
seed: pip
seedless: 5 navel
variety: 5 blood, navel, osage 7 seville

Orange Bowl site: 5 Miami

orange-flower oil: 6 neroli

orange-shaped: 6 oblate

orangeat: 9 orangeade

orangeberry: 9 cranberry

orangebird: 7 tanager

orangeleaf: 6 karamu

orangelike fruit: bel 9 tangerine

orangewood: 5 Osage

orangutan: ape 4 mias 5 orang, pongo, satyr 7 primate 11 orangoutang

orate: 5 plead, speak, spiel, spout 7 address, declaim, lecture 8 harangue 9 discourse, speechify 10 filibuster 11 expostulate

oration: 6 sermon 7 concion 9 panegyric
funeral: 5 eloge 6 eulogy 7 elogium, encomia(pl.) 8 encomium

orator: 6 rhetor 7 demagog, speaker 8 cicerone, ciceroni(pl.) 9 demagogue, plaintiff 10 petitioner 11 rhetorician, spellbinder

oratorian: 6 priest

oratorical: 8 eloquent 10 rhetorical

oratorio: 7 Messiah, Seasons
  coda in: 7 stretta

oratory: 6 chapel 9 elocution, eloquence

orb: eye, sun 4 ball, moon, star 5 earth, globe 6 circle, planet, sphere 7 circuit, enclose 8 encircle, surround

orbed: 5 lunar, round

orbit: 4 path 5 track 6 socket 7 circuit, ellipse
  point: 5 apsis, syzygy 6 apogee, epigee 7 apsides(pl.), perigee

orc: 4 orca 5 whale 7 grampus

orchard: 5 arbor 6 arbour, garden 8 arbustum 9 enclosure 10 plantation

orchestra: 4 band 5 group 8 ensemble
  section: 4 wind, wood 5 brass 6 string 7 timpany

orchestra bells: 12 glockenspiel

orchestra circle: 7 parquet 8 parterre

orchestrate: 5 score 7 arrange, compose

orchid: 5 faham, petal, vanda 6 purple 7 aerides, calypso, lycaste, pogonia, vanilla 8 arethusa, labellum
  appendage: 8 caudicle
  dried tubers: 5 salep
  genus of: 5 vanda 6 laelia 10 gymnadenia 14 gymnadeniopsis
  leaves: 4 faam 5 faham
  meal: 5 salep
  petal: 8 labellum
  tuber: 5 salep 7 cullion

Orcus: 5 Hades

ordain: 4 deem 5 allot, enact, order 6 decree 7 adjudge, appoint, arrange, behight, command, destine, install, prepare 9 establish, prescribe 10 adjudicate, commission, constitute

ordeal: 4 gaff 5 trial 10 experience

order: ban, bid 4 boon, fiat, form, ordo, rank, rule, sect, will 5 align, array, class, dight, edict, genus, grade, guide 6 billet, charge, cosmos, decree, degree, demand, direct, enjoin, genera(pl.), graith, kilter, manage, method, ordain, police, series, system 7 adjudge, arrange, bespeak, bidding, command, compose, dispose, embargo, mandate, ordines(pl.), precept, process, society 8 decision, neatness, organize, regulate 9 direction, directive, procedure 10 injunction, succession 11 appointment, instruction
  back: 6 remand 8 recommit
  connected: 8 seriatim
  cosmic: tao 4 rita

good: 6 eutaxy 7 eutaxie

grammar: 5 taxis

lacking: 5 amiss, messy, mussy 7 chaotic, unkempt 8 confused 10 disarrayed

law: 4 writ 7 summons 8 subpoena
  Parliamentary: 9 procedure
  writ: 7 precipe

orderly: 4 aide, tidy, trim 6 batman 7 regular 8 decorous, obedient 9 peaceable, regularly, shipshape 10 law-abiding 11 well-behaved

ordinal: 4 book 6 number 7 orderly, regular

ordinance: law 4 doom, fiat, rite 5 bylaw, edict 6 assize, decree 7 control, decreta(pl.), statute 8 decretum 9 direction, sacrament 10 management, regulation 11 appointment

ordinary: 4 lala, ruck, soso 5 nomic, plain, prose, usual 6 common, normal 7 average, natural, prosaic, trivial, vulgate 8 everyday, habitual, mediocre 9 customary 11 commonplace

ordinate: 7 appoint, orderly, regular 8 moderate 9 temperate 10 methodical

ordnance: 4 guns 5 armor, orgue 6 petard 7 weapons 8 basilisk 9 artillery, torpedoes 10 ammunition, serpentine

ordo: 5 order 7 almanac

ore (see also **mineral**): tin 4 gold, iron, lead 5 favor, glory, grace, honor, mercy, metal 6 copper 7 respect, seaweed 8 clemency 9 reverence
  crusher: 5 dolly
  deposit: 4 lode 5 scrin 7 bonanza
  fusing: 8 smelting
  horizontal layer: 5 stope
  impure: 6 speiss
  iron: 5 ocher, ochre 8 hematite 9 magnetite
  layer: 4 seam 5 stope
  lead: 6 galena
  loading platform: 4 plat
  mercury: 8 cinnabar
  refuse: 6 scoria 8 tailings
  separator: 6 vanner
  silver: 10 stephanite
  sluice: 5 trunk
  tin: 5 scove
  tungsten: 4 cals
  washing trough: 6 strake
  worthless: 5 matte

oread: 5 nymph

Oregon: *capital:* 5 Salem
  coin: 6 beaver
  county: 4 Coos 5 Curry 7 Gilliam, Klamath, Malheur, Wallowa, Yamhill 8 Umatilla 9 Deschutes, Multnomah, Tillamook
  crab apple: 7 powitch
  fabled monster: 7 Big Foot 9 Sasquatch
  Indian tribe: 4 Coos

mountain: 4 Hood 5 Coast 7 Cascade
river: 5 Rogue 7 Klamath 8 Columbia 9 Deschutes 10 Willamette
town: 4 Bend 7 Medford 8 Portland
university site: 6 Eugene
wind: 7 chinook
oreortyx: 5 quail
Orestes: *father:* 9 Agamemnon
friend: 7 Pylades
mother: 12 Clytemnestra
sister: 7 Electra
wife: 8 Hermione
orf, orfe: ide 4 fish
orfevrerie: 7 jewelry
organ: 6 medium 9 equipment 10 instrument
auricular: ear
barrel: 8 autophon
bristle-like: 4 seta
cactus: 7 saguaro
desk: 7 console
elongated: 8 tentacle
essential: 5 brain, heart, liver, lungs 6 viscus 7 viscera(pl.)
fish: 8 drumfish
flutter device: 7 tremolo
footlike: pes
gallery: 4 loft
interlude: 6 verset
lymphoid: 6 tonsil
note: 9 tremolant
of insect: 7 stinger
of living bodies: 8 organism
of motion: 6 muscle
of volition: 5 manas
olfactory: 4 nare, nose
opening: os; ora(pl.)
optical: eye
part: 4 reed, stop
piano: 9 melopiano
pipe: 4 reed 5 flute 7 mixture
portable: 5 regal
prelude: 6 verset
reed: 9 harmonium
respiratory: 4 lung
sawlike: 5 serra
secreting: 5 gland
sensory: ear, eye 4 nose
speech: lip 6 throat, tongue
tactile: 6 feeler
organ stop: 5 quint, viola 7 celesta, tertian 8 diapason, dulciana, gemshorn, register 9 rohrflute 10 quindecima
adjust: 10 registrate
bell-like: 8 carillon
labial: 7 melodia
reed: 4 oboe 7 bassoon 8 possaune
storm-imitating: 5 orage
string: 5 gamba

two banks of pipes: 7 tertian
organic: 6 inborn 7 natural 8 inherent 9 organlike 11 fundamental 12 instrumental 14 constitutional
body: 5 zooid
compound: 5 amine, ketol
radical: 5 ethyl
organism: 5 plant 6 aerobe, animal
bacterial: 4 germ 7 microbe
body: 4 soma 6 somata(pl.)
elementary: 5 monad
minute: 5 ameba, monad, spore
pelagic: 6 nekton
process: 6 miosis 7 meiosis
vegetable: 4 tree 5 plant
organization: 5 setup 11 association, disposition 12 constitution
business: 4 firm 5 guild 11 cooperative, corporation, partnership 13 establishment
college: 4 frat 5 alumna, alumni(pl.) 7 alumnus 8 sorority 10 fraternity
political: 4 bloc 5 party
secret: K.C.; K.O.P., P.E.O., W.O.W. 4 B.P.O.E., Elks, frat 5 lodge, mafia, Moose 6 apache, maffia, Masons 8 sorority 9 Foresters, Maccabees 10 fraternity, Freemasons 11 underground
skeleton: 5 cadre
social: 4 club 5 forum
veterans: A.V.C., D.A.V., G.A.R., S.A.R., V.F.W. 5 Fidac 6 AMVETS 14 American Legion 21 Veterans of Foreign Wars
women's: D.A.R., W.A.F., W.R.C. 8 sorority
organize: 4 form 5 edify 6 embody 7 arrange 8 regiment
organized: 7 organic 10 systematic
organized body: 4 army, navy 5 corps, posse
organology: 10 phrenology 12 splanchnology
organophone: 9 harmonium
organoscopy: 10 phrenology
orgueil: 5 pride 11 haughtiness
orgy: 4 lark, romp 5 revel, spree 6 frolic, shindy 7 revelry, wassail 8 carousal, ceremony 10 observance 11 celebration, merrymaking
Oriana: *father:* 8 Lisuarte
lover: 6 Amadis
oribi: 8 antelope, bleekbok
oriel: bay 6 recess, window 7 balcony, gallery, portico 8 corridor
orient: 4 dawn 5 adapt, place 6 adjust, locate 7 sunrise 11 accommodate
Orient: 4 Asia, East 6 Levant
animal: 4 zebu
archangel: 5 Uriel
bearer: 5 hamal
beverage: 6 arrack

bow: 6 salaam
cap: 7 calpack
caravansary: 4 khan 5 serai 6 imaret
carriage: 10 jinricksha 11 jinrickshaw
cart: 5 araba
chief: 4 khan
Christian: 4 Uniat
coin: sen, yen 5 dinar
commander: ras 4 amir, emir, rais, reis 5 ameer, emeer
corn: 4 para
cosmetic: 4 kohl
council: 5 Divan
cymbal: zel
deity: Bel
destiny: 6 Kismet
disease: 8 beri-beri
dish: 5 pilau, pilaw
drug: 6 heroin 7 hashish
drum: 7 anacara
dulcimer: 6 santir
dwelling: dar
emperor: 6 sultan
fan: ogi
fish: tai
food: 4 rice 5 salep
garment: aba
gate: dar
guitar: 5 sitar
inn: 5 serai
liquor: 4 sake, saki
litter: 5 dooli, dooly 6 dooley, doolie
lute: tar
manservant: 5 hamal
mansion: 5 yamen
market: 5 bazar 6 bazaar
measure: dra, mao
measure of weight: 4 kati, rotl, tael 5 abbas, bhaar, catty, picul 6 cantar, kantar, miskal
money of account: rin
monkey: 7 macaque
musical instrument: tar 5 sitar, surna, suray 6 santir 7 samisen
name: Ali
nomad: 5 Tatar 6 Tartar
nurse: 4 amah, ayah
oboe: 5 surna, suray
pagoda: tea
people: Tai, Tho 4 Sere 5 Asian, Tatar 6 Indian, Korean, Muslim, Tartar 7 Chinese, Eastern 8 Japanese 9 Easterner, Levantine 10 Mohammedan
pine: 5 matsu
pipe: 7 nargile 8 harghile, nargileh
plane-tree: 7 cheenar
porter: 5 hamal
rest house: 4 khan 5 serai
rice dish: 5 pilaf, pilau, pilaw

rice paste: ame
ruler: 4 amir, emir, khan, shah 5 ameer, calif, emeer 6 caliph, sultan
saber: 6 tulwar 7 tulwaur 8 scimitar
sailing ship: 4 dhow
sailor: 6 lascar
salutation: 5 saheb, salam 6 kowtow, salaam
sash: obi
sauce: soy
sea captain: ras 4 rais, reis
shoe: 6 sandal
silkworm: 6 tussah, tusseh, tusser 7 tussore
slipper: 7 baboosh 8 babouche
smoking apparatus: 7 nargile 8 narghile, nargileh
tamarisk: 4 atle 5 atlee
tambourine: 5 daira
taxi: 7 ricksha 8 rickshaw
tea: cha
title: aga 4 amir, baba 5 pasha 6 huzoor
tower: 6 pagoda
tree: 4 atle 5 atlee
vessel: 4 dhow, saic
wagon: 5 araba
weight: 4 mann, tael 5 artal(pl.)
whip: 6 chabuk 7 chabouk
wind: 7 monsoon
worker: 5 cooly
oriental: 5 pearl 6 bright, ortive, rising 7 eastern, shining 8 lustrous, pellucid, precious 9 ascending, brilliant 11 resplendent
Oriental rug: 4 Baku, Kali 5 Herez, Mahal, Saruk, Senna, Sumak 6 Kashan, Kerman, Kirman, Meshed, Pamiri, Sarouk, Shiraz, Soumak, Tabriz 7 Bokhara, Bukhara, Chinese, Hamadan, Isfahan, Ispahan, Karajas, Meshhed 8 Lerestan, Sedjadeh 9 Kurdistan 10 Kermanshah
pattern: 7 ainaleh
orifice: 4 hole, vent 5 inlet, mouth 6 cavity, outlet 7 chimney, opening, ostiole 8 aperture
in brain: 4 lura
origin: nee 4 rise, root, seed 5 birth, cause, start 6 nature, parent, source 7 genesis, lineage 8 nascence, nascency 9 beginning, inception, naissance, parentage 10 extraction, incunabula(pl.) 11 incunabulum, provenience 12 commencement, fountainhead
foreign: 7 ecdemic
on earth: 7 epigene
original: new 5 first, novel 6 fontal, native, primal, primer 7 primary 8 pristine 9 authentic, inventive, primitive 10 aboriginal 11 fundamental, primigenial
originally: 5 first 9 initially, primarily 10 inherently

originate: 4 coin, make, open, rise 5 arise, begin, breed, cause, found, start 6 create, derive, devise, invent 7 causate, emanate, produce 8 commence, contrive, discover, generate, initiate 9 construct, establish, institute

origination: 7 genesis 9 etymology

originator: 6 author

oriole: *family:* 9 icteridae
golden: 5 pirol 6 loriot

Orion: 5 Rigel 13 constellation
hound: 6 Aratus
slayer: 7 Artemis

orison: 6 prayer, speech 7 praying

oristic: 10 definitive 11 determinate

Orkney Island: *capital:* 8 Kirkwall
fishing ground: 4 haaf
hut: 4 skio
inlet: voe
island: Hoy 6 Pomona, Sanday
land: 4 odal, udal 6 udaler 7 udalman 8 udalborn
largest: 6 Pomona
tower: 5 broch

orle: 6 border, fillet, wreath 7 bearing, chaplet

orlean: 7 annatto

orlop: 4 deck

ormer: 7 abalone

ormolu: 4 gilt, gold 5 alloy 7 varnish

ornament (see also **decoration**): dub, fob, pin 4 etch, gaud, gear, tool, trim, waly 5 adorn, braid, chase, decor, gutta, inlay, wally 6 amulet, attire, bedaub, bedeck, billet, brooch, edging, emboss, enrich, finery, flower 7 agremen, engrave, garnish, spangle, trinket 8 agrement, applique, decorate, flourish, lavalier 9 arabesque, billiment, embellish, embroider, lavaliere 10 decorament, furnishing, habiliment, lavalliere 11 garnishment 13 embellishment
apex: 6 finial
bell-shaped: 9 clochette
Biblical: 4 Urim
boat-shaped: nef
claw-like: 6 griffe
crescent-shaped: 6 lunula 7 lunette, lunulae(pl.)
delicate: 7 tracery
diamond-shaped: 10 epigonatia(pl.) 11 epigonation
dress: 4 frog, lace 5 jabot 6 sequin, zequin 7 spangle 8 chequeen, zecchino 10 embroidery
flowerlike: 7 rosette
hanging: 6 bangle, fringe, tassel 7 pendant
magical: 6 amulet
mantel: 7 bibelot

neck: 5 chain 6 choker, gorget 8 necklace
pagoda: tee
pendant: 6 anadem, bangle, tassel 7 earring 8 lavalier 9 lavaliere 10 lavalliere
protuberant: 4 boss
scroll-like: 6 volute
silver: 6 tinsel
spiral: 5 helix 7 helices(pl.)
terminal: 6 finial
tufted: 6 pompon, tassel 7 pompoon, rosette

ornamental: 7 elegant 8 fanciful 10 decorative

ornamented: 6 ornate, tawdry 9 elaborate

ornate: gay 4 fine 5 fancy, showy 6 florid 7 aureate, flowery 9 elaborate, unnatural 10 flamboyant 11 overadorned

ornery: 4 mean 7 crabbed 8 stubborn 9 irritable 12 cantankerous

ornithologist: 7 Audubon, birdman

ornithon: 6 aviary

orogeny: 8 upheaval

orotund: 4 full 5 clear, showy 6 mellow, strong 7 pompous 8 resonant 9 bombastic

Orozco specialty: 5 mural

orp: 4 fret, weep

orphan: 5 Annie 9 foundling

orpheum: 7 theater

Orpheus: *birthplace:* 6 Pieria
father: 6 Apollo
instrument: 4 lyre
mother: 8 Calliope
wife: 8 Eurydice

orphrey: 4 band 10 embroidery

orpiment: 7 arsenic

orpit: 7 fretful

orra: odd 10 occasional, unemployed 13 miscellaneous

orris: 4 gimp, lace 5 braid 7 galloon

ort: bit 5 crumb, scrap 6 morsel, refuse 7 leaving, remnant 8 fragment

orthodox: 4 good 6 proper 7 canonic, correct 8 accepted, standard 9 canonical, customary 12 conventional

orthographer: 7 speller

ortive: 7 Eastern

ortolan: 4 bird, rail 7 bunting 8 bobolink, wheatear

ortstein: 7 hardpan

oryx: 7 gazelle, gemsbok 8 antelope

os: 4 bone 5 eskar, esker, mouth 7 opening

Osaka Bay port: 4 Kobe

oscillate: wag 4 rock, sway, vary 5 swing, waver, weave 7 vibrate 9 fluctuate, vacillate

oscillation: 11 trepidation

oscine: 9 scopoline

oscitant: 4 dull 6 drowsy, gaping, sleepy, stupid 7 yawning 8 careless, sluggish 9 apathetic

osculate: 4 buss, kiss
ose: 6 glucid **7** glucide **13** monosaccharid **14** monosaccharide
osier: rod **5** wand **6** basket, sallow, willow **7** dogwood, wilgers
Osiris: *brother:* Set **4** Seth
　crown: **4** atef
　enemy: Set **4** Seth **7** brother
　father: Geb, Keb, Seb
　mother: Nut
　recorder: **5** Thoth
　sister: **4** Isis
　son: **5** Horus **6** Anubis
　wife: **4** Isis
Osmanli: 4 Turk
osmesis: 8 smelling **9** olfaction
osprey: 4 bird, hawk, ossi
ossature: 8 skeleton
osse: 4 dare **7** attempt, presage, promise **8** prophesy **9** recommend, utterance
osseous: 4 bone, bony **6** osteal **10** ossiferous
ossianic: 7 flowery, pompous **9** bombastic
ossicle: 4 bone **5** incus **6** stapes **7** bonelet, malleus
ossifrage: 5 eagle **6** osprey **11** lammergeier
ossify: 6 harden
ossuary: urn **4** tomb **5** vault **10** depository, receptacle
ostend: 4 show **6** reveal **7** exhibit **8** manifest **11** demonstrate
ostensible: 7 seeming **8** apparent, specious **9** pretended, professed
ostensorium: pix, pyx **10** monstrance
ostent: air **4** mien **5** token **7** display, portent **10** appearance **13** manifestation
ostentation: 4 show **5** eclat, flare **6** parade **7** display, flutter, pageant, portent, presage **8** flourish, pretense **9** showiness, spectacle **10** exhibition **11** fanfaronade
ostentatious: 4 arty, loud **5** gaudy, showy **6** sporty **7** obvious, pompous **8** fastuous **9** elaborate, flaunting **11** pretentious
osteoma: 5 tumor
osteria: inn **6** tavern
ostiole: 4 pore **5** stoma **7** orifice, stomata(pl.) **8** aperture
ostler: 7 hostler **9** stableman
ostracize: bar **4** snub **5** exile **6** banish, reject **7** exclude **9** blackball, proscribe **10** expatriate
ostracon: 8 potsherd
ostreger: 8 falconer
ostrich: 4 rhea **5** nandu
　extinct: moa
　feather: boa, boo **5** plume
ostrichlike bird: emu **4** emeu
Otaheite: 6 Tahiti
otalgia: 7 earache
otary: 4 seal

Othello: 4 Moor
　character in play: **6** Bianca, Cassio, Emilia
　friend: **4** Iago
　wife: **9** Desdemona
other: 4 else, more **5** ither(Sc.) **6** former **7** further **9** distinct **9** different **10** additional
　combining form: **5** heter **6** hetero
other-worldly: fey **9** imaginary, spiritual
otherness: 8 alterity **9** diversity
others: 4 rest
　and: **4** et al **6** et alii
otherwise: or **4** else **5** alias **6** aliter **11** differently
otic: 5 aural **8** auditory, oracular **9** auricular
otiose: 4 idle, lazy, vain **6** futile, otiant **7** sterile, useless **8** inactive, indolent, reposing **10** unemployed **11** ineffective, superfluous
otium: 7 leisure
otologist: 6 aurist
ottavino: 7 piccolo
otter: fur **4** fish **6** tackle **7** annatto **8** paravane
　genus: **5** lutra
　sea: **5** kalan
ottoman: 4 pouf, seat **5** couch, divan, stool **6** fabric **9** footstool
Ottoman (see also **Turkey**): **4** Turk **5** Osman **6** Othman
　court: **5** porte
　governor: **5** pasha
　imperial standard: **4** alem
　leader of: **5** Osman
　poetry couplet: **4** beyt
　province: **7** Vilayet
　subject: **4** Raia **5** Rayah
ouachitite: 4 dike
ouakari: 6 monkey
oubliette: 7 dungeon
ouch: oh **5** adorn, bezel, clasp **6** brooch, fibula **7** fibulae(pl.) **8** ornament **11** exclamation
ought: 4 bood, must, zero **6** cipher, naught, nought, should **7** behoove
ouija board part: 10 planchette
ounce: ure **6** weight **7** measure
　sixteenth of: **4** dram
oundy: 4 wavy **5** curly **6** waving
ouphe: elf **6** goblin
our: wir(Sc.) **5** notre(F.) **7** pronoun **10** possessive
ourie: 4 cold **5** dingy **6** dreary
ousia: 6 nature **7** essence **9** substance
oust: bar **5** eject, evict, expel **6** banish, remove **7** dismiss **8** forjudge **9** forejudge **10** dispossess
out: 4 away **5** forth **6** absent, begone, issued **8** external **9** published **12** disadvantage
　at elbows: **5** seedy

of: 4 from 6 dehors

of date: old 5 passe 10 antiquated

of kilter: 4 alop, awry 6 broken

of line: 4 awry 5 askew

of order: 5 amiss, kaput 6 faulty 9 deficient

of place: 5 inept 13 inappropriate

of play: 4 dead, foul

of, prefix for: ec, ex; ect, exo 4 ecto

of sight: 5 great 6 hidden 7 extreme

of sorts: 5 cross 7 peevish

of the ordinary: odd 5 novel 6 unique 7 strange, unusual 8 peculiar, uncommon 9 different

of the way: 5 aside 6 afield, remote 10 farfetched

of this world: 4 fine 6 superb

out-and-out: 5 sheer, utter 6 arrant, wholly 8 absolute, complete

outage: 4 vent 6 outlet 10 suspension 12 interruption

outas: 6 clamor, outcry

outback: 7 country 10 wilderness

outbear: 4 bear, lead 7 sustain 8 outcarry

outbearing: 8 arrogant, demeanor 10 projection

outbraid: 4 draw 5 eject 7 upbraid

outbreak: fit 4 riot 5 burst 6 bust-up, emeute(F.), ruckus, tumult 7 boutade, outcrop, ruction 8 eruption 12 insurrection

new: 13 recrudescence

sudden: 5 spurt

outbreeding: 7 exogamy

outbuilding: 4 barn, shed 5 privy 6 barton, garage, hemmel 8 outhouse 9 backhouse

outburst: 4 fume, gale, gust, rage, tiff 5 blast, brunt, flare 6 blower, blow-up, tirade 7 outcrop, tantrum, torrent 8 eruption, outbreak 9 explosion 10 ebullition, outpouring

outcast: 5 exile, leper, ronin 6 outlet, pariah 7 missile 8 castaway, chandala, rejected, vagabond 10 expatriate

outclass: 5 excel 6 outwit 7 surpass 8 outcraft

outcome: 4 fate 5 issue 6 effect, exitus, outlet, result, sequel, upshot 7 emanate 9 aftermath, emanation 10 conclusion, denouement 11 consequence

outcraft: 8 outclass

outcrop: 5 ledge

outcry: ga; cry, hue, yip 4 bawl, bray, yell 5 alarm, boast, noise, shout 6 clamor, racket, shriek, steven 7 calling, clamour, exclaim, protest, screech, shil-loo 8 proclaim 9 objection 11 lamentation 12 vociferation

outdate: 7 outmode 9 antiquate

outdistance: 7 surpass 8 outstrip

outdo: cap, cow 5 excel 6 defeat, exceed 7 nonplus, surpass 8 overcome

outdoors: 5 forth 7 outside

outer: 5 alien, ectad, ectal, utter 7 foreign, outside 8 exterior, external 10 extraneous

Outer Mongolia capital: 4 Urga 9 Ulan Bator

outermost: 5 final, utter 6 utmost 7 extreme, outward 8 farthest, remotest 9 extremest, outermost, uttermost

outface: 4 defy 6 resist, subdue 8 overcome

outfield: 6 garden 7 pasture 8 moorland

outfit: kit, rig 4 gang, gear, suit, team, unit 5 equip 6 attire, fitout 7 furnish 8 equipage 9 equipment, furniture, grubstake 12 organization 13 paraphernalia

outflow: 4 flux 5 drain 6 efflux, escape

outgo: 4 exit 5 excel, issue, outdo 6 efflux, egress, exceed, outlay, outlet, outrun 7 outcome, outflow, product, surpass 11 expenditure, outdistance

outgrowth: 8 offshoot 9 emergence 11 excrescence

outhouse: 4 shed 5 privy 6 biggin 7 latrine

outing: 4 stay, trip 6 picnic 7 holiday 8 vacation 9 excursion

outknee: 6 bowleg

outlandish: 5 alien 6 exotic, remote 7 bizarre, foreign, strange, uncouth 8 peculiar 9 barbarous, fantastic, grotesque 10 tramontane

outlaw: ban 4 caco 5 exile, exlex, fleme, ronin 6 arrant, bandit, banish 8 fugitate, fugitive, prohibit 9 proscribe 10 disqualify, expatriate

outlawed: 7 illegal, illicit

outlay: 4 cost 7 expense 11 expenditure 12 disbursement

outlet: 4 exit, vent 5 issue 6 egress, escape, exitus 7 opening, outcast, outcome 9 avoidance

outline: map 4 form, plan 5 brief, chart, draft, frame, shape, trace 6 design, figure, sketch 7 contour, profile, summary 8 describe, skeleton, synopsis 9 delineate, perimeter 10 compendium, figuration, silhouette 11 delineation 13 configuration

outlive: 7 outlast, survive

outlook: 4 view 5 vista 6 aspect 7 purview 8 frontage, prospect 10 perception 11 expectation

medical: 9 prognosis

outlying district: 7 purlieu

outmoded: 5 dated, passe 7 antique 8 obsolete, outdated

outpeer: 8 outclass

outpost: 7 station 8 forepost 10 settlement

outpour: 4 flow 7 outflow 8 outburst

output: cut **5** expel, power, yield **6** energy **10** production

outrage: 4 rape **5** abuse **6** insult, offend, ravish **7** abusion, affront, offense, violate

outrageous: 5 enorm **7** heinous, obscene, ungodly **8** flagrant, shocking **9** atrocious, desperate, execrable, monstrous **10** exorbitant

outre: 7 bizarre, strange **9** eccentric **11** exaggerated, extravagant

outreach: 5 cheat **6** exceed, extend, outwit, search **7** deceive, project, surpass **8** protrude **9** overreach

outright: 5 total, whole **6** direct, openly, wholly **8** complete, entirely **9** downright **15** straightforward

outrival: 5 excel **6** outvie **7** eclipse

outroot: 9 eradicate, extirpate

outrun: 4 beat, cote **6** exceed **7** forerun **9** forespeed

outset: 5 start **9** beginning

outshine: 5 blind, excel **6** dazzle, deface **7** distain, surpass

outside: 4 bout, free **8** exterior, external *comb. form:* ect **4** ecto

outsider: 5 alien **8** stranger **9** extranean(Sc.), foreigner

outspoken: 4 bold, free **5** bluff, blunt, broad, frank **6** candid, direct **7** artless **8** explicit **10** unreserved **12** unrestrained

outstanding: big **4** arch, rare **5** famed, noted **6** famous, heroic, marked, unpaid **7** eminent **9** principal, prominent, unsettled **10** noticeable, pre-eminent, projecting **11** conspicuous, exceptional, uncollected, unfulfilled **13** distinguished

outstretched: 5 stent(Sc.) **8** extended

outstrip: cap, top, win **4** best, cote, lead, pass **5** excel, out do **6** exceed **7** devance, surpass **8** distance **9** transcend

outvie: 8 outstrip

outward: 5 ectad, outer, overt **6** exodic, extern, formal **7** extreme, visible **8** apparent, exterior, external, obsolete **9** extrinsic **11** superficial

outweighing: 8 dominant **12** preponderant

outwit: fox **4** balk, best, foil **5** block, check, cross **6** baffle, jockey, thwart **9** checkmate, frustrate **10** circumvent, disappoint

outwork: 6 tenail **7** defense, lunette, ravelin **8** tenaille

ouzel: 4 piet **5** colly, ousel **6** thrush **8** whistler **9** blackbird

oval: 7 ellipse, stadium **8** avelonge **10** elliptical **11** ellipsoidal

ovary: 6 germen

ovate: 9 egg-shaped *inversely:* **7** obovate

ovation: 8 applause **10** exultation

oven: 4 kiln, oast **5** baker **6** calcar **7** furnace *annealing glass:* **4** leer, lehr *goddess of:* **6** Fornax

oven mop: 6 scovel

over: oer, sur(F.), too **4** also, anew, done, uber(G.), upon **5** above, again, clear, ended, extra, vault **6** across, beyond, excess **7** surplus, through **8** finished **9** completed, excessive **10** terminated **11** consummated, superfluous *and above:* **7** besides **11** therewithal *combining form:* sur **5** hyper, super, supra *prefix:* sur **5** super, supra

overabundance: 6 excess **7** surplus **8** plethora

overact: 5 emote **9** burlesque **10** exaggerate

overage: 6 excess **7** surplus

overalls: 5 chaps **10** chaparajos, chapareras, chaparejos **11** chaparreras

overassuming: 4 bold

overbalance: 8 dominate

overbearing: 5 proud **6** lordly **7** haughty **8** arrogant, bullying, insolent, snobbish, subduing **9** imperious **10** disdainful, high-handed **11** dictatorial, domineering, magisterial **12** overpowering, supercilious

overburden: 8 encumber **9** surcharge

overbusy: 5 fussy

overcast: dim, sew **4** bind, dark, dull **5** cloud, heavy **6** cloudy, darken, gloomy, lowery **7** accloud, becloud, clouded

overcharge: gyp **6** excise **9** extortion

overcloud: dim **6** darken **7** obscure

overcoat: 5 benny **6** capote, raglan, slipon(Sc.), ulster **7** paletot(F.), surtout, topcoat **9** balmacaan, greatcoat, inverness **12** chesterfield *close fitting:* **7** surtout *loose:* **6** raglan **7** paletot *sleeveless:* **9** inverness

overcome: awe, get, win **4** beat, best **5** charm, crush, daunt, fordo **6** appall, beaten, craven, defeat, exceed, foredo, master **7** confute, conquer **8** convince, encumber, outstrip, overbear, overturn, suppress, surmount, vanquish **9** overpower, overthrow, overwhelm, prostrate

overcrowded: 9 congested

overdo: 6 exceed **7** exhaust, fatigue **8** overcook, overwork **9** burlesque **10** caricature, exaggerate

overdue: 4 late **5** tardy **7** arrears, belated, delayed

overeager: 8 feverish

overeat: 5 gorge **7** satiate **8** gourmand **10** gluttonize

overfed: 7 fulsome

overflow: 4 slop, swim, teem, vent **5** float, flood, spate, spill **6** abound, debord, deluge, outlet **7** overrun **8** alluvion, inundate

9 abundance, cataclysm 10 ebullience, exuberance

overflowing: 5 awash 7 copious

overgrown: 7 fulsome

overhang: jut 6 beetle 7 project, suspend

overhasty: 4 rash 6 daring 8 headlong

overhaul: 7 examine 8 renovate 9 forereach

overhead: 5 above, aloft 7 expense

overissue: 9 inflation

overjoyed: 6 elated 8 jubilant 9 delighted

overlapping: 8 obvolute 9 imbricate

overlay: cap, lap 4 ceil, coat 5 couch, cover, glaze, plate 6 cravat, spread, veneer 7 encrust, oppress, overlie 8 covering 10 overburden 11 superimpose

overload: 4 glut 6 charge 8 encumber

overloaded: 9 plethoric

overlook: 4 balk, miss, omit, skip 5 forgo 6 acquit, excuse, forego, forget, ignore, manage 7 absolve, condone, inspect, neglect 9 disregard

overlord: 5 liege 6 despot, satrap, tyrant 8 suzerain

overlying: 8 brochant

overman (see also **overseer**): 5 chief 6 leader 7 arbiter, foreman, referee 8 overseer 9 overpower

overmatch: 4 best 6 exceed 7 surpass 8 vanquish

overmodest: 4 prim 7 prudish

overmuch: too 6 excess 7 surplus 9 excessive

overnice: 5 fussy 7 precise 8 dentical 10 fastidious

overplus: 6 excess 7 surplus 9 advantage

overpower: awe 4 rout 5 crush, whelm 6 compel, defeat, deluge, master, subdue 7 conquer 8 convince, entrance, overbear, overcome, vanquish 9 enrapture, overthrow, overwhelm

overpowering: 4 dire 6 fierce 8 dazzling, stunning

overreach: do 5 cheat 6 grease, nobble, outwit 10 circumvent

overready: 7 forward

override: 4 veto 6 defeat 7 nullify

overrule: 4 veto 8 abrogate

overrun: 5 crush 6 infest, ravage, spread 7 destroy 9 overwhelm

overs: 5 boots

overseas address: APO

oversee: 5 watch 6 survey 7 examine, inspect 9 supervise 11 superintend

overseer (see also **overman**): 4 boss 5 ephor(Gk.), grave, reeve 6 bishop, censor, driver, gaffer, grieve 7 baliff, caporal, curator, foreman, manager 8 banksman, martinet 9 inspector 10 acequiador, supervisor 14 superintendent

agricultural: 8 agronome

spiritual: 6 pastor, priest

overshadow: dim 5 cover, dwarf 6 darken 7 eclipse, obscure 8 dominate 9 adumbrate

overshoe: gum 4 boot 6 arctic, galosh, golosh, patten, rubber 7 flapper

overshoot: 6 exceed

oversight: 4 care 5 error, lapse, watch 6 charge 7 blunder, control, mistake 8 omission 9 direction 10 inspection, negligence 11 supervision 12 surveillance 15 superintendence

overskirt: 6 peplum 7 pannier

oversleeve: 6 armlet

overspread: 4 deck, pall 5 brede, cloud, cover 6 deluge

overstate: 7 magnify 10 exaggerate

overstep: 6 exceed 10 transgress

overt: 4 open 6 patent, public 7 obvious 8 apparent, manifest

overtake: 5 catch 6 attain, detect 7 ensnare 9 apprehend, captivate

overtask: 5 drive

overtax: 6 exceed

overthrow: tip 4 dash, down, fell, foil, fold, hurl, raze, rout, ruin, rush 5 allay, evert, fling, upset, worst, wrack 6 defeat, unseat 7 afflict, conquer, destroy, dismiss, ruinate, unhorse 8 confound, demolish, overcome, overturn, reversal, supplant, vanquish 9 discomfit, overpower, overwhelm, prostrate 10 defeasance 11 destruction 12 discomfiture

overtime: 8 extended

overtire: tax

overture: 5 offer, proem 7 opening, prelude 8 aperture, proposal 11 proposition

opera: 8 sinfonia

overturn: tip 4 cave, coup, tilt 5 throw, upset 6 topple 7 capsize, destroy, pervert, reverse, subvert 8 overcome 9 overthrow, overwhelm

overweening: 8 arrogant

overwhelm: 4 bury 5 amaze, cover, crush, drouk, swamp 6 defeat, deluge, engulf, quench 7 confute, conquer, engross, oppress 8 astonish, inundate, overturn, submerge 9 overpower, overthrow

overword: 7 refrain

Ovid: *birthplace:* 5 Sulmo

burial place: 4 Tomi 5 Tomis

work: 5 Fasti 7 Tristia 13 Metamorphoses

ovine: 5 sheep 9 sheeplike

female: ewe

ovoid: 5 ovate 7 egg-like, obovoid, oviform

ovule: egg 4 seed 6 embryo 7 gemmule, seedlet

integument: 7 primine

ovum: *egg:* 4 seed 5 spore

combining form: ova
owala tree: 4 bobo
owe: due, own 7 possess 9 attribute
ower: 6 debtor
owl: 4 lulu, momo 5 wekau 7 boobook, harfang, woolert 8 billy-wix, moreport 10 gillhooter, hob-houchin
  barn: 5 madge
  call: 4 hoot
  genus of: 5 ninox
  pert. to: 8 strigine
  plumed eye area of: 4 disk
  short-eared: 4 momo
  small: 4 utum 6 howlet
  young: 4 utum 5 owlet
Owl and Pussycat author: 4 Lear
own: ain(Sc.), owe 4 avow, have, hold, nain(Sc.) 5 admit 7 concede, confess, possess 9 recognize 11 acknowledge
ownership: 5 title 7 tenancy 8 dominium 11 condominium 14 proprietorship
owse: 8 quagmire
ox: yak 4 anoa, aver, beef, buff, gaur, musk, reem, zebu 5 bison, bugle, gayal, steer, tsine 6 bovine 7 banteng, buffalo 8 seladang 9 quadruped
  extinct: 4 urus
  harness: 4 yoke
  pert. to: 5 bovid 6 bovine 7 taurine
  small: 4 runt
  stall: 5 boose
  wild: 4 gaur 8 seladang
oxalis: oca 5 plant 6 sorrel
oxen: 6 cattle
  yoke: 4 span
oxeye: 4 boce 5 aster 6 dunlin
oxford: 4 shoe 5 cloth 7 college 10 saddleshoe, university
Oxford: *Earl of:* 6 Harley 7 Asquith
  examination: 6 greats
  library: 8 Bodleian
  officer: 5 bedel 6 beadle

  scholar: 4 demy
  scholarship: 6 Rhodes
oxhead: 4 dolt 9 blockhead
oxidation: 4 rust
oxide: *aluminum:* 7 alumina
  barium: 6 baryta
  calcium: 4 lime
  hydrocarbon radical: 5 ether
  iron: 4 rust
  sodium: 4 soda
  strontium: 8 strontia
oxidize: 4 rust 7 calcine
oxlike: 6 bovine 7 taurine
oxlip: 8 primrose
oxter: arm 6 armpit
oxtongue: 7 alkanet, bugloss
oxyacantha: 8 hawthorn
oxygen: gas
  acid: 7 chloric 9 sulphuric
  allotropic: 5 ozone
  binary: 5 oxide
oxygenate: 6 aerate
oyez: 4 hear 6 attend 9 attention
oyster: 6 huitre 7 bivalve, mollusk
  bed: 4 park, stew 5 layer 6 clair 9 oysterage
  eggs: 5 spawn
  fossil: 9 ostracite
  gatherer: 7 tongman
  genus: 6 ostrea
  kind of: 6 native 9 bluepoint
  phylum: 8 mollusca
  rake: 5 tongs
  shell: 4 husk, test 5 shuck
  spawn: 5 culch 6 cultch
  tree: 8 mangrove
  young: 4 spat
oyster catcher: 4 bird 5 tirma
oyster grass: 4 kelp
oyster plant: 7 salsify
oysterfish: 6 tautog 8 toadfish
Oz books author: 4 Baum
Ozark State: 8 Missouri
ozone: air

P

pa, pah: dad, paw 4 fort, papa 5 daddy 6 father 7 village 8 stockade 10 settlement

pabulum: 4 food, fuel, prog 6 cereal 7 aliment, support 9 nutriment 10 sustenance

pac, pack 4 boot 8 moccasin

paca: 4 cavy, lava 5 agout, labba 6 rodent

pace: way 4 clip, gait, lope, pass, rack, rate, step, trot, walk 5 amble, canto, speed, tempo, tread 6 canter, gallop, strait 7 channel, chapter, dogtrot, measure, passage 8 platform 10 passageway

pacer: 5 horse 9 pacemaker

pachisi: 4 game, ludo

pachyderm: 8 elephant 10 rhinoceros 12 hippopotamus

pacific: 4 calm, meek, mild 5 irene 6 irenic, placid, serene 8 irenical, peaceful, tranquil 9 appeasing, peaceable 12 conciliatory

Pacific coast state: 6 Oregon 10 California, Washington

Pacific Islands: *archipelago:* Aru 4 Sulu 5 Malay, Samoa 6 Tulagi

bird: 4 kagu

cloth: 4 tapa

collective name: 7 Oceania

grass: 4 neti

military base: 4 Guam

region: 9 Polynesia

tree: kou 4 ipil, taro 7 dasheen, madrona, madrono 8 eddyroot

Pacific Ocean: *archipelago:* 4 Sulu 5 Malay, Samoa

discoverer: 6 Balboa

island: Ie; Lae, Yap 4 Guam, Truk, Wake 5 Leyte, Samoa 6 Tahiti 8 Tasmania 9 Carolines, Marquesas

shark: 4 mako

"stepping stones": 9 Aleutians

pacifier: sop 4 ring 6 nipple

pacifist: 8 appeaser, peacenik

pacify: 4 calm, ease, lull 5 abate, allay, quiet, still 6 serene, soften, soothe 7 appease, assuage, mollify, placate 8 mitigate 9 alleviate, reconcile 10 conciliate, propitiate 11 tranquilize

pack: wad 4 bale, cram, gang, load, stow, tamp 5 crowd, flock, horde, steve, store, truss 6 barrel, bundle, duffle, embale, encase, fardel, impact, wallet 8 knapsack

of cards: 4 deck

pack animal: ass 4 mule 5 burro, camel, horse, llama 6 donkey

package: pad 4 bale 6 bundle, packet, parcel

packer: 5 baler, roper 6 canner

packet: 4 boat 6 bundle, parcel

packing: 4 rags 5 gauze, paper, straw, waste 7 stowage

box: 5 crate

clay: 4 lute

material: 6 gasket, baline 9 excelsior

water-tight: 6 gasket

packing plant: 7 cannery

Pacolet: 5 dwarf, horse

pact: 6 cartel, treaty 7 bargain, compact 8 alliance, contract, covenant 9 agreement

Pactolian: 6 golden

pad: mat, wad, way 4 boss, path, road, walk 5 quilt, stuff, tramp 6 basket, buffer, jockey, pillow, tablet, trudge 7 bolster, bombast, cushion, footpad 8 footfall 10 highwayman

padcloth: 7 housing 11 saddlecloth

padding: 7 packing, robbery, wadding 8 stuffing

paddle: oar, row 4 spud, wade 5 aloof 6 dabble, toddle 8 lumpfish

paddlefish: 9 spadefish 10 shovel-fish

paddock: lot 4 frog, park 5 field 6 sledge 9 enclosure

paddockstone: 10 greenstone

paddockstool: 9 toadstool

Paddy: 8 Irishman

paddywhack: 4 beat, blow 9 thrashing

Paderewski opera: 5 Manru

padlock: 4 lock 6 fasten 7 closing 8 fastener

padre: 4 monk 6 cleric, father, priest 8 chaplain

padrona: 8 landlady, mistress

padrone: 6 master, patron 8 landlord 9 innkeeper

paean, pean: ode 4 hymn, song 6 praise

pagan: 6 ethnic, paynim 7 heathen, infidel 8 idolator 10 idolatrous, unbeliever 11 nonbeliever

god: 4 Baal, idol

page: boy 4 call, leaf 5 child, folio, sheet 6 donzel, summon, varlet 7 footboy, servant 8 henchboy, henchman 9 attendant, messenger

beginning: 4 leaf 7 flyleaf

book: 5 folio 6 cahier

lady: 8 escudero

left-hand: vo 5 verso

number: 5 folio 10 pagination

paper: 5 sheet

reverse: 5 verso

right-hand: 5 recto

title: 5 unwan 6 rubric

pageant: 4 pomp, show 6 parade 7 tableau 8 aquacade 9 spectacle 10 exhibition, procession

pageantry: 8 splendor 11 ostentation

Pagliacci: *character:* 5 Nedda, Tonio

composer: 11 Leoncavallo

pagoda: taa 6 temple 10 kryailteyo 11 summerhouse

finial or ornament: tee

pagurian: 4 crab

pah: pa 5 nasty 6 humbug 8 improper

paha: 4 hill 5 ridge

Pahlavi's realm: 4 Iran

paideutics: 8 pedagogy

pail: can, cog(Sc.), pan, soa, soe 4 beat, bowk, gawn, meal, trug, 5 bowie, cogue(Sc.), eshin, skeel 6 bucket, coggie(Sc.), harass, piggin, situla(L.), thrash, vessel 7 collock, situlae(pl.) 8 cannikin

paillette: 7 spangle

pain: 4 ache, agra, care, cark, harm, hurt, pang 5 agony, cramp, grief, sting, thraw(Sc.), throe, wound 6 grieve, twinge 7 afflict, algesis, anguish, penalty, torture, travail, trouble 8 disquiet, distress 9 suffering 10 affliction, algophilia, discomfort, punishment

comb. form: 5 algia

darting: 6 twinge

dull: 4 ache

pert. to: 6 asonal 7 algetic

relayer: 5 nerve

sensitiveness to: 7 algesia

painful: 4 sare, sore 5 angry 6 bitter 7 irksome 8 exacting 9 difficult, laborious 11 painstaking

painkiller: 6 opiate 7 anodyne, aspirin 8 reliever 9 analgesic, paregoric

pains: 4 care, work 5 labor 6 effort 7 trouble 8 exertion

painstaking: 4 busy 7 careful 8 diligent, exacting 9 assiduous, elaborate, laborious

paint: 4 coat, daub, gaud, limn 5 color, feign, fucus, rouge, stain 6 bedaub, depict, enamel 7 besmear, portray, pretend 8 decorate, disguise

combining form: 5 picto

glossy: 6 enamel

painted: 5 pinto 6 fucate 10 artificial, variegated

painter: 6 artist 7 artiste, panther, workman 9 decorator

painting: oil 5 mural 6 canvas 10 watercolor

equipment: 5 brush, easel, paint 6 canvas, pallet 7 palette

medium: oil 7 gouache, tempera 10 watercolor

one-color: 8 monotint 10 monochrome

plaster: 5 secco 6 fresco

sacred: 5 pieta

scenic: 5 scape 8 seascape 9 cityscape, landscape

small: 9 miniature

style: 5 genre

three panels: 8 triptych

wall: 5 mural, panel 6 fresco

pair: duo, two 4 case, diad, duad, dyad, mate, span, team, yoke 5 brace, match, unite 6 couple

paisano: 7 peasant 10 countryman

Paisley: 5 shawl 6 design, fabric 7 pattern

Pakistan: *city or town:* Dir 6 Lahore, Multan, Quetta

province: 4 Sind, Swat 5 Kalat, Sindh 6 Khelat 11 Baluchistan

pass: 5 Bolan

pal: 4 ally, chum, pard 5 buddy, crony 6 cobber, digger, friend 7 comrade, partner 9 associate, companion 10 accomplice 11 confederate

palace: 5 court, serai 6 castle, palais(F.) 7 alcazar, edifice, mansion 8 Alcalzar 9 pretorium 10 praetorium

officer: 7 paladin 8 palatine

papal: 7 Lateran

paladin: 4 hero, peer 6 knight 8 champion, douzeper

palaestra: 6 school 9 gymnasium

palamate: 9 web-footed

Palamedes: *enemy:* 7 Ulysses

father: 8 Nauplius

mother: 7 Clymene

war: 6 Trojan

Palamon: *rival:* 6 Arcite

wife: 6 Emelye

palanquin: 4 kago 5 dooli, dooly, palki, sedan 6 doolee, dooley, doolie, litter, palkee 10 conveyance

palatable: 5 sapid, tasty 6 savory 8 delicate, pleasing 9 agreeable, delicious 10 acceptable

render: 4 salt 5 spice 6 season

palatal: 5 front, velar 8 gutteral 9 consonant

palate: 5 taste 6 relish 7 gourmet

pert. to: 6 uranic

soft: 4 cion, vela(pl.) 5 uvula, velum

palatial: 5 large 6 ornate 7 stately 11 magnificent

palantine: 4 cape 7 officer, paladin 8 palatial

palaver: 4 talk 6 debate, glaver, parley 7 chatter, flatter, wheedle 8 cajolery, flattery 10 conference 12 conversation

pale: dim, wan 4 ashy, fade, grey, gull, lily, pall, sick 5 ashen, blake, blate, bleak, faint, fence, livid, lurid, stake, stick, white 6 anemic, blanch, chalky, feeble, pallid, pastel, picket, region, sickly, whiten 7 anaemic, enclose, ghastly, haggard, insipid, obscure, whitish 8 encircle, etiolate 9 colorless

paleness: 6 pallor

Palestine: *animal:* 5 daman

ancient city: 8 Ashkelon

coin: mil 5 pound

conquerors: 5 Turks

country: 4 Edom 9 Philistia

god: 4 Baal

Jewish: 5 Erets, Eretz 7 Yisrael, Yisroel

lake: 5 Merom 7 Galilee 8 Tiberias

landmark: Dan

language: 7 Aramaic

mammal: 5 daman

measure: 5 cubit, donum 6 sacred

mountain: 4 Ebal, Nebo, Zion 6 Carmel, Gilead, Hermon, Moriah, Olives, Pisgah 7 Gerizim 8 Jebel Tur

part: 4 Gaza 5 Haifa 6 Canaan, Ghazze

people: 7 Amorite

plain: 6 Sharon

port: 4 Acre 5 Haifa, Jaffa

province: 7 Galilee

region: 5 Perea 6 Bashan

river: 6 Jordan

town: Tob 4 Bire, Cana, Gaza 5 Endor 6 Ghazze 7 Samaria 9 Jerusalem

weight: 4 rotl, zuza

palestra, palaestra: 6 school 9 gymnasium

palet: 5 quoit

paletot: 8 overcoat 9 greatcoat

palfrey: 5 horse

palimpsest: 6 tablet 9 parchment

palindrome: 7 sotadic

paling: 4 pale 5 fence, flake, limit, stake 6 picket 7 fencing 9 enclosure

palinode: 10 retraction 11 recantation

Palinurus: 9 steersman

palisade: 5 cliff, fence, stake 7 barrier, enclose, fortify, furnish 8 espalier, surround 9 implement

pall: 4 bore, cloy, pale, sate 5 cloak, cloth, faint, qualm, stale, weary 6 mantle, nausea 7 disgust, satiate 8 animetta, covering

Pall Mall site: 7 West End

palladium symbol: Pd

pallbearer: 6 bearer

pallet: bed, cot, pad 5 couch, quilt 7 blanket 8 mattress, plancher 9 headpiece

palliard: 6 beggar, lecher, rascal 8 vagabond

palliasse: 6 pallet 8 mattress

palliate: 4 ease, hide 5 cloak, cover, gloss, gloze 6 lessen, soften 7 conceal, shelter 8 disguise, mitigate 9 alleviate, exculpate, extenuate

pallid: wan 4 ashy, pale, paly 5 bleak, white 7 ghastly 9 colorless

pallion: bit 5 piece 6 pellet

pallium: 4 band, pall 5 cloak 6 mantle 8 himation

palm: 4 hide 6 palmus(Lat.), thenar, trophy 7 conceal

betel nut: 5 areca, bonga

beverage: 5 assai

cabbage: 8 palmetto

climbing: 6 rattan

coconut: 4 coco

fan-leafed: 7 talipat, talipot, taliput 8 palmetto

feather: 5 howea 6 gomuti 7 urucuri, urucury

fiber: tal 4 buri 6 raffia

food: nut 4 sago 5 fruit

juice: 4 nipa, sura 5 taree, toddy

kind: ti 4 jara 5 assai, royal, tucum 6 bacaba, tucuma 7 babassu, jaggery, tokopat 8 bangalow

leaf: ola, ole 4 olay, olla 5 frond

low: 5 bussu 6 trooly, trouie, ubussu

palmyra: ola, ole, tal 4 brab, olla 6 ronier

pert. to: 6 palmar 8 frondous 10 palmaceous

pith: 4 sago

reader: 7 palmist

sap: 5 toddy

seeds: 4 nipa

spiny: 6 grigri, grugru

starch: 4 sago

stem: 4 cane 5 ratan 6 rattan

stemless: 5 curua

thatch: 4 nipa 9 barriguda

wing-leaved: 6 cohune

palm-leaf mat: 4 yapa

palm off: 5 foist
palma: 5 yucca
palmary: 5 chief, palmy 6 palmar 8 superior 9 principal 10 pre-eminent, victorious
palmate: 4 flat 5 broad, lobed 6 palmed, webbed
palmed: 7 palmate
palmer: 5 louse 6 stroll, travel, votary, wander 7 pilgrim 15 prestidigitator
Palmetto State: 13 South Carolina
palmistry: 10 chirognomy, chiromancy
practicer: 11 chiromancer
palmodic: 5 jerky
palms down: 7 pronate
palmy: 7 palmary 10 prosperous, triumphant 11 flourishing
Palmyra's queen: 7 Zenobia
palmyra tree: 4 brab 7 talipot
palp: 6 feeler, palpus 7 flatter 8 tentacle
palpable: 4 rank 5 plain 6 patent 7 audible, evident, obvious, tactile 8 apparent, distinct, manifest, tangible 10 noticeable, perceptive 12 recognizable
palpebra: 6 eyelid
palpebrate: 4 wink
palpitation: 4 beat, pant 7 flicker, flutter 9 pulsation, quivering, throbbing, trembling
palsied: 5 shaky 7 shaking 9 paralyzed, tottering, trembling
palter: fib, lie 6 babble, haggle, mumble, trifle 7 chatter, quibble 10 equivocate 11 prevaricate
paltock: 6 jacket 7 doublet
paltry: 4 bald, bare, base, mean, puny, vile 5 footy, petty, trash 6 chetif, flimsy, trashy 7 pitiful, rubbish, trivial 8 picayune, trifling 9 worthless 10 despicable 12 contemptible 13 insignificant
paludal: 6 marshy 8 paludine
pampas: 6 plains
cat: 6 pajero
pamper: pet 4 baby, cram, delt(Sc.), glut 5 spoil 6 caress, cocker, coddle, cosher, cosset, cuddle, dandle, fondle, posset 7 cherish, cockney, gratify, indulge, satiate, forwean
pamphagous: 10 omnivorous
pamphlet: 5 tract 6 folder 7 booklet, catalog, leaflet 8 brochure 9 catalogue
pan: fit, tab 4 part, wash 5 agree, basin, unite 6 frache(F.), lappet, vessel 7 cranium, hardpan, portion, subsoil 8 brainpan, ridicule 9 criticize 10 acetabulum
coal burner: 5 grill 7 brazier
frying: 6 spider 7 skillet
gold-washing: 4 tina 5 batea
Pan: 6 Faunus
father: 6 Hermes

instrument: 4 pipe, reed
place of worship: 7 Arcadia
son: 7 Silenus 8 Seilenos
panacea: 4 cure 6 elixir, remedy 7 allheal, cure-all, heal-all 8 nepenthe 10 catholicon 11 panchreston
panache: 5 plume
panachure: 8 mottling
panal: 7 biscuit
Panama: hat 6 Darien
city: 5 Colon 6 Panama 9 Aspinwall, Cristobal
coin: 6 balboa
gulf: 6 Darien
measure: 7 celemin
river: 5 Sambu, Tuira 7 Chagres
rubber: 8 Castilla
tree: 4 yaya 6 alfaje, cativo
Panama Canal: *dam and locks:* 5 Gatun 10 Miraflores
engineer: 9 de Lesseps
lake: 5 Gatun
port: 5 Colon 9 Cristobal
panatela: 5 cigar
panax: 4 herb
pancake: 5 arepa(Sp.), flawn 6 blintz, fraise, froise 7 blintze, fritter, hotcake 8 flapjack 11 griddlecake
delicate: 5 crepe
panda: wah 6 animal 7 bearcat
pandemonium: 5 noise 6 tumult, uproar 8 disorder 9 confusion
pander: 4 bawd, pimp 5 cater 7 whiskin 8 procurer 9 go-between, procuress
Pandora: *brother:* 10 Prometheus
daughter: 6 Pyrrha
husband: 10 Epimetheus
pane: 5 glass 7 section
panegyric: 5 eloge, elogy 6 eulogy, praise 7 encomia(pl.), oration, tribute, writing 8 encomium 9 discourse, laudation
panel: 4 jury 5 group 6 tympan 8 decorate
paneling: 4 wall 7 ceiling
panfish: 4 crab, king 9 horseshoe
pang: 4 ache, cram, fill, gird, pain, tang 5 agony, spasm, stuff, throe 6 twinge 7 anguish, travail 8 paroxysm 9 heartache
Pangim native: 4 Goan
pangolin: 5 manis 8 anteater, edentate
order: 9 pholidota
panhandle: beg 5 cadge
Panhandle State: 12 West Virginia
panic: 4 fear, fray, funk 5 alarm, chaos, scare 6 fright, terror 8 stampede 13 consternation
panjandrum: 7 magnate 9 personage
pannier, panier: bag, ped 5 seron 6 basket, dorsel, dorser, dosser, pantry 9 overskirt

horse: **6** curagh **7** currach, currack, curragh, currock

panoply: 5 armor **6** armour

panorama: 4 view **5** scene, sweep, vista **7** picture, scenery **9** cyclorama

panpipe: 6 syrinx **8** zampogna

pansy: 9 heartease **10** heartsease

pant: 4 ache, beat, blow, gasp, puff **5** heave, throb, yearn **7** pulsate **9** palpitate **11** palpitation

Pantagruel: *companion:* **7** Panurge
father: **9** Gargantua
mother: **7** Badebec

pantalan: 5 wharf **8** platform

Panthea's husband: 9 Abradatus

pantheon: 6 temple

panther: cat **4** pard, puma **6** cougar, jaguar **7** leopard, painter

pantile: 4 tile **7** biscuit **8** hardtack

panting: 8 anhelose, anhelous **10** anhelation

pantomimist: 4 mime **5** actor **7** Marceau

pantry: 4 cave **5** ambry **6** closet, larder **7** buttery, pannier, pantler **8** cupboard

pants: 5 jeans **7** drawers **8** trousers **10** pantaloons
leather: **5** chaps **10** chaparajos, chapareras, chaperejos, lederhosen(G.) **11** chaparreras

panuelo: 6 collar, ruffle **8** kerchief **9** neckcloth

pap: 4 teat **6** nipple **8** emulsion, mammilla

papa pa; dad, paw, pop **6** baboon, father, potato, priest **7** vulture

papal (see also **Pope**): **9** apostolic **10** pontifical

papal court: see **5** curia

papaya: 5 papaw **6** pawpaw

paper: 5 essay, theme **6** cartel, report **7** journal, writing **8** document **9** monograph, newspaper, wallpaper **10** periodical **11** credentials, examination **12** dissertation **13** unsubstantial
absorbent: **7** blotter **9** towelling
case: **4** file **5** folio **6** binder
collection: **7** dossier
currency: **5** scrip
damaged: **5** broke, casse, salle **6** cassie
design: **9** watermark
detachable: tab **4** stub **6** coupon
fine: **5** linen **6** vellum
folded once: **5** folio
gummed: **5** label, stamp **6** paster **7** sticker
hard: **6** pelure
large-size: **5** atlas
legal: **4** writ
medicinal: **6** charta
official: **5** targe **8** document
pad: **6** tablet
piece: **5** scrip, sheet

postage-stamp: **6** pelure
pulp: **4** ulla
quantity: **4** page, ream **5** quire, sheet **6** bundle
scroll: **9** parchment
size: cap **4** copy, demi, demy, pott **5** atlas, crown, folio, legal **7** bastard, emperor **8** foolscap, imperial **9** colombier
thin: **6** pelure, tissue **9** onionskin
untrimmed edge: **6** deckle
writing-size: cap **8** foolscap

paper money: 4 bill, cash **7** lettuce **8** frogskin **9** greenback

papilla: bud **6** pimple

papist: 8 Catholic

papoose: 4 baby

pappy: pa; dad, paw **4** papa, soft **5** mushy **6** father

papule: 6 pimple

papyrus: 4 reed **6** biblos, biblus, scroll **7** bulrush
repository: **5** capsa

par: by **5** equal **6** normal **7** average **8** equality **9** enclosure **11** equivalence

par value: 4 face **7** nominal

parable: 4 myth, tale **5** fable, story **6** apolog, byword **7** byspell **8** allegory, apologue, forbysen **10** comparison, similitude

parabola: arc **5** curve

parachute: *material:* **4** silk **5** nylon
part: **4** pack **6** canopy **7** harness, ripcord

paraclete: 6 helper **7** pleader **8** advocate, consoler **9** comforter **11** intercessor

parade: 4 pomp, show, walk **5** march, strut **6** flaunt, review, stroll **7** cortege, display, exhibit, marshal **8** ceremony, flourish, grandeur, splendor **9** advertise, pageantry, promenade, strollers **10** callithump, pretension, procession **12** magnificence

paradigm: 5 model **7** example, pattern

Paradise: 4 Eden **5** bliss **6** Aidenn, heaven **7** Elysium
Buddhist: **4** Jodo
fool's: **5** limbo
Muslim: **5** Jenna
river: **5** Gihon

Paradise Lost angel: 5 Ariel, Uriel

paraffin: 6 alkane

paragon: gem **4** type **5** ideal, model **7** pattern **9** nonpariel

paragram: pun

paragraph: 4 item, sign **5** caput **7** initial **8** material

Paraguay: *city:* Ita **8** Asuncion(c.) **9** Paraguari, Villa Rica
coin: **4** peso
Indian: **7** Guarani

measure: pie 4 line, lino, vara 5 legua, linea 6 cordel, cuadra, cuarta, fanega, league

money: 7 guarani

river: Apa 6 Parana 8 Paraguay 9 Tibiquare

tea: 4 mate 5 yerba

weight: 7 quintal

parakeet: 6 parrot, wellat 8 paraquet 10 budgerygah 11 budgereegah

parallel: 4 even 5 along, equal, match 8 analogue 10 collateral 11 counterpart

render: 9 collimate

parallelism: 6 simile 10 similarity 11 resemblance 14 correspondence

parallelogram: 5 rhomb 6 oblong, square 9 rectangle

paralogist: 7 sophist

paralysis: 5 cramp, palsy 7 paresis 10 holoplexia 11 monoparesis

with: 7 paretic 9 paralytic

paralyzed: 4 numb 7 palsied 8 benumbed, crippled

paramount: 5 above, chief, ruler 7 capital, supreme 8 dominant, superior, suzerain 10 pre-eminent, proprietor

lord: 5 liege

paramour: 5 leman, lover, wooer 6 amoret, friend 10 sweetheart

female: 7 hetaera, hetaira 8 mistress

paranomasia: pun

paranymph: 10 bridesmaid

parapet: 4 butt, wall 5 redan 7 bulwark, railing, rampart 10 breastwork 12 embattlement 13 fortification

part of: 5 crete

V-shaped: 5 redan

paraphernalia: 4 gear 9 apparatus, equipment, trappings 10 belongings 11 furnishings

paraphrase: 6 reword 7 version 9 translate 11 translation

parasite: bug, bur 4 burr, moss 5 leech, toady, virus 6 fungus, sponge 7 sponger 8 hanger-on 9 mistletoe, sycophant

animal: 8 entozoan

blood: 4 tryp

marine: 6 remora, sponge

plant: 9 entophyte

trout: sug

parasol: 8 sunshade, umbrella 11 bumbershoot

paratrooper cry: 8 Geronimo

paravane: 5 otter

Parcae: See **Fates**

parcel: lot 4 deal, mete, pack, part 5 bulse, bunch, group, piece 6 bundle, divide, packet 7 package, portion 8 fragment 10 collection, distribute

parch: dry 4 burn, sear 5 roast, toast 6 scorch 7 bristle, brustle, graddan, shrivel

parched: 4 arid, sere 5 fiery 6 gizzen, torrid

parchment (see also **paper, scroll**): 6 charta

book cover: 5 forel 6 forrel

fine: vel 6 vellum

manuscript: 10 palimpsest

piece: 8 membrane

roll: 4 pell 6 scroll

pard: pal 4 chum 5 tiger 7 leopard, panther, partner 9 companion 10 camelopard

pardesi: 9 foreigner, outlander

pardie, pardi: 6 indeed, surely, verily 9 certainly

pardo: 7 mulatto

pardon: 5 mercy, remit, spare 6 assoil, excuse 7 absolve, amnesty, condone, forgive 8 reprieve, tolerate 9 exculpate, remission 10 absolution, indulgence 11 forgiveness

general: 7 amnesty

stall: 12 confessional

pardonable: 6 venial 9 excusable

pare: cut 4 chip, peel, skin 5 shave 6 reduce, remove, resect 7 curtail, whittle 8 diminish 11 decorticate

paregoric: 7 anodyne

pareil: 4 mate 5 equal 8 equality

parel: 7 apparel 11 mantelpiece

parella, parelle: 6 lichen

parent: dad, dam 4 mama, papa, sire 5 daddy, mater(L.), pater 6 author, father, mother, origin 7 forbear, genitor 8 ancestor, begetter, forebear, guardian, producer 10 forefather, progenitor

parentage: 5 birth 6 family, origin 10 extraction, parenthood

parget: 4 coat 6 gypsum 7 plaster 8 decorate 9 whitewash

pariah: 7 Ishmael, outcast

parian: 6 marble, market 9 porcelain

Paris: *airport:* 4 Orly

district: 7 Auteuil

father: 5 Priam

first bishop: 5 Denis, Denys

mother: 6 Hecuba

palace: 6 Elysee, Louvre 9 Tuileries

police: 5 flics 6 Surete

river: 5 Seine

Roman name: 7 Lutetia

stock exchange: 6 bourse

suburb: 5 Passy

subway: 5 metro

thug: 6 apache

wife: 6 Oenone

parish: 12 congregation

head: 6 pastor, priest 8 minister

officer: 10 borsholder

official: 9 vestryman

paristhmion: 6 tonsil

parity: 7 analogy 8 equality 10 similarity 11 resemblance

park: hay 4 stop 7 commons, paddock 10 playground

parlance: 4 talk 7 diction 9 discourse 11 phraseology 12 conversation

parlay: 5 wager 6 paroli

parley: 5 speak, treat, utter 6 confer, paroli 7 discuss, palaver 9 discourse 10 conference, discussion 12 conversation

parliament: 4 diet 5 senat(F.) 7 council 8 congress, converse 9 parleying 10 conference

member: 4 lord

parlous: 4 keen 5 risky 6 clever, shrewd 7 cunning 8 perilous 9 dangerous 11 exceedingly, excessively, mischievous 13 disconcerting

parnassian: 4 poet

paroch: 9 clergyman

parody: 4 skit 6 satire 8 travesty 9 burlesque, imitation 10 caricature

paroemia: 7 proverb

parole: 6 pledge 7 promise

paronomasia: pun 12 agnomination

paroxysm: fit 4 pang 5 agony, spasm, throe 6 access, attack, orgasm 8 epitasis, outburst 9 agitation 10 convulsion 12 exacerbation

parrot: ara 4 copy, echo, jako, lory 5 arara, mimic, polly 6 repeat, tiriba 7 corella 8 cockatoo, lorikeet, lovebird, parakeet 9 cockateel, cockatiel

disease: 11 psittacosis

genus: 9 psittacus

gray: 4 jako

green: 5 cagit

hawk: hia

like: 5 arine 11 psittaceous

long-tailed: 5 macaw

monk: 4 loro

owl: 4 kaka 6 kakapo

part of bill: 4 cere

sheep-killing: kea

small: 8 lovebird, parakeet

parrot fish: 4 scar 5 lania 6 scarus 9 labroidea

parry: 4 fend, ward 5 avoid, block, evade 6 thwart 7 deflect, evasion

parse: 7 analyse, analyze, diagram 8 construe

Parsee: See **Parsi**

Parsi: 11 Zoroastrian

holy book: 6 Avesta

priest: 5 mobed 6 dastur 7 destour, dustoor

parsimonious: 4 mean, near 5 close, scant, spare 6 frugal, narrow, skimpy, sordid, stingy 7 miserly, sparing 8 covetous, grasping, wretched 9 illiberal, mercenary, niggardly, penurious 10 avaricious, economical, ungenerous 17 narrowheartedness

parsley: 5 cumin 6 eltrot

derivative: 5 apiol 6 apiole

genus: 12 petroselinum

relative: 6 celery

parsley camphor: 6 apiole

parson: 6 rector 8 minister, preacher 9 clergyman, guidepost

parson bird: poe, tui 4 rook

parson-in-the-pulpit: 10 cuckoopint

parsonage: 5 manse 7 rectory 9 pastorium

part (see also **parts**): 4 deal, dole, half, role, rove, side, some, twin 5 piece, quota, sever, share 6 behalf, canton, cleave, depart, detail, divide, member, sunder 7 disjoin, element, portion, section, segment 8 alienate, disperse, dissever, disunite, division, estrange, fraction, fragment, separate 9 abteilung(G.), apportion, dismember 10 department 11 constituent

baglike: sac

basic: 4 core, pith 7 essence

central: 4 core 5 focus, solar 6 nuclei(pl.) 7 nucleus

choice: 5 cream, elite 6 marrow 7 essence

coarse: 5 dregs

comb. form: 4 demi, hemi, meri, semi

distinct: 4 unit 7 article

essential: 4 core, gist, pith 6 factor

final: 5 shank

hardest: 5 brunt

highest: top 4 apex 5 crest 6 summit

inmost: 4 core 5 heart 6 center

main: 4 body 5 trunk

minor: bit, cog

moving: 5 rotor

narrow: 4 neck

revolving: 5 rotor 7 rotator

root-like: 7 radicle

small: bit, jot 4 atom, iota, mite 5 tithe 6 detail, moiety 7 snippet

suddenly: 4 rend, snap

uppermost: top 4 peak 6 upside 7 topside

part with: 4 give, lose, sell 5 leave 6 donate 7 abandon

partage: 4 part 5 share 7 portion 8 division

partake: 4 bite 5 share 6 divide 11 participate

of: use

partan: 4 crab

parted: 7 partite

parten: 6 impart 7 partake

Parthian ruler: 7 Arsaces

parti-colored: 4 pied 7 piebald 10 variegated

partial: 4 half, part 6 biased, unfair 7 colored, halfway 8 coloured, inclined, one-sided, partisan 10 fractional, incomplete, prejudiced 11 predilected, predisposed
prefix: 4 demi, semi
participant: 5 party 8 partisan 10 accomplice 12 participator 13 participating
participate: 4 join, side 5 enter, share 7 compete, partake 9 cooperate
particle: ace, bit, dot, gru, jot 4 atom, grue, iota, mite, mote, whit 5 fleck, grain, shred, speck 6 smidge, tittle 7 smidgen, smidgin 8 smidgeon, smitchin
affirmative: yes
burnt: 6 cinder
co-ordinating: or
cosmic: 5 meson
electrified: ion 5 anion 6 proton
incandescent: 5 spark
minute: jot, ort, ray 4 atom, iota, mite, mote 5 grain, speck 7 granule, ramenta(pl.) 8 molecule, ramentum 9 scintilla
negative: nor, not
pluvial: 4 drop
small: see *minute* above
particular: 4 item, nice 5 fussy, thing 6 detail, minute 7 article, careful, correct, precise, special, unusual 8 accurate, concrete, detailed, especial, exacting, itemized, specific 10 fastidious, noteworthy 11 scrumptious 12 circumstance 13 extraordinary 14 circumstantial
particularly: 9 expressly
parting: 5 death 8 farewell 11 leavetaking
parting shot: 5 taunt
partisan: 4 pike 5 staff 6 biased, fautor 7 devotee 8 adherent, follower, partizan 9 truncheon 10 factionary, factioneer, interested
unwavering: 6 zealot 8 stalwart
partite: 6 parted 7 divided 9 separated
partition: 4 wall 5 septa(pl.) 6 divide, screen, septum 7 enclose, portion, scantle 8 cleavage, division 9 severance 10 distribute, enterclose, separation 11 compartment 13 apportionment
partitioned: 7 septate
partlet: hen 5 woman
partner: pal 4 ally, half, mate, wife 5 butty 6 fellow, sharer 7 comrade, consort, husband 8 camarada 9 associate, coadjutor, colleague, companion 10 accomplice 11 confederate, participant
comedian's: 6 stooge
paid: 6 gigolo
partnership: hui 4 firm 7 cahoots, company 14 compagnieschap(D.)
partridge: 4 yutu 5 titar 6 chukar, chukor, seesee 7 tinamou 9 francolin

flock: 5 covey
young: 7 cheeper 8 squealer
partridgeberry: 9 snowberry
parts (see also **part**): *innermost:* 10 penetralia
together: 9 adhesions
totality: 5 unity
two: 6 binary
parturition: 7 travail 8 delivery 10 childbirth
party (see also **political party**): bal(F.) 4 clan, drum, sect, side 5 cabal, group 6 comite, fiesta, person 7 company, faction 9 gathering 10 detachment 11 association, combination 12 participator
afternoon: tea 9 reception
evening: 4 ball 6 soiree
guilty: 7 culprit
men's: 4 stag 6 smoker
reconnaissance: 6 patrol
seashore: 6 picnic 8 clambake
party man: 8 partisan
parure: 5 adorn 6 paring 7 apparel, peeling 8 ornament
parvenu: 4 snob 6 arrive 7 upstart 9 arriviste 12 nouveauriche, nouvellerich
Pascal work: 7 Pensees
Pasch, Pascha: 6 Easter 8 Passover 10 Good Friday
paschal: 4 lamb 6 supper 8 Passover 11 celebration
pasear: 4 walk 6 airing 9 promenade
pasha: dey 4 emir
territory: 8 pachalic, pashalic, pashalik
Pashur's father: 9 Malchijah
Pasiphae: *children:* 7 Ariadne, Phaedra
husband: 5 Minos
pasqueflower: 6 badger 10 badgerweed
pasquinade: 5 squib 6 satire 7 lampoon, pasquil
pass: go; col, end, gap 4 abra, beal(Sc.), comp, cove, fare, ghat, hand, lane, pace, step, wend 5 canto, enact, ghaut, gorge, hurry, kotal, lapse, lunge, occur, relay, smite, spend, utter, yodel 6 billet, convey, defile, elapse, exceed, happen, passus, permit, ticket, twofer 7 allonge, approve, devolve, passage, undergo 8 beallach, surmount 10 abjudicate, permission 11 Annie Oakley 13 complimentary
slowly: 4 drag
without touching: 5 clear
pass around: 5 skirt 6 detour
pass away: die 6 expire, perish, vanish 8 transfer 9 disappear, surrender
pass by: 4 cote, omit, skip 6 forego, ignore 8 overlook 9 disregard
pass off: con 5 foist

pass over: die 4 omit, skip 5 cross 6 elapse, expire, excuse, ignore 8 overlook, transfer, traverse 9 disregard
lightly: 4 skim
quickly: 4 scan, scud
smoothly: 5 elide
pass through: 5 cross 6 pierce 7 pervade 8 permeate, traverse 9 penetrate
pass up: 6 reject 7 decline 9 disregard
passable: fit 4 fair, soso 7 genuine 8 adequate, mediocre, moderate, traveled 9 navigable, navigated, tolerable, traversed 10 admissable
passage: gat, gut, wro 4 adit, belt, door, duct, exit, fare, flue, ford, gang, gate, hall, iter, lane, pass, pawn, race, ramp, slip 5 aisle, allee, alley, alure, atria(pl.), entry, going, gorge, meuse 6 access, arcade, atrium, avenue, burrow, course, defile, egress, strait, travel, tunnel, voyage 7 channel, couloir, estuary, gangway, itinera(pl.), journey, transit 8 aqueduct, corridor, crossing 9 ventiduct 10 bottleneck 12 thoroughfare
air: 4 flue 9 ventiduct
between two walls: 5 slype
covered: 6 arcade
literary: 4 text 7 excerpt 9 quotation
mine: 5 stope
one outlet: 7 impasse 8 cul-de-sac
scripture: 4 text
subterranean: 4 mine 6 tunnel 8 cuniculi(pl.) 9 cuniculus
passageway: 5 aisle
passant: 4 past 7 current, cursory, passing, walking 9 ephemeral, excelling 10 proceeding, surpassing, transitory
passe: 4 aged, past, worn 5 faded 7 demoded 8 obsolete, outmoded 10 antiquated 12 old-fashioned 13 superannuated
passementerie: 8 trimming
passenger: 4 fare 8 ferryman, traveler, wayfarer
passerby: 9 saunterer
passerine bird: 7 sparrow 8 starling
passing: 7 cursory 8 elapsing, fleeting 9 departing, ephemeral, exceeding 10 pre-eminent, transitory, surpassing
passion (see also **mania**): ire 4 fire, fury, heat, love, lust, raga, rage, zeal 5 anger, ardor 6 affect, choler, desire, fervor 7 emotion, feeling, fervour 8 appetite 9 calenture, martyrdom 10 affliction, enthusiasm
passion flower: 6 maypop
family: 14 passifloraceae
passionate: 4 fond 6 fervid, fierce 7 amorous, flaming, peppery 8 frenetic 9 irascible, phrenetic 11 impassioned 12 affectionate

passionless: 4 cold 6 freddo(It.)
passive: 5 inert, stoic 6 stolid 7 patient 8 inactive, yielding 9 apathetic, impassive 10 submissive
passover: 5 phase
Passover: 5 Pesah 6 Pesach
bread: 5 matzo 6 matzos 7 matzoth 8 afikomen
festival: 5 Seder
pert. to: 7 paschal
songs of praise: 6 hallel
story: 7 haggada 8 haggadah
passport: 5 conge 6 dustuk 7 dustuck 8 furlough
endorsement: 4 visa, vise
passus: 4 pace, part, step 5 canto 8 division
password: 11 countersign
past: by; ago 4 gone, yore 5 after, agone, aside, ended, since 6 behind, bygone 8 foregone 9 completed, foregoing 11 antecedents
immediate: 9 yesterday
pert. to: 8 historic
tense: 11 perteritive
pasta: 7 ravioli 8 macaroni 9 spaghetti
paste: hit, pap 4 beat, blow, duff, glue, pate 5 cream, dough, false, punch, stick 6 attach, batter, fasten, strass 7 filling 8 adhesive, mucilage 9 imitation
aromatic: 6 pastil 7 pastile 8 pastille
dried: 7 guarana
pasteboard: 4 card, sham 6 flimsy
pastel: 6 crayon 7 picture
pastern: 6 hobble, hopple, tether 7 shackle
Pasternak novel: 7 Zhivago
pasticcio: 4 olio 6 jumble, medley 9 patchwork, potpourri 10 hodgepodge
pastime: 4 game 5 hobby, sport 9 amusement, diversion 10 yesteryear 13 entertainment
pastor: 4 herd 5 angel, rabbi 6 curate, keeper, priest, rector 7 dominie 8 guardian, minister, shepherd 9 clergyman
pastoral: 4 poem 5 drama, rural 7 bucolic, idyllic, romance
god: Pan
pert. to: 8 agrestic, geoponic
pipe: 4 reed
place: 7 Arcadia
poem: 4 idyl 5 idyll 7 eclogue, georgic
pastry (see also **cake, pie**): pie 4 flan, huff, tart 6 eclair 7 carcake(Sc.), strudel 8 napoleon, turnover
garnish: 5 cream, fruit 8 meringue
shell: 7 dariole, timbale
pasturage: 4 gang 6 eatage, forage 7 herbage

pasture: hag, ham, ing, lea 4 heaf, hoga 5 agist, drift, grass, graze, veldt 6 meadow, saeter 7 grazing, vaccary 8 herdwick 9 grassland 10 agostadero

god: Pan

pasturer: 7 grazier 8 herdsman

pasty: pie 6 doughy

pasty cement: 6 mastic

pat: apt, dab, tap 4 blow 5 fitly, fixed, impel, throw 6 caress, soothe, strike, stroke, timely 7 apropos, fitting, readily 8 suitable 9 immovable, opportune, pertinent 10 seasonable 12 commendation

Patagonia: *cavy:* 4 mara

deity: 7 Setebos

rodent: 4 cavy, mara

tree: 6 alerce, alerse

patamar: 7 courier 9 messenger

patand: 4 base 6 plinth

patch: bit 4 mend, vamp 5 bodge, clout, clump, cover, piece, scrap 6 blotch, cobble, dollop, parcel, revamp, solder 7 clobber, remnant

of woods: 5 motte

patchwork: 5 cento 6 jumble, scraps 9 fragments 10 hodgepodge

pate: pie, top 4 head 5 crown, paste, pasty, patty 6 badger, noggin

patella: pan 4 dish, vase 7 kneecap, kneepan

paten: 4 arca, disc, dish, disk 5 plate 6 vessel

patent: 4 arca, open 6 berat(Orient), overt, plain 7 evident, license, obvious 8 apparent, archives, enduring, manifest 9 available, franchise 10 accessible, university 12 unobstructed

notice: 6 caveat

pater: 6 father, priest

paterissa: 7 crosier

paternal: 8 fatherly

kinsman: 6 agnate

paternity: 6 father, origin 10 authorship, fatherhood 12 fatherliness

path: pad, rut, way 4 fare, lane, line, road, walk 5 alley, byway, going, piste, route, track, trail 6 camino, casaun, comino, course, groove 7 footway, highway, towpath

hill: 4 berm 5 berme 6 roddin 7 borstal, rodding 8 borstall

math: 5 locus

pathetic: sad 5 teary 7 pitiful 8 stirring 9 affecting

pathic: 7 passive 8 catamite 9 suffering

pathological: 4 sick 6 morbid

pathway: run 4 lane, path 6 course, roddin 7 rodding

patience: 4 calm 8 stoicism 9 composure, endurance, fortitude 10 submission 11 forbearance, resignation 12 acquiescence

patient: 4 case, meek 6 bovine

patinize: 6 patine

patio: 5 court 9 courtyard

patisserie: 4 shop 6 pastry

patois: 6 Creole 7 dialect

patriarch: 4 Enos, Levi, Nasi, Noah 5 elder 7 ancient 9 venerable

patrician: 5 noble 10 aristocrat 12 aristocratic

patrimony: 8 ancestry, heritage

patriot: 10 chauvinist, countryman 11 compatriate

song: 6 anthem 7 America

patrocinium: 9 patronage 10 protection

patrol: 5 guard, scout, watch 7 protect 10 detachment

patrolman: cop 5 guard 9 inspector, policeman

patron: 5 buyer, guest 6 client, fautor 7 sponsor 8 advocate, champion, customer, defender, guardian 9 protector, supporter 10 benefactor

stock exchange: 5 buyer 6 seller, trader

patron saint: *of beggars:* 5 Giles

of children: 8 Nicholas

of cripples: 5 Giles

of England: 6 George

of Ireland: 7 Patrick

of lawyers: 4 Ives, Yves

of musicians: 7 Cecilia

of sailors: 5 Elmo

of Scotland: 6 Andrew

patronage: 5 aegis, favor 6 custom, favour 7 auspice, fomento 8 business 10 assistance 13 encouragement

patronize: 5 deign 10 condescend

patroon: 5 tract 6 patron 9 supporter 10 proprietor

land: 5 manor

patten: 4 base, clog, foot, shoe 5 skate, stand, stilt 6 sandal 7 support 8 overshoe, snowshoe

patter: 4 cant, talk 5 lingo 6 jargon 7 blatter, chatter

pattern: 4 form, norm, plan 5 bysen, draft, epure, guide, ideal, model, plaid 6 checks, design, format, former, sample, stripe 7 example,, project, stencil, templet 8 exemplar, forbysen, paradigm, specimen, template 9 archetype, ensampler, precedent

patulous: 4 open 8 expanded 9 distended, spreading

paucity: 4 lack 6 dearth 7 fewness 8 exiguity, scarcity 13 insufficiency

paughty: 4 pert 5 saucy 7 haughty

Paul: *associate:* 5 Demas, Titus

birthplace: 6 Tarsus

companion: 5 Silas 7 Artemas 8 Barnabas

original name: 4 Saul

place of conversion: 8 Damascus
pauldron: 5 armor 6 splint
paunch: 5 belly, rumen 7 abdomen, stomach 8 potbelly 10 disembowel, eviscerate
pauper: 6 beggar 8 indigent
pause: 4 halt, lull, rest, stop, wait 5 abide, break, cease, delay, demur, dwell, hover, selah, tarry 6 breach, breath, falter, stance 7 caesura, respite 8 breather, caesurae(pl.), hesitate, intermit 9 cessation 10 hesitation 12 intermission, interruption
paut: paw 4 poke 5 stamp 6 finger
pavane: 5 dance
pave: lay 4 path, stud, tile 5 cover, floor 6 causey, cobble, smooth 7 overlay, prepare 10 facilitate, macadamize
pavid: 5 timid 6 afraid 7 fearful
pavilion: 4 flag, tent 5 kiosk 6 canopy, ensign, litter 8 covering 9 gloriette
paving: 4 flag, sett 5 block, brick, dalle, paver, stone 6 cobble, Tarmac 7 asphalt 9 flagstone
pavis: 5 cover 6 shield 7 protect
pavo: 7 peacock 13 constellation
paw: pud, toe 4 foot, gaum, hand, maul, paty 5 patte 6 fumble, handle, pattee 7 crubeen, flipper 8 forefoot
pawky: sly 4 arch, bold 5 canny, saucy 6 crafty, lively, shrewd 7 cunning, forward
pawl: cog, dog 4 bolt, sear, tent, trip 5 catch, click 6 detent, pallet, tongue 7 ratchet
pawn: 4 gage, hock, soak 6 lumber, pledge 7 counter, hostage, peacock 8 chessman, guaranty 11 impignorate
pawnbroker: 6 broker
Pawnee: 6 Indian
rite: 4 hako
pawnie: 7 peacock
pawpaw: 5 papaw 6 papaya 7 immoral, naughty 8 indecent 11 bushwhacker 15 euphemistically
pax: 5 board, peace 6 friend, tablet 10 friendship, osculatory
pay: fee, tip 4 ante, foot, meet, rent, wage 5 repay 6 defray, reward, salary 7 imburse, requite, satisfy, stipend, tribute 9 indemnify, reimburse 10 compensate, recompense, remunerate 11 retribution 12 compensation
attention: 4 heed 6 listen
back: 6 rebate, refund 9 reimburse, retaliate
extra: 5 batta, bonus 8 kickback
for: buy 4 rent 8 purchase
homage: 5 adore, honor
out: 5 spend 6 expend 8 disburse 10 distribute
up: 4 ante 6 settle 9 liquidate

payable: due 5 owing 11 outstanding
paying: 10 profitable
paymaster: 6 bakshi, bukshi, purser 7 bukshee(Ind.) 8 buckshee 9 treasurer
payment: cro, fee, tax 4 bill, dole, dues, duty, feal, fine, gale, levy, toll 5 gavel, price 6 pledge, rebate, return, reward, tariff 7 alimony, annuity, customs, pension, stipend, trewage, tuition 8 defrayal, requital 9 acquittal, allowance, discharge, honoraria(pl.) 10 honorarium, recompense, remittance 12 compensation, contribution
demand: dun 4 bill
evade: 4 bilk 7 default
failure: 13 nonredemption
immediate: 4 cash 9 alcontado(Sp.)
on delivery: COD
press for: dun
without: 4 free 6 gratis
paynim: 5 pagan 7 heathen, infidel 10 Mohammedan
payoff: fix 5 bribe 6 climax 9 reckoning 10 settlement
payola: 5 bribe
payong: 8 umbrella
paysage: 7 picture 9 landscape
Pb: 4 lead
pea: dal 4 gram, seed 5 arhar, chick, cicer, pease 6 gandul, legume, pigeon 7 carmele, catjang 8 garvanro 12 peavetchling
dove: 7 zenaida
family: 8 fabaceae
finch: 9 chaffinch
flour: 9 Erbswurst
pod: 5 quash
sausage: 9 Erbswurst
seeds: 5 pulse
shaped: 8 pisiform
vine: 8 earthpea
peaberry: 11 coffeeberry
peabird: 6 oriole 7 wryneck
peace: pax(L.), paz(Sp.) 4 calm, ease, liss, rest 5 amity, grith, lisse, quiet 6 repose 7 concord, harmony 8 ataraxia, security, serenity 9 armistice, heartease 10 heartsease 11 tranquility
goddess: 5 Irene
pledge: 11 Frankpledge
symbol: 4 dove, toga 5 olive
peace pipe: 7 calumet
peaceable: 6 gentle 7 pacific, solomon 11 undisturbed
peaceful: 4 calm 5 still 6 irenic, placid 7 halcyon 8 irenical 11 undisturbed
peach: 4 blab 6 accuse, betray, indict, inform 7 impeach, whittle
family: 12 amygdalaceae
grafted on quince: 9 melocoton

kind: 6 Carman, Crosby, Salwey 7 Elberta 8 Crawford, quandang, quandong, quantong 9 freestone, nectarine 10 clingstone
origin: 5 China
stone: 7 putamen
peachwort: 9 persicary
peachy: 4 fine, nice 9 beautiful, excellent
peacock: mao 4 pavo, pawn
fan: 9 flabellum
feather fiber: 4 marl
female: 6 peahen
pert. to: 8 pavonine
tail spot: eye
peacock bittern: sun
peacock blue: 4 paon 7 pigment
peacock butterfly: io 4 kiho
peacock fish: 6 wrasse
peacock flower: 9 poinciana
peacock heron: 7 bittern
peacock ore: 7 bornite 12 chalcopyrite
peafowl: 6 peahen 7 peacock
peag, peage: tax 4 toll 5 beads 6 pedage, wampum
peak: Alp, ben, pic(F.), top, tor 4 acme, apex, cima, cusp, dent, dolt, pico(Sp.) 5 crest, crown, point, slink, sneak, steal 6 shrink, summit 7 epitome, maximum 8 aiguille, headland, pinnacle 9 ascendant, ascendent, simpleton 10 promontory
ice: 5 serac
ornament: epi 6 finial
rocky: alp 4 crag
snow-capped: 7 calotte
peaked: wan 4 pale, thin 5 drawn 6 picked, sickly 9 emaciated
peal: 4 clap, ring, toll 5 chime 6 appeal, shovel 7 resound, summons, thunder 8 carillon
Peale Island: 4 Habe
pean, paean: ode 4 hymn, song
peanut: 4 mani 5 pinda 6 goober, pindal 7 beennut 8 earthnut, earthpea, grassnut, katchung
pear: 4 bosc 5 melon 6 beurre, burrel, warden, winter 7 kieffer, prickly 8 ambrette, Bartlett, bergamot 9 alligator 10 chaumontel
squash: 5 perry 7 chayote
pear-shaped: 8 pyriform
pearl: gem 5 nacre, onion 6 bouton, orient 9 margarite
artificial: 6 olivet
of great luster: 6 orient
seed: 7 aliofar
pearl blush: 7 rosetan
pearl moss: 9 carrageen
Pearl of Antilles: 4 Cuba
pearl opal: 9 cacholong
pearlbird: 6 barbet

pearlweed: 6 sagina 8 sealwort
pearlwort: 6 sagina
pearly: 8 nacreous
peart: 4 pert
peasant: 4 bond, boor, hind, kern(Ir.), kopi, peon, ryot, serf 5 churl, kerne(Ir.), knave, kulak, swain 6 cotman, cottar, cotter, farmer, fellah, rascal, rustic 7 bondman, laborer, paisano(Sp.) 9 chopstick, contadino(It.) 10 countryman
crop sharing: 7 metayer
pease: pea 5 quiet 6 pacify 7 appease 9 reconcile
pease brose: 7 pottage 8 porridge
peaseweep: See **peesweep**
pease crow: 4 tern
peashooter: 6 blower 7 blowgun 11 beanshooter
peat: gor(Ir.), pet 4 fuel, turf 6 lawyer, minion 7 darling 8 favorite 11 combustible
bog: 4 cess, moss
cutter: 5 piner(Sc.)
spade: 5 slane
peatwood: 11 loosestrife
peau d'ange: 6 fabric, finish 9 angelskin
peavey, peavy: 4 hook 5 lever
peba: 9 armadillo
pebble: 5 scree, stone 6 gravel, quartz, sycite 7 chuckie, crystal 10 chuckstone
pebble-shaped: 9 calciform
peccadillo: 5 fault 7 offense 8 mischief
peccant: 6 morbid, sinner 7 corrupt, sinning 9 incorrect, unhealthy
peccary: 6 warree 7 tagassu, tayassu 8 javelina
pech: 4 pant, sigh 6 breath 7 breathe
pecht: 4 pict 5 fairy, gnome, pygmy
peck: dab, dot, nip 4 bill, carp, food, hole, jerk, kiss 5 pitch, prick, throw 6 nibble, stroke 7 chimble, measure
at: nag 4 twit 5 tease 6 attack, harass
four: bu. 6 bushel
pecker: 4 nose 5 eater 6 feeder 7 courage, spirits 10 resolution, woodpecker
pectase: 6 enzyme
peculate: 5 steal 6 misuse 8 embezzle 11 appropriate
peculiar: odd 5 queer 6 unique 7 curious, special, strange, unusual 8 especial, singular 9 eccentric, exclusive 10 particular 11 distinctive 14 characteristic
combining form: 4 idio
peculiarity: 4 kink 5 quirk, trait, twist 6 idiasm 9 attribute 12 idiosyncracy
of expression: 5 idiom 6 idioma, idiome
pecuniary: 9 financial
ped: 6 basket, hamper, panier 7 pannier
pedagogue: 5 tutor 6 pedant 7 dominie, teacher 12 schoolmaster

pedal: 5 lever 7 treadle
coupler: 7 tirasse
piano: 7 celeste
pedant: 4 prig 5 dunce, tutor 6 dorbel, purist, tassel 9 pedagogue 12 bluestocking, schoolmaster
pedantic: 7 bookish 8 teaching 10 didascalic, moralistic
peddle: 4 hawk, sell 5 cadge, trant 6 higgle, meddle, piddle, retail 7 colport
peddler: 5 faker 6 broker, coster, duffer, hawker, seller 7 camelot, chapman 8 huckster, pitchman 12 carpetbagger, costermonger
pedestal: 4 anta, base 6 pillar, podium 7 support 10 foundation
part: die 4 dado 5 socle 6 plinth, quadra
put on: 7 idolize 8 enshrine
pedestrian: ped 4 dull, slow 6 hoofer, walker 7 footman, prosaic 11 commonplace 13 unimaginative
pedicel: ray 4 stem 5 scape, stalk 8 peduncle 9 footstalk
umbel: ray
pedigree: 6 stemma 7 descent, lineage 8 ancestry, stemmata 9 genealogy
pedometer: 8 odograph 12 perambulator
pedum: 5 crook, staff
peduncle: 7 pedicel
peek: 4 peep
peekaboo: 4 game 6 bopeep, peep-bo 7 peep-eye
peel: 4 bark, harl, hull, pare, rind, skin 5 flipe, slipe, stake, strip 6 shovel 7 undress 8 palisade, stockade 11 decorticate
peeler: 4 crab 5 bobby, corer 7 hustler 8 pillager 9 policeman
peeling: 4 rind, skin 6 paring
peep: pry, spy 4 peek, peer, pule, skeg 5 cheep, chirp, dekko, glint, snoop, tweet 6 glance, squeak
hawk: 7 kestrel
show: 5 raree
peeper: eye, Tom 4 frog
peepeye: 8 peekaboo
peephole: 4 hole 6 eyelet 7 crevice, eyehole
peeping: 4 nosy 5 nosey 11 inquisitive
peer: pry, vis. 4 duke, earl, fear, fere, gaze, look, lord, mate, peep 5 baron, equal, feere, gloze, match, noble, rival, stare, stime(Sc.), styme(Sc.), thane(Sc.) 6 appear, fellow 7 compeer, comrade, marquis 8 nobleman, superior, viscount 9 associate, companion 12 contemporary
residence: 6 barony
Peer Gynt: *author:* 5 Ibsen
character: 4 King 6 Anitra
composer: 5 Grieg
mother: Ase

peerage: 4 rank 7 dignity
peerdom: 8 equality
peerless: 9 matchless, nonpareil, unrivaled 11 superlative
peesoreh: 7 meminna
peesweep: 5 pewit 7 lapwing 10 greenfinch
peetweet: 9 sandpiper
peeve: irk 6 grudge, nettle 8 irritate 9 annoyance
peevish: 5 cross, techy, testy, wemod 6 crusty, hipped, snarly, sullen, touchy 7 crabbed, frecket, fretful, froward, pettish, spleeny, waspish 8 captious, choleric, crotched, frampoid, petulant, sawshach, snappish 9 fractious, impatient, irascible, irritable, plaintive, splenetic 10 ill-humored 11 caper-noited, contentious, disgruntled
peewee: 4 bird, lark 7 lapwing
peg: fix, hob, nob, nog, pin 4 plug, scob, step 5 cleat, dowel, drink, perch, piton, prong, spill, stake, throw, tooth 6 degree, dowell, marker, reason 7 pretext, support 8 fastener
pega, pagador: 6 remora
pegall: 6 basket
Pegasus: *rider:* 11 Bellerophon
source: 6 Medusa
Peggotty's niece: 5 Emily
Pego: See **Burma**
peho: 8 morepork
peignoir: 4 gown 5 dress 6 kimono 7 wrapper 8 negligee 9 housecoat 12 dressing-gown
peise: 4 blow 5 force, poise 6 impact, weight 7 balance, measure, oppress
pelage: fur 4 hair, pelt
pelagic: 6 marine 7 aquatic, oceanic 9 thalassic
Peleg: *father:* 4 Eber
son: Reu
Peleus: *brother:* 7 Telamon
father: 6 Aeacus
son: 7 Pelides 8 Achilles
wife: 6 Thetis
pelf: rob 4 gain 5 booty, lucre, money, spoil, trash 6 pilfer, refuse, riches, wealth 7 despoil, rubbish
pelham: bit
Pelican State 9 Louisiana
pelike: jar 4 vase 7 amphora 8 amphorae
pell: 4 pelt
pellar: 6 wizard 8 conjurer
pellet: wad 4 ball, pill, shot 5 bolus, stone 6 bullet, pilule 7 granule
pellicle: 4 film, scum, skin 5 crust 7 cuticle
pellock: 8 porpoise
pellucid: 5 clear 6 bright, limpid 7 crystal 11 crystalline, translucent, transparent

pelmet: 7 valance
Peloponnesus: *city:* **6** Sparta
people: **7** Moreote
river god: **7** Alpheus
Pelops: *father:* **8** Tantalus
son: **6** Atreus **8** Thyestes
wife: **10** Hippodamia
pelota: 7 jai-alai
pelt: fur **4** beat, blow, cast, dash, fell, hide,
hurl, pell, push, skin **5** fitch, flung, hurry,
stone **6** gallop, hasten, pelage, refuse,
strike, thrust **7** rawhide, rubbish **8** woolfell
dealer: **7** furrier
peltast: 7 soldier
peltmonger: 7 furrier
peltry: 4 furs **5** pelts
peludo: 9 armadillo
pelvis: *bone:* **4** ilia **5** ilium, pubes **7** ischium
pert. to: **5** iliac
pen: cot, cub, get, mew, pin, sty **4** bolt, cage,
coop, fold, jail, yard **5** bught, crawl, hutch,
kraal, quill, write **6** bought, corral, cruive,
fasten, hurdle, indite, record, stylus, zareba **7** calamus, compose, confine, zareeba
9 enclosure **12** penitentiary
kind: ink **8** fountain **9** ball-point **12** stylo-
graphic
point: neb, nib **4** stub
seller: **9** stationer
pen-like: 7 styloid
pen name (see also **nickname, pseud-**
onym)**: 6** anonym **9** pseudonym **10** nom de
plume
Francois Arouet: **8** Voltaire
Henri Beyle: **8** Stendhal
Charlotte Bronte: **10** Currer Bell
Emily Bronte: **9** Ellis Bell
Samuel Clemens: **9** Mark Twain
Charles Dickens: Boz
Charles Dodgson: **12** Lewis Carroll
Amandine Dupin: **10** George Sand
Mary Ann Evans: **11** George Eliot
Benjamin Franklin: **11** Poor Richard
Charles Lamb: **4** Elia
Alexei Peshkov: **10** Maxim Gorky
Jean Baptiste Poquelin: **7** Moliere
William S. Porter: **6** O. Henry
Jacques Thibault: **13** Anatole France
Louis Viaud: **10** Pierre Loti
pen text: 5 ronde
penal: 8 punitive, punitory
penalize: 4 fine **5** mulct **6** punish
penalty: 4 fine, loss, pain **5** mulct **6** amende,
amerce **7** forfeit **8** hardship **10** forfeiture,
punishment **12** disadvantage
pay: aby **4** abye

penance: 6 sorrow **7** remorse **9** atonement,
penitence, suffering **10** contrition, repentance
pencel: 4 flag **6** pennon **8** streamer **9** pen-
noncel
penchant: 4 bent **5** taste **6** liking **7** leaning
8 fondness **10** attraction **11** inclination
pencil: red, wad **4** blue, lead, wadd **8** charcoal **9** eversharp **10** mechanical
pert. to: **6** desmic
worn-down: **4** stub
pendant, pendent: bob, jag **4** jagg, pend,
tail **5** aglet **6** aiglet, tassel **7** pensile, support **8** gamaliel, lavalier **9** lavaliere, pendulous, suspended, undecided
pending: 6 during
pendulous: lop **7** hanging **8** swinging
Penelope: *father:* **7** Icarius
father-in-law **7** Laertes
husband: **7** Ulysses **8** Odysseus
suitor: **7** Agelaus
penetralia: 6 secret **7** privacy
penetrate: 4 bore, dive, gore, stab **5** break,
enter, imbue **6** fathom, ficche, pierce **7** discern, pervade **8** permeate **9** insinuate, perforate **10** understand
penetrating: 5 acute, sharp **6** astute,
shrewd, shrill, subtle **7** knowing **8** incisive
9 sagacious **10** insightful **11** clairvoyant **14**
discriminating
penetration: 6 acumen **13** understanding
penguin: auk **6** Johnny
genus: **9** eudyptula
home: **4** pole **7** rookery **10** penguinery
large: **7** emperor
small: **6** Adelie
peninsula: 4 neck **6** penile **10** chersonese
penitence: rue **6** regret **7** remorse **10** contrition, repentance **11** compunction
season of: **4** Lent
penitent: 4 ruer **5** sorry **6** humble
penitentiary: jug, pen **4** jail, stir **5** tench **6**
prison **8** big-house
penman: 6 author, scribe, writer **10** amanu-
enses, amanuensis **12** calligrapher
penmanship: 4 hand **6** script **7** writing
pennant: 4 fane, flag, whip **5** roger **6** cornet,
banner, pennon, pinion **8** streamer **9** banderole
yacht: **6** burgee
pennate: 9 penniform
penniless: 4 poor **5** broke, needy **8** bankrupt
9 insolvent **11** impecunious
pennon: 4 flag, wing **6** banner, pinion **7**
feather, pennant
Pennsylvania: *borough:* **5** Avoca, Sayre **9**
Homestead
coal-mining town: **6** Jermyn
county: **7** Venango

founder of: 4 Penn
people: 5 Amish
port: 4 Erie
sect: 5 Amish
river: 6 Beaver, Lehigh 9 Allegheny, Connemaugh 10 Schuylkill 11 Monongahela, Susquehanna
town: Ono 4 Erie, York 5 Avoca 6 Easton, Sharon 7 Lebanon, Reading 8 Steelton
penny: 5 brown, pence 6 copper, saltee, stiver
penny-pinching: 6 stingy 7 miserly
penology: 11 criminology
Pensees author: 6 Pascal
pensile: 7 pendent
pension: 7 payment, stipend, subsidy, tribute 8 gratuity 9 allowance 10 exhibition
pensive: 5 sober 6 dreamy, musing 7 wistful 10 meditative, melancholy, reflective, thoughtful 13 contemplative
pent: 5 caged 8 confined, enclosed
pentacle: 4 star
pentastitch: 4 poem 6 stanza 7 strophe
Pentateuch: law 4 tora 5 Bible, torah
first book: 7 Genesis
pentene: 7 amylene
Pentheus: *grandfather:* 6 Cadmus
mother: 5 Agave
penthouse: 4 roof, shed 5 aerie 6 hangar 7 pentice 8 dwelling 9 apartment, treehouse
pentyl: 4 amyl
penurious: 4 mean, poor 6 barren, scanty, stingy 7 miserly, wanting 8 indigent 9 destitute 10 avaricious 12 parsimonious
penury: 7 beggary, poverty 9 privation
peon: 4 hand, pawn, serf 5 slave 6 thrall 7 footman, laborer, peasant, soldier 9 attendant, constable, messenger, policeman
state of: 7 peonage
peony: 4 piny 5 plant 6 flower, mouton
people (see also **person**): kin, men 4 folk, gens, herd, pais(law) 5 demos, gentée(Sp.), laity, stock 6 daoine, gentry 7 tilikum-(Ind.) 8 canaglia(It.), canaille(F.), populate, tillicum(Ind.) 11 inhabitants
aggregation: 5 tribe
ancient: 4 Seba 5 Itali, Medes 6 Greeks, Romans 7 Sabines 8 Grecians 9 Assyrians, Egyptians, Etruscans
ape-shaped skull: 9 proghathi
body: 4 race 6 nation 7 society 8 assembly, populace 9 citizenry, community 10 public Rais
group: mob 4 army, band, team 5 corps, crowd, posse 6 chorus, troupe, throng 7 company, coterie 8 assembly 9 orchestra 11 association
headless: 8 Acephali
mythical: 8 Acephali

pert. to: 6 ethnic 7 demotic
present: 5 class, crowd 10 assemblage, attendance 12 congregation
well-bred: 9 gentility
pep: go; vim 4 dash 5 verve, vigor 6 energy, ginger 7 animate, quicken 9 animation, briskness, encourage, stimulate 10 initiative, invigorate, liveliness
peplos: 5 scarf, shawl
peplum: 5 shawl 8 kerchief 9 overskirt
pepo: 5 gourd, melon 6 squash 7 pumpkin 8 cucumber
pepper ava, hot, red 4 kava, siri 5 betel, green, sirih, sweet 7 paprica, paprika 8 capsicum, kavakava, pimiento
beverage: 4 kava 8 kavakava
grass: 5 cress
package: 6 robbin
shrub: 4 cava, kava
species: 5 betel 7 cayenne
pepper-and-salt: 4 gray 7 mottled
pepper picker: 5 Peter, Piper
pepper plant: ava 5 chile, chili 6 chilli
peppermint camphor: 7 menthol
peppery: hot 5 fiery 7 piquant, pungent 8 choleric, spirited, stinging 9 irritable 10 passionate
Pequod's captain: 4 Ahab
per: by 4 each 7 through
per se: 6 itself 8 directly 11 essentially 13 intrinsically
peract: 7 perform
peradventure: hap 5 doubt, maybe 6 chance, mayhap 7 happily, perhaps 8 possibly 11 uncertainty
perambulate: 4 walk 6 ramble, stroll 8 traverse 9 promenade
perambulator: 5 buggy 12 baby-carriage, pushwainling
perceive: see 4 feel, hear, know, note 5 scent, sense, smell, taste, touch 6 behold, descry, divine, notice 7 discern, observe, realize, sensate 8 comprise, comprize 9 apprehend, recognize 10 articulate, comprehend, understand 11 distinguish 12 discriminate
perceivable: 11 perceptible
perceiving: 5 acute
percentage: 4 agio, part 5 share 6 profit 7 portion, rake-off 9 advantage
perceptible: 7 tactile, visible 8 palpable, sensible, tangible 10 cognizable 11 appreciable, discernible, perceivable 12 intelligible
perception: 6 acumen 9 sensation 13 animadversion, consciousness
capable of: 8 sentient
perceptor: 5 tutor
perch: bar, peg, rod, sit 4 fish, jook, mado, okow, pike, pole, pope 5 barse, light, roost,

ruffe, staff **6** alight, sauger, settle, weapon, zingel **9** trumpeter

perchance: 5 haply, maybe **7** perhaps **8** possibly

Percheron: 5 horse

perchers: 7 rooster **10** Incessores

percolate: 4 ooze, seep, sift, silt **5** exude, leach **6** filter, strain

percolator: 6 biggin

percussion instrument: 4 drum, gong, trap **6** cymbal **7** marimba **8** triangle **9** xylophone **10** tambourine **12** glockenspiel

percylite: 7 boleite

perdition: 4 hell, loss, ruin **9** damnation **11** destruction

perdrigon: 4 plum

perdue, perdu: 6 hidden **9** concealed

perdurable: 7 durable, eternal, lasting **8** enduring **9** permanent **11** everlasting

Pere Goriot author: 6 Balzac

peregrinate: 6 travel, wander **7** journey, sojourn **8** traverse

peregrine: 4 hawk **5** alien **6** exotic, falcon **7** foreign, pilgrim, strange

perempt: 5 quash **6** defeat **7** destroy

peremptory: 5 final, utter **7** express **8** absolute, decisive, dogmatic, positive **9** arbitrary, imperious **10** conclusive, imperative **11** dictatorial **13** authoritative

perennial: rue **4** tree **5** carex, liana, liane, peony, plant, sedum **6** banana **8** enduring, geophyte, toadflax **9** continual, permanent, perpetual, unceasing **12** neverfailing

perfect: all **4** fill, fine, holy, pure **5** exact, ideal, right, ripen, sheer, sound, utter, whole **6** entire, finish **7** concoct, correct, improve, plenary, precise, sinless, spheral **8** absolute, accurate, circular, complete, finished, flawless, thorough **9** blameless, elaborate, exquisite, faultless, righteous **10** accomplish, consummate, immaculate, satisfying

combining form: **5** teleo

perfection: 4 acme, pink **5** ideal **7** fulness, paragon **8** fullness, maturity **10** excellence

realm of: **6** Utopia

perfectly: 5 quite **10** altogether

perfecto: 5 cigar

perfervid: 6 ardent

perficient: 6 actual **10** proficient

perfidious: 5 false, snaky **8** disloyal, spiteful **9** dishonest, faithless, felonious **10** traitorous **11** disaffected, treacherous

perfidy: 7 treason **8** apostasy **9** defection, treachery **10** disloyalty, infidelity **13** faithlessness

perforate: eat **4** dock **5** drill, punch **6** pierce, pounce, riddle **9** penetrate, torebrate **10** foraminate

perforation: 4 bore, hole **6** broach, eyelet, tresis **7** stencil **8** aperture

perform: do; act **4** char, fill, full, play **5** chare, dight, enact, exert **6** effect, fulfil, render **7** achieve, execute, exhibit, exploit, fulfill, furnish, gesture **8** transact **10** accomplish, perpetrate

again: **7** re-enact

inadequately: **6** bungle

while moving about: **11** peripatetic

with ceremony: **9** solemnise, solemnize

performance: act **4** deed, feat, show, test, work **5** stunt **6** acting, action, effect **7** benefit, concert, exploit, matinee **8** feasance, function **9** discharge, execution, rendition **10** completion, fulfilment **11** fulfillment **12** consummation **14** accomplishment

daytime: **7** matinee

first: **8** premiere

individual: **4** soli, solo

standard: **5** bogey

performer: 4 doer, moke **5** actor, shine **6** artist, worker **7** artiste **8** executor, thespian

company: **6** troupe

diligent: **5** plier **6** drudge **7** plugger

low-grade: **9** hamfatter

supplementary: **7** ripieno

top-notch: ace **4** star

perfume: 4 atar, nose, otto **5** aroma, attar, cense, irone, myrrh, ottar, scent, smell **6** chypre, flavor **7** essence, flavour, incense, odorize, sweeten **8** bergamot, fumigate **9** fragrance

base: **4** musk **5** civet **6** neroli **9** ambergris

container: **4** vial **5** phial **6** censer

medicated: **6** pastil **7** pastile **8** pastille

oriental: **5** myrrh

pad: **6** sachet

shrub source: **8** abelmosk

with burning spice: **5** cense

perfumed cherry: 7 mahaleb

perfumer: 6 censer, sachet **8** atomizer, pomander, thurible

perfunctory: 8 careless **10** mechanical **11** indifferent, superficial

pergola: 5 arbor, bower **6** arbour **7** balcony, trellis **9** colonnade

perhaps: 4 haps **5** maybe **6** ablins, belike, happen, mayhap **7** ablings **8** doubtful, possibly, probably **9** perchance

peri: elf **5** fairy, houri **6** sprite

periapt: 5 charm **6** amulet

pericarp: pod **4** boll **5** berry

Pericles: *consort:* **7** Aspasia

ward: **10** Alcibiades

pericranium: 4 head 5 brain

periculum: 4 risk 5 peril 6 danger

peril: 4 risk 6 crises, crisis, danger, hazard, menace 7 apperil, imperil 8 jeopardy 9 adventure 10 insecurity

perilous: 8 doubtful 9 desperate

perimeter: rim 7 outline 8 boundary 9 periphery 13 circumference

period: age, dot, end, eon, era 4 aeon, span, stop, term, time 5 avail, close, cycle, epact, epoch, spell, stage 6 season 8 duration, semester 10 conclusion 11 termination
critical: 6 crises, crisis
festive: 7 holiday 8 vacation
holding: 6 tenure
infinite: 8 eternity
penitential: 4 Lent
playing: 4 half, hand 5 frame, round 6 inning 7 chukkar, chukker, quarter
sleep: 6 godown 11 hibernation
tertiary: 6 eocene 7 neocene
time: day 4 hour, week, year 5 month 6 decade, minute, second 7 century 9 fortnight

periodic: 4 eral 6 annual 7 etesian, regular 8 seasonal 12 intermittent

periodical: 5 daily, paper 6 annual, review, Tatler 7 etesian, journal, tabloid 8 bulletin, magazine 9 ephemeris, newspaper, Spectator

peripatetic: 8 rambling 9 itinerant, wandering

peripheral: 5 outer 6 distal 7 distant 8 confined, external

periphery: lip, rim 4 brim, edge 5 ambit, limit 6 areola, areole, border 7 areolae, outside 8 environs 9 perimeter 13 circumference

periphrastic: 14 circumlocutory

perique: 7 tobacco

perish: die 4 fade, fall, ruin 6 depart, expire 7 consume, crumble, forfare, succumb

perishable: 6 caduke 7 brittle

peristyle: 9 colonnade 10 peripteral

perite: 7 skilled

peritomy: 12 circumcision

peritoneum: 8 covering, membrane
fold of: 7 omentum

peritroch: 5 larva 6 embryo

periwig: wig 6 peruke, toupee 10 periwinkle

periwinkle: 5 color, snail 6 mussel, myrtle

perjink: 4 neat, nice 7 precise

perjure: 8 forswear 9 aperjurer

perk: 5 preen, prink 7 smarten 8 animated 9 percolate 10 perquisite

perkin: 5 cider

permanent: 5 fixed 6 stable 7 abiding, durable, lasting 8 constant, enduring 9 continual, headdress, perennial 10 continuing

permeable: 6 porous

permeate: 4 fill 5 bathe, imbue 6 drench 7 pervade 8 saturate 9 penetrate

permirific: 8 wondrous

permission: 5 leave 7 consent, license
to use: 4 loan

permit: let 4 leve, pass 5 admit, allow, conge, favor, grace, grant, leave 6 accord, beteem, dustuk, entree, favour, suffer 7 consent, dustuck, license, pompano, warrant 8 furlough, tolerate 9 authorize 10 permission
travel: 8 passport

permutation: 6 change 10 alteration 11 interchange 13 rearrangement

pern: 7 buzzard

pernicious: bad 4 evil 5 fatal 6 deadly, malign, wicked 7 baleful, baneful, harmful, hurtful, noisome, noxious, ruinous 10 villainous 11 deleterious, destructive, detrimental

pernio: 9 chilblain

peronate: 5 mealy, wooly

perorate: 7 address, declaim 8 harangue

perpendicular: 4 sine 5 erect, plumb, sheer 6 abrupt 7 apothem, upright 8 binormal, vertical 9 downright

perpetrate: do 6 commit, effect 7 perform

perpetual: 5 etern 7 endless, eternal 8 constant, unending 9 continual, incessant, perennial, permanent, unceasing 10 continuous 11 everlasting 14 unintermittent

perpetually: 4 ever 6 always 7 forever

perpetuate: 8 continue, eternize, maintain, preserve

perplex: cap 4 clog, doze 5 amaze, beset 6 baffle, boggle, bother, cumber, darken, gravel, hamper, harass, hobble, muddle, pother, puzzle, twitch 7 bedevil, confuse, diffuse, embroil, mystify, nonplus 8 babulyie, bewilder, confound, distract, distress, entangle 9 bamboozle, obfuscate 10 complicate

perplexed: 4 asea 5 upset 7 anxious 8 troubled 10 distraught

perplexing: 4 hard 6 crabby 7 carking, complex, crabbed 9 equivocal 11 complicated

perplexity: fog 4 knot 6 tangle 7 anxiety, trouble 9 intricacy 11 encumbrance 13 embarrassment

perquisite: fee, tip 6 income 7 adjunct, apanage 8 appanage, appenage, gratuity 9 accessory 11 appointment, prerogative 12 appurtenance 13 accompaniment
presidential: 4 veto

perquod: 7 whereby

Perry Mason creator: 7 Gardner

perse: 4 blue

Perse: *daughter:* 5 Circe 8 Pasiphae

father: **7** Oceanus
husband: **6** Helios
son: **6** Aeetes, Perses
persecute: 4 bait **5** annoy, harry, hound,
wrack, wrong **6** harass **7** afflict, oppress,
torment, torture
persecuted: 7 refugee
Persephone: 4 Kore **8** Despoina
daughter: **4** Cora, Kore
father: **4** Zeus
husband: **5** Hades, Pluto
mother: **7** Demeter
Perseus: *father:* **4** Zeus
grandfather: **8** Acrisius
mother: **5** Danae
star of: **4** Atik **5** Algol
victim: **8** Acrisius
wife: **9** Andromeda
perseverance: 4 grit **8** patience, tenacity **9**
assiduity, constancy, diligence, endurance
10 insistence, steadiness **11** continuance,
persistence, pertinacity **12** continuation
13 indefatigable, steadfastness
persevere: 4 tore
persevering: 4 busy **11** unremitting
Persia (see also **Iran**): *ancient inhabitant:* **4**
Mede
apple: **6** citron
assembly: **6** majlis, meklis
bug: **5** miana
carpet: see *rug* below
cat: **6** Angora
chief officer: **5** dewan, diwan
deer: **5** maral **6** fallow
elf or fairy: **4** peri
gate: bab
gazelle: **4** cora
goddess: **7** Anahita
measure: gaz, guz, zer
lynx: **7** caracal
mightingale: bulbul
old coin: **5** daric
poet: **4** Omar, Sadi **5** Hafiz
rug: **4** Kali **5** Saruk, Senna **6** Sarouk **7** Isfahan, Ispahan, Teheran **8** Serabend
ruler: **4** shah
scriptures: **5** Koran
tick: **8** miana bug
wheel: **5** noria **7** tympana **8** tympanum
Persian Gulf: *kingdom:* **7** Chaldea
port: **7** Bushire
province: **4** Fars
wind: **6** shamal, sharki **7** shurgee
persiennes: 6 blinds
persiflage: 6 banter **8** raillery
persimmon: 7 chapote
family: **5** ebony **9** ebenaceae
persist: 4 last **6** endure, insist, remain **8** continue **9** persevere

persistent: 4 dree, hard **6** gritty **7** durable **8**
constant, enduring, frequent, holdfast, ob-
durate, resolute, stubborn **9** assiduous,
continued, tenacious **10** consistent, continuing, determined, relentless **11** persevering **13** indefatigable
person (see also **people**): guy, man, one, urf
4 body, chap, self, soul **5** being, child, human, wight, woman **6** entity, fellow **10** individual
amusing: **8** comedian, comedien **10** comedienne
bad-luck carrier: **4** jinx **5** jonah
baptized: **10** illuminato **11** illuminatus
base: **7** caitiff, hangdog
bearing the blame: **4** goat
beatified: **6** beatus
betrothed: **6** fiance **7** fiancee
blamed for others: **4** butt, goat **9** scapegoat
brilliant: **6** genius **10** mastermind
callow: **6** gorlin, smarty **7** gosling
canonized: **5** saint
careless: **6** tassel **11** pococurante
charitable: **9** samaritan
cheery: **8** optimist
*contemptible:*cad, yap **4** heel, toad **7**
bauchle
cunning: **8** slyboots
deranged: nut **7** lunatic **10** monomaniac,
psychopath
despicable: **5** hound **6** rotter **10** blackguard
detested: **8** anathema
disgruntled: **8** sorehead
dull: **5** dunce, moron **8** imbecile **9** blockhead, defective
eighty-year old: **12** octogenarian
enterprising: **8** go-getter
fearless: **10** fearnaught, fearnought **11**
dreadnaught, dreadnought
fifty-year old: **15** quinquagenarian
foolish: sop **4** zany **5** clown **6** dotard **7** half-
wit **9** simpleton
forty-year-old: **14** quadragenarian
good-luck carrier: **6** mascot
gray-headed: **7** grisard
guilty: **7** culprit
half-grown: **6** haflin **8** halfling **9** stripling
held as pledge: **7** hostage
holy: ste.(F.) **5** saint
horned: **7** cornute
ill: **7** invalid, patient
indefinite: one **6** anyone **7** anybody, so and
so, someone **8** somebody
indifferent to pleasure or pain: **5** stoic
injured: **6** victim **8** casualty
learned: **6** pundit, savant **7** scholar **9** professor **12** intellectual
left-handed: **9** portsider
loud-voiced: **7** stentor

married: 4 wife 6 spouse 7 husband
middle-class: 9 bourgeois 11 bourgeoisie
mischievous: imp 4 pest
named after another: 8 namesake
ninety-year-old: 12 nonagenarian
non-Jewish: 7 gentile
of distinction: VIP 4 star 7 notable
of mixed blood: 7 mestizo, mulatto 8 octoroon 9 half-breed
one-hundred-year-old: 11 centenarian
overnice: 4 prig
perfidious: 5 snake 7 serpent, traitor
proposed for office: 7 nominee
rapacious: 4 wolf 5 harpy, shark
representing another: 5 mimic, proxy 9 alternate
rude: 4 boor 7 caveman
scolding: 9 catamaran
second: you 4 thou
seventy-year-old: 14 septuagenarian
shiftless: bum 7 drifter
sick: 5 ailer 7 invalid, patient 9 aegrotant
sixty-year-old: 12 sexagenarian
skilled: 5 adept 6 artist, master, talent 7 artisan 8 mechanic
small: 5 dwarf 6 midget, poppet
sponsored by another: 7 protege
studious: 5 grind, porer
stupid: ass 4 boob, clod, coot, dolt, fool, gump, moke 5 bucca, clout, moron, stirk, stock, stupe, sumph 6 boodle, duffer, gander 7 dullard 8 bonehead, dumbbell, gamphrel 9 boeoetian, simpleton
timid: 11 milquetoast
trustworthy: 7 standby
unmarried: 6 maiden 8 bachelor, celibate, spinster
unusual: 4 oner
wealthy: 5 nabob 9 plutocrat 10 capitalist 11 millionaire 12 millionnaire
white: fay 4 ofay 5 haole 6 albino 7 abiculi, redneck
young: 8 chipling 9 stripling 14 whippersnapper
personable: 6 comely 7 shapely 8 handsome 10 attractive 11 good-looking, well-favored
personage: 6 shogun, tycoon 7 magnate
personal: own 7 private 8 intimate
comb. form: 4 idio
personality: ego 4 self 8 selfhood 11 disposition 13 individuality
split: 13 schizophrenia
personate: See **impersonate**
personification: 10 embodiment 11 incarnation 14 representation
of rumor: 4 Fama
of truth: Una
personified: 9 incarnate

personify: 6 embody 9 represent 11 impersonate
personnel: 5 staff 9 employees
perspicacious: 4 keen 5 acute 6 shrewd 10 discerning, perceptive 11 penetrating
perspicacity: 6 acumen
perspicuous: 5 clear, lucid, plain 8 manifest 11 conspicuous, translucent, transparent 12 intelligible
perspiration: 5 sudor, sweat 8 hidrosis, sweating 9 exudation 10 ephidrosis
pert. to: 7 sudoric
sheep: 5 suint
persuade: get, win 4 coax, gain, sway, urge 5 argue, suade 6 allure, assure, engage, entice, induce 7 entreat 8 convince, inveigle 9 influence
persuaded: 7 pliable 8 gullible 9 credulous
persuasion: 6 belief
persuasive: 6 cogent 8 eloquent 9 impelling
pert: 4 bold 5 alert, alive, bardy, brisk, cocky, quick, sassy, saucy, smart 6 active, clever, cocket, comely, dapper, frisky, lively 7 forward, paughty 8 handsome, impudent, insolent, petulant 9 exquisite, officious, sprightly 11 flourishing
pert girl: 4 minx
pertain: 5 belie 6 befall, belong, relate 7 concern 9 accessory, appertain
pertaining to: For all definitions beginning with this phrase, see under following main word or phrase, EXAMPLES: "pertaining to gold": see **gold** *pert. to;* "pertaining to the sun": see **sun** *pert. to.*
suffix: ac, ar, ic; ese, ile
pertinacious: 4 firm 6 dogged 8 adhering, stubborn 9 obstinate, tenacious 10 determined, inflexible, persistent, unyielding
pertinent: apt, fit, pat 6 proper, timely 7 adapted, apropos, germane, telling 8 apposite, relative, relevant 10 applicable, felicitous 11 appropriate 12 appurtenance
pertinentia: 6 things 8 fixtures
perturb: 5 upset, worry 7 agitate, confuse, derange, disturb, trouble 8 disorder 10 discompose, disconcert
perturbation: 6 flight, pother 7 turmoil 9 commotion 10 uneasiness 12 irregularity
pertuse: 7 pierced, punched 10 perforated
pertussis: 5 cough 13 whooping cough
Peru: *animal:* 5 llama 6 alpaca
bark: 8 cinchona
city: Ica 4 Lima(c.) 5 Cuzco, Paita 6 Callao 7 Iquitos 8 Arequipa
coin: sol 5 libra 6 dinero 7 centavo
cormorant: 6 Guanay
dance: 5 cueca
department: Ica, Yca 4 Lima 5 Cusco, Cuzco, Piura, Tacna, Tagna

emblem of nobility: 6 llautu
empire: 4 Inca, Ynca
fog: 5 garua
goddess: 4 Mama
hillock: 4 loma
inn: 5 tambo
king: 7 cacique
lake: 8 Titicaca
liquor: 5 pisco
llama: 4 paco 6 alpaca
mark of nobility: 6 llautu
measure: 4 topo, vara 5 galon 7 celemin 8
  fanegada
partridge: 4 yutu
people: 4 Ande, Cana, Inca, Inka, Peba,
  Yutu 5 Boros, Campa, Carib, Panos 6 Aymara, Jibaro, Jiyaro, Kechua, Lamano 7
  Quechau
plant: oca 6 ulluco 7 rhatany
relic: 5 huaco
river: Ica 5 Rimac, Santa 7 Maranon,
  Ucayale 8 Apurimac, Huallaga, Uru-
  bamba 11 Paucartambo
rodent: 10 chinchilla
ruler: 4 Inca, Inka
shrub: 6 shansa
skin disease: uta
tableland: 4 puna
tavern: 5 tambo
tinamou: 4 yutu
tree: 6 bucare 8 cinchona
tuber: oca
volcano: 5 Misti
weight: 5 libra 7 quintal
wind: 4 puna 5 sures
peruke: wig 6 toupee 7 periwig
perukier: 8 wigmaker
perula: 6 mentum
peruse: con 4 read, scan 5 study 6 handle,
  survey 7 examine, inspect 9 supervise
pervade: 4 fill 5 bathe, imbue 6 occupy 8
  permeate, traverse 9 penetrate
pervading: 9 prevalant, universal 10 widespread
perverse: awk 4 awry, wogh, wraw 6 divers,
  wicked, wilful 7 awkward, distort, diverse,
  forward, froward, wayward 8 backward,
  camshach, contrary, crotched, petulant 9
  camsteary, camsteery, difficult, fractious
  10 determined 11 contentious, contrarious, disobedient, intractable 12 cantankerous, contumacious
perversely: 7 athwart
pervert: 4 ruin, skew 5 abuse, twist, upset 6
  debase, divert, garble, invert, misuse, poison 7 contort, corrupt, deprave, distort, vitiate 8 apostate, misapply, overturn, renegade 9 misdirect 10 demoralize 12 misinterpret

perverted: bad 6 wicked 7 vicious
pervious: 9 permeable 10 accessible
pervulgate: 7 publish
Pescadores: *island:* 4 Hoko
  town: 4 Mako
peshkar: 5 agent 7 steward 8 minister 10
  accountant
peshkash: tax 7 present, tribute 8 offering
pesky: 6 plaguy 8 annoying 9 pestering, vexatious 11 troublesome 12 disagreeable
peso: 4 coin
  silver: 4 duro
pess: 7 hassock
pessimism: 5 gloom 7 despair 8 cynicism
pessimistic: 6 gloomy 7 alarmed, cynical
pessoner: 4 boat, ship 10 fishmonger
pest: 4 bane, weed 5 mouse 6 insect, plague,
  vermin 8 epidemic, nuisance 10 pestilence
pester: dun, nag, rib 5 annoy, devil, tease,
  worry 6 badger, bother, harass, molest 7
  torment, trouble 9 aggravate
pestiferous: 4 evil 11 mischievous
pestilence: 4 pest 5 death 6 plague 7 disease
  8 epidemic
pestilent: 6 deadly 7 noxious 9 poisonous 10
  contagious, infectious
pestle: 4 bray 5 grind 6 beetle, bettle, muller
  vessel: 6 mortar
pet: cat, dog 4 coax, daut(Sc.), dawt(Sc.),
  dear, duck, huff, neck, sulk, tiff 5 drunt,
  humor, quiet, spoil 6 caress, coddle,
  cosher, cuddle, dautie(Sc.), dawtie(Sc.),
  faddle, fantad, fantod, fondle, pamper,
  stroke 7 cherish, darling, indulge, tantrum 8 favorite, fondling 9 cherished,
  favourite
petal: ala 4 alae
petal-bearing: 8 petalous
petals: 7 corolla
  without: 9 apetalous
petard: 11 firecracker
petasus, petasos: cap, hat
peteman: 9 cracksman 10 safeblower
peter: 4 fade, fail, wane 5 cease 7 dwindle,
  exhaust 8 diminish
Peter: 4 czar, rock 5 saint, Simon
  father: 5 Jonas
Peter Pan: *author:* 6 Barrie
  dog: 4 Nana
  pirate: 4 Smee
peterman: 5 thief 7 burglar 9 fisherman
petiole: 4 stem 5 stalk 8 peduncle 9 leafstalk
  10 mesopodium
petit: 4 mean 5 minor, small 6 little 13 insignificant
petite: 4 trim 6 demure 10 diminutive
petition: ask, beg, sue 4 bill, boon, plea,
  pray, suit, wish 5 apply, orate, plead 6 appeal, prayer, steven 7 address, entreat, implore, oration, request, solicit 8 entreaty

10 supplicate 11 application, deprecation 12 supplication 13 contemplation

petitioner: 5 asker 6 beggar, seeker 8 appealer, beadsman, bedesman 9 applicant
chancery: 7 relator

petitor: 10 petitioner

peto: 5 wahoo

Petrarch's love: 5 Laura

petrean: 5 rocky

petrel: 4 titi 5 mitty 7 assilag 8 allamoth 9 allamonti, allamotti, mallemuck

petrifying: 7 numbing 9 deadening, hardening 10 petrescent, terrifying 11 fossilizing

Petrograd: 9 Leningrad

petrol: gas 8 gasoline

petroleum: oil 10 illuminant
by-product: 6 butane, deisel 7 propane 9 propylene
product: wax 4 coke 5 ethyl 6 petrol 7 alcohol, asphalt, canadol, naphtha 8 gasoline, kerosene, paraffin 9 righolene

petrosal: 4 hard 5 stony 7 petrous

petticoat: 4 kilt, slip 5 jupon, pagne 6 kirtle 7 whittle 8 basquine, halfslip, vasquine 9 undercoat, waistcoat 10 fustanella, underskirt 11 farthingale
tails: 7 teacake 9 shortcake

pettifogger: 6 lawyer 7 shyster 8 attorney

pettish: 8 petulant

pettle: 6 cuddle, nestle, potter 7 cherish, indulge

petty: 4 base, mean, orra, puny 5 minor, small 6 paltry, puisne 7 trivial 8 childish, inferior, nugatory, trifling 9 frivolous, minuscule 10 diminutive 11 subordinate, unimportant 12 contemptible 13 insignificant 14 inconsiderable
fault: 10 peccadillo
matter: 6 fidfad
morel: 9 spikenard 10 nightshade
whin: restharrow

petulant: 4 pert 5 cross, huffy, saucy, short, testy 6 petted, sullen, wanton, wilful 7 forward, fretful, peevish, wayward 8 contrary, immodest, insolent, perverse 9 impatient, irascible, irritable, plaintive, querulous 10 ill-humored

pew: 4 desk, seat, slip 5 bench, bught, stall 6 bought

pewee: 10 flycatcher

pewter: tra 5 bidri, bidry 6 bidery, bidree 7 biddery

peyote: 5 plant 6 cactus, mescal, peyotl

Phaedo's school: 5 Elian

Phaedra: *father:* 5 Minos
husband: 7 Theseus
stepson: 10 Hippolytus

phaeton: 8 carriage

phalacrocorax: 4 coot 9 cormorant

phalacrosis: 8 alopecia, baldness

phalanger: 5 tapoa

phalera: 4 boss, disk 5 cameo

phantasm: 5 dream, fancy, vapor 7 phantom 8 delusion

phantasmal: 6 unreal 10 transitory

phantasy: 5 fancy

phantom: 4 idol 5 bogle, ghost, idola, image, shade, umbra 6 eidola(pl.), idolon, idolum, spirit 7 eidolon, fantasy, specter, spectre 8 illusion, phantasm 10 apparition

Phaon's consort: 6 Sappho

Pharaoh: 7 Rameses
ancestor: Ra

Pharaoh's chicken: 7 vulture

Pharaoh's fig: 8 sycamore

Pharaoh's mouse: 9 ichneumon

phare: 6 pharos

pharisaical: 12 hypocritical

pharmaceutical: dia 7 mellite

pharmacist: 8 druggist 9 dispenser 13 pharmaceutist

pharmacy weight: 5 obole 6 obolus

pharos: 5 cloak 6 beacon 7 lantern 10 chandelier, lighthouse

phase: 4 side 5 angle, facet, stage 6 aspect 8 passover 13 manifestation

phasm: 6 meteor 7 phantom 10 appearance

pheasant: 5 cheer, monal 6 monaul, moonal, pukras 7 kallege 8 fireback, tragopan
breeding-place: 4 stew
brood: 3 nid, nye 4 nide
nest: 4 nide

pheasant cuckoo: 6 coucal

pheasant duck: 7 pintail 9 merganser

pheasant finch: 7 waxbill

phenate: 9 phenolate

Phenicia: See **Phoenicia**

phenol: 6 orcine, thymol 9 germicide
derivative: 4 anol

phenolate: 7 phenate

phenomenal: 7 unusual 13 extraordinary

phenyl salicylate: 5 salol

pheon: 7 bearing

phial: cup 4 bowl, vial 6 bottle, vessel

Phidias' statue: 6 Athena

philabeg: 4 kilt

philander: 5 flirt 10 flirtation

philanthropic: 6 humane 10 altruistic, benevolent, charitable 12 humanitarian

philanthropist: 5 donor 10 benefactor

philanthropy: 4 alms 10 almsgiving
universal: 15 omnibenevolence

philippic: 6 screed, tirade 8 diatribe

Philippines: *animal:* 5 civet, lemur
ant: 4 anai, anay
archipelago: 4 Sulu
attendant: 5 alila

banana: **7** saguing
barracks: **7** cuartel
beer: **7** pangasi
bird: **6** abacay
boat: **5** balsa, banca **8** balangay, barangay
breadfruit: **4** rima **8** casmansi
brigand: **7** ladrone
buffalo: **7** carabao, timarau, timerau
canoe: **5** banca, vinta **6** baroto
capital: **8** cabecera
carriage: **9** carretela, carromata
chief: **4** dato **5** datto, Iloco **7** Ilocano, Ilokano
Christianized tribe: **5** Bicol, Bikol, Tagal, Vicol **7** Bisayan, Tagalog, Visayan
city: Iba **4** Agoa, Cebu, Naga **5** Albay, Davao **6** Aparri, Baguio, Cavite, Ilagan, Manila(c.) **7** Dagupan
coconut meat: **5** copra
coin: **4** peso **7** centavo
cyclone: **6** baguio
dagger: **4** itac **7** balarao
deity: **5** Dagon
discoverer: **8** Magellan
drink: **4** beno, vino **5** bubud **7** pangasi
farmer: lao, tao
fern: **4** nito
fetish: **5** anito
fiber: **4** eruc **6** buntal **9** pineapple
fish: **8** langaray
food: **4** baha, taro
forest: **5** gubat
fort: **4** Gota **10** Corregidor
garment: **4** saya
grass: **5** cogon
guerrilla: Huk
gulf: **5** Davao, Ragay
hardwood: **4** ipil **5** narra
hat: **7** salacot
hemp: **5** abaca **6** manila
house: **5** bahay
idol: **5** anito
island: **4** Cebu **5** Batan, Bohol, Leyte, Luzon, Panay, Samal, Samar **6** Negros **7** Masbate, Mindora, Palawan, Paragua **8** Mindanao
kitchen: **5** calan
knife: **4** bolo, itac **7** balarao, machete
lake: **4** Taal **5** Lanao
language: **4** Moro **5** Bicol, Tagal **6** Ibanag **7** Ilocano, Tagalog, Visayan
lighthouse: **4** faro
liquor: **4** beno **7** pangasi
litter: **7** talabon
lizard: **4** ibid
mammal: **7** tarsier
mango: **5** bauno **7** pahutan
market-day: **7** tiangue
measure: **4** loan **5** braza, caban, cavan, chupa, ganta **6** apatan, balita, quinon

measure of weight: **5** catty, fardo, picul, punto **6** lachsa **7** quilate **8** chinanta
mother: ina
mountain: Apo, Iba **5** Mayon
mountaineer: **8** mentesco
mudfish: **5** dalag
muskmelon: **6** atimon
Muslim: **4** Moro
native: see *people* below
nut: **4** pili
oil: **5** cebur
pagan: **6** Italon
palm: **4** nipa **6** anahao, anahau
parrot: **5** cagit
peasant: tao
people: Ata, Ati, Ita, Tao **4** Aeta, Atta, Etas, Moro, Sulu **5** Bicol, Bikol, Tagal, Vicol **6** Igorot, Timaua, Timawa **7** Bisayan, Tagalog, Visayan **8** Filipino, Igorrote **10** Philippino
plant: aga **4** alem **5** abaca, baroi, batad **6** agamid
plum: **6** sapote
port: **4** Cebu **6** Cavite, Iloilo
priest: **7** pandita
province: **4** Abra **5** Albay **6** Iloilo
raft: **5** balsa
reptile: **6** python
rice: **4** paga **5** barit, bigas, macan
river: **4** Abra, Agno **5** Pasig **7** Cagayan **8** Mindanao, Pampanga
road: **4** daan
rope tree: **4** nabo **5** anabo
sapodilla: **5** chico
sarong: **8** padadion
sea: **4** Sulu
sentinel: **6** bantay
servant: **4** bata **5** alila
shirt: **4** baro
shrub: **4** alem, nabo **6** anilao
silk: **10** alcaiceria
skirt: **4** saya
slave: **6** alipin
slipper: **7** chinela
soap vine: **4** gogo
spirit: **5** anito
stream: **4** ilog
sword: **6** barong **8** campilan
termite: **4** anai, anay
textile: **4** pina, saba **7** sina-may
thatch: **4** nipa
timber: **5** cahuy
tree: dao, iba, tua, tui **4** acle, anam, ates, bogo, dita ifil, ipil, supa **5** almon, amaga, anabo, balao, balau, bayok, betis, bulak, guijo, ligas, tabog, yacal **6** alagao, alagau, alupag, amuyon, anagap, aranga, bancal, banuyo, bataan, batino, botong, dungon, lanete, marang, molave **7** amuguis, amuyong, anabong, apitong, banilad,

binukau, hapiton, mambong, tindalo 8 al-
maciga, bitanhol, macaasim, malapaho,
tanguile 9 alintatad, batikulin, batitinan
10 batikuling 11 alibangbang, balinghasay
tree bark: aga 6 agamid
vine: iyo
volcano: Apo 4 Mayo
watchtower: 7 atalaya 8 bantayan
water buffalo: 7 carabao
water-jar: 5 bango
weapon: 4 bolo
white man: 7 cachila
wine: 4 beno
wood: 4 teak 5 ebony, narra 6 sandal
yam: ubi, uve
Philistine: 9 barbarian, hypocrite
city: 4 Gath
giant: 7 Goliath
god: 4 Baal 5 Dagan, Dagon
foe: 6 Samson
philomel: 11 nightingale
Philomela: 11 nightingale
father: 7 Pandion
sister: 6 Procne
philosopher: 4 Kant, sage 5 Plato, Renan,
Solon 6 Nestor, Seneca 7 Emerson 8 Socrates, Voltaire 9 Epictetus
disciples: 4 sect 6 school
of Syracuse: 4 Dion
philosophical: 4 wise 8 rational 9 temperate, unruffled
philosophy: 4 yoga 7 dualism 8 stoicism 9
esoterics 10 empiricism, esthetics, pragmatism 17 transcendentalism
philter, philtre: 5 charm 6 potion 7 amatory 9 fascinate
phlebotomize: 5 bleed 8 venesect
phlegm: 5 gleet 10 equanimity
phlegmasia: 12 inflammation
phlegmatic: 4 calm, cool, dull, slow 5 inert
6 watery 7 viscous 8 composed, sluggish 9
apathetic, impassive 13 imperturbable
phloem: 4 bast
phlogistic: 5 fiery 6 heated 7 burning, flaming 11 impassioned 12 inflammatory
phoca: 4 seal
Phoebad: 7 seeress 9 priestess 10 prophetess
phoebe: 4 bird 5 pewee, pewit 6 peewee 10
flycatcher
Phoebe: 5 Diane 6 Selene 7 Artemis
Phoebus: Sol, sun 6 Apollo
Phoenicia: *city:* 4 Tyre 5 Sidon
colony: 8 Carthage
dialect: 5 Punic
god: 4 Baal
goddess: 5 Tanit 6 Baltis, Tanith 7 Astarte
goddess of love: 7 Astarte

king: 6 Agenor
seaport: 5 Sidon
phonetic: 4 oral 5 vocal
notation system: 5 romic
sound: 7 palatal
phonograph record: 4 disk 7 platter
phony: 4 fake, sham 5 bogus, false 8 impostor, spurious 9 charlatan 10 fictitious 11
counterfeit
Phorcys: *child:* 5 Ladon 6 Gorgon, Grae-
ae(pl.)
father: 6 Pontus
mother: 4 Gaea
phosphate: 6 ehlite 7 apatite 9 wavellite
photocopy: 4 stat 5 print
photoengraving: 15 heliotypography
photograph: mug 4 film, snap, X-ray 7 picture, tintype 8 likeness, portrait, snapshot
9 ferrotype, pictorial 10 cheesecake, helio-
graph 13 daguerreotype
bath: 5 fixer, toner 7 reducer 9 developer
chemical: 5 metal, toner
color tool: 5 blimp
developer: 5 ortol 6 amidol 9 revelator
fixing agent: 4 hypo
instrument: 8 enlarger
inventor: 6 Niepce, Talbot 8 Daguerre
kind: 5 panel, still 6 motion 7 boudoir, cabinet, diamond 8 imperial, passport, portrait 9 pictorial 10 commercial, scientific
12 composograph 13 carte de visite
negative: 4 film
printing: 7 ozotype
photographer: 9 cameraman
photology: 6 optics 7 photics
photometric unit: pyr, rad
phrase: mot 4 term, word 5 idiom, state 6
clause, cliche, saving, slogan 7 adjunct,
diction, epigram, epithet, thought 8 acrostic 9 catchword, leitmotif 10 expression
phraseology: 7 dialect, diction, wording 8
parlance
phratry: 4 clan
phrenetic: 8 frenetic
phrenic: 6 mental
Phrixos: *father:* 7 Athamus
mother: 7 Nephele
sister: 5 Helle
Phrygia: *enthusiast:* 9 Montanist
god: 4 Atys 5 Attis 8 Sabazios
king: 5 Midas
river: 7 Meander
town: 5 Ipsus
phylactery: 5 charm 6 amulet 8 talisman
phyletic: 6 racial 12 phylogenetic
phyma: 5 tumor 6 nodule
physic: 5 purge 9 cathartic
physical: 6 bodily 7 natural, somatic 8 material 9 corporeal, somatical

physician: asa, doc 5 curer, medic, quack 6 doctor, intern, healer, medico 7 interne 8 restorer 10 consultant, medicaster 11 aesculapian, philosopher 12 practitioner
association: AMA
combining form: 5 iatro
group: AMA 5 panel, staff
symbol: 8 caduceus
physicist: 10 naturalist
physiognomy: mug 4 face 8 portrait 11 countenance
physique: 4 body 6 figure 8 strength 10 appearance 12 constitution
physostigmine: 5 esere 6 eserin 7 eserine
piacle: sin 5 crime, guilt 7 offense 8 piaculum
pian: 4 yaws 9 frambesia 10 framboesia
piano: 5 grand 6 softly, spinet 7 clavial, quietly, upright 8 pianette 10 anemochord, pianoforte
dumb keyboard: 9 digitoria 10 digitorium 11 finger board
early: 6 spinet
key: 7 digital
keyboard: 7 clavier
notes: 6 octave
pedal: 7 celeste
pedal keyboard: 8 pedalier
piatti: 7 cymbals
piazza: 5 porch 7 gallery, portico, veranda
pic: 4 peak 8 picayune
picacho: 4 hill 5 butte
picador: wit 6 jester 7 debater 11 bullfighter
picadura: 7 tobacco
picaro: 5 knave, rogue, tramp 7 sharper 8 vagabond
picaroon: 5 rogue, thief 6 bandit, pirate, rascal 7 brigand, corsair 9 hooka-roon 10 adventurer
Picasso painting: 8 Guernica
picayune: 4 mean 5 small 6 little
pichiciago: 9 armadillo
pick: 4 gaff, pike, wale 5 adorn, beele, cavil, elect, elite, pluck 6 choice, gather, pickax, twitch 7 bargain, diamond 8 plectrum
on: 5 abuse, annoy, tease 9 criticize
out: 4 cull, sort 5 glean 6 assort, choose, select
pickax: 4 bill, pick 6 tubber, twibil 7 mattock, twibill
picked: 4 trim 5 spiny 6 dainty, peaked, spruce 7 pointed 8 stripped 10 fastidious
picket: peg 4 pale, post 5 fence, stake 6 fasten, paling, tether 7 enclose, fortify
pickle: 4 alec, dill, mess, peck 5 achar, brine 6 capers, dawdle(Sc.), muddle, nibble, pid-

dle, pilfer(Sc.), trifle(Sc.) 7 chutney, condite, confect, gherkin, vitriol 8 marinate 11 predicament
mixed: 6 higdon
pickled: 5 drunk, soust 6 soused 11 intoxicated
pickling herb: 4 dill
pickpocket: dip 4 bung, hook, wire 5 diver, filer, thief 6 buzzer, cannon, dipper, figboy, hooker, ratero(Sp.), robber 7 foister, mobsman, stealer 8 clyfaker 11 fingersmith
helper: 4 duke 5 shill, stall 6 bulker
pickup: 5 truck 6 bracer, chippy 8 recovery 9 stimulant 10 hitchhiker 11 improvement, stimulation 12 acquaintance
again: 6 resume
Pickwick Papers author: 7 Dickens
picnic: 5 gipsy, gypsy 6 junket, outing
picot: 4 loop
picotee: 9 carnation
pictograph: 5 glyph
picture (see also **motion picture**): oil 4 copy, icon, idea, ikon 5 ikono, image, photo, print, scene, vinet 6 chromo, crayon, depict, marine, pastel 7 diorama, etching, explain, imagine, paysage(F.), portray, porture, reflect, tableau 8 describe, likeness, makimono, painting, panorama, portrait, seascape, triptych, vignette 9 delineate, landscape, miniature 10 illustrate, impression, photograph, watercolor 16 chromolithograph
border: mat 5 frame
composite: 7 montage
drawn with heated instrument: 11 pyrogravure
painted on wall: 5 mural
section: 7 gravure
small: 5 cameo 9 miniature 15 microphotograph
stand: 5 easel
viewer: 9 projector 11 alethoscope, stereoscope
Picture of Dorian Gray author: 5 Wilde
picture puzzle: 5 rebus 6 jigsaw
pictured: 11 counterfeit
picturesque: 5 vivid 6 quaint, scenic 7 graphic 8 informal, scenical, striking
picuda: 9 barracuda
piddle: toy 4 pick, play 6 dawdle, putter, trifle
piddling: 6 paltry 7 trivial, useless 13 insignificant
pie: 4 mess, tart 5 chaos, flawn, graft, patty, pasty 6 jumble, magpie, pastry, tourte 7 cobbler, dessert, mixture 8 crustade, turnover 9 blackbird, confusion
meat: 5 pasty 7 rissole

with ice cream: 7 a la mode

piebald: 4 pied, piet, pyot 5 mixed, motly, pinto 6 bauson 7 mongrel, mottled 10 variegated 12 multicolored 13 heterogeneous

piece: bat, bit, cob, eke 4 chip, gare, hunk, join, mend, part, slab, slat, snip, stub, tate(Sc.) 5 crumb, flake, patch, pezzo(It.), scrap, sheet, shred, slice, strip 6 cantle, gobbet, morsel, parcel, sliver 7 cantlet, driblet, flinder, flitter, morceau(F.), oddment, portion, section, segment, snippet 8 assemble, dribblet, fraction
tapering: 4 gore, shim 6 gusset

piece of eight: 4 peso(Sp.) 6 escudo(Sp.)

piece out: eke 10 supplement

piece together: 4 form, make 5 unite

pied: 7 piebald

pied antelope: 8 bontebok

pieplant: 7 rhubarb

pier: cob 4 cobb, dock, mole, pile, quai, quay 5 groin, stilt, wharf 6 bunder 7 landing, support 8 buttress, pilaster 10 breakwater
architectural: 4 anta
base: 5 socle

pierce: dag, rit 4 bear, bite, bore, brod, cloy, dirl, gore, hole, stab, tang 5 break, drill, enter, gride, lance, probe, smite, spear, spike, stick, sting 6 broach, cleave, empale, ficche, impale, riddle 7 discern, poniard 8 puncture 9 intersect, lancinate, penetrate, perforate 10 comprehend
with horn: 4 gore
with stake: fix 6 impale

pierced: 5 ajour

piercer: awl

piercing: 4 fell, high, keen, tart 5 clear, sharp 6 shrill 7 cutting, pungent 8 poignant 9 searching 10 foraminate

Pierus: *consort:* 4 Clio
son: 10 Hyacinthus

piet: 5 ouzel 6 magpie 10 chatterbox, chattering

piety: 4 pity 7 loyalty 8 devotion, holiness, religion 9 godliness, reverence 10 compassion, devoutness

pig (see also **hog**): far, ham, hog, sow 4 boar, pork 5 bacon, chuck, crock(Sc.), ingot, shoat, shote, swine 6 farrow, gussie, porker 7 casting, dogboat, glutton, grumphy(Sc.) 8 grumphie(Sc.), pressman, sixpence
female: sow 4 gilt
lead: 6 fother
litter: far 6 farrow
male: 4 boar 6 barrow
metal: bar 5 ingot
pert. to: 7 porcine
pickled feet of: 5 souse
red variety: 5 Duroc

tender: 9 swineherd
young: elt 4 gilt, runt 5 grice(Sc.), piggy, shoat, shote, snork 6 bonham, farrow, piggie, piglet 7 teatman 9 gruntling

pig bed: sty 4 sand

pig deer: 8 babirusa 9 babirussa 10 babiroussa

pig hickory: 6 pignut

pig iron ballast: 9 kentledge

pig latin: 5 argot

pig potato: 7 cowbane

pig rat: 9 bandicoot

pigboat: sub 9 submarine

piggy bank: 6 pishke 7 knippel, pushkeh

pigs and whistles: 4 ruin 8 fragment, wreckage

pigeon: 4 barb, bird, dodo, dove, dupe, gull 5 decoy, pluck, squab, wonga 6 coward, culver, cushat, dodlet, fleece, isabel, pouter, turbit 7 cropper, fantail, jacobin, namaqua, pintado, swallow, tumbler 8 squealer 9 frillback, harlequin 10 sweetheart, turbitteen, turtledove, wonga-wonga
call: coo
carrier: 5 homer 6 homing 8 horseman 10 scandaroon
clay: 5 skeet 6 target
domestic: nun 4 barb, ruff, runt, spot 9 satinette, trumpeter
extinct: 4 dodo 9 passenger
feed: 7 saltcat
genus of: 7 columba
hawk: 6 falcon, merlin
pert. to: 9 columboid 12 peristeronic
short-beaked: 4 barb
tooth-billed: 6 dodlet
young: 5 piper 8 squealer

pigeon blood: red 6 garnet

pigeon grass: 7 foxtail 9 crabgrass 12 bristlegrass

pigeon hawk: 6 merlin

pigeon house: 7 dovecot 9 columbary

pigeon-livered: 4 meek, mild 6 gentle

pigeon pea: dal, tur 4 herb, seed 5 arhar 6 gandul 7 cajanus, catjang

pigeon woodpecker: 7 flicker

pigeonberry: 8 pokeweed 9 Juneberry 11 coffeeberry

pigeonhearted: 5 timid 8 cowardly 14 chickenhearted

pigeonhole: 6 shelve 7 arrange, cubicle 8 classify

pigeonry: 7 dovecot 8 dovecote

piggery: 4 pigs 6 pigsty 8 crockery(Sc.)

piggish: 4 mean 6 filthy, greedy 7 selfish 8 stubborn 10 gluttonous

pigheaded: 7 willful 8 perverse, stubborn 9 obstinate 10 determined

piglike animal: 7 peccary
pigment: 4 lake 5 color, paint 8 colorant
absence of: 8 alphosis
applied to canvas: 7 impasto
black: tar 5 sepia 7 melanin
blood: 10 hemoglobin
blue: 4 bice 5 smalt 7 veriter
blue-gray: 4 bice
blue-white: 4 zinc
brown: 5 sepia, umber 6 bister, bistre, sienna 7 melanin
green: 4 bice 7 veriter
kind: 7 aniline, rubiate 8 alizarin, massicot 9 alizarine
red: 7 amatito, realgar, turacin
yellow: 5 ocher, ochre 7 etiolin 8 orpiment
pigmy: See **pgymy**
pignus: 4 pawn 6 pledge
pigpen: sty
pigsconce: 7 pighead
pigskin: 5 glove 6 saddle 8 football
pigsney: 4 dear 7 darling 10 sweetheart
pigsticker: 4 sled 5 sword 7 butcher 11 pocketknife
pigtail: 5 braid, queue
pigwash: 5 swill 7 hogwash
pika: 6 rodent
pike: ged(Sc.) 4 dore, fish, gedd(Sc.), luce, pick, road 5 cairn, point, spike, tower 6 beacon, pickax, summit 7 highway 8 poulaine 9 spearhead 11 muskallonge, muskallunge, muskellunge
pike perch: 4 dory 6 sauger
pikel, pikle: 7 hayfork 9 pitchfork
pikelet: 7 crumpet
piker: 5 thief, tramp 6 coward 7 gambler, quitter, shirker, vagrant 8 pilferer, tightwad 10 speculator
pilar: 5 downy, hairy
pilaster: 4 anta 5 antae 6 column
Pilate: 10 procurator
prisoner: 8 Barabbas
tribunal: 8 Gabbatha
wife: 7 Claudia
pilchard: 7 sardine
smoked: 6 fumado
pile: cop, mow, nap 4 bank, bing, cock, dass(Sc.), dess(Sc.), heap, mass, mole, pier, rick, sess, shag 5 amass, crowd, spile, stack, stake 6 pillar 7 fortune 8 buttress 10 accumulate, breakwater, coacervate
funeral: 4 pyre 5 mound
hay: 4 cock, rick 5 stack
rubbish: 4 dump
stone: 5 cairn, scree
pile driver: 6 beetle
weight: tup
pile up: 5 amass, stack
pileup: 4 heap, mass 8 accident 9 collision

pilewort: 6 ficary
pilfer: rob 4 hook, loot, pelf, take 5 filch, sneak, steal, swipe 6 finger, snitch 7 purloin 8 scrounge
pilgrim: 5 ihram 6 palmer 8 crusader, traveler, wanderer, wayfarer 9 sojourner 12 peregrinator
bottle: 7 ampulla, costrel
garb at Mecca: 5 ihram
ship: 9 Mayflower, Speedwell
to Holy Land: 6 palmer
Pilgrim's Progress: *author:* 6 Bunyan
character: 5 Demas
pilgrimage: 4 hadj, trip 7 journey
pill: 4 ball, goli, pare, peel, pool 5 bolus, creek, strip 6 pellet, pilule 7 capsule, granule, pitcher, placebo 11 decorticate
pill bug: 5 louse 6 slater
pillage: 4 flay, loot, prey, sack 5 booty, foray, harry, rifle, spoil, strip 6 maraud, rapine, ravage 7 despoil, plunder 8 expilate, spoliate 9 depredate, devastate
pillager: 6 peeler 10 freebooter
of Rome: 6 Alaric
pillaging: 9 predatory
pillar: lat 4 pile, post 5 cippi(pl.), pylon, shaft, stela, stele 6 cippus, column, stelae(pl.), steles 7 obelisk, osiride, support 8 pilaster, pillaret 9 totem pole
capital: 7 chapter
pert. to: 6 stelar
resembling: 6 stelar
series of: 9 colonnade
without: 7 astylar
pillar-like: 6 stelar
pillar saint: 7 stylite
pillar-stone: 8 monument 11 cornerstone
pillarist: 7 stylite
Pillars of Hercules: 5 Abila, Calpe 9 Gibraltar
pillbox: cap, hat 7 shelter 8 brougham 11 emplacement 13 fortification
pilled: 4 bald, bare 6 barked, peeled, shaven 8 tonsured 12 decorticated
pillion: 6 saddle 7 cushion
pillory: 4 joug(Sc.), thew 5 stock, trone
pillow: cod, pad 5 block 7 bolster, cushion, support
stuffing: 5 eider, kapok 6 dacron
pillowcase: 4 sham, slip 5 cover, linen 8 flanerie
pilm: 4 dust
pilon: 4 gift 5 bonus 7 present 8 gratuity, lagnappe 9 lagniappe
pilose: 5 hairy
pilot: ace, fly 4 lead 5 flyer, guide, steer 6 leader 7 aviator, conduct, hobbler 8 chap-

lain, coxswain, director, governor, helms- man, preacher **9** clergyman, cockswain, steersman **10** cowcatcher

test for: **4** solo

pilot bird: 6 plover

pilot fish: 6 remora, romero **9** whitefish

pilot snake: 4 bull **10** copperhead

pilot whale: 9 blackfish

pilotweed: 7 compass **9** rosinweed

pilous: 5 hairy **6** pilose

pilum: 6 pestle **7** javelin

Piman Indian: 5 Opata

pimento: 7 paprika **8** allspice

pimple: 4 blob, burl, flaw **6** burble, papule **7** bubukle

pin: fed, fix, hob, nog, peg, pen, tit **4** axle, bolt, coak, dart, join, lill, scob **5** affix, arrow, badge, dowel, preen, rivet, spile, stake, style **6** bobbin, broach, brooch, cotter, fasten, pintle, secure, skewer **7** confine, enclose, eyebolt, gudgeon, jewelry, skittle, spindle, trenail **8** fastener, kingbolt, linchpin, ornament, spilikin, transfix **9** spillikin **10** chatelaine

for fastening meat: **6** skewer

machine: **6** cotter

oar: **5** thole

rifle: **4** tige

wooden: fid, peg **5** dowel

pin grass: 9 alfilaria

pin plant: 5 tacca

pin-wing: 6 pinion

pinafore: 4 slip **5** apron, dress, smock **6** daidly(Sc.) **8** sundress **9** gaberdine

Pinafore: *author:* **7** Gilbert **8** Sullivan

Pinales: 5 trees **6** shrubs **11** Coniferales

pinbone: 7 hipbone

pince-nez: 5 specs **7** glasses, lorgnon **10** eyeglasses, spectacles

pincers: tew **5** chela **6** pliers, tenail **7** forceps **8** tenaille

pinch: nip, rob, wry **4** bite, raid **5** cramp, gripe, hinch, steal, stint, tweak **6** arrest, crisis, extort, snatch, snitch, twince **7** confine, squeeze **8** contract, straiten **9** emergency, vellicate

pinch bar: pry **5** lever

pinchbeck: 4 sham **5** alloy, cheap **8** spurious **11** counterfeit

pinchpenny: 4 carl **5** miser, stint **9** niggardly

Pindaric: ode

pine: ara, fir, iva, lim **4** ache, flag, hone, tree **5** cedar, droop, dwine, kauri, kaury, larch, pinon, vacoa, waste, white, yearn **6** balsam, grieve, lament, pandan, repine, spruce, totara, vacona, vacoua, wither **7** dwindle **8** galagala, languish, Northern **9** evergreen, Norwegian

acid: **5** pinic

exudation: **5** resin, rosin

fruit: **4** cone

grove: **7** pinetum

leaf: **6** needle

mahogany: **6** totara

product: tar **5** resin **10** turpentine

pine bark aphid: 10 phylloxera

pine family: 8 pinaceae

pine gum: 8 sandarac

pine knot: 7 dovekie

pine siskin: 5 finch

pine tar: 6 retene

Pine Tree State: 5 Maine

pine tulip: 10 pipsissewa

pineapple: 4 bomb, pina(Sp.) **5** anana(It.) **7** grenade **8** ornament **10** decoration

family: **12** bromeliaceae

genus of: **6** ananas

segment: pip

pineapple weed: 8 marigold

pinecone: 4 clog **8** strobile

pinfold: 4 jail **5** pound

ping: 4 push, urge **5** prick

pinguid: fat **5** fatty

pinguin: 7 aguamas

pinguitude: 7 fatness, obesity **8** oiliness **10** greasiness

pinhead: 4 fool **5** clown

pinion: pin, tie **4** bind, gear, wing **5** quill **7** confine, disable, feather, pennant, shackle, trundle **8** cogwheel, restrain

pink: cut **4** deck, rose, rosy, stab, tint **5** adorn, color, coral, prick **6** flower, minnow, pastel, pierce, salmon **7** blossom, radical **8** decorate, grayling **9** carnation, embellish

family: **15** caryophyllaceae

genus of: **6** silene

pink needle: 9 alfilaria

pink pill: 7 cure-all

pinkeen: 6 minnow

pinkeye: 14 conjunctivitis

pinnace: 4 boat, ship **5** woman **6** tender **9** procuress **10** prostitute

pinnacle: epi, tee, top, tor **4** acme, apex, peak **5** crest, crown, serac **6** finial, needle, summit **8** gendarme

glacial: **5** serac

rocky: tor

pinnate: 9 feathered **11** featherlike

pinniped: 4 seal **6** walrus

pinnula: 4 barb

Pinocchio author: 7 Collodi **9** Lorenzini

pinochle score: 4 meld

pinpoint: aim, dot, fix **5** exact, point **6** trifle **7** precise

pintado: 4 cero, fish, sier **6** chintz, pigeon, sierra **7** siering

pintail: 4 duck, smee
pintle: 4 bolt 5 hinge, dowel
pinto: 4 pied, pony 5 horse 6 calico 7 mottled, painted, piebald
pinxter flower: 6 azalea 11 honeysuckle
pion: dig 8 excavate
pioneer: 5 miner 6 digger 7 settler 8 colonist, explorer 9 excavator
pious: 4 good, holy 5 froom, godly, loyal 6 devout, devine, pietic 7 canting, goddard, godlike, piteous 8 faithful 9 religious 11 reverential 13 sanctimonious
pip: 4 paip, peep, seed, spot 5 cheep, chirp, speck
pipe: oat 4 cask, duct, flue, lead, main, reed, tube 5 briar, canal, drain, spout, stack 6 dudeen, leader, outlet, tubule 7 calumet, conduit, fistula, larigot 8 mirliton(F.)
ashes: 6 dottle
bend: el 5 elbow
clay: TD 4 tile 5 straw 12 churchwarden
connection: ell, tee 5 cross, elbow
end: 4 taft 6 nozzle
joint: "T", "Y"; ell, tee, wye 5 cross, elbow 7 calepin 8 coupling
Oriental: 5 hooka 6 hookah 7 nargile 8 narghile, nargileh 12 hubble-bubble
part: 4 bowl, stem
pastoral: oat 4 reed
pert. to: 6 tubate
player: 5 fifer 8 shepherd
smoke: 5 tewel
steam: 5 riser
stove: 4 flue 5 tewel 7 chimney
pipe dream: 4 hope 7 chimera 8 illusion
pipe wrench: 8 Stillson
pipeline: 7 channel, conduit
Piper's son: Tom
piperly: 7 trivial 9 worthless
pipette: 6 taster 7 dropper
measuring: 11 stactometer
piping: 6 edging, tubing
pipistrel, pipistrelle: bat
pipit: 6 wekeen 7 titlark
pippin: 5 apple
piquancy: 4 salt 6 flavor, ginger 7 flavour
piquant: 4 racy, tart 5 salty, sharp, spicy, tasty, zesty 6 biting, bitter 7 peppery, pungent 8 poignant, stinging 11 provocative, stimulating
pique: 4 fret, goad 5 annoy, pride, spite, sting 6 excite, grudge, harass, malice, nettle, offend, pritch, strunt 7 dudgeon, offense, provoke, umbrage 8 irritate, vexation 9 annoyance, displease 10 irritation, resentment 11 displeasure
piqued: 5 pouty
piquet: *score:* pic
tricks: 5 capot

pirate: 4 Kidd 5 rover 6 robber 7 brigand, corsair, omnibus 8 algerine, marauder, picaroon, predator 9 buccaneer, privateer 10 freebooter, plagiarize
flag: 5 Roger
gallows: 7 yardarm
piripiri: 4 weed 5 birch, mapau
pirl: 4 spin 5 twine, twist
pirn: 4 reel 5 spool 6 bobbin
pirogue: 5 canoe
pirol: 6 oriole
piscation: 7 fishery, fishing
piscator: 6 angler 9 fisherman 11 piscatorian
piscina: 4 tank 5 basin 8 fishpond 9 reservoir
piscine appendage: fin
Pisgah summit: 4 Nebo
pishogue, pishoge: 5 spell 7 sorcery 10 witchcraft
pismire: ant 5 emmet
pismo: 4 clam
piste: 4 path 5 spoor, track, trail
pistil: 6 carpel
pistle: 4 tale 5 story 7 epistle
pistol: dag, gat, gun, rod 6 barker, buffer 7 dungeon 8 bulldoze 9 automatic, derringer
case: 7 holster
lock: 5 rowet
piston: 7 plunger
pit: 4 butt, delf, foss, hell, hole, mine, pool, seed, sump, trap, weem, well 5 abyss, chasm, delft, delve, fossa, fosse, fovea, grave, shaft, snare, stone 6 cavern, cavity, fossae, hollow, oppose 7 abaddon, cockpit 8 downfall 9 barathron, barathrum, waterhole 10 depression, excavation 11 indentation
bottomless: 7 Abaddon
of peach: 4 seed 7 putamen
of theater: 7 parquet
small: 7 alveola, foveola 8 alveolus, foveolae
pit viper: 4 habu 8 lachesis 10 bushmaster, copperhead
pitch: dip, key, tar 4 cant, cast, hurl, line, roll, send, tone, toss 5 fling, heave, lunge, lurch, resin, rosin, throw 6 accent, encamp, patter, plunge, totter 7 asphalt, bitumen 8 alkitran 9 alchitran
above: 5 sharp
apple: 5 copei, cupay
below: 4 flat
high in: alt
pipe: 9 epitonion
pitch-color: 7 piceous
pitchblende: 6 radium 7 uranium
pitcher: jar 4 ewer, olla, olpe, toby 5 buire, gorge, gotch, ollae, olpae 6 carafe, heaver, hurler, tosser, urceus 7 canette, creamer 8

cruisken, oenochoe **9** container, cruiskeen **10** ballplayer

false move: **4** balk

left-handed: **8** southpaw

motions: **6** windup

place: **5** mound

pitcher plant: 8 nepenthe **10** cephalotus, sarracenia **12** chrysamphora, darlingtonia

pitcher-shaped: 9 urceolate **10** ascidiform

pitchfork: 4 evil **5** pikel, pikle **8** sheppeck, sheppick

pitchhole: 5 cahot

piteous: 5 pious **6** devout, moving, tender **7** pitiful, pitying **8** pitiable, touching **13** compassionate

pitfall: 4 lure, trap **5** snare **6** danger **10** difficulty

pith: jet, nub **4** core, crux, gist, meat, pulp **5** force, vigor **6** kernel, marrow **7** essence, medulla, nucleus **8** strength

full of: **5** heady, meaty, terse **7** concise

pith helmet: 5 topee

pith tree: 7 ambatch

pithy: 5 crisp, meaty, terse **7** compact, concise, laconic **11** sententious **12** apothegmatic

plant: **4** sola

saying: mot **5** maxim **9** witticism

pitiful: sad **4** mean **6** rueful, woeful **7** forlorn, piteous **8** pathetic, pitiable **9** miserable, sorrowful **10** despicable, lamentable **12** contemptible

pitiless: 4 grim **5** cruel, stony **6** savage **8** ruthless **9** ferocious, merciless **10** despiteous, dispiteous, relentless **11** hardhearted

pitpit: 8 guitguit

pittance: bit **4** alms, dole, gift, mite, song **6** trifle **7** bequest

pitted: 7 foveate, opposed, scarred **9** alveolate **10** pockmarked **11** honeycombed

pity: 4 ruth **5** mercy, piety **6** pathos **8** clemency, sympathy **10** compassion, condolence, tenderness **11** commiserate **13** commiseration

Pius: 4 Pope

Pius II: 6 Aeneas **7** Silvius

pivot: toe **4** slew, slue, turn **5** hinge, swing **6** evener, swivel **7** gudgeon

pivot pin: 6 pintle **8** kingbolt

pivotal: 5 polar **7** central, crucial **8** cardinal

pixie, pixy: elf **5** fairy **6** sprite

pixilated: 5 dotty

placable: 4 calm **8** peaceful **9** agreeable, forgiving, peaceable

placard: 4 bill, post, sign **6** poster **7** affiche **9** manifesto **12** proclamation **13** advertisement

placate: 4 calm **5** quiet, sooth **6** pacify, please, soothe **7** appease **10** conciliate

place: lay, put, set **4** area, calm, city, lieu, loci, post, room, seat, site, spot, town **5** being, court, estre, locus, plant, posit, siege, situs, space, stead **6** bestow, locale, locate, region, repose, square **7** allodge, bestead, demesne, deposit, dispose, situate, village **8** dwelling, location, locality, position **9** collocate, residence, situation

again: **6** reseat **7** replace

apart: **6** enisle **8** separate

before: **6** appose, prefix

beneath: **9** infrapose

between: **6** insert **9** interpose

business: **5** plant, store **6** office

by itself: **7** isolate

camping: **5** etape

combining form: gea **4** gaea

end for end: **7** reverse

hiding: mew **4** cave

holy: **6** shrine

in a row: **5** align, aline

in the sun: **5** glory **11** recognition

intermediate: **5** limbo

little hiding: **5** niche

market **4** mart **5** agora

meeting: **5** tryst **10** rendezvous

one inside another: **4** nest

side by side: **9** collocate, juxtapose

trial: **5** venue

placebo: 8 medicine **11** preparation

placed: 7 bestead

placid: 4 calm, even, mild **5** downy, quiet, suant **6** gentle, serene **8** peaceful, tranquil **9** unruffled **11** undisturbed **13** imperturbable

placket: 4 slit **6** pocket **7** opening

pladaroma: 5 tumor

plage: 4 zone **5** beach **6** region **7** country **8** transept

plagiarism: 4 crib **5** theft **6** piracy

plagiarize: rob **4** crib **5** steal **6** borrow, pirate, thieve **7** purloin

plague: dun, pox, vex **4** fret, pest, twit **5** annoy, harry, tease, worry **6** harass, hector, pester, wanion **7** scourge, torment, trouble **8** calamity, epidemic, irritate, nuisance **9** annoyance **10** affliction, pestilence **11** infestation

carrier: rat

pert. to: **6** loimic

plaguy: 6 vexing **9** vexatious **12** disagreeable

plaice: 8 flounder

plaid: 4 maud **5** cloth **6** design, tartan **7** bracken, garment, pattern **9** checkered **11** crossbarred

plain: lea **4** bald, bare, chol, down, even, fair, mead, mere, mesa, moor, open, vega, wold

5 blair, blunt, broad, camas, campo, clear, corah, frank, gross, heath, homey, llano, veldt **6** camass, cammas, coarse, cuesta, graith, homely, humble, lenten, meadow, pampas, simple, steppe, tundra, undyed **7** artless, certain, evident, genuine, glaring, legible, obvious, prairie, quamash, savanna **8** apparent, campagna(It.), campaign, distinct, explicit, flatland, homemade, homespun, ordinary, savannah, tailored **9** champaign, downright, outspoken, primitive, unadorned, unfigured, untwilled **10** unaffected **11** perspicuous, transparent, undisguised **12** altiplanicie **13** unembellished **15** straightforward

depression **5** swale
elevated: **4** mesa **7** plateau
Olympic games: **4** Elis
salt-covered: **5** flats **6** salada
treeless: **5** llano, pampa, veldt **6** tundra **7** prairie, savanna **8** savannah
upland: **4** wold **5** weald

plainstone: 6 paving **9** flagstone
plaint: 6 lament **9** complaint **11** lamentation
plaintiff: 4 suer **7** accuser **9** recoverer **11** complainant
plaintive: sad **5** cross **7** elegiac, fretful, peevish, pettish **8** dolorous, mournful, petulant, repining **9** lamenting, sorrowful **10** melancholy **11** complaining **12** discontented
plait: cue **4** fold, knit **5** braid, brede, crimp, pleat, weave **6** border, gather, goffer, pleach, plight, wimple **7** gauffer **8** complect **9** gathering **10** interweave
plaited: 7 browden
plan: aim, map **4** card, dart, form, game, idea, plat, plot **5** draft, epure, ettle, frame **6** budget, decoct, design, devise, intend, layout, method, policy, scheme, sketch, system **7** arrange, concert, diagram, draught, drawing, outline, program, project, purpose **8** conspire, contrive, engineer, platform, prepense, schedule **9** calculate, machinate, stratagem **10** concoction **11** arrangement, contemplate, contrivance, preconceive, precontrive, premeditate
planate: 5 plane **9** flattened
plancher: bed **4** slab **5** board, floor, plank **6** pallet **7** ceiling **8** planking, platform
plancier: 6 soffit
plane (see also **airplane**)**: 4** even, flat, soar **5** glide, level **6** aequor, chinar, smooth **7** surface **8** sycamore
block: **5** stock
handle: **4** toat, tote
inclined: **5** chute, shute

kind of: **4** iron, jack **5** block **6** router **8** grooving, tounging
on same: **8** coplanar
plane figure: *boundary:* **9** perimeter
four angles: **8** tetragon
nine-sided: **7** nonagon
plane iron: bit **5** blade
plane-tree: 8 sycamore
planer: 6 shaper **8** surfacer
planet: orb **4** Mars, moon, star **5** Earth, Pluto, Venus **6** Saturn, sphere, Uranus **7** Jupiter, Mercury, Neptune **8** asteroid, terrella, wanderer **9** satellite
brightest: **5** Venus
cone: **8** strobile
course: **5** orbit
nearest sun: **7** Mercury
newest: **5** Pluto
orbit: **7** ellipse
orbit point: **5** apsis, nadir **6** apogee, zenith **8** parigree
path: **5** orbit
period: **9** alfridary
red: **4** Mars
relation to another: **5** trine **7** sextile **10** opposition **11** conjunction
ruling: **9** dominator
satellite: **4** moon
shadow: **5** umbra
planeta: 5 cloak
planetarian: 10 astrologer
planetarium: 6 orrery
planetary: 7 erratic **9** wandering, worldwide **10** astrologer **11** terrestrial
planeticose: 9 wandering
planetoid: 8 asteroid
plangor: 4 wail **11** lamentation
planisphere: 9 astrolabe
plank: 4 deal, slab **5** board, slate, stone **6** lumber, timber **8** plancher **10** gravestone
breadth: **6** strake
increasing bearing surface: **5** shole
lengthwise: **8** stringer
plank down: pay **7** advance, deposit
planking: 8 flooring
planner: 9 architect
plant: fix, set, sow, spy **4** arum, bush, fern, herb, hide, rape, root, seed, slip, trap, tree, weed, wort **5** berry, clote, decoy, found, fruit, grain, place, shoot, shrub, sotol, spice, trick, works **6** annual, clover, flower, legume, scheme, settle, teasel **7** alyssum, aquatic, creeper, cutting, factory, furnish, pungent, sapling **8** aromatic, building, business, geophyte, narcotic, radicate **9** detective, establish, perennial, seasoning, succulent, swindling, vegetable **13** establishment

acid-juice: **5** ribes **6** nettle **8** knotweed **9** smartweed
aconite: **4** bikh
amaryllis family: **5** agave
ambrosia genus: **7** ragweed
ammoniac: **5** oshac
apiaceous: **4** ache
apoplexy: **4** esca
appendage: **7** stipule
aquatic: see **aquatic plant**
arboreal: **4** tree
aromatic: see **aromatic**
arrowroot-yielding: **7** curcuma
arum family: **4** arad, taro **5** aroid, calla
aster family: **5** oxeye, tansy **8** fleabane
asteraceous: **5** daisy
bayonet: **5** datil
bean family: **6** lupine **8** licorice **9** liquorice
benthonic: **6** enalid
bitter: ers, rue **9** colicroot
blue-blossomed: **6** lupine **8** ageratum
body: **6** cormus
bog genus: **5** abama **10** narthecium
bramble: **5** briar, furze, gorse, thorn
branched: **4** bush, tree **5** shrub
breathing organ: **5** stoma **7** stomata(pl.)
bulbous: **5** camas **6** camass, cammas, nerine **7** quamash
cabbage family: **4** rape
cactus family: **5** dildo **6** cereus, mescal
cactus-like: **8** stapelia **9** xerophyte
capsule: pod
carrot-like: **7** parsnip
cassia genus: **5** senna
catnip family: nep **6** nepeta
celery family: **5** anise
celery-like: udo
cell: **6** gamete
chlorophyll-rich: **4** alga **5** algae(pl.)
chromatophore-lacking: **6** albino
class: **4** alga **5** algae(pl.)
climbing: ive, ivy **4** bine, vine **5** liana, liane, vetch **6** byrony, smilax **7** creeper
clover-like: **5** medic **7** calomba
coloring matter: **8** clorofil **10** endochrome **11** chlorophyll
corn lily: **4** ixia
crocus family: **4** irid
crossbred: **6** hybrid
crowfoot family: **5** peony **8** clematis
cruciferous: **5** cress **7** alyssum
cryptogamous: **4** moss
cuticle: **5** cutin
cyperaceous: **5** sedge
decorative: ivy **4** bush, fern **6** flower
desert: **5** agave **6** alhagi, cactus
dipsacus genus: **6** teasel
disease: **4** scab, smut **5** ergot **7** blister
division: **15** archichlamydeae

dock-like: **6** sorrel
dry-climate: **5** xerad **9** xerophyte **10** ombrophobe
dwarf: **5** cumin
dye: **4** anil, weld, woad, wold **5** henna, woald, would **6** kamala, madder, wurras, wurrus **7** alhenna, orselle
dye-yielding: **4** anil, woad **5** henna, sumac **6** madder **7** alkanet
ebony family: **6** ebenad
embryo: **8** plantule
environmentally modified: **4** ecad
erica genus: **5** heath **7** heather
Euphorbia genus: **6** spurge
exudation: gum, sap **4** milk **5** latex, resin, rosin
fabaceous: pea
family: **7** araceae
fernlike: **8** filicoid
fiber: see **fiber**
flag-family: **4** irid
floating: **7** frogbit
flowering: see **flowering plant**
forgetfulness-causing: **5** lotus
fragrant: **5** orris **8** angelica
garden: **4** geum, iris, ixia, rose **5** aster, calla, canna, daisy, pansy, phlox, poppy, stock, viola **6** bellis, bletia, celery, clivia, cosmos, crocus, lupine, oxalis, zinnia **7** agathea, alyssum, anchusa, anemone, begonia, celosia, clarkia, gazania, gerbera, godetia, lettuce, lobelia, muscari, petunia, primula, statice, verbena **8** ageratum, arctotis, cyclamen, daffodil, dianthus, herebell, hyacinth, larkspur, marigold, myosotis, scabiosa, sparaxis, sweet pea, tithonia, watsonia **9** amaryllis, calendula, campanula, candytuft, carnation, centaurea, cinararia, coreopsis, digitalis, gladiolus, hollyhock, linararia, narcissus, nicotiana, penstemon, portulaca **10** delphinium, gaillardia, gypsophila, marguerite, ranunculus, snapdragon, sweet basil, wallflower **11** dusty miller, forget-me-not, helichrysum, hunnemannia, Madonna Lily, shasta daisy **12** nierembergia, rhododendron, salpiglossis, sweet William **13** chrysanthemum, dimorphotheca, glory of the sun **14** canterbury bell **15** Star of Bethlehem **16** spring snowflakes
genus: **4** dion
geography: **14** phytogeography
gourd family: **5** melon
grain: oat, rye **4** corn **5** wheat **6** barley
grass: **5** avena
grass cloth: **5** ramee, ramie
grass-like: **5** sedge
grassland: **6** baccar **7** bacchar

growing from inside: **7** endogen **9** endogenae(pl.)
growing from outside: **6** exogen
growth layer: **7** cambium
growth on: **4** gall
habitat: **4** ecad
hawthorn: **7** azarole **9** mayflower
head: bud, bur **4** burr **5** fruit **6** flower
healing: **7** sanicle
heather family: **4** ling **5** erica
herbaceous: see **herb**
honey-secreting organ: **7** nectary
house: see **houseplant**
interior chaff: **5** palea, palet
iridaceae: **4** irid
iris family: **4** irid, ixia **7** freesia
joined to another: **5** graft
joint: **4** node
juice: see *exudation* above
leguminous: see **legume**
liliaceous: **4** aloe, leek **5** onion **9** birthroot
lily family: **4** aloe, sego **5** lotos, lotus, yucca **6** camass
linen-producing: **4** flax
main axis: **4** stem **5** stalk, trunk
male: mas **16** androgametophore
mallow family: **5** altea **6** escoba
manufacturing: **4** mill
marine: see **aquatic plant**
marsh: **4** fern, reed **7** bulrush, cattail
masculine: see *male* above
medicinal: hop, oak **4** aloe, dill, flax, herb, lime, sage **5** buchu, elder, erica, guaco, jalap, peony, poppy, senna, tansy **6** arnica, carrot, catnep, catnip, fennel, garlic, ipecac, kousso, laurel, nettle **7** aconite, boneset, calamus, camphor, caraway, catechu, copaiba, ephedra, gentian, hemlock, henbane, juniper, lobelia, mullein, mustard, parsley, rhubarb, saffron **8** barberry, camomile, crowfoot, foxglove, licorice, plantain, rosemary, valerian, wormwood **9** asparagus, bearberry, buckthorn, chamomile, colchicum, coltsfoot, dandelion, liquorice, monkshead **10** assafetida, pennyroyal, peppermint, stavesacre **11** assafoetida, bittersweet
microscopic: **5** spore
millet: **5** hirse
mock orange: **7** syringa
modified by environment: **4** ecad
moss-like: **6** orpine **7** hepatic
mottled leaf: **8** ratsbane
multicellular: **9** metaphyte
mushroom-type: **6** fungus
mustard family: **4** woad **5** cress **6** radish **7** alyssum
native: **8** indigene
nettle family: **4** hemp

nightshade family: **6** tomato
oil-yielding: **4** odal **6** sesame
old-world: **5** lotus
one-seeded fruit: **9** olacaceae
onion family: **4** leek
onion-like: **5** chive **7** shallot
opening: **5** stoma **7** stomata(pl.)
packing: **7** cannery
painful to touch: **5** briar, thorn **6** nettle **8** knotweed **9** smartweed
parsley family: **4** dill **5** anise
part: **6** stamen, stipel **7** tendril
pert. to: **6** agamic **7** botanic, vegetal **9** botanical **10** vegetative
pigment-lacking: **6** all ino
poaceae: **5** grass
pod: **4** boll
poisonous: **4** atis **6** datura **7** amanita **8** oleander
poisonous to cattle: **4** loco **8** calfkill, locoweed
poisonous to fowls: **7** henbane
poppy family: **9** celandine
pore: **8** lenticel
potato-like: oca
preserving: **4** dill **7** cannery
prickly: **5** briar, brier, cacti(pl.), thorn **6** cactus, nettle, teasel **7** thistle **9** tearthumb
rat poison: **8** oleander
reproductive organ: **5** spore
root: **5** radix
rope: **4** hemp
rose family: **5** avens
round-leaved: **9** pennywort
salad: **5** cress **6** celery, endive, greens **7** lettuce, romaine **8** purslane **10** watercress
scented: **4** mint **6** catnip **7** catmint
science: **6** botany
seasoning: **8** tarragon
sedge family: **5** carex
seed: nut, pip **4** bulb **5** grain **6** button **7** putamen
seedless: **4** fern
seller: **7** florist
shoot: rod **4** cion **5** scion, sprig **6** stolon
silk: **5** floss
soap: **5** amole
solanaceous: **7** tobacco
sour-juice: **6** sorrel
starch: pia **4** arum, taro **7** cassava
stem: **4** bine **5** shaft **6** caulis
stem joint: **4** node
stem tissue: **4** pith **6** phloem
tanning: **5** sumac
tapioca-yielding: **6** casava, casave, casavi **7** cassava
tequila-yielding: **5** agave
thistle family: **5** aster
thorny: see *prickly* above

three-leaved: 9 trifolium
trailing: 7 arbutus
tropical: 4 arum, palm, taro 5 agave, altea, canna, liana, liane, yucca, zamia 6 pepino 7 dasheen, hamelia 8 mangrove, redwithe
tufted: 4 moss
twining: see *climbing* above
type: 6 exogen
urticaceous: 6 nettle
valerian genus: 4 nard
verbenaceous: 7 lantana
vetch family: ers
vine: ivy 5 liana
wall: ivy
water-side: 5 sedge
wild-growing: 9 agrestial
woody: 4 bush, tree, vine 5 shrub
woody-vine genus: 5 vitis
xyloid: 4 tree
young: 4 cion 5 scion, shoot 6 sprout 7 vinelet 8 seedling
yucca-like: 5 sotol
plant life: 5 flora 10 vegetation
plant louse: 5 aphid
secretion: 4 laap, lerp 5 laarp
plant raising: *pert. to:* 13 floricultural
Plantagenets: 7 Angevin
plantain: 4 weed 6 banana, wabron 8 balisier
family: 14 plantaginaceae
plantain eater: 7 touraco
plantation: 4 farm 6 estate 8 hacienda
cacti: 7 nopalry
coffee: 5 finca 7 cafetal, fazenda
coniferous tree: 7 pinetum
oak tree: 9 quercetum
sugar: 8 trapiche
trees: 6 forest 7 orchard
willow: 4 holt 6 osiery
planter: 5 sower 6 farmer, grower, seeder 7 pioneer, settler 8 colonist 13 agriculturist
government by: 11 plantocracy
planting stick: 6 dibble
plantling: 8 plantlet
plaque: pin 5 medal 6 broach, brooch
plash: 4 pool 5 blash, hedge 6 pleach, puddle, splash 9 bespatter
plashy: wet 6 marshy
plasm: 4 mold 6 matrix
plasma: 5 lymph 11 trophoplasm
plaster: 4 daub, harl, teer, tere 5 cleam, cover, gatch, gesso, grout, salve, smalm, smear 6 mortar, parget
artist's: 5 gesso
coarse: 5 grout 6 parget, stucco
of Paris: 6 gypsum
stone: 6 gypsum
support: 4 lath
tool: 7 spatula

wax: 6 cerate
plastered: 5 drunk 11 intoxicated
plasterer: 5 mason
plastic: 4 soft 5 gesso 7 ductile, fictile, flexile, pliable 8 flexible 9 formative 14 impressionable
cotton-sizing: 7 viscose
dentist's: 6 cement
plastosome: 12 chondriosome
plastron: 7 calipee 8 trimming 11 breastplate
plat: lot, map 4 boat, flat, plan, slap 5 braid, chart, level, plain, plait 6 buffet 7 flatten, plateau 8 straight 9 tableland 10 interweave 15 straightforward
platanist: 4 susu
platano: 6 banana
plate: cut, gib 4 coat, disc, dish, disk, lame, tile 5 aglet, armor, facia, scute, stove 6 aiglet, discus, lamina, platen, tagger, veneer 7 lamella, laminae, overlay 8 assiette, lamellae, laminate 9 silverize
communion: 5 paten 6 patina
cooking: 4 grid
for throwing: 6 discus
from matrix: 6 stereo 10 stereotype
glass: 4 pane
horny: 5 scute
perforated: dog 4 grid 7 stencil
pitcher's: 4 slab
ship-shaped: nef
stereotype: 6 cliche
thin: 6 lamina 7 lamella
plate bone: 7 scapula
plate mark: 8 hallmark
plateau: 4 dish, mesa, seir 5 fjeld 6 hamada, plaque, salver 7 hammada, uplands 9 altiplano, tableland 12 altiplanicie
plateholder: 8 cassette
platen: 6 roller
platform: map 4 bank, bema, dais, deck, plan 5 bench, chart, floor, stage 6 bemata(pl.), podium, pulpit 7 estrade, program, rostrum, tribune 8 chabutra, plancher 9 banquette, gangplank, vestibule
church: 5 solea
fort: 8 barbette
mining: 6 sollar, soller
nautical: 7 maintop
reloading: 6 staith
salt-manufacturing: 6 hurdle
ship: 7 foretop, maintop 9 gangplank
sleeping: 4 kang
temple: 5 dukan
theater: 7 logeion
wheeled: 5 float
platic: 9 imperfect
platinum: *combining form:* 6 platin 7 platino

crude: **7** platina
symbol: Pt
wire: **4** oese
platitude: 6 cliche, truism **7** bromide **8** dullness, flatness **9** staleness, triteness **10** triviality **11** commonplace **15** commonplaceness
Plato: *idea:* **5** eidos
knowledge: **6** noesis
school: **7** Academe
work: **4** Meno **5** Crito **6** Phaedo **7** Apology, Gorgias, Sophist, Timaeus **8** Republic
platoid: 4 flat **5** broad
platonic: 9 spiritual, visionary **10** idealistic **11** impractical, theoretical
body: **4** cube **10** hexahedron, octahedron **11** icosahedron, tetrahedron **12** dodecahedron
philosophy follower: **9** academist
platoon: set **4** team, unit **5** squad **6** volley **7** coterie **8** division **9** formation
Platoon School: 4 Gary
platter: 4 dish, lanx(L.) **5** ashet(Sc.), grail, plate **7** charger
platter-shaped: 10 scutellate
platyfish: 8 moonfish
platypus: 8 duckbill
plaudit: 4 clap **6** praise **8** applause, approval, encomium **11** acclamation, approbation
plausible: 4 oily **6** glossy **7** colored **8** coloured, credible, specious **10** applausive, ostensible, plauditory
Plautus: *character:* **5** miles(L.) **7** soldier
forte: **6** comedy
language: **5** Latin
play: act, fun, jeu(F.), hit, toy **4** game, jeux(F.), move, romp **5** charm, dally, drama, enact, flirt, sport **6** cavort, frolic, gambol, rollix **7** disport, execute, perform **9** amusement, dalliance, diversion, pantomime **10** recreation **13** entertainment
badly: err **4** miff **6** bobble
ball: **5** begin **6** resume **9** cooperate
complication: **4** node
festival: **9** festspiel
kind: **4** auto **5** farce **6** comedy, one-act **7** musical, tragedy **8** burletta **9** melodrama, pantomime **13** curtain-raiser
musical: **5** opera **8** burletta, operetta
on words: pun
outline: **8** scenario
part: act, bit **4** acte(F.), role **5** exode, scene **7** prelude **8** epilogue, epitasis, prologue
possum: **4** sham **5** feign **7** pretend
put on: **5** stage **7** produce
silent: **9** pantomime
playa: 4 lake **5** basin, beach

playboy: 4 fool **5** clown, idler **6** madcap **7** buffoon
playday: 7 holiday
play out: 6 finish, unreel
played out: 5 tired **8** finished **9** exhausted
player: man **4** cast, star **5** actor **6** leader **7** enactor, gambler **8** gamester, thespian **10** competitor, contestant
card: **4** pone **6** dealer, eldest
leading: **4** star
poor: dub, dud, sub **12** second-string
strolling: **9** serenader, troubador **10** troubadour **11** barnstormer
player piano: 7 pianola
playful: 5 merry **6** frisky, joking, lusory, wanton **7** jocular **8** gamesome, humorous, playsome, sportive **10** frolicsome
playground: 4 park, yard
playhouse: 5 house, movie **6** cinema **7** theater
playing cards: 4 deck **6** tarots
hand: cat **4** deal
playlet: 4 skit
playman: 7 gambler **8** gamester
playmate: pal **6** friend
playock: 9 plaything
playroom: den, gym **7** nursery
playsome: 7 playful
plaything: die, toy **4** hoop **6** bauble, trifle
playtime: 6 recess
playwright: 6 author **9** dramatist
plea: sue **4** suit **6** abater, answer, appeal, excuse, prayer **7** apology, pretext, request, solicit **8** argument, entreaty, petition, pretense **12** supplication **14** nolo contendere
to end: **6** abater
pleach: 5 plait, plash **9** interlace
plead: beg, sue **5** orate **6** allege, assert **7** beseech, entreat, implore, solicit **8** advocate, appealed, petition **9** importune, intercede **10** supplicate
pleading: 4 oyer **6** answer **8** demurrer **9** suppliant **10** litigation **12** supplication
pleasant: gay **4** bien(F.), fine, good, hend, joli, nice, waly **5** bigly, cushy, douce(F.), hende, hoddy, jolie, lepid, merry, sweet, wally **6** genial **7** amiable, amusing, farrand, farrant, jesting, jocular, leesome(Sc.), playful, winsome **8** delicate, gracious, humorous, pleasing, sportive **9** agreeable, appealing, diverting, enjoyable, laughable, sprightly **10** acceptable, delightful, gratifying
pleasantness: 7 amenity
pleasantry: fun **4** jest, joke **6** banter **7** jesting **10** jocularity **11** gauloiserie **13** facetiousness

please: 4 suit 5 agree, amuse, elate, humor 6 arride, humour 7 aggrate, appease, content, delight, gladden, gratify, indulge, placate, satisfy

pleased: 4 fain 5 apaid, happy 8 gladsome

pleaseship: 10 litigation

pleasing: 4 glad, lief 5 amene, sooth 6 comely, eesome(Sc.), liking 7 roseate 8 fetching, pleasant 9 desirable, favorable, palatable 10 attractive, delectable, favourable 11 pleasureful

pleasurable: 7 hedonic 8 pleasant

pleasure: fun, joy 4 ease, este, gree, will 5 bliss, mirth, sport, treat 6 gaiety 7 delight, jollity 8 delicacy, fruition, gladness, hilarity 9 amusement, diversion, enjoyment, happiness, merriment 10 beneplacit 11 beneplacity, contentment, delectation 12 cheerfulness 13 gratification

god: Bes

ground: 4 park 9 pleasance

insensitiveness to: 9 anhedonia

pert. to: 7 hedonic

philosophy of: 8 hedonism

seeker: 5 sport 7 epicure, playboy 8 hedonist

pleat: 4 fold, kilt, shir 5 braid, prank 7 plicate

pleater: 8 plicator

plebe: 5 toast 8 commoner, freshman

plebeian: 4 snob 6 coarse, common, vulgar 7 illbred, lowborn 8 baseborn, ordinary

plebiscite: 4 vote 6 decree 7 mandate 10 referendum

pleck: 4 spot 5 speck, stain 9 enclosure

plectrum: 4 pick 5 uvula 6 fescue, tongue 7 malleus

pledge: bet, vas(L.), vow 4 adhi, band, bond, gage, hand, hest, hock, oath, pawn, seal, wage, word 5 siker, skoal, toast, troth 6 arrest, assure, borrow, commit, engage, lumber, parole, plight, sicker 7 betroth, earnest, espouse, hostage, promise 8 affiance, contract, guaranty, mortgage 9 assurance, certainty, sacrament 11 association, impignorate

security for: 5 gager

pledger, pledgor: 6 pawner

pledget: 4 swab 8 compress

Pleiad of Alexandria: 5 Homer 6 Aratus 8 Nicander 9 Lycophron 10 Apollonius, Theocritus 11 Callimachus

Pleiades: 4 Maia 6 Merope 7 Alcyone, Celaeno, Electra, Sterope, Taygeta 8 Asterope

constellation: 6 Taurus

father: 5 Atlas

mother: 7 Pleione

Pleione's offspring: 8 Pleiades

plenary: 4 full 6 entire 7 perfect 8 absolute, complete 11 unqualified

plenipotentiary: 5 envoy 8 minister 10 ambassador

plenitude: 6 plenty

plenteous: 9 plentiful

plenteously: 6 freely

plentiful: 4 full, rich, rife 5 ample, sonsy 6 galore, plenty, sonsie 7 copious, fertile, liberal, opulent, profuse 8 abundant, affluent, fruitful, generous, prolific 9 abounding, bounteous, bountiful, exuberant, plenteous 10 productive

plenty: 4 enow, heap, raff 5 ample, cheap, fouth 6 enough, foison, scouth 7 copious(L.) 8 fullness, opulence 9 abundance, affluence, plenitude, plenteous 10 exuberance, luxuriance, perfection, sufficient 11 copiousness, sufficiency 12 completeness

goddess: Ops

horn of: 10 cornucopia

plenum: 5 space 8 assembly, fullness, plethora

pleon: 6 telson 7 abdomen

pleonasm: 8 fullness 10 redundancy

plethora: 4 glut 6 excess 8 fullness 9 repletion 13 overabundance 14 superabundance

plethoric: 6 turgid 8 inflated, overfull 9 bombastic 10 overloaded

pleurapophysis: rib

pleurocarpous: 11 cladanthous, cladogenous

plexiform: 4 rete 5 retia 7 complex 9 intricate 11 complicated

plexus: 4 rete 5 retia 6 tangle 7 network

pliable: 4 easy, limp, soft, waxy 5 lithe 6 limber, pliant, supple 7 bending, ductile, flaccid, flexile, plastic, tensile 8 flexible, fluxible, informal, tractile, workable, yielding 9 adaptable, compliant, malleable, tractable 10 applicable 13 unconstrained

pliant: 4 flip 7 willowy 8 cheverel, cheveril 10 sequacious

plicate: 4 fold 5 pleat

plight: 4 fold, risk 5 array, braid, plait, state 6 engage, pledge, status 7 betroth, embrace, promise 8 position 9 betrothal, condition 10 difficulty 11 predicament

plinth: 4 base, orlo 5 block, couch, stone, table 6 course 8 skirting 9 baseboard

flat: 4 orlo

Pliny's birthplace: 4 Como 5 Comum

plod: dig, mog, peg 4 grub, slog, toil, tore, vamp, work 6 drudge, trudge

plop: 5 plump

plot: map 4 land, plan, plat 5 cabal, chart, draft, story 6 design, devise, scheme, secret 7 compact, connive, diagram, outline

8 conspire, contrive, engineer, intrigue, scenario 9 insidiate, machinate 10 conspiracy 11 machination
garden: bed 8 parterre
ground: lot 5 grave 7 terrain
inventor: 8 schemist
play: 4 node
plouk, plook: 4 knob 6 pimple
plounce: 6 plunge 8 flounder
plout: 4 dash 5 plash 6 splash
plover: 4 bied, crab, dupe 5 drome, sandy 6 kildee, piping 7 collier, killdee, lapwing 8 dotterel, killdeer, Wilson's 9 courtesan, turnstone 10 beetle-head, blacksmith
plow, plough: dig, ear 4 farm, mole, rove, till 5 break 6 digger, furrow 9 cultivate
handle: 5 stilt
kind of: 4 snow 5 sulky 6 gopher, lister, rotary, shovel 7 breaker 8 stirring, turnplow 9 moldboard 14 prairiebreaker
knife: 6 colter 7 coulter
part: 4 hale 5 sheth, slade, stilt 6 sheath 9 plowshare, sharebeam
plow spade: 9 plowstaff
plowgang: 4 area, land 6 bovate(Sc.), oxgang
plowhead: 4 beam 5 frame 6 clevis
plowing: 7 aration
plowland: 4 area 7 measure 8 carucate
plowman: 6 farmer, rustic, tiller 7 acreman, husband 10 clodhopper, countryman
command: gee, haw
plowman's-spikenard: 4 herb 8 aromatic 12 cinnamonroot
plowshare, ploughshare: 6 colter 7 coulter
bone: 5 vomer
ploy: 4 bend, joke 5 sport, trick 6 frolic, tactic 7 pastime 8 escapade 11 merrymaking
pluck: rob, tug 4 grit, jerk, pick, pull, sand, tear 5 cheek, nerve, spunk, strip, twang 6 daring, finger, fleece, gather, snatch, spirit, twitch 7 bravery, courage, deplume, plunder 8 decision, gameness, 9 endurance, fortitude, hardihood 10 resolution
plug: peg, tap, tit 4 blow, bung, calk, cork, slog 5 boost, caulk, estop, knock, punch, shoot, spile, spill 6 dottle, tampon 7 bouchon, pledget, stopper, stopple, tampeon, tampion, tampoon 9 advertise
cannon muzzle: 7 tampion
clay: bod 4 bott
medical: 4 clot 7 embolus
wall: 6 outlet
water: 7 hydrant
plug bib: 6 spigot
plug cock: 6 spigot
plug hat: 4 tile 5 gibus 6 topper
plug-ugly: 4 thug 5 rowdy, tough 7 ruffian 8 gangster

plugboard: 11 switchboard
plum: hog 4 amra, coco, gage, sloe 5 drupe, duhat, icaco, prune 6 damson, jambul, sapote 7 bullace, jambool 9 greengage 10 amatungula
date: 6 sapote
dried: 5 prune
family: 12 amygdalaceae
sapodilla: 5 chico
seed: pit 7 putamen
wild: 4 sloe
plum-colored: 4 puce
plum curculio: 6 weevil
plum duff: 7 pudding
plum weevil: 8 curculio
plumage: 4 down 5 dress 6 hackle 7 floccus 8 feathers 9 adornment
plumb: 4 bung 5 delve, probe, solve 6 chunky, fathom, plunge 7 explore, plummet 8 absolute, complete, entirely, vertical 9 downright 10 absolutely, straighten, understand 13 perpendicular
plumbago: ore 4 lead 5 plant 8 graphite, leadwort
plumbeous: 4 dull 6 leaden
plumber: 5 piper
plume: 4 tuft 5 crest, egret, preen, pride, prize, prune 6 aigret, plumet 7 feather, panache 8 aigrette, plumelet 9 plumicorn
plummet: 4 drop, fall, lead 5 plumb 6 weight
plump: fat 4 back, drop, fall, plop, sink, tidy 5 bonny, buxom, obese, plunk, stout 6 bonnie, chubby, dilate, flatly, fleshy, portly, rotund 7 bluntly, distend, fulsome, support 9 downright
plunder: gut, rob 4 boot, loot, pelf, prey, raid, sack, swag 5 booty, cheat, harry, pluck, poach, raven, reave, rifle, spoil, steal, strip 6 bezzle, boodle, creach(Sc.), creagh(Sc.), dacoit, maraud, pilfer, pirate, rapine, ravage, ravish, spoils 7 despoil, pillage, ransack 8 predator, spoliate 9 depredate, devastate
plunderer: 5 thief 6 bandit, vandal 8 marauder, predator 10 freebooter
plunge: bet, dig, dip 4 cave, dive, duck, dump, pool, sink 5 douse, dowse, drive, fling, lunge, merse, plumb, souse 6 absorb, emerge, footer, gamble, thrust 7 immerge, immerse 8 submerge
plunger: ram 6 risker 10 speculator
plunk: 4 drop, flop, pull, push, sink, toss 5 drive, pluck, plump, sound, throw 6 dollar, strike
plunther: 4 plod 8 flounder
plurality: 8 majority 9 multitude
plus: add 4 more, over 5 extra 6 excess 8 addition, positive
Plutarch work: 5 Lives

Pluto: Dis **5** Hades
 kingdom: **5** Hades
 wife: **10** Persephone, Proserpina
plutocrat: **5** nabob
plutonium symbol: Pu
Plutus: *father:* **6** Iasion
 mother: **7** Demeter
ply: web **4** bend, fold, mold, sail, urge, work
 5 beset, layer, plait, wield **6** double, handle, travel **7** belabor, shuttle **8** belabour,
 exercise **9** importune, thickness
 with drink: **5** birle
pneuma: **4** soul **5** neume **6** breath, spirit **9**
 breathing
pneumonia: **5** lobar, viral **9** bronchial
Po tributary: **4** Adda **9** Cispadane
poach: ram **4** boil, cook, poke, push, stab,
 stir **5** drive, force, shirr, spear, steal,
 steam **6** pierce, thrust **7** trample **8** encroach, trespass
poacher: **7** lurcher, stalker, widgeon
Pocahontas: *father:* **8** Powhatan
 husband: **5** Rolfe
pochard: **4** duck, fowl, smee **6** dunker
pochette: **6** violin **7** handbag **8** envelope
pock: pit **4** scar **6** pimple **7** pustule
pocket: bin, cly, fob **4** poke, prat, sack **7** cantina, conceal, confine, enclose
 ore: **4** lode **7** bonanza
 water: **6** tinaja **7** alberca
pocketbook: bag, fob, lil **4** poke **5** burse,
 pouch, purse **6** wallet **8** billfold **12** portemonnaie
poco: **6** little **8** slightly, somewhat
pococurante: **9** apathetic **10** nonchalant **11**
 indifferent
pocosin, pocoson, pocosen: **5** marsh,
 swamp
pod: bag, bur, cod, kid, sac **4** aril, boll, hull,
 swad **5** belly, carob, pouch, shell, shuck **6**
 legume, loment **7** silicle
podesta: **5** judge, mayor **8** executor, governor, official **10** magistrate
podgy: fat **5** pudgy, squat
podium: **4** base, dais, wall **8** pedestal, platform **12** substructure
Poe: *bird* **5** raven
 house: **5** Usher
 poem: **5** Raven **6** Lenore **7** Ulalume
poem: ode **4** duan, epic, raff, rann(Ir.), rime,
 song, vers(F.) **5** canto, ditty, elegy, ionic,
 lyric, poesy, raffe, stave, verse **6** ballad,
 carmen, epopee, eulogy, iambic, jingle, poetry, screed, sonnet, tercet **7** ballade, dim-
 eter, sestina, triolet, virelay **8** acrostic,
 doggerel, hexapody, senarius, trimeter **9**
 hexameter, hexastich, monometer, octameter, soliloquy **10** tetrameter **11** acatalec-
 tic

break in rhythm: **6** cesura **7** caesura
bucolic: **8** pastoral
division of: see *part* below
eight-line: **7** triolet
foot: **4** iamb **6** iambus **7** anapest, spondee
four-line: **8** quatrain
fourteen-line: **6** sonnet
heroic: **4** epic
line: **8** trimeter **9** hexameter **12** decasyl-
 labic
love: **6** erotic
lyric: **4** alba
medieval: lai **4** alba
melodic: **5** lyric
moral: dit
mournful: **5** elegy
narrative: **4** epos
node: **4** plot
nonsensical: **8** doggerel, limerick
part: fit **4** feet, foot, line **5** canto, epode,
 stich, verse **6** epilog, prolog, stanza **7** refrain **8** epilogue, prologue
pastoral: **4** idyl
pert. to: **4** odic
religious: **4** hymn **5** psalm
rural: **7** eclogue, georgic
satirical: dit(F.) **6** iambic, parody
seven-line: **10** heptastich
short: dit(F.) **5** ditty **6** sonnet **7** epigram **8**
 rondelet
six-line: **9** hexastich
six-stanza: **7** sestina
ten-line: **6** dizain **7** dizaine **9** decastich
poems: **5** poesy, verse **6** poetry
 collection: **5** sylva
poesy: **4** poem **5** motto, verse **7** nosegay
poet: **4** bard, fili, scop **5** odist, rishi **6** lyrist
 7 dreamer, imagist, metrist **8** idyllist, minstrel **9** bucoliast, **13** cinque-centist
 humorous: **4** Lear, Nash
 inferior: **5** rimer **6** rhymer **8** rimester **9** poetaster, poeticule, rhymester, versifier
 inspiration: **4** Muse
poetic: **4** odic **5** lyric **6** dreamy **8** romantic **9**
 beautiful **11** imaginative
poetical: **8** sonnetic
poetry: *accented foot:* **5** arsis
 god: **5** Bragi
 inspiring to: **7** helicon
 muse: **5** Erato **6** Thalia **8** Calliope
pogonip: fog
pogrom: **6** attack **8** massacre **9** slaughter
pogy: **8** menhaden
poi: **4** food **5** paste
 source: **4** taro
poietic: **8** creative
poignant: **4** keen, tart **5** acute, sharp **6** biting, bitter, moving **7** cutting, piquant,
 pointed, pungent **8** piercing, pricking

poind: 4 sell 5 seize 7 impound

point: aim, dot, jag, jet, jot, neb, nib, res, tip, wit 4 apex, barb, cape, crux, cusp, foci, gist, horn, peak, pith, pole, show, spit, spot 5 angle, focus, issue, level, prong, refer, sense, taper 6 allude, apices, cruces(pl.), degree, direct, tittle 7 apicula(L.), apiculi(L.), article, feature, meaning 8 apiculae(L.), apiculus(L.), emphasis, indicate, salience 10 promontory

cardinal: 4 east, west 5 north, south

compass: E., N., S., W.; N.E., N.W., S.E., S.W.; E.N.E., E.S.E., N.N.E., N.N.W., S.S.E., S.S.W., W.N.W., W.S.W. 4 airt 5 airth

final: dot, end 6 period

finishing: 4 tape

highest: sum 4 acme, apex, noon, peak 6 apices, apogee, maxima, summit, zenith 7 maximum 8 meridian, pinnacle

land: 4 hook, spit

law: res

lowest: 4 zero 5 nadir 6 bottom, pergee

pert. to: 6 apical

scoring: ace, run 5 punto 6 sponge

spear: gad

strong: 5 forte

supporting: 5 pivot 7 fulcrum

to the: 8 relevant 9 pertinent

turning: 4 tide 6 crisis, crises

utmost: 7 extreme

vibration: 4 node

weak: 4 flaw 5 fault 6 foible

point-blank: 7 blankly, bluntly, exactly 8 directly 9 perfectly, precisely 10 completely 13 unqualifiedly

point of view: eye 5 angle, sight, slant

pointed: 5 acute, tangy, terse 6 acuate, marked, picked 7 actuate, capapie, concise 8 aculeate, piercing, poignant, spicated, stinging 9 acuminate, apiculate, fastigate 11 conspicuous

pointer: arm, dog, tip 4 clue, hand, hint 5 index 6 fescue, gnomon 7 indices 9 indicator

pointless: 4 dull 5 blunt, inane, silly, vapid 6 stupid 7 insipid

points: *three:* 11 tricuspidal

twelve: 4 pica

pointsman: 7 flanker 9 switchman

poise: tee 5 carry, weigh 6 aplomb 7 balance, ballast, bearing, support, suspend 8 calmness, carriage, liberate, maintain 9 equipoise, stability 10 equanimity 11 equilibrium 12 counterpoise 14 counterbalance

poison: fig 4 bane, drab, gall 5 atter, taint, venin, venom, virus 6 amarin, infect, mi-

asma 7 amarine, arsenic, corrupt, pervert, vitiate 8 empoison, ptomaine 11 contaminate

ant: 10 formmicide 11 formicicide

arrow: 4 haya, inee, upas 5 urali, urare, urari 6 curare, curari

comb. form: 5 toxic 6 toxico

hexapod: 11 insecticide

kind: 4 bikh 5 abrin, nabee, ricin 6 antiar 7 arsenic, tanghin

pert. to: 9 arsenious

tree: 4 upas

poison ash: 5 sumac 6 sumach 9 torchwood

poison dogwood: 5 sumac 6 sumach

poison fish: 4 fugu 6 weever 8 scorpion, toadfish

poison flag: 4 iris

poison flower: 11 bittersweet

poison ivy: 5 sumac 6 laurel

poison tobacco: 7 henbane

poisoned: 6 sepsis

poisonous: 5 toxic 6 virose 7 noxious 8 virulent 9 malignant 11 destructive

fish: 4 fugu

fungus: 7 amanita

gas: 6 arsine 8 phosgene

herb: 8 aconitum

lizard: 4 gila

plant: 8 mandrake 10 nightshade

weed: 4 loco

poisonwood: 5 sumac 10 manchineel

poisson bleu: 7 blue cat, catfish 8 grayling

poitrel: 5 armor, plate 6 armour 9 stomacher 11 breastplate

poke: bag, dig, hat, jab, jog 4 blow, bore, brod, prod, root, sack 5 nudge, probe, punch, purse 6 bonnet, dawdle, loiter, meddle, pocket, potter, putter, sleeve, thrust, wallet 7 dawdler, intrude, tobacco 8 slowpoke 10 pocketbook

poker: rod 4 dart, game

drawing by: 10 pyrography

forerunner: 7 primero

form: 4 draw, stud

stake: pot 4 ante 5 chips

pokeweed: 5 pocan 6 garget 8 inkberry

family: 14 phytolaccaceae

pokey, poky: 4 dull, mean, slow 5 dowdy 6 narrow, shabby, stuffy 7 tedious 8 trifling

Poland: 7 Polonia 8 Sarmatia

cake: 4 baba

carriage: 7 britska

city: 4 Lodz 5 Brest, Posen, Vilna 6 Cracow, Gdynia, Grodno, Krakow, Lublin, Tarnow, Warsaw 7 Beuthen, Lemberg, Litovsk 8 Gleiwitz, Tarnopol 9 Bialystok, Bielostok, Byelostok

coin: 5 ducat, grosz, marka, zloty 6 fennig, halerz, korona

commune: 4 Ruda 5 Plock, Radom
composer: 6 Chopin
dance: 7 mazurka 9 krakowiak, polonaise 11 cracovienne
dollar: 5 dalar
dynasty: 5 Piast
island: 5 Wolin
measure: cal 4 mila, morg, pret 5 linja, morga, sazen, stopa, vloka, wloka 6 cwierc, korzec, kwarta, lokiec 7 garniec 9 kwarterka
nobleman: 7 starost
parliament: 4 Seim, Sejm, Seym 5 Senat
people: 4 Slav 5 Marur 8 Silesian
river: San 4 Styr 5 Dwina, Seret 6 Niemen, Pripet, Strypa 7 Vistula 8 Dniester, South Bug
scientist: 5 Curie
szlachta: 6 gentry 8 nobility 9 landowner
title of address: 4 Pani
weight: lut 4 funt 5 uncya 6 kamian 7 centner, skrupul
polar: 6 Arctic 7 pivotal 8 opposite
polar explorer: 4 Byrd
polar plant: 9 rosinweed
pole: bar, pew, poy, rod, xat 4 axis, boom, brog, mast, palo(Sp.), pike, prop, spar, wand 5 caber, guide, nader, perch, sprit, staff, stake, stick, stool, sweep, totem 6 crotch 7 barling
circle: 11 circumpolar
electric: 5 anode 7 cathode, kathode 9 electrode
fishing: rod
pert. to: 5 polar
tribal: xat 5 totem
vehicle: 4 cope, neap 5 thill
pole fluke: 8 flounder
pole horse: 7 wheeler
pole strip: 8 template
polecat: 5 skunk, zoril 6 ferret, musang 7 fitchet, fitchew, foumart
polehead: 7 tadpole
polemic: 8 argument 9 disputant 10 discussion 11 disputation 12 disputatious 13 argumentative, controversial
polenta: 4 mush 8 porridge
polestar: 5 guide 8 lodestar 10 tramontane
police: 5 guard, watch 6 govern, patrol 7 protect, rurales 8 officers 11 carabinieri(It.) 12 constabulary
headquarters: 4 tana 7 station 8 bargello, barracks 9 marshalcy
line: 6 cordon
officer: 6 kotwal 8 bargello
organization: PAL
vehicle: car, van 7 cruiser 8 prowl car, squad car
policeman: cop 4 bull 5 bobby, bulky, burly, rural, sepoy 6 bobbie, copper, peeler 7

crusher, gumshoe, officer, trooper 8 flatfoot, gendarme(F.) 9 burkundaz, constable, patrolman 11 burkundauze, carabiniere(It.)
badge: 6 buzzer, shield
club: 5 billy 9 espantoon, truncheon 10 nightstick
policy: wit 4 plan 6 wisdom 8 contract, prudence, sagacity 9 diplomacy, principle 10 artfulness, management, shrewdness 14 administration
polish: rub 4 buff 5 frush, glaze, gloss, grind, rabat, scour, sheen, shine, slick 6 finish, luster, lustre, rabbat, refine, smooth 7 burnish, culture, furbish 8 brighten, civilize, elegance, lapidate, levigate, urbanity 10 refinement
polish off: end 4 kill 6 finish
polished: 4 fine 5 compt, suave 6 polite 7 gallant
polisher: 5 rabat(F.) 8 abrasive
polishing: 8 frottage, limation
polishing material: 4 sand 5 emery, rabat 6 pumice
polite: 5 civil, suave 6 gentle, smooth, urbane 7 correct, courtly, cunning, gallant, genteel, refined 8 cultured, debonair, decorous, discreet, polished 9 courteous, debonaire 10 cultivated, debonnaire 11 complaisant
politesse: 10 politeness 11 cleanliness, courtliness 12 decorousness
politic: 4 wary, wise 5 suave 6 artful, crafty, shrewd 7 prudent 8 discreet 9 expedient, politique, provident, sagacious 10 diplomatic 12 unscrupulous
political: *division:* 4 city, town, ward 5 shire, state 6 county 8 province 9 community
gathering: 5 rally 6 caucus
group: 4 bloc, ring 5 cadre, party 6 caucus 7 faction, machine
hanger-on: 6 heeler
incumbents: ins
influence: 5 lobby
list: 5 slate
political party: G.O.P. 4 Tory, Whig 5 labor 9 Communist, Socialist 10 Democratic, Republican 12 Conservative
principles: 8 platform
program article: 5 plank
unit: 4 city, East, ward, West 5 state 6 county, parish 7 borough, hundred, kingdom 8 district 9 sultanate
politician: 7 schemer, senator, statist 9 intriguer, president, statesman 16 congressionalist
politico: 9 statesman 10 politician
polka dot: 4 spot 6 circle

poll: cow 4 clip, coll, head, list, trim 5 count, shave, shear 6 fleece, survey 7 canvass, despoil, listing 8 counting, register 9 enumerate

pollack: 4 fish, pool 6 billet 7 baddock(Sc.) 8 coalfish

pollan: 9 whitefish

pollard: cow 4 bran, deer, goat, stag, tree 5 sheep

polled: 8 hornless

pollen: 4 dust, meal 5 flour

pollen brush: 5 scopa 6 scopae

pollen grain: *mass:* 8 pollinia 9 pollinium

pollenization: 5 xenia

poller: 6 barber 9 plunderer 11 extortioner, taxgatherer

pollex: 4 inch 5 digit, thumb 7 phlange

pollicitation: 7 promise 8 proposal

pollinate: 9 fecundate

pollinosis: 8 hay fever

polliwog: 7 tadpole

pollute: 4 foul, soil 5 dirty, smear, stain, sully, taint 6 befoul, defile, ravish 7 corrupt, debauch, profane, violate, vitiate 9 desecrate 11 contaminate

pollution: 5 filth 8 impurity 11 uncleanness

Pollux: *brother:* 6 Castor

father: 4 Zeus

mother: 4 Leda

polo: *division:* 7 chucker, chukker

mount: 4 pony 5 horse

stick: 6 mallet

team: 4 four

Polonius: *daughter:* 7 Ophelia

son: 7 Laertes

Polony: 6 Polish 7 sausage 9 polonaise

polt: 4 blow, club 5 knock, thump

poltergeist: 5 ghost 6 spirit

poltfoot: 8 clubfoot

poltroon: cad 4 idle, lazy 6 coward, craven 7 dastard 8 cowardly, sluggard 9 dastardly

polverine: 6 potash 8 pearlash

polyandrium: 8 cemetery

polychromatic: 10 variegated 12 multicolored

polygamy: 6 bigamy

polygon: 4 ngon 6 square 7 decagon, hexagon, nonagon, octagon 8 pentagon, triangle

equal sides: 6 isagon

nine sides: 7 nonagon

twelve sides: 9 dodecagon

Polynesia: *apple:* 4 hevi

baking pit: umu

banana: fei

beverage: 4 kava, kawa

breech cloth: 4 malo

burial place: ahu

butterfly: io

chestnut: 4 rata

cloth: 4 tapa

dance: 4 siva

dragon: ati

fern: 4 tara

garment: 5 pareu

god: Oro 4 Tane, Tiki

goddess: 4 Pele

herb: pia

homeland: 7 Havaiki

island: 4 Fiji 5 Samoa 7 Phoenix, Tokelau

language: 7 Tagalog

magical power: 4 mana

memorial: ahu

oven: umu

people: Ati 5 Malay, Maori 6 Kanaka, Samoan, Tongan 8 Hawaiian, Tahitian 9 Marquesan

pepper plant: 4 avas

pigeon: 4 lupe

pine: ara 4 hala

plant: 4 taro

ruler: 7 faipule

sky: 5 langi

sling: ma

spirit: 4 Atua

statue: 4 Tiki

tree: ti 4 ahia, rata

wages: utu

yam: ube, ubi, uve, uvi

polyp: 5 hydra, tumor 6 seapen 7 anemone, hydroid

skeleton: 5 coral

polytrophic: 9 versatile

Polyxena: *father:* 5 Priam

lover: 8 Achilles

mother: 6 Hecuba

pomade: 5 salve 7 pomatum, unguent 8 cosmetic, ointment

pome: 4 ball, pear 5 apple, fruit, globe 6 quince, sphere

pomegranate: 6 granet 7 granate, grenade

sirup: 9 grenadine

pomelo: 8 shaddock 10 grapefruit

Pomerania: *capital:* 7 Stettin

city: 6 Anklam

island: 5 Rugen 6 Usedom

river: 4 Oder

Pomeranian: dog

pomme de terre: 6 potato

pommel: bat 4 beat, knob 6 handle 12 protuberance

bag: 7 cantina

pomp: 4 fare 5 boast, pride, state 6 estate, parade 7 cortege, display, pageant 8 ceremony, grandeur, splendor 9 pageantry, spectacle 10 ceremonial 11 ostentation 12 magnificence

Pomp and Circumstance composer: 5 Elgar

pompano: 4 fish 7 alewife 9 poppy fish

Pompeii: *archeologist:* Mau

heroine: 4 Ione

pom-pom: gun 6 cannon

pompon: 4 ball, tuft 8 ornament 13 chrysanthemum

pompous: big 7 bloated, fustian, orotund, stately, stilted 9 bombastic, flatulent, grandiose 10 altisonant, pontifical 11 altiloquent, dictatorial, magnificent, pretentious, stateliness 12 ostentatious 13 grandiloquent, self-important

Ponchielli opera: 8 Gioconda

pond: dam, lum 4 delf, dike, dyke, lake, mere, pool, tarn 5 delft 6 lagoon 7 lakelet

fish: 7 aquaria, pisoina 8 aquarium

frog: 7 ranaria 8 ranarium

oyster: 6 claire

pond dogwood: 10 buttonbush

pond duck: 7 mallard

pond hen: 4 coot

ponder: 4 chaw, mull, muse, pore 5 brood, opine, weigh 6 reason 7 reflect, revolve 8 appraise, cogitate, consider, evaluate, meditate, ruminate 10 deliberate 11 contemplate

ponderous: 5 bulky, grave, heavy, hefty, massy 7 awkward, massive, weighty 8 unwieldy 9 important, momentous 11 elephantine

pondfish: 7 sunfish

pondokkie: hut 5 hovel

pone: 4 lump, turf 8 swelling 10 johnnycake

pongee: 4 silk 5 cloth 6 fabric 8 shantung

pongy: 4 monk 6 priest 8 Buddhist

poniard: 4 kill, stab 6 bodkin, dagger, pierce, stylet 8 stiletto

pont: 5 ferry, float 6 bridge 7 caisson, pontoon 9 ferryboat

pontiff: 4 pope 6 bishop

pert. to: 5 papal 7 sistine

pontifical: 5 papal 7 pompous 8 dogmatic

pontoon: 4 boat 5 barge, float 6 bridge, vessel 7 caisson

plank: 5 chess

pony: cab, cob, nag 4 crib 5 glass, horse 6 garran, liquor 7 hackney, measure

kind: 5 pinto, tatoo 6 cayuse, Exmoor 8 Shetland

student's: 4 crib, trot

pooch: dog 6 barbet 7 mongrel

pooh-pooh: 8 ridicule 9 denigrate

pook: 4 heap, pile, pull 5 pluck, stack

pooka: 6 goblin 7 specter

pool: car, dib(Sc.), dub(Sc.), lin, pit, pot 4 carr, dike, dyke, game, jeel, linn, loch, mear, meer, mere, pond, tank, tarn 5 flash, flush, funds, kitty, lough, plash, stake, trunk, trust 6 cartel, charco, flodge, lagoon, plunge, puddle, salina 7 alberca, carline, combine, jackpot, plashet 8 monopoly 9 billabong, billiards, reservoir, resources 10 natatorium 11 combination

ball: cue 4 spot 6 ringer

poon tree: 4 dilo 5 domba, keena 8 mastwood

poonghie: See **pongy**

poop: 4 deck, fool, gulp, seat 5 cheat, cozen, stern 8 hinddeck 10 nincompoop 11 information

poor: bad, ill 4 bare, base, lean, mean 5 cheap, dinky, naked, needy, seedy 6 abject, barren, feeble, humble, hungry, paltry, pilled, scanty, shabby 7 hapless, sterile, unlucky 8 indigent, inferior 9 defective, destitute, emaciated, imperfect, infertile, penurious 10 inadequate, ungenerous 11 impecunious, inefficient, unfortunate 12 contemptible, insufficient 13 improverished, insignificant 14 unsatisfactory

Poor Clare: nun 6 sister

poor joe: 5 heron

poor John: cod 4 food, hake

poor man's pepper: 9 stonecrop 11 peppergrass

poor man's soap: 8 hardhack

poor man's weatherglass: 9 pimpernel

poor soldier: 9 friarbird

poor-spirited: 4 base 8 cowardly

poorer: 5 worse 8 inferior

poorhouse: 9 almshouse, workhouse

poorly: 13 disparagingly

pop: 4 dart 8 beverage 9 explosion

popadam: 4 cake 5 wafer 6 cookie

popdock: 8 foxglove

pope: 4 ruff 6 bishop, priest, puffin, shrike 7 pontiff 9 bullfinch, patriarch

answer: 8 rescript

cape: 5 fanon 7 mozetta 8 mozzetta

collar: 5 orale

court: 5 Curia

court office: 6 datary 7 dataria

court officer: 6 datary

crown: 5 tiara 9 triregnum

envoy: 6 legate 7 nuntius 8 ablegate

epistle: 8 decretal

headdress: 5 miter, mitre

letter: 4 bull

line: 6 papacy

name: Leo 4 John, Pius 5 Peter, Ratti, Urban 6 Adrian 7 Gregory, Zachary 8 Benedict

palace: 7 Lateran, Vatican

pert. to: 5 papal

seal: 5 bulla

veil: 5 orale 6 fannel

Popeye's sweetheart: Oyl 5 Olive
popinac: 8 huisache
popinjay: 6 parrot 8 parakeet 10 woodpecker
poplar: 4 liar 5 abele, alamo, aspen, bahan, bolle, garab 7 populus 9 tacamahac 10 cottonwood
  white: 4 abele, aspen
Poppaea's husband: 4 Nero
poppy: 5 plant 6 blaver, canker, flower 7 coprose, papaver, ponceau 8 foxglove 10 coquelicot
  herb family: 9 celandine
  seed: maw
poppycock: rot 4 bosh, dung 8 nonsense
populace: mob 4 mass 5 demos, plebs 6 people
popular: lay, pop 6 common, simple 7 demotic, favored 8 accepted, favorite 9 prevalent, well-liked 11 proletarian 12 nontechnical
popularity: 5 vogue
populate: 6 occupy, people 7 inhabit
population: 9 habitancy 11 inhabitants
  count: 6 census
  study: 10 larithmics
porbeagle: 5 shark
porcelain: 4 frit 5 china 7 biscuit
  ancient: 5 murra
  clay: 6 kaolin 7 kaoline
  furnace: 5 hovel
  kind of: 6 Sevres 7 Celadon, Dresden, Limoges 8 Haviland 9 Wedgewood
porch: 4 door, stoa 5 lanai, plaza, stoae(pl.), stoop 6 harbor, loggia, piazza 7 balcony, galilee, gallery, portico, terrace, veranda 8 entrance 9 colonnade
  church: 7 galilee
  sun: 7 solaria(pl.) 8 solarium
  swing: 6 glider
porcine: 7 piglike
porcupine: 5 urson 7 cawquaw 8 hedgehog
  disease: 10 ichthyosis
  genus of: 7 hystrix
  spine: 5 quill
porcupine anteater: 7 echidna
porcupine fish: 6 diodon
porcupine grass: 5 stipa
  quill: pen
pore: con 4 gaze 5 gloze, stare, stoma, study 6 ponder 7 foramen, opening, orifice, ostiole, stomata(pl.) 8 lenticel, meditate
  plant: 8 lenticel
porgy: tai(Jap.) 4 fish, scup 6 besugo, pagrus 7 margate, pinfish 8 menhaden 9 spadefish
pork: ham, pig 5 bacon, money, swine 6 hamhog 7 griskin, sausage 8 position
porker: hog, pig 5 swine

porkfish: 4 sisi
porky: fat, pig 6 greasy 9 porcupine
pornographic: 4 lewd 7 obscene 10 licentious
porphyry: 4 rock
porpoise: 4 inia 6 seahog 7 dolphin, pellock(Sc.) 8 gairfish
porrect: 6 extend, tender 7 present
porret: 4 leek 5 onion 6 garlic 8 scallion
porridge: 4 samp 5 atole, brose(Sc.), grout, gruel 6 burgoo 7 brochan, burgout, oatmeal, polenta, pottage 9 stirabout 11 skilligalee
  container: 6 bicker
port: 4 gate, toal, left, wine 5 carry, haven 6 apport, harbor, market, portal, refuge 7 bearing, harbour, meaning, purport, shelter 8 carriage, demeanor, larboard 9 demeanour, transport 10 deportment 11 destination
portable: 6 mobile 7 movable 8 bearable
  bathtub: 4 tosh
  bed: cot 8 rollaway
  chair: 5 sedan
  lamp: 7 lantern
  stove: 4 etna
portal: 4 arch, door, gate 7 gateway 8 entrance
portance: 7 bearing, conduct 8 carriage, demeanor
portcullis: bar 4 door, gate, shut 5 grate, herse 7 grating, lattice
porte-monnaie: 5 purse 10 pocketbook
portefeuille: 9 portfolio
portend: 4 bode 5 augur 6 divine 7 betoken, forbode, predict, presage 8 forebode, foretell, prophesy 10 foreshadow
portent: 4 omen, sign 5 event 6 marvel, ostent, wonder 7 meaning, prodigy 8 ceremony 10 prognostic 11 forewarning
portentous: 4 dire 5 fatal, grave 6 solemn 7 fateful, ominous 10 impressive 11 significant
porter: ale 5 carry, hamal, stout 6 bearer, durwan, hamaul, hammal, khamal, redcap, suisse 7 bailiff, carrier, durwaun, dvornik(Russ.), gateman, hummaul, janitor 8 beverage, cargador, janitrix 9 attendant, concierge, janitress, transport 10 doorkeeper
porteress: See **portress**
Portia: *alias:* 9 Balthazar
  lover: 8 Bassanio
  maid: 7 Nerissa
portia tree: 5 bendy
portico: 4 stoa(Gr.), xyst 5 porch, stoae(Gr., pl.) 6 atrium, piazza, xystus 7 narthex, pteroma, terrace, veranda 9 colonnade, pteromata(pl.) 10 ambulatory, antetemple

long: 6 xystus 7 veranda

potiere: 5 drape 7 curtain

portion: bit, cut, dab, dot, jag, lot, nip 4 chaw, deal, dole, dunt, fate, jagg, part, some 5 allot, allow, divvy, dower, dowry, endow, piece, quota, ratio, share 6 canton, divide, dowery, gobbet, moiety, parcel, rasher, ration 7 destiny, helping, scruple, section, segment, serving 8 legitime, quantity 9 allotment, allowance, apportion 10 distribute 13 apportionment

portly: fat 5 obese, stout 6 goodly 7 stately 8 imposing, majestic 9 corpulent, dignified

portmanteau: bag 4 case 6 valise 8 suitcase 9 carpetbag, gladstone

Porto Rico: See **Puerto Rico**

portoise: 7 gunwale 8 portlast

portrait: 4 copy, icon, ikon 5 image 7 picture 8 likeness 10 similitude

pert. to: 6 iconic

sitting: 6 seance

portray: act 4 draw, form, limn, mime, show 5 enact, frame, graph, image, paint 6 depict 7 fashion, picture 8 describe 9 delineate, pantomime, represent 11 demonstrate

portrayal: 8 portrait

portreeve: 5 mayor 7 bailiff, officer

portress, porteress: 6 porter 9 charwoman 10 doorkeeper

Portugal: *brandy:* 11 aguardiente

city: 4 Ovar 5 Braga, Evora 6 Guarda, Lisbon, Oporto 7 Coimbra 8 Braganca

coin: rei 4 peca, real 5 conto, coroa, dobra, indio 6 dobrao, escudo, macuta, macute, pataca, pataco, testao, tostao, vintem 7 centavo, crusado, moidore, patacao 8 equipaga

colony: Diu, Goa 5 Damao, Macao, Timor 6 Angola, Guinea 8 Principe, Sao Thome 10 Mozambique 11 Cape de Verde

commune: 5 Braga

district: 4 Tete 5 Evora

explorer: Cao 4 Diaz

festival: 9 chamarita

former money: 5 dobra

guitar: 7 machete

harbor: 4 Faro, Ovar 5 Macao 6 Aveiro, Lisbon, Oporto, Vianna 7 Setubal 8 Figueira

island: 6 Angola, Azores 7 Madeira 8 Principe, Sao Thome

Jew: 8 Sephardi 9 Sephardim(pl.)

legislature: 6 cortes

liquid measure: 6 canada

measure: pe 4 alma, bota, meio, moio, pipa, vara 5 almud, braca, fanga, geira, legoa, linha, milha, palmo 6 almude, covado,

quarto 7 alquier, estadio, ferrado, selamin 8 alqueire, tonelada 9 pollegada, quartilho

money: rei 4 peca 5 dobra 8 johannes

mountain: 15 Serra d'Estrella

navigator: 4 Gama 8 Magellan

noble: see *title* below

people: 7 Iberian

poet: 7 Camoens

province: 4 Ovar 5 Beira, Minho 6 Azores 7 Algarve, Madeira 8 Alemtejo 11 Estremadura 12 Traz-os-Montes

river: 4 Sado 5 Douro, Duero, Minho, Tagus 7 Mondego 8 Guadiana

saint: Sao

song: 4 fado

title: dom 4 dona 6 senhor 7 fidalgo, senhora 9 senhorita

vessel: 7 caravel

weight: 4 grao, onca, once 5 libra, marco 6 arroba, oitava 7 arratel, quintal 9 escropulo

porwigle: 7 tadpole

posada: inn 5 hotel

posaune: 8 trombone

pose: set, sit 4 airs 5 model, place 6 baffle, puzzle, stance 7 nonplus, posture 8 attitude, position, propound 9 mannerism 10 disconcert, expression 11 affectation, impersonate 12 attitudinize

Poseidon: 7 Neptune(L.)

father: 6 Cronus

mother: 4 Rhea

scepter: 7 trident

servant: 7 Proteus

son: 6 Albion, Triton 7 Alebion, Antaeus, Antaios

wife: 10 Amphitrite

poser: 5 facer 6 puzzle 7 problem 8 question

posh: 5 smart 6 spruce, swanky 7 elegant 9 luxurious

posit: 6 affirm, assert, assume 9 postulate

position (see also **place**): job, lie, set 4 loci(pl.), pose, post, rank, site 5 cense, coign, locus, place, situs, stand 6 billet, coigne, estate, locale, office, plight, stance, status 7 calling, posture 8 attitude, doctrine, location, sinecure, statuses(pl.) 9 condition, gradation, situation 11 affirmation, appointment, disposition 12 circumstance

change: 4 move

correct: 8 oriented

defensive: 4 fort 10 bridgehead

relative: 5 grade 8 standing

with little work: 8 sinecure

positional: 6 situal

positive: set 4 plus, sure 6 actual, thetic 7 assured, certain 8 absolute, complete, constant, dogmatic, emphatic, explicit 9 assertive, confident, downright, empirical, practical 10 peremptory 11 affirmative, dictatorial, opinionated, unqualified **13** authoritative, overconfident

positively: 5 truly 6 really 8 actually 9 certainly, obviously 11 indubitably

positivism: 7 Comtism 11 materialism
founder: 5 Comte

positure: 7 posture 11 arrangement, disposition 13 configuration

poss: 4 beat, dash, push 5 drive, knock, pound, stamp 6 thrust

posse: 4 band

possess: get, owe, own 4 have 5 reach 6 occupy 7 inhabit 8 dominate, maintain

possessed: mad 8 demoniac

possession: 4 aver, hold 5 aught 6 havior, seisin, wealth 7 control, dewanee, haviour, mastery 8 property 9 ownership
family: 8 heirloom
legal: 5 title 6 estate
of goods by finding: 6 trover
take: 5 seise
time: 5 lease

possessions: 5 goods 6 graith

possessor: 10 proprietor

posset: 4 turn 6 curdle, pamper 8 beverage 9 balductum, coagulate

possibility: 11 eventuality

possible: may 6 likely 8 feasible, probable 9 potential 10 contingent 11 practicable

possibly: may 5 maybe 7 perhaps

possum: 7 opossum 9 marsupial, phalanger
comic strip: 4 Pogo
play: 4 sham 5 feign 7 pretend

post: set 4 dole, dool, fort, mail, pole, ride, send 5 cippi(pl.), newel, place, stake, stock 6 assign, cippus, column, inform, office, pillar, travel 7 courier, placard, station 8 announce, dispatch, garrison, position 9 advertise, situation, sternpost 11 publication
airplane race: 5 pylon
boat rope: 7 bollard, capstan
easy: 4 pipe, snap 8 sinecure
middle: 8 kingpost

post chaise: 4 jack 5 coach 8 carriage

post office: 6 correo(Sp.)
letter box: 8 apartado(Sp.)

postage: 5 stamp
stamp design: 6 burele 8 burelage, spandred

postbox: 7 mailbox

postboy: 7 courier, yamshik(Russ.) 8 yemschik 9 postilion, yamstchik(Russ.)

postdate: 9 afterdate

postea: 5 entry 6 record

poster: 4 bill, clap, sign 7 affiche, courier, placard, sticker 10 billposter 13 advertisement

posterior: 4 back, hind, rear 6 behind, caudal, dorsal, hinder 10 subsequent

posterity: 6 sequel 10 generation 11 descendants

postern: 4 door, exit, gate 7 private 8 entrance 10 undercover

postfix: 6 append 7 suffix

postiche: wig 6 switch, toupee 8 pretense 9 imitation 14 counterfeiting

postil: 6 homily 7 comment 10 commentary

postilion: 7 postboy

postpone: 4 stay, wait 5 defer, delay, remit, table 6 remand, retard, shelve 7 adjourn, prolong 10 pigeonhole 11 subordinate 13 procrastinate

postponement: 4 mora 5 morae(pl.) 7 respite 8 reprieve 10 ampliation

postprandial: 11 after-dinner

postulant: 9 applicant, candidate 10 petitioner

postulate: 5 claim, posit 6 assume, demand 7 premise, require 10 hypotheses(pl.), hypothesis 11 proposition 12 prerequisite

posture: 4 pose 6 stance 7 bearing, gesture 8 attitude, carriage, position 9 composure
erect: 11 orthostatic

posy: 5 motto, verse 6 flower, legend 7 bouquet, nosegay 9 sentiment 11 composition

pot: bag, pan, win 4 dixy, pool 5 abyss, crewe, dixie, drink, kitty, shoot 6 aludel, basket, cruset, posnet, secure, vessel 7 caldron, capture, cuvette 8 cauldron, crucible, potation 11 deteriorate
arch: 4 kiln
earthen: 4 olla 5 crock, cruse 6 chytra
handle: 4 bool
hat: 5 derby 6 bowler
lead: 8 graphite
wheel: 5 noria

pot-au-feu: 4 soup, stew

pot liquid: 6 brewis

pot-rustler: 4 cook

potable: 5 drink 8 beverage 9 drinkable

potage: 4 soup 5 broth

potash: 4 kali 5 niter, nitre, salin 6 alkali, saline 8 pearlash

potassium: *compound:* 4 alum 6 chrome, potash
sulphate: 4 alum

potation: 4 bout, dram 5 draft, drink 6 liquid, liquor 7 spirits 8 beverage, drinking

potato: 4 ima, oca, yam 4 chat, papa, spud 5 rural, tuber 6 murphy 7 manroot
beetle: 8 hardback
bud: eye
disease: pox 4 curl
dish: 8 au gratin 9 lyonnaise, scalloped
family: 10 solanaceae
planting ridge: 4 ruck

seed part: eye
starch: 6 farina
sweet: 6 batata, comote, patata 7 batatas, ocarina
Potato State: 5 Idaho, Maine
potbank: 7 pottery
potboiler: 4 book 8 painting 9 potwaller
potboy: 8 Ganymede 9 cupbearer
pote: 4 kick, poke, push 6 thrust
poteen, potheen: 6 whisky
potence: 5 cross 6 gibbet 7 gallows
potency: vis 5 force, might, power, vigor 6 energy 8 efficacy, strength, vitality 9 fertility
potent: 4 able 6 cogent, mighty 7 dynamic 8 powerful, puissant, virulent 9 effective, efficient 10 convincing 11 influential
potentate: 4 amir, emir 5 ameer, emeer, mogul, ruler 6 moghul, prince 7 monarch 9 sovereign
potential: 6 latent, mighty 8 possible 10 unrealized 11 influential, possibility, undeveloped
potentiality: 5 power
potgun: 6 pistol, popgun 8 braggart
pothead: 9 blackfish
pother: ado, row, vex 4 fuss, stir 5 worry 6 bother, bustle, harass, muddle, uproar 7 fluster, perplex, trouble 9 commotion, confusion 11 disturbance 12 perturbation
potherb: 4 kale, mint, wort 5 chard 6 greens 7 mustard, spinach
pert. to: 7 olitory
pothole: 6 tinaja
pothook: rod 4 hake, nine 5 crook 6 collar, scrawl
pothouse: 6 tavern 8 alehouse
potiche: jar 4 vase
potion: 4 brew, dose, drug 5 draft, drink 6 drench 7 draught, philter, philtre 8 nepenthe
sleeping: 5 dwale 6 opiate 8 narcotic 9 soporific 10 belladonna
potlatch: 4 gift 5 feast
potomania: 10 dipsomania
potpie: 4 stew 9 fricassee
potpourri: jar 4 olio, stew 6 medley 7 mixture 9 anthology 10 miscellany 11 salamagundi
potrero: 6 meadow 7 pasture
potsherd: bit 4 chip 5 shard 8 fragment
potshot: 5 shoot 6 assail, attack
potstone: 8 steatite
pottage: 4 soup 6 brewis 8 porridge
pottah: 4 deed 5 lease 11 certificate
potted: 5 drunk 11 intoxicated
potter: fad, pry 4 fuss, mess, poke, push 6 cotter, dabble, dacker, daiker, dawdle, dodder, fiddle, footer, footle, loiter, meddle, putter, tamper, tinker, trifle 7

cloamer, fossick, saunter 8 ceramist 10 ceramicist
potter's clay: 5 argil
potter's field: 8 Aceldama, cemetery
potter's wheel: 4 disk 5 lathe, palet, throw 6 jigger, pallet
pottery: 4 bank, ware 5 china, delft 7 Keramos(F.) 8 ceramics 9 delftware, Keramikos(Gr.), stoneware 11 earthenware
decorating paste: 9 barbotine
dish: 7 ramekin
enameled: 8 majolica
firing box: 6 saggar, sagger 7 saggard
fragment: 5 shard, sherd
kind: uda(Ind.) 4 delf 5 delft 6 basalt 7 aretine, bocraro 8 bucchero, Majolica, vitreous 9 delftware, sigillate 12 buccheronero
maker: 6 potter 8 ceramist
mineral: 8 feldspar
pert. to: 7 ceramic
pottle: pot 6 basket, liquor 7 tankard
potty: pot 5 crazy, dotty, petty 7 foolish, haughty, trivial 9 eccentric 12 supercilious
pouch: bag, cod, pod, sac 4 cyst, sack 5 bulge, bursa, purse 6 budget, gipser, pocket, sporan 7 alforja, gipsire, mailbag, saccule, silicle, sporran 9 spleuchan 10 pocketbook
Highlander's: 7 sporran
pouch bone: 9 marsupial
pouched: 9 sacculate
dog: 4 wolf
marmot: 8 squirrel 11 spermophile
pouf: 4 bang, puff 7 ottoman 9 hairdress
poule: 6 wanton 10 prostitute
poulp, poulpe: 7 octopus
poultry: 4 fowl 5 ducks, geese 7 pigeons, turkeys 8 chickens 9 pheasants 10 guinea fowl
breed: 6 Ancona 7 Dorking, Leghorn 12 Plymouth Rock 14 Rhode-Island Red
dealer: 6 eggler
disease: pip 4 roup
dish: 9 galantine
farm: 7 hennery
yard: 6 barton
pounamu: 4 jade 8 nephrite 10 greenstone
pounce: nab 4 leap, pink, poke, stab 5 pound, prick, punch, stamp, swoop, talon 6 emboss, spring, thrust 8 ornament 9 comminute, perforate
pound: lb. 4 beat, bray, ding, maul, pond, tamp, unit 5 knock, thump 6 bruise, hammer, powder, weight 7 contuse 9 enclosure, pulverize
poundage: 6 charge, weight 8 distrain 9 constrain, enclosure 11 confinement
pounder: 6 pestle
pour: 4 emit, flow, gush, hale, lave, pass, rain, teem, tide, toom(Sc.), vent, well 5

birle, drain, empty, heald, hield, issue, spout, utter 6 affuse, decant, effuse, libate, stream 8 downpour 9 discharge

pourboire: fee, tip 7 douceur 8 gratuity 9 buona-mani(pl.), buona-mano

pout: bib, mop 4 moue, sulk 5 boody, pique 7 catfish, eelpout 8 bullhead 9 sulkiness

poverty: 4 lack, need, want 6 dearth, penury 7 paucity, tenuity 9 indigence 10 inadequacy, scantiness 11 destitution, inferiority

powder: 4 abir(Ind.), dust, kish, mull, talc 5 boral, boron, flour, grind 6 empasm, pollen, pounce, yttria 7 araroba, aristol, malarin, saponin, tripoli 8 cosmetic, sprinkle, tannigen 9 pulverize 10 epiplastic
case: 9 bandolier
container: 4 horn 7 arsenal 8 magazine
make: 4 bray 5 grind 7 calcine 9 pulverize
smokeless: 6 filite, poudre 7 cordite 8 amberite

powdered: 4 seme 5 semee 6 floury

power: arm, art, vis 4 bulk, dint, gift, hand, iron, rial, sway, thew 5 force, might, state, steam, vigor, vires(pl.), wield 6 agency, effort, empire, energy, foison, throne 7 ability, command, control, potence, potency, stamina 8 capacity, efficacy, momentum, strength, virility 9 authority, dominator, influence, intensity, puissance 10 domination, efficiency 12 jurisdiction, potentiality
comb. form: 4 dyna
deprive of: 4 maim 7 impeach 8 dethrone 12 deparliament
intellectual: wit 5 brain 6 genius
lack: 5 atony
natural: od 4 odyl 5 odyle
partnership: 9 champerty
provide with: 5 endue, endow
superior: 10 prepotency 12 predominance
symbol: 5 sword 7 scepter, sceptre
third: 4 cube
unit of: HP; RPM 4 watt
unlimited: 11 omnipotence

power of attorney: 5 agent 10 procurator

powerboat: 5 yacht 9 motorboat

powerful: 4 able, bold, deep 5 stout 6 brawny, cogent, heroic 7 feckful, leonine 9 effective, effectual 10 dominating 11 efficacious

powerless: 4 weak 6 feeble, unable 8 helpless, impotent, lifeless

Powhatan: *daughter:* 10 Pocahontas

pownie: 4 pony

powwow: 6 confer, priest 7 meeting 8 assembly, ceremony, congress, conjurer 10 conference

poyou: 6 peludo 9 armadillo

praam: 4 pram

prabble: 7 quarrel 8 squabble

prabhu: 4 lord 5 chief 6 writer

practic: 6 artful, shrewd 7 cunning 8 decision(Sc.) 9 practical, practiced

practical: 5 utile 6 actual, beaten, usable, useful 7 practic, working 8 feasible, possible, workable 9 available, practiced, pragmatic 11 pragmatical, utilitarian
example: 6 praxis
joke: 4 hoax 5 prank, trick

practically: 6 almost, nearly 9 virtually 13 substantially

practice: do; ply, rut, try, use 4 plot, rote 5 apply, canon, cause, drill, habit, trade, train, usage 6 custom, follow, praxic 7 perform 8 exercise, intrigue, rehearse 9 construct, negotiate 10 experience
pert. to: 9 pragmatic
sharp: 4 game 5 dodge, fraud, usury 6 deceit 9 chicanery

practiced: 7 practic, skilled, veteran 10 conversant

practico: 5 guide 7 skilled 11 experienced

practitioner: 5 agent 6 artist, healer, novice 7 learner, plotter, schemer 8 civilian 9 assistant

prad: 5 horse

praenomen: 4 name 5 Caius, Gaius, Titus 9 first-name

pragmatic: 7 skilled 8 dogmatic, meddling 9 conceited, empirical, officious, practical 10 meddlesome, systematic 11 dictatorial, opinionated, pragmatical

Prague: 4 Prag 5 Praha
river: 6 Moldau, Vltava

prairie: bay 5 camas, llano, plain 6 camass, cammas, steppe 7 quamash 9 grassland 10 prairillon
clump of trees in: 5 motte
mud: 5 gumbo
plant: 5 camas 6 camass

prairie anemone: 12 pasqueflower

prairie antelope: 9 pronghorn

prairie apple: 9 breadroot

prairie berry: 9 trompillo

prairie breaker: 4 plow

prairie chicken: 6 grouse

prairie crocus: 12 pasqueflower

prairie dog: 6 marmot 11 wishton-wish

prairie dog weed: 8 marigold

prairie pigeon: 6 plover 9 sandpiper

prairie potato: 9 breadroot

prairie schooner: ark 5 wagon

Prairie State: 8 Illinois

prairie wolf: 6 coyote

prairieweed: 10 cinquefoil

praise: 4 hery, laud, tout 5 adore, allow, alose, bless, extol, glory, honor, kudos, roosa, roose 6 eulogy, extoll, kudize 7 acclaim, adulate, applaud, commend, encomia(pl.), glorify, hosanna, magnify, plaudit, tribute 8 applause, appraise, blessing, encomium, eulogize, macarism 9 adulation, celebrate, panegyric 10 compliment, panegyrize 11 approbation 12 commendation 13 glorification

ascription of: 6 Gloria

praiseworthy: 9 exemplary 13 complimentary

praising: 9 laudative

Prakrit: 7 Bahlika 8 language 11 Dakshinatya

praline: 5 candy 10 confection

pram, praam: 4 boat, cart 5 barge 8 carriage, stroller 12 perambulator

prana: 9 principle

prance: 5 brank, caper, dance, strut 6 cavort, frolic 7 swagger

prancer: 5 horse, rider

prandium: 4 meal 6 dinner, repast

prank: jig 4 dido, fold, lark, prat 5 adorn, antic, caper, freak, pleat, shine, trick 6 curvet, fegary, frolic, gambol 8 capricci(pl.), escapade, mischief 9 capriccio 11 monkeyshine

prase: 6 quartz 10 chalcedony

prat: 4 push 5 nudge, prank, trick

prate: gab 4 blab, buck, bukh, carp, chat, talk 5 blate, boast, clack, clash 6 babble, claver, tattle, tongue 7 blatter, chatter, deblate, prattle, twaddle 8 harangue 11 deblaterate

prattle: 4 gaff, lisp 5 prate 6 cackle 7 blather, blether, clatter 9 bavardage 11 confabulate

prawn: 10 crustacean

praxis: 6 action, custom 8 practice

pray: ask, beg, bid, sue 5 daven(Heb.) 6 appeal, invite, invoke 7 beseech, conjure, entreat, implore, request 8 petition 10 supplicate

praya: 4 road 5 beach 6 strand 9 esplanade 10 waterfront

prayer: ave 4 bead, bede, bene, boon, plea, suit 5 grace, matin 6 appeal, ectene, ektene, errand, orison 7 Angelus, bidding, collect, complin, gayatri, oration, request, savitri 8 compline, entreaty, petition 9 competory, precation 10 paratheses(pl.), parathesis, requiescat 11 benediction, paternoster 12 intercession, supplication

call: 4 adan, azan, bell 5 chime 6 oremus

chancery: 7 relator

day's last: 7 complin 8 compline

form of: 5 chant 6 litany

group: 12 comprecation

nine-day: 6 novena

set: 9 akoluthia

short: 5 grace 11 benediction

prayer bead: 6 rosary

prayer book: 6 missal, portas, ritual 7 brevary, portass 9 porthouse

prayer desk: 8 prie-dieu

prayer rug: 5 asana

prayer shawl: 5 orale 7 tallith

prayer tower: 7 minaret

praying figure: 5 orant

preach: 4 sugh 5 sough, teach 6 exhort, inform 8 advocate, homilize, instruct, moralize, proclaim 9 discourse, predicate, sermonize 10 concionate

preacher: 6 parson, rector 8 minister 9 clergyman, predicant, pulpiteer

preachment: 6 sermon 7 lecture 9 discourse 11 exhortation

preachy: 8 didactic 10 moralistic

preamble: 7 preface

preannounced: 10 annunciate

prebend: 4 land 7 stipend 9 allowance

prebendary: 5 canon

precarious: 5 risky 7 assumed, dubious 8 insecure, perilous, unstable 9 dangerous, hazardous, uncertain, unsettled 11 unwarranted

precative: 10 beseeching 12 supplicating

precaution: 4 care 6 cautel 7 caution

precede: 4 lead 5 usher 6 forego 7 forerun, predate, preface 8 antecede, antedate 9 introduce

precedence: pas 8 priority

right: pas

precedent: 5 model, usage 7 example 8 decision, standard

preceding: 5 first 8 anterior

precentor: 6 cantor

precept: law 4 hest, rule, tora, writ 5 adage, axiom, breve, brief, maxim, order, sutra, torah 6 lesson 7 caution, command, mandate 8 doctrine, document, teaching 9 direction, principle 10 injunction 11 commandment, instruction

preceptive: 8 didactic 9 mandatory 11 instructive

preceptor: 5 tutor

precinct: 5 ambit, bound 6 hieron 7 temenos 8 boundary, district, environs 9 enclosure

precious: 4 dear, rare, very 5 chere(F.), loved 6 costly, valued 7 beloved 8 affected, esteemed, valuable 9 extremely 10 fastidious 11 overrefined

precious stone: See gem

precipice: lin 4 crag, drop, linn, pali, scar 5 bluff, brink, cliff, steep 7 clogwyn 8 downfall 9 declivity

precipitate: 4 fall, floc, hurl, rash 5 hasty, heady, hurry, speed, throw 6 abrupt, hasten, sudden, tumble, unwary **8** headlong, settling, slapdash **9** desperate, impetuous, impulsive **11** precipitous

precipitation: dew **4** hail, mist, rain, snow **5** haste, sleet **8** downpour **9** hastening **10** deposition **11** impetuosity **12** acceleration

precipitous: 5 sheer, steep **6** steepy **7** pre- rupt **11** precipitate

rock: **4** crag, scar **5** steep

precis: 7 epitome, summary **8** abstract **11** abridgement

precise: 4 even, nice, prim **5** exact, stiff **6** formal, minute, strict **7** buckram, certain, correct, finicky, literal, starchy **8** accu- rate, definite, delicate, explicit, overnice, priggish **9** faultless, veracious **10** ceremo- nial, fastidious, particular, scrupulous **11** ceremonious, painstaking, punctilious **14** circumstantial

preclude: bar **4** stop **5** avert, close, debar, estop **6** forbid, hinder, impede **7** obviate, prevent **9** foreclose

precocious: 6 unripe **7** forward **9** premature

preconceive: 5 dream **6** ideate, scheme **8** foreknow

precursor: 6 herald **8** ancestor, foregoer **9** harbinger, messenger **10** forefather, fore- runner **11** predecessor

precursory: 11 preliminary, premonitory **12** introductory

predatory: 7 robbing **9** pillaging, piratical, rapacious, raptorial **10** plundering, preda- cious

bird: owl **4** hawk **5** eagle

insect: **6** mantis

predestine: 4 doom, fate **6** decree, ordain **7** destine, predoom **8** foredoom **9** determine, forepoint, preordain **10** foreordain **11** foredestine **12** predetermine

predetermine: 4 bias **6** decree **7** destine, predict **8** forecast **9** prejudice **10** prepos- sess

predicament: fix **4** hole, stew **5** state **6** pickle, plight **7** scrape **8** dilemma **8** quan- dary **9** condition, situation

predicant: 5 friar **8** preacher **9** dominican

predicate: cry **4** aver **5** imply **6** affirm, as- sert, preach **7** commend, declare, foresee, involve, predict **8** foretell, proclaim

predict: 4 bode, dope, omen **5** augur, weird **6** divine, halsen **7** forbode, presage **8** fore- bode, forecast, prophesy, soothsay **9** auspi- cate, predicate **13** prognosticate

prediction: 5 weird **7** bodword **12** forespeak- ing, vaticination

predictor: 4 seer

predilection: 4 bent, bias **8** fondness, ten- dency **9** prejudice **10** partiality, prefer- ence, propensity **11** inclination **14** predis- position, susceptibility

predisposed: 5 prone **6** biased **7** partial

predisposition: 12 predilection

predominant: 6 ruling **8** dominant, reign- ing, superior **9** ascendant, ascendent, heg- emonic, prevalent **10** dominating, notice- able, prevailing **11** controlling, outstand- ing **12** preponderant

predominate: 6 domine, exceed **8** domineer

pree: try **5** taste **6** sample

preeminent: big **4** star **5** grand **7** capital, palmary, ranking, supreme **8** dominant, superior **9** excellent, prominent **10** sur- passing **11** outstanding

preempt: 5 usurp **9** establish **10** monopolize **11** appropriate

preen: pin, sew **4** perk, trim **5** adorn, clasp, dress, plume, press, primp, prink, prune **6** bodkin, brooch, smooth, spruce, stitch

preface: 5 front, proem **6** herald **7** forerun, precede, prelude **8** exordium, foreword, preamble, prologue **9** introduce **11** prelim- inary **12** forespeaking, introduction, intro- ductory

prefect, praefect: 4 dean **7** monitor, officer **8** director, minister, official **9** president **10** magistrate

prefecture: 7 eparchy(Gr.) **8** district

prefer: opt **4** like **5** elect, favor **6** desire, fa- vour, rather, select

preferable: 6 better

preference: 6 choice **8** appetite, priority **11** alternative **12** predilection

prefigure: 4 type **6** ideate, typify **7** forerun **8** foretell **10** foreshadow

prefix (see also **combining form, suffix**): For all definitions beginning with this word, look under main word or phrase. EXAMPLES: "prefix for two": see **two:** *pre- fix;* "prefix for within": see **within:** *prefix.*

pregnable: 10 assailable, expugnable, vul- nerable **11** conquerable

pregnancy: 6 cyesis

pregnant: big **5** heavy **6** gravid **7** fertile, teeming, weighty **8** enceinte, fruitful, pro- lific **9** abounding, gestating, potential **10** germinable

prehend: 5 seize

prehistoric: 10 immemorial

preindicate: 7 presage **8** prophesy

prejudice: 4 bent, bias, harm, hurt **6** dam- age, hatred, impair **7** bigotry **9** suspicion **10** partiality, prepossess **11** inclination, in- tolerance **12** disadvantage, predetermine, predilection, prejudgement **13** prejudica- tion

prejudicial: 8 contrary 9 injurious 11 contrarious, detrimental

prelate: 4 head 5 chief 6 abbess, bishop, priest 7 primate 8 superior 9 dignitary 10 archbishop 12 ecclesiastic

prelector: 6 reader 8 lecturer 9 professor 10 discourser, praelector

preliminary: 5 prior 7 preface 8 entrance, previous, proemial 9 prefatory, threshold 10 antecedent 11 preparatory

prelude: 6 verset 7 descant, intrada, opening, preface 8 overture, ritornel 10 ritornelle 12 introduction

premature: 6 unripe 8 immature, untimely 10 precocious 12 unseasonable

premeditate: See **meditate**

premeditation: 11 forethought 12 aforethought

premier: 5 chief 7 leading 8 earliest, foremost 9 principal

premise: 6 ground 9 postulate 10 assumption 11 proposition

premium: 4 agio 5 bonus, prize, spiff 6 bounty, deport, reward 8 lagnappe 9 lagniappe 10 recompense

premonition: 4 omen 5 hunch 6 notice 7 bodword, warning 9 forescent 10 foreboding 11 forewarning, information 12 apprehension, presentiment

preoccupied: 4 lost, rapt 6 absent, filled 8 absorbed 9 engrossed

preordain: 10 predestine

preparation: 5 array 7 extract, product 8 cosmetic 9 condiment, decoction 10 confection 11 arrangement 12 introduction

place of: 10 laboratory, paratorium

without: 5 ad lib 8 careless 9 impromptu

prepare: arm, fit, fix, get, set 4 bush, busk, gibe, gird, make, pave, suit, tibe 5 adapt, alert, coach, curry, dight, equip, ettle, frame, groom, prime, ready, train 6 adjust, devise, graith 7 address, affaite(F.), apparel, arrange, concoct, confect, dispose, furnish, provide, qualify 8 accustom, compound, instruct, rehearse 9 calculate, condition, construct 10 concinnate

for the press: 4 edit 6 redact, revise

prepared: apt 4 yare

prepaschal period: 4 Lent

prepense: 8 designed 11 forethought 12 aforethought, premeditated

preponderance: 6 weight 9 dominance 10 ascendancy, ascendency, prevalence 12 predominance

preponderate: 4 sink 7 incline, surpass

prepose: 6 prefix 7 preface

preposition: at, by, in, on, to, up; but, for, off, out, tae(Sc.) 4 from, into, onto, over, unto, upon, with 5 about

prepossess: 12 predetermine

prepossessing: 10 attractive

prepossession: 4 bent, bias 9 prejudice 10 absorption 11 inclination 12 predilection 14 predisposition

preposterous: 6 absurd, screwy 7 foolish 9 grotesque, senseless 10 irrational, ridiculous 11 nonsensical

prerequisite: 9 postulate

prerogative: 5 right 7 apanage 8 appanage, appenage, priority 9 privilege 10 precedence

eldest son's: 6 esnecy

prerupt: 11 precipitous

presage: 4 bode, omen, osse, sign 5 augur, token 6 augury, betide, divine, import 7 betoken, forbode, meaning, portend, portent, predict, warning 8 forebode, foretell, prophecy, prophesy 9 foretoken, harbinger 10 foreboding, prediction, prognostic 11 foreknowing, preindicate 12 apprehension, presentiment 13 prognosticate

presbyter: 5 elder 6 priest 7 prester 8 minister 9 clergyman

presbytery: 5 court 7 council, rectory 9 residence

prescience: 9 foresight 11 omniscience 13 foreknowledge

prescind: 6 detach 7 isolate 8 abstract, separate

prescribe: set 5 allot, guide, limit, order 6 define, direct, ordain, outlaw 7 appoint, command, control, dictate 9 prescript 10 invalidate

prescribed: 6 thetic

prescript: 9 prescribe

prescription: rx 6 recipe

presence: 4 mien 5 being 6 spirit 7 bearing, company, dignity, spectre 8 assembly 9 influence 10 apparition, attendance, deportment

prefix: oxy

present: now 4 boon, gift, give, here 5 adsum(L.), being, bonus, cuddy, grant, nonce, offer, ready, today 6 adduce, allege, bestow, bounty, confer, donate, render, tender 7 cumshaw, display, exhibit, largess, perform 8 donation, gratuity, lagnappe 9 collected, introduce, lagniappe, personate 10 exhibition 11 benefaction, efficacious

again: 5 rerun

pert. to: 6 modern 7 current 12 contemporary

to guest or stranger: 6 xenium

with another: 8 collocal

present-day: 7 current 12 contemporary

presentiment: 10 foreboding 11 premonition 12 apprehension

presently: 4 anon, enow, soon 7 shortly 8 directly 9 forthwith 11 immediately

preservation: 11 safekeeping

preservative: 4 salt 5 spice 7 alcohol, vinegar 8 creosote 12 conservative

preserve: can, dry, jam, tin 4 corn, cure, keep, salt, save 5 bless, guard, jelly, spare, store, uvate 6 athold, comfit, defend, govern, retain, secure, shield, uphold 7 compote, condite, confect, forfend, protect, succade, sustain 8 conserve, forefend, maintain 9 confiture, safeguard

preside: 6 direct 7 control 8 moderate, regulate

president: mir 4 head 5 ruler 8 governor 9 sovereign

successor: 9 designado(Mex.)

President (U.S.): (1, 1789-97) George Washington; (2, 1797-1801) John Adams; (3, 1801-09) Thomas Jefferson; (4, 1809-17) James Madison; (5, 1817-25) James Monroe; (6, 1825-29) John Quincy Adams; (7, 1829-37) Andrew Jackson; (8, 1837-41) Martin Van Buren; (9, 1841) William Henry Harrison; (10, 1841-45) John Tyler; (11, 1845-49) James K. Polk; (12, 1849-50) Zachary Taylor; (13, 1850-53) Millard Fillmore; (14, 1853-57) Franklin Pierce; (15, 1857-61) James Buchanan; (16, 1861-65) Abraham Lincoln; (17, 1865-69) Andrew Johnson; (18, 1869-77) Ulysses S. Grant; (19, 1877-81) Rutherford B. Hayes; (20, 1881) James A. Garfield; (21, 1881-85) Chester A. Arthur; (22, 1885-89) Grover Cleveland; (23, 1889-93) Benjamin Harrison; (24, 1893-97) Grover Cleveland; (25, 1897-1901) William McKinley; (26, 1901-09) Theodore Roosevelt; (27, 1909-13) William H. Taft; (28, 1913-21) Woodrow Wilson; (29, 1921-23) Warren G. Harding; (30, 1923-29) Calvin Coolidge; (31, 1929-33) Herbert Hoover; (32, 1933-1945) Franklin D. Roosevelt; (33, 1945-1953) Harry S. Truman; (34, 1953-1961) Dwight D. Eisenhower; (35, 1961-1963) John F. Kennedy; (36, 1963-1969) Lyndon B. Johnson; (37, 1969-1974) Richard M. Nixon; (38, 1974-1977) Gerald R. Ford; (39, 1977-) Jimmy Carter
last name: 4 Ford, Polk, Taft 5 Adams, Grant, Hayes, Nixon, Tyler 6 Arthur, Carter, Hoover, Monroe, Pierce, Taylor, Truman, Wilson 7 Harding, Jackson, Johnson, Kennedy, Lincoln, Madison 8 Buchanan, Coolidge, Fillmore, Garfield, Harrison, McKinley, Van Buren 9 Cleveland, Jefferson, Roosevelt 10 Eisenhower, Washington

nickname: Abe, Cal, Ike 5 Teddy

presignify: 7 presage 8 intimate 9 foretoken

press: hug 4 bale, bear, bind, cram, dint, iron, mash, spur, thew, urge 5 brize, brizz, chest, chirt, crowd, crush, drive, force, knead, preen, serry, wring 6 compel, crunch, impact, roller, smooth, throng 7 armoire, embrace, entreat, flatten, impress, imprint, scrunge, smasher, squeeze 8 calender, compress, straiten, wardrobe 9 constrain, embarrass, emphasize, importune 10 constipate, newspapers

corrector: 11 proofreader

critic: 6 censor

press down: 4 tamp

pressed: 5 dense 7 compact, serried

presser: 5 baler 6 ironer, mangle

of skins: 7 sammier

pressing: 6 urgent 7 exigent 8 exacting 9 imperious 10 imperative 11 importunate

pressman: 7 printer

pressure: 4 heat, push 5 force 6 duress, stress 7 bearing, squeeze 8 exigency, instancy 10 affliction, constraint, impression, oppression 11 compression

equal: 8 isobaric

gauge: 9 manometer, manoscope

unit: 4 atmo, dyne 5 barad 7 mesobar

pressure group: 5 lobby

pressure measuring instrument: 10 piezometer

prest: 4 duty, loan 7 advance, pressed

prester: 4 vein 5 snake 6 priest 7 serpent 9 hurricane, presbyter, whirlwind

prestidigitator: 6 palmer 7 juggler 8 conjurer, magician

prestige: 6 renown 7 sorcery 8 illusion 9 deception, influence 10 importance, prominence

presto: 7 passing, quickly 8 suddenly 11 immediately 13 instantaneous

presumably: 8 probably 10 ostensibly, supposedly

presume: 5 guess 6 impose 7 daresay, suppose, venture 8 arrogate 9 postulate 10 conjecture, presuppose

presumptuous: 4 bold 5 fresh 7 forward, haughty, icarian 8 arrogant, assuming, familiar, impudent, insolent 9 audacious, confident, foolhardy 11 adventurous, venturesome

presuppose: 6 assume

pretend: act 4 pose, seem, sham 5 claim, feign 6 affect, allege, assume, gammon 7 profess 8 disguise, simulate 11 dissimulate, make-believe

pretended: 4 fake 5 false 7 colored, reputed 8 coloured, intended, proposed 10 fictitious, ostensible

pretender: fop 4 fake, idol, snob 5 cowan(Sc.), faker, quack 6 poseur, seemer 8 aspirant, claimant, deceiver, impostor 9 charlatan 10 mountebank 11 fourflusher 12 dissimulator

pretense, pretence: act, peg 4 brag, cant, flam, plea, ruse, sham, show 5 claim, cloak, cover, feint, gloze, study, trick 6 excuse, humbug, tinsel 7 fiction, grimace, potiche, pretext 8 artifice, occasion 9 deception, moonshine, semblance 10 appearance, assumption, subterfuge 11 affectation, fabrication, make-believe, ostentation 13 stalking-horse

pretentious: big 4 arty 5 gaudy, showy 7 pompous 8 affected, assuming 11 highfaluten, highfalutin 12 highfaluting, ostentatious

pretermit: 4 omit 6 ignore 7 neglect, suspend 8 intermit 9 disregard, interrupt

preternatural: 6 gousty 7 goustie 8 abnormal, uncommon 9 irregular 12 supernatural

pretext: 8 pretense

pretty: gay, toy 4 cute, deft, fair, gent, joli 5 bonny, jolie, lindo(Sp.) 6 bonita, bonito, bonnie, clever, comely 7 dollish 8 betcheri, budgeree 9 beautiful, ingenious 10 attractive, knickknack, moderately

prevail: win 5 reign 6 induce, obtain 7 persist, succeed, triumph 8 dominate 11 predominate

prevail: *upon:* 4 urge 6 allure, induce 7 entreat 8 persuade

prevalent: 4 rife 6 common, potent 7 current, general 8 dominant, powerful 9 extensive 10 prevailing, successful, victorious, widespread 11 efficacious, influential

prevaricate: fib, lie 5 evade 7 quibble, shuffle 10 equivocate

prevarication: 10 subterfuge

prevene: 7 prevent

prevent: bar, gag, let 4 balk, bind, save, stop, warn 5 avert, debar, deter, estop 6 defend, forlet, hinder, impede, resist, thwart 7 forfend, impeach, obviate, prevent 8 antevert, forefend, preclude, prohibit, restrain 9 foreclose, forestall, frustrate 10 anticipate, circumvent

by law: 5 estop

preventive: 12 prophylactic 13 precautionary

previous: ere 4 erst, fore, past 5 prior, supra 6 before, bygone, former 7 earlier 8 anterior, foregone, untimely 9 foregoing, preceding, premature 10 antecedent, beforehand, heretofore 11 unwarranted

prevision: 8 forecast 9 foresight 10 prescience, prevoyance 13 foreknowledge 15 prognostication

prewar: 10 antebellum

prey: 4 feed 5 booty, raven, ravin, seize, spoil 6 quarry, ravage, ravine, victim 7 capture, plunder 9 victimize

living on: 9 predatory

prey upon: 4 feed 5 seize 9 victimize

Priam: *daughter:* 6 Creusa 8 Polyxena 9 Cassandra

grandfather: 4 Ilus

servant: 7 Agelaus

son: 5 Paris 6 Hector 7 Helenus, Troilus 9 Deiphobus, Polydorus

wife: 6 Hecuba

price: fee 4 cost, fare, fiar(Sc.), fier(Sc.), hire, rate 5 cheap, value, worth 6 charge, ransom, reward 7 expense 8 appraise, evaluate 10 estimation, excellence 12 preciousness 13 consideration

maintain: peg

reduced: 4 sale 7 bargain

rising: 4 boom 9 inflation

priceless: 4 rare 6 absurd, costly, unique 7 amusing 8 valuable 10 invaluable 11 inestimable

prick: dot, jag 4 brod, brog, cloy, drob, goad, jagg, ping, pink, prod, stab, tang 5 briar, point, smart, spine, sting, thorn 6 broach, cactus, incite, nettle, pierce, skewer, tingle 7 bramble, pricker, prickle 8 puncture

prick song: 7 descant

pricket: 4 buck 5 spike 11 candlestick

pricking: 8 poignant

prickle: 4 seta 5 setae(pl.), sieve 6 basket 7 acantha, aculeus, spicula(pl.) 8 spiculum

prickly: 5 burry 8 echinate

animal: 8 hedgehog 9 porcupine

plant: 6 cactus, nettle

seed coat: bur 4 burr

shrub: 4 rose 5 briar

prickly heat: 4 rash 8 eruption

prickly pear: 4 tuna 5 nopal 7 opuntia

pride: 5 glory, pique, plume, valor 6 egoism, esteem, spirit, vanity 7 conceit, disdain, egotism, elation, hauteur, respect 8 nobility, splendor, valiancy 9 arrogance, insolence, loftiness 10 lordliness, self-esteem 11 haughtiness, self-conceit, self-respect 12 independence 15 self-approbation 16 superciliousness

Pride and Prejudice: *author:* 6 Austen

character: 5 Darcy 9 Elizabeth

prier, pryer: 10 inquisitor

priest: en; fra 4 abbe, club, cura, cure(F.), imam, lama, papa(It.), pere(F.) 5 clerk, druid, hotar(Ind.), imaum, mulla, padre(Sp.), rabbi, sarip, vicar 6 bhikku, bishop, cleric, dastur, divine, father, gallah(Heb.), mullah, oblate, rector, vestal, wahabi 7 cassock, destour, dustoor, prester, tuhunga, wahabee, wahhabi 8 minister 9 clergyman, dignitary, orato-

rian, priesteen 10 hierophant, priestling
12 ecclesiastic
army: 5 padre 8 chaplain
assistant: 7 acolyte
cap: 7 biretta
garment: alb 4 cope, robe 5 ephod, habit 8
scapular 9 vestments
habit ornament: 4 urim
headdress: 9 saghavart
high: Eli 5 Aaron 7 pontiff
neckpiece: 5 amice, stole
pert. to: 10 sacerdotal
scarf: 5 rabat 7 maniple
server: 7 acolyte
surplice: 5 ephod
voodoo: 5 mambu 6 hungan 7 gangang
priesthood: 9 sacerdocy 11 sacerdotage
priestly: 10 sacerdotal
prig: beg, fop, pan 4 buck 5 dandy, filch,
plead, prink, prude, steal, thief 6 haggle,
pilfer, purist, tinker 7 bargain, entreat,
pitcher 8 pilferer 9 precision 10 pickpocket
prigger: 5 thief
priggish: 4 prim, smug 8 thievish 11 overprecise
prill: 4 rill 6 button, nugget, pellet, stream
prim: mim, set 4 neat, nice 5 stiff 6 demure,
formal, proper 7 correct, precise, prudish
8 accurate, decorous 10 ceremonial
prima donna: 4 diva, lead, star 6 singer 7
actress
famous: 4 Lind 5 Patti 7 Russell 13 Schu-
mann-Heink
primary: 4 main 5 chief, first, prime 6 primal 7 capital, central, initial 8 earliest,
original, primeval, pristine 9 elemental,
primitive, principal 10 elementary, pre-
eminent, primordial 11 fundamental
primate: ape, man 5 lemur, orang 6 bishop,
monkey 8 marmoset 9 orangutan 10 anthropoid, archbishop 11 orangoutang
prime: 4 size 5 coach 7 prepare, primary 9
copacetic, excellent, undercoat
of life: 5 bloom 6 heyday
prime minister: 7 premier
primer: 8   hornbook,   textbook   11
abecedarium
primeval: 6 primal 7 ancient, ogygian 8
original, pristine 9 primitive
primitive: 5 basic, crude, first, rough 6 simple 7 ancient, archaic, primary, priscan,
radical 8 barbaric, original, pristine 9 un-
derived 10 aboriginal, antiquated 11 uncivilized 12 old-fashioned
primogenial: 6 primal 7 primary 8 original
9 primitive
primordial: 5 first 7 primary 9 elemental 11
fundamental

primordium: 6 embryo, origin 8 rudiment
primp: 5 adorn, dress, preen, prink
primrose: 5 oxlip, spink(Sc.) 7 cowslip,
primula 8 auricula
family: 11 primulaceae
primus: 5 first, stove
prince: bey, ras 4 amir, emir, raja, rial 5
alder, ameer, emeer, ruler 6 despot, dynast, satrap 7 dynasty, monarch 8 archduke 9 potentate, princekin, princelet,
sovereign 10 princeling
allowance: 8 appenage
pine: 10 pipsissewa
title: 6 serene
Prince of: *Apostles:* 8 St. Peter
Darkness: 5 devil, Satan 7 Ahriman 9 Beelzebub
Destruction: 6 Timour 9 Tamerlane
Evil Spirits: 7 Sammael
Liars: 5 Pinto
Peace: 7 Messiah
the Ode: 7 Ronsard
the Sonnet: 15 Joachim du Bellay
princedom: 4 rank 11 sovereignty 12 jurisdiction
princely: 5 noble, regal, royal 6 kingly 10
munificent 11 magnificent
princeps: 4 head 5 first, pagus 7 headman
princess: 5 begum(Muslim), ranee (Muslim)
loved by Cupid: 6 Psyche
loved by Zeus: 6 Europa
mythological: 8 Atalanta
Princeton symbol: 5 tiger
principal: top 4 arch, head, high, main, star
5 chief, first, grand, major, prime 6 leader,
staple 7 capital, captain, chattel, leading,
palmary, primary, stellar 8 cardinal, dominant, foremost 9 important, preceptor 10
headmaster 11 outstanding
comb. form: 4 arch 5 archi
principle: law 4 rule 5 axiom, canon, dic-
ta(pl.), maxim, prana, tenet 6 dictum 7
brocard, essence, precept, theorum 8 doctrine 9 integrity 11 fundamental, uprightness
accepted: 5 axiom
embodiment: 6 avatar
first: 4 base, seed 5 basis 8 rudiment 10
fundamenta(pl.) 11 fundamentum
general: 9 generalia 12 generalities
statement: 5 credo, creed, motto
vital: 4 soul 5 anima
principles: 5 creed
princox: fop 7 coxcomb
prink: 4 deck, perk, wink 5 adorn, dress,
preen, primp, prune 6 bedeck, glance

print: 4 copy, film 5 issue, stamp 6 fabric 7 edition, engrave, impress, publish 8 negative 9 engraving, newspaper 10 impression

printer: 4 typo 8 letterer, pressman 11 typographer 12 lithographer

aid: 5 devil

cross stroke: 5 serif 6 ceriph

direction: tr.; cut 6 delete

printing: *block:* 4 wood 7 edition 8 linoleum

blurred appearance: 5 macul

color: 17 chromolithography

error: pi; pie 6 errata(pl.) 7 erratum

form: cut, die, mat 5 frame 6 matrix 7 matrice

implement: 5 biron 6 brayer, dabber, dauber

ink spreader: 6 brayer

mark: 4 dash, dele, list, stet 5 caret, obeli, tilde 6 dagger, diesis, obelus 7 obelisk 8 ellipses

measure: em, en 4 pica 5 agate, empen

metal block: 4 quad

plate: 6 stereo 10 stereotype

press part: 6 platen, roller, rounce 7 frisket

process: 6 offset 7 braille, typeset 8 cerotype 10 photolitho 11 lithography 14 photoengraving

second: 7 reissue

space block: 4 quad

system for the blind: 7 braille

type for spacing: 4 quad, slug

prion: 6 petrel

prionid: 6 beetle

prior: ex; ere 4 fore, past 5 elder 6 before, former 7 earlier 8 anterior, previous 10 antecedent 11 retroactive

priority: 8 position 9 privilege 10 precedence, preference 11 superiority

priory: 5 abbey 7 nunnery 8 cloister 9 monastery, sanctuary

priscan: 7 ancient 9 primitive

prism device: 8 iriscope

prismatic: 9 brilliant 10 iridescent 12 orthorhombic

prison: gib, jug 4 brig, cell, gaol, hell, hole, jail, keep, quod, rock, stir 5 bagne, clink, grate 6 bagnio, carcel, carcer, cooler, lockup 7 Atlanta, Bocardo, college, dungeon, Gehenna, hoosgow, kidcote, Newgate 8 Alcatraz, Bastille, hoosegaw, hoosegow, Sing Sing 9 Bridewell, calaboose, enclosure 10 guardhouse, panopticon 11 Leavenworth 12 penitentiary

guard: 5 screw

keeper: 5 guard 6 gaoler, jailer, jailor, keeper, warden 7 turnkey

naval or ship: 4 brig

room: 4 cell, hole, tank 7 dungeon 8 solitary

sentence: rap

spy: 6 mouton

prisoner: con 5 lifer 6 detenu(F.), inmate 7 caitiff, captive, convict, detenue(F.), parolee 9 collegian 10 emancipist 11 probationer

exchange agreement: 6 cartel

Prisoner of the Vatican: 4 Pope

prisoner of war: PW; P.O.W. 7 kriegie

prissy: 4 prim 5 fussy 7 finicky, precise, prudish 9 sissified 11 over-refined

pristav, pristaw: 8 official, overseer 12 commissioner

pristine: new 4 pure 5 early, fresh 7 ancient, primary 8 original 9 primitive, unspoiled, untouched 11 uncorrupted

pritch: 5 prick, spike, staff 6 pierce

privacy: 7 privity, retreat, secrecy 8 darkness, solitude 9 seclusion 10 penetralia 12 hugger-mugger

privado: 6 friend 8 intimate 9 confidant

private: 6 closet, covert, secret 7 soldier 8 esoteric, homefelt, personal, secluded, solitary 10 unofficial 12 confidential, unpublicized

comb. form: 4 idio

private eye: 6 tailer 9 detective, operative 12 investigator

privateer: 4 Kidd 5 caper 6 pirate 7 corsair, drumler 8 drumbler

privately: 5 aside

privation: 4 loss, want 6 misery 8 hardship 11 deprivation, destitution

privet: 5 hedge, ibota, shrub 7 alatern, ibolium 9 houseleek

privilege: law, soc, use 4 soke 5 favor, grace, grant, right 6 favour, patent 7 charter, liberty 8 easement, immunity 9 advantage, exemption, franchise 10 concession 11 prerogative

privy: wc 4 gong 6 cloaca, hidden, secret, toilet 7 cloacae(pl.), furtive, private 8 familiar, intimate, out-house 9 backhouse, confidant, necessary 11 clandestine, water-closet 12 confidential 13 surreptitious

prix: 5 prize

prize: cup, pry 4 gree(Sc.), prix(F.), tern 5 award, bacon, booty, lever, medal, plate, purse, stake, value 6 esteem, glaive, reward, trophy 7 capture, premium, seizure 8 estimate, leverage, purchase, treasure 10 appreciate

prizefight: go 4 bout 5 match 7 contest

customer demand: K.O.

ring: 5 arena

prized: 4 dear 5 chary

pro: for 8 advocate, favoring 9 favouring 12 professional

probability: 4 odds 6 chance 10 appearance, likelihood, likeliness 11 credibility

probable: 6 likely 8 credible, feasible

probably: 6 belike, likely

probation: 4 test 5 trial 6 parole 9 novitiate 11 examination

probe: 4 acus, tent, test 5 grope, sound 6 pierce, search, seeker, stylet, tracer 7 examine, explore 9 penetrate 10 ankylomele, instrument, scrutinize 11 exploration, investigate 13 investigation

probity: 7 honesty 9 integrity, rectitude 11 uprightness

problem: nut, sum 4 crux, knot 5 hydra, poser 6 enigma, riddle 8 question 9 situation

problematical: 8 doubtful 9 ambiguous, equivocal, uncertain, unsettled 12 questionable

proboscis: 4 nose 5 snout, trunk

proboscis monkey: 4 kaha

procacious: 4 pert 8 impudent, insolent, petulant

Procas' son: 7 Amulius, Numitor

procavia: 5 hyrax 10 hyracoidea

procedure: 6 tactic 7 process, program, routine

proceed: go 4 fand, fare, move, pass, wend 5 arise, frame, issue 6 derive 7 advance, emanate, forthgo 8 continue, progress 9 originate

laboriously: mog 4 plod, plow, slog, wade 6 trudge

rapidly: run 5 speed 6 gallop

proceeding: 4 acta(pl.), step 5 actum, doing 6 affair, afflux, course 7 conduct, measure 9 affluxion, procedure 11 transaction

proceeds: 4 loot 5 booty 6 income, profit, return 8 stealage

procerity: 6 height 8 tallness

process: 4 cook, writ 5 lapse, order 6 capias, course, manner, method, notice, system 7 advance, mandate, summons 8 progress 9 operation, procedure, sterilize 10 injunction

procession: 4 file 5 march 6 course, exequy, litany, parade 7 cortege, pageant 9 cavalcade, formation, recession

prochein: 4 next 7 nearest

proclaim: bid, cry 4 call, deem, toot, tout 5 blare, blast, blaze, claim, grede, knell, voice 6 blazon, bounce, defame, herald, indict, outcry, preach 7 declare, divulge, enounce, publish 8 announce, denounce, forspeak 9 advertise, celebrate, enunciate, forespeak 10 promulgate

proclamation: ban 4 bans, fiat 5 bando(Sp.), banns, blaze, edict, ukase 6 notice 7 bid-

ding, placard 9 manifesto 11 publication 12 announcement, annunciation, denunciation, notification, promulgation

proclivity: 4 bent 6 talent 7 leaning 10 propensity 11 disposition, inclination

Procne: *husband:* 6 Tereus

sister: 9 Philomela

procrastination: 5 delay, stall 9 deferment 10 cunctation, inactivity 12 dilatoriness, postponement

procreant: 8 fruitful 9 producing 10 generating

procreate: 4 sire 5 beget 7 produce 8 engender, generate

procreation: 8 virility 9 offspring 10 generation, production

Procris: *father:* 10 Erechtheus

husband: 8 Cephalus

proctor: 5 agent, proxy 6 patron 7 steward 8 advocate, attorney

procumbent: 5 prone

procurable: 10 accessible

procure: get 4 fang, find, gain 5 bring 6 effect, obtain, secure, suborn 7 acquire, chevise, receive 8 contrive 9 impetrate

procurer: 4 bawd, pimp

procuress: 4 bawd, hack 7 commode

prod: egg, jab 4 brog, goad, poke, urge 6 incite, thrust

prodigal: 5 flush 6 lavish 7 liberal, profuse, spender, wastrel 8 abundant, generous, wasteful 10 profligate, squanderer 11 extravagant, spendthrift, squandering

prodigious: 4 huge 5 giant 7 amazing, immense 8 enormous, gigantic 9 marvelous, monstrous, wonderful 10 portentous, tremendous 11 astonishing 13 extraordinary

prodigy: 4 omen, sign 6 marvel, ostent, wonder 7 miracle, portent 8 ceremony

prodition: 7 treason 8 betrayal 15 treacherousness

prodrome: 7 symptom

produce: do 4 bear, form, make, show 5 breed, carry, cause, shape, stage, yield 6 create, effect, fruits 7 exhibit 8 engender, generate 9 fabricate, offspring 10 production, vegetables 11 manufacture

new: 6 create, invent 9 originate

producer: 6 author, farmer, grower, parent 7 creator 8 director 12 manufacturer

product: 4 item 5 fruit 6 number, result 9 offspring, outgrowth

production: 4 work 5 fruit 6 output 11 performance

productive: 4 rich 6 active, parous 7 fertile 8 creative, fruitful, sonorous 10 generative 11 originative

proem: 7 preface, prelude 8 foreword, overture, preamble 12 introduction

profanation: 9 sacrilege

profane: hoa 4 foul 5 abuse 6 debase, defile, defoil, defoul, unholy, vulgar, wicked 7 godless, impious, obscene, secular, ungodly, violate, worldly 8 temporal 9 desecrate, vulgarize 10 irreverent, unhallowed 11 blasphemous 12 unsanctified

profanity: 4 oath 5 curse 9 blasphemy

profess: own 4 avow 5 admit, claim 6 affect, affirm, allege 7 confess, declare, protest 8 proclaim 11 acknowledge

professed: 9 pretended 10 ostensible

profession: art 5 craft, faith, forte, trade 6 avowal, career, metier(F.) 7 calling 8 function, vocation 9 following 10 employment, occupation

professional: pro 4 paid 5 hired 6 expert 7 artiste, skilled, trained 8 finished

professor: don, fly 7 teacher

proffer: bid 4 give, hand 5 offer 6 extend, tender 11 countenance

proficiency: 5 skill 7 ability, aptness 9 adeptness 10 capability, competence, efficiency, expertness 14 accomplishment

proficient: 6 actual, versed 9 effective, effectual 10 conversant

profile: 4 form 6 figure 7 contour, drawing, outline 10 silhouette 14 representation

profit: net, pay, use 4 boot, gain, good, help, mend, nett 5 avail, frame, lucre, melon 6 behoof, return 7 account, benefit, bestead, revenue, utility 8 increase, interest 9 advantage, emolument 12 remuneration

receiver of: 6 pernor

profitable: fat 8 repaying 9 expedient

profitless: 9 fruitless 12 unprofitable

profligate: 6 rioter 7 corrupt, riotous, spender, vicious, wastrel 8 depraved, flagrant, prodigal, rakehell, wasteful 9 abandoned, dissolute, reprobate 10 licentious 11 extravagant

profound: low 4 deep, sage, wise 5 heavy 7 abysmal, intense 8 abstruse, unbroken 9 recondite, sagacious 10 acroamatic, exhaustive 11 far-reaching 12 unfathomable

profuse: 4 lush 5 frank 6 galore, hearty, lavish 7 copious, liberal 8 abundant, generous, prodigal, wasteful 9 bountiful, exuberant, luxuriant, plentiful 10 munificent 11 extravagant, overflowing

profusion: 6 galore 8 opulence 9 affluence 11 prodigality

prog: 4 food 5 prick, prowl, tramp 6 forage 7 vagrant 8 supplies 9 provender

progenitor: 4 sire 6 parent 8 ancestor 10 forefather, foreparent, forerunner

progeny: imp, son 4 race, seed 5 breed, brood, brook, child, issue, scion, shoot 6 family, strain 8 children, daughter 9 genealogy, offspring 10 generation 11 descendants

prognostic: 4 omen, sign 5 token

prognosticate: 4 bode 5 augur 6 divine 7 betoken, forbode, forerun, portend, predict, presage 8 forebode, forecast, foreshow, foretell, prophesy 9 foretoken, hariolate

prognosticator: 4 seer 5 augur 6 divine 7 augurer, diviner, prophet 9 predictor 10 soothsayer

program: 4 card, list, show 5 draft, edict 6 agenda, notice 7 agendum, catalog, outline 8 bulletin, playbill, schedule, syllabus 9 broadcast 10 prospectus 12 proclamation

programma: 5 edict 6 decree 7 preface 12 prolegomenon

progress: 4 fare, flow, grow, tour, wend 5 march 6 course, growth, motion 7 advance, circuit, develop, headway, improve, journey, proceed 10 betterment, expedition 11 development, furtherance, improvement

planned: 7 telesia, telesis

progression: 5 stage 8 sequence 10 succession

progressive: 6 active, onward 7 forward, liberal 9 advancing, ascensive 12 enterprising

prohibit: ban, bar, bid 4 stop, veto 5 debar, estop, fence 6 defend, enjoin, forbid, hinder, outlaw 7 forfend, forwarn, prevent 8 disallow, forefend 9 interdict, proscribe 11 countermand

prohibited: 4 tabu 5 taboo 7 illegal, illicit 8 unlawful, verboten(G.)

prohibiting: 8 vetitive

prohibition: ban, nay 4 veto 7 embargo 8 estoppel 12 interdiction

prohibitionist: dry

project: jet, jut, lap 4 abut, apse, barb, butt, game, idea, plan, send, task 5 filip, shoot 6 beetle, design, device, fillip, scheme 7 extrude, imagine, pattern, problem 8 contrive, proposal, protrude 9 intention 10 enterprise 11 contrivance, proposition, undertaking

projectile: 4 bomb, dart, rock, shot 5 arrow, shell 6 bullet, rocket 7 missile, torpedo 8 shrapnel 9 cartridge

curve: 8 parabola

pert. to: 9 ballistic

projecting: 6 beetle 7 salient

projection: arm, cam, ell, hob, hub, jag, lee, lug, toe 4 apse, barb, croc, fang, lobe 5 bulge, crena, redan, socle, tenon, tooth 6 corbel, crenae(pl.), dormer, lobule, tappet 7 cornice, empathy 8 abutment, ejection, eminence **9** crenation **10** protrusion **12** protuberance

projector: **8** bioscope **13** cinematograph, kinematograph

projet: **4** plan **5** draft

prolapse: **7** falling

prolate: **9** elongated
opposite of: **6** oblate

proletarian: **4** mean, rude **6** coarse, vulgar **7** laborer, working

prolific: **6** birthy, fecund **7** fertile, teeming **8** fruitful **9** abounding, plentiful **10** generative **11** propagative **12** reproductive

prolix: **5** wordy **7** diffuse, prosaic, tedious, verbose **8** tiresome **9** prolonged, wearisome **10** longwinded, protracted **11** displeasing **13** uninteresting

prolocutor: **6** orator **7** speaker **8** advocate, chairman **9** spokesman **10** mouthpiece

prolong: **5** defer **6** extend **8** continue, lengthen

prolonged: **5** great **6** prolix **7** chronic, delayed, dilated **8** extended **9** continued, postponed, sostenuto, sustained **10** lengthened, protracted

prom: **4** ball **5** dance

promenade: **4** deck, hall, mall, walk **5** prado(Sp.) **6** avenue, marina, parade, pasear(Sp.) **7** alameda, gallery **9** boardwalk, esplanade

Prometheus: *father:* **7** Iapetus
gift to man: **4** fire
mother: **7** Clymene

promethium symbol: Pm

prominence: **4** cusp **5** agger **8** eminence, prestige, salience **10** colliculus, promontory **11** distinction

prominent: **5** chief **6** marked, signal **7** capital, eminent, notable, obvious, salient **8** aquiline, manifest **9** egregious **10** celebrated, noticeable, projecting **11** conspicuous, distinctive **13** distinguished

promise: vow **4** band, hest, hote, oath, osse, sure, word **5** agree, grant, hight **6** assure, behest, engage, parole, pledge, plight **7** behight, betroth, fianced **8** affiance, contract, covenant **9** assurance, betrothal, foretoken **10** convenable, engagement, obligation **11** declaration
oral stipulation: **6** cautio **9** cautiones(pl.)

Promised Land: **6** Canaan

promissory note: I.O.U. **5** check **6** pledge

promontory: hoe **4** bill, cape, head, mull, nase, naze, ness, peak, scaw, skaw, spit **5** mount, point **8** headland **10** projection, prominence

promote: aid **4** help **5** boost, exalt, nurse, raise, speed **6** better, foster, prefer **7** advance, dignify, elevate, forward, further **9** advantage, encourage, patronize **10** aggrandize

promoter: **5** agent **7** abetter, abettor, booster, hustler **8** broacher, lobbyist

promotion: **6** brevet **7** advance **10** graduation, preferment **11** advancement, furtherance

prompt: apt, cue **4** move, yare(Sc.) **5** alert, quick, ready, yeder **6** active, assist, excite, nimble, remind **7** animate, forward **8** punctual **11** expeditious

prompter: aid **4** cuer **7** readier

promptly: **4** soon, tite(Sc.) **8** directly

promptness: **8** alacrity, dispatch

promulgate: **7** declare, publish **8** announce, proclaim **9** advertise

prone: apt **4** bent, flat **5** buxom **6** agroof, agrufe, agruif, supine **7** passive **8** addicted, disposed, inclined, pronated **9** declivous, groveling, prostrate, recumbent **10** decubitous

prong: nib, peg **4** fang, fork, horn, tine **5** point, tooth **6** branch

prongbuck: **9** pronghorn, springbok

prong key: **7** spanner

pronghorn: **4** deer **6** cabree, cabret, cabrie, cabrit **8** berrendo

pronoun: he, it, me, my, we, ye; any, her, him, his, its, one, our, she, thy, you **4** mine, ours, that, thee, them, they, this, thou, your **5** their, these, thine, those **6** itself, myself **7** herself, himself, oneself, ourself **8** yourself **9** ourselves **10** themselves, yourselves
demonstrative: **4** that, this **5** these, those
interrogative: who **4** whom **5** whose
substantive: who **7** whoever **9** whosoever

pronounce: **4** pass **5** speak, utter **6** affirm **7** behight, declare, deliver, enounce **8** announce **9** enunciate **10** articulate
indistinctly: **4** slur

pronounced: **6** marked **7** decided, howling **12** unmistakable

pronouncement: **5** dicta(pl.) **6** dictum **9** manifesto, statement **11** declaration **12** announcement

pronto: **5** quick **7** quickly **8** promptly **11** immediately

pronunciation: **4** burr, lisp, slur **5** drawl, twang
correct: **8** orthoepy **9** phonology
incorrect: **7** cacoepy **8** psellism **9** psellisum

pronunciation mark: **5** tilde **8** dieresis **9** diacritic

proof: **4** test **5** trial **6** result **7** approof, probate, exhibit, outcome **8** argument, evidence **9** testimony **10** indication **11** approbation **12** confirmation, impenetrable, verification **13** certification, demonstration

proofreader mark: lc, tr; cap **4** dele, stet **5** caret, space

prop: leg, nog **4** stay **5** appui, brace, shore, sprag, staff, stell(Sc.), stilt **6** scotch, shorer **7** fulcrum, support, sustain **8** buttress **10** strengthen

propaganda: **4** plan **5** ideas **6** scheme, system **8** doctrine **12** brainwashing

propagation: **12** continuation

propagate: **5** breed **7** diffuse **8** engender, generate, increase, multiply **9** circulate **11** disseminate

propel: gun, row **4** flip, move, pole, push, send, urge **5** drive, flick, force, impel, shove **7** project

propeller: fan, fin, oar **4** vane **5** screw **6** driver, paddle

arm: **4** vane

propensity: yen **4** bent, bias **6** liking **7** aptness, avidity **8** appetite, tendency **9** affection, proneness **10** proclivity, propension **11** disposition, inclination **12** predilection

proper: due, fit **4** fair, fine, good, meet, prim **5** right, stiff **6** behove, chaste, comely, decent, honest, modest, sedate, seemly, strict **7** behoove, correct, fitting, seeming **8** accurate, decorous, formular, suitable **9** advisable, allowable, befitting, beseeming, excellent **10** commodious, convenient, scrupulous **11** appropriate, respectable

properly: **6** featly, gladly **7** gradely

property: lot, res **4** acre, alod, aver, bona, dhan(Ind.), gear **5** addle, allod, asset, aught, glebe, goods, manor **6** domain, estate, havier, realty, wealth **7** acquest, alodium, chattel, haviour, holding **8** allodium **9** acensuada, attribute, homestead **11** appropriate, possessions **14** characteristic

act to regain: **8** replevin

bride's gift to husband: dos **5** dowry

charge against: **4** lien

conveyor of: **7** alienor, grantor

deceased wife's gift to husband: **8** courtesy

destruction of: **8** sabotage

found on the thief: **6** mainor

personal: **7** chattel

real: **4** land **7** acreage

receiver: **7** alienee

settle: **6** entail

settlement: dos

stolen: **4** loot, pelf **5** booty, lucre, spoil

suit for: **6** trover

transferring party: **7** alienor

wanton destruction of: **5** arson **8** sabotage **9** vandalism

property right: **4** lien **8** easement

prophecy: **5** weird **6** oracle **8** bodement **9** utterance **10** prediction **11** declaration, foretelling **12** vaticination

pert. to: **9** vatical

prophesy: **4** dope, osse, spae **5** aread, areed, augur **6** divine **7** predict, presage **8** ariolate, forecast, foreshow, foretell **10** vaticinate **11** preindicate **13** prognosticate

prophet: **4** Amos, John, seer **5** augur, Elias, fatal, Hosea, Syrus **6** divine, Elijah, Elisha, leader, mantis, oracle **7** augurer, diviner, Malachi, teacher **8** Mohammed, Muhammed, presager **9** John Smith **10** soothsayer **11** vaticinator

prophetess: **5** Sibyl **7** Pythian, seeress **9** Cassandra

prophetic: **5** vatic **6** mantic **7** fateful, fatidic, vatical **8** foretell, oracular **9** prescient **10** divinatory, predictive, presageful, signifying **11** fatiloquent, foretelling, nostradamic **12** vaticinatory **14** interpretative

propine: **5** offer **6** pledge **7** present, propose

propinquity: **7** kinship **8** affinity, nearness, vicinity **9** proximity **12** neighborhood, relationship **13** appropinquity, neighbourhood

propitiate: **5** atone **6** pacify **7** appease, expiate, satisfy **9** reconcile **10** conciliate

propitious: **4** rosy **5** happy, lucky **6** benign **8** benedict **9** benignant, favorable, opportune, promising **10** auspicious, benevolent, favourable, prosperous **12** advantageous

proponent: **6** backer **8** advocate

proportion: **4** part, rate **5** quota, ratio, share **7** analogy, portion, prorate **8** relation **9** dimension

proportionate: **5** equal **7** ratable **8** adequate **10** answerable, equivalent **11** symmetrical **12** commensurate, proportional

proportionately: **6** fairly **7** prorata **10** adequately

proposal: bid **4** plan **5** offer **6** design, feeler, motion, scheme **7** project **8** overture **10** nomination, suggestion **11** proposition

propose: **4** give, moot, move **5** state **6** allege, design **8** propound **11** contemplate

proposition: **5** axiom, offer, point **6** affair, porism **7** premise, project, theorem **8** offering, overture, proposal, question **9** corollary, postulate, situation, statement **11** affirmation, undertaking

antecedent: **6** premise **7** premiss

preliminary: **5** lemma **7** lemmata(pl.)

propound: **4** pose **5** posit, state **7** propose

proprietor: **5** owner **6** master, tanist **7** lairdie

propriety: See also **proper 4** code, rule **7** customs, manners, quality **8** behavior, elegance, standard **9** attribute, etiquette **13** possessorship

propugnator: **8** defender **10** vindicator

propulsion: jet **5** drift **8** ejection **9** expulsion

prorate: **5** allot **6** assess, divide **9** apportion **10** distribute, proportion

prorogue: **5** defer **6** extend **7** adjourn, prolong **8** postpone, protract

prosaic: **4** drab, dull, flat **5** prosy **6** prolix, stolid, stupid **7** humdrum, insipid, tedious **8** tiresome, unpoetic **10** unexciting **11** commonplace **12** matter-of-fact **13** unimaginative, uninteresting

proscenium: **5** stage
front area: **5** apron

proscribe: ban **4** tabu **5** exile, taboo **6** banish, forbid, outlaw **8** prohibit **9** interdict, ostracize

prose form: **5** novel, story, tract **7** fiction, romance **8** treatise **10** nonfiction

prosecute: sue **4** urge **5** carry, chase, hound **6** accuse, charge, follow, indict, pursue **7** enforce **8** continue

prosecutor: D.A. **7** accuser, relator

proselyte: **5** alien **7** convert **8** neophyte, newcomer
to Judaism: ger

Proserpine: See **Persephone**

proseuche: **7** oratory **9** synagogue

prosit: **5** toast **10** salutation

prosody: **5** meter

prospect: **4** hope, mine, view **5** buyer, scene, vista **6** aspect **7** outlook **8** customer, exposure **9** applicant, candidate, foretaste **10** contestant

prospective: **5** lofty **6** future, likely **7** eminent **8** expected, prospect **9** provident **11** anticipated, perspective

prospector: **9** sourdough

prosper: dow, hie, wax **4** fare **5** cheve, edify, frame, speed **6** thrive **7** blossom **8** flourish

prosperity: up; hap, ups **4** boom, weal **5** ikbal **6** thrift, wealth **7** fortune, success, welfare **9** happiness, well-being
god: **4** Frey
goddess: **5** Salus
symbol: **9** turquoise

Prospero: *daughter:* **7** Miranda
servant: **5** Ariel
slave: **7** Caliban

prosperous: up **4** bein, bien, boon **5** flush, happy, lucky, palmy, sonsy **6** sonsie **7** well-off **8** thriving **9** favorable, fortunate **10** auspicious, propitious, successful **11** flourishing

prostitute: bat, cat **4** aunt, drab, hack, trug **5** broad, venal, whore **6** callet, debase, harlot **7** baggage, brothel, corrupt, Cyprian, hackney **8** berdache, commoner, cus-

tomer, infamous, occupant **9** courtesan, courtezan **10** crosha-bell, hobby-horse, licentious **12** streetwalker **13** commercialize
customer: **4** john
reformed: **8** Magdalen

prostitution house of: **6** bordel **7** brothel **8** bordello

prostrate: bow **4** fell, flat **5** prone **6** fallen, supine **7** exhaust **8** dejected, helpless, overcome **9** collapsed, flattened, overthrow, recumbent **10** subjugated, submissive

prosy: dry **4** dull **6** jejune **7** humdrum, prosaic, tedious **11** commonplace, displeasing **13** unimaginative

protagonist: foe **4** hero **5** actor, agent, enemy **6** leader **7** heroine **8** advocate, champion, defender **9** contender, principal, spokesman

protasis: **11** conditional, proposition **12** introduction

protean: **10** changeable

protect: arm **4** bind, hill, save, wear **5** bield, bless, guard, hedge, shade **6** assert, defend, insure, patent, police, screen, shield **7** bulwark, cherish, forfend, shelter, tuition **8** champion, conserve, forefend, preserve **9** copyright

protecting: **7** tutelar **8** tutelary

protection: bib, lee **4** egis, fort, moat, pass **5** aegis, apron, armor, frith, guard, shell, smock **6** amulet, armour, patent, safety **7** auspice, defence, defense, parapet, shelter, tuition, umbrage **8** passport, security **12** preservation

protector: **5** guard **6** fautor, patron, shield **8** defender, guardian **9** custodian

protectorate: **11** condominium

protege: **4** ward

proteid: **6** alexin **7** albumin **9** legumelin

Proteida family: olm **7** proteus **8** necturus **11** salamanders, typhlomolge

protein: **6** avidin, casein, fibrin **7** albumin, edestin, mucedin **8** aleurone, creatine, prolamin
group: **8** globulin
poison: **5** abrin, ricin **6** ricine
source of: egg **4** bean, meat, milk **6** cheese, lentil

protest: **4** aver, beef, deny, kick **5** demur **6** affirm, assert, assure, holler, object, plaint **7** contest, declare, dissent, testify **8** complain **9** complaint, objection, stipulate **10** asseverate **11** expostulate, remonstrate **12** remonstrance

Protestant: **9** dissenter
sect: **9** orangeist

proteus: olm **6** amoeba

Proteus: *friend:* 9 Valentine
love: 6 Silvia
wife: 5 Julia

protograph: 7 writing 9 holograph 12 illustration

protoplasm: 5 ameba, spore 6 amoeba 7 sarcade
outer layer: 9 ectoplasm
substance: gel

protoplasmic: 10 archetypal, primordial

prototype: 5 model 6 emblem 7 pattern 8 antetype, original 9 archetype

protozoan: 5 ameba 6 amoeba 8 rhizopod
genus of: 7 arcella
order: 6 lobosa
parasitic: 5 ameba 6 amoeba 8 amoebida

protract: 4 spin 5 defer, delay 6 dilate, extend 7 detract, prolong 8 continue, elongate, lengthen, protrude

protrude: jut 5 blear, bulge 7 extrude, project 9 interfere

protruded: 6 extant

protuberance: nub, wen 4 boll, boss, bulb, bump, heel, hump, knob, knot, lobe, lump, node, snag, umbo 5 bulge, bunch, caput, hunch, torus 8 eminence, swelling 9 gibbosity 10 projection, prominence, protrusion
rounded: 4 hump, umbo

protuberant: 6 convex, extant 7 bottled, gibbous 8 blubbery

proud See also **pride**): 4 ikey 5 brant, chuff 7 haughty, stately, valiant 8 imposing 9 cockhorse 10 impressive 11 magisterial, overbearing 12 presumptuous, supercilious

prove: try 4 aver, fand, pree, test 5 argue, essay, nurse, prive(Sc.) 6 argify, argufy, evince, verify 7 confirm, justify, probate 8 identify, manifest 9 ascertain, establish 11 corroborate, demonstrate

provenance: 6 origin, source 10 derivation 11 provenience

provender: hay 4 corn, feed, food, oats, prog 5 grain, straw 6 fodder 7 prebend 10 provisions

provenience: 10 provenance

proverb: saw 4 word 5 adage, axiom, maxim, motto 6 ballad, byword, enigma, saying 7 byspell, parable 8 allegory, aphorism, forbysen

proverbial: 11 sententious

provide: 5 cater, equip, stock, store, yield 6 afford, foison, purvey, ration, render, supply 7 chevise, furnish 8 accouter, accoutre 9 stipulate 10 contribute

provided: if; but 5 boden, found 6 sobeit 8 afforded, supplied 9 furnished 13 conditionally

provided that: if, so

providence: 8 function, guidance

provident: 4 wise 6 frugal, saving 7 careful, prudent, thrifty 8 cautious, discreet 9 farseeing 10 economical, farsighted 11 foresighted

providential: 5 lucky 9 fortunate

province: 4 area, nome 5 arena, range, realm, shire, tract 6 colony, domain, eparch, region, sphere 7 country, emirate 8 district, division 9 bailiwick, territory 10 department, palatinate 12 jurisdiction
pert. to: 5 nomic

provincial: 4 rude 5 crude, local 6 narrow, rustic 7 insular, limited 9 parochial 10 uncultured 11 countrified 15 unsophisticated

provision: 4 fare, food 5 board, cater, grist, stock, store 6 clause, supply, wraith 7 proviso 9 condition
seller: 6 sutler

provisional: 4 iffy 7 aeolian 9 provisory, temporary, tentative 10 contingent 11 conditional

provisions: 4 cate, chow, fare, food 5 board, bouge, terms 6 forage, stocks, stores, viands 7 rations 9 provender 10 chevisance
search for: 6 forage
stock of: 6 larder 8 magazine

proviso: 5 salvo 6 clause 7 article, caution 9 condition 11 stipulation

provisory: 11 provisional

provocative: 7 agacant 8 agacante 9 provoking 10 aggressive 11 stimulating

provoke: ire, vex 4 bait, move, spur, stir 5 anger, annoy, cause, eager, evoke, frump, pique, start, tease 6 arouse, excite, harass, incite, invite, invoke, nettle, summon 7 affront, incense, quicken 8 irritate 9 aggravate, challenge, displease, forthcall, stimulate 10 exasperate

provost: 4 head 5 chief 6 jailer, keeper 7 prefect 8 director, official 10 magistrate 13 administrator 14 superintendent

prow: bow 4 beak, nose, stem 5 brave, prore 6 steven 7 gallant, rostrum, valiant 9 honorable 10 courageous

prowess: 5 skill, valor 6 valour 7 bravery, courage 9 ingenuity 10 excellence

prowl: 4 lurk, roam 6 brevit, ramble, wander

proximal: 4 next 7 nearest 9 proximate 12 conterminous

proximate: 4 next 6 direct 8 proximal 9 immediate

proximity: 8 nearness, nighness, vicinage, vicinity 9 adjacence, closeness 10 contiguity 11 propinquity 13 approximation, juxtaposition

proxy: 5 agent, power, vicar 6 agency, deputy 7 proctor 8 function 9 authority 10 procurator, substitute

prudence: 10 management 11 calculation

prudent: 4 sage, wary, wise 5 canny, chary, douce, siker 6 frugal, sicker 7 careful 8 cautious, discreet, sensible 9 advisable, cautelous, provident, sagacious 10 economical, forehanded 11 circumspect, considerate, foresighted 14 forethoughtful

prudish: 4 nice, prim 8 priggish 10 overmodest

prune: cow, cut, lop 4 clip, coll, frog, geld, plum, sned(Sc.), trim 5 dress, fruit, plume, preen, purge, rasee, razee, shave 6 anoint 7 tonsure 8 castrate 9 simpleton

pruning knive: 8 serpette

prurient: 4 lewd 7 itching, longing, lustful 10 lascivious

pruritis: 4 itch

Prussia: *bay:* 4 Kiel 6 Danzig 10 Pomeranian

city: 4 Kiel 5 Essen 6 Aachen, Altena, Berlin, Tilsit 7 Breslau, Hanover, Munster, Stettin 9 Frankfort, Magdeburg 10 Dusseldorf, Konigsberg 14 Charlottenburg

district: 7 Stettin

island: 5 Rugen 6 Usedom, Wollin 7 Frisian

lagoon: 4 haff 7 Frische 8 Kurische 11 Pommerische

lancer: 4 Ulan 5 Uhlan

land-holding aristocracy: 6 Junker

legislature upper house: 10 Herrenhaus

measure: 4 fuss, rute, zoll 5 fuder, meile 6 morgen, oxhoft 8 scheffel

mountain: 4 Harz 7 Sudeten 11 Schneekoppe 13 Riesengebirge

province: 5 Posen 6 Berlin, Saxony 7 Hanover, Prussia, Silesia 9 Pomerania, Rhineland 10 Westphalia 11 Brandenburg, East-Prussia, Hesse-Nassau, West-Prussia 12 Hohenzollern 17 Schleswig-Holstein

river: Ems 4 Alle, Eder, Elbe, Oder, Saar 5 Memel 6 Niemen, Pregel 7 Vistula 8 Passarge, Weichsel

seaport: 4 Kiel 5 Emden

spa: Ems

university town: 5 Halle

weight: 4 mark 9 quentchen

prussiate: 4 salt 7 cyanide 12 ferricyanide, ferrocyanide

pry: spy 4 gaze, lift, move, nose, peek, peep, peer 5 jemmy, jimmy, lever, mouse, prize, raise, snoop 6 potter 7 crowbar 8 leverage, scrounge 10 scrutinize

prying: 4 nosy 5 nosey 7 curious 11 inquisitive

psalm: ode 4 hymn, poem, song 11 composition

collection: 6 hallel 7 psalter

kind: 4 laud 6 hallel, Venite 7 Cantate, introit 8 Miserere

opening communion: 7 introit

sign: 5 selah

word of punctuation: 5 selah

psalmist: 5 David 6 cantor, writer 8 composer 9 precentor

psalterium: 4 lyra 6 omasum 7 stomach 9 manyplies

psammite: 9 sandstone

pseudo: 4 fake, mock, sham 5 bogus, false 7 feigned 8 spurious 9 pretended, simulated 11 counterfeit

pseudologist: 4 liar

pseudonym (see also **nickname, pen name**): 5 alias 6 anonym 7 anonyme

Lev Bronstein: 11 Leon Trotsky

Josip Broz: 4 Tito

Iosif Dzhugashvili: 12 Joseph Stalin

Adolf Schicklgruber: 11 Adolf Hitler

Vladimir Ulyanov: 13 Vladimir Lenin

psittaceous: 10 parrotlike

psyche: 4 mind, soul 6 spirit

psychiatrist: 4 Jung 5 Adler, Freud 6 shrink 7 analyst 8 alienist

psychic: 9 animastic

psychic power: ESP

psychotic: mad 5 crazy 6 insane 10 disordered 12 unreasonable

Ptah's wife: 6 Sekhet

ptarmica: 10 sneezewort

ptarmigan: 4 bird, ripa, rype 6 grouse

pteric: 4 alar 8 winglike

pteroid: 8 fernlike, winglike

ptisan: tea 5 drink 6 tisane 9 decoction

Ptolemy: *astronomy work:* 8 almagest

wife: 12 Philadelphia

ptomaine: 6 poison

pub: bar, inn 5 hotel 6 boozer, tavern

pubble: fat 5 plump

public: inn 4 open 5 overt, state 9 community

discussion: 5 forum

record office: 7 archion 8 archives

service: 7 railway, utility 9 telegraph, telephone 10 waterworks

way: 4 road 5 alley 6 bridge, tunnel 7 highway 8 turnpike 9 boulevard

publican: 6 farmer, keeper 9 catchpole, catchpoll, collector

publication: 4 book 5 paper 6 annals, blazon, digest 7 booklet 8 pamphlet 9 ephemeris 10 periodical 12 notification, proclamation, promulgation

examiner: 6 censor

make-up: 6 format

permit: 7 release

preliminary: 9 prodromus

prepare for: 4 edit
regular: 10 periodical
publicist: 5 agent, solon 6 writer 10 journalist
publicity: air 7 buildup 9 promotion 11 advertising, information
publish: air 4 blow, edit, vent 5 issue, print 6 blazon, defame, delate, expose 7 diffuse, divulge, release 8 announce, evulgate, forspeak, proclaim, promulge 9 advertise, forespeak 10 promulgate 11 disseminate
without authority: 6 pirate 10 plagiarize
publisher: 6 editor, issuer 7 printer 8 broacher 10 journalist
copy: 5 blurb 8 colophon 12 announcement
Puccini: *heroine:* 4 Mimi
opera: 7 La Tosca
puck: elf 4 disk 5 fairy 6 roller, sprite, strike 9 hobgoblin 10 goatsucker
pucker: 4 fold 5 bulge, purse, reeve, smock 6 cockle, cotter, lucken 7 wrinkle 8 contract
puckered: 7 bullate
puckfist: 8 braggart, puffball
puckish: 8 annoying, pucklike 10 mysterious 11 mischievous
pud: paw 4 hand 7 pudding 8 forefoot
pudding: 4 duff, mush, sago 6 burgoo, hackin, haggis(Sc.), panada 7 burgout, custard, dessert, hacking, sausage, tapioca 8 roly-poly 9 stir-about
puddle: dub 4 plud, pond, pool 5 plash, swamp 6 charco, flodge 7 plashet 8 quagmire
puddock: 7 paddock
pudency: 7 modesty 11 bashfulness, prudishness 13 embarrassment 14 shamefacedness
pudgy: fat 5 dumpy, plump, squat 7 bulging 8 roly-poly
peublo: 4 town 7 village
Pueblo: 4 Hopi
assembly hall: 6 estufa
ceremonial chamber: 4 kiva
village: 4 taos
puerile: 4 weak 5 silly, young 7 babyish, foolish, trivial 8 childish, immature, juvenile, unworthy, youthful 10 unthinking
Puerto Principe: 8 Camaguey
Puerto Rico: *bark:* 4 mabi
beverage: 4 mabi
bird: 4 rola 7 yeguita
breadfruit: 7 castana
city: 5 Ponce 6 Dorado 7 Arecibo, San Juan(c.) 8 Mayaguez
conqueror of: 5 Miles
fish: 4 sama, sisi
island: 4 Mona
measure: 6 cuerda 10 caballeria

person of mixed blood: 6 gibaro
tree: 4 mora 5 yagua, yaray 8 guayroto 9 guaraguao
puff: 4 blow, chug, flam(Sc.), flan, fuff, gust, pant, pegh(Sc.), pouf, waff, waft 5 fluff, whiff
puff up: 5 bloat, swell 6 tumefy 7 distend, inflate
puffball: 4 fist, fuzz 8 fuzzball
puffbird: 6 barbet 8 barbacou
genus: 6 monasa
puffed up: 5 large 6 astrut 7 souffle 8 bouffant, imposing, inflated 9 bombastic, bouffante 11 pretentious
puffer: 6 blower 8 blowfish
puffin: auk 4 bird
puffy: 4 soft 5 pursy 6 flabby
pug: dog, elf 4 clay, plug, poke, puck 5 boxer, chaff, churn, dwarf, knead, track 6 harlot, refuse, sprite, thrust 7 trample 8 mistress, pugilist 9 footprint, hobgoblin
pug-nosed: 5 camus
puggy 6 monkey(Sc.) 10 sweetheart
pugilist: lug 5 boxer 7 battler, bruiser, fighter
assistant: 6 second 7 handler
pugilistic: 6 fistic
pugnacious: 7 warlike 8 fighting 9 bellicose, combative 10 aggressive 11 belligerent, contentious, quarrelsome
puisne: 4 puny 5 judge, later, petty 6 feeble, junior 10 subsequent 11 subordinate 13 insignificant
puissance: 4 army, host 5 force, might, power, vigor 8 potency 8 strength 12 forcefulness
puissant: 6 mighty, strong 8 powerful
puke: 4 wool 5 vomit
pukka, pucka: 4 good, real 7 genuine 8 complete 9 authentic 11 substantial 13 thoroughgoing
pulchritude: 5 grace 6 beauty 10 comeliness, excellence, loveliness
pule: cry 4 peep 5 cheep, whine 6 repine, snivel 7 whimper 8 complain
puling: 4 puly 6 sickly 7 babyish 8 childish, delicate
pull: lug, tew, tit, tow, tug, wap 4 claw, drag, draw, duct, hale, haul, jerk, yank, yerk 5 bouse(naut.), heave(naut.), hitch, pluck, tweak 6 arrest, twitch 7 attract, revulse, stretch 9 influence
apart: rip 4 rend, tear 8 separate
away: 5 wrest 6 remove 8 withdraw
down: 4 raze 7 destroy 8 demolish
off: pug 6 avulse, manage 7 succeed
one's freight: 5 leave 6 depart
one's leg: 4 hoax 7 deceive 8 hoodwink
out: 7 extract 9 extirpate 10 deracinate

through: **7** recover, succeed
up: **5** elate, trice
pullet: hen **4** fowl **5** frier **6** earock(Sc.) **7** pollard **8** poullard
pulley: **4** ring **5** fusee, fuzee, wheel **6** sheave
part: **4** arse, drum **6** rigger
Pullman: car **5** coach **7** sleeper
pullulate: bud **4** teem **5** swarm **9** germinate
pulp: pap **4** marc, mash, mass, pith **5** chyme, magma **6** pomace **7** bagasse
machine: **9** macerater
pulpit: **4** ambo, bema, desk **5** chair, stage **7** lectern, rostrum **8** platform, scaffold
pulpy: **6** fleshy
pulque: **5** drink **6** liquor, mescal
pulsate: **4** beat, move, pant **5** throb **6** quiver, strike, thrill **7** vibrate
pulsation: **5** ictus
pulsatory: **8** rhythmic **9** pulsatile, pulsative, systaltic, throbbing
pulse: mug **7** battuta **8** sphygmus
pulverize: **4** bray, meal, mull **5** crush, grind **6** bruise **7** atomize **8** demolish, levigate **9** comminute, triturate **12** contriturate
pulverized: **4** fine
pulverizer: **13** disintegrator
pulverulent: **5** dusty **7** crumbly, powdery **8** powdered
puly: **6** puling
puma: cat **6** cougar **7** panther **9** carnivore
pumice: **8** abrasive
pummel: fib **4** beat, maul **5** thump **6** batter, hammer
pump: gin, ram **4** jack **6** racker **7** stirrup, syringe **10** pulsometer
handle: **5** sweep, swipe
pumpernickel: **5** bread
pumpkin: **4** pepo **6** citrul, squash
head: **4** dolt **7** Puritan **9** blockhead
pumpkinseed: **7** sunfish **8** bluegill **10** butterfish
pun: mot **4** beat, joke **5** knock, pound **7** quibble **8** paragram **9** calembour, conundrum **11** paronomasia
punch: ade, jab **4** glog, poke, prod **5** douse, dowse, drink, negus, paste **6** pierce, strike **7** mattoir **8** beverage, puncture **9** perforate
Punch: **5** clown **7** buffoon, journal **8** magazine **10** periodical
first editor of: **5** Lemon
puncheon: die **4** cask, post, stud, tool **5** punch, stamp **6** timber
puncher: **6** cowboy **7** cowpoke **10** cowpuncher, perforator
Punchinello: **5** clown **7** buffoon
punctilious: **4** nice **5** exact **6** formal, proper **7** careful, correct, precise **8** exacting **10** ceremonial, scrupulous **11** ceremonious **13** conscientious

punctual: **6** prompt
punctuate: **4** mark **9** emphasize **11** distinguish
punctuation mark: dot **4** dash **5** colon, comma, quote **6** hyphen, period **8** ellipsis **9** semicolon **10** apostrophe **11** parenthesis
puncture: **4** bite, hole, stab, vent **5** prick, wound **6** pierce **9** perforate **11** perforation
pundit: **4** sage **5** swami **6** nestor **7** Brahman, scholar, teacher
pung: **4** sled **6** sleigh
pungent: hot **4** fell, keen, racy, tart **5** acrid, acute, cress, minty, salty, sharp, smart, spicy, tangy **6** biting, bitter, pepper **7** caustic, peppery, piquant **8** aromatic, piercing, poignant, stinging **10** expressive, irritating **11** acrimonious, stimulating
pungi: bin **4** pipe **5** flute
pungled: **8** shrunken **9** shriveled
Punic: **7** dialect **9** faithless **11** treacherous **12** Carthaginian
Punic faith: **8** betrayal **9** treachery
punish: **4** beat, fine, whip **5** abuse, mulct, scold, slate, smite, spank, strap, wreak **6** amerce, strike **7** chasten, correct, corrige, revenge, scourge **8** chastise, penalize **9** castigate **10** discipline **13** excommunicate
punishing: **8** grueling **9** gruelling
punishment: **4** loss, pain **5** peine(law), wrack **6** desert, dirdum, ferule **9** suffering **13** animadversion
device: rod **6** stocks
freedom from: **8** impunity
spare: **6** acquit **7** absolve **9** exculpate, exonerate
punitive: **5** penal **8** punitory **9** punishing **10** vindictive
Punjab: See **India**
punk: bad **4** fuel, poor **5** conch, tramp **6** amadou, tinder **8** beginner, elephant, inferior, strumpet **9** beginning, miserable, touchwood, worthless **10** prostitute
punkah: fan
punt: **4** boat, kick **6** gamble
punter: **5** poler **6** bettor **7** scalper
puny: **4** weak **5** dawny, frail, petty, small **6** feeble, puisne, sickly, slight **8** droghlin, inferior **9** unskilled **13** inexperienced, insignificant
pupa: **9** chrysalis
case: **5** theca
pupil: **4** tyro **5** cadet, eleve(F.), minor, plebe, youth **6** junior, senior **7** ecolier(F.), learner, scholar, student **8** disciple, neophyte, freshman **9** sophomore
pupilage: **6** nonage **10** immaturity
puppet: **4** baby, doll, tool **5** image **8** drollery **9** neuropast **10** marionette
show: **6** wajang, wayang

puppy: fop 5 whelp

pur: 4 purr

purblind: 5 blind 6 bisson, obtuse

purchasable: 5 venal 7 corrupt, salable 9 available 10 marketable

purchase: buy 5 acate, cheap, yield 6 emptio, income, obtain, return 7 acquire, bargain, emption 11 acquisition
back: 6 redeem, regain

purchaser: 5 buyer 6 emptor, patron, vendee 8 co-emptor, customer 9 acquereur 13 adjudicataire

purdah: 6 screen 7 curtain 9 seclusion

pure: 4 fine, good, mear, meer, mere, neat, nice, pute, true 5 clean, clear, fresh, moral, sheer, utter 6 candid, chaste, simple, vestal, virgin 7 cleanly, genuine, perfect, refined, sincere, sinless, unmixed 8 absolute, complete, dovelike, filtered, innocent, virtuous, zaccheus(Heb.) 9 authentic, blameless, downright, elemental, faultless, guiltless, stainless, unalloyed, undefiled, unsullied 10 immaculate 11 crystalline, unblemished, uncorrupted, unqualified 13 unadulterated 15 unsophisticated

puree: 4 mush, soup 8 porridge

purely: 6 solely, wholly

purfle: hem 6 border 7 outline 8 decorate, ornament, trimming

purgative: 5 jalap 6 physic 8 evacuant 9 cathartic 10 alviducous

purgatory: 5 limbo

purge: rid 5 clear 6 physic, purify, remove, seethe 7 cleanse, deterge 8 absterge 9 exculpate, expurgate

purification: 9 catharsis

purify: 5 clean, clear, purge 6 bleach, filter, refine 7 baptize, clarify, cleanse, distill, epurate 8 depurate, lustrate, renovate 9 elutriate

Puritan: 9 Roundhead

puritanic: 6 strict 7 denying 8 rigorous

purl: rib 4 eddy, knit 5 frill, swirl 6 murmur, purfle, stitch

purlieu: 5 haunt 7 environ 12 neighborhood

purloin: 4 crib 5 filch, steal, swipe 6 finger, pilfer, pirate 7 cabbage 8 abstract 10 plagiarize

purple: 4 plum 5 grape, lilac, mauve, royal 6 blatta, emblem, maroon, ornate, tyrian, violet 7 cassius 8 amaranth, imperial, lavender 9 cathedral, elaborate
dye: 7 cassius
land of: 4 Tyre
seller of: 5 Lydia

purple coneflower: 9 echinacea

purple copper ore: 7 bornite

Purple Heart: 5 award, medal, order

purple ragwort: 4 herb 6 jacoby

purport: 4 feck, gist, mean 5 drift, sense, tenor 6 effect, import, intent, object 7 bearing, meaning 9 intention, substance

purpose: aim, end, use 4 bent, goal, main, mean, plan, sake 5 avail 6 design, intend, intent, motive 7 mission 9 intention, objective, predesign 10 cogitation, conception, employment, resolution 13 determination
alleged: 7 pretext
lackin: 9 driftless

purposive: 5 telic 12 teleological

purpure: 6 purple

purr: hum 5 noise, sound 6 murmur

purse: bag, cly 4 bung, poke 5 bulse, burse, money, pouch 6 pucker, wallet 7 almoner, handbag 8 coco-wort, finances, treasury 9 exchequer 10 pocketbook 12 portemonnaie

purse crab: 5 ayuyu

purser: 6 bursar 7 boucher, cashier 9 paymaster, treasurer

pursue: run 4 hunt, seek 5 chase, chevy, chivy, hound, stalk 6 chivey, chivvy, follow, gallop 7 proceed 8 continue 9 prosecute

pursuer: 6 hunter 8 huntress

pursuit: 5 scent 7 calling 10 occupation
means: 7 dragnet

pursy: fat 5 obese, puffy 7 swollen, wealthy 9 asthmatic

purulent: 4 foul 5 pussy

purvey: tax 5 cater 6 supply 7 furnish, procure, provide 10 assessment

purveyor: 6 seller, sutler 7 caterer 9 victualer

push: go; pop, por 4 birr, bore, bunt, butt, ding, dush, pelt, ping, pole, porr, poss, prod, urge 5 bevel(Sc.), boost, crowd, drive, elbow, force, heave, hunch, impel, nudge, press, shove 6 clique, effort, energy, expand, extend, hustle, jostle, potter, propel, thrust 7 advance, promote 10 enterprise 14 aggressiveness
along: 4 prod 5 nudge
down: 7 detrude
in: 5 stove

pushy: 5 bossy 7 forward 9 officious

pusillanimous: 4 tame 5 timid 6 afraid 8 cowardly 10 irresolute 12 fainthearted

puss: cat 4 face, girl, hare 5 mouth, woman 8 baudrons(Sc.)

pustule: 4 blob, burl 5 achor, blain 6 blotch, pimple 7 blister 8 eruption, swelling

put (see also **place**): lay, set 4 cast, push, urge 5 clink, drive, fixed, force, impel place, state, throw **6** appose, attach, bestow, incite, thrust **7** deposit, express **9** attribute, constrain

away: **4** kill **5** store **6** murder **7** consume

back: **6** demote **7** replace, restore

before: **7** apposed, present

by: **4** save **5** store **6** reject

down: **6** humble, record **7** degrade, depress **8** suppress **9** deposited

forth: **4** show **5** exert, offer **7** extrude, propose, publish **9** circulate

forward: **7** prepose, propone

in: **4** ante **5** defer, delay, elude **6** baffle, divert, insert **7** discard, enclose **8** postpone **9** frustrate

off: fob **4** doff, haft **5** defer, delay, evade, table **6** divert, shelve **7** discard **8** deferred, postpone

on: act, don **5** apply, endue, indue **7** assumed, feigned, pretend **10** exaggerate

out: irk, vex **4** oust **5** anger, annoy, eject, evict, exile, expel **6** banish, deport, retire **7** publish **8** displace, distress **9** ostracize **10** discompose, disconcert, expatriate, extinguish **14** discountenance

over: **4** bilk, hoax **5** cheat, trick **7** deceive

together: add **5** piece, unite **6** gather, muster **7** collect **8** assemble **9** construct **10** congregate

up: can **4** post **5** build, erect

up with: **4** bear, take **5** brook, stand **6** endure **7** stomach **8** tolerate

putrefy: rot **5** decay **6** fester **7** corrupt **9** decompose **12** disintegrate

putrid: **4** foul **7** friable, noisome, vicious **8** depraved **10** putrescent **11** displeasing **12** disagreeable

puttee: **4** spat **6** gaiter **7** legging

putting area: **5** green

putty: **6** cement

puxy: **6** swampy **8** quagmire

puzzle: cap, get **5** glaik, griph, pinon, poser, rebus, stick **6** baffle, enigma, fickle, riddle **7** anagram, charade, confuse, foitter, griphus, mystery, mystify, nonplus, paradox, perplex **8** acrostic, bewilder, distract, entangle, intrigue **9** conundrum **10** difficulty, disconcert, palindrome

puzzled: **4** asea

puzzling: **9** equivocal

pygarg: **5** addax **6** osprey

Pygmalion: *sister:* **4** Dido

offspring: **6** Paphos, Paphus

sister's husband: **8** Sichaeus

statue: **7** Galatea

victim of: **8** Sichaeus

pygmy, pigmy: elf **4** pixy, runt **5** atomy, dwarf, gnome, minim, short **8** dwarfish **9** dandiprat **10** chimpanzee

pygmy musk deer: **10** chevrotain

pygostyle: **4** bone **5** vomer

pyknic: **5** solid, squat **6** stocky, sturdy **8** muscular **9** endomorph, squatness **11** endomorphic

pylon: **4** post **5** tower **6** marker **7** gateway **8** monument

Pylos' king: **6** Nestor

pyramid: **4** heap **6** accrue **8** increase

builder of largest: **6** Cheops

inhabitant: **5** Khufu **6** Cheops

site: **4** Giza **7** Cholula

pyramidal: **4** huge **8** enormous, imposing

pyre: **4** bale, bier **6** suttee

pyrene: pip **4** seed **5** stone

Pyrenees: *bandit:* **8** miquelet

chamois: **5** izard

mountain peak: **5** Aneto

people: **6** Basque

republic: **7** Andorra

resort: Pau

pyriform: **10** pear-shaped

pyromaniac: **7** firebug **8** arsonist

pyrotechnics: **9** fireworks

pyrotechnical device: **8** pinwheel

pyroxene: **6** augite **8** diopside **11** schefferite **12** hedenbergite

Pythagoras' birthplace: **5** Samos

Pythias' friend: **5** Damon

python: **5** snake **7** serpent

slayer: **6** Apollo

pythonic: **4** huge **8** inspired, oracular **9** monstrous

pyx, pix: box **4** case, test, vase **5** assay, capsa, carry, chest **6** casket, coffer, vessel **8** binnacle, ciborium, preserve **10** tabernacle

Q

Q: cue 5 queue
Qatar's capital: 4 Doha
q.e.d.: 21 quod erat demonstrandum
qua: as 4 bird 5 heron 7 quabird
quabird: 5 heron
quack: cry 5 couch, faker, fraud 6 crocus 8 impostor 9 charlatan, pretender 10 mountebank
quad: 4 quod 5 block 6 campus, person 7 sibling, quadrat 10 quandrangle
quadra: 6 fillet, listel, plinth
quadragenarian: 8 fortyish
quadragesimal: 5 forty 6 Lenten
quadrangle: 5 court 8 tetragon
quadrant: 4 gill 6 fourth 8 farthing 9 antimeter 10 instrument
quadrate: 4 suit 5 agree, ideal 6 square 7 perfect, squared 8 balanced 9 rectangle 10 correspond 13 correspondent
quadriga: 4 cart 6 horses 7 chariot
quadrille: 5 cards, dance
quadroon: 6 hybrid 7 mulatto
quadrumane: ape 6 monkey 7 gorilla 10 chimpanzee
quadruped: 6 mammal 10 fourlegged
quaere: 5 query 7 inquiry 8 question
quaff: sip 5 draft, drink 6 waught
quag: 5 quake 6 quiver 8 quagmire
quaggy: 4 miry, soft 5 boggy 6 flabby, spongy 7 queachy 8 yielding
quagmire: bog, gog, hag 5 marsh, swamp 6 morass
quahog: 4 clam
quail: cow 4 bird 5 colin, cower, quake, shake 6 blench, cringe, curdle, flinch, recoil, shrink, tremor, turnix 7 massena, tremble 8 bobwhite 9 coagulate, courtesan, partridge
  flock of: 4 bevy 5 covey
  young: 7 cheeper 8 squealer
quail snipe: 9 dowitcher
quaint: odd 4 nice 6 crafty 7 antique, curious, strange, unusual 8 fanciful, graceful, peculiar, singular 9 whimsical

quake: 4 quag, rese 5 shake, waver 6 quiver, shiver, tremor 7 shudder, tremble, vibrate 10 earthquake
Quaker: Fox 4 Penn 6 Friend 9 broadbrim
Quaker City: 12 Philadelphia
Quaker gray: 5 acier
Quaker-ladies: 5 bluet 11 meadowsweet
Quaker State: 12 Pennsylvania
Quaker's founder: 9 George Fox
quaking: 5 aspen, quaky 6 trepid 9 trepidity
qualification: 7 ability 8 aptitude 9 condition, endowment, knowledge, requisite 10 adaptation, capability, competence, experience 11 acquirement, designation, restriction 12 capacitation, modification
qualified: 8 eligible
qualify: fit 5 abate, adapt, equip, limit 6 enable, modify, soften, temper 7 assuage, entitle, prepare 8 diminish, mitigate, moderate, restrain, restrict 10 habilitate
quality: 4 cost, kind, rank, rate, sort, thew, tone 5 class, grade, power, quale, taste, trait 6 nature, status, strain, virtue 7 caliber, calibre, element 8 capacity, nobility, property 9 attribute, character 10 excellence 11 superiority 14 accomplishment, characteristic
  of tone: 6 timbre 9 resonance
qualm: 4 drow, pall 5 spasm 6 attack, nausea, regret, twinge 7 scruple 8 sickness 9 faintness, misgiving 11 compunction 16 faintheartedness
quamash: 5 camas 6 camass, cammas 7 prairie
quandary: fix 4 pass 6 pickle 7 dilemma, nonplus 11 predicament 12 bewilderment
quannet: 4 file
quant: 4 pole
quantity (See also **amount**): ace, any, bit, jag, jot, lot, sea, sum 4 atom, bulk, dash, dose, dram, drop, feck, iota, lick, lots, mass, mort, much, raff, raft, slew, unit 5 batch, bunch, grist, hoard, scads, stack, store 6 amount, capful, degree, extent, hir-

sel, morsel, number, weight **7** average, handful, modicum, portion, slather **8** dribblet **9** allowance **10** pennyworth
fixed: **8** constant
full: **10** complement
irrational: **4** surd
per unit: **4** rate
prescribed: **4** dose **6** dosage
without direction: **6** scalar
Quantrill's men: 7 raiders
quantum: 4 unit **6** amount **7** portion **8** quantity
quarantine: ban **7** exclude, isolate **8** restrain **9** interdict
quaranty: 5 court
quarentene: 4 rood **7** furlong
quark: caw **5** croak, quawk
quarl, quarle: 4 tile **5** brick
quarrel: row **4** feud, fuss, spat, tiff **5** brawl, broil, cavil, flite, flyte, scene, scrap **6** affray, barney, bicker, breach, breeze, cangle, chisel, debate, fracas, fratch, hassle, jangle, quarry, strife **7** contend, dispute, faction, rhubarb, wrangle **8** argument, disagree, squabble **9** upscuddle **10** contention **11** altercation, controversy **13** collie-shangie **16** misunderstanding
quarrelsome: 7 fratchy, hostile **8** brawling, choleric, frampoid, petulant **9** bellicose, irascible, irritable, litigious **10** discordant, pugnacious **11** belligerent, contentious **12** disputatious **13** argumentative
quarry: 4 delf, game, prey **5** chase, delft **6** latomy, object, ravine **7** latomia, quarrel
quart: 6 fourth **7** measure
four: **6** gallon
metric: **5** liter, litre
one-eighth: **4** gill
two: **6** flagon
quartan: 5 fever **7** malaria
quarter: 4 coin, span **5** allot, grith, house, lodge, tract **6** assign, bestow, canton, charge, fourth, harbor, supply **7** bearing, furnish, harbour, shelter **8** clemency, contrada, contrade(pl.), district, division **9** apportion, dismember **11** forbearance
quarters: 4 camp, room **7** billets, lodging, shelter **8** barracks **9** dormitory
nautical: **6** fo'c'sle **7** gunroom **8** steerage, wardroom **10** forecastle
winter: **10** hibernacle
women's: **5** harem
quarter note: 8 crotchet
quartz: 4 onyx, sand, sard **5** agate, flint, prase, silex, topaz **6** jasper, silica **7** citrine, crystal, rubasse, sinople **8** amethyst **9** carnelian **10** calchedony
quartzite: 9 itabarite, sandstone
quash: 4 cass, drop, void **5** abate, annul, crush, quell, shake **6** cancel **7** abolish, cas-

sare, destroy, pumpkin, shatter **8** abrogate, suppress **9** overthrow
quat: 4 boil, glut, quit(Sc.) **5** squat **6** pimple, squash **7** blister, pustule, satiate
quaternion: 6 tetrad **8** quatrain
turning factor: **6** versor
quaver: 5 shake, trill **6** quiver **7** tremble, tremolo, vibrate **9** vibration
quaw: 8 quagmire
quawk: caw **5** heron **7** screech
quay: key **4** bund, dock, mole, pier, wall **5** levee, quell, wharf **6** bunder, subdue **7** landing **10** embankment
quean: 4 jade **5** hussy, wench **6** harlot
queach: fen **7** thicket
queachy: 5 boggy, bushy **6** marshy, quaggy, swampy
queasy: 5 timid **8** delicate, qualmish, ticklish, troubled **9** hazardous, nauseated, squeamish, uncertain, unsettled **10** fastidious **11** embarrassed **13** uncomfortable
Quebec: *acre:* **6** arpent
cape: **5** Gaspe
county: **5** Laval
patron saint: **4** Anne
peninsula: **5** Gaspe
town: **5** Sorel
vehicle: **7** caleche
quebrada: gap **5** brook, creek, gorge **6** ravine, stream **7** fissure **8** brooklet
Quechua: 4 Inca **6** Indian
queechy: 4 puny, weak **5** small **6** feeble, sickly
queen: 4 fers, rani(Ind.) **5** ranee(Ind.), reine(F.) **6** regina **7** monarch **9** sovereign
widowed: **7** dowager
queen it: 8 domineer **9** tyrannize
queen of fairies: Mab, Pam, Una **7** Titania **8** Gloriand
Queen Anne's lace: 6 carrot
Queen City: 10 Cincinnati
Queen of the Adriatic: 6 Venice
Queen of the Antilles: 4 Cuba
Queen of the East: 7 Zenobia
queen of gods: 4 Hera, Juno, Sati
Queen of Hearts: 9 Elizabeth
Queen of Heaven: 4 Hera, Mary, moon **7** Astarte
Queen of Isles: 6 Albion
Queen of Palmyra: 7 Zenobia
Queen of Sheba: 6 Balkis
queen of spades: 5 basta
Queen of Thebes: 5 Dirce
queen of underworld: Hel **4** Hela
queen's arm: 6 musket
queen's-delight: oil **4** herb **9** perennial, queenroot
queen's-flower: 6 myrtle **9** bloodwood
queenly: 5 noble, regal, royal **7** reginal

Queensland: *river:* 8 Brisbane
seaport: 8 Brisbane

queer: odd, rum 4 sham 5 comic, droll, drunk, faint, funny, giddy, rally, spoil 6 banter, insane 7 comical, erratic, strange, unusual 8 abnormal, doubtful, fanciful, humorous, peculiar, qualmish, ridicule, singular, spurious 9 dishonest, eccentric, fantastic 10 homosexual, suspicious 11 counterfeit, intoxicated 12 questionable

queest: 8 ringdove

queet: 4 coot

quell: 4 calm, cool, damp, dash, kill, quay 5 allay, check, crush, quash, quiet, still 6 obtund, pacify, reduce, soothe, spring, stanch, stifle, subdue 7 assuage, destroy, repress, satisfy 8 fountain, suppress 9 overpower, overwhelm 10 extinguish

quelque-chose: 6 trifle

queme: fit 4 neat, snug, tidy 5 handy, quiet 6 comely 7 fitting, satisfy 8 pleasant, suitable 9 agreeable

quench: 5 delay, slake

quenelle: 8 meatball 9 forcemeat

quercus: oak 4 tree 9 evergreen

querent: 8 inquirer 9 plaintiff 11 complainant

querida: 5 lover 10 sweetheart

querist: 8 inquirer 10 questioner

querken: 5 choke 6 stifle

querl: 4 coil 5 twirl, twist

quern: 4 mill 7 grinder

quernstone: 9 millstone

querulous: 7 fretful, peevish, whining 9 complaint, plaintive, quizzical 11 complaining 12 querimonious

query: ask 5 doubt 6 demand, quaere 7 inquire, inquiry 8 question 9 challenge 11 interrogate

quest: ask 4 hunt, seek 6 search 7 examine, inquest, journey, pursuit, seeking 9 adventure 10 enterprise, expedition

question: ask 4 crux, quiz 5 doubt, grill, poser, query, scout, targe(Sc.) 6 appose, cruces(pl.), debate, demand, quaere, riddle, shrive 7 dispute, inquire, inquiry, problem, scruple, stumper 9 catechise, catechize, challenge, interview 10 discussion 11 examination, interrogate, proposition 12 interpellate 13 interrogation, interrogative, investigation
denoting: 15 interrogational
rhetorical: 10 eperotesis

question mark: 7 erotema, eroteme

questionable: 4 moot 7 dubious, suspect 9 ambiguous, equivocal, uncertain

questionnaire: 4 form, poll

quetch: 4 stir 6 twitch

quetzal: 6 trogon

queue: cue 4 line 5 braid 7 pigtail

quey: 6 heifer

quiaquia: 4 scad 9 cigarfish

quibble: cog, pun 4 carp, quib 5 cavil, cheat, evade 6 ambage, baffle, haffle 7 brabble, evasion, shuffle 9 previcate 10 equivocate 12 equivocation

quica: 7 opossum, sarigue

quick: apt, yap 4 deft, fast, flit, lish, live, spry, vite(F.), yare 5 acute, agile, alert, alive, apace, brisk, fiery, fleet, hasty, rapid, ready, sharp, swift, tosto(It.), yeder 6 abrupt, active, lively, moving, nimble, prompt, speedy, sudden, volant 7 intense 8 animated, dextrous, shifting, vigorous 9 dexterous, impatient, sensitive, sprightly 10 celeritous, perceptive 11 expeditious 12 invigorating

quick bread: 7 muffins 8 biscuits 9 cornbread

quicken: 4 whet 5 hurry, speed 6 arouse, excite, hasten, incite, revive, vivify 7 animate, enliven, provoke, refresh, sharpen 8 expedite, inspirit 9 reanimate, stimulate 10 accelerate 11 resuscitate 12 reinvigorate

quicker than: ere

quicklime: 5 rusma

quickly: 4 fast, rath, soon, vite(F.) 5 alive, apace 6 belive, hourly, presto, pronto 7 rapidly 8 promptly, speedily, vigorous

quickness: 6 acumen 7 acidity 8 dispatch, progress, pungency, sagacity 9 acuteness 10 expedition

quicksand: 4 flow, syrt, trap 6 danger, syrtis

quickset: 5 hedge 7 thicket 8 hawthorn

quicksilver: 7 mercury 9 heautarit

quid: cud, fid 4 chaw, chew 5 pound, trade 6 barter, return 8 exchange, quiddity 9 sovereign

quiddany: 5 jelly, sirup

quiddit: 7 quibble 8 subtlety

quiddle: 6 dawdle, trifle

quidnunc: 5 frump 6 gossip, tatler 8 busybody

quiescent: 5 quiet, still 6 latent, static 7 dormant, resting 8 inactive, sleeping 10 motionless

quiet: sh; coy, pet 4 calm, cosh, dead, ease, fair, hush, lull, mild, rest, tame 5 allay, downy, inert, peace, privy, sober, still 6 gentle, hushed, merely, modest, placid, repose, secret, sedate, serene, settle, silent, smooth, soothe, static, stilly 7 appease, compose, halcyon, restful, retired, silence 8 composed, decorous, peaceful, secluded, tranquil 9 alleviate, contented, noiseless, peaceable, placidity, quiescent, reposeful, unruffled 10 motionless, silentness, unmolested **11** clandestine, tranquilize, undisturbed

quietus: 5 death **6** repose **8** mittimus **11** acquittance

quiff: 4 girl, puff **5** whiff **8** forelock

quill: cop, pen **5** remex, spina **6** bobbin, pinion **7** remiges(pl.), spindle

porcupine: pen **5** spine

quillet: 4 tube **5** tract **7** quibble

quilt: pad, sew **4** gulp **5** eider **6** caddow, pallet, stitch **7** blanket, comfort, swallow **8** coverlet **9** comforter **11** counterpane

quink: 5 brant

quinoa: 5 seeds **7** pigweed

quinoline derivative: 7 analgen

quintuplets: 6 Dionne **7** Fischer

quip: mot, pun **4** gibe, jest, joke **5** sally, taunt **6** saying **7** quibble

quire: 4 fold **5** choir, paper

quirk: 4 kink, quip, turn **5** clock, knack, sally, trait, twist **6** groove, strike **7** caprice, evasion **8** flourish **9** deviation **10** subterfuge **11** peculiarity **12** equivocation

quirquincho: 5 pichi **6** peludo **9** armadillo

quirt: 4 whip **5** romal

quis: 8 woodcock

quisling: rat **7** traitor

quit: rid **4** free, stop **5** avoid, cease, clear, forgo, leave, repay **6** acquit, depart, desist, forego, resign, vacate **7** abandon, forsake, release, relieve **8** abdicate, absolved, liberate, renounce **9** surrender **10** relinquish **11** discontinue

quitclaim: 6 acquit **7** release **14** relinquishment

quite: all **4** very **5** stark, truly **6** really, wholly **7** totally, utterly **8** entirely **10** altogether, completely, positively **12** considerably

quite so: 7 exactly **9** precisely

quittance: 5 repay **6** return **7** requite **8** reprisal, requital **9** departure, discharge, repayment **10** recompense **11** acquittance

quitter: 4 seal, slag **5** piker **6** coward **7** shirker

quiver: 4 case, quag, tirl(Sc.) **5** bever, quake, quick, shake, thirl(Sc.), trill **6** active, arrows, bicker, cocker, dindle, lively, nimble, quaver, sheath, shiver, tremor **7** frisson, tremble, vibrate **8** flichter **9** palpitate, vibration

quivering: 5 aspen **6** ashake, didder **7** aquiver **8** blubbery

quiverleaf: 5 aspen

quixotic: 7 utopian **9** visionary **10** chivalrous, idealistic **11** impractical **13** impracticable

quiz: ask **4** exam, hiss, hoax, jest, joke, mock, test, whiz **5** chaff, probe **7** examine **8** instruct, question, ridicule **11** examination, questioning

quizzical: odd **7** amusing, comical, teasing **9** bantering, eccentric, perplexed

quizzing glass: 7 monocle **8** eyeglass

quod: jug **4** jail **5** court **6** prison

quodlibet: 6 debate, medley **8** fantasia, subtlety

quoin: 4 coin **5** angle, wedge **6** corner **8** keystone, voussoir

quoit: 4 disc, ring **5** throw **6** discus **8** cromlech

mark aimed at: tee

pin: hob

quomodo: 5 means **6** manner

quondam: 6 former **7** onetime **8** sometime

quonset hut: 6 prefab

British type: **6** Nissen

quop: 5 throb

quorum: 5 group **7** council **8** majority

quota: 4 part **5** share **6** divide, rating **8** dividend **10** contingent, proportion

quotation: 5 price, quote

quotation mark: 9 guillemet(F.)

quote: 4 cite, cote, name, note **5** motto, refer **6** adduce, allege, allude, notice, repeat, select **7** excerpt, extract, passage **9** quotation, reference, selection **10** memorandum

quoth: 4 said **5** spoke

quotha: 6 indeed **8** forsooth

quotidian: 5 daily **7** trivial **8** everyday, ordinary **9** recurring **11** commonplace

quotient: 6 result

quotity: 5 group **10** collection

R

R: ar; rho 6 letter
Ra: Re; Shu, Tem, Tum 4 Aten 5 Horus 7
Chepera, Khepera, Sokaris 9 Harmachis
bull form: 5 Bacis
child: Mu; Mat, Shu 4 Maat 5 Athor
parent: Geb, Keb, Nut, Seb 5 Neith
wife: 4 Mout
raad: 7 catfish
rab: 6 beater
rabat: 5 rabbi 8 polisher
rabato, rebato: 4 ruff 6 collar
rabban: 6 master 7 teacher
rabbet: 5 check 6 groove, recess 7 channel
rabbi: 4 lord 5 amora 6 master, rabbin 7
amoraim, tannaim, teacher 8 sabaraim,
saboraim 9 clergyman
assistant: 6 cantor
school: 7 yeshiva 8 yeshibah, yeshivah 9
yeshiboth(pl.)
wife: 9 rebbetzin
rabbit: bun, doe 4 buck, cony, hare, tyro 5
bunny, capon, coney, lapin(F.) 6 coward,
novice, rodent, tapeti
fur: 4 cony, rack, scut 5 coney, lapin
genus: 5 lepus
shelter: 5 hutch 6 burrow, warren 7 clapper
tail: fud(Sc.) 4 scut
young: 4 rack 6 gazabo, gazebo 7 starter
rabbit-ear: 6 cactus 8 toadflax
rabbit fever: 9 tularemia
rabbit flower: 8 foxglove, toadflax
rabbit-foot: 5 charm 8 talisman
rabbit-meat: 9 archangel
rabbit tobacco: 10 balsamweed
rabbit vine: 9 groundnut
rabbitfish: 8 chimaera
rabbitmouth: 10 harelipped
rabbitry: 5 hutch 6 warren
rabbit's-mouth: 10 snapdragon
rabbit's-root: 12 sarsaparilla
rabble: mob 4 herd, raff, rout 5 crowd 6 ragtag 7 bobtail 8 canaglia, canaille, riffraff 9
confusion 10 clamjamfry, hubble-shoo,
hubble-show 11 commonality

rabble-rouser: 6 ragtag 8 agitator 9 demagogue
Rabelaisian: 5 bawdy 6 earthy
rabid: mad 6 raging 7 frantic, furious, violent, zealous 8 frenzied, virulent 9 fanatical 12 enthusiastic
rabies: 5 lyssa, lytta 7 madness 11 hydrophobia
raccoon: 4 coon 6 mapach 7 mapache
related animal: 5 coati, panda
race: cut, ilk, run 4 dash, gest, herd, kind,
lane, line, root, rush, slit, sort, stem, stud
5 blood, breed, brood, caste, chevy, chivy,
class, corso, flesh, geste, hurry, relay,
speed, stock, track, tribe 6 arroyo, bicker,
broose, chivvy, course, family, groove, hasten, hurdle, nation, people, slalom, sprint,
stirps, strain 7 bombast, channel, contend,
contest, dynasty, lineage, regatta, running, scamper, scratch 8 marathon 9 ho-
lethnos, 10 freeforall, generation, passageway 11 competition, descendants, watercourse
combined form: 4 gend, geno
division: 7 Negroid 9 Caucasian, Mongolian
human: man 7 mankind 9 mortality
mixed: see **person:** *of mixed blood*
murder: 8 genocide
pert. to: 6 ethnic
series: 7 regatta
science: 9 athletics, ethnology
starting line: 7 scratch
race board: 9 gangplank
race ginger: 10 gingerroot
raceabout: 5 sloop 8 roadster
racecourse: 4 heat, oval 6 career, circus,
course 7 raceway
marker: 4 meta 5 pylon
racehorse: 6 maiden, mantis, plater
racer: 4 crab 5 miler, snake 6 runner 7
courser, serpent 8 sprinter 9 turntable 10
blacksnake
racetrack: 4 oval, turf 10 hippodrome
tipster: 4 tout

raceway: 5 canal **7** channel, fishway **8** mill-race

Rachel: *children:* **6** Joseph **8** Benjamin
father: **5** Laban
husband: **5** Jacob
sister: **4** Leah

rachis: 4 stem **5** spine **8** backbone

rachitis: 7 rickets

rack: bar, fly, gin, jib **4** bink, crib, gait, pace, path, scud, skin, tree **5** airer, brake, creel, flake, horse, stand, touse, trace, track, vapor **6** course, cratch, gantry, harass, strain, wrench **7** agonize, grating, oppress, pathway, stretch, torment, torture, vestige **9** framework **10** excruciate, foresaddle

racket: bat, din **4** shoe **5** bandy, dodge, noise, trick **6** bustle, clamor, crosse, hubbub, outcry, scheme, strike **7** clangor, clatter, pattern, revelry **8** snowshoe **10** battledore, turbulence **11** merrymaking
jai alai: **5** cesta

rackle: 5 clank **6** rattle **7** clatter **8** reckless **9** impetuous **10** headstrong

raconteur: 8 narrator **11** storyteller

racy: 5 brisk, fresh, smart, spicy, swift **6** lively, risque **7** piquant, pungent, zestful **8** indecent, spirited, stirring, vigorous **10** suggestive **12** exhilarating

rad: 5 eager, quick, ready **6** afraid, elated **11** exhilarated

Radames' love: 4 Aida

raddle: rod **4** beat **5** color, ocher, twist **6** branch, cudgel, thrash **10** interweave

radial: ray **8** quadrant

radian: arc **7** auroral

radiance: 4 beam, glow **5** glare, gleam, glory, nitor, sheen, shine **6** luster **7** glitter, glowing, shining **8** lambency, splendor **9** brilliant **10** brightness, brilliancy, effulgence, refulgence

radiant: 7 auroral **11** resplendent

radiate: 4 beam, emit **5** shine **6** spread **7** diffuse, emanate **9** coruscate, irradiate **10** illuminate

radiating: 6 radial **8** stellate **11** centrifugal

radiation detector: 6 geiger

radiator: 6 heater

radical: red **4** root, surd **5** basal, basic, rebel, ultra **7** capital, drastic, extreme, forward, leftist, organic, support **8** cardinal, complete **9** extremist **10** foundation, iconoclast **11** fundamental **12** intransigent **13** revolutionary
chemical: ion **4** amyl, aryl **6** acetyl, adenyl, adipyl **7** tartryl **8** aluminyl

radicate: 9 establish

radicle: 7 rootlet

radio: set **8** portable, wireless **9** broadcast, radiogram **10** transistor **12** walkie-talkie
detector: **5** radar
frequency: **5** audio
interference: **6** static
operator: ham **6** sparks **11** broadcaster
part: **5** diode **8** detector, selector
rating: **6** Hooper
signal check: **7** monitor
wave: **5** micro, short

radish: 5 radis(F.) **7** cadlock

radium: *discoverer:* **5** Curie
emanation: **5** niton, radon
source: **7** uranite

radius: ken **5** orbit, range, spoke, sweep **6** extent, length
pert. to: **6** radial

radix: 4 root **6** etymon **7** radical

raff: 4 heap, raft, rake **5** trash **6** huddle, jumble, litter, lumber, rabble, timber **7** rubbish **8** leavings, riffraff

raffish: low **5** cheap **6** flashy, frowsy, tawdry **7** unkempt **9** worthless **11** disgraceful **12** disreputable

raffle: 4 raff **6** jumble, rabble, refuse, tangle **7** drawing, lottery, rubbish, serrate **8** entangle, riffraff

raft: cow **4** crib, floe, heap, moki, raff, spar **5** balsa, barge, float **6** rafter **9** catamaran, transport **10** collection
part: **5** brail

raft-breasted: 6 ratite

raft duck: 5 scaup **7** redhead **8** bluebill

rafter: 4 balk, beam, firm, raft, viga **7** carline, chevron

rafty: 4 damp **5** musty, stale **6** rancid

rag: jag **4** mock, rail, rate, tune **5** annoy, dance, scold, scrap, shred, tease **6** banter, harass, rumpus, tatter, uproar **7** quarrel, ragtime, remnant, wrangle

ragamuffin: 14 tatterdemalion

rage: fad, ire **4** beef, fret, fume, funk, fury, heat, rant, rave, tear **5** anger, chafe, craze, furor, mania, storm, wrath **6** choler, fervor, frenzy, furore, temper **7** amentia, bluster, bombast, emotion, fashion, fervour, passion, thunder **8** insanity, violence **9** vehemence **10** enthusiasm

ragged: 5 harsh, rough **6** jagged, shaggy, uneven **7** shreddy, unkempt **8** strident, tattered **9** defective, dissonant, imperfect, irregular **10** straggling, unfinished **11** dilapidated

ragged jacket: 4 seal

ragged lady: 5 guara **11** love-in-a-mist

ragged sailor: 10 bluebottle, cornflower

raggedy doll: Ann **4** Andy, Anne

raggle: cut **6** groove

raggy: 6 ragged

raging: 4 grim 5 rabid 6 fierce 7 fervent, rageous 8 furibund 9 ferocious

raglan: 6 sleeve 8 overcoat

ragout: 4 hash, stew 5 salmi 6 salmis 7 goulash, haricot 8 salpicon 10 capilotade 11 gallimaufry

ragpicker: 6 bunter 10 chiffonier(F.) 11 chiffonnier(F.)

ragshag: 11 masquerader

ragwort: 5 plant 8 ambrosia

rah: 5 cheer 6 hurrah

raid: 4 tala 5 foray 6 attack, creach(Sc.), creagh(Sc.), forage, harass, inroad, invade, maraud, piracy 7 chappow, despoil, hership 8 invasion 9 chevachie, incursion, roadstead, cavalcade

rail: bar, jaw 4 coot, flow, gush, jest, rant, rate, slat, sora 5 abuse, array, chide, cloak, crake, dress, guard, heron, plank, scoff, scold, soree, track 6 banter, berate, callet, revile, septum 7 arrange, bidcock, bilcock, clocker, footrest, garment, inveigh 8 decorate, Rallidae(pl.), reproach 9 spectator
genus of: 4 sora 6 rallus

railing: bar 5 fence 7 barrier, parapet 8 balconet, banister, espalier, rabulous 9 guardrail 10 balconette, balustrade 12 vituperation

raillery: 4 gaff 5 chaff, sport 6 banter, blague 8 badinage, ridicule 10 persiflage

railly: 4 jest, mock 5 rally 8 ridicule

railroad: 4 herd, line, push, rush 5 hurry, track 8 ceinture, monorail 9 transport
branch: 4 stub 6 feeder
bridge: 7 trestle, viaduct
car: 5 diner 6 parlor 7 caboose, coal-car, parlour, Pullman, sleeper
center: 7 station 8 terminal, terminus 10 roundhouse
cross rail: 4 frog
flare: 5 fusee
signal: 5 fusee 9 semaphore
station: 4 gare(F.) 5 depot
switch: 4 frog
tie: 6 timber 7 sleeper
worker: 6 boomer, porter 7 fireman 8 engineer, strapper 9 conductor

railway: 5 train 6 subway 8 elevated, jackstay, monorail 9 funicular

raiment: See **dress**

rain: dag, fog 4 mist, pour 5 blizz, blout, misle, plash, spate, storm 6 deluge, mizzle, serein, shower 7 drizzle 8 downpour, sprinkle 10 cloudburst 13 precipitation
check: 4 stub 12 postponement
fine: 4 mist 7 drizzle
god: 8 Parjanya
icy: 4 hail, snow 5 sleet
pert. to: 7 pluvial

unit of measure: 4 inch

rain bird: 6 plover

rain cloud: 5 nimbi(pl.) 6 nimbus

rain forest: 5 selva

rain gage: 8 udometer 10 hyetometer 11 pluviograph, pluviometer 15 hyetometrograph

rain glass: 9 barometer

rain leader: 9 downspout

rain-loving: 12 ombrophilous

rain tree: 5 saman, zaman 6 zamang 8 genisaro

rainbow: arc, bow 4 iris
goddess: 4 Iris
measuring device: 12 spectrometer
pert. to: 6 iridal

rainbow chaser: 9 visionary 11 doctrinaire

rainbow-like: 6 iridal 10 iridescent

raincoat: 4 mino 6 poncho, ulster 7 slicker 10 mackintosh, trenchcoat

rainfall: *pert. to:* 6 hyetal

rainfowl: 6 cuckoo 10 woodpecker 11 channelbill

rainspout: 4 rone(Sc.) 10 waterspout

rainworm: 8 nematode 9 earthworm

rainy: wet 4 damp 5 moist 7 flooded 8 cluttery
season: 7 monsoon

rais, reis: 4 head 5 chief, ruler 7 captain

raise: up; end 4 buoy, grow, hain, heft, hike, levy, lift, rear, rise, stir 5 arear, boost, breed, crane, dight, elate, exalt, hance, heave, heeze, hoist, horse, rouse, set-up, start, trice 6 arouse, ascend, assume, awaken, cantle, create, emboss, excite, gather, incite, leaven, muster, obtain, remove, uplift 7 address, advance, chevise, collect, elevate, enhance, ennoble, lighten, present, procure, produce, promote 8 heighten, increase 9 cultivate, establish, institute, intensify, originate, propagate 10 aggrandize, appreciate, invigorate

raised: 4 hove 6 arrect, enleve(F.)

raisin: 5 lexia, zibeb 7 currant

raj: 4 rule 5 reign 11 sovereignty

rajah: 4 king 5 chief 6 prince 9 dignitary
wife: 4 rani 5 ranee

Rajmahal creeper: 4 jiti, vine

rake: gad, rue, rut 4 path, raff, roue, rove, trip 5 claut, glean, track 6 gather, groove 7 collect, gleaner, scratch 8 enfilade, rakehell 9 debauchee 11 inclination
with gunfire: 8 enfilade

rakehell: 4 rake 7 immoral 9 debauched, debauchee, dissolute 10 profligate

rake-off: 4 take 6 profit, rebate 10 commission, percentage

rakish: 4 lewd, pert 7 roguish 9 dissolute

rale: 6 rattle

rallidae: 5 coots, rails, wekas 6 crakes 10 gallinules

rally: 4 drag, mock 5 chaff, noise, rouse 6 arouse, attack, banter, deride, revive 7 recover, reunite 8 assemble, raillery, ridicule 10 recuperate, strengthen 11 concentrate

rallying cry: 6 slogan

ram: hit, pun, tup, wad 4 buck, butt, tamp, teap 5 Aries, crash, sheep, stuff 6 batter, beetle, chaser, rancid, strike, wether 7 collide, plunger 8 bulldoze

ram cat: tom 4 male

Rama's bride: 4 Sita

ramage: 4 wild 5 bough, rough 6 unruly 7 untamed 8 branches, frenzied, wildness

ramage hawk: 8 brancher

ramass: 6 gather 7 collect

ramate: 8 branched

ramble: gad 4 roam, rove, walk 5 jaunt, prowl, range 6 stroll, travel, wander 7 saunter 8 straggle 9 excursion

rambling: 7 cursory, devious 9 desultory, wandering 10 circuitous, discursive 11 peripatetic 12 disconnected

rambunctious: 4 wild 6 unruly 10 boisterous, disorderly, rampageous 12 obstreperous 14 uncontrollable

ramekin: pan 4 dish 9 casserole

ramentum: 5 palea, palet 6 paleae(pl.), scales 7 shaving 8 particle

ramhead: arm 4 hook 5 lever 8 clodpate

ramie, ramee: 4 hemp, rhea 5 fiber

ramification: arm 4 rami(pl.) 5 ramus 6 branch, spread 8 division, offshoot 9 branching 10 divergence 12 embranchment

rammack: 4 rush

rammel: 5 trash 9 brushwood 11 undergrowth

rammish: 4 rank 5 rammy

Ramona author: 7 Jackson

ramose: 7 cladose 8 branched 9 branching

ramp: rob 4 bank, rage, walk 5 crawl, creep, slope, storm 6 dupery, unruly 7 incline, rampage, swindle 8 gradient, platform 9 helicline 10 cuckoopint

rampageous: 4 wild 6 unruly 9 rampaging 10 boisterous

rampant: 4 rife 6 fierce 7 violent 9 unchecked 10 rampageous, widespread 11 extravagant, flourishing, threatening 12 unrestrained 14 uncontrollable

rampart: 4 wall 5 agger, mound, redan 6 vallum 7 barrier, bulwark, parapet, ravelin 10 embankment 13 fortification

part: 4 spur

ramper: 7 lamprey

rampire: dam 7 fortify, rampart 10 embankment, strengthen

Ramses' goddess: 4 Anta

ramshackle: 5 loose, shaky 7 rickety 10 disorderly, dissipated, tumble-down

ramstam: 8 headlong, reckless 10 headstrong 11 thoughtless

ramus: 6 branch 10 branchlike

rance: 5 stone 6 marble

rancel: 6 search 7 ransack

ranch: 4 casa, farm, tear 5 finca, pluck 7 acreage, scratch 8 estancia, hacienda 9 estantion

worker: 4 hand 5 owner 6 cowboy, farmer 7 cowpoke, rancher 8 herdsman, ranchero(Sp.), ranchman

rancho: 5 ranch

rancid: 4 rank, sour 5 musty, stale 6 frowsy 7 spoiled 8 stinking 9 obnoxious, offensive 10 unpleasant

rancor, rancour: ire 4 gall, hate 5 spite 6 enmity, hatred, malice 8 rankling 9 animosity, antipathy, hostility 10 bitterness

rand: 4 edge 5 ridge, strip 6 border, margin

randan: row 4 boat 5 spree 7 rampage

random: 5 loose, stray 6 casual, chance 7 aimless 9 desultory, haphazard 10 accidental, fortuitous 11 purposeless

randy: 5 crude, revel, shrew 6 beggar, coarse, frolic, virago, vulgar 7 canvass 8 carousal 9 festivity 10 disorderly 12 unmanageable

range: ken, row 4 ally, area, farm, line, rank, roam, rove 5 align, aline, blank, class, field, gamut, order, reach, ridge, scope, space, stove, stray 6 extent, ramble, series, sphere, stroll, tether, wander 7 arrange, compass, explore, habitat, saunter 8 classify, distance 9 cookstove, grassland 11 systematize

range-finder: 6 stadia 9 mekometer, telemeter 10 trekometer

ranger: 4 seal 5 rover, sieve 6 keeper, warden 8 commando, rangeman, wanderer

Rangoon's state: 4 Pegu

rangy: 8 spacious

rank: row 4 army, file, foul, line, rate, sort, tier 5 array, caste, cense, class, frank, genus, grade, gross, order, proud, range, space 6 barony, coarse, degree, estate, fertid, gentry, mighty, rancid, rating, series, status, strong 7 caliber, calibre, calling, compeer, copious, corrupt, dignity, extreme, fertile, froward, glaring, haughty, noisome, overfed, peerage, quality, rammish, station, stratum, swollen, violent 8 absolute, abundant, classify, division, eminence, estimate, flagrant, gentrice, headlong, indecent, palpable, position, powerful, vigorous 9 condition, downright, excessive, exuberant, formation, gradua-tion, hierarchy, luxuriant, offensive, over-grown, plentiful 10 coordinate 11 arrange-ment, distinction 14 classification

deprive of: 4 bust 5 break 6 depose 7 cashier

mark of: 6 stripe

military: PFC 5 major 7 captain, colonel, general, private 8 banneret, corporal, ser-geant 10 lieutenant

rankle: 4 fret, gall 6 fester, rancor 7 inflame 8 irritate, ulcerate

rann: 5 verse 6 stanza, strain

ransack: 4 loot, rake, sack 5 rifle, steal 6 search 7 pillage, rummage

ransom: buy, fee 5 atone, price 6 redeem, rescue 7 deliver, expiate, release 9 re-deeming 13 consideration

money: 10 redemptory

rant: 4 fume, rage, rail, rand, rave, riot, song, tune 5 dance, revel, scold, spout 6 frolic, speech, steven 7 bluster, bombast, carouse, declaim, fustian 9 discourse 11 merrymaking, rodomontade 13 jollifica-tion

rantipole: 4 wild 6 rakish, unruly 9 terma-gant

ranty: 4 wild 7 excited

ranula: 4 cyst 8 swelling

rap: bob, box, con, hit, tap 4 blow, chap, grab, knap, tirl 5 blame, clink, clout, knock, seize, smite, steal, utter 6 snatch, strike, thwack 7 deliver 8 sentence 9 criti-cize, criticism, enrapture, transport 10 punishment

rapacious: 6 greedy 8 covetous, grasping, revening, ravenous 9 ferocious, voracious 10 avaricious, predacious

rapacity: 5 ravin 7 edacity 8 appetite 9 ex-tortion

rape: 4 file, rasp 5 abuse, haste, hasty, hurry, quick, seize 6 defile, pomace, rav-ish, turnip 7 dispoil, hastily, pillage, plun-der, robbery, scratch, violate 9 violation 10 plundering, spoliation

rapeseed: 5 colza

Raphael: 5 angel 9 archangel

conqueror of: 8 Asmodeus

raphe: 4 line, seam 5 joint 6 suture

rapid: 4 fast 5 chute, fleet, quick, steep, swift 6 abrupt, moving, speedy 10 fastmov-ing 11 expeditions

rapidity: 5 haste 8 celerity, velocity

rapidly: 5 apace

rapier: 5 bilbo, sword 6 verdun 7 ricasso

blade heel: 7 ricasso

part of: 5 forte 6 foible

rapine: 4 rape

rapparee: 6 robber 8 vagabond 9 plunderer 10 freebooter

rappee: 5 snuff

rapport: 6 accord 7 harmony 8 affinity, rela-tion 9 agreement 12 relationship

rapscallion: 5 rogue 6 rascal, wretch 8 ras-cally 11 ne'er-do-well 14 good-for-nothing

rapt: 4 deep 5 tense 6 intent 8 absorbed, ecstatic 9 comprised, enchanted, en-grossed, entranced, transport 10 enrap-tured 11 preoccupied, transported

raptorial: 11 accipitrine

raptorial bird: owl 4 hawk 5 eagle 7 vulture

rapture: 5 bliss 6 trance 7 delight, ecstasy 8 rhapsody 9 enrapture, happiness, trans-port 10 exultation

rare: odd, raw 4 fine, good, nice, thin 6 choice, dainty, geason, scarce, seldom, unique 7 antique, capital, curious, ex-treme, special, tenuous, unusual 8 pre-cious, uncommon, unwonted 9 beautiful, excellent, exclusive, exquisite, scattered, underdone 10 infrequent 11 distinctive, exceptional 13 distinguished, extraordi-nary

rarefied: 4 thin 7 diluted, ethered, gaseous, refined 8 aethered 10 attenuated

rarity: 5 curio, relic 6 geason 7 antique 8 rareness

ras: 4 cape 6 prince 8 headland 9 commander

rascal: boy, cad, imp 4 file, loon 5 foist, gipsy, gypsy, knave, rogue, scamp 6 ablach, budzat, coquin, harlot 7 budzart, glutton 8 hosebird, scalawag, sealpeen, widdifow 9 miscreant, reprobate, scal-lawag, scoundrel, trickster 11 rapscallion

rascally: 4 base, mean 6 arrant 9 dishonest, worthless 11 furciferous, mischievous

rase: 4 raze

rash: cut, mad 4 bold 5 brash, erase, hardy, hasty, heady, hives, scamp, shave, slash, uredo 6 daring, eczema, scrape, unwary 7 foolish, hotspur, icarian, scratch 8 care-less, eruption, headlong, heedless, reck-less, temerous 9 desperate, exanthema, foolhardy, foreright, impetuous, impru-dent, overhasty, urticaria, venturous 10 headstrong, hotspurred, incautious, indis-creet, unthinking 11 adventurous, fur-thersome, harum-scarum, precipitate, precipitous, temerarious, thoughtless, venturesome 13 adventuresome, efflores-cence

rasher: 5 slice 7 portion 8 rockfish

rashness: 4 rese 5 folly 6 acrisy 8 temerity

Rasores: 8 Columbae, Gallinae

rasorial: 10 scratching

rasp: rub 4 file 5 belch, eruct, grate 6 scrape 8 bogberry, irritate 9 raspberry

rasping: 5 harsh, raspy, rough 6 hoarse, rasion 7 raspish, raucous 8 guttural 9 offensive

rasse: 5 civet

rasure: cut 6 filing 7 erasing, erasure, rasping, scratch, shaving 8 scraping 12 obliteration

rat: pad 4 scab 6 rodent, vermin 8 betrayer, deserter, informer, renegade, squealer 9 councilor, counselor 11 stool-pigeon 13 doublecrosser
genus: 6 spalax
kind: 5 metad, zemmi, zemni 6 tosher
poison: 8 ratsbane

rat hare: 4 pika

ratafia: 4 noyau 7 biscuit, cordial, liqueur

rataplan: 8 drumbeat

ratch: bar 4 rend 7 ratchet, stretch 8 distance

ratchet: 4 pawl 5 click 6 bobbin, detent

rate: fee, tax 4 fare, file, pace, rank 5 abuse, blame, chide, grade, price, scold, score, tempo, value 6 assess, assize, charge, reckon, regard, tariff 7 account, censure, chasten, despise, quality, reprove 8 appraise, classify, consider, estimate, evaluate 10 proportion 14 classification

rate of exchange: 4 agio 5 batta

ratel: 6 badger

ratfish: 8 chimaera

rathe, rath: 4 soon 5 eager, early, quick 6 prompt, speedy 7 betimes 8 promptly, speedily

rather: ere 4 erer 5 prior 6 before, choice, liever, sooner 7 earlier, quickly 8 somewhat 10 preferably, preference 11 immediately

rather than: ere

ratify: 4 amen, pass, seal 6 affirm, enseal, verify 7 approve, confirm 8 roborate, sanction 9 authorize, establish

ratihabition: 8 sanction 12 ratification

rating: 4 rank 5 cense, class, grade 6 rebuke 8 estimate, scolding, standing 9 reprimand 10 evaluation 14 classification

ratio: pi; cos 4 rate, sine 5 quota, share 6 cosine, degree, ration 7 average, portion 8 relation 10 percentage, proportion 11 capacitance

ratiocination: 5 logic 7 thought 8 argument 9 reasoning

ration: 4 dole, food, mete 5 allot, ratio, share 6 divide 7 portion 8 relation 9 allotment, allowance 10 distribute 11 calculation

rational: 4 sane 5 sober 7 logical 8 sensible 10 reasonable 11 intelligent 13 philosophical

rational integer: 4 norm

rational principle: 5 logos

rations: 8 buckshee 10 provisions

ratite: emu, moa 4 bird, emeu 7 ostrich 9 cassowary
genus: 7 apteryx 8 dinornis

ratoon: 5 shoot, stalk 6 spring, sprout

rattail: 5 braid 7 pigtail

rattan: 4 cane, lash, palm, sega, whip 5 noose, thong 6 punish, switch, wicker

ratter: cat, dog 8 betrayer

rattle: din 4 birl, rale, rick, stun, tirl 5 addle, annoy, clack, rouse, scold, upset 6 assail, racket, uproar 7 agitate, chatter, clapper, clatter, clitter, confuse, fluster, gnatter, maracas 9 crepitate, embarrass 10 disconcert

rattlebrained: 5 giddy 9 frivolous 11 empty-headed, harebrained

rattlemouse: bat

rattlepate: ass 4 dolt 9 chatterer 11 rattlebrain

rattleroot: 7 bugbane

rattlesnake: 8 cascavel, crotalus 9 sistrurus 10 crotalidae(pl.) 11 massasaugas

rattlesnake-bite: rue

rattlesnake fern: 9 sporangia

rattlesnake herb: 9 baneberry

rattlesnake pilot: 10 copperhead

rattle-top: 7 bugbane

rattletrap: 5 ratty 7 gewgaws, rickety 10 ramshackle 11 knickknacks

ratton: rat

ratty: 4 mean 6 shabby 10 rattletrap 11 dilapitated

ratwa: 7 muntjac

raucous: dry 4 loud 5 harsh, noisy, rough 6 coarse, hoarse 7 braying, rasping 8 strident 11 cacophonous

raun: roe 5 spawn

raupo: 7 cattail

ravage: eat 4 loot, prey, ruin, sack 5 foray, harry, havoc, spoil, waste 6 forage 7 despoil, destroy, overrun, pillage, plunder, violate 8 deflower, desolate 9 devastate 10 depopulate, desolation 11 despoilment, devastation

rave: 4 rage, rant 5 blurb, crush, storm 7 bluster, bombast, declaim 8 harangue 11 infatuation 12 commendation

ravel: run 4 comb, fray, rail 5 snarl 6 runner, sleave, tangle, unwind 7 crumble, involve, railing, unravel, untwist, unweave 8 entangle, separate 11 disentangle

ravelin: 8 demilune 13 fortification

raveling: 4 lint 6 thread

raven: 4 crow 5 black 9 blackbird
genus: 5 corvus
of Odin: 5 Hugin

Raven: *author:* Poe
character: 6 Lenore

ravenous: 6 greedy, hungry, lupine, toothy 8 edacious 9 cormorant, ferocious, rapacious, voracious 10 catawampus, gluttonous 12 catawampious 13 catawamptious

ravine: den, gap, lin 4 dell, ghyl, gill, linn, sike, wadi, wady 5 canon, chine, clove, ditch, flume, glack, gorge, goyal, goyle, griff, grike, gulch, gully, kloof, strid 6 arroyo, canyon, cleuch, clough, coulee, gulley, hollow, nullah 8 barranca, barranco, quebrado 10 depression

raving: 6 raging 8 frenzied 9 delirious 10 incoherent, irrational 12 arreptitious

ravish: rob 4 rape 5 abuse, charm, force, harry, seize 6 defile, snatch 7 afforce, corrupt, delight, despoil, enchant, plunder, violate 8 deflower, entrance 9 captivate, constrain, enrapture

ravishment: 7 ecstasy, rapture

raw: 4 cold, damp, dazy(Sc.), lash, nude, rare 5 bawdy, bleak, chill, crude, green, harsh, naked 6 abrade, chilly, unfair 7 cutting, natural, obscene 8 immature, indecent, uncooked 9 inclement, unexposed, unrefined, unskilled, untrained 10 indelicate, unfinished, unprepared, unseasoned 11 uncivilized, unpracticed, unprocessed 12 uncultivated 13 inexperienced

rawboned: 4 lean 5 gaunt 7 angular, scrawny

rawhide: 4 pelt, whip 5 knout, quirt, thong

ray: 4 beam, beta, dorn, soil 5 array, dress, flair, gleam, gleed, light, manta, order, shine, sight, skate 6 defile, glance, obispo, radial, streak, stripe, vision 7 besmear, homelyn, radiate, raiment 9 irradiate, selachian 10 perception, vertebrate 11 arrangement, irradiation

fish: 4 dorn 5 skate

penetrating: 5 gamma

rayon: 5 moire, ninon, tulle 6 faille, pongee 7 taffeta

yarn size: 6 denier

raze, rase: cut, rub 4 rage, ruin, tear 5 erase, graze, growl, level, shave 6 efface, incise, scrape 7 destroy, scratch, subvert 8 demolish, dismantle 9 depredate, overthrow, prostrate 10 obliterate

razee: cut 5 prune 6 reduce 7 abridge

razor: 4 clam 6 shaver

kind: 7 rattler 8 electric

sharpen: 4 hone 5 strop

razorback: hog 5 ridge 10 roustabout

razorbill: auk 7 skimmer

razor stone: 10 novaculite

razz: 5 chaff, tease 6 banter, deride, heckle 8 ridicule

razzia: 4 raid 5 foray 9 incursion

razzle-dazzle: 5 spree 6 dazzle 7 confuse 8 hilarity 9 confusion

re: 5 anent 9 regarding 10 concerning

Re: See **Ra**

reach: toe 4 come, gain, hawk, hent, ryke(Sc.), seek, span, spit 5 grasp, retch, scope, vomit 6 advene, affect, amount, arrive, attain, extend, extent, strive 7 achieve, expanse, possess, stretch 9 culminate, penetrate 10 accomplish

under: 7 subtend

reachable: 10 accessible

reaching: 6 effort 8 profound

reaction: 4 kick 5 start 6 answer 7 tropism 8 response 9 influence 10 impression, opposition

read: con 4 lire(F.), pore, scan, skim, tell 5 aread, areed, drone, guess, solve, study 6 advise, browse, peruse, relate 7 counsel, declare, discern, foresee, learned 8 decipher, describe, foretell, indicate 9 interpret, supervise

ability to: 8 literacy

inability to: 6 alexia

metrically: 4 scan

superficially: 4 skim

readable: 7 legible

reader: 6 lector, lister, primer 7 reciter 8 lectrice, lecturer 9 assistant 10 instructor 11 proofreader 12 elocutionist

readiness: art 4 ease, gift 6 graith 7 address, freedom 8 alacrity, facility, goodwill, volition 9 dexterity, eagerness, quickness 10 promptness 12 preparedness

reading: 6 lesson 7 lection, lecture, perusal, recital, version 9 collation 10 prelection

ready: apt, fit 4 free, glib, here, pret(F.), ripe 5 alert, apert, bound, eager, handy, happy, point, quick 6 active, adroit, facile, fluent, prompt 7 forward, willing 8 cheerful, dextrous, handsome, prepared, skillful 9 agreeable, available, dexterous 10 convenient 11 expeditious 12 unhesitating

real: 4 very, true, vrai(F.) 5 being, loyal 6 actual, hearty 7 certain, cordial, factual, genuine, gradely, literal, sincere 8 existent, faithful, tangible 9 authentic, effective, heartfelt, intrinsic, unfeigned, veritable 10 unaffected

real estate: 4 alod 5 allod, lands 6 realty 8 freehold, premises, property, tenement 13 hereditaments

claim: tax 8 mortgage 9 trust deed 11 encumbrance

pert. to: 7 predial

realistic: 5 vivid 8 lifelike

realization: 8 fruition

realize: get **4** gain, know **5** sense **6** effect, obtain **7** achieve, acquire, convert, fulfill **8** complete, conceive **9** apprehend **10** accomplish, appreciate, understand

really: ara **5** quite, sooth **6** indeed **8** actually

realm: 4 land **5** bourn, clime **6** bourne, circle, domain, empire, region, sphere **7** country, demesne, dynasty, kingdom, terrene **8** division, dominion, province **9** territory **10** department **11** sovereignty **12** jurisdiction

realty: 7 honesty, loyalty, royalty **8** fidelity, property **10** possession

ream: 4 bore, draw, foam, scum **5** bevel, cream, froth, widen **7** enlarge, stretch **11** countersink

reamer: 5 drift **6** broach

reanimate: 5 rally, renew **6** revive **11** resuscitate **12** reinvigorate

reap: cut **4** crop, rake **5** glean **6** garner, gather **7** acquire, collect, harvest

rear: aft, end, fix **4** back, buck, cave, grow, last, lift, rere, tail **5** abaft, breed, build, erect, nurse, raise, stern, train **6** astern, behind, foster, nursle **7** arriere(F.), educate, elevate, nurture **9** construct, establish, posterior **10** background, forthbring

toward: aft **5** abaft **6** astern

rearing by horse: 5 stend **6** pesade

rearhorse: 6 insect, mantis

rearward: 8 backward **10** retrograde

reason: peg **4** mind, nous **5** argue, brain, cause, logic, sense, think **6** debate, ground, motive, ponder, sanity **7** meaning **8** argument, converse **9** discourse, intellect, rationale, wherefore **10** moderation, understand **11** expostulate, ratiocinate, rationality, rationalize **12** plausibility **13** consideration, understanding

alleged: **7** pretext

deprived of: **8** demented

pert. to: **6** noetic

want of: **5** folie **7** amentia, madness **8** insanity

reasonable: 4 fair, just **8** feasible **9** equitable **11** inexpensive

reasoning: 5 logic **8** argument **10** conclusion **13** argumentation

basis of: **7** premise

reassure: 6 assure **7** comfort, hearten **8** reinsure **9** encourage

reata, riata: 4 rope **5** lasso **6** lariat

reave: rob **4** tear **5** burst, seize, split **7** bereave, pillage, plunder

reb: 5 rebel

rebate: 5 check **6** lessen, reduce, refund, weaken **8** diminish, discount **9** abatement, deduction, reduction, remission

rebec: 4 lyre **5** sarod, rebab **6** fiddle, violin

Rebekah: *brother:* **5** Laban

father: **7** Bethuel

husband: **5** Isaac

mother: **6** Milcah

sister: **5** Laban

son: **4** Esau **5** Jacob

rebel: 4 rise **6** oppose, revolt **8** renegade **9** insurgent

rebellion: 6 mutiny, putsch, revolt **8** defiance, sedition, uprising **10** resistance, revolution **12** disobedience, insurrection, renunciation **15** insubordination

rebellious: 10 refractory **12** contumacious, recalcitrant

rebirth: 7 revival **10** conversion, renascence **11** renaissance **13** reincarnation

reboant: 7 echoing **13** reverberating

rebound: dap **4** echo, stot **5** bound, carom **6** bounce, carrom, recoil, re-echo, resile, return, spring **7** reflect, resound **8** ricochet **9** boomerang **11** reverberate

rebuff: cow **4** scat, slap, snub **5** check, chide, fling, repel, scold, spurn **6** lesson **7** censure, refusal, reprove, repulse **9** rejection, reprimand

rebuke: nip, tsk, tut **4** beat, snub, tush **5** barge, blame, check, chide, scold **6** berate, dirdum, lesson, rating **7** downset, lecture, repress, reproof, reprove **8** admonish, chastise, reproach, restrain **9** criticism, criticize, reprehend, reprimand **10** correction **11** comeuppance, reprobation

rebus: 6 enigma, puzzle, riddle

rebut: 5 reply **6** oppose, rebuff, refute, revile **7** repulse **8** disprove **10** contradict

recalcitrant: 5 rebel **6** unruly **7** defiant **9** obstinate **10** calcitrant, rebellious, refractory

recall: 5 annul **6** cancel, encore, remind, repeal, revoke **7** abolish, bethink, rescind, retrace, retract, summons **8** remember, withdraw **9** recollect, reminisce **11** countermand

recant: 6 abjure, revoke **7** abandon, disavow, retract **8** renounce, withdraw **9** repudiate **10** contradict

recapitulate: sum **5** essay **6** repeat, review **7** restate **8** argument **9** enumerate, reiterate, summarize

recapture: 6 recall, regain, retake **7** recover **9** reacquire

recede: ebb **6** depart, retire **7** deviate, regress, retreat **8** withdraw **10** retrograde

receipt: 4 stub, take **6** acquit, apocha, binder, recipe **7** formula **11** acquittance **15** acknowledgement

receive: get **4** take **5** admit, adopt, greet, reset **6** accept, assume, derive, obtain **7** acquire, procure **9** affiliate

receiver: 4 host 5 donee, fence 6 pernor, porter 7 breaker, catcher, hostess, rentier 8 cymaphen, receptor 9 collector, condenser, treasurer 12 receptionist
of property in trust: 6 bailee 7 trustee
of stolen goods: 5 fence

recense: 6 review, revise

recension: 6 review 8 revising 9 reviewing 11 enumeration, examination

recent: new 4 late 5 fresh 6 modern 7 current 8 neoteric
comb. form: neo

recently: 4 anew 8 latterly

receptacle: bin, box, can, cup, fat, pan, pot, tub, urn, vat 4 case, cell, cist, crib, etus, font, inro, pail, tray, vase, well, tank 5 basin, chest, etwee, torus 6 basket, bottle, bucket, carton, holder, hopper, trough 7 capcase, cistern, hanaper, humidor, pitcher 8 canister, receiver 9 cannister, container, continent, reservoir 11 chalkotheke

reception: tea 5 levee, party 6 accoil, durbar, soiree 7 accueil, ovation, receipt, welcome 8 greeting 9 admission, collation 10 admittance 13 entertainment
morning: 5 levee
place: 4 hall 5 atria(pl.), foyer, salon 6 atrium, parlor 7 parlour 9 vestibule

receptive: 9 acceptant, recipient 10 hospitable

receptor: 5 basin 8 receiver 10 dispositor

recess: ala, bay 4 apse, cave, cove, grot, hole, nook 5 ambry, cleft, crypt, niche, sinus 6 alcove, closet, grotto, rabbet, retire 7 adjourn, conceal, retreat, seclude 8 interval, vacation 9 cessation, embrasure, recession, remission, seclusion 10 retirement, suspension 11 withdrawing 12 intermission

recessive: 8 backward, receding

Rechab's son: 7 Jonadab

recherche: 4 rare 6 choice 8 uncommon 9 exquisite 10 farfetched

recidivation: 7 relapse 8 apostasy 11 backsliding

recipe: 7 formula, pattern, receipt 12 prescription

recipient: 4 heir 5 donee 7 alienee, devisee, legatee 8 receiver 9 receiving, receptive

reciprocal: 6 mutual 9 alternate 11 convertible, correlative
comb. form: 6 allelo

reciprocate: 5 bandy, repay 6 return 8 exchange 9 alternate 10 recompense 11 countervail, interchange

recital: 4 saga, tale 5 story 6 report 7 account, concert, program 8 relation 9 narration, narrative, rehearsal, statement 10 recitation, repetition 11 declamation, description, enumeration

recitation: 7 reading, recital

recitative: 5 scena 9 narrative

recite: say 4 carp, scan, tell 5 chant, spout 6 intone 7 recount 9 enumerate 10 cantillate 12 recapitulate

reciter: 6 anteri, diseur(F.) 7 diseuse(F.) 8 narrator 12 elocutionist

reck: 4 care, deem, heed, mind 7 concern 8 estimate

reckless: 4 bold, rash 5 blind, folle, perdu 6 madcap, perdue 7 hotspur 8 careless, headlong, heedless 9 blindfold, bodacious, daredevil, desperate, dissolute, hotheaded, imprudent 10 neglectful, regardless 11 adventurous, extravagant, harum-scarum, indifferent, thoughtless 13 inconsiderate, irresponsible

reckon: 4 aret, date, deem, rate, rely, tell 5 audit, count, think 6 arette, impute, number, regard, repute 7 account, ascribe, compute, include, suppose 8 consider, estimate, numerate 9 calculate, enumerate 10 adjudicate 11 connumerate

reckoner: 5 abaci, brain 6 abacus 9 tabulator 10 calculator 11 comptometer

reckoning: 4 rate, scot, shot 5 chalk, score 6 compot, esteem
machine: I.B.M. 5 adder, brain 6 abacus 9 tabulator 10 calculator

reclaim: 4 save, tame 5 train 6 ransom, recall, redeem, reform, repair, rescue, revoke 7 recover, restore, salvage 8 civilize, empolder 10 regenerate 11 domesticate

reclaimed land: 6 polder

recline: lay, lie, sit 4 lean, loll, rest 6 repose 7 incline

reclining: 5 lying 6 supine 7 leaning, lolling, passive, resting 8 reposing 9 accumbent, recumbent

recluse: nun 4 monk 6 hermit, hidden, secret 7 eremite 8 anchoret, secluded, solitary 9 anchoress, anchorite, cloistral 10 cloistered 11 sequestered

recognizance: 4 rank 5 badge, token 6 avowal, pledge, symbol 10 cognizance, obligation, profession 11 recognition

recognize: ken, own, see 4 avow, know, note, spot 5 admit, greet 6 accept, acknow, agnize, beknow, recall, review, revise, salute 7 consent, correct, recover 8 identify, perceive 9 apprehend 10 appreciate 11 acknowledge, distinguish

recoil: shy 4 kick 5 quail, wince 6 flinch, shrink 7 rebound, retreat, reverse 8 withdraw 12 repercussion

recollect: 6 recall 7 bethink 8 remember

recollection: 4 mind 6 memory 8 memorial 9 anamnesis 11 remembrance 12 reminiscence

recommence: 6 resume

recommend: 4 tout 5 refer 6 advise, commit, denote 7 commend, consign, counsel, entrust 8 advocate

recommit: 6 remand

recompense: fee, pay 5 repay 6 amends, bounty, reward, salary 7 premium, requite 8 requital 9 gratulate, indemnify, reimburse, repayment 10 compensate, remunerate 11 reciprocate, restitution, retribution 12 compensation, remuneration 13 consideration, gratification
without: 4 free 6 gratis

reconcile: 4 wean 5 agree, atone 6 accord, adjust, pacify, regain, settle, shrive, square 7 absolve, conform, expiate, explain, restore, reunite, satisfy 9 harmonize 10 conciliate, propitiate

recondite: 4 dark, deep 6 hidden, mystic, occult 7 cryptic, obscure 8 abstract, abstruse, esoteric, profound 9 concealed

reconnaissance: 6 survey

reconnoiter: spy 5 scout 6 survey 7 examine, explore, inquire 8 discover

record: log, tab 4 acta(pl.), book, dope, file, memo, note, past, roll 5 actum, annal, chart, diary, enrol, enter, entry, graph, score 6 agenda, enroll, legend, memoir, postea, report 7 account, archive, blotter, calends, catalog, dossier, estreat, history, journal, kalends, rotulet 8 calendar, memorial, register 9 catalogue, chronicle, itinerary, narration 10 background, chronology, memorandum, transcribe, transcript
historical: 6 annals
holder: 4 file 6 binder 7 cabinet
keeper: 8 recorder 9 registrar
of arrest: 7 blotter
of ship: log
of travel: 9 itinerary
official: 4 acta(pl.) 5 actum
personal: 5 diary 7 journal

recorded proceeding: 4 acta(pl.) 5 actum

recorder: 5 flute, judge 8 greffier, register 9 cartulary, registrar 10 chartulary

recording device: 4 tape 5 meter

recount: 4 deem, tell 5 count 6 recite, reckon, relate, repeat, retail 7 account, include, narrate 8 describe, rehearse 9 enumerate

recoup: 7 recover 9 indemnify, reimburse 10 compensate, recuperate

recover: get 5 amend, rally, upset 6 obtain, recoup, reform, regain, rescue, resume, retake 7 reclaim, recruit, restore, salvage 8 overcome, retrieve 9 repossess 10 convalesce, recuperate

recovery: 13 convalescence
law: 6 trover

recreant: 5 false 6 coward, craven, crying, wretch, yellow 7 traitor 8 apostate, betrayer, cowardly, deserter, disloyal, yielding 10 traitorous, unfaithful 11 disaffected 12 mean-spirited

recreation: 4 meal, play 5 dance, hobby, sport 6 picnic 7 renewal 9 amusement, avocation, diversion 10 relaxation 11 delassement, refreshment 12 regeneration 13 divertisement, entertainment
time: 6 recess 7 holiday 8 vacation

recrement: 4 scum 5 dregs, dross, spume 6 refuse, scoria

recruit: 4 bleu(F.), boot 5 raise, rooky 6 gather, muster, revive, rookie, supply 7 draftee, private, recover, refresh, restore, soldier 8 assemble, bezonian, inductee 9 reinforce, replenish 10 recuperate, strengthen

rectangle: 6 oblong, square

rectifier: 5 diode

rectify: 5 amend, emend, right 6 adjust, better, purify, refine, reform, remedy 7 correct, distill 8 emendate, regulate 10 straighten

rectitude: 6 equity, virtue 7 fitness, honesty 10 straitness 11 uprightness 12 straightness

rector: 4 head 5 chief, ruler 6 leader, priest 7 proctor 8 director, governor, minister 9 clergyman, conrector 10 headmaster, proproctor

rectory: 5 manse 8 benefice 9 parsonage

recumbent: 4 idle 5 lying 7 leaning, resting 8 inactive, reposing 9 reclining

recuperate: 4 heal, rest 5 rally 6 recoup, regain 7 recover 9 reimburse 10 convalesce

recur: 6 advert, repeat, return 7 rearise, reoccur 8 reappear

recurrent: 9 recurring, returning 11 reappearing 12 intermittent

recusant: 9 dissenter 11 dissentient 12 nonconformer

red: 4 lake, puce, rosy, ruby 5 canna, color, coral, fiery, gules, peony, roset, ruddy 6 cerise, cherry, claret, garnet, maroon, rubric, sienna, titian 7 carmine, crimson, glowing, leftist, magenta, nacarat, radical, roseate, Russian, scarlet 8 amaranth, blushing, inflamed, rubicund 9 anarchist, bloodshot, Bolshevik, communist, Muscovite, vermilion 10 erubescent 12 bloodstained

antique: **5** canna
brown: **5** sepia **6** russet, sorrel
dye: aal, lac **4** chay, choy **5** aurin, eosin **6** aurine **8** morindin
marked with: **6** rubric
purplish: **4** lake **6** claret
yellow: **4** lama **5** aloma, brass, ochre, tenne **6** alesan, orange **7** saffron **9** alabaster, peachblow
red ape: 9 orangutan
red arsenic: 7 realgar
red-backed sandpiper: 6 dunlin
red bell: 9 columbine
red-bellied snipe: 9 dowitcher
red benjamin: 9 birthroot
red blotch: 10 adustiosis
red box: 8 official **12** bureaucratic
red bug: 7 chigger
red cedar: 5 savin **6** sabine, savine **7** juniper **8** flindosa
red cell: 11 erythrocyte
red chalk: 6 ruddle
red cobalt: 9 erythrite
red copper ore: 7 cuprite
red corpuscle deficiency: 6 anemia
Red Cross founder: 6 Barton
Red Cross Knight: 6 George
wife: Una
red deer: roe **4** hart, hind, spay, stag
red-faced: 7 blowzed, flushed **8** blushing
red fever: 10 erysipelas
red fir: 4 pine **6** spruce **7** Douglas
red gum: 10 eucalyptus, strophulus
red honeysuckle: 5 sulla
red lead ore: 8 corcoite
red man: 6 Indian
red pepper: 5 chile, chili **6** chilli
red perch: 8 rosefish
Red Planet: 4 Mars
Red Sea: 9 Erythrean
gulf: **4** Suez **5** Aqaba
island: **5** Perim
peninsula: **5** Sinai
port: **9** Leningrad
red viper: 10 copperhead
red willow: 5 osier **6** cornel
redact: 4 edit **5** draft, frame **6** reduce, revise
redan: 7 rampart **8** fortress **10** breastwork **13** fortification
redargue: 6 accuse, refute **7** confute, convict, reprove **8** disprove, reproach
redbelly: 4 char **7** grouper **8** terrapin
redbird: 7 tanager **8** cardinal **9** bullfinch
redbird cactus: 7 jewbush
redbreast: 5 robin
redbud tree: 5 judas
redcap: 6 porter **7** carrier, specter, spectre **8** tarboosh **9** goldfinch, policeman
redden: 5 blush, flush, rouge

rede: saw **4** plan, tale, tell **5** story **6** advice, advise, relate, scheme **7** counsel, explain, narrate, predict, proverb **9** interpret, narration **10** prediction **11** explanation **14** interpretation
redeem: buy **4** save **6** ransom, regain, rescue **7** deliver, fulfill, reclaim, recover, release, restore **8** liberate **10** repurchase
redeye: 4 rudd **5** vireo **6** whisky **7** sunfish **10** copperhead
redhead: 5 finch **7** pochard **10** woodpecker
redmouth: 4 fish **5** grunt
redolence: 4 balm, odor **5** aroma, odour, scent, smell **7** perfume **9** fragrance, sweetness
redouble: 6 reecho, repeat **7** reprise, retrace **10** ingeminate
redoubt: 6 schanz **10** breastwork **13** fortification
redoubtable: 5 dread **8** fearsome **10** formidable
redound: 5 react **6** accrue, recoil, return **7** conduce, resound **11** reverberate
redress: 5 amend, emend **6** adjust, relief, remedy **7** correct, relieve **10** compensate, reparation **12** compensation, satisfaction
redshank: 4 bird, clee
redshirt: 9 anarchist **11** Garibaldian **13** revolutionist
reduce: cut **4** bant, bate, bust, diet, ease, pare, raze, thin **5** abase, abate, annul, break, level, lower, scale, slash, smelt **6** appall, change, debase, demote, depose, derate, dilute, equate, humble, impair, lessen, rebate, refine, subdue, weaken **7** abridge, assuage, commute, conquer, curtail, degrade, deplete, whittle **8** attemper, condense, contract, decrease, diminish, discount, emaciate, minimize, retrench **9** subjugate **10** annihilate, bantingize, depreciate
to half: **9** dimidiate
sail: **4** reef
reduced: 6 broken **7** dwarfed **9** vestigial
reduction: cut **5** slice **6** rebate **7** cutting, meiosis **8** analysis, discount **11** contraction, degradation **12** annihilation
redundancy: 7 nimiety **8** pleonasm, verbiage **8** plethora **9** verbosity **11** periphrasis
redundant: 5 wordy **6** lavish, prolix **7** copious, diffuse, verbose **9** excessive, exuberant **10** pleonastic **11** overflowing, superfluous **12** overabundant, tautological **13** superabundant **17** circumlocutionary
redwing: 6 thrush **9** blackbird, francolin
redwood: 7 Sequoia
ree: 4 bird, ruff **9** sandpiper, sheepfold
Ree: 7 Arikara

re-echo: **7** redoubt, resound **8** resonate **11** reverberate

reed: sag **4** dart, junk, pipe, sley, stem **5** arrow, grass, spear, stalk **7** bulrush, calamus, fistula
loom: **4** sley

reed organ: **9** harmonium

reedbird: **7** warbler **8** bobolink

reedbuck: kob **4** koba **5** bohor, nagor **7** reitbok **8** antelope **9** waterbuck

reeder: **8** thatcher

reedy: **4** thin **11** arundineous

reef: bar, cay, key **4** cayo, itch, lode, vein **5** atoll, mange, shoal **6** boiler **7** shorten **8** eruption
mining: **4** lode, vein
sail: **4** furl **7** shorten

reefer: **4** coat, eton **5** miner **6** jacket, oyster **9** cigarette **10** midshipman

reek: rig **4** emit, fume, heap, pile, vent **5** equip, exude, smell, smoke, steam, vapor **6** exhale, stench **7** seaweed **8** mountain **10** exhalation

reel: **4** drum, pirn(Sc.), roll, spin, sway, swim, wind **5** dance, lurch, spool, swift, swing, waver, whirl, wince **6** bobbin, hammer, teeter, totter, wintle **7** stagger **8** titubate, windlass
fishing: **4** pirn

reelrall: **9** confusion **10** topsy-turvy **11** disturbance

reem: **4** uris **7** unicorn

reese: **6** scorch

reeve: pen **4** pass, wind **5** twist **6** pucker, thread **7** bailiff, wrinkle **9** enclosure, sheepfold

refection: **4** food **5** drink, lunch **6** repast **11** refreshment

refectory: **4** mess **10** dining hall
monastery: **6** frater

refel: **6** refute, reject **7** deceive, repulse **8** disprove **9** discredit

refer: **4** cite, harp, send **5** recur **6** advert, allude, appeal, assign, charge, commit, direct, impute, regard, relate, return **7** ascribe, consult, mention, specify **8** identify **9** affiliate, appertain, attribute

referee: **5** judge **6** decide, umpire **7** arbiter **8** mediator **10** arbitrator
decision: nod

reference: **5** quote **6** aspect **7** respect **9** relevance **10** connection, pertinence **12** relationship **13** recommendation **14** recommendation

reference book: **5** atlas **7** almanac **8** handbook, syllabus **10** dictionary **12** encyclopedia

referendum: **4** vote **7** mandate **10** plebiscite

refine: **5** exalt, smelt **6** decoct, filter, finish, polish, purify **7** clarify, cleanse, concoct, elevate, improve, perfect **8** chastise, separate **9** cultivate, elaborate, subtilize **12** spiritualize

refined: **4** nice **5** civil **6** artful, chaste, polite, urbane **7** courtly, elegant, genteel **8** delicate, graceful, highbred **9** courteous, exquisite **10** fastidious

refinement: **7** finesse

refining cup: **5** cupel

reflect: **4** echo, muse, pore **5** think **6** divert, mirror, ponder **7** bethink, deflect **8** cogitate, consider, meditate, ruminate **9** reproduce **10** deliberate **11** contemplate, reverberate

reflected: **8** specular

reflection: **4** idea **5** image **6** musing **7** thought **8** likeness **10** cogitation, meditation, rumination **12** deliberation **13** consideration, contemplation
measuring device: **11** albedograph

reflective: **7** pensive

reflex: **4** bend, fold, turn **7** reflect **11** involuntary

reflux: ebb **6** ebbing, euripi(pl.), reflow **7** euripus **9** refluence, returning

refont: **6** recast

reform: **4** mend, trim **5** amend, emend, prune, renew **6** better, direct, punish, remass, repair, revise **7** censure, correct, improve, rebuild, reclaim, rectify, redress, reprove, reshape, restore **8** instruct **10** regenerate **11** reformation

refract: **6** dimish, impair **7** deflect, reflect

refraction: *device:* **4** lens **5** prism **9** telescope
pert. to: **10** anaclastic

refractory: **6** immune, unruly **7** froward, restive **8** contrary, perverse, stubborn **9** camsteary, camsteery, obstinate **10** rebellious, unyielding **11** contrarious, disobedient, intractable **12** contumacious, ungovernable, unmanageable, unresponsive **13** insusceptible

refrain: bob **4** curb, shun **5** avoid, cease, check, epode, forgo **6** chorus, forego, govern **7** abstain, forbear **8** forebear, response, restrain, withhold
music: fa, la **4** aria, song **5** derry

refresco: **5** drink **11** refreshment

refresh: **4** rest **5** bathe, cheer, renew, slake **6** caudle, revise, revive **7** comfort, enliven, freshen, hearten, quicken, restore **8** recreate, renovate **9** reanimate, replenish **10** invigorate, strengthen **12** reinvigorate

refreshing: **4** dewy **5** balmy, tonic **11** refectorial, refrigerant

refreshment: **8** refresco

refrigerant: ice **6** cooler **7** ammonia, coolant, cooling

refrigerate: ice 4 cool 5 chill 6 freeze

reft: 5 cleft 7 divided, forlorn 8 bereaved, divested

refuge: ark 4 home, port, rock 5 haven 6 asylum, bilbie, covert, harbor, resort 7 crannog(Sc.), harbour, retreat, shelter 8 crannoge(Sc.), hospital 9 sanctuary 10 protection, rendezvous, subterfuge

refugee: d.p. 5 exile 6 emigre 8 fugitive

refulgent: 6 bright 7 glowing, radiant, shining 8 splendid 9 brilliant 11 resplendent

refund: 5 repay 6 rebate 9 reimburse, repayment

refurbish: 5 renew 6 polish, revamp 7 freshen 8 brighten, renovate

refusal: no; nay, vee

refuse: nay, ort 4 balk, coom, culm, deny, dirt, dreg, junk, marc, nite, pelf, pelt, veto 5 chaff, coomb, crawm, debar, drast, drest, dross, grith, offal, renig, repel, scrap, trash, waste, wrack 6 debris, forbid, garble, litter, lumber, reject, renege 7 backing, baggage, decline, disavow, forsake, garbage, gubbins, leaving, mullock, rubbish, repulse 8 disclaim, renounce, withhold 9 excrement, repudiate

coffee beans: 6 triage

grape: 4 marc

metal: 4 slag 5 dross 6 scoria

table: ort 5 scrap

wine: 4 lees

refute: 4 deny, meet 5 avoid, rebut, refel 6 assoil 7 confute 8 disprove, infringe, redargue 9 overthrow 10 contradict

serving to: 8 elenctic 10 elenctical

regain: 6 recoup 7 recover 8 retrieve

regal: 5 jewel, royal 6 groove, kingly 7 channel, stately 8 imperial, majestic, splendid

regale: 4 dine, fete 5 feast, treat 7 delight, gratify 9 entertain

regalia: 5 crown, dress 6 finery 7 emblems, ensigns, scepter, symbols 8 costumes, insignia 11 decorations 13 paraphernalia

regality: 5 right 7 country, kingdom, royalty 8 kingship 9 privilege, territory 11 sovereignty 12 jurisdiction

regalo: 4 gift 6 dainty 7 banquet, present 8 delicacy

Regan: *father:* 4 Lear

sister: 7 Goneril 8 Cordelia

regard: air, awe, con, eye 4 care, deem, gaze, heed, hold, look, mind, note, rate, sake, view, yeme 5 honor, think, treat, watch 6 admire, aspect, attend, behold, esteem, glance, homage, notice, remark, repute, revere 7 adjudge, concern, observe, respect 8 consider, estimate, interest, relation 9 adoration, affection, attention, deference, reference 10 admiration, appearance, attendance, estimation, veneration

11 contemplate 13 consideration, contemplation

regarding: 5 about, anent 6 anenst

regardless: 9 negligent 10 neglectful

regatta: 4 race

regency: 4 rule 8 dominion 10 government

regenerate: 5 renew 6 reborn, redeem, reform, revive 7 convert, newborn, reclaim, restore 8 gracious, recreate, renovate

regent: 5 ruler 6 ruling 7 regnant, teacher 8 governor 9 governing

of sun: 5 Uriel

regimen: 4 diet, rule 6 system 7 control, hygiene 10 government, regulation 14 administration

regiment: 4 alai 5 cadre, order 11 systematize

flag: 6 pennon

member: 9 grenadier

nucleus: 5 cadre

officer: 5 boots 7 colonel

regina: 5 queen

region: des, erd, gay 4 area, belt, zone 5 clime, place, realm, space, tract 6 locale, sphere 7 climate, country, demesne, kingdom 8 district, division, latitude, province, vicinity 9 territory 12 neighborhood 13 neighbourhood

comb. form: 5 nesia

infernal: 5 Hades 7 Avernus 8 Tartarus 10 underworld

pert. to: 5 areal

surrounded by alien power: 7 enclave

upper: 5 ether

warm: 7 tropics

woodless: 4 wold 5 llano, plain, weald 6 desert, meadow, steppe 7 pasture, savanna 8 savannah

regional: 5 local 9 sectional 10 provincial

register: lid 4 book, list, roll, rota 5 album, annal, diary, enrol, enter, entry, slate 6 agenda, docket, enlist, enroll, record, roster 7 ascribe, calends, catalog, certify, coucher, kalends, license, stopper 8 archives, bookmark, calendar, recorder, registry, schedule 9 catalogue, chronical, inventory, registrar 10 enrollment 11 certificate, matriculate 12 authenticate, registration

cash: 6 damper

legal: 6 docket

of deaths: 9 necrology

registrar: 8 greffier, recorder, register

regius: 4 king 5 royal 13 professorship

regle: 4 rule 6 govern 10 regulation

reglet: 5 strip 7 molding

regnal: 5 royal 6 kingly

regnant: 6 regent, ruling 8 dominant, reigning 9 prevalent 10 widespread 11 predominant

regorge: 5 vomit 8 disgorge

regress: 6 egress, return 10 retrograde, withdrawal 13 retrogression 14 retrogradation

regressive: 8 backward

regret: rew, rue 4 miss, ruth 5 grief, mourn, sorry, spurn 6 lament, repent, repine, sorrow 7 bethink, deplore, dislike, remorse 8 aversion, distress, forthink 9 penitence 10 misgivings, repentance 11 compunction, lamentation 14 disappointment

regular: 4 even 5 exact, sober, usual 6 formal, normal, proper, serial, stated, steady 7 amiable, correct, ordered, orderly, typical, uniform 8 complete, constant, decorous, formular, habitual, ordinary, ordinate, periodic, pleasant, rhythmic, rotative, standard, thorough 9 continual, customary, isometric 10 consistent, dependable, methodical, systematic 11 symmetrical

regulate: set 4 pace, rule, time 5 frame, guide, order 6 adjust, behave, direct, govern, settle 7 arrange, compose, conduct, control, correct, dispose, rectify 8 attemper, modulate 9 establish 10 discipline 11 standardize

regulating box: 8 rheostat

regulation: law 5 bylaw, canon, regle 6 assize, normal 7 precept, regimen, repulse, statute 8 ordinary 9 ordinance 14 administration

regulator: 5 valve
electricity: 9 rheometer

regulus: 4 king, star 5 matte, ruler

rehash: 7 restate 9 rechauffe

rehearse: say 4 cite, tell 5 drill, quote, speak, train 6 detail, recite, relate, repeat 7 mention, narrate, recount 8 describe, instruct 9 enumerate 12 recapitulate

rehoboam: hat 4 bowl 6 flagon 8 jeroboam

Rehoboam: *father:* 7 Solomon
son: 6 Abijah

reif: 7 plunder, robbery

reign: raj 4 rule, sway 5 guide, power, realm 6 empire, govern 7 kingdom, prevail 8 dominate, dominion 9 authority, dominance 10 prevalence 11 predominate, sovereignty
pert. to: 6 regnal

reimburse: pay 5 repay 6 defray, recoup, refund 7 replace 9 indemnify 10 compensate, recompense, remunerate

reimkennar: 8 sorcerer 9 sorceress

Reims: 4 Loin, Remi

rein: 4 curb, slow, stop, turn 5 check, guide, leash, strap 6 bridle, direct, govern,

haunch, kidney 7 control, repress 8 restrain 9 hindrance

reindeer: 6 tarand 7 caribou
genus: 8 rangifer
Santa's: See **Santa Claus** *reindeer*

reinforce: 4 back 5 brace, reman 6 second 7 afforce, support 10 strengthen

reinforcement: 4 sput 9 accession

reinstate: 6 revest

reinvigorate: 7 quicken, refresh

reit: 5 sedge 7 seaweed

reiterate: 4 drum, harp 6 repeat, resume 8 rehearse 10 ingeminate 12 recapitulate

reject: 4 defy, snub 5 eject, repel, scorn, scout, spurn, vomit 6 abjure, disown, rebuff, recuse, refuse 7 cashier, decline, discard, dismiss, disobey, forsake 8 abnegate, castaway, disallow, forswear, relegate, renounce 9 blackball, ostracize, reprobate, repudiate 10 disapprove, disbelieve 13 excommunicate

rejoice: 5 cheer, elate, exult 6 please 7 delight, gladden 8 jubilate 10 exhilarate, tripudiate

rejoin: 5 reply 6 answer 7 respond, reunite

rekindle: 6 revive 7 relight

relache: 10 relaxation 12 intermission

relapse: 4 fall, sink, slip 5 lapse 7 setback, subside 9 backslide 10 recurrence 11 backsliding 12 recidivation

relate: 4 ally, tell 5 apply, refer, state 6 allude, detail, recite, report 7 connect, declare, narrate, pertain, recount, restore 8 describe, rehearse 9 appertain, associate, correlate, enumerate

related: kin 4 akin 7 cognate, germane, kindred 9 affiliate, connected 10 becousined 11 appropriate
on father's side: 6 agnate
on mother's side: 5 enate 6 enatic 7 cognate

relation: sib 5 blood, ratio 6 degree, family, status 7 account, bearing, history, kinship 8 affinity, relative, standing 10 connection, friendship 12 relationship 13 consanguinity
local: 6 ubiety
mutual: 11 correlation
second term of: 7 relatum

relative: pa; eme, kin 4 aunt, mama, papa 5 aunty, niece, uncle 6 auntie, cousin, father, friend, mother, nephew, sister 7 brother, kindred, kinsman, sibling 8 ancestor, apposite, relation, relevant 9 connected, kinswoman, pertinent 10 pertaining 11 comparative 13 corresponding, proportionate
female line: 6 bandju
maternal: 5 enate

relative amount: 5 ratio 6 ration

relatives: 7 kinfolk 8 cousinry, kinsfolk
favoritism to: 8 nepotism

relax: 4 ease, open, rest 5 abate, loose, remit
6 divert, lessen, loosen, reduce, soften, unbend 7 mollify, release, relieve, slacken 8
mitigate

relaxation: 6 repose 7 detente(F.), relache 9
amusement 10 recreation 11 delassement

relaxed: 4 lash 7 lenient 8 flexuous

relay: 4 post, race 5 spell 6 remuda(Sp.),
supply 7 forward, relieve, station 8 avantlay, transmit

release: 4 bail, drop, free, liss, trip, undo,
vent 5 lisse, relay, remit, slake, untie 6
acquit, assoil, demise, exempt, loosen, parole, remise, rescue, spring 7 absolve, deliver, disband, freedom, manumit, publish, relieve, unleash, unloose 8 liberate,
mitigate, unfasten 9 acquittal, discharge,
disengage, eliminate, exculpate, extricate
10 emancipate, liberation, relinquish 11
acquittance, deliverance 12 emancipation

relegate: 5 exile 6 banish, commit, deport,
remove 7 consign, dismiss

relent: 4 melt 5 abate, yield 6 soften 7 abandon, liquefy, mollify, slacken 8 dissolve 10
deliquesce

relentless: 4 grim, hard 5 harsh, stern,
stony 6 strict 8 pitiless, rigorous 9 ferocious, immovable, merciless 10 inexorable, inflexible, persistent 11 unremitting

relevant: apt 6 timely 7 apropos, germain,
germane 8 apposite 9 connected, pertinent
10 applicable 11 appropriate, referential

relevate: 5 raise 7 relieve, restore

reliable: 4 true 5 tried 6 dinkum, honest,
steady, trusty 7 certain 9 authentic 10 dependable 11 trustworthy

reliance: 4 hope 5 trust 6 belief 8 affiance 10
confidence, dependence

relic: 5 curio, mummy 6 corpse, hallow, remain 7 antique, leaving, memento, remnant, residue 8 memorial, souvenir
pert. to: 9 reliquary

relic cabinet: 6 etager 7 etagere, whatnot

relict: 5 widow 7 widower 8 survivor

relief: bot 4 alms, boot, bote, dole 15 indemnification
ornamental: 4 fret 7 relievo

relieve: aid 4 beet, ease, free, help, liss 5
abate, allay, beete, erase, lisse, raise, relay, slake, spare, spell 6 assist, lessen, remedy, remove, succor 7 assuage, comfort,
console, deliver, lighten, redress, release,
support, sustain, unloose 8 diminish, mitigate 9 alleviate, debarrass, disburden, discharge, exonerate

religieuse: nun 6 sister

religieux: 4 monk 5 pious 9 religious

religion (see also next entry): 4 cult, sect 5
piety 6 voodoo 7 service, worship 8 devotion, fidelity 9 adoration, voodooism 10
conformity, observance, profession 17 con-
scientiousness
sect: 5 alogi
study of: 8 theology
system of: 5 faith

religion: See also under specific religions.
EXAMPLES: "Jewish god", see **Judaism:**
god of: "Islamic priest," see **Islam:** *priest*

religious: 4 holy 5 exact, godly, pious 6 devout, divine 7 fervent, godlike, zealous 8
devouted, faithful, monastic 9 pietistic,
spiritual 10 devotional, scrupulous 13 conscientious
belief: 5 credo, creed
brotherhood: 8 sodality
denomination: 4 sect
devotion: 6 novena
directory: 4 ordo 7 ordines(pl.)
festival: 6 Easter 8 Passover
formally: 5 rigid 6 strict 8 orthodox 9
pharasaic
image: 4 icon
military order member: 7 Templar
observance: 4 fast, Lent 5 Purim
offering: 5 tithe 7 deodand 8 oblation
reformer: 4 Huss, Knox 6 Luther
sayings: 5 logia

relinquish: 4 cede, drop, quit 5 demit, forgo,
grant, leave, waive, yield 6 desert, forego,
remise, resign 7 abandon, dispose, forsake
8 abdicate, abnegate, disgorge, renounce 9
surrender

reliquary: box 4 apse, arca 5 apsis, arca-
e(pl.), chest 6 casket, chasse, shrine 7
chorten

reliquiae: 6 relics 7 remains

relish: 4 dash, gust, like, tang, zest 5 achar,
enjoy, gusto, sauce, savor, taste 6 canape,
degust, flavor, palate, savour 7 delight,
flavour 8 appetite, hautgout 9 appetizer,
degustate, enjoyment, seasoning 11 inclination
kind: 5 achar, curry 6 catsup, caviar 7
botargo, chutney, mustard

relucent: 6 bright 7 radiant, shining 9 refulgent

reluct: 5 fight 6 revolt 8 struggle

reluctance: 6 revolt 8 aversion 9 adversion,
hesitancy 10 opposition, repugnance, resistance 13 indisposition, unwillingness
14 disinclination

reluctant: 4 loth 5 loath 6 averse, forced 7
adverse 8 backward, grudging, hesitant,
opposing 9 resisting, unwilling 11 disinclined

reluctate: 5 repel 6 oppose 9 repudiate

rely: 4 bank, base, hold, hope, lean, rest 5 count, rally, trust 6 belong, cleave, depend, expect, lippen, reckon, repose 7 believe, confide

Remagen's river: 5 Rhine

remain: be; lie 4 bide, last, rest, stay, wait 5 abide, dwell, hover, stand, tarry, thole 6 endure, linger, reside 7 persist 8 continue

remainder: 4 rest, stub 5 stump 7 balance, remanet, remnant, residue, surplus 8 leavings, residual, residuum 9 leftovers

remains: 4 dust 5 ashes, relic, ruins, trace 6 corpse, fossil 7 vestige 9 remainder

remand: 6 commit 7 consign 8 recommit

remanent: 7 further, lasting, remains 8 enduring 9 permanent, remainder 10 additional 13 supplementary

remark: say 4 barb, heed, note, word 5 aside, gloss, state, write 6 notice, regard 7 comment, descant, express, observe 8 indicate, perceive 9 aspersion, platitude 10 animadvert, annotation, commentary, expression 11 distinguish, observation

embarrassing: 5 boner, break 7 blooper, faux pas

witty: gag, mot 4 quip 5 sally 7 sarcasm 9 witticism

remarkable: 7 notable, strange, unusual 8 uncommon 9 egregious, wonderful 11 exceptional 12 considerable 13 extraordinary

remble: 4 move, stir 6 remove

remedy: aid, bot 4 balm, boot, bote, cure, drug, gain, hale, heal, help 5 amend, salve, topic 6 arcana(pl.), relief, repair 7 arcanum, correct, cure-all, nostrum, panacea, placebo, rectify, redress, relieve 8 antidote, curative, medicine 9 treatment 10 assistance, catholicon, chevisance, corrective, reparation 13 counteractive

imaginary: 6 elixir 7 panacea

quack: 7 nostrum, placebo

soothing: 4 balm 6 balsam

remember: 6 ideate, recall, record, remind, reward 7 bethink, mention 9 recollect, reminisce 11 commemorate

remembrance: 4 gift, mind 5 token 6 memory, minnie, notice, trophy 7 memento, mention 8 allusion, keepsake, memorial, souvenir 9 discourse, reference 10 impression 11 inscription 12 recollecting

remex: 5 quill 7 feather

remind: 6 recall

reminder: cue 4 hint, memo, note, prod, twit 7 memento, monitor 10 admonition

reminiscence: act 4 fact 5 power 6 memory 9 recalling 10 experience 11 memorabilia, remembering, remembrance 12 recollection

remise: 4 deed 5 remit 6 giving, return 7 release, replace, respite 8 granting 9 remission, surrender 10 remittance

remiss: lax 4 lazy, mild, pale 5 slack, tardy 6 gentle 7 diluted, languid, lenient, relaxed 8 careless, derelict, dilatory, heedless, moderate 9 dissolved, liquefied, negligent 10 neglectful 11 inattentive, thoughtless 13 irresponsible

remission: 4 liss 5 lisse 6 rebate 9 abolition, cessation, lessening 10 diminution

remit: pay 4 bate, send 5 abate, defer, enter, refer, relax 6 cancel, excuse, insert, pardon, resign, return, submit 7 abandon, absolve, forgive, forward, readmit, release, restore, slacken, suspend 8 abrogate, liberate, mitigate, moderate, postpone, recommit, transmit 9 exculpate, surrender

remittance: 9 allowance

remnant: bit, end, ort, rag 4 dreg, fent, left, part, rest, stub 5 crumb, piece, relic, scrap, trace, wrack 7 leaving, portion, remains, residue 8 fragment 9 remainder 10 suggestion

remodel: 6 change, recast 7 rebuild 11 reconstruct

remolade: 5 sauce 8 dressing, ointment

remonstrance: 10 benedicite 13 expostulation

remonstrate: 5 argue 6 object 7 declare, profess, protest 8 complain 11 demonstrate, expostulate

remora: 4 clog, drag, fish, pega 5 delay 7 pegador 9 hindrance 10 impediment

remord: 5 taint 6 excite, ponder, rebuke 7 afflict, censure, remorse 8 remember

remorse: rue 4 pity, ruth 5 grief, qualm 6 regret, sorrow 7 penance 8 distress 9 penitence, repentent 10 compassion, contrition 11 compunction

remote: far, off 4 afar, cool 5 alien, aloof, faint, vague 6 forane, slight 7 distant, faraway, foreign, removed 8 secluded, separate 10 abstracted, impersonal, unfriendly 12 inaccessible

goal or end: 5 Thule

more: 7 endmost, further 8 ulterior

most: 6 ultima 9 diametric

remove: rid 4 bate, dele, doff, fire, free, kill, move, oust, pare, raze, rend, sack, void, weed 5 amove, apart, avoid, elide, eloin, erase, evict, expel, strip 6 betake, cancel, change, convey, deduct, delete, depose, disbar, distal, eloign, recall, remble, retire, uproot 7 deprive, despoil, dismiss, extract, uncover, whittle 8 abstract, disclose, discover, dislodge, displace, relegate, separate, supplant, transfer **9** eliminate, eradicate, translate **10** disconnect **11** assassinate

clothing: **5** strip **7** disrobe, undress
from office: **4** oust **6** depose
ice: **7** defrost
impurities: **5** smelt **6** filter, refine
legally: **4** oust **6** disbar
to another place: **8** transfer

removed: off **4** away, move **5** aloof, apart **6** remote **7** distant **10** abstracted

remover: **6** porter **7** carrier, drayman, solvent **9** scavenger **10** contractor

remuneration: pay **5** wages **6** reward **7** payment, stipend **8** requital **9** emolument, repayment **10** recompense **12** compensation, satisfaction **13** consideration, gratification, reimbursement

remunerative: **10** beneficial, profitable

Remus: *brother:* **7** Romulus
father: **4** Mars
foster mother: **4** wolf
mother: **4** Rhea
slayer: **7** Romulus

renable: **4** glib **5** ready **6** fluent **8** eloquent

renaissance: **7** rebirth, revival **10** renascence

renal: **7** nephric **9** nephritic

Renard: See **Reynard**

rencounter: **4** duel, meet **5** clash, fight **6** action, battle, combat, debate **7** collide, contest, meeting **8** conflict **9** collision, encounter

rend: cut, rip **4** pull, rent, rive, slit, tear **5** break, burst, sever, split, wrest **6** breach, cleave, divide, enrive, pierce, remove, screed, sunder **7** abscind, dispart, disrupt, rupture **8** fracture, lacerate, separate **9** dismember **12** disintegrate

render: do; pay, put, try **4** emit, give, make, melt **5** treat, yield **6** depict, recite, repeat, return, submit **7** clarify, deliver, exhibit, extract, furnish, inflict, payment, perform, present, requite, restore **8** transmit **9** interpret, represent, surrender, translate **10** contribute

rendezvous: **4** date, meet **5** place, tryst **6** refuge **7** hangout, meeting, retreat **8** assemble, mobilize **9** agreement, gathering **11** appointment

rendition: **8** delivery **9** surrender **11** deliverance, performance, translation **14** interpretation

renegade: rat **5** rebel **6** bolter **7** traitor **8** apostate, deserter, fugitive, renegado, turncoat **10** changeling

renege, renig: **4** deny **5** welsh **6** desert, refuse, revoke **7** decline **8** renounce

renew: **4** beet **5** beete **6** extend, refill, repair, repeat, resume, revamp, revive **7** freshen,

rebuild, refresh, replace, restore **8** reassume, re-create, renovate **9** replenish **10** invigorate, recommence, regenerate, rejuvenate **11** re-establish, resuscitate **12** redintegrate

renitent: **7** opposed **8** opposing **9** obstinate, resistant **12** recalcitrant

rennet: lab **5** apple **6** curdle, keslop **7** earning(Sc.) **8** cheeslep, cheeslip, earnings(Sc.), membrane **9** coagulate
ferment: **6** enzyme, rennin

renomme: **8** renowned **10** celebrated

renounce: **4** cede, defy, deny **5** cease, forgo, renay, renig, waive **6** abjure, desert, disown, forego, forlet, forsay, recant, reject, renege, repeal, resign **7** abandon, disavow, forsake, retract **8** abdicate, abnegate, disclaim, forspeak, forswear, renounce **9** repudiate, surrender **10** abrenounce, relinquish **12** abrenunciate

renovate: **4** redo **5** alter, clean, renew **6** purify, repair, resume, revive **7** cleanse, furbish, refresh, replace, restore **10** invigorate, regenerate

renown: rap **4** fame, note **5** eclat, glory, kudos, rumor **6** report **7** acclaim **8** eminence **9** celebrity **10** reputation **11** celebration, distinction

renowned: **5** known **11** illustrious

rent (see also **rend**): let, pay **4** gape, hire, hole, rime, toll **5** censo, chink, cleft, crack, cuddy, gavel, gorge, lease, share, split, yield **6** breach, engage, income, profit, return, reward, schism **7** fissure, opening, revenue, rupture, tribute
high: **8** rackrent
paid: tac
transfer: **6** attorn

rental: **4** cost, list **5** house **8** schedule **9** apartment

rente: **6** income **7** annuity, revenue

renter: **6** lessee, tenant **8** occupant

renverse: **7** reverse **8** overturn **9** overthrow

reopen: **6** resume **10** recommence

rep: **5** cloth **6** fabric

repair: fix **4** darn, heal, help, mend **5** amend, patch, piece, refit, renew **6** remedy, return, revamp, revive **7** correct, rebuild **8** renovate

repairman: **6** tinker **7** cobbler **8** mechanic

repand: **4** bent, wavy **6** uneven

reparation: **4** bote **6** amende, amends, reward **7** damages, redress **8** requital **9** amendment, atonement, indemnity, repairing **10** recompense **11** restitution **12** compensation, distribution, partitioning **14** redistribution

repartee: wit **5** reply **6** retort **7** riposte

repast: tea **4** bait, feed, food, meal **5** bever, feast, snack, treat **6** dinner **7** banquet **8**

mealtime **9** collation, refection **11** refreshment

pert. to: **8** prandial

repatriation: 6 return **11** restoration

repay: pay **4** meed **5** appay **6** avenge, profit, punish, refund, return, reward **7** deserve, requite, restore **9** gratulate, reimburse, retaliate **10** compensate, recompense, remunerate **11** reciprocate

repeal: 5 amend, annul, emend **6** appeal, cancel, recall, revoke **7** abolish, rescind, retract, reverse **8** abrogate, derogate, renounce, withdraw

repeat: bis(It.), din **4** cite, echo, rame **5** ditto, quote, recap, recur **6** encore, parrot, resume, retell **7** iterate, recount, reprise, restate **8** redouble **9** duplicate, reiterate **10** ingeminate, repetition **11** battologize **12** recapitulate

music: bis

performance: **6** encore

sign in music: **5** segno

repeatedly: oft **5** often **10** frequently **11** continually **12** continuously

repeater: gun **5** rifle, watch **6** pistol **7** firearm **10** recidivist

repel: 4 beat, stop **5** check, debar, force **6** combat, defend, oppose, rebuff, refuse, reject, remove, resist **7** decline, disgust, repulse **8** vanquish **10** extinguish

repellent: 4 grim **5** harsh **9** repugnant **10** forbidding

repent: rue **5** atone **6** grieve, lament, regret **7** reptant **8** crawling, creeping, forthink, penitent

repentance: 4 pity, ruth **5** shame **7** penance, remorse **9** attrition, penitence **10** contrition **11** compunction

repentant: 11 penitential

repercussion: 4 blow **6** impact, recoil **7** rebound **8** reaction **10** reflection **11** reiteration **12** ballottement **13** reverberation

repertory: 4 list **5** index **7** theater, theatre **8** calendar, magazine, treasury **9** catalogue **10** collection, storehouse

repetition: bis **4** copy, echo, rote **5** rondo **6** dilogy, encore **7** replica, tremolo **9** iteration, rehearsal **10** redundancy **12** reproduction

mechanical: **4** rote **8** anaphora

of homologous parts: **6** merism

of idea: **8** pleonasm **9** tautology

of others: **7** echolia, mimicry **9** echolalia

of sound: **4** echo

repine: 4 fail, fret, pine, wane **5** mourn **6** grouse, lament, regret **7** grumble, whimper **8** complain, languish

replace: 4 stet **5** reset, stead **6** follow **7** relieve, restore, succeed **8** supplant **9** reimburse, supersede **10** substitute

replacement: 6 ersatz **9** successor **10** substitute

replenish: 4 feed, fill **5** renew, store

replete: fat **4** full, rife **5** sated, stout **6** filled, gorged **7** bloated, implete, stocked, stuffed **8** complete **9** abounding, surfeited

replevy: 5 seize **6** attach, redeem **7** recover

replica: 5 image **6** carbon, ectype **8** likeness **9** facsimile **10** repetition **12** reproduction

replicate: 4 bend, fold **5** reply **6** repeat **8** manifold, repeated **9** duplicate, multifold

reply: 4 echo, fold, sass **5** rebut **6** answer, oracle, re-echo, rejoin, repeat, retort, return **7** respond, retract, riposte **8** repartee, response **9** rejoinder **11** replication

report: pop **4** fame, tell, word **5** bruit, noise, rumor, state, story **6** breeze, cahier(F.), delate, digest, recite, relate, repeat, return, rumour **7** account, crackle, hansard, hearing, hearsay, inkling, narrate, recital, summary **8** announce, describe **9** circulate, grapevine, narration, narrative

false: fib, lie **6** canard **7** slander **8** tall-tale **12** misstatement

reporter: cub **6** legman, writer **7** newsman **9** columnist **10** journalist

symbol: **6** thirty

repose: lay, lie, set, sit **4** calm, ease, rely, rest, seat **5** peace, place, quiet, sleep **6** relief **7** compose, confide, deposit, dignity, recline, replace, restore, support **8** calmness, serenity **9** composure, quietness **10** relaxation, repository **11** downsitting **12** requiescence, tranquillity

reposit: 7 deposit, replace

repository: ark, box **4** bank, file, safe, shop **5** ambry, capsa, chest, vault **6** closet, museum **7** arsenal, capsule, granary, storage **8** magazine, treasury **9** confidant, reliquary, sepulcher, warehouse **10** depository, storehouse

reposoir: 5 altar

repossess: 6 regain **7** recover

reprehend: 4 warn **5** blame, chide **6** rebuke **7** censure, reprove **8** admonish, disprove **9** reprimand

reprehensible: 8 criminal, culpable

represent: act **4** show **5** enact **6** clothe, denote, depict, typify **7** exhibit, express, picture, portray, produce, profess **8** describe, simulate **9** delineate, designate, exemplify, reproduce, symbolize **10** substitute **11** impersonate **12** characterize

representation: map **4** icon, idol, ikon **5** chart, graph, image, model **6** avowal, blazon, sample **7** account, diagram **8** likeness, notation **9** portrayal, statement **10** simili-

tude **11** histrionics, performance, portraiture
favorable: **14** recommendation
representative: 4 heir **5** agent, envoy **6** consul, deputy, legate **7** tribune **8** delegate, executor, exponent, salesman **10** ambassador **12** illustrating, illustrative **13** administrator
repress: 4 bury, curb, hush, rein, stop **5** check, choke, crush, daunt, press, quell **6** bridle, deaden, reduce, stifle, subdue **7** depress **8** compress, restrain, suppress, withhold **9** constrain, overpower
reprieve: 5 defer, delay **6** escape **7** respite, suspend **8** postpone **12** postponement
reprimand: 4 call **5** check, chide, slate **6** rebuff, rebuke **7** censure, chapter, chasten, repress, reproof, reprove **9** reprehend **12** reprehension
reprint: 4 copy
reprisal: 7 revenue **8** requital
reprise: 8 reassume **10** compensate, recommence, repetition **12** reprehension
reproach: 4 blot, slur, twit **5** abuse, blame, braid, chide, shame, shend, sully, taunt **6** accuse, infamy, rebuke, revile, stigma, vilify **7** censure, condemn, reprove, traduce, upbraid **8** besmirch, disgrace, dishonor **9** bespatter, challenge, contumely, descredit, disrepute, invective **10** correction, exprobrate, opprobrium, scurrility **11** impeachment **12** vilification **13** animadversion **15** discommendation
old word of: **4** raca
reprobate: 4 hard **5** Satan, scamp **6** disown, rascal, reject **7** abandon, condemn, corrupt, vicious **8** castaway, denounce, hardened **9** blameable, reprehend, scoundrel **10** censurable, condemned, disallowed **11** blameworthy, disapproved **12** unprincipled **13** reprehensible
reproduce: 4 copy, draw **6** repeat **7** imitate **8** multiply **9** duplicate, propagate, represent **11** reconstruct
asexually: **5** clone
reproduction: 6 ectype **7** fission, replica **8** likeness **9** photostat **11** counterpart **13** proliferation
reproductive: 8 prolific
reproductive cell: 6 gamete
reprove: 4 flay, rate, slam **5** blame, check, chide, roast, scold, shame **6** berate, rebuff, rebuke, refute, reject **7** censure, confute, correct, lecture, upbraid **8** admonish, carritch, chastise, disgrace, disprove, redargue, reproach **9** castigate, challenge, objurgate, reprehend, reprimand, reprobate **10** administer, animadvert, carritches **11** epostulate

reptant: 8 crawling, creeping
reptile: 4 croc, worm **5** snake **6** turtle **8** dinosaur, tortoise **9** alligator, crocodile, pterosaur **10** dinosauria(pl.), predentate **11** pterodactyl, pterosauria(pl.)
age: **8** Mesozoic
edible: **6** iguana, turtle
legless: **4** apod **5** snake
pert. to: **7** saurian **8** ophidian
scale: **5** scute
study of: **11** herpetology
reptiles: *age of:* **8** Mesozoic
group: **6** sauria
reptilian: low **4** mean **5** snaky **6** lizard, sneaky **7** reptant, saurian, serpent **8** crawling, creeping, ophidian **9** groveling, malignant **10** despicable
republic: 5 state **9** democracy **10** commonweal, government **12** commonwealth
imaginary: **7** Oceania
world's smallest: **5** Nauru
Republic author: 5 Plato
repudiate: 4 defy, deny **6** abjure, disown, recant, refuse, reject **7** decline, disavow, discard, divorce, retract **8** abrogate, disclaim, renounce **9** disaffirm
repugn: 6 oppose, resist
repugnance: 5 odium **6** enmity, hatred **7** disgust, dislike **8** aversion, distaste, loathing **9** antipathy, hostility, repulsion **10** abhorrence, antagonism, opposition, reluctance **11** abomination, contrariety, incongruity **13** inconsistency **14** disinclination **15** incompatibility **16** disagreeableness **17** contradictoriness
repugnant: 8 inimical **9** offensive, repellent **10** refractory **12** disagreeable **14** irreconcilable
repulse: 4 deny, foil, rout **5** check, fling, rebut, refel, repel **6** defeat, denial, rebuff, refuse, reject **7** exclude, refusal **9** rejection
repulsion: ug(Sc.) **7** dislike **8** aversion, distaste **10** repugnance
repulsive: 4 dain, evil, loth, ugly, vile **5** loath, toady **6** odious **7** fulsome, hateful, loathly **9** offensive, repellent, repugnant **10** disgusting, forbidding **11** distasteful, gorgonesque
repurchase: 6 redeem
reputable: 4 good **8** credible **10** creditable **11** responsible
reputation: 4 fame, lose, name, note, odor **5** glory, honor, izzat, odour, stamp **6** credit, honour, renown, repute **7** respect **9** attribute, character **11** distinction **13** consideration
loss of: **7** scandal
repute: 4 fame **5** honor, worth **6** credit, esteem, regard, revere **7** account, respect,

suppose **9** character **10** ascription, estimation

reputed: dit **8** putative

request: ask, beg, sue **4** plea, pray, suit, wish **5** apply, crave, order **6** appeal, behest, demand, invite **7** entreat, prithee, solicit **8** entreaty, petition, rogation **11** application **12** solicitation, supplication

formal: **8** rogation

requiem: 4 hymn, mass, rest, song **5** chant, dirge, peace, quiet **7** service

requiescat: 4 wish **6** prayer

requiescence: 6 repose

requin: 5 shark **8** man-eater

require: ask **4** lack, need **5** claim, crave, exact, force **6** behove, compel, demand, enjoin, entail, expect, oblige **7** behoove **9** postulate **11** necessitate

requirement: 4 duty **9** formality, requisite

requisite: 4 need **7** needful **9** condition, essential **11** requirement **13** indispensable

requisition: 5 order **6** billet, demand **9** embargo, request **11** application, requirement

requital: 7 guerdon **8** reprisal **9** vengeance **11** antapodosis, retribution

requite: pay **5** atone, repay **6** acquit, avenge, defray, return, reward **7** deserve, gratify, revenge **9** retaliate **10** compensate, recompense

reredos: 4 wall **6** screen **7** drapery **9** backplate, partition

reree: 7 cattail

reremouse: bat

rerun: 6 replay, reshow

res: 5 point, thing **6** matter

resale: 8 exchange

resay: 6 repeat **7** iterate

rescind: 4 void **5** annul **6** cancel, repeal, revoke **7** abolish, retract **8** abrogate **11** countermand

rescissible: 9 revokable **11** rescindable

rescript: 5 order **6** answer, decree **9** rewriting **11** counterpart

rescue: 4 free, save **6** ransom, redeem, succor **7** deliver, reclaim, recover, release, salvage **8** delivery, liberate **9** extricate **11** deliverance

rese: 4 rage, rush **5** hurry, onset, quake, shake **7** impulse, tremble **8** rashness

research: 7 inquiry **11** examination **13** investigation **15** experimentation

reseau: net **6** ground **7** network **10** foundation

resect: 6 excise

reseda: 10 mignonette

resemblance: 5 image **6** simile, symbol **7** analogy **8** affinity, likeness, vicinity **9**

agreement, imitation, semblance **10** comparison, similarity, similitude **12** assimilation **14** representation

one bearing: **6** ringer

resembling: 4 like **5** alike **11** approximate

resentment: ire **4** gall **5** anger, depit, pique, spite **6** animus, choler, enmity, grudge, hatred, malice, rancor, spleen **7** dudgeon, umbrage **8** acrimony **9** animosity, annoyance, hostility, malignity **10** irritation **11** displeasure, indignation

reserve: 4 cash, cave, fund, keep, save **5** spare, stock, store **6** assets, retain, supply **7** backlog, bespeak, caution, modesty, shyness, silence, surplus **8** coldness, distance, forprise, preserve, withhold **9** exception, reservoir, restraint, retention, reticence **10** constraint, diffidence, discretion, limitation, substitute **11** reservation, taciturnity

reserved: coy **4** cold **5** aloof, staid, taken **6** sedate **8** backward, cautious **15** incommunicative, uncommunicative

reservoir: vat **4** font, pond, pool, sump, tank **5** basin, fount, stope, store **6** cenote, supply **7** cistern, favissa, forebay, piscina, reserve **8** favissae(pl.), fountain

re-set: 4 help **5** abode, alter **6** harbor, refuge, resort, succor **7** receipt, receive, replace, secrete, shelter **9** receiving **10** receptacle

resiance: 5 abode **9** residence

reside: big, lie **4** bigg, live, room, stay **5** abide, dwell, habit, lodge **6** remain, settle **7** inhabit, sojourn, subside **8** habitate

residence: 4 home, seat, shed **5** abode, house, villa **6** biding, castle, palace **7** habitat, mansion **8** domicile, residuum, sediment **9** apartment **10** habitation, villanette **13** collectorship

resident: cit **6** lessee, tenant **7** burgess, citizen **8** inherent, occupant

residue: ash **4** dreg, lees, marc, orts, rest, silt, slag **5** ashes, dregs **6** cinder, excess, relics, sludge, sordes **7** balance, remains, remnant **8** leavings, remanent, residuum, sediment **9** remainder

residuum: 8 hangover **9** remainder

resign: 4 cede, quit **5** demit, remit, yield **6** devote, submit **7** abandon, consign, deliver **8** abdicate, renounce **9** surrender **10** relinquish

resignation: 8 patience **9** endurance **12** acquiescence

resile: 6 recede, return **7** rebound, retract, retreat **8** withdraw

resiliency: 4 tone **8** buoyancy **10** elasticity

resilient: 5 toned **7** buoyant, elastic, springy **8** bouncing, stretchy **9** recoiling, returning **10** rebounding

resin, rosin: alk, gum, lac, tar 4 aloe, balm, tolu 5 amber, anime, animi, copal, damar, elemi, gugal, gugul, loban, myrrh, pitch 6 balsam, charas, dammar, derrid, elemin, googul, salban, storax 7 acouchi, ambrite, aroiera, copaiba, copaiva, derride, exudate, fluavil, galipot, hartite, ladanum, retinol 8 alkitran, bdellium, fluavile, gedanite, glessite, guaiacum, labdanum, retinite, sandarac 9 alchitran, colophony, elaterite 11 colophonium 12 frankincense
fossil: 5 amber 8 glessite
gum: 5 gugal 6 mastic
incense: 8 sandarac
purified: 7 shellac
varnish: 5 anime, copal

resinous tree: fir 4 pine 6 balsam

resist: 4 buck, fend 5 rebel, repel 6 baffle, combat, defeat, defend, impugn, oppose, wither 7 contest, prevent 9 frustrate, gainstand, withstand

resistance: 6 rebuff 7 defence, defense 9 hostility, renitence 10 antagonism, oppugnance 13 recalcitrance

resistance box: 8 rheostat

resistant: 4 hard 8 obdurate, renitent

resolute: 4 bold 5 fixed 7 animose, animous 8 positive, resolved, stalwart, unshaken 9 unbending 10 unwavering

resolution: vow 4 grit, thew 5 heart, nerve 7 purpose, resolve, verdict 8 analysis, backbone, decision, firmness, proposal, strength 9 assurance, certainty, constancy, fortitude, hardihood, statement, sternness, stoutness 10 conviction, separation, steadiness 11 intrepidity, persevering 12 deliberation, faithfulness, perseverance, resoluteness 13 determination, inflexibility, steadfastness 14 simplification 15 disentanglement

resolve: 4 free, melt 5 relax, untie 6 answer, assoil, dispel, inform, loosen, reduce, remove, settle 7 appoint, dispose, explain, liquefy, scatter, unravel 8 conclude, dissolve, enfeeble, persuade, separate

resonant: 7 ringing, vibrant 8 sonorous, sounding 10 resounding 11 reverberant

resort: go; spa 4 howf 5 crowd, haunt, howff, joint, place, visit 6 betake, casino, refuge, return, revert, throng 7 company 8 frequent, habitual, recourse 10 assemblage, honkeytonk
health: spa 9 sanatoria(pl.) 10 sanatorium, sanitarium
place of: 5 haunt 7 purlieu

resound: 4 echo, peal, ring 5 clang 6 reecho 11 reverberate

resounding: 8 plangent

resourceful: apt 5 sharp 7 fertile

resources: 5 funds, means, money 6 assets, stocks, stores 7 resorts 8 reserves, supplies, supports 10 expedients 12 contrivances
guardian: 15 conservationist

respect: awe 4 heed 5 defer, honor, value 6 admire, esteem, homage, regard, revere 7 concern, neglect, observe, respite, tribute, worship 8 postpone, venerate 9 attention, deference, reference, reverence 10 admiration
act of: 6 devoir
pay: 5 greet 6 salute

respectable: 4 good 6 decent, honest, proper 7 fausant 9 estimable, honorable, reputable 10 creditable 11 presentable

respectful: 5 civil 7 careful, duteous 11 ceremonious

respective: 4 each 6 sundry 7 partial 9 regardful 10 individual, particular

respiration: 6 breath 7 eupnoea 9 breathing
difficulty: 4 rale 5 cough 7 dyspnea 8 dyspnoea
normal: 7 eupnoea

respire: 4 live, sigh 6 exhale, inhale 7 breathe

respite: 4 lull, rest 5 delay, pause 6 recess 7 leisure 8 interval, reprieve, surcease 9 cessation 10 suspension 12 intermission, postponement

resplendent: 6 bright 7 aureate, blazing, radiant, shining 8 dazzling, glorious, gorgeous, lustrous, splendid 9 brilliant, refulgent 10 epiphanous, flamboyant

respond: 4 echo, feel 5 react, reply, write 6 accord, answer, pillar, rejoin, retort, return 8 response 10 correspond

response: 4 word 5 verse 6 anthem, chorus, phrase 7 refrain 8 sentence

responsible: 8 amenable 9 accordant, reputable 10 answerable, dependable, sufficient 13 correspondent

responsibility: 4 care, onus 6 burden, charge 9 liability 10 obligation 11 reliability 14 accountability 15 trustworthiness

responsive: 6 mutual 8 amenable 9 sensitive 11 sympathetic

res publica: 5 state 8 republic 10 commonweal 12 commonwealth

rest: lay, lie, set, sit 4 calm, ease, hang, lair, lean, liss, prop, rely, seat, slip, stay, stop 5 abide, ceast, found, lisse, pause, peace, quiet, relax, renew, repos(F.), sleep, stand 6 alight, cesura, depend, desist, remain, repose, settle 7 balance, caesura, comfort, leisure, refresh, remains, remnant, reposal, residue, respite, shelter, support, surplus 8 breather, interval, lodgment, vacation 9 cessation, establish, quietness, remainder, stillness 10 immobility, inactivity, relaxation 11 refreshment 12 intermission, peacefulness, tranquillity

in reading: 7 caesura

noonday: nap 6 siesta

rest house: inn 4 chan, khan 5 hotel, serai 6 abalam, hostel, tavern 7 chhatri

restate: 6 reword 8 reassert

restaurant: inn 4 cafe 5 diner, hotel 6 bistro, tavern 7 automat, beanery, cabaret, tearoom 9 cafeteria, chophouse, hashhouse 10 rotisserie, steakhouse 11 rathskeller(G.)

restful: 5 quiet 8 peaceful

resting: 4 abed 6 asleep, latent 7 dormant

restitution: 6 amends, return 8 recovery 10 recompense, reparation 11 restoration 12 compensation 13 reimbursement

restive: 5 balky 6 uneasy, unruly 7 fidgety, nervous 8 restless, stubborn 9 impatient 10 refractory 12 unmanageable

restless: 6 fidget, fitful, haunty, hectic, roving, uneasy 7 agitato(It.), fidgety, fretful, inquiet, restive, unquiet 8 agitated, feverish, stirring 9 disturbed, impatient, sleepless, unsettled, wandering 10 disquieted, reposeless 12 discontented

restoration: 10 reparation 11 restitution

restorative: 7 anodyne 8 salutary

restore: 4 cure, heal, mend 5 amend, atone, renew, repay, right 6 redeem, refund, repair, return, revive 7 convert, rebuild, recover, replace 8 renovate 9 reinstate, resurrect 10 regenerate 11 reconstruct, re-establish, resuscitate 12 redintegrate, rehabilitate

printer's mark: 4 stet

restrain: bar, dam 4 bate, bind, calm, clog, curb, hold, rein, rule, stay, stop 5 chain, check, cramp, deter, guard, limit, still, stint 6 arrest, behave, bridle, coerce, detain, fetter, forbid, govern, halter, hamper, hinder, pinion, tether 7 abridge, abstain, chasten, command, confine, contain, control, deprive, forbear, inhibit, prevent, repress, shackle, trammel 8 attemper, compesce, compress, conclude, imprison, prohibit, restrict, suppress, withhold 9 constrain, detention 12 circumscribe

restrained: 6 severe 8 reserved 9 hidebound 11 disciplined

restraint: bit 5 force 7 barrier, durance, reserve 9 avoidance, reticence 10 internment

restrict: bar 4 curb 5 bound, cramp, limit, scant, stint 6 censor, coerce, hamper, modify, ration 7 astrict, confine, repress, tighten 8 contract, derogate, prohibit, restrain, straiten 9 constrict 12 circumscribe

restricted: 5 local 6 finite, narrow, strait 9 parochial 10 provincial

restriction: 10 regulation 11 reservation 13 qualification

restrictive: 7 binding 8 limiting 9 stringent

resty: 5 quiet 6 rancid 7 restive 8 sluggish

result: go; end, sum 4 leap, rise 5 ensue, event, fruit, issue, score, total 6 accrue, effect, follow, sequel, spring, upshot 7 outcome, proceed, redound 8 aftering, decision 9 aftermath, eventuate, terminate 10 conclusion 11 achievement, consequence, termination

result in: 5 cause

resume: 5 renew 6 reopen, repeat, review 7 epitome, summary 8 continue, reoccupy, synopsis 9 epitomize, reiterate, summarize 10 abridgment, recommence 12 recapitulate 14 recapitulation

resurrection: 7 rebirth, revival 11 restoration

resuscitate: 6 revive 7 quicken, restore 8 revivify

ret: rot, sop 4 soak 5 steep 6 dampen

retable: 5 ledge, shelf 6 gradin 9 framework

retail: 4 hawk, sell vent 5 trade 6 barter, peddle, relate, repeat

retailer: 6 dealer 8 huckster, merchant

retain: 4 hire, hold, keep, save 6 adhere, athold, behold, employ 7 contain, prevent, reserve 8 maintain, preserve, remember, restrain 9 entertain, recollect

retainer: fee 4 cage, hewe 5 frame 6 menial, minion, vassal 7 hobbler 8 follower 9 burkundaz 11 burkundauze

retaining: 9 retentive

retaliate: 5 repay 6 avenge, punish, retort 7 requite, revenge

retaliation: 6 talion 8 reprisal, requital 11 retribution

retard: 4 slow 5 brake, catch, defer, delay, deter, trash 6 belate, deaden, detain, hinder, impede 8 encumber, obstruct, postpone, restrain 10 decelerate

retardant: 8 obstacle

retardation: lag

retch: gag 4 hawk, spit 5 reach, vomit 6 expand, extend, strain 7 stretch

rete: 6 plexus 7 network

retem: 7 juniper

retention: 6 memory 7 holding, keeping 8 learning 10 retainment 11 maintenance, remembering

retepore: 8 bryozoan

rethe: 5 cruel 6 ardent, fierce, severe

retiarius: 9 gladiator

retiary: 6 meshed, telary 7 netlike

reticent: 4 dark 6 silent 7 sparing 8 discreet, reserved, retiring, taciturn 9 secretive 10 mysterious 15 uncommunicative

reticule: bag 4 etui 5 cabas, etwee 6 pocket, sachet 7 handbag, reticle, workbag

reticulum: net 7 network, stomach 8 meshwork

retinaculum: 6 frenum

retinue: 4 band, crew, ging, rout, suit, tail 5 harem, meiny, suite, train 6 attend, escort 7 cortege, service 8 equipage 9 entourage, retainers 10 attendance, attendants

retire: go; ebb 5 leave 6 depart, recede, recess, remove, vanish 7 pension, retreat 8 withdraw 9 disappear, sequester

retired: 4 abed, lone 5 quiet 6 secret 7 private, recluse 8 abstruse, emeritus, reserved, secluded, solitary 9 recondite

retiring: shy 5 timid 6 modest 7 bashful, fugient 8 reserved 9 diffident 11 unobtrusive

retort: mot 4 quip, turn 5 facer, repay, reply, sally 6 answer, recoil, return, ripost 7 alembic, cornute, respond, riposte 8 blizzard, repartee 9 retaliate

retortion, retorsion: 7 bending 8 reprisal, twisting 10 reflection

retract: 4 bend 6 abjure, cancel, disown, recall, recant, remove, repeal, retire, revoke 7 disavow, prevent, rescind, retreat 8 restrain, withdraw 9 repudiate

retraction: 8 palinode

retral: 8 backward 9 posterior 10 retrograde

retreat: den 4 abri, cave, holt, lair, nest, nook, rout 5 arbor, bower 6 arbour, asylum, harbor, recede, recess, refuge, retire 7 harbour, privacy, retiral, shelter 8 solitude, withdraw 9 departure, hibernate, sanctuary, seclusion 10 rendezvous, retirement, sanitarium, withdrawal
underground: 4 abri, cave

retrench: cut 4 bate, omit, pare 6 delete, excise, lessen, reduce, remove 7 abridge, curtail, repress 8 decrease, diminish 9 economize, intercept

retrenchment: 5 ditch 7 parapet, rampart 8 traverse 10 breastwork 12 entrenchment

retribution: pay 6 return, reward 7 nemesis, revenge, tribute 8 requital 9 vengeance 10 punishment, recompense
goddess of: Ate

retrieve: 6 recall, regain, revive 7 recover, restore 8 discover 10 recuperate

retrograde: 4 slow 6 recede, retral 7 decline, inverse, opposed, regress 8 backward, contrary, decadent, inverted, rearward, withdraw 9 catabolic, reversely 10 degenerate, retrogress 11 deteriorate

retrogression: 7 regress 8 fallback 9 decadence 12 degeneration 14 retrogradation

retrogressive: 8 backward

retrospective: 6 review 8 backward 11 retroactive 13 contemplative

retund: 4 dull 5 blunt 6 refute, subdue 9 attenuate

return: lob 4 bend, turn 5 recur, remit, repay, yield 6 advert, answer, profit, render, report, retort, revert 7 regress, replace, reprise, requite, respond, restore, revenue, reverse 8 requital, response 9 repayment, retaliate, reversion 10 recompense, recurrence 11 reciprocate, replacement, restoration 12 reappearance 13 reciprocation

Return of the Native author: 5 Hardy

Reuben: *brother:* 6 Joseph
father: 5 Jacob
mother: 4 Leah

Reuel's father: 4 Esau

reunite: 6 rejoin 9 reconcile

reus: 9 defendant

revamp: 5 renew

reveal: bid 4 bare, blab, jamb, open, show, tell, wray 5 exert 6 betray, bewray, descry, detect, expose, impart, unveil 7 confide, develop, display, divulge, exhibit, uncover 8 announce, decipher, develope, disclose, discover, evidence, manifest, revelate 11 communicate

reveille: 4 call, dian 5 diana, levet 6 signal

revel: joy 4 orgy, riot, wake 5 feast, randy, spree, watch 6 bezzle, gavall, high-go 7 carouse, delight, revelry, roister 8 carnival, carousal, domineer, festival 9 celebrate, festivity 11 celebration, merrymaking 12 conviviality

revelant: 9 pertinent

revelation: 4 tora 5 torah 9 discovery 10 disclosure 13 manifestation

reveler, reveller: 8 bacchant 9 bacchanal, roisterer 10 merrymaker
cry: 4 evoe

revenant: 5 ghost 7 specter 9 recurring 10 apparition

revendicate: 7 reclaim, recover

revenge: 6 avenge 7 requite 8 requital 9 retaliate 11 retribution

revenue: 4 rent 5 yield 6 income, profit, rental, return 7 finance 8 interest

reverberate: 4 echo, ring 6 re-echo, return 7 reflect, resound

reverberating: 7 reboant 8 resonant 12 repercussive 13 reverberatory

revere: 4 love 5 adore, honor 6 admire, esteem, regard, repute 7 respect, worship 8 venerate

reverence: awe 4 fear 5 dread, piety 6 homage 8 devotion 9 deference, obeisance, solemnity
gesture of: 8 kneeling 11 genuflexion 12 genuflection
reverend: sri 4 holy 5 abbot 6 clergy, sacred 9 clergyman, monsignor
reverent: 6 humble 7 dutiful
reverie: 5 dream 6 musing, vision 7 fantasy 8 daydream
revers: 5 lapel
reverse: 5 annul, upset 6 defeat, invert, regard, repeal, revoke 7 abolish, backset, convert, subvert 8 backward, contrary, converse, disaster, opposite, overturn 9 disaffirm, overthrow, transpose 10 misfortune 11 countermand
reversion: 6 return
to state: 7 escheat
to type: 7 atavism
reversional: 9 atavistic
revert: 5 react 6 advert, return, revive 7 escheat, recover, reverse 9 backslide 11 antistrophe
revest: 4 robe 5 dress 6 attire, clothe 8 reinvest 9 reinstate
review: 4 edit 5 recap 6 parade, resume, survey 7 account 8 ceremony, critique 9 criticise, criticism, criticize, re-examine 10 certiorari, inspection, periodical, reconsider, retrospect 11 examination
revile: 4 hate, rail 5 abuse, blame, brawl, scold 6 debase, malign, vilify 7 deprave 8 reproach 9 blaspheme 10 calumniate
revince: 6 refute
revise: 4 edit 5 alter, amend, emend 6 change, redact 7 correct, improve, recense 8 readjust 9 castigate, reexamine, supervise
reviser, revisor: 10 diaskeuast
revival: 6 recall 7 rebirth 11 renaissance 12 reproduction 13 recrudescence
revive: daw 4 wake 5 rally, renew, rouse 6 return 7 enliven, freshen, quicken, recover, refresh, restore 8 reawaken, recreate, rekindle, revivify 9 reanimate, refreshen, resurrect 10 regenerate, rejuvenate 11 resuscitate 12 reinvigorate
revoice: 4 echo 5 refit 7 restore
revoke: 5 adeem, annul, check, renig 6 cancel, recall, recant, renege, repeal 7 abolish, fenagle, finagle, prevent, repress, rescind, retract, reverse 8 abrogate, restrain, withdraw 9 fainaigue 11 countermand
revolt: 5 rebel, repel 6 mutiny, offend 7 retreat 8 renounce, sedition, uprising 9 rebellion 12 insurrection, renunciation

revolting: 4 ugly 6 horrid 7 hateful, hideous 8 shocking 9 loathsome, offensive, repellent, repulsive 10 disgusting, nauseating
revolution: 4 gyre, turn 5 cycle 7 circuit 8 disorder, rotation, uprising 9 overthrow, rebellion 12 renunciation
revolutions per minute: RPM 4 revs
revolve: con 4 birl, roll, spin, turn, whir 5 recur, swing, trend, twirl, wheel, whirl, whirr 6 circle, gyrate, ponder, rotate 7 agitate, reflect, trundle 8 consider, meditate 10 deliberate
revolver: gat 6 pistol 7 firearm
revolving: 4 orby 6 rotary
part: 5 rotor 7 rotator
revue: 4 show 9 burlesque 13 entertainment
revulsion: 4 fear 6 change 8 reaction 9 reversion 10 withdrawal
reward: fee, pay, utu 4 heed, hire, meed, rent 5 ameed, award, bonus, check, crown, merit, medal, prize, repay, wages, yield 6 bounty, gersum, notice, profit, regard, return, salary, trophy 7 guerdon, premium, success 8 requital 9 honoraria(pl.) 10 compensate, honorarium, recompense, remunerate 11 retribution 12 compensation, remuneration 13 gratification
rewarding: 7 helpful 10 beneficial
rewrite: 4 edit 6 revise
rex: 4 king
Reynard: fox
rezai: 8 coverlet
rhamn: 9 buckthorn
rhapontic: 7 rhubarb 8 pieplant 9 knapweeds
rhapsodic: 8 ecstatic, effusive 9 emotional
rhea: emu 4 emeu 5 nandu 8 avestruz(Sp.)
Rhea: Ops
child: 4 Hera, Zeus 5 Hades 6 Hestia 7 Demeter 8 Poseidon
father: 6 Uranus
husband: 6 Cronus
rhema: 4 term, verb, word
rheoscope: 12 galvanoscope
rheotome: 11 interrupter
rhesus: 6 monkey 7 macaque
rhetor: 6 master, orator 7 teacher
rhetorical: 6 florid 8 forensic 10 figurative, oratorical
rhetorician: 6 master, orator, writer 7 speaker, teacher
rhetorics: *digression:* 6 ecbole
diminution: 7 litotes
figure of speech: 6 aporia, simile 7 epandos 8 metaphor 10 apostrophe 12 alliteration, onomatopoeia 15 personification
rheum: 4 cold 7 catarrh 8 rhinitis
rheumatism remedy: 5 salol 9 salacetol
rheumatism weed: 10 pipsissewa

rhexis: 7 rupture
rhinal: 5 nasal 6 narial
rhine: 5 ditch, drain 6 runnel
Rhine: *city:* 8 Mannheim
  magic hoard: 9 Rheingold, Rhinegold
  nymph: 7 Lorelei
  pert. to: 7 Rhenish
  tributary: Aar, Ill 4 Aare, Lahn, Main, Ruhr, Waal
  wine: 7 Moselle
rhino: 4 cash 5 money 10 rhinoceros
rhinoceros: 5 abada, topan 6 borele, umhofo 7 keitloa, upeygan
  black: 6 borele
  cousin of: 5 tapir
  feature: 4 horn
rhinoceros beetle: 4 uang
rhinoceros bird: 9 beefeater
rhipidion: 8 flabella(pl.) 9 flabellum
rhizoid: 8 rootcell
rhoda: 4 rose
Rhode Island founder: 13 Roger Williams
Rhodes: *ancient wonder:* 8 Colossus
  festival: 10 Chelidonia
Rhodesia: *language:* Ila
  people: 10 Balokwakwa
rhododaphne: 8 oleander
rhoeadales: 5 poppy
rhomboid: 13 parallelogram
rhonchus: 4 rale 7 snoring 8 croaking 9 whistling
Rhone: *town:* 5 Arles
  tributary: 5 Isere, Saone
rhubarb: 5 error 6 hassle 7 mistake, yawweed 8 argument, pieplant 9 butterbur, rhapontic 10 discussion
  derived from: 5 rheic
  genus: 5 rheum
rhus tree: 5 sumac 6 sumach
rhyme: 5 verse 9 harmonize
rhymester: 4 poet 6 rhymer 8 rimester 9 poetaster
rhyptic: 9 detergent
rhythm: 4 beat, lilt, time 5 clink, meter, pulse, swing, tempo 7 cadence, measure
  break in: 7 caesura 8 caesurae(pl.)
  instrument: 4 drum 7 cymbals 8 triangle 9 tamborine
  monotonous: 8 singsong
rhythmic: 6 poetic 8 metrical 9 recurrent
ria: bay 5 creek, inlet
rial: 4 king 5 great, noble, power, royal 6 prince 8 splendid 9 excellent 11 magnificent
rialto: 4 mart 6 bridge, market 8 exchange
rialty: 4 pomp 5 power, state 6 estate 8 grandeur 10 ceremonial
riant: gay 6 bright 8 cheerful, laughing, smiling

riata: 4 rope 5 lasso, reata 6 lariat
rib: 4 bone, hair, purl, stay, wale 5 costa, ridge, tease 6 costae(pl.), lierne 7 bristle, support 9 cotelette, tierceron
  pert. to: 6 costal 7 costate
ribald: low 6 coarse, rascal, vulgar 7 obscene 9 offensive 10 irreverent, scurrilous 11 blasphemous
riband: 6 ribbon
ribband: bar 4 spar 5 plank, strip 6 bridge, timber 9 scantling
ribbed: 6 barred, corded 7 costate
  fabric: rep 5 twill 6 faille
ribbet: 5 rybat 6 rabbet, rebate
ribble row: 6 string 9 rigmarole
ribbon: bow 4 tape 5 braid, corse, padou, reins, shred, snood, strip, taste 6 cordon, fillet, riband, silver, taenia, tatter 7 binding, taeniae(pl.) 8 banderol, decorate, tressour, tressure 9 banderole
  badge: 6 cordon
  binding: 6 lisere
ribbon-fish: 4 fish 7 cutlass, oarfish 8 bandfish, dealfish
ribbon gum: 8 eucalypt
ribbon-like: 8 taeniate, taenioid
ribbon worm: 9 nemertine
ribless: 8 ecostate 9 decostate
ribwort: 8 hardhead, plantain
rice: 4 boro, chit, paga, twig 5 arroz(Sp.), bigas, canin, macan, pilaf, pilau, stick 6 branch 7 risotto 9 brushwood
  boiled with meat: 5 pilaf, pilau
  drink: 4 sake 5 bubud 7 pangasi
  field: 4 padi 5 paddy
  husk: 4 shud 5 shood
  inferior: 4 chit
  milk: 5 gruel 7 pudding 8 porridge
  paste: ame
  polishings: 5 darac
rice rail: 4 sora
ricebird: 7 bunting, sparrow 8 bobolink 9 gallinule
riceroot grass: 9 broomroot
rich: fat 4 dear, oofy 5 ample, opime 6 absurd, costly, creamy, daedal, fruity, greasy, hearty, mellow, mighty, oofier, potent 7 copious, fertile, moneyed, opulent, orotund, pinguid, wealthy 8 abundant, affluent, generous, luscious, powerful, valuable, well-to-do 9 abounding, bountiful, elaborate, laughable, luxuriant, plentiful, sumptuous 10 productive 12 concentrated, preposterous
  man: 5 Midas, nabob 7 Croesus 9 plutocrat
richard: 9 plutocrat
richdom: 6 wealth 8 richness
riche: 4 rule 5 realm, reign 9 authority
Richelieu's successor: 7 Mazarin

607

riches: 4 gold, pelf, weal 5 lucre, worth 7 fortune 8 treasure
demon of: 6 Mammon
region of: 8 Eldorado
worship of: 10 plutomania
rick: 4 goaf, heap, pile 5 noise, scold, stack, twist 6 jingle, rattle, sprain, wrench 7 chatter
rickety: 4 weak 5 crazy, shaky 6 feeble, senile 7 unsound 8 unstable 9 tottering 10 ramshackle
rickmatic: 6 affair 7 concern 8 business
rickshaw: 6 samlor
ricochet: 4 skip 5 carom 6 bounce, glance 7 rebound
rictus: 4 gape, mask
rid: 4 free 5 clear, empty 6 assoil, remove, rescue 7 deliver, relieve 8 dispatch, liberate 9 eradicate 11 disencumber
ridder: 4 sift 5 sieve
riddle: ree 4 crux, sift 5 aread, areed, griph, rebus, sieve 6 enigma, pierce, puzzle 7 griphus, mystery, perplex 8 disprove, separate 9 conundrum, criticize, perforate
riddler: 8 screener
ride: 4 dosa 5 drive, float, motor, tease 6 harass 7 hagride, journey, torment 8 ridicule 9 carrousel, cavalcade, excursion 12 merry-go-round
to hounds: 4 hunt
without power: 5 coast, glide
rideau: 5 mound, ridge
rident: 5 riant 7 smiling 8 grinning, laughing
rider: 6 clause, cowboy, jockey, knight 7 allonge 8 addition, bucaayro, buckaroo, cavalier, desultor, horseman 9 amendment, performer, straddler 10 equestrian, freebooter, highwayman, horsewoman 11 endorsement, mosstrooper 12 bronco-buster, equestrienne(fem.)
ridge: as, os; aas, rib, top 4 aret, asar, back, balk, bank, barb, bult, dene, dune, gold, kame, lira, loma, osar(pl.), rand, reef, ring, ruck, ruga, seam, spur, wale, wave, weal, welt 5 arete, arris, bargh, chine, costa, crest, eskar, esker, hause, oesar(pl.), rugae(pl.), serac, spine, stria, varix, wheal, whelk 6 costae(pl.), crista, rideau, striae(pl.) 7 annulet, costula, cristae(pl.), hogback, porcate, varices(pl.), wrinkle, yardang 8 costulae(pl.), headland, sastrugi, zastrugi 9 elevation, razorback
anatomical: 5 spine, stria
cloth: 4 wale
glacial: 5 esker
pert. to: 7 cardinal
shell: 5 varix 7 varices(pl.)
skin: 4 wale, welt

ridge oak: 9 blackjack
ridged and furrowed: 7 porcate
ridicule: guy, pan 4 gibe, jeer, mock, quiz, razz, twit 5 borak, chaff, irony, roast, scout, sneer, taunt 6 banter, deride, expose, satire 7 asteism, buffoon, lampoon, mockery, pillory, sarcasm 8 derision, raillery, satirize 9 burlesque
deity: 5 Momus
object of: 13 laughingstock
ridiculous: 5 droll 6 absurd 7 amusing 8 farcical 9 laughable, ludicrous 10 irrational, outrageous 12 preposterous
riding: 9 chevachie 10 equitation
costume: 5 habit
pants: 8 jodhpurs
shoe: 8 solleret
riding school: 6 manege
riding whip: 4 crop 5 quirt
ridotto: 6 resort 7 redoubt, retreat 8 festival 9 gathering 10 masquerade 11 abridgement, arrangement 13 entertainment
riem: 5 strap, strip, thong
Rienzi composer: 6 Wagner
rier: 4 cask
rife: 5 brief 7 current, replete 8 abundant, numerous 9 abounding, plentiful, prevalent 10 prevailing, widespread
riff: 6 riffle, ripple 7 midriff 9 diaphragm
Riff: 6 Berber
riffle: 4 plow, reef 5 rapid, shoal 6 rattle 7 shallow, shuffle 11 obstruction
riffraff: mob 4 raff, scum 5 trash 6 rabble, refuse 7 rubbish 9 sweepings
rifle: arm, gun, rob 4 tige 5 reeve, steal 6 furrow, groove, weapon 7 bundock, carbine, despoil, escopet, firearm, pillage, plunder, ransack 8 bandhook 9 chassepot, escopette
accessory: 6 ramrod
ball: 5 minie
instrument: 7 bayonet
kind of: 6 Garand, Mauser 7 Enfield 9 Remington 10 Winchester 11 Springfield
magazine: 6 Mauser
pin: 4 tige
rifleman: 5 jager, yager
rift: lag 4 flaw, rive 5 belch, break, chasm, cleft, crack, rapid, split 6 breach, cleave, divide 7 blemish, fissure, opening, shallow 8 division
rig: fig, fit, fix 4 fool, gear, hoax, wind 5 dress, equip, rifle, storm, trick 6 lateen, outfit, square, tackle 7 arrange, costume, derrick, ransack, swindle, turnout 8 accouter, accoutre, carriage, equipage 9 apparatus, equipment 10 manipulate 11 contraption
part of: 4 spar

riga: 6 balsam

Riga Gulf island: 5 Oesel

Riga native: 4 Lett 7 Latvian

rigadoon: 5 dance

rigescence: 8 numbness 9 stiffness

rigging part: 4 gear, spar 5 ropes

right: fit, gee, hak 4 fair, good, hakh, real, sane, soke, true 5 droit, sound 6 angary, dexter, equity, lawful, normal, patent, proper 7 correct, derecho, fitting, genuine, liberty, rectify, redress, upright 8 becoming, courtesy, easement, interest, straight, suitable, usufruct, virtuous 9 authority, equitable, faultless, franchise, privilege 11 appropriate, certificate, prerogative

comb. form: 6 dextro

exclusive: ex 7 patents 10 concession

law: 5 droit

of way: 8 easement

proprietary: 8 interest

royal: 7 regalia

right-angled: 10 orthogonal, rectangled 11 rectangular

right down: 4 very 8 complete, thorough 10 positively, thoroughly

right hand: 6 dextra 7 dextera

right-hand page: 5 recto

right-handed: 7 dextral 8 dextrous 9 dexterous

righteous: 4 good, holy, just 5 godly, moral, pious, zadoc, zadok 6 devout, worthy 7 perfect, sinless, upright 8 virtuous 9 blameless, equitable, guiltless

righteousness: 9 rectitude

rightful: due 4 fair, just, true 5 legal 6 honest, lawful, proper 7 fitting, upright 9 righteous 11 appropriate

rightist: 4 Tory 11 reactionary 12 conservative

rigid: set 4 firm, hard, taut 5 fixed, stark, stern, stiff, stony, tense 6 marbly, severe, strait, strict 7 austere 8 rigorous 9 immovable, stringent, unbending 10 inflexible, motionless, unyielding

rigmaree: 4 coin 6 trifle

rigmarole: 8 nonsense 10 balderdash

rignum: 9 horsemint

rigol: 4 ring 6 circle, furrow, groove 7 channel

Rigoletto: *composer:* 5 Verdi

role: 5 Gilda

rigor, rigour: 4 fury 7 cruelty 8 asperity, hardship, rigidity, severity, violence 9 austerity, harshness, rigidness, sharpness, stiffness 10 difficulty, exactitude, puritanism, strictness 13 inflexibility

rigorous: 5 angry, rigid, stern 6 severe, strait, strict, strict 7 correct, drastic, precise 8 accurate 9 inclement 10 inexorable, oppressive, relentless

rikk: 10 tambourine

rile: vex 4 roil 5 anger, annoy, upset 7 agitate, disturb 8 irritate 9 turbidity

rill: 5 brook, creek, crick, ditch 6 course, furrow, groove, runnel, trench 7 rillock, rivulet 8 brooklet 9 arroyuelo(Sp.), streamlet

rim: lip 4 bank, brim, edge, orle, ring, tire 5 basil, bezel, bezil, brink, somma, verge 6 border, flange, margin, shield 7 enclose, horizon 8 boundary 9 perimeter

horseshoe: web

pipe: 6 flange

rail: 6 flange

wheel: 4 tire 5 felly, 6 felloe

rima: 5 cleft 7 fissure 8 aperture 10 breadfruit

rimash: 9 hackberry

rimate: 8 fissured

rime: ice 4 hoar, poem, rent, rung, step 5 chink, crack, frost, rhyme, verse 6 freeze 7 fissure, versify 8 aperture 9 cranreuch(Sc.), hoarfrost

rimple: 4 fold 6 crease, ripple, rumple 7 wrinkle

rimption: lot 9 abundance

Rinaldo's steed: 6 Bayard 7 Bajardo

rind: 4 bark, husk, melt, peel, skin 5 crust, waste 6 cortex 7 clarify, epicarp, peeling 8 cortices(pl.)

rindle: 5 brook 6 runnel 7 rivulet

ring: bee, cut, rim, set 4 bail, band, cric, ding, dirl, echo, gyre, halo, hank, hoop, link, lute, peal, toll, tore 5 anlet, arena, bague, bezel, chime, clang, group, knell, longe, ridge, rigol 6 arenae, border, brough(Sc.), chaton, circle, circus, clique, collar, collet, corona, dindle, dingle, famble, gasket, girdle, terret, tingle, tinkle, toroid 7 annulet, annulus, circlet, coterie, curette, ferrule, grommet, resound, ringlet, tanbark, vibrate 8 bracelet, cincture, encircle, surround 9 archivolt, enclosure, encompass 10 racecourse 11 reverberate 14 tintinnabulate

carrier: 9 go-between

comb. form: 4 gyro

gem setting: 5 bezel 6 chaton

of chain: 4 link

of rope: 7 grommet

pert. to: 7 annular

stone: gem

to hold reins: 6 terret

to tighten joint: 6 washer

wedding: 4 band

ring finger: 5 third

ring ouzel: 6 thrush
ring plover: 5 sandy
ring-shaped: 7 annular 8 annulate 9 annulated
ring-tailed cat: 8 cacomixl 9 cacomixle 10 cacomistle
ring-worm: 5 tinea 7 serpigo 8 milleped 9 millepede
ringdove: 4 dove 6 cushat, pigeon 10 turtledove
ringed: 6 wedded 7 engaged, married 8 annulate, circular 9 annulated, decorated, encircled 10 surrounded
ringed worm: 7 annelid
ringent: 6 gaping
ringing: 4 clam 6 bright 7 orotund 8 resonant
ringle-eye: 7 walleye
ringleader: 10 instigator
ringlet: 4 curl, lock, ring 5 tress
rings: *interlocking:* 6 gimmal
    series: 4 coil
rink: man 4 hero, race, ring 9 encounter
rinner: 6 runner
rinse: 4 lave, sind(Sc.), wash 5 douse 6 douche, gargle, sluice 7 cleanse
rinthereout: 5 tramp 7 vagrant 8 vagabond
rio: 5 river 6 coffee, stream
riot: din 4 clem 5 brawl, feast, melee, revel 6 affray, bedlam, clamor, excess, pogrom(-Russ.), tumult, uproar 7 dispute, quarrel, revelry 8 carousal, debauche, disorder, outburst, sedition, uprising 9 commotion, confusion, luxuriate 10 donnybrook 11 dissolution, disturbance
riotous: 4 loud, wild 5 loose 6 wanton 10 boisterous, profligate 11 saturnalian 12 contumacious, unrestrained
rip: hag, rit 4 rend, rent, rive, tear 6 sunder 8 disunite, harridan, lacerate 9 debauchee 10 laceration
rip-roaring: 5 noisy 6 lively 8 exciting 9 hilarious 10 boisterous, uproarious
ripa: 4 bank 5 beach, shore 6 strand
ripe: fit, rob 4 aged, bank 5 adult, ready, rifle 6 addled, august, mature, mellow 7 plunder 8 complete, finished, seashore 9 developed, full-grown, perfected, riverbank 10 consummate, seasonable 11 intoxicated
    early: 8 rareripe
ripen: age 4 grow 6 mature, mellow 7 develop, improve, perfect, prepare
riposte, ripost: 5 reply 6 retort, return, thrust 8 repartee
ripper: 7 bobsled 9 bobsleigh
rippet: 4 romp 6 uproar 7 quarrel
ripping: 4 fine 8 splendid 9 admirable, excellent 10 remarkable

ripping iron: 8 ravehook
rippit: 5 fight
ripple: cut, lap 4 curl, fret, purl, riff, tear, wave 5 acker, graze 6 cockle, dimple, rimple 7 crinkle, scratch, wavelet, wrinkle 8 undulate
ripple grass: 7 ribwort
rise: 4 flow, grow, hulk, loom, rare, rear, soar, stem, well 5 arise, begin, climb, issue, mount, reach, rebel, stand, start, surge, swell, tower 6 amount, appear, ascend, ascent, aspire, assume, attain, derive, emerge, growth, mature, revolt, spring, thrive 7 adjourn, advance, elevate, emanate, prosper, succeed 8 eminence, flourish, increase, levitate 9 ascension, beginning, elevation, originate
    again: 7 resurge 9 resurrect
    and fall: 4 tide 5 heave 6 welter
riser: 4 pipe, step
risible: 5 funny 7 amusing 9 laughable, ludicrous
rising: 5 arist 6 orient, ortive 7 montant, nearing 8 gradient, uprising 9 ascendant, ascendent, ascension 11 approaching 12 extumescence, insurrection
risk: 4 dare, gage, wage 5 peril, stake 6 chance, danger, expose, gamble, hazard, injury, plight, plunge 7 imperil, venture 8 exposure, jeopardy 9 adventure 12 disadvantage
risky: 7 parlous
risley: 7 acrobat
risp: bar, rub 4 file, rasp, stem, tirl, wisp 5 grass, stalk 7 bulrush, scratch
risper: 11 caterpillar
risque: 4 racy 5 risky 6 daring 9 audacious, hazardous 10 suggestive
rissle: 4 pole 5 staff, stick
rist: 4 mark 5 wound 6 ascent 7 engrave, scratch 8 increase 12 insurrection, resurrection
risus: 5 laugh 8 laughter
rit: cut, rip 4 slit, tear 5 split 6 pierce 7 scratch
ritardando: 9 retarding 11 rallentando
rite: 4 cult, form, orgy 5 sacra 6 augury, exequy, novena, prayer, ritual 7 liturgy, obsequy 8 accolade, accolate, ceremony 9 ordinance, procedure, sacrament, solemnity 10 ceremonial, initiation, observance
Ritter: 6 knight
ritual: 4 cult, form, rite 7 liturgy, obsequy 8 ceremony 9 obsequies(pl.) 10 ceremonial
ritus: 5 usage 6 custom
ritzy: 6 modish 7 elegant 9 expensive, luxurious 11 fashionable
rivage: 4 bank, duty 5 coast, shore
rival: vie 4 even, peer 5 equal, match 7 compete, emulate, feuding 8 corrival, emula-

tor, opponent **9** adversary, competing **10** antagonist, competitor, contending **11** comparative

rivalry: 11 competition

rive: rip, rob **4** bank, plow, pull, rend, rent, rift, tear **5** break, cleft, shore, split, steal **6** arrive, cleave, pierce, sunder, thieve, thrust **7** dispart **8** lacerate **9** disembark

rivel: 6 shrink **7** shrivel, wrinkle

river: ea; ree, ria(Sp.), rio(Sp.), run **4** wadi, wady **5** bayou, waddy **6** stream **7** channel **8** effluent **9** abundance **11** watercourse

arm: **7** estuary **9** tributary

bank: **4** rand, ripa **5** levee

channel: bed **6** alveus

comb. form: **6** potamo

current: **4** eddy **6** rapids

dam: **4** weir

gauge: **9** nilometer

god: **7** Alpheus, Inachus **8** Achelous

horse: **5** hippo

ice: **7** glacier

inlet: **5** bayou **6** slough

island: ait **4** holm

Kubla Khan's: **4** Alph

land: **5** carse(Sc.), flats

living in: **9** amphibian, rheophile

log run: **9** sluiceway

mouth: **4** beal(Sc.), lade **5** delta **7** estuary

mythical: **4** Styx

nymph: **4** nais **5** naiad

obstruction: **4** snag **5** gorce

of oblivion: **5** Lethe

passage: **4** ford **7** estuary

pert. to: **5** amnic **6** rivery **7** fluvial, potamic **8** riverine **9** fluminose, fluminous

sacred: **5** Ganga **6** Ganges

siren: **7** Lorelei

small: **5** brook, creek, tchai **6** stream **7** rivulet **8** riverlet **9** streamlet

thief: **6** ackman

underworld: **4** Styx **5** Lethe **7** Acheron

winding part: ess

river dog: 10 hellbender

river duck: 4 teal

river horse: 5 hippo **12** hippopotamus

river mussel: 4 unio

River of Forgetfulness: 5 Lethe

River of Hate: 4 Styx

River of Sorrows: 7 Acheron

riverbank: 4 ripa, ripe **5** levee

riverbed: 4 wadi, wady **5** waddy

riverboat: ark **5** barge **7** rowboat, towboat **8** flatboat

riverside: 4 bank **5** shore

riverweed family: 13 podostemaceae

rivet: fix **4** bolt, brad **6** clinch, fasten **8** fastener

riviere: 8 necklace

rivose: 5 brook **6** gutter **7** channel

rivulet: 4 burn, rill **5** bache, bayou, bourn, brook, creek **6** bourne, rindle(Sc.), runlet, runnel, stream **7** channel **9** streamlet

rix: 4 reed, rush

rixatrix: 5 scold **6** virago

rixy: 4 tern

rizzar: dry **4** cure **6** drying **7** currant

rizzom: ear **5** stalk, straw **8** particle

roach: bug, cut **4** fish, hill, rock, roll, soil, spot **6** braise **7** sunfish **9** cockroach

road: way **4** fare, gang, iter, path, raid, ride **5** agger, bargh, going, itero(pl.), route **6** avenue, camino, career, causey, chemin, course, street **7** calzada(Sp.), estrada, gangway, highway, itinera(pl.), journey, passage, railway **8** beallach, causeway, chaussee(F.), cul-de-sac, pavement, railroad **9** direction, incursion, roadstead **10** expedition

bend: **7** hairpin

character: **4** hobo **5** tramp **10** hitchhiker

country: **4** lane

edge: **4** berm **8** shoulder

machine: **4** harl **5** paver **6** grader **9** bulldozer

menace: **7** speeder

military: **5** agger

surface: tar **6** bricks, gravel, stones **7** macadam **8** concrete, pavement

road book: map **9** gazetteer, itinerary

road goose: 5 brant

road runner: 6 cuckoo **7** paisano(Sp.)

roadhouse: inn **6** tavern

roadman: 7 drummer, peddler **8** salesman **9** canvasser

roadster: 5 horse **7** bicycle **8** runabout

roadtrack: 9 roadstead

roadweed: 8 plantain

roam: err, gad **4** roil, rove **5** prowl, range, stray **6** bangle, ramble, stroll, travel, wander **7** meander **8** straggle **9** gallivant

roamer: 5 gipsy, gypsy, nomad **8** fugitive **12** peregrinator

roan: bay **5** horse **9** sheepskin

Roanoke bell: 7 cowslip

roar: cry, din **4** beal, bell, bere, boom, bray, clap, hurl, rote, rout, yell **5** blart, brool, fream, laugh **6** bellow, buller, outcry, steven **7** thunder **8** shouting

roaring: 4 loud **5** aroar, brisk, noisy **7** riotous **10** boisterous, disorderly, stentorian

roaring game: 7 curling

roaring Meg: 6 cannon

roast: fry **4** bake, cook, razz, roti(F.) **5** asado(Sp.), brede, grill, parch **6** assate, banter **7** torrefy, torrify **8** ridicule **9** criticize

meat on stick: **5** cabob, kabob

prepare: **5** truss

roasting stick: 4 spit 6 skewer

rob: cop 4 fake, flap, loot, pelf, take 5 bribe, filch, harry, pilch, pinch, pluck, raven, reave, rifle, spoil, steal, strip, touch 6 burgle, pilfer, pirate, ravish, shrive, snatch, snitch, thieve 7 bereave, defraud, deprive, despoil, pillage, plunder 10 plagiarize

Rob Roy: 5 canoe

robber: 4 goul, yegg 5 ghoul 6 arrant, bandit, dacoit, pirate 7 brigand, corsair, footpad, ladrone, yeggman 8 marauder 9 bandolero, buccaneer, privateer 10 depredator, highwayman

robe (see also **dress, gown**): aba 4 skin, vest, wrap 5 array, camis, camus, cloak, cover, cymar, simar, talar, tunic 6 caftan, chimer, clothe, dolman, invest, kimono, mantle, revest 7 chimere, costume, garment, vesture 8 clothing, covering, vestment 10 sticharion

robin: 4 lout, tody 6 oriole, thrush 7 bumpkin, chewink 8 trimming 10 cuckoopint, toxalbumin

Robin Goodfellow: 4 Puck 5 fairy 6 sprite 9 hobgoblin

Robin Hood: *chaplain:* 9 Friar Tuck
follower: 4 John 9 Friar Tuck
sweetheart: 6 Marian

robin sandpiper: 9 dowitcher

robinet: 6 cannon 9 chaffinch

Robinson Crusoe: *author:* 5 Defoe
companion: 6 Friday

roborant: 5 tonic 13 strengthening

roborate: 6 ratify 10 strengthen 11 corroborate

roborean: 5 oaken, stout 6 strong

robot: 5 golem 7 android 9 androides, automaton
drama about: RUR

robust: 4 hale, hard, iron, rude 5 hardy, lusty, rough, sound, stout, wally 6 brawny, coarse, hearty, rugged, sinewy, strong, sturdy 7 healthy 8 athletic, muscular, vigorous 10 boisterous

roc: 4 bird 6 simurg 7 simurgh, soldier

rocca: 4 hold, keep 6 donjon 8 fortress

rochet: 5 cloak, frock 7 camisia, garment, gurnard 8 vestment

rock: dag, ore, tor 4 clay, crag, lull, peak, reef, reel, roll, scar, shog, spar, sway, trap, tufa, tuff, wash 5 agate, brack, candy, chert, cliff, earth, flint, geest, lytta, prase, scree, shake, shale, shaul, slate, stane(Sc.), stone, wacke 6 aplite, basalt, dacite, egeran, gneiss, gravel, issite, oolite, pebble, refuge, rognon, schist, silica, sinter, teeter, totter 7 adinole, akerite, alunite, defense, diamond, gondite, granite, griesen, support, tremble, vibrate 8 andesite, banakite, dolomite, laterite, obsidian,

porphyry, psephite, rhyolite 9 epidosite, flagstone, oscillate, phanerite 10 greenstone, promontory 11 petrography
boring tool: 6 trepan
cavity: vug 4 vugg 5 druse, geode
clay: 8 ganister
comb. form: 5 petro
debris: 5 talus 8 detritus
decomposed: 6 gossan
discarded: 5 attle
finely broken: 4 sand
fissile: 5 shale
flintlike: 5 chert 6 quartz
fold: 8 syncline 9 anticline
fragments: see *debris* above
glacier deposit: 7 moraine
glacier-transported: 7 erratic
igneous: 4 boss, sial, sima, trap, tufa 5 trass 6 basalt, domite, latite 7 diabase, diorite, felsite, ijolite, peridot 8 extaxite, ijussite, porphyry 11 agglomerate
laminated: 4 mica 5 shale, slate
liquid: aa 4 lava
mythical: 6 Scylla
nodule: 5 geode
pert. to: 6 petric 7 petrean
point: 4 crag, peak
science: 9 petrology
strata: see *fold* above
suffix: ite, yte
volcanic: 4 lava, tufa, tuff

rock badger: 4 cony

rock bass: 6 red-eye

rock bottom: 6 lowest 8 cheapest

rock dove: 9 guillemot 10 rockpigeon

rock eel: 6 gunnel

rock falcon: 6 merlin

rock geranium: 8 alumroot

rock goat: 4 ibex

rock grouse: 9 ptarmigan

rock hind: 7 grouper

rock hopper: 7 penquin

rock kangaroo: 7 wallaby

rock oak: 8 chestnut 10 California, chinquapin

rock oil: 9 petroleum

rock plant: 4 moss 6 lichen

rock rabbit: 5 hyrax

rock snake: 5 krait 6 phthon

rock starling: 5 ouzel

rock tar: 9 petroleum

rock tripe: 6 lichen

rock wren: 4 bird

rockaway: 8 carriage

rockbell: 9 columbine

rockbird: 5 murre 9 sandpiper

rocker: 5 chair, skate 6 cradle

rocket: 4 weld, wold 5 slate, woald, would 9 satellite 11 firecracker

end of combustion: 7 burnout
landing: 7 reentry 10 splashdown
launcher: 7 bazooka
launching: 4 shot 8 blastoff
rockfish: 4 bass, rena 5 perch 7 grouper 9 killifish 10 priestfish
rockling: 4 fish, gade
rockrose: 6 cistus
rocky: 4 hard, weak 5 dizzy, shaky, stony 6 cliffy 7 petrean 8 obdurate, unsteady 9 unfeeling
Rocky Mountain: *goat:* 8 antelope
park: 5 Estes
peak: 5 Logan, Pikes
range: 5 Teton 7 Wasatch
sheep: 7 bighorn
wind: 7 chinook
rococo: 4 arty 9 fantastic
rod: bar, gad, guy, rab, rib 4 axle, bolt, came, cane, crop, goad, I-bar, lath, pole, prod, race, scob, spit, wand, wire 5 arrow, baton, board, lytta, osier, perch, power, scion, spoke, staff, stick, stock, strip, tribe 6 baculi(pl.), batten, broach, carbon, etalon, eyebar, ferule, needle, pistol, piston, pontil, raddle, skewer, switch, toggle 7 baculus, caliper, crowbar, distaff, measure, scepter, sceptre, spindle, stemmer, support, tringle, tyranny 8 arrester, offshoot, revolver 9 authority 10 oppression 12 chastisement
bundle: 6 fasces
divination by: 7 dowsing 11 rhabdomancy
movable: 6 piston
square: 5 perch
rod-like: 6 rhabdo 7 virgate
rodd: 8 crossbow
rode goose: 5 brant
rodent: jap, rat 4 cavy, cony, cypu, degu, hare, mole, paca, pica, pika, utia, vole 5 aguti, hutia, jutia, lerot, mouse, ratel, zokor 6 agouti, agouty, beaver, biting, cururo, gerbil, gopher, gundie, jerboa, marmot, murine, rabbit, weasel 7 chincha, hamster, leveret, muskrat 8 capibara, capybara, dormouse, gerbille, leporide, sewellel, squirrel, viscacha, vizcacha 9 porcupine 10 chinchilla
aquatic: 6 beaver 7 muskrat
genus: mus
jumping: 6 jerboa
pert. to: 8 rosorial
rodeo: 7 roundup 9 enclosure 10 exhibition
rodge: 7 gadwall
rodman: 4 thug 10 highwayman
rodney: 5 idler 7 shirker 8 vagabond
rodomontade: 4 brag, rant 5 boast, empty 7 bluster, bombast 8 boastful, boasting, braggart

rodster: 6 angler 9 fisherman
roe: ra; ova, pea 4 deer, eggs, hart, hind 5 coral, spawn 6 caviar 7 caviare
roebuck: 4 girl 9 chevreuil
Roentgen's discovery: 4 X-ray
roestone: 6 oolite
rog: 4 pull, stir 5 shake 6 jumble
rogan: 4 bowl 10 receptacle
rogation: law 6 decree, litany, prayer 7 inquiry, request 8 petition 12 supplication
rogue: boy, gue, imp, wag 4 hemp, kite 5 catso, cheat, crank, decry, gipsy, gypsy, hempy, knave, scamp, shark, tramp 6 beggar, canter, coquin, harlot, pirate, rascal, wander 7 corsair, erratic, hellion, sharper, vagrant, villain, waggish 8 picaroon, swindler, vagabond 9 scoundrel, trickster 10 frolicsome, stigmatize 11 rapscallion
pert. to: 10 picaresque
roguery: 5 fraud 8 mischief, trickery 15 mischievousness
roguish: sly 4 arch 5 pawky 6 wanton 7 playful, puckish 8 espiegle, sportive 9 dishonest, fun-loving 12 unscrupulous
roid: 5 rough 6 severe 7 riotous, roguish 10 frolicsome 12 unmanageable
roil vex 4 foul, roam, romp, rust, stir 5 anger, annoy, muddy, rouse 6 cloudy, fidget, ruffle, wander 7 blunder, disturb 8 irritate 9 displease, unsettled
roily: 6 turbid
roister: 4 brag, rude 5 bully, revel, spree 7 bluster, boorish, reveler, swagger, violent 9 gilravage
roistering: 6 hoiden, hoyden
rojo: 6 Indian 7 redskin
roke: fog 4 mist, stir 5 smoke, steam, vapor 8 moisture
roker: ray 8 rockling 9 thornback
roky: 4 damp 5 foggy, misty, smoky 6 hoarse
Roland: *beloved:* 4 Aude
emperor: 11 Charlemagne
enemy: 4 Gano 7 Ganelon
friend: 6 Oliver
horn: 7 Olivant
horse: 10 Veillantif
sword: 8 Durendal
role: bit 4 cast, duty, part 6 office 8 business, function 9 character 13 impersonation 16 characterization
leading: 4 star
roll: bun, gad, rob 4 bolt, coil, file, flow, furl, list, pell, roam, rota, seel, sway, turn, wind, wrap 5 cadre, frisk, lurch, shift, surge, swing, trill, troll 6 bundle, enroll, enwrap, goggle, grovel, roster, rotate, scroll, spiral, tumble, wallow, wander, welter, whelve, wintle 7 biscuit bri-

oche, revolve, rissole, stagger, swagger, trundle 8 cylinder, flounder, register, undulate
of hair: bun 7 chignon
roll back: 5 lower 6 reduce 7 repulse
roll in: 4 flow 6 arrive, wallow, welter
roll up: 4 furl 5 amass 6 arrive, gather 10 accumulate
roller: 4 band, wave 5 finer, inker, swath 6 canary, caster, fascia, fillet, pigeon, platen, rowlet, sponge 7 bandage, breaker, presser, sirgang, tumbler 8 cylinder 9 surcingle
rolleyway: 4 road 5 track 7 gangway, tramway
rollick: 4 romp 5 sport 6 frolic
rollicking: gay 6 jovial, lively 8 careless 9 hilarious
rolling stock: 4 cars 7 coaches, engines 8 cabooses, Pullmans, sleepers 11 locomotives
rolling weed: 10 tumbleweed
rollix: 7 rollick
rolltop: 4 desk
roly-poly: 5 dumpy, pudgy, round 6 portly, rotund 7 pudding
rom: 4 buzz 5 gipsy, gypsy
romaine: cos 5 plant 7 lettuce
romal: 5 thong
Roman: 5 brave, Latin 6 frugal, honest, simple 7 Italian
Roman Catholic: *cassock:* 7 soutane, zimarra
 church: 7 lateran
 ecclesiastic: 7 Rosmini
 priest: 4 abbe(F.) 6 father 8 sacerdos 9 monsignor
 skullcap: 9 zucchetto
 society: 7 Jesuits
romance: woo 4 gest, tale 5 court, dream, fable, fancy, feign, geste, novel, story 6 affair 7 chimera, fantasy, fiction, romanza 9 falsehood, sentiment 10 exaggerate 12 exaggeration
Romance language: 6 French 7 Catalan, Italian, Spanish 8 Rumanian 9 Provencal 10 Portuguese
Romanese: 7 gypsies 9 Walachian
romantic: 6 poetic, unreal 8 quixotic 9 imaginary, visionary 10 idealistic 11 extravagant
Romany, Rommany: 5 gipsy, gypsy
 tongue: 7 Romanes
romanza: 7 fiction, romance
Rome (see also **Latin**): 4 Roma
 abode of gods: 7 Olympus
 adviser to king: 6 Egeria
 amphitheater: 9 colosseum
 apostle: 4 Neri, Paul

army unit: 6 cohort
army wing: ala
assembly: 5 forum 6 senate 7 comitia
attendant: 7 aliptes 8 aleiptes
augur: 6 auspex
author(see also *biographer, historian, poet,* below): 5 Pliny, Varro
authority symbol: 6 fasces
basilica: 7 lateran
barracks: 6 canaba
battle array: 5 acies
biographer: 5 Nepos 9 Suetonius
boy: 4 puer 8 camillus
brothers: 5 Remus 7 Romulus
building: 5 aedes
Caesar's title: 9 imperator
captain: 9 centurion
carriage: 5 essed
chief god: 4 Jove 7 Jupiter
citadel: arx
clans: 4 gens
cloak: 4 toga
coin: as; aes 5 asses(pl.), aurei(pl.), semis 6 aureus, dinder, solidu, triens 7 denarii(pl.), siliqua 8 decussis, denarius, sesterce, sesteria(pl.) 9 sesterium 10 sestertius, victoriate 11 victoriatus
comedy: 5 exode
comedy writer: 6 Cicero 7 Plautus, Terence
concert hall: 5 odeum
conqueror: 6 Alaric
conspirator: 8 Catiline
contract: 5 nexum
couch: 9 accubitum
court: 5 atria(pl.) 6 atrium
custodian: 10 neocorates
date: 4 Ides
district: 5 Pagus 7 Pontine 8 Pomptine
diviner: 5 augur 6 auspex
division: 5 curia
earthwork: 5 agger
emperor: 4 Nero, Otho, Otto 5 Galba, Nerva, Titus 6 Caesar, Julian, Trajan 7 Hadrian 8 Augustus, Claudius, Domitian, Tiberius 9 Vespasian 10 Elagabalus 11 Constantine
empress: 7 Eudocia
encampment: 7 castrum
entrance hall: 5 atria(pl.) 6 atrium
family: 7 familia
farmer: 7 colonus 8 agricola
Fate: 4 Nona 5 Morta, Parca 6 Decuma, Parcae(pl.)
fighter: 9 gladiator
fortress: 7 castrum
founder: 5 Remus 7 Romulus
galley: 6 bireme 7 trireme
garment: 4 toga 5 palla, sagum, stola, stole, togae(pl.), tunic

general: 5 Sulla, Titus 6 Antony, Marius, Scipio 8 Agricola

god: Dis, Lar, Sol 4 Amor, Jove, Mars 5 Comus, Cupid, Fauns, Janus, Lares, manes, Orcus, Pluto 6 Faunus, Vulcan 7 Jupiter, lemures, Neptune, penates, Phoebus, Vatican 8 Dispater, Morpheus, Quirinus 11 Aesculapius

god of dead: 5 Orcus

god of death: 4 Mors

god of fire: 6 Vulcan

god of love: 4 Amor

god of mirth: 5 Comus

god of sea: 7 Neptune

god of sleep: 8 Morpheus

god of sun: Sol

god of underworld: Dis 5 Pluto

god of war: 4 Mars

god of wind: 5 Eurus 6 Boreas

god of wine: 7 Bacchus

goddess: dea(L.), Lua, Nox, Ops, Pax 4 Caca, Juno, Luna, Maia, Paca 5 Ceres, Diana, Epona, Terra, Venus, Vesta 6 Aestas, Annona, Aurora, Lucina, Rumina, Tellus, Vacuna 7 Bellona, Fortuna, Minerva 8 Libitina 9 Abudantia, Discordia, Felicitas

goddess of agriculture: Ops 5 Ceres

goddess of beauty: 5 Venus

goddess of flowers: 5 Flora

goddess of hearth: 5 Vesta

goddess of hope: 4 Spes

goddess of hunting: 5 Diana

goddess of love: 5 Venus

goddess of marriage: 4 Juno

goddess of moon: 4 Luna

goddess of night: Nox

goddess of peace: Pax

goddess of plenty: Ops

goddess of underworld: 10 Proserpina

goddess of vegetation: 5 Ceres

goddess of war: 7 Bellona, Minerva

goddess of wisdom: 7 Minerva

greeting: ave

guard: 6 lictor

hall: 5 atria(pl.) 6 atrium

hat: 7 petasos, petasus

helmet: 5 galea 6 galeae(pl.)

highway: via 4 iter 5 itero(pl.) 6 Appian, 7 itinera(pl.)

holiday: 4 ides 5 feria 6 feriae(pl.)

hill: 7 Caelian, Viminal 8 Aventine, Palatine, Quirinal 9 Esquiline 10 Capitoline

historian: 4 Livy 5 Nepos

javelin: 4 pile 5 aclys, pilum

judge: 5 edile 6 aedile

jurist: 5 Gaius

king: 7 Romulus, Servius, Tullius 12 Ancus Martius 13 Numa Pompilius 15 Tullus Hostilius 18 Tarquinius Superbus

lake: 4 Nemi

language: 5 Latin

law: fas, lex 4 cern

leader: dux

magistrate: 5 edile 6 aedile, censor, pretor 7 praetor, tribune

marble: 7 cipolin

measure: pes, urn 4 mile, pace, urna 5 actus, clima, cubit, juger 6 culeus, dolium, gradus, hemina, modius, palmus, passus, saltus, versus 7 amphora, congius, cyathus, digitus, stadion, stadium 8 centuria, hereduim, quadrant 9 decempeda, millarium, sextarius 10 acetabulum, quartarius

measure of weight: as; bes 4 pood 5 asses(pl.), libra, uncia 6 duella 7 dodrans, sextula, solidus 8 sicilium 9 scrupulus, scrupulum

military formation: ala 6 alares(pl.) 7 phalanx

military machine: 7 terebra

military unit: 6 cohort, legion 7 maniple

military vessel: 6 bireme 7 trireme

naturalist: 5 Pliny

nymph: 6 Egeria

official: 5 augur, edile 6 aedile, lictor 7 prefect, tribune 8 irenarch 9 nestorian

ox: 4 urus

palace: 5 chigi 7 lateran

palace troops: 9 palatines

peace: 5 Irene

people: 5 Laeti 7 Sabines 8 plebians 10 patricians

pert. to: 9 classical

philosopher: 4 Cato 6 Seneca

physician: 9 archiater 11 Aesculapius

pillager: 6 Alaric

pin: 4 acus

poet: 4 Ovid 5 Cinna, Lucan 6 Horace, Vergil, Virgil 7 Juvenal, Terence 8 Catullus, Tibullus 10 Propertius

port: 5 Ostia

praenomen: 5 Aulus, Caius, Gaius, Titus 6 Appius 7 Quintus, Spurius 8 Tiberius

priest: 5 epulo 6 flamen 7 luperci

priestess: 6 vestal

procurator: 5 Felix 6 Pilate

province: 5 Dacia 7 Cilicia

queen of goddesses: 4 Juno

regulator: 6 censor

religious law: fas

river: Po 5 Tiber

road: 4 iter

room: ala 5 atria(pl.) 6 atrium 7 tablina(pl.) 8 fumarium, tablinum

rural deity: 6 Faunus

saint: 4 Neri

section: 5 Ostia

senate division: **5** curia
senate emblem: **9** laticlave
senate house: **5** curia
shield: scuta(pl.) **6** ancile, scutum **7** ancilia(pl.), clypeus
spirits of dead: **5** manes
standard: **7** labarum, vexilla(pl.) **8** vexillum
standard-bearer: **9** vexillary
statesman: **4** Cato **5** Pliny **6** Caesar, Cicero, Seneca **7** Agrippa **8** Maecenas
tax gatherer: **8** publican
temple: **4** naos **5** cella **8** pantheon
treasurer: **8** quaestor
veteran: **7** emeriti(pl.) **8** emeritus
weight: see *measure of weight* above
writing tablet: **7** diptych
Romeo: *beloved:* **6** Juliet
enemy: **6** Tybalt
father: **8** Montague
friend: **8** Mercutio
rival: **5** Paris
rommack: **4** play, romp **7** rummage
romp: **4** hoit, play, roil **6** frolic, hoiden, hoyden **7** carouse, courant, gammock **8** carousal, courante
Romulus: *brother:* **5** Remus
father: **4** Mars
rond: **4** rand **5** shred **6** border
rondure: **5** round **6** circle, sphere **9** plumpness, roundness
rone: **5** brake **7** thicket **9** brushwood
rood: **5** cross **7** measure **8** crucifix
roodebok: **6** impala
roof: **5** cover **7** palate, shelter **8** covering
border: **4** eave
comb. form: **5** stego
style: hip **4** dome, flat, nave, sark **5** gable, spire **6** cupola **7** cricket, gambrel, mansard **9** penthouse, pyramidal **10** jerkinhead
timber: **6** after⟩ rafter
window: **6** dormer
roofing material: tar, tin **4** tile **5** paper, slate, straw, terne **6** copper, gravel, shakes, thatch **7** pantile **8** shingles
rook: **4** bird, crow **5** cheat, raven, steal **6** castle **7** defraud, sharper, swindle **8** swindler
rookery: **8** building
rookie, rooky: **4** tyro **6** novice **7** recruit, trainee **8** beginner
rooky: **4** roky **5** foggy **6** rookie, untidy **8** rascally **9** swindling **10** disheveled
room: ala, ben, den **4** aula, cell, hall, loge, sala(Sp.), seat **5** atria(pl.), aulae(pl.), cubby, divan, kiosk, lodge, place, salle(F.), salon, scope, space **6** atrium, casino, leeway, reside, saloon, scouth **7** boudoir, cabi-

net, chamber, cubicle, expanse, gallery, lodging, rotunda, theater **9** apartment, garderobe **10** auditorium
conversation: **6** exedra **7** exedrae(pl.) **11** drawing room
eating: **4** nook **7** cenacle, kitchen **8** cenacula(pl.) **9** cenaculum, refectory
private: **7** boudoir
provision: **4** ewry **5** ewery **6** larder **7** pantry **8** cupboard
reading: den **5** study **7** library
sleeping: **5** lodge **6** dormer **7** barrack, bedroom **8** roomette **9** dormitory
storage: **4** loft, shed **5** attic **6** cellar **9** storeroom
roomer: **5** guest **6** lodger, tenant **7** boarder
rooms: **4** flat **5** suite **9** apartment
roomy: **5** ample, broad, spacy **8** spacious **9** capacious **10** commodious
roorback, roorbach: lie **4** hoax **6** canard **7** fiction **9** falsehood
roose: **5** boast, extol, vaunt **6** praise
Roosevelt, F. D.: *dog:* **4** Fala
mother: **4** Sara
roost: sit **4** nest, pole, rest **5** abode, perch, sleep **6** alight, garret **7** lodging, support
rooster: **4** cock **5** gallo(Sp.) **11** chanticleer
root: dig **4** base, bulb, core, grub, moot, rout, stem **5** basis, cheer, grout, plant, radix, shout, tuber **6** bottom, etymon, ground, origin, settle **7** radical, radices(pl.), rootlet, support **9** beginning, establish **10** foundation
dyeing: **6** madder
edible: oca, roi, rue, uva, yam **4** beet, eddo, taro **5** orris, tania **6** carrot, ginger, orrice, radish, turnip **7** parsnip **8** rutabaga **9** sassafras
fragrant: **5** orris
outer layer: **7** exoderm
pert. to: **7** radical
principal: **7** taproot
pungent: **11** crinkleroot
starch: **4** arum
root out: **4** stub **6** evulse **9** eradicate, extirpate **10** deracinate
rooted: **10** inveterate
rooter: fan **10** enthusiast
rootlet: **7** radicle, rhizoid
rootstock: **6** stolon
rope: gad, guy, tie, tow **4** bind, cord, hemp, line, stay **5** cable, longe, riata, sheet, widdy **6** binder, fasten, halter, hawser **7** aweband, binding, bobstay, bollard, cordage, halyard, marline, painter **8** inveigle, prolonge
animal's: **5** leash **6** halter, tether
fiber: **4** coir, flax, jute **5** istle, sisal **6** cotton, Manila

holder: 6 becket

loop: 5 bight, noose 6 becket, parral, parrel

restraining: 6 tether

ship's: tye 4 colt, rode, stay, vang 5 sheet 6 hawser, inhaul, parral, parrel, ratlin, shroud 7 halyard, lanyard, painter, ratline

throwing: 5 lasso, reata, riata 6 lariat

ropedancer: 7 acrobat 9 funambulo 11 funambulist

roper: 6 cowboy, packer

ropery: 6 banter 7 roguery

roque: 7 croquet

roric: 4 dewy, rory 5 roral 6 roscid

rosaceous: 4 rosy 5 rosal 8 blushing

rosary: 4 bede 5 beads 7 chaplet, garland 8 beadroll

rose (see also **rise**): ris 5 delta, flush 6 flower, nozzle 7 rambler, rosette 9 hellebore

family: 8 rosaceae

kind of: dog 4 moss, musk

oil: 4 atar, otto 5 attar, ottar

part: 5 petal

Rose City: 8 Pasadena, Portland

rose of Sharon: 6 althea

rose parakeet: 7 rosella

rose pogonia: 10 snakemouth

rosebay: 8 oleander

rosemary: 9 rosmarine

rosette: 7 cockade 8 ornament

rosilla: 10 sneezeweed

rosin: See **resin**

Rosinante: nag 4 jade, plug 5 horse, steed

rosiness: 5 blush, flush

ross: 4 bark, peel 5 waste 8 exterior

roster: 4 list, roll, rota 5 slate

rostrum: 4 beak, dais 5 snout, stage 6 pulpit 7 lectern, tribune 8 platform 9 proboscis

rosy: red 4 pink 5 ruddy 6 bright, florid 7 auroral, flushed, roseate 8 blooming, blushing, cheerful, rubicund 9 favorable, promising, rosaceous 10 favourable, optimistic

rot: ret 4 bosh, dote, doze, joke 5 chaff, decay, spoil, tease, trash 6 banter, fester, perish 7 corrupt, putrefy, rubbish, twaddle 8 nonsense 9 decompose, poppycock 10 degenerate 13 decomposition

rot grass: 9 flukewort 10 butterwort

rota: 4 list, roll 5 court, round 6 course, roster 8 register

rotate: 4 pass, roll, spin, turn 5 twirl, wheel, whirl 6 gyrate 7 perform, revolve, trundle 8 rotiform 9 alternate

rotation: 4 eddy 6 torque, vortex 9 pirouette

part: cam 4 axle 5 rotor, wheel

rote: 4 list 5 learn 6 course, custom, memory, repeat, system 7 routine 8 practice 9 automatic, condition 10 memorizing, repetition

rotiform: 6 rotate

rotor: 7 spinner 8 impeller

rotten: bad 4 evil, foul 5 fetid, nasty 6 putrid 7 carrion, corrupt, decayed, spoiled, tainted, unsound 8 depraved, unstable 9 offensive, putrefied 10 abominable, decomposed, putrescent, undermined 12 disagreeable 13 disintegrated 14 unsatisfactory

comb. form: 4 sapr 5 sapro

rotter: cad 7 shirker, slacker 10 blackguard

rotula: 6 troche 7 kneepan, lozenge, patella

rotund: 5 obese, plump, round, stout 6 chubby, portly 7 rounded 8 rolypoly, sonorous 9 spherical

roturier: 7 freeman 8 commoner

roue: rip 4 rake 9 debauchee, libertine

rouge: red 5 blush, color, flush, paint, score 6 redden, ruddle 8 cosmetic

rough: 4 hard, rude 5 acrid, brute, crude, hairy, harsh, husky, lumpy, raggy, rowdy, seamy, stern, surly, uncut 6 abrupt, broken, choppy, coarse, crabby, craggy, hoarse, jagged, rugged, severe, shaggy, uneven 7 austere, boorish, bristly, brusque, grating, hirsute, inexact, jarring, raucous, ruffian, ruffled, uncivil 8 churlish, clownish, gangster, impolite, obdurate, unplaned 9 imperfect, inclement, turbulent, unrefined 10 boisterous, discordant, incomplete, tumultuous, unpleasant, unpolished 11 approximate, tempestuous

roughen: 4 chap, fret, shag 5 feaze 7 engrail 10 exasperate

roughneck: 4 boor 5 rowdy, tough 7 sweater

roughness: 7 crudity 8 acrimony, asperity

rouky: 4 roky 5 foggy, misty

roulade: run 8 arpeggio, division, flourish

roulette: 10 epicycloid 11 epitrochoid 12 hypotrochoid

bet: bas 4 noir 5 carre, rouge 6 milieu 7 dernier, encarre, enplein

rounceval: 5 giant, large 6 virago 9 termagant

round: 4 beat, bout, full, rung 5 group, large, orbed, plump 6 circle, curved, period, rotund 7 bulbous, circuit, liberal 8 circular, complete, globular, rolypoly 9 spherical 11 cylindrical

round clam: 6 quahog

round dance: hay, ray 5 polka, waltz 7 roundel 9 roundelay, schottish 11 schottische

round robin: 6 letter 7 contest 8 document, petition 9 cigarfish 10 tournament

Round Table knight: Kay 6 Gawain 7 Caradoc, Cradock, Gaheris, Galahad 8 Lancelot, Tristram 9 Percivale

roundabout: 5 about, dance 6 detour 7 devious 8 circular, indirect, tortuous 10 circuitous, farfetched 13 approximately 14 circumlocution, circumlocutory

rounded: 4 oval 5 bombe, ovate 6 convex, rotund 7 arrondi, bunting, gibbous 8 circular 10 labialized

roundel: 4 guze

rounder: 4 roue 5 sport 8 criminal, drunkard, preacher 11 spendthrift

roundhead: 5 Swede 7 Puritan

roundup: 5 rodeo 9 gathering

roundworm: 4 nema 7 ascaris

roup: 4 sale 6 clamor 7 auction 8 shouting

rouse: daw, hie 4 call, move, stir, wake, whet 5 alarm, amove, awake, raise, rally, start, toast, upset, waken 6 arouse, awaken, bestir, bumper, excite, foment, frolic revive 7 actuate, agitate, animate, disturb, enliven, startle 8 carousal, festival, inspirit 9 stimulate

Rousseau hero: 5 Emile

roussette: 5 shark 7 dogfish

roust: 4 roar, stir, tide 5 rouse 6 bellow, tumult 7 current, roaring 9 bellowing

rout: ado, low, mob 4 band, beat, bray, dart, fuss, roar, root 5 crowd, knock, noise, scoop, shout, snore, snort, troop 6 bellow, clamor, defeat, furrow, rabble, search, strike, throng, tumult, uproar 7 company, confuse, debacle, repulse, retinue, retreat, rummage, slumber, trouble 8 assemble, assembly, confound, disperse, shouting, stampede, vanquish 9 bellowing, discomfit, hurricane, overpower, overthrow, overwhelm 11 disturbance 12 dicomfiture

route: way 4 gest, lane, line, path, road 5 geste, march, trail 6 course, skyway 7 circuit, journey 9 direction, itinerary

circuitous: 6 detour

straight: 7 beeline

routh: 6 plenty 8 abundant 9 abundance, plentiful

routine: rut 4 rote 5 grind, habit, round, troll 6 course, groove, system 8 habitual 9 treadmill

rove: go; gad 4 move, part, pass, plow, roam, turn 5 prowl, range, stray 6 maraud, pierce, ramble, stroll, wander 8 straggle

rover: 5 nomad 6 pirate 7 corsair, Ishmael, migrant, vagrant 8 gadabout 9 itinerant

roving: 6 errant 7 cursory, devious 9 desultory 10 discursive

row: air, oar 4 bank, dust, file, fuss, line, list, rank, spat, tier 5 align, aline, brawl, broil, garry, noise, scull, swath 6 barney, clamor, paddle, pother, propel, rumpus, swathe 7 dispute, quarrel, ruction 8 argument, squabble 9 catalogue, commotion, excursion 11 disturbance 13 collieshangie

form in: 4 line 5 align, aline

rowan tree: ash 4 sorb

rowboat: cog, gig 4 dory, skif 5 canoe, cobil, coble, scull, skiff, skift 6 caique, galley, randan, wherry

stern: 7 transom

rowdy: 4 b'hoy, rude 5 rough, tough 6 roarer, tricky 7 hoodlum, vicious 8 larrikin 9 obstinate 10 boisterous

rowel: 4 spur 5 wheel 6 circle

rowen: 5 field 9 aftermath

rower: oar 6 punter 7 oarsman

rowing: 6 randan 8 sculling

royal: 4 real, rial, stag, true 5 basil, regal 6 august, kingly 7 stately 8 imperial, majestic, princely, splendid 9 excellent, sovereign 11 magnificent, monarchial

royal agaric: 8 mushroom

Royal Canadian Mounted Police: 7 Mountie

royal rock snake: 6 python

royal standard: 4 flag 6 banner, emblem

royalist: 4 Tory 8 Cavalier

royalty: 5 share 6 emblem 7 kingdom 8 kingship, nobility 10 kingliness, percentage 11 sovereignty

denoting: 5 crown 6 ermine, purple 7 scepter

symbol: 6 ermine

royet: 4 wild 6 unruly 7 romping 11 mischievous

rub: 4 bark, bray, buff, fret, rasp, wear, wipe 5 chafe, dight, feeze, grind, scour, smear 6 abrade, anoint, fridge, polish, scrape, smooth, stroke 7 burnish, massage 8 friction, irritate, obstacle 9 hindrance, triturate 10 difficulty, impediment

rub down: 4 comb 5 curry 7 massage

rub elbows: 9 associate 10 fraternize

rub out: 4 kill 5 elide, erase 6 cancel, efface, murder 7 expunge 10 obliterate

rubber: 4 band 5 brick 6 caucho, cutter, eraser 7 ebonite, masseur 8 masseuse, overshoe, polisher 9 vulcanite 10 caoutchouc

juice: 6 achete

source: 5 latex

substitute: 7 factice

synthetic: 4 buna

tree: 7 seringa

Rubber City: 5 Akron

rubber tree: ule 4 para 6 caucho 7 seringa 10 caoutchouc

rubbish: ket(Sc.), 4 flam, gear, junk, mull, pelf, pelt, raff, ross 5 crawm, dross, offal, trash, waste, wrack 6 colder, debris, garble, litter, refuse, rubble, trashy 7 baggage, beggary, mullock, rummage 8 nonsense, trumpery 9 worthless 10 clamjamfry 11 foolishness

rube: 4 hick, jake 6 rustic 7 bumpkin, hayseed 10 countryman

rubedity: 7 redness 9 ruddiness

rubellite: 10 tourmaline

rubeola: 7 measles, rubella

rubescent: red 4 pink 8 blushing, flushing 9 reddening 10 erubescent

rubicund: red 4 rosy, ruby 5 ruddy 6 florid 7 flushed, reddish, redness 11 fullblooded

rubor: 9 hyperemia

rubric red 5 title 6 redden

book: 4 ordo 7 ordines(pl.)

ruby: gem, red 5 balas, jewel, stone 6 spinel 7 rubasse

ruck: rut, sit 4 fold, heap, mass, pile, rake, rick 5 cower, crowd, squat, stack 6 crease, crouch, furrow, pucker 7 crumple, wrinkle 9 multitude

ruckus: ado, row 6 rumpus, uproar 7 ruction 9 confusion 11 disturbance

ruction: 4 fray 5 fight, melee 6 uproar 7 quarrel 8 fraction, outbreak 11 disturbance

rudder: *control:* 4 helm 6 tiller

edge: 8 bearding

part: 4 yoke

ruddle: 5 rouge 6 redden

ruddy: red 4 rosy 5 fresh 6 florid, tanned 7 reddish 8 blushing

rude: 4 bold, curt, lewd 5 bluff, crude, harsh, rough, rowdy 6 bloody, borrel, brutal, clumsy, coarse, fierce, rugged, rustic, savage, severe, vulgar 7 artless, boorish, brutish, country, jarring, loutish, uncivil, uncouth, violent 8 churlish, clownish, homespun, ignorant, impolite, impudent, insolent, ungentle, untaught 9 barbarian, barbarous, ferocious, impetuous, inclement, inelegant, insulting, makeshift, truculent, turbulent, unskilled, untrained 10 boisterous, discordant, tumultuous, uncultured, ungracious, unmannerly, unpolished 11 acrimonious, impertinent, uncivilized 12 contumelious, discourteous

rudeness: 6 ferity

rudiment: 4 germ

rudimentary: 7 initial 9 elemental, vestigial 10 elementary 11 abecedarian, fundamental

rue: rew 4 pity, rake 5 dolor, grief, mourn 6 bewail, grieve, lament, regret, repent, sorrow, street, suffer 7 afflict, deplore, remorse 8 penitent 10 bitterness, compassion, repentance 14 disappointment

rueful: 5 sorry 8 penitent

ruff: ree 4 bird, fish 5 perch, plait, reeve, stamp, trump 6 collar, fraise, hackle, pigeon, rabato, rebato, ruffle, tippet 7 applaud, sunfish 8 disorder, drumbeat 9 sandpiper

female: ree 5 reeve

ruffian: 4 pimp, rage, thug 5 bully, cruel, rowdy 6 brutal, cutter, cuttle, pander, roarer, stormy 7 lawless, lustful, violent 8 assassin, gangster, hooligan, paramour 9 cutthroat, desperado, murderous 10 boisterous, licentious

ruffle: vex 4 beat, fret, roil, rool 5 annoy, brawl, crimp, frill, jabot, shake 6 nettle, riffle, ripple, tousel, tousle, tumult 7 agitate, derange, disturb, flounce, flutter, panuelo, roughen, swagger, wrinkle 8 brandish, dishevel, disorder, drumbeat, furbelow, irritate 9 balayeuse, carfuffle, commotion, confusion 10 disarrange, discompose 12 irregularity

neck: 5 jabot, ruche

ruffler: 5 bully, tramp 6 beggar 7 boaster, ruffian 8 braggart 10 attachment

rufous: 5 rusty, tawny 7 reddish

rug: dog, mat, tug 4 Agra, cozy, haul, pull, snug, tear, wrap 5 Herat 6 afghan, carpet, frieze, kaross, liquor, runner, wrench 7 bargain, blanket, drugget, laprobe 8 Akhissar, Amritsar, covering, portiere 9 Samarkind 11 comfortable

Persian: see **Oriental rug**

ruga: 4 fold 6 crease 7 wrinkle 8 membrane

rugby: *formation:* 5 scrum

score: try

rugged: 4 hard, rude, sour 5 asper, hardy, harsh, rough, stern surly 6 craggy, fierce, horrid, robust, seamed, severe, shaggy, stormy, strong, sturdy, uneven 7 austere, crabbed, gnarled, uncivil, unkempt 8 obdurate, vigorous, wrinkled 9 irregular, turbulent 10 ungracious, unpolished 11 tempestuous

rugose: 6 ridged 8 wrinkled 10 corrugated

Ruhr river: 4 Eder

ruin: gin 4 bane, bust, dash, doom, fall, fate, fell, harm, loss, undo 5 blast, break, decay, exile, fordo, havoc, spoil, wrack, wreck 6 beggar, blight, damage, deface, defeat, diddle, dismay, foredo, impair, injure, perish, ravage 7 decayed, despoil, destroy, pervert, ruinate, subvert 8 bankrupt, calamity, demolish, desolate, disaster, downfall 9 overthrow, perdition, ruination 10 bankruptcy, desolation, subversion 11 destruction, devastation, dissolution, ecroulement 12 delapidation

ruined: 4 dead 5 kaput 6 shabby forlorn 10 tumbledown 11 dilapidated

ruinous: 10 pernicious

ruins: 5 ashes 6 debris 7 remains

rule: law 4 lord, norm, sway 5 by-law, canon, guide, maxim, order, regle, reign 6 course, decide, decree, direct, domine, empire, govern, manage, method, regime, screed 7 alidade, brocard, command, conduct, control, counsel, formula, precept, prevail, regency, regimen, theorem 8 behavior, decision, doctrine, domineer, dominion, persuade, practice, regulate, standard 9 authority, criterion, direction, enactment, influence, principle 10 convention, government, regulation 11 aristocracy, predominate 12 prescription 14 administration

pert. to: 5 rutic

rule out: bar 5 debar 6 forbid, refuse 7 prevent, scratch 8 preclude, prohibit

rule over: 6 manage 7 oversee 8 dominate 11 superintend

ruler: dey, min 4 amir, czar, emir, king, lord, tsar, tzar 5 alder, ameer, emeer, prior 6 archon, author, despot, dynast, ferule, gerent, prince, regent, satrap, sultan, tyrant 7 emperor, monarch, regulus, viceroy 8 autocrat, dictator, governor, hierarch, interrex 9 dominator, governail, imperator, matriarch, potentate, sovereign, yardstick 10 interreges(pl.) 12 straightedge

family: 7 dynasty

former: Nhu 4 czar, Diem, tsar, tzar 5 Lenin 6 Fuhrer, Hitler, Stalin 7 Batista, Fuehrer, Leopold 8 Napoleon, Nicholas 9 Alexander, Mussolini

one of three: 7 triarch 8 triumvir

one of two: 6 duarch

wife: 4 rani 5 queen, ranee 7 czarina, empress, tzarina

rules: 4 code

infraction: 4 foul 8 cheating

ruling: law 7 average, current, inkling, regnant, statute 8 decision, dominant 9 ascendant, ascendent, hegemonic, prevalent 10 prevailing 11 predominant 13 predominating

rum: bad, odd 4 good, grog, poor 5 queer, tafia 6 liquor 7 Bacardi, cachaca, strange 8 beverage, peculiar 9 excellent

rumal: 8 kerchief

Rumania: *capital:* 8 Bucurest 9 Bucharest, Bukharest

coin: ban, leu, ley, lei 4 bani(pl.)

conservative: 5 boyar

king: 5 Carol 7 Michael

mountain: 5 Negoi

queen: 5 Marie

river: Alt, Jiu 5 Aluta, Arges, Schyl, Siret 6 Sereth

river port: 6 Galati, Galatz

town: 4 Arad, Iasi 5 Bacau, Jassy, Neamt, Turnu 6 Braila, Brasov, Galati, Galatz 7 Craiova, Focsani, Ploesti, Severin 8 Cernauti, Irongate, Kishenef, Kolsovar, Temesvar 9 Constanta, Cronstadt, Kronstadt, Nagyvarad, Timisoara 10 Czernovitz, Czernowitz 11 Klausenburg 12 Grosswardein

rumble: 4 seat 5 growl, rumor 6 murmur, polish, ramble, report, ripple, uproar 7 grumble 9 complaint 11 disturbance

rumbo: 4 grog

rumen: cud 6 paunch 7 stomach

ruminant: ox; yak 4 deer, goat 5 bison, camel, llama, moose, okapi, sheep, steer 6 alpaca, cattle, vicuna 7 buffalo, chewing, giraffe 8 antelope 10 meditative

female: cow, doe, ewe 5 nanny

genus: bos 5 capra

male: ram 4 buck, bull

stomach: 4 read, reed 5 rumen 6 omasum 8 abomasum, abomasus, roddikin 9 reticulum

ruminate: 4 chaw, chew, mull, muse 5 think, weigh 6 ponder 7 reflect 8 cogitate, consider, meditate

rummage: 4 rout, stow 6 gather, litter, search 7 collect, confuse, derange, examine, fossick, ransack, rubbish, stowage, turmoil 8 upheaval 9 confusion, searching 10 disarrange 11 derangement

rummer: cup 5 glass 6 better

rummy: rum 4 chap, game 5 drunk 8 drunkard

rumor: 4 buzz, sugh, talk, tell, word 5 bruit, noise, sough, story, voice 6 clamor, furphy, gossip, murmur, norate, report, spread, uproar 7 hearsay, message, tidings, whisper 9 grapevine, statement 10 reputation 11 scuttlebutt

personification: 4 Fama

repeat: 5 noise

rump: 4 dock 6 behind, insult 7 hurdies, plunder, remnant 8 bankrupt, buttocks 11 legislature

rump bone: 6 sacrum 8 edgebone 9 aitchbone

rumple: 4 fold, muss, rool, rump, tail 5 plait, touse 6 crease, frowse, tousle 7 crinkle, crumple, wrinkle

rumpus: row 5 brawl 6 barney, fracas, hubbub, uproar 9 confusion 11 disturbance

rumshop: bar 6 saloon, tavern 7 barroom, taproom

run: go; fly, gad, ply, rin(Sc.), sew 4 butt, cast, dart, dash, emit, flow, fuse, gait, grow, hare, hunt, melt, mold, move, pass, pour, race, roam, rove, sail, scud, tear, tend, trip, trot, turn, work **5** blend, brook, carry, climb, cover, creep, drive, enter, going, hurry, range, ravel, reach, recur, river, route, scoot, score, scour, speed, stand, trace, treat **6** ascend, bicker, career, charge, course, elapse, extend, gallop, govern, hasten, manage, output, pursue, refine, rotate, scurry, spread, spring, sprint, stream, thrust **7** conduct, contend, descend, develop, diffuse, journey, liquefy, migrate, operate, proceed, process, roulade, scamper, scutter, scutttle, smuggle, stretch, trickle **8** continue, dissolve, function, sequence, stampede, traverse **9** discharge, suppurate, transport **11** watercourse

run across: 4 meet **9** encounter **10** transverse

run aground: 7 founder

run away: 4 bolt, flee **5** elope **6** decamp, desert, escape

run down: hit **4** kill, sink, stop **5** crush, decry **6** pursue **7** capture, decline, traduce **8** overbear **9** disparage, exhausted, overthrow **11** dilapidated

run for office: 5 stand

run-in: 4 tiff **5** fight **7** quarrel **11** altercation

run-of-the-mill: 6 common **7** average **8** ordinary

run off: 5 print, waste **7** impress

run out: 4 flow **5** expel, lapse, peter, spill, spilt, waste **6** elapse, expire, spread **8** squander

run over: 6 exceed, strike **8** overflow, rehearse

run through: 4 stab **6** pierce **7** examine, inspect, pervade **8** transfix

run up: 4 grow, rise **5** erect **7** enlarge **8** increase **9** construct **10** accumulate

runagate: 7 runaway **8** deserter, fugitive, renegade, vagabond, wanderer

runaway: 7 escapee **8** fugitive, runagate

rundle (see also **runnel**): **4** ball, drum, rung, step **5** round **6** circle, sphere

rundlet: tun **4** cask **6** barrel

rune: wen **5** magic **6** secret **7** mystery

rung: 4 rod **5** spar, step **5** round, spoke, staff, stair, stake, stave, tread **6** cudgel, degree, rundle **7** girdled

runlet: 4 rush **5** brook **6** barrel, runnel **7** rivulet **9** streamlet

runnel: 4 rill **5** brook, creek, rhine **6** runlet, stream **7** channel, rivulet **9** streamlet **11** watercourse

runner: rug, ski **4** skee **5** agent, miler, racer, ravel, scarf **6** cursor, stolon **8** operator, smuggler, sprinter **9** collector, detective, messenger, solicitor

running: 4 care, trip **6** attack **7** contest, current, cursive, journey **8** skirmish **10** management, successive

running birch: 9 snowberry

running board: 9 footboard

running knot: 5 noose

running toad: 10 natterjack

runt: 4 chit, wrig **5** dwarf, pigmy, pygmy **6** durgan, durgen, titman

runty: 4 puny **5** small **7** stunted **8** dwarfish **10** diminutive, undersized **12** contemptible

runway: 4 file, path, ramp, road **5** chute, strip, track, trail **6** bridge, groove, trough **7** channel **8** platform **10** passageway

rupee, rupia: re., rs.(pl.)

rupia 8 eruption

rupture: 4 part, rend, rent **5** break, burst, split **6** breach, hernia, rhexis **7** ruction, ruption **8** fraction, fracture **10** disruption, separating

rural: 6 rustic **7** bucolic, country **8** agrestic, Arcadian, geoponic, pastoral **11** countrified

life: **7** bucolic, georgic **8** pastoral

rurales: 9 policemen **12** constabulary

ruse: 4 fall, hoax, slip, wile **5** dodge, feint, fraud, shift, trick **6** deceit **8** artifice **9** stratagem **10** subterfuge

rush: sag **4** birr, dart, dash, junk, race, rout, scud, tear **5** break, brook, chute, feeze, haste, hurry, onset, press, sally, scoot, spate, sprat, sprot, straw, surge **6** attack, bustle, charge, combat, defeat, fescue, hasten, hurtle, hustle, runlet, sortie, trifle **7** assault, bulrush, cattail, destroy, rampage, repulse, tantivy **8** eruption, stampede **9** overthrow **11** undergrowth **13** precipitation

family: **9** juncaceae

load: **5** barth, gavel

rush hour: 4 peak

rush nut: 5 chufa

rush toad: 10 natterjack

rusk: 4 cake **5** bread, crisp, toast **7** biscuit

Russ: 7 Russian

Russia (see also **Soviet Union**): **4** USSR **7** Muscovy

alcoholic beverage: **5** kvass, quass, vodka **9** slivovitz

antelope: **5** saiga

apple: **9** astrachan

aristocrat: **5** Boyar **6** Boyard

automobile: Zis

bondman: **4** serf

braid: **8** soutache

cabinet member: **9** commissar

cactus: **7** thistle

calendar: **6** Julian

cap: 4 aska
carriage: 6 drosky, troika 8 tarantas
cathedral: 5 sobor
caviar: 4 ikra 5 ikary
citadel: 7 Kremlin
city: 4 Kiev, Omsk, Orel, Perm 5 Gomel,
   Kasan, Kazan, Minsk, Pensa, Pskov 6
   Kertch, Moscow(c.), Moskva, Nizhni,
   Odessa, Rostov, Samara, Sartov 7 Bataisk,
   Ivanovo, Kalinin, Rybinsk 8 Kostroma,
   Orenburg, Smolensk, Taganrog, Tashkent, Vladimir, Voronezh, Yaroslaf 9
   Archangel,   Astrakhan,   Kuibishev,
   Petrograd 10 Michurinsk, Sebastopol, Sevastopol,   Voznesensk   11   Cheliabinsk,
   Vladivostok 12 Ekaterinburg 13 Yekate-
   rinburg 14 Nizhni Novgorod 15 Saint Petersburg
coal area: 6 Donets
coin: 5 altin, copec, kopek, ruble 6 copeck,
   grivna, kopeck 9 altininck, poltinnik 10
   chervonets
collective farm: 6 kolhoz 7 kolkhos
commune: 6 kolhoz 7 kolkhos, kolkhoz
composer: Cui 9 Prokofiev 10 Stravinsky 12
   Tschaikovsky   13   Shostakovitch   14
   Rimsky-Korsakov
cossack: 6 Tartar
council: 4 Duma
country house: 5 dacha
dance: 7 ziganka
decree: 5 ukase
delicacy: 6 caviar 7 caviare
despot: 4 czar, tsar, tzar
devil: 5 chort
diplomat: 5 Malik, Zorin 6 Stalin 7 Gro-
   myko, Molotov, Sobolev 8 Malenkov 9
   Kuznetzov,   Tsarapkin,   Vishinsky   11
   Shcherbakov
district: 7 Karelia
dog: 4 alan 6 borzoi 7 owtchah 9 wolfhound
dress: 7 sarafan
emperor: 4 czar, Ivan, tsar, tzar 5 Peter
empress: 7 czarina, tsarina, tzarina 8 tsa-
   ritza, tzaritza
exclamation: 7 nichevo 8 nitchevo
farmer: 5 kulak
fish: 6 beluga
flax: 6 bobbin
folk song: 6 bylina
forest: 6 tundra
fox: 6 corsac 7 karagan
gambling game: 6 coocoo
general: 10 Timoshenko 14 Tukhashchev-
   ski
government group: 4 duma, rada, tsik 6 soviet 7 zemstvo 9 Politburo, Presidium 10
   Praesidium 11 Politbureau
grandmother: 8 babushka

gulf: 4 Azov
hood: 7 bashlik, bashlyk
horse: 6 tarpan
house: 4 isba 5 dacha
image: 4 icon, ikon 5 ikono
imperial order: 5 ukase
kerchief: 6 analav
labor association: 5 artel
lagoon: 5 liman
lake: 4 Aral, Neva, Sego 5 Elton, Ilmen,
   Onega
language: 4 Russ
leader: 5 Lenin 6 Stalin 7 Molotov 8 Brezh-
   nev 10 Khrushchev
measure: fut, lof 4 duim, fass, loof, stof 5
   duime, foute, korec, ligne, osmin, pajak,
   stoff, vedro, verst 6 arshin, charka, liniya,
   osmina, paletz, sagene, tchast, versta,
   verste 7 arsheen, botchka, chkalik, gar-
   netz, verchoc, verchok 8 boutylka, chet-
   vert, krouchka, kroushka 9 chetverik 10
   dessiatine 11 polugarnetz
mile: 5 verst
money: 5 ruble
monk: 7 starets 8 Rasputin
mountain range: 4 Alai, Ural
musical instrument: 5 gudok, gusla, gusle 9
   balalaika
name: 4 Igor, Ivan, Olga 5 Peter, Sonya
naval academy: 6 Frunze
news agency: 4 Tass
newspaper: 6 Pravda 8 Izvestia
novelist: 5 Gorki 7 Chekhov, Tolstoi, Tolstoy 10 Dostoevsky
peasant: 5 kulak 6 muzhik, muzjik
peninsula: 4 Kola 6 Crimea 7 Karelia
people: Red 4 Lett, Russ, Slav 5 Ersar 7
   Cossack,   Russine   9   Muscovite   12
   Byelorussian
plain: 6 steppe
poet: 6 Jehuda 7 Pushkin 9 Aleksandr, Pasternak, Sholokhov 11 Sergyeevich, Vozne-
   sensky, Yevtushenko
port: 4 Eisk 5 Anapa 6 Odessa 9 Archangel
   10 Sevastapol 11 Vladivostok
prince: 4 knez 5 knais, knyaz
revolutionist: 5 Lenin, Rykov 6 Stalin,
   Tomsky 7 Trotsky
river: Ik, Ob; Don, Ili, Ner, Oka, Ros, Ufa 4
   Amur, Duna, Kara, Lena, Neva, Orel,
   Sura, Svir, Ural 5 Dnepr, Dvina, Onega,
   Terek, Tobol, Volga 6 Donets, Irtish, Ir-
   tysh 7 Dnieper
saint: 4 Olga
satellite: 7 sputnik
sea: 4 Aral, Azof, Azov 6 Baikal
soup: 5 shchi 6 borsch 7 borscht
spa: Ems
stockade: 5 etape

tavern: 6 caback
urn: 7 samovar
villa: 5 dacha
village: mir
violinist: 5 Elman
weight: 4 dola, pood
whip: 5 knout
worker: 7 dvornik 12 Stakhanovite
youth organization: 8 Comsomol, Komsomol

russud: 5 grain 6 forage

rust: eat 5 erode 6 aecium, aerugo, blight, canker, patina 7 corrode, erosion, oxidize 9 corrosion, oxidation, verdigris

rustic: hob 4 boor, carl, dull, hick, hind, jake, rube, rude 5 bacon, carle, chuff, churl, clown, doric, hodge, plain, rough, rural, swain, yokel 6 coarse, gaffer, honest, simple, sturdy, sylvan 7 artless, awkward, boorish, bucolic, bumpkin, bushman, Corydon, country, hayseed, peasant, plowboy, plowman, uncouth 8 agrestic, churlish, clownish, pastoral 9 agrestian, campesino, chawbacon, unadorned 10 clodhopper, countryman, unaffected, unpolished

rustle: 5 steal 6 fissle, fistle, scroop 7 crinkle

Rustum: *father:* Zal
son: 6 Sohrab

rut: rat, rit 4 brim 5 ditch, track 6 furrow, groove, strake 7 routine, wrinkle

rutabaga: 6 turnip

ruth: woe 4 pity 5 grief, mercy 6 regret, sorrow 7 remorse, sadness 10 compassion, repentance, tenderness 17 compassionateness

Ruth: *husband:* 4 Boaz
mother-in-law: 5 Naomi
son: 4 Obed

ruthless: 4 grim 5 cruel 6 savage 9 ferocious

rutter: 4 plow 5 guide 7 trooper 8 horseman

ruttle: 6 gurgle, rattle

rye: ree, rie 5 grain, grass 6 whisky 9 gentleman
disease: 5 ergot

ryke: 5 reach(Sc.)

ryot, raiyat: 6 farmer, tenant 7 peasant 10 cultivator

rytina: 12 hydrodamalis

Ryukyu island: 7 Okinawa

S

S-shaped: 4 ogee 7 sigmate, sigmoid
sabana: See **savanna**
sabbat: 8 assembly
saber, sabre: 8 scimitar, scimiter, yataghan
Sabine: *goddess:* 6 Vacuna
   people: 7 Vestini
sable: sad 4 dark, ebon 5 black, brush, saber
  6 dismal, gloomy, marten, pellet 8 antelope, darkened 10 mysterious 11 threatening
  genus of: 7 mustela
  pert. to: 8 zibeline 9 zibelline
sablefish: cod 6 beshow 10 candlefish
sabot: 4 shoe
sabotage: 7 destroy 9 undermine 11 destruction
sabre: See **saber**
Sabrina River: 6 Severn
sabulous: 5 dusty, sandy 6 floury, gritty 10 arenaceous
sabutan: 5 fiber, straw
sac: bag, pod 4 cyst, sack 5 ascus, bursa, pouch, theca 6 cavity, saccus 7 cistern, utricle, vesicle 8 sacculus
Sacar's son: 5 Ahiam
sacaton: 5 grass
saccadic: 5 jerky 9 twitching
saccharin: 7 gluside
saccharine: 5 sweet 10 sweetening
saccos: See **sakkos**
sacculate: 7 pouched
sacerdotal: 8 clerical, priestly
sachem: 4 boss 5 chief 8 sagamore
sachet: bat, pad 4 oris 5 pouch, scent 8 reticule
sack (see also **sac**): bag, bed 4 base, fire, loot, poke, ruin 5 bursa, gunny, harry, pouch, purse, waste 6 budget, burlap, jacket, ravage, wallet 7 boucher, dismiss, musette, pillage, plunder 8 desolate 9 container, discharge, dismissal
  fiber: 4 jute 5 gunny 6 burlap
sackbut: 8 trombone

sackless: 4 weak 7 bashful 8 harmless, innocent 9 guiltless, peaceable 10 dispirited, unmolested
sacque: 4 sack 6 jacket
sacrament: 4 sign 5 token 6 pledge, symbol 7 baptism, penance, promise, unction 8 ceremony, covenant 9 communion, Eucharist, matrimony 12 confirmation
sacrarium: 5 ambry 6 chapel, shrine 7 oratory 9 sanctuary 10 tabernacle
sacred: 4 holy 5 huaca, santo 6 divine 7 blessed 8 hallowed, reverend 9 geistlich, inviolate, venerated 10 inviolable, sacrosanct 11 consecrated 13 sanctimonious
  combining form: 5 hagio, hiero
  make: 8 enshrine
  most: 10 sacrosanct
sacred bean: 5 lotus
sacred beetle: 10 scarabaeus
sacred bo tree: 5 pipal
sacred fig: 5 pipal
sacred weed: 7 vervain
sacrifice: 4 host, loss 6 corban, homage, korban, victim 8 hecatomb, immolate, oblation, offering 9 holocaust, martyrdom, privation, surrender 10 immolation 11 destruction
sacrilege: 9 blasphemy 11 desecration, profanation
sacristy: 6 vestry
  pert. to: 7 vestral
sacrosanct: 6 sacred
sad: bad 4 blue, dark, dram, dull 5 dusky, grave, sober, sorry, trist 6 dismal, dreary, gloomy, solemn, somber, sombre, triste(F.), wicked, woeful 7 doleful, dolente(It.), pensive, serious, unhappy 8 dejected, desolate, dolorous, downcast, grievous, mournful, pathetic, pitiable 9 afflicted, cheerless, depressed, plaintive, sorrowful 10 calamitous, deplorable, despondent, lugubrious 11 distressing, melancholic 12 disconsolate, heavyhearted
  combining form: 5 tragi 7 tragico
sadden: 7 attrist

saddle: 4 load 5 ridge 6 howdah 7 aparejo, pillion 8 encumber
blanket: 6 corona, tilpah
bow: 6 pommel
maker: 7 knacker, saddler
pad: 5 panel 7 housing
part: 4 horn, tore 5 arson, cinch, croup, girth, panel, pilch, skirt 6 cantle, corona, crutch, latigo, pommel 7 stirrup 8 sudadero 9 saddlebow
rear part: 6 cantle
saddle horse: 4 pony 5 mount
saddle rock: 6 oyster
saddleback: 4 hill 5 ridge
saddlebag: sag(Sc.) 4 jagg(Sc.) 7 alforja, pannier
saddlecloth: 5 panel 7 housing 8 shabrack 9 shabraque
saddler: 4 seal 5 horse 7 cobbler, knacker, lorimer, loriner 9 shoemaker 11 saddlemaker
sadness: 5 blues, dumps
saeter: 6 meadow 7 pasture
safari: 4 hunt, trek 7 caravan, journey 9 excursion 10 expedition
safe: box 4 sure 5 chest, siker, sound, vault 6 armory, closet, coffer, holder, secure, sicker, unhurt 8 cupboard, unharmed 9 strongbox, untouched 10 depository 11 gardeviance, trustworthy
safe-conduct: 4 pass 5 cowle, guard 6 convoy 10 permission, protection
safecracker: 4 yegg 7 peteman
safeguard: 4 pass 5 guard 6 convoy, escort, safety 7 defense, protect 10 protection
safekeeping: 4 care 7 custody, storage 10 protection
safety: 6 surete(F.) 9 assurance
place of: ark 4 port 5 haven 6 asylum, refuge 7 retreat, sanctum
zone: 6 island
safety lamp: 4 Davy
safety pin: 5 clasp 6 fibula
safety rail: 9 guardrail
saffron: 6 crocus, yellow 9 safflower
sag: 4 bend, flag, reed, rush, sink, wilt 5 drift, droop, sedge, slump 6 settle, weaken
saga: 4 edda, epic, myth, tale 5 story 6 legend 7 history, recital 9 narrative
narrator: 7 sagaman
sagaciate: 4 fare 6 thrive
sagacious: 4 sage, wise 5 acute, quick 6 argute, astute, shrewd 7 knowing, politic, prudent, sapient 9 judicious 10 discerning, farsighted, hardheaded 11 clairvoyant, penetrating 13 perspicacious
sagacity: 6 acumen 8 sapience
sagamore: 5 chief 6 sachem
sage: 4 herb, mint, seer, wise 5 clary, grave, rishi(Ind.), solon, spice 6 pundit, salvia,

shrewd, solemn 7 learned, prudent, sapient 8 sagebush 9 counselor, judicious, venerable 10 counsellor, discerning, perceptive 11 philosopher
Sage: *of Chelsea:* 13 Thomas Carlyle
of Concord: 17 Ralph Waldo Emerson
of Emporia: 5 White
of Ferney: 8 Voltaire
of Monticello: 15 Thomas Jefferson
of Pylos: 6 Nestor
sage cheese: 7 cheddar
sage cock: 6 grouse
sage hen: 6 grouse 7 Nevadan
Sagebrush State: 6 Nevada
saginate: 6 fatten
Sagittarius: 6 archer, bowman
sago: 6 starch
sago palm: 7 coontie
sagoin: 8 marmoset
saguaro: 6 cactus
sagum: 5 cloak
Sahara: *people:* 4 Arab 5 nomad 6 Tuareg
plateau: 6 hamada 7 hammada
wind: 5 leste
saic: 4 boat 5 ketch
said (see also **say**): dit(F.) 5 quoth 6 spoken, stated 7 reputed, uttered 8 supposed
Saida: 5 Sidon
saiga: 4 coin 8 antelope
sail: awe, awn, fly, rig, van 4 dart, duck, haul, keel, luff, move, scud, skim, soar, swim, trip 5 fleet, float, glide, sheet 6 canvas, depart, embark, voyage 7 journey 8 navigate 9 excursion
kind of: jib 5 royal 6 lateen, mizzen, square 7 balloon, lugsail, skysail, spanker, topsail, trysail 8 foresail, mainsail, staysail, studding 9 crossjack, foreroyal, spinnaker 10 topgallant 12 forestaysail
nearer wind: 4 luff
part: 4 bunt, clew, yard 5 leach, leech, sheet 6 earing 7 earring, yardarm
pert. to: 5 velic
prepare to: 4 trim
triangular: jib
sail yard: rae(Sc.) 4 spar
sailboat: 4 bark, yawl 5 skiff, sloop, yacht 7 caravel 9 caravelle
sailcloth: 4 duck 6 canvas
sailfish: 8 billfish
sailing: 4 asea
sailing ship: cog 4 bark, brig, saic, yawl 5 sloop 6 barque, cutter, galley, sampan, vessel 7 frigate, galleon 8 schooner 10 barkentine, brigantine 11 barquentine
scoop: 5 skeet

sailor: gob, hat, tar, tot 4 salt 5 Jacky 6 hearty, lascar, ratiny 7 mariner, seafman 8 coxswain, seafarer, waterman 10 bluejacket, lobscouser
assent: aye
associate: 8 messmate
call: 4 ahoy
carving: 9 scrimshaw
chapel: 6 bethel
group: 4 crew 5 hands
jacket: 6 reefer
mess tub: kid
old: 4 salt
patron saint: 4 Elmo
patroness: 11 Mother Carey
potion: 4 grog
song: 6 chanty 7 chantey 9 barcarole
saint (see also **patron saint**): St.; Sao(Port.), Ste. 4 holy 5 santa(Sp.), santo 6 hallow 7 beatify 8 canonize, enshrine
biography: 11 hagiography
image: 5 santo
invocation of: 10 hagiolatry
worship: 10 hagiolatry, hierolatry
Saint Andrew's cross: 7 saltier, saltire
Saint Anthony's cross: tau 4 ankh
Saint Barnabas' prayer: 8 Ave Maria
Saint Catherine's home: 5 Siena
Saint Elmo's fire: 5 flame 6 furole 9 corposant
Saint Francis' birthplace: 6 Assisi
Saint John's-bread: 5 carob
Saint Martin's: *bird:* 7 harrier
feast: 9 Martinmas
Saint Paul: *birthplace:* 6 Tarsus
companion: 4 Luke
Saint Peter: 5 Simon
Saint-Saens opera: 6 Samson
Saint Veronica's handkerchief: 8 sudarium
Saint Vitus' dance: 6 chorea
saintly: 4 holy 5 pious 6 devout 7 angelic 9 angelical 13 sanctimonious
sake: end 5 cause, drink 6 behalf, motive, regard 7 account, benefit, concern, purpose 8 beverage 13 consideration
saker: 6 falcon
saki: 5 drink, yarke 6 monkey, yarkee 8 beverage
sakkos, saccos: 8 vestment
sal: 4 salt
sala: 4 hall
salaam, salam: bow 4 bend 6 salute 8 greeting 9 obeisance 10 compliment, salutation
salacious: 4 lewd 7 lustful, obscene 8 scabrous 9 lecherous 12 pornographic

salad ingredient: 5 cress 6 celery, endive, greens, tomato, 7 cabbage, lettuce, parsley, romaine 8 scallion 9 dandelion 10 watercress
salad tree: 6 redbud
Saladin's foes: 9 Crusaders
salamander: eft, olm 4 evet, newt 6 triton 7 axoloti, axolotl, caudata, urodela, urodele 10 hellbender
order: 7 caudata, urodela
salami: 7 sausage
store: 4 deli
Salammbo author: 8 Flaubert
salary: fee, pay 4 hire 5 wages 6 reward 7 stipend 8 pittance 9 allowance, emolument 10 exhibition, honorarium, recompense 12 compensation, remuneration 13 consideration
sale: net 4 deal, hall, vend 5 bower 6 market, palace, vendue, willow 7 auction, bargain, chamber, rummage 8 contract, transfer 9 utterance, vendition 10 conveyance 11 transaction
sales talk: 4 line 5 pitch, spiel 6 patter
salesman: 5 agent, clerk 6 hawker, pedlar, seller, sutler, vendor 7 drummer, hustler, peddler 8 pitchman, vendeuse(fem.) 9 solicitor 14 representative
salience: 5 point 7 agility 8 emphasis 9 highlight 10 prominence
salient: 4 line 5 cabre, redan 6 trench 7 jumping, leaping 8 bounding, extended, striking 10 noticeable 11 conspicuous
salient angle: 5 arris
salient point: 5 heart 6 detail, source 7 feature
salientia: 5 anura, frogs, toads 7 aglossa, costata 8 Amphibia, linguata
salina: 4 lake, pond 5 marsh 6 salada 9 saltworks
saline: 4 tear 5 brine, briny, salty 8 brackish 10 saliferous
Salisbury steak: 9 hamburger
saliva: 4 spit 7 spittle
salix: 5 genus 6 osiers 7 sallows, willows
salle: 4 room
sallet, salade: 6 helmet
sallow: wan 4 pale, twig 5 muddy, osier, shoot 6 pallid, willow 9 yellowish
sally: 4 leap, quip, rush, trip 5 dance, issue, jaunt, start 6 attack, escape, retort, sortie, spring 7 darting, rushing 8 escapade, outbreak, outburst 9 excursion, witticism 10 liveliness
salmagundi: 4 hash, olio 5 salad 6 medley 7 mixture 9 potpourri
salmi: 6 ragout
salmon: gib, lax 4 chum, coho, kelt, keta, mort, pike, pink, raun, slat 5 color, haddo, holia, nerka, smolt, tecon 6 baggit, kipper,

laurel, sauqui, taimen 7 gilling, saumont, shedder 8 schoodic, springer, weakfish 9 ceratodus 10 barramunda
enclosure: 4 weir, yair, yare
female: 4 raun 6 baggit
male: 6 kipper
pool: 5 stell
silver: 4 coho
smoked: lox
trap: 4 slap
young: 4 parr
salmon trout: 5 sewen
salmonoid: 4 ahyu 5 nelma, powan
Salome: *father:* 8 Herodias
grandfather: 5 Herod
salon: 4 hall, room 7 gallery 9 apartment, reception 10 assemblage, exhibition
saloon: bar 4 hall, room 5 cabin, coach, cuddy, divan, sedan 6 tavern 7 barroom, cantina(Sp.) 8 alehouse, groggery 9 apartment, brasserie(F.)
saloop: 5 drink, salep 9 sassafras
salpa, salp: 8 tunicate
salse: 7 volcano
salt: sal, tar, wit 4 alum, corn, cure 5 brine, briny, ester, salic, sharp, witty 6 alkali, flavor, halite, harden, lively, sailor, saline, seaman, season 7 bromate, piquant, pungent, seadust 8 brackish, halinous 9 seasoning
combining form: 4 sali
deposit: 6 saline
oleic acid: 6 oleate
resembling: 5 halid 6 halide, haloid
rock: pig
working: 7 halurgy
salt-like: 6 haloid
salt marsh: 6 salina
salt pit: vat
salt tree: 4 atle 8 tamarisk
salt water: 5 brine
saltate: 4 jump, leap 5 bound, dance
saltcellar: 5 saler
salted: 4 alat 5 cured 6 corned
saltpeter, saltpetre: 5 niter, nitre
saltworks: 7 saltern, saltery
salty: See **salt**
salubrious: 8 salutary 9 benignant, healthful, wholesome 10 beneficial
salutary: 4 good 6 benign 7 healthy, helpful 8 curative 9 desirable, healthful, medicinal, wholesome 10 beneficial 11 restorative
salutation: hi; ave, bow 4 beck, hail 5 aloha, hello, howdy, salam, skoal 6 curtsy, kowtow, Mizpah, Mizpeh, prosit, salaam, salute 7 address, welcome, slainte 8 accolade, chin-chin, farewell, greeting

salute: nod 4 hail 5 greet, halse, salvo 6 accost 7 address 10 salutation
salvage: 4 save 6 rescue 7 reclaim 12 compensation
salvager: 6 salvor
salvation: 6 rescue 10 redemption 12 preservation
pert. to: 8 soterial 9 soterical
salve: 4 balm 6 anoint, cerate, soothe 7 assuage, unguent 8 flattery, ointment, palliate
salver: 4 tray 6 waiter
salvo: 6 excuse, salute 7 pretext, proviso, quibble 9 exception 11 reservation
samadh: 4 tomb 6 shrine
samaj: 6 church 7 society 12 congregation
Samaritan: *alphabet:* i; ba, in, it; jud, mim, nun, phi, sen, tav, tit 4 alaf, bith, goph, kaph, rish, sadi, shan 5 dalat, gaman, labad 6 simcat
god: 6 Tartak
people: 8 Assyrian 9 Israelite
sambar, sambur: elk 4 deer, maha, rusa
same: id; ilk, one 4 ibid, idem, like, meme(F.), self 5 alike, ditto, equal 7 identic 9 identical, unchanged 10 invariable
comb. form: iso 4 homo
sameness: 8 monotony 10 similarity 11 resemblance 14 correspondence
Samhain Eve: 9 Halloween
Samian philosopher: 10 Pythagoras
samisen: 5 banjo
samlet: 4 parr 6 salmon 10 fingerling
sammy: 5 ninny 6 clammy, sodden, watery 9 simpleton
Samoa (see also **Polynesia**): *capital:* 4 Apia
fish: 6 ataata, sesele
hostess: 5 taupo 6 taupou
island: 5 Upolu 6 Savaii
mollusk: asi
mudworm: ipo
owl: 4 lulu
red: 4 mumu
warrior: toa
samovar: urn 6 teapot
samp: 4 meal, mush, soup 6 cereal, hominy 8 porridge
sampaloc: 8 tamarind
sampan: 4 boat 5 skiff
sample: 4 test 5 taste 6 swatch 7 example, pattern 8 specimen 12 illustration
sampleman: 6 taster 12 demonstrator
sampler: 5 model 6 taster 7 example, hanging, pattern 8 original, specimen 9 archetype
Samson: *betrayer:* 7 Delilah
deathplace: 4 Gaza
vulnerable place: 4 hair
Samuel: *home:* 5 Ramah

mentor: Eli
parent: 6 Hannah 7 Elkanah
son: 5 Abiah
victim: 4 Agag, Agog
Samurai: 7 warrior
ostracized: 5 Ronin
San Francisco hill: Nob
San Simeon name: 6 Hearst
sanative: 6 curing 7 healing 8 curative, sanatory 9 healthful
sanatorium: spa 8 hospital
sanatory: 8 sanative
Sancho Panza: *island:* 9 Barataria
master: 10 Don Quixote
mule: 6 Dapple
sanctify: 8 dedicate 10 consecrate
sanctimonious: 4 holy 5 pious 6 devout, sacred 7 saintly 10 sanctified
sanctimoniousness: 4 cant
sanction: 4 amen, fiat 5 allow 6 assent, avouch, permit, placet, ratify 7 approve, confirm, endorse, indorse, support 8 accredit, approval 9 allowance, approbate, authority, authorize, encourage, subscribe 10 imprimatur 11 approbation, countenance, countersign, endorsement 12 ratification 13 authorization, encouragement
sanctity: 5 rites 6 purity 7 halidom 8 halidome, holiness, recesses 9 godliness, solemnity 10 sacredness 11 obligations, saintliness 13 inviolability
place of: 4 fane 5 altar, hiera 6 chapel, church, hieron, shrine, temple 7 chaitya 9 synagogue
sanctuary: ark 4 bema, fane, holy, naos 5 abbey, adyta(pl.), bamah, grith, haven 6 adytum, asylum, bemata, chapel, church, haikal, priory, refuge, shrine, temple 7 alsatia, chancel, convent, halidom, retreat, sanctum, shelter 8 cloister, halidome, holiness 9 monastery 10 penetralia, protection, tabernacle 11 reservation
sanctum: den 5 study 6 adytum, office 9 sanctuary
sand: 4 grit 5 nerve 6 abrade, desert, gravel, smooth 7 courage 8 alluvium, asbestic
and clay: 4 loam
particle: 5 grain
particles: 4 silt
resembling: 7 arenoid
sand cock: 8 redshank
sand dune: 5 towan
sand eel: 4 grig 5 lance 6 launce
sand flea: 6 chigoe 7 chigger
sand flounder: 5 fluke 10 windowpane
sand hill: 4 dene, dune
sand lob: 7 lugworm
sand widgeon: 7 gadwall

sandal (see also **moccasin**): 4 clog, shoe 6 buskin, caliga, charuk 7 rullion, slipper, talaria 9 alpargata 10 espadrille
winged: 7 talaria(pl.)
wooden: 6 patten
sandalwood: 5 algum, almug, maire
Sandalwood Island: 5 Sumba 6 Soemba
sandarac: 7 realgar
tree: 4 arar
wood: 6 alerce, alerse
sandbank: 4 dune, meal
sandbar: 4 dene, dune, reef, spit 5 beach, shelf, shoal
sandia: 10 watermelon
sandpiper: ree 4 bird, knot, ruff 5 reeve, terek 6 dunlin, teeter, tiltup 7 brownie, chorook, fiddler, haybird 8 triddler, redshank 10 canderling
sandstone: 4 grit 5 hazel 6 arkose 8 ganister 9 gritstone
block: 6 sarsen
pert. to: 10 arenilitic
sandy: 6 gritty, plucky 7 arenose, arenous 8 shifting, unstable 9 arenulous 10 arenaceous 13 uninteresting
pert. to: 6 eremic
Sandy: 8 Scotsman
sane: 4 wise 5 lucid, sober, sound 6 normal 7 healthy, sapient 8 rational, sensible 10 reasonable
sang (see also **sing**): 5 blood
sangfroid: 8 calmness, coolness 9 composure 16 imperturbability
sanglier: 4 boar
Sangraal: See **Holy Grail**
sanguinaria: 6 yarrow 9 bloodroot
sanguine: red 4 fond, gory, warm 5 cruel, ruddy 6 ardent, bloody, crayon, savage, yarrow 7 buoyant, hopeful 8 cheerful, hematite 9 confident, ferocious, murderous 10 bloodstone, ensanguine, optimistic, sanguinary 12 bloodthirsty
sanitary: 8 hygienic
sanity: 6 reason 7 balance 8 lucidity, saneness 9 soundness 13 wholesomeness
sans: 7 without
Sanskrit: *dialect:* 4 Pali
dictionary: 10 amara-kosha
division of literature: 5 Sruti 6 Shruti
epic: 8 Ramayana
epic character: 4 Sita
school: tol
soul: 5 atman
verse: 5 sloka
Santa Barbara island: 8 Catalina
Santa Claus's reindeer: 5 Comet, Cupid, Vixen 6 Dancer, Dasher, Donder, Donner 7 Blitzen, Prancer
santo: 5 image, saint

santon: 4 monk 5 image, saint 6 hermit 7 dervish

sap: lac 4 dupe, fool, milk, mine, seve(F.), upas 5 drain, juice, latex, lymph, vigor 6 energy, trench, weaken 7 exhaust, saphead 8 enervate, vitality, weakling 9 exudation, schlemiel, schlemihl, screwball, undermine 10 debilitate, devitalize

dried: gum

lose: 5 bleed

spout: 5 spile

sapajou: 6 monkey

sapanwood, sappanwood: 4 tree 10 brazilwood

saphead: See **sap**

saphie, saffi: 5 charm 6 amulet 8 talisman

sapid: 5 tasty 6 savory 7 savoury 8 engaging 9 palatable 10 flavorable

sapient: 4 sage, sane, wise 6 shrewd 7 knowing 9 sagacious 10 discerning

sapiutan: 4 anoa

sapless: dry 7 insipid 8 withered 9 exsuccous 11 devitalized

sapling: 5 plant, youth

sapo: 4 soap 8 toadfish

sapodilla, sapotilha, sapotilla: 5 chico 6 sapota, sapote, zapote 7 nispero 9 naseberry

saponaceous: 5 soapy 7 elusive 8 slippery

sapor: 5 gusto, savor, taste 6 flavor, relish 7 flavour

sapper: 5 miner 6 digger

Sappho: *consort:* 5 Phaon

home: 6 Lesbos

sappy: 5 juicy, moist, pithy, plump, silly 6 sodden 7 fatuous, foolish 8 vigorous 9 energetic, succulent 11 sentimental

sapsago: 6 cheese

sapsucker: 10 woodpecker

sapwood: 8 alburnum

Saracen: 4 Arab 5 nomad 6 Moslem

knight: 6 Rogero 8 Ruggiero

leader: 7 Saladin

Sarah: *husband:* 7 Abraham

slave: 5 Hagar

son: 5 Isaac

sarcasm: 4 gibe, jeer 5 fling, irony, taunt 6 attack, rebuke, satire 7 mockery 8 acridity, reproach, ridicule 9 criticism

pert. to: 8 ironical

sarcastic: dry 6 biting 7 cutting, mordant 8 incisive, sardonic

sarcenet, sarsenet: 4 silk, soft 6 smooth 8 tempered

sarcina: 8 bacteria 9 bacterium

sarcophagus: 4 tomb 6 coffin, cooler

sard: 7 sardine, sardius 9 carnelian 10 chalcedony

sardine: 4 bang 8 pilchard

Sardinia: *city:* 8 Cagliari

duchy: 5 Savoy 6 Savoie

language: 7 Catalan

seaport: 8 Cagliari

sardonic: 8 derisive 9 sarcastic

Sargon capital: 5 Accad

sarkinite: 8 arsenate

sarment: 4 cion 6 runner 7 cutting

sarong: 6 comboy

sarpler: 4 bale 6 weight 7 wrapper 8 covering

sarrazin: 9 buckwheat

sarsen: 5 block 8 monument 9 sandstone

sartor: 6 tailor

sash: obi 4 band, belt, benn(Sc.) 5 scarf 6 fascia, girdle 8 casement 9 waistband 10 cummerbund

sasin: 4 buck 8 antelope

Saskatchewan capital: 6 Regina

sassaby: 8 antelope

sassafras tea: 6 saloop

Satan: 4 Nick 5 demon, devil, eblis, fiend 6 Belial 7 Lucifer, tempter 8 diabolus 9 archenemy, archfiend 14 Mephistopheles

associate: 9 Beelzebub

son: Imp

satanic: 4 evil 6 wicked 8 devilish, diabolic, infernal 10 diabolical

satchel: bag 4 case, grip 5 cabas 6 valise

sate: 4 cloy, cram, glut 5 gorge, stuff 7 gratify, satiate, surfeit

satellite: Io 4 luna, moon, Rhea, vein 5 Ariel, Dione, Mimas, Titan 6 Europa, planet, Tethys 7 Japetus 8 Callisto, follower, Ganymede, Hyperion 9 attendant, dependent, Enceladus

man-made: Oso 4 Anna, Echo, Mars 5 Ariel, Faith, Lunik, Midas, Relay, Samos, Tiros 6 Cosmos, Flight, Ranger, Syncom, Vostok 7 Courier, Mariner, Pioneer, Sputnik, Telstar, Transit 8 Alouette, Explorer, Telestar, Vanguard 9 Vela-Hotel 10 Discoverer 12 Mercury-Atlas, Project-Score

weather: 5 Tiros

satiat: 7 replete

satiate: 4 cloy, fill, glut, pall, sate 5 gorge, slake 6 pamper 7 content, gratify, overeat, satisfy

satiating: 4 rich 6 stodgy 7 fulsome

satiety: 7 surfeit

satin imitation: 6 sateen 7 satinet 9 satinette

satin pod: 7 honesty

satiny: 6 glossy 8 lustrous

satire: 5 grind, irony 6 banter, parody, satura 7 lampoon, mockery, sarcasm 8 ridicule, travesty

satiric: dry 6 bitter, ironic 7 abusive, atellan, caustic, cutting 8 ironical, poignant 10 censorious 11 reproachful

satirist: 4 Pope, Shaw 5 Swift 8 Voltaire

satirize: 4 lash 5 grind 6 attack, expose 8 denounce 9 criticize

satisfaction: 4 ease, gree 6 amends 7 content, payment 8 pleasure 9 atonement, enjoyment 10 bloodmoney, recompense, reparation, settlement 11 complacence, contentment 12 compensation, propitiation, remuneration 13 gratification 15 indemnification

combat for: 4 duel

payment for killing: cro

satisfactory: pat 4 good 6 enough 8 adequate 9 allowable, expiatory 10 acceptable, satisfying

satisfied: fed 4 paid, smug 5 proud 9 contented, gratified 10 complacent

satisfy: do; pay 4 cloy, feed, fill, free, meet, sate, suit 5 appay, atone, repay, serve, slake 6 defray, please, supply 7 appease, assuage, content, expiate, fulfill, gratify, requite, satiate, suffice, surfeit 8 convince, reparate 9 discharge 10 compensate, remunerate

satrap: 5 ruler 6 prince, tyrant 8 governor, official, overlord

sattva: 5 truth 6 purity, wisdom 8 goodness 12 tranquillity

saturate: ret, sog, sop, wet 4 fill, glut, soak 5 imbue, souse, steep 6 dampen, drench, imbibe, imbrue, seethe 7 ingrain, satiate, satisfy 8 permeate 9 penetrate 10 impregnate

saturated: 6 sodden

Saturday: 7 Sabbath

pert. to: 9 sabbatine

Saturn: 6 Cronus, planet

in alchemy: 4 lead

ring part: 4 ansa 5 ansae(pl.)

satellite: 4 Rhea 5 Dione, Mimas, Titan 6 Tethys 7 Japetus 8 Hyperion 9 Enceladus

temple treasury: 8 aerarium

wife: Ops

saturnalia: 4 orgy 5 feast 7 revelry 8 carnival, festival

saturnine: 4 dull 5 grave, heavy 6 gloomy, morose, sullen 8 sluggish, taciturn

satyr: 4 faun, idol 5 deity 7 demigod 9 butterfly

sauce: dip 5 gravy 6 flavor, relish 8 dressing, matelote 9 condiment

kind: soy 4 alec, lear 5 garum 6 catsup 7 catchup, gascony, ketchup, mustard 8 chawdron, remolade 9 genevoise, remoulade 10 Bordelaise, mayonnaise 11 Hollandaise

sauciness: 10 effrontery

saucy: 4 bold, coxy, pert, rude 5 brash, fresh 6 bantam, cocket 7 forward 8 impudent, malapert 9 audacious, sprightly 11 impertinent

Saudi Arabia (see also **Arabia**): *capital:* 5 Mecca 6 Riyadh

desert: 5 Nefud

port: 5 Jidda

religious center: 5 Mecca 6 Medina

state: 4 Asir, Nejd

sauger: 4 fish 5 perch

Saul: *concubine:* 6 Rizpah

daughter: 6 Michal

father: 4 Kish

grandfather: Ner

herdsman: 4 Doeg

successor: 5 David

uncle: Ner

wife: 7 Ahinoam

Saul of Tarsus: 4 Paul

Sault Sainte Marie: Soo

saumont: 6 salmon

sauna: 4 bath 9 bathhouse

saunter: lag 4 idle, roam, rove, walk 5 range, shool, stray 6 dander, dawdle, loiter, lounge, potter, ramble, stroll, wander 8 ruminate

saunterer: 8 passerby

saurel: 4 fish, scad 5 xurel

saurian: 6 lizard 8 dinosaur

saury: 4 fish

sausage: 5 gigot 6 salame, salami, wiener 7 balloon, balogna, baloney, savely 8 cervelat, drisheen, rollejee, rolliche 9 andouille, bratwurst, rollichie 11 wiernerwurst 12 andouillette

casing: 4 bung

poisoning: 11 allantiasis

sausage-shaped: 9 allantoid 11 allantoidal

savage: 4 fell, grim, rude, wild 5 brute, crude, cruel, feral 6 brutal, ferine, fierce 7 brutish, furious, howling, inhuman, untamed 8 pitiless, ruthless 9 aborigine, atrocious, barbarian, barbarous, ferocious, merciless, primitive, truculent 10 unpolished 11 uncivilized 12 uncultivated, unrestrained

Savage Island people: 5 Niuan

savanna, savannah: 5 plain 9 grassland

savant: 4 sage 5 Solon 6 pedant 7 scholar 9 scientist

savarin: 7 brioche 10 coffeecake

save: bar, but 4 hain, keep 5 amass, catch, guard, hoard, salve, spare, store 6 defend, except, redeem, rescue, retain, scrimp, unless 7 deliver, husband, protect, reclaim, reserve, salvage 8 conserve, preserve 9 economize, excepting 10 accumulate

savin, savine: 7 juniper
saving: 6 frugal, thrift 7 thrifty 9 frugality
savings: 7 account, addlins 8 addlings
savoir faire: 4 tact 10 adroitness 11 worldliness 14 sophistication
savor, savour: 4 odor, zest 5 sapor, scent, smack, smell, taste, tinge 6 degust, flavor, relish, season 9 degustate
savory: 5 gusty, salty, sapid, tasty 7 piquant 8 pleasing 9 agreeable, palatable 10 appetizing, delightful
saw (see also **see**): cut 4 talk, word 5 adage, axiom, maxim, motto, rumor 6 cliche, saying 7 proverb 8 aphorism, apothegm 9 platitude 10 apophthegm
combining form: 5 serri
kind: 5 briar, edger, serra 6 stadda, trapan, trepan 8 trephine
part: 4 tine 5 redan, tooth
surgical: 6 trapan, trepan 8 trephine
saw-like: 8 serrated
sawbelly: 7 alewife
sawbones: 7 surgeon
sawder: 7 flatter
sawfish: ray
sawhorse: 4 buck 7 sawbuck
sawyer: 6 beetle, logman 9 lumberman 10 woodcutter
saxhorn: 4 alto, tuba
saxifrage: 6 seseli
Saxon: 9 Sassenach
chief: 5 Horsa
city: Ave
king: Ine 6 Harold
lady: 6 Godiva, Rowena
serf: 4 esne
swineherd: 5 Gurth
warrior: 5 Thane
Saxony city: 7 Dresden
say: 4 aver, deem, silk, tell, wool 5 speak, state, utter 6 advise, allege, answer, assert, bucket, direct, fabric, recite, relate, remark, repeat, report 7 declare, dictate, express, iterate, testify 8 announce, indicate 9 pronounce 10 asseverate
again: 6 repeat 9 reiterate
further: add
saying: mot, saw 4 quip, word 5 adage, axiom, logia, maxim, motto 6 byword, phrase 7 epigram, proverb 8 aphorism, apothegm 9 statement 11 declaration
apt: 6 bon mot
collection: ana 9 gnomology
distinguishing: 10 shibboleth
scab: 5 crust, mange 6 eschar, ratter 8 blackleg 9 scoundrel 13 strike-breaker
scabbard: 4 case 6 sheath, tsubas 7 holster
put in: 7 sheathe
tip: 7 crampit

scabby: low 4 base, mean 5 mangy 6 scurvy, shabby, stingy 12 contemptible
scabies: 4 itch 5 mange
scaddle: 4 wild 6 fierce 7 nervous 8 skittish 11 mischievous
scads: 4 lots 6 oodles
scaffie: 9 scavenger
scaffold: 4 cage, loft 5 easel, stage 7 gallery 8 platform
scalage: 8 estimate 9 allowance 10 percentage
scalar: 10 ladderlike
scalawag, scallawag: 4 pony, runt 5 scamp 6 rascal 10 scapegrace
scald: vex 4 burn 5 worry 6 blanch, excite, scorch 7 inflame, torment
scale: cup, hut 4 bowl, film, husk, peel, rate, rule, scut, shed, size 5 climb, flake, gamut, lepis, palea, scute, shive, weigh 6 ascend, lamina, rament, spread, vessel, weight 7 balance, clamber, coating, compare, lamella, measure, scatter, vernier 8 covering, disperse, separate 9 gradation, steelyard 12 incrustation
bony: 6 scutum
comb. form: 5 lepid 6 lepido
having: 7 leprose, scutate
note: do, fa, la, mi, re, ti; sol 8 dominant 10 supertonic
scale-like: 6 scurfy 7 leprose
scaling device: 6 ladder
scallion: 4 leek 5 onion 7 shallot
scallop: 4 quin 5 crena, notch 7 crenate, mollusk
scalp: rob 4 skin 5 cheat 6 defeat, denude, profit, trophy
disease: 5 favus, scurf 8 dandruff
scalpel: 5 knife 6 lancet 8 bistoury
scalper: 6 punter, trader 10 speculator
scaly: low 4 mean 6 stingy 8 squamous 10 despicable
scamble: 6 sprawl 7 collect, shamble, trample 8 scramble
scamp: imp 5 cheat, knave, rogue 6 rascal 8 scalawag, spalpeen, widdifow 9 scallawag, scoundrel 10 highwayman
scamper: run 4 race 5 speed 6 frolic, hasten, scurry 7 brattle, skitter 9 skedaddle
scan: eye 5 study, watch 6 behold, peruse, survey 7 examine, observe 10 scrutinize 11 contemplate
scandal: 5 eclat, odium, shame 6 gossip 7 calumny, outrage, slander 8 disgrace, ignominy 9 discredit 10 backbiting, defamation, detraction, opprobrium
scandalize: 5 shock 6 malign, offend, vilify
scandalous: 6 unholy 8 libelous, shocking 9 offensive 10 flagitious 11 furciferous
scandent: 8 climbing

Scandinavia (see also **Norse; Teuton**): **4** Dane, Lapp **5** Norse, Swede **8** Norseman, Suiogoth **9** Icelandic, Norwegian
alphabetical character: **4** rune
bard: **5** scald **7** sagaman
division: amt
explorer: **4** Eric
hero's place: **8** Valhalla
king: **4** Atli
land: **4** odal
legend: **4** edda, saga
legendary creature: nis **5** nisse, troll **6** Kraken
measure: ass, lod, ort, vog **4** last, mark, pund, sten, untz **5** carat **6** nylast **7** centner, lispund **8** lispound, skalpund, skeppund, skippund **9** shippound, skaalpund, skibslast **10** bismerpund
minstrel: see *bard* above
money: **5** krone
navigator: **4** Eric
nobleman: **4** jarl
pert. to: **5** Norse
plateau: **5** fjeld
rulers: Ros **10** Varangians
ship: **4** aesc
small bay: **5** fjord
trumpet: **4** lure
scant: few **4** lean **5** chary, stint **6** geason, meager, meagre, narrow, scrimp, slight, sparse **7** limited, sparing, wanting **12** parsimonious
scantling: 4 beam, stud **6** timber
scanty: 4 bare **5** close, small, spare **6** meager, meagre, scarce, sparse **7** limited, niggard, scrimpy, sparing **8** exiguous **9** niggardly **12** insufficient, parsimonious
scape: 4 slip, stem **5** fault, shaft **8** escapade, peduncle
scapegoat: 4 dupe **6** victim **10** substitute
scapegrace: 5 rogue, scamp **6** madcap, rascal **8** scalawag **9** reprobate, scallawag **10** profligate
scar: arr, mar, shy **4** mark, rock, seam, slit, wild **5** chink, cliff, crack, wound **6** cinder, deface, scared **7** blemish, catface, clinker **8** cicatrix, mountain, pockmark **9** disfigure **13** disfigurement
pert. to: **5** uloid
tissue: **6** keloid
scarab: 5 charm **6** beetle
scaramouch, scaramouche: 4 fool **5** scamp **6** rascal **7** buffoon
scarce: 4 dear, rare **5** scant, short **6** geason, meager, meagre, scanty, sparse **8** uncommon **9** deficient **10** infrequent **12** insufficient
scarcely: 6 barely, hardly, merely
scarcity: 4 lack, need, want **6** dearth, famine, penury, rarity **7** paucity, poverty **8** rareness **9** parsimony **10** deficiency, scarcensss **11** infrequency, sparingness **12** uncommonness **13** insufficiency, niggardliness
scare: awe, shy **4** fleg **5** alarm, dread, gliff, gloff, panic **6** fright **7** scarify, startle, terrify **8** affright, frighten
scarecrow: 5 bogle
scared: 6 afraid
scarf: boa, tie **4** band, sash, wrap **5** adorn, ascot, barbe, cloud, cover, orale, shawl, stole, unite **6** cravat, groove, rebozo, runner, tapalo, tippet **7** dopatta(Ind.), muffler, necktie **8** liripipe, liripoop **9** comforter, cormorant **10** fascinator **11** comfortable, neckerchief
feathered: boa
head: **8** babushka
scarfskin: 7 cuticle **9** epidermis
scarify: See **scare**
scarlet: red **4** lewd **5** bawdy **8** flagrant
Scarlett O'Hara: *home:* **4** Tara
husband: **5** Rhett
scarp: cut **5** cliff, slope **6** escarp **7** descent **8** fragment **9** declivity
scart: 4 mark **6** scrape **7** scratch **9** cormorant
scarves: See **scarf**
scary: 4 eery **5** eerie, timid, weird **6** spooky **7** ghostly, uncanny **8** alarming
scat: bop, tax **4** beat, riff, shoo **5** smash **6** begone, rebuff, shower **7** getaway, scatter, tribute, vamoose
scathe: 4 harm, hurt, sear **5** blast **6** assail, damage, injure, injury, scorch, wither **8** denounce **10** misfortune
scathing: 6 biting, severe **7** mordant **8** blasting, injuring, wounding **9** scorching, truculent, withering
scatter: sow, ted **4** deal, rout **5** fling, spray, strew, waste **6** dispel, shower, splash, spread **7** bestrew, confuse, diffuse, disband, fritter, radiate **8** dishevel, disperse, distract, separate, sprinkle, squander **9** bespatter, circulate, discomfit, dissipate **10** disconnect, distribute **11** disseminate
scatter-gun: 7 shotgun
scatterbrained: 5 giddy **7** flighty **9** frivolous
scattered: 6 sparse **7** erratic, strawed **8** rambling, sporadic **9** irregular **10** straggling
scatterer: 6 tedder
scattering: 7 vagrant, wastrel
scatula: box
scaup: 4 duck **8** grayback **10** canvasback
scavage: tax **4** duty, toll
scavenger: rat **7** vulture
scaw: 8 headland **10** promontory
scena: 10 recitative
scenario: 4 plot **6** script **10** continuity
scend: 4 lift **5** heave

scene: act 4 site, view 5 sight, vista 6 blow-up, locale 7 diorama, display, episode, picture, quarrel, tableau 8 prospect 9 landscape, spectacle
last: 6 finale

scenery: 4 view 7 picture 9 landscape 14 representation

sceneshifter: 4 grip

scenic: 8 dramatic 9 panoramic 10 theatrical 11 picturesque

scenite: 5 nomad

scent: 4 nose, odor 5 aroma, odour, savor, smell, sniff, spoor, track 6 breath, flavor 7 bouquet, essence, flavour, inkling, perfume 8 effluvia 9 emanation, fragrance

scented: 5 olent

scepter, sceptre: rod 4 mace 5 baton, staff 6 emblem 7 trident 8 caduceus 9 authority 11 sovereignty

scerne: 7 discern

schedule: 4 card, list, plan, time 5 slate, table 6 tariff 7 catalog, routine, writing 8 calendar, document, register, tabulate 9 catalogue, inventory, timetable

schefferite: 8 pyroxene

schelm: 5 rogue 6 rascal

schema: 4 plan 6 figure, scheme 7 diagram, outline

scheme: aim, gin, web 4 dart, list, plan, plot 5 angle, cabal, cadre, draft, drift, table 6 design, device, devise, figure, racket 7 complot, concoct, diagram, epitome, outline, program, project 8 conspire, contrive, forecast, gimcrack, intrigue 9 statement 10 concoction, conspiracy 11 contrivance, machination, proposition

schemer: 6 artist

scheming: 6 artful, crafty, tricky 8 fetching 9 designing 10 intriguing

schism: 4 rent 5 split 6 breach 8 division 10 separation

schist: 5 slate

schizocarp: 5 fruit, regma

schlemiel: dub, oaf 4 clod, goof 5 chump 7 saphead

schmaltz: 4 corn 14 sentimentality

scholar: 5 clerk, pupil 6 pedant, savant 7 bookman, learner, student 8 disciple 11 academician, philologist
day: 6 extern
servant: 7 famulus

scholarly: 7 erudite, learned 8 studious 10 scholastic

scholarship: 7 bursary 8 learning 9 allowance, education, erudition, knowledge 10 fellowship 11 instruction

scholiast: 9 annotator 10 glossarist 11 commentator 13 glossographer

school: gam, pod 4 cult, sect 5 drill, ecole(F.), flock, group, lycee(F.), shoal, teach, train 6 manege 7 academy, college, company, convent, educate, seminar 8 atheneum, document, exercise, instruct, seminary 9 athenaeum, cultivate 10 realschule(G.), university 11 institution, schoolhouse
grounds: 6 campus
group: PTA
kind: 4 high, prep 5 grade 7 primary 8 military 9 finishing, secondary 10 elementary, vocational 11 preparatory
of fish: 5 shoal
of thought: ism
of whales: gam
official: 9 principal, scholarch 10 headmaster 14 superintendent
pert. to: 8 academic
religious: 5 heder 6 cheder 8 seminary
riding: 6 manege
task: 6 lesson 7 problem 10 assignment 11 composition
term: 7 quarter 8 semester 9 trimester

schoolbook: 4 text 5 atlas 6 primer, reader 7 speller 9 geography

schoolfellow: 11 condisciple

schoolmaster: 4 caji, head 7 dominie, manager, pedagog 9 pedagogue

schooner: 4 boat, brig, tern 5 glass 6 vessel 7 measure
builder: 14 Andrew Robinson

schottische: 5 dance, polka

schout: 7 bailiff, sheriff

schrik: 5 panic 6 fright

science: art, sci 5 ology 9 knowledge 10 technology
of crop production: 8 agronomy
of healing: 9 iatrology
of human behavior: 6 ethics 10 psychology
of mountains: 7 orology
of plants: 6 botany
of words: 9 semantics
principle: 7 logic

scient: 4 able 7 knowing 8 skillful 9 knowledge

sciential: 4 able 7 capable 9 competent

scientific: 8 skillful 9 technical

scilicet: 6 namely 9 videlicet

scimitar, scimiter: 4 snee 5 saber, sword

scintilla: 4 atom, iota 5 spark, trace 8 particle

scintillate: 5 flash, gleam, spark 7 glitter, sparkle, twinkle 9 coruscate

scion, cion: bud, son 4 heir, twig 5 shoot, sprig 6 sprout 8 offshoot 9 offspring 10 descendant

scissor: cut 4 clip, trim 5 shear

scissors: 6 shears

scleroid: 4 hard 8 hardened 9 indurated

scoff: 4 food, gibe, gird, jeer, leer, meal, mock, rail 5 fleer, flout, gleek, scout, sneer, steal, taunt 6 deride 7 mockery, plunder 8 ridicule

scoffer: 5 clown 6 jester 10 unbeliever

scoke: 8 pokeweed

scold: nag, yap 4 haze, jump, rail, rant, rate 5 abuse, barge, boast, brawl, chide, score, shrew, slate 6 berate, bounce, rebuff, rebuke, revile 7 reprove, upbraid 8 chastise 9 objurgate 10 vituperate

scolding: 6 dirdum, rating, rebuke 7 combing, hearing, reproof 8 dressing

scombroid fish: 4 tuna 6 bonito 8 mackerel

sconce: 4 fine, fort, head 5 cover, skull 7 bracket, bulwark, lantern, shelter 8 entrench 10 protection 11 candlestick

scone: 4 farl 5 farle 7 biscuit

scoop: dig 4 bail, beat, lade 5 didle, empty, gouge, ladle, skeet, spoon 6 bucket, chisel, dipper, dredge, gather, hollow, shovel, vessel 7 curette 8 excavate

scoot: 4 dart, dray, scud 5 shoot, slide 6 begone, decamp, scurry 9 skedaddle

scooter: toy 4 boat, plow 6 glider

scop: 4 bard, poet

scope: 4 area, goal, room 5 range, reach, theme, tract 6 domain, extent, import, intent, length, object, sphere, target 7 liberty 8 distance, latitude 9 dimension, extension, intention

  having: 13 comprehensive
  large: 7 general

scopic: 6 visual

scoptical: 7 jeering, jesting 8 scoffing

scorch: cut 4 burn, char, flay, sear, skin 5 adust, parch, score, singe, slash, sting, toast 6 birsle, scathe, wither 7 blister, scratch, shrivel

scorched: 4 sere 5 adust

score: cut, run, tab, taw 4 goal, line, mark, rate 5 chalk, chase, corge, count, judge, notch, scold, slash, tally 6 abrade, barter, berate, furrow, grudge, number, reason, record, scotch, twenty, weight 7 account, arrange, scratch, upbraid 8 incision 9 criticize, grievance, reckoning 10 obligation 11 enumeration, orchestrate 12 indebtedness

scoria: aa 4 lava, slag 5 dross 6 refuse

scorify: 5 smelt

scoring point: ace, hit, run 4 down, goal 5 tally 6 basket

scorn: 4 geck, jeer, mock 5 scoff 6 deride, reject, slight 7 condemn, despise, disdain 8 contempt, derision 9 contumely

scornful: 5 aloof 7 haughty, stuckup 8 arrogant, insolent 10 disdainful, fastidious

scorpion: 4 nepa 6 onager, weapon 7 scourge 8 arachnid, catapult 10 vinegaroon

  stinger: 6 telson

Scorpion's Heart: 7 Antares

scorse: 5 trade 6 barter 8 exchange

scot: tax 4 levy 6 assess 7 payment 9 reckoning 10 assessment

Scot: 4 Gael, Pict 10 Caledonian, Highlander

scotch (see also **Scotland**): cut 4 stop 5 check, chock, notch, score, wedge 6 hinder, stingy, whisky 7 scratch, scruple 8 hesitate 9 frustrate

Scotchman: Mac 4 Gael, Scot 7 bluecap, Scottie 10 Highlander

scoter: 4 coot, duck, fowl

  genus: 7 oidemia 9 melanitta

Scotland: *accent:* 4 birr, burr
  askew or awry: 4 agee 5 agley
  at all: ava
  author: 5 Scott 6 Barrie
  beg: 4 sorn
  bird: gae 4 hern 6 grouse, snabby 7 snabbie 8 throstle 9 swinepipe
  blessing: 6 rebuke 8 scolding
  blood money: cro
  bluebell: 8 harebell
  boat: 4 zulu 6 scaffy, sexern 7 coracle, skaffie
  bonfire: 6 tandle
  brain: 4 harn
  bread: 5 briar 6 tammie 7 bannock
  bread dish: 4 saps
  briar: 4 rose
  brook: 4 sike
  broth: 4 soup
  bucket: 5 stoop, stoup
  bull: 4 stot
  bushel: fou
  buxom: 6 sonsie
  cake: 5 scone
  camp follower: 6 gudget
  cap: tam 6 bonnet, tassel, toorie 8 Balmoral 9 Glengarry 11 Tam O'Shanter
  cap tassel: 6 toorie
  cascade: lin 4 linn 5 force
  cat: 6 malkin
  cattle: 8 Ayrshire
  celebration: 4 kirn
  chafing dish: 7 choffer
  chair: 5 regal
  chief: 5 thegn
  child: 4 dalt 5 bairn 6 scuddy 8 smatchet
  church: 4 kirk
  city: Ayr 5 Alloa, Leith, Perth, Troon 6 Dundee 7 Glasgow, Grunock, Paisley 8 Aberdeen, Stirling 9 Edinburgh, Inverness, St. Andrews 10 Kilmarnock

cloth: 4 kelt 6 tartan
coin: 4 demy 5 bodle, groat 6 baubee, bawbee
colt: 4 stag
congress: Mod
corner: 4 neuk
county: Ayr 4 Bute, Fife, Ross 5 Angus,
Banff, Moray, Nairn, Perth 6 Argyll, Lan-
ark, Orkney 7 Berwick, Kinross, Peebles,
Renfrew, Selkirk, Wigtown 8 Aberdeen,
Ayrshire, Dumfries, Roxburgh, Shetland,
Stirling 9 Caithness, Dumbarton, Inverness 10 Kincardine, Midlothian, Suther-
land 11 Clackmannan, West Lothian 13
Kirkcudbright
court officer: 5 macer
cross: 8 crantara 9 crostarie
cuddy: 6 draper 7 peddler
cup: 4 tass
curlies: 4 kale
dagger: 5 skean
dance: bob 4 reel 7 walloch 9 ecossaise 10
strathspey 13 Highland-fling
destiny: 5 weird
devil: 4 deil
district: Ayr 5 Rinns 6 Atholl 7 Lothian 8
Galloway 9 Tweeddale 11 Breadalbane
donkey: 5 cuddy
drapery: 4 pand
drinking bout: 6 screed
drinking vessel: 4 tass 6 quaich, quaigh
duck: 10 bufflehead
elm: 4 wych
endure: 4 dree
excuse: 6 sunyie
explorer: Rae
eye: ee
fairy: 4 fane
farmer: 6 cottar, cotter 7 crofter
fashion: 7 Scotice
festival: Mod 7 Uphelya
fiddle: 4 itch
fingering: 4 wool, yarn
fireplace: 5 ingle
firth: Tay 4 Loch, Lorn 5 Clyde, Forth,
Moray 6 Linnhe 8 Cromarty
fish: 4 sile 7 sillock 8 spalding
fish trap: 4 yare 5 yaire
fishing expedition: 5 drave
fog: 4 haar
fort: 4 dune 10 roundabout
game: 6 shinty
garment: tam 4 kilt, maud 5 toosh 6 fecket,
tartan 7 arisard 8 Balmoral 11 Tam o'
Shanter
garter: 8 wooer-bab
ghost: 6 taisch
girl: 4 lass 5 quean 6 lassie, towdie 7 win-
klot

give: gie
grandchild: oe, oy; oye
grandfather: 8 gudesire
granite: 5 gowan
guess: 4 rede
gutter: 5 siver
hands: 8 paddling
have: hae
hazelnut: nit
heater: 7 choffer
heath: 7 heather
heavy: 5 tharf
hill: 6 strone
hillside: 4 brae
historian: 4 Hume 5 Skene
hoppers: 9 Hopscotch
icicle: 7 shoggle
inlet: gio
island: 4 Iona 5 Arran 6 Orkney 8 Hebrides,
Shetland
kale: 8 borecole
king: 6 Robert
kiss: 8 smoorich
lake: dee 4 loch
lament: 6 ochone
land: 6 carses
land tax: 4 cess
landholder: 5 laird, thane
language: 4 Erse 6 Lallan 7 Lalland
liquor: 5 scour 6 athole 8 whittier
lord: 5 laird
loyal: 4 leal
maurauder: 7 cateran
measure: cop 4 cran, fall, mile, peck, pint,
rood, rope 5 crane, crans, lippy 6 firlot,
lippie 7 auchlet, chalder, choppin 8
mutchkin, stimpart, stimpert 9 particate,
shaftment, shaftmont
mist: ure
money: 6 siller
monk: 6 culdee
mountain: 8 Ben Nevis 9 Grampians
muddled: ree
music festival: Mod
musical instrument: 5 pipes 7 bagpipe
musician: 5 piper
must: 4 maun
negative: nae
odd: 4 orra
pastry: 5 scone 7 carcake
patron saint: 6 Andrew
peasant: 6 cottar, cotter
peninsula: 5 Rinns
people: 8 Damnonii 9 Dammonian
person: 4 Gael, Pict, Scot 7 Scottie 9 Lowlander, Scotchman 10 Highlander
physicist: 4 Watt
plaid: 4 maud
poet: 4 Hogg, Moir 5 Burns

pole: 5 caber
pool: lin 4 linn
porridge: 5 brose
proprietor: 5 laird
pouch: 6 sporan 7 sporran
pudding: 6 haggis
queen: 4 Mary
ridge: run
river: Ayr, Dee, Don, Esk, Tay 4 Doon, Find, Norn, Nith, Spey 5 Afton, Annan, Clyde, North, Tweed 6 Teviot 7 Deveron
sausage: 9 whitehass 10 whitehawse
schoolmaster: dux
scurvy grass: 8 seabells
seaport: 4 Leth 5 Alloa 6 Dundee
sect: 9 Buchanite
self: sel
servant: 5 gilly 6 gillie
sheepfold: ree
small: sma
snow: sna 4 snaw
soldier: 7 cateran
song: 6 strowd
student: 5 bejan 6 nejant
tenure: 6 sorren 7 sorehon
tinker: 5 caird
tithe: 5 teind
title: 5 laird
to: tae
toad: ted 4 taed
tobacco: 5 elder
toe: tae
toil: 4 darg
topaz: 6 tassel 9 cairngorm
tourist resort: 4 Oban
tower: 7 toorock
town hall: 8 tolbooth 9 tollbooth
tree: arm
trousers: 5 trews
uncle: eme
unit: ane
vigor: vir
warrior: 4 kemp
water spirit: 5 kelpy 6 kelpie
waterfall: lin 4 linn 5 force
weakling: 4 ribe 5 shilp 7 shilpit
weapon: 5 skean 8 claymore, skeandhu
weight: 4 boll, drop 5 trone 6 bushel
whine: 4 yirn
whirlpool: 7 swilkie 8 swelchie
whisky: 6 athole 9 Glenlivat, Glenlivit 10 Usquebaugh
whitefish: 7 vendace
window: 7 winnock
woodcock: 4 eggs
world: 4 warl
yell: 4 gowl
youth: 5 chiel 7 callant

Scott: *character:* 5 Norna 7 Ivanhoe 9 Lochinvar
   novel: 6 Rob Roy 7 Ivanhoe 8 Talisman
   poem: 7 Marmion
Scottish: See **Scotland**
scoundrel: cad 4 scab 5 cheat, filth, knave, scamp 6 rascal, varlet 7 glutton, villain, warlock 8 bezonian 9 miscreant, reprobate 10 blackguard
scoup: run 4 leap, skip 7 scamper
scour: rub, run 4 beat, rake, rush, wash 5 clean, purge, scrub 6 decamp, polish, punish, remove 7 cleanse, roister 8 brighten, traverse
scourge: 4 bane, flay, flog, lash, whip 5 harry, shoot, slash 6 plague, punish, swinge, switch 7 afflict, torment 8 chastise 9 devastate 10 affliction, discipline, flagellate, infliction, punishment
Scourge of God: 6 Attila
scout: guy, spy 4 chap, jeer, look 5 scoff, watch 6 fellow, search 7 despise, explore, lookout, observe 8 emissary, informer, ridicule, watchman 11 reconnoiter, reconnoitre
   unit: den 4 pack 5 troop
scouth: 4 room 5 range, scope 6 plenty
scovy: 7 blotchy, smeared, streaky
scow: 4 acon(F.), boat 5 barge, float 6 garvey 7 gabbard, gabbart, lighter
scowl: 5 frown, glare, glout, lower 6 glower
scrab: 7 scratch
scraffle: 7 wrangle 8 scramble, struggle
scraggly: 5 rough 6 jagged, ragged 7 unkempt 9 irregular 10 splintered
scraggy: 4 bony, lean, thin 5 rough, weedy 6 meager, rugged, skinny 7 knotted, scrawny
scram: 4 shoo 6 benumb 7 vamoose 8 paralyze, withered
scramble: mix 4 push 5 climb, crowd, crush 6 jostle, sprawl, spread, strive 7 clamber, pushing, scatter 8 struggle
scrambled: 4 pied
scran: 4 grub 6 morsel, refuse 9 leftovers 10 provisions
scrannel: dry 4 lean, poor, thin, weak 5 harsh 6 slight 7 scrawny 11 unmelodious
scrap: bit, end, jag, ort, rag 4 chip, item, junk 5 fight, grain, piece, shred, waste 6 cullet, morsel, refuse 7 cutting, discard, extract, oddment, quarrel, remnant 8 fraction, fragment
scrape: bow, hoe, row, rub, saw 4 claw, grit, harl, rake, rasp, scud, trap 5 claut, erase, grate, graze, gride, hoard, order, shave 6 abrade, dredge, fiddle, gather, harass, re-

fine, remove, sclaff 7 collect, corrode, scratch 9 situation 10 difficulty 11 predicament

scraped linen: 4 lint

scraper: 6 barber, rasper, xyster 7 fiddler, strigil 8 grattoir

scraping: 6 rasion, rasure

scrapper: 5 boxer 7 fighter 8 pugilist

scraps: 5 scran
literary: ana

scratch: dig, mar, rat, rit, rub, wig 4 claw, draw, feed, heap, line, mark, race, rake, rist, tear 5 break, claut, clawk, erase, expel, fluke, frush, score, wound 6 cancel, furrow, gather, injury, rasure, scotch, scrape, scrawl 7 expunge, roughen, scarify, scorify 8 incision, scribble, scrobble, withdraw 12 scratchbrush

scratcher: 6 forger 13 counterfeiter

scratching: 8 rasorial

scratchy: 6 uneven 10 straggling

scrawk: 6 squeak, squawk 7 scratch, screech

scrawl: 4 teem 5 crawl 7 scratch, writing 8 scribble

scrawm: 5 climb 7 clamber 8 scramble

scrawny: 4 lean, poor, thin 7 scraggy, scranny, scrubby 8 rawboned

scrawny animal: 5 scrag

screak: 4 rasp 5 creak, grate 7 screech

scream: cry 4 wail, yarm, yaup, yawl, yell, yowt 6 shriek, squall, yammer 7 screech

screamer: 5 chaja

scree: 5 stone, talus 6 pebble

screech: cry 4 yell 5 quawk 6 outcry, scream, shriek 7 ululate

screed: say 4 land, rend, rent, tear 5 board, shred, strip 6 scrape, smooth, tirade 7 leveler 8 diatribe, fragment, harangue 9 discourse

screen: 4 cage, hide, mask, mesh, reja, sept, sift, veil 5 arras, blind, chick(Ind.), cloak, cover, grill, purda, scarf, shade, sieve, speer, spier 6 defend, filter, grille, purdah, settle, shield 7 conceal, curtain, protect, reredos, shelter 8 bescreen, covering, separate 9 breakwind, partition 10 protection
architectural: 5 spier
chancel: 4 jube 7 reredos
chimney: 6 bonnet
mesh: 4 laun 5 sieve
wind: 8 paravent

screw: key, pay 4 turn, wind, worm 5 cheat, guard, horse, miser, twist 6 gimlet, keeper, salary, spiral 7 contort, distort, robbery, squeeze, tighten, turnkey 9 bargainer, propeller, skinflint 10 contortion, crustacean, instructor

screw-like: 6 spiral, spirod 7 helical

screw pine: 5 vacoa 6 vacona, vacoua 8 pandanus

screw-pine family: 11 pandanaceae

screwball: nut, sap 5 crank, crazy, dippy, goose 7 fanatic, galloot, saphead 8 crackpot, dumbbell 9 blockhead, eccentric 10 crackbrain, muttonhead

screwed: 5 drunk 11 intoxicated

screwy: 5 crazy, wacky 6 absurd, whacky 7 winding 8 freakish, peculiar 9 eccentric, fantastic 10 irrational, misleading, unbalanced 11 impractical 12 crackbrained, preposterous

scribal: 7 clerkly

scribble: 5 write 6 scrawl 7 scratch 8 scrabble

scribe: 5 clerk, write 6 author, copier, doctor, notary, penman, scrive, writer 7 copyist, graffer, teacher 8 inscribe 9 draftsman, scenarist, scrivener, secretary 10 amanuensis, journalist 11 transcriber 13 bibliographer

scriggle: 5 twist 6 squirm, wiggle 7 wriggle 8 curlicue

scrimmage: 4 play 6 battle, splore, tussle 8 football, practice

scrimp: 4 save 5 stint 6 meager, scanty 9 economize

scrimping: 7 miserly, sparing 9 niggardly

scringe: net 4 flog 5 glean, seine 6 cringe, flinch, search

scrip: bag 4 list 6 wallet 7 satchel, writing 8 schedule 11 certificate

script: 5 ronde 8 scenario 10 penmanship 11 chirography, handwriting
Arabic: 5 neski
round: 5 ronde
Syriac: 5 serta

scriptor: See **scribe**

scriptural: 8 Biblical

scripture: 4 text, word, writ 5 Bible, motto 7 passage, writing 10 manuscript, penmanship 11 composition, handwriting, inscription
interpreter: 7 exegete
Moslem: 7 Alcoran
occult interpretation: 6 cabala
part: 6 lesson
version: Vul 4 Vulg 5 Douay, Itala 7 Vulgate

scrive: cut 5 score, write 6 scribe 7 carving, scratch, writing 8 inscribe 11 handwriting

scrivello: 4 tusk

scrivener: See **scribe**

scrofula: 4 evil 6 struma 9 king's evil

scrofulous: 7 corrupt 10 degenerate 12 contaminated

scroll: 4 list, roll 5 draft 6 escrol, record, scrawl, spiral, volute 7 escroll, outline, writing 8 enscribe, inscribe, schedule, streamer
Hebrew: 6 mezuza 7 mezuzah
writing: 8 makimono
scrooch: 6 crouch, huddle
scroop: 5 creak, grate 6 scrape, squeak
scrouge: 5 crowd, press 7 squeeze
scrounge: 5 cadge, steal 6 pilfer, search, sponge
scroyle: 6 fellow, wretch 9 scoundrel
scrub: mop, rub 4 mean, poor, runt, wash 5 clean, dwarf, scour, small 6 drudge, paltry, shabby 7 cleanse 8 inferior 10 undersized 14 undernourished
scrub turkey: 6 leipoa 8 megapode
scrubby: 5 runty, small 7 stunted 8 inferior
scruff: 4 film, nape, scum 5 crust, dross 6 refuse 7 coating 8 covering, dandruff
scrump: 6 shrink 7 shrivel, squeeze
scrumptious: 4 fine, nice 5 dandy 7 capital, elegant 8 splendid 9 delicious
scrunch: 5 crush 6 crunch, huddle 7 squeeze
scruple: 4 part 5 demur, doubt, qualm 6 amount, boggle, weight 7 anxiety, portion 8 question 9 disbelief, misgiving 10 uneasiness
one-half: 5 obole
scrupulous: 4 nice 5 chary, exact 6 honest, proper, strict 7 careful, correct, precise, upright 8 accurate, cautious 9 reluctant 11 punctilious 13 conscientious
to excess: 7 finical, finicky, prudish 9 finicking 10 fastidious
scrutinize: eye, pry 4 scan, sift 5 probe 7 examine, inspect, observe
scrutiny: 4 gaze, look
scrutoire: 10 escritoire
scruze: 5 crush 7 squeeze
scry: cry 4 gaze, look 5 shout 6 descry, outcry
scryer: 4 seer
scud: ale, fly, run 4 beer, blow, foam, gust, mist, move, scum, skim, slap 5 hurry, spank, spray 6 scrape, shower 7 rushing 10 crustacean
scuff: 4 blow, cuff, drag, gust, toss, wipe 5 brush, evade, graze, rowdy, slare, touch, tread 6 buffet, rabble, scruff, shower, slight 7 scatter, shuffle, slipper 9 roughened, scratched
scuffle: 4 cuff 5 amble, fight, melee, scuff, shool 6 affray, bustle, clinch, combat, sclaff, strive, tussle 7 contend, shamble, shuffle 8 struggle
scug: 5 shade 6 shadow 7 protect, shelter 8 pretense, squirrel 9 schoolboy
sculch: 6 cultch, refuse

scull: oar 4 boat 6 basket, propel, wherry 7 rowboat 8 scullion
scullery: 5 ewery
scullion: 4 base 5 gippo, onion 6 menial, wretch 7 servant 8 scallion 10 blackguard
sculp: 4 pelt, skin 5 break, carve, scalp 6 sculpt 7 engrave 9 engraving, sculpture
sculptor: 6 artist, graver, imager
famous: 5 Rodin 7 Phidias 12 Michelangelo
tool: 6 graver
sculpture: 4 bust, head 5 carve, grave, torso 6 emboss, relief, statue 7 engrave, relievo
framework: 8 armature
pert. to: 7 glyphic, glyptic 9 glyptical
slab: 6 metope
scum: 4 brat, foam, scud, silt, skim 5 dross, froth, range, scour, spume, sweep 6 bubble, rabble, refuse, scoria 10 impurities 12 offscourings
scumfish: 5 choke 9 discomfit, overpower, suffocate
scup: 4 fish 5 bream, porgy
scuppernong: 4 wine 5 grape 9 muscadine
scurrilous: low 4 foul, vile 5 gross 6 ribald, vulgar 7 abusive 8 indecent, scurrile 9 insulting, offensive 11 foulmouthed, opprobrious
scurry: hie, run 4 race 5 harry, scoot, scour, skirr 6 flurry, hasten 7 scamper, scuttle, skelter 9 skedaddle
scurvy: low 4 mean 6 shabby 7 disease 8 scorbute 12 contemptible, discourteous
preventative: 6 citrus 13 antiscorbutic
scutage: fee, tax 4 levy 6 impost
scutate: 5 scaly 7 peltate
scuttle: hod, run 4 dish, sink, veto 5 scoot 6 basket, bucket, scotch, scurry, shovel 7 octopus, platter 8 hatchway 10 cuttlefish
scuttlebutt: 5 rumor 6 gossip
scutum: 5 plate, scute 6 shield
Scylla: *father:* 5 Nisus
lover: 5 Minos
scythe: sy(Sc.); lea 6 sickle
handle: 5 snath, thole 6 snathe
sweep: 5 swath
sea: mer(F.) 4 meer(G.)
anemone: 5 polyp 7 actinia
approach: 7 seagate
arm: bay 4 gulf 5 bayou, firth, fjord, frith, inlet, lough 7 estuary
at: 4 asea
bottom: bed
combining form: mer
current: 4 tide 8 undertow
deity: Ler, Ran 5 Aegir, Doris 6 Nereus, Triton 7 Neptune, Phorcus, Phorcyn, Phorcys, Phorkys, Proteus 8 Palaemon, Poseidon
delicacy: roe 4 nori

description: 11 haliography
god: 7 Neptune 8 Poseidon
goddess: Ran 4 Nina 8 Eurynome 9 Leucothea 10 Amphitrite
king: Ler 5 chief 6 pirate, viking
land in: 6 island
life of: 8 halibios
little: 6 sealet
mammal: 4 seal 5 whale
open: 6 midsea
periodic motion: 4 tide
pert. to: 4 vast 5 naval 6 marine 7 oceanic, pelagic 8 maritime, nautical 9 aequoreal, thalassic
plant: 6 enalid
prophetic god: 7 Proteus
roughness: 5 swell, waves 6 lipper
route: 4 lane
spray: 9 spindrift 10 spoondrift
swell: 4 surf
term: 4 ahoy 5 avast, belay, trice
sea biscuit: 7 galette(F.) 8 hardtack
sea cow: 6 dugong, rytina, walrus 7 manatee 8 sirenian 12 hippopotamus
sea cucumber: 6 pedata 7 trepang 11 holothurian
sea dog: tar 4 seal 6 pirate, sailor 7 breaker, dogfish 9 privateer
sea duck: 5 eider 6 scoter 7 scooter
sea eagle: ern 4 erne, tern 6 osprey
sea-ear: 7 abalone
sea eel: 6 conger 7 lamprey
sea-foam: 5 froth 9 sepiolite 10 meerschaum
sea gate: 5 beach 7 channel
sea goose: 7 dolphin 9 phalarope
sea gull: cob, mew 4 cobb, gore
sea hog: 8 porpoise
sea horse: 6 walrus 8 whitecap 11 hippocampus
sea kale: 4 cole
sea lettuce: 5 laver 7 seaweed
sea nettle: 6 medusa 9 jellyfish
sea nymph: 5 siren 6 Nereid 7 Galatea, Oceanid
sea raven: 7 sculpin 9 cormorant 10 squaretail
sea robber: 6 jaeger, pirate 7 corsair 9 buccaneer, privateer
sea slug: 6 trepan 8 cucumber 10 nudibranch
sea soldier: 6 marine
sea squirt: 5 salpa 8 ascidian, tunicate
sea swallow: 4 tern 6 petrel
sea unicorn: 7 narwhal
sea urchin: 6 repkie 7 echinid, echinus 8 echinoid 10 echinoderm
rock hole: 5 geode
sea wolf: 4 seal 6 pirate 7 wolfish 9 privateer, submarine

sea worm: sao 7 annelid
seabird: auk, ern 4 duck, erne, gull, smew, tern 5 solan, yager 6 gannet, petrel 7 pelican 9 albatross 10 shearwater
seaboard: 5 coast 9 coastland, tidewater
seadog: 6 fogbow, fogdog 8 fogeater
seafarer: gob, tar 4 salt 6 sailor, seaman 7 mariner 9 navigator
seagoing: 5 naval 7 capable 9 seafaring 13 weatherbeaten
seal: cap, fix, hem, set, wax 4 bind, bull, cere, lute, rope, seel, shut, sign 5 bulla, chain, close, sigil, stamp, swile, token, wafer 6 attest, cachet, clinch, fasten, pledge, ranger, ratify, scarab, secure, signet 7 closure, confine, confirm, leather 8 breloque, document, guaranty, imprison, sealskin, validate 9 assurance, carnivore, guarantee, sigillate 10 obligation 12 authenticate 14 authentication
bearded: 5 ursuk 6 makluk
decorated with: 9 sigillate
eared: 5 otary
eared genus: 8 zalophus
letter: 6 cachet
limb: 7 flipper
official: 6 signet
pelt: 5 sculp
pert. to: 7 phocine
place: LS 7 rookery
polar: 5 otary, phoca, Ross's, ursal, ursuk 6 makluk 8 bedlamer, Ross seal, seecatch 9 sterrinck
school: pod
young: pup 6 beater, hopper 7 quitter, saddler 11 flipperling, holluschick
seal skin: 5 sculp
sealing wax: lac
seam: sew 4 fash, fold, join, line, load, mark, scar 5 cleft, joint, layer, raphe, ridge, strip, unite 6 groove, streak, suture 7 crevice, fissure, stratum, wrinkle 8 cicatrix 10 packsaddle
pert. to: 7 sutural, suturic
seaman: See sailor, seafarer
seamark: 6 beacon 8 landmark 10 lighthouse
seamer: 5 sewer 6 seamer 8 stitcher 10 dressmaker, seamstress
seamless: 5 whole 7 unsewed 12 araphorostic
seamy: 5 rough 8 degraded, wrinkled 12 disreputable
seance: 7 meeting, session, sitting
holder: 6 medium
seaport: 4 port 6 harbor
sear (see also **sere**): 4 burn, mark, scar 5 brand, brown, catch, parch, singe 6 braise, deaden, scorch, wither 9 cauterize

search: 4 comb, grub, hunt, look, nose, rout, seek 5 delve, frisk, probe, quest 6 brevit, ferret, forage, pierce, sphere, survey 7 canvass, examine, explore, inquire, inquiry, inspect, ransack, rummage 8 research, scrounge, scrutiny 9 penetrate 10 scrutinize 11 exploration, investigate

searching: 4 keen 5 acute, sharp 10 discerning

searing: 7 cautery

seascape: 6 marine

seashell: 4 clam 5 conch, snail 7 scallop

seashore: 5 beach, coast, shore 7 seaside 8 seabeach, seacoast

pert. to: 8 littoral

season: age, dry, tid, ver 4 beek, fall, salt, sele, tide, time 5 devil, imbue, inure, ripen, savor, spice, taste, tinge 6 autumn, embalm, flavor, mature, period, soften, spring, steven, summer, temper, winter 7 condite, flavour, Maytide, weather 8 accustom, marinate, occasion 9 habituate 10 impregnate 11 acclimatize, opportunity

religious: 4 Lent 6 careme

seasonable: pat 4 ripe 6 timely 7 apropos 8 suitable 9 opportune 11 appropriate

seasonably: 7 betimes

seasonal: 8 periodic

seasoned: 7 veteran 8 finished

seasoning: 4 herb, mace, sage, salt 5 cumin, onion, spice, thyme 6 celery, cloves, cummin, garlic, nutmeg, pepper, relish 7 caraway, cuminos, mustard, oregano, paprika, vinegar 8 allspice, cardamom, marjoram, rosemary, turmeric 9 condiment, coriander

seasons: 5 Horae

goddess: 4 Dike 5 Horae 6 Eirene, Eunomi

seat: fix, pew, see 4 apse, bank, form, hold, home, loge, room, site 5 asana, bench, chair, floor, place, sella(L.), siege, stool, usher 6 exedra, grange, howdah, locate, sedile, settee, settle, throne 7 capital, install, ottoman, situate, station, taboret, tendoor, tendour 8 bleacher, locality, location, tabouret 9 banquette, establish, residence, situation

chancel: 6 sedile

high: 5 roost

of judgment: 8 tribunal

of justice: 4 banc

on elephant: 6 houdah, howdah

tier of: 6 gradin

seat bone: 7 ischium

seat worm: 7 pinworm

seawan: See **sewan**

seaweed: ore 4 agar, alga, kelp, nori 5 algae, dulse, laver, varec, vraic, wrack 6 delisk, desmid, fucoid, varech 7 oreweek 8 agar-agar, hempweed, sargasso 9 desmidian

culture medium: 4 agar

edible: 5 dulse

extract: 4 agar

genus of: 6 alaria

pert. to: 6 algous

purple: 4 nori 5 laver

red: 5 dulse 6 delisk

study: 6 algology

seaweedy: 6 algous

Seb: See **Geb**

sebaceous: 5 fatty

sec: dry

secant: 7 cutting 12 intersecting

secede: 8 withdraw

seceder: 8 apostate

secern: 7 secrete 8 separate 11 distinguish 12 discriminate

seckel: 4 pear

seclude: bar 4 deny, hide 5 debar, expel 6 recess, remove, retire, screen 7 exclude, isolate, protect, retreat 8 prohibit, separate, withdraw 9 segregate, sequester

secluded: 5 aloof, apart 6 remote, secret 7 private 8 excepted, solitary

second: aid 4 abet, back, echo, time 5 other 6 assist, attend, backer, handle, moment 7 another, confirm, endorse, forward, further, instant, succeed, support, sustain 8 inferior 9 assistant, encourage, imperfect, prototype, reinforce, secondary, viscosity 10 additional 11 corroborate, subordinate 13 supplementary

comb. form: 6 deuter 7 deutero

second childhood: 6 dotage 8 senility

second-rate: 6 shabby 8 inferior, mediocre

second sight: ESP 9 intuition 12 clairvoyance

second-sighted: fey 7 psychic 9 intuitive, visionary 11 clairvoyant 12 precognitive

second-story man: 5 thief 7 burglar

second team: 6 scrubs 9 yannigans 11 substitutes

secondary: bye 5 minor 6 deputy 8 delegate, inferior 9 auxiliary, satellite 10 accidental 11 subordinate

color: 5 green 6 orange, purple

proposition: 5 lemma

secondary school: 4 high, prep 5 lycee(F.) 7 academy 10 realschule(G.), vocational

secondhand: 4 used, worn 6 resold 7 derived 8 borrowed 10 unoriginal

dealer: 6 ragman 7 junkman

secret: 4 dark, dern, hide, rune 5 blind, cabal, close, inner, privy 6 arcane, arcana, closet, covert, hidden, occult, remote, stolen 7 arcanum, cryptic, furtive, mystery, privacy, private, privity, retired, unknown 8 discrete, esoteric, intimate, mystical, reticent, secluded, stealthy **9** clancular, concealed, recondite, seclusion, secretive, underhand **10** confidence **11** clandestine, concealment **12** confidential, hugger-mugger **13** surreptitious

secret agent: spy **8** emissary, saboteur **10** counterspy

secret place: 6 adytum **7** sanctum

secretaire: 9 secretary **10** escritoire

secretary: 4 desk **5** clerk **9** confidant **10** amanuensis

secrete: 4 bury, hide, ooze, stow **5** exude **7** conceal

secretion: gum, sap **4** bile, laap, lerp, milk **5** juice, latex, mucus, resin, sudor, sweat **6** saliva **9** exudation

secretly: 4 inly **5** aside **13** clandestinely

sect: 4 clan, cult, part **5** class, group, order, party **6** school **7** faction, section **9** following **10** philosophy **12** denomination

distinguishing word: **10** shibboleth

sectarian: 7 bigoted, heretic, sectary **8** apostate **9** dissenter **12** narrow-minded **17** denominationalist

sectary: 4 sect **6** votary **8** adherent, disciple, follower, partisan **9** dissenter, sectarian **11** independent **13** non-conformist

section: 4 pane, part **5** piece, slice **6** canton **7** portion, segment **8** division **9** signature **11** subdivision

concluding: **8** epilogue

section hand: 6 worker **7** crewman, laborer

sector: 4 area **8** division

secular: lay **4** laic **5** civil **6** carnal, laique(F.), vulgar **7** earthly, profane, worldly **8** temporal **9** temporary **17** nonecclesiastical

secure: buy, get, pot, tie **4** bail, bind, bolt, easy, fast, firm, gird, moor, nail, safe, sure, tape **5** chain, guard, siker, spike, trice, truss **6** anchor, assure, clinch, defend, ensure, fasten, obtain, sicker, stable, strong **7** acquire, assured, certain, forfend, procure, protect **8** conserve, forefend **9** confident, constrain, guarantee **10** dependable **11** trustworthy, undisturbed **13** overconfident

security: 4 bail, bond, ease, gage **5** frith, grith, guard **6** pledge, safety, surety **7** defense, hostage, shelter **8** guaranty, warranty **9** assurance, certainty, guarantee, insurance **10** confidence, protection

sedan: car **4** auto **5** chair **10** automobile

sedate: 4 calm, cool, dope, drug **5** douce, grave, quiet, sober, staid **6** demure, proper, serene **7** earnest, serious, settled **8** composed, decorous **9** dignified, unruffled **12** tranquillize **13** contemplative, dispassionate

sedative: 6 remedy **7** aconite, bromide, chloral, nervine **8** barbital, lenitive, soothing **9** paregoric **10** palliative **13** tranquillizer

sedent: 6 seated **7** sitting

sedentary: 7 settled, sitting **8** inactive, slothful, tranquil **10** deliberate, motionless, stationary

sederunt: 7 session, sitting **8** assembly

sedge: sag **5** brood, flock **7** bulrush, hassock

genus of: **5** carex **7** scirpus

sediment: lee **4** crap, silt **5** dregs, magma, waste **6** bottom, refuse **7** deposit, grounds **8** settling

sedition: 6 revolt, strife, tumult **7** treason **9** commotion, rebellion **10** dissention, turbulence **12** insurrection

seditionary: 7 inciter **8** promoter **9** seditious **10** factitious, treasonist **12** contumacious

seduce: 4 lure **5** charm, decoy, tempt **6** allure, betray, entice **7** corrupt, debauch, mislead **8** inveigle

seducer: 8 Lothario

sedulous: 4 busy **8** diligent, untiring **9** assiduous, laborious, unwearied **10** persistent **11** industrious, persevering, unremitting

see: spy **4** espy, hear, ibid, look, meet, rank, scry, seat, view **5** besee, chair, power **6** attend, behold, descry, detect, escort, notice, office, throne **7** diocese, discern, examine, inspect, observe, undergo, witness **8** cathedra, consider, discover, perceive **9** accompany, apprehend, authority, bishopric, encounter, interview, visualize **10** comprehend, experience, scrutinize, understand

above: vs(L.) **5** supra

below: vi(L.) **5** infra

seeing: 6 ocular **13** introspective

seed: ben, egg, pea, pip, pit, sow **4** germ, milt, tare **5** acorn, drupe, grain, ovule, plant, spore, stock **6** acinus, bubble, kernel, origin, samara, source **7** capsule, progeny, seedlet **8** ancestry **9** beginning, inoculate, offspring, posterity **10** descendant

apple: pip

aromatic: **5** anise **6** nutmeg **7** aniseed **9** anise-seed

case: pod **4** burr

cell: **4** cyst

coat: **4** aril, bran **5** testa

comb. form: **5** sperm **7** spermat **8** spermato

container: bur, pod **6** carpel, legume, loment

edible: pea **4** bean **6** lentil

expansion: ala

flavoring: **5** anise, cumin **6** cummin, sesame **7** caraway

immature: **5** ovule

organ: **6** pistil

part: pod 4 aril 5 testa 6 tegman, tunica 9 endosperm
part with: 4 core
poisonous: 7 calabar 9 jequirity
remove: gin, pit 5 picul
scar: 4 hila(pl.) 5 hilum
vessel: pod 6 carpel, legume
seed leaf: 9 cotyledon
seedless: 7 agamous
seedy: 4 worn 5 tacky 6 shabby 7 scruffy 11 debilitated
seek: beg, sue, try, woo 4 busk, fand, hunt, sick 5 court, crave, essay, probe, quest, scout, trace 6 aspire, follow, fraist, pursue, search 7 attempt, beseech, entreat, examine, explore, inquire, request, solicit 8 endeavor 9 importune 11 investigate
seeker: 6 prober, tracer 7 pursuer, zetetic 9 applicant 10 petitioner
seel: 5 blind 8 hoodwink
seem: 4 look 5 feign 6 appear, beseem 7 pretend 8 manifest
seeming: 6 proper 9 befitting
seemingly: 5 quasi
seemliness: 5 grace 7 decorum
seemly: fit 6 comely, decent, proper, rather, suited 7 fitting 8 decently, decorous, graceful, handsome, passably, suitable, suitably 10 becomingly 13 appropriately
seen (see also **see**): 7 visible
seep: run 4 leak, ooze 5 exude 8 transude 9 percolate 10 infiltrate
seer: 4 sage 5 augur, sybil 6 mystic, oracle, scryer 7 augurer, diviner, prophet 9 predictor 10 forecaster, foreteller, soothsayer 11 clairvoyant, Nostradamus 14 prognosticator
seesaw: 6 teeter, tilter, totter 9 alternate, crossruff, vacillate 10 reciprocal
seethe: hum 4 boil, soak, stew, teem 5 steep 6 bubble, buller, decoct 7 blubber 8 saturate
segment: arc 4 part 5 piece, tmema 6 cantle, divide, somite 7 isomere, portion, section 8 division, fragment, metamere, separate
body: 8 somatome
of crustacean: 6 telson
segment-shaped: 5 toric
segregate: 4 part 5 sever 6 divide, select 7 isolate, seclude 8 classify, separate
seine: net 5 trawl
Seine tributary: 4 Aube, Eure, Oise 5 Marne
seise: See **seize**
seism: 10 earthquake
seity: 8 selfhood 13 individuality
seize: bag, cap, cly, cop, hap, nab, net 4 bind, bite, claw, fang, grab, grip, hent, hook, prey, take, trap 5 annex, catch, clink, grasp, reave, ravin, usurp, wrest 6 affect,

arrest, attach, attack, betake, clinch, clutch, collar, fasten, ravene, snatch, strike 7 afflict, capture, grabble, grapnel, possess, prehend 8 arrogate 9 apprehend, deprehend, raptorize 10 comprehend, confiscate, understand
for debt: 6 attach 8 distrain 9 garnishee
seizure: fit 6 stroke 10 androlepsy 11 androlepsia, manucapture
Sekhet's husband: 4 Ptah
selachian: ray 5 shark 7 dogfish
seladang: 4 gaur 6 animal 7 buffalo
selcouth: 7 strange, unusual 9 marvelous, wonderful
seldom: 4 rare 6 rarely 10 infrequent 12 infrequently
sele: 4 time 6 season 7 welfare 8 occasion 9 happiness 11 opportunity
select: opt 4 cull, draw, name, pick, wale 5 allot, elect, elite 6 assign, choice, choose, chosen, exempt, picked, prefer 8 eximious 9 excellent, exclusive, segregate 10 fastidious 11 outstanding
selection: 5 piece 7 analect, passsage 10 collection
selective: 6 choosy 7 choosey 8 electric 9 demanding
Selene: 4 Luna, moon
selenium: *compound:* 7 selenid 8 selenide
soft acid: 8 selenate
self: ego, own, sel(Sc.), soi(F.) 4 same, very 5 being 6 myself 7 himself 8 personal 9 identical 10 particular 11 personality
combining form: 4 auto
killing of: 7 suicide 8 felo-de-se
pert. to: 8 personal
self-acting: 9 automatic
self-assertion: 6 egoism, vanity
self-centered: 6 stable 7 selfish 10 egocentric, stationary 11 independent
self-confidence: 5 poise 6 aplomb 8 presence 9 composure
self-contained: 4 calm, cool 8 composed, reserved 9 collected 15 uncommunicative
self-control: 4 will 8 calmness 11 forbearance
self-defense: 6 boxing 7 fencing, j(i)ujitsu, j(i)ujutsu 8 fighting
self-denial: 10 abstinence, asceticism, puritanism 11 forbearance
self-esteem: 5 pride 6 egoism, vanity, 7 egotism 9 assurance
self-evident: 5 clear 7 obvious 8 truistic 9 axiomatic 11 postulation
self-examination: 13 introspection
self-generated: 11 spontaneous
self-government: 8 autonomy 12 independence
self-important: 7 pompous

self-love: 6 egoism 7 egotism

self-possessed: 4 calm, cool 6 cooler 8 composed 11 undisturbed

self-reproach: rue 6 regret 7 remorse 9 penitence 10 contrition

self-respect: 5 pride

self-righteous: 11 pharisaical

self-satisfied: 4 smug 6 jaunty 10 complacent

self-subsistence: 12 independence

self-worship: 9 autolatry

selfish: 6 stingy 7 hoggish 9 dissocial, egotistic 10 egocentric 11 egotistical 12 self-centered

selfishness: 12 ego-centricity

selfsameness: 8 identity

sell: 4 bilk, cant, deal, dump, dupe, give, gull, hand, hawk, hoax, vend 5 cheat, trade, trick, yield 6 barter, betray, impose, market, peddle, retail 7 auction, bargain, deceive, deliver, dispose 8 convince, persuade, transfer 9 negotiate, wholesale
over official rate: 5 scalp

seller: 6 dealer, seller, sutler, trader, vender, vendor 7 peddler 8 salesman 9 tradesman 10 saleswoman, saltcellar

selling place: See **market**

selvage: 4 edge, list 5 gouge 6 border, margin 8 sticking

semblable: 7 seeming 8 suitable 10 ostensible

semblance: air 4 copy, face, form, look 5 guise, image 6 aspect, figure 7 pretext 8 likeness, pretense 10 apparition, appearance, conformity, likelihood, similarity, similitude, simulacrum 11 countenance, presumption, resemblance 14 representation

Semele: *father:* 6 Cadmus
husband: 4 Zeus
sister: Ino
son: 7 Bacchus 8 Dionysos 9 Dionysius

semester: 4 half, term 6 course, period

semi: 4 half

semiape: 5 lemur

semidiameter: 6 radius

seminar: 6 course, school 7 meeting

seminary: 6 school 7 academy, college 11 institution

Seminole Indian chief: 7 Osceola

semiopaque: 5 horny 11 translucent

Semiramis' husband: 5 Ninus

Semite: Jew 4 Arab 6 Hebrew 7 Moabite 8 Aramaean, Assyrian 9 Caucasian 10 Babylonian, Phoenician
god: 4 Baal 5 Anath, Hadad 6 Moloch 7 Shamash
language: 4 Geez 6 Arabic, Hebrew, Syrian 7 Hebraic, Maltese

people: 6 Shagia 7 Shaigia 9 Shaikiyeh

semolina: 4 meal, suji 5 flour, sujee 6 groats

semper: 6 always

sempiternal: 4 ever 7 endless, eternal 11 everlasting

senate: 5 boule, divan 7 council 8 assembly 11 legislature

senator: 5 solon 8 lawmaker 10 legislator

senatorship: 4 toga

send: 4 haul, mail, ship 5 drive, grant, impel, issue, relay, speed 6 bestow, commit, convey, depute, ordain, propel 7 address, consign, deliver, dismiss, forward, inflict, project 8 delegate, dispatch, transmit 9 discharge, vouchsafe 10 commission
back: 5 remit 6 remand, return
down: 5 demit
for: 5 order 6 summon
forth: 4 emit 6 effuse
out: 4 emit 5 exile 6 deport, export
to obscurity: 8 relegate
packing: 7 dismiss 9 discharge
up: 4 jail 8 imprison

Senegal: *capital:* 5 Dakar
gazelle: 5 korin
timber: 9 cailcedra

senescent: 5 aging

senile: old 4 aged, weak 5 aging 6 daffle, dotard, infirm 7 ancient, elderly, rickety 8 decrepit 9 doddering 13 deteriorating

senility: 6 dotage 8 caducity

senior: 4 aine, dean 5 elder, older 7 ancient, student 8 alderman, superior 13 undergraduate

seniority: age 5 state 6 status 7 quality 8 priority 10 precedence
by birth: 13 primogeniture

Sennacherib: *father:* 6 Sargon
son: 8 Sharezer

sensation: 5 sense 7 emotion, feeling 8 interest 10 appearance, experience, perception 11 sensibility
lacking: 4 numb

sensational: 5 lurid 6 yellow 8 exciting 9 emotional, startling, thrilling 12 melodramatic

sense: 4 feel, mind 5 touch 6 import, intuit, reason, sanity, wisdom 7 feeling, meaning 8 judgment, perceive, prudence 9 apprehend, awareness, sensation, sentience, soundness 10 appreciate, cognizance, comprehend, perception 11 sensibility 12 intelligence 13 consciousness, sensitiveness, understanding 14 susceptibility

Sense and Sensibility author: 6 Austen

sense organ: ear, eye 4 nose, skin 5 nerve 6 tongue 8 receptor

senseless: mad 4 dumb 5 blind, inane 6 stupid, unwise 7 foolish, idiotic 9 insensate, unfeeling 10 half-witted, insensible, irrational 11 meaningless, nonsensical, purposeless, unconscious 12 unreasonable 13 unintelligent

senselessness: 5 folly

sensible: 5 privy 7 prudent 8 rational 10 responsive

sensitive: raw 4 nice, sore 5 acute, alive 6 tender, touchy 8 delicate 9 receptive 10 compatible, responsive 11 susceptible 14 impressionable

plant: 6 mimosa

sensual: 4 lewd 5 alive, gross 6 carnal, coarse, fleshy 7 bestial, brutish, fleshly, lustful, worldly 9 seductive 10 licentious, voluptuous

sent: See **send**

sentence: rap 4 doom 5 award, axiom, maxim, motto 6 decide, decree, saying 7 adjudge, condemn, opinion, passage, proverb 8 aphorism, decision, judgment 9 destinate, statement 12 adjudication 13 determination

consisting of one word: 7 monepic

construction: 6 syntax

describe: 5 parse

part: 6 clause, phrase, object 7 subject 9 predicate

same backwards and forwards: 10 palindrome

type: 6 simple 7 complex 8 compound

sententious: 5 pithy, short, terse 7 compact, concise, laconic 10 moralistic, proverbial

sentient: 5 alive 6 animal, living 7 feeling 8 sensible 9 conscious

sentiment: 5 maxim, toast 6 lyrics, saying 7 emotion, feeling, meaning, opinion 9 sensation, substance 10 perception 11 sensibility 14 sentimentality, susceptibility

sentimental: 5 gushy 7 maudlin, mawkish, schmalz 8 romantic, schmaltz 9 fantastic 10 idealistic 11 susceptible 13 lackadaisical

sentinel: 5 guard, vedet(Sp.), videt(Sp.), watch 6 bantay(P.I.), sentry, warder 7 soldier 8 watchman 10 factionary, watchtower

sepal: 4 leaf

separate: 4 bolt, cull, deal, free, part, rend, rift, shed, sift, slay, sley, sort 5 alone, aloof, apart, aside, break, hedge, ravel, sever, space, strip 6 assort, breach, cleave, decide, deduct, depart, detach, divide, refine, remove, secede, secern, sejoin, single, sleave, sleeve, sunder, winnow 7 analyse, analyze, disjoin, dispart, diverse, divorce, expanse, isolate, segment, sejunct 8 abstract, alienate, detached, discrete, disperse, dissolve, distinct, disunite, prescind, secluded, solitary, withdraw 9 demarcate, different, disengage, dismember,

disparate, eliminate, segregate, withdrawn 10 disconnect, dispossess, dissociate, distribute, individual, sejunctive 11 disembodied, distinctive, distinguish, fractionate, independent, precipitate, unconnected 12 disassociate, disconnected, disintegrate

separated: 4 free, lone 5 alone

separation: 4 gulf 6 schism, tmesis 7 diacope 8 distance 9 cessation, partition 14 discontinuance

prefix; di; dis

separatists: 8 Pilgrims, Zoarites 9 Bimmelers

Sephardim: 4 Jews

country of origin: 5 Spain 8 Portugal

dialect: 6 Ladino

sepia: dun 7 pigment 10 cuttlebone, cuttlefish

sepiment: 5 hedge 7 defense 9 enclosure

sepiolite: 10 meerschaum

sepoy: 9 policeman

seps: 5 snake 6 lizard 7 serpent

sept: 4 clan 5 seven, tribe

septic: 6 putrid, rotten 9 infective

septum: 4 wall 9 partition

sepulcher: 4 bury, tomb 5 grave, inter, vault 6 entomb 8 monument 10 repository

subterranean vault: 8 catacomb

sepulchral: 6 gloomy, hollow 7 charnel 8 funereal

sequacious: 6 pliant 7 ductile, servile 9 attendant, compliant, dependent, following, malleable

sequel (see also **sequence**): 4 next 5 issue 6 effect, result, upshot 7 outcome 8 follower, sequitur 9 aftermath, following, inference 10 conclusion 11 consequence, continuance 12 continuation

sequence (see also **sequel**): run, set 5 gamut, order, suite 6 course, series, tenace 8 straight 10 succession 11 progression

sequent: 8 follower 9 attendant, following 10 succeeding

sequential: 9 following 10 continuous, processive, succeeding 11 consecutive

sequester: 5 seize 6 enisle 7 isolate, seclude 10 confiscate

sequestered: 5 alone 6 lonely, seized 7 private, recluse, removed, retired 8 isolated, secluded, solitary, withdrew 9 renounced, separated, withdrawn 10 cloistered, disclaimed, segregated 11 confiscated 12 appropriated

sequin: 4 disk 7 spangle

sequoia: 7 redwood

serac: 5 block 8 pinnacle

seraglio: 5 harem, serai 6 zenana 8 lodgings 9 enclosure, warehouse

serai: 5 harem 8 lodgings, seraglio 11 caravansary 12 caravanserai

serape: 5 cloak, shawl 7 blanket

seraph: 5 angel 6 cherub

seraphic: 4 pure 7 angelic, refined, sublime 8 cherubic 9 unworldly

seraphim: 5 angel 6 cherub

seraphine: 8 melodeon 10 instrument

Serapis' temple: 7 serapea(pl.) 8 serapeum

Serb: 4 Slav

Serbia: *coin:* 5 dinar
  combining form: 5 Serbo
  measure: 4 ralo
  prince: 4 Cral

sere, sear: dry, wax 4 worn 5 dried, talon 6 yellow 7 parched, several, various 8 scorched, separate, withered 10 desiccated, threadbare

serein: dew 4 mist, rain

serenade: 6 aubade 8 nocturne, serenata
  burlesque: 8 shivaree 9 charivari 10 callithump

serenata: 6 serena 7 cantata 8 serenade

serene: 4 calm, cool, damp 5 clear, light, quiet 6 bright, pacify, placid, sedate, serein, steady 7 pacific 8 composed, decorous, peaceful, tranquil 9 collected, impassive, unruffled 10 unobscured 11 tranquilize, undisturbed 13 dispassionate, imperturbable

serenity: 6 repose 7 balance 10 equanimity

serf: 4 esne, peon 5 churl, helot, slave 6 servus, thrall, vassal 7 bondman, peasant, villein 8 bondsman, hireling
  female: 5 neife 6 colona

serge: 7 worsted

sergeant: 6 chiaus, tenant 7 esquire, servant, surgeon 9 attendant

sergeant fish: 5 cobia

seriation (see also **series**): 8 position 9 formation 11 arrangement

series: set 4 list 5 chain, gamut, suite, train 6 catena, course 8 beadroll, category, sequence, seriatim 9 gradation 10 succession
  arranged in: 6 serial 7 seriate 11 installment

serious: 4 deep, grim, keen 5 grave, heavy, sober, staid 6 demure, sedate, severe, solemn 7 austere, capital, earnest, weighty 9 important, momentous 10 thoughtful 11 considerate

serment: 4 oath 9 sacrament

sermon: 4 talk 5 psalm, speak 6 homily 7 address, lecture 8 harangue 9 collation, discourse, preaching 10 admonition
  study of: 10 homiletics
  subject: 4 text

sermonic: 5 grave

sermonize: 6 advise, preach 8 admonish

seroon: 4 bale 7 package

serotine: bat

serous: 4 thin 6 watery

serow: 5 goral, jagla

serpent (see also **snake**): 7 entwine, reptile
  comb. form: 4 ophi 5 ophio
  elapine: 4 naia, naja
  mythological: Ahi 5 Apepi, Dahak, Hydra 6 ellops, dragon 8 basilisk 11 Amphisbaena
  nine-headed: 5 Hydra
  pert. to: 5 anguine
  thousand-headed: 5 Sesha 6 Ananta
  victim: 7 Laocoon
  worship of: 6 ophism

serpentine: 4 file, wily, worm 5 snaky 7 sinuous, turning, winding 8 tempting 10 circuitous, meandering
  variety: 10 antigorite

serpigo: 5 tinea 6 herpes, tetter 8 ringworm

serrate: 5 notch, tooth 11 denticulate

serried: 5 dense 6 massed, packed 7 compact, crowded

serum: 4 whey 5 fluid 9 antitoxin

serum-like: 6 serous

servable: 6 usable 10 functional

servant: dey, gyp 4 amah, bata, cook, dasi, esne, girl, help, hewe, hind, maid, maty, mozo, syce 5 alila, biddy, boots, chela, gilly, groom, hamal, nurse, scout, slave, usher, valet 6 abigal, batman, bearer, bildar, butler, chakar, ewerer, flunky, garcon, gillie, hamaul, hammal, harlot, helper, khamal, menial, tenant, varlet, vassal 7 bondman, famulus, flunkey, footman, hummaul 8 chasseur, domestic, sergeant, servitor 9 atriensis 11 chamberlain
  female: 4 maid 5 wench 6 slavey
  garment: 5 apron 6 livery 7 uniform
  head: 6 butler
  male: 5 valet 6 butler, lackey
  of God: 4 monk, pope 5 friar, rabbi 6 bishop, priest 8 chaplain, minister, preacher 10 Holy Father, missionary
  of nobleman: 7 equerry
  pert. to: 8 famulary
  retired: 8 emeritus

serve: do; act, aid 4 abet, give, help, mess, pass, suit, tend, wait 5 avail, cater, frame, ladle 6 answer, assist, attend, succor 7 advance, benefit, bestead, deliver, forward, further 8 function, minister 9 officiate 10 distribute

server: urn 4 tray 6 salver, waiter 7 caterer 9 assistant, lazy-Susan

Servia: See **Serbia**

service: use 4 mass, rite 5 avera, favor, wages 6 employ, fealty, homage, repair, supply 7 chakari, retinue, slavery, utility

8 kindness, ministry 9 servitude 10 recompense 11 maintenance 12 installation, ministration
military: 4 duty 5 hitch 7 stretch 10 enlistment 12 conscription
public: 7 utility
service charge: fee, tip
service tree: 4 sorb
serviceable: 4 kind 6 useful 7 durable, helpful, lasting 8 obliging 9 available 10 beneficial, commodious
serviette: 6 napkin
servile: 4 base, bond, mean 6 abject, menial, sordid 7 fawning, slavish 8 cringing, enslaved 9 dependent, parasitic, truckling 10 obsequious, sequacious, submissive 11 subservient, sycophantic
Servite: 5 friar 9 mendicant
servitor: 6 beadle, menial, squire 7 servant, soldier 8 adherent, follower 9 assistant, attendant 10 apprentice 12 exhibitioner
servitude: 4 yoke 7 bondage, peonage, serfdom, service, slavery 8 sentence 9 captivity, vassalage
sesame: til 4 herb, teel 5 benne 7 passkey 8 ajonjoli, password
seed: 7 gingili, tilseed
session: 4 term 7 meeting, sitting 8 sederunt 10 assemblage
set: fix, gel, lay, put, sit 4 bent, clan, club, cock, crew, gang, laid, park, port, pose, prim, ring, seat, stud, suit 5 align, aline, brood, elect, elite, embed, fixed, group, imbed, place, plant, posit, range, ready, rigid, staid, stake, stand, suite 6 adjust, assign, cement, circle, clique, define, formal, harden, impose, impost, ordain, series, settle 7 appoint, arrange, company, confirm, congeal, coterie, decline, deposit, dispose, instate, platoon, station, stiffen 8 attitude, decorate, exchange, immobile, moveless, regulate, solidify 9 coagulate, collocate, designate, determine, establish, immovable, obstinate, prescribe, stabilize 10 assortment, collection, constitute, stationary
about: 5 begin, start
afloat: 6 launch
apart: 5 elect 6 exempt 7 isolate, reserve, seclude 8 allocate, dedicate, separate 9 segregate, sequester
aside: 4 void 5 annul, table 6 except, reject 7 discard, dismiss, earmark, exclude, reserve 8 overrule, separate
at naught: 4 defy 7 despise 9 disregard
back: 4 loss 5 check 6 hinder 7 backset, relapse, reverse, setback
down: fix 4 seat 5 abase, enter, place, write 6 depose, encamp, ordain, reckon, record, regard, relate 7 appoint, descend, resolve,

slacken 8 consider, estimate, register 9 attribute, determine, establish, humiliate, prescribe
forth: 5 adorn, offer, state 6 expone, expose 7 arrange, commend, display, enounce, exhibit, explain, expound, present, promote, propone, publish 8 announce, decorate, manifest 9 interpret, translate 10 promulgate
free: See **liberate**
fresh: 5 relay
in motion: 6 excite 8 activate
in operation: 4 jump, move, skip 5 slide, start 6 launch, plunge, spring
in order: 4 file, tidy 5 align, aline 6 adjust 7 arrange
of players: 4 team 5 squad
of rules: 4 code
on end: 5 upend 10 topsyturvy
on fire: 4 tind 5 light 6 kindle
out: 4 plan 5 adorn, allot, equip, extol, issue, limit, start 6 embark, outfit, recite 7 publish, started 8 describe, proclaim 9 embellish 10 promulgate
right: 4 file 5 align, aline, amend, order 6 adjust, repair 7 arrange, correct, ordered 11 systematize
thickly: 4 stud
to: go 4 bout 5 fight 6 fracas 7 contest 8 struggle
up: 4 post 5 build, erect, exalt, found, hoist, raise, treat 7 appoint, arrange, elevate 8 organize 9 establish
upon: 7 browden
Set, Seth (see also **Seth** below): god 5 deity
brother: 6 Osiris
father: Geb
mother: Nut
victim: 6 Osiris
wife: 8 Nephthys
seta: 6 chaeta 7 bristle
setacceous: 7 bristly
setal: 7 bristly
seth: 6 banker 8 merchant
Seth (see also **Set, Seth** above):
brother: 4 Abel, Cain
descendant: 4 Enos 7 Sethite
father: 4 Adam
son: 4 Enos
seton: 6 suture
setose: 7 bristly 9 setaceous
setout: 4 fuss 6 outfit 7 costume, display, exhibit 10 excitement 13 entertainment
settee: 4 seat, sofa 5 bench, divan
setter: dog 5 Irish 6 Gordon 7 English 10 compositor

setting: 4 eggs, trap, pave 5 decor, scene, snare, scena(It.) 6 locale 7 scenery 8 mounting 10 background 11 environment 12 surroundings

settle: fix, pay, sag, set 4 calm, dais, firm, lend, nest, root, seat, sink, toit 5 affix, agree, audit, bench, clear, couch, lodge, order, perch, plant, quiet, serve, solve 6 accord, adjust, alight, assign, decide, locate, purify, reduce, render, secure, soothe 7 appoint, arrange, clarify, compone, compose, confirm, conform, deposit, depress, dispose, provide, resolve, silence, subside 8 colonize, compound, conclude, ensconce, regulate 9 conjobble, designate, determine, establish, habituate, liquidate, shrinkage 10 accomodate, adjudicate, administer, strengthen 11 tranquilize

strike: 7 mediate

settled: 4 alit, fast 5 fixed, staid 6 formed, sedate 7 certain, decided, peopled, statary, testate 8 decorous 9 inerratic, sedentary, steadfast 10 consistent, determined, unchanging 11 established

in advance: 13 predetermined

settlement: dos 4 camp, lees 5 abode, dregs 6 colony, hamlet 7 payment, village 8 decision, disposal, fixation, sediment 9 aldeament, community, residence 10 adjustment, conclusion, occupation, regulation 11 arrangement 12 colonization, satisfaction 13 clarification, determination, establishment

arrange: 9 negotiate

settler: 6 sooner, vessel 7 planter, pioneer 8 colonist, emigrant 9 colonizer, immigrant 10 forehearth, receptacle

American: 7 Pilgrim, Puritan

seugh, seuch: rut 5 ditch, drain 6 furrow

seven: 4 zeta

combining form: 5 hepta

days and nights: 8 sennight

deadly sins: 4 envy, lust 5 anger, pride, sloth 8 gluttony 12 covetousness

group of: 6 heptad, septet 8 hebdomad

Seven Against Thebes: 6 Tydeus 8 Adrastus, Capaneus 9 Polynices 10 Hippomedon 13 Parthenopaeus

Seven Churches: 6 Sardis, Smyrna 7 Ephesos 8 Laodicea, Pergamos, Thyatira 12 Philadelphia

Seven Dwarfs: Doc 5 Dopey, Happy 6 Grumpy, Sleepy, Sneezy 7 Bashful

seven-faced: 11 heptahedral

seven-fold: 8 septuple

seven hills: See **Rome:** *hill*

seven-sided: 10 heptagonal

sever: cut 4 deal, part, rend, slit 5 break 6 breach, cleave, depart, detach, divide, except, exempt, sunder 7 disjoin, dispart, divorce, scatter 8 disunite, separate 9 dismember, segregate 10 disconnect, dissociate 12 disassociate

from neck: 6 behead 9 decollate 10 decapitate

several: few 4 some 6 divers, single, sundry 7 diverse, various 8 distinct, peculiar 9 different 10 individual, respective

minimum: 5 three

severe: bad 4 dear, dere, dour, dure, hard, keen, sore, tart 5 acute, breme, cruel, grave, gruff, harsh, rethe, rigid, rough, sharp, sober, stark, stern, stiff 6 biting, bitter, chaste, coarse, hetter, sedate, simple, solemn, strict, trying, unkind 7 ascetic, austere, caustic, chronic, condign, crucial, cutting, drastic, extreme, intense, serious, spartan, violent 8 captious, exacting, grievous, rigorous, scathing 9 difficult, draconian, inclement, strenuous, stringent, unsparing 10 afflictive, astringent, censorious, forbidding, methodical, oppressive, restrained 12 unornamented

severed: 5 apart

severity: 8 acerbity, acrimony, asperity

Seville cathedral tower: 7 Giralda

sew: hog, sow 4 bind, darn, join, mend, seam 5 baste, broth, drain, sewer, shirr, smock, unite 6 fasten, needle, stitch, suture 7 pottage

up: end 6 settle 8 conclude 10 monopolize

with gathers: 4 full 5 shirr

sewan: 5 beads, money 6 wampum

Seward's Folly: 6 Alaska

sewer: 5 drain 7 conduit, servant 10 seamstress

opening: 7 manhole

sewing machine: *inventor:* 9 Elias Howe

part: 8 plicator 10 zipperfoot

sex: 6 gender

combining form: 4 geno

hormone: 7 steroid

sexless: 6 neuter 7 epicene

sexton: 6 verger 7 sacrist 9 sacristan 12 underofficer

sextuplet: 7 sestole 8 sestolet

sexual: 5 gamic 6 carnal

continence: 8 chastity

inclination: 4 urge 6 libido

sexy: 5 spicy 6 carnal, erotic 7 amatory, earthly

Seychelles: 4 Mahe 7 La Digue, Praslin

capital: 8 Victoria

sha: 5 sheep, urial 6 nahoor, oorial

shab: 4 itch, scab 7 scratch

shabby: old 4 base, mean, worn 5 dowdy, faded, seedy 6 paltry, ragged, scurvy 7 outworn, unkempt 8 shameful, tattered, unworthy **9** beggardly **10** despicable, threadbare **11** disgraceful **12** contemptible, deteriorated

shack (see also **shuck**): coe, hut **4** feed, plug **5** cabin, catch, chase, hovel, tramp **6** lean-to, refuse, shanty, wander **7** stubble **8** brakeman, retrieve, vagabond

shackle: tie **4** band, bind, bolt, bond, curb, gird, gyve, idle, iron, loaf, ring **5** chain, gyves **6** fetter, hamper, hinder, hobble, pinion, secure **7** confine, manacle, trammel **8** coupling, restrain **10** fetterlock

shad: 5 alose **6** allice **7** crappie, mojarra

shaddock: 5 fruit **6** pomelo **10** grapefruit

shade: bar, dim, hue **4** dark, dull, tint, tone, veil **5** color, cover, ghost, hatch, tinge, trace, umbra, vault **6** awning, canopy, darken, degree, nuance, screen, shadow, spirit, sprite, shield **7** curtain, eclipse, foliage, obscure, parasol, phantom, protect, shelter, spector, shutter, umbrage, vestige **8** clearing, darkness, ornament **9** adumbrate, variation **10** apparition, difference, overshadow, protection, silhouette

light: **6** pastel

lines: **5** hatch

of cap: **5** visor

of meaning: **6** nuance

shaded: 10 umbrageous

shaded walk: 4 mall **6** arcade **8** cloister

shadetail: 8 squirrel

shadow (see also **shade**): dog **4** blot, omen, tail **5** cleek, cloud **6** attend, follow, shroud, symbol **7** remnant **8** penumbra **10** indication, overspread **13** prefiguration

dark cone of: **5** umbra

dispelling: **9** scialytic

figure: **10** silhouette

of death: **5** gloom, Sheol

outline: **10** silhouette

person without: **6** ascian

shadowbox: 4 spar

shadowy: dim **5** faint, vague **6** opaque, shaded, umbral, unreal **7** obscure, retired **8** adumbral **10** impalpable, indistinct, overspread, transitory **12** inaccessible **13** unsubstantial

Shadrach: *companion:* **7** Meshach **8** Abednego

persecutor: **14** Nebuchadnezzar

shady: 7 shadowy, umbrous **11** underhanded **12** disreputable, questionable

shaffle: 4 limp **5** shirk **6** hobble, loiter **7** shuffle

shaft: bar, pit, ray, rod **4** axle, beam, bolt, cone, fust, hole, pole, stem, tige, tole **5** arbor, arrow, helve, heuch, heugh, irony, lance, scape, shank, spear, spire, stalk, stele, thill, trunk **6** arbour, column, groove, handle, pillar, tongue, upcast **7** chamber, chimney, Maypole, missile, obelisk, spindle **8** gatepost **9** flagstaff

column: **4** fust **5** scape, verge

feather: **5** scape

part: **4** orlo

plant: **4** axis

vehicle: **5** thill

shag: mat, nap **4** hair, mane, mass, pile, toss, wool **5** chase, fiber, shake **6** follow, rascal, refuse **7** garment, tobacco **9** cormorant **10** blackguard

shaggy: 5 bushy, furry, nappy, rough **7** hirsute, scrubby, unkempt, villous **8** straggly **10** unpolished

shagreen: 4 skin **7** leather, rawhide **8** galuchat

shaitan, sheitan: 5 devil, fiend

shake: go; **4** bob, jar, jog, wag **4** free, jolt, move, pass, rese, rock, shog, stir, sway, toss, wave **5** churn, drink, eject, quake, shock, steal, swing, trill **6** depart, dither, dodder, goggle, hustle, joggle, quaver, quiver, rattle, shiver, totter, tremor, weaken **7** agitate, chatter, concuss, disturb, fluster, tremble, unnerve, vibrate **8** brandish, convulse, dislodge, enfeeble, flourish **9** agitation, dismissal **10** earthquake

down: bed, con **5** dance **6** extort, settle **9** blackmail

off: **4** shed **6** excuss **8** disagree

Shaker: 4 sect

founder: Lee

Shakespeare: *actor:* **4** Ward **5** Booth **6** Burton **7** Garrick, Geilgud, Olivier, Sothern **8** Modjeska **9** Barrymore

alternate author: **5** Bacon

character: **4** Bone, Iago, Iras, Lear, Snug **5** Biron, Cleon, Henry, Regan, Romeo, Speed, Timon **6** Banquo, Juliet, Oberon, Portia, Simple **7** Antonio, Cassius, Othello, Salerio, Shylock, Silence, Slender, Titania **8** Falstaff

elf: **4** Puck

forest: **5** Arden

home: **4** Avon

play: **4** Lear **6** Caesar, Hamlet **7** Macbeth, Othello **9** Cymbeline

theater: **5** Globe

wife: Ann

shaking: 4 ague **9** tremulant, tremulous **10** concussion

shako: cap **9** headdress

decoration: **6** pompon

shakti: 5 force, power

shaky: 4 weak **5** dicky **6** dickey, groggy, infirm, wabbly, wobbly **7** casalty, caselty, unsound 8 insecure 9 tottering, trembling, tremulous, uncertain 10 unreliable 12 questionable

shale: cod 4 husk, rock 5 metal, scale, shell, slate 7 shuffle 8 impurity

shall: may 4 must, will 5 would 7 obliged

shallop: 4 boat 6 dinghy, vessel

shallot: 4 tube 5 onion 8 eschalot

shallow: hat 4 cart, tray, weak 5 shoal 6 basket, flimsy, slight 7 cursory, trivial 9 depthless, frivolous 11 superficial

shalom: 5 peace

sham: 4 fake, hoax, mock 5 bogus, cheat, dummy, false, feign, fraud, trick 6 assume, bunyip, chouse, deceit, delude, device, duffer, humbug, shoddy 7 deceive, feigned, forgery, grimace, pretend 8 pretense, trickery 9 brummagem, deception, imitation, imposture, pretended, trickster 10 artificial, factitious, simulacrum, substitute 11 counterfeit, make-believe

shamal: 4 wind

shaman: 4 monk 6 beggar, priest 8 conjurer

Shamash: *consort:* Ai; Aya
  messenger: 6 Bunene
  worship center: 5 Larsa 6 Sippar

shamble: 5 bandy, bench, stall, stool, table 7 bauchle, butcher, counter, shuffle 9 footstool, malformed, slaughter

shambles: 8 abattoir

shame: 5 abase, abash 6 ashame, assume, bemean, bismer 7 degrade, mortify 8 contempt, disgrace, dishonor 9 embarrass, humiliate 10 repentance 11 degradation, shortcoming 12 illegitimacy 13 embarrassment, mortification

shamefaced: 6 humble, modest 7 bashful 9 diffident

shameful: 4 base, mean 5 gross 7 ignoble 8 flagrant, improper, indecent, infamous 9 degrading, dishonest 10 outrageous, scandalous, slanderous 11 disgraceful, ignominious, opprobrious 12 contumelious, dishonorable, disreputable, vituperative 13 dishonourable

shameless: 6 arrant, brazen 8 immodest, impudent 9 abandoned, audacious, barefaced 10 unblushing 11 brazenfaced

shammer: 4 aper 5 fraud 8 imposter

shammock: 4 loaf 6 dawdle, slouch

shampoo: 4 lave, wash 5 clean

shamrock land: 4 Eire, Erin 5 Irena 7 Ireland

shandrydan: gig 6 chaise 7 vehicle

shandy: 4 wild 5 drink 9 visionary 11 unrealistic

Shang dynasty: Yin

shanghai: 4 drug, ship 6 kidnap

Shangri-la: 6 utopia 8 paradise

shank: leg 4 gamb, shin, stem, tang 5 gambe, knife, ladle, ridge, shaft 8 leggings, stocking
  pert. to: 6 crural

shanny: shy 4 fish 5 giddy, silly 6 blenny

shantung: 4 silk 6 pongee, tussah

Shantung's capital: 6 Tsinan

shanty: hut 5 cabin, hovel, hutch, shack 6 leanto 8 chantier, dwelling

shape: fit, hew 4 bend, cast, form, knap, make, mold, plan, tool, trim 5 block, boast, build, carve, feign, frame, guise, model, mould, state, torus 6 create, decree, design, devise, figure, format, happen, ordain 7 appoint, arrange, conform, contour, fashion, incline, phantom, posture, whittle 8 attitude, contrive 9 condition, determine, structure 10 apparition, appearance, figuration 11 arrangement 13 configuration
  different: 8 variform
  garden: 7 topiary
  in: 4 trim

shapeless: 6 deform 8 deformed, formless 9 amorphous, contorted, distorted, misshapen, unshapely

shapely: fit 4 neat, trim 6 decent, gainly 8 suitable 11 symmetrical

shaping machine: 5 edger, lathe 6 shaper

shard: 5 scale, shell 8 fragment

share: cut, lot 4 cant, deal, dole, hand, part, rent 5 divvy, enter, quota, ratio, shear 6 cleave, divide, impart, moiety, ration 7 partake, portion 8 dividend, division 9 allotment, allowance, apportion, communion, plowshare 10 distribute 11 participate
  widow's: 5 dower, dowry, terce, third 6 dowery

sharecropper: 7 metayer

Shari River: See Cameroon

shark: 4 gata, haye, mako, tope 5 adept 6 expert, lawyer, usurer 7 dogfish, sharper, sponger 8 drunkard, maneater, parasite, swindler, thrasher, thresher 9 porbeagle, selachian, trickster 10 hammerhead
  blue pointer: 4 mako
  genus of: 11 carcharodon
  nurse: 4 gata
  pilot: 6 remora
  small: 4 tope 5 lamia
  young: 8 sharklet

sharp: 4 acid, cold, cute, edgy, fell, gash, gleg, gnib, high, keen, nice, sour, tart 5 acrid, acute, adept, alert, breme, brisk, crisp, eager, edged, fiery, harsh, salty, steep, tangy, witty 6 abrupt, active, acuate, astute, barbed, biting, bitter, clever, crafty, crispy, expert, peaked, severe, shrewd, shrill, snelly(Sc.) 7 angular, austere, caustic, cunning, cutting, gingery, grating, intense, lyncean, nipping, painful, piquant, pointed, pungent, rasping, sharper, violent, waspish 8 aculeate, distinct, handsome, incisive, piercing, poignant, vigilant, vigorous 9 attentive, beautiful, designing, impetuous, merciless, penetrant, sagacious, sarcastic, trenchant 10 discerning 11 acrimonious, intelligent, penetrating, underhanded

comb. form: oxy

to taste: 4 acid 5 acrid

sharp-sighted: 6 astute

sharpen: nib, ted 4 edge, hone, whet 5 grind, point, reset, strop 6 acuate 7 enhance, quicken 9 intensify 10 cacuminate

sharper: gyp 4 bite 5 cheat, rogue 6 cogger, keener 7 cheater, gambler 8 deceiver, swindler 9 trickster

sharpness: 6 acumen

sharpshooter: 6 sniper 8 marksman

shastra class: 5 sruti 6 purana, smriti, tantra

shatter: 4 blow, dash 5 blast, break, burst, crash, smash, split, wreck 6 batter, damage, impair 7 clatter, derange, destroy, disable, scatter 8 disorder, disperse, splinter 9 dissipate

shattered: 6 broken 8 broozled, doddered

shave: ace, cut 4 pare, poll, trim 5 graze, skive 6 rasure, scrape 7 tonsure, whittle

shaveling: 4 monk 5 youth 6 priest 9 hypocrite, stripling

shaven: 4 bald 6 pilled 8 tonsured

shaver: boy, lad 4 chap 5 cheat 6 barber, fellow, tonsor 8 swindler 9 bargainer, youngster 11 extortioner

shavetail: 4 mule 10 lieutenant

shavie: 4 joke 5 prank, trick

shaving: 5 spale 8 ramentum

shaw: 4 wood 5 copse, grove 7 thicket

shawl (see also **vestment**): 4 maud, wrap 5 manta, orale 6 serape(Mex.) 7 amlikar, paisley 8 epiblema

Shawnee Indian chief: 8 Tecumseh, Tecumtha

shay: 6 chaise 8 carriage

Shea player: Met

sheaf: 4 kern, kirn 5 bunch 6 bundle 7 cluster

group: 6 thrave

shear: cut 4 clip, gnaw, reap, rend, snip, trim 5 carve, force, mince, prune, sever, shave, strip 6 cleave, divest, fleece, nibble, pierce, remove 7 deprive, scissor, whittle 10 circumcise

shearing machine: 7 cropper

shears: 6 forfex 8 scissors, secateur

sheartail: 4 tern 11 hummingbird

shearwater: 4 crew 6 hagdon, haglet

sheatfish: 4 wels 7 catfish

sheath: cot 4 boot, case 5 dress, forel, ocrea, theca, stall 6 forrel, spathe 8 covering, envelope, scabbard

sheathe: 4 bury, case, ceil, dull 5 blunt, cover, glove 6 plunge 7 enclose, envelop

sheave: 5 wheel 6 pulley

sheaves: See **sheaf**

Sheba: 4 Saba

shebang: 4 deal 6 affair, outfit 7 concern 8 business 11 contrivance 13 establishment

Shechem god: 10 Baalberith

shed: cut, hut 4 abri(F.), byre, cast, cote, drop, emit, hull, lair, molt, nest, part, pour 5 booth, cabin, hovel, repel, scale, spill, tease 6 belfry, dingle, divide, effuse, hangar, hemmel, impart, lean-to, slough 7 cottage, diffuse, emanate, radiate, scatter, shelter, testudo 8 disperse, outhouse, separate, sprinkle, woodshed, workshop 9 irradiate, penthouse 11 intersperse, out-building

skin: 7 ecdysis

shedder: 4 crab 6 peeler, salmon 7 lobster

sheen: 4 fair 5 gleam, gloss, shine, shoes 6 bright, glossy, luster 7 exalted, glisten, glitter, radiant, shimmer, shining 8 brightly, lustrous, splendid, splendor 9 beautiful, shininess 10 brightness, glittering 11 beautifully, illustrious, resplendent

sheep: mug, sha 5 argal, dumba, ovine, urial 6 aoudad, argali, wether 7 bighorn, bleater, karakul, mouflon 8 karakule, moufflon, ruminant 9 blackface

breed: 4 Horn 6 Dorset, Exmoor, Merino, Romney 7 Cheviot, Delaine, Lincoln, Suffolk 8 Cotswold, Dartmoor 9 Leicester, Southdown, Teeswater 10 Corriedale, Oxford Down, Shropshire

caretaker: 8 shepherd

coat: 6 fleece

cry: maa 5 bleat

dead: 5 braxy, traik

disease: coe, gid, rot

feed: 5 graze 7 pasture

female: ewe 6 gimmer, sheder

head: 5 jemmy

head broth: 9 powsowdy

kidney extract: 5 venes

male: ram, tup 5 heder 6 wether 10 bell-wether

mark: 4 smit 5 brand

pathway: 6 roddin 7 rodding

pen: 5 bught(Sc.) 6 bought(Sc.)

pert. to: 5 ovine

second year: tag, teg

wild: sha 4 arui, udad 5 argal, audad, urial 6 aoudad, argali, bharal, nahoor, nayaur 7 mouflon 8 moufflon

young: hog, teg 4 lamb, tegg 5 heder 6 bident, gimmer, hogget, sheder 7 twinter 8 hoggerel, shearhog 9 four-tooth, shearling

sheep dog: 6 collie 8 shepherd

sheep-like: 4 meek 5 ovine 6 docile

sheepfaced: See **sheepish**

sheepfold: cot, pen, ree(Sc.) 4 cote, fold 7 sheppey 8 sheepcot 9 sheepcote, sheepfold 10 sheephouse

sheepheaded: 5 silly 6 stupid 12 simple-minded

sheepish: shy 4 meek 5 blate, silly, timid 7 abashed, awkward, bashful, daffish 11 embarrassed

sheepskin: 4 bond, cape 5 basil 7 diploma 9 parchment

leather: 4 roan

sheepwalk: run 5 range, slait 7 pasture

sheer: 4 fine, mere, pure, thin, turn 5 brant, clear, steep, utter 6 abrupt, bright, swerve 7 deviate, shining, unmixed, utterly 8 absolute, outright 9 deviation, downright, undiluted 10 diaphanous 11 transparent, unqualified 13 perpendicular

sheet: air 4 fine, page, rope, sail 5 chain, daily, linen, paper, plate 6 expand, lamina, shroud 7 tabloid 8 pamphlet 9 newspaper

twelvemo: 9 duodecimo

sheeting: 5 linen 7 percale

sheldrake, shelldrake: 4 duck

shelf: 4 bank, berm, bink, reef, sill 5 altar, berme, ledge, shoal 6 gradin, mantel 7 bedrock, bracket, gradine, retable, sandbar, stratum 8 credence, credenza, sandbank 9 banquette 10 pigeonhole

shell: hud, pod 4 boat, bomb, coin, hull, husk, lyre, swad, test 5 balat, cameo, conch, cowry, crust, money, murex, scale, shuck, spoon, testa, troca 6 coffin, concha, cowrie, crusta, dolite, dugout, lamina, lorica, strafe 7 abalone, admiral, bombard, capsule, caracol, dariole, grenade 8 caracole, carapace, covering, exterior, frustule 9 cartridge 10 projectile, schoolroom

beads: 4 peag 6 wampum

casing: 5 gaine

defective: dud

explosive: 4 bomb 7 grenade

hole: 6 crater

large: 5 conch

measuring device: 11 conchometer

money: 4 peag 5 cowry, peage, sewan, uhllo 6 cowrie, seawan, wampum

protected with: 8 loricate

ridge: 4 lira 5 varix 7 varices(pl.)

unexploded: dud

shellac: lac 5 resin

shellacking: 6 defeat 7 beating 8 flogging, whipping

shellapple: 9 chaffinch, crossbill

Shelley: *drama:* 5 Cenci

poem: 7 Adonais

shellfire: 6 strafe 7 barrage

shellfish: 5 nacre 6 limpet 7 mollusk 10 crustacean

shelter: cot, hut, lee 4 abri, barn, camp, cote, fold, gite(F.), herd, howf, port, roof, shed, skug, tent 5 benab, bield, boist, bower, cloak, cover, embay, haven, house, hovel, howff, hutch, shack 6 asylum, burrow, covert, defend, garage, hangar, harbor, hostel, refuge, sconce, sconse, screen, shield, trench 7 carport, cottage, defense, embosom, foxhole, harbour, hospice, imbosom, nacelle, pillbox, protect, retreat, trailer, umbrage 8 bescreen, ensconce, mantelet, quarters, security 9 coverture, harbinger, harborage, sanctuary 10 harbourage, protection

sheltered side: 7 leeward

on: 4 alee

shelve: tip 4 tilt 5 defer, ledge, shelf, table 6 mantel, retire 7 dismiss, project 8 overhang, platform 10 pigeonhole

Shem: *father:* 4 Noah

son: Lud 4 Aram, Elam 6 Asshur

shenanigan: 5 trick 7 evasion, foolery 8 mischief, nonsense, trickery

shend: mar 4 harm, lose, ruin 5 blame, shame, spoil, worst 6 damage, defeat, defend, injure, punish, revile, shield 7 degrade, destroy, protect 8 confound, disgrace, dishonor, reproach 10 discomfort

Sheol: 4 hell 5 grave, Hades 10 underworld

shepherd: 4 herd, lead, tend 5 drive, guard, watch 6 attend, escort, feeder, gather, herder, leader, pastor, shadow 8 guardian, minister

band of: 10 pastoureau

clock: 7 salsify 9 pimpernel

dog: 6 Collie 8 Cebalrai

god: Pan 5 Pales

pert. to: 8 pastoral

pipe: 4 reed 7 musette 11 flageolette

purse: 4 herb 9 blindweed

staff: 4 kent 5 crook

shepherdess: 7 bergere 9 Amarillis, Amaryllis

sherbet: ice

sherd: See **shard**

Sheridan play: 6 Rivals

sheriff: 6 grieve 7 bailiff, officer

aides: 5 posse

deputy: 6 elisor 7 bailiff

jurisdiction: 9 bailiwick
Sherlock Holmes: *companion:* 6 Watson
  creator: 5 Doyle
sherry: 4 wine 5 tokay 6 Solera 7 oloroso 11
  amontillado
Shetland Island: *inlet:* voe
  land: 4 odal, udal 6 udaler 7 udalman
  measure: ure
  musical instrument: gue
  ounce: ure
  tax: 4 scat
sheugh, sheuch: 5 ditch, gully 6 furrow,
  ravine, trench
sheyle: 6 squint 7 grimace
shibboleth: 4 test 8 password 9 criterion,
  watchword
shield: ecu(F.), rim 4 egis, hide, umbo 5 aegis, armor, avert, badge, board, cloak,
  cover, guard, shade, targe 6 blazon,
  brooch, canopy, defend, forbid, screen, target 7 buckler, conceal, defense, lirelle, prevent, protect, rotella, shelter, testudo 8
  conserve, rondache 9 protector 10 escutcheon, protection
  band across: 4 fess
  boss: 4 umbo
  knob: 4 umbo
  large: 5 pavis
  Minerva's: 4 egis 5 aegis
  on insect's head: 7 clypeus
  part of: 4 boss, ente, orle, umbo 6 pointe 7
  bordure, impresa
  rim: 4 orle
  small: ecu
  strap: 6 enarme
shield-bearer: 8 escudero
shield-shaped: 7 peltate, scutate 9 clypeo-
  lar
shieling: hut 7 cottage, pasture
shift: rid 4 deal, eddy, fend, jibe, move, quit,
  ruse, stir, tour, turn, veer 5 avoid, dodge,
  evade, feint, hours, order, shunt, slide 6
  assign, bestir, change, device, divide, period 7 arrange, dispose, evasion, replace,
  shuffle 8 artifice, exchange, mutation,
  transfer 9 apportion, expedient 10 equivocate, subterfuge, transplant 11 contrivance 12 redistribute 13 transposition
shifting: 6 shifty 8 ambulant, drifting, floating
shiftless: 4 lazy 8 feckless 10 thriftless 11
  inefficient
shifty: 4 haft 6 fickle, tricky 7 devious, hangdog 8 shifting 9 changeful, faithless 10
  changeable
shikar: 4 hunt 5 sport 7 hunting
shikari, shikaree: 5 guide 6 hunter 9
  sportsman
shillelagh: 4 club 6 cudgel

shillibeer: 6 hearse 7 omnibus
shilling: bob
shilly-shally: 5 hedge, waver 6 trifle 8 hesitate 9 vacillate
shilpit: 4 flat, puny, thin, weak 6 feeble,
  sickly 7 insipid
shim: hoe 5 image, level, wedge 6 shadow,
  streak, washer 7 glimpse, shingle
Shimei's father: 4 Gera
Shimel's father: Ela
shimmer: 5 flash, light 7 glimmer, glisten
shimmy: 5 dance, shake 6 quiver 7 chemise,
  tremble, vibrate 10 shimmering
shin: run 4 kick, walk 5 climb, ridge, shank,
  tibia 6 cnemis, strike
  pert. to: 7 cnemial
shindy: row 4 jump, lark, orgy, romp 5
  brawl, dance, party, revel, spree 6 fracas,
  frolic, rumpus, uproar 7 shindig, wassail 8
  carousal 9 commotion 11 disturbance,
  merrymaking
shine: ray 4 beam, beek(Sc.), glow, star 5
  black, blaze, blink, excel, glaik, gleam,
  glent, glint, gloss, gloze, prank, sheen 6
  liking, polish 7 glimpse, glisten, glister,
  glitter, radiate 8 eradiate, fondness, illumine 9 coruscate, irradiate, transluce
shiner: hat 4 chub 6 bruise 8 blackeye 9
  bootblack
shingle: 4 sign, whip 7 haircut 9 signboard
  splitting tool: 6 prower
shingles: 4 zona 6 herpes
shining: 4 glad, gold 5 aglow, glary, lucid,
  nitid, sleek 6 ardent, argent, bright,
  fulgid, glossy, lucent 7 beaming, eminent,
  fulgent, glowing, radiant 8 flashing,
  gleaming, luminous, lustrous, radiance,
  splendid 9 brilliant, effulgent, refulgent,
  sparkling, unclouded 10 glistening, glittering, remarkable 11 illustrious, irradiat-
  ing, resplendent
shinplaster: 5 scrip
Shinto: *deity:* 8 Hachiman
  gateway: 5 torii
  temple: sha 5 Jinja 6 Jinsha 7 Yashiro
shiny: See **shining**
ship: 4 boat, pink 5 setee 7 hagboat 8 balin-
  ger
  abandoned: 8 derelict
  ancient: 7 galleon
  Arabian: 6 boutre
  arctic: 6 sealer
  Argonaut's: 4 Argo
  armored: 7 carrack, cruiser 9 destroyer,
  ironsides, submarine
  ascent: 5 scend
  attendant: 7 steward
  auxiliary: 6 tender
  beak: bow, ram 4 prow

berth: 4 dock, slip
biscuit: 8 hardtack
boarding device: 6 ladder 9 gangplank
boat: 4 dory, life 5 barge, dingy 6 dingey, dinghy, tender 7 pinnace
body: 4 hull
breadth of: 4 beam
brutally disciplined: 8 hell ship
burden: 5 cargo
cabin: 6 saloon 9 stateroom
canvas: 4 sail
capacity: 7 tonnage
capacity unit: ton
cargo: 7 gaiassa
cargo invoice: 8 manifest
carpenter: 5 Chips
channel: gat 5 canal 6 narrow, strait
clean: 6 careen
clerk: 6 purser
clock: nef
coast guard: 6 cutter
coastal: hoy 4 dhow, grab 6 droger, trader 7 drogher
codfishing: 6 banker 8 walloper
commercial: 6 trader
company of: 4 crew 5 fleet, hands 6 armada
compass housing: 8 binnacle
cook: 6 slushy
course: 7 sealane
crane: 5 davit
crew leader: 5 bosun
curved planking: sny
desert: 5 camel
deserter: rat
direction: 4 atry 5 abeam
drain: 7 scupper
enemy-watching: 7 vedette
employee: 5 oiler 6 purser, sailor 7 steward 8 deckhand, engineer, helmsman, steerman 9 navigator
fishing: 5 smack 6 hooker, lugger 7 trawler
flat-bottom: 4 keel 5 barge
fleet of: 6 armada
floor: 4 deck
fuel: 5 barge, oiler 6 coaler, tanker 7 collier
fur-hunting: 6 sealer
group: 4 navy 5 fleet 6 armada
hoist: 4 boom 5 dairt 7 capstan
jail: 4 brig
kitchen: 6 galley
lateral movement: 6 leeway
left side: 4 port
lifting device: 5 crane, davit 7 capstan
line: 7 marline, ratline
merchant: 6 argosy, galiot, holcad 7 galliot
middle: 9 amidships
mortgage: 8 bottomry
movement: 6 leeway

oar: 6 bireme, galley, sampan 7 pinnace, rowboat, trireme
officer: 4 mate 5 bosun 6 purser 7 steward 9 boatswain
part: bow 4 beam, brig, deck, helm, hold, hull, keel, mast, prow 5 bilge, stern, waist, wheel 6 bridge, galley, rudder, steven 7 lazaret, scupper 8 binnacle 9 lazarette, lazaretto, sternpost
partition: 8 bulkhead
personnel: 4 crew 5 hands
pirate: 8 gallivat
planking: sny 6 strake
prison: 4 brig
privateer: 10 brigantine
prow: 5 prore
quarters: 6 fo'c'sle 8 steerage 10 forecastle
record: log
repair: 6 careen
repairing device: 7 drydock
rescue: ark
room: 4 brig 5 cabin, salon 6 galley 7 caboose 10 forecastle
rope: 4 line 6 hawser 7 halyard, lanyard, painter, ratline
sailing: 4 buss, dhow, proa, yawl 5 ketch, setee, sloop, smack, xebec 6 caique, chebec, hooker, lugger, mistic, saltie 7 galleon, Geordie, polacre
shovel: 5 skeet
side: 5 abeam
station: 5 berth
structure frame: 7 carcass
table frame: 6 fiddle
tender: 7 collier, pinnace
third-class: AE
tiller: 4 helm
timber: rib 4 bitt, keel, mast, spar 5 stick 7 bollard
twin-hulled: 9 catamaran
unseaworthy: 4 hulk 5 wreck 8 ballahoo, ballahou, derelict
upward movement: 5 scend
Venetian: 9 frigatoon
voyage record: log
war (see also **warship**): sub 7 cruiser, flat-top 8 corvette 9 destroyer, submarine 11 dreadnaught
wheel: 4 helm
windless: 7 capstan 8 becalmed
window: 4 port 8 porthole
wood for: 4 teak
worm: 5 borer 6 teredo
Ship of Fools author: 6 Porter
ship out: 6 enlist, export
shipboard: 5 board
shipment: 5 cargo 7 carload 8 delivery
shipping center: 7 seaport
shipshape: 4 neat, taut, tidy, trim 7 orderly

shipwright (launching slide marker): **6** wayman

shire: 5 derby, horse **6** county, region **8** district, province **11** subdivision

shirk: 4 duck, funk **5** avoid, dodge, evade, slack **6** desert **7** neglect **9** fainaigue

shirker: 6 loafer, truant **8** embusque

shirl: 4 slip **5** glide, slide

shirr: 6 gather

shirt: tee **4** jupe, polo, sark **5** dress, haire, kamis, parka, sport **6** camisa, camise, cilice, parkee
button: **4** stud

shirtfront: 5 dicky **6** dickey

shirtwaist: 6 blouse **9** garibaldi

shiver: 4 grue **5** chill, quake, shake **6** dither, quiver, tremor, twitch **7** flicker, frisson, shatter, shudder, tremble, vibrate **8** fragment, splinter
fit: **4** ague **6** chills **10** goosebumps

shivoo: 7 banquet, shindig **9** gathering **13** entertainment

shoal: bar **4** bank, mass, reef **5** barra, crowd, flock **6** school, throng **7** shallow **9** multitude

shoat: hog, pig **5** shote

shock: jar, lot **4** blow, heap, jolt, pile, stun **5** appal, brunt, bushy, gliff, gloff, scare, shake **6** fright, impact, offend, parcel, shaggy, stroke, trauma **7** astound, collect, disgust, horrify, startle, terrify **8** paralyze **9** agitation, collision **10** assemblage, concussion
mental: **6** trauma
to reality: **5** sober

shock absorber: 7 snubber

shocking: 5 awful, lurid **6** horrid, unholy **7** fearful, ghastly, hideous **8** dreadful, horrible **9** egregious, revolting **10** disgusting

shod: 5 soled **6** booted **7** ensoled

shoddy: 4 poor **5** cheap **6** shabby **8** inferior

shoe (see also **overshoe**): cue **4** boot, clog, flat, pump **5** gilly, sabot **6** brogan, brogue, buskin, caliga, crakow, gaiter, galosh, gillie, oxford, patten, sandal **7** blucher, flattie, slipper, sneaker **8** colonial, Congress, mocassin, moccasin, solleret **9** brodequin, pampootee **10** clodhopper, veldschoen
aid: **4** horn
baby: **6** bootee
fix: **5** retap **6** polish, resole
form: **4** last, tree
grip: **5** cleat
gym: **7** sneaker
house: **4** mule **7** slipper
mule's: **6** planch

part: box, cap, toe, top **4** heel, lift, pull, rand, vamp, welt **5** shank, strap **6** insole, tongue **7** counter, outsole **8** backstay, slipsole
paste: **7** clobber
piked: **6** cleats, crakow
repair: tap **5** retap **6** reheel, resole, stitch
rolling: **5** skate
rubber: **6** arctic, galosh **7** galoshe **8** overshoe
wooden: **5** sabot **6** patten
worker: **6** laster **7** cobbler
worn: **7** bauchle

shoebill: 5 stork

shoelace: tie **5** lacet **7** latchet
tip: **5** aglet **6** aiglet

shoemaker: 4 snob **5** soler, sutor(L.) **7** cobbler, crispin, farrier **10** cordonnier(F.)
apprentice: **4** snob
patron saint: **7** Crispin
tool: **4** butt **5** elsin **6** elshin

shoes (see also **shoe**): **5** sheen, shoon
winged: **7** talaria

shoeshine: 9 bootblack

shog: jog **4** jerk, jolt, rock **5** shake **6** jostle

shoggie: 4 sway **5** swing

shoggle: 6 dangle, joggle

Shogun title: 6 tycoon

shole: 5 plank, plate

shoneen: 4 snob **5** toady

shoo: 4 away, scat

shooi: 4 bird, skua **6** jaeger

shook: See **shake**

shool: 4 idle **6** loiter, scrape, shovel **7** saunter, scuffle, shamble, shuffle

shoot: bud, pot **4** bine, cast, chit, cion, dart, emit, film, fire, grow, move, plug, push, twig **5** bough, chute, drive, eject, plant, scion, snipe, spear, spout, spray, sprig, spurt, throw, tuber, utter, wound **6** branch, inject, propel, sprout, stolon, strike, thrust **7** burgeon, project **9** discharge **10** photograph **11** precipitate
objective: **6** target

shooting match: tir(F.) **5** skeet

shooting star: 5 comet **6** meteor **8** fireball

shop: 5 store **6** market, prison, tienda **7** bottega, factory **8** boutique, workshop
coffee: **4** cafe **6** bistro **9** estaminet
dairy: **8** cremerie
kind: **5** stith **6** smithy, stithy **7** mercery **8** saddlery, smithery **12** haberdashery
meat: **7** shamble **10** rotisserie **11** charcuterie
wine: **4** cafe **6** bistro

shophar: 4 horn

shopkeeper: cit **8** merchant, retailer **9** tradesman **11** businessman, storekeeper

shoplifter: 7 booster

shopper: 5 buyer 8 customer
shore: 4 bank, edge, land, prop 5 beach, brink, coast, drain, offer, scold, sewer 6 rivage, strand 7 seaside, support 8 threaten 9 foreshore
pert to: 8 littoral
poetic: 6 strand
recess: bay 4 cove 5 bayou, inlet
shore up: 4 prop
shorebird: ree 4 ruff 5 snipe 6 curlew, plover 9 sandpiper
shorn: See **shear**
short: 4 bain, curt, rude 5 bluff, brief, brusk, crisp, fubsy, harsh, scant, terse 6 abrupt, scanty, scarce 7 briefly, brusque, concise, crisply, curtail, friable, summary 8 abruptly, succinct 9 concisely, crumbling, deficient, shortstop 11 compendious 12 insufficient
and stout: 5 bunty, dumpy 6 stocky, stodgy, stubby 8 rolypoly, thickset
comb. form: 5 brevi 6 brachy
short-breathed: 5 pursy 6 winded 7 puffing
short-lived: 9 ephemeral
short-sighted: 6 myopic
short-spoken: 4 curt 5 gruff 7 laconic
shortage: 7 deficit 10 deficiency 13 insufficiency
shortcoming: 4 flaw 5 fault 6 defect 7 failure 10 deficiency, inadequacy 12 imperfection
shortcut: 5 alley 6 byroad 8 diagonal, gain cope
shorten: bob, cut, lop 4 clip, furl, reef 5 check 6 lessen, reduce 7 abridge, curtail, curtate, deprive 8 condense, contract, decrease, diminish 9 apocopate, decurtate 10 abbreviate 11 incapsulate
shorthand: 11 stenography 12 brachygraphy, speedwriting
system: 5 Gregg 6 Pitman
shortly (see also **short**)**:** 4 soon 7 quickly 9 presently
shortness: 7 brevity
shortsighted: 4 dull 6 myopic, obtuse 11 nearsighted 13 opportunistic
Shoshone Indian: Ute 4 Hopi, Otoe, Utah 5 Piute 6 Paiute 8 Comanche
shot (see also **shoot**)**:** pop, try 5 blank, carom, drink, guess, masse, photo, range, reach, sally, tired, weary 6 bullet, pellet, stroke 7 attempt, missile 8 marksman, snapshot 9 exhausted, reckoning 10 conjecture, projectile 11 intoxicated
size: B; BB, FF, FT, TT; BBB 4 dust 8 air-rifle, buckshot
shou: 4 deer
should: 5 ought

shoulder: 4 berm, edge 5 bough, raise 6 axilla
angle: 6 epaule
belt: 4 sash 7 baldric
bone: 7 scapula
combining form: omo
muscle: 7 deltoid
ornament: tab 7 epaulet 9 epaulette
pain: 7 omalgia
pert to: 4 alar 7 humeral 8 scapular
protection for: 8 pauldron
to shoulder: 7 serried
shoulder blade: 7 scapula
shout: boo, cry, hoy, hue 4 bark, bawl, call, crow, hoot, roar, root, roup, scry, yell, yelp 5 cheer, huzza, noise, whoop, yodel, yodle 6 clamor, gollar, goller, halloo, hurrah, outcry, yammer 7 acclaim 10 vociferate 11 acclamation
hunting: 5 hallo, holla 6 yoicks 7 tallyho 9 view-haloo
shove: 4 cast, push 5 drive, eject, elbow, hunch, shunt 6 hustle, jostle, propel, thrust
shovel: van 4 pale, peel 5 scoop, shool, skeet, spade 6 thrust 7 shuffle 8 strockle
shoveler: 9 broadbill
shovelfish: 9 spadefish 10 paddlefish
shovelhead: 5 shark 7 catfish 8 flathead, sturgeon
show: 4 bosh, dash, fair, lead, pomp 5 coach, farce, gloss, guide, movie, plead, prove, raree, revue, teach, train 6 accuse, afford, allege, assign, bestow, blazon, cinema, circus, confer, denote, detect, escort, evince, expose, flaunt, gaiety, gayety, inform, locate, parade, reveal, tinsel, unveil, veneer 7 bespeak, betoken, bravura, declare, display, divulge, exhibit, explain, perform, present, produce 8 ceremony, disclose, evidence, flourish, indicate, instruct, manifest 9 barnstorm, burlesque, designate, rareeshow, represent, semblance 10 appearance, exhibition, exposition, expression 11 countenance, demonstrate, performance 13 demonstration
false: 6 tinsel
forth: 7 publish 8 manifest, proclaim 9 publicize
stylized: 4 mime 6 parade 7 pageant 9 cavalcade, pantomime
way: 5 guide, usher, 6 direct, escort 7 conduct
show up: 5 strip 6 appear, arrive, expose 7 display
showcase: 7 vitrine

shower: wet 4 bath, rain, sump, wash 5 bathe, party, spray, water 6 bestow, deluge 7 drizzle, scatter 8 revealer, sprinkle 9 exhibitor
meteor: 6 Leonid

showery: wet 4 damp 5 moist 7 tearful

showing: 4 sign 6 aspect 7 account 10 apocalypse, appearance
first: 8 premiere

showy: gay 4 arty, loud 5 dashy, gaudy, grand 6 flashy, garish, ornate, swanky 7 dashing, gallant, gaudful, pompous 8 gorgeous, splendid, striking 9 brillante, sumptuous 10 pretensive 11 pretentious 12 ostentatious

shrab: 5 drink 6 spirit 8 beverage

shrapnel: 10 projectile

shred: bit, cut, hew, jag, rag 4 fell, jagg, snip, tear, twig, wisp 5 blype, grate, piece, prune, scrap, sever, shard, strip 6 divide, screed, sliver, tailor, tatter 7 fritter, parings, vestige 8 fragment, particle

shrew: 5 curse, scold, vixen 6 mammal, tartar, virago 7 muskrat, villain 9 scoundrel, termagant
long-tailed: 5 sorex

shrewd: bad, sly 4 cagy, cute, evil, foxy, hard, keen, sage, wily 5 acute, canny, harsh, sharp, smart, stern 6 argute, artful, astute, biting, clever, crafty, subtle, wicked 7 abusive, cunning, gnostic, hurtful, knowing, parlous, politic, sapient 8 depraved, grievous, piercing, shrewish 9 gnostical, ingenious, injurious, sagacious 10 discerning, farsighted, hardheaded 11 distressing, mischievous, penetrating, sharpwitted 13 perspicacious

shrewish: 7 nagging 8 vixenish 9 termagant

shriek: cry, yip 4 yell 6 holler, outcry, scream 7 screech

shrift (see also **shrive**): 10 absolution, confession, disclosure 12 confessional 14 acknowledgment

shrill: 4 high, keen 5 acute, sharp 6 argute, biting, piping, shriek, squeak 7 screech 8 piercing, poignant, strident 11 high-pitched, penetrating

shrimp: kid 5 dwarf 6 shaver 9 stripling 10 crustacean
large: 5 prawn

shrine box 4 case, naos, tomb 5 altar, caaba, chest, kaaba, huaca 6 abaton, adytum, chapel, chasse, dagaba(Ind.), dagoba(Ind.), entomb, hallow, temple 7 chaitya, enclose, memoria 8 canonize, enshrine 9 container, reliquary 10 receptacle
goddesses: 9 anaktoran
visitor: 7 pilgrim

shrink: shy 4 fawn, funk, shun, wane 5 cling, cower, quail, rivel, shrug, wizen 6 blench, boggle, cotter, cringe, flinch, gizzen, huddle, humble, lessen, recoil, retire, wither 7 atrophy, dwindle, retract, shrivel 8 condense, contract, decrease, withdraw 9 constrict 10 depreciate

shrinking: shy 5 timid 6 afraid 9 diffident

shrive: rob 4 free 5 purge 6 pardon 7 absolve, confess 8 disclose 9 reconcile

shrivel: 5 blast, crine, parch, rivel, wizen 6 cotter, scrump, shrink, weazen, wither

shriveled: 4 wede

shroff: 6 banker, expert 7 changer, inspect 8 separate 12 moneychanger

shrogs: 9 brushwood

shroud: lop 4 hide, trim, veil 5 array, cloak, cover, crypt, dress, shade, sheet, vault 6 branch, clothe, screen, shadow 7 conceal, curtain, envelop, foliage, garment, plumage, protect, shelter 8 cerement, clothing, covering, envelope 9 cerecloth 10 protection

Shrove Tuesday: 10 Pancake Day

shrub: lop, tea, tod 4 bago, bush, cade, coca, gumi, majo, nabo, olea, sida, sola 5 elder, lilac, prune, punch, salal 6 cudgel, frutex 7 arboret, buckeye, chamise, chamiso, heather, scratch, tarbush 8 abelmosk, barberry, beverage, huisache 9 chaparral, manzanita
aromatic: tea 4 mint, sage 5 batis, thyme 8 rosemary
bean family: 4 ulex
collection: 10 fruticetum
desert: 5 retem 6 alhagi, raetam
evergreen: box 4 ilex, moss, titi 5 furze, heath, salal, savin 6 laurel, myrtle 7 jasmine, juniper 8 oleander 9 mistletoe
fence: box 5 hedge
flowering: 5 lilac, tiara 6 azalea, laurel, myrtle, spirea 7 lantana, rhodora, spiraea, syringa 8 japonica, oleander, oleaster 9 mistletoe 10 mignonette
fruit: 5 salal
genus of: 4 inga 5 erica, ledum 6 aralia
hardy: 7 althaea, heather
indigo: 4 anil
myrtle-like: 7 cajeput, cajuput
ornamental: 6 privet
parasitic: 9 mistletoe
pert. to: 9 fruticose, fruticous
poisonous: 5 sumac 6 sumach
prickly: 4 whin 5 briar, brier, gorse 7 bramble 8 allthorn, hawthorn
rubber: 7 guayule
stunted: 5 scrag, scrub
tea-like: kat 4 coca
tropical: 5 henna 6 olacad 7 lantana 10 frangipane, frangipani
yercum-yielding: 5 madar

shrubbery: 7 boscage, boskage

shruff: 5 dross 7 rubbish

shrug: don, tug 5 hitch 6 fidget, shiver, shrink 7 gesture, shudder 8 contract, hitching 9 handshake 10 convulsion

shrunken (see also **shrink**): 4 lank

Shu: *parent:* Ra 6 Hathor

  sister: 6 Tefnut

  wife: 6 Tefnut

shuck: pod 4 husk 5 shell, strip 6 recoil, remove 7 discard

shudder: 4 grue 5 quake, shake 6 agrise, shiver 7 frisson, tremble

shuffle: mix 4 gait, plod 5 dance, scuff 6 huddle, juggle, jumble, mingle, remove, sclaff 7 evasion, quibble, scuffle, shamble 8 artifice 10 equivocate 11 prevaricate 12 equivocation

shuffling: 6 shifty 7 evasive 9 deceitful 13 opportunistic

shun: 4 balk, flee, hide 5 avert, avoid, evade, evite 6 eschew 7 forbear, forsake, refrain 8 forebear

shunt: 5 shift, shove 6 divert, remove, switch 9 conductor, rechannel, sidetrack

shut: bar, rid 4 free 5 close 6 climax, fasten, forbid 7 confine, exclude 8 prohibit 10 portcullis

  in: hem, pen 4 cage, pent, wall 5 embar, embay, fence 6 bottle, hemmed 7 bottled, confine, enclose, impound 8 imprison 10 quarantine, surrounded

shut-in: 7 invalid, recluse 12 convalescent

shut out: bar 7 exclude 8 preclude

shut up: end, gag 7 seclude 8 conclude 9 terminate

shutter: 5 blind, cover 6 screen 7 buckler 8 jalousie

shuttle: 6 looper

shuttlecock: 4 bird 6 birdie

shy: coy, mim 4 jump, shun, wary 5 aloof, avoid, chary, scant, start, throw, timid 6 anerly, boggle, demure, modest, recoil, shrink 7 bashful, lacking 8 farouche, hesitant, reserved, retiring, secluded, sheepish, skittish 9 diffident, reluctant, shrinking 10 shamefaced, suspicious, unassuming 11 distrustful, unobtrusive 14 unostentatious

Shylock: *coin:* 5 ducat

  daughter: 7 Jessica

  friend: 5 Tubal

shyster: 11 pettifogger

si: yes

Siam: See **Thailand**

Siamese twin: Eng 5 Chang

sib: kin 4 akin 6 allied, sister 7 brother, kindred, kinship, kinsman, related, sibling 8 friendly, relation, relative 9 congenial, kinswoman, relatives 12 well-disposed

Siberia: *antelope:* 5 saiga

  carnivore: 5 sable

  city: 4 Enna, Omsk 5 Chita, Tomsk 7 Barnaul, Irkutsk 11 Krasnoyarsk, Vladivostok 15 Blagovestchensk

  dog: 7 Samoyed 8 Samoyede

  Eskimo: 4 Yuit

  fish: 5 nelma

  forest: 5 Urman

  fur: 7 calabar

  gulf: Ob

  hunters and fishers: 6 Giliak, Gilyak 7 Samoyed 8 Samoyede

  hut: 8 barabara, barabora

  leopard: 5 ounce

  mountains: 5 Altai

  peninsula: 6 Taimir 9 Kamchatka

  people: 5 Sagai, Tatar, Yakut 6 Kirgiz, Tartar 7 Kirghis, Kirghiz, Yukagir 8 Yukaghir 9 Mongolian

  plain: 6 steppe, tundra

  region: 5 taiga

  river: Ob, Om; Ili, Tom 4 Amur, Lena, Maya, Onon 5 Sobol, Tobol 6 Olenek 7 Yenisei

  squirrel: 7 miniver

  squirrel-skin: 7 calabar

  storm: 5 buran

  tanning plant: 5 badan

  tent: 4 yurt 5 yurta

  wild cat: 5 manul

  wild sheep: 6 argali

sibilant: s, z; ch, sh, zh; ess 7 hissing

sibling (see also **sib**): 6 sister 7 brother

sibness: 7 kinship 10 connection 12 relationship

sibyl: 5 witch 6 Libyan, Samian, Trojan 7 Cumaean, seeress 8 Delphian, Phrygian 9 Cimmerian, Erythrean, sorceress, Tiburtine 10 prophetess 13 fortuneteller, Hellespontine

sibylline: 6 occult 7 cryptic 8 oracular 9 ambiguous, equivocal, prophetic 10 exorbitant, mysterious 11 prophetical

sic: so; set 4 seek, such, thus, urge 5 chase 6 attack, incite

sice: six 8 sixpence

Sicilian: 10 Trinacrian

Sicily: *cape:* 4 Boeo, Faro 7 Passaro

  city: 4 Gela 5 Aetna, Bidis 6 Alcamo, Modica, Ragusa 7 Catania, Marsala, Messina, Palermo, Trapani 8 Girgenti 13 Caltanissetta

  composer: 7 Bellini

  crime society: 5 Mafia

god: 7 Adranus
harbor: 7 Palermo
island: 11 Pantelleria
king: 4 Eryx
measure: 5 salma 7 caffiso
mountain: 4 Etna
people: 5 Elymi, Sicel
river: 5 Salso 6 Belice, Simeto 7 Platani
seaport: Aci 7 Messina
secret society: 5 Mafia
volcano: 4 Etna
whirlpool: 9 Charybdis
youth: 4 Acis

sick: bad, ill, set, wan 4 abed, pale, seek, urge, weak 5 badly, chase, crank, cronk, fed-up, unfit, weary 6 ailing, attack, incite, unwell 7 unsound 8 impaired 9 crapulous, depressed, disgusted, instigate, nauseated, surfeited, unhealthy 10 indisposed 11 exasperated
deathly: 5 amort 7 alamort
person: 7 invalid, patient
sickbay: 6 clinic 8 hospital 9 infirmary 10 dispensary
sicken: 6 affect 8 languish
sickening: 7 fulsome 9 revolting 10 disgusting, nauseating
sicker (see also **sick**): 4 fast, firm, safe, sure 5 fixed 6 assure, pledge, safely, secure, stable 7 assured, certain 8 securely 9 assuredly, certainly, confident 10 dependable 11 established, trustworthy
sickish: 6 sickly 9 sickening
sickle: 6 scythe
sickly: ill, wan 4 flue, pale, puny, weak 5 cothy, faint, frail 6 ailing, cranky, feeble, infirm, weakly 7 cothish, insipid, invalid, languid, mawkish, queechy 8 diseased 9 sickening, unhealthy
sickness: 6 malady, nausea 7 ailment, disease, disgust, illness 9 distemper, infirmity, weariness 12 qualmishness 13 indisposition
feign: 8 malinger
mental: See **mental disorder**
side: far 4 edge, face, line, part, team, wall, wide 5 agree, ample, costa, facet, flank, latus, party, phase, place, proud, shore, slope, space, width 6 aspect, behalf, border, margin, region, severe 7 conceit, distant, faction, lateral, support, surface 8 district, position, spacious 9 declivity, direction, outskirts 10 collateral 15 pretentiousness
on the: 5 apart
pain in: 6 stitch
pert. to: 7 lateral
piece: rib 5 stave
sheltered: lee 4 alee

side arm: 5 sword 6 pistol, weapon 7 bayonet 8 revolver
side by side: 8 parallel, together
side view: 7 profile
sideboard: 6 buffet 8 credence, credenza, cupboard, dressoir
sidekick: pal 4 chum 6 friend 7 partner 8 follower 9 assistant, companion, satellite 11 confederate
sideline: 5 bench 9 avocation
sideling, sidling: 5 askew, slope, steep 7 lateral, sloping 8 inclined, sidelong, sideways 9 inclining, laterally, obliquely
sidelong: 6 subtle 7 lateral, oblique, sloping 8 indirect, sideways, slanting 9 laterally, obliquely
sidepiece: rib 6 border
sidereal: 6 astral, starry 7 stellar 8 starlike
siderite: ore
sideroad: 5 byway
siderolite: 9 meteorite
sideshow: 10 attraction
attraction: 5 freak
sideslip: 4 skid 5 slide 10 digression
sidestep: 4 duck 5 avoid, evade
sidetrack: 4 spur 5 shunt 6 divert, switch
sidewalk: 6 causey 9 banquette, boardwalk
part: 4 curb, kerb 5 crack 6 paving
sideway: 5 byway 6 bypath 7 postern 8 sidewalk, sideways
sideways: 5 aside 6 askant 7 askance, athwart, lateral 8 indirect, sidewise 9 laterally, obliquely
Sidi's wife: 5 Amine
sidle: 4 edge 6 loiter 7 saunter
Sidon's modern name: 5 Saida
sie: 4 drip, drop, sift 6 strain
siege: see 4 rank, seat 5 bench, beset, flock, place, privy 6 attack, throne 7 besiege, sitting, station 8 blockade 9 beleaguer 13 beleaguerment
Siegfried: *mother:* 8 Sieglind
slayer: 5 Hagen
sword: 7 Balmung
vulnerable spot: 4 back 8 shoulder
wife: 9 Kriemhild
sierra: 5 range, ridge
Sierra Nevada: *fog:* 7 pogonip
peak: 4 Dana 7 Whitney
siesta: nap 4 rest 5 sleep
sieve: 4 lawn, sift 5 tamis, temse 6 basket, bolter, filter, ranger, riddle, screen, sifter, strain 7 chaffer, cribble, measure 8 colander, separate, strainer
for clay: 4 laun
sievelike: 8 cribrate
sift: ree, sie, sye 4 bolt, cull, scry, seek 5 sieve, temse 6 dredge, filter, riddle, screen,

search, strain, winnow **7** canvass, examine, inspect, scatter **8** separate **10** scrutinize

sifter: **5** sieve **6** bolter **8** strainer

sigh: sob **4** moan, sugh, wail **5** mourn, sithe, sough, yearn **6** grieve, lament **7** suspire **11** respiration

sight: aim, ken, sum **4** bone, espy, gaze, look, show, vane, view **5** scene **6** aspect, behold, descry, glance, vision **7** discern, display, glimpse, insight, suspire **8** eyesight, quantity **9** spectacle **10** appearance, exhibition, inspection, perception **11** examination, observation, suspiration

defect: **7** anopsia

gun: **4** bead

loss: **9** amaurosis

obscurity: **6** caligo

offending: **7** eyesore

out of: **11** disappeared

pert. to: **6** ocular, visual

second: fey, ESP **7** psychic

sightless: **5** blind **6** unseen **9** invisible

sigil: **4** seal, sign, word **6** device, signet **9** signature

sigmoid: ess

Sigmund: *father:* **7** Volsung

son: **6** Sigurd

sword: **4** Gram

wife: **7** Hiordis

sign (see also **signal**): ad; cue, nod **4** hire, mark, note, omen **5** badge, image, segno(It.), sigil, spoor, token, trace **6** banner, beacon, beckon, caract, effigy, emblem, engage, ensign, figure, motion, notice, poster, signet, symbol, wigwag **7** auspice, endorse, gesture, initial, insigne, message, picture, portent, prodigy, vestige, warning **8** password, pretense, standard **9** character, semaphore, semblance, subscribe, watchword **10** denotation, expression, forerunner, indication, prognostic, underwrite **11** countersign **13** advertisement, constellation, demonstration, foreshadowing

astrological: **5** Aries **6** Gemini, Pisces, Taurus **8** Aquarius **9** Capricorn

diacritical: **5** hamza, tilde **6** hamzah, tittle, umlaut **7** cedilla

direction: **5** arrow

illuminated: ad **4** neon **6** lights

liturgical: **5** selah **6** shelah

magic: **5** sigil

music: **5** presa, segno

pert. to: **5** semic **8** semantic

Zodiac: See **Zodiac** *sign*

sign language: **11** dactylology

sign off: out **6** thirty

sign on: **4** hire, ship **6** engage, enlist, enroll **8** register

signal (see also **sign**): **4** flag **6** buzzer, ensign, notify, sennet **7** betoken, eminent, lantern, notable, presage, signify **9** memorable, prominent, semaphore, symbolize **10** remarkable **11** communicate, conspicuous **13** extraordinary

distress: SOS **6** mayday

electric: **8** teleseme

system: **4** code

warning: **5** alarm, alert, flare, siren **6** alarum, beacon, tocsin **7** blinker

signature: **4** hand, mark, name, sign, visa, vise **5** sigil, stamp **9** allograph, autograph, birthmark, designate **10** directions, impression **11** countersign

signet: **4** mark, seal, sign **5** sigil, stamp **10** impression **12** authenticate

significance: **7** bearing, purport **13** signification

significant: **4** sign **5** grave, token **6** symbol **7** ominous, weighty **8** eloquent, sinister **9** important, momentous **10** expressive, indicative, meaningful, portentous, suggestive **13** consequential

signification: **4** sign **5** sense, token **7** meaning **10** importance, indication **11** consequence **12** apprehension, notification

signify: nod **4** mean, show, sign **5** augur, imply, spell, utter **6** amount, denote, import, inform, matter, signal **7** betoken, compare, declare **8** announce, foreshow, indicate, intimate, manifest **11** communicate

signor: man **4** lord **5** title **9** gentleman

signpost: **5** guide **6** beacon **9** guidepost

signum: **4** bell, mark, sign **9** signature

Sigurd: *father:* **7** Sigmund

foster father: **5** Regin **6** Reginn

horse: **5** Grani

slayer: **5** Hogni

wife: **6** Gudrun

Sigyn's husband: **4** Loki

sike: **4** rill **5** brook, ditch, drain, gully **6** ravine, stream, trench

siker: **4** safe **6** secure **7** assured **9** confident **10** dependable **11** trustworthy

Sikkim (see also **India**): *capital:* **7** Gangtok

people: **4** Rong

silage: **4** feed **6** ensile, fodder **8** ensilage

Silas Marner author: **5** Eliot

sile: fry **4** beam, drop, fall, flow, pour, soil **5** glide, sieve, spawn **6** filter, rafter, strain **8** strainer

silence: gag **4** hush, mute, rest, stun **5** choke, floor, quiet, still, tacet **6** muffle **7**

campion, confute, repress, secrecy **8** muteness, suppress **9** obscurity, reticence, stillness **10** silentness
  goddess: **8** Angerona
  music: **5** tacet
silencer: **4** mute **5** gavel **7** muffler
silene: **7** campion **8** catchfly
silent: mum **4** dumb, flat, mute **5** quiet, still,
tacit **8** inactive, overcome, reserved, reticent, taciturn, unspoken **9** noiseless, secretive, unuttered **10** flavorless, speechless,
unrecorded **11** unexpressed, unmentioned
15 uncommunicative
Silesian town: **4** Oels **5** Opava, Opole
silex: **5** flint **6** quartz, silica
silica: **4** opal **5** silex **7** dioxide
silicate: **4** mica **6** cerite, iolite **7** epidote **8**
calamine, severite, wellsite
silicon derivative: **5** monox
silk: **5** pekin, surah, tulle **7** foulard **8** florence, sarcenet, sarsenet
  corded: **6** faille
  embroidery thread: **5** floss **8** arrasene
  fabric: **4** gros **5** caffa, China, crepe, moire,
ninon, pekin, satin, surah, tabby, tulle **6**
cendal, faille, mantua, pongee, samite,
sendal, tussah, tusser, tussur **7** alamode,
marabou, sarsnet, taffeta, tsatlee, tussore
8 sarcenet, sarsenet
  fishline: **4** gimp
  hank: **4** hasp
  hat: **4** tile **6** topper
  Indian moth: **4** muga
  raw: **5** grege
  refuse: **6** strass
  source: **6** cocoon
  substitute: **5** nylon, rayon
  thread: **4** filo
  unspun: **6** sleave
  waste: **4** noil **5** floss **6** frison
  watered: **5** moire
  worker: **7** thrower **9** throwster
  yarn: **4** tram **7** schappe
  yarn size: **6** denier
silk-stocking: **4** ride **5** elite **7** elegant,
wealthy **9** exclusive, luxurious **10** Federal-
ist **12** aristocratic
silken: **4** fine, soft **5** quiet, silky, sleek,
suave, sweet **6** gentle, glossy, smooth, tender **7** elegant **8** delicate, lustrous, silklike
9 luxurious, sericeous **10** effeminate **12** ingratiating
silkworm: eri **4** eria **6** tussah, tusser, tussur
7 tussore **8** bombycid
silkworm rot: **7** calcino
sill: **4** beam, seat, sile **5** bench, frame, ledge,
shelf, stone **6** timber **9** threshold
silliness: **5** folly **6** betise(F.)
silly: mad **4** bete, daft, fond, fool, idle, simp,
weak **5** anile, apish, barmy, dazed, dense,

frail, goofy, goose, inane, plain **6** absurd,
cranky, cuckoo, dotard, dottle(Sc.), feeble,
footle, humble, infirm, paltry, rustic,
sickly, simple, stupid, unwise **7** asinine,
fatuous, foolish, foppish, shallow, witless **8**
childish, fopperly, ignorant, imbecile, innocent **9** brainless, childlike, ludicrous,
pointless, senseless, simpleton **10** half-witted, indiscreet **12** simple-minded **15** unsophisticated
silt: **4** scum **5** dregs **7** deposit, moraine, residue **8** sediment **9** percolate
silver: **4** pale **5** money, plate, sweet **6** argent,
gentle **7** bullion, silvery **8** argentum, eloquent, lustrous, peaceful, precious, sterling **9** tableware **10** silverware **11** resplendent **13** argentiferous
  comb. form: **6** argyro **7** argento
  containing: **5** lunar
  lace: **8** filigree
  pert. to: **9** argentine, argentous
  reducing kettle: **4** cazo(Sp.)
  symbol: Ag
silver and gold: *ornament:* **5** orris
silver-fox fur: **7** platina
silver oak: **11** flannelbush
silver plover: **4** knot(Sc.)
silver thaw: ice **4** rime **5** glaze
silver thistle: **8** acanthus
silver-tongued: **8** eloquent
silverfish: **6** insect, tarpon
silversmith: **9** artificer
silverware: **5** vases **6** dishes **8** platters **9** ornaments, tableware
  ornament: **7** gadroon
silverweed: rue **5** tansy **9** jewelweed
silvery: **7** frosted **9** argentine **10** argenteous
silviculture: **8** forestry
simar: **4** robe **6** jacket **7** garment **12** undergarment
Simeon: *father:* **5** Jacob
  mother: **4** Leah
simian: ape **6** monkey **7** apelike
similar: sib **4** akin, like, such **5** alike **6**
evenly **7** uniform **8** analogic, parallel **9**
semblance **9** analogous, resembling **11**
counterpart, homogeneous, resemblance
13 correspondent
  comb. form: **4** homo **5** homeo **6** homoeo
simile: **10** comparison
similitude: **4** form **5** image **6** simile, symbol
7 analogy, parable **8** allegory, likeness **9**
facsimile, semblance **10** similarity **11**
counterpart, resemblance **14** representation
similize: **5** liken **7** compare
simmer: **4** boil, stew **6** braise
simmon: **9** persimmon

simnel: 5 bread 7 biscuit 8 cracknel 9 fruit-cake

Simon: 5 Peter

Simon Legree: 6 driver 10 taskmaster

simon-pure: 4 real, true 7 genuine 9 authentic 11 unqualified

simony: 8 barratry

simoom, simoon: 4 wind 5 storm 6 tebbad

simper: 5 mince, smile, smirk 7 whimper

simple: 4 bald, bare, dull, easy, fond, mere, poor, pure, real, true, weak 5 folly, lowly, naive, naked, plain, Roman, silly 6 common, Dorian, homely, humble, oafish, rustic, severe, single, stupid 7 artless, austere, babyish, foolish, idyllic, natural, onefold, sincere, Spartan, unmixed 8 absolute, arcadian, childish, complete, gullible, homemade, ignorant, innocent, modestly, ordinary, tailored, trifling 9 childlike, elemental, ingenuous, primitive, unadorned 10 elementary, unaffected, uninvolved 11 homogeneous, undesigning, unimportant 12 inartificial, uncompounded, unpretending 13 insignificant, uncomplicated, unconstrained, unembellished 15 straightforward, undistinguished, unsophisticated

simple-minded: 6 simple, stupid 12 feeble-minded, unsuspecting 13 simple-hearted 15 unsophisticated

simpleton: ass, daw 4 boob, dolt, fool, gaby, gawk, gawp, gowk, lout, simp, tony, zany 5 dunce, goose, idiot, ninny, noddy, sammy 6 dawkin, gander, gawney, gulpin, nincom, nincum, nitwit, noodle 7 gomeral, gomerel, gomeril, muggins, widgeon 8 Abderite, fondling, numskull, omadhaun 10 changeling, nincompoop 11 ninnyhammer

simplify: 7 clarify, expound 9 elucidate, interpret

simulacrum: 4 sham 5 image 7 phantom 8 likeness, pretense, travesty 9 imposture, semblance 11 assemblance, counterfeit

simulate: act, ape 4 fake, mock, sham 5 feign, feiut 6 affect, assume 7 feigned, imitate, pretend 9 dissemble, personate, pretended 10 fictitious 11 counterfeit

simulation: 9 hypocrisy

simurgh, simurg: roc

sin: err 4 debt, envy, evil, lust, vice 5 anger, blame, crime, error, fault, folly, guilt, pride, sloth, wrong 6 acedia, felony 7 offense, violate 8 gluttony, iniquity, peccancy 9 deviation 10 immorality, peccadillo, transgress, wickedness, wrongdoing 11 misdemeanor, ungodliness, viciousness 12 covetousness 13 transgression

canonical: 6 heresy, murder 8 adultery, idolatry

Sinai mountain: 5 Horeb

sinapis: 7 mustard

Sinbad's bird: roc

since: as; ago, for, fro, now 4 ergo, gone, past, sith, syne(Sc.) 5 after, hence, later 7 already, because, whereas 8 inasmuch 9 afterward, therefore, thereupon 11 considering 12 continuously, subsequently

sincere: 4 open, pure, real, true 5 frank, whole 6 candid, devout, hearty, honest 7 cordial, correct, earnest, genuine, unmixed, upright 8 faithful, truthful, virtuous 9 authentic, blameless, heartfelt, unfeigned, veracious 10 unaffected 11 unvarnished 12 wholehearted 13 unadulterated 15 straightforward

sinciput: 8 forehead

Sinclair Lewis character: 7 Babbitt

sind: 5 rinse 6 drench, quench

sinecure: 4 pipe, snap 5 cinch, gravy

sinew: 5 snare 6 tendon

sinewy: 4 firm, wiry 5 thewy, tough 6 brawny, robust, strong 7 fibrose, nervous, stringy 8 forceful, muscular, powerful, vigorous 9 tendinous

sinful (see also **sin**): bad 4 evil 6 wicked 7 immoral, ungodly, vicious 10 iniquitous 11 unrighteous

sing: hum 4 cant, lilt, pipe, ring 5 carol, chant, chirl, croon, ditty, yodel, yodle 6 betray, intone, warble 7 chortle, confess, descant, rejoice, roulade, tweedle

as a round: 5 troll

softly: hum 5 croon

with trills: 6 warble 7 roulade

singable: 7 lyrical, melodic, tuneful 9 cantabile

singe: 4 burn, char, sear 6 scorch

fiber: 6 genapp

singer: 4 alto, bard, bass, diva 5 basso, buffa, buffo, tenor 6 artist, cantor 7 artiste, chanter, crooner, soloist, songman, soprano 8 minstrel, vocalist 9 chanteuse, chorister, contralto, descanter 10 cantatrice 11 entertainer

comic opera: 5 buffa

female: 9 chanteuse

opera: 4 diva

singerie: 6 design 7 picture 10 decoration

singing: 4 cant 5 charm 9 cantation

group: 4 duet, trio 5 choir, octet 6 chorus, sextet 7 octette, quartet 8 chanters, sextette 9 quartette

pert. to: 6 choral 9 cantative

trio: 9 tricinium

single: one 4 lone, only, part, sole, unit 5 alone, unwed 6 unique 7 onefold, unusual 8 celibate, separate, singular, solitary,

withdraw 9 sequester, unmarried 10 individual, particular 11 unsupported
combining form: uni

single out: 6 choose

singlet: 5 shirt 6 jersey 9 waistcoat 10 undershirt

singly: 4 once 5 alone 6 merely, solely 7 unaided 8 honestly 9 severally, sincerely 12 individually, particularly, single-handed

singsong: 5 chime

singular: odd 4 each, rare, sole 5 queer 6 single, unique 7 eminent, private, strange, unusual 8 isolated, peculiar, separate, superior, uncommon 9 eccentric, fantastic, whimsical 10 individual, remarkable, unexampled 11 exceptional 12 unparalleled 13 extraordinary, unprecedented

singult: sob 4 sigh

singultus: hic

sinister: car(Sc.) 4 dark, evil, grim, left 5 wrong 7 adverse, baleful, corrupt, ominous 9 dishonest, injurious, malicious, underhand 10 disastrous, portentous 11 prejudicial, unfortunate 12 inauspicious

sink: bog, dip, ebb, sag 4 cave, drop, fail, fall, ruin, wane 5 avale, drain, droop, embog, heald, hield, lower, plump, sewer, slope 6 debase, dolina, doline, drench, extend, gutter, plunge, settle 7 decline, degrade, depress, descend, destroy, immerse, relapse, subside 8 decrease, diminish, submerge, suppress 9 penetrate
below horizon: set
ship: 7 scuttle

sinker: 6 weight 8 doughnut

Sinkiang: *capital:* 7 Urumchi
river: 5 Tarim

sinking: 10 depression

sinless: 7 perfect 8 innocent 9 righteous

sinner: 5 scamp 8 evildoer, offender, penitent 9 reprobate, wrongdoer 10 backslider, trespasser 12 transgressor

sinning: 7 peccant

sinuous: 4 wavy 5 snaky 7 bending, crooked, curving, devious, sinuate, winding 9 deviating, intricate 10 circuitous, serpentine 11 anfractuous

sinus: bay 4 bend, fold 5 bosom, curve 6 cavity, hollow, recess 7 channel 10 depression
pert. to: 5 sinal 7 sinusal

Sioux: Kaw, Oto 4 Crow, Iowa, Otoe 5 Brule, Omaha, Osage, Sioux 6 Dakota, Santee, Tutelo 8 Catawaba 9 Winnebago
division: 5 Teton

sip: bib, lap, sup 5 draft, drink, quaff, taste 8 toothful

sipe: 4 seep, soak 9 percolate

sipper: 4 tube 5 straw

sir: 4 lord 5 title 6 knight, master 9 gentleman

sirdar: 5 chief, noble 6 bearer 7 officer, servant

sire: 4 lord 5 title 6 father, master, parent 8 ancestor, begetter 10 forefather, procreator, progenitor

siren: 5 lurer 7 charmer, foghorn, Lorelei, mermaid 9 Cleopatra 10 bewitching 11 fascinating
of Nile: 4 Cleo 9 Cleopatra

sirenian: 6 dugong 7 manatee

sirenic: 8 alluring 9 deceptive, melodious 11 fascinating

siriasis: 9 sunstroke

Sirius' master: 5 Orion

sirocco: 4 wind

sisal: 4 hemp 5 sizal

Sisera: *enemy:* 5 Barak
murderer: 4 Jael

siskin: 5 finch, tarin

sissy: 7 girlish 11 mollycoddle

sister: nun, sis 4 girl 5 soror(L.) 7 sibling
murder: 10 sororicide
pert. to: 5 soral 8 sororate, sororial
younger: 7 cadette(F.)

Sister Superior: 6 abbess

sisterhood: 8 sorority

sistrum: 6 rattle

sistrusus: 11 rattlesnake

sit: lie, set 4 meet, pose, rest, seat 5 brood, dwell, model, perch, press, roost, squat 6 occupy, remain, repose 7 convene 8 incubate
carelessly: 4 loll 6 sprawl

sit in: 6 attend 7 protest 11 participate

sit on: 6 confer, rebuke 7 repress, squelch 8 suppress 9 reprimand 11 investigate

site: 4 ruin, seat, spot 5 locus(L.), place, scene, venue 6 locale, locate 8 location, position 9 situation

sitfast: 5 fixed, stone 9 immovable 10 stationary

sithe: 4 sigh

Sitsang: 5 Tibet

sitter: 5 model, rider

sitting: 4 seat 5 abode, place 6 clutch, posing, seance, sedent, sejaul 7 sejeant, session 8 sederunt
court: 6 assize 7 session

Sitting Bull: *enemy:* 6 Custer
tribe: 5 Sioux

sitting duck: 5 decoy 6 target

situated: 4 seat 5 basal 6 nether, placed, plight 7 located, station 8 marginal 13 circumstanced
between folds: 11 interplical
in the middle: 6 medial, median

on membrane enveloping the brain: 8 epidural

on right: 6 dexter

toward rear: 6 astern 7 postern 9 posterior

situation: job 4 case, need, post, seat, site 5 berth, place, siege, situs(L.), state 6 estate, locale, morass, plight, scrape, strait 7 bargain, dilemma, station, vantage 8 locality, location, position, quandary 9 condition, emergency, imbroglio 11 predicament, whereabouts 12 circumstance

situla: 4 pail, vase 6 bucket 10 receptacle

situs: 5 place 8 location, position 9 situation

Siva: *consort:* Uma 4 Devi

son: 6 Skanda

trident: 6 trisul 7 trisula

wife: 4 Sati

six: 6 senary, sestet 7 digamma, sestole 8 senarius

group: 5 hexad 6 hexade, senary, sextet 8 sextette

pert. to: 6 senary

prefix: 4 hexa, hexo

series of: 5 hexad 6 hexade

six-eyed: 9 senocular

six-footed: 7 hexaped 9 hexapodal, hexapodan

six-line stanza: 6 sestet

six on dice: 4 sice

six sheets: 7 sextern

sixfold: 8 sextuple

sixpence: 6 bender 7 cripple, fiddler

size: 4 area, bore, bulk, mass 5 cover, glaze, grade 6 adjust, amount, candle, extent, format, volume 7 arrange, stiffen 8 classify, standard 9 dimension, magnitude 11 measurement

book page: 9 duodecimo

hosiery: 4 pope

indefinite: nth

paper: cap 4 copy, demi, demy, pott 5 atlas, crown, felic, folio, legal 6 bagcap 7 bastard, emperor 8 foolscap, imperial 9 colombier

separation device: 6 grader

type: 4 pica, ruby 5 agate, canon, elite, pearl 6 minion, primer 7 brevier, diamond, English, paragon 9 bourgeois, columbian, nonpareil

yarn: lea 5 forty 6 denier

sizing: 4 glue 6 starch

sizy: 7 viscous 9 glutinous

sizz: 4 hiss

sizzle: fry 4 burn, sear, siss 7 shrivel

sizzling: hot 6 torrid

sjambok: 4 flog, whip

skag: 4 boat, skeg, tear 5 split, wound

skate: jag, ray 4 fish, plug, shoe, skid 5 flair, glide, horse

order: 4 raja 5 raiae 7 rajidae

skate blade: 6 runner

skating arena: 4 rink

skean: 4 dirk 5 sword 6 dagger

skedaddle: 4 bunk, flee 5 scoot 6 scurry 7 scamper

skeeg: 4 flog, lash, slap

skeel: tub 4 pail 6 bucket

skeesicks: 6 rascal 9 skinflint

skeet: 12 trapshooting

skegger: 4 parr

skeigh, skeich: shy 5 proud 10 mettlesome

skein: rap 4 hank, wind 5 flock 6 flight, hurdle, sleeve 7 spireme, thimble

skelder: 5 cheat 7 vagrant 9 panhandle

skelet: 5 mummy 8 skeleton

skeletal: 4 bony

skeleton: 4 past 5 atomy, bones, coral, ilium, mummy 6 sketch 7 outline, remains 9 framework

disease: 7 rickets

hiding place: 6 closet

organization: 5 cadre

sea animal: 5 coral, shell 6 sponge

skeleton key: 4 gilt 5 screw 7 twirler

skell: 5 twist, upset 6 squint

skellum: 5 rogue, scamp 6 rascal

skelly: 4 chub 6 squint 9 chaffinch

skelp: say 4 beat, blow, kick, pare, push, rain, slap, walk 5 write 6 basket, colony, squall, stride, strike 7 beehive, measure, perform, quickly, scratch, scuttle 8 splinter, suddenly

skeppist: 8 apiarist 9 beekeeper

skeptic, sceptic: 7 doubter, infidel 10 pyrrhonist, unbeliever 11 disbeliever, freethinker, nullifidian

skeptical, sceptical: 8 doubting 9 faithless 11 questioning

skerrick: bit 5 scrap, trace 6 morsel

skerry: 4 isle, punt, reef, rock 6 potato

sketch: dot, jot, map 4 draw, limn, plan, play, skit 5 draft, paint, skate, story, trace 6 apercu, design, pastel 7 cartoon, croquis, drawing, outline, schizzo(It.) 8 describe 9 delineate, summarize 11 composition, delineation, description

sketchy: 5 rough, vague 10 inadequate, unfinished

skew: cup, cut, set 4 awry, fail, make, shun, slip, turn 5 askew, avoid, flunk, slant, stone, throw, twist 6 coping, escape, eschew, gauche, glance, offset, squint, swerve 7 blunder, distort, drizzle, oblique, pervert 8 slanting 9 deviating, distorted 12 misrepresent

skewer: pin, rod 5 prick, truss 6 fasten, pierce 7 hairpin 9 brochette

ski: *fall marker:* 8 sitzmark

race: 6 slalom

run: 6 schuss

skid: bar 4 clog, curb, drag, hook, rail, scud, shoe, slip, trig 5 brake, check, slide 6 fender, runner, timber, twitch 7 protect, skidpan, support 8 platform, sideslip

skiff: 4 boat, skif, skim 5 canoe, glide, graze, skift, touch 6 caique, flurry 7 currane, rowboat

skiing salutation: 4 heil

skill: art, can 5 craft, haunt, knack, virtu 7 ability, address, aptness, cunning, finesse, justice, mastery, science 8 artifice, capacity, deftness, facility, industry, judgment, rhetoric, training 9 adeptness, dexterity, knowledge, readiness 10 adroitness, artfulness, astuteness, capability, cleverness, competence, efficiency, experience, expertness 11 discernment, information, proficiency 12 skillfulness 13 judiciousness, understanding

skilled: 5 adept 6 astute, expert, versed 7 capable 10 conversant, proficient

government: 9 statesman

skillful: apt 4 able, deft, fine, good, hend, just 5 adept, handy 6 adroit, artful, aufait, clever, crafty, daedal, expert, habile, proper 7 capable, cleanly, cunning 8 dextrous, tactical 9 daedalian, dexterous, ingenious, righteous 10 proficient, reasonable 11 intelligent 12 accomplished

skillfulness: 5 craft

skilligalee: 5 broth 8 porridge

skim: cut 4 film, flit, sail, scud, scum, skip 5 clear, cover, fleet, glide, graze, ready, study, throw 6 glance, refuse 7 examine

skim over: 5 skirr 6 passim

skimmings: 9 fleetings

skimp: 6 meager, scanty, scrimp 9 economize

skimpy: 5 chary, skimp, spare 6 scanty, stingy 9 niggardly 12 parsimonious

skin: 4 bark, derm, dole, fell, film, flay, hide, pare, peel, pell, pelt, rack, rind, scum 5 balat, cheat, cutis, derma, fraud, layer, plica, purse, scalp, shell, strip, sweep 6 callus, escape, fleece, scrape, spoils 7 callous, cuticle, defraud, plating, profits, sharper, surface, swindle 8 covering, membrane, pellicle, planking 9 epidermis, skinflint 10 integument, pocketbook 11 decorticate, outdistance

animal: fur 4 coat, hide, pelt, plew, rack, robe, vair 5 coney, sculp 6 hackle, peltry

beaver: 4 plew

burning sensation: 5 uredo

comb. form: 4 derm 5 derma 6 dermis

decoration: 6 tattoo

deeper layer: 5 cutis

depression: 6 dimple

disease: 4 acne 5 hives, mange, psora, rupia, tinea 6 eczema, tetter

dressed: fur

dryness: 7 xerosis

excessive pigment: 8 melanism

exudation: 5 sudor, sweat 12 perspiration

fold: 5 plica 7 dewlaps

fruit: 7 epicarp

layer: 4 derm 5 cutis, derma

oil: 5 sebum

opening: 4 pore

pert. to: 5 deric 6 dermal 9 cuticular, epidermal

piece: 5 blype

prepare: taw

presser: 7 sammier

protuberance: 4 mole, wart

remover: 5 parer

resembling: 7 dermoid

sensitive layer: 5 cutis 7 enderon

tan: taw

unsheared pelt: 8 woolfell

without: 8 apellous

worn by Dionysus: 6 nebris

skin game: 5 bunco, bunko, fraud 7 swindle

skinflint: 5 flint, miser 6 huddle 7 niggard

skink: 4 adda, draw, hock, shin 5 drink, serve 6 liquor, lizard

skinker: 7 tapster

skinking: 4 thin 6 watery

skinkle: 5 strew 7 glitter, scatter, sparkle 8 sprinkle

skinned: *dark:* 7 melanic, swarthy

thick: 9 pachyderm 11 pachydermic

skinner: bet, gyp 5 cheat 6 driver 8 swindler

skinny: 4 bony, lean, thin 5 scant 6 meanly, stingy 9 emaciated, niggardly 10 membranous

skip: dap, hip, hop 4 balk, gait, jump, leap, miss, omit, skep, trip 5 bound, caper, elide, frisk, leave, salto, scout, vault 6 basket, bucket, escape, gambol, lackey, spring 7 abscond, captain, footman, servant 8 ricochet

along a surface: 7 skitter

school: tib

skip over: 5 elide

lightly: 4 skim

water: dap

skipjack: fop 4 fish 6 bonito, elater, jockey 7 upstart 8 sailboat 9 stripling 10 butterfish

skipper: ihi 5 saury 6 master 7 captain 9 butterfly

East Indian: 6 serang

skippet: box 4 boat 5 ladle, scoop, skiff 6 basket 8 envelope

skipping: 4 balk

skirl: fly 4 pipe, rain, snow 5 sweep, whirl 6 scream, shriek

skirling: 5 trout 6 salmon

skirmish: 5 brush, fence, fight, melee 6 action, battle, bicker, combat, effort 7 contest 8 conflict, flourish 9 encounter 10 velitation

skirp: 6 splash 7 spatter

skirr: fly, run 4 move, skim, tern 5 scour, whirr 6 scurry

skirt: lie, rim 4 edge, flap, girl 5 trend, woman 6 border, fringe 8 envelope, environs 9 outskirts, periphery, petticoat 10 underskirt

ballet: 4 tutu

coat: 6 lappet

divided: 7 culotte

hoop: 6 peplum 9 crinoline, krinoline 11 farthingale

medieval armor: 4 tace 5 tasse 6 tasset

section: 4 gore 5 panel

short: 4 kilt 6 kirtle

steel: 7 lamboys

velvet: 4 base

skit: act 4 gibe, girl, gust, hoax, jeer, jest, slap 5 caper, pound, revue, story, taunt, trick 6 parody, shower, sketch, splash 7 asperse, flounce 8 ridicule 9 enclosure 10 caricature, reflection

skite: 4 blow, dart, dash, fall, slip 5 boast, smite, trick 6 shower, squirt, strike 7 boaster 9 buffeting, squirting 12 yellow-hammer

skitter: 4 pass, skim, skip 5 glide 7 scamper, scatter 8 sprinkle

skittish: coy, shy 5 jumpy 6 fickle, lively 7 nervous, playful, restive 8 spirited 9 excitable, frivolous 10 capricious 12 undependable

skittle: 4 play 5 trash 7 ninepin 8 nonsense, squander 9 enjoyment

skive: 4 dart, pare, skim 5 shave, wheel

skiver: 6 impale, skewer 7 leather, scatter

skivvy: 9 underwear 10 undershirt

sklent: fib 5 slant 7 untruth 8 slanting

skoal: 5 toast 10 salutation 11 exclamation

skua: 4 gull 5 jager 6 jaeger

skulduggery: 8 trickery 10 craftiness, wickedness

skulk: 4 hide, lurk 5 dodge, evade, hedge, miche, shirk, slink, sneak 8 malinger

skull: 4 bean, head, mind 5 brain 6 cobbra, crania(pl.) 7 cranium, harnpan

back part: 7 occiput

bone: 5 vomer 6 zygoma 7 frontal, maxilla 8 mandible, sphenoid

cavity: 5 fossa 7 foramen

pert. to: 5 inial 7 cranial

protuberance: 5 inion

soft spot: 8 fontanel

skull cap: 5 calot 6 beanie 7 calotte 8 capeline, yarmulke, yarmelke(Yid.) 9 zucchetto

Arabian: 7 chechia

cardinal's: 10 berrettino

defensive: 4 coif 9 coiffette

ecclesiastical: 6 callot 7 calotte 9 zucchetto

felt: 6 pileus

skunk: 5 snipe 6 putois(F.) 7 polecat 8 betrayer

skunk-like animal: 5 civet 7 zorille

sky: 4 blue 5 azure, ether 6 welkin 7 heavens 9 firmament

comb. form: 4 uran 5 urano

god: Anu 4 Anat 5 Dyaus

goddess: 5 Frigg 6 Frigga

highest point: 6 zenith

pert. to: 6 coelar 9 celestial

sky-blue: 5 azure 6 celeste 8 cerulean

sky pilot: 8 chaplain, preacher 9 clergyman 10 missionary

skylark: run 4 bird, jump, lark, play, skip, yerk 5 pipit 6 frolic

genus: 6 alauda

skylight: 6 dormer, window 8 abat-jour(F.)

skyline: 7 horizon

slab: 4 tile 5 dalle, plate, slice, stela, stele 6 tablet

slab-like: 6 stelar 7 stelene

slack: lax 4 dull, idle, lull, slow, soft 5 chaff, evade, loose, relax, shirk, slake, tardy 6 abated, loosen, remiss 7 slacken 8 careless, dilatory, inactive, listless, sluggish, unsteady 9 dissolute, impudence, looseness, negligent 10 diminished, inadequate, neglectful 11 inattentive, indifferent

slacken: 4 ease, slow 5 abate, delay, relax 6 loosen, reduce, relent, retard 8 decrease, moderate

slackening: 7 detente(F.)

slacker: 4 spiv 7 coucher, shirker 8 embusque

slacks: 8 trousers

slade: den 4 cave, glen 5 glade, glide, slide 6 ravine, valley 7 peat bog 8 hillside

slag: 4 lava 5 dross, waste 6 cinder, debris, refuse, scoria 7 scoriae(pl.) 9 recrement 11 agglomerate

slain: 4 dead 6 fallen, killed 8 murdered 11 slaughtered 12 assassinated

slainte: 6 health 8 greeting 10 salutation

slaister: 4 idle, mess 5 smear 6 bedaub

slaistery: 4 dirt, miry 6 refuse, sloppy

slake: mud, wet 4 cool, daub, flag, free, lick, mire, sate 5 abate, algae, allay, gully, loose, slack, slime, smear, yield 6 aslake, deaden, lessen, quench, ravine, reduce 7 appease, assuage, crumble, refresh, relaxed, release, relieve, satisfy, slacken 8 decrease, mitigate, moderate **10** extinguish **12** disintegrate

slam: hit **4** bang, beat, blow, cuff, dash, push, shut, vole **5** abuse, clash, close, noise, throw **6** impact **7** flounce **9** criticize

in cards: **4** vole

slammock, slummock: 6 sloven **8** slattern, slipshod, ungainly

slander: 4 tale **5** belie, libel, shame **6** defame, malign, report, vilify **7** asperse, blacken, distort, scandal, traduce **8** derogate, disgrace, dishonor, reproach **10** defamation, depreciate, detraction, scandalize **12** misrepresent

slanderous: 8 libelous, shameful **11** disgraceful

slang: 4 cant **5** abuse, argot **6** jargon, rakish, vulgar **7** license, swindle

slant: tip **4** bend, bias, cant, skew, slab, tilt, turn, view **5** bevel, point, slope **6** biased, breeze, glance, sklent **7** incline, opinion **8** attitude, occasion **10** hypotenuse **11** inclination, opportunity

slanted angle: 5 bevel

slanting: 4 bias, skew **5** askew, aside, atilt **6** askile, aslant, aslope **7** athwart, crooked

slap: box, hit, lap **4** beat, blow, clap, cuff, nick, pass, scud, snub, spat **5** click, clink, cluff, notch, plump, skelp, smack **6** break, buffet, insult, rebuff, slight, strike **7** attempt **8** suddenly

slapdash: 5 abuse, hasty **8** careless **9** impetuous, roughcast **10** abruptness **11** haphazardly **12** carelessness **13** precipitately

slape: 6 crafty, smooth **8** slippery **9** deceitful

slapjack: 7 pancake **11** griddlecake

slapstick: 4 joke **6** comedy

slare: 4 slur **5** scuff, smear, sneer

slash: cut **4** dash, gash, lash, slit **5** crack, slosh, wound **6** attack, defeat, lessen, reduce, splash, strike, stripe **7** censure, scourge, slitter **9** criticize

slasher 5 knife, sword **6** dagger **8** billhook **9** swordsman **12** swashbuckler

slashing: 4 huge **6** severe **7** dashing, driving, immense, violent **8** spirited **9** merciless **10** tremendous **11** criticizing

slat: bar, dab, rib **4** beat, blow, flap, hide, hurl, lath, slab, slap, toss **5** crack, split, throw **6** pummel, strike **8** fragment, splinter

slate: rag **4** list, rock, tile **5** board, color, flesh, hound, plank, scold **6** berate, pummel, punish, pursue, record, roster, tablet, thrash **7** censure, roofing **8** nominate, register, schedule **9** criticize, reprimand, thrashing

break into slabs: **5** sculp

clean: **10** tabula rasa

tool: sax, zax

slater: 5 louse **6** critic **7** hellier

slath: 6 basket

slattern: daw **4** drab, frow, slut **5** dolly, idler, moggy, waste **6** blowze, faggot, sloppy **7** trifler, trollop **8** careless, slovenly

slatternly: 5 dirty, dowdy **6** blowzy, sordid, untidy **8** slovenly

slaty: 6 clayey **7** grayish **9** argillous **12** argillaceous

slaughter: 4 gash, kill, slay **6** battue, murder, pogrom, reduce **7** butcher, carnage, killing **8** butchery, hecatomb, massacre **9** bloodshed, reduction **10** butchering **11** destruction

slaughterhouse: 8 abattoir, butchery, matadero(Sp.)

waste: **7** tankage

Slav: 4 Pole, Serb, Sorb, Wend **5** Croat, Czech, Sider **6** Sclave, Slovak **7** Russian, Serbian, Servian **8** Bohemian, Croatian, Moravian, Silesian **9** Bulgarian **12** Czechoslovak

slave: 4 bond, esne, neif, peon, serf **5** chela, dasir, helot, thane **6** addict, cumhal, drudge, penest(Gr.), thrall, toiler, vassal, wretch **7** bondman, captive, chattel, enslave, odalisk, servant **9** gallerian, hierodule, odalisque

block: **7** catasta

comedy: **5** Davus(L.)

dealer: **5** bichy

free: **7** manumit **10** emancipate

fugitive: **6** maroon

pen: **5** crawl

ship: **6** slaver

The Tempest: **7** Caliban

traveling group: **6** coffle

slave driver: 6 despot, tyrant **8** martinet **11** Simon Legree

Slave States: 5 Texas **7** Alabama, Florida, Georgia **8** Arkansas, Delaware, Kentucky, Maryland, Missouri, Virginia **9** Carolinas, Louisiana, Tennessee **11** Mississippi **13** North Carolina, South Carolina

slaver: 5 drool, smear **6** drivel, saliva **7** slabber, slobber

slavery: 7 bondage, service **8** drudgery **9** captivity, servitude, thralldom, vassalage **11** enslavement **12** enthrallment

release from: **8** liberate **10** emancipate **11** affranchise, enfranchise

Slavic: See **Slav**

slavish: low **4** base, bond, vile **6** abject, menial **7** servile **8** despotic, enslaved **9** barbarous, dependent, imitative **10** oppressive, tyrannical

slaw: 8 coleslaw

slay: 4 kill 5 smite 6 murder, strike 7 butcher, destroy, execute 9 slaughter 10 annihilate 11 assassinate, exterminate
by suffocation: 5 burke

slayer: 4 bane 6 killer 8 criminal, genocide, murderer, regicide, vaticide 9 matricide, patricide, regicidal 10 fratricide, sororicide

sleave: 4 sley 6 cleave, divide, reduce, tangle 8 separate, untangle 11 disentangle

sleazy: 4 thin 6 flimsy

sled: 4 pung 6 jumper, sleigh 7 clipper, coaster, sledger, travois, vehicle 8 toboggan 10 conveyance
log: 4 tode 7 travois

sledge: 4 dray, sled 5 break 6 hammer, hurdle, sleigh, strike

sleech: 4 ooze, silt 5 slime

sleek: nap 4 oily 5 gloss, preen, shiny, slick, smart, suave 6 finish, glossy, polish, smooth, soigne 7 flatter, mollify, soignee 8 polished, unctuous 10 flattering 11 insinuating

sleekit: 5 sleek 6 crafty, smooth 9 deceitful

sleep: nap 4 doss, doze 5 death, sopor 6 drowse, repose, snooze, stupor 7 slumber 8 lethargy 10 somnipathy 11 hibernation 15 unconsciousness
comb. form: 4 hypn 5 hypno
deep: 4 coma 5 sopor 6 stupor
god: 4 Soma 8 Morpheus
inability to: 8 insomnia
inducer of: 6 opiate 7 sandman, sopient 8 sedative
midday: 6 siesta
pert. to: 7 somnial

sleeper: bet, tie 4 beam 5 horse, shark 6 rafter, rester, timber 7 dormant, earmark, Pullman, reposer 8 dormouse 9 dowitcher, slumberer 11 stringpiece

sleepiness: 10 drowsiness, somnolence

sleeping: 4 abed 6 latent 7 dormant 8 dormient, inactive 9 quiescent
place: bed 4 bunk, doss 5 berth, couch 6 pallet 7 cubicle 9 cubiculum, dormitory
sickness: 12 encephalitis

sleepless: 5 alert 7 unquiet, wakeful 8 restless, watchful 9 ceaseless

sleepwalker: 12 noctambulist, somnambulist

sleepy: 4 dull 5 tired 6 drowsy 8 sluggish, soporose, soporous 9 lethargic, somnolent 10 phlegmatic, slumberous

Sleepy Hollow author: 6 Irving

sleet: 5 glaze

sleeve: 5 gigot 6 armlet
bar on: 7 chevron
hole for: 4 scye

sleigh: 4 pung, sled 6 cutter 7 cariole 8 carriole, toboggan
runner: 4 shoe

sleight: sly 5 craft, knack, skill, trick 6 crafty, wisdom 7 agility, conjure, cunning 8 artifice, deftness, prudence, trickery 9 dexterity, dexterous, quickness, stratagem 10 nimbleness

sleight-of-hand: 11 legerdemain
performer: 4 mage 8 conjurer, magician 15 prestidigitator

slender: 4 lean, slim, thin, weak 5 exile, gaunt, lanky, lithe, petit, reedy, small, sylph, wispy 6 feeble, lissom, meager, slight, svelte 7 gracile, tenuous, willowy 8 ethereal 9 attenuate, elongated 10 abstemious

slenderize: 4 slim

slenderness: 7 exility, tenuity

slent: 4 tear 5 slope, split 6 glance 9 declivity

sleuth: tec 6 tracer 7 tracker, trailer 9 detective, operative 12 investigator

slew: lot 4 slue, turn 5 twist 6 slough

sley: 4 part, reed 8 guideway

slice: cut, saw 4 jerk, part 5 carve, piece, share, shave, whang 6 cantle, divide, rasher, shiver, sliver 7 portion 8 separate, splinter
of bacon: 6 rasher
of meat: 6 collop

slick: 4 fine, neat, oily, tidy 5 alert, preen, sleek 6 adroit, chisel, clever, crafty, glossy, paddle, polish, smooth 7 smarten, thicket 8 slippery 9 enjoyable, excellent, ingenious 10 attractive, glistening 12 accomplished

slicker: 4 dude 5 cheat 7 gambler 8 raincoat 9 trickster

slide: 4 fall, skid, sled, slew, slip, slue 5 chute, coast, glide, hurry, scoot 6 sledge 7 incline, slither, sluther 8 glissade, ornament 9 avalanche, backslide, landslide
fastener: 6 zipper

slideway: 8 guideway

slight: cut 4 fine, slap, snub, thin 5 frail, leger(L.), light, minor, scant, scorn, sleek, small 6 flimsy, ignore, meager, scanty, simple, slight, smooth 7 distain, fragile, gracile, neglect, nominal, shallow, slender, trivial 8 careless, delicate 9 disesteem, disparage, disregard, indignity 10 immaterial 11 discourtesy, superficial, unimportant 12 contemptuous 13 disparagement, imperceptible, insignificant, unsubstantial
convexity: 6 camber
sound: 4 peep
variation: 6 nuance 7 shading

slightest: 5 least

slighting remark: 4 slur

slim: sly 4 lean, slur, thin 5 gaunt, small, spare 6 adroit, crafty, meager, meagre, scanty, slight, svelte 7 cunning, slender, tenuous 9 worthless 10 slenderize

slime: mud 4 gore, ooze 5 cover, gleet, smear 6 mucous

slimer: 8 toadfish

slimsy: 5 frail 6 flimsy

slimy: 4 vile 6 filthy, vulgar 7 viscous 9 glutinous, offensive, repulsive 10 disgusting

sling: 4 cast, hurl 5 drink, fling, throw 7 bandage 9 slingshot

slink: 4 lurk 5 crawl, sneak, steal

slip: err, imp 4 balk, clay, fall, omit, pier, shed, skid, slue 5 chute, elude, error, fault, frock, glide, lapse, leash, scion, shoot, slide 6 elapse, miscue 7 blunder, cutting, delapse, descend, faux pas, illapse, misstep, mistake, neglect, slither, sluther 8 pinafore 9 gaucherie 12 undergarment 13 transgression

slip away: die 4 pass 5 steal 6 elapse

slip back: 7 relapse

slip by: 4 pass 6 elapse

slip-up: 5 error 6 miscue 9 oversight

slipe: 4 pare, peel, slip 5 glide, slice, sneak, split, strip 6 sledge, sleigh

slipknot: 5 noose

slipper: 4 mule, shoe 5 moyle, scuff 6 juliet, pliant, sandal 7 bauchle, scuffer, shuffle, willowy 8 babouche, slippery

slippery: 4 eely, glib 5 slick 6 crafty, shifty, tricky, wanton 7 elusive, evasive, glidder 8 glibbery, unstable 9 deceitful, uncertain 10 unreliable 13 untrustworthy

slipshod: 8 careless, slommack, slovenly, slummock 10 disorderly

slipslop, slip-slop: 5 inane, slops 6 gabble 7 blunder, twaddle 10 wishy-washy 11 malapropism

slit: cut, rit 4 fent, gash, kerf, nick, race, rent, tear 5 sever, slash, split, unrip 6 cleave 7 fissure, opening 8 aperture, incision

slither: 4 slip 6 rubble 7 rubbish 8 slippery

slive: cut 4 slip 5 slice, slide, sneak, split 6 cleave, stroke

sliver: cut 5 shred, slice, slops, split 6 strand 7 slobber 8 fragment, splinter

slob: ice, mud 4 mire, ooze, snow 6 sloven, sludge

slobber: mud 4 gush, kiss, slob, slop 5 drool, slime, smarm 6 drivel, slaver, sloven 7 blubber, slabber

slobby: 5 boggy, muddy 8 slobbery

slock: bog 4 lure 5 drink 6 drench, entice, pilfer, quench 7 swallow

slocken: 5 slake 6 quench 8 saturate

sloe: haw 4 plum 10 blackthorn

slog: hit 4 blow, plod, plug, slam, slug, toil, work 5 drive 6 strike

slogan: cry 4 word 5 motto 6 phrase 9 catchword

sloop: 9 raceabout

slop: mud 4 gush, mash 5 slush, smock, spill, swill, waste 6 puddle, refuse, splash 7 cassock, clothes, garment, slobber 8 breeches, clothing, trousers

slope: dip, lie 4 bank, brae(Sc.), brow, cant, hang, ramp, rise, tilt 5 bevel, cliff, hield, scarp, slant, talus 6 ascent, aslant, aslope, bajada, depart, escarp, glacis 7 descent, incline, terrace, versant 8 gradient, hillside 9 acclivity, declivity, obliquely 10 declension 11 inclination

angle-measuring device: 10 clinometer

protective: 6 glacis

sloping: 6 aslant, aslope 7 oblique 8 inclined, slanting 9 declivous, inclining

sloppy: 5 messy 6 slushy 7 splashy 8 careless, slovenly 12 disagreeable

slosh: mud 5 slash, slush, spill, throw 6 wallow 8 flounder

slot: bar, cut 4 bolt, slat, stab 5 track, trail 6 groove, hollow, keyway, spline 7 keyhole, opening 8 aperture, guideway 10 depression

sloth: ai 4 idle, lazy, pack, slow, unau 5 delay 6 acedia, animal 7 accidie, inertia, neglect 8 edentate, idleness, laziness, slowness 9 indolence, tardiness 11 sleuthhound 12 sluggishness, wastefulness

three-toed: ai

two-toed: 4 unau

slothful: 4 argh, idle, lazy 5 inert 8 inactive, indolent, sluggish 9 sedentary

slouch: hat 4 gait, lout, pipe 5 droop 6 bonnet, loafer, lubber 7 posture 8 drooping, laziness 9 pendulous 13 shiftlessness

slough, slew, slue: bog, mud 4 fall, husk, mire, molt, ooze, plod, road, shed, skin, slew, slue 5 bayou, inlet, swamp 6 eschar, sheath, strike 7 channel, discard, mudhole 8 imprison

sloughing: 7 ecdysis

slounge: 4 idle, loaf 6 lounge

sloven: 4 slob 5 besom, clart 6 loafer 7 hallion 8 slovenly 9 scoundrel 11 undeveloped 12 uncultivated

slovenly: 4 lazy 5 dowdy, messy 6 blowzy, frouzy, frowsy, frowzy, grubby, sloppy, untidy 7 unkempt 8 careless, slattern, slipshod, sluttish 9 negligent 10 disorderly, slatternly

slow: lax 4 dull, late, poky 5 brosy, delay, grave, hooly, inert, pokey, slack, tardy 6 boring, hamper, hinder, retard, stolid, strike, stupid 7 dronish, gradual, laggard,

slacken 8 boresome, dilatory, diminish, inactive, sluggard, sluggish 9 leisurely, lingering, slowgoing, unhurried 10 decelerate, deliberate, phlegmatic, retrograde 13 unprogressive
comb. form: 5 brady
music: 5 largo, lento, tardo 6 adagio
slow down: lap 4 idle 6 retard 7 decline 10 decelerate, deliberate
slow loris: 5 kokam
slow-witted: 4 dull 6 stupid
slowness: 6 lentor
slowpoke: 5 snail 7 dawdler
slubber: 4 daub, mire, slur 5 billy, botch, slime, smear, stain 6 darken 7 obscure, slabber
slud: mud 4 mire 5 slush 7 sludder
sludge: ice, mud 4 mire, ooze, slob 5 waste 7 deposit, mixture 8 sediment 9 settlings
slue, slew, slough: 4 turn, veer 5 pivot, swing, twist
sluff: 7 discard
slug: bat, hit 4 blow, dram, slow, snag, stud 5 delay, drink, limax, snail 6 bullet, hinder, loiter, nugget, strike 7 draught, mollusk, trepang 8 sluggard, sluggish 9 gastropod 11 caterpillar, obstruction
genus of: 4 doto 5 limax 6 elysia
pert. to: 8 limacine
sea: 7 trepang 10 nudibranch
sluggard: daw 4 idle, lazy, slug 5 drone 8 faineant, sluggish
slugger: bat 4 goon 5 boxer 6 hitter, mauler 7 batsman 8 operator
sluggish: 4 dull, lazy, logy, slow 5 brosy, faint, heavy, inert 6 bovine, drowsy, leaden, supine, torpid 7 dronish, languor, lumpish 8 dilatory, inactive, indolent, slothful, sluggard, stagnant 10 tardigrade 15 procrastinating
sluice: 4 gash, gote, gout, pipe, race 5 flume, sasse, valve 6 breach, stream, trough 7 channel, launder, opening, passage 8 irrigate 9 floodgate
sluit: 5 ditch, gulch, gully
slum: 4 junk, room 5 alley 6 barrio, ghetto
slumber: 4 coma, doze 5 sleep 6 drowse, repose
slumberous: 4 calm 5 quiet 6 drowsy, sleepy 8 peaceful, tranquil 9 somnolent, soporific 10 slumbering
slump: sag 4 drop, fall, sink, slip 6 settle 7 decline 8 collapse 10 depreciate, depression
slur: 4 blot, blur, slip, soil 5 cheat, decry, elide, glide, slare, slide, smear, stain, sully, trick 6 insult, macule, slight, smirch, stigma 7 blemish, calumny, dimness, traduce 8 besmirch, disgrace, innuendo, reproach 9 aspersion, criticize, dis-

credit, disparage, indignity 10 calumniate 11 contaminate 12 imperfection
slush: mud, wet 4 gush, mire, pulp, slud, wash 5 grout 6 drench, drivel, sloven, sluice, splash 7 mixture, sludder
slut: 4 jade 5 bitch, filth, quean 6 befoul, harlot 8 slattern 9 dratchell
sluther: 4 slip 5 slide 7 shuffle
sluttish: 4 lewd 5 gross 6 filthy, sordid 8 slovenly 10 disorderly
sly: 4 arch, cagy, foxy, ruse, slee, wily 5 coony, snaky 6 artful, clever, crafty, feline, secret, shrewd, slinky, sneaky, subtle, tricky 7 cunning, evasive, furtive, roguish 8 skillful, sneaking 9 cautelous, deceitful, secretive 10 fallacious 11 clandestine, dissembling, mischievous, underhanded 12 hugger-mugger
look: 4 leer, ogle
slyly spiteful: 5 catty
smack: bit, hit 4 blow, boat, buss, kiss, slap, tang 5 crack, savor, sloop, taste, touch, trace 6 cutter, flavor, strike, vessel 7 vestige 8 mouthful, sailboat 10 suggestion
smacking: 5 brisk, sharp 6 lively 8 spanking, vigorous
smaik: 6 rascal 9 scoundrel
small: dab, sma(Sc.), tot, wad, wee(Sc.) 4 cute, lite, mean, puny, thin, tiny, whit, wisp 5 dawny, minim, petty, scant 6 atomic, dapper, grubby, humble, little, mignon, minute, modest, petite(F.), slight 7 minimal, slender, trivial 8 atomical, picayune, trifling 9 miniature, minuscule, thumbnail 10 diminutive 13 insignificant
amount: mot 4 atom, chip, drop, iota, mote, tate 5 speck 6 detail, morsel 7 driblet, handful, modicum, morceau(F.), snippet 8 modecule
bunch: 4 wisp
coin: 4 mite
combining form: 5 lepto, micro
prefix: 5 micro
small-fry: 4 kids, tots 8 children 10 youngsters
small-minded: 4 mean 5 petty 6 narrow 7 selfish 10 prejudiced, ungenerous, vindictive
small talk: 6 babble 7 prattle 8 chitchat
smallage: 6 celery 7 parsley
smaller: 4 less 5 minor 6 lesser
combining form: mi; mio 4 meio
smallest: 5 least
smallness: 7 exility, paucity
smallpox: 7 variola
smalt: 4 flux
smaragd: 7 emerald
smarm: 4 gush 7 slobber
smart: 4 bite, braw, chic, neat, posh, smug, trig, wily, wise 5 acute, alert, brisk, clean,

fresh, natty, nifty, quick, sharp, sting, witty **6** active, astute, bright, cheesy, clever, dressy, jaunty, lively, shrewd, spruce, suffer, swanky **7** capable, knowing, pungent, stylish **8** spirited, talented, vigorous **9** competent, dexterous **10** precocious **11** fashionable, intelligent

smarten: 6 spruce **7** improve **8** brighten, titivate

smash: hit **4** bash, blow, bung, dash, ruin **5** break, crash, crush, stave, wreck **7** destroy, shatter, smash-up, success **8** collapse, stramash(Sc.) **9** collision **10** bankruptcy

smashup: 4 ruin **5** wreck **6** defeat **7** failure **8** collapse **9** collision **10** bankruptcy

smatter: 4 smut, spot **5** break **6** babble, dabble, defile **7** chatter, clatter, crackle, shatter, spatter **9** fragments

smatterer: 7 dabbler **8** sciolist

smear: dab, rub **4** blot, blur, daub, gaum, soil, spot, stop **5** clart, cleam, slake, slare, stain, sully **6** anoint, bedaub, blotch, defame, defeat, defile, grease, malign, smirch, smudge, spread, thwart **7** besmear, plaster, pollute, slander, splatch **8** besmirch, ointment, slaister **9** overwhelm **10** overspread

smearcase: 6 cheese

smeared: 4 foul **6** greasy

smeary: 6 greasy, soiled, sticky **7** smeared

smectic: 9 detergent, purifying

smeddum: 4 dust **5** flour, vigor **6** powder, spirit

smeech: 4 dust **5** smell, smoke, stink, vapor

smeek: 4 reek **5** smoke

smell: 4 funk, fust, odor, olid, reek **5** aroma, fetor, flair, scent, sniff, trace **6** breath **7** hircine, noisome, perfume **9** fragrance **10** suggestion **11** graveolence

comb. form: **4** osmo

having a disagreeable: bad **4** foul, olid, **5** fetid **10** malodorous

loss of sense: **7** anosmia

offensive: **4** reek **5** fetor, nidor, stink **6** stench

pert. to: **9** olfactory

pleasant: **5** aroma **7** perfume

stale: **5** fusty, musty

smell-feast: 7 sponger **8** parasite

smeller: 4 nose **6** feeler **7** antenna, bristle

smelling salts: 9 hartshorn

smelt: 4 fish, flux, fuse, melt, prim **6** iuanga(N.Z.), reduce, refine **7** scorify

smelting: *by-product:* **4** slag

cone: **4** pina

smew: 4 duck **9** merganser

smicker: 5 smile, smirk

smidge, smidgen: bit **4** mite

smile: 4 beam, grin **5** smirk, sneer **6** arride, simper

smirch: 4 blot **5** asoil, smear, stain, sully, taint **6** blotch, smudge, smutch **7** begrime, blacken, blemish, tarnish **8** besmirch, discolor, dishonor

smirched: 5 dingy

smirk: 4 leer, trim, yirn **5** quick, smart, smile **6** simper, spruce **7** grimace, smiling

smit: cut, hit **4** blow, smut, spot **5** brand, stain **6** infect, smirch, stroke, struck **7** tarnish **8** disgrace, punished

smite: hit **4** blow, clap, cuff, gird, hurl, kill, pass, slap, slay, swat **5** blast, knock, skite **6** attack, buffet, defeat, hammer, pierce, punish, strike **7** afflict, chasten, collide, destroy, disease, impress, inspire **8** distress

smith: 6 forger **7** farrier **10** blacksmith **11** metalworker

smithcraft: 6 smithy **8** smithery

smithereens: 4 bits **5** atoms **6** pieces **8** flinders **9** fragments

smithy: 6 forger **7** farrier **10** blacksmith

smitten: 8 affected, enamored, stricken **9** afflicted, enamoured

smock: 5 kamis, shift, tunic **6** camise **7** chemise **11** overgarment

smog: fog **4** mist

smoke: 4 floc, fume, funk, haze, mist, pipe, smog **5** cigar, cubeb, segar, smook(Sc.), vapor **6** smudge **7** cheroot, cigaret **9** cigarette

fragrant: **7** incense

outlet: **7** chimney **8** fumeduct, fumiduct

wisp: **4** floc

smoke out: 5 flush **6** reveal **8** discover

smokejack: 6 funnel

smokeless powder: 6 poudre

smoker: car **4** stag **5** party

smokestack: 4 pipe **6** funnel **7** chimney

smoking equipment: 7 nargile, tabagie

smoky: 4 hazy **5** dingy, fumid **6** fumish **9** fumacious

smolder, smoulder: 5 choke, smoke **6** smudge **7** smother **9** suffocate

smolt: 4 calm **5** clear **6** bright, salmon, smooth

smoodge, smooge: pat **6** pamper **7** wheedle

smooth: 4 clam, ease, easy, even, gleg, glib, iron, lene, mild, pave, sand **5** bland, brent, furry, glace, glary, gloze, level, plane, preen, press, quiet, silky, sleek, slick, soapy, suave **6** creamy, evenly, fluent, glassy, glossy, mangle, serene, sleeky **7** amiable, equable, erugate, flatten, plaster, sadiron **8** explicit, friendly, glabrous, levigate, palliate, pleasant, polished,

soothing 9 courteous, unruffled 10 flattering 11 alabastrine 12 frictionless, ingratiating 13 mellifluently, uninterrupted
combining form: lio
phonetically: 4 lene
smoother: 7 abraser
smorgasbord item: 4 eels
smot: 4 mark 5 brand, stain
smote: hit 7 chasten
smother: 5 choke, smoor, smore 6 stifle, welter 7 overlie, smolder, turmoil 8 suppress
9 suffocate
smudge: 4 blot, blur, smug, smut, soil, soot
5 laugh, prink, smear, smile, stain 6
smutch 7 begrime, chuckle, smolder
smug: dig 4 neat, prig, tidy, trim 5 clean,
grind, smart, steal, suave 6 pilfer, spruce
7 correct 9 confident 10 blacksmith, complacent 13 selfsatisfied
smuggler: 6 runner
smurr, smur: 4 mist 5 cloud 7 drizzle
smut: 4 bunt, coom, mark, soil, spot 5 coomb,
grime, stain, sully, taint 6 blight, defile,
smudge 8 colbrand 9 obscenity
smutch: 4 blot, dirt, smut, soot, spot 5 grime,
stain, sully, taint, tinge, touch, trace 6 defile, smudge 7 blacken
smutty: 5 dirty, dusky, sooty 6 soiled, sordid
7 obscene, tainted 8 indecent
Smyrna: 5 Izmir
fig: 5 eleme, elemi
smytrie: 6 litter 10 collection
snack: bit, sip 4 ball, bite, jibe, part, snap 5
acute, alert, chack, lunch, quick, seize,
share, smack, taste 6 adroit, morsel, repast, snatch 7 portion, quickly, sharply,
teatime 8 grasping, snappish
snaffle: bit 4 loot 5 check, steal 6 pilfer 7
saunter, snuffle 8 restrain 9 restraint
snafu: 4 awry 6 muddle 8 disorder, entangle
9 confusion
snag: cut, hew, nag, nub 4 base, carp, knot,
part, slug, tear, tine, tree, trim, unit 5
break, catch, point, snail, stump, tooth 6
branch, damage, hazard, tongue 8 obstacle
9 hindrance 10 difficulty, impediment 11
obstruction 12 protuberance
snagger: 8 billhook
snail: 4 slug, snag, wilk 5 drone, mitra 6
dodman, tritou, winkle 7 driller, mollusk,
testudo 8 escargot, neritine, sluggard 9
gastropod 10 hoddy-doddy
clam-killing: 6 winkle
genus of: 5 fusus 6 nerita 9 clausilia
pond: 5 coret
shell: 7 cochlea
snailflower: 7 caracol
snake: asp, boa, bom, esp, nag 4 bind, boma,
curl, drag, draw, naga, skid, tail, turn,
wind, worm 5 aboma, adder, arrow, braid,

cobra, coral, crawl, cribo, filch, kriat,
mamba, racer, sneak, steal, viper 6
katuka, python 7 bokadam, camoodi, elapine, hagworm, ingrate, meander, rattler,
reptile, serpent 8 anaconda, bungarum,
camoodie, moccasin, ophidian, ringhals 9
whipsnake 10 blacksnake, bushmaster,
copperhead, massasauga, sidewinder 11
cottonmouth, rattlesnake 12 schaapsteker
big: boa 6 python 8 anaconda 11 constrictor
comb. form: 4 ophi 5 ophio
expert: 13 herpetologist
genus of: boa 7 ophidia
horned: 8 cerastes
killer: 7 mongoos 8 mongoose
marine: 6 chital
movement: 7 slither
mythological: See **serpent**
poison: 5 venom
resembling: 8 viperine
sea: 6 kerril
sound: 4 hiss 6 rattle
suborder: 6 asinea
snake charmer's flute: 5 pungi
snake dancers: 4 Hopi, Taos 5 Moqui
snake doctor: 9 dragonfly 12 hellgrammite
snake-haired woman: 6 Gorgon, Medusa,
Stheno 7 Euryale
snake killer: 7 mongoos 8 mongoose
snake-shaped: 9 anguiform
snakeberry: 6 byrony 9 baneberry 11 bittersweet 14 partridge-berry
snakebird: 7 anhinga, wryneck
snakebite antidote: 5 guaco
snakeflower: 7 campion 8 blueweed 10 star-
flower, stitchwort
snakehead: 7 figwort 10 turtlehead
snakelike: 5 snaky 8 ophidian 9 colubrine
10 anguineous
fish: eel
snakemouth: 6 orchid
snakeroot: 6 seneca, senega 7 sangrel 9
birthwort 10 bitter-bush
snakeskin: 6 exuvia
snakestone: 8 ammonite
snaky: sly 4 evil, wavy 5 angry 6 touchy 7
anguine, sinuous, winding, wriggly 8
spiteful, twisting, venomous 9 snakelike
10 perfidious, serpentine 11 exasperated,
treacherous
snap: bit, rod 4 bark, bite, knap, lirp, pass,
shut 5 break, catch, chack, cheat, cinch,
close, crack, filip, flask, flick, ganch,
grasp, hanch, quick, scrap, seize, sever,
smart, snack, spell, stamp, steal, vigor,
wafer 6 biting, cloyer, cookie, energy, fillip, morsel, report, retort, snatch 7 capture, cozener, crackle, project, sharper,
sparkle 8 interval, puncheon, sinecure,
snapshot 9 crackling, crispness, fastening,

handcuffs, interrupt, smartness, snatching 10 gingersnap 11 scintillate
with finger: 6 fillip

snape: nip 4 snub 5 bevel, check, stint, taper 6 rebuke 7 snaping 8 beveling 10 disappoint

snapper: 4 bean, sesi 5 error 6 beetle, bonbon, turtle 7 cosoque, stumble, whopper 8 cachucho, fastener 9 castanets 10 stitchwort, woodpecker 11 firecracker, glassworker, phainopepla
black-fin: 4 sesi

snappish: 4 edgy, tart 5 crisp, cross, short, testy 7 brittle, cutting, peevish, uncivil 8 petulant 9 fractious, irascible, irritable 12 sharp-tongued

snappy: 4 frim 5 brisk, quick, sharp, smart 6 strong, sudden 7 stylish 8 pungency 9 briskness, copacetic, smartness

snapshot: 4 shot 5 photo 10 photograph

snare: bag, gin, net, pit, web 4 fang, grin, lure, mesh, toil, trap 5 benet, brake, catch, grasp, noose, steal 6 ambush, cobweb, entice, entoil, entrap, gilder, tangle, trapan, trepan 7 ensnare, involve, overnet, pitfall 8 entangle, inveigle 9 deception 12 entanglement

snarer: 6 spider 7 trapper

snark: 6 boojum

snarl: arr, gin 4 carl, girn, gnar, harl, hurr, knot, yarr, yirr 5 anvil, catch, ganch, gnarl, gnarr, growl, noose, scold, snare 6 tangle 7 confuse, ensnare, grizzle, grumble, involve, quarrel 8 complain, entangle 9 confusion 10 complicate 12 complication

snarly: 5 cross, surly 7 peevish, snarled, tangled 8 confused, snarling 10 illnatured 11 bad-tempered

snash: 5 abuse 6 gibing 9 insolence

snatch: bit, get, hap, nab 4 grab, snap, take, trap, yerk 5 braid, catch, clawk, cleek, erept, grasp, gripe, pluck, seize, snare, spell, stint, swipe, wrest 6 clutch, kidnap, remove, twitch 7 excerpt, grabble 8 fragment

snatchy: 9 irregular, spasmodic 11 interrupted 12 disconnected

snath, snathe: lop 5 prune, shaft, snead 6 handle

sneak: 4 lurk 5 filch, miche, peach, skulk, slink, snoop, steal 6 coward, cringe, pilfer, snudge, tattle 9 fefnicute

sneaking: sly 4 mean, poor 5 craven, hidden, paltry, secret 7 furtive, hangdog 8 cowardly, stealthy 9 dastardly, niggardly, underhand 12 contemptible 13 surreptitious

sneap: spy 5 check, chide, snape, sneak

sneb: bar 4 bolt, snub 6 fasten, rebuke 9 reprimand

sneck: 5 catch, click, close, latch 6 fasten

sned: lop 5 prune

snee: cut 4 dirk 5 knife 6 dagger

sneer: 4 gibe, gird, grin, jeer, mock 5 fleer, fling, flird, flout, flurn, scoff, slare, snirl, snort 7 grimace, snicker 8 belittle, ridicule

sneesh: 5 snuff

sneeze: 5 neese(Sc.) 7 kerchoo 12 sternutation
pert. to: 7 errhine 12 sternutatory

sneezewort: 8 ptarmica, ptarmite 10 gesundheit

snell: 4 hard, keen 5 acute, eager, harsh, quick, sharp, smart, snood, swift 6 active, biting, clever, leader, severe 7 caustic, extreme, pungent, quickly, swiftly 8 piercing 10 vigorously

snib: bar 4 bolt, snub 5 catch, check, snuff 6 entrap, fasten, rebuff, rebuke 7 capture 8 restrain 9 fastening, reprimand

snick: cut, hit 4 blow, draw, kink, knot, move, nick, snip 5 click, notch, share, shoot, snack 6 pierce, strike 8 snicking

snicker: 5 knife, laugh, neigh, sneer, snirl 6 giggle, nicker, titter, whinny

snide: low, sly 4 base, mean 6 tricky 8 inferior, spurious 9 malicious

sniff: 4 nose 5 scent, smell, snuff 6 detect, inhale 7 sniffle 8 perceive 9 recognize

sniffy: 8 scornful 10 disdainful 12 contemptuous, supercilious

snifter: 4 blow, dram, good 5 drink, sniff, snort, storm 6 moment, snivel 7 dilemma, reverse 9 excellent

snig: eel, lop 4 chop, drag, jerk 5 snake, sneak 6 pilfer

snigger: 6 giggle 7 snicker

sniggle: 7 broggle

snip: bit, cut 4 clip, curb, snap 5 check, filch, notch, piece, shred, snack 6 snatch, stripe, stroke, tailor 8 fragment, incision, particle 9 disfigure

snipe: 4 bird, butt, fool 5 skunk 10 sharpshoot
cry: 5 scape
flock: 5 whisp

snipe hawk: 7 harrier

sniper: 8 ambusher

snippy: 4 curt, mean, tart 5 brief, sharp 6 sniffy, stingy 8 snappish, snippety 11 closefisted, fragmentary 12 supercilious

snirl: 5 gnarl, snare, sneer, snort 6 tangle 7 snicker, wrinkle

snirt: 5 sneer, snort 7 snicker

snitch: 4 nose, tell 5 catch, peach, pinch, steal, thief 6 betray, inform, pilfer, smitch, snatch 8 informer, particle snivel: cry 4 cant, fret 5 sniff, whine 6 pathos 7 emotion, snuffle 8 complain

snivy, snivey: 4 mean, ugly 8 contrary

snob: sob 4 aper, scab 5 toady 6 flunky 7 cobbler, cricket, flunkey, parvenu, plebian, shoneen, upstart 8 blackleg, bluenose, commoner, parvenue, townsman 9 pretender, shoemaker 10 fivestones

snobbish: 7 high-hat 11 overbearing

snod: 4 neat, snug, trim 6 smooth 7 cunning, trimmed 9 plausible

snood: bad, hat, tie 4 bind 5 braid 6 fasten, fillet, ribbon 7 hairnet

snook: pry 5 smell, sneak, sniff 6 follow, robalo, search 7 snuffle 9 barracuda

snool: cow 4 snub 6 craven, cringe

snoop: pry 4 look, nose, peek, peep 5 sneak 6 search 8 busybody

snooper: 7 marplot, meddler 8 busybody

snoot: 4 face, nose 7 grimace

snooty: 7 haughty 8 snobbish 10 hoity-toity 12 contemptuous, supercilious

snooze: nap 4 doze 5 sleep 6 drowse, siesta 7 snoozle

snoozle: 4 doze 5 sleep 6 cuddle, nuzzle, snooze 7 snuggle

snore: 4 rout 5 snork, snort

snoring: 5 stiff 7 roaring, stertor 10 stertorous

snork: pig 5 grunt, snore, snort

snort: 4 rout 5 drink, grunt, laugh, snirl, snore, snork

snotty: 5 dirty, nasty, slimy 6 offish, snooty 7 haughty, viscous 8 impudent, snotlike 9 offensive 12 contemptible, supercilious

snouch: 4 jibe, snub 5 taunt

snout: neb 4 mull, nose 5 groin, spout, trunk 6 nozzle 7 rostrum, tobacco

snout-nose: 7 gruntle 9 proboscis

snow: sna 4 grue, snaw(Sc.) 5 blizz, cover, opium 6 heroin 7 cocaine 8 obstruct 9 whiteness

  glacial: 4 firn, neve
  granular: 4 corn
  half-melted: 5 slush
  house: 4 iglu 5 igloo
  living in: 5 neval
  mushy: 4 slob
  resembling: 7 niveous
  slide: 8 glissade 9 avalanche
  vehicle: 4 pung, sled 6 sleigh
  wedding: 4 rice

snow and rain: 5 sleet

snow flurry: 5 skirl

snow goose: 4 chen 5 brant, wavey

snow grouse: 9 ptarmigan

snow mass: 9 avalanche

snow ridges: 8 sastrugi, zastrugi

snow runner: ski 4 skee

snowflake: 4 bird 5 finch 7 crystal

snowshoe: pac, ski 4 skee

snowstorm: 8 blizzard

snowy: 4 pure 5 nival, white 8 spotless, unsoiled

snub: cut, nip 4 chip, curb, slap, stop 5 check, frump, quell, scold, snool 6 ignore, rebuff, rebuke, remark, retort, slight, tauten 7 affront, neglect, repress, upbraid 8 restrain 9 interrupt, reprimand

snudge: 4 sulk 5 miser, sneak

snuff: 4 odor 5 pinch, pique, scent, smell, sniff, snort 6 detect, inhale 7 offense, umbrage 10 extinguish

  kind of: 5 musty 6 rappee 8 bergamot, Maccaboy 10 blackguard, Copenhagen

snuff box: 4 mill, mull 9 tabatiere

snuffy: 5 sulky, vexed 6 horrid 7 annoyed 10 displeased 12 disagreeable, unattractive

snug: 4 bein, bien, cosh, cozy, neat, safe, tidy, trim, warm 5 close, quiet, tight 6 modest, secure, silent 7 compact, snuggle 8 reticent, secreted 9 concealed, seaworthy, secretive 10 prosperous 11 comfortable

snuggery: den

snuggle: 4 nest 6 cuddle, nestle

snugly: 6 cosily

sny: 4 bend 5 swarm 6 abound

so: sae, sic, sua 4 ergo, thus, very 5 hence 7 because 9 therefore 11 accordingly 12 consequently

so be it: 4 amen

so far: yet 4 thus

soak: dip, hit, ret, sog, sop, sot, wet 4 bate, blow, bowk, buck, hurl, ooze, pawn, sock 5 drink, drouk, imbue, punch, souse, spree, steep 6 drench, imbibe, imbrue, seethe 8 drunkard, macerate, permeate, saturate 9 distemper, percolate 10 impregnate, instructor, overcharge

  flax: ret
  in brine: 4 corn, salt 8 marinate

soaked: wet 6 sodden

soaking: 4 slow 6 gentle 7 soakage

soap: 4 sape, sapo 5 money, savon 6 lather 7 cleanse, flatter 8 flattery 9 detergent

  convert into: 8 saponify
  frame bar: 4 sess
  mottled: 7 castile 8 eschwege
  pharmaceutical: 4 sapo
  plate: 4 sess
  substitute: 5 amole, borax

soap plant: 5 amole 8 soapwort

soapmaking substance: lye

soapstone: 4 talc 8 steatite

  full of: 7 talcose

soapweed: 5 yucca

soapy: 4 oily, soft 5 suave 6 smooth 7 saponic 8 lathered, unctuous 9 soapsuddy 10 latherable 11 saponaceous 12 ingratiating

soar: fly 4 lift, rise, sail 5 float, glide, hover, mount, plane 6 ascend, aspire 9 transcend

sob: cry, yex 4 sigh, soak, wail, weep 6 boohoo 7 whimper 8 frighten

sober: 4 calm, cool, poor, sane 5 douce, grave, quiet, staid 6 ailing, feeble, gentle, humble, sedate, severe, simple, solemn, somber, steady, subdue, temper 7 chasten, earnest, regular, serious, subdued 8 composed, decorous, moderate, peaceful, rational 9 abstinent, collected, temperate 10 abstemious 11 indifferent 13 unimpassioned, unpretentious

soberly: sad 5 grave 8 demurely

sobol: 5 sable 6 marten

soboles: 5 shoot 6 stolon, sucker

sobriety: 7 gravity 9 restraint, soberness, solemnity, soundness 10 abstinence, moderation, sedateness, temperance 11 seriousness 14 reasonableness

sobriquet, soubriquet: 4 name 5 alias, chuck, title 6 byname 7 affront, epithet 8 nickname 11 appellation

soc: 12 jurisdiction

soccer player: 6 booter

sociability: 10 affability

sociable: 4 cozy, sofa 6 chummy, social 7 affable 8 carriage, familiar, friendly, informal, tricycle 9 aeroplane, agreeable, reception 10 accessible, gregarious 13 communicative, companionable

social: tea 4 stag 5 party 6 smoker 9 agreeable, convivial, gathering 10 gregarious 13 companionable

affair: tea 4 ball 6 soiree 9 reception

career beginning: 5 debut

climber: 4 snob 7 parvenu, upstart

gathering: bee, tea 4 club, stag 5 party 6 smoker 7 reunion 9 reception

group: 4 clan, club 5 caste, class, lodge, tribe 6 estate, family 7 coterie

insect: bee

outcast: 5 leper 6 pariah

person: 4 host 5 mixer 7 hostess

system: 6 feudal, modern, regime, tribal 11 traditional

worker: 7 analyst 8 do-gooder 9 clinician

socialism: 9 Communism 10 utopianism 13 Manchesterism

socialist: Red 9 Anarchist, communist 10 Bolshevist 11 nationalist 12 collectivist

socialize: 6 mingle

society (see also **organization**): 4 bund, clan, gild 5 guild, order, union 6 menage 7 academy, company, hetaera, hetaira 8 academie, alliance 9 accademie, community 10 connection 11 association, coopera-

tion, intercourse, partnership 12 denomination, relationship 13 companionship, confederation, confraternity, participation

girl: deb

low (member): 4 raff 8 riff-raff

kind of: 4 SPCA, frat, Tong 5 elite, order, choir 7 societe 8 sorority 10 fraternity

secret: Hui 4 tong, egbo 5 mafia, lodge 6 maffia, ogboni 7 Camorra 9 Carbonari

symbol: 7 regalia

Society Island: 6 Tahiti

tree: 5 aitoa

Society of Friends: 7 Quakers

founder: Fox

sociology: 8 demotics

sock: hit, sew, udo 4 beat, blow, hurl, shoe, sigh, vamp 5 drive 6 anklet, buskin, comedy, sandal, strike 7 slipper, socking 8 drainage, stocking 9 plowshare

symbol of tragedy: 6 buskin

sockdolager: 4 oner 8 finisher

socket: 5 lance, spear 6 budget, cavity, collet, hollow 7 opening 9 plowshare

kind of: pan 4 birn 5 orbit 8 alveolus

Socrates: *biographer:* 5 Plato

dialogue: 4 Meno 6 Phaedo 8 Apologia

escape plotter: 5 Crito

love: 10 philosophy, Alcibiades

wife: 8 Xantippe 9 Xanthippe

sod: 4 delf, dove, flag, peat, soak, turf 5 delft, divot, glebe, soggy, sward 6 saddle, sodden 7 stratum 9 fermented

pert. to: 8 alkaline

soda: sal 8 beverage 9 saleratus

sodalite: 5 lenad

sodality: 5 union, unity 6 chapel 10 fellowship, fraternity 11 association, brotherhood 13 companionship

sodden: 5 drunk, heavy, moist, sammy, soggy 6 boiled, dulled, soaked, stewed, stupid 7 bloated, drunken, steeped 8 spirited 9 saturated 11 intoxicated

sodium: 7 natrium

carbonate: 4 soda 5 borax, trona 6 natron 7 salsoda

chlorate: 5 NaClo

chloride: sal, tar 4 salt 7 saltcat

compound: 4 soda

nitrate: 5 niter

tetraborate: 5 borax

Sodom: *king:* 4 Bera

neighbor: 8 Gomorrah

sodomite: 6 bugger

sofa: 5 boist, couch, divan 6 lounge, settee 7 bergere, dosados 8 causeuse 9 davenport 12 chesterfield

soft: coy, low 4 feil, fine, limp, mild, saft(Sc.), waxy, weak 5 bland, cushy, downy, dolce, dulce, faint, givey, hooly, mushy, piano, sooth 6 clammy, dreamy, fluffy, gentle, gently, placid, silken, smooth, tender 7 clement, ductile, lenient, lightly, quietly, squashy, subuded 8 delicate, feminine, flexible, tranquil 9 temperate, tractable, untrained 10 effeminate, peacefully 11 sympathetic 12 nonalcoholic 13 compassionate

and smooth: 5 furry, silky, soapy 6 mellow, supple 7 cottony

and sweet: 5 dolce 6 dulcet

and wet: 5 mushy 7 squashy

food: pap

mass: 4 pulp

music: 5 dulce, piano

palate: 4 cion 5 uvula, velum

soap: 4 gush 7 blarney, flatter, wheedle 8 flattery 9 wheedling

soft drink: ade, pop 4 soda 5 tonic

softa: 7 student 8 beginner

soften: 4 ease, melt 5 allay, malax, relax, yield 6 anneal, gentle, pacify, relent, soothe, subdue, temper, weaken 7 amolish, appease, assuage, mollify 8 attemper, enervate, enfeeble, lenitive, macerate, mitigate, modulate 9 alleviate, emolliate, meliorate 10 emasculate, intenerate 11 tranquilize

softening: 7 lenient 8 emulsive 9 demulcent 11 melioration

of brain: 8 dementia

of decayed fruit: 4 blet

soft-spoken: 4 mild 5 bland, suave 6 gentle, smooth 12 ingratiating

softhearted: 6 tender 13 tenderhearted

softheartedness: 4 pity

softly: low 4 soft 5 piano, sotto 6 fairly, gentle, gently 7 foolish, quietly 10 spiritless 13 unobtrusively

softness: 10 tenderness

sog: 4 soak 6 drowse 8 saturate

soggy: wet 4 damp 5 heavy 6 soaked, sodden, watery 9 saturated

soigne, soignee: 4 neat, tidy 5 sleek 11 well-groomed

soil: 4 blot, blur, daub, dirt, foil, grit, land, moil, mool, slur, spot 5 dirty, earth, filth, glebe, grime, smear, solum, stain, sully 6 assoil, bedaub, befile, befoul, bemire, defile, grease, ground, refuse, sewage, smirch, smudge 7 begrime, benasty, besmear, corrupt, pollute, tarnish 8 alluvium, besmirch, disgrace 9 bedraggle, bespatter, droppings, excrement 11 contaminate

claylike: 4 marl

comb. form: geo 4 agro

goddess of: 7 Demeter

kind of: 4 clay, loam, marl, lair, malm, moss 5 adobe, loess, groot, humus

organic: 5 humus

soiled: 4 foul 5 dingy, grimy 6 smeary

soilure: 5 stain 6 smirch

soiree: 5 party 6 affair

sojourn: 4 bide, howf, rest, stay 5 abide, abode, delay, dwell, howff, lodge, tarry, visit 6 reside, travel 7 allodge, mansion 8 abidance 9 residence 11 peregrinate

sojourner: 7 boarder 8 comeling

sol: sun 4 gold 6 sun-god 7 Phoebus

solace: 5 allay, amuse, cheer 6 lessen, relief, soothe 7 assuage, comfort, console 9 alleviate, diversion, entertain 10 recreation, relaxation 11 alleviation, consolation

solacing: 6 dulcet

solan: 4 fowl 5 goose 6 gannet

solar, soler, sollar: 4 room 5 floor, story 6 garret, heliac, tropic 7 chamber 8 heliacal 9 apartment

deity: Su; Shu

disk: 4 aten, aton

excess over lunar year: 5 epact

solar system: *member:* 6 planet

model: 6 orrery

sold (see also **sell**): 8 marketed

solder: 4 fuse, join, mend 5 braze, patch, unite 6 cement

soldering: *flux:* 5 resin, rosin

piece: lug

soldier: man, vet 4 fogy, swad 5 fogey, guffy, poilu, sammy, shirk 6 galoot, marine, Zouave 7 brigand, feedman, fighter, hobbler, hotspur, palikar, private, regular, trooper, veteran, warrior 8 buffcoat, cavalier, gendarme, malinger, servitor, tolpatch, shackman 9 grenadier, musketeer

detachment: 4 file

drinking flask: 7 canteen

female: 6 W.A.C.

foreign: 4 peon, kern 5 nezam, poilu, sepoy, kerne, spahi 6 sapper, lascar, askari 7 cateran, hoplite, Billjim 8 grognard, miquelet 10 base wallah, carmagnole, carabineer

group of: 4 band, file 5 corps, force, squad, troop 7 brigade, caterva, company, platoon 8 division 9 battalion

mercenary: 7 Hessian, Swisser, Switzer

newly-trained: 5 cadet, plebe, rooky 6 rookie 7 chicken, recruit, trainee 8 bezonian 11 replacement

of fortune: 10 adventurer

old: vet 7 veteran

overcoat: 6 capote

quarters: 7 billets 8 barracks

special functions: 6 lancer, sapper 7 velites, dragoon, trooper 8 fencible, fugleman 9 fantassin, targeteer, flugelman 10 cuirassier, velitation, carabineer, carabinier 12 antesignanus

trenching tools: 8 burgoyne

vacation: 4 pass 5 leave 8 furlough

soldierly: 5 brave 6 heroic 7 martial

sole: 4 dish, fish, foot, lone, mere, only, yoke 5 afald, alone, floor, plate, slade 6 bottom, entire, furrow, halter, hearth, lonely, single, unique, valley 7 outsole, subsoil 8 desolate, flatfish, isolated, solitary, unshared 9 exclusive, threshold, unmarried, unmatched 10 foundation, underframe, unsharable, windowsill

foot: 4 vola 5 pelma

part: 5 shank

pert. to: 7 plantar

solecism: 9 barbarism, deviation 11 impropriety

solely: all 4 only 5 alone 6 merely, singly 8 entirely 9 allenarly 11 exclusively

solement: 4 only 6 solely

solemn: sad 5 budge, grave, sober, usual 6 august, devout, formal, gloomy, ritual, sacred, severe, somber 7 earnest, serious, stately 8 funereal, splendid 9 customary, dignified, sumptuous 10 ceremonial, devotional, noteworthy 11 reverential 13 distinguished

solemnity: 7 gravity 8 ceremony

solemnization: 9 celebrity

solemnize: 5 exalt, marry 7 dignify, glorify, observe 9 celebrate 11 commemorate

solenodon: 6 agouta 7 almique

soler: 7 cobbler 9 shoemaker

solert: 6 crafty 8 skillful

solicit: ask, beg, woo 4 bark, plea, seek, tout 5 court, crave, mooch, tempt 6 accost, entice, incite, invite, manage 7 beseech, canvass, entreat, forward, implore, request 8 campaign, disquiet, petition 9 importune, panhandle, prosecute 10 supplicate

solicitor: 4 tout 6 barker 8 attorney

chambers: 4 inns

solicitous: 5 eager 7 careful 8 desirous, troubled 9 attentive, concerned 10 thoughtful 12 apprehensive

solicitude: 4 care, coda, ease, fear, heed, yeme 7 anxiety, concern 8 business 11 carefulness 12 apprehension

solid: 4 cone, cube, firm, full, hard 5 cubic, dense, level, sound, stiff 6 bodily, sphere, stable, strong 7 bedrock, compact, uniform, weighty 8 constant, reliable, sterling, unbroken 9 estimable 10 consistent, dependable, inflexible 11 homogeneous, responsible, substantial, trustworthy

comb. form: 6 stereo

geometrical: 4 cone, cube 5 prism 7 pyramid 8 cylinder 11 heptahedron, pentahedron 12 dodecahedron

solidified: 8 hardened

solidify: gel, set 4 cake 6 cement, harden 7 compact 8 concrete, condense 9 coagulate 11 consolidate, crystallize

solidity: 8 firmness, hardness 9 solidness, soundness, stability 11 compactness, consistency 13 dependability

solidly: 10 completely

solidum: sum 4 dado

soliloquy: 4 poem 9 discourse, monologue, utterance

solitaire: 4 game 6 hermit, lonely 7 diamond, recluse 8 Canfield, patience, solitary 9 neckcloth

solitary: 4 hole, lone, monk, sole 5 alone 6 hermit, lonely, remote, simple, single 7 dungeon, eremite, recluse 8 desolate, lonesome, solitary 10 individual 12 unfrequented

combining form: 5 eremo

solitude: 6 dearth, desert 7 expanse, privacy, retreat 8 soleness 9 isolation, seclusion 10 loneliness, remoteness, retirement, uniqueness, wilderness 12 solitariness

solo: air 4 aria 5 alone, scena, radel 6 strain

accompaniment: 8 obligato 9 obbligato

soloist: 6 cantor, singer 7 aviator

Solomon: *ally:* 5 Hiram

father: 5 David

gold obtained from: 5 Ophir

mother: 9 Bathsheba

son: 8 Rehoboam

temple: 6 shamir

Solomon Islands: 4 Buka, Gizo, Savo

gulf: 4 Huon, Kula

volcano: 5 Balbi

Solon: 4 sage 7 senator 8 lawmaker 9 publicist 10 legislator

soluble: 4 frim 6 solute

solus: 5 alone

solute: 4 free 5 loose, solve 7 arrange, soluble 8 dissolve, separate 9 dissolved 13 disintegrated

solution: key 6 answer 8 analysis 9 discharge, releasing 10 denouement, resolution 11 deliverance, explanation 14 disintegration 15 disentanglement.

kinds of: lye 5 brine, eusol, iodin, titer, sirup, syrup 6 iodine, phenol

strength of: 5 titer

solve: 4 free, undo 5 break 6 assoil, fathom, unfold 7 explain, resolve, unravel 8 dissolve 9 interpret 11 disentangle

solvent: 8 solution 9 detergent

Somaliland: *city:* 7 Berbera 8 Mogdisho

coin: 4 besa

measure: top 4 caba 5 chela, darat, tabla 6 cubito

weight: 8 parsalah

Somalis division: 6 Hawiya

Somalis Proper: 4 Asha

somatic: 5 somal 6 bodily 8 parietal, physical 9 corporeal 13 somatopleuric

somber, sombre: sad 4 dark, dern, dull 5 dusky, gloom, grave, sober 6 dismal, gloomy, lenten, severe, solemn 7 austere 9 depressed 10 depressing, melancholy

sombrero: hat 8 headgear, sunshade

some: any, few, one 4 part 5 about 7 portion, several 13 approximately

somersault: 4 flip

something: 5 drink 6 liquor 7 aliquid 8 beverage, somewhat

sometime: 4 late, once 6 former 7 quondam 8 formerly 12 occasionally

somewhat: 6 rather 7 aliquid 9 something

Somme city: 6 Amiens

sommelier: 6 butler 9 cellarman

somnambulism: 12 noctambulism

somnolent: 6 drowsy, sleepy

somnus: 5 sleep

son: ben 4 fils 5 child, scion 6 filius, Jesuit, native 8 disciple, follower 9 offspring 10 descendant

as in Welsh names: ap

foster: 7 alumnus

pert. to: 6 filial

Scot.: Mac

youngest: 5 cadet

son-in-law: 5 gener 8 beau-fils

Son of God: 6 Savior 7 Saviour

sonance: 4 tune 5 sound

sonant: 4 oral 5 tonic, vocal 6 voiced 8 sounding 9 intonated

sonata: *closing:* 4 coda

part: 5 rondo 7 scherzo

song: dit, lay, uta 4 aria, cant, dite, duan, fuss, glee, hymn, lied, lilt, noel, poem, tune 5 blues, canto, carol, chant, charm, ditty, lyric, melos, music, psalm, verse 6 ballad, cantic, cantus, canzon, carmen, chanty, clamor, himene, himine, melody, poetry, shanty, sonnet, strain, trifle 7 cancion, cantion, canzone, chantey, descant, shantey 8 canticle, pittance 9 cabaletta 11 composition

baby's: 7 lullaby

choral muse: 11 Terpischore

Christmas: 4 noel 5 carol

college: 4 glee

collection: 9 anthology 10 cancionero

evening: 6 vesper 8 evensong, serenade

folk: 5 blues 6 ballad

funeral: 5 dirge, elegy, elogy 6 elegie, lament, threne 7 elogium, epicede 8 epicedia, threnody 9 epicedium

gay: 4 lilt

German: 4 lied 6 lieder(pl.)

gypsy: 10 zingaresca

love: 6 amoret, ballad, serena 8 serenade

mountaineer's: 5 yodel

mourning: see *funeral* above

obscure: 4 rune

operatic: 4 aria

part: 5 canon, round 8 madrigal

pert. to.: 5 melic

sacred: 4 hymn 5 chant, motet, psalm 6 anthem 7 polymny

sailor's: 6 chanty, shanty 7 chantey, shantey 8 rumbelow 9 barcarole 10 barcarolle

simple: 5 ditty

solo: 4 glee

triumphal: 5 paean

wedding: 5 hymen

song-like: 6 ariose, arioso 7 lyrical

Song of Bernadette author: 6 Werfel

songbird: 4 lark, wren 5 mavie, mavis, robin, veery, vireo 6 canary, linnet, mocker, oriole, oscine, thrush 7 mocking, warbler 8 redstart

songman: 6 singer 7 gleeman 8 minstrel

songster: 4 poet 6 singer 7 chanter, warbler 8 songbird

songstress: 9 chantress

sonnet: 4 poem, song 5 octet, verse 6 sestet

conclusion: 6 sestet

sonority: 9 resonance

sonorous: 7 ringing 8 imposing, resonant 10 impressive

sons, sonse: 6 health 7 fortune 8 felicity 10 prosperity

sonsie, sonsy: 5 buxom, happy, lucky 6 comely 8 handsome, pleasing 9 plentiful 10 prosperous 11 comfortable

soodle: 6 stroll 7 saunter

soodly: 4 slow 9 leisurely

soogan: 4 rope 7 blanket

sook: 4 call 5 booth 6 market

soon: ere 4 anon, yern 5 early, later, quick, yerne 6 belive, rather, speedy 7 betimes, erelong, quickly, readily, shortly 8 directly, promptly, speedily 9 presently, willingly 10 beforetime 11 immediately

sooner: 4 erer, erst 6 before 9 Oklahoman

Sooner State: 8 Oklahoma

soot: 4 coom, smut, stup 5 colly, coomb, grime, sweet, smoke 6 carbon, gentle, smudge 7 blacken 9 melodious

particle: 4 isel, izle

pert. to: 10 fuliginous

sooth: 4 fact, real, soft, true 5 being, sweet, truly, truth 6 augury, smooth 7 comfort, genuine, present, proverb, reality 8 cajol-

ery, pleasing, pleasure, soothing, truthful
10 delightful 11 soothsaying, trustworthy
12 blandishment

soothe: coy, pat, pet 4 balm, calm, dill, ease,
lull 5 accoy, allay, charm, dulce, quiet 6
pacify, soften, solace, stroke 7 appease, assuage, comfort, compose, console, de-
mulce, flatter, mollify, placate, relieve 8
mitigate, palliate 9 alleviate, attempter 10
demulceate 11 tranquilize

soother: 4 balm 5 salve 9 emollient

soothing: 4 mild 5 balmy, downy, dulce 6
dreamy, dulcet, gentle 7 anodyne, calming
8 lenitive, sedative 9 appeasing, assuasive,
demulcent 13 tranquilizing

soothsay: 4 omen 7 portent, predict, proverb 8 foretell

soothsayer: 4 seer 5 augur, weird, vates 6
ariole, mantis 7 augurer, diviner, prophet,
seeress 8 haruspex, chaldean 10 hariolizer
14 prognosticator

sooty: 4 dark 5 black, colly, dusky 6 brokie
9 blackened 10 fuliginous

sop: 4 dunk, gift, heap, lump, mass, mess,
soak, tuft 5 bribe, cloud, clump, steep 7
advance, milksop 8 saturate

sophism: 7 fallacy 8 argument

sophist: 7 casuist, teacher, thinker 10
paralogist 11 philosopher

sophistical: 8 captious 9 deceptive 11 adulterated

sophisticate: 5 alter, spoil 6 debase, garble
7 corrupt, falsify, mislead 10 adulterate

sophisticated: 4 wise 7 amended, refined,
worldly 11 adulterated

sophistry: 6 deceit 7 fallacy, quibble, sophism 8 argument, trickery 9 deception

Sophocles play: 7 Oedipus

sophy: 4 sage 5 ruler, skill 6 wisdom 7 science 8 religion 9 personage 10 philosophy

sopie: 4 dram 5 drink

sopite: 5 draft, quash, quiet, sleep 6 drowsy
8 drooping

sopor: 5 sleep 6 stupor

soporific: 5 dwale 6 drowsy, opiate 8 hypnotic, narcotic 11 somniferous 12 somnifacient, somnivolency

soppy: wet 5 rainy 6 soaked 7 mawkish 8
drenched 11 sentimental

soprano: 6 singer, treble

operatic: 4 Lind 5 Freni, Patti 6 Callas 7
Nilsson

sora: 4 rail

sorcerer: 4 mage, magi 5 boyla, brujo, Go-
eta 6 boolya, wizard 7 warlock 8 conjurer,
magician 11 necromancer, thaumaturge
13 thaumaturgist

sorceress: 5 Circe, Lamia, sibyl, witch 6
Gorgon 11 enchantress

sorcery: art, obe, obi 5 magic, obeah, spell 6
fetich, fetish, voodoo 8 pishogue, prestige
9 diablerie, diabolism 10 necromancy,
witchcraft 11 enchantment

sordellina: 7 bagpipe

sordid: low 4 base, mean, vile 5 dirty, gross
6 chetif, filthy, menial 7 ignoble, selfish,
servile, squalid 8 churlish, covetous,
grasping, grewsome, gruesome, sluttish,
wretched 9 mercenary, niggardly 10 avaricious, despicable, slatternly 12 contemptible

sordo: low 4 deaf, dull 5 muted

sordor: 5 dregs 6 refuse 10 sordidness

sore: 4 boil, buck, evil, harm, kibe, pain, sair
5 angry, blain, botch, grief, ulcer, vexed,
wound, wrong 6 bitter, bruise, fester, severe, sorrel, sorrow, tender, touchy 7 angered, annoyed, disease, extreme, grieved,
painful, penance, trouble, violent 8 abrasion, grievous, inflamed, offended, sickness 9 detriment, irritated, sensitive, suffering, ulcerated, vexatious 10 affliction,
afflictive, contrition, difficulty, distressed,
unpleasant 11 disgruntled, distressing 13
temperamental, oversensitive

sorehead: 5 loser 6 griper 10 malcontent

sorely: 7 greatly 8 severely, urgently 9 extremely, painfully, violently 10 grievously

soreness: 4 ache 8 severity, vexation, violence 11 painfulness 12 irritability

sorghum: 4 cush, dura, milo 5 batad, darso,
durra, sorgo 7 shallu 8 feterita

sorite: 4 heap 10 collection

sorority: 4 club 7 society 10 fraternity, sisterhood

sorrel: oca 5 brown, horse, plant 6 oxalis 7
roselle

sorrow: rue, woe 4 bale, care, dole, harm,
loss, sigh, teen, weal 5 devil, dolor, grief,
mourn, rogue, scamp 6 grieve, lament,
misery, plague, regret 7 sadness, trouble,
waeness 8 calamity, distress, egrimony,
mourning 9 adversity, penitence, suffering 10 affliction, compassion, contrition,
discomfort, melancholy 11 lamentation,
tribulation, unhappiness 12 wretchedness

over: 6 bemoan, bewail, lament 7 deplore

sorrowful: sad 4 teen 5 drear, sadly 6
dismal, dolent, dreary, rueful 7 doleful,
grieved, unhappy 8 contrite, dolesome, dolorous, grievous, mournful 9 afflicted,
plaintive 10 lamentable, melancholy 11
distressing 12 disconsolate

sorrowing: 11 penitential 13 commiserat-
ing

sorry: bad 4 hurt, mean, poor 5 vexed 6
dismal, gloomy, regret, repent 7 chagrin,
painful, pitiful 8 contrite, grievous,
mournful, penitent, wretched 9 afflicted,

chagrined, miserable, mortified, regretful, worthless **10** apologetic, melancholy **12** contemptible, disappointed

sort: ilk, ill, lot, set, way **4** cull, gere, kind, part, race, rank, sift, suit, type **5** adapt, allot, batch, befit, breed, class, crowd, flock, genus, grade, group, order, swarm, vexed **6** adjust, assign, choose, garble, gender, manner, nature, punish, select **7** arrange, company, conform, fashion, quality, species, stripes, variety **8** classify, separate **9** character, disturbed **10** collection, distribute **11** accommodate, description

sorted: **6** chosen **8** assorted, selected **9** separated **10** classified

sortie: **4** knot **5** foray, sally **6** attack

sortilege: **7** sorcery **8** witchery **11** enchantment

sosh: jag **4** dash **5** drunk **11** intoxicated

soso: bad **4** poor **6** unwell **8** mediocre, middling, passable **9** tolerable **11** indifferent

soss: lap **4** mess, slop **5** plump, swill **6** muddle **7** heavily

sossle: **4** mess, slop **10** intoxicate

sot: **4** fool **5** child, fixed, toper, waste **6** befool, guzzle, tipple **7** dastard, foolish, sottish, stupefy, tippler, tosspot **8** drunkard, innocent, squander, stubborn **9** immovable, inebriate, obstinate, simpleton, swillbowl **10** winebibber

sotted: **5** bousy **8** besotted

sottish: **4** dull **6** stupid **7** doltish, drunken, foolish **9** senseless

sotto: **5** below, under

soubise: **5** sauce

soubrette: **4** maid **7** actress **11** entertainer, maidservant

soucar: **6** banker **8** merchant, straight **9** honorable

souchong: tea

soud: pay **4** join **5** unite **6** amount, enlist, fasten, solder **8** quantity **10** strengthen

soudagur: **8** merchant **10** shopkeeper

sough: die, sob **4** moan, sigh, whiz **5** chant, ditch, drain, rumor, whizz **6** murmur, report **7** breathe, moaning, whistle **8** singsong **9** murmuring

soul: ba; ame, God, ker **4** alma **5** atman, force, heart, saint **6** dibbuk, esprit, fervor, leader, pneuma, spirit **7** courage, essence **8** inspirer **10** embodiment, heartiness **11** anilopyrine **15** personification

 loss: **9** perdition

 personification: **6** Psyche

souled: **5** vital

soulless: **5** brute

sound: cry, din **4** birr, blow, bray, firm, good, hail, hale, rime, safe, sane, test, tone, true **5** alarm, blare, bruit(F.), chang, clang, fresh, grope, hoddy, inlet, legal, loyal, noise, plumb, probe, rhyme, solid, valid, whole **6** bedlam, bratte, clamor, entire, fathom, hearty, honest, hubbub, intact, measure, outcry, racket, report, robust, secure, stable, steven, strong, sturdy, tumult, uproar **7** bluster, clamour, clangor, clatter, clitter, clutter, examine, explore, healthy, hearing, measure, perfect, sonance, sputter **8** complete, flawless, orthodox, profound, reliable, shouting, splutter, thorough **9** honorable, undamaged **10** dependable, hullabaloo, scrutinize **11** trustworthy, undisturbed

amorous: coo

atonic: **4** surd

beating drum: **8** rataplan

bell-like: **4** ding **5** clang, knell **6** tinkle

breathing: **5** snore

bullet: zip **4** ping

buzzing: **4** whiz **5** whirr, whizz

cat's: mew **4** meow, mewl, purr

comb. form: **4** audi, phon **5** audio, phono

contemptuous: **5** snort

contented: **4** purr

derisive: boo **7** catcall

detection instrument: **10** hydrophone

discordant: **6** jangle **9** cacophony

distinctive: **6** timbre

donkey's: **4** bray **6** heehaw

dove's murmuring: **4** curr

drum: **4** roll

dry leaves: **6** rustle

elephant's: **4** roar **7** trumpet

engine: **4** chug, ping

explosive: pop **4** bang, boom, clap, roar **5** blast **6** report

guttural: **4** burr **5** grunt

harsh: **4** bray **5** creak, twang **9** cacophony

high-pitched: **4** ping, ting

hissing: zip **4** siss

hoarse: caw **4** bray

in doctrine: **8** orthodox

in mind: **4** sane

insect's: **5** chirr

jingling: **16** tintinnabulation

light: **5** swish **7** pitapat

loud: **4** boom, peal **5** blare, clang

magnifying device: **9** megaphone **11** loudspeaker

measurement of: bel

menacing: **5** growl, snarl

mentally: **4** sane **5** lucid **6** normal

metallic: **4** ping, ting **5** clang, clank **6** tinkle

monotonous: hum **4** moan **5** drone

mournful: sob

murmuring: **4** purr **5** groan

musical: **4** note

nasal: **5** snore, whine **7** stridor

of bell: **4** ding

of disapproval: boo, bah 4 hiss
of drinking: 4 glub
of hoofbeat: 4 clop
of pain: 4 moan, ouch, yell 5 groan
of rising birds: 5 whirr
of surf: 4 rote
pert. to: 5 tonal 6 sonant 10 acoustical
pleasing in: 8 euphonic
respiratory: 4 rale
ringing: 5 clang 7 tinitus
shallow: 6 lagoon, laguna, lagune
shrill: 5 reedy, skirl
sibilant: 4 hiss, siss
small: 4 peep
solemn: 4 peal
speech: 5 vowel 8 phonetic
splashing: 5 swash
syllabic: 6 sonant
throat: 8 guttural
transposition: 10 spoonerism
trumpet: 5 blare 7 clarion
unvaried: 8 monotone
vibrant: 4 birr
vocal: 4 tone 6 hiccup 8 hiccough
warning: 5 alarm 6 alarum, tocsin
water: 4 klop, rote 5 plash, swish 6 splash
whispering: 8 susurrus
whizzing: 4 ping 5 swish
yelping: yip
sound out: 5 study 7 explore 11 investigate
sounded: 4 blew, rang, rung 5 oaten 6 tooted 7 clanged 8 syllabic
sounding: 6 sonant 8 plangent, resonant, sonorous, strident 9 bombastic 11 mellisonant 12 grandisonant, grandisonous
soundless: 5 quiet 9 noiseless 12 unfathomable
soundly: 6 deeply 7 healthy 8 securely 9 violently 10 completely, forcefully, profoundly, thoroughly
soundness: 5 truth 6 sanity 8 solidity, strength 9 integrity, rectitude 10 heartiness 11 healthiness
sounds: *having melody and rhythm:* 5 music
succession of: 4 peal
vocal symbols: 6 sonant
soup: 5 broth, puree, shchi, slash, stchi 6 borsch, borsht, oxtail 7 garbure, shtchee 8 consomme, gazpacho 12 mulligatawny
dish: 6 tureen
ingredient: 4 lalo, okra 7 noodles
spoon: 5 ladle
thick: 4 bisk 5 hoosh, puree 6 bisque, burgoo 7 burgout, pottage 8 minestra 10 minestrone
thickener: 7 tapioca
thin: 5 broth 8 consomme

soupcon: 5 taste, trace 7 modicum, portion 9 suspicion 10 suggestion
sour: wry 4 acid, dour, grim, hard, tart 5 acerb, acrid, cross, eager, gruff 6 acetic, bitter, cruety, morose, sullen 7 acetose, acetous, acidify, austere, crabbed, painful, peevish 8 acerbate, acescent, embitter 9 acidulate, acidulent, acidulous 10 afflictive, astringent, unpleasant 11 distasteful 12 disagreeable
source: 4 fons, font, germ, head, rise, root, seed 5 fount 6 ascent, origin, parent, spring 7 edition 8 fountain 9 beginning 10 wellspring 12 fountainhead
of caoutchouc: ule
of contrary action: 7 reagent
of gum arabic: 6 acacia
of income: 7 revenue
of indigo: 4 anil
of inspiration: 4 Muse
of iodine: 4 kelp
of knowledge: 7 organon
of metal: ore
of phosphorus: 7 apatite
of vitamin C: 6 orange
of vitamin E: 5 grain
sourdine: 4 mute
sourdook: 10 buttermilk
sourdough: 7 settler 10 prospector
sourness: 7 acidity 8 acerbity, acrimony, asperity 10 moroseness 16 disagreeableness
soursop: 9 guanabana
souse, souce, sowce, sowse: ear, jag 4 blow, cuff, duck, fall, prop, soak, wash 5 bathe, brine, douse, drink, swoop, thump 6 drench, pickle, plunge, pounce, strike, thwack 7 heavily, immerse, tippler 8 clumsily, drunkard, saturate, steeping, submerge 9 drenching
soused: 5 drunk 11 intoxicated
soutache: 5 braid 8 trimming
soutane: 5 cloak 7 cassock, zimarra
souter: 7 cobbler 9 shoemaker
South: (see also **Confederacy**): 5 Dixie
crop: 6 cotton 7 tobacco
dish: 4 okra 5 gumbo 7 hoecake
inlet: 5 bayou
novelist: 5 Welty 8 Faulkner
South Africa: *animal:* das 5 nenta 8 suricate
antelope: gnu 5 eland, leche, oribi, peele 6 lechee, lechwe, rhebok 7 blaubok, blesbok, boshbok, grysbok, rheeboc, rheebok, sassaby 8 blesbuck, bontebok, boschbok
armadillo: 4 para
ass: 6 quagga
assembly: 4 raad
aunt: 5 tanta
blaubok: 5 etaac

breastwork: 6 scherm
bushman: 4 Qung
camp: 5 lager 6 laager
caterpillar: 6 risper
cattle enclosure: 5 kraal
city: 6 Durban 8 Cape Town, Pretoria 9 Germiston 12 Johannesburg
cliff: 4 klip
club: 10 knobkerrie
coin: 4 cent, pond, rand 6 florin
colonist: 4 Boer
conference: 6 indaba
cony: das
corn: 5 mealy 6 mealie
council: 4 raad
criminal: 8 amalaita
dialect: 4 Taal
diamond: 4 jager 9 schlenter
Dutch: 4 Boer, Taal
Dutch speech: 9 Afrikaans
ferry: 4 pont
foreigner: 9 uitlander
fox: 4 asse 5 caama
garment: 6 caross, kaross
goldfield: 4 rand
government: 8 republic
grass country: 4 veld 5 veldt
greenhorn: 5 ikona
gully: 5 donga
gun: 4 roer
hill: kop 8 spitzkop
hillock: 5 kopje
hippopotamus: 6 zeekoe
hog: 9 boschvark
hut: 8 rondavel, rondawel
javelin: 7 assagai
laborer: 4 togt
legislative assembly: 4 raad
lowland: 4 vlei, vley
monkey: 4 vervet 8 talapoin
mountain: kop
pass: nek
pasture: 5 veldt
people: 4 Xosa 5 Bantu, Namas, Pondo 6 Damara 7 Swahili 8 Bechuana 9 Hottentot
plain: 5 veldt
plant: 4 aloe
plot: erf
polecat: 6 musang
policeman: 4 zarp
province: 9 Transvaal
race: see *people* above
racial policy: 9 apartheid
region: 5 congo
river: 4 Vaal 6 Orange 7 Limpopo
rodent: 5 ratel
settler: 4 Boer
shrub: 6 protea

simpleton: 5 ikona
snake: 5 elaps 8 eggeater
spirit: 8 tikolosh
starling: 5 sprew 7 spreeuw
stream: aar
sumac: 6 karree
thong: 4 riem 7 riempie
tick: 6 tampan
tract: 9 zuurveldt
trader: 7 Swahili
tree: 5 tenio 7 assagai 8 gamdeboo
tribe: see *people* above
village: 5 kraal
warrior: 4 impi
weaverbird: 4 taha
whip: 7 sjambok
South African: 4 Boer 10 Afrikander
South America: *aborigine:* 6 Arawak
animal: ai 4 paca 5 coati, coypu, llama, sloth, tapir 6 alpaca, jaguar, nutria, vicuna 8 anteater 9 armadillo
ant: 5 sauba, sauva
anteater: 7 tamandu
arbor: 6 ramada
armadillo: 4 apar 7 tatouay 10 pichiciago
arrow poison: 6 curara, curare
balsam: 4 tolu
beast of burden: 5 llama
beef: 6 tasajo
beverage: 4 mate
bird: 4 aura, guan, mitu, myna, rara, taha, yeni 5 agami, arara, chaja, mynah 6 barber, barbet 7 aracari, jacamar, oilbird, seriema, tinamou 8 bellbird, boatbill, curassow, guacharo, puffbird, screamer, terutero
blanket: 6 serape
boat: 6 cayuco
cactus: 7 airampo
catfish: 5 dorad
cattle ranch: 8 estancia 9 estantion
country: 4 Peru 5 Chile 6 Brazil 7 Bolivia, Ecuador 8 Colombia 9 Argentina, Patagonia, Venezuela
cowboy: 6 gaucho 7 llanero, planero
cowboy's weapon: 5 bolas
dance: 5 mambo, samba 6 cha-cha
deer: 6 guemal, guemul
dove: 9 talpacoti
estuary: 4 Para 5 Plata
fish: 4 paru 6 aimara, caribe 7 scalare 8 arapaima
fox: 4 asse
game: 6 pelota
garment: 6 serape
gold: oro
griddle cake: 5 arepa
hare: 6 tapeti
hawk: 8 caracara

herb: 9 romerillo
herdsman: 7 llanero
Indian: Ges, Ona 5 Auca, Inca, Tama 5 Carib, Tapas 6 Arawak, Jivaro 7 Cayapos, Goyanas, Guatoan, Pampero, Tapuyan 8 Camacans, Coroados, Timbiras 9 Caingangs, Chavantes 10 Patagonian
Indian hut: 5 toldo
Indian medicine man: 4 peai 6 shaman
Indian poison: 6 curara, curare, curari
island: 5 Aruba
knife: 7 machete 8 machette
language: Ona
lapwing: 8 terutero
liberator: 7 Bolivar
limestone: 5 tosca
liquor: 6 chicha
lizard: 4 teju 5 coati
mammal: ai 4 paca 5 coati, llama, tapir 6 alpaca, guanco 8 kinkajou, pacarana 10 coati-mondi, coati-mundi
marmoset: 7 tamarin
measure: 4 vara 7 manzana
mineral: 4 urso
monkey: sai 4 saki, titi 5 acari, araba 6 grison, teetee 7 ouakari, sapajou 8 marmoset, orabassu 9 barrigudo, beelzebub
mountains: 5 Andes
native: 5 Carib
opossum: 5 quica 7 sarigue
ostrich: 4 rhea
palm: 5 assai, bussu, datil, troly 6 tooroo, ubussu 7 troolie
parrot: 5 macaw
plain: 5 llano, pampa
plains dweller: 7 llanero
plant: 6 ipecac 8 crassula 10 tillandsia
porridge: 5 atole
rabbit: 6 tapeti
raccoon: 5 coati 10 coatimundi
rancher: 10 estanciero
republic: 5 Chile 8 Colombia 9 Argentina, Venezuela
river: 4 Para 5 Plata 6 Amazon 7 Orinoco
rodent: 4 degu, mara, paca 5 coypu 6 agouti, agouty 8 viscacha, vizcacha 10 chinchilla
root: oca
rubber tree: 4 para
ruminant: 5 llama 6 alpaca
scarf: 5 manta
serpent: 5 aboma
shrub: 4 coca
slaughterhouse: 11 frigorifico
snake: bom 4 lora 5 aboma 8 anaconda 10 bushmaster
sorrel: oca
stock: Ona
strait: 8 Magellan
tapir: 5 danta

tiger cat: 5 chati
toucan: 4 toco 7 aracari
tree: 4 fotu, lana, mora, para, vera 5 balsa, cacao, cebil, couma, pekea 6 chicha, simaba, yachan 7 bebeeru, quayabi 9 balaustre, couvatari 11 chichicaste
tribe: Ona
trumpeter: 5 agami
tuber: oca
turtle: 8 matamata
ungulate: 5 tapir
vulture: 6 condor
walnut: 9 conacaste
weapon: 4 bola 5 bolas
wild cat: 4 eyra
wind: 7 pampero
South American: 5 Latin
South Australia: See **Australia**
South Carolina: *county:* Lee 4 York 5 Aiken, Horry, Union 6 Dillon, Saluda, Sumter
dam: 6 Saluda
fort: 6 Sumter
native: 6 weasel
river: 6 Peedee, Saluda, Santee
state tree: 8 palmetto
South Dakota: *capital:* 6 Pierre
county: Day 4 Clay, Hand, Hyde, Lake, Todd 5 Brule, Deuel, Tripp
dam: 4 Oahe
Indian: 5 Brule
state animal: 6 coyote
state flower: 6 pasque
South India: See **India**
South Pacific: *island:* 4 Fiji 5 Samoa, Tonga 7 Society 8 Pitcairn, Woodlark
sea: 5 Coral, Timor 6 Tasman
star: 5 Pinza 6 Martin
South Pole: See **Antarctica**
South Sea: *canoe:* 4 proa
island: 4 Bali, Siam, Sulu
island drink: ava
island food: 5 taros
island money: 6 wakiki
islander: 5 Maori 6 Kanaka, Samoan
plant: 4 taro
product: 5 copra
staple: 4 taro
South Vietnam: *capital:* 6 Saigon
city: Hue 5 Dalat 6 Da Nang
guerillas: 8 Vietcong
holiday: Tet
monetary unit: 7 piastre
river: 6 Mekong
south wind: 5 notus 6 auster
South Wind author: 7 Douglas
Southeast Asia (see also **Asia**): 4 Laos, Siam 5 Burma 6 Ceylon 7 Vietnam 8

Cambodia, Malaysia, Pakistan, Thailand
9 Indonesia 10 Bangladesh 11 Philippines
southeast wind: 5 eurus
southerly: 8 austrine
southern: 7 austral
Southern California: See **California**
Southern dish: See **South:** *dish*
Southern France: 4 Midi
Southern tonic: 4 dope
southernwood: 9 abrotanum
Southwark inn: 6 Tabard
Southwest: *cowboy:* 7 llanero
  Indian: 4 Cree
Southwest Pacific island: 5 Samoa
southwest wind: 4 afer
southwester: hat 5 squam, storm
souvenir: 5 curio, relic 6 memory 7 memento 8 keepsake, reminder 12 recollection, remembrancer
sovereign: 4 king 5 chief, liege, royal, ruler
  6 couter, Mikado, prince 7 emperor, highest, monarch, supreme 8 autocrat, greatest, princely, reigning, superior, suzerain
  9 effectual, excellent, paramount, potentate 11 controlling, efficacious, independent
  female: 7 empress 11 autocratrix
  petty: 8 tetrarch
sovereign authority: 8 dominion
sovereign power: 6 throne
sovereign prerogative claim: 11 seigniorage
sovereignty: 4 rule, sway 5 realm 6 diadem,
  empery, empire, status 7 dynasty, majesty, scepter, sceptre 8 dominion 9 supremacy 10 ascendancy, ascendency, domination
  absolute: 8 autarchy
  joint: 11 condominium
Soviet: 7 council, Russian
Soviet Union (see also **Russia**): 4 USSR
  administrative committee: 9 presidium
  founder: 5 Lenin
  government farm: 7 sovkhos, sovkhoz 8
  sovkhose
  hero: 5 Lenin 6 Stalin
  money: 5 ruble
  news agency: 4 Tass
  newspaper: 5 Pravda 8 Izvestia
  republic: 5 Uzbek 6 Latvia 7 Armenia,
  Georgia, Kirghiz, Turkmen, Ukraine
  secret police: 4 NKVD, OGPU
sow: hog, pig 4 heap, seed, shed 5 ditch,
  drain, drill, plant, stack, swine 6 runner,
  sluice, spread 7 channel, furnish, grumphy, implant, scatter 8 disperse, grumphie
  9 broadcast, inoculate 10 salamander 11
  disseminate
  wild: 8 javelina

young: elt 4 gilt
sower: 7 seedman
  of dragon's teeth: 6 Cadmus
soy: 4 silk
soy bean: 4 soja
soya: 4 dill 6 fennel 7 soybean
spa: 5 oasis, oases 6 resort, spring 8 Saratoga
  10 sanatorium
  place: Ems 4 Bath 5 Baden
space: gap 4 area, path, rank, roam, room,
  rove, void, walk 5 ambit, plena(pl.), range,
  track 6 course, divide, extent, plenum, region 7 areolae, arrange, expanse 8 capacity, distance, duration, interval, quantity
  11 reservation 14 accommodations
  agency: 4 NASA
  architectural: 8 pediment
  between eyes: 4 lore
  between two intersecting lines: 5 angle
  between two points: 8 distance
  blank: 6 lacuna 7 lacunae(pl.)
  breathing: 6 recess
  cleared: 5 glade
  coin: 7 exergue
  docking: 6 linkup
  empty: 4 void 5 blank, inane 6 vacuum
  forest: 5 glade
  hallowed: 7 mortice, mortise
  included: 8 contents
  limitless: 8 infinite
  occupied: 6 volume
  on surface: 4 area
  partitioned: 4 room
  pert. to: 5 areal
  portion of: 5 place
  safekeeping: 7 storage
  small: 6 areola, areole 7 aerolae
  storage: 4 shed 5 attic 6 cellar 9 storeroom,
  warehouse
  void: 5 chasm 7 inanity
  wall: 5 niche
  white: 6 margin
space for goods: 7 storage
space full of matter: 6 plenum
space of time: 8 interval
space theory: 7 plenism
spacecraft: 6 rocket 9 satellite
  first: 7 Sputnik
  part: 6 module 7 capsule
  to moon: 6 Apollo
spaceman: 9 astronaut, cosmonaut
spacer: bar
spacious: 4 vast 5 ample, broad, great,
  large, rangy, roomy 9 capacious, expansive, extensive 13 comprehensive
spack: 7 forward, knowing 11 intelligent
spad: 4 nail
Spad: 7 biplane
spadassin: 5 bravo 7 duelist 9 swordsman

spade: dig **5** graft **6** shovel
  Irish: **5** slane
  kind of: **6** scavel
  narrow: loy
  plasterer's: **6** server
  sharp: **4** spud
  triangular: **5** didle
  turf: **5** slane
spadger: boy **7** sparrow
spae: **6** divine **8** foretell, prophecy
spaghetti: **5** pasta
  sauce spice: **7** oregano
spahi, spahee: **7** cavalry
Spain: **6** Iberia
  adventurer: **9** almogaver
  article: el, la, un; las, los, una
  aunt: tia
  author: **9** Cervantes
  bayonet: **5** yucca
  beach: **5** plays
  belle: **4** maja
  blanket: **6** serape
  boat: **5** aviso
  brandy: **11** aguardiente
  bull: **4** toro
  cape: **9** Trafalgar
  cart: **7** carreta **8** carretta
  cathedral city: **7** Seville
  cedar: **6** acajou
  celery: **4** apio
  cellist: **6** Casals
  champion: Cid
  channel: **4** Cano
  chaperone: **6** duenna
  cheer: ole
  city: See *town* below
  clerk: **11** escribiente
  cloak: **4** capa **5** manta **6** mantle
  coat: **7** zamarra, zamarro
  coin: **5** dobla **6** cuarto, doblon, peseta **7** Alfonso, centimo, piaster **8** cuartino **9** cuartillo
  conqueror: Cid **7** Pizarro **12** conquistador
  contract: **7** asiento **8** assiento
  council: **5** junta
  count: **5** conde
  dance: **4** jota **5** danza, tango **6** bolero, gitano **8** fandango, saraband **9** zapateado **10** seguidilla
  dish: **6** posole
  district: **5** Xeres
  dollar: **4** duro, peso, pezo **7** piaster, piastre
  dumpling: **6** tamale
  earth: **6** tierra
  exclamation: **6** carajo **7** caramba
  execution: **7** garotte, garrote **8** garrotte
  explorer: **7** Mendoza **8** Coronado
  fabric: **5** tiraz
  fleet: **6** armada

  friend: **5** amigo
  frigate: **5** zabra
  game: **5** omber **6** pelota **7** jai-alai
  gentleman: don **5** senor **8** cavalier **9** caballero
  god: **4** dios
  goddess: **5** Diosa
  gold: oro
  governor: **10** idelantado
  grass: **5** spart **7** esparto
  greeting: **4** hola
  griddlecake: **5** arepa
  gunboat: **5** barca
  gypsy: **7** zincalo
  hall: **4** sala
  head covering: **8** mantilla
  herdsman: **8** ranchero
  hero: Cid
  hill: **5** cerro, morro
  holiday: **6** fiesta
  horse: **7** caballo
  hotel: **5** venta **6** posada
  house: **4** casa
  instrument: **8** castanet, zambomba
  judge: **7** alcalde
  kettle: **4** cazo
  king: rey
  kingdom: **4** Leon **6** Aragon **7** Castile
  lady: **4** dona **6** senora
  lagoon: **6** laguna
  lake: **4** lago
  lariat: **5** reata, riata
  leather: **8** cordovan
  legislature: **6** cortes
  letter: **5** carta
  letter carrier: **6** correo
  linen cloth: **4** crea
  lute: **7** vihuela
  magic: **8** brujeria
  man: don **6** hombre
  mausoleum: **8** Escorial
  mayor: **6** alcade **7** alcalde
  measure: pie **4** codo, copa, dedo, moyo, paso, vara **5** aroba, braza, cafiz, cahiz, legua, linea, medio, milla, palmo, sesma **6** cordel, cuarta, estado, fanega, league, racion, yugada **7** azumbre, cantara, celemin, estadel, pulgada **8** aranzada, fanegada **9** cuarteron, cuartilla, cuartillo **10** caballeria
  miss: **8** senorita
  money: **4** duro **6** dinero
  monk: **5** padre
  mountain: **8** Asturian, Pyrenees **9** Mulahacem **10** Cantabrian, Guardarrama, Pic de Netou **11** La Maladetta **12** Sierra Morena **14** Sierra de Toledo
  mouth: **4** boca
  muleteer: **7** arriero
  native: **7** Catalan, Iberian

nobleman: don **7** grandee, hidalgo
now: **5** ahora
nun: **6** Teresa
officer: **8** alguacil, alguazil
operetta: **8** zarzuela
other: **4** otro
oyster: **5** pinna
painter: **4** Cano, Dali, Goya, Miro, Sert **6** Ribera **7** Murillo, Picasso, Zuloaga **9** Velasquez
palace: **8** Escorial
pancake: **5** arepa
parliament: **6** cortes
pear: **7** avocado
peasant: **7** paisano
peninsula: **6** Iberia
pepper: **5** chili **7** pimento
pickpocket: **6** ratero
plant: aji
poet: **6** Encina
porridge: **5** atole
port: **5** Palos
post office: **6** correo
pot: **4** olla
priest: **4** cura **5** padre
promenade: **5** paseo
pronunciation mark: **5** tilde
raisin: **4** pasa
province: **4** Jaen, Leon, Lugo, Vigo **5** Alava, Avila, Cadiz, Soria **6** Burgos, Coruna, Cuenca, Gerona, Huelva, Huesca, Lerida, Madrid, Malaga, Murcia, Orense, Oviedo, Teruel, Toledo, Zamora **7** Almeria, Badajoz, Caceres, Cordova, Granada, Logrono, Navarra, Segovia, Seville, Vizcaya **8** Albacete, Alicante, Palencia, Valencia **9** Barcelona, Guipuscoa, Salamanca, Santander, Saragossa, Tarragona **10** Ciudad Real, Pontevedra, Valladolid **11** Guadalajara **15** Balearic Islands **18** Castellon de la Plana
rice: **5** arroz
rider: **8** herisson
river: ria, rio **4** Ebro **5** Douro, Tagus **8** Guadiana **12** Guadalquivir
road: **6** camino
room: **4** sala
seaport: **4** Adra **5** Palos
sentinel: **5** vedet, videt **7** vedette, vidette
shawl: **5** manta **6** serape
sherry: **5** Xeres **11** Amontillado
silk: **5** tiraz
sorcerer: **5** brujo
south: sur
stanza: **10** seguidilla
street: **5** calle
sword: **5** bilbo
tax: **8** alcabala
title: don **5** senor **6** senora **7** hidalgo **8** senorita

tomorrow: **6** manana
town: **4** Irun, Jaen, Leon, Olot **5** Cadiz, Gijon, Lorca, Ronda, Siero, Xeres **6** Bilbao, Madrid(c.), Malaga, Murcia, Toledo **7** Cordoba, Cordova, Granada, Seville **8** Valencia, Zaragoza **9** Barcelona, Cartegena, Salamanca, Santander, Saragossa **10** Carthagena, Valladolid **18** Jerez de la Frontiera
trail: **6** camino
trefoil: **7** alfalfa, lucerne
uncle: tio
vase: **4** urna
vehicle: **7** tartana
very: muy
watchword: **6** alerta
water: **4** agua
watercourse: **6** arroyo
weight: **4** onza **5** frail, grano, libra, marco, tomin **6** adarme, arroba, dinero, dracma, ochava **7** arienzo, quilate, quintal **8** caracter, tonelada **9** escrupulo **10** castellano
white: **6** blanco
wind: **6** solano
window: **7** ventana
witchcraft: **8** brujeria
woman: **6** senora
spalpeen: boy, fop, lad **5** scamp **6** rascal **7** laborer, workman **8** braggart **9** youngster
spald: **4** limb, open **5** joint, splay, split **8** shoulder, splinter
spale: bar **4** chip, fine, lath, rail **5** brace, spall **6** timber **7** shaving **8** splinter
spall: **4** chip, fall **5** break **6** reduce **7** breakup, crumble **8** fragment, shoulder
spalt: **4** chip, tear **5** crisp, split **7** brittle
span: **4** cock, pair, rope, swim, team, time **5** cover, grasp, reach, seize **6** attach, bridge, extend, fasten, fetter, hobble, inspan, spread **7** confine, matched, measure, stretch **8** distance, duration, encircle **9** encompass, perfectly **10** completely
spancel: tie **4** clog **6** fetter, hobble
spang: **4** bang, hurl, jump, kick, leap, yoke **5** clasp, crack **6** stride **7** spangle **8** abruptly, directly, ornament, straight
spangle: set **4** boss **5** adorn, aglet, gleam, plate **6** aiglet, sequin, zequin **7** glisten, glitter, sparkle **8** sprinkle, zecchino
spangly: **9** sparkling **10** glittering
Spaniard: **5** Latin **7** Espanol **9** Castilian
imaginary: **9** Espriella
spaniel: **5** trasy **6** cocker **8** springer **9** sycophant
spank: **4** prat, whip **6** strike **8** chastise
spanker: **4** sail
spanking: **4** fine **5** brisk, fresh, large, stout **6** lively, strong **7** dashing **8** vigorous
spanner: **6** wrench

spar: bar, box, rod 4 beam, bolt, boom, gaff, mast, pole, raft, rung, shut, yard 5 close, fight, lunge, sprit, steve 6 barite, bicker, charge, fasten, rafter, strike, thrust, timber 7 contest, dispute, enclose, wrangle, yardarm 8 dolomite, lazulite

end: 7 yardarm

spare: 4 bear, free, gain, hain, lean, part, save, slim, slit, slow, stop, thin 5 avoid, chary, extra, favor, gaunt, grant, lanky, stint 6 desist, endure, favour, frugal, meager, scanty 7 deprive, forbear, forgive, haggard, leisure, opening, placket, refrain, relieve, reserve, sparing 8 dilatory, forebear, preserve, tolerate 9 duplicate, parsimony 11 replacement, superfluous 12 parsimonious

spare time: 7 leisure

sparge: 6 splash 8 sprinkle 9 bespatter

sparing: 5 chary, gnede, scant 6 frugal, meager, saving, scanty 7 careful, limited, thrifty 8 merciful, reticent, stinting 9 scrimping 12 parsimonious

spark: arc, woo 4 beau, funk, soil 5 aizle, belle, blade, court, flash, grain, lover 7 diamond, gallant, sparkle, spatter 8 sparklet 9 scintilla 10 sweetheart 11 scintillate

igniting property: 11 incendivity

sparked: 5 arced 7 courted, spotted 8 streaked 10 variegated

sparker: 5 lover 7 gallant 8 firework

sparkle: 5 blink, flash, gleam, glent, glint, shine, spark, strew, trace 7 diffuse, glisten, glitter, radiate, reflect, scatter, showing, spangle 8 disperse, sprinkle, vivacity 9 coruscate 10 effervesce, illuminate, liveliness 11 coruscation, scintillate 13 scintillation

sparkling: 4 dewy 5 crisp 6 bright, lively, starry 7 shining 8 animated, flashing, gleaming 9 brillante, brilliant, twinkling 10 glittering, reflecting 12 effervescent, effervescing

sparoid fish: 4 scup 5 porgy 10 sheepshead

sparple: 4 rout 7 scatter 8 disperse, sprinkle 11 disseminate

sparrer: 5 boxer 7 sparrow

sparrow: 7 chanter

sparse: 4 thin 5 scant 6 meager, meagre, scanty, thinly 7 scatter 8 disperse 9 scattered 10 distribute, infrequent

Sparta (see also **Attica, Greece**): *army:* 4 mora

bondman: 5 helot

commander: 7 lochage

dog: 10 bloodhound

festival: 6 Carnea 7 Carneia

governor: 7 harmost

king: 8 Leonidas, Menelaus

king's wife: 4 Leda

lawgiver: 8 Lycurgus

magistrate: 5 ephor

method of cipher writing: 7 scytale

native: 8 Laconian

queen: 5 Helen

serf: 5 helot

tyrant: 5 Nabis

spartan: 5 brave, hardy 6 frugal, heroic, severe 7 laconic 9 undaunted 10 courageous

sparver: 4 tent 6 canopy, tester

spasm: fit, tic 4 grip 5 crick 8 paroxysm 10 convulsion 11 contraction

muscle: 5 cramp

of distress: 4 pang

of pain: 5 throe

spasmodic: 6 fitful, sudden 7 snatchy, violent 9 excitable 12 intermittent

disease: 7 tetanus

spat: row 4 blow, clap, fuss, slap, tiff 5 eject 6 gaiter, oyster, splash, strike 7 dispute, legging, quarrel

spate: 4 gush, rain 5 flood 7 freshet, outflow, torrent 9 overwhelm, rainstorm 10 waterspout

spatial: 5 areal 6 steric 8 sterical

spatter: jet 4 dash, drop, soil, spot 5 slart, spurt 6 dabble, defame, injure, splash, spread 7 scatter, spatule, sputter 8 splutter, sprinkle

spatterdash: 7 legging

spatula: 4 tool 5 spade 6 thible

spatulate: 6 lyrate

spawn: roe 4 eggs, germ, seed, spot 5 fungi 6 bulbis, source 7 cormels, deposit, produce 8 generate, mycelium

ascending river to: 10 anadromous

spay: 4 geld 8 castrate 9 sterilize

speak: say 4 carp, chat, hail, talk, tell 5 extol, honor, orate, utter 6 reveal 7 address, bespeak, declaim, declare, deliver, express, publish 8 converse, harangue, manifest, proclaim 9 celebrate, discourse, pronounce 10 articulate

affectedly: 4 mimp 5 mince

against: 6 oppose

at length: 9 expatiate

comb. form: 4 lalo

curtly: 4 snap, birk

evasively: 5 hedge, stall

foolishly: 6 drivel

from memory: 6 recite

imperfectly: 4 lisp 7 stutter

in undertone: 6 mumble, murmur

inability to: 6 alalia, mutism 7 aphasia 8 aglossia

incoherently: 6 gabble, gibber

noisily: 4 fume, rant, rave

of: 4 call 7 mention
offhand: 11 extemporize
oracularly: 11 pontificate
pert. to: 10 oratorical
profusely: 6 dilate 7 palaver
rapidly: 5 troll 6 patter 8 splutter
rhetorically: 5 orate 7 declaim
slightingly: 8 backbite 9 disparage
slowly: 5 drawl
softly: 7 whisper
thoughtlessly: 4 blat 8 splutter
through nose: 9 nasillate
to: 5 greet 6 accost 7 address
under breath: 6 mumble, mutter
with interruption: haw, hem
speaker: 5 drone, sayer 6 lisper, orator, proser, ranter, talker 7 demagog, utterer 8 lecturer 9 demagogue 10 mouthpiece, prolocutor 11 entertainer, spellbinder
inspired: 7 prophet
of many languages: 8 linguist, polyglot
speaker's hammer: 5 gavel
speaking: *style:* 8 staccato, fluently
without preparation: 13 extemporizing
spean: 4 test, wean 5 prong 6 nipple
spear: gad, rod 4 dart, fram, reed, shut, spar 5 apine, blade, lance, shoot, stalk 6 aprout, glaive, impale, pierce, strike 7 feather, harpoon, javelin, missile, trident 9 penetrate
grass: 5 blade
kind of: 4 gaff 5 gidia, gidya 6 bident, fizgig, gidgea, gidgee, gidjee, gidyea 7 assagai, assegai, bourdon, harpoon, leister, trident
three-pronged: 7 trident
spear-shaped: 7 hastate
spearfish: 8 billfish
spearhead: 4 gaff
spearwort: 8 crowfoot
special: 4 dear, rare 5 chief, extra, local 6 unique 7 limited, unusual 8 concrete, detailed, favorite, intimate, paramour, peculiar, personal, specific, uncommon 9 specially 10 especially, individual, noteworthy, particular, restricted 11 distinctive, exceptional 12 particularly 13 distinguished, extraordinary
ability: 6 talent
edition: 5 extra
specialist: *atomic:* 9 physicist
city planning: 8 urbanist
ear: 6 aurist
eye: 7 oculist
medical(see also **doctor**): 7 oculist, surgeon 9 otologist 11 orthopedist 12 obstetrician, orthopaedist, pediatrician 13 paediatrician
mineral: 12 mineralogist
money management: 9 economist

surgical: see **doctor**
specialty: 5 forte, skill 8 aptitude 13 particularity
specie: 4 cash, coin 5 money
species: 4 kind, race, sort, type 5 breed, brood, class, genre, image 7 mankind, variety 8 category, humanity 9 spectacle 10 exhibition, reflection
modified by environment: 4 ecad
spider: 5 acera
various: 5 genus 6 genera
specific: 5 exact 7 precise, special 8 concrete, definite, explicit, peculiar 10 particular, restricted, specifying 11 determinate
specifically: 6 namely 9 specially
specify: 4 name, tell 5 allot, state 6 assign, define, detail 7 mention 8 describe, nominate 9 designate, stipulate 10 articulate
in detail: 4 item 7 itemize
singly: 9 enumerate
specimen: 4 mark 5 model, relic, token 6 cotype, sample, swatch 7 example, pattern 11 examination
specious: gay 4 fair 5 showy 6 glossy, hollow 7 colored 8 coloured 9 colorable, plausible 10 ostensible 12 hyprocritical
speck: bit, dot, nit 4 blot, iota, mark, mite, mote, spot, whit 5 glebe, stain 7 blemish, blubber 8 particle
speckle: dot 5 fleck 7 stipple
speckled: 6 menald 7 bracket
specs: 10 eyeglasses, spectacles
spectacle: 4 show 5 bysen, model, scene, sight 6 mirror 7 display, diorama, example, pageant, pattern 8 panorama, spyglass 9 cyclorama 10 exhibition 14 representation
structure for: 5 arena 7 stadium, theater, theatre 8 coliseum
spectacles: 7 glasses
part of: 6 bridge, temple
spectator: 4 eyer 6 espier 7 witness 8 beholder, kibitzer, looker-on, observer, onlooker
specter, spectre: 4 bogy 5 bogey, bogie, bogle, ghost, shade, spook 6 boggle, spirit, wraith 7 boggart, bugaboo, bugbear, phantom 8 boggle-bo, guytrash, phantasm, revenant 10 apparition
spectral: 6 ghosty, spooky 7 ghostly, phantom 12 apparitional 13 insubstantial
spectrum: 8 infrared
speculate: 5 guess, think 6 gamble, mirror, ponder, wonder 8 consider, meditate, ruminate, theorize 10 conjecture, deliberate, philosophy 11 contemplate
speculation: 6 bubble, vision 7 surmise 8 decision 9 guesswork, intuition 10 conclusion, conjecture

speculator: spy 4 lamb 7 lookout, scalper 8 explorer, observer, theorist 12 contemplator, investigator

speculum: 6 mirror 7 diopter

sped: 4 hied 5 raced 6 darted, dashed 8 galloped, hastened 11 accelerated

speech: 4 talk 5 idiom, voice, slang 6 dilogy, epilog, orison, steven, tongue 7 address, dialect, oration, oratory, vinegar 8 colloquy, epilogue, harangue, language 9 utterance

abusive: 6 tirade

art: 8 rhetoric

blunder: 8 solecism

conclusion: 9 episcopal 10 peroration

defect: 4 lisp 6 alogia 7 stammer, stutter

denunciation: 5 frump 6 tirade 8 filippic 9 philippic

difficulty: 9 baryphony 10 baryphonia

element: 4 surd

expert: 9 phonetist

figure of: 5 irony, trope 6 aporia, simile 7 imagery 8 metaphor

goddess: Vac

hesitation: haw 7 stutter

impassioned: 6 tirade 9 dithyramb

insane: 9 bedlamism

local: 6 patois 7 dialect

long: 5 spiel

loss: 6 alalia 7 aphasia 8 muteness

part: 4 noun, verb 6 adverb 9 adjective 11 conjunction, preposition 12 interjection

peculiar: 5 idiom

provincial: 6 patois 7 dialect

readiness: 9 facundity

religious: 6 sermon 9 preaching

representing: 8 phonetic

reserved: 8 reticent

summary: 5 notes

violent: 6 tirade

voiceless element: 4 surd 7 spirate

world language: 7 volapuk 9 esperanto

speechify: 5 orate 8 harangue

speechless: mum 4 dumb, mute 6 silent 9 voiceless

speed: go; hie, rip 4 fare, flee, help, race, rate 5 haste, hurry 6 assist, career, hasten, profit, succor 7 execute, prosper 8 celerity, dispatch, expedite, rapidity, velocity 9 advantage, discharge, quickness, swiftness 10 accelerate, expedition, facilitate 12 precipitance

full: 5 amain

great: 4 zoom 5 haste, spurt, amain 6 career 9 posthaste

measuring device: 11 speedometer, velocimeter

note: 4 time 5 clock

rate of: RPM 4 pace 5 tempo

ratio: 4 Mach

speeder: 5 racer 11 accelerator

speedful: 5 rapid 6 expert, speedy 9 efficient, favorable 10 successful

speedily: 4 fast, soon 5 apace 6 presto 7 betimes, hastily, quickly, rapidly 8 promptly 13 expeditiously

speediness: 5 haste 8 dispatch, rapidity 9 quickness 10 promptness

speedometer: 5 clock 8 odometer 10 tachometer

speedy: 4 fast 5 fleet, hasty, quick, rapid, swift 6 active, prompt 7 helpful 12 advantageous

speel: 5 climb, mount 8 splinter

speer: ask 4 seek 5 query 6 screen 7 inquire 9 partition

spell: bar, peg 4 chip, form, lath, mean, rung, save, tale, talk, tell, trap, turn, snap 5 brief, charm, curse, magic, relay, shift, spare, speak, spell, story, utter, weird 6 glamor, gospel, import, period, relate, relief, splint, trance 7 bewitch, cantrip, compose, glamour, relieve, shaving, signify, sorcery, drought, syncope 8 pishogue, splinter 9 discourse 10 constitute, demonifuge 11 conjuration, enchantment, fascination, abracadabra 12 entrancement 13 orthographize, prognosticate

in another alphabet: 13 transliterate

spellbind: 5 orate 7 enchant 9 fascinate

speller (according to pronunciation): 9 phonetist 11 phoneticist

poor: 11 cacographer

spelt: 5 grain, wheat 6 cereal

spelter: 4 zinc

spelunk: den 4 cave, lair 6 cavern

spence, spense: 6 larder, pantry 7 buttery 9 apartment

spencer: wig 4 coat 6 butler, jacket, pantry 7 buttery, steward, trysail

spend: run, use 4 blow, dash, flow, give, jump, pass, span 5 beset, exert, grasp, waste 6 attach, bestow, beware, devote, elapse, expend, fasten, lavish, manage, spread, spring, weaken 7 consume, dispend, exhaust, fatigue, perform 8 confound, disburse, squander 9 dissipate, sacrifice 10 distribute

spend the summer: 8 estivate 9 aestivate

spendful: 8 wasteful 11 extravagant

spendthrift: 6 waster 7 wastrel 8 prodigal, wasteful 10 dingthrift, profligate

Spenserian character: Una

spent: 4 beat, paid, used 5 weary 6 effete, wasted 8 lavished 9 exhausted 10 squandered

speos: 4 cave, tomb 6 grotto, temple

sperm: 4 seed 5 semen 12 spermatozoon

sperm whale: 8 cachalot

spet: 9 barracuda

spetch: 4 mend 5 patch 6 refuse 7 parings

spew, spue: bog 4 ooze, slip 5 eject, exude, strew, vomit 7 extrude, scatter 8 disgorge 10 afterswarm

sphacelate: 7 decayed, mortify 8 withered 9 mortified

sphenic: 11 wedge-shaped

spheral: 7 perfect 10 harmonious 11 symmetrical

sphere: orb, sky 4 ball, rank, star 5 ambit, arena, class, field, globe, orbit, order, range, scope 6 domain, orblet, planet 7 circuit, compass, heavens, stratum, station, theatre, terella 8 idiosome, position, province 9 idioblast 10 atmosphere, department 12 jurisdiction
  of action: 5 arena
  perforated: 4 bead

spheric: 8 globular 11 globe-shaped

spherical: 5 orbic, round 6 rotund 7 globate, globose 8 globated, globular, obrotund 9 globulous, orbicular

sphericity: 9 rotundity, roundness

spheroid: 4 ball 5 earth

spherule: 7 globule

sphinx: 4 moth 6 enigma 7 monster, prophet
  land of: 5 Egypt
  mother: 7 Echidna
  query of: 6 riddle
  site of: 4 Giza 5 Luxor

sphinxian: 10 mysterious 11 enigmatical, inscrutable

sphygmus: 5 pulse

spial: spy 5 scout, watch 6 espial

spica: 7 bandage

spice: 4 dash, kind, mace, mull, nard, odor, sort, vein 5 aroma, taste, touch 6 embalm, flavor, relish, season 7 modicum, perfume, portion, species, variety 8 quantity, specimen 9 admixture, condiment, seasoning 10 appearance
  kind of: 4 mace, mull, sage 5 anise, cumin, curry, thyme 6 cloves, ginger, nutmeg, pepper, stacte, tamara 7 cayenne, mustard, oregano, paprika, pimento 8 allspice, cinnamon, marjoram, pimiento, turmeric
  mill: 5 quern
  package for: 6 robbin

Spice Islands: 6 Indies 7 Molucca

spices: 9 aromatics

spicier: 4 racy 7 nuttier

spick: fat 5 split 6 grease 7 blubber 8 lavender, titmouse

spick-and-span: 4 neat, trim 5 clean, fresh 6 spruce 8 brand-new

spicknel: 9 baldmoney

spicule: rod 4 dart, nail, toxa 5 aster, spine 6 actine 7 prickle, rhabdus 8 sclerite, spikelet
  sponge: 5 cymba

spicy: hot 4 keen, racy 5 balmy, natty, showy, smart 6 active, risque 7 gingery, peppery, piquant, pungent 8 aromatic, fragrant, spirited

spider: cob, cop, hub, pan 5 arain 6 eresid, epeira, snarer, tripod, trivet 7 pokomoo, skillet, retiary 8 arachnid, attercop, telarian 9 tarantula 12 candleholder
  comb. form: 6 arachn 7 arachno
  family of: 7 attidae 9 drassidae 10 citigradae
  genus of: 6 aranea, epeira
  three-legged: 6 trivet
  venomous: 9 tarantula 10 black widow
  web-spinning organ: 9 spinneret

spider bug: 5 emesa

spider crab: 4 maia

spider monkey: 9 belzebuth

spider nest: web 5 nidus

spider species: 5 acera

spider web: 8 attercop
  resembling: 9 arachnoid
  spinner: 9 spinneret

spieler: 5 crier 6 barker, talker 7 sharper, speaker 8 lecturer 9 announcer 11 spellbinder

spiff: PM 5 bonus 7 premium 8 gratuity

spiffy: 4 neat 5 smart 6 spruce

spifflicate, spifflicate: 4 beat, kill 6 stifle 8 astonish, bewilder, confound

spigot: peg, pin, tap 4 cock, plug 5 spile, spout 6 dossil, faucet, pierce

spike: cut, cob, ear, gad 4 brob, chat, nail, tine, umbo 5 ament, block, prong 6 antler, cereal, earlet, fasten, finish, impale, pierce, secure, thwart 7 bayonet, disable, fortify, trenail 8 mackerel 9 frustrate, merganser 10 spadix-tine 13 inflorescence

spike hole: 5 spile

spike let: 4 chat, nail 7 spinule

spikenard: 4 nard 8 ointment

spile: pin, rod, tap 4 bung, heap, pile, plug, rule, tube 5 spill, spout, stake 6 spigot 8 forepole, splinter

spiler: 6 burler

spilikin: peg 7 pushpin 10 jackstraws

spill: die, mar, peg, pin, rod 4 disk, fail, fall, flow, kill, roll, ruin, shed, slip, slop 5 flosh, spile, spoil, spool, waste 6 injure, perish, punish, reveal, sheath, tumble, wasted 7 correct, destroy, divulge, scatter 8 chastise, downpour, gratuity, overflow, spillway, splinter, squander 11 deteriorate

Spillane's hero: 6 Hammer

spiloma: 5 nevus 9 birthmark

spin: 4 birl, burl, gyre, pirl, reel, turn **5** spurt, swirl, twirl, twist, whirl **6** gyrate, rotate **7** prolong, revolve **8** protract

spin a yarn: 7 narrate

spina: 4 wall **5** spine **8** backbone

spinach: 7 epinard, potherb

   mountain: **5** orach, savoy **6** orache

spinal: 5 balas

   area: **6** dorsal, lumbar, sacral **8** cervical

   column: **5** spine **8** backbone **9** vertebrae

   cord: **4** alba **6** myelon

   disease: **5** polio **8** myelitis

   layer: **4** dura

   muscle: **5** psoas

spindle: pin, rod **4** axis, axle, hasp, stem **5** arbor, fusee, shaft, stalk, xeres **6** arbour, broach, fuseau, rachis **7** mandrel

spindling: 5 leggy **7** slender

spine (see also **spinal**): awn **4** back, seta, turf **5** chine, ridge, sward, thorn **6** chaeta, needle, spirit **7** acantha, acicula, courage, prickle, spicule **8** backbone, spiculum **9** vertebrae

spine bone: 6 sacrum

spine-tingling: 4 eery **5** eerie **7** ghostly

spinel: gem **5** balas

spinet: 5 piano **7** giraffe **11** harpsichord

spinnaker: 4 sail

spinner: cap, top **5** spoon **6** spider, weaver **8** narrator **10** goatsucker

spinney: 5 copse, grove **7** thicket

spinning: 5 areel **6** rotary **8** whirling **9** revolving

   device: **7** distaff

   machine: **4** mule **5** jenny **8** throstle

   rod: **7** distaff

spinning wheel: 6 charka **7** charkha

spinous: 5 spiny **7** spinose **9** acanthoid, spinelike

Spinoza work: 6 Ethics

spinule: 8 backbone, spikelet

spiny: 6 picked, thorny **7** prickly **9** acanthoid, difficult

spiny-footed: 10 acanthopod **13** acanthopodous

spiny shrub: 4 ulex

spiracles: 4 hole **5** pores, vents **6** breath, spirit **8** blowhole, orifices **9** apertures

spiral: 4 coil, curl **5** curve, helix **7** coiling, curving, helical, winding **8** circling, helicoid **9** corkscrew **11** anfractuous

   combining form: **5** helic, helix

spirate: 9 voiceless

spire: 4 coil, curl **5** blade, stalk, tower, twist, whorl **6** fleche, spiral, sprout **7** sapling, steeple

   finial: epi **4** epis

   ornament: **6** finial

spirit: hag, vim **4** aitu, alma, dash, dook, elan, fire, gimp, life, mood, soul, wind **5** angel, ardor, bugan, dhoul, ethos, fairy, fling, ghost, haunt, metal, pluck, shade, spook, verve, vigor **6** ardour, asuang, breeze, elixir, energy, esprit, ginger, mettle, morale, pneuma, temper, yaksha (mas.), yakshi(fem.) **7** animate, bravery, courage, entrain, hearten, loyalty **8** folletto, phantasm, vivacity **9** animation, encourage **10** apparition, enterprise, enthusiasm **11** disposition, inspiration **12** cheerfulness, entrainement

   air: **5** Ariel

   animating: **6** animus

   animation: pep **4** dash

   avenging: Ate **6** alecto, erinys **7** megaera, nemesis **9** tisiphine

   evil: Ate, imp, Ker **4** baka, beng, boko, drow, gyre **5** bugan, demon, devil **6** animus, asuang, daemon, daitya, dibbuk, Erynes, Lilith **9** cacodemon **10** cacodaemon

   female: **6** undine **7** banshee, banshie

   fire: **4** Agni

   good: **5** genie, genus **7** eudemon **8** eudaemon

   heralding death: **7** banshee, banshie

   kinds of: Po; akh, imp, lar, nat **4** arac, gimp, Kuei, Kwei, soul **5** angel, Ariel, duffy, duppy, dusio, ethos, genie, jinni, manes, rakee, shade **6** animus, fulgja, jinnee, mammon, tangie, Undine **7** banshee

   lose: **7** despond

   mischievous: imp **4** Puck **6** goblin **7** gremlin **11** poltergeist

   of censure: **5** Momus

   of people: **5** ethos

spirit lamp: 4 etna

spirit-land: 9 fairyland

spirit-leaf: 8 manyroot

spirited: 4 fell, gamy **5** brisk, eager, fiery **6** active, audace, birkie, ginger, lively, spunky **7** animato, dashing **8** animated, desirous, frampoid, generous, vigorous **9** audacious, energetic, spiritoso, sprightly **10** mettlesome

   horse: **5** steed **7** charger

spiritedness: 9 animation, animosity

spiritless: 4 cold, dead, meek **5** amort, blate, vapid **6** flashy **7** daviely, hilding **8** dejected, feckless, flagging, lifeless, listless, thewless **9** depressed, exanimate, heartless **10** dispirited

spiritlike: 8 ethereal

spiritous: 6 active, ardent **8** animated **9** vivacious

spirits: *dash of:* **5** lacer

   dead: **5** manes

   dwelling place of: Po **5** Hades **7** Elysium

kinds of: 6 furies, uplift 7 elation, Sammael 9 firewater 13 aquacaelestis

lift: 5 elate 7 gladden

low: 5 blues, dumps, gloom 6 gloomy 8 doldrums

spirits and water: 4 grog

spirits of hartshorn: 7 ammonia

spiritual: 4 holy, pure, song 5 witty 6 clever, devout, divine, sacred 7 ghostly 8 churchly, internal, platonic, spirited 9 alcoholic, animastic, geistlich, unwordly 10 devotional, immaterial, spirituous 11 animastical, disembodied, incorporeal 14 ecclesiastical

apathy: 6 acedia

being: ens 5 angel, entia(pl.) 6 seraph

darkness: 4 Hell 5 tamas

spiritualistic meeting: 6 seance

spiritualize: 5 endow 6 purify, refine 7 animate 8 idealize 11 etherealize

spirituous: gay 4 airy, hard 5 vivid 6 active, ardent, lively 8 ethereal 9 alcoholic 10 immaterial 11 incorporeal

spiry: 4 tall 6 coiled, curled, spiral 7 slender 8 tapering, wreathed 10 serpentine

spit: dig, fix, rod 4 emit, hang, rain, reef, snow 5 eject, image, light, plant, reach, retch, shoal, spade, stick, sword, utter 6 broach, dagger, impale; saliva, skewer, sputum, thrust 7 spindle, spittle 8 broacher, likeness, sandbank, spadeful, sprinkle 9 brochette, secretion 11 counterpart, expectorate

spital: den 6 refuge, resort 7 shelter 8 hospital 9 lazaretto

spite: vex 4 hate, hurt, mood 5 annoy, depit, pique, shame, venom 6 enmity, grudge, hatred, injury, malice, mauger, maugre, rancor, thwart 7 chagrin, despite, dislike, ill-will, mortify 8 disgrace, dishonor 9 animosity, frustrate, humiliate 10 resentment 11 disposition, malevolence 12 spitefulness 13 mortification

spiteful: 4 mean 5 catty, snaky 6 sullen 7 waspish 8 annoying, venomous 9 malicious, malignant 10 dispiteous, irritating, vindictive 11 troublesome

spitfire: 9 brimstone

spitter: 4 deer 5 spade 7 brocket 8 spitball 12 expectorater

spitting: 6 saliva 10 exspuition

spittle: 4 spit 6 saliva

spittle insect: 10 froghopper

spittoon: 8 crachoir, cuspidor

spiv: 7 slacker

splash: lap 4 dash, daub, gout, lave, plop, pond, pool, spot 5 bathe, blash, plash, slart, slash, spray 6 blotch, dabble, flouse,

floush, strike 7 display, scatter, spatter 8 splatter 9 dashingly 10 appearance, excitement 14 ostentatiously

splashboard: 4 gate, trap 5 board, plank 6 fender, screen 8 mudguard

splashy: wet 5 muddy, showy 6 blashy, slushy 8 striking 11 sensational, spectacular 12 ostentatious

splat: 4 open, plot, spot 5 patch 6 blotch 7 flatten

splatter: dab 4 dash, rush 6 hubbub, splash 7 cluster, spatter 9 splashing

splay: hem 4 awry, turn 5 adorn, bevel, carve, slant, slope 6 clumsy, expand, spread 7 awkward, display, sloping 8 ungainly 9 dislocate, expansion, obliquely, slopingly, spreading 10 slantingly 11 enlargement

spleen: fit 4 fire, milt, mood, whim 5 anger, ardor, freak, humor, mirth, organ, spite 6 malice, temper 7 caprice, dislike, impulse 8 laughter 9 lienculus, merriment 10 melancholy 11 impetuosity

pert. to: 6 lienal

spleeny: 5 angry 7 fretful, peevish 9 irritable 10 melancholy

splendent: 6 glossy 7 beaming, shining 8 lustrous, splendid 9 brilliant 11 conspicuous, illustrious, magnificent, resplendent

splendid: gay 4 braw, fine, good, rial 5 grand, regal, showy, tinny 6 bright, candid, costly, superb 7 gallant, ripping, shining, sublime 8 glorious, gorgeous 9 brilliant, excellent, sumptuous 11 illustrious, magnificent, resplendent

splendor, splendour: 4 gite, pomp 5 blaze, eclat, gleam, glory, sheen 6 bright, fulgor, luster, parade 7 display, fulgour 8 elegance, grandeur, radiance, richness 9 pagaentry, showiness 10 brightness, brilliance, brilliancy, effulgence 12 gorgeousness, magnificence, resplendence 14 impressiveness

splenetic: 6 sullen 7 fretful, peevish, splenic 8 spiteful 9 depressed, irritable, malicious, spleenful 10 melancholy

spleuchan: 5 pouch

splice: 4 join 5 marry, unite 6 fasten 7 wedding 8 marriage 10 interweave

spliced: wed 6 joined, united 7 married

splint: 4 coal, lath, tace, scob 5 brace, plate, split, strip, tasse 6 fasten, shiver, tasset 7 confine 8 splinter

splinter: 4 chip, rend 5 break, broom, slice, smash, spale, split 6 fasten, shiver, sliver 7 confine, flinder, shatter 8 fragment

split: cut, rit 4 chap, rend, rent, rive, ruin, tear 5 break, burst, clave, cleft, crack, peach, reave, riven, share, wedge 6 betray, bisect, bottle, breach, broken, cleave, cloven, dilute, divide, rifted, schism, sliver, sunder **7** destroy, dispart, divided, fissure, portion, rupture, shatter **8** fragment, informer, separate, splinter **9** fractured, separated **10** separation

in two parts: **5** bifid **6** cloven, halved **8** bisected **9** bipartite

split pea: dal

splitfruit: **10** schizocarp

splitting: **5** funny **6** severe **7** comical, fission, rending **8** piercing

of mind: **13** schizophrenia

sploit: **5** spout **6** squirt

splore: **4** bout, brag, riot **5** boast, broil, revel **6** frolic **7** debauch, display **8** carousal, escapade **9** commotion, festivity, scrimmage **11** merrymaking

splotch: dab **4** blob, blot, dash, daub, spot **5** smear, stain **6** blotch, splash

splother: **6** splash **8** splutter

splurge: **6** effort **7** display **11** ostentation **13** demonstration

splutter: **4** fuff **5** hurry, noise, stuff **6** bustle, splash **7** dispute, glutter, quarrel, scatter, spatter, sputter, stammer **8** nonsense **9** confusion

Spode: **5** china **6** potter **9** porcelain

Spohr opera: **8** Jessonda

spoil: mar, rob, rot **4** blad, boot, loot, pelf, prey, ruin, swag **5** bitch, blend, booty, carve, cheat, decay, harry, prize, seize, strip, taint, waste **6** coddle, damage, deface, divest, forage, impair, infuse, injure, pamper, perish, ravage **7** connach, corrump, corrupt, estrepe, deprive, despoil, destroy, indulge, pillage, plunder, violate, vitiate **8** confound, unclothe **10** chevisance, corruption, impairment

eggs: **5** addle

spoiled: bad **5** dazed, musty **6** addled, marred, molded, petted, preyed, rotted **7** botched, decayed, tainted **8** pampered, pillaged **9** plundered

spoiler: **6** robber **7** marplot **8** pillager **9** despoiler, plunderer **10** depredator

spoilsport: **10** wet-blanket

spoke: bar **4** clog, grip, rung, tale, talk **5** block, check, drone, round, spake, stake, stick **6** radius, speech **7** mention, uttered **8** handhold **10** impediment **11** enchantment

spoken: **4** oral, said **5** parol **7** uttered **9** declaimed

spoliate: rob **7** despoil, pillage, plunder

spoliation: **6** rapine **7** pillage, plunder, robbery **8** pillaged **12** despoliation

spondulix: **5** funds, money

spondyl: **8** vertebra

sponge: bum, wet **4** form, swab, wipe **5** ascon, cadge, dough, erase, mooch **6** absorb, ascula, efface, rhagon **7** badiaga, cleanse,

destroy, drinker, scrunge, zimocca **8** drunkard, parasite, scrounge

calcareous: **6** leucon

orifice: **6** oscula(pl.) **7** osculum

pen: **5** kraal

pert. to: **9** poriferal

spicule: **4** toxa

vegetable: **5** loofa **6** loofah

sponge tree: **8** huisache

sponger: **6** cadger **8** parasite

spongewood: **4** sola

spongy: **4** fozy **5** rainy **6** porous, quaggy **9** absorbent

sponsor: **4** back **5** angel **6** backer, gossip, patron, surety **9** godfather, godmother, introduce

sponsorship: **4** egis **5** aegis **8** auspices

spontaneous: **4** free, wild **6** native **8** careless, untaught **9** automatic, impulsive **10** indigenous, self-acting **11** instinctive, involuntary

spontoon: **4** club, pike **7** halberd, pantoon **8** spantoon **9** espantoon, truncheon

spoof: guy **4** fool, hoax, joke **5** trick **7** deceive, swindle **8** nonsense **9** deception

spook: **5** ghost, haunt **6** spirit, wraith **7** specter **9** hobgoblin **10** apparition

spooky: **4** eery **5** eerie, weird **7** ghostly, haunted, uncanny **8** spectral

spool: **4** reel, wind **6** bobbin, broach **7** spindle **8** cylinder

spoon: **4** chip, neck **5** ladle, labis, lover, ninny **6** nestle, shovel, spoony **7** student **8** cochlear, splinter **9** simpleton

spoon-fed: **7** coddled **8** pampered

Spoon River poet: **7** Masters

spoon-shaped: **8** cochlear

spoonbill: **5** ajaja **10** paddlefish

spoondrift: **5** spray **9** spindrift

spoony: **5** silly **7** foolish **11** sentimental

spoor: **5** piste, scent, trace, track, trail

spore: **4** germ, seed

spore sac: **5** ascus

sport (see also **game** *official*): bet, fun, gig, toy **4** game, gaud, glee, jest, joke, mock, play, polo, romp **5** dally, freak, mirth, wager **6** frolic, gamble, racing, shikar **7** contest, gambler, jesting, mockery, pastime **8** derision, raillery **9** amusement, diversion, plaything **10** pleasantry, recreation **13** entertainment

attendance: **4** gate

event: **4** game, meet, race

shirt: tee **4** polo

shoe: **6** loafer **7** sneaker

site: gym **4** grid, oval, pool, ring, rink **5** arena, court, field, links, track **6** course **7** diamond, stadium **8** coliseum **10** hippodrome *summer:* **6** diving, hiking, quoits, rowing, skiing **7** fishing, sailing **8** swimming

winter: **6** hockey, skiing **7** skating **8** sledding **11** tobogganing

sportive: gay 5 merry **6** frisky, lusory, wanton **7** amorous, festive, jocular, playful **8** frolicky, gamesome, playsome, pleasant **9** lecherous **10** frolicsome

sportiveness: 7 knavery

sports-minded: 8 athletic

sports official: 5 coach, judge **6** umpire **7** referee **8** linesman **10** timekeeper

sportsman: 6 hunter **7** shikari **8** shikaree

sportula: 4 gift **7** largess, present

sporty: 4 loud **5** showy **6** flashy

spot: bit, dab, dot **4** blot, blur, fish, flaw, mark, site **5** blaze, fault, fleck, nevus, patch, place, point, ready, speck, stain, sully, tache, taint **6** blotch, defect, detect, locate, macula, macule, naevus, remove **7** asperse, blemish, freckle, splotch **8** discolor, disgrace, handicap, locality, location, maculate, position, quantity, reproach **9** bespatter, recognize

kinds of: ace, dot, pip, tee **4** blet, fret, gall, rone, spil, wems **5** macle, oasis **6** alcove, bethel, mascle, mottle, mouche **7** freckle **8** bethesda, fenestra, fontanel

on animal's face: **4** star **5** blaze

on playing card: pip

spotless: 5 clean, snowy **9** blameless, unspotted, unsullied **10** immaculate **11** unblemished, untarnished **14** irreproachable

spotlight: arc **4** beam

spotted: 6 bauson, calico, espied, marked, notate, sanded, ticked **7** bracket, dappled, guttate, mottled, noticed, stained, sullied **9** blemished, suspected, tarnished

animal: **4** paco, pard **6** chital, ocelot **7** cheetah, leopard

fever: **6** typhus

spotter: 7 watcher **9** detective

spotty: 5 dotty **6** uneven **9** irregular

spousal: 7 wedlock **8** ceremony, marriage, nuptials

spouse: wed **4** give, join, mate, wife **5** annar, bride, marry, unite **6** fiance **7** consort, espouse, fiancee, husband, partner, promise, wedlock **8** affiance, espousal, marriage **9** companion **10** bridegroom

spout: jet, jut, lip **4** dale, flow, geat, gush, lift, pawn, pipe, rant **5** eject, issue, orate, shoot, speak, spile, spurt, utter **6** pledge, recite, spigot, spring, squirt, stream, trough **7** conduit, declaim **8** downpour, gargoyle, pawnship **9** discharge, waterfall **10** waterspout

sprack: 4 deft **5** alert **6** active, lively, nimble, shrewd

sprag: 4 prop **6** billet

sprain: 5 chink **6** weaken **10** overstrain

sprang: 5 arose, spray **6** branch

sprangle: 5 spray **6** sprawl, spread **8** straggle, struggle

sprat: 5 bleak **6** garvie **7** herring **8** sixpence

sprattle: 6 sprawl **8** scramble, struggle

sprauchie: 6 sprawl **7** clamber **8** scramble

sprawl: 4 loll **7** grabble **8** struggle **9** sprauchie

spray: jet **4** chap, twig **5** bough, shoot, spree, sprig, water **6** boquet, branch, sparge, spread **7** atomize, bouquet, scatter **8** sprinkle **9** aspersion, discharge, spindrift

spread: fan, jam, ted **4** emit, meal, span, taft **5** cover, flare, jelly, reach, smear, splay, strew, widen **6** anoint, dilate, expand, extend, extent, ramify, unfold, unfurl **7** broaden, compass, diffuse, distend, diverge, divulge, enlarge, exhibit, expanse, overlay, overrun, prolong, protect, publish, radiate, scatter, slather, stretch **8** diffused, dispense, disperse, expanded, extended, increase, multiply, permeate, straddle **9** broadcast, circulate, dispersed, displayed, expansion, expatiate, propagate **10** distribute, generalize **11** disseminate

abroad: **5** bruit, noise, libel, rumor **6** delate, rumour, spring **7** delated, radiate **9** broadcast, publicize **11** disseminate

as plaster: **4** teer

for drying: ted

loosely: **5** strew **7** scatter

out: fan, lap, ted **4** bray, open, span **5** flare, widen **6** deploy, flange, sprawl, unfold

spreader: 6 tedder

spreading of light: 8 halation

spreading out: 6 radial

spree: bat, jag **4** bout, bust, gell, lark, orgy, romp, toot, jagg **5** beano, binge, booze, revel **6** bender, buster, bust-up, frolic, high-go, shindy **7** carouse, debauch, wassail **8** carousal **10** indulgence

sprig: 4 brad, nail, trim, twig **5** bough, scion, shoot, smart, spray, youth **6** active, branch, spruce **7** tendril **9** stripling

sprightliness: 6 gaiety, gayety **8** airiness, alacrity, buoyancy **9** animation

sprightly: gay, tid **4** airy, pert **5** agile, alive, brisk, canty, crank, desto, elfin, peart **6** active, blithe, lively **7** briskly, buoyant, chipper, ghostly, quickly **8** animated, vigorous **10** enlivening, spiritedly, spiritlike **11** incorporeal

spring: ain, fly, hop, spa **4** bend, dart, font, head, jump, leap, lilt, rise, warp, well **5** arise, atart, bound, flirt, glent, issue, lymph, shoot, spurt, therm, tower, vault **6** accrue, bounce, emerge, therme, venero **7**

diffuse, estuary, thermae 8 fountain 10 intoxicate

abruptly: 4 bolt

back: 6 recoil, resile 7 rebound

deposit: 4 urao 5 trona

hot: 7 balneum, thermae, gipsies

kind of: ain, cee, spa, ver, hop, ojo 4 font 5 lymph 6 geyser, charco, source, saline 7 gambado 9 Castalian

pert. to: 6 vernal

up: 5 arise

spring-like: 6 vernal

springboard: 5 wagon 6 batule

springbok: 7 gazelle

springe: gin, set 4 trap 5 agile, catch, noose, snare 6 supple 7 ensnare

springer: 7 grampus, spaniel 9 springbok

springing back: 7 elastic 9 renascent

springtime: May 8 germinal

springy: wet 6 spongy 7 elastic 8 flexible 9 resilient

sprinkle: deg, dot, wet 4 dart, rain, spot 5 color, flour, spray, strew, twist, water 6 affuse, bedrop, dabble, dredge, sparge 7 asperge, asperse, drizzle, scatter, spairge, sparkle, spatter 8 disperse 9 bespangle, bespatter 10 besprinkle, intoxicate

with flour: 6 dredge

with grains of mustard: 8 sinapize

with grit: 4 sand

with moisture: 5 bedew

with mud: 9 bespatter

with powder: 4 dust

with water: deg

sprinkler: 7 dredger 11 aspergillum

sprinkling: 4 seme 9 aspersion

sprint: run 4 dash, race 5 snare 6 bicker 7 springe

sprinter: 5 racer 6 runner 7 athlete

sprit: bud 4 dart, pole, rush, spar 5 shoot, speck, sprat 6 sprint, sprout 8 bowsprit 9 germinate

sprite: elf, fay, hob, imp 4 elve, life, mind, mood, peri, soul 5 Ariel, bucca, fairy, genie, ghost, gnome, nisse, pixie, shade, vital 6 goblin, person, spirit 7 essence 9 germinate, hobgoblin 10 apparition, woodpecker 11 disposition, inspiration

kind of: nix 5 ariel, demon, Holda, naiad, nixie 6 Kelpie 8 coltpixy 9 coltpixie 10 leprechaun, shoopiltie

sprocket: cam 5 tooth

sproil: 6 active, energy 7 agility 8 activity 9 energetic

sprout: bud, eye, son 4 cion, brod, chit, chun, germ, malt 5 achar, brode, chine, shoot, spire, spout, sprig, spurt 6 braird, expand, germen, growth, ratoon 7 burgeon 8 offshoot 9 germinate

comb. form: 5 blast 6 blasto 7 blastic

spruce: gim 4 deft, neat, posh, smug, trig, trim 5 compt, fussy, natty, Picea, smart, sprig 6 dapper, picked 7 dandify, finical, smarten 8 overnice, titivate

tree: 5 larch 8 epinette

sprue: 4 hole 5 dross 7 opening 8 psilosis 9 asparagus

sprunt: 4 hill, leap 5 brisk, steep 6 active, spring, spruce 8 struggle

spry: 5 agile, brisk, quick, smart 6 active, clever, nimble, spruce 7 knowing 8 vigorous 9 sprightly

spud: dig, man 4 hand 5 child, dough, drill, knife, money, spade 6 dagger, paddle, potato, reamer, remove, shovel 10 projection

spume: 4 foam, scum 5 froth

spumescent: 7 foaming 8 frothing

spumy: 5 foamy 6 frothy 7 spumous

spun: See **spin**

spunk, sponk: 4 punk 5 anger, flame, gleam, match, nerve, pluck, spark 6 kindle, mettle, spirit, sponge, tinder 7 courage, passion 9 touchwood

spunky: 4 game 5 quick 6 plucky, touchy 8 spirited 9 irritable 10 courageous, mettlesome

spur: egg 4 calk, gaff, goad, move, prod, prop, urge 5 arete, brace, drive, hurry, impel, press, prick, range, ridge, rowel, spine, spoor, strut, tower 6 arouse, broach, calcar, digger, excite, foment, griffe, hasten, incite, motive 7 gablock, provoke, publish 8 buttress, stimulus 9 incentive, instigate, stimulate 10 blockhouse 11 publication

having: 7 spicate

of mountain: 5 arete

on gamecock: 4 gaff

railroad: 6 siding

wheel: 5 rowel

spur wheel: 5 rowel

spurge: 4 weed 5 purge 6 purify 8 milkweed 9 euphorbia

spurious: 4 fake 5 bogus, false, phony, snide 6 forced 7 bastard 10 adulterate, apocryphal, artificial, fictitious, fraudulent 11 counterfeit, superficial 12 illegitimate 14 supposititious

spurl: 6 sprawl 8 scramble

spurn: hit 4 blow, dash, kick, rush, spur 5 haste, scorn 6 affray, incite, pillar, rebuff, refuse, reject, scrape, strike 7 contemn, decline, despise, disdain, scratch, stumble 10 engagement

spurt: bud, jet, jut 4 dart, gush 5 expel, shoot, spell, spout 6 sprout, squirt 8 increase, outbreak

Sputnik: 9 satellite

dog: 5 Laika
sputter: ado 4 fuss, spit
sputum: 4 spit 6 saliva 7 spittle
spy: see 4 case, espy, keek, note, tout 5 scout, sneak, snoop, watch 6 behold, descry, detect,. espial, gaycat, mouton, search 7 discern, examine, hi-carra, inspect, observe, snooper 8 discover, emissary, hi-carrah, informer, perceive 10 discoverer, scrutinize 13 intelligencer
famous: 4 Hari 5 Andre, Caleb, Fuchs 6 Arnold, Cavell 8 Mata Hari
spying: 9 espionage 16 counter-espionage
spyri's heroine: 5 Heidi
squab: coy, fat, shy 4 drop, fall, flop, slop, sofa 5 couch, crush, piper, plump, short, thick 6 callow, pigeon, squash 7 cushion, ottoman 8 nestling 9 fledgling, unfledged, upholster
squabble: 5 brawl 6 bicker, jangle 7 bobbery, contend, dispute, quarrel, wrangle 13 collie-shangie
squabbling: 8 bangling
squad: 4 team 5 group, troop
leader of: 8 sergeant
squadron: 6 armada 10 escadrille
squalid: 4 foul, mean, poor 5 dirty, nasty 6 filthy, sordid 7 unclean 8 wretched 9 miserable, repellant, repellent, repulsive
squall: cry, pet 4 dear, drow, gush, gust, wawl 5 storm 6 flurry, scream, shower, squawk, wretch 7 borasca, borasco, dispute, trouble 8 borasque 9 windstorm 11 disturbance
squalor: mud 4 dirt, mire 5 filth 9 roughness 10 filthiness 11 squalidness 12 wretchedness
squander: 4 burn, lash 5 spend, waste 6 befool, lavish, wander 7 consume, debauch, dispend, scatter 8 disperse, embezzle, misspend 9 dissipate
squanderer: 5 loser 7 wastrel
square: 4 even, parc, park, rule, true 5 agora, carre, clear, exact, hunky, plaza 6 dinkum, direct, honest, settle 7 commons, pattern, quarrel, upright 8 justness. quadrate, standard 9 carre-four, criterion, principle 11 unequivocal 13 parallelogram 15 straightforward
public: 5 plaza 6 common
square dance: 4 reel 7 hoedown, lancers
squared circle: 4 ring 5 arena
squarehead: 4 dolt 5 Swede 6 German 8 numskull 9 screwball 12 Scandinavian
squares: 5 panes
squaring tool: 5 edger
squarish: 4 boxy
squark: 5 croak 6 squawk
squarrose: 5 scaly

squash: 4 beat, fall, ooze, pepo, stop 5 crush, press, quash 7 cymling, flatten, pumpkin, squeeze, squelch 8 suppress 9 discomfit 10 disconcert
kind of: 6 banana, cushaw, simnel, summer, turban 7 cymling, Hubbard, Italian 8 cymbling, patty pan, zucchini 9 crookneck
squashy: wet 4 soft 5 boggy, muddy, mushy 8 overripe
squat: sit 4 fall, quat, sink, stub 5 cower, crush, dumpy, pinch, pudgy, quash, quiet, stoop 6 bruise, crouch, fodgel, hurkle, settle, splash, stubby 7 descend, silence, squatty, squeeze 8 thickset
squatter: 4 flap 5 squat 6 crouch, nester, plunge 7 confuse, flutter, nestler, scatter, settler 8 bewilder, squander 9 sandpiper
Squatter State: 6 Kansas
squatting: 8 couchant
squatty: 5 dumpy, squat 8 thickset
squaw: 6 mahala, coween 10 klootchman
husband: 4 buck 6 sannup
squawbush: 5 sumac
squawfish: 4 chub 8 chappaul
squeak: cry, wee 4 peep 5 cheep, creak, noise, speak 6 betray, escape, shrill 7 confess, disturb
squeal: yip 4 blab, sing 5 broil, frail, weary 6 betray, inform 7 dispute, protest, quarrel 8 complain
squealer: 4 duck, fink 5 quail, swift 6 grouse, pigeon, plover 7 traitor 8 informer 9 partridge
squeamish: shy 4 helo, nice, stir 5 dizzy, heloe 6 bustle, dainty, dauncy, modest, queasy 7 finical, prudish 8 overnice, qualmish 9 dizziness, giddiness, reluctant, sensitive 10 fastidious, scrupulous 13 oversensitive
squeeze: eke, hug, jam 4 gain, mull, neck, silk 5 chirt, creem, crowd, crush, force, pinch, press, wring 6 corner, escape, extort, scrump, scruze, thrust, twitch 7 extract, oppress, procure, scrunch, scrunge 8 compress, condense, pressing, pressure, scrounge 9 constrict, influence 10 commission, constraint 11 compression
squeezer: 5 drier, noose 6 juicer, reamer 7 wringer 8 squeegee 9 extractor
squeezy: 7 cramped 8 confined
squelch: 4 blow, fall 5 crush, quash, quell, stamp 6 rebuke, subdue 7 silence, washrag 8 suppress 9 discomfit 10 disconcert
squelcher: 8 blizzard
squib: jet 4 ball, bomb, mote, pipe, skit, tube 5 candy, match, throw, write 6 speech, squirt, writer 7 dispute, explode, lampoon, pasquil, publish, torpedo, writing 9 bespatter 10 pasquinade 11 firecracker

squid: 6 loligo 7 mollusk, octopus 8 cala-
mary 10 cuttlefish
arm: 8 tentacle
pen: 5 quill
secretion: ink
shell: pen
squiffer: 10 concertina
squiggle: 4 curl, line 5 shake, twist 6 squirm
7 wriggle 8 curlicue
squiggly: 4 wavy 8 twisting 9 wriggling
squilla: 5 prawn 6 shrimp
squinch: 4 arch 5 twist 6 lintel, quince,
squint, wrench 7 squeeze, squench 9 cor-
beling
squint: 4 bent, cast, glee, gleg, gley, skew 5
glent, trend 6 gledge, goggle 7 deviate 10
hagioscope, strabismus
squint-eyed: 5 gleed, gleyd
squire: 5 lover, title 6 donzel, escort 7 gallant 8 henchman, servitor 9 accompany,
attendant, gentleman, landowner
squirrel: bun 5 sisel, xerus 6 chippy, gyrate
7 assapan 8 archilla, jelerang 9 assapanic,
chickaree, shadetail
burrowing: 6 gopher
flying: 7 assapan
genus of: 7 sciurus
nest: 4 dray, drey
shrew: 4 tana
skin: 4 vair
squirrellike: 8 sciuroid
animal: 8 dormouse
squirt: 5 chirt, skite, slirt, spout, spurt 14
whippersnapper
sri: 4 holy 7 Lakshmi 8 glorious, reverend 9
fortunate
stab: dag, jab, jag, try 4 gore, jagg, pink,
yerk 5 chive, drive, knife, knive, lunge,
prick, sound, stake, stick, stool, stump,
wound 6 broach, dagger, pierce, strike,
stroke, thrust 7 attempt, poniard, roughen
8 puncture 9 penetrate
in fencing: 4 pink 8 stoccado
stability: 5 poise 7 balance 8 firmance, firmness 9 constancy, fixedness 10 permanence, stableness, steadiness 12 immov-
ability, immutability 13 steadfastness 15
indissolubility
stabilize: fix, set 5 poise 6 steady 8 regulate
stabilizer: 7 ballast
stable: 4 barn, fast, firm, shed, sure 5 fixed,
set-up, solid, sound, stall 6 hangar, secure,
steady, strong, sturdy 7 durable, equerry,
lasting 8 constant, enduring, immobile 9
confirmed, establish, permanent, resistant, steadfast, unabashed, unvarying 10
stationary, unwavering 11 established,
trustworthy 12 unchangeable
compartment: 5 stall

range: 4 mews
royal: 4 mews
stableman: 5 groom 6 ostler 7 hostler
stack: set 4 bike, heap, pile, rick, pike, stow,
tier 5 group, hovel, mound, scroo, shock 7
chimney, conduit 9 fireplace
stack up: 4 tier 5 total
stackyard: 7 haggard 10 stackgarth
stad: 4 town 7 village
staddle: row 4 cane, tree 5 staff, stain, swath
6 crutch 7 sapling, support
stade: 7 furlong, stadium
stadium: 4 oval 5 arena, stade, stage 7 furlong 8 coliseum
staff: bar, gad, rod 4 cane, club, line, mace,
maul, pole, prod, rung, wand 5 aides, baton, crook, lance, pedum, perch, spear,
stave, stick, suite 6 baston, cudgel, stanza
7 attache, bailiff, caducei(pl.), scepter,
sceptre, support 8 caduceus 9 constable,
entourage, personnel 10 assistants, associates 12 quarter-staff
bearer: 5 macer
kinds of: 4 kent, wand 5 filch 6 croche, muleta 7 baculus, bourdon, cambuca, crosier,
crozier, distaff, rhabdos 10 alpenstock
officers: 5 aides, cadre
staff of life: 5 bread
stag: 4 colt, hart 7 pollard, shorten 8 informer
horn: 4 rial 9 bezantler
stage: era 4 dais, gest, step, tier 5 board,
coach, floor, grade, level, phase, shelf,
stair, story 6 degree, stadia 7 display, exhibit, produce, rostrum, stadium, theater
8 platform, scaffold 9 condition, gradation
10 proscenium, stagecoach 11 subdivision
extra: 4 supe 5 super
hanging: 7 scenery
on: 7 en scene
part: 4 role
pert. to: 6 scenic
raised: 4 dais 7 estrade
stage direction: all 4 exit, sola 5 aside, enter, manet, omnes, solus 6 exeunt, sennet
8 loquitur
stage whisper: 5 aside
stagecoach: 9 diligence
stager: 5 actor 6 player
stagger: 4 reel, rock, stun, sway 5 lurch,
shake, waver 6 hobble, totter, wintle(Sc.) 7
tremble, vibrate 8 hesitate, titubate, unsettle
stagnant: 4 dull, foul 5 inert, stale, still 8
sluggish, standing 10 motionless 13 unprogressive
stagnate: 4 dull 5 inert 10 motionless
stagnation: 6 stasis, stases, torpor
stagy: 8 affected 10 theatrical

staid: set 5 fixed, grave, sober 6 demure, sedate, steady 7 earnest, serious, settled 8 decorous 9 dignified, steadfast 10 coolheaded

stain: dye 4 blot, blur, soil, spot, tint 5 cloud, paint, smear, sully, tache, taint, tinge, trace 6 blotch, infamy macula, smirch, smudge, stigma, vilify 7 blemish, corrupt, tarnish 8 discolor, disgrace, dishonor, maculate, tincture 9 bespatter, pollution 10 attainture 11 contaminate

stainless: 4 pure

stair: 4 step 5 stage, stile 6 degree
face: 5 riser
post: 5 newel
series of: 6 flight

staircase: 5 grece, grice 6 griece
moving: 9 escalator
on ship: 12 companionway
outdoor: 6 perron
part of: 4 rung 5 newel, riser, tread
portable: 6 ladder
spiral: 8 caracole

stake: bet, peg, pin, pot, set 4 ante, back, gage, pale, pile, pole, pool, post, risk, spit, stob 5 anvil, prize, spile, stick, teest, wager 6 chance, gamble, hazard, picket 7 venture 9 grubstake
driver: 4 maul
pert. to: 5 palar

stale: old 4 flat, hoar, lure, rung, worn 5 banal, blown, corny, decoy, frowy, moldy, musty, shaft, trite, vapid, waugh(Sc.) 7 insipid 9 hackneyed, tasteless 10 flavorless, prostitute 11 commonplace 13 uninteresting

stalemate: 4 draw 7 impasse 8 deadlock 10 standstill

stalk: bun 4 axis, halm, hunt, mote, risp, seta, stem 5 haulm, spear, stipe, straw 6 pursue, ratoon, stride 7 pedicel, petiole 8 peduncle
having: 9 petiolate
remove: 5 strig

stalker: 6 hunter

stalking-horse: 5 blind, decoy 7 pretext

stalkless: 7 sessile

stall: bin, cot, pew 4 crib, loge, mire, seat, stop 5 boose, boosy, booth, check, crame, decoy, delay, stand 6 manger, stable 7 pretext, station 8 hesitate 9 enclosure 10 dilly-dally 11 compartment, confederate

stallion: 6 cooser(Sc.)

stalwart: 4 firm 5 brave, stout 6 brawny, robust, strong, sturdy 7 valiant 8 partisan, resolute 10 unyielding

stamina: gut 4 grit 5 vigor 7 essence 8 backbone, capacity, strength 9 endurance, fortitude

stammer: 4 hack, stut 6 falter, hacker 7 fribble, stumble, stutter 8 hesitate

stamp: die 4 beat, coin, form, kind, mark, seal, tool, type 5 brand, class, crush, drive, pound, press, print, stomp 6 signet, strike, thresh 7 impress, imprint, postage, sticker 8 inscribe 9 character 10 impression 11 distinguish
collecting: 9 philately
fencing: 5 appel
madness for: 11 timbromania
paper: 6 pelure
space: 8 spandrel

stampede: 4 bolt, rout, rush 5 panic 6 flight 7 debacle

stamping plate: die

stance: 4 pose 7 posture, station 8 position

stanch, staunch: 4 firm, stem, stop, true 5 allay, check, close, loyal, quell, sound 6 hearty, quench, steady, strong, trusty 7 zealous 8 constant, faithful, resolute 9 steadfast 10 extinguish, unswerving, unwavering, watertight 11 substantial, trustworthy

stanchion: bar 4 beam, post, prop 5 brace, piton 7 confine, support, upright

stand: set 4 bear, dais, ease, halt, hold, last, rack, stop 5 abide, arise, booth, cease, erect, pause, table 6 afford, endure, podium, remain, resist, tripod, trivet 7 etagere, station, sustain, support, taboret, undergo 8 attitude, continue, hesitate, maintain, position, tabouret, tolerate 9 withstand
candles: 7 epergne 10 candelabra
cuplike: 4 zarf
for: 4 mean 8 tolerate 9 represent
for election: run
in awe of: 4 fear 5 dread 7 respect
on end: 5 upend
on hind legs: 4 ramp, rear
opposite: 4 face
ornamental: 7 atagere, etagere
out: jut 6 beetle 7 project 8 overhang, protrude
painter's: 5 easel
small: 7 taboret 8 tabouret
still: ho 4 stop, whoa
three-legged: 6 tripod, trivet

stand-in: 10 substitute

standard: cup, par, set 4 fiar(Sc.), flag, mark, norm, suit, type, unit 5 canon, chest, grade, gauge, ideal, level, model 6 assize, banner, beacon, coffer, ensign, goblet, normal, sample, signal 7 classic, example, labarum(L.), pattern, support, upright 8 accepted, brattach(Sc.), gonfalon, orthodox, vexillum 9 criterion, oriflamme, yardstick 10 touchstone 11 candlestick

bearer: 11 gonfalonier
golf: 5 bogey, bogie
of measurement: 6 metric
Turkish: 4 alem, toug
standardize: 9 calibrate
standing: 4 rank 5 being, erect, fixed 6 estate, stable, stance, status 7 lasting, settled, statant, station, upright 8 constant, duration, location, position, stagnant 9 permanent, situation 10 reputation, stationary
upright: 11 orthostatic
standing room only: S.R.O.
standstill: 4 halt, rest, stop 5 stand, state 8 deadlock 9 cessation, stalemate
stang: bar 4 ache, pang, pole 5 sting, throb
stanhope: 5 buggy
stank: 4 pond, pool 5 ditch
stanza: 5 envoi, stave, verse 7 strophe 8 division 9 apartment
eight line: 6 huitan, octave 7 triolet
five line: 8 cinquain
four line: 8 quatrain
irregular: 13 alloeostropha
six line: 6 sestet
ten line: 6 dizain 7 dizaine
three line: 8 tristich
staple: 4 city, town 5 chief, fiber, shaft 7 chaplet, support 8 fastener 9 principal 10 foundation
star (see also **constellation**): ace, orb, sun 4 hero, lead 5 actor, badge, shine 6 etoile 7 actress, estoile, heroine, ingenue, stellar 8 asterisk, luminary, pentacle, twinkler 9 bespangle, headliner, principal 10 preeminent, topnotcher
apple: 7 caimito
brightest in constellation: 5 alpha
combining form: 5 astro 6 sidero
difference in direction: 8 parallax
divination: 9 astrology
evening: 5 Venus 6 Hesper, Vesper 7 Evestar 8 Hesperus
evil: 8 sidereal
exploding: 4 nova
five-pointed: 8 pentacle
group: 6 galaxy 13 constellation
in Aquila: 6 Altair
in Bootes: 8 Arcturus
in Canis Major: 6 Sirius
in Carina: 7 Canopus
in Centaurus: 5 Agena
in Cetus: 4 Mira
in Cygnus: 5 Deneb 7 Albireo
in Draco: 6 Alsafi 7 Al Rakis, Eltanin
in Gemini: 5 Wasat 6 Alhena, Castor, Pollux
in Leo: 7 Regulus
in Lyra: 4 Vega

in Orion: 5 Rigel, Saiph
in Perseus: 5 Algol
in Scorpius: 7 Antares
in Taurus: 8 Pleiades
in Ursa Major: 5 Alcor, Mizar 6 Alkaid
in Ursa Minor: 7 Polaris
in Virgo: 5 Spica
morning: 4 Mars 5 Venus 6 Saturn 7 Daystar, Jupiter, Mercury
north: 7 polaris 8 loadstar, lodestar, polestar
pert to: 6 astral 7 astrean, stellar 8 sidereal, stellate
representation: 6 etoile
resembling: 8 stellate 9 stellated
shooting: 5 comet 6 Leonid, meteor
six-pointed: 8 hexagram
suddenly flaring: 4 nova
two: 9 bistellar
variable: 4 Mira
worshiper: 7 sabaist
star cluster: 6 nebula
star facet: 4 pane
star-like: 8 stellate
starch: vim 4 arum, sago 5 tikor, vigor 6 amylum, energy, farina, strong 7 cassava, precise, stiffen 8 activity, glycogen, strength 9 arrowroot, formality, stiffness 12 carbohydrate
combining form: 4 amyl
starchy: 5 rigid, stiff 6 formal 7 precise 9 unbending
stare: 4 gape, gaup, gawk, gawp, gaze, gouk, gowk, gype, look, ogle, peer 5 glare, glaze, glore 6 glower, goggle 7 bristle 8 starling
starfish: 7 sun star 8 asteroid
limb: ray
stargazer: 4 fish 10 astrologer, astronomer
staring: 6 astare, gazing 7 glaring 8 wide-eyed
stark: 4 bare, firm, hard, pure 5 bleak, harsh, quite, rigid, rough, sheer, stern, stiff, tense, utter 6 barren, severe, strong, wholly 7 violent 8 absolute, complete, desolate, entirely, obdurate, powerful, stalwart, stripped, vigorous 9 downright, unadorned 10 absolutely, unyielding 11 intractable
starling: 6 pastor
starnose: 4 mole
starry: 6 astral, bright 7 shining, stellar 8 sidereal, starlike, stellate 9 sparkling
Star-Spangled Banner author: 15 Francis Scott Key
start: fit, run, shy 4 dart, head, jerk, jump, lead, rush 5 alarm, begin, dodge, enter, flush, glent, lever, onset, rouse, sally, shock, wince 6 boggle, broach, flinch, fright, loosen, outset, spring, twitch 7 disturb, get away, impulse, provoke, retreat,

startle 8 commence, displace, handicap, outburst 9 advantage, dislocate, introduce, originate

starter: 5 drill, punch 7 entrant 8 official 10 controller

startle: 5 alarm, rouse, scare, shock, start 6 excite 8 affright, frighten, surprise 9 electrify

startling: 7 rousing 8 alarming, restless, skittish 10 surprising

starvation: 6 famine

starve: 4 fast 6 famish, hunger

starveling: 4 lean 6 hungry, pining, wasted

starwort: 5 aster 9 chickweed, colicroot

stash: end 4 stop 5 store

stashie: 6 clamor

state: say 4 acme, aver, etat(F.), mode, pomp, rank, seat, tell, term, weal 5 chair, posit, style, utter 6 affirm, allege, assert, avouch, degree, empire, estate, height, nation, polity, recite, relate, report, status, throne 7 account, country, declare, dignity, enounce, express, narrate 8 ceremony, eminence, grandeur, position, property, propound, standing 9 community, condition, enunciate, pronounce, situation, territory 10 asseverate, possession 11 stateliness 12 circumstance, commonwealth

based on honor: 9 timocracy

bound by treaty: 4 ally

explicitly: 6 define 7 itemize, specify 13 particularize

ideal: 6 Utopia

member: 7 citizen

of balance: 9 equipoise

of excitement: 7 ferment

of mind: 4 mood 5 humor 6 morale

office of: 11 secretariat

pert. to: 7 federal

relating to: 6 statal

under foreign control: 12 protectorate

State Fair author: 5 Stong

state police: 7 trooper

stated: 5 fixed 6 avowed 7 regular 8 declared 10 formulated 11 established

statehouse: 7 capitol

stately: 5 grand, lofty 6 august, formal, superb 7 courtly, gallant, haughty 8 imperial, imposing, majestic 9 dignified 10 deliberate 11 ceremonious, magisterial, magnificent

music: 5 largo

woman: 4 Juno

statement: 4 bill, word 5 audit, dicta 6 dictum, precis, remark, report, resume 7 account, address, article, bromide, epitome, invoice, recital, summary 8 abstract, averment(law), relation, sentence, schedule 9 affadavit, agreement, manifesto, narrative 10 allegation, deposition, expression 11 abridgement, affirmation, assertation, certificate, declaration 12 presentation 13 prevarication 14 circumspection

assumed true: 7 premise

authoritative: 6 dictum

defamatory: 5 libel

formal: 9 affidavit 10 deposition

introductory: 5 proem 6 prolog 7 preface, prelude 8 foreword, prologue

mathematical: 7 theorem

of belief: 5 credo, creed

of facts: 4 case

self-contradictory: 7 paradox

self-evident: 6 truism

stateroom: 5 cabin

statesman: 7 statist 10 politician

static: 7 resting 8 inactive 9 quiescent 10 stationary

station: fix, run, set 4 camp, halt, post, rank, seat, spot, stop 5 berth, depot, field, place, serai, siege 6 assign, church, degree, region, stance 7 appoint, calling, cuartel(Sp.), dignity, habitat, posture 8 attitude, location, position 9 condition, homestead, situation 10 constitute 11 equilibrium, institution

stationary: set 4 fast 5 fixed 6 stable, static 8 immobile, moveless 9 immovable, sedentary 10 unchanging

stationer: 9 publisher 10 bookseller

stationery: ink, pen 4 book 5 blank, paper 6 pencil 10 papeteries

statist: 9 statesman 10 politician

statistics collector: 7 statist 12 statistician

statue: 4 bust, icon, ikon, nude 5 image, orant 6 bronze 7 Madonna 8 Colossus, figurine, likeness, monument

at Thebes: 6 Memnon

base: 6 plinth

gigantic: 8 colossus

in London Guildhall: Gog 5 Magog

praying: 5 orant

primitive: 6 xoanon

that came to life: 7 Galatea

upper part of: 4 bust 5 torso

weeping: 5 Niobe

Statue of Liberty: *poet:* 7 Lazarus

sculptor: 9 Bartholdi

statuesque: 7 stately 8 graceful

statuette: 8 figurine

stature: 6 height

status: 4 rank 5 state 6 aspect, classe(F.) 8 position, relation, standing 9 condition

statute: act, law 4 rule 5 edict 6 assize, decree 9 enactment, ordinance 10 regulation

heading of: 5 title

volume of: 4 code 5 codex 7 codices

staunch: See **stanch**

stave: bar 4 beat, rung, slat, stap(Sc.) 5 break, knock, lathi, staff, stick 6 baculi(pl.), cudgel 7 baculus 8 puncture
bundle of: 5 shook
staver: 6 totter 7 saunter
stavesacre: 8 larkspur
stay: dam, guy, lie, rib 4 bide, calm, halt, hold, live, prop, rely, rest, rope, stem, stop, tack, wait 5 abide, allay, avast, await, brace, cable, cease, check, delay, demur, dwell, pause, quell, stand, stare, tarry 6 arrest, depend, detain, endure, fasten, linger, pacify, remain, reside, resist, secure, shroud, status 7 appease, control, incline, refrain, satisfy, sojourn, support, sustain, triatic 8 continue, restrain 9 anchorage, cessation, hindrance, residence 10 impediment, permanence 12 postponement
staying power: 7 stamina 9 endurance
stead: 4 farm, help, lieu, site, spot 5 avail, beset, place, trace, track 6 assist, behalf 7 benefit, bestead, impress, involve, replace, service, support 8 bedstead, locality, position 9 advantage, farmstead, situation, successor 10 substitute
steadfast, stedfast: 4 fast, firm, true 5 fixed, staid 6 stable, stanch, steady 7 certain, settled, staunch 8 constant, faithful, resolute 9 immovable 10 unchanging, unswerving 11 established, unalterable
steadiness: 5 nerve 7 balance 8 firmness 9 constancy
steading: 9 farmhouse, homestead
steady: 4 calm, even, firm 5 fixed, grave, sober, staid 6 direct, stable, sturdy 7 assured, equable, regular, uniform 8 constant, diligent, faithful, reliable, resolute 9 incessant, steadfast 10 continuous, controlled, invariable, sweetheart, unswerving 11 unfaltering, unmitigated 13 unfluctuating, uninterrupted
steak: 4 club 5 chuck, flank, round, shell, t-bone 7 griskin, New York, sirloin 9 entrecote 11 porterhouse
steal: bag, cly, cop, gyp, nim, rap 4 crib, gain, glom, hook, lift, stem, take 5 bribe, creep, fetch, filch, harry, pinch, poach, shaft, stalk, swipe 6 abduct, burgle, convey, divert, extend, handle, kidnap, pilfer, pirate, rustle, snitch 7 purloin 8 embezzle, peculate 9 condiddle 10 plagiarize 11 appropriate 14 misappropriate
stealage: 5 theft 7 larceny 8 burglary
stealer: 5 thief 6 robber 7 burglar 10 plagiarist 11 biblioklept
cattle: 7 abactor, rustler
stealthy: sly 6 artful, secret 7 catlike, cunning, furtive 11 clandestine 13 surreptitious

walk: 5 stalk
steam: 4 boil, fume, reek 5 force, power, smoke, vapor 6 energy 8 vaporize, vexation 10 exhalation, irritation
jet: 8 soffione, soffioni
pipe: 5 riser
steamer: 4 boat, ship 5 liner 6 vessel 9 steamship
cabin: 5 texas
steaming: 5 aboil
steamship: 5 liner 7 steamer
route: 4 lane
smokestack: 6 funnel
stearic acid: 8 stearate
steatite: 4 talc 9 soapstone
stech: 4 cram 5 gorge 10 gormandize
steed: 4 Arab 5 horse 7 charger, courser
steek: 4 shut 5 close 6 fasten, stitch
steel: 4 rail 5 acier(F.), inure, press 6 damask, harden, smooth, toledo 8 Bessemer, Damascus 10 strengthen
process: 8 Bessemer 11 cementation
steelhead: 5 trout
steely: 10 unyielding
steelyard: 7 balance
steep: ret 4 bate, bath, bold, bowk, brew, buck, high, soak, stew, tall 5 bathe, brant, brent, heavy, hilly, imbue, lofty, proud, sharp, sheer 6 abrupt, bright, clifty, decoct, drench, imbibe, imbrue, infuse, seethe 7 arduous, extract, extreme, immerse 8 elevated, headlong, macerate, saturate, solution 9 difficult, distemper, excessive, precipice 10 exorbitant, impregnate 11 precipitous 13 perpendicular
steeper: vat 6 teapot, vessel 7 cistern
steeple: 5 spire, tower 6 cupola 8 pinnacle 9 campanile
steeply: 5 brant
steepness: 6 height
steer: ox; con, tip 4 conn, helm, lead, stot 5 guide, pilot 6 bovine, direct, govern, manage 7 bullock, control, oversee
close to wind: 4 luff
steerage: 8 guidance 9 direction 10 management, regulation
steering: aim 9 direction, mangement 10 government
apparatus: 4 helm 5 wheel 6 rudder, tiller
part: 10 rudderhead
superintend: con 4 conn
steery: 4 stir 6 tumult
steeve: 4 pack, stow 5 store, stuff
stein: mug 4 toby
steinbock: 8 antelope
steinkirk, steenkirk: 6 cravat 9 neckcloth
stela, stele: 4 slab 6 pillar 8 monument 10 gravestone
stelar: 10 columnlike

stellar: 5 chief 6 astral, starry 7 leading 8 starlike, stellate 9 principal

stellate: 8 starlike 10 star-shaped

Steller's sea cow: 6 rytina

stem: bow, bun, dam, ram 4 axis, base, body, bole, cane, culm, halt, hold, load, prow, race, reed, rise, risp, root, stop, tamp 5 check, haulm, shaft, stalk, steer, stipe, stock, trunk 6 branch, derive, oppose, stanch 7 lineage, pedicel, petiole, spindle 8 ancestry, contract, peduncle, restrain 9 originate, petiolule

bulblike: 4 corm 5 tuber 7 rhizome

climbing: 4 bine 7 tendril

comb. form: 4 caul 5 caulo

fungus: 5 stipe

joint: 4 node

part: 4 pith 5 stele

pert. to: 7 cauline 8 stipular

sheath: 5 ocrea

stemless: 11 acaulescent

stemma: 7 descent, lineage 8 ancestry, pedigree

stemmer: bar

stem-winder: 5 watch

stench: 4 fogo, odor, reek 5 fetor, smell, stink 6 foetor

Stendhal hero: 5 Sorel

stenographer: 5 steno

stenography: 9 shorthand 12 brachygraphy

stent: 5 tight 6 extend, extent 7 stretch 12 outstretched

stentor: 6 roarer

stentorian: 4 loud

step: sty, way 4 gait, pace, rank, rest, rung, walk 5 break, crush, dance, grade, ledge, level, plane, round, shelf, space, stage, stair, stalk, strut, stufe(G.), trace, tread 6 action, degree, manner, squash, stride 7 advance, deprive, imprint, measure 8 distance, footfall, foothold, footrest, footstep, movement 9 footprint, gradation, procedure, promotion 10 proceeding, stepladder 11 translation

dance: pas 5 coule 6 chasse 8 glissade

introductory: 8 rudiment 10 initiative

ladder's: 4 rime, rung

measuring device: 10 passimeter

over fence: 5 stile

part: 5 riser, tread 6 nosing

recording device: 8 odograph

rope ladder: 7 ratline

series of raised: 6 gradin 7 gradine

step up: rev

step-by-step: 8 gradatim(L.)

step-in: 4 shoe 7 slipper

step-ins: 10 underpants

stepbrother: 9 beau-frere(F.) 11 beaux-freres

stepdame: 10 stepmother

steppe: 5 plain 7 prairie 9 wasteland

storm: 5 buran

stepper: 6 dancer

steps: See **step, staircase**

stepson: 8 beau-fils(F.) 9 beaux-fils

stere: 9 kiloliter

sterotype: 6 repeat 7 hackney

sterotyped: 5 trite

sterile: dry 4 arid, dead, geld 6 barren, meager, meagre, otiose 7 aseptic, useless 8 impotent 9 fruitless, infertile 10 unfruitful 11 ineffective 12 unproductive

sterility: 7 asepsis

sterilize: 9 disinfect

sterling: 5 penny 7 genuine 9 excellent

stern: 4 back, dour, firm, grim, hard, helm 5 harsh, rough, steer, stout 6 fierce, gloomy, mighty, rudder, savage, severe, strict, strong, sturdy, sullen, tiller, unkind 7 austere, massive 8 exacting, resolute, rigorous 9 unbending, unfeeling 10 astringent, forbidding, inexorable, inflexible, relentless, uninviting, unyielding 11 hard-hearted 14 uncompromising

toward: aft 5 abaft 6 astern

Sterne character: 4 Slop, Toby, Trim 6 Shandy 8 Tristram

sternforemost: 7 awkward 8 backward

sternness: 5 rigor 7 cruelty 8 hardness, severity 9 austerity, harshness, rigidness, stiffness 10 strictness 12 exactingness 13 inflexibility

sternutation: 6 sneeze 8 sneezing

sternward: aft 5 abaft 6 astern

sterol: 7 alcohol

stertor: 5 snore

stevdore: 6 loader, stower 8 cargador 12 longshoreman

steven: din 4 roar 5 noise, voice 6 outcry

Stevenson: *character: Jim* 4 Hyde

home: 5 Samoa

stew: 4 boil, cook, dive, fret, mess, olio 5 bathe, cloud, imbue, steep, study, sweat, worry 6 burgoo, ragout, seethe, simmer 7 brothel, haricot, swelter 8 hothouse 9 Brunswick, confusion 10 capilotade, excitement, hodgepodge, hotchpotch 11 predicament

steward: 4 hind 5 dewan, diwan, graff, grave 6 factor, grieve, waiter 7 bailiff, curator, foreman, granger, manager, officer, proctor 8 bhandari, employee 9 custodian, dispenser, seneschal 10 magistrate 11 chamberlain

monastery: 8 cellarer

ship: 6 flunky 7 flunkey

stewed: 5 drunk 10 inebriated 11 intoxicated

stey: 5 steep

sthenic: 6 active, strong

stib: 6 dunlin 9 sandpiper

stich: 4 line 5 verse

stick: bat, bow, cue, gad, gum, put, rod, set 4 bind, cane, clag, clam, club, fife, glue, kill, mast, poke, pole, push, shut, spit, stab, stem, stop, twig, wand 5 affix, baton, cheat, cleam, cling, close, delay, demur, flute, mount, paste, place, prick, shoot, shove, staff, stalk, stall, stave, trunk 6 adhere, attach, baffle, ballow, billet, branch, cement, cleave, cohere, cudgel, endure, fasten, ferule, fescue, impale, mallet, pierce, puzzle, rammer, strike, thrust 7 confine, defraud, drummer 8 bludgeon, clarinet, hesitate, puncture, revolver, tolerate 9 crabstick, drumstick

bamboo: 5 lathi 6 lathee

bundle of: 5 fagot 6 fasces 7 fascine

conductor's: 5 baton

crooked: 5 caman 7 cammock, gambrel

jumping: 4 pogo

measuring: 5 ruler 7 ellwand 8 yardwand 9 yardstick

mountain climbing: 10 alpenstock

stick out: 7 extrude

stick up: 6 hold up

sticker: bur 4 burr 5 knife, label, poser, thorn 6 paster, puzzle, weapon 7 bramble

sticking: 6 viscid 8 adhering, cohesive 12 stonewalling

stickit: 6 failed 7 botched 9 imperfect 12 unsuccessful

stickle: 5 demur, rapid, rough, steep 6 higgle, pacify 7 contend, current, scruple 8 separate 9 agitation, altercate, intervene 10 perplexity 11 participate 12 perturbation

stickleback: 6 bandie(Sc.)

stickler: 6 purist, second, umpire 7 arbiter, meddler 8 mediator

sticky: 4 clit 5 gluey, gooey, humid, messy 6 claggy, clammy, clarty, slushy, viscid, wooden 7 viscous 8 adhesive 9 difficult, glutinous 10 saccharine 13 uncomfortable

stife: 4 fume 5 smell

stiff: bum 4 deep, firm, hard, high, hobo, taut 5 brave, budge, clung, dense, fixed, grave, harsh, horse, money, rigid, steep, tense, thick, tramp, woody 6 clumsy, corpse, formal, loafer, proper, robust, severe, stanch, strong, sturdy 7 awkward, buckram, cadaver, precise, starchy 8 absorbed, exacting, resolute, rigorous, stalwart, starched, stubborn 9 difficult, laborious, obstinate, unbending 10 ceremonial, consistent, inflexible, unyielding 12 pertinacious 14 uncompromising

stiff-necked: 8 stubborn 9 obstinate 12 contumacious

stiffen: set 5 brace 6 benumb, harden, starch 10 inspissate

stiffness: 5 rigor 8 rigidity 10 constraint 11 starchiness

stifle: gag 4 stop 5 check, choke 6 muffle, quench 7 repress, smother 8 strangle, suppress, throttle 9 suffocate 10 extinguish

stigma: 4 blot, mark, scar, spot 5 brand, cloud, odium, stain, taint 6 defect 7 blemish 10 projection

stigmatize: 5 brand 8 denounce

stile: 4 step 5 style 6 gnomon 9 turnstile

stiletto: 4 kill, stab 6 bodkin, dagger, stylet 9 eyeleteer

still: but, een, low, mum, tho, yet 4 also, calm, cosh, drip, even, ever, hush, lull, stop 5 allay, check, inert, quiet 6 always, distil, gentle, hushed, pacify, serene, soothe 7 appease, however, silence, subdued 8 habitual, inactive, restrain, suppress, tranquil 9 noiseless, uniformly 10 constantly, distillery, motionless, stationary, uneventful 11 continually 12 nevertheless

stillicide: 4 drip, drop

stillness: 5 peace, quiet 7 silence 8 calmness 9 quietness 11 taciturnity

stilly: 4 calm 5 quiet 7 quietly 8 silently

stilt: 4 limp, pile, pole, post 5 shaft 6 crutch

stilted: 6 formal 7 awkward, pompous 8 affected 9 bombastic, dignified 11 sententious

Stilton: 6 cheese

feature: 4 mold

Stilwell's nickname: 10 Vinegar Joe

stimulant: kat 5 drink, tonic 6 bracer 8 beverage 9 sassafras

heart: 8 cardiant, thialdin 9 digitalis, thialdine 10 adrenaline, epinephrin 11 epinephrine

in coffee: 7 caffein

in tea: 5 thein

stimulate: fan, jog, pep 4 goad, move, spur, stir, urge, whet 5 brace, elate, filip, impel, rouse, sting 6 affect, arouse, excite, fillip, incite 7 animate, enliven, inspire, provoke, quicken 8 irritate, motivate 9 encourage, galvanize, instigate 10 exhilarate, invigorate

stimulating: 5 brisk 9 innerving 12 invigorating

stimulus: 4 goad, spur 5 filip, sting 6 fillip, motive 7 impetus 9 incentive

threshold: 5 limen

sting: 4 bite, dupe, goad, mast, pain, pike, pole, post, tang, urge 5 cheat, prick, shaft, smart, wound 6 impale, incite, nettle, pierce, tingle 7 stimuli 8 irritate, stimulus 9 stimulate 10 incitement

stinger: 4 blow 5 drink

stinginess: 9 closeness, frugality, parsimony 13 niggardliness

stinging: 6 biting, bitter 7 caustic, piquant, pungent 8 piercing 10 irritating 11 acrimonious

stingo: ale, vim, zip 4 beer, zest 6 energy

stingray: 6 obispo

stingy: 4 dree(Sc.), hard, mean 5 cheap, light, sharp, stint, tight 6 biting, greedy, meager, scanty 7 miserly, niggard, nipping, selfish 8 covetous 9 illiberal, penurious 10 avaricious 11 closefisted 12 parsimonious

stinking: 4 foul, rank 5 drunk, fetid 6 putrid, rancid 7 noisome 9 offensive 10 malodorous

stint, stent: 4 duty, stay, stop, task 5 bound, cease, check, chore, delay, limit, scant, serve, spare, stunt 6 assign, desist, divide, scrimp 7 confine 8 quantity, restrain, restrict, stoppage 9 cessation, economize, restraint 10 assignment, limitation, proportion 11 restriction

stinting: 7 sparing 8 scanting

stipe: 4 stem 5 stalk 6 caudex 7 petiole

stipend: ann, fee, pay 4 hire, wage 5 annal 6 income, salary 7 payment, prebend 9 allowance 12 compensation, remuneration

stipendiary: 4 beak 7 soldier, teacher 9 clergyman, mercenary 10 magistrate

stipple: dot 6 render 7 engrave, speckle

stipulate: 5 agree 7 bargain, specify 8 contract, covenant

stipulation: 4 bond, item 6 clause, detail 7 article, bargain, proviso 8 contract, covenant 9 agreement, condition, situation 11 arrangement, undertaking

stipule of leaflet: 6 stipel

stir: ado, fan, gog, jog, mix, sir 4 busk, fuss, jail, move, plow, poke, roil, to-do 5 amove, budge, churn, doing, hurry, rally, rouse, shake, shift, shove, stoke, waken 6 arouse, awaken, bestir, bustle, excite, flurry, foment, hubbub, incite, motion, muddle, pother, prison, quetch, tumult 7 agitate, animate, blunder, disturb, flutter, inflame, provoke, trouble 8 activity, brandish, displace, movement 9 commotion, exagitate, stimulate 10 manipulate 12 penitentiary

together: 6 stodge

stirabout: 8 porridge

stirk: cow 4 bull 6 heifer 7 bullock

stirless: 10 motionless

stirps: 4 race 5 stock 6 branch

stirra: boy 6 sirrah 9 stripling

stirring: 5 astir 6 moving, tumult, uproar 7 rousing 8 activity, exciting, movement 9 agitation, animating, inspiring, thrilling 10 incitement 11 stimulating

stirrup: bar 4 ring, rope 5 clamp, strap 6 stapes 7 support 8 footrest

hood: 8 tapadera(Sp.)

straps: 8 chapelet

stirrup bone: 6 stapes

stitch: bit, hem, sew 4 loop, pain, purl 5 baste, picot, ridge, unite 6 pierce, suture, tailor 8 distance 9 embroider

knitting: 4 purl 6 feston

stitchbird: ihi

sticher: 5 sewer 6 seamer 10 dressmaker

stitchwort: 9 chickweed

stithy: 5 anvil, forge 6 smithy 8 smithery

stive: 6 stifle 9 suffocate

stiver: 4 coin 5 money 7 bristle, stagger 8 struggle

stivy: 5 close 8 stifling

stoa: 7 portico 9 colonnade

stoat: 6 ermine, weasel 8 clubster 9 clubstart

stob: 4 post, stab 5 stake 6 pierce

stock: bar, cop, log 4 band, bond, butt, fund, hive, line, post, race, rail, stem 5 banal, block, blood, brace, breed, broth, estoc, flesh, frame, hoard, stake, stick, store, stump, swell, trite, trunk 6 assets, budget, common, cravat, handle, holder, pillar, strain, supply 7 cabbage, capital, catasta, descent, extract, lineage, provide, rhizome, support 8 ancestry, bitstock, colewort, material, ordinary, stoccado 9 extirpate, hackneyed, livestock, provision, replenish, stockfish 10 foundation 11 commonplace, certificate 12 accumulation

framed on: 5 ramed

of food: 5 foray

of goods: 4 line

pair of: 5 cippi 6 cippus

preliminary: 5 scrip

racial: 8 pedigree

stockade: pen 5 etape, pound 6 corral, kennel 7 barrier, fortify, protect 8 poundage 9 enclosure

Africa: 4 boma 5 kraal 6 keddah, zareba 7 zareeba

stock exchange: 6 bourse(F.)

business: 9 arbitrage

patron: 5 buyer 6 seller, trader

stockfish: cod 4 hake, ling 5 torsk 7 haddock

stock-in-trade: 4 tool, ware 5 goods 7 capital 8 material 11 merchandise

stocked: 7 replete

stockholder: 8 investor, stockman
stocking: bas(F.) 4 hose 7 hosiery
　bishop's: 6 buskin, caliga
　cotton: 5 lisle
　footless: 7 hushion
　ornament: 5 clock
　run: 6 ladder
　soleless: 7 traheen
　worsted: 7 scogger
stockjobbing: 8 agiotage
stockman: 6 herder 7 rancher 8 beastman
stocky: fat 4 cold, stub 5 cobby, stiff 6
　chumpy, formal, stubby, sturdy 7 bunting,
　defiant 8 thickset 10 boisterous, head-
　strong
stodge: 6 trudge 7 satiate, satisfy
stodgy: 4 dull 5 bulky, heavy, thick 6 packed
　7 crammed, lumpish, stuffed, tedious 8
　thickset 9 satiating 10 uninspired 13 unin-
　teresting
stogy: 4 boot, shoe 5 cigar 6 brogan, clumsy,
　coarse
stoic: 5 porch 7 ascetic, passive 9 impassive
Stoic School: 4 Stoa
　founder: 4 Zeno
stoicism: 8 patience 11 impassivity 13 im-
　passiveness
stoit: 5 lurch 7 stagger, stumble
stoke: 4 coal, fire, fuel, poke, stab, tend 5
　stick 6 supply, thrust
stoker: 5 firer 7 fireman, greaser
　glassworks: 6 teaser
stole: fur 5 scarf 7 garment, orarion 8 vest-
　ment 13 epitrachelion
stolen: 5 shoot 6 branch, runner 9 rootstock
stolen property: 4 loot, pelf
　buyer of: 5 fence
stolid: 4 dull, firm, slow 5 beefy 6 stupid 7
　brutish, clumpse, clumpst, passive 9 im-
　passive, inanimate, unfeeling 10 impass-
　able 12 unexciteable
stolon: 6 runner 7 rhizome
stoma: 4 pore 5 mouth 7 opening, orifice
stomach: gut, maw 4 bear, craw, crop, kyte,
　vell 5 anger, belly, bingy, brook, pride, ru-
　men 6 bingey, desire, endure, gebbie(Sc.),
　resent, spirit, temper 7 abdomen, gizzard,
　gizzern 8 appetite, tolerate 9 arrogance 10
　resentment 11 inclination
　acidity: 4 acor
　bird's: maw 4 craw, crop
　comb. form: 6 gastro
　lower opening of: 7 pylorus
　pert. to: 7 gastric
　ruminant's first: 5 rumen
　ruminant's fourth: 4 read, reed 8 aboma-
　　sum, roddikin(Sc.)
　ruminant's second: 6 bonnet 9 reticulum

　ruminant's third: 6 omasum 9 manyplies
　　10 psalterium
　used as food: 5 tripe
stomach ache: 5 colic 7 gullion
stomacher: 4 gimp 7 echelle 8 forepart
stomachy: 5 proud 8 paunched, spirited 9
　irritable, obstinate, resentful 10 potbel-
　lied
stomp: See **stamp**
stone (see also **rock**): gem, pit, rub 4 bone,
　pelt, rock 5 block, brick, lapis(L.), scour,
　scrub 6 chaton, cobble, domino, harden,
　marble, mirror 7 diamond, dornick, scru-
　ple, sharpen 8 gunflint, lapidate, memo-
　rial, monolith, testicle 9 hailstone, hema-
　chate, milestone, millstone, whetstone 10
　gravestone, grindstone
　abrasive: 5 emery
　and clay: 4 sere
　architectural 6 abacus
　artificial: 8 albolite, albolith 9 granolith
　base: 6 plinth
　Biblical: 4 ezel
　broken: 6 rubble
　carved: 5 cameo
　chip of: 5 spall 6 gallet
　combining form: 5 litho
　convert into: 7 petrify
　druid: 6 sarsen
　drupe: 6 nutlet
　eagle: 5 etite
　engraving: 8 intaglio
　famous: 4 Hope, Pitt 5 Green, Mogul,
　　Sancy, Scone 6 Jonker, Nassak, Orloff, Re-
　　gent, Vargas 7 Blarney, Dresden, Jubilee,
　　Kohinur, Stewart, Tiffany 8 Braganza,
　　Cullinan, Kohinoor 9 Excelsior, Polar
　　Star 10 Florentine, Great Mogul 12 Plym-
　　outh Rock, Star of Africa 14 Star of the
　　South
　fruit: pit 4 paip 5 drupe 6 pyrene 7 putamen
　gem cutting: 6 adamas
　granitic: 6 gneiss
　grave: 5 stela, stele 6 marker, stelae, steles
　　8 memorial, monument
　grinding: 6 metate
　hammering: 8 lapstone
　hand grinding: 4 mano
　hard: 5 flint 6 quartz 7 adamant 9 chatoy-
　　ant
　heap: 4 karn 5 cairn
　hoist: 5 lewis
　hollow: 5 druse, geode
　hurling device: 9 trebucket
　implement: 4 celt 5 arrow 7 neolith
　kidney: 8 calculus
　loose: 6 gibber
　maize grinding: 4 mano
　meteoric: 8 aerolite, aerolith

monumental: 4 lech 6 menhir
of arch: 8 keystone
paving: 4 flag, slab, slat
pert. to: 7 lithoid
philosopher's: 6 carmot, elixir
precious: gem 4 keas, onyx, opal, ruby 5 beryl, pearl, topaz 6 garnet, jasper, lazuli, ligure 7 diamond, peridot 8 astroite, sapphire, tigereye 9 aromatite
pyramid-shape: 6 benben
shaped into pillars: 7 obelisk 9 monoliths
sharpening: oil 4 hone, whet
seam: dry
semiprecious: 4 jade, onyx, sard 5 agate, lapis 6 garnet, lazule, lazuli 7 olivine 8 murrhine 11 lapis lazuli
small: 6 pebble
squared: 6 ashlar
suffix: ith
to death: 8 lapidate
uncut: 4 naif
upright: 5 bauta 6 menhir
used for cameos: 4 onyx
woman turned into: 5 Niobe
worker: 5 mason 6 slater
writing: 5 slate
Stone Age tool: 4 celt 6 eolith 7 neolith 10 palaeolith
stonecrop: 5 orpin 6 orpine
stonecutter: 6 jadder
chisel: 5 drove
disease: 9 silicosis
wooden receptacle of: 7 sebilla
stonelike: 7 lithoid
stoneman: 5 cairn 9 stonehand
stones: *fine* 4 sand
heap of: 5 scree
loose: 6 eratum 8 erratice
mass of loose: 7 clitter
mound of: 4 carn, karn 5 cairn
pile of: 7 warlock
stonewall: 8 stubborn 9 obstinate 10 determined, filibuster
stonewalling: 8 sticking
stoneware: 4 gres 7 ceramic, pottery 11 earthenware
stonework: 7 masonry
stoneworker: 5 mason
stony: 4 cold, hard 5 fixed, rigid, still 7 adamant 8 obdurate, pitiless 9 petrified, unfeeling 10 inexorable, inflexible, petrifying, relentless, stupefying, unyielding 14 expressionless 15 uncompassionate
stood: 5 arose 7 endured
stooge: 4 foil
stook: 5 shock 6 pillar 12 handkerchief
stookie: 4 fool
stool: 4 base, mora, pole, seat, thew 5 bench, chair, decoy, morae, stand, stump 6 buffet, growth, throne, tiller, tripod 7 commode,

creepie, taboret, trestle 8 kingship, platform, standard, tabouret 9 footstool 10 foundation 11 chieftaincy
stoolpigeon: spy 5 decoy, narks 7 peacher 8 betrayer, informer, observer
stoop: bow, lay 4 bend, bode, lean, post, sink, tilt 5 deign, lower, porch, slant, souse, stake, stump, swoop, yield 6 alight, boggle, coorie, crouch, debase, gamble, huckle, humble, patron, pillar, pounce, submit 7 decline, degrade, descend, descent, subject, succumb, veranda 8 adherent, overcome, platform, stairway 9 prostrate, supporter 10 condescend 11 humiliation 13 condescension
stop: ho; bar, dam, end, inn, pug, wad 4 bait, bode, bung, call, calk, clog, drop, fill, halt, mend, pawl, plug, quit, stay, stem, stum, wear, weir, whoa 5 avast, basta, block, break, caulk, catch, cease, check, choke, close, delay, embar, estop, holla, hollo, parry, pause, point, repel, stall, stuff, tarry 6 alight, anchor, arrest, behold, boggle, defeat, desist, detain, finish, gravel, hinder, period, reside, scotch, stanch, stench 7 caesura, confine, counter, prevent, sojourn, station, staunch, stopper, suspend 8 caesurae(pl.), obstacle, obstruct, obturate, pinblock, preclude, prohibit, restrain, stoppage, suppress, withhold 9 barricade, cessation, hindrance, intercept, interrupt, punctuate 10 constipate 11 countermand, discontinue, obstruction 12 intermission, interruption, lodginghouse
legally: 5 estop
organ: 5 orage, viola 7 posaune 8 dulciana, gemshorn 9 rohrflote
short: 5 delay, pause 7 respite 8 interval 9 cessation 12 intermission
temporary: 5 pause
stop watch: 5 timer
stopcock: 5 valve 6 faucet
stope: 8 excavate 10 excavation
stopgap: 5 shift 6 resort 9 expedient, makeshift 10 substitute
stoppage: 4 halt 5 block, choke, hitch 6 arrest, devall, strike 7 embargo, seizure 9 cessation, detention 10 arrestment, congestion 11 obstruction
body fluid: 6 stasis
debate: 7 cloture
temporary: 5 delay, pause 6 arrest, recess 10 arrestment 12 interception, intermission, interruption
stopper: wad 4 bung, cork, plug 6 fipple 7 bouchon
stopping: 4 halt 5 block, check 7 seizure 9 detention 11 obstruction
device: 5 brake

stopple: 4 bung, cork, plug 7 stopper

storage: 4 dump 11 safekeeping
battery plate: 4 grid
bin: mow 4 loft 7 granary 8 elevator
charge: 9 demurrage
place: bin 4 shed, silo 5 attic, depot 6 cellar,
closet 7 arsenal, granary 8 cupboard, elevator 9 blood bank, reservoir, warehouse
prepare for: can
room: 6 closet, larder 7 lastage, lazaret 9
lazarette, lazaretto

storax: 5 resin 6 balsam

store: bin 4 cave, deck, deep, dose, fond,
fund, hold, mass, save, shop, stow 5 amass,
breed, cache, hoard, stock 6 amount, budget, garner, repair, shoppe, supply 7 bhandar, collect, deposit, furnish, husband,
provide, restore 8 emporium, reserves,
supplies, treasure 9 abundance, chandlery, livestock, replenish, reservoir, resources, sweetshop, warehouse 10 accumulate, collection, provisions, storehouse
12 accumulation
cargo: 5 steve
fodder: 6 ensile 8 ensilate
food: 6 market 9 sweetshop 12 delicatessen
fruit: 12 greengrocery
hidden: 5 cache
Hindu: 7 bhandar
in ground: 5 cache
in silo: 6 ensile
large: 4 raff, raft
lumber camp: van
military: PX 7 canteen 10 commissary
milk: 5 dairy
slang: 5 stash
up: 4 hive 6 garner

storehouse: mow 4 barn, bike, crib, shed,
silo 5 cache, depot, etape 7 arsenal, bhandar, camalig, camarin, granary 8 building,
magazine, treasury 9 repertory, warehouse 10 commissary 11 chalkotheke
military: 5 depot 7 arsenal 10 commissary
public: 5 depot, etape
rural: mow 4 barn, crib, shed, silo 7 granary
wool: 6 lanary

storekeeper: 6 grocer 8 bhandari, merchant, storeman 10 shopkeeper 11 al-
macenista, stockkeeper

storeroom: 4 cave, gola, loft 6 bodega, cellar
7 buttery, genizah, granary 8 basement 10
repository

stork: 4 ibis 6 simbil 7 marabou 12 xenor-
hynchus
kin of: 4 ibis 5 heron 10 hammerhead

storken: 7 congeal, stiffen

storklike: 8 pelargic

storm: wap 4 birr, blow, bura, fume, gale,
gust, hail, rage, rain, rand, rant, rave,
snow, wind 5 blizz, brash, orage 6 attack,

burran, expugn, shamal, shower, simoom,
simoon, tumult, Wester 7 assault, bluster,
borasca, borasco, bravado, cyclone, rampage, tempest, tornado, trouble 8 calamity, eruption, outburst, upheaval, violence
9 agitation, bourasque, commotion, hurricane 10 hurly-burly 11 disturbance
god: Zu 5 Rudra
revolving: 7 cyclone
sand: 6 tebbad
snow: 5 buran

stormcock: 6 petrel, thrush 9 fieldfare 10
woodpecker

stormy: 4 foul 5 dirty, gusty 6 raging 7 furious, riotous, violent 8 agitated, cluttery 9
inclement, turbulent 10 blustering, passionate, tumultuous 11 tempestuous

story: fib, lie 4 myth, plot, saga, tale, tier,
yarn 5 etage, fable, floor, rumor, solar,
soler 6 fabula, legend, record, report, sollar 7 account, article, episode, history,
narrate, parable, recital 8 anecdote, intrigue 9 falsehood, happening, narration,
narrative, statement, tradition 11 description
complication in: 4 node 5 nodus
continued: 6 serial, sequel
correspondent's: 8 dispatch
exclusive: 4 beat 5 scoop
heroic: 4 gest, saga 5 geste
kind of: 4 epic, saga, tale, yarn 5 conte, fable 6 canard, legend, script 7 mystery, no-
vella, parable, romance 8 allegory, scenario
short: 5 conte
traditional: 4 myth 6 legend
upper: 5 attic 6 garret

storyteller: 4 liar 5 Aesop 6 disour, fibber 8
narrator 9 raconteur

stot: ox 4 bull 5 bound, horse, steer 6 bounce
7 rebound, stagger, stammer, stumble,
stutter

stound: 4 ache, beat, blow, pain, pang, stun,
time 5 grief, shock, sight, smart, swoon,
throb 6 attack, benumb, bruise, moment,
period, season, sorrow, thrill, twinge 7 assault, instant, stupefy 8 astonish, occasion
10 apparition 12 astonishment, stupefaction

stoup, stoop: cup 4 cask, pail 5 basin 6
bucket, flagon, vessel 7 measure, tankard
10 aspersoria 11 aspersorium
holy-water: 8 benitier 11 cantharus-ri(pl.)
12 kantharos-roi(pl.)

stour: fit, fog 4 dust, gale, gush, hard, huge,
loud, move, pour, rise, rude, stir, vast 5
agony, chaff, drive, great, hardy, hurry,
onset, rough, shock, spray, stern, stiff,
storm, throe 6 breeze, coarse, combat,
fierce, hoarse, robust, severe, strife,

strong, tumult **7** assault, austere, conflict, meeting, quarrel, turmoil, violent **8** hardship, numerous, paroxysm **9** agitation, commotion, encounter **10** affliction, difficulty, excitement, inflexible, opposition

stourness: 7 bigness **9** greatness **10** sturdiness

stoush: 4 beat, blow **6** attack, strike, tirade **7** assault

stout: ale, fat **4** beer, bold, firm, gnat, hard **5** brave, bulky, burly, cobby, frack, freck, hardy, obese, plump, proud, shock, solid, tough **6** active, flagon, fleshy, liquor, porter, portly, robust, rotund, stable, stanch, stocky, stouty, strong, sturdy **7** defiant, haughty, violent **8** arrogant, bouncing, enduring, forceful, forcible, horsefly, insolent, powerful, resolute, stalwart, stubborn, thickset, vigorous **9** corpulent, energetic, obstinate, undaunted **10** courageous, determined, persistent **11** substantial **14** uncompromising

and rough: **5** burly

and short: **6** stocky **8** thickset

stout-hearted: 4 bold, good **5** brave **10** courageous

stoutly: 7 hardily

stoutness: 8 strength **9** hardihood

stove: 4 dent, etna, kiln **5** grate, plate, range, stave **6** cockle, heater **7** furnace **10** calefactor, glasshouse **12** conservatory

alcohol: **4** etna

charcoal: hod

grated: **8** chauffer

part: **4** oven **7** firebox, griddle

stovepipe: hat **4** flue **7** silk hat

stow: box, cut **4** cram, crop, hide, hold, mass, pack, stop, trim **5** cease, crowd, douse, dowse, grant, lodge, place, shoot, slice, stack, store, stump **6** bestow, commit **7** arrange, contain, entrust, secrete **8** restrain

cargo: **5** steve(var.) **6** steeve

stowage: 6 charge **7** packing

Stowe character: Eva, Tom **5** Topsy **6** Legree

stower: 9 stevedore

strabismus: 6 squint **8** cross-eye

Strad, Stradivarius: 6 violin

straddle: 5 hedge **6** option, sprawl **7** astride, bracket **8** bestride **11** noncommital

straddler: 5 rider

strafe: 4 waif **5** shell, stray **6** punish **7** bombard **9** castigate

straggle: 4 rove **5** stray **6** ramble, wander **7** meander

straggler: 5 tramp **8** vagabond, wanderer

straight: 4 neat **5** brant, erect, euthy, frank, ortho, plain, recti, rigid, stern **6** aright, candid, direct, graith, honest, severe **7** rightly, sincere, stretch, through, un-mixed, upright **8** accurate, directly, honestly, reliable, rigorous, sequence, unbroken, virtuous **9** correctly, honorably, undiluted **10** continuous, methodical, unmodified **11** immediately, straightway, undeviating, unqualified **12** continuously, unswervingly **13** unaccompanied, uninterrupted **15** straightforward

combining form: **5** euthy

straight course: 7 beeline

straight edge: 5 ruler

straight-faced: 7 deadpan **9** impassive

straight-haired: 12 leiotrichous **13** lissotrichous

straight man: 4 foil **6** stooge

partner: **8** comedian

straight-out: 6 direct **8** outright **11** unqualified **12** unrestrained **13** thorough-going

straight up and down: 15 perpendicularly

straighten: 5 align, aline, level, order, plumb **7** compose, rectify, unravel **11** disentangle

straightforward: 4 even, open **5** apert, frank **6** aright, candid, dexter, direct, honest **7** sincere **8** directly, outright, straight **9** foreright, outspoken **10** forthright **11** undeviating

straightforwardly: 8 directly

straightness: 9 rectitude

straightway: 4 anon **6** aright, bedene **8** directly **9** downright, forthwith **10** forthright **11** immediately

strain: air, hug, sie, sye, tax, try **4** balk, barb, bend, bind, curb, dash, gain, heft, kind, line, mood, note, ooze, race, sift, solo, sort, tone, tune, turn, urge, vein **5** begte, breed, clasp, class, exert, force, music, press, raise, shade, sieve, stock, style, tenor, touch, trace, track, trail, wield **6** burden, colate, effort, extend, extort, family, fasten, filter, injure, manner, melody, obtain, sprain, strand, stread, stress, strive, temper, thread, weaken, wrench **7** confine, descent, element, embrace, lineage, overtax, progeny, quality, squeeze, stretch, tension, trickle, variety **8** ancestry, brandish, compress, eliquate, exertion, restrain, tendency **9** begetting, character, constrain, constrict, percolate **10** distortion, generation **11** deformation, disposition

blood: **4** race **5** breed, stock **6** family **7** lineage

chief: **5** brunt

combining form: **4** tono

great: tax, tug **5** tense **6** stress **7** tension **8** exertion, overbear **11** tenterhooks

measuring device: **9** telemeter

strained: 4 taut 5 tense 6 forced 7 intense 8 weakened, wrenched 9 distorted 10 far-fetched

strainer: 4 cage, sile 5 sieve, strum, tamis 6 filter, milsey, milsie, sifter 8 colander, colature, huckmuck 10 colatorium

strait: 4 area, neck, pass 5 phare 6 narrow 7 channel, isthmus
between Labrador and Newfoundland: 9 Belle Isle

Strait of Gibraltar: 17 Pillars of Hercules

Strait of Messina rock: 6 Scylla

straits: 5 pinch, rigor 7 narrows, poverty 10 difficulty

Straits Settlements: 6 colony
city: 7 Malacca 9 Singapore 10 Georgetown
coin: 4 cent 6 dollar 13 Straits dollar
measure: pau, tun 4 para, pipe 5 parah 6 chupak, parrah 7 gantang
native state: 5 Perak 6 Johore, Pahang 8 Selangor 11 Sungei Ujong 13 Negri Sembilan
weight: 4 chee, hoon, saga 5 bedur, bhara, catty, koyan, picul, tahil

straiten: 5 limit 6 hamper 7 confine 8 contract, distress, restrict 9 embarrass

strait-jacket: 8 camisole

strait-laced: 5 stiff 6 severe, strict 8 stubborn 9 obstinate, puritanic 10 restricted 11 constrained 14 overscrupulous

strake: rut 4 band 5 crack 6 loiter, streak, stripe, stroll, trough, wander 7 stretch

stramineous: 6 chaffy, strawy 9 straw-like, valueless

strand: sea 4 bank, quay, wire 5 beach, fiber, shore, wharf 6 gutter, maroon, region, stream, thread 7 channel, current 8 filament

stranded: 6 ashore 7 aground, beached 8 castaway, marooned

strange: odd 4 fell, rare, unco 5 alien, droll, eerie, fremd, novel, queer 6 exotic, quaint 7 curious, distant, erratic, foreign, uncanny, unknown, unusual 8 abnormal, estrange, fanciful, peculiar, reserved, singular, uncommon 9 couthless, different, eccentric, unnatural 10 outlandish, unfamiliar, unfriendly 12 unaccustomed, unacquainted 13 extraordinary, inexperienced, preternatural
combining form: xen 4 xeno
language: 4 cant 5 lingo 6 jargon 7 dialect

strangely: 5 oddly 6 featly

stranger: goy 5 alien, guest, odder 6 ganger, novice 7 comical, visitor 8 emigrant, estrange, intruder, newcomer, outsider 9 estranger, foreigner, outlander 10 tramontane 12 intermeddler
comb. form: 4 xeno

strangle: 4 kill, slay 5 choke, grane 6 stifle 7 garrote, repress 8 garrotte, suppress, throttle 9 suffocate

strangulate: 5 choke 8 compress, obstruct, strangle 9 constrict

strap: bar, fit, tie 4 band, beat, belt, bind, hang, rein, riem, whip 5 girth, groom, strip, strop, thong 6 billet, chaser, credit, enarme, fillet, halter, latigo, ligule, punish, secure 7 furnish, laniard, lanyard, sharpen 8 chastise
kind of: 4 jess, taws 5 guige, leash, strop, tawse, thong 6 chaser, enarme 8 bretelle 10 boondoggle

strap-shaped: 6 lorate 7 ligular 8 ligulate 9 ligulated

strapping: 6 robust, strong 7 beating 9 thrashing

strass: 5 glass, paste

strata (see also **stratum**): *geological:* 4 lias
later: 7 neozoic
social: 7 classes

stratagem: 4 coup, ruse, wile 5 cheat, fetch, fraud, trick 6 blench, device, humbug, scheme 7 finesse 8 artifice, maneuver 9 chicanery, deception, execution, slaughter 10 artfulness
smart: 8 liripipe, liripoop

strategic: 9 favorable 12 advantageous

strategy: 8 artifice, intrigue, maneuver

stratification: 7 bedding

stratum: bed 5 layer, level 6 couche 7 section 8 division
thin: 4 seam

Strauss work: 5 waltz 6 Salome 7 Electra

stravagant: 7 vagrant 11 extravagant, irrelevance

stravage, stravaig: 6 stroll, wander 7 saunter

Stravinsky work: 8 Firebird 10 Petrouchka

straw: hat, wap 4 gloy, mote, pipe, rush 5 chaff, strae, stree 6 fescue, litter, trifle 9 worthless, yellowish 11 meaningless 12 churchwarden
bed: 6 pallet
bundle of: 6 batten
coat: 4 mino
color: 6 flaxen
colored: 11 stramineous
for hats: 6 sennit
half rotten: 5 mulch
load of: 5 barth
plaited: 6 sennit
threshing floor: 6 bhossa
to protect plants: 5 mulch
used for hats: 7 sabutan
waxed: 6 strass
weaving: 5 rafia

straw in the wind: 4 omen, sign 7 portent
straw vote: 4 poll
strawberry: 6 fraise, runner 8 fragaria
strawlike: 11 stramineous
stray: err, gad 4 cavy, roam, rove, waif 5
  range 6 casual, course, errant, estray, random, stroll, swerve, wander 7 decline, deviate, digress, forlorn, habitat, saunter 8
  detached, distract, isolated, straggle 9
  straggler, unrelated 10 incidental, occasional 12 unenumerated
  calf: 4 dogy 5 dogie
straying: 6 astray 7 erratic 8 aberrant 9
  deviation, erroneous
streak: rub 4 line, rung, vein, wale 5 fleck,
  freak, garle, hurry, layer, lined, round,
  smear, spell, trace, trait 6 period, polish,
  smooth, strain, strake, stripe, stroke 7
  stratum, striped 8 discolor
  mottled: roe
  narrow: 5 stria 6 striae
  regular: 6 stripe
streaked: 4 liny 6 marked 7 alarmed, brin-
  dle, striped, worried 8 brindled 10 variegated
streaky: 4 liny 5 liney, mixed 6 uneven 8
  variable
stream: ea; run 4 burn, flow, flux, ford, gote,
  gush, rill, rush 5 bache, bayou, bourn,
  brook, creek, fleam, floss, flume, fluor,
  force, issue, river, speed, trend 6 amount,
  bourne, course, fluent, runnel 7 channel,
  current, rivulet 8 affluent 9 anabranch 11
  watercourse
  diminutive: run 4 race 5 brook 6 rillet 7
  rivulet 9 streamlet
  dry bed: 6 arroyo
  lava: 6 coulee
  living in: 9 amphibian, rheophile
  ravine: 4 ghyl, gill
  rushing: jet 7 torrent
  small: run 4 rill, sike 5 brook, siket 6 rillet,
  runlet
  sound: 4 purl 6 murmur
  underground: aar
  upper part of: 6 source 9 headwater
streamer: jet 4 flag 5 strip 6 guidon, ribbon
  7 feather, pendant, pennant 8 banderol,
  headline 9 banderole
streamlet: 4 rill 5 brook 6 rillet, runlet, runnel 7 freshet, rivulet
streamline curve: 10 lissoneoid
streck: 6 direct 8 straight
streel: 7 saunter 8 slattern, straggle
street: rew(Sc.), way 4 char, lane, road 5
  calle, chare 6 avenue, causey, spread 7 estreat, highway, roadway, strasse(G.) 8
  chaussee, contrada, contrade(pl.), notebook 9 boulevard 12 thoroughfare

  Chinese: 6 hutung
  degraded: 4 slum
  ditch: 6 gutter
  India: 5 chawk, chowk
  narrow: 5 alley, place
street roister: mun
street urchin: 4 arab 5 gamin
streetcar: 4 tram 7 trolley
  driver: 8 motorman
streetwalker: 6 hooker 10 prostitute
strength: arm 4 beef, iron, thew 5 brawn,
  force, might, power, vigor 6 energy, foison
  7 ability, potency, stamina, sthenia 8 capacity, firmness, solidity 9 coherence, endurance, fortitude, intensity, lustiness,
  puissance, stoutness, toughness, vehemence 10 heartiness, robustness, stronghold 14 impregnability
  deprive of: 7 unnerve
  diminish: 6 dilute
  electric current: 8 amperage
  liquor: 5 proof
  loss: 8 asthenia
  military: 8 armament
  of character: 4 guts, sand 9 fortitude
  poetic: 9 puissance
  regain: 5 rally
  solution: 5 titer, titre
  source of: 5 asset
strengthen: 4 back, bind, frap, help, prop 5
  brace, nerve, steel 6 clench, deepen, endure 7 afforce, comfort, confirm, depthen,
  educate, fortify, toughen 8 roborate 9 encourage, reinforce 10 invigorate 11 consolidate
  with alcohol: 5 spike 7 fortify
strengthener: 6 gusset
strengthening: 7 bracing 8 roborant 10
  nourishing, supporting, sustaining 11 corroborant
strenuous: 4 hard 5 eager 6 active, ardent,
  severe 7 arduous, zealous 8 vigorous 9 energetic
strepent: 4 loud 5 noisy
streperous: 4 loud 5 harsh, noisy 7 noisily 9
  turbulent 10 boisterous
strepitant: 5 noisy 9 clamorous 10 strepi-
  tous
stress: 5 brunt, force, labor 6 accent, strain
  7 afflict, amplify, overtax, tension, urgency 8 ampliate, distrain, distress, emphasis, exertion, pressure 9 emphasize, intensity 10 constraint, importance, overstrain, resistence 12 significance 13 inconvenience
  mechanical: 8 erossure
  metrical: 5 ictus
  music: 6 accent
  voice: 5 arsis 6 accent

stretch: eke 4 hang, span, walk 5 reach, retch, space, toise, tract 6 course, dilate, effort, expand, extend, period, spread, strain 7 distend, enlarge, execute, expanse, tension 8 elongate, sentence 9 direction, extension 10 exaggerate
injuriously: 6 sprain
out: eke, lie, out
the neck: 5 crane

stretched: *out:* 6 craned 7 porrect 8 extended, prolated 9 elongated
tight: 4 taut 5 tense
while drying: 8 tentered

stretcher: 6 litter, racker 8 ringhead
neck: 6 craner

stretchy: 7 elastic, rubbery 9 resilient

strew: 6 litter, spread 7 diffuse, scatter 8 disperse, sprinkle 9 bespatter, broadcast 10 besprinkle 11 disseminate

strewing: 4 seme

stria: 4 band, line 5 ridge 6 fillet, furrow, groove, hollow, streak, stripe 7 channel 9 striation

striate: 5 lined 7 grooved 8 furrowed

stricken (see also **strike**): 7 smitten, wounded 13 incapacitated

strickle: 5 rifle 7 pattern 8 template

strict: 4 blue, hard 5 close, exact, harsh, rigid, stern, tense, tight 6 entire, narrow, severe 7 ascetic, austere, binding, correct, perfect, precise 8 absolute, accurate, intimate, limiting, rigorous, straight 9 confining, puritanic, stringent 10 compressed, forbidding, inexorable, inflexible, relentless, scrupulous 11 constricted, punctilious, puritanical, restricting, straitlaced, undeviating 14 uncompromising
disciplinarian: 8 martinet
discipline: 13 regimentation

striction: 12 constriction

strictly: 6 narrow 7 closely 9 precisely 10 positively, rigorously 11 stringently

strictness: 5 rigor 9 closeness
in law: 8 legalism

stricture: 4 sign 5 spark, touch, trace 7 binding, censure, closing 9 criticism 11 contraction 13 animadversion

strid: 5 gorge 6 ravine

stride: 4 step, walk 5 stalk 7 advance 8 bestride, progress, straddle 11 advancement

strident: 5 harsh 6 shrill 7 grating, raucous, yelling 11 cacophonous

stridor: 5 noise

stridulate: 5 cheep, chirk, chirp, creak, crick 7 clitter

strife: war 4 bait, bate, feud 5 fight, flite, flyte, noise, strow 6 combat, debate, estrif 7 contest, discord, hurling, quarrel 8 conflict, endeavor, exertion, struggle 9 emulation 10 contention 11 altercation, competition, controversy
about mere words: 9 logomachy
civil: 6 stasis

striffen: 4 skin 8 membrane

strigil: 7 fluting

strigose, strigous: 5 sharp 6 hispid

strike: bat, bob, box, cob, cop, dab, dad, hew, hit, lam, pat, ram, rap, wap 4 baff, bang, bash, bean, beat, biff, bill, bump, bunt, chap, cope, coup, cuff, dash, daub, daud, dint, dunt, fist, flap, flog, frap, gird, gowf, hurl, hurt, knap, lash, pelt, rout, slap, slay, swat 5 clash, clink, clout, douse, dowse, dunch, fight, filch, gowff, impel, knock, punch, skelp, skite, slash, smear, smite, spank, swipe, touch, trend, whang 6 assail, attack, attain, bounce, buffet, fettle, hammer, hartal, punish, strike, stroke 7 afflict, cacanny, collide, impinge, impress 8 discover, struggle
a balance: 5 agree 6 settle 10 compromise
a mean: 7 average
against: 4 bump 5 crash 7 collide
and rebound: 5 carom 6 carrom 9 carambole
demonstrator: 6 picket
down: 4 fell, kill 5 floor 7 disable
dumb: 4 stun
feature: 7 lockout
gently: dab, pat 4 bump, putt
heavily: lam, ram 4 bash, slog, slug
obliquely: 5 carom
on head: 4 bean
out: fan 4 dele 5 elide, erase 6 cancel, delete 9 eliminate
prepare to: 4 coil
producing musical sound: 5 chime
series of blows: 4 pelt
settler: 8 mediator
together: 5 clash, crash 7 collide
up: 5 begin, start 8 commence
violently: ram 4 slam
with fist: 4 plug 5 punch, pound
with head: 4 butt
with wonder: awe 7 astound

strikebreaker: rat 4 fink, goon, scab

striker: 4 scab, tern 6 batman, batter, helper, hitter, smiter 7 batsman, clapper, mobster 8 blackleg 9 assistant, harpooner

striking: 4 dint 7 salient 8 stunning 9 arresting, effective 10 noticeable, remarkable, surprising 11 conspicuous
effect: 5 eclat

strind: 4 cast, race 6 strain 7 kindred, progeny 9 offspring 10 generation 11 disposition

string: 4 band, cord, hoax, josh, line 5 bound, braid, chain, jolly, strip, twine 6 series, thread 10 conditions, succession 14 qualifications

course: 6 guidon

kinds of: 4 wire 5 lacet, snare 6 amenta, hypate, lachet 7 amentum, langate

of beads: 6 rosary 8 necklace

up: 4 hang, lace 5 lynch

string instrument: uke 4 harp, lute, lyre 5 banjo, cello, piano, viola 6 fiddle, guitar, spinet, violin, zither 7 ukalele, ukelele 8 mandolin 11 harpsichord

old: 4 lute, lyre 6 spinet 8 psaltery 11 harpsichord

stringency: 5 force, rigor 7 cogency 8 scarcity, severity 9 tightness 10 strictness

stringent: 4 hard, ropy 5 rigid, tense, tight 6 cogent, severe, strict 7 binding, extreme 10 convincing 11 restrictive

stringer: tie 4 rope, vein, wire 5 irons 6 string, timber 8 filament 9 handcuffs, libertine 11 stringpiece

stringy: 4 ropy 5 gluey 6 sinewy, viscid 7 fibrous, viscous 11 filamentous

strip: bar, rob, tab, tag, top 4 band, bare, bark, belt, doff, flay, hull, husk, peel, pull, skin, tear 5 clear, flake, fleck, pluck, shred, spoil, swath, unrig 6 border, denude, devest, divest, expose, flense, reduce, remove, runway, swathe 7 bandage, bandeau, bereave, degrade, deprive, despoil, disrobe, pillage, plunder, uncloak, uncover, undress, unleave 8 bandeaux(pl.), denudate, disarray, headland, outstrip, separate 9 dismantle, excoriate 10 disfurnish, dispossess 11 debenzolize, decorticate

blubber: 6 flense

kinds of: 4 came, cove, lead, rand, riem, tirr 5 cleat, ridge, stave 6 inwale, reglet 7 gunwale

leather: 4 welt 5 thong 6 latigo 7 belting

narrow: 4 slat, tape 5 reeve, strap 7 bandeau 8 bandeaux(pl.)

wooden: rib 4 lath, slat 5 stave 6 reglet

strip tease dancer: 9 ecdysiast

stripe: bar, roe 4 band, beat, belt, blow, kind, lash, line, mark, sort, type, wale, weal, welt, zone 5 chest, stria, strip 6 border, frenum, streak, strike, stroke, thrust 7 chevron, fraenum, lineate, pattern, rivulet 8 division 9 character

striped: 5 bandy 6 banded, barred 7 lineate, vittate 8 bayadere, streaked

animal: 5 bongo, zebra

cloth: 6 madras

stripling: boy, lad 5 chiel, youth 6 chield

stripped: 4 bare, nude 6 picked

by trickery: 7 buncoed, bunkoed, fleeced

strive: aim, hie, tew, try, tug, vie 4 seek, toil 5 bandy, ensue, fight, labor, rival 6 battle,

buffet, resist, strain 7 compete, contend, contest, emulate 8 contrast, endeavor, struggle

striving: 5 nisus

strobile: 4 chat, cone

strobilophyta: 4 cone

strockle: 6 shovel

stroil: 5 grass, power, weeds 9 dexterity 10 capability

stroke: bat, coy, fit, hew, hit, pat, pet, rub 4 baff, beat, blow, chap, coup, dash, ding, dint, flip, gowf, hurt, lash, mark, milk, oner, shot, walk, whet 5 chare, douse, dowse, flack, fluke, gowff, ictus, knock, power, pulse, rower, strut, throb, trait 6 attack, caress, effort, fondle, ictuse, impact, injury, soothe, stride 7 seizure, sharpen, whample 8 apoplexy, disaster 9 influence

brilliant: ace 4 coup

cutting: 4 chop 5 slice

golf: 4 baff

kinds of: 5 eagle, cerif, serif, wedge 6 birdie 7 virgule

of luck: 8 windfall

short: 4 flip, putt 5 whisk

stroll: 4 mosy, roam, rove, walk 5 mosey, range, stray, tramp 6 dacker, daiker, dander, ramble, soodle, wander 7 saunter 8 flanerie

stroller: 4 cart, pram 5 actor, tramp 6 beggar, gocart, player, shuler 7 peddlar, peddler, shuiler, vagrant 8 bohemian, carriage, wanderer 9 saunterer

strolling: 7 roaming 8 flanerie, fugitive

Stromboli: 6 island 7 volcano

stromming: 7 herring

strone: 4 hill 5 spout 6 stream

strong: fit, hot 4 able, bold, dure, elon, fere, firm, fort, hale, hard, rank, warm, wiry 5 bonny, clear, eager, frack, freck, fresh, great, gross, hardy, heavy, large, lusty, solid, sound, stout, tough, yauld 6 active, ardent, bonnie, brawny, buckra, cogent, feckle, mighty, potent, robust, rugged, sinewy, stable, stouty, strict, sturdy 7 buirdly, durable, fertile, greatly, huffcap, humming, intense, sthenic, violent, zealous 8 athletic, distinct, flagrant, forceful, forcible, muscular, powerful, puissant, resonant, rigorous, severely, stalwart, strongly, vehement, vigorous 9 Atlantean, difficult, effective, impetuous, important, strapping, violently 10 boisterous, forthright, nourishing, outrageous, passionate, persuasive, productive, pronounced, remarkable 11 excessively 12 concentrated

upward movement: 5 surge

strong-arm: rob 4 beat, thug 5 force, power
  7 assault, violent 8 violence
  man: 4 goon 7 bouncer
strong cloth: 5 scrim
strong man: *Biblical:* 6 Samson 7 Sampson
  legendary: 5 Atlas
strong point: 5 forte
strong-smelling: 4 foul, rank 5 fetid 6 foetid
  8 mephitic, stinking
strongbox: 4 case, safe 5 chest, vault
stronghold: 4 fort, hold, keep 5 tower 6 castle 7 citadel, fortify 8 fasthold, fastness,
  fortress 13 fortification
strongly: 5 bigly 6 stably 8 heartily
strop: 4 hone, whet 7 sharpen
strophe: 6 stanza 10 heptastich
stroud: 5 harsh 6 morose 7 blanket
strow: 5 strew 6 strife 7 turmoil 9 confusion
  11 disturbance
stroygood: 7 wastrel 11 spendthrift
strub: rob 5 strip 7 despoil
strubbly: 6 untidy 7 unkempt
struck: 4 smit 5 smote 7 smitten 8 punished
  with amazement: 6 aghast
  with small missiles: 6 pelted
  with sudden fear: 7 alarmed
  with terror: 6 aghast
  with wonder: 6 aghast
struck out: 5 deled 6 elided, erased, fanned
  7 deleted
struck smartly: 9 percussed
structural quality: 7 texture
structure: dam 4 form 5 frame 6 bridge,
  format, make-up 7 edifice, texture 8 building, bulkhead 9 formation 11 arrangement, composition, fabricature 12 constitution, construction
  abnormal: 12 malformation
  calcareous: 5 coral
  conical: 7 pyramid
  crown-like: 6 corona
  curved: 4 arch
  filamentous: 4 hair
  floating: 4 raft
  funeral: 10 catafalque
  hallowed: 6 bethel, chapel, church, temple
    8 basilica 9 cathedral, synagogue 10 taber-
    nacle
  high: 5 tower
  human: 8 physique
  keel-like: 6 carina
  latticework: 7 trellis
  looplike: 4 ansa
  monumental: 5 pylon
  on roof: 6 cupola, dormer 9 penthouse
  Oriental: 6 pagoda
  original: 6 isogen
  osseous: 4 bone
  over obstacles: 6 bridge

  pergola-like: 6 ramada
  pert. to: 8 tectonic
  projecting into water: 4 jiti 5 jetty 6 jettee
  raised: 4 dais 5 altar, stage 8 platform
  sacrificial: 5 altar
  sheltering: cot 4 cote
  supporting: 4 pier
  tall: 5 tower 7 steeple 9 campanile
  tent-like: 10 tabernacle
  white: 6 albedo
strudel: 6 pastry
struggle: tug, vie 4 agon, cope, frab, wade 5
  fight, heave, labor 6 battle, buckle, bustle,
  combat, effort, Peniel, strife, strike, strive,
  throes, tussle, widdle 7 bargain, barrace,
  contend, contest, flounce, scuffle, warfare,
  wauchle, wrestle 8 conflict, endeavor, exertion, flounder, scraffle, scramble 10 contention, difficulty
  a deux: 4 duel
  helplessly: 8 flounder
struggling: 12 colluctation
struma: 6 goiter, goitre
strummed: 8 thrummed
strumpet: 4 brim 5 belie, wench 6 blowen,
  harlot 7 cocotte, debauch, slander 8 harridan 10 prostitute
strung: 6 beaded
  highly: 5 tense 7 nervous
strunt: 4 dock 5 pique, strut, stump 6 liquor
  7 stubble
strut: 4 brag, cock, gait, step, walk 5 brace,
  bulge, swell 6 parade, stride, strife, strunt,
  thrust 7 distend, peacock, provide, stiffen,
  stretch, support, swagger, wrangle 8 protrude 10 contention 11 protuberant
struthious: 4 emus 5 rheas 6 ratite 9 os-
  triches
stub: pen 4 beat, dolt 5 crush, drive, squat,
  stump 6 coupon, stocky 7 feather, remnant 8 thickset 9 blockhead, extirpate 11
  counterfoil
stubble: bun 6 strunt 7 gratten, gratton 8
  eelgrass
  field: 5 rowen
stubborn: set 4 rude 5 fixed, hardy, harsh,
  rough, tough 6 coarse, dogged, mulish,
  sturdy 7 restive 8 obdurate, perverse, resolute, starkish, vigorous 9 camsteary, camsteery, difficult, obstinate, pigheaded 10
  bullheaded, calcitrant, determined, hardheaded, headstrong, inflexible, refractory,
  unyielding 11 intractable 12 pertinacious
stubborness: 8 tenacity 9 contumacy, obsti-
  nacy 12 perverseness
stubby: 5 squat 6 stocky, stumpy 8 thickset
stuck: See **stick**
stuck in the mud: 7 bemired

stuck-up: 4 vain 7 haughty 8 arrogant, snobbish 9 conceited 12 supercilious 13 self-important

stud: dot, pin, rod 4 boss, knob, post, stem, stub 5 adorn, aglet, beset, brace, haras, study, stump 6 aiglet, button, pillar 7 chaplet, support 9 studhorse 10 besprinkle
farm: 5 haras
for shoe: 7 hobnail
with jewels: 5 engem
with radiating bodies: 6 enstar

student: 5 eleve(F.), pupil 6 bursar 7 educand, learner 8 disciple, observer
according to grade: 6 termer
agricultural college: 5 Aggie
college: 4 soph 6 junior, senior 8 freshman 9 sophomore
divinity: 9 theologue 10 theologian
fellow: 9 classmate
first-year: 5 Fuchs(G.)
former: 7 dropout 8 graduate
fourth-year: 6 senior
girl: 4 coed
group: 5 class
hall: 5 burse 9 dormitory
in charge: 7 monitor
law: 8 stagiary
medical: 6 intern 7 interne
military: 5 cadet, plebe
naval academy: 5 cadet 10 midshipman
of birds: 13 ornithologist
of crime: 10 penologist 13 criminologist
of heavens: 13 uranographist
of proverbs: 14 paroemiologist
of punishment: 10 penologist
of relics: 13 archaeologist
of reptiles: 13 herpetologist
of spiders: 13 arachnologist
Oxford: 8 commoner
residence: 5 house 6 hostel 9 dormitory
room: 7 seminar
second-year: 9 sophomore
stipend paid: 6 bursar
third-year: 6 junior
West Point: 5 cadet, plebe

studied: 5 pored 6 intent 7 learned, planned 8 designed, inclined, reasoned 10 ceremonial, deliberate 12 premeditated

studies: *academic:* 4 arts 7 science 10 humanities
advanced: 7 seminar 8 graduate
chosen by students: 9 electives
series of: 6 course

studio: 7 atelier, bottega 8 botteghe, workshop 11 ergasterion

studious: 5 booky 7 bookish, devoted, studied 8 diligent, sedulous 9 assiduous, scholarly 10 deliberate 13 contemplative

study: con, den, mug 4 bone, muse, muzz, pore, read, scan 5 grind 6 lesson, peruse, ponder 7 analyse, analyze, canvass, croquis, examine 8 consider, meditate 11 contemplate 13 consideration, contemplation
animals: 9 zoography
bees: 8 apiology
Bible: 9 isagogics
by lamplight: 9 lucubrate
closely: con 4 pore 7 examine
course: 7 seminar
fingerprints: 13 dactylography
fixed course: 4 rote
flowers: 12 anthoecology
handwriting: 10 graphology
hard: 4 bone
horses: 9 hippology
human generations: 15 anthropogenesis
insect's habits: 10 entomology
laborious: 11 lucubration
mountains: 7 orology
musical: 5 etude
optional: 8 elective
population: 10 larithmics
punishment: 8 penology
sacred edifices: 7 naology
sacred images: 9 iconology
sermons: 10 homiletics
wines: 7 enology
words: 9 etymology

stufe: 4 step 6 degree

stuff: pad, ram, wad 4 copy, cram, fill, gaum, junk, pang 5 crowd, farce, force, grain, pulse, steve 6 amount, fabric, graith, matter, refuse, stifle, supply 7 bombast, element, essence, filling, mixture, portion 8 material, medicine, nonsense, overload, stuffing 9 character, principle, substance, suffocate
full: 4 glut 5 gorge 6 stodge 7 satiate
harvested grain: 7 stubble
sticky: goo
worthless: 4 gear 7 hogwash

stuffed: 6 bourre, stodgy 7 bombast, replete 8 farctate

stuffing: 7 padding 8 dressing 9 forcemeat
prepare with: 8 marinate

stuffy: fat 4 dull, prim 5 angry, close, fubsy, fuggy, stout, sulky 6 froust, frowst, stodgy 8 resolute 9 obstinate 10 mettlesome, old-fogyish 11 strait-laced 12 conservative, old-fashioned

stuggy: 5 short 6 stodgy, sturdy 8 thickset

Stuka: 6 bomber

stulm: 4 adit 8 entrance

stultiloquy: 4 talk 6 babble

stum: 4 must 5 grape, juice

stumble: err 4 fall, slip, trip 5 lurch 6 boggle, chance, faffle, falter, happen, offend 7 blunder, failure, founder, perplex, scrupple, stagger 8 confound, flounder

stumbling: 7 hurting
stumbling block: 8 obstacle 9 hindrance 10 impediment 11 obstruction
stump: cob, lop 4 butt, dare, foil, grub, snag, stab, stub 5 block, clump 6 baffle, corner, hobble, pillar, puzzle, strunt, thwart, travel 7 canvass, nonplus, perplex, rostrum, stumble 8 platform 9 challenge 11 electioneer
stumps: 4 legs
stumpy: 5 bunty 6 stubby 8 thickset
stun: 4 bowl, daze, tear 5 amaze, aston, daunt, daver, deave, dizzy, dover, shock 6 appall, astone, astony, benumb, bruise, crease, deaden, deafen 7 astound, dammish, scratch, stupefy 8 astonish, bewilder 9 dumbfound, overpower, overwhelm
stung (see also **sting**): 7 smarted
stunned: 10 astonished
stunning: 7 stylish 8 dazzling 9 beautiful 10 foudroyant
stunt: act 4 feat 5 angry, blast, blunt, check, cramp, crowl, dwarf, stamp, whale 6 abrupt, hinder 7 curtail, exploit 8 stubborn 10 undersized 11 performance
gymnastic: kip 4 kipp 10 handspring
stunted: 4 runt
stunty: 5 short 6 flashy, stocky 7 dwarfed
stupa: 5 mound, tower 6 shrine
lamaism: 7 chorten
stupe: 6 foment
stupefacient: 4 drug 8 narcotic 10 stupefying
stupefied: 8 benumbed 9 inebriate
stupefy: fox, sot 4 baze, daze, dope, doze, drug, dull, dunt, numb, stun 5 amaze, aston, besot, blunt, daunt, daver, deave, shock 6 astone, bedaze, bemuse, benumb, muddle 7 astound, confuse 8 astonish, bewilder, confound 10 incrassate
with drink: 6 fuddle
stupefying: 8 bemusing
stupend: 4 stun 7 astound, stupefy 10 stupendous
stupendous: 5 great 7 amazing, immense 8 enormous 9 monstrous, wonderful 10 astounding 11 astonishing 12 overpowering, overwhelming
stupent: 9 stupefied 11 dumbfounded
stupid: 4 bete, clod, dull, dumb, dunt, guam, lewd, slow 5 besot, blunt, booby, crass, dazed, dense, dizzy, goosy, heavy, inane, sumph 6 assish, barren, beetle, boring, bovine, dawkin, doiled, doited, drowsey, goosey, hebete, lurdan, oafish, obtuse, simple, stolid, torpid 7 asinine, brutish, buzzard, calvish, daffish, doldrum, doltish, duffing, dullard, fatuous, foolish, foppish, glaiket, glaikit, gomerel, goosish, gullish, lurdane, prosaic, stunned, vacuous, witless 8 anserine, anserous, backward, bayardly, blockish, boeotian, cloddish, deadened, footless, headless, retarded, sluggish 9 blocklike, bourgeois, brainless, codheaded, inanimate, insensate, insipient, plumbeous, pointless, senseless, stupefied 10 hardwitted, hulver-head, irrational, slow-witted 11 claybrained, heavy-headed 12 buffleheaded 13 unintelligent, uninteresting
person: ass, sap 4 clod, clot, coot, dolt, dope, fool, jerk, loon 5 dunce, goose, idiot, moron, ninny 7 dullard, fathead 8 numskull 9 blockhead
render: 8 hebetate
stupidity: 6 betise, stupor 7 density, fatuity 8 dullness, hebetude, idiotism, numbness 9 crassness 12 astonishment, indifference, stupefaction 13 insensibility
stupidly: 10 bullheaded
stupor: fog 4 coma, damp, dote 5 sopor 6 trance 8 lethargy
comb. form: 5 narco
pert. to: 7 carotic, narcose
stuprate: 6 ravish 7 debauch
sturdy: gid, set 4 buff, firm 5 felon, hardy, harsh, lusty, sound, stern, stiff, stout 6 brawny, robust, rugged, rustic, stable, steady, strong 7 violent 8 obdurate, resolute, stalwart, stubborn, vigorous 9 rigidness, obstinate 10 courageous, determined, unyielding 12 stupefaction
sturdy and stout: 5 burly
sturgeon: 6 beluga
small: 7 sterlet
white: 6 beluga
roe: 6 caviar
sturt: vex 4 stir 5 annoy 6 strife 7 startle, trouble 11 disturbance
sturtin, sturtan: 9 staggered 10 frightened
stutter: 7 stammer
stuttering: 8 psellism 9 psellisum
sty, stye: pen 4 boil, soar 5 climb, lodge, mount, stair, steps, stile 6 ascend, aspire, ladder 8 swelling 9 enclosure
stygian: 6 gloomy 7 hellish 8 infernal
style: air, dub, pen, pin, ton 4 call, garb, gere, kind, mode, name, sort, term, type 5 vogue 6 format, gnomon, graver, manner, method, needle, phrase, stylus 7 alamode, diction, entitle, fashion, variety 8 demeanor 9 designate, execution 10 denominate 12 characterize, construction
architecture: 5 Doric, Greek, Ionic, Roman, Saxon 6 Gothic, Norman 7 Italian 8 Colonial, Georgian, Monterey 9 Byzantine 10 Corinthian, Romanesque 11 Elizabethan, Renaissance 13 Mediterranean
art: 5 genre

artistic: **5** gusto
dress: **5** get-up
fantastic: **6** rococo **7** baroque
furniture: **6** Empire
lofty: **4** epic
oratorical: **10** rhetorical
out of: **5** dated, passe
painting: **5** genre
penmanship: **4** hand
performance: **9** execution
styled: 5 named **6** called, formed, yclept
stylet: pro **5** organ, probe **6** dagger **7** poniard **8** stiletto **9** appendage
surgical: **6** trocar
stylish: 4 chic, tony **5** dashy, nifty, smart, swell **6** classy, dressy, jaunty, modish, spiffy, swanky **7** alamode, dashing, doggish, genteel, knowing, swagger **11** fashionable
stylist: 7 modiste
stylites: 7 hermits **8** ascetics
styloid: 8 belonoid
stymie, stymy: 5 block **6** hinder, impede **8** obstruct
Stymphalus: *daughter:* **10** Parthenope
enemy: **6** Pelops
father: **6** Elatus
mother: **7** Laodice
son: **6** Gortys **8** Agamedes
styptic: 4 alum **10** astringent
Styx: 5 nymph, river
father: **7** Oceanus
ferryman: **6** Charon
locale: **5** Hades
mother: **6** Tethys
pert. to: **7** stygian
suant: 4 even **5** grave, quiet **6** demure, placid, smooth, steady **7** equable, regular **9** agreeable, following
suasion: 10 persuasion
suasive: 10 convincing, persuasive
suave: 4 easy, oily, smug **5** bland, civil, soapy, sweet **6** polite, smooth, urbane **7** fulsome **8** gracious, mannered, pleasant, polished, unctuous **9** agreeable **12** ingratiating
suavity: 6 comity **7** amenity **8** urbanity **10** politeness **12** complaisance
sub: 9 auxiliary, submarine
sub rosa: 8 covertly, secretly
subarctic forest: 5 taiga
subbase: 6 plinth
subdivide: 5 carve, mince **8** separate
subdivision: 6 sector, suburb **10** department
defensive position: **6** sector
lateral: **5** aisle
rocks: **5** range
subdue: cow **4** bend, quay, tame **5** accoy, allay, amate, atill, break, charm, crush,

daunt, dompt, lower, quell, sober **6** adaunt, bridle, disarm, dismay, evince, master, mellow, reduce, soften, steady, subact **7** affaite, chasten, conquer, control, repress, squelch **8** convince, diminish, overcome, suppress, surmount, vanquish **9** captivate, castigate, overpower, subjugate
suber: 4 cork
subjacent: 10 underlying
subject: try **4** text **5** basis, cause, prone, theme, topic **6** liable, matter, motive, phrase, reason, submit, vassal **7** article, citizen, conquer, exposed, reality **8** disposed, incident, inferior, obedient **9** dependent, subjugate, substance **10** contingent, predispose, submissive, substratum **11** conditional, subordinate
of discourse: **5** theme, topic
of disease: **4** case **7** patient
of lawsuit: res
of verb: **4** noun
to abuse: **6** revile
to argument: **4** moot
to authority: **6** master
to be taught: **10** didascalic
to change: **7** mutable
to choice: **8** elective
to control: **7** rulable
to death: **6** mortal
to depression: **5** moody
to discussion: **4** moot **9** debatable
to dislike: **8** aversion
to ill treatment: **6** misuse
to mistakes: **7** erratic
to taxation: **8** reteable
to whirling action: **11** centifugate
subjection: 8 thirling **9** captivity
subjoin: add **5** affix, annex **6** append, attach
subjugate: 6 compel, master, reduce, subdue **7** conquer, depress, overawe **8** overcome
sublate: 4 deny **6** cancel, negate, remove **9** eliminate
sublime: 5 exalt, grand, great, lofty, noble, proud **6** purify, refine **7** emotion, exalted, haughty, supreme **8** elevated, empyreal, heavenly, heighten, majestic, splendid, upraised **9** expletive
sublimity: 7 majesty **8** grandeur **12** magnificence
submarine: sub **4** boat **5** diver **9** periscope **11** submersible
detector: **5** sonar
projectile: **7** missile, Polaris, torpedo
submerge: dip **4** bury, dive, hide, sink **5** souse **6** deluge, drench, engulf, plunge **8** inundate, suppress
submerged: 4 sunk **5** awash **6** sunken

continent: 8 Atlantis

submiss: low 6 humble 7 subdued 10 obsequious, submissive

submission: 8 meekness 9 deference, obedience, surrender 10 compliance, confession 11 resignation 13 nonresistance

act of: 5 kneel 6 curtsy 7 curtsey

to destiny: 8 fatalism

submissive: 4 meek 5 buxom 6 docile, humble 7 dutiful, passive, servile 8 obedient, resigned, yielding 9 childlike, compliant

to wife: 8 uxorious

submit: bow 4 bend, obey 5 abide, agree, avale, defer, heald, hield, lower, stoop, yield 6 assent, comply, delate, resign, soften, subdue, suffer, temper 7 exhibit, knuckle, propose, succumb, suggest 8 moderate 9 acquiesce, surrender 10 condescend

for consideration: 5 remit

proposal to: 4 move

to: 4 obey

subordinate: 5 minor, under 6 puisne, subdue 7 control 8 inferior, obedient, servient 9 ancillary, assistant, auxiliary, dependent, secondary, underling 10 accidental, collateral, incidental, submissive 11 subservient

activity: 8 parergon

adjunct: 9 appendage

officer: 4 exon

suborn: 5 adorn, bribe, equip, foist 6 father, incite, induce 7 furnish, procure, provide 9 instigate

subpoena: 4 writ 6 summon

subreption: 6 secret, snatch, unfair 8 unlawful 9 deduction 11 underhanded

subrogate: 10 substitute

subscribe: 5 favor 6 assent, attest 7 ascribe, consent, support 8 sanction 10 acceptance, underwrite

subscriber of newspaper: 6 abonne

subscription to newspaper: 10 abonnement

subsequent: 5 after, later 6 puisne 7 ensuing 8 retainer 9 attendant, companion, following

to birth: 9 postnatal

subsequently: 5 later, since 10 afterwards, thereafter

subservient: 6 vassal 7 duteous, servile 9 accessory, ancillary, auxiliary, truckling 10 obsequious, submissive 11 subordinate

subside: ebb 4 bate, fall, lull, sink, wane 5 abate, cease, lower 6 settle 7 descend, flatten, relapse 8 decrease, withdraw

subsidence: 5 dregs

subsidiary: 7 reserve 9 accessory, assistant, auxiliary, tributary 10 collateral 13 supplementary

subsidy: aid 4 gift, help 5 bonus, grant 6 bounty 7 pension, reserve, support, tribute 10 assistance, subvention

subsist: be 4 feed, hold, live, stay 5 abide, exist, stand 6 obtain, remain 7 support, continue, maintain

subsistence: 6 living 9 allowance, inherency, substance 10 livelihood, provisions 11 persistence

subsoil: bed, pan 4 sole 7 stratum

animal: 4 mole

substance: sum 4 body, core, gist, mass, meat 5 basis, metal, stuff 6 estate, ground, import, matter, realty, spirit, supply, wealth 7 aliment, essence, meaning, purport 8 hardness, majority, material, property, solidity 9 actuality, affluence, resources, solidness 11 consistency

amorphous: 5 resin, rosin 7 ferrite

animal: 7 gelatin

bitter: 4 acid 5 aloes, aloin, linin 6 ilicin 7 amarine, emetine 8 elaterin

dissolving: 9 resolvent

drying: 8 desicant

expansive: gas

reaction-inducing: 7 reagent

rubber-like: 5 gutta

simple: 7 element

sour: 4 acid 7 vinegar

starch-like: 6 inulin, olivil 8 alantine

sticky: goo, gum, tar 4 glue 5 paste

transparent: 9 celluloid

unctuous: oil 6 grease

vegetable: 4 peat 5 resin, rosin

white: 4 alba 6 inulin 7 alanine 8 elaterin

substantial: 4 firm, real, true 5 ample, large, meaty, solid, sound, stout 6 actual, bodily, hearty, stable, strong, sturdy 7 genuine, wealthy 8 tangible 9 corporeal, important 12 considerable

substantiality: See **substance**

substantiate: 5 prove 6 assure, embody, verify 7 confirm 9 establish 11 corroborate

substantive: 4 noun 6 actual, entity 7 pronoun 9 essential 13 self-contained

substitute: 5 extra, fudge, proxy, vicar 6 deputy, ersatz(G.), ringer 7 commute, replace 8 exchange, nominate 9 alternate, makeshift, surrogate 10 viceregent 11 succedaneum 13 succenturiate

for a name: 6 dingus, doodad, widget 9 doohickey 11 thingamabob

temporary: 7 stopgap 9 expedient

substructure: 4 base 6 podium 10 foundation

[handwritten note in left margin: WILE]

subsume: 6 assume, deduce 7 contain 8 classify 9 summarize

subterfuge: 4 plan, ruse 5 blind, trick 6 device, escape, refuge 7 evasion 8 artifice, pretense 9 deception 13 prevarication 14 tergiversation
use: 7 chicane 12 tergiversate

subterranean: 4 cave 6 cavern, hidden, secret

subtile: See subtle

subtilize: 5 exalt 9 sublimate

subtle: sly 4 deft, keen, nice, wily 5 acute 6 artful, clever, crafty, expert, shrewd 7 cunning, elusive, refined, tenuous 8 abstruse, analytic, delicate, rarefied, skillful 9 beguiling, designing, ingenious, intricate 10 mysterious, perceptive 11 penetrating 14 discriminating
emanation: 4 aura
variation: 6 nuance

subtlety: 7 exility, finesse

subtract: 5 minus 6 deduct, remove 7 detract 8 withdraw, withhold

suburb: 8 environs 9 dissolute, outskirts, periphery

subvention: aid 4 help 5 grant 7 subsidy, support 9 endowment 10 assistance 13 appropriation

subvert: sap 4 ruin 5 evert, upset 6 uproot 7 corrupt, destroy, pervert 8 alienate, overturn 9 overthrow, undermine

subway: 4 tube 5 metro 6 tunnel 11 underground
entrance: 5 kiosk

succade: 8 preserve 10 confection

succedaneum: 6 remedy 8 medicine 10 substitute

succeed: win 4 fare 5 fadge, occur 6 attain, follow, happen, thrive 7 achieve, descend, inherit, prevail, prosper, replace 8 approach, flourish 10 accomplish

succeeding: 7 ensuing, sequent

success: go; hit, wow 4 luck 7 fortune 8 accolade 9 happiness 11 consequence

succession: row, run 6 course, series 7 dynasty 8 sequence 9 gradation
next in line: 4 heir

successive: 9 inherited 10 hereditary 11 consecutive

successor: 4 heir 5 heres 6 haeres, tanist 9 designado(Sp.)

succin: 5 amber

succinct: 4 curt 5 brief, short, terse 6 girded 7 compact, concise, laconic, summary 10 compressed

succor: aid 4 abet, cure, help 5 serve 6 assist, refuge, relief, rescue 7 comfort, deliver, provide, sustain 8 befriend, mitigate 9 alleviate 10 strengthen

succory: 7 chicory

succulent: 4 aloe, lush 5 fresh, juicy, pappy, tasty, vital 6 cactus, tender
fruit: uva

succumb: die 5 yield 6 perish, submit

succursal: 6 branch 9 auxiliary 10 subsidiary

such: as, so; sic(L.) 4 kind, like, some 7 certain, similar

suck: rob, sip 4 draw, lick, swig 5 bleed, draft, drain, drink, nurse 6 absorb, adsorb, imbibe, inhale, suckle 7 consume, extract, suction 14 disappointment

sucker: 4 dupe 5 leech 6 victim 8 lollipop 9 simpleton

sucking fish: 6 remora 7 lamprey

suckle: 4 feed, rear, suck 5 nurse 6 foster 7 nourish 11 honeysuckle

sucrose: 5 sugar 10 saccharose

suction: 6 intake 7 drawing, lifting

sud: 4 foam 6 bubble

Sudan: *animal:* 4 dama 6 oterop
beer: 4 dolo
capital: 7 Khartum
lake: No
language: Ga, Mo; Ewe, Ibo, Kru 4 Efik, Mole, Tshi 6 Yoruba 8 Mandingo
mountain: 4 Nuba
people: 4 Daza, Golo, Sere 5 Fulah, Hausa, Mossi
stockade: 6 zareba, zereba, zeriba 7 zareeba
stretcher: 7 angareb, angarep 8 angareeb
weapon: 8 trombash, trumbash

sudarium: 6 napkin 7 veronica 12 handkerchief

sudden: 4 rash, soon 5 brief, early, ferly, hasty, short, swift 6 abrupt, speedy 7 prerupt, violent 8 headlong, meteoric 9 alertness, impetuous, impromptu 10 unexpected, unforeseen, unprepared 11 precipitate, precipitous

suddenly: 6 presto

suddle: 4 soil 5 stain

Sudra caste member: 5 palli

suds: bog 4 beer, foam 5 dregs, filth, froth 6 lather, refuse 7 bubbles

sue: beg, woo 4 seek, urge 5 chase, court, ensue, plead 6 appeal, follow, guided, pursue 7 beseech, contest, entreat, proceed, request, solicit 8 continue, governed, petition, practice 9 prosecute

suer: 9 plaintiff

suet: fat 6 tallow

Suez Canal: *builder:* 9 de Lesseps
port: 4 Said

suffer: get, let 4 bear, bide, dree(Sc.) 5 admit, allow, groan, thole 6 endure, grieve, permit, submit 7 agonize, undergo 8 tolerate 10 experience

sufferance: 4 pain 6 misery 7 consent, respite 8 patience, sanction 9 passivity, suffering 11 forbearance 12 postponement

sufferer: 3 martyr, victim

suffering: ill 4 bale, dree(Sc.), loss, pain 5 agony 6 ailing, injury 8 distress, sickness 9 adversity 10 affliction 11 tribulation

comb. form: 4 path 5 patho

reliever of: 9 Samaritan

suffice: do 5 serve 6 answer 7 appease, content, satisfy

sufficiency: 4 fill 7 ability, conceit 8 adequacy, capacity 9 abundance 10 capability, competency

sufficient: due, fit 4 able, enow, good 5 ample, valid 6 enough, plenty 7 suffice 8 abundant, adequate 9 competent, effectual, efficient, qualified 11 responsible, substantial 12 satisfactory 13 well-qualified

suffix (see also **combining form, prefix**): For all definitions beginning with this word, look under main word or phrase. EXAMPLES: "suffix for inhabitant": see **inhabitant:** *suffix;* "suffix for sugar": see **sugar:** *suffix.*

sufflate: 7 inflate, inspire

suffocate: 4 kill 5 burke, choke 6 stifle 7 destroy, smother 8 compress, strangle, suppress, throttle 10 asphyxiate, extinguish

suffocation: 8 asphyxia

suffragan: 4 help 5 agent 6 bishop, deputy 9 assistant, auxiliary 11 subordinate

suffrage: aid 4 help, vote 5 right, voice 6 assent, ballot, prayer 7 witness 8 petition 9 franchise, testimony 10 assistance 12 intercession, supplication

suffuse: 4 fill, pour 5 embay 7 diffuse 10 overspread

sugar: gur, ose 4 cane 5 biose, candy, maple, money, oside 6 acrose, aldose, fucose, gulose, hexose, ketose, talose, triose 7 caramel, chitose, glucide, maltose, sucrose, sweeten, tetrose, threose 8 rhodeose 9 muscovado, raffinose, sweetness 10 digitoxose, piloncillo, saccharose 12 carbohydrate 13 dissaccharide 14 monosaccharide

artificial: 6 allose 7 glucose 9 saccharin

boiling kettle: 8 flambeau

burnt: 7 caramel

crystals: 5 candy

fruit: 8 fructose, levulose

liquid: 5 sirup, syrup

lump: 4 cube, loaf

measure: 13 saccharimeter

milk: 7 lactose

mixture: 5 syrup

preparation device: 10 granulator

raw: 9 cassonade

source: sap 4 beet, cane 5 maple

substitute: 5 honey 9 saccharin

syrup: 7 treacle 8 molasses

sugar apple: 6 biriba 8 sweetsop

sugar sand: 5 niter

sugarcane: *disease:* 5 sereh

pulp: 4 marc 6 megass 7 bagasse, megasse

refuse: 4 marc 6 begass 7 bagasse, begasse

stalk: 6 ratoon

sugarloaf: 4 hill 8 conoidal, mountain

sugarplum: 6 bonbon 9 sweetmeat

sugary: 5 sweet 7 honeyed 8 pleasant 10 flattering, saccharine 11 mellifluous

suggest: 4 hint, move 5 imply 6 allude, broach, prompt 7 connote, inspire, mention, propose 8 indicate, intimate 9 insinuate

suggestion: 4 idea 5 tinge, touch, trace 6 advice 7 inkling, remnant, soupcon 8 proposal 9 complaint 10 accusation, incitement, intimation, temptation 11 information

sui juris: 5 adult 11 responsible

suicidal: 4 rash 5 fatal 6 deadly, lethal

suidae: hog 5 swine

suing: 11 prosecution

suint: 5 sweat 6 grease 12 perspiration

suit: do 4 case(law), kind, plea, sort 5 adapt, agree, apply, cards, class, dress, fadge, group, habit, match, order, serve, tally 6 accord, adjust, answer, appeal, assort, attire, behove, outfit, please, prayer, series, trover, wooing 7 arrange, behoove, clothes, comport, conform, costume, request, satisfy, uniform 8 classify, courting, entreaty, petition, sequence 9 harmonize 10 correspond, litigation, succession 11 accommodate 12 solicitation

maker: 6 sartor, tailor

suitable: apt, due, fit, pat 4 able, fair, good, meet 5 right 6 comely, gainly, proper 7 a propos, seeming 8 adequate, apposite, becoming, coherent, eligible, feasible, idoneous, matching 9 competent, congruent, congruous, consonant, expedient 10 commodious, compatible, consistent, convenient, equivalent 11 appropriate 12 commensurate

render: 5 adapt 7 prepare

suitcase: bag 4 grip 6 valise 9 gladstone

suite: set 4 band 5 abode, group, staff, train 6 series 7 retinue 8 equipage 9 apartment, entourage 10 collection

member of: 7 attache

musical: See **musical composition**

suited: See **suitable**

suiting: 4 wool 5 serge

suitor: 4 beau 5 wooer 7 gallant 8 follower 10 petitioner

sukey: 9 teakettle

sulcate: 6 fluted 7 grooved

sulfate: 5 treat 7 convert, sulphur 9 brimstone 10 impregnate
 kind: 4 alum 5 hepar, matte 6 barite, blende 7 ilesite, loweite

sulfur: 9 brimstone
 substance containing: 5 hepar

sulfuric acid: 7 vitriol

sulk: 4 dort(Sc.), mope, pout 5 grump 6 grouch

sulky: 4 cart, dull, weak 5 chuff, dorty, inert 6 gloomy, gocart, grouty, sullen 7 doggish, peevish 8 carriage, inactive 10 unyielding

sullage: mud 4 silt 5 filth 6 refuse, scoria, sewage 8 drainage 9 pollution 10 filthiness

sullen: sad 4 dour, dull, glum, grim, sour 5 alone, black, cross, felon, gruff, heavy, moody, pouty, stern, sulky, surly 6 crusty, dismal, dogged, gloomy, grouty, morose, silent, somber 7 baleful, boorish, crabbed, peevish, serious 8 churlish, lowering, petulant, solitary 9 obstinate, saturnine 10 depressing, ill-humored, ill-natured, refractory, unsociable 11 intractable, threatening 12 unpropitious

Sullivan's collaborator: 7 Gilbert

sully: 4 blot, blur, foul, soil 5 cloud, dirty, grime, smear, stain, taint 6 darken, defile, smirch 7 attaint, blacken, blemish, corrupt, pollute, tarnish 8 besmirch 9 bespatter 11 contaminate

sulphate: See **sulfate**

sultan: 5 ruler 8 padishah 9 sovereign
 decree: 5 irade

sultanate: 4 Oman

sultry: hot 5 close, fiery, humid, lurid 6 coarse, smutty, torrid 7 sensual 8 inflamed 10 oppressive, sweltering 13 uncomfortable

Sulu island: 6 Siassi

sum: add, end, tot 4 gist, host 5 count, gross, issue, total, whole 6 amount, degree, height, number, result, summit 7 integer, numeral, problem, summary 8 addition, assembly, entirety, perorate, quantity 9 aggregate, calculate, gathering, magnitude, substance, summarize, summation 11 epilogation 12 recapitulate
 forfeited: 5 dedit
 large: gob, pot
 small: 4 drab 7 driblet 8 dribblet 11 chickenfeed
 subtracted: 9 deduction
 unexpended: 7 savings
 up: add 9 summarize 12 recapitulate

sumac, sumach: 4 anam 7 dogwood 8 shoemake 11 balinghasay
 genus of: 4 rhus

Sumatra: *animal:* 4 balu, tanu 5 orang
 ape: 5 orang 6 ourang 9 orangutan
 city: 5 Achin, Jambi, Medan 6 Padang 8 Bonkulin 9 Bencoolen, Indrapoor, Palembang
 deer: 4 napu
 fiber: 6 caloee
 lake: 4 Toba
 language: 4 Nias
 measure: 4 paal
 raft: 5 rakit
 river: 4 Musi 5 Jambi, Rokan 9 Indragiri
 wildcat: 4 balu

Sumer deity: Abu

summarize: sum 5 recap 6 digest 8 abstract 9 epitomize

summary: sum 4 gist 5 brief, recap, short 6 digest, precis, resume, summit 7 concise, epitome, extract, general, medulla 8 abstract, argument, breviate, succinct, synopsis 9 condensed 10 compendium 11 abridgement 13 comprehension 14 recapitulation

summation: See **sum**

summer: ete(F.) 8 estivate 9 aestivate
 ailment: 8 heat rash
 beverage: ade
 pass: 8 estivate
 pert. to: 7 estival 8 aestival

summer teal: 8 garganey

summerhouse: 5 kiosk 6 casino, gazebo 7 cottage 8 pavilion 9 belvedere

summery: 5 light 7 estival 8 delicate

summing up: See **sum**

summit (see also **mountain, peak**): bow, cap, tip, top, van 4 acme, apex, knap, roof 5 crest, crown, ridge 6 climax, comble, height, vertex, zenith 8 pinnacle 9 fastigium(L.) 11 culmination
 pert. to: 6 apical

summon: ban, bid 4 call, page 5 charm, evoke, rally, rouse 6 accite, appeal, arouse, compel, demand, gather, muster 7 collect, command, convoke, provoke
 to court: 4 cite, sist

summoner: 6 beadle 9 apparitor

summons: 4 writ 6 venire 7 command, warning 8 citation 9 challenge 12 notification

sump: mud, pit 4 dirt, pool, pump, tank, well 5 drain 6 puddle, shower 7 cistern, depress 8 cesspool 9 reservoir 10 depression, excavation, receptacle

sumpter: 4 pack 6 burden

sumptuous: 5 grand 6 costly, lavish, superb 8 splendid 9 expensive, luxurious 11 magnificent

sun: orb, sol 4 bask, star 5 Titan 6 bleach 7 daystar, Phoebus 8 luminary 9 Harmachis
combining form: 5 helio
crossing equator: 7 equinox
god: Ra; Tem, Utu 4 Baal, Lleu, Llew, Utug 6 Apollo, Helios 7 Chepera, Khepara, Shamash, Sokaris 8 Hyperion
luminous envelope of: 6 corona
measuring device: 13 pyrheliometer
mock: 9 parhelion
near: 6 heliac
outer layer: 6 corona
part: 6 corona
path: 8 ecliptic
pert. to: 5 solar 6 heliac
protective devices: 7 parasol 8 blindage, havelock
satellite: 6 planet
worshiper: 5 Parsi 6 Parsee 10 heliolater

sun-clock: 7 sundial

sun disk: 4 Aten

sun dog: 4 halo 7 rainbow 9 parhelion

sun room: 7 solaria(pl.) 8 solarium

sun watch: 7 sundial 9 timepiece

sunburn: tan 8 heliosis

sunburst: 6 brooch, ensign

Sunda Island: 4 Bali, Java, Nias 6 Borneo, Lombok 7 Celebes, Sumatra

Sunday: *following Easter:* Low 9 Quasimodo
mid-Lent: 7 Laetare
pert. to: 9 dominical
special: 4 Palm 6 Easter

sunder: rip 4 part, rend, rive 5 break, split 6 divide, severe 7 disjoin, disrupt, divorce 8 dissever, disunite, separate

sundial part: 6 gnomon

sundown: See **sunset**

sundowner: 5 drink, tramp 7 captain 8 nightcap

sundry: 5 apart 6 divers 7 asunder, diverse, several, various 8 distinct, frequent, manifold, numerous, separate, sundered 9 different, disunited 10 respective, separately 12 multifarious 13 miscellaneous
companion of: all

sunfall: See **sunset**

sunfish: 5 bream 8 pondfish
genus of: 4 mola

sunflower: 4 marigold, rockrose 10 balsamroot, heliotrope
maid turned into: 6 Clytie

Sunflower State: 6 Kansas

Sungkiang capital: 6 Harbin

sunk (see also **sink**): pad 4 bank, seat, turf, 5 couch 6 abject, hollow 8 absorbed, overcome 9 depressed

sunken: 6 hollow 9 depressed
fence: 4 ha-ha

sunket: 4 food 6 dainty 8 delicacy

sunless: 4 dark

sunny: gay 4 warm 5 clear, happy, merry 6 bright, golden, sunlit 8 cheerful 9 sparkling, vivacious

sunrise: 4 dawn
song: 6 aubade

sunset: e'en, eve 4 dusk 7 evening, sundown, sunfall 8 twilight
pert. to: 9 acronical
reflection: 9 alpenglow

Sunset State: 6 Oregon 7 Arizona

sunshade: 5 visor 6 awning 7 parasol

sunshine: 5 cheer, light 6 warmth 8 sunburst 9 happiness, sunniness 11 fairweather 12 cheerfulness

Sunshine State: 9 New Mexico 11 South Dakota

sunspot: 6 facula 7 freckle

sunstroke: 8 siriasis 9 calenture

sunwise: 6 deasil, dessil 7 deiseal 9 clockwise

Suomi: 7 Finland

sup: eat, sip 4 dine 5 drink, feast 6 absorb, amount, liquor 7 consume, swallow 8 mouthful, quantity, spoonful

supawn: 4 mush 12 hasty pudding

super: 5 actor, watch 6 square 7 janitor 9 excellent, first-rate

superable: 12 surmountable

superabundance: 5 flood 6 excess 8 plethora 10 exuberance 11 superfluity

superabundant: 4 rank 6 lavish 9 redundant 11 overflowing

superannuate: 6 retire 7 outlast 8 obsolete 9 out-of-date 10 disqualify

superannuated: 5 passe 8 obsolete, outdated 10 antiquated 12 old-fashioned

superb: 4 fine, rich 5 grand, noble, proud 6 lordly 7 elegant, haughty, stately 8 enormous, majestic, splendid 9 excellent, luxurious, sumptuous 13 extraordinary

superbity: 9 arrogance 11 haughtiness

supercilious: 5 lofty, proud 6 uppish 7 haughty 8 arrogant, cavalier, snobbish 9 arbitrary 11 overbearing 12 contemptuous 13 hypercritical

superficial: 4 glib 5 hasty 6 casual, flimsy, slight 7 cursory, outward, shallow, surface 8 external

superfine: 4 luxe, nice, rich 5 extra, plush, prime 6 choice, subtle 8 delicate, overnice 9 excellent

superfluity: 6 excess, luxury 9 abundance 11 prodigality

superfluous: 4 over 5 spare 6 de trop(F.) 7 surplus, useless 8 abnormal, needless, wasteful 9 excessive, redundant, worthless 10 gratuitous, inordinate 11 extravagant, unnecessary 12 nonessential 13 superabundant

superhuman: 6 divine 8 superman 9 herculean 12 supernatural 13 extraordinary

superhumeral: 5 amice

superimpose: 7 overlay

superintend: 4 boss 5 guide 6 direct, manage 7 conduct, control, inspect, oversee 8 engineer 9 supervise 10 administer

superintendence: 4 care 9 authority 14 responsibility

superintendent: 4 boss 6 bishop 7 captain, curator, manager 8 director, minister, overseer 9 inspector 10 supervisor 11 chamberlain

superior: 4 fine, head, lord, over, peer 5 above, eigne, extra, liege, upper 6 better, higher, senior 7 exalted, greater, haughty, palmary, prelate, ranking 8 alderman, arrogant, assuming, dominant, elevated, masterly 9 ascendant, ascendent, excellent, paramount, spiritual 10 preeminent, surpassing 11 predominant 12 supercilious, supernatural 13 comprehensive

superiority: 4 gree(Sc.) 8 priority 9 advantage, meliority, seniority 13 preponderance

position of: 10 domination

superlative: 4 acme, best, peak 6 utmost 7 supreme 8 peerless 9 excessive 11 exaggerated

absolute: 7 elative

suffix: est

Superman's friend: 4 Lois

supernal: 6 divine 8 ethereal, heavenly 9 celestial

supernatural: 5 magic 6 divine 9 marvelous 10 miraculous, superhuman 13 preternatural

supernatural being: elf, god 4 atua 5 angel, deity, demon, fairy, gnome, nymph, troll 6 cherub, seraph, spirit 7 banshee, goddess 10 leprechaun

supernatural happening: 6 vision 7 miracle

supernumerary: 4 supe 5 actor, extra, super

superpower: USA 4 USSR

superscribe: 5 write 6 direct 7 address, engrave

superscription: 5 title 9 direction 11 description, inscription

supersede, supercede: 7 replace, succeed 8 displace, override, supplant

supersensory: 12 extrasensory 13 supersensible

supersonic noise: 4 boom

superstition: 5 freet, freit, magic 6 fetish, voodoo 8 idolatry

supervene: 5 ensue 6 follow, happen 9 supersede

supervise: 4 boss, edit, read, scan 5 check 6 direct, govern, manage, peruse, revise 7 conduct, correct, inspect, oversee 11 superintend

supervisor: 7 foreman 8 alytarch(G.) 9 spectator 10 roadmaster

supine: 5 inert, prone 6 abject, drowsy 7 leaning, passive, sloping, unalert 8 inactive, inclined, indolent, listless, sluggish 9 negligent 11 inattentive, indifferent

supper: tea 4 meal

supplant: 5 upset, usurp 6 follow, remove, uproot 7 replace, succeed 8 displace 9 extirpate, overthrow, supersede, undermine

supple: sly 4 bain, oily 5 agile, lithe 6 limber, lissom, nimble, pliant, swanky 7 cunning, elastic, fawning, lissome, pliable, servile 8 flexible, yielding 9 adaptable, compliant, resilient 10 obsequious, responsive 11 complaisant

supplement: add 8 addendum, addition, appendix 9 accessory 10 complement 13 reinforcement

supplemental: 12 adscititious 13 succenturiate

suppliant: 6 beggar 10 beseeching, entreating, petitioner

supplicate: beg, sue 4 knee, pray 5 crave, plead 6 appeal, invoke, obtest 7 beseech, conjure, entreat, implore, request, solicit 8 petition 9 importune, obsecrate

supplication: 6 litany 8 rogative

supply: aid, fit 4 feed, fill, fund, give, help, load 5 cache, cater, equip, hoard, relay, stock, store, yield 6 afford, employ, foison, purvey, relief, succor 7 fraught, furnish, granary, nourish, plenish, provide, replace, reserve, satisfy 8 minister, ordnance 9 profusion, reinforce, replenish, reservoir 10 administer, assistance, compensate, contribute

support: aid, arm, guy, leg, peg, rib 4 back, base, beam, bear, bibb, fend, help, keep, limb, pier, prop, stay 5 boost, brace, carry, cheer, cleat, easel, favor, found, hinge, shore, sling, staff, strut, truss 6 anchor, behalf, better, defend, endure, lintel, pillar, second, shield, splint, spring, suffer, tripod, trivet, uphold, verify 7 bolster, cherish, comfort, confirm, console, endorse, espouse, fulcrum, nourish, nurture,

protect, provide, reserve, sustain, trestle 8
approval, baluster, befriend, evidence,
maintain, pedestal, sanction, tolerate, underlie 9 adminicle, encourage, reinforce,
stanchion, vindicate 10 assistance, foundation, strengthen 11 corroborate, countenance 12 alimentation, substantiate
for statue: 5 socle 8 pedestal
one-legged: 6 unipod
slab: 4 tray 6 planch

supporter: 4 ally, knee 6 bearer, patron,
rooter 7 abetter, abettor, booster, founder,
support 8 adherent, advocate, assertor,
follower, henchman, partisan 9 auxiliary

suppose: 4 deem, trow, ween 5 allow, imply,
judge, opine, think 6 assume, expect, repute 7 believe, imagine, incline, opinion,
presume, suspect 8 conceive, conclude,
consider, obligate, supposal 9 apprehend,
intention 10 conjecture, presuppose, substitute 11 expectation, supposition

supposed: See **supposititious**

supposition: if 6 notion, theory 7 forgery,
surmise 9 postulate 10 alteration, assumption, conjecture, estimation, hypothesis
11 expectation, proposition, uncertainty

supposititious: 7 feigned 8 fabulous, putative, spurious, supposed 9 imaginary, pretended 10 artificial 11 counterfeit 12 hypothetical, illegitimate

suppress: 4 hide, keep, kill, stop 5 check,
choke, crush, elide, quash, quell 6 arrest,
bridle, censor, harass, ravish, retard, stifle, subdue 7 abolish, conceal, destroy, exclude, oppress, prevent, refrain, repress,
silence, smother, squelch 8 compress, prohibit, restrain, withhold 9 interdict, overpower, overthrow 10 dissolving, extinguish

suprarenal: 7 adrenal

supremacy: 4 sway 5 power 7 control, mastery 8 dominion 9 authority, autocracy,
dominance, influence 10 ascendancy, ascendency, domination 11 sovereignty 12
predominance 13 preponderance

supreme: 4 last 5 chief, final 6 utmost 7
crucial, highest 8 foremost, greatest, lofti-
est, peerless, ultimate 9 paramount 10
preeminent

supreme being: 5 Allah, monad 7 creator

surcease: end 4 rest, stay, stop 5 defer, delay
6 desist, relief 7 refrain, respite, suspend
8 postpone 9 cessation

surcharge: tax 4 cost, fill, load 6 burden,
impost 7 surfeit 8 overload, surprint 9
overcrowd, overprint, overstock 10 impregnate, overburden, overcharge

surcingle: 4 band, belt 6 girdle 8 cincture

surcoat: 5 jupon 6 cyclas 7 garment

surd: 7 radical 9 insensate, voiceless 10 irrational

sure: 4 fast, firm, safe, true 5 siker(Sc.) 6
indeed, secure, sicker(Sc.), stable, steady,
strong 7 assured, certain 8 enduring, positive, reliable, unerring 9 authentic, betrothed, confident, convinced, steadfast,
undoubted, unfailing 10 dependable, infallible 11 indubitable, trustworthy, unfaltering 12 indisputable 13 incontestable 14
unquestionable

surely: 6 atweel(Sc.), really

sureness: 9 certitude

surety: 4 bail 6 backer, pledge 7 engager,
sponsor 8 bailsman, bondsman, security 9
assurance, certainty, guarantee, guarantor 10 confidence
post: 4 bond

surf: 4 foam, wave 5 spray, swell 7 breaker
sound of: 4 rote

surface: 4 area, face, pave, side, skin 5 facet,
plane 6 facing, finish, patina 7 outside 8
boundary, exterior 11 superficial
flat: 4 area 5 plane, sheet 7 lateral
geometrical: 5 nappe 6 toroid
inclined: 4 cant, ramp
mellowed: 6 patina
pert. to: 6 facial
rounded: 9 concavity, convexity
toward: 5 ectad

surfacing: 6 gravel 7 asphalt, macadam

surfeit: 4 cloy, feed, glut, sate 6 excess, nausea, supply 7 disgust, replete, satiate, satiety, satisfy 8 disorder 9 satiation 10 discomfort 11 extravagant, overindulge, superfluity 13 overabundance 14 overindul-
gence

surfeited: 4 sick 5 blase, fed up 8 complete

surge: 4 rise, rush, tide, wave 5 gurge, swell
6 billow 7 estuate, rolling 8 sweeping,
swelling

surgeon: 10 chirurgeon

surgeonfish: 4 tang

surgery: 9 operation, resection
appliance: 5 brace 6 crutch, splint
compress: 5 stupe
father of: 4 Pare
instrument: 5 fleam, lance, probe, scala 6
bilabe, gorget, lancet, splint, stylet, trapan, trepan, trocar, vectis 7 forceps, levator, ligator, rongeur, scalpel, trilabe, trochar 8 bistoury, ecraseur, trephine, tweezers 9 goosebill, tenaculum, vulsellum 10
abaptiston, abaptistum, terebellum, tour-
niquet
perform: 7 operate
plug: 6 tampon
puncture: 8 centesis
roller: 6 fascia 7 fasciae

stitch: 5 seton 6 suture
thread: 6 catgut
Surinam: *capital:* 10 Paramaribo
hut: 5 benab
measure: 7 ketting
toad: 4 pipa 5 pipal
tribe: 4 Boni 5 Djuka
surly: 4 glum, grum, rude 5 bluff, chuff, cross, gruff, gurly 6 abrupt, grumpy, morose, sullen 7 boorish, crabbed, haughty, uncivil 8 arrogant, churlish, growling 10 ill-natured 11 intractable
surmise: 4 deem 5 guess, infer, trace 6 charge 7 imagine, presume, suppose 9 suspicion 10 allegation, assumption, conclusion, conjecture 11 supposition
surmount: top 4 pass, rise, tide 5 climb, crown, excel, mount, total 6 ascend, exceed, hurdle, subdue 7 conquer, surpass 8 overcome 9 negotiate, transcend
surmountable: 9 superable
surmounting: 4 atop
surname: 6 byname 7 agnomen 8 cognomen 11 appellation
surpass: cap, cob, top 4 beat, flog 5 amend, excel, outdo 6 better, exceed, outvie 7 eclipse, outrank, outsoar 8 outclass, outreach, outstrip, surmount 9 transcend
surpassing: 4 fine 6 banner 9 excellent 10 inimitable, preeminent
surplice: 5 cotta, ephod
surplus: 4 over, rest 5 extra 6 excess 7 backlog, reserve 8 overplus 10 redundancy
surprise: awe, cap 5 alarm, amaze, catch, seize, shock 6 dazzle, detect, strike, wonder 7 astound, capture, gloppen, perplex, startle, uncover 8 astonish, bewilder, confound, dumfound, overcome 9 amazement, overwhelm 11 flabbergast
surprised: 5 agape
surprising: 10 unexpected 13 extraordinary
surrealist: 4 Dali
surrender: 4 cede, fall, give 5 remit, yield 6 remise, resign, tender, waiver 7 abandon, cession, concede, deliver, forsake 8 dedition, remittal 9 rendition 10 abdication, capitulate, compromise, relinquish 11 divestiture 12 cancellation
surreptitious: sly 6 secret 7 bootleg 8 sneaking, stealthy 9 underhand 11 clandestine
surrey: 8 carriage
Surrey parish: Kew
surrogate: 6 deputy 8 delegate 9 subrogate 10 substitute
surround: bar, hem 4 belt, fold, gird, ring 5 beset, embay, flood, hedge 6 circle, corral, encase, enring, invest 7 besiege, embosom, enclose, environ, imbosom 8 encircle, en-

velope, inundate, overflow 9 beleaguer, encompass 12 circumscribe 14 circumnavigate
with water: 4 isle 6 enisle
surrounded: in; mid 4 amid 5 among 6 amidst 7 bounded
surrounding: 5 about, midst 7 context, setting 8 ambiance 9 entourage 11 environment 12 circumjacent, circumstance
surtax: 4 agio, levy 5 extra
surtout: 4 coat, hood 7 garment 8 overcoat
survey: 4 pool, scan, view 5 study 6 regard, review, search 7 examine, history, inspect, oversee 8 consider, traverse 9 delineate, determine, treatment 10 exposition, scrutinize 11 description, reconnoiter, superintend 13 triangulation 14 reconnaissance
surveyor: 6 gauger 9 arpenteur, inspector 14 superintendent
helper: 6 rodman 7 lineman, poleman 8 chainman
instrument: 11 stratameter
nail: 4 spad
tool: 6 alidad 7 alidade, transit 10 theodolite 12 perambulator
survival: 5 relic
survive: 7 outlast, outlive
Susa inhabitant: 7 Elamite
Susanna: *accusers:* 6 elders
husband: 7 Joachim
susceptible: 4 easy, open 6 liable 7 exposed, subject 8 allergic, sensible 9 receptive, sensitive 10 responsive, vulnerable 11 softhearted, unresistant 13 tenderhearted 14 impressionable
to error: 8 fallible
susceptibility: 5 sense 7 emotion, feeling 11 sensibility 13 affectibility
suscitate: 5 rouse 6 excite 7 animate 9 stimulate
suslik: 5 sisel 8 squirrel 11 spermophile
suspect: 4 fear 5 doubt, guess 7 dubious, imagine, inkling, presume, suppose, surmise 8 conceive, distrust, mistrust 9 discredit 10 disbelieve, intimation, suspicious 12 apprehension
suspend: bar 4 hang, hold, oust, stop 5 cease, debar, defer, demur, expel 6 dangle, recess 7 adjourn, exclude 8 intermit, postpone, withhold 9 pretermit
suspended: 4 hung 6 latent 7 abeyant, pendent, pensile 8 inactive 11 inoperaive
suspender: 5 brace 6 garter 7 galluse 9 supporter
suspense: 7 anxiety 8 cautious, hesitant, withheld 11 tenterhooks, uncertainty 12 apprehension 14 indecisiveness
in: 7 pending

suspension: 4 stop 5 delay 7 failure 8 abeyance, buoyancy, stoppage 9 remission 11 withholding 12 intermission, interruption
in air: 5 vapor
of court sentence: 9 probation
of hostilities: 5 truce 9 armistice, cease-fire

suspicion: 4 hint 5 doubt, touch, trace 7 askance, inkling 8 distrust, jealousy, mistrust 9 misgiving 10 diffidence, intimation, suggestion, uneasiness 11 expectation, 12 apprehension

suspicious: 5 fishy, leery 8 doubtful 9 equivocal 11 mistrustful 12 questionable

suspire: 4 sigh 7 respire

Sussex borough: 4 Hove

sustain: 4 abet, back, bear, buoy, dure, feed, help, prop 5 abide, carry 6 assist, endure, foster, second, succor, suffer, supply, uphold 7 comfort, confirm, console, contain, nourish, prolong, provide, support, undergo 8 befriend, continue, maintain 9 encourage, withstand 10 strengthen 11 corroborate

sustenance: 4 food, meat 5 bread, viand 6 living, upkeep 7 aliment, support 9 nutrition, provision 10 exhibition 11 maintenance, nourishment, subsistence 12 alimentation

sustentation: 6 upkeep 7 support 10 sustenance 11 maintenance 12 preservation

susurrus: 6 murmur, rustle 7 whisper

sutler: 9 vivandier 10 vivandiere

suttee: 7 suicide 10 immolation

suture: 4 line, seam 6 stitch 9 arthrosis 12 articulation

suzerain: 8 overlord 9 paramount, sovereign

svelte: 4 slim 5 lithe 6 lissom 7 lissome, slender 8 graceful

swab: mop 4 lout 5 brush, clean 7 epaulet, plunger 8 medicate

swack: 4 blow 5 whack 6 nimble, pliant, supple

swad: pod 4 mass 5 clown, crowd, shell 7 bumpkin, soldier

swaddle: 4 beat, bind, wrap 6 cudgel, swathe 7 bandage 8 restrict, surround

swag: pit, sag, tip 4 list, loot, sway 5 booty, lurch, spoil, swing, tramp 6 bundle, hollow 7 plunder, swagger 10 decoration

swage: 4 tool 5 shape 6 border, groove 7 assuage

swagger: 4 brag 5 bluff, boast, bully, lurch, strut, swell 6 cuttle, hector, prance 7 bluster, gauster, panache, quarrel, roister, ruffler, stagger, stylish 11 braggadocio, fanfaronade 16 ultrafashionable

swaggering: 6 gascon 7 huffcap

swagman: 9 sundowner

bundle: 5 bluey

swain: boy 5 lover, youth 6 rustic, suitor 7 admirer, gallant, peasant, servant 8 shepherd 9 attendant 10 countryman

swale: fen 4 moor, sway 5 marsh, shade, slash, sweal, swing, swirl 6 hollow, meadow, valley 8 coolness 10 depression

swallow: eat, sip, sup 4 bear, bolt, gaup, gawp, glut, gulp, tern 5 drink, merge, quilt, swift 6 absorb, accept, englut, engulf, go-down, gullet, imbibe, ingest, martin, recant, resorb, throat, vanish 7 believe, consume, engorge, retract 8 aperture, suppress, tolerate, withdraw 9 esophagus

swamp: bog, fen 4 mire, moor, muck, ruin, sink, slew, sloo, slue, thin, wham 5 clear, empty, flood, marsh 6 deluge, engulf, hollow, morass, slough 7 cienaga, pocosin, pocoson, slender 8 overcome, quagmire, submerge 9 overwhelm 10 Everglades
gas: 6 miasma 7 methane
grass: 5 sedge
pert. to: 7 miasmal, paludal

swan: cob, elk, pen 5 swear 6 cygnet 7 declare 8 surprise 9 trumpeter
female: pen
genus: 6 cygnus
male: cob
young: 6 cygnet

Swan river: 4 Avon

swank: 6 active, lively 7 stylish, swagger

swanky: ale 4 beer 5 cider 6 active

Swann's Way author: 6 Proust

swap: 4 bang, blow, move, slap 5 fling, smack, swoop, throw, trade 6 barter, dicker, pounce, strike, stroke 8 exchange

swape: bar, oar 4 pole

sward: sod 4 lawn, skin, turf 8 covering 10 greensward

swarm: fry, sny 4 bike(Sc.), byke(Sc.), host, move, shin, swim, teem 5 climb, cloud, crowd, flock, group, horde, mount 6 abound, throng 7 migrate 8 assemble 9 multitude 10 congregate

swarming: 6 aswarm 10 emigration

swart: 4 dark 6 dismal, gloomy 7 baneful, swarthy 8 blackish 9 malignant

swarthy: dun 4 dark 5 dusky 8 blackish

swash: bar 4 blow, move 5 noise, sound 6 strike 7 bluster, channel, dashing, swagger 9 splashing 12 swashbuckler

swashbuckler: 5 bravo 6 gascon 7 ruffian, slasher, soldier 9 daredevil, swaggerer

swashy: 4 weak 6 watery 7 insipid

swastika, svastika, swastica: 5 cross 6 fylfot 9 Gammadion

swat: bat, hit 4 blow 5 clout 6 strike

swatch: 5 swash 6 sample

swath, swathe: row 4 band, crop 5 strip, sweep, 6 stroke 7 windrow

swathe: 4 band, bind, wrap 6 enfold 7 envelop, swaddle 8 surround

sway: 4 bend, bias, lean, move, reel, rock, rule, veer 5 force, grace, guide, lurch, power, shake, swing, waver, wield 6 direct, divert, govern, swerve, totter, waddle 7 command, control, deflect, shoggie 8 dominion, rotation 9 dominance, influence, oscillate, vacillate 10 ascendancy, ascendency 11 fluctuation, inclination, sovereignty 13 lithesomeness

swaying: 5 asway

sweal: 4 burn, melt 5 singe, waste 6 scorch

swear: vow 4 bind 5 curse, utter 6 adjure, affirm, assert, pledge, threat 7 declare, promise 8 execrate 9 blaspheme 10 administer, asseverate

falsely: 7 perjure, slander

to secrecy: 4 tile

sweat: dry 4 emit, ooze, work 5 bleed, exude, hoist, labor, sudor(L.) 6 drudge, fleece 7 excrete, extract, ferment, putrefy, soldier 8 condense, overwork, perspire, transude

sweater: 5 shell 8 cardigan, pullover

Sweden: *artist:* 4 Zorn

botanist: 5 Fries 9 Bromelius

bread: 10 knackebrod

city: 5 Boras, Edane, Falun, Gavle, Malmo, Ystad 6 Orebro, Upsala 7 Uppsala 8 Goteborg, Nykoping 9 Falkoping, Jonkoping, Stockholm 10 Eskilstuna, Gottenburg, Norrkoping 11 Halsingborg

clover: 6 alsike

coin: ore 5 krona

county: lan

dance: 6 polska

division: amt 4 Laen 5 Skane 8 Gotaland, Gothland, Norrland, Swealand

dynasty: 4 Vasa

explorer: 5 Hedin

farm: 4 torp

gulf: 7 Bothnia

island: 5 Oland 6 Oeland 8 Gotaland, Gothland

king: 4 Eric, Wasa 5 Oscar 10 Bernadotte

lake: 5 Asnen, Malar, Wener 6 Siljan, Varern, Vatter, Wennen, Wetter 7 Hielmar, Malaren, Vattern

manual training: 5 sloyd

match: 12 taendstikker

measure: am; aln, fot, mil, ref, tum 4 famn, last, stop 5 carat, foder, kanna, kappe, linje, nymil, spann, stang, tunna 6 fathom, jumfru 7 kollast, oxhuvud, tunland 8 fjarding, kappland, koltunna, tunnland

money: 8 skilling

motion-picture director: 7 Bergman

mountain: 6 Sarjek

noble title: 4 graf

parliament: 7 Riksdag

philologist: 5 Ihre

physicist: 5 Dalen

province: 6 Kalmar, Orebro, Upsala 7 Gotland, Halland 8 Blekinge, Elfsborg, Jemtland, Malmohus, Wermland 9 Gefleborg, Jonkoping, Kronoberg, Skaraborg, Stockholm 10 Kopparberg, Norrbotten 11 Westmanland 12 Oster Gotland, Sodermanland, Westerbotten 13 Christianstad 14 Westernorrland 18 Gottenborgoch Bohus

river: 4 Gota, Klar, Umea 5 Kalix, Lulea, Pitea, Ranea 6 Lainio, Ljusne, Tornea, Windel 7 Ljungan

soprano: 7 Nilsson 10 Jennie Lind

sour milk: 8 tatmjolk

state religion: 8 Lutheran

tribe: 6 Geatas

weight: ass, lod, ort 4 last, mark, pund, sten, untz 5 carat 6 nylast 7 centner, lispund 8 lispound, skalpund, skeppund 9 ship pound

writer: 6 Carlen 7 Bellman 8 Lagerlof 10 Strindberg

Swedish Nightingale: 4 Lind 5 Jenny

sweep: oar 4 line 5 besom, broom, brush, clean, clear, drive, range, scope, scour, strip, surge, swath 6 extend, remove 7 contour, stretch 8 traverse

sweeping: 8 complete 9 extensive 13 comprehensive, thoroughgoing

sweepings: 6 fulyie(Sc.), fulzie(Sc.)

sweer: 4 slow 5 loath 8 indolent 9 reluctant

sweet: 4 dear, fair 5 bonny, candy, dolce, douce(F.), fresh, soave 6 dulcet, gentle, lovely, pretty, sugary, syrupy 7 beloved, caramel, darling, honeyed, musical, winning 8 aromatic, fetching, fragrant, pleasant, pleasing, preserve 9 agreeable, ambrosial, melodious 10 attractive, confection, harmonious 11 mellisonant

sweet flag: 7 calamus

sweet potato: yam 6 batata 7 ocarina

sweetbread: 9 ris de veau

sweetbrier: 9 eglantine

sweeten: 4 mull 5 sugar 6 purify, refine, soften, solace 7 appease, cleanse, freshen, mollify, perfume, relieve 9 disinfect 10 edulcorate

sweetfish: ayu

sweetheart: jo(Sc.); gra 4 agra, beau, dear, doll, doxy, gill, girl, jill, lass, love 5 bully, court, flame, leman 6 adorer, fellow, orpine 8 truelove

sweetly: 8 smoothly 10 pleasantly 11 comfortably 13 mellifluently

sweetmeat: 4 cake **5** candy, goody **6** comfit, dragee, pastry **7** caramel, dessert **8** confetti, conserve, hardbake, marzipan, preserve **9** marchpane, sugarplum **10** confection

sweetsop: 4 ates

swell: nob, sea **4** bell, bulb, bulk, grow, huff, rise, surf, toff, wave **5** bloat, bulge, grand, surge **6** billow, dilate, expand, extend, roller, tiptop, tumefy **7** augment, distend, enlarge, inflate, sea-gate, stylish **8** increase **9** elevation, excellent, first-rate, intumesce **10** prominence, thickening **11** fashionable **12** protuberance **16** ultrafashionable

swelled head: 6 egoist **7** conceit

swellfish: 6 puffer **8** puff-fish

swelling: sty **4** bleb, bubo, node **5** blain, botch, bouge, bunch, edema, tumor **6** aswell, gather, growth **7** gibbous, turgent **8** windgall **9** gibbosity

on plants: **4** gall

pert. to: **5** nodal **9** edematose, edematous

swelt: die **5** broil, faint, swoon **6** perish, scorch **9** suffocate

swelter: 4 fret, heat, rush **5** exude, faint, roast, sweat **6** wallow, welter **8** perspire

swerve: bow **4** skew, turn, veer **5** stray, yield **6** totter **7** deflect, deviate, digress

sweven: 5 dream, sleep **6** vision

swift: 4 cran(Sc.), fast, reel **5** alert, fleet, hasty, quick, rapid, ready **6** lizard, prompt, speedy, winged

Swift: 4 Dean **8** satirist

brute: **5** Yahoo

flying island: **6** Laputa

hero: **8** Gulliver

lady friend: **6** Stella

pen name: **7** Draper **11** Bickerstaff

swiftly: 4 fast **5** apace

swiftness: 5 haste **8** celerity

swig: 4 gulp, rock, sway **5** draft, drink, hoist, swash **6** tackle

swile: 4 seal

swill: 4 fill, wash **5** flood, rinse, swash, waste **6** basket, drench, guzzle, refuse **7** garbage, hogwash

swillbowl: sot **8** drunkard

swim: 4 reel **5** float, swoon **9** dizziness **13** forgetfulness **15** unconsciousness

pert. to: **8** natatory

swimmer: 7 natator

of the English Channel: **6** Ederle

of the Hellespont: **7** Leander

of Tiber river: **7** Cloelia

swimming: 5 aswim **6** filled, naiant, natant **7** flooded, vertigo **9** dizziness

swimming pool: 4 tank **10** natatorium

swimming stroke: 4 back, side **5** crawl **6** breast **9** butterfly

swindle: con, gyp **4** bilk, dupe, fake, mace, rook **5** bunco, bunko, cheat, foist, fraud, spoof, trick **6** diddle, trepan **7** defraud **8** flimflam

swindler: fob **5** biter, cheat, crook, knave, rogue, shark **6** chiaus, chouse, shaver **7** sharper **8** blackleg

swine: hog, pig, sow **4** boar **7** peccary

breed of: **8** Cheshire, Tamworth **9** Berkshire, Hampshire, Yorkshire **11** Duroc-Jersey, Poland China **12** Chester White

feeding of: **7** pannage **8** slopping

female: sow **4** gilt

fever: **6** rouget **7** cholera

flesh: **4** pork

litter of: **6** farrow

male: **4** boar

pert. to: **7** porcine

young: pig **5** shoat **6** piglet

swinelike: 7 porcine

swing: 4 beat, bent, blow, hang, hurl, lilt, slew, slue, sway, whip **5** fling, power, shake, throw, trend, waver **6** dangle, manage, rhythm, stroke, totter **7** flutter, shoggie(Sc.), suspend, trapeze, vibrate **8** brandish, undulate **9** fluctuate, oscillate

swing around: 4 slue

swinge: 4 beat, lash, whip **5** whirl **6** thrash **7** impetus, revolve, scourge

swinish: 5 gross **6** coarse **7** beastly, boarish, piggish, sensual

swink: 4 toil **5** labor, slave **8** drudgery

swipe: cut, hit **4** blow, glom **5** draft, drink, lever, steal, swape, sweep **6** pilfer, snatch, strike

swirl: ess **4** curl, eddy **5** curve, gurge, twist, whirl, whorl

swirly: 7 knotted, tangled, twisted

swish: 4 cane, flog, hiss, lash, whip **5** birch, smart, sound **6** rustle, strike

Swiss: See **Switzerland**

switch: gad, rod **4** beat, flog, lash, turn, twig, wand, whip **5** shift, shunt, swing **6** change, divert, strike **7** scourge **8** transfer **10** disconnect

switchboard: 5 panel

switchman: 7 shunter

Switzerland: 6 Suisse(F.) **7** Schweiz(G.) **8** Helvetia

ax: **6** piolet

bay: Uri

canton: Uri, Zug **4** Bern, Genf, Vaud **5** Basel, Basle, Waadt **6** Aargau, Geneva, Geneve, Glaris, Glarus, Luzern, St. Gall, Schwyz, Tessin, Ticino, Valais, Wallis, Zurich **7** Grisons, Lucerne, Schwytz, Soleure, Thurgau **8** Freiberg **9** Appenzell, Neuchatel, Neuenberg, Solothurn **10** Graubunden

11 Sankt Gallen, Schaffhouse, Unterwalden 12 Schaffhausen
card game: 4 jass
cheese: 7 Gruyere, sapsago 9 schweizer 10 Emmentaler 13 schweizer-kase
city: 4 Bale, Bern, Chur, Genf, Sion 5 Basel, Basle, Berne 6 Geneva, Schwyz, Zurich 7 Fyzabad, Locarno, Lucerne 8 Faizabad, Lausanne, Montreux, St. Gallen 9 Constance, Neuchatel 10 Farukhabad, Winterthur
coin: 5 franc, rappe 6 rappen 7 angster, centime, duplone 8 blaffert
commune: Zug 4 Biel, Wald 5 Aarau, Morat
composer: 4 Raff
district: 6 canton
food: 12 bernerplatte
herdsman: 4 senn
hero: 11 Wilhelm Tell
lake: Uri, Zug 4 Joux, Thon 5 Leman 6 Bienne, Brienz, Geneva, Lugano, Sarnen, Zurich 7 Lucerne, Lungern 8 Viervald 9 Constance, Neuchatel, Sarnersee, Thunersee 10 Stattersee 11 Brienzersee
language: 5 Ladin 6 French, German 7 Italian, Romansh 8 Romansch, Roumansh 14 Switzerdeutsch
legislature: 8 grossrat 9 grosserat, grossrath
measure: imi, pot 4 aune, elle, fuss, immi, muid, pied, saum, zoll 5 lieue, ligne, linie, maass, moule, pouce, schuh, staab, toise 6 perche, setier, strich 7 juchart, klafter, viertel 9 quarteron 11 holzklafter
money: 4 batz
mountain: 4 Alps, Jura, Rigi, Rosa 5 Blanc, Cenis, Genis 7 Pilatus 8 Jungfrau 9 St. Gothard 10 Matterhorn 11 Burgenstock
mountain pass: 5 Furka 7 Gothard, Grimsel, Simplon 8 Lotschen 13 Saint Gotthard
officer: 5 amman
painter: 4 Klee
people: 4 muff 5 French, German 7 Italian, Romansh 8 Rhaetian, Romansch, Roumansh 9 Helvetian
pert. to: 5 Alpen
pine: 6 arolla
psychologist: 4 Jung
resort: 5 Davos
river: Aar, Inn 4 Aare 5 Doubs, Reuss, Rhone
sled: 4 luge 5 luger
song: 5 yodel
tunnel: 5 Cenis 7 Gothard, Simplon 11 Loetschberg
weight: 5 pfund 7 centner, quintal 11 zugtierlast 12 zugthierlast
wind: 4 bise
wine: 7 Dezaley

valley: Aar
swivel: 4 turn
swollen: 4 blub 5 blown, pursy, tumid 6 turgid 7 blubber, bulbous, bulging, pompous 8 enlarged, inflated, varicose 9 distended, increased, tumescent
swoon: fit 4 dwam 5 dwalm(Sc.), faint, sleep, spell 6 attack 7 ecstasy, syncope 8 languish
swoop: cut 5 seize, sweep 6 pounce 7 descend
sword: sax 4 dirk, epee, foil, pata 5 bilbo, brand, estoc, glawe, gully, kukri, saber, sabre 6 barong, creese, cutlas, Damask, dusack, espada, floret, parang, rapier, spatha, Toledo 7 ascalon, askelon, baslard, curtana, curtein, cutlass, espadon, estoque, shabble, simitar 8 acinaces, camplian, claymore, Damascus, falchion, flamberg, scimitar, schlager, whinyard 9 achiavone, flamberge
blade of: 5 forte
cross guard: 7 quillon
curved: 5 saber, sabre 8 scimitar
fencing: 4 epee, foil
handle: 4 haft, hilt
of the Cid: 6 Colada
short: 4 dirk
two-edged: 4 pata
sword lily: 9 gladiolus
swordfish: 6 espada 7 espadon 9 broadbill
swordlike: 5 xypho 6 ensate 8 ensiform, gladiate
swordsman: 6 fencer 7 epeeist
swore: 5 curst 6 cursed
sworn: 7 devoted 8 affirmed, attested 9 confirmed 10 determined, inveterate
swot (see also **swat**): 5 grind, labor, sweat
syagush: 7 caracal
sybarite: 7 epicure 10 voluptuary
Sybil: See **Sibyl**
syce: 5 groom
sycophant: 5 toady 7 fawning, spaniel 8 informer, parasite 9 charlatan, flatterer 10 footlicker, talebearer
sycophantic: 7 servile, slavish
sye: sy; sie 4 fall, sink 7 descend
Syleus' slayer: 8 Heracles, Hercules
syllable: *added:* 6 prefix
deletion: 7 apocope
final: 6 ultima
lacking at end: 10 catalectic
musical: do, fa, la, mi, re, so, ti
next to last: 6 penult
second before last: 10 antepenult
short: 4 mora 5 breve
shortening: 7 apocope, elision, systole
stressed: 5 arsis
unaccented: 6 atonic

syllabus: 7 outline, summary 8 headnote, synopsis 9 statement 10 compendium

sylloge: 10 collection, compendium

syllogism: 7 Sorites 8 argument 9 reasoning 10 epichirema 11 epicheirema

sylph: elf, fay 5 fairy 6 undine

sylphlike: 7 lissome, slender 8 graceful

sylvan: 5 woody 6 rustic, wooded 8 woodsman 10 forestlike

sylvan deity: Pan 4 faun 6 Faunus

sylvatic: 4 rude 11 uncivilized

symbol (see also **element**): 4 icon, ikon, sign, type, word 5 badge, creed, crest, cross, image, token, totem 6 caract, emblem, ensign, figure, letter 7 diagram 9 character, hierogram, trademark 10 expression, similitude 12 abbreviation, contribution

achievement: 5 medal 6 ribbon
comedy: 4 sock
early Christian church: 5 orant
immortality: 6 phenix 7 phoenix
mourning: 5 crepe 7 cypress
peace: 4 dove
put into: 6 notate
saintliness: 4 halo
servitude: 4 yoke
victory: 4 palm 6 laurel
wisdom: owl

symbolical: 7 typical 8 mystical 11 allegorical, sacramental 14 representative

symbolize: 5 agree 6 concur, typify 7 betoken, combine, express, signify 9 harmonize, represent

symmetrical: 7 regular, spheral 13 commensurable

symmetry: 7 balance, harmony 9 congruity 10 conformity, consistency, proportion

sympathetic: 4 soft 6 humane, tender 7 pietoso, piteous 8 affected 9 condolent, congenial, expansive, sensitive 10 responsive 13 compassionate

sympathize: 6 bemoan 7 condole 11 commiserate

sympathy: 4 pity 6 accord, liking 7 harmony 8 interest 9 agreement 10 compassion, condolence, tenderness 13 commiseration, understanding

expression of: 8 clemency 10 condolence
lack of: 8 dyspathy

symphonious: 9 accordant 10 harmonious

symphony: 5 music 7 concord, harmony

division: 8 movement
for Napoleon: 6 Eroica
form: 6 sonata

symposium: 4 talk 7 banquet 8 dialogue 9 symposiac 10 conference, discussion 11 compotation

symptom: 4 mark, note, sign 5 token 10 indication

synagogue: 4 shul 5 group 8 assembly, building, religion 9 communion, community 12 congregation

officer: 6 parnas
platform: 7 almemar
pointer: yad
Sephardic: 5 anoga
singer: 6 cantor, chazan 7 chazzan

synaxis: 7 meeting, service 12 congregation

synchronize: 7 arrange 8 regulate 12 contemporize

synchronous: 8 existing 10 concurrent 11 concomitant 12 contemporary, simultaneous 15 contemporaneous

syncope: 4 loss 5 faint, swoon 7 elision 9 cessation, haplology 10 suspension 11 contraction, hyphaeresis 15 unconsciousness

syndetic: 10 connective

syndic: 5 agent, judge, mayor 7 manager, officer, trustee 8 advocate, official 10 magistrate

syndicate: 4 sell 5 chain, group, trust, unite 6 cartel 7 censure, council 8 monopoly 9 committee 11 association 12 organization

synod: 4 body 5 court 7 council, meeting 8 assembly 10 convention 11 convocation

syne: ago 5 since

synonymous: 4 like 5 alike 10 equivalent

synopsis: 4 plan 7 summary 8 abstract 9 statement 10 compendium, conspectus 11 abridgement

syntax: 5 order 6 system 9 structure 11 arrangement

analyze: 5 parse
mistake: 8 solecism

synthesis: 5 summa 7 complex 11 combination, composition 13 incorporation

syphilis: pox 4 lues

lesion: 7 chancre
old remedy: 9 Salvarsan

Syracuse: *conqueror:* 4 Rome
founder: 7 Archias
tyrant: 5 Gelon

Syria: *ancient name:* 4 Aram
animal: 5 addax, daman
bear: 4 dubb
bishop: 4 abba
buried city: 4 Dura
church plan: 8 triconch
city: 4 Homs 5 Calno, Derra 6 Aleppo, Balbec, Calneh 7 Antioch 8 Damascus, Seleucia 12 Alexandretta
deity: El 4 Baal 5 Allat 6 Mammon 7 Resheph
district: 6 Aleppo, Hauran
goat: 6 angora
grass: 7 Johnson

gypsy: **5** Aptal
lake: **5** Merom **8** Tiberias
mallow: **4** okra
measure: **5** makuk **6** garava
money: **5** pound **6** talent **7** piaster
mountain: **6** Carmel **7** Libanus
peasant: **6** fellah
people: **5** Druse **7** Ansarie, Saracen
plant: **5** cumin
religious sect: **5** Druse
river: **6** Jordan **7** Orontes
script: **5** serta
silk: **4** acca
tetrarchy: **7** abilene
weight: **4** cola, rotl **5** artal, artel, ratel **6** talent
wind: **6** simoon
syringa: 5 lilac, shrub

syrinx: 7 panpipe **8** panpipes
syrt: bog **9** quicksand
syrup: 4 karo, sapa **6** orgeat **7** dhebbus, glucose, sarghum
system: ism **4** code **5** group **6** circle, method, regime, theory **7** regimen **8** religion, treatise, universe **9** procedure **10** assemblage, hypothesis, philosophy, regularity **11** aggregation, arrangement, orderliness
of rules: **4** code
of weights: **4** troy
of worship: **4** cult
systematic: 4 neat **7** orderly, regular **9** organized **10** methodical
systematics: 8 taxonomy
systematize: 6 adjust **7** arrange, catalog **8** organize, regiment **9** catalogue
syzygy: 6 dipody
Szechwan capital: 7 Chengtu

T

t-shaped: tau

taa: 6 pagoda

Taal: 9 Afrikaans

tab: pan, tag **4** bill, drop, flap, loop **5** aglet, check, index, label, score, strap, strip **6** aiglet, eartab, record **7** account, latchet, officer **9** appendage, reckoning **10** accounting

tabac: 5 snuff **7** tobacco

tabanid: 8 horsefly

tabard: inn **4** cape, coat **5** cloak **6** chimer, jacket, mantle **7** pendant

tabasco: 5 sauce

tabatiere: 8 snuffbox

tabby: cat, pad **4** gown, silk **5** dress **6** fabric, gossip, moreen **7** padding, taffeta **8** brindled

tabella: 6 tablet **7** lozenge

taberna: 4 shop, tent **5** booth **7** shelter

tabernacle: 4 tent **5** abode, dwell, hovel, niche **6** church, recess, reside, temple **7** deposit, shelter, support **8** enshrine **9** sanctuary, structure **10** habitation, receptacle

tabes: 7 atrophy **10** emaciation **11** consumption **12** tuberculosis

tabetless: 4 numb **7** foolish **9** senseless

table: hem **4** fare, feed, food, slab, wash **5** bench, board, canon, index, panel, plate, treat **6** indius, lamina, record, repast, tablet **7** console, surface **8** credence, feasting, postpone, schedule, synopsis, tabulate **10** collection **11** concentrate **12** stringcourse
centerpiece: **7** epergne
communion: **5** altar **8** credence, credenza
cover: **5** baize, cloth, tapis
decorative cloth: **6** runner
dish: **6** tureen
game: **4** pool **8** Ping-Pong **9** billiards
linen: **6** napery **7** napkins **11** tablecloths
philosophers: **14** deipnosophists
small: **5** stand, wagon **6** teapoy **7** taboret, tendoor, tendour
working: **5** bench
writing: **4** desk **10** escritoire

table tennis: 8 Ping-Pong

tableland: 4 mesa **5** karoo **6** karroo **7** plateau **8** balaghat, plateaux, plateaus **9** balaghaut **12** altiplanicie

tableau: 7 picture **8** register, schedule **14** representation

tablet: pad **4** bred, slab **5** facia, panel **6** troche **7** lozenge **10** receptacle
medicine: **6** troche
sculptured: **5** stela, stele **6** stelae, steles
stone: **4** slab **5** stele
three-leaved: **8** triptych
two-leaved: **7** diptych
writing: pad **5** slate

tableware item: cup **4** bowl, dish, fork **5** knife, plate, spoon **6** saucer

tablinum: 4 room **6** alcove, recess

tabloid: 5 short **9** condensed **12** concentrated

taboo, tabu: ban **5** debar **6** forbid **8** prohibit **9** forbidden **12** interdiction
opposed to: noa

tabor, tabour: 4 drum **6** atabal **7** attabal, eardrum, timbrel

taboret, tabouret: 4 drum, seat **5** stand, stool, tabor **6** tabour

tabu: See taboo

tabulate: 4 list **7** arrange **8** schedule

tabulation: *grammatical:* **8** paradigm
of the year: **8** calendar

taccaceous herb: pia

taccada: 9 fanflower

tache: pan, tie **4** spot **5** clasp, fault, habit, stain **6** attach, buckle **7** blemish, tarnish **11** disposition **14** characteristic

tacit: 6 silent **7** implied **8** implicit, unspoken, wordless **9** noiseless **10** understood

taciturn: 6 silent **8** reserved, reticent **9** saturnine **15** uncommunicative

tack: 4 beat, busk, clap, gear, haul, join, link, nail, rope, slap, trim **5** baste, catch, fetch, rider, spell, strip, tying, unite **6** attach, course, fasten, handle, method, secure, tackle **7** clothes, connect, payment **8**

contract 9 agreement, endurance, fastening 10 stickiness, supplement 12 adhesiveness
glazier: 4 brad
nautical: 5 board
to: 4 jibe
to windward: 4 trip
two-pointed: 6 staple
tackle: rig 4 arms, food, gear, tack 5 angle,
drink, seize, stuff 6 attach, collar, secure 7
grapple, harness, rigging, weapons 8 mistress, windlass 9 apparatus, encounter,
equipment, undertake
football: 4 stop 5 throw
fishing: tew
single and double block: 6 burton
strong: cat
tacky: 5 crude, dowdy, seedy 6 shabby,
sticky, untidy 8 adhesive, slovenly
tact: 5 poise, touch 6 stroke 7 address, feeling 8 delicacy, graceful 9 appendage, diplomacy 10 adroitness, cleverness, discretion, perception 11 discernment 14 discrimination
tactfully: 7 happily
tactics: 6 method, system 9 procedure
tactless: 5 brash
tactlessness: 9 gaucherie
tad: 5 child 6 urchin
tadpole: 8 polliwog
taenia: 4 band 6 fillet 8 headband
taffy: 5 gundy 7 glaggum 8 flattery
Taffy: 8 Welshman
tag: dog, end, tab 4 flap, game, join, lock 5
aglet, label, shred, strip, touch 6 aiglet,
append, attach, eartab, fasten, follow, rabble 7 refrain, taglock 9 appendage, catchword 11 aiguillette
metal: 5 aglet 6 aiglet
Tagalog (see also **Philippine Islands**): 8
Filipino
child: 4 bata 5 Anacs
deity: 6 Batala 7 Bathala
gambling game: 10 panguingui
learn: 4 aral
mother: Ina
peasant: Tao
race: Ita
wine: 4 alac
tagrag: rag, tag 6 rabble, tatter 8 vagabond
tagtail: 9 sycophant
taha: 4 baya 10 weaverbird
Tahiti: *canoe:* 4 pahi
capital: 7 Papeete
centipede: 4 veri
coronation robe: 4 maro
food plant: 4 taro
god: Oro 6 Taaroa
loincloth: 4 malo, maro

mulberry: 4 aute
old name: 8 Otaheite
people: 10 Polynesian
resident painter: 7 Gauguin
seaport: 7 Papeete
woman: 6 vahine, wahine
Tai, Thai: 7 Siamese
race: Lao
taigle: 4 drag 5 catch, delay, trail 6 entrap,
hinder loiter 7 fatigue
tail: bun, cue, end 4 arse, back, bunt, last,
rear 5 cauda 6 follow, shadow, switch 7
limited, pendant, reduced 8 abridged, buttocks, encumber, entailed 9 appendage,
curtailed, extremity, fundament
having a: 7 caudate
kinds of: bob, bun, fud 4 bunt, scut 5 cauda,
plume, stern, twist 6 strunt, wreath 8
streamer 9 empennage
pert. to: 6 caudal
plane: 10 stabilizer
short: bun 4 scut
tailed: 7 caudate
tailing: 5 chaff, waste 6 refuse
taille: fit, tax 4 form 5 build, shape, style,
waist 6 figure 10 imposition
tailless: 7 acaudal, anurous 8 acaudate,
ecaudate 9 excaudate
tailor: 4 snip 6 darzee, draper, sartor 7 cabbage 9 bushelman 11 bushelwoman
goose: 8 flatiron
iron: 5 goose
lap board: 5 panel
pert. to: 9 sartorial
tailzie: cut 5 agree, shape, slice, tally 6 entail 7 account, appoint, arrange 9 reckoning
taint: dip, dye, hit, hue 4 blow, evil, hogo,
spot, tint 5 cloud, color, imbue, prove,
spoil, stain, sully, tinge, touch, trace,
wound 6 accuse, defile, infect, poison,
stigma 7 attaint, blemish, convict, corrupt, debauch, deprave, pollute, vitiate 8
disgrace, empoison, hautgout, tincture 10
conviction, corruption, impregnate 11
contaminate
tainted: bad 5 blown
taipo: 5 demon, devil 10 theodolite
taisch: 5 ghost, voice
taissle: 6 puzzle, tangle 8 disorder
tait: 5 sport 6 lively 8 sportive 9 marsupial
12 cheerfulness
taivers, tavers: 6 babble, shreds 7 tatters
Taiwan: See **Formosa**
taj: cap 8 Taj Mahal
Taj Mahal site: 4 Agra
tajo: 6 trench
take: get, hit, win 4 doff, fang, glom, grip,
haul, lead, trap 5 adopt, atone, avail,
carry, catch, charm, cheat, check, fetch,

glaum, grasp, infer, seize, snare, spell, steal, swear, touch, trick 6 absorb, accept, affirm, amount, arrest, assume, attach, attack, borrow, choose, convey, deduce, deduct, derive, employ, endure, engage, number, obtain, profit, remove, secure, select, strike, submit, tenure 7 capture, conduct, detract, extract, promise, receive, undergo 8 abstract, contract, proceeds, quantity, receipts, subtract 9 apprehend, interrupt 11 appropriate

aback: 5 check 7 startle 8 astonish, confound, surprise

account of: 6 notice, regard

advantage of: 5 abuse 6 misuse 7 exploit

advice: 4 hear, heed, mind 6 listen

aim: 5 level

another's place: sub 9 alternate 10 substitute

apart: 4 ruin 7 destroy 9 dismantle

as actual: 5 posit

as one's own: 5 adopt 6 borrow

away: 5 adeem, reave 6 adempt, deduct, devest, recant, remove 7 deprive, detract, retract 8 subtract

back: 6 recant 7 retract 8 withdraw

beforehand: 7 pre-empt

bold attitude: 5 brisk

by craft: 6 entoil

by force: 5 erept 8 ereption

by storm: 5 seize 6 attack

by stratagem: 4 trap

care: 4 mind, reck 5 nurse, watch 6 beware, cuiado

care of: 4 tend 5 nurse

chair: sit

cognizance of: 4 note 6 notice

comb from beehive: 4 geld

delight: 5 revel

direction: 5 steer

down: 5 abase, lower 6 escort, humble, record, reduce 7 swallow 8 emaciate, withdraw 10 distribute

evening meal: sup 4 dine

exception: 5 demur 6 object

fire: 5 spunk

first: 7 preempt

five: 4 rest

for granted: 6 assume 7 presume

forcibly: 5 seize

from: 5 wrest 6 deduct, divest 7 deprive, derived, detract 8 derogate, subtract

heed: 4 mind, reck, ware

hold: 5 grasp 6 obtain

in: 4 furl, open 5 admit, annex, brail, cheat, fence, trick, visit 6 attend, escort 7 deceive, embrace, enclose, explore, include,

observe, receive 8 commence, comprise, contract 9 encompass 10 comprehend, understand

in hand: 5 seize 7 attempt 9 undertake

in sail: 4 reef

into custody: 6 arrest 9 apprehend

it ill: 6 resent

it easy: 4 rest 5 relax

leave: 6 decamp, depart

legal possession of: 5 seise, seize

liberties: 7 presume

meals for pay: 5 board

no notice of: 9 disregard

notice: NB; see

off: 4 copy, doff, soar 5 abate, begin, deter, mimic, start 6 deduct, depart, lessen, remove 7 detract 8 discount, distract, subtract, withdraw 9 burlesque, calculate, determine, reproduce

off suspended list: 9 reinstate

offense of: 6 resent

on: 4 hire 6 assume, employ, engage, oppose, tackle 7 consort, receive 8 arrogate 9 associate, undertake

on cargo: 4 lade

one's way: 4 wend

orders: 4 obey 5 yield

out: 4 copy, dele, omit 5 elide 6 deduct, delete, efface, escort, except, remove 7 extract, scratch, unhitch 8 overall, separate 9 eliminate

out by roots: 9 extirpate

out curves and bends: 10 straighten

out of pawn: 6 redeem

over: 5 seize 6 assume, convey

part: 4 join 5 share

part in contest: 7 compete

part of: 4 side 5 enact

place: 5 occur

place again: 5 recur

place of: 4 else 8 supplant 9 supersede

pleasure in: 5 enjoy, fancy

positive opinion: 4 side

possession of: 5 enter, seise

rise: 7 emanate

root: 4 grow 6 settle

service as seaman: 4 ship

shape: 4 form 11 crystallize

shelter: 6 nestle

some of: 7 partake

stock: 5 count 6 survey 8 appraise, estimate 9 inventory

the stick: 5 steer

to court: sue

turns: 9 alternate

umbrage at: 6 resent

unawares: 5 seize 7 astound, capture, startle 8 astonish, confound, overcome, surprise 9 overwhelm *unlawfully:* rob 5 steal, usurp 6 pilfer

up: buy 4 fill, lift 5 adopt, allow, check, enter, exact, mount, raise, seize 6 absorb, accept, arrest, assume, borrow, employ, gather, occupy, remove, resume 7 collect, dissent, elevate, engross, receive 9 extirpate, reprimand 10 comprehend, understand

up again: 5 renew 6 resume

up weapons: arm 4 rise

with: 4 like 5 brook 6 accept 7 confess 11 acknowledge

without authority: 5 usurp

taken: 8 occupied

in all: 7 overall 9 inclusive

by twos: 5 duple

taker: 5 thief 6 captor 7 catcher 8 pilferer, purveyor 10 plagiarist

of court action: 4 suer

of income or profits: 6 pernor

takin: 7 gazelle 8 antelope

taking: 4 take 5 catch, palsy 6 arrest, attack, blight, plight 7 capture, malefic, seizing, seizure 8 alluring, capitious, catching, engaging, grasping, receipts 9 accepting, rapacious, receiving, reception 10 attachment, attractive, contagious, infectious 11 captivating 12 apprehension

different form: 7 protean 11 metamorphic

precedence: 7 ranking

unauthorized leave: 4 A.W.O.L.

takt: 4 beat 5 beats, pulse, tempo 7 measure

tala: 4 raid, ruin 11 destruction

talapoin: 4 monk 6 monkey 7 poongee 8 poonghee, poonghie

talc: 6 talcum 7 agalite 8 steatite 9 soapstone

tale: lie 4 gest, myth, saga, talk, tell, yarn 5 count, fable, geste, speak, story, tally, total 6 esteem, gossip, legend, reckon, report, speech 7 account, fiction, history, parable, recital 8 anecdote, category, consider, counting, relation 9 discourse, falsehood, narration, narrative, numbering, reckoning 11 declaration, enumeration, information 12 conversation

adventure: 4 gest 5 geste

kind of: lai 4 gest, saga, yarn 5 bourd, geste, roman 6 legend 7 romance 8 allegory, jeremiad 9 storiette

medieval: lai, lay

Tale of Two Cities: *author:* 7 Dickens

hero: 6 Carton

heroine: 5 Lucie

talebearer: 6 buzzer, gossip 7 tattler 8 talepyet, telltale 10 newsmonger 13 scandalmonger

talent: 4 gift 5 anger, dowry, flair, gifts, knack, money, skill, talon 6 custom, desire, flavor, genius, powers, riches, wealth 7 ability, betters, faculty, feature, longing, passion 8 appetite, aptitude, capacity, gamblers, property 9 abilities, abundance, attribute 10 endowments 11 disposition, inclination 14 accomplishment

sale: 8 venality

special: 5 forte

talented: 4 able 5 smart 6 clever, gifted 8 addicted, disposed, inclined

talenter: 4 hawk

talents: 9 endowment

talesman: 5 juror 8 narrator

taletelling: 4 blab

taliation: 5 tally 10 adjustment

taliera: 4 tara

talion: 11 retaliation

talipot: 4 palm

talisman: 4 tara 5 charm, saffi, safie 6 amulet, fetich, fetish, grigri, saphie, scarab, telesm 8 greegree

talitol: 7 alcohol

talk: yap 4 buck, bukh, carp, chat, gaff, knap, talk, word 5 bazoo lingo, parle, prate, rumor, speak, theme, utter 6 confer, debate, gabble, gossip, reason, report, speech, steven, tongue 7 address, chatter, consult, council, dialect, express, meeting, mention, palabra 8 causerie, chitchat, collogue, colloquy, converse, parlance, verbiage 9 dalliance, discourse 10 conference, discussion 11 communicate 12 conversation

about: 6 gossip 7 discuss

abusive: 5 hoker

back: 4 sass 6 retort, ripost 7 riposte 8 repartee

big: 4 brag 5 boast

boastful: 4 gaff, rant

ceremonious: 8 chin-chin

chatty: gab 6 gossip

common: 7 hearsay

complaining: 4 carp

confused: 10 galimatias

desultorily: 6 ramble

deliriously: 4 rave

down: 7 outtalk, silence

down to: 9 patronize 10 condescend

effusively: 4 gush, rave

familiar: 6 confab

fast and idly: 7 gnatter

flattering: 7 palaver

flippant: 10 persiflage

fluent: 7 verbose, voluble

foolish: gab, gas 4 bosh, buff, bunk, gash 5 spiel 6 babble, bunkum, claver, fraise, patter 7 blabber, twaddle 8 buncombe, wishwash 9 poppycock, rigmarole 11 goosecackle, stultiloquy

formal: 7 address, lecture

from pulpit: 6 homily, sermon
glib: 6 patter 7 palaver
idly: gab, gas 5 prate 6 tattle 7 chatter, twaddle
imperfectly: 4 lisp 7 stutter
in sleep: 15 somniloquacious
indiscreetly: 4 blab
indistinctly: 7 sputter
irrationally: 4 rant, rave
light: 5 chaff 6 banter 8 raillery
persuasively: 6 reason
pert: lip 4 sass
profuse: 4 chat 6 patter 7 palaver 10 persiflage
slowly: 5 drawl
small: gab 4 chat, chin 7 prattle 8 chitchat
table: ana 9 symposiac
tediously: 5 prose
to no purpose: 4 blat
together: 4 chat 8 converse
turgid: 4 cant, rant
unintelligible: 6 drivel, jargon, patter 9 gibberish
wildly: 4 rave
with passion: 4 rave
talkative: 4 cozy, gash, glib 5 gabby 6 chatty, clashy, fluent 7 verbose, voluble 8 flippant 9 garrulous 10 babblative, loquacious
talkativeness: 9 garrulity, garrulous, loquacity
talker: 6 proser, ranter, rhetor 7 babbler, spieler 17 conversationalist
incessant: 6 gasbag, magpie 10 chatterbox 12 blabbermouth
talkfest: 9 gathering 10 discussion
talking iron: gun 5 rifle
tall: 4 bold, deft, fine, high, lank, long 5 brave, grand, great, lanky, large, lofty, quick, rangy, ready, steep, tally 6 comely, docile, seemly 7 doughty, skyhigh, unusual 8 obedient, towering, yielding 9 excellent 10 courageous, incredible 11 exaggerated 13 grandiloquent
tallage: aid, due, fee, tax 4 toll 6 custom, impost, tarage
tallet: 5 attic 7 hayloft
talliar: 8 watchman
tallness: 9 procerity
tallote: 5 gourd 7 chayote 8 calabash
tallow: fat 4 suet 5 sevum, smear 6 fatten, grease
pert. to: 7 stearic
pot: 7 fireman
refuse: 9 crackling
sediment: 7 greaves
tallow-berry: 11 locustberry
tally: run, tab, tag 4 deal, goal, mark, mate, suit 5 agree, check, count, grade, label, match, notch, score 6 accord, reckon, re-

cord 7 account, compare, loftily 8 estimate 9 agreement, elegantly, reckoning 10 becomingly, correspond, resolutely 11 counterpart 14 correspondence
tallyho: cry 5 coach
crier of: 6 hunter
talma: 4 cape, coat
Talmud commentary: 6 Gemara
Talmudic academy: 7 Yeshiva 8 Yeshibah, Yeshivah 9 Yeshiboth
student: 5 bahur
talon: 4 claw, heel, sere 6 clutch, hallux 7 molding 11 certificate
Talos' slayer: 8 Daedalus
talter: 4 hang
taluk: 5 tract 6 estate 10 dependency 11 subdivision 12 collectorate
talukdar: 9 collector, tahsildar 10 landholder, proprietor
talus: 4 ankle, scree, slope 6 debris 8 clubfoot 9 anklebone 11 knucklebone
tam: cap, hat 5 beret 8 headgear 11 tam-o-shanter
tamarack: 10 hackmatack
tamarind: 8 sampaloc
tamarisk: sal 4 atle, jhow 5 atlee
tamas: 7 inertia 8 dullness 9 ignorance
tamasha: 4 fuss, show 7 pageant 9 commotion, spectacle 10 excitement 13 entertainment
tambo: inn 6 corral, stable, tavern 7 station
tambour: cup 4 desk, drum 5 frame 7 drummer 8 buttress, ornament 9 embroider 10 embroidery, projection
tambourin: 4 drum 5 dance, tabor
tambourine: 4 dove, drum, taar 5 daira 7 timbrel, travale
tambreet: 8 duckbill
tame: cut 4 bust, dead, dull, mild 5 accoy, begin, break, daunt, prune 6 broach, docile, gentle, humble, soften, subdue 7 affaite, crushed, insipid, servile 8 cicurate, civilize, familiar, harmless 9 deficient, tractable 10 accustomed, cultivated, submissive 11 domesticate, ineffectual 12 domesticated 13 pusillanimous
animal: pet 4 cade 6 cosset
poison: 11 swallowwort
tamed: 6 broken, gentle
tameness: 10 mansuetude
Tamil: 9 Dravidian
caste member: 7 Vellala
Taming of the Shrew character: Sly 4 Kate 6 Bianca, Tranio 8 Baptista
tamis: 5 sieve, tammy 8 strainer
Tammany Society: *officer:* 8 Wiskinky 9 Wiskinkie
leader: 6 sachem
Tammuz: *love:* 6 Ishtar

sister: 6 Belili

tamp: ram 5 drive

tamper: fix 4 fool, plot, tool 6 dabble, meddle, potter, scheme 7 machine 9 influence, interfere

Tampico fiber: 5 istle

tampion, tempeon, tampoon: 4 bung, plug 5 cover 7 stopper, turnpin

tampon: 4 plug 6 tympan 9 drumstick
nasal: 9 rhinobyon

tan: dun, taw 4 beat, camp, ecru, flog, tent, whip 5 brown, color, toast 6 almond, bronze, switch, tannin, thrash 7 embrown, imbrown, sunburn, tanbark
derived from: 5 tanic

tana: 8 banxring

tanager: 4 yeni
genus of: 7 piranga

tanbark: 4 bark

tancel: 4 beat 5 abuse 6 thrash

tang: nip 4 butt, capt, fang, foil, odor, pang, pike, ring, root, spur, tine, zest 5 knife, prick, prong, shank, smack, sting, taste, tinge, trace, twang 6 branch, flavor, pierce, tangle, tongue 7 flavour, seatang, seaweed 8 rockweed 10 suggestion 11 surgeonfish

Tanganyika: See **Tanzania**

tangent: 8 touching

tangible: 4 real 6 actual 7 tactile 8 definite, palpable 9 objective, touchable 11 perceptible, substantial

Tangiers measure: 4 kula, mudd

tangle: bar, cot, mat 4 fank, harl, kink, knot, mesh, trap 5 frame, gnarl, ravel, snare, snarl 6 balter, entrap, icicle, medley, muddle, sleave 7 ensnare, involve, quandry 8 obstruct, scrobble 9 embarrass 10 intertwine, perplexity
of thread: 5 snarl

tangle-foot: 5 aster, drink 6 whisky 8 deerweed

tangled: 11 complicated

tango: 5 bingo, dance

tania: 5 aroid

Tanis: 4 Zoan

tank: hit, vat 4 bang, lake, pond, pool 5 basin, knock, trunk 7 cistern, cuvette, drinker, pachuca, piscina, stomach 9 container, reservoir
part: 5 tread 6 turret

tankard: 5 facer, hanap 6 pottle 7 goddard

tanker: 5 oiler

tanned: 5 brown, tawny 8 sixpence, sunburnt

tanner: 6 barker 8 sixpence

Tannhauser composer: 6 Wagner

tannic acid salt: 7 tannate

tannin: 10 astringent

tanning: *extract:* 5 cutch 7 amaltas
material: 5 sumac 6 sumach
method: 4 napa
pert. to: 11 scytodepsic
plant: 5 alder, sumac 6 sumach

tansy: 9 tanacetum

tanta: 4 aunt

tantadlin: 4 tart 6 dainty 8 dumpling

tantalize: 4 grig 5 taunt, tease 6 harass 7 torment

tantalus: toy 4 case 8 cellaret

Tantalus: *children:* 5 Niobe 6 Pelops
father: 4 Zeus

tantamount: 5 equal 9 identical 10 equivalent

tantara, tantarara: 5 blare 7 fanfare

tantieme: 5 bonus, share 10 percentage

tantivy: cry 4 call, ride, rush, Tory 5 rapid, swift 6 gallop, speedy 7 swiftly 8 headlong, Royalist

tantrum: pet 4 rage

tantum: 5 stint 9 allowance

Tanzania: *island:* 5 Pemba
mountain: 4 Meru
part: 8 Zanzibar 10 Tanganyika
peak: 4 Kibo
people: 4 Goma 6 Wagogo, Wagoma 7 Swahili, Wabunga
title: 5 sayid
weight: 8 farsalah

Taoism: Tao 12 cosmic reason
right conduct: te

tap: bob, cut, hob, pat, rap, tit, vat 4 beat, blow, cock, flip, heat, hole, open, pipe, plug 5 break, fever, flirt, knock, leach, spile, touch, valve 6 broach, faucet, repair, signal, spigot, strike, tapnet 7 censure, connect, penance, reprove
down: 4 tamp

tape: gin, tie 4 band, bind, mole 5 scale, strip 6 fillet, liquor, ribbon, secure 7 bandage, binding
kind of: 4 lear, wick 5 inkle 6 ferret
needle: 6 bodkin

taper: 4 ream, wick 5 light, point, snape 6 candle, cierge, lessen, narrow, trowel 7 conical, dwindle, trindle 8 decrease, diminish 9 acuminate 11 pyramidical

tapered: 7 conical

tapering: 5 conic 6 terete 7 conical 9 acuminate
blades: 6 spires
four-sided pillar: 7 obelisk
piece: 4 gore, shim 5 miter 6 gusset
solid: 4 cone
with circular cross section: 6 terete

tapestry: 5 arras, tapis 6 bayeux, dorser, dosser 7 dossier, gobelin 8 dossiere
comb: 4 reed

kind: 7 Gobelin
warp thread: 5 lisse

tapeworm: 6 taenia 7 taeniae
embryonic form: 10 oncosphere
segments: 8 strobila 9 strobilae
hanging: 5 tapis
provide: 6 arrase

taphouse: bar, inn 6 saloon, tavern 7 taproom

tapioca-like food: 5 salep
source: 7 cassava

tapir: 4 anta 5 danta 8 anteater, ungulate

tapirus Americanus: 4 anta

tapis: 4 band, hide, sash 6 carpet 7 hanging 8 tapestry 10 tablecloth

taplet: 5 block

tapnet: 5 frail 6 basket

tapper: 6 dancer 7 workman 9 decoherer, innkeeper 10 woodpecker

tappet: cam 5 lever 10 projection

taproom: bar, pub 6 saloon, tavern

tapster: 7 barmaid, skinker 9 barkeeper, bartender

Tapuyan: Ge; Ges 5 Gesan 6 Cayapo, Goyana, Timbra 7 Camacan, Coroado 8 Botocudo, Caingang, Chavante

tar: gob 4 brea, salt 5 black, pitch, tease 6 cresol, incite, sailor, seaman 7 blacken, mariner, provoke 8 alkitran, irritate, seafarer, telegram 9 alchitran 10 bluejacket

tar and feathers: 12 plumeopicean

taradiddle: fib, lie 8 nonsense

Taranaki volcano: 6 Egmont

tarantula: 6 spider

tarbet: 7 isthmus, portage

tarboosh: cap, fez

tarde: 4 late, slow 7 evening 9 afternoon

tardigrade: 8 sluggish

tardy: lag, lax 4 late, slow 5 delay, slack 6 remiss, retard 7 belated, lagging, overdue 8 dilatory 10 behindhand, unprepared 11 cunctatious

tare: 4 weed 5 vetch, weigh 6 darnel 7 leakage 9 allowance 13 counterweight

targe: 4 beat 5 paper, scold 6 harass, shield, targer, target 7 buckler, censure 8 document 9 reprimand 10 protection

targer: 5 scold, shrew

target: cut, tee 4 butt, coin, mark, vane 5 shred, sight, slice 6 cymbal, object, shield, tassel, tatter 7 buckler, pendant 8 bullseye, ornament, ridicule 9 indicator, objective, criticism
center: eye 5 clout
shooting gallery: 4 duck

target finder: 5 radar, sonar

Tarheel State: 13 North Carolina

tariff: tax 4 duty, list, rate 5 scale 6 charge, scheme, system 7 average, tribute 8 schedule
favorer: 13 protectionist

Tarkington title: 6 Penrod 9 Seventeen

tarn: 4 lake, pool

tarnish: dim 4 blot, dull, soil, spot 5 cloud, dirty, spoil, stain, sully, taint 6 canker, darken, defile, smirch 7 asperse, blemish, destroy, distain, obscure 8 besmirch, diminish, discolor

taro: 4 coco, eddo, gabi 5 aroid, cocgo, eddoe, tania 7 dasheen 8 caladium
paste: poi
root: edo 4 eddo 6 eddoes

tarpaulin: hat, tar 4 coat, tarp 5 cover 6 sailor 7 sea-bred 10 sailorlike

tarpon: 9 savanilla 10 silverfish

Tarquin's avenger: 7 Porsena

tarriance: 5 delay 7 sojourn 8 awaiting, tarrying 9 hindrance

tarrock: 4 gull, tern

tarrow: 5 delay, tarry 6 linger 7 grumble

tarry: lag, vex 4 bide, loll, rest, stay, stop, wait 5 abide, await, black, dally, defer, delay, demur, dwell, lodge, pause, weary 6 arrest, bundle, hinder, linger, loiter, remain, retard, soiled, tarred, tarrow 7 fatigue, outstay, sojourn, unclean 8 irritate

tarrying: 6 arrest

tarsus: 5 ankle
fore: 4 pala

tart: pie 4 acid, flan, girl, keen, sour 5 acrid, acute, bowla, sharp 6 pastry, pielet, severe, tender, tourte 7 caustic, cutting, painful, piquant, pungent 8 piercing, poignant, turnover 9 acidulous, endearing, sensitive 10 astringent, prostitute

tartan: 4 sett, ship 5 plaid

tartar: 5 argol, shrew, valet 12 incrustation

Tartar: See Tatar

tartarean: 8 infernal

Tartarus: 4 hell 5 Hades

Tartary prince: 4 Agib

tartness: 7 acidity 8 acerbity, acrimony, asperity, piquancy, sourness

Tartuffe: *author:* 7 Moliere
maid: 6 Dorine

tarve: 4 bend, turn

tarweed: 5 Madia

Tarzan's mate: 4 Jane

tash: 4 soil 5 stain 7 fatigue 8 disgrace

task: job, tax 4 busk, char, darg, duty, test, toil, work 5 chare, chore, labor, stent, stint, study 6 amount, burden, dargue, devoir, impost, lesson, strain 7 aufgabe, censure, oppress, overtax 8 quantity 10 accounting, assignment, employment 11 undertaking

easy: 4 pipe, snap 5 cinch 8 sinecure
taskmaster: 6 driver 8 overseer
Tasmania: *animal:* 6 wombat
  cape: 4 Grim
  capital: 6 Hobart
  devil: 7 dasyure
  discoverer: 6 Tasman
  lake: 12 Westmoreland
  mountain: 4 Grey 5 Brown, Drome, Nevis 6 Barrow 8 Humboldt 9 Ben Lomond 10 Wellington
  phalanger: 5 tapoa
  river: 4 Huon 5 Tamar 6 Arthur, Jordan 7 Derwent
  thylacine: 5 tiger
  town: 6 Hobart 10 Launceston
  wolf: 9 thylacine
tass: cup, mow 4 bowl, heap 5 draft 6 goblet
tassel: 4 tuft 5 adorn, label 6 fringe, toorie, zizith 7 pendant 8 ornament
taste: bit, eat, gab, goo, sip, try 4 bent, dash, gout, gust, heed, hint, rasa, tang, test 5 drink, flair, gusto, prove, sapor, savor, scent, shade, smack, smell, spice, touch, trace 6 degust, flavor, liking, little, palate, relish, relush, ribbon, sample, savour 7 flavour, soupcon, thought 8 appetite, delicacy, elegance, fondness 9 attention, degustate, judgement 10 experience, suggestion 11 discernment, inclination 14 discrimination
  absence of: 7 ageusia 8 aguestia
  fundamental: 4 acid, salt 5 sweet 6 bitter
  kind of: nip, sip 4 tang 5 prose, sapor, savor, smack 8 penchant
  lacking in: 4 rude 8 ungentle 9 inelegant 10 unpolished 11 inaesthetic
  pert. to: 7 palatal 9 gustative, gustatory
  perversion: 7 malacia
  refined: 7 elegant
  strong: 4 tang
tasted: 4 sipt
tasteful: 4 neat 5 tasty 6 savory 7 elegant
tasteless: 4 dull, flat 5 vapid 7 insipid 8 lifeless 9 savorless 10 inartistic
tasty: 5 sapid 6 savory 7 palatal 8 tasteful 9 flavorful, palatable, toothsome 10 delectable
tat: die, rag, tap 4 pony 5 touch 6 tangle 7 crochet 8 absolute 9 embroider
Tatar, Tartar: Hun 6 ataman, hetman 7 Cossack
  dynasty: Kin, Wei
  horseman: 7 Cossack
  king: 4 khan
  militiaman: 4 Ulan 5 Uhlan
  mounted band: 4 ulan 5 horde, uhlan 7 chambul
  nobleman: 5 murza

principality: 7 Khanate
republic capital: 5 Kazan
tribe: Hun 5 Alani, Alans 7 Shortzy
tatou, tatu: 9 armadillo
tatter: jag, rag 4 jagg, stir, tear 5 hurry, scold, scrap, shred, testy 6 bustle, gabble, ribbon, tattle 7 chatter, flitter, peevish 8 guenille 14 tatterdemalion
tatterdemalion: 6 ragged 8 tattered 10 ragamuffin
tattered: 4 torn 6 broken, jagged, ragged, shaggy 7 slashed 9 disrupted 10 disheveled 11 dilapidated
tattle: 4 blab, chat, gash, talk, tell 5 cheep, clash, clype, prate 6 gossip 7 chatter, clatter, prattle, stammer
tattler: 6 gossip 8 telltale 9 sandpiper 10 talebearer
tattletale: 6 gossip 7 tattler 8 telltale 10 talebearer
tau cross: 4 ankh, crux
Taube: 9 monoplane
taught: See **teach**
taunt: 4 bob 4 dare, gibe, jeer, jibe, mock, quip, tall, twit 5 check, fleer, glaik, reply, slare, slart, sneer, tease, tempt 6 banter, deride, flaunt, rejoin 7 provoke, upbraid 8 reproach, ridicule 9 aggravate
taurine: 4 bull 6 bovine
taurocol: 4 glue
Taurus: 4 bull
taut: 4 firm, neat, snug, tidy, trim 5 rigid, stiff, tense, tight, tough 6 severe, strict 9 distended, shipshape
tauten: 5 tense 7 tighten
tautog: 9 blackfish
tautological: 9 redundant
tave: 4 rage, toss 5 hurry, labor 6 sprawl 8 struggle
tavern: bar, hut, inn, pub 4 bush, howf 5 booth, hotel, house, howff 6 saloon 7 cabaret, gasthof 8 alehouse, gasthaus, hostelry
tavert: 5 tired 6 stupid 8 confused
taw: tan, tew 4 beat, whip 5 agate 6 harass, marble 7 scourge, shooter, torment, toughen
tawdry: 5 cheap, gaudy, showy 6 sleazy, tinsel
tawny, tawney: tan 5 brown, dusky, olive, swart, tenne 6 Indian, tanned 7 fulvous, tigrine 8 brindled 9 bullfinch
tawse, taws: 4 whip 5 strap
tax: 4 cess, duty, feel, fine, levy, rate, scat, scot, task, toll 5 abuse, agist, exact, order, scatt, stent, stint, tithe, touch, value 6 accuse, assess, avania, burden, charge, demand, excise, extent, handle, hidage, impose, impost, settle, strain 7 censure, dispute, finance, gabelle, license, tailage, tallage, tollage, tribute 8 estimate, exaction,

overtire, reproach **9** prescribe **10** assessment, imposition **12** contribution

assessment: **7** doomage

church: **5** tithe

feudal: **7** tailage, tallage

gatherer: **9** catchpole, catchpoll

hide: **6** hidage

kind of: cro, soc **4** cess, geld, scat **5** finta, tithe **6** abkari, excise, pavage, surtax, taille, vinage **7** boscage, chevage, patente, prisage, scewing, tailage **8** auxilium, carucage **9** surcharge **10** chaukidari

rate: **5** ratal **10** assessment

salt: **7** gabelle

taxable: 10 assessable, censurable

taxation: tax **6** charge **7** finance, reproof, revenue **9** valuation **10** accusation, assessment

degree of: **5** ratal

taxi: cab **4** hack **5** jixie **6** litter **7** vehicle

parking place: **5** stand

taximeter: 5 clock

taxing: 10 accusation

taxman: 8 publican

taxpayer: 9 ratepayer

tazza: cup **4** bowl, vase

tchai: 5 brook, river **6** stream

tea: 5 party **6** repast, supper **8** beverage, function **9** collation, decoction, reception

cake: **5** scone

constituent: **8** caffeine

container: **8** canister

drug: see *stimulant* below

expert: **6** taster

family: **8** Theaceae

genus: **4** thea

kind of: cha **4** chaa, chia, tsia **5** assam, black, bohea, congo, chias, Emesa, green, hyson, Ledum, oopak, pekoe, salop **6** congue, oolong, saloop **7** cambric **8** bouillon, go-widdie **9** gunpowder

plant: **4** thea

receptacle: **8** canister

room: **5** kiosk

serve: **4** pour

stimulant: **5** thein **6** theine

table: **5** tepoy **6** teapoy

urn: **7** samovar

weak: **5** blash

Tea House location: 4 Naha **7** Okinawa

teach: 4 show **5** coach, edify, endue, guide, point, train, tutor **6** commit, direct, lesson, preach, school **7** apprise, apprize, beteach, conduct, educate **8** accustom, amaister, document, instruct **9** enlighten **10** discipline **11** demonstrate

teachable: apt **6** pliant **7** fitting **8** amenable

teacher: 5 coach, guide, Plato, tutor **6** docent, doctor, mentor, pedant, pundit, reader, regent **7** adjunct, edifier, maestro, sophist, trainer **8** civilian, director, educator, gamaliel, moralist, preacher **9** pedagogue, preceptor **10** instructor

Alexandria: **6** Origen

association: NEA

fee: **8** minerval

Indian religion: **4** guru

Jewish: **5** rabbi

Mohammedan: pir **4** alim, imam **5** imaum, molla, mulla **6** mollah, mullah

of eloquence: **6** rhetor **7** sophist

of the deaf: **7** oralist

Russia: **7** starets

teaching: **5** moral **6** docent **7** precept **10** discipline **11** instruction

of a fable: **5** moral

of the Twelve: **7** Didache

pert. to: **9** pedagogic

teakettle: 4 suke, suky **5** sukey, sukie

teal: 5 crick **8** garganey

team: 4 crew, gang, join, pair, race, span, yoke **5** brood, chain, flock, group, wagon **6** convey, couple, number **7** lineage, progeny, vehicle **8** carriage **9** associate, stationed

baseball: **4** nine

kinds of: duo **4** crew **6** scrubs **7** varsity

supporter: fan **6** rooter

two animals: **4** pair, yoke

teamed with: 5 yoked **6** paired **7** matched

teamster: 6 carter, driver **7** carrier

tear: ram, rip, rit, run **4** claw, drag, fine, pull, rage, rend, rent, rive, rush, skag, snag, weep **5** break, claut, larme, reave, split, spree, touse, unrip, waste **6** cleave, dainty, damage, divide, flurry, lament, pierce, remove, screed, tatter, wrench **7** agitate, chatter, consume, destroy, disrupt, fritter, passion, shatter, torment **8** carousal, delicate, lacerate, lachryma, separate

apart: **4** rend **9** dismember

down: **4** rase, raze **11** disassemble

heraldry: **5** larme

into: rip **6** attack

limb from limb: **9** dismember

off: rip, run **4** rush **5** start

to pieces: **6** tatter **10** dilacerate

up by the roots: **6** arache **9** eradicate, extirpate

tearcat: 7 ranting **9** blusterer **10** swaggering

teardrop design: 5 larme

tearful: sad **6** watery **7** flebile, snively, weeping **8** lacrimal

mother: **5** Niobe

tearing: 4 rage **5** hasty, hurry **7** furious, violent **8** splendid **9** furiously, harrowing, impetuous **10** impressive

tearpit: 7 larmier

tears: 5 grief
inducing: 9 rheumatic
pert. to: 8 lacrimal
poetic: 5 rheum

tease: beg, guy, irk, nag, rag, tew, vex 4 card, coax, comb, drag, fret, hare, razz, stir, tear, twit 5 annoy, chevy, chivy, devil, taunt, wrack 6 badger, bother, caddle, chivvy, harass, heckle, molest, pester, plague, teasel 7 disturb, hatchel, provoke, scratch, torment 8 irritate, separate 9 aggravate, importune, tantalize 11 disentangle
wool: tum 4 comb, toom

teasel: 4 comb

teaser: 4 gull 6 carder, curler, sniper, stoker, willow 7 curtain, fireman, problem 8 operator, pesterer, willower

teasing: 11 importunate

teaty: 5 cross 7 fretful, peevish

tebbad: 6 simoom 9 sandstorm

tebeldi: 6 baobab

technology of agriculture: 10 agrotechny

techy: 4 spot 5 habit 6 touchy, vexing 7 blemish, fretful, peevish, quality 9 irascible, irritable

teck: 6 cravat

tectonic: 7 builder, plastic 9 carpenter 10 structural 13 architectural

ted: 4 toad, turn 5 waste 6 spread 7 scatter

tedge: 6 ingate, runner

tedious: dry 4 dead, dree, dull, long, slow 5 bored, prosy 6 boring, borish, elenge, prolix 7 irksome, noxious, peevish, prosaic 8 dilatory, slowness, tiresome 9 exhausted, irritable, laborious, prolixity, wearisome 10 monotonous 11 displeasing, everlasting 13 uninteresting

tedium: 5 ennui 7 boredom, doldrum 11 irksomeness, tediousness 13 wearisomeness

tee: 5 mound

teem: go 4 bear, fill, gush, lead, pour, rain, swim 5 bring, drain, empty, fetch, swarm 6 abound, resort, seethe, summon 7 produce 8 abundant, conceive, generate, prolific

teeming: 4 full 5 agush 7 pouring, replete 8 crowding, prolific 9 abounding 11 overflowing 13 overabounding

teen: vex 4 harm, hate, keen, lose, pain, shut, tell, tind, tune 5 abuse, anger, grief, vexed 6 damage, injure, injury, sorrow 7 provoke, trouble 8 announce, distress, irritate, reproach, vexation 9 vexatious 10 affliction, calumniate

teeny: wee 4 tiny 5 small 7 fretful, peevish 9 malicious

teeny-weeny: 4 tiny 5 small 6 minute

teer: 4 daub 7 plaster

teeter: 4 rock 5 waver 6 jiggle, quiver, seesaw 7 rocking, rolling, tremble 9 sandpiper, vacillate

teeter board: 6 seesaw

teeth: 5 tines 7 canines
decay of: 6 caries
false: 5 plate 8 dentures
grinding of: 7 bruxism
hard tissue: 7 dentine
having all alike: 7 isodont
incrustation on: 6 tartar
large: 4 buck 5 snags
long: 5 fangs 6 tushes
outer covering of: 6 enamel
pert. to: 5 molar 6 dental
serpent: 5 fangs
socket: 7 alveoli(pl.) 8 alveolus
sower of dragon's: 6 Cadmus
without: 10 edentulate, edentulous

teethy: 5 cross 6 biting 7 crabbed 9 irritable

teeting: 7 titlark

teetotal: 6 entire 7 abstain 8 complete

teetotaller: dry 7 nonuser 9 abstainer, rechabite, refrainer

teetotum: top, toy

teewhapp: 7 lapwing

teg: doe 5 sheep, woman 6 fleece

tegmen: 5 cover, plate 6 elytra 8 covering, fore-wing, tegument

tegua: 6 sandal

teguexin: 4 teju 6 lizard

tegula: 4 tile

tegument: 4 coat 5 cover, testa 6 testae 10 integument

tegurium: hut 5 cabin 6 shrine

tehee: 6 giggle, titter 7 snicker

Tehuantepec Gulf Indian: 5 Huave

teicher: 4 ooze 5 bleed

teiidae: 4 teju 7 lizards

teind: 5 tithe

teju: 6 lizard 8 teguexin

tekke: rug 6 carpet 7 convent 9 monastery

tela: web 6 tissue 7 bristle 8 membrane

telamon: 8 atlantes, caryatid

Telamon: *brother:* 6 Peleus
father: 6 Aeacus
friend: 8 Heracles, Hercules
son: 4 Ajax 6 Teucer

teledu: 6 badger

telega: 4 cart 5 wagon

telegraph: 4 wire 5 cable
code: 5 Morse
inventor: 5 Morse
key: 6 tapper
signal: dot 4 dash 9 semaphore

telegraphic communication: 10 lettergram

Telemachus: *father:* 7 Ulysses 8 Odysseus
mother: 8 Penelope

teleost fish: eel 5 apoda
telephone: 4 buzz, call, dial 5 phone
book: 9 directory
inventor: 4 Bell
receiver: 8 cymaphen
Telephus' mother: 4 Auge
telescope: jam 5 glass 7 shorten 8 collapse, condense, simplify
object seen with: 11 debilissima
site: 7 Palomar
telescopic: 9 farseeing
television: TV 4 tube 5 telly, video
award: 4 Emmy
broadcast: 8 telecast
cable: 7 coaxial
camera platform: 5 dolly
comedienne: 4 Lucy
commercial cat: 6 Morris
dragon: 5 Ollie
interference: 4 snow
lens: 4 zoom
network: ABC, CBS, NBC, NET
picture tube: 9 kinescope
type of show: 4 live, news, quiz 5 movie, rerun 6 sitcom, sudser
telic: 9 purposive 10 purposeful 12 teleological
tell: bid, say 4 chat, deem, hill, know, tale, talk, tole, toll 5 aread, areed, breve, count, mound, order, speak, state, utter, value 6 decide, direct, impart, inform, number, recite, reckon, regard, relate, repeat, report, reveal, tattle 7 account, command, dictate, discern, divulge, express, mention, narrate, publish, recount, request 8 acquaint, announce, disclose, rehearse 9 calculate, discourse, enumerate, recognize 11 communicate 12 discriminate
in advance: 4 warn
on: 4 sing 5 peach 6 snitch, squeal
revelatory facts: 6 debunk
romances: 4 gest 5 geste
secrets: 5 clype
stories: 4 yarn 6 tattle
thoughtlessly: 4 blab, blat
without authority: 5 rumor
Tell's home: Uri
teller: 4 blow 5 shoot 6 remark, sprout 8 informer, narrator 9 describer 11 annunciator
telling: 5 valid 6 cogent 8 forceful, relation, striking 9 effective, pertinent 10 convincing
telltale: 4 blab, hint 7 tattler 8 betrayer, informer 9 betraying, indicator 10 indication, talebearer
telltruth: 7 honesty 9 frankness
telluride: 7 altaite
telson: 6 somite 7 segment

of king crab: 5 pleon
temblor: 10 earthquake
temerarious: 4 rash 6 chance 8 heedless, reckless 9 venturous 10 fortuitous, headstrong 11 venturesome
temerity: 4 gall 5 check, nerve 8 audacity, boldness, rashness 9 hardihood 10 effrontery 12 recklessness 13 foolhardiness 15 venturesomeness
temper: fit, ire, mix 4 bait, bate, coll, curb, cure, heal, mean, mood, neal, rage, tone 5 adapt, anger, birse, blend, delay, humor 6 adjust, animus, anneal, attune, church, dander, direct, govern, harden, manage, medium, mingle, modify, puddle, reduce, season, soften, soothe, steady 7 assuage, chasten, control, moisten, mollify, qualify, restore, toughen 8 attemper, chastise, compound, mitigate, moderate, modulate, regulate, restrain 9 composure 10 equanimity, irritation 11 accommodate, disposition
display: 5 scene 7 tantrum
even: 4 calm 5 staid 6 sedate
kind of: ire 4 huff, mood 6 choler, spleen
temperament: 4 mood 5 gemut, humor 6 crasis, crases(pl.), humour, nature, temper 7 caprice, climate, emotion 10 adjustment 11 disposition, temperature 12 constitution
temperance: 8 sobriety 10 abstinence, moderation
temperate: 4 calm, cool, mild 5 sober 6 soften, temper 8 moderate 9 continent 10 abstemious, restrained 13 dispassionate
temperature: 4 heat 5 fever, state 6 temper 7 mixture 8 compound, mildness 10 moderation, proportion 11 disposition, temperament 12 constitution
tempest: 4 gale, wind 5 orage, storm 6 tumult 7 agitate, borasca, borasco, turmoil 9 agitation, bourasque, commotion, hurricane 12 thunderstorm
Tempest characters: 5 Ariel 7 Caliban, Miranda 8 Prospero
tempestuous: 5 galey, gusty 6 stormy 7 violent 9 turbulent
template, templet: 4 beam, mold 5 basil, bezel, bezil, gauge 7 pattern
temple: 4 fane, naos, rath 5 candi, cella, edile, huaca, kovil, ratha, speos 6 aedile, chandi, church, haffet, haffit, hieron
basin: 5 laver
for all gods: 8 pantheon
kind of: sha, taj, wat 4 deul, Rath 5 jinja, Ratha 6 church, jinsha, pagoda 7 capitol 8 pantheon 9 Parthenon
part: 5 cella
sanctuary: 10 penetralia

tempo: 4 pace, rate, time 6 rhythm, timing
pert. to: 6 agogic
rapid: 6 presto
slow: 5 lento
very slow: 5 grave

temporal: 4 laic 5 civil, scale 6 carnal, muscle 7 earthly, secular, worldly 9 ephemeral, political, temporary 10 transitory 11 impermanent 13 chronological

temporarily: 5 nonce

temporary: 6 acting, timely 7 interim, secular, topical 8 temporal 9 adinterim, ephemeral 10 transitory 11 provisional
contrivance: 9 makeshift

temporize: 5 delay, humor, yield 6 demand, parley, soothe 9 negotiate 13 procrastinate

tempt: try 4 defy, fand, lead, lure, test 5 decoy, probe, prove, taunt 6 allure, assail, entice, incite, induce, seduce 7 assault, attempt, attract, provoke 8 endeavor, persuade 9 endeavour, seduction 10 inducement

temptation: 4 bait 5 trial 7 testing 9 seduction 10 allurement, enticement, inducement

tempter: 5 devil, Satan 6 baiter

tempting: 8 alluring 9 seductive 10 attractive

temptress: 4 vamp 5 Circe, siren 7 Delilah, Lorelei, mermaid 10 Parthenope 11 enchantress

temse, tems: 4 sift 5 sieve

temulence: 12 intoxication

ten: 4 iota(Gk.) 5 decad 6 decade, denary
ares: 6 decare
decibels: bel
dollars: 7 sawbuck
group of: 6 decade
prefix: dec 4 deca

Ten Commandments: 7 Decalog 9 Decalogue

ten-footed: 7 decapod

ten-gallon hat: 8 sombrero

ten-sided figure: 7 decagon

ten-stringed: 9 decachord

ten-year periods: 7 decades 9 decenniad, decennium

tenable: 10 defensible 12 maintainable

tenacious: 5 tough 6 cledgy, dogged, grippy, sticky 7 gripple, miserly, viscous 8 adhesive, cohesive, holdfast, sticking, stubborn 9 glutinous, niggardly, retentive 10 persistent 11 closefisted 12 pertinacious

tenaciously: 8 doggedly 10 persistent

tenacity: 8 firmness 9 toughness 11 miserliness, persistence, persistency 12 adhesiveness, cohesiveness, perseverance 13 glutinousness, retentiveness

tenancy: 6 estate, tenure 7 holding 9 occupancy 10 possession

tenant: 4 leud 5 ceile, dreng 6 bordar, drengh, geneat, holder, leaser, lessee, occupy, renter, vassal 7 chakdar, cottier, dweller 8 occupant 9 bordarius, collibert 10 inhabitant
feudal: 4 leud 6 vassal 7 socager

tend: 4 burn, care, lead, move, wait, work 5 apply, await, guard, nurse, offer, reach, serve, swing, treat, watch 6 attend, direct, expect, extend, foster, intend, kindle, listen, manage, supply 7 conduce, hearken, incline, oversee, provide, purpose, stretch, tending 8 minister, tendency 9 accompany, attentive, co-operate, cultivate, gravitate
a fire: 5 stoke
to rise: 8 levitate
toward one point: 8 converge

tendency: set 4 bent, bias, tide 5 drift, drive, tenor, trend 6 course, effect, object, result 7 aptness, bearing, leaning 8 appetite, movement, relation 9 affection, direction, proneness, readiness 10 proclivity, propension, propensity 11 disposition, inclination
monistic: 11 unitariness
structural: 7 peloria

tender: bid, tid 4 boat, dear, fond, gift, keen, kind, mild, nice, soft, sore, thin, warm, weak 5 chary, frail, light, offer, young 6 delate, feeble, gentle, humane, loving, touchy, vessel, waiter 7 amabile, amatory, amorous, careful, fragile, pitiful, present, proffer, slender, sparing, steamer, subdued, tenuous, vehicle 8 delicate, feminine, immature, merciful, precious, proposal, ticklish 9 brotherly, sensitive, succulent 10 charitable, effeminate, scrupulous 11 considerate, softhearted, susceptible, sympathetic, warmhearted 12 affectionate 13 compassionate 14 impressionable
animals: 6 herder 10 husbandman
cattle: 6 cowboy, herder 7 byreman 8 neatherd 9 byrewoman
for cloth: 9 stenterer
horse: 5 groom 6 ostler 7 hostler, stabler
music: 7 amoroso
ship: gig 5 barge, dingy 6 dingey, dinghy 7 collier, pinnace

tenderfoot: 6 novice 7 greenie 8 beginner, neophyte, newcomer 9 cheechaco, cheechako, greenhorn

tenderhearted: 6 humane

tenderloin: 5 steak

tenderness: 4 love, pity 6 cherte 8 kindness, softness, sympathy, weakness 9 affection 10 compassion, gentleness 13 sensitiveness

tendon: 4 band, cord 5 chord, nerve, sinew 11 aponeurosis
comb. form: 4 teno

tendour, tendoor: 4 seat 5 table

tendril: 4 curl 5 clasp, sprig 6 branch, cirrus 7 ringlet, stipule

tendron: bud 5 shoot 6 sprout

tenebrous: 4 dark 5 dusky 6 gloomy 7 obscure 8 darkness

tenement: 5 abode 8 building, dwelling 9 apartment 10 habitation

tenet: ism 4 view 5 adoxy, canon, creed, dogma, maxim 6 belief, decree 7 opinion, paradox 8 doctrine 9 principle

tenfold: 6 denary 7 decuple

tengere: sky 7 heavens

teniente: 6 deputy 7 headman 10 lieutenant

tenmantale: tax 7 tithing 8 carucage

tenne: 5 brown, color

Tennessee: *capital:* 9 Nashville
city: 7 Memphis 11 Chattanooga
county: 4 Clay, Dyer, Knox, Lake, Polk, Rhea
dam: 6 Norris
federal agency: TVA
first governor: 6 Sevier
national park: 6 Shiloh
state flower: 4 iris

tennis: *between four persons:* 7 doubles
between two persons: 7 singles
champion: 4 Ashe, King 5 Budge, Perry, Riggs 6 Gibson, Tilden 8 Gonzalez
cup 5 Davis
game series: set
no score: 4 love
old form: 5 bandy
points: 4 aces
prize cup: 5 Davis
racket: bat
related game: 6 squash 8 handball
score: ace 4 love 5 deuce
shoe: 7 sneaker
stroke: cut, let, lob 4 chop 8 backhand
term: ace, cut, let, lob, set 4 love 5 deuce, fault, serve 6 volley 7 receive, service 9 advantage
trophy donor: 5 Davis

Tennyson: *character:* 4 Enid 5 Arden 6 Elaine
heroine: 4 Enid
"In Memoriam" subject: 6 Hallam

tenon: cog 4 coak 8 dovetail

tenor: 4 copy, feck, gist 5 drift, stamp, trend 6 course, intent, nature, singer 7 holding, purport, writing 8 tendency 9 character, condition, direction, discourse, procedure 10 transcript
falsetto: 8 tenorino

tens of thousands: 7 myriads

tense: 4 rapt, taut, time 5 rigid, stiff, tight 6 intent, tauten 7 intense 8 strained 9 stretched 10 breathless
past: 9 preterite
verb: 4 past 6 aorist, future 7 perfect, present 9 preterite 10 pluperfect 11 conditional

tenseness: 5 rigor

tensile: 6 pliant 7 ductile 8 tensible

tension: 4 bent 6 strain, stress 7 closure 8 pressure

tent: hut 4 camp, care, heed, show, stop, tend, test, wine 5 crame, frame, lodge, probe, teach, tempt 6 attend, beware, encamp, hinder, intent, pulpit, tender 7 observe, prevent, proffer, shelter 9 attention, attentive 10 habitation
dweller: 4 Arab 5 nomad 6 camper, Indian 7 scenite, tourist
flap: fly
kind: 4 pawl, yurt 5 darry, shool, tepee, toldo, yurta 6 abbacy, tienda, wigwam 7 balagan, kibitka, marquee, sparver 8 pavilion 9 pretorium 10 praetorium
large: 8 pavilion

tentacle: 6 feeler 7 tendril 10 tentaculum
animal with: 5 squid 7 octopus 10 cuttlefish
without: 7 acerous

tentage: 5 camps

tentamen: 5 trial 7 attempt

tentative: 9 temporary 11 impermanent, provisional 12 experimental

tenter: 5 frame

tenterhooks: 6 strain 8 suspense

tenth: 5 tithe 6 decima 7 decimae 8 decimate
comb. form: 4 deci
part: 5 tithe

Tentmaker: 4 Omar

tents: 4 camp 7 baggage 10 encampment

tenty: 7 careful 8 watchful 9 attentive, carefully 10 watchfully

tenuity: 6 rarity 7 exility, poverty 8 delicacy, fineness, rareness, thinness 9 faintness, indigence 10 meagerness, slightness 11 slenderness

tenuous: 4 fine, rare, slim, thin 6 flimsy, slight 7 gaseous, slender, subtile 8 delicate, ethereal 13 insignificant, unsubstantial

tenure: 4 term 5 lease 6 manner 8 courtesy 9 condition

tepee, teepee: 6 wigwam

tepid: 4 warm 8 lukewarm

tepidness: 5 tepor

tepor: 9 tepidness
tequila: 5 drink 6 liquor, mescal
tera: 6 church 9 monastery
Terah: *father:* 5 Nahor
  son: 7 Abraham
teraph: 4 idol 5 image
teras: 7 monster
teratosis: 11 monstrosity
terceron: 7 mulatto
tercet: 7 triplet
tere, teer: 4 daub 7 plaster
terebene: 10 antiseptic 12 disinfectant
terebra: 5 auger, drill
terebrate: 4 bore 9 perforate
teredo: 7 mollusk 8 shipworm
teres: 6 muscle
terete: 7 centric 8 columnar 11 cylindrical
Tereus: *son:* 4 Itys 6 Itylus
  wife: 6 Procne
tergal: 6 dorsal
tergiversate: lie 5 shift 7 shuffle 10 apostatize, equivocate
tergiversation: 6 deceit 7 evasion 8 apostasy 10 subterfuge
tergum: 4 back
term: end 4 call, date, half, name, time, word 5 bound, limit, state 6 period, tenure 7 article, entitle, epithet, session 8 boundary, duration, semester 9 condition, extremity 10 definition, expression 11 appellation, termination
  cricket: off, ons 6 yorker
  fencing: hai, hay 4 bind 5 coupe 6 touche 8 tacautac
  golf: lie, par, tee 4 baff, fore, hook 5 bogey, bogie, divot, eagle, green, slice, stimy 6 birdie, stroke, stymie 7 gallery
  grammar: 6 phase, simile, syntax
  heraldry: 4 ente, urde
  Hindu, of respect: sri
  Jewish, of reproach: 4 raca
  mathematics: 4 nome, root, sine 6 cosine
  of address: sir 4 sire 6 milady, milord, sirrah
  of endearment: 5 astor 8 ashstore
  of life: age 5 sands
  of office: 6 regime
  printer: 4 dele, stet
  rugby: try 5 scrum
  school: 7 seminar 8 semester 9 trimester
  science: ame, azo 4 beta 5 stoss
  sea: 4 ahoy 5 avast, belay
termagant: 5 shrew 6 Amazon, tartar, virago 7 furious 8 scolding 9 turbulent 10 boisterous, tumultuous 11 quarrelsome
termed: 5 named 6 called, styled, yclept 7 ycleped
terminable: 6 finish, finite 9 limitable 12 determinable 13 discontinuing

terminal: end 5 anode, depot, final, limit 6 finish 7 cathode, closing, limital, station 8 desinent, terminus, ultimate 9 electrode, extremity 10 concluding 11 desinential, termination
  negative: 7 cathode, kathode
  positive: 5 anode
terminate: end 4 call, halt, stop 5 bound, cease, close, limit 6 define, direct, expire, finish, result 7 achieve, confine, destine, perfect 8 complete, conclude, restrict
terminating: 5 final 6 ending
  distinct point: 9 apiculate
  trefoil: 6 botone
termination: end 4 amen 5 bound, close, event, limit 6 ending, expiry, finale, finish, period, result, upshot 7 outcome, purpose 8 boundary, decision, finality, terminus 9 extremity 10 completion, concluding, conclusion, expiration 13 determination
  malady: 5 lysis
terminative: 8 absolute, bounding, definite 10 concluding 11 determining, terminating
terminus: end 4 goal, post 5 depot, stone 6 marker 8 boundary, terminal 9 extremity 11 termination
termite: ant 4 anai, anay
termless: 8 infinite, nameless, unending 9 boundless, limitless 13 indescribable, inexpressible, unconditional, unconditioned
terms: 9 agreement 10 conditions, provisions 11 limitations 12 propositions 13 circumstances
  come to: 5 agree
  make: 5 treat 9 negotiate
tern: 4 darr, gull 9 wide-awake
  genus: 5 anous 6 sterna
ternary: 6 treble, triple 7 ternion, trinity 9 threefold
ternate: 12 trifoliolate
terne: 8 tinplate
terpsichore: 6 dancer 7 dancing
terra: 5 earth
terra alba: 4 clay 6 gypsum, kaolin
terra cotta: 4 clay 6 statue 7 pottery 11 earthenware
terra firma: 5 earth 6 estate 8 mainland
terrace: 4 bank, dais, mesa, step 5 bench 7 balcony, gallery, portico 8 chabutra, platform 9 colonnade
  in series: 8 parterre
  wall: 6 podium
terrage: tax 4 toll 7 payment
terrain: 4 terr 5 tract 6 milieu, region 7 estrial, terrane, terrent 11 environment

terrapin: 4 emyd, emys 6 coodle, emydea, heifer, potter, slider, turtle 8 emydidae, emydinae

terrar: 6 bursar

terrene: 4 land 5 earth, realm 6 earthy 7 earthly, mundane, terrain, worldly 11 terrestrial

terrestrial: 6 earthy, layman, mortal 7 earthly, mundane, terrene, worldly 9 planetary

terret: 4 ring 7 cringle

terrible: 4 dire, gast 5 awful, lurid 6 severe, tragic 7 direful, extreme, fearful, ghastly, hideous, intense, painful 8 almighty, dreadful, horrible, terrific 9 appalling, atrocious, excessive, frightful 10 formidable, terrifying, tremendous, unpleasant 12 disagreeable

Terrible one: 4 Ivan

terribly: 4 very 5 felly 6 grisly 9 extremely 11 exceedingly

terrier: fox 4 Bull, Skye 5 Irish, Welsh 6 Boston 8 Scottish, Sealyham 10 Bedlington, Clydesdale

terrific: 7 extreme 8 dreadful, exciting, terrible 9 appalling, excessive, frightful 10 terrifying, tremendous

terrified: 4 awed 6 afraid, aghast 7 ghastly

terrifier: 5 haunt 7 haunter

terrify: awe, cow, hag 4 bree, fray 5 alarm, annoy, appal, daunt, deter, drive, haunt, impel, scare, shock, tease 6 affirm, afread, agrise, appall, bother, dismay, injure 7 torment 8 affright, frighten 9 importune

terrifying: 6 horrid 7 hideous 8 terrible

terrigenous: 9 earthborn 13 autochthonous

terrine: jar 4 stew 6 ragout

territorial division: amt 6 canton 7 commune 10 department 14 arrondissement

territory: 4 area, land 5 field, scope, state, tract 6 extent, ground, region, sphere 7 country, portion 8 district, environs, province 12 neighborhood

kind of: 5 banat 6 canton 7 banlieu, enclave 8 banlieue, Pashalic 10 palatinate

shut in: 7 enclave

terror: awe 4 fear, fray, pest 5 alarm, dread, panic 6 affray, dismay, fright, horror 8 dreddour 12 terribleness 13 consternation

terrorism: 11 subjugation 12 intimidation

terrorist: 5 rebel 8 alarmist 11 scaremonger

terrorize: awe 5 abash, appal, scare 6 appall, coerce 8 frighten 9 embarrass 10 intimidate

terry: 4 loop

terse: 4 curt, neat 5 brief, pithy 6 abrupt, claret, rubbed, smooth 7 compact, concise,

laconic, pointed, refined 8 polished, succinct, unprolix 11 sententious, tightlipped 12 accomplished

tertiary period: 7 neocene

tertulia: 4 club 5 party

tervee: 6 writhe 8 struggle

terzina: 6 tercet 7 triplet

terzo: 6 legion 7 brigade

tessel: 11 checkerwork

tessellated: 6 mosaic

tessera: 4 cube, tile 5 glass, label, token 6 billet, marble, pledge, tablet, ticket 7 voucher 8 password 9 rectangle 11 certificate

test: pot, try 4 exam, fand, feel, will 5 assay, check, cupel, grope, proof, prove, shell, taste, testa, trial, weave 6 ordeal, refine, sample 7 approof, approve, examine, witness 8 cupeling, evidence, potsherd, standard 9 construct, criterion, determine, testament, testimony 10 experience, experiment, touchstone 11 examination, performance 12 authenticate

in fineness and weight: pyx

kind: 4 acid

operation: 9 shakedown

ore: 5 assay

series: 7 gantlet

value: 5 assay

testa: 7 coating 8 covering, episperm, tegument 10 integument

testament: Job 4 will 8 covenant, landbook

testator: 7 legator, witness 9 testatrix

beneficiary of: 4 heir 7 heiress, heritor 9 inheritor

tester: 5 crown 6 canopy, conner, helmet, prover, teston 7 assayer, candler, sparver 9 chauffeur, headpiece

testicle: cob 6 testis, testes(pl.)

deer: 6 doucet, dowcet, dowset

testificate: 11 certificate, testimonial

testified under oath: 7 deponed

testifier: 7 witness 8 deponent

testify: 6 affirm, attest, depone, depose 7 declare, express, profess, protest 8 indicate, manifest, proclaim

testimonial: 4 sign 5 token 7 warrant, writing 8 evidence 9 testimony 10 credential 11 certificate

testimony: say 6 attest, avowal 7 witness 8 evidence 10 deposition, profession 11 affirmation, attestation, certificate, declaration 14 recommendation

testing: 5 assay 11 examination

testudo: 4 lyre, shed 5 cover, talpa, tumor, vault 6 screen 7 ceiling

testy: 6 touchy 7 crabbed, fretful, peevish, waspish 8 petulant, snappish 9 impatient, irascible, irritable, obstinate 10 headstrong

tetanus: 7 lockjaw

tetchy: 6 touchy 7 peevish 9 irritable, sensitive

tête-a-tête: 4 chat, seat, sofa 8 causeuse 12 conversation

tetel: 5 torah

tether: tie 4 band, rope 5 cable, chain, leash, limit, noose 6 fasten, picket 7 confine 8 restrain

Tethys: 5 Titan 8 Titaness
 brother: 6 Cronus
 father: 6 Uranus
 husband: 7 Oceanus

tetragon: 6 square 7 rhombus 10 quadrangle

tetric: 5 harsh 6 gloomy 7 austere

tetter: 4 fret 6 eczema, herpes, lichen

Teuton: 4 Goth 6 German

Teutonic: 5 Dutch 6 German, Gothic 7 English 12 Scandinavian
 alphabet character: 4 rune
 barbarian: 4 Goth
 deity: As, Er; Eir, Hel, Tiu, Tyr, Ull 4 Erda, Frea, Frig, Norn, Odin, Thor 5 Aesir, Baldr, Brage, Bragl, Donar, Othin, Tiwaz, Wodin, Wotan 6 Balder, Frigga, Saeter 7 Forseti 8 Heimdall
 homicide: 5 morth
 land: 4 odal
 law: 5 Salic
 legendary hero: 4 Offa
 race: 4 Ubii 5 Danes, Goths, Jutes 6 Angles, Franks, Saxons 7 Germans, Vandals 8 Lombards 10 Norwegians 11 Burgundians, 13 Scandinavians
 water nymph: nis

tew: taw, tow, vex 4 beat, fuss, pull, work 5 knead, tease, tools 6 incite, strive, tackle, tuyere 7 fatigue 8 struggle

tewel: 4 bore, hole, pipe, tool, vent 6 funnel, tuyere 7 chimney, trumpet

tewer: 4 lane 5 alley

tewit: 7 lapwing

tewly: 6 sickly 8 delicate, qualmish

tewsome: 8 restless 11 troublesome

Texas: *battle:* 5 Alamo
 bronco, broncho: 7 mustang
 capital: 6 Austin
 citadel: 5 Alamo
 city: 4 Waco 5 Cuero, Mexia, Paris 6 Austin, Dallas, El Paso, Laredo, Odessa 7 Abilene, Denison, Houston, Lubbock 8 Amarillo
 cottonwood: 5 alamo
 county: Bee 4 Leon, Polk, Rusk 5 Nolan, Starr, Tyler 6 Harris, Sutton, Walker 7 Houston, Madison, Navarro, Trinity 8 Anderson, Angelina, Cherokee 9 Freestone, Limestone 11 Nacogdoches
 cowboy jacket: 8 chaqueta
 fever carrier: 4 tick
 fortress: 5 Alamo
 founder: 6 Austin
 hat: 7 Stetson 9 ten-gallon
 itch: 5 mange 7 scabies
 massacre site: 5 Alamo
 mission: 5 Alamo
 poplar: 5 Alamo
 river: Red 5 Pecos 6 Neches, Nueces 9 Rio Grande
 shrine: 5 Alamo
 shrub: 6 anagua, anaqua
 state police: 6 ranger
 university: SMU, TCU 4 Rice 6 Baylor

text: 4 copy 5 theme, topic 7 passage, subject 11 handwriting
 operatic: 8 libretto
 pen: 5 ronde
 pert. to: 7 textual
 revision: 9 recension
 set to music: 8 oratorio
 variation: 7 lection

textbook: 6 manual

textile: *dealer:* 6 mercer
 goods: 7 mercery
 ornament: 8 fagoting
 plant refuse: 5 hurds
 ring device: 6 poteye
 worker: 4 dyer 6 reeder

texture: web 4 wale 5 grain 6 dobweb, fabric, tissue 7 textile 9 structure 11 composition, fabrication
 cloth: 4 wale, warp, woof

tez: 7 pungent, violent

tezkirah: 7 license 8 passport 11 certificate

thack: 4 roof, that 5 thump 6 thatch, thwack 8 thatched

Thackeray: *tale country:* 10 Paflagonia
 tale hero: 9 Pendennis

Thailand: 4 Siam
 cab: 5 samlo 6 samlaw, samlor
 canal: 5 klong
 city: 6 Bankok 7 Ayuthia, Ayuthya, Bangkok 9 Sukhothai
 coin: at; att 4 baht 5 fuang, tical 6 pynung, salung, satang
 demon: nat
 dialect: Lao
 dress: 6 panung
 fabric: 8 siamoise
 fruit: 5 mango 6 papaya, pumelo
 island: 6 Phuket
 isthmus: Kra
 king: 4 Rama
 measure: wa; ken, niu, nmu, rai, sat, sen, sok, wah, yot 4 keup, ngan, tang, yote 5 kwien, laang, sesti, tanan 6 kabiet, kam

745   **thelium**

meu, kanahn **7** chai meu, roeneng **8** chang
awn **9** anukabiet
native: Lao
people: Tai **4** Thai **7** Siamese
provincial capital: **5** Muang
river: **6** Mekong, Meping **7** Meklong **10**
Chaophraya
spirit: nat
state: **6** Patani
temple: wat
town: **5** Puket **7** Ayuthia, Bangkok, Lop-
buri, Singora, Songkla **8** Kiangmai **9**
Chiengmai
weight: hap, pai, sen, sok **4** baht, haph,
klam, klom **5** catty, chang, coyan, picul,
tical **6** fluang, salung, sompay **7** tamlung
Thais composer: 8 Massenet
thalassic: 6 marine **7** oceanic, pelagic
Thalia: *sisters:* **6** Aglaia, Graces **7** Gratiae **8**
Charites(Gk.) **10** Euphrosyne
slayer: **5** Erato
Thames: 4 Isis
town: **4** Eton
tributary: **6** Tyburn
Thanatopsis author: 6 Bryant
Thanatos: 5 death
mother: Nyx
thane: 5 churl **7** servant, warrior **8** follower
9 attendant
estate: **5** manor
thank: 7 aggrate **11** acknowledge
thankful: 8 grateful **11** meritorious, thank-
worthy **12** appreciative
thankfulness: 9 gratitude
thankless: 10 ungrateful **13** unappreciated
person: **7** ingrate
thanks: 7 cumshaw **8** gramercy **9** gratitude
11 gratulation **12** appreciation **15** acknowledgement
thapes: 12 gooseberries
thar: 4 need **7** behoove
tharf: 5 heavy, stiff **9** unbending
tharm: gut **5** belly **6** catgut **9** intestine
that: yon **6** yonder **7** because
that is: e.g., i.e.
to say: **6** namely
that not: 4 lest
thatch: 4 nipa
peg: **4** scob
support: **6** wattle
thatched: 6 reeded, roofed
thatcher: 6 reeder **7** crowder, hellier
thaumaturgists: 6 Goetae **7** wizards **9** magi-
cians, sorcerers
thaumaturgy: 5 magic **11** legerdemain
thaw: 4 melt **6** unbend **8** dissolve
the: se
French: la, le; les
German: der, die, das

Italian: i; il, la, le **4** egli, ella
Spanish: el, la; las, los
the same: 4 idem **5** ditto
theater, theatre: 5 arena, house, odeon,
odeum, stage **8** coliseum **9** playhouse
audience: **5** house
award: **4** Tony
box-office sign: SRO
curtain: **4** drop **6** teaser
district: **6** Rialto
Elizabethan: **5** Globe
entrance hall: **5** foyer, lobby
full: SRO
Greek: **5** odeon, odeum
group: **4** ANTA
low-class: **4** gaff
motion-picture: **5** movie **6** cinema **8** bioscope **13** cinematograph
outdoor: **5** arena **7** drive-in, open-air
part: box, pit **4** loge **5** foyer, stage **7** balcony,
gallery, parquet **8** parterre **9** orchestra **10**
proscenium
pit: **6** circle **7** parquet **8** parterre
sports: **5** arena
theater box: 4 loge
theater-in-the-round: 5 arena
theater stall: 4 loge
theatrical: 5 showy, stagy **6** scenic **7** pompous **8** affected, dramatic **10** artificial, his-
tronic **11** declamation **12** melodramatic
company: **6** troupe
extra: **4** supe **5** super
profession: **5** stage
sign: S.R.O.
spectacle: **7** pageant
star: **4** hero, lead **7** heroine
valet **7** dresser
Thebes: *acropolis:* **6** Cadmea
blind soothsayer: **8** Tiresias
deity: **4** Amon **5** Ament
district: **7** Thebiad
founder: **6** Cadmus
king: **5** Laius **7** Amphion, Oedipus **8** Eteocles, Pentheus
poet: **6** Pindar
prince: **7** Oedipus
queen: **5** Aedon, Niobe **7** Jocasta
statute: **6** Memnon
wicked queen: **5** Dirce
theca: sac, sad **4** case **7** capsule
thee: tha **4** grow **6** thrive **7** prosper **8** increase
theft: 6 furtum, piracy **7** bribery, larceny,
robbery **8** burglary **10** conveyance, plagiarism **12** embezzlement
theft-like: 7 piratic
theine: 8 caffeine
source: tea
thelium: 6 nipple **7** papilla

them: 5 hemen

thema: 5 theme, topic 6 thesis 7 subject 12 dissertation

theme: 4 base, text 5 ditty, essay, motif, topic 6 matter, theses, thesis 7 subject 9 discourse 11 composition, proposition 12 dissertation

literary: 5 motif

musical: 4 tema

title: 5 lemma

Themis: *concern of:* law 7 harmony

father: 6 Uranus

mother: 4 Gaea

then: 4 next 5 alors(F.) 7 besides 8 formerly, moreover 9 therefore 11 accordingly

music: poi

then too: 5 again

thence: 4 away 9 elsewhere, therefore 10 henceforth 11 thenceforth

theodolite: 7 alidade

theologian: 6 divine

authority: 4 imam 5 ulema

famous: 5 Arius 6 Calvin, Luther 13 Thomas Aquinas

study of unity: 7 irenics

theorbo: 4 lute

theoreum: 4 rule

theoretical: 5 ideal 8 platonic 11 speculation, speculative, unpractical 12 hypothetical

theorist: 10 ideologist

theorize: 9 postulate, speculate

theory: ism 4 plan 5 guess 6 scheme 7 formula 8 analysis, doctrine 9 principle 10 conjecture, hypothesis 11 explanation, speculation 13 contemplation

kind of: 7 plenism 9 Platonism 13 phenomenalism

theow: 4 bond 5 slave 7 servile

there: ibi(L.), yon 4 able 5 ready 6 yonder 7 thither 8 equipped, reliable 10 dependable

thereafter: 9 afterward 11 accordingly 12 subsequently

thereat: 7 thither

therefore: as, so 4 ergo, then, thus 5 hence, since 6 frothy, thence 9 wherefore 11 accordingly 12 consequently

thereto: 4 also 7 besides 8 moreover

therewith: mit 6 withal 7 besides, thereat 8 moreover 9 forthwith, thereupon

therm, therme: 4 bath, pool

thermal: hot 4 warm

thermal unit: btu 7 calorie

thermometer: 7 Reaumur 8 pyrostat 9 pyrometer 10 Centigrade, Fahrenheit

thesaurus: 7 lexicon 8 treasury 10 dictionary, repository, storehouse 12 encyclopedia

Thesaurus compiler: 5 Roget

Theseus: *father:* 6 Aegeus

lover: 7 Ariadne

wife: 7 Antiope, Phaedra 9 Hippolyte

thesis: 5 essay, point, theme 7 premise 9 postulate, statement 10 assumption, conception 11 affirmation, proposition 12 dissertation

opposed to: 5 arsis

thespian: 5 actor 6 player 7 actress 9 tragedian

Thessaly: *king:* 7 Admetus

mountain: Ida, Osa 4 Ossa 6 Pelion 9 Psiloriti

valley: 5 Tempe

witch: 7 Aganice

thetic: 8 positive 9 arbitrary 10 prescribed

Thetis: *husband:* 6 Peleus

son: 8 Achilles

theurgy: 5 magic 7 miracle, sorcery 9 occultism

thew: 4 form, mode 5 habit, power, press, sinew, stool, trait 6 custom, manner, muscle, virtue 7 oppress, pillory, quality 8 strength 10 discipline, resolution

thewless: 4 lazy 6 feeble 10 spiritless

thewy: 6 sinewy 8 muscular

thick: fat 4 dull, hazy 5 broad, brosy, burly, close, crass, dense, gross, heavy, husky, plump, solid 6 coarse, filled, greasy, hoarse, obtuse, shaggy, stodgy, stupid 7 blubber, compact, crowded, grumous, muffled, thicket, viscous 8 abundant, familiar, friendly, guttural, intimate, profound, thickset 9 excessive, luxuriant 10 indistinct 11 inspissated, marticulate, thickheaded 12 impenetrable

and short: 5 squat

soup: 5 puree 7 pottage

thick-skinned: 4 cold 7 callous 9 pachyderm 11 pachydermic

thicken: gel 4 clot, crud, curd 5 cloud, crowd, flock 6 curdle, deepen, harden 7 confirm, congeal, stiffen 8 condense 9 intensify 10 incrassate, inspissate, strengthen

thicket: 4 bosk, bush, rone, shaw 5 brake, clump, copse, grove, hedge, shola 6 bosket, covert, greave 7 boscage, boskage, bosquet, coppice, spinney 9 brushwood 10 underbrush

kind: 5 brake, hedge, shola 7 chamise, chamiso, coppice, spinney 8 chamisal 9 chaparral

thickheaded: 4 dull 5 dense 6 stupid 7 doltish 11 blockheaded

thickness: ply 5 layer, sheet 8 diameter 9 curdiness, denseness, dimension, heaviness 11 consistency

thickset: 4 stub 5 squat, stout 6 chumpy, chunky, stocky, stodgy, stubby

thickskulled: 4 dull, slow 5 heavy 6 stupid 11 thickheaded

thicky: fat

thief (see also **stealer**): 4 chor, gilt 5 budge, scamp 6 ackman, arrant, bandit, cannon, cloyer, hooker, looter, nimmer, rascal, robber, sucker, waster 7 bramble, brigand, burglar, grifter, sneaker, stealer 8 cutpurse, gangster, larcener 9 larcenist, scoundrel 10 depredator, freebooter, highwayman, plagiarist

crucified beside Christ: 6 Desmas, Dismas, Dysmas

kind of: gun 5 ganef, ganof, gonof, snoop 6 ackman, angler, gonoph, pirate, swiper 7 gorilla, mercury, rustler 9 drawlatch 10 pickpocket

thieveless: 4 cold 5 bleak 6 frigid 7 aimless 8 bootless, listless 10 forbidding

thieves' Latin: 5 slang

thievish: sly 7 furtive, kleptic 8 stealthy 9 Hungarian

thig: ask, beg 6 borrow 7 beggary

thigh: ham 4 hock 5 carve, femur, flank, meros, merus 6 femora(pl.), gammon

armor: 5 cuish

bone: 5 femur, iluim

comb. form: mer 4 mero

muscle: 9 sartorius

pains: 8 sciatica

pert. to: 6 crural

thill: 5 plank, shaft 6 thwart 8 planking, wainscot

thimble: *conjurer:* 6 goblet

machine: 6 sleeve

thimblerigger: 5 cheat 8 swindler

thin: dim 4 bony, flue, lank, lean, pale, poor, rare, slim, weak 5 exile, faint, gaunt, lanky, lathy, scant, sheer, spare, washy, wizen 6 dilute, flimsy, hollow, meager, meagre, papery, rarefy, reduce, scanty, scarce, skinny, slight, slinky, sparse, watery, weaken, weazen 7 gracile, haggard, scrawny, slender, tenuous 8 araneous, gossamer, rarefied, scantily 9 attenuate, emaciated, extenuate, infertile, subtilize 10 inadequate 11 transparent 12 unbelievable, unconvincing 13 unsubstantial

and delicate: 8 araneous

and haggard: 5 gaunt

and slender: 4 lean 5 lanky

and vibrant: 5 reedy

and weak: 6 watery

and withered: 5 wizen 6 weezen

coating or layer: 4 film 6 veneer

disk: 5 wafer

out: 5 peter

plate: 4 leaf, shim 5 wedge 6 lamina, tegmen

scale: 5 flake 6 lamina 7 lamella

Thin Man: dog: 4 Asta

wife: 4 Nora

thin-skinned: 6 touchy 9 sensitive

thine: 4 tuum

thing: act 4 deed, idea, item 5 cause, chose, court, event, point 6 affair, detail, matter, notion, object, reason, wealth 7 article, council 8 assembly, incident, property 9 happening 11 transaction 12 circumstance

accomplished: 4 acta, deed 5 actum, actus

added: ell 6 insert 7 addenda(pl.) 8 addendum, addition, appendix 9 insertion 10 additament, complement, supplement

admitted: 4 fact 5 datum 7 element 9 principle

aforesaid: 5 ditto

assumed: 7 premise, premiss 9 postulate 11 implication, stipulation 14 presupposition

brought into existence: 8 creation

capable of spontaneous motion: 8 automata 9 automaton

complete in itself: 5 unity

consecrated to a deity: 6 hieron, sacrum 8 anathema

cursed: 8 anathema

extra: 5 bonus 6 bounty, lanyap 7 premium 8 lagnappe 9 lagniappe

following: 6 sequel

forfeited to crown: 7 deodand

found: 5 trove

given as security: 4 gage 6 pledge

indefinite, unnamed: 7 so and so 11 nondescript

invariable: 8 constant

known by reasoning: 7 noumena 8 noumenon

known by senses: 9 phenomena 10 phenomenon

of no value: 4 bean 5 nihil 6 fillip, nought, stiver, trifle 7 bauchle, nothing, pinhead, trinket 8 picayune 9 nonentity, resnihili 10 resnullius

of remembrance: 5 token

personal property law: 5 chose

precious: 4 oner 5 curio, relic 6 pippin, rarity 8 treasure

small: dot, jot 4 atom, iota, whit 6 tittle 8 particle, scuddick

to be done: 5 chore 6 agenda 7 agendum

unusual: 5 freak 6 oddity 11 monstrosity 12 malformation

thingamajig: 6 device, gadget, widget 9 doohickey, doohickus, doohinkey, doohinkus, thingummy 10 thingumbob

things: res 4 gear 5 goods 7 clothes, effects 10 belongings 13 appurtenances
between extremes: 13 intermediates
done: 9 res gestae
for sale: 5 goods, wares 8 services 11 merchandise
gained by purchase: 10 acquirenda
hidden: 10 penetralia
holy: 5 hagia
jumble of: 4 mess, muss 14 conglomeration
linked in nature: 8 cognates
movable: 8 chattels 10 resmobiles
obtained from other things: 11 derivatives
prohibited: 7 vetanda
suitable for eating: 9 esculents
to see: 6 sights
worth remembering: 11 memorabilia
thingumbob: See **thingamajig**
think: wis 4 deem, feel, muse, seem, trow, ween 5 judge, opine 6 appear, esteem, expect, intend, reason, repute, scheme 7 believe, bethink, concoct, imagine, purpose, reflect, resolve, suppose, surmise 8 cogitate, conceive, consider, meditate, ruminate 9 calculate, determine, speculate 10 conjecture, deliberate, reconsider 11 contemplate
alike: 5 agree
for: 7 suppose, suspect
logically: 6 reason
out: 4 plan 5 solve 6 devise 7 develop, perfect 8 cogitate, contrive, discover 10 excogitate
over: 5 brood
thinker: 4 mind 5 brain 7 student 9 meditator 11 philosopher
Thinker sculptor: 5 Rodin
thinking: 7 opinion 9 judgement 10 cogitation, reflection 13 ratiocination 17 intellectualizing
marked by exact: 13 ratiocinative
thinly: 6 airily 8 sparsely 14 insufficiently
metallic: 5 tinny
scattered: 6 sparse
thinner: 5 rarer 7 sheerer 10 turpentine
thinness: 6 rarity 7 exility, tenuity 11 attenuation
third: *combining form:* 4 trit
figure mood: 7 ferison
in number: 8 tertiary
music: 6 tierce
power of number: 4 cube
Third Man author: 6 Greene
thirl: 4 hole, hurl, thin 5 drill, gaunt, whirl, wound 6 hungry, hurtle, pierce, sucken, thrill, tingle, window 7 enslave, nostril, opening, vibrate 8 enthrall, restrict, thirlage, traverse 9 penetrate, perforate, shriveled 11 perforation

thirlage: fee, pay 4 dues 5 right 7 multure, service 8 mortgage 9 servitude, thralldom
thirling: 7 bondage 10 subjection
thirst: 4 long 5 crave, dryth 6 desire 7 aridity, craving, longing
absence of: 7 adipsia
excessive: 9 anadipsia
thirsty: dry 4 adry, arid avid 6 desire, drouth 7 athirst, craving, drought, longing, parched 8 droughty
thirty: 6 lambda(Gr.), trente(F.)
thirty nine and thirty seven hundredths inches: 5 meter
this: yis 4 esta(Sp.), haec(L.)
this way: 4 here
Thisbe's love: 7 Pyramus
thistle: 4 weed 7 bedegar, caltrop 8 bedeguar 10 acanaceous
genus of: 5 layia
thistle-like plants: 7 carlina
thistledown: 6 pappus
thither: end, yon 5 hence, there 6 result, yonder 7 farther, thereat
thivel: 5 stick 7 spatula
thixle: ax; adz 7 hatchet
Thjazi: *daughter:* 6 Skathi
home: 9 Thrymheim
tho: 5 still
thole: peg, pin 4 bear 5 allow 6 endure, remain, suffer 7 undergo 8 tolerate
Thomas' opera: 6 Mignon
thong: 4 lace, lash, rein, riem 5 lasso, leash, romal, strap, strip, whang 6 twitch 7 amentum, laniard, lanyard, latchet 8 whiplash
thong-shaped: 6 lorate
Thor: *father:* 4 Odin
hammer: 8 Mjollnir
noise: 7 thunder
stepson: Ull
wife: Sif
thorax: 5 chest
thorn: 4 brod, goad 5 briar, brier, spine, worry 7 acantha 8 vexation 9 annoyance 10 irritation
apple: 5 metel 6 datura
combining form: 5 spini
Egyptian: 5 babul 6 gonake 7 gonakie
full of: 6 briery
small: 7 spinule
thorny: 5 sharp, spiny 6 spinal 7 brambly, bristly, prickly 8 spinated 9 acanthoid, difficult, vexatious 11 contentious
thorough: 4 deep, full 6 arrant 7 through 8 absolute, accurate, complete, finished 9 downright, intensive 10 exhaustive, throughout 11 painstaking 13 thorough-going
thorough-going: 6 arrant 7 radical

thoroughbred: 5 horse **7** trained **8** cultured, educated, well-bred **11** full-blooded

thoroughfare: 4 road **5** alley **6** avenue, street **7** highway, passage, transit **8** waterway **9** boulevard

thoroughly: all **4** inly **6** deeply **9** downright, intensive **10** absolutely, altogether

thoroughwort: 7 boneset

thorp, thorpe: 4 dorp **6** hamlet **7** village **9** community

Thoth: god **6** Tehuti
  head: **4** ibis

thou: tha

though: 7 however **12** nevertheless

thought: 4 care, hope, idea, mind, view **5** trace **6** deemed, opined **7** anxiety, concept, judging, opinion **9** cogitated, reasoning **10** cogitation, conception, meditation, melancholy, reflection **11** cerebration, expectation, imagination **12** deliberation, recollection **13** concentration, consideration, ratiocination **16** intellectualized
  continuous: **10** meditation
  deep in: **10** cogitabund
  form: **6** ideate
  inability to express: **6** asemia
  reader: **8** telepath
  transference: **9** telepathy

thoughtful: 4 kind **5** moody **7** careful, earnest, heedful, mindful, pensive, prudent, serious **9** attentive, designing, regardful **10** cogitabund, meditative, melancholy, reflective, ruminative, solicitous **11** circumspect, considerate

thoughtfulness: 14 circumspection

thoughtless: 4 dull, rash **6** remiss, stupid **7** glaiket, glaikit **8** careless, heedless, reckless **9** brainless **10** unthinking **11** harum-scarum, inattentive, lightheaded **13** inconsiderate

thoughtlessness: 12 inadvertence

thousand: *combining form:* **4** kilo **5** mille
  one: **mil 5** grand **7** chiliad

thousand-headed snake: 5 Sesha **6** Shesha

thousandth: 10 millesimal
  of an inch: mil

Thrace: *goddess:* **6** Bendis
  king: **6** Tereus
  mountaineers: **5** Bessi
  musician: **7** Orpheus
  people: **6** Satrae **8** Bisaltae
  river: **6** Hebrus
  town: **6** Sestos

thrall: 4 esne, serf **5** slave, theow **7** bondage, bondman, captive, enslave, slavery, subject **8** enslaved, enthrall **9** suffering **10** oppression, subjugated

thralldom: 7 bondage, slavery **9** captivity, servitude

thrangity: 6 bustle **8** business

thrash: lam, tan **4** bang, beat, bray, ding, drub, flax, flog, lash, rush, sail, whip, yerk **5** array, baste, bless, flail, pound, swing, threp, whang **6** anoint, defeat, fettle, raddle, strike, threap, threep, threip, threpe, thresh, thwack **7** trounce **8** belabour, blathery, vanquish **9** triturate **10** flagellate

thrashing: 4 bean **7** beating, milling **8** drubbing, flogging, whipping

thrast: 5 press **9** constrain

thrave: 4 bind **5** crowd **6** bundle, number, throng **8** quantity

thrawart: 7 adverse, crooked, peevish, twisted **8** backward, perverse, stubborn **9** reluctant **12** unpropitious

thrawn: 7 crooked **8** perverse **9** misshapen **10** unpleasant

thread: ray **4** filo, line, vein, yarn **5** fiber, reeve, weave **6** strata, stream, string **7** quality, stratum **8** filament, fineness, raveling **9** ravelling **11** composition
  a needle: **5** reeve
  ball of: **4** clew, clue
  bits of: **4** lint **9** ravelings
  cell: **5** cnida
  combining form: nem
  cone: cop
  division of: **4** beer
  in weaving shuttle: **4** weft
  inserted beneath skin: **5** seton
  kind of: **4** bast, bave, film, silk, yarn **5** floss, linen, lisle, rayon, seton, trame **6** cotton, lingel, lingle **8** arrasene
  knot in: **4** burl
  on spindle: cop
  pert. to: **5** filar
  raveled: **6** sleave
  shoemaker's: **6** lingel
  silk: bur **4** bave, burr **5** floss, trame **9** filoselle
  skein of: **4** hasp
  surgical: **6** catgut
  tape: **5** inkle
  tester: **9** serimeter
  used as core for tinsel: **4** poil
  winding tube: cop

thread-like: 5 filar **6** filose

threadbare: 4 bare, sere, worn **5** stale, trite **6** frayed, pilled, shabby **9** hackneyed

threads: 4 beer, weft, woof **6** filler **8** clothing
  combining form: **4** byss

threadworm: 7 filaria **8** nematode

thready: 4 ropy, thin, weak **7** fibrous, stringy

threap, threep, threip, threp, threpe: 4 beat, urge 5 chide, press, scold 6 affirm, assert, haggle, insist, thrash 7 dispute, quarrel, wrangle 8 complain, maintain

threat: vex 4 fail, lack, urge, want, warn 5 chide, crowd, peril, press, troop 6 compel, menace, misery, throng 7 oppress, portend, reprove, trouble, warning 8 maltreat, threaten 10 compulsion 12 denunciation

threaten: 4 brag 5 boast, lower, utter 6 charge, menace 7 portend, promise 8 denounce

threatening: big 6 greasy, lowery 8 lowering, menacing 9 impending 10 formidable

three: 4 drei(G.) 5 crowd, gamma(Gr.), trias 7 Trinity
combination of: 7 triplet, ternary
combining form: ter, tri
consisting of: 7 ternate
group of: tre 4 trio 5 triad, trine 8 triumvir
months: 7 quarter 9 trimester
prefix: tri
ruling group: 11 triumvirate
set of: 4 trio 5 triad 7 ternion

Three B's (in music): 4 Bach 6 Brahms 9 Beethoven

three-card monte: 9 montebank

three-cleft: 6 trifid

three-dimensional: 5 cubic 6 stereo 7 cubical

three-flowered: 9 trifloral

Three Graces: job 5 bloom 6 Aglaia, Thalia 10 brilliance, Euphrosyne

three-headed goddess: 6 Hecate

three-hundredth anniversary: 13 tercentennial, tricentennial

three in one: 6 triune 7 trinity

Three Kingdoms: Wu; Shu, Wei

three L's: 4 lead 7 lookout 8 latitude

three-layered: 10 trilaminar

three-legged stand: 6 tripod, trivet

three-lined: 9 trilinear

three-masted vessel: 5 xebec 8 schooner

Three Musketeers: 5 Athos 6 Aramis 7 Porthos
author: 5 Dumas
friend: 9 D'Artagnan

three-piled: 4 best 6 costly 11 extravagant

three-pointed: 11 tricuspidal

three-score: 5 sixty

three-seeded: 11 trispermous

three-sided figure: 6 trigon 8 triangle

three-spot: 4 trey

three-square: 5 cross 9 irritable, three-fold

three-styled: 10 trystylous

three-toed sloth: ai

Three Wise Men: 6 Gaspar 8 Melchior 9 Balthasar

threefold: 4 tern 5 trine 6 ternal, thrice, treble, trinal, triple, triply
combining form: ter

threescore: 5 sixty

threesome: 4 trio

threne: 5 dirge 8 threnody 11 lamentation

threnody: 4 song 5 dirge 6 hearse

thresh (see also **thrash**): cob 4 beat, flog, lump, rush 5 berry, flail 6 thrash

thresh out: 5 argue 6 debate 7 discuss

threshed grain husks: 5 straw

threshel: 5 flail

thresher: 5 flail; shark 6 beater 7 combine

thresher shark: 6 sea fox 7 foxfish
genus: 7 alopias

threshing: *refuse:* 6 colder
tool: 5 flail

threshold: eve 4 gate, sill 5 limen 6 outset 8 doorsill, entrance 9 beginning

thribble: 6 triple 9 threefold

thrice: 4 very 9 threefold

thrift: 4 work 5 labor 7 economy 9 frugality, husbandry 10 employment, occupation, prosperity, providence 14 forehandedness

thriftily: 4 near

thriftless: 6 lavish 8 prodigal, wasteful 11 extravagant, improvident

thrifty: 4 near 5 fendy, small 6 frugal, narrow, proper, saving, useful, worthy 7 careful, sparing 8 thriving 9 befitting, estimable, provident 10 economical, forehanded, prospering 11 flourishing, serviceable

thrill: 4 bore, cast, dirl, girl, hurl 5 drill, elate, flush, thirl, throw 6 dindle, pierce, quiver, tremor 7 frisson, tremble, vibrate 8 fremitus, transfix 9 penetrate, perforate, throbbing, vibration

thrilling: 9 throbbing, vibrating

thrilly: 8 stirring 11 sensational

thrimble: 6 fumble 7 squeeze, wrestle 8 hesitate

thrimp: 5 press 7 squeeze

thring: 4 cast 5 crowd, crush, press 6 batter, pierce, throng, thrust 7 squeeze

thrive: dow 4 gain, grow 5 addle, moise 6 batten, fatten 7 improve, prosper, succeed 8 flourish, increase

thriven: 4 wise 5 adult, grown 7 prudent 8 thriving 10 prosperous 11 experienced

thriving: 4 bein, bien 10 prosperous, successful 11 flourishing
in shade: 11 sciophilous

thrivingly: 5 gaily, gayly

throat: maw 4 crag, crop, gowl, hals, lane, tube 5 halse 6 groove, gullet, guzzle, weason 7 channel, orifice, weasand 8 guttural
armor: 6 gorget
combining form: 4 lemo
covering: 4 barb

infection: 5 croup 6 angina, quinsy 8 cynan-
che 9 squinancy 11 strep throat
irritation: 4 frog
lozenge: 6 pastil, troche 7 pastile 8 pastille
part: 7 glottis
pert. to: 5 gular 7 jugular 8 guttural
protector: 5 scarf 7 muffler
sore: 6 housty
swelling: 6 goiter
to clear: hem 4 hawk
upper: 4 gula
throat skin: 6 dewlap
throaty: 6 hoarse 8 guttural 9 voracious
throb: 4 ache, beat, drum, pant 5 flack,
pulse 7 flacker, pulsate, vibrate 9 palpitate, pulsation
throbbing: 4 beat
throdden: 4 grow 6 thrive
throddy: 5 plump 6 active 9 well-grown
throe: 4 pang 5 agony 6 effort 7 anguish 8
struggle
thrombus: 4 clot 6 fibrin
throne: see 4 apse, seat 5 asana, chair, exalt,
gaddi, gadhi, power, siege 7 anguish, dignity 8 cathedra, enthrone 11 sovereignty
remove from: 6 depose
throng: 4 busy, crew, heap, host, push, rout
5 close, crowd, horde, peril, press, swarm
6 busily, bustle, strain, stress 7 company,
hurried 8 distress, familiar, hardship, intimate 9 confusion, frequency, multitude 10
affliction, constantly
thronged: 5 alive 7 peopled 10 celebrious
throttle: gun 5 check, choke 6 throat 7 garrote 8 compress, garrotte, strangle, suppress, windpipe 9 suffocate 11 accelerator
open: gun
through, thru: by; per 4 over 5 athro, ended
6 across, coffin 7 perpend 8 athrough, finished 9 completed, tombstone 11 sarcophagus 12 thoroughfare, unobstructed
comb. form: di; dia
the agency of: per
the mouth: 7 peroral
throughgang: 5 labor 6 energy 11 overhauling 12 thoroughfare
throughgoing: 9 reprimand 11 examination, overhauling 12 thoroughfare
throughout: 5 about 6 bedene, during, sempre 7 perfect 8 thorough 10 completely,
everywhere
comb. form: per
throw: boa, cob, don, hit, lob, pat, peg, put,
shy, wap 4 bail, bear, blow, cast, dash, fall,
form, hike, hove, hurl, pelt, rack, risk,
shed, time, toss, turn, yerk 5 check, chuck,
chunk, crank, drive, flick, fling, flirt,
force, frame, heave, impel, pitch, place,
scarf, sling, start, strip, trice, twist,
whang, while, whirl 6 change, defeat, di-

vest, elance, hinder, inject, retard, sprain,
spread, spring, strike, stroke, thrust,
thwart, wrench, writhe 7 advance, discard, fashion, present, produce, project,
revolve, venture 8 catapult, coverlet, distance, obstruct 9 prostrate 10 flagellate
a fit: 5 angry 7 excited 9 disturbed, irritated
a scare into: 5 scare 7 terrify
about: 4 tack 5 slosh 6 thrash
at quoits: 6 leaner, ringer
away: 5 waste 6 refuse, reject 7 discard,
leaflet 8 handbill, squander
back: 5 check, delay, repel 6 refuse, reject,
retort, revert 8 reversal 9 reversion
dice: 4 cast, main, roll
double one at dice: 7 ambsace
down: 4 cast 5 fling 6 defeat, reject 7 refusal, subvert 9 overthrow, rejection 11
precipitate
down the gauntlet: 4 defy 9 challenge
dust in one's eyes: 7 deceive, mislead
from saddle: 7 unhorse
in: add 4 join 6 inject 10 contribute
in the towel: 4 cede, quit 5 yield 9 surrender
into confusion: 4 riot 5 snafu 7 disturb 8
stampede 10 demoralize
into disorder: pif 4 pied 7 derange
into ecstasy: 6 enrapt
into shade: 7 eclipse
lazily: lob
light upon: 6 illume
lightly: 4 toss
obliquely: 4 deal, skew, toss
off: 4 cast, emit, free, molt, shed 5 abate,
expel, moult 6 reject 7 abandon, deflect,
discard 8 discount 10 disconnect
off the track: 6 derail
one's weight around: 4 push, urge 8 domineer
out: 4 emit, lade 5 egest, eject, evict, expel,
utter 6 extend, reject 7 confuse, discard,
excrete, project 8 distance 9 eliminate
out of order: 7 derange
over: 4 jilt 7 abandon
overboard: 8 jettison
six at dice: 4 sise 5 sises
stones at: 8 lapidate
together: 7 collect 8 assemble
underhand: lob
up: 4 rise 5 demit, vomit 10 relinquish
water upon: 5 douse
with force: 4 bung
throwing rope: 5 lasso, reata, riata 6 lariat
throwing-stick: 6 atlatl 9 boomerang
thrown: 4 cast 6 hurled 7 twisted 8 unseated
thrum: bit 4 drum, lout, purr, tuft 5 strum,
waste 6 fringe, recite, repeat, tangle,
thatch 8 particle 10 threepence
thrush: dig 4 bear, birr, bore, butt, dash,
ding 5 barge, mavie, mavis, ouzel, robin,

veery 6 missel, oriole, shrike 7 bearing 8 bluebird, throstle 9 blackbird
disease: 4 soor 5 aptha 6 aphtha
European: 4 osel 5 mavis, ossel, ousel, ouzel 6 missel, shrite
ground: 5 pitta
migratory: 5 robin
thrust: dig, jab 4 bear, birr, bore, butt, dush, gird, jerk, pelt, poke, prop, push, stab 5 barge, clash, crowd, drive, force, hunch, impel, longe, lunge, onset, press, shove 6 attack, detude, extend, hustle, pierce, plunge, repost, ripost, spread, stress, throng 7 allonge, assault, collide, extrude, intrude, riposte 8 estocade, pressure, protrude 9 interject, interpose
against wall: 5 crush, mured
aside: 5 shove, shunt
back: 4 rout 6 defeat 7 repulse
thrutch: 4 push 5 crowd, press 6 throng, thrust
thrutchings: 4 whey
thud: 4 baff, blow, gust, move, push 5 press 6 strike 7 tempest 9 windstorm
thug: 5 rough 6 attack, cuttle, gunman 7 ruffian 8 assassin, gangster 9 cutthroat
thuggery: 6 murder 7 thuggee 10 ruffianism
thumb: 6 pollex, thenar 9 peachwort
part: 6 thenar
Thummim's partner: 4 Urim
thump: cob, dad, dub, hit 4 bang, beat, blow, bump, daud, ding, dird, drub, dunt, polt, whip, yerk 5 blaff, bunch, clour, crump, knock, pound, throb 6 bounce, cudgel, hammer, strike, thrash, thunge
thumping: 5 large 6 tattoo 7 bumping 8 whopping
thunder: 4 peal, rage, roar 6 bronte 7 fouldre 9 Fulminate
comb. form: 5 bront 6 bronto
god: 4 Thor, Zeus
witch: 4 baba
thunder and lightning: 8 ceraunic 9 fulminous
thunder-smitten goddess: 6 Semele
thunderbolt: 4 bolt 6 fulmen 7 fouldre 9 fulminant
thunderhead: 4 omen 5 cloud 7 warning
thundering: 5 large 8 thumping, whopping 10 foudroyant
thunderpeal: 4 clap 11 thunderclap
thunderstorm: *Cuba:* 6 bayamo
West Indies: 7 houvari
thunge: 4 bang 5 sound, thump
thurible: 6 censer
Thuringia: *castle:* 8 Wartburg
city: 4 Gera, Jena 5 Gotha 6 Weimar
Thursday: *god of:* 4 Thor

Holy: 5 Skire
thus: so; sae, sic 4 fiat 5 hence 9 therefore 12 consequently
thwack: rap 4 bang, blow, pack 5 crump, crush, drive, force, knock, whack 6 defeat, strike, thrash 7 belabor 8 belabour
thwart: 4 balk, foil, pert, seat 5 bench, block, brace, clash, cross, parry, saucy, spite, zygon 6 across, baffle, defeat, hinder, oppose, outwit, resist 7 athwart, oblique, prevent, quarrel 8 contrair, obstruct, perverse, stubborn, thwartly 9 frustrate, interpose 10 contravene, disappoint, opposition, transverse 11 intractable, obstruction
thy: tha
Thyestes: *brother:* 6 Atreus
father: 6 Pelops
son: 9 Aegisthus
thylacine: 4 wolf 5 tiger, yabbi
thyme: 8 hillwort
thymus: 5 gland
thyroid enlargement: 6 goiter
thyrsus: 5 staff, stick
tiara: 5 crown 6 diadem, fillet 7 cidares, cidaris, coronet 8 frontlet 9 headdress
Tiber county: 7 Etruria
tibert: cat
Tibet: 7 Sitsang
animal: 5 panda
antelope: goa, sus
ass: 5 kiang
banner: 5 tanka
beast of burden: yak
beer: 5 chang
capital: 5 Lassa, Lhasa
city: Noh 5 Lassa, Lhasa
coin: 5 tanga
deer: 4 shou
dialect: 9 Bhutanese
ecclesiastic: 4 lama 5 dalai
food: 6 tsamba
gazelle: goa
goat fleece: 5 pashm
kingdom: 5 Nepal
lama: 5 Dalai
language: 7 Bodskad
leopard: 5 ounce
monastery: 8 lamasery
monk: 4 lama
ox: yak
oxlike animal: 4 zebu
people: 6 Bhotia 7 Bhotiya
pony: 6 tangum, tangun 7 tanghan
priest: 4 lama
religion: Bon
river: 5 Indus
ruminant: 5 takin
sheep: sha 6 bharal, nahoor, nayaur
wild ass: 5 kiang

wildcat: 5 manul
Tibetan: 6 Tangut
tibia: 5 flute 6 cnemis 8 shinbone
  pert. to: 7 cnemial
tiburon: 5 shark
Tiburon Island Indian: 4 Seri
tic: 4 jerk 5 spasm 9 twitching 11 vellication
tice: 6 entice, yorker 10 enticement
tichel: lot 5 troop 6 number
tick: dot, fag, ked, pat, tag, tap 4 beat, case,
  dash, kade, mark, mite, note, pest 5 acari,
  chalk, click, count, cover, flirt, speck,
  touch, trust 6 acarid, acarus, credit, fondle, insect, moment, record, second, tampon, talaje 7 acarina, instant, ticking 8
  acaridan, arachnid, garapata, indicate,
  mattress, tickbean 10 pajahuello, pajaro-
  ello
  fowl: 5 argas
  genus of: 5 argas
  sheep: ked
ticker: 5 clock, heart, watch
ticket: bid, tag 4 book, card, list, note, slip,
  tick 5 check, ducat, fiche, label, score,
  sight, slate, token 6 ballot, billet, notice,
  permit, record 7 license, placard, voucher,
  warrant 8 document 9 cardboard, discharge, etiquette 10 memorandum 11 certificate
  complimentary: 4 comp, pass 11 Annie
  Oakley
  of leave: 6 parole
  receiver of free: 8 deadhead
  season: 6 abonne 10 abonnement
  sell above cost: 5 scalp
  speculator: 7 scalper
tickey, tickie: 10 threepence
tickle: do 4 beat, nice, play, stir, take, whip
  5 amuse, annoy, frail, tease, touch 6
  arouse, cuitle, divert, excite, please, thrill,
  tingle, touchy, wanton 7 capture, cuittle,
  delight, gratify, operate, passage, portray,
  provoke, tickler 8 chastise, delicate, insecure, tickling, ticklish, unstable, unsteady
  9 difficult, squeamish, titillate, vellicate
  10 insecurely
tickled: 6 amused 7 pleased 9 gratified
tickler: pad, sip 4 book, cane, file 5 flask,
  knife, prong, strap 6 pistol, puzzle, record,
  weapon 7 problem
tickling: 7 craving 13 gratification
ticklish: 4 nice 5 risky 6 fickle, queasy,
  touchy 7 comical 8 critical, delicate, unstable, unsteady 9 uncertain 10 changeable,
  precarious, unreliable 13 oversensitive
tid: 4 fond, mood 5 humor, silly 6 lively, tender 8 childish, ill-humor 9 sprightly
tidal: *bore:* 5 eagre
  creek: 6 estero

  current: 8 tiderace
  flow: 4 bore 5 eagre
  wave: 5 aigre, eagre
tidbit, titbit: 5 goody 7 saynete 8 beatille
tiddle: 4 rear 6 fidget, fondle, pamper, potter, tickle
tiddley: 5 small 7 trivial
tiddy: 4 girl, tiny 5 child 7 babyish, trivial 8
  childish
tide: sea 4 fair, flow, hour, pass, time 5
  carry, drift, drive, flood, point, space,
  surge, tidal 6 befall, betide, endure, happen, moment, period, season, stream 7
  current, freshet, proceed 8 continue, festival, occasion, surmount, tendency 11 anniversary, opportunity
  low: 4 neap
  lowest of high: 4 neap
  pert. to: 4 neap
tidewater: 8 seaboard
tidily: 5 fitly 7 smartly 8 cleverly, suitable
  9 shipshape
tiding, tidings: ebb 4 flow, news 5 event 6
  advice, gospel 7 account, message 9 happening 11 information 12 intelligence
tidy: 4 cosh, fair, good, meet(obs.), neat,
  redd, smug, tosh, trig, trim 5 clean, douce,
  great, groom, large, natty, plump 6
  comely, fettle, sleeky, tidily, timely, worthy 7 healthy, orderly, upright 8 diligent,
  pinafore, skillful 9 shipshape 10 receptacle, seasonable 12 antimacassar, considerable, satisfactory
tie: ty; rod, sag 4 band, beam, beat, bind,
  bond, cord, draw, duty, even, join, knot,
  lace, link, post, rope, teck 5 angle, ascot,
  brace, cadge, chain, equal, hitch, marry,
  nexus, sheaf, trice, union, unite 6 attach,
  cement, connex, couple, cravat, enlace,
  fasten, pledge, string, tether, tiewig 7 confine, connect, necktie, oxfords, sleeper 8
  alligate, restrain, restrict, shoelace 9 constrain, constrict, influence, stalemate 10
  allegiance, obligation
  down: 7 confine 8 restrain, restrict
  fast: 5 belay
  off: 4 snub 5 belay
  ornament: pin 4 clip
  securely: 4 lash 5 truss 7 shackle, trammel
  tightly: 4 bind, lash
  up: 4 bind, moor, stop 5 truss 6 hinder,
  tether 8 obstruct
tie-up: 5 delay 6 strike 7 mooring 10 connection
tied 4 even
tienda: 4 shop, tent 5 booth 6 awning
tier: row 4 bank, rank 5 layer, place, stack,
  story 6 degree 7 antenna, arrange 8 pinafore

tierce: 4 cask 5 lunge, parry, third 7 measure 8 sequence

Tierra del Fuego Indian: Ona 4 Agni

tiff: fit, pet, sip 4 huff, mood, spat 5 draft, dress, drink, humor, lunch, order, scent, smell, sniff, spell, state, taste 6 liquor 7 quarrel 8 outburst 9 condition 11 altercation

tiffin: 5 lunch 6 eating 8 drinking

tiffle: 4 fray, idle 6 potter, trifle, tumble 7 unravel 8 entangle 10 disarrange

tift: 4 gust, pant, puff 5 hurry, sniff, whiff 6 flight 14 breathlessness

tig: pat, tag, tap 5 touch

tiger: cat, cub 4 howl, rake, yell 5 bully, groom 6 feline, jaguar 7 leopard 9 carnivore, swaggerer, thylacine 12 organization

family: 7 felidae

tiger finch: 8 amadavat

tiger-hunting dog: 5 dhole

tigerish: 5 cruel 6 fierce, flashy 9 ferocious 10 swaggering 12 bloodthirsty

tigers-mouth: 8 foxglove, toadflax 10 snapdragon

tight: 4 fast, firm, hard, held, neat, snug, taut, tidy, trim 5 alert, bound, cheap, close, dense, drawn, drunk, fixed, ready, smart, solid, tense, tipsy 6 climax, comely, firmly, packed, severe, steady, stingy, strait, strict 7 capable, compact, concise, quickly, shapely, soundly, ummoved 8 constant, exacting, faithful 9 competent, condensed, energetic, mercernary, niggardly 10 impervious, vigorously 11 closefisted, intoxicated, restraining 12 parsimonious

making: 7 tensing

tight-fisted: 6 stingy 11 closefisted 12 parsimonious

tight-lipped: 5 terse 9 secretive

tighten: 5 tense 6 tauten 9 constrict

strings of drum: 4 frap

tightness: 9 closeness

tightwad: 4 fist 5 miser, piker 7 niggard 9 skinflint

tigrine: 5 tawny

Tigris River city: 7 Nineveh

til: 6 sesame

tile: hat 5 brick, drain, plate, slate 6 tegula 7 carreau, quarrel

composed of: 7 tegular 9 tessellar

curved: 7 pantile

malting floor: 6 pament 7 pamment

mosaic: 7 tessera 8 abaculus

pert. to: 7 tegular

used in game: 6 domino

tile-like: 5 slaty

tiler: cat 4 kiln 5 field, thief 7 hellier 10 doorkeeper

tilery: 4 kiln

tiles: 8 ceramics

till: at, by, of; box, far, for, get, hoe, sow 4 draw, earn, farm, gain, plow, tray 5 charm, dress, labor, train, while 6 casket, drawer, entice, strive, whilst 7 develop, prepare 9 cultivate 10 concerning

tillable: 6 arable 7 earable

tillage: 7 aration, culture 11 cultivation

fit for: 6 arable

tilled land: 5 arada

tiller: bar, bow 4 helm, hoer 5 lever, stalk, stick 6 farmer, handle, sprout 7 husband, rancher 10 cultivator, husbandman

tilt: tip 4 cant, duel, heel, lean, list, rush, tent 5 argue, fight, forge, heald, hield, joust, pitch, poise, slant, slope, speed, upend, upset 6 awning, canopy, careen, combat, hammer, oppose, seesaw, stroke, thrust, topple 7 contest, dispute, incline 8 covering, tiltyard 10 tournament 11 altercation

hammer: 6 oliver

skyward: 5 upend

tilter: 5 sword 6 avocet, seesaw 7 jouster 9 sandpiper

tilting: 5 alist 7 swaying 8 slanting

tilting match: 5 joust

timarau, timerau: 7 buffalo

timbal: 10 kettledrum

timber: log, rib 4 beam, fuel, gate, land, raff, stay, wood 5 build, cahuy, cover, fence, frame, gripe, spile, stile, trees 6 forest, lumber 7 support 8 building, contrive 9 construct, structure, underpier

bend: sny 6 camber, rafter

central portion: 7 duramen 9 heartwood

cut: 4 bunk 6 lumber 7 fallage 8 teakwood

decay: 4 conk, dote, doze

defect: lag 4 conk, doze

end: 5 tenon

estimator: 6 scaler 7 cruiser

joining peg: 7 trenail, trunnel 8 treenail

partially decayed: 4 doty

parts of building: rib 4 sill 5 joist, spale 6 purlin, rafter 7 purline 8 stringer

peg: 4 coak

ship: bao, rib 4 bibb, bitt, keel, mast, spar, wale 5 snape, spale 7 stemson 8 sternson

sloping: 6 rafter

standing: 4 stud 5 spile 6 forest 8 puncheon, studding, stumpage

tree: ash, fir 4 pine 5 birch, cedar, maple 6 walnut 7 redwood 8 mahogany

wolf: 4 lobo

timber-jack: 10 lumberjack

timberman: 6 sawyer 7 cruiser 8 woodsman 9 carpenter, lumberman

timbre: 4 tone 5 crest, miter 7 coronet, quality, timbrel 9 character

timbrel: 4 drum 5 tabor 10 tambourine

time: age, day, eld, era, tid 4 date, fuss, hint, hour, sele, term, week, year 5 clock, epoch, month, tempo, tense, watch 6 during, indeed, minute, moment, period, season, second, steven 8 duration, occasion, regulate, schedule, yuletide 9 foresooth 13 demonstration

ahead of: 5 early 9 premature

allowed for payment: 6 usance

another: 5 again

at no: 5 never 9 nevermore

before: eve

blossom: 9 blutezeit

break in: 6 hiatus

brief: 4 span 6 moment

Christmas: 8 yuletide

devoted to religion: 8 holytide

error in order of: 11 anachronism

fast: 4 Lent

gone by: 4 yore 10 yesteryear

granted: 4 stay 5 delay, frist 8 reprieve

happy: 4 bust, lark 5 revel, spree 6 soiree 8 jamboree

intervening: 7 interim 8 meantime 9 meanwhile

length: age, eon, era 6 moment, period

long ago: 4 yore

music: 6 presto

musical marker: 9 metronome

of great depression: 5 nadir

of highest strength: 6 heyday

olden: eld 4 syne(Sc.), yore

period of: age, day, eon, era 4 aeon, date, hour, span, term, week, year 5 epoch, month, spell, trice 6 decade, ghurry, minute, moment, recess, season, second 7 century, instant 8 azoic age 9 fortnight

pert. to: 4 eral 8 temporal

present: 5 nonce

right: tid(Sc.)

single: 4 once

to come: 5 tabor

waste: 4 idle, loaf 5 dally 6 dwadle, diddle, loiter 8 flanerie

wrong: 13 anachronistic

time being: 5 nonce

time clock: 8 recorder

Time Machine author: 5 Wells

time out: 4 five 5 break 6 recess

timeless: 4 true 5 valid 6 eterne 7 ageless, eternal, undated 8 dateless, unending, untimely 9 co-eternal, premature 11 everlasting 12 interminable

timeliness: 9 relevance

timely: apt, pat 4 soon 5 early 6 prompt 8 temporal 9 opportune, pertinent 10 forehanded, seasonally 11 opportunity

timepiece: 4 dial 5 clock, watch 8 sunwatch 9 horologue 11 chronometer 17 chronothermometer

water: 9 clepsydra

times: many: oft 5 often 10 frequently

olden: eld 9 yesterday 10 yesteryear

prosperous: ups 5 booms

timetable: 8 schedule

timid: shy 4 argh, eery 5 arghe, bauch, blate, eerie, faint, mousy, pavid, scary 6 afraid 7 bashful, fearful, gastful, nervous 8 cowardly, fearsome, ghastful, hesitant, retiring, timorous 9 diffident, shrinking 12 fainthearted 13 pusillanimous 14 chicken-hearted

timidity: 4 fear 7 shyness 9 funkiness 10 diffidence 11 fearfulness

timish: 6 modish 11 fashionable

timon: 4 helm 5 cynic 6 rudder 11 misanthropy

Timon of Athens character: 5 Titus 6 Caphis, Lucius 7 Flavius

timor: 5 dread

Timor: capital: 4 Dili

coin: avo 6 pataca

island: 4 Leti

timorous: 5 faint, timid 6 afraid, cowish, sheepy 7 fearful 8 fearsome, hesitant, terrible 9 shrinking 12 fainthearted

timpani: 11 kettledrums

tin: box, can, pan 5 money, terne 6 latten 7 stannic, stannum 8 preserve, prillion 9 container

pert. to: 7 stannic, stranic

rubbish: 5 stent

sheet: 6 latten

symbol: Sn

tin and copper alloy: 6 pewter

Tin Can Island: 7 Niuafoo

tin dioxide: 8 tinstone

tin foil: 4 tain

Tin Pan Alley group: 5 ASCAP

tin-pot: 4 poor 6 paltry 8 inferior, wretched

tinamou: 4 bird, yutu 6 ynambu

tincal: 5 borax

tinct: dye 4 tint 5 color, imbue, tinge 6 tinged, tinted 7 colored 8 coloured, tincture 10 impregnate

tincture: or 4 cast 5 color, gules, imbue, myrrh, smack, stain, taint, tenne, tinge, trace 6 elixir, imbrue 7 vestige 8 coloring 9 admixture, suspicion 10 extraction 12 modification

for sprains: 6 arnica

of opium: 9 paregoric

tinder: punk: 6 amadou

vegetable: 6 amadou

tine: tub, vat 4 fine, fork, lose, pain, shut, teen 5 grief, prong, spike, tooth 6 harrow, perish, repair 7 destroy, enclose, forfeit, trouble

tine branch: 4 snag

tinea: 8 ringworm

tinean: 4 moth

tineoidea: 5 moths

tinge: dye, hue 4 cast, odor, tint 5 color, imbue, savor, shade, smack, stain, touch, trace 6 affect, flavor 7 glimpse, quality 8 coloring, discolor, tincture 9 influence 10 suggestion

tinged with purple: 10 violaceous

tinglass: tin 7 bismuth

tingle: 4 dirl, girl, nail, ring, tack 5 alive, patch, sting 6 dindle, tinkle 7 support, tremble, vibrant 9 fastening, sensation, stimulate

tinker: auk 4 fuss, mend, work 5 caird, gypsy, murre, patch, rogue, skate, tramp 6 mender, mugger, potter, putter, rascal, repair, wander 7 botcher, bungler, vagrant 8 mackerel 11 silversides

tinkle: 5 clink 6 dindle, dingle, tingle

tinner: 6 canner 8 tinsmith

tinny: 4 hard, rich, thin 5 cheap 6 bright 7 brittle, wealthy 8 metallic, tinsmith

tinplate: 5 terne

tinsel: 4 sham 5 gaudy, showy 6 tawdry 8 specious, splendor 9 clinquant 10 forfeiture, glittering

tinseled: 9 clinquant 10 glittering

tint: dye, hue 5 blush, color, stain, taste, tinge, trace 6 nuance 9 foretaste

cheeks: 5 rouge

Tintagel Head's prince: 6 Arthur

tinter: 4 dyer

tintinnabulum: 4 bell 5 rhyme 7 rhythem 8 rhymster

tintype: 9 ferrotype

tiny: wee 5 child, small, teeny 6 atomic, infant, minute 9 miniature 10 diminutive 13 infinitesimal

tip: cap, cue, end, fee, neb, tap, toe, top 4 apex, barb, blow, cant, cave, clue, dump, fall, heel, hint, keel, lean, list, pile, tilt, vail 5 aglet, alist, chape, crown, drink, empty, point, slant, snick, spire, steer, touch, upset 6 aiglet, apices, arista, careen, corona, nozzle, summit, topple, unload 7 crampit, crumshaw, ferrule, incline 8 bakshish, bonamano, gratuity, overturn 9 baksheesh, buona-mano, buona-mani, extremity, overthrow, pourboire, protector 10 intoxicate

near to: 6 apical

off: 4 tell, warn 5 alarm 8 forewarn

over: 5 upset 8 overturn

tip-off: tip 4 hint 7 warning

tiple: 6 fuddle, guitar

tippet: boa, fur 4 barb, cape, hood, rope, ruff 5 amice, scarf, snell 6 almuce, sindon 7 hanging, muffler, patagia(pl.) 8 liripipe, liripoop, palatine, patagium 9 comforter, victorine

tipping: 5 alist 7 ripping, topping

up: 5 atilt

tipple: bib, nip, sip, tip 4 drip, gill, lose, suck, whet 5 drink, spend, upset 6 fuddle, liquor, sipple, tumble 8 overturn

tippled: 5 drank 6 beered

tippler: sot 4 souse, toper, winer 6 tipper, tipple, tumble 7 drinker, whetter 9 draftsman 11 draughtsman

tippy: 5 smart 6 tiptop 7 stylish 8 unsteady

tipstaff: 7 bailiff 9 attendant, constable

tipster: 4 tout 8 dopester 10 forecaster

tipsy: ree 4 awry 5 bosky, drunk, shaky, tippy 6 bungfu, groggy 7 crooked, ebriose, ebrious, foolish, fuddled, muddled, puddled, tipsify 8 unsteady 10 staggering 11 intoxicated

tiptoe: 5 alert, eager 6 roused, warily 7 eagerly, exalted, quietly 8 cautious, stealthy 10 cautiously 11 expectantly

tiptop: 4 best 9 first-rate 11 galumptious

tirade: 6 screed, speech 7 censure 8 harangue, jeremiad 9 philippic

tirailleur: 10 skirmisher 12 sharpshooter

tire: fag, lag, rim 4 band, bore, gnaw, hoop, jade, pall, prey, pull, shoe, tear, tier 5 dress, recap, seize, spare, weary 6 attire, casing, harass, satiate, tucker 7 apparel, exhaust, fatigue, frazzle, vesture 8 decorate, enginery, overwork, pinafore 9 adornment, discharge, equipment, furniture, headdress, tiredness, weariness 12 accouterment

burst: 4 flat 7 blowout

casing: 4 shoe

saver: 5 recap 7 retread

tired: 5 blown, spent, weary 6 aweary, fagged, sleepy 7 wearied 8 fatigued 9 exhausted

out: 5 jaded, spent

tireless: 4 busy 8 untiring 10 unwearying 13 indefatigable

Tiresias: 4 seer 10 soothsayer

blinded by: 6 Athena, Athene

home: 6 Thebes

tiresome: dry 4 dull, tame 6 boring, borish, dreary, prolix 7 irksome, prosaic, tedious 8 annoying, ennuyant 9 fatiguing, wearisome 10 irritating, monotonous 13 uninteresting

tirl: rap, tap 4 bout, turn 5 strip, twirl, twist, whirl 6 divest, rattle, thrill, unroof 7 uncover 9 vibration

tiro: See **tyro**

tirr: 5 strip 6 unroof 7 uncover, undress

tirrivee: 7 tantrum 9 commotion

tirve: 5 strip 6 unroof 7 uncover

tissue: gum, web 4 tela 5 gauze, sheer, telae, weave 6 girdle, ribbon 7 network 8 meshwork 9 embroider, gauzelike 10 interweave

  animal: fat, gum 4 bone, seur, suet 6 paxwax 7 keratin 8 gelatine

  connective: 6 stroma, tendon

  horny: 7 keratin

  human: fat, gum 4 suet, tela 5 fiber 6 albedo, diploe, keloid, stroma, tendon 7 tonsils 8 ligament, stromata 10 aerenchyma

  layer of: 6 strata 7 stratum

  nerve: 8 ganglion

  oily: fat

  pert. to: 5 telar

  resembling: 7 histoid

  vegetable: 4 bast 5 xylem 6 lignin 7 endarch 8 meristem

  wasting away of: 8 phthisis

tissue-like: 5 telar

tit: nag, pap, pin, tap, tee, tug 4 bird, blow, draw, girl, jade, jerk, plug, pull, teat, tite, twit 5 horse, woman 6 nipple, twitch 7 titlark 8 titmouse

Titan: Ge 4 Bana, Leto, Rhea 5 Coeus, Creus, Dione, giant, Theia 6 Cronus, Kronos, Pallas, Phoebe, Tethys, Themis 7 Iapetus, Oceanus 8 gigantic, Hyperion 9 extensive, Mnemosyne

  father: 6 Uranus

  mother: Ge 4 Gaia

Titania's husband: 6 Oberon

titanic: 4 huge 5 great 7 immense 8 colossal, gigantic

titanite: 6 sphene 7 ijolite

tite: 4 soon 7 quickly 8 promptly 11 immediately

tithe: tax 5 teind, tiend, tenth 6 decima 7 decimae, decimal

  pert. to: 7 decimal

tithing: 6 borrow, decime, denary 8 decenary 9 decennary

titi: 6 monkey

titillate: 6 excite, tickle 9 stimulate, vellicate

titlark: 4 bird 5 pipit

title: Bey, sir 4 Czar, dame, deed, Duke, Earl, Emir, Khan, King, name, Raja, Shah 5 Baron, claim, Count, friar, Major, Mayor, Noble, right 6 assign, Ensign, Kaiser, Knight, legend, madame, Mikado, notice, Prince, record, squire, Sultan 7 Admiral, ascribe, Baronet, Captain, caption, Emperor, epithet, Esquire, General, heading, Justice, Khedive, Marquis, placard, Viceroy 8 Archduke, document, Governor, Viscount 9 Commander, Commodore, designate, President 10 appelation, capitulate, Lieutenant 11 designation 12 championship, denomination 13 Generalissimo

  ecclesiastic: dom, fra 4 abba 8 reverend 10 excellency 11 monseigneur

  feminine: 4 dame, lady 5 hanum, madam 6 hanoum, milady, missis, missus 8 mistress

  foreign: aga, aya, Dan, don, mir, sha, sri 4 baba, Herr, lars, sidi, shri 5 basha, mirza, mpret, pasha, sayid, senor, shree, sieur 6 bashaw, shogun, squire 7 dominus, effendi 8 monsieur

  of Athena: 4 Alea

  pert. to: 7 titular

  royal: hon., sir 4 sire 5 Grace 8 banneret 9 honorable

titled person: 4 peer 5 noble

titmouse: mag, nun, tit 6 fuffit, puffer, titmal, tomtit, verdin 7 jacksaw, titmall, tomnoup 8 heckimal 9 chickadee, mumruffin

  pert. to: 6 parine

titter: 5 laugh 6 giggle, rather, seesaw, sooner, totter, wobble 7 tremble

tittered: 7 giggled, teeheed 9 snickered

tittle: dot, jot 4 iota, sign, whit 5 point, tilde 6 accent, gossip, tattle 7 cedilla, whisper 8 particle

tittup: 5 caper, frisk

titubate: 4 reel 6 totter 7 stagger 8 unsteady 11 vacillating

titular: 7 nominal

Titus Andronicus: *daughter:* 7 Lavinia

  queen: 6 Tamora

Tivoli's ancient name: 5 Tibur

tizzy: 4 snit 6 dither 7 anxiety

tmema: 7 section, segment

TNT: 6 trotyl 8 dynamite 14 trinitrotoluol 15 trinitrotoluene

to (see also **next entries**): tae, 4 till, unto 5 until 6 toward 7 forward

  a conclusion: out

  a place on: 4 onto

  a point on: 4 onto

  an end: out

  be: 4 esse(L.), etre(F.), sein(G.) 5 einai(Gk.) 6 essere(It.)

  be sure: 6 indeed

  no extent: not

  one side: 5 abeam

  position into: 4 into

  sheltered side: 4 alee

  that time: 5 until

  the left: haw 5 aport

  the opposite side: 6 across

the point that: **5** until
the rear: **5** arear **6** astern
the victor: **4** aboo
this: **6** hereto
this place: **4** here **6** hither
which: **7** whereto
wit: viz. **6** namely **8** scilicet **9** videlicet
your health: **5** skoal **6** prosit
to-deal, to-dele: 6 divide **8** separate **10** distribute **11** distinguish
to-do: ado **4** fuss, stir **6** bustle **9** commotion
to-draw: 4 pull, tear **7** detract **8** postpone, protract
toa: 7 warrior
toad: ted **4** agua, bufo, hyla, pipa, tade **6** anuran, peeper **7** crapaud, paddock, quilkin **9** amphibian, spadefoot
genus of: **4** bufo, hyla **6** alytes
larva: **7** tadpole **8** polliwog
order: **5** anura
tongueless suborder: **7** aglossa
toadeater: 5 toady **8** hanger-on, parasite **9** dependent, sycophant
toadfish: 4 sapo **6** angler, grubby, puffer, slimer **8** frogfish **10** midshipman
toadflax: 7 ransted **8** gallwort, ramstead, ranstead
toady: 4 fawn, snob, ugly, zany **6** flunky **7** flunkey, hideous, shoneen, truckle **8** bootlick, parasite, truckler **9** flatterer, repulsive, sycophant, toadeater
toast: dry, tan **4** soak, warm **5** brede, brown, drink, melba, parch, roast, skoal, worst **6** birsle, pledge, prosit **7** bristle, carouse, drinker, propose, swindle, tippler **8** cinnamon
kind of: **4** rusk **5** melba **8** zwieback
toasted bread: 6 sippet
toastmaster: M.C. **5** emcee
tobacco: *chewing:* **4** quid
coarse: **7** caporal
disease: **6** calico **7** walloon
flavor mixture: **6** petune
holder: **4** pipe **7** humidor
hookah smoking: **7** goracco
ingredient: **8** nicotine
in pipe-bowl: **6** dottel, dottle
juice: **6** ambeer, ambier
kind of: **4** capa, shag **5** bogie, fogus, tabac **6** Burley, cowpen **7** caporal, henbane, Latakia, perique, Turkish **8** domestic, Virginia **9** salvadora
leaf moistener: **5** caser
low grade: **4** shag
paste: **7** goracco
pile: **4** bulk
receptacle: **4** pipe **7** humidor
roll: **5** cigar, segar **7** carotte

small portion: cud, fid, fig **4** quid **6** dottel, dottle **7** carotte
Tobacco Road: *author:* **8** Caldwell
character: **5** Pearl **6** Jeeter
tobacco smoke hater: 11 misocapnist
Tobias: *father:* **5** Tobit
wife: **4** Sara
Tobit: *place of captivity:* **7** Nineveh
son: **6** Tobias
wife: **4** Anna
toboggan: 4 sled **7** coaster, decline
toby: jug, mug, way **5** cigar, stein **6** street **7** highway, pitcher, robbery
toby-man: 10 highwayman
tocher: dot **5** dower **7** portion
toco: 6 toucan **8** flogging **9** thrashing
tocology, tokology: 9 midwifery **10** obstetrics
tocsin: 4 bell, sign **5** alarm **6** alarum, signal
tod: fox, mat **4** bush, load, pack **5** clump, shrub **6** bundle, weight
today: now **4** here, oggi(It.) **7** present
pert. to: **7** diurnal **9** hodiernal
toddle: go **4** walk **5** dance **6** daddle, diddle, stroll **7** saunter
toddler: tot **4** trot **5** child
tode: 4 boat, haul, sled
toe: paw, tae, tai, tip **5** digit, pivot, reach, touch **7** journal **10** projection
comb. form: **6** dactyl
great: **6** hallux
little: **7** minimus
pert. to: **7** digital
thickening of skin: **4** corn **6** callus
without: **10** adactylous
toehold: 7 footing
toff: 5 bloke, dandy, swell
toffish: 5 smart **7** stylish
tog: 4 coat **5** dress **7** clothes, garment
toga: **4** gown, robe **5** tunic **7** garment
togated: 7 stately **9** dignified
together: mix **5** along, chain, union **6** bedene, fasten, unison **7** alongst, concert, contact, harmony **8** ensemble **9** cojointly, collision, courtship **11** association **12** cohabitation, coincidently **13** companionship, consecutively **14** simultaneously
prefix: co; com, con, syn
toggery: set **4** kind **5** dress **7** clothes, harness **9** trappings **12** haberdashery
toggle, toggel: pin, rod **4** bolt **6** cotter **10** crosspiece
Togo: *capital:* **4** Lome
language: Ewe **4** Mina **6** French
tribe: Ewe **4** Mina **6** Cabrai
togs: 7 clothes **8** clothing
togt: 5 draft, labor **7** drawing **10** enterprise **11** undertaking
togue: 9 namaycush**

toil: fag, net, tug 4 drag, mesh, moil, plod, pull, rend, roll, task, trap, work 5 broil, cloth, graft, labor, slave, snare, weary 6 battle, canvas, drudge, effort, entrap, harass, strife, writhe 7 contend, ensnare, network, travail, turmoil 8 distress, drudgery, overwork, struggle, writhing 9 enclosure, wallowing 10 accomplish, contention, employment, occupation

toiler: 7 laborer, plodder, workman

toilet: 5 cloth, dress 6 attire 7 costume 8 bathroom, grooming, toilette 9 cleansing
  case: 4 etui 5 etwee

toilsome: 4 hard 7 arduous 9 laborious, wearisome

toise: eye 4 look 6 extend 7 stretch

toit: 4 seat 6 dawdle, settle, totter 7 hassock, saunter

tokalon: 6 beauty 9 beautiful

Tokay: 4 wine 5 grape

token: 4 gift, mark, omen, sign 5 badge, check, medal, merit, proof 6 amulet, emblem, hansel, ostent, pledge, signal, symbol 7 betoken, betroth, feature, handsel, memento, portent, presage, signify 8 accolade, evidence, forbysen, keepsake, souvenir, tessella 9 character, symbolize 10 denotation, expression, indication, prognostic 14 characteristic
  affection: 6 amoret, mascot 7 handsel 8 accolade
  office: 5 badge
  servitude: 4 yoke
  victory: 4 palm

toko: 4 shop 5 store 8 flogging

Tokyo: Edo 4 Yedo

tolbooth, tollbooth: 4 city, hall, jail, town 5 burgh 6 prison 9 tollhouse 11 customhouse

toldo: hut 4 tent

tole: 5 decoy 6 allure, entice

tolerable: gey 4 fair, so-so 8 bearable, passable 9 allowance, endurable 10 sufferable 11 comportable, supportable, translation 13 entertainment

tolerably: 5 geyah 6 fairly, pretty 7 gaylies, geylies 10 moderately

tolerance: 9 allowance, endurance, variation 10 indulgence 11 forbearance 13 understanding

tolerant: 5 broad 7 lenient, patient 8 enduring 9 indulgent 10 ecumenical 11 forebearing

tolerate: 4 bear, bide 5 abide, allow, broad, brook, stand 6 endure, permit, resist, suffer

toll: due, tax 4 chum, drag, draw, duty, lure, peal, pull, rent, ring 5 annul, decoy, knell, sound 6 allure, charge, custom, entice, excise, impost, invite, vacate 7 scatter, trew-

age 8 announce, exaction 10 assessment 12 compensation
  gatherer: 8 customer, publican 9 collector 11 taxgatherer
  kind of: 6 caphar 7 tronage 9 chiminage 10 ballastage
  weight: 7 tronage

tolls: 4 dues

tolly: 4 cane 5 spire 6 candle

Toltec: 7 Nahuatl 9 Nahuatlan
  site of ruins: 4 Tula

tolu: 6 balsam

toluic acid: 7 toluate

tolypeutine: 4 apar 9 armadillo

Tom of Lincoln: 4 bell

Tom Sawyer: *aunt:* 5 Polly
  author: 5 Twain
  brother: Sid
  girl friend: 5 Becky
  pal: 15 Huckleberry Finn

Tom Thumb: 5 dwarf 6 midget

Tom Tulliver's river: 5 Floss

tomahawk: ax; axe, cut 4 kill 6 assail, attack, strike 7 hatchet 9 criticize

toman: 4 coin 5 mound 6 weight 7 hillock 8 division

tomato: 9 loveapple
  relish: 6 catsup 7 ketchup
  sauce: 6 catsup 7 ketchup
  soup: 8 bisque 8 gazpacho

tomb: 4 bury 5 grave, house, huaca, speos, vault 6 burial, casket, cavity, entomb, hearse 7 chamber 8 catacomb, cenotaph, monument 9 sepulcher, tombstone
  empty: 8 cenotaph
  for bones: 7 ossuary
  kind of: 4 cist 7 tritaph 8 cistvaen, kistvaen 9 mauseleum 11 sarcophagus
  saint's: 6 shrine

tombe: 4 drum

tomboy: meg 5 rowdy 6 harlot, hoiden, hoyden 8 strumpet

tombstone: 5 stele 8 monument 9 headstone 10 gravestone

Tombstone marshal: 4 Earp 5 Wyatt

tomcat: gib

tome: 4 book 5 atlas 6 ledger, letter, volume 12 encyclopedia

tomfool: 4 fool 5 clown 6 stupid 7 buffoon, doltish, foolish, half-wit 8 rainbird 9 blockhead 10 flycatcher

tomfoolery: 8 nonsense 9 silliness

tommyrot: 8 nonsense 9 silliness

tomorrow: 6 domani(It.), manana(Sp.)

ton: 4 lots, mode 5 heaps, style, tunny, vogue 7 fashion

tonant: 7 blatant

tonca, tonka: 4 bean
  wood: 6 camara

tone: 4 mood, note, tint 5 pitch, shade, sound, trend 6 accent, effect, intone, modify, temper, timbre 7 quality 8 coloring, mitigate, modulate 9 character, harmonize 10 atmosphere, inflection, intonation, modulation 12 modification
down: 4 mute 6 soften
lacking: 5 atony 6 atonal, atonic
musical: 5 siren, syren 6 sirene
of cord: 8 concento
quality: 6 timbre
rapid: 7 tremolo
sharp: 4 tang
single: 8 monotone
singsong: 4 sugh 5 sough
succession: 5 melos
system of: 6 tonart
thin: 7 sfogato
third of diatonic scale: 7 mediant
vibrant: 5 twang
tone arm: 6 pickup
tone color: 6 timbre
toneless: 5 atony
tones: *combination of:* 5 chord
series of: 5 scale
Tonga island: Ono
tongs: 5 clamp 6 tenail 7 forceps, pincers, tueiron 8 tenaille
tongue: gab 4 bark, chib, fame, flap, howl, pole, sole, vote 5 chide, clack, lingo, prate, scold, speak, utter 6 report 7 beeweed, dialect, feather, lingula 8 language, lingulae, reproach, suffrage 9 pronounce
bone: 5 hyoid
classical: 5 Greek, Latin 6 Hebrew
comb. form: 6 glosso
disease: 5 agrom
Jesus': 7 Aramaic
mother: 10 vernacular
oxcart: 4 cope
pert. to: 7 glossal, lingual
pivoted: 4 pawl
projection: 7 papilla 8 papillae(pl.)
sacred: 4 Pali
seam: 5 raphe
serpent: 4 fang
tip of: 6 corona
wagon: 4 neap, pole
tongue-lash: 5 baste, scold
tongue-like: 7 lingual
tongued: 6 prated
tongueless: 4 dumb, mute 10 speechless
tonic: 5 aloes 6 bracer 7 bracing 8 medicine, roborant 9 sassafras, stimulant 10 refreshing 11 corroborant 12 invigorating
kind of: 4 dope 6 catnip 7 boneset, nervine
tonic leaf: 4 coca
toning down: 10 modulation
Tonkin See **North Vietnam**

tonlet: 4 band
tonsil: 5 gland 8 amygdala
inflammation: 6 quinsy
operation: 12 tonsilectomy 13 tonsillectomy
tonsorialist: 6 barber
tonsure: 5 shave 6 barber 7 haircut
tonsured: 4 bald 5 shorn 6 pilled, shaven 7 clipped
tony: 5 smart 7 stylish
too: and, tae 4 also, over, very 6 overly 7 besides 8 likewise 9 extremely 11 exceedingly, excessively 13 superfluously
bad: 4 alas
late: 5 tardy 7 belated
much: 7 nimiety
small to matter: 13 inappreciable
soon: 9 premature
tool (see also **instrument**): ax; adz, axe, saw 4 adze, draw, dupe, file, form, ride 5 drive, plane, shape, sword 6 convey, device, finish, hammer, manage, puppet, weapon 7 cat's-paw, hatchet, utensil 8 ornament 9 appliance, implement 10 manipulate
abrading: 4 file
biting edge: bit
bookbinding: 5 gouge
boring: awl, bit 5 auger, drill 6 gimlet, reamer 7 bradawl
box: see *chest* below
bricklayer: 4 hock 5 float, level 6 hammer, trowel
butcher: saw 5 knife, steel 6 skewer, skiver 7 cleaver
carpenter: ax; bit, saw 4 rasp 5 auger, level, plane, punch 6 chisel, gimlet, hammer, pliers, square 7 handsaw, hatchet, scriber
chest: kit
chopping: 7 dolabra
cobbler's: awl 6 hammer
cultivating: 4 plow 6 harrow, plough 7 leveler
cutting: ax, adz, axe, bit, hob, saw 4 adze 5 bezel, bezil, gouge, knife, plane, razor 6 chisel, graver, reamer, shears
edged: ax; axe 4 adze 5 knife, razor 6 chisel, reamer
engraver's: 5 burin
excavating: 4 pick 6 pickax, shovel
flat: 7 spatula
garden: hoe 4 rake 5 edger, mower 6 sickle, trowel, weeder
gripping: 4 vise 5 clamp, tongs 7 pincers
hole-making: 6 dibble
kind of: awl, fid, fro, loy, tap, zax 4 celt, file, lute, sley 5 burin, edger, flail, lathe, loper, peavy, peevy, punch 6 chisel, cranny, eo-

lith, flange, lifter, peavey, peevey, pommel, taster, trepan, trowel 7 setiron 8 burgoyne 12 straightedge
marble worker's: 6 fraise
mason's: 6 chisel
mining: gad 4 pick
molding: die
pointed: awl, fid, gad 4 barb, brod, brog, pick 6 gimlet, stylet
pounding: 6 pestle
prehistoric: 4 celt 6 eolith 9 paleolith 10 palaeolith
set: kit
shaping: 5 lathe, swage
slate-measuring: 7 scantle
smoothing: 4 file 5 plane 7 sleeker
splitting: 4 froe, frow
temperer: 8 hardener
trimming: ax; axe, saw 6 shears 8 clippers, scissors
woodworking: adz 4 adze 7 edgeman, grainer, scauper, scriber 10 spokeshave
tool handle: *end* 4 butt
fitted part: 4 tang
tools: tew 4 gear 7 gibbles(Sc.)
toom: 4 lank, lean, pour 5 empty 7 leisure
toomly: 4 idly 6 vainly 7 emptily 9 leisurely
toorie: 4 heap, knob 5 tower 6 tassel
toorock: 4 heap 5 tower
toosh: 4 gown, robe 9 nightgown
toot: pry, spy 4 blow, fool, gaze, peep 5 blast, draft, drink, shout, sound, spree 6 spread, sprout 7 carouse, trumpet, whistle 8 carousal, eminence, proclaim 9 elevation
tooter: spy 7 lookout 8 watchman 9 trumpeter
tooth (see also **teeth**): cog, jag 4 bite, dent, fang, jagg, snag, tine, tusk 5 molar, point, prong 6 cuspid, indent 7 consume, grinder, incisor, snaggle 10 projection
canine: 4 tush 6 cuspid, holder 7 laniary
combining form: 6 odonto
diminutive: 13 denticulation
double: 5 molar
drawer: 7 dentist
edge: 7 dentate
facing: 6 enamel
fore: 5 biter 6 cutter
gear wheel: cog 4 dent, tine
grinding surface: 5 mensa
having but one: 8 monodont
tooth covering: 6 enamel
tooth decay: 6 caries 8 cavities 11 saprodontia
tooth for tooth: 6 talion
toothache: 4 worm(Sc.) 8 dentagra 10 odontalgia
toothed: *irregularly:* 5 erose
on edge: 8 serrated

toothful: sip 4 bite 5 drink 6 tipple 9 toothsome
toothless: 4 weak 6 futile 7 edental 8 decrepit, edentate 9 infantile 10 agomphious, edentulate
toothsome: 5 tasty 8 pleasing 9 agreeable, delicious, palatable
toozoo: 8 ringdove
top: ace, cap, fid, lid, tip, toy 4 acme, apex, crop, head, knap, lead, peak, pick, tent, tilt, tuft 5 caput, cream, crest, crown, drain, drink, equal, excel, outdo, prune, ridge, upset 6 apices(pl.), better, capote, culmen, exceed, finial, summit, swells, topple, tumble, upside, vertex, zenith 7 gyrator, highest, surpass, topmost 8 covering, dominate, forelock, foremost, pinnacle, surmount, vertexes(pl.), vertices(pl.) 9 uppermost 10 pre-eminent 11 aristocrats
altar: 5 mensa
head: 4 pate 5 scalp
of card suit: ace
of wave: 5 crest
toy: 8 teetotum
wooden stand: 5 criss
top-hole: 6 tiptop 9 excellent 10 first-class
top kick: 8 sergeant
top-notch: 4 best 6 tiptop 7 highest 9 first-rate 11 unsurpassed
topaz: gem 5 stone
symbol of: 8 fidelity
topaz humming bird: ani, ava 4 avas(pl.), aves(pl.)
topcoat: 6 reefer 8 overcoat
tope: 4 butt, wren 5 clump, drink, grove, shark, stupa 6 guzzle 7 dogfish, orchard
topechee: 12 artilleryman
topee, topi: cat, hat 6 helmet
toper: sot 5 shark 6 boozer, bouser 7 tippler, tosspot 8 drunkard
tophaceous: 5 rough, sandy, stony 6 gritty
tophet, topheth: 4 hell 5 chaos 8 darkness 9 confusion
topi: cap, hat 5 topee 6 helmet 8 antelope
topic: 4 item, text 5 issue, thema, theme 6 reason, remedy 7 heading, subject, themata 8 argument 11 application 13 consideration
topic of discourse: 5 theme
topical: 5 local 9 temporary
topknot: 4 hair, head, tuft 5 crest, onkos 7 commode 8 flounder 9 headdress
toplofty: 5 lofty 7 haughty 10 disdainful 12 contemptuous, supercilious
topmost: 6 apical 7 highest 9 uppermost
topnotcher: ace 4 hero, star
topper: hat 5 cover, float 6 stower 7 cheater, snuffer, topcoat 10 high-rigger 11 highclimber

toppiece: 4 head 6 toupee 11 masterpiece

topping: 4 bran, fine, good 5 icing, proud 6 refuse, tiptop 7 forlock, gallant, highest, topknot, topmost 8 arrogant, pleasant, superior 9 excellent, first-rate, skimmings 11 pretentious

topple: tip 4 fall, tilt 5 pitch, upset 6 totter, tumble 7 overset 8 overhang, overturn 9 overthrow 10 somersault 11 overbalance

toppy: 5 showy 7 stylish

tops: 4 A-one, aces, best 7 supreme

topsman: 5 chief 6 drover 7 hangman, headman

topsy-turvy: 8 confused 10 disordered 11 widdershins, withershins

toque: hat 6 bonnet 9 headdress

tor: taw 4 crag, hill, peak 5 mound 8 pinnacle

tora, torah: law 5 tetel 7 precept 10 hartebeest, Pentateuch, revelation 11 instruction

torch: 4 lamp 5 blaze, brand, flare, fusee 7 lucigen 8 flambeau 8 flambeaux(pl.) 10 flashlight
frame: 7 cresset

tore: 4 knob, plod 5 grass 6 pommel 9 persevere

toreador: 11 bullfighter

torero: 11 bullfighter

torii: 7 gateway

torment: rib, vex 4 bait, pain, rack 5 agony, annoy, chevy, chivy, devil, force, grill, harry, tease, wrack 6 badger, chivvy, harass, harrow, hector, misery, pester, plague, strain 7 afflict, agitate, anguish, bedevil, crucify, distort, hagride, hatchel, tempest, torture, travail 8 distress, vexation 9 martyrdom, suffering, tantalize 10 cruciation 11 persecution

tormenting: 6 plaguy, vexing 9 harassing 11 troublesome

tormina: 5 colic, pains 6 cramps

torn: 4 rent 5 riven 6 broken, ripped 9 lacerated

tornado: 4 wind 6 squall 7 cyclone, thunder, twister 9 hurricane, whirlwind, windstorm 12 thunderstorm

Tornado Junction: 8 Trinidad

toro: 4 bull, tree 7 cavalla, cowfish

torous, torose: 6 brawny 7 bulging, knobbed, swollen 8 muscular 11 protuberant

torpedinous: 9 benumbing 10 stupefying

torpedo: 4 mine, ruin 5 wreck 6 attack, benumb, damage, gunman 7 destroy, explode, shatter 8 firework, gangster, numbfish, paralyze 9 crampfish, detonator
front end: 4 nose

torpedo fish: ray

torpid: 4 boat, dull, numb 5 inert 6 stupid 7 dormant, torpent 8 benumbed, inactive, lifeless, sluggish 9 apathetic, lethargic

torpor: 4 coma 5 sleep 6 acedia, apathy, stupor 7 accidie 8 dormancy, dullness, lethargy 10 inactivity, stagnation 12 sluggishness 13 insensibility

torque: bee 5 chain, sarpe, twist 6 collar

torrefy, torrify: dry 5 parch, roast 6 scorch

torrent: 4 flow, rush 5 flood, parch, roast, spate 6 stream 7 burning, channel, consume, current, roaring, rushing 8 downpour 9 impetuous

torrential: 10 outpouring 12 overwhelming

torrid: hot 4 arid 5 dried 6 ardent 7 burning, parched, zealous 8 inflamed, parching, scorched 9 scorching 10 oppressive, passionate

Torrid Zone boundary: 6 Tropic

tortoise: 6 turtle 8 terrapin 9 chelonian
genus: 4 emys
kind: 4 emyd 5 giant 9 Galapagos
marsh: 6 gopher 7 elodian
order of: 8 chelonia
pert. to: 9 chelonian
shell: 8 carapace

tortuosity: 4 bend, turn 5 twist 7 flexure, winding 9 sinuosity 10 distortion 11 crookedness, deviousness

tortuous: 6 cranky, spiral 7 crooked, devious, immoral, sinuate, sinuous, winding, wriggly 8 wrongful 9 deceitful, injurious 10 circuitous, roundabout 11 anfractuous 12 labyrinthine

torture: 4 pain, rack 5 agony, twist, wheel 6 punish, wrench 7 agonize, anguish, crucify, distort, torment 8 distress, twisting 9 martyrdom 10 affliction, cruciation, distortion, excruciate, perversion, punishment
device: 4 rack

torus: 6 baston 7 molding 9 elevation 12 protuberance

torvity: 8 grimness, severity 9 sternness

torvous: 4 grim 5 stern 6 severe

tory: 6 bandit, outlaw, Papist 8 loyalist, marauder, Royalist 11 reactionary 12 conservative

Tosca's love: 5 Mario

tosh: 4 bath, bosh, neat, tidy 5 souse, trash 6 drench, neatly 7 bathtub 8 familiar, intimate, nonsense 10 intimately

toss: cob, cup, lob 4 cast, cave, flip, hike, hurl, rear, roll 5 chuck, flick, fling, flirt, heave, pitch, raise, serve, throw, wager 6 buffet, chance, fillip, harass, tossup, totter, uplift 7 agitate, disturb 8 disquiet 9 agitation, commotion 10 excitement
a coin: 4 flap, flip

about: 5 bandy 6 thrash, thresh
carelessly: 4 flip
head in derision: 4 geck
side to side: 6 careen
together confusedly: 8 scramble

tosspot: sot 5 toper 7 drinker 8 drunkard
  bottle: 6 flagon

tosticate: 6 harass 8 distract 10 intoxicate

tosto: 4 fast 5 quick

tosy: 4 snug 10 comforting 11 intoxicated

tot: add, cup 4 item, note 5 child, count, drink, total, totum 6 amount, toddle, totter, tottum 7 jotting, toddler 8 exercise

tota: 6 grivet, monkey

total: add, all, sum, tot 4 full 5 gross, utter, whole 6 abrupt, amount, entire 7 concise, perfect, summary 8 absolute, complete, entirety 9 aggregate, undivided 10 accumulate

totality: all, sum 6 amount 7 allness 8 entirety 9 aggregate, wholeness 10 altogether

totally: 5 quite 6 wholly 8 entirely 10 altogether, completely

tote: all, lug, tot 4 bear, haul, lead, load 5 carry, count, total 6 handle, reckon 7 conduct 9 abstainer, transport

totem: 6 emblem, fetich, fetish, figure

totem post: xat

toto: 4 baby

totter: 4 fall, hang, reel, rock, sway, toss 5 pitch, shake, swing, waver 6 dodder, falter, quiver, seesaw, staver(Sc.), toddle 7 fribble, stagger, tremble 8 titubate, unstable, unsteady 9 vacillate

tottering: 4 fall 5 shaky 6 groggy 7 adverse, rickety, shaking 8 collapse, unsteady, wavering 9 faltering 10 changeable 11 threatening, vacillating

tottery: 4 weak 5 shaky 8 unsteady 9 tottering

tottle: 4 boil, purl 5 count, total 6 reckon, simmer, toddle, topple, totter 9 reckoning

tottlish: 7 tottery 8 unsteady

tottum, totum: all, tot 5 child, whole

totty: 4 weak 5 child, dotty, shaky 7 tottery 8 unsteady 9 befuddled

toty: 7 laborer 9 messenger

toucan: 4 toco 7 aracari 8 hornbill 13 constellation

touch: dab, hit, rap, rob, tag, tap, tig, toe, use 4 abut, blow, feel, meet, rape 5 equal, reach, rival, steal, taste, trait 6 accuse, adjoin, affect, attain, border, borrow, extend, handle, molest, rebuke, strike, stroke 7 attinge, censure, contact, impinge, palpate, partake 8 perceive 9 mishandle
  boundary line: 4 abut

closely: 8 osculate
clumsily: paw
combining form: tac
for medical diagnosis: 7 palpate
lightly: 5 brush 7 attinge, twiddle
measuring device: 10 haptometer
off: 4 fire 5 start
organ of: 4 palp 6 feeler 7 antenna
perceptible by: 7 tactile 8 palpable
pert. to: 6 haptic 7 tactile, tactual

touching: 4 upon 6 moving 7 contact, meeting, tangent 8 adjacent, pathetic 9 affecting, attingent, conjoined 10 contacting, contiguous, contingent
a single point: 7 tangent

touchstone: 4 test 8 basanite, standard 9 criterion

touchwood: 4 funk, punk 5 sponk, spunk 6 amadou, tinder 8 punkwood

touchy: 4 sore 5 cross, risky, snaky, techy, testy 7 peevish 8 ticklish 9 irascible, irritable, sensitive 10 precarious 11 inflammable 13 over-sensitive

tough: 4 thug, wiry 5 hardy, rigid, rough, rowdy, stiff 6 brutal, robust, sinewy, sticky, strong 7 hickory, ruffian, violent, viscous 8 cohesive, enduring, hardened, leathery, rowdyish, stubborn, sturdily, toilsome, vigorous 9 difficult, glutinous, obstinate, ruffianly 10 aggressive, unyielding
and lean: 5 scrag 6 sinewy

tough-minded: 6 shrewd 7 willful 8 stubborn 9 practical, realistic 10 hardheaded 13 unsentimental

toughen: 5 inure 6 anneal, endure, temper

toughened: 5 clung 8 hardened, tempered

toupee: wig 6 peruke 7 periwig

tour: go 4 trip, turn 5 cover, drive, range, round, shift, spell, trick, watch 6 course, travel 7 circuit, compass, journey, proceed 9 barnstorm, excursion 10 appearance, revolution

tourbillion: 5 whirl 6 vortex 8 firework 9 whirlwind

tourelle: 5 tower 6 turret

tourist: 8 traveler

tourmaline: 6 schorl 9 rubellite

tournament: 4 tilt 5 joust, sport, trial 6 battle 7 contest, tourney 9 encounter

tourney: 10 tournament

tournure: pad 6 bustle

touse: 4 fuss, pull, rack, tear 5 worry 6 handle, rumple, tousel, tousle, tussle 7 turmoil 8 dishevel 11 disturbance

tousle, tousel: 4 drag, muss, pull, tear 5 touse 6 ruffle, rumple, tussle 7 rummage 8 dishevel, disorder

tousy: 5 rough 6 shaggy 7 tangled, tousled

tout: spy, vex 4 peep, peer, puff, toot 5 tease, thief, watch 6 praise 7 canvass, lookout, solicit, tipster, touting 8 informer, proclaim, smuggler 9 importune, recommend

tove: 4 emit 5 smoke

tow: tew, tug 4 drag, draw, flax, haul, lead, pull, rope 5 barge, chain 6 hawser 7 towboat, towrope, tugboat 8 cordelle

tow-row: 6 rumpus, uproar 9 racketing

toward: by; tae(Sc.) 4 near 5 anent 6 anenst, coming, future, onward 7 forward, willing 8 imminent, obliging 9 compliant, promising, tractable 11 approaching

  center: 5 entad

  exterior: 5 ectad

  mouth: 4 orad

  prefix: ob, oc

  stern: aft 5 abaft 6 astern

towardly: 6 docile, gentle, kindly 7 affable 9 compliant, favorable, tractable 10 propitious

towel: dry, rub 5 cloth 6 napkin 8 vesperal 9 handcloth

  fabric: 4 huck 5 linen, terry

tower: 4 rise, silo, soar 5 broch, exalt, mount, pylon, raise, reach, sikar, spire, stupa 6 ascend, belfry, castle, donjon, pagoda, prison, turret 7 bastile, bulwark, citadel, clocher, defense, elevate, mansion, minaret, mirador, overtop, shikara, steeple, surpass, zikurat 8 bastille, domineer, fortress, zuggurat, zikkurat 9 campanile 10 protection, stronghold

  bell: 6 belfry 9 campanile

  castle: 6 donjon

  church: 5 spire 7 steeple

  famous: 4 Pisa 5 Babel, Minar 6 Eiffel, London

  glacier ice: 5 serac

  kind of: 5 ivory

  mosque: 7 minaret

  signal: 6 beacon

  small: 6 turret

towering: 4 high, tall 5 great, lofty, steep 7 eminent, intense, violent 11 overweening

towhee: 7 bunting, chewink

town: 4 burg, city, dorp, farm, stad, vill, yard 5 bourg, burgh, court, derby, house, manor, ville(F.), voter 6 ciudad(Sp.), garden, hamlet, parish, podunk, staple 7 borough, burgess, citizen, cluster, village 8 bourgade, township 9 enclosure, farmstead 10 electorate, metropolis 11 aggregation

  Attic: 4 deme

  official: 6 grieve

  pert. to: 5 civic, urban 7 oppidon

  plan: 4 plat

  small: 11 whistle-stop

  witch: 5 Salem

townsman: cit 7 citizen, oppidan 9 selectman 10 inhabitant

township: 4 area 8 district

toxic: 9 poisonous

toxophilite: 6 archer

toy: pet, top 4 ball, daff, doll, fool, play, whim 5 antic, dally, fancy, flirt, panda, sport 6 bauble, finger, gewgaw, hoople, rattle, trifle 7 caprice, conceit, pastime, trinket 8 aversion, flirting, gimcrack, interest, mistress, ornament, teetotum, weakling 9 bandalore, dalliance, headdress, plaything, rattlebox, teddybear 10 knickknack

toyish: 6 wanton 7 playful, trivial, useless 8 sportive, trifling 9 fantastic, frivolous, whimsical 13 unsubstantial

toze: 4 comb, pull 5 tease 11 disentangle

trabant: 9 attendant, bodyguard

trabea: 4 toga

trabeation: 6 beamed 11 entablature

trabuco: 5 cigar 11 blunderbuss

trace: 4 clew, clue, copy, draw, fall, file, hint, line, mark, nose, path, road, seek, sign, step, tang, walk 5 grain, march, probe, route, shade, tinge, track, trail, tread 6 amount, deduce, derive, detect, follow, locate, ramble, sketch, trudge 7 conduct, glimpse, impress, imprint, inquire, outline, remnant, soupcon, uncover, vestige 8 discover, evidence, quantity, traverse 9 ascertain, attribute, delineate, establish, footprint, scintilla 10 indication, procession 11 investigate

tracer: 5 horse 6 bullet, gilder, stylus 7 stainer 9 draftsman

trachea: 4 duct 8 windpipe

trachyte: 6 domite

tracing: 4 copy 6 record 8 ergogram 10 cardiogram

track: rut, way 4 drag, draw, hunt, line, mark, oval, path, rail, road, wake 5 march, route, scent, sight, spoor, trace, trail, tread 6 course, follow, infuse, pursue, teapot, travel 7 circuit, conduct, vestige 8 guideway, sequence, speedway, trackage, traverse 9 ascertain, footprint, spectacle 10 cinder path, succession

  animal: run 4 slot 5 spoor

  down: 4 hunt 6 pursue, search

  official: 5 judge, timer 7 referee, starter

  race: 4 mile 5 relay 6 sprint

  ship: 4 wake

  train: 4 rail 6 siding

tracker: 5 guide, tower

tract (see also **land**)**:** 4 area, mark, path, zone 5 campo, clime, essay, lapse, range, trace, track 6 course, estate, extent, region 7 country, expanse, leaflet, pteryla, quarter, stretch 8 brochure, district, duration, pamphlet, sequence, treatise 9 lineament, narrative, territory 10 exposition 11 subdivision 12 dissertation

tractable: 4 easy 6 docile, gentle, pliant 7 ductile, flexile 8 amenable, flexible, obedient, workable 9 adaptable, compliant, malleable 10 governable

tractate: 5 essay, tract 8 handling, treatise 9 treatment 10 discussion 12 dissertation

tractile: 6 pliant 7 ductile, tensile

traction: 5 power 7 drawing, utility 8 friction 9 influence 10 attraction

tractor: 9 agrimotor

trade: buy, way 4 chap, chop, deal, fuss, path, sell, swap, work 5 cheap, craft, habit, track, trail, tread 6 action, barter, bother, course, employ, manner, method, metier, scorse 7 bargain, calling, dealing, pursuit, traffic 8 activity, business, commerce, exchange, practice, purchase 10 handicraft, occupation, profession 11 intercourse, nundination

association: NAM 5 hansa, hanse

combination: 4 gild 5 guild, hanse 6 cartel, merger

pert. to: 10 emporeutic

unlawful: 10 contraband

votes: 7 logroll

trademark: 5 brand

trader: 6 dealer, monger, seller, slaver, sutler 7 chapman 8 barterer, merchant 9 tradesman 10 shopkeeper

tradesman: 5 buyer 7 artisan, workman 8 merchant 9 craftsman 10 shopkeeper 11 storekeeper

supply: 4 line 5 stock 9 inventory

trading post: P.X. 7 station

trading stamp: 7 premium

tradition: 4 code, lore 6 belief, custom, legend 8 practice 9 surrender 10 convention

traduce: 4 slur 5 abuse, belie 6 debase, defame, malign, vilify 7 asperse, blacken, detract, pervert, slander 8 disgrace 10 calumniate

traffic: buy 4 coup, sell 5 trade 6 barter, market 7 chaffer, dealing 8 business, commerce, exchange 11 intercourse

in holy offices: 6 simony

violator: 9 jaywalker

trafficker: 6 dealer, trader 8 merchant

in narcotics: 6 pusher

tragacanth: gum 4 tree 5 shrub

tragedy: 6 buskin, misery 8 calamity, disaster 10 misfortune

Muse: 9 Melpomene

tragic: sad 4 dire 5 fatal 7 doleful 8 mournful, pathetic, terrible

tragopan: 8 pheasant

tragule: 4 deer 10 chevrotain

trail: lag 4 drag, draw, hang, hunt, mark, path, slot, tail, wake 5 blaze, drail, piste, route, scent, spoor, trace, track, train, tramp, troll 6 camino(Sp.), course, follow, trapse 7 draggle, dwindle, traipse 8 footpath, straggle

blazer: 7 pioneer

marker: 5 cairn

trailer: 4 vine

truck: 4 semi

train: row 4 bait, drag, draw, file, form, gait, lead, line, lure, rack, rank, rear, tail, trap 5 breed, coach, decoy, drawl, drill, flier, guide, local, seine, snare, suite, teach, trace, trail 6 allure, coffle, convoy, cradle, direct, entice, ground, scheme, school, series, shaped 7 caravan, conduct, cortege, educate, prepare, retinue 8 accustom, artifice, equipage, instruct, protract, rehearse, sequence, trickery 9 condition, entourage, following, strategem, treachery 10 attendants, conveyance, discipline, procession 11 streamliner 13 accommodation

end car of: 7 caboose

fast: 7 express, limited

horses: 6 manege

men: 4 crew

of attendants: 5 suite 7 retinue 9 entourage

overhead: el 8 elevated, monorail

slow: 5 local

underground: 4 tube 5 metro(F.) 6 subway

trained: 4 bred 5 aimed 8 educated

trainee: 5 pupil 6 novice 10 apprentice

trainer: 5 tamer 7 lanista 11 gymnasiarch

training: 4 diet 5 drill 8 breeding, exercise 9 education 10 background, discipline 11 supervision

lack of: 11 inappetence

manual: 5 sloid, sloyd

traipse, trapes: gad 4 walk 5 trail, tramp, tread 6 trudge, wander 8 gadabout, slattern

trait: 4 line, mark, note, thew 5 touch 6 streak, stroke 7 feature, quality 9 lineament, mannerism 11 peculiarity 14 characteristic

traitor: 5 Judas 8 betrayer, Iscariot, renegade

Norweigian: 8 Quisling

traitorous: 5 false 9 faithless, felonious 11 disaffected, treacherous, treasonable

traject: way 4 cast 5 ferry, route, throw 6 course 7 passage 8 transmit

trajet: way 5 route 6 course 7 passage, traject

tralatitious: 12 metaphorical

tram, trame: car, leg 4 beam, haul, limb 5
bench, shaft, wagon 6 thread 7 tramcar,
trammel, tramway, trolley 9 streetcar 10
conveyance

tier: 4 deck

trammel: net, tie 4 clog, lock 5 check, gauge
6 braids, fasten, fetter, hamper, impede 7
compass, confine, pothook, prevent,
shackle, tresses 8 restrain 9 intercept,
plaitings 10 instrument

tramontane: 4 boor 5 alien 7 foreign 8
stranger 9 barbarous 10 outlandish 11
transalpine

tramp: bo; boe, bum, vag 4 hike, hobo, hoof,
prog, step, tart, vamp, walk 5 caird, jaunt,
tread 6 gaycat, trapes, travel, trudge, waffie, wander 7 steamer, traipse, vagrant 8
vagabond 9 excursion 10 prostitute 11 bindle stiff

baggage: 6 bindle

offering to: 7 handout

trample: 4 foil, hurt 5 crush, tread 6 injure
7 destroy, violate

trance: 4 coma, daze 5 spell, swoon 6 prance,
raptus, stupor 7 ecstasy, enchant, passage
8 entrance 9 catalepsy, enrapture 10 passageway

traneen: bit 6 trifle

tranquil: 4 calm, cool, easy, even, mild 5
equal, quiet, still 6 gentle, placid, serene,
steady 7 equable, pacific, restful 8 composed, peaceful 9 sedentary 10 motionless
11 undisturbed 13 imperturbable

tranquility, tranquillity: kef, kif 5 peace,
quiet 8 serenity 10 equanimity 12 peacefulness

tranquilize: 4 lull 5 allay 6 settle, soften,
soothe 7 appease, assuage 9 alleviate

transact: do 5 treat 7 conduct, perform 8
complete, transfer 9 negotiate

transaction: 4 deal, sale 6 action, affair 7
bargain 8 business 10 proceeding 11 proposition

unlawful: 10 chevisance

Transcaspian capital: 9 Ashkhabad

Transcaucasia: See **Armenia,
Azerbaijan, Georgia**

transcend: 5 climb, excel, mount, raise 6
ascend, exceed 7 elevate, surpass 8 outstrip, overstep, surmount

transcendent: 8 superior 13 extraordinary

transcendental: 5 ideal 8 ethereal 10 superhuman 12 metaphysical, supersensual, su-
pranatural

transcribe: 4 copy 5 write 6 impute, record
7 ascribe, imitate 9 reproduce, translate
10 paraphrase

transcript: 6 record 8 apograph 9 duplicate
12 reproduction

transfer: 4 cede, deed, move, pass, sale, send
5 carry, grant, shift 6 assign, attorn,
change, convey, decant, demise, depute,
remove 7 dispose 8 alienate, delegate 9
translate, transport 10 abalienate 12
transmission 13 transposition

bus or train: 6 ticket

design: 5 decal

of court suit: 7 remover

property: 4 deed 5 grant 6 convey

transference: 7 passage 10 conveyance

transfigure: 5 exalt 7 glorify 8 idealize 9
transform 12 metamorphose

transfix: fix, pin 5 spear, stick 6 fasten, impale, pierce 11 transpierce

transform: 4 turn 5 alter 6 change 7 convert
9 transmute 11 transfigure 12 metamorphose, transmogrify

transformation: 10 conversion 13 metamorphosis

into human form: 17 anthropomorphosis

transfuse: 5 imbue 6 infuse 7 instill 8 transfer, transmit

transgress: err, sin 5 break, cross 6 offend
7 disobey, violate 8 overstep

transgression: 5 crime, fault 7 misdeed 8
trespass 10 infraction 12 infringement 13
contravention

transient: 8 fleeting, fugitive 9 ephemeral,
itinerant, migratory, momentary, temporary, transeunt 10 evanescent, shortlived,
transitory 11 impermanent

transit: 6 change 7 passage 10 conveyance,
transition 12 thoroughfare

coach: bus

transition: 5 phase, shift 9 metabasis 10
conversion

transitive: 7 flowing 12 transitional

transitory: 5 brief, fleet 8 caducous, temporal 9 ephemeral, temporary 10 evanescent

translate: 4 read, rede 6 change, decode, remove, render 7 convert 8 construe, decipher, entrance, transfer 9 enrapture, interpret 10 paraphrase

translation: 4 pony, trot 7 version 9 rendition 10 paraphrase 14 interpretation 15
transliteration

translucent: 6 limpid 9 alabaster 11 perspicuous, transparent

transmigration: 7 samsara

transmit: 4 emit, hand, send 5 carry, relay
6 convey, render 7 conduct, devolve, forward 8 bequeath 11 communicate

transmutation: 9 evolution

transmute: 6 change 7 convert 8 transfer 9
transform

transom: 5 trave 6 louver, window

transparent: 4 open 5 clear, frank, gauzy,
lucid, sheer 6 candid, limpid, lucent 7 obvi-

ous, pelucid 8 luminous, lustrous 9 colorless 10 diaphanous 11 crystalline, perspicuous, translucent

transpierce: 6 pierce 8 transfix 9 penetrate

transpire: 6 happen

transport: dak 4 bear, boat, buss, haul, move, send, ship, tote 5 bring, carry, ferry, flute, truck 6 banish, convey, deport, ravish 7 convict, ecstasy, emotion, fraught, freight, passion, portage, rapture, smuggle 8 entrance, horsecar, overcome, palander, transfer 9 captivate, enrapture, happiness

transportation: *business:* 4 mail 7 air line, express 8 shipping 9 steamship 11 railroading

means: 7 rockets

system: 4 line

transpose: 5 shift 6 change, remove 7 convert, disturb, reverse 8 exchange, transfer 9 rearrange, transform, translate, transmute 11 interchange

transposition: 7 anagram 10 spoonerism 11 permutation

Transvaal: *capital:* 8 Pretoria

district: 4 Rand

policeman: 4 zarp

transverse: bar, way 4 bank, over, pass, rung, turn 5 argue, cross, pivot, route, shift, trace 6 across, denial, stripe, survey, swivel, thwart, travel 7 barrier, discuss, examine, impeach, oblique, pervade, quarrel 9 alternate, crossbeam 10 crosspiece 11 controversy

Transylvania: *city:* 4 Cluj

fabled resident: 7 Dracula, vampire

trap: bag, get, gin, net, pit 4 cage, lure, nail 5 brake, buggy, catch, goods, mouth, rocks, snare, steps, trick 6 ambush, corner, detect, enmesh 7 capture, cunning, ensnare, luggage, pitfall, springe 8 carriage, confound, covering, deadfall, separate, trapball 9 caparison, detective, policeman, stratagem 10 belongings, stepladder

animal: pot, web 4 weir 5 creel 6 bownet, eelpot

police: 7 dragnet 9 roadblock

trapdoor: 4 drop

trapes: See **traipse**

trapeze: bar

trapping: 4 gear 5 cloth 7 harness 8 catching, covering, ornament 9 adornment, caparison, coverture 10 decoration 12 accouterment, accoutrement 13 embellishment, paraphernelia

theatrical: 4 prop 7 scenery 8 property

Trappist: 4 monk

cheese: oka

writer: 6 Merton

traps: 5 bells, drums 7 cymbals

trapshooting: 5 skeet

target: 10 clay pigeon

trash: jog, lop 4 bosh, clog, crop, dirt, jade, pelf, plod, raff, tosh 5 leash, money, tramp, waste, wrack 6 bushwa, debris, halter, hinder, rabble, refuse, retard, rubble, trudge 7 baggage, beggary, blather, rubbish 8 encumber, flummery, nonsense, restrain, riffraff, trumpery 10 balderdash 11 sleuthhound

trashy: 9 worthless

trauma: 5 shock, wound 6 injury

travail: 4 pain, pang, task, toil 5 agony, drive, labor 6 effort, travel 7 journey, torment, trouble 8 exertion 9 suffering 11 parturition

trave: 9 crossbeam

travel: go; run 4 fare, move, mush, post, ride, tour, trek, trip, walk, wend 5 coast 6 motion 7 commute, journey, migrate, passage, proceed, sojourn, torment, travail 8 traverse 9 gallivant, itinerate 10 locomotion 11 peregrinate

company: 7 caravan

pert. to: 6 viatic

yen for: 10 wanderlust

traveler: 5 farer, tramp 6 viator 7 drummer, pilgrim, swagman, tourist, voyager 8 salesman, wanderer, wayfarer 9 itinerant 12 globe-trotter

aid of: 5 guide 7 courier 8 cicerone

commercial: 5 agent 7 drummer 8 salesman

refuge: inn 5 oasis, motel 7 hospice

travels: 7 odyssey

traverse: 4 deny, ford, pass 5 cross, range, rebut 6 patrol, refute, thwart

travesty: 6 parody, satire 8 disguise 9 burlesque, imitation 10 caricature

writer: 8 parodist

trawl: net 4 fish, line 7 boulter, dragnet

tray: hod 4 font 6 hurdle, salver, server 7 coaster

treacherous: 5 false, punic, snaky 6 fickle, hollow 8 disloyal, insecure, plotting, unstable 9 faithless, insidious 10 fraudulent, perfidious, traitorous, unreliable 11 disaffected 12 Machiavelian 13 Machiavellian, untrustworthy

treachery: 5 guile 6 deceit 7 perfidy, treason, untruth 8 betrayal

treacle: 4 cure 6 remedy 7 claggum 8 molasses

treaclewort: 4 herb 10 pennycress

tread: rut 4 gait, mark, pace, rung, step, volt, walk 5 clump, crush, labor, press, stair, stamp, trace, track, trail, tramp 6 balter, course, quench, subdue, trapes 7 conquer, repress, traipse, trample 8 copulate, footfall **9** footprint **10** employment, occupation

treadle: **5** pedal **7** chalaza

treason: **7** perfidy **8** betrayal **9** treachery

treasure: **4** roon **5** cache, hoard, pearl, prize, store, trove, value **6** gersum, riches, supply, wealth **7** cherish, finance **8** treasury **9** thesaurus(L.) **10** appreciate, collection **12** accumulation

Treasure State: **7** Montana

treasured: **5** chary

treasurer: **7** cashier, curator **8** bhandari, cofferer, deftedar, guardian, receiver **11** chamberlain

college: **6** bursar

treasury: **4** fisc, fund **5** chest, hoard **6** coffer **7** bursary, revenue **9** exchequer **10** repository, storehouse

Roman: **6** fiscus

treat: use **4** deal, dose, lead, urge **5** argue, besee, Dutch, feast, guide, touch **6** attend, confer, demean, doctor, govern, handle, parley, regale, regard, repast **7** address, bargain, control, discuss, entreat, expound **8** consider, transact, treatise **9** discourse, entertain, negotiate **10** manipulate

improperly: **4** snub **5** flout, scout, spite **6** ill-use, misuse **8** dishonor

tenderly: **5** spare **6** coddle, pamper

treatise: **5** essay, tract **6** thesis, treaty **7** account, grammar **8** brochure **9** discourse, narration, treatment **10** commentary **11** description **12** dissertation

elementary: **6** primer **7** grammar

opening part: **8** exordium

preface: **7** isagoge

treatment: **4** care **5** usage **7** therapy **8** demeanor, entreaty, handling **10** management **13** entertainment

before doctor's arrival: **8** first aid

compassionate: **5** mercy

harsh: **5** abuse **8** misusage, severity

treaty: **4** pact **7** article, concord, entente **8** contract, treatise **9** agreement, discourse **10** convention, discussion **11** arrangement, negotiation **13** understanding

treaty-bound: **6** allied

treble: **6** shrill, triple **7** soprano **9** threefold **11** high-pitched

treble clef: gee

tree (see also next entry): ach, ber, dal, dao, ebo, elm, fir, hur, iba, kou, lin, mee, oak **4** acle, alan, alof, anam, asak, asok, ates, ausu, bael, biti, bogo, bola, dali, dhak, dita, ipil, mabi, mora, odal, palm, pole, post, ship, toon, trap, wood, yaya **5** areca, asoka, betis, bongo, bulak, bumbo, cacao, carob, catch, cebil, couma, dadap, dalli, fulwa, genip, ligas, mahua, neeba, nepal, niepa, nitta, oodal, rohan, roman, salai, sassy, shaft, shift, siman, sissu, spade, staff, stake, stick, tikur, yacca **6** bahera, banyan, barbas, bariba, brauna, bucare, cativo, cedron, chalta, chogak, chupon, cocuyo, colima, corner, cudgel, design, gibbet, gomart, illupi, jarrah, locust, marane, marara, ramoon, sabino, simaba, sissoo, stemma, tikoor, timber **7** anubing, araraba, arboret, assagai, assegai, azarole, capture, champac, champak, cocullo, dhamnoo, diagram, gallows, guaraba, gumihan, hautboy, hollong, madrona, madrono, malpaho, mambong **8** ahueuete, cockspur, gamdeboo, ironbark, magnolia, mangrove, mokihana, phulwara, seedling, tamarack **9** bandoline, betel-palm, bitanhole, canadulce, couratari, currajong, genealogy, sassywood **10** bunyabunya, chaulmugra **11** balinghasay, chaulmaugra, chaulmoogra, guachipilin, hursinghair

alder: arn **5** alnus, birch **12** ament-bearing

algarroba: **5** carob **6** calden

allspice: **7** pimento

apple: **4** sorb

aromatic: **9** sassafras

balsam: fir **9** torchwood

bark: **4** ross, tapa

basswood: **6** linden

bead: nim

bean: **5** sapan

bearing samara: ash

beefwood: **5** belah, belar

betel: **5** areca

bignoniacious: **7** catalpa

blinding sap: **7** alipata

boxwood: **5** seron

breadnut: **6** capomo

buckthorn: **7** cascara

buckwheat: **4** titi **6** teetee

Buddha's: **6** botree

bully: see *gum* below

burned, broken: **7** rampick, rampike

buttonball: **5** plane **8** sycamore

cabbage: **7** angelin

camphor: **5** kapur

candlenut: ama

caoutchouc: ule **6** rubber

caucho-yielding (see also *rubber* below): ule

cemetery: yew

chestnut: **10** chinqua pin

chocolate: **5** cacao

cinchona: **7** quinine **9** quinidine

cinnamon family: **6** cassia

clump: **4** tump **5** motte

coconut: **4** coco

coffee: **6** chicot

conebearing: fir, yew **4** pine **5** alder, cedar, larch **7** conifer **8** gnetales

coral: **6** gabgab

cottonwood: **5** alamo

covering: **4** bark

cranberry: **7** pembina

derivative: **5** pinic

devil: **4** dita

drumstick: **11** canafistolo, canafistula, canafistulo

drupe bearing: **4** bito

dwarf: **5** scrub **7** abuscle **10** chinquapin

dwelling: **4** nest

dye yielding: tua, tui **4** mora **7** annatto **10** hursinghar

ebony: **9** diospyros

elder: **7** trammon

eucalyptus: **4** yati **6** mallee

evergreen: fir, yeu **4** pine, tawa **5** carob, cedar, holly, larch, ocote, olive **6** balsam, carobe, cazaba, coigue, tarata **7** bebeery, juniper, madrona, madrono, taratah

exudation: gum, lac, sap, tar **5** resin, rosin, xylan

fabacious: **5** agati

fiber: **5** bulak, simal, terap **7** bentang

fig family: **4** upas **5** pipal **7** gondang

flowering: **5** agati, elder, titis **6** mimosa, redbud **8** cleaster, oleaster

fodder: **5** mahoe **9** tagasaste

food: **4** akee

fruit: bel, fig, gab **4** gaub, lime **5** araca, lemon, mahis, olive, papaw, topes **6** annona, banana, bearer, biriba, litchi, medlar, pawpaw, sapota **7** avocado, capulin, genipap, tangelo **8** bakupari, tamarind **9** tangerine **12** custard apple

gaucho: ule

group: **4** bosk **5** copse, grove, woods **6** forest **7** coppice, orchard

grower: **8** arborist

gum: **5** babul, balta **6** balata, sapota, sapote, tupelo, zapote **8** banildad **9** sapodilla, sapotilha, sapotilla **10** bansalague, eucalyptus

gum genus: **6** owenia

hardwood: **4** poon **5** aalii, gidia, gidya, mabee, maple, narra, ngaio **6** gidgea, gidgee, gidjee, gidyea, walnut **7** hickory, tindalo **8** macaasin, mahogany **9** quebracho

heartwood: **7** duramen

health: **5** briar, brier

hickory: **5** pecan

holly: **4** ilex

honeberry: **5** genip

horseradish: **4** behn **5** behen

jobber: **10** woodpecker

juniper: **4** cade **5** cedar

kino: **4** bija

koranic: **6** zaggum

laurel: bay **7** tarairi

limb: **5** bough **6** branch

lime: lin **4** linn, teil **6** linden **9** tilicetum

linden: lin **4** lime, teil **8** basswood

locust: **6** acacia **9** courbaril

lotus: sad **4** lote

mafurra: **6** elcaja

magnolia: **5** yulan

mahogany: **4** toon

maple: **4** acer

margosa: **4** neem

marmalade: **5** mamey, mamie **6** mammee, sapote

medicinal: **5** sumac **6** sumach, wahahe

mimosaceous: **5** siris

monkeybread: **6** baobab

mountain ash: **4** sorb **5** rowan **7** service

mulberry: **4** more

nut: **4** cola **6** akhrot, chicha **9** almendron

nymph turned into: **6** Daphne

oil: **5** mahua, mahwa **9** candlenut

old-yielding: bel, ben **4** eboe, shea

olive: **4** olea

olive family: ash

orange-like: **5** osage

palm: ti; tal **4** coco **6** arengs

paradise: **8** aceituna

part: **4** bark, bole, knot, leaf, root, twig **5** shade, trunk **6** branch

pert. to: **8** arboreal

pine: see *evergreen* above

pipal: **6** botree

plane: **8** sycamore **10** buttonwood

plantain: **4** pala

pod-bearing: **7** catalpa

poisonous: **4** upas

poon: **4** dilo **5** keena

poplar: **5** abele, alamo, aspen, tulip **10** cottonwood

pottery: **7** caraipe, caraipi

rain: **5** saman, zaman **6** zamang **8** genisaro **9** algarroba

rare: **6** Joshua

resin: **4** arar

ribbon: **6** akaroa **7** houhere

rowan: see *mountain ash* below

rubber: ule **4** para **6** caucho **7** seringa **10** caoutchouc

rutaceous: **4** lime

salt: **4** atle **5** atlee

sandarac: **4** arar

sandbox: **6** assacu

science: **7** silvics

shade: ash, elm, lin, oak **5** maple **6** linden, poplar **7** catalpa **8** sycamore

smoke: **6** fustet **9** zante-wood

soft-wood: lin **5** ambay, balsa, linde

sour gum: **5** nyssa **6** tupelo

sprout: **5** sprig **7** sapling

streaked wood: 5 baria

stunted: 5 scrub

tallow: 4 cera

tamarisk: see *salt* above

tea: 6 manuka

teak: 4 teca

thorny: bel 4 bael, bito, brea 7 colorin 9 barriguda 11 chichicaste

timber: ash, dar, eng, koa, saj, sal, yew 4 coco, cuya, ipil, pelu, pine, poon, rata, tala, teak, toon, ulmo 5 acana, almon, amate, balao, balau, bayok, beech, birch, cedar, culla, dalli, ebano, fotui, guijo, icica, kauri, kaury, maple, narra, pekea, penda, rauli, tenio, timbo, uadal, yacal, zorro 6 alerce, alerse, alfaje, ausubo, bacury, banaba, banago, banaki, bancal, banuyo, bataan, batino, dagame, dungon, lanete, molave, satine, totara, walnut 7 batulin, becuiba, billian, camagon, capulin, cypress, gateado, gomavel, guacimo, hapiton, redwood 8 flindosa, flindosy, mahogany, zapetero 9 balaustre, guaraguao 10 batikuling

treatise: 5 silva

tropical genus: 8 bauhinia

trunk: 4 bole 5 shaft

tulip: 6 poplar

Turkey oak: 6 cerris

turpentine: 6 tarata 7 taratah 9 terebinth

walnut see *nut* above: 6 akhrot

wattle: 5 boree

wide-spreading: 5 cedar 7 juniper

willow: 5 osier

worship: 11 dendrolatry

yellow alder: 8 sagerose

tree: For trees of specific countries or regions, see under that country or region. EXAMPLES: "African tree", see under **Africa:** *tree;* "American tree," see under **America:** *tree*

tree bear: 7 raccoon

tree runner: 8 nuthatch

tree toad: 4 hyla 6 peeper

treelike: 11 arborescent

treeless: 6 barren

plain: 5 llano, pampa 6 steppe 7 prairie, savanna 8 savannah

treen: 6 wooden

treenail: nog, peg, pin 5 spike 7 trunnel

trefoil: 6 claver, clover

tregetour: 7 juggler 8 magician

treillage: 5 grill 7 trellis 8 espalier 11 latticework

trek: 4 draw, pull 5 march 6 travel 7 journey, migrate 10 expedition

trellis: 5 bower, cross 7 lattice, pergola 8 espalier 10 interweave 11 latticework

trematode worms: 8 cercaria 9 flatworms

tremble: 5 bever, quake, shake 6 didder, dither, dodder, falter, quaver, quiver, shiver, totter, tremor 7 flacker, flicker, shudder, vibrate 9 trepidate

trembling: 7 fearful, twitter 9 tremulous

tremendous: big 5 awful, giant, great, large 7 amazing 8 dreadful, enormous, horrible, powerful, terrific 9 frightful, momentous, monstrous 10 terrifying 13 extraordinary

tremolo: 6 quaver

tremor: 5 quake, shake 6 quiver, shiver, thrill 7 tremble 9 vibration

tremplin: 11 springboard

tremulous: 5 aspen, timid 7 fearful, nervous, palsied 8 timorous, unsteady, wavering 9 quavering, sensitive 11 palpitating

trench: cut, gaw 4 bury, gash, moat, sike 5 carve, ditch, drain, fosse, fossa(L.), graff, graft, slash, slice 6 furrow, groove, gutter 7 acequia 8 encroach, entrench, infringe 10 excavation

digger: 6 sapper

digging from within: sap

trenchant: 4 keen 5 acute, sharp 6 biting 7 cutting 8 clear-cut, distinct, forceful, incisive, vigorous 9 energetic 11 penetrating

trencher: 5 board, plate 7 platter 9 parasitic 11 sycophantic

trencherman: 7 sponger 8 hanger-on, parasite 11 gormandizer

trend: run 4 bend, bent, tone, turn, vein 5 drift, swing, tenor 6 extend, strike 7 incline 8 movement, tendency 9 direction 11 inclination

trendle: tub 6 trough

trepan: 4 lure, tool, trap 5 snare, trick 6 entrap 7 deceive, ensnare, swindle 9 perforate, stratagem

trepang: 10 beche-de-mer 22 holothurian-sea-cucumber

trepid: 7 quaking 8 timorous 9 trembling

trepidation: 4 fear 5 alarm, dread 6 dismay, tremor 7 quaking 9 agitation, confusion 11 disturbance 12 perturbation 13 consternation

trespass: sin 5 poach 6 breach, invade, offend 7 intrude 8 encroach, entrench, infringe 9 interlope 10 infraction, transgress 11 misfeasance

tress: 4 curl, hair, lock 5 braid, plait 7 ringlet

tressure: 4 band, caul 6 border, fillet, ribbon 9 headdress

trestle: leg 5 bench, horse, stand, stool 6 tripod, trivet 7 support, viaduct 9 framework

tret: 9 allowance

trew: 5 trust 7 believe

trews: 8 breeches, trousers 9 stockings

triad: 5 three, trine 6 triune 7 trinity 9 trivalent

trial: go; try 4 bout, case, pain, test 5 assay, cross, essay, grief, proof 6 assize, effort, ordeal, sample 7 approof, attempt, contest, hearing, inquiry 8 endeavor, evidence, hardship 10 experience, experiment, tournament 11 examination, tribulation 13 investigation

inconclusive: 8 mistrial

pert. to: 7 empiric

scene of: 5 court

severe: 6 ordeal

trial balloon: 4 kite, test 6 feeler

triangle: 5 delta 6 trigon 7 scalene, trigone 9 isosceles 11 equilateral

draw circle touching: 7 escribe

in heraldry: 5 giron

side: leg 11 hypothenuse

unequal sided: 7 scalene

triangular: 7 deltoid 13 three-cornered

piece: 4 gore 5 miter, mitre, wedge 6 gusset

sail: jib 6 lateen 9 spinnaker

triangular muscle: 7 deltoid

triarchy: 11 triumvirate

tribe: rod 4 band, clan, kind, race, sept 5 class, firca(Ind.), group 6 family 9 community

emblem: 5 totem

Germanic: 8 Alamanni, Alemanni

head: 5 chief 9 patriarch

New Zealand: ati

Roman: 5 Latin 6 Sabine 8 Etruscan

tribulation: 5 agony, trial 6 misery, sorrow 8 distress 9 suffering 10 affliction

tribunal: bar 4 banc, seat 5 bench, court, forum 7 tribune 8 assembly 10 consistory

tribune: 4 dais 6 throne 8 platform 10 magistrate

tributary: 5 ruler, state 6 feeder 7 subject 9 auxiliary, subsidary 11 subordinate 12 contributory

tribute: fee, tax 4 cain, dues, duty, gift, levy, rent, scat 5 grant 6 assign, eulogy, impost, praise, tariff 7 chevage, ovation, payment, respect 8 encomium 9 attribute, gratitude, laudation, panegyric 10 obligation 11 testimonial

tricar: 8 tricycle

trice: 4 bind, gird, haul, lash, pull 5 jiffy 6 moment, secure 7 instant 9 twinkling

trichome: 4 hair 7 bristle, prickle

trichord: 4 lyre

trick: bob, boy, cog, dor, fob, fox, fub, gag, gum, toy 4 bilk, dupe, feat, flam, fool, gaff, gaud, girl, gull, hoax, jest, joke, prat, ruse, trap, turn, wile 5 catch, child, cully, dodge, feint, fraud, gleek, guile, knack, prank, shift, skite, spell, stunt 6 begunk, chouse, delude, humbug, palter, trepan, trifle 7 be-

guile, cantrip, deceive, defraud, finesse, gimmick, pretext, sleight, swindle 8 artifice, flimflam, illusion, maneuver 9 bamboozle, capriccio, chicanery, diablerie, imposture, mannerism, stratagem 10 subterfuge 11 hornswoggle, legerdemain

trickery: art 5 fraud, hocus 6 cautel, deceit, japery 7 knavery, roguery, slyness 8 cheating, trumpery 9 deception, duplicity 10 hanky-panky

trickle: 4 drip, flow, sipe(Sc.) 5 exude 6 distil 7 distill, dripple

trickster: 5 cheat 6 rascal 7 slicker

tricksy: 5 smart 6 spruce 7 evasive, playful, roguish 8 prankish, sportive 9 deceiving, deceptive, uncertain 11 embellished, mischievous

tricky: sly 5 dodgy 6 artful, catchy 7 devious 8 ticklish 9 deceitful, intricate

tricycle: 6 tricar

trident: 5 spear

bearer: 7 Neptune

tried: 6 ettled(Sc.), proved, select, tested 8 faithful, reliable 11 trustworthy

trier: 5 judge 7 refiner 8 examiner, renderer 12 experimenter, investigator

Trieste measure: 4 orna, orne(pl.)

trifle: bit, fig, rap, toy 4 bean, doit, fike, jest, mock, mote, play 5 dally, flirt, straw, trick 6 bauble, coquet, dabble, dawdle, delude, dibble, doodle, fiddle, fidget, footer, footle, frivol, gewgaw, potter 7 deceive, dessert, fribble, nothing, traneen 8 flimflam, gimcrack, raillery 9 bagatelle 10 equivocate, knickknack, triviality

trifler: 7 flaneur

trifling: 4 airy, idle, mere 5 inane, petty 6 futile, little 7 shallow, wasting 8 badinage, frippery 9 dalliance 10 immaterial 13 insignificant

trifoliolate: 7 ternate 11 three-leaved

plant: 6 clover 8 shamrock

trifolium: 6 clover 8 shamrock

trig: run 4 chic, cram, deck, fill, firm, full, line, neat, prim, prop, stop, tidy, trim, trot 5 brisk, dandy, natty, smart, sound, stiff, stone, stuff, wedge 6 active, lively, spruce, steady, strong, trench 7 distend, foppish, precise, support 10 methodical

trigo: 5 wheat

trigon: 4 harp, lyre 5 trine 8 triangle

trigonometry function: 4 sine 6 cosine, secant 7 tangent

Trilby: *author:* 9 du Maurier

character: 8 Svengali

trill: 4 flow, move, turn 5 shake, twirl 6 gruppo, quaver, quiver, warble 7 mordent, trickle, vibrate, vibrato 8 grupetto 10 coloratura

trim: bob, cut, gay, lop 4 beat, chic, clip, crop, deft, dink, edge, fine, firm, neat, nice, snod(Sc.), snug, tidy, trig 5 adorn, braid, cheat, chide, dress, equip, fitty, natty, nifty, preen, prune, ready, shave, shear 6 adjust, dapper, defeat, modify, petite, punish, spruce, thrash 7 balance, compact, defraud, furnish, orderly 8 chastise, decorate, ornament, pleasant, tailored 9 condition, embellish, excellent, shipshape 10 compromise 11 disposition

coin: nig

dress: 4 gimp 5 ruche 6 sequin

lace: 5 jabot 6 ruffle

trimmer: 5 finer

trimming: 4 gimp, lace 5 braid, ruche 6 frieze, fringe, piping 7 falbala, ruching 8 furbelow, ornament, rick-rack 9 garniture 10 decoration 13 passementerie

trinal: 5 trial 9 threefold

trindle: 4 roll 5 wheel 7 trundle

trine: go 4 hang 5 march, triad 6 trigon, triple, triune 7 Trinity 9 favorable, threefold 10 auspicious

Trinidad: *gulf:* 5 Paria

music: 7 calypso

tree: 4 mora

trinitrotoluene: TNT 6 trotyl 14 trinitrotoluol

trinity: 5 three, triad 6 triune 9 threeness 10 spiderwort

trinket: toy 4 bead, gaud, ring 5 bijou, jewel 6 bangle, bauble, gewgaw, trifle 7 bibelot 8 gimcrack, intrigue, ornament 10 knick-knack

trinkle: 4 drip, flow 7 trickle

trio: 9 threesome

trip: run 4 gait, halt, hike, pawl, skip, slip, spin, tour 5 brood, caper, catch, danse, error, flock, jaunt, lapse, tread, wedge 6 cruise, falter, voyage 7 blunder, failure, journey, misstep, mistake, release, stumble 8 obstruct 9 excursion 10 expedition

trip-hammer: *operator:* 6 tilter

tripe: 5 trash 7 rubbish

triple: 5 trine 6 treble 9 threefold

triplet: 4 trin, trio

tripletail: 9 berrugate, spadefish

triplicate: 6 treble, triple 9 threefold

tripod: cat 5 easel, stand 6 trivet

Tripoli ruler: dey

trippet: cam

tripping: 5 quick 6 nimble 7 walking 8 trippant

triptych: *wing:* 5 volet

trisaccharide: 6 triose

trismus: 7 lockjaw, tetanus

Tristam, Tristan: *beloved:* 5 Isolt 6 Iseult, Isolde

uncle: 4 Mark

villain: 5 Melot

wife: 6 Isolde

Tristram Shandy author: 6 Sterne

triste: sad 4 dull 6 dismal 9 sorrowful 10 depressing, melancholy

trite: 4 worn 5 banal, corny, stale, vapid 6 common, jejune 7 bromide, trivial 9 hackneyed 10 threadbare, unoriginal 11 commonplace, stereotyped 12 conventional 13 platitudinous

trite expression: 6 cliche 7 bromide

triton: eft 4 newt 7 demigod 10 salamander

triturate: rub 5 crush, grind 6 bruise 9 comminute, pulverize

triumph: win 4 gain 5 exult, glory 6 defeat, hurrah 7 conquer, prevail, rejoice, success, victory 8 flourish 11 achievement, celebration

triumvirate: *first:* 6 Caesar, Pompey 7 Crassus

second: 6 Antony 7 Lepidus 8 Octavius

trivet: 5 stand 6 tripod 7 support

trivial: 5 banal, fluff, inane, petty, small, trite 6 common, paltry, slight 7 nominal, piperly 8 doggerel, ordinary, trifling 9 frivolous 11 unimportant 13 insignificant 14 inconsiderable

trocar: 6 stylet 7 trochar

troche: 6 pastil, rotula, tablet 7 lozenge, pastile 8 pastille

trochilus: 7 warbler 9 goldcrest 11 hummingbird

trod: 4 path, walk 5 trace, track, tread 8 footpath, footstep

trogon: 4 bird 7 quetzal

Troilus: *beloved:* 8 Cressida

father: 5 Priam

Trojan: 9 Dardanian

epic: 5 Iliad

king: 5 Priam

prince: 5 Eneas, Paris 6 Aeneas, Hector

prisoner: 5 Sinon

serpent victim: 7 Laocoon

soothsayer: 7 Helenus 9 Cassandra

Trojan horse: 8 saboteur 10 subversive

builder: 5 Epeus

Trojan War: *cause:* 5 Helen

hero: 4 Ajax 5 Eneas 6 Aeneas, Agenor, Hector 9 Palamedes

troll: run, wag 4 bowl, fish, lure, reel, roll, sing, song, turn 5 angle, catch, chant, dwarf, giant, gnome, round, spoon 6 trolly 7 revolve, trolley, trollop 9 circulate

trolley: car 4 cart, tram 5 block 6 barrow, sledge 8 handcart 9 streetcar

trollop: 4 hang 5 slump 6 dangle, slouch 8 slattern 10 bedraggled, prostitute

trombone: 7 sackbut

trommel: 5 sieve 6 screen

tronk: 4 jail 6 lockup, prison

troop: lot 4 army, band, ging, line, rout, wave 5 crowd, group 6 number, troupe 7 battery, cavalry, company, echelon, militia, phalanx 8 quantity, soldiers 9 associate, gathering 10 congregate

Anglo-Indian: 6 risala 7 ressala, risalah

arrangement: 7 echelon

assembling: 6 muster

concealed: 6 ambush

German: 6 Panzer

raise: 4 levy 5 draft 9 conscript

sellers to: 6 sutler 10 vivandiere

trooper: 6 hussar 7 soldier 9 policeman, troopship 10 cavalryman

trop: too 4 many

trope: 8 metaphor

trophy: cup 4 palm 5 prize 6 laurel, reward 7 memento 8 memorial, ornament

tropic: 5 limit 8 boundary

animal: 4 alco, eyra 5 agama, coati, potto 6 agouti, iguana 7 peccary

bird: ani 4 tody 5 jalap 7 jacamar

fish: 4 toro 6 salema 7 squetee

fruit: 4 date 5 guava, mango, papaw 6 banana, papaya 8 tamarind

genus of herb: 4 evea, sida 5 tacca, urena 8 laportea

helmet: 4 topi

plant: dal 4 aloe, arum, sida, taro 5 agave 6 alacad 7 cowhage, lantana 8 gardenia

plant genus: 5 rhoeo 6 cannas 7 bomarea, geonoma, hamelia

tree: ebo 4 ceba, coco, dali, eboe, etua, guao, mabi, palm 5 acapu, amate, artar, assai, balsa, banak, bongo, cacao, dalli, guama, guava, icica, nepal, nitta, njave, papaw, seron, zorro 6 baboen, bacury, banana, barbas, cazaba, chupon, dagame, espave, mammee, pawpaw, sapota 7 anubing, gateado, guacimo 8 amarillo, mangrove, sweetsop, tamarind 9 huamuchli, quebracho, sapodilla, sapotilha, sapotilla 10 frangipane, frangipani, manchineel 11 guachipilin

trot: jog, run, tot 4 gait 5 child, hurry 6 hasten 7 toddler 11 translation

troth: 5 certy, faith 6 certie, pledge 8 fidelity 9 betrothal

trottoir: 8 footpath, pavement, sidewalk

trotty: 5 brisk 6 lively

trotyl: TNT 14 trinitrotoluol 15 trinitrotoluene

troubadour, troubador: 4 poet 6 singer 8 minstrel, musician

trouble: ado, ail, irk, vex, woe 4 busy, care, cark, fike, fuss, harm, pain, sore, stir 5 anger, annoy, grief, labor, tease, worry 6 bother, burble, caddle, cumber, dither, effort, harass, impair, matter, mishap, molest, pester, plague, pother, sorrow, unrest 7 afflict, agitate, anxiety, chagrin, concern, disease, disturb, embroil, illness, perturb, travail 8 aggrieve, calamity, disorder, disquiet, distress, exertion 9 adversity, incommode, interfere 10 difficulty, disarrange, discomfort, discommode, misfortune, perplexity, uneasiness 11 displeasure, encumbrance 13 inconvenience

troubled: 6 queasy 12 heart-scalded

troublemaker: 6 gossip 8 agitator

troublesome: 5 pesky 6 fashious 9 pestilent, turbulent, wearisome 10 burdensome, oppressive

troublous: 6 stormy, turbid 7 unquiet 8 restless 9 unsettled

trough: bin 4 boat, bosh, bowl, dale, tank, tomb 5 bakie, basin, canoe, chute 6 buddle, coffin, dugout, gutter, sluice 7 channel, conduit

between waves: 6 valley

inclined: 5 chute

trounce: sue 4 beat, flog 5 scold, tramp 6 cudgel, defeat, indict, punish, ramble, thrash 7 censure, journey

troupe: 4 band 5 group 7 company 9 cuadrilla(Sp.)

trouper: 5 actor

troupial: 6 oriole 7 cacique, cowbird 9 blackbird 10 meadowlark

trousers: 5 pants 6 skilts, slacks 8 breeches, culottes 9 pantalets, shintiyan 10 pantaloons

foreign: 7 shalwar 9 shaksheer, shulwaurs 10 calzoneras(Sp.)

trout: 4 char, peal 5 brook, sewen 6 finnac, grilse 7 gilaroo, rainbow 8 finnacle 9 steelhead 10 squeteague

lake: 9 namaycush

troutlet: 10 fingerling

trovatore: 10 troubadour

trove: 9 discovery

trow: 4 boat, hope 5 faith, fancy, smack, think, troll, trust 6 belief, expect 7 believe, imagine, suppose 9 catamaran

trowing: 5 creed 6 belief 7 opinion

Troy (see also **Trojan, Trojan horse, Trojan War**)**:** 5 Iliac, Ilian, Ilion, Ilium, Troas, Troad 8 Teucrian

defender: 6 Aeneas

founder: 4 Ilus, Tros

king: 5 Priam

mountain: Ida

pert. to: 5 Iliac 6 Trojan

region: 5 Troad

troy weight: 5 grain, ounce, pound 11 pennyweight

truant: 4 idle 5 stray 6 beggar, errant 7 shirker, vagrant 8 vagabond, wanderer 9 shiftless

play: 5 miche

truce: 5 pause, treve(F.) 7 respite 9 armistice, cessation 12 intermission

truck: van 4 deal, dray 5 lorry, trade, trash 6 barrow, barter, camion, peddle, potter 7 bargain, rubbish, traffic, trundle 8 business, exchange, handcart 9 negotiate, transport, vegetable 10 handbarrow 11 association, intercourse

with trailer: 4 semi

truckle: 4 fawn 5 toady, wheel 6 caster, cheese, cringe, submit 7 trundle

truckling: 7 servile

truculent: 4 mean, rude 5 cruel, harsh 6 fierce, savage 8 ruthless, scathing 9 barbarous, ferocious 11 destructive

trudge: pad 4 plod, walk 5 stoge, tramp 6 trapes 7 traipse

true: 4 just, leal(Sc.), pure, real, vera(L.), vrai(F.) 5 align, aline, exact, level, loyal, plumb, right, valid 6 actual, adjust, honest, lawful, proper, steady 7 certain, correct, devoted, factual, genuine, germane, precise, sincere, staunch, upright 8 accurate, bonafide, constant, faithful, reliable, unerring, virtuous 9 authentic, steadfast, truepenny, unfeigned, veracious, veritable 10 legitimate 11 unfaltering

true blue: 5 loyal 7 staunch

truelove: 10 sweetheart

trueness: 7 reality 8 veracity 9 exactness 11 genuineness 12 faithfulness

truffle: 5 tuber 8 earthnut

trug: 4 caul, cawl, pail, tray 5 wench 6 basket, trough 7 measure 10 prostitute

truism: 5 axiom

Truk island: Tol 4 Moen, Udot, Uman 6 Dublon

trull: 4 dell, girl, lass 5 demon, fiend, giant, wench 6 blowze, callet 7 trollop 8 strumpet 10 prostitute

truly: 4 iwis 6 atwee, dinkum, indeed, verily 13 realistically

trump: cap, pam 4 beat, ruff 5 outdo, pedro 7 nonplus, surpass, trumpet 8 jew's-harp

trumpery: 5 fraud, showy, trash, weeds 6 deceit, paltry 7 rubbish 8 gimcrack, nonsense, trickery 9 worthless

trumpet: 4 horn 5 blare 6 bucina(Lat.), funnel, kerana, summon 7 begonia, clarion, publish 8 denounce, proclaim

belt: 7 baldric

blare: 6 sennet 7 fanfare, tantara

caller: 7 Gabriel

muffler: 4 mute

stage direction: 6 sennet

trumpet creeper: 5 plant 6 tecoma

trumpet shell: 6 triton

trumpeter: 4 bird, swan 6 herald, pigeon, tooter 7 yakamik

truncate: cut, lop 6 lessen 7 shorten

truncheon: 4 club, stem 5 baton, staff 6 cudgel 8 fragment, splinter

trundle: bed 4 bowl, cart, hoop, roll 5 truck, twirl, wheel, whirl 6 barrow, caster, pinion, rotate 7 revolve, trindle 11 wheelbarrow

trundler: 6 bowler

trunk: box 4 body, bole, pipe, stem, tank, tube 5 chest, snout, stock, torso 6 caudex, coffer, corpse, thorax 7 baggage 9 proboscis

animal: 4 soma 5 torso, snout

trunkless: 8 bodiless

truss: tie, wap 4 bind, furl, gird, hang, lade, pack 6 bundle, fasten 7 arrange, bracket, enclose, package, support, tighten 10 strengthen

trust: 4 affy, care, duty, hope, task 5 faith 6 belief, cartel, charge, credit, depend, merger 7 believe, confide, consign, custody, keeping, loyalty 8 affiance, commenda, credence, reliance, security 9 assurance, coalition, fiduciary, syndicate 10 commission, confidence 11 combination

trustee: 6 bailee 7 sindico 8 director, guardian 9 garnishee 13 administrator

trustful: 5 liege 7 devoted 9 confiding 13 unquestioning

trustless: 10 unreliable 11 distrustful, treacherous

trustworthy: 4 safe 5 siker, solid, tried 6 honest, sicker 7 certain 8 credible, fiducial, reliable 9 authentic, confiding 10 dependable 12 confidential

trusty: 8 faithful, trustful 9 confiding

truth: 4 fact 5 sooth, troth 6 certes, verity 7 honesty, loyalty 8 accuracy, fidelity, veracity 9 agreement, constancy, integrity, principle, sincerity 11 correctness, genuineness, uprightness 12 faithfulness 14 verisimilitude

goddess: 4 Maat

personification of: Una

seeming: 14 verisimilitude

self-evident: 5 axiom 6 truism

truthful: 6 honest 7 correct 9 veracious, veridical

try: do 4 cull, sift, test 5 annoy, assay, essay, ettle(Sc.), found, prove, trial 6 choose, effort, hansel, harass, purify, refine, render, sample, screen, select, strain, strive 7 adjudge, afflict, approve, attempt, contest, extract, handsel, subject, torment, venture 8 audition, endeavor, irritate, separate, struggle 9 ascertain, undertake 10 experience, experiment 11 demonstrate, investigate

trying: 6 severe 7 irksome, painful 8 annoying 12 exasperating

tryst: 4 fair 5 visit 6 market 7 bespeak, meeting 9 agreement, gathering 10 engagement, rendezvous 11 appointment, assignation

tsamba: 5 flour 6 barley

tsar: 4 czar, Ivan, tzar 5 Peter 6 despot 8 autocrat

tsetse fly: 4 kivu 6 muscid

tsine: 6 wild ox 7 banteng

tuatara, tuatera: 6 lizard 16 rhynchocephalian

tub (see also **barrel, cistern, vat, vessel**): box, kid, soe, vat 4 bath, boat, cask, cool, ship, tram 5 barge, bathe, bowie(Sc.), eshin, keeve, skeel 6 bucket, pulpit, vessel 7 bathtub, cistern, tubfish 9 container
  wooden: soe

tuba: 7 helicon
  mouthpiece: 5 bocal

tubal: 8 pipelike

Tubal's father: 7 Japheth

Tubalcain's father: 6 Lamech

tubbal: 7 mattock

tubber: 6 cooper, pickax

tubby: 5 squat 6 chubby, portly

tube: 4 duct, hose, lull, pipe 5 chute, diode 6 cannon, siphon, tremie, triode, tunnel 7 cannula, conduit, fistula, pipette, tetrode 8 adjutage, bombilla(Sp.), cylinder 9 telescope
  anatomical: 7 salpinx
  flexible: 4 hose
  for winding silk: cop
  glass: 6 sipper 7 pipette
  remove by: 6 siphon, syphon
  system of: 6 pipage
  underground: 6 subway, tunnel

tuber: oca, yam 4 beet, bulb, clog, eddo, root, taro, yamp 5 jalap, salep 6 potato 8 swelling 9 tubercule 10 tuberosity 12 protuberance
  orchid: 5 salep

tubercle: 6 nodule 10 prominence

tubiform: 6 tubate

Tubuai island: 4 Rapa

tubular: 4 pipy 5 round 11 cylindrical

tuck: eat, jam, nip 4 cram, draw, fold, hang, poke 5 cramp, feast, pinch, press, scold, stuff, sword 6 energy, gather, hamper, rapier, upraid 7 consume, shorten, tighten 9 sweetmeat

tucked up: 7 cramped 8 hampered 9 exhausted

tucker: bib 4 food, meal, tire 5 board, weary 6 ration 7 fatigue 10 chemisette

Tudesque: 6 German

Tuesday: 5 mardi(F.)
  god of: Tiu, Tyr
  Shrove: 9 Mardi Gras

tufa: 5 trass

tufan: 5 storm

tuft: 4 beat, coma, disk 5 beard, bunch, clump, crest 6 button, comose, dollop, goatee, pompon, tassel 7 cluster, fetlock, scopula 8 imperial
  pert. to: 5 comal

tuft-hunter: 4 snob

tug: lug, tit, tow 4 drag, draw, haul, maul, pull, rope, toil, yank 5 chain, exert, hitch, labor, strap, trace 6 drudge, effort, strain, strife, strive, tussle 7 contend, contest, tugboat, wrestle 8 struggle 11 counterpull

tuition: 4 care 5 watch 6 charge 7 custody 8 teaching 10 protection 11 instruction 12 guardianship

tule: 7 bulrush

tumble: 4 fall, leap, roll, trip, veer 5 pitch, slope, spill, whirl 6 rumple, spring, tousle 7 stumble 8 collapse, dishevel, disorder 9 confusion, overthrow 10 disarrange, handspring, somersault 11 precipitate
  down: 10 dilapidate

tumbler: dog 4 cart, pupa 5 glass 6 dunker, pigeon, roller, vessel 7 acrobat, gymnast, tippler, tumbrel

tumbrel, tumbril: 4 cart 5 wagon 8 dumpcart

tumefy: 4 puff 5 swell 7 inflate

tumid: 6 turgid 7 bloated, bulging, fustian, pompous, swollen, teeming 8 bursting, enlarged, inflated 9 bombastic, distended, plethoric 11 protuberant

tumor: wen 4 beal, wart 5 edema, gumma 6 ambury, anbury, glioma, lipoma 7 bombast 8 blastoma, ganglion, hepatoma, neoplasm, papiloma, sarocele, swelling 10 distending 12 adamantinoma, protuberance
  brain: 6 glioma
  operation: 8 ancotomy
  small: wen 7 papilla
  suffix: oma

tumorous: 5 tumid 7 swollen 8 inflated 9 bombastic

tump: 4 heap 5 clump 7 hillock, tumulus

tumult: din, mob 4 fray, fuss, riot 5 babel, brawl, broil, noise 6 affray, babble, bedlam, bustle, dirdum(Sc.), emeute, hubbub, uproar 7 bluster, bobbery, ferment, tempest, turmoil 8 disorder, outbreak, outburst, uprising 9 agitation, commotion, confusion, distemper, hurlement 10 convulsion, excitement, turbulence 11 disturbance

tumultuous: 4 high, wild 5 rough 6 stormy 7 furious, violent 10 boisterous, hurly-burly

tumulus: 4 tump 5 mound 6 barrow 7 hillock

tun: cup, jar, tub, vat 4 cask 5 drink 6 guzzle, vessel 7 chimney

tune: air, key, pat 4 lilt, port, song, tone 5 dirge, drant, sound 6 choral, draunt, melody, string 7 chorale, concord, harmony, sonance 8 anglaise 9 agreement 10 adjustment
out: 6 detune

tuneful: 7 musical, tunable 9 melodious 10 concordant, euphonious, harmonious

tungsten ore: cal

tunic: 4 coat, jama, jupe, robe, toga 5 acton, frock, gippo, jamah 6 kirtle 8 colobium 10 cote-hardie, sticharion 11 houppelande

tunicate: 4 salp 5 salpa 12 marine animal

Tunisia: *cape:* bon
capital: 5 Tunis
cities: 4 Sfax, Susa 5 Gabes, Gafsa, Tunis 6 Mateur, Nabeul 7 Bizerte 8 Tebourba, Zaghouan 9 Grombalia 10 Ferryville
gulf: 5 Gabes, Tunis 8 Hammamet
island: 6 Djerba
measure: saa, sah 4 saah 5 cafiz, whiba 6 mettar 9 millerole
river: 8 Medjerda
ruler: bey, dey
weight: saa 4 rotl 5 artal, artel, ratel, uckia 6 kantar

tunk: rap 5 thump

tunnel: net 4 adit, bore, flue, tube 6 burrow, funnel 10 smokestack
long: 5 Otira 6 Hoosac, Severn, Spiral 7 Arlberg, Detroit, Gothard, Holland, Lincoln, Mont D'Or, St. Clair, Simplon 8 Gunnison 9 Baltimore, Cascade Mt., Connaught, Gallitzin, Montcenis, Mt. Roberts 10 Bitterroot, Cumberland, Lotschberg, St. Gotthard, Wasserfluh 11 Busk-Ivanhoe, Loetschberg, Trans-Andine

tunny: 4 tuna 8 albacore

tup: ram 5 cover, sheep 6 mallet 7 cuckold

tupelo: gum 4 tree 5 nyssa

tur: pea 4 goat

turb: 5 clump, crowd

turban: cap, fez, hat 4 pata 5 scarf 6 fillet, mandil 9 headdress

turbid: 4 dark, dull 5 dense, gumly(Sc.), muddy, roily, thick 6 cloudy, grumly(Sc.), impure 7 muddled 8 confused, polluted 9 perplexed
render: 4 roil

turbine: *part:* 6 stator
wheel: 5 rotor

turbot: 5 brill 8 flatfish

turbulence: 4 fury 6 tumult, uproar 7 bluster, ferment, rioting 8 disorder 9 agitation, commotion 11 disturbance

turbulent: 4 wild 5 rough 6 stormy, unruly 7 furious, violent 9 clamorous 10 boisterous, tumultuous 11 tempestuous

turdine bird: 6 thrush

turf: sod 4 flag, peat, vell 5 divot, grass, sward

Turgenev character: 5 Elena

turgid: 5 tumid 7 bloated, pompous, swollen, turgent 8 inflated, swelling 9 bombastic, distended, flatulent, grandiose 12 magniloquent 13 grandiloquent

Turk: aga 5 Tatar 7 Osmanli, Ottoman 9 Kizilbash

turkey: tom 5 poult 7 bustard, failure, gobbler
buzzard: 7 vulture
male: tom
young: 5 poult

Turkey: *agent:* 6 Kehaya
army corps: 4 ordu 8 seraglio
army regiment: 4 alai
bath: 6 hamman
boat: 4 sail 6 mahone
cabinet: 5 divan
camp: 7 palanka
capital: 6 Ankara
carpet: 6 Smyrna
cavalryman: 5 spahi 6 spahee
chief (see also *ruler* below)*:* aga 6 kehaya 7 chambul
city: bir 4 Homs, Sert 5 Adana, Brusa, Izmir, Konya, Siirt, Sivas 6 Aintab, Ankara, Edessa, Edirne, Elaziz, Marash, Samsun, Smyrna 7 Broussa, Erzurum, Kayseri, Scutari, Skutari, Uskudar 8 Istanbul, Stamboul 9 Eskisehir 10 Adrianople, Diyarbekir 14 Afyonkarahisar, Constantinople
commander: 4 amir, emir 5 ameer, emeer, pacha, pasha 6 sirdar 9 seraskier
council: 5 divan, diwan
court: 5 porte
decree: 5 irade 11 hatti-sherif 12 hatti-humaiun, hatti-humayum
deputy: 6 kahaya
dignitary: 5 pasha
district: 4 Pera 7 Beyoglu, Cilicia
division: 4 caza 5 adana 6 eyalet 7 vilayet 8 villayet
drink: 5 airan
dynasty: 6 seljuk
empire: 7 Ottoman
fig: 5 eleme, elemi
flag: 4 alem, toug 9 horsetail
general: 5 kamal
gold coin: 4 lira 6 mahbub

gulf: Cos
hat: fez **6** calpac
infidel: **6** giaour
inn: **6** imaret **7** cafenet
javelin: **5** jerid **6** jeered
judge: **4** cadi
liquor: **4** raki **5** rakee **6** mastic
man-of-war: **6** carvel **7** caravel **9** caravelle
measures: dra, oka, oke, pic, pik **4** alma, draa, hatt, khat, kile, zira **5** almud, berri, donum, kileh, zirai **6** almude, arshin, chinik, djerib, fortin, halebi, parmak **7** arsheen, arshine, nocktat, parmack **9** pik halebi
military camp: **4** ordu
military rank: **6** chiaus **7** chaoush **8** bimbashi, binbashi
minister: **5** vizir **6** vizier
money: **4** lira, lire, para **5** akcha, asper, attun, pound, rebia **6** akcheh, sequin, zequin **7** altilik, beshlik, chequin, chiquin, pataque, piaster **8** medjidie, zecchino **9** medjidieh
mosque: **4** jami
mountain: **6** Ararat
musical instrument: **5** canum, kanum **7** kussier
musket: **8** tophaike
oak: **6** cerris
official: **4** amir, emir **5** ameer, emeer **6** vizier **7** osmanli, subashi **8** subbassa
palace: **5** serai
policeman: **7** zaptiah, zaptieh
prayer rug: **5** kulah, melas, meles
province: **4** Sert **5** Siirt **6** Angora, Eyalet
religious war: **11** crescentade
reservist: **5** redif
river: **5** Mesta, Sarus **6** Seihun, Seyhan
rug: **5** konia
ruler: bey, dey **4** khan **5** mudir **6** sultan **7** chambul **9** president
saber: **6** odolus
sailor: **8** galionji **9** galiongee
seaport: **4** Enos
slave: **8** mameluke
soldier: **6** nizami **8** janizary **9** janissary **11** bashi-bazouk
statue: **8** tanzimat
storage place: **5** ambar
sultan: Ali **5** Ahmed, calif, Selim **6** caliph **7** Ilderim, Saladin
sword: **7** yatagan **8** yataghan
tambourine: **5** daira
tax: **5** vergi **6** caphar, avania
title: ali **4** amir, baba **5** ameer, basha, pasha **6** bashaw **7** effendi
tobacco: **7** chibouk, Latakia **9** chibouque
treasurer: **8** deftedar
tribe: **4** Kurd

veil: **7** yashmac, yashmak **8** maharmah
vilayet: **4** Urfa
weight: oka, oke **4** dram, kile, ocha, rotl **5** artal, artel, cequi, cheke, kerat, kileh, maund, obolu, ratel **6** batman, dirhem, kantar, miskal **7** drachma, quintal, yusdrum
wheat: **6** bulgar
woman's clothing: **6** jelick **8** charshaf
turkey buzzard: **4** aura **9** gallinazo
Turkish: **7** Osmanli
Turkistan: *cities:* **6** Kokand **7** Andijan **9** Samarkand
highland: **6** Pamirs
land: **5** takyr
moslem: **5** salar
mountain: **4** Alai
peoples: **4** Sart **5** Tatar, Uigur, Usbeg, Usbek, Uzbeg, Yakut **6** Tartan
regiment: **4** alai
river: Ili
salt lake: **4** Shov
sea: **4** Aral
Turkmen: *capital:* **9** Ashkhabad
carpet: **5** Tekke, Yomud **6** Afghan **7** Bokhara
tribe: **5** Ersar **7** Viddhal
turmeric: rea
turmoil: ado, din **4** hurl, toil, toss **5** hurly, labor, touse, upset, worry **6** harass, tumult, unrest, uproar, welter **7** ferment, quarrel, tempest, trouble **8** disquiet, drudgery **9** agitation, commotion, confusion **10** turbulence **11** disturbance **12** perturbation
turn: bow, lap, rev **4** airt, bend, bent, bout, cant, char, head, plow, roll, slew, slue, spin, veer, vert **5** alter, avert, cramp, crook, curve, hinge, pivot, quirk, screw, tarve, wheel, whirl, whorl **6** bought, change, direct, divert, gyrate, invert, ponder, rotate, swerve, swivel, wimple(Sc.), zigzag **7** convert, derange, ferment, meander, rebound, reverse, revolve **8** exchange, nauseate, persuade **9** cinclamen, influence, pirouette, transform, translate **11** disposition **12** metamorphose
about: **9** alternate
another way: **6** obvert
inside out: **5** evert **6** invert
inward: **9** introvert
left: haw **4** port, wynd, wyne
outward: **5** evert, splay **8** extrorse **9** extrovert
rapidly: **4** spin **5** twirl, whirl
right: gee **9** starboard
sour: **5** blink **8** acescent
to one side: **4** awry, skew
turn around: **4** gyre, slue, spin

turn aside: 4 veer 5 shunt 6 detour, divert, swerve

turn away: shy 5 avert, avoid, deter, evade, repel, shunt 6 depart, divert 7 decline, deflect, deviate, dismiss, diverge, swerve

turn back: 4 fold 5 repel 6 return, revert 7 evolute, retrace 9 inversion 10 retroverse

turn down: 4 fold, veto 6 invert, refuse, reject 7 decline

turn off: 4 hang 5 marry, shunt 6 detour, divert 7 consign, deflect, dismiss, putrefy 9 discharge

turn out: 4 oust, trig 5 array, evert, expel, prove 6 outfit, output, siding 7 abandon, dismiss, produce, reverse, striker 8 equipage 9 discharge, equipment, eventuate

turn over: 4 keel 5 spill, upset 6 invert, ponder, reform 7 evolute 8 delegate, overturn, transfer 10 relinquish

turn up: 6 appear, arrive

turnabout: 8 reversal 9 about-face, volte-face

turncoat: 8 apostate, renegade 10 changeling

turned up: 9 retrousse

turner: 7 gymnast, tumbler

turning (see also **turn** above): 6 rotary 7 flexion, winding 8 flection, rotative, twisting 10 revolution 11 sinistrorse, vertiginous

turning point: 6 crisis 8 decision, landmark

turnip: 4 neep(Sc.) 5 watch 8 rutabaga 9 blockhead

turnip-shaped: 8 napiform

turnkey: 5 screw 6 jailer, warder

turnover: 4 tart

turnpike: 7 highway 8 tollgate

   gatekeeper: 7 pikeman

turnstile: 5 stile

turnstone: 4 bird 6 plover, redleg

turpentine: 4 thus 5 resin, rosin 9 oleoresin

   residue: 5 resin, rosin

   tree: 4 pine 6 tarata 9 terebinth

turpitude: 6 fedity 8 baseness, vileness 9 depravity

turquoise: 10 chalchuite

turret: 5 tower 8 gunhouse

turse: 4 load, pack 6 bundle

turtle: 5 arrau, caret, torup 6 cooter, emydea, jurara 7 snapper 8 chelonia, emydidae, matamata, shagtail, terrapin, tortoise 10 loggerhead, thalassian 11 leatherback

   genus of: 4 emys 7 caretta, testudo 9 chelodina

   giant: 5 arrau

   part: 7 calipee

   shell: 8 carapace

Tuscany: *city:* 4 Pisa

   commune: 5 Greve

   island: 4 Elba

   river: 4 Arno

   wine: 7 chianti

tusk: 4 fang 5 tooth 9 scrivello

tusker: 8 elephant

tussis: 5 cough

tussle: 5 fight 6 tousel, tousle 7 contend, contest, scuffle, wrestle 8 struggle 9 scrimmage

tussock: 4 tuft 5 bunch, clump 7 hassock

tut: 4 hush 6 rebuke

tutelage: 7 nurture 8 teaching 9 tutorship 11 instruction 12 guardianship

tutelar: 8 guardian

tutelary: 10 protecting

   gods: 5 Lares

tutor: 5 coach, drill, guide, train, watch 6 ground, mentor, school 7 grinder, pedagog, teacher 8 guardian, instruct 9 pedagogue, preceptor 10 discipline

tutta: all 5 whole

tuyere: tew 4 pipe 5 tewel 6 nozzle

TV: See **television**

twaddle: rot 4 bunk 5 haver, prate 6 babble, drivel, footle, gabble 8 nonsense

twangy: 5 nasal

tweak: 4 pull 5 pinch, twist 6 twitch

tweet: 4 peep 5 chirp 7 chirrup

tweezers: 7 pincers 9 merganser

twenty: 5 corge, kappa, score

twenty-faced: 11 icosahedral

twibil: 6 chisel 7 mattock

twice: bis(L.) 6 doubly

   prefix: di; dis

twig: 4 beat, mode, pull 5 birch, bough, scion, shoot, spray, sprig, style, tweak, withe 6 branch, fescue, notice, sallow, switch, twitch, wattle 7 fashion, observe 8 perceive 10 comprehend, understand

   bundle: 5 fagot 6 barsom

twiggy: 4 thin 6 slight 7 slendor 8 delicate

twilight: 4 dusk 5 gloam 6 dimmet 8 gloaming, glooming 9 cocklight 10 crepuscule

   of the Gods: 8 Ragnarok 17 Goetterdaemmerung

   pert. to: 11 crepuscular

twill: rib 5 quill, weave

twin: two 4 dual, pair, part 5 gemel, sever, twain 6 couple, double, sunder 7 twofold 8 didymous 11 counterpart

   crystal: 5 macle

   one: 5 gemel

   Siamese: Eng 5 Chang

   stars: 6 Castor, gemini, Pollux

twinge: 4 ache, pain, pang 5 pinch, qualm, tweak 6 twitch

twine: ran 4 coil, turn, vine, warp, wind, wrap 5 braid, snarl, twist 6 encurl, enfold, enlace, infold, string, tangle, thread 7 anamite, embrace, entwine, wreathe 8 encircle 9 interlace 10 intertwine, interweave 11 convolution, intermingle

twink: 4 wink 6 punish, thrash 7 twinkle 9 chaffinch

twinkle: 4 wink 5 blink, flash, gleam, shine 7 flicker, flutter, glimmer, glitter, sparkle 11 scintillate

twinkler: 4 star 8 sparkler

twinkling: 4 wink 5 flash, gleam, trice 6 moment 7 instant 13 scintillation

twire: 4 gaze, look, peer 5 gleam 6 glance 7 twinkle

twirl: 4 coil, curl, move, spin, turn 5 querl, twist, whirl 6 gyrate 7 revolve, twizzle 8 flourish, rotation 11 convolution

twist: 4 bend, coil, cord, curl, hang, hurl, silk, skew, slew, slue, spin, tirl(Sc.), turn, wind, yarn 5 crink, crook, curve, gnarl, hinge, quirk, reeve, screw, snarl, swirl, tweak, twine, twirl, unite, wrest, wring 6 branch, enlace, hankle, rotate, spiral, squirm, thread, torque, wrench, writhe 7 confuse, contort, distort, entwine, flexure, meander, perplex, pervert, revolve, scatter, tendril, torment, torsion, torture, twizzle, wreathe 8 appetite, encircle, entangle, separate 9 constrain, deviation, insinuate 10 intertwine, interweave 11 convolution, peculiarity

twisted: cam, wry 6 warped 7 complex, tortile

twister: 4 roll, turn 7 cruller, cyclone, mallard, tornado 8 doughnut 10 somersault, waterspout

twistical: sly 7 evasive 11 underhanded

twistle: 5 twist 6 wrench

twisty (see also **twist** above): 6 tricky 7 bending, evasive, winding 9 dishonest

twit: guy 4 gibe 5 blame, chirp, taunt, tease 7 upbraid 8 reproach, ridicule

twitch: nip, tic, tie, tug 4 draw, jerk, pick, pull, skid, yank 5 pluck, start, thong, tweak 6 fasten, snatch 9 vellicate 11 contraction

twitter: 5 chirp, shake 6 giggle, titter 7 chatter, chitter, flutter, tremble 9 agitation

twizzle: 5 twirl

two: twa(Sc.) 4 beta(Gr.), both, duet, dyad, pair 5 twain, twins 6 couple 7 twosome

chambered: 9 biacameral

edged: 9 ancipital

headed: 11 dicephalous

metrical feet: 6 dipody

months: 8 bi-mester

parts: 6 bident 9 bifurcate 11 dichotomous

pert. to: 4 dual 6 dyadic

prefix: bi, di 5 dioxy

winged: 7 bialate 8 dipteral 9 dipterous

two-bit: 5 cheap

two-faced: 5 false 9 deceitful 11 treacherous 12 hypocritical

god: 5 Janus

two-fisted: 6 virile 8 vigorous

two-foot: 5 biped 7 bipedal

two-pronged: 6 bident

two-sided: 9 bilateral 12 hypocritical

two-spot: 5 deuce

two-time: 5 cheat 7 deceive

two-tone: 7 bicolor

twofold: 4 dual 5 duple 6 bifold, binary, double, duplex 9 bifarious, duplicate

twopenny: ale 4 mean 5 cheap

twosome: 4 duet, pair 6 couple

tycoon: 7 magnate 9 financier 13 industrialist

tyddyn: 4 farm 9 homestead

tydie: 4 bird, wren 8 titmouse

tye: 4 case, rope, wash 5 chain, close 6 common 7 pasture 9 enclosure

tyee: 5 chief

tyke, tike: cur, dog 5 child 6 shaver 7 bumpkin

tylopod: 5 camel

tympan: 4 drum 8 membrane

tympanum: 6 tympan 7 eardrum

tympany: 7 bombast, conceit 9 inflation 10 distention, turgidness

Tyndareus' wife: 4 Leda

typal: 8 symbolic

type: pi; gem 4 font, form, kern, kind, mark, norm, pica, sign, slug, sort 5 agate, class, doric, elite, genre, group, ideal, ionic, metal, model, order, pearl, roman, stamp, token 6 emblem, italic, minion, nature, symbol 7 brevier, English, example, impress, paragon, pattern, species 8 antetype, boldface, classify 9 archetype, bourgeois, character, condensed, nonpareil 11 Baskerville

block: 4 quad 7 quadrat

frame: 5 chase

line: 4 slug

measure: em, en

mixed: pi

mold: 6 matrix

size: 4 pica, ruby 5 pearl 6 minion 7 brevier, diamond 9 nonpareil

slanting: 6 italic

stroke: 5 serif

tray: 6 galley

typeset: 7 compose

typesetter: 8 linotype, monotype 10 compositor

typewriter part: key 6 platen, spacer 9 tabulator

typhoon: 4 wind 5 storm 7 cyclone

typical: 5 typal 6 normal 7 regular 9 schematic 10 emblematic, figurative 13 prefigurative 14 characteristic, representative

typify: 6 embody 9 prefigure, represent, symbolize

typographer: 7 printer

tyrannical: 5 cruel, harsh 6 lordly, unjust 7 slavish 8 despotic 9 arbitrary, imperious 10 oppressive 11 domineering

tyrannosaurus: 8 dinosaur

tyrannous: 5 cruel, harsh 6 severe, unjust 8 despotic 10 tyrannical

tyranny: 5 rigor 8 severity 9 despotism, harshness

tyrant: 4 czar, Ivan, Nero, tsar, tzar 6 despot 7 monarch, usurper 8 martinet 9 oppressor
murder: 11 tyrannicide

Tyre: *king:* 5 Belus, Hiram
noble: 7 Acerbas
prince: 8 Pericles
princess: 4 Dido

tyro: 4 tiro 5 pupil 6 novice 7 amateur 8 beginner, neophyte 9 commencer 10 apprentice 11 abecedarian

tzar, czar, tsar: 4 king 5 ruler 6 tyrant

tzigane: 5 gypsy

U

U-boat: sub 9 submarine
uang: 6 beetle
ubermensch: 8 superman
uberous: 7 copious 8 abundant, fruitful
ubiety: 8 location, position, relation 9
  whereness
ubiquitous: 10 everywhere 11 omnipresent
ubiquity: 12 omnipresence
uca: 4 crab
Uffizi site: 8 Florence
Uganda: *capital:* 7 Entebbe
  cattle: 6 ankoli
  people: 7 Bunyoro
ughten: 4 dawn, dusk 7 evening, morning 8
  twilight
ugly: bad 4 vile 5 awful, cross, snivy, toady
  6 cranky, homely, snivey 7 crabbed, hideous, ominous 8 grewsome, gruesome, horrible, terrible, unlovely 9 dangerous, fractious, frightful, graceless, loathsome, offensive, repulsive, unsightly 10 ill-favored, ill-natured, unpleasant 11
  ill-tempered, quarrelsome, threatening 12
  cross-grained, disagreeable 13 objectionable
ugliness symbol: 4 toad
Ugrian: 4 Avar
ugsome: 6 horrid 9 abhorrent, frightful,
  loathsome
uhlan: 6 lancer 7 soldier 10 cavalryman
uitlander: 9 foreigner, outlander
ukase: 5 edict, order 6 decree 7 command 12
  proclamation
ukelele, ukulele: uke
Ukraine: *assembly:* 4 rada
  coin: 6 grivna 7 schagiv
  dance: 5 gopak
  holy city: 4 Kiev
  Mother of Cities: 4 Kiev
  seaport: 6 Odessa
Ulalume author: Poe
ulcer: 4 noma, sore 7 egilops 8 aegilops, fossette 9 cacoethes
  kind of: 6 peptic
ulceration: 8 helcosis

ule: 6 caucho
uliginous: wet 4 oozy 5 moist, muddy 6
  swampy
ullage: 7 wantage 8 shortage 10 deficiency
ulna: 4 bone 7 cubitus
  end of: 5 ancon
ulster: 4 coat 8 overcoat
ulterior: 5 later 6 future 7 further, remoter
  10 subsequent, succeeding 11 undisclosed
ultimate: end 4 dire, last 5 final, telos(Gr.)
  6 remote 7 extreme, maximum, primary 8
  eventful, eventual, farthest 9 elemental
  10 conclusive 11 fundamental
ultimatum: 5 order 6 demand
ultra: 6 beyond 7 extreme, forward, radical
  9 excessive, extremist, fanatical 11 extravagant 14 uncompromising
ulu: 5 knife
ululate: bay 4 hoot, howl, wail, yelp 6 lament 7 screech
Ulysses: *antagonist:* 4 Irus
  author: 5 Joyce
  character: 5 Bloom, Molly
  dog: 5 Argos
  enchantress of: 5 Circe
  enemy: 8 Poseidon
  father: 7 Laertes
  friend: 6 Mentor
  kingdom: 6 Ithaca
  mother: 8 Anticlea
  plant: 4 moly
  son: 9 Telegonus 10 Telemachus
  swineherd: 7 Eumaeus
  temptress: 5 Circe
  voyage: 7 odyssey
  wife: 8 Penelope
umber: 5 brown, shade, visor 6 darken,
  shadow 7 protect, umbrere 8 grayling, umbrette
umbles: 7 numbles 8 entrails
umbra: 4 fish 5 ghost, shade 6 shadow 7
  phantom, vestige
umbrage: 5 cloak, doubt, pique, shade, trace
  6 offend, shadow 7 foliage, offense, pretext, shelter 8 disfavor, disgrace, disguise
  9 disesteem, semblance, suspicion 10 over-

shadow, protection, resentment 11 displeasure

umbrageous: 5 shady 6 shaded

umbrella: 4 gamp 5 blind, guard, shade 6 brolly, chatta, payong, pileus, screen 7 parasol, protect, shelter 8 disguise 11 bumber-shoot

umbrella tree: 8 magnolia

umbrette: 9 hammerkop

Umbrian river: 6 Tevere

umbrous: 5 shady

umiak: 4 boat

umpire: ump 5 judge 6 decide, oddman 7 arbiter, daysman, oddsman, referee 9 supervise 10 arbitrator

Una boat: 7 catboat

unable: 6 cannot 7 disable 8 helpless, impotent 9 incapable 11 incompetent, inefficient, unqualified 13 incapacitated

unaccented: 4 lene 6 atonic

unaccompanied: 4 bare, solo 5 alone

unaccountable: 7 strange 9 countless 10 mysterious 12 inexplicable, unfathomable 13 irresponsible

unaccustomed: new 7 strange 8 uncommon, unwonted 10 unfamiliar

unacquainted: 7 strange, unusual 10 unfamiliar 13 inexperienced

unadorned: 4 bald, bare 5 naked, plain, stark 6 rustic 7 austere

unadulterated: 4 pure 5 clean 6 honest 7 genuine, sincere, unmixed 9 immutable

unaffected: 4 easy, naif, real 5 naive, plain 6 rustic, simple 7 artless, genuine, natural, sincere, unmoved 8 unbiased 9 ingenuous, unaltered, untouched 12 uninfluenced

unaging: 7 eternal

Unalaska native: 5 Aleut

unalike: 9 different

unalleviated: 4 hard

unalloyed: 4 pure 7 genuine, unmixed 11 unqualified

unambiguous: 8 explicit

unanchored: 6 adrift

unanimous: 5 solid 6 united 8 agreeing 11 consentient

unanimously: 7 una voce

unanswerable: 5 final 10 conclusive

unappeasable: 10 implacable

unarmed: 4 bare 5 inerm 11 defenseless

unaspirated: 4 lene

unassailable: 12 invulnerable

unassuming: shy 6 modest 7 natural 8 retiring 9 diffident 14 unostentatious

unattached: 4 free 5 loose 6 single 9 unmarried 11 independent 13 noncollegiate

unattractive: 4 rude, ugly 10 ungracious

unau: 5 sloth

unavailing: 6 futile 8 bootless, gainless

unavowed: 8 ulterior

unaware: 6 unwary 8 heedless, ignorant 11 thoughtless

unbalanced: 6 uneven 8 deranged, lopsided, one-sided

unbecoming: 4 rude 5 inept 8 improper, unseemly, unworthy 10 indecorous, unsuitable 11 disgraceful 12 unattractive

unbefitting: 5 below 10 unsuitable

unbelief: 9 disbelief 10 skepticism 11 agnosticism, incredulity

unbelievable: 9 fantastic 10 incredible 13 inconceivable

unbeliever: 5 pagan 7 atheist, doubter, heretic, infidel, scoffer, skeptic 8 agnostic 11 freethinker

unbend: 4 rest, thaw 5 relax, untie, yield 6 loosen, uncock 7 slacken 8 unfasten

unbending: 5 rigid, stern, stiff 8 obdurate, resolute 10 inexorable, inflexible

unbiased: 4 fair, just 8 detached 9 impartial 12 unprejudiced

unbind: 4 free, undo 5 untie 6 detach, loosen 7 absolve, deliver, release 8 dissolve, unfasten

unbleached: 4 blae, ecru 5 beige 7 natural

unblemished: 4 pure 8 spotless

unblushing: 9 shameless

unbolt: 4 open 5 unbar, unpin 6 unlock 8 unfasten

unbosom: 4 tell 6 reveal

unbound: 4 free 5 loose 10 unconfined

unbounded: 4 open 9 limitless, unchecked, unlimited 11 measureless 12 uncontrolled, unrestrained

unbrace: 4 free, undo 5 carve, relax 6 loosen, reveal, weaken 8 disjoint, enfeeble

unbranched antler: dag

unbridled: 4 free 5 loose 7 violent 9 dissolute, unchecked 10 licentious, ungoverned 12 uncontrolled, unrestrained

unbroken: one 4 flat 5 undug, whole 6 entire, intact 7 untamed 8 unplowed 9 continual, undivided, unsubdued 10 continuous 13 uninterrupted

unburden: 4 ease 5 empty, untax 6 unload 7 disload, relieve

unbury: 6 exhume

uncanny: 4 eery 5 eerie, scary, weird 6 spooky 7 awkward, ghostly, strange 8 careless 9 dangerous, unnatural 10 mysterious

uncanonical: 10 apocryphal

unceasing: 6 eterne 7 endless, eternal 9 continual, incessant, perennial 11 everlasting 14 unintermittent

unceasingly: 7 forever 11 continually, incessantly

unceremonious: 4 curt 5 bluff, blunt 6 abrupt 8 familiar, informal 14 unconventional

uncertain: 4 asea, dark, hazy 5 fluky, vague 6 chancy, fitful, queasy 7 dubious 8 aleatory, doubtful, unsteady, variable 9 ambiguous, equivocal, hazardous, undecided 10 changeable, indefinite, precarious 12 questionable 13 indeterminate, problematical, untrustworthy

uncertainty: 4 were 6 gamble, wonder 7 dubiety 8 suspense 9 dubiosity 10 skepticism

unchanging: 7 eternal, forever, settled, uniform 9 immutable, steadfast, unvarying 10 invariable, stationary

unchaste: 4 lewd 5 bawdy 6 coarse, impure 7 haggard, obscene 8 immodest

unchecked: 4 free 5 loose 7 rampant 9 unbounded, unbridled

unchurch: 13 excommunicate

uncia: 4 coin, inch 5 ounce 7 twelfth

uncivil: 4 rude 5 bluff 7 ill-bred 8 clownish, impolite 9 barbarous 10 indecorous, ungracious, unsuitable 11 uncivilized 12 discourteous 13 disrespectful

uncivilized: 4 rude, wild 5 feral 6 brutal, ferine, savage 8 barbaric 9 barbarian, barbarous, primitive 10 unmannerly 13 unenlightened

uncle: eme, oom, unk 5 nunks 6 nuncle 10 pawnbroker
pert. to: 9 avuncular

Uncle Remus: *author:* 6 Harris
rabbit: 4 Brer

Uncle Tom's Cabin author: 5 Stowe
character: Eva 5 Eliza, Topsy 6 Legree

unclean: 4 foul, tref, vile 5 black, dirty 6 common, filthy, impure 7 defiled, obscene 8 polluted, unchaste 11 unwholesome

unclose: ope 4 open 6 reveal 8 disclose 10 unreserved

unclothe: 5 spoil, strip 6 divest, expose 7 despoil, uncover, undress

unclothed: 4 bare, nude 5 naked

unclouded: 4 open 5 clear, sunny

unco: 5 great, weird 7 foreign, strange, uncanny, unknown 13 extraordinary

uncoil: 6 unwind

uncombined: 4 free 5 loose 10 elementary

uncomfortable: 6 uneasy

uncommon: odd 4 rare 5 novel 6 choice, scarce, unique 7 special, strange, unusual 8 especial, unwonted 10 infrequent, remarkable 11 exceptional 12 unaccustomed 13 extraordinary, preternatural

uncommunicative: 6 silent 8 reserved, reticent

uncompassionate: 5 stony

uncomplaining: 5 stoic 7 stoical

uncomplicated: 5 plain 6 simple

uncompromising: 4 firm 5 rigid, stern 6 strict 9 unbending 10 determined, inflexible, unyielding 12 intransigent

unconcealed: 4 bare, open 5 overt

unconcerned: 4 cool, easy 8 careless, detached 9 apathetic 10 insouciant 11 indifferent 12 uninterested

unconditional: 4 free 8 absolute, explicit

unconfined: lax 4 free 5 loose 9 boundless, limitless, unlimited

unconfused: 4 calm 5 clear 6 steady

unconnected: 5 gappy 6 abrupt 8 detached, rambling, separate 10 incoherent 12 disconnected

unconscious: out 6 asleep, torpid 7 stunned, unaware 8 comatose, ignorant, mindless 9 inanimate, lethargic 10 insensible
render: 4 stun
state: 5 swoon 8 apsychia

unconsciousness: 4 coma 5 faint 6 torpor

unconstrained: 4 easy, free 7 natural 8 familiar 11 spontaneous 12 unrestrained

uncontrollable: 4 wild 11 intractable

uncontrolled: 4 free, wild 5 loose 9 irregular, unbounded, unmanaged 10 hysterical, licentious, ungoverned 11 unregulated 12 unrestrained

unconventional: 5 loose, outre 6 casual 7 devious 8 Bohemian, informal 13 unceremonious

uncooked: raw 6 rawish

uncorrupted: 4 pure 8 pristine

uncouple: 5 loose 8 unfasten 10 disconnect

uncouth: odd 4 rare, rude 5 crude 6 clumsy, dismal, rugged 7 awkward, boorish, loutish, strange, uncanny, unknown 8 desolate, dreadful, ignorant, uncommon, ungainly 9 couthless, unknowing, unrefined, untrained 10 mysterious, outlandish, uncultured, unfamiliar, unpolished 11 comfortless 12 unacquainted, uncultivated

uncouth person: oaf 4 boor, lout 5 yokel 6 bumkin, rustic 7 bumpkin

uncover: 4 bare, open, tirl(Sc.), tirr(Sc.) 6 denude, detect, divest, expose, remove, reveal, unveil 7 display, divulge, undrape, unearth 8 disclose, discover

uncovered: 4 bald, nude, open 5 naked 6 cuerpo 9 developed 10 bareheaded

uncrystallized: 9 amorphous

unction: oil 7 suavity, unguent 8 ointment
give extreme: 5 anele

unctuous: fat 4 oily 5 bland, fatty, soapy, suave 6 fervid, greasy 7 gushing, pinguid, plastic 10 oleaginous

uncultivated: 4 arid, wild 5 feral 6 desert, fallow 7 deserty 9 barbarous

uncultured: 4 rude 7 artless, boorish 9 unrefined

uncurbed: 12 uncontrolled

undamaged: 5 whole 6 intact

undaunted: 4 bold 5 brave 7 spartan 8 fearless, intrepid, undashed 9 confident, dauntless, turbulent, unbridled, unchecked 10 courageous, undismayed 11 unconquered

undecayed: 5 fresh, green

undeceive: 8 disabuse 11 disillusion

undecided: 4 moot, pend 7 pending 8 doubtful, wavering 9 unsettled 10 inconstant, irresolute, unresolved 13 problematical

undefiled: 4 pure 6 chaste 8 innocent, virtuous 9 unlimited 10 immaculate

undemonstrative: 4 calm, cold, cool 8 reserved 10 restrained

undeniable: 4 true 7 certain 12 indisputable 13 incontestable

undependable: 7 erratic 13 irresponsible

under: 4 alow 5 below, neath, sotto(It.) 6 nether 7 beneath 10 underneath 11 subordinate

obligation: 5 owing 8 beholden, indebted

prefix: hyp, sub

the weather: 4 sick 5 drunk 6 ailing

under-set: 4 prop 6 sublet 7 provide, support 8 maintain, underlet 10 strengthen

underbrush: 6 covert 7 abature

undercover: 6 secret 13 surreptitious

man: spy 5 agent 9 detective 10 counterspy

underdone: 4 rare

underestimate: 8 minimize 9 underrate 10 undervalue

undergarment: bra 4 slip 5 teddy 6 cilice, corset, flimsy, shorts, stepin 7 chemise 9 brassiere, chemilonn, nairshirt, petticoat, teddybear, underwear 10 foundation 11 camiknicker, combination

undergo: 4 bear, pass 5 carry 6 endure, suffer 7 sustain 10 experience

undergraduate: 4 coed 6 junior, senior 7 student 8 freshman 9 sophomore

underground: 5 train 6 hidden, secret, subway 7 beneath 10 undercover 15 surreptitiously

burial place: 5 crypt 8 catacomb

dweller: 5 dwarf, gnome, troll

fighter: 6 maquis 8 partisan

fungus: 7 truffle 8 earthnut

worker: 5 miner 6 mucker, pitman, sapper

undergrowth: 4 rush 5 brush 10 hypotrophy, underbrush

underhanded: sly 4 dern, mean 5 shady 6 byhand, secret, sneaky, unfair 8 sneaking, unfairly 9 deceitful 10 circuitous, fraudulent 11 clandestine, shorthanded, unobtrusive 13 unobtrusively 15 surreptitiously

underlie: 4 bear 7 support

underline: 4 mark 6 stress 9 emphasize

underling: 6 menial, minion 8 inferior 11 subordinate

underlying: 5 basic 7 obscure 8 cardinal 11 fundamental

undermine: sap 4 cave 5 drain, erode 6 impair, weaken 7 founder, subvert 8 discover, enfeeble, excavate 10 demoralize

underneath: 5 below, under 6 secret 7 beneath 13 surreptitious

underpin: 7 justify, support 8 maintain 9 vindicate 12 substantiate

underprop: 4 prop 6 uphold 7 support 8 underpin

underrate: 5 decry 9 extenuate 10 undervalue 13 underestimate

underscore: 9 emphasize, italicize

undersea boat: sub 5 U-boat, wreck 9 submarine 11 submersible

eye: 9 periscope

undershirt: 4 vest 7 chemise

undershrub: 4 bush 7 heather

undersized: 4 puny 5 runty, small 7 scrubby

underskirt: 4 slip 9 petticoat

understand: con, dig, get, ken, see 4 know, sabe, twig 5 grasp, infer, sabby, savey, savvy, sense 6 follow, reason, savvey 7 discern, realize 8 conceive, perceive 9 apprehend, interpret, penetrate 10 comprehend

understandable: 5 clear, lucid

understanding: ken 4 feet, idea, news 5 amity, brain 6 humane, kindly, treaty 7 compact, concept, empathy, entente, knowing 8 attitude, contract, footwear, judgment, skillful, sympathy 9 agreement, diagnosis, knowledge, tolerance 10 acceptance 11 intelligent, sympathetic 12 intelligence

understatement: 7 litotes

understeward: 7 bailiff

understood: 5 clear, lucid, tacit 8 implicit

undertake: try 4 dare, fand, fang 5 chide, grant, seize 6 accept, assume, engage, incept 7 attempt, emprise, emprize, execute, perform, promise, receive, reprove 8 contract, covenant, endeavor, overtake 9 guarantee, underfong

undertaker: 4 bant 5 cerer 6 surety 7 rebuker, sponsor 8 embalmer 9 mortician 12 entrepreneur

undertaking: 4 task 6 charge, pledge 7 calling, project, promise, venture 8 covenant 9 adventure, guarantee 10 enterprise 11 proposition

written: 6 cautio 9 cautiones

undertone: 5 aside

undertow: 4 eddy 6 vortex 7 current, riptide

undervalue: 5 decry 8 disprize, disvalue 10 depreciate

underwater: *apparatus:* 6 tremie 7 caisson
captain: 4 Nemo
chamber: 4 cave 7 caisson
craft: sub 5 U-boat 7 pigboat 9 submarine
missile: 7 torpedo
sound detector: 5 sofar, sonar

underwear: 6 skivvy 7 dessous(F.), stepins 8 lingerie, skivvies 12 underclothes

underwood: 5 frith 7 boscage, coppice 10 underbrush 11 undergrowth

underworld: 4 hell 5 Hades, Orcus, Sheol 6 Amenti, Erebus 7 xibalba 8 gangland 9 antipodes
boatman: 6 Charon
deity: Dis 4 Bran 5 Hades, Pluto 6 Osiris 8 Dispater 9 Enmeshara 11 Ningishzida
goddess: 6 Allatu, Belili, Hecate, Trivia
organization: 5 Mafia
pert. to: 8 chthonic 9 chthonian
river: 4 Styx 5 Lethe 7 Acheron
watchdog: 8 Cerberus

underwrite: 6 insure 7 assure, finance, sponsor 9 subscribe

undesigned: 6 chance 10 accidental

undesigning: 6 simple 7 artless, sincere

undetermined: 5 vague 7 dubious 8 aoristic, doubtful 9 equivocal

undeveloped: 5 crude 6 latent 8 immature

undeviating: 4 even 8 straight

undigested: 5 crude

undiluted: 4 mear, meer, mere, neat, pure 8 straight

undiminished: 6 entire

undine: 5 nymph

undirected: 6 misled 7 aimless 11 misdirected

undisciplined: 4 wild 6 unruly, wanton 9 untrained

undisclosed: 6 secret 8 ulterior

undisguised: 4 bald 5 frank, overt 9 barefaced

undisturbed: 4 calm 5 quiet 6 placid, secure, serene 9 unruffled

undivided: one 5 total, whole 6 entire, intact 8 complete, unbroken 10 continuous

undo: 4 open, ruin 5 annul, fordo, loose, solve 6 betray, cancel, defeat, diddle, foredo, unlash, unwrap 7 defease, destroy, disjoin, explain, nullify, release, uncover, unravel 8 unfasten 10 disappoint, disconnect, invalidate

undoing: 4 ruin 8 downfall 9 overthrow

undomesticated: 4 wild 5 feral 6 ferine

undone: raw 9 neglected 10 defeasible

undoubted: 4 sure 7 certain 8 accepted, admitted 11 indubitable

undraped: 4 bare, nude

undress: 4 doff 5 strip 6 devest, divest 7 disrobe 8 unclothe 10 dishabille

undressed skin: kip 4 pelt

undue: 7 extreme 8 improper 9 excessive 10 exorbitant, immoderate, inordinate, unsuitable 11 unwarranted 12 unreasonable 13 inappropriate

undulant: 7 aripple, sinuous 10 undulating, undulatory

undulate: 4 roll, wave 5 swing 6 billow 9 fluctuate

undulation: 5 crimp, swell 8 waviness

undutiful: 7 impious

undying: 6 eterne 7 ageless, endless, eternal 8 immortal, unending 9 continual, deathless 12 imperishable

unearth: dig 5 learn 6 exhume, expose 7 uncover 8 disclose, discover

unearthly: 4 eery 5 eerie, weird 7 awesome, uncanny, ungodly 8 terrific 9 appalling, fantastic 10 mysterious, outlandish 12 preposterous, supernatural 13 preternatural

uneasiness: 5 worry 6 unrest 7 anxiety, disease, trouble 8 disquiet 10 constraint, discomfort, discontent 11 displeasure, disturbance 12 apprehension 13 inconvenience 15 dissatisfaction

uneasy: 5 stiff 7 anxious, awkward, fidgety, unquiet, restive 8 restless 9 difficult, perturbed, unsettled 13 uncomfortable

uneaten: 5 waste, whole 6 scraps

uneducated: 8 ignorant 10 illiterate, unlettered, unschooled

unemotional: 4 cold 5 stony, stoic 7 stoical 10 phlegmatic

unemployed: 4 idle 6 otiant, otiose 8 inactive, leisured

unenclosed: 4 open 9 fenceless

unencumbered: 4 free

unending: 7 endless, eternal, undying 8 timeless 9 ceaseless 12 interminable

unendurable: 10 impassible, unbearable 11 intolerable

unenthusiastic: 4 cool 9 apathetic 12 uninterested

unequal: 5 impar 6 uneven, unfair, unjust 8 variable 9 disparate, irregular 11 fluctuating 16 disproportionate
comb. form: 5 aniso
condition: 4 odds

unequaled: 7 supreme 9 matchless, unmatched, unrivaled 10 surpassing 12 unparalleled

unequivocal: 5 clear, plain 7 sincere 8 definite, explicit 9 certainly 11 categorical 15 straightforward

unerring: 4 sure, true 5 exact 7 certain 8 inerrant 9 inerrancy, unfailing 10 infallible

unethical: 5 wrong 6 amoral

uneven: odd 5 erose, gobby, haggy, rough 6 hobbly, rugged, unfair, unjust, unlike 7 unequal, varying 9 irregular 10 ill-matched 11 fluctuating, ill-assorted

unevenness: 8 asperity

unexamined: 7 apriori

unexcelled: 8 champion, superior

unexceptional: 5 usual 7 regular 8 ordinary

unexcitable: 6 stolid

unexcited: 4 calm 7 stoical

unexciting: 4 dead, tame 6 boring 7 prosaic 13 uninteresting

unexpected: 6 abrupt, sudden 9 inopinate, unguarded 10 accidental, unforeseen

unexpended: 6 saving 7 reserve, surplus

unexpired: 5 alive, valid 9 operative

unexpressed: 5 tacit

unextinguished: 5 alive

unface: 6 unmask

unfadable: 4 fast 9 memorable

unfaded: 5 fresh 6 bright

unfading flower: 8 amaranth

unfailing: 4 sure 7 certain 8 reliable, unerring 10 infallible, unflagging, unyielding 13 inexhaustible

unfair: 4 foul, hard 5 wrong 6 biased, uneven, unjust 8 unseemly, wrongful 9 dishonest, unethical 11 inequitable, underhanded, unfavorable 12 dishonorable

unfaithful: 7 infidel, traitor 8 derelict, disloyal, recreant, turncoat 9 dishonest, faithless 10 adulterous, inaccurate, traitorous 13 untrustworthy

unfaltering: 4 true 5 brave 6 steady

unfamed: 5 lowly 6 humble 7 obscure

unfamiliar: new 7 strange, unknown 12 unaccustomed

unfashionable: 5 dated 9 distorted, unshapely

unfast: 6 unfirm, untrue 8 insecure

unfasten: 4 free, open, undo 5 loose, unbar, unfix, unpin, untie 6 detach, loosen, unlace, unlock 8 untether

unfathomable: 10 bottomless 12 impenetrable

unfavorable: bad, ill 4 foul 6 averse 7 adverse 8 contrary 15 disadvantageous

unfeeling: 4 dull, hard 5 cruel, harsh, stern, stony 6 brutal, marble, stolid 7 callous 8 numbness, obdurate 9 apathetic, bloodless, heartless, insensate, senseless 10 impassible, insensible 11 hardhearted, insensitive 13 unsusceptible 16 unimpressionable

unfeigned: 4 real, true 6 hearty 7 genuine, natural, sincere

unfermented grape juice: 4 stum

unfertile: 4 arid 6 barren

unfetter: 6 loosen

unfettered: 4 free 5 broad, loose

unfilled: 5 blank, empty

unfilled cavity: 4 vugg

unfinished: raw 5 crude, rough 7 sketchy 8 immature 9 imperfect 10 incomplete

unfit: bad 4 sick 5 inept, pasul(Heb.) 6 faulty 8 disabled, improper 10 unsuitable 11 handicapped, incompetent, unqualified 12 disqualified 13 incapacitated

unfix: 6 detach, loosen 8 dissolve, unfasten, unsettle

unfixed: 6 adrift, afloat 8 drifting, shifting

unflagging: 8 tireless

unflattering: 4 open 5 blunt, frank 6 candid 10 derogatory, unbecoming

unfledged: 5 green 6 callow 8 immature 11 undeveloped, unfeathered

bird: 4 eyas 8 nestling

unflinching: 4 firm 6 stanch 8 resolute 9 steadfast 10 unwavering, unyielding

unfold: ope 4 open 6 deploy, evolve, expand, explat, flower, reveal, spread, unfurl, unwrap 7 develop, display, divulge, evolute, explain, explate, release 8 develope, disclose 9 explicate

unforced: 4 easy 7 natural, willing 9 voluntary

unforeseen: 6 casual 10 accidental

unformed: 6 callow 9 shapeless, uncreated 11 undeveloped

unfortunate: bad, ill 4 poor 5 worst 6 dismal, wretch 7 hapless, unhappy, unlucky 8 luckless, wretched 9 graceless 10 calamitous, prostitute, ungracious 12 inauspicious, infelicitous, unsuccessful

unfounded: 4 idle, vain 8 baseless 10 chimerical, groundless

unfragrant: 4 olid 5 fetid

unfrequented: 6 lonely 8 isolated, solitary

unfriendly: 4 cool 6 remote 7 asocial, hostile 8 inimical, unsocial 9 dissocial

terms: 4 outs

unfruitful: 5 blunt 6 barren, wasted 7 sterile, useless 9 fruitless, infertile 12 unproductive, unprofitable

unfurl: 4 open 5 enrol 6 enroll, expand, spread, unfold, unroll 7 develop 8 develope

unfurnished: 4 bare 6 vacant

ungainly: 5 lanky 6 clumsy 7 awkward, boorish, uncouth 8 clownish, slammock, slummock 11 elephantine

ungenerous: 4 mean 5 harsh, nasty 6 stingy

ungentlemanly: 7 ill-bred 9 illiberal

ungirt: 5 loose, slack 7 unbound

ungodly: 6 sinful, wicked 7 impious 8 dreadful 9 atheistic, atrocious, unearthly 11 unbelieving 12 hypocritical

ungovernable: 4 wild 6 unruly 7 froward 9 unbridled 10 disorderly, headstrong, licentious, rebellious 11 intractable 13 irrepressible 14 uncontrollable

ungraceful: 6 clumsy 7 angular, awkward 9 inelegant

ungracious: 4 hard, rude 6 wicked 8 churlish, disliked, impolite 9 graceless, offensive 10 unmannerly, unpleasant 11 unfortunate 12 discourteous, unattractive

ungrateful: 9 thankless

ungrounded: 8 baseless 9 unfounded 10 uninformed 12 uninstructed

ungrudging: 8 cheerful

ungual: 4 claw, hoof, nail 6 ungula

unguarded: 6 unwary 8 careless 9 imprudent 10 incautious 11 defenseless, thoughtless, unprotected

unguent: 4 balm 5 salve 6 cerate, ceroma, chrism 8 ointment 9 lubricant

unguinous: 4 oily 8 unctuous

ungula: 4 claw, hoof, nail 6 ungual

ungulate: hog, pig 4 deer 5 horse, tapir 6 hoofed 8 elephant 10 rhinoceros

unhallowed: 6 impure, unholy, wicked 7 impious, profane 10 desecrated

unhamper: 5 loose

unhandsome: 4 mean, rude 5 plain 6 homely, stingy 10 unbecoming

unhandy: 6 clumsy 7 awkward 12 inconvenient

unhap: 6 mishap 7 ill-luck

unhappiness: woe 5 blues, dolor, grief, worry 6 misery, unrest

unhappy: sad 4 evil 6 dismal 7 unlucky 8 dejected, illfated, wretched 9 miserable, sorrowful, woebegone 10 calamitous 11 melancholic, mischievous, unfavorable, unfortunate 12 inauspicious, unsuccessful 13 inappropriate

unharmed: 4 safe 6 unhurt 8 harmless 10 scatheless

unharmonious: 9 dissonant

unharness: 6 disarm, divest, ungear 7 unhitch, unhorse

unhasp: 8 unfasten

unhealthy: ill 4 sick 6 sickly 11 unwholesome

unheard of: 7 strange, unknown 13 unprecedented

unheated: 4 cold

unheeding: 4 deaf 8 careless 12 disregarding

unhesitating: 5 ready

unhidden: 5 overt

unholy: 6 impure, wicked 7 impious, profane 8 dreadful, shocking 9 frightful 10 scandalous, unhallowed

unhonored: 12 dishonorable 13 dishonourable

unhorse: 5 throw 8 dislodge, dismount 9 overthrow, unharness

unhurried: 4 easy, slow 10 deliberate

unhurt: 4 safe 8 unharmed 9 uninjured

unicellular animal: 5 ameba 6 amoeba 9 protozoan 10 paramecium

unicellular plant: 5 spore

unicorn: 4 reem

unicorn fish: 4 unie 7 narwhal 8 filefish

unidentified flying object: UFO

uniform: 4 even, flat, suit 5 equal, level 6 livery, outfit, steady 7 regular, similar 8 constant, equiform 9 continual, equitable, unvarying 10 consistent, equiformal, invariable, monotonous, unchanging 11 homogeneous

cord: 11 aiguillette

in color: 4 flat, flot

servant's: 6 livery

shoulder ornament: 7 epaulet 9 epaulette

uniformly: 6 always

unify: 5 merge, unite 8 coalesce 9 correlate, integrate 11 consolidate

unimaginative: 4 dull 7 literal, prosaic

unimpaired: 4 free 5 fresh 6 entire, intact

unimpassioned: 6 steady

unimpeachable: 9 blameless, faultless 14 irreproachable, unquestionable 15 unexceptionable

unimpeded: 4 free

unimportant: 5 minor, petty, small 6 little, paltry 7 trivial 10 negligible

unimpressed: 6 unawed

uninflected: 7 aptotic

uninformed: 8 ignorant

uninhabited: 5 empty 6 vacant 8 deserted, desolate

uninspired: 4 dull 6 stodgy

unintelligent: 4 dumb 5 brute 6 obtuse, stupid, unwise 7 foolish 8 ignorant 9 senseless 10 irrational

unintentional: 10 accidental 11 inadvertent

uninteresting: dry 4 arid, drab, dull, flat 5 stale 6 boring, jejune, prolix, stupid 7 humdrum, insipid, prosaic, tedious 8 tiresome 9 colorless 10 unexciting

uninterrupted: 7 endless, eternal 9 continual 10 continuous 11 everlasting

unio: 6 mussel

union: AFL, CIO, one, UAW 4 bloc 5 artel, ILGWU, unity 6 accord, copula, fusion, gremio(Sp.), league, merger, unicum 7 amalgam, concord, contact, entente, meeting, oneness, society 8 alliance, junction, knitting, marriage **9** coalition, coherence, composure **10** connection, copulation, federation, fellowship **11** association, coalescence, combination, concurrence, confederacy, conjunction, consistency

political: **4** bloc **9** coalition

trade: **5** guild, hanse

union jack: 4 flag

Union of South Africa: See **South Africa**

Union of Soviet Socialist Republics (see also **Russia, Soviet Union**): **4** USSR **6** Russia, Soviet

unique: odd, one **4** rare, sole **5** alone, queer **6** single **7** notable, special, unequal, unusual **8** peculiar, singular **9** matchless **13** extraordinary

unison: 5 union **6** accord **7** concord, harmony **9** agreement, consonant, identical, unanimity, unisonant, unisonous **10** concordant, consonance, equivalent

unit: ace, one **4** item **5** digit, group, monad, whole **6** entity **10** individual

conductivity: mho

discord: **4** word

fluidity: rhe

flux density: **5** gauss

force: **4** dyne, volt **5** kinit, tonal

hypothetical: **6** pangen **7** pangene

illumination: **4** phot

inductance: **5** henry

light: lux, pyr **5** lumen

magnetic: **5** weber

measure: are, mil, rod **4** pint **5** meter, stere

measuring sound: **7** decibel

metrical: **4** dyne, mora **5** liter, morae

military: **4** army **5** corps, squad **7** brigade, company, platoon **8** division, regiment **9** battalion

physical: erg **7** atomerg

power: HP; bel **4** watt **5** dynam, horse

pressure: **5** barad, barye

reluctance: rel

resistance: ohm

social: **4** clan, sect **6** family

speed: **4** velo

stellar: **6** parsec

tale: **4** rees

telegraphic: **4** baud

thermal: **6** calory **7** calorie

time: day **4** bell, hour, week, year **5** month **6** minute, season, second

ultimate: **5** monad

velocity: kin **4** kine, velo

volume: oz, pd; cwt, ton **5** ounce, pound **13** hundredweight

weight: ton **4** dram, gram **5** carat, ounce, pound

work: erg **5** ergon, joule **6** kilerg

unite: add, fay, pan, sew, tie, wed **4** ally, band, bind, club, fuse, hasp, join, knit, link, meld, pair, seam, weld **5** affix, annex, blend, graft, hitch, marry, merge, piece, rally **6** adhere, adjoin, attach, cement, cohere, concur, couple, embody, mingle, pleach, solder, splice **7** combine, conjoin, connect, consort, convene **8** assemble, coalesce, compound, concrete, condense, conspire, continue, federate, regelate **9** affiliate, aggregate, associate, colleague **10** amalgamate, articulate, consociate, federalize **11** concentrate, compaginate, consolidate, incorporate **12** conglutinate

united: one **9** concerted, conjugate, corporate **10** corporated

United Nations Organization: UNO

United Provinces: 7 Holland, Utrecht, Zeeland **9** Friesland, Groningen **10** Gelderland, Overijssel

United States (see also **America**): *admiral:* **4** King, Sims **5** Dewey **6** Halsey, Nimitz **8** Farragut

artist: **4** Pyle, Wood **5** Flagg, Homer, Marin, Moses, Peale, Ryder, Sloan, Wyeth **6** Benton, Eakins, Hopper, Stuart

author: Ade, Poe, Roe **4** Ames, Baum, Buck, Dana, Grey, Pyle, Uris, Ward, Wolf **5** Alger, Barth, Beach, Davis, Field, Harte, Hurst, Lewis, James, Quinn, Stowe, Tripp **6** Alcott, Bellow, Bryant, Cabell, Cooper, Ferber, Hersey, Holmes, Irving, London, Lowell, Jewett, Kantor, O. Henry, O'Neill, Porter, Snyder **7** Barrett, Clemens, Dreiser, Emerson, Hayward, Malamud, Parkman, Saroyan, Stewart, Thoreau, Vaughan, Wallace, Whitman **8** Faulkner, Salinger, Sinclair, Whittier **9** Cenedella, Hawthorne, Hemingway **10** Longfellow, Tarkington

bandleader: **5** Sousa

canal: **4** Erie **6** Panama

capital city: **5** Boise, Dover, Salem **6** Albany, Austin, Boston, Denver, Helena, Juneau, Pierre, St. Paul, Topeka **7** Atlanta, Augusta, Concord, Jackson, Lansing, Lincoln, Madison, Olympia, Phoenix, Raleigh, Santa Fe, Trenton **8** Bismarck, Cheyenne, Columbia, Columbus, Hartford, Honolulu, Richmond **9** Annapolis, Des Moines, Frankfort, Nashville **10** Baton Rouge, Carson City, Charleston, Harrisburg, Little Rock, Montgomery, Montpelier, Providence, Sacramento **11** Springfield, Tallahassee **12** Indianapolis, Oklahoma City, Salt Lake City **13** Jefferson City

cartoonist: **4** Arno, Capp, Nast **5** Petty **6** Addams, Disney **7** Mauldin **8** Herblock

chemist: **4** Urey **5** Moore **7** Pauling

coin: bit **4** cent, dime **5** eagle, penny **6** dollar, nickel **7** quarter

colonists: **5** Dutch **8** Pilgrims, Puritans

composer: **4** Foss, Kern **5** Foote, Grofe, Nevin **6** Berlin, Foster, Porter **7** Copland, Rodgers **8** Gershwin **9** Bernstein

deer: elk **6** wapiti

dramatist: **4** Inge, Rice **5** Barry, Odets **6** Crouse, Miller, O'Neill **8** Crothers, Williams

editor: Bok **4** Dana, Ochs **5** White **7** Greeley

emblem: **5** eagle

essayist: Poe **5** Mabie **6** Lowell, Morley **7** Emerson, Thoreau

explorer: **4** Byrd, Long, Pike **5** Boone, Clark, Lewis, Logan, Perry

falls: **7** Niagara **8** Yosemite **9** Multnomah

flagmaker: **9** Betsy Ross

frontiersman: **4** Cody **5** Boone, Clark, Lewis **8** Crockett

general: Lee, Ord **4** Otis, Pope **5** Bragg, Grant, Meade **7** Bradley, Jackson **8** Burnside, Pershing, Stilwell **10** Eisenhower

historian: **4** Dodd

horse: **5** pinto **6** bronco, morgan **7** mustang

humorist: Ade, Day, Nye **4** Cobb, Nash, Neal **5** Twain **6** Rogers **7** Lardner, Thurber

illustrator: **5** Flagg

Indian: See under **Indian**

inventor: Hoe **4** Bell, Howe **5** Fiske, Fitch, Morse **6** Edison, Fulton **7** Whitney

journalist: **4** Dana, Ochs, Pyle, Reid, Riis **5** Alsop, Block, Broun, White **6** Reston **7** Lorimer **8** Brisbane

jurist: Jay **4** Hand, Reed, Taft **5** Chase, Stone, Story, Taney **6** Holmes **8** Marshall **11** Frankfurter

legendary hero: **6** Bunyan

lexicographer: **4** Funk **7** Webster

measure: lea, mil, rod, ton, tub, vat **4** acre, bolt, cord, drum, foot, gill, hand, hank, heer, inch, iron, last, line, link, mile, nail, pace, palm, peck, pint, pipe, pole, pool, roll, sack, span, typp, vara, yard **5** block, carat, chain, labor, minim, perch, point, prime, quart, skein, stran **6** barrel, basket, bushel, fathom, gallon, league, pottle, square, strand, thread **7** quarter, section, spindle **8** hogshead, quadrant, standard, township **9** board foot, decillion, fluid dram **10** fluid ounce **11** teaspoonful **13** tablespoonful **16** Winchester bushel

measure of weight: bag, keg, kip, ton **5** carat, flask, grain, ounce, pound **6** denier **7** long ton, quarter, quintal **9** troy ounce, troy pound **11** metric carat **13** hundredweight

mountain: **4** Hood **6** Cumbre, Elbert, Helena, Shasta **7** Massive, Rainier, Whitney **8** Katahdin, McKinley

mountain lion: **4** puma **6** cougar

naturalist: **4** Muir **5** Baird, Beebe, Seton **7** Thoreau

novelist: see *author* above

opera singer: **4** Alda **5** Price, Sills **6** Callas, Farrar, Tucker **7** Stevens

orator: **4** Otis **5** Bryan, Henry

ornithologist: **7** Audubon

painter: see *artist* above

personification: **8** Uncle Sam

philanthropist: **4** Ford, Riis **5** Lenox **8** Carnegie **11** Rockefeller

philosopher: **5** James **6** Edmans **7** Thoreau

physician: **4** Mayo, Reed, Rush, Salk **5** Minot

physicist: **5** Tesla **6** Teller **7** Nichols

pianist: **5** Watts **6** Duchin, Levant **7** Cliburn

pioneer: see *frontiersman* above

pirate: **4** Kidd

plains: **7** prairie **8** savannah

poet: Poe **4** Nash **5** Benet, Field, Moore, Reese, Riley, Stein, Towne, Wylie **6** Bryant, Holmes, Kilmer, Lanier, Lowell, Millay **7** Whitman **8** Whittier **10** Longfellow

polar explorer: **4** Byrd **5** Perry

President: See **President (U.S.)**

publisher: **4** Luce, Ochs **6** Cowles, Fields, Hearst, Howard **9** McCormick, Patterson

racetrack: **5** Bowie **6** Goshen, Laurel **7** Hialeah, Jamaica, Pimlico **8** Aqueduct

river: **4** Ohio **6** Hudson, Wabash **8** Missouri **9** Merrimack **11** Mississippi

rodent: **6** beaver, gopher **8** squirrel

sculptor: **6** Calder **7** Borglum

socialist: **4** Debs **6** Thomas

statesman: Jay **5** Baker, Lodge, Logan **6** Baruch, Blaine **7** Acheson, Stimson **9** Stevenson

suffragist: **4** Catt **7** Anthony

Vice President: See **Vice President (U.S.)**

violinist: **5** Stern

units: *aggregate distance:* **7** mileage

biological: **6** idants

unity: one **5** union **6** accord **7** concord, harmony, oneness **8** alliance, identity **9** agreement, communion **10** singleness, solidarity, uniformity **11** conjunction, unification

universal: all **5** local, total, whole **6** common, cosmic, entire, public **7** general **8** catholic, constant **9** continual, unlimited **12** allpervading

language: Ro; ido **9** Esperanto

military training: **5** draft

universe: **5** earth, monad, world **6** cosmos, nature, system **8** creation

comb. form: 5 cosmo
controlling principle: 4 tien 5 logos
pert. to: 6 cosmic
science: 9 cosmology
university (see also **college**): 6 patent 7 academy, college 8 academie 9 accademie
division: 6 school 7 college
grounds: 6 campus
Ivy League: 4 Yale 5 Brown 7 Cornell, Harvard 8 Columbia 9 Dartmouth, Princeton 12 Pennsylvania
official: 4 dean 6 regent
rank: 6 docent 9 professor 10 instructor
team: 7 varsity
univocal: 7 uniform 9 unanimous, unisonous 11 indubitable 12 unmistakable
unjust: 5 cruel 6 unfair 8 improper, wrongful 9 dishonest, faithless 10 inaccurate, iniquitous, unfaithful
unked, unkid: odd 5 weird 6 lonely 7 awkward, ghastly, strange, uncanny, uncouth, unknown 8 desolate 12 inconvenient 13 uncomfortable
unkeeled: 6 ratite
unkempt: 5 crude, messy, rough 6 frouzy, frowsy, frowzy, shaggy, untidy 7 ruffled, squalid, tousled 9 unrefined 10 disarrayed, disheveled, unpolished
unkind: bad, ill 4 vile 5 cruel, harsh, rough, stern 6 severe, wicked 7 foreign, strange 8 ungenial 9 inclement, undutiful, unnatural 10 degenerate, ungenerous, ungracious, ungrateful, unsuitable 11 unfavorable
unknit: 4 undo 5 ravel, relax, untie 6 unknot 7 unravel 8 disperse, dissolve, disunite
unknowable: 8 mystical, noumenon 9 enigmatic
unknown: 4 unco 7 inconnu(F.), strange 9 anonymous, incognito 10 unfamiliar 12 incalculable 13 inexpressible
unlace: 4 undo 5 loose 6 carver 7 undress, unravel 8 unfasten, untangle
unlawful: 7 bastard, illegal, illicit 8 wrongful 9 irregular 10 contraband 12 illegitimate
hunting: 8 poaching
intrusion: 8 trespass
unlearned: 4 lewd 5 gross 6 borrel 7 natural 8 ignorant, untaught 9 untutored 10 illiterate, uneducated 11 instinctive, instinctual
unleashed: 4 free 5 loose 8 released
unleavened: 7 azymous
bread: 4 azym 5 azyme, matzo 7 matzoth(pl.)
unless: 4 lest, nisi(L.), save 6 except 9 excepting, provision 11 reservation

unlettered: 4 lewd 8 ignorant 9 barbarian 10 illiterate, uneducated
unlike: 6 uneven 7 difform, diverse 8 unlikely 9 different, irregular 10 dissimilar, improbable 13 heterogeneous
unlikely: 5 unfit 10 improbable, unsuitable 11 unpromising 12 disagreeable, unattractive 13 objectionable
unlikeness: 8 contrast 12 disagreement 13 dissimilarity
unlimited: 4 vast 9 boundless, limitless, unbounded, undefined, universal 10 indefinite, unconfined 11 illimitable, untrammeled 12 immeasurable, unrestricted 13 indeterminate
unlit: 4 dark
unload: 4 dump 5 empty, trash 6 decant, remove 7 deplete, discard, lighten, relieve 9 disburden, discharge, liquidate, sacrifice
unlock: ope 4 open 5 solve 6 reveal
unlooked for: 6 chance 10 unexpected
unlucky: bad, fey, ill 7 hapless 8 illfated 9 illomened 11 unfortunate
unman: 5 crush 7 monster, unnerve 8 castrate
unmanageable: 5 randy 8 churlish 10 disorderly
unmanly: 8 childish
unmannerly: 4 rude 7 boorish, uncivil 8 impolite 10 ungracious 12 discourteous
unmarried: one 4 lone 6 chaste, single
in law: 4 sole
unmask: 6 expose, reveal, unface 7 uncloak 8 disclose 9 dismantle
unmatched: odd 5 alone 9 matchless
unmeasured: 4 huge, vast 7 immense 9 boundless 12 unrestrained
unmelodious: 9 dissonant 11 cacophonous
unmerciful: 5 cruel 8 pitiless, ruthless 9 inclement 10 relentless
unmethodical: 7 cursory, erratic 9 desultory
unmindful: 8 careless, heedless 9 forgetful, negligent 10 neglectful
unmistakable: 4 open 5 clear, plain 6 patent 7 evident, obvious 8 apparent, definite
unmitigated: 4 mere 5 sheer 6 arrant 8 absolute, clearcut 10 unmodified
unmixed: 4 deep, mear, mere, pure 5 blank, sheer, utter 7 sincere
unmoved: 4 calm, cool, firm 5 stony 6 serene 7 adamant 8 obdurate, stubborn, unshaken 9 apathetic
unmoving: 5 inert
unnatural: 4 eery 5 eerie 7 strange, uncanny 8 abnormal, affected, farcical 9 irregular 10 artificial, factitious 11 counterfeit

unnecessary: 7 useless 8 needless 11 superfluous

unnerve: 5 unman 6 weaken 8 enervate 10 dishearten

unnoble: 7 ignoble

unobservant: 8 heedless

unobstructed: 4 free, open 9 panoramic

unobtrusive: 6 modest 8 retiring

unobtrusively: 9 underhand

unoccupied: 4 idle, void 5 empty 6 vacant 7 leisure 10 unemployed

unofficial: 7 private 8 informal

unorganized: 5 messy 7 chaotic 10 disorderly

unoriginal: 4 copy 5 trite 10 secondhand

unorthodox: 9 heretical

unostentatious: 5 quiet 6 lenten, modest 10 restrained

unpaid: due 6 arrear 10 unrevenged

unpaired: odd

unpalatable: 10 unpleasant 11 distasteful

unparalleled: 5 alone 6 unique 7 unequal 8 peerless 9 matchless, unmatched 10 inimitable

unplaned: 5 rough

unpleasant: bad 7 irksome 9 offensive 10 abominable, forbidding, illfavored, ungracious 11 displeasing, distasteful 12 disagreeable

most: 5 worst

unplowed: lea 6 fallow 8 untilled

unpolished: 5 bruit, crude, rough 6 coarse, rugged 8 agrestic, impolite 9 barbarous 10 agrestical

unpopularity: 5 odium

unprecedented: new 5 novel 10 unexampled

unprejudiced: 4 fair 9 impartial 13 dispassionate

unpremeditated: 6 casual 9 extempore 10 accidental

unprepared: raw 5 unfit

unprepossessing: 4 ugly 5 plain 6 homely 11 unappealing 12 unattractive

unpretentious: 5 plain 6 homely, humble, modest, simple 10 unaffected

unprincipled: 4 lewd 9 abandoned 10 perfidious 12 unscrupulous

unprocessed: raw 5 crude

unproductive: 4 arid, dead, lean 6 barren, geason 7 sterile 10 unfruitful

unprofessional: lay 6 laical 7 amateur 9 unskilled 15 nonprofessional

unprofitable: dry 4 dead 6 barren 7 inutile, useless 8 bootless, gainless 9 fruitless, frustrate 10 unfruitful 12 frustraneous 15 disadvantageous

unpropitious: 4 evil 7 adverse, ominous, opposed 12 inauspicious

unprotected: 7 exposed 8 helpless 9 unguarded

unqualified: 4 bare, mear, meer, mere 5 sheer, unfit 6 entire, unable 7 plenary 8 absolute, complete, definite 9 categoric, downright, incapable 11 categorical, incompetent

unquestionable: 7 certain, decided, evident 8 implicit, positive 12 indisputable

unravel: 4 undo 5 feaze, ravel, solve 6 unfold, unlace 8 disorder, disunite, separate, untangle 9 disengage 11 disentangle

unready: 4 slow 5 unfit 6 clumsy 7 awkward 8 hesitant 9 undressed

unreal: 5 false, ideal 6 aerial 7 fancied, fatuous, nominal 8 aeriform, fanciful, illusive, illusory, spurious 9 deceptive, fantastic, imaginary, pretended, visionary 10 apocryphal, artificial, barmecidal, fictitious, mandacious 11 counterfeit, imaginative 13 insubstantial, unsubstantial

unreality: 7 fantasy 9 fantastry

unreasonable: mad 6 absurd 9 excessive, senseless 10 exorbitant, immoderate, irrational 11 extravagant, impractical

unreasonableness: 5 alogy

unrecognized: 6 unsung 7 unknown 13 unappreciated

unrefined: raw 4 dark, loud, rude 5 broad, crass, crude, gross 6 coarse, common, earthy, vulgar 7 uncouth 12 uncultivated

unregenerate: 6 carnal, sinful 9 shameless 10 impenitent 11 unrepentent

unrelated: 5 fremd

unrelaxed: 4 taut 5 tense

unrelenting: 4 grim, hard, iron 5 cruel, stern 6 severe 8 rigorous 9 merciless 10 inexorable, inflexible, relentless, unyielding

unreliable: 5 fishy 6 fickle 7 casalty 10 capricious 12 undependable 13 irresponsible, untrustworthy

unremitting: 4 busy, hard 9 assiduous, continual, incessant 10 persistent 11 persevering

unrepentent: 10 impenitent 12 unregenerate

unreserved: 4 free 5 frank 6 candid 9 outspoken, unlimited

unresponsive: 4 cold, cool

unrest: 5 alarm 6 bustle, motion 8 disquiet 9 commotion 10 uneasiness 12 restlessness

unrestrained: lax 4 free, wild 5 broad, loose 6 wanton 7 riotous 9 abandoned, dissolute, expansive, unbounded, unbridled, unlimited 10 licentious, unmeasured 11 extravagant 12 uncontrolled

unrestraint: 7 license 8 immunity

unrevealed: 6 hidden, latent, masked 7 covered 9 concealed

unripe: 5 crude, green 6 callow 7 uncured, unready 8 immature 9 premature 10 precocious, unseasoned 12 unseasonable 13 inexperienced

unrobe: 7 disrobe, undress

unroll: 6 evolve, unfold 7 display 8 disclose

unruffled: 4 calm, cool 5 quiet 6 placid, poised, sedate, serene, smooth 8 decorous 11 undisturbed 13 dispassionate, philosophical

unruly: 6 haunty, ramage 7 lawless, restive 9 fractious, obstinate, turbulent 10 disorderly, headstrong, licentious, refractory 11 disobedient, intractable 12 recalcitrant, ungovernable, unmanageable

unsafe: 7 exposed 8 insecure, perilous 9 dangerous, hazardous 10 unreliable

unsatisfactory: 9 defective, imperfect 10 inadequate 11 inefficient

unsatisfied: 9 insatiate 15 dissatisfaction

unsatisfying: 6 hollow

unsavory: 7 insipid 9 offensive, tasteless 10 unpleasant 11 distasteful 12 disagreeable

unscrupulous: 8 rascally 9 dishonest, miscreant 12 unprincipled 13 untrustworthy

unseal: ope 4 open 8 disclose

unseasonable: 6 unripe 8 untimely 9 premature 11 inopportune

unseasoned: raw 5 bland, green 8 untimely

unseat: 6 remove 7 unhorse 9 overthrow

unseemly: 8 improper, indecent, unworthy 10 indecorous, unbecoming 13 inappropriate

unseen: 9 invisible, unnoticed 10 unobserved 11 unperceived 12 undiscovered

unselfish: 6 heroic 8 generous 10 altruistic, benevolent

unserviceable: 7 useless

unsettle: 5 upset 7 commove, derange, disturb 8 disorder, displace, disquiet 10 disarrange, discompose

unsettled: 4 moot 6 fickle, queasy 7 dubious 8 restless, unstable 9 ambiguous, desultory, itinerant, uncertain, unquieted 10 changeable, precarious, unoccupied 11 unpopulated 12 undetermined 13 problematical

unshaken: 4 firm 6 steady

unshapely: 8 deformed

unsheathe: 4 draw 6 remove

unsightly: 4 ugly 5 messy 6 homely

unskilled: 4 rude 5 green 6 puisne 7 artless 8 ignorant, malapert

unskillful: 5 inept 6 bungly, clumsy 7 awkward 10 inexpertly 13 inexperienced

unskillfully: 5 badly

unsociable: shy 8 reserved 9 withdrawn

unsocial: 7 asocial 9 dissocial, nonsocial 10 antisocial

unsoiled: 5 clean 10 immaculate

unsophisticated: 4 naif, pure 5 frank, green, naive 6 callow, simple 7 artless, genuine 8 innocent 9 ingenuous, untutored

unsorted flour: 4 atta

unsound: bad 4 evil, sick, weak 5 crazy, dotty, false, frail, risky, shaky 6 addled, fickle, flawed, hollow, rotten, weakly 7 decayed, wracked 8 diseased, impaired, insecure, weakened 9 defective, imperfect, tottering 10 illfounded

unspeakable: bad 4 vile 6 wicked 7 heinous 9 ineffable 11 unutterable

unspoiled: 4 racy 5 fresh

unspoken: 4 oral 5 tacit 6 silent 9 ineffable, unuttered

unspotted: 8 spotless 10 immaculate

unstable: 5 loose, sandy 6 fickle, fitful, flitty, labile 7 astatic, dwaible, dwaibly, erratic, flighty, plastic 8 insecure, ticklish, unhinged, unsteady, variable 9 eccentric, faithless, irregular, unsettled 10 changeable, inconstant, precarious, unreliable 11 fluctuating, vacillating

unstained: 8 spotless 10 immaculate

unsteady: 5 dizzy, fluky, shaky, tippy 6 fickle, flicky, fluffy, groggy, wabbly, wobbly 7 erratic, quavery, rickety, unsound, wayward 8 titubate, unstable, variable, wavering 9 desultory, irregular, uncertain 10 capricious, changeable, flickering, inconstant 11 fluctuating, lightheaded, vacillating

unstinted: 5 ample 8 generous

unstudied: 7 natural 8 careless, unforced, unversed 9 unlearned 10 colloquial, unaffected 11 spontaneous

unsubstantial: 4 airy, slim 5 filmy, light, paper 6 aerial, flimsy, papery, slight, unreal 7 folious, gaseous, nominal, shadowy 8 filigree, footless 9 visionary 10 immaterial

unsuccessful: 6 losing 7 failing, unlucky 8 abortive 9 fruitless 10 disastrous 11 ineffectual, unfortunate

unsuitable: bad 5 inapt, inept, undue, unfit 10 unbecoming 13 inappropriate

unsullied: 4 pure 8 spotless 10 immaculate

unsure: 4 weak 5 timid 6 infirm 8 doubtful 9 dangerous, hazardous 10 precarious 11 vacillating 13 untrustworthy

unsusceptible: 6 immune 8 obdurate

unsweetened: dry, sec 4 sour

unswerving: 4 firm, true 5 loyal 8 straight 9 steadfast

unsymmetrical: 8 lopsided 9 irregular 15 disproportional

unsympathetic: 4 hard 5 stony 6 frozen 7 hostile 9 heartless 11 hardhearted 12 unresponsive

untainted: 4 pure 9 unsullied

untalented: 8 mediocre 11 incompetent

untamed: 4 wild 5 feral 6 ferine, ramage, ramish, savage 9 unsubdued

untangle: 4 free 6 sleave 9 extricate 11 disentangle

untanned skin: kip 4 hide, pelt 8 shagreen

untarnished: 5 clean 8 spotless

untaught: 5 naive 7 natural 8 ignorant 9 unlearned 10 illiterate, uneducated 11 spontaneous 12 uninstructed

untenanted: 5 empty 6 vacant

untended: 9 neglected

untested: new 5 green 7 untried

unthinking: 4 rash 5 brute 6 casual 8 careless, heedless 9 impetuous 11 thoughtless 13 inconsiderate

unthrifty: 6 wanton 7 foolish, profuse 8 prodigal 10 profitless, profligate 11 extravagant

unthrone: 6 unseat 7 decrown 9 overthrow

untidiness: 4 mess, muss 6 litter

untidy: 5 dowdy, messy 7 bunting 8 careless, littered, slovenly 10 disheveled, disordered, slatternly 11 disarranged

untidy person: pig 4 slob 6 sloven 8 slattern

untie: 4 free, undo 5 loose 6 loosen, unbind, unlash 8 disunite, unfasten 9 disengage

until: to; til 4 till, unto

untimely: 8 immature 9 premature 11 inopportune 12 unseasonable

untiring: 4 busy 8 sedulous, tireless 13 indefatigable

unto: to 4 till 5 until

untold: 4 vast 9 boundless, unrelated 10 uninformed, unrevealed 12 immeasurable, incalculable

untouchable: 8 chandala 10 intangible

untouched: 6 intact 9 insensate

untoward: 6 unruly 7 awkward, froward, unlucky 8 improper, perverse, stubborn, unseemly 9 vexatious 10 indecorous, ungraceful 11 troublesome, unfavorable, unfortunate 12 inconvenient, unpropitious

untrained: raw 4 wild 5 green 7 awkward, untamed 8 undocile 9 unskilled 10 amateurish, unprepared

untrammeled: 4 free 5 loose 9 unlimited 10 unhampered

untransferable: 11 inalienable

untraversed: 6 untrod

untried: new 5 fresh, green 8 immature 13 inexperienced

untrue: 4 flam 5 false, wrong 8 disloyal 9 erroneous, faithless, incorrect 10 fallacious, unfaithful 11 disaffected

untrustworthy: 6 tricky 8 slippery 9 dishonest, uncertain 10 perfidious 12 undependable

untruth: lie 5 fable 7 falsity 9 falsehood, mendacity, treachery 11 fabrication, tarradiddle

untutored: 5 naive 6 simple 7 artless 8 clownish, ignorant, untaught 9 barbarian, unlearned 10 illiterate 15 unsophisticated

untwine: 5 frese, untie 6 unwind 11 disentangle

untwist: 4 free, open 5 ravel 7 unravel, untwine 8 separate 11 disentangle

Unungun: 5 Aleut

unutterable, inutterable: 7 extreme 9 ineffable 11 unspeakable 13 inexpressible 15 unpronounceable

unused: new 4 idle 5 fresh 8 unwonted 12 unaccustomed

unusual: odd 4 rare 5 novel, queer, weird 6 quaint, unique 7 strange 8 abnormal, uncommon, unwonted 9 anomalous, different, eccentric 10 remarkable 11 exceptional 12 illegitimate 13 extraordinary

unusual person or thing: 4 oner

unvaried: 10 monotonous

unvarnished: 4 bald 5 plain 6 simple 8 unglazed 9 unadorned, unglossed 13 unembellished

unvarying: 7 uniform 8 constant

unveil: 6 reveal 7 uncover 9 disclose

unvitiated: 4 pure 8 pristine

unvoiced: 4 surd 5 tacit 6 secret 9 unuttered

unwarranted: 5 undue 11 unjustified

unwary: 4 rash 7 unaware 8 careless, heedless 9 unguarded 10 groundless 11 precipitate

unwavering: 4 firm 5 solid 6 stable 8 constant 9 steadfast

unwearied: 4 busy 8 tireless 9 assiduous 13 indefatigable

unweave: 4 undo 5 ravel 6 unfold

unwed: 6 single

unwelcome: 8 non grata, unwanted 9 intruding, intrusive

unwell: ill 4 evil, sick 5 badly 6 ailing, wicked

unwholesome: 4 evil 6 impure 7 corrupt, harmful, immoral, noisome, noxious, unclean 11 unhealthful

unwieldy: 5 bulky 6 clumsy 7 awkward, hulking 8 cumbrous, ungainly 9 ponderous 10 cumbersome 12 hippopotamic, unmanageable

unwilling: 4 loth 5 loath 6 averse, mauger, maugre 7 loathly 8 backward 9 eschewing, reluctant 11 disinclined

unwind: 5 ravel 6 uncoil 8 untangle 11 disentangle

unwise: 5 inane 6 simple 7 foolish, witless 9 brainless, impolitic, imprudent, senseless 10 irrational 11 injudicious 12 undiplomatic 13 unintelligent

unwonted: 4 rare 6 unused 7 unusual 8 uncommon 10 infrequent 12 unaccustomed

unworldly: 4 eery 5 eerie, naive, weird 9 spiritual, unearthly

unworthy: 4 base 7 beneath 8 shameful, unseemly 10 despicable, unbecoming 12 contemptible, dishonorable

unwrinkled: 5 brent(Sc.) 6 smooth

unwritten: 4 oral 5 blank, vocal 6 verbal

unwrought: 8 unworked

unyielding: set 4 fast, firm, grim, hard, iron 5 rigid, stern, stiff, stith, stony 6 frozen, steely 7 adamant 8 obdurate, stubborn 9 inelastic, obstinate, unbending 10 determined, immaleable, inexorable, relentless 12 contumacious, unsubmissive 14 uncompromising

unyoke: 4 free, part 5 loose 6 remove 7 disjoin, release 8 separate 10 disconnect

up: 4 busy, rise 5 aloft, astir, raise 6 active 7 success 9 according

up and down: 5 erect 6 direct, uneven 7 upright 8 vertical 9 downright, irregular 10 undulating 13 perpendicular

up to: 5 until

date: new 6 modern 7 stylish 11 fashionable

this time: 6 hereto 8 hitherto

Upanishad: 4 Isha

upas tree gum: 6 antiar

upbraid: 4 draw, twit 5 abuse, blame, braid, chide, scold, score, taunt, twist 6 accuse, charge 7 censure, reprove 8 denounce, reproach 9 exprobate 10 denunciate

upbuilding: 8 increase 11 edification

Updike novel: 7 Centaur, Couples

upeygan: 6 borele 10 rhinoceros

upgrade: 5 raise, slope 6 ascent 7 incline

upheavel: 5 storm 6 revolt 7 rummage 9 agitation, cataclysm, commotion

upheave: 4 lift, rear, rise

uphill: 6 rising, tiring 9 ascending, difficult, laborious

uphold: aid 4 abet, back, bear, stay 5 favor, raise 6 assert, defend, favour, second 7 confirm, support, sustain 8 conserve, maintain 9 encourage 11 countenance

upholder: 6 dealer 8 adherent 9 tradesman 10 undertaker 11 upholsterer

upholstered: 9 cushioned

upholstering material: 6 damask, lampas, mohair 7 valance 8 tapestry

upkeep: 4 cost 6 repair 7 support 8 maintain 11 maintenance

upland: 4 wold 6 coteau 7 plateau

uplift: 4 head, lift, rock 5 erect, raise, tower 7 collect, improve 8 elevated, ennobled, upheaval 9 elevation

Upolu: *city:* 4 Apia

island group: 5 Samoa

upon: on; oer, sur(law) 4 atop 5 about, above 8 touching 10 concerning

prefix: ep; epi

that: 7 thereat 9 thereupon

which: 7 whereat 9 whereupon

upper: 4 bunk, over, vamp 5 above, berth 8 superior

upper case: 7 capital

upper crust: 5 elite 7 segment

upper lips part: 5 flews

upperclassman: 6 junior, senior

uppermost: 5 first 6 upmost, uptown 7 topmost 8 farthest, foremost 9 outermost 11 predominant

uppish: 5 proud 6 elated 7 haughty, peevish 8 arrogant, assuming, snobbish

upraised: 5 atilt 6 lifted, raised 7 erected 8 elevated, extolled, improved 10 encouraged

uprear: 5 erect, exalt, raise

upright: 4 good, just, true 5 erect, moral, piano, right, stela, stele, stile 6 honest, square 7 endwise, sincere 8 straight, vertical, virtuous 9 elevation, equitable, honorable, righteous 10 pianoforte, scrupulous 11 unambiguous 13 perpendicular

comb. form: 5 ortho

support: 4 jamb, stud

uprightness: 9 rectitude

uprising: 4 riot 6 ascent, mutiny, putsch, revolt 7 ensuing 8 reaction 9 ascending, commotion, rebellion 10 increasing, insurgency, revolution 12 insurrection 17 counterrevolution

uproar: din 4 riot, rout 5 brawl, hurly, noise 6 bedlam, bustle, clamor, dirdum, fracas, habble, hubble, hubbub, rattle, tumult 7 clamour, ferment, turmoil 8 outbreak 9 commotion, confusion 10 convulsion, donnybrook, hurlyburly, rumbullion, tintamarre 11 disturbance, pandemonium

uproot: 8 supplant 9 eradicate, extirpate 11 exterminate

upscuddle: 7 quarrel

upset: irk 4 cave, coup, keel, rile 6 defeat, refund, topple 7 capsize, confuse, derange, disturb, outcome, pervert, quarrel, reverse, subvert 8 capsized, overturn 9 discomfit, embarrass, overthrow, perturbed 10 discompose, disconcert, disordered, distressed, overturned 11 disorganize

upshot: end 5 issue, limit 6 result, sequel 7 outcome 10 conclusion 11 termination 12 consummation

upside: top

upstage: shy 5 aloof 6 offish 8 backward, outshine, snobbish 9 conceited 12 supercilious

upstart: 4 snob 6 origin 7 dalteen, parvenu, saffron 8 parvenue 9 cockhorse

upstir: 6 incite 7 agitate 9 stimulate

upsurge: 4 boom 9 inflation

uptake: 4 flue, tube 5 shaft 6 upcast 10 collection, comprehend 13 comprehension, understanding

upupoid bird: 6 hoopoe

upward: 4 more, over 5 above, lofty 7 airward, skyward 8 airwards 9 ascending
comb. form: ano

uraeus: asp 10 decoration

uralite: 9 amphibole

Urania's son: 5 Hymen

uranian: 6 uranic 8 heavenly 9 celestial 12 astronomical

uranium dioxide: 10 ianthinite

Uranus: *children:* 4 Rhea 5 Titan 7 Cyclops
moon: 5 Ariel 6 Oberon 7 Titania, Umbriel
mother: Ge 4 Gaea, Gaia
satellite: 5 Ariel
wife: Ge 4 Gaea, Gaia

urare: rat 6 curare

urban: 5 civic 7 oppidan

urban division: 4 ward

urbane: 5 bland, civil, suave 6 polite, smooth 7 affable, elegant, refined 8 polished 9 courteous 13 sophisticated

urbanity: 6 comity 12 complaisance

urchin: boy, elf, imp, tad 4 arab, brat 5 child, elfin, gamin 8 cylinder, hedgehog, hurcheon 9 dandiprat, hunchback, youngster

ure: use 4 haze, mist 6 custom 8 exercise, practice

urease: 6 enzyme

uredo: 5 hives 9 urticaria

Urfa: 6 Edessa

urge: dun, egg, ert(Sc.), hie, ply, sue 4 brod, coax, goad, prod, push, spur 5 broad, drive, filip, force, hurry, impel, plead, press 6 allege, compel, demand, desire, excite, exhort, fillip, incite, induce, insist 7 animate, augment, commove, entreat, impulse, provoke, solicit 8 advocate, persuade 9 flagitate, importune, influence, prosecute, stimulate 10 exasperate

urgency: 4 need 5 haste, hurry 6 crisis, stress 8 exigency, pressure 10 insistence 11 importunity

urgent: hot 5 grave 7 clamant, exigent 8 critical, pressing 9 important 10 solicitous 11 importunate

Uriah's wife: 9 Bathsheba

urial, oorial: sha 5 sheep

Uriel: 5 angel 9 archangel

Urim's partner: 7 Thummim

Uris novel: 5 QBVII 6 Exodus

urisk: 7 brownie

urn: jar, run 4 bury, ewer, urna, vase 5 grave, inurn, steen, theca 6 spring 7 capsule, cistern, pitcher, samovar, vaselet 8 fountain 9 container 10 jardiniere 11 watercourse
for bones: 7 ossuary
tea: 7 samovar

urn-shaped: 9 urceolate

Urne-Buriall author: 6 Browne

urodela: 5 newts, order 7 Caudata 8 amphibia 10 salamander

Ursa: 4 Bear

ursine: 6 ursoid 8 bearlike

ursine baboon: 6 chacma

ursoid: 6 ursine 8 bearlike

Urth: 4 Norn

urticaria: 5 hives, uredo

urubu: 7 vulture

Uruguay: *city:* 4 Melo 5 Minas 6 Rivera 7 Durazno, Florida 8 Paysandu 9 Maldonado 10 Montevideo
coin: 4 peso 9 centesimo
estuary: 5 Plata
lake: 5 Merin, Mirim
measure: 4 vara 6 cuadra, suerte
river: 4 Malo 5 Negro 6 Ulimar 7 Uruguay 9 Cebollary 10 Tacaurembo
weight: 7 quintal

urus: ox; tur 7 aurochs

us: uns(Gr.) 4 nous(Fr.)

usable: fit 8 servable 9 available, practical 10 convenient, functional 11 serviceable, utilitarian

usage: use 4 wont 5 habit, haunt, idiom 6 custom, method 7 conduct, manners, utility 8 behavior, interest, practice 9 treatment 10 convention, employment, experience

usance: use 5 usage, usury 6 custom, income

use: try 4 boot, hire, vail, wont 5 apply, avail, guide, habit, right, spend, stead, treat, trope, usage, value, wield 6 behoof, custom, employ, expend, handle, hansel, occupy 7 benefit, consume, exhaust, exploit, utility, utilize 8 accustom, exercise, frequent, function, handling, practice 9

habituate, privilege, treatment 10 employment, manipulate 11 application, consumption, utilization
as example: 4 cite
refrain from: 7 boycott
to be of: 5 avail
up: eat 4 tire 5 spend 7 consume, deplete, exhaust, outwear
wastefully: 7 fritter 8 squander 9 dissipate
used: 10 secondhand 11 experienced
useful: 4 good 5 utile 7 helpful 9 practical 10 beneficial, commodious, profitable 11 serviceable 12 advantageous
usefulness: 5 avail, value 6 profit 7 utility
useless: 4 idle, null, vain 6 futile, otiose 7 inutile 8 bootless, hopeless 9 fruitless, worthless 11 ineffectual, inefficient, superfluous 12 unprofitable 13 unserviceable 14 good-for-nothing
user: 4 usee 8 consumer
usher: 4 lead, page 5 guide 6 beadle, escort, herald 7 chobdar, conduct, officer, precede, preface, servant, teacher 9 announcer, assistant, attendant, harbinger, introduce, precursor 10 doorkeeper, forerunner, inaugurate
usings: 8 property 10 belongings
usquebaugh: 6 whisky 7 cordial, whiskey
U.S.S.R.: See **Union of Soviet Socialist Republics**
ustion: 7 burning 13 cauterization
usual: 6 common, normal, wonted 7 average, general, regular, typical 8 familiar, frequent, habitual, ordinary, orthodox 9 customary 10 accustomed, prevailing 11 stereotyped 12 conventional
usurer: 5 shark 6 loaner 11 moneylender
usurp: 4 take 5 seize 6 assume 8 accroach, arrogate
usury: 7 gombeen
Utah: *lake:* 4 Salt, Swan, Utah 6 Sevier
mountain range: 5 Uinta 7 Wasatch
resident: 6 Mormon
river: 5 Grand, Green, Weber 6 Jordan, Sevier 8 Colorado
state tree: 6 spruce
state flower: 4 sego
town: 4 Lehi 5 Delta, Heber, Kanab, Logan, Ogden, Provo 6 Beaver, Eureka, Payson, Tooele 7 Milford 9 Richfield
utensil: pan, pot 4 tool 5 sieve 6 grater, vessel 7 skillet 8 strainer 9 collander, imple-

ment 10 instrument
cleaning: mop 5 broom, brush 6 Hoover, ramrod, vacuum 7 Bissell, sweeper
utensils: 7 baggage
Uther's son: 6 Arthur
utile: 6 useful 9 practical 10 profitable 12 advantageous
utilitarian: 5 plain 6 useful 8 economic 9 practical 10 functional 12 matter-of-fact
utility: use 5 avail 6 profit 7 benefit, service
utilize: use 6 employ 9 economize
utmost: end 4 best, last 5 final 7 extreme 8 farthest, greatest 9 uttermost
Uto-Aztecan Indian: 4 Pima 7 Nahuatl 8 Shoshone
Utopia: 4 Eden 9 Shangri La
author: 4 More
Harrington's: 6 Oceana
Utopian: 5 ideal 8 idealist, Quixotic 9 visionary 10 chimerical
utricle: sac 7 vesicle
Uttar Pradesh capital: 7 Lucknow
utter: add, say 4 blat, bray, emit, gasp, pipe, pray, rail, roar, tell, vent 5 blurt, clack, croak, drawl, final, issue, mince, sheer, speak, spill, spout, trill, stark, state, total, voice 6 assert, direct, entire, mumble, reveal, warble 7 bluster, deliver, divulge, enounce, express, extreme, iterate, publish 8 abnormal, absolute, complete, disclose 9 enunciate, pronounce 10 articulate, peremptory 11 unqualified 13 unconditional
utterance: gab 4 osse.5 aside, dicta, ditty 6 dictum, oracle, speech 7 calling 8 effusion, monotone, phonesis, rhapsody 9 phonation 10 expression, forthgoing 12 articulation
soft: 6 breath, murmur 7 whisper
voiced: 6 sonant
voiceless: 4 surd 7 spirate
uttered: 4 oral 5 spake
utterly: 5 fully, stark 6 merely 7 totally 8 entirely 10 absolutely, allutterly, completely 11 diametrally 13 diametrically 17 straightforwardly
uttermost: 5 final 6 utmost 7 extreme, outmost
utu: 6 reward 12 compensation, satisfaction
uva: 5 fruit, grape
ux: 4 uxor(L.), wife
uxorial: 6 wifely
Uzbek capital: 8 Tashkent

V

V: vee **4** five
symbol of: **7** victory
V-shaped piece: **5** wedge
vacancy: gap **5** break, chasm, space **6** cavity, hollow **7** interim, vacuity **10** hollowness, interstice **11** vacuousness
vacant: **4** free, idle, open, void **5** blank, empty, fishy, inane, silly **6** barren, devoid, hollow, lonely **7** foolish, lacking, leisure, vacuous, wanting **8** unfilled **9** destitute **10** disengaged, unemployed, unoccupied, untenanted **12** unencumbered, unreflecting **14** expressionless
vacate: **4** quit, void **5** annul, avoid, empty, leave **7** abandon, abolish **8** abdicate, abrogate, evacuate
vacation: **4** rest **5** leave, spell **6** outing, recess **7** holiday, leisure, nonterm, respite **8** furlough **9** justitium **12** intermission
place: spa **4** city, lake, park **5** beach **6** forest, resort **7** seaside **9** mountains
vacationist: **6** camper **7** tourist
vaccinate: **9** inoculate
vaccination: *inventor:* **6** Jenner
vaccine: **4** sera **5** serum
discoverer of: **4** Salk **6** Jenner
vacillate: **4** sway **5** waver **6** dacker, daiker, seesaw, teeter, totter **7** flutter, stagger **8** hesitate, titubate **9** fluctuate, oscillate
vacillation: **5** doubt **7** halting, swaying **8** wavering **9** faltering, hesitancy, infirmity **10** fickleness, indecision, unsureness **11** uncertainty **12** irresolution **14** changeableness
vacuity: **7** inanity, vacancy
vacuous: **4** dull, idle **5** blank, empty **6** stupid **8** unfilled **9** evacuated, senseless **11** purposeless **13** unintelligent
vacuum: **4** void
opposite of: **6** plenum
vacuum tube: **5** diode **7** tetrode **9** electrode
vacuum pump: **10** pulsometer
vade mecum: **6** manual **8** handbook
vadimonium: **4** bond **6** pledge **8** contract, security

vadium: **4** bail, pawn **6** pledge
vagabond: vag **4** rove **5** scamp **6** beggar, canter, jockey, rascal **7** erratic, gadling, nomadic, vagrant, wayward **8** bohemian, brodyaga, drifting, fugitive, wanderer **9** shiftless, straggler, wandering, worthless **10** blackguard, ne'er-do-well **12** hallanshaker **14** good-for-nothing
vagarious: **7** erratic **13** unpredictable
vagary: **4** roam, whim **5** caper, fancy, freak, jaunt, prank, stray, trick, waver **6** action, breach, notion, oddity, ramble, totter, whimsy **7** caprice, conceit **8** flagarie, rambling **9** departure, excursion, procedure, wandering **10** digression, divergence **13** manifestation
vagrant: bum, vag **4** hobo, prog **5** caird, rogue, tramp **6** arrant, roving, shuler, truant, vagrom **7** devious, drifter, nomadic, prowler, roaming, shuiler **8** brodyaga, vagabond **9** itinerant **10** capricious, circuitous **11** extravagant
vague: dim **4** dark, hazy **5** loose, misty, stray **6** dreamy, vagary **7** obscure, shadowy, sketchy, unfixed, vagrant **8** confused, nebulous, vagabond, wanderer **9** ambiguous, uncertain, unsettled, wandering **10** ill-defined, indefinite, indistinct, intangible **13** indeterminate
vail: tip, use **4** doff, dole, veil **5** avail, bribe, lower, yield **6** humble, profit, return, submit **7** benefit, decline, descend, descent, subside **8** downflow, gratuity, proceeds **9** advantage **10** beneficial, profitable **12** advantageous
vain: **4** idle **5** empty, flory, petty, proud, silly **6** flimsy, futile, hollow, otiose, snooty **7** foolish, stuckup, trivial, useless **8** gorgeous, hopeless, ignorant, nugatory **9** conceited, emptiness, fruitless, frustrate, unfounded, worthless **10** chimerical, evanescent, unavailing, unrewarded **11** empty-headed, ineffectual, overweening, unimportant **12** unprofitable, vainglorious

vain boasting: 11 fanfaronade
vain person: fop 5 dandy 7 coxcomb
vainglorious: 4 vain 8 boastful 9 selfproud
vair: fur
Vaishnavas: *deity:* 6 Vishnu
 priest: 6 gosain, gusain
Vaisya caste: 6 Aroras
vakass: 5 amice
valance: 5 drape 6 pelmet 7 curtain, drapery, hanging
vale: 4 dale, dean, dell, dene, glen 5 bache, glade 6 dingle, valley 8 farewell
valediction: 5 adieu 7 address 8 farewell
Valence's river: 5 Rhone
valency: 5 power, value 10 importance
valentine: 4 card, gift, love 8 greeting
valerian: 4 drug 5 plant 7 allheal, panacea, setwall
valet: man 4 goad 5 stick 6 andrew, tartar 7 dresser 9 attendant, cameriere, chamberer 10 manservant
Vali's mother: 4 Rind 5 Rindr
valiant: 4 bold, prow 5 aught, brave, proud 6 heroic, robust, strong, sturdy 7 doughty 8 galliard, intrepid, powerful, stalwart, vigorous, virtuous 9 bounteous, excellent, steadfast 10 chivalrous, courageous 11 meritorious 12 stouthearted
valid: 4 good, just, true 5 legal, sound 6 cogent, lawful, robust, strong 7 binding, healthy, telling, weighty 8 forcible, powerful 9 authentic, effective, efficient 10 conclusive, convincing, sufficient 11 efficacious 12 well-grounded
 opposite of: 4 null, void
validate: 7 confirm 9 establish
valise: bag 4 case, grip 7 baggage 8 suitcase
Valjean: *discoverer:* 6 Javert
 friend: 6 Marius
 protege: 7 Cosette
Valkyrie: 8 Brynhild 10 Brunnhilde
vallecula: 6 furrow, groove 7 channel 10 depression
Valletta people: 7 Maltese
valley: dip 4 brae, comb, coom, cove, dale, dean, dell, dene, ghyl, gill, glen, rill, vale, wadi, wady 5 atrio, basin, combe, coomb, dhoon, glack, gorge, goyal, goyle, gully, kloof, swale, waddy 6 bolson, canada, canyon, clough, coombe, coulee, dingle, gutter, hollow, ravine, rincon, strath, trough 7 blowout 10 depression
 between volcanic cones: 5 atrio
 deep: 5 canon 6 canyon
vallum: 4 wall 7 rampart
valor, valour: 5 arete, merit, value, worth 6 bounty, virtue 7 bravery, courage, heroism, prowess 8 position 9 valuation 10 importance 11 distinction 12 fearlessness 13 signification
valuable: 4 dear 5 asset 6 costly, prized, useful, worthy 8 precious 9 estimable, excellent, treasured 10 worthwhile 11 serviceable
valuable discovery: 4 find
value: use 4 cost, feck(Sc.), rate 5 avail, cheap, price, prize, worth 6 assess, assize, esteem, extend, moment 7 account, apprise, apprize, average, cherish, compute, opinion, respect, utility 8 appraise, estimate, evaluate, treasure 9 inventory, valuation 10 appreciate, estimation, importance
 anything of little: 5 plack(Sc.) 6 trifle
 equal: 6 parity
 mathematical limit of: 8 derivate
 mean: 7 average
 net: 7 reserve
 nominal: par
 reduction: 12 depreciation
valued: 4 dear
valve: tap 4 cock, gate 6 faucet, outlet, piston, spigot 7 petcock
 heart: 6 mitral
 sliding: 6 piston
vamoose: lam 4 scat 5 leave, scram 6 decamp, depart
vamp: 4 hose, plod, sock 5 patch, tramp 6 invent, repair, seduce 7 beguile, concoct, fireman 9 fabricate, improvise
vampire: bat 5 lamia 6 alukah, corpse, usurer 7 seducer 11 blackmailer, bloodsucker, extortioner 12 extortionist
 famous: 7 Dracula
van: fan 4 fore, lead, wing 5 front, truck, wagon 6 shovel, summit, winnow 7 fourgon, vehicle 9 forefront
Van Gogh town: 5 Arles
vandal: hun 9 plunderer
vandalize: mar 6 deface
Vandyke: 5 beard 6 artist 7 picture
vane: arm 5 blade 7 feather 11 weathercock
 feather: web 8 vexillum
vanguard: 10 avantgarde
vanilla substance: 8 coumarin
vanish: 4 fade, melt 8 disperse, evanesce 9 disappear
vanity (see also **vain**): 4 airs 5 pride 6 egoism 7 compact, conceit, egotism, falsity 8 futility, idleness 9 dizziness, emptiness 10 hollowness 11 fatuousness, foolishness, self-conceit
 symbol of: 7 peacock
vanity case: 4 etui 7 compact
Vanity Fair character: 5 Becky 6 Amelia
vanquish: get, win 4 beat, best, rout 5 expel, floor 6 defeat, expugn, master, subdue 7

confute, conquer **8** confound, overcome, suppress, surmount **9** overthrow

vanquisher: **6** victor

vantage: fee **4** gain **6** chance, profit **9** advantage **10** perquisite **11** opportunity, superiority

place of: **5** coign **6** coigne

vapid: dry **4** dull, flat, pall **5** inane, stale, trite **7** insipid, mawkish **8** lifeless **9** pointless, tasteless **10** flavorless, spiritless, unanimated, unexciting **13** uninteresting

vapor: fog, gas **4** fume, haze, idea, mist **5** boast, brume, cloud, ewder, fancy, humor, smoke, steam **6** breath, bubble, humour, nimbus, notion **7** halitus **8** contrail, humidity, phantasm **9** evaporate **10** blustering **11** braggadocio

comb. form: atm **4** atmo

frozen: **4** hail, rime, snow **5** frost, sleet

pressure indicator: **9** tonometer

vaporizable: **8** volatile

vaporize: **5** steam **9** evaporate

vaporous: **8** fleeting **13** unsubstantial

vaquero: **6** cowboy **8** herdsman, horseman **10** equestrian

varec, varech: **4** kelp **7** seaweed

variable (see also **vary**): **6** fickle, fitful **7** protean, unequal, variant, varying **8** floating, unstable, unsteady **9** irregular, uncertain **10** capricious, inconstant

variance (see also **vary**): **7** discord, dispute **10** contention **11** discrepancy

variate: **4** vary **6** varied **8** variable

variation (see also **vary**): **7** variety **8** heterism, mutation **9** tolerance **10** aberration, deflection **11** distinction

varicolored: **6** varied **7** mottled **11** diversified

varicose: **7** dilated, swollen **8** enlarged

varied: **6** daedal **7** several, various **10** variegated

variegate: **9** diversify

variegated: **4** pied, shot **5** lyard(Sc.), lyart(Sc.) **6** daedal, menald, motley, varied **7** dappled, flecked, mottled, painted, piebald, tissued **8** speckled **9** different, enamelled **11** diversified

variety: **4** kind, sort **5** breed, class **7** species **9** diversity, variation **10** difference **16** multifariousness

variola: **6** cowpox **8** horsepox, smallpox

various: **4** many **6** divers, sundry **7** diverse, several **8** manifold, variable **9** different, uncertain, versatile **10** changeable, inconstant

varlet: boy **4** page **5** gippo, knave, noble, youth **6** menial, rabble, rascal, vassal **7** bailiff, footman, servant **8** coistrel, coistril **9** attendant, scoundrel

varmint, varment: **5** sharp **6** clever **7** amateur, cunning, dashing **8** sporting

varnish: **4** spar **5** japan **7** lacquer **8** brighten **9** embellish

ingredient: lac **5** copal, elemi, resin, rosin **6** dammar

vary: **5** alter, range, shift **6** change, depart, differ, modify, swerve **7** deviate, dispute, dissent, diverge, quarrel, variate **8** disagree **9** alternate, diversify, fluctuate, oscillate

vas: **4** duct **6** pledge, surety, vessel

vase: jar, urn **4** asci, vaso **5** ascus, askos, echea, tazza **6** crater, deinoi, deinos, krater **7** amphora **8** amphorae **10** cassolette, jardiniere

handle: **4** ansa

vassal: man **4** bond, esne, rule, serf **5** ceile, helot, liege, slave **6** varlet **7** bondman, feedman, feodary, geneate, homager, servant, servile, subject **8** dominate **9** dependent, feudatory **11** beneficiary, subordinate, subservient

pert. to: **6** feudal

vassalage: **5** valor **6** fealty, homage **7** courage, loyalty, prowess **8** dominion, services **9** authority, servitude

vast: **4** huge **5** broad, great, large, vasty **6** cosmic, lonely, mighty, untold **7** immense **8** colossal, enormous, gigantic, spacious **9** boundless, cyclopean, extensive **11** farreaching, illimitable

vastness: **7** expanse **8** grandeur **9** magnitude

vat (see also **barrel, tub, vessel**): bac, fat, pit, tub, tun, wit **4** back, beck, cask, coom, gyle, keel, kier, tank **5** coomb, keeve, kieve, press **6** barrel, kettle, vessel **7** caldron, chessel, cistern **8** cauldron, chessart

bleaching: **4** keir, kier

vatic: **8** inspired, oracular **9** prophetic **11** prophetical

Vatican: *chapel:* **7** Sistine

guards' nationality: **5** Swiss

official: **6** datary

statuary group: **7** Laocoon

vaticanism: **9** curialism

vaticinate: **8** foretell

vaticinator: **4** seer **7** prophet

vaudeville: **5** revue

act: **4** skit, song, turn **5** dance

vaudevillist: **5** actor **6** dancer, hoofer, singer **7** acrobat, juggler **9** performer

vaudy: gay **5** gaudy, showy **6** elated, sturdy **8** cheerful

vault: box, pit **4** arch, bend, cave, cope, dome, jump, leap, over, roof, room, safe, tomb **5** bound, croft, crypt, curve, floor, groin, shade **6** cavern, cellar, crater, cupola, curvet, flaunt, grotto, hurdle, spring, welkin **7** ceiling, chamber, dungeon, glorify, testudo **8** flourish **9** concavity, staircase **10** depository, repository, testudines(pl.)

vaunt: van **4** brag, font **5** boast, roosa, roose **6** avaunt **11** ostentation

vaunty: 4 vain **5** brave, proud

veal: 4 calf, meat, veau(F.)
cutlet: **9** schnitzel
larded: **8** fricando **10** fricandeau

vector: 4 host **7** carrier
opposite of: **6** scalar

vedette: 5 vigil, watch **8** sentinel

Vedic: *artisans of gods:* **6** Ribhus
cosmic order: **4** Rita
fire god: **4** Agni
god: **6** Aditya
hymn: **6** mantra
language: **4** Pali **8** Sanskrit
sky serpent: ahi
sun god: **7** Savitar
text: **5** Sakha, Shaka

veer: yaw **4** slue, sway, turn **5** alter, shift **6** broach, careen, change, swerve **7** deviate, digress **9** fluctuate

veery: 6 thrush

vega: 5 tract **6** meadow

Vega's constellation: 4 Lyra

vegetable: pea, yam **4** bean, beet, corn, kale, leak, ocra, okra, soya **5** onion, pease, plant **6** carrot, celery, lentil, pepper, potato, radish, squash, tomato, turnip **7** brocoli, cabbage, lettuce, parsley, parsnip, peascod, rhubarb, spinach **8** broccoli, cucumber, eggplant, peasecod, rutabaga **9** artichoke **11** cauliflower **15** Brussels sprouts
carbonized: **7** lignite
dealer: **8** huckster **11** greengrocer **12** costermonger
decayed: **4** duff **5** humus
dish: **6** zimmis **10** chiffonade
esculent: **6** legume
exudation: lac, sap **5** resin
ferment: **5** yeast
green: **5** sabzi
grown for sale: **5** truck
oil: **8** macassar
onionlike: **4** leek **7** shallot
pepsin: **6** caroid
pod: **4** hull **8** peasecod
poison: **5** abrin
purple: **8** eggplant
rubbish: **5** wrack
salad: **4** leak **5** chard **6** endive **7** lettuce, romaine, shallot **8** scallion
sponge: **5** loofa **6** loofah
stunted: **5** scrub
sugar-yielding: **4** beet
tinder: **6** amadou

vegetable caterpillar: 5 aweto

vegetable pear: 7 chayote

vegetant: 7 vegetal **9** animating **12** invigorating

vegetation: 6 growth **7** verdure
floating: **4** sadd, sudd
god: **4** Atys, Esus **5** Attis

vegete: 6 lively **7** healthy **11** flourishing

vehement: hot **5** angry, eager, fiery, hefty, irked, yeder **6** ardent, fervid, flashy, heated, raging, urgent **7** animose, animous, fervent, furioso, furious, intense, violent **8** forceful, vigorous **9** impetuous **10** boisterous, passionate

vehemently: 5 amain

vehicle (see also **aircraft, ship**): ark, bus, car, van **4** auto, shay, wain **5** araba, brake, break, buggy, dilly, sedan, sulky, wagon **6** barrow, charet, device, hansom, landau, troika **7** chariot, kibitka(Russ.), tallyho **8** carriage, charette **9** buckboard, velociman **10** automobile, conveyance
army: **4** jeep, tank **9** ambulance
child's: **4** pram **5** buggy **6** walker **7** scooter **8** carriage, stroller, tricycle **10** velocipede
display: **5** float
hauling: van **4** dray, lory, sled **5** truck **7** tractor, trailer
parade: **5** float
passenger: bus, cab **4** hack, taxi, tram **5** train **6** hansom **7** minibus, omnibus, tramcar, trolley **9** charabanc
public: bus, cab, car **4** taxi, tram **5** train **7** omnibus, ricksha **8** rickshaw **10** jinricksha, jinrikisha
snow: **4** pung, sled **6** sleigh
two-wheeled: **4** cart **5** sulky, tonga **6** cisium **7** bicycle, caleche **9** carromata(Fil.) **11** vinaigrette
wheelless: **4** ship, sled **6** cutter, sledge, sleigh

veil: dim **4** caul, film, hide, mask **5** cloak, cover, orale, velum, volet **6** bumble, fannel, masque, screen, shroud, soften **7** conceal, curtain, watcher **8** calyptra, disguise, headrail **11** amphithyron
head: **4** caul
in botany: **5** velum

veiling: 4 veil **5** tulle, voile **7** curtain **10** obvelation

vein: bed, rib **4** dash, hilo, lode, mood, seam, tang, vena, wave **5** costa, crack, scrin, shade, smack, spice, tinge, touch, trend, venae **6** cavity, costae, strain, streak **7** bonanza, channel, crevice, fissure, stratum **8** tendency **11** inclination, variegation
arrangement of: **9** neuration
enlarged: **5** varix
fluid: **4** icor **5** ichor

inflammation: 9 phlebitis
leaf: rib
mining: 4 lode
pert. to: 6 veinal, venous
small: 6 venule 7 veinlet, veinule 8 veinulet
throat: 7 jugular
veinless: 7 avenous
veinstone: 6 gangue, matrix 9 lodestuff
velamen: 5 velum 8 membrane
velar: 7 palatal 8 guttural
velarium: 4 veil 6 awning 8 covering
veldt, veld: 6 meadow, plains 9 grassland
velitation: 7 contest, dispute 8 skirmish
velleity: 4 hope, wish 6 desire 8 volition 11
    inclination
vellicate: nip 4 pull 5 pinch, pluck 6 tickle,
    twitch 9 titillate
veloce: 7 dashing, rapidly 9 direction
velocious: 4 fast 6 speedy
velocipede: 4 ride 7 bicycle, dicycle 8 tricy-
    cle 11 quadricycle
velocity: 4 pace 5 speed 8 celerity, rapidity
    9 quickness, swiftness
    instrument: 11 cinemograph
velum: 4 veil 6 awning, palate 8 membrane
velutinous: 7 velvety
velvet: 4 gain 5 drink 6 birodo(Jap.), profit
    7 surplus 8 winnings
    fabric like: 5 panne 6 velure
    knife: 6 trevet
velvet dock: 6 mullen 7 mullein 10 elecam-
    pane
velvetbreast: 9 merganser
venal: 6 venous 7 corrupt, salable 8 saleable,
    vendible 9 mercenary
vend: 4 hawk, sell 5 utter 6 market, peddle
    7 publish 8 transfer
vendetta: 4 feud
vendeuse: 9 salesgirl 10 saleswoman
vendible: 5 venal 7 salable 8 saleable 9 mer-
    cenary 10 marketable
vendition: 4 sale
vendor, vender: 6 seller 7 alienor, butcher
    8 merchant, salesman
vendue: 4 sale 7 auction
veneer: lac 4 coat, face, show 5 glaze, gloss,
    layer, plate 6 enamel, facing 7 overlay
venenate: 6 poison 8 poisoned 9 poisonous
venerable: old 4 aged, hoar, sage 5 hoary 6
    august 7 ancient, antique, classic
veneration: awe 4 fear 6 esteem 7 respect,
    worship 8 devotion, idolatry 9 adoration,
    reverence
    of saints and angels: 5 dulia
venerer: 6 hunter 8 huntsman
venery: 5 chase 7 hunting
Venetian: See Italy, Venice
Venezuela: *city:* 4 Aroa, Coro 6 Atures,
    Cumana 7 Barinas, Caracas(c.), Guanare,
    Maracay, Maturin, Ocumare, San Juan 8

Tacupita, Trujillo, Valencia 9 Barcelona,
Los Teques, San Carlos, San Filepe 10 La
Asuncion 11 San Fernando 12 Barquisi-
meto, San Cristobal
coin: 4 real 5 medio 6 fuerte 7 bolivar, cen-
    timo 8 morocota 10 venezolano
dam: 4 Guri
fiber: 5 erizo
Indian: 6 Timote
lake: 9 Maracaibo, Tacarigua
language: 4 Pume 7 Spanish
measure: 5 galon, milla 6 fanega 7 estadel
measure of weight: bag 5 libra
mountain: 5 Andes, Icutu 6 Concha,
    Cuneva, Parima 7 Imutaca, Roraima 9
    Pacaraima 20 Sierra-Nevada-de-Merida
patriot: 7 Bolivar
people: 5 Carib 6 Timote 7 Timotex 8
    Guarauno
plain: 5 llano
port: 8 La Guayra 9 Maracaibo 13 Ciudad
    Bolivar, Puerto-Cabello
revolutionist: 7 Miranda
river: 5 Apure, Caura 6 Arausa, Caroni 7
    Orinoco, Ventuar
snake: 4 lora
state: 4 Lara 5 Apure, Sucre, Zulia 6 Ara-
    gua, Falcon, Merida, Zamora 7 Bolivar,
    Cojedes, Guarico, Monagas, Tachira,
    Yaracuy 8 Carabobo, Trujillo 10 An-
    zoategui, Portuguesa 12 Nueva Esparta
tree: 6 balata
vengeance: 5 wrack 6 wanion 7 revenge 8
    reprisal, requital 10 punishment 11 retali-
    ation, retribution
    god of: 6 Erinys 7 Alastor
    goddess of: Ara, Ate 7 Nemesis
venial: 7 trivial 9 allowable, excusable, tol-
    erable 10 pardonable 13 insignificant 15
    unobjectionable
Venice: *beach:* 4 Lido
    boat: 7 gondola 9 bucentaur
    bridge: 6 Rialto
    coin: 5 betso, bezzo, ducat 6 sequin 8
        bagatino, gazzetta
    court: 8 quaranty
    district: 6 Rialto
    island: 6 Rialto
    magistrate: 4 doge
    medal: 5 osela, osele 6 osella, oselle 7 os-
        cella
    old silver coin: 5 betso
    painter: 6 Titian 7 Bellini 8 Veronese 9 Gi-
        orgione 10 Tintoretto
    resort: 4 Lido
    river: 6 Brenta
    traveler and writer: 5 Conti 9 Marco Polo
    wine measure: 6 anfora
Venice of the North: 9 Stockholm

venin: 6 poison

venireman: 5 juror

venison: 7 pemican 8 pemmican

vennel: 4 lane 5 alley, sewer 6 gutter

venomous: 5 snaky, toxic 6 attern, deadly 7 baneful, noxious 8 poisoned, spiteful, virulent 9 envenomed, malicious, malignant, poisonous, rancorous 11 mischievous

vent: 4 draw, emit, exit, hole, slit 5 brand, eject 6 cancel, outlet, report 7 fissure, opening, release 8 aperture, avacuate, disgorge, emission 9 discharge, embrasure 10 escapement

ventilate: air, fan 6 aerate, aerify, winnow 9 oxygenate

ventilation: 6 aerage 9 breathing

ventilator: 6 blinds, louver

ventral: 7 sternal

ventriloquist: 12 engastrimyth 13 gastriloquist

venture: hap, try 4 dare, luck, risk, wage 5 brave, essay, stake 6 chance, danger, feeler, hazard 7 attempt, courage, flutter, fortune, risking 8 trespass 9 adventure, speculate 10 enterprise 11 contingency, presumption, speculation, undertaking

ventured: 5 durst

venturesome: 4 bold, rash 5 hardy 6 heroic 8 fearless, heedless, reckless 9 audacious, dangerous, foolhardy, hazardous, venturous 11 adventurous, furthersome, temerarious

venturesomeness: 8 temerity

venturous: 11 venturesome

venue: hit 4 bout, site 5 lunge, match, onset 6 coming, ground, thrust 7 arrival, assault 9 encounter

Venus: 6 Hesper, Vesper 8 Hesperus
  as morning star: 7 Lucifer
  girdle: 6 cestus
  island: 5 Melos
  mother: 5 Dione
  son: 5 Cupid
  sweetheart: 6 Adonis
  tree sacred to: 6 myrtle

Venus flytrap: 5 plant 7 dionaea

venust: 6 comely 7 elegant 8 graceful 9 beautiful

veracious: 9 measuring, veridical 10 estimating

veracity: 5 truth 7 honesty 8 accuracy, trueness 9 judgement, precision, sincerity 11 correctness 12 faithfulness, truthfulness

veranda: 5 lanai, porch, stoep 6 loggia, piazza 7 gallery, portico 8 verandah

verb: *auxiliary:* had, has, may, was 4 hast, will 5 might, shall, shalt, would
  form: 5 tense
  suffix: le; ire, ise 4 esce

  table: 8 paradigm
  tense: 8 aorist

verbal: 4 oral 5 wordy 7 verbose 9 talkative 10 articulate

verbatim: 6 orally 7 literal 8 verbally

verbena: 7 aloysia

verberate: 4 beat 5 shake 6 quiver, strike 7 tremble

verbiage: 4 talk 7 chatter, diction, fustian, wording 9 verbosity, wordiness 10 redundancy

verbose: 5 windy, wordy 6 prolix 7 diffuse 9 redundant

verboten: 4 tabu 5 taboo 9 forbidden 10 prohibited

verdant: raw 5 fresh, green 8 immature, innocent 13 inexperienced 15 unsophisticated

Verdi: *character:* 7 Amneris, Radames
  opera: 4 Aida 6 Ernani, Otello 7 Othello 8 Traviata 9 Rigoletto

verdict: 4 word 7 finding, opinion 8 decision, judgment

verdigris: 6 aerugo

Verdun river: 5 Meuse

verdure: 4 odor 5 scent, smell 6 flavor 7 acidity 8 greenery, strength, tapestry, tartness 9 freshness, greenness

verecund: shy 6 modest 7 bashful

Verein: 7 society 11 association 12 organization

verge: lip, rim, rod 4 edge, tend, twig, wand 5 bound, brink, limit, marge, range, scope, shaft, staff, stick, watch 6 border, margin 7 incline, virgate 8 approach, boundary, yardland 9 extremity, timepiece 13 circumference

verger: 4 dean 6 garden 7 justice, orchard 8 official 9 attendant

Vergil: See **Virgil**

veridical: 7 genuine 8 accurate, truthful 9 veracious 12 truthtelling

verification: 8 averment 12 confirmation 14 authentication

verify: 4 aver, back, test 5 audit, check, prove 6 affirm, ratify, second 7 certify, collate, confirm, support 8 maintain 9 establish 11 certificate 12 authenticate, substantiate

verily: yea 4 amen 5 parde, pardi, pardy, truly 6 certes, indeed, pardie, really 9 certainly 11 confidently

verisimilitude: 5 truth 10 likelihood 11 probability

veritable: 4 real, true 6 actual, gospel, honest 7 genuine 9 authentic, veracious

verity: 12 faithfulness

verjuice: 5 juice 7 acidity 8 sourness, tartness

vermiform: 4 long, thin 7 sinuous, slender 8 wormlike 10 vermicular

vermifuge: 12 anthelmintic

vermilion: red 8 cinnabar

vermin: 4 lice, mice, rats 5 filth, fleas, flies 7 bedbugs, rodents, weasels

verminous: 5 dirty 6 filthy 7 noxious 9 offensive

Vermont: *city:* 5 Barre 10 Montpelier(c.)
  county: 5 Essex 6 Orange 7 Addison, Rutland 8 Lamoille 10 Bennington, Chittenden
  mountain range: 7 Taconic

vernacular: 5 lingo 6 jargon, patois 7 dialect

vernal: 4 mild, warm 5 fresh, young 8 youthful 10 springlike

Verne: *character:* 4 Nemo
  submarine: 8 Nautilus

verneuk: 5 cheat 6 humbug 7 swindle

verrel: 7 ferrule

versate: 4 turn 7 revolve

versatile: 5 handy 6 fickle 7 flexile 8 unsteady, variable 10 changeable, inconstant, reversible

verse (see also **poem**): 4 turn 5 meter, stave, stich 6 stanza 7 revolve, stichos 8 consider 11 familiarize
  Bible: 4 text
  foot: 4 iamb
  pert. to: 6 poetic
  stress: 5 ictus

verse-maker: 8 meterist

versed: 5 adept 6 beseen 7 erudite, learned, skilled 8 familiar 9 practiced 10 acquainted, conversant, proficient

verset: 7 prelude 8 versicle 9 interlude

versification: 5 rhyme 6 poetry

versifier: 4 poet 5 rimer 6 verser 7 poetess 9 poetaster

versify: 6 berime 7 berhyme

version: 7 edition, turning 9 rendition 10 conversion, paraphrase 11 translation 14 transformation

verso: vo

versus: vs.; con 4 agin 7 against

vertebra: 4 axis 6 spondy 7 spondyl

vertebrae: 5 spine

vertebrate: ray 9 backboned
  class: 4 aves
  division: 6 somite
  feathered: 4 bird
  group: 9 amnionata

vertex: top 4 apex 6 summit 11 culmination

vertical: 4 acme 5 apeak, erect, plumb, sheer 6 abrupt, height, summit, vertex 7 upright 13 perpendicular

verticil: 5 whorl

vertiginate: 5 twirl, whirl

vertiginous: 5 dizzy, giddy 6 rotary 8 rotating, unstable, whirling 9 dizziness, giddiness, revolving 10 inconstant 11 vacillating

vertigo: 6 megrim 9 dizziness, giddiness

verve: pep 4 dash, elan 5 ardor, vigor 6 bounce, spirit, talent 7 ability 8 aptitude, vivacity 9 animation 10 enthusiasm

vervet: 6 monkey

very: so; too 4 fell, real, same, tres(F.), true, unco(Sc.) 5 assai(It.), molto(It.), truly, utter 6 actual, lawful, mighty, really 7 dimolto(It.), exactly, genuine 8 absolute, complete, especial, peculiar, rightful, truthful 9 extremely, identical, precisely, veracious, veritable 10 legitimate, mortacious 11 exceedingly
  combining form: eri

vesica: 6 vessel 7 bladder

vesicate: 7 blister

vesicle: sac 4 bleb, cell, cyst 5 bulla 6 cavity, vessel 7 bladder, blister, utricle
  air: 8 aerocyst

vesper: 7 evening 8 eventide

Vesper: 4 star 5 Venus 8 Hesperus

vespers: 6 prayer 7 service 8 ceremony, evensong

vessel: (see also **aircraft, boat, container, pail, ship**): can, cog, cup, jar, pan, tub, urn, vas 4 bell, cadi, drum, duct, ewer, olla, olpe, tank, tube, vase 5 bocal, cadus, canoe, cogue, craft, cruse, laver, liner, paten 6 aftaba, aludel, barrel, cootie, crater, firkin, funnel, goblet, goulah, holmos, krater, patera, situla, yetlin 7 aleyard, blickey, blickie, cistern, cresset, gabbard, gabbart, paterae, pinnace, pitcher, situlae, steamer, utensil, yetling 8 aiguiere, ciborium 9 alcarraza 10 receptacle
  anatomical: vas 4 vasa(pl.), vein 6 artery
  assaying: 5 cupel
  comb. form: vas 4 vaso
  drinking: cup, mug 4 toby 5 flask, glass, gourd, jorum, stein, stoup 6 dipper, flagon, seidel 7 tankard, tumbler 8 schooner
  earthen: 5 crock
  oil: 5 cruse, cruet
  pert. to: 5 vasal
  sacred: ama, pix, pyx
  small: nog 4 pony, shot 6 noggin
  wooden: soe 5 cogue, skeel 6 piggin

vest: 4 robe 5 dress, endow, gilet 6 accrue, clothe, invest, jacket, jerkin, linder, weskit 7 furnish, garment 9 waistcoat 10 undershirt

vesta: 5 match

Vesta: 6 Hestia

vestal: nun 4 pure 6 chaste, virgin

vestibule   **804**

vestibule: 4 hall 5 entry, lobby, porch 7
   chamber, narthex, passage 8 anteroom,
   entrance, vestibule 10 antechapel
vestige: bit 4 mark, sign 5 relic, shred,
   smack, trace, track, umbra 8 footstep,
   tincture 9 vestigium
vestiture: 4 garb 5 dress 8 clothing
vestment (see also dress): 4 garb, gear,
   gown, hood, robe 5 cotta, dress, orale 6
   chimer, chimre, gloves, rochet, tippet 7
   cassock, garment, sandals 8 cincture,
   clothing, covering 10 habiliment
   ecclesiastical: alb, cap 4 alba, cope 5 albae,
   amice, ephod, fanon, miter, orale, stole 6
   lappet, palium, saccos 7 cassock, maniple,
   tunicle 8 chasuble, dalmatic, surplice
   pert. to: 8 vestiary
vestry: 4 room 7 meeting 8 sacristy
vesture: 4 corn 5 cover, crops, grass 6 clothe,
   seizin 7 apparel, envelop, raiment, stubble, wrapper 8 garments, vestment 9 underwood 11 investiture
vesuvian: 5 fusee, match 8 volcanic
vet: 7 veteran 10 veterinary 12 veterinarian
vetch: ers 4 akra, tare, weed 5 fetch 7 arve-
   jon
   bitter: ers
veteran: old 7 oldster 8 seasoned 9 practiced
   11 experienced
veterinarian: 7 farrier
vetiver: 5 grass 6 cuscus 8 khuskhus
veto: 6 forbid 7 message 8 document, negative, overrule, prohibit 11 disapproval, forbiddance, prohibition 12 interdiction
vettura: 5 coach 8 carriage
veuve: 4 bird 6 whydah
vex: ire, irk, tew 4 cark, chaw, fret, fuss, gall,
   miff, rile, roil, toss 5 anger, annoy, chafe,
   harry, shake, spite, tease, worry, wrack 6
   bother, cumber, harass, madden, molest,
   nettle, offend, plague, pother, ruffle 7 afflict, agitate, discuss, dispute, disturb, perplex, provoke, torment, trouble 8 disquiet,
   irritate, vexation 9 annoyance, displease,
   infuriate 11 disturbance
vexation: 5 pique, thorn 7 fatigue 9 weariness 13 mortification
vexatious: 4 chaw, sore, vexy 5 pesky 8 annoying, cumbrous, frampoid, untoward 9
   disturbed, pestilent 10 afflictive 11 contrarious, troublesome
vexed: 5 sorry 7 grieved
vexillum: web 4 flag, vane 6 banner 8 standard
via: way 4 road 5 right 7 passage, through
viaduct: 6 bridge 7 trestle
vial: 5 ampul, cruet, phial 6 bottle, caster,
   vessel 7 ampoule

viand: 4 fare, food 6 edible 7 aliment 8 victuals 10 provisions
   choice: 4 cate
viaticum: 5 money 8 supplies 9 allowance
   10 provisions
viator: 8 traveler, wayfarer
Viaud's pen name: 4 Loti
vibrant: 5 alive, ringy 8 sonorous, vigorous
   9 vibrating
vibrate: jar, wag 4 beat, cast, dirl, rock,
   whir 5 pulse, quake, shake, swing, throb,
   throw, trill, waver, whirr 6 dindle, launch,
   quaver, quiver, shimmy, shiver, thrill 7
   agitate, resound, tremble 8 brandish,
   flichter, resonate 9 fluctuate, oscillate,
   vacillate
vibration: 4 dirl(Sc.), tirl(Sc.) 5 thirl(Sc.) 6
   dingle, quaver, quiver, thrill, tremor 7
   flutter 8 stirring 11 oscillation, vacillation
   14 changeableness
   musical: 5 trill 7 sonance, tremolo, vibrato
   8 overtone
   point without: 4 node
vicar: 5 proxy 6 deputy, priest 8 minister 9
   clergyman 10 substitute, vicegerent
   assistant: 6 curate
Vicar of Wakefield author: 9 Goldsmith
vicarage: 4 dues 5 house 6 salary, tithes 8
   benefice 9 household, pastorate, rectorate,
   residence
vice: sin 4 evil, grip, hold, turn 5 crime,
   fault, force, grasp, place, proxy, stead,
   taint 6 defect 7 blemish, failing, squeeze,
   stopper 8 iniquity, stairway 9 deformity,
   depravity 10 corruption, substitute, wickedness 11 harmfulness, viciousness 12 imperfection
Vice President (U.S.): 4 Burr, Ford, King 5
   Adams, Agnew, Dawes, Gerry, Nixon, Tyler 6 Arthur, Colfax, Curtis, Dallas, Gar-
   ner, Hamlin, Hobart, Morton, Truman,
   Wilson 7 Barkley, Calhoun, Clinton, John-
   son, Sherman, Wallace, Wheeler 8 Coo-
   lidge, Fillmore, Marshall, Tompkins, Van
   Buren 9 Fairbanks, Hendricks, Jefferson,
   Roosevelt, Stevenson 11 Rockefeller 12
   Breckinridge
   Adams, J.: 9 Jefferson
   Adams, J.Q.: 7 Calhoun
   Arthur: none
   Buchanan: 12 Breckinridge
   Cleveland: 9 Hendricks(1), Stevenson(2)
   Coolidge: 5 Dawes
   Eisenhower: 5 Nixon
   Fillmore: none
   Ford: 11 Rockefeller
   Garfield: 6 Arthur
   Grant: 6 Colfax(1), Wilson(2)
   Harding: 8 Coolidge

Harrison, B.: 6 Morton
Harrison, W.H.: 5 Tyler
Hayes: 7 Wheeler
Hoover: 6 Curtis
Jackson: 7 Calhoun(1) 8 Van Buren(2)
Jefferson: 4 Burr(1) 7 Clinton(2)
Johnson, A.: none
Johnson, L.B.: 8 Humphrey
Kennedy: 7 Johnson
Lincoln: 6 Hamlin(1) 7 Johnson(2)
Madison: 5 Gerry(2) 7 Clinton(1)
McKinley: 6 Hobart(1) 9 Roosevelt(2)
Monroe: 8 Tompkins
Nixon: 4 Ford(2) 5 Agnew(1)
Pierce: 4 King
Polk: 6 Dallas
Roosevelt, F.D.: 6 Garner(1), Truman(3) 7 Wallace(2)
Roosevelt, T.: 9 Fairbanks
Taft: 7 Sherman
Taylor: 8 Fillmore
Truman: 7 Barkley
Tyler: none
Van Buren: 7 Johnson
Washington: 5 Adams
Wilson: 8 Marshall
viceroy: 5 nabob, nazim 6 exarch, satrap 8 governor 9 butterfly
vicinity: 6 region 8 nearness, vicinage 9 proximity 11 propinquity, resemblance 12 neighborhood 13 neighbourhood
vicious: bad, ill 4 evil, foul, lewd, mean, vile 6 faulty, wicked 7 corrupt, immoral, noxious 8 debasing, depraved, infamous, spiteful 9 dangerous, defective, dissolute, malicious, malignant, nefarious, perverted 10 corrupting, iniquitous, villainous
vicissitude: 6 change 8 mutation 10 difficulty, revolution, succession 11 alternation, interchange
victim: 4 dupe, goat, gull, prey 6 sucker
  list: 4 toll
victor: 6 captor, winner 7 conquer 8 bangster, unbeaten 9 conqueror 10 vanquisher, victorious
victory: win 7 mastery, success, triumph 8 conquest 9 landslide, supremacy 11 superiority
  celebrating: 9 epinician
  crown: bay 6 laurel
  goddess: 4 Nike
  memorial: 4 arch 6 spoils, trophy
  ruinous: 7 Pyrrhic
  sign: vee
  song: 9 epinicion
  symbol: 4 palm
Victory heroine: 4 Lena

victrola: 9 turntable 10 phonograph 12 record player
victualler: 6 sutler 9 innkeeper
victuals: bit 4 bite, food, grub, meat 6 viands 7 vittles 11 nourishment
videlicet: viz 6 namely 8 scilicet
vie: bet, run 4 cope 5 bandy, rival, stake, wager 6 endure, hazard, oppose, strive 7 compete, contend, contest, emulate 8 panorama, prospect, struggle 9 challenge
Vienna: 4 Wien
  palace: 10 Schonbrunn
  park: 6 Prater
Vietnam: See **North Vietnam, South Vietnam**
view: aim, eye, ken, see, vue(F.) 4 goal, look, scan 5 aview, scape, scene, sight, slant, tenet, vista, watch 6 admire, apercu(F.), aspect, behold, belief, object, regard, sketch, survey, vision 7 examine, inspect, opinion, picture, profile, summary, thought, witness 8 attitude, consider, panorama, prospect, synopsis 9 apprehend 10 appearance, inspection, perception, photograph, scrutinize, standpoint 11 contemplate, examination, expectation 13 contemplation
  extended: 8 panorama
  mentally: 8 envision
  obstruct: 4 hide 7 conceal
  open to: 4 bare 5 overt 6 expose
viewer: 9 spectator 11 stereoscope 14 superintendent
viewing instrument: 5 scope 9 telescope 10 binoculars
viewy: 5 showy 8 fanciful 9 visionary 11 spectacular, unpractical 12 ostentatious
vigil: eve 4 wake 5 guard 7 prayers, service 8 devotion, watchman
vigilant: 4 agog, wary 5 alert, awake, aware 7 careful, wakeful 8 cautious, watchful 9 attentive, observant, sleepless 11 circumspect
vigilant person: 5 Argus
vigilantes: 5 posse
vigneron: 10 winegrower 13 viticulturist
vignettist: 6 artist, author, writer 7 painter 8 engraver 12 photographer
vigor, vigour: pep, vim, vir(Sc.), vis 4 birr, zeal 5 flush, force, nerve, power 6 energy, foison, growth, health 7 impetus, potency, stamina 8 activity, boldness, strength, virility, vitality 9 animation, fraicheur, hardihood, intensity, vehemence 10 invigorate
  deprive of: sap 6 deaden 8 enervate
  lose: fag, sag 4 fail, flag, pine 6 weaken 7 decline
  period of: 6 heyday
vigoroso: 8 vigorous 9 direction, energetic

vigorous: yep 4 able, cant, fell, hale, spry, yepe 5 eager, frank, hardy, hefty, lusty 6 florid, hearty, lively, robust, rugged, sturdy 7 cordial 8 athletic, muscular 9 effective, energetic, strenuous 11 efficacious, energetical

vigorously: 5 amain

Viking: 4 Eric 5 rover 6 pirate 8 Norseman, Northman 12 Scandinavian

vilayet: 6 region 8 division

vile: bad, low 4 base, evil, foul, mean 5 cheap, lowly 6 abject, coarse, drasty, filthy, impure, odious, sinful, sordid, wicked 7 bestial, carrion, corrupt, debased, ignoble, unclean, vicious 8 baseborn, befouled, depraved 9 abandoned, degrading, loathsome, nefarious, obnoxious, offensive, repulsive, worthless 10 abominable, despicable, disgusting 12 contaminated

vileness: 6 fedity 9 turpitude

vilify: 5 abuse, avile, libel 6 bemean, debase, defame, malign, revile, slight 7 asperse, blacken, cheapen, debauch, degrade, despise, detract, slander, traduce 8 belittle, disgrace, dishonor, reproach, vilipend 9 blaspheme, disparage 10 calumniate, depreciate

vility: 8 vileness

vill: 4 town 7 village 8 division, township

villa: 5 aldea, dacha(Russ.), house 8 villakin 9 residence, villaette 10 villanette

village: gav, mir(Russ.), rew(Sc.) 4 dorp, home, stad(African), town, vici 5 aldea, bourg, kraal, thorp, vicus 6 bustee, castle, hamlet, pueblo, thorpe 7 borough, caserio(Sp.), endship 8 bourgade, villaget, villakin 9 aldeament 10 settlement 11 aggregation

villain: 4 boor, Iago, lout, serf 5 churl, demon, devil, heavy, knave, rogue 6 rascal 8 scelerat 9 miscreant, scoundrel 10 villainous

mythological: 4 ogre 5 giant 6 dragon
nemesis of: 4 hero

villainous: bad, low 4 base, evil, mean, vile 6 common, slight, vulgar, wicked 7 boorish 8 clownish, criminal, depraved, flagrant, wretched 9 dastardly, felonious 10 detestable, flagitious, iniquitous 12 disagreeable 13 objectionable

villainy: 5 crime 7 knavery 9 depravity

villatic: 5 rural 6 rustic

villein: 4 carl, serf 5 ceorl, churl 7 bondman, cottier

vim: zip 4 gimp 5 force, vigor 6 energy, ginger, spirit 8 strength

vina: 10 instrument

vinaigrette: box 6 bottle 7 vehicle 8 carriage

vincible: 11 conquerable 12 surmountable

vinculum: 4 band, bond 5 brace, union 6 frenum

vindicate: 4 free 5 clear 6 acquit, assert, avenge, defend, excuse, uphold 7 absolve, deliver, justify, propugn, revenge, support, sustain 8 advocate, maintain 9 exculpate, exonerate

vindication: 7 apology

vindicative: See **vindictive**

vindictive: 7 hostile 8 punitive, spiteful, vengeful 10 revengeful 11 retaliatory, retributive, vindicative, vindicatory

vine: hop, ivy 4 akas, bine, gogo, odal, soma 5 betel, buaze, bwazi, guaco, liana, liane 6 maypop 7 creeper, cupseed, trailer 8 clematis 9 grapevine 10 chilicothe

comb. form: 4 viti
covered with: 5 ivied 7 lianaed
fruit-bearing: 5 grape 7 cupseed
parasite: 5 aphid, aphis
twining: 4 bine

vinegar: 4 acid 5 eisel 6 acetum, alegar, eisell 8 vinaigre(F.)

bottle: 5 cruet
dregs: 6 mother
ester: 7 acetate
pert. to: 6 acetic
preserve in: 6 pickle
salt: 7 acetate
spice: 8 tarragon

vinegary: 4 sour 7 acetose, crabbed 9 unamiable 11 ill-tempered

vineyard: cru
protector: 7 Priapus

vinous: 4 winy 9 vinaceous

vintage: 4 crop, wine 5 cuvee, yield

vintner: 8 merchant

viol: 5 gigue, rebec 6 rebeck, vielle 7 quinton 9 violaalta
progenitor: 5 rebec

viola: 4 alto 5 gamba 7 pomposa 12 viola pomposa

Viola's brother: 9 Sebastian

violate: 4 flaw, rape 5 abuse, break, force, harry, spoil, wrong 6 betray, broach, defile, defoil, defoul, injure, insult, invade, offend, ravage, ravish 7 corrupt, debauch, disturb, falsify, outrage, pollute, profane 8 deflower, dishonor, infringe, mistreat 9 constrain, desecrate, disregard 10 contravene, transgress

violation: 5 crime, error 6 breach 10 infraction 11 delinquency 13 nonobservance
sentence structure: 11 anacoluthon

violence: 4 fury 5 ardor 6 bensel, bensil, fervor, hubris, hybris 7 assault, bensail, bensall, bensell, outrage 8 ferocity 9 bloodshed 11 desecration, profanation 12 infringement

violent: 4 high, loud 5 acute, fiery, great, heady, heavy, hefty, rabid, rough, sharp, vivid 6 fierce, mighty, raging, savage, severe, stormy, strong 7 extreme, furious, hotspur, intense, rammish 8 flagrant, forceful, forcible, frenetic, vehement 9 atrocious, impetuous, phrenetic, turbulent 10 headstrong, hotspurred, immoderate, passionate, tumultuous 11 tempestuous

violently: 5 amain 8 slambang

violet: 5 mauve 6 blaver, flower, purple
  perfume: 5 irone

violet root: 9 orrisroot

violet tip: 9 butterfly

violin: kit 4 alto, bass 5 Amati, cello, Rocta, Strad 6 fiddle 7 Cremona 8 Guarneri 10 Guadagnini, Guarnerius, Stradivari 11 violincello 12 Stradivarius
  city: 7 Cremona
  direction: 4 arco 9 pizzicato
  forerunner: 5 rabab
  part: peg 4 hole, neck 6 string 7 eclisse
  rare: 5 Amati, Strad 10 Guarnerius

violin-shaped: 7 waisted

violinist (first): 13 concertmaster 14 concertmeister
  comic: 5 Benny
  fabled: 4 Nero
  famous: 4 Auer 5 Elman, Stern, Ysaye 7 Heifetz, Menuhin 8 Kreisler

V.I.P.: 7 notable

viper: asp 5 adder, snake 8 cerastes 10 bushmaster, copperhead, fer-de-lance 11 rattlesnake
  genus of: 5 echis

viperish: 8 spiteful, venomous 9 malicious

vir: 5 green

virago: 5 randy, scold, vixen, woman 6 Amazon, beldam, callet 7 beldame 9 brimstone, termagant

vireo: 7 grasset 8 greenlet, songbird

Virgil: *birthplace:* 6 Mantua
  character: 5 Amata, Damon 7 Corydon
  family name: 4 Maro
  friend: 8 Maecenas
  hero: 5 Aneas, Eneas 6 Aeneis
  language: 5 Latin
  poem: 4 epic 5 Eneid 6 Aeneid
  queen: 4 Dido

virgin: new 4 maid, pure 5 first, fresh 6 chaste, maiden, modest, vestal 7 initial 8 maidenly, spinster, virginal 9 unalloyed, undefiled, unsubdued, unsullied, untouched 10 uncaptured 11 undisturbed 12 uncultivated, unfertilized 13 unadulterated

Virgin Island coin: bit 5 daler, franc

Virgin Mary: *flower:* 8 marigold
  image: 5 Pieta
  mother: 4 Anna, Anne

virginal: 6 spinet, virgin 11 harpsichord

Virginia: *aristocrats:* FFV
  dam: 4 Kerr
  motto: 17 Sic semper tyrannis
  mountain: 5 Cedar
  pine: 8 loblolly
  quail: 8 bobwhite
  river: Dan 5 James 7 Potomac, Rapidan
  signature: 4 R. Lee
  swamp: 6 Dismal
  town: 5 Luray 8 Danville 11 Falls Church

Virginia creeper: ivy 5 plant 8 woodbine 10 ampelopsis

Virginia goat's rue: 6 catgut

Virginia snakeroot: 7 sangrel 9 birthwort 11 sangree-root

Virginia willow: iva 4 itea

Virginian author: 6 Wister

virgularian: 6 searod

viridity: 5 youth 7 verdure 8 verdance 9 freshness, greenness 10 liveliness

virile: 4 male 5 manly 7 lustful 8 forceful, powerful, vigorous 9 masculine, masterful

virl: 7 ferrule

virose: 5 fetid 8 virulent 9 poisonous 10 malodorous

virtu: 5 curio 7 antique

virtually: 6 nearly 7 morally, totally 11 practically

virtue: 4 thew 5 arete, grace 6 bounty, purity 7 probity, quality 8 chastity, efficacy, goodness, morality 9 rectitude, excellence 11 uprightness 13 righteousness
  cardinal: 4 hope 5 faith 7 charity, justice 8 prudence 9 fortitude 10 temperance
  paragon of: 5 saint

virtuoso: 6 expert, savant 7 scholar 8 aesthete, esthetic 10 empiricist 11 connoisseur, philosopher

virtuous: 4 good, pure 5 brave, moral 6 chaste, honest, potent 7 goddard, thrifty, upright, valiant 8 valorous 9 righteous 11 efficacious, industrious

virulent: 5 acrid, rabid 6 bitter, deadly, potent 7 hostile, noxious 8 spiteful, venomous 9 festering, injurious, malignant, poisonous 10 infectious 12 antagonistic

virus: 5 venom 6 poison 8 acrimony

vis: 5 force, power, vigor, visit 6 visual 7 potency 8 strength

vis-a-vis: 4 seat, sofa 8 carriage, opposite

visage: 4 face, look, show 5 image 6 aspect 8 portrait 9 semblance 10 appearance 11 countenance

viscera: 4 guts 6 vitals 8 entrails 10 intestines

viscid: 7 viscous

viscount: 4 peer 6 deputy 7 sheriff 8 nobleman

viscous: 4 limy, ropy, sizy 5 gobby, gummy, tarry, thick 6 mucous, sirupy, sticky, viscid 7 stringy 8 adhering, sticking 9 glutinous, semisolid

vise: 5 clamp
part: jaw

Vishnu: *bearer:* 6 Garuda
consort: Sri 7 Lakshmi
epithet: 8 Bhagavat
incarnation: 4 Rama 6 avatar 7 Krishna 8 Balarama 11 Ramachandra
serpent: 4 Naga

visible: 4 seen 6 extant 7 evident, glaring, obvious 8 apparent, manifest 9 available 11 conspicuous, discernible, perceivable, perceptible

Visigoth king: 6 Alaric

vision: eye 5 dream, fancy, image, sight 6 beauty, seeing 7 fantasy, imagine
combining form: 4 opto
defect: 6 anopia, myopia 14 metamorphopsae, metamorphopsia
double: 8 diplopia
illusory: 6 mirage
instrument of: 6 retina
lacking in: 8 purblind
measuring device: 9 optometer
pertaining to: 5 optic 6 ocular, visual

visionary: fey 4 aery, airy, wild 5 ideal 6 unreal 7 dreamer, fantast, laputan, utopian 8 delusive, idealist, quixotic, romantic 9 fantastic, imaginary 10 chimerical, ideologist 11 imaginative, impractical, speculative

visit: gam, see, vis 4 call, chat, hawk, slum, stay 5 apply, haunt 6 assail, attend, avenge 7 afflict, ceilidh(Sc.), inflict, sojourn 8 converse 10 inspection, visitation 12 conversation

visitant: 7 visitor

visitation: 8 disaster, visiting 9 migration 10 affliction

visitor: 5 guest 6 caller 7 company 8 visitant

visne: 4 jury, hood 5 venue 8 neighbor, vicinage

vison: 4 mink

vista: 4 view 5 scene 7 outlook 8 panorama, prospect

Vistula tributary: Bug, San

visual: 5 optic 6 ocular, scopic 7 optical, visible 11 perceptible

visualize: 6 ideate 7 imagine, picture 8 envisage 13 conceptualize

vita: 4 life

Vita Nuova author: 5 Dante

vital: 4 live 5 basic, chief, fatal 6 deadly, lively, living, souled, viable 7 animate, capital, exigent, supreme 8 vigorous 9 elemental, energetic, essential, important, necessary, requisite 10 imperative 11 fundamental 13 indispensable

vital fluid: sap 5 blood, lymph

vitality: sap, vim 6 biosis, foison

vitalize: 7 animate

vitals: 7 viscera

vitamin, vitamine: 6 biotin, citrin 7 choline 8 ascorbic, carotene, inositol, thiamine 10 calciferol, pyridoxine, riboflavin, tocopherol

vitellus: 4 yolk

vitiate: 5 pical, spoil, taint 6 debase, faulty, impair, impure, poison, weaken 7 corrupt, deprave, envenom, pervert, pollute 9 defective 10 adulterate, invalidate, neutralize 11 contaminate, ineffective

viticulturist: 8 vigneron 10 winegrower

vitiosity: 4 vice 5 fault 6 defect 9 depravity 11 viciousness 13 defectiveness

vitrella: 11 retinophore

vitrify: 5 glaze

vitrine: 8 showcase

vitriol: 4 acid, sory 7 caustic

vitriolic: 5 sharp 6 biting, bitter 7 caustic 8 scathing, virulent 9 sarcastic

vituperate: 4 rail 5 abuse, curse, scold 6 berate, revile 7 censure

vituperative: 10 scurrilous 10 opprobrious

vivace: 9 direction, vivacious

vivacious: gay 4 airy 5 brisk, merry 6 active, breezy, lively, vivace(It.) 7 buoyant, zestful 8 animated, cheerful, spirited, sportive 9 long-lived, sprightly 12 lighthearted

vivacity: 4 fire, zeal 5 ardor, force, verve, vigor 6 gaiety, gayety 7 gayness 9 longevity 10 liveliness

vivandier: 6 sutler

vivarium: box, zoo 4 cage 6 vivary, warren 9 enclosure

vive: 5 brisk, vivid 6 lively, living 8 forcible, lifelike 9 perceived

vivers: 4 food 8 victuals

vivid: 4 keen, live, rich 5 clear, fresh, sharp 6 active, bright, lively, living, strong 7 eidetic, flaming, glaring, glowing, graphic, intense 8 animated, colorful, distinct, dramatic, spirited, striking, vigorous 9 brilliant

vivificate: 6 vivify

vivify: 5 endue 6 revive 7 animate, enliven, quicken 10 invigorate, vivificate

vivres: 9 foodstuff 10 provisions

vixen: fox, nag 4 fury 5 scold, shrew, woman 9 termagant

viz: 5 to-wit 6 namely 9 videlicet

vizard: 4 mask 5 guise, visor 8 disguise

vizcacha, viscacha: 6 rodent

vocabulary: 5 words 7 diction, lexicon 8 glossary, wordbook 10 dictionary

vocabulist: 13 lexicographer

vocal: 4 oral 5 vowel 9 unwritten

vocalist: 4 alto 5 basso, tenor 6 artist, singer 7 soprano 8 songster 9 performer 10 coloratura

vocalization: 11 melismatics

vocation: 4 call 5 trade 6 career 7 calling, summons 8 business 9 following 10 employment, occupation, profession

vociferate: cry 4 bawl, roar 5 shout, utter 6 assert, bellow, clamor 7 clamour

vociferation: 6 outcry

vociferous: 4 loud 5 noisy 7 blatant 8 brawling, strident 9 turbulent 10 boisterous 11 loud-mouthed, openmouthed 12 obstreperous

voe: bay 5 creek, inlet

vogie: 4 vain 5 merry, proud 6 elated

vogue: cut, ton(F.) 4 mode 5 style 6 custom 7 fashion 8 practice 10 popularity

in: 10 prevailing

voice: say, vox(L.) 4 emit, voce(It.), vote, wish 5 rumor, utter 6 choice, report, speech, steven, tongue 7 divulge, express, opinion 8 announce, falsetto, proclaim 9 utterance 10 expression 12 articulation

handicap: 4 lisp 7 stutter

loss of: 7 anaudia, aphonia

loud: 12 megalophonic 13 megalophonous

male: 4 bass 5 basso, tenor 8 baritone, barytone 12 countertenor

natural singing: 7 dipetto

part: 7 glottis

pert. to: 8 phonetic

principal: 6 cantus

quality: 6 timbre

quiet: 5 sotto

sound: 5 vowel 6 symbol

stop: 9 affricate

stress: 5 arsis

voice box: 6 larynx

voiced: 6 sonant

voiceless: mum 4 dumb, mute, surd 6 atonic, flated, silent 7 aphonic, spirate 8 aphonous 10 speechless

void: gap 4 free, idle, lack, null, vain, want 5 abyss, annul, blank, egest, eject, empty, leave, space 6 devoid, hollow, remove, vacant, vacate, vacuum 7 invalid, lacking, leisure, nullify, opening, useless, vacuity,

wanting 8 evacuate 9 destitute, discharge, emptiness, frustrate 10 unemployed, unoccupied 11 ineffective, ineffectual

voile: 5 ninon

voiture: 5 wagon 8 carriage

volage: 5 giddy 6 fickle 7 flighty 8 fleeting

volant: 5 agile, light, quick 6 flying, nimble 7 flounce 8 volitant

volary: 4 cage 6 aviary

volatile: 4 airy, bird 5 ether 6 fickle, figent, flying, lively, volage, volant 7 alcohol, ammonia, buoyant, essence, gaseous, volatic 8 fleeting, fugitive, vaporous 9 fugacious, transient 10 capricious, changeable, transitory 11 hairbrained 12 lighthearted

volatilize: 9 evaporate

volcano: Apo 4 Etna 5 Askja, Pelee 6 Ranier, Shasta 8 Cotopaxi, Krakatao, Krakatau, Mauna Loa, Vesuvius 9 Stromboli 12 Popocatepetl

crater: 4 maar

matter: aa, oo 4 lava, tufa 5 trass 6 pumice

mud from: 5 salse

opening: 5 mouth 6 crater 8 fumarole

rock: 5 trass 6 dacite 8 tephrite

scoria: 4 slag

steam from: 5 stufa

vole: 6 craber, rodent

Volga: Rha

volition: 4 will 6 choice 13 determination

volley: 5 crowd, volee 6 flight 7 barrage, company, platoon

volplane: 5 coast, glide

Volpone character: 5 Mosca

Volsunga Saga: *dragon:* 6 Fafnir

hero: 6 Sigurd

king: 4 Atli

Voltaire: *character:* 8 Pangloss

estate: 6 Ferney

novel: 5 Zadig 7 Candide

real name: 6 Arouet

voluble: 4 glib 5 wordy 6 fickle, fluent 8 rotating, unstable 9 garrulous, revolving, talkative 10 changeable, loquacious

volume: 4 book, bulk, coil, mass, roll, tome, turn 6 amount, cubage, scroll 8 capacity, document, fullness, loudness, quantity, strength 9 aggregate 10 crassitude 11 convolution

large: 4 tome

measure: 11 stereometer

voluminous: 4 full 5 bulky, large

Volund's brother: 4 Egil 5 Egill

voluntary: 4 free 6 freely 7 willful, willing 8 elective 9 volunteer, willingly 10 deliberate, unimpelled 11 intentional, spontaneous 13 unconstrained

volunteer: 5 offer 6 enlist, worker 7 proffer

Volunteer State: 9 Tennessee

voluptuous: 7 sensual 8 sensuous 9 luxurious 11 pleasurable

volute: 4 turn 5 whorl 6 cilery, scroll 7 cillery

volution: 4 coil, turn 5 twist, whorl 7 rolling 9 revolving 11 convolution

vomit: 4 boke, bolk, puke, spew 5 braid, brake, reach, retch 6 emetic 8 disgorge 10 egurgitate 11 regurgitate

vomiting: 6 emesis 12 anacatharsis

voodoo: obe, obi 5 magic, obeah 6 fetish 8 sorcerer

charm: 4 mojo

voracious: 5 eager 6 greedy, hungry 8 esurient, ravening, revenous 9 cormorant, rapacious 10 gargantuan, gluttonous, immoderate, insatiable

voracity: 7 edacity 10 greediness 12 ravenousness

vorago: 4 gulf 5 abyss

vortex: 4 apex, eddy, gyre 5 whirl 7 tornado 9 waterpool, whirlpool, whirlwind 10 waterspout

votary: 6 zealot 7 devoted, devotee 8 adherent, follower, promised 10 enthusiast

vote: aye, con, nay, pro, vow, yes 4 anti, poll, wish 5 elect, grant 6 assign, ballot, choice, confer, prayer 7 declare, opinion 8 dedicate, suffrage 10 plebiscite, referendum

group: 4 bloc

method: 4 hand 5 proxy, straw, voice 6 ballot, secret 7 write-in

of assent: aye, nod, yea 6 placet

of dissent: nay

receptacle: 6 situla 7 situlae

right to: 8 suffrage 9 franchise

solicitation of, for bill: 5 lobby

voter: 6 poller 7 elector 8 balloter, chooser 11 constituent

illegal: 8 repeater, underage 11 nonresident

voters (body of): 10 electorate

votive: 11 consecrated

vouch: vow 4 aver, back, bail, call, pray 6 affirm, allege, assure, attest, second, summon 7 certify, confirm, declare, resolve, support, warrant 8 accredit, maintain, sanction 9 assertion, establish, guarantee 11 attestation 12 authenticate

voucher: 4 chit 7 receipt 9 debenture, statement 10 credential

vouchsafe: 4 give 5 deign, yield 6 assure, bestow, beteem 7 concede 9 guarantee 10 condescend

voussoir: 5 wedge 8 keystone

projection: ear

voust: 5 boast, vaunt

vow: vum 4 bind, hote, oath, wish 5 swear 6 behest, devote, pledge 7 behight, declare, promise 8 dedicate 9 assertion 10 consecrate, obligation 12 asseveration, supplication

dedicated by: 6 votive

vowel: 5 vocal

contraction: 6 crasis, crases 9 diphthong

gradation: 6 ablaut

group of two: 6 digram 7 digraph

mark: 5 breve, tilde 6 umlaut 8 dieresis 10 circumflex

omission: 7 aphesis

sound: 6 dental, labial 7 palatal

unaspirated: 4 lene

vox: 5 voice

voyage: 4 trip 6 cruise, travel 7 journey, passage, passing, project 8 proceeds 9 excursion 10 enterprise, expedition, pilgrimage 11 undertaking

voyageur: 7 boatman, trapper 8 traveler, woodsman

voyaging: 4 asea

vraic: 7 seaweed

vrouw: 4 frow 5 woman 8 mistress 9 housewife

vug, vugg, vugh: 6 cavity, hollow

Vulcan: 5 smith 10 blacksmith, Hephaestus

consort: 4 Maia 5 Venus

epithet: 8 Mulciber

son: 5 Cacus 8 Caeculus

workshop: 4 Etna

vulcanite: 7 ebonite

vulcanize: 4 cure

vulgar: 4 lewd, rude 5 crude, gross 6 coarse, common, public, slangy 7 boorish, general, obscene, popular, profane 8 churlish, ordinary 9 customary, earthbred, inelegant, unrefined

vulgarian: 4 snob

vulgarism: 4 cant 9 vulgarity

Vulgate translator: 6 Jerome

vulnerable: 6 liable 7 exposed 9 pregnable, untenable 10 assailable 11 defenseless, susceptible

point: 12 Achilles heel

vulnerate: 4 hurt 5 wound

vulpine: fox 4 foxy 6 artful, clever, crafty, tricky 7 cunning 9 alopecoid

vult: 4 mien 6 aspect 10 expression 11 countenance

vulture: 4 papa 5 arend, grape, gripe, griph, urubu 6 condor, griphe 8 aasvogel, zopilote 9 gallinazo 11 lammergeier

genus of: 4 gyps

vum: vow

W

waag: 6 grivet, monkey
wabble: See **wobble**
wabby: 4 loon
wabeno: 6 shaman
wachna: cod
wacky, whacky: 5 crazy 6 screwy 7 eratic 9 eccentric 10 irrational
wad: bat, gag, pad, ram 4 cram, heap, lead, line, lump, mass, plug, roll, tuft 5 crowd, money, stuff, trace, track, would 6 bundle, insert, pledge, wealth 7 stopper 8 bankroll, compress, graphite
of paper money: 4 roll
Wadai Muslim: 4 Maba
wadding: 4 hemp 5 kapok 6 cotton
waddle: 5 tread 6 hoddle, toddle, widdle 7 trample
waddy: 4 beat, cane, club 5 stick 6 attack, cowboy
wade: go 4 ford, pass 6 paddle 7 proceed 8 struggle
wader: 4 boot, coot, hern ibis, rail 5 crane, heron, snipe, stork 6 jacana 9 sandpiper
wadi, wady: 5 oasis, river 6 ravine, stream, valley 7 channel 11 watercourse
wading bird: See **bird:** *wading*
wadset: 4 pawn 6 pledge 8 mortgage
wady: See **wadi**
wafer: 4 cake, disk, ring, seal, snap 5 close 6 fasten 7 biscuit, cracker
container for: pix, pyx
waff: wag 4 flap, gust, odor, puff, wave 5 ghost, whiff 6 paltry, wraith 7 flutter, lowborn 8 inferior 9 worthless 12 disreputable
waffie: 5 tramp 7 vagrant 8 vagabond
waffle: 4 cake
waft: 4 blow, buoy, flag, gust, odor, puff, turn, wave, weft 5 carry, drift, float, gleam, sound, taste, whiff 6 beckon, breath, direct, propel, signal, wraith 7 glimpse, pennant 9 transport
wag: wit 4 card, move, stir, sway 5 joker, leave, nudge, rogue, shake, swing 6 beckon, depart, signal 7 farceur, vibrate 8 brandish, flourish, humorist, jokester 9 oscillate
wagang: 5 death 9 departure 11 leavetaking
wage (see also **wager**)**:** fee, pay, utu 4 hire, levy, pawn 5 bribe, fight, incur 6 employ, engage, reward, salary 7 attempt, conduct, contend, stipend 9 emolument 10 recompense 12 compensation
deduct: 4 dock
insurance: 7 chomage
wage earner: 6 worker 7 laborer 8 employee, mechanic 11 proletarian
wager: bet, bid, lay, vie 4 gage, risk 5 prize, sport, stake 6 gamble, hazard, parlay, pledge 7 venture
made in bad faith: 6 levant
waggery: 4 jest, joke 7 foolery 10 pleasantry 11 waggishness
waggish: 4 arch 5 droll, merry 7 jesting, jocular, parlous, playful, roguish 8 humorous, sportive 10 frolicsome 11 mischievous
waggle: wag 6 waddle, wobble
waggly: 8 unsteady
Wagner: *character:* Eva 4 Elsa, Erda 5 Hagen, Senta, Wotan 8 Parsifal
opera: 6 Rienzi 9 Lohengrin 15 Gotterdammerung
wife: 6 Cosima
wagon: bin, van 4 cart, dray, tram, wain 5 araba, aroba, dilly, gilly, lorry, lurry, tonga 6 camion, telega 7 caisson, chariot, fourgon, vehicle 8 carryall, schooner 12 perambulator
maker: 10 wainwright
part: 4 neap, pole, rave 5 thill 6 tongue
shaft: 5 thill
wagon-lit: 7 sleeper
wagonload: 6 fother 8 wagonful
wagonmaker: 10 wagonsmith, wainwright 11 wagonwright
wah: 5 panda
wahine: 4 wife 5 woman 8 mistress 10 sweetheart

wahoo: elm 4 fish, peto 8 nonsense, tommy-rot 9 buckthorn, guarapucu

waif: 4 flag 5 stray 7 pennant, vagrant 8 castaway, homeless, wanderer 9 foundling

wail: cry, wow 4 howl, moan, waul, weep, yarm 5 croon, mourn 6 bemoan, bewail, grieve, lament, plaint 7 deplore, ululate 9 complaint 11 lamentation

wain: 4 cart 5 fetch, wagon 6 convey 7 chariot, vehicle

wainscot: 4 line 6 lining 7 ceiling 8 paneling 9 partition

waist: 4 belt, wasp 5 shirt 6 basque, blouse, bodice, camisa, girdle 7 corsage 8 camisole 10 undershirt 12 undergarment
circumference: 5 girth

waistband: 4 sash

waistcoat: 4 vest 5 benjy, gilet 6 fecket, jacket, jerkin
unlined: 7 singlet

wait: 4 bide, rest, stay, stop, tend 5 await, cater, court, dally, defer, delay, guard, serve, tarry, watch 6 ambush, attend, escort, expect, follow, harken, linger, remain 7 hautboy, hearken, observe 8 hesitate, inactive, postpone 9 accompany 10 stationary 11 expectation 12 watchfulness

waiter: spy 4 tray 6 garcon, salver, server, vessel 7 messboy, messman, servant, steward, watcher 8 servitor, watchman, waylayer 9 attendant

waive: put 4 cast, turn 5 cease, defer, forgo, leave, swing, yield 6 desert, forego, refuse, reject, vacate 7 abandon, forbear, forsake, neglect 8 postpone 9 disregard 10 relinquish

waka: 5 canoe

Wakashan: 6 Nootka

wake: 4 call, stir, wauk(Sc.) 5 guard, revel, rouse, track, trail, vigil, waken, watch 6 arouse, awaken, excite, revive 7 passage

wakeful: 5 alert 8 restless, vigilant 9 sleepless

Walden author: 7 Thoreau

Waldensian: 7 Leonist

wale: rib 4 best, flog, mark, pick, weal, welt 5 ridge, wheal 6 choice, choose, select, streak, stripe 7 timber 8 choicest

Wales (see also **Welsh**): 5 Cymru 7 Cambria
bard: 5 ovate
boat: 7 coracle
city: 6 Amlweh, Bangor 7 Cardiff, Rhondda, Swansea 8 Hereford, Holyhead, Pembroke 9 Carnarvon, Worcester 13 Kidderminster
cheese: 10 Caer-philly
deity: 4 Bran 5 Dylan
dog: 5 corgi
emblem: 4 leek
fine: 6 saraad
lake: 4 Bala
language: 6 Cymric, Kymric 7 Cymraeg
law: 7 galanas
legendary prince: 5 Madoc
marriage fee: 6 amober
measure: 5 cover 7 cantred, cantref, lestrad, listred 8 crannock
musical instrument: 7 pibcorn
patron saint: 5 David
people: 5 Cymry, Kymry
person: 5 Taffy 8 Welshman
poet: 6 Thomas
port: 7 Cardiff
river: Dee, Wye 4 Teme 5 Teifi 6 Severn

walk: mog, pad, wag 4 foot, gait, hike, hoof, limp, mall, pace, path, plod, ramp, reel, roam, roll, step, turn, wade 5 allee, amble, haunt, mince, scuff, stalk, stram, stray, strut, stump, trail, tramp, tread 6 arcade, hobble, loiter, lumber, pasear, prance, ramble, resort, stride, stroll, toddle, totter, trapes, trudge, wander 7 alameda, saunter, shuffle, traipse 8 ambulate, frescade, traverse 9 esplanade, promenade, tilicetum 11 perambulate, somnabulate 14 constitutional
a beat: 6 patrol
affectedly: 5 mince
inability to: 6 abasia
lamely: 4 limp
public: 4 mall 6 arcade 7 alameda 9 esplanade, promenade
reeling: 5 lurch

walk off: 5 leave 6 depart

walk off with: win 5 steal

walk-out: 6 strike

walk out on: 5 leave 6 desert 7 abandon

walker: 6 ganger 7 footman 8 stroller 10 pedestrian

walking: 7 passant(her.) 8 ambulant 10 ambulation 11 peripatetic
like a bear: 11 plantigrade

walking meter: 9 pedometer

walking stick: 4 cane 5 kebby, staff, stilt, waddy 6 kebbie

wall: 4 dike, ha-ha 5 fence, levee, redan, scarp 6 bailey, cashel, escarp, haw-haw, paries, podium, septum 7 barrier, bastion, curtain, defense, enclose, parapet, rampart 9 barricade, enclosure, encompass, partition, revetment 13 fortification
bracket: 6 corbel
covering: 4 tile 5 cloth, paint, paper 8 paneling 9 calcimine, draperies, kalsomine, wallpaper
dividing: 5 septa(pl.) 6 septum 9 partition
enclose within: 4 mure 6 immure
hanging: 5 arras
lining: 8 wainscot

masonry: 9 revetment
on: 5 mural
opening: 4 bole, door 6 window 7 scupper
ornament: 4 dado 6 mirror, plaque 7 hanging, molding, picture, placque 8 moulding, tapestry
part: 4 dado, pier 5 bahut, gable 6 coping, plinth 7 cornice
pert. to: 5 mural 8 parietal
plug: 6 outlet
up: 6 immure
wallaba tree: apa
wallaby: 8 kangaroo
wallah, walla: 5 agent, owner 6 fellow, master, person, worker 7 servant
wallet: bag, jag 4 jagg, pack, poke, sack 5 purse, scrip 6 budget 8 billfold, knapsack 10 pocketbook
wallop: 4 beat, blow, flog, lick, whip, whop 6 defeat, strike, thrash
walloping: 5 large 6 strong 8 enormous
wallow: pit 4 fade, mire 5 surge 6 billow, grovel, hollow, trough, welter, wither 7 founder 8 flounder, kommetje 10 depression
wallowish: 4 flat 7 insipid
wallpaper measure: 4 bolt
wally: 4 fine 6 robust, strong, sturdy 8 pleasant, pleasing, splendid 9 agreeable, excellent, first-rate
walnut: 6 bannut
skin: 4 zest
walrus: 5 morse 6 seacat 9 rosmarine
flock: pod
limb: 7 flipper
order: 5 bruta
tooth: 4 tusk
walt: 8 unsteady
waltz: 5 dance, valse
kind of: 6 Boston, Vienna
wambly: 5 faint, shaky 8 unsteady 9 nauseated, squeamish
wame: 5 belly
wampish: 5 swing 9 fluctuate
wampum: 4 peag 5 beads, money 7 roanoke
wamus: 6 jacket 7 doublet 8 cardigan
wan: dim, one, sad 4 dark, fade, pale, sick 5 dusky, faint, livid 6 dismal, feeble, gloomy, pallid, pallor, peaked, sickly 7 ghastly, languid, wanness 8 paleness 9 colorless, sorrowful 10 lusterless
wand: rod 4 pole, twig 5 baton, shoot, staff, stick 6 switch 7 pointer, rhabdos, scepter, sceptre 8 caduceus 9 horsewhip
royal: 4 mace 7 scepter
wand-shaped: 7 virgate
wander: err, gad 4 haik, hake, prog, rave, roam, roil, rove, wind 5 drift, prowl, range, shift, stray 6 cruise, dander, depart, ramble, stroll, trapes, travel 7 deviate, digress,

meander, saunter, traipse 8 divagate, straggle, traverse 11 peregrinate
aimlessly: gad 5 stray 7 traipse
wanderer: vag 4 Arab, waif 5 gypsy, nomad 6 truant 7 migrant, pilgrim, vagrant 9 itinerant 11 extravagant
religious: 6 palmer
wandering: 5 vagus(anat.) 6 astray, errant 7 devious, erratic, journey, odyssey 8 aberrant 9 aberrance, planetary 10 circuitous, incoherent 11 noctivigant, perambulant
wandering Jew: ivy 5 plant 7 zebrina
Wandering Jew author: Sue
wanderlust: 8 nomadism 12 restlessness
wanderoo: 6 langur, monkey 7 macaque
wandle: 5 agile, lithe 6 supple
wane: go; ebb 4 fail, làck, sink, want 5 abate, decay, peter 6 absent, defect, repine 7 decline, dwindle, subside 8 decrease, diminish 10 defervesce
opposite of: wax
wang: 4 king 5 ruler 6 prince
wanga: 5 charm, spell 6 voodoo 7 philter, sorcery
wangle: 4 fake 5 shake 6 adjust, change, juggle, totter, wiggle 7 falsify, wriggle 8 contrive 9 extricate 10 manipulate
wanhap: 6 mishap 10 misfortune
wanion: 5 curse 6 plague 9 vengeance
wankle: 6 feeble, fickle, sickly 8 unstable, unsteady 10 irresolute
want: gap 4 hole, lack, lose, miss, mole, need, void, wish 5 crave, fault 6 besoin, dearth, desire, forget, hunger, penury 7 absence, beggary, blemish, craving, lacking, missing, poverty, require, straits, vacancy 8 exigency, scarcity, shortage 9 deficient, indigence, necessary, necessity, privation 10 deficiency, inadequacy 11 deprivation, destitution 12 difficulties
wanted man: 6 outlaw 7 escapee
wanting: 4 less 5 minus 6 devoid 7 without, witless 12 feeble-minded
wanton: gay 4 lewd 5 cadgy, dally, frisk, merry, revel 6 frisky, frolic, giglet, harlot, lavish, trifle, unruly 7 fulsome, haggard, ill-bred, immoral, lustful, playful, sensual, wayward 8 arrogant, flagrant, inhumane, insolent, prodigal, spiteful, sportive, unchaste 9 dissolute, lecherous, luxuriant, luxurious, malicious, merciless 10 capricious, effeminate, frolicsome, gratuitous, lascivious, licentious, refractory, voluptuous 11 extravagant, mollycoddle 12 disregardful, unmanageable, unrestrained 13 undisciplined, unjustifiable
wantwit: 4 fool
wanty: tie 4 rope 5 girth 9 bellyband, surcingle

wap: 4 beat, bind, blow, whop, wrap 5 blast, fight, knock, storm, truss 6 bundle, strike 8 wrapping

wapiti: elk 4 deer, stag

war: *alarm:* 4 flap

club: 4 mace 5 nulla 6 nullah

correspondent: 4 Pyle

fleet: 6 armada

god of: Ira, Tyr 4 Ares, Coel, Mars, Thor 6 Nergal

goddess: 4 Alea 5 Anath, Bella 6 Anunit, Ishtar 7 Bellona

instrument: 7 caltrap, caltrop 9 relocator

machine: ram 4 bomb, tank 6 rocket 7 missile 8 catapult

religious: 7 crusade

restriction: 8 blockade

trophy: 4 star 5 medal, scalp 6 ribbon

vehicle: 4 jeep, tank

vessel: sub 6 corvet 7 cruiser 8 corvette 9 destroyer, submarine 11 dreadnaught

War and Peace author: 7 Tolstoy

war hawk: 5 jingo

war-horse: 5 steed 6 leader 7 charger, standby 8 partisan 10 campaigner, politician

warbird: 7 aviator, tanager 8 airplane

warble: 4 sing 5 carol, chant, chirl, shake, trill, yodel 7 descant, twitter, vibrate

warbler: 4 wren 5 pipit, robin 6 singer, thrush 8 blackcap, grosbeak, redstart, songbird, songster 9 beccafico 10 bluethroat 11 whitethroat

ward: 4 care, jail, rule, warn 5 watch 6 charge, defend, govern, prison, warden, warder 7 counsel, custody, defense, enclose, fortify, keeping, protect 8 district, garrison, guardian, watchman 9 safeguard, storeroom 10 protection 11 confinement 12 guardianship 14 arrondissement(F.)

pert. to: 9 pupillary

ward off: end 4 fend 5 avert, guard, parry, repel 7 forfend, prevent

warden: 4 caid 5 guard, nazir 6 disdar, dizdar, jailer, jailor, keeper, ranger, regent, sexton 7 alcaide, alcayde, turnkey, viceroy 8 director, governor, guardian, overseer, watchman 9 castellan, concierge, constable, custodian 10 doorkeeper, gatekeeper, supervisor

warder (see also **warden**): 5 staff 7 bulwark 8 sentinel 9 caretaker, truncheon 10 stronghold

wardrobe: 4 room 5 privy 6 closet 7 apparel, armoire, bedroom, cabinet, chamber, clothes 8 costumes 9 garderobe 12 clothespress

ware: 4 host, sage, shun, wary, wise 5 avoid, aware, china, goods, ready, spend, stuff,

waste 6 people, shrewd 7 careful, chaffer, heedful, pottery, prudent, seaweed 8 cautious, products, squander, vigilant 9 cognizant, conscious, porcelain 11 commodities, earthenware, inhabitants, merchandise

warehouse: 4 silo 5 depot, etape, store 6 fonduk, godown 7 almacen, fondouk, funduck, storage 8 elevator, entrepot, magazine 10 storehouse

fee: 7 storage

warfare: See **war**

warily (see also **wary**): 8 gingerly

warkloom: 4 tool 7 utensil 9 implement

warlike: 7 hostile, martial 8 militant, military 9 bellicose, Bellonian, soldierly 10 battailous, pugnacious 11 belligerent

warlock: 6 wizard 8 conjuror, magician, sorcerer 9 enchanter

warm (see also **hot**): 4 avid, beek, heat, keen, kind, mild 5 angry, brisk, calid, chafe, eager, fiery, fresh, tepid, toast 6 ardent, devout, genial, hearty, heated, kindly, lively, loving, strong, tender, toasty 7 amorous, clement, cordial, earnest, enliven, excited, fervent, glowing, irksome, sincere, thermal, zealous 8 animated, friendly, generous, grateful, vehement, vigorous 9 irascible, irritated, sprightly, strenuous 10 harrassing, overheated, passionate, responsive 11 sympathetic 12 affectionate, disagreeable, enthusiastic 13 uncomfortable

warman: See **warrior**

warming: 7 heating 11 calefacient

warmth: 4 elan, zest 6 spirit

pert. to: 7 thermal

warn: 4 rede 5 alarm, alert 6 advise, exhort, inform, notify 7 apprise, apprize, caution, counsel 8 admonish, threaten 9 reprehend

warning: 4 omen 5 knell 6 alarum, beware, caveat, lesson, signal 7 sematic 13 animadversion

sound of: 4 bell 5 alarm, siren 6 alarum, tocsin

warp: abb, end, hit, mud, wry 4 beat, bend, bias, cast, emit, hurl, line, rope, silt, sway, turn, warf 5 eject, expel, fling, quirk, throw, twist 6 buckle, deform, devise, fasten, swerve 7 contort, deflect, distort, falsify, pervert 8 sediment 9 fabricate 10 aberration, intertwine 12 misinterpret

thread for loom: 6 stamen

warragal, warrigal: 5 dingo, horse

warrant: act 4 earn, save, writ 5 berat, guard, order, right 6 assert, defend, ensure, ground, permit, reason, refuge, safety 7 behight, command, defense, justify, precept, protect, voucher, writing 8 document, guaranty, mittimus, sanction 9 authority, authorize, guarantee, protector, safeguard **10** commission, foundation, instrument, obligation, protection **11** certificate **13** authorization, justification

warranty: 8 guaranty, sanction **9** assurance, guarantee **13** authorization, justification

warren: 5 hutch **8** rabbitry, tenement

warrener: 10 gamekeeper

warrior: toa **4** hero, impi **5** brave **6** Amazon **7** fighter, martial, soldier
  group: **4** army
  mythical: **6** Amazon **7** Aslauga
  professional: **7** Hessian **9** gladiator, mercenary
  Trojan: **6** Agenor, Hector

Warsaw suburb: 5 Praga

warship: sub **5** razee **6** bireme **7** cruiser, dromond, frigate, onebank, trireme **8** corvette **9** destroyer, submarine **10** battleship **11** dreadnaught
  deck: **5** orlop
  fleet: **6** armada
  pert. to: **5** naval
  quarters: **7** gunroom
  squadron: **10** escadrille
  three-bank: **7** trireme
  two-bank: **6** bireme

warsle, warstle: 6 tussle **7** wrestle **8** flounder, struggle

wart: 5 tumor **7** verruca **9** subaltern **10** midshipman

wary: shy **5** alert, cagey, canny, chary, leery **7** careful, guarded, knowing, prudent **8** cautious, discreet, stealthy, watchful **9** cautelous, provident **10** economical **11** circumspect

was: See **is**

wase: pad **4** wisp **6** bundle

wash: lap, mud, pan **4** lave, silt, soap **5** bathe, clean, creek, drift, float, leach, rinse, scour, scrub **6** buddle, debris, purify, sperge **7** cleanse, launder, shampoo **8** ablution, alluvium **9** lixiviate
  away: **5** erode, purge
  out: **4** fail **5** elute, erase, flush **7** discard, launder
  up: **6** finish **7** discard, dismiss

washbowl: 4 sink **5** basin **6** lavabo **8** lavatory **9** aljofaina

washed-out: wan **4** pale **5** faded, tired **8** depleted **9** exhausted **10** dispirited, spiritless

washer: 4 rove **5** clove

washing: 8 ablution
  chemical: **6** eluate

Washington, D.C.: 7 capital
  art gallery: **5** Freer **8** National
  hostess: **5** Howar, Mesta
  original planner: **7** L'Enfant
  river: **7** Potomac

section: NE, NW, SE, SW **10** Georgetown
  seeress: **5** Dixon

Washington, George: *portraitist:* **6** Stuart
  wife: **6** Martha

Washington, State of: *city:* Roy **4** Yelm **5** Twist **6** Tacoma, Yakima **7** Everett, Hoquiam, Olympia, Rainier, Seattle, Spokane **8** Aberdeen, Chelalis **9** Wenatchee **10** Bellingham, Walla Walla
  county: **4** King **5** Adams, Ferry, Lewis **6** Pierce, Yakima
  falls: **10** Snoqualmie
  fort: **5** Lewis
  river: **6** Yakima **8** Quinault **9** Snohomish **10** Snoqualmie
  sound: **5** Puget **7** Rosario
  volcano: **7** Rainier
  wind: **7** chinook

Washington palm: 7 fanleaf

washout: 5 gulch, gully **6** fiasco **7** erosion, failure

washy: 4 oozy, thin, weak **5** loose **6** feeble, watery **7** diluted, insipid **8** slippery **9** frivolous, worthless

wasp: 5 whamp **6** dauber, hornet, insect, vespid **12** hymenopteron, yellow jacket
  genus of: **5** sphex
  pert. to: **6** vespal **7** vespine

waspish: 5 testy **7** peevish, slender **8** choleric, petulant, snappish, spiteful **9** fractious, irascible, irritable

wassail: 4 lark, orgy, romp **5** drink, revel **6** frolic, shindy **7** carouse **8** carousal **9** festivity, merriment **10** salutation **11** celebration

waste (see also **refuse, wasteland**)**: 4** fail, idle, loss, pine, ruin, sack **5** decay, dwine, havoc **6** barren, bezzle, devour, molder, ravage **7** atrophy, consume, corrode, destroy, dwindle, exhaust, fritter **8** confound, decrease, demolish, desolate, enfeeble, misspend, squander **9** condiddle, devastate, dissipate, emanciate **11** consumption, destruction, devastation, dissipation, prodigality, superfluous, uninhabited **12** extravagance, improvidence, uncultivated
  allowance: **4** tret
  lay: **4** sack **5** havoc, spoil **6** ravage

waste matter: 5 ashes, dregs, dross **6** debris **7** garbage

wasted: 7 haggard **8** impaired, phthisic

wasteful: 6 lavish **8** prodigal **10** thriftless **11** extravagant, improvident

wasteland: fen **4** burn, moor **5** heath, marsh, swamp, wilds **6** desert, morass **8** badlands

wasting: 5 tabes **6** awaste **8** cachexia, marasmus **12** malnutrition

wastrel: 4 waif 5 idler 6 waster 8 vagabond 10 profligate 11 spendthrift

wat: 6 temple

watch: eye, spy 4 espy, glom, heed, mark, mind, tend, view, wait 5 await, guard, timer, vigil 6 ambush, behold, defend, patrol, police, regard, sentry 7 bivouac, lookout, observe 8 horologe, meditate, sentinel 9 ambuscade, timepiece 11 observation 13 sleeplessness

crystal rim: 5 basil, bezel, bezil

maker: 10 horologist

part: fob 7 crystal

watchdog: 8 guardian

Hel's: 4 Garm 5 Garmr

underworld: 8 Cerberus

watcher: spy 5 scout 8 observer, watchman

watchful: 4 wary 5 alert, aware 7 careful, wakeful 8 cautious, open-eyed 9 attentive 10 unsleeping 11 circumspect

watchman: 5 guard, scout 6 sentry, warder 8 sentinel 10 gatekeeper

watchtower: 6 beacon, garret 7 lookout, mirador 8 bantayan 10 lighthouse

watchword: 5 motto 6 ensign, signal, parole 8 consign 10 shibboleth 11 countersign

watchworks: 8 movement

arrangement: 7 caliper

mechanism: 10 escapement

water: eau(F.), wet 4 agua(Sp.), aqua(L.), brim, broo, burn, hose, pani 5 brine, fluid, flume, laver, lough, lymph, spray 6 dilute, liquid 7 moisten 8 calender, beverage, irrigate, sprinkle 10 citronelle

body: (see also **watercourse**): bay, see sea 4 deep, gulf, lake, mear, mere, pind, pool, tank, well 5 oasis, ocean 6 lagoon, strait 7 springs 9 reservoir

carrier: 4 duct, pipe 5 barge, canal, flume, zanja 7 aguador 8 aqueduct

comb. form: 5 hydro

congealed: ice 5 glace 6 icicle

covered by: 5 awash 7 flooded

draw: 4 lade

element: 6 oxygen 8 hydrogen

goddess: 4 Nina 7 Anahita

hog: 8 capybara

hole: 5 oasis 7 alberca

living in: 9 amphibian

mineral: 5 Vichy 6 selter, Shasta 7 seltzer

neck: 6 strait

obstruction: bar, dam 4 reef

pert. to: 6 marine 7 aquatic

play in: 5 plash

pure: 8 aqua pura(L.)

raising apparatus: 4 pump 5 sweep 6 siphon 7 shadoof 10 water wheel

rough: rip, sea 4 eddy 5 waves 6 rapids 8 breakers

search for: 5 dowse

soapy: 4 suds

sound: 4 drip 5 plash 6 murmur, splash

still: 6 lagoon

surface: 4 ryme

vessel: jug 4 cowl, ewer, lota, pail 5 cruse, flask, lotah 6 bottle, bucket, goglet 7 pitcher, stamnos 8 decanter

Water Bearer: 8 Aquarius

water bird: 4 coot, loon 5 diver 9 waterfowl

water bottle: 4 lota, olla 6 tinaja

water buffalo: ox 7 carabao

water carrier: 4 pipe 7 aguador(Sp.), bheesty(Ind.), channel 8 bheestie(Ind.)

water cavy: 8 capybara

water centipede: 12 hellgrammite

water chicken: 9 gallinule

water clock: 9 clepsydra

water cooler: 4 icer, olla, tank 11 refrigerant

water cow: 7 manatee

water crow: 4 coot 9 snakebird

water crowfoot: 4 herb 9 buttercup

water cure: 10 hydropathy 12 hydrotherapy 17 hydrotherapeutics

water deep: 10 chevrotain

water eagle: 6 osprey

water elephant: 12 hippopotamus

water gate: 6 sluice 9 floodgate 11 watercourse

water germander: 4 mint

water glass: 6 goblet 7 tumbler 9 clepsydra

water grampus: 12 hellgrammite

water hog: 7 bushpig 8 capybara

water hole: pit 4 lake, pond, pool 5 oasis 7 alberca

water horse: 6 kelpie 11 hippocampus 12 hippopotamus

water ice: 7 sherbet

water lift: 4 pump 5 noria 6 siphon 7 shadoof

water lily: 5 lotos, lotus 6 bobbin, nuphar 7 nelumbo 8 nenuphar

water meter: 7 venturi

water moccasin: 5 snake, viper

water mole: 6 desman 8 duckbill, platypus

water nymph: nix 4 lily 5 Ariel, naiad, nixie 6 flower, kelpie, nereid, Undine 7 goddess, hydriad, Oceanid 9 dragonfly

water on the brain: 13 hydrocephalus

water ouzel: 4 bird 6 dipper, thrush

water pig: 7 gourami 8 capybara

water pipe: 4 duct, hose, tube 6 hookah 8 nargileh

water plant: 7 aquatic 10 hydrophyte

water plug: tap 6 spigot 7 hydrant 8 fireplug

water pocket: 6 tinaja

water rat: 4 vole 7 muskrat

water sprite: See **water nymph**

water thief: 6 pirate

watercourse (see also **water** *body*): run 4 dike, dyke, race, wadi, wady 5 brook, canal, chute, creek, drain, gully, river 6 arroyo(Sp.), course, gutter, nullah, ravine, sluice, stream 7 channel, trinket 8 barranca(Sp.)

watercraft: See **boat; ship**

watercress: 9 brooklime

watered: 5 moire

waterfall: lin 4 linn 5 force 7 cascade, chignon, Niagara 8 cataract, Victoria, Yosemite

waterfowl: 4 coot, loon 5 diver

waterfront worker: 5 navvy 9 stevedore

Watergate judge: 6 Sirica

waterhead: 6 source 9 headwater 12 fountainhead 13 hydrocephalus

watering device: 4 hose, pump 5 spray 6 nozzle

watering place: spa 4 pool 5 oasis 6 aguada(Sp.), battis, resort, spring

waterless: dry 4 arid

watermelon: 6 citrul, sandia 7 anguria

waters: See **watering place**
primeval: 4 Apsu

watershed: 5 ridge 6 divide

waterspout: 5 canal, spate 8 gargoyle 9 hurricano

waterwheel: 5 noria, sakia 6 sakieh 7 sakiyeh 8 tympanum

watery: wet 4 soft, thin, weak 5 fluid, sammy, soggy 6 blashy, serous, soaked, sweaty 7 aqueous, insipid, tearful, weeping 8 humorous 11 transparent

wattle: rod 4 beat, bind, flog, gill, twig, wand 5 cooba, fence, stick, twist, withe 6 acacia, coobah, dewlap, hurdle, lappet 9 boobyalla, framework, hackthorn 10 intertwine, interweave

waugh: 4 weak 5 faint, stale 7 insipid 8 nauseous

wave: ola(Sp.), sea, set, wag 4 bore, curl, flap, surf, sway, tide, vein 5 bless, crimp, curve, eager, eagre, float, flood, ridge, shake, surge, swell, swing, tilde, water, waver 6 beckon, billow, comber, fickle, flaunt, marcel, ripple, roller, signal 7 breaker, flutter, ripplet, seagate, tsunami, vibrate, wavelet 8 brandish, flourish, undulate, whitecap 9 fluctuate, permanent, vibration 10 undulation, unevenness
comb. form: 4 ondo
top: 5 crest
upward motion: 5 scend

waver: 4 reel, sway, twig 5 quake, swing 6 change, falter, teeter, totter, wiggle 7

flicker, flitter, flutter, sapling, stagger, tremble, vibrate 8 hesitate 9 fluctuate, oscillate, vacillate

wavering: 6 fickle 7 lambent 8 doubtful, flexuous, unsteady 9 desultory 10 irresolute

wavy: 4 ente(her.), onde(her.), unde(her.), undy(her.) 5 crisp, curly, snaky, undee(her.) 6 flying 7 billowy, sinuate, sinuous 8 undulant 9 undulated 10 undulating

wawl, waul: 4 howl, wail 6 squall

wax: 4 cere, grow, pela 5 putty 6 become 7 cerumen, suberin 8 adhesive, increase, paraffin 11 zietriskite
candle: 5 taper 6 cierge
cobbler's: 4 code
comb. form: cer
figure: 9 ceroplast
match: 5 vesta
mixture: 6 cerate
myrtle: 8 bayberry
ointment: 6 cerate
opposite of: 4 wane
pert. to: 5 ceral
preparation: 6 cerate
substance: 5 cerin
used for skis: 7 klister
yellow: 7 ceresin

waxbill: 7 astrild

waxen: 4 soft, waxy 6 pallid, viscid 7 cerated, pliable 8 yielding 11 impressible 14 impressionable

waxwing: 9 cedarbird

waxy: 5 angry, vexed

way: via 4 cost, fore, gait, lane, mode, path, plan, road, room 5 alley, going, habit, milky, route, space, style, track 6 ambage, arcade, avenue, career, causey, chemin, course, detour, device, manner, method, scheme, street 7 advance, fashion, highway, opening, passage 8 causeway, contrada, progress 9 banquette, direction, procedure 12 idiosyncrasy
in: 7 contact 8 entrance
on: 7 en route
open: 7 pioneer
out: 4 exit 6 egress, escape

waybill: 8 manifest

wayfarer: 6 viator 8 traveler

waygate: 4 path 9 departure 10 passageway

waylay: 5 await, belay, beset 6 ambush 7 forelay 8 surprise 9 ambuscade

waymark: ahu 5 arrow 9 milestone

wayward: 6 unruly 7 erratic, froward, naughty, willful 8 contrary, perverse, stubborn, unsteady, untoward 9 irregular 10 capricious, headstrong, refractory, self-willed 11 disobedient, fluctuating, intractable 13 unpredictable

waywiser: 8 odometer 9 pedometer 12 perambulator

we: nos(L.) 8 ourselves

weak: 4 puny, soft, thin, worn 5 anile, bauch, chirp, crank, crimp, dicky, faint, frail, seely, washy, waugh, young 6 caduke, debile, dickey, dotish, faulty, feeble, flabby, flaggy, flimsy, foible, infirm, scream, sickly, squeak, tender, unwise, watery 7 brittle, doatish, dwaible, dwaibly, foolish, fragile, pliable 8 childish, decrepit, feckless, feminine, flagging, helpless, impotent 9 childlike, dissolute, enfeebled, nerveless, powerless 10 effeminate, inadequate 11 ineffective 12 unconvincing

weaken: go; sap 4 thin, tire 5 appal, break, craze, delay 6 appall, deaden, defeat, dilute, impair, lessen, rebate, reduce, soften 7 cripple, decline, depress, disable, exhaust, unnerve 8 enervate 9 attenuate, extenuate, undermine 10 debilitate, demoralize

weakling: 5 puler, sissy 6 softie 7 crybaby

weakness: 4 flaw 6 defect, foible 7 acratia, ailment, failing 8 debility, fondness 9 inability 11 attenuation 12 imperfection
of organ or muscle: 5 atony

weal: 4 line, mark, pomp, wale, welt 5 ridge, state, wheal 6 choice, choose, riches, stripe, wealth 7 welfare 9 happiness, wellbeing 10 commonweal, prosperity

wealth: 4 dhan, gear, gold, good, weal 5 money 6 assets, graith, mammon, riches 7 capital, fortune, welfare 8 opulence, property, treasure 9 abundance, affluence, wellbeing 10 prosperity 11 possessions
comb. form: 5 pluto
gained: 8 chevance 9 chievance
god of: 6 Plutus
income from: 6 usance
person of: 5 Midas, nabob 7 Croesus, magnate 9 moneybags, plutocrat

wealthy: 4 full 5 ample, pursy

wean: 4 baby 5 child 6 detach, infant 8 alienate, estrange 9 reconcile

weanie: 4 baby

weanly: 6 feeble 8 childish

weapon: arm, dag, gun 4 beak, bola, bolo, celt, claw, dart, dirk, epee, foil, pike 5 arrow, bolas, glave, knife, lance, rifle, saber, sabre, shaft, sling, spear, sword, talon, vouge 6 bomber, dagger, eolith, glaive, mortar, pistol, poleax, rapier 7 bazooka, carbine, gisarme, halberd, halbert, machete, missile, poleaxe, trident 8 catapult, crossbow, fauchard, leeangle, revolver, stiletto, tomahawk 9 artillery, derringer 11 blunderbuss
lay down: 6 disarm 9 surrender

storage place: 7 arsenal
without: 7 unarmed

wear: don, rub 4 fray, tire 5 chafe, erode, grind, sport, weary 6 abrade, attire, endure, impair 7 apparel, clothes, consume, corrode, display, exhaust, exhibit, fatigue 8 diminish 11 deteriorate
away: 5 erode 6 abrade

wearable: 6 usable 7 garment 8 clothing

weariful: See **wearisome**

weariness (see also **weary**): 5 ennui 6 tedium 7 fatigue 8 vexation 9 lassitude

wearish: 4 weak 5 faint 6 sickly 7 insipid 8 unsavory 9 squeamish

wearisome: 4 hard 6 boring, dismal, dreary, prolix, tiring 7 irksome, tedious 8 tiresome 9 fatiguing, laborious, vexatious 10 monotonous 11 displeasing, everlasting

weary: bad, fag, irk, sad 4 bore, jade, puny, tire, weak, worn 5 annoy, bored, curse, spent, timid, tired 6 harass, plague, sickly 7 exhaust, fatigue, irksome, tedious 8 fatigued, grievous, tiresome 9 forjaskit, forjesket, surfeited 10 defatigate, disastrous 11 unfortunate

Weary Willie: 5 tramp 7 shirker, vagrant 13 featherbedder

weasand: 6 gullet, throat 7 trachea 8 windpipe 9 esophagus

weasel: 4 cane, stot, vare 5 ratel, stoat 6 ermine, ferret 10 equivocate
family: 6 ermine, ferret, marten

weasel cat: 7 linsang

weasel-like: 9 musteline

weather: dry 4 hail, rain, snow, wind 5 erode, sleet 7 climate 8 discolor, windward 12 disintegrate

weather map line: 6 isobar

weather satellite: 5 Tiros

weathercock: 4 fane, vane

weathered: 5 faded 6 tanned 7 bronzed, stained 8 bleached, hardened 9 roughened, toughened

weatherman: 13 meteorologist

weave: 4 darn, knit, lace, spin 5 braid, drape, plait, unite 6 devise, enlace, wattle 7 canille, entwine, fashion 8 cannelle, contrive 9 fabricate, interlace, interwind 10 intertwine, intertwist
twigs: 6 wattle

weaver's tool: 4 loom, reed, sley

weaverbird: 4 baya, taha 6 whidah

weaving: *cylinder:* 4 beam
goddess: 6 Ergane
machine: 4 loom 6 carder 8 jacquard
product: 4 cloth 7 textile

weazen: See **wizen**

web: mat, net, ply 4 caul, trap, veil, warp 5 snare 6 fabric, tissue 7 ensnare, network, texture, webbing 8 entangle, gossamer, membrane, vexillum 11 fabrication 12 entanglement

pert. to: 6 telary 7 retiary

web-footed: 7 palmate 11 totipalmate

web-like: 4 lacy 7 spidery

half: 11 semi-palmate

webbing: 7 binding

Weber opera: 6 Oberon

wed: 4 join 5 elope, marry, mated, unite 6 joined, pawned 7 espouse, pledged, spliced 9 mortgaged

pert. to: 7 marital

wedding: 6 splice 8 ceremony, espousal, marriage, nuptials 11 anniversary

anniversary: See **wedding anniversary**

attendant: 5 usher 10 bridesmaid

canopy: 5 chupa 6 huppah 7 chuppah

party: 9 breakfast, reception

proclamation: 5 banns

ring: 4 band

wedding anniversary: *fifteenth:* 7 crystal

fifth: 4 wood

first: 5 paper

kind of: tin 4 ruby 5 candy, china, coral, linen, paper, pearl, straw 6 floral, golden, silver, wooden 7 crystal, diamond, emerald, leather

seventy-fifth: 7 diamond

tenth: tin

thirtieth: 5 pearl

twentieth: 5 china

twenty-fifth: 6 silver

wedge: jam 4 club, heel, lump, shoe 5 cleat, crowd, ingot, piece, split 6 cleave, sector, wedgie 7 niblick 8 separate, triangle, voussoir 9 formation

wedge-shaped: 6 cuneal 7 cuneate 8 cuneated, cuniform 9 cuneiform

wedgie: 4 shoe

wedlock (see also **wedding**): 4 wife 9 matrimony

Wednesday (source of name): 5 Woden

wee: 4 tiny 5 bitty, small, teeny 6 little, minute 10 diminutive

weed: 4 band, garb, loco, milk, sida, tare 5 armor, cheat, dress, horse, vetch 6 darnel, datura, nettle, remove, sarcle, spurge 7 allseed, clothes, costume, garment, illness, mallows, purloin, ragweed, relapse, thistle, tobacco 8 clothing, plantain, purslane, sealwort, toadflax, trumpery 9 alfilaria, dandelion, eradicate 11 undergrowth

weed killer: 9 herbicide

weeds: 8 mourning

weedy: 4 foul, lean 5 lanky 7 scraggy 8 ungainly

week: 8 hebdomad

weekday: 5 feria

weekly: 5 aweek 10 hebdomadal, periodical 11 hebdomadary, publication

weeks (two): 9 fortnight

weel: 4 eddy, pool, trap 6 basket 9 whirlpool

weem: pit 4 cave 6 cavern

ween: 4 hope 5 fancy, think 6 expect 7 believe, imagine, suppose 8 conceive

weep: cry, sob 4 leak, tear, wail 5 exude, greet, mourn 6 bewail, beweep, boohoo, lament 7 blubber

Weeping Philosopher: 10 Heraclitus

weeping statue: 5 Niobe

weepy: 5 moist, seepy 6 oozing 7 tearful, weeping 8 mournful

weeshy, weeshie: wee 4 tiny 5 weeny

weet: wet, wit 4 know

weevil: 4 boll, lota 8 circulio

weeze: 4 ooze

weft: web 4 film, warp, woof, yarn 5 shoot, shute 7 filling 12 crossthreads

weigh: 4 bear, lift, tare, test 5 carry, hoist, poise 6 esteem, ponder, regard 7 balance, examine, measure, portion, support 8 consider, dispense, meditate 9 apportion 14 counterbalance

weigh down: sit 4 lade, load 7 depress, oppress

weigher: 5 trone 6 potdar, scaler 7 balance, trutine 8 computer 9 steelyard

weighing machine: 5 scale, trone 7 balance 9 steelyard

weight: bob, CWT, keg, lot, mol, tod, tom, ton, tup 4 beef, dram, gram, heft, lade, last, load, mina, onus, pari, rati, shot, tola 5 carat, clove, flask, grain, ounce, pfund, poise, pound, power, ratti, rider, scale, stein 6 barrel, burden, cental, charge, denier, fother, fotmal, gramme, grivna, import, moment 7 centner, drachma, gravity, oppress, plummet, quarter, quintal, scruple, tonnage 8 decagram, encumber, kilogram, micogram, pressure, vierling, vamfront, vammazsa 9 authority, centigram, hectogram, heaviness, influence, liespfund, milligram, myriagram, quentchen, zollpfund 12 significance 13 hundredweight, ponderability

allowance: 4 tare 7 scalage

comb. form: 4 baro

inspector: 6 sealer

kind of: net 4 troy 5 gross 6 metric 8 jeweler's 10 apothecary 11 avoirdupois

of container: 4 tare

of 100 pounds: 6 cental

of 2000 pounds: ton

official: 6 metage

pert. to: 5 baric 8 ponderal

sash cord: 5 mouse

system of: 4 troy 5 avoir 11 avoirdupois 12 apothecaries

weighted: 5 laden 6 loaded 8 burdened 9 evaluated, oppressed

weightiness: 4 pomp 7 dignity, gravity 9 solemnity

weighty: fat 5 bulky, heavy, hefty, large, massy, obese, solid 6 severe, solemn 7 capital, massive, onerous, serious, telling 8 forcible, grievous, powerful 9 corpulent, momentous, ponderous 10 burdensome, chargeable, cumbersome, impressive, oppressive

weir: dam 4 bank 5 fence, garth, levee 7 barrier, milldam 11 obstruction

weird: lot, odd 4 eery, fate, unco, wild 5 charm, eerie, queer, scary, spell 7 awesome, curious, destine, destiny, fortune, ghostly, macabre, predict, strange, uncanny, unusual 8 foretell, prophecy 9 unearthly 10 mysterious, prediction, soothsayer

weka: 4 bird, rail

welcome: 4 hail 5 adopt, greet 7 acclaim, embrace 8 greeting 9 agreeable, bienvenue, desirable 10 acceptable, salutation

weld: 5 unite 11 consolidate

welding gas: 9 acetylene

welfare: 4 sele, weal 10 prosperity
goddess: 5 Salus

welkin: air, sky 10 atmosphere

well: fit, pit 4 bene(It., L.), bien(F.), fair, flow, gush, hole, sump 5 aweel(Sc.), fount 6 gusher, hearty, spring 7 cistern, gaylies, geylies, gradely, healthy 8 artesian, expertly, fountain 10 gratifying 11 excellently 12 satisfactory
comb. form: 4 bene
drill device: jar
lining: 5 steen
pit: 4 sump
pole: 5 sweep
prefix: eu

well-behaved: 4 good

well-being: 4 good, weal 6 health 7 comfort 8 eucrasia, felicity 9 eudaemony, happiness 10 prosperity

well-bred: 5 civil 6 polite 7 genteel, refined 8 cultured, wellborn 9 pedigreed 10 cultivated 11 gentlemanly 12 thoroughbred

well-defined: 8 distinct 11 distinctive

well-founded: 4 firm

well-groomed: 4 neat 5 clean, sleek 6 soigne 7 soignee

well-grounded: 4 firm 5 valid

well-heeled: 4 rich 7 moneyed 10 prosperous

well-known: 6 famous 7 eminent 8 familiar 9 notorious

well-liked: 7 popular

well-made: 9 affabrous

well-nigh: 6 almost, nearly

well-off: 5 lucky 8 thriving 10 prosperous

well-timed: 6 timely 9 opportune

well-versed: 7 erudite

Welland: 4 city 5 canal, river

wellaway: woe 4 alas 5 alack 6 regret 9 alackaday

wellborn: 4 rich 5 noble 7 eugenic

wellhead: 6 source, spring 8 fountain 12 fountainhead

welsh, welch: 5 cheat, evade, renig 6 renege 7 swindle

Welsh, Welch (see also **Wales**): 6 Cymric 8 Cambrian

welsh drake: 7 gadwale, gadwall, gadwell

Welsh onion: 5 cibol

Welsh Rabbit: 7 rarebit

welt: 4 mark, turn, wale 5 ridge, upset 6 stripe, thrash 8 overturn

welter: 4 reel, roll, toss, wilt 5 upset 6 grovel, tumble, wallow, wither 7 stagger, turmoil 8 overturn 9 confusion

wem: 4 flaw, scar, spot 5 stain

wen: 4 cyst, rune 5 tumor 7 blemish 11 excrescence 12 imperfection, protuberance

wench: 4 dell, doxy, drab, gill, girl 5 child, gouge, trull, woman 6 blowen, blowze, damsel, maiden 7 consort, servant 8 strumpet 11 maidservant

wend: go; bow 4 fare, pass 5 alter, shift 6 depart, travel 7 circuit, journey, proceed 9 disappear

Wend: 4 Slav, Sorb 7 Sorbian

Wendy: *brother:* 5 Peter
dog: 4 Nana

went (see also **go**): 4 lane, road 5 alley 7 passage 9 crossroad

wenzel: 4 jack 5 knave

were (see also **are**): 5 check, doubt, dread, guard 10 perplexity 11 uncertainty 12 apprehension

wergild: cro 4 eric

Wessex king: Ine, Ini

West: 8 frontier, Occident

West Africa: See **Africa**

West Germany capital: 4 Bonn

West Indies: 7 Bahamas 8 Antilles
bird: 4 arar, tody 6 mucaro
boat: 6 droger 7 drogher 9 catamaran
coin: 5 daler
fiber: 5 cajun
fish: 4 paru, pega, sesi 5 pelon 6 testar 7 pegador 8 scirenga 9 picudilla
fleas: 7 chigoes
fruit: 4 tuna 5 papaw 6 papaya, pawpaw 7 genipap
handkerchief: 7 malabar

herb: 4 ocra 6 vanglo 7 vangloe
island: 4 Cuba 5 Aruba, Haiti, Nevis 6 Bahama 7 Jamaica 8 Antilles, Barbados, Trinidad
king: 7 Cacique
liquor: 5 mobby, tafia 6 mobbie, taffia
lizard: 6 arbalo
mistletoe: 7 gadbush
palm: 5 yagua, yaray 6 grigri, grugru
people: Ebo 4 Eboe 5 Cuban 6 Creole
pert. to: 9 Antillean
plum: 4 jobo
region: 7 Malabar
republic: 5 Haiti
rodent: 5 hutia, jutia 6 agouti
shrub: 4 anil 7 joewood
snuff: 8 maccaboy, maccoboy
sorcery: ob; obe, obi 6 voodoo
sugar work: 5 usine
taro: 5 tania
tortoise: 7 hicatee 8 hiccatee
tree: 4 ausu, cera 5 acana, acapu, ebony, genip, papaw, yacca 6 aralie, ausubo, balata, cocuyo, gomart, pawpaw, ramoon 7 cocullo 8 aceituna, cockspur, drumwood 9 cocuswood, sapodilla
treewood: 5 galba
volcano: 5 Pelee
West Point: *island:* 4 Iona
mascot: 4 mule
student: 4 pleb 5 cadet, plebe 8 yearling
West Virginia city: 5 Logan 10 Charleston(c.)
Western treaty alliance: 4 NATO
Westminster clock: Ben
Westphalian city: 7 Munster
wet: lax, off 4 damp, dank, dewy, lash, mire, rain, soak 5 bedew, bewet, dabby, foggy, humid, leach, misty, moist, mushy, rainy, soggy, soppy, sweat, wrong 6 clashy, dampen, drench, humect, imbrue, jarble, liquor, shower, soaked, sodden, watery 7 flotter, moisten, splashy, squashy 8 dampened, irrigate, moisture, sprinkle 9 misguided 11 intoxicated 18 anti-prohibitionist
wet blanket: 6 dampen 7 depress, killjoy 8 deadhead, dispirit 10 discourage, spoilsport
wet flax: ret
wet one's whistle: 5 drink
weta: 6 insect
wetbird: 9 chaffinch
wether: ram 4 wool 5 sheep 6 eunuch 7 dinmont
whack: hit, try 4 bang, beat, belt, blow 5 share, thump, trial, whang 6 chance, strike, stroke, thwack 7 attempt, portion 8 division 9 allowance, condition

whacking: 5 large 8 whopping 10 tremendous
whale: hit, orc 4 beat, cete, drub, lash, orca, wale, whip, whop 5 poggy, sperm, whack 6 baleen, beluga, blower, strike, thrash 7 Cetacea, grampus, ripsack 8 cachalot, hardhead 9 blackfish, mysticete, mysticeti, zeuglodon 10 bottlehead, zeuglodont 13 sulphur-bottom
blue: 9 sibbaldus
carcass: 5 kreng
constellation: 5 Cetus
cry: 4 fall
fat: 7 blubber
female: cow
food: 4 brit
iron: 7 harpoon
order: 4 cete 7 Cetacea
pert. to: 5 cetic
school: gam, pod
secretion: 9 ambergris
skin: 6 muktuk
strip blubber from: 6 flense
tail part: 5 fluke
young: 4 calf 5 stunt 9 shorthead
whale oil: 10 spermaceti
cask: 4 rier
whaleback: 9 steamship 10 turtleback 12 grain-carrier
whalebird: 4 gull 6 petrel 9 phalarope, turnstone
whalebone: 5 stiff 6 baleen, severe 10 inflexible
whalehead: 8 shoebill
whaler: 4 ship 7 bushman, swagman, whopper 8 whaleman 9 sundowner, whaleboat
visit: gam
whaling: 4 huge 8 whopping
cask: 4 rier 6 cardel
profit: lay
spear: 7 harpoon
whaling ship: 6 Pequod, whaler
whample: 4 blow 6 stroke
whang: 4 bang, beat, blow, chop 5 chunk, slice, thong, throw, whack 6 assail, strike, thrash
whangee, wanghee: 4 cane 5 stick 6 bamboo
wharf: 4 dock, pier, quai(F.), quay 7 landing
space: 7 quayage
worker: 9 stevedore
wharf fish: 6 cunner
wharfmaster: 10 wharfinger
whatnot: 7 etagere
whaup: 4 fuss 6 curlew, outcry
wheal: 4 mark, mine, wale, weal 5 whelk 6 stripe 7 postule 9 suppurate
wheat: 5 durum, spelt, trigo 6 imphee 7 einkorn, semoule

chaff: 4 bran

disease: 4 bunt, rust, smut 5 ergot 6 aecium, fungus

gritty part: 8 semolina

head: ear

outer coat: 4 bran

processed: 4 suji 5 grits 6 bulgur 9 middlings

repository: bin 8 elevator

state: 4 Ohio 5 Idaho 6 Dakota, Kansas 7 Indiana, Montana 8 Illinois, Missouri, Nebraska, Oklahoma 9 Minnesota 10 Washington 12 Pennsylvania

stubble: 6 arrish

wheat duck: 7 widgeon 8 baldpate

wheat louse: 5 aphid

wheat smut: 4 bunt 8 colbrand

wheatbird: 4 lark

wheatear: 4 bird 5 chack 8 chickell 10 gorsehatch

wheedle: cog 4 cant, coax 5 carny, tease, whine 6 banter, butter, cajole, carney, fleech, whilly 7 blarney, cuittle, flatter 8 persuade 9 influence

wheel (see also **gear**): cam, cog 4 bike, disk, helm, roll, turn 5 pivot, rotor, rowel, skeif, skive 6 caster, circle, roller, rotate, sheave 7 bicycle, chukkar, chukker, pedrail, revolve 10 revolution, waterwheel

comb. form: 5 troch 6 trocho

furniture: 6 caster

part: cam, cog, rim 4 tire 5 felly, spoke, sprag 6 felloe 8 sprocket

pert. to: 5 rotal

potters: see **potter's wheel**

rim: 5 felly 6 felloe

shaft: 4 axle

spinning: see **spinning wheel**

spurred: 5 rowel

stopper: 5 brake

toothed: cog

water-raising: see **waterwheel**

wheel-shaped: 6 rotate 8 circular, rotiform

wheelbarrow: hod 10 hurlbarrow

wheeler (see also **wheelman**): 7 cyclist, vulture 11 wheelwright

wheelman: 5 pilot 7 cyclist, steerer, wheeler 8 helmsman, pedalist 9 bicyclist

wheeze: gag 4 hint, joke 5 adage, dodge, hoose, hooze, trick 6 cliche, coghle(Sc.), device, saying 9 witticism

wheezy: 9 asthmatic

whelk: 4 acne 5 snail 6 papule, pimple, winkle 7 pustule

whelm (see also **overwhelm**): 5 cover, crush 9 drainpipe

whelp: cub, dog, pup 4 bear, fawn, lion, wale, welt, wolf 5 child, puppy, tiger, youth 7 leopard

whemmel, whemmle: 5 upset 6 tumble 8 overturn 9 confusion

when: as 5 until 7 whereas 8 although, whenever

where: 7 whither

whereas: as 5 since

wherefore: 5 cause 6 reason 9 therefore 11 accordingly

whereness: 6 ubiety

wherewithal: 5 means 9 resources

wherret: box, hit 4 slap

wherry: 4 boat 5 barge, carry, scull 7 lighter, rowboat, vehicle 9 transport

whet: 4 hone 5 grind, rouse, strop 6 excite 7 quicken, sharpen 9 stimulate

whether: if

whetstone: bur 4 buhr, burr, hone 5 stone 9 sharpener

whewl: cry 4 howl 5 whine

whey: 5 serum

which: who 4 that, whom

which was to be shown: QED

whicker: 5 neigh 6 whinny

whid: fib, lie 4 word 5 frisk

whiff: fan 4 flag, fuff, guff, gust, odor, puff, waft, wave 5 expel, fluff, jiffy, smell 6 breath, exhale, inhale, stench 7 instant 10 inhalation

whiffle: 4 blow, emit, idle, turn, veer, wave 5 expel, shake, shift 6 change, trifle 7 flicker, flutter, scatter 8 disperse 9 vacillate

whig: jog 4 whey 8 beverage 10 buttermilk

Whig poet: Og 8 Shadwell

while: as; yet 5 until 6 whenas 7 whereas

whilly: 4 gull 6 cajole 7 wheedle

whilom: 4 erst, once, past 6 former 8 erewhile, formerly 9 erstwhile

whim: fad, fit, gig 4 idea, mood 5 fancy, humor, winch 6 megrim, notion, trifle, vagary, whimsy 7 boutade, caprice, capstan, whimsey 8 crotchet

whimper: cry, sob 4 mewl, moan, pule, weep 5 whine 6 murmur, yammer 7 grizzle, sniffle

whimsical: odd 5 droll, queer 6 cockle 7 bizzaro, comical 8 fanciful, freakish, notional 9 conceited, eccentric, fantastic, grotesque 10 capricious 11 fantastical

whimsy: See **whim**

whin: 4 rock, whim 5 furze, gorse 9 whinstone

whinchat: 9 gorsechat, grasschat

whine: wow 4 cant, girn, moan, pule 5 croon, whewl 6 snivel, yammer 7 whimper 8 complain

whinnock: 7 whimper

whinny: 4 bray 5 hinny, neigh

whinyard: 5 sword

whip: cat, gad, tan 4 beat, cane, crop, flay, flog, jerk, lace, lash, urge, wind, wrap 5 birch, flick knout, outdo, quirt, spank, strap, swish 6 defeat, punish, stitch, strike, swinge, switch, thrash 7 belabor, chicote, conquer, overlay, scourge, sjambok 8 chawbuck, coachman, hunstman 9 bullwhack, flagellum 10 discipline, flagellate

mark: 4 wale, weal, welt

part: 4 crop 5 snead 6 handle, socket

whir: bur, fly 4 birl, burr, move, whiz 5 hurry, skirr, swirl, whizz 6 bustle, hurtle 7 revolve, vibrate 9 commotion

whirl: 4 eddy, reel, spin, stir, tirl, turn 5 drill, twirl 6 bustle, circle, gyrate, rotate, swinge, tumult, uproar, vortex 7 revolve 9 commotion, pirouette

whirlbone: 7 kneepan, patella 10 hucklebone

whirlpool: 4 eddy 5 gorce, swirl 6 gurges, vortex 9 Charybdis, maelstrom

whirlwind: oe 7 cyclone, tornado 9 maelstrom

whirr: See whir

whisht: 4 hush 7 silence

whisk: 4 tuft, whip, wisp 5 flisk

whiskers (see also beard): 6 growth 7 stubble 9 sideburns, vibrissae 11 muttonchops

fish: 7 barbels

whiskey, whisky: rye 4 corn 6 poteen, redeye, rotgut, Scotch 8 blockade, busthead 9 moonshine 10 usquebaugh

maker: 9 distiller

punch: 5 facer

whiskin: 4 bowl

whisper: 4 buzz 5 rumor 6 breeze, murmur

whisperer: 7 tattler 9 backbiter, slanderer 10 talebearer

whist: 4 game, hush, mute 5 cards, quiet, still 6 silent 7 silence 8 silently

declaration: 6 misere

dummy: 4 mort

hand: 6 tenace 10 Yarborough

whistle: 4 hiss, pipe, sugh, toot 5 siren, sough

whistle duck: 9 goldeneye

whistle-pig: 9 woodchuck

whistlewing: 9 goldeneye

whit: bit, jot 4 atom, doit, haet, hate, iota 5 speck 8 particle

white: wan 4 ashy, bawn, hoar, pale, pure 5 ashen, happy, hoary, ivory 6 albino, argent, blanch, chalky, grayed, honest, pallid, pearly 7 ivorine, silvery 8 harmless, innocent, spotless 9 colorless, fortunate, honorable 10 auspicious

becoming: 9 canescent

egg's: 5 glair 7 albumen

with age: 4 hoar 5 hoary

white ant: 4 anai, anay 7 termite

white antimony: 11 valentinite

white cell: 9 leukocyte

white cliffs' site: 5 Dover

white-collar: 5 clerk 6 typist 8 salesman 9 secretary 10 bookkeeper

white crow: 7 vulture

white elephant (land of): 4 Siam 5 Burma, India 6 Ceylon 8 Thailand

white feather: 4 fear 9 cowardice

white flag: 5 truce 9 surrender

white gentian: 9 feverroot

white grouse: 9 ptarmigan

white heat: 13 incandescence

white horse nettle: 9 trompillo

White House: *designer:* 5 Hoban

dog: 4 Fala

feature: 7 portico

first resident: 5 Adams

initials: FDR, HST

nickname: Abe, Ike

white Indian hemp: 8 milkweed

white iron pyrites: 9 marcasite

white jade: 9 alabaster

white lead: 6 ceruse

white lead ore: 9 cerussite

white-livered: 8 cowardly 13 pusillanimous

white magic: 7 theurgy

white merganser: 4 smew

white mica: 9 muscovite

White Monk: 10 Cistercian

White Mountain: 5 Adams

white mule: gin 6 liquor, whisky 7 whiskey 9 moonshine

white mundic: 12 arsenopyrite

white nun: 4 smew

white partridge: 9 ptarmigan

white plague: 8 phthisis 11 consumption 12 tuberculosis

white plantain: 9 pussytoes

white poplar: 5 abele, aspen

white pudding: 7 sausage 9 whitehass

white pyrite: 9 marcasite

white sanicle: 9 snakeroot

white snipe: 6 avocet 10 sanderling

White Sunday: 10 Whitsunday

white walnut: 8 shagbark, sycamore 9 butternut

white whale: 6 beluga

white widgeon: 4 smew

whitebelly: 6 grouse, pigeon

whiteboy: pet 8 favorite

whitecap: 4 wave 5 crest

whited sepulcher: 9 hypocrite

whitefish: 5 cisco 6 beluga 8 menhaden

whiten: 4 pale 5 chalk 6 blanch, bleach 8 etiolate

whiteside: 9 goldeneye

whitewash: 6 blanch, defeat, parget 7 conceal

whiteweed: 5 daisy

whitewing: 4 sail 6 scoter 7 sweeper 9 chaffinch

whither: 4 blow, hurl, rush, whiz 5 hurry, shake, throw, where 6 flurry, totter 7 bluster, tremble 8 wherever

whiting: 4 fish 5 chalk

whitlow: 4 sore 5 felon 6 fetlow 12 inflammation

whitster: 8 bleacher

Whitsunday: 9 Pentecost

whittaw: 7 saddler

whitten: 5 rowan

whitterick: 6 curlew

whittle: cut 4 pare, whet 5 knife, shape, shave, shawl 6 mantle, reduce, remove 7 blanket 9 petticoat, whetstone

whiz: go; hum 4 buzz, hiss, pirr, whir 5 hurry 6 corker, rotate 7 bargain

who: quo(L.), Wer(G.), wha(Sc.) 13 interrogative

whoa: 4 halt, stop

whole: all, sum 4 full, hail, hale, sole, unit 5 gross, total 6 entire, healed, intact, wholly 7 perfect 8 absolute, complete, ensemble, entirely, entirety, thorough, unbroken 9 unanimous, undamaged, undivided 10 unimpaired

comb. form: 4 toti, toto

whole note: 9 semibreve

whole number: 7 integer

whole-souled: 7 devoted, sincere, zealous 8 generous 12 whole-hearted

wholehearted: 6 hearty 7 devoted, earnest, sincere 8 complete 10 unreserved 11 unmitigated

wholesale: 4 bulk, lots 7 massive 8 abundant, sweeping 9 extensive

wholesome: 5 sound 6 benign, hearty, robust 7 healthy 8 benedict, halesome, salutary, vigorous 9 favorable, healthful 10 beneficial, healthsome, propitious, salubrious

wholly: 5 quite 7 algates 10 altogether 11 exclusively

comb. form: 4 toto

whoop: 4 hoot, urge, yell 5 cheer, shout 6 halloo

whooping cough: 9 pertussis

whop: 4 beat, blow, bump, flop 5 knock, throw 6 strike, stroke

whopper: lie 5 story 6 bender, bumper 7 bouncer

whopping: 5 great, large 7 banging

whore: 4 drab 5 wench 6 harlot 8 strumpet 9 courtesan 10 prostitute

whorl: 5 spire

why: 9 wherefore

whyo: 6 robber 7 footpad 8 gangster

wick: bay 4 bend, town 5 angle, creek, inlet 6 corner, hamlet, inwick 7 borough, village 9 farmstead

wicked: bad, ill 4 evil, vile 6 fierce, guilty, horrid, sinful, unjust 7 beastly, harmful, heinous, hellish, painful, profane, vicious 8 criminal, depraved, devilish, diabolic, felonous, fiendish, flagrant, indecent 9 atrocious, difficult, malicious, nefandous, nefarious, perverted 10 diabolical, flagitious, impassable, iniquitous, villainous 11 mischievous 12 inaccessible

wicker: 4 twig 5 osier, withe

wicker basket: 4 kish

wicker cradle: 8 bassinet

wicker hut: 5 jacal

wicket: 4 arch, door, gate, hoop 5 hatch 6 window 7 guichet, opening

wickiup: hut 7 shelter

widdershins, withershins: 10 contrarily, topsy-turvy 12 contrariwise

widdle: 7 wriggle 8 struggle

widdrim: 4 fury 7 madness 9 confusion 10 excitement

widdy: 4 rope 5 noose, widow, withy 6 halter 7 gallows

wide: 5 ample, broad, loose, roomy 6 opened 8 expanded, spacious 9 capacious, distended, expansive, extensive 12 farspreading 13 comprehensive

wide-awake: hat 4 keen, tern 5 alert 7 knowing 8 watchful 10 interested

widely: far 4 afar 6 abroad

widen: 4 ream 6 dilate, expand, extend, spread 7 amplify, broaden, enlarge 10 generalize

widespread: 4 rife 7 allover, diffuse, general 8 diffused, sweeping 9 extensive, pervasive, prevalent, universal 13 comprehensive

widgeon: 4 duck 5 goose 8 baldpate 9 simpleton

genus: 6 mareca

widow: 5 widdy 6 relict 7 dowager 8 bereaved

in cards: 4 skat

right: 5 dower 10 quarantine

suicide: 6 suttee

widow monkey: 4 titi

widow's mite: 5 lepta(pl.) 6 lepton

widowhood: 7 viduage

widowman: 7 widower

width: 5 girth 7 breadth 8 diameter, latitude, wideness

wield: ply 4 bear, cope, deal, rule 5 power, swing 6 direct, employ, handle, manage, ordain 7 control 8 brandish 9 determine 10 manipulate

wife: ux(L.); hen 4 frau, frow, mate, uxor(L.) 5 donna, mujer 6 gammer, spouse 7 consort 8 gudewife(Sc.), guidwife(Sc.), helpmate, helpmeet

bequest to: dot 5 dowry

clergyman's: 8 curatess

killer: 9 uxoricide

lord's: 4 lady

pert. to: 7 uxorial

rajah's: 4 rani 5 ranee

slave's: 9 broadwife

wig: 4 gizz 5 busby, caxon, jasey, judge, scold 6 baguio, peruke, rebuke, toupee 7 censure, periwig, spencer 8 Chedreux 9 dignitary, Gregorian, reprimand

repair: 6 careen

wiggle: 5 shake 6 waggle, wobble 7 stagger, wriggle

wight: man 4 loud 5 brave, swift, witch 6 active, nimble, strong 7 swiftly, valiant 8 creature, powerful, strongly

wigwag: 6 signal

wigwam: 4 home, tipi 5 tepee 6 teepee

wild: mad, ree 4 daft, wowf(Sc.) 5 feral, rough, waste, weird 6 desert, ferine, ramage, savage, stormy, unruly 7 bestial, haggard, riotous, skeered(Sc.), untamed, wilsome 8 aberrant, agrestal, desolate, dramatic, farouche, frenetic, hellicat, reckless, untilled 9 agrestial, barbarian, barbarous, dissolute, disturbed, ferocious, hellicate, imprudent, primitive, turbulent, unbridled, visionary 10 chimerical, dissipated, irrational, licentious, tumultuous, wilderness 11 extravagant, harumscarum, uncivilized, uninhabited 12 obstreperous, uncontrolled, uncultivated 14 uncontrollable

wild alder: 8 goutweed

wild allspice: 9 spicebush

wild arum: 10 cuckoopint

wild ass: 6 onager

wild banana: 5 papaw 6 pawpaw

wild carrot: 8 hilltrot

wild coffee: 9 feverroot

wild crocus: 12 pasqueflower

wild dog: 5 dingo

Wild Duck author: 5 Ibsen

wild flower: See **flower**

wild goat: 4 ibex

wild goose: 7 greylag 8 Jacobite

wild hog: 4 boar

wild horse: 7 mustang

wild hyacinth: 6 camass

wild Irishman: 10 tumatakura

wild jalap: 8 mayapple

wild kale: 6 radish 8 charlock

wild masterwort: 8 goutweed

wild musk: 9 alfilaria

wild mustard: 8 charlock

wild passionflower: 6 maypop

wild pineapple: 7 pinguin

wild plum: 4 sloe

wild pumpkin: 11 calabazilla

wild sage: 5 clary

wild sago: 7 coontie

wild sheep: See **sheep**

wild succory: 7 chicory

wild sweet potato: 7 manroot

wild turnip: 6 radish 8 rutabaga 9 breadroot

wildcat: cat 4 balu, eyra 6 ocelot, serval 7 panther 9 promotion

wildebeast: gnu

wilder (see also **wild**): 5 stray 6 wander 7 perplex 8 bewilder

wilderness: 5 waste 6 desert, forest

wildfowl: 4 duck 5 goose, quail 8 pheasant 9 partridge

flight: 5 skein

wildness: 6 ramage 8 ferocity 12 extravagance

wile: art 4 lure, ruse 5 fraud, guile, trick 6 allure, deceit, entice 7 beguile, cunning 8 artifice, trickery 9 stratagem

Wilkes Island: 4 Ashi

will: 4 lust, wish 6 animus, choose, decree, desire, devise, prefer 7 command, longing 8 appetite, pleasure, volition 9 intention, testament 11 disposition, inclination, self-control 13 determination

appendix: 7 codicil

having no: 9 intestate

maker of: 8 testator

proof of: 7 probate

valid: 7 testacy

willful: mad 4 rash 5 heady 7 wayward 8 stubborn 9 camsteary, camsteery, impetuous, obstinate, voluntary 10 hardheaded 11 intentional

willies: 6 creeps 7 jitters

William II's residence: 5 Doorn

William Tell: *canton:* Uri

composer: 7 Rossini

hero: 4 Egil

William The Conqueror's burial place: 4 Caen

willing: apt 4 bain 5 prone, ready 6 minded 7 tending 8 desirous, disposed, unforced 9 agreeable 10 volitional

willingly: 4 fain, lief 5 lieve 6 freely, gladly

willingness: 7 consent 8 alacrity

willow: iva 4 itea 5 osier, salix 6 teaser

willow basket: 7 prickle

willow wren: 10 chiffchaff

willowy: 5 lithe 6 pliant 7 slender 8 flexible, graceful

willpower: 7 purpose 10 resolution 12 resoluteness 13 determination

loss of: 6 abulia 7 aboulia

willy: 4 trap 6 basket, willow

Wilson's thrush: 5 veery

wilt: sag 4 fade, flag 5 droop, quail 6 wither 8 languish

wily: sly 4 foxy 5 canny, smart 6 artful, astute, crafty, shrewd, subtle 7 cunning, subtile 9 cautelous

wimble: awl 4 bore 5 auger, brace, scoop, twist 6 active, gimlet, pierce 9 penetrate, sprightly, whimsical

Wimbledon event: 6 tennis

wimick: cry 7 whimper

wimple: 4 bend, fold, turn, veil, wind 5 curve 6 ripple 7 meander, wriggle 9 headdress

win: get, pot 4 earn, gain, take 5 charm 6 allure, attain, defeat, entice, obtain, secure 7 achieve, acquire, capture, conquer, prevail, succeed, triumph 8 vanquish 9 captivate, influence 10 accomplish, conciliate

all tricks: 4 slam

back: 7 recover 8 retrieve

over: 6 defeat 8 persuade 10 conciliate

wince: 4 crab, reel 5 start 6 cringe, flinch, recoil, shrink 8 windlass

wind: oe; air 4 birr, bise, bora, coil, flaw, gale, gust, kona, reel, wend, wrap 5 belay(naut.), blast, buran, crank, curve, foehn, noser, reeve, samum, siroc, storm, trade, twine, twist, wield 6 boreas, bought, breath, breeze, buster, gibleh, simoom, simoon, solano, squall, writhe, zephyr 7 chamsin, chinook, cyclone, entwine, entwist, etesian, gregale, khamsin, meander, monsoon, pampero, revolve, sirocco, tempest, tornado, typhoon, wreathe, wriggle, wulliwa 8 blizzard, khamseen, libeccio, williwaw, willywaw 9 harmattan, hurricane, libecchio, noreaster 10 euroclydon, tramontana, tramontane

combining form: 5 anemo

desert: 6 simoon 7 sirocco

god of: 4 Adda, Adad, Vayu 5 Eolus 6 Aeolus, Eecatl

periodic: oe 7 etesian, monsoon

personification: 6 Caurus 7 Caecias 8 Favonius

pertaining to: 6 eolian 7 aeolian

summer: 6 breeze, zephyr

wind gauge: 4 vane 10 anemometer 11 weathercock

wind instrument: sax 4 fife, horn, oboe, tuba 5 flute, organ 6 cornet 7 hautboy 8 clarinet

wind up: end 4 coil 5 close 6 finish 8 conclude

windfall: 4 boon, vail 7 bonanza, fortune 8 buckshee

windflower: 7 anemone

windhover: 7 kestrel

windiness: 7 conceit 9 puffiness 11 verboseness 12 boastfulness

winding: 4 wily 6 screwy, spiral, tricky 7 coiling, crinkle, devious, pliable, sinuous, twining, wriggly 8 flexible, rambling, tortuous, twisting 9 deceitful, intricate, meandrous, sinuosity 10 anfracture, circuitous, meandering, serpentine 11 amortisseur, anfractuous

winding device: 4 reel 7 capstan 8 windlass

winding sheet: 6 shroud

windjammer: 4 ship 6 bugler, sailor, talker 8 musician 9 trumpeter

windlass: 4 crab, reel 5 hoist, winch 7 capstan

windle: 7 measure, redwing

windmill: *blade:* 4 vane

fighter of: 7 Quixote

pump: gin

sail: awn, ban

window: bay 5 gable, glaze, oriel 6 dormer 7 balcone, fenetre, lucarne, mirador, opening, winnock(Sc.) 8 aperture, casement

arrangement: 12 fenestration

bay: 5 oriel

frame: 4 sash

leading: 4 came

ledge: 4 sill

part: 4 came, sill

pert. to: 9 fenestral

recess: 6 exedra

roof: 6 dormer 8 skylight

sash weight: 5 mouse

ship's: 4 port

ticket: 6 wicket 7 guichet

worker: 7 glazier

window glass (to supply): 7 impanel

windpipe: 6 artery, gullet, throat, weason 7 trachea, weasand, weazand 9 esophagus

pert. to: 8 ttrachean

windrow: 5 swath 6 furrow, swathe

windshake: 8 anemosis

windstorm (see also storm; wind): 4 gale 7 cyclone, typhoon 9 hurricane

windward: 5 aloof 8 aweather

Windward Island: 7 Grenada

windy: 4 airy 5 empty, gusty, huffy, swift 6 breezy, stormy 7 gustful, pompous, verbose 8 boastful, skittish 9 aeolistic, bombastic 10 boisterous, changeable, intangible 11 harebrained, tempestuous 13 unsubstantial

Windy City: 7 Chicago

wine: vin(F.) 4 alac, Asti, Bual, cote, deal, port, tent 5 Baden, Casel, drink, liane, Medoc, merum(L.), Rhine, Tinta, tokay, Yquem 6 Barolo, Barsac, Beaune, canary, claret, Malaga, Massic, Muscat, Saumur, sherry 7 Alicant, Banyals, Bastard, Chablis, chacoli, Chateau, Chianti, Conthey, Dezaley, Falerno, hollock, Madeira, Margaux, Marsala, Medeira, Moselle, Orvieto 8 Alicante, Ambonnay, beverage, Bordeaux, Bucellas, Burgundy, Florence, Marsalla, muscadel, Muscatel, Rulander, Riesling, Ruchelle, Rulander, sauterne 9 Gladstone, hermitage, teneriffe, Zeltinger, zinfandel 10 Beaujolais, Calon-Segur, Hockheimer, Roussillon 11 Niersteiner, scuppernong 12 Geisenheimer 15 scharlachberger

apple: 5 cider
bag: 8 wineskin
bibber: sot 5 toper 7 tippler 8 drunkard
bottle: 6 fiasco, magnum 8 decanter, jeroboam
cask: tun 4 pipe
cask deposit: 6 tartar
cellar: 6 bodega
comb. form: oen 4 oeno
cruet: 7 burette
cup: ama 5 amula 6 goblet 7 chalice
deposit: 6 tartar
discoverer: 4 Noah
disorder: 5 casse
drink: 5 clary, mulse, negus, punch
dry: 4 brut
film: 8 beeswing
god: 4 Soma 7 Bacchus 8 Dionysus
list: 4 card
lover: 11 oenophilist
maker: 6 abkari, abkary
measure: aam, aum 4 orna, orne
medicinal preparation: 5 mosto
merchant: 6 bistro(F.) 7 vintner 8 gourmand
new: 4 must
pert. to: 5 vinic 6 vinous
pitcher: 4 olpe 5 olpae 8 oenochoe
residue: 4 marc
rice: 4 sake
scene of miracle: 4 Cana
shop: 6 bodega
spiced: 9 hippocras
stock: 6 cellar
study of: 7 enology
strength: 4 seve

sweet: 4 port 5 lunel, tokay 7 malmsey, Moselle 8 Alicante, muscatel
unfermented: 4 must
vessel: ama 5 amula 7 chalice
year: 7 vintage

wine and dine: 4 fete 6 regale

wineberry: 5 grape 7 currant 8 bilberry, makomako 9 raspberry 10 gooseberry

winegrower: 8 vigneron 13 viticulturist

Winesburg Ohio author: 8 Anderson

wineshop: bar 6 bistro, bodega

wineskin: 5 askos

wing: ala, arm, ell, fin, fly, van 4 limb 5 aisle, alula, pinna, shard, speed, volet, wound 6 hasten, pennon, pinion 7 flutter
arrangement: 7 alation
building: ell
pert to: 4 alar 6 pteric
under: 8 subalary
vestigial: 5 alula

wing cover: 7 elytron

wing-footed: 5 swift 6 aliped 9 mercurial

wing-like: 4 alar 5 alary, alate 6 pteric 7 aliform, pteroid
part: ala 4 alae 7 aileron

winged: 4 aile, alar 5 alary, alate, lofty, rapid, swift 6 alated 7 bialate, sublime, wounded 9 aliferous, aligerous, feathered
in heraldry: 4 aile

Winged Horse: 7 Pegasus

wingless: 7 apteral 8 apterous

wingless locust: 4 weta

wings: *being with:* 5 angel 6 cherub, seraph 7 Mercury
conjoined: vol(her.)

wink: bat, nap, nod 4 hint 5 blink, flash, gleam, prink, sleep 6 signal 7 flicker, instant, nictate, slumber, sparkle, twinkle 9 nictation, nictitate, twinkling 10 periwinkle

winking: 13 blepharospasm

winks (forty): nap 6 catnap

winner: 6 earner, reaper, victor 7 faceman, sleeper 8 bangster 9 conqueror 11 breadwinner

Winnie-the-Pooh: *author:* 5 Milne
character: Owl, Roo 5 Kanga 6 Piglet, Rabbit, Tigger

winning (see also **win; winsome**): 5 shaft 6 profit 7 victory

winning three numbers: 4 tern

winninish, winnonish: 6 salmon 10 ouananiche

winnock: 6 window

winnow: fan, van 4 beat, flap, sift 5 dight 6 assort, select 7 analyze, examine, scatter 8 brandish, disperse, separate 9 eliminate

winsome: gay 5 bonny, merry 6 blithe, bonnie 7 likable, winning 8 charming, cheerful, engaging, pleasant 9 agreeable 10 attractive 11 captivating 12 lighthearted

winter: 9 hibernate

pear: 6 seckel, warden

pert. to: 6 brumal, hiemal

winter quarters: 10 hibernacle 12 hibernaculum

winter teal: 9 greenwing

Winter's Tale character: 4 Dion 5 Mopsa 6 Dorcas 7 Camillo, Leontes, Perdita

winterbloom: 6 azalea

wintergreen: 10 pipsissewa

wintle: 4 reel, roll 7 stagger, wriggle

wintry: icy 4 aged, cold 5 snowy, white 6 frigid, hiemal, stormy 8 chilling, hibernal, wintered 9 cheerless

winy: 6 vinous 7 drunken

wipe: dry, hit, mop, rub 4 beat, blow, draw, gibe, jeer, pass 5 brand, cheat, clean, dight, erase, stain, swipe, towel, trick 6 cancel, defeat, remove, sponge, strike, stroke 7 abolish, defraud, exhaust, sarcasm 8 disgrace 10 annihilate, obliterate 11 exterminate 12 handkerchief

wire: 4 coil 5 cable 6 fasten 8 telegram 9 cablegram, telegraph

bundle of: 5 cable

cutters: 6 pliers

measure: mil 5 stone

system: 7 network, reticle

wire cutter: 5 wirer 8 secateur

wiredraw: 5 wrest 7 distort, prolong 8 protract 9 attenuate 10 overrefine

wireless: 5 radio

wirework: 8 filigree

wireworm: 8 myriapod 9 millepede

wiry: 4 lean 5 hardy, stiff, tough 6 sinewy, strong

wis: 4 deem, know 5 think 7 believe, imagine, suppose

Wisconsin: *city:* 6 Beloit, Racine, Sparta 7 Kenosha, Madison(c.), Necedah, Oshkosh 10 Oconomowoc

county: 4 Dane, Polk, Rusk, Sauk 5 Dodge, Pepin, Vilas 6 Barron 7 Kenosha, Ozaukee 8 Bayfield, Walworth, Waushara

native: 6 Badger

wisdom (see also **wise**)**:** 4 lore 8 judgment

god of: 4 Nabu, Nebo 6 Ganesa 7 Ganesha

goddess of: 6 Athena, Pallas 7 Minerva

man of: 6 Nestor

wisdom tooth: 5 molar

wise: 4 mode, sage, sane, show, wary 5 aware, smart, sound, witty 6 advise, crafty, direct, inform, manner, shrewd, subtle, versed, witful 7 beguile, cunning, erudite, explain, fashion, heedful, knowing, learned, politic, prudent, sapient,

skilled 8 discreet, informed, instruct, persuade, profound, sensible, skillful 9 cognizant, dexterous, expedient, judicious, provident, sagacious 10 discerning, omniscient 11 calculating, circumspect, enlightened, intelligent, well-advised 13 sophisticated

infinitely: 10 omniscient

wise man: 4 sage 5 magus, solon 6 Casper, Gasper, Nestor, wizard 8 magician, Melchior 9 Balthasar, Balthazar, councilor

Wise Men: 4 Magi

wise saying: saw 5 adage, maxim

wiseacre: 5 dunce 7 prophet 9 simpleton 10 mastermind 11 wisenheimer

wiselike: 6 decent 7 fitting 8 becoming, sensible 9 judicious 11 appropriate

wish: 4 hope, long, want 5 crave, yearn 6 behest, desire, invoke 7 longing, propose, request 8 petition, yearning 10 aspiration, invocation 11 imprecation

grammatical mood expressing: 8 optative

wishbone: 8 furculum 10 fourchette

wishful: 8 desirous 9 desirable 10 attractive

wisht: 5 eerie 6 dismal, dreary 7 uncanny 8 wretched 10 melancholy

wishy-washy: 4 pale, sick, thin, weak 5 tepid 6 feeble, trashy, watery 7 insipid 13 unsubstantial

wisket: 6 basket

wisp: 4 band, ring, wase 5 broom, brush, bunch, clean, flock, shred, torch, whisk 6 bundle, parcel, rumple, wreath 7 crumple, handful 8 fragment

wispy: 5 filmy 6 slight 7 slender 8 gossamer

wissel: 5 money 6 change 8 exchange 11 retribution

wist: 4 know

wistaria 4 bush, fuji 6 purple, violet

wistful: 6 intent 7 longing, pensive 8 yearning 9 attentive, nostalgic

wistfulness: rue 6 regret

wit: wag 4 know 5 humor, irony, learn 6 acumen, esprit(F.), namely, reason, satire, wisdom 7 cunning, faculty, punster 8 comedian, drollery, funnyman, repartee 9 intellect 12 intelligence, perspicacity 13 understanding

low form of: pun

witch: hag, hex 4 baba 5 charm, crone, lamia, woman 6 cummer, kimmer, wizard 7 bewitch 9 fascinate, sorceress

cat: 9 grimalkin

city: 5 Salem

famous: 5 Circe 6 Lilith

male: 7 warlock

means of transportation: 5 broom

witch hazel: 4 tree 5 shrub 8 hornbeam 10 astringent

witchcraft: 5 charm, magic 7 cunning, hex-erei, sorcery 8 brujeria(Sp.), pishogue, witchery, wizardry 9 sortilege 11 enchantment, fascination 12 invultuation
goddess of: 5 Obeah 6 Hecate
practice: hex 7 bewitch
witchman: 6 shaman, wizard 8 sorcerer
wite: 4 fine 5 blame, fault 6 accuse 7 censure 8 reproach 9 exemption 14 responsibility
with: wi(Sc.); con(It.), cum(L.), mit(G.) 4 avec(F.), near 5 along 9 alongside 12 accompanying
prefix: col, com, cyn, pro, syn
withdraw: go 4 void 5 avoid 6 absent, depart, detach, divert, recall, recant, recede, remove, retire, secede 7 abscond, decline, detract, extract, forbear, forsake, refrain, retract, retreat, subduce, subside 8 abstract, alienate, derogate, distract, evacuate, renounce, restrain, withhold 9 disengage, sequester 10 relinqish, retrograde
withdrawal (see also **withdraw**): 7 regress
withe: 4 band, bind, herb, rope, twig 5 osier, snare, withy 6 branch, fasten, halter, wattle, willow
wither: age, die, dry 4 fade, pine, sear, sere, wilt 5 blast, cling, daver, decay, wizen 6 blight, cotter, shrink, weaken 7 shrivel, wrinkle 8 languish
withered: 4 arid, sere 7 sapless 10 marcescent 11 sphacelated
withhold: 4 curb, deny, hide, keep 5 check 6 desist, detain, refuse, retain 7 abstain, forbear, prevent, refrain, repress, reserve 8 maintain, postpone, restrain
within: in, on; ben 4 inly, into 5 among 6 during, herein, inside 7 indoors 8 inwardly 10 underneath
comb. form: ent, eso 4 endo, ento
prefix: 5 intra
without: 4 bout, sans, sine(L.) 6 beyond 7 lacking, outside 9 outwardly 10 externally
prefix: se; ect, exo 4 ecto
without this: 7 sine hoc
withstand: 4 bear, bide, defy 5 abide 6 combat, endure, oppose, resist 7 gainsay 8 confront 9 gainstand 10 contradict, controvert
withy: 4 turn, twig, wind, wiry 5 agile, braid 6 branch, willow 8 flexible
witless: mad 5 crazy, gross 6 insane, stupid 7 foolish, unaware 8 heedless 9 brainless, pointless, unknowing 10 dullwitted, indiscreet
witness: eye, see, wit 4 know 5 teste 6 attest, beheld, behold, martyr 7 observe, sponsor, testify 8 beholder, evidence, observer, onlooker 9 spectator, subscribe, testifier, testimony 11 attestation 13 understanding

Witt's planetoid: 4 Eros
witter: tee 4 barb
witticism: mot, pun 4 gibe, jeer, jest, joke, quip 5 sally 11 gauloiserie
witting: 7 tidings 8 judgment 9 knowledge 10 deliberate 11 information, intentional 12 intelligence
wittol: 4 fool 7 cuckold 8 wheatear
witty: 4 gash, wise 5 comic 6 bright, clever, facete, jocose, jocund, versed 7 amusing, comical, jocular, knowing 8 humorous, informed 9 facetious 11 intelligent
witty remark: mot, pun 4 quip
witty reply: 7 riposte 8 repartee
wive: 5 marry
wivern: 6 dragon
wizard: 4 mage, sage 5 fiend 6 genius, Merlin 7 magical, prodigy, warlock 8 charming, conjurer, magician, sorcerer 10 enchanting 11 necromancer, thaumaturge 12 thaumaturgus 13 thaumaturgist
wizardry: art 5 magic 7 sorcery 10 witchcraft
wizen, weazen: dry 6 wither 7 shrivel, wizened
woad: 8 dyestuff
wobble, wabble: 4 boil 5 shake, waver 6 quaver 7 tremble 9 vacillate
wobbly: 5 loose, shaky
woe: 4 bale, bane 5 grief 6 misery, sorrow 7 trouble 8 calamity, disaster 9 dejection 10 affliction, desolation, melancholy, misfortune
tale of: 8 jeremiad 11 lamentation
woeful: sad 4 dire 6 paltry 7 direful, pitiful, unhappy 8 mournful, wretched 9 miserable, sorrowful, woebegone 10 deplorable, dispirited 12 disconsolate
wolaba: 8 kangaroo
wold: lea 5 plain 6 meadow
wolf: 4 lobo 6 canine, chanco, coyote 9 thylacine 10 ladykiller 11 philanderer
cry: 4 howl
gait: 4 lope
genus: 5 canis
pert. to: 6 lupine
young: pup 5 whelp
wolf-like: 6 lupine 9 rapacious
wolfhound: 4 alan 6 borzoi
wolfsbane: 7 aconite 9 monkshood
Wolsey's birthplace: 7 Ipswich
wolverine: 8 carcajou
genus of: 4 gulo
Wolverine State: 8 Michigan
woman (see also **girl; mother**): gin, hen 4 bint, dame, dona, lady, maid, rani 5 begum, broad, chick, donna, femme, madam, mujer, ranee, skirt, squaw 6 calico, cummer, domina, female, heifer, kimmer, maness, senora 7 alewife, servant, signora 8

mistress, senorita 10 klootchman, sweetheart 11 gentlewoman

affected: 5 prude 7 cockney

attractive: 4 doll, peri 5 filly, pin-up, siren, sylph, Venus 6 beauty, looker 7 charmer, Zenobia 8 Musidora

beloved: 9 inamorata

brave: 7 hellcat, heroine

celibate: 7 agapeta

comb. form: gyn 4 gyno

domain: 7 distaff

kept: 8 mistress 9 concubine 12 demimondaine

lawyer: 6 Portia

learned: 4 blue 7 basbleu(F.), seeress 12 bluestocking

little: 4 wife 7 ladykin

loose: tib 4 drab, flap, jilt, slut 5 hussy, quean, queen 6 chippy, giglet, giglot, harlot, wanton 7 cocotte, Jezebel, trollop 9 courtesan, courtezen, dratchell

married: 4 frau, frow, wife 5 vrouw 6 matron

mythical: 6 Gorgon

objectionable: hag 5 fagot, shrew, witch 6 faggot, gorgon, virago 8 harridan 9 grimalkin, termagant

old: gib, hag 4 baba, dame, trot 5 crone, frump 6 carlin, gammer, granny 7 carline, dowager, grandam 8 grandame, spinster 9 cailleach, cailliach

organization: DAR, WAC, WSP 4 AMVS, WAAC, WAVE, Wren 5 Ebell 6 circle 7 sorosis 8 sorority 10 sisterhood

pert. to: 7 gynecic 8 gynaecic 9 muliebral

patient: 8 Griselda

physicist: 5 Curie 7 Meitner

ruler: 5 queen 9 matriarch

sailor: 4 Spar, Wave

serving: See **servant**

single (see also **maiden**): 6 virgin 8 mistress, spinster

soldier: Wac 4 Waac

staid: 4 lady 6 beldam, matron 7 beldame

state of: 10 muliebrity

strong: 6 Amazon, virago 8 titaness

suffragist: 4 Mott 5 Stone 7 Anthony, Stanton

talkative: cat, gad, hen 5 dolly, flirt, scold, shrew, vixen 6 fizgig, virago 7 hellcat 9 termagant

theater: 6 dancer 7 actress, chorine 9 soubrette

unattractive: bag, dog 4 drab 5 crone, dowdy, witch 8 slattern

young (see also **girl**): tib 4 burd, dell, drab, lass 5 filly, trull, wench 6 lassie 7 damozel 10 demoiselle

woman chaser: 4 wolf 8 lothario 10 sheepbiter 11 philanderer

woman hater: 10 misogynist

womanish: 5 anile 6 effete, female 8 feminine 10 effeminate

womb: bag 5 belly 6 uterus

wombat: 6 badger 9 marsupial

won (see also **win**): 4 live 5 abide, dwell 7 inhabit

wonder: awe 4 evil, harm, sign 5 grief, wrong 6 esteem, marvel 7 curious, miracle, prodigy 8 surprise 9 amazement, speculate, uncertain 10 admiration, wonderment 11 destruction 12 astonishment

of the world: 6 Pharos 8 pyramids, Colossus

performance: See **magic**

worker of: See **wizard**

Wonder State: 8 Arkansas

wonderful: 4 fine, good 5 super 6 lovely 7 amazing, amusing, corking, mirific, strange 8 wondrous 9 admirable, excellent, marvelous 10 miraculous, surprising 11 astonishing, interesting 13 extraordinary

wong: 5 field 6 meadow

wonky: off 4 awry 5 shaky 6 feeble 7 tottery 8 unsteady 9 tottering

wont: use 5 dwell, habit, usage, usual 6 custom, reside 8 inclined, practice 10 accustomed

woo: beg, sue 4 coax, seek 5 court, spark 6 assail, invite, splunt(Sc.) 7 address, beseech, entreat, solicit 9 importune

wood: hag, keg, mad 4 bois(F.), bosk, bowl, cask, holt, wold 5 angry, cahuy, grove, hurst, trees, xylem 6 forest, insane, lumber, timber 7 enraged, furious, violent 8 woodland

ash: 6 potash

black: 5 ebony

bundle of: 5 fagot

burned: ash 4 brae 8 charcoal

comb. form: 4 hylo, xylo 5 ligni

core: ame

dealer: 10 xylopolist

derivative: tar 5 turps 6 balsam 10 turpentine

distillation from: tar 5 turps 10 turpentine

edge: 8 woodrime, woodside

fine-grained: yew 6 brauna

firing easily: 4 punk 5 sponk, spunk 6 tinder 8 kindling, punkwood 9 touchwood

flexible: 5 edder, osier 6 willow

fragrant: 5 aloes, cedar

god: See **woodland:** *deity*

growth: 7 coppice

gum: 5 resin, xylan

hard: ash, elm, eng, oak **4** lana, poon, rata, teak **5** ebony, maple, zante **6** walnut **7** hickory **8** mahogany

juice: sap

kind: See **tree**

knot: nur **4** burl, knag, knar **5** gnarl

light: **4** cork **5** balsa

overlaying: **6** veneer

part: fid, nog, peg, rib **4** lath, shim, slat **5** dowel, spile, sprag, stave, tenon **6** batten, billet, reglet, splint **7** dingbat

pert. to: **5** treen

prefix: **4** xylo

steward: **9** woodreeve

strip: **4** lath, slat **6** batten, spline

striped: roe

supporting: **5** cleat

valuable: sal **4** teak

worker: **6** joiner, sawyer **7** paneler **9** carpenter

wood alcohol: 6 methyl **8** methanol

wood-ash salt: 6 potash

wood nymph: 4 moth **5** dryad **8** grayling **11** hummingbird

wood pigeon: 4 dove **6** cushat **8** ringdove

wood pussy: 5 skunk

wood sorrel: oca **6** oxalis **7** begonia **8** haremeat

wood stork: 4 ibis

woodbine: 11 honeysuckle

woodchuck: 6 marmot **9** groundhog

woodcock: 4 dupe, fool **5** pewee **7** becasse(F.) **9** simpleton **10** woodpecker

woodcutter: 6 axeman, logger, sawyer **7** chopper **8** woodsman **9** lumberman

wooded: 6 sylvan

wooden: dry **4** dull, wood **5** oaken, stiff, treen **6** clumsy, stolid **7** awkward **8** lifeless **10** spiritless **11** insensitive **14** expressionless

wooden shoe: 4 clog, geta **5** sabot **6** patten

wooden-headed: 4 dull **6** stupid **8** blockish

Wooden Horse: See **Trojan horse**

woodkern: 6 outlaw, robber

woodland: 6 forest **7** woodlot **10** timberland

burnt over: **6** brulee

deity: Pan **4** faun **5** Diana, satyr, Silen **7** Silenus **8** Seilenos

landscape: **7** boscage

woodness: 4 fury, rage **7** madness **8** insanity

woodpecker: 4 chab **5** picus **6** picule, yaffle, yockel, yuckle, yukkel **7** flicker, piculet, whetile, wryneck, yaffler **8** hickwall, woodcock, woodhack **9** sapsucker, woodchuck, woodspite **10** carpintero, woodhacker, woodjobber **11** hickoryhead, woodknacker

genus: **5** picus

type: **5** downy, hairy **8** imperial, pileated **9** redheaded

pert. to: **6** picine

woods: 6 forest

love of: **9** nemophily

pert. to: **6** sylvan **7** nemoral

woodsman: 5 scout **6** hunter **7** bushman, trapper **8** forester **10** woodcutter **11** woodchopper

woodwind: 4 oboe **5** flute **7** bassoon. piccolo **8** clarinet **9** saxophone

woodworker: 6 joiner, turner **9** carpenter **12** cabinetmaker

machine: saw **5** edger, lathe **6** planer, router, shaper **7** sticker

tool: adz, saw **4** adze **5** plane **6** hammer

woody: 5 bosky **6** sylvan, xyloid **8** ligneous

woody fiber: 4 bast, hemp **5** xylem

wooer: 4 beau **6** suitor **8** courtier

woof: abb **5** cloth, weave **6** fabric **7** filling, texture **9** essential

wool: fur **4** hair, lamb **5** llama, sheep **6** fleece, mohair **8** barragan, barragon **9** cordillas

blemish: **4** mote

clean: **7** garnett

cloth: **5** baize, duroy, tweed **6** alpaca, angora, baline, duffel, frieze, hodden, kersey, melton, merino, mohair, vicuna **7** flannel, ratteen, stammel **8** cashmere, casimire **9** cassimere, hauberget **10** broadcloth, fearnaught, fearnought **11** dreadnaught, dreadnought

comb. form: **4** lani

fat: **5** suint **7** lanolin **8** lanoline

fibers: nep

grower: **5** sheep **7** rancher

implement: **6** carder, shears, teaser **7** distaff, spindle

inferior: **7** cleamer

kind: **4** noil, shag **8** mortling **9** downright, shearling

lock: **5** flock

mixed hues: tum

nap-raising plant: **5** tease

package: **5** fadge

piece: **4** frib, tate(Sc.) **7** cleamer

pulled: **5** slipe

rag: **5** mungo **6** shoddy

reclaimed: **5** mungo **6** shoddy

refuse: **7** backing

spun: **4** yarn

tease: tum **4** card

texture: nap

twisted roll: **4** slub

unravel: **5** tease

waste: fud

weight: tod **5** clove

worker: **8** shedhand

yarn: abb, eis 7 eiswool
wool-colored: 5 beige, camel
wool-dryer: 5 fugal
woolfell: 4 pelt
woolly: 6 fleecy, lanate, lanose 7 lanated 8 peronate
woozy: 5 drunk, shaky 7 muddled, strange, trembly 9 befuddled
word: 4 fame, news, talk, term 5 adage, honor, maxim, motto, order, parol, voice 6 assent, avowal, phrase, pledge, remark, report, repute, saying, signal, speech 7 account, adjunct, command, comment, dispute, message, promise, proverb, tidings 8 acrostic, language, password 9 direction, discourse, statement, watchword 10 expression 11 affirmation, declaration, information 12 intelligence 13 communication
battle 9 logomachy
colorful: 5 slang
complex of ideas: 10 holophrase 11 holophrasis
containing all vowels: 6 oiseau(F.) 7 eulogia, miaoued, sequoia 12 ambidextrous 14 undiscoverably 15 uncopyrightable
containing all vowels in reverse sequence: 10 duoliteral
containing all vowels in sequence: 8 caesious
containing four letters: 9 tetragram
containing no vowels: cwm, nth 5 crwth
containing uu: 6 mutuum, vacuum 7 duumvir, triduum 8 residuum 9 continuum, menstruum, perpetuum, zuurveldt 10 duumvirate
contraction: 9 haplology
corresponding: 8 analogue
derived from another: 7 paronym
figurative use: 5 trope 7 metonym
group: 6 clause, phrase 8 sentence
hard to pronounce: 10 jawbreaker
imitative: 9 onomatope
improper use: 8 solecism
inventor: 6 coiner 9 neologist
last sound omitted: 7 apocope
longest: 45 pneumonoultramicroscopicsilicovolcanokoniosis
magical: 6 presto, sesame 11 abracadabra
meaning: 9 semantics
misuse of: 11 catachresis, malapropism
mystical: 7 anagoge
new: 9 neologism, neoterism
of action: 4 verb
of naming: 4 noun
of opposite meaning: 7 antonym
of same meaning: 7 synonym
pretentious: 10 lexiphanic
root: 6 etymon

sacred: om, um 5 selah 6 sesame, shelah
same backward and forward: 10 palindrome
same sound: 7 homonym 9 homophone
same spelling: 7 homonym 9 homograph
scrambled: 7 anagram
separation: 6 tmesis 7 diacope
square: 10 palindrome
substituted: 5 trope 7 metonym
transposition: 7 anagram
use of imitative: 12 onomatopoeia
use of new: 7 neology
use of unnecessary: 8 pleonasm
very long: 13 sesquipedalia(pl.)
word blindness: 6 alexia
word for word: 7 exactly 8 verbatim 9 literally
Word of God: 5 Logos
word of honor: 6 parole 7 promise
word puzzle: 5 rebus 7 anagram, charade 8 acrostic 9 crossword
word-sign: 8 ideogram, logogram 10 hieroglyph, pictograph
wordbook: 7 lexicon, speller 8 libretto 9 thesaurus 10 cyclopedia, dictionary, vocabulary
wordiness: 8 verbiage
wording: 8 phrasing 9 wrangling 10 expression
wordless: 5 tacit 6 silent
words: 4 text 6 lyrics 7 quarrel 8 libretto
depiction in: 8 vignette
excessive interest in: 10 verbomania
meaningless: 6 drivel 9 gibberish
misuse: 11 catachresis, heterophemy
put into: 5 state 6 phrase 7 express
written: 4 copy, text
wordy: 6 prolix 7 diffuse, verbose 9 garrulous, redundant
wore: See **wear**
work: go; act, job, tew 4 beat, duty, feat, move, opus, plan, task, worm 5 chore, craft, draft, ergon, exert, graft, grind, knead, solve, stint, trade 6 arbeit(G.), design, effort, puddle, strive 7 belabor, ferment, operate, pattern, perform, travail 8 activity, belabour, business, drudgery, exertion, function, industry, struggle 10 accomplish, employment, manipulate, occupation, profession 11 achievement, performance, undertaking
agreement: 4 code, pact 8 contract
aimlessly: 6 potter, putter
aversion to: 10 ergophobia
by day: 4 char 5 char
defensive: See **fortification**
divine: 7 theurgy
excess: 6 overdo 8 overwork
evade: 4 snib 9 goldbrick

hard: peg, ply 4 char, moil, plod, plug, toil 5 chare, delve, drill, labor, sweat 6 drudge 7 travail 8 scrabble 9 lucubrate

incomplete: 7 ebauche

labored: 11 lucubration

lover of: 9 ergophile

musical: See **musical composition**

period: day 4 hour, turn, week 5 month, shift, spell, trick, watch 8 schedule

slowly: 6 potter, putter 7 cacanny

steadily: ply

together: 4 team 5 co-act 9 co-operate 11 collaborate

unit: erg 5 ergon, joule 7 calorie

women's: 7 distaff

work-a-day: 8 everyday, ordinary 11 commonplace

work-brittle: 11 industrious

work for: 4 earn 5 serve

work of art: 4 song 6 statue 7 classic, etching, picture 8 painting

work on: 6 affect 9 influence

work out: 5 erase, solve 6 efface 7 arrange, develop, exhaust 9 calculate, elaborate 10 accomplish

work over: 6 recast, rehash, revamp 8 persuade 9 brainwash, elaborate, influence

work up: irk 5 raise, rouse 6 arouse, excite, expend 7 advance, develop 9 elaborate 10 manipulate

workable: 4 ripe 6 mellow, pliant 8 feasible 9 practical 11 practicable

workbag: 8 reticule

worked: 7 wrought

worker: 4 arry, doer, hand, hind 5 navvy 6 earner, toiler 7 artisan, laborer 8 operator, opificer 9 artificer, craftsman, operative, performer 11 breadwinner

fellow: 5 buddy, butty 7 comrade 8 confrere

group: 4 crew, gang, team 5 corps, shift, staff 9 personnel

hard: 6 beaver, drudge, fagger

head: 4 boss 5 super 6 ganger 7 foreman 8 employer, overseer 14 superintendent

kind: 5 diver, mason, miner, smith, tuner 6 barman, cocker, hopper, joiner, laster, sapper, sawyer, slater, smithy, tanner, warper, wright 7 analyst, cobbler, collier, geordie, glazier, paneler, plumber, reedman, riveter, sandhog, spinner 8 chaffman, chuckler, enameler, mechanic, shedhand, strapper 9 carpenter, groundhog, machinist, stevedore

migrant: 4 hobo, Okie 5 Arkie 6 boomer 7 floater, wetback

objectionable: 4 scab 7 botcher, bungler 11 scissorbill 13 featherbedder

unskilled: 4 peon 6 coolie 7 laborer

workful: 8 diligent

workhorse: 4 peon, serf 5 slave 6 drudge, toiler 7 trestle 8 sawhorse

workhouse: 6 prison 8 workshop 9 almshouse, poorhouse

working (see also **work**): 4 busy 5 alert 6 active, decree, effort 7 halurgy 8 employed, endeavor 9 ordinance, practical 10 contortion

not: off 4 idle 6 broken 10 unemployed

working-class: 7 laborer 11 proletariat

workman: See **worker**

workman-like: 4 deft 5 adept 8 skillful 10 proficient

workroom: den, lab 4 mill, shop 5 plant, study 6 studio 7 atelier, bottega, factory, library 10 laboratory 11 ergasterion

works: 5 plant

worktable: 5 bench, siege

world: 5 globe, realm 6 cosmos, domain, people, public 7 kingdom, mankind 8 creation, humanity, universe

antedating creation of: 10 premundane

bearer of: 5 Atlas

external: 6 nonego

lower: See **underworld**

miniature: 9 microcosm

pert. to: 7 mundane, secular 11 terrestrial

World War I: *battle:* 5 Marne, Somme, Ypres 6 Verdun 7 Jutland

general: 8 Pershing

hero: 5 York

marshal: 4 Foch

World War II: *battle:* 4 Orel 5 Anzio, Bulge 6 Bataan, Sicily, Tarawa, Warsaw 7 Cassino, Okinawa 8 Normandy

correspondent: 4 Pyle

craft: LST

famous nickname: Ike 5 Monty

worldly: 6 carnal, laical 7 earthen, earthly, mundane, secular, sensual, terrene 11 terrestrial 13 sophisticated

worldwide: 6 global 8 ecumenic, pandemic 9 planetary, universal 10 ecumenical 13 international

worm: bob, eel, eri, ess, ipo, loa, lug, pin 4 grub, nais, nema 5 borer, larva, tinea 6 looper, maggot, palolo, teredo 7 annelid, ascarid, ipomoea, reptile, sagitta, serpent, tagtail 8 cercaria, helminth 9 angleworm, earthworm, nemertina, nemertine, nemertini, trematode 10 nemertinea, serpentine 13 platyhelminth

aquatic: sao 4 naid, nais, nema 5 cadew, leech 6 nereis 7 achaeta, annelid 8 annelida

bait: mad 4 lurg

eye-infecting: loa

genus of: 6 nereis 8 geoplana

parasitic: **5** fluke **7** ascarid, cestode, pinworm **8** tapeworm, trichina **9** roundworm
segment: **6** somite **8** metamere
threadlike: **7** filaria

worm-eaten: old **6** ragged, shabby **7** worn-out **8** decrepit **9** out-of-date, worthless

worm-eating mammal: 4 mole

wormlike: 7 vermian **11** helminthoid

wormweed: 8 pinkroot

wormwood: 4 moxa

wormy: 6 rotten **8** diseased, crawling

worn: See **wear**

worn down: 5 erose **6** eroded **7** abraded, attrite **8** attrited

worn-out: 4 sere, used **5** jaded, passe, seedy, spent, stale, trite **6** frayed, shabby **7** haggard **8** consumed, decrepit, impaired, weakened **9** enfeebled, exhausted, hackneyed **10** bedraggled, threadbare **11** commonplace

worricow: 5 devil **7** bugaboo **9** hobgoblin

worry: hox, nag, vex **4** bait, care, cark, faze, fear, fike, fret, fuss, hare, stew **5** annoy, brood, choke, gally, harry, hurry, touse **6** badger, bother, caddle, fidget, harass, hatter, hector, pester, plague, pother **7** anxiety, bedevil, chagrin, concern, disturb, perturb, torment, trouble **8** distress, strangle **9** worriment **10** disconcert, uneasiness

worse: 8 pejority

worsen: 8 pejorate **10** retrogress **11** deteriorate

worship: 4 cult, fame, love **5** adore, dulia, honor, worth **6** credit, homage, latria, renown, repute, revere **7** dignity, idolism, idolize, liturgy, respect **8** blessing, devotion, hierurgy, idolatry, venerate **9** adoration, deference, monolatry, reverence, theolatry **10** admiration, allotheism, hagiolatry, hierolatry, hyperdulia, reputation, veneration, worthiness
form of: **4** rite **6** ritual
house of: dom **6** chapel, church, mosque, shrine, temple **9** cathedral, synagogue **10** tabernacle
nature: **11** physiolatry
of angels and saints: **5** dulia
object of: 4 icon, idol **5** totem **6** fetich, fetish
pert. to: **8** liturgic **10** liturgical
place of: **5** altar
system of: **4** cult **6** cultus

worshiper: 6 adorer, bhakta, votary **7** devotee **8** disciple, idolater

worshipful: 7 notable **8** esteemed **9** honorable, respected **10** venerating **11** worshipping **13** distinguished

worst: bad **4** beat, best **6** defeat **9** discomfit, overthrow

worsted: 4 garn, yarn **5** serge **6** tamine **8** whipcord **9** gabardine
yarn: 6 caddis, crewel **7** caddice, genappe **9** fingering

wort: 4 herb **8** fleabane

worth: 5 merit, price, value **6** bounty, desert, esteem, riches, virtue, wealth **7** account, fitting **8** eminence **9** deserving, desirable **10** excellence, importance, possession, usefulness
sense of: **5** pride **7** dignity, respect
thing of little: rap **6** stiver, trifle

worthless: bad, rap **4** base, evil, idle, vain, vile **5** inane **6** cheesy, drossy, futile, hollow, paltry, putrid, rotten, trashy **7** fustian, inutile, useless **8** feckless, unworthy **9** frivolous, valueless **11** undeserving **12** contemptible **14** good-for-nothing

worthy: 4 dear, good **7** condign **8** deserved, eligible, meriting, valuable **9** competent, deserving, estimable, excellent, qualified **11** appropriate, meritorious

wound: cut **4** gore, harm, hurt, pain, stab, wing **5** break, ganch, sting **6** breach, damage, grieve, harrow, injury, trauma **7** afflict, attaint **8** distress, puncture
discharge from: pus **5** ichor, serum
dressing: **7** bandage, pledget
in heraldry: **4** vuln
lint to dilate: **4** tent
mark: **4** scab, scar, welt **7** blister
sign: **4** scar **5** blood

woundwort: 7 allheal

wove: See **weave**

woven (see also **weave**): **4** lacy **7** damasse
raised figures: **6** broche **7** brocade

wow: hit, mew **4** howl, rave, wail **5** whine **7** success

wowf: 4 wild **6** crazed

wrack: 4 kelp, rack, ruin **5** goods, trash, weeds, wreck **6** avenge, defeat, injury **7** destroy, seaweed, torment, unsound **8** calamity, mischief, wreckage **9** overthrow, shipwreck, vengeance **10** punishment **11** destruction, persecution

wraith: 5 ghost, spook **7** specter, spectre **10** apparition

wrangle (see also **quarrel**): **4** spar **5** argue, brawl, chide **6** bicker, debate, haggle **7** contend, dispute **11** altercation, controversy **12** disagreement

wrangler: 6 cowboy, hafter **7** student **8** herdsman, opponent **9** disputant **10** antagonist

wrangling: 11 belligerent, contentious

wrap: hap, rug, wap **4** cere, coil, fold, furl, hide, roll, wind **5** cloak, cover, nubia, twine **6** afghan, encowl, enfold, infold, invest, swathe 7 blanket, conceal, enclose, envelop, package 8 enshroud, enswathe, surround 9 encompass

wrapper: 4 gown 6 fardel 8 galabeah 9 undervest 10 undershirt

wrapping: wap 8 cerement

wrasse: 6 ballan

wrath: ire 4 fury, rage 5 anger 6 choler, felony 7 passion 8 violence 10 turbulence 11 indignation 12 exasperation

wrathful: 5 wroth 8 incensed 9 malignant

wreak: 5 exact 6 avenge, punish 7 gratify, indulge, inflict, revenge 9 vengeance

wreath, wreathe: lei 4 bank, coil, orle, roll, turn 5 crown, drift, torse(her.), twine, twist, whorl 6 anadem, corona, crants, crease, laurel, spirea, wrench 7 chaplet, contort, coronet, crownal, entwine, festoon, garland, spiraea, wrinkle 8 encircle, surround

in heraldry: 5 torse

wreck: 4 hulk, ruin 5 crash, ruins, smash, wrack 6 damage, defeat, thwart 7 destroy, disable, founder, shatter 8 demolish, derelict, sabotage 9 overthrow, shipwreck 11 destruction

wreckage: 7 flotsam 8 driftage

wrench (see also **wrest**)**:** 4 jerk, pipe, pull, rack, tear, tool, turn 5 twist, wring 6 injury, monkey, sprain, strain, twinge 7 distort, spanner 8 Stillson 9 alligator, epitonion 10 distortion

wrest: 4 rend, ruse 5 exact, force, fraud, seize, trick, usurp, wring 6 elicit, extort, snatch 7 pervert, wrestle

wrestle: tug 6 squirm, strive, tussle, wraxle 7 contend, grapple, wriggle 8 struggle

wrestler: 6 mauler

wrestling: *ceremonial:* 4 sumo

hold: 4 lock 6 nelson 8 scissors

pad: mat

place: 4 ring 5 arena 8 palestra 9 palaestra

score: 4 fall

throw: 4 hipe

wretch: bum, dog 5 exile, loser 6 beggar, pauper 7 hilding, scroyle 8 derelict, recreant 9 miscreant 11 rapscallion

wretched: 4 base, foul, lewd, mean, poor 5 dawny 6 dismal, paltry, pilled, woeful 7 baleful, caitiff, forlorn, unhappy 8 dejected, grievous, inferior 9 afflicted, execrable, miserable, niggardly 10 calamitous, deplorable, depressing, despicable, distressed 11 unfortunate 12 contemptible, parsimonious 14 unsatisfactory

wriggle: 4 frig, turn, wind 5 dodge, evade, snake, twist 6 fitter, squirm, widdle, wiggle, wintle, writhe 7 meander 10 equivocate

wriggly: 8 tortuous

wring: 4 fret, rack 5 press, twist 6 elicit, extort, squirm, wrench 7 extract, squeeze, wrestle 8 compress, struggle

wrinkle: fad, rut 4 fold, idea, knit, lirk, ruck, ruga, seam 5 crimp, fancy, knack, reeve, ridge, rivel 6 cockle, crease, device, furrow, notion, pucker, rimple 7 crimple, crinkle, crumple, frumple, novelty, winding 8 contract 9 corrugate 10 prominence

facial: 4 line

wrinkled: 6 crepey, rugate, rugose, rugous 7 savoyed 8 ruglose

free from being: 6 smooth 7 erugate

wrist: 5 joint 6 carpus

bone: 4 ulna 5 carpi(pl.) 6 carpal, carpus 7 carpale 8 carpalia(pl.) 9 capitatum

mark: 7 rasceta

ornament: 4 band 8 bracelet

pert. to: 6 carpal

wristband: 4 cuff 6 bracer

wristlet: 4 band 5 strap 8 bracelet, handcuff 9 wristband 11 comfortable

writ: 5 breve, brief, tales 6 capias, elegit, extent, venire 7 exigent, process, writing 8 detainer, document, mittimus, replevin, subpoena 10 certiorari, distringas, injunction, instrument 11 fierifacias

of execution: 5 outre

write: pen 5 clerk, enrol 6 direct, enface, enroll, indite, record, scrawl, scribe 7 compose, engross, scratch 8 inscribe, scribble 9 character

letters: 10 correspond

write down: 4 list, note 6 record

write off: 4 drop 6 cancel, deduct, remove

writer: 4 hack, poet 5 clerk, odist 6 author, critic, glozer, lawyer, penman, scribe 7 copyist, glosser, hymnist, penster, realist, tropist 8 annalist, composer, gazeteer, literate, lyricist, novelist, parodist, prefacer, scriptor 9 annotater, columnist, craftsman, dramatist, glossator, scrivener, solicitor 10 amanuensis, chronicler, glossarist, journalist 12 calligrapher, epistolarian 13 glossographer

inferior: 4 hack 8 rhymster 9 poetaster, scribbler

prose: 8 prosaist

unscrupulous: 10 plagiarist

verse: 4 bard, poet 5 odist 7 elegist 9 sonneteer

writhe: 4 bend, bind, curl, turn 5 twist, wrest, wring 6 squirm 7 agonize, contort, distort, shrivel 8 encircle, enswathe 9 convolute, insinuate 10 contortion, intertwine

writhing: 4 eely 9 wriggling

writing: ms; ola 4 book, deed, olla, poem, writ 5 diary, essay, prose, verse 6 script 7

epistle, pothook 8 contract, covenant, document, makimono, pleading, spelling 9 allograph, cerograph, enrolment, esoterics 10 enrollment, instrument, literature, penmanship 11 chirography, composition, handwriting, inscription, orthography, pornography, publication
alternate: 13 boustrophedon
ancient manuscript: 6 uncial
character: (see also **word-sign**): 4 sign 6 letter, symbol 9 cuneiform
comb. form: 5 graph 6 grapho
desk: 9 secretary 10 escritoire
excessive interest in: 11 graphomania
master: 7 stylist
material: pad 5 board, paper, slate 6 tablet 7 papyrus 9 parchment 10 stationery
on the wall: 4 mene 5 tekel 8 upharsin
pert. to: 7 scribal
sacred: 5 Bible, Koran 6 psalms, Talmud 9 hagiology, testament 10 scriptures
secret: 4 code 6 cipher 10 cryptogram 12 cryptography
tool: pen 5 chalk, stick 6 pencil, stylus 9 ballpoint
wrizzled: 8 wrinkled 9 shriveled
wrong: bad, car, ill, off, out, sin 4 awry, evil, harm, tort 5 abuse, agley, amiss, crime, error, false, grief, malum, unfit 6 astray, faulty, injure, injury, malign, seduce, sinful, unfair, unjust, wicked 7 crooked, defraud, immoral, misdeed, twisted, violate 8 dishonor, improper, iniquity, mistaken, tortuous, wrongful, wrongous 9 erroneous, incorrect, injurious, injustice, violation 10 dispossess, inaccurate, iniquitous, unsuitable 11 malfeasance, misfeasance 12 illegitimate 14 unsatisfactory
civil: 4 tort
prefix: mis

wrongdoer: 6 sinner 8 criminal, violator 10 malefactor, tort-feasor, trespasser 12 transgressor

wroth: 5 angry, irate 7 violent 8 incensed, wrathful, wrothful 9 turbulent

wrought (see also **work**): 4 agog, made 5 eager 6 formed, shaped, worked 7 excited, operose 9 decorated, disturbed, fashioned, processed 10 elaborated, ornamented, stimulated 11 embroidered 12 manufactured

wrung: See **wring**

wry: 4 awry, bend, bias, sour, tend, turn 5 avert, pinch, twist, wring 6 swerve, warped 7 contort, crooked, deflect, deviate, distort, incline 8 contrary, perverse

wryneck: 5 loxia 9 snakebird 10 woodpecker 11 torticollis
genus: 4 jynx

Wurttemberg: *city:* Ulm 9 Esslingen, Heilbronn, Stuttgart
river: 6 Danube, Neckar
measure: imi

Wuthering Heights author: 6 Bronte
wych: elm
Wycliffe disciple: Hus 4 Huss 7 Lollard

wyliecoat: 9 petticoat, undervest 10 nightdress
wynd, wyne: haw 4 lane 5 alley, close, court
Wyoming: *capital:* 8 Cheyenne
cavern: 8 Shoshone
county: 5 Uinta 6 Goshen, Platte, Weston 7 Natrona 8 Sublette, Washakie
mountain: 5 Moran, Teton
national park: 11 Yellowstone
river: 5 Teton
town: 4 Cody 7 Laramie, Jackson, Rawlins 8 Cheyenne

X

X: chi, ten 4 mark 5 cross 9 signature
X-shaped: 8 cruciate
Xanadu's river: 4 Alph
xanthic: 6 yellow 9 yellowish
Xanthippe: 5 scold, shrew 6 nagger, virago 9 termagent
 husband: 8 Socrates
xanthous: 6 yellow 9 Mongolian
xebec: 4 boat, ship 6 vessel
 user: 6 pirate 7 corsair
xema: 4 gull
xenagogue: 5 guide
xenagogy: 9 guidebook
xenium: 4 gift 7 present
xenodochy: 11 hospitality
xenogamy: 13 fertilization
xenon: Xe
Xenophanean: 7 eleatic
Xenophon: *teacher:* 8 Socrates
 work: 8 Anabasis
Xeres: 4 wine 5 Jerez 6 sherry
xerophyte: 6 cactus
xerosis: 7 dryness
xerotic: dry, sec
Xerox: 4 copy 6 copier 9 duplicate

xerus: 8 squirrel
Xerxes: *composer:* 6 Handel
 parent: 6 Atossa, Darius
 wife: 6 Esther
Xhosa, Xosa: 5 Bantu, tribe 8 language
xiphoid: 8 ensiform
Xmas: 9 Christmas
X-ray: *inventor:* 8 Roentgen
 measuring device: 11 quantimeter
 science: 12 rontgenology 13 roentgenology
 source: 6 target
 type: 8 grenzray
Xtian: 8 Christian
xurel: 4 scad 6 saurel
xylograph: 5 print 9 engraving 10 impression
xyloid: 5 woody 8 ligneous
Xylonite: 9 celluloid
xylophone: 5 saron 6 gender 7 gambang, gamelan, marimba 8 gamelang, gigelira, sticcado
xyrid: 4 iris
xyst, xystos, xystus: 4 stoa, walk 5 porch 7 portico
xyster: 7 scraper 10 instrument

Y

yabber: 4 talk 6 jabber 8 language 12 conversation

yabby, yabbie: 8 crayfish

yacht: 4 boat, race, sail, ship 5 craft 6 cruise, sonder

yacht basin: 6 marina

yacht flag: 6 burgee

yaff: yap 4 bark, yelp

yaffle: 4 yaff 6 armful 7 handful 10 woodpecker

yahoo: 4 lout 5 brute 6 savage 7 bumpkin
creator: 5 Swift

Yahweh: God 4 YHVH, YHWH 5 Yahwe 7 Jehovah

yak: ox 4 zobo 6 sarlak, sarlyk 7 buffalo
cross-bred: 6 yakalo 9 yakattalo

yakamik: 9 trumpeter

yakka: 4 work 5 labor

yaksha: god 4 jinn, ogre 5 angel, demon, dryad, fairy, gnome 6 spirit

Yakut river: 4 Lena

Yale: Eli 4 lock 10 University

Yalta: *conference member:* 6 Stalin 9 Churchill, Roosevelt
location: 6 Crimea

yam: ube, ubi 5 tugui 6 buckra, igname, potato, uviyam 7 boniata 8 cush-cush 9 posthouse 11 sweetpotato

yamen: 6 office 7 mansion 9 residence 12 headquarters

yammadji: 6 native 11 blackfellow

yammer: cry 4 yell 5 crave, shout, whine, yearn 6 clamor, desire, lament, scream 7 chatter, grumble, stammer, whimper 8 complain

yamp: 5 tuber

yang: cry 4 honk

yang-kin: 8 dulcimer

Yangtze River tributary: Han, Kan, Min

yank: 4 blow, jerk, pull 5 hoick 6 twitch

Yank, Yankee: 8 American 10 Northerner

yannigan: 5 scrub

yap: apt, cur, dog, gab 4 bark, keen, talk, yelp 5 cheep, eager, mouth, quick, ready, rowdy, scold 6 active, hungry, jabber 7 bumpkin, chatter, hoodlum 9 greenhorn

Yap Island money: fei 5 stone

yapock, yapok: 6 monkey 7 opossum

yapp: 7 binding

Yaqui: 5 river 6 Indian

yard: rod 4 lawn, spar, wand 5 garth, staff, stick 7 confine 9 courtyard, curtilage, enclosure 10 correction, playground
enclosed: 5 garth, patio
part of: 4 foot, inch
sixteenth of: 4 nail

yards: *five and one-half:* rod
119.6 square: ar
600: 4 heer
two hundred twenty: 7 furlong

yardage: 6 length 8 distance

yardland: 7 virgate

yare: 4 well 5 brisk, eager, quick, ready 6 active, lively, prompt 8 entirely, prepared 10 manageable

yarm: 4 wail, yell 5 whine 6 scream

yarn: abb, eis, tow 4 garn, sley, tale 5 fiber, story 6 caddis, crewel 7 caddice, eiswool, genappe, schappe 9 fingering
ball: 4 clew
croft: 8 ropeyard
holder: cop
quantity: cop, lea 4 clew, clue, hank, hasp 5 skein 7 spangle
reel: 4 pirn
size: 6 denier
spindle: 4 hasp
waste: 5 thrum

yarr: 7 spurrey

yarrow: 7 allheal, milfoil

yashmak, yasmak: 4 veil

yataghan: 5 knife, saber

yatter: 7 chatter

yaud: 4 jade, mare

yauld: 4 mare 5 alert, sharp 6 active, nimble, strong 7 healthy 8 vigorous 10 able-bodied

yaupon: 5 holly 7 cassena, cassina 9 evergreen

yaw: 4 turn, veer 5 steer 6 swerve 7 deviate

yawl: 4 boat, howl 6 scream, vessel

yawn: 4 galp, gant(Sc.), gape, yaup, yawp 5 chasm 7 opening 8 oscitate

yawp: bay, cry, yap 4 bawl, call, gape, yelp 6 bellow, scream 8 complain

yaws: 9 frambesia

yawweed: 7 rhubarb

yclept: 5 named 6 called

ye: you 4 thee, thou

yea: ay; aye, yes 5 truly 6 assent, indeed, verily 11 affirmative

yean: ean 4 bear, lamb 7 produce

yeanling: kid 4 lamb 7 newborn

year: 5 annus(L.)

  designation: 4 leap 5 lunar, solar 6 fiscal 7 natural 8 calendar, sidereal, tropical 12 astronomical

  difference between lunar and solar: 5 epact

  division: 5 raith(Sc.) 6 season

  of plenary indulgence: 7 jubilee

  one-fourth of calendar: 9 trimester

  one-half of academic: 8 semester

  one-third of academic: 9 trimester

  record: 5 annal 8 calendar

yearbook: 7 almanac

yearling: 4 colt 9 hornotine

Yearling: *author:* 8 Rawlings

  boy: 4 Jody

yearly: 6 annual 7 etesian 8 annually

yearn: beg, vex, yen 4 ache, long, pine, sigh 5 crave 6 desire, grieve, hanker, yammer, 7 request

yearning: 4 wish 5 eager 7 anxious

years: age, eon, era 4 time

  eight: 9 octennial

  fifteen: 9 indiction

  five: 6 pentad 7 lustrum

  hundred: 9 centenary

  ninety: 10 nonagenary

  seventy: 12 septuagenary

  ten: 6 decade 8 decenary 9 decennary, decenniad, decennium

  thousand: 7 chiliad 10 millennium

  two: 8 biennium

yeast: bee 4 barm, foam, rise 5 froth 6 leaven 7 ferment 9 agitation 14 tumultuousness

  brewer's: 4 barm

yeasty: 5 light 8 restless 9 frivolous, unsettled 11 superficial

yegg: 5 thief 6 robber 7 burglar 8 criminal 11 safebreaker, safecracker

yell: cry 4 gowl, howl, roar, yarm, yowl 5 cheer, shout, whoop 6 outcry, scream, shriek, yammer 7 yelloch

yelling: 8 strident 9 clamorous

yelloch: 4 yell

yellow: or(her.) 4 gull, mean, sere, turn, yolk 5 amber, blake, color, favel, lemon, ochre, tinge 6 butter, canary, fallow,

flavic, flavid, flaxen, golden, sallow 7 xanthic 8 cowardly, recreant 9 flavicant, jaundiced, lutescent 10 flavescent, melancholy 11 sensational, treacherous 12 contemptible, dishonorable 13 dishonourable, untrustworthy

  brown: dun 4 bran 5 aloma, amber, pablo, straw 6 manila

  comb. form: 5 luteo, xanth 6 xantho

  dyestuff: 5 morin 6 orlean 7 annatto, annotto, arnatto

  egg's: 4 yolk

  gray: 4 drab

  green: 5 olive 6 privet 8 glaucous, tarragon 10 chartreuse, serpentine

  orange: 9 grenadine

  red: 4 lava, roan 5 sandy 6 orange 7 nacarat

yellow alloy: 5 brass

yellow bird: 6 canary 7 warbler 9 goldfinch

yellow copper ore: 12 chalcopyrite

yellow copperas: 9 copiapite

yellow jacket: 4 wasp 8 eucalypt

yellow mustard: 8 charlock

yellow ocher: sil

yellow pigment: 7 etiolin 8 orpiment

yellow race: 6 Mongol 9 Mongolian

Yellow River: 7 Hwang Ho

yellow star: 10 sneezeweed

yellow starwort: 10 elecampane

yellowhammer: 4 bird, yite 5 ammer, finch, skite 6 gladdy 7 yeldrin 8 yeldrine, yeldring, yeldrock, yeorling, yoldring 10 woodpecker

Yellowhammer State: 7 Alabama

yellowlegs: 4 bird 9 sandpiper

Yellowstone Park attraction: 4 deer 5 bears 6 geyser 11 Old Faithful

yelp: cry, yip 4 bark, brag 5 boast, cheep, shout 6 greedy, outcry, shriek, squeal 7 ululate 8 complain 9 criticize

yeme: 4 care, heed 5 guard 6 govern, regard 7 observe 10 solicitude

Yemen: *people:* 4 Arab 7 Arabian

  seaport: 5 Mocha, Mukha

  town: 4 Sana 5 Damar

yen: 4 coin, urge 5 yearn 6 desire 7 longing 10 propensity

  one-hundredth: sen

yeoman: 5 clerk 6 butler 8 retainer 9 assistant, attendant 10 freeholder, journeyman, manservant 11 subordinate

  of guard officer: 4 exon

yeomanly: 6 sturdy 8 faithful

yerk: 4 carp, cast, gird, goad, jerk, kick, lash, pull, stab 5 crack, throw, thump 6 snatch, thrash, wrench 7 lashing

yes: da(Russ.), ja(G.), si(It., Sp.); aye, iss, oui(F.), yeh, yep 4 yeah 5 agree 6 assent 9 assuredly 11 affirmation, affirmative

yesterday: 6 yester

yet: but 4 also 5 still 7 algates, besides, further, however 10 eventually 11 nonetheless 12 nevertheless 15 notwithstanding

yeti: 7 monster, snowman

yew: ew 4 tree 7 conifer 9 evergreen
genus: 5 taxus

Yiddish: 6 Jewish
pray: 5 daven
synagogue: 4 shul

yield: bow, net, pay, sag 4 bear, bend, cede, cess, elde, fold, give, obey, vail 5 addle, admit, agree, allow, avale, defer, grant, heald, hield, repay, stoop, waive 6 accede, afford, comply, impart, profit, relent, render, return, reward, soften, submit, supply 7 abandon, concede, consent, deliver, produce, revenue, succumb 9 acquiesce, surrender 10 capitulate, recompense, relinquish 11 acknowledge

yielding: 4 meek, soft, waxy 5 buxom 6 feeble, flabby, pliant, supple 7 flaccid 8 flexible, recreant 9 tractable 10 manageable

yill: ale

yin: one 8 feminine, negative

yip: 4 yelp

yird: 5 earth

yirr: 5 growl, snarl

Ymir, Ymer: 5 giant
slayer: Ve 4 Odin, Vili

yodel: 4 call, sing 5 carol, shout 6 warble 7 refrain

yogi: 4 yoga 5 fakir, yogin 6 fakeer 7 ascetic

yoke: tie 4 bail, bond, join, link, pair, span, team 5 bangy, fight(Sc.), marry, seize(Sc.) 6 attack(Sc.), banghy, couple, inspan, tackle(Sc.) 7 bondage, carrier, enslave, harness, oppress, service, slavery 8 restrain 9 associate, servitude
comb. form: 4 zygo

yoked: 9 conjugate

yokefellow: 4 mate, wife 6 spouse 7 husband, partner 9 associate, companion

yokel: oaf 4 boor, clod, lout, rube 6 obtuse, rustic 7 bumpkin, hayseed, plowboy 8 Abderite, gullible 10 countryman, slowwitted

yoking: 4 bout 7 contest, mugging

yolk: 6 yellow 7 essence 8 vitellus

yon: 6 yonder

yond: 4 past 6 raging, yonder

yonder: yon 4 away 5 there 6 beyond 7 distant, farther, further, thither

yore: 4 past

Yorkshire: *district:* 5 Otley, Selby
river: Ure
town: 5 Leeds

you: te, tu(F.), yi; sie(G.), yez

young: fry, raw 4 tyro, weak 5 brood, fetus, fresh, green 6 active, foetus, litter, strong, tender 7 pliable 8 childish, ignorant, immature, juvenile, newcomer, vigorous, workable, youthful 9 offspring, succulent 13 inexperienced
bring forth: ean 4 yean 5 calve, whelp
with: 6 gravid 8 pregnant

young animal: cub, kid, pup 4 calf, colt, fawn, joey 5 chick, puppy 6 kitten 7 tadpole

young hare: 7 leveret

young herring: 4 brit

younger: 6 junior

younger son: 5 cadet

youngling: 5 youth 6 novice 7 student 8 beginner, neophyte

youngster (see also **child**): boy, cub, lad, tad, tot 4 baby, calf, colt, girl, lass, tike 5 filly, youth 6 moppet, shaver, urchin 7 stripling 10 midshipman

younker: 6 knight 7 gallant 8 nobleman 9 gentleman, youngster

your: thy

youth: bud 4 chap 5 chiel(Sc.), chabo 6 hoiden, hoyden 7 callant(Sc.), ephebos, ephebus, gossoon 9 youngster 10 adolescent 11 adolescence, hobbledehoy
goddess of: 4 Hebe
mythological: 5 Etana 6 Adonis, Apollo, Icarus
time of: 9 salad days

youth shelter: 6 hostel

youthful: new 5 early, fresh, young 6 active 7 puerile 8 immature, juvenile, vigorous

yowl: cry 4 howl, wail, yell

yowt: 4 howl, yell, yelp 6 scream

yttrium: Yt

Yucatan: *people:* 4 Maya 5 Mayan
tree: 6 yaxche

yucca: 5 palma

Yugoslavia: *brandy:* 5 rakia 9 slivovitz
city: Nis 5 Agram 6 Morava, Mostar, Prilep, Skopje, Vardar, Zagrab, Zagreb 7 Cattaro 8 Belgrade, Monastir, Sarajevo, Subotica 9 Ljubljana, Subotitsa
coin: 4 para 5 dinar
commune: Pec 4 Stip 5 Veles
island: Rab, Vis 4 Cres, Hvar 5 Solta, Susak
measure: rif 4 akov, ralo 5 donum, khvat, lanaz, stopa 6 motyka, palaze, ralico 9 dan oranja
monarch: 5 Peter
people: 4 Serb 5 Croat 7 Slovene
region: 5 Banat 6 Banate, Bosnia
river: 4 Sava 5 Drava, Drina 6 Danube, Morava, Vardar
weight: oka, oke 5 dramm, tovar, wagon 7 satlijk

yule: 9 Christmas 13 Christmastide

Z

Z: zed 6 izzard
zac: 4 goat, ibex
zacate: hay 5 grass 6 forage
Zacchaeus, Zaccheus: 4 pure 8 innocent
Zadok: 4 just 9 righteous
  son: 7 Ahimaaz
Zagreb: See **Yugoslavia**
zaguan: 4 gate 8 entrance 11 entranceway
Zaire: *animal:* 5 okapi
  capital: 8 Kinshasa
  cool season: 7 cacimba
  lake: 5 Tumba
  official language: 6 French
  people: 5 Bantu, Pygmy 7 Hamitic, Nilotic
  8 Sudanese
  river: 4 Uele 5 Congo, Zaire 7 Aruwimi
  snake: 8 amphiuma
  wet season: 6 kundey
Zambales (see also **Philippine Islands**):
  capital: Iba
  language: 4 Tino
zamia: 4 tree 5 cycad, shrub
Zamindar: *chief:* 6 mirdha 7 mirdaha
  overseer: 6 mirdha 7 mirdaha
zampogna: 7 bagpipe, panpipe
zanja: 5 canal, ditch, gully 6 arroyo
zanni: 5 clown
zany: 4 dolt, fool 5 clown, crazy, dotty, nutty,
  toady 7 acrobat, buffoon, idiotic 8 clownish, follower, imitator 9 assistant, attendant, simpleton 10 lieutenant 11 merry-andrew
Zanzibar: See **Tanzania**
zarf: cup 5 stand 6 holder
zati: 6 monkey
zeal: 4 fire 5 ardor 6 desire, fervor 7 passion
  8 devotion, interest 9 eagerness 10 enthusiasm, fanaticism
Zealand: *city:* 10 Copenhagen
zealot: 5 bigot 6 votary 7 devotee, fanatic 8
  partisan, votaress 10 enthusiast
zealous: 4 warm 5 rabid 6 ardent, fervid,
  hearty 7 devoted, earnest, fervent 8 frenetic, vigorous 9 phrenetic, strenuous 12
  enthusiastic

Zebedee's son: 4 John 5 James
zebra: 4 dauw
  extinct: 6 quagga
zebrawood: 7 arariba 9 nakedwood 10 mar-
  blewood
zebu: 8 Brahmany
Zebulon, Zebulun: *brother:* 4 Levi 5 Judah
  6 Simeon
  father: 5 Jacob
  mother: 4 Leah
zecchino: 6 sequin, zequin
Zelus: *brother:* Bia 6 Cratus
  father: 6 Pallas
  mother: 4 Styx
  sister: 4 Nike
zenana: 5 harem 8 seraglio
zenith: 4 acme, peak 6 summit 11 culmination
  opposite of: 5 nadir
Zeno: *city:* 4 Elea
  follower: 5 Stoic
Zenobia: *country:* 7 Palmyra
  husband: 9 Odenathus
zephyr: 4 aura, wind 6 breeze
zeppelin: 5 blimp 9 dirigible
zequin: 6 sequin 8 zecchino
zero: nil 6 cipher, naught, nought 7 nothing
Zeruiah's son: 7 Abishai
zest: 4 tang 5 gusto, savor 6 flavor, relish 8
  piquancy 9 enjoyment 10 enthusiasm
zestful: 4 racy 6 hearty 7 pungent
Zeus: 7 Alastor, Jupiter
  attendant: 4 Nike
  beloved of: Io 6 Europa
  brother: 5 Hades 8 Poseidon
  cupbearer: 4 Hebe 8 Ganymede
  daughter: Ate 4 Hebe, Kore 5 Irene 6
  Athena, Athene 7 Artemis, Astraea 8 Despoina 9 Aphrodite 10 Persephone, Proserpina, Proserpine 11 Persephassa
  epithet: 5 soter 7 Alastor
  form assumed by: 4 bull, swan
  messenger: 4 Iris 6 Hermes
  mother: 4 Rhea
  nurse: 4 goat 8 Amalthea, Cynosura

oracle: 6 Dodona
parent: 4 Rhea 6 Cronus, Kronos
shield: 5 aegis
sister: 4 Hera
son: Gad 4 Ares 5 Arcas, Argus 6 Aeacus, Apollo, Hermes, Tityus 7 Perseus 8 Dardanus, Dionysos, Dionysus, Heracles, Herakies, Hercules, Tantalus 10 Hephaestus
victim: 4 Idas
wife: 4 Hera 5 Danae, Metis 6 Semele
ziarat, ziara: 4 tomb 6 shrine
ziggurat: 5 tower 7 pyramid
zigzag: 4 tack, turn 5 angle, crank, weave 8 flexuous
Zillah: *husband:* 6 Lamech
son: 9 Tubal-cain
Zilpah's son: Gad 5 Asher
zimarra: 5 cloak 7 cassock, soutane
zimb: bug, fly 6 insect
zinc: Zn 7 adamine, adamite, spelter, tutenag 9 galvanize, tutenague
ore: 6 blende
sulphate: 7 ilesite
zing: pep, vim, zip 4 dash, snap 5 force, vigor 6 energy, spirit, stingo 10 enthusiasm
zingaro: 5 gypsy
zingel: 4 fish 5 perch
zinnia: 5 aster 6 flower
Zion: 4 hill 6 heaven
Zionism founder: 5 Herzl
zip: 4 zing
zipper: 8 fastener
Zipporah's father: 6 Jethro
zippy: 5 brisk 6 snappy
zizany: 4 weed 5 tares 6 darnel
zizith: 7 fringes, tassles
Zoan: 5 Tanis
Zobeide's sister: 5 Amina
zodiac sign: Leo, Ram 4 Bull, Crab, Fish, Goat, Lion 5 Aries, decan, Libra, Scale, Twins, Virgo 6 Archer, Cancer, Fishes,

Gemini, Pisces, Taurus, Virgin 7 Balance, Scorpio 8 Aquarius, Scorpion 9 Capricorn 11 Capricornus, Sagittarius, Waterbearer
Zola: *defender of:* 7 Dreyfus
character: 4 Nana
work: 4 Nana 6 Verite 7 J'accuse 8 Germinal
zone: 4 area, band, belt, path, zona(L.) 5 layer, tract 6 course, girdle, region, stripe 7 circuit 8 cincture, encircle, engirdle
geological succession: 6 assise
marked by: 6 zonate
zoom: 9 chandelle
zoo: 8 vivarium 9 menagerie
floating: ark
zoophyte: 5 coral
zoril: 7 polecat
Zoroaster's works: 6 Avesta
Zoroastrian: 5 Parsi 6 gheber, ghebre, Parsee
demon: 4 deva
god: 5 Ahura, Mazda 10 Ahura-Mazda
zoster: 4 belt 6 girdle
Zouave: 4 Zuzu
zounds: 4 egad
zoysia: 5 grass
zucchetto: 7 calotte 8 skullcap
zucchini: 5 gourd 6 squash
zufolo: 5 flute 9 flageolet
zuisin: 4 duck 7 widgeon 8 baldpate
Zulu: *boy:* 6 umfaan
headman: 6 induna
language family: 5 Bantu
regiment: 4 impi
spear: 7 assegai
Zuni: 6 Indian, Pueblo
zwieback: 4 rusk 5 toast 7 biscuit
zygomatic bone: 9 cheekbone
zygote: 7 oosperm
zymase: 6 enzyme
source: 5 yeast
zymogen activating substance: 6 kinase
zymosis: 12 fermentation
zythum: 4 beer